A Concordance to the
Complete Poems of
E. E. CUMMINGS

THE CORNELL CONCORDANCES

S. M. Parrish, *General Editor*

Supervisory Committee

M. H. Abrams

Donald D. Eddy

Ephim Fogel

Alain Seznec

POEMS OF MATTHEW ARNOLD, *edited by Stephen Maxfield Parrish* (out of print)

POEMS OF W. B. YEATS, *edited by Stephen Maxfield Parrish*

POEMS OF EMILY DICKINSON, *edited by S. P. Rosenbaum*

WRITINGS OF WILLIAM BLAKE, *edited by David V. Erdman* (out of print)

BYRON'S *DON JUAN*, *edited by Charles W. Hagelman, Jr., and Robert J. Barnes*

THÉÂTRE ET POÉSIES DE JEAN RACINE, *edited by Bryant C. Freeman* (out of print)

BEOWULF, *edited by J. B. Bessinger, Jr.*

PLAYS OF W. B. YEATS, *edited by Eric Domville*

POEMS OF JONATHAN SWIFT, *edited by Michael Shinagel*

PLAYS OF WILLIAM CONGREVE, *edited by David Mann*

POEMS OF SAMUEL JOHNSON, *edited by Helen Harrold Naugle*

FABLES AND TALES OF JEAN DE LA FONTAINE, *edited by J. Allen Tyler*

POEMS OF OSIP MANDELSTAM, edited by Demetrius J. Koubourlis

POEMS OF SIR PHILIP SIDNEY, *edited by Herbert S. Donow*

PLAYS AND POEMS OF FEDERICO GARCÍA LORCA, *edited by Alice M. Pollin*

PASCAL'S *PENSÉES*, *edited by Hugh M. Davidson and Pierre H. Dubé*

COMPLETE WRITINGS OF GEORGE HERBERT, *edited by Mario A. Di Cesare and Rigo Magnani*

THE ANGLO-SAXON POETIC RECORDS, *edited by J. B. Bessinger, Jr.* (out of print)

POEMS OF BEN JONSON, *edited by Mario A. Di Cesare and Ephim Fogel*

PLAYS, POEMS, AND TRANSLATIONS OF CHRISTOPHER MARLOWE, *edited by Robert J. Fehrenbach, Lea Ann Boone, and Mario A. Di Cesare*

COMPLETE ENGLISH POEMS OF JOHN SKELTON, *edited by Alistair Fox and Gregory Waite*

COMPLETE POEMS OF E. E. CUMMINGS, *edited by Katharine Winters McBride*

A Concordance to the
Complete Poems of
E. E. CUMMINGS

Edited by

KATHARINE WINTERS MCBRIDE

Cornell University Press

ITHACA AND LONDON

This concordance is based on *E. E. Cummings: Complete Poems 1913–1962* (New York: Harcourt Brace Jovanovich, Inc., 1972), copyright © 1923, 1925, 1931, 1935, 1938, 1939, 1940, 1944, 1945, 1946, 1947, 1948, 1949, 1950, 1951, 1952, 1953, 1954, 1955, 1956, 1957, 1958, 1959, 1960, 1961, 1962 by E. E. Cummings, copyright © 1961, 1963, 1968 by Marion Morehouse Cummings, by permission of Harcourt Brace Jovanovich, Inc., Liveright Publishing Corporation, and Grafton Books.

First published 1989 by Cornell University Press.

Library of Congress Cataloging-in-Publication Data

McBride, Katharine Winters, 1956–
  A concordance to the complete poems of E. E. Cummings / edited by Katharine Winters McBride.
      p. cm.—(The Cornell concordances)
  ISBN 0-8014-2239-6 (alk. paper)
  1. Cummings, E. E. (Edward Estlin), 1894–1962—Concordances. I. Cummings, E. E. (Edward Estlin), 1894–1962. II. Title. III. Series.
PS3505.U334Z76   1989   811'.52—dc19   89-31058

Printed in the United States of America

CONTENTS

Preface	vii
Abbreviations	xi
Concordance to the Complete Poems of E. E. Cummings	1
Appendix: Index Words in Order of Frequency	939

PREFACE

This concordance is based on *E. E. Cummings: Complete Poems 1913–1962*, first American edition published by Harcourt Brace Jovanovich in 1972, but it can be used with any edition of Cummings's poems. On the concordance page each indexed word, or key word, is shown in a context provided by the computer, which was programmed to center the word and to string out some four words before it and up to four words after it, depending on available room. Following the context is the pertinent page number in *Complete Poems*, an abbreviated poem title, and the number of the line at which the key word begins.

In a Cummings poem, of course, a "word" is not always something a computer can be taught to recognize—that is, a group of letters arrayed horizontally and set off by spaces or punctuation. A Cummings word can be made up of physical elements that are typographically separated—trailing letter by letter, or syllable by syllable, down the page, for example. It can be interrupted by other words inserted into it; it can be run right into a stream of other words; it can be submerged in dialect, or in a pun. In all such cases the word has to be extracted or constructed for the index, which makes this concordance a unique combination of machine labor and human ingenuity. All constructed words are marked with a + to discriminate them from index words that occur in straightforward order in their normal form. Thus +ACTION emerges from line 13 in poem 12 of *New Poems* (page 474 of *Complete Poems*): "yewrety oride lesgo eckshun," and +AFRAID can be found in three lines of poem 33 in *95 Poems* (page 705):

(eyeaintu)

s

(hfraiduh

Constructing words out of scattered elements or buried parts is frequently a matter of judgment, and certain principles have been followed. To begin

vii

with, a word that is distorted by eccentric spelling is not indexed in its raw form but under the normal conventional spelling of the word. Thus Cummings's "applaws" will be found indexed under + APPLAUSE. When a recognizable word stands at the beginning of a sequence of letters, like "almost" in "almostclean," it is not separated out as a constructed entry, since the reader can readily find it by scanning the index entries. When a word is buried behind another word, however, so that it does not show up among the index entries (like the "clean" in "almostclean") it is presented as a constructed key word, preceded by +. Similarly, the second portion of a hyphenated compound is automatically pulled out and made into an index word. Index entries also include terms in which a given word can easily be picked out even though it is very slightly distorted—as, for example, ACROBATA or ADJUSTIN. The reader will further discover among the index entries a number of distinctive compounds or variants, or strings of real words, like ALEAK, or ABSITIVELY, or ALBUTNOTQUITEMOST. Word fragments that make no sense standing alone, however, have been dropped from the index (though preserved, of course, in quoted contexts and in the computer-compiled list of frequencies), thus sparing the reader such index entries as ULAR, GH, UCH, and the like. Pieces of language that resist analysis or cannot be broken into intelligible parts have been indexed as they stand, and readers are invited to try their ingenuity on such terms as "sirkusricky" or "radarw leschin" or "ahlbrhoon." Prefixes that have been separated from a word are rejoined to the word to make an index entry (as with + UNGOD); it was not thought necessary, however, to reattach suffixes. Repeated words in a line are not indexed separately.

Just as words sometimes have to be constructed, so do Cummings's contexts. For example, contexts that run vertically down the page have to be arrayed horizontally so that they can stand in a concordance line. For constructed words, even when a context is fairly simple, the reader is normally directed to the full setting with the instruction FOR CONTEXT SEE . . . and the pertinent page and line numbers.

An example may help to make our creative procedures clear. Page 673 of *Complete Poems* contains the first poem in the collection *95 Poems*:

l(a

le
af
fa

ll

s)

one

l

iness

Written out horizontally, with the material inside parentheses set apart, the poem comes into focus: "loneliness (a leaf falls)". In the concordance, these words are made into index entries marked with + .

A few other principles of format need to be explained. (1) The computer was programmed to space at the end of each line and after each mark of punctuation; the words thus (sometimes artificially) formed are not, however, regarded as constructed. (2) While all punctuation is preserved (although not separately indexed), accents are omitted. (3) A series of slashes—up to four, depending on space available—marks the end or the beginning of a poem in the line of context. (4) Single letters that are judged to be in some way significant are indexed; those judged to be accidental are dropped. (5) Empty pointed brackets <> signal a stretch of language omitted from the context owing to its length. (6) Greek words are transliterated within brackets, and the dollar sign and equals sign are similarly spelled out within brackets. (7) Numbers deemed significant are concorded after the alphabetical list of words. (8) Common words such as AM, AND, THIS, and the like are listed in the index as DELETED, with their frequencies of occurence, but without contexts. (9) The Appendix lists all words in the index in descending order of frequency.

ACKNOWLEDGMENTS

Encouraged by the hope expressed by Rushworth Kidder, an authority on the poetry of E. E. Cummings, that a concordance would be of great value to students and readers of the poet, I began work on this project under his direction. From the beginning, Professor Kidder's advice on interpreting a large part of the poetry, and on accommodating Cummings's language to the computer, has been invaluable.

Carroll Gunter, scientific programmer at Wichita State University, designed the computer program, and Wichita State funded the initial stages of the concordance with a series of research grants. Their generous contributions over a lengthy period ensured that the project would be completed. The final computer processing and the preparation of camera-ready copy were carried out at Brigham Young University by Randall Jones, whose unfailingly intelligent and good-humored support made publication possible.

Compiling a concordance, even a computer concordance, involves hun-

dreds of hours of proofreading and checking. Many people helped in this process, but I especially thank my mother, Flavia McBride, my friend Tom Miville, and the students at Cornell drawn into the project. Finally, I thank Stephen Parrish for sticking with me through years of work and giving me the opportunity to publish the concordance in the series of which he is General Editor.

KATHARINE WINTERS McBRIDE

Vancouver, B.C.

ABBREVIATIONS

Complete Poems, on which the concordance is based, includes the contents of twelve volumes. Within each volume, abbreviated section titles and poem numbers are added to the abbreviated volume title, as shown in the following lists (in which numbers and the ampersand precede the alphabet). Cummings gave titles to about a dozen of his poems; words in these titles have all been indexed and indicated with a "T" in place of a line number.

Concordance Abbreviation	*Volume, Section, Poem Nos.*	*Pages in Complete Works*
1 X 1 1–54	*1 X 1* (1944) I–LIV	541–594
50 POEMS 1–50	*50 Poems* (1940) 1–50	487–538
73 POEMS 1–73	*73 Poems* (1963) 1–73	773–845
95 POEMS 1–95	*95 Poems* (1958) 1–95	673–769

♭ (1925)

& POST IMPR 1–14	A: POST IMPRESSIONS I–XIV	89–104
& PORTRAIT 1–12	PORTRAITS I–XII	105–121
& SEVEN POEMS 1–7	N: &: SEVEN POEMS I–VII	122–129
& SON REAL 1–22	D: SONNETS—REALITIES I–XXII	130–151
& SON ACTU 1–24	SONNETS—ACTUALITIES I–XXIV	152–175
{CHAIRE} 1–71	*XAIPE* (1950) 1–71	599–669

is 5 (1926)

IS 5 ONE LIZ	ONE LIZ	225
IS 5 ONE MAME	ONE MAME	226
IS 5 ONE GERT	ONE GERT	227
IS 5 ONE MARJ	ONE MARJ	228
IS 5 ONE FRAN	ONE FRAN	229
IS 5 ONE 2–34	ONE II–XXXIV	230–265
IS 5 TWO 1–10	TWO I–X	266–276
IS 5 THREE 1–7	THREE I–VII	277–283
IS 5 FOUR 1–18	FOUR I–XVIII	284–301
IS 5 FIVE 1–5	FIVE I–V	302–306

NEW POEMS 1–22   *New Poems* (1938) 1–22   463–484

NO THANKS 1–71   *No Thanks* (1935) 1–71   381–456

Tulips and Chimneys (1923)
Tulips

T&C EPITHALAM   EPITHALAMION 1–3   3–7
T&C OF NICOL   OF NICOLETTE   8
T&C SONGS 1–6   SONGS I–VI   9–16
T&C PUELLA MEA   PUELLA MEA   17–23
T&C CHANSONS 1–3   CHANSONS INNOCENTES I–III   24–26
T&C ORIENTALE 1–6   ORIENTALE I–VI   27–35
T&C AMORES 1–8   AMORES I–VIII   36–44
T&C LA GUERRE 1–2   LA GUERRE I–II   45–46
T&C IMPRESS 1–5   IMPRESSIONS I–V   47–51
T&C PORTRAIT 1–10   PORTRAITS I–X   52–63
T&C POST IMPR 1–6   POST IMPRESSIONS I–VI   64–69

Chimneys

T&C SON REAL 1–6   SONNETS—REALITIES I–VI   70–75
T&C SON UNRE 1–6   SONNETS—UNREALITIES I–VI   76–81
T&C SON ACTU 1–5   SONNETS—ACTUALITIES I–V   82–86

VIVA 1–70   *W [ViVa]* (1931) I–LXX   309–379

XLI Poems (1925)

XLI SONGS 1–12   SONGS I–XII   179–190
XLI CHANSONS 1–2   CHANSONS INNOCENTES I–II   191–192
XLI PORTRAIT 1–9   PORTRAITS I–IX   193–202
XLI LA GUERRE 1–2   LA GUERRE I–II   203–204
XLI SONNETS 1–16   SONNETS I–XVI   205–220

A Concordance to the
Complete Poems of
E. E. CUMMINGS

A

  WORD DELETED, APPEARED 1921 TIMES
+A
  FOR CONTEXT, SEE . . . . 200 XLI PORTRAIT 8   30
+A 1
  FOR CONTEXT, SEE . . . . 248 IS 5 ONE 19   18
+A.M.
  FOR CONTEXT, SEE . . . . 787 73 POEMS 15   1
A-LIVE
  Of ; elate shyly a-live keen parallel specks float-ing . . . 447 NO THANKS 62   3
+A-MOTION-UPO-NMOTIO-N
  rouNdly)ftblac kl(ness)y a-motion-upo-nmotio-n Less? . . . . 429 NO THANKS 46   6
A'S
  th e (s e a's; m e, m (or. . . . . 447 NO THANKS 62   18
ABDOMENS
  to lie upon our abdomens for greater privacy and . . . . . . 261 IS 5 ONE 31   13
ABDOMINOUS
  by midnight the flyspecked abdominous female indubitably . . 116 & PORTRAIT 9   3
ABE
  tooked out his C.O.D. Abe tucks it up back . . . . 321 VIVA 13   8
ABERDEEN
  or are, good luck! aberdeen plato-rabelais peter jack / . . . 605 (CHAIRE) 7   16
ABIDE
  lovers are (whose selves abide under whatever shall . . . . . 446 NO THANKS 61   9
ABLAZE
  and o each living ablaze greenly thing ; may . . . . 583 1 X 1 43   13
  of the sky is ablaze with their voices) all . . . . 841 73 POEMS 69   7
ABLE
  (whom i meet anywhere able to be and seem . . . . 367 VIVA 58   3
  through these each illimit able to speak very softly . . . . 600 (CHAIRE) 2   14
ABOARD
  first put right sleuthfully aboard all to--mendaciously . . . 334 VIVA 25   5
ABOMINABLE
  with tipsy tables the abominable floor belches smoky laughter 55 T&C PORTRAIT 3   3
ABORTED
  and when which was aborted what was dead dead . . . . 401 NO THANKS 18   6
ABOUT
  thy long sinful arms about me dream shall my . . . .   9 T&C SONGS 1   34
  seeds of dead song about home and love from . . . . 55 T&C PORTRAIT 3   14
  clustered like bright lice about god's capable dull important 85 T&C SON ACTU 4   4
  crying to nobody something about les roses les bluets . . . . 102 & POST IMPR 12   16
  dearie we should worry about the rain huh dearie? . . . . . . 109 & PORTRAIT 5   8
  or if it talks about you somewhere behind your . . . . 126 & SEVEN POEMS 5   18
  Chair he kept talking about eyes / / / . . . . 145 & SON REAL 16   14
  to heave and twine about me, and to kiss . . . . 147 & SON REAL 18   14
  of dimension to occur about us and birds known, ... 205 XLI SONNETS 1   13
  a fellow's twistandtwirl talk about your Sal- Sal- Sal-, . . 235 IS 5 ONE 6   19
  Sal- Sal- Sal-, talk about your Salo -mes but . . . . 235 IS 5 ONE 6   23
  some guys talks big about Lundun Burlin an gay . . . . 237 IS 5 ONE 8   5
  never never to wonder about guys you used to . . . . 242 IS 5 ONE 13   4
  to have no doubts about why you put the . . . . 242 IS 5 ONE 13   11
  really wonder i mean about the smell of babies . . . . 242 IS 5 ONE 13   17
  it didn't Ruskin says about you got the haven't . . . . 257 IS 5 ONE 27   35
  &) & chatters about Peacepeacepeace (to droppingly descend . 267 IS 5 TWO 2   7
  tiny cane and, mazurkas about tweak- ing his wing . . . . . . 274 IS 5 TWO 9   32
  to become hoarse talking about how it was a . . . . 276 IS 5 TWO 10   16
  what does he think about, i wonder as over . . . . 286 IS 5 FOUR 3   2
  with knowing --and all about herself the sprouting largest . 301 IS 5 FOUR 18   14
  Of (without more ado about less than nothing) 2 . . . . 317 VIVA 9   22
  asong tohim self all about the desertbyIts elf while) . . . . 318 VIVA 10   13
  dimly remarked some- thing about "stuffed fauna" . . . . . . 326 VIVA 18   32
  everywhere beneath thee and about thyself a small hoping . . 351 VIVA 42   9
  which is why something about me reminded him of . . . . 355 VIVA 46   20
  know what it is about you that closes and . . . . 366 VIVA 57   17
  criminal (hears Darwin; asks about Death) concept O . . . . . 398 NO THANKS 15   14
  finger is) what's right about the g.o. world what's . . . . . 411 NO THANKS 28   8
  may my mind stroll about hungry and fearless and . . . . . . 481 NEW POEMS 19   5
  them kings you read about and on him sings . . . . 568 1 X 1 28   13

                                    1

	PAGE	TITLE	LINE
ABOUT (CONTINUED)			
/ / (nothing whichful about thick big this friendly	658	(CHAIRE) 60	1
+ABOUT			
FOR CONTEXT, SEE	318	VIVA 10	23
FOR CONTEXT, SEE	332	VIVA 23	2
FOR CONTEXT, SEE	495	50 POEMS 9	24
FOR CONTEXT, SEE	567	1 X 1 27	9
ABOVE			
ladies do not care, above Cambridge if sometimes in	70	T&C SON REAL 1	11
peregrinate, a cigar-stub disintegrates, above, underdrawers	144	& SON REAL 15	5
of air wonderfully stumbled above the square, little	173	& SON ACTU 22	3
by god i want above fourteenth fifth's deep purring	220	XLI SONNETS 16	1
Lydia E. Pinkham, land above all of Just Add	230	IS 5 ONE 2	12
and is a kewpie above the ears (but my	253	IS 5 ONE 24	10
gondola signore gondola and above me pass loudly and	256	IS 5 ONE 27	25
pimples, correctly dressed, cleanshaven above the nombril, .	262	IS 5 ONE 32	8
country and for Yale above his blond determined head	273	IS 5 TWO 8	13
tidiyum chins, and just above their very tidiyum ears	274	IS 5 TWO 9	13
small lady upon earth above; to whom i cry, ...	360	VIVA 51	33
which night hoists miraculously above the always beyond such	378	VIVA 69	12
with the cohn) down above all with love and	466	NEW POEMS 4	21
/ / you shall above all things be glad	484	NEW POEMS 22	1
not some under's mere above but breathing yes which	538	50 POEMS 50	1
or un-) proudly depths above why's first because (faith's . .	574	1 X 1 34	9
to have been what above did was always fall	634	(CHAIRE) 36	9
am and we are (above and under all possible	664	(CHAIRE) 66	17
parasol, so she may above people walk in the	762	95 POEMS 89	8
become more than alive) above anybody and fate and	762	95 POEMS 89	11
greatness is alone-- one (above nevermoving all nowhere) . .	808	73 POEMS 36	5
truth of patience heard above the everywhereing fact of . . .	821	73 POEMS 49	6
ABRAHAM			
i sing: land of Abraham Lincoln and Lydia E.	230	IS 5 ONE 2	11
ABRUPT			
cold jolts of lovecrazed abrupt flesh split "Pretty Baby" . .	106	& PORTRAIT 2	11
ABRUPTLY			
(the new moon fills abruptly with sudden silver these	93	& POST IMPR 5	14
from a pissoir enters abruptly Notre Dame (whereas de	245	IS 5 ONE 16	23
and smother; until autumn abruptly wholly hugs our dying . .	305	IS 5 FIVE 4	8
dignity square feet turned abruptly Miss Gay away: "on . . .	326	VIVA 18	26
ABSENCE			
mean that the blond absence of any program except	264	IS 5 ONE 33	17
can quite endure the absence of that moment when	812	73 POEMS 40	11
utterly that timelessness whose absence would make your whole	817	73 POEMS 45	13
ABSITIVELY			
maybe sing and be absitively posolutely dead, like Coney . .	72	T&C SON REAL 3	14
ABSOLUTE			
hands emboss, betwixt whose absolute feet anoint with calm .	3	T&C EPITHALAM	30
curtained with wordless worship absolute, unto the certain .	6	T&C EPITHALAM	115
crumbling flight into the absolute stars the gods are	112	& PORTRAIT 6	83
silent greens serenely lingering, absolute lights like baths	208	XLI SONNETS 4	4
it more than mildly Absolute destructivity to non- entities .	391	NO THANKS 8	22
through never's always until absolute un gulps the first . .	517	50 POEMS 31	12
of black because your absolute courage with its legs	522	50 POEMS 35	14
snowily sailing perfect silence. Absolute ocean / / /	586	1 X 1 46	20
--that screech of space) absolute (my soul tastes If	639	(CHAIRE) 41	6
fol ding int o absolute gone & positive quite	646	(CHAIRE) 48	13
where (chr ist) what absolute nothing / / /	823	73 POEMS 51	20
and gently (very whiteness: absolute peace, never imaginable	839	73 POEMS 67	14
ABSOLUTELY			
me and the night absolutely into me.... a wise	302	IS 5 FIVE 1	8
or just a handful absolutely doesn't matter and whether . . .	549	1 X 1 9	5
+ABSOLUTELY			
FOR CONTEXT, SEE	72	T&C SON REAL 3	14
ABSORBED			
of t oo vertiginously absorbed which a la /	465	NEW POEMS 3	12
ABSORBS			
worlds: immortal yonder collidingly absorbs eternal near) day	376	VIVA 67	13

		PAGE	TITLE	LINE

ABSURD
common purple soul the absurd eyelids sulked enormous sobs . 52 T&C PORTRAIT 1 26
skilfully, teasing its lips, absurd eyes, the hair). Creasing 164 & SON ACTU 13 9
and luminous (here the absurd I; life, to peer . . . . 281 IS 5 THREE 5 18
i am alive this absurd fraction in its lowest . . . . 295 IS 5 FOUR 12 18
the smallening world became absurd; him did an archer . . . . 360 VIVA 51 14
through whose foul windows absurd clouds cruise nobly . . . . 442 NO THANKS 57 12
(extremely like but quite absurd gloved fist on hip . . . . . 640 {CHAIRE} 42 8
+ABSURD
FOR CONTEXT, SEE . . . . 262 IS 5 ONE 32 3
ABSURDITY
the enormous rhythm of absurdity. skin like the poisonous . . 103 & POST IMPR 13 11
ABUNDANT
richly scattered by the abundant sun invades the new . . . . 5 T&C EPITHALAM 83
ABUSE
whose very minuteness doth abuse reason, why then the . . . . 22 T&C PUELLA MEA 218
dreams thy strangeness must abuse....) Time being not for . . 213 XLI SONNETS 9 14
ABUSES
it's the people that abuses it you can git . . . . 567 1 X 1 27 11
ABYSS
aeronaut down, into the abyss --and wonderfully i fell . . . 360 VIVA 51 17
dooms conceive an oceaning abyss of orange dream larger . . . 599 {CHAIRE} 1 3
AC
hardboil guys frum duh A.C. fulla hooch kiddin eachudder . . 332 VIVA 23 1
ACCELERATOR
avenue i touched the accelerator and give her the . . . . . . 248 IS 5 ONE 19 22
ACCEPT
take his hands, saying, Accept all happiness from me. . . . . 76 T&C SON UNRE 1 12
others wrote in steel, accept all praise of after . . . . . . 209 XLI SONNETS 5 10
is now let us accept (the time forever, and . . . . 504 50 POEMS 18 14
will becauseless ultimate earth accept and primeval whyless . 745 95 POEMS 73 6
ACCEPTANCE
(yes by microscopic yes) acceptance of irrevocable time . . . 821 73 POEMS 49 4
ACCIDENT
in twilight is an accident whose niceness betters easily . . 162 & SON ACTU 11 2
wherefore yon mob an accident? somebody got concus- sion . . 245 IS 5 ONE 16 17
ACCLAIM
even deafanddumb thy sons acclaim your glorious name by . . . 268 IS 5 TWO 3 7
ACCOMPLISH
i are accustomed to accomplish two or three times, ... 236 IS 5 ONE 7 14
ACCORDING
do you get me?) according to such supposedly indigenous . . . 230 IS 5 ONE 2 30
the same place. Why according to tomorrow's paper the . . . . 262 IS 5 ONE 32 18
wispily is to say according to his perfect satisfaction . . . 516 50 POEMS 30 13
ACCOUNT
may or may not account for the fact that . . . . 239 IS 5 ONE 10 7
ACCROST
tuh duh whole gang accrost duh table-- "fellers have . . . . 332 VIVA 23 20
ACCURATE
sins perfectly gesticulate the accurate strenuous lips of . . 43 T&C AMORES 7 36
a beautiful suppression the accurate boy mouth now droops . . 54 T&C PORTRAIT 2 8
muscles into nervous and accurate silence.... But first you) 67 T&C POST IMPR 4 16
/ / by little accurate saints thickly which tread . . . . . . 85 T&C SON ACTU 4 1
my mouth, taste the accurate demure ferocious rhythm of . . . 162 & SON ACTU 11 11
cherie, j'en doute. the accurate key to a palace . . . . . . 169 & SON ACTU 18 14
pale fracas upon the accurate moon.... Across the important . 214 XLI SONNETS 10 9
machinery is the more accurate, yes it delivers the . . . . 264 IS 5 ONE 33 11
wishless melancholy, suddenly looming) accurate undaunted . . 305 IS 5 FIVE 4 14
through man -ufactured harmlessly accurate gloom "I think he 464 NEW POEMS 2 19
ACCURATELY
doucement le soir (ladies accurately dead les anglais sont . 120 & PORTRAIT 12 25
electric solidity remembers some accurately profuse . . . . . 197 XLI PORTRAIT 5 18
hypnotism . i am accurately parsed by this gorgeous . . . . . 201 XLI PORTRAIT 9 27
cricks where a hurdy-gurdy accurately pants. and pompous . . 219 XLI SONNETS 15 8
or by doomful connivance accurately thither and hither myself 299 IS 5 FOUR 16 8
now with blood now accurately wan) keenly, to dreamings . . . 344 VIVA 35 6
ACCUSE
distinctly walk your smiles accuse the dusk with an . . . . . 138 & SON REAL 9 4

3

	PAGE	TITLE	LINE
ACCUSE (CONTINUED)			
to make an acorn--valleys accuse their mountains of having .	520	50 POEMS 34	10
(though flesh and blood accuse him of coercion or	683	95 POEMS 11	3
ACCUSTOMED			
you and i are accustomed to accomplish two or	236	IS 5 ONE 7	13
ACERB			
intent stars circling the acerb pole poises, smiling, the . .	3	T&C EPITHALAM	31
ACH			
devil ouch the devil ach the great green dancing	25	T&C CHANSONS 2	24
ACHED			
but how dat baby ached." and when i timidly	226	IS 5 ONE MAME	11
ACHES			
in tickling intuitive flight aches, just, simply, into, her.	130	& SON REAL 1	11
clean through me tickling aches, and the weak noise	147	& SON REAL 18	7
ACHIEVE			
and go) may i achieve another steepest thing-- how	558	1 X 1 18	10
+ACHIEVE			
FOR CONTEXT, SEE	785	73 POEMS 13	13
ACHIEVES			
small hoping insect, humanity, achieves (moult beyond	351	VIVA 42	10
ACHILLES			
upon an almostclean plate "Achilles" said Nicho' "and did . .	194	XLI PORTRAIT 2	35
ACHING			
nearness. (peers: body of aching toys in unsmooth sexual . .	159	& SON ACTU 8	12
ACOLD			
withers; thy hair is acold with dreams, love thou	190	XLI SONGS 12	16
ACORN			
birch to make an acorn--valleys accuse their mountains of . .	520	50 POEMS 34	10
ACRES			
young with rain, spiral acres of bloated rose coiled	93	& POST IMPR 5	5
ACROBATA			
pinkthisgreen acr) o) greenthatpink) acrobata mong trees . .	385	NO THANKS 2	44
ACROBATIC			
spontaneous clumsy trivi- al acrobatic edgeless gesture of .	193	XLI PORTRAIT 1	20
ACROSS			
air stooped with fear, across the harvest whitely peer . . .	11	T&C SONGS 2	23
am who wanders imminently across the renewed world" to . . .	91	& POST IMPR 3	18
wet, warm lips limp, across my bruising smile; as	137	& SON REAL 8	8
him on her knees across the locked room. he	145	& SON REAL 16	3
sunlight falls and, cruelly, across the grass Comes the . . .	190	XLI SONGS 12	9
steeds moving to war across the smiling meads; thou	209	XLI SONNETS 5	5
upon the accurate moon.... Across the important gardens her .	214	XLI SONNETS 10	10
moments go and go across this dirtied pane where	218	XLI SONNETS 14	10
tumbles; rolling in sand. across this water, crowding tints:	281	IS 5 THREE 5	5
/ / swi (across! gold's rouNdly) ftblac	429	NO THANKS 46	2
/ mrs & mr across the way are kind	501	50 POEMS 15	2
+ACROSS			
FOR CONTEXT, SEE	171	& SON ACTU 20	2
FOR CONTEXT, SEE	332	VIVA 23	20
ACRUISE			
grim yessing childflesh perpetually acruise and her quick way	337	VIVA 28	7
ACT			
worthy in the fragile act of doing her eyebrows.	228	IS 5 ONE MARJ	12
"kill" killing is an act of christian love. "Nothing"	636	(CHAIRE) 38	8
ACTED			
see how nice she acted right up to the	248	IS 5 ONE 19	26
+ACTION			
FOR CONTEXT, SEE	474	NEW POEMS 12	13
ACTIONS			
astonished should from their actions and speeches sawdust . .	261	IS 5 ONE 31	4
ACTUAL			
feels the keen ecstatic actual tread (and thereto perfectly .	19	T&C PUELLA MEA	125
findingly new textures of actual cool stupendous is nor . . .	373	VIVA 64	15
i'm and you are actual either hand is when	538	50 POEMS 50	10
all numerable mosts the actual more minds ignorant of	556	1 X 1 16	4
ACTUALITIES			
/ / / / SONNETS--ACTUALITIES a thing most new	82	T&C SON ACTU 1	T
/ / / / SONNETS--ACTUALITIES when my love comes	152	& SON ACTU 1	T

4

ACTUALITY
    intrinsic frag- ment of actuality), an orchid whose velocity 193 XLI PORTRAIT 1   25
ACTUALLY
    horribly scared i would actually fall off the rail . . . . . 263 IS 5 ONE 32   62
    these, your crisp eyes actually shall contain new faeries . . 294 IS 5 FOUR 11   9
    colour strike into form (actually) realness kill (make . . . 422 NO THANKS 39   7
    of all nothing will actually lift a luminous whole; . . . . . 649 (CHAIRE) 51   5
+ACTUALLY
    FOR CONTEXT, SEE . . . . 790 73 POEMS 18   14
ACUTE
    legs. painful ankles large acute brutal feet propped on . . . 103 & POST IMPR 13   7
    of a doomed impetuous acute sentience whose whitehot lips . . 193 XLI PORTRAIT 1   10
    tree among sunset dream acute from root to leaf) . . . . . . 362 VIVA 53   8
    only in the tide's acute weaving murmur / / . . . . 369 VIVA 60   21
    of with his gradual acute lusting glance an alert . . . . . . 374 VIVA 65   5
ADD
    weeness of boots tiny add death what shall? / . . . . 105 & PORTRAIT 1   10
    above all of Just Add Hot Water And Serve-- . . . . 230 IS 5 ONE 2   12
    necks begin) let us add that there are 50 . . . . 274 IS 5 TWO 9   16
    Gadgets murder squawk and add, the cult of Same . . . . 438 NO THANKS 54   11
    the least) except to add an A? henceforth he . . . . 650 (CHAIRE) 52   8
ADDED
    and be it needlessly added my Uncle Sol's farm . . . . 239 IS 5 ONE 10   13
ADDING
    thens by nows and adding and (i understand) is . . . . 500 50 POEMS 14   7
ADDRESS
    --tomorrow is our permanent address and there they'll . . . . 579 1 X 1 39   12
ADDS
    should say goodmorning trouble adds up all sorts of . . . . . 287 IS 5 FOUR 4   2
ADHUC
    / / / / ADHUC SUB JUDICE LIS when . . . . 706 95 POEMS 34   T
ADJUSTIN
    not exacly fat "father" (adjustin his robe) who now . . . . . 240 IS 5 ONE 11   4
ADMIRAL
    (bubs) where's Jim Soon Admiral Soon the saviour of . . . . . 642 (CHAIRE) 44   12
ADMIT
    pants have a hunch admit in threedimensional distress these . 150 & SON REAL 21   6
    moves.... and also, i'll admit--) till, at the corner . . . . 174 & SON ACTU 23   13
    me to decline to admit i've died) seeing your . . . . 329 VIVA 20   2
ADMITTING
    which i despise, frankly admitting i have been true . . . . . 43 T&C AMORES 7   21
ADO
    memory Of (without more ado about less than nothing) . . . . 317 VIVA 9   22
ADOLESCENT
    hell a song of adolescent ivory. / / / . . . . 214 XLI SONNETS 10   14
ADORABLE
    heartlike ears have flown adorable him self tail and . . . . 631 (CHAIRE) 33   5
ADORATION
    Lady of my unkempt adoration if i have made . . . . 43 T&C AMORES 7   2
ADORES
    the unspeaking watcher who adores perceived sails whose . . . 79 T&C SON UNRE 4   8
ADORING
    one amazing thing (secretly adoring shyly tiny winging . . . 591 1 X 1 51   21
ADORN
    nearly solved we dare adorn the whole with a . . . . 650 (CHAIRE) 52   14
ADROIT
    flesh doth entertain the adroit blood's mysterious skein (but 21 T&C PUELLA MEA 186
ADVANCING
    hugely) wish firmly. splendidly advancing colour strike into 422 NO THANKS 39   4
ADVANTAGE
    / / the great advantage of being alive (instead . . . . 664 (CHAIRE) 66   1
ADVENTURE
    is a more minute adventure) lady. The clumsy dark . . . . . . 98 & POST IMPR 9   12
    begins a whole verbal adventure to illimitably Grow / . . . . 557 1 X 1 17   15
    and even (we'll adventure the into most immemorial . . . . . 577 1 X 1 37   17
    green trance, would not adventure soon a deeper magic: . . . 675 95 POEMS 3   10
    much than littlest they adventure (wish by terror) steep . . 757 95 POEMS 85   20
    birds; unders of dream adventure truths of skies-- darling . 761 95 POEMS 88   8

		PAGE	TITLE	LINE

ADVENTURES
each (both and) Self adventures deathlessness / / / . . . . . 721 95 POEMS 49   14
ADVENTURING
most not imagined life adventuring who would feel if . . . . 450 NO THANKS 65   12
known swim ignorant fire (adventuring and time's dead which; 533 50 POEMS 45   17
not themselves believing eyes adventuring, enormous nowhere . 669 {CHAIRE} 71   4
+ADVENTURING
FOR CONTEXT, SEE . . . . 403 NO THANKS 20   3
ADVISE
give roses who will advise even yourself, lady in . . . . . . 294 IS 5 FOUR 11   3
AEONS
tree of jubilee: with aeons of (trivial merely) existence, . 763 95 POEMS 90   33
AERONAUT
this he shot the aeronaut down, into the abyss . . . . 360 VIVA 51   17
AESTHETE
preacher gargles jesus the aesthete indulges his soul for . . 108 & PORTRAIT 4   28
AFAR
one bird sing terribly afar in the lost lands. . . . . 76 T&C SON UNRE 1   14
AFFECTIONATE
that the pout And affectionate leer interminable pyramidal, . 243 IS 5 ONE 14   5
AFFIRM
Heaven.... i do signore affirm that all gondola signore . . . 256 IS 5 ONE 27   23
AFFIRMATION
enormous nowhere from) querying affirmation; virginal . . . . 669 {CHAIRE} 71   5
AFFORDS
of flanging shop-girls impersonally affords furnished a soft 197 XLI PORTRAIT 5   5
AFLAME
and over them this aflame with dreams incredible is) . . . . 832 73 POEMS 60   15
AFLICKF
where mil (lions of aflickf) litter ing brightmillion ofS . . 265 IS 5 ONE 34   3
AFLOAT
each why of star (afloat on not quite less . . . . 575 1 X 1 35   19
+AFLOAT
FOR CONTEXT, SEE . . . . 571 1 X 1 31   1
AFLUTTER
through the bruised air aflutter with pearls they are . . . . 34 T&C ORIENTALE 6 106
AFRAID
whose body words are afraid perfectly beautiful is, forgive . 22 T&C PUELLA MEA 240
under stones.) Don't be afraid and we will pass . . . . . . 86 T&C SON ACTU 5   10
a pen is dreadfully afraid of her of this . . . . 141 & SON REAL 12   3
would, only don't be afraid look the spangles that . . . . . 192 XLI CHANSONS 2   12
/ / who's most afraid of death? thou art . . . . 215 XLI SONNETS 11   1
art of him utterly afraid, i love of thee . . . . 215 XLI SONNETS 11   3
and not to be afraid. / / / / . . . . 264 IS 5 ONE 33   32
the poet who is afraid only to mistranslate a . . . . 291 IS 5 FOUR 8   9
vain: Nor am i afraid that this, which we . . . . 293 IS 5 FOUR 10   22
ever so very little afraid") i say "along this . . . . 303 IS 5 FIVE 2   7
knowing that you are afraid "go first" of dreams . . . . . . 353 VIVA 44   26
a little further--why be afraid-- here's the earliest star . 357 VIVA 48   1
eats moves remembers is afraid) each hates a Man . . . . . . 394 NO THANKS 11   8
strange? Married and lies afraid; aggressive and: American / 406 NO THANKS 23   15
they're old (kumrads aren't afraid to die kumrads don't . . . 413 NO THANKS 30   3
i (because they are afraid to love / / . . . . 413 NO THANKS 30   18
be damned with whomever's afraid down with ought with . . . . 424 NO THANKS 41   8
way are kind of afraid) afraid of what (of . . . . 501 50 POEMS 15   3
are kind of afraid) afraid of what (of a . . . . 501 50 POEMS 15   3
really really kind of afraid of) these (down pull . . . . . . 501 50 POEMS 15   24
any jerk who was afraid to dare to answer . . . . 636 {CHAIRE} 38   4
same because you aren't afraid to kiss the dirt . . . . 679 95 POEMS 7   5
dancing are they possibly afraid that life is running . . . . 724 95 POEMS 52   13
+AFRAID
FOR CONTEXT, SEE . . . . 469 NEW POEMS 7   18
FOR CONTEXT, SEE . . . . 705 95 POEMS 33   13
AFRICAN
waist continually with an African gesture utters a frivolous 95 & POST IMPR 7   6
AFT
be off duty wanderfuling aft spits) int o immensity . . . . . 465 NEW POEMS 3   4

		PAGE	TITLE	LINE

AFTER

solemn blinky eyeswhichneversmile and after he has caught a,   69   T&C POST IMPR 6   15
it is at moments after i have dreamed of   78   T&C SON UNRE 3   1
as silence, because Whirl's after all: (after me) love, . . . 160   & SON ACTU 9   12
because Whirl's after all: (after me) love, and after 160   & SON ACTU 9   13
(after me) love, and after you. I occasionally feel 160   & SON ACTU 9   13
link clauses of warmth (after dream who knows?) a 168   & SON ACTU 17   16
/ / / / after five times the poem 184   XLI SONGS 6   1
flesh I will rise After a thousand years lipping 189   XLI SONGS 11   14
accept all praise of after ages, and of hungering 209   XLI SONNETS 5   11
before the really train after all arrived. If i 263   IS 5 ONE 32   63
i say that even after April by God there 264   IS 5 ONE 33   7
whittles life to eternity --after which our separating selves 297   IS 5 FOUR 14   14
dreams to live on) after all, kid you might 298   IS 5 FOUR 15   12
his hat) go wandering after it with fingers; till 298   IS 5 FOUR 15   22
moves --climbing (past light after light) to turn, disappears 300   IS 5 FOUR 17   4
/ / / / after all white horses are 302   IS 5 FIVE 1   1
wor shipped her) who after not coming once in 320   VIVA 12   11
(carefully climbing carpeted flight after carpeted flight. in 375   VIVA 66   12
thick stickingly un stride after glide massacre monday did . 522   50 POEMS 35   4
/ / / / after screamgroa ning. ish: ly; 656   (CHAIRE) 58   1
mind with none) boy after girl each brings a 716   95 POEMS 44   10
mercy of perfect sunlight after days of dark, will 735   95 POEMS 63   12
(sEe) locked in gOLd after- gLOw are t ReMbLiN 838   73 POEMS 66   7

AFTERDAY

sweet heels of passed afterday, clothe thy soul's coming . .   10   T&C SONGS 1   39

AFTERGLOW

bells; perfectly outlined against afterglow are all amazing . 750   95 POEMS 78   3

+AFTERGLOW

FOR CONTEXT, SEE 838   73 POEMS 66   7

AFTERNOON

surmise she dreamed one afternoon ....or maybe read? of . . .   72   T&C SON REAL 3   9
decently hanged himself, one afternoon. The last thing he . . 170   & SON ACTU 19   4
a moon in the afternoon and warm air turning 279   IS 5 THREE 3   1
a typewriter, in the afternoon sky. goats and sheep 281   IS 5 THREE 5   7
the sea, in the afternoon. rapidly a reddish ant 281   IS 5 THREE 5   10
gives me, on this afternoon; i am a shape 360   VIVA 51   3
in his death at afternoon? (kow dow r 2 409   NO THANKS 26   2
(alone) in some autumnal afternoon: breathing a fatal 674   95 POEMS 2   2
/ / one winter afternoon (at the magical hour 802   73 POEMS 30   1

AFTERWARD

worms rushing through loam. (afterward i'll climb by tall . .   67   T&C POST IMPR 4   13

AFTERWARDS

lady, whose name is Afterwards she is sitting beside 102   & POST IMPR 12   24
assuming the laughter of afterwards-- i spirally understand . 356   VIVA 47   17

AGAIN

people saw their once again victorious Pantarkes (whose grace   4   T&C EPITHALAM   34
dark svelte and urgent (again love i slowly gather   37   T&C AMORES 2   16
not know thy smile again, lingering a little while   75   T&C SON REAL 6   4
told returned gather the Again: who danc ing goes   89   & POST IMPR 1   10
hope he'll do it again or if it talks 126   & SEVEN POEMS 5   17
the dance all over again and you, feel all 127   & SEVEN POEMS 5   36
and you, feel all again all over the way 127   & SEVEN POEMS 5   36
Bed --eh? I'm not. Again. Hush. God. Please hold. 130   & SON REAL 1   15
of me somewhere begins again, shares the year's perfect . . . 156   & SON ACTU 5   11
and which i will again and again and again 175   & SON ACTU 24   8
i will again and again and again kiss, i 175   & SON ACTU 24   8
again and again and again kiss, i like kissing 175   & SON ACTU 24   8
body turns toward thee again for the stars have 184   XLI SONGS 6   10
in neutral tried and again slo-wly; bare, ly nudg. 248   IS 5 ONE 19   15
the tea regressed. Kipling again H.G. Wells, and Anatole . . 263   IS 5 ONE 32   43
Anatole France shook hands again and yet again shook 263   IS 5 ONE 32   44
hands again and yet again shook again hands again, ... 263   IS 5 ONE 32   44
and yet again shook again hands again, the former 263   IS 5 ONE 32   44
again shook again hands again, the former coachman with . . . 263   IS 5 ONE 32   45
a pipewrench of the again latter then opening a 263   IS 5 ONE 32   46
you. I understand. Once again....) sliding a little downward, 282   IS 5 THREE 6   33
for because dear whispered again in never's ear (i'm 316   VIVA 8   4

AGAIN (CONTINUED)

	PAGE	TITLE	LINE
hoped we might "meet again sometime") vanished, gunwale . . .	326	VIVA 18	36
skirt exhumes (which buries again quick- ly its self	341	VIVA 32	15
high look (it's back again there therehere And) i	353	VIVA 44	23
by death: drowned only again carefully through deepness to .	369	VIVA 60	11
feet hands poising to again utterly disappear; rushing gently	369	VIVA 60	15
what ghostly nevers of again) silent not night by	432	NO THANKS 49	11
the hearse, see you again. Love (having found) wound	451	NO THANKS 66	8
and ask and ask again and) ask a brittle	498	50 POEMS 12	11
then a single hair again" marvels "and liars kill	572	1 X 1 32	17
trudges up to ignorance again: but winter's not forever, . .	579	1 X 1 39	2
are offering jonquils) down again who but zooms through . . .	585	1 X 1 45	17
a down up around again fly) forever was never	594	1 X 1 54	26
(let's remember) day died again and again; whose golden, . .	599	(CHAIRE) 1	1
day died again and again; whose golden, crimson dooms	599	(CHAIRE) 1	2
i'm certain they're (look again) flowers." "Don't worlds open	603	(CHAIRE) 5	6
lowing spewnonspew clutch) pers again & again (jukejog mist .	629	(CHAIRE) 31	18
clutch) pers again & again (jukejog mist & strict)	629	(CHAIRE) 31	18
mist & strict) & again (ly infin) It's Snowing	629	(CHAIRE) 31	20
if, when we meet again, little he (having flown	631	(CHAIRE) 33	7
have died am alive again today, and this is	663	(CHAIRE) 65	5
which will never happen again, a miracle which has	667	(CHAIRE) 69	6
earth puts on immortality again --her murdered selves	818	73 POEMS 46	4
they put on here again --to livingest one star	819	73 POEMS 47	16
not conceive--let ocean grow again / / / /	843	73 POEMS 71	14

AGAINING

deathless earth's innumerable doom: againing (yes by	821	73 POEMS 49	3

AGAINLESS

stirs as never (in againless depths of silence) and	758	95 POEMS 85	40

AGAINS

(s r BIRDS BECAUSE AGAINS emarkable s) h? y	421	NO THANKS 38	22
be, gi N s agAins t b ecomin gsky?	423	NO THANKS 40	9
/ ! blac k agains t (whi) te sky	487	50 POEMS 1	3
we no (smiling) strike agains De Big Boss (crying)	618	(CHAIRE) 20	9

AGAINST

trembling and smooth Unstrength, against the strong silences	11	T&C SONGS 2	9
my mouth petals danced against my eyes and down	39	T&C AMORES 4	19
feet and wings mounts against the margins of steep	59	T&C PORTRAIT 7	14
The trees, suddenly wait against the moon's face. /	80	T&C SON UNRE 5	17
(put your smallest ear against yester- day My Lady	110	& PORTRAIT 6	31
problem of colour floating against the clever deadly heaven .	112	& PORTRAIT 6	106
who buttons his coat against the wind / /	115	& PORTRAIT 8	28
the unmitigated systole purrs against my mind, the eyes' . .	136	& SON REAL 7	6
to. lean.... a little against me, when for two	148	& SON REAL 19	13
curving colour (say orange) against silence, or darkness....	152	& SON ACTU 1	5
/ / / fabulous against , a, fathoming jelly	159	& SON ACTU 8	1
i make me stern against your charming strength O	182	XLI SONGS 4	13
put on purple thought against the magnificent clamor of . . .	188	XLI SONGS 10	3
closed eyes to dash against darkness in the sleeping	189	XLI SONGS 11	7
street-lamps were turning snowy against a west of robin's . .	194	XLI PORTRAIT 2	3
the death of light, against whose enormous curve of	214	XLI SONNETS 10	3
Or with thy mind against my mind, to hear	215	XLI SONNETS 11	12
and less moonlight ourselves against the worms hate laugh . .	238	IS 5 ONE 9	20
sawdust chucks and rolls against the tent his thick	259	IS 5 ONE 29	6
his bunged hinging victim against the giving ropes amid . . .	259	IS 5 ONE 29	16
red pieces of day (against which and quite silently	278	IS 5 THREE 2	4
leans its dreamy spine against thick sunset i perceive . . .	279	IS 5 THREE 3	4
fat colour reared itself against the sky and the	283	IS 5 THREE 7	19
of my necktie wandered against my shirt and into	284	IS 5 FOUR 1	6
sunset it should, leaning against me, smile; or (between . .	285	IS 5 FOUR 2	13
me courage so that against myself the sharp days	293	IS 5 FOUR 10	20
their; puLLing: bright futures against the deep sky in . . .	314	VIVA 6	16
shaped object vomits cleverly against a quai wall almost . .	324	VIVA 16	7
of crowing gold) nuzzle against summer thunder (together) . .	340	VIVA 31	18
at nightfall; and because against this wall his white	355	VIVA 46	13
for Ills (a recipe against Laughing Virginity Death) then . .	359	VIVA 50	9
but more fleet) herself against the air--and whose do	378	VIVA 69	5
y <> Less? thE (against is) Swi mming	429	NO THANKS 46	9

	PAGE	TITLE	LINE
AGAINST (CONTINUED)			
flattened arms complain steadily against the west one Clock .	434	NO THANKS 51	13
vines (my heart pursues against the little moon a	434	NO THANKS 51	17
of dark voices sing against the awful mystery of	454	NO THANKS 69	14
is protected by cellophane against anything (because nothing	470	NEW POEMS 8	19
because do not stand against yes which is built	512	50 POEMS 26	29
work his shoulders marched against the dark his sorrow . . .	521	50 POEMS 34	44
and rainbows are insured against old age when every	620	(CHAIRE) 22	4
stand with me, love! against these its until you	633	(CHAIRE) 35	6
A D "can stand against the argument of mil	636	(CHAIRE) 38	10
prevail a million questionings against the silence of his . .	714	95 POEMS 42	13
of bells; perfectly outlined against afterglow are all . . .	750	95 POEMS 78	3
hearts have set saint against sinner; put gain over	769	95 POEMS 95	15
the rain) un til against my (where three dreams	785	73 POEMS 13	20
he StandS lift ing against the shrieking sky such	826	73 POEMS 54	11
+AGAINST			
FOR CONTEXT, SEE	333	VIVA 24	6
FOR CONTEXT, SEE	423	NO THANKS 40	9
FOR CONTEXT, SEE	487	50 POEMS 1	3
FOR CONTEXT, SEE	618	(CHAIRE) 20	9
FOR CONTEXT, SEE	687	95 POEMS 15	5
AGE			
of Mann's righteousness the age of dollars and no	266	IS 5 TWO 1	4
SPEED ASTERN) m usil (age) ini sticks tuh de	325	VIVA 17	3
are insured against old age when every thrush may	620	(CHAIRE) 22	4
generous --for youth read age-- read for sheer wonder	689	95 POEMS 17	2
/ / / old age sticks up Keep Off	729	95 POEMS 57	1
yanks them down (old age cries No Tres) &	729	95 POEMS 57	7
youth laughs (sing old age scolds Forbid den Stop	729	95 POEMS 57	12
it left; at the age of 8 ysomethi ng	792	73 POEMS 20	11
AGED			
/ / EPITHALAMION Thou aged unreluctant earth who dost	3	T&C EPITHALAM	1
o the sweet & aged people who rule this	250	IS 5 ONE 21	2
the town is so aged the ocean wanders the	505	50 POEMS 19	4
AGES			
fingers young the caving ages curiously con) --but the . . .	77	T&C SON UNRE 2	4
all praise of after ages, and of hungering days	209	XLI SONNETS 5	11
AGGRESSIVE			
Married and lies afraid; aggressive and: American / /	406	NO THANKS 23	15
AGILE			
which is filthy with agile swarming sonal crea- tures	69	T&C POST IMPR 6	5
I Want a Doll, wispish-agile feet with slid steps	140	& SON REAL 11	14
AGLOW			
immaculate perfume--whereby (with fear aglow) my soul is wont	19	T&C PUELLA MEA	108
all his hearty soul aglow) his nightly supper sups	254	IS 5 ONE 25	21
AGO			
of Herod's silence, long ago. If she a little	17	T&C PUELLA MEA	32
it perhaps a year) ago i found staring me	296	IS 5 FOUR 13	15
and ask and ask ago and) ask a simple	498	50 POEMS 12	27
stifles forests in white ago? Blow hope to terror;	560	1 X 1 20	12
/ / no time ago or else a life	648	(CHAIRE) 50	1
(the others have long ago laid them) i never	695	95 POEMS 23	13
name myself) one long ago who had died , ...	828	73 POEMS 56	6
AGONIZING			
is the sacred and agonizing proximity to its desire	193	XLI PORTRAIT 1	9
AGONY			
crimson years arched with agony i reined them in	30	T&C ORIENTALE 4	36
becoming garden of her agony / / / /	48	T&C IMPRESS 2	18
sags in frolicsome wooden agony). / / / /	134	& SON REAL 5	16
the jiggled norm of agony my grunting eyes pin	137	& SON REAL 8	10
hair-thin strands of magic agony ....by day this lady	146	& SON REAL 17	8
shares the year's perfect agony. Waiting (always) upon a . .	156	& SON ACTU 5	12
fatal tools in an agony of sensual chisels i	199	XLI PORTRAIT 7	5
metaphor opens the simple agony of time --small wonder . . .	842	73 POEMS 70	12
AGREE			
had (maybe they couldn't agree) not happened (and floating- .	652	(CHAIRE) 54	15
call their cowardice quite agree) shall never discover our .	664	(CHAIRE) 66	14
the chappy who doesn't agree (if you can't dentham	791	73 POEMS 19	4

9

AGREEABLE
    to lie a sharp agreeable flower between my amused . . . . . . 172 & SON ACTU 21   11
AGREEABLY
    imagine never mind Joe agreeably cheerfully remarked when . . 241 IS 5 ONE 12   2
AGREED
    alive all glories we've agreed with nothing deeper than . . . 741 95 POEMS 69   8
    which you've and i've agreed and we've (with one . . . . . 741 95 POEMS 69   12
AGREEMENT
    wisdom cancels conflict and agreement --saharas have their . 683 95 POEMS 11   6
AGRIN
    smoothness--and leave the bed agrin with memories (this white 164 & SON ACTU 13   10
AH
    for -gotten some- thing ah (my necktie / / . . . . 232 IS 5 ONE 3   17
    a forgotten prisoner --"Ici?" --"Ah non, mon cheri; il . . . 304 IS 5 FIVE 3   10
    rea- disa) ular, (ppear ah! Star whycol our ed . . . . . . 349 VIVA 40   10
    kemeruh daretoi nig) Ah, Soul / / / . . . . 474 NEW POEMS 12   16
    ns; unli, gh; t: "ah gwonyuhdoanfool me" toitselfw. hispering 710 95 POEMS 38   6
AHLBRHOON
    . (musically-who? pivoting) SmileS "ahlbrhoon / / / / . . . . 430 NO THANKS 47   31
AID
    fuzzy language with the aid of an exclamatory tooth-pick . . 194 XLI PORTRAIT 2   26
AIM
    an archer spy (whose aim had erred never) and . . . . 360 VIVA 51   15
    lilacs who proclaim the aim of waking is to . . . . 688 95 POEMS 16   5
AIMING
    of ridiculous molecules) nakedest (aiming for hugely the . . 373 VIVA 64   6
    for stalin was he aiming ; spare the child . . . . 643 (CHAIRE) 45   4
AIMS
    ungenerous who ape deftly aims they dare not share) . . . . 440 NO THANKS 56   21
AIN'T
    doesn't take your choice. Ain't freedom grand / / . . . . . 636 (CHAIRE) 38   14
+AIN'T
    FOR CONTEXT, SEE . . . . 310 VIVA 2   10
AINT
    day of their lives aint you, oo-oo. dearie not . . . . . . 109 & PORTRAIT 5   19
    some noive all right. Aint much on looks but . . . . 226 IS 5 ONE MAME   11
    "daughter" uv eve (who aint precisely slim) sim ply . . . . 240 IS 5 ONE 11   1
    my particular pal funny aint it we was buddies . . . . . . 270 IS 5 TWO 5   8
    god help me it aint no ews eye like . . . . 405 NO THANKS 22   10
    people well youknow kindof) aint & even (not having . . . . 412 NO THANKS 29   9
    was which the radio aint (proov -ing that the . . . . 425 NO THANKS 42   7
    born alive) some folks aint born somes born dead . . . . . 426 NO THANKS 43   10
    places on such babies aint plenty good enough for . . . . . 476 NEW POEMS 14   8
    to smoke and we aint got nothing to smoke: . . . . 489 50 POEMS 3   2
    to Sing and we aint got nothing to sing; . . . . 489 50 POEMS 3   6
    to die and we aint got Nothing to die, ... 489 50 POEMS 3   10
    to dream and we aint got nothing to dream . . . . 489 50 POEMS 3   14
    big as the world aint square with room for . . . . 568 1 X 1 28   17
    you red says it aint his daughter her father . . . . 707 95 POEMS 35   20
+AINT
    FOR CONTEXT, SEE . . . . 705 95 POEMS 33   13
AIR
    man forth into bright air, for now the red . . . . 4 T&C EPITHALAM   61
    of snow tickles the air to golden tears, and . . . . 5 T&C EPITHALAM   74
    When through the thin air stooped with fear, across . . . . . 11 T&C SONGS 2   22
    rare Slowness of gloried air... The flute of morning . . . . 12 T&C SONGS 2   45
    with indefinable flowering, the air is deep with desirable . 31 T&C ORIENTALE 5   11
    building he takes the air in a howdah of . . . . 32 T&C ORIENTALE 6   4
    depart through the bruised air aflutter with pearls they . . 34 T&C ORIENTALE 6 106
    fills with peacefully leaping air the minute mind of . . . . 62 T&C PORTRAIT 10   8
    into the flower- stricken air which is filthy with . . . . . 69 T&C POST IMPR 6   5
    it cleverly from, the air and stuff it seriously . . . . . . 69 T&C POST IMPR 6   10
    the final brain of air!) Let us as we . . . . 80 T&C SON UNRE 5   12
    lazily carved on sharpening air. Fields lying miraculous in . 86 T&C SON ACTU 5   6
    angels sharpen: themselves (on air) don't speak A white . . . 99 & POST IMPR 10   17
    b etw ee nch air st ott er s . . . . 104 & POST IMPR 14   16
    dangerous womb of cringing air) the largest hour push . . . . 115 & PORTRAIT 8   11
    placing an inch of air there) and without breaking . . . . . 124 & SEVEN POEMS 3 18

		PAGE	TITLE	LINE

AIR (CONTINUED)
```
sweetly to the mangling air muchness of buds mattered.   . . . 135 & SON REAL 6      13
club the faintly sweating air with pinkness, one pale  . . . . 144 & SON REAL 15      6
of flower strike the air in utterable coolness deeds   . . . . 163 & SON ACTU 12     7
from my window, night air bothered with a rustling   . . . . . 171 & SON ACTU 20     3
a clumsy brightness of air wonderfully stumbled above the . . 173 & SON ACTU 22     2
leap into the ripe air Alive with closed eyes . . . . . . . . 189 XLI SONGS 11       4
o'clock in the oblong air, from which a singular  . . . . . . 202 XLI PORTRAIT 9     50
with the astounding everlasting air-- but if i like,  . . . . 212 XLI SONNETS 8      12
the afternoon and warm air turning into January darkness  . . 279 IS 5 THREE 3      2
cries drifting through high air a sail a fishing  . . . . . . 283 IS 5 THREE 7       6
went creeping along the air over houses roofs And . . . . . . 284 IS 5 FOUR 1        14
the sprouting largest final air plunges inward with hurled  . 301 IS 5 FOUR 18       16
and leaves, filling the air with fear and sweetness. . . . . . 304 IS 5 FIVE 3       12
pale miles of perishing air, haunted with huddling infinite . 305 IS 5 FIVE 4        12
er (Er camef romth AIR / / / /  . . . . . . . . . . . . . . . 320 VIVA 12            25
(apparition.) WITH (THE ROUND AIR IS FILLED) OPENING /  . . . 348 VIVA 39            16
me a little: the air darkens and is alive-- . . . . . . . . . 357 VIVA 48            8
now hills invent the air) breathe simply my each  . . . . . . 372 VIVA 63            3
fleet) herself against the air--and whose do you suppose  . . 378 VIVA 69            5
little joe lives on air Harvard Brevis Est for  . . . . . . . 410 NO THANKS 27       4
And (night climbs the air / / / /. . . . . . . . . . . . . . . 428 NO THANKS 45      18
and strewed the black air with writhing alive skies--and  . . 432 NO THANKS 49      17
(whose feet almost walk air). now who stops. Smiles.  . . . . 437 NO THANKS 53       17
( here, inven ting air U ) sing tw  . . . . . . . . . . . . . 448 NO THANKS 63       3
inin -gness Am root air rock day) : you;  . . . . . . . . . . 449 NO THANKS 64       13
births of mind if air is throbbing prayers whom . . . . . . . 450 NO THANKS 65       6
poor how colding hereless. air theres what immense live . . . 491 50 POEMS 5        4
that if (so timid air is firm) under his  . . . . . . . . . . 520 50 POEMS 34       7
/ / / / air, be comes or (a)  . . . . . . . . . . . . . . . . 532 50 POEMS 44        1
while his maples wept air to blood, asked "something  . . . . 555 1 X 1 15          12
of tremendous darkness into air) / / / /  . . . . . . . . . . 559 1 X 1 19          14
mayflowers: quite eyes of air not with twilight's first . . . 577 1 X 1 37          5
man) nic he like wint-air nic like ot-am sum-air  . . . . . . 618 (CHAIRE) 20       23
wint-air nic like ot-am sum-air (young old nic) like  . . . . 618 (CHAIRE) 20       25
nic) like spring yoo un-air-stan? me crazy me like  . . . . . 618 (CHAIRE) 20       28
(fro on stiffening greenly air and to ghosts go . . . . . . . 633 (CHAIRE) 35       4
false, in earth in air in water and in  . . . . . . . . . . . 651 (CHAIRE) 53       7
welcoming sweet miracles of air (and joyfully all truths  . . 659 (CHAIRE) 61       2
/ / / now air is air and thing  . . . . . . . . . . . . . . . 675 95 POEMS 3        1
/ now air is air and thing is thing:  . . . . . . . . . . . . 675 95 POEMS 3        1
people walk in the air with almost breathing me)  . . . . . . 762 95 POEMS 89       8
swim love is the air the ocean and the  . . . . . . . . . . . 768 95 POEMS 94       4
and leaps upon the air) / / / /. . . . . . . . . . . . . . . . 774 73 POEMS 2        16
a web so subtle air is comparatively crude; an  . . . . . . . 799 73 POEMS 27       17
```
+AIR
```
FOR CONTEXT, SEE  . . . . . . . . . . . . . . . . . . . . . . 100 & POST IMPR 11    25
FOR CONTEXT, SEE  . . . . . . . . . . . . . . . . . . . . . . 755 95 POEMS 83       9
```
AIRY
```
turn O turn that airy hurdysturdygurdy but when will  . . . . 233 IS 5 ONE 4        2
```
AL-DOWN
```
and (th e moon's al-down) most whis per (here)  . . . . . . . 423 NO THANKS 40      7
```
ALARM
```
stale shriek like an alarm-clock) / / / /  . . . . . . . . . .  49 T&C IMPRESS 3     28
like POF goes the alarm off and the little  . . . . . . . . . 126 & SEVEN POEMS 5  10
at six exactly the alarm tore two slits in  . . . . . . . . . 132 & SON REAL 3      12
regard their roses with alarm and rainbows are insured  . . . 620 (CHAIRE) 22       3
her does not occur (alarm ing notion for idealists?  . . . . . 790 73 POEMS 18       10
```
ALARM-CLOCK
```
stale shriek like an alarm-clock) / / / /. . . . . . . . . . .  49 T&C IMPRESS 3     28
```
ALAS
```
weepings soundless, saying of "alas we were chaste on . . . .   9 T&C SONGS 1       21
with and leaves say alas, much is to do . . . . . . . . . . . 181 XLI SONGS 3       2
"Paul" a harvard boy alas! (who simply wor shipped  . . . . . 320 VIVA 12           8
```
ALBUTNOTQUITEMOST
```
/ / / / albutnotquitemost lost (in this br  . . . . . . . . . 695 95 POEMS 23       1
```
ALCHEMIST
```
are lost the divine alchemist, the magus of creation,  . . . .   6 T&C EPITHALAM    133
```

		PAGE	TITLE	LINE

ALE
din thinking drinking the ale, which never lets you . . . . . 96 & POST IMPR 8   23
+ALE
FOR CONTEXT, SEE . . . . 233 IS 5 ONE 4   6
ALEAK
this world is all aleak; and lifepreservers there are . . . . 438 NO THANKS 54   25
ALERT
creatures of idiom (beings alert and innocent very deftly . . 19 T&C PUELLA MEA   94
and-cling of stuffs the alert willing myth of body, ... 155 & SON ACTU 4   9
god why on the alert neck of this brittle . . . . 229 IS 5 ONE FRAN   2
still; we were two alert lice in the blond . . . . 289 IS 5 FOUR 6   24
acute lusting glance an alert clumsily foolishwise (tracking 374 VIVA 65   6
so is your heart alert, of languages there's none . . . . . . 575 1 X 1 35   26
alive --that is, completely alert and miraculously whole; . . 802 73 POEMS 30   15
+ALERT
FOR CONTEXT, SEE . . . . 430 NO THANKS 47   14
ALGEBRAIC
occasionally budding a flabby algebraic odour jigs et tout . 134 & SON REAL 5   8
exquisitely in- secure sharp algebraic music. For the first . 201 XLI PORTRAIT 9   20
ALGEBRAS
slightly joggled sink through algebras of proud inwardlyness 311 VIVA 3   10
ALGERNON
of Amy Sandburg of Algernon Carl Swinburned. Waiter a . . . . 233 IS 5 ONE 4   19
ALICE
shove of hiding pleasure. Alice, stinging quips of flesh. . . 138 & SON REAL 9   14
her men? buried with Alice in her hair, (but . . . . 183 XLI SONGS 5   4
pal dropped o god alice yells but who shot . . . . 496 50 POEMS 10   7
man. Up sam (down! alice) a hole in the . . . . 513 50 POEMS 27   23
ALIGHT
her slim lascivious arms alight in skilful wrists which . . . 20 T&C PUELLA MEA   157
ALIGHTING
the king & queen alighting from their limousine inhabit . . . 245 IS 5 ONE 16   3
of imprecision, you'll (silently alighting) and i'll sing . . 659 (CHAIRE) 61   12
+ALIGHTING
FOR CONTEXT, SEE . . . . 833 73 POEMS 61   6
ALIKE
some old none look alike the flics rush batter . . . . 274 IS 5 TWO 9   5
ALIMONY
perceive or minus news alimony blackmail whathavewe and . . . 391 NO THANKS 8   11
ALINGWAYSING
the ant (al ways alingwaysing) go to the ant . . . . 403 NO THANKS 20   20
ALIVE
day my lady utterly alive, to me is a . . . . 17 T&C PUELLA MEA   24
tail which is allbyitself alive. (and he has a . . . . 69 T&C POST IMPR 6   40
clock strikes, in the alive coolness, very faintly and . . . 92 & POST IMPR 4   14
rounded. if she were alive, death was amusing / . . . . 103 & POST IMPR 13   17
as if they were alive and number two took . . . . 117 & PORTRAIT 10   14
been Effie who isn't alive just imagine it I . . . . 117 & PORTRAIT 10   24
me wonder if i'm alive (eye pries, not open. . . . . 166 & SON ACTU 15   10
clumsy smelloftheworld. We intricately alive, cleaving the . 174 & SON ACTU 23   4
into the ripe air Alive with closed eyes to . . . . 189 XLI SONGS 11   5
flowers (stealthily) in the alive west begin requiescat this 277 IS 5 THREE 1   3
being, that i am alive this absurd fraction in . . . . 295 IS 5 FOUR 12   17
(who are so perfectly alive) my shame: lady through . . . . 306 IS 5 FIVE 5   12
air darkens and is alive-- o live with me . . . . 357 VIVA 48   9
that which we who're alive in spite of mirrors . . . . 386 NO THANKS 3   1
deathfuls) awaits yes this alive secretly i frantic this . . 415 NO THANKS 32   21
emptied. hills. listen. ,not, alive, trees, dream(ev: ery: . 416 NO THANKS 33   2
of pride and loneliness alive like some dream giving . . . . 418 NO THANKS 35   3
mys teriouSly ("i am alive") brave ly and . . . . 423 NO THANKS 40   3
/ / theys sO alive (who is ? niggers) . . . . 426 NO THANKS 43   1
jes livin not Jes alive But So alive (they . . . . 426 NO THANKS 43   6
Jes alive But So alive (they s born alive) . . . . 426 NO THANKS 43   7
alive (they s born alive) some folks aint born . . . . 426 NO THANKS 43   9
dead an somes born alive (but niggers is all . . . . 426 NO THANKS 43   12
is all born so Alive) ump-A-tum ; tee-die uM-tuM . . . . . . 426 NO THANKS 43   18
black air with writhing alive skies--and in death's place . . 432 NO THANKS 49   18
immeasurable into the mightily alive the dear beautiful . . . 464 NEW POEMS 2   35

	PAGE	TITLE	LINE

ALIVE (CONTINUED)

	PAGE	TITLE	LINE
from totally sprouted by alive green each very lifting . . .	480	NEW POEMS 18	23
yours mine . We're alive and shall be: cities	491	50 POEMS 5	11
one unsellable not buyable alive one i say human	524	50 POEMS 36	45
win less never than alive less bigger than the	530	50 POEMS 42	10
arrive (silent) one by (alive) from (into disappear and . . .	557	1 X 1 17	2
with pitying terrible some alive individual ten centuries of	561	1 X 1 21	5
wisping tinily the silverest alive silentness god ever . . .	572	1 X 1 32	9
heartbeat which i am alive to kiss / /	577	1 X 1 37	20
when, whatever is less alive than never begins to	580	1 X 1 40	21
them sing the dark alive but) look: begins to	582	1 X 1 42	7
brave bright cry of alive with a trill like	587	1 X 1 47	22
alone there's nobody else alive (such a sky and	591	1 X 1 51	12
(with a spin leap alive we're alive) we're wonderful	594	1 X 1 54	44
spin leap alive we're alive) we're wonderful one times . . .	594	1 X 1 54	44
queries of self pouring (alive twice) and becomes eithering .	613	(CHAIRE) 15	9
-ness) nine souls only alive with a single mys-	627	(CHAIRE) 29	13
never was death so alive: chaos so (hark --that	639	(CHAIRE) 41	5
five) neither dead nor alive (in real the rain)	640	(CHAIRE) 42	15
eagerly wandering (equally all alive in miraculous day) . . .	661	(CHAIRE) 63	6
of forever come riding alive down while crylessly drifting .	661	(CHAIRE) 63	12
catastrophe april might make alive filthy some past imagining	662	(CHAIRE) 64	4
who have died am alive again today, and this	663	(CHAIRE) 65	5
great advantage of being alive (instead of undying) is . . .	664	(CHAIRE) 66	1
and nothing and nonsense --alive; we're alive, dear: it's . .	665	(CHAIRE) 67	11
and nonsense --alive; we're alive, dear: it's (kiss me . . .	665	(CHAIRE) 67	11
person is (my love) alive than every world can	667	(CHAIRE) 69	4
& worlds are less alive than dolls & dream	680	95 POEMS 8	31
the dearest little women alive (but jim stood still	709	95 POEMS 37	14
by far than you're alive or i'm-- crying to	716	95 POEMS 44	32
a dream larger than alive any star goes round	735	95 POEMS 63	4
easily beyonds than timelessly alive all glories we've agreed	741	95 POEMS 69	7
(spilling his rings) threeing alive pasture and hills / . .	751	95 POEMS 79	7
prodigious Selves both now alive creatures (bright if by . .	757	95 POEMS 85	9
(are become more than alive) above anybody and fate	762	95 POEMS 89	11
lovetree! least the rose alive must three, must four	764	95 POEMS 90	50
poisoned mouse still who alive is asking What have	784	73 POEMS 12	5
i've no word except alive --that is, completely alert	802	73 POEMS 30	14
nowhere) goldenly whole, prodigiously alive most mercifully .	808	73 POEMS 36	6
her trillion secrets touchably alive --while and all	809	73 POEMS 37	4
as makes his moon alive sing more will wonderfully	811	73 POEMS 39	13
Must be your" perfectly alive blossom of a bliss	837	73 POEMS 65	11
away (as far as alive) lies april; and i	839	73 POEMS 67	5

+ALIVE

	PAGE	TITLE	LINE
FOR CONTEXT, SEE	444	NO THANKS 59	6
FOR CONTEXT, SEE	447	NO THANKS 62	3
FOR CONTEXT, SEE	471	NEW POEMS 9	16
FOR CONTEXT, SEE	528	50 POEMS 40	5
FOR CONTEXT, SEE	532	50 POEMS 44	5
FOR CONTEXT, SEE	534	50 POEMS 46	8
FOR CONTEXT, SEE	607	(CHAIRE) 9	8
FOR CONTEXT, SEE	740	95 POEMS 68	3
FOR CONTEXT, SEE	803	73 POEMS 31	18

ALIVEING

	PAGE	TITLE	LINE
or an amoral morality sort-of-aliveing by innumerable	410	NO THANKS 27	12

ALL

	PAGE	TITLE	LINE
is the time when all occasional things close into	6	T&C EPITHALAM	121
NICOLETTE dreaming in marble all the castle lay like	8	T&C OF NICOL	1
up her delicate silk) all white, with shining feet, ...	8	T&C OF NICOL	27
moment which shall seek all blossoms that do learn, ...	9	T&C SONGS 1	17
make early flowers of all things. thy hair mostly	13	T&C SONGS 3	2
/ / / / All in green went my	14	T&C SONGS 4	1
lucky hunter sang before. All in green went my	14	T&C SONGS 4	31
with her face and all the while shall my	16	T&C SONGS 6	13
like sudden flowers and all her body filled with	17	T&C PUELLA MEA	22
of Paris would not all the Troys of Helen's	18	T&C PUELLA MEA	67
with the twinge of all living intense things. Never	19	T&C PUELLA MEA	101
(past the luck of all dead men and loving)	19	T&C PUELLA MEA	103

ALL (CONTINUED)

scrupulous enchanted fronds toward all things intrinsic . . . 19 T&C PUELLA MEA 112
thereto perfectly responds) of all things exquisite and dead, 19 T&C PUELLA MEA 127
things exquisite and dead, all living things and beautiful. . 19 T&C PUELLA MEA 128
most beauteous, being for all things amorous fashioned very . 20 T&C PUELLA MEA 136
smile and quail) of all things perfect the most . . . . 20 T&C PUELLA MEA 162
body do distinctly live all sweet cities passed away-- . . . 22 T&C PUELLA MEA 257
me your ladies are all one-- keep your dead . . . . 23 T&C PUELLA MEA 264
beautiful ladies. Eater of all things lovely--Time! upon . . 23 T&C PUELLA MEA 266
gesticulates, and disappears-- of all dainties which do crowd 23 T&C PUELLA MEA 271
harem are queens of all the earth and the . . . . 33 T&C ORIENTALE 6 46
nakedness he nods and all depart through the bruised . . . . 34 T&C ORIENTALE 6 105
while the queens of all the earth writhe upon . . . . 35 T&C ORIENTALE 6 115
each fragrant night, when all my days shall have . . . . . . 39 T&C AMORES 4 31
dwells the breath of all persisting stars / / . . . . 40 T&C AMORES 4 47
is the passing of all shining things therefore we . . . . . 41 T&C AMORES 5 10
is the passing of all shining things no lingering . . . . . . 41 T&C AMORES 5 25
silence. I have seen all the silence filled with . . . . . . 45 T&C LA GUERRE 1 10
of the earth and all the trees are put . . . . 61 T&C PORTRAIT 9 21
flowers, and most of all i hear your stepping . . . . 61 T&C PORTRAIT 9 33
roofs are talking rapidly all together there happens . . . . 62 T&C PORTRAIT 10 18
of heaven full of all dreams, draws down. cover . . . . 65 T&C POST IMPR 2 6
have roses darling, it's all i ask of you-- . . . . 71 T&C SON REAL 2 6
faintly, wishes you with all her fragile might to . . . . . . 72 T&C SON REAL 3 8
his hands, saying, Accept all happiness from me. Then . . . . 76 T&C SON UNRE 1 12
god Is The Sea. All terrors of his being . . . . 77 T&C SON UNRE 2 10
the sky away and all the leaves away, and . . . . 80 T&C SON UNRE 5 2
large road crosses and all the people are minutely . . . . . 86 T&C SON ACTU 5 13
the Dark on us all; stories told returned gather . . . . . . 89 & POST IMPR 1 6
myself and Paris and all things) the bright rain . . . . . . 92 & POST IMPR 4 4
with its blue hair (all is eaten by yester- . . . . 112 & PORTRAIT 6 77
e n) 1- ing all go BlacK wh-eel-ing oh . . . . 122 & SEVEN POEMS 1 18
and I was hot all Hot and the bar . . . . 123 & SEVEN POEMS 2 5
) with your head. all big / / / . . . . 123 & SEVEN POEMS 2 15
kittens and pennies they all sit there looking at . . . . . 126 & SEVEN POEMS 5 6
stuff the poor thing all full of fingers dead . . . . 126 & SEVEN POEMS 5 13
than you so that's all you see but you . . . . 126 & SEVEN POEMS 5 26
like the way underclothes All so differ- ently solemn . . . 126 & SEVEN POEMS 5 27
hours and you take all your prickley-clothes off and . . . . 127 & SEVEN POEMS 5 33
give you, the dance all over again and you, ... 127 & SEVEN POEMS 5 36
again and you, feel all again all over the . . . . 127 & SEVEN POEMS 5 36
you, feel all again all over the way men . . . . 127 & SEVEN POEMS 5 37
you (but that's not all) because largeness tells you . . . . 127 & SEVEN POEMS 5 38
goes land- ing away all by himself on somebody's . . . . . . 127 & SEVEN POEMS 5 42
go up higher with all the pretty people than . . . . 129 & SEVEN POEMS 7 8
h get: breath once, all over, all how, funny . . . . 136 & SON REAL 7 14
night before Christmas when all through the house not . . . . 142 & SON REAL 13 12
a vine that's spent all of its life on . . . . 147 & SON REAL 18 11
in the hundred ands All the chips would kid . . . . 149 & SON REAL 20 10
becomes less. And then all her beauty is a . . . . 152 & SON ACTU 1 10
it's funny. They will all be dead knead of . . . . 153 & SON ACTU 2 4
be and i and all the days and nights . . . . 153 & SON ACTU 2 10
us see if that's all. Bit into you as . . . . 154 & SON ACTU 3 1
silence, because Whirl's after all: (after me) love, and . . 160 & SON ACTU 9 12
worn upon my mind all night, quitting only in . . . . 165 & SON ACTU 14 3
like little kittens are all the leaves which open . . . . . 191 XLI CHANSONS 1 7
the spangles that sleep all the year in a . . . . 192 XLI CHANSONS 2 14
and i'll give them all to you to hold . . . . 192 XLI CHANSONS 2 18
because you unflinchingly applaud all songs containing the . 204 XLI LA GUERRE 2 6
wrote in steel, accept all praise of after ages, ... 209 XLI SONNETS 5 10
caving stem. But of all most would i be . . . . 215 XLI SONNETS 11 9
pitiful: because i've travelled all alone through the forest 216 XLI SONNETS 12 11
duh woild; some noive all right. Aint much on . . . . 226 IS 5 ONE MAME 10
E. Pinkham, land above all of Just Add Hot . . . . 230 IS 5 ONE 2 12
now sing each and all fortissimo A- mer i . . . . 230 IS 5 ONE 2 36
there're a <> like all of you successfully if . . . . 231 IS 5 ONE 3 43
of (if you please) all the glory that or . . . . 233 IS 5 ONE 4 11
or which was Greece all the grandja that was . . . . 233 IS 5 ONE 4 12

	PAGE	TITLE	LINE
ALL (CONTINUED)			
/ / even if all desires things moments be	237	IS 5 ONE 8	1
/ / nobody loses all the time i had	239	IS 5 ONE 10	1
possibly most inexcusable of all to use a highfalootin . . .	239	IS 5 ONE 10	9
and i remember we all cried like the Missouri	239	IS 5 ONE 10	32
Lowell got up and all the little schoolchildren sat	249	IS 5 ONE 20	4
neck up is lead all over Brattle Street by	253	IS 5 ONE 24	14
wondrous fine sonofabitch (to all purposes and intents) in .	254	IS 5 ONE 25	6
his uncorrupted arse with all his hearty soul aglow)	254	IS 5 ONE 25	21
do signore affirm that all gondola signore day below	256	IS 5 ONE 27	23
puke i put him all into my arms and	258	IS 5 ONE 28	22
Paws of careful time all of which is extremely	260	IS 5 ONE 30	11
i had first of all really made quite a	262	IS 5 ONE 32	5
mistake in being at all born, seeing that i	262	IS 5 ONE 32	6
could be clearer to all concerned than that i	263	IS 5 ONE 32	40
hands from the tennisracket. All was over. One brief	263	IS 5 ONE 32	55
the really train after all arrived. If i should	263	IS 5 ONE 32	63
new frock coat (scrambling all up over the tribune	267	IS 5 TWO 2	4
the bugs crawling right all up all everywhere over	272	IS 5 TWO 7	10
crawling right all up all everywhere over you all	272	IS 5 TWO 7	11
all everywhere over you all me everyone that's been	272	IS 5 TWO 7	11
tidiyum reassuringly similar, they all have very tidiyum . .	274	IS 5 TWO 9	11
one (I) communist and all the flics are very	274	IS 5 TWO 9	19
memory faint -er than all the whys which lurk	282	IS 5 THREE 6	21
very middle of fire all the world becoming bright	283	IS 5 THREE 7	26
goodmorning trouble adds up all sorts of quickly things . . .	287	IS 5 FOUR 4	3
should say Now the all saucers but cups if	287	IS 5 FOUR 4	15
lady i swear by all flowers. Don't cry --the	290	IS 5 FOUR 7	10
--listen, for (out of all things) dream is noone's	292	IS 5 FOUR 9	9
under and thoroughly into all beautiful things) winter, whom	293	IS 5 FOUR 10	30
your heart softly; not all but the beginning of	294	IS 5 FOUR 11	19
shadows --what does it all come down to? love?	295	IS 5 FOUR 12	21
to live on) after all, kid you might as	298	IS 5 FOUR 15	12
most exquisite of cities) all of the long night	300	IS 5 FOUR 17	11
smile with knowing --and all about herself the sprouting . .	301	IS 5 FOUR 18	14
/ / / after all white horses are in	302	IS 5 FIVE 1	1
or to sum it All Up god being Dead	315	VIVA 7	9
the He-in-her (& both all hopped up) prettily then	317	VIVA 9	33
syriansang asong tohim self all about the desertbyIts elf . .	318	VIVA 10	12
n.y. the way of (all flesh is grass) with	320	VIVA 12	5
dribbling from the table all which seemed sweet deep	322	VIVA 14	7
ourselves two solids in (all one it) solution (of	323	VIVA 15	2
it doesn't look at all like what you and	323	VIVA 15	27
" aureally (yawning while all the dominoes) fall: down; . . .	331	VIVA 22	8
put right sleuthfully aboard all to--mendaciously speaking--a	334	VIVA 25	6
packed and released for all this very diminishing vicarious .	337	VIVA 28	10
instruments-- Olaf (being to all intents a corpse and	339	VIVA 30	15
hurriedly to shave) but--though all kinds of officers (a . .	339	VIVA 30	22
w : theraIncomIng o all the roofs roar drownInsound(. . . .	347	VIVA 38	18
; s (--sing)all are aLl (cry alL	347	VIVA 38	33
(--sing)all are aLl (cry alL See) o	347	VIVA 38	33
)all are aLl (cry alL See) o (ver All)	347	VIVA 38	33
alL See) o (ver All) Th (e grEEn ?eartH)	347	VIVA 38	33
to dare: prouder than all mountains, more than all	351	VIVA 42	6
all mountains, more than all oceans various and while	351	VIVA 42	6
heavens my mother will (all by herself) have one.	352	VIVA 43	1
the innocently Doomed brief all which somewhere is	356	VIVA 47	11
Out) & first of all foam -like hair spatters	358	VIVA 49	2
or none let's feel all) mind in mind flesh	364	VIVA 55	15
take you away --and all the clocks would run	365	VIVA 56	14
eyes is deeper than all roses) nobody, not even	366	VIVA 57	19
my dreams last night, all of your body with	369	VIVA 60	18
little more than twice all that so gently while	370	VIVA 61	12
/ / granted the all saving our young kiss	373	VIVA 64	1
no refuge keep though all the weird worlds must	377	VIVA 68	14
some bird which is all birds but more fleet)	378	VIVA 69	4
the thrilling least of all (for love's secret supremely . . .	379	VIVA 70	4
no (w ove (r all; o ver pinkthisgreen acr)	385	NO THANKS 2	41

15

ALL (CONTINUED)

dead seem generous) don't All suspect each (nor have	391	NO THANKS 8	4
like a grave) with all his toys (money men	394	NO THANKS 11	3
than the fear of all hearts never which have	397	NO THANKS 14	6
every nonelastic male-- uplook, all joybegotten whelps whom .	398	NO THANKS 15	18
/ / / IN) all those who got athlete's	404	NO THANKS 21	2
are of vicians and all the world howls stadesmen	405	NO THANKS 22	3
eye like the steak all ried but eye certainly	405	NO THANKS 22	11
and death knows whie (all good kumrads you can	413	NO THANKS 30	7
than wars of feet all things whose slendering sweetness . . .	414	NO THANKS 31	4
renown) suddenly themselves if all dreams unmake (when in . .	414	NO THANKS 31	5
dream giving more than all life's busy little dyings	418	NO THANKS 35	3
are mountains; and beyond all hurt of praise the	418	NO THANKS 35	13
enters my soul feels all small facts dissolved by	419	NO THANKS 36	5
unstrange learn (nor could all earth's rotting scholars guess	420	NO THANKS 37	8
the fly) for know all men ({CHAIRETE}) as it	425	NO THANKS 42	9
alive (but niggers is all born so Alive) ump-A-tum	426	NO THANKS 43	15
that heartbeat) mightily forgetting all which will forget him	428	NO THANKS 45	13
i win (like touch all stars or to live	433	NO THANKS 50	11
cult of Same is all the chic; by instruments, ...	438	NO THANKS 54	12
Christ, this world is all aleak; and lifepreservers there . .	438	NO THANKS 54	25
their blind fear --haunts all unsleep this cry of	439	NO THANKS 55	6
scheme to harness: let all unfools of unbeing set	439	NO THANKS 55	15
war whose naught and all sun are and moon	440	NO THANKS 56	25
(with brightness of peace) all places yes is a	443	NO THANKS 58	5
yes live (skilfully curled) all worlds / / /	443	NO THANKS 58	10
being wishless; but love, all of wishing) though life's . . .	446	NO THANKS 61	2
time totters, light droops, all measures bend nor marvel . .	446	NO THANKS 61	6
/ / / come (all you mischief- hatchers hatch	452	NO THANKS 67	1
mischief- hatchers hatch mischief) all you guilty scamper . .	452	NO THANKS 67	3
of doom rush (which all ghosts of life became)	454	NO THANKS 69	10
and lives imperishably feast all timeless souls (the not . .	456	NO THANKS 71	3
ver me you & all those & that "I	464	NEW POEMS 2	9
hell and heaven and all the religious fuss infinity	466	NEW POEMS 4	14
the cohn) down above all with love and everything	466	NEW POEMS 4	21
feel more better when all ought to feel less	466	NEW POEMS 4	24
kindest of ring & all one two three rings	470	NEW POEMS 8	17
is patient is (patiently all the eyes of these	478	NEW POEMS 16	10
infinite corner of love, all that i am easily	479	NEW POEMS 17	18
who could fail pulling all the sky over him	481	NEW POEMS 19	12
new (dark we all findingly Spring the Fragrance	482	NEW POEMS 20	8
/ you shall above all things be glad and	484	NEW POEMS 22	1
-prison a woman for all her now: but we've	491	50 POEMS 5	14
cheers for labor give all things to enni one	492	50 POEMS 6	11
the Ergo perished later all hands (you may recall)	494	50 POEMS 8	7
who stop damned fall all we go spill and	496	50 POEMS 10	14
strut-mince and stink-brag have all come to town some	497	50 POEMS 11	4
to vote for me (all decent mem and wonens	500	50 POEMS 14	21
lousy eyes roaming) wonderful all sky (a little mouth) . . .	501	50 POEMS 15	8
every tree or than all life more death begins	502	50 POEMS 16	8
dark around) five (are all dancesing singdance all are . . .	507	50 POEMS 21	4
(are all dancesing singdance all are three with faces	507	50 POEMS 21	4
singdance six dancesing three all around around all clouds .	507	50 POEMS 21	18
three all around around all clouds singing three and	507	50 POEMS 21	18
three menandwomen three and all around all and all	507	50 POEMS 21	22
three all around all and all around five	507	50 POEMS 21	22
all around all and all around five all around	507	50 POEMS 21	23
and all around five all around five around) five	507	50 POEMS 21	23
in a room's dark) all five are one flowers	507	50 POEMS 21	27
flowers five flowers and all one is fire /	507	50 POEMS 21	28
flower an hour in all, all) o yes to	509	50 POEMS 23	6
an hour in all, all) o yes to flower	509	50 POEMS 23	6
wholes not parts but all these hundreds upon thousands . . .	510	50 POEMS 24	9
will the impure think all things pure and hornets	511	50 POEMS 25	13
for us spilled) than all mankind something more small	514	50 POEMS 28	10
bring the kiddies let's all have fun / /	514	50 POEMS 28	14
for anyone not at all they sowed their isn't	515	50 POEMS 29	6
still anyone's any was all to her someones married	515	50 POEMS 29	16

	PAGE	TITLE	LINE

ALL (CONTINUED)

and was by was all by all and deep	515	50 POEMS 29	29
by was all by all and deep by deep	515	50 POEMS 29	29
looks and the is all floatful and remembering /	516	50 POEMS 30	18
am though dull were all we taste as bright, ...	521	50 POEMS 34	61
taste as bright, bitter all utterly things sweet, maggoty . .	521	50 POEMS 34	62
minus and dumb death all we inherit, all bequeath	521	50 POEMS 34	64
death all we inherit, all bequeath and nothing quite	521	50 POEMS 34	64
whole and more than all / / / /	521	50 POEMS 34	68
and began to sing all here is hands machine	523	50 POEMS 36	9
big even a thing all small and sad man, ...	526	50 POEMS 38	3
hope meets most despair? all knowing's having and have . . .	528	50 POEMS 40	10
it shall unbe than all the sea which only	530	50 POEMS 42	7
it cannot die than all the sky which only	530	50 POEMS 42	15
the, of each where all was is to be	533	50 POEMS 45	7
which now drop who all dreamlike (im / /	536	50 POEMS 48	20
your are birds our all and one gone away	541	1 X 1 1	6
are (yes they're gravensteins) all as red as to	543	1 X 1 3	4
/ / / of all the blessings which to	544	1 X 1 4	1
thumb a plus fingers all with blind him of	546	1 X 1 6	10
took his breath away all history oped her teeming	552	1 X 1 12	21
exactly nothing's soon; scream, all ye screamers, till your .	555	1 X 1 15	9
any quantity; but than all numerable mosts the actual	556	1 X 1 16	4
fiends and angels sing: all murdering lies by mortals	556	1 X 1 16	10
only rides his year. All lose, whole find /	556	1 X 1 16	15
come until (over dull all nouns) begins a whole	557	1 X 1 17	14
as easily creation up all sky (really unreal world, ...	558	1 X 1 18	13
snowingly enfolding glory is all angry common things to . . .	559	1 X 1 19	3
than the year (if all her most first little	559	1 X 1 19	13
blow death to was) --all nothing's only our hugest	560	1 X 1 20	23
with toys (than are all unworlds hollow silence has	565	1 X 1 25	7
come crashing into go (all than were nevers ugly	565	1 X 1 25	15
gone into what like all them kings you read	568	1 X 1 28	12
born to go let all go--the big small middling	569	1 X 1 29	15
really the biggest and all things--let all go dear	569	1 X 1 29	18
biggest and all things--let all go dear so comes	569	1 X 1 29	19
window saying if that's all, just if" "that's all	572	1 X 1 32	3
all, just if" "that's all there is to say"	572	1 X 1 32	4
life's the deathboard where all now turns when (love's . . .	574	1 X 1 34	6
ourselves continue to outgrow all whose mosts if you	574	1 X 1 34	13
not quite less than all of time) gives you	575	1 X 1 35	21
hearts live longer than all which and every who;	576	1 X 1 36	2
disprove by proving true (all doubts, all certainties, as . .	576	1 X 1 36	5
proving true (all doubts, all certainties, as villains strive	576	1 X 1 36	5
ask into his was all shall, their eyes would	576	1 X 1 36	14
/ / / / all ignorance toboggans into know	579	1 X 1 39	1
the game, what then? all history's a winter sport	579	1 X 1 39	5
i'd still insist that all history is too small	579	1 X 1 39	6
to grow more than all real, all imagining; and	582	1 X 1 42	9
more than all real, all imagining; and we who	582	1 X 1 42	9
gay earth opening is all the flowers of his	583	1 X 1 43	6
into if shall climb all the blue heaven green	588	1 X 1 48	2
(live live) spring with all beautiful things when to	589	1 X 1 49	11
wonder (beingest growingest) over all under all hate all . .	590	1 X 1 50	21
growingest) over all under all hate all fear --all	590	1 X 1 50	22
all under all hate all fear --all perfectly dyingest	590	1 X 1 50	22
all hate all fear --all perfectly dyingest my and	590	1 X 1 50	23
and viva sweet love" (all the merry little birds	591	1 X 1 51	5
more each than living's all multiplied with infinity sans . .	592	1 X 1 52	4
each around we go all) there's somebody calling who's	594	1 X 1 54	35
you were wrong --then all the way from perfect	599	(CHAIRE) 1	12
a particular tree are all breathing bright darkness to . . .	600	(CHAIRE) 2	8
to gether are slowly all together very magically smiling . .	600	(CHAIRE) 2	9
--but" lifting "flowers" more all stars than eyes "only . . .	603	(CHAIRE) 5	13
your breakfast every night all day) a 3ringbrain you	605	(CHAIRE) 7	5
wholly wallendas) ready were all erect your yous to	605	(CHAIRE) 7	11
undeluded notselfpitying lover of all things excellently . .	607	(CHAIRE) 9	10
is more much than all of timely space (was	608	(CHAIRE) 10	3

	PAGE	TITLE	LINE

ALL (CONTINUED)

	PAGE	TITLE	LINE
yet man can, being all, escape from none) so	609	(CHAIRE) 11	4
(is miraculous like tomorrow) all around the self of	617	(CHAIRE) 19	7
/ / jake hates all the girls (the shy	619	(CHAIRE) 21	2
meek proud sloppy sleek) all except the cold ones	619	(CHAIRE) 21	6
cold ones paul scorns all the girls (the bright	619	(CHAIRE) 21	8
slim plump tiny tall) all except the dull ones	619	(CHAIRE) 21	13
dull ones gus loves all the girls (the warped	619	(CHAIRE) 21	15
the mad moronic maimed) all except the dead ones	619	(CHAIRE) 21	20
dead ones mike likes all the girls (the fat	619	(CHAIRE) 21	22
mean kind dirty clean) all except the green ones	619	(CHAIRE) 21	27
new moon in if all screech-owls have not okayed	620	(CHAIRE) 22	6
some cannot pay at all he never seems to	624	(CHAIRE) 26	11
and he's clever) "for all, yes for all sweet	625	(CHAIRE) 27	7
"for all, yes for all sweet things are until"	625	(CHAIRE) 27	7
-nto wintry twi- light (all together a manying one	627	(CHAIRE) 29	8
than silence even tells) all the earth has turned	630	(CHAIRE) 32	9
him self tail and all (and his tail's red	631	(CHAIRE) 33	6
sink last things (least all turns almost now; now	633	(CHAIRE) 35	9
am quick i they'll all not conceive less who	634	(CHAIRE) 36	15
/ / / & (all during the dropsin king	646	(CHAIRE) 48	1
--from the reality of all nothing will actually lift	649	(CHAIRE) 51	4
(kneeling in doubt: while all skies fall) and then	650	(CHAIRE) 52	2
grandiloquent deep D; while all skies fall at last	650	(CHAIRE) 52	16
a single wish, receive all i am and dream	651	(CHAIRE) 53	4
nothing, and feels everything; all around whom is perfectly	657	(CHAIRE) 59	3
of air (and joyfully all truths of wing resuming)	659	(CHAIRE) 61	3
sunlight (side by side all in a singing wonder	661	(CHAIRE) 63	3
proudest eagerly wandering (equally all alive in miraculous	661	(CHAIRE) 63	6
reve and geoffrey and all) come up from the	661	(CHAIRE) 63	11
from the no of all nothing--human merely being doubt	663	(CHAIRE) 65	11
world (as timorous itsters all to call their cowardice	664	(CHAIRE) 66	13
are (above and under all possible worlds) in love	664	(CHAIRE) 66	18
and cringing --it's spring (all our night becomes day)	665	(CHAIRE) 67	18
day) o, it's spring! all the pretty birds dive	665	(CHAIRE) 67	19
heart of the sky all the little fish climb	665	(CHAIRE) 67	20
mind of the sea (all the mountains are dancing;	665	(CHAIRE) 67	21
our so right is, all (each thing most lovely)	666	(CHAIRE) 68	2
/ / / now all the fingers of this	667	(CHAIRE) 69	1
(darling) have hands, and all the hands have people;	667	(CHAIRE) 69	2
have no you: and all trees are (any more	667	(CHAIRE) 69	11
that white sleep wherein all human curiosity we'll spend	675	95 POEMS 3	12
& loathing for (dull all regular righteous comfortable)	677	95 POEMS 5	6
i can turn immense all time's because to why	679	95 POEMS 7	14
singing but more than all (as all your more	683	95 POEMS 11	13
more than all (as all your more than eyes	683	95 POEMS 11	13
good and kind to all" "o no no no	684	95 POEMS 12	12
yes in time of all sweet things beyond whatever	688	95 POEMS 16	10
brief (rose here&gone) flesh all is If all blood	690	95 POEMS 18	7
flesh all is If all blood And When /	690	95 POEMS 18	8
mad) fly (ly who all at) stops (once /	692	95 POEMS 20	7
we fell-- how have all time and space bowed	694	95 POEMS 22	5
(for no reason at all) reminds me the cheerfulest	699	95 POEMS 27	10
hell upon you and all filthy men come annabel	707	95 POEMS 35	21
announces night & day "all poor little peoples that	711	95 POEMS 39	7
her and marathon and all prehuman history and finally	711	95 POEMS 39	15
so rah-rah-rah democracy let's all be as thankful as	711	95 POEMS 39	26
smile --whose only secret all creation sings / /	714	95 POEMS 42	14
joy! joy) and whiteliest all wonderings are silence is	715	95 POEMS 43	15
the hell are we all morticians? / / /	727	95 POEMS 55	21
wintry me) that not all matterings of mind equal	736	95 POEMS 64	7
beyonds than timelessly alive all glories we've agreed with	741	95 POEMS 69	7
the amazing miracle of all / / / /	741	95 POEMS 69	14
the blessed eachness of all beautiful selves wholly which	745	95 POEMS 73	11
/ / / / all nearness pauses, while a	750	95 POEMS 78	1
a star can grow all distance breathes a final	750	95 POEMS 78	2
outlined against afterglow are all amazing the and peaceful	750	95 POEMS 78	4
takes (and he takes all) nor any marvel finds	750	95 POEMS 78	12

18

			PAGE	TITLE	LINE

ALL (CONTINUED)

	PAGE	TITLE	LINE
world ends more than all worlds begin to (see?)	750	95 POEMS 78	16
awaited by leaves with all their trees and by	754	95 POEMS 82	13
and by forests with all their mountains) / /	754	95 POEMS 82	14
that himself out of all silence strolls) nearness awakened, .	756	95 POEMS 84	10
fearless and complete love, all safely small big wickedly . .	761	95 POEMS 88	11
worlds of world disappear all and (like any these	761	95 POEMS 88	13
song to see: whose all (you're a sight to	763	95 POEMS 90	3
of (trivial merely) existence, all when may not measure . . .	763	95 POEMS 90	34
seize each nothing which all soulless wraiths proclaim . . .	765	95 POEMS 91	3
soulless wraiths proclaim substance; all heartless spectres,	765	95 POEMS 91	4
mind revealed (more than all dying life, all living	765	95 POEMS 91	7
than all dying life, all living death) and never	765	95 POEMS 91	7
be told sings only--and all lovers are the song.	765	95 POEMS 91	9
land (do lovers suffer? all divinities proudly descending put	768	95 POEMS 94	5
is the voice under all silences, the hope which	768	95 POEMS 94	9
the opening sky (the all the any merry every	773	73 POEMS 1	2
truth follow no path all paths lead where truth	775	73 POEMS 3	3
young (big little and all worlds) merely have the	776	73 POEMS 4	6
keen; big little and all) but lose or win	776	73 POEMS 4	12
they've (big little and all) no power beyond the	776	73 POEMS 4	22
bright; big little and all) whereas (my sweet) our	776	73 POEMS 4	28
both (big little and all) / / / /	776	73 POEMS 4	40
/ the first of all my dreams was of	777	73 POEMS 5	1
(with wonder into colours all into singing) may wonder . . .	778	73 POEMS 6	4
the earth more moving (all gay fair brave tall	778	73 POEMS 6	9
where soulless our (with all their minds) eyes blindly . . .	780	73 POEMS 8	7
love's every truth beyond all since and why asking	783	73 POEMS 11	4
whose form less form all goodness truth and beauty	790	73 POEMS 18	9
for idealists? so what) all politicians like the sight . . .	790	73 POEMS 18	12
stranger 'some people have all the luck; since our	800	73 POEMS 28	10
chary the wary (as all as con each) they	801	73 POEMS 29	8
/ / / / all which isn't singing is	804	73 POEMS 32	1
is mere talking and all talking's talking to oneself	804	73 POEMS 32	2
deafened every mother's son-- all is merely talk which . . .	804	73 POEMS 32	11
which isn't singing and all talking's to oneself alone . . .	804	73 POEMS 32	12
christ but they're few all (beyond win or lose)	805	73 POEMS 33	2
alone-- one (above nevermoving all nowhere) goldenly whole, .	808	73 POEMS 36	5
touchably alive --while and all mysteries which i or	809	73 POEMS 37	5
sun, my moon, and all my stars / /	810	73 POEMS 38	14
heart's each whisper wear all never guessed unknowable most .	811	73 POEMS 39	7
life who's your --when all fears hopes beliefs doubts	812	73 POEMS 40	13
lifts his life from all the dark who wings	815	73 POEMS 43	4
subhuman superminds declare --nor all their times encompass .	817	73 POEMS 45	4
near (one silent pasture, all a heartbeat dares; that	818	73 POEMS 46	8
green meteors swim signals all some world's millionary mind .	818	73 POEMS 46	12
star as small these all these thankful (hark) birds	819	73 POEMS 47	19
doom of sky (silently all then known things or	822	73 POEMS 50	7
/ / / of all things under our blonder	825	73 POEMS 53	1
ness as con founds all itcreating winds / /	826	73 POEMS 54	17
and a chickadee to all the world, but to	828	73 POEMS 56	4
wonderful tree smiling stand (all realms of where and	832	73 POEMS 60	6
more by most endure all that you never were	834	73 POEMS 62	12
since brave are cowards all) therefore despair, my heart . .	834	73 POEMS 62	22
will stop it With All The Policemen In The	835	73 POEMS 63	31
wind-- scatter his nothing all over what angry skies	839	73 POEMS 67	12
sun moon stars the all, & a (big ger	840	73 POEMS 68	12
ablaze with their voices) all shallbe and was are	841	73 POEMS 69	8
(undering proudly humbly overing) all bright all things swim	841	73 POEMS 69	27
humbly overing) all bright all things swim climb minds . . .	841	73 POEMS 69	27
shall turn; and from all selfsubtracting hugely doom	843	73 POEMS 71	7
/ / / / all worlds have halfsight, seeing	845	73 POEMS 73	1
climb can time with all his years) he's free	845	73 POEMS 73	8

+ALL

	PAGE	TITLE	LINE
FOR CONTEXT, SEE	109	& PORTRAIT 5	13
FOR CONTEXT, SEE	237	IS 5 ONE 8	11
FOR CONTEXT, SEE	251	IS 5 ONE 22	17
FOR CONTEXT, SEE	265	IS 5 ONE 34	6

		PAGE	TITLE	LINE

+ALL (CONTINUED)

FOR CONTEXT, SEE . . . . 265 IS 5 ONE 34   8

FOR CONTEXT, SEE . . . . 310 VIVA 2   9

FOR CONTEXT, SEE . . . . 445 NO THANKS 60   2

FOR CONTEXT, SEE . . . . 474 NEW POEMS 12   13

ALL'S

poppies, the dears; when all's done and said, and . . . . . . 181 XLI SONGS 3   11

sages say and fools, all's well / / / . . . . 768 95 POEMS 94   14

ALLABOUT

Kishcam elscasta? netsits Elf allaBout. (chic) -kchi cK, / . 318 VIVA 10   23

ALLBYITSELF

remarkable tail which is allbyitself alive. (and he has . . . 69 T&C POST IMPR 6   40

ALLEGIANCE

while kindred intellects evoke allegiance per blunt . . . . . 339 VIVA 30   14

ALLEMAND

knows? Who knows? Some "allemand" ....? of Goethe, since . . 158 & SON ACTU 7   6

ALLEN

my eyes go into Allen street the dark long . . . . 100 & POST IMPR 11   2

ALLEY

softly, in the hot alley, a nigger's voice feels . . . . . . 167 & SON ACTU 16   17

ALLEZCIRCULEZ

processions of minions <> "allezcirculez") --my he's . . . . 275 IS 5 TWO 9   39

ALLGOTUPFITTOKILL

/ <> this noN allgotupfittokill She with the & . . . . . . 726 95 POEMS 54   3

ALLL

shybrigHteyes is crum bs (alll) if, ey Es / . . . . 265 IS 5 ONE 34   8

ALLNESS

if than each known allness disappears lovers are mindless . . 563 1 X 1 23   6

ALLOFHER

brakes Bothatonce and brought allofher tremB -ling to a: . . 248 IS 5 ONE 19   34

ALLONS

fini pRaW, lT; O: allons 9 & . (musically-who? . . . . . . 430 NO THANKS 47   24

ALLOTTED

quivering, upon the sternly allotted sandpile --how silently 231 IS 5 ONE 3   51

ALLOWED

being taken out and allowed to shine, the balls . . . . . . 192 XLI CHANSONS 2   15

ALLOWS

mem and wonens will allows which if they don't . . . . . . 500 50 POEMS 14   22

ALLS

mirrors; sprung dimensionless new alls of joy: quietly & . . 480 NEW POEMS 18   21

ALLWHERE

fluttercrimbs are floatfallin, g; allwhere: a: . . . . . . 265 IS 5 ONE 34   5

ALMIGHTY

we thank thee god almighty for dying (forgive us, ... 604 (CHAIRE) 6   24

ALMOND

i got a Bad almond chick. thepinkisht artskiDs... with . . . 318 VIVA 10   17

ALMOST

in particular she gasped almost loudly i'm so drunG . . . . 53 T&C PORTRAIT 1   46

in singing--hands fragile whom almost tire the sleepshaped . 85 T&C SON ACTU 4   11

an eye winks). and almost i refrain from jumbling . . . . . 131 & SON REAL 2   6

putrid window every day almost leans a lady whose . . . . 144 & SON REAL 15   13

not too frail lips almost discussed; between her and . . . . 146 & SON REAL 17   12

rather than anything have (almost when hugeness will shut . . 163 & SON ACTU 12   20

hugeness will shut quietly) almost, your kiss / / . . . . . . 163 & SON ACTU 12   21

are eyeing, as with almost melancholy delicacy night gargles 168 & SON ACTU 17   18

the whole of life almost do guess) if god . . . . 205 XLI SONNETS 1   8

maturely childish, more beautiful almost than you. Yet if . . 211 XLI SONNETS 7   5

between you and me almost succeeds while toddle rings . . . 227 IS 5 ONE GERT   7

is this pale softish almost round young man to . . . . . . 245 IS 5 ONE 16   6

infantile phenomenon) George Washington almost incompletely . 262 IS 5 ONE 32   11

and buried eye) the almost large he- shaped object . . . . . 324 VIVA 16   5

against a quai wall almost spray -ing threecoloured puke . . 324 VIVA 16   7

were once knees) does almost ceaselessly repeat "there is . . 339 VIVA 30   32

no servants. We could almost live at the top . . . . 365 VIVA 56   6

a free room. We almost could go (you and . . . . 365 VIVA 56   8

dreamhorse moving (whose feet almost walk air). now who . . . 437 NO THANKS 53   17

who dares to stroll almost this god this surely . . . . . . 441 NO THANKS 56   48

not eyes quite try almost their mind immeasurably roots . . . 479 NEW POEMS 17   5

ALMOST (CONTINUED)
    more is are mostly almost are feebler than feeble . . . . . . 505 50 POEMS 19   22
    unless and children of almost) never shall guess the . . . . 512 50 POEMS 26   3
    be thrushes climbing through almost (do they beautifully . . 582 1 X 1 42   1
    wigglesome whisperful body and almost isn't (grabbed into . . 585 1 X 1 45   10
    the stupidest teacher will almost guess (with a run . . . . . 594 1 X 1 54   5
    things excellently rare; obsolete almost that phenomenon (too 607 (CHAIRE) 9   11
    say to sing you'd almost cut your thumb so . . . . 624 (CHAIRE) 26   15
    Tew Mee as somebody's almost moth er folds (but . . . . 629 (CHAIRE) 31   14
    things (least all turns almost now; now almost swims . . . . 633 (CHAIRE) 35   9
    turns almost now; now almost swims into a hair's . . . . . . 633 (CHAIRE) 35   9
    a by no means almost white morethanPerson; who (riding . . . 697 95 POEMS 25   18
    / out of night's almosT Floats a colour (in . . . . 719 95 POEMS 47   1
    ghostly doll of an almost vanished me (for whom . . . . 720 95 POEMS 48   9
    a why as i'm (almost too small for death's . . . . 735 95 POEMS 63   2
    as i'm a why (almost too small for dying's . . . . 735 95 POEMS 63   10
    until No least leaf almost stirs as never (in . . . . 758 95 POEMS 85   38
    in the air with almost breathing me) --look up: . . . . 762 95 POEMS 89   9
    effigy or seeming (an almost someone always who's noone) . . 812 73 POEMS 40   4
    smallest as perfect this (almost invisible where of a . . . . 827 73 POEMS 55   8
+ALMOST
    FOR CONTEXT, SEE . . . . 388 NO THANKS 5   13
    FOR CONTEXT, SEE . . . . 423 NO THANKS 40   7
    FOR CONTEXT, SEE . . . . 695 95 POEMS 23   1
    FOR CONTEXT, SEE . . . . 704 95 POEMS 32   11
    FOR CONTEXT, SEE . . . . 723 95 POEMS 51   16
    FOR CONTEXT, SEE . . . . 725 95 POEMS 53   3
    FOR CONTEXT, SEE . . . . 753 95 POEMS 81   7
ALMOSTCLEAN
    than street-lamps upon an almostclean plate "Achilles" said . 194 XLI PORTRAIT 2   33
ALMOSTNESS
    the sacred witchery of almostness which May makes follow . .   10 T&C SONGS 1   38
ALONE
    with pearls they are alone he beckons, she rises . . . . . .   35 T&C ORIENTALE 6 108
    because i've travelled all alone through the forest of . . . 216 XLI SONNETS 12   11
    a smile, one thought alone: to do or die . . . . 273 IS 5 TWO 8   11
    fewness of these colours; alone who slightly always are . . . 357 VIVA 48   12
    terrible than to be alone in the house, with . . . . 375 VIVA 66   2
    perfectly whO flOat newly alOne is dreamest oNLY THE . . . . 383 NO THANKS 1   7
    come foul he goes alone daring to dare for . . . . 440 NO THANKS 56   28
    calm star big yEs alone (wHo Yes near deep . . . .   455 NO THANKS 70   9
    near deep whO big alone soft near deep calm . . . . 455 NO THANKS 70   12
    ????Ht ?????T) Who (holy alone) holy (alone holy) alone . . . 455 NO THANKS 70   15
    Who (holy alone) holy (alone holy) alone / / . . . . 455 NO THANKS 70   15
    alone) holy (alone holy) alone / / / / . . . . 455 NO THANKS 70   15
    o a child who alone st and s (not . . . . 469 NEW POEMS 7   16
    to jack leave her alone she's not your gal . . . . 496 50 POEMS 10   2
    any two are perfectly alone there's nobody else alive . . . . 591 1 X 1 51   12
    is most lonely man alone (his briefest breathing lives . . . 609 (CHAIRE) 11   9
    / / to stand (alone) in some autumnal afternoon: . . . . . .   674 95 POEMS 2   1
    universe we'd (and we alone had) made --yes; or . . . . 675 95 POEMS 3   8
    and as large as alone. For whatever we lose . . . . 682 95 POEMS 10   10
    heartless spectres, happiness) lovers alone wear sunlight. .   765 95 POEMS 91   5
    all talking's to oneself alone but the very song . . . . . . 804 73 POEMS 32   12
    serenely truly himself; and alone only as greatness is . . . 808 73 POEMS 36   4
    only as greatness is alone-- one (above nevermoving all . . . 808 73 POEMS 36   4
    and my love are alone / / / / . . . .   813 73 POEMS 41   12
    tide at poise, love alone understands: only for whom . . . . 843 73 POEMS 71   5
ALONG
    wings flutters and flops along the grass collides with . . .   47 T&C IMPRESS 1   8
    min chb yi nch along the whirl- ingPeaceful furious . . . . . 100 & POST IMPR 11   38
    And The Moon came! along-along to the waggy silver . . . . . 125 & SEVEN POEMS 4 24
    And The Moon came! along-along to the waggy silver . . . . . 125 & SEVEN POEMS 4 24
    <> tables) while softly along Kirkland Street the infantile . 232 IS 5 ONE 3   11
    step smoothly and rapidly along this pole over five . . . . . 279 IS 5 THREE 3   15
    are driven by somebody along a curve of road . . . . 281 IS 5 THREE 5   8
    fall she went creeping along the air over houses . . . . . . 284 IS 5 FOUR 1   14
    beyond a little instant, along with rhyme and with . . . . . 293 IS 5 FOUR 10   11

		PAGE	TITLE	LINE

ALONG (CONTINUED)
little afraid") i say "along this particular road the . . . . 303 IS 5 FIVE 2   9
don't believe? look back. (Along the sand behind us, ... 303 IS 5 FIVE 2   11
/ / / / along the brittle treacherous bright . . . . 304 IS 5 FIVE 3   1
froid"-- they are gone: along these gardens moves a . . . . . 304 IS 5 FIVE 3   11
one's own memory (but) along perhaps the By invisibilities . 317 VIVA 9   19
+ALONG
FOR CONTEXT, SEE . . . . 319 VIVA 11   3
FOR CONTEXT, SEE . . . . 616 (CHAIRE) 18   11
ALONG-ALONG
And The Moon came! along-along to the waggy silver . . . . . 125 & SEVEN POEMS 4   24
ALOTTA
duh koib" --you know alotta sweet bull like dat . . . . 332 VIVA 23   12
ALREADY
to frail (whose grave already three or two young . . . . . . 115 & PORTRAIT 8   2
who as you've guessed already is the poorbuthonest workingman 254 IS 5 ONE 25   15
ALSEEP
gently while we were alseep while we were each . . . . 370 VIVA 61   15
ALSO
little sorry Another comes also picking flowers / / . . . . . 26 T&C CHANSONS 3   9
shining things therefore we also blandly into receptive . . . 41 T&C AMORES 5   11
and have comfortable minds (also, with the church's . . . . . 70 T&C SON REAL 1   3
she is Lust.... mine also, little painted poem of . . . . . . 75 T&C SON REAL 6   14
an intaglio. Nothing has also carved upon her much . . . . . 116 & PORTRAIT 9   9
mouth's coy rooting dies also. (my loveFist in her . . . . . 131 & SON REAL 2   8
bad laughters, smiles unbold) also, tomorrow the daily papers 142 & SON REAL 13   9
ball, i think and also i think of you, ... 169 & SON ACTU 18   5
you move.... moves.... and also, i'll admit--) till, at . . . 174 & SON ACTU 23   13
did you perhaps wish also shishkabob?" / / / . . . . 194 XLI PORTRAIT 2   38
your eyes, present me also with the terror of . . . . 285 IS 5 FOUR 2   15
as skilfully.) But carry also, with that indolent and . . . . 294 IS 5 FOUR 11   15
being "very interesting"... we also discussed the . . . . . . 326 VIVA 18   33
i guessed that he also had climbed the pincian . . . . 355 VIVA 46   12
our merely universe, love's also there: and being here . . . 377 VIVA 68   6
over (moving) you beautifully also; at denfert the fat . . . 384 NO THANKS 2   18
involved (this i who's also you) and nothing less . . . . . . 650 (CHAIRE) 52   10
beautiful my blossoming) for also then's until / / . . . . . 667 (CHAIRE) 69   14
world vanishes, teach disappearing also me the keen . . . . . 669 (CHAIRE) 71   13
/ / / but also dying (as well as . . . . 686 95 POEMS 14   1
moon are we're; but also nowhere / / / . . . . 686 95 POEMS 14   20
shines they are our also my darling) but should . . . . 728 95 POEMS 56   8
mistfully whispering rainlife) infinite also ourselves exist 755 95 POEMS 83   13
y are (mi dnite also conce als 2 ph . . . . 795 73 POEMS 23   13
her-and-his nonexistence vanishes with also earth's --"dying" 808 73 POEMS 36   13
ALTAR
absolute, unto the certain altar at whose head stands . . . .   6 T&C EPITHALAM   116
ALTER
(& mischievous tenderly phoebeing alter) clown of an angel . 678 95 POEMS 6   7
ALTERED
i cleverly am being altered that i slightly am . . . . 199 XLI PORTRAIT 7   8
ALTHOUGH
think will do it although the glad monosyllable jounce . . . 227 IS 5 ONE GERT   1
/ / but observe; although once is never the . . . . 282 IS 5 THREE 6   1
not spend my fortune (although endlessness should end) / . . 394 NO THANKS 11   14
why or because or although (and buds know better . . . . . . 594 1 X 1 54   10
without a little innocence, although it were as red . . . . . 649 (CHAIRE) 51   10
man will partly understand (although the wisest man am . . . 685 95 POEMS 13   11
singing welcome your coming although winter may be everywhere 717 95 POEMS 45   5
ALTITUDE
their mountains of having altitude--and march denounces april 620 (CHAIRE) 22   11
ALTOGETHER
faintly and finally through altogether delicate gestures of . 92 & POST IMPR 4   16
wear clothes. i am altogether foolish, i suddenly make . . . 281 IS 5 THREE 5   19
his buttonhole he is altogether a queer fellow as . . . . . . 296 IS 5 FOUR 13   3
+ALTOGETHER
FOR CONTEXT, SEE . . . . 600 (CHAIRE) 2   15
ALTOONA
rapidly denizens of Omaha Altoona or what not enthusiastic . 256 IS 5 ONE 27   26

	PAGE	TITLE	LINE

ALTRUISTIC
| can tell by their altruistic smell moscow pipes good . . . . | 413 | NO THANKS 30 | 8 |

ALWAYS
/ / / / Always before your voice my	11	T&C SONGS 2	1
feet crisply are straying. Always thy moist eyes are	13	T&C SONGS 3	9
(of her voice which always dwells beside the vivid	19	T&C PUELLA MEA	115
mind) --the vocal fern, always which feels the keen	19	T&C PUELLA MEA	124
eyes and lips consists --always upon the mouth there	20	T&C PUELLA MEA	148
my lady, in that always beyond this poem or	22	T&C PUELLA MEA	238
minstrel between them is always a pleasant song my	29	T&C ORIENTALE 3	14
behind whose ear sits always a crowned king twir-	32	T&C ORIENTALE 6	10
my hands herself to always keep" always? the young	57	T&C PORTRAIT 5	20
herself to always keep" always? the young man sitting	57	T&C PORTRAIT 5	21
Dick Mid's Place asked "always" Death said "then as	57	T&C PORTRAIT 5	26
the street unchangingly the always old lady always sitting .	58	T&C PORTRAIT 6	20
the always old lady always sitting in her gentle	58	T&C PORTRAIT 6	21
at whose gate smile always the chosen flowers of	58	T&C PORTRAIT 6	26
quite too large lips always clenched faintly, wishes you . .	72	T&C SON REAL 3	7
chunklike nose on which always the four tablets of	73	T&C SON REAL 4	8
1", white, prostitute. ducking always the touch of must . . .	74	T&C SON REAL 5	2
SONNETS--UNREALITIES it may not always be so; and i	76	T&C SON UNRE 1	1
(it was through tears always) and silence moulds such	78	T&C SON UNRE 3	7
man, whose here is always worse than naught, feels	81	T&C SON UNRE 6	11
floating snake upon itself always and slowly which upward . .	95	& POST IMPR 7	9
on his head flowers, always crying to nobody something . . .	102	& POST IMPR 12	15
nobody's ever visited, where always it's Spring) and	129	& SEVEN POEMS 7	13
just to see how always squirms the skilful mystery	130	& SON REAL 1	6
love.... do you? and always (i simply understand the	133	& SON REAL 4	9
et tout en face always wiggles the perfectly dead	134	& SON REAL 5	11
a thud of scarlet. always. More interesting, as i	143	& SON REAL 14	6
year's perfect agony. Waiting (always) upon a fragile instant	156	& SON ACTU 5	13
sudden body atop which always quivers the electric Distinct .	193	XLI PORTRAIT 1	2
make us shrill presents always shut in the sumptuous	195	XLI PORTRAIT 3	6
o'clock I stare only always into the tremendous canyon . . .	202	XLI PORTRAIT 9	43
the , tremendous canyon always only exhales a climbing . .	202	XLI PORTRAIT 9	44
rich slovenly obscene procession always floats through the .	202	XLI PORTRAIT 9	46
these haunters of dreams always demurely halfsmiling from .	211	XLI SONNETS 7	7
the grey and perpendicular Always-- or possibly there drift .	218	XLI SONNETS 14	11
in its three- cornered always moist mouth) --jazz, for . . .	227	IS 5 ONE GERT	5
wot's well behaved" ...and always try to not wonder	229	IS 5 ONE FRAN	11
dodderingly goddly toothless always-so-much-interested-in-. .	250	IS 5 ONE 21	13
A collarbutton which had always not nothurt me not	262	IS 5 ONE 32	16
program except last and always and first to live	264	IS 5 ONE 33	18
chain securely to this always talking individual, mysterious	279	IS 5 THREE 3	11
suspected (but wherein silently always are kneeling the . . .	285	IS 5 FOUR 2	19
us a new terror always which shall brighten carefully	289	IS 5 FOUR 6	10
have perhaps forgotten how, always (from these hurrying . . .	297	IS 5 FOUR 14	9
i am a beggar always who begs in your	298	IS 5 FOUR 15	1
cling to my mind always But now she sharpens	301	IS 5 FOUR 18	11
(Halfwhispering.... halfsinging stirs the always smiling . .	304	IS 5 FIVE 3	14
(ghost) Who screams Faintly always who Is bluish; next . . .	312	VIVA 4	8
is aunt death did always teethe / / /	316	VIVA 8	22
colours; alone who slightly always are beyond the reach . . .	357	VIVA 48	13
to speak are they always which creep budgingly over	359	VIVA 50	15
a neverish subchemistry of alWays)fiercely live whom on . .	361	VIVA 52	29
as fingers, you open always petal by petal myself	366	VIVA 57	7
Dreaming) somewhere behind us always trying (or sometimes . .	368	VIVA 59	10
at least i beat --always think i am gone	372	VIVA 63	7
hoists miraculously above the always beyond such wheres and .	378	VIVA 69	12
by you my heart always moves / / /	379	VIVA 70	14
dog? piglike big! sorrows always; finally and always, the . .	384	NO THANKS 2	12
sorrows always; finally and always, the iflike moon over . .	384	NO THANKS 2	12
run the world) A always don't there B being	390	NO THANKS 7	2
most ever lived people always) don't die (becoming most . . .	412	NO THANKS 29	14
unto men who are always men while a man	414	NO THANKS 31	13
a disappearing poet of always, snow and to morning;	424	NO THANKS 41	5
my mind, woven by always upon sunset, crickets within	435	NO THANKS 51	35
free truly which live always shall be may never	441	NO THANKS 56	63

23

	PAGE	TITLE	LINE

ALWAYS (CONTINUED)

then it's Spring immortal Always & lewd shy New	442	NO THANKS 57	20
realness bring-- ask the always impossible of me and	454	NO THANKS 69	2
/ may my heart always be open to little	481	NEW POEMS 19	1
away flimsy which but) always (they're more much further . .	501	50 POEMS 15	15
disappears they will disappear always who are filled with . .	505	50 POEMS 19	19
us home through never's always until absolute un gulps . . .	517	50 POEMS 31	12
is a flower of always their flowers of stone	525	50 POEMS 37	8
silent than silence these always children forever singing . .	525	50 POEMS 37	12
tree listens forever to always children singing forever a . .	525	50 POEMS 37	21
sea love is less always than to win less	530	50 POEMS 42	9
mr lipshits pres (who always nothing says) and he	552	1 X 1 12	27
a soul sunlight? yes (always we have heard them	582	1 X 1 42	6
merry in the blossoming always joyful selves are singing) . .	591	1 X 1 51	24
smiled "was and will always remain: who i am.	626	{CHAIRE} 28	6
what above did was always fall (yes but behind	634	{CHAIRE} 36	10
robbed of day) puts always on by always dream, ...	674	95 POEMS 2	8
puts always on by always dream, is to taste	674	95 POEMS 2	8
colossal (& daunted by always nothing) you darling diminutive	678	95 POEMS 6	2
try to fool has always failed to fool your	679	95 POEMS 7	8
or a me) it's always ourselves we find in	682	95 POEMS 10	12
only the truest things always are true because they	697	95 POEMS 25	31
me than i but always everything which only dies	718	95 POEMS 46	5
never grows old) is always beau tiful and that	724	95 POEMS 52	19
(when flowers) in credibly (always are beautiful) ugly" / . .	738	95 POEMS 66	16
glory a little more always less believably so than	748	95 POEMS 76	8
and still that singing's always his eyes can feel	760	95 POEMS 87	4
(only here) is freedom: always here no then of	765	95 POEMS 91	10
whatever a moon has always meant and whatever a	766	95 POEMS 92	8
whatever a sun will always sing is you here	766	95 POEMS 92	9
became silence: in huger always whom two tiny selves	777	73 POEMS 5	10
blue can be sky always (through fragrance and singing) . . .	778	73 POEMS 6	21
this darkness (in whom always i do nothing) deepens	785	73 POEMS 13	4
what does do, has always done ; & will	793	73 POEMS 21	19
it is now and always will be or the	803	73 POEMS 31	14
the teachable imposture of always arriving at the place . . .	807	73 POEMS 35	3
seeming (an almost someone always who's noone) a noone . . .	812	73 POEMS 40	4
of rain; and of always and of nowhere) and	816	73 POEMS 44	3
more than thanks of always merest me / /	821	73 POEMS 49	14
is a miracle" his always not imaginably morethanmostgenerous	823	73 POEMS 51	11
death's: any world must always half perceive. Only whose . .	845	73 POEMS 73	4

+ALWAYS

FOR CONTEXT, SEE	96	& POST IMPR 8	25
FOR CONTEXT, SEE	280	IS 5 THREE 4	28
FOR CONTEXT, SEE	345	VIVA 36	15
FOR CONTEXT, SEE	403	NO THANKS 20	12
FOR CONTEXT, SEE	403	NO THANKS 20	18
FOR CONTEXT, SEE	403	NO THANKS 20	20
FOR CONTEXT, SEE	611	{CHAIRE} 13	4
FOR CONTEXT, SEE	715	95 POEMS 43	7
FOR CONTEXT, SEE	793	73 POEMS 21	21

+ALWAYS-SO-MUCH-INTERESTED-

| dodderingly godly toothless always-so-much-interested- . . . | 250 | IS 5 ONE 21 | 13 |

AM

WORD DELETED, APPEARED 110 TIMES

AMARANTH

| bug fainarain wee celibate amaranth clutch owch so chuck . . | 333 | VIVA 24 | 21 |

AMASS

| urgent urn which doth amass for whoso drinks, a . . . . | 21 | T&C PUELLA MEA | 198 |

AMAYING

| fear, we will go amaying. thy whitest feet crisply . . . . . | 13 | T&C SONGS 3 | 7 |
| nor he that will amaying go with my lord . . . . | 20 | T&C PUELLA MEA | 169 |

AMAZE

| time of roses (who amaze our now and here . . . . | 688 | 95 POEMS 16 | 7 |

AMAZED

| whose imperishable smile the amazed doves flicker upon sunny | 6 | T&C EPITHALAM | 138 |

AMAZEMENT

| quite undo such first amazement as a leaf--here's one . . . . | 762 | 95 POEMS 89 | 5 |

AMAZING
    remember of this night amazing ecstasies slowly, in the . . .   36 T&C AMORES 1   22
    a whiskey-sour-- whose least amazing smile is the most   . . .   74 T&C SON REAL 5   14
    (moult beyond difficult moult) amazing doom who standest as . 351 VIVA 42   11
    / but being not amazing: without love separate, ... 374 VIVA 65   1
    your any most very amazing now or here) let . . . . 580 1 X 1 40   3
    thousands mean only one amazing thing (secretly adoring shyly 591 1 X 1 51   20
    welcoming dream: is amazing) a world. and in . . . . 657 (CHAIRE) 59   9
    God for most this amazing day: for the leaping . . . . 663 (CHAIRE) 65   1
    to call most the amazing miracle of all / . . . . 741 95 POEMS 69   14
    against afterglow are all amazing the and peaceful hills . . 750 95 POEMS 78   4
    steep) deep rush through amazing day it's brains without . . 769 95 POEMS 95   14
    one strict here of amazing most now, with what . . . . 840 73 POEMS 68   28
    how many moments must (amazing each how many centuries) . . . 843 73 POEMS 71   1
AMAZINGLY
    go out in pairs: amazingly, one pair is white . . . . 171 & SON ACTU 20   9
+AMAZINGLY
    FOR CONTEXT, SEE . . . . 827 73 POEMS 55   13
AMBER
    dust the ghastly warriors amber with lust breathe together .   34 T&C ORIENTALE 6 98
AMBIGUOUS
    incense for in the ambiguous faint aspirings the indolent . .   31 T&C ORIENTALE 5 15
AMBITIOUS
    gonorrhea Oldeyed child, to ambitious weeness of boots tiny . 105 & PORTRAIT 1   7
AMBROSIAL
    twain perfect roses whose ambrosial grace, goddess, thy . . .   6 T&C EPITHALAM   148
AMEN
    B.V.D. let freedom ring amen. i do however protest, ... 230 IS 5 ONE 2   15
AMERICA
    why granted who discovered America ether the movies may . . . 238 IS 5 ONE 9   14
    to of course god america i love you land . . . . 268 IS 5 TWO 3   1
    you were going to America. Then moving was a . . . . 289 IS 5 FOUR 6   21
    The) United States Of America unde negant redire quemquam . . 392 NO THANKS 9   19
+AMERICA
    FOR CONTEXT, SEE . . . . 230 IS 5 ONE 2   36
AMERICAINS
    anglais m'aiment tous, les americains aussi.... "bon dos, bon 120 & PORTRAIT 12   13
    sont gentils et les americains aussi, ils payent bien . . . . 120 & PORTRAIT 12   26
    ils payent bien les americains dance exactly in my . . . . . 120 & PORTRAIT 12   27
AMERICAN
    (as one merely terricolous American an instant doubts the . . 116 & PORTRAIT 9   12
    in brief : an American, if you understand that . . . . 262 IS 5 ONE 32   13
    youth the upper class American unsullied stands, before the . 273 IS 5 TWO 8   16
    lies afraid; aggressive and: American / / / / . . . . 406 NO THANKS 23   15
+AMERICAN
    FOR CONTEXT, SEE . . . . 200 XLI PORTRAIT 8   13
    FOR CONTEXT, SEE . . . . 708 95 POEMS 36   5
AMERICANS
    / / / FIVE AMERICANS LIZ with breathing as . . . . 225 IS 5 ONE LIZ   T
    ladies) --pretty littleliverpill- ◇ americans (who . . . . . 231 IS 5 ONE 3   48
    the coming of the Americans particularly the brand of . . . . 256 IS 5 ONE 27   13
AMERIQUE
    thy your ear: en amerique on ne boit que . . . . 233 IS 5 ONE 4   6
    sort-of-aliveing by innumerable kind-of-deaths (Amerique Je . 410 NO THANKS 27   13
AMETHYST
    clay clothed with incognizable amethyst. Lady at whose . . .   6 T&C EPITHALAM   136
AMIABLE
    / / / an amiable putrescence carpenters the village . . . . . 136 & SON REAL 7   1
    exposed his hibernative contours, amiable immensity . . . . . 197 XLI PORTRAIT 5   10
AMID
    it I say God amid a monstrous din watch . . . . 117 & PORTRAIT 10   26
    saw was you naked amid unnaked things, your flesh, ... 170 & SON ACTU 19   6
    O sweetly melancholy trillers amid the thrillers these . . . 230 IS 5 ONE 2   25
    Royce swoops smoothly outward (amid ◇ tables) while softly . 232 IS 5 ONE 3   8
    against the giving ropes amid screams of deeply bulging . . . 259 IS 5 ONE 29   17
    Peacepeacepeace (to droppingly descend amid thunderous . . . 267 IS 5 TWO 2   9
+AMMUNITIONS
    FOR CONTEXT, SEE . . . . 405 NO THANKS 22   7

AMONG
    shadow of secret bowers) among the curves of that . . . . . .   3 T&C EPITHALAM   23
    the emperor, exerting himself among his pillows throws jewels   34 T&C ORIENTALE 6 100
    of Her green body among unseen things, things obscene . . . .   77 T&C SON UNRE 2   2
    kew-ri-ous-ly a mong Them (among their stomachs andtheir . . 101 & POST IMPR 11   63
    sit, ata little roundtable among otherlittle roundtables Her, 104 & POST IMPR 14   3
    hair; feeling your knees among the supercilious chimneys, my   169 & SON ACTU 18   7
    They here enraptured, as among the slow deep trees . . . . .   208 XLI SONNETS 4   12
    thrillers these crepuscular violinists among my and your . .   230 IS 5 ONE 2   26
    Mr Tom Larsen twirls among pale lips the extinct . . . . . .   252 IS 5 ONE 23   5
    man who had fallen among thieves lay by the . . . .   258 IS 5 ONE 28   1
    / / / / Among these red pieces of . . . .   278 IS 5 THREE 2   1
    very (therefore and) softly among one's own memory (but) . .   317 VIVA 9   18
    children but men speaks (among leaves Easily through voices .   356 VIVA 47   3
    and once only, Queen among centuries universes between Who .   358 VIVA 49   12
    half daemon half tree among sunset dream acute from . . . . .   362 VIVA 53   7
    child 's shy foot among cool ferns) therefore . . . .   371 VIVA 62   13
    creature of shadow, that among first light groping washes . .   374 VIVA 65   14
    mov -ing ing ing among who dreams whom mutterings . . . . . .   384 NO THANKS 2   6
    put (only) a Leaf among dark ness. sunlight's thenlike? . . .   397 NO THANKS 14   16
    create voice if therefore among foul pains appears an . . . .   425 NO THANKS 42   13
    someone will lie (glued among familiar things newly which . .   428 NO THANKS 45   3
    touch less stillness (seized among what ghostly nevers of . .   432 NO THANKS 49   11
    cries nine, i stride among the vines (my heart . . . .   434 NO THANKS 51   15
    field (and i pause among the smell of minute . . . .   434 NO THANKS 51   24
    sp, arrow, s wince among those skeletons of these . . . . . .   442 NO THANKS 57   9
    and shall who wave among your deepening thighs a . . . . . .   454 NO THANKS 69   3
    excu se (in use among pu rposive pu nks) . . . .   477 NEW POEMS 15   6
    their mind immeasurably roots among much soundless rubbish of   479 NEW POEMS 17   6
    feet which is prayer among) float withins he upclimbest . . .   482 NEW POEMS 20   5
    or thrushes toward dusk among whippoorwills or tree field . .   512 50 POEMS 26   25
    star nicked ends next among broken odds of yes . . . .   522 50 POEMS 35   6
    each was of whom among not numerable ams (leaving . . . . . .   558 1 X 1 18   6
    (dreaming out of dreams among) no year will fall . . . . . .   573 1 X 1 33   11
    / / / if (among silent skies bluer than . . . .   583 1 X 1 43   1
    Strange known Face (whylaughing! among: skydiamonds / / / .   628 (CHAIRE) 30   13
    mystery of freedom? yet, among their loud exactitudes of . .   659 (CHAIRE) 61   10
    even the laziest creature among us a wisdom no . . . .   769 95 POEMS 95   8
    such a lay-- whom, among her dollies, dad first . . . .   794 73 POEMS 22   3
+AMONG
    FOR CONTEXT, SEE . . . .   101 & POST IMPR 11   63
    FOR CONTEXT, SEE . . . .   319 VIVA 11   1
    FOR CONTEXT, SEE . . . .   347 VIVA 38   12
    FOR CONTEXT, SEE . . . .   385 NO THANKS 2   44
AMONGOTHER
    a surely! little, roundtable amongother; littleexactly round. 104 & POST IMPR 14   21
AMONGS
    nd ArE GLIB SCARCELYEST AMONGS FLOWERING / / / . . . .   421 NO THANKS 38   31
AMOR
    with wormS eyes writhe amor (Though through our hearts . . .   361 VIVA 52   7
AMORAL
    chiefly submerged or an amoral morality sort-of-aliveing by .   410 NO THANKS 27   11
AMORES
    / / / / AMORES consider O woman this . . . .   36 T&C AMORES 1   T
AMOROUS
    on her flesh the amorous strain of gradual hands . . . . . .   4 T&C EPITHALAM   53
    dim slow perfect body amorous (whiter than lilies which . . .   5 T&C EPITHALAM   99
    being for all things amorous fashioned very curiously of . .   20 T&C PUELLA MEA   136
    the emperor is very amorous he reclines upon the . . . . . .   33 T&C ORIENTALE 6   54
    in the blue night amorous of waters tremulous, blinded . . .   37 T&C AMORES 2   5
    is like a woman amorous to be known; and . . . .   81 T&C SON UNRE 6   10
    a little uncouth and amorous in memory of Cleopatra . . . . . 111 & PORTRAIT 6   57
    i fall back, quietly amorous of, through the autumn . . . . . 158 & SON ACTU 7   12
    unkind dawn its muscle amorous pricks with minute odour . . . 165 & SON ACTU 14   4
    above the square, little amorous-tadpole people wiggled . . . 173 & SON ACTU 22   4
    floats through the thin amorous enormous only lips of . . . . 202 XLI PORTRAIT 9   47
AMOROUS-TADPOLE
    above the square, little amorous-tadpole people wiggled . . . 173 & SON ACTU 22   4

	PAGE	TITLE	LINE
+AMOROUSLY			
FOR CONTEXT, SEE	361	VIVA 52	7
AMOUNT			
by an impregnable Because (amount of inter -vening) anyway .	335	VIVA 26	14
AMPLE			
to grasp the belly's ample vase (that urgent urn	21	T&C PUELLA MEA	197
incorruptible Nothing under the ample sun, under the	43	T&C AMORES 7	38
AMPLIFY			
bump off or otherwise amplify others) the so to	391	NO THANKS 8	16
AMPUTATE			
little gould used to amputate his appetite with bad	410	NO THANKS 27	3
AMS			
ar pin g dre ams whichful sarcasms papery deathfuls)	415	NO THANKS 32	17
-tured together- ly singing ams trample (they flyingly . . .	482	NEW POEMS 20	11
whom among not numerable ams (leaving a perfectly distinct .	558	1 X 1 18	6
-it- eness dre (is) ams a the o f	820	73 POEMS 48	9
and who (2 little ams and over them this	832	73 POEMS 60	13
AMUS			
g toe hip popot amus Back gen teel-ly lugu-	107	& PORTRAIT 3	7
AMUSE			
like two elves incredibly amuse themselves) with a look . . .	17	T&C PUELLA MEA	40
AMUSED			
Sixteen you corking brute amused from time to time	74	T&C SON REAL 5	10
agreeable flower between my amused legs kissing with little .	172	& SON ACTU 21	12
your slim lips are amused, no wisest painter of	294	IS 5 FOUR 11	10
AMUSING			
were alive, death was amusing / / / /	103	& POST IMPR 13	17
his right slapped the amusing big vital vicious vegetable . .	148	& SON REAL 19	5
wax. Something, distinct and. Amusing, brittle / / /	164	& SON ACTU 13	17
AMUSINGLY			
/ / utterly and amusingly i am pash possibly	155	& SON ACTU 4	1
AMY			
and Old days: of Amy Sandburg of Algernon Carl	233	IS 5 ONE 4	18
curse and a frown Amy Lowell got up and	249	IS 5 ONE 20	3
AN			
WORD DELETED, APPEARED 149 TIMES			
ANAESTHETIZE			
murmur wink at kid anaesthetize marry bump off or	391	NO THANKS 8	15
ANARCHIST			
vivid voltaire you beautiful anarchist (i salute thee / . . .	677	95 POEMS 5	15
ANATOLE			
again H.G. Wells, and Anatole France shook hands again . . .	263	IS 5 ONE 32	43
ANATOMY			
joke on my passionate anatomy oh yes! Large legs	146	& SON REAL 17	6
ANCHORED			
/ not time's how (anchored in what mountaining roots	517	50 POEMS 31	1
ANCIENT			
accurately pants. and pompous ancient jews obscurely twitch .	219	XLI SONNETS 15	9
lay a wreath from ancient greath on insulated brows	500	50 POEMS 14	13
the streets are so ancient the houses enter the	505	50 POEMS 19	6
+ANCIENT			
FOR CONTEXT, SEE	616	(CHAIRE) 18	1
AND			
WORD DELETED, APPEARED 2145 TIMES			
AND-CLING			
eyes beyond a fit- and-cling of stuffs the alert	155	& SON ACTU 4	9
ANDDARK			
tend: ing: hush) andDark IshbusY ing-roundly-dis tinct; . .	416	NO THANKS 33	5
ANDS			
operated in the hundred ands All the chips would	149	& SON REAL 20	9
ANDSOFORTH			
and God's In His andsoforth do you get me?)	230	IS 5 ONE 2	29
ANDTHEIR			
Them (among their stomachs andtheir sexes) stomachsofold pe	101	& POST IMPR 11	64
ANDWHYEVERNOT			
with me he says (andwhyevernot) into the round well	127	& SEVEN POEMS 5	45
ANENT			
i do however protest, anent the un -spontaneous and	230	IS 5 ONE 2	15

ANENT (CONTINUED)
of pyro -technic blurb anent the (hic) hero dead . . . . . . 266 IS 5 TWO 1   12
with brushes recently employed anent this muddy toiletbowl, . 339 VIVA 30   12
ANGEL
your eyes half- thrush half-angel and your drowsy lips . . . 186 XLI SONGS 8   11
mediately. Thumbprints of an angel named Frederick found on . 262 IS 5 ONE 32   30
tinsel; silently yes before angel curvings upon a mostless . 480 NEW POEMS 18   12
generous completely light, an angel; or (as various worlds . 562 1 X 1 22   7
black skin of an angel named imagination / / . . . . 639 (CHAIRE) 41   14
alter) clown of an angel everywhere welcome (but chiefly . . 678 95 POEMS 6   8
A hummingbird princess FlOaTs doll-angel-life from Bet: To; . 747 95 POEMS 75   5
some neither ape nor angel called a man is . . . . 807 73 POEMS 35   7
+ANGEL
FOR CONTEXT, SEE . . . . 631 (CHAIRE) 33   1
ANGEL'S
upon the night, like angel's tears, the syllables of . . . . 8 T&C OF NICOL   10
the splendor of an angel's fart came one trembling . . . . . 506 50 POEMS 20   11
ANGELFACES
light of paradise-- by angelfaces clustered like bright lice 85 T&C SON ACTU 4   3
ANGELS
use for their youngest angels (whose praising bodies in . . . 20 T&C PUELLA MEA 142
Thick silence) blacktreesthink tiny, angels sharpen: . . . . 99 & POST IMPR 10   15
a score of youngest angels suddenly should stretch neat . . . 130 & SON REAL 1   5
the darkness) stood sharp angels with faces like Jim . . . . 241 IS 5 ONE 12   9
Loggia where are we angels by O yes beautiful . . . . 257 IS 5 ONE 27   31
song which fiends and angels sing: all murdering lies . . . . 556 1 X 1 16   9
fiends speak truth; if angels burn by their own . . . . 562 1 X 1 22   5
the devil and his angels too yes, sir what . . . . 568 1 X 1 28   19
with summitless younger than angels are mountains rivery . . 586 1 X 1 46   6
create precision more than angels fear to learn and . . . . . 842 73 POEMS 70   4
ANGER
dooms of feel; his anger was as right as . . . . 520 50 POEMS 34   35
ANGLAIS
suis belle cheri? les anglais m'aiment tous, les americains . 120 & PORTRAIT 12   12
(ladies accurately dead les anglais sont gentils et les . . . 120 & PORTRAIT 12   25
ANGLE
this taxi smile or angle we do not sell . . . . 238 IS 5 ONE 9   6
(eyes do bang hands angle scoot bulbs marry a . . . . 309 VIVA 1   12
+ANGLE
FOR CONTEXT, SEE . . . . 97 & POST IMPR 8   36
ANGLES
compose curves and yellows, angles or silences to a . . . . . 291 IS 5 FOUR 8   4
ANGLEWORM
june-bug and the frivolous angleworm thou dost persuade to . 61 T&C PORTRAIT 9   3
ANGLICAN
budge from kew a anglican was who (with a . . . . 552 1 X 1 12   7
ANGRILY
sunset their chimneys converse angrily, their roofs are . . . 62 T&C PORTRAIT 10 13
ANGRY
like a fragment of angry candy / / / . . . . 70 T&C SON REAL 1   14
cleverly-crinkling -water pursues the angry dream of the . . 160 & SON ACTU 9   5
describe what mimicry, with angry seasalt and indignant . . . 376 VIVA 67   4
enfolding glory is all angry common things to disappear . . . 559 1 X 1 19   3
nothing all over what angry skies and gently (very . . . . . 839 73 POEMS 67   12
+ANGRY
FOR CONTEXT, SEE . . . . 711 95 POEMS 39   19
ANGUISH
in trembling thirds of anguish quivers to your words, ... 11 T&C SONGS 2   17
whiten befall saith rain anguish of dream-send is hushed . . 90 & POST IMPR 2   5
-selves-U pcurv E, into: anguish (clim b) ing s-p-i-r-a- . . 278 IS 5 THREE 2   10
knows not if any anguish struck how thin a . . . . 414 NO THANKS 31   7
star could give that anguish room; but likes it . . . . 414 NO THANKS 31   10
remember love by frequent anguish (imagine Her least never . 453 NO THANKS 68   9
than most how immeasurable anguish pregnant one fearless one 523 50 POEMS 36   37
(most common, for each anguish is his grief; and, ... 562 1 X 1 22   3
fury: through joy and anguish) who've made her, outglory . . 742 95 POEMS 70   8
with its rapture and anguish) at peace with nature . . . . . 749 95 POEMS 77   14

	PAGE	TITLE	LINE

ANGUISHED
sun fingers numb) with anguished each their me brains . . . . 822 73 POEMS 50   3
ANIMAL
in the sweet slow animal bottomless eyes importantly banal, . 74 T&C SON REAL 5   6
flesh, a succinct wandlike animal, a little strolling with . 170 & SON ACTU 19   7
sixteen years of rapid animal whose swir -ling (not . . . . . 341 VIVA 32   12
Without a heart the animal is very very kind . . . . 544 1 X 1 4   25
we touched a shy animal called where and she . . . . 612 (CHAIRE) 14   10
there's your mineral general animal (five foot five) neither 640 (CHAIRE) 42   12
+ANIMAL
FOR CONTEXT, SEE . . . . 544 1 X 1 4   3
FOR CONTEXT, SEE . . . . 620 (CHAIRE) 22   14
ANIMALS
on these long talkative animals are laid fists of . . . . . 45 T&C LA GUERRE 1   8
moving, suddenly is three animals. The minute waist . . . . . 95 & POST IMPR 7   4
surrounded by fat stupid animals the jewess shrieked the . . 241 IS 5 ONE 12   3
into the world the animals continued eating. And i . . . . . 241 IS 5 ONE 12   6
to say to the animals and the animals had . . . . 326 VIVA 18   29
the animals and the animals had nothing to say . . . . 326 VIVA 18   29
marrying to themselves Life's animals) but not darkness shall 376 VIVA 67   5
ANISETTES
i sit, sipping singular anisettes as. One opaque big . . . . 220 XLI SONNETS 16   14
ANKLE
any monarch please.) Each ankle is divinely shy; as . . . . . 21 T&C PUELLA MEA 215
ANKLES
thy feet upon thy ankles are flowers in vases . . . . 29 T&C ORIENTALE 3   29
of queens comes forth ankles musical with large pearls . . . 33 T&C ORIENTALE 6   66
keenly lascivious legs. painful ankles large acute brutal . . 103 & POST IMPR 13   7
ANKUS
king twir- ling an ankus of ebony the fountains . . . . 32 T&C ORIENTALE 6   13
ANN
"so you're hunting for ann well i'm looking for . . . . 707 95 POEMS 35   1
darling come annie come ann" "she's coming right now . . . . 707 95 POEMS 35   22
ANNABEL
i just heard your annabel screech have you hunted . . . . . . 707 95 POEMS 35   5
all filthy men come annabel darling come annie come . . . . . 707 95 POEMS 35   22
ANNIE
as there's ladies my annie is one nor she . . . . 707 95 POEMS 35   11
come annabel darling come annie come ann" "she's coming . . . 707 95 POEMS 35   22
/ / / / annie died the other day . . . . 794 73 POEMS 22   1
your mother") had; making annie slightly mad but very . . . . 794 73 POEMS 22   5
ANNIHILATION
scatter pink propaganda of annihilation / / / / . . . . 150 & SON REAL 21   15
i wait the sweet annihilation of swift flesh i . . . . 182 XLI SONGS 4   11
+ANNIHILATION
FOR CONTEXT, SEE . . . . 197 XLI PORTRAIT 5   6
ANNIHILATOR
charming strength O haste annihilator drawing into you my . . 182 XLI SONGS 4   16
ANNOUNCE
our selves. create (suddenly announce: hurl) blind full steep 422 NO THANKS 39   15
ANNOUNCES
having ceased the captain announces that as three dimes . . . 196 XLI PORTRAIT 4   8
the voice-with-a-smile of democracy announces night & day . . 711 95 POEMS 39   6
ANNOYED
gave) responds, without getting annoyed "I will not kiss . . 339 VIVA 30   18
ANNOYS
a star or three annoys me, but the stink . . . . 169 & SON ACTU 18   2
ANNUAL
with exact death the annual brain clotted with loosely . . . 99 & POST IMPR 10   5
+ANNUAL
FOR CONTEXT, SEE . . . . 99 & POST IMPR 10   21
ANOINT
betwixt whose absolute feet anoint with calm of intent . . . 3 T&C EPITHALAM 30
where in tense starlessness anoint with ardor the yellow . . 37 T&C AMORES 2   10
ANON
hears in the frail anon the shovings and the . . . . 77 T&C SON UNRE 2   8
ANONYMITY
come? o come, terrible anonymity; enfold phantom me with . . 839 73 POEMS 67   9

	PAGE	TITLE	LINE

ANONYMOUS

and perfectly) nowhere vivid anonymous mythical guests of Is   557 1 X 1 17   5

+ANONYMOUS

FOR CONTEXT, SEE . . . . 449 NO THANKS 64   16

ANOTHER

eyes a little sorry Another comes also picking flowers . . .   26 T&C CHANSONS 3   8
whose deep squirm nibbles. another couches, weary, upon a . . 143 & SON REAL 14   11
lady called death get another man with firmer lips . . . . . 161 & SON ACTU 10   2
a finishes Helmar lights another x and y play, ...   200 XLI PORTRAIT 8   16
prefer this face to another and why do i . . . . 295 IS 5 FOUR 12   15
as fingers, loving one another gradually into hands) and . . 305 IS 5 FIVE 4   2
go) may i achieve another steepest thing-- how more . . . . . 558 1 X 1 18   10
(so easily one in another hides; yet man can, ... 609 (CHAIRE) 11   3
him with a smile another with a tear some . . . . 624 (CHAIRE) 26   10
boys" "he'll give me another if i let him . . . . 684 95 POEMS 12   9
quite --come such perfection-- another i and you, is . . . . 798 73 POEMS 26   24
finally released flee one another like the pest thus . . . . 799 73 POEMS 27   31

ANOTHER'S

have loved, should touch another's, and your dear strong . .   76 T&C SON UNRE 1   3
far away; if on another's face your sweet hair . . . .   76 T&C SON UNRE 1   5

ANSWER

and thou didst not answer thy mouth is as . . . .   27 T&C ORIENTALE 1   3
mcsorley's It, did not answer. outside. (it was New . . . . .   97 & POST IMPR 8   44
nod like buddha or answer modestly i am dying . . . . 198 XLI PORTRAIT 6   29
i would receive the answer more or less deserved, ... 229 IS 5 ONE FRAN   7
found" and smiling you answer "everything turns into . . . . 303 IS 5 FIVE 2   4
of not and same answer, beginning, ecstasy, to dare: . . . . 351 VIVA 42   5
mine should overhear and answer Who with the useless . . . . 374 VIVA 65   11
question my roses will answer" "but dying's meanwhile" (mind 625 (CHAIRE) 27   14
afraid to dare to answer "no"? quote citizens unquote . . . . 636 (CHAIRE) 38   4
every question time can't answer: and such vivid nothing . . 818 73 POEMS 46   10

+ANSWER

FOR CONTEXT, SEE . . . . 468 NEW POEMS 6   4

ANSWERED

and my love slowly answered I think so. But . . . . 102 & POST IMPR 12   22
it" their, hands minutely answered / / / / . . . . 255 IS 5 ONE 26   11

ANSWEREST

thy rhythmic lover thou answerest them only with spring) . .   46 T&C LA GUERRE 2   25

ANSWERING

recedes into weather without answering / / / / . . . . 279 IS 5 THREE 3   24

ANSWERS

stroke for now stroke answers (but now don't you're . . . . . 343 VIVA 34   4
summer puts on fur answers eats moves remembers is . . . . . 394 NO THANKS 11   8
(generalissimo e) and echo answers "there is no appeal . . . 636 (CHAIRE) 38   12
eagerly sweet carolling self answers me) "i could not . . . . 836 73 POEMS 64   9

ANT

afternoon. rapidly a reddish ant travels my fifth finger. . . 281 IS 5 THREE 5   11
the negro because he ant but Coolitch wiped his . . . . 321 VIVA 13   12
are) go to the ant (al ways alingwaysing) go . . . . 403 NO THANKS 20   17
alingwaysing) go to the ant thou go (inging) to . . . . 403 NO THANKS 20   21
go (inging) to the ant, thou ant- eater / . . . . 403 NO THANKS 20   24
to the ant, thou ant- eater / / / . . . . 403 NO THANKS 20   24

+ANTEATER

FOR CONTEXT, SEE . . . . 403 NO THANKS 20   24

ANTHOLOGIST

missed who as an anthologist sold the many on . . . . 551 1 X 1 11   2

ANTHROPOID

droppingly descend amid thunderous anthropoid applause) . . . 267 IS 5 TWO 2   9

ANTIBOLSHEVISTIC

of large immaculate unmute antibolshevistic gents (each . . . 266 IS 5 TWO 1   9

ANTICS

colossus whose irrefutable spiral antics involve me with the 201 XLI PORTRAIT 9   25
its soullessness by lonely antics of ridiculous molecules) . 373 VIVA 64   5

ANTIMERE

swim and who's myself's Antimere Should words carry weapons) 395 NO THANKS 12   9

ANTIQUITIES

of these antiquities--relaxing hurries elsewhere. . . . . . . 116 & PORTRAIT 9   14

		PAGE	TITLE	LINE

ANTONY

of Cleopatra and of Antony and we will confuse . . . . 111 & PORTRAIT 6   59

ANUS

every of a park anus stick some quote statue . . . . 636 {CHAIRE} 38   2

ANY

a little lovelier than any of your ladies were. . . . . 17 T&C PUELLA MEA   4
a little lovelier than any of those ladies were.) . . . . . . 20 T&C PUELLA MEA 134
ladies nothing care nor any lady dead and gone.) . . . . . . 21 T&C PUELLA MEA 180
sensual knees well might any monarch please.) Each ankle . . 21 T&C PUELLA MEA 214
beyond this poem or any poem she of whose . . . . 22 T&C PUELLA MEA 239
upon oblivion sweeter than any there is one; to . . . . 23 T&C PUELLA MEA 273
it is not like any songs (the singers the . . . . 43 T&C AMORES 7   6
/ / / / any man is wonderful and . . . . 68 T&C POST IMPR 5   1
little derricks of gesture any skyscraper bulges in the . . . 68 T&C POST IMPR 5   5
in the hoisting light any woman is smooth and . . . . . . 68 T&C POST IMPR 5 13
and who--touches--the hills without any reason (i have spoken 91 & POST IMPR 3   5
not suppose these without any reason and otherwise roses . . 91 & POST IMPR 3 15
a hurry beyond that any this taxi smile or . . . . 238 IS 5 ONE 9   5
simple, terse, seated like any king or prince upon . . . . . 254 IS 5 ONE 25 19
the blond absence of any program except last and . . . . . 264 IS 5 ONE 33 17
will not rub, like any other pastel. (While you . . . . . . 264 IS 5 ONE 33 24
to know the reason any more than.) But look: . . . . 282 IS 5 THREE 6   4
is first who pays any attention to the syntax . . . . 290 IS 5 FOUR 7   2
am i content should any by me carven thing . . . . . . 291 IS 5 FOUR 8 18
your gesture possibly or any painting (for its own . . . . 291 IS 5 FOUR 8 21
corner) never bother you any more. / / / . . . . 298 IS 5 FOUR 15 28
who may you be any how? down to smoking . . . . 314 VIVA 6 27
a corpse and wanting any rag upon what God . . . . 339 VIVA 30 16
i have seen on any man-- a little fluttering, ... 344 VIVA 35   8
thou shalt stand. Nor any dusk but kneelingly believes . . . 351 VIVA 42 13
/ if there are any heavens my mother will . . . . 352 VIVA 43   1
am a birdcage without any bird, a collar looking . . . . . . 360 VIVA 51 25
lips; a prayer lacking any knees but something beats . . . . 360 VIVA 51 27
never travelled, gladly beyond any experience, your eyes have 366 VIVA 57   2
are your eyes (shall any dream come a more . . . . 367 VIVA 58   9
by what neither is any echo of dream nor . . . . 368 VIVA 59   4
echo of dream nor any flowering of any echo . . . . 368 VIVA 59   6
nor any flowering of any echo (but the echo . . . . 368 VIVA 59   6
wheres and fears or any when unwondering immense . . . . . 378 VIVA 69 13
day) i mean, should any curious dawn discuss our . . . . . 379 VIVA 70   6
bathe who must or any dream means more than . . . . 390 NO THANKS 7 10
minds (but never had any to lose) and a . . . . 410 NO THANKS 27   8
which knows not if any anguish struck how thin . . . . . . 414 NO THANKS 31   7
man can 't hurt any more h u sh . . . . 472 NEW POEMS 10 15
some not every but any) heart--wholly, idiotically--before . 480 NEW POEMS 18   3
her only love whose any mystery makes every man's . . . . . 484 NEW POEMS 22   7
total sun oceaning than any this tear jumping from . . . . 502 50 POEMS 16   3
is a toe and any courage is a fear . . . . 511 50 POEMS 25 11
stir by still anyone's any was all to her . . . . 515 50 POEMS 29 16
say i have not any never no vacation here . . . . 523 50 POEMS 36 17
say the world yes any world is much too . . . . 523 50 POEMS 36 30
brightness with your eyes any illimitable star / / . . . . 526 50 POEMS 38 12
day are worlds collapsing? any was a glove but . . . . . . 538 50 POEMS 50   9
occur no death and any quantity; but than all . . . . . . 556 1 X 1 16   3
(mercifully) touch deathful earth's any which Weavingly now . 557 1 X 1 17 10
/ / / as any (men's hells having wrestled . . . . 558 1 X 1 18   1
a forever is love's any now and her each . . . . 576 1 X 1 36   9
each your least your any most very amazing now . . . . . . 580 1 X 1 40   3
not you behold nor any breathing creature this? nothing . . 582 1 X 1 42 11
or this (young trembling any) into flame twig or . . . . . 583 1 X 1 43 10
come awandering awondering but any two are perfectly alone . 591 1 X 1 51 11
miss them more than any bright word may cry . . . . 605 {CHAIRE} 7   7
aristide maillols occurred with any ticking of a clock . . . 617 {CHAIRE} 19 14
okayed his voice --and any wave signs on the . . . . . . 620 {CHAIRE} 22   7
than small is dirtiest any city's least street) of . . . . 623 {CHAIRE} 25   3
(there--see?) children" nor might any earth's first morning . 626 {CHAIRE} 28 13
that a hero equals any jerk who was afraid . . . . 636 {CHAIRE} 38   3
see now no not any christ but you must . . . . 638 {CHAIRE} 40 13

	PAGE	TITLE	LINE

ANY (CONTINUED)

	PAGE	TITLE	LINE
touching hearing seeing breathing any--lifted from the no of	663	{CHAIRE} 65	10
every leaf opens without any sound and wishing is	665	{CHAIRE} 67	8
and all trees are (any more than each leafless)	667	{CHAIRE} 69	11
them) i never (selves any than every more silent	695	95 POEMS 23	15
loveless some world not any un god manufacture might	698	95 POEMS 26	3
& i don't mean any thing real Ly what	701	95 POEMS 29	16
nothing's exAct ly what any one Living (or some	702	95 POEMS 30	3
perfectly blue) i am any (while around him streets	720	95 POEMS 48	4
our (home means if any moon or possibly sun	728	95 POEMS 56	5
/ / / when any mortal (even the most	731	95 POEMS 59	1
dream larger than alive any star goes round --a	735	95 POEMS 63	4
improbable world and without any doubt of impossible ours . .	748	95 POEMS 76	3
and crying) children whose any sadness or joy is	749	95 POEMS 77	8
he takes all) nor any marvel finds quite disappearance . . .	750	95 POEMS 78	12
silence strolls) nearness awakened, any bird should sing: and	756	95 POEMS 84	11
disappear all and (like any these my) words of	761	95 POEMS 88	13
a person; joyful your any new (every more only	764	95 POEMS 90	45
and an every (who's any who's some) one who's	769	95 POEMS 95	28
sky (the all the any merry every pretty each	773	73 POEMS 1	3
/ / / for any ruffian of the sky	774	73 POEMS 2	1
did & never will) any damn thing : far	793	73 POEMS 21	11
to err inhuman) or any thine a mine --dingdong:	798	73 POEMS 26	5
lend to borrow) or any foe a friend --cry	798	73 POEMS 26	19
and why? because without any doubt he was whatever	802	73 POEMS 30	10
fate and mine (or any truth beyond perceive) quivers	809	73 POEMS 37	2
to her eyes, not any longer blinded with a	811	73 POEMS 39	5
of (nothing i or any somebody or you can	816	73 POEMS 44	11
heartbeat dares; that mountain, any god) while leaf twig . .	818	73 POEMS 46	9
of fear; and under any silence of each bird	821	73 POEMS 49	7
/ i never guessed any thing (even a universe)	827	73 POEMS 55	3
"though your sorrows not any tongue may name, three	837	73 POEMS 65	2
you five hopes for any fear, but it Must	837	73 POEMS 65	9
dies to be at any moment born-- some for	842	73 POEMS 70	2
of things appear) death's: any world must always half	845	73 POEMS 73	4

+ANY

	PAGE	TITLE	LINE
FOR CONTEXT, SEE	493	50 POEMS 7	16

ANYBODY

	PAGE	TITLE	LINE
of life or did anybody Open a moment are	395	NO THANKS 12	4
/ if i or anybody don't know where it	475	NEW POEMS 13	2
by the by has anybody seen little you-i who	593	1 X 1 53	2
more than alive) above anybody and fate and even	762	95 POEMS 89	12
so damn sweet when Anybody-- yes; no matter who, ...	779	73 POEMS 7	2

ANYBODYELSES

	PAGE	TITLE	LINE
teen or sixty 000,000 anybodyelses-- but for once (imag . . .	779	73 POEMS 7	27

ANYHOW

	PAGE	TITLE	LINE
looked at whom first, anyhow dancing" (a moon swims	338	VIVA 29	20
child (& therefore invisible) anyhow you 've (whoever we . .	668	{CHAIRE} 70	14

ANYONE

	PAGE	TITLE	LINE
howling moves off will anyone tell him why he	196	XLI PORTRAIT 4	20
is hardly surprising if anyone hardly should call exactly . .	263	IS 5 ONE 32	35
mouse) Won derfully is anyone else entirely who doesn't . . .	397	NO THANKS 14	3
/ / / / anyone lived in a pretty	515	50 POEMS 29	1
and small) cared for anyone not at all they	515	50 POEMS 29	6
bells down) one day anyone died i guess (and	515	50 POEMS 29	25
their sleep noone and anyone earth by april wish	515	50 POEMS 29	31
floated a blossoming (while anyone might slowly count to . .	599	{CHAIRE} 1	9
beautiful darling) more than anyone on the earth and	717	95 POEMS 45	2
/ / never could anyone who simply lives to	718	95 POEMS 46	1
dear) is this --how anyone so gay possibly could	825	73 POEMS 53	5

+ANYONE

	PAGE	TITLE	LINE
FOR CONTEXT, SEE	492	50 POEMS 6	11
FOR CONTEXT, SEE	702	95 POEMS 30	3

ANYONE'S

	PAGE	TITLE	LINE
and stir by still anyone's any was all to	515	50 POEMS 29	16
to his earth; so anyone's world does -n't interest	676	95 POEMS 4	4
/ --laughing to find anyone's blind (like me like	716	95 POEMS 44	2

	PAGE	TITLE	LINE

ANYTHING
- nor am aware of anything save that these houses . . . . 98 & POST IMPR 9 — 15
- CAT WITH is there anything my ears love it's . . . . 100 & POST IMPR 11 — 33
- cOOl i didn't have anything on and I was . . . . 123 & SEVEN POEMS 2 — 4
- there) and without breaking anything. / / / . . . . 124 & SEVEN POEMS 5 — 19
- you lie still as anything in largeness and this . . . . . . 127 & SEVEN POEMS 5 — 35
- i should rather than anything have (almost when hugeness . . 163 & SON ACTU 12 — 19
- you stood thinking of anything, maybe the world.... But . . . 172 & SON ACTU 21 — 8
- a little love preferably, anything which you can't pass . . . 298 IS 5 FOUR 15 — 16
- perish (believe that not anything which has ever been . . . . 357 VIVA 48 — 5
- because he knows (that anything is bad which you . . . . . . 406 NO THANKS 23 — 4
- man, should he have anything would give a little . . . . . . 420 NO THANKS 37 — 1
- the human soul and anything else uncanned for everyone . . . 466 NEW POEMS 4 — 6
- dwo we know of anything which can be as . . . . 468 NEW POEMS 6 — 2
- protected by cellophane against anything (because nothing . . 470 NEW POEMS 8 — 19
- glad; nobody ever earns anything, everything little looks big 514 50 POEMS 28 — 8
- it you can git anything you like out of . . . . 567 1 X 1 27 — 12
- a song like not anything under skies over grass . . . . 587 1 X 1 47 — 10
- books don't grow) one's anything old being everything new . . 594 1 X 1 54 — 14
- calling who's we we're anything brighter than even the . . . 594 1 X 1 54 — 37
- old. Old may mean anything which everyone would rather . . . 626 (CHAIRE) 28 — 3
- H, and smile could anything be pleasanter (some big . . . . . 650 (CHAIRE) 52 — 5
- who why which (or anything) / / / . . . . 797 73 POEMS 25 — 24
- a word who was anything but dumb; since the . . . . 802 73 POEMS 30 — 26
- i should tell you anything" (that eagerly sweet carolling . . 836 73 POEMS 64 — 7

+ANYTHING
- FOR CONTEXT, SEE . . . . 594 1 X 1 54 — 18
- FOR CONTEXT, SEE . . . . 594 1 X 1 54 — 41
- FOR CONTEXT, SEE . . . . 701 95 POEMS 29 — 16
- FOR CONTEXT, SEE . . . . 827 73 POEMS 55 — 3

ANYTHING'S
- can't be done (and anything's righter than books could . . . 594 1 X 1 54 — 2

ANYWAY
- perfect life, dollies of anyway VIOLIN / / / . . . . 101 & POST IMPR 11 — 83
- nobody expects you to anyway dead says come with . . . . . . 127 & SEVEN POEMS 5 — 44
- april the twenty nellie anyway and it's flutters everything . 251 IS 5 ONE 22 — 3
- has are leap, which, anyway give rapid lapfulls of . . . . . 251 IS 5 ONE 22 — 21
- (amount of inter -vening) anyway You know Separated what . . 335 VIVA 26 — 15

ANYWHERE
- flower (whom i meet anywhere able to be and . . . . 367 VIVA 58 — 2
- two-made-of-one & nothing tells anywhere "snow will come . . 483 NEW POEMS 21 — 7
- am never without it (anywhere i go you go, ... 766 95 POEMS 92 — 2
- with not credible the anywhere eclipsing of a spirit's . . . 843 73 POEMS 71 — 9

APART
- sleepy morning) gently draws apart her curtains, and lays . . 8 T&C OF NICOL — 14
- like they would fall apart and masturbate with dynamite . . . 427 NO THANKS 44 — 11
- that's keeping the stars apart i carry your heart . . . . . . 766 95 POEMS 92 — 14

APE
- or creep ungenerous who ape deftly aims they dare . . . . . . 440 NO THANKS 56 — 21
- namely that some neither ape nor angel called a . . . . 807 73 POEMS 35 — 7

APISH
- & spurred with an apish grin (extremely like but . . . . . . 640 (CHAIRE) 42 — 6

APPALLING
- yearhour tree- spires shout appalling deathmoney into spiralS 346 VIVA 37 — 15

+APPARELED
- FOR CONTEXT, SEE . . . . 232 IS 5 ONE 3 — 2

APPARELLING
- solemnly and per rules apparelling its soullessness by lonely 373 VIVA 64 — 4

APPARITION
- darkness holds the genuine apparition of your smile (it . . . 78 T&C SON UNRE 3 — 6
- trois der die Stood (apparition.) WITH (THE ROUND AIR . . . . 348 VIVA 39 — 15

APPEAL
- answers "there is no appeal from reason" (freud) --you . . . 636 (CHAIRE) 38 — 12

+APPEAL
- FOR CONTEXT, SEE . . . . 492 50 POEMS 6 — 3

APPEAR
- to me there shall appear than a rose more . . . . 21 T&C PUELLA MEA — 175
- ivory if naked she appear to me my flesh . . . . 22 T&C PUELLA MEA — 231

APPEAR (CONTINUED)
    beneath a clumsiest disguise, appear capable of fragility and 91 & POST IMPR 3   12
    my treasure, when violets appear love is a deeper . . . . . . 578 1 X 1 38   8
    the guise of things appear) death's: any world must . . . . . 845 73 POEMS 73   3
APPEARANCE
    offspring has that largo appearance of somebody who was . . . 326 VIVA 18   9
APPEARED
    beloved i dreamed it appeared that you thought to . . . . . . 30 T&C ORIENTALE 4   4
    light her nice concupiscence appeared rounded. if she were . 103 & POST IMPR 13 15
    w the how dis (appeared cleverly) world iS Slapped: . . . . . 347 VIVA 38   4
    night clothed in sealace appeared to me your mind . . . . . . 369 VIVA 60   3
APPEARING
    a thingish o crashdis appearing con ter fusion ror . . . . . 646 (CHAIRE) 48   5
    to a lmost) dis appearing how patiently be coming . . . . . . 753 95 POEMS 81   9
APPEARS
    therefore among foul pains appears an if emerges a . . . . . 425 NO THANKS 42   13
    are full of eyes) appears. Because only the truest . . . . . 697 95 POEMS 25   30
APPEASE
    whose spiral hunger may appease what merely riches of . . . . 456 NO THANKS 71   4
    mere unmiracle can quite appease-- humbly in their imagined . 714 95 POEMS 42   5
APPETITE
    used to amputate his appetite with bad brittle candy . . . . 410 NO THANKS 27   3
    --gifted with every keener appetite than mere unmiracle can . 714 95 POEMS 42   4
APPLAUD
    and because you unflinchingly applaud all songs containing . 204 XLI LA GUERRE 2 6
    People stare, the drunker applaud while twilight takes the . 279 IS 5 THREE 3   17
APPLAUSE
    hast taken thy last applause, and when the final . . . . . . 75 T&C SON REAL 6   1
    descend amid thunderous anthropoid applause) pronounced by . 267 IS 5 TWO 2   9
+APPLAUSE
    FOR CONTEXT, SEE . . . . 548 1 X 1 8   1
APPLE
    maenads knows,-- having Discordia's apple in thy hands, which 6 T&C EPITHALAM   151
    picked you as an apple is picked by the . . . . 30 T&C ORIENTALE 4 42
APPLES
    plums of tangerines and apples it will, Gorge indistinct . . 100 & POST IMPR 11 26
    over this) wall the apples are (yes they're gravensteins) . 543 1 X 1 3   3
APPLIED
    by means of skilfully applied bayonets roasted hot with . . . 339 VIVA 30   29
APPRECIATE
    climbed the pincian to appreciate rome at nightfall; and . . 355 VIVA 46   13
APPRECIATION
    with my curiously instant appreciation exposed his . . . . . 197 XLI PORTRAIT 5   9
APPROACH
    whose armpits is the approach of spring thy thighs . . . . . 29 T&C ORIENTALE 3 10
+APPROACHED
    FOR CONTEXT, SEE . . . . 193 XLI PORTRAIT 1 11
APPROACHES
    and y play, effendi approaches, sets down coffee withdraws . 200 XLI PORTRAIT 8 18
    perceives (as the ego approaches) painfully sterilized . . . 319 VIVA 11   27
APPROACHING
    gnarled lips totter Therefore, approaching my twentysix . . . 255 IS 5 ONE 26   5
APPROVE
    to dream of you, approve these firm unsated eyes . . . . . . 36 T&C AMORES 1   9
    way-- (nervously Whose eyes approve the blessed while His . . 117 & PORTRAIT 10 35
APPROVES
    the world my blood approves, and kisses are a . . . . 290 IS 5 FOUR 7   7
APRIL
    the wild trump of April: witchery of sound and . . . .   4 T&C EPITHALAM   59
    the uncertain morning, with April feet like sudden flowers . 17 T&C PUELLA MEA 21
    body to me is April in whose armpits is . . . . 29 T&C ORIENTALE 3   9
    the correct fingers of April resolved into a clutter . . . . 47 T&C IMPRESS 1   3
    briefness Life: handorgans and April darkness, friends i . . 66 T&C POST IMPR 3 3
    / / Paris; this April sunset completely utters utters . . . . 93 & POST IMPR 5   1
    with little dints of april, making the obscene shy . . . . . 172 & SON ACTU 21   14
    / / / one April dusk the sallow street-lamps . . . . 194 XLI PORTRAIT 2   1
    a new turd in April his legs are brittle . . . . 198 XLI PORTRAIT 6 20
    on the Madam's best april the twenty nellie anyway . . . . . 251 IS 5 ONE 22   1

APRIL (CONTINUED)
say that even after April by God there is . . . . 264 IS 5 ONE 33   7
small clumsy feet of April came into the ragged . . . . 306 IS 5 FIVE 5   14
and anyone earth by april wish by spirit and . . . . 515 50 POEMS 29   31
the first who, his april touch drove sleeping selves . . . . 520 50 POEMS 34   10
whose moving is more april than the year (if . . . . 559 1 X 1 19   12
and soul november and april) who younger than begin . . . . . 575 1 X 1 35   36
if a look should april me, down isn't's own . . . . 580 1 X 1 40   6
if a look should april me, some thousand million . . . . . . 580 1 X 1 40   11
if a look should april me for half a . . . . 580 1 X 1 40   19
if a look should april me (though such as . . . . 580 1 X 1 40   22
having altitude--and march denounces april as a saboteur then 620 (CHAIRE) 22   12
sunlight and mountains) in april (but if he should . . . . . 660 (CHAIRE) 62   24
human the most catastrophe april might make alive filthy . . 662 (CHAIRE) 64   4
doubting and never --it's april (yes, april; my darling) . . 665 (CHAIRE) 67   4
never --it's april (yes, april; my darling) it's spring! . . 665 (CHAIRE) 67   4
sing (like april's own april and awake's awake) / . . . . . . 735 95 POEMS 63   14
to young (winter goodbye) april hello, / / / . . . . 737 95 POEMS 65   8
i some times call april) must often have wondered . . . . . . 738 95 POEMS 66   9
sun and rain make april my life is the . . . . 749 95 POEMS 77   4
far as alive) lies april; and i ◇ some . . . . 839 73 POEMS 67   6
+APRIL
FOR CONTEXT, SEE . . . . 782 73 POEMS 10   8
APRIL'S
of Maeterlinck now that April's here? (ask the man . . . . . 233 IS 5 ONE 4   22
my sweet one (and april's where we're) / / . . . . : 578 1 X 1 38   12
of his eyes : april's they this if now . . . . 583 1 X 1 43   7
blossom: will sing (like april's own april and awake's . . . 735 95 POEMS 63   14
now of spring; but april's day transcends november's year . . 765 95 POEMS 91   12
APRILS
and more much (as aprils elsewhere stroll) exhumed most . . . 546 1 X 1 6   3
APT
winsome thing and strange; apt in my hand warmly . . . . . . 21 T&C PUELLA MEA 195
explain how children are apt to forget to remember . . . . . 515 50 POEMS 29   23
AQUEDUCT
--consider well this ruined aqueduct lady, which used to . . 260 IS 5 ONE 30   22
ARCHED
a thousand crimson years arched with agony i reined . . . . . 30 T&C ORIENTALE 4 36
moan of jazz whose arched occasional steep youth swallows . . 140 & SON REAL 11   5
ARCHER
absurd; him did an archer spy (whose aim had . . . . 360 VIVA 51   15
ARCHITECTURE
to defend a sunbeam's architecture with his life: and . . . . 562 1 X 1 22   12
ARDENSTEIL
ardensteil-henarub-izabeth) this noN allgotupfittokill. . . . 726 95 POEMS 54   1
ARDENT
from fragrant shoulders small, ardent, and perfectly withal . 20 T&C PUELLA MEA 154
ARDOR
tense starlessness anoint with ardor the yellow lover stands   37 T&C AMORES 2   10
ARE
WORD DELETED, APPEARED 466 TIMES
AREN'T
before they're old (kumrads aren't afraid to die kumrads . . 413 NO THANKS 30   3
finding Holes where pockets aren't lucky 's to spend . . . . 467 NEW POEMS 5   3
dream-- here's, wherever you aren't or are, good luck! . . . 605 (CHAIRE) 7   15
the same because you aren't afraid to kiss the . . . . 679 95 POEMS 7   5
makes you feel you aren't 6 or 6 teen . . . . 779 73 POEMS 7   23
+AREN'T
FOR CONTEXT, SEE . . . . 795 73 POEMS 23   25
AREN'TS
cold stones (o-l-d) names aren'ts) L iv es . . . . 417 NO THANKS 34   9
ARGO
investigator of paper sailors--argonauta argo harmoniously . 326 VIVA 18   6
ARGONAUTA
renowned investigator of paper sailors--argonauta argo . . . 326 VIVA 18   6
ARGOS
there no kings in Argos, that the song is . . . .   4 T&C EPITHALAM   49

	PAGE	TITLE	LINE

ARGUE
    are legs think wrists argue) short (eyes do bang . . . . . . 309 VIVA 1   11
ARGUES
    lithe indolent prostitute Night, argues with certain houses / 93 & POST IMPR 5   17
ARGUMENT
    "can stand against the argument of mil itary necessity" . . . 636 (CHAIRE) 38   10
ARISE
    crackles upon the gloom arise purple pencils fluent spires . 31 T&C ORIENTALE 5 4
    kiss) where everything's nothing --arise, my soul; and sing . 834 73 POEMS 62   30
+ARISE
    FOR CONTEXT, SEE . . . . 388 NO THANKS 5   27
ARISING
    a tiny dust finely arising at the integration of . . . . . . 197 XLI PORTRAIT 5 23
    this uncouth enchanted person, arising from a restaurant, . . 300 IS 5 FOUR 17   2
ARISTIDE
    (as calmly as if aristide maillols occurred with any . . . . 617 (CHAIRE) 19   13
ARITHMETHICS
    collide spirally with iron arithmethics and mesh witH Which . 311 VIVA 3   11
+ARITHMETIC
    FOR CONTEXT, SEE . . . . 464 NEW POEMS 2   7
ARM
    order of The Artificial Arm and Limb) --or, since . . . . . . 266 IS 5 TWO 1   28
    puerile moving of your arm will do suddenly that . . . . . . 302 IS 5 FIVE 1   9
+ARM
    FOR CONTEXT, SEE . . . . 263 IS 5 ONE 32   48
ARMED
    marriageable nymph which is armed with large legs rancid . . 256 IS 5 ONE 27   15
ARMENIAN
    y play, b starts armenian record pho nographisrunn ingd . . . 200 XLI PORTRAIT 8 . 24
ARMIES
    winter cowers, seeing green armies steadily expand hearing . 4 T&C EPITHALAM 71
    tread of those vast armies of the marching dead, ... 209 XLI SONNETS 5   3
    themselves unmade makes love armies (than hate itself and . . 580 1 X 1 40   15
    and no meanness unsmaller) armies can immensely meet for . . 580 1 X 1 40   16
ARMOR
    dressed in various tremulous armor stun the eyes of . . . . . 4 T&C EPITHALAM 68
ARMOUR
    heroes beautifully in shrill armour colliding on huge blue . 302 IS 5 FIVE 1   13
ARMPITS
    is April in whose armpits is the approach of . . . . 29 T&C ORIENTALE 3 10
ARMS
    betwixt whose cool incorrigible arms impaled upon delicious . 7 T&C EPITHALAM 156
    of thy long sinful arms about me dream shall . . . . 9 T&C SONGS 1   34
    tree, her slim lascivious arms alight in skilful wrists . . . 20 T&C PUELLA MEA 157
    has lain with empty arms upon the giddy hills . . . . 36 T&C AMORES 1   6
    doll-like face and hairy arms like an ogre and . . . . 69 T&C POST IMPR 6 38
    my once more illustrious arms are filled with fascination, . 78 T&C SON UNRE 3   9
    ders, sprouted the extraordinary arms through an an- gle . . 97 & POST IMPR 8   36
    of picture hat. the arms hung ugly. , the . . . . 103 & POST IMPR 13 5
    of wise lust whose arms and legs like white . . . . 110 & PORTRAIT 6   6
    in your legs Your arms under me around; my . . . . 123 & SEVEN POEMS 2 10
    a caret of clenched arms a delicately elephantine face . . . 143 & SON REAL 14   1
    i (having in my arms caught the picture) hurry . . . . 162 & SON ACTU 11   9
    is stirringofbirds between my arms; but i should rather . . . 163 & SON ACTU 12 18
    put up your little arms and i'll give them . . . . 192 XLI CHANSONS 2 17
    slowly with pinkish ponderous arms bedecked whose white thick 225 IS 5 ONE LIZ   7
    him all into my arms and staggered banged with . . . . 258 IS 5 ONE 28   22
    their hats legs & arms brush dirt coats smile . . . . 275 IS 5 TWO 9   45
    proud fingers and your arms tremble remembering something . . 279 IS 5 THREE 3 22
    mouths fears hearts lungs arms hopes feet hands under . . . . 283 IS 5 THREE 7   2
    leaning back in my arms for life's not a . . . . 290 IS 5 FOUR 7   14
    my careful how careful arms created this at length . . . . . 295 IS 5 FOUR 12   6
    shut by our mingling arms through a darkness where . . . . . 297 IS 5 FOUR 14   2
    KILLED her (in his arms) Self & Him self . . . . 317 VIVA 9   13
    to your (in my arms flowering so new) self . . . . 424 NO THANKS 41   2
    are silent their flattened arms complain steadily against the 434 NO THANKS 51 12
    bed these ends of arms which pinch that purple . . . . 506 50 POEMS 20   2
    green as grain septembering arms of year extend less . . . . 521 50 POEMS 34 37

		PAGE	TITLE	LINE
ARMS (CONTINUED)				
with its legs and arms / / / /	. . . .	522	50 POEMS 35	14
stranger takes in his arms my very life who's	. . . .	812	73 POEMS 40	12
+ARMS				
FOR CONTEXT, SEE	. . . .	94	& POST IMPR 6	22
ARMS'				
youth wounded by my arms' bothness (say a twilight	. . . . .	218	XLI SONNETS 14	3
ARMY				
thy shoulders is an army with victory and with	. . . .	29	T&C ORIENTALE 3	20
through me as one army. From her nostrils to	. . . .	135	& SON° REAL 6	2
world quickly from rises army the gradual of unbeing	. . . .	633	(CHAIRE) 35	3
AROAM				
forests frolicsome, fleetly mystical, aroam with keen	. . . .	19	T&C PUELLA MEA	92
+AROMAS				
FOR CONTEXT, SEE	. . . .	94	& POST IMPR 6	12
AROSE				
with life this poet arose nor hate nor grief	. . . .	441	NO THANKS 56	42
AROUND				
sits Down. pigeons circle around and around and around	. . .	62	T&C PORTRAIT 10	29
pigeons circle around and around and around the irresponsible		62	T&C PORTRAIT 10	29
around and around and around the irresponsible toys circle	.	62	T&C PORTRAIT 10	29
is building a building around you, a frail slippery	. . . . .	83	T&C SON ACTU 2	2
(building thatandthis into Thus, Around the reckless magic of		83	T&C SON ACTU 2	8
upon the huge neck around whose unwashed sonorous muscle	. .	96	& POST IMPR 8	30
kegs they curl loving around beers the world has	. . . . . .	114	& PORTRAIT 7	11
Your arms under me around; my head fits (my	. . . .	123	& SEVEN POEMS 2	11
mind breathing beside under around myself) by and by	. . . .	283	IS 5 THREE 7	17
you are a house around which i am a	. . . .	292	IS 5 FOUR 9	3
i am prowls carefully around this house of you	. . . .	292	IS 5 FOUR 9	12
from the shut house (around and around which a	. . . .	292	IS 5 FOUR 9	19
shut house (around and around which a poor wind	. . . .	292	IS 5 FOUR 9	19
(pulling Its shawl carefully around it) "things i mean	. . .	328	VIVA 19	19
grassblade Thinks beyond or around (as poems are made)	. . .	364	VIVA 55	8
it mayn't be twirled around your little finger is)	. . . . .	411	NO THANKS 28	7
spasm rise we you-with-me around (me) you IYou /	. . . . . .	442	NO THANKS 57	24
but draw a line around the spot and call	. . . .	500	50 POEMS 14	3
in a room's dark around) five (are all dancesing	. . . . . .	507	50 POEMS 21	2
in a room's dark around) five (six are in	. . . .	507	50 POEMS 21	9
six dancesing three all around around all clouds singing	. .	507	50 POEMS 21	18
dancesing three all around around all clouds singing three	.	507	50 POEMS 21	18
menandwomen three and all around all and all around	. . . .	507	50 POEMS 21	22
around all and all around five all around five	. . . .	507	50 POEMS 21	23
all around five all around five around) five flowers	. . . .	507	50 POEMS 21	24
five all around five around) five flowers five (six	. . . .	507	50 POEMS 21	24
him starrily her and around ing swim snowing ly	. . . . . .	584	1 X 1 44	10
(with a run skip around we go yes) there's	. . . .	594	1 X 1 54	8
(with a what which around we come who) one's	. . . .	594	1 X 1 54	17
(with a down up around again fly) forever was	. . . .	594	1 X 1 54	26
(with a shout each around we go all) there's	. . . .	594	1 X 1 54	35
miraculous like tomorrow) all around the self of this	. . .	617	(CHAIRE) 19	7
everyone is noone dance around the snowman / /	. . . .	630	(CHAIRE) 32	16
and feels everything; all around whom is perfectly a	. . . .	657	(CHAIRE) 59	3
blossoms a newborn babe: around him, eyes --gifted with	. . .	714	95 POEMS 42	3
i am any (while around him streets taking moment	. . . . . .	720	95 POEMS 48	4
grief or my gladness around me surges a miracle	. . . .	749	95 POEMS 77	9
kindness of fragrance opens around them) and whisper their	.	754	95 POEMS 82	10
and thus-- but look around you, friends and foes	. . . . . .	799	73 POEMS 27	39
i lay (with everywhere around) me (the great dim	. . . . . .	816	73 POEMS 44	1
+AROUND				
FOR CONTEXT, SEE	. . . .	122	& SEVEN POEMS 1	3
FOR CONTEXT, SEE	. . . .	237	IS 5 ONE 8	18
FOR CONTEXT, SEE	. . . .	332	VIVA 23	25
FOR CONTEXT, SEE	. . . .	342	VIVA 33	6
+AROUNDING				
FOR CONTEXT, SEE	. . . .	385	NO THANKS 2	63
FOR CONTEXT, SEE	. . . .	719	95 POEMS 47	17
ARRANGED				
flics are very organically arranged and their nucleus	. . . .	274	IS 5 TWO 9	20

37

	PAGE	TITLE	LINE
+ARRANGED
FOR CONTEXT, SEE	267	IS 5 TWO 2	12
ARRANGING
carefully out of Nowhere) arranging a window, into which . .	124	& SEVEN POEMS 3	3
look (while people stare arranging and changing placing . . .	124	& SEVEN POEMS 3	6
the handmirror. "Look at" arranging before me a mellifluous .	226	IS 5 ONE MAME	1
two, countenances seated in arranging; sunlight with-ered . .	255	IS 5 ONE 26	2
ARRAY
were. In her perfectest array my lady, moving in	17	T&C PUELLA MEA	5
ARRIVAL
day and welcome earth's arrival with a soul sunlight?	582	1 X 1 42	4
everything real is the arrival of everything true) and . . .	720	95 POEMS 48	11
ARRIVE
believe me that strangers arrive when i have kissed	295	IS 5 FOUR 12	8
which somewhere is fragrantly, arrive (when Rain comes; . . .	356	VIVA 47	13
/ / one (Floatingly) arrive (silent) one by (alive)	557	1 X 1 17	1
kill more mostful to arrive each (futuring snowily which . .	639	(CHAIRE) 41	10
he to nowhere from arrive human the most catastrophe	662	(CHAIRE) 64	2
+ARRIVE
FOR CONTEXT, SEE	444	NO THANKS 59	6
ARRIVED
really train after all arrived. If i should have	263	IS 5 ONE 32	63
and how this has arrived your mind may guess	285	IS 5 FOUR 2	11
ARRIVES
into young Now entirely arrives gesture past fragrance . . .	456	NO THANKS 71	8
and overing grief nothing arrives a so prodigious am	517	50 POEMS 31	10
every where a miracle arrives (yes) you and i	835	73 POEMS 63	24
ARRIVING
hurry in a gently arriving gloom and see! (the	93	& POST IMPR 5	12
of Briggs by Kitty) arriving in an exhausted condition, . . .	326	VIVA 18	15
will include --there by arriving magically here-- an	741	95 POEMS 69	11
that himself the sun --arriving truly, faithfully who goes .	756	95 POEMS 84	2
teachable imposture of always arriving at the place you . . .	807	73 POEMS 35	4
+ARRIVING
FOR CONTEXT, SEE	396	NO THANKS 13	11
FOR CONTEXT, SEE	676	95 POEMS 4	19
ARROW
gold valley the famished arrow sang before. Bow at	14	T&C SONGS 4	20
built like a smooth arrow or a fleet pillar	110	& PORTRAIT 6	2
pillar or a smooth arrow Cleopatra is eaten by	111	& PORTRAIT 6	47
texture of Now the arrow and the pillar pursue	112	& PORTRAIT 6	81
you land of the Arrow Ide and Earl &	230	IS 5 ONE 2	7
hings (whi, le sp, arrow, s wince among those	442	NO THANKS 57	8
ARROWS
Now- spears and The Then-arrows making do our mouths	160	& SON ACTU 9	16
ARSE
prince upon his uncorrupted arse with all his hearty	254	IS 5 ONE 25	20
for pu tting the arse before the torse /	477	NEW POEMS 15	9
i'll kiss a stalinist arse in hitler's window on	514	50 POEMS 28	12
a politician is an arse upon which everyone has	550	1 X 1 10	1
ART
day) for which girl art thou flowers bringing? To	13	T&C SONGS 3	14
a sword and thou art silent thy breast is	27	T&C ORIENTALE 1	24
with dreams, love thou art frail --walk the longness	190	XLI SONGS 12	18
afraid of death? thou art of him utterly afraid, ...	215	XLI SONNETS 11	2
such supposedly indigenous throstles Art is 0 World 0	230	IS 5 ONE 2	32
pr gress verily thou art m mentous superc lossal	392	NO THANKS 9	2
give a fart for art they kill like you	427	NO THANKS 44	15
pull but practicing the art of swot to preach	500	50 POEMS 14	19
the god's truth stands art-naked: you and the fact	605	(CHAIRE) 7	3
Big pastmaster of the Art of Jigajig sitting pretty	642	(CHAIRE) 44	23
+ART
FOR CONTEXT, SEE	409	NO THANKS 26	3
ART-NAKED
the god's truth stands art-naked: you and the fact	605	(CHAIRE) 7	3
ARTIFICER
reason, why then the artificer did most exquisitely err.) . .	22	T&C PUELLA MEA	219
shortly comprehend a marvellous artificer now Ugly was the .	799	73 POEMS 27	7

ARTIFICIAL
   large, unclever. hair genuinely artificial, unpleasantly . . 103 & POST IMPR 13   14
   the order of The Artificial Arm and Limb) --or, ... 266 IS 5 TWO 1   28
   The Expectant stutter (upon artificial limbs, with faces like 280 IS 5 THREE 4   33
   is strictly scientific & artificial & evil & legal) . . . . . 604 {CHAIRE} 6   20
ARTISTIC
   way Pay the extremely artistic <> fla -me of . . . . 267 IS 5 TWO 2   11
ARTISTS
   grace the prince of artists made him bold to . . . .   4 T&C EPITHALAM   35
   of prowst but respects artists if they are sincere . . . . . 499 50 POEMS 13   11
ARTSKIDS
   Bad almond chick. thepinkisht artskiDs... with thema Tiss . . 318 VIVA 10   19
ARTY
   so spry concernin questions arty each has his tastes . . . . 247 IS 5 ONE 18   2
AS
   WORD DELETED, APPEARED 367 TIMES
+ASCENDING
   FOR CONTEXT, SEE . . . . 100 & POST IMPR 11   25
ASCENDS
   in sweet unserious dress ascends the golden crocus from . . .   4 T&C EPITHALAM   64
ASCENSIONS
   aspirings the indolent frail ascensions, of thy smile rises . 31 T&C ORIENTALE 5   16
ASH
   and thrown on the ash-heap where lies what was . . . . . . 203 XLI LA GUERRE 1   16
+ASH
   FOR CONTEXT, SEE . . . . 726 95 POEMS 54   13
ASH-HEAP
   and thrown on the ash-heap where lies what was . . . . . . 203 XLI LA GUERRE 1   16
ASHAMED
   genius-- painting wholly feels ashamed before this music, and 162 & SON ACTU 11   5
ASHBARREL
   buried upsidedown in an ashbarrel so of course dominic . . . 680 95 POEMS 8   9
ASHES
   perfume only, from the ashes then thou wilt rise . . . . . 40 T&C AMORES 4   37
   hello: (of solongs and, ashes) / / / / . . . . 66 T&C POST IMPR 3 17
ASININE
   of rich frail firm asinine life (i pant for . . . . 220 XLI SONNETS 16   4
ASK
   darling, it's all i ask of you-- but that . . . . 71 T&C SON REAL 2   6
   near to me, i ask of shad- ow won't . . . . 97 & POST IMPR 8   40
   hair, (but if you ask the rain he'll not . . . . 183 XLI SONGS 5   5
   FRAN should i entirely ask of god why on . . . . 229 IS 5 ONE FRAN   1
   now that April's here? (ask the man who owns . . . . 233 IS 5 ONE 4   23
   man who owns one ask Dad, He knows). / . . . . 233 IS 5 ONE 4   24
   photographed, ourselves yawning will ask ourselves ou sont . 237 IS 5 ONE 8   2
   / / / some ask praise of their fellows . . . . 291 IS 5 FOUR 8   1
   you disappear solemnly myselves ask "life, the question how . 295 IS 5 FOUR 12   14
   (and who does not ask for more than just . . . . 298 IS 5 FOUR 15   9
   one father of one (ask super-) wonderful (mother) child . . . 398 NO THANKS 15   5
   give and realness bring-- ask the always impossible of . . . 454 NO THANKS 69   2
   straighter than a needle) ask her ask when (ask . . . . . . 498 50 POEMS 12   4
   a needle) ask her ask when (ask and ask . . . . 498 50 POEMS 12   6
   ask her ask when (ask and ask and ask . . . . 498 50 POEMS 12   8
   ask when (ask and ask and ask again and) . . . . 498 50 POEMS 12   9
   (ask and ask and ask again and) ask a . . . . 498 50 POEMS 12   10
   and ask again and) ask a brittle little person . . . . . . 498 50 POEMS 12   11
   nipples like pink thimbles) ask him ask who (ask . . . . . . 498 50 POEMS 12   20
   pink thimbles) ask him ask who (ask and ask . . . . 498 50 POEMS 12   22
   ask him ask who (ask and ask and ask . . . . 498 50 POEMS 12   24
   ask who (ask and ask and ask ago and) . . . . 498 50 POEMS 12   25
   (ask and ask and ask ago and) ask a . . . . 498 50 POEMS 12   26
   and ask ago and) ask a simple crazy thing . . . . 498 50 POEMS 12   27
   a crazy man) don't ask me how i know . . . . 501 50 POEMS 15   6
   boys) mine is yours ask me the name of . . . . 513 50 POEMS 27   19
   massacre monday did more) ask a lifelump buried by . . . . . 522 50 POEMS 35   5
   sooner to biz don't ask me what it's pliz) . . . . 552 1 X 1 12   5
   / i've come to ask you if there isn't . . . . 572 1 X 1 32   1
   and if time should ask into his was all . . . . 576 1 X 1 36   13

	PAGE	TITLE	LINE

ASK (CONTINUED)

   while leaf twig limb ask every question time can't . . . . . 818 73 POEMS 46   10

ASKED

   in Dick Mid's Place asked "always" Death said "then . . . . . 57 T&C PORTRAIT 5   25

   her a shove and asked Eddie did he care . . . . 145 & SON REAL 16   12

   / / / you asked me to come: it . . . . 173 & SON ACTU 22   1

   & by the way asked sis breath of brud . . . . 316 VIVA 8   19

   wept air to blood, asked "something a little child . . . . . 555 1 X 1 15   12

   'twas me that she asked would it hurt too . . . . 707 95 POEMS 35   24

   roses-- "and who" i asked my love " could . . . . 748 95 POEMS 76   12

ASKING

   with an occult shrug asking Through her Muteness will . . . . 137 & SON REAL 8   5

   "ladies&gentlemen" --under glass-- are: asking. ? each oth? . 319 VIVA 11   35

   / / / i'm asking you dear to what . . . . 638 {CHAIRE) 40   2

   but your daughter i'm asking yes who but that . . . . 707 95 POEMS 35   13

   all since and why asking no favor but (while . . . . 783 73 POEMS 11   5

   still who alive is asking What have i done . . . . 784 73 POEMS 12   6

ASKS

   will tell who softly asks in love, am i . . . . 295 IS 5 FOUR 12   2

   a criminal (hears Darwin; asks about Death) concept O . . . . 398 NO THANKS 15   14

   Spring comes (no- one asks his name) a mender . . . . 660 {CHAIRE) 62   4

   this bell 's whisper asks (of a world born . . . . 787 73 POEMS 15   14

ASKYUH

   datswut eesez tuhmih. (Nowoi askyuh woodundat maik yurarstoin 310 VIVA 2   5

ASLEEP

   / / Doll's boy's asleep under a stile he . . . . 15 T&C SONGS 5   1

   are mine. Doll's boy's asleep under the stile for . . . . . 15 T&C SONGS 5   17

   beyond the brittle towns asleep i look where stealing . . . . 64 T&C POST IMPR 1   1

   side as i lie asleep my eyes go into . . . . 100 & POST IMPR 11   2

   old man 3 thirds asleep, on his head flowers, ... 102 & POST IMPR 12   14

   what we stroke maybe asleep? do you know? or . . . . 191 XLI CHANSONS 1   12

   to mark, how that asleep whitely she seems whose . . . . . 205 XLI SONNETS 1   7

   (crossing them slowly) "I'm asleep. Yep. Youse is asleep . . 228 IS 5 ONE MARJ   4

   asleep. Yep. Youse is asleep kid and everybody is." . . . . . 228 IS 5 ONE MARJ   4

   mind. awake being not asleep, elsewhere our dreams began . . 304 IS 5 FIVE 3   7

   daytime, when who is asleep with only several faces . . . . . 312 VIVA 4   5

   "I may say professor" asleep wop "shapley has compared . . . 464 NEW POEMS 2   11

   sit creatures of quills (asleep who must go . . . . 483 NEW POEMS 21   11

   awake what waking calls asleep) so never is most . . . . . . 609 {CHAIRE) 11   8

   yas buy gad) nor asleep booted & spurred with . . . . 640 {CHAIRE) 42   4

+ASLEEP

   FOR CONTEXT, SEE . . . . 347 VIVA 38   25

   FOR CONTEXT, SEE . . . . 691 95 POEMS 19   7

   FOR CONTEXT, SEE . . . . 733 95 POEMS 61   6

ASPIRINE

   a garret and eat aspirine) but who is this . . . . 245 IS 5 ONE 16   5

ASPIRINGS

   in the ambiguous faint aspirings the indolent frail . . . . . 31 T&C ORIENTALE 5   15

+ASPROUT

   FOR CONTEXT, SEE . . . . 445 NO THANKS 60   10

ASQUIRM

   croon mime nakedly hurl asquirm the dip & giveswoop . . . . . 445 NO THANKS 60   25

+ASS

   FOR CONTEXT, SEE . . . . 254 IS 5 ONE 25   20

   FOR CONTEXT, SEE . . . . 310 VIVA 2   6

   FOR CONTEXT, SEE . . . . 477 NEW POEMS 15   9

   FOR CONTEXT, SEE . . . . 492 50 POEMS 6   3

   FOR CONTEXT, SEE . . . . 514 50 POEMS 28   12

ASSASSINATING

   may overflow (am was) assassinating whole grassblades, five . 491 50 POEMS 5   12

ASSAULT

   is a ghost whom assault these whispering fists of . . . . . . 299 IS 5 FOUR 16   12

ASSEMBLES

   mad magnificent herald Spring assembles beauty from . . . . . 4 T&C EPITHALAM   58

ASSERTIONS

   president, being of which assertions duly notified threw the 339 VIVA 30   35

ASSERTS

   fear denies, what hope asserts, what falsest both disprove . 576 1 X 1 36   3

	PAGE	TITLE	LINE

ASSIDUOUSLY
legs nice to pinch assiduously which justgraze each other). . 150 & SON REAL 21   9
ASSISTANCE
upon the most crimson assistance of my com- forter . . . . . 197 XLI PORTRAIT 5   15
ASSUME
when thy bashful hands assume silence beyond the mystery . . 210 XLI SONNETS 6   14
ASSUMING
Rain comes; predicating forever, assuming the laughter of . . 356 VIVA 47   16
ASTERN
/ / FULL SPEED ASTERN) m usil (age) ini . . . . 325 VIVA 17   1
ASTERS
who so thumb o'clock asters miggle dim a ram . . . . 333 VIVA 24   16
ASTIR
the new world scarce astir my fragile lady wandering . . . . 17 T&C PUELLA MEA   12
knowledge can kill is astir-- now dull eyes are . . . . . . 769 95 POEMS 95   9
ASTONISHED
us not be continually astonished should from their actions . 261 IS 5 ONE 31   3
+ASTONISHING
FOR CONTEXT, SEE . . . . 354 VIVA 45   14
ASTONISHMENT
chained to a grave astonishment feel in my being . . . . . . 79 T&C SON UNRE 4   11
and much to my astonishment much impressed by having . . . . 262 IS 5 ONE 32   9
ASTOUNDING
be free with the astounding everlasting air-- but if . . . . 212 XLI SONNETS 8   12
ASTUTE
puerperal face and with astute fatuous swallowed eyes smiles, 151 & SON REAL 22   13
AT
WORD DELETED, APPEARED 187 TIMES
ATE
disdain picKles, once, it, ate a scarlet pepper and . . . . . 100 & POST IMPR 11   30
failed because the chickens ate the vegetables so my . . . . 239 IS 5 ONE 10   16
farm till the skunks ate the chickens when my . . . . 239 IS 5 ONE 10   19
ATHANOR
magnificence. In heaven's intolerable athanor inimitably . .   6 T&C EPITHALAM   129
ATHLETE'S
is a WELL KNOWn ATHLETE'S BRIDE (lullaby) & z . . . . 317 VIVA 9   1
all those who got athlete's mouth jumping on&off bandwaggons 404 NO THANKS 21   3
ATHWART
droops with things dead athwart the narrowing hours and . . . 207 XLI SONNETS 3   6
ATILT
became a great lily atilt on insolent waters but . . . . . . 30 T&C ORIENTALE 4   6
ATLANTIS
pink suspenders c reads Atlantis x and y play . . . . 200 XLI PORTRAIT 8   8
ATMOSPHERE
cafes, the more dissolute atmosphere of a street . . . . . . 197 XLI PORTRAIT 5   2
ATOM
without or until no atom couldn't die (how and . . . . . . 634 {CHAIRE} 36   13
ATOMIES
scramble faintly tickling putrescent atomies, and i feel the 69 T&C POST IMPR 6 30
ATOMS
grind me into lifeless atoms various ab- surd thoughts . . . 262 IS 5 ONE 32   3
ATOMY
dares partly seem one atomy once, and every cannot . . . . . 559 1 X 1 19   10
ATONE
dead) Whoshout (Ghost) atOne (voiceless) O ther or . . . . . 347 VIVA 38   22
ATOP
the composed sudden body atop which always quivers the . . . 193 XLI PORTRAIT 1   2
ATRICKLING
-less un- (wonderful) story atrickling a -rithmetic o- ver . 464 NEW POEMS 2   7
ATROCIOUS
a trembly mist of atrocious melody.... tiniest dead tunes . . 69 T&C POST IMPR 6 27
chauvesouris-- whose grammar is atrocious; but so what . . . 504 50 POEMS 18   10
ATTACHED
padded pole; a monkey attached by a chain securely . . . . . 279 IS 5 THREE 3   10
ATTACKS
too far and: she attacks her Lobster without feet . . . . . . 243 IS 5 ONE 14   13
lightheavy twic twoc ingly attacks landing a onetwo which . . 259 IS 5 ONE 29   13

	PAGE	TITLE	LINE
ATTEND			
O hairlesschested females, well attend! list, every	398	NO THANKS 15	17
ATTENTION			
the subject of our attention; to speak even less	263	IS 5 ONE 32	61
first who pays any attention to the syntax of	290	IS 5 FOUR 7	2
ATTIC			
squirrel-stairs into a mid-victorian attic which is known as	194	XLI PORTRAIT 2	8
ATTITUDE			
proud of his scientific attitude and liked the prince	499	50 POEMS 13	1
of his scientif ic attitude and liked the king	499	50 POEMS 13	13
ATTRACTED			
Divine Average who was attracted by the inspired sister's . .	196	XLI PORTRAIT 4	17
AUDIBLE			
immaculate of god's evasive audible great rose! Lover, lead .	5	T&C EPITHALAM	112
AUGUST			
hugs whom) as the august evening mauls Kneeland, and	217	XLI SONNETS 13	7
Dragon st one fine August night, i just happened	313	VIVA 5	2
AUNT			
my sweet old etcetera aunt lucy during the recent	276	IS 5 TWO 10	2
brud breathe how is aunt death did always teethe	316	VIVA 8	21
AUSPICIOUS			
to him upon the auspicious occasion of his decease	239	IS 5 ONE 10	29
AUSSI			
m'aiment tous, les americains aussi.... "bon dos, bon cul . .	120	& PORTRAIT 12	14
gentils et les americains aussi, ils payent bien les	120	& PORTRAIT 12	27
AUTHENTIC			
the brutal dew, --the authentic scroll of fairie hands . . .	5	T&C EPITHALAM	87
find beyond the white authentic springs, beyond the sweet . .	19	T&C PUELLA MEA	120
make it serious something authentic and delirious you know .	407	NO THANKS 24	11
AUTHENTICITY			
an instant doubts the authenticity of these ◇ hurries . . .	116	& PORTRAIT 9	13
AUTHOR			
headwaiters bow so? hush--the author of Women By Night . . .	245	IS 5 ONE 16	8
AUTOMATON			
they shied at the automaton moon from the transplendent . . .	30	T&C ORIENTALE 4	39
AUTUMN			
light. it is the autumn of a year: When	11	T&C SONGS 2	21
i too have known autumn too long (and what	80	T&C SON UNRE 5	4
/ / / / autumn is: that between there	158	& SON ACTU 7	1
amorous of, through the autumn indisputably roaming death's .	158	& SON ACTU 7	13
cannot grieve nor the autumn, as i grieve, faint	165	& SON ACTU 14	9
that sways in the autumn she will never guess.	183	XLI SONGS 5	14
cruelly, love walk the autumn long; the last flower	190	XLI SONGS 12	2
moon love, walk the autumn love, for the last	190	XLI SONGS 12	13
--walk the longness of autumn smile dustily to the	190	XLI SONGS 12	19
when unto nights of autumn do complain earth's ghastlier . .	207	XLI SONNETS 3	1
this, which we call autumn, cleverly dies and over	293	IS 5 FOUR 10	23
he is old when autumn comes, who twiddles his	296	IS 5 FOUR 13	5
starve and smother; until autumn abruptly wholly hugs our . .	305	IS 5 FIVE 4	8
bells down) spring summer autumn winter he sang his	515	50 POEMS 29	3
as up they grew autumn winter spring summer) that	515	50 POEMS 29	11
dong and ding) summer autumn winter spring reaped their . . .	515	50 POEMS 29	34
some perpetually roaming whylessness-- autumn has gone: will	839	73 POEMS 67	8
+AUTUMN			
FOR CONTEXT, SEE	618	(CHAIRE) 20	24
FOR CONTEXT, SEE	696	95 POEMS 24	10
AUTUMN'S			
than it away (his autumn's winter being summer's spring . . .	420	NO THANKS 37	3
AUTUMNAL			
/ / / noone" autumnal this great lady's gaze	626	(CHAIRE) 28	1
stand (alone) in some autumnal afternoon: breathing a fatal .	674	95 POEMS 2	2
AVEC			
brain voulez- vous coucher avec moi? Non? pourquoi?) ladies .	120	& PORTRAIT 12	29
Henri Mounier voulez-vous coucher avec moi? te ferai Mimi . .	121	& PORTRAIT 12	36
AVENUE			
the corner of Divinity avenue i touched the accelerator . . .	248	IS 5 ONE 19	22
of the old sixth avenue el; in the top	553	1 X 1 13	23
cars pour into sixth avenue) "then" my voice marvels	800	73 POEMS 28	20

	PAGE	TITLE	LINE

AVENUES
hurled dream down eager avenues of lifelessness consider for   81 T&C SON UNRE 6   6
AVERAGE
dollar whereupon the Divine Average who was attracted by . . 196 XLI PORTRAIT 4   16
AWAIT
Of curvish (,males await she patiently 1) . . . . 342 VIVA 33   17
AWAITED
(here is that rain awaited by leaves with all . . . . 754 95 POEMS 82   13
AWAITETH
without, the street darkling awaiteth her whose feet have . . 75 T&C SON REAL 6   10
AWAITS
whichful sarcasms papery deathfuls) awaits yes this alive . . 415 NO THANKS 32   19
AWAKE
wifeless and only half awake, cursed with pimples, correctly 262 IS 5 ONE 32   7
though not as yet awake, of ourselves which shout . . . . . . 264 IS 5 ONE 33   13
policeman of my mind. awake being not asleep, elsewhere . . . 304 IS 5 FIVE 3   6
expensively democratic tyrannically dumb Awake, chaos: we . . 337 VIVA 28   15
each will kissed breast awake) slow tottering visions bigly . 565 1 X 1 25   12
twilight's first thrushes may awake more secretly than our . 577 1 X 1 37   6
of flesh and so awake what waking calls asleep) . . . . 609 (CHAIRE) 11   8
are growing stones (neither awake are goddesses nor sleeping) 617 (CHAIRE) 19   8
/ / / neither awake (there's your general yas . . . . 640 (CHAIRE) 42   1
ears of my ears awake and now the eyes . . . . 663 (CHAIRE) 65   13
own april and awake's awake) / / / / . . . . 735 95 POEMS 63   14
AWAKE'S
april's own april and awake's awake) / / / . . . . 735 95 POEMS 63   14
AWAKEN
(and a few windows awaken certain faces busily horribly . . . 299 IS 5 FOUR 16   13
AWAKENED
as if our souls, awakened from summer's green trance, ... 675 95 POEMS 3   9
all silence strolls) nearness awakened, any bird should sing: 756 95 POEMS 84   11
AWAKENING
if you and i awakening discover that (somehow in . . . . . . 370 VIVA 61   1
stranger who is i awakening am. Living no single . . . . . . 559 1 X 1 19   8
AWANDERING
go and lovers come awandering awondering but any two . . . . 591 1 X 1 51   10
AWARE
waters but i was aware of fragrance and i . . . . 30 T&C ORIENTALE 4   8
nor think nor am aware of anything save that . . . . 98 & POST IMPR 9   14
gammon boards i was aware of an entirely dirty . . . . 194 XLI PORTRAIT 2   18
yon motheaten forum be aware notice what hath remained . . . 260 IS 5 ONE 30   2
are (less who are aware) than of my books . . . . 386 NO THANKS 3   3
poor not rich (only aware) kind neither nor cruel . . . . . . 564 1 X 1 24   5
+AWARE
FOR CONTEXT, SEE . . . . 724 95 POEMS 52   16
AWASH
again sometime") vanished, gunwale awash. I thereupon . . . . 327 VIVA 18   37
wraith's progress or mainly awash while chiefly submerged or 410 NO THANKS 27   11
AWAY
all sweet cities passed away-- in her flesh at . . . . 22 T&C PUELLA MEA 257
stiff-ly throw the shell away with a small bored . . . . . . 69 T&C POST IMPR 6 19
curtain strikes the world away, leaving to shadowy silence . 75 T&C SON REAL 6   2
in time not far away; if on another's face . . . . 76 T&C SON UNRE 1   4
has blown the rain away and blown the sky . . . . 80 T&C SON UNRE 5   1
and blown the sky away and all the leaves . . . . 80 T&C SON UNRE 5   2
and all the leaves away, and the trees stand. . . . . 80 T&C SON UNRE 5   2
has blown the rain away and the leaves and . . . . 80 T&C SON UNRE 5   14
eyes can take day away more softly horribly suddenly; . . . . 98 & POST IMPR 9   4
never sold and couldn't-be-given-away because Who?. . . . . . 101 & POST IMPR 11   67
had once i was away up in the sky . . . . 123 & SEVEN POEMS 2   1
the best time tickling away every- body's brain so . . . . . 126 & SEVEN POEMS 5 11
which goes land- ing away all by himself on . . . . 127 & SEVEN POEMS 5 42
and clouds: go sailing away and away sailing into . . . . . . 129 & SEVEN POEMS 7 11
go sailing away and away sailing into a keen . . . . 129 & SEVEN POEMS 7 11
<> (will BigMorning get away with them? j'en doute,) . . . . 169 & SON ACTU 18   11
/ when you went away it was morning (that . . . . 172 & SON ACTU 21   1
to juggle Kandinsky gold-fish away from the gripping gigantic 180 XLI SONGS 2   14
maybe did something go away ever so quietly when . . . . . . 191 XLI CHANSONS 1   14

		PAGE	TITLE	LINE
AWAY (CONTINUED)

very sorry to come away? see i will comfort . . . . 192 XLI CHANSONS 2   6
/ because you go away i give roses who . . . . 294 IS 5 FOUR 11   2
found what was thrown away himself taptaptaps out of . . . . 298 IS 5 FOUR 15 24
something else, and slips away.... (these leaves are Thingish 303 IS 5 FIVE 2   5
turned abruptly Miss Gay away: "on the whole" (if . . . . . . 326 VIVA 18 26
is takin fellers' goils away frum dem" --"somebody hung . . . 332 VIVA 23   6
buttons) would take you away --and all the clocks . . . . . . 365 VIVA 56 13
little more than it away (his autumn's winter being . . . . . 420 NO THANKS 37   2
world: & toss it away; or cause one causeless . . . . 433 NO THANKS 50   3
its of mind chucks away flimsy which but) always . . . . . . 501 50 POEMS 15 14
fades) is here and away (but born are maids . . . . 509 50 POEMS 23   3
all and one gone away the they leaf of . . . . 541 1 X 1 1   8
that took his breath away all history oped her . . . . 552 1 X 1 12 20
me while i am away?) / / / / . . . . 558 1 X 1 18 15
they do, we'll move away still further: into now . . . . . . 579 1 X 1 39 14
bluest took it our away beyond where what a . . . . 593 1 X 1 53 18
how) so here is away and so your is . . . . 594 1 X 1 54 23
(1Y) & & & away wanders: exact ly; as . . . . 655 {CHAIRE} 57 10
a world crylaughingly float away leaving just this strolling 720 95 POEMS 48   7
that life is running away from them (i wonder) . . . . 724 95 POEMS 52 14
(and dance your death away at this wedding) never . . . . . . 732 95 POEMS 60 12
here there where) and away we go in even . . . . 769 95 POEMS 95   7
one a third face, away in the sky finally . . . . 813 73 POEMS 41   9
makes a crash --far away (as far as alive) . . . . 839 73 POEMS 67   5
+AWAY

FOR CONTEXT, SEE . . . . 10 T&C SONGS 1 44
FOR CONTEXT, SEE . . . . 632 {CHAIRE} 34   1
FOR CONTEXT, SEE . . . . 632 {CHAIRE} 34   7
FOR CONTEXT, SEE . . . . 660 {CHAIRE} 62 16
AWE

between the feet of awe), thunderer whose omnipotent brow . .   4 T&C EPITHALAM 36
AWFUL

peacefully, lifted into the awful beauty of sunset the . . . 48 T&C IMPRESS 2 13
up into itself, an awful big light squoits down . . . . 332 VIVA 23 27
voices sing against the awful mystery of light / . . . . . . 454 NO THANKS 69 14
AWKWARD

as some smooth and awkward foal, whereof young moons . . . . 11 T&C SONGS 2   3
Through the young and awkward hours my lady perfectly . . . . 17 T&C PUELLA MEA 10
old and with his awkward eyes pushing sleep under . . . . . . 293 IS 5 FOUR 10 27
AWOKE

a soul until i awoke for the beautiful sake . . . . 587 1 X 1 47 19
AWONDERING

and lovers come awandering awondering but any two are . . . . 591 1 X 1 51 10
AWRY

and yanks immortal stars awry? Blow king to beggar . . . . . 560 1 X 1 20   4
AX

phonograph x wins exeunt ax: by; c, Goo dnightef . . . . . . 200 XLI PORTRAIT 8 30
AXE

The Distinct your brain's axe only chops hugest inherent . . 195 XLI PORTRAIT 3 18
AXIS

truth; and strolls the axis of the universe --love. . . . . . 845 73 POEMS 73 10
AYS

ins tead, smiles alw ays a trifl e w . . . . 611 {CHAIRE} 13   5
eyes eyes looking (alw ays) while earth and sky . . . . 715 95 POEMS 43   8
& will do alw -ays something is (guess) yes . . . . 793 73 POEMS 21 22
AZURES

come and go, frail azures fluttering from night's outer . . . 208 XLI SONNETS 4   2
B

a has gold teeth b pink suspenders c reads . . . . 200 XLI PORTRAIT 8   6
x and y play b cries "effendi" "Uh" "coffee" . . . . 200 XLI PORTRAIT 8   9
x and y play b spits x and y . . . . 200 XLI PORTRAIT 8 21
x and y play, b starts armenian record pho . . . . 200 XLI PORTRAIT 8 24
w, n phonograph stopS. b swears in persian at . . . . 200 XLI PORTRAIT 8 29
A always don't there B being no such thing . . . . 390 NO THANKS 7   2
+B

FOR CONTEXT, SEE . . . . 200 XLI PORTRAIT 8 30

	PAGE	TITLE	LINE

+B.O.
    FOR CONTEXT, SEE . . . . 425 NO THANKS 42   15
BABBITT
    wid i (check undublcheck) babbitt (GOD SAVE THE . . . . 325 VIVA 17   21
BABBLE
    tooth (and the wholly babble open at blessed are . . . . . 635 {CHAIRE} 37   19
BABE
    not swell (get me) babe not (understand me) lousy . . . . . . 475 NEW POEMS 13   23
    night blossoms a newborn babe: around him, eyes --gifted . . 714 95 POEMS 42   3
BABIES
    about the smell of babies and how you know . . . . 242 IS 5 ONE 13   18
    do do neighbours re babies while; / / / . . . . 309 VIVA 1   35
    going places on such babies aint plenty good enough . . . . . 476 NEW POEMS 14   8
BABOON
    colours stroll.... and the Baboon sniggering insipidities . . 220 XLI SONNETS 16   12
    white mice, and a baboon. O a monkey with . . . . 279 IS 5 THREE 3   8
    the skull of a baboon (where once good lips . . . . 360 VIVA 51   1
BABY
    abrupt flesh split "Pretty Baby" to numb rhythm before . . . 106 & PORTRAIT 2   13
    the face of a baby smeared with beautiful jam . . . . 166 & SON ACTU 15   13
    looks but how dat baby ached." and when i . . . . 226 IS 5 ONE MAME   11
    gas and the oh baby shrapnel or my feet . . . . 272 IS 5 TWO 7   7
    but Death ? o baby i wouldn't like Death . . . . 604 {CHAIRE} 6   3
    / open his head, baby & you'll find a . . . . 637 {CHAIRE} 39   1
+BABY
    FOR CONTEXT, SEE . . . . 100 & POST IMPR 11   5
    FOR CONTEXT, SEE . . . . 705 95 POEMS 33   5
BABYBREASTED
    their sunday flower. The babybreasted broad "kitty" twice . . 74 T&C SON REAL 5   12
BABYLON
    are the cries of Babylon.) Diarmuid Paris and Solomon, . . . 23 T&C PUELLA MEA   261
    / / / / Babylon slim -ness of evenslicing . . . . 106 & PORTRAIT 2   1
BABYPOUT
    balanced upon one broken babypout (pretty teeth wander into . 406 NO THANKS 23   10
BACCHANT
    sinuous riot the flashing bacchant. partedpetaled mouth, face 185 XLI SONGS 7   12
BACHELOR
    to my position. A bachelor incapable of occupation, he . . . 263 IS 5 ONE 32   37
BACK
    my round red hat back on my head i . . . . 69 T&C POST IMPR 6   34
    toe hip popot amus Back gen teel-ly lugu- bri . . . . 107 & PORTRAIT 3   7
    dread lift the sheet back in this way. here . . . . 118 & PORTRAIT 10   42
    you somewhere behind your back it makes your neck . . . . . 126 & SEVEN POEMS 5   18
    he'd bumped a bloke back in fifteen. Then she . . . . 145 & SON REAL 16   2
    dreaming --and i fall back, quietly amorous of, through . . . 158 & SON ACTU 7   12
    cards and smack of back- gammon boards i was . . . . 194 XLI PORTRAIT 2   17
    index down- dragging yanks back skin "see" (i, seeing, . . . 226 IS 5 ONE MAME   6
    next minute i was back in neutral tried and . . . . 248 IS 5 ONE 19   14
    the last minute coming back down by the Public . . . . . . 248 IS 5 ONE 19   27
    the roadside on his back dressed in fifteenthrate ideas . . . 258 IS 5 ONE 28   2
    to which, considering the back- ground, it is hardly . . . . 263 IS 5 ONE 32   34
    into a pink cliff back and up leaning out . . . . 281 IS 5 THREE 5   9
    other: then laugh, leaning back in my arms for . . . . . . 290 IS 5 FOUR 7   14
    You don't believe? look back. (Along the sand behind . . . . 303 IS 5 FIVE 2   11
    Abe tucks it up back inley clamored Clever Rusefelt . . . . 321 VIVA 13   8
    sidesteps im an draws back huly jeezus" --an-- "my . . . . 332 VIVA 23   5
    too high look (it's back again there therehere And) . . . . . 353 VIVA 44   23
    his wheel upon his back and off he goes . . . . 624 {CHAIRE} 26   20
    the (dropp ingspinson his back mad) fly (ly who . . . . . . 692 95 POEMS 20   5
+BACK
    FOR CONTEXT, SEE . . . . 275 IS 5 TWO 9   38
BACKGAMMON
    Helmar cigarettes 2 play backgammon, 3 watch a has . . . . . 200 XLI PORTRAIT 8   4
+BACKGAMMON
    FOR CONTEXT, SEE . . . . 194 XLI PORTRAIT 2   17
+BACKGROUND
    FOR CONTEXT, SEE . . . . 263 IS 5 ONE 32   34

45

BACKWARD
    whispers primeval and throw backward their foreheads to the .   5 T&C EPITHALAM   77
    things no lingering no backward- wondering be unto us . . . .   41 T&C AMORES 5   26
    but when will turn backward O backward Time in . . . . 233 IS 5 ONE 4   3
    will turn backward O backward Time in your no . . . . 233 IS 5 ONE 4   3
    though the stars walk backward) honour the past but . . . . . 732 95 POEMS 60   8
BACKWARDSPINNING
    its english the Forwardflung backwardSpinning hoop returns . 311 VIVA 3   5
BAD
    huddling nuts and the bad candies my, mouth loves . . . . . . 100 & POST IMPR 11   22
    that stumbling in gloom, bad laughters, smiles unbold) also,   142 & SON REAL 13   8
    and i got a Bad almond chick. thepinkisht artskiDs. . . . . . 318 VIVA 10   17
    a soft desert smoked bad me whilepin Kishcam elscasta? . . . 318 VIVA 10   21
    ng like like, like bad, like candy: & you . . . . 389 NO THANKS 6   14
    knows (that anything is bad which you think good) . . . . . . 406 NO THANKS 23   4
    amputate his appetite with bad brittle candy but just . . . . 410 NO THANKS 27   3
    not being felt as bad, itself thinks goodness what . . . . . 438 NO THANKS 54   3
    Ever-Ever Land for a bad cigar is a woman . . . . 466 NEW POEMS 4   27
    whispers jill mopping too bad dear sh not yet . . . . 496 50 POEMS 10   17
BADLY
    a palping wreaths of badly Yep cigars who jim . . . .   96 & POST IMPR 8   16
    his ghost-lips gradually) remembering badly, softly your . . 300 IS 5 FOUR 17   22
BADNESS
    worship Much and Quick; badness not being felt as . . . . . . 438 NO THANKS 54   3
BAEDEKERS
    large legs rancid voices Baedekers Mothers and kodaks --by . 256 IS 5 ONE 27   16
BAGDAD
    in the city of Bagdad-- mine is a little . . . .   20 T&C PUELLA MEA   132
    in the city of Bagdad.) Keep your dead beautiful . . . . . .   23 T&C PUELLA MEA   288
BAGS
    these twin imminent lisping bags of flesh; became eyes . . . 115 & PORTRAIT 8   22
    condition, i purchased two bags of lukewarm peanuts with . . 326 VIVA 18   15
BAIT
    al -ly jiggle the bait of dawn and be . . . .   49 T&C IMPRESS 3   19
    (transparent or science must bait laws with stars to . . . . 478 NEW POEMS 16   5
BAKED
    curl, bloat, are newly baked and swaggering cookies of . . . 226 IS 5 ONE MAME   13
BALANCED
    pale slippery small eyes balanced upon one broken babypout . 406 NO THANKS 23   10
BALD
    from bushy obscurity a bald greenish foetal head established   96 & POST IMPR 8   28
    i've died) seeing your bald intellect collywobbling on its . 329 VIVA 20   3
    he drinks and) not bald. (Coughs.) Two pale slippery . . . . 406 NO THANKS 23   9
    hopes dance best on bald men's hair and every . . . . 511 50 POEMS 25   9
BALDNESS
    bounds gently from his baldness a smile masturbates softly . 259 IS 5 ONE 29   21
BALL
    mounts from the fireman's ball, i think and also . . . . . . 169 & SON ACTU 18   4
    rouNdar (round) ounDing ; ball balll ballll balllll / . . . . 385 NO THANKS 2   64
BALLOON
    if the moon's a balloon, coming out of a . . . .   129 & SEVEN POEMS 7   2
    take you into their balloon, why then we'd go . . . . 129 & SEVEN POEMS 7   6
    like an old toy balloon) heavily swims to Strunsky's, ... 219 XLI SONNETS 15   12
    slowly in a tight balloon until the smallening world . . . . 360 VIVA 51   13
BALLOONMAN
    luscious the little lame balloonman whistles far and wee . .   24 T&C CHANSONS 1   4
    puddle-wonderful the queer old balloonman whistles far and .   24 T&C CHANSONS 1   12
    spring and the goat-footed balloonMan whistles far and wee .   24 T&C CHANSONS 1   21
BALLOONS
    tell better how the balloons move (as her ghost . . . . 227 IS 5 ONE GERT   3
+BALLOONS
    FOR CONTEXT, SEE . . . . 104 & POST IMPR 14   17
BALLS
    allowed to shine, the balls the chains red and . . . . 192 XLI CHANSONS 2   16
    the click of ivory balls.... noting flies, which jerk . . . . 217 XLI SONNETS 13   2
+BALLS
    FOR CONTEXT, SEE . . . . 315 VIVA 7   16

BAM
    umptyumpty (OO-- ! ting Bam- : do) , chippity. . . . . . . 426 NO THANKS 43   27

BANAL
    animal bottomless eyes importantly banal, Kitty. a whore. . . 74 T&C SON REAL 5   7

BANANA
    it insensible with a banana, establishing meanwhile a re- . . 262 IS 5 ONE 32   24

BAND
    ever hear a jazz Band? or unnoise men don't . . . . 141 & SON REAL 12   17
    in the civil war band and can play the . . . . 253 IS 5 ONE 24   3

BANDWAGGONS
    athlete's mouth jumping on&off bandwaggons (MEMORIAM / / / . 404 NO THANKS 21   4

BANDY
    While permanent faces coyly bandy scandal of Mrs. N . . . . . 70 T&C SON REAL 1   9

BANG
    argue) short (eyes do bang hands angle scoot bulbs . . . . . 309 VIVA 1   12
    honestly now who go (BANG (BANG / / / . . . . 317 VIVA 9   38
    now who go (BANG (BANG / / / / / . . . . 317 VIVA 9   38
    (slopped givers of not) bang spurting mesh (faith -ful . . . 388 NO THANKS 5   11
    world system universe and bang --fear buries a tomorrow . . . 531 50 POEMS 43   2
    no sunbeam ever lies Bang is the meaning of . . . . 570 1 X 1 30   6
    you like" a strawberry bang this blueeyed world (on . . . . . 585 1 X 1 45   3

+BANG
    FOR CONTEXT, SEE . . . . 107 & PORTRAIT 3   15

BANGAROOM
    ram flat hombre sin bangaroom slim guesser goose pin . . . . 333 VIVA 24   17

BANGBELLS
    (things) men selves-them inghurl) bangbells (yawnchurches . . 444 NO THANKS 59   13

BANGED
    my arms and staggered banged with terror through a . . . . . 258 IS 5 ONE 28   23

+BANGED
    FOR CONTEXT, SEE . . . . 347 VIVA 38   12

+BANGLESSLY
    FOR CONTEXT, SEE . . . . 797 73 POEMS 25   8

BANGOFPIANO
    thumPing colours like a bangofpiano colours which, are, the, 100 & POST IMPR 11   10

BANGS
    tones intimate tumult (Into) bangs minds into dream (An) . . 348 VIVA 39   8

BANGUP
    de woild one swell bangup time wen nobody wore . . . . 237 IS 5 ONE 8   16

BAR
    on ceiling- flatness the Bar. tinking luscious jigs dint . . 96 & POST IMPR 8   11
    in a stinking joyman bar a cockney is buying . . . . 108 & PORTRAIT 4   10
    sky Blue, everything: a bar the bar was made . . . . 123 & SEVEN POEMS 2   2
    everything: a bar the bar was made of brass . . . . 123 & SEVEN POEMS 2   2
    was lying on the bar it was cOOl i . . . . 123 & SEVEN POEMS 2   4
    all Hot and the bar was COOl O My . . . . 123 & SEVEN POEMS 2   5

BARBAROUS
    their foreheads to the barbarous bright sky, and suddenly . . 5 T&C EPITHALAM   77
    in spring, the little barbarous Greenwich perfumed fake And . 220 XLI SONNETS 16   10

BARBER
    / (one!) the wisti-twisti barber -pole is climbing people . . 128 & SEVEN POEMS 6   2

BARE
    her curtains, and lays bare her trembling heart, with . . . . 8 T&C OF NICOL   15
    tried and again slo-wly; bare, ly nudg. ing (my . . . . 248 IS 5 ONE 19   15

+BARELY
    FOR CONTEXT, SEE . . . . 248 IS 5 ONE 19   15

BARGAIN
    / / when serpents bargain for the right to . . . . 620 (CHAIRE) 22   1

BARK
    creasing fragility --. Dogs bark children play -ing Are . . . 63 T&C PORTRAIT 10   33
    will kiss your cool bark and hug you safe . . . . 192 XLI CHANSONS 2   9

BARKS
    (listen) this a dog barks and how crazily houses . . . . . . 835 73 POEMS 63   2

BARN
    with north over the barn / / / / . . . . 512 50 POEMS 26   36
    swallows tryst in your barn be glad; nobody ever . . . . . . 514 50 POEMS 28   7
    small facts of hilltop (barn house wellsweep forest & . . . . 755 95 POEMS 83   3

	PAGE	TITLE	LINE

BARN'S
which) he reaches the barn's immense doorway and halts . . . 754 95 POEMS 82 7
BARNS
newly murdered flowers whispering barns bulge a tiniest . . . 340 VIVA 31 12
BARRAGES
i have seen between barrages, the night utter ripe . . . . . 45 T&C LA GUERRE 1 14
+BARREL
FOR CONTEXT, SEE . . . . 680 95 POEMS 8 9
BASE
athanor inimitably tortured the base day utters at length . . 6 T&C EPITHALAM 130
+BASEBALL
FOR CONTEXT, SEE . . . . 392 NO THANKS 9 26
BASED
a re- ligious cult based on consubstantial intangibility. . . 262 IS 5 ONE 32 25
BASH
fists of idiot futures bash the bragging breasts, puppy-faces 151 & SON REAL 22 6
BASHFUL
nothing and when thy bashful hands assume silence beyond . . 210 XLI SONNETS 6 14
BASKET
writhes... A.. lit. tleora basket of RipeBlackbeRRies emptied 101 & POST IMPR 11 53
BASSOON
noon-- noon the implacable bassoon-- now Twilight seeks the . 12 T&C SONGS 2 47
BASTARD
showed billy how" "your bastard boy must have learned . . . . 707 95 POEMS 35 15
BASTARDS
you guilty scamper (you bastards throw dynamite) let knowings 452 NO THANKS 67 5
+BASTARDS
FOR CONTEXT, SEE . . . . 547 1 X 1 7 14
BAT
"we can see a bat in this twilight") there . . . . 353 VIVA 44 4
BATH
jolts of delapida- tion bath-houses whose opened withins . . 94 & POST IMPR 6 4
BATH-HOUSES
jolts of delapida- tion bath-houses whose opened withins . . 94 & POST IMPR 6 4
BATHE
swim who can and bathe who must or any . . . . 390 NO THANKS 7 10
BATHS
lingering, absolute lights like baths of golden snow. This . 208 XLI SONNETS 4 4
BATS
of dreams and little bats & mice (and you, ... 353 VIVA 44 27
BATTENING
Work most old Whose battening gesture prophecies a freeing . 77 T&C SON UNRE 2 12
BATTER
alike the flics rush batter the crowd sprawls collapses . . . 274 IS 5 TWO 9 6
BATTERED
ecstasy while in the battered bodies the odd unlovely . . . . 55 T&C PORTRAIT 3 17
gush clumsily from the battered box fattish and mysterious . 69 T&C POST IMPR 6 23
little amorous-tadpole people wiggled battered by stuttering 173 & SON ACTU 22 5
BATTLE
and wed to valor, battle with heroic breeds; thou, ... 209 XLI SONNETS 5 8
the hero of the Battle of Because he's squatting . . . . . . 642 {CHAIRE} 44 3
BATTLING
cruel-littleness of cold (when battling street-lamps fail . . 142 & SON REAL 13 3
BAY
before the spirit at bay; if this should be, ... 76 T&C SON UNRE 1 8
BAYONETS
means of skilfully applied bayonets roasted hot with heat-- . 339 VIVA 30 30
BE
WORD DELETED, APPEARED 257 TIMES
BEACH
/ I remark this beach has been used too. . . . . 94 & POST IMPR 6 1
so far on the beach below me a little . . . . 281 IS 5 THREE 5 3
went down to the beach (to play one day) . . . . 682 95 POEMS 10 2
stroll some never deepening beach locked in foreverish time's 843 73 POEMS 71 3
BEADS
her trembling heart, with beads of dew made jewels . . . . . 8 T&C OF NICOL 16
frequently fingering the exact beads of a faultless languor . 193 XLI PORTRAIT 1 6

                                                    PAGE   TITLE   LINE
BEAK
   terror of whose furious beak (as sweetly singing creatures . 774 73 POEMS 2   5
+BEAK
   FOR CONTEXT, SEE . . . . 697 95 POEMS 25   23
BEALE
   Tristram slowly dote, La beale Isoud whose leman was. . . . . 17 T&C PUELLA MEA   37
BEAR
   subtle throne twain sphinxes bear each with a writhing . . .   4 T&C EPITHALAM   42
   sing (heart, could we bear the marvel of this . . . . 205 XLI SONNETS 1   15
   bridge rugged as a bear slickern a weazel how . . . . 568 1 X 1 28   7
   bid a good kind bear is angary we fear . . . . 711 95 POEMS 39   19
BEARD
   tiny motheaten old manwhose Beard rests. onthetopwhose silly, 101 & POST IMPR 11   47
   totters, life has a beard" i say to you . . . . 102 & POST IMPR 12   9
BEARS
   jew stands beside his teddy-bears the sailor shuffles the . . 108 & PORTRAIT 4   24
BEAST
   He then, And every beast of the field / . . . . 267 IS 5 TWO 2   20
   clumsily foolishwise (tracking the beast Tomorrow by her . . 374 VIVA 65   7
   clown, traitor, idiot, dreamer, beast-- such was a poet . . . 562 1 X 1 22   9
   down with the fascist beast boom boom) two eyes . . . . 635 {CHAIRE} 37   14
   machine turns less than beast at 6 this bell . . . . 787 73 POEMS 15   12
+BEAST
   FOR CONTEXT, SEE . . . . 544 1 X 1 4   5
BEASTS
   a procession of deep beasts coming with keen ridiculous . . . 112 & PORTRAIT 6   100
   where strove the droll god-beasts do thou distinctly bring . 213 XLI SONNETS 9   9
   wild (at our first) beasts uttered human words --our . . . . 844 73 POEMS 72   1
BEAT
   of mountains ceased to beat? Wind beautifully who wanderest .   3 T&C EPITHALAM   16
   the dew: right wildly beat her heart at every . . . .   8 T&C OF NICOL   28
   knocked her cold and beat it for Chicago. Eddie . . . . 145 & SON REAL 16   4
   her how my least heart-beat becomes less. And then . . . . . 152 & SON ACTU 1   9
   because at least i beat --always think i am . . . . 372 VIVA 63   6
   of scheming how to beat the noblest game a . . . . 679 95 POEMS 7   2
+BEAT
   FOR CONTEXT, SEE . . . . 135 & SON REAL 6   8
BEATIFIC
   Upwardlooking Serene Illustrious and Beatific Lord of . . . . 315 VIVA 7   12
BEATITUDE
   ultimate pose! O visible beatitude sweet sweet intolerable! .   5 T&C EPITHALAM   110
BEATS
   native, who in revenge beats it insensible with a . . . . . . 262 IS 5 ONE 32   23
   any knees but something beats within my shirt to . . . . . . 360 VIVA 51   28
   be nor every partialness beats one entirety neither may . . . 425 NO THANKS 42   11
BEAU
   her ghost lurks, a Beau Brummell sticking in its . . . . . . 227 IS 5 ONE GERT   4
BEAUTEOUS
   while the moving of beauteous dead mouths throughout that . .   6 T&C EPITHALAM   141
   from her cheek the beauteous colour went with every . . . . .   8 T&C OF NICOL   30
   Her body is most beauteous, being for all things . . . . . . 20 T&C PUELLA MEA   135
BEAUTIES
   never boast your dead beauties, you greatest lovers in . . . 22 T&C PUELLA MEA   243
   never boast your dead beauties, mine being unto me . . . . . 22 T&C PUELLA MEA   249
   when) roses complain their beauties are in vain but . . . . . 744 95 POEMS 72   4
BEAUTIFUL
   your voice my soul half-beautiful and wholly droll is . . . . 11 T&C SONGS 2   2
   Hafiz keep your dead beautiful ladies. Mine is a . . . . . . 17 T&C PUELLA MEA   2
   all living things and beautiful. (Caliph and king their . . . 19 T&C PUELLA MEA   128
   words are afraid perfectly beautiful is, forgive these words 22 T&C PUELLA MEA   241
   one-- keep your dead beautiful ladies. Eater of all . . . . . 23 T&C PUELLA MEA   265
   Bagdad.) Keep your dead beautiful ladies Harun Omar and . . . 23 T&C PUELLA MEA   289
   poise a wounding a beautiful suppression the accurate boy . . 54 T&C PORTRAIT 2   7
   -ing Are in the beautiful nonsense of twilight and . . . . . 63 T&C PORTRAIT 10   38
   a time when the beautiful most of her (this . . . . 72 T&C SON REAL 3   11
   make a possible and beautiful sound: if a (perhaps) . . . . . 92 & POST IMPR 4   13
   careful and furious and beautiful elephants (mingled in . . . 95 & POST IMPR 7   14
   a baby smeared with beautiful jam or my invincible . . . . . 166 & SON ACTU 15   13

BEAUTIFUL (CONTINUED)

mind is its own beautiful prisoner. Mine looked long . . . . 170 & SON ACTU 19   1
looking up at our beautiful tree we'll dance and . . . . . . 192 XLI CHANSONS 2   26
more maturely childish, more beautiful almost than you. Yet . 211 XLI SONNETS 7   5
and because she is beautiful / / / / . . . . 216 XLI SONNETS 12   15
angels by O yes beautiful we now pass through . . . . 257 IS 5 ONE 27   32
umbrella. It seemed too beautiful. Let us perhaps excuse . . 263 IS 5 ONE 32   58
and thoroughly into all beautiful things) winter, whom Spring 293 IS 5 FOUR 10   30
grammatical errors "is dead" beautiful Warren Gamaliel . . . 336 VIVA 27   6
A leaf and, Opening beautiful earth put (only) a . . . . . . 397 NO THANKS 14   15
morning; and to morning's beautiful friend twilight (and a . 424 NO THANKS 41   6
for happens only and beautiful there is a ragged . . . . . . 437 NO THANKS 53   9
upward --to have tasted Beautiful to have known Only . . . . 437 NO THANKS 53   12
mightily alive the dear beautiful eternal night / / . . . . . 464 NEW POEMS 2   36
somebody or you are beautiful or deep or generous . . . . . . 475 NEW POEMS 13   13
too busy being her beautiful yes. The place is . . . . 504 50 POEMS 18   12
than were nevers ugly beautiful most is now) / . . . . 565 1 X 1 25   16
ever breathed upon beginning) "beautiful o most beautiful" . 572 1 X 1 32   11
beginning) "beautiful o most beautiful" her, my life worships 572 1 X 1 32   12
and (night) then "everything beautiful can grow" my, her . . 572 1 X 1 32   14
zooms through one perfectly beautiful bow "my home ionian . . 585 1 X 1 45   20
i awoke for the beautiful sake of a grave . . . . 587 1 X 1 47   20
live) spring with all beautiful things when to me . . . . . . 589 1 X 1 49   11
and be will) from beautiful obvious to Mere but . . . . 608 (CHAIRE) 10   6
magical gaiety makes your beautiful name-- i feel that . . . 631 (CHAIRE) 33   12
to here, never to beautiful: a little innocence creates . . . 649 (CHAIRE) 51   7
without, completely dare be beautiful one if should sing . . 666 (CHAIRE) 68   15
fear (my own, my beautiful my blossoming) for also . . . . . 667 (CHAIRE) 69   13
& vivid voltaire you beautiful anarchist (i salute thee . . . 677 95 POEMS 5   15
/ / / / Beautiful is the unmea ning . . . . 713 95 POEMS 41   1
love you much (most beautiful darling) more than anyone . . . 717 95 POEMS 45   1
certainly would (my most beautiful darling) believe in . . . 717 95 POEMS 45   14
in credibly (always are beautiful) ugly" / / / . . . . 738 95 POEMS 66   16
blessed eachness of all beautiful selves wholly which and . . 745 95 POEMS 73   11
fleet and profound this) beautiful kindness sweet such (past 763 95 POEMS 90   24
want no world (for beautiful you are my world, ... 766 95 POEMS 92   7
love by whom (my beautiful friend) the gift to . . . . 776 73 POEMS 4   18
human plane) someone completely beautiful; and Beautiful, who 799 73 POEMS 27   11
someone completely beautiful; and Beautiful, who (truth to . 799 73 POEMS 27   12
dark) laugh long at Beautiful and Brave --wildly who . . . . 799 73 POEMS 27   28
or lose) good true beautiful things god how he . . . . 805 73 POEMS 33   4
the night, bring this beautiful wanderer home to a . . . . . 811 73 POEMS 39   9
night this is a beautiful way) / / / . . . . 824 73 POEMS 52   8

+BEAUTIFUL
FOR CONTEXT, SEE . . . . 268 IS 5 TWO 3   9
FOR CONTEXT, SEE . . . . 500 50 POEMS 14   4
FOR CONTEXT, SEE . . . . 724 95 POEMS 52   5
FOR CONTEXT, SEE . . . . 724 95 POEMS 52   19
FOR CONTEXT, SEE . . . . 724 95 POEMS 52   22

BEAUTIFUL-CURVEOFHUNGER
stomachsClenche Dtoth beautiful-curveofhunger, cHuBbY . . . . 101 & POST IMPR 11 71

BEAUTIFULLY
ceased to beat? Wind beautifully who wanderest over smooth .   3 T&C EPITHALAM   17
bright rain occurs deeply, beautifully and i (being at . . . 92 & POST IMPR 4   7
was New York and beautifully snowing. Inside snug and . . . . 96 & POST IMPR 8   2
was New York and beautifully, snowing.... / / . . . . 97 & POST IMPR 8   45
Ladies you who move beautifully in the winds of . . . . 112 & PORTRAIT 6   95
perfect hunger Yes) how beautifully swims the fooling world . 157 & SON ACTU 6   10
when these thy lips beautifully embrace nothing and when . . 210 XLI SONNETS 6   12
do more than heroes beautifully in shrill armour colliding . 302 IS 5 FIVE 1   12
motif smites truly to Beautifully retire through its english 311 VIVA 3   3
life will shut very beautifully, suddenly, as when the . . . 366 VIVA 57   10
g over (moving) you beautifully also; at denfert the . . . . 384 NO THANKS 2   18
through almost (do they beautifully wandering in merciful . . 582 1 X 1 42   2
and given is how beautifully snow) now i lay . . . . 816 73 POEMS 44   9

+BEAUTIFULLY
FOR CONTEXT, SEE . . . . 657 (CHAIRE) 59   11
FOR CONTEXT, SEE . . . . 715 95 POEMS 43   18

	PAGE	TITLE	LINE

BEAUTY

magnificent herald Spring assembles beauty from forgetfulness	4	T&C EPITHALAM	58
of Spring (with her beauty more than snow dexterous	17	T&C PUELLA MEA	16
(as sometimes the improbable beauty of my lady will)	18	T&C PUELLA MEA	44
But should my lady's beauty play at not speaking	18	T&C PUELLA MEA	61
the Troys of Helen's beauty: never did Lord Jason	18	T&C PUELLA MEA	68
shall not lack for beauty there, nor he that	20	T&C PUELLA MEA	168
ladies goodly store whose beauty did in nothing err.	21	T&C PUELLA MEA	174
of silver in thy beauty is the dilemma of	29	T&C ORIENTALE 3	31
supple flower of thy beauty, my heart discovers thee	31	T&C ORIENTALE 5	28
perfect breasts darkness and beauty of stars was on	39	T&C AMORES 4	17
of science prodded thy beauty . how often have	46	T&C LA GUERRE 2	13
lifted into the awful beauty of sunset the young	48	T&C IMPRESS 2	13
of silver dig) by beauty i declare to you	115	& PORTRAIT 8	4
And then all her beauty is a vise whose	152	& SON ACTU 1	10
he'll not tell where.) beauty makes terms with time	183	XLI SONGS 5	7
feet sun-sheer the smarting beauty of dawn) / /	187	XLI SONGS 9	18
slowly which on thy beauty dreams (proud through the	205	XLI SONNETS 1	5
/ / POEM, OR BEAUTY HURTS MR. VINAL take	230	IS 5 ONE 2	T
gum why talk of beauty what could be more	268	IS 5 TWO 3	9
or Silently Flowers resembles beauty less than our breathing	363	VIVA 54	11
than guessed more than beauty begins the most not	450	NO THANKS 65	11
overlove & underwish of beauty; before keen if dim	480	NEW POEMS 18	7
love whose doom is beauty and its fate to	538	50 POEMS 50	4
higher than have --but beauty is more each than	592	1 X 1 52	4
they call men --but beauty is more now than	592	1 X 1 52	14
better than to grow beauty knows no their goal	742	95 POEMS 70	6
thinking forever's long let beauty touch a blunder (called .	742	95 POEMS 70	13
all goodness truth and beauty lurk, simply to her	790	73 POEMS 18	9
triumphed over vice and beauty bowed to ugliness and	799	73 POEMS 27	37
for the deathlessness who's beauty: reoccurs so magically,	818	73 POEMS 46	6
precise thrill of your beauty, then my lost my	819	73 POEMS 47	13
he's free into the beauty of the truth; and	845	73 POEMS 73	9

+BEAUTY

FOR CONTEXT, SEE	474	NEW POEMS 12	10

BECAME

to escape me and became a great lily atilt	30	T&C ORIENTALE 4	5
to thwart me and became a little bird and	30	T&C ORIENTALE 4	18
have deceived me and became a star in the	30	T&C ORIENTALE 4	32
i without fail entered became and was these twin	115	& PORTRAIT 8	21
lisping bags of flesh; became eyes moist lithe shuddering . .	115	& PORTRAIT 8	23
for her, merrily we became each other humped to	119	& PORTRAIT 11	11
courtesy of five o'clock became the omen of his	197	XLI PORTRAIT 5	11
until the smallening world became absurd; him did an	360	VIVA 51	14
all ghosts of life became) and does our fatally	454	NO THANKS 69	10
head; if every friend became his foe he'd laugh	521	50 POEMS 34	47
that mere fury soon became silence: in huger always	777	73 POEMS 5	9
vanquished instinct and matter became the slave of mind; . .	799	73 POEMS 27	35
as one whole buck became his (believe it or	800	73 POEMS 28	14

BECAUSE

of this it is because you have loved me, ...	39	T&C AMORES 4	5
lover sumptuously being kind because i trust him to	42	T&C AMORES 6	22
i paused a moment because on the frying curb	52	T&C PORTRAIT 1	12
if They were ideas?" "because, sir things which in	91	& POST IMPR 3	10
never sold and <> because Who? wanted them, stomachslikEDead	101	& POST IMPR 11	67
dead it means nearer because deeper firmer since darker . . .	126	& SEVEN POEMS 5	1
having the fastest time because they've never met before . .	126	& SEVEN POEMS 5	7
duced you say Yes because you know you want	126	& SEVEN POEMS 5	21
(but that's not all) because largeness tells you so	127	& SEVEN POEMS 5	38
i am pash possibly because . dusk and if	155	& SON ACTU 4	2
and let's as silence, because Whirl's after all: (after . . .	160	& SON ACTU 9	12
poetry cannot go near because perfectly fearful. meanwhile .	162	& SON ACTU 11	7
i will comfort you because you smell so sweetly	192	XLI CHANSONS 2	8
Humanity i love you because you would rather black	204	XLI LA GUERRE 2	2
for both parties and because you unflinchingly applaud all .	204	XLI LA GUERRE 2	5
Humanity i love you because when you're hard up	204	XLI LA GUERRE 2	9
the pawn shop and because you are continually committing . .	204	XLI LA GUERRE 2	14
Humanity i love you because you are perpetually putting . . .	204	XLI LA GUERRE 2	17

51

BECAUSE (CONTINUED)

down on it and because you are forever making . . . . 204 XLI LA GUERRE 2   22
say--let him be pitiful: because i've travelled all alone . . 216 XLI SONNETS 12   11
and the peaceful, and because she is beautiful / . . . . . . 216 XLI SONNETS 12   15
gone into vaudeville perhaps because my Uncle Sol could . . . 239 IS 5 ONE 10   5
Uncle Sol's farm failed because the chickens ate the . . . . 239 IS 5 ONE 10   15
Uncle Sol's coffin lurched because somebody pressed a button 239 IS 5 ONE 10   33
stand at no window because i can't sleep (smoking . . . . . . 242 IS 5 ONE 13   21
sought newer pastures or because swaddled with a frozen . . . 258 IS 5 ONE 28   12
the slim hinging you --because it's five o'clock and . . . . 282 IS 5 THREE 6   9
drifts (nobody can tell because Nobody knows, or why . . . . 286 IS 5 FOUR 3   6
further than of old because you fooled the doctors, ... 289 IS 5 FOUR 6   15
/ / / because you go away i . . . . 294 IS 5 FOUR 11   1
take the train for because dear whispered again in . . . . . 316 VIVA 8   3
couldn't free the negro because he ant but Coolitch . . . . . 321 VIVA 13   12
expressing "as for myself, because i am slender and . . . . . 328 VIVA 19   15
jerkily) not toucH- ing because separated by an impregnable . 335 VIVA 26   13
separated by an impregnable Because (amount of inter -vening) 335 VIVA 26   14
and Olaf, too preponderatingly because unless statistics lie 339 VIVA 30   40
rome at nightfall; and because against this wall his . . . . 355 VIVA 46   13
which i cannot touch because they are too near . . . . 366 VIVA 57   4
/ / / because i love you) last . . . . 369 VIVA 60   1
i am not heart, because at least i beat . . . . 372 VIVA 63   6
than (if Green invents because where might Where live . . . . 395 NO THANKS 12   6
not have to feel because he thinks (the thoughts . . . . . . 406 NO THANKS 23   1
not have to think because he knows (that anything . . . . . . 406 NO THANKS 23   3
which you think good) because he knows, he cannot . . . . . . 406 NO THANKS 23   5
he knows he owes) because he cannot understand, he . . . . . 406 NO THANKS 23   7
/ / kumrads die because they're told) kumrads die . . . . . . 413 NO THANKS 30   1
and so do i (because they are afraid to . . . . 413 NO THANKS 30   18
! (s r BIRDS BECAUSE AGAINS emarkable s) h? . . . . 421 NO THANKS 38   22
down with ought with because with every brain which . . . . . 424 NO THANKS 41   9
rand handsomely who did because she could what the . . . . . 425 NO THANKS 42   5
movies try to do because they can't i mean . . . . 425 NO THANKS 42   6
for ifs diving under because) only who'll say "and . . . . . 439 NO THANKS 55   24
less unminds must fear because and why what filth . . . . . . 440 NO THANKS 56   6
things without name beyond because things over blame things . 441 NO THANKS 56   58
thunderbolt compose poems not because harm symmetry . . . . . 452 NO THANKS 67   15
symmetry earthquakes starfish (but because nobody can sell . 452 NO THANKS 67   17
by cellophane against anything (because nothing really exists 470 NEW POEMS 8   19
not earn his bread because he would not sell . . . . 473 NEW POEMS 11   3
miss nobody's probably handbag) because i say that's not . . 475 NEW POEMS 13   22
/ beware beware beware because because because equals . . . . 478 NEW POEMS 16   2
beware beware beware because because because equals . . . . . 478 NEW POEMS 16   2
beware beware beware because because because equals (transparent or 478 NEW POEMS 16   2
it beautifool to multiply because and why dividing thens . . 500 50 POEMS 14   5
Mountain) whycoloured worlds of because do not stand against 512 50 POEMS 26   28
were why men breathe-- because my father lived his . . . . . 521 50 POEMS 34   67
and out of black because your absolute courage with . . . . . 522 50 POEMS 35   13
shall see the not because and why but (who . . . . 523 50 POEMS 36   4
eye dissected to mere because and why? take this . . . . . . 527 50 POEMS 39   15
her why she his because / / / / . . . . 533 50 POEMS 45   24
why smashed it into because / / / / . . . . 566 1 X 1 26   8
depths above why's first because (faith's last doubt and . . 574 1 X 1 34   9
will shy wings of because; each why of star . . . . 575 1 X 1 35   17
/ / / darling! because my blood can sing . . . . 580 1 X 1 40   1
are those eyes every because is murdered twice / . . . . . . 588 1 X 1 48   8
hasn't a why or because or although (and buds . . . . 594 1 X 1 54   10
you must understand why because i am dead / . . . . 638 (CHAIRE) 40   15
of the Battle of Because he's squatting in the . . . . 642 (CHAIRE) 44   3
yes: love; and give because the why --gracious wanderer, . . 651 (CHAIRE) 53   11
/ / / / because you take life in . . . . 679 95 POEMS 7   1
will do the same because you aren't afraid to . . . . 679 95 POEMS 7   5
to climb the sky) because a mind no other . . . . 679 95 POEMS 7   7
(without the smallest doubt) because no best is quite . . . . 679 95 POEMS 7   9
conceive a better; and because no evil is so . . . . 679 95 POEMS 7   11
turn immense all time's because to why / / . . . . 679 95 POEMS 7   14
dear) our birth's the because of a why but . . . . 686 95 POEMS 14   11

BECAUSE (CONTINUED)
    stars 14th st dis (because my tears are full . . . . 697 95 POEMS 25   29
    full of eyes) appears. Because only the truest things . . . . 697 95 POEMS 25   30
    things always are true because they can't be true . . . . . . 697 95 POEMS 25   32
    the statue of liberty (because it begins to smell) . . . . . 711 95 POEMS 39   28
    who found forgiveness hard because my (as it happened) . . . 730 95 POEMS 58   3
    too small for death's because to find) may, given . . . . . . 735 95 POEMS 63   2
    small for dying's huge because) given much mercy more . . . . 735 95 POEMS 63   10
    sings birds sing gay-be-gay because today's today) the romp . 773 73 POEMS 1   5
    his friends he loves because he cannot fear (you . . . . . . 774 73 POEMS 2   14
    / / / / because it's Spring thingS dare . . . . 782 73 POEMS 10   1
    the other way round) because it 's A pril . . . . 782 73 POEMS 10   7
    and they die for because though the bell in . . . . 801 73 POEMS 29   4
    but myself; and why? because without any doubt he . . . . . . 802 73 POEMS 30   9
    wings his why beyond because and sings an if . . . . 815 73 POEMS 43   6
+BECAUSE
    FOR CONTEXT, SEE . . . . 604 (CHAIRE) 6   12
    FOR CONTEXT, SEE . . . . 727 95 POEMS 55   14
    FOR CONTEXT, SEE . . . . 782 73 POEMS 10   19
BECAUSELESS
    breathe) wounded us will becauseless ultimate earth accept . 745 95 POEMS 73   5
BECKON
    twilight will dissolve reintegrate beckon through me, i think 379 VIVA 70   12
BECKONED
    and (by octobering flame beckoned) as earth will downward . . 521 50 POEMS 34   42
BECKONINGLY
    thy freedom: star isful beckoningly fabulous crumb / / . . . 456 NO THANKS 71   15
BECKONS
    couch of couches and beckons with the little finger . . . . . 33 T&C ORIENTALE 6   56
    they are alone he beckons, she rises she stands . . . . 35 T&C ORIENTALE 6   109
BECOME
    before a certain face become white perfume only, from . . . . 39 T&C AMORES 4   33
    then did my servant become of the company of . . . . 57 T&C PORTRAIT 5   36
    too much and am become perfectly and simply Lustful... . . . . 157 & SON ACTU 6   2
    fare much better-- what's become of (if you please) . . . . . 233 IS 5 ONE 4   10
    or three drinks what's become of Maeterlinck now that . . . . 233 IS 5 ONE 4   21
    my father used to become hoarse talking about how . . . . . . 276 IS 5 TWO 10   16
    brain hands merely to become the jumping puppets of . . . . . 295 IS 5 FOUR 12   4
    which our separating selves become museums filled with . . . 297 IS 5 FOUR 14   14
    scoot bulbs marry a become) ened (to is see! . . . . 309 VIVA 1   13
    / / sunset) edges become swiftly corners (Besides which, . . 345 VIVA 36   1
    And what may have become of with his gradual . . . . 374 VIVA 65   4
    you wear it will become you; and if you . . . . 484 NEW POEMS 22   3
    whatever's living will yourself become. Girlboys may nothing 484 NEW POEMS 22   4
    cordially invite me to become noone except yourselves r . . . 504 50 POEMS 18   4
    only mystery of love become while every sun goes . . . . . . 510 50 POEMS 24   14
) more dream than become more am than imagine . . . . 571 1 X 1 31   15
    everyone would rather not become; but growing is" erect . . . 626 (CHAIRE) 28   4
    side swoop mountains flimsying become if who'd) me under . . 634 (CHAIRE) 36   4
    wheres which never may become one (wholly strange; familiar . 659 (CHAIRE) 61   6
    are their whys stones become eyes locks open keys . . . . . . 716 95 POEMS 44   23
    by moment day thankfully become each other) one who . . . . . 720 95 POEMS 48   6
    until she and he become (on tiptoe at the . . . . 758 95 POEMS 85   44
    and you; high (are become more than alive) above . . . . . . 762 95 POEMS 89   11
    four and (to quite become nothing) five times, proclaim . . . 764 95 POEMS 90   51
    known things or dreamed become un- / / / . . . . 822 73 POEMS 50   8
    if day has to become night this is a . . . . 824 73 POEMS 52   7
    and yes: if they've become the same it's time . . . . 834 73 POEMS 62   17
+BECOME
    FOR CONTEXT, SEE . . . . 396 NO THANKS 13   15
    FOR CONTEXT, SEE . . . . 448 NO THANKS 63   13
    FOR CONTEXT, SEE . . . . 463 NEW POEMS 1   17
BECOMES
    morning but in twilight becomes unutterably crisp a thing, . 68 T&C POST IMPR 5   7
    how my least heart-beat becomes less. And then all . . . . . 152 & SON ACTU 1   9
    now she sharpens and becomes crisper until i smile . . . . . 301 IS 5 FOUR 18   12
    meaning; or how dreaming becomes if your heart's mine) . . . 364 VIVA 55   4
    way freezes a serpent becomes a rod smiles the . . . . 384 NO THANKS 2   22

BECOMES (CONTINUED)
   you-i as the hill becomes nil) and will somebody . . . . . . 593 1 X 1 53   22
   pouring (alive twice) and becomes eithering dreams the secret 613 {CHAIRE} 15   10
   spring (all our night becomes day) o, it's spring! . . . . . 665 {CHAIRE} 67   18
   gone is who. since becomes why: old turns to . . . . 737 95 POEMS 65   5
   (as what was dusk becomes darkness) innumerably singular . . 741 95 POEMS 69   1
   die to breathe, itself becomes her wonder --and wonderful . . 742 95 POEMS 70   15
   not sorry when silence becomes singing winter by spring, . . 749 95 POEMS 77   16
   magical hour when is becomes if) a bespangled clown . . . . 802 73 POEMS 30   3
   each my deeper death becomes your kiss losing through . . . 810 73 POEMS 38   8
   reoccurs so magically, farthest becomes near (one silent . . 818 73 POEMS 46   7
+BECOMES
   FOR CONTEXT, SEE . . . . 342 VIVA 33   20
   FOR CONTEXT, SEE . . . . 471 NEW POEMS 9   4
   FOR CONTEXT, SEE . . . . 532 50 POEMS 44   2
   FOR CONTEXT, SEE . . . . 581 1 X 1 41   8
BECOMING
   instruct him silently with becoming steps to seek your . . . 42 T&C AMORES 6   12
   a blush enters the becoming garden of her agony . . . . 48 T&C IMPRESS 2   18
   / / my strength becoming wistful in a glib . . . . 131 & SON REAL 2   1
   that i slightly am becoming something a little different, . . 199 XLI PORTRAIT 7 9
   fire all the world becoming bright and little melted. . . . . 283 IS 5 THREE 7   27
   people always) don't die (becoming most buried unbecomingly . 412 NO THANKS 29 15
+BECOMING
   FOR CONTEXT, SEE . . . . 423 NO THANKS 40 10
   FOR CONTEXT, SEE . . . . 715 95 POEMS 43   16
   FOR CONTEXT, SEE . . . . 753 95 POEMS 81   10
BECOMINGLY
   still occur; birds disappear becomingly: a thunderbolt . . . 452 NO THANKS 67 14
BED
   which rising from thy bed steals to his wife . . . . 3 T&C EPITHALAM   5
   thy love unto that bed prepared by whitest hands . . . . . . 6 T&C EPITHALAM 113
   with Egypt went to bed, whom white-thighed Semiramis put . . 22 T&C PUELLA MEA 246
   man is in his bed the city sleeps with . . . . 50 T&C IMPRESS 4 28
   from being brought to bed of crocuses When you . . . . 61 T&C PORTRAIT 9 17
   Nicer To Lie In Bed --eh? I'm not. Again. . . . . 130 & SON REAL 1 13
   / / / the bed is not very big . . . . 134 & SON REAL 5   1
   we grimly go to bed with these legs she . . . . 147 & SON REAL 18 12
   it go rapidly to bed: i will get in . . . . 164 & SON ACTU 13 7
   its smoothness--and leave the bed agrin with memories (this . 164 & SON ACTU 13 10
   white horses are in bed will you walking beside . . . . . . 302 IS 5 FIVE 1   1
   One a on Dirty bed Mangy from person Porous . . . . 312 VIVA 4   18
   the middle of a bed bed bed) when each . . . . 401 NO THANKS 18 3
   middle of a bed bed bed) when each other . . . . 401 NO THANKS 18 3
   of a bed bed bed) when each other courted . . . . 401 NO THANKS 18 4
   death come (in one bed. / / / / . . . . 433 NO THANKS 50 16
   girls with boys to bed will go, / / . . . . 451 NO THANKS 66 16
   perhaps than a newengland bed these ends of arms . . . . . . 506 50 POEMS 20   1
   & you'll find a bed in it (fact) open . . . . 637 {CHAIRE} 39   5
   it (fact) open this bed, sibyl & you'll find . . . . 637 {CHAIRE} 39   7
   if in one little bed she and he lie . . . . 694 95 POEMS 22   7
   but very wonderful in bed --saints and satyrs, go . . . . . 794 73 POEMS 22   6
BEDAD
   traffic get so jammed? bedad it is the famous . . . . 245 IS 5 ONE 16 13
BEDBUGS
   so. maybe: somebody?) or, bedbugs / / / / . . . . 312 VIVA 4   24
BEDDINGS
   is it between such beddings and bumpings of ourselves . . . . 261 IS 5 ONE 31   6
BEDECKED
   with pinkish ponderous arms bedecked whose white thick wrists 225 IS 5 ONE LIZ 7
BEDFELLOWS
   fire is cool took bedfellows for moons mountains for . . . . 420 NO THANKS 37 12
BEDROOM
   the mantelpiece of a bedroom) begins to croon more . . . . . 813 73 POEMS 41   4
BEDTIME
   sort of) A soursweet bedtime -less un- (wonderful) story . . 464 NEW POEMS 2   4
BEE
   million years (while a bee dozes on the poppies, ... 181 XLI SONGS 3   9

		PAGE	TITLE	LINE
BEE (CONTINUED)				
/ / / un (bee) mo vi n (in)		691	95 POEMS 19	1
BEEN				
the others they have been faithful to many things		43	T&C AMORES 7	8
which die i have been sometimes true to Nothing		43	T&C AMORES 7	11
frankly admitting i have been true only to the		43	T&C AMORES 7	21
face lay which had been dorothy and once permitted		52	T&C PORTRAIT 1	17
remark this beach has been used too. much Too.		94	& POST IMPR 6	1
with the others i've been Effie who isn't alive		117	& PORTRAIT 10	24
for the stars have been finished in the nobler		184	XLI SONGS 6	10
and ten pennies have been deposited upon the drum		196	XLI PORTRAIT 4	10
invariably commendable room has been forever subject his . .		197	XLI PORTRAIT 5	21
remark the walls have been repapered he will nod		198	XLI PORTRAIT 6	26
Gillette Razor Blades having been used and reused to		230	IS 5 ONE 2	21
it entirely would have been not my fault. /		263	IS 5 ONE 32	65
all me everyone that's been there knows what i		272	IS 5 TWO 7	12
fragile and which had been presented unto you by		279	IS 5 THREE 3	23
a cliff) what had been something else carefully slowly . . .		283	IS 5 THREE 7	24
since my heart has been with yours shut by		297	IS 5 FOUR 14	1
feel how myself has been coarse and dull compared		301	IS 5 FOUR 18	8
lullabylullaby (I could have been You, You might have		317	VIVA 9	7
You, You might have been I) "?" quoth the		317	VIVA 9	9
hardly never not have been unsorry, perhaps / /		336	VIVA 27	11
children (if he had been playing a fiddle i		355	VIVA 46	18
a fiddle i had been dancing: which is why		355	VIVA 46	19
anything which has ever been invented can spoil this		357	VIVA 48	5
dark) this world has been Picked, like a piece		370	VIVA 61	3
this (which might have been a man and kept		479	NEW POEMS 17	8
than truly there's never been quite such a fool		481	NEW POEMS 19	11
between what hands had been before they died squirming: . . .		506	50 POEMS 20	3
merry bells) Someone has been born everyone is noone		630	(CHAIRE) 32	14
Love only has ever been, is, and will ever		631	(CHAIRE) 33	14
than never to have been what above did was		634	(CHAIRE) 36	8
than was lost has been found has been found		665	(CHAIRE) 67	15
has been found has been found and having is		665	(CHAIRE) 67	15
have and i 've been doing as long as		686	95 POEMS 14	7
Nothing (which would have been Something) what got him . . .		702	95 POEMS 30	22
universe to might have been, and stop ten thousand		714	95 POEMS 42	10
and never which has been or will be told		765	95 POEMS 91	8
a bird. Mostpeople have been heard screaming for		802	73 POEMS 30	29
BEER				
teeth snowy, stick to beer and lime, wear dark, ...		71	T&C SON REAL 2	4
broad "kitty" twice eight --beer nothing, the lady'll have .		74	T&C SON REAL 5	13
BEERS				
they curl loving around beers the world has these		114	& PORTRAIT 7	12
BEES				
are swarms of white bees upon the bough of		29	T&C ORIENTALE 3	7
BEFALL				
tomb rosily gods whiten befall saith rain anguish of		90	& POST IMPR 2	4
BEFORE				
/ / / Always before your voice my soul		11	T&C SONGS 2	1
of the snow, and before your dead face which		11	T&C SONGS 2	29
the merry deer ran before. Fleeter be they than		14	T&C SONGS 4	5
the cruel bugle sang before. Horn at hip went		14	T&C SONGS 4	10
the level meadows ran before. Softer be they than		14	T&C SONGS 4	15
the famished arrow sang before. Bow at belt went		14	T&C SONGS 4	20
the sheer peaks ran before. Paler be they than		14	T&C SONGS 4	25
the lucky hunter sang before. All in green went		14	T&C SONGS 4	30
my heart fell dead before. / / / /		14	T&C SONGS 4	35
reined them in tottering before the throne and as		30	T&C ORIENTALE 4	37
carven of chalcedony and before every door a naked		33	T&C ORIENTALE 6	35
my days shall have before a certain face become		39	T&C AMORES 4	32
skipping high-heeled flames courtesied before my eyes or . .		44	T&C AMORES 8	7
uttering overmuch, stand helplessly before the spirit at bay;		76	T&C SON UNRE 1	8
of his being quake before this its hideous Work		77	T&C SON UNRE 2	11
serenely silently a cathedral before whose upward lean . . .		93	& POST IMPR 5	3
Baby" to numb rhythm before christ / / /		106	& PORTRAIT 2	15
because they've never met before dead's more even than . . .		126	& SEVEN POEMS 5	7

BEFORE (CONTINUED)

and "'Twas the night before Christmas when all through . . .	142	& SON REAL 13	12
cleaned up a few times--before she got the info	145	& SON REAL 16	6
really enough pulled one before one the vague tough	154	& SON ACTU 3	7
i loved....? you) sheath before sheath stripped to the . . .	154	& SON ACTU 3	12
/ / / / before the fragile gradual throne	156	& SON ACTU 5	1
will do to me before shutting.... understand i love	157	& SON ACTU 6	5
painting wholly feels ashamed before this music, and poetry .	162	& SON ACTU 11	6
eternity as Nicho' laid before me bread more downy	194	XLI PORTRAIT 2	31
his queer hands twitter before him, like foolish butterflies	198	XLI PORTRAIT 6	23
send the morning; and before my doubting window leaves . . .	205	XLI SONNETS 1	9
handmirror. "Look at" arranging before me a mellifluous idiot	226	IS 5 ONE MAME	2
Evil sold 69 carloads before publication the girl who	245	IS 5 ONE 16	9
/ / / slightly before the middle of Congressman	249	IS 5 ONE 20	1
fall off the rail before the really train after	263	IS 5 ONE 32	63
and then ◇ and before you can ! &	269	IS 5 TWO 4	7
class American unsullied stands, before the world: with manly	273	IS 5 TWO 8	17
only-just- shined buttons tidiyum before and behind) has a .	274	IS 5 TWO 9	26
smooth entirely our minds --before leaving my room i	288	IS 5 FOUR 5	6
(but we read that beFore) of Course life being	315	VIVA 7	6
prowls, its nose winces before a dissonance of Rish	319	VIVA 11	12
a wish?) touch me, before we perish (believe that	357	VIVA 48	4
and stones; lifted, and (before my eyes sinking) inward, . .	369	VIVA 60	7
/ / / who before dying demands not rebirth	402	NO THANKS 19	1
they're told) kumrads die before they're old (kumrads aren't	413	NO THANKS 30	2
carve time so we'll before what's death come (in	433	NO THANKS 50	14
pu tting the arse before the torse / /	477	NEW POEMS 15	10
every but any) heart--wholly, idiotically--before such . . .	480	NEW POEMS 18	4
& underwish of beauty; before keen if dim quiveringly	480	NEW POEMS 18	7
spangle & thingless & before flashing soft neverwheres & . .	480	NEW POEMS 18	10
gushing tinsel; silently yes before angel curvings upon a . .	480	NEW POEMS 18	12
your exploding my) heart before how worlds delicate of . . .	480	NEW POEMS 18	16
of joy: quietly & before illimitably spiralling candy of . .	480	NEW POEMS 18	21
what hands had been before they died squirming: now	506	50 POEMS 20	3
We've Met subhuman rights Before / / / /	549	1 X 1 9	14
known complexity was born before the moon before God	577	1 X 1 37	14
born before the moon before God wished Himself into	577	1 X 1 37	15
immemorial of whens) before each heartbeat which i	577	1 X 1 37	19
i and every world, before silence begins a star	601	(CHAIRE) 3	19
which has never happened before-- and shining this our . . .	667	(CHAIRE) 69	7
edge, of life (inquiry before snow / / /	712	95 POEMS 40	9
a failing year --now, before quite your whisper's whisper . .	821	73 POEMS 49	9

BEFRIENDED

her troubles, and milly befriended a stranded star whose . .	682	95 POEMS 10	5

BEFRIENDING

it's no good pretending befriending means loving" (sighs . .	625	(CHAIRE) 27	5

BEGAN

the three trickling chins began to traipse into the	73	T&C SON REAL 4	11
and impertinently dead. expression began with the early . . .	103	& POST IMPR 13	6
jerkily, themselves quietly they began playing with a button	284	IS 5 FOUR 1	9
asleep, elsewhere our dreams began which now are folded: . .	304	IS 5 FIVE 3	7
steam be- ginning and began to sing all here	523	50 POEMS 36	9
predicted end who never began of god and fiend?	527	50 POEMS 39	6
a circustent and everything began when man determined to . .	566	1 X 1 26	4

+BEGAN

FOR CONTEXT, SEE	472	NEW POEMS 10	2

BEGET

sing a rose shall beget the spring that maidens	16	T&C SONGS 6	6

BEGGAR

/ i am a beggar always who begs in	298	IS 5 FOUR 15	1
awry? Blow king to beggar and queen to seem	560	1 X 1 20	5

BEGGARS

lousy full. of. rain beggars yaw: nstretchy: awn) then, . . .	442	NO THANKS 57	15
is the winner (and beggars are rich but misers	769	95 POEMS 95	4
far near blue if beggars are rich (and a	769	95 POEMS 95	22

BEGGING

pockets of lame and begging colour) while there and	93	& POST IMPR 5	15

	PAGE	TITLE	LINE
BEGIN			
foal, whereof young moons begin the newness of his	11	T&C SONGS 2	4
just as smaller stars begin to husk heaven) you, ...	71	T&C SON REAL 2	11
young mouth whose lips begin a smile exactly strange-- . . .	85	T&C SON ACTU 4	8
when the jolly shells begin dropping jolly fast you	269	IS 5 TWO 4	4
their very tidiyum necks begin) let us add that	274	IS 5 TWO 9	15
in the alive west begin requiescat this six feet	277	IS 5 THREE 1	4
to their knees. people begin crossing people) and hErE . . .	280	IS 5 THREE 4	8
saucers but cups if begin to spoons dance every-	287	IS 5 FOUR 4	16
you believe it? i begin to and that doesn't	289	IS 5 FOUR 6	9
darkness where new lights begin and increase, since your . .	297	IS 5 FOUR 14	3
with birds seriously i begin to climb the best	434	NO THANKS 51	5
such life could not begin to live id est	510	50 POEMS 24	6
of isn't shall never begin to begin to imagine	512	50 POEMS 26	15
shall never begin to begin to imagine how (only	512	50 POEMS 26	16
only the snow can begin to explain how children	515	50 POEMS 29	22
moon singing desire into begin joy was his song	520	50 POEMS 34	20
bigger than the least begin less littler than forgive	530	50 POEMS 42	11
miracle peace: or (if begin the colours of your	559	1 X 1 19	5
only we our least begin to guess / /	574	1 X 1 34	14
april) who younger than begin are, the worlds move	575	1 X 1 35	38
stopping to think) you begin to feel of it, ...	604	(CHAIRE) 6	10
keen illimitable secret of begin / / /	669	(CHAIRE) 71	14
plati -num fl- oozey begin to (a -lm- ost)	704	95 POEMS 32	11
darkness noone can quite begin to guess (except my	717	95 POEMS 45	7
my love " could begin to imagine quite such	748	95 POEMS 76	12
more than all worlds begin to (see?) begin /	750	95 POEMS 78	16
worlds begin to (see?) begin / / / /	750	95 POEMS 78	16
a moment ceasing to begin the mystery of day	756	95 POEMS 84	3
love did no more begin than love will end;	768	95 POEMS 94	2
it was in the begin ning it is now	803	73 POEMS 31	13
somebody or you can begin to begin to imagine)	816	73 POEMS 44	12
you can begin to begin to imagine) something which	816	73 POEMS 44	12
big gest could even begin to be) dream of;	840	73 POEMS 68	17
+BEGIN			
FOR CONTEXT, SEE	421	NO THANKS 38	9
FOR CONTEXT, SEE	421	NO THANKS 38	9
FOR CONTEXT, SEE	536	50 POEMS 48	4
BEGINNING			
a strong fragile house (beginning at the singular beginning .	83	T&C SON ACTU 2	4
(beginning at the singular beginning of your smile) a	83	T&C SON ACTU 2	4
a gradual stir of beginning muscle, and what it	157	& SON ACTU 6	4
let us mildly contemplate beginning with his wellfilled pants	266	IS 5 TWO 1	32
once is never the beginning of enough, is it	282	IS 5 THREE 6	2
not all but the beginning of mySelf / /	294	IS 5 FOUR 11	20
made of thing in beginning corners dawn smirks and	322	VIVA 14	13
not and same answer, beginning, ecstasy, to dare: prouder . .	351	VIVA 42	5
it was in the beginning it (rejoice) was and	425	NO THANKS 42	10
briefness dig for love beginning means return seas who . . .	526	50 POEMS 38	5
god ever breathed upon beginning) "beautiful o most	572	1 X 1 32	10
/ / if in beginning twilight of winter will	808	73 POEMS 36	1
+BEGINNING			
FOR CONTEXT, SEE	523	50 POEMS 36	7
FOR CONTEXT, SEE	803	73 POEMS 31	13
BEGINNINGLESS			
if) swallowing is everywhere beginningless a Magic of green .	757	95 POEMS 85	14
BEGINNINGLY			
muchmouthed) her way of beginningly finishing (and such hair)	337	VIVA 28	12
+BEGINNINGLY			
FOR CONTEXT, SEE	444	NO THANKS 59	4
BEGINNINGS			
the rule) and dark beginnings are his luminous ends	420	NO THANKS 37	10
BEGINS			
when the spent day begins to frail (whose grave	115	& PORTRAIT 8	1
largeness and this largeness begins to give you, the	127	& SEVEN POEMS 5	35
bore --When The Sun Begins To (with a phrasing	130	& SON REAL 1	3
with these legs she begins to heave and twine	147	& SON REAL 18	13
of her obsolete gaze begins to. lean.... a little	148	& SON REAL 19	12

	PAGE	TITLE	LINE

BEGINS (CONTINUED)

mind of me somewhere begins again, shares the year's	156 & SON ACTU 5	11
hills an edged nothing begins to prune let's live	160 & SON ACTU 9	9
i says the mmmoon, begins to, drool softly, in	167 & SON ACTU 16	16
silk wrinkling loth stocking begins queerly to do a	225 IS 5 ONE LIZ	4
tree flights an Sam begins boxin im on duh	332 VIVA 23	9
/ An (fragrance) Of (Begins) millions Of Tints (and)	348 VIVA 39	2
ing ? mind (moon begins The) now, est	350 VIVA 41	10
did <> did) who begins stuttering each sentence we	398 NO THANKS 15	10
eyelands) sin uously&them&twi tching, begins unununun? . . .	445 NO THANKS 60	13
guessed more than beauty begins the most not imagined	450 NO THANKS 65	11
all life more death begins to grow end's ending	502 50 POEMS 16	8
face goes (if how begins a pillow's green means	506 50 POEMS 20	9
(over dull all nouns) begins a whole verbal adventure	557 1 X 1 17	14
if strangers meet life begins-- not poor not rich	564 1 X 1 24	3
less alive than never begins to yes but if	580 1 X 1 40	21
dark alive but) look: begins to grow more than	582 1 X 1 42	8
every world, before silence begins a star / /	601 {CHAIRE} 3	20
of liberty (because it begins to smell) / /	711 95 POEMS 39	28
knows a mindless he begins to guess what no	716 95 POEMS 44	16
tells (such as ourselves) begins to sing an only	716 95 POEMS 44	19
yes the speckled strut begins to scretch and scratch-scrutch	773 73 POEMS 1	13
until my second dream begins-- the sky is wild	777 73 POEMS 5	5
with wind (and hark begins to Rain) a house	785 73 POEMS 13	7
out of climbing whom begins to spill such golden	811 73 POEMS 39	12
mantelpiece of a bedroom) begins to croon more particularly .	813 73 POEMS 41	4

+BEGINS

| FOR CONTEXT, SEE . . . . | 423 NO THANKS 40 | 9 |

+BEGOTTEN

| FOR CONTEXT, SEE . . . . | 398 NO THANKS 15 | 18 |

BEGS

kneeling, your frequent mercy begs, sharply believe me, . . .	115 & PORTRAIT 8	8
Mounier a little love begs, Mimi with the body	121 & PORTRAIT 12	48
a beggar always who begs in your mind (slightly	298 IS 5 FOUR 15	2
close when the oak begs permission of the birch	620 {CHAIRE} 22	9

BEGUILES

| bliss of heavenly earth beguiles our spirits, whose . . . . . | 675 95 POEMS 3 | 2 |

BEGUN

| unserious twilight) shadows have begun the hair's worm huge, | 84 T&C SON ACTU 3 | 10 |

BEHAVED

| "a bloke wot's well behaved" ...and always try to . . . . . . | 229 IS 5 ONE FRAN | 11 |

BEHELD

| unsated eyes which have beheld night's speechless carnival . | 36 T&C AMORES 1 | 12 |
| by well- drawn icecakes beheld being too strong, in . . . . . | 262 IS 5 ONE 32 | 12 |

BEHEMOTH

| gargle to jip hug behemoth truly pseudo yours podia . . . . . | 333 VIVA 24 | 24 |

BEHIND

like a song heard behind a golden door, poet	22 T&C PUELLA MEA	222
elephant twelve feet high behind whose ear sits always . . .	32 T&C ORIENTALE 6	9
squats with quiveringgold body behind the emperor ten elected	34 T&C ORIENTALE 6	74
may watch together how behind the doomed exact smile	43 T&C AMORES 7	29
joy pathetic dress fluttering behind her a mothermonster with	56 T&C PORTRAIT 4	5
talks about you somewhere behind your back it makes	126 & SEVEN POEMS 5	18
pinkness, one pale dog behind a slopcaked shrub painstakingly	144 & SON REAL 15	7
voice the kingdomofheaven up behind and crazily skating . . .	259 IS 5 ONE 29	3
buttons tidiyum before and behind) has a nucleolus: the . . .	274 IS 5 TWO 9	26
there are old men behind me I tell you;	281 IS 5 THREE 5	24
back. (Along the sand behind us, a big yellow	303 IS 5 FIVE 2	12
Shame as (out from behind Nowhere) creeps the deep	330 VIVA 21	13
sit dying thinking huddled behind dir ty glass mind	354 VIVA 45	5
And sit huddling dumbly behind three or two partly	354 VIVA 45	18
flower of Dreaming) somewhere behind us always trying (or . .	368 VIVA 59	9
my sharpening life are (behind each no) touching every . . .	373 VIVA 64	18
(stuck in a spanked behind / / / /	408 NO THANKS 25	16
a cross in her behind they do not give	427 NO THANKS 44	6
village does not move behind my eye the windmills	434 NO THANKS 51	8
know him (and while behind death's death whenless voices . .	450 NO THANKS 65	17
disappear finally what's left behind is (just a head	501 50 POEMS 15	18

                                                          PAGE   TITLE   LINE
BEHIND (CONTINUED)
  are am (beyond when behind where under un) / . . . . 505 50 POEMS 19   24
  when till it rolled behind forever, we touched a . . . . . . 612 (CHAIRE) 14   9
  dream's eternity (you feel behind this man earth's first . . 617 (CHAIRE) 19   4
  always fall (yes but behind yes) without or until . . . . . 634 (CHAIRE) 36   11
+BEHIND
  FOR CONTEXT, SEE . . . . 469 NEW POEMS 7   1
BEHOLD
  space god worships God-- (behold! where chaste stars writhe . 77 T&C SON UNRE 2   16
  as now i love behold this fool who, in . . . . 360 VIVA 51   11
  lean from the window, behold ghosts, a man hugging . . . . . 375 VIVA 66   6
  not i not you behold nor any breathing creature . . . . 582 1 X 1 42   11
+BEHOLD
  FOR CONTEXT, SEE . . . . 392 NO THANKS 9   11
BEHOLDING
  cling & kiss neither beholding a nor seen by . . . . 698 95 POEMS 26   7
BEING
  born and cease for being whiter than this world) . . . . . .   5 T&C EPITHALAM   101
  is to stroke my being with numbing forests frolicsome, . . . 19 T&C PUELLA MEA   90
  body is most beauteous, being for all things amorous . . . . 20 T&C PUELLA MEA   136
  a blossom is, which being a little while caressed . . . . . . 21 T&C PUELLA MEA   191
  your dead beauties, mine being unto me sweeter (of . . . . . 22 T&C PUELLA MEA   250
  as your lover sumptuously being kind because i trust . . . . 42 T&C AMORES 6   20
  a sloppy body from being brought to bed of . . . . 61 T&C PORTRAIT 9   17
  All terrors of his being quake before this its . . . . 77 T&C SON UNRE 2   10
  of your eyes, when (being fool to fancy) i . . . . 78 T&C SON UNRE 3   3
  astonishment feel in my being the delirious smart of . . . . 79 T&C SON UNRE 4   12
  me said the) wind being A lady in a . . . .   91 & POST IMPR 3   19
  deeply, beautifully and i (being at a window in . . . . . .   92 & POST IMPR 4   8
  the low ceiling my being pleasantly was punctuated by . . . . 96 & POST IMPR 8   25
  / / / PORTRAITS being twelve who hast merely . . . . 105 & PORTRAIT 1   1
  pin tailored flames Her being at this instant commits . . . . 137 & SON REAL 8   11
  nothing as much as being by her seen, which . . . . 141 & SON REAL 12   14
  rain- darkness, the sunset being sheathed i sit and . . . . . 186 XLI SONGS 8   3
  dark box dreaming of being taken out and allowed . . . . . . 192 XLI CHANSONS 2   15
  imperceptible content my friend's being, out of the . . . . . 193 XLI PORTRAIT 1   19
  that i cleverly am being altered that i slightly . . . . . . 199 XLI PORTRAIT 7   8
  mysticism of entire vertical being, i am skilfully construed 201 XLI PORTRAIT 9   24
  Whose favour nothing is (being of men called Love) . . . . . 210 XLI SONNETS 6   4
  strangeness must abuse....) Time being not for us, purple . . 213 XLI SONNETS 9   15
  peace. which i do, being as Dick Mid once . . . . 229 IS 5 ONE FRAN   9
  / / / she being Brand -new; and you . . . . 248 IS 5 ONE 19   1
  oh and her gears being in A 1 shape . . . . 248 IS 5 ONE 19   17
  quite a mistake in being at all born, seeing . . . . 262 IS 5 ONE 32   6
  well- drawn icecakes beheld being too strong, in brief . . . 262 IS 5 ONE 32   12
  petal confutes... to exist being a peculiar form of . . . . 264 IS 5 ONE 33   4
  which shout and cling, being for a little while . . . . 264 IS 5 ONE 33   14
  and no sense. Which being quite beyond dispute as . . . . . . 266 IS 5 TWO 1   5
  im -peccable cravat directing being shooting his cuffs . . . 275 IS 5 TWO 9   34
  / / / if being mortised with a dream . . . . 285 IS 5 FOUR 2   1
  their fellows but i being otherwise made compose curves . . . 291 IS 5 FOUR 8   2
  house of you love being such, or such, the . . . . 292 IS 5 FOUR 9   13
  / / / you being in love will tell . . . . 295 IS 5 FOUR 12   1
  they cry "to be, being, that i am alive . . . . 295 IS 5 FOUR 12   17
  you i say (it being Spring and night) "let . . . . 303 IS 5 FIVE 1   1
  of my mind. awake being not asleep, elsewhere our . . . . . . 304 IS 5 FIVE 3   7
  / / / Space being (don't forget to remember) . . . . 315 VIVA 7   1
  beFore) of Course life being just a Reflex you . . . . 315 VIVA 7   7
  it All Up god being Dead (not to mention . . . . 315 VIVA 7   9
  deep and inexplicable not being dollars toenails or ideas . . 322 VIVA 14   8
  paper sailors--argonauta argo harmoniously being with his . . 326 VIVA 18   7
  thing about "stuffed fauna" being "very . . . . 326 VIVA 18   33
  raiment with phenomena: such being a conduct worthy of . . . 328 VIVA 19   6
  whose vast one function being to enter a Toy . . . . 337 VIVA 28   2
  per blunt instruments-- Olaf (being to all intents a . . . . 339 VIVA 30   15
  not eat" our president, being of which assertions duly . . . 339 VIVA 30   34
  bigly climb what (love being some- thing possibly more . . . 358 VIVA 49   7
  it Will come (we being unwound & gone into . . . . 361 VIVA 52   3

59

	PAGE	TITLE	LINE
BEING (CONTINUED)			
/ / / but being not amazing: without love	374	VIVA 65	1
absorbs eternal near) day being come, Love, put on	376	VIVA 67	14
love's also there: and being here imprisoned, tortured here .	377	VIVA 68	7
always don't there B being no such thing for	390	NO THANKS 7	2
and give than lend --being through failures born who	394	NO THANKS 11	12
timidly, throb; which hints being; suggests identity)	402	NO THANKS 19	10
away (his autumn's winter being summer's spring who moved . .	420	NO THANKS 37	3
(establish new) come, what Being! open us open our	422	NO THANKS 39	12
and Quick; badness not being felt as bad, itself	438	NO THANKS 54	3
Hearts are sick, Hearts being sick, Minds nothing can: . . .	438	NO THANKS 54	22
this mind made war being generous this heart could	440	NO THANKS 56	2
to fabricate unknownness (known being wishless; but love, all	446	NO THANKS 61	2
catch telescopes) why. Being is patience is patient	478	NEW POEMS 16	8
/ / / must being shall one only thing	480	NEW POEMS 18	1
hands (you may recall) being lost including captain Pater .	494	50 POEMS 8	7
who's much too busy being her beautiful yes. The	504	50 POEMS 18	12
wise the people remember being born) when and if	505	50 POEMS 19	16
just so long will being pay the rent of	511	50 POEMS 25	5
one i say human being) one goldberger / /	524	50 POEMS 36	46
doom yea (fresh complexions being oke with him) one	552	1 X 1 12	23
than sleep illimitably my --being so very born no	558	1 X 1 18	12
grow) one's anything old being everything new (with a	594	1 X 1 54	14
to wit a human being --let's remember that /	607	(CHAIRE) 9	15
hides; yet man can, being all, escape from none)	609	(CHAIRE) 11	4
the self of this being are growing stones (neither	617	(CHAIRE) 19	8
of all nothing--human merely being doubt unimaginable You? .	663	(CHAIRE) 65	11
the great advantage of being alive (instead of undying) . . .	664	(CHAIRE) 66	1
transcends november's year (eternity being so sans until . .	765	95 POEMS 91	13
/ / / / being to timelessness as it's	768	95 POEMS 94	1
vainly who strive; and being finally released flee one . . .	799	73 POEMS 27	30
love equals mob love being youamiare (2) the holy	803	73 POEMS 31	8
can create the whole (being forever born a foolishwise . . .	845	73 POEMS 73	6
+BEING			
FOR CONTEXT, SEE	101	& POST IMPR 11	65
FOR CONTEXT, SEE	471	NEW POEMS 9	4
BEINGALIVE			
& (5) unbeingdead isn't beingalive / / / / /	803	73 POEMS 31	18
BEINGEST			
what of the wonder (beingest growingest) over all under . . .	590	1 X 1 50	20
BEINGS			
keen creatures of idiom (beings alert and innocent very . . .	19	T&C PUELLA MEA	94
BELCH			
soft right old feller belch the chap hic sum-	96	& POST IMPR 8	21
BELCHES			
tables the abominable floor belches smoky laughter into the .	55	T&C PORTRAIT 3	4
BELIEFS			
(laws clocks fears hopes beliefs compulsions doubts &	755	95 POEMS 83	17
--when all fears hopes beliefs doubts disappear. Everywhere .	812	73 POEMS 40	13
BELIEVABLE			
of orish mind --nothing believable inhabits here: overs of .	761	95 POEMS 88	5
(blinded by merely things believable) could only fancy we . .	809	73 POEMS 37	6
BELIEVABLY			
a Toy and emerging (believably enlarged) make how many . . .	337	VIVA 28	3
little more always less believably so than (how should . . .	748	95 POEMS 76	8
+BELIEVABLY			
FOR CONTEXT, SEE	827	73 POEMS 55	6
BELIEVE			
/ / if i believe in death be sure	39	T&C AMORES 4	1
unscented shapeless spirited) they believe in Christ and . .	70	T&C SON REAL 1	5
frequent mercy begs, sharply believe me, wholly, well --did .	115	& PORTRAIT 8	9
it from me kiddo believe me my country, 'tis	230	IS 5 ONE 2	2
if we are to believe these gently O sweetly	230	IS 5 ONE 2	24
Bent fer election makin believe dey was chust born	237	IS 5 ONE 8	19
the first ride and believe i we was happy	248	IS 5 ONE 19	25
way up the Campanile, believe thou me cocodrillo-- mine . . .	256	IS 5 ONE 27	8
what i say i believe my most intimate friends	262	IS 5 ONE 32	14
what i and you believe; not for philosophy does	264	IS 5 ONE 33	19

		PAGE	TITLE	LINE

BELIEVE (CONTINUED)

eat sunlight (do you believe it? i begin to . . . . 289 IS 5 FOUR 6   9
go from several persons: believe me that strangers arrive . . 295 IS 5 FOUR 12   8
yellow dog. You don't believe? look back. (Along the . . . . 303 IS 5 FIVE 2   11
be ele- vating" Miss (believe it or) Gay is . . . . 327 VIVA 18   42
me, before we perish (believe that not anything which . . . . 357 VIVA 48   5
must deny mind: may believe in brains. / / . . . . 402 NO THANKS 19   15
don't and kumrads won't believe in life) and death . . . . . 413 NO THANKS 30   6
told him: he couldn't believe it (jesus told him; . . . . . . 553 1 X 1 13   3
told him; he wouldn't believe it) lao tsze certainly . . . . 553 1 X 1 13   5
mam) sherman; and even (believe it or not) you . . . . 553 1 X 1 13   14
told him (he didn't believe it, no sir) it . . . . 553 1 X 1 13   19
we're everyanything more than believe (with a spin leap . . . 594 1 X 1 54   41
a saboteur then we'll believe in that incredible unanimal . . 620 (CHAIRE) 22   13
uppercut but everybody (i believe) else thought lucinda . . . 706 95 POEMS 34   3
is have doubt and believe (like me like you) . . . . 716 95 POEMS 44   26
(my most beautiful darling) believe in nothing but love . . . 717 95 POEMS 45   14
nearer than each our heartbeat--believe that love (and only . 741 95 POEMS 69   5
whole buck became his (believe it or don't) by . . . . 800 73 POEMS 28   15
of am perceive (but believe scarcely may) certainly while . . 808 73 POEMS 36   9
not guests of seem) believe me, dear, clocks have . . . . . 817 73 POEMS 45   7
world deny may or believe / / / / . . . . 845 73 POEMS 73   14

+BELIEVE

FOR CONTEXT, SEE . . . . 600 (CHAIRE) 2   11

BELIEVED

this nobody would have believed would they no kidding . . . . 270 IS 5 TWO 5   4

BELIEVES

deep nakedness death most believes, perpetual girls marching 138 & SON REAL 9   10
/ / / memory believes fragrance of a town . . . . 340 VIVA 31   1
any dusk but kneelingly believes thy secret and each . . . . 351 VIVA 42   13

BELIEVING

its feeble stem is believing science=(2b)-n herr professor m 329 VIVA 20   4
Were your eyes: lost, believing; hushed with when / . . . . . 432 NO THANKS 49   20
silent skies bluer than believing) a little gay earth . . . . 583 1 X 1 43   3
these my not themselves believing eyes adventuring, enormous 669 (CHAIRE) 71   3
proportion with generosities beyond believing (though flesh . 683 95 POEMS 11   2
gay (today tomorrow, doubting believing and to lend to . . . 798 73 POEMS 26   17
the universe --love. Each believing world denies, whereas . . 845 73 POEMS 73   11

BELL

midnight (and did occur bell beyond fiercely spurting bell . 115 & PORTRAIT 8   18
bell beyond fiercely spurting bell a jetted music splashing . 115 & PORTRAIT 8   18
while toddle rings the bell. But if her tall . . . . 227 IS 5 ONE GERT   7
dream-- flaming a coolly bell touches most mere until . . . . 601 (CHAIRE) 3   13
man reminding with his bell to disappear a sun . . . . 624 (CHAIRE) 26   3
gone reminding with his bell to reappear a moon . . . . 624 (CHAIRE) 26   23
life where the young bell tolled and the old . . . . 647 (CHAIRE) 49   14
beast at 6 this bell 's whisper asks (of . . . . 787 73 POEMS 15   13
for because though the bell in the steeple says . . . . . . 801 73 POEMS 29   5

+BELL'S

FOR CONTEXT, SEE . . . . 787 73 POEMS 15   13

BELLE

pas que je suis belle cheri? les anglais m'aiment . . . . . 120 & PORTRAIT 12   11

BELLES

will He buy? Les belles bottes--oh hear ,pas cheres") . . . . 102 & POST IMPR 12   20

BELLOW

in the slot and bellow like a bool to . . . . 500 50 POEMS 14   12

BELLOWING

you imagine His surprise bellowing through the general noise 117 & PORTRAIT 10   9

BELLOWINGS

lilac shrieks and scarlet bellowings. / / / / . . . . 199 XLI PORTRAIT 7   12

BELLS

are the betrayal of bells comprehended through incense / . . 29 T&C ORIENTALE 3   33
the litanies the great bells are ringing with rose . . . . . 51 T&C IMPRESS 5   6
rose the lewd fat bells and a tall wind . . . . 51 T&C IMPRESS 5   7
flowers were pulling upon bells of gold i looked . . . . . . 58 T&C PORTRAIT 6   10
filled with fear people bells) i say your eyes . . . . 98 & POST IMPR 9   2
(1) ing of just bells (touch) ing ? mind . . . . 350 VIVA 41   8
up so floating many bells down) spring summer autumn . . . . 515 50 POEMS 29   2

61

		PAGE	TITLE	LINE

BELLS (CONTINUED)
up so floating many bells down) one day anyone . . . . . . 515 50 POEMS 29 24
we (pretty twinkle merry bells) Someone has been born . . . . 630 (CHAIRE) 32 13
godtown (kissed bigly by bells) / / / / . . . . 681 95 POEMS 9 16
a final dream of bells; perfectly outlined against afterglow 750 95 POEMS 78 2
faith! ! life love! bells cry bells (the sea . . . . 841 73 POEMS 69 5
life love! bells cry bells (the sea of the . . . . 841 73 POEMS 69 5
cities to eyes) drift bells glide seethe glow (undering . . . 841 73 POEMS 69 22
+BELLS
FOR CONTEXT, SEE . . . . 444 NO THANKS 59 1
FOR CONTEXT, SEE . . . . 444 NO THANKS 59 7
FOR CONTEXT, SEE . . . . 444 NO THANKS 59 13
FOR CONTEXT, SEE . . . . 444 NO THANKS 59 17
FOR CONTEXT, SEE . . . . 444 NO THANKS 59 18
FOR CONTEXT, SEE . . . . 444 NO THANKS 59 31
FOR CONTEXT, SEE . . . . 444 NO THANKS 59 31
FOR CONTEXT, SEE . . . . 444 NO THANKS 59 33
FOR CONTEXT, SEE . . . . 444 NO THANKS 59 34
FOR CONTEXT, SEE . . . . 444 NO THANKS 59 36
FOR CONTEXT, SEE . . . . 444 NO THANKS 59 37
FOR CONTEXT, SEE . . . . 444 NO THANKS 59 38
FOR CONTEXT, SEE . . . . 444 NO THANKS 59 40
BELLY
/ the poem her belly marched through me as . . . . 135 & SON REAL 6 1
to peek into the belly whose deep squirm nibbles. . . . . . . 143 & SON REAL 14 10
BELLY'S
whereby to grasp the belly's ample vase (that urgent . . . . 21 T&C PUELLA MEA 197
kiss of her riant belly's fooling bore --When The . . . . . 130 & SON REAL 1 2
crust (only feeling the belly's merry thrust Boost my . . . . 132 & SON REAL 3 7
BELLYFUL
or everybody gets a bellyful without lifting my finger . . . 475 NEW POEMS 13 8
BELONG
O thou to whom belong the hearts of lovers! . . . . 7 T&C EPITHALAM 166
bodies big and boozing belong to Marj the greenslim . . . . . 114 & PORTRAIT 7 16
BELONGING
grace, in an engraving belonging to my friend. Whom . . . . 158 & SON ACTU 7 8
by these (particularly belonging to a retired general) . . . 341 VIVA 32 7
BELOVED
/ / / listen beloved i dreamed it appeared . . . . 30 T&C ORIENTALE 4 2
upon my mouth listen beloved i dreamed in my . . . . 30 T&C ORIENTALE 4 16
upon my blood listen beloved i dreamed i thought . . . . . 30 T&C ORIENTALE 4 30
then your dancesong soul. rarely-beloved a single star is . . 186 XLI SONGS 8 18
--i shall not smile beloved; i shall not weep: . . . . . . 210 XLI SONNETS 6 8
i love of thee (beloved) this and truly i . . . . 215 XLI SONNETS 11 4
whisper This is my beloved my (suddenly in sunlight . . . . . 352 VIVA 43 15
+BELOVED
FOR CONTEXT, SEE . . . . 339 VIVA 30 4
BELOW
mysteries , life. Far below myself the lunging leer . . . . . 202 XLI PORTRAIT 9 35
(i pant for what's below. the singer. Wall. i . . . . 220 XLI SONNETS 16 6
all gondola signore day below me gondola signore gondola . . 256 IS 5 ONE 27 24
far on the beach below me a little girl . . . . 281 IS 5 THREE 5 3
faintly playing moving far below us perhaps one villa . . . . 283 IS 5 THREE 7 9
doubt and humbly heights below) kneeling, we--true . . . . . 574 1 X 1 34 10
BELOWTRY
whisper sum blinked he belowtry eye nowbrow sangsung nee . . 333 VIVA 24 9
BELT
sang before. Bow at belt went my love riding . . . . 14 T&C SONGS 4 21
BEN
yessir wheel no sendwisp ben jiffyclaus bug fainarain wee . . 333 VIVA 24 19
+BEN
FOR CONTEXT, SEE . . . . 342 VIVA 33 9
BEND
ouredRoom and, my ears bend to the little silent . . . . . 101 & POST IMPR 11 45
gradually into hands) and bend into the huge disaster . . . . 305 IS 5 FIVE 4 3
light droops, all measures bend nor marvel if a . . . . . . 446 NO THANKS 61 6
BENDING
touch wishing by willows, bending upon streams? / / . . . . . 211 XLI SONNETS 7 18

+BENDING
    FOR CONTEXT, SEE . . . . 278 IS 5 THREE 2   7
    FOR CONTEXT, SEE . . . . 389 NO THANKS 6   10
BENEATH
    breasts My strong fingers beneath the snow Into strenuous . . 16 T&C SONGS 6   9
    a kingdom wholly is. Beneath her thighs such legs . . . . . . 21 T&C PUELLA MEA 207
    miraculous inflected oral devious, beneath the body's . . . . 21 T&C PUELLA MEA 211
    a howdah of jasper beneath saffron umbrellas upon an . . . . 32 T&C ORIENTALE 6   5
    mind blossom will stumble beneath a clumsiest disguise, . . . 91 & POST IMPR 3   12
    of a solemn mechanism. beneath her drab tempo of . . . . . . 103 & POST IMPR 10
    of gold delicately crouching beneath silver youths the . . . 110 & PORTRAIT 6   35
    what's beyond logic happens beneath will; nor can these . . . 264 IS 5 ONE 33   5
    various and while everywhere beneath thee and about thyself . 351 VIVA 42   9
    beyond sound down (slowly beneath sight fall ing) fall . . . 432 NO THANKS 49   5
    than even death's what beneath breathing selves transported . 454 NO THANKS 69   5
    and me a moon; beneath, bombed the by ocean . . . . 639 {CHAIRE} 41   3
BENEVOLENT
    careful) O, the darling benevolent mindless He--and She-- . . 250 IS 5 ONE 21   7
BENT
    every bough that reverently bent to touch the yellow . . . . 8 T&C OF NICOL   31
    ports of costlier commerce bent / / / / . . . . 79 T&C SON UNRE 4   16
    say elation causes the bent eyes thickly to protrude-- . . . 229 IS 5 ONE FRAN   13
    aroun wid eachudder Hell Bent fer election makin believe . . 237 IS 5 ONE 8   19
    erect cursing hatless who (bent by wind) slammed hard- . . . 277 IS 5 THREE 1   10
    her a fragile light bent gatheringly / / / . . . . 284 IS 5 FOUR 1   18
    etc (as the boodle's bent is the crowd inclined . . . . . . 635 {CHAIRE} 37   22
+BENT
    FOR CONTEXT, SEE . . . . 408 NO THANKS 25   10
BENTHAM
    you can't dentham comma bentham; or 1 law for . . . . 791 73 POEMS 19   6
BEQUEATH
    all we inherit, all bequeath and nothing quite so . . . . . 521 50 POEMS 34   64
BEREAVES
    poison of sure sleep bereaves us of our slow . . . . 210 XLI SONNETS 6   2
BERINGED
    rosenbloom picks strawberries with beringed hands) but if i . 287 IS 5 FOUR 4   9
+BERLIN
    FOR CONTEXT, SEE . . . . 237 IS 5 ONE 8   5
BESEECH
    hearts of lovers! --I beseech thee bless thy suppliant . . . 7 T&C EPITHALAM 167
BESIDE
    unsheared fleece is mean beside its lovelier friends, between 11 T&C SONGS 2   13
    voice which always dwells beside the vivid magical impetuous 19 T&C PUELLA MEA 116
    Afterwards she is sitting beside young death, is slender; . . 102 & POST IMPR 12   25
    smiles the jew stands beside his teddy-bears the sailor . . . 108 & PORTRAIT 4   24
    your flesh mind breathing beside under around myself) by . . 283 IS 5 THREE 7   17
    bed will you walking beside me, my very lady, ... 302 IS 5 FIVE 1   2
    there is a ragged beside the who limps man . . . . 437 NO THANKS 53   10
    and what were summer's beside their glories downward if . . . 573 1 X 1 33   5
BESIDES
    edges become swiftly corners (Besides which, i note how . . . 345 VIVA 36   2
BESPANGLED
    is becomes if) a bespangled clown standing on eighth . . . . 802 73 POEMS 30   4
BEST
    girls smoothanduseless i, like, best, the, stomachs, of the . 101 & POST IMPR 11   76
    little striker having the best time tickling away every- . . 126 & SEVEN POEMS 5   11
    / on the Madam's best april the twenty nellie . . . . 251 IS 5 ONE 22   1
    in spite of the best overseeing) i mean that . . . . 264 IS 5 ONE 33   16
    flowers. Don't cry --the best gesture of my brain . . . . . 290 IS 5 FOUR 7   11
    is curved since the best he can do is . . . . 292 IS 5 FOUR 9   7
    to demonstrate the biggest best busiest city and presently . 326 VIVA 18   11
    than truth untrue, the best mouth i have seen . . . . 344 VIVA 35   8
    begin to climb the best hill, driven by black . . . . 434 NO THANKS 51   6
    whom for worst or best (and proudly things only . . . . . . 441 NO THANKS 56   52
    grow or hopes dance best on bald men's hair . . . . 511 50 POEMS 25   9
    hail sam done the best he kin till they . . . . 568 1 X 1 28   3
    who made the world's best one hand snatch / . . . . 645 {CHAIRE} 47   4
    smallest doubt) because no best is quite so good . . . . . . 679 95 POEMS 7   10

| | PAGE | TITLE | LINE |

BESTIAL
of strangling breasts and bestial grovelling hands rasps the   28 T&C ORIENTALE 2   7
between the breasts of bestial Marj lie large men . . . . . . 114 & PORTRAIT 7   2
between the breasts of bestial Marj for the strong . . . . . 114 & PORTRAIT 7   26
BET
kum een, dare ease Bet, an Leelee, an dee . . . . 73 T&C SON REAL 4   13
the elevator but I bet two bits come seven . . . . 125 & SEVEN POEMS 4   10
princess FlOaTs doll-angel-life from Bet: To; Bouncing, Bet . 747 95 POEMS 75   7
from Bet: To; Bouncing, Bet the ruby&emerald zigging HE . . . 747 95 POEMS 75   7
+BETH
FOR CONTEXT, SEE . . . . 73 T&C SON REAL 4   13
BETRAYAL
thy eyes are the betrayal of bells comprehended through . . . 29 T&C ORIENTALE 3   32
BETTER
seberries, it, loves these better than, cubesandovalsof . . . 100 & POST IMPR 11   28
(not knowing how much better than me will you . . . . 153 & SON ACTU 2   12
frail, peace (dreaming is better) murdering coolness slowly . 168 & SON ACTU 17   12
new a thing. Muscles better and nerves more. i . . . . 175 & SON ACTU 24   3
whitely live by? or better, queens, queens laughing lightly . 211 XLI SONNETS 7   13
jounce possibly can tell better how the balloons move . . . . 227 IS 5 ONE GERT   3
we scarcely fare much better-- what's become of (if . . . . . 233 IS 5 ONE 4   9
and kisses are a better fate than wisdom lady . . . . 290 IS 5 FOUR 7   8
makes some feel more better when all ought to . . . . 466 NEW POEMS 4   23
whatever they sing is better than to know and . . . . 481 NEW POEMS 19   3
inquires is your cough better today? nn-nn went head . . . . 506 50 POEMS 20   8
and round early to better is wiser for worse. . . . . 513 50 POEMS 27   10
sir what may be better or what may be . . . . 568 1 X 1 28   21
although (and buds know better than books don't grow) . . . . 594 1 X 1 54   11
mean worlds may have better luck, some day?" "Or . . . . . . 603 (CHAIRE) 5   11
you don't conceive a better; and because no evil . . . . . . 679 95 POEMS 7   11
and i like you better than everything in the . . . . 717 95 POEMS 45   3
fail and cease --but better than to grow beauty . . . . 742 95 POEMS 70   5
eye cue unquote. Much better than which, every woman . . . . 807 73 POEMS 35   9
BETTERS
an accident whose niceness betters easily the intent of . . . 162 & SON ACTU 11   3
BETTY
/ / / goodby Betty, don't remember me pencil . . . . 71 T&C SON REAL 2   1
so pale: pale) for betty was born to never . . . . 509 50 POEMS 23   19
BETTYANDISBEL
far and wee and bettyandisbel come dancing from hop-scotch . 24 T&C CHANSONS 1   14
BETWEEN
him bold to imitate between the feet of awe), ...   4 T&C EPITHALAM   36
(thee will i praise between those rivers whose white . . . .   9 T&C SONGS 1   1
beside its lovelier friends, between your thoughts more white 11 T&C SONGS 2   13
world will dance upon Between my lips which did . . . . 16 T&C SONGS 6   5
passion wastes will lay between their little breasts My . . . 16 T&C SONGS 6   8
bodies in a row between slow glories fleetly go.) . . . . . . 20 T&C PUELLA MEA   144
a brown god smiles between greentwittering smokes from broken 28 T&C ORIENTALE 2   4
of a good minstrel between them is always a . . . . 29 T&C ORIENTALE 3   14
when my heart sang between your perfect breasts darkness . . 39 T&C AMORES 4   15
Roupy i have seen between barrages, the night utter . . . . . 45 T&C LA GUERRE 1   14
/ / / / between nose-red gross walls sprawling . . . . 55 T&C PORTRAIT 3   1
of Woman and how between her hips India is . . . . 95 & POST IMPR 7   18
piece of money held between his thumb and first . . . . 102 & POST IMPR 12   4
eaten by yester- day between the nibbling timid teethful . . 112 & PORTRAIT 6   79
/ / / / between the breasts of bestial . . . . 114 & PORTRAIT 7   1
large men who lie between the breasts of bestial . . . . . . 114 & PORTRAIT 7   25
strong men who sleep between the legs of Lil . . . . 114 & PORTRAIT 7   29
dizzily grips. Querying greys between mouthed houses curl . . 139 & SON REAL 10   12
the mouth who sits between her cheeks utters a . . . . 143 & SON REAL 14   5
frail lips almost discussed; between her and ourselves a . . 146 & SON REAL 17   13
-colour. Hair. he put between her lips a moist . . . . 148 & SON REAL 19   9
/ autumn is: that between there and here gladness . . . . . . 158 & SON ACTU 7   1
your smile is stirringofbirds between my arms; but i . . . . 163 & SON ACTU 12   18
a little puppy hopping between skipping children (It is . . . 167 & SON ACTU 16   8
a sharp agreeable flower between my amused legs kissing . . . 172 & SON ACTU 21   11
/ / / / between green mountains sings the . . . . 185 XLI SONGS 7   1
squeak of planes or between squeals of Nothing grabbed . . . 195 XLI PORTRAIT 3   13

BETWEEN (CONTINUED)
    n'est-ce pas effendi drifts between tables like an old   . . . 198 XLI PORTRAIT 6   15
    like an old leaf between toadstools he is the . . . . 198 XLI PORTRAIT 6   17
    i like, i'll take between thy hands what no . . . . 212 XLI SONNETS 8   13
    for whose twitching lips, between you and me almost . . . . . 227 IS 5 ONE GERT   6
    leak rather is it between such beddings and bumpings . . . . 261 IS 5 ONE 31   6
    willowing out and in between bottles, who step smoothly . . . 279 IS 5 THREE 3   14
    the whys which lurk between your naked shoulderblades. --Here 282 IS 5 THREE 6   23
    souls inhabit whatever is between them) knowing my lips . . . 285 IS 5 FOUR 2   5
    against me, smile; or (between dawn and twilight) giving   . . 285 IS 5 FOUR 2   14
    the year a cigarette between his ghost-lips gradually) . . . 300 IS 5 FOUR 17   20
    hither and) softly thither between (tumb ling) houses (as . . 319 VIVA 11   6
    ideas thoroughly's stolen (somewhere between our unlighted . 322 VIVA 14   9
    like a dream (and between houses, really a kind . . . . 353 VIVA 44   9
    Queen among centuries universes between Who out of deeplyness 358 VIVA 49   12
    world what's wrong with (between me and we) the . . . . 411 NO THANKS 28   9
    (sometimes in Spring somewhere between what is and what . . . 428 NO THANKS 45   9
    pinch that purple book between what hands had been . . . . . 506 50 POEMS 20   3
    a dead house clutch between eyes emptiness toss one . . . . . 522 50 POEMS 35   2
    n skyline on earth between whose d owdy hou . . . . 788 73 POEMS 16   8
    the holy miraculous difference between firstrate & second . . 803 73 POEMS 31   9
+BETWEEN
    FOR CONTEXT, SEE . . . . 104 & POST IMPR 14   16
    FOR CONTEXT, SEE . . . . 201 XLI PORTRAIT 9   2
    FOR CONTEXT, SEE . . . . 384 NO THANKS 2   3
    FOR CONTEXT, SEE . . . . 581 1 X 1 41   4
BETWIXT
    sun's white hands emboss, betwixt whose absolute feet anoint   3 T&C EPITHALAM   30
    shuddering sacrament of sleep, betwixt whose cool . . . . . .   7 T&C EPITHALAM   156
BEWAIL
    may envy neither; nor bewail (would rather make than . . . . 394 NO THANKS 11   10
BEWARE
    the world howls stadesmen beware of politisions beware of . . 405 NO THANKS 22   4
    stadesmen beware of politisions beware of folks with missians 405 NO THANKS 22   5
    / / / / beware beware beware because because . . . . 478 NEW POEMS 16   1
    / / / beware beware beware because because because . . . . . 478 NEW POEMS 16   1
    / / beware beware beware because because because equals . . . 478 NEW POEMS 16   1
    stern miraculous this every truth--beware of heartless them . 556 1 X 1 16   6
    tale concludes herewith: soldier, beware of mrs smith / . . . 799 73 POEMS 27   41
BEWITCH
    it is wholly to bewitch my smallest thought with . . . . . .   18 T&C PUELLA MEA   78
BEYOND
    fond soul seriously yearns beyond this fern of sunset . . . .   12 T&C SONGS 2   42
    Thee i call rich beyond wishing if this thou . . . .   13 T&C SONGS 3   17
    its leaves inimitable find beyond the white authentic . . . .   19 T&C PUELLA MEA   120
    the white authentic springs, beyond the sweet instinctive . .   19 T&C PUELLA MEA   121
    lady, in that always beyond this poem or any . . . .   22 T&C PUELLA MEA   238
    house silently sits looking beyond the kissing and the . . .   57 T&C PORTRAIT 5   8
    / / POST IMPRESSIONS beyond the brittle towns asleep . . . .   64 T&C POST IMPR 1   1
    When what's in velvet beyond doomed thought is like . . . . .   81 T&C SON UNRE 6   9
    of wallowing male (shock beyond shock blurted) strokes, . . . 115 & PORTRAIT 8   13
    (and did occur bell beyond fiercely spurting bell a . . . . . 115 & PORTRAIT 8   18
    stiffening slow shrill eyes beyond a fit- and-cling of . . . 155 & SON ACTU 4   8
    stars are opening one beyond one immaculate curving cool . . 156 & SON ACTU 5   3
    the flinger of fire beyond red rivers of fair . . . . 185 XLI SONGS 7   5
    bashful hands assume silence beyond the mystery of rhyme . . 210 XLI SONNETS 6   15
    sexual smell of lilies.... beyond night's silken immense . . 214 XLI SONNETS 10   12
    is in a hurry beyond that any this taxi . . . . 238 IS 5 ONE 9   5
    form of sleep what's beyond logic happens beneath will; . . . 264 IS 5 ONE 33   5
    sense. Which being quite beyond dispute as prove from . . . . 266 IS 5 TWO 1   5
    painter of your voice-- beyond these elements remarkably . . 291 IS 5 FOUR 8   16
    and since nothing lingers beyond a little instant, along . . 293 IS 5 FOUR 10   10
    go a very little beyond the last road--there's something . . 303 IS 5 FIVE 2   2
    it's nothing paradoxically enough beyond mere personal pride 329 VIVA 20   1
    of twi -light pale beyond soft- liness than dream . . . . . . 349 VIVA 40   5
    insect, humanity, achieves (moult beyond difficult moult) . . 351 VIVA 42   11
    who slightly always are beyond the reach of death . . . . . . 357 VIVA 48   13
    me this fear (which beyond night shall go) remembering . . . 362 VIVA 53   2

BEYOND (CONTINUED)

    guess a grassblade Thinks beyond or around (as poems   . . . . 364 VIVA 55   7
    have never travelled, gladly beyond any experience, your eyes 366 VIVA 57   1
    wear your dearest fears beyond their ceaselessness (nor has . 372 VIVA 63   10
    dear (and worlds whirl beyond worlds: immortal yonder . . . 376 VIVA 67   12
    miraculously above the always beyond such wheres and fears . 378 VIVA 69   13
    say that both precisely beyond either were-- so in . . . . . 379 VIVA 70   2
    of mirrors (have died beyond the clock) we, of . . . . . . 386 NO THANKS 3   2
    girth are mountains; and beyond all hurt of praise . . . . . 418 NO THANKS 35   13
    darkly taking rain) drown, beyond sound down (slowly beneath 432 NO THANKS 49   3
    snow things without name beyond because things over blame . . 441 NO THANKS 56   58
    New and upon the beyond imagining spasm rise we . . . . . . 442 NO THANKS 57   21
    A trifle less (merely beyond how very) closely than . . . . . 453 NO THANKS 68   6
    immeasurable dream wherelessly spiralling) beyond time's sky 454 NO THANKS 69   8
    is who are am (beyond when behind where under . . . . 505 50 POEMS 19   24
    moving are twilight they beyond near) girlest she slender . . 518 50 POEMS 32   5
    keen as midsummer's keen beyond conceiving mind of sun . . . 520 50 POEMS 34   25
    (death and life safely beyond) plays with the bigness . . . . 554 1 X 1 14   3
    when (love's a universe beyond obey or command, reality . . . 574 1 X 1 34   7
    only love immortally occurs beyond the mind) such a . . . . . 576 1 X 1 36   8
    one merely opening leaf (beyond whose nearness there is . . . 592 1 X 1 52   8
    nearness there is no beyond) or does some littler . . . . . . 592 1 X 1 52   8
    took it my far beyond far and high beyond . . . . 593 1 X 1 53   14
    beyond far and high beyond high bluer took it . . . . 593 1 X 1 53   15
    took it our away beyond where what a wonderful . . . . 593 1 X 1 53   18
    times earth: a flame beyond soul immemorially forevering am-- 599 (CHAIRE) 1   4
    holiness a pilgrim from beyond the future's future; and . . . 601 (CHAIRE) 3   9
    is to taste not (beyond death and life) imaginable . . . . . 674 95 POEMS 2   11
    of proportion with generosities beyond believing (though . . 683 95 POEMS 11   2
    of all sweet things beyond whatever mind may comprehend, . . 688 95 POEMS 16   10
    dream and (through stillness beyond conceiving) dream until . 757 95 POEMS 85   35
    of prose mind utterly beyond is brief that how . . . . 763 95 POEMS 90   20
    and all) no power beyond the trick to seem . . . . 766 95 POEMS 92   23
    sings love's every truth beyond all since and why . . . . . . 783 73 POEMS 11   4
    but they're few all (beyond win or lose) good . . . . 805 73 POEMS 33   2
    mine (or any truth beyond perceive) quivers this miracle . . 809 73 POEMS 37   2
    find selves unimaginably mine; beyond sorrow's own joys and . 810 73 POEMS 38   10
    most joy) faithfully blossoming beyond to breathe suns of . . 811 73 POEMS 39   8
    who wings his why beyond because and sings an . . . . 815 73 POEMS 43   6
    of where and when beyond) now and here (far . . . . 832 73 POEMS 60   7
+BEYOND
    FOR CONTEXT, SEE . . . . 447 NO THANKS 62   9
BEYONDS
    love) comprehends huger easily beyonds than timelessly alive 741 95 POEMS 69   6
+BIBLE
    FOR CONTEXT, SEE . . . . 635 (CHAIRE) 37   19
BICEPS
    fourteenth fifth's deep purring biceps, the mystic screech of 220 XLI SONNETS 16   2
BID
    do as you are bid a good kind bear . . . . 711 95 POEMS 39   18
BIDDY
    earth like a tipsy biddy with an old mop . . . . 203 XLI LA GUERRE 1   2
BIEN
    americains aussi, ils payent bien les americains dance . . . 120 & PORTRAIT 12   27
BIG
    violets dandelions And the big bullying daisies through the . 26 T&C CHANSONS 3   5
    glide. I into the big vermilion departure swim, sayingly; . . 66 T&C POST IMPR 3   11
    funny hat with a big feather is tied under . . . . 69 T&C POST IMPR 6   42
    face scribbled with a big grin. her sow- eyes . . . . 73 T&C SON REAL 4   6
    twitter wickedly whereas the big and firm legs moving . . . . 95 & POST IMPR 7   13
    money fuzzily mouths take big wobbly foot-steps every goggle 96 & POST IMPR 8   19
    hands but their bodies big and boozing belong to . . . . . . 114 & PORTRAIT 7   15
    eyes moist lithe shuddering big, the luminous laughter, and . 115 & PORTRAIT 8   23
    sister could with our big brother who is would . . . . 117 & PORTRAIT 10   19
    in your Brain--my, head's big she (said laughing) . . . . . 123 & SEVEN POEMS 2   13
    with your head. all big / / / / . . . . 123 & SEVEN POEMS 2   15
    bed is not very big a sufficient pillow shoveling . . . . . . 134 & SON REAL 5   1
    right slapped the amusing big vital vicious vegetable of . . 148 & SON REAL 19   5

BIG (CONTINUED)

a week with a big toothless girl in Yonkers.	149 & SON REAL 20	12
smoke: remembering, two pink big lips curl.... how Jimmie	149 & SON REAL 20	15
Horizontal Business (set on big legs nice to pinch	150 & SON REAL 21	8
autumn indisputably roaming death's big rotten particular	158 & SON ACTU 7	14
who eye sO neatly big / / / /	159 & SON ACTU 8	17
says to me you big fool she says i	167 & SON ACTU 16	12
was morning (that is, big horses; light feeling up	172 & SON ACTU 21	2
parting flesh.... And eyes big love-crumbs, and possibly i	175 & SON ACTU 24	12
forgot to shut your big eyes. where did you	191 XLI CHANSONS 1	4
my mind is a big hunk of irrevocable nothing	199 XLI PORTRAIT 7	2
anisettes as. One opaque big girl jiggles thickly hips	220 XLI SONNETS 16	15
blunt unslender, what her big unkeen "Business is rotten"	225 IS 5 ONE LIZ	11
and how these wooden big two feet conclude happeningly	229 IS 5 ONE FRAN	4
neiges.... some guys talks big about Lundun Burlin an	237 IS 5 ONE 8	4
rapid lapfulls of idiotic big hands / / /	251 IS 5 ONE 22	23
evangelist buttons with his big gollywog voice the	259 IS 5 ONE 29	2
kilt last with the big eyes i loved like	271 IS 5 TWO 6	9
six feet of Breton big good body, which terminated	277 IS 5 THREE 1	6
the least matter. The big fear Who held us	289 IS 5 FOUR 6	2
follows us like a big yellow dog. You don't	303 IS 5 FIVE 2	10
sand behind us, a big yellow dog that's.... now	303 IS 5 FIVE 2	12
now it's red a big red dog that may	303 IS 5 FIVE 2	13
tho nithe steered his big was) thither to thence	316 VIVA 8	12
e (wut) hova in big cumbine wid i (check	325 VIVA 17	17
duh clap an talkin big how dey could kill	332 VIVA 23	3
into itself, an awful big light squoits down my	332 VIVA 23	27
of Olaf glad and big whose warmest heart recoiled	339 VIVA 30	1
into a together whitely big there is but if	365 VIVA 56	9
& one dog? piglike big! sorrows always; finally and	384 NO THANKS 2	11
unkindness exit little mr Big notbusy Busi ness notman	389 NO THANKS 6	3
lie bravely down sleep big rain big snow big	393 NO THANKS 10	13
down sleep big rain big snow big sun big	393 NO THANKS 10	14
big rain big snow big sun big moon (enter	393 NO THANKS 10	15
big snow big sun big moon (enter us) /	393 NO THANKS 10	16
/ brIght bRight s??? big (soft) soft near calm	455 NO THANKS 70	2
near sta? calm star big yEs alone (wHo Yes	455 NO THANKS 70	8
Yes near deep whO big alone soft near deep	455 NO THANKS 70	12
thin very much more big & kinder of ring	470 NEW POEMS 8	13
that spell that out big (bigger than cosmic rays	475 NEW POEMS 13	18
forehead. No body loved big that quick sharp thick	490 50 POEMS 4	8
keep up with how big very them) now (it	501 50 POEMS 15	10
anything, everything little looks big in a mist and	514 50 POEMS 28	8
much too not quite big enough to hold one	523 50 POEMS 36	31
earth so glad and big even a thing all	526 50 POEMS 38	2
kind of a blind big sound on the ground	543 1 X 1 3	30
is worse squats a big dove on g w's	545 1 X 1 5	11
from a funeral eyes "big thing" / / /	567 1 X 1 27	23
a whippoorwill; heart was big as the world aint	568 1 X 1 28	16
go let all go--the big small middling tall bigger	569 1 X 1 29	16
of a whisper so (big with innocence) forgivingly a	601 (CHAIRE) 3	3
(smiling) strike agains De Big Boss (crying) jew wop	618 (CHAIRE) 20	10
bub? (bubs) where's John Big Doughgob Big pastmaster of	642 (CHAIRE) 44	21
where's John Big Doughgob Big pastmaster of the Art	642 (CHAIRE) 44	22
anything be pleasanter (some big dark little day which	650 (CHAIRE) 52	6
(nothing whichful about thick big this friendly himself of	658 (CHAIRE) 60	2
whippoorwill this moonday into (big with unthings) tosses	751 95 POEMS 79	3
the Lovestar grows most big a voice comes out	752 95 POEMS 80	1
love, all safely small big wickedly worlds of world	761 95 POEMS 88	12
old worlds and young (big little and all worlds)	776 73 POEMS 4	6
(dull worlds or keen; big little and all) but	776 73 POEMS 4	12
until: but pitiful they've (big little and all) no	776 73 POEMS 4	22
(dim worlds or bright; big little and all) whereas	776 73 POEMS 4	28
glad sorry or both (big little and all) /	776 73 POEMS 4	40
in his kind sweet big voice: then a slender	813 73 POEMS 41	2
mi (dreamlike) st makes big each dim inuti ve	829 73 POEMS 57	3
the all, & a (big ger than big gest	840 73 POEMS 68	13
a (big ger than big gest could even begin	840 73 POEMS 68	15

+BIG

FOR CONTEXT, SEE . . . . 73 T&C SON REAL 4   13
FOR CONTEXT, SEE . . . . 646 (CHAIRE) 48   15

BIGGER

tiniest smile? may Be bigger than the fear of . . . . 397 NO THANKS 14   6
spell that out big (bigger than cosmic rays war . . . . . . 475 NEW POEMS 13   18
a this world into bigger much some out of . . . . 516 50 POEMS 30   14
never than alive less bigger than the least begin . . . . . 530 50 POEMS 42   11
an a: fear no bigger th an a hope) . . . . 532 50 POEMS 44   14
he took one breath bigger than a circustent and . . . . . . 566 1 X 1 26   3
big small middling tall bigger really the biggest and . . . . 569 1 X 1 29   17
every new bird no bigger than to sing) leaf . . . . 583 1 X 1 43   17
a little star no bigger than not to understand . . . . . . 622 (CHAIRE) 24   3
petals of silence) hole bigger than never to have . . . . . 634 (CHAIRE) 36   7
(see the) with the bigger much than biggest (little . . . . 715 95 POEMS 43   13
each (a wish no bigger than) in roguish am . . . . 763 95 POEMS 90   8

+BIGGER

FOR CONTEXT, SEE . . . . 840 73 POEMS 68   13

BIGGEST

thumbs: picture His peering biggest whey coloured face on . . 117 & PORTRAIT 10   32
from whose living and biggest bodies lopped of every . . . . 195 XLI PORTRAIT 3   20
his wellfilled pants earth's biggest grafter, nothing less; . 266 IS 5 TWO 1   33
offering to demonstrate the biggest best busiest city and . 326 VIVA 18   11
more than very much biggest & thickest & kindest . . . . . . 470 NEW POEMS 8   16
tall bigger really the biggest and all things--let all . . . 569 1 X 1 29   18
the bigger much than biggest (little is) now (dancing . . . . 715 95 POEMS 43   13

+BIGGEST

FOR CONTEXT, SEE . . . . 840 73 POEMS 68   15

BIGGISH

me. The eyes which biggish loll the hands' will . . . . . . 131 & SON REAL 2   13

BIGLY

Findingest whispers understand sobs bigly climb what (love . 358 VIVA 49   7
awake) slow tottering visions bigly come crashing into go . . 565 1 X 1 25   13
the by ocean earth bigly shudders) never was death . . . . . 639 (CHAIRE) 41   4
man's thingfulest godtown (kissed bigly by bells) / / . . . . 681 95 POEMS 9   16

BIGMORNING

play with ◇ (will BigMorning get away with them? . . . . . . 169 & SON ACTU 18   11

BIGNESS

/ LA GUERRE the bigness of cannon is skilful, ... 45 T&C LA GUERRE 1   1
beyond) plays with the bigness of his littleness --electrons 554 1 X 1 14   4

BIGTWITTERING

canounchir p ing the bigtwittering zither-and the mealy, . . 100 & POST IMPR 11   42

BILL

diamond he gave her. Bill was put wise that . . . . 145 & SON REAL 16   9
some tricks with my bill as long as there's . . . . 707 95 POEMS 35   9

+BILL

FOR CONTEXT, SEE . . . . 24 T&C CHANSONS 1   6

BILL'S

/ / / Buffalo Bill's defunct who used to . . . . 60 T&C PORTRAIT 8   1
/ it started when Bill's chip let on to . . . . 145 & SON REAL 16   1

BILLIARD

sex squeaked like a billiard-cue chalking itself, as not . . 170 & SON ACTU 19   9

BILLIARD-CUE

sex squeaked like a billiard-cue chalking itself, as not . . 170 & SON ACTU 19   9

BILLIARDBALLS

terrific quadruped swoons into billiardBalls! / / / / . . . . 315 VIVA 7   16

BILLIARDS

playing with Lord Rothermere billiards very well by moonlight 262 IS 5 ONE 32   21

BILLIKEN

the stomach like A billiken with hisknees huggedtogether it, 101 & POST IMPR 11   60

BILLION

terror through a million billion trillion stars / / . . . . . 258 IS 5 ONE 28   24
right impatiently replied two billion pubic lice inside one . 473 NEW POEMS 11   5
worlds) in love a billion brains may coax undeath . . . . . . 664 (CHAIRE) 66   19
with a million flaming billion kinds of nameless silence) . . 786 73 POEMS 14   15

BILLS

read Papernapkin no laundry bills likes People preferring . . 410 NO THANKS 27   6

BILLY

bitch could have showed billy how" "your bastard boy . . . . 707 95 POEMS 35   14

BINGBONGWHOM

/ from the cognoscenti bingbongwhom chewchoo laugh dingle . . 333 VIVA 24   2

BIPEDS

godly toothless ◇ ◇ bipeds) OH the bothering dear . . . . . 250 IS 5 ONE 21   15

BIRCH

begs permission of the birch to make an acorn--valleys . . . 620 {CHAIRE} 22   9

dreamsoul floatstands oak by birch by maple pine by . . . . . 658 {CHAIRE} 60   18

BIRD

the sweet strong final bird transcends the sight, O . . . . . 7 T&C EPITHALAM   165

a wistful and precarious bird.) Springing from fragrant . . . 20 T&C PUELLA MEA 152

and became a little bird and hid in a . . . . 30 T&C ORIENTALE 4   19

face, and hear one bird sing terribly afar in . . . . 76 T&C SON UNRE 1   13

was thinking why the girl-and-bird of you move.... moves.... 174 & SON ACTU 23   12

sensible night a quick bird (tenderly upon the dark's . . . . 187 XLI SONGS 9   8

my fifth finger. a bird chirps in a tree, ... 281 IS 5 THREE 5   12

pulls a trigger a bird flies into a mirror) . . . . 338 VIVA 29   24

flag" straightway the silver bird looked grave (departing . . 339 VIVA 30   20

/ twi- is -Light bird ful -ly dar kness . . . . 350 VIVA 41   2

a birdcage without any bird, a collar looking for . . . . . . 360 VIVA 51   25

as your hair what bird has perfect fear (of . . . . 367 VIVA 58   5

lifts (skilfully like some bird which is all birds . . . . . 378 VIVA 69   4

a -live a , bird ! O & j . . . . 471 NEW POEMS 9   18

rather learn from one bird how to sing than . . . . 484 NEW POEMS 22   13

she cried his grief bird by snow and stir . . . . 515 50 POEMS 29   15

so very born no bird can sing as easily . . . . 558 1 X 1 18   12

(by yes every new bird no bigger than to . . . . 583 1 X 1 43   17

heard a certain a bird i dreamed i could . . . . 587 1 X 1 47   2

a dream of a bird with a song like . . . . 587 1 X 1 47   9

or does some littler bird than eyes can learn . . . . 592 1 X 1 52   9

silence only made of, bird / / / . . . . 612 {CHAIRE} 14   14

brook -bright flower- soft bird -quick voice loves children . 660 {CHAIRE} 62   20

day) younger than young bird first for joy, he's . . . . . 666 {CHAIRE} 68   19

. is a looking bird: the turn ing; edge, ... 712 95 POEMS 40   5

voice is more than bird) and when no am . . . . 752 95 POEMS 80   6

dream wing tree leaf bird sun & singing &) . . . . 753 95 POEMS 81   17

strolls) nearness awakened, any bird should sing: and our . . 756 95 POEMS 84   11

than we) is a bird singing in a tree, ... 760 95 POEMS 87   2

high low and the bird on the bough) how? . . . . 767 95 POEMS 93   4

merry every pretty each bird sings gay-be-gay . . 773 73 POEMS 1   4

(gifted with illimitable joy) bird sings love's every truth . 783 73 POEMS 11   3

self sang like a bird. Mostpeople have been heard . . . . . 802 73 POEMS 30   28

any silence of each bird who dares to not . . . . 821 73 POEMS 49   7

+BIRD

FOR CONTEXT, SEE . . . . 429 NO THANKS 46   14

BIRDCAGE

occurred: i am a birdcage without any bird, a . . . . 360 VIVA 51   25

BIRDS

a flight of thirty birds shakes with a thickening . . . . . 11 T&C SONGS 2   18

the snow Into strenuous birds shall go my love . . . . . . 16 T&C SONGS 6   10

forest filled with sleeping birds thy breasts are swarms . . 29 T&C ORIENTALE 3   6

she is softer than birds when the emperor is . . . . 33 T&C ORIENTALE 6   52

with this thou hangest canary-birds in parlor windows spring 61 T&C PORTRAIT 9   10

her with intricate faint birds by daisies and twilights . . . 65 T&C POST IMPR 2   9

there is where strange birds purr / / / . . . . 180 XLI SONGS 2   20

occur about us and birds known, scarcely to sing . . . . . 205 XLI SONNETS 1   14

s U n: starT birDs (lEap) Openi ng t . . . . 347 VIVA 38   30

where truth grows why birds fly and especially who . . . . 368 VIVA 59   20

bird which is all birds but more fleet) herself . . . . . . 378 VIVA 69   4

of) ! (s r BIRDS BECAUSE AGAINS emarkable s) . . . . 421 NO THANKS 38   22

Light is filled with birds seriously i begin to . . . . . . 434 NO THANKS 51   3

treebodies wobbly- ing thing -birds) sing- u (cities are . . 436 NO THANKS 53   12

the rain's wings the birds of snow things without . . . . . 441 NO THANKS 56   56

/ / / / birds (here, inven ting . . . . 448 NO THANKS 63   1

Is will still occur; birds disappear becomingly: a . . . . . 452 NO THANKS 67   13

be open to little birds who are the secrets . . . . 481 NEW POEMS 19   2

soon" & pretending they're birds sit creatures of quills . . 483 NEW POEMS 21   9

	PAGE	TITLE	LINE

BIRDS (CONTINUED)
my are your are birds our all and one . . . . 541 1 X 1 1   6
you gave gave darling birds are in (trees are . . . . 589 1 X 1 49   15
(all the merry little birds are flying in the . . . . 591 1 X 1 51   5
is a bough (and birds sing sweeter than books . . . . 594 1 X 1 54   20
/ / / nine birds (rising through a gold . . . . 627 (CHAIRE) 29   1
earth are leapandswooping tinily birds whose magical gaiety . 631 (CHAIRE) 33   11
spring! yes the pretty birds frolic as spry as . . . . 665 (CHAIRE) 67   5
spring! now the pretty birds hover so she and . . . . 665 (CHAIRE) 67   12
spring! all the pretty birds dive to the heart . . . . 665 (CHAIRE) 67   19
substances and wings are birds; unders of dream adventure . . 761 95 POEMS 88   7
pretty each bird sings birds sing gay-be-gay because today's 773 73 POEMS 1   4
sing more will wonderfully birds than are / / . . . . 811 73 POEMS 39   14
all these thankful (hark) birds singing wholly are / . . . . 819 73 POEMS 47   20
made stones sing like birds-- but o the starhushed . . . . . 844 73 POEMS 72   2
+BIRDS
FOR CONTEXT, SEE . . . . 163 & SON ACTU 12   18
BIRTH
organ of imperception gave birth to which i should . . . . . 263 IS 5 ONE 32   33
to be born) his birth is their fear is . . . . 439 NO THANKS 55   5
hole in it that birth was wicked and life . . . . 545 1 X 1 5   10
birthday; this is the birth day of life and . . . . 663 (CHAIRE) 65   6
deeply less conceivable than birth or death or even . . . . . 720 95 POEMS 48   13
in such mysteries as birth and death a day . . . . 743 95 POEMS 71   13
a miracle of unceasing birth and glory and death . . . . . . 749 95 POEMS 77   10
BIRTH'S
(and longer dear) our birth's the because of a . . . . 686 95 POEMS 14   11
BIRTHDAY
this is the sun's birthday; this is the birth . . . . 663 (CHAIRE) 65   6
/ / / your birthday comes to tell me . . . . 734 95 POEMS 62   1
will be and my birthday is / / / . . . . 734 95 POEMS 62   4
+BIRTHDAY
FOR CONTEXT, SEE . . . . 663 (CHAIRE) 65   6
BIRTHDAYS
earth was playing at birthdays each (a wish no . . . . 763 95 POEMS 90   6
BIRTHS
flowering than stars whitely births of mind if air . . . . . 450 NO THANKS 65   5
BISCUIT
a" pause "uh" cough "Biscuit" (& so on & . . . . 464 NEW POEMS 2   25
BISHOP
told by is it Bishop Taylor who needs hanging . . . . 167 & SON ACTU 16   4
pliz) then up rose bishop budge from kew a . . . . 552 1 X 1 12   6
BIT
and a formula a bit of tobacco and gladness . . . . 68 T&C POST IMPR 5 3
nights and chews a two-bit cigar waiting for the . . . . . . 149 & SON REAL 20   2
see if that's all. Bit into you as teeth, ... 154 & SON ACTU 3   2
the brain? --Not a bit of it, my dears . . . . 245 IS 5 ONE 16   19
every kumrad is a bit of quite unmitigated hate . . . . 413 NO THANKS 30   13
it took a nipponized bit of the old sixth . . . . 553 1 X 1 13   21
BITCH
oneeyed son of a bitch invents an instrument to . . . . 264 IS 5 ONE 33   27
chairs tables the and bitch whispers jill mopping too . . . . 496 50 POEMS 10   16
but that sly little bitch could have showed billy . . . . . . 707 95 POEMS 35   14
+BITCH
FOR CONTEXT, SEE . . . . 254 IS 5 ONE 25   5
FOR CONTEXT, SEE . . . . 339 VIVA 30   36
FOR CONTEXT, SEE . . . . 699 95 POEMS 27   13
BITE
skyscraper in me i bite on the eyes' brittle . . . . 132 & SON REAL 3   6
know Had you as bite teeth; i stood with . . . . 154 & SON ACTU 3   14
nibble now And then bite) candy others fly, their; . . . . . 314 VIVA 6   12
girls who buck and bite they do not give . . . . 427 NO THANKS 44   2
come with girls who bite and buck who cannot . . . . 427 NO THANKS 44   9
BITES
doom of a dream bites this universe in two, ... 560 1 X 1 20   18
BITS
but I bet two bits come seven come eleven . . . . 125 & SEVEN POEMS 4 10
not speak) tumbled hushingly bits of downward flower flowing 168 & SON ACTU 17   7

	PAGE	TITLE	LINE

BITS (CONTINUED)
he should blow two bits for the coming of . . . . 196 XLI PORTRAIT 4   21
+BITS
FOR CONTEXT, SEE . . . . 94 & POST IMPR 6   11
BITTER
we taste as bright, bitter all utterly things sweet, ... 521 50 POEMS 34   62
BITTEREST
be loved by his bitterest enemies" is dead the . . . . 336 VIVA 27   2
BLACK
microscopic whithering ...(that's the Black People, cherie, . 86 T&C SON ACTU 5   9
pond on whoseswooning edge black trees think (hear little . . 99 & POST IMPR 10   11
buttoned with pain THE BLACK CAT WITH is there . . . . 100 & POST IMPR 11   32
fucking eyes the great black preacher gargles jesus the . . . 108 & PORTRAIT 4   27
even Nile the kind black great god) Cleopatra you . . . . . . 112 & PORTRAIT 6   88
l- ing all go BlacK wh-eel-ing oh ver mYveRylitTle . . . . . 122 & SEVEN POEMS 1   18
simplicity (out of the black unbunged Something gushes . . . 195 XLI PORTRAIT 3   10
because you would rather black the boots of success . . . . . 204 XLI LA GUERRE 2   2
with tall boys in black gloves and flowers and . . . . 239 IS 5 ONE 10   31
language trickling pried his black mouth with fat jibing . . 277 IS 5 THREE 1   14
Satanic and blase a black goat lookingly wanders There . . . 278 IS 5 THREE 2   16
tonight's erect everywhere of black muscles fools a . . . . . 299 IS 5 FOUR 16   2
seen trees (in whose black bod ies leaves hide . . . . 354 VIVA 45   27
legthelessne sssuc kedt oward black, this) roUnd . . . . . . 385 NO THANKS 2   62
sockets and strewed the black air with writhing alive . . . . 432 NO THANKS 49   17
best hill, driven by black wine. a village does . . . . 434 NO THANKS 51   7
darkness who moves in black light dancing isn'ts on . . . . . 439 NO THANKS 55   20
crown he dressed in black candy she veiled with . . . . 470 NEW POEMS 8   4
magic out of the black this which of one . . . . 493 50 POEMS 7   10
why and out of black because your absolute courage . . . . . 522 50 POEMS 35   13
brightest than hate's more black keenest than dying's keener 565 1 X 1 25   10
that life is a black cannonadin g into silenc . . . . 628 (CHAIRE) 30   2
eyes, and touch the black skin of an angel . . . . 639 (CHAIRE) 41   13
bi g screeching new black perfectly isn 't) one . . . . 646 (CHAIRE) 48   16
white eye and one black eye and the eyes . . . . 647 (CHAIRE) 49   18
daughter her father lays" "black hell upon you and . . . . . 707 95 POEMS 35   21
a total stranger one black day knocked living the . . . . . . 730 95 POEMS 58   1
pool A so of Black er than est if . . . . 759 95 POEMS 86   4
+BLACK
FOR CONTEXT, SEE . . . . 487 50 POEMS 1   1
+BLACKBERRIES
FOR CONTEXT, SEE . . . . 101 & POST IMPR 11   53
BLACKENING
sparrows, the cathedral shudders blackening; the sky is . . . 282 IS 5 THREE 6   13
BLACKER
windy torches each is blacker than oblivion the ladies . . . 33 T&C ORIENTALE 6   42
sit into a moon) blacker than dreams are round . . . . 483 NEW POEMS 21   3
+BLACKER
FOR CONTEXT, SEE . . . . 759 95 POEMS 86   4
+BLACKEST
FOR CONTEXT, SEE . . . . 759 95 POEMS 86   4
BLACKISH
dream who knows?) a blackish cat and a bluish . . . . 168 & SON ACTU 17   17
BLACKMAIL
or minus news alimony blackmail whathavewe and propaganda (it 391 NO THANKS 8   11
BLACKNESS
threatens the tubular downward blackness occasionally from . 201 XLI PORTRAIT 9   9
+BLACKNESS
FOR CONTEXT, SEE . . . . 429 NO THANKS 46   4
BLACKRED
be a heaven of blackred roses my father will . . . . 352 VIVA 43   4
BLACKSHIRT
/ red-rag and pink-flag blackshirt and brown strut-mince and 497 50 POEMS 11   2
BLACKSNAKE
the whipping of a blackSnake cu tSudden ly in . . . . 101 & POST IMPR 11   52
BLACKTREESTHINK
sof a. Thick silence) blacktreesthink tiny, angels sharpen: . 99 & POST IMPR 10   14
BLADE
reap and on Death's blade lie many a flower . . . . 208 XLI SONNETS 4   10

71

		PAGE	TITLE	LINE

+BLADE
FOR CONTEXT, SEE . . . . 364 VIVA 55   6
FOR CONTEXT, SEE . . . . 554 1 X 1 14   5
FOR CONTEXT, SEE . . . . 656 (CHAIRE) 58   10
BLADES
rhymes, like Gillette Razor Blades having been used and . . . 230 IS 5 ONE 2   20
+BLADES
FOR CONTEXT, SEE . . . . 282 IS 5 THREE 6   23
FOR CONTEXT, SEE . . . . 491 50 POEMS 5   12
BLAME
loss or gain from blame or praise) but many . . . . 372 VIVA 63   12
beyond because things over blame things under praise glad . . 441 NO THANKS 56 59
BLANDLY
things therefore we also blandly into receptive earth, O . . 41 T&C AMORES 5 12
BLANK
red goes green --groping blank sky with a blind . . . . . . 800 73 POEMS 28   23
BLASE
and, disappear) Satanic and blase a black goat lookingly . . 278 IS 5 THREE 2 15
BLAST
mind without soul may blast some universe to might . . . . 714 95 POEMS 42   9
BLAZE
is most (windows where blaze naLOVEme crazily ships bulge . . 436 NO THANKS 52   3
BLAZED
light to flame and blazed with snowy fire) unfolding, ... 8 T&C OF NICOL   18
BLAZING
/ out of midsummer's blazing most not night as . . . . . . 818 73 POEMS 46   1
+BLEATS
FOR CONTEXT, SEE . . . . 442 NO THANKS 57   7
BLEND
smiting sky tense with blend ing the tree leaps . . . . . . 182 XLI SONGS 4   4
each morning stoops to blend her star with what . . . . . . 351 VIVA 42   14
most : locking foreverfully blend we a universe of . . . . . 371 VIVA 62   20
BLESS
lovers! --I beseech thee bless thy suppliant singer and . . .   7 T&C EPITHALAM 167
BLESSED
Whose eyes approve the blessed while His ears are . . . . . 117 & PORTRAIT 10   36
Requiescat. carry carefully the blessed large silent him into 277 IS 5 THREE 1 23
wholly babble open at blessed are the peacemuckers) $ . . . . 635 (CHAIRE) 37   20
may reverently share the blessed eachness of all beautiful . 745 95 POEMS 73   11
it cruel fair or blessed evil-- it is you . . . . 804 73 POEMS 32   7
BLESSINGS
with the church's protestant blessings daughters, unscented . 70 T&C SON REAL 1 3
/ of all the blessings which to man kind . . . . 544 1 X 1 4   1
BLEST
fragrance makes the lover blest.) Her waist is a . . . . . . 21 T&C PUELLA MEA 192
BLIND
the sea through her blind miles of crumbling silence . . . . 81 T&C SON UNRE 6 13
bright their eyes a blind irisher fiddles a scotch . . . . . 108 & PORTRAIT 4   8
sign on his breast BLIND) yes i am this . . . . 298 IS 5 FOUR 15   6
sky-- nor (as a blind, how timidly, throb; which . . . . . 402 NO THANKS 19   9
create (suddenly announce: hurl) blind full steep love / . . 422 NO THANKS 39   16
their fear is their blind fear --haunts all unsleep . . . . . 439 NO THANKS 55   5
the seeing are the blind and robins never welcome . . . . . 511 50 POEMS 25   15
confound the wise? doubt blind the brave? does mask . . . . 538 50 POEMS 50   5
with kind of a blind big sound on the . . . . 543 1 X 1 3   29
plus fingers all with blind him of who) i . . . . 546 1 X 1 6   10
terror; blow seeing to blind (blow pity to envy . . . . . . 560 1 X 1 20   13
deaf dumb church and blind with an if in . . . . 647 (CHAIRE) 49   11
--laughing to find anyone's blind (like me like you) . . . . 716 95 POEMS 44   2
which sleep and move) blind sands, at pitiless the . . . . . 743 95 POEMS 71   8
burned earth but a blind blissfully seething gift wandering . 754 95 POEMS 82   3
blank sky with a blind stare, he whispers "i . . . . 800 73 POEMS 28   23
where seeing eyes go blind (where lips forget to . . . . . . 834 73 POEMS 62   27
BLINDED
amorous of waters tremulous, blinded with silence the . . . . 37 T&C AMORES 2   7
which i or you (blinded by merely things believable) . . . . 809 73 POEMS 37   6
eyes, not any longer blinded with a world; and . . . . 811 73 POEMS 39   5

		PAGE	TITLE	LINE

BLINDLY
all their minds) eyes blindly stare life herSelf stands . . . 780 73 POEMS 8   8
BLINDMAN
quietly) life was a blindman / / / / . . . . 699 95 POEMS 27   21
BLINDS
fragrance to rickety unclosed blinds inslants peregrinate, a 144 & SON REAL 15   3
everywhere exploding maims and blinds (but surely does not . 377 VIVA 68   8
yells they f-oo-l (whom, blinds; blood) pa-nt stab are . . . 388 NO THANKS 5   9
BLINK
i sit up and blink at you with my . . . . 69 T&C POST IMPR 6   35
BLINKED
button of whisper sum blinked he belowtry eye nowbrow . . . . 333 VIVA 24   8
BLINKING
lets you grow old blinking at the low ceiling . . . . 96 & POST IMPR 8   24
BLINKY
you with his solemn blinky eyeswhichneversmile and after he . 69 T&C POST IMPR 6   14
BLISS
the year has perfect bliss-- for each breast a . . . . . . 21 T&C PUELLA MEA   189
whose dome the trembling bliss of a kingdom wholly . . . . . 21 T&C PUELLA MEA   205
gimme the he-man's solid bliss for youse ideas i'll . . . . . 247 IS 5 ONE 18   5
heart the queen --incalculable bliss! Picture it gents: our . 254 IS 5 ONE 25   13
i have had some bliss of one small lady . . . . 360 VIVA 51   32
thing is thing: no bliss of heavenly earth beguiles . . . . . 675 95 POEMS 3   1
of briefer each our bliss-- where seeing eyes go . . . . . . 834 73 POEMS 62   26
alive blossom of a bliss "seven heavens for just . . . . . . 837 73 POEMS 65   12
BLISSFUL
and (stealing toward the blissful pair) skilfully wafted over 799 73 POEMS 27   20
BLISSFULLY
earth but a blind blissfully seething gift wandering deeply . 754 95 POEMS 82   3
shameless gaiety of blossom --blissfully nonchalant wise and 764 95 POEMS 90   39
BLITHE
a pair of companions blithe and fair; who to . . . . 20 T&C PUELLA MEA   165
to flower until so blithe a doer a wooer . . . . 509 50 POEMS 23   8
now of your treasure blithe each shameless blithe each . . . 763 95 POEMS 90   37
treasure blithe each shameless blithe each shameless gaiety . 764 95 POEMS 90   37
BLOAT
the eyes outstart, curl, bloat, are newly baked and . . . . . 226 IS 5 ONE MAME   13
BLOATED
rain, spiral acres of bloated rose coiled within cobalt . . . 93 & POST IMPR 5   5
happeningly the unfirm drooping bloated calves i would . . . 229 IS 5 ONE FRAN   5
BLOB
/ / / nonsun blob a cold to skylessness . . . . 541 1 X 1 1   1
BLOCK
falling in a singular block her, rain-warm-naked exquisitely 133 & SON REAL 4   1
BLOCKS
whimpered how girllike laughtering blocks when builds its . . 371 VIVA 62   5
BLOKE
bulls he'd bumped a bloke back in fifteen. Then . . . . 145 & SON REAL 16   2
(here's to youse) "a bloke wot's well behaved" ...and . . . . 229 IS 5 ONE FRAN   11
BLOKES
us into rissions and blokes with ammunicions who tend . . . . 405 NO THANKS 22   7
BLOND
i mean that the blond absence of any program . . . . 264 IS 5 ONE 33   17
for Yale above his blond determined head the sacred . . . . . 273 IS 5 TWO 8   13
alert lice in the blond hair of nothing / . . . . 289 IS 5 FOUR 6   24
a moment" The is blond with small hands "& . . . . 338 VIVA 29   15
brave than me: more blond than you. / / . . . . 339 VIVA 30   42
/ / squints a blond job at her diamond . . . . 545 1 X 1 5   1
BLONDE
with a carroty youth blonde whis (gorgedis reswal lowing . . 629 {CHAIRE} 31   17
who, some total (preferably blonde of course) or on . . . . . 779 73 POEMS 7   6
BLONDER
all things under our blonder than blondest star the . . . . . 825 73 POEMS 53   2
BLONDEST
under our blonder than blondest star the most mysterious . . 825 73 POEMS 53   2
BLOOD
the sharp and thirsty blood of Paris would not . . . . 18 T&C PUELLA MEA   66
the keys of thy blood thy feet upon thy . . . . 29 T&C ORIENTALE 3   28

	PAGE	TITLE	LINE
BLOOD (CONTINUED)			
broke you upon my blood listen beloved i dreamed	30	T&C ORIENTALE 4	28
smile wan, and his blood stopped hears in the	77	T&C SON UNRE 2	8
just throttled my seeing blood, her heart's chatter riveted .	132	& SON REAL 3	3
of new mingling: deeper: blood of my blood: with	139	& SON REAL 10	5
deeper: blood of my blood: with upwardcringing swiftness . .	139	& SON REAL 10	5
world in my huge blood, cracking brains A swiftlyenormous . .	157	& SON ACTU 6	11
the futile purr of blood; your sex squeaked like	170	& SON ACTU 19	9
the rivers of our blood, miss by how terrible	174	& SON ACTU 23	9
smile looking hands spit blood teeth the Communists have .	275	IS 5 TWO 9	47
in the world my blood approves, and kisses are	290	IS 5 FOUR 7	7
these hurrying crudities of blood and flesh) Love coins . . .	297	IS 5 FOUR 14	11
reacts (sharp now with blood now accurately wan) keenly, . .	344	VIVA 35	6
they f-oo-l (whom, blinds; blood) pa-nt stab are (slopped .	388	NO THANKS 5	9
skill each world of blood is made (whose fatal	424	NO THANKS 41	13
me whisper whose erect blood finally trembles, emerging to .	435	NO THANKS 51	38
not yet jesus what blood darling i said /	496	50 POEMS 10	19
if (by Him Whose blood was for us spilled)	514	50 POEMS 28	9
flesh was flesh his blood was blood: no hungry	520	50 POEMS 34	29
flesh his blood was blood: no hungry man but	520	50 POEMS 34	29
which cannot share, let blood and flesh be mud	521	50 POEMS 34	54
maples wept air to blood, asked "something a little	555	1 X 1 15	12
/ darling! because my blood can sing and dance	580	1 X 1 40	1
sharpening freedom lifts our blood as if whole supreme . . .	675	95 POEMS 3	6
believing (though flesh and blood accuse him of coercion . .	683	95 POEMS 11	3
all is If all blood And When / /	690	95 POEMS 18	8
to spill such golden blood as makes his moon	811	73 POEMS 39	13
no (silence is the blood whose flesh is singing)	839	73 POEMS 67	1
BLOOD'S			
doth entertain the adroit blood's mysterious skein (but like	21	T&C PUELLA MEA	186
BLOODBEAT			
to feel. Unwieldy.... the bloodbeat in her fierce laziness .	135	& SON REAL 6	8
+BLOODED			
FOR CONTEXT, SEE	407	NO THANKS 24	3
BLOODIES			
truth to summer's lie; bloodies with dizzying leaves the . .	560	1 X 1 20	3
BLOODLIGHT			
colour (in -to day's bloodlight climbs the onlying world) . .	719	95 POEMS 47	2
BLOODSHED			
and Limb) --or, since bloodshed and kindred questions inhibit	266	IS 5 TWO 1	29
BLOOMING			
tiny troubadours, and (phantom-white) dumb-blooming boughs .	8	T&C OF NICOL	6
BLOSSOM			
whose tremendous hair that blossom stands whereof is most . .	6	T&C EPITHALAM	146
for each breast a blossom is, which being a	21	T&C PUELLA MEA	190
which in my mind blossom will stumble beneath a	91	& POST IMPR 3	11
even than breathing shall blossom a first star) one	720	95 POEMS 48	14
dark, will climb; will blossom: will sing (like april's . . .	735	95 POEMS 63	13
each shameless gaiety of blossom --blissfully nonchalant wise	764	95 POEMS 90	38
be your" perfectly alive blossom of a bliss "seven	837	73 POEMS 65	12
+BLOSSOM			
FOR CONTEXT, SEE	347	VIVA 38	10
BLOSSOMING			
ghost-flower born of night blossoming in white towers to . .	8	T&C OF NICOL	3
children of stone with blossoming eyes know if a	525	50 POEMS 37	16
strikes my your our blossoming sphere / / /	582	1 X 1 42	16
are winging in the blossoming) lovers go and lovers	591	1 X 1 51	8
floating merry in the blossoming always joyful selves are . .	591	1 X 1 51	23
knows?) eternity floated a blossoming (while anyone might . .	599	(CHAIRE) 1	8
/ / / / blossoming are people nimbler than	630	(CHAIRE) 32	1
a singing wonder of blossoming yes riding) to him	661	(CHAIRE) 63	3
rags strode earth ignorantly blossoming a scarecrow demongod	662	(CHAIRE) 64	7
own, my beautiful my blossoming) for also then's until . . .	667	(CHAIRE) 69	14
ilthi es t sidewalk blossoming glory / / /	668	(CHAIRE) 70	25
sorry while these were blossoming) roses which really are . .	748	95 POEMS 76	10
and dance you suddenly blossoming tree --i'll sing /	767	95 POEMS 93	23
you and i are blossoming / / / /	777	73 POEMS 5	16
unknowable most joy) faithfully blossoming beyond to breathe	811	73 POEMS 39	8

PAGE   TITLE   LINE

BLOSSOMS
which shall seek all blossoms that do learn, scents . . . . . 9 T&C SONGS 1   17
steal slowly in dumb blossoms of new mingling: deeper: . . . 139 & SON REAL 10   4
the prettiest wrath of blossoms dishevelling made a pale . . 214 XLI SONNETS 10   8
singing wreathed with singing blossoms children of stone with 525 50 POEMS 37   15
flutter to and swim blossoms of person) through musical . . 586 1 X 1 46   12
earth's most prodigious night blossoms a newborn babe: around 714 95 POEMS 42   3
BLOUSE
stout fellow in a blouse just outside this window, ... 282 IS 5 THREE 6   24
in) while a transparent blouse even recklessly juggles the . 341 VIVA 32   18
BLOW
hear the purple trumpets blow horses of gold delicately . . . 110 & PORTRAIT 6   34
<> hurries elsewhere; to blow incredible wampum / / . . . . . 116 & PORTRAIT 9   16
him why he should blow two bits for the . . . . 196 XLI PORTRAIT 4   21
garden: pursed lips do blow upon cool flutes within . . . . . 208 XLI SONNETS 4   5
yanks immortal stars awry? Blow king to beggar and . . . . . 560 1 X 1 20   5
and queen to seem (blow friend to fiend: blow . . . . 560 1 X 1 20   6
(blow friend to fiend: blow space to time) --when . . . . . . 560 1 X 1 20   6
forests in white age? Blow hope to terror; blow . . . . 560 1 X 1 20   13
Blow hope to terror; blow seeing to blind (blow . . . . 560 1 X 1 20   13
blow seeing to blind (blow pity to envy and . . . . 560 1 X 1 20   14
with me and you? Blow soon to never and . . . . 560 1 X 1 20   21
and never to twice (blow life to isn't: blow . . . . 560 1 X 1 20   22
(blow life to isn't: blow death to was) --all . . . . 560 1 X 1 20   22
BLOWING
which raced sideways while blowing bubbles: and may came . . 682 95 POEMS 10   8
BLOWN
lips wisely minced for blown kisses, condemnatory fingers . . 9 T&C SONGS 1   12
/ a wind has blown the rain away and . . . . 80 T&C SON UNRE 5   1
the rain away and blown the sky away and . . . . 80 T&C SON UNRE 5   1
integration........ a wind has blown the rain away and . . . 80 T&C SON UNRE 5   13
a sidewalk out of (blown never quite to -gether . . . . . . 442 NO THANKS 57   3
BLOWS
the harder the wind blows the taller i am" . . . . 439 NO THANKS 55   27
/ / / hate blows a bubble of despair . . . . 531 50 POEMS 43   1
BLUBBERING
(the crowd howls faintly blubbering pointing see yes) It . . 280 IS 5 THREE 4   15
BLUE
moon sole in the blue night amorous of waters . . . . 37 T&C AMORES 2   3
are troubled. A sharp blue day fills with peacefully . . . . 62 T&C PORTRAIT 10 7
face, gashed by hair's blue cold jolts of lovecrazed . . . . 106 & PORTRAIT 2   9
her nakedness with its blue hair (all is eaten . . . . 112 & PORTRAIT 6   76
up in the sky Blue, everything: a bar the . . . . 123 & SEVEN POEMS 2 2
/ / / a blue woman with sticking out . . . . 167 & SON ACTU 16   1
a flight in the blue; when love's had his . . . . 181 XLI SONGS 3   5
west of robin's egg blue when i entered a . . . . 194 XLI PORTRAIT 2   3
tear within his stern blue eye, upon his firm . . . . 273 IS 5 TWO 8   9
armour colliding on huge blue horses, and the poets . . . . . 302 IS 5 FIVE 1   13
(together) smell only such blue slender hands of god . . . . 340 VIVA 31   20
hop point at red blue yellow violet white orange . . . . . . 437 NO THANKS 53   14
c-urlin-g noworld Silent is blue (sleep! new girlgold / . . . 503 50 POEMS 17   10
/ the silently little blue elephant shyly (he was . . . . . 516 50 POEMS 30   1
was painted in round blue but quite now it's . . . . 516 50 POEMS 30   6
only through) the little blue elephant at the zoo . . . . . 516 50 POEMS 30   7
you) has (elephant the blue) put some just a . . . . 516 50 POEMS 30   9
as a sun with blue true two man neral . . . . 567 1 X 1 27   4
a sunrise fresh with blue come true from a . . . . 567 1 X 1 27   19
/ these (whom; pretends blue nothing) are built of . . . . 584 1 X 1 44   2
shall climb all the blue heaven green earth neither . . . . 588 1 X 1 48   3
threw his wish at blue with a swoop and . . . . 593 1 X 1 53   6
singing like a flame blue took it my far . . . . 593 1 X 1 53   13
of trees and a blue true dream of sky; . . . . 663 (CHAIRE) 65   3
/ / / / blue the triangular why of . . . . 668 (CHAIRE) 70   1
/ / crazy jay blue) demon laughshriek ing at . . . . 677 95 POEMS 5   1
how look at it blue is the high is . . . . 695 95 POEMS 23   18
silent upon new perfectly blue) i am any (while . . . . . . 720 95 POEMS 48   3
which of slim of blue of here will who . . . . 746 95 POEMS 74   5
not here but neither's blue most both) and history . . . . . 750 95 POEMS 78   5

	PAGE	TITLE	LINE

BLUE (CONTINUED)
  thing found one old blue wheel in a pasture . . . . 753 95 POEMS 81   21
  fall into far near blue if beggars are rich . . . . 769 95 POEMS 95   21
  may under more a blue than blue can be . . . . 778 73 POEMS 6   19
  more a blue than blue can be sky always . . . . 778 73 POEMS 6   20
+BLUE
  FOR CONTEXT, SEE . . . . 108 & PORTRAIT 4   13
BLUEANDGREEN
  silently hills made of blueandgreen paper scorchbend ingthem 278 IS 5 THREE 2   6
BLUEDMUFFLETOMBEN
  7th s o howpale) bluedmufFletomben outerly jeT ting lip . . . 342 VIVA 33   9
BLUEEYED
  do you like your blueeyed boy Mister Death / . . . . 60 T&C PORTRAIT 8   10
  one, i am this blueeyed Finn emerging from a . . . . 115 & PORTRAIT 8   26
  officers (a yearning nation's blueeyed pride) their passive . 339 VIVA 30   23
  a strawberry bang this blueeyed world (on which are . . . . . 585 1 X 1 45   4
BLUENESS
  to the power of blueness) whos (ex- plore my . . . . 612 {CHAIRE} 14   4
BLUER
  us the unspeaking Mediterranean bluer than we had imagined . 283 IS 5 THREE 7   3
  if (among silent skies bluer than believing) a little . . . . 583 1 X 1 43   3
  and high beyond high bluer took it your but . . . . 593 1 X 1 53   16
  call old frank go bluer still as (shifting his . . . . 754 95 POEMS 82   6
BLUES
  hardslippery greens and helplessbaby blues and stic-ky . . . 100 & POST IMPR 11   5
BLUEST
  took it your but bluest took it our away . . . . 593 1 X 1 53   17
  deeply through godthanking ground) bluest whos of this snowy 754 95 POEMS 82   5
BLUETS
  about les roses les bluets yes, will He buy? . . . . 102 & POST IMPR 12   17
BLUISH
  frieze of smoking Face Bluish-old and choked pat of . . . . . 142 & SON REAL 13   5
  / Dick Mid's large bluish face without eyebrows sits . . . . 149 & SON REAL 20   1
  blackish cat and a bluish cat are eyeing, as . . . . 168 & SON ACTU 17   17
  Faintly always who Is bluish; next Door but two . . . . 312 VIVA 4   9
+BLUISH
  FOR CONTEXT, SEE . . . . 434 NO THANKS 51   32
BLUISH-OLD
  frieze of smoking Face Bluish-old and choked pat of . . . . . 142 & SON REAL 13   5
BLUISHSUSPENDERS
  rather fat man in bluishsuspenders half-reading the Evening . 166 & SON ACTU 15   6
BLUNDER
  certain faces busily horribly blunder through new light hush 299 IS 5 FOUR 16   14
  let beauty touch a blunder (called life) we die . . . . 742 95 POEMS 70   13
BLUNDERING
  but (while down come blundering proud hugenesses of hate . . 783 73 POEMS 11   6
BLUNT
  sure of this) her blunt unslender, what her big . . . . 225 IS 5 ONE LIZ   11
  intellects evoke allegiance per blunt instruments-- Olaf . . 339 VIVA 30   14
BLUR
  there drift a pulseless blur of paleness; the unswift . . . . 218 XLI SONNETS 14   12
  falls off and eyes blur And thighs forget (when . . . . 359 VIVA 50   1
+BLUR
  FOR CONTEXT, SEE . . . . 723 95 POEMS 51   2
BLURB
  brand of pyro -technic blurb anent the (hic) hero . . . . . . 266 IS 5 TWO 1   12
BLURTED
  male (shock beyond shock blurted) strokes, vibrant with the . 115 & PORTRAIT 8   14
BLURTING
  s olemnandputrid vast, stomachs bLurting and cHuckling like . 101 & POST IMPR 11   69
BLUSH
  off dimension with a blush enters the becoming garden . . . . 48 T&C IMPRESS 2   16
BLUSHING
  And i hazarded "god" (blushing slightly) --"O damn ginks . . 228 IS 5 ONE MARJ   6
BO
  p.s. the most successful b.o. fully speaking concession at . 425 NO THANKS 42   15
+BOARD
  FOR CONTEXT, SEE . . . . 574 1 X 1 34   6

		PAGE	TITLE	LINE

BOARDS
    smack of back- gammon boards i was aware of . . . . 194 XLI PORTRAIT 2   18
BOAST
    have made. And never boast your dead beauties, you . . . . . 22 T&C PUELLA MEA 243
    to wholly kiss-- never boast your dead beauties, mine . . . . 22 T&C PUELLA MEA 249
    confused with fact, fish boast of fishing and men . . . . . . 446 NO THANKS 61   4
BOAT
    a sail a fishing boat somebody an invisible spectator, . . . 283 IS 5 THREE 7   7
BOCCA
    of sudden nothing.... la bocca mia "he kissed wholly . . . . 84 T&C SON ACTU 3   15
BOCCACCIO
    go with my lord Boccaccio-- whoso knocketh at the . . . . . . 20 T&C PUELLA MEA 170
BODIES
    feet of mowers whose bodies strong with love through . . . . 11 T&C SONGS 2   34
    youngest angels (whose praising bodies in a row between . . . 20 T&C PUELLA MEA 143
    ten elected warriors with bodies of lazy jade and . . . . . . 34 T&C ORIENTALE 6   77
    while in the battered bodies the odd unlovely souls . . . . . 55 T&C PORTRAIT 3   18
    with faces painteaten and bodies lightly desperate certainly . 57 T&C PORTRAIT 5   38
    hotly our moreover irrevocable bodies while the infinite . . 111 & PORTRAIT 6   62
    men's hands but their bodies big and boozing belong . . . . . 114 & PORTRAIT 7   15
    marching to love whose bodies kiss me with the . . . . 138 & SON REAL 9   12
    the luminous stammer of bodies (eagerly just not each . . . . 174 & SON ACTU 23   4
    whose living and biggest bodies lopped of every prettiness . 195 XLI PORTRAIT 3   21
    mouth, steer our lost bodies carefully downward) / / . . . . 215 XLI SONNETS 11   17
    thoughts kiss -ing wishes bodies) squirm-of-frightened shy . 437 NO THANKS 53   7
    humbly in their imagined bodies kneel (over time space . . . 714 95 POEMS 42   6
+BODIES
    FOR CONTEXT, SEE . . . . 354 VIVA 45   27
    FOR CONTEXT, SEE . . . . 436 NO THANKS 52   10
BODILY
    village of her mind bodily which ravelling, to a . . . . . . 136 & SON REAL 7   2
BODY
    and dim slow perfect body amorous (whiter than lilies . . . . 5 T&C EPITHALAM 99
    when god lets my body be From each brave . . . . 16 T&C SONGS 6   1
    flowers and all her body filled with May) --moving . . . . . 17 T&C PUELLA MEA 22
    day who with Egypt's body lay. Lovely as those . . . . 18 T&C PUELLA MEA 74
    those ladies were.) Her body is most beauteous, being . . . . 20 T&C PUELLA MEA 135
    doth from my lady's body grow; as morning may . . . . 21 T&C PUELLA MEA 183
    most frail parting my body hears the cry of . . . . 22 T&C PUELLA MEA 234
    poem she of whose body words are afraid perfectly . . . . . . 22 T&C PUELLA MEA 240
    in whose warm superlative body do distinctly live all . . . . 22 T&C PUELLA MEA 256
    the bough of thy body thy body to me . . . . 29 T&C ORIENTALE 3   8
    of thy body thy body to me is April . . . . 29 T&C ORIENTALE 3   9
    mile deep but the body of the queen of . . . . 33 T&C ORIENTALE 6   49
    player squats with quiveringgold body behind the emperor ten . 34 T&C ORIENTALE 6   73
    is dancing her subtle body weaving insinuating upon the . . . 34 T&C ORIENTALE 6   86
    sudden lust her stealing body ex- pending gathering pouring . 34 T&C ORIENTALE 6   91
    O woman this my body. for it has lain . . . . 36 T&C AMORES 1   3
    fingers drooped your shining body when my heart sang . . . . 39 T&C AMORES 4   13
    the kindly lips and body fatherly of a romantic . . . . 57 T&C PORTRAIT 5   31
    you have a sloppy body from being brought to . . . . 61 T&C PORTRAIT 9   16
    and shall, whose slippery body is Death's littlest pal, . . . 74 T&C SON REAL 5   3
    reachings of Her green body among unseen things, things . . . 77 T&C SON UNRE 2   2
    of flesh, makes my body sorry when the minute . . . . 82 T&C SON ACTU 1   4
    and say Perhaps her body touched me; and to . . . . 82 T&C SON ACTU 1   14
    lilies-- should my lady's body with these frail ladies . . . 85 T&C SON ACTU 4   13
    simplicity of her hipless body, pausing to invent im- . . . . 103 & POST IMPR 13   2
    heels. Her gasping slippery body moved with the hideous . . . 103 & POST IMPR 13   9
    horrible stops of her body Cleopatra had a body . . . . 110 & PORTRAIT 6   13
    body Cleopatra had a body it was thick slim . . . . 110 & PORTRAIT 6   15
    i salute you whose body is Egypt whose hair . . . . 113 & PORTRAIT 6   110
    praise Marj's cleancornered strokable body these men's . . . 114 & PORTRAIT 7   6
    begs, Mimi with the body like une boite a . . . . 121 & PORTRAIT 12   48
    your shall i say body? follows truly through a . . . . 140 & SON REAL 11   3
    the nifty, ruffian-rogue, laughing body with wise breasts . . 140 & SON REAL 11   11
    to do the posed body luckily made a pen . . . . 141 & SON REAL 12   2
    flame of her indomitable body uses a careful fierceness. . . 146 & SON REAL 17   2
    is her long hard body filled with surprise like . . . . . . 147 & SON REAL 18   4

	PAGE	TITLE	LINE
BODY (CONTINUED)			
god hurried a boy's body on unsuspicious legs of	148	& SON REAL 19	2
alert willing myth of body, which will make oddly	155	& SON ACTU 4	10
you.... feel your suddenly body reach for me with	157	& SON ACTU 6	6
with is nearness. (peers: body of aching toys in	159	& SON ACTU 8	11
your smile over his body squirms kissingly, i will	161	& SON ACTU 10	6
/ i like my body when it is with	175	& SON ACTU 24	1
it is with your body. It is so quite	175	& SON ACTU 24	2
more. i like your body. i like what it	175	& SON ACTU 24	4
the spine of your body and its bones, and	175	& SON ACTU 24	6
cloaked with renewal my body turns toward thee again	184	XLI SONGS 6	8
winsome cage of thy body rose through the sensible	187	XLI SONGS 9	3
sleeping curves of my body Shall enter fingers of	189	XLI SONGS 11	1
enjoy the composed sudden body atop which always quivers . .	193	XLI PORTRAIT 1	2
the important gardens her body will come toward me	214	XLI SONNETS 10	10
if her tall corpsecoloured body seat itself (with the	227	IS 5 ONE GERT	8
of Breton big good body, which terminated in fists	277	IS 5 THREE 1	7
shirt and into my body the sharp things fingered	284	IS 5 FOUR 1	6
i separated from your body smile brain hands merely	295	IS 5 FOUR 12	3
thing to oh no body will (can you give	314	VIVA 6	21
night, all of your body with its spirit floated	369	VIVA 60	19
rock of forehead. No body loved big that quick	490	50 POEMS 4	6
twilight : never, no (body. Nothing / / /	490	50 POEMS 4	21
by its wigglesome whisperful body and almost isn't (grabbed .	585	1 X 1 45	9
one Living (or some body Dead like even a	702	95 POEMS 30	5
i ob serve no body wants Most (not putting	727	95 POEMS 55	9
mind with out a body (turn ing silently to	753	95 POEMS 81	6
+BODY			
FOR CONTEXT, SEE	100	& POST IMPR 11	15
FOR CONTEXT, SEE	100	& POST IMPR 11	40
BODY'S			
that fee her eager body's unimmortal flower knew in	4	T&C EPITHALAM	55
oral devious, beneath the body's breathing noun (moreover the	21	T&C PUELLA MEA	211
time tickling away every- body's brain so everybody just . .	126	& SEVEN POEMS 5	12
where sits rigidly her body's doll gay exactly perishing . .	131	& SON REAL 2	16
embrace me with your body's suddenly curving entire warm . .	282	IS 5 THREE 6	34
is sculptor of your body's idiom: the musician of	291	IS 5 FOUR 8	7
less firm than your body's whitest song upon my	306	IS 5 FIVE 5	4
BODYFEE			
the Street of her bodyfee l inga ro undMe	122	& SEVEN POEMS 1	3
BOG			
and slap tremendous sorrydaze bog triperight election who so	333	VIVA 24	14
+BOIL			
FOR CONTEXT, SEE	332	VIVA 23	1
BOIS			
always smiling chevaux de bois) when you were in	304	IS 5 FIVE 3	14
BOIT			
en amerique on ne boit que de Jingyale. things	233	IS 5 ONE 4	6
BOITE			
the body like une boite a joujoux, want nice	121	& PORTRAIT 12	49
BOLD			
of artists made him bold to imitate between the	4	T&C EPITHALAM	35
(the shy ones, the bold ones; the meek proud	619	(CHAIRE) 21	3
BOLDEST			
a look the very boldest man can scarcely dare	685	95 POEMS 13	2
+BOLSHEVISTIC			
FOR CONTEXT, SEE	266	IS 5 TWO 1	9
BOMBAST			
how worlds delicate of bombast--papery what & vast	480	NEW POEMS 18	17
BOMBED			
me a moon; beneath, bombed the by ocean earth	639	(CHAIRE) 41	4
+BOMBS			
FOR CONTEXT, SEE	500	50 POEMS 14	15
BON			
tous, les americains aussi.... "bon dos, bon cul de	120	& PORTRAIT 12	14
americains aussi.... "bon dos, bon cul de Paris" (Marie . . .	120	& PORTRAIT 12	14
BONE			
a rag and a bone and a hank of	552	1 X 1 12	8

		PAGE	TITLE	LINE

BONES
your body and its bones, and the trembling -firm-smooth . . . 175 & SON ACTU 24   6
+BONG
FOR CONTEXT, SEE . . . . 333 VIVA 24   2
BONNET
nose and coquettishly- cocked bonnet having ceased the . . . 196 XLI PORTRAIT 4   5
BOO
fu -gaces Postu- me boo who) / / / . . . . 236 IS 5 ONE 7   20
His Royal Highness said "peek-a-boo" and thirty tame fleas . 262 IS 5 ONE 32   27
hope must coo or boo may strut or creep . . . . 440 NO THANKS 56   18
BOOBS
slaves will click; where Boobs are holy, poets mad, ... 438 NO THANKS 54   19
BOODLE'S
$ etc (as the boodle's bent is the crowd . . . . 635 {CHAIRE} 37   22
BOOK
this lady in some book had read / / . . . . 225 IS 5 ONE LIZ   16
which pinch that purple book between what hands had . . . . 506 50 POEMS 20   2
out of a red book) on a proud round . . . . 631 {CHAIRE} 33   4
BOOKS
aware) than of my books could even be your . . . . 386 NO THANKS 3   4
(and anything's righter than books could plan) the stupidest 594 1 X 1 54   3
buds know better than books don't grow) one's anything . . . 594 1 X 1 54   12
birds sing sweeter than books tell how) so here . . . . 594 1 X 1 54   21
you love me (and books are shuter than books . . . . 594 1 X 1 54   29
books are shuter than books can be) and deep . . . . 594 1 X 1 54   30
(we're everything greater than books might mean) we're . . . 594 1 X 1 54   39
BOOL
and bellow like a bool to lay a wreath . . . . 500 50 POEMS 14   12
BOOM
sibl y (ShoutflowereD flowerish boom b el Lsb El . . . . . . 444 NO THANKS 59   30
with the fascist beast boom boom) two eyes for . . . . 635 {CHAIRE} 37   15
the fascist beast boom boom) two eyes for an . . . . 635 {CHAIRE} 37   16
BOOMING
les Of, CleaN a booming smell waddles toward, me, ... 94 & POST IMPR 6   15
BOOST
the belly's merry thrust Boost my huge passion like . . . . . 132 & SON REAL 3   8
BOOSTS
/ / / life boosts herself rapidly at me . . . . 151 & SON REAL 22   1
BOOTED
buy gad) nor asleep booted & spurred with an . . . . 640 {CHAIRE} 42   5
BOOTS
to ambitious weeness of boots tiny add death what . . . . . . 105 & PORTRAIT 1   8
would rather black the boots of success than enquire . . . . 204 XLI LA GUERRE 2   2
their clarion voices and boots were much the worse, ... 339 VIVA 30   26
BOOZING
their bodies big and boozing belong to Marj the . . . . 114 & PORTRAIT 7   15
BORE
her riant belly's fooling bore --When The Sun Begins . . . . 130 & SON REAL 1   2
BORED
away with a small bored gesture that makes the . . . . . . 69 T&C POST IMPR 6   19
BORN
than lilies which are born and cease for being . . . . 5 T&C EPITHALAM   100
like some gigantic ghost-flower born of night blossoming in . 8 T&C OF NICOL   2
leans at a lady whose still-born smile involves the comedy . . . 144 & SON REAL 15   13
believe dey was chust born / / / / . . . . 237 IS 5 ONE 8   19
Sol who was a born failure and nearly everybody . . . . . . 239 IS 5 ONE 10   3
in being at all born, seeing that i was . . . . 262 IS 5 ONE 32   6
die which was not born of dream while wings . . . . 372 VIVA 63   13
lend --being through failures born who cannot fail having . . 394 NO THANKS 11   12
So alive (they s born alive) some folks aint . . . . 426 NO THANKS 43   9
alive) some folks aint born somes born dead an . . . . . . 426 NO THANKS 43   10
folks aint born somes born dead an somes born . . . . 426 NO THANKS 43   11
born dead an somes born alive (but niggers is . . . . 426 NO THANKS 43   12
(but niggers is all born so Alive) ump-A-tum ; . . . . . . 426 NO THANKS 43   16
whose death's to be born) his birth is their . . . . 439 NO THANKS 55   4
& there was is born: one face who. and . . . . 479 NEW POEMS 17   13
the people remember being born) when and if nothing . . . . . 505 50 POEMS 19   16
here and away (but born are maids to flower . . . . 509 50 POEMS 23   4

BORN (CONTINUED)

pale) for betty was born to never say nay . . . . 509 50 POEMS 23   19
work since i am born is good but there . . . . 523 50 POEMS 36   21
grow our can'ts were born to happen our mosts . . . . 537 50 POEMS 49   9
not a world of born--pity poor flesh and trees, ... 554 1 X 1 14   10
a gift called dying born) must grow deep in . . . . 556 1 X 1 16   12
my --being so very born no bird can sing . . . . 558 1 X 1 18   12
them go they were born to go let all . . . . 569 1 X 1 29   13
never known complexity was born before the moon before . . . 577 1 X 1 37   14
soon carved of to born of be One : . . . . 584 1 X 1 44   5
you leap and i'm born we 're sunlight of . . . . 589 1 X 1 49   19
bells) Someone has been born everyone is noone dance . . . . 630 (CHAIRE) 32   14
little horse is newlY Born) he knows nothing, and . . . . . 657 (CHAIRE) 59   2
not imaginable which instant born, a (who is neither . . . . 721 95 POEMS 49   13
miracle drift killed swim born a dream and (through . . . . 757 95 POEMS 85   33
dream of a deed, born not to die) but . . . . 776 73 POEMS 4   36
asks (of a world born deaf) "heaven or hell" . . . . 787 73 POEMS 15   15
one, handsome strong and born to dare --a fighter . . . . . . 799 73 POEMS 27   3
by which my spirit's born: yours is the darkness . . . . . . 810 73 POEMS 38   12
be at any moment born-- some for whom crumbs . . . . 842 73 POEMS 70   2
of reeking innocence are born. Then, with not credible . . . 843 73 POEMS 71   8
the whole (being forever born a foolishwise proudhumble . . . 845 73 POEMS 73   6
BORNE
youths the leaneyed Caesars borne neatly through enormous . . 111 & PORTRAIT 6   37
BORROW
slender and fragile i borrow contact from that you . . . . . 328 VIVA 19   17
and to lend to borrow) or any foe a . . . . 798 73 POEMS 26   18
BOSOMS
jouncing fruit of eager bosoms" Wing Wong / / . . . . 341 VIVA 32   21
+BOSOMY
FOR CONTEXT, SEE . . . . 792 73 POEMS 20   1
BOSS
strike agains De Big Boss (crying) jew wop rich . . . . . . 618 (CHAIRE) 20   10
BOSTON
when i am in Boston, i do not speak. . . . . 217 XLI SONNETS 13   1
of the Cluett Shirt Boston Garter and Spearmint Girl . . . . 230 IS 5 ONE 2   5
found on a lightning-rod, Boston, Mass. such were the . . . 262 IS 5 ONE 32   31
less than nothing) 2 boston Dolls; found with Holes . . . . 317 VIVA 9   24
+BOSTON
FOR CONTEXT, SEE . . . . 200 XLI PORTRAIT 8   13
BOTH
think yourself delivered into both my hands herself to . . . 57 T&C PORTRAIT 5   19
in Christ and Longfellow, both dead, are invariably . . . . . 70 T&C SON REAL 1   5
and, whose distended immense Both paws slowly loved a . . . . 97 & POST IMPR 8   38
would be embarrassing for both parties and because you . . . 204 XLI LA GUERRE 2   4
the silent shoulders are both slowly with pinkish ponderous . 225 IS 5 ONE LIZ   6
rai -ned on people (both male and female created . . . . . . 267 IS 5 TWO 2   18
unremembered (rememberingly with in both pockets curled hands 299 IS 5 FOUR 16   10
mesh witH Which when both march outward into the . . . . . . 311 VIVA 3   13
man and his wife: Both very young noisily who . . . . 312 VIVA 4   11
many a vow but both made sense in when's . . . . 316 VIVA 8   15
with the He-in-her (& both all hopped up) prettily . . . . . 317 VIVA 9   33
seem puzzling but we both might have found the . . . . 323 VIVA 15   18
this caress that laugh both quickly signify life's only . . . 364 VIVA 55   11
is moonlight: say that both precisely beyond either were-- . 379 VIVA 70   2
hates a Man whom both would call their friend . . . . 394 NO THANKS 11   9
stuttering each sentence we both consid (notb- notbr- notbre- 398 NO THANKS 15   10
when each other courted both was very very thwarted) . . . . 401 NO THANKS 18   4
the chic; by instruments, both span and spic, are . . . . . 438 NO THANKS 54   13
like a spoon are both making silence two-made-of-one & . . . 483 NEW POEMS 21   5
of this earth whose both eyes love this now . . . . 512 50 POEMS 26   9
did. Women and men (both little and small) cared . . . . . . 515 50 POEMS 29   5
yes. Women and men (both dong and ding) summer . . . . 515 50 POEMS 29   33
/ newlys of silence (both an only moon the . . . . 518 50 POEMS 32   2
more than enough for both of us darling. And . . . . 531 50 POEMS 43   13
dead which; falling falling both locked in each down . . . . 533 50 POEMS 45   20
door we are so both and oneful night cannot . . . . 537 50 POEMS 49   13
not since not why) both didn't know exeunt they . . . . . . 542 1 X 1 2   4

	PAGE	TITLE	LINE

BOTH (CONTINUED)
yon gilty ceiling per both pale orbs thus excluding . . . . . 546 1 X 1 6 — 5
hope asserts, what falsest both disprove by proving true . . 576 1 X 1 36 — 4
nor mere death nor both who is la guerre) . . . . 577 1 X 1 37 — 10
let's open the year both is the very weather . . . . 578 1 X 1 38 — 5
twisted laws) it comes both prigged and canted / . . . . . . 644 {CHAIRE} 46 — 6
/ / / / both eaching come ghostlike (inch) . . . . 681 95 POEMS 9 — 1
(who is neither each both and) Self adventures deathlessness 721 95 POEMS 49 — 14
but neither's blue most both) and history immeasurably is . . 750 95 POEMS 78 — 5
more most prodigious Selves both now alive creatures (bright 757 95 POEMS 85 — 9
goodbye: glad sorry or both (big little and all) . . . . . . 776 73 POEMS 4 — 39
this stranger went on both knees" green turns red . . . . . . 800 73 POEMS 28 — 16
your lover (looking through both life and death) timelessly . 845 73 POEMS 73 — 12

BOTHATONCE
internalexpanding & externalcontracting brakes Bothatonce and 248 IS 5 ONE 19 — 33

BOTHER
turning a corner) never bother you any more. / . . . . 298 IS 5 FOUR 15 — 28

BOTHERED
my window, night air bothered with a rustling din . . . . . . 171 & SON ACTU 20 — 3

BOTHERING
<> bipeds) OH the bothering dear unnecessary hairless o . . . 250 IS 5 ONE 21 — 16

BOTHING
laugh matching onceupons each bothing (if) creep (by if) . . 681 95 POEMS 9 — 9

BOTHNESS
wounded by my arms' bothness (say a twilight lifting . . . . 218 XLI SONNETS 14 — 3

BOTHS
fair friends and the boths and neithers--you must let . . . . 569 1 X 1 29 — 11

BOTTES
He buy? Les belles bottes--oh hear ,pas cheres") and . . . . 102 & POST IMPR 12 — 20

BOTTLE
it him good a bottle she quick who stop . . . . 496 50 POEMS 10 — 12

BOTTLES
neck to neck of bottles, cats smoothly willowing out . . . . 279 IS 5 THREE 3 — 13
out and in between bottles, who step smoothly and . . . . . . 279 IS 5 THREE 3 — 14

BOTTOM
and why (at the bottom of this trunk, under . . . . 296 IS 5 FOUR 13 — 11
he's swooning at the bottom of the ocean of . . . . 642 {CHAIRE} 44 — 15

BOTTOMLESS
the sweet slow animal bottomless eyes importantly banal, . . 74 T&C SON REAL 5 — 7

BOTTOMS
privacy and lest punished bottoms interrupt philosophy / / . 261 IS 5 ONE 31 — 14

BOUGH
colour went with every bough that reverently bent to . . . . 8 T&C OF NICOL — 31
white bees upon the bough of thy body thy . . . . 29 T&C ORIENTALE 3 — 8
such fruit from what bough that someone called they . . . . . 543 1 X 1 3 — 22
so tree is a bough (and birds sing sweeter . . . . 594 1 X 1 54 — 19
the bird on the bough) how? why --we never . . . . 767 95 POEMS 93 — 4

BOUGHS
troubadours, and (phantom-white) dumb-blooming boughs let . . 8 T&C OF NICOL — 6

BOUGHT
freedom a drug that's bought and sold giving to . . . . 521 50 POEMS 34 — 56

BOULDER
friendly himself of a boulder) nothing mean in tenderly . . . 658 {CHAIRE} 60 — 5

+BOULDER
FOR CONTEXT, SEE . . . . 830 73 POEMS 58 — 17

BOULEVARD
/ i walked the boulevard i saw a dirty . . . . 56 T&C PORTRAIT 4 — 1

BOULEVARDS
and frisks down the boulevards without his coat and . . . . . 296 IS 5 FOUR 13 — 7

+BOULEVARDS
FOR CONTEXT, SEE . . . . 332 VIVA 23 — 18

BOUNCE
ments, waltzing; undigestibly: groans. bounce ! o-ras-ourh . 442 NO THANKS 57 — 6

BOUNCELESS
nations sic item a bounceless period unshy the empty . . . . 499 50 POEMS 13 — 7

BOUNCING
doll-angel-life from Bet: To; Bouncing, Bet the ruby&emerald 747 95 POEMS 75 — 7
no sharp shrill shower bouncing up off burned earth . . . . . 754 95 POEMS 82 — 2

BOUND
    lovers, two and two bound for themselves, when passionately . 71 T&C SON REAL 2   9
BOUNDING
    whipped the top leaps bounding upon other tops to . . . . . . 311 VIVA 3   6
BOUNDS
    candidate's new silk lid bounds gently from his baldness   . . 259 IS 5 ONE 29   21
BOUQUET
    candy white carrying a bouquet of pretend flowers this   . . . 470 NEW POEMS 8   6
BOW
    famished arrow sang before. Bow at belt went my . . . . 14 T&C SONGS 4   21
    man to whom headwaiters bow so? hush--the author of . . . . . 245 IS 5 ONE 16   7
    in sunlight he will bow, & the whole garden . . . . 352 VIVA 43   17
    the whole garden will bow) / / / / . . . . 352 VIVA 43   18
    dark rain snow rain -bow & a moon 's . . . . 512 50 POEMS 26   19
    through one perfectly beautiful bow "my home ionian isles . . 585 1 X 1 45   20
    his tail's red christmas bow) --and if, when we . . . . 631 {CHAIRE} 33   6
    they pray and they bow to a must though . . . . 801 73 POEMS 29   28
BOWED
    all time and space bowed to immortal us if . . . . 694 95 POEMS 22   6
    over vice and beauty bowed to ugliness and logic . . . . . . 799 73 POEMS 27   37
BOWERS
    greener shadow of secret bowers) among the curves of   . . . . 3 T&C EPITHALAM   22
BOWING
    but now, as Mr bowing Cockatoo proffers the meaning . . . . . 697 95 POEMS 25   27
BOWL
    i burn incense the bowl crackles upon the gloom . . . . 31 T&C ORIENTALE 5   3
    spires of fragrance the bowl seethes a flutter of . . . . . . 31 T&C ORIENTALE 5   6
+BOWL
    FOR CONTEXT, SEE . . . . 339 VIVA 30   12
BOWS
    of our fathers' fathers bows to a which that . . . . 711 95 POEMS 39   3
BOX
    turns the crank; the box sprouts fairies, out of . . . . . . 69 T&C POST IMPR 6   2
    tumble clumsily, the little box is spilling rancid elves . . 69 T&C POST IMPR 6   3
    clumsily from the battered box fattish and mysterious the . . 69 T&C POST IMPR 6   23
    if sometimes in its box of sky lavender and . . . . 70 T&C SON REAL 1   12
    year in a dark box dreaming of being taken . . . . 192 XLI CHANSONS 2   14
    latter then opening a box of newly without exaggeration . . . 263 IS 5 ONE 32   46
    a new nice pine box (collect / / / . . . . 270 IS 5 TWO 5   20
    Here Comes a glass box which the exhumed hand . . . . 280 IS 5 THREE 4   2
    hErE cOmEs a glass box: surrounded by priests moving . . . . 280 IS 5 THREE 4   9
    here comes A Glass Box and incense with and . . . . 280 IS 5 THREE 4   22
    in that face a box of skin lay eyes . . . . 355 VIVA 46   9
BOXES
    window, touching the glass boxes one by one with . . . . . . 282 IS 5 THREE 6   26
BOXIN
    flights an Sam begins boxin im on duh koib" . . . . 332 VIVA 23   9
BOY
    curves of that delicious boy whose serious grace one   . . . . 3 T&C EPITHALAM   23
    whose charms the tall boy god of everlasting war . . . . 7 T&C EPITHALAM   154
    beautiful suppression the accurate boy mouth now droops the . 54 T&C PORTRAIT 2   8
    you like your blueeyed boy Mister Death / / . . . . 60 T&C PORTRAIT 8   10
    first twitch of crisp boy flesh dips my height . . . . 140 & SON REAL 11   7
    kilt and my youngest boy was kilt last with . . . . 271 IS 5 TWO 6   8
    clean upstanding well dressed boy that with his peers . . . . 273 IS 5 TWO 8   6
    one "Paul" a harvard boy alas! (who simply wor . . . . 320 VIVA 12   7
    one notHard) not boys boy- ish (a stopped A) . . . . 388 NO THANKS 5   23
    (Than girl 's tears boy Dream's) forge tful: e . . . . 447 NO THANKS 62   12
    wurl no gal no boy (day simbully loves id) . . . . 519 50 POEMS 33   20
    it now when the boy who gave it to . . . . 684 95 POEMS 12   7
    billy how" "your bastard boy must have learned what . . . . . 707 95 POEMS 35   15
    for mind with none) boy after girl each brings . . . . 716 95 POEMS 44   10
    ends-- this girl and boy who're littler than (day . . . . . . 757 95 POEMS 85   2
    whirl over a frightened boy and girl) but that . . . . 777 73 POEMS 5   8
+BOY
    FOR CONTEXT, SEE . . . . 200 XLI PORTRAIT 8   12
    FOR CONTEXT, SEE . . . . 200 XLI PORTRAIT 8   14

                                                    PAGE   TITLE   LINE
BOY'S
    / / / Doll's boy's asleep under a stile . . . . 15 T&C SONGS 5   1
    eyes are mine. Doll's boy's asleep under the stile . . . . . 15 T&C SONGS 5   17
    Marjorie god hurried a boy's body on unsuspicious legs   . . . 148 & SON REAL 19   2
BOYGIRLS
    may nothing more than boygirls need: i can entirely . . . . . 484 NEW POEMS 22   5
+BOYISHNESS
    FOR CONTEXT, SEE . . . . 388 NO THANKS 5   23
BOYS
    filled with vivid noiseless boys at Roupy i have . . . . . . 45 T&C LA GUERRE 1   11
    with the tall tight boys at Tabari' s, keep . . . . 71 T&C SON REAL 2   3
    like moths and like boys and like incense and . . . . 111 & PORTRAIT 6   63
    fill her hips with boys and girls / / . . . . 148 & SON REAL 19   14
    splendiferous funeral with tall boys in black gloves and . . 239 IS 5 ONE 10   31
    hard one notHard) not boys boy- ish (a stopped . . . . . .   388 NO THANKS 5   23
    / / / / the boys i mean are not . . . . 427 NO THANKS 44   1
    shit for wit the boys i mean are not . . . .   427 NO THANKS 44   8
    masturbate with dynamite the boys i mean are not . . . . . . 427 NO THANKS 44   13
    in their pants the boys i mean are not . . . . 427 NO THANKS 44   19
    while daisies grow (and boys and girls have whispered . . . . 451 NO THANKS 66   13
    so) and girls with boys to bed will go, ... 451 NO THANKS 66   15
    a pie (it's try, boys) mine is yours ask . . . .   513 50 POEMS 27   17
    the why (it's now, boys) here we come / . . . . 513 50 POEMS 27   35
    the tallest of the boys" "he'll give me another . . . . 684 95 POEMS 12   8
+BOYS
    FOR CONTEXT, SEE . . . . 484 NEW POEMS 22   5
BRAG
    and brown strut-mince and stink-brag have all come to . . . . 497 50 POEMS 11   3
BRAGGING
    idiot futures bash the bragging breasts, puppy-faces to mouth 151 & SON REAL 22   7
BRAIN
    whirling in the final brain of air!) Let us . . . . 80 T&C SON UNRE 5   11
    exact death the annual brain clotted with loosely voices . . 99 & POST IMPR 10   5
    white idea, drenching. earth's brain detaches clottingsand . 99 & POST IMPR 10   20
    elephants through our single brain in memory of Cleopatra . . 111 & PORTRAIT 6   71
    dance exactly in my brain voulez- vous coucher avec . . . . . 120 & PORTRAIT 12   28
    (my head) in your Brain--my, head's big she (said . . . . . . 123 & SEVEN POEMS 2   12
    tickling away every- body's brain so everybody just puts . . 126 & SEVEN POEMS 5   12
    in her cheeks. A brain peered at the dawn. . . . . 132 & SON REAL 3   13
    light stick on my brain harder than can twitch . . . . 136 & SON REAL 7   7
    a stream does. the brain of cleverly-crinkling -water pursues 160 & SON ACTU 9   4
    it is for the brain irrevocably frigid to touch . . . . 193 XLI PORTRAIT 1   15
    concus- sion of the brain? --Not a bit of . . . . 245 IS 5 ONE 16   18
    best gesture of my brain is less than your . . . . 290 IS 5 FOUR 7   11
    from your body smile brain hands merely to become . . . . . . 295 IS 5 FOUR 12   3
    taptaptaps out of your brain, hopes, life to (carefully . . . 298 IS 5 FOUR 15   26
    with because with every brain which thinks it thinks, ... 424 NO THANKS 41   9
    by prodigious time's mere brain contrived: a spook of . . . . 558 1 X 1 18   9
    most vast (unmind by brain) more than machine turns . . . . . 787 73 POEMS 15   10
+BRAIN
    FOR CONTEXT, SEE . . . . 605 {CHAIRE} 7   6
BRAIN'S
    of The Distinct your brain's axe only chops hugest . . . . . 195 XLI PORTRAIT 3   17
BRAINS
    little Effie's head whose brains are made of gingerbread . . 117 & PORTRAIT 10   2
    little Effie's head whose brains are made of gingerbread . . 118 & PORTRAIT 10   44
    my huge blood, cracking brains A swiftlyenormous light --and 157 & SON ACTU 6   12
    hun dred doomed hurrying brains (by twos or threes . . . . . 354 VIVA 45   21
    trivial labelling of punctual brains... --Who wields a poem   377 VIVA 68   11
    mind: may believe in brains. / / / / . . . . 402 NO THANKS 19   15
    in love a billion brains may coax undeath from . . . . 664 {CHAIRE} 66   19
    through amazing day it's brains without hearts have set . . . 769 95 POEMS 95   15
    anguished each their me brains of that this and . . . . 822 73 POEMS 50   4
BRAINY
    made three) brawny and brainy they sing and they . . . . . . 709 95 POEMS 37   9
BRAKES
    the internalexpanding & externalcontracting brakes Bothatonce 248 IS 5 ONE 19   33

		PAGE	TITLE	LINE

+BRAMBLIEST
FOR CONTEXT, SEE . . . . 695 95 POEMS 23   2

BRAND
/ / she being Brand -new; and you know . . . . 248 IS 5 ONE 19   1
the Americans particularly the brand of marriageable nymph . 256 IS 5 ONE 27   14
word his own unrivalled brand of pyro -technic blurb . . . . 266 IS 5 TWO 1   11

BRASS
bar was made of brass hangIng from strings (or) . . . . 123 & SEVEN POEMS 2   2

BRATTLE
is lead all over Brattle Street by a castrated . . . . 253 IS 5 ONE 24   15

BRAVE
man's poor soul superlatively brave. Surely from robes of . .   5 T&C EPITHALAM   96
body be From each brave eye shall sprout a . . . . 16 T&C SONGS 6   2
and writhe like caught. brave: flies; / / / . . . . 55 T&C PORTRAIT 3   20
◇ "allezcirculez") --my he's brave.... the communists pick . 275 IS 5 TWO 9   40
lie he was more brave than me: more blond . . . . 339 VIVA 30   42
("i am alive") brave ly and (th e . . . . 423 NO THANKS 40   5
wise? doubt blind the brave? does mask wear face? . . . . . . 538 50 POEMS 50   5
of a grave gay brave bright cry of alive . . . . 587 1 X 1 47   21
a gay of a brave and a true of . . . . 606 {CHAIRE} 8   7
--we never we know-- brave! brave (the earth and . . . . . . 767 95 POEMS 93   13
never we know-- brave! brave (the earth and the . . . . 767 95 POEMS 93   13
moving (all gay fair brave tall young come they) . . . . . . 778 73 POEMS 6   10
long at Beautiful and Brave --wildly who rage, vainly . . . . 799 73 POEMS 27   28
the only right since brave are cowards all) therefore . . . . 834 73 POEMS 62   22

BRAVELY
by thy tremulous grace bravely to fling Implacable death's . 206 XLI SONNETS 2   3
i would die etcetera bravely of course my father . . . . . . 276 IS 5 TWO 10   15
who have cried) lie bravely down sleep big rain . . . . 393 NO THANKS 10   11

+BRAVELY
FOR CONTEXT, SEE . . . . 423 NO THANKS 40   5

BRAVER
of peril heedless, each braver than the other, each . . . . . 266 IS 5 TWO 1   19

BRAVEST
were the cleanest keenest bravest killers you'd care to . . . 709 95 POEMS 37   5

BRAVING
now passionately remember how-- braving the worst, of peril . 266 IS 5 TWO 1   18

BRAWNY
its life made three) brawny and brainy they sing . . . . . . 709 95 POEMS 37   9

BRAZEN
youth caught to her brazen breasts, whose foot-stool tells .   4 T&C EPITHALAM   43

BREAD
strong men are digging bread and i see the . . . . 50 T&C IMPRESS 4   13
Nicho' laid before me bread more downy than street-lamps . . 194 XLI PORTRAIT 2   31
we break the precious bread of dear communion with . . . . . 209 XLI SONNETS 5   6
could not earn his bread because he would not . . . . 473 NEW POEMS 11   2
was as true as bread: no liar looked him . . . . 521 50 POEMS 34   45

BREADCRUMB
discreetly (masturbates one honest breadcrumb) say "i . . . . 546 1 X 1 6   12

BREAK
in her flesh at break of day are the . . . . 22 T&C PUELLA MEA   258
a watersmooth-silver stallion and break onetwothreefourfive . 60 T&C PORTRAIT 8   6
--w hee e; seasays. Break snice-Ly in-twin K les . . . . . . 94 & POST IMPR 6   14
graceful oath, upsoarings the break on ceiling- flatness the 96 & POST IMPR 8   9
by whose page we break the precious bread of . . . . 209 XLI SONNETS 5   6
while and which easily break in spite of the . . . . 264 IS 5 ONE 33   15
nor dingsters die at break of dong and common's . . . . 511 50 POEMS 25   18
it's un lucky to break one) whole with sky . . . . 623 {CHAIRE} 25   7
earth and sky should break in two he'd make . . . . 760 95 POEMS 87   7

+BREAK
FOR CONTEXT, SEE . . . . 310 VIVA 2   5
FOR CONTEXT, SEE . . . . 398 NO THANKS 15   12

BREAKFAST
(while scotch was your breakfast every night all day) . . . . 605 {CHAIRE} 7   5

BREAKFASTFOOD
as freedom is a breakfastfood or truth can live . . . . 511 50 POEMS 25   1

BREAKING
with sleep.... love, the breaking of your soul upon . . . . . 38 T&C AMORES 3   15

	PAGE	TITLE	LINE

BREAKING (CONTINUED)
air there) and without breaking anything. / / / . . . . 124 & SEVEN POEMS 3 19
+BREAKING
FOR CONTEXT, SEE . . . . 94 & POST IMPR 6 7
FOR CONTEXT, SEE . . . . 94 & POST IMPR 6 7
FOR CONTEXT, SEE . . . . 94 & POST IMPR 6 7
BREAKS
of defeat, her heart breaks in a smile--and she . . . . 75 T&C SON REAL 6 13
and when the string breaks (or something) my uncle . . . . . 253 IS 5 ONE 24 8
something) my uncle Frank breaks into tears. my uncle . . . . 253 IS 5 ONE 24 8
BREAST
gold over the infinite breast in bright degrees, whose . . . 4 T&C EPITHALAM 39
and gone.) Each tapering breast is firm and smooth . . . . . 21 T&C PUELLA MEA 181
perfect bliss-- for each breast a blossom is, which . . . . . 21 T&C PUELLA MEA 190
thou art silent thy breast is as a tomb . . . . 27 T&C ORIENTALE 1 25
with fascination, when my breast wears the intolerant . . . . 78 T&C SON UNRE 3 10
a sign on his breast BLIND) yes i am . . . . 298 IS 5 FOUR 15 5
keener each will kissed breast awake) slow tottering visions 565 1 X 1 25 12
than this (mere most) breast spring's million (who are . . . 573 1 X 1 33 18
+BREASTED
FOR CONTEXT, SEE . . . . 74 T&C SON REAL 5 12
BREASTS
caught to her brazen breasts, whose foot-stool tells how . . 4 T&C EPITHALAM 43
lay between their little breasts My strong fingers beneath . 16 T&C SONGS 6 8
a sound of strangling breasts and bestial grovelling hands . 28 T&C ORIENTALE 2 7
with sleeping birds thy breasts are swarms of white . . . . . 29 T&C ORIENTALE 3 7
with ecstasy my palpitating breasts inhale the slow supple . 31 T&C ORIENTALE 5 24
sang between your perfect breasts darkness and beauty of . . 39 T&C AMORES 4 16
sobs puckered the foolish breasts the droll mouth wilted . . 52 T&C PORTRAIT 1 29
the jostle of thy breasts and the slobber of . . . . 61 T&C PORTRAIT 9 24
and where your meeting breasts are round have roses . . . . . 71 T&C SON REAL 2 5
teeth and small important breasts (is it the Frolic . . . . . 72 T&C SON REAL 3 2
bulgings of the pretended breasts, forked in surprisable . . 103 & POST IMPR 13 3
/ / between the breasts of bestial Marj lie . . . . 114 & PORTRAIT 7 1
who lie between the breasts of bestial Marj for . . . . 114 & PORTRAIT 7 25
transparency. the harsh erecting breasts and uttering tits . 137 & SON REAL 8 13
laughing body with wise breasts half-grown, lisping flesh . . 140 & SON REAL 11 11
could) eyes say the breasts look very good: firmlysquirmy . . 150 & SON REAL 21 3
futures bash the bragging breasts, puppy-faces to mouth her . 151 & SON REAL 22 7
woman with sticking out breasts hanging clothes. On the . . . 167 & SON ACTU 16 1
making the obscene shy breasts tickle, laughing when i . . . 172 & SON ACTU 21 15
softly your face smile breasts gargled by death: drowned . . 369 VIVA 60 9
and up come who breasts will be breasts thighs . . . . 511 50 POEMS 25 24
who breasts will be breasts thighs will be thighs . . . . . 511 50 POEMS 25 24
BREATH
clear candle whose expecting breath exults upon the tongue . 6 T&C EPITHALAM 117
wings, where dwells the breath of all persisting stars . . . 40 T&C AMORES 4 46
hide them in thy breath drive them in nothingness . . . . . . 41 T&C AMORES 5 21
ploop. --OOc h get: breath once, all over, kid . . . . . . 136 & SON REAL 7 13
/ / nearer: breath of my breath: take . . . . 139 & SON REAL 10 1
nearer: breath of my breath: take not thy tingling . . . . 139 & SON REAL 10 1
the way asked sis breath of brud breathe how . . . . 316 VIVA 8 19
possibly more intricate) i (breath in breath) have nicknamed 358 VIVA 49 8
intricate) i (breath in breath) have nicknamed ecstasy and . 358 VIVA 49 9
such life could its breath would stink and as . . . . 510 50 POEMS 24 7
desdemonial that took his breath away all history oped . . . 552 1 X 1 12 20
everything he took one breath bigger than a circustent . . . 566 1 X 1 26 3
-ble flame is lives breath es (over- ing un . . . . 719 95 POEMS 47 13
BREATHE
warriors amber with lust breathe together the emperor, . . . 34 T&C ORIENTALE 6 98
chuckles seeing the Greeks breathe) / / / / . . . . 220 XLI SONNETS 16 16
(i, seeing, ceased to breathe). The plump left fist . . . . 226 IS 5 ONE MAME 7
that i laugh and breathe is oh love and . . . . 295 IS 5 FOUR 12 24
sis breath of brud breathe how is aunt death . . . . 316 VIVA 8 20
/ / / / breathe with me this fear . . . . 362 VIVA 53 1
hills invent the air) breathe simply my each how . . . . . 372 VIVA 63 4
most secret i will breathe such crude perfection as . . . . 428 NO THANKS 45 10
not money lucky are Breathe grow dream die love . . . . . . 467 NEW POEMS 5 7

	PAGE	TITLE	LINE
BREATHE (CONTINUED)			
to live id est breathe but if such life	510	50 POEMS 24	7
hate were why men breathe-- because my father lived	521	50 POEMS 34	66
where (no) when may breathe so sky so	584	1 X 1 44	17
leap, no soul can breathe but by the sizeless	664	(CHAIRE) 66	21
or if where shall breathe a new (silverly rare	666	(CHAIRE) 68	7
life) we die to breathe, itself becomes her wonder	742	95 POEMS 70	14
than every miracle's to breathe) wounded us will becauseless	745	95 POEMS 73	4
now dreams are to breathe / / / /	755	95 POEMS 83	20
where nothing is to breathe to stroll to swim	768	95 POEMS 94	3
faithfully blossoming beyond to breathe suns of the night, .	811	73 POEMS 39	8
BREATHE-MOVE-AND-SEEM			
april;and i breathe-move-and-seem some perpetually	839	73 POEMS 67	6
BREATHED			
alive silentness god ever breathed upon beginning) "beautiful	572	1 X 1 32	9
you and everybody never breathed quite so many kinds	591	1 X 1 51	15
hell) and never have breathed such miracle murdered we . . .	639	(CHAIRE) 41	9
BREATHES			
spite of everything which breathes and moves, since Doom . .	288	IS 5 FOUR 5	2
from a restaurant, looks breathes or moves --climbing (past .	300	IS 5 FOUR 17	3
hints being; suggests identity) breathes fleet perfectly far	402	NO THANKS 19	10
can grow all distance breathes a final dream of	750	95 POEMS 78	2
+BREATHES			
FOR CONTEXT, SEE	719	95 POEMS 47	13
BREATHING			
devious, beneath the body's breathing noun (moreover the . .	21	T&C PUELLA MEA	211
a) slEEping neck a breathing a , lies (slo	104	& POST IMPR 14	7
i lie at length, breathing with shut eyes the	184	XLI SONGS 6	15
FIVE AMERICANS LIZ with breathing as (faithfully) her	225	IS 5 ONE LIZ	1
Honorable Mr. (guess) who, breathing on the ear of	266	IS 5 TWO 1	35
kisses your flesh mind breathing beside under around myself)	283	IS 5 THREE 7	16
(and every brittle marvelous breathing thing) since i and . .	293	IS 5 FOUR 10	13
beauty less than our breathing / / / /	363	VIVA 54	12
and forever with each breathing (i do not know	366	VIVA 57	16
we, entirely whose least breathing may surprise ourselves . .	368	VIVA 59	14
on seas of iron breathing height eating steepness the	419	NO THANKS 36	13
be) whose ignorant each breathing dares to hide more	446	NO THANKS 61	11
feel if spring's least breathing should cause a colour . . .	450	NO THANKS 65	13
even death's what beneath breathing selves transported are .	454	NO THANKS 69	5
childmoon smile to your breathing doll / / /	518	50 POEMS 32	12
under's mere above but breathing yes which fear will	538	50 POEMS 50	2
you perhaps do the breathing for me while i	558	1 X 1 18	15
why their stride and breathing to limp and prove	580	1 X 1 40	10
you behold nor any breathing creature this? nothing except .	582	1 X 1 42	11
particular tree are all breathing bright darkness to gether .	600	(CHAIRE) 2	8
man alone (his briefest breathing lives some planet's year, .	609	(CHAIRE) 11	10
never (by breathless one breathing) be" soul "more" cries: .	625	(CHAIRE) 27	23
tasting touching hearing seeing breathing any--lifted from .	663	(CHAIRE) 65	10
of the ground and breathing is wishing and wishing	665	(CHAIRE) 67	2
in some autumnal afternoon: breathing a fatal stillness; . .	674	95 POEMS 2	3
death or even than breathing shall blossom a first	720	95 POEMS 48	13
am (life to life; breathing to breathing flaming dream . . .	721	95 POEMS 49	2
to life; breathing to breathing flaming dream to dreaming . .	721	95 POEMS 49	2
which) a marvel every breathing creature feels (but none . .	735	95 POEMS 63	7
propped on a pitchfork (breathing) lovers like rej and . . .	754	95 POEMS 82	8
the air with almost breathing me) --look up: and	762	95 POEMS 89	9
+BREATHING			
FOR CONTEXT, SEE	349	VIVA 40	17
FOR CONTEXT, SEE	657	(CHAIRE) 59	12
BREATHING'S			
living's to give so breathing's to steal-- five wishes . . .	543	1 X 1 3	16
BREATHINGS			
Do tell ....sweat, succeeds breathings stopped to hear, in .	136	& SON REAL 7	15
BREATHLESS			
divine! O singular and breathless pearl! O indefinable frail	5	T&C EPITHALAM	108
the surrounded smile hangs breathless / / / /	83	T&C SON ACTU 2	17
and wealthy vermilion and breathless-scarlet, dark colours .	100	& POST IMPR 11	7
firm fragile stinging weather, (breathless with sharp	140	& SON REAL 11	9

BREATHLESS (CONTINUED)
   forever could never (by breathless one breathing) be" soul . 625 {CHAIRE} 27   22
BREATHLESS-SCARLET
   and wealthy vermilion and breathless-scarlet, dark colours . 100 & POST IMPR 11   7
BREATHS
   rap idly with their breaths.) "people are walking deaths . . 354 VIVA 45   11
   rapidly pass with their breaths) in win ter you . . . . 354 VIVA 45   23
BRED
   (trig westpointer most succinctly bred) took erring Olaf soon 339 VIVA 30   5
BREEDING
   thick (cringing they brood breeding they wince) his laugh . . 439 NO THANKS 55   10
BREEDS
   valor, battle with heroic breeds; thou, Froissart, for that . 209 XLI SONNETS 5   8
BRETON
   this six feet of Breton big good body, which . . . . 277 IS 5 THREE 1   6
BREVIS
   lives on air Harvard Brevis Est for Handkerchief read . . . . 410 NO THANKS 27   5
BREWED
   that rotgut never was brewed which could knock you . . . . . 605 {CHAIRE} 7   4
BRIDE
   a WELL KNOWn ATHLETE'S BRIDE (lullaby) & z = ... 317 VIVA 9   1
   / / this little bride & groom are standing) . . . . 470 NEW POEMS 8   1
   with this candy little bride & little groom in . . . . 470 NEW POEMS 8   9
BRIDEGROOMS
   over me are like bridegrooms Naked and luminous (here . . . . 281 IS 5 THREE 5   16
BRIDGE
   long door golf slam bridge train shriek chewing whistles . . 309 VIVA 1   18
   man stout as a bridge rugged as a bear . . . . 568 1 X 1 28   6
BRIDGES
   isn'ts on why, digging bridges with mirrors from whispers . . 439 NO THANKS 55   21
BRIEF
   when on a green brief gesture of twilight trembles . . . . . 156 & SON ACTU 5   8
   being too strong, in brief : an American, if . . . . 262 IS 5 ONE 32   12
   All was over. One brief convulsive octopus, and then . . . . 263 IS 5 ONE 32   56
   comprehend the innocently Doomed brief all which somewhere is 356 VIVA 47   11
   memory shrink from such brief selves as fiercely seek . . . . 373 VIVA 64   13
   "dearest we" unsigned: remarkably brief but covering one . . 504 50 POEMS 18   2
   so must most lily brief (rose here&gone) flesh all . . . . 690 95 POEMS 18   5
   mind utterly beyond is brief that how infinite (deeply . . . 763 95 POEMS 90   21
+BRIEF
   FOR CONTEXT, SEE . . . . 282 IS 5 THREE 6   11
BRIEFER
   do not worry if briefer days grow briefest, i . . . . 749 95 POEMS 77   3
   this endless end of briefer each our bliss-- where . . . . . 834 73 POEMS 62   26.
BRIEFEST
   lonely man alone (his briefest breathing lives some planet's 609 {CHAIRE} 11   10
   if briefer days grow briefest, i am not sorry . . . . 749 95 POEMS 77   3
BRIEFNESS
   draws down. cover her briefness in singing close her . . . . 65 T&C POST IMPR 2   8
   / into the strenuous briefness Life: handorgans and April . . 66 T&C POST IMPR 3   1
   man, may his mighty briefness dig for love beginning . . . . 526 50 POEMS 38   4
BRIGGS
   harmless quips, out of Briggs by Kitty) arriving in . . . . . 326 VIVA 18   14
BRIGHT
   the infinite breast in bright degrees, whose pillow is . . . 4 T&C EPITHALAM   39
   thing man forth into bright air, for now the . . . . 4 T&C EPITHALAM   61
   foreheads to the barbarous bright sky, and suddenly from . . 5 T&C EPITHALAM   77
   drift murmurous things divinely bright; it is foolingly to . 18 T&C PUELLA MEA   81
   by angelfaces clustered like bright lice about god's capable 85 T&C SON ACTU 4   3
   is a Lady with bright slender eyes (who moves) . . . . 91 & POST IMPR 3   2
   and all things) the bright rain occurs deeply, beautifully . 92 & POST IMPR 4   5
   loves melons slitted with bright knives, it stains itself, . 100 & POST IMPR 11   23
   the unspontaneous streets make bright their eyes a blind . . 108 & PORTRAIT 4   6
   tremendously floats in the bright shouting street of time . . 112 & PORTRAIT 6   75
   my hug presto! the bright rile of jovial hair . . . . 137 & SON REAL 8   16
   perpetually meticulous concupiscence the bright large . . . . 193 XLI PORTRAIT 1   23
   roll) i spill my bright incalculable soul. / / . . . . 206 XLI SONNETS 2   15
   quickly into the very bright spittoon / / / . . . . 252 IS 5 ONE 23   12

BRIGHT (CONTINUED)

      poorbuthonest workingman (by that bright flame whose myriad . 254 IS 5 ONE 25   17
      whom areEyes shy-dodge is bright cruMbshandful, quick-hurl . 265 IS 5 ONE 34   4
      truth unfurled, in the bright heyday of his youth . . . . . . 273 IS 5 TWO 8   15
      all the world becoming bright and little melted. / . . . . . 283 IS 5 THREE 7   27
      this floor (quietly with bright eyes) drifts (nobody can . . 286 IS 5 FOUR 3   5
      along the brittle treacherous bright streets of memory comes 304 IS 5 FIVE 3   1
      looming) accurate undaunted moon's bright third tumbling . . 305 IS 5 FIVE 4   15
      others fly, their; puLLing: bright futures against the deep . 314 VIVA 6   14
      pass ignorantly into sleep's bright land / / / . . . . 358 VIVA 49   15
      inhabited by roamingly stern bright faeries if you love . . . 363 VIVA 54   4
      with what ease that bright how plural tide measures . . . . . 418 NO THANKS 35   10
      by silently unday life's bright less dwindled to a . . . . . 432 NO THANKS 49   13
      let knowings magic with bright credos each divisible fool . 452 NO THANKS 67   7
      / / / / brIght bRight s??? big (soft) . . . . 455 NO THANKS 70   1
      / / / brIght bRight s??? big (soft) soft . . . . 455 NO THANKS 70   2
      (soft) soft near calm (Bright) calm st?? holy (soft . . . . . 455 NO THANKS 70   5
      calm st?? holy (soft briGht deep) yeS near sta? . . . . 455 NO THANKS 70   7
      all we taste as bright, bitter all utterly things . . . . . . 521 50 POEMS 34   61
      thousand million hundred more bright worlds than merely by . 580 1 X 1 40   13
      a grave gay brave bright cry of alive with . . . . 587 1 X 1 47   22
      tree are all breathing bright darkness to gether are . . . . 600 (CHAIRE) 2   8
      them more than any bright word may cry --even . . . . 605 (CHAIRE) 7   7
      all the girls (the bright ones, the dim ones; . . . . 619 (CHAIRE) 21   10
      thing sil -very ; bright, &: mys (a . . . . 632 (CHAIRE) 34   6
      way (and whose brook -bright flower- soft bird -quick . . . . 660 (CHAIRE) 62   19
      celestial wish (whying diminutive bright deathlessness to . . 669 (CHAIRE) 71   2
      face & mended his bright torn trousers (quite as . . . . . . 680 95 POEMS 8   16
      both now alive creatures (bright if by shadowy if) . . . . . . 757 95 POEMS 85   10
      wrong (dim worlds or bright; big little and all) . . . . . . 776 73 POEMS 4   27
      where climbing was and bright is darkness and to . . . . . . 834 73 POEMS 62   19
      proudly humbly overing) all bright all things swim climb . . 841 73 POEMS 69   27

+BRIGHT
      FOR CONTEXT, SEE . . . . 265 IS 5 ONE 34   6
      FOR CONTEXT, SEE . . . . 265 IS 5 ONE 34   8
      FOR CONTEXT, SEE . . . . 455 NO THANKS 70   14
      FOR CONTEXT, SEE . . . . 455 NO THANKS 70   14

BRIGHTEN
      terror always which shall brighten carefully these things we 289 IS 5 FOUR 6   11

BRIGHTENING
      unspeaking tower within whose brightening strictness Danae .   4 T&C EPITHALAM   51
      stars writhe captured in brightening fright) / / / . . . . . 77 T&C SON UNRE 2   17

BRIGHTER
      love god's terrible face, brighter than a spoon, collects . . 360 VIVA 51   21
      who's we we're anything brighter than even the sun . . . . . 594 1 X 1 54   37
      and song wonderingly come (brighter than prayers) riding . . 778 73 POEMS 6   14

BRIGHTEST
      purest than fear's obscener brightest than hate's more black 565 1 X 1 25   10

BRIGHTMILLION
      of aflickf) litter ing brightmillion ofS hurl; edindodg: ing 265 IS 5 ONE 34   3

BRIGHTNESS
      breast wears the intolerant brightness of your charms: one . 78 T&C SON UNRE 3   11
      perceived sails whose mighty brightness dumbs the utterance . 79 T&C SON UNRE 4   9
      the spring; a clumsy brightness of air wonderfully stumbled . 173 & SON ACTU 22   2
      silently into crocuses of brightness. (That is enough of . . 282 IS 5 THREE 6   31
      of love move (with brightness of peace) all places . . . . . 443 NO THANKS 58   4
      whispered were, completes its brightness with your eyes any . 526 50 POEMS 38   11

BRIGHTSHADOWFULLY
      through (slapsoothed by sundark) brightshadowfully . . . . . 681 95 POEMS 9   14

BRILLIANT
      with his probably most brilliant pupil mated, let us . . . . 326 VIVA 18   7

BRILLIANTLY
      of hasteful futility lived brilliantly the enormous rhythm of 103 & POST IMPR 13   11

BRING
      roses and spring will bring her worms rushing through . . . . 67 T&C POST IMPR 4   11
      squirms kissingly, i will bring you every spring handfuls . . 161 & SON ACTU 10   7
      eye laughs, i will bring you every year something . . . . . . 161 & SON ACTU 10   12
      god-beasts do thou distinctly bring thy footstep, and the . . 213 XLI SONNETS 9   10

	PAGE	TITLE	LINE

BRING (CONTINUED)
no excuse for May --bring forth your flowers and . . . . . . 264 IS 5 ONE 33 9
rose give a damn... bring on your fireworks, which . . . . . 264 IS 5 ONE 33 21
others give and realness bring-- ask the always impossible . 454 NO THANKS 69 1
next at 1 E.S.T. bring the kiddies let's all . . . . 514 50 POEMS 28 14
have shadowless they? i bring you peace the moon . . . . . . 527 50 POEMS 39 3
move may rest --you bring (out of dark the . . . . 575 1 X 1 35 6
's hand) very carefully bring -ing to you and . . . . 652 (CHAIRE) 54 4
suns of the night, bring this beautiful wanderer home . . . . 811 73 POEMS 39 9
BRINGING
girl art thou flowers bringing? To be thy lips . . . . 13 T&C SONGS 3 14
gardens moves a wind bringing rain and leaves, filling . . . 304 IS 5 FIVE 3 11
maids mothers widows wives bringing this visitor their very . 624 (CHAIRE) 26 7
+BRINGING
FOR CONTEXT, SEE . . . . 256 IS 5 ONE 27 29
FOR CONTEXT, SEE . . . . 403 NO THANKS 20 12
BRINGS
themselves, when passionately dusk brings softly down the . . 71 T&C SON REAL 2 10
nudging into neglected sentiments brings to light dusty . . . 203 XLI LA GUERRE 1 7
boy after girl each brings a world to build . . . . 716 95 POEMS 44 11
BRISKLY
usual hither, thither who briskly busily carry the as . . . . 354 VIVA 45 14
+BRITISH
FOR CONTEXT, SEE . . . . 492 50 POEMS 6 5
BRITTLE
this man with the brittle legs winces swiflty out . . . . . . 62 T&C PORTRAIT 10 24
POST IMPRESSIONS beyond the brittle towns asleep i look . . . 64 T&C POST IMPR 1 1
huge and its chords brittle eager eternal luminous firmly . . 110 & PORTRAIT 6 26
bite on the eyes' brittle crust (only feeling the . . . . . 132 & SON REAL 3 6
Something, distinct and. Amusing, brittle / / / . . . . . . 164 & SON ACTU 13 17
kiss was a distinct brittle flower, and the flesh . . . . . 173 & SON ACTU 22 9
which easily trickles a brittle fuss of fragile huge . . . . 174 & SON ACTU 23 6
April his legs are brittle and small his feet . . . . 198 XLI PORTRAIT 6 21
alert neck of this brittle whore delicately wobbles an . . . 229 IS 5 ONE FRAN 2
ring of people a brittle swoon of centrifugally expecting . . 279 IS 5 THREE 3 6
my lady (and every brittle marvelous breathing thing) since . 293 IS 5 FOUR 10 13
/ / along the brittle treacherous bright streets of . . . . . 304 IS 5 FIVE 3 1
his appetite with bad brittle candy but just (nude . . . . . 410 NO THANKS 27 3
through its cluttered and brittle emblems, or a field . . . . 434 NO THANKS 51 23
again and) ask a brittle little person fiddling in . . . . . 498 50 POEMS 12 12
BRITTLER
shrivel and hearts grow brittler every Instant (when of . . . 359 VIVA 50 4
BRITTLEST
(◇ ! throughwhich! brittlest! whitewhom! f l o . . . . . . 416 NO THANKS 33 12
BROAD
sunday flower. The babybreasted broad "kitty" twice eight . . 74 T&C SON REAL 5 12
the info from a broad that knew Eddie in . . . . 145 & SON REAL 16 7
BROADWAY
the mystic screech of Broadway, the trivial stink of . . . . 220 XLI SONNETS 16 3
BROGUE
the tousle of saxophonic brogue. / / / / . . . . 140 & SON REAL 11 15
BROKE
caught you strained you broke you upon my blood . . . . . . 30 T&C ORIENTALE 4 28
to please my musn't broke) life Is like that . . . . 343 VIVA 34 2
with madness wind and broke oceans and tore mountains . . . . 432 NO THANKS 49 16
him) one william shakespeare broke the silence of the . . . . 552 1 X 1 12 24
BROKEN
between greentwittering smokes from broken eyes a sound of . 28 T&C ORIENTALE 2 5
eyes balanced upon one broken babypout (pretty teeth wander . 406 NO THANKS 23 10
nicked ends next among broken odds of yes terday's . . . . . 522 50 POEMS 35 6
it go--the smashed word broken open vow or the . . . . 569 1 X 1 29 2
be to sing if broken hearts were whole and . . . . 798 73 POEMS 26 8
BROMFIELD
and at tremont and bromfield i paused a moment . . . . 52 T&C PORTRAIT 1 11
BRONX
well known suburb the bronx (enlivening an otherwise dead . . 326 VIVA 18 13
BROOD
dreams thick (cringing they brood breeding they wince) his . 439 NO THANKS 55 9

	PAGE	TITLE	LINE
BROOK			
swaddled with a frozen brook of pinkest vomit out	258	IS 5 ONE 28	13
field rock hollyhock forest brook chickadee mountain.	512	50 POEMS 26	26
/ hair your a brook (it through are gaze	613	(CHAIRE) 15	1
a- way (and whose brook -bright flower- soft bird	660	(CHAIRE) 62	18
BROOKS			
dead. Hills jump with brooks: trees tumble out of	580	1 X 1 40	27
BROTHER			
could with our big brother who is would don't	117	& PORTRAIT 10	19
seduced by Life; whose brother married Heart, now Mrs	621	(CHAIRE) 23	3
my lover has a brother who is good and	684	95 POEMS 12	11
right from wrong, took brother Fearless by the eyes	799	73 POEMS 27	14
+BROTHER			
FOR CONTEXT, SEE	316	VIVA 8	20
BROUGHT			
zone of her that brought forth tall Hippolytus, lord	4	T&C EPITHALAM	45
hills by darkness softly brought-- (be with me in	9	T&C SONGS 1	36
sloppy body from being brought to bed of crocuses	61	T&C PORTRAIT 9	17
externalcontracting brakes Bothatonce and brought allofher .	248	IS 5 ONE 19	34
weep my father's fingers brought her sleep: vainly no	520	50 POEMS 34	14
BROW			
awe), thunderer whose omnipotent brow showers its curls of .	4	T&C EPITHALAM	37
eyes a memory this brow five or three dreamfuls	402	NO THANKS 19	6
+BROW			
FOR CONTEXT, SEE	333	VIVA 24	10
BROWN			
in the silence a brown god smiles between greentwittering . .	28	T&C ORIENTALE 2	3
and pink-flag blackshirt and brown strut-mince and stink-brag	497	50 POEMS 11	2
BROWNS			
this water, crowding tints: browns and whites shoving, the .	281	IS 5 THREE 5	5
BROWS			
ancient greath on insulated brows (while tossing boms at . .	500	50 POEMS 14	14
BRUD			
asked sis breath of brud breathe how is aunt	316	VIVA 8	20
BRUISED			
all depart through the bruised air aflutter with pearls . . .	34	T&C ORIENTALE 6	106
through the evening in bruised narrow questioning faces) / .	275	IS 5 TWO 9	50
crouch (lunge)ing bruiseD Suddenly by thousand starings . .	388	NO THANKS 5	5
BRUISING			
lips limp, across my bruising smile; as rapidly upon	137	& SON REAL 8	8
BRUMMELL			
ghost lurks, a Beau Brummell sticking in its three-	227	IS 5 ONE GERT	4
BRUSH			
come to her and brush the mischief from her	40	T&C AMORES 4	40
lies flat on the brush / / / /	231	IS 5 ONE 3	55
hats legs & arms brush dirt coats smile looking	275	IS 5 TWO 9	45
BRUSHES			
which others stroke with brushes recently employed anent this	339	VIVA 30	11
BRUSHING			
a button solemnly inert. Brushing from whom the stiffened . .	258	IS 5 ONE 28	21
BRUTAL			
spun to snare the brutal dew, --the authentic scroll	5	T&C EPITHALAM	87
and i see the brutal faces of people contented	50	T&C IMPRESS 4	14
a nudging bulb silkenly brutal a devout flexion /	68	T&C IMPR 5	15
painful ankles large acute brutal feet propped on	103	& POST IMPR 13	8
fiercely shy and gently brutal, the prettiest wrath of . . .	214	XLI SONNETS 10	7
simplicity a more intensively brutal futility" And sit . . .	354	VIVA 45	17
BRUTE			
whore. Sixteen you corking brute amused from time to	74	T&C SON REAL 5	9
BRUTEBEAK			
tweak S with his brutebeak one fatal faded (pinkish	697	95 POEMS 25	23
BRYANT			
negro son, Henry Wadsworth Bryant. By this time, however, . .	263	IS 5 ONE 32	53
BUB			
forgotten full of why (rub-her-bub) bub? (bubs) where's Jim .	642	(CHAIRE) 44	8
never in his fly (rub-her-bub) bub? (bubs) where's John . . .	642	(CHAIRE) 44	18
up a wench's rock-a-bye (rub-her-bub) bub? (bubs) / /	642	(CHAIRE) 44	28

90

BUBBIES
   with o man what bubbies going places on such . . . . 476 NEW POEMS 14   6
BUBBLE
   people trickle curselaughgroping shrieks bubble squirmwrithed 330 VIVA 21   3
   / hate blows a bubble of despair into hugeness . . . . 531 50 POEMS 43   1
BUBBLES
   friendless dingy female frenzy bubbles / / / / . . . . 151 & SON REAL 22   18
   willing bulb of flame bubbles) see here and here . . . . . . 282 IS 5 THREE 6   28
   raced sideways while blowing bubbles: and may came home . . . 682 95 POEMS 10   8
+BUBBLES
   FOR CONTEXT, SEE . . . . 100 & POST IMPR 11 25
   FOR CONTEXT, SEE . . . . 495 50 POEMS 9   23
BUBS
   of why (rub-her-bub) bub? (bubs) where's Jim Soon Admiral . . 642 {CHAIRE} 44   10
   his fly (rub-her-bub) bub? (bubs) where's John Big Doughgob . 642 {CHAIRE} 44   20
   wench's rock-a-bye (rub-her-bub) bub? (bubs) / / / / . . . . 642 {CHAIRE} 44   30
BUCH
   Lydia E. McKinley when Buch tooked out his C.O.D. . . . . . . 321 VIVA 13   7
+BUCHANAN
   FOR CONTEXT, SEE . . . . 321 VIVA 13   7
BUCK
   go with girls who buck and bite they do . . . . 427 NO THANKS 44   2
   girls who bite and buck who cannot read and . . . . 427 NO THANKS 44   9
   but as one whole buck became his (believe it . . . . 800 73 POEMS 28   14
BUCK'
   to get one whole buck' not a word this . . . . 800 73 POEMS 28   12
BUCKS
   hold down the fifty bucks per job with one . . . . 242 IS 5 ONE 13   8
BUD
   this recalls hat gestures bud plumptumbling hand voices Eye . 330 VIVA 21   6
   heer we kum dearie) bud hooz gwine ter hate . . . . 519 50 POEMS 33   14
   ydoan o nudn LISN bud LISN dem gud am . . . . 547 1 X 1 7   10
   were in (give give) bud when to me you . . . . 589 1 X 1 49   3
   the humble proud youngest bud testified "giving (and giving . 763 95 POEMS 90 16
   the root and the bud of the bud and . . . . 766 95 POEMS 92 11
   the bud of the bud and the sky of . . . . 766 95 POEMS 92 11
+BUD
   FOR CONTEXT, SEE . . . . 423 NO THANKS 40   22
BUDDHA
   he will nod like buddha or answer modestly i . . . . 198 XLI PORTRAIT 6 28
BUDDIES
   aint it we was buddies i used to know . . . . 270 IS 5 TWO 5   10
BUDDING
   neckless nudity (very occasionally budding a flabby algebraic 134 & SON REAL 5   7
BUDGE
   then up rose bishop budge from kew a anglican . . . . 552 1 X 1 12   6
BUDGINGLY
   they always which creep budgingly over some numbered face . . 359 VIVA 50   15
BUDS
   mangling air muchness of buds mattered. a valley spilled . . 135 & SON REAL 6 14
   and do not wait) buds imitate upward each first . . . . 573 1 X 1 33   22
   because or although (and buds know better than books . . . . 594 1 X 1 54   11
BUFFALO
   / / / / Buffalo Bill's defunct who used . . . . 60 T&C PORTRAIT 8   1
BUFFETING
   scraggy knees squeezing and buffeting thee that thou mightest 46 T&C LA GUERRE 2 17
BUG
   crossing sidewalks the unwary june-bug and the frivolous . . 61 T&C PORTRAIT 9   3
   no sendwisp ben jiffyclaus bug fainarain wee celibate . . . . 333 VIVA 24   20
+BUG
   FOR CONTEXT, SEE . . . . 127 & SEVEN POEMS 5 47
BUGGER
   things to enni one bugger thy nabor (neck and . . . . 492 50 POEMS 6   12
BUGGY
   in spite of his buggy of lady godiva & . . . . 699 95 POEMS 27   7
BUGLE
   white water the cruel bugle sang before. Horn at . . . . . . 14 T&C SONGS 4   10

	PAGE	TITLE	LINE

BUGS

water or with the bugs crawling right all up . . . . 272 IS 5 TWO 7　10

+BUGS

FOR CONTEXT, SEE . . . . 126 & SEVEN POEMS 5　5
FOR CONTEXT, SEE . . . . 127 & SEVEN POEMS 5　51
FOR CONTEXT, SEE . . . . 312 VIVA 4　24

BUILD

foe he'd laugh and build a world with snow. . . . . 521 50 POEMS 34　48
silence) such hands can build a (who are like . . . . 617 (CHAIRE) 19　3
brings a world to build our clown --shouting to . . . . . . 716 95 POEMS 44　12

BUILDING

was a million years building he takes the air . . . . 32 T&C ORIENTALE 6　3
/ my love is building a building around you, ... 83 T&C SON ACTU 2　1
love is building a building around you, a frail . . . . . . 83 T&C SON ACTU 2　1
a precise clumsy prison (building thatandthis into Thus, . . 83 T&C SON ACTU 2　7
mouth) my love is building a magic, a discrete . . . . . . 83 T&C SON ACTU 2　9
tongue sits the Woolworth building a serene pastile-shaped . 201 XLI PORTRAIT 9　15
yellowgreen water. they are building a house down there . . . 281 IS 5 THREE 5　10
rest to these children building this rainman out of . . . . . 390 NO THANKS 7　14

BUILDS

girllike laughtering blocks when builds its invisibly skil . 371 VIVA 62　6

BUILT

/ / / Cleopatra built like a smooth arrow . . . . 110 & PORTRAIT 6　1
thick slim warm moist built like an organ and . . . . 110 & PORTRAIT 6　18
column of Egypt , built like a fleet pillar . . . . 111 & PORTRAIT 6　45
can be and was built that way on purpose . . . . 466 NEW POEMS 4　11
against yes which is built by forever & sunsmell . . . . . . 512 50 POEMS 26　29
pretends blue nothing) are built of soon carved of . . . . . 584 1 X 1 44　4

BULB

silent planes a nudging bulb silkenly brutal a devout . . . . 68 T&C POST IMPR 5　15
the madam was a bulb stuck in the door. . . . . 73 T&C SON REAL 4　2
(in which a willing bulb of flame bubbles) see . . . . 282 IS 5 THREE 6　28

BULBOUS

cheerful man with majestic bulbous lips and forlorn piggish . 56 T&C PORTRAIT 4　11

BULBS

bang hands angle scoot bulbs marry a become) ened . . . . . . 309 VIVA 1　13

BULGE

heart be With the bulge and nuzzle of the . . . . 16 T&C SONGS 6　14
we have got a bulge on death, silence, and . . . . 84 T&C SON ACTU 3　13
save that these houses bulge like memories in one . . . . . . 98 & POST IMPR 9　16
give us Things which bulge: grunting lungs pumped full . . . 195 XLI PORTRAIT 3　4
murdered flowers whispering barns bulge a tiniest street or . 340 VIVA 31　13
blaze naLOVEme crazily ships bulge hearts by darts pierced . 436 NO THANKS 52　7

BULGES

of gesture any skyscraper bulges in the looseness of . . . . 68 T&C POST IMPR 5　6

BULGILY

into someone's kitchenette) wheezing bulgily world of genial 607 (CHAIRE) 9　4

BULGING

approaching my twentysix selves bulging in immortal Spring . 255 IS 5 ONE 26　6
amid screams of deeply bulging thousands i too omit . . . . . 259 IS 5 ONE 29　18

BULGINGS

to invent im- perceptible bulgings of the pretended breasts, 103 & POST IMPR 13　3

BULL

--you know alotta sweet bull like dat ...suddenly i . . . . . 332 VIVA 23　12

+BULL

FOR CONTEXT, SEE . . . . 409 NO THANKS 26　3
FOR CONTEXT, SEE . . . . 500 50 POEMS 14　12

BULL'S

valley forge with Sitting Bull's T.P. and the duckbilled . . 321 VIVA 13　14

BULLET

Summer Time. My gorgeous bullet in tickling intuitive flight 130 & SON REAL 1　10

BULLIED

are no more unjoyously bullied of vilest mind and . . . . . . 213 XLI SONNETS 9　2

BULLS

let on to the bulls he'd bumped a bloke . . . . 145 & SON REAL 16　2
cigar waiting for the bulls to pull his joint. . . . . 149 & SON REAL 20　4
of circumstance whom the bulls nabbed at 33rd) pulled . . . . 266 IS 5 TWO 1　39

BULLYING
    dandelions And the big bullying daisies through the field . . 26 T&C CHANSONS 3   5
    will do in my bullying fingers) as for the . . . . 164 & SON ACTU 13   14
BUM
    squinting who's a wink bum-nothing and money fuzzily mouths . 96 & POST IMPR 8   19
    seen by some that bum who's every one / . . . . 698 95 POEMS 26   8
BUM-NOTHING
    squinting who's a wink bum-nothing and money fuzzily mouths . 96 & POST IMPR 8   19
BUMP
    at kid anaesthetize marry bump off or otherwise amplify . . . 391 NO THANKS 8   15
BUMPED
    to the bulls he'd bumped a bloke back in . . . . 145 & SON REAL 16   2
BUMPING
    tottered to a glass bumping things. she picked wearily . . . 132 & SON REAL 3   16
    obscurely twitch through the bumping teem of Grand. a . . . . 219 XLI SONNETS 15   10
BUMPINGS
    between such beddings and bumpings of ourselves to be . . . . 261 IS 5 ONE 31   7
BUMPS
    from which detaching itself bumps clumsily into the throat . 201 XLI PORTRAIT 9   10
BUMS
    / / / twentyseven bums give a prostitute the . . . . 150 & SON REAL 21   1
    <> tosses like thin bums dream ing i'm thick . . . . 469 NEW POEMS 7   2
BUNCH
    fact; who threw the bunch of violets into the . . . . 125 & SEVEN POEMS 4 14
BUNCHA
    / / / / buncha hardboil guys frum duh . . . . 332 VIVA 23   1
+BUNCHES
    FOR CONTEXT, SEE . . . . 100 & POST IMPR 11   24
+BUNDLE
    FOR CONTEXT, SEE . . . . 472 NEW POEMS 10   13
BUNG
    laugh dingle nails personally bung loamhome picpac obviously 333 VIVA 24   4
BUNGED
    doubles up suddenly his bunged hinging victim against the . . 259 IS 5 ONE 29   15
BUOYANT
    than dream more sing (buoyant & who silently shall . . . . 349 VIVA 40   7
BUOYED
    a morsel prettily wanders buoyed on the murderous saliva . . 201 XLI PORTRAIT 9   5
BURIED
    Madge and her men? buried with Alice in her . . . . 183 XLI SONGS 5   3
    a policeman's majestic and buried eye) the almost large . . . 324 VIVA 16   4
    don't die (becoming most buried unbecomingly very by most) . 412 NO THANKS 29   16
    trembles, emerging to perceive buried in cliff precisely at . 435 NO THANKS 51   40
    / / / Jehovah buried, Satan dead, do fearers . . . . 438 NO THANKS 54   1
    his face) busy folk buried them side by side . . . . 515 50 POEMS 29   27
    more) ask a lifelump buried by the star nicked . . . . 522 50 POEMS 35   5
    little clown whom somebody buried upsidedown in an ashbarrel 680 95 POEMS 8   8
BURIES
) skirt exhumes (which buries again quick- ly its . . . . . . 341 VIVA 32   15
    universe and bang --fear buries a tomorrow under woe . . . . 531 50 POEMS 43   3
BURN
    victorious impossibly) so wholly burn, to undertake Medea's . 18 T&C PUELLA MEA 71
    / unto thee i burn incense the bowl crackles . . . . 31 T&C ORIENTALE 5   2
    litanies unto thee i burn incense, over the dim . . . . 31 T&C ORIENTALE 5 21
    thee unto whom i burn olbanum / / / . . . . 31 T&C ORIENTALE 5 31
    gripping for a decision: burn the terrific fingers which . . 146 & SON REAL 17   4
    speak truth; if angels burn by their own generous . . . . . . 562 1 X 1 22   5
BURNED
    shower bouncing up off burned earth but a blind . . . . 754 95 POEMS 82   3
BURNING
    the darkness a more burning rain? And still the . . . .   4 T&C EPITHALAM   56
    thighs are steeped in burning flowers I will take . . . . . . 189 XLI SONGS 11   2
BURNS
    coming whom her soul burns to embrace--and didst thou . . . .   3 T&C EPITHALAM   12
    they smoked a robert burns cigerr to the god . . . . 552 1 X 1 12   29
BURRS
    mind, the eyes' shuddering burrs of light stick on . . . . . 136 & SON REAL 7   6

	PAGE	TITLE	LINE

BURST
oh don't you makes burst want to dear somehow . . . . 251 IS 5 ONE 22   12
sun: who music wear burst icy known swim ignorant . . . . . . 533 50 POEMS 45   15
over and which under burst lurch things phantoms curl . . . . 565 1 X 1 25   2
through merciful sunlight) to burst in a thunder of . . . . . 841 73 POEMS 69   34
+BURST
FOR CONTEXT, SEE . . . . 49 T&C IMPRESS 3   25
BURSTING
playful immortal hands the bursting of the wafted stars . . . 36 T&C AMORES 1   19
seem) "stetti" and willbeishfully bursting un- eats wasvino . 387 NO THANKS 4   17
this eternal mere one bursting soul why, then comes . . . . . 414 NO THANKS 31   11
+BURSTING
FOR CONTEXT, SEE . . . . 159 & SON ACTU 8   9
FOR CONTEXT, SEE . . . . 739 95 POEMS 67   4
BURSTS
hold his whose unlife bursts only so; only if . . . . 479 NEW POEMS 17   16
BURY
griefs wide (it shall bury much stench) and a . . . . 439 NO THANKS 55   12
thankful as hell and bury the statue of liberty . . . . . . 711 95 POEMS 39   27
BUSHSCYTHEBLADE
(s a) mu) ddied bushscytheblade "pud-dih-gud") S creang . . 656 (CHAIRE) 58   10
BUSHY
soiling light yanKing from bushy obscurity a bald greenish . 96 & POST IMPR 8   28
BUSIEST
demonstrate the biggest best busiest city and presently found 326 VIVA 18   11
BUSILY
windows awaken certain faces busily horribly blunder through 299 IS 5 FOUR 16   14
hither, thither who briskly busily carry the as tonishing . . 354 VIVA 45   14
some thing else kisses busily a memory, which how . . . . . . 370 VIVA 61   24
darlingest who (on this busily nowhere rollingest it) 's . . 590 1 X 1 50   10
BUSINESS
of a romantic tired business man somewhat tweaked and . . . . 57 T&C PORTRAIT 5   32
huge passion like a business and the Y her . . . . 132 & SON REAL 3   8
were made for Horizontal Business (set on big legs . . . . . 150 & SON REAL 21   7
what her big unkeen "Business is rotten" the face . . . . . . 225 IS 5 ONE LIZ   12
so-much-interested-in-everybody-else's-business . . . . 250 IS 5 ONE 21   14
(to instigate constructive Horizontal business.... even so, . 260 IS 5 ONE 30   21
+BUSINESS
FOR CONTEXT, SEE . . . . 552 1 X 1 12   4
FOR CONTEXT, SEE . . . . 708 95 POEMS 36   7
+BUSINESSMAN
FOR CONTEXT, SEE . . . . 389 NO THANKS 6   5
BUSTED
/ (ponder, darling, these busted statues of yon motheaten . . 260 IS 5 ONE 30   1
into sunset, playin uh busted harmonica / / / . . . . 332 VIVA 23   32
BUSY
a girlish whore with busy rhythmic mouth and silly . . . . . 56 T&C PORTRAIT 4   14
more than all life's busy little dyings may possess) . . . . 418 NO THANKS 35   4
thing who's much too busy being her beautiful yes. . . . . . 504 50 POEMS 18   12
to kiss his face) busy folk buried them side . . . . 515 50 POEMS 29   27
he is much too busy sitting the horse / . . . . 545 1 X 1 5   15
/ / pity this busy monster, manunkind, not. Progress . . . . 554 1 X 1 14   1
titty and lisps "i'm busy right now" so rah-rah-rah . . . . . 711 95 POEMS 39   24
glory says Who the busy the millions (as you're . . . . 801 73 POEMS 29   13
+BUSY
FOR CONTEXT, SEE . . . . 389 NO THANKS 6   4
+BUSYING
FOR CONTEXT, SEE . . . . 416 NO THANKS 33   6
BUT
WORD DELETED, APPEARED 345 TIMES
+BUTS
FOR CONTEXT, SEE . . . . 445 NO THANKS 60   4
BUTTERCUPS
/ Tumbling-hair picker of buttercups violets dandelions And . 26 T&C CHANSONS 3   2
you know it's snowing buttercups / / / / . . . . 254 IS 5 ONE 25   24
BUTTERFLIES
young girls and like butterflies and like money and . . . . . 111 & PORTRAIT 6   66
before him, like foolish butterflies he is the most . . . . . 198 XLI PORTRAIT 6   24

	PAGE	TITLE	LINE
+BUTTERFLY			
FOR CONTEXT, SEE	320	VIVA 12	1
BUTTING			
hunched over swill; one butting trolley imposingly empty; . .	172	& SON ACTU 21	4
BUTTON			
will sew a nagging button of candlelight (halfstooping to . .	164	& SON ACTU 13	3
because somebody pressed a button (and down went my	239	IS 5 ONE 10	34
mute trouserfly confessed a button solemnly inert. Brushing .	258	IS 5 ONE 28	20
began playing with a button the moon smiled she	284	IS 5 FOUR 1	9
exudes thursday fasters by button of whisper sum blinked . .	333	VIVA 24	8
+BUTTON			
FOR CONTEXT, SEE	262	IS 5 ONE 32	16
BUTTONED			
and my eyes were buttoned with pain THE BLACK	100	& POST IMPR 11	31
BUTTONHOLE			
yellow flower in his buttonhole he is altogether a	296	IS 5 FOUR 13	2
BUTTONS			
from a lovehouse who buttons his coat against the	115	& PORTRAIT 8	28
/ / this evangelist buttons with his big gollywog	259	IS 5 ONE 29	2
-uniforms with only-just- shined buttons tidiyum before and .	274	IS 5 TWO 9	24
white wig and polished buttons) would take you away	365	VIVA 56	13
BUTTS			
and houses and finally, butts into the river /	47	T&C IMPRESS 1	11
down to smoking found Butts / / / /	314	VIVA 6	33
+BUTTS			
FOR CONTEXT, SEE	194	XLI PORTRAIT 2	20
BUY			
(i say "will he buy flowers" to you and	102	& POST IMPR 12	6
bluets yes, will He buy? Les belles bottes--oh hear	102	& POST IMPR 12	19
pawn your intelligence to buy a drink and when	204	XLI LA GUERRE 2	11
electric When In Doubt Buy Of (but a roof	217	XLI SONNETS 13	5
do not sell and buy things so necessary as	238	IS 5 ONE 9	7
pigs do it it buy uh cupl un wait	325	VIVA 17	8
/ / / / buy me an ounce and	513	50 POEMS 27	1
(there's your general yas buy gad) nor asleep booted	640	{CHAIRE} 42	3
they sell and they buy and they die for	801	73 POEMS 29	3
BUYABLE			
souldoll one unsellable not buyable alive one i say	524	50 POEMS 36	45
BUYING			
bar a cockney is buying whiskies for a turk	108	& PORTRAIT 4	12
BUYS			
"uh" enter paperboy, c buys Bawstinamereekin, exit paperboy a	200	XLI PORTRAIT 8	13
BUZZ			
people are flies who buzz on) -lar (windows called	436	NO THANKS 52	16
BUZZSQUEAKING			
zagflash king poUnc es buzzsqueaking th ey tangle in	747	95 POEMS 75	13
BVD			
And Serve-- from every B.V.D. let freedom ring amen.	230	IS 5 ONE 2	13
BY			
WORD DELETED, APPEARED 338 TIMES			
BYE			
censored up a wench's rock-a-bye (rub-her-bub) bub? (bubs) /	642	{CHAIRE} 44	27
C			
teeth b pink suspenders c reads Atlantis x and	200	XLI PORTRAIT 8	7
"coffee" "uh" enter paperboy, c buys Bawstinamereekin, exit .	200	XLI PORTRAIT 8	12
coffee withdraws a and c discuss news in turkish	200	XLI PORTRAIT 8	20
wins exeunt ax: by; c, Goo dnightef fendi	200	XLI PORTRAIT 8	30
to a Y. W. c. a. she suddenly luffed	326	VIVA 18	35
no such thing for C can't casts no shadow	390	NO THANKS 7	3
C'EST			
to Slivers of (unthinking. c'est l'heure exquise) i remind .	94	& POST IMPR 6	18
fort le negre esn7othingish8s c'est fini pRaW, 1T; 0:	430	NO THANKS 47	22
CA			
yearnswoons; &Isdensekil- ◇ ruptingly) ca-y-est droppe5 . .	430	NO THANKS 47	16
here) swing low sweet ca rr y on (pass	641	{CHAIRE} 43	4
CA-Y-EST			
yearnswoons; &Isdensekil- ◇ ruptingly) ca-y-est droppe5 . .	430	NO THANKS 47	16

		PAGE	TITLE	LINE

CADENCE
   hark to the sheer cadence of our gray flesh . . . . 9 T&C SONGS 1   23
   sound, newly one moving cadence may release the fragrance . . 842 73 POEMS 70   6
CAESARS
   silver youths the leaneyed Caesars borne neatly through . . . 111 & PORTRAIT 6   37
CAFE
   death sits in a cafe smiling, a piece of . . . . 102 & POST IMPR 12   3
CAFES
   not find him in cafes, the more dissolute atmosphere . . . . 197 XLI PORTRAIT 5   1
   in the darkness of cafes people drink smile if . . . . 340 VIVA 31   8
CAGE
   Silence from the winsome cage of thy body rose . . . . . . 187 XLI SONGS 9   2
   way in the soiled canary-cage of largest existence. (when . . 197 XLI PORTRAIT 5   12
   p, s this dingy cage: then with a ghost . . . . 697 95 POEMS 25   10
+CAGE
   FOR CONTEXT, SEE . . . . 360 VIVA 51   25
CAIRO
   from Troy (N.Y.) to Cairo (Egypt) the luminous dithyrambs . . 266 IS 5 TWO 1   6
CAKE
   two three rings are cake & everything is protected . . . . . 470 NEW POEMS 8   18
+CAKE
   FOR CONTEXT, SEE . . . . 217 XLI SONNETS 13   9
+CAKED
   FOR CONTEXT, SEE . . . . 144 & SON REAL 15   7
+CAKES
   FOR CONTEXT, SEE . . . . 262 IS 5 ONE 32   12
CALCHIDAS
   of this hill at Calchidas, in the sunlight? down . . . . . . 281 IS 5 THREE 5   2
CALENDARS
   hoax of clocks and calendars / / / / . . . . 659 (CHAIRE) 61   14
CALIFORNIAN
   and such hair) the Californian handpicked thrill mechanically 337 VIVA 28   9
CALIPH
   living things and beautiful. (Caliph and king their ladies . 20 T&C PUELLA MEA 129
   poet and sage and caliph had to love them . . . . 22 T&C PUELLA MEA 223
CALL
   small. Death, Thee i call rich beyond wishing if . . . . . . 13 T&C SONGS 3   17
   if anyone hardly should call exactly extraordinary. We refer, 263 IS 5 ONE 32   36
   that this, which we call autumn, cleverly dies and . . . . . 293 IS 5 FOUR 10   23
   Man whom both would call their friend and who . . . . 394 NO THANKS 11   9
   hock who dares to call himself a man? go . . . . 438 NO THANKS 54   8
   kike who dares to call himself a man? loudly . . . . 438 NO THANKS 54   16
   fuck who dares to call himself a man? King . . . . 438 NO THANKS 54   24
   walk Who dares to call Himself a man. / . . . . 438 NO THANKS 54   28
   around the spot and call it beautifool to multiply . . . . . 500 50 POEMS 14   4
   nonsense which itself must call a state submicroscopic is-- . 561 1 X 1 21   2
   on some ? i call twilight you 'll see . . . . 571 1 X 1 31   4
   everything) death, as men call him, ends what they . . . . . 592 1 X 1 52   13
   him, ends what they call men --but beauty is . . . . 592 1 X 1 52   13
   timorous itsters all to call their cowardice quite agree) . . 664 (CHAIRE) 66   14
   and i some times call april) must often have . . . . 738 95 POEMS 66   8
   than our minds to call the stars. And (darling) . . . . . . 741 95 POEMS 69   9
   more than kiss) to call most the amazing miracle . . . . . . 741 95 POEMS 69   13
   of that nonexistence millions call life, you and i . . . . . 745 95 POEMS 73   9
   this snowy head we call old frank go bluer . . . . 754 95 POEMS 82   5
   merely what dying must call life are you / . . . . 818 73 POEMS 46   14
   cries the (whom we call rose a) mystery "but . . . . 837 73 POEMS 65   16
CALLED
   own land he is called death. / / / . . . . 42 T&C AMORES 6   25
   the song, might i'm called and did no wrong . . . . 117 & PORTRAIT 10   16
   sleep with a lady called death get another man . . . . 161 & SON ACTU 10   1
   little kittens who are called spring, is what we . . . . . . 191 XLI CHANSONS 1   10
   is (being of men called Love) upward doth leap . . . . 210 XLI SONNETS 6   4
   everybody was kilt they called them the kilties / . . . . . . 271 IS 5 TWO 6   12
   g to yonder s called newsreel s called theatre . . . . 392 NO THANKS 9   9
   s called newsreel s called theatre & with your . . . . 392 NO THANKS 9   10
   (and a first dream called ocean) and let must . . . . 424 NO THANKS 41   7
   buzz on) -lar (windows called sidewalks of houses called . . 436 NO THANKS 52   16

CALLED (CONTINUED)

called sidewalks of houses called cities) spring most . . . . 436 NO THANKS 52   17
lies, the foetal grave called progress, and negation's dead . 484 NEW POEMS 22   12
joy; praising a forehead called the moon singing desire . . . 520 50 POEMS 34   19
each of those creatures called one's self so we'll . . . . . 528 50 POEMS 40   12
what bough that someone called they made him pay . . . . . . 543 1 X 1 3   23
we (by a gift called dying born) must grow . . . . 556 1 X 1 16   12
how should a loudness called mankind unteach whole infinite . 603 (CHAIRE) 5   3
open) if that fool called everyone (or you or . . . . 603 (CHAIRE) 5   10
touched a shy animal called where and she disappeared. . . . 612 (CHAIRE) 14   10
a silence by noises called people called sunlight (elsewhere 658 (CHAIRE) 60   10
by noises called people called sunlight (elsewhere flat the . 658 (CHAIRE) 60   10
/ / when faces called flowers float out of . . . . 665 (CHAIRE) 67   1
clumsy some dull cowardice called a world vanishes, teach . . 669 (CHAIRE) 71   12
beauty touch a blunder (called life) we die to . . . . 742 95 POEMS 70   14
sky of a tree called life; which grows higher . . . . 766 95 POEMS 92   12
a Dream like fire called flowers over green the . . . . 778 73 POEMS 6   16
hugenesses of hate sometimes called world) to sing / . . . . 783 73 POEMS 11   8
neither ape nor angel called a man is measured . . . . 807 73 POEMS 35   7
home to a dream called time: and give herself . . . . 811 73 POEMS 39   10

CALLING

go all) there's somebody calling who's we we're anything . . 594 1 X 1 54   36

CALLS

deep thing everybody sometimes calls morning / / / . . . . . 330 VIVA 21   14
so awake what waking calls asleep) so never is . . . . 609 (CHAIRE) 11   8
should a fool that calls him "I" presume to . . . . 609 (CHAIRE) 11   13
year-- and if what calls itself a world should . . . . 717 95 POEMS 45   9

CALM

absolute feet anoint with calm of intent stars circling . . .   3 T&C EPITHALAM   30
big (soft) soft near calm (Bright) calm st?? holy . . . . . . 455 NO THANKS 70   4
soft near calm (Bright) calm st?? holy (soft briGht . . . . . 455 NO THANKS 70   6
deep) yeS near sta? calm star big yEs alone . . . . 455 NO THANKS 70   8
alone soft near deep calm deep ????Ht ?????T) Who . . . . . . 455 NO THANKS 70   13
no their goal (in calm and fury: through joy . . . . 742 95 POEMS 70   7

CALMLY

the mere worshipping (as calmly as if aristide maillols . . . 617 (CHAIRE) 19   13

CALVES

the unfirm drooping bloated calves i would receive the   . . . 229 IS 5 ONE FRAN   6

CAMBRIDGE

/ / SONNETS--REALITIES the Cambridge ladies who live in . . . 70 T&C SON REAL 1   1
and Professor D ....the Cambridge ladies do not care, ... 70 T&C SON REAL 1   11
do not care, above Cambridge if sometimes in its . . . . . . 70 T&C SON REAL 1   12
a Young Woman of cambridge, mass. to whom nobody . . . . . . 326 VIVA 18   1
instruction at radcliffe college, cambridge, mass. i try if . 327 VIVA 18   44

CAME

of fragrance and i came riding upon a horse . . . . 30 T&C ORIENTALE 4   9
distinguished singing and i came riding upon a scarlet . . . 30 T&C ORIENTALE 4   22
your eyes and i came riding upon a thousand . . . . 30 T&C ORIENTALE 4   35
voice Over the wires came leaping and i felt . . . . 44 T&C AMORES 8   2
/ / her flesh Came at meassandca V ingint . . . . 119 & PORTRAIT 11   3
sorry And The Moon came! along-along to the waggy . . . . . . 125 & SEVEN POEMS 4   24
dog and the moon came and the Moon said . . . . 125 & SEVEN POEMS 4   26
in fifteen. Then she came toward him on her . . . . 145 & SON REAL 16   3
her. He laughed. She came. he gave her a . . . . 145 & SON REAL 16   11
clumsy feet of April came into the ragged meadow . . . . . . 306 IS 5 FIVE 5   14
of ourselves) as Nobody came slowly over the town . . . . . 355 VIVA 46   21
(out of sheer nothing) came a huger than fear . . . . 432 NO THANKS 49   15
so unto canned swoonsong came "I wish you good" . . . . 464 NEW POEMS 2   28
of an angel's fart came one trembling out of . . . . 506 50 POEMS 20   12
sowing and went their came sun moon stars rain . . . . 515 50 POEMS 29   35
voice until and who came with a song like . . . . 587 1 X 1 47   7
way from perfect nowhere came (as easily as we . . . . 599 (CHAIRE) 1   12
blowing bubbles: and may came home with a smooth . . . . . . 682 95 POEMS 10   9
throat of one two came hurrying home to the . . . . 709 95 POEMS 37   13

CAMEF

smelt rath er (Er camef romth AIR / / . . . . 320 VIVA 12   23

CAMELS

while) nextto Mesmoked eleven camels ! and i got . . . . . . 318 VIVA 10   15

	PAGE	TITLE	LINE
+CAMELS			
FOR CONTEXT, SEE	318	VIVA 10	21
+CAMERA			
FOR CONTEXT, SEE	474	NEW POEMS 12	14
CAMMIN'			
elevator nel mezzo del cammin' that means half- way	256	IS 5 ONE 27	7
CAMPANILE			
half- way up the Campanile, believe thou me cocodrillo-- . .	256	IS 5 ONE 27	8
CAN			
i say your eyes can take day away more	98	& POST IMPR 9	3
(want a match or can you see?) which the	117	& PORTRAIT 10	29
wants to and it can dance and Whocares dead's	126	& SEVEN POEMS 5	22
have somebody play who can but you know you	126	& SEVEN POEMS 5	31
you know you never can and why have to?	126	& SEVEN POEMS 5	31
tells you so you can feel what you made, ...	127	& SEVEN POEMS 5	39
my brain harder than can twitch its terrors; the, ...	136	& SON REAL 7	7
sleep upstairs. And you can see their ears. Ears	171	& SON ACTU 20	7
SONGS the sky was can dy lu minous edible	179	XLI SONGS 1	4
glad monosyllable jounce possibly can tell better how the . .	227	IS 5 ONE GERT	2
goil and she coitnly can shimmie when you see	235	IS 5 ONE 6	6
civil war band and can play the triangle like	253	IS 5 ONE 24	3
happens beneath will; nor can these moments be translated: . .	264	IS 5 ONE 33	6
so forth oh say can you see by the	268	IS 5 TWO 3	3
<> and before you can ! & we're NOT	269	IS 5 TWO 4	8
and who replies "I can!" --yon clean upstanding well	273	IS 5 TWO 8	5
bright eyes) drifts (nobody can tell because Nobody knows, .	286	IS 5 FOUR 3	6
fist is no longer, can you imagine it i	289	IS 5 FOUR 6	4
since the best he can do is to peer	292	IS 5 FOUR 9	7
/ / but mr can you maybe listen there's	314	VIVA 6	1
oh no body will (can you give a) listen	314	VIVA 6	22
"elevating--that is, if dancing CAN be ele- vating" Miss . .	327	VIVA 18	40
were a child "we can see a bat in	353	VIVA 44	4
has ever been invented can spoil this or this	357	VIVA 48	6
am a shape that can but eat and turd	360	VIVA 51	4
flesh or swim who can and bathe who must	390	NO THANKS 7	10
where might Where live can fisherMen swim and who's	395	NO THANKS 12	8
(all good kumrads you can tell by their altruistic	413	NO THANKS 30	7
fate and (if you can withholding nothing) World, conceive . .	420	NO THANKS 37	13
being sick, Minds nothing can: if Hate's a game	438	NO THANKS 54	22
heart could dare) unhearts can less unminds must fear	440	NO THANKS 56	4
nor hate nor grief can go where goes this	441	NO THANKS 56	44
starfish (but because nobody can sell the Moon to	452	NO THANKS 67	18
as simple as simple can be and was built	466	NEW POEMS 4	10
know of anything which can be as dull as	468	NEW POEMS 6	2
e of what man can 't hurt any more	472	NEW POEMS 10	14
enough for i eu can have you rope /	476	NEW POEMS 14	12
than boygirls need: i can entirely her only love	484	NEW POEMS 22	6
whole grassblades, five ideas can swallow a man; three . . .	491	50 POEMS 5	13
a breakfastfood or truth can live with right and	511	50 POEMS 25	2
cannot dream what dreams can do --time is a	511	50 POEMS 25	25
(and only the snow can begin to explain how	515	50 POEMS 29	22
terday's tomorrow (than today can guess or fears to	522	50 POEMS 35	7
i say no world can hold a you you shall	523	50 POEMS 36	2
as small as me can do or be?" god	555	1 X 1 15	13
very born no bird can sing as easily creation	558	1 X 1 18	12
that abuses it you can git anything you like	567	1 X 1 27	11
(night) then "everything beautiful can grow" my, her life . .	572	1 X 1 32	14
well she knows; and can perfectly speak (snowflake and . . .	575	1 X 1 35	30
darling! because my blood can sing and dance (and	580	1 X 1 40	1
go ghostly they doubting can turn men's see to	580	1 X 1 40	8
no meanness unsmaller) armies can immensely meet for	580	1 X 1 40	16
such as perfect hope can feel only despair completely	580	1 X 1 40	23
until into flame i can feel how the earth	587	1 X 1 47	14
yes) not a tree can count his leaves each	591	1 X 1 51	17
littler bird than eyes can learn look up to	592	1 X 1 52	9
are shuter than books can be) and deep in	594	1 X 1 54	31
himself: who's we --nor can you die or i	601	{CHAIRE} 3	18
will be goes was) can travel this or i	608	{CHAIRE} 10	12

CAN (CONTINUED)
    another hides; yet man can, being all, escape from . . . . . 609 (CHAIRE) 11   4
    pure silence) such hands can build a (who are . . . . 617 (CHAIRE) 19   2
    he goes but we can hear him still if . . . . 624 (CHAIRE) 26   21
    gaze enters a sunset "can grow (gracefully or otherwise) . . 626 (CHAIRE) 28   2
    his destiny) mountains! how can each" while flame crashed . . 626 (CHAIRE) 28   9
    in 1944 A D "can stand against the argument . . . . 636 (CHAIRE) 38   10
    that mind no more can disprove than prove what . . . . 664 (CHAIRE) 66   3
    spaceful time-- no heart can leap, no soul can . . . . . . 664 (CHAIRE) 66   21
    can leap, no soul can breathe but by the . . . . 664 (CHAIRE) 66   21
    frolic as spry as can fly yes the little . . . . 665 (CHAIRE) 67   5
    gambol as glad as can be (yes the mountains . . . . 665 (CHAIRE) 67   6
    alive than every world can understand and now you . . . . . 667 (CHAIRE) 69   4
    of a silence who can guess ex- actly what . . . . 676 95 POEMS 4   10
    noblest game a man can proudly lose, or playing . . . . . . 679 95 POEMS 7   3
    one mortally immortal i can turn immense all time's . . . . 679 95 POEMS 7   14
    the very boldest man can scarcely dare to meet . . . . . . 685 95 POEMS 13   3
    so that she never can (kno wledge is po . . . . 700 95 POEMS 28   8
    ully lee -r- ing) can this plati -num fl- . . . . 704 95 POEMS 32   8
    there's haymows you never can tell" "as long as . . . . . . 707 95 POEMS 35   10
    ow) dinary a meri can b usiness soca lled . . . . 708 95 POEMS 36   7
    appetite than mere unmiracle can quite appease-- humbly in . 714 95 POEMS 42   5
    such a darkness noone can quite begin to guess . . . . . . 717 95 POEMS 45   7
    only dies to grow can guess and as for . . . . 718 95 POEMS 46   7
    (even the most odd) can justify the ways of . . . . 731 95 POEMS 59   2
    strange that normal mortals can not justify the ways . . . 731 95 POEMS 59   3
    creature feels (but none can think) a learning under . . . 735 95 POEMS 63   8
    pauses, while a star can grow all distance breathes . . . . 750 95 POEMS 78   1
    singing's always his eyes can feel but ears may . . . . . . 760 95 POEMS 87   5
    each leaf newer than can be: and for his . . . . 760 95 POEMS 87   10
    grows higher than soul can hope or mind can . . . . 766 95 POEMS 92   13
    can hope or mind can hide) and this is . . . . 766 95 POEMS 92   13
    a wisdom no knowledge can kill is astir-- now . . . . 769 95 POEMS 95   9
    as an earth which can never do wrong does . . . . 769 95 POEMS 95   17
    a blue than blue can be sky always (through . . . . 778 73 POEMS 6   20
    2 or per (who can and do fat pigeons . . . . 787 73 POEMS 15   6
    of work while she can swarm. To doubt that . . . . 790 73 POEMS 18   8
    science) Q: how numb can an unworld get? A: . . . . 791 73 POEMS 19   9
    people (as if as can yes) they sell and . . . . 801 73 POEMS 29   2
    wary (as all as can each) they don't and . . . . 801 73 POEMS 29   8
    millions (as you're as can i'm) they flock and . . . . . . 801 73 POEMS 29   14
    craven (as think as can feel) they when and . . . . 801 73 POEMS 29   20
    tender (as doubt as can trust) they work and . . . . 801 73 POEMS 29   26
    more than selfless i can quite endure the absence . . . . . 812 73 POEMS 40   10
    n OthI n g can s urPas s the . . . . 814 73 POEMS 42   4
    any somebody or you can begin to begin to . . . . 816 73 POEMS 44   12
    whom crumbs of colour can create precision more than . . . 842 73 POEMS 70   3
    perceive. Only whose vision can create the whole (being . . . 845 73 POEMS 73   5
    more steep than climb can time with all his . . . . 845 73 POEMS 73   8
+CAN
    FOR CONTEXT, SEE . . . . 474 NEW POEMS 12   12
    FOR CONTEXT, SEE . . . . 568 1 X 1 28   3
    FOR CONTEXT, SEE . . . . 703 95 POEMS 31   16
CAN'S
    kindness sweet such (past can's every can't) immensest . . . 763 95 POEMS 90   25
CAN'T
    no window because i can't sleep (smoking sawdust cigarettes . 242 IS 5 ONE 13   21
    i loved like you can't imagine Harry was o . . . . 271 IS 5 TWO 6   9
    you imagine it i can't which doesn't matter and . . . . . . 289 IS 5 FOUR 6   5
    preferably, anything which you can't pass off on other . . . 298 IS 5 FOUR 15   16
    real flowers, but I can't imagine real flowers for . . . . . 338 VIVA 29   8
    such thing for C can't casts no shadow D . . . . 390 NO THANKS 7   3
    w. isn't that it can't exist (and is that . . . . 411 NO THANKS 28   11
    / most (people simply can't) won't (most parent people . . . 412 NO THANKS 29   3
    to do because they can't i mean move yes . . . . 425 NO THANKS 42   6
    / / If you can't eat you got to . . . . 489 50 POEMS 3   1
    to sleep if you can't smoke you got to . . . . 489 50 POEMS 3   5
    to sleep if you can't sing you got to . . . . 489 50 POEMS 3   9

		PAGE	TITLE	LINE
CAN'T (CONTINUED)				
to sleep if you can't die you got to		489	50 POEMS 3	13
(a little mouth) stumbling (can't keep up with how		501	50 POEMS 15	9
if everything happens that can't be done (and anything's . .		594	1 X 1 54	1
seem to realize i can't make it clearer war		638	{CHAIRE} 40	7
that me isn't me can't you see now no		638	{CHAIRE} 40	12
are true because they can't be true / /		697	95 POEMS 25	32
d e l'echelle) die can't quite poison God's sunlight		708	95 POEMS 36	15
ess of her selves) can't u -nderstan- d my		739	95 POEMS 67	12
such (past can's every can't) immensest mysteries contradict		763	95 POEMS 90	26
doesn't agree (if you can't dentham comma bentham; or		791	73 POEMS 19	5
no in- deed; money can't do (never did &		793	73 POEMS 21	9
ask every question time can't answer: and such vivid		818	73 POEMS 46	10
+CAN'T				
FOR CONTEXT, SEE		472	NEW POEMS 10	14
CAN'TS				
cowards into grow our can'ts were born to happen		537	50 POEMS 49	9
CANARY				
with this thou hangest canary-birds in parlor windows spring		61	T&C PORTRAIT 9	10
way in the soiled canary-cage of largest existence. (when . .		197	XLI PORTRAIT 5	12
CANARY-BIRDS				
with this thou hangest canary-birds in parlor windows spring		61	T&C PORTRAIT 9	10
CANARY-CAGE				
way in the soiled canary-cage of largest existence. (when . .		197	XLI PORTRAIT 5	12
CANCELLED				
lowest terms with everything cancelled but shadows --what . .		295	IS 5 FOUR 12	19
mightiest meditations of mankind cancelled are by one merely		592	1 X 1 52	7
CANCELS				
(feel) pauseless immeasurably Now cancels the childfully . .		402	NO THANKS 19	4
nor unreasoned, his wisdom cancels conflict and agreement . .		683	95 POEMS 11	6
to nothingness (cruel now cancels kind; friends turn to . . .		834	73 POEMS 62	3
CANDIDATE'S				
response to howjedooze the candidate's new silk lid bounds .		259	IS 5 ONE 29	20
CANDIES				
nuts and the bad candies my, mouth loves melons		100	& POST IMPR 11	22
CANDLE				
head stands that clear candle whose expecting breath exults .		6	T&C EPITHALAM	117
poems on earth a candle is extinguished the city		50	T&C IMPRESS 4	4
dusk on earth a candle is lighted and it		50	T&C IMPRESS 4	25
fingers) as for the candle, it'll turn into a		164	& SON ACTU 13	15
the spittoon by a candle furnished by courtesy of		263	IS 5 ONE 32	49
of this road, a candle in a shrine: its		435	NO THANKS 51	43
sit (holding a red candle over his head by		631	{CHAIRE} 33	2
CANDLELIGHT				
a nagging button of candlelight (halfstooping to exactly kiss		164	& SON ACTU 13	3
CANDLES				
/ / / lean candles hunger in the silence		28	T&C ORIENTALE 2	1
/ / / / candles and Here Comes a		280	IS 5 THREE 4	1
CANDY				
a fragment of angry candy / / / /		70	T&C SON REAL 1	14
now And then bite) candy others fly, their; puLLing:		314	VIVA 6	12
like, like bad, like candy: & you are dead		389	NO THANKS 6	15
appetite with bad brittle candy but just (nude eel)		410	NO THANKS 27	4
he dressed in black candy she veiled with candy		470	NEW POEMS 8	4
candy she veiled with candy white carrying a bouquet		470	NEW POEMS 8	5
of pretend flowers this candy crown with this candy		470	NEW POEMS 8	8
candy crown with this candy little bride & little		470	NEW POEMS 8	8
& before illimitably spiralling candy of tiniest		480	NEW POEMS 18	22
+CANDY				
FOR CONTEXT, SEE		179	XLI SONGS 1	4
CANE				
daintily twiddling his tiny cane and, mazurkas about tweak- .		374	VIVA 65	31
CANNED				
maost faolks rally demannd canned saounds) gloats upon the .		331	VIVA 22	3
pooped universe (of croons canned a la vallee and		425	NO THANKS 42	2
on & so unto canned swoonsong came "I wish		464	NEW POEMS 2	26
CANNIBAL				
the scowl of a cannibal) there's your mineral general		640	{CHAIRE} 42	10

	PAGE	TITLE	LINE
CANNON			
GUERRE the bigness of cannon is skilful, but i	45	T&C LA GUERRE 1	1
CANNONADIN			
life is a black cannonadin g into silenc e	628	{CHAIRE} 30	2
+CANNONADING			
FOR CONTEXT, SEE	628	{CHAIRE} 30	2
CANNOT			
this music, and poetry cannot go near because perfectly . . .	162	& SON ACTU 11	6
and the empty twilight cannot grieve nor the autumn, ...	165	& SON ACTU 14	8
shirts neckties trousers we cannot wear it out no	238	IS 5 ONE 9	11
me, or which i cannot touch because they are	366	VIVA 57	4
not forget, perish, sleep cannot be photographed, measured; .	377	VIVA 68	10
through failures born who cannot fail having no wealth . . .	394	NO THANKS 11	12
because he knows, he cannot understand (why Jones don't . . .	406	NO THANKS 23	5
he owes) because he cannot understand, he drinks (and	406	NO THANKS 23	7
bite and buck who cannot read and cannot write	427	NO THANKS 44	10
who cannot read and cannot write who laugh like	427	NO THANKS 44	10
are not refined they cannot chat of that and	427	NO THANKS 44	14
/ / much i cannot) tear up the world:	433	NO THANKS 50	1
s v p" she cannot read or write, la	504	50 POEMS 18	6
will be thighs deeds cannot dream what dreams can	511	50 POEMS 25	25
let men kill which cannot share, let blood and	521	50 POEMS 34	53
sunly and more it cannot die than all the	530	50 POEMS 42	14
both and oneful night cannot be so sky sky	537	50 POEMS 49	14
be so sky sky cannot be so sunful i	537	50 POEMS 49	15
atomy once, and every cannot stir imagining; while you . . .	559	1 X 1 19	10
with a tear some cannot pay at all he	624	{CHAIRE} 26	11
miracle murdered we whom cannot kill more mostful to	639	{CHAIRE} 41	10
most lovely) sweet things cannot spring but we be	666	{CHAIRE} 68	4
he loves because he cannot fear (you see it	774	73 POEMS 2	14
i hear eng (which cannot sing) lish sparrows say	787	73 POEMS 15	3
timelessness and time. Time cannot children, poets, lovers .	817	73 POEMS 45	9
CANOE			
marvels "here'll be a canoe and a whole world	572	1 X 1 32	15
CANOPENERS			
uncanned for everyone carries canopeners in Ever-Ever Land .	466	NEW POEMS 4	7
CANOUNCHIR			
into Hassan's place the canounchir p ing the bigtwittering .	100	& POST IMPR 11	41
CANTED			
comes both prigged and canted / / / /	644	{CHAIRE} 46	6
CANYON			
always into the tremendous canyon the , tremendous canyon . .	202	XLI PORTRAIT 9	43
canyon the , tremendous canyon always only exhales a	202	XLI PORTRAIT 9	44
CAP			
ching this crump led cap mumble some thing to	314	VIVA 6	19
CAPABLE			
bright lice about god's capable dull important head-- by . .	85	T&C SON ACTU 4	4
a clumsiest disguise, appear capable of fragility and	91	& POST IMPR 3	13
from woolworthian pinnacle a capable millennium of faces . .	197	XLI PORTRAIT 5	8
over some numbered face capable of a largest nonglance . . .	359	VIVA 50	16
CAPERING			
music of the innumerable capering damned) --staring wildly up	118	& PORTRAIT 10	38
CAPTAIN			
bonnet having ceased the captain announces that as three . .	196	XLI PORTRAIT 4	7
you are dead you captain) Memo 1 wife in	389	NO THANKS 6	17
recall) being lost including captain Pater / / /	494	50 POEMS 8	8
is a ship which captain am sails out of	781	73 POEMS 9	2
CAPTAINS			
their nucleus (composed of captains in freshly-creased . . .	274	IS 5 TWO 9	22
CAPTIVATING			
/ "Gay" is the captivating cognomen of a Young	326	VIVA 18	1
CAPTURED			
where chaste stars writhe captured in brightening fright) / .	77	T&C SON UNRE 2	17
was invented but why (captured by a policeman's majestic . .	324	VIVA 16	3
out of final towers; captured: in the narrow light	345	VIVA 36	8
CAR			
deep expels (over Selene's car closing uncouth) of Helios . .	4	T&C EPITHALAM	47

		PAGE	TITLE	LINE

CARBURETOR
went right to it flooded-the-carburetor cranked her . . . . . 248 IS 5 ONE 19   9

CARCASS
dawn. Inane, the poetic carcass of a girl / . . . . 139 & SON REAL 10   14

CARD
Tramp who played each card as if it were   . . . . 194 XLI PORTRAIT 2   23

CARDS
the snick- er of cards and smack of back- . . . . 194 XLI PORTRAIT 2   17

CARE
for those ladies nothing care nor any lady dead . . . . 21 T&C PUELLA MEA   179
Cambridge ladies do not care, above Cambridge if sometimes . 70 T&C SON REAL 1   11
sun, nor will rain care cautiously who prolongs unserious . . 84 T&C SON ACTU 3   8
goat but we don't care do we dearie we   . . . . 109 & PORTRAIT 5   6
by the chimney with care in hopes that Saint . . . . 142 & SON REAL 13   14
asked Eddie did he care to ride her? ....she   . . . . 145 & SON REAL 16   12
for winter who crookedly care. / / / / . . . . 190 XLI SONGS 12   22
if he did not care to rise one hand . . . . 258 IS 5 ONE 28   16
rerum first having taken care to lie upon our . . . . 261 IS 5 ONE 31   12
side up handle with care fragile and send him . . . . 270 IS 5 TWO 5   16
worms (love may not care if time totters, light . . . . 446 NO THANKS 61   5
(sing ing) He no care so what yoo-gointa-doo? (ice   . . . . . 618 (CHAIRE) 20   16
he never seems to care he sharpens is to   . . . . 624 (CHAIRE) 26   12
keenest bravest killers you'd care to see (while a . . . . . 709 95 POEMS 37   6
gladness and joy under care-- let's do as an   . . . . 769 95 POEMS 95   16
without an i) be care ful (touch noth ing)   . . . . 797 73 POEMS 25   4

+CARE
FOR CONTEXT, SEE . . . . 330 VIVA 21   8

CARED
(both little and small) cared for anyone not at . . . . . . 515 50 POEMS 29   6

CAREENS
How replies the upsquirtingly careens the to collide   . . . . 330 VIVA 21   9

CAREF
/ ondumonde" (first than caref ully; pois edN-o wt   . . . . . 430 NO THANKS 47   2

CAREFUL
known musics in whose careful eyes are dinned; and   . . . . . 9 T&C SONGS 1   18
only certain dead and careful painters love to use . . . . . 20 T&C PUELLA MEA   141
i'll climb by tall careful muscles into nervous and . . . . . 67 T&C POST IMPR 4   15
legs moving solemnly like careful and furious and beautiful . 95 & POST IMPR 7   14
rain-warm-naked exquisitely hashed (little careful   . . . . 133 & SON REAL 4   4
/ / / her careful distinct sex whose sharp . . . . 137 & SON REAL 8   1
indomitable body uses a careful fierceness. Her lips study . 146 & SON REAL 17   3
existence, continually whittles keen careful futile flowers . 193 XLI PORTRAIT 1   21
flat minute gallop of careful hugeness i am conjugated . . . 201 XLI PORTRAIT 9   22
little stiff i was careful of her and (having . . . . 248 IS 5 ONE 19   5
if we're not very careful) O, the darling benevolent . . . . 250 IS 5 ONE 21   5
Them Greediest Paws of careful time all of which . . . . . . 260 IS 5 ONE 30   10
with a near and careful smile in his mouth . . . . 293 IS 5 FOUR 10   25
entirely having in my careful how careful arms created . . . 295 IS 5 FOUR 12   5
in my careful how careful arms created this at . . . . 295 IS 5 FOUR 12   6
love (a little) More careful Than of everything guard . . . . 453 NO THANKS 68   2
we are not perfectly careful be lieve me you . . . . 600 (CHAIRE) 2   11

+CAREFUL
FOR CONTEXT, SEE . . . . 797 73 POEMS 25   4

CAREFULLY
of the Princess Salome carefully dancing in the noise . . . . 17 T&C PUELLA MEA   31
plus innocuous winking hands, carefully inhabits number 1 on 62 T&C PORTRAIT 10   3
someThing street and trickles carefully into the park sits . 62 T&C PORTRAIT 10   26
skilfully with his, mouth carefully holding, it, in his . . . 69 T&C POST IMPR 6   17
in my head ladies carefully dead / / / . . . . 121 & PORTRAIT 12   61
perhaps hand (which comes carefully out of Nowhere) arranging 124 & SEVEN POEMS 3   2
arranging and changing placing carefully there a strange . . 124 & SEVEN POEMS 3   7
here) and changing everything carefully spring is like a . . 124 & SEVEN POEMS 3   9
Hand in a window (carefully to and fro moving . . . . 124 & SEVEN POEMS 3   12
things, while people stare carefully moving a perhaps . . . . 124 & SEVEN POEMS 3   15
excitation, whose careless movements carefully scatter pink . 150 & SON REAL 21   14
steer our lost bodies carefully downward) / / / . . . . 215 XLI SONNETS 11   17
Gawd" opening slowlyslowly them--then carefully the rolypoly 228 IS 5 ONE MARJ   8
forgets) time Requiescat. carry carefully the blessed large . 277 IS 5 THREE 1   23

	PAGE	TITLE	LINE

CAREFULLY (CONTINUED)
    a sharp face waddling carefully the length of this . . . . . 279 IS 5 THREE 3   9
    had been something else carefully slowly fatally turning into 283 IS 5 THREE 7   25
    always which shall brighten carefully these things we . . . . 289 IS 5 FOUR 6   12
    who i am prowls carefully around this house of . . . . 292 IS 5 FOUR 9   12
    brain, hopes, life to (carefully turning a corner) never . . 298 IS 5 FOUR 15   27
    perhaps nothing, he murmurs carefully lying down) / / . . . . 299 IS 5 FOUR 16   16
    imitation of (perhaps) myself carefully wanders streets dark 300 IS 5 FOUR 17   13
    and that you had carefully ourselves decided what this . . . 323 VIVA 15   23
    what i (of course) carefully had decided oh no . . . . 323 VIVA 15   29
    exquisite" (pulling Its shawl carefully around it) "things i 328 VIVA 19   19
    the Geddup curb leans carefully spewing into her own . . . . 330 VIVA 21   12
    me) distance is mind carefully luminous with innumerable . . 363 VIVA 54   6
    flower imagines the snow carefully everywhere descending; . . 366 VIVA 57   12
    death: drowned only again carefully through deepness to rise 369 VIVA 60   11
    somebody coming up stairs, carefully (carefully climbing . . 375 VIVA 66   11
    coming up stairs, carefully (carefully climbing carpeted . . 375 VIVA 66   12
    child 's hand) very carefully bring -ing to you . . . . 652 (CHAIRE) 54   3
    (whoever we are) stepped carefully o ver (& i) . . . . 668 (CHAIRE) 70   16
+CAREFULLY
    FOR CONTEXT, SEE . . . . 430 NO THANKS 47   2
CARELESS
    of unmarketable excitation, whose careless movements . . . . 150 & SON REAL 21   14
CARES
    love each other, who cares?) They pull the morning . . . . . 171 & SON ACTU 20   11
    to sing with who cares if some oneeyed son . . . . 264 IS 5 ONE 33   27
+CARES
    FOR CONTEXT, SEE . . . . 126 & SEVEN POEMS 5   23
CARESS
    reason with the deep caress of every most shy . . . . 19 T&C PUELLA MEA   98
    Our picking it. this caress that laugh both quickly . . . . . 364 VIVA 55   10
CARESSED
    being a little while caressed its fragrance makes the . . . . 21 T&C PUELLA MEA   191
    however slenderly by it caressed will explode and spill . . . 193 XLI PORTRAIT 1   16
CARET
    sits dropping on a caret of clenched arms a . . . . 143 & SON REAL 14   1
CARING
    through its indolent lascivious caring eyes watches; truly, . 344 VIVA 35   4
CARL
    Amy Sandburg of Algernon Carl Swinburned. Waiter a drink . . 233 IS 5 ONE 4   19
CARLOADS
    Of Evil sold 69 carloads before publication the girl . . . . 245 IS 5 ONE 16   9
CARNIVAL
    have beheld night's speechless carnival the painting of the . 36 T&C AMORES 1   13
    life's placid obscure palpable carnival where to a normal . . 43 T&C AMORES 7   32
CARNIVOROUS
    (table but three) hero's carnivorous (smile by lipstick smell 546 1 X 1 6   8
CAROLLING
    anything" (that eagerly sweet carolling self answers me) "i . 836 73 POEMS 64   8
CAROMING
    upon other tops to caroming off persist displacing Its . . . 311 VIVA 3   6
CAROUSE
    recently discovered cave, the carouse of geomet- rical . . . 197 XLI PORTRAIT 5   19
CARPENTERS
    / an amiable putrescence carpenters the village of her . . . 136 & SON REAL 7   1
CARPET
    has put down his carpet from which rise slim . . . . 384 NO THANKS 2   20
CARPETED
    of the emperor is carpeted with gold cloth from . . . . 32 T&C ORIENTALE 6   21
    stairs, carefully (carefully climbing carpeted flight after . 375 VIVA 66   12
    climbing carpeted flight after carpeted flight. in stillness, 375 VIVA 66   13
    in stillness, climbing the carpeted stairs of terror) and . . 375 VIVA 66   14
CARRIES
    else uncanned for everyone carries canopeners in Ever-Ever . 466 NEW POEMS 4   7
+CARRION
    FOR CONTEXT, SEE . . . . 641 (CHAIRE) 43   4
CARROTY
    up the with a carroty youth blonde whis (gorgedis . . . . . . 629 (CHAIRE) 31   17

CARROTY (CONTINUED)

couldn't well miss willy's carroty hair" "it seems like . . . 707 95 POEMS 35   4

CARRY

signifi- cant stomachs: Who carry-tadpole! s,, stomachs of . 101 & POST IMPR 11   75
colourless forgets) time Requiescat. carry carefully the . . 277 IS 5 THREE 1   22
made as skilfully.) But carry also, with that indolent . . . 294 IS 5 FOUR 11   14
thither who briskly busily carry the as tonishing & . . . . . 354 VIVA 45   14
myself's Antimere Should words carry weapons) are not Less . 395 NO THANKS 12   10
/ / / i carry your heart with me . . . . 766 95 POEMS 92   1
heart with me (i carry it in my heart) . . . . 766 95 POEMS 92   1
the stars apart i carry your heart (i carry . . . . 766 95 POEMS 92   15
carry your heart (i carry it in my heart) . . . . 766 95 POEMS 92   15

CARRY-TADPOLE

signifi- cant stomachs: Who carry-tadpole! s,, stomachs of . 101 & POST IMPR 11   75

CARRYING

(who slenderly descends, daintily carrying in her eyes the . 93 & POST IMPR 5   10
is an old man carrying flowers on his head. . . . . 102 & POST IMPR 12   2
veiled with candy white carrying a bouquet of pretend . . . . 470 NEW POEMS 8   6

CARS

through west ninth slowly cars pour into sixth avenue) . . . 800 73 POEMS 28   19

+CARTS

FOR CONTEXT, SEE . . . . 100 & POST IMPR 11   25

CARVE

this pith of darkness: carve an evilfringing flower of . . . 139 & SON REAL 10   8
a while) and shall carve time so we'll before . . . . 433 NO THANKS 50   14
with his life: and carve immortal jungles of despair . . . . 562 1 X 1 22   13

CARVED

rune of road lazily carved on sharpening air. Fields . . . . 86 T&C SON ACTU 5   6
where night gathers morte carved smiles cloud-gloss is at . . 90 & POST IMPR 2   11
intaglio. Nothing has also carved upon her much too . . . . . 116 & PORTRAIT 9   9
are built of soon carved of to born of . . . . 584 1 X 1 44   4

CARVEN

there are thrice-three-hundred doors carven of chalcedony and 33 T&C ORIENTALE 6   34
should any by me carven thing provoke your gesture . . . . . 291 IS 5 FOUR 8   19

CARVES

upon her tit one carves a cross in her . . . . 427 NO THANKS 44   6

+CARVING

FOR CONTEXT, SEE . . . . 342 VIVA 33   14

CASE

Not To Be Resharpened. (Case in point if we . . . . 230 IS 5 ONE 2   23
doctors know a hopeless case if--listen: there's a hell . . . 554 1 X 1 14   14

CASKET

thy head is a casket of the cool jewel . . . . 29 T&C ORIENTALE 3   16

CASSIOPEIA'S

yes chair but not Cassiopeia's might those be stockings . . . 322 VIVA 14   5

+CASTANETS

FOR CONTEXT, SEE . . . . 318 VIVA 10   4
FOR CONTEXT, SEE . . . . 318 VIVA 10   21

CASTLE

in marble all the castle lay like some gigantic . . . .   8 T&C OF NICOL   1
of lustre from the castle wall glided, a drop . . . .   8 T&C OF NICOL   23

CASTLES

languages) she smokes three castles He looks jewish , ... 312 VIVA 4   16

CASTRATED

Brattle Street by a castrated pup / / / . . . . 253 IS 5 ONE 24   15

CASTS

thing for C can't casts no shadow D drink . . . . 390 NO THANKS 7   3

CASUAL

not my tower, laborious, casual where the surrounded smile . 83 T&C SON ACTU 2   14
jumbling her flesh whose casual mouth's coy rooting dies . . 131 & SON REAL 2   7

CAT

his lady the musical tom-cat, thou stuffest the parks . . . . 61 T&C PORTRAIT 9   5
with pain THE BLACK CAT WITH is there anything . . . . 100 & POST IMPR 11   32
normal window. and a cat. A cat waiting for . . . . 166 & SON ACTU 15   8
and a cat. A cat waiting for god knows . . . . 166 & SON ACTU 15   9
who knows?) a blackish cat and a bluish cat . . . . 168 & SON ACTU 17   17
cat and a bluish cat are eyeing, as with . . . . 168 & SON ACTU 17   17
distinctly move, a yellowandbluish cat (perched why Curvingly 434 NO THANKS 51   32

	PAGE	TITLE	LINE

+CAT
FOR CONTEXT, SEE . . . . 655 {CHAIRE} 57   1
CATASTROPHE
arrive human the most catastrophe april might make alive . . 662 {CHAIRE} 64   3
CATCH
wishing if this thou catch, else missing. (though love . . . 13 T&C SONGS 3   18
and vainly tried to catch one funny hand opening . . . . . . 53 T&C PORTRAIT 1   43
Sometimes he does not catch a piece of money . . . . 69 T&C POST IMPR 6   12
laws with stars to catch telescopes) why. Being . . . . . . 478 NEW POEMS 16   6
heart if the seas catch fire (and live by . . . . 732 95 POEMS 60   6
CATCHING
the harbouring dark, and (catching up her delicate silk) . .   8 T&C OF NICOL   26
CATHEDRAL
utters serenely silently a cathedral before whose upward lean 93 & POST IMPR 5   2
which sprouting gently, the cathedral leans its dreamy spine 279 IS 5 THREE 3   3
by a mystery? ...the cathedral recedes into weather without . 279 IS 5 THREE 3   24
nonsense of sparrows, the cathedral shudders blackening; the 282 IS 5 THREE 6   12
ourselves decided what this cathedral ought to look like) . . 323 VIVA 15   24
little church (no great cathedral) far from the splendor . . 749 95 POEMS 77   1
CATHEDRALS
fishermen are prevented by cathedrals / / / / . . . . 478 NEW POEMS 16   12
CATS
devours a man, three cats, five white mice, and . . . . 279 IS 5 THREE 3   7
individual, mysterious witty hatless. Cats which move . . . . 279 IS 5 THREE 3   13
to neck of bottles, cats smoothly willowing out and . . . . . 279 IS 5 THREE 3   13
CAUGHT
with a writhing youth caught to her brazen breasts, ...   4 T&C EPITHALAM   43
shrieking from splintering foam caught you clutched you upon   30 T&C ORIENTALE 4   13
shocked impossible tower i caught you strained you broke . . 30 T&C ORIENTALE 4   26
slowly and writhe like caught. brave: flies; / / . . . . . . 55 T&C PORTRAIT 3   20
a thing, which tightens caught in the hoisting light . . . . 68 T&C POST IMPR 5   11
and after he has caught a, penny or three, ... 69 T&C POST IMPR 6   15
(having in my arms caught the picture) hurry it . . . . 162 & SON ACTU 11   9
farm but the skunks caught cold and died and . . . . 239 IS 5 ONE 10   22
us perhaps one villa caught like pieces of a . . . . 283 IS 5 THREE 7   10
tugs weakly at twilight, caught in thickening fear our . . . 305 IS 5 FIVE 4   6
fishing and men are caught by worms (love may . . . . 446 NO THANKS 61   5
one day a nigger caught in his hand a . . . . 622 {CHAIRE} 24   2
single mys- tery (liftingly caught upon falling) silent! ly . 627 {CHAIRE} 29   15
CAUSE
an end (the silly cause of trivial which thinkless . . . . . 411 NO THANKS 28   3
toss it away; or cause one causeless cloud to . . . . 433 NO THANKS 50   4
spring's least breathing should cause a colour and i . . . . 450 NO THANKS 65   13
's miraculous why? be cause dying is perfectly natural; . . . 604 {CHAIRE} 6   13
much) may be be cause ever ybody wants more . . . . 727 95 POEMS 55   15
CAUSELESS
away; or cause one causeless cloud to purely grow . . . . . . 433 NO THANKS 50   4
CAUSES
how let's say elation causes the bent eyes thickly . . . . . 229 IS 5 ONE FRAN   13
item: a water- melon causes indigestion to William Cullen . . 263 IS 5 ONE 32   52
CAUSING
common things to disappear causing through mystery miracle . 559 1 X 1 19   4
CAUTION
ecstasy --for poem prose-- caution for curiosity (and close . 689 95 POEMS 17   7
CAUTIOUSLY
nor will rain care cautiously who prolongs unserious . . . . 84 T&C SON ACTU 3   9
(he, slightly whom or cautiously this person and this . . . . 300 IS 5 FOUR 17   17
CAVALIERS
parks with overgrown pimply cavaliers and gumchewing giggly . 61 T&C PORTRAIT 9   7
CAVE
in a recently discovered cave, the carouse of geomet- . . . . 197 XLI PORTRAIT 5   19
CAVEAT
terror strawberries democ ra (caveat emptor) cy superfluous . 549 1 X 1 9   13
CAVING
(Whose fingers young the caving ages curiously con) --but . . 77 T&C SON UNRE 2   4
murdered petals. with the caving stem. But of all . . . . . . 215 XLI SONNETS 11   8
+CAVING
FOR CONTEXT, SEE . . . . 119 & PORTRAIT 11   5

CCCOME

  go slow said she (cccome? said he ummm said . . . . 399 NO THANKS 16   29

CE

  throat Marie Louise Lallemand n'est-ce pas que je suis . . . 120 & PORTRAIT 12   11

  the playthings for dust n'est-ce pas effendi drifts between . 198 XLI PORTRAIT 6   14

  millionaires a cute idea n'est-ce pas? (whereas, upon the . . 245 IS 5 ONE 16   14

  stroll living spawn imitate) ce (re peat credo fais . . . . . 309 VIVA 1   32

  <> ruptingly) ca-y-est droppe5 qu'est-ce que tu veux Dwrith . 430 NO THANKS 47   18

CEASE

  which are born and cease for being whiter than . . . .   5 T&C EPITHALAM 100

  happens Something, and They cease (and one by one . . . . . . 62 T&C PORTRAIT 10 20

  smiles cloud-gloss is at moon-cease soon verbal mist-flowers 90 & POST IMPR 2   12

  flower flowing without or cease or time; a naming . . . . . . 168 & SON ACTU 17   8

  coward waiting clumsily to cease whom every perfect thing . . 360 VIVA 51   6

  for lives (may never cease views with smooth vigilant . . . . 386 NO THANKS 3   9

  must wither fail and cease --but better than to . . . . 742 95 POEMS 70   4

CEASED

  furious hearts of mountains ceased to beat? Wind beautifully   3 T&C EPITHALAM 16

  coquettishly- cocked bonnet having ceased the captain . . . . 196 XLI PORTRAIT 4   6

  skin "see" (i, seeing, ceased to breathe). The plump . . . . 226 IS 5 ONE MAME   6

  flight of crows had ceased. I withdrew my hands . . . . 263 IS 5 ONE 32   54

CEASELESSLY

  once knees) does almost ceaselessly repeat "there is some . . 339 VIVA 30   32

CEASELESSNESS

  dearest fears beyond their ceaselessness (nor has a syllable 372 VIVA 63   10

CEASING

  goes (never a moment ceasing to begin the mystery . . . . . . 756 95 POEMS 84   3

CECILE

  square crime of life.... Cecile, the oval shove of . . . . . 138 & SON REAL 9   13

CEILING

  gold cloth from the ceiling (one diamond timid with . . . . . 32 T&C ORIENTALE 6 24

  upsoarings the break on ceiling- flatness the Bar. tinking . 96 & POST IMPR 8   9

  blinking at the low ceiling my being pleasantly was . . . . . 96 & POST IMPR 8   25

  my feet on the ceiling inhaling six divine inches . . . . . . 194 XLI PORTRAIT 2   14

  hangs at yon gilty ceiling per both pale orbs . . . . 546 1 X 1 6   5

CELEBRATE

  in merciful miracles wonderingly celebrate day and welcome . 582 1 X 1 42   3

CELEBRATES

  life and death) timelessly celebrates the merciful wonder no 845 73 POEMS 73   13

CELESTIAL

  and sing (of harps celestial to the quivering string) . . . . 208 XLI SONNETS 4   7

  have snarled threads of celestial silence huger than . . . . 555 1 X 1 15   5

  / luminous tendril of celestial wish (whying diminutive . . . 669 {CHAIRE} 71   1

  (human one; and one celestial) stand soul to soul: . . . . . 721 95 POEMS 49   8

  illustrious scientist petitions the celestial host to . . . . 799 73 POEMS 27   24

CELIBATE

  jiffyclaus bug fainarain wee celibate amaranth clutch owch so 333 VIVA 24   20

CELLOPHANE

  everything is protected by cellophane against anything . . . 470 NEW POEMS 8   19

CELLOS

  breathless-scarlet, dark colours like 'cellos keen fiddling . 100 & POST IMPR 11   7

CEMENT

  oA chute i had cement for her, merrily we . . . . 119 & PORTRAIT 11   9

CENSORED

  of notwithstanding with his censored up a wench's rock-a-bye 642 {CHAIRE} 44   26

CENT

  wobbly foot-steps every goggle cent of it get out . . . . . . 96 & POST IMPR 8   20

  never gave me one cent in his life but . . . . 707 95 POEMS 35   17

CENTRIFUGALLY

  a brittle swoon of centrifugally expecting faces clumsily . . 279 IS 5 THREE 3   6

  wisdom in thirtytwo seconds centrifugally is refuted by these 341 VIVA 32   5

CENTRIPETAL

  producing sixtyfour maxims whose) centripetal wisdom in . . . 341 VIVA 32   4

CENTS

  of just twenty five cents dear friends to make . . . . 196 XLI PORTRAIT 4   12

  as and some six cents hit the whigh shaped . . . . 602 {CHAIRE} 4   4

  'could you spare three cents please' --why guesswho nearly . 800 73 POEMS 28   6

	PAGE	TITLE	LINE

CENTURIES
superbly limp the ostensible centuries therefore let us be . 111 & PORTRAIT 6 55
my country 'tis of centuries come and go and . . . . 268 IS 5 TWO 3 4
once only, Queen among centuries universes between Who out . 358 VIVA 49 12
some alive individual ten centuries of original soon or . . . 561 1 X 1 21 6
can immensely meet for centuries and (except nothing) . . . 580 1 X 1 40 17
agreement --saharas have their centuries; ten thousand of . . 683 95 POEMS 11 7
(amazing each how many centuries) these more than eyes . . . 843 73 POEMS 71 2
CENTURY
the Frolic or the Century whirl? one's memory indignantly . . 72 T&C SON REAL 3 3
CERTAIN
worship absolute, unto the certain altar at whose head . . . 6 T&C EPITHALAM 116
is such as only certain dead and careful painters . . . . . . 20 T&C PUELLA MEA 140
shall have before a certain face become white perfume . . . . 39 T&C AMORES 4 32
and i entreat, by certain foolish perfect hours dead . . . . 42 T&C AMORES 6 15
have made a fragile certain song under the window . . . . . . 43 T&C AMORES 7 4
swiftly take my fragile certain song that we may . . . . . . 43 T&C AMORES 7 27
had long on a certain taut precarious holiday frighteningly . 52 T&C PORTRAIT 1 5
i was passing a certain gate, rain fell (as . . . . 58 T&C PORTRAIT 6 2
prostitute Night, argues with certain houses / / / . . . . . 93 & POST IMPR 5 18
indulges his soul for certain things which died it . . . . . 108 & PORTRAIT 4 29
try; i have watched certain petals rapidly wish in . . . . . 214 XLI SONNETS 10 5
i would suggest that certain ideas gestures rhymes, like . . 230 IS 5 ONE 2 19
death is more than certain a hundred these sounds . . . . . . 238 IS 5 ONE 9 2
i i likes a certain party gimme the he-man's . . . . 247 IS 5 ONE 18 4
an invisible spectator, maybe certain nobodies laughing . . . 283 IS 5 THREE 7 8
sweeter frailer you whom certain flowers resemble but . . . . 293 IS 5 FOUR 10 4
a few windows awaken certain faces busily horribly blunder . 299 IS 5 FOUR 16 13
man who (at a certain corner, suddenly) meets the . . . . . 304 IS 5 FIVE 3 4
or) Gay is a certain Young Woman unacquainted with . . . . . 327 VIVA 18 42
of June, having of certain stars and planets heard, ... 360 VIVA 51 12
imagine your sorrow a certain reckoning demands... marvelling 374 VIVA 65 3
you suppose possibly are certain hands, terse and invisible, 378 VIVA 69 6
well naturally i und certain i o posi but . . . . 400 NO THANKS 17 10
and i heard a certain a bird i dreamed . . . . 587 1 X 1 47 2
"Worlds? o no: i'm certain they're (look again) flowers." . . 603 (CHAIRE) 5 5
rose, roses (you feel certain) will only smile / . . . . . . 744 95 POEMS 72 8
a woman knows; and certain men quite possibly may . . . . . . 807 73 POEMS 35 12
CERTAINLY
and bodies lightly desperate certainly wherefrom departed is 57 T&C PORTRAIT 5 39
you; or if i certainly create, lady, one of . . . . 92 & POST IMPR 4 20
and slowly which upward certainly is pouring) emits a . . . . 95 & POST IMPR 7 10
lady in the most certainly (of what we everywhere . . . . . . 294 IS 5 FOUR 11 4
all ried but eye certainly hate the juse / . . . . 405 NO THANKS 22 12
and here's to silent certainly mountains; and to a . . . . . 424 NO THANKS 41 4
most magical maybes of certainly never the iswas . . . . . . 495 50 POEMS 9 14
believe it) lao tsze certainly told him, and general . . . . 553 1 X 1 13 8
your each nearerness) everyone certainly would (my most . . . 717 95 POEMS 45 13
means that when the certainly roof leaks it 's . . . . 728 95 POEMS 56 2
(but believe scarcely may) certainly while mute each inch . . 808 73 POEMS 36 9
dreams, less into heaven certainly earth swims than each . . 810 73 POEMS 38 7
no mind contrives (but certainly each spirit is) and . . . . 842 73 POEMS 70 8
+CERTAINLY
FOR CONTEXT, SEE . . . . 235 IS 5 ONE 6 6
FOR CONTEXT, SEE . . . . 400 NO THANKS 17 10
CERTAINTIES
true (all doubts, all certainties, as villains strive and . . 576 1 X 1 36 5
CESSATION
began with the early cessation of her skirt. fleshless . . . 103 & POST IMPR 13 6
CETERA
the deep mud et cetera (dreaming, et cetera, of . . . . 276 IS 5 TWO 10 21
et cetera (dreaming, et cetera, of Your smile eyes . . . . . 276 IS 5 TWO 10 24
CEZANNE
a wet dream by Cezanne / / / / . . . . 246 IS 5 ONE 17 13
CEZANNE'S
gripping gigantic muscles of Cezanne's logic, oho. a street . 180 XLI SONGS 2 15
CHAIN
nine ladies they must chain his foot for his . . . . 15 T&C SONGS 5 11

CHAIN (CONTINUED)
    soul dangles from his watch-chain which would be embarrassing 204 XLI LA GUERRE 2   4
    monkey attached by a chain securely to this always . . . . . 279 IS 5 THREE 3   11
CHAINED
    soul--so even i wholly chained to a grave astonishment   . . . 79 T&C SON UNRE 4   11
CHAINS
    shine, the balls the chains red and gold the . . . . 192 XLI CHANSONS 2   16
CHAIR
    exactly-mutilated ghost of a chair, a; domeshaped interval of 96 & POST IMPR 8   34
    of love in The Chair he kept talking about . . . . 145 & SON REAL 16   14
    is it oh yes chair but not Cassiopeia's might . . . . 322 VIVA 14   5
+CHAIR
    FOR CONTEXT, SEE . . . . 259 IS 5 ONE 29   9
CHAIRETE
    for know all men ((CHAIRETE)) as it was in . . . . 425 NO THANKS 42   9
CHAIRS
    ing; nake; D and chairs wait under the trees . . . . 104 & POST IMPR 14   13
    we go spill and chairs tables the and bitch . . . . 496 50 POEMS 10   15
+CHAIRS
    FOR CONTEXT, SEE . . . . 104 & POST IMPR 14   16
    FOR CONTEXT, SEE . . . . 385 NO THANKS 2   48
CHALCEDONY
    thrice-three-hundred doors carven of chalcedony and before . 33 T&C ORIENTALE 6   34
CHALKING
    squeaked like a billiard-cue chalking itself, as not to . . . 170 & SON ACTU 19   10
CHALLENGE
    / / structure, miraculous challenge, devout am upward deep . 351 VIVA 42   1
CHAMBERS
    / opening of the chambers close quotes the microscopic . . . 267 IS 5 TWO 2   1
CHAMPYCHUMPCHOMPS
    stimpstamps) the grintgrunt wugglewiggle champychumpchomps . 773 73 POEMS 1   12
CHANCEL
    0 thou within the chancel of whose charms the . . . .   7 T&C EPITHALAM   153
CHANGE
    the sea does not change and she goes forth . . . . 38 T&C AMORES 3   10
    worth than death to change their coat --which something . . . 544 1 X 1 4   12
    hero is quite without change, you're going to get . . . . . . 800 73 POEMS 28   11
CHANGELESS
    endowed him with a changeless grin whereon a dozen . . . . . 258 IS 5 ONE 28   8
CHANGING
    people stare arranging and changing placing carefully there a 124 & SEVEN POEMS 3   6
    known thing here) and changing everything carefully spring is 124 & SEVEN POEMS 3   9
CHANSONS
    / / / / / CHANSONS INNOCENTES in Just- spring . . . . 24 T&C CHANSONS 1   T
    / / / / / CHANSONS INNOCENTES why did you . . . . 191 XLI CHANSONS 1   T
CHANTS
    upon the spires silver chants the litanies the great . . . . 51 T&C IMPRESS 5   5
CHAOS
    a freeing of ghostly chaos in this dangerous night . . . . . 77 T&C SON UNRE 2   13
    democratic tyrannically dumb Awake, chaos: we have napped. / 337 VIVA 28   15
    was death so alive: chaos so (hark --that screech . . . . . . 639 {CHAIRE} 41   5
CHAP
    old feller belch the chap hic sum- more eh . . . . 96 & POST IMPR 8   21
CHAPPY
    to hell with the chappy who doesn't agree (if . . . . 791 73 POEMS 19   3
CHARGE
    April darkness, friends i charge laughing. Into the hair-thin 66 T&C POST IMPR 3   5
    issingupperc uts-lurc hhurt-re coil charge &) swooN . . . . . 388 NO THANKS 5   18
CHARIOT
    horses yoked to a chariot of kings they are . . . . 29 T&C ORIENTALE 3   11
+CHARLES
    FOR CONTEXT, SEE . . . . 611 {CHAIRE} 13   1
CHARLIE
    night something odd occurred" charlie confessed (halting) "a 800 73 POEMS 28   2
CHARMING
    me stern against your charming strength O haste annihilator . 182 XLI SONGS 4   14
    mark is a remarkably charming person personally they tell . . 246 IS 5 ONE 17   6

		PAGE	TITLE	LINE

CHARMS
the chancel of whose charms the tall boy god . . . .   7 T&C EPITHALAM   153
intolerant brightness of your charms: one pierced moment . . 78 T&C SON UNRE 3   11
as i think, her charms en repos.... a fattish . . . . 143 & SON REAL 14   7
CHARY
steeple says Why the chary the wary (as all . . . . 801 73 POEMS 29   7
CHAS
/ / / / chas sing does (who , ... 611 (CHAIRE) 13   1
CHASED
with slavver of spring chased two flights of squirrel-stairs 194 XLI PORTRAIT 2   7
were; and molly was chased by a horrible thing . . . . . . 682 95 POEMS 10   7
CHASM
yous to cross the chasm of time lessness; but . . . . 605 (CHAIRE) 7   12
CHASSISED
in the head keen chassised like a Rolls Royce . . . . 232 IS 5 ONE 3   5
CHASTE
of "alas we were chaste on earth we ghosts: . . . .   9 T&C SONGS 1   22
worships God-- (behold! where chaste stars writhe captured in 77 T&C SON UNRE 2   17
CHASTENESS
of smooth mastery with chasteness of sea-girls Will i . . . . 189 XLI SONGS 11   10
CHAT
not refined they cannot chat of that and this . . . . 427 NO THANKS 44   14
CHATOUILLE
la voix fragile qui chatouille Des Italiens the putain . . . 120 & PORTRAIT 12   7
CHATOUILLER
dance si vous voulez chatouiller mon lezard ladies suddenly . 121 & PORTRAIT 12   41
CHATTER
flecks of and a chatter sobbings intersect with which . . . .   96 & POST IMPR 8   8
seeing blood, her heart's chatter riveted a weeping . . . . . 132 & SON REAL 3   3
CHATTERING
its eyeless miles the chattering sunset ludicrously dies, i .   64 T&C POST IMPR 1   9
through, prismatic, whims, the chattering self perceives with 157 & SON ACTU 6   14
+CHATTERING
FOR CONTEXT, SEE . . . .   94 & POST IMPR 6   12
CHATTERISH
humble. Over thin earths chatterish strut cuddle & shrink: . 346 VIVA 37   3
CHATTERS
& &) & chatters about Peacepeacepeace (to droppingly . . . . 267 IS 5 TWO 2   7
CHAUCER
in the tale of Chaucer knoweth many a pair . . . . 20 T&C PUELLA MEA 164
CHAUVESOURIS
--name unless i'm mistaken chauvesouris-- whose grammar is . 504 50 POEMS 18   9
CHEAP
left to guess: the cheap intelligent thighs, the electric . . 173 & SON ACTU 22   14
the wonderless city's sublime cheap distinct mouth) do the . 218 XLI SONNETS 14   7
too much o much cheap me i work i . . . . 523 50 POEMS 36   15
good but there this cheap this suit too quick . . . . 523 50 POEMS 36   22
CHEAPLY
and And spills smile cheaply thick --who therefore Thee . . . 358 VIVA 49   10
CHECK
big cumbine wid i (check undublcheck) babbitt (GOD SAVE . . . 325 VIVA 17   19
+CHECK
FOR CONTEXT, SEE . . . . 325 VIVA 17   20
CHEEK
leaps in the maple's cheek, and suddenly by shining . . . . .   4 T&C EPITHALAM   62
daisy-cup, and from her cheek the beauteous colour went . . .   8 T&C OF NICOL   30
mysterious shepherd lifts a cheek teartroubled to the . . . .   9 T&C SONGS 1   10
CHEEKS
to traipse into the cheeks "eet smeestaire steevensun kum . . 73 T&C SON REAL 4   12
two slits in her cheeks. A brain peered at . . . . 132 & SON REAL 3   13
who sits between her cheeks utters a thud of . . . . 143 & SON REAL 14   5
your face your little cheeks the streets of smiles . . . . . 186 XLI SONGS 8   7
sel is i. Vast cheeks enclose me. a gigantic . . . . 201 XLI PORTRAIT 9   7
drizzle untidily from released cheeks "I'll tell duh woild; . 226 IS 5 ONE MAME   10
it understood my eyes cheeks mouth its hands (slipping) . . . 284 IS 5 FOUR 1   4
CHEERFUL
the father a thick cheerful man with majestic bulbous . . . .   56 T&C PORTRAIT 4   10

109

	PAGE	TITLE	LINE

CHEERFULEST
toadstools he is the cheerfulest of men his peaked . . . . . 198 XLI PORTRAIT 6 18
/ / if a cheerfulest Elephantangelchild should sit (holding . 631 {CHAIRE} 33 1
all) reminds me the cheerfulest goddamned sonofabitch i ever 699 95 POEMS 27 12
CHEERFULLY
never mind Joe agreeably cheerfully remarked when surrounded 241 IS 5 ONE 12 2
CHEERING
smoothly onward(amid tinkling-cheering-hammering tables). . . 232 IS 5 ONE 3 9
CHEERS
the millenni um three cheers for labor give all . . . . . . 492 50 POEMS 6 10
+CHEMISTRY
FOR CONTEXT, SEE . . . . 361 VIVA 52 28
CHERES
belles bottes--oh hear ,pas cheres") and my love slowly . . . 102 & POST IMPR 12 21
CHERI
que je suis belle cheri? les anglais m'aiment tous, ... 120 & PORTRAIT 12 12
kissed and i .... cheri.... nous sommes / / . . . . 133 & SON REAL 4 23
--"Ici?" --"Ah non, mon cheri; il fait trop froid"-- . . . . 304 IS 5 FIVE 3 10
CHERIE
...(that's the Black People, cherie, who live under stones.) 86 T&C SON ACTU 5 9
with them? j'en doute,) cherie, j'en doute. the accurate . . 169 & SON ACTU 18 13
CHERISHED
image my proud heart cherished as fair. (The child-head . . . 207 XLI SONNETS 3 13
CHERRIES
itself, with currants and cherries it (swallow s bun . . . . 100 & POST IMPR 11 23
+CHESTED
FOR CONTEXT, SEE . . . . 398 NO THANKS 15 16
CHEVAUX
stirs the always smiling chevaux de bois) when you . . . . . 304 IS 5 FIVE 3 14
CHEWCHOO
from the cognoscenti bingbongwhom chewchoo laugh dingle nails 333 VIVA 24 2
CHEWED
patter of kisses, the chewed stump of a mouth, ... 133 & SON REAL 4 14
their faces like cigarettebutts, chewed with disdain, led by 194 XLI PORTRAIT 2 20
CHEWING
slam bridge train shriek chewing whistles hugest to morrow . 309 VIVA 1 19
+CHEWING
FOR CONTEXT, SEE . . . . 61 T&C PORTRAIT 9 7
CHEWS
the kitchen nights and chews a two-bit cigar waiting . . . . 149 & SON REAL 20 2
CHIC
elscasta? netsits Elf allaBout. (chic) -kchi cK, / / . . . . 318 VIVA 10 24
Same is all the chic; by instruments, both span . . . . 438 NO THANKS 54 12
CHICAGO
and beat it for Chicago. Eddie was waiting for . . . . 145 & SON REAL 16 4
+CHICAGO
FOR CONTEXT, SEE . . . . 237 IS 5 ONE 8 7
CHICK
thecas-tanets in 5/4; Time chick. chick but: that Mat . . . . 318 VIVA 10 6
in 5/4; Time chick. chick but: that Mat isse . . . . 318 VIVA 10 6
got a Bad almond chick. thepinkisht artskiDs... with thema . 318 VIVA 10 18
+CHICK
FOR CONTEXT, SEE . . . . 318 VIVA 10 24
FOR CONTEXT, SEE . . . . 318 VIVA 10 25
CHICKADEE
rock hollyhock forest brook chickadee mountain. Mountain) . . 512 50 POEMS 26 26
"be you?" and a chickadee to all the world, ... 828 73 POEMS 56 3
CHICKEN
Uncle Sol had a chicken farm till the skunks . . . . 239 IS 5 ONE 10 18
CHICKENS
farm failed because the chickens ate the vegetables so . . . 239 IS 5 ONE 10 15
the skunks ate the chickens when my Uncle Sol . . . . 239 IS 5 ONE 10 19
CHICKS
to his mate his chicks his friends he loves . . . . 774 73 POEMS 2 13
CHIEF
eyebrows the 3 rd chief something or must be . . . . 465 NEW POEMS 3 3
CHIEFLY
of your fragility (but chiefly of your smile, most . . . . . 293 IS 5 FOUR 10 16

CHIEFLY (CONTINUED)
   intricate imperfect various things chiefly which wrong your . 306 IS 5 FIVE 5   2
   or mainly awash while chiefly submerged or an amoral   . . . . 410 NO THANKS 27   11
   angel everywhere welcome (but chiefly at home in snowily . . 678 95 POEMS 6   10
CHILD
   i saw a dirty child skating on noisy wheels . . . . 56 T&C PORTRAIT 4   2
   how she was with child / / / / . . . .   56 T&C PORTRAIT 4   16
   thequeer hopping ghosts of child- ren. my, ears know . . . . 100 & POST IMPR 11   35
   hast merely gonorrhea Oldeyed child, to ambitious weeness of 105 & PORTRAIT 1   6
   extended to the pumping Child, and "'Twas the night . . . . . 142 & SON REAL 13   11
   cherished as fair. (The child-head poised with the serious . 207 XLI SONNETS 3   14
   and make me a child, a pretty dribbling child, ... 233 IS 5 ONE 4   4
   child, a pretty dribbling child, a little child. In . . . . . 233 IS 5 ONE 4   4
   dribbling child, a little child. In thy your ear: . . . . . . 233 IS 5 ONE 4   4
   dada? make me a child, stout hurdysturdygurdyman waiter, make 233 IS 5 ONE 4   14
   waiter, make me a child. So this is Paris. . . . . 233 IS 5 ONE 4   15
   and so (an erring child of circumstance whom the . . . . . . 266 IS 5 TWO 1   38
   only man woman or child who wrote a simple . . . . 336 VIVA 27   3
   if i were a child "we can see a . . . . 353 VIVA 44   4
   this was of a child 's shy foot among . . . . 371 VIVA 62   12
   forget relax wait (little child who have tried who . . . . . 393 NO THANKS 10   7
   (ask super-) wonderful (mother) child is a good Husband . . . 398 NO THANKS 15   5
   toe ingt o a child who alone st and . . . . 469 NEW POEMS 7   16
   h u sh nor child) / / / / . . . . 472 NEW POEMS 10   18
   each tree (and every child was sure that spring . . . . 521 50 POEMS 34   51
   one true one generous child- man -god one eager . . . . 523 50 POEMS 36   41
   asked "something a little child who's just as small . . . . . 555 1 X 1 15   12
   aiming ; spare the child and spoil the rod . . . . 643 (CHAIRE) 45   5
   maybe god is a child 's hand) very carefully . . . . 652 (CHAIRE) 54   2
   like face of the child who's every child (& . . . . 668 (CHAIRE) 70   11
   the child who's every child (& therefore invisible) anyhow . 668 (CHAIRE) 70   13
   one heartbeat of this child; nor shall even prevail . . . . . 714 95 POEMS 42   11
   this father and his child are watching snowflakes (falling . 715 95 POEMS 43   4
   e) e yes are (chIld) and wh (g o . . . . 740 95 POEMS 68   6
   white rose of a child" / / / / . . . . 748 95 POEMS 76   17
   found a by lost child and a (float through . . . . 757 95 POEMS 85   26
   sleeping firsts of wonder) child unbreathingly share (huge . 757 95 POEMS 85   28
   (myself's own self who's) child will dance! and when . . . . 843 73 POEMS 71   12
+CHILD
   FOR CONTEXT, SEE . . . . 631 (CHAIRE) 33   1
   FOR CONTEXT, SEE . . . . 715 95 POEMS 43   21
CHILD-HEAD
   cherished as fair. (The child-head poised with the serious . 207 XLI SONNETS 3   14
CHILD'S
   singless on- ly a child's eyes float silently down . . . . . 491 50 POEMS 5   6
CHILDFLESH
   drooling unmind grim yessing childflesh perpetually acruise . 337 VIVA 28   7
CHILDFULLY
   immeasurably Now cancels the childfully diminishing earth . . 402 NO THANKS 19   4
   more miracle may grow --childfully serious flower of holiness 601 (CHAIRE) 3   7
CHILDHOOD
   redstone mouth renews his childhood and He said "willingly . 57 T&C PORTRAIT 5   12
   well recognised regime of childhood is reversed meantime in . 261 IS 5 ONE 31   9
CHILDISH
   were something more maturely childish, more beautiful almost 211 XLI SONNETS 7   5
CHILDLOST
   g Is poet iS (childlost so; ul) foundclown . . . . 471 NEW POEMS 9   14
CHILDMOON
   (softlying wisdoms enter guess) childmoon smile to your . . . 518 50 POEMS 32   11
CHILDREN
   fragility --. Dogs bark children play -ing Are in . . . . . . 63 T&C PORTRAIT 10   34
   swarming sonal crea- tures --Children, stand with circular . 69 T&C POST IMPR 6   7
   gesture that makes the children laugh. But i don't, ... 69 T&C POST IMPR 6   19
   the street and the children and the monkeyandtheorgan and . . 69 T&C POST IMPR 6   25
   puppy hopping between skipping children (It is the . . . . . 167 & SON ACTU 16   10
   A new curve of children gladly cricks where a . . . . 219 XLI SONNETS 15   7
   / / listen my children and you shall hear . . . . 236 IS 5 ONE 7   1
   not less than sixteen children and of course you . . . . . . 254 IS 5 ONE 25   11

CHILDREN (CONTINUED)

did-not-move exquisitely ,like dead children (if he had been 355 VIVA 46   17
rain whom fear not children but men speaks (among . . . . . . 356 VIVA 47   2
rise slim curving mighty children while a python over . . . . 384 NO THANKS 2   21
my rest to these children building this rainman out . . . . . 390 NO THANKS 7   14
and hornets wail by children stung or as the . . . . 511 50 POEMS 25   14
sons of unless and children of almost) never shall . . . . 512 50 POEMS 26   3
sun moon stars rain children guessed (but only a . . . . . . 515 50 POEMS 29   9
begin to explain how children are apt to forget . . . . 515 50 POEMS 29   23
death's wandering guess) while children climb their eyes to . 517 50 POEMS 31   14
/ / / these children singing in stone a . . . . 525 50 POEMS 37   1
of stone these little children wound with stone flowers . . . 525 50 POEMS 37   3
these silently lit tle children are petals their song . . . . 525 50 POEMS 37   6
than silence these always children forever singing wreathed . 525 50 POEMS 37   13
wreathed with singing blossoms children of stone with . . . . 525 50 POEMS 37   15
listens forever to always children singing forever a song . . 525 50 POEMS 37   21
poets grow; and (there--see?) children" nor might any earth's 626 (CHAIRE) 28   12
bird -quick voice loves children and sunlight and mountains) 660 (CHAIRE) 62   22
most nothing's own nothing children go of dust / . . . . . . 661 (CHAIRE) 63   14
if) timelessly foundlost glad (children of) dirtpoor (popes . 681 95 POEMS 9   11
silence are cries poems children dreams & through slowquickly 719 95 POEMS 47   6
and laughing and crying) children whose any sadness or . . . 749 95 POEMS 77   7
conceiving who comforts his children, if he disappears; till 756 95 POEMS 84   6
and time. Time cannot children, poets, lovers tell- measure . 817 73 POEMS 45   9

+CHILDREN

FOR CONTEXT, SEE . . . . 100 & POST IMPR 11   35
FOR CONTEXT, SEE . . . . 249 IS 5 ONE 20   4

CHIME

/ / / (hills chime with thrush) A hummingbird . . . . 747 95 POEMS 75   1

CHIMNEY

were hung by the chimney with care in hopes . . . . 142 & SON REAL 13   14

CHIMNEYS

in the sunset their chimneys converse angrily, their roofs . 62 T&C PORTRAIT 10   12
fire-escapes and roofs and chimneys and while roofs and . . . 62 T&C PORTRAIT 10   16
roofs and fire-escapes and chimneys and while chimneys and . 62 T&C PORTRAIT 10   17
and chimneys and while chimneys and fire-escapes and roofs . 62 T&C PORTRAIT 10   17
knees among the supercilious chimneys, my nerves sumptuously 169 & SON ACTU 18   7

CHIN

is tied under myhis chin.) that climbs and cries . . . . . . 69 T&C POST IMPR 6   42

CHINESE

Mat isse like -with-the-chinese-eyebrowsMan gave me,A, . . . 318 VIVA 10   8

+CHINOISERIES

FOR CONTEXT, SEE . . . . 747 95 POEMS 75   17

CHINS

Mid's the three trickling chins began to traipse into . . . . 73 T&C SON REAL 4   11
mustaches, and very tidiyum chins, and just above their . . . 274 IS 5 TWO 9   13
and a multitude of chins: next door but three . . . . 312 VIVA 4   6

CHIP

it started when Bill's chip let on to the . . . . 145 & SON REAL 16   1

CHIPMUNK

oul der a drea (chipmunk) ming / / / . . . . 830 73 POEMS 58   21

CHIPPING

sight keep hitting and chipping with sharp fatal tools . . . 199 XLI PORTRAIT 7   4

CHIPPITY

Bam- : do) , chippity. / / / / . . . . 426 NO THANKS 43   29

CHIPS

hundred ands All the chips would kid Jimmie to . . . . 149 & SON REAL 20   10
played for timelessness with chips of when) that's yours; . . 451 NO THANKS 66   4

+CHIRPING

FOR CONTEXT, SEE . . . . 100 & POST IMPR 11   41

CHIRPS

fifth finger. a bird chirps in a tree, somewhere . . . . . . 281 IS 5 THREE 5   12

CHISEL

squirming with light insane chisel the killing flame that . . 139 & SON REAL 10   11

CHISELED

diadumenos in whose young chiseled eyes the people saw . . . 4 T&C EPITHALAM   33

CHISELS

of evenslicing eyes are chisels scarlet Goes with her . . . . 106 & PORTRAIT 2   4

		PAGE	TITLE	LINE

CHISELS (CONTINUED)
  an agony of sensual chisels i perform squirms of . . . . . . 199 XLI PORTRAIT 7 5
CHIVALRY
  he's the soul of chivalry in terror of whose . . . . 774 73 POEMS 2 4
+CHOCOLATES
  FOR CONTEXT, SEE . . . . 179 XLI SONGS 1 10
CHOICE
  you doesn't take your choice. Ain't freedom grand / . . . . . 636 (CHAIRE) 38 14
CHOKE
  Large legs pinch, toes choke-- hair-thin strands of magic . . 146 & SON REAL 17 7
  a town (whose dormers choke and snore the steeples . . . . . 340 VIVA 31 3
CHOKED
  smoking Face Bluish-old and choked pat of going soles . . . . 142 & SON REAL 13 6
CHOKES
  life's lived wrongsideout, sameness chokes oneness truth is . 446 NO THANKS 61 3
+CHOMPS
  FOR CONTEXT, SEE . . . . 773 73 POEMS 1 12
CHOOSE
  minute of evening. We'll choose the way to the . . . . 86 T&C SON ACTU 5 3
CHOPPED
  in surprisable unliving eyes chopped by a swollen inanity . . 103 & POST IMPR 13 4
CHOPS
  your brain's axe only chops hugest inherent Trees of . . . . 195 XLI PORTRAIT 3 18
CHORD
  mouth is as a chord of crimson music Come . . . . 27 T&C ORIENTALE 1 5
CHORDS
  they (writhe they, struggleinweird chords of humorous, fury . 100 & POST IMPR 11 12
  witty huge and its chords brittle eager eternal luminous . . 110 & PORTRAIT 6 25
CHORES
  his grin done his chores laid him down. Sleep . . . . 568 1 X 1 28 28
CHOSEN
  gate smile always the chosen flowers of reminding / . . . . . 58 T&C PORTRAIT 6 26
CHREYESAKE
  say b ut for chreyesake how ca n i . . . . 703 95 POEMS 31 16
CHRIST
  spirited) they believe in Christ and Longfellow, both dead, . 70 T&C SON REAL 1 5
  to numb rhythm before christ / / / / . . . . 106 & PORTRAIT 2 15
  for the coming of Christ Jesus ? ?? ??? . . . . 196 XLI PORTRAIT 4 21
  lambs, of Sumner Volstead Christ and Co. the epoch . . . . . 266 IS 5 TWO 1 2
  dungeon, where he died Christ (of His mercy infinite) . . . . 339 VIVA 30 38
  himself a man? King Christ, this world is all . . . . 438 NO THANKS 54 25
  now no not any christ but you must understand . . . . 638 (CHAIRE) 40 13
  the dark i met christ jesus) my heart flopped . . . . 648 (CHAIRE) 50 4
  / / / / christ but they're few all . . . . 805 73 POEMS 33 1
+CHRIST
  FOR CONTEXT, SEE . . . . 823 73 POEMS 51 18
+CHRIST'S
  FOR CONTEXT, SEE . . . . 310 VIVA 2 9
  FOR CONTEXT, SEE . . . . 703 95 POEMS 31 16
CHRISTIAN
  is an act of christian love. "Nothing" in 1944 . . . . 636 (CHAIRE) 38 8
CHRISTMAS
  "'Twas the night before Christmas when all through the . . . 142 & SON REAL 13 12
  little tree little silent Christmas tree you are so . . . . . 192 XLI CHANSONS 2 2
  in dem daze kid Christmas meant sumpn youse knows . . . . . . 237 IS 5 ONE 8 13
  (and his tail's red christmas bow) --and if, when . . . . . . 631 (CHAIRE) 33 6
CHRISTOPHER
  On My Couch at Christopher Street For my stomach . . . . . . 101 & POST IMPR 11 58
CHROMATIC
  one unhurried muscled huge chromatic fist skilfully modeling 82 T&C SON ACTU 1 8
CHROME
  i perform squirms of chrome and execute strides of . . . . . 199 XLI PORTRAIT 7 6
CHROMES
  helplessbaby blues and stic-ky chromes and pretty- lemons and 100 & POST IMPR 11 5
CHRYSELEPHANTINE
  goddess loved too well? Chryselephantine Zeus Olympian . . . 3 T&C EPITHALAM 25
CHUBBY
  empty stomachsClenche Dtothe <> cHuBbY stomachs which have . 101 & POST IMPR 11 72

113

	PAGE	TITLE	LINE
CHUCK			
creases of screaming warmth chuck pil- lows are noise	96	& POST IMPR 8	4
amaranth clutch owch so chuck slop hight evolute my	333	VIVA 24	22
andDark IshbusY ing-roundly-dis tinct; chuck lings, laced ar:	416	NO THANKS 33	8
CHUCKING			
have i observed some chucking some legally into Oblivion . .	391	NO THANKS 8	6
+CHUCKING			
FOR CONTEXT, SEE	445	NO THANKS 60	20
CHUCKLED			
its fellow five crumbs chuckled as if they were	117	& PORTRAIT 10	14
CHUCKLES			
hic sum- more eh chuckles skulch.... and i was	96	& POST IMPR 8	22
me suddenly grips in chuckles of supreme sex. In	130	& SON REAL 1	8
the kanoon but Hassan chuckles seeing the Greeks breathe) . .	220	XLI SONNETS 16	16
say solong my tailor chuckles like a woman in	287	IS 5 FOUR 4	12
CHUCKLING			
vast, stomachs bLurting and cHuckling like uninteresting- . .	101	& POST IMPR 11	69
a grim epitome of chuckling flesh. Weak thirsty fists	151	& SON REAL 22	5
your mind drifting with chuckling rubbish of pearl weed . . .	369	VIVA 60	5
+CHUCKLING			
FOR CONTEXT, SEE	350	VIVA 41	7
+CHUCKLINGS			
FOR CONTEXT, SEE	416	NO THANKS 33	8
CHUCKS			
hither in filthy sawdust chucks and rolls against the	259	IS 5 ONE 29	5
rag its of mind chucks away flimsy which but)	501	50 POEMS 15	14
+CHUMP			
FOR CONTEXT, SEE	773	73 POEMS 1	12
CHUNKLIKE			
from thick lids. the chunklike nose on which always	73	T&C SON REAL 4	8
CHURCH			
Thursdays, opposite which a church stood perfectly upright .	263	IS 5 ONE 32	50
procession: and Enters this church. toward which The	280	IS 5 THREE 4	31
is a deaf dumb church and blind with an	647	(CHAIRE) 49	11
i am a little church (no great cathedral) far	749	95 POEMS 77	1
i am a little church (far from the frantic	749	95 POEMS 77	13
CHURCH'S			
minds (also, with the church's protestant blessings	70	T&C SON REAL 1	3
CHURCHES			
without effort while hungering churches (topped with effigies	340	VIVA 31	16
+CHURCHES			
FOR CONTEXT, SEE	444	NO THANKS 59	13
CHURNING			
ing goes utter ly churning witty, twitters upon Our	89	& POST IMPR 1	13
CHUTE			
meassandca V ingint oA chute i had cement for	119	& PORTRAIT 11	8
CI			
/ / / / ci-git 1 Foetus (unborn to	394	NO THANKS 11	1
CI-GIT			
/ / / / ci-git 1 Foetus (unborn to	394	NO THANKS 11	1
CIGAR			
blinds inslants peregrinate, a cigar-stub disintegrates, . .	144	& SON REAL 15	4
and chews a two-bit cigar waiting for the bulls	149	& SON REAL 20	3
pale lips the extinct cigar) at which this (once	252	IS 5 ONE 23	7
Land for a bad cigar is a woman but	466	NEW POEMS 4	27
+CIGAR			
FOR CONTEXT, SEE	552	1 X 1 12	29
CIGAR-STUB			
blinds inslants peregrinate, a cigar-stub disintegrates, . .	144	& SON REAL 15	4
CIGARETTE			
with the year a cigarette between his ghost-lips gradually) .	300	IS 5 FOUR 17	20
something inhaling gently a cigarette (in a mirror /	375	VIVA 66	16
CIGARETTEASH			
nts (while showe ring cigaretteash O ver that scre	726	95 POEMS 54	13
CIGARETTEBUTTS			
habitues their faces like cigarettebutts, chewed with	194	XLI PORTRAIT 2	20
CIGARETTES			
5 ⟨⟩ smoke Helmar cigarettes 2 play backgammon, 3	200	XLI PORTRAIT 8	3

PAGE   TITLE   LINE

CIGARETTES (CONTINUED)
    can't sleep (smoking sawdust cigarettes in the middle of . . 242 IS 5 ONE 13   22
CIGARS
    wreaths of badly Yep cigars who jim him why . . . . 96 & POST IMPR 8   16
CIGARSTINKING
    is persuasive the editor cigarstinking hobgoblin swims upward 259 IS 5 ONE 29   8
CINCINGONDOLANATI
    God only, gondola knows Cincingondolanati i gondola don't . . 256 IS 5 ONE 27   28
+CINCINNATI
    FOR CONTEXT, SEE . . . . 256 IS 5 ONE 27   28
CINDERCOLOURED
    i gaze on the cindercoloured little {MEGA} {HELLENIKON . . . 217 XLI SONNETS 13   14
CINQ
    la guerre j'm'appelle Manon, cinq rue Henri Mounier . . . . . 121 & PORTRAIT 12   35
    Louise with queenly legs cinq rue Henri Mounier a . . . . . . 121 & PORTRAIT 12   46
CIRCLE
    park sits Down. pigeons circle around and around and   . . . . 62 T&C PORTRAIT 10   28
    around the irresponsible toys circle wildly in the slow-ly-in 63 T&C PORTRAIT 10   31
    of an entirely dirty circle of habitues their faces . . . . . 194 XLI PORTRAIT 2   19
CIRCLING
    calm of intent stars circling the acerb pole poises, ...   3 T&C EPITHALAM   31
CIRCULAR
    tures --Children, stand with circular frightened faces   . . . 69 T&C POST IMPR 6   7
    of Nothing grabbed with circular shrieking tightness solid . 195 XLI PORTRAIT 3   14
+CIRCULEZ
    FOR CONTEXT, SEE . . . . 275 IS 5 TWO 9   39
CIRCUMSTANCE
    (an erring child of circumstance whom the bulls nabbed   . . . 266 IS 5 TWO 1   38
CIRCUSHEART
    you had and a circusheart and we miss them . . . . 605 {CHAIRE} 7   6
CIRCUSTENT
    breath bigger than a circustent and everything began when . . 566 1 X 1 26   3
CISEL
    is thatofa fly. pre cisel Yhalf (squashe) d with, ... 94 & POST IMPR 6   27
CITHAREDE
    taut neck of the citharede wags in the dust . . . . 34 T&C ORIENTALE 6   96
CITHERN
    of the emperor a cithern- player squats with quiveringgold . 34 T&C ORIENTALE 6   70
CITIED
    / / / when citied day with the sonorous . . . . 79 T&C SON UNRE 4   1
CITIES
    the currency of faint cities eternal--ere the sinless taint .   9 T&C SONGS 1   33
    distinctly live all sweet cities passed away-- in her . . . . 22 T&C PUELLA MEA   257
    this most exquisite of cities) all of the long . . . . 300 IS 5 FOUR 17   11
    thing -birds) sing- u (cities are houses people are . . . . . 436 NO THANKS 52   14
    sidewalks of houses called cities) spring most singular- ly . 436 NO THANKS 52   17
    spring most singular- ly (cities are houses are) is . . . . . 436 NO THANKS 52   19
    alive and shall be: cities may overflow (am was) . . . . . . 491 50 POEMS 5   11
    and squalor of hurrying cities --i do not worry . . . . 749 95 POEMS 77   2
    streets into faces and cities to eyes) drift bells . . . . . 841 73 POEMS 69   20
CITIZEN
    born a foolishwise proudhumble citizen of ecstasies more . . 845 73 POEMS 73   7
CITIZENS
    dozen staunch and leal citizens did graze at pause . . . . . 258 IS 5 ONE 28   10
    to answer "no"? quote citizens unquote might otherwise forget 636 {CHAIRE} 38   5
+CITIZENS
    FOR CONTEXT, SEE . . . . 548 1 X 1 8   4
    FOR CONTEXT, SEE . . . . 600 {CHAIRE} 2   17
CITY
    and mad, in the city of Bagdad-- mine is . . . . 20 T&C PUELLA MEA   132
    and frail, in the city of Bagdad.) Keep your . . . . 23 T&C PUELLA MEA   288
    of sunset the young city putting off dimension with . . . . . 48 T&C IMPRESS 2   15
    candle is extinguished the city wakes with a song . . . . . . 50 T&C IMPRESS 4   5
    in his bed the city sleeps with death upon . . . .   50 T&C IMPRESS 4   29
    out of a keen city in the sky--filled with . . . . 129 & SEVEN POEMS 7   2
    sailing into a keen city which nobody's ever visited, ... 129 & SEVEN POEMS 7   12
    and by a gestured city stilled in the framing . . . . 158 & SON ACTU 7   10
    of you the holy city which is your face . . . . 186 XLI SONGS 8   6

CITY (CONTINUED)
  life that his fair city might not die. / . . . . 209 XLI SONNETS 5   14
  if scarcely the somewhat city wiggles in considerable . . . . 302 IS 5 FIVE 1   3
  the biggest best busiest city and presently found himself . . 326 VIVA 18   11
  seething of this raving city screamingly street wonderful . . 437 NO THANKS 53   3
CITY'S
  joining with the wonderless city's sublime cheap distinct . . 218 XLI SONNETS 14 7
  small is dirtiest any city's least street) of mirror . . . . 623 (CHAIRE) 25   3
+CIVIC
  FOR CONTEXT, SEE . . . . 258 IS 5 ONE 28   11
CIVIL
  Daniel fought in the civil war band and can . . . . 253 IS 5 ONE 24   2
CIVILIZATION
  more distorting than socalled civilization i'll kiss a . . . 514 50 POEMS 28   12
+CIVILIZE
  FOR CONTEXT, SEE . . . . 547 1 X 1 7   16
CLAIM
  ether the movies may claim general importance to me . . . . . 238 IS 5 ONE 9   15
CLAIMS
  Paree an some guys claims der never was nutn . . . . 237 IS 5 ONE 8   6
CLAMOR
  thought against the magnificent clamor of day tortured in . . 188 XLI SONGS 10   5
CLAMORED
  it up back inley clamored Clever Rusefelt to Theodore . . . . 321 VIVA 13   9
CLAMORS
  and sag of planes clamors of collision collapse As . . . . . 48 T&C IMPRESS 2   8
CLAMPS
  the dainty destroyed hero clamps the hearty sharp column . . 111 & PORTRAIT 6   42
CLAP
  to war with trumpets clap and syphilis / / . . . . 273 IS 5 TWO 8   24
  kiddin eachudder bout duh clap an talkin big how . . . . . . 332 VIVA 23   2
CLAPPED
  the whole he suddenly clapped a tiny sunset of . . . . 148 & SON REAL 19   7
CLARION
  until for wear their clarion voices and boots were . . . . . 339 VIVA 30   25
CLASS
  his youth the upper class American unsullied stands, before . 273 IS 5 TWO 8   16
+CLASS
  FOR CONTEXT, SEE . . . . 339 VIVA 30   27
CLATTERED
  hard- over the tiller; clattered forward skidding in . . . . 277 IS 5 THREE 1   11
CLAUS
  The kid) er Santa Claus a criminal (hears Darwin; . . . . . . 398 NO THANKS 15   14
+CLAUS
  FOR CONTEXT, SEE . . . . 333 VIVA 24   19
CLAUSES
  withs of star link clauses of warmth (after dream . . . . . . 168 & SON ACTU 17   15
CLAY
  is the world's insufferable clay clothed with incognizable .   6 T&C EPITHALAM 135
CLEAN
  in-twin K les Of, CleaN a booming smell waddles . . . . 94 & POST IMPR 6 14
  commenting upon an un- clean table. and, whose distended . . 97 & POST IMPR 8 38
  Eddie in Topeka, went clean daffy, and which was . . . . . . 145 & SON REAL 16   7
  sometimes makes gaily go clean through me tickling aches, . . 147 & SON REAL 18   7
  the, clothes which are clean --this is twilight, a . . . . . 167 & SON ACTU 16   6
  replies "I can!" --yon clean upstanding well dressed boy . . 273 IS 5 TWO 8   6
  fearlessly obscene but really clean get what I mean . . . . . 407 NO THANKS 24   7
  ones;the mean kind dirty clean) all except the green . . . . 619 (CHAIRE) 21   26
  meet mr universe (who clean and jerked 300 lbs) . . . . 645 (CHAIRE) 47   1
+CLEAN
  FOR CONTEXT, SEE . . . . 194 XLI PORTRAIT 2 33
CLEANCORNERED
  men who praise Marj's cleancornered strokable body these . . 114 & PORTRAIT 7   5
CLEANED
  for him, and they cleaned up a few times--before . . . . . . 145 & SON REAL 16   5
CLEANERS
  dictaphones wireless subways vacuum cleaners pianolas . . . . 237 IS 5 ONE 8   10

+CLEANERS
   FOR CONTEXT, SEE . . . . 549 1 X 1 9   12
CLEANEST
   him) two were the cleanest keenest bravest killers you'd . . 709 95 POEMS 37   5
CLEANSHAVEN
   with pimples, correctly dressed, cleanshaven above the . . . 262 IS 5 ONE 32   8
CLEAR
   whose head stands that clear candle whose expecting breath .   6 T&C EPITHALAM   117
   have made this perfectly clear, it entirely would have . . . 263 IS 5 ONE 32   64
CLEARER
   opposite? Nothing could be clearer to all concerned than . . 263 IS 5 ONE 32   40
   i can't make it clearer war just isn't what . . . . 638 {CHAIRE} 40   8
CLEARING
   house wellsweep forest & clearing) gone are enormous near . . 755 95 POEMS 83   4
CLEAT
   of silence. The inspired cleat of her glad leg . . . . 135 & SON REAL 6   3
CLEAVING
   smelloftheworld. We intricately alive, cleaving the luminous 174 & SON ACTU 23   4
CLENCHED
   too large lips always clenched faintly, wishes you with . . . 72 T&C SON REAL 3   7
   street's DarkcOOllonGBody windows, are. clenched. fists of . 100 & POST IMPR 11   16
   on a caret of clenched arms a delicately elephantine . . . . 143 & SON REAL 14   1
   the hairy notching of clenched thighs a friendless dingy . . 151 & SON REAL 22   17
   my life; the grim clenched mind of me somewhere . . . . 156 & SON ACTU 5   11
   vest its wideflung friend clenched weakly dirt while the . . 258 IS 5 ONE 28   18
+CLENCHED
   FOR CONTEXT, SEE . . . . 101 & POST IMPR 11   71
CLEOPATRA
   / / / / Cleopatra built like a smooth . . . . 110 & PORTRAIT 6   1
   stops of her body Cleopatra had a body it . . . . 110 & PORTRAIT 6   14
   or a smooth arrow Cleopatra is eaten by yester- . . . . 111 & PORTRAIT 6   48
   amorous in memory of Cleopatra and of Antony and . . . . . . 111 & PORTRAIT 6   58
   brain in memory of Cleopatra while easily tremendously floats 111 & PORTRAIT 6   71
   kind black great god) Cleopatra you are eaten by . . . . . . 112 & PORTRAIT 6   89
   and your skyscrapers--Helen & Cleopatra were Just Too Lovely, 230 IS 5 ONE 2   27
CLERK
   and nun merchant frere clerk somnour miller and reve . . . . 661 {CHAIRE} 63   10
CLEVER
   i have seen death's clever enormous voice which hides . . . . 45 T&C LA GUERRE 1   4
   time to time by clever drolls fearsomely who do . . . . 74 T&C SON REAL 5   10
   may not confuse the clever hair nor rout the . . . . 85 T&C SON ACTU 4   7
   colour floating against the clever deadly heaven i salute . . 112 & PORTRAIT 6   107
   in the morning dead's clever too like POF goes . . . . 126 & SEVEN POEMS 5   10
   up back inley clamored Clever Rusefelt to Theodore Odysseus . 321 VIVA 13   9
   smoothly gesturing stars are clever to persuade even silence: 376 VIVA 67   8
   seem not quite so clever as the pratfall of . . . . 414 NO THANKS 31   2
   (sighs mind: and he's clever) "for all, yes for . . . . 625 {CHAIRE} 27   6
   / / handsome and clever and he went cruising . . . . 709 95 POEMS 37   1
CLEVEREST
   yes Will that was cleverest he was kilt and . . . . 271 IS 5 TWO 6   6
CLEVERJERK
   dark tool. With a cleverjeRk in itlike the motionofa . . . . 101 & POST IMPR 11   50
CLEVERLY
   he will pick it cleverly from, the air and . . . . 69 T&C POST IMPR 6   10
   does. the brain of cleverly-crinkling -water pursues the . . 160 & SON ACTU 9   4
   i feel that i cleverly am being altered that . . . . 199 XLI PORTRAIT 7   8
   rush of upward lips.... cleverly perching on the sudden . . . 201 XLI PORTRAIT 9   29
   Kneeland, and a waiter cleverly lugs indigestible honeycake . 217 XLI SONNETS 13   8
   which we call autumn, cleverly dies and over the . . . . . . 293 IS 5 FOUR 10   23
   he- shaped object vomits cleverly against a quai wall . . . . 324 VIVA 16   6
   the how dis (appeared cleverly) world iS Slapped: with; . . . 347 VIVA 38   4
CLEVERLY-CRINKLING
   does. the brain of cleverly-crinkling -water pursues the . . 160 & SON ACTU 9   4
CLICHES
   one cocked eyebrow) subtracting cliches un by un till . . . . 605 {CHAIRE} 7   2
CLICK
   my com- forter a click of deciding glory inflicted . . . . . 197 XLI PORTRAIT 5   16
   i sit in the click of ivory balls.... noting . . . . 217 XLI SONNETS 13   2

	PAGE	TITLE	LINE

CLICK (CONTINUED)
  a secondhand set which click) little gould used to . . . . . 410 NO THANKS 27   2
  for Freedom slaves will click; where Boobs are holy, ... 438 NO THANKS 54   18
+CLICK
  FOR CONTEXT, SEE . . . . 180 XLI SONGS 2   4
CLICKING
  grin. her sow- eyes clicking mischief from thick lids. . . . 73 T&C SON REAL 4   7
CLIFF
  eats into a pink cliff back and up leaning . . . . 281 IS 5 THREE 5   9
  in grass upon a cliff) what had been something . . . . . . 283 IS 5 THREE 7   24
  to perceive buried in cliff precisely at the Ending . . . . . 435 NO THANKS 51   40
CLIMB
  through loam. (afterward i'll climb by tall careful muscles . 67 T&C POST IMPR 4 14
  whispers understand sobs bigly climb what (love being some- . 358 VIVA 49   7
  seriously i begin to climb the best hill, driven . . . . . . 434 NO THANKS 51   6
  my spirit you tumble climb and mightily fatally i . . . . . . 434 NO THANKS 51   28
  firm swirl hips whirling climb to GIVE (yoursmine mineyours . 445 NO THANKS 60   27
  wandering guess) while children climb their eyes to touch . . 517 50 POEMS 31   14
  as earth will downward climb, so naked for immortal . . . . . 521 50 POEMS 34   42
  it into if shall climb all the blue heaven . . . . 588 1 X 1 48   2
  through a gold moment) climb: ing i -nto wintry . . . . . . 627 (CHAIRE) 29   2
  all the little fish climb through the mind of . . . . 665 (CHAIRE) 67   20
  (and consequently dare to climb the sky) because a . . . . 679 95 POEMS 7   6
  you and did i climb (crazily kissing) till into . . . . . . 694 95 POEMS 22   2
  days of dark, will climb; will blossom: will sing . . . . . 735 95 POEMS 63   13
  (spiralling as luminous they climb oblivion) voices who are . 810 73 POEMS 38   6
  bright all things swim climb minds (down slowly swoop . . . . 841 73 POEMS 69   28
  ecstasies more steep than climb can time with all . . . . . 845 73 POEMS 73   8
+CLIMB
  FOR CONTEXT, SEE . . . . 423 NO THANKS 40   30
CLIMBED
  that he also had climbed the pincian to appreciate . . . . 355 VIVA 46   12
  crazy they drink who've climbed steeper than hopes are . . . 563 1 X 1 23   2
  a fish but it climbed like a dream) throbbing . . . . 593 1 X 1 53   10
CLIMBI
  / / / mortals) climbi ng i nto eachness . . . . 536 50 POEMS 48   2
CLIMBING
  huge trudging kiss moistly climbing hideously with large . . 67 T&C POST IMPR 4   25
  wisti-twisti barber -pole is climbing people high, up-in . . 128 & SEVEN POEMS 6   3
  always only exhales a climbing dark exact walloping human . . 202 XLI PORTRAIT 9 44
  looks breathes or moves --climbing (past light after light) . 300 IS 5 FOUR 17   4
  up stairs, carefully (carefully climbing carpeted flight . 375 VIVA 66   12
  carpeted flight. in stillness, climbing the carpeted stairs . 375 VIVA 66   13
  greenthatpink) acrobata mong trees climbing on A pi llarofch 385 NO THANKS 2   46
  from whispers to stars; climbing silence for ifs diving . . . 439 NO THANKS 55   23
  love loved whose his climbing shoulders queerly twilight : . 490 50 POEMS 4   19
  fear much than more climbing hope meets most despair? . . . . 528 50 POEMS 40   9
  might these be thrushes climbing through almost (do they . . 582 1 X 1 42   1
  unworld's most rightful wrong climbing, my love (till . . . . 745 95 POEMS 73   2
  while this dream is climbing sky (until his voice . . . . . . 752 95 POEMS 80   5
  a true) and a climbing fall into far near . . . . 769 95 POEMS 95   21
  star, if out of climbing whom begins to spill . . . . 811 73 POEMS 39   12
  time you unbecame where climbing was and bright is . . . . 834 73 POEMS 62   19
+CLIMBING
  FOR CONTEXT, SEE . . . . 278 IS 5 THREE 2   10
CLIMBINGLY
  he most him --the climbingly fallingest fool in this . . . . 590 1 X 1 50   14
CLIMBS
  under myhis chin.) that climbs and cries and runs . . . . . 69 T&C POST IMPR 6   43
  eating steepness the ship climbs murmuring silver mountains . 419 NO THANKS 36   15
  outthunders silence. And (night climbs the air / / . . . . . 428 NO THANKS 45   18
  perfectly their imperfect gaze climbs this steep fragrance of 450 NO THANKS 65   8
  (in -to day's bloodlight climbs the onlying world) whose . . 719 95 POEMS 47   2
CLIMBSCR
  hows of whi ne climbscr e AM e xploding . . . . 795 73 POEMS 23   21
CLINCHED
  Distinct face haughtily vital clinched in a swoon of . . . . 193 XLI PORTRAIT 1   3

		PAGE	TITLE	LINE

CLING
```
  eyes beyond a fit- and-cling of stuffs the alert  . . . . . .  155   & SON ACTU 4     9
  which do so frailly cling....) i who am but  . . . . . . . . .  215   XLI SONNETS 11  10
  ourselves which shout and cling, being for a little  . . . . .  264   IS 5 ONE 33     14
  silently who are and cling to my mind always  . . . . . . .    301   IS 5 FOUR 18    10
  was and that was cling) on win ter sc  . . . . . . . . . . . .  415   NO THANKS 32     4
  one who are) lovers cling & kiss neither beholding  . . . . .  698   95 POEMS 26      6
```
CLINGING
```
  remained --the stone cringes clinging to the stone, how . . .  260   IS 5 ONE 30      5
  touching hearts slenderly comprehend (clinging as fingers, .   305   IS 5 FIVE 4      2
  are these (wraith a clinging with a wraith) ghosts  . . . . .  639   (CHAIRE) 41      1
```
+CLINGING
```
  FOR CONTEXT, SEE  . . . . . . . . . . . . . . . . . . . . . .  632   (CHAIRE) 34     15
```
CLINGS
```
  pale meaning of heaven clings, (whose million leaves in . . .    6   T&C EPITHALAM  124
  love, my love! soul clings and heart conceives and  . . . . .  386   NO THANKS 3     12
```
CLINK
```
  think of you, getting mandolin-clink mixed with your hair;  .  169   & SON ACTU 18    5
```
CLOAKED
```
  that by responding ways cloaked with renewal my body  . . . .  184   XLI SONGS 6      7
```
CLOCK
```
  stale shriek like an alarm-clock) / / / / .  . . . . . . . . .   49   T&C IMPRESS 3   28
  sound: if a (perhaps) clock strikes, in the alive . . . . . .   92   & POST IMPR 4   14
  and there was a clock. tac-tic. tac-toc. Time and . . . . . .  133   & SON REAL 4     7
  invitation is like a clock striking in a dark . . . . . . . .  229   IS 5 ONE FRAN   15
  of a cloud a clock strikes midnight a finger  . . . . . . . .  338   VIVA 29         22
  (have died beyond the clock) we, of ourselves who . . . . . .  386   NO THANKS 3      2
  against the west one Clock dimly cries nine, i  . . . . . . .  434   NO THANKS 51    14
  any ticking of a clock / / / /  . . . . . . . . . . . . . . .  617   (CHAIRE) 19     14
```
CLOCKS
```
  And thighs forget (when clocks whisper and night shouts)  . .  359   VIVA 50          2
  house of my mind. Clocks strike. The moon's round,  . . . . .  365   VIVA 56          3
  away --and all the clocks would run down the  . . . . . . . .  365   VIVA 56         14
  stares colossal hoax of clocks and calendars / /  . . . . . .  659   (CHAIRE) 61     14
  shallbe or was (laws clocks fears hopes beliefs compulsions .  755   95 POEMS 83     16
  seem) believe me, dear, clocks have enough to do  . . . . . .  817   73 POEMS 45      7
```
CLOGS
```
  nudging froth of faces clogs Second as Mrs. Somethingwich . .  219   XLI SONNETS 15  11
```
CLOSE
```
  when all occasional things close into silence, only one . . .    6   T&C EPITHALAM  122
  space i saw you close your eyes and i . . . . . . . . . . . .   30   T&C ORIENTALE 4 34
  her briefness in singing close her with intricate faint . . .   65   T&C POST IMPR 2  9
  moon-cease soon verbal mist-flowers close ghosts on prowl . .   90   & POST IMPR 2   14
  commemoration, (from whose faint close as some grave  . . . .  206   XLI SONNETS 2   12
  opening of the chambers close quotes the microscopic  . . . .  267   IS 5 TWO 2       1
  possession of quotes keltyer close " " aureally (yawning . .   331   VIVA 22          6
  your wish be to close me, i and my  . . . . . . . . . . . . .  366   VIVA 57          9
  whom did merely day close) opens if more than . . . . . . . .  450   NO THANKS 65     2
  open for you and close will shy wings of  . . . . . . . . . .  575   1 X 1 35        15
  while your sweet eyes close have disappeared a million  . . .  588   1 X 1 48         5
  worlds open and worlds close?" "Worlds do, but differently; .  603   (CHAIRE) 5       7
  to understand they'd never close (and open) if that . . . . .  603   (CHAIRE) 5       9
  ocean is compelled to close when the oak begs . . . . . . . .  620   (CHAIRE) 22      8
  while he passed (as close as i'm to you . . . . . . . . . . .  648   (CHAIRE) 50      9
  caution for curiosity (and close your eyes) / / . . . . . . .  689   95 POEMS 17      8
```
CLOSED
```
  roses he laughed, and closed his eyes as a  . . . . . . . . .  170   & SON ACTU 19   13
  ripe air Alive with closed eyes to dash against . . . . . . .  189   XLI SONGS 11     6
  me though i have closed myself as fingers, you  . . . . . . .  366   VIVA 57          6
```
CLOSELY
```
  (merely beyond how very) closely than Nothing, remember love  453   NO THANKS 68     7
```
CLOSER
```
  i'm to you yes closer made of nothing except  . . . . . . . .  648   (CHAIRE) 50     10
```
CLOSES
```
  eyes as a girl closes her left hand upon  . . . . . . . . . .  170   & SON ACTU 19   13
  for the swallow, that closes a flight in the  . . . . . . . .  181   XLI SONGS 3      4
  is about you that closes and opens; only something  . . . . .  366   VIVA 57         17
```

CLOSING
    expels (over Selene's car closing uncouth) of Helios the ..   4 T&C EPITHALAM   47
CLOTH
    is carpeted with gold cloth from the ceiling (one ...... 32 T&C ORIENTALE 6 22
    insinuating upon the gold cloth incessantly creates patterns 34 T&C ORIENTALE 6 87
CLOTHE
    heels of passed afterday, clothe thy soul's coming merely, . 10 T&C SONGS 1   40
CLOTHED
    the world's insufferable clay clothed with incognizable ...   6 T&C EPITHALAM 136
    finger of thitherhithering gas. clothed with a luminous fur . 134 & SON REAL 5   13
    love you) last night clothed in sealace appeared to ..... 369 VIVA 60   2
    with its spirit floated (clothed only in the tide's ..... 369 VIVA 60   20
CLOTHES
    you take all your prickley-clothes off and squeeze- ..... 127 & SEVEN POEMS 5 33
    sticking out breasts hanging clothes. On the line. not ... 167 & SON ACTU 16   2
    dirty wind, twitches the, clothes which are clean --this .. 167 & SON ACTU 16   6
    unlocked by white-grub faces) clothes in delicate hubbub as . 172 & SON ACTU 21   7
    to peer and wear clothes. i am altogether foolish, ... 281 IS 5 THREE 5   18
    (for love's secret supremely clothes herself with day) i . 379 VIVA 70   5
    whats are a (piercing clothes thoughts kiss -ing wishes ... 437 NO THANKS 53   6
    was young Up floatingly clothes tumbledish olD (with sprouts 534 50 POEMS 46   5
+CLOTHES
    FOR CONTEXT, SEE .... 237 IS 5 ONE 8   17
CLOTHS
    the weak colour of table-cloths, the electric When In .... 217 XLI SONNETS 13   4
CLOTTED
    death the annual brain clotted with loosely voices look ... 99 & POST IMPR 10   6
CLOTTINGSAND
    drenching. earth's brain detaches clottingsand from a a nnual 99 & POST IMPR 10   21
CLOUD
    gathers morte carved smiles cloud-gloss is at moon-cease soon 90 & POST IMPR 2   12
    swims out of a cloud a clock strikes midnight .... 338 VIVA 29   21
    or cause one causeless cloud to purely grow but, ... 433 NO THANKS 50   4
    with faces made of cloud dancing and three singing .... 507 50 POEMS 21   6
    on a proud round cloud in a white high .... 631 {CHAIRE} 33   4
CLOUD-GLOSS
    gathers morte carved smiles cloud-gloss is at moon-cease soon 90 & POST IMPR 2   12
CLOUDS
    houses and steeples and clouds: go sailing away and .... 129 & SEVEN POEMS 7   9
    to illimitable dissipation unhurried clouds of incense ... 206 XLI SONNETS 2   14
    is tumbling in sand Clouds over me are like .... 281 IS 5 THREE 5   15
    are Made leaves open Clouds take sun mountains stand .... 359 VIVA 50   12
    murders. cries: hopes; houses, clouds. kisses, lice; .... 361 VIVA 52   19
    each (shyly) other, what clouds do or Silently Flowers ... 363 VIVA 54   10
    whose foul windows absurd clouds cruise nobly ridiculous .. 442 NO THANKS 57   13
    all around around all clouds singing three and and .... 507 50 POEMS 21   19
CLOVEN
    the imprint of whose cloven feet the shrieking dryad ....   3 T&C EPITHALAM   13
CLOVER
    like a piece of clover, from the green meadow .... 370 VIVA 61   5
    angry seasalt and indignant clover marrying to themselves .. 376 VIVA 67   4
    and what may be clover clover clover (nobody'll know) .... 568 1 X 1 28   23
    what may be clover clover clover (nobody'll know) sam .... 568 1 X 1 28   24
    may be clover clover clover (nobody'll know) sam was .... 568 1 X 1 28   24
    "spring follows winter: as clover knows, maybe" (heart makes 625 {CHAIRE} 27   10
CLOVERISH
    the truth) enter a cloverish silence of thrushsong (and ... 745 95 POEMS 73   3
CLOWN
    the pratfall of a clown (should stink of failure ..... 414 NO THANKS 31   2
    fail immeasurable fate) coward, clown, traitor, idiot, ... 562 1 X 1 22   9
    mischievous tenderly phoebeing alter) clown of an angel ... 678 95 POEMS 6   8
    truck a wistful little clown whom somebody buried upsidedown 680 95 POEMS 8   7
    world to build our clown --shouting to see what ...... 716 95 POEMS 44   12
    becomes if) a bespangled clown standing on eighth street .. 802 73 POEMS 30   4
    fine not a coarse clown (no mob, but a .... 802 73 POEMS 30   23
+CLOWN
    FOR CONTEXT, SEE .... 342 VIVA 33   20
    FOR CONTEXT, SEE .... 471 NEW POEMS 9   16

CLOWN'S
   / / / a clown's smirk in the skull . . . . 360 VIVA 51   1
CLOWNLIKE
   a very crazily how clownlike that this quickly ghost . . . . 504 50 POEMS 18   7
CLUB
   cigar-stub disintegrates, above, underdrawers club the . . . 144 & SON REAL 15   5
   wields easily the pale club of the wind and . . . . 163 & SON ACTU 12   5
+CLUCKING
   FOR CONTEXT, SEE . . . . 350 VIVA 41   7
CLUE
   furnished a soft first clue to his innumerable whereabouts . 197 XLI PORTRAIT 5   5
CLUETT
   you, land of the Cluett Shirt Boston Garter and . . . . . . 230 IS 5 ONE 2   4
CLUMSIEST
   will stumble beneath a clumsiest disguise, appear capable of 91 & POST IMPR 3   12
CLUMSILY
   it sour gnomes tumble clumsily, the little box is . . . . . 69 T&C POST IMPR 6   3
   and frantic fairies gush clumsily from the battered box . . . 69 T&C POST IMPR 6   22
   which detaching itself bumps clumsi- into the throat A . . . 201 XLI PORTRAIT 9   10
   of centrifugally expecting faces clumsily which devours a . . 279 IS 5 THREE 3   7
   morning Memory stands, with clumsily wilted fingers emptying 359 VIVA 50   6
   gird, a coward waiting clumsily to cease whom every . . . . . 360 VIVA 51   6
   / / item: is Clumsily with of what manshaped . . . . 371 VIVA 62   2
   lusting glance an alert clumsily foolishwise (tracking the . 374 VIVA 65   6
   sorry) creatures out of (clumsily shining out of) instru- . . 442 NO THANKS 57   5
   prayers of earth's own clumsily striving (finding and losing 749 95 POEMS 77   6
CLUMSY
   uncouth prison, a precise clumsy prison (building thatandthis 83 T&C SON ACTU 2   6
   minute adventure) lady. The clumsy dark threatens (and i . . 98 & POST IMPR 9   13
   and the spring; a clumsy brightness of air wonderfully . . . 173 & SON ACTU 22   2
   lewdly the murmurous minute clumsy smelloftheworld. We . . . 174 & SON ACTU 23   2
   out of the spontaneous clumsy trivi- al acrobatic edgeless . 193 XLI PORTRAIT 1   19
   lips the sweet small clumsy feet of April came . . . . 306 IS 5 FIVE 5   14
   your sweet innocence refuted) clumsy some dull cowardice . . 669 {CHAIRE} 71   11
CLUSTERED
   of paradise-- by angelfaces clustered like bright lice about 85 T&C SON ACTU 4   3
CLUTCH
   your dear strong fingers clutch his heart, as mine . . . . . 76 T&C SON UNRE 1   3
   her up, slipped the clutch (and then somehow got . . . . . . 248 IS 5 ONE 19   11
   fainarain wee celibate amaranth clutch owch so chuck slop . . 333 VIVA 24   21
   & were who skies clutch an of poor how . . . . 491 50 POEMS 5   3
   into a dead house clutch between eyes emptiness toss . . . . 522 50 POEMS 35   2
   (gorgedis reswal lowing spewnonspew clutch) pers again & . . 629 {CHAIRE} 31   18
   als 2 ph antoms clutch ed in a writhewho . . . . 795 73 POEMS 23   15
CLUTCHED
   splintering foam caught you clutched you upon my mouth . . . 30 T&C ORIENTALE 4   13
   fists of shrill colour, clutched the dull volume of . . . . . 73 T&C SON REAL 4   5
   puppet of once man (clutched by immense the-seat-of-the pants 616 {CHAIRE} 18   5
   rind with a photograph clutched in the half of . . . . 647 {CHAIRE} 49   3
+CLUTCHED
   FOR CONTEXT, SEE . . . . 795 73 POEMS 23   15
CLUTCHING
   whom of girl) dolls clutching their dolls wallow toys . . . . 565 1 X 1 25   5
CLUTTER
   April resolved into a clutter of trite jewels now . . . . . . 47 T&C IMPRESS 1   6
CLUTTERED
   with red grumbling face cluttered in pursuit pleasantly . . . 56 T&C PORTRAIT 4   7
   graveyard dreams through its cluttered and brittle emblems, . 434 NO THANKS 51   23
CO
   un der, a lo co mo tive s pout . . . . 179 XLI SONGS 1   15
   Sumner Volstead Christ and Co. the epoch of Mann's . . . . . 266 IS 5 TWO 1   2
   it was a goodly co which paid to make . . . . 552 1 X 1 12   1
COACH
   shall --and Love's a coach with gilt hopeless wheels . . . . 131 & SON REAL 2   15
COACHMAN
   hands again, the former coachman with a pipewrench of . . . . 263 IS 5 ONE 32   45
COAL
   so what yoo-gointa-doo? (ice coal wood man) nic he . . . . . 618 {CHAIRE} 20   20

		PAGE	TITLE	LINE
+COAL				
FOR CONTEXT, SEE	680	95 POEMS 8	5
COARSE				
how myself has been coarse and dull compared with	301	IS 5 FOUR 18	8
a fine not a coarse clown (no mob, but	802	73 POEMS 30	23
COAST				
sank just off the coast of Sum precisely where	494	50 POEMS 8	4
COAT				
has a little red coat with i have a	69	T&C POST IMPR 6	41
lovehouse who buttons his coat against the wind /	115	& PORTRAIT 8	28
in a new frock coat (scrambling all up over	267	IS 5 TWO 2	4
the boulevards without his coat and hat --(and i	296	IS 5 FOUR 13	8
death to change their coat --which something as you'll . . .	544	1 X 1 4	12
COATS				
& arms brush dirt coats smile looking hands spit	275	IS 5 TWO 9	45
COAX				
a billion brains may coax undeath from fancied fact	664	(CHAIRE) 66	19
COBALT				
bloated rose coiled within cobalt miles of sky yield	93	& POST IMPR 5	6
and execute strides of cobalt nevertheless i feel that . . .	199	XLI PORTRAIT 7	6
COCKATOO				
now, as Mr bowing Cockatoo proffers the meaning of	697	95 POEMS 25	27
COCKED				
crimson nose and coquettishly- cocked bonnet having ceased .	196	XLI PORTRAIT 4	5
jack--tactfully you (with one cocked eyebrow) subtracting . .	605	(CHAIRE) 7	1
COCKNEY				
stinking joyman bar a cockney is buying whiskies for	108	& PORTRAIT 4	11
COCODRILLO				
Campanile, believe thou me cocodrillo-- mine eyes have seen .	256	IS 5 ONE 27	9
COD				
Buch tooked out his C.O.D. Abe tucks it up	321	VIVA 13	7
CODIFIED				
originally spontaneous twurls-of-excrement inanely codified .	94	& POST IMPR 6	3
COEDS				
netsam our spinsters and coeds) thoroughly bretish they scout	492	50 POEMS 6	4
COERCION				
blood accuse him of coercion or mind and soul	683	95 POEMS 11	3
COFFEE				
in together and drink coffee covered with froth half-mud . .	198	XLI PORTRAIT 6	32
b cries "effendi" "Uh" "coffee" "uh" enter paperboy, c . . .	200	XLI PORTRAIT 8	10
effendi approaches, sets down coffee withdraws a and c . . .	200	XLI PORTRAIT 8	19
men ....one perfectly smooth coffee tasting of hellas, i . .	217	XLI SONNETS 13	10
COFFIN				
when my Uncle Sol's coffin lurched because somebody pressed .	239	IS 5 ONE 10	33
COFFIN'S				
it's just like a coffin's inside when you die, ...	198	XLI PORTRAIT 6	1
COFFINLID				
crumbs stooping by the coffinlid waiting for something to . .	117	& PORTRAIT 10	5
COGITATING				
the nearest 1; surreptitiously cogitating the dictum of a . .	327	VIVA 18	38
COGNOMEN				
"Gay" is the captivating cognomen of a Young Woman	326	VIVA 18	1
COGNOSCENTI				
/ / from the cognoscenti bingbongwhom chewchoo laugh dingle .	333	VIVA 24	1
COHERENT				
hugging with the rash, coherent light) only to	155	& SON ACTU 4	6
COHN				
lies down with the cohn) down above all with	466	NEW POEMS 4	20
COHORTS				
or what not enthusiastic cohorts from Duluth God only, . . .	256	IS 5 ONE 27	27
COIL				
ightsm issingupperc uts-lurc hhurt-re coil charge &) swooN .	388	NO THANKS 5	18
COILED				
acres of bloated rose coiled within cobalt miles of	93	& POST IMPR 5	6
COIN				
you toss him a coin he will pick it	69	T&C POST IMPR 6	10
little thickness of the coin comes here a man	531	50 POEMS 43	8

	PAGE	TITLE	LINE

COINS
blood and flesh) Love coins His most gradual gesture, ... 297 IS 5 FOUR 14   12
COITNLY
a goil and she coitnly can shimmie when you . . . . 235 IS 5 ONE 6   6
COLD
gashed by hair's blue cold jolts of lovecrazed abrupt . . . . 106 & PORTRAIT 2   9
to the cruel-littleness of cold (when battling street-lamps . 142 & SON REAL 13   2
room. he knocked her cold and beat it for . . . . 145 & SON REAL 16   4
Yes to wind and cold; and how much earth . . . . 183 XLI SONGS 5   11
hair, thy lips are cold with songs for which . . . . 190 XLI SONGS 12   4
dreams (proud through the cold perfect night whisperless to . 205 XLI SONNETS 1   6
hours and hope (by cold espoused unto fear) in . . . . 207 XLI SONNETS 3   7
Time storms and rough cold, wind's menace and leaf's . . . . 207 XLI SONNETS 3   10
but the skunks caught cold and died and so . . . . 239 IS 5 ONE 10   22
ly (goes folds? folds) cold stones (o-l-d) names aren'ts . . 417 NO THANKS 34   7
/ nonsun blob a cold to skylessness sticking fire . . . . . . 541 1 X 1 1   2
sleek) all except the cold ones paul scorns all . . . . 619 (CHAIRE) 21   6
scream and a keen cold groan while the gadgets . . . . 647 (CHAIRE) 49   8
souls sit round with cold three (huddling a- gainst . . . . . 687 95 POEMS 15   4
the murdering minus of cold --open this ghost with . . . . . 839 73 POEMS 67   10
COLDING
an of poor how colding hereless. air theres what . . . . . . 491 50 POEMS 5   4
COLLAPSE
planes clamors of collision collapse As peacefully, lifted . 48 T&C IMPRESS 2   10
+COLLAPSED
FOR CONTEXT, SEE . . . . 710 95 POEMS 38   2
COLLAPSES
gold, which presently crumpled collapses. exhaling a red soul 188 XLI SONGS 10   10
batter the crowd sprawls collapses singing knocked down . . . 274 IS 5 TWO 9   6
(the roar of traffic collapses: through west ninth slowly . . 800 73 POEMS 28   18
COLLAPSING
of day are worlds collapsing? any was a glove . . . . 538 50 POEMS 50   9
forevering am-- and as collapsing that grey mind by . . . . . 599 (CHAIRE) 1   6
+COLLAPSING
FOR CONTEXT, SEE . . . . 646 (CHAIRE) 48   5
+COLLAPSINGLY
FOR CONTEXT, SEE . . . . 330 VIVA 21   4
COLLAR
the filth of a collar hung gently. (spattered) by . . . . . . 96 & POST IMPR 8   31
tweak- ing his wing collar pecking at his im . . . . 274 IS 5 TWO 9   33
I thereupon loosened my collar and dove for the . . . . 327 VIVA 18   37
just by the dirty collar of his jacket were . . . . 355 VIVA 46   6
without any bird, a collar looking for a dog, ... 360 VIVA 51   26
COLLARBUTTON
never have gathered. A collarbutton which had always not . . 262 IS 5 ONE 32   16
COLLARS
and Earl & Wilson Collars) of you i sing: . . . . 230 IS 5 ONE 2   10
WEAR earl & wilson COLLARS / / / / . . . . 244 IS 5 ONE 15   5
trunk, under some dirty collars) only a moment (or . . . . . 296 IS 5 FOUR 13   12
COLLECT
new nice pine box (collect / / / / . . . . 270 IS 5 TWO 5   21
COLLECTIVE
a heart. Huge this collective pseudobeast (sans either pain . 544 1 X 1 4   5
too small. Swoop (shrill collective myth) into thy grave . . 579 1 X 1 39   9
COLLECTS
brighter than a spoon, collects the image of one . . . . . . 360 VIVA 51   22
COLLEGE
of instruction at radcliffe college, cambridge, mass. i try . 327 VIVA 18   44
man should go to college is so that she . . . . 700 95 POEMS 28   7
+COLLEGE
FOR CONTEXT, SEE . . . . 700 95 POEMS 28   15
COLLIDE
impact with the inutile collide once more with the . . . . . 289 IS 5 FOUR 6   7
of proud inwardlyness to collide spirally with iron . . . . . 311 VIVA 3   11
upsquirtingly careens the to collide flatfooting with . . . . 330 VIVA 21   10
+COLLIDE
FOR CONTEXT, SEE . . . . 347 VIVA 38   14

COLLIDES
   flops along the grass collides with trees and houses . . . . 47 T&C IMPRESS 1   9
COLLIDING
   dusty heroisms and finally colliding with the most expensive 203 XLI LA GUERRE 1   11
   beautifully in shrill armour colliding on huge blue horses, . 302 IS 5 FIVE 1   13
COLLIDINGLY
   beyond worlds: immortal yonder collidingly absorbs eternal . 376 VIVA 67   13
COLLISION
   of planes clamors of collision collapse As peacefully, lifted 48 T&C IMPRESS 2   9
COLLYWOBBLING
   seeing your bald intellect collywobbling on its feeble stem . 329 VIVA 20   3
COLON
   son a woopsing queer colon hobby photography never has . . . 499 50 POEMS 13   10
COLONEL
   his fearless derriere sturdily seated--Colonel Needless To . 266 IS 5 TWO 1   22
   conscientious object-or his wellbeloved colonel (trig . . . . 339 VIVA 30   4
COLOSSAL
   deafly a most stares colossal hoax of clocks and . . . . . . 659 (CHAIRE) 61   14
   / / / spirit colossal (& daunted by always . . . .   678 95 POEMS 6   1
COLOSSUS
   Chryselephantine Zeus Olympian sceptred colossus of the . . .   3 T&C EPITHALAM   26
   a delicately experi- menting colossus whose irrefutable . . . 201 XLI PORTRAIT 9   25
COLOUR
   her cheek the beauteous colour went with every bough . . . .   8 T&C OF NICOL   30
   two fists of shrill colour, clutched the dull volume . . . .   73 T&C SON REAL 4   4
   instrument yours the preposterous colour unbeheld --mine the   84 T&C SON ACTU 3   2
   this: if to the colour of midnight to a . . . .   92 & POST IMPR 4   2
   gestures of rain a colour comes, which is morning, ...   92 & POST IMPR 4   17
   of lame and begging colour) while there and here . . . . . .   93 & POST IMPR 5   15
   wincing upon a single colour, i know only that . . . .   98 & POST IMPR 9   7
   cool tunnel of raving colour, on either side the . . . . . . 100 & POST IMPR 11   3
   a sinuous problem of colour floating against the clever . . . 112 & PORTRAIT 6   105
   tiny streets shrugging with colour) the mouth who sits . . . 143 & SON REAL 14   4
   this wilting wall the colour drub souring sunbeams, of . . . 144 & SON REAL 15   1
   tiny sunset of vermouth -colour. Hair. he put between . . . . 148 & SON REAL 19   9
   little more like curving colour (say orange) against silence, 152 & SON ACTU 1   3
   jerk upon the weak colour of table-cloths, the electric . . . 217 XLI SONNETS 13   4
   and by a fat colour reared itself against the . . . . 283 IS 5 THREE 7   19
   wilted fingers emptying youth colour and what was into . . . 359 VIVA 50   7
   compels me with the colour of its countries, rendering . . . 366 VIVA 57   15
   as rain is unto colour; create me gradually (or . . . . 372 VIVA 63   1
   joists hewn from hugest colour (and which night hoists . . . 378 VIVA 69   10
   wish firmly. splendidly advancing colour strike into form .   422 NO THANKS 39   4
   breathing should cause a colour and i do not . . . . 450 NO THANKS 65   14
   night's almosT Floats a colour (in -to day's bloodlight . . . 719 95 POEMS 47   1
   for whom crumbs of colour can create precision more . . . . . 842 73 POEMS 70   3
COLOURED
   yellow dawn, into the women-coloured twilight i smilingly . .   66 T&C POST IMPR 3   8
   His peering biggest whey coloured face on which a . . . . . . 117 & PORTRAIT 10   33
   this dome of many coloured glass, and see his . . . . 273 IS 5 TWO 8   2
   that face) large one coloured nonthings of gluttonous sky-- . 402 NO THANKS 19   8
+COLOURED
   FOR CONTEXT, SEE . . . .   69 T&C POST IMPR 6   39
   FOR CONTEXT, SEE . . . . 101 & POST IMPR 11   44
   FOR CONTEXT, SEE . . . . 111 & PORTRAIT 6   53
   FOR CONTEXT, SEE . . . . 217 XLI SONNETS 13   11
   FOR CONTEXT, SEE . . . . 227 IS 5 ONE GERT   8
   FOR CONTEXT, SEE . . . . 311 VIVA 3   16
   FOR CONTEXT, SEE . . . . 324 VIVA 16   8
   FOR CONTEXT, SEE . . . . 349 VIVA 40   10
   FOR CONTEXT, SEE . . . . 512 50 POEMS 26   28
COLOURLESS
   the sea heaving indolent colourless forgets) time Requiescat. 277 IS 5 THREE 1   20
COLOURS
   turbans of a hundred colours in their hands scimitars . . . .   33 T&C ORIENTALE 6 38
   vermilion and breathless-scarlet, dark colours like 'cellos . 100 & POST IMPR 11   7
   like 'cellos keen fiddling colours colours cOOler than harps 100 & POST IMPR 11   8
   'cellos keen fiddling colours colours cOOler than harps . . . 100 & POST IMPR 11   8

COLOURS (CONTINUED)

colours cOOler than harps colours p r i c . . . . 100 & POST IMPR 11   8
n glike piccolos thumPing colours like a bangofpiano colours 100 & POST IMPR 11   9
colours like a bangofpiano colours which, are, the, flowery . 100 & POST IMPR 11   10
pluckings of a harpsichord colours of Pure percussion . . . . 100 & POST IMPR 11   11
colours of Pure percussion colours- like-trumpets they . . . 100 & POST IMPR 11   11
smooth, fruits of eager colours of the little, huddling . . . 100 & POST IMPR 11   21
/ / the dirty colours of her kiss have . . . . 132 & SON REAL 3   1
this is the garden: colours come and go, frail . . . . 208 XLI SONNETS 4   1
lightly crowned with far colours, thinking very much of . . . 211 XLI SONNETS 7   15
fooling labyrinth where noisy colours stroll.... and the . . 220 XLI SONNETS 16   12
priests moving in fifty colours , sensuously (the crowd . . . 280 IS 5 THREE 4   11
the crash of the colours (of the oh silently . . . . 280 IS 5 THREE 4   25
into the streets and colours of a town-- that . . . . 297 IS 5 FOUR 14   7
the fewness of these colours; alone who slightly always . . . 357 VIVA 48   11
ter a, strut: do; colours; are: m, ove o . . . . 444 NO THANKS 59   24
or (if begin the colours of your voice) from . . . . 559 1 X 1 19   5
the (with wonder into colours all into singing) may . . . . . 778 73 POEMS 6   3
COLUMN
clamps the hearty sharp column of Egypt , built . . . . 111 & PORTRAIT 6   43
COMB
sex whose sharp lips comb my mumbling gropeofstrength . . . . 137 & SON REAL 8   1
COMBINE
the grapes of heaven combine with earth's madness) --'tis . . 21 T&C PUELLA MEA 200
+COMBINE
FOR CONTEXT, SEE . . . . 325 VIVA 17   17
COMBINING
whose kiss is the combining of kings thy wrists . . . . 29 T&C ORIENTALE 3 25
COME
and wee and eddieandbill come running from marbles and . . . 24 T&C CHANSONS 1   6
and wee and bettyandisbel come dancing from hop-scotch and . 24 T&C CHANSONS 1   14
chord of crimson music Come hither O thou, is . . . . 27 T&C ORIENTALE 1   6
vase of divine silence Come hither O thou, is . . . . 27 T&C ORIENTALE 1 13
locked in white fragrance Come hither O thou, is . . . . . . 27 T&C ORIENTALE 1 20
tomb softer than flowers Come hither O thou, is . . . . 27 T&C ORIENTALE 1 27
stars (in time to come you shall remember of . . . . 36 T&C AMORES 1   21
rise and thou wilt come to her and brush . . . . 40 T&C AMORES 4   40
too, if that he come receive him as your . . . . 42 T&C AMORES 6   18
street where you will come, at twi li ght . . . . 122 & SEVEN POEMS 1 24
I bet two bits come seven come eleven m . . . . 125 & SEVEN POEMS 4 11
two bits come seven come eleven m m make . . . . 125 & SEVEN POEMS 4 11
to anyway dead says come with me he says . . . . 127 & SEVEN POEMS 5 45
(like that) sure i'll come with you you say . . . . 127 & SEVEN POEMS 5 49
you asked me to come: it was raining a . . . . 173 & SON ACTU 22   1
you very sorry to come away? see i will . . . . 192 XLI CHANSONS 2   6
dying so let us come in together and drink . . . . 198 XLI PORTRAIT 6   31
is the garden: colours come and go, frail azures . . . . . . 208 XLI SONNETS 4   1
/ / / / come nothing to my comparable . . . . 212 XLI SONNETS 8   1
gardens her body will come toward me with its . . . . 214 XLI SONNETS 10   11
mind that i am come by little countries to . . . . 216 XLI SONNETS 12   7
questions inhibit unprepared digestions, come: let us mildly 266 IS 5 TWO 1   31
country 'tis of centuries come and go and are . . . . 268 IS 5 TWO 3   4
/ / / / come, gaze with me upon . . . . 273 IS 5 TWO 8   1
--what does it all come down to? Love . . . . 295 IS 5 FOUR 12   21
/ / / / come a little further--why be . . . . 357 VIVA 48   1
It will it Will come (we being unwound & . . . . 361 VIVA 52   2
/ lady will you come with me into the . . . . 365 VIVA 56   1
eyes (shall any dream come a more millionth mile . . . . . . 367 VIVA 58   10
eternal near) day being death come, Love, put on your . . . . 376 VIVA 67   14
(wears pain at joy, come summer puts on fur . . . . 394 NO THANKS 11   7
strangely) known (establish new) come, what Being! open us . 422 NO THANKS 39   11
are not refined they come with girls who bite . . . . 427 NO THANKS 44   9
we'll before what's death come (in one bed. / . . . . 433 NO THANKS 50   16
sun are and moon come fair come foul he . . . . 440 NO THANKS 56   27
and moon come fair come foul he goes alone . . . . 440 NO THANKS 56   27
eLl s? bE -ginningly) come-swarm: faces ar; rive go. . . . . 444 NO THANKS 59   5
ness. Be) look now (come soul; & : and . . . . 448 NO THANKS 63   15
/ / / / come (all you mischief- hatchers . . . . 452 NO THANKS 67   1

		PAGE	TITLE	LINE

COME (CONTINUED)

whos est people be come un / / /	463 NEW POEMS 1	18
a twitch like kingdom come (moon The sq uirmwri	469 NEW POEMS 7	5
tells anywhere "snow will come soon" & pretending they're . .	483 NEW POEMS 21	8
got nothing to smoke: come on kid let's go	489 50 POEMS 3	3
got nothing to sing; come on kid let's go	489 50 POEMS 3	7
got Nothing to die, come on kid let's go	489 50 POEMS 3	11
got nothing to dream (come on kid Let's go	489 50 POEMS 3	15
(as gallant as they come) until she hit a	494 50 POEMS 8	2
and stink-brag have all come to town some like	497 50 POEMS 11	4
go which and up come who breasts will be	511 50 POEMS 25	23
now, boys) here we come / / / /	513 50 POEMS 27	36
last shore and home come young so truly perfectly	526 50 POEMS 38	8
wonder (on twilight) they come until (over dull all	557 1 X 1 17	13
slow tottering visions bigly come crashing into go (all . . .	565 1 X 1 25	14
sunrise fresh with blue come true from a funeral	567 1 X 1 27	19
/ / / i've come to ask you if	572 1 X 1 32	1
thing ; may has come love (by yes every	583 1 X 1 43	14
(on wingfeet of thingfear) come ships go snowily sailing . .	586 1 X 1 46	17
lovers go and lovers come awandering awondering but any . . .	591 1 X 1 51	9
what which around we come who) one's everyanything so	594 1 X 1 54	17
and dreaming drift hundreds come swimming (Each a keener . .	630 (CHAIRE) 32	6
screamgroa ning. ish: ly; come (s gruntsqueak , while, . . .	656 (CHAIRE) 58	3
and geoffrey and all) come up from the never	661 (CHAIRE) 63	11
the never of when come into the now of	661 (CHAIRE) 63	12
the now of forever come riding alive down while	661 (CHAIRE) 63	12
this our now must come to then our then	667 (CHAIRE) 69	8
/ / both eaching come ghostlike (inch) wraithish (by	681 95 POEMS 9	1
no let the roses come and go for kindness	684 95 POEMS 12	14
moon sun fall rise come go rain snow) remembers	693 95 POEMS 21	19
and all filthy men come annabel darling come annie	707 95 POEMS 35	22
men come annabel darling come annie come ann" "she's	707 95 POEMS 35	22
annabel darling come annie come ann" "she's coming right . .	707 95 POEMS 35	22
and here of freedom. Come / / / /	745 95 POEMS 73	14
green solitude (go marvels come) as littler much than	757 95 POEMS 85	17
but lose or win (come heaven, come hell) precisely	776 73 POEMS 4	14
or win (come heaven, come hell) precisely ours is	776 73 POEMS 4	14
fair brave tall young come they) through the may	778 73 POEMS 6	11
fragrance and song wonderingly come (brighter than prayers) .	778 73 POEMS 6	13
(through fragrance and singing) come lovers with slender . .	778 73 POEMS 6	22
favor but (while down come blundering proud hugenesses of . .	783 73 POEMS 11	6
and i'd be quite --come such perfection-- another i	798 73 POEMS 26	23
(leaves; flowers) dreams , come quickly come run run	835 73 POEMS 63	14
dreams , come quickly come run run with me	835 73 POEMS 63	14
gone: will winter never come? o come, terrible anonymity; . .	839 73 POEMS 67	8
winter never come? o come, terrible anonymity; enfold phantom	839 73 POEMS 67	9

+COME

FOR CONTEXT, SEE	73 T&C SON REAL 4	13
FOR CONTEXT, SEE	399 NO THANKS 16	29
FOR CONTEXT, SEE	421 NO THANKS 38	14
FOR CONTEXT, SEE	519 50 POEMS 33	14

COME-SWARM

| eLl s? bE -ginningly) come-swarm: faces ar; rive go. . . . . | 444 NO THANKS 59 | 5 |

COMEDY

| flesh. Loretta, cut the comedy kid.... Fran Mag Glad . . . . | 138 & SON REAL 9 | 15 |
| still-born smile involves the comedy of decay, / / . . . . . | 144 & SON REAL 15 | 14 |

COMELY

| do the exact human comely thing? (or will the . . . . | 218 XLI SONNETS 14 | 8 |

COMES

a little sorry Another comes also picking flowers /	26 T&C CHANSONS 3	8
the queen of queens comes forth ankles musical with	33 T&C ORIENTALE 6	64
on something street Spring comes the lean and definite . . .	62 T&C PORTRAIT 10	5
of rain a colour comes, which is morning, 0	92 & POST IMPR 4	17
when the judgment day comes God will find six	117 & PORTRAIT 10	3
a perhaps hand (which comes carefully out of Nowhere)	124 & SEVEN POEMS 3	2
SONNETS--ACTUALITIES when my love comes to see me it's . . .	152 & SON ACTU 1	1
electric fur, and what-is-it comes over parting flesh.... And	175 & SON ACTU 24	11
cruelly, across the grass Comes the moon love, walk	190 XLI SONGS 12	10

                                                         PAGE   TITLE   LINE
COMES (CONTINUED)
  violetflavoured nuisance: Odor? ono. comes out like a ribbon 231 IS 5 ONE 3   55
  refers ter Satter Nailyuh (comes but once er year) . . . . . 237 IS 5 ONE 8   15
  / candles and Here Comes a glass box which . . . . 280 IS 5 THREE 4   2
  crossing people) and hErE cOmEs a glass box: surrounded . . . 280 IS 5 THREE 4   9
  see yes) It here comes A Glass Box and . . . . 280 IS 5 THREE 4   20
  your naked shoulderblades. --Here comes a stout fellow in . . 282 IS 5 THREE 6   24
  is old when autumn comes, who twiddles his white . . . . . . 296 IS 5 FOUR 13   5
  bright streets of memory comes my heart, singing like . . . . 304 IS 5 FIVE 3   2
  from-soft quits (now) ly Comes: : lush ly-smooTHdumb . . . . 342 VIVA 33   22
  into spiralS and Now (comes un, season of in: . . . . 346 VIVA 37   19
  fragrantly, arrive (when Rain comes; predicating forever, . . 356 VIVA 47   15
  know) but what it comes to (listen you don't . . . . 400 NO THANKS 17   5
  bursting soul why, then comes peace unto men who . . . . . 414 NO THANKS 31   13
  distinct and natural he comes to his disappearance; as . . . 418 NO THANKS 35   6
  Little ness be (ing) comes ex -pert- Ly expand: . . . . . . 471 NEW POEMS 9   6
  (a he of head comes to some dirty window . . . . 501 50 POEMS 15   7
  of merely not nothing comes only one snowflake (and . . . . 502 50 POEMS 16   13
  under woe and up comes yesterday most green and . . . . . . 531 50 POEMS 43   4
  thickness of the coin comes here a man would . . . . 531 50 POEMS 43   9
  / / air, be comes or (a) new (live) . . . . 532 50 POEMS 44   3
  neither could say (it comes so slow not since . . . . 542 1 X 1 2   2
  you not i) it comes so who / / . . . . 542 1 X 1 2   8
  all go dear so comes love / / . . . . 569 1 X 1 29   21
  mountain of his soul comes a keen pure silence) . . . . . . 617 (CHAIRE) 19   1
  sharpens every dull here comes the only man reminding . . . . 624 (CHAIRE) 26   2
  i am dreams until comes vast dark until sink . . . . 633 (CHAIRE) 35   8
  some twisted laws) it comes both prigged and canted . . . . 644 (CHAIRE) 46   6
  / / in Spring comes (no- one asks his . . . . 660 (CHAIRE) 62   2
  if he should Smile) comes nobody'll know / / . . . . 660 (CHAIRE) 62   26
  / / your birthday comes to tell me this . . . . 734 95 POEMS 62   1
  most big a voice comes out of some dreaming . . . . 752 95 POEMS 80   2
  / / / now comes the good rain farmers . . . . 754 95 POEMS 82   1
  / O the sun comes up-up-up in the opening . . . . 773 73 POEMS 1   1
+COMES
  FOR CONTEXT, SEE . . . . 417 NO THANKS 34   12
COMEST
  me Hollers for thou comest and your hands are . . . . 61 T&C PORTRAIT 9   28
COMFORT
  a pale world gathers comfort to her soul, hope . . . .   5 T&C EPITHALAM   82
  away? see i will comfort you because you smell . . . . 192 XLI CHANSONS 2   7
COMFORTABLE
  are unbeautiful and have comfortable minds (also, with the . 70 T&C SON REAL 1   2
  not. Progress is a comfortable disease: your victim (death . 554 1 X 1 14   2
  (dull all regular righteous comfortable) unworlds thief crook 677 95 POEMS 5   8
+COMFORTER
  FOR CONTEXT, SEE . . . . 197 XLI PORTRAIT 5   15
COMFORTS
  splendors past conceiving who comforts his children, if he . 756 95 POEMS 84   6
COMIC
  with hysterical fright a comic tadpole wriggling in delicious 157 & SON ACTU 6   15
COMICS
  mind's poor pretend --grim comics of duration: only love . . 576 1 X 1 36   7
COMING
  in token of his coming whom her soul burns . . . .   3 T&C EPITHALAM   11
  afterday, clothe thy soul's coming merely, with a croon . . . 10 T&C SONGS 1   40
  procession of deep beasts coming with keen ridiculous silks . 112 & PORTRAIT 6   101
  with keen ridiculous silks coming with sharp languid perfumes 112 & PORTRAIT 6   102
  with sharp languid perfumes coming with the little profound . 112 & PORTRAIT 6   103
  the moon's a balloon, coming out of a keen . . . . 129 & SEVEN POEMS 7   2
  wise that she was coming with his kid inside . . . . 145 & SON REAL 16   10
  silence, or darkness.... the coming of my love emits . . . . 152 & SON ACTU 1   6
  two bits for the coming of Christ Jesus ? . . . . 196 XLI PORTRAIT 4   21
  to the last minute coming back down by the . . . . 248 IS 5 ONE 19   27
  the glory of the coming of the Americans particularly . . . . 256 IS 5 ONE 27   12
  her) who after not coming once in seven years . . . . 320 VIVA 12   11
  in "take hands" smiling "coming up these dark stairs. . . . . 353 VIVA 44   31
  i am hearing somebody coming up stairs, carefully (carefully 375 VIVA 66   11

                                   127

COMING (CONTINUED)

his my next meal's coming from i say to . . . . 475 NEW POEMS 13   4

/ hush) noones are coming out in the gloam . . . . 600 (CHAIRE) 2   3

annie come ann" "she's coming right now in the . . . . . . 707 95 POEMS 35 23

and singing welcome your coming although winter may be . . . 717 95 POEMS 45   4

appearing how patiently be coming some (& merciful ly . . . . 753 95 POEMS 81 11

joy under entirely the coming quitenotimaginable . . . . . . 754 95 POEMS 82 11

miracle which is the coming of pure joyful your . . . . . . 761 95 POEMS 88 10

human words --our second coming made stones sing like . . . . 844 73 POEMS 72   2

+COMING

FOR CONTEXT, SEE . . . . 347 VIVA 38   17

FOR CONTEXT, SEE . . . . 812 73 POEMS 40   1

FOR CONTEXT, SEE . . . . 812 73 POEMS 40   1

FOR CONTEXT, SEE . . . . 840 73 POEMS 68   9

COMMA

doctors won't let her comma considers frood whom he . . . . . 499 50 POEMS 13   3

(if you can't dentham comma bentham; or 1 law . . . . 791 73 POEMS 19   6

COMMAND

universe beyond obey or command, reality or un-) proudly . . 574 1 X 1 34   8

COMMEMORATION

dim shrine of intangible commemoration, (from whose faint . . 206 XLI SONNETS 2 11

COMMENDABLE

putrescence whereto my invariably commendable room has been . 197 XLI PORTRAIT 5 20

COMMENTING

gle of ridiculous velocity commenting upon an un- clean . . . 97 & POST IMPR 8 37

COMMERCE

frailer ports of costlier commerce bent / / / . . . . 79 T&C SON UNRE 4 16

COMMITS

being at this instant commits an impenetrable transparency. . 137 & SON REAL 8 11

COMMITTING

because you are continually committing nuisances but more . . 204 XLI LA GUERRE 2 14

COMMON

twenty iron men her common purple soul the absurd . . . . . . 52 T&C PORTRAIT 1 24

is the most great common divisor of unequal souls. . . . . . 74 T&C SON REAL 5 15

a singular ribbon of common sunset is hanging, snow . . . . . 202 XLI PORTRAIT 9 51

glory is all angry common things to disappear causing . . . . 559 1 X 1 19   3

man is this (most common, for each anguish is . . . . 562 1 X 1 22   3

freedom from freedom the common man wants) honey swoRkey . . 635 (CHAIRE) 37 25

COMMON'S

break of dong and common's rare and millstones float . . . . 511 50 POEMS 25 19

COMMUNICATE

eyes are You will communicate a little more than . . . . . . 370 VIVA 61 11

COMMUNION

precious bread of dear communion with the past, and . . . . . 209 XLI SONNETS 5   7

COMMUNIST

for every one (I) communist and all the flics . . . . 274 IS 5 TWO 9 18

COMMUNISTS

16 heures l'Etoile the communists have fine Eyes some . . . . 274 IS 5 TWO 9   3

--my he's brave.... the communists pick up themselves friends 275 IS 5 TWO 9 42

spit blood teeth the Communists have (very) fine eyes . . . . 275 IS 5 TWO 9 48

COMPANION

return voyage, my pensive companion dimly remarked some- . . 326 VIVA 18 31

COMPANIONS

many a pair of companions blithe and fair; who . . . . 20 T&C PUELLA MEA 165

COMPANY

that very proud transparent company of quivering . . . . . . 6 T&C EPITHALAM 142

servant become of the company of those ladies with . . . . . 57 T&C PORTRAIT 5 36

+COMPANY

FOR CONTEXT, SEE . . . . 552 1 X 1 12   1

COMPARABLE

come nothing to my comparable soul which with existence . . . 212 XLI SONNETS 8   1

COMPARATIVELY

so subtle air is comparatively crude; an indestructible . . . 799 73 POEMS 27 17

COMPARED

been coarse and dull compared with you, silently who . . . . 301 IS 5 FOUR 18   9

asleep wop "shapley has compared the universe to a . . . . . 464 NEW POEMS 2 13

a state submicroscopic is-- compared with pitying terrible . 561 1 X 1 21   4

COMPASSIONATE
    least crooking of Whose compassionate digit, earth's most . . 315 VIVA 7   15
COMPEL
    pride which tends to compel me to decline to . . . . 329 VIVA 20   2
COMPELLED
    dears-- or even is compelled to fight itself from . . . . . . 544 1 X 1 4   17
    else an ocean is compelled to close when the . . . . 620 {CHAIRE} 22   8
COMPELS
    intense fragility: whose texture compels me with the colour . 366 VIVA 57   15
COMPLACENT
    teeth deliriously sprouting from complacent gums, a morsel . 201 XLI PORTRAIT 9   4
COMPLAIN
    nights of autumn do complain earth's ghastlier trees by . . . 207 XLI SONNETS 3   1
    to him let me complain, whose seat is where . . . . 212 XLI SONNETS 8   10
    silent their flattened arms complain steadily against the . . 434 NO THANKS 51   13
    than not entitled to complain --plunged in eternal now . . . 561 1 X 1 21   8
    if (and when) roses complain their beauties are in . . . . . 744 95 POEMS 72   3
COMPLAINED
    "nothing" the unjust man complained "is just" ("or un-" . . . 806 73 POEMS 34   1
COMPLETE
    with silver several tears complete the perfumed paraphrase of   6 T&C EPITHALAM   120
    thing more nimble and complete) than ever to Judea's . . . . 17 T&C PUELLA MEA   26
    a thing most new complete fragile intense, which wholly . . . 82 T&C SON ACTU 1   1
    a; domeshaped interval of complete plasticity, shoul- ders, . 97 & POST IMPR 8   35
    of sea-girls Will i complete the mystery of my . . . . 189 XLI SONGS 11   11
    myself surveys safely the complete important profane frantic 201 XLI PORTRAIT 9   31
    sunlight (everywhere sunlight keen complete silent and . . . 283 IS 5 THREE 7   14
    with innumerable gnomes Of complete dream if we love . . . . 363 VIVA 54   8
    woman in a park. Complete. and slightly (why? or . . . . . . 375 VIVA 66   8
    ing dead but not complete -ly not (not as . . . . 387 NO THANKS 4   12
    untouch meaningless precision and complete fate (he must deny 402 NO THANKS 19   14
    brief but covering one complete miracle of nearest far . . . 504 50 POEMS 18   3
    measureless our pure living complete love whose doom is . . . 538 50 POEMS 50   3
    your voice) from some complete existence of to dream . . . . 559 1 X 1 19   6
    of to dream into complete some dream of to . . . . 559 1 X 1 19   7
    neither nor cruel (only complete) i not not you . . . . 564 1 X 1 24   8
    if whole supreme this complete doubtless universe we'd (and . 675 95 POEMS 3   7
    / / joyful your complete fearless and pure love . . . . 761 95 POEMS 88   1
    joyful your fearless and complete love, all safely small . . 761 95 POEMS 88   11
COMPLETELY
    no reason feel deeply completely conscious of the rain . . . 92 & POST IMPR 4   11
    Paris; this April sunset completely utters utters serenely . 93 & POST IMPR 5   1
    him doll self) hay completely thus or that wispily . . . . . 516 50 POEMS 30   12
    and should some why completely weep my father's fingers . . . 520 50 POEMS 34   13
    fearless one good yes completely kind mindheart one true . . . 524 50 POEMS 36   40
    by their own generous completely light, an angel; or . . . . 562 1 X 1 22   6
    can feel only despair completely strikes forests of mind, . . 580 1 X 1 40   24
    up to silence and completely sing? futures are obsolete; . . 592 1 X 1 52   10
    your and) self without, completely dare be beautiful one . . 666 {CHAIRE} 68   14
    merely human plane) someone completely beautiful; and . . . . 799 73 POEMS 27   11
    except alive --that is, completely alert and miraculously . . 802 73 POEMS 30   15
    but should this namelessness (completely fleetly) vanish, at 819 73 POEMS 47   10
+COMPLETELY
    FOR CONTEXT, SEE . . . . 387 NO THANKS 4   12
COMPLETES
    folded: but the year completes his life as a . . . . 304 IS 5 FIVE 3   8
    merciful love whispered were, completes its brightness with . 526 50 POEMS 38   11
COMPLEXIONS
    to doom yea (fresh complexions being oke with him) . . . . . 552 1 X 1 12   23
COMPLEXITY
    this creative never known complexity was born before the . . 577 1 X 1 37   14
COMPLEXLY
    with which vast my complexly wisdoming friend's --a fingery . 517 50 POEMS 31   5
COMPLICATED
    to the serene the complicated and the obvious they . . . . . 43 T&C AMORES 7   16
COMPOSE
    i being otherwise made compose curves and yellows, angles . . 291 IS 5 FOUR 8   3
    disappear becomingly: a thunderbolt compose poems not because 452 NO THANKS 67   14

	PAGE	TITLE	LINE

COMPOSED
    particularly to enjoy the composed sudden body atop which . . 193 XLI PORTRAIT 1   2
    arranged and their nucleus (composed of captains in . . . . . 274 IS 5 TWO 9   21
COMPREHEND
    pardon, possibly you will comprehend. and how this has . . . 285 IS 5 FOUR 2   10
    our touching hearts slenderly comprehend (clinging as . . . . 305 IS 5 FIVE 4   1
    motion deeply to wickedly comprehend the innocently Doomed . 356 VIVA 47   10
    him "I" presume to comprehend not numerable whom? / . . . . . 609 (CHAIRE) 11   14
    beyond whatever mind may comprehend, remember seek . . . . . 688 95 POEMS 16   11
    one least ignorance may comprehend more than shall ever . . 761 95 POEMS 88   2
    but as you'll shortly comprehend a marvellous artificer now . 799 73 POEMS 27   6
COMPREHENDED
    the betrayal of bells comprehended through incense / / . . . 29 T&C ORIENTALE 3   33
COMPREHENDS
    love (and only love) comprehends huger easily beyonds than . 741 95 POEMS 69   6
COMPRISE
    as not imagined secrecies comprise goldenly huge whole the . 750 95 POEMS 78   8
COMPRISES
    ours --God's heaven perhaps comprises poems (my mother's . . 748 95 POEMS 76   5
+COMPRISES
    FOR CONTEXT, SEE . . . . 789 73 POEMS 17   7
COMPULSIONS
    clocks fears hopes beliefs compulsions doubts & corners) . . 755 95 POEMS 83   17
COMPULSORY
    supernod where freedom is compulsory and only man is . . . . 544 1 X 1 4   23
+COMRADE
    FOR CONTEXT, SEE . . . . 413 NO THANKS 30   13
+COMRADES
    FOR CONTEXT, SEE . . . . 413 NO THANKS 30   1
    FOR CONTEXT, SEE . . . . 413 NO THANKS 30   2
    FOR CONTEXT, SEE . . . . 413 NO THANKS 30   3
    FOR CONTEXT, SEE . . . . 413 NO THANKS 30   4
    FOR CONTEXT, SEE . . . . 413 NO THANKS 30   5
    FOR CONTEXT, SEE . . . . 413 NO THANKS 30   7
    FOR CONTEXT, SEE . . . . 413 NO THANKS 30   9
    FOR CONTEXT, SEE . . . . 413 NO THANKS 30   10
CON
    the caving ages curiously con) --but the lunge of . . . . . 77 T&C SON UNRE 2   4
    nonth inkable enormousness by con trast with the tiny . . . . 803 73 POEMS 31   11
CONAREFETTI
    crumbles hand (ful released conarefetti) ev eryflitter, inga. 265 IS 5 ONE 34   2
CONCEALED
    earth's first morning have concealed so unimaginably young a 626 (CHAIRE) 28   13
+CONCEALS
    FOR CONTEXT, SEE . . . . 795 73 POEMS 23   13
CONCEIVABLE
    no (if deeply less conceivable than birth or death . . . . . 720 95 POEMS 48   12
CONCEIVABLY
    fancy be more not conceivably future than mrs somethingwitz . 790 73 POEMS 18   5
CONCEIVE
    thee that thou mightest conceive gods (but true to . . . . . 46 T&C LA GUERRE 2   17
    / / / / conceive a man, should he . . . . 420 NO THANKS 37   1
    can withholding nothing) World, conceive a man / / . . . . . 420 NO THANKS 37   14
    selves yet younger selves conceive here's music's music and . 538 50 POEMS 50   7
    whose golden, crimson dooms conceive an oceaning abyss of . . 599 (CHAIRE) 1   2
    i they'll all not conceive less who than love) . . . . 634 (CHAIRE) 36   15
    so good you don't conceive a better; and because . . . . . . 679 95 POEMS 7   10
    as men do not conceive--let ocean grow again / . . . . 843 73 POEMS 71   14
CONCEIVES
    soul clings and heart conceives and mind leaps (and . . . . . 386 NO THANKS 3   12
    (and whose what he conceives to be Love did . . . . 398 NO THANKS 15   6
CONCEIVING
    as midsummer's keen beyond conceiving mind of sun will . . . 520 50 POEMS 34   26
    with silver splendors past conceiving who comforts his . . . 756 95 POEMS 84   5
    and (through stillness beyond conceiving) dream until No . . 757 95 POEMS 85   36
CONCENTRIC
    first into different deaths Concentric geometries of . . . . 311 VIVA 3   9

		PAGE	TITLE	LINE

CONCEPT
   Darwin; asks about Death) concept 0 hairlesschested females, 398 NO THANKS 15 15
CONCERNED
   be clearer to all concerned than that i am . . . . 263 IS 5 ONE 32 40
CONCERNIN
   needn't be so spry concernin questions arty each has . . . . 247 IS 5 ONE 18 2
CONCERNING
   and much could understand concerning no and yes: if . . . . . 834 73 POEMS 62 16
CONCESSION
   successful b.o. fully speaking concession at the recent . . . 425 NO THANKS 42 15
CONCLUDE
   wooden big two feet conclude happeningly the unfirm drooping 229 IS 5 ONE FRAN 4
CONCLUDES
   foes my tragic tale concludes herewith: soldier, beware of . 799 73 POEMS 27 40
CONCRETE
   pulled the sluice emerging. concrete / / / / . . . . 119 & PORTRAIT 11 18
CONCUPISCENCE
   of light her nice concupiscence appeared rounded. if she . . 103 & POST IMPR 13 15
   (isolating with perpetually meticulous concupiscence the . . 193 XLI PORTRAIT 1 22
+CONCUSSION
   FOR CONTEXT, SEE . . . . 245 IS 5 ONE 16 17
CONDEMNATORY
   minced for blown kisses, condemnatory fingers thinned of . .   9 T&C SONGS 1 13
CONDITION
   arriving in an exhausted condition, i purchased two bags . . 326 VIVA 18 15
CONDOMS
   if it sells hate condoms education snakeoil vac uumcleaners . 549 1 X 1 9 11
CONDUCT
   phenomena: such being a conduct worthy of more ponderous . . 328 VIVA 19 6
CONEY
   absitively posolutely dead, like Coney Island in winter / . .   72 T&C SON REAL 3 15
CONFESSED
   while the mute trouserfly confessed a button solemnly inert. 258 IS 5 ONE 28 19
   something odd occurred" charlie confessed (halting) "a tall . 800 73 POEMS 28 2
CONFESSIO
   with Master Gower in Confessio doth prefer shall not . . . .   20 T&C PUELLA MEA 167
+CONFETTI
   FOR CONTEXT, SEE . . . . 265 IS 5 ONE 34 2
CONFINE
   uncultured (who Very distinctly confine their omnipotent . . 391 NO THANKS 8 20
CONFLICT
   unreasoned, his wisdom cancels conflict and agreement . . . . 683 95 POEMS 11 6
CONFORM
   a disease of same, conform the pinnacle of am . . . . 521 50 POEMS 34 60
CONFOUND
   to grow shall hate confound the wise? doubt blind . . . . . . 538 50 POEMS 50 5
+CONFOUNDS
   FOR CONTEXT, SEE . . . . 826 73 POEMS 54 15
CONFUSE
   mother) but may not confuse the clever hair nor . . . .   85 T&C SON ACTU 4 6
   Antony and we will confuse hotly our moreover irrevocable . . 111 & PORTRAIT 6 61
   and others please don't confuse. Some people 's future . . . 314 VIVA 6 6
CONFUSED
   chokes oneness truth is confused with fact, fish boast . . . 446 NO THANKS 61 4
CONFUSING
   enough to do without confusing timelessness and time. Time . 817 73 POEMS 45 8
+CONFUSION
   FOR CONTEXT, SEE . . . . 646 {CHAIRE} 48 5
CONFUTE
   --it is distinctly to confute my reason with the . . . . . .   19 T&C PUELLA MEA 97
CONFUTES
   this and that petal confutes... to exist being a . . . . . . 264 IS 5 ONE 33 3
CONGRESSMAN
   before the middle of Congressman Pudd 's 4th of . . . . 249 IS 5 ONE 20 1
CONJUGATED
   careful hugeness i am conjugated by the sensual mysticism . . 201 XLI PORTRAIT 9 23
CONJURERS
   By handless hints do conjurers rule? do mannikins forbid . . 527 50 POEMS 39 18

131

	PAGE	TITLE	LINE

CONNIVANCE
received) or by doomful connivance accurately thither and . . 299 IS 5 FOUR 16   7
CONNOTATION
/ / / a connotation of infinity sharpens the . . . . 81 T&C SON UNRE 6   1
CONQUERS
west's numerous dun magnificence conquers magnificence. In .   6 T&C EPITHALAM 128
CONSCIENCE
with manly heart and conscience free, upon the front . . . . 273 IS 5 TWO 8   18
CONSCIENTIOUS
recoiled at war: a conscientious object-or his wellbeloved . 339 VIVA 30   3
CONSCIOUS
reason feel deeply completely conscious of the rain or . . . 92 & POST IMPR 4 11
CONSCIOUSNESS
had in return for consciousness endowed him with a . . . . . 258 IS 5 ONE 28   7
CONSEQUENTLY
-new; and you know consequently a little stiff i . . . . . . 248 IS 5 ONE 19   3
kiss the dirt (and consequently dare to climb the . . . . . . 679 95 POEMS 7   6
CONSIDER
/ / / AMORES consider O woman this my . . . . 36 T&C AMORES 1   1
eager avenues of lifelessness consider for how much . . . . . 81 T&C SON UNRE 6 7
a glib girl i consider her as a leaf . . . . 131 & SON REAL 2   2
let us make haste --consider well this ruined aqueduct . . . 260 IS 5 ONE 30   22
carefully these things we consider life. Dear i put . . . . . 289 IS 5 FOUR 6   12
i wonder never mind consider rather heavenly things and . . . 322 VIVA 14   2
remembering only dare (Wholly consider how these immaculate . 362 VIVA 53   4
wholly imagining fire) only consider How / / / . . . . 362 VIVA 53   16
sea --but if yourself consider wonderful that your (how . . . 379 VIVA 70   10
+CONSIDER
FOR CONTEXT, SEE . . . . 398 NO THANKS 15   11
CONSIDERABLE
somewhat city wiggles in considerable twilight touch (now) . 302 IS 5 FIVE 1   4
CONSIDERED
molle dancers, whom he considered "elevating--that is, if . . 327 VIVA 18   40
CONSIDERING
/ / i was considering how within night's loose . . . . 49 T&C IMPRESS 3   1
have objected to which, considering the back- ground, it . . 263 IS 5 ONE 32   34
CONSIDERS
won't let her comma considers frood whom he pronounces . . . 499 50 POEMS 13   3
CONSISTS
in eyes and lips consists --always upon the mouth . . . . . . 20 T&C PUELLA MEA 147
CONSTITUTES
swear (to noone everyone) constitutes undying; or whatever . 264 IS 5 ONE 33   2
CONSTRUCTIVE
momentary partnership (to instigate constructive Horizontal . 260 IS 5 ONE 30   19
CONSTRUED
being, i am skilfully construed by a delicately experi- . . . 201 XLI PORTRAIT 9 24
CONSUBSTANTIAL
ligious cult based on consubstantial intangibility. Personne 262 IS 5 ONE 32   25
CONSULT
faultless languor when invisibly consult with some delicious 193 XLI PORTRAIT 1   7
CONSUMMATION
children (It is the consummation of day, the hour) . . . . . 167 & SON ACTU 16   11
CONTACT
and fragile i borrow contact from that you and . . . . 328 VIVA 19   17
CONTAIN
crisp eyes actually shall contain new faeries (and if . . . . 294 IS 5 FOUR 11   9
of) Life, dost Thou contain a marvel than this . . . . 406 NO THANKS 23   12
CONTAINING
unflinchingly applaud all songs containing the words country 204 XLI LA GUERRE 2 7
CONTAINS
tiniest street or three contains these prettiest deaths . . . 340 VIVA 31   14
CONTEMPLATE
come: let us mildly contemplate beginning with his wellfilled 266 IS 5 TWO 1   31
freudian wish; when i contemplate her uneyes safely ensconced 326 VIVA 18   4
poco putrido when we contemplate her uneyes safely ensconced 327 VIVA 18   46
still doth our hero contemplate in raptures of undream . . . 544 1 X 1 4   19
CONTEMPTUOUS
unbeheld --mine the unbought contemptuous intent till this . 84 T&C SON ACTU 3   3

CONTENT
    giggly girls and not content Spring, with this thou . . . . . 61 T&C PORTRAIT 9   8
    spill the immediate imperceptible content my friend's being, 193 XLI PORTRAIT 1   18
    therefore, lady am i content should any by me . . . . 291 IS 5 FOUR 8   18
CONTENTED
    brutal faces of people contented hideous hopeless cruel happy 50 T&C IMPRESS 4   15
    than dream-- how should contented fools of fact envision . . 659 (CHAIRE) 61   9
CONTENTMENT
    (then turn the page) contentment read for ecstasy --for . . . 689 95 POEMS 17   5
CONTINUAL
    who dost with quivering continual thighs invite the thrilling   3 T&C EPITHALAM   2
    ravelling, to a proud continual stitch of the unmitigated . . 136 & SON REAL 7   3
CONTINUALLY
    animals. The minute waist continually with an African gesture 95 & POST IMPR 7   5
    edgeless gesture of existence, continually whittles keen . . 193 XLI PORTRAIT 1   20
    and because you are continually committing nuisances but more 204 XLI LA GUERRE 2 14
    let us not be continually astonished should from their . . . 261 IS 5 ONE 31   3
    stairs of terror) and continually i am seeing something . . . 375 VIVA 66   15
CONTINUE
    be deciphered selves merely Continue to experience a neverish 361 VIVA 52   27
    that us will ourselves continue to outgrow all whose . . . . 574 1 X 1 34   12
CONTINUED
    the world the animals continued eating. And i imagine . . . . 241 IS 5 ONE 12   6
CONTINUOUS
    curling thing, yet holds continuous intercourse--through . .   5 T&C EPITHALAM   91
CONTINUUM
    expanded Newton's law preserved conTinuum (but we read that . 315 VIVA 7   6
CONTOURS
    think is the slippery contours of a vase inexpressibly . . . 193 XLI PORTRAIT 1   14
    appreciation exposed his hibernative contours, amiable . . . 197 XLI PORTRAIT 5   9
    ego approaches) painfully sterilized contours; within which . 319 VIVA 11   28
+CONTRACTING
    FOR CONTEXT, SEE . . . . 248 IS 5 ONE 19   32
CONTRADICT
    every can't) immensest mysteries contradict a deathful realm 763 95 POEMS 90   27
CONTRARY
    dead) whereupon mary quite contrary didn't die (may be . . . 401 NO THANKS 18   9
+CONTRAST
    FOR CONTEXT, SEE . . . . 240 IS 5 ONE 11   3
    FOR CONTEXT, SEE . . . . 803 73 POEMS 31   11
CONTRIVE
    doom create is now contrive; imagined, merely know (freedom: 834 73 POEMS 62   7
CONTRIVED
    prodigious time's mere brain contrived: a spook of stop . . . 558 1 X 1 18   9
CONTRIVES
    of Life, himself occasionally contrives an unreal precise . . 193 XLI PORTRAIT 1   24
    freedom which no mind contrives (but certainly each spirit . 842 73 POEMS 70   8
CONTRIVING
    encompass true) while your contriving fate, my sharpening . . 373 VIVA 64   17
CONTROL
    speak or one name control more incredible splendor than . . . 377 VIVA 68   5
CONVENTIONS
    old mop punching underneath conventions exposes hidden . . . 203 XLI LA GUERRE 1   4
CONVERSATION
    / / / PORTRAITS conversation with my friend is . . . . 193 XLI PORTRAIT 1   1
CONVERSE
    the sunset their chimneys converse angrily, their roofs are . 62 T&C PORTRAIT 10 12
CONVERSED
    which with existence has conversed in vain, O scrupulously . 212 XLI SONNETS 8   2
CONVICT
    or mind and soul convict him of deceiving) whose . . . . . . 683 95 POEMS 11   4
CONVULSED
    / / notice the convulsed orange inch of moon . . . . 86 T&C SON ACTU 5   1
CONVULSIVE
    was over. One brief convulsive octopus, and then our . . . . 263 IS 5 ONE 32   56
CONWAY
    Fist) drifts a long conway 's unstreet with treadwatering . . 616 (CHAIRE) 18   12

COO

    pinks shy lemons greens coo l choc olate s. . . . . 179 XLI SONGS 1   10

    hope of hope must coo or boo may strut . . . . 440 NO THANKS 56   18

    and do fat pigeons coo) haps even 4 now . . . . 787 73 POEMS 15   7

COOK

    mean me a Irish, cook but well oh don't . . . . 251 IS 5 ONE 22   11

    --O Education: O thos cook & son (O to . . . . 257 IS 5 ONE 27   38

COOKIE

    to a uh" pause "Cookie but" nonvisibly smi- ling . . . . . . 464 NEW POEMS 2   16

COOKIES

    newly baked and swaggering cookies of indignant light / . . . 226 IS 5 ONE MAME   14

COOL

    of sleep, betwixt whose cool incorrigible arms impaled upon .   7 T&C EPITHALAM 156

    scintillant space, with the cool writhe of gloom truly . . . 18 T&C PUELLA MEA 84

    a casket of the cool jewel of thy mind . . . . 29 T&C ORIENTALE 3 17

    incense is tangled a cool moon there are thrice-three-hundred 32 T&C ORIENTALE 6 32

    street the dark long cool tunnel of raving colour, ... 100 & POST IMPR 11   3

    the bar it was cOOl i didn't have anything . . . . 123 & SEVEN POEMS 2   4

    and the bar was cOOl O My lover, there's . . . . 123 & SEVEN POEMS 2   6

    the well it's too cool to be crooked and . . . . 126 & SEVEN POEMS 5   3

    beyond one immaculate curving cool treasures of silence . . . 156 & SON ACTU 5   4

    nigger's voice feels curiously cool (suddenly-Lights go! on, 167 & SON ACTU 16 18

    i will kiss your cool bark and hug you . . . . 192 XLI CHANSONS 2   9

    lips do blow upon cool flutes within wide glooms, ... 208 XLI SONNETS 4   6

    always demurely halfsmiling from cool faces, moving purely . 211 XLI SONNETS 7   8

    trivial toll, for whose cool feet this frantic heart . . . . 212 XLI SONNETS 8   4

    's shy foot among cool ferns) therefore togethering . . . . 371 VIVA 62   13

    new textures of actual cool stupendous is nor may . . . . . 373 VIVA 64   15

    than a fire is cool took bedfellows for moons . . . . 420 NO THANKS 37   11

+COOL

    FOR CONTEXT, SEE . . . . 100 & POST IMPR 11   15

    FOR CONTEXT, SEE . . . . 179 XLI SONGS 1   10

COOLER

    keen fiddling colours colours cOOler than harps colours p . . 100 & POST IMPR 11   8

+COOLIDGE

    FOR CONTEXT, SEE . . . . 321 VIVA 13   13

COOLISH

    heart my the halfgloom coolish of The what are . . . . 251 IS 5 ONE 22   18

COOLITCH

    because he ant but Coolitch wiped his valley forge . . . . . 321 VIVA 13   13

COOLLY

    remembered dream-- flaming a coolly bell touches most mere . 601 {CHAIRE} 3   13

COOLNESS

    strikes, in the alive coolness, very faintly and finally . . 92 & POST IMPR 4   15

    the air in utterable coolness deeds of green thrilling . . . 163 & SON ACTU 12   7

    and sing And the coolness of your smile is . . . . 163 & SON ACTU 12   17

    (dreaming is better) murdering coolness slowly in peopling . 168 & SON ACTU 17   13

+COOLNESS

    FOR CONTEXT, SEE . . . . 104 & POST IMPR 14   15

COON

    one slipslouch twi tterstamp coon wid a plon kykerplung . . . 519 50 POEMS 33   3

+COON

    FOR CONTEXT, SEE . . . . 387 NO THANKS 4   8

COOS

    die) "gedup" the gentscoon coos gently: tug? g (ing . . . . 387 NO THANKS 4   8

COP'S

    her waist said the cop's rung for the wagon . . . . 53 T&C PORTRAIT 1   37

COPIOUS

    wai ter lugs his copious whichwhat skilfully here & . . . . . 629 {CHAIRE} 31   9

COPPERS

    furious street people drop, coppers into, the littletin-cup . 100 & POST IMPR 11   39

COPS

    dey could kill sixereight cops-- "I sidesteps im an . . . . . 332 VIVA 23   4

COQUETTISHLY

    the crimson nose and coquettishly- cocked bonnet having . . . 196 XLI PORTRAIT 4   4

CORAL

    rubbish of pearl weed coral and stones; lifted, and . . . . . 369 VIVA 60   6

	PAGE	TITLE	LINE

CORDIALLY
of nearest far "i cordially invite me to become . . . . 504 50 POEMS 18   4
CORKING
a whore. Sixteen you corking brute amused from time . . . . . 74 T&C SON REAL 5   9
CORKSCREW
(having dreamed of a corkscrew) studied with Freud a . . . . 236 IS 5 ONE 7   6
CORN
silky and lewd) like corn s l e n . . . . 101 & POST IMPR 11   77
CORNER
admit--) till, at the corner of Nothing and Something, . . . 174 & SON ACTU 23   14
will sit in the corner and drink thinks and . . . . 233 IS 5 ONE 4   16
as we turned the corner of Divinity avenue i . . . . 248 IS 5 ONE 19   21
to (carefully turning a corner) never bother you any . . . . 298 IS 5 FOUR 15   28
who (at a certain corner, suddenly) meets the tall . . . . . 304 IS 5 FIVE 3   4
should turn the infinite corner of love, all that . . . . . 479 NEW POEMS 17   18
CORNERED
sticking in its three- cornered always moist mouth) --jazz, . 227 IS 5 ONE GERT   5
+CORNERED
FOR CONTEXT, SEE . . . . 114 & PORTRAIT 7   5
CORNERLESS
of sky lavender and cornerless, the moon rattles like . . . . 70 T&C SON REAL 1   13
exquisitely flutters in the cornerless tomorrow / / / . . . . 370 VIVA 61   28
CORNERS
unto fear) in dreadful corners hideously cowers-- i do . . . 207 XLI SONNETS 3   8
rapidly wish in the corners of her youth; whom, ... 214 XLI SONNETS 10   6
or such, the normal corners of your heart will . . . . 292 IS 5 FOUR 9   14
of thing in beginning corners dawn smirks and there's . . . . 322 VIVA 14   13
sunset) edges become swiftly corners (Besides which, i note . 345 VIVA 36   2
beliefs compulsions doubts & corners) worlds are to dream . . 755 95 POEMS 83   18
+CORNERS
FOR CONTEXT, SEE . . . . 311 VIVA 3   17
CORNUCOPIOUSLY
it horribly smith spouts cornucopiously not unrecognizable . 465 NEW POEMS 3   10
CORPSE
me, but of my corpse the tool her smile . . . . 152 & SON ACTU 1   12
to all intents a corpse and wanting any rag . . . . 339 VIVA 30   16
CORPSECOLOURED
But if her tall corpsecoloured body seat itself (with . . . . 227 IS 5 ONE GERT   8
CORRECT
silver dissonance by the correct fingers of April resolved . 47 T&C IMPRESS 1   2
that's) but listen here's (correct you said it yeah) . . . . 400 NO THANKS 17   12
CORRECTLY
awake, cursed with pimples, correctly dressed, cleanshaven . 262 IS 5 ONE 32   8
+CORRUPTINGLY
FOR CONTEXT, SEE . . . . 430 NO THANKS 47   14
CORRUPTION
/ / / honour corruption villainy holiness riding in . . . . . 661 {CHAIRE} 63   1
COSMIC
out big (bigger than cosmic rays war earthquakes famine . . . 475 NEW POEMS 13   18
COST
where a craft of cost the Ergo perished later . . . . 494 50 POEMS 8   5
COSTLIER
on frailer ports of costlier commerce bent / / . . . . 79 T&C SON UNRE 4   16
COSTLY
moment (futile, proud, a costly morsel of sweet tears) . . . 23 T&C PUELLA MEA 269
COSTUME
of Siam in native costume, who emerging from a . . . . 245 IS 5 ONE 16   21
COUCH
drowsy-fair (when from her couch of poppy petals peers . . . 8 T&C OF NICOL   13
he reclines upon the couch of couches and beckons . . . . . . 33 T&C ORIENTALE 6   55
true to the incomparable couch of death thy rhythmic . . . . 46 T&C LA GUERRE 2   22
to Lie On My Couch at Christopher Street For . . . . 101 & POST IMPR 11   58
COUCHER
my brain voulez- vous coucher avec moi? Non? pourquoi?) . . . 120 & PORTRAIT 12   29
rue Henri Mounier voulez-vous coucher avec moi? te ferai . . 121 & PORTRAIT 12   36
COUCHES
upon the couch of couches and beckons with the . . . . 33 T&C ORIENTALE 6   55
deep squirm nibbles. another couches, weary, upon a flabby . 143 & SON REAL 14   11

		PAGE	TITLE	LINE

COUGH

i lie down i cough too much). How did . . . . 245 IS 5 ONE 16   11
as a" pause "uh" cough "Biscuit" (& so on . . . . 464 NEW POEMS 2   24
who inquires is your cough better today? nn-nn went . . . . . 506 50 POEMS 20   7

COUGHED

was mussed, and she coughed while tying strings / . . . . . . 132 & SON REAL 3   18
of my soul i coughed , naturally / / . . . . 197 XLI PORTRAIT 5   24

COUGHING

self fee (bly Perpetually coughing And thickly spi) tting . . 312 VIVA 4   20

+COUGHING

FOR CONTEXT, SEE . . . . 488 50 POEMS 2   21

COUGHS

drinks and) not bald. (Coughs.) Two pale slippery small . . . 406 NO THANKS 23   9

COULD

is my little sister could with our big brother . . . . . . 117 & PORTRAIT 10   18
would see if it could) eyes say the breasts . . . . 150 & SON REAL 21   2
scarcely to sing (heart, could we bear the marvel . . . . . 205 XLI SONNETS 1   15
Do- nothing Do -nothing could do nothing which you . . . . 236 IS 5 ONE 7   11
because my Uncle Sol could sing McCann He Was . . . . 239 IS 5 ONE 10   5
meaning its opposite? Nothing could be clearer to all . . . . 263 IS 5 ONE 32   40
talk of beauty what could be more beaut- iful . . . . 268 IS 5 TWO 3   9
during the recent war could and what is more . . . . 276 IS 5 TWO 10   3
and if only he could meanwhile my self etcetera . . . . . 276 IS 5 TWO 10   18
ultrawrists who lullabylullaby (I could have been You, You . 317 VIVA 9   7
talkin big how dey could kill sixereight cops-- "I . . . . . 332 VIVA 23   3
flowers for if I could, they would somehow not . . . . . . 338 VIVA 29   9
have no servants. We could almost live at the . . . . 365 VIVA 56   6
free room. We almost could go (you and i) . . . . 365 VIVA 56   8
than of my books could even be your shelves . . . . 386 NO THANKS 3   4
nor some edgeless star could give that anguish room; . . . . 414 NO THANKS 31   9
mind unstrange learn (nor could all earth's rotting scholars 420 NO THANKS 37   8
who did because she could what the movies try . . . . 425 NO THANKS 42   5
being generous this heart could dare) unhearts can less . . . 440 NO THANKS 56   3
and spat (this life could dare freely to give . . . . 440 NO THANKS 56   12
pretty toys as themselves could not know: the earth . . . . 451 NO THANKS 66   10
said a man (who could not earn his bread . . . . 473 NEW POEMS 11   2
such a fool who could fail pulling all the . . . . 481 NEW POEMS 19   11
or feethands; nobody ever could ever had love loved . . . . 490 50 POEMS 4   17
shuts more than open could that every tree or . . . . 502 50 POEMS 16   7
say nay but lucy could learn and lily could . . . . 509 50 POEMS 23   21
could learn and lily could pray and fewer were . . . . . . 509 50 POEMS 23   22
took life such life could not begin to live . . . . 510 50 POEMS 24   6
but if such life could its breath would stink . . . . 510 50 POEMS 24   7
multiplied by twice infinity could never equal one) which . . 510 50 POEMS 24   11
might cry for he could feel the mountains grow. . . . . . . 520 50 POEMS 34   16
of star by him could steer and pure so . . . . 520 50 POEMS 34   22
/ / you which could grin three smiles into . . . . 522 50 POEMS 35   1
humbly thank you which could grin may stern particular . . . 522 50 POEMS 35   9
means return seas who could sing so deep and . . . . 526 50 POEMS 38   6
/ / / neither could say (it comes so . . . . 542 1 X 1 2   1
bird i dreamed i could sing but like nothing . . . . 587 1 X 1 47   3
anything's righter than books could plan) the stupidest . . . 594 1 X 1 54   4
never was brewed which could knock you down (while . . . . . 605 (CHAIRE) 7   4
if now than forever could never (by breathless one . . . . 625 (CHAIRE) 27   22
dear to what else could a no but it . . . . 638 (CHAIRE) 40   4
them to see who could not learn to look . . . . 649 (CHAIRE) 51   3
upon H, and smile could anything be pleasanter (some . . . . 650 (CHAIRE) 52   5
forest &; wh o could be so ! f! . . . . 653 (CHAIRE) 55   8
than earth hers elf could silent more no be . . . . 654 (CHAIRE) 56   12
"o how how how could i ever wear it . . . . 684 95 POEMS 12   6
round a so moon could dream (i sus pect) . . . . 698 95 POEMS 26   1
like even a Poet) could hardly express what i . . . . 702 95 POEMS 30   7
that sly little bitch could have showed billy how" . . . . 707 95 POEMS 35   14
/ / / never could anyone who simply lives . . . . 718 95 POEMS 46   1
hurl snow suppose we could not love, dear; imagine . . . . 743 95 POEMS 71   4
asked my love " could begin to imagine quite . . . . 748 95 POEMS 76   12
let's love until noone could quite be (and young . . . . . 769 95 POEMS 95   24
/ / / nobody could in superhuman flights of . . . . 790 73 POEMS 18   1

	PAGE	TITLE	LINE

COULD (CONTINUED)

who (truth to sing) could never quite tell right . . . . . . 799 73 POEMS 27   13
over, stopped me by 'could you spare three cents . . . . . . 800 73 POEMS 28   6
by merely things believable) could only fancy we should . . . 809 73 POEMS 37   7
anyone so gay possibly could die / / / . . . . 825 73 POEMS 53   6
/ / / / "could that" i marvelled "be . . . . 828 73 POEMS 56   1
so wise; and much could understand concerning no and . . . . 834 73 POEMS 62   15
self answers me) "i could not sing" / / . . . . 836 73 POEMS 64   10
ger than big gest could even begin to be) . . . . 840 73 POEMS 68   16

COULDN'T

Theodore Odysseus Graren't we couldn't free the negro because 321 VIVA 13   11
like a soul and couldn't use a mind / . . . . 544 1 X 1 4   28
plato told him: he couldn't believe it (jesus told . . . . . 553 1 X 1 13   2
or until no atom couldn't die (how and am . . . . 634 (CHAIRE) 36   13
poppa but who just couldn't help it no matter . . . . 635 (CHAIRE) 37   5
something had (maybe they couldn't agree) not happened (and . 652 (CHAIRE) 54   14
sang so sweetly she couldn't remember her troubles, and . . . 682 95 POEMS 10   4
looked there" "and you couldn't well miss willy's carroty . . 707 95 POEMS 35   4

COULEUR

eclate ta voix fragile couleur de pivoine?) with the . . . . 121 & PORTRAIT 12   56

COUNT

otherlittle roundtables Her, eyes count slow (ly obstre . . . 104 & POST IMPR 14   3
not a tree can count his leaves each herself . . . . 591 1 X 1 51   17
(while anyone might slowly count to soon) rose--did you . . . 599 (CHAIRE) 1   9
you (kiss me) quickly count to never? you were . . . . 599 (CHAIRE) 1   11

COUNTED

the sorrowful hour, thy counted petals O tremendous flower . 79 T&C SON UNRE 4   3

COUNTENANCES

weazened Irrefutable unastonished two, countenances seated in 255 IS 5 ONE 26   2

COUNTING

of pity--so he stands counting the moved myriads wonderfully   9 T&C SONGS 1   14

COUNTLESS

blossoming a scarecrow demongod countless in hatred pity fear 662 (CHAIRE) 64   9

COUNTRIES

am come by little countries to the yes of . . . . 216 XLI SONNETS 12   7
the colour of its countries, rendering death and forever . . 366 VIVA 57   15
glory escorted through infinite countries be my darling (open 811 73 POEMS 39   3

COUNTRY

songs containing the words country home and mother when . . . 204 XLI LA GUERRE 2   7
kiddo believe me my country, 'tis of you, land . . . . 230 IS 5 ONE 2   3
the dawn's early my country 'tis of centuries come . . . . . 268 IS 5 TWO 3   4
die for God for country and for Yale above . . . . 273 IS 5 TWO 8   12
to me the distinct country of your eyes, gifted . . . . 291 IS 5 FOUR 8   26
yes is a pleasant country: if's wintry (my lovely) . . . . . 578 1 X 1 38   1

COUNTRY'S

in token of their country's love received my dears . . . . . 266 IS 5 TWO 1   26

COUPLE

some lips plus a couple of) holes probably that's . . . . . 501 50 POEMS 15   20

+COUPLE

FOR CONTEXT, SEE . . . . 325 VIVA 17   8

COURAGE

marriage) you give me courage so that against myself . . . . 293 IS 5 FOUR 10   19
despise what is not courage my darling (for only . . . . . . 368 VIVA 59   17
a toe and any courage is a fear --long . . . . 511 50 POEMS 25   11
black because your absolute courage with its legs and . . . . 522 50 POEMS 35   14
must) immortal and the courage to receive time's mightiest . 675 95 POEMS 3   14
merrily humble your livingest courage / / / / . . . . 678 95 POEMS 6   16

COURSE

sixteen children and of course you know their mother, ... 254 IS 5 ONE 25   11
extraordinary. We refer, of course, to my position. A . . . . 263 IS 5 ONE 32   36
/ "next to of course god america i love . . . . 268 IS 5 TWO 3   1
die etcetera bravely of course my father used to . . . . . . 276 IS 5 TWO 10   15
read that beFore) of Course life being just a . . . . 315 VIVA 7   7
one it) solution (of course you must shake well) . . . . . . 323 VIVA 15   5
and what i (of course) carefully had decided oh . . . . 323 VIVA 15   28
libido and pursuing a course of instruction at radcliffe . . 327 VIVA 18   44
sure why not yuh course yeh well naturally i . . . . 400 NO THANKS 17   9
i know yes of course) but what i mean . . . . 400 NO THANKS 17   18

	PAGE	TITLE	LINE

COURSE (CONTINUED)

but it doesn't of course but you don't seem . . . . 638 (CHAIRE) 40   6

an ashbarrel so of course dominic took him home . . . . . . 680 95 POEMS 8   10

to meet in the course of a shall we . . . . 699 95 POEMS 27   16

total (preferably blonde of course) or on the other . . . . . 779 73 POEMS 7   7

COURSELESS

(fail me not) whose courseless waters are a gloat . . . . . . 9 T&C SONGS 1   3

COURTED

bed) when each other courted both was very very . . . . . . 401 NO THANKS 18   4

COURTEOUS

he is the most courteous of men should you . . . . 198 XLI PORTRAIT 6   25

+COURTEOUS

FOR CONTEXT, SEE . . . . 326 VIVA 18   17

COURTESIED

wee skipping high-heeled flames courtesied before my eyes or   44 T&C AMORES 8   7

COURTESY

immensity impeccably extending the courtesy of five o'clock . 197 XLI PORTRAIT 5   11

a candle furnished by courtesy of the management on . . . . . 263 IS 5 ONE 32   49

COVER

all dreams, draws down. cover her briefness in singing . . . 65 T&C POST IMPR 2   8

COVERED

together and drink coffee covered with froth half-mud and . . 198 XLI PORTRAIT 6   32

even whose recktie are covered by lloyd's / / . . . . 492 50 POEMS 6   16

COVERING

unsigned: remarkably brief but covering one complete miracle 504 50 POEMS 18   2

COW

way to hump a cow is not to get . . . . 500 50 POEMS 14   1

way to hump a cow is not to elevate . . . . 500 50 POEMS 14   9

way to hump a cow is not to push . . . . 500 50 POEMS 14   17

+COW

FOR CONTEXT, SEE . . . . 409 NO THANKS 26   3

COWARD

him vastly gird, a coward waiting clumsily to cease . . . . . 360 VIVA 51   6

than fail immeasurable fate) coward, clown, traitor, idiot, . 562 1 X 1 22   9

but fear-- mind's a coward; lies are laws) laugh, ... 651 (CHAIRE) 53   9

COWARDICE

all to call their cowardice quite agree) shall never . . . . 664 (CHAIRE) 66   14

refuted) clumsy some dull cowardice called a world vanishes, 669 (CHAIRE) 71   12

COWARDS

flowers resemble but trembling (cowards which fear to miss . 293 IS 5 FOUR 10   5

are such shoulders as cowards will scheme to harness: . . . . 439 NO THANKS 55   14

people into eachs and cowards into grow our can'ts . . . . . 537 50 POEMS 49   8

hearts were whole and cowards heroes (the popular the . . . . 798 73 POEMS 26   9

right since brave are cowards all) therefore despair, my . . 834 73 POEMS 62   22

COWER

nan they tremble and cower so pale: pale) for . . . . 509 50 POEMS 23   17

COWERS

from his kingdom winter cowers, seeing green armies steadily   4 T&C EPITHALAM 70

in dreadful corners hideously cowers-- i do excuse me, . . . 207 XLI SONNETS 3   8

COWS

hows to hump a cows the way to hump . . . . 500 50 POEMS 14   8

hows to hump a cows the way to hump . . . . 500 50 POEMS 14   16

hows to hump a cows / / / / . . . . 500 50 POEMS 14   24

COY

flesh whose casual mouth's coy rooting dies also. (my . . . . 131 & SON REAL 2   7

COYLY

perhaps. While permanent faces coyly bandy scandal of Mrs. . 70 T&C SON REAL 1   9

+CRABS

FOR CONTEXT, SEE . . . . 336 VIVA 27   10

+CRACK

FOR CONTEXT, SEE . . . . 347 VIVA 38   8

CRACKED

vow or the oath cracked length wise--let it go . . . . 569 1 X 1 29   4

a heart in it (cracked) open that heart, mabel . . . . 637 (CHAIRE) 39   3

CRACKING

in my huge blood, cracking brains A swiftlyenormous light . . 157 & SON ACTU 6   12

CRACKLE

graze of splintered normality crackle and sag of planes . . . 48 T&C IMPRESS 2   6

| | PAGE | TITLE | LINE |

CRACKLE (CONTINUED)
of houses--Lisboa. Like the crackle of a typewriter, in . . . 281 IS 5 THREE 5   6
CRACKLES
burn incense the bowl crackles upon the gloom arise . . . . . 31 T&C ORIENTALE 5   3
CRACKLING
may cry --even the crackling spark of (hung in . . . . 605 {CHAIRE} 7   8
CRACKSMAN
necessary lips) kid female cracksman of the nifty, ... 140 & SON REAL 11   10
CRADLE
foot and rock a cradle with the other) it . . . . 242 IS 5 ONE 13   10
CRADLES
pronounces young mistaken and cradles in rubbery one somewhat 499 50 POEMS 13   5
CRADLING
girlest she slender is cradling in joy her flower . . . . . . 518 50 POEMS 32   7
CRAFT
Sum precisely where a craft of cost the Ergo . . . . 494 50 POEMS 8   5
CRAFTY
veers the vast most crafty crow your kingbird doesn't . . . . 774 73 POEMS 2   8
CRAMMED
while His ears are crammed with the strenuous music . . . . . 117 & PORTRAIT 10   36
likely twice that (once crammed into someone's kitchenette) . 607 {CHAIRE} 9   3
CRANK
fattish hand turns the crank; the box sprouts fairies, . . . 69 T&C POST IMPR 6   2
in whose hand the crank goes desperately, round and . . . . 69 T&C POST IMPR 6   8
But i don't, the crank goes round desperate elves . . . . . 69 T&C POST IMPR 6   21
CRANKED
right to it ◇ cranked her up, slipped the . . . . 248 IS 5 ONE 19   9
CRANKIN
slowlywith, the handle ofa crankin It The L's roar . . . . . 101 & POST IMPR 11   48
CRAPS
have eaten them Yapenese Craps somebody might hardly never . 336 VIVA 27   10
CRASH
and oh sunlight-- the crash of the colours (of . . . . . . 280 IS 5 THREE 4   24
el Ls) -to sun (crash). Streets glit ter a, ... 444 NO THANKS 59   21
some im probably unworld crash to 1 nonillion (& . . . . . . 728 95 POEMS 56   11
leaf stirring makes a crash --far away (as far . . . . . . 839 73 POEMS 67   4
CRASHDIS
kly a thingish o crashdis appearing con ter fusion . . . . 646 {CHAIRE} 48   4
CRASHED
to joe 's left crashed pal dropped o god . . . . 496 50 POEMS 10   5
can each" while flame crashed "be so am and . . . . 626 {CHAIRE} 28   10
CRASHING
exroper of horned suddenly crashing things) man spits quickly 252 IS 5 ONE 23   11
tottering visions bigly come crashing into go (all than . . . 565 1 X 1 25   14
CRAVAT
at his im -peccable cravat directing being shooting his . . . 275 IS 5 TWO 9   34
CRAVEN
Be the cunning the craven (as think as can . . . . 801 73 POEMS 29   19
CRAWL
melody.... tiniest dead tunes crawl upon my face my . . . . . 69 T&C POST IMPR 6   27
us how we drink crawl eat walk die fly . . . . 528 50 POEMS 40   4
CRAWLED
room swung roun an crawled up into itself, an . . . . 332 VIVA 23   25
CRAWLING
or with the bugs crawling right all up all . . . . 272 IS 5 TWO 7   10
+CRAZED
FOR CONTEXT, SEE . . . . 106 & PORTRAIT 2   11
CRAZILY
kingdomofheaven up behind and crazily skating thither and . . 259 IS 5 ONE 29   3
over the tribune dances crazily & &) & . . . . 267 IS 5 TWO 2   5
(windows where blaze naLOVEme crazily ships bulge hearts by . 436 NO THANKS 52   5
through (stepp) this (ing) crazily seething of this raving . 437 NO THANKS 53   2
spiralling candy of tiniest forever--crazily from totally . . 480 NEW POEMS 18   23
moon. Employs a very crazily how clownlike that this . . . . 504 50 POEMS 18   7
of a dream (with crazily eyes of window) may . . . . 668 {CHAIRE} 70   3
and did i climb (crazily kissing) till into themselves . . . 694 95 POEMS 22   3
dog barks and how crazily houses eyes people smiles . . . . . 835 73 POEMS 63   3

	PAGE	TITLE	LINE

CRAZY

girl How i was crazy how i cried when . . . . 44 T&C AMORES 8   19
from dumb summer? O crazy daddy of death dance . . . . 80 T&C SON UNRE 5   9
make my pain their crazy meal letting thy tigers . . . . . . 139 & SON REAL 10   2
newness --and then. My crazy fingers liked your dress . . . . 173 & SON ACTU 22   8
and) ask a simple crazy thing singing in the . . . . 498 50 POEMS 12   29
of what (of a crazy man) don't ask me . . . . 501 50 POEMS 15   5
a spring at which crazy they drink who've climbed . . . . . . 563 1 X 1 23   2
spring yoo un-air-stan? me crazy me like evry-ting / . . . . 618 (CHAIRE) 20   29
/ / / / crazy jay blue) demon laughshriek . . . . 677 95 POEMS 5   1
went cruising into a crazy dream two were a . . . . 709 95 POEMS 37   2
--i thank heaven somebody's crazy enough to give me . . . . . 802 73 POEMS 30   32

CREASE

To (with a phrasing crease of hot subliminal lips, ... 130 & SON REAL 1   3
longest hands neatening each crease) will smooth entirely our 288 IS 5 FOUR 5   4

CREASED

(composed of captains in freshly-creased -uniforms with . . . 274 IS 5 TWO 9   22

CREASES

walls filthily push witless creases of screaming warmth chuck 96 & POST IMPR 8   4

CREASING

wildly in the slow-ly-in creasing fragility --. Dogs bark . . 63 T&C PORTRAIT 10   31
absurd eyes, the hair). Creasing its smoothness--and leave . 164 & SON ACTU 13   9
foam -like hair spatters creasing pillow next everywhere . . 358 VIVA 49   3

CREATE

or if i certainly create, lady, one of the . . . . 92 & POST IMPR 4   20
your lips slenderly should create one least smile (shyly . . 291 IS 5 FOUR 8   23
death"-- you only will create (who are so perfectly . . . . . 306 IS 5 FIVE 5   11
rain is unto colour; create me gradually (or as . . . . 372 VIVA 63   1
us open our selves. create (suddenly announce: hurl) blind . 422 NO THANKS 39   14
flesh neither may vibration create voice if therefore among . 425 NO THANKS 42   12
and cry) who dream, create and kill while the . . . . 446 NO THANKS 61   13
keen parallel specks float-ing create height, liv- ing ly . . 447 NO THANKS 62   3
will share for whom create is less than have . . . . 664 (CHAIRE) 66   8
don a doer's doom create is now contrive; imagined, ... 834 73 POEMS 62   7
crumbs of colour can create precision more than angels . . . 842 73 POEMS 70   3
Only whose vision can create the whole (being forever . . . . 845 73 POEMS 73   5

CREATED

(both male and female created He then, And every . . . . . . 267 IS 5 TWO 2   19
for, my sister isabel created hundreds (and hundreds) of . . 276 IS 5 TWO 10   8
careful how careful arms created this at length inexcusable, 295 IS 5 FOUR 12   6

CREATES

the gold cloth incessantly creates patterns of sudden lust . 34 T&C ORIENTALE 6   88
but" her, my "love creates love only" our / . . . . 572 1 X 1 32   18
beautiful: a little innocence creates a day. And something . 649 (CHAIRE) 51   8
only you) most emanation creates creation lovetree! least the 764 95 POEMS 90   48

CREATING

through hoops of fire, creating smoothness. People stare, the 279 IS 5 THREE 3   16

+CREATING

FOR CONTEXT, SEE . . . . 826 73 POEMS 54   17

CREATION

soul whose eagle frights creation, in whose palm Nike . . . . 3 T&C EPITHALAM   27
alchemist, the magus of creation, lifts a flower-- whence . . 6 T&C EPITHALAM   134
and Beatific Lord of Creation, MAN: at a least . . . . 315 VIVA 7   13
can sing as easily creation up all sky (really . . . . 558 1 X 1 18   13
--whose only secret all creation sings / / / . . . . 714 95 POEMS 42   14
you) most emanation creates creation lovetree! least the rose 764 95 POEMS 90   48
disappear, that hugest whole creation may be less . . . . . . 809 73 POEMS 37   13

CREATIVE

, darling sweet this creative never known complexity was . . 577 1 X 1 37   13

CREATURE

haunts the lyre, a creature of white hands, who . . . . 8 T&C OF NICOL   22
the house not a creature was stirring, not even . . . . 142 & SON REAL 13   12
Police (a dapper derbied creature, swaggers daintily . . . . 274 IS 5 TWO 9   29
pale naked very poor) creature of shadow, that among . . . . 374 VIVA 65   14
tOwns mOOn whisper less creature huge grO pingness whO . . . 383 NO THANKS 1   3
behold nor any breathing creature this? nothing except the . 582 1 X 1 42   11
through pasture wom an creature whom than earth hers . . . . 654 (CHAIRE) 56   8
enormous this how patient creature (who's never by never . . 674 95 POEMS 2   6

140

CREATURE (CONTINUED)

a marvel every breathing creature feels (but none can . . . . 735 95 POEMS 63   7
one more than each creature new (except your fear . . . . . . 762 95 POEMS 89   6
in even the laziest creature among us a wisdom . . . . 769 95 POEMS 95   8
exist --whereas that delicate creature is most herself while 813 73 POEMS 41   7
a thing: of a creature who's O cean (everywhere . . . . 840 73 POEMS 68   19

CREATURES

mystical, aroam with keen creatures of idiom (beings alert . 19 T&C PUELLA MEA 93
-gether by large sorry) creatures out of (clumsily shining . 442 NO THANKS 57   4
pretending they're birds sit creatures of quills (asleep who 483 NEW POEMS 21   10
kill each of those creatures called one's self so . . . . . 528 50 POEMS 40   12
Selves both now alive creatures (bright if by shadowy . . . . 757 95 POEMS 85   10
beak (as sweetly singing creatures know) cringes the hugest . 774 73 POEMS 2   6

+CREATURES

FOR CONTEXT, SEE . . . . 69 T&C POST IMPR 6   5

CREDIBLE

plore my unreal in -credible true each new self) . . . . . . 612 (CHAIRE) 14   6
born. Then, with not credible the anywhere eclipsing of . . . 843 73 POEMS 71   9

CREDIBLY

so (when flowers) in credibly (always are beautiful) ugly" . 738 95 POEMS 66   15

CREDO

imitate) ce (re peat credo fais do do neighbours . . . . . . 309 VIVA 1   34

CREDOS

knowings magic with bright credos each divisible fool (life . 452 NO THANKS 67   7

CREED

high estate whose mongrel creed is Might Makes Right . . . . 774 73 POEMS 2   11

CREEP

are they always which creep budgingly over some numbered . . 359 VIVA 50   15
boo may strut or creep ungenerous who ape deftly . . . . . . 440 NO THANKS 56   19
food; no cripple wouldn't creep one mile uphill to . . . . . 520 50 POEMS 34   31
of ghosts some few creep there here or on . . . . 541 1 X 1 1   10
onceupons each bothing (if) creep (by if) timelessly . . . . 681 95 POEMS 9   9

CREEPED

find But the moon creeped into the pink hand . . . . 125 & SEVEN POEMS 4 21

CREEPING

last light thread the creeping shores as out of . . . . . . 64 T&C POST IMPR 1   4
not fall she went creeping along the air over . . . . 284 IS 5 FOUR 1   14
disappear; rushing gently swiftly creeping through my dreams 369 VIVA 60   16

CREEPS

(out from behind Nowhere) creeps the deep thing everybody . . 330 VIVA 21   13

CREPT

ab- surd thoughts slyly crept into my highly sexed . . . . . 262 IS 5 ONE 32   4
go my vest and crept through the window she . . . . 284 IS 5 FOUR 1   11

CREPUSCULAR

amid the thrillers these crepuscular violinists among my and 230 IS 5 ONE 2   26

CRESCENDO

stars and flowers gold crescendo and silver muting of . . . . 39 T&C AMORES 4   8

CRICKETS

by always upon sunset, crickets within me whisper whose . . . 435 NO THANKS 51   37

CRICKS

curve of children gladly cricks where a hurdy-gurdy . . . . . 219 XLI SONNETS 15   7

CRIED

was crazy how i cried when i heard over . . . . 44 T&C AMORES 8   19
and did no wrong cried the third crumb, i . . . . 117 & PORTRAIT 10   17
i remember we all cried like the Missouri when . . . . 239 IS 5 ONE 10   32
have failed who have cried) lie bravely down sleep . . . . . 393 NO THANKS 10   10
laughed his joy she cried his grief bird by . . . . 515 50 POEMS 29   14
will freely die" she cried so high thermopylae heard . . . . 711 95 POEMS 39   13
might less frenziedly have cried eev mahmah hadn chuzd . . . 790 73 POEMS 18   15

+CRIED

FOR CONTEXT, SEE . . . . 405 NO THANKS 22   9

CRIES

is gone are the cries of Babylon.) Diarmuid Paris . . . . . . 23 T&C PUELLA MEA 261
chin.) that climbs and cries and runs and floats . . . . . . 69 T&C POST IMPR 6 43
flat pavements with icy cries of this and that . . . . 142 & SON REAL 13   7
and y play b cries "effendi" "Uh" "coffee" "uh" . . . . 200 XLI PORTRAIT 8   10
or sometimes two remarking cries of paklavah meeah. (Very . . 217 XLI SONNETS 13   12
had imagined a few cries drifting through high air . . . . . 283 IS 5 THREE 7   5

	PAGE	TITLE	LINE

CRIES (CONTINUED)

/ / / don't cries to please my musn't . . . . 343 VIVA 34 — 1

whens, wheels; wonders: murders. cries: hopes; houses, . . . 361 VIVA 52 — 18

west one Clock dimly cries nine, i stride among . . . . 434 NO THANKS 51 — 14

breathing) be" soul "more" cries: with a smile / . . . . . . 625 (CHAIRE) 27 — 24

world) whose silence are cries poems children dreams & . . . 719 95 POEMS 47 — 5

them down (old age cries No Tres) & (pas) . . . . 729 95 POEMS 57 — 8

today's today) the romp cries i and the me . . . . 773 73 POEMS 1 — 6

i'll give you" silently cries the (whom we call . . . . . . 837 73 POEMS 65 — 16

+CRIES

FOR CONTEXT, SEE . . . . 697 95 POEMS 25 — 13

CRIESWHICHAREWINGS

(hundreds of) millions of CriesWhichAreWings / / / / . . . . 840 73 POEMS 68 — 32

CRIGHT

pity the fool who cright god help me it . . . . 405 NO THANKS 22 — 9

CRIMBFLITTERINGISH

floatfallin, g; allwhere: a: crimbflitteringish is . . . . . 265 IS 5 ONE 34 — 6

CRIME

me with the square crime of life.... Cecile, the . . . . . . 138 & SON REAL 9 — 12

CRIMINAL

er Santa Claus a criminal (hears Darwin; asks about . . . . . 398 NO THANKS 15 — 14

CRIMSON

as a chord of crimson music Come hither O . . . . 27 T&C ORIENTALE 1 — 5

riding upon a thousand crimson years arched with agony . . . 30 T&C ORIENTALE 4 — 36

leatherfaced woman with the crimson nose and coquettishly- . 196 XLI PORTRAIT 4 — 3

cularity upon the most crimson assistance of my com- . . . . 197 XLI PORTRAIT 5 — 15

and again; whose golden, crimson dooms conceive an oceaning . 599 (CHAIRE) 1 — 2

CRINGE

s ofC omeg o CRINGE WITHS lilt (-ing- . . . . 421 NO THANKS 38 — 15

CRINGES

hath remained --the stone cringes clinging to the stone, . . 260 IS 5 ONE 30 — 4

sweetly singing creatures know) cringes the hugest heartless 774 73 POEMS 2 — 7

CRINGEWILTDROOLERY

yell itfulls o f cringewiltdroolery i mean really th . . . . 646 (CHAIRE) 48 — 7

CRINGING

a dangerous womb of cringing air) the largest hour . . . . . 115 & PORTRAIT 8 — 11

the useless flanks and cringing feet is this (shivering . . . 374 VIVA 65 — 12

a thousand dreams thick (cringing they brood breeding they . 439 NO THANKS 55 — 9

darkness and winter and cringing --it's spring (all our . . . 665 (CHAIRE) 67 — 17

+CRINGING

FOR CONTEXT, SEE . . . . 94 & POST IMPR 6 — 11

FOR CONTEXT, SEE . . . . 139 & SON REAL 10 — 5

CRINKLING

does. the brain of cleverly-crinkling -water pursues the . . 160 & SON ACTU 9 — 4

CRIPPLE

wished him food; no cripple wouldn't creep one mile . . . . . 520 50 POEMS 34 — 31

CRIPPLED

ambrosial grace, goddess, thy crippled thunder-foraging groom 6 T&C EPITHALAM — 149

CRISP

little stranger thing than crisp Sheba with her king . . . . 17 T&C PUELLA MEA — 8

of ivory. The immaculate crisp head is such as . . . . 20 T&C PUELLA MEA — 139

syllable its leaves go crisp with miracle. Love!--maker of . 22 T&C PUELLA MEA — 236

and love ladies with crisp eyes and frail, in . . . . 23 T&C PUELLA MEA — 287

in twilight becomes unutterably crisp a thing, which tightens 68 T&C POST IMPR 5 — 8

with the tightened eyes crisp ogling shoulders and the . . . 72 T&C SON REAL 3 — 6

your first twitch of crisp boy flesh dips my . . . . 140 & SON REAL 11 — 7

flower, and the flesh crisp set my love-tooth on . . . . . . 173 & SON ACTU 22 — 10

so tinily these, your crisp eyes actually shall contain . . . 294 IS 5 FOUR 11 — 8

washed panes into a crisp todo of murdering uncouth . . . . . 354 VIVA 45 — 9

CRISPER

she sharpens and becomes crisper until i smile with . . . . . 301 IS 5 FOUR 18 — 12

CRISPING

lips and eyes inwardly crisping for my friend, feeling . . . 193 XLI PORTRAIT 1 — 8

CRISPLY

amaying. thy whitest feet crisply are straying. Always thy . 13 T&C SONGS 3 — 8

when his scythe takes crisply the whim of thy . . . . 215 XLI SONNETS 11 — 6

CRITICS

measures her guest (as critics will upon a poet . . . . . . 418 NO THANKS 35 — 11

142

		PAGE	TITLE	LINE

CROCODILE
    with Lord Rothermere. A crocodile eats a native, who . . . . 262 IS 5 ONE 32   23
CROCUS
    dress ascends the golden crocus from the dead. On . . . . . .   4 T&C EPITHALAM   64
CROCUSES
    brought to bed of crocuses When you sing in . . . . 61 T&C PORTRAIT 9   17
    they explode silently into crocuses of brightness. (That is . 282 IS 5 THREE 6   31
CRONE
    gai -te. a sharp crone dodders be- tween taxis . . . . 384 NO THANKS 2   3
CROOK
    righteous comfortable) unworlds thief crook cynic . . . . . . 677 95 POEMS 5   9
CROOKED
    like memories in one crooked street of a mind . . . . 98 & POST IMPR 9   17
    too cool to be crooked and it's too firm . . . . 126 & SEVEN POEMS 5   3
    some distance from the crooked town) a harbour fools . . . . 319 VIVA 11   17
CROOKEDLY
    people, for winter who crookedly care. / / / . . . . 190 XLI SONGS 12   22
CROOKING
    MAN: at a least crooking of Whose compassionate digit, . . . 315 VIVA 7   14
CROON
    coming merely, with a croon of mingling robes musically . . . 10 T&C SONGS 1   40
    what does little Ernest croon in his death at . . . . 409 NO THANKS 26   1
    eyes grip live loop croon mime nakedly hurl asquirm . . . . . 445 NO THANKS 60   24
    a bedroom) begins to croon more particularly at just . . . . 813 73 POEMS 41   4
CROONS
    subprincestures pooped universe (of croons canned a la . . . 425 NO THANKS 42   2
CROSS
    are now judgment day cross the threshold have no . . . . . . 118 & PORTRAIT 10   41
    tit one carves a cross in her behind they . . . . 427 NO THANKS 44   6
    erect your yous to cross the chasm of time . . . . 605 {CHAIRE} 7   12
CROSSES
    where a large road crosses and all the people . . . . 86 T&C SON ACTU 5   12
CROSSING
    thou dost inveigle into crossing sidewalks the unwary . . . . 61 T&C PORTRAIT 9   2
    with radishred legs said (crossing them slowly) "I'm asleep. 228 IS 5 ONE MARJ   3
    their knees. people begin crossing people) and hErE cOmEs . . 280 IS 5 THREE 4   8
CROUCH
    (meet) t (touch) ems crouch (lunge)ing bruiseD . . . . . . 388 NO THANKS 5   3
CROUCHED
    dawn. four lean hounds crouched low and smiling the . . . . . 14 T&C SONGS 4   4
    dawn. four lean hounds crouched low and smiling the . . . . . 14 T&C SONGS 4   14
    dawn. four lean hounds crouched low and smiling the . . . . . 14 T&C SONGS 4   24
    dawn. four lean hounds crouched low and smiling my . . . . . 14 T&C SONGS 4   34
    vacant eyes, painfully perpetually crouched, quivering, upon 231 IS 5 ONE 3   50
+CROUCHED
    FOR CONTEXT, SEE . . . . 795 73 POEMS 23   3
CROUCHING
    horses of gold delicately crouching beneath silver youths the 110 & PORTRAIT 6   35
CROW
    the vast most crafty crow your kingbird doesn't give . . . . 774 73 POEMS 2   8
CROWD
    all dainties which do crowd gaily upon oblivion sweeter . . . 23 T&C PUELLA MEA   271
    a woman in the crowd whinnied and a man . . . . 53 T&C PORTRAIT 1   34
    flics rush batter the crowd sprawls collapses singing knocked 274 IS 5 TWO 9   6
    colours , sensuously (the crowd howls faintly blubbering . . 280 IS 5 THREE 4   13
    boodle's bent is the crowd inclined it's freedom from . . . . 635 {CHAIRE} 37   23
CROWDING
    sand. across this water, crowding tints: browns and whites . 281 IS 5 THREE 5   5
+CROWDING
    FOR CONTEXT, SEE . . . . 100 & POST IMPR 11   14
CROWDLOOMROAR
    coil charge &) swooN Crowdloomroar: ing; diskface, es (are . 388 NO THANKS 5   19
CROWDS
    a hundred these sounds crowds odours it is in . . . . 238 IS 5 ONE 9   3
    tween taxis swirl hues crowds mov -ing ing ing . . . . 384 NO THANKS 2   4
CROWING
    (topped with effigies of crowing gold) nuzzle against summer 340 VIVA 31   17

143

+CROWINGLY
    FOR CONTEXT, SEE . . . . 423 NO THANKS 40   8
CROWN
    palm Nike presents the crown sweetest to man, whose . . . . .   3 T&C EPITHALAM   28
    in a kind of crown he dressed in black . . . . 470 NEW POEMS 8   3
    pretend flowers this candy crown with this candy little . . . 470 NEW POEMS 8   8
+CROWN
    FOR CONTEXT, SEE . . . . 342 VIVA 33   19
CROWNED
    ear sits always a crowned king twir- ling an . . . . 32 T&C ORIENTALE 6 10
    queens, queens laughing lightly crowned with far colours, . . 211 XLI SONNETS 7   15
    not move ; is .crowned the with shrill Nonleaf . . . . 346 VIVA 37   26
CROWS
    however, the flight of crows had ceased. I withdrew . . . . . 263 IS 5 ONE 32   54
    green field watchin four crows drop into sunset, playin . . . 332 VIVA 23   31
CRUCIFIX
    expensive furniture upsets a crucifix which smashes into . . 203 XLI LA GUERRE 1 14
CRUDE
    i will breathe such crude perfection as divides by . . . . . 428 NO THANKS 45   10
    subtle air is comparatively crude; an indestructible occult . 799 73 POEMS 27   17
CRUDITIES
    always (from these hurrying crudities of blood and flesh) . . 297 IS 5 FOUR 14   10
CRUEL
    a white water the cruel bugle sang before. Horn . . . . 14 T&C SONGS 4   10
    people contented hideous hopeless cruel happy and it is . . . 50 T&C IMPRESS 4   15
    i turn to the cruel-littleness of cold (when battling . . . . 142 & SON REAL 13   2
    giving to steal and cruel kind, a heart to . . . . 521 50 POEMS 34   57
    aware) kind neither nor cruel (only complete) i not . . . . . 564 1 X 1 24   7
    and smiles name it cruel fair or blessed evil-- . . . . 804 73 POEMS 32   7
    the path to nothingness (cruel now cancels kind; friends . . 834 73 POEMS 62   3
CRUEL-LITTLENESS
    i turn to the cruel-littleness of cold (when battling . . . . 142 & SON REAL 13   2
CRUELLY
    daddy of death dance cruelly for us and start . . . . 80 T&C SON UNRE 5 10
    / / / / cruelly, love walk the autumn . . . . 190 XLI SONGS 12   1
    of sunlight falls and, cruelly, across the grass Comes . . . 190 XLI SONGS 12   8
CRUELTY
    suspicious madder, importing the cruelty of roses. The . . . 103 & POST IMPR 13   1
CRUISE
    foul windows absurd clouds cruise nobly ridiculous skies . . 442 NO THANKS 57   13
+CRUISE
    FOR CONTEXT, SEE . . . . 337 VIVA 28   7
CRUISING
    clever and he went cruising into a crazy dream . . . . 709 95 POEMS 37   1
+CRUISING
    FOR CONTEXT, SEE . . . . 361 VIVA 52   11
    FOR CONTEXT, SEE . . . . 421 NO THANKS 38   2
CRUMB
    am may the first crumb said whereupon its fellow . . . . . . 117 & PORTRAIT 10   12
    wrong cried the third crumb, i am should and . . . . 117 & PORTRAIT 10   17
    good; and the last crumb with some shame whispered . . . . . 117 & PORTRAIT 10   21
    star isful beckoningly fabulous crumb / / / / . . . . 456 NO THANKS 71   15
    per F ectl y crumb ling eye -holes oUt . . . . 534 50 POEMS 46   16
    which sprints for the crumb of our Now) twiceuponatime . . . 639 (CHAIRE) 41   12
+CRUMB
    FOR CONTEXT, SEE . . . . 546 1 X 1 6   12
CRUMBLE
    (whom fairies hate) shall crumble the mouth-flower fleet . . 83 T&C SON ACTU 2   12
    (people tumble down. people crumble to their knees. people . 280 IS 5 THREE 4   6
CRUMBLES
    earth withers the moon crumbles one by one stars . . . . . . 38 T&C AMORES 3   6
    life hurl my yes, crumbles hand (ful released conarefetti) . 265 IS 5 ONE 34   2
CRUMBLING
    her blind miles of crumbling silence seriously smiles / . . . 81 T&C SON UNRE 6 14
    pillar pursue curiously a crumbling flight into the absolute 112 & PORTRAIT 6   83
    is the season of crumbling & folding hopes, hark; . . . . . . 345 VIVA 36   13
+CRUMBLING
    FOR CONTEXT, SEE . . . . 319 VIVA 11   2

	PAGE	TITLE	LINE

+CRUMBLING (CONTINUED)

FOR CONTEXT, SEE . . . . 534 50 POEMS 46   16

FOR CONTEXT, SEE . . . . 723 95 POEMS 51   3

CRUMBS

God will find six crumbs stooping by the coffinlid . . . . . 117 & PORTRAIT 10   4

whereupon its fellow five crumbs chuckled as if they . . . . 117 & PORTRAIT 10   14

which the six subjunctive crumbs twitch like mutilated . . . 117 & PORTRAIT 10   30

flesh.... And eyes big love-crumbs, and possibly i like . . . 175 & SON ACTU 24   12

(theys) the : se! crumbs things? Its noyesiyou he-she . . . . 417 NO THANKS 34   22

born-- some for whom crumbs of colour can create . . . . . . 842 73 POEMS 70   3

+CRUMBS

FOR CONTEXT, SEE . . . . 265 IS 5 ONE 34   5

FOR CONTEXT, SEE . . . . 265 IS 5 ONE 34   5

FOR CONTEXT, SEE . . . . 265 IS 5 ONE 34   8

FOR CONTEXT, SEE . . . . 725 95 POEMS 53   6

CRUMBSHANDFUL

areEyes shy-dodge is bright cruMbshandful, quick-hurl edinwho 265 IS 5 ONE 34   4

CRUMP

mine's tou ching this crump led cap mumble some . . . . 314 VIVA 6   18

CRUMPLE

fragile splendors from us crumple them hide them in . . . . . 41 T&C AMORES 5   20

CRUMPLED

in gold, which presently crumpled collapses. exhaling a red . 188 XLI SONGS 10   9

+CRUMPLED

FOR CONTEXT, SEE . . . . 314 VIVA 6   18

CRUSHING

(and quite with out crushing) the papery weightless . . . . . 652 {CHAIRE} 54   8

CRUSOELIKE

their master's spirit stooping, Crusoelike examines fearingly 344 VIVA 35   13

CRUST

on the eyes' brittle crust (only feeling the belly's . . . . 132 & SON REAL 3   6

CRY

my body hears the cry of Spring, and with . . . . 22 T&C PUELLA MEA 234

move, the old trumpets cry; who gavest as one . . . . 209 XLI SONNETS 5   12

and the small spiritual cry of spring utters a . . . . 213 XLI SONNETS 9   6

immortal Spring express a cry of How do you . . . . 255 IS 5 ONE 26   6

by all flowers. Don't cry --the best gesture of . . . . 290 IS 5 FOUR 7   10

wonder. oh and they cry "to be, being, that . . . . 295 IS 5 FOUR 12   17

--sing)all are aLl (cry alL See) o (ver . . . . 347 VIVA 38   33

above; to whom i cry, remembering her face, i . . . . 360 VIVA 51   34

r O wing; ly: cry. be, gi N s . . . . 423 NO THANKS 40   9

--haunts all unsleep this cry of one fiend, a . . . . 439 NO THANKS 55   7

is here unlives do cry on him they shat . . . . 440 NO THANKS 56   8

is here unpoets do cry unfools unfree undeaths who . . . . . 440 NO THANKS 56   32

Lsb El l s! cry) (be llsbe lls) b . . . . 444 NO THANKS 59   32

see (who laugh and cry) who dream, create and . . . . 446 NO THANKS 61   13

no smallest voice might cry for he could feel . . . . 520 50 POEMS 34   15

too-nearishness and shall we cry and shall we laugh . . . . . 528 50 POEMS 40   6

trees, it's they shall cry hello to the spring . . . . 560 1 X 1 20   16

a truth is a cry of a whole of . . . . 587 1 X 1 47   16

grave gay brave bright cry of alive with a . . . . 587 1 X 1 47   22

any bright word may cry --even the crackling spark . . . . . 605 {CHAIRE} 7   7

(i have none) "don't cry dear violet you may . . . . 684 95 POEMS 12   3

(as well as to cry and sing, my love . . . . 686 95 POEMS 14   3

she gave a terrible cry "no slave's unlife shall . . . . . . 711 95 POEMS 39   10

any foe a friend --cry nay: cry yea-- november . . . . 798 73 POEMS 26   20

a friend --cry nay: cry yea-- november would be . . . . . . 798 73 POEMS 26   20

jump shout (laugh dance cry sing) for it's Spring . . . . . . 835 73 POEMS 63   18

! life love! bells cry bells (the sea of . . . . 841 73 POEMS 69   5

+CRY

FOR CONTEXT, SEE . . . . 774 73 POEMS 2   3

FOR CONTEXT, SEE . . . . 774 73 POEMS 2   12

CRYING

his head flowers, always crying to nobody something about . . 102 & POST IMPR 12   15

the who limps man crying silence upward --to have . . . . . . 437 NO THANKS 53   11

agains De Big Boss (crying) jew wop rich poor . . . . 618 {CHAIRE} 20   11

and there's time for crying-- for hoping for despair . . . . 683 95 POEMS 11   9

you're alive or i'm-- crying to lose (as down . . . . 716 95 POEMS 44   33

CRYING (CONTINUED)

losing and laughing and crying) children whose any sadness . 749 95 POEMS 77   7

CRYINGLY

through the sharp light cryingly as the knights flew. . . . . 302 IS 5 FIVE 1   15

CRYINGS

their everyones laughed their cryings and did their dance . . 515 50 POEMS 29   18

CRYLAUGHINGLY

who feels a world crylaughingly float away leaving just . . . 720 95 POEMS 48   7

CRYLESSLY

riding alive down while crylessly drifting through vast most 661 {CHAIRE} 63   13

CUBE

taste of this squirming cube of undimishied silence, supports 201 XLI PORTRAIT 9   18

CUBES

curve of flesh exactly cubes of tiny fragrance try; . . . . . 214 XLI SONNETS 10   4

CUBESANDOVALSOF

loves these better than, cubesandovalsof sweetness but it . . 100 & POST IMPR 11   28

CUBICAL

one--onion for. putrescence is Cubical sliced-nicelybits Of,   94 & POST IMPR 6   10

CUDDLE

thin earths chatterish strut cuddle & shrink: as through . . 346 VIVA 37   4

CUDDLED

glass mind muddled and cuddled by dreams (or some . . . . . . 354 VIVA 45   7

CUE

sex squeaked like a billiard-cue chalking itself, as not . . 170 & SON ACTU 19   9

by his quote eye cue unquote. Much better than . . . . 807 73 POEMS 35   8

CUED

/ / the surely Cued motif smites truly to . . . . 311 VIVA 3   2

CUFFS

directing being shooting his cuffs saluted everywhere . . . . 275 IS 5 TWO 9   35

CUL

aussi.... "bon dos, bon cul de Paris" (Marie Vierge . . . . . 120 & PORTRAIT 12   14

invin cible nod oc cul t ke ylike writhe . . . . 349 VIVA 40   16

CULARITY

the innovation of mus- cularity upon the most crimson . . . . 197 XLI PORTRAIT 5   15

CULLEN

causes indigestion to William Cullen Longfel- low's small . . 263 IS 5 ONE 32   52

CULT

meanwhile a re- ligious cult based on consubstantial . . . . 262 IS 5 ONE 32   25

squawk and add, the cult of Same is all . . . . 438 NO THANKS 54   12

CULTIVATE

/ / i will cultivate within me scrupulously the . . . . 328 VIVA 19   1

+CULTURE

FOR CONTEXT, SEE . . . . 331 VIVA 22   6

CUMBINE

(wut) hova in big cumbine wid i (check undublcheck) . . . . . 325 VIVA 17   17

CUNNING

were the shapely sharp cunning and withal delirious feet . . 17 T&C PUELLA MEA   28

his eyelashes-- the other, cunning ugly lame; but as . . . . 799 73 POEMS 27   5

joy with him then Cunning forged a web so . . . . 799 73 POEMS 27   16

silence say Be the cunning the craven (as think . . . . 801 73 POEMS 29   19

CUP

at every kiss of daisy-cup, and from her cheek . . . .   8 T&C OF NICOL   29

drop, coppers into, the littletin-cup His wrappedupbody . . . 100 & POST IMPR 11   40

CUPBOARD

skeleton stepped from his cupboard gallantly offering to . . 326 VIVA 18   10

CUPIDOERGOSUM

anc & e & --cupidoergosum spun= flash omiepsicronlonO-- . . . 431 NO THANKS 48   23

CUPS

the all saucers but cups if begin to spoons . . . . 287 IS 5 FOUR 4   16

CURB

because on the frying curb the quiet face lay . . . . 52 T&C PORTRAIT 1   14

the, rocker by the, curb, tipping and tipping, the . . . . . 166 & SON ACTU 15   3

girl-flops to the Geddup curb leans carefully spewing into . 330 VIVA 21   11

+CURB

FOR CONTEXT, SEE . . . . 257 IS 5 ONE 27   36

FOR CONTEXT, SEE . . . . 332 VIVA 23   10

CURE

marriage is a sure cure for masturbation). A dirty . . . . . 167 & SON ACTU 16   5

	PAGE	TITLE	LINE

CURE (CONTINUED)
    disease which quacks will cure when pimps may please? . . . . 527 50 POEMS 39   23
    merely my fourth will cure the laziest self of . . . . . . 537 50 POEMS 49   2
CURIOSITY
    sleep wherein all human curiosity we'll spend (gladly, as . . 675 95 POEMS 3   12
    poem prose-- caution for curiosity (and close your eyes) . . 689 95 POEMS 17   7
CURIOUS
    the hovering high perfume curious of that one month . . . . . 5 T&C EPITHALAM 102
    me is a more curious thing (a thing more . . . . 17 T&C PUELLA MEA 25
    gles a few mildly curious rai -ned on people . . . . 267 IS 5 TWO 2   17
    i mean, should any curious dawn discuss our mingling . . . . 379 VIVA 70   6
+CURIOUS
    FOR CONTEXT, SEE . . . . 477 NEW POEMS 15   2
CURIOUSLY
    things amorous fashioned very curiously of roses and of . . . 20 T&C PUELLA MEA 137
    the moon) --fashioned very curiously of roses and of . . . . 22 T&C PUELLA MEA 229
    young the caving ages curiously con) --but the lunge . . . . 77 T&C SON UNRE 2   4
    and the pillar pursue curiously a crumbling flight into . . . 112 & PORTRAIT 6   82
    a nigger's voice feels curiously cool (suddenly-Lights go! . 167 & SON ACTU 16   18
    faces meshing with my curiously instant appreciation exposed 197 XLI PORTRAIT 5   8
+CURIOUSLY
    FOR CONTEXT, SEE . . . . 101 & POST IMPR 11   63
CURL
    sacks spin kegs they curl loving around beers the . . . . . . 114 & PORTRAIT 7   9
    greys between mouthed houses curl thirstily. Dead stars . . . 139 & SON REAL 10   12
    two pink big lips curl.... how Jimmie was framed . . . . . . 149 & SON REAL 20   15
    "novocaine?" the eyes outstart, curl, bloat, are newly baked 226 IS 5 ONE MAME   13
    burst lurch things phantoms curl (mouth seekingly lips wander 565 1 X 1 25   2
CURLED
    was a tendril fleetly curled upon frailness) used to . . . . 23 T&C PUELLA MEA 279
    you exactly paled and curled with mystic lips take . . . . . 71 T&C SON REAL 2   12
    hands flowers of silence curled upon a wish, to . . . . 205 XLI SONNETS 1   3
    lie many a flower curled, in other lands where . . . . 208 XLI SONNETS 4   10
    with in both pockets curled hands moves) why then . . . . . . 299 IS 5 FOUR 16   10
    of yes live (skilfully curled) all worlds / / . . . . 443 NO THANKS 58   9
CURLING
    in every curved and curling thing, yet holds continuous . . . 5 T&C EPITHALAM 90
    small hands and with curling infantile fingers it understood 284 IS 5 FOUR 1   3
+CURLING
    FOR CONTEXT, SEE . . . . 395 NO THANKS 12   15
    FOR CONTEXT, SEE . . . . 503 50 POEMS 17   7
CURLS
    omnipotent brow showers its curls of unendured eternal gold . 4 T&C EPITHALAM 38
CURRANTS
    it stains itself, with currants and cherries it (swallow . . 100 & POST IMPR 11   23
CURRENCY
    flesh silver, like the currency of faint cities eternal--ere 9 T&C SONGS 1   32
CURSE
    turn into a little curse of wax. Something, distinct . . . . 164 & SON ACTU 13   16
    July oration, with a curse and a frown Amy . . . . 249 IS 5 ONE 20   2
    prey did kick and curse until for wear their . . . . 339 VIVA 30   24
CURSED
    / / / light cursed falling in a singular . . . . 133 & SON REAL 4   1
    and only half awake, cursed with pimples, correctly dressed, 262 IS 5 ONE 32   7
CURSELAUGHGROPING
    proregress heandshe-ingly people trickle curselaughgroping . 330 VIVA 21   3
CURSING
    fists hair wood erect cursing hatless who (bent by . . . . . 277 IS 5 THREE 1   9
CURTAIN
    microscopic stage whose jouncing curtain. , rises upon one . 55 T&C PORTRAIT 3   7
    and when the final curtain strikes the world away, ... 75 T&C SON REAL 6   2
    lost thing (like a curtain on which tiny the . . . . 516 50 POEMS 30   5
CURTAINED
    hands of waiting years, curtained with wordless worship . . . 6 T&C EPITHALAM 115
CURTAINING
    --let but the incurious curtaining dusk be drawn surpassing . 5 T&C EPITHALAM 85
CURTAINS
    gently draws apart her curtains, and lays bare her . . . . . 8 T&C OF NICOL 15

CURTAINS (CONTINUED)

smacked me: pummeling the curtains, drooped to a purr... . . 228 IS 5 ONE MARJ 14
/ / / / curtains part) the peacockappareled prodigy . . . . . 232 IS 5 ONE 3 1

CURVE

handorgan prop- ping the curve of the tiny motheaten . . . . 101 & POST IMPR 11 46
light, against whose enormous curve of flesh exactly cubes . 214 XLI SONNETS 10 3
neatest distance.... A new curve of children gladly cricks . 219 XLI SONNETS 15 7
by somebody along a curve of road which eats . . . . 281 IS 5 THREE 5 8

+CURVE

FOR CONTEXT, SEE . . . . 278 IS 5 THREE 2 9

CURVECORNERS

uPDownwardishly find everywheres noisecoloured curvecorners . 311 VIVA 3 17

CURVED

of desire in every curved and curling thing, yet . . . . . . 5 T&C EPITHALAM 90
strangely my life is curved since the best he . . . . 292 IS 5 FOUR 9 6
(don't forget to remember) Curved (and that reminds me . . . 315 VIVA 7 1

CURVEDSHIP

uddenl Y totouch the curvedship of Her- ....kIss her: . . . . 122 & SEVEN POEMS 1 7

CURVEOFHUNGER

empty stomachesClenche beautiful-curveofhunger, ... 101 & POST IMPR 11 71

CURVES

secret bowers) among the curves of that delicious boy . . . . 3 T&C EPITHALAM 23
darkness in the sleeping curves of my body Shall . . . . . . 189 XLI SONGS 11 8
being otherwise made compose curves and yellows, angles or . 291 IS 5 FOUR 8 3

CURVING

a little more like curving colour (say orange) against . . . 152 & SON ACTU 1 3
one beyond one immaculate curving cool treasures of silence . 156 & SON ACTU 5 3
with your body's suddenly curving entire warm questions / . . 282 IS 5 THREE 6 35
from which rise slim curving mighty children while a . . . . 384 NO THANKS 2 20
/ into a truly curving form enters my soul . . . . 419 NO THANKS 36 2
lenses extend unwish through curving wherewhen till unwish . 554 1 X 1 14 7

CURVINGLY

the mouth there trysts curvingly a fragile smile which . . . 20 T&C PUELLA MEA 149
occasional steep youth swallows curvingly the keenness of my 140 & SON REAL 11 6
caring eyes watches; truly, curvingly while reacts (sharp now 344 VIVA 35 5
yellowandbluish cat (perched why Curvingly at this) window; . 434 NO THANKS 51 33

CURVINGS

silently yes before angel curvings upon a mostless more . . . 480 NEW POEMS 18 12

CURVISH

rletlycaR v Ingharness Of curvish (,males await she . . . . 342 VIVA 33 16

CUSPIDOR

squeaky songs into the cuspidor-col ouredRoom and, my ears . 101 & POST IMPR 11 44

CUSS

him lift the poor cuss tenderly this side up . . . . 270 IS 5 TWO 5 14

CUSSING

lled me n dis cussing "parity" in l'ho tel . . . . 708 95 POEMS 36 11

CUT

quips of flesh. Loretta, cut the comedy kid.... Fran . . . . 138 & SON REAL 9 15
to sing you'd almost cut your thumb so right . . . . 624 {CHAIRE} 26 15

+CUT

FOR CONTEXT, SEE . . . . 101 & POST IMPR 11 52

CUTE

in quick softness. Unspontaneous. cute. the signal perfume of 74 T&C SON REAL 5 4
monkeyglands in millionaires a cute idea n'est-ce pas? . . . 245 IS 5 ONE 16 14

CYNIC

comfortable) unworlds thief crook cynic (swimfloatdrifting . 677 95 POEMS 5 9

CYTHEREA

flower of unchastity, imperial Cytherea, from frail foam . . 7 T&C EPITHALAM 161

D

Mrs. N and Professor D ....the Cambridge ladies do . . . . . 70 T&C SON REAL 1 10
can't casts no shadow D drink and E eat . . . . 390 NO THANKS 7 3
omiepsicronlonO-- megaeta? p aul D-as-in-tip-toe r apeR / / . 431 NO THANKS 48 28
"Nothing" in 1944 A D "can stand against the . . . . 636 {CHAIRE} 38 9
a distinct grandiloquent deep D; while all skies fall . . . . 650 {CHAIRE} 52 16

D-RE-A-MI-N-GL-Y

/ / / / D-re-a-mi-N-gl-Y leaves (sEe) locked in . . . . 838 73 POEMS 66 1

D'OEUVRES

mercy. (exit the hors d'oeuvres) / / / / . . . . 243 IS 5 ONE 14 16

	PAGE	TITLE	LINE

DAD

who owns one ask Dad, He knows). / / . . . . 233 IS 5 ONE 4   24
hooz gwine ter hate dad hurt fool wurl no . . . . 519 50 POEMS 33   18
i rather suppose" "will's dad never gave me one . . . . 707 95 POEMS 35   17
whom, among her dollies, dad first ("don't tell your   . . . . 794 73 POEMS 22   3

DADA

the grandja that was dada? make me a child, ... 233 IS 5 ONE 4   13

DADDY

dumb summer? O crazy daddy of death dance cruelly . . . . . . 80 T&C SON UNRE 5   9

DAEMON

immaculate thin things half daemon half tree among sunset . . 362 VIVA 53   6

DAEMONS

the with shrill Nonleaf daemons and large The downlife   . . . 346 VIVA 37   27
shadows while hunted by daemons seethe luminous leopards (on 586 1 X 1 46   14

DAFFODILS

/ in time of daffodils (who know the goal . . . . 688 95 POEMS 16   1

DAFFY

in Topeka, went clean daffy, and which was very . . . . 145 & SON REAL 16   8

DAILY

unbold) also, tomorrow the daily papers will feature Peace   . 142 & SON REAL 13   9

DAINTIES

and disappears-- of all dainties which do crowd gaily . . . . 23 T&C PUELLA MEA 271

DAINTILY

twilight (who slenderly descends, daintily carrying in her   . 93 & POST IMPR 5   10
dapper derbied creature, swaggers daintily twiddling his tiny 274 IS 5 TWO 9   29

DAINTY

listen well how the dainty destroyed hero clamps the   . . . . 111 & PORTRAIT 6   41

+DAINTY

FOR CONTEXT, SEE . . . . 831 73 POEMS 59   2

DAISIES

the grave frailty of daisies--by what rare unease revealed   . 5 T&C EPITHALAM   94
And the big bullying daisies through the field wonderful   . . 26 T&C CHANSONS 3   5
intricate faint birds by daisies and twilights Deepen her,   . 65 T&C POST IMPR 2   10
earth tinily whirls; while daisies grow (and boys and . . . . 451 NO THANKS 66   12

DAISY

at every kiss of daisy-cup, and from her cheek . . . . 8 T&C OF NICOL   29
suggestion) "or even a daisy-- your thorniest question my . . 625 (CHAIRE) 27   12
/ / once White&Gold daisy in the Dust (trite . . . . 690 95 POEMS 18   2
to give me a daisy / / / / . . . . 802 73 POEMS 30   33

DAISY-CUP

at every kiss of daisy-cup, and from her cheek . . . . 8 T&C OF NICOL   29

DAM

slim hot queens with dam next to nothing on) . . . . 242 IS 5 ONE 13   5
how you know the dam rent's going to and . . . . 242 IS 5 ONE 13   19

DAME

pissoir enters abruptly Notre Dame (whereas de gustibus non . 245 IS 5 ONE 16   23
hat off to this dame: he won't be out . . . . 790 73 POEMS 18   7

DAMN

"god" (blushing slightly) --"O damn ginks like dis Gawd"   . . 228 IS 5 ONE MARJ   6
this rose give a damn... bring on your fireworks, ... 264 IS 5 ONE 33   20
give a soft white damn Whom it touches / . . . . 328 VIVA 19   23
kingbird doesn't give a damn-- his royal warcry is . . . . . 774 73 POEMS 2   2
kingbird doesn't give a damn for murderers of high . . . . 774 73 POEMS 2   9
/ / it's so damn sweet when Anybody-- yes; . . . . 779 73 POEMS 7   2
& never will) any damn thing : far from . . . . 793 73 POEMS 21   12

+DAMN

FOR CONTEXT, SEE . . . . 242 IS 5 ONE 13   19
FOR CONTEXT, SEE . . . . 519 50 POEMS 33   8

DAMNED

of the innumerable capering damned) --staring wildly up and . 118 & PORTRAIT 10   38
i mean a god damned lot of people don't . . . . 272 IS 5 TWO 7   13
where say over the damned table and we hold . . . . 287 IS 5 FOUR 4   17
must or if be damned with whomever's afraid down . . . . . 424 NO THANKS 41   8
she quick who stop damned fall all we go . . . . 496 50 POEMS 10   13
the dull are the damned / / / / . . . . 499 50 POEMS 13   14
your whole (yes god damned) life is a Flop . . . . 702 95 POEMS 30   13

DAN

it gents: our hero, Dan who as you've guessed . . . . 254 IS 5 ONE 25   14

DAN (CONTINUED)

a nda n-saint dance! Dan Sai ntd anc & . . . . 431 NO THANKS 48   20

DANAE

within whose brightening strictness Danae saw the night . . .   4 T&C EPITHALAM   51

DANCE

the purpled world will dance upon Between my lips . . . . . . 16 T&C SONGS 6   4
melody of probable violins dance the square virtues and . . . 43 T&C AMORES 7   33
get me?) will maybe dance and maybe sing and . . . . 72 T&C SON REAL 3   13
crazy daddy of death dance cruelly for us and . . . . 80 T&C SON UNRE 5   10
(knows and WhoEver would)? dance lewd dollies pretty and . . 101 & POST IMPR 11   80
more than dead exactly dance in my head, precisely . . . . . 120 & PORTRAIT 12   2
in my head, precisely dance where danced la guerre. . . . . . 120 & PORTRAIT 12   4
payent bien les americains dance exactly in my brain . . . . 120 & PORTRAIT 12   27
ladies skilfully dead precisely dance where has danced la . . 121 & PORTRAIT 12   32
ferai Minette, dead exactly dance si vous voulez chatouiller 121 & PORTRAIT 12   39
and hot men precisely dance in my head ladies . . . . 121 & PORTRAIT 12   60
you want it to dance with you and it . . . . 126 & SEVEN POEMS 5   22
to and it can dance and Whocares dead's fine . . . . 126 & SEVEN POEMS 5   22
dead's nice like a dance where you danced simple . . . . . . 127 & SEVEN POEMS 5   32
to give you, the dance all over again and . . . . 127 & SEVEN POEMS 5   36
it?) and this shall dance upon the nude and . . . . 155 & SON ACTU 4   14
our beautiful tree we'll dance and sing "Noel Noel" . . . . . 192 XLI CHANSONS 2   27
is when frost to dance maketh the sagest pane . . . . 207 XLI SONNETS 3   3
if begin to spoons dance every- should where say . . . . . . 287 IS 5 FOUR 4   16
the year and trees dance (and i guess though . . . . 372 VIVA 63   14
but if a living dance upon dead minds why, ... 377 VIVA 68   1
moscow pipes good kumrads dance) kumrads enjoy s. freud . . . 413 NO THANKS 30   9
the mountains when they dance / / / / . . . . 427 NO THANKS 44   20
(G1Y) a nda n-saint dance! Dan Sai ntd anc . . . . 431 NO THANKS 48   20
to have smelled Happens--skip dance kids hop point at . . . . 437 NO THANKS 53   13
stars how not to dance / / / / . . . . 484 NEW POEMS 22   14
peachtrees grow or hopes dance best on bald men's . . . . . . 511 50 POEMS 25   9
cryings and did their dance (sleep wake hope and . . . . . . 515 50 POEMS 29   18
who sing small thing dance little joy (shine most . . . . . . 535 50 POEMS 47   11
blood can sing and dance (and does with each . . . . 580 1 X 1 40   2
born everyone is noone dance around the snowman / . . . . . . 630 (CHAIRE) 32   16
welcome the future (and dance your death away at . . . . . . 732 95 POEMS 60   11
were less than dead) dance, i and you; high . . . . 762 95 POEMS 89   10
(forever is now) and dance you suddenly blossoming tree . . . 767 95 POEMS 93   23
wild with leaves; which dance and dancing swoop (and . . . . 777 73 POEMS 5   6
now jump shout (laugh dance cry sing) for it's . . . . 835 73 POEMS 63   18
self who's) child will dance! and when he's plucked . . . . . 843 73 POEMS 71   12

+DANCE

FOR CONTEXT, SEE . . . . 431 NO THANKS 48   13
FOR CONTEXT, SEE . . . . 431 NO THANKS 48   21
FOR CONTEXT, SEE . . . . 507 50 POEMS 21   4
FOR CONTEXT, SEE . . . . 507 50 POEMS 21   17

DANCED

on my mouth petals danced against my eyes and . . . .   39 T&C AMORES 4   18
head, precisely dance where danced la guerre. Mimi a . . . . 120 & PORTRAIT 12   4
precisely dance where has danced la guerre j'm'appelle Manon, 121 & PORTRAIT 12   33
a dance where you danced simple hours and you . . . . 127 & SEVEN POEMS 5   32
sang his didn't he danced his did. Women and . . . . 515 50 POEMS 29   4
was sure that spring danced when she heard my . . . . 521 50 POEMS 34   52

DANCER

indignantly protests) this little dancer with the tightened .   72 T&C SON REAL 3   5

DANCERS

re the helen molle dancers, whom he considered . . . . 327 VIVA 18   40

DANCES

up over the tribune dances crazily & &) . . . . 267 IS 5 TWO 2   5
roguish am of fragrance dances a honeydunce; whirling's a . . 763 95 POEMS 90   10

DANCESING

around) five (are all dancesing singdance all are three . . . 507 50 POEMS 21   4
white (three singdance six dancesing three all around around 507 50 POEMS 21   17

DANCESONG

hair and then your dancesong soul. rarely-beloved a single . 186 XLI SONGS 8   17

DANCIN

t hrough his dream; dancin g you Star / . . . . 733 95 POEMS 61   10

	PAGE	TITLE	LINE

DANCING
the Princess Salome carefully dancing in the noise of . . . . 17 T&C PUELLA MEA 31
wee and bettyandisbel come dancing from hop-scotch and . . . 24 T&C CHANSONS 1 14
ach the great green dancing devil devil devil devil . . . . . 25 T&C CHANSONS 2 26
queen of queens is dancing her subtle body weaving . . . . . 34 T&C ORIENTALE 6 84
and tossed into delicious dancing up Up with the . . . . . 44 T&C AMORES 8 12
and the man are dancing slowly are tottering up . . . . . . 69 T&C POST IMPR 6 26
zither-and the mealy, ladies dancing thicklyfoolish, with, . 100 & POST IMPR 11 42
delirious. indivisible grace of dancing / / / . . . . 185 XLI SONGS 7 17
considered "elevating--that is, if dancing CAN be ele- . . . 327 VIVA 18 40
at whom first, anyhow dancing" (a moon swims out . . . . . . 338 VIVA 29 20
fiddle i had been dancing: which is why something . . . . . . 355 VIVA 46 19
moves in black light dancing isn'ts on why, digging . . . . . 439 NO THANKS 55 21
immense live without every dancing. singless on- ly a . . . . 491 50 POEMS 5 5
faces made of cloud dancing and three singing with . . . . . 507 50 POEMS 21 6
three and and three dancing earths three menandwomen three . 507 50 POEMS 21 20
(yes the mountains are dancing together) when every leaf . . 665 {CHAIRE} 67 7
(now the mountains are dancing, the mountains) when more . 665 {CHAIRE} 67 14
(all the mountains are dancing; are dancing) / / . . . . . . 665 {CHAIRE} 67 21
mountains are dancing; are dancing) / / / / . . . . 665 {CHAIRE} 67 21
biggest (little is) now (dancing yes for) white ly . . . . . 715 95 POEMS 43 14
sing an only grin-- dancing to feel nots are . . . . 716 95 POEMS 44 21
morning) fly instead of dancing are they possibly afraid . . 724 95 POEMS 52 11
leaves; which dance and dancing swoop (and swooping whirl . . 777 73 POEMS 5 7
+DANCING
FOR CONTEXT, SEE . . . . 89 & POST IMPR 1 11
FOR CONTEXT, SEE . . . . 493 50 POEMS 7 17
FOR CONTEXT, SEE . . . . 534 50 POEMS 46 1
FOR CONTEXT, SEE . . . . 615 {CHAIRE} 17 3
+DANCINGLY
FOR CONTEXT, SEE . . . . 431 NO THANKS 48 15
DANDELIONS
picker of buttercups violets dandelions And the big bullying 26 T&C CHANSONS 3 4
DANGEROUS
ghostly chaos in this dangerous night through moaned space . 77 T&C SON UNRE 2 14
in her eyes the dangerous first stars) people move . . . . 93 & POST IMPR 5 10
(wisely suddenly into a dangerous womb of cringing air) . . . 115 & PORTRAIT 8 11
ladies firmly lewd on dangerous slabs of tilting din . . . . 138 & SON REAL 9 2
kike is the most dangerous machine as yet invented . . . . . 644 {CHAIRE} 46 1
DANGEROUSLY
with these frail ladies dangerously respire: impeccable girls 85 T&C SON ACTU 4 14
DANGLE
lips of Lucienne which dangle the old men and . . . . 120 & PORTRAIT 12 21
lips of Lucienne which dangle the old men and . . . . 121 & PORTRAIT 12 59
DANGLES
a tree fruit that dangles therefrom the purpled world . . . . 16 T&C SONGS 6 3
than enquire whose soul dangles from his watch-chain which . 204 XLI LA GUERRE 2 3
DANGLING
his swivelchair one fist dangling scandal while five other . 259 IS 5 ONE 29 9
DANIEL
/ / my uncle Daniel fought in the civil . . . . 253 IS 5 ONE 24 2
DANIELLI
l'Europe Grand and Royal Danielli their numbers are like . . 256 IS 5 ONE 27 20
DANSENT
petites femmes exactes qui dansent toujours in my head . . . 121 & PORTRAIT 12 51
DAPPER
Prefect of Police (a dapper derbied creature, swaggers . . . 274 IS 5 TWO 9 28
DAPPLED
from the dead. On dappled dawn forth rides the . . . . 4 T&C EPITHALAM 65
Fleeter be they than dappled dreams the swift sweet . . . . . 14 T&C SONGS 4 6
DARE
smeestaire steevensun kum een, dare ease Bet, an Leelee, . . 73 T&C SON REAL 4 13
town whose spires softly dare. Will take the houseless . . . 86 T&C SON ACTU 5 4
answer, beginning, ecstasy, to dare: prouder than all . . . . 351 VIVA 42 5
shall go) remembering only dare (Wholly consider how these . 362 VIVA 53 3
generous this heart could dare) unhearts can less unminds . . 440 NO THANKS 56 3
spat (this life could dare freely to give as . . . . 440 NO THANKS 56 12
ape deftly aims they dare not share) such make . . . . 440 NO THANKS 56 22

	PAGE	TITLE	LINE

DARE (CONTINUED)

	PAGE	TITLE	LINE
goes alone daring to dare for joy of joy)	440	NO THANKS 56	29
each Forever its freedom (Dare until a flower, understanding	453	NO THANKS 68	13
roun' who does not dare to stand or sit	466	NEW POEMS 4	3
loves id) fer ids dare pain dares un no	519	50 POEMS 33	22
budy elses un ids dare dare joy (eye kinely	519	50 POEMS 33	26
elses un ids dare dare joy (eye kinely thank	519	50 POEMS 33	26
guess or fears to dare whatever dares to fear)	522	50 POEMS 35	8
this than, a least dare of snow less quite	573	1 X 1 33	14
who was afraid to dare to answer "no"? quote	636	{CHAIRE} 38	4
problem nearly solved we dare adorn the whole with	650	{CHAIRE} 52	14
and) self without, completely dare be beautiful one if . . .	666	{CHAIRE} 68	14
the dirt (and consequently dare to climb the sky)	679	95 POEMS 7	6
boldest man can scarcely dare to meet no matter	685	95 POEMS 13	3
(day disappears) their heartbeats dare some upward world of .	757	95 POEMS 85	5
because it's Spring thingS dare to do people (&	782	73 POEMS 10	4
strong and born to dare --a fighter to his	799	73 POEMS 27	3
wisdom knowledge fears to dare, how the (myself's own	843	73 POEMS 71	11

DAREN'T

	PAGE	TITLE	LINE
people mustn't shouldn't) most daren't (sortof people well .	412	NO THANKS 29	6

DARES

	PAGE	TITLE	LINE
thinks it thinks, nor dares to feel (but up	424	NO THANKS 41	10
hang in hock who dares to call himself a	438	NO THANKS 54	8
Jew turn kike who dares to call himself a	438	NO THANKS 54	16
Love's a fuck who dares to call himself a	438	NO THANKS 54	24
He may walk Who dares to call Himself a	438	NO THANKS 54	28
a loneliest road who dares to stroll almost this	441	NO THANKS 56	47
whose ignorant each breathing dares to hide more than	446	NO THANKS 61	11
fer ids dare pain dares un no budy elses	519	50 POEMS 33	23
fears to dare whatever dares to fear) i very	522	50 POEMS 35	8
Living no single thing dares partly seem one atomy	559	1 X 1 19	9
pasture, all a heartbeat dares; that mountain, any god) . . .	818	73 POEMS 46	8
of each bird who dares to not forsake a	821	73 POEMS 49	8

DARETOI

	PAGE	TITLE	LINE
oride lesgo eckshun kemeruh daretoi nig) Ah, Soul	474	NEW POEMS 12	14

DARING

	PAGE	TITLE	LINE
foul he goes alone daring to dare for joy	440	NO THANKS 56	29

DARK

	PAGE	TITLE	LINE
she sought the harbouring dark, and (catching up her	8	T&C OF NICOL	26
hands rasps the purple dark- ness a worshipper prostrate . .	28	T&C ORIENTALE 2	10
the painting of the dark with meteors streaming from	36	T&C AMORES 1	15
stands in the dumb dark svelte and urgent (again	37	T&C AMORES 2	12
lighted and it is dark. the people are in	50	T&C IMPRESS 4	26
the hovering at the dark portals of hurt girl	54	T&C PORTRAIT 2	3
beer and lime, wear dark, and where your meeting	71	T&C SON REAL 2	5
night featherly swifts the Dark on us all; stories	89	& POST IMPR 1	5
adventure) lady. The clumsy dark threatens (and i do	98	& POST IMPR 9	13
into Allen street the dark long cool tunnel of	100	& POST IMPR 11	2
wealthy vermilion and breathless-scarlet, dark colours like .	100	& POST IMPR 11	7
east Side in a. dark street a hur- DygurdY	100	& POST IMPR 11	34
the, Jab: of a dark tool. With a cleverjeRk	101	& POST IMPR 11	50
/ / whereas by dark really released, the modern	146	& SON REAL 17	1
Jimmie was a dude. Dark hair and nice hands.	149	& SON REAL 20	5
gross fuzzy-pash --dead--and the dark gold delicately	153	& SON ACTU 2	7
red soul into the dark so duneyed master enter	188	XLI SONGS 10	11
the year in a dark box dreaming of being	192	XLI CHANSONS 2	14
be a single place dark or unhappy then when	192	XLI CHANSONS 2	20
only exhales a climbing dark exact walloping human noise . .	202	XLI PORTRAIT 9	45
clock striking in a dark house / / /	229	IS 5 ONE FRAN	15
somehow quickyes when (now, dark dear oh) the iceman	251	IS 5 ONE 22	13
my wonderful jealousy is dark if light should flower:	292	IS 5 FOUR 9	16
myself carefully wanders streets dark and, deep with rain....	300	IS 5 FOUR 17	14
smiling "coming up these dark stairs. / / /	353	VIVA 44	32
of death love earth dark) and thousand thrusts squirms . . .	356	VIVA 47	5
that (somehow in the dark) this world has been	370	VIVA 61	3
(only) a Leaf among dark ness. sunlight's thenlike? now . . .	397	NO THANKS 14	16
/ / / how dark and single, where he	418	NO THANKS 35	1
find the rule) and dark beginnings are his luminous	420	NO THANKS 37	10

DARK (CONTINUED)

opens sharp holes in dark places paints eyes touches	437	NO THANKS 53	5
(yawnchurches suck people) reel (dark- ly) whirling in (b . .	444	NO THANKS 59	14
a small million of dark voices sing against the	454	NO THANKS 69	13
) open new (dark we all findingly Spring	482	NEW POEMS 20	8
this light is so dark the mountains grow up	505	50 POEMS 19	9
are in a room's dark around) five (are all	507	50 POEMS 21	2
are in a room's dark around) five (six are	507	50 POEMS 21	9
are in a room's dark) all five are one	507	50 POEMS 21	26
shall be were dawn dark rain snow rain -bow	512	50 POEMS 26	18
shoulders marched against the dark his sorrow was as	521	50 POEMS 34	44
must grow deep in dark least ourselves remembering love . . .	556	1 X 1 16	13
forever (and so to dark) / / / /	564	1 X 1 24	17
--you bring (out of dark the earth) a procession	575	1 X 1 35	7
heard them sing the dark alive but) look: begins	582	1 X 1 42	7
than particle of perfect dark-- how should a loudness	603	{CHAIRE} 5	2
dreams until comes vast dark until sink last things	633	{CHAIRE} 35	8
life walking in the dark i met christ jesus)	648	{CHAIRE} 50	3
/ who were so dark of heart they might	649	{CHAIRE} 51	1
be pleasanter (some big dark little day which seems	650	{CHAIRE} 52	6
Be thou gay by dark and day: gay as	651	{CHAIRE} 53	5
(two faces at a dark window) this father and	715	95 POEMS 43	2
sunlight after days of dark, will climb; will blossom: . . .	735	95 POEMS 63	13
of more much than dark most nowhere no particle	756	95 POEMS 84	7
shining realms of regions dark) laugh long at Beautiful . . .	799	73 POEMS 27	27
the wind in the dark) whispers. And i and	813	73 POEMS 41	11
life from all the dark who wings his why	815	73 POEMS 43	4
love) how more than dark i am, no song	819	73 POEMS 47	5
receive (undaunted guest of dark most downwardness and . . .	821	73 POEMS 49	11
nothing but light and dark; but never forever &	840	73 POEMS 68	24

+DARK

| FOR CONTEXT, SEE . . . . | 681 | 95 POEMS 9 | 13 |

DARK'S

| bird (tenderly upon the dark's prodigious face thy voice . . | 187 | XLI SONGS 9 | 10 |

DARKCOOLLONGBODY

| either side the street's DarkcOOllonGBody windows, are. . . . | 100 | & POST IMPR 11 | 15 |

DARKENS

| a little: the air darkens and is alive-- o . . . . | 357 | VIVA 48 | 9 |

DARKER

because deeper firmer since darker than little round water .	126	& SEVEN POEMS 5	2
as a tear is darker than a mile. /	371	VIVA 62	27
mindscream into life; possibly darker than a spinster's heart	506	50 POEMS 20	6
/ / pieces (in darker than small is dirtiest	623	{CHAIRE} 25	1

DARKESTNESS

| what a gently welcoming darkestness-- now i lay me . . . . . | 816 | 73 POEMS 44 | 4 |

+DARKISH

| FOR CONTEXT, SEE . . . . | 416 | NO THANKS 33 | 5 |

DARKLING

| last; without, the street darkling awaiteth her whose feet . | 75 | T&C SON REAL 6 | 10 |

DARKLY

over hate has triumphed darkly love and the small	213	XLI SONNETS 9	5
the great world (in darkly taking rain) drown, beyond	432	NO THANKS 49	2
merely by doubting have darkly themselves unmade makes love .	580	1 X 1 40	14
lena smile (while looming darkly a kindness of fragrance . .	754	95 POEMS 82	10

+DARKLY

| FOR CONTEXT, SEE . . . . | 444 | NO THANKS 59 | 14 |

DARKNESS

flower knew in the darkness a more burning rain?	4	T&C EPITHALAM	56
the sensual dome of darkness, and the sweet strong	7	T&C EPITHALAM	165
soft sighed the passionate darkness to the tune of	8	T&C OF NICOL	4
the people of perfect darkness fills his mind who	9	T&C SONGS 1	19
from steep hills by darkness softly brought-- (be with . . .	9	T&C SONGS 1	36
the king whereof is darkness thy forehead is a	29	T&C ORIENTALE 3	3
between your perfect breasts darkness and beauty of stars . .	39	T&C AMORES 4	17
into the serious steep darkness / / / /	41	T&C AMORES 5	37
i -mal- ly devours darkness the hungry star which	49	T&C IMPRESS 3	11
Life: handorgans and April darkness, friends i charge	66	T&C POST IMPR 3	4
, the reckless oral darkness raging with thin impulse	67	T&C POST IMPR 4	4

DARKNESS (CONTINUED)

	PAGE	TITLE	LINE
moments when the glassy darkness holds the genuine apparition	78	T&C SON UNRE 3	5
whose huge heart prospecting darkness roams torture my spirit	79	T&C SON UNRE 4	4
to a more than darkness (which is myself and	92	& POST IMPR 4	3
a dinted mug gone Darkness it was so near	97	& POST IMPR 8	40
the fragrant unspeaking ignorant darkness of New Lady whose .	112	& PORTRAIT 6	98
stopped to hear, in darkness, water the lips of	136	& SON REAL 7	17
ream this pith of darkness: carve an evilfringing flower . .	139	& SON REAL 10	8
orange) against silence, or darkness.... the coming of my . .	152	& SON ACTU 1	5
flowers, whom hardens richly, darkness. On the whole possibly	154	& SON ACTU 3	10
/ in the rain- darkness, the sunset being sheathed	186	XLI SONGS 8	2
eyes to dash against darkness in the sleeping curves	189	XLI SONGS 11	7
/ SONNETS if learned darkness from our searched world	205	XLI SONNETS 1	1
slobber and in the darkness) stood sharp angels with	241	IS 5 ONE 12	8
air turning into January darkness up through which sprouting	279	IS 5 THREE 3	2
to squat in first darkness --a little moon thinner	282	IS 5 THREE 6	16
mingling arms through a darkness where new lights begin . . .	297	IS 5 FOUR 14	3
to that patch of darkness there's a what is	322	VIVA 14	4
or huddled in the darkness of cafes people drink	340	VIVA 31	7
live whom on Large Darkness And The Middle Of	361	VIVA 52	31
Life's animals) but not darkness shall quite outmarch forever	376	VIVA 67	6
either were-- so in darkness ourselves go, mind in	379	VIVA 70	3
wanders through only white darkness who moves in black . . .	439	NO THANKS 55	19
rise out of tremendous darkness into air) / /	559	1 X 1 19	14
are all breathing bright darkness to gether are slowly . . .	600	(CHAIRE) 2	8
living-- but keeping is darkness and winter and cringing . .	665	(CHAIRE) 67	17
then shall be some darkness during which fingers are	667	(CHAIRE) 69	9
silence and such a darkness noone can quite begin	717	95 POEMS 45	6
what was dusk becomes darkness) innumerably singular strictly	741	95 POEMS 69	2
light and proudly His darkness) / / / /	749	95 POEMS 77	20
/ o nly this darkness (in whom always i	785	73 POEMS 13	3
born: yours is the darkness of my soul's return	810	73 POEMS 38	13
was and bright is darkness and to fall (now	834	73 POEMS 62	20

+DARKNESS

	PAGE	TITLE	LINE
FOR CONTEXT, SEE	350	VIVA 41	4
FOR CONTEXT, SEE	397	NO THANKS 14	16

DARKS

	PAGE	TITLE	LINE
s groupingThe 6around one darks to 7th s o	342	VIVA 33	7

DARLING

	PAGE	TITLE	LINE
are round have roses darling, it's all i ask	71	T&C SON REAL 2	6
very careful) O, the darling benevolent mindless He--and . .	250	IS 5 ONE 21	7
isn't this wellcurb simply darling" --O Education: O thos . .	257	IS 5 ONE 27	36
/ / / (ponder, darling, these busted statues of	260	IS 5 ONE 30	1
/ / / my darling since you and i	368	VIVA 59	1
is not courage my darling (for only Nobody knows	368	VIVA 59	18
yet jesus what blood darling i said / /	496	50 POEMS 10	20
for both of us darling. And if i sing	531	50 POEMS 43	14
simplify my you , darling sweet this creative never	577	1 X 1 37	12
/ / / / darling! because my blood can	580	1 X 1 40	1
me you gave gave darling birds are in (trees	589	1 X 1 49	14
rose--did you see her? darling, did you (kiss me)	599	(CHAIRE) 1	10
touch --the great (my darling) happens to be that	664	(CHAIRE) 66	5
april (yes, april; my darling) it's spring! yes the	665	(CHAIRE) 67	4
fingers of this tree (darling) have hands, and all	667	(CHAIRE) 69	1
by always nothing) you darling diminutive person jovial ego .	678	95 POEMS 6	3
the far o my darling) of (down / /	695	95 POEMS 23	21
filthy men come annabel darling come annie come ann"	707	95 POEMS 35	22
you much (most beautiful darling) more than anyone on	717	95 POEMS 45	1
would (my most beautiful darling) believe in nothing but . .	717	95 POEMS 45	14
are our also my darling) but should some im	728	95 POEMS 56	9
call the stars. And (darling) never fear: love, when	741	95 POEMS 69	9
adventure truths of skies-- darling of darlings! by that . .	761	95 POEMS 88	9
is your doing, my darling) i fear no fate	766	95 POEMS 92	4
am) to sing, my darling: while old worlds and	776	73 POEMS 4	4
what's wholly marvellous my Darling is that you &	782	73 POEMS 10	16
infinite countries be my darling (open the very secret . . .	811	73 POEMS 39	4
a thousand poems my darling but nobody will stop	835	73 POEMS 63	29

	PAGE	TITLE	LINE
DARLINGEST			
you're by far the darlingest who (on this busily	590	1 X 1 50	9
DARLINGS			
including flu) my little darlings, let us now passionately .	266	IS 5 TWO 1	16
of skies-- darling of darlings! by that miracle which	761	95 POEMS 88	9
DART			
a swoop and a dart out flew his wish	593	1 X 1 53	7
DARTING			
adoring shyly tiny winging darting floating merry in the . .	591	1 X 1 51	22
DARTS			
ships bulge hearts by darts pierced lazily writhe lurch . . .	436	NO THANKS 52	8
DARWIN			
Claus a criminal (hears Darwin; asks about Death) concept . .	398	NO THANKS 15	14
DASH			
with closed eyes to dash against darkness in the	189	XLI SONGS 11	7
DAT			
on looks but how dat baby ached." and when	226	IS 5 ONE MAME	11
not disagreeable contras tuh dat not exacly fat "father" . .	240	IS 5 ONE 11	3
alotta sweet bull like dat ...suddenly i feels so	332	VIVA 23	12
DATE			
man and kept a date and played a tune)	479	NEW POEMS 17	9
DATSWUT			
oidoughwuntuh doot, butoiguttuh braikyooz, datswut eesez . .	310	VIVA 2	5
DAUGHTER			
/ / now dis "daughter" uv eve (who aint	240	IS 5 ONE 11	1
Yes of guk rooms daughter item son a woopsing	499	50 POEMS 13	9
"and who but your daughter i'm asking yes who	707	95 POEMS 35	13
says it aint his daughter her father lays" "black	707	95 POEMS 35	20
DAUGHTER'S			
/ my (his from daughter's mother's zero mind fahrenheit) . .	546	1 X 1 6	1
DAUGHTERS			
the church's protestant blessings daughters, unscented . . .	70	T&C SON REAL 1	4
/ / wherelings whenlings (daughters of ifbut offspring of . .	512	50 POEMS 26	2
DAUNTED			
/ spirit colossal (& daunted by always nothing) you	678	95 POEMS 6	2
DAUNTING			
Paler be they than daunting death the sleek slim	14	T&C SONGS 4	26
DAVE			
and mabel dick and dave --tomorrow is our permanent	579	1 X 1 39	11
DAWN			
the dead. On dappled dawn forth rides the pungent	4	T&C EPITHALAM	65
hands and vanishing with dawn). Spring, that omits no	5	T&C EPITHALAM	88
gold into the silver dawn. four lean hounds crouched	14	T&C SONGS 4	3
down into the silver dawn. four lean hounds crouched	14	T&C SONGS 4	13
down into the silver dawn. four lean hounds crouched	14	T&C SONGS 4	23
gold into the silver dawn. four lean hounds crouched	14	T&C SONGS 4	33
jiggle the bait of dawn and be jerked into	49	T&C IMPRESS 3	20
stars and it is dawn into the street of	50	T&C IMPRESS 4	2
eyes and it is dawn the world goes forth	50	T&C IMPRESS 4	9
hair-thin tints of yellow dawn, into the women-coloured . . .	66	T&C POST IMPR 3	7
brain peered at the dawn. she got up with	132	& SON REAL 3	13
thirstily. Dead stars stink. dawn. Inane, the poetic carcass	139	& SON REAL 10	13
fail upon the gold dawn, where teeth of slowturning	142	& SON REAL 13	4
only in the unkind dawn its muscle amorous pricks	165	& SON ACTU 14	4
while east deserves of dawn. i lie at length, ...	184	XLI SONGS 6	14
the smarting beauty of dawn) / / / /	187	XLI SONGS 9	18
of nothing and whom dawn loves most to touch	211	XLI SONNETS 7	17
me, smile; or (between dawn and twilight) giving your	285	IS 5 FOUR 2	14
thing in beginning corners dawn smirks and there's the . . .	322	VIVA 14	13
a gate; the prisoner dawn embraces hugely some few	376	VIVA 67	10
mean, should any curious dawn discuss our mingling spirits, .	379	VIVA 70	6
you good" the mechanical dawn "morning") & that those	464	NEW POEMS 2	29
are shall be were dawn dark rain snow rain	512	50 POEMS 26	18
spring what if a dawn of a doom of	560	1 X 1 20	17
DAWN'S			
you see by the dawn's early my country 'tis	268	IS 5 TWO 3	3
DAY			
pungent sun with hooded day preening upon his hand	4	T&C EPITHALAM	66

DAY (CONTINUED)

	PAGE	TITLE	LINE
inimitably tortured the base day utters at length her	6	T&C EPITHALAM	130
(though love be a day) do not fear, we	13	T&C SONGS 3	6
(though love be a day) for which girl art	13	T&C SONGS 3	13
(though love be a day and life be nothing, ...	13	T&C SONGS 3	20
lady, moving in the day, is a little stranger	17	T&C PUELLA MEA	6
--moving in the unskilful day my lady utterly alive, ...	17	T&C PUELLA MEA	23
swooned the white egyptian day who with Egypt's body	18	T&C PUELLA MEA	73
flesh at break of day are the smells of	22	T&C PUELLA MEA	258
in her eyes when day is gone are the	23	T&C PUELLA MEA	260
kingdom of heaven through day and space i saw	30	T&C ORIENTALE 4	34
worms. in the eligible day under the unaccountable sun) . . .	43	T&C AMORES 7	23
sun, under the insufficient day under the noise of	43	T&C AMORES 7	40
happy and it is day, in the mirror i	50	T&C IMPRESS 4	16
/ but the other day i was passing a	58	T&C PORTRAIT 6	2
troubled. A sharp blue day fills with peacefully leaping . .	62	T&C PORTRAIT 10	7
the roses of the day grow deep. / /	78	T&C SON UNRE 3	14
/ / when citied day with the sonorous homes	79	T&C SON UNRE 4	1
through the stopped entire day horribly and seriously thrills	82	T&C SON ACTU 1	10
at the edge of day) i surely make a	92	& POST IMPR 4	18
your eyes can take day away more softly horribly	98	& POST IMPR 9	4
god knows when every day of their lives aint	109	& PORTRAIT 5	17
smallest ear against yester- day My Lady hear the	110	& PORTRAIT 6	32
is eaten by yester- day) O i tell you	111	& PORTRAIT 6	50
is eaten by yester- day between the nibbling timid	112	& PORTRAIT 6	78
are eaten by yester- day (and O My Lady	112	& PORTRAIT 6	92
/ when the spent day begins to frail (whose	115	& PORTRAIT 8	1
gingerbread when the judgment day comes God will find	117	& PORTRAIT 10	3
we are now judgment day cross the threshold have	118	& PORTRAIT 10	40
sews and grows every day paler-paler she sits sewing	125	& SEVEN POEMS 4	4
Europe has --. One day i felt a mountain	135	& SON REAL 6	11
a putrid window every day almost leans a lady	144	& SON REAL 15	12
of magic agony ....by day this lady in her	146	& SON REAL 17	9
sagging debris of exploded day the hulking perpendicular . .	151	& SON REAL 22	2
will be dead some day. By you the mouth	153	& SON ACTU 2	1
is the consummation of day, the hour) she says	167	& SON ACTU 16	12
/ / and this day it was Spring.... us	174	& SON ACTU 23	1
the magnificent clamor of day tortured in gold, which	188	XLI SONGS 10	6
the mysterious high futile day an enormous stride (and . . .	215	XLI SONNETS 11	14
that all gondola signore day below me gondola signore	256	IS 5 ONE 27	24
these red pieces of day (against which and quite	278	IS 5 THREE 2	4
this) only imagine, when day has thrilled you are	292	IS 5 FOUR 9	2
this window just as day dissolves when it is	301	IS 5 FOUR 18	2
/ / (one fine day) let's take the train	316	VIVA 8	1
the zoo were that day inclined to be uncouthly	326	VIVA 18	23
run down the next day. / / / /	365	VIVA 56	14
your faces, Death: for day is over (and such	376	VIVA 67	1
over (and such a day as must remember he	376	VIVA 67	2
collidingly absorbs eternal near) day being come, Love, put .	376	VIVA 67	14
supremely clothes herself with day) i mean, should any . . .	379	VIVA 70	5
Am root air rock day) : you; smile, hands	449	NO THANKS 64	13
(and whom did merely day close) opens if more	450	NO THANKS 65	1
/ a pretty a day (and every fades) is	509	50 POEMS 23	1
many bells down) one day anyone died i guess	515	50 POEMS 29	25
no gal no boy (day simbully loves id) fer	519	50 POEMS 33	21
peace the moon of day predicted end who never	527	50 POEMS 39	4
sunlight with a firm day in it you will	529	50 POEMS 41	8
music's music and the day of day are worlds	538	50 POEMS 50	8
and the day of day are worlds collapsing? any	538	50 POEMS 50	8
merciful miracles wonderingly celebrate day and welcome . . .	582	1 X 1 42	3
/ this (let's remember) day died again and again;	599	(CHAIRE) 1	1
have better luck, some day?" "Or worse! poor worlds;	603	(CHAIRE) 5	11
breakfast every night all day) a 3ringbrain you had	605	(CHAIRE) 7	5
/ / one day a nigger caught in	622	(CHAIRE) 24	1
little innocence creates a day. And something thought or . .	649	(CHAIRE) 51	8
(some big dark little day which seems a lifetime	650	(CHAIRE) 52	6
gay by dark and day: gay as only truth	651	(CHAIRE) 53	5
all alive in miraculous day) merrily moving through sweet . .	661	(CHAIRE) 63	6

	PAGE	TITLE	LINE

DAY (CONTINUED)

for most this amazing day: for the leaping greenly . . . . . 663 (CHAIRE) 65 — 2
this is the birth day of life and of . . . . 663 (CHAIRE) 65 — 7
(all our night becomes day) o, it's spring! all . . . . 665 (CHAIRE) 67 — 18
sing (at yes of day) younger than young bird . . . . 666 (CHAIRE) 68 — 17
by never robbed of day) puts always on by . . . . 674 95 POEMS 2 — 8
beach (to play one day) and maggie discovered a . . . . 682 95 POEMS 10 — 2
for silence and a day for singing but more . . . . 683 95 POEMS 11 — 12
democracy announces night & day "all poor little peoples . . 711 95 POEMS 39 — 6
moment off by moment day thankfully become each other) . . . 720 95 POEMS 48 — 5
total stranger one black day knocked living the hell . . . . 730 95 POEMS 58 — 1
birth and death a day (or maybe even less) . . . . 743 95 POEMS 71 — 14
spirits and with illimitable day (shrived of that . . . . . 745 95 POEMS 73 — 8
begin the mystery of day for someone's eyes) with . . . . . 756 95 POEMS 84 — 4
boy who're littler than (day disappears) their heartbeats . . 757 95 POEMS 85 — 4
of spring; but april's day transcends november's year . . . . 765 95 POEMS 91 — 12
deep rush through amazing day it's brains without hearts . . 769 95 POEMS 95 — 14
the new earth a day of may under more . . . . 778 73 POEMS 6 — 18
annie died the other day never was there such . . . . 794 73 POEMS 22 — 1
sings an if of day to yes / / . . . . 815 73 POEMS 43 — 8
sunlight is (life and day are) only loaned: whereas . . . . . 816 73 POEMS 44 — 7
floats a more than day whose sun is moon, ... 818 73 POEMS 46 — 2
(and feeling: that if day has to become night . . . . 824 73 POEMS 52 — 6

+DAY

FOR CONTEXT, SEE . . . . 10 T&C SONGS 1 — 39
FOR CONTEXT, SEE . . . . 618 (CHAIRE) 20 — 2
FOR CONTEXT, SEE . . . . 751 95 POEMS 79 — 2

DAY'S

a colour (in -to day's bloodlight climbs the onlying . . . . 719 95 POEMS 47 — 2
by a single sweet day's death: as not imagined . . . . 750 95 POEMS 78 — 7

DAYS

pass) and these my days their sounds and flowers . . . . . . 11 T&C SONGS 2 — 31
night, when all my days shall have before a . . . . 39 T&C AMORES 4 — 31
i and all the days and nights that matter . . . . 153 & SON ACTU 2 — 10
minute odour these gross days when i think of . . . . 165 & SON ACTU 14 — 6
ages, and of hungering days for whom the old . . . . 209 XLI SONNETS 5 — 11
to use in other days (drawing my Mes from . . . . 213 XLI SONNETS 9 — 13
the Grand and Old days: of Amy Sandburg of . . . . 233 IS 5 ONE 4 — 17
against myself the sharp days slobber in vain: Nor . . . . . 293 IS 5 FOUR 10 — 21
in the hoe tell days are teased: let (however) . . . . . . 317 VIVA 9 — 15
fer duh good ole days we spent in '18 . . . . 332 VIVA 23 — 14
months & weeks & days & years & nights . . . . 702 95 POEMS 30 — 19
--each luckiest of lucky days i've loved, shall love, ... 734 95 POEMS 62 — 2
of perfect sunlight after days of dark, will climb; . . . . . 735 95 POEMS 63 — 12
not worry if briefer days grow briefest, i am . . . . 749 95 POEMS 77 — 3

+DAYS

FOR CONTEXT, SEE . . . . 237 IS 5 ONE 8 — 12
FOR CONTEXT, SEE . . . . 237 IS 5 ONE 8 — 13

DAYTIME

who Talks in the daytime, when who is asleep . . . . 312 VIVA 4 — 4

DAZE

superior to the genuine daze of unmarketable excitation, . . 150 & SON REAL 21 — 12
gimme de good ole daze.... in dem daze kid . . . . 237 IS 5 ONE 8 — 12
ole daze.... in dem daze kid Christmas meant sumpn . . . . . 237 IS 5 ONE 8 — 13
said to us Kid. daze nutn like it. / . . . . 259 IS 5 ONE 29 — 28

+DAZE

FOR CONTEXT, SEE . . . . 333 VIVA 24 — 14

DAZED

then my lost my dazed my whereful selves they . . . . 819 73 POEMS 47 — 15

DDAANNCCIINN

a: nC. eda: Nci; ddaanncciinn (GlY) a nda n-saint . . . . . 431 NO THANKS 48 — 15

DE

"bon dos, bon cul de Paris" (Marie Vierge Priez . . . . . . 120 & PORTRAIT 12 — 14
ta voix fragile couleur de pivoine?) with the long . . . . . 121 & PORTRAIT 12 — 56
on ne boit que de Jingyale. things are going . . . . 233 IS 5 ONE 4 — 6
as fer i gimme de good ole daze.... in . . . . 237 IS 5 ONE 8 — 12
er year) i'll tell de woild one swell bangup . . . . 237 IS 5 ONE 8 — 16
abruptly Notre Dame (whereas de gustibus non disputandum est 245 IS 5 ONE 16 — 24

157

	PAGE	TITLE	LINE

DE (CONTINUED)

felicitous vicinity of the de l'Europe Grand and Royal . . . 256 IS 5 ONE 27 — 18
the always smiling chevaux de bois) when you were . . . . . . 304 IS 5 FIVE 3 — 14
at present (l'on parle de repapering; i don't think . . . . . 312 VIVA 4 — 23
(age) ini sticks tuh de mans 1 (hutch) hutchinson . . . . . . 325 VIVA 17 — 5
me" --dey was petrified. De room swung roun an . . . . 332 VIVA 23 — 25
2 bul retoinis wus de woids uf lil Oinis . . . . 409 NO THANKS 26 — 4
no (smiling) strike agains De Big Boss (crying) jew . . . . . 618 (CHAIRE) 20 — 10

+DE

FOR CONTEXT, SEE . . . . 708 95 POEMS 36 — 13

DEAD

golden crocus from the dead. On dappled dawn forth . . . . . 4 T&C EPITHALAM — 64
the moving of beauteous dead mouths throughout that very . . 6 T&C EPITHALAM — 141
snow, and before your dead face which sleeps, a . . . . 11 T&C SONGS 2 — 29
smiling my heart fell dead before. / / / . . . . 14 T&C SONGS 4 — 35
Master Hafiz keep your dead beautiful ladies. Mine is . . . . 17 T&C PUELLA MEA — 2
that i am wholly dead: nor ever did on . . . . 17 T&C PUELLA MEA — 34
the luck of all dead men and loving) as . . . . 19 T&C PUELLA MEA — 103
all things exquisite and dead, all living things and . . . . 19 T&C PUELLA MEA — 127
such as only certain dead and careful painters love . . . . 20 T&C PUELLA MEA — 140
care nor any lady dead and gone.) Each tapering . . . . 21 T&C PUELLA MEA — 180
And never boast your dead beauties, you greatest lovers . . . 22 T&C PUELLA MEA — 243
kiss-- never boast your dead beauties, mine being unto . . . 22 T&C PUELLA MEA — 249
all one-- keep your dead beautiful ladies. Eater of . . . . . 23 T&C PUELLA MEA — 265
of Bagdad.) Keep your dead beautiful ladies Harun Omar . . . 23 T&C PUELLA MEA — 289
last immortal leaf is dead and the gold year . . . . 41 T&C AMORES 5 — 5
my lips for a dead thing, i shall instruct . . . . 42 T&C AMORES 6 — 10
certain foolish perfect hours dead too, if that he . . . . . 42 T&C AMORES 6 — 17
who spits seeds of dead song about home and . . . . 55 T&C PORTRAIT 3 — 13
of atrocious melody.... tiniest dead tunes crawl upon my . . 69 T&C POST IMPR 6 — 27
Christ and Longfellow, both dead, are invariably interested . 70 T&C SON REAL 1 — 5
and be absitively posolutely dead, like Coney Island in . . . 72 T&C SON REAL 3 — 14
the people are minutely dead. Then you will slowly . . . . . 86 T&C SON ACTU 5 — 13
hands sharp and impertinently dead. expression began with the 103 & POST IMPR 13 — 5
little ladies more than dead / / / / . . . . 108 & PORTRAIT 4 — 37
is Effie who was dead? --to God in a . . . . 117 & PORTRAIT 10 — 10
little ladies more than dead exactly dance in my . . . . . . 120 & PORTRAIT 12 — 2
le soir (ladies accurately dead les anglais sont gentils . . 120 & PORTRAIT 12 — 25
Non? pourquoi?) ladies skilfully dead precisely dance where . 121 & PORTRAIT 12 — 32
Mimi te ferai Minette, dead exactly dance si vous . . . . . . 121 & PORTRAIT 12 — 39
my head ladies carefully dead / / / / . . . . 121 & PORTRAIT 12 — 61
like to think of dead it means nearer because . . . . 126 & SEVEN POEMS 5 — 1
all full of fingers dead has a smile like . . . . 126 & SEVEN POEMS 5 — 14
and stoopid and if dead says may i have . . . . 126 & SEVEN POEMS 5 — 20
sitting on one string dead never says my dear, ... 126 & SEVEN POEMS 5 — 29
expects you to anyway dead says come with me . . . . 127 & SEVEN POEMS 5 — 45
always wiggles the perfectly dead finger of thitherhithering 134 & SON REAL 5 — 11
mouthed houses curl thirstily. Dead stars stink. dawn. Inane, 139 & SON REAL 10 — 13
funny, you will be dead some day. By you . . . . 153 & SON ACTU 2 — 1
They will all be dead knead of lustfulhunched deeplytoplay . 153 & SON ACTU 2 — 4
stare the gross fuzzy-pash --dead--and the dark gold . . . . 153 & SON ACTU 2 — 7
year droops with things dead athwart the narrowing hours . . 207 XLI SONNETS 3 — 6
armies of the marching dead, with standards and the . . . . 209 XLI SONNETS 5 — 3
nostrils of the fervent dead, feed with felicities me . . . . 212 XLI SONNETS 8 — 6
tremB -ling to a: dead. stand- ; Still) / . . . . 248 IS 5 ONE 19 — 36
shaped waxworks filled with dead ideas (the oh quintillions . 250 IS 5 ONE 21 — 10
my uncle Ed that's dead from the neck up . . . . 253 IS 5 ONE 24 — 13
anent the (hic) hero dead that gladly (sic) in . . . . 266 IS 5 TWO 1 — 13
than these heroic happy dead who rushed like lions . . . . . 268 IS 5 TWO 3 — 10
in the face a dead yellow small rose / . . . . 296 IS 5 FOUR 13 — 16
your living or probably dead" so Jones was murdered . . . . . 313 VIVA 5 — 8
All Up god being Dead (not to mention inTerred) . . . . 315 VIVA 7 — 9
bronx (enlivening an otherwise dead silence with harmless . . 326 VIVA 18 — 13
spine like i was dead er sumpn: next i . . . . 332 VIVA 23 — 28
his bitterest enemies" is dead the only man woman . . . . . . 336 VIVA 27 — 2
seven grammatical errors "is dead" beautiful Warren Gamaliel 336 VIVA 27 — 5
Warren Gamaliel Harding "is" dead he's "dead" if he . . . . . 336 VIVA 27 — 7
Harding "is" dead he's "dead" if he wouldn't have . . . . . . 336 VIVA 27 — 9

DEAD (CONTINUED)

& (we (are like) dead) Whoshout (Ghost) atOne . . . . 347 VIVA 38   21
fingers did-not-move exquisitely ,like dead children (if he . 355 VIVA 46   17
a living dance upon dead minds why, it is . . . . 377 VIVA 68   1
refuse; just, look) ing dead but not complete -ly . . . . . . 387 NO THANKS 4   12
candy: & you are dead you captain) Memo 1 . . . . 389 NO THANKS 6   16
/ the (Wistfully dead seem generous) don't All . . . . 391 NO THANKS 8   3
imploring threaten) the wistFully dead you directly perceive 391 NO THANKS 8   10
so to speak wistfulLy dead are not relatively speaking . . . 391 NO THANKS 8   17
shave that Ghost is dead (whom noone might inter . . . . . . 394 NO THANKS 11   5
was aborted what was dead dead dead) whereupon mary . . . . . 401 NO THANKS 18   7
aborted what was dead dead dead) whereupon mary quite . . . . 401 NO THANKS 18   7
what was dead dead dead) whereupon mary quite contrary . . . 401 NO THANKS 18   7
aint born somes born dead an somes born alive . . . . 426 NO THANKS 43   11
/ Jehovah buried, Satan dead, do fearers worship Much . . . . 438 NO THANKS 54   1
called progress, and negation's dead undoom. I'd rather learn 484 NEW POEMS 22   12
three smiles into a dead house clutch between eyes . . . . . 522 50 POEMS 35   1
fire (adventuring and time's dead which; falling falling both 533 50 POEMS 45   18
/ / / / dead every enormous piece of . . . .   561 1 X 1 21   1
who death is killed dead. Hills jump with brooks: . . . . . 580 1 X 1 40   27
maimed) all except the dead ones mike likes all . . . . . . 619 (CHAIRE) 21   21
his mind in it (dead) / / / / . . . . 637 (CHAIRE) 39   12
why because i am dead / / / / . . . . 638 (CHAIRE) 40   17
(five foot five) neither dead nor alive (in real . . . . . 640 (CHAIRE) 42   14
a jew a few dead dollars and some twisted . . . . 644 (CHAIRE) 46   5
that death should be dead humblest and proudest eagerly . . . 661 (CHAIRE) 63   4
proudly lose, or playing dead and hoping death himself . . . 679 95 POEMS 7   3
Living (or some body Dead like even a Poet) . . . . 702 95 POEMS 30   5
like living neither nor dead these (or many thousand . . . . 743 95 POEMS 71   5
what were less than dead) dance, i and you; . . . . 762 95 POEMS 89   10
hugest how hush, one dead leaf stirring makes a . . . . . . 839 73 POEMS 67   4

+DEAD

FOR CONTEXT, SEE . . . . 101 & POST IMPR 11   51
FOR CONTEXT, SEE . . . . 101 & POST IMPR 11   68
FOR CONTEXT, SEE . . . . 122 & SEVEN POEMS 1   11
FOR CONTEXT, SEE . . . . 726 95 POEMS 54   6
FOR CONTEXT, SEE . . . . 803 73 POEMS 31   18

DEAD'S

they've never met before dead's more even than how . . . . . 126 & SEVEN POEMS 5   8
has in the morning dead's clever too like POF . . . . 126 & SEVEN POEMS 5   10
can dance and Whocares dead's fine like hands do . . . . . . 126 & SEVEN POEMS 5   24
you don't want to dead's happy like the way . . . . 126 & SEVEN POEMS 5   27
and why have to? dead's nice like a dance . . . . 127 & SEVEN POEMS 5   32
when, you touched, them dead's sorry like a . . . . 127 & SEVEN POEMS 5   41

DEADFROMTHENECKUP

/ / / yonder deadfromtheneckup graduate of a somewhat . . . . 234 IS 5 ONE 5   1

DEADLY

floating against the clever deadly heaven i salute you . . . 112 & PORTRAIT 6   107

DEADS

of gently smell of deads (lovers grip sprawl twitch . . . . . 384 NO THANKS 2   9

DEAF

dined this is a deaf dumb church and blind . . . . 647 (CHAIRE) 49   11
(of a world born deaf) "heaven or hell" / . . . . 787 73 POEMS 15   15

DEAFANDDUMB

in every language even deafanddumb thy sons acclaim your . . 268 IS 5 TWO 3   6

DEAFENED

with haranguing --you are deafened every mother's son-- all . 804 73 POEMS 32   10

DEAFER

is mine either was deafer than neither was dumb. . . . . . . 513 50 POEMS 27   28

DEAFLY

while at us very deafly a most stares colossal . . . . 659 (CHAIRE) 61   13

+DEAL

FOR CONTEXT, SEE . . . . 410 NO THANKS 27   4

DEAR

the unshapeful hour making dear moan in tones of . . . . . .   9 T&C SONGS 1   6
and the Humorous moon dear girl How i was . . . .   44 T&C AMORES 8   18
i'm so drunG k, dear / / / / . . . .   53 T&C PORTRAIT 1   51
me pencil your eyes dear and have a good . . . .   71 T&C SON REAL 2   2

DEAR (CONTINUED)

		PAGE	TITLE	LINE
touch another's, and your dear strong fingers clutch his	. .	76	T&C SON UNRE 1	3
dearie not so hard dear you're killing me /		109	& PORTRAIT 5	22
dead never says my dear, Time for your musiclesson	. . . . .	126	& SEVEN POEMS 5	29
salute, by what is dear to us; and by		158	& SON ACTU 7	9
unsmooth sexual luminosity spree. --dear) the uncouthly Her.		159	& SON ACTU 8	14
just twenty five cents dear friends to make it		196	XLI PORTRAIT 4	13
and not too wide dear god there's a portrait		198	XLI PORTRAIT 6	6
the precious bread of dear communion with the past, ...		209	XLI SONNETS 5	7
bipeds) OH the bothering dear unnecessary hairless o ld . . .		250	IS 5 ONE 21	17
makes burst want to dear somehow quickyes when (now, ...		251	IS 5 ONE 22	12
quickyes when (now, dark dear oh) the iceman how, ...		251	IS 5 ONE 22	13
morning) kiss this pillow, dear where our heads lived		288	IS 5 FOUR 5	9
are not going to, dear. You are not going		289	IS 5 FOUR 6	1
does is possibly this dear, that we may resume		289	IS 5 FOUR 6	6
things we consider life. Dear i put my eyes		289	IS 5 FOUR 6	13
too isn't it different dear from moving as we, ...		289	IS 5 FOUR 6	18
the train for because dear whispered again in never's		316	VIVA 8	3
hidinglyseek no o god dear wait sh please o		358	VIVA 49	5
have never loved you dear as now i love		360	VIVA 51	10
have never loved you dear as now i love		360	VIVA 51	20
have never loved you dear as now i love.		360	VIVA 51	30
have never loved you dear as now i love		360	VIVA 51	35
few most rare perfectly dear (and worlds whirl beyond		376	VIVA 67	11
the mightily alive the dear beautiful eternal night /		464	NEW POEMS 2	36
jill mopping too bad dear sh not yet jesus		496	50 POEMS 10	18
all things--let all go dear so comes love /		569	1 X 1 29	20
/ open green those (dear) worlds of than great		573	1 X 1 33	2
/ i'm asking you dear to what else could		638	{CHAIRE} 40	3
nonsense --alive; we're alive, dear: it's (kiss me now) . . .		665	{CHAIRE} 67	11
have none) "don't cry dear violet you may take		684	95 POEMS 12	3
(yes) forget (and longer dear) our birth's the because . . .		686	95 POEMS 14	10
we could not love, dear; imagine ourselves like living . . .		743	95 POEMS 71	4
own (his love) his dear he sings till everywhere		760	95 POEMS 87	11
go you go, my dear; and whatever is done		766	95 POEMS 92	3
sweet eagerly my most dear (die! live) the new		767	95 POEMS 93	8
young is the year, dear) as living as i'm		769	95 POEMS 95	25
of seem) believe me, dear, clocks have enough to		817	73 POEMS 45	7
most mysterious (eliena, my dear) is this --how anyone . . .		825	73 POEMS 53	4

DEAREST

Laughing Virginity Death) then dearest the way trees are	. .	359	VIVA 50	10
throat) i wear your dearest fears beyond their ceaselessness		372	VIVA 63	10
ecco a letter starting "dearest we" unsigned: remarkably	. .	504	50 POEMS 18	1
(wholly strange; familiar wholly) dearest more than reality	.	659	{CHAIRE} 61	7
hurrying home to the dearest little women alive (but	. . . .	709	95 POEMS 37	13

DEARIE

the shade will youse dearie? rain wouldn't that get		109	& PORTRAIT 5	2
don't care do we dearie we should worry about		109	& PORTRAIT 5	7
about the rain huh dearie? yknow i'm sorry for		109	& PORTRAIT 5	10
lives aint you, oo-oo. dearie not so hard dear		109	& PORTRAIT 5	20
(now heer we kum dearie) bud hooz gwine ter		519	50 POEMS 33	14

DEARLY

love each other very dearly , more than raindrops		577	1 X 1 37	1

DEARS

on the poppies, the dears; when all's done and		181	XLI SONGS 3	10
bit of it, my dears merely the prime minister		245	IS 5 ONE 16	19
country's love received my dears the order of The		266	IS 5 TWO 1	27
loss of liberty my dears-- or even is compelled		544	1 X 1 4	16

DEATH

the perfumed paraphrase of death). Now is the time		6	T&C EPITHALAM	120
sweet thing and small. Death, Thee i call rich		13	T&C SONGS 3	17
be they than daunting death the sleek slim deer		14	T&C SONGS 4	26
thou, is love not death? / / / /		27	T&C ORIENTALE 1	28
if i believe in death be sure of this		39	T&C AMORES 4	2
sea i knew thee death. and when i have		39	T&C AMORES 4	28
land he is called death. / / / /		42	T&C AMORES 6	25
time and tide and death leaping Sweetly your voice		44	T&C AMORES 8	21
the incomparable couch of death thy rhythmic lover thou . . .		46	T&C LA GUERRE 2	22

DEATH (CONTINUED)

upon her mouth having death in her eyes and	50	T&C IMPRESS 4	8
the city sleeps with death upon her mouth having	50	T&C IMPRESS 4	30
Mid's Place said to Death teach me of her	57	T&C PORTRAIT 5	4
Mid's Place asked "always" Death said "then as i	57	T&C PORTRAIT 5	27
and thought to myself Death and will You with	58	T&C PORTRAIT 6	14
your blueeyed boy Mister Death / / / /	60	T&C PORTRAIT 8	11
i know: proving to Death that Love is so	71	T&C SON REAL 2	14
O crazy daddy of death dance cruelly for us	80	T&C SON UNRE 5	10
i guess) when Farmer Death (whom fairies hate) shall	83	T&C SON ACTU 2	11
got a bulge on death, silence, and the keenly	84	T&C SON ACTU 3	13
, Rinsing with exact death the annual brain clotted	99	& POST IMPR 10	4
pretty and putrid dollies of-love-and-of-death dollies of . .	101	& POST IMPR 11	81
on his head. young death sits in a cafe	102	& POST IMPR 12	3
flowers" to you and "Death is young life wears	102	& POST IMPR 12	7
is sitting beside young death, is slender; likes flowers. . .	102	& POST IMPR 12	25
if she were alive, death was amusing / /	103	& POST IMPR 13	17
of boots tiny add death what shall? / /	105	& PORTRAIT 1	11
water the lips of death / / / /	136	& SON REAL 7	17
On whose deep nakedness death most believes, perpetual girls	138	& SON REAL 9	10
with a lady called death get another man with	161	& SON ACTU 10	1
in the lap of death Humanity i hate you	204	XLI LA GUERRE 2	24
excuse me, love, to Death and Time storms and	207	XLI SONNETS 3	9
its fellows in the death of light, against whose	214	XLI SONNETS 10	2
who's most afraid of death? thou art of him	215	XLI SONNETS 11	1
a few gestures to death, the silent shoulders are	225	IS 5 ONE LIZ	5
/ / / / death is more than certain	238	IS 5 ONE 9	1
so necessary as is death and unlike shirts neckties	238	IS 5 ONE 9	9
not a paragraph And death i think is no	290	IS 5 FOUR 7	16
is of love and death a marriage) you give	293	IS 5 FOUR 10	18
music stole nothing from death"-- you only will create . . .	306	IS 5 FIVE 5	10
breathe how is aunt death did always teethe /	316	VIVA 8	21
Me please you're killing) death is like now That	343	VIVA 34	6
voices womenlike telling of death love earth dark) and . . .	356	VIVA 47	5
beyond the reach of death and the English /	357	VIVA 48	13
recipe against Laughing Virginity Death) then dearest the way	359	VIVA 50	9
ere with the dirt death shall him vastly gird, ...	360	VIVA 51	5
of its countries, rendering death and forever with each . . .	366	VIVA 57	16
smile breasts gargled by death: drowned only again carefully	369	VIVA 60	10
put off your faces, Death: for day is over	376	VIVA 67	1
: the moon over death over edgar the moon	384	NO THANKS 2	7
(hears Darwin; asks about Death) concept O hairlesschested .	398	NO THANKS 15	14
a marvel than this death named Smith less strange?	406	NO THANKS 23	13
Ernest croon in his death at afternoon? (kow dow	409	NO THANKS 26	2
believe in life) and death knows whie (all good	413	NO THANKS 30	6
so we'll before what's death come (in one bed.	433	NO THANKS 50	15
is as round as) Death / / / /	436	NO THANKS 52	25
least; and less, that death should end) how lucky	446	NO THANKS 61	8
(and while behind death's death whenless voices sing	450	NO THANKS 65	17
/ / / / death (having lost) put on	451	NO THANKS 66	1
than all life more death begins to grow end's	502	50 POEMS 16	8
maggoty minus and dumb death all we inherit, all	521	50 POEMS 34	63
forbid the soul? is death a whore with life's	527	50 POEMS 39	21
would have from madame death neverless now and without . . .	531	50 POEMS 43	9
of something worth than death to change their coat	544	1 X 1 4	12
comfortable disease: your victim (death and life safely . . .	554	1 X 1 14	3
reintegrating, shall occur no death and any quantity; but . .	556	1 X 1 16	3
life to isn't: blow death to was) --all nothing's	560	1 X 1 20	22
(nor madness nor mere death nor both who is	577	1 X 1 37	10
which of his who death is killed dead. Hills	580	1 X 1 40	27
nothing's more than everything) death, as men call him, . . .	592	1 X 1 52	13
dying is fine) but Death ? o baby i	604	{CHAIRE} 6	1
baby i wouldn't like Death if Death were good:	604	{CHAIRE} 6	6
wouldn't like Death if Death were good: for when	604	{CHAIRE} 6	6
it mildly lively (but Death is strictly scientific &	604	{CHAIRE} 6	17
life! the sin of Death / / / /	604	{CHAIRE} 6	25
married Heart, now Mrs Death. Poor Mind / /	621	{CHAIRE} 23	4
/ quick i the death of thing glimpsed (and	634	{CHAIRE} 36	1

		PAGE	TITLE	LINE
DEATH (CONTINUED)				
bigly shudders) never was death so alive: chaos so	. . . .	639	{CHAIRE} 41	5
proud power of himself death immense is not so	. . . . . .	649	{CHAIRE} 51	13
him who died that death should be dead humblest	. . . . . .	661	{CHAIRE} 63	4
than life (or than death) is on f ilthi	. . . .	668	{CHAIRE} 70	20
to taste not (beyond death and life) imaginable mysteries	. .	674	95 POEMS 2	12
playing dead and hoping death himself will do the	. . . . .	679	95 POEMS 7	4
silence eyes love laughter death (dreams hopes despairs) Once	693	95 POEMS 21	4
-derfully & a- rounding death) L o v e	. . . .	719	95 POEMS 47	19
conceivable than birth or death or even than breathing	. . .	720	95 POEMS 48	13
future (and dance your death away at this wedding)	. . . . .	732	95 POEMS 60	11
wonder --and wonderful is death; but more, the older	. . . .	742	95 POEMS 70	16
mysteries as birth and death a day (or maybe	. . . . . .	743	95 POEMS 71	14
birth and glory and death and resurrection: over my	. . . .	749	95 POEMS 77	10
a single sweet day's death: as not imagined secrecies	. . . .	750	95 POEMS 78	7
dying life, all living death) and never which has	. . . . . .	765	95 POEMS 91	7
most by more-- if death is the loser and	. . . .	769	95 POEMS 95	3
mrs somethingwitz nay somethingelsestein. Death should take	.	790	73 POEMS 18	6
seventy were young and death uncommon (forgiving not divine,	798	73 POEMS 26	2
than each my deeper death becomes your kiss losing	. . . .	810	73 POEMS 38	8
is given (night and death and the rain are	. . . .	816	73 POEMS 44	8
through both life and death) timelessly celebrates the	. . .	845	73 POEMS 73	12
+DEATH				
FOR CONTEXT, SEE	. . . .	650	{CHAIRE} 52	4
DEATH'S				
peer empty of surprise death's faultless eyes (whose hand	. .	11	T&C SONGS 2	25
but i have seen death's clever enormous voice which	. . . .	45	T&C LA GUERRE 1	4
whose slippery body is Death's littlest pal, skilled in	. . .	74	T&C SON REAL 5	3
the autumn indisputably roaming death's big rotten particular	158	& SON ACTU 7	14
bravely to fling Implacable death's mysteriously sable robe	.	206	XLI SONNETS 2	4
surely reap and on Death's blade lie many a	. . . .	208	XLI SONNETS 4	10
writhing alive skies--and in death's place new fragrantly	. .	432	NO THANKS 49	18
for them, them; whose death's to be born) his	. . . .	439	NO THANKS 55	4
him (and while behind death's death whenless voices sing	. .	450	NO THANKS 65	17
greedier wand than even death's what beneath breathing selves	454	NO THANKS 69	4
and played a tune) death's dollhead wandering under weakening	479	NEW POEMS 17	10
the first knowledge of death's wandering guess) while	. . . .	517	50 POEMS 31	13
(almost too small for death's because to find) may,	. . . . .	735	95 POEMS 63	2
guise of things appear) death's: any world must always	. . .	845	73 POEMS 73	4
DEATHBOARD				
of may: life's the deathboard where all now turns	. . . . . .	574	1 X 1 34	6
DEATHFUL				
descend -ing (mercifully) touch deathful earth's any which	.	557	1 X 1 17	10
immensest mysteries contradict a deathful realm of fact --by	763	95 POEMS 90	28
proudly descending put on deathful flesh: are lovers glad?	.	768	95 POEMS 94	6
DEATHFULS				
ams whichful sarcasms papery deathfuls) awaits yes this alive	415	NO THANKS 32	19
DEATHLESS				
at every pore a deathless life with magic until	. . . .	428	NO THANKS 45	16
standing erect in the deathless truth of His presence	. . . .	749	95 POEMS 77	19
at twilight voice of deathless earth's innumerable doom:	. .	821	73 POEMS 49	2
DEATHLESSNESS				
whys of such a deathlessness) remembrance might no patient	.	420	NO THANKS 37	6
wish (whying diminutive bright deathlessness to these my not	669	{CHAIRE} 71	2
both and) Self adventures deathlessness / / / /	. . . .	721	95 POEMS 49	14
exchanging swiftly for the deathlessness who's beauty:	. . .	818	73 POEMS 46	6
DEATHMONEY				
tree- spires shout appalling deathmoney into spiralS and Now	346	VIVA 37	16
DEATHS				
are kneeling the various deaths which are your lover	. . . .	285	IS 5 FOUR 2	20
and first into different deaths Concentric geometries of	. .	311	VIVA 3	8
three contains these prettiest deaths without effort while	. .	340	VIVA 31	15
breaths.) "people are walking deaths in this season" think	.	354	VIVA 45	11
morality sort-of-aliveing by innumerable kind-of-deaths	. . .	410	NO THANKS 27	12
DEBRIS				
at me through sagging debris of exploded day the	. . . . . .	151	& SON REAL 22	2
DECAY				
involves the comedy of decay, / / / /	. . . .	144	& SON REAL 15	14

	PAGE	TITLE	LINE

DECEASE
auspicious occasion of his decease a scrumptious not to . . . 239 IS 5 ONE 10   29
DECEIVE
true than reason will deceive (more secret or than . . . . . 592 1 X 1 52   1
DECEIVED
thought you would have deceived me and became a . . . . . . 30 T&C ORIENTALE 4   31
DECEIVER
pastime --each joy a deceiver, and sorrow a system-- . . . . 625 {CHAIRE} 27   19
DECEIVING
soul convict him of deceiving) whose ways are neither . . . . 683 95 POEMS 11   4
DECENT
vote for me (all decent mem and wonens will . . . . 500 50 POEMS 14   21
DECENTLY
her new wings then decently hanged himself, one afternoon. . 170 & SON ACTU 19   4
DECIDED
you had carefully ourselves decided what this cathedral ought 323 VIVA 15   24
(of course) carefully had decided oh no (but / . . . . 323 VIVA 15   29
/ / when god decided to invent everything he . . . . 566 1 X 1 26   1
DECIDING
forter a click of deciding glory inflicted to the . . . . . . 197 XLI PORTRAIT 5   16
DECIPHERED
our Not to be deciphered selves merely Continue to . . . . . 361 VIVA 52   25
DECISION
head gripping for a decision: burn the terrific fingers . . . 146 & SON REAL 17   4
DECLARATIVE
who wrote a simple declarative sentence with seven . . . . . 336 VIVA 27   4
DECLARE
dig) by beauty i declare to you if what . . . . 115 & PORTRAIT 8   4
or so subhuman superminds declare --nor all their times . . . 817 73 POEMS 45   3
DECLINE
to compel me to decline to admit i've died) . . . . 329 VIVA 20   2
DECOMPOSING
i find myself gently decomposing in the mouth of . . . . . . 201 XLI PORTRAIT 9   2
DEDUCTION
and you, is a deduction which (be it false . . . . 798 73 POEMS 26   25
DEE
Bet, an Leelee, an dee beeg wun" her handless . . . . 73 T&C SON REAL 4   13
DEED
(a dream of a deed, born not to die) . . . . 776 73 POEMS 4   35
, o no in- deed; money can't do (never . . . . 793 73 POEMS 21   7
eyes and did the deed of joy with him . . . . 799 73 POEMS 27   15
DEEDS
air in utterable coolness deeds of green thrilling light . . 163 & SON ACTU 12   8
swordgreat story shine the deeds of history her heroes, . . . 209 XLI SONNETS 5   1
thighs will be thighs deeds cannot dream what dreams . . . . 511 50 POEMS 25   25
DEEM
mated, let us not deem it miraculous if their . . . . 326 VIVA 18   8
DEEMED
to fancy) i have deemed with your peculiar mouth . . . . . . 78 T&C SON UNRE 3   3
DEEP
on whose pedestal the deep expels (over Selene's car . . . . 4 T&C EPITHALAM   46
reeking of the whispered deep, deliberate groping ocean . . . 7 T&C EPITHALAM   158
my reason with the deep caress of every most . . . . 19 T&C PUELLA MEA   98
flowering, the air is deep with desirable flowers i . . . . . 31 T&C ORIENTALE 5   12
from mines a mile deep but the body of . . . . 33 T&C ORIENTALE 6   48
the earth writhe upon deep rugs / / / . . . . 35 T&C ORIENTALE 6   116
hands infinite the erect deep upon me in the . . . . 64 T&C POST IMPR 1   6
of the day grow deep. / / / / . . . . 78 T&C SON UNRE 3   14
is a procession of deep beasts coming with keen . . . . . . 112 & PORTRAIT 6   100
the largest hour push deep his din of wallowing . . . . . . 115 & PORTRAIT 8   12
immense lips On whose deep nakedness death most believes, . . 138 & SON REAL 9   10
into the belly whose deep squirm nibbles. another couches, . 143 & SON REAL 14   11
grins nudge smiles push--. deep into the edgeless gloaming . 202 XLI PORTRAIT 9   37
as among the slow deep trees perpetual of sleep . . . . . . 208 XLI SONNETS 4   13
mute hugeness of depriving deep, with thunder of those . . . 210 XLI SONNETS 6   5
the rushing of thy deep hair and the smiting . . . . 213 XLI SONNETS 9   11
want above fourteenth fifth's deep purring biceps, the mystic 220 XLI SONNETS 16   2
deliver promptly to a deep lap enormous mindless hands. . . . 225 IS 5 ONE LIZ   9

DEEP (CONTINUED)
   lay quietly in the deep mud et cetera (dreaming, ... 276 IS 5 TWO 10   20
   everywhere do not touch) deep things; remembering ever so . . 294 IS 5 FOUR 11   5
   wanders streets dark and, deep with rain.... (he, slightly . 300 IS 5 FOUR 17   14
   eyes (frailer than most deep dreams are frail) songs . . . . 306 IS 5 FIVE 5   3
   bright futures against the deep sky in May mine's . . . . . . 314 VIVA 6   16
   all which seemed sweet deep and inexplicable not being . . . 322 VIVA 14   7
   into the street) this deep immediate mask and expressing . . 328 VIVA 19   14
   behind Nowhere) creeps the deep thing everybody sometimes . . 330 VIVA 21   13
   challenge, devout am upward deep most invincible unthing . . 351 VIVA 42   2
   my father will be (deep like a rose tall . . . . 352 VIVA 43   5
   life's only half (through deep weather then or none . . . . . 364 VIVA 55   13
   thin a ghost so deep and he might live) . . . . 414 NO THANKS 31   8
   i remark how through deep lifted fields Oxen distinctly . . . 434 NO THANKS 51   30
   and Am the glad deep the living from nowh . . . . 449 NO THANKS 64   7
   st?? holy (soft briGht deep) yeS near sta? calm . . . . 455 NO THANKS 70   7
   alone (wHo Yes near deep whO big alone soft . . . . 455 NO THANKS 70   12
   big alone soft near deep calm deep ????Ht ?????T) . . . . . . 455 NO THANKS 70   13
   soft near deep calm deep ????Ht ?????T) Who (holy . . . . . . 455 NO THANKS 70   13
   you are beautiful or deep or generous what i . . . . 475 NEW POEMS 13   14
   all by all and deep by deep and more . . . . 515 50 POEMS 29   29
   all and deep by deep and more by more . . . . 515 50 POEMS 29   29
   who could sing so deep and strong one queerying . . . . 526 50 POEMS 38   6
   dying born) must grow deep in dark least ourselves . . . . . 556 1 X 1 16   13
   once if strangers (who deep our most are selves) . . . . . . 564 1 X 1 24   14
   books can be) and deep in the high that . . . . 594 1 X 1 54   32
   with a distinct grandiloquent deep D; while all skies . . . . 650 {CHAIRE} 52   16
   a- gainst one immense deep hell -o of keen . . . . 687 95 POEMS 15   7
   the high is the deep is the far o . . . . 695 95 POEMS 23   20
   gay and a steep) deep rush through amazing day . . . . 769 95 POEMS 95   14
   may wonder a with deep (A so wonder pure) . . . . 778 73 POEMS 6   5
   me (the great dim deep sound of rain; and . . . . 816 73 POEMS 44   2
DEEP'S
   hope most innocent (so deep's the mind of flesh . . . . 609 {CHAIRE} 11   7
DEEPEN
   the hills the pines deepen to whispers primeval and . . . . .   5 T&C EPITHALAM   76
   by daisies and twilights Deepen her, Recite upon her . . . . 65 T&C POST IMPR 2   11
DEEPENING
   who wave among your deepening thighs a greedier wand . . . . 454 NO THANKS 69   3
   and stroll some never deepening beach locked in foreverish . 843 73 POEMS 71   3
DEEPENS
   always i do nothing) deepens with wind (and hark . . . . . . 785 73 POEMS 13   5
DEEPER
   it means nearer because deeper firmer since darker than . . . 126 & SEVEN POEMS 5   1
   blossoms of new mingling: deeper: blood of my blood: . . . . 139 & SON REAL 10   5
   thee perchance to me deeper. / / / / . . . . 213 XLI SONNETS 9   17
   of your eyes is deeper than all roses) nobody, ... 366 VIVA 57   19
   sea which only is deeper than the sea love . . . . 530 50 POEMS 42   8
   lips smash unimagined sky deeper than heaven is hell . . . . 563 1 X 1 23   12
   unworlds hollow silence has deeper eyes purest than fear's . 565 1 X 1 25   8
   appear love is a deeper season than reason; my . . . . 578 1 X 1 38   9
   than madness did reveal) deeper is life than lose: . . . . . 592 1 X 1 52   3
   not adventure soon a deeper magic: that white sleep . . . . . 675 95 POEMS 3   11
   we've agreed with nothing deeper than our minds to . . . . . 741 95 POEMS 69   8
   swims than each my deeper death becomes your kiss . . . . . . 810 73 POEMS 38   8
DEEPEST
   me) like these first deepest rare quite who are . . . . 367 VIVA 58   7
   you here is the deepest secret nobody knows (here . . . . . . 766 95 POEMS 92   10
DEEPLY
   let thy twain eyes deeply wield a noise of . . . . 10 T&C SONGS 1   42
   the bright rain occurs deeply, beautifully and i (being . . . 92 & POST IMPR 4   7
   for no reason feel deeply completely conscious of the . . . . 92 & POST IMPR 4   11
   ropes amid screams of deeply bulging thousands i too . . . . 259 IS 5 ONE 29   18
   fear Who held us deeply in His fist is . . . . 289 IS 5 FOUR 6   3
   with its Own motion deeply to wickedly comprehend the . . . . 356 VIVA 47   9
   / / / move deeply, rain (dream hugely) wish . . . . 422 NO THANKS 39   2
   moon by sun i deeply greet this fool and . . . . 441 NO THANKS 56   67
   and i'm no (if deeply less conceivable than birth . . . . . . 720 95 POEMS 48   12

DEEPLY (CONTINUED)
   blissfully seething gift wandering deeply through godthanking 754 95 POEMS 82   4
   brief that how infinite (deeply immediate fleet and profound 763 95 POEMS 90   22
DEEPLYNESS
   between Who out of deeplyness rose to undeath) salute. . . . 358 VIVA 49   13
DEEPLYTOPLAY
   dead knead of lustfulhunched deeplytoplay lips and stare the 153 & SON ACTU 2   5
DEEPNESS
   only again carefully through deepness to rise these your . . 369 VIVA 60   11
   small wish into upward deepness of less fear much . . . . . . 528 50 POEMS 40   8
+DEEPNESS
   FOR CONTEXT, SEE . . . . 395 NO THANKS 12   14
DEER
   and smiling the merry deer ran before. Fleeter be . . . . . . 14 T&C SONGS 4   5
   dreams the swift sweet deer the red rare deer. . . . . 14 T&C SONGS 4   7
   deer the red rare deer. Four red roebuck at . . . . 14 T&C SONGS 4   8
   sleep the lean lithe deer the fleet flown deer. . . . . 14 T&C SONGS 4   17
   deer the fleet flown deer. Four fleet does at . . . . 14 T&C SONGS 4   18
   death the sleek slim deer the tall tense deer. . . . . 14 T&C SONGS 4   27
   deer the tall tense deer. Four tall stags at . . . . 14 T&C SONGS 4   28
DEFEAT
   one warrior innocent of defeat thy hair upon thy . . . . . . 29 T&C ORIENTALE 3 19
   on the lintel of defeat, her heart breaks in . . . . 75 T&C SON REAL 6 12
DEFEND
   depths of horror to defend a sunbeam's architecture with . . 562 1 X 1 22   11
DEFERENCE
   my frank qualms in deference to her not inobvious . . . . . 326 VIVA 18   21
DEFINITE
   comes the lean and definite houses are troubled. A . . . . . 62 T&C PORTRAIT 10 6
   world. The lean and definite houses are troubled. in . . . . 62 T&C PORTRAIT 10 11
DEFT
   since but through spontaneous deft strictly horrors which . . 386 NO THANKS 3   7
DEFTLY
   alert and innocent very deftly upon which indolent miracles . 19 T&C PUELLA MEA 95
   little normal worms. Dress deftly your flesh in stupid . . . 161 & SON ACTU 10 9
   perhaps that and this, deftly propping on smallest hands . . 282 IS 5 THREE 6   6
   fools a weightless slowness (deftly muting the world's . . . 299 IS 5 FOUR 16   3
   creep ungenerous who ape deftly aims they dare not . . . . . 440 NO THANKS 56 21
DEFUNCT
   / / Buffalo Bill's defunct who used to ride . . . . 60 T&C PORTRAIT 8   2
   that and this radically defunct periodical. i would suggest . 230 IS 5 ONE 2   18
   rapidly through mist a defunct king as linotypes gobblehobble 259 IS 5 ONE 29 11
   limbs, with faces like defunct geraniums) / / / . . . . 280 IS 5 THREE 4 34
DEGREES
   infinite breast in bright degrees, whose pillow is the . . . 4 T&C EPITHALAM 39
DEIFY
   of his littleness --electrons deify one razorblade into a . . 554 1 X 1 14   5
DEITY
   gush to it as deity or devil --toss in . . . . 804 73 POEMS 32   5
DEL
   pause elevator nel mezzo del cammin' that means half- . . . . 256 IS 5 ONE 27   7
+DELAPIDATION
   FOR CONTEXT, SEE . . . . 94 & POST IMPR 6   3
DELETE
   g.o.w. is full of) delete / / / / . . . . 411 NO THANKS 28 12
DELETED
   smile.... remark a few deleted of texture or meaning . . . . 260 IS 5 ONE 30   8
DELIBERATE
   of the whispered deep, deliberate groping ocean fondled o'er 7 T&C EPITHALAM 159
DELIBERATED
   by oaks and roses deliberated.) / / / / . . . . 181 XLI SONGS 3   15
DELICACY
   as with almost melancholy delicacy night gargles windows. / . 168 & SON ACTU 17 19
DELICATE
   and (catching up her delicate silk) all white, with . . . . . 8 T&C OF NICOL   27
   and finally through altogether delicate gestures of rain a . 92 & POST IMPR 4 16
   remind Me of HerThe delicate-swill tints of hair Whose . . . 94 & POST IMPR 6 20
   more intricately in the delicate scorn with which in . . . . 144 & SON REAL 15 11

	PAGE	TITLE	LINE
DELICATE (CONTINUED)			
white-grub faces) clothes in delicate hubbub as you stood . .	172	& SON ACTU 21	7
heart before how worlds delicate of bombast--papery what & .	480	NEW POEMS 18	16
fellow'll exist --whereas that delicate creature is most . .	813	73 POEMS 41	7
DELICATE-SWILL			
remind Me of HerThe delicate-swill tints of hair Whose . . .	94	& POST IMPR 6	20
DELICATELY			
blow horses of gold delicately crouching beneath silver . . .	110	& PORTRAIT 6	35
of clenched arms a delicately elephantine face (It is	143	& SON REAL 14	2
--dead--and the dark gold delicately smash.... grass, and the	153	& SON ACTU 2	7
skilfully construed by a delicately experi- menting colossus	201	XLI PORTRAIT 9	24
of this brittle whore delicately wobbles an improbably . . .	229	IS 5 ONE FRAN	3
of you successfully if delicately gelded (or spaded)	231	IS 5 ONE 3	44
DELICIOUS			
the curves of that delicious boy whose serious grace	3	T&C EPITHALAM	23
incorrigible arms impaled upon delicious mystery, with gaunt	7	T&C EPITHALAM	157
subliminal fern of her delicious voice (of her voice	19	T&C PUELLA MEA	114
breathing noun (moreover the delicious frown of the grave . .	21	T&C PUELLA MEA	212
sweeter (of whose shy delicious glance things which never . .	22	T&C PUELLA MEA	251
whirled and tossed into delicious dancing up Up with	44	T&C AMORES 8	12
comic tadpole wriggling in delicious mud / / /	157	& SON ACTU 6	15
invisibly consult with some delicious image the a little . .	193	XLI PORTRAIT 1	7
DELIGHT			
her pale flesh with delight) --immortally whence are the . .	3	T&C EPITHALAM	7
DELIGHTED			
writing one still finds delighted fingers knitting for the .	70	T&C SON REAL 1	8
DELIGHTFUL			
a turbulence of forms delightful with indefinable flowering,	31	T&C ORIENTALE 5	10
DELIRIOUS			
sharp cunning and withal delirious feet of the Princess . . .	17	T&C PUELLA MEA	29
in my being the delirious smart of thrilled ecstasy, ...	79	T&C SON UNRE 4	12
bacchant. partedpetaled mouth, face delirious. indivisible .	185	XLI SONGS 7	15
serious something authentic and delirious you know something	407	NO THANKS 24	11
DELIRIOUSLY			
its supple financial teeth deliriously sprouting from	201	XLI PORTRAIT 9	3
DELIRIUM			
light the droll snowing delirium (we do not speak)	168	& SON ACTU 17	5
DELIVER			
whose white thick wrists deliver promptly to a deep	225	IS 5 ONE LIZ	8
DELIVERED			
was i think yourself delivered into both my hands	57	T&C PORTRAIT 5	18
muckers pimps and tratesmen delivered are of vicians and . .	405	NO THANKS 22	2
DELIVERS			
more accurate, yes it delivers the goods, Heaven knows . . .	264	IS 5 ONE 33	12
DEM			
good ole daze.... in dem daze kid Christmas meant	237	IS 5 ONE 8	13
fellers' goils away frum dem" --"somebody hung uh gun	332	VIVA 23	7
kickin duh guts outa dem doity frogeaters an humpin	332	VIVA 23	15
yunnuhstan ydoan o yunnuhstan dem yguduh ged yunnuhstan dem .	547	1 X 1 7	5
dem yguduh ged yunnuhstan dem doidee yguduh ged riduh	547	1 X 1 7	7
nudn LISN bud LISN dem gud am lidl yelluh	547	1 X 1 7	11
DEMAND			
but let us next demand wherefore yon mob an	245	IS 5 ONE 16	15
an eagerest strict flame) demand the metaphor of our	362	VIVA 53	11
+DEMAND			
FOR CONTEXT, SEE	331	VIVA 22	3
+DEMANDE			
FOR CONTEXT, SEE	430	NO THANKS 47	1
DEMANDING			
over --it's no use demanding that lending be giving;	625	(CHAIRE) 27	2
DEMANDS			
sorrow a certain reckoning demands... marvelling And what may	374	VIVA 65	3
/ who before dying demands not rebirth of such	402	NO THANKS 19	1
DEMOCRACY			
the world safe for democracy it never fails and	125	& SEVEN POEMS 4	12
but the voice-with-a-smile of democracy announces night & day	711	95 POEMS 39	5
right now" so rah-rah-rah democracy let's all be as	711	95 POEMS 39	25

	PAGE	TITLE	LINE

+DEMOCRACY
  FOR CONTEXT, SEE . . . . 549 1 X 1 9   12
  FOR CONTEXT, SEE . . . . 635 (CHAIRE) 37   11
DEMOCRATIC
  such hair) the expensively democratic tyrannically dumb . . . 337 VIVA 28   13
  funereally hilarious (or otherwise democratic) but . . . . . 802 73 POEMS 30   20
DEMON
  her teeming womb said demon for to doom yea . . . . 552 1 X 1 12   22
  / crazy jay blue) demon laughshriek ing at me . . . . 677 95 POEMS 5   2
DEMONGOD
  ignorantly blossoming a scarecrow demongod countless in . . . 662 (CHAIRE) 64   8
DEMONS
  it out of which demons with wings would be . . . . 652 (CHAIRE) 54   13
DEMONSTRATE
  cupboard gallantly offering to demonstrate the biggest best . 326 VIVA 18   11
DEMONSTRATING
  logic of annihi- lation demonstrating from woolworthian . . . 197 XLI PORTRAIT 5   7
DEMOTIC
  savouring slightly of the demotic) Miss Gay had nothing . . . 326 VIVA 18   28
DEMURE
  mouth, taste the accurate demure ferocious rhythm of precise 162 & SON ACTU 11   11
DEMURELY
  haunters of dreams always demurely halfsmiling from cool . . 211 XLI SONNETS 7   7
DEN
  old age scolds Forbid den Stop Must n't Don't . . . . 729 95 POEMS 57   14
DENFERT
  you beautifully also; at denfert the fat strongman has . . . 384 NO THANKS 2   19
DENIED
  / / / / denied night's face have shadowless . . . . 527 50 POEMS 39   1
DENIES
  who; despite what fear denies, what hope asserts, what . . . 576 1 X 1 36   3
  --love. Each believing world denies, whereas your lover . . . 845 73 POEMS 73   11
DENIZENS
  loudly and gondola rapidly denizens of Omaha Altoona or . . . 256 IS 5 ONE 27   26
  perturba- tions unhappily, the denizens of the zoo were . . . 326 VIVA 18   23
DENOUNCES
  of having altitude--and march denounces april as a saboteur . 620 (CHAIRE) 22   12
+DENSE
  FOR CONTEXT, SEE . . . . 430 NO THANKS 47   13
DENTHAM
  agree (if you can't dentham comma bentham; or 1 . . . . 791 73 POEMS 19   5
DENY
  complete fate (he must deny mind: may believe in . . . . . . 402 NO THANKS 19   15
  merciful wonder no world deny may or believe / . . . . 845 73 POEMS 73   14
DEPAOLA
  my wonderful friend dominic depaola gives me a most . . . . . 680 95 POEMS 8   24
DEPART
  the flowers --didst e'er depart upon more exquisite quest? . 3 T&C EPITHALAM   20
  he nods and all depart through the bruised air . . . . 34 T&C ORIENTALE 6 106
DEPARTED
  we loved the far- departed mouth sweetly-saluted lingers. if 42 T&C AMORES 6   6
  lightly desperate certainly wherefrom departed is youth's . . 57 T&C PORTRAIT 5   40
DEPARTING
  the green- greeting pale- departing irrevocable sea i knew . 39 T&C AMORES 4   26
  silver bird looked grave (departing hurriedly to shave) . . . 339 VIVA 30   21
DEPARTS
  and when a kiss departs our lips are made . . . . 322 VIVA 14   12
DEPARTURE
  into the big vermilion departure swim, sayingly; (Do you . . 66 T&C POST IMPR 3   11
  me (for whom the departure of everything real is . . . . . . 720 95 POEMS 48   10
DEPEND
  which thinkless unwishing doth depend upon the texture of . . 411 NO THANKS 28   4
DEPENDING
  even a few more depending on the remu- nerativeness . . . . . 236 IS 5 ONE 7   16
DEPOSITED
  ten pennies have been deposited upon the drum there . . . . . 196 XLI PORTRAIT 4   10
DEPRIVING
  the mute hugeness of depriving deep, with thunder of . . . . 210 XLI SONNETS 6   5

<pre>
                                                           PAGE   TITLE   LINE
DEPTHS
  my father moved through depths of height this motionless . . 520 50 POEMS 34   4
  is --who'll solve the depths of horror to defend . . . . . . 562 1 X 1 22   11
  reality or un-) proudly depths above why's first because . . 574 1 X 1 34   9
  as never (in againless depths of silence) and forever . . . . 758 95 POEMS 85   40
  of known descend through depths of guess, shadows are . . . . 761 95 POEMS 88   6
DERANGE
  loud most howish time derange the silent whys of . . . . . . 420 NO THANKS 37   5
DERBIED
  of Police (a dapper derbied creature, swaggers daintily . . . 274 IS 5 TWO 9   28
DERBIES
  up streets; heels taking derbies (where?) a pup hurriedly . . 172 & SON ACTU 21   3
  .... five men in derbies / / / / . . . . 200 XLI PORTRAIT 8   33
DERRICKS
  and gladness plus little derricks of gesture any skyscraper .   68 T&C POST IMPR 5   4
DERRIERE
  reach) upon his fearless derriere sturdily seated--Colonel . 266 IS 5 TWO 1   21
DES
  voix fragile qui chatouille Des Italiens the putain with . . 120 & PORTRAIT 12   7
  ladies suddenly j'm'en fous des negres (in the twilight . . . 121 & PORTRAIT 12   43
DESCEND
  and the glowing throng descend, felt on her flesh . . . . . .   4 T&C EPITHALAM   53
  earth, O let us descend take shimmering wind these . . . . .   41 T&C AMORES 5   16
  her eyes the hours descend, putting on stars.... in . . . .   50 T&C IMPRESS 4   31
  about Peacepeacepeace (to droppingly descend amid thunderous 267 IS 5 TWO 2   9
  here who there who) descend -ing (mercifully) touch deathful 557 1 X 1 17   8
  here: overs of known descend through depths of guess, ... 761 95 POEMS 88   6
  now does our world descend the path to nothingness . . . . . 834 73 POEMS 62   1
  peace, never imaginable mystery) descend / / / / . . . . . . 839 73 POEMS 67   16
+DESCEND
  FOR CONTEXT, SEE . . . . 421 NO THANKS 38   7
  FOR CONTEXT, SEE . . . . 421 NO THANKS 38   9
DESCENDING
  and how gradually which descending are suddenly received) or 299 IS 5 FOUR 16   6
  the snow carefully everywhere descending; nothing which we . 366 VIVA 57   12
  suffer? all divinities proudly descending put on deathful . . 768 95 POEMS 94   6
DESCENDS
  of twilight (who slenderly descends, daintily carrying in her   93 & POST IMPR 5   9
  and this imitation resemble, descends into the earth with . . 300 IS 5 FOUR 17   19
DESCRIBE
  he who watched unhands describe what mimicry, with angry . . 376 VIVA 67   3
  now be inclined to describe it rather as a" . . . . 464 NEW POEMS 2   21
DESDEMONIAL
  she gave him a desdemonial that took his breath . . . . 552 1 X 1 12   19
DESERT
  Rowspeach es a soft desert smoked bad me whilepin . . . . . . 318 VIVA 10   21
DESERTBYITS
  self all about the desertbyIts elf while) nextto Mesmoked . . 318 VIVA 10   13
DESERVED
  answer more or less deserved, Young fellow go in . . . . . . 229 IS 5 ONE FRAN   8
DESERVES
  eventual perfection while east deserves of dawn. i lie . . . 184 XLI SONGS 6   14
DESIRABLE
  air is deep with desirable flowers i think thou . . . .   31 T&C ORIENTALE 5 12
DESIRE
  omits no mention of desire in every curved and . . . .   5 T&C EPITHALAM   89
  stands whereof is most desire, yet less than those . . . . .   6 T&C EPITHALAM   147
  my dream you had desire to thwart me and . . . .   30 T&C ORIENTALE 4   18
  a white thorn of desire the taut neck of . . . .   34 T&C ORIENTALE 6   95
  agonizing proximity to its desire of a doomed impetuous . . . 193 XLI PORTRAIT 1   10
  had long suppressed the desire to suppress the suppressed . . 263 IS 5 ONE 32   38
  to suppress the suppressed desire of shall we say: . . . . . 263 IS 5 ONE 32   39
  called the moon singing desire into begin joy was . . . . . . 520 50 POEMS 34   20
DESIRES
  / even if all desires things moments be murdered . . . . . . 237 IS 5 ONE 8   1
DESPAIR
  a wild and thin despair of violin / / . . . .   12 T&C SONGS 2   50
  there is laughter and despair impersonates a street i . . . . 375 VIVA 66   5
</pre>

		PAGE	TITLE	LINE

DESPAIR (CONTINUED)

or three dreamfuls of despair that face) large one . . . . . 402 NO THANKS 19   7

climbing hope meets most despair? all knowing's having and . 528 50 POEMS 40   9

blows a bubble of despair into hugeness world system . . . . 531 50 POEMS 43   1

carve immortal jungles of despair to hold a mountain's . . . 562 1 X 1 22   13

hope can feel only despair completely strikes forests of . . 580 1 X 1 40   24

crying-- for hoping for despair for peace for longing . . . . 683 95 POEMS 11   10

each ignorant gladness--unteaches what despair preaches . . . 764 95 POEMS 90   42

hope doubt (wonder mistrust) despair and right where soulless 780 73 POEMS 8   4

are cowards all) therefore despair, my heart and die . . . . 834 73 POEMS 62   23

and partially imagine whose despair when every silence will . 842 73 POEMS 70   9

DESPAIRING

luminous whole; turn sheer despairing to most perfect gay, . 649 {CHAIRE} 51   6

DESPAIRS

laughter death (dreams hopes despairs) Once happened nowhere 693 95 POEMS 21   5

DESPERATE

painteaten and bodies lightly desperate certainly wherefrom . 57 T&C PORTRAIT 5   39

the crank goes round desperate elves and hope- less . . . . . 69 T&C POST IMPR 6   21

DESPERATELY

hand the crank goes desperately, round and round pointing . . 69 T&C POST IMPR 6   9

+DESPERATELY

FOR CONTEXT, SEE . . . . 703 95 POEMS 31   9

DESPISE

faithful and which i despise, frankly admitting i have . . . 43 T&C AMORES 7   19

surprise ourselves --let's then despise what is not courage . 368 VIVA 59   17

DESPITE

a swoon of synopsis despite a sadistic modesty his . . . . . 193 XLI PORTRAIT 1   5

mama had generously provided (despite courte- ous . . . . . . 326 VIVA 18   17

which and every who; despite what fear denies, what . . . . . 576 1 X 1 36   3

which, every woman who's (despite the ultramachinations of . 807 73 POEMS 35   10

DESPOT'S

from himself ye duskiest despot's goldenest gal did wring . . 552 1 X 1 12   16

DESTINIES

somewhat hand the paper destinies of nations sic item . . . . 499 50 POEMS 13   6

DESTINY

only and illimitably his destiny) mountains! how can each" . 626 {CHAIRE} 28   9

DESTROY

when man determined to destroy himself he picked the . . . . 566 1 X 1 26   5

DESTROYED

well how the dainty destroyed hero clamps the hearty . . . . 111 & PORTRAIT 6   41

DESTRUCTIVITY

more than mildly Absolute destructivity to non- entities e. . 391 NO THANKS 8   23

DETACHES

idea, drenching. earth's brain detaches clottingsand from a a 99 & POST IMPR 10   20

DETACHING

blackness occasionally from which detaching itself bumps . . 201 XLI PORTRAIT 9   10

DETERMINE

a wheel turns doesn't determine its roundness: if swallows . 514 50 POEMS 28   6

DETERMINED

Yale above his blond determined head the sacred flag . . . . 273 IS 5 TWO 8   13

everything began when man determined to destroy himself he . 566 1 X 1 26   5

DEUX

(An) quickly Not un deux trois der die Stood . . . . 348 VIVA 39   12

DEVIL

for she knows the devil ooch the devil ouch . . . . 25 T&C CHANSONS 2   21

the devil ooch the devil ouch the devil ach . . . . 25 T&C CHANSONS 2   22

the devil ouch the devil ach the great green . . . . 25 T&C CHANSONS 2   23

the great green dancing devil devil devil devil wheeEEE . . . 25 T&C CHANSONS 2   27

great green dancing devil devil devil devil wheeEEE / . . . . 25 T&C CHANSONS 2   28

green dancing devil devil devil devil wheeEEE / / . . . . . . 25 T&C CHANSONS 2   29

dancing devil devil devil devil wheeEEE / / / . . . . 25 T&C CHANSONS 2   30

the triangle like the devil) my uncle Frank has . . . . 253 IS 5 ONE 24   4

with room for the devil and his angels too . . . . 568 1 X 1 28   18

it as deity or devil --toss in sobs and . . . . 804 73 POEMS 32   5

DEVIOUS

verb, miraculous inflected oral devious, beneath the body's . 21 T&C PUELLA MEA 210

DEVOURING

undimishied silence, supports while devouring the firm tumult 201 XLI PORTRAIT 9   19

		PAGE	TITLE	LINE

DEVOURS
tes- i -mal- ly devours darkness the hungry star . . . . . . 49 T&C IMPRESS 3   10
expecting faces clumsily which devours a man, three cats, . . 279 IS 5 THREE 3   7
DEVOUT
bulb silkenly brutal a devout flexion / / / . . . . 68 T&C POST IMPR 5   16
/ structure, miraculous challenge, devout am upward deep most 351 VIVA 42   1
DEW
to snare the brutal dew, --the authentic scroll of . . . . . 5 T&C EPITHALAM   87
heart, with beads of dew made jewels by the . . . . 8 T&C OF NICOL   16
went forth into the dew: right wildly beat her . . . . 8 T&C OF NICOL   28
used to yield with dew when the world was . . . . 18 T&C PUELLA MEA   53
of laughter and of dew, was a flight, a . . . . 23 T&C PUELLA MEA   277
shrieks Yew May n't Dew Thiz Tew Mee as . . . . 629 (CHAIRE) 31   13
+DEXTERITY
FOR CONTEXT, SEE . . . . 403 NO THANKS 20   9
DEXTEROUS
beauty more than snow dexterous and fugitive my very . . . . 17 T&C PUELLA MEA   17
DEY
fer election makin believe dey was chust born / . . . . . . 237 IS 5 ONE 8   19
an talkin big how dey could kill sixereight cops-- . . . . . 332 VIVA 23   3
have some on me" --dey was petrified. De room . . . . 332 VIVA 23   24
DIADUMENOS
pole poises, smiling, the diadumenos in whose young chiseled   3 T&C EPITHALAM   32
DIAMOND
from the ceiling (one diamond timid with nesting incense) . . 32 T&C ORIENTALE 6   25
very silly hocked the diamond he gave her. Bill . . . . 145 & SON REAL 16   9
blond job at her diamond solitaire while guesswho nibbles . . 545 1 X 1 5   3
+DIAMONDS
FOR CONTEXT, SEE . . . . 628 (CHAIRE) 30   13
DIAPHANOUS
sings drifting in slow diaphanous faint rout), queen in . . .   6 T&C EPITHALAM   144
DIARMUID
world was young and Diarmuid looked in Grania's eyes.) . . . 18 T&C PUELLA MEA   60
the cries of Babylon.) Diarmuid Paris and Solomon, Omar . . . 23 T&C PUELLA MEA   262
DICK
young man sitting in Dick Mid's Place said to . . . . 57 T&C PORTRAIT 5   3
young man sitting in Dick Mid's Place asked "always" . . . . 57 T&C PORTRAIT 5   23
when you rang at Dick Mid's Place the madam . . . . 73 T&C SON REAL 4   1
they knew you at Dick Mid's the three trickling . . . . 73 T&C SON REAL 4   10
/ / / / Dick Mid's large bluish face . . . . 149 & SON REAL 20   1
Jimmie's sister worked for Dick. And had some rows . . . . 149 & SON REAL 20   7
toothless girl in Yonkers. Dick Mid's green large three . . . 149 & SON REAL 20   14
i do, being as Dick Mid once noted lifting . . . . 229 IS 5 ONE FRAN   9
(hprettyw) ith) mr jeff dick son fec i (m . . . . 388 NO THANKS 5   29
Tom, your Tom is Dick; while Gadgets murder squawk . . . . . 438 NO THANKS 54   10
every madge and mabel dick and dave --tomorrow is . . . . . 579 1 X 1 39   11
+DICKSON
FOR CONTEXT, SEE . . . . 388 NO THANKS 5   29
DICTAPHONES
York an San Fran dictaphones wireless subways vacuum cleaners 237 IS 5 ONE 8   8
DICTUM
1; surreptitiously cogitating the dictum of a new england . . 327 VIVA 18   r39
DID
more exquisite quest? and did thy fortunate fingers sometime   3 T&C EPITHALAM   21
Between my lips which did sing a rose shall . . . . 16 T&C SONGS 6   5
wholly dead: nor ever did on such a throat . . . . 17 T&C PUELLA MEA   35
of Helen's beauty: never did Lord Jason (in impossible . . . 18 T&C PUELLA MEA   68
goodly store whose beauty did in nothing err. If . . . . . . 21 T&C PUELLA MEA   174
why then the artificer did most exquisitely err.) When . . . 22 T&C PUELLA MEA   220
tweaked and dinted then did my servant become of . . . . . . 57 T&C PORTRAIT 5   35
wun" her handless wrists did gooey severe shapes. / . . . . . 73 T&C SON REAL 4   14
to say, wind wind wind--did you love somebody and . . . . . . 80 T&C SON UNRE 5   6
ejaculate. obscenity the tide Did dl es a, fad . . . . 94 & POST IMPR 6   5
sitting in mcsorley's It, did not answer. outside. (it . . . 97 & POST IMPR 8   44
believe me, wholly, well --did (wisely suddenly into a . . . 115 & PORTRAIT 8   10
mesh of following tone: did this and this spire . . . . 115 & PORTRAIT 8   16
spire strike midnight (and did occur bell beyond fiercely . . 115 & PORTRAIT 8   17
as the other somethings did-- you imagine His surprise . . . 117 & PORTRAIT 10   7

		PAGE	TITLE	LINE

DID (CONTINUED)
might i'm called and did no wrong cried the	117	& PORTRAIT 10	16
as i think , did you ever hear a	141	& SON REAL 12	16
shove and asked Eddie did he care to ride	145	& SON REAL 16	12
you a little dizzy did the world's smell (but	174	& SON ACTU 23	11
/ CHANSONS INNOCENTES why did you go little fourpaws?	191	XLI CHANSONS 1	1
your big eyes. where did you go? like little	191	XLI CHANSONS 1	5
you know? or maybe did something go away ever	191	XLI CHANSONS 1	13
"Achilles" said Nicho' "and did you perhaps wish also	194	XLI PORTRAIT 2	38
/ as usual i did not find him in	197	XLI PORTRAIT 5	1
a mountain of gum did something like a whisper, ...	228	IS 5 ONE MARJ	9
cough too much). How did the traffic get so	245	IS 5 ONE 16	12
staunch and leal citizens did graze at pause then	258	IS 5 ONE 28	10
looked as if he did not care to rise	258	IS 5 ONE 28	16
to rise one hand did nothing on the vest	258	IS 5 ONE 28	17
the roaring slaughter they did not stop to think	268	IS 5 TWO 3	12
and what is more did tell you just what	276	IS 5 TWO 10	4
through the window she did not fall she went	284	IS 5 FOUR 1	13
how is aunt death did always teethe / /	316	VIVA 8	22
up) prettily then which did lie Down, honestly now	317	VIVA 9	35
pride) their passive prey did kick and curse until	339	VIVA 30	24
with their guessing fingers did-not-move exquisitely ,like .	355	VIVA 46	16
world became absurd; him did an archer spy (whose	360	VIVA 51	15
skeleton of life or did anybody Open a moment	395	NO THANKS 12	4
conceives to be Love did <> did) who begins	398	NO THANKS 15	7
be Love did <> did) who begins stuttering each	398	NO THANKS 15	9
sally rand handsomely who did because she could what	425	NO THANKS 42	5
by silently not night did the great world (in	432	NO THANKS 49	2
night's mostness (and whom did merely day close) opens . . .	450	NO THANKS 65	1
fiddling in the rain (did you kiss a girl	498	50 POEMS 12	17
their shadows if which did not do the losing	502	50 POEMS 16	12
didn't he danced his did. Women and men (both	515	50 POEMS 29	4
laughed their cryings and did their dance (sleep wake	515	50 POEMS 29	18
after glide massacre monday did more) ask a lifelump	522	50 POEMS 35	4
(on radios and raddios) did save man from himself	552	1 X 1 12	15
duskiest despot's goldenest gal did wring that dragon's tail	552	1 X 1 12	17
by love love said did o no yes earth	589	1 X 1 49	6
never knew and neither did you and everybody never	591	1 X 1 51	14
secret or than madness did reveal) deeper is life	592	1 X 1 52	2
slowly count to soon) rose--did you see her? darling, ...	599	(CHAIRE) 1	10
you see her? darling, did you (kiss me) quickly	599	(CHAIRE) 1	10
me white" so she did and now stars shine	622	(CHAIRE) 24	7
have been what above did was always fall (yes	634	(CHAIRE) 36	9
this her and him did you and did i	694	95 POEMS 22	2
him did you and did i climb (crazily kissing)	694	95 POEMS 22	2
i'm looking for will" "did you look for him	707	95 POEMS 35	2
it's to time, love did no more begin than	768	95 POEMS 94	2
no-she-yes-he fluffies tittle tattle did-he-does-she) & the .	773	73 POEMS 1	17
money can't do (never did & never will) any	793	73 POEMS 21	10
by the eyes and did the deed of joy	799	73 POEMS 27	15
like the pest thus did immortal jealousy quell divine	799	73 POEMS 27	32
very falling most (there: did you see it?) star	809	73 POEMS 37	12

DID-HE-DOES-SHE
| no-she-yes-he fluffies tittle tattle did-he-does-she) & the . | 773 | 73 POEMS 1 | 17 |

DID-NOT-MOVE
| with their guessing fingers did-not-move exquisitely ,like . | 355 | VIVA 46 | 16 |

+DIDDLES
| FOR CONTEXT, SEE . . . . | 94 | & POST IMPR 6 | 5 |

DIDN'T
it was cOOl i didn't have anything on and	123	& SEVEN POEMS 2	4
into the tree? I didn't said the little lady	125	& SEVEN POEMS 4	3
foliage what is it didn't Ruskin says about you	257	IS 5 ONE 27	34
whereupon mary quite contrary didn't die (may be seen	401	NO THANKS 18	9
winter he sang his didn't he danced his did.	515	50 POEMS 29	4
since not why) both didn't know exeunt they (not	542	1 X 1 2	4
we told him (he didn't believe it, no sir)	553	1 X 1 13	19
of finding what you didn't lose (existing's tricky: but . . .	807	73 POEMS 35	1

		PAGE	TITLE	LINE

DIDST
soul burns to embrace--and didst thou know the god . . . . . 3 T&C EPITHALAM 12
theorems of the flowers --didst e'er depart upon more . . . . 3 T&C EPITHALAM 20
a smile and thou didst not answer thy mouth . . . . 27 T&C ORIENTALE 1 2
a song and thou didst not listen thine eyes . . . . 27 T&C ORIENTALE 1 10
a soul and thou didst not wonder thy face . . . . 27 T&C ORIENTALE 1 17
Froissart, for that thou didst love the pen while . . . . . . 209 XLI SONNETS 5 9
and the smiting smile didst love to use in . . . . 213 XLI SONNETS 9 12
DIE
many things and which die i have been sometimes . . . . 43 T&C AMORES 7 10
merci.... i want to die nous sommes heureux my . . . . 133 & SON REAL 4 17
and is going to die. When we grimly go . . . . 147 & SON REAL 18 12
coffin's inside when you die, pretentious and shiny and . . . 198 XLI PORTRAIT 6 2
fair city might not die. / / / . . . . 209 XLI SONNETS 5 14
alone: to do or die for God for country . . . . 273 IS 5 TWO 8 11
hoped that i would die etcetera bravely of course . . . . . 276 IS 5 TWO 10 14
un deux trois der die Stood (apparition.) WITH (THE . . . . 348 VIVA 39 14
win ter you think, die slow ly "toc tic" . . . . 354 VIVA 45 24
many a thought shall die which was not born . . . . 372 VIVA 63 13
shelves (that which we die for; not when or . . . . 386 NO THANKS 3 5
wince) that which we die for lives (may never . . . . 386 NO THANKS 3 9
(and that which we die for lives as wholly . . . . 386 NO THANKS 3 13
too sick to rightly die) "gedup" the gentscoon coos . . . . 387 NO THANKS 4 6
Foetus (unborn to not die safely whose epoch fits . . . . . 394 NO THANKS 11 1
mary quite contrary didn't die (may be seen to . . . . . . 401 NO THANKS 18 10
lived people always) don't die (becoming most buried . . . . 412 NO THANKS 29 15
/ / / kumrads die because they're told) kumrads . . . . . 413 NO THANKS 30 1
because they're told) kumrads die before they're old (kumrads 413 NO THANKS 30 2
(kumrads aren't afraid to die kumrads don't and kumrads . . . 413 NO THANKS 30 3
so Alive) ump-A-tum ; tee-die uM-tuM tidl -id umptyumpty . . 426 NO THANKS 43 20
are Breathe grow dream die love not Fear eat . . . . 467 NEW POEMS 5 9
sing you got to die and we aint got . . . . 489 50 POEMS 3 10
aint got Nothing to die, come on kid let's . . . . 489 50 POEMS 3 11
sleep if you can't die you got to dream . . . . 489 50 POEMS 3 13
wales wife wants to die but the doctors won't . . . . 499 50 POEMS 13 2
is round nor dingsters die at break of dong . . . . 511 50 POEMS 25 18
drink crawl eat walk die fly do? a notalive . . . . 528 50 POEMS 40 4
and more it cannot die than all the sky . . . . 530 50 POEMS 42 14
you're which as to die (each green of a . . . . 543 1 X 1 3 9
home; the most who die, the more we live . . . . 560 1 X 1 20 24
we --nor can you die or i and every . . . . 601 {CHAIRE} 3 18
until no atom couldn't die (how and am quick . . . . 634 {CHAIRE} 36 13
only man who'll never die / / / / . . . . 685 95 POEMS 13 16
(rue d e l'echelle) die can't quite poison God's . . . . . 708 95 POEMS 36 15
for i will freely die" she cried so high . . . . 711 95 POEMS 39 12
who simply lives to die dream that your valentine . . . . . 718 95 POEMS 46 2
blunder (called life) we die to breathe, itself becomes . . . 742 95 POEMS 70 14
more than life must die to merely Know / . . . . 759 95 POEMS 86 10
eagerly my most dear (die! live) the new is . . . . 767 95 POEMS 93 9
in the spring) live! die (forever is now) and . . . . 767 95 POEMS 93 21
deed, born not to die) but worlds are made . . . . 776 73 POEMS 4 36
they buy and they die for because though the . . . . 801 73 POEMS 29 4
so gay possibly could die / / / / . . . . 825 73 POEMS 53 6
despair, my heart and die into the dirt but . . . . 834 73 POEMS 62 24
much to live) must die" "if i should tell . . . . 836 73 POEMS 64 5
DIED
for certain things which died it is eighteen hundred . . . . 108 & PORTRAIT 4 29
skunks caught cold and died and so my Uncle . . . . 239 IS 5 ONE 10 23
stop to think they died instead then shall the . . . . . . 268 IS 5 TWO 3 12
decline to admit i've died) seeing your bald intellect . . . 329 VIVA 20 2
a dungeon, where he died Christ (of His mercy . . . . 339 VIVA 30 37
spite of mirrors (have died beyond the clock) we, ... 386 NO THANKS 3 2
sky screamed the sun died) the ship lifts on . . . . 419 NO THANKS 36 10
of trousers (which had died) / / / / . . . . 473 NEW POEMS 11 6
had been before they died squirming: now withered and . . . 506 50 POEMS 20 3
down) one day anyone died i guess (and noone . . . . 515 50 POEMS 29 25
happen our mosts have died in more our twentieth . . . . . 537 50 POEMS 49 10
this (let's remember) day died again and again; whose . . . 599 {CHAIRE} 1 1

172

	PAGE	TITLE	LINE

DIED (CONTINUED)
   is a girl who died in her mind with . . . . 647 (CHAIRE) 49 6
   riding) to him who died that death should be . . . . 661 (CHAIRE) 63 4
   yes (i who have died am alive again today, ... 663 (CHAIRE) 65 5
   / / / annie died the other day never . . . . 794 73 POEMS 22 1
   long ago who had died , replied / / . . . . 828 73 POEMS 56 7
DIES
   whom the whole year dies, risen at length from . . . . 5 T&C EPITHALAM 103
   the chattering sunset ludicrously dies, i hear only tidewings 64 T&C POST IMPR 1 10
   casual mouth's coy rooting dies also. (my loveFist in . . . . 131 & SON REAL 2 8
   we call autumn, cleverly dies and over the ripe . . . . . 293 IS 5 FOUR 10 24
   strictly fiercely and wholly dies his impeccable feathered . 344 VIVA 35 1
   which we live for dies) / / / / . . . . 386 NO THANKS 3 14
   always everything which only dies to grow can guess . . . . . 718 95 POEMS 46 6
   how illimitable plight who dies to be at any . . . . 842 73 POEMS 70 2
DIFFER
   way underclothes All so differ- ently solemn and inti . . . . 126 & SEVEN POEMS 5 27
   doubt a mind, to differ a disease of same, ... 521 50 POEMS 34 59
DIFFERENCE
   else makes no more difference than if it sells . . . . . . 549 1 X 1 9 10
   (2) the holy miraculous difference between firstrate & second 803 73 POEMS 31 9
DIFFERENT
   otherwise roses and mountains different from the i am . . . . 91 & POST IMPR 3 17
   becoming something a little different, in fact myself . . . . 199 XLI PORTRAIT 7 9
   smile or move. It's different too isn't it different . . . . 289 IS 5 FOUR 6 17
   different too isn't it different dear from moving as . . . . 289 IS 5 FOUR 6 18
   slowly and first into different deaths Concentric geometries 311 VIVA 3 8
   hellas dwelt two very different sons of zeus: one, ... 799 73 POEMS 27 2
   by every star a different time, and each most . . . . 817 73 POEMS 45 2
DIFFERENTLY
   close?" "Worlds do, but differently; or as if worlds . . . . 603 (CHAIRE) 5 7
+DIFFERENTLY
   FOR CONTEXT, SEE . . . . 126 & SEVEN POEMS 5 27
DIFFICULT
   humanity, achieves (moult beyond difficult moult) amazing . . 351 VIVA 42 11
   tonishing & spontaneous & difficult ugliness of themselves . 354 VIVA 45 15
DIFFICULTY
   exaggeration shot with some difficulty sardines. Mr. Wiggin . 263 IS 5 ONE 32 47
   inunderstood re with some difficulty one father of one . . . 398 NO THANKS 15 3
DIG
   with spades of silver dig) by beauty i declare . . . . 115 & PORTRAIT 8 3
   may his mighty briefness dig for love beginning means . . . . 526 50 POEMS 38 4
DIGESTIBLE
   walloping human noise of digestible mill- ions whose rich . . 202 XLI PORTRAIT 9 45
DIGESTION
   such freedom such intense digestion so much greenness only . 491 50 POEMS 5 15
DIGESTIONS
   kindred questions inhibit unprepared digestions, come: let us 266 IS 5 TWO 1 30
DIGGED
   he kin till they digged his hole : sam . . . . 568 1 X 1 28 4
DIGGING
   where strong men are digging bread and i see . . . . 50 T&C IMPRESS 4 13
   dancing isn'ts on why, digging bridges with mirrors from . . 439 NO THANKS 55 21
DIGIT
   crooking of Whose compassionate digit, earth's most terrific 315 VIVA 7 15
DIGNITY
   Was irrevocably emanates a dignity of papyruscoloured faces . 111 & PORTRAIT 6 53
   the primates--from which with dignity square feet turned . . 326 VIVA 18 25
DIKE
   fluttering, at the enchanted dike of whose lean lips, ... 344 VIVA 35 9
DILEMMA
   thy beauty is the dilemma of flutes thy eyes . . . . 29 T&C ORIENTALE 3 31
DIM
   and undiscovered eyes and dim slow perfect body amorous . . . 5 T&C EPITHALAM 99
   burn incense, over the dim smoke straining my lips . . . . . 31 T&C ORIENTALE 5 22
   dreams of parted lips dim upon the syrinx / . . . . 54 T&C PORTRAIT 2 12
   dreams--O Love! upon thy dim shrine of intangible . . . . . . 206 XLI SONNETS 2 10
   or my feet getting dim freezing or up to . . . . 272 IS 5 TWO 7 8

	PAGE	TITLE	LINE

DIM (CONTINUED)
thumb o'clock asters miggle dim a ram flat hombre . . . . . . 333 VIVA 24   16
of the heart's eager dim enormous language loss or . . . . . 372 VIVA 63   11
beauty; before keen if dim quiveringly spangle & thingless . 480 NEW POEMS 18   8
time lessness; but two dim disks of stare are . . . . 605 (CHAIRE) 7   13
(the bright ones, the dim ones; the slim plump . . . . 619 (CHAIRE) 21   10
hi llside) a few dim tombstones try to re . . . . 695 95 POEMS 23   6
/ / / / dim i nu tiv e . . . . 696 95 POEMS 24   1
and right goes wrong (dim worlds or bright; big . . . . 776 73 POEMS 4   27
around) me (the great dim deep sound of rain; . . . . 816 73 POEMS 44   2
st makes big each dim inuti ve turns obv . . . . 829 73 POEMS 57   3
DIME
lukewarm peanuts with the dime which her mama had . . . . . . 326 VIVA 18   17
DIMENSION
young city putting off dimension with a blush enters . . . . 48 T&C IMPRESS 2   16
o'er --and frailties of dimension to occur about us . . . . . 205 XLI SONNETS 1   12
never shall guess the dimension of him whose each . . . . . . 512 50 POEMS 26   4
+DIMENSIONAL
FOR CONTEXT, SEE . . . . 150 & SON REAL 21   6
DIMENSIONLESS
dizzily & mirrors; sprung dimensionless new alls of joy: . . 480 NEW POEMS 18   20
DIMES
announces that as three dimes seven nickels and ten . . . . . 196 XLI PORTRAIT 4   9
DIMINISHING
eager eternal luminous firmly diminishing have swoopingly . . 110 & PORTRAIT 6   27
for all this very diminishing vicarious ughhuh world (the . . 337 VIVA 28   10
Now cancels the childfully diminishing earth --never whose . 402 NO THANKS 19   4
DIMINUTIVE
crushing) the papery weightless diminutive world with a hole 652 (CHAIRE) 54   9
of celestial wish (whying diminutive bright deathlessness to 669 (CHAIRE) 71   2
always nothing) you darling diminutive person jovial ego (& . 678 95 POEMS 6   4
(riding through space to diminutive this opened drawer) tweak 697 95 POEMS 25   21
spring, i lift my diminutive spire to merciful Him . . . . . 749 95 POEMS 77   17
downwardness and marvellously self diminutive whose universe 821 73 POEMS 49   12
+DIMINUTIVE
FOR CONTEXT, SEE . . . . 696 95 POEMS 24   1
FOR CONTEXT, SEE . . . . 829 73 POEMS 57   3
DIMLY
within the eyes is dimly heard a wistful and . . . . 20 T&C PUELLA MEA   151
voyage, my pensive companion dimly remarked some- thing about 326 VIVA 18   31
the west one Clock dimly cries nine, i stride . . . . 434 NO THANKS 51   14
DIMMER
whim poke if inch dimmer twist on permament and . . . . . . 333 VIVA 24   12
DIMNESS
willows wail, a slender dimness in the unshapeful hour . . . 9 T&C SONGS 1   5
DIN
was sitting in the din thinking drinking the ale, ... 96 & POST IMPR 8   23
hour push deep his din of wallowing male (shock . . . . 115 & PORTRAIT 8   12
God amid a monstrous din watch your step and . . . . 117 & PORTRAIT 10   26
dangerous slabs of tilting din whose mouths distinctly walk . 138 & SON REAL 9   2
bothered with a rustling din sort of sublimated tom-tom . . . 171 & SON ACTU 20   3
DINE
write what they are dine to live / / . . . . 334 VIVA 25   7
DINED
purred and the gangsters dined this is a deaf . . . . 647 (CHAIRE) 49   10
DING
men (both dong and ding) summer autumn winter spring . . . . 515 50 POEMS 29   33
+DING
FOR CONTEXT, SEE . . . . 798 73 POEMS 26   6
DINGDONG
any thine a mine --dingdong: dongding-- to say would . . . . 798 73 POEMS 26   6
DINGLE
cognoscenti bingbongwhom chewchoo laugh dingle nails . . . . 333 VIVA 24   3
DINGSTERS
world is round nor dingsters die at break of . . . . 511 50 POEMS 25   18
DINGY
clenched thighs a friendless dingy female frenzy bubbles / . 151 & SON REAL 22   18
a, p, s this dingy cage: then with a . . . . 697 95 POEMS 25   10

DINNED
whose careful eyes are dinned; and the people of . . . . . .   9 T&C SONGS 1   18
DINT
Bar. tinking luscious jigs dint of ripe silver with . . . . . 96 & POST IMPR 8   11
DINTED
man somewhat tweaked and dinted then did my servant . . . . . 57 T&C PORTRAIT 5   33
paws slowly loved a dinted mug gone Darkness it . . . . 97 & POST IMPR 8   39
DINTS
legs kissing with little dints of april, making the . . . . . 172 & SON ACTU 21   13
DIP
liontamer nearby hieroglyphs soar dip dip soar equalling . . 384 NO THANKS 2   25
nearby hieroglyphs soar dip dip soar equalling noise solemn . 384 NO THANKS 2   26
nakedly hurl asquirm the dip & giveswoop & swoon . . . . . . 445 NO THANKS 60   26
DIPS
of crisp boy flesh dips my height in a . . . . 140 & SON REAL 11   7
DIRECTING
his im -peccable cravat directing being shooting his cuffs . 275 IS 5 TWO 9   34
DIRECTIONLESS
any when unwondering immense directionless horizon) --do you 378 VIVA 69   14
DIRECTLY
the wistFully dead you directly perceive or minus news . . . 391 NO THANKS 8   10
DIRT
wideflung friend clenched weakly dirt while the mute . . . . 258 IS 5 ONE 28   18
legs & arms brush dirt coats smile looking hands . . . . . . 275 IS 5 TWO 9   45
turd ere with the dirt death shall him vastly . . . . 360 VIVA 51   5
afraid to kiss the dirt (and consequently dare to . . . . . 679 95 POEMS 7   5
and die into the dirt but from this endless . . . . 834 73 POEMS 62   24
DIRTIED
and go across this dirtied pane where softly preys . . . . . 218 XLI SONNETS 14 10
what was into a dirtied glass) Pills for Ills . . . . 359 VIVA 50   8
DIRTIEST
darker than small is dirtiest any city's least street) . . . 623 {CHAIRE} 25   2
DIRTPOOR
foundlost glad (children of) dirtpoor (popes emperors) . . . 681 95 POEMS 9   11
DIRTY
boulevard i saw a dirty child skating on noisy . . . . 56 T&C PORTRAIT 4   2
of seasons you have dirty legs and a muddy . . . . 61 T&C PORTRAIT 9   12
minute terrif iceffort one dirty squeal of soiling light . . 96 & POST IMPR 8   27
/ / / the dirty colours of her kiss . . . . 132 & SON REAL 3   1
cure for masturbation). A dirty wind, twitches the, clothes . 167 & SON ACTU 16   6
aware of an entirely dirty circle of habitues their . . . . . 194 XLI PORTRAIT 2 19
this trunk, under some dirty collars) only a moment . . . . . 296 IS 5 FOUR 13   12
but One a on Dirty bed Mangy from person . . . . 312 VIVA 4   18
(but just by the dirty collar of his jacket . . . . 355 VIVA 46   6
head comes to some dirty window every) twilight i . . . . . . 501 50 POEMS 15   7
lean ones;the mean kind dirty clean) all except the . . . . . 619 {CHAIRE} 21   26
dominic washed his sweet dirty face & mended his . . . . . . 680 95 POEMS 8   14
+DIRTY
FOR CONTEXT, SEE . . . . 332 VIVA 23   16
FOR CONTEXT, SEE . . . . 354 VIVA 45   5
FOR CONTEXT, SEE . . . . 547 1 X 1 7   7
DIS
toujours in my head dis-donc, Paris ta gorge mysterieuse . . 121 & PORTRAIT 12 52
--"O damn ginks like dis Gawd" opening slowlyslowly . . . . . 228 IS 5 ONE MARJ   7
/ / / now dis "daughter" uv eve (who . . . . 240 IS 5 ONE 11   1
(o) w the how dis (appeared cleverly) world iS . . . . 347 VIVA 38   4
hush) andDark IshbusY ing-roundly-dis tinct; chuck lings, . 416 NO THANKS 33   7
the stars 14th st dis (because my tears are . . . . 697 95 POEMS 25   29
DISAGREEABLE
woid sin in not disagreeable contras tuh dat not . . . . . . 240 IS 5 ONE 11   3
DISAPPEAR
ing s-p-i-r-a- l and, disappear) Satanic and blase a . . . . 278 IS 5 THREE 2   14
since and if you disappear solemnly myselves ask "life, . . . 295 IS 5 FOUR 12   11
flesh In flesh succeeding disappear / / / / . . . . 364 VIVA 55   16
poising to again utterly disappear; rushing gently swiftly . 369 VIVA 60   15
of sun perfectly should disappear moon's utmost magic, or . . 377 VIVA 68   3
mingling spirits, you would disappear unreally; as this . . . 379 VIVA 70   7
murmuring silver mountains which disappear (and only was . . 419 NO THANKS 36   18

DISAPPEAR (CONTINUED)

will still occur; birds disappear becomingly: a thunderbolt . 452 NO THANKS 67   13
further these those three disappear finally what's left . . . 501 50 POEMS 15   17
nothing disappears they will disappear always who are filled 505 50 POEMS 19   19
by (alive) from (into disappear and perfectly) nowhere vivid 557 1 X 1 17   3
angry common things to disappear causing through mystery . . 559 1 X 1 19   3
secretly than our (if disappear should some world) selves . . 577 1 X 1 37   7
every joy) --wholly now disappear night's not eternal terrors 582 1 X 1 42   14
with his bell to disappear a sun and out . . . . 624 (CHAIRE) 26   4
shall fail and dully disappear-- but the proud power . . . . 649 (CHAIRE) 51   12
wickedly worlds of world disappear all and (like any . . . . 761 95 POEMS 88   12
see it?) star to disappear, that hugest whole creation . . . 809 73 POEMS 37   12
fears hopes beliefs doubts disappear. Everywhere and joy's . 812 73 POEMS 40   13

+DISAPPEAR

FOR CONTEXT, SEE . . . . 349 VIVA 40   7
FOR CONTEXT, SEE . . . . 797 73 POEMS 25   7

DISAPPEARANCE

he comes to his disappearance; as a mind full . . . . 418 NO THANKS 35   6
any marvel finds quite disappearance but some keener makes . 750 95 POEMS 78   13

DISAPPEARED

for maybe what was Disappeared into ourselves who (look) . . 286 IS 5 FOUR 3   22
we were each other disappeared: but i slightly smiling, . . . 370 VIVA 61   16
sweet eyes close have disappeared a million whys; but . . . . 588 1 X 1 48   6
mind by wave doom disappeared, out of perhaps (who . . . . . 599 (CHAIRE) 1   7
called where and she disappeared. Out of more (fingeryhands . 612 (CHAIRE) 14   10

+DISAPPEARED

FOR CONTEXT, SEE . . . . 347 VIVA 38   4
FOR CONTEXT, SEE . . . . 472 NEW POEMS 10   3

DISAPPEARING

and skilfully which is disappearing / / / / . . . . 98 & POST IMPR 9   18
mountains; and to a disappearing poet of always, snow . . . . 424 NO THANKS 41   5
mind feeling throughout ignorant disappearing me hurling . . 428 NO THANKS 45   7
will pray so (unlove disappearing) only your less than . . . 450 NO THANKS 65   10
eternity) stupendous if discoverably disappearing floats at . 517 50 POEMS 31   3
a world vanishes, teach disappearing also me the keen . . . . 669 (CHAIRE) 71   13

+DISAPPEARING

FOR CONTEXT, SEE . . . . 646 (CHAIRE) 48   4
FOR CONTEXT, SEE . . . . 753 95 POEMS 81   8

+DISAPPEARINGLY

FOR CONTEXT, SEE . . . . 445 NO THANKS 60   23

DISAPPEARS

sweet tears) gesticulates, and disappears-- of all dainties . 23 T&C PUELLA MEA 270
after light) to turn, disappears the very swift and . . . . . 300 IS 5 FOUR 17   5
ness. sunlight's thenlike? now Disappears some thing (silent: 397 NO THANKS 14   19
that i am easily disappears (leaving no proof not . . . . . . 479 NEW POEMS 17   19
when and if nothing disappears they will disappear always . . 505 50 POEMS 19   18
than each known allness disappears lovers are mindless they . 563 1 X 1 23   6
his children, if he disappears; till of more much . . . . . . 756 95 POEMS 84   6
who're littler than (day disappears) their heartbeats dare . 757 95 POEMS 85   4

+DISAPPEARS

FOR CONTEXT, SEE . . . . 697 95 POEMS 25   29

DISASTER

bend into the huge disaster of the year: like . . . . 305 IS 5 FIVE 4   4

DISCIPLE

or seeking master or disciple sheep or wolf) gush . . . . . . 804 73 POEMS 32   4

DISCOBOLUS

what was once the discobolus of one Myron / . . . . 203 XLI LA GUERRE 1   19

DISCORDIA'S

skipping maenads knows,-- having Discordia's apple in thy . . 6 T&C EPITHALAM 151

DISCOVER

you and i awakening discover that (somehow in the . . . . . . 370 VIVA 61   2
what thousandth why and discover laughing) / / / . . . . . . 453 NO THANKS 68   16
quite agree) shall never discover our touch and feel . . . . 664 (CHAIRE) 66   15

DISCOVERABLY

mere eternity) stupendous if discoverably disappearing floats 517 50 POEMS 31   3

DISCOVERED

scratchings in a recently discovered cave, the carouse of . . 197 XLI PORTRAIT 5   19
is why granted who discovered America ether the movies . . . 238 IS 5 ONE 9   13

		PAGE	TITLE	LINE
DISCOVERED (CONTINUED)				
abide under whatever shall discovered be) whose ignorant each	446	NO THANKS 61		10
one day) and maggie discovered a shell that sang	682	95 POEMS 10		3
DISCOVERS				
the exquisite failure uncouth discovers a trembling and . . .	11	T&C SONGS 2		8
thy beauty, my heart discovers thee unto whom i	31	T&C ORIENTALE 5		28
DISCREETLY				
him of who) i discreetly (masturbates one honest breadcrumb)	546	1 X 1 6		11
DISCRETE				
building a magic, a discrete tower of magic and	83	T&C SON ACTU 2		9
of thing silent spits discrete lumps of noise.... furniture .	159	& SON ACTU 8		7
DISCUSS				
withdraws a and c discuss news in turkish x	200	XLI PORTRAIT 8		20
should any curious dawn discuss our mingling spirits, you . .	379	VIVA 70		6
DISCUSSED				
too frail lips almost discussed; between her and ourselves .	146	& SON REAL 17		12
"very interesting"... we also discussed the possiblility of .	326	VIVA 18		33
+DISCUSSING				
FOR CONTEXT, SEE	708	95 POEMS 36		10
DISDAIN				
sugaredellipses it does not disdain picKles, once, it, ate .	100	& POST IMPR 11		30
like cigarettebutts, chewed with disdain, led by a Jumpy . .	194	XLI PORTRAIT 2		21
DISDAINS				
cannot be photographed, measured; disdains the trivial . . .	377	VIVA 68		10
DISEASE				
the bright large undeniable disease of Life, himself	193	XLI PORTRAIT 1		23
mind, to differ a disease of same, conform the	521	50 POEMS 34		59
a whore with life's disease which quacks will cure	527	50 POEMS 39		22
Progress is a comfortable disease: your victim (death and . .	554	1 X 1 14		2
+DISEASE				
FOR CONTEXT, SEE	552	1 X 1 12		3
DISENCHANTED				
our spirits, whose miraculously disenchanted eyes live the .	675	95 POEMS 3		3
+DISGORGE				
FOR CONTEXT, SEE	629	(CHAIRE) 31		1
FOR CONTEXT, SEE	629	(CHAIRE) 31		17
DISGUISE				
stumble beneath a clumsiest disguise, appear capable of . . .	91	& POST IMPR 3		12
+DISH				
FOR CONTEXT, SEE	534	50 POEMS 46		5
DISHES				
red washing things and dishes) and to never, never	242	IS 5 ONE 13		16
DISHEVELLING				
prettiest wrath of blossoms dishevelling made a pale fracas .	214	XLI SONNETS 10		8
DISHONOURED				
never were hide, poor dishonoured mind who thought yourself .	834	73 POEMS 62		13
DISINTEGRATES				
inslants peregrinate, a cigar-stub disintegrates, above, . .	144	& SON REAL 15		5
+DISINTEGRATION				
FOR CONTEXT, SEE	94	& POST IMPR 6		16
DISINTERESTEDLY				
ourselves a nearly-opaque perfume disinterestedly obscene. /	146	& SON REAL 17		14
DISKFACE				
&) swooN Crowdloomroar: ing; diskface, es (are two notSoft .	388	NO THANKS 5		19
DISKS				
intersect with which distinct disks of graceful oath, ...	96	& POST IMPR 8		8
lessness; but two dim disks of stare are still	605	(CHAIRE) 7		13
DISMAL				
thinking) rests upon a dismal misconception; namely that some	807	73 POEMS 35		6
DISMAY				
to shadowy silence and dismay that stage which shall	75	T&C SON REAL 6		3
DISPLACING				
to caroming off persist displacing Its own and their	311	VIVA 3		7
DISPLEASURE				
not sinned in whose displeasure lives a kiss) kneeling, . . .	115	& PORTRAIT 8		7
DISPOSES				
it false or true) disposes me to shoot dogooding	798	73 POEMS 26		27

DISPROVE
    asserts, what falsest both disprove by proving true (all . . 576 1 X 1 36   4
    mind no more can disprove than prove what heart . . . . . . 664 (CHAIRE) 66   3
    than shall ever provingly disprove eithering vastnesses of . 761 95 POEMS 88   3
DISPUTANDUM
    (whereas de gustibus non disputandum est my lady is . . . . 245 IS 5 ONE 16   24
DISPUTE
    Which being quite beyond dispute as prove from Troy . . . . . 266 IS 5 TWO 1   5
DISSECT
    (given the scalpel, they dissect a kiss; or, sold . . . . . . 556 1 X 1 16   7
DISSECTED
    space? love's murdered eye dissected to mere because and . . 527 50 POEMS 39   14
DISSIPATION
    hymn pledged to illimitable dissipation unhurried clouds of . 206 XLI SONNETS 2   13
DISSOLUTE
    in cafes, the more dissolute atmosphere of a street . . . . 197 XLI PORTRAIT 5   1
DISSOLVE
    life toward twilight will dissolve reintegrate beckon through 379 VIVA 70   12
DISSOLVED
    feels all small facts dissolved by the lewd guess . . . . . . 419 NO THANKS 36   6
DISSOLVES
    window just as day dissolves when it is twilight . . . . . . 301 IS 5 FOUR 18   2
DISSONANCE
    the sky a silver dissonance by the correct fingers . . . . . 47 T&C IMPRESS 1   2
    nose winces before a dissonance of Rish and Foses) . . . . . 319 VIVA 11   12
DISSONANT
    hear the screech of dissonant flowers, and most of . . . . . 61 T&C PORTRAIT 9 32
DISTANCE
    looped straightens, into neatest distance.... A new curve of 219 XLI SONNETS 15 6
    one's self at some distance from the crooked town) . . . . . 319 VIVA 11   16
    dar kness eats a distance a c (h) luck . . . . 350 VIVA 41   6
    if you love me) distance is mind carefully luminous . . . . . 363 VIVA 54   6
    who and who) The distance is more much than . . . . 608 (CHAIRE) 10   2
    star can grow all distance breathes a final dream . . . . . . 750 95 POEMS 78   2
DISTANT
    possiblility of rain... in distant proximity to a Y. . . . . 326 VIVA 18   35
    perfect nothing: millionary wherewhens distant, as reckoned . 721 95 POEMS 49   5
DISTENDED
    clean table. and, whose distended immense Both paws slowly . 97 & POST IMPR 8 38
DISTINCT
    would espy the little distinct foot (if whose very . . . . . 22 T&C PUELLA MEA 217
    / / / 0 Distinct Lady of my unkempt . . . . 43 T&C AMORES 7   1
    under the unaccountable sun) Distinct Lady swiftly take my . 43 T&C AMORES 7   25
    sobbings intersect with which distinct disks of graceful . . 96 & POST IMPR 8   8
    / / her careful distinct sex whose sharp lips . . . . 137 & SON REAL 8   1
    curse of wax. Something, distinct and. Amusing, brittle / . . 164 & SON ACTU 13 17
    your kiss was a distinct brittle flower, and the . . . . . . 173 & SON ACTU 22 9
    always quivers the electric Distinct face haughtily vital . . 193 XLI PORTRAIT 1   3
    whisper.) Lumberman of The Distinct your brain's axe only . . 195 XLI PORTRAIT 3 16
    leer of horizontal large distinct ecstasy wags and. rages . . 202 XLI PORTRAIT 9 36
    wonderless city's sublime cheap distinct mouth) do the exact 218 XLI SONNETS 14 7
    it were a kiss) distinct entirely melting sinuous lean... . . 225 IS 5 ONE LIZ   15
    delicately wobbles an improbably distinct face, and how these 229 IS 5 ONE FRAN 3
    and intents) in which distinct and rich portrait should . . . 254 IS 5 ONE 25   7
    lift to me the distinct country of your eyes, ... 291 IS 5 FOUR 8   26
    knitting the structure of distinct sunset driving white . . . 378 VIVA 69   8
    possess) how sincere large distinct and natural he comes . . 418 NO THANKS 35   5
    ams (leaving a perfectly distinct unhe; a ticking phantom . . 558 1 X 1 18   7
    the whole with a distinct grandiloquent deep D; while . . . . 650 (CHAIRE) 52   15
+DISTINCT
    FOR CONTEXT, SEE . . . . 416 NO THANKS 33   7
DISTINCTLY
    very frail lady drifting distinctly, moving like a myth . . . 17 T&C PUELLA MEA 19
    miracles impinge) --it is distinctly to confute my reason . . 19 T&C PUELLA MEA 97
    warm superlative body do distinctly live all sweet cities . . 22 T&C PUELLA MEA 256
    one sheet on which distinctly wags at times the . . . . 134 & SON REAL 5   4
    tilting din whose mouths distinctly walk your smiles accuse . 138 & SON REAL 9   3
    pity me whom (god distinctly has) the weightless svelte . . . 140 & SON REAL 11 1

DISTINCTLY (CONTINUED)
    smiles, one grin very distinctly wobbles from the thinning . 151 & SON REAL 22   15
    droll god-beasts do thou distinctly bring thy footstep, and . 213 XLI SONNETS 9   10
    fragrant sag of fruit distinctly grouped. I have not   . . . . 219 XLI SONNETS 15   1
    speaking uncultured (who Very distinctly confine their . . . 391 NO THANKS 8   20
    deep lifted fields Oxen distinctly move, a yellowandbluish . 434 NO THANKS 51   31
DISTINGUISHED
    a great way i distinguished singing and i came . . . . 30 T&C ORIENTALE 4   21
DISTORTING
    occurs or something more distorting than socalled . . . . . . 514 50 POEMS 28   11
DISTRESS
    hunch admit in threedimensional distress these hips were made 150 & SON REAL 21   6
DITHYRAMBS
    Cairo (Egypt) the luminous dithyrambs of large immaculate . . 266 IS 5 TWO 1   7
DIVE
    waked) & perfectingly We dive out of tinying time . . . . . . 373 VIVA 64   9
    all the pretty birds dive to the heart of . . . . 665 (CHAIRE) 67   19
    / / / / dive for dreams or a . . . . 732 95 POEMS 60   1
DIVED
    flew his wish (it dived like a fish but . . . . 593 1 X 1 53   9
DIVER
    McCann He Was A Diver on Xmas Eve like . . . . 239 IS 5 ONE 10   6
DIVERSIFIED
    shall we say somewhat diversified (putting it quietly) life . 699 95 POEMS 27   17
+DIVES
    FOR CONTEXT, SEE . . . . 585 1 X 1 45   7
DIVIDES
    such crude perfection as divides by timelessness that . . . . 428 NO THANKS 45   11
DIVIDING
    multiply because and why dividing thens by nows and . . . . . 500 50 POEMS 14   6
DIVINE
    primeval hands, frivolous feet divine! O singular and . . . .   5 T&C EPITHALAM   108
    and are lost the divine alchemist, the magus of . . . . . .   6 T&C EPITHALAM   133
    as a vase of divine silence Come hither O . . . . 27 T&C ORIENTALE 1   12
    the ceiling inhaling six divine inches of Haremina in . . . . 194 XLI PORTRAIT 2   14
    even dollar whereupon the Divine Average who was attracted . 196 XLI PORTRAIT 4   16
    one (Everywhere Why) as divine poesy per that and . . . . . . 230 IS 5 ONE 2   17
    ummm said she) you're divine! said he (you are . . . . 399 NO THANKS 16   31
    is human; to forgive divine) that if the quote . . . . 636 (CHAIRE) 38   7
    death uncommon (forgiving not divine, to err inhuman) or . . 798 73 POEMS 26   3
    did immortal jealousy quell divine generosity, thus reason . 799 73 POEMS 27   33
    / POEM (or "the divine right of majorities, that . . . . . . 803 73 POEMS 31   2
    illegitimate offspring of the divine right of kings" Homer . 803 73 POEMS 31   4
DIVINELY
    slowly drift murmurous things divinely bright; it is . . . . 18 T&C PUELLA MEA   81
    please.) Each ankle is divinely shy; as if for . . . . 21 T&C PUELLA MEA   215
DIVING
    climbing silence for ifs diving under because) only who'll . 439 NO THANKS 55   24
    ex prince of whoses diving into a whatses to . . . . 475 NEW POEMS 13   20
DIVINITIES
    (do lovers suffer? all divinities proudly descending put on . 768 95 POEMS 94   5
DIVINITY
    turned the corner of Divinity avenue i touched the . . . . . 248 IS 5 ONE 19   21
DIVISIBLE
    with bright credos each divisible fool (life imitate gossip . 452 NO THANKS 67   7
DIVISOR
    the most great common divisor of unequal souls. / . . . . . . 74 T&C SON REAL 5   15
DIZZIER
    for whoso drinks, a dizzier wine than should the . . . . . . 21 T&C PUELLA MEA   199
DIZZILY
    sun- light is thickening dizzily is reeling gently the . . . 69 T&C POST IMPR 6   24
    the killing flame that dizzily grips. Querying greys between 139 & SON REAL 10   11
    & vast solidities, unwinding dizzily & mirrors; sprung . . . 480 NEW POEMS 18   19
    nto eachness begi n dizzily swingthings of speeds of . . . . 536 50 POEMS 48   6
    rollingest it) 's the dizzily he most him --the . . . . 590 1 X 1 50   12
DIZZIZ
    enslaved by a dread dizziz and the sooner it's . . . . 552 1 X 1 12   3

                                                          PAGE   TITLE   LINE
DIZZY
  and i felt suddenly dizzy With the jostling and . . . .   44 T&C AMORES 8   4
  made you a little dizzy did the world's smell . . . . 174 & SON ACTU 23   11
  else drive dumb mankind dizzy with haranguing --you are . . . 804 73 POEMS 32   9
DIZZYING
  summer's lie; bloodies with dizzying leaves the sun and . . . 560 1 X 1 20   ·3
  eager a (twice by Dizzying eyeplums pun ctured) moo . . . . . 615 (CHAIRE) 17   7
DO
  seek all blossoms that do learn, scents of not . . . .   9 T&C SONGS 1   17
  while on faint hills do frailly go The peaceful . . . .   11 T&C SONGS 2   27
  love be a day) do not fear, we will . . . .   13 T&C SONGS 3   7
  whose warm superlative body do distinctly live all sweet . .   22 T&C PUELLA MEA   256
  of all dainties which do crowd gaily upon oblivion . . . . .   23 T&C PUELLA MEA   271
  her nose what she'll do to yer nobody knows . . . .   25 T&C CHANSONS 2   19
  to know is how do you like your blueeyed . . . .   60 T&C PORTRAIT 8   10
  vermilion departure swim, sayingly; (Do you think?) the i . .   66 T&C POST IMPR 3   13
  you think?) the i do, world is probably made . . . .   66 T&C POST IMPR 3   14
  D ....the Cambridge ladies do not care, above Cambridge . . .   70 T&C SON REAL 1   11
  (this here and This, do you get me?) will . . . .   72 T&C SON REAL 3   12
  clever drolls fearsomely who do keep their sunday flower. . .   74 T&C SON REAL 5   11
  are the poems i do not write. In this . . . .   84 T&C SON ACTU 3   12
  the wind?" "Yes" "why do you touch flowers as . . . .   91 & POST IMPR 3   8
  of fragility and indecision --do not suppose these without .   91 & POST IMPR 3   14
  which is morning, O do not wonder that (just . . . .   92 & POST IMPR 4   17
  dark threatens (and i do not speak nor think . . . .   98 & POST IMPR 9   13
  you who are silent. --"Do you see Life? he . . . . 102 & POST IMPR 12   10
  but we don't care do we dearie we should . . . . 109 & PORTRAIT 5   6
  don't but really you do see and you are . . . . 126 & SEVEN POEMS 5   16
  winked and hope he'll do it again or if . . . . 126 & SEVEN POEMS 5   17
  dead's fine like hands do you see that water . . . . 126 & SEVEN POEMS 5   24
  i like kittens i do and jackknives i do . . . . 127 & SEVEN POEMS 5   50
  do and jackknives i do and pennies i do . . . . 127 & SEVEN POEMS 5   50
  do and pennies i do and rosebugs i do . . . . 127 & SEVEN POEMS 5   50
  do and rosebugs i do / / / / . . . . 127 & SEVEN POEMS 5   51
  lilacs.... minutes and love.... do you? and always (i . . . . 133 & SON REAL 4   8
  over, kid how, funny Do tell ....sweat, succeeds breathings . 136 & SON REAL 7   14
  pencil has fear to do the posed body luckily . . . . 141 & SON REAL 12   2
  very frail enormous star (do you see it?) and . . . . 155 & SON ACTU 4   13
  and shall the (i do but touch you) timid . . . . 155 & SON ACTU 4   16
  and what it will do to me before shutting.... . . . . 157 & SON ACTU 6   4
  and The Then-arrows making do our mouths something red, . . . 160 & SON ACTU 9   16
  feel what it will do in my bullying fingers) . . . . 164 & SON ACTU 13   13
  think of you and do not live: and the . . . . 165 & SON ACTU 14   7
  droll snowing delirium (we do not speak) tumbled hushingly . 168 & SON ACTU 17   6
  alas, much is to do for the swallow, that . . . . 181 XLI SONGS 3   3
  we stroke maybe asleep? do you know? or maybe . . . . 191 XLI CHANSONS 1   13
  whole of life almost do guess) if god should . . . . 205 XLI SONNETS 1   8
  unto nights of autumn do complain earth's ghastlier trees . . 207 XLI SONNETS 3   1
  corners hideously cowers-- i do excuse me, love, to . . . . . 207 XLI SONNETS 3   9
  the garden: pursed lips do blow upon cool flutes . . . . . . 208 XLI SONNETS 4   5
  roses. Perfume? for i do forget.... or mere Music . . . . . 211 XLI SONNETS 7   1
  strove the droll god-beasts do thou distinctly bring thy . . 213 XLI SONNETS 9   10
  the hurt heart which do so frailly cling....) i . . . . 215 XLI SONNETS 11   10
  am in Boston, i do not speak. and i . . . . 217 XLI SONNETS 13   1
  sublime cheap distinct mouth) do the exact human comely . . . 218 XLI SONNETS 14   8
  stocking begins queerly to do a few gestures to . . . . 225 IS 5 ONE LIZ   4
  joggle i think will do it although the glad . . . . 227 IS 5 ONE GERT   1
  in peace. which i do, being as Dick Mid . . . . 229 IS 5 ONE FRAN   9
  freedom ring amen. i do however protest, anent the . . . . . 230 IS 5 ONE 2   15
  God's In His andsoforth do you get me?) according . . . . . . 230 IS 5 ONE 2   30
  true story of Mr Do -nothing the wellknown parvenu . . . . . 236 IS 5 ONE 7   3
  Freud got through with Do- nothing Do -nothing could . . . . 236 IS 5 ONE 7   9
  through with Do- nothing Do -nothing could do nothing . . . . 236 IS 5 ONE 7   10
  nothing Do -nothing could do nothing which you and . . . . . 236 IS 5 ONE 7   11
  smile or angle we do not sell and buy . . . . 238 IS 5 ONE 9   6
  a cry of How do you find the sun, ... 255 IS 5 ONE 26   7
  stars of Heaven.... i do signore affirm that all . . . . . . 256 IS 5 ONE 27   22
  one thought alone: to do or die for God . . . . 273 IS 5 TWO 8   11

180

		PAGE	TITLE	LINE
DO (CONTINUED)

lovingly, our lady what do you think of this? . . . . 279 IS 5 THREE 3   21
you think of this? Do your proud fingers and . . . . 279 IS 5 THREE 3   21
enough, is it (i do not pretend to know . . . . 282 IS 5 THREE 6   3
love, and eat sunlight (do you believe it? i . . . . 289 IS 5 FOUR 6   8
the best he can do is to peer through . . . . 292 IS 5 FOUR 9   7
(of what we everywhere do not touch) deep things; . . . . . 294 IS 5 FOUR 11   5
flower wholly whom you do not ever fear, me . . . . 294 IS 5 FOUR 11   16
"life, the question how do i drink dream smile . . . . 295 IS 5 FOUR 12   14
dream smile and how do i prefer this face . . . . 295 IS 5 FOUR 12   15
to another and why do i weep eat sleep--what . . . . 295 IS 5 FOUR 12   16
the reason that i do not fall into this . . . . 295 IS 5 FOUR 12   25
of your arm will do suddenly that will do . . . . 302 IS 5 FIVE 1   10
do suddenly that will do more than heroes beautifully . . . . 302 IS 5 FIVE 1   11
wrists argue) short (eyes do bang hands angle scoot . . . . . 309 VIVA 1   11
(re peat credo fais do do neighbours re babies . . . . 309 VIVA 1   34
peat credo fais do do neighbours re babies while; . . . . . . 309 VIVA 1   35
happened to meet "how do you do" she smiling . . . . 313 VIVA 5   5
meet "how do you do" she smiling said "thought . . . . 313 VIVA 5   5
says sweet guinea pigs do it it buy uh . . . . 325 VIVA 17   8
on the head him) do through icy waters roll . . . . 339 VIVA 30   9
rain) faces (at windows) do not speak and are . . . . 340 VIVA 31   5
mountains stand And oceans do Not sleep matters nothing; . . 359 VIVA 50   13
(shyly) other, what clouds do or Silently Flowers resembles . 363 VIVA 54   10
with each breathing (i do not know what it . . . . 366 VIVA 57   17
against the air--and whose do you suppose possibly are . . . 378 VIVA 69   5
unwondering immense directionless horizon) --do you perhaps . 378 VIVA 69   16
knows why) and so do i (because they are . . . . 413 NO THANKS 30   17
the movies try to do because they can't i . . . . 425 NO THANKS 42   6
! ting Bam- : do) , chippity. / / . . . . 426 NO THANKS 43   28
buck and bite they do not give a fuck . . . . 427 NO THANKS 44   3
in her behind they do not give a shit . . . . 427 NO THANKS 44   7
that and this they do not give a fart . . . . 427 NO THANKS 44   15
on their mind they do whatever's in their pants . . . . . . 427 NO THANKS 44   18
Jehovah buried, Satan dead, do fearers worship Much and . . . 438 NO THANKS 54   2
filth is here unlives do cry on him they . . . . 440 NO THANKS 56   8
stink is here unpoets do cry unfools unfree undeaths . . . . 440 NO THANKS 56   32
be may never have) do i salute (by moon . . . . 441 NO THANKS 56   65
glit ter a, strut: do; colours; are: m, ove . . . . 444 NO THANKS 59   24
/ / / / Do. omful relaxing -ly) i . . . . 449 NO THANKS 64   1
a colour and i do not know him (and . . . . 450 NO THANKS 65   15
young and may myself do nothing usefully and love . . . . . 481 NEW POEMS 19   9
if which did not do the losing spectres mime . . . . 502 50 POEMS 16   12
dream what dreams can do --time is a tree . . . . 511 50 POEMS 25   25
whycoloured worlds of because do not stand against yes . . . 512 50 POEMS 26   28
tear. By handless hints do conjurers rule? do mannikins . . . 527 50 POEMS 39   18
hints do conjurers rule? do mannikins forbid the soul? . . . 527 50 POEMS 39   19
eat walk die fly do? a notalive undead too-nearishness . . . 528 50 POEMS 40   4
you're he as to do what must (whispers) be . . . . 543 1 X 1 3   12
small as me can do or be?" god whispered . . . . 555 1 X 1 15   13
world, will you perhaps do the breathing for me . . . . . . 558 1 X 1 18   14
million (who are and do not wait) buds imitate . . . . 573 1 X 1 33   21
find us (if they do, we'll move away still . . . . 579 1 X 1 39   13
thrushes climbing through almost (do they beautifully . . . . 582 1 X 1 42   1
and worlds close?" "Worlds do, but differently; or as . . . . 603 (CHAIRE) 5   7
lying are each (why do people say it's un . . . . 623 (CHAIRE) 25   6
excellent E will exactly do next (our great problem . . . . . 650 (CHAIRE) 52   12
nothing times nothing to do (for love are in . . . . 664 (CHAIRE) 66   11
actly what life will do) loves nothing as much . . . . 676 95 POEMS 4   15
hoping death himself will do the same because you . . . . . . 679 95 POEMS 7   4
for kindness and goodness do not make a fellow . . . . 684 95 POEMS 12   15
as well as i do) what it takes; & . . . . 701 95 POEMS 29   12
quiet little hungary and do as you are bid . . . . 711 95 POEMS 39   18
o (rounD) moon, how do you (rouNd er than . . . . 722 95 POEMS 50   3
/ / / why do the fingers of the . . . . 724 95 POEMS 52   2
i've loved, shall love, do love you, was and . . . . 734 95 POEMS 62   3
of hurrying cities --i do not worry if briefer . . . . 749 95 POEMS 77   3
peace with nature --i do not worry if longer . . . . 749 95 POEMS 77   15

	PAGE	TITLE	LINE

DO (CONTINUED)

poor worlds must merely do, which than are done; . . . . . . 762 95 POEMS 89　3
ocean and the land (do lovers suffer? all divinities . . . . 768 95 POEMS 94　5
more last than star --do lovers love? why then . . . . 768 95 POEMS 94　13
joy under care-- let's do as an earth which . . . . 769 95 POEMS 95　17
earth which can never do wrong does (minute by . . . . 769 95 POEMS 95　17
and the when to do is exactly theirs (dull . . . . 776 73 POEMS 4　9
Spring thingS dare to do people (& not the . . . . 782 73 POEMS 10　4
(in whom always i do nothing) deepens with wind . . . . . . 785 73 POEMS 13　5
per (who can and do fat pigeons coo) haps . . . . 787 73 POEMS 15　6
omprises 6 twirls of do gsh it m uch . . . . 789 73 POEMS 17　10
in- deed; money can't do (never did & never . . . . 793 73 POEMS 21　9
friend. But what does do, has always done ; . . . . 793 73 POEMS 21　18
done ; & will do alw -ays something is . . . . 793 73 POEMS 21　21
they don't and they do and they turn to . . . . 801 73 POEMS 29　9
clocks have enough to do without confusing timelessness and . 817 73 POEMS 45　7
such mysteries as men do not conceive--let ocean grow . . . . 843 73 POEMS 71　14

+DO

FOR CONTEXT, SEE . . . . 259 IS 5 ONE 29　20
FOR CONTEXT, SEE . . . . 468 NEW POEMS 6　1
FOR CONTEXT, SEE . . . . 618 {CHAIRE} 20　19
FOR CONTEXT, SEE . . . . 629 {CHAIRE} 31　13

+DO'S

FOR CONTEXT, SEE . . . . 259 IS 5 ONE 29　20

DOANCARE

denly immense impotently Eye Doancare Eye And How replies . . 330 VIVA 21　8

DOANGIVUH

plumptumbling hand voices Eye Doangivuh sud- denly immense . 330 VIVA 21　7

DOCILE

papillae expertly drink the docile perpendicular taste of . . 201 XLI PORTRAIT 9　17

DOCTOR

it is the famous doctor who inserts monkeyglands in . . . . . 245 IS 5 ONE 16　13

DOCTORS

because you fooled the doctors, i touch you with . . . . . . 289 IS 5 FOUR 6　15
to die but the doctors won't let her comma . . . . 499 50 POEMS 13　3
of hypermagical ultraomnipotence. We doctors know a hopeless 554 1 X 1 14　13

+DODDERING

FOR CONTEXT, SEE . . . . 100 & POST IMPR 11　37

DODDERINGLY

oh quintillions of incredible dodderingly godly toothless ◇ 250 IS 5 ONE 21　12

DODDERS

-te. a sharp crone dodders be- tween taxis swirl . . . . . . 384 NO THANKS 2　3

DODGE

edindodg: ing whom areEyes shy-dodge is bright cruMbshandful, 265 IS 5 ONE 34　4

DODGING

(hurl flicker handful in) dodging are shybrigHteyes is crum . 265 IS 5 ONE 34　8

+DODGING

FOR CONTEXT, SEE . . . . 265 IS 5 ONE 34　3

DODREAMING

Less than (that by doDreaming heteronomously metameric me are 395 NO THANKS 12　12

DODREAMINGLY

more slowly than trees) dodreamingly phantoms (exchanging) e 681 95 POEMS 9　5

DOER

until so blithe a doer a wooer some limber . . . . 509 50 POEMS 23　9

DOER'S

dream and don a doer's doom create is now . . . . 834 73 POEMS 62　6

DOES

flown deer. Four fleet does at a gold valley . . . . 14 T&C SONGS 4　19
dust but the sea does not change and she . . . . 38 T&C AMORES 3　10
minute pocket) Sometimes he does not catch a piece . . . . . 69 T&C POST IMPR 6　12
have made songs it does not greatly matter to . . . . 84 T&C SON ACTU 3　7
s greedily sugaredellipses it does not disdain picKles, once, 100 & POST IMPR 11　30
simply. well fussed flesh does surely to mesh. New . . . . . 136 & SON REAL 7　12
eminent fragility. Well and when--Does susceptibility imply . 141 & SON REAL 12　7
huge light as she does not stand-ing. unsits her . . . . . . 159 & SON ACTU 8　3
hands.... is swig it does who eye sO neatly . . . . 159 & SON ACTU 8　17
honest trees, a stream does. the brain of cleverly-crinkling 160 & SON ACTU 9　4
i like what it does, i like its hows. . . . . 175 & SON ACTU 24　4

	PAGE	TITLE	LINE
DOES (CONTINUED)			
it's flutters everything queer; does smells he smiles is . .	251	IS 5 ONE 22	5
believe; not for philosophy does this rose give a	264	IS 5 ONE 33	20
little mouse) and what does he think about, i	286	IS 5 FOUR 3	2
doesn't matter and what does is possibly this dear, ...	289	IS 5 FOUR 6	6
i weep eat sleep--what does the whole intend" they	295	IS 5 FOUR 12	16
cancelled but shadows --what does it all come down	295	IS 5 FOUR 12	21
i wonder what he does) and why (at the	296	IS 5 FOUR 13	10
wholly rid (and who does not ask for more	298	IS 5 FOUR 15	9
what were once knees) does almost ceaselessly repeat "there .	339	VIVA 30	32
of him (every) who does (where) not move ;	346	VIVA 37	23
touching means or What does a hand with your	356	VIVA 47	21
and blinds (but surely does not forget, perish, sleep	377	VIVA 68	9
exact victim, how he does not stir) O love, ...	386	NO THANKS 3	11
/ / / he does not have to feel	406	NO THANKS 23	1
be it understood) he does not have to think	406	NO THANKS 23	3
/ / / what does little Ernest croon in	409	NO THANKS 26	1
/ / / / does yesterday's perfection seem not	414	NO THANKS 31	1
wondering why this star does not fall into his	428	NO THANKS 45	5
black wine. a village does not move behind my	434	NO THANKS 51	8
of life became) and does our fatally unshadowing fate	454	NO THANKS 69	11
morons gather roun' who does not dare to stand	466	NEW POEMS 4	3
so near the earth does not open her eyes	505	50 POEMS 19	11
doubt blind the brave? does mask wear face? have	538	50 POEMS 50	6
either pain or joy) does nothing except preexist its	544	1 X 1 4	7
sing and dance (and does with each your least	580	1 X 1 40	2
is no beyond) or does some littler bird than	592	1 X 1 52	9
in the high that does nothing but fall (with	594	1 X 1 54	32
/ / chas sing does (who , ins tead, ...	611	{CHAIRE} 13	1
earth; so anyone's world does -n't interest him (by	676	95 POEMS 4	5
can never do wrong does (minute by second and	769	95 POEMS 95	17
and the gentle who-horns says-does moo-woo (the prance with .	773	73 POEMS 1	8
no-she-yes-he fluffies tittle tattle did-he-does-she) & the .	773	73 POEMS 1	17
suppose one 's wife) --does doesn't unsays says looks	779	73 POEMS 7	19
/ Me up at does out of the floor	784	73 POEMS 12	1
lurk, simply to her does not occur (alarm ing	790	73 POEMS 18	10
my friend. But what does do, has always done	793	73 POEMS 21	17
world) more my life does not leap than with	810	73 POEMS 38	3
/ / / now does our world descend the	834	73 POEMS 62	1
DOESN'T			
and i but that doesn't in the least matter.	289	IS 5 FOUR 6	2
it i can't which doesn't matter and what does	289	IS 5 FOUR 6	5
begin to and that doesn't matter) which i suggest	289	IS 5 FOUR 6	9
into you but that doesn't matter further than of	289	IS 5 FOUR 6	13
going to (but that doesn't matter) when you thought	289	IS 5 FOUR 6	20
that) that seems important doesn't it and doesn't that . . .	323	VIVA 15	15
important doesn't it and doesn't that seem puzzling but . . .	323	VIVA 15	17
to look like) it doesn't look at all like	323	VIVA 15	25
of persons the snow doesn't give a soft white	328	VIVA 19	22
anyone else entirely who doesn't move (Moved more suddenly .	397	NO THANKS 14	3
lost his teeth and doesn't know where to find	410	NO THANKS 27	1
hell with that that doesn't matter (and if he	475	NEW POEMS 13	6
that i say that doesn't matter) but if somebody	475	NEW POEMS 13	11
so what princess selene doesn't know a thing who's	504	50 POEMS 18	11
times a wheel turns doesn't determine its roundness: if . . .	514	50 POEMS 28	6
just a handful absolutely doesn't matter and whether it's . .	549	1 X 1 9	5
your money and you doesn't take your choice. Ain't	636	{CHAIRE} 38	14
a no but it doesn't of course but you	638	{CHAIRE} 40	5
the sky your kingbird doesn't give a damn-- his	774	73 POEMS 2	2
crafty crow your kingbird doesn't give a damn for	774	73 POEMS 2	9
one 's wife) --does doesn't unsays says looks smiles	779	73 POEMS 7	19
with the chappy who doesn't agree (if you can't	791	73 POEMS 19	4
+DOESN'T			
FOR CONTEXT, SEE	611	{CHAIRE} 13	1
FOR CONTEXT, SEE	676	95 POEMS 4	5
DOG			
dunno said the silver dog, with ripe eyes and	125	& SEVEN POEMS 4	16
to the waggy silver dog and the moon came	125	& SEVEN POEMS 4	25

DOG (CONTINUED)
with pinkness, one pale dog behind a slopcaked shrub . . . . 144 & SON REAL 15   7
like a big yellow dog. You don't believe? look . . . . 303 IS 5 FIVE 2   10
us, a big yellow dog that's.... now it's red . . . . 303 IS 5 FIVE 2   12
red a big red dog that may be owned . . . . 303 IS 5 FIVE 2   13
collar looking for a dog, a kiss without lips; . . . . 360 VIVA 51   26
twitch lovers) & one dog? piglike big! sorrows always; . . . 384 NO THANKS 2   11
silenc e go lliw og-dog) life ? tree3ghosts are . . . . 628 {CHAIRE} 30   6
twined this is a dog of no known kind . . . . 647 {CHAIRE} 49   16
/ (listen) this a dog barks and how crazily . . . . 835 73 POEMS 63   2
+DOG
FOR CONTEXT, SEE . . . . 789 73 POEMS 17   10
DOGOODING
disposes me to shoot dogooding folk on sight / . . . . 798 73 POEMS 26   28
DOGS
slow-ly-in creasing fragility --. Dogs bark children play . . 63 T&C PORTRAIT 10   32
DOIDEE
yguduh ged yunnuhstan dem doidee yguduh ged riduh ydoan . . . 547 1 X 1 7   7
DOING
the fragile act of doing her eyebrows. --Marj's laughter . . 228 IS 5 ONE MARJ   13
me what am i doing on top of this . . . . 281 IS 5 THREE 5   2
it seems to be doing nicely / / / . . . . 401 NO THANKS 18   21
world) selves . No doing shall undo (nor madness . . . . . . 577 1 X 1 37   9
and i 've been doing as long as to . . . . 686 95 POEMS 14   8
done; and whose last doing shall not quite undo . . . . 762 95 POEMS 89   4
only me is your doing, my darling) i fear . . . . 766 95 POEMS 92   4
DOITY
duh guts outa dem doity frogeaters an humpin duh . . . . . . 332 VIVA 23   16
DOLL
rises upon one startling doll undressed in unripe green . . . 55 T&C PORTRAIT 3   8
with a little oldish doll-like face and hairy arms . . . . . 69 T&C POST IMPR 6   38
sits rigidly her body's doll gay exactly perishing sexual, . 131 & SON REAL 2   16
of I Want a Doll, wispish-agile feet with slid . . . . 140 & SON REAL 11   13
fewer were shyer than doll. doll / / / . . . . 509 50 POEMS 23   24
were shyer than doll. doll / / / / . . . . 509 50 POEMS 23   24
his magical shoulders him doll self) hay completely thus . . 516 50 POEMS 30   11
smile to your breathing doll / / / / . . . . 518 50 POEMS 32   12
/ dominic has a doll wired to the radiator . . . . 680 95 POEMS 8   2
how dominic has a doll & every now & . . . . 680 95 POEMS 8   21
just this strolling ghostly doll of an almost vanished . . . 720 95 POEMS 48   8
A hummingbird princess FlOaTs doll-angel-life from Bet: To; . 747 95 POEMS 75   5
two tiny selves sleep (doll by doll) motionless under . . . . 777 73 POEMS 5   11
selves sleep (doll by doll) motionless under magical . . . . 777 73 POEMS 5   11
+DOLL
FOR CONTEXT, SEE . . . . 524 50 POEMS 36   44
DOLL-ANGEL-LIFE
A hummingbird princess FlOaTs doll-angel-life from Bet: To; . 747 95 POEMS 75   5
DOLL-LIKE
with a little oldish doll-like face and hairy arms . . . . . 69 T&C POST IMPR 6   38
DOLL'S
/ / / / Doll's boy's asleep under a . . . . 15 T&C SONGS 5   1
his eyes are mine. Doll's boy's asleep under the . . . . . . 15 T&C SONGS 5   17
DOLLAR
Who threw the silver dollar up into the tree? . . . . 125 & SEVEN POEMS 4   2
make it an even dollar whereupon the Divine Average . . . . . 196 XLI PORTRAIT 4   15
DOLLARBRINGING
gondola don't --the substantial dollarbringing virgins "from 256 IS 5 ONE 27   29
DOLLARFULL
by" sold! to the dollarfull shea with a weakness . . . . . . 546 1 X 1 6   14
DOLLARS
me, when for two dollars i fill her hips . . . . 148 & SON REAL 19   14
righteousness the age of dollars and no sense. Which . . . . 266 IS 5 TWO 1   4
and inexplicable not being dollars toenails or ideas . . . . 322 VIVA 14   8
jew a few dead dollars and some twisted laws) . . . . 644 {CHAIRE} 46   5
+DOLLARS
FOR CONTEXT, SEE . . . . 244 IS 5 ONE 15   2
FOR CONTEXT, SEE . . . . 792 73 POEMS 20   6

DOLLHEAD
played a tune) death's dollhead wandering under weakening . . 479 NEW POEMS 17   10
DOLLIES
WhoEver would)? dance lewd dollies pretty and putrid dollies 101 & POST IMPR 11   81
dollies pretty and putrid dollies of-love-and-of-death   . . . 101 & POST IMPR 11   81
and putrid dollies of-love-and-of-death dollies of perfect . 101 & POST IMPR 11   82
dollies of perfect life, dollies of anyway VIOLIN / . . . . . 101 & POST IMPR 11   83
lay-- whom, among her dollies, dad first ("don't tell . . . . 794 73 POEMS 22   3
DOLLS
or meaning monuments and dolls resist Them Greediest Paws . . 260 IS 5 ONE 30   9
put to sleep by dolls let us not be . . . . 261 IS 5 ONE 31   2
than nothing) 2 boston Dolls; found with Holes in . . . . . . 317 VIVA 9   25
soar equalling noise solemn dolls re -volve whirlswans   . . . 384 NO THANKS 2   28
end's ending then these dolls of joy and grief . . . . 502 50 POEMS 16   9
finding whom of girl) dolls clutching their dolls wallow . . 565 1 X 1 25   5
girl) dolls clutching their dolls wallow toys playing writhe 565 1 X 1 25   5
are less alive than dolls & dream / / . . . . 680 95 POEMS 8   32
DOLORES
of Flo's midnight Frolic dolores small in the head   . . . . 232 IS 5 ONE 3   4
DOMAINS
perfectly far from tangible domains rare with most early . . 402 NO THANKS 19   11
+DOMAINS
FOR CONTEXT, SEE . . . . 347 VIVA 38   14
DOME
star perfects the sensual dome of darkness, and the . . . . .   7 T&C EPITHALAM   164
shapely thighs) in whose dome the trembling bliss of . . . . 21 T&C PUELLA MEA   205
with me upon this dome of many coloured glass, ... 273 IS 5 TWO 8   1
DOMESHAPED
of a chair, a; domeshaped interval of complete plasticity, . 97 & POST IMPR 8   35
DOMINIC
/ / / / dominic has a doll wired . . . . 680 95 POEMS 8   1
ashbarrel so of course dominic took him home & . . . . 680 95 POEMS 8   10
him home & mrs dominic washed his sweet dirty . . . . 680 95 POEMS 8   13
so that 's how dominic has a doll & . . . . 680 95 POEMS 8   21
then my wonderful friend dominic depaola gives me a . . . . . 680 95 POEMS 8   24
DOMINOES
(yawning while all the dominoes) fall: down; in, rows . . . . 331 VIVA 22   8
DON
lament, my dream and don a doer's doom create . . . . 834 73 POEMS 62   6
DON'T
children laugh. But i don't, the crank goes round . . . . . 69 T&C POST IMPR 6   21
/ / goodby Betty, don't remember me pencil your . . . . 71 T&C SON REAL 2   1
who live under stones.) Don't be afraid and we . . . . 86 T&C SON ACTU 5   10
sharpen: themselves (on air) don't speak A white idea, . . . 99 & POST IMPR 10   18
yer goat but we don't care do we dearie . . . . 109 & PORTRAIT 5   6
brother who is would don't punish us for we . . . . 117 & PORTRAIT 10   20
and you pretend you don't but really you do . . . . 126 & SEVEN POEMS 5   16
you see but you don't want to dead's happy . . . . 126 & SEVEN POEMS 5   26
Band? or unnoise men don't make soup who drink. . . . . 141 & SON REAL 12   18
vague how vague i don't know tenuous Now- spears . . . . . . 160 & SON ACTU 9   15
your mother would, only don't be afraid look the . . . . . . 192 XLI CHANSONS 2   12
precisely slim) sim ply don't know duh meanin uv . . . . . . 240 IS 5 ONE 11   2
cook but well oh don't you makes burst want . . . . 251 IS 5 ONE 22   11
knows Cincingondolanati i gondola don't --the substantial . . 256 IS 5 ONE 27   28
damned lot of people don't and never never will . . . . 272 IS 5 TWO 7   14
never will know, they don't want to no / . . . . 272 IS 5 TWO 7   17
swear by all flowers. Don't cry --the best gesture . . . . . 290 IS 5 FOUR 7   10
big yellow dog. You don't believe? look back. (Along   . . . 303 IS 5 FIVE 2   11
parle de repapering; i don't think so. maybe: somebody?) . . 312 VIVA 4   24
people and others please don't confuse. Some people 's . . . 314 VIVA 6   5
/ / Space being (don't forget to remember) Curved . . . . . . 315 VIVA 7   1
now we muthn't pleathe don't as pop weird up . . . . 316 VIVA 8   9
/ / / / don't cries to please my . . . . 343 VIVA 34   1
stroke answers (but now don't you're hurting o Me . . . . . . 343 VIVA 34   5
self int o eighteen) Don't (for) Please (tnights, on . . . . 343 VIVA 34   14
the world) A always don't there B being no . . . . 390 NO THANKS 7   2
Wistfully dead seem generous) don't All suspect each (nor . . 391 NO THANKS 8   3
is incredible But others don't scream murmur wink at   . . . 391 NO THANKS 8   13

	PAGE	TITLE	LINE

DON'T (CONTINUED)

she (tiptop said he don't stop said she oh	399	NO THANKS 16	26
comes to (listen you don't have to i mean	400	NO THANKS 17	6
Reely) but (no listen don't be sil why sure)	400	NO THANKS 17	7
cannot understand (why Jones don't pay me what he	406	NO THANKS 23	6
ever lived people always) don't die (becoming most buried . .	412	NO THANKS 29	14
afraid to die kumrads don't and kumrads won't believe	413	NO THANKS 30	4
if i or anybody don't know where it her	475	NEW POEMS 13	2
allows which if they don't to hell with them)	500	50 POEMS 14	23
(of a crazy man) don't ask me how i	501	50 POEMS 15	5
the sooner to biz don't ask me what it's	552	1 X 1 12	5
know better than books don't grow) one's anything old	594	1 X 1 54	13
they're (look again) flowers." "Don't worlds open and worlds	603	{CHAIRE} 5	6
of course but you don't seem to realize i	638	{CHAIRE} 40	6
quite so good you don't conceive a better; and	679	95 POEMS 7	10
rose (i have none) "don't cry dear violet you	684	95 POEMS 12	3
it takes; & i don't mean It-- & i	701	95 POEMS 29	13
mean It-- & i don't mean any thing real	701	95 POEMS 29	15
den Stop Must n't Don't &) youth goes right	729	95 POEMS 57	16
many thousand hearts which don't and dream or many	743	95 POEMS 71	6
whisper it Selves but don't look down and to	762	95 POEMS 89	13
/ / / why don't be sil ly , ...	793	73 POEMS 21	2
her dollies, dad first ("don't tell your mother") had; . . .	794	73 POEMS 22	4
his (believe it or don't) by god down this	800	73 POEMS 28	15
as can each) they don't and they do and	801	73 POEMS 29	9

+DON'T

FOR CONTEXT, SEE	310	VIVA 2	3
FOR CONTEXT, SEE	310	VIVA 2	4
FOR CONTEXT, SEE	330	VIVA 21	7
FOR CONTEXT, SEE	330	VIVA 21	8
FOR CONTEXT, SEE	343	VIVA 34	17
FOR CONTEXT, SEE	392	NO THANKS 9	6
FOR CONTEXT, SEE	547	1 X 1 7	2
FOR CONTEXT, SEE	547	1 X 1 7	4
FOR CONTEXT, SEE	547	1 X 1 7	9
FOR CONTEXT, SEE	710	95 POEMS 38	7

DONC

| toujours in my head dis-donc, Paris ta gorge mysterieuse . . | 121 | & PORTRAIT 12 | 52 |

DONE

the dears; when all's done and said, and under	181	XLI SONGS 3	11
my uncle Frank has done nothing for many years	253	IS 5 ONE 24	5
at this) a 75 done this nobody would have	270	IS 5 TWO 5	2
rain or hail sam done the best he kin	568	1 X 1 28	2
man grinned his grin done his chores laid him	568	1 X 1 28	28
happens that can't be done (and anything's righter than . . .	594	1 X 1 54	1
And something thought or done or wished without a	649	{CHAIRE} 51	9
a job to be done) while a wisp of	709	95 POEMS 37	10
do, which than are done; and whose last doing	762	95 POEMS 89	3
dear; and whatever is done by only me is	766	95 POEMS 92	3
asking What have i done that You wouldn't have	784	73 POEMS 12	7
does do, has always done ; & will do	793	73 POEMS 21	19

DONG

| die at break of dong and common's rare and . . . . | 511 | 50 POEMS 25 | 18 |
| Women and men (both dong and ding) summer autumn . . . . . | 515 | 50 POEMS 29 | 33 |

+DONG

| FOR CONTEXT, SEE . . . . | 798 | 73 POEMS 26 | 6 |

DONGDING

| thine a mine --dingdong: dongding-- to say would be . . . . | 798 | 73 POEMS 26 | 6 |

DOO

| no care so what yoo-gointa-doo? (ice coal wood man) . . . . | 618 | {CHAIRE} 20 | 19 |

DOOM

gave thee for his doom-- O thou within the	6	T&C EPITHALAM	152
be immortal is our doom; but a rain frailly	9	T&C SONGS 1	24
time extract his inconsiderable doom, when these thy lips .	210	XLI SONNETS 6	11
breathes and moves, since Doom (with white longest hands . .	288	IS 5 FOUR 5	2
beyond difficult moult) amazing doom who standest as thou . .	351	VIVA 42	11
having worshipped for my doom pass ignorantly into sleep's .	358	VIVA 49	14
mile shyly to its doom than you will smile)	367	VIVA 58	11

		PAGE	TITLE	LINE

DOOM (CONTINUED)
  universe will wraiths of doom rush (which all ghosts . . . . 454 NO THANKS 69   10
  and shall entirely our doom steer his great small . . . . . . 528 50 POEMS 40   7
  living complete love whose doom is beauty and its . . . . . . 538 50 POEMS 50   4
  said demon for to doom yea (fresh complexions being . . . . . 552 1 X 1 12   22
  a dawn of a doom of a dream bites . . . . 560 1 X 1 20   17
  grey mind by wave doom disappeared, out of perhaps . . . . . 599 (CHAIRE) 1   7
  radiator of his ZOOM DOOM icecoalwood truck a wistful . . . . 680 95 POEMS 8   4
  a why but our doom is to grow (remember . . . . 686 95 POEMS 14   12
  kneel (over time space doom dream while floats the . . . . 714 95 POEMS 42   7
  of deathless earth's innumerable doom: againing (yes by . . . 821 73 POEMS 49   2
  try to seize the doom of sky (silently all . . . . 822 73 POEMS 50   6
  and don a doer's doom create is now contrive; . . . . 834 73 POEMS 62   6
  from all selfsubtracting hugely doom treasures of reeking . . 843 73 POEMS 71   7
DOOM'S
  we have seen see doom's integration......... a wind has . . . 80 T&C SON UNRE 5 13
DOOMED
  together how behind the doomed exact smile of life's . . . . 43 T&C AMORES 7   29
  what's in velvet beyond doomed thought is like a . . . . . . 81 T&C SON UNRE 6   9
  its desire of a doomed impetuous acute sentience whose . . . 193 XLI PORTRAIT 1 10
  from a hun dred doomed hurrying brains (by twos . . . . 354 VIVA 45   21
  wickedly comprehend the innocently Doomed brief all which . . 356 VIVA 47   10
DOOMFUL
  suddenly received) or by doomful connivance accurately . . . 299 IS 5 FOUR 16   7
+DOOMFUL
  FOR CONTEXT, SEE . . . . 449 NO THANKS 64   1
DOOMS
  my father moved through dooms of love through sames . . . . . 520 50 POEMS 34   1
  my father moved through dooms of feel; his anger . . . . . 520 50 POEMS 34   34
  again; whose golden, crimson dooms conceive an oceaning abyss 599 (CHAIRE) 1   2
  (huge Perhaps by hugest) dooms of miracle drift killed . . . 757 95 POEMS 85   31
DOOR
  whoso knocketh at the door of Marie and of . . . . 20 T&C PUELLA MEA 171
  heard behind a golden door, poet and sage and . . . . 22 T&C PUELLA MEA 222
  chalcedony and before every door a naked eunuch watches . . . 33 T&C ORIENTALE 6 35
  hand then the ◇ door is opened by the . . . . 33 T&C ORIENTALE 6 62
  bulb stuck in the door. a fang of wincing . . . . 73 T&C SON REAL 4   2
  a portrait over the door very notable of the . . . . 198 XLI PORTRAIT 6   8
  tired of this a door opens by itself woman.) . . . . 243 IS 5 ONE 14   8
  is see! so long door golf slam bridge train . . . . 309 VIVA 1   17
  are 6 doors. Next door (but four) gentlemen are . . . . . . 312 VIVA 4   2
  multitude of chins: next door but three dwells; a . . . . . 312 VIVA 4   6
  who Is bluish; next Door but two occupy a . . . . 312 VIVA 4   10
  looks jewish , next door but One a on . . . . 312 VIVA 4   17
  spi) tting But next door nobody seems to live . . . . 312 VIVA 4   21
  hotel this is the door (opening it i think . . . . 353 VIVA 44   13
  wide a wide open door we are so both . . . . 537 50 POEMS 49   12
  a good universe next door; let's go / / . . . . 554 1 X 1 14   15
DOORS
  moon there are thrice-three-hundred doors carven of . . . . . 33 T&C ORIENTALE 6 34
  imposingly empty; snickering shop doors unlocked by . . . . . 172 & SON ACTU 21   6
  is like Out of doors he's a with eyes . . . . 251 IS 5 ONE 22   6
  / there are 6 doors. Next door (but four) . . . . 312 VIVA 4   1
DOORWAY
  reaches the barn's immense doorway and halts propped on . . . 754 95 POEMS 82   8
DOOT
  oi sez. Tom oidoughwuntuh doot, butoiguttuh braikyooz, . . . 310 VIVA 2   4
DOOYUH
  duh woil doi sez dooyuh unnurs tanmih eesez pullih . . . . . 310 VIVA 2   2
DORMERS
  of a town (whose dormers choke and snore the . . . . 340 VIVA 31   3
DOROTHY
  lay which had been dorothy and once permitted me . . . . . 52 T&C PORTRAIT 1 17
  kid.... Fran Mag Glad Dorothy / / / / . . . . 138 & SON REAL 9   17
DOS
  les americains aussi.... "bon dos, bon cul de Paris" . . . . 120 & PORTRAIT 12 14
DOST
  aged unreluctant earth who dost with quivering continual . .   3 T&C EPITHALAM   1

DOST (CONTINUED)
   spring omnipotent goddess thou dost inveigle into crossing . 61 T&C PORTRAIT 9   1
   the frivolous angleworm thou dost persuade to serenade his . 61 T&C PORTRAIT 9   4
   and out of) Life, dost Thou contain a marvel . . . . 406 NO THANKS 23   12
DOTE
   lips of Tristram slowly dote, La beale Isoud whose . . . . . 17 T&C PUELLA MEA   36
DOTH
   silence of her face doth immediately make in my . . . . 18 T&C PUELLA MEA   64
   strangeness of her face doth float, which in eyes . . . . . . 20 T&C PUELLA MEA   146
   Master Gower in Confessio doth prefer shall not lack . . . . 20 T&C PUELLA MEA   167
   in a lovely fashion doth from my lady's body . . . . 21 T&C PUELLA MEA   182
   know, her petaled flesh doth entertain the adroit blood's . . 21 T&C PUELLA MEA   185
   (that urgent urn which doth amass for whoso drinks, ... 21 T&C PUELLA MEA   198
   (if whose very minuteness doth abuse reason, why then . . . . 22 T&C PUELLA MEA   218
   men called Love) upward doth leap from the mute . . . . 210 XLI SONNETS 6   4
   every perfect thing meanwhile doth miss; a hand's impression 360 VIVA 51   7
   trivial which thinkless unwishing doth depend upon the . . . 411 NO THANKS 28   4
   to man kind progress doth impart one stands supreme . . . . . 544 1 X 1 4   2
   tame to teem) still doth our hero contemplate in . . . . . . 544 1 X 1 4   19
DOTING
   how often have the doting fingers of prurient philosophers . 46 T&C LA GUERRE 2   4
   giving-- but keeping is doting and nothing and nonsense . . . 665 {CHAIRE} 67   10
DOTTED
   wave signs on the dotted line or else an . . . . 620 {CHAIRE} 22   7
DOTTING
   and whites shoving, the dotting millions of windows of . . . 281 IS 5 THREE 5   5
+DOUBLE
   FOR CONTEXT, SEE . . . . 325 VIVA 17   20
DOUBLES
   landing a onetwo which doubles up suddenly his bunged . . . . 259 IS 5 ONE 29   15
DOUBLEYOU
   at the end of doubleyou 4th) reminds me in . . . . 699 95 POEMS 27   5
DOUBT
   the electric When In Doubt Buy Of (but a . . . . 217 XLI SONNETS 13   5
   purely grow but, never doubt my weakness makes more . . . . . 433 NO THANKS 50   6
   heart to fear, to doubt a mind, to differ . . . . 521 50 POEMS 34   58
   hate confound the wise? doubt blind the brave? does . . . . . 538 50 POEMS 50   5
   first because (faith's last doubt and humbly heights below) . 574 1 X 1 34   10
   to stop (kneeling in doubt: while all skies fall) . . . . . . 650 {CHAIRE} 52   2
   all nothing--human merely being doubt unimaginable You? (now 663 {CHAIRE} 65   12
   most (without the smallest doubt) because no best is . . . . 679 95 POEMS 7   9
   keys haven't is have doubt and believe (like me . . . . 716 95 POEMS 44   26
   world and without any doubt of impossible ours --God's . . . 748 95 POEMS 76   3
   Magic dust expect hope doubt (wonder mistrust) despair and . 780 73 POEMS 8   2
   she can swarm. To doubt that in whose form . . . . 790 73 POEMS 18   8
   timid the tender (as doubt as can trust) they . . . . 801 73 POEMS 29   26
   why? because without any doubt he was whatever (first . . . . 802 73 POEMS 30   10
   some world (we marvel) doubt, for just sweet terrifying . . . 809 73 POEMS 37   9
DOUBTING
   morning; and before my doubting window leaves softly to . . . 205 XLI SONNETS 1   10
   isn't go ghostly they doubting can turn men's see . . . . . . 580 1 X 1 40   8
   worlds than merely by doubting have darkly themselves unmade 580 1 X 1 40   13
   keeping is downward and doubting and never --it's april . . . 665 {CHAIRE} 67   3
   were gay (today tomorrow, doubting believing and to lend . . 798 73 POEMS 26   17
DOUBTLESS
   whole supreme this complete doubtless universe we'd (and we . 675 95 POEMS 3   7
DOUBTS
   terricolous American an instant doubts the authenticity of . 116 & PORTRAIT 9   12
   never to have no doubts about why you put . . . . 242 IS 5 ONE 13   11
   by proving true (all doubts, all certainties, as villains . . 576 1 X 1 36   5
   fears hopes beliefs compulsions doubts & corners) worlds are 755 95 POEMS 83   18
   all fears hopes beliefs doubts disappear. Everywhere and . . 812 73 POEMS 40   13
DOUCEMENT
   hot men se promenent doucement le soir (ladies accurately . . 120 & PORTRAIT 12   24
DOUGH
   pullih nizmus tash, oi dough un giv uh shid . . . . 310 VIVA 2   3
DOUGHGOB
   (bubs) where's John Big Doughgob Big pastmaster of the . . . 642 {CHAIRE} 44   22

DOUTE
  away with them? j'en doute,) cherie, j'en doute. the   . . . . 169 & SON ACTU 18   12
  j'en doute,) cherie, j'en doute. the accurate key to   . . . . 169 & SON ACTU 18   13
DOVE
  loosened my collar and dove for the nearest 1; . . . . 327 VIVA 18   38
  worse squats a big dove on g w's wig . . . . 545 1 X 1 5   12
DOVES
  imperishable smile the amazed doves flicker upon sunny wings   6 T&C EPITHALAM   138
DOW
  death at afternoon? (kow dow r 2 bul retoinis . . . . 409 NO THANKS 26   3
  : seized (tatterdemalion dow nupfloatsw oon InG s . . . . . 495 50 POEMS 9   8
+DOWDY
  FOR CONTEXT, SEE . . . . 788 73 POEMS 16   8
DOWN
  thinking twilight momently) as down the oblivious west's . .   6 T&C EPITHALAM   127
  riding riding the echo down into the silver dawn. . . . . . . 14 T&C SONGS 4   12
  riding riding the mountain down into the silver dawn. . . . . 14 T&C SONGS 4   22
  the waters i rode down the red horse shrieking . . . . 30 T&C ORIENTALE 4   11
  against my eyes and down the singing reaches of . . . . 39 T&C AMORES 4   20
  into the park sits Down. pigeons circle around and . . . . . 62 T&C PORTRAIT 10   28
  of all dreams, draws down. cover her briefness in . . . . . . 65 T&C POST IMPR 2   7
  are tottering up and down in a trembly mist . . . . 69 T&C POST IMPR 6   26
  passionately dusk brings softly down the perfume of the . . . 71 T&C SON REAL 2   10
  earth's a hurled dream down eager avenues of lifelessness . . 81 T&C SON UNRE 6   6
  RipeBlackbeRRies emptied suddenl (y down the squirming sPine 101 & POST IMPR 11   54
  luck somebody else says down the hatch the nigger . . . . . . 108 & PORTRAIT 4   21
  --staring wildly up and down the here we are . . . . 118 & PORTRAIT 10   39
  play, effendi approaches, sets down coffee withdraws a and . 200 XLI PORTRAIT 8   19
  it's there and sitting down on it and because . . . . 204 XLI LA GUERRE 2   20
  / MAME she puts down the handmirror. "Look at" . . . . 226 IS 5 ONE MAME   1
  flesh). A thumblike index down- dragging yanks back skin . . 226 IS 5 ONE MAME   5
  pressed a button (and down went my Uncle Sol . . . . 239 IS 5 ONE 10   35
  feller tries to hold down the fifty bucks per . . . . 242 IS 5 ONE 13   8
  (whereas when i lie down i cough too much). . . . . 245 IS 5 ONE 16   11
  last minute coming back down by the Public Gardens . . . . . 248 IS 5 ONE 19   27
  the little schoolchildren sat down / / / / . . . . 249 IS 5 ONE 20   4
  sprawls collapses singing knocked down trampled the kicked by 274 IS 5 TWO 9   7
  miraculously inhabits. (people tumble down. people crumble to 280 IS 5 THREE 4   6
  Calchidas, in the sunlight? down ever so far on . . . . 281 IS 5 THREE 5   3
  are building a house down there by the sea, ... 281 IS 5 THREE 5   10
  fingers voices rise from down ever so far-- hush. . . . . . . 281 IS 5 THREE 5   21
  does it all come down to? love? Love if . . . . 295 IS 5 FOUR 12   21
  white thumbs and frisks down the boulevards without his . . . 296 IS 5 FOUR 13   7
  he murmurs carefully lying down) / / / / . . . . 299 IS 5 FOUR 16   16
  you be any how? down to smoking found Butts . . . . 314 VIVA 6   29
  then which did lie Down, honestly now who go . . . . 317 VIVA 9   37
  all the dominoes) fall: down; in, rows / / . . . . 331 VIVA 22   8
  Marcus"-- "duh Swede rolls down tree flights an Sam . . . . . 332 VIVA 23   8
  an wid tears streamin down my face i hauls . . . . 332 VIVA 23   19
  awful big light squoits down my spine like i . . . . 332 VIVA 23   27
  he shot the aeronaut down, into the abyss --and . . . . 360 VIVA 51   17
  the clocks would run down the next day. / . . . . 365 VIVA 56   14
  wish and world go down, one poem yet shall . . . . 372 VIVA 63   15
  fat strongman has put down his carpet from which . . . . . . 384 NO THANKS 2   20
  have cried) lie bravely down sleep big rain big . . . . 393 NO THANKS 10   11
  fear might faithfully lie down to so much sleep . . . . 418 NO THANKS 35   7
  and (th e moon's al-down) most whis per (here) . . . . 423 NO THANKS 40   7
  damned with whomever's afraid down with ought with because . 424 NO THANKS 41   9
  entirety neither may shadow down flesh neither may vibration 425 NO THANKS 42   12
  rain) drown, beyond sound down (slowly beneath sight fall . . 432 NO THANKS 49   4
  may take it lying down) down with the human . . . . 466 NEW POEMS 4   4
  take it lying down) down with the human soul . . . . 466 NEW POEMS 4   5
  simple people like we) down with hell and heaven . . . . . . 466 NEW POEMS 4   13
  and the hitler lies down with the cohn) down . . . . 466 NEW POEMS 4   20
  down with the cohn) down above all with love . . . . 466 NEW POEMS 4   21
  child's eyes float silently down more than two those . . . 491 50 POEMS 5   6
  of afraid of) these (down pull & who'll shades . . . . 501 50 POEMS 15   24
  if the people sit down) and this light is . . . . 505 50 POEMS 19   8

	PAGE	TITLE	LINE
DOWN (CONTINUED)			
but joy's the voice down shall go which and	511	50 POEMS 25	23
the man. Up sam (down! alice) a hole in	513	50 POEMS 27	22
so floating many bells down) spring summer autumn winter . .	515	50 POEMS 29	2
only a few and down they forgot as up	515	50 POEMS 29	10
so floating many bells down) one day anyone died	515	50 POEMS 29	24
will go (kiss me down into your memory and	529	50 POEMS 41	10
both locked in each down a thief by a	533	50 POEMS 45	21
his chores laid him down. Sleep well / /	568	1 X 1 28	29
look should april me, down isn't's own isn't go	580	1 X 1 40	7
hands are offering jonquils) down again who but zooms . . .	585	1 X 1 45	17
a my (with a down up around again fly)	594	1 X 1 54	24
which could knock you down (while scotch was your	605	(CHAIRE) 7	4
guess) quite half way down to the earth are	631	(CHAIRE) 33	10
of mocra c (sing down with the fascist beast	635	(CHAIRE) 37	14
forever come riding alive down while crylessly drifting . . .	661	(CHAIRE) 63	13
molly and may went down to the beach (to	682	95 POEMS 10	2
o my darling) of (down / / /	695	95 POEMS 23	21
you look for him down by the old swimminghole"	707	95 POEMS 35	2
no" "than look you down through the old swimminghole	707	95 POEMS 35	27
years and then lay down with a smile) /	709	95 POEMS 37	16
crying to lose (as down someone who's we ungrows)	716	95 POEMS 44	34
& youth yanks them down (old age cries No	729	95 POEMS 57	6
we who have wandered down from fragrant mountains of	743	95 POEMS 71	11
Selves but don't look down and to -morrow and	762	95 POEMS 89	13
no favor but (while down come blundering proud hugenesses . .	783	73 POEMS 11	6
or don't) by god down this stranger went on	800	73 POEMS 28	16
now i lay me down (in a most steep	816	73 POEMS 44	5
now i lay me down to dream of (nothing	816	73 POEMS 44	10
now i lay me down to dream of Spring	816	73 POEMS 44	14
therefore, my life, lie down and more by most	834	73 POEMS 62	10
things swim climb minds (down slowly swoop wholly up	841	73 POEMS 69	29
+DOWN			
FOR CONTEXT, SEE	200	XLI PORTRAIT 8	27
FOR CONTEXT, SEE	445	NO THANKS 60	7
FOR CONTEXT, SEE	495	50 POEMS 9	8
FOR CONTEXT, SEE	680	95 POEMS 8	9
DOWNDOWN			
toyTown which upups to dowNdown (and only where remembers . .	371	VIVA 62	9
DOWNDOWNDOWN			
up upup: go ing downdowndown com; ing won der	840	73 POEMS 68	8
DOWNLIFE			
daemons and large The downlife gods of shut)	346	VIVA 37	27
DOWNRISE			
omful relaxing -ly) i downrise outwrithein- ing upfall and .	449	NO THANKS 64	5
DOWNWARD			
tumbled hushingly bits of downward flower flowing without or	168	& SON ACTU 17	8
gesticulations threatens the tubular downward blackness . . .	201	XLI PORTRAIT 9	9
our lost bodies carefully downward) / / / /	215	XLI SONNETS 11	17
again....) sliding a little downward, embrace me with your .	282	IS 5 THREE 6	34
plunges inward with hurled downward thousands of enormous . .	301	IS 5 FOUR 18	19
beckoned) as earth will downward climb, so naked for	521	50 POEMS 34	42
summer's beside their glories downward if they'll or goldenly	573	1 X 1 33	7
having-- but keeping is downward and doubting and never . . .	665	(CHAIRE) 67	3
+DOWNWARD			
FOR CONTEXT, SEE	311	VIVA 3	15
DOWNWARDNESS			
guest of dark most downwardness and marvellously self	821	73 POEMS 49	11
DOWNY			
before me bread more downy than street-lamps upon an	194	XLI PORTRAIT 2	32
DOZEN			
changeless grin whereon a dozen staunch and leal citizens . .	258	IS 5 ONE 28	9
DOZES			
years (while a bee dozes on the poppies, the	181	XLI SONGS 3	9
DRAB			
solemn mechanism. beneath her drab tempo of hasteful futility	103	& POST IMPR 13	10
DRAGGED			
over which of earth dragged once -ful leaf. &	491	50 POEMS 5	2

	PAGE	TITLE	LINE

DRAGGED (CONTINUED)
thief by a whore dragged goes to meet her . . . . 533 50 POEMS 45   22
DRAGGING
a tall wind is dragging the sea with dream . . . . 51 T&C IMPRESS 5   10
A thumblike index down- dragging yanks back skin "see" . . . 226 IS 5 ONE MAME   6
DRAGON
/ myself, walking in Dragon st one fine August . . . . 313 VIVA 5   1
DRAGON'S
gal did wring that dragon's tail (for men must . . . . 552 1 X 1 12   17
DRANK
mute?" He. spoke. And drank rapidly a glass of . . . . 268 IS 5 TWO 3   14
+DRAPER
FOR CONTEXT, SEE . . . . 431 NO THANKS 48   28
DRAW
yourself a stool but draw a line around the . . . . 500 50 POEMS 14   3
DRAWER
to diminutive this opened drawer) tweak S with his . . . . . 697 95 POEMS 25   22
DRAWERS
Turn Your Shirttails Into Drawers and If It Isn't . . . . . . 230 IS 5 ONE 2   34
DRAWING
strength O haste annihilator drawing into you my enchanting . 182 XLI SONGS 4   17
use in other days (drawing my Mes from sleep . . . . 213 XLI SONNETS 9   13
an enormous stride (and drawing thy mouth toward my . . . . . 215 XLI SONNETS 11   16
DRAWN
incurious curtaining dusk be drawn surpassing nets are . . . 5 T&C EPITHALAM   85
incompletely surrounded by well- drawn icecakes beheld being 262 IS 5 ONE 32   12
DRAWS
the sleepy morning) gently draws apart her curtains, and . . 8 T&C OF NICOL   14
full of all dreams, draws down. cover her briefness . . . . . 65 T&C POST IMPR 2   7
"I sidesteps im an draws back huly jeezus" --an-- . . . . . . 332 VIVA 23   4
DREA-MINGLY
and if it perhaps drea-mingly Is (not- quite trees . . . . . 155 & SON ACTU 4   4
DREAD
the threshold have no dread lift the sheet back . . . . 118 & PORTRAIT 10   41
is enslaved by a dread dizziz and the sooner . . . . 552 1 X 1 12   3
DREADFUL
espoused unto fear) in dreadful corners hideously cowers-- i 207 XLI SONNETS 3   8
DREADFULLY
made a pen is dreadfully afraid of her of . . . . 141 & SON REAL 12   3
DREADS
should weigh a star --dreads dying least; and less, ... 446 NO THANKS 61   8
DREAM
sinful arms about me dream shall my love wholly . . . . 9 T&C SONGS 1   34
face which sleeps, a dream shall pass) and these . . . . . . 11 T&C SONGS 2   30
and utter ponds of dream; and very secret food . . . . 19 T&C PUELLA MEA   118
slender ladies made of dream (in the lazy world . . . . 23 T&C PUELLA MEA   284
face is as a dream locked in white fragrance . . . . 27 T&C ORIENTALE 1   18
i dreamed in my dream you had desire to . . . . 30 T&C ORIENTALE 4   17
the giddy hills to dream of you, approve these . . . . 36 T&C AMORES 1   8
dragging the sea with dream -S / / / . . . . 51 T&C IMPRESS 5   14
i will have a dream i think it shall . . . . 67 T&C POST IMPR 4   8
this earth's a hurled dream down eager avenues of . . . . . . 81 T&C SON UNRE 6   5
saith rain anguish of dream-send is hushed in moan-loll . . . 90 & POST IMPR 2   6
i'll tell you a dream i had once i . . . . 123 & SEVEN POEMS 2   1
these leopards of white dream in the glad flesh . . . . 139 & SON REAL 10   6
her sails filled with dream-- when on a green . . . . 156 & SON ACTU 5   7
of Spring.... and the dream of dreaming --and i . . . . 158 & SON ACTU 7   11
-water pursues the angry dream of the shore. By . . . . 160 & SON ACTU 9   5
clauses of warmth (after dream who knows?) a blackish . . . . 168 & SON ACTU 17   16
goes he's a wet dream by Cezanne / / . . . . 246 IS 5 ONE 17   12
measure Spring with? each dream nascitur, is not made...) . . 264 IS 5 ONE 33   29
being mortised with a dream myself speaks (whispering, . . . 285 IS 5 FOUR 2   1
a woman in a dream (but if i should . . . . 287 IS 5 FOUR 4   13
(out of all things) dream is noone's fool; if . . . . 292 IS 5 FOUR 9   10
jumping puppets of a dream? oh i mean: entirely . . . . 295 IS 5 FOUR 12   4
how do i drink dream smile and how do . . . . 295 IS 5 FOUR 12   14
(Into) bangs minds into dream (An) quickly Not un . . . . . . 348 VIVA 39   10
beyond soft- liness than dream more sing (buoyant & . . . . . 349 VIVA 40   6

	PAGE	TITLE	LINE

DREAM (CONTINUED)

now, est hills er dream; new . oh if	350	VIVA 41	12
it goes like a dream (and between houses, really	353	VIVA 44	8
half tree among sunset dream acute from root to	362	VIVA 53	7
innumerable gnomes Of complete dream if we love each	363	VIVA 54	8
your eyes (shall any dream come a more millionth	367	VIVA 58	9
is any echo of dream nor any flowering of	368	VIVA 59	5
was not born of dream while wings welcome the	372	VIVA 63	13
who dreams whom mutterings dream & : the moon	384	NO THANKS 2	6
who must or any dream means more than sleep	390	NO THANKS 7	10
listen. ,not, alive, trees, dream(ev: ery: wheres: ex: . . .	416	NO THANKS 33	2
loneliness alive like some dream giving more than all	418	NO THANKS 35	3
/ move deeply, rain (dream hugely) wish firmly. splendidly .	422	NO THANKS 39	3
twilight (and a first dream called ocean) and let	424	NO THANKS 41	7
this god this surely dream perhaps this ghost) humbly	441	NO THANKS 56	49
laugh and cry) who dream, create and kill while	446	NO THANKS 61	13
(only more than immeasurable dream wherelessly spiralling) .	454	NO THANKS 69	7
lucky are Breathe grow dream die love not Fear	467	NEW POEMS 5	8
tosses like thin bums dream ing i'm thick in	469	NEW POEMS 7	2
a. Not one smallest dream) / / / /	479	NEW POEMS 17	20
die you got to dream and we aint got	489	50 POEMS 3	14
aint got nothing to dream (come on kid Let's	489	50 POEMS 3	15
recent memories of future dream these perhaps who have . . .	502	50 POEMS 16	10
be thighs deeds cannot dream what dreams can do	511	50 POEMS 25	25
nevers they slept their dream stars rain sun moon	515	50 POEMS 29	20
more by more they dream their sleep noone and	515	50 POEMS 29	30
us) whom only his dream ing own soul looks	516	50 POEMS 30	15
eyes to touch his dream / / / /	517	50 POEMS 31	14
hugely) stood my father's dream his flesh was flesh	520	50 POEMS 34	28
mothery same rotting keen dream? i rise which am	527	50 POEMS 39	30
tell us why we dream and will it tell	528	50 POEMS 40	3
reason, they undream a dream) one is the song	556	1 X 1 16	8
complete existence of to dream into complete some dream . . .	559	1 X 1 19	6
dream into complete some dream of to exist a	559	1 X 1 19	7
a doom of a dream bites this universe in	560	1 X 1 20	17
is the) more dream than become more am	571	1 X 1 31	15
a song like a dream of a bird with	587	1 X 1 47	8
it climbed like a dream) throbbing like a heart	593	1 X 1 53	10
oceaning abyss of orange dream larger than sky times	599	(CHAIRE) 1	3
like some newly remembered dream-- flaming a coolly bell . .	601	(CHAIRE) 3	12
stunt was really a dream-- here's, wherever you aren't . . .	605	(CHAIRE) 7	14
as time turned to dream "and poets grow; and	626	(CHAIRE) 28	11
all i am and dream and have. Be thou	651	(CHAIRE) 53	4
erywhere (a welcom ing dream: is amazing) a worlD.	657	(CHAIRE) 59	9
reality of more than dream-- how should contented fools . . .	659	(CHAIRE) 61	8
and a blue true dream of sky; and for	663	(CHAIRE) 65	3
sizeless truth of a dream whose sleep is the	664	(CHAIRE) 66	22
triangular why of a dream (with crazily eyes of	668	(CHAIRE) 70	2
always on by always dream, is to taste not	674	95 POEMS 2	9
to receive time's mightiest dream / / / /	675	95 POEMS 3	14
alive than dolls & dream / / / /	680	95 POEMS 8	33
-o of keen moon) dream unthings silent three like	687	95 POEMS 15	9
of waking is to dream, remember so (forgetting seem)	688	95 POEMS 16	5
a so moon could dream (i sus pect) only	698	95 POEMS 26	1
cruising into a crazy dream two were a hundred	709	95 POEMS 37	2
(over time space doom dream while floats the whole	714	95 POEMS 42	7
who's we ungrows) a dream in the rain /	716	95 POEMS 44	36
simply lives to die dream that your valentine makes	718	95 POEMS 46	3
breathing to breathing flaming dream to dreaming flame) . . .	721	95 POEMS 49	3
(dreaming flame by flaming dream) merge--at not imaginable .	721	95 POEMS 49	11
e t hrough his dream; dancin g you Star	733	95 POEMS 61	10
perfect mercy, live a dream larger than alive any	735	95 POEMS 63	3
star goes round --a dream sans meaning (or whatever	735	95 POEMS 63	5
hearts which don't and dream or many million minds	743	95 POEMS 71	6
distance breathes a final dream of bells; perfectly outlined	750	95 POEMS 78	2
me and while this dream is climbing sky (until	752	95 POEMS 80	5
(star rain snow moon dream wing tree leaf bird	753	95 POEMS 81	16
corners) worlds are to dream now dreams are to	755	95 POEMS 83	19

192

		PAGE	TITLE	LINE

DREAM (CONTINUED)
```
killed swim born a dream and (through stillness beyond  . . .  757  95 POEMS 85    34
(through stillness beyond conceiving) dream until No least  .  757  95 POEMS 85    36
are birds; unders of dream adventure truths of skies--  . . .  761  95 POEMS 88     8
this only truth (a dream of a deed, born  . . . . . . . . . .  776  73 POEMS  4    35
land until my second dream begins-- the sky is  . . . . . . .  777  73 POEMS  5     5
she quickly dreamed a dream of spring --how you  . . . . . . .  777  73 POEMS  5    15
prayers) riding through a Dream like fire called flowers  . .  778  73 POEMS  6    15
of sleep steering for dream / / / .  . . . . . . . . . . . .  781  73 POEMS  9     4
wanderer home to a dream called time: and give  . . . . . . .  811  73 POEMS 39    10
lay me down to dream of (nothing i or . . . . . . . . . . . .  816  73 POEMS 44    10
lay me down to dream of Spring / / .  . . . . . . . . . . . .  816  73 POEMS 44    14
enemies) therefore lament, my dream and don a doer's  . . . .  834  73 POEMS 62     5
even begin to be) dream of; a thing: of . . . . . . . . . . .  840  73 POEMS 68    17
a thunder of oneness dream! ! joy truth! !  . . . . . . . .  841  73 POEMS 69    37
will not make a dream speak; or if to . . . . . . . . . . . .  842  73 POEMS 70    10
```
+DREAM
```
FOR CONTEXT, SEE  . . . . . . . . . . . . . . . . . . . . . .  610  {CHAIRE} 12    16
```
DREAM-SEND
```
saith rain anguish of dream-send is hushed in moan-loll  . . .   90  & POST IMPR 2    6
```
DREAM'S
```
girl 's tears boy Dream's) forge tful: e ver  . . . . . . .  447  NO THANKS 62    12
are like ocean patient) dream's eternity (you feel behind  . .  617  {CHAIRE} 19     3
```
DREAMED
```
/ listen beloved i dreamed it appeared that you . . . . . . .   30  T&C ORIENTALE 4     3
mouth listen beloved i dreamed in my dream you  . . . . . . .   30  T&C ORIENTALE 4    17
blood listen beloved i dreamed i thought you would  . . . . .   30  T&C ORIENTALE 4    30
to not surmise she dreamed one afternoon ....or maybe . . . .   72  T&C SON REAL 3     9
moments after i have dreamed of the rare entertainment  . . .   78  T&C SON UNRE 3     1
wellknown parvenu who (having dreamed of a corkscrew) studied  236  IS 5 ONE 7     6
/ / supposing i dreamed this) only imagine, when  . . . . . .  292  IS 5 FOUR 9     1
certain a bird i dreamed i could sing but . . . . . . . . . .  587  1 X 1 47     3
to Feel how Everything (dreamed & hoped & prayed  . . . . . .  702  95 POEMS 30    16
and so she quickly dreamed a dream of spring  . . . . . . . .  777  73 POEMS  5    15
then known things or dreamed become un- / / . . . . . . . . .  822  73 POEMS 50     8
```
DREAMER
```
coward, clown, traitor, idiot, dreamer, beast-- such was a  .  562  1 X 1 22     9
snow. And then this dreamer wept: and so she  . . . . . . . .  777  73 POEMS  5    14
```
DREAMERS
```
swarm their fates woke dreamers to their ghostly roots  . . .  520  50 POEMS 34    12
```
DREAMEST
```
flOat newly alOne is dreamest oNLY THE MooN o . . . . . . . .  383  NO THANKS 1     8
```
+DREAMFULLY
```
FOR CONTEXT, SEE  . . . . . . . . . . . . . . . . . . . . . .  423  NO THANKS 40    16
```
DREAMFULS
```
brow five or three dreamfuls of despair that face)  . . . . .  402  NO THANKS 19     7
```
DREAMHORSE
```
/ what a proud dreamhorse pulling (smoothloomingly) through .  437  NO THANKS 53     1
o what a proud dreamhorse moving (whose feet almost . . . . .  437  NO THANKS 53    16
```
DREAMIN
```
(fea therr ain : dreamin g field o ver  . . . . . . . . . . .  653  {CHAIRE} 55     4
```
DREAMING
```
/ / OF NICOLETTE dreaming in marble all the . . . . . . . . .    8  T&C OF NICOL     1
are the trees of dreaming whose fruit is the  . . . . . . . .   29  T&C ORIENTALE 3    22
see a frail man dreaming dreams dreams in the . . . . . . . .   50  T&C IMPRESS 4    20
and the dream of dreaming --and i fall back,  . . . . . . . .  158  & SON ACTU 7    11
girl lasciviously frail, peace (dreaming is better) murdering  168  & SON ACTU 17    12
in a dark box dreaming of being taken out . . . . . . . . . .  192  XLI CHANSONS 2    15
deep mud et cetera (dreaming, et cetera, of Your  . . . . . .  276  IS 5 TWO 10    22
must shake well) indolently dreaming puzzling over that one .  323  VIVA 15     6
the meaning; or how dreaming becomes if your heart's  . . . .  364  VIVA 55     3
of the flower of Dreaming) somewhere behind us always . . . .  368  VIVA 59     9
or goldenly float so (dreaming out of dreams among) . . . . .  573  1 X 1 33    10
return by millions and dreaming drift hundreds come swimming   630  {CHAIRE} 32     5
breathing flaming dream to dreaming flame) united by perfect   721  95 POEMS 49     3
utmost secrecies and his (dreaming flame by flaming dream) .   721  95 POEMS 49    11
comes out of some dreaming tree (and how i'll . . . . . . . .  752  95 POEMS 80     2
forever of his loneliness dreaming their eyes have opened . .  812  73 POEMS 40     7
```

		PAGE	TITLE	LINE
+DREAMING				
FOR CONTEXT, SEE	. . . .	395	NO THANKS 12	12
FOR CONTEXT, SEE	. . . .	516	50 POEMS 30	15
FOR CONTEXT, SEE	. . . .	830	73 POEMS 58	21
+DREAMINGLY				
FOR CONTEXT, SEE	. . . .	155	& SON ACTU 4	4
FOR CONTEXT, SEE	. . . .	681	95 POEMS 9	5
FOR CONTEXT, SEE	. . . .	838	73 POEMS 66	1
DREAMINGS				
accurately wan) keenly, to dreamings more than truth untrue,		344	VIVA 35	7
DREAMLESS				
himself a man? go dreamless knaves on Shadows fed,	. . . . .	438	NO THANKS 54	9
+DREAMLESSNESSES				
FOR CONTEXT, SEE	. . . .	488	50 POEMS 2	5
DREAMLIKE				
now drop who all dreamlike (im / / /	. . . .	536	50 POEMS 48	20
/ / / mi (dreamlike) st makes big each	. . . .	829	73 POEMS 57	1
DREAMS				
be they than dappled dreams the swift sweet deer	. . . . .	14	T&C SONGS 4	6
goes forth to murder dreams.... i see in the	. . . .	50	T&C IMPRESS 4	11
a frail man dreaming dreams dreams in the mirror	. . . . . .	50	T&C IMPRESS 4	21
frail man dreaming dreams dreams in the mirror and	. . . .	50	T&C IMPRESS 4	22
now the intimate flower dreams of parted lips dim	. . . . .	54	T&C PORTRAIT 2	10
eyes are sticky with dreams and you have a	. . . .	61	T&C PORTRAIT 9	15
heaven full of all dreams, draws down. cover her	. . . . . .	65	T&C POST IMPR 2	6
hair is acold with dreams, love thou art frail	. . . .	190	XLI SONGS 12	17
which on thy beauty dreams (proud through the cold	. . . .	205	XLI SONNETS 1	5
are keeping their exquisite dreams--O Love! upon thy dim	. .	206	XLI SONNETS 2	10
be these haunters of dreams always demurely halfsmiling from	211	XLI SONNETS 7	7
ladies, ladies of my dreams justly touching roses their	. . .	211	XLI SONNETS 7	10
from sleep whose stranger dreams thy strangeness must	. . . .	213	XLI SONNETS 9	14
is reversed meantime in dreams let us investigate thoroughly	261	IS 5 ONE 31	10
more than just enough dreams to live on) after	. . . . . .	298	IS 5 FOUR 15	10
downward thousands of enormous dreams / / / /	301	IS 5 FOUR 18	19
not asleep, elsewhere our dreams began which now are	. . . .	304	IS 5 FIVE 3	7
(frailer than most deep dreams are frail) songs less	. . . .	306	IS 5 FIVE 5	3
is loneliness, these unique dreams never shall soil their	. .	328	VIVA 19	3
afraid "go first" of dreams and little bats &	353	VIVA 44	26
muddled and cuddled by dreams (or some times vacantly	. . . .	354	VIVA 45	7
swiftly creeping through my dreams last night, all of	. . . .	369	VIVA 60	17
ing ing among who dreams whom mutterings dream &	. . . .	384	NO THANKS 2	6
suddenly themselves if all dreams unmake (when in a	. . . .	414	NO THANKS 31	5
thread invisible) A graveyard dreams through its cluttered	.	434	NO THANKS 51	22
one fiend, a thousand dreams thick (cringing they brood	. . .	439	NO THANKS 55	8
a moon) blacker than dreams are round like a	. . . .	483	NEW POEMS 21	3
deeds cannot dream what dreams can do --time is	. . . . . .	511	50 POEMS 25	25
be welcomes welcomes her dreams his face (her face	. . . . .	533	50 POEMS 45	10
face (her face his dreams rejoice rejoice) --opens the	. . .	533	50 POEMS 45	11
so (dreaming out of dreams among) no year will	. . . .	573	1 X 1 33	11
older with ships than dreams more hands are offering	. . . .	585	1 X 1 45	16
twice) and becomes eithering dreams the secret of /	613	(CHAIRE) 15	11
and until i am dreams until comes vast dark	633	(CHAIRE) 35	7
eyes love laughter death (dreams hopes despairs) Once	693	95 POEMS 21	5
are cries poems children dreams & through slowquickly opening	719	95 POEMS 47	6
/ / dive for dreams or a slogan may	732	95 POEMS 60	1
roses which really are dreams of roses-- "and who"	748	95 POEMS 76	10
are to dream now dreams are to breathe /	755	95 POEMS 83	20
first of all my dreams was of a lover	777	73 POEMS 5	1
against my (where three dreams live) fore head is	785	73 POEMS 13	21
oblivion) voices who are dreams, less into heaven certainly .	810	73 POEMS 38	6
them this aflame with dreams incredible is) / /	832	73 POEMS 60	15
o-p-e-n-i-n-g are (leaves; flowers) dreams , come quickly . .	835	73 POEMS 63	13
+DREAMS				
FOR CONTEXT, SEE	. . . .	415	NO THANKS 32	16
FOR CONTEXT, SEE	. . . .	820	73 POEMS 48	9
DREAMSEEMS				
moo nface swimming ly dreamseems (vivi d an O	615	(CHAIRE) 17	12

DREAMSLENDER
    twilight's mystery made flesh-- dreamslender exquisite white 669 (CHAIRE) 71   9
DREAMSOUL
    a livingly free mysterious dreamsoul floatstands oak by birch 658 (CHAIRE) 60   17
DREAMTREE
    their precision evolving vision dreamtree, truthtree tree of 763 95 POEMS 90   31
DREAMY
    the cathedral leans its dreamy spine against thick sunset . . 279 IS 5 THREE 3   4
DRENCHED
    nearaway from huge trees drenched by a rounding moon) . . . . 10 T&C SONGS 1   45
DRENCHES
    a white idea (Listen drenches: earth's ugly) mind. , ... 99 & POST IMPR 10   3
DRENCHING
    speak A white idea, drenching. earth's brain detaches . . . . 99 & POST IMPR 10   20
DRESS
    hordes in sweet unserious dress ascends the golden crocus . .   4 T&C EPITHALAM   63
    wheels of joy pathetic dress fluttering behind her a . . . . 56 T&C PORTRAIT 4   4
    lady in a green dress, who; touches: the fields . . . . 91 & POST IMPR 3   20
    / / / the dress was a suspicious madder, ... 103 & POST IMPR 13   1
    leaks obscenely from the dress. one nipple tries. playfully . 143 & SON REAL 14   9
    keeping silence on her dress, good for sleeping is . . . . . 147 & SON REAL 18   3
    of little normal worms. Dress deftly your flesh in . . . . . 161 & SON ACTU 10   9
    crazy fingers liked your dress ....your kiss, your kiss . . . 173 & SON ACTU 22   8
    as (faithfully) her lownecked dress a little topples and . . 225 IS 5 ONE LIZ   2
DRESSED
    untimid final flowers (which dressed in various tremulous . .   4 T&C EPITHALAM   68
    smell waddles toward, me, dressed like a Plum grinning . . . 94 & POST IMPR 6   15
    then when you're quite dressed you'll stand in the . . . . . 192 XLI CHANSONS 2   21
    roadside on his back dressed in fifteenthrate ideas wearing . 258 IS 5 ONE 28   3
    cursed with pimples, correctly dressed, cleanshaven above the 262 IS 5 ONE 32   8
    --yon clean upstanding well dressed boy that with his . . . . 273 IS 5 TWO 8   6
    kind of crown he dressed in black candy she . . . . 470 NEW POEMS 8   3
    strong young finelooking fellow, dressed well but not over, . 800 73 POEMS 28   4
DREW
    it was Spring.... us drew lewdly the murmurous minute . . . . 174 & SON ACTU 23   2
    string of pretty medals drew (while messrs jack james . . . . 266 IS 5 TWO 1   24
DRIBBLES
    it get out ears dribbles soft right old feller . . . . 96 & POST IMPR 8   21
DRIBBLING
    follows truly through a dribbling moan of jazz whose . . . . 140 & SON REAL 11   4
    a child, a pretty dribbling child, a little child. . . . . . 233 IS 5 ONE 4   4
    might those be stockings dribbling from the table all . . . . 322 VIVA 14   6
DRIFT
    swift radiance wherein slowly drift murmurous things divinely 18 T&C PUELLA MEA   80
    Always-- or possibly there drift a pulseless blur of . . . . 218 XLI SONNETS 14   12
    a universe of gulls' drift Of thickly starhums wherefore . . 371 VIVA 62   22
    by millions and dreaming drift hundreds come swimming (Each . 630 (CHAIRE) 32   6
    and to ghosts go drift slippery hands tease slim . . . . . 633 (CHAIRE) 35   5
    hugest) dooms of miracle drift killed swim born a . . . . . . 757 95 POEMS 85   33
    and cities to eyes) drift bells glide seethe glow . . . . . . 841 73 POEMS 69   21
+DRIFT
    FOR CONTEXT, SEE . . . . 655 (CHAIRE) 57   6
DRIFTED
    the world's texture with drifted gifts of featheriest . . . . 299 IS 5 FOUR 16   4
DRIFTING
    ghosts-of-love which scarcely sings drifting in slow . . . .   6 T&C EPITHALAM   144
    my very frail lady drifting distinctly, moving like a . . . . 17 T&C PUELLA MEA   18
    has) the weightless svelte drifting sexual feather of your . 140 & SON REAL 11   2
    imagined a few cries drifting through high air a . . . . . . 283 IS 5 THREE 7   5
    to me your mind drifting with chuckling rubbish of . . . . . 369 VIVA 60   4
    alive down while crylessly drifting through vast most . . . . 661 (CHAIRE) 63   13
+DRIFTING
    FOR CONTEXT, SEE . . . . 677 95 POEMS 5   10
DRIFTS
    dust n'est-ce pas effendi drifts between tables like an . . . 198 XLI PORTRAIT 6   15
    (quietly with bright eyes) drifts (nobody can tell because . 286 IS 5 FOUR 3   5
    pants inani nvisible Fist) drifts a long conway 's . . . . . 616 (CHAIRE) 18   10

DRINK
    nine ladies his lips drink water but his heart . . . . 15 T&C SONGS 5   7
    won't you have a drink? (the eternal perpetual question) . . 97 & POST IMPR 8 41
    don't make soup who drink. / / / / . . . . 141 & SON REAL 12 18
    come in together and drink coffee covered with froth . . . . 198 XLI PORTRAIT 6 32
    sentience whose papillae expertly drink the docile . . . . . 201 XLI PORTRAIT 9 17
    intelligence to buy a drink and when you're flush . . . . . . 204 XLI LA GUERRE 2 11
    tasting of hellas, i drink, or sometimes two remarking . . . 217 XLI SONNETS 13 11
    in the corner and drink thinks and think drinks, ... 233 IS 5 ONE 4   16
    Carl Swinburned. Waiter a drink waiter two or three . . . . . 233 IS 5 ONE 4   20
    question how do i drink dream smile and how . . . . 295 IS 5 FOUR 12 14
    darkness of cafes people drink smile if here there . . . . . 340 VIVA 31   8
    casts no shadow D drink and E eat of . . . . 390 NO THANKS 7   3
    tell us how we drink crawl eat walk die . . . . 528 50 POEMS 40   4
    at which crazy they drink who've climbed steeper than . . . . 563 1 X 1 23   2
DRINKING
    in the din thinking drinking the ale, which never . . . . . . 96 & POST IMPR 8 23
DRINKS
    water but his heart drinks wine the tenth lady . . . . 15 T&C SONGS 5   8
    doth amass for whoso drinks, a dizzier wine than . . . . . . 21 T&C PUELLA MEA 199
    drink thinks and think drinks, in memory of the . . . . . . 233 IS 5 ONE 4   16
    waiter two or three drinks what's become of Maeterlinck . . . 233 IS 5 ONE 4   20
    he cannot understand, he drinks (and he drinks and . . . . 406 NO THANKS 23   7
    he drinks (and he drinks and he drinks and . . . . 406 NO THANKS 23   8
    he drinks and he drinks and he drinks and) . . . . 406 NO THANKS 23   8
    he drinks and he drinks and) not bald. (Coughs.) . . . . . 406 NO THANKS 23   8
DRIPPED
    mad street whose mouth dripped with slavver of spring . . . . 194 XLI PORTRAIT 2   5
DRIVE
    them in thy breath drive them in nothingness for . . . . . . 41 T&C AMORES 5   21
    (ne i) nobody else drive dumb mankind dizzy with . . . . . . 804 73 POEMS 32   9
DRIVEN
    goats and sheep are driven by somebody along a . . . . 281 IS 5 THREE 5   8
    climb the best hill, driven by black wine. a . . . . 434 NO THANKS 51   7
DRIVES
    of sound and odour drives the wingless thing man . . . . . .   4 T&C EPITHALAM 60
DRIVING
    structure of distinct sunset driving white spikes of silence 378 VIVA 69   9
DRIZZLE
    gas. Flynn" the words drizzle untidily from released cheeks . 226 IS 5 ONE MAME 9
DROLL
    soul half-beautiful and wholly droll is as some smooth . . . 11 T&C SONGS 2   2
    the foolish breasts the droll mouth wilted and not . . . . . 52 T&C PORTRAIT 1 30
    of shadowy light the droll snowing delirium (we do . . . . . 168 & SON ACTU 17   5
    just where strove the droll god-beasts do thou distinctly . . 213 XLI SONNETS 9   9
DROLLS
    to time by clever drolls fearsomely who do keep . . . . 74 T&C SON REAL 5 10
DRONE
    to thread the fattish drone of I Want a . . . . 140 & SON REAL 11 12
DROOL
    the mmmoon, begins to, drool softly, in the hot . . . . 167 & SON ACTU 16 16
+DROOL
    FOR CONTEXT, SEE . . . . 303 IS 5 FIVE 2   6
+DROOLERY
    FOR CONTEXT, SEE . . . . 646 (CHAIRE) 48   7
DROOLING
    (now -fed infantile eyes drooling unmind grim yessing . . . . 337 VIVA 28   6
+DROOLINGLY
    FOR CONTEXT, SEE . . . . 408 NO THANKS 25   8
DROOP
    truth (from hang from droop w ar pin g . . . . 415 NO THANKS 32 12
DROOPED
    when in my fingers drooped your shining body when . . . . . . 39 T&C AMORES 4 13
    me: pummeling the curtains, drooped to a purr... i . . . . . 228 IS 5 ONE MARJ 14
DROOPING
    conclude happeningly the unfirm drooping bloated calves i . . 229 IS 5 ONE FRAN   5
DROOPNEW
    Comes; : lush ly-smooTHdumb droopnew-gree N. lyestmostsaresl 342 VIVA 33   24

		PAGE	TITLE	LINE
DROOPS				
accurate boy mouth now droops the faun head now		54	T&C PORTRAIT 2	9
longness of the year droops with things dead athwart		207	XLI SONNETS 3	6
lark who; rises, and; droops as if upon a		434	NO THANKS 51	20
if time totters, light droops, all measures bend nor		446	NO THANKS 61	6
DROP				
castle wall glided, a drop of radiance, to the		8	T&C OF NICOL	24
ingPeaceful furious street people drop, coppers into, the . .		100	& POST IMPR 11	39
field watchin four crows drop into sunset, playin uh		332	VIVA 23	31
elevate your tool but drop a penny in the		500	50 POEMS 14	11
d fall which now drop who all dreamlike (im		536	50 POEMS 48	20
DROPP				
off a pane) the (dropp ingspinson his back mad)		692	95 POEMS 20	2
DROPPED				
's left crashed pal dropped o god alice yells		496	50 POEMS 10	6
if out of midnight dropped more suns than are		576	1 X 1 36	12
+DROPPED				
FOR CONTEXT, SEE		430	NO THANKS 47	17
FOR CONTEXT, SEE		487	50 POEMS 1	10
DROPPE5				
&Isdensekil- ◇ ruptingly) ca-y-est droppe5 qu'est-ce que tu		430	NO THANKS 47	17
DROPPING				
of a mouth, huge dropping of a flesh from		133	& SON REAL 4	15
/ / she sits dropping on a caret of		143	& SON REAL 14	1
the jolly shells begin dropping jolly fast you hear		269	IS 5 TWO 4	4
+DROPPING				
FOR CONTEXT, SEE		692	95 POEMS 20	2
DROPPINGLY				
chatters about Peacepeacepeace (to droppingly descend amid .		267	IS 5 TWO 2	8
DROPS				
off and a faint piddle-of-drops she says I ploc		96	& POST IMPR 8	14
when the first guy drops you know everybody feels		272	IS 5 TWO 7	4
having wrestled with) man drops into his own paradise		558	1 X 1 18	2
DROPSIN				
& (all during the dropsin king god my sic		646	(CHAIRE) 48	2
DROVE				
who, his april touch drove sleeping selves to swarm		520	50 POEMS 34	11
DROWN				
while the slippery eyes drown in surging flesh). A		226	IS 5 ONE MAME	4
(in darkly taking rain) drown, beyond sound down (slowly . .		432	NO THANKS 49	3
DROWNED				
breasts gargled by death: drowned only again carefully . . .		369	VIVA 60	10
ghost goes under, his drowned girth are mountains; and . . .		418	NO THANKS 35	12
are hanged and oceans drowned, the single secret will		560	1 X 1 20	7
shallbe and was are drowned by prodigious a now		841	73 POEMS 69	10
DROWNING				
subtle manner or by drowning himself in the watertank		239	IS 5 ONE 10	26
thus excluding a leanderless drowning in sub (at the		546	1 X 1 6	7
with a wraith) ghosts drowning in supreme thunder? ours . . .		639	(CHAIRE) 41	2
DROWNINSOUND				
all the roofs roar drownInsound(& (we (are like)		347	VIVA 38	19
DROWNS				
unimaginable upward lark and drowns the earth and passes . .		5	T&C EPITHALAM	80
DROWSY				
as an opening lily drowsy-fair (when from her couch		8	T&C OF NICOL	12
and a muddy petticoat, drowsy is your mouth your		61	T&C PORTRAIT 9	13
thrush half-angel and your drowsy lips where float flowers .		186	XLI SONGS 8	11
DROWSY-FAIR				
as an opening lily drowsy-fair (when from her couch		8	T&C OF NICOL	12
DRUB				
wilting wall the colour drub souring sunbeams, of a		144	& SON REAL 15	1
DRUG				
passion willed, freedom a drug that's bought and sold		521	50 POEMS 34	56
DRUM				
been deposited upon the drum there is need of		196	XLI PORTRAIT 4	11
DRUNK				
n i s ell drunk if i be pencils		703	95 POEMS 31	19

	PAGE	TITLE	LINE

+DRUNK
    FOR CONTEXT, SEE 53   T&C PORTRAIT 1   50
    FOR CONTEXT, SEE 705   95 POEMS 33   8
DRUNKARD
    sawdust Voices a: whispering drunkard passes who knows if . . 128   & SEVEN POEMS 6   6
DRUNKEN
    idiot, whispering like a drunken man who (at a 304   IS 5 FIVE 3   3
+DRUNKENLY
    FOR CONTEXT, SEE 695   95 POEMS 23   9
DRUNKENNESS
    up with laughing and drunkenness) here's to one 424   NO THANKS 41   11
DRUNKER
    smoothness. People stare, the drunker applaud while twilight 279   IS 5 THREE 3   17
DRYAD
    cloven feet the shrieking dryad sought her leafy goal, . . . 3   T&C EPITHALAM   14
DU
    the triple starred Hotel du Golf... that notable structure . 319   VIVA 11   22
DUCKBILLED
    Bull's T.P. and the duckbilled platitude lays & lays 321   VIVA 13   15
DUCKING
    5' 1", white, prostitute. ducking always the touch of 74   T&C SON REAL 5   2
DUDE
    joint. Jimmie was a dude. Dark hair and nice 149   & SON REAL 20   5
DUH
    released cheeks "I'll tell duh woild; some noive all 226   IS 5 ONE MAME   10
    sim ply don't know duh meanin uv duh woid 240   IS 5 ONE 11   2
    know duh meanin uv duh woid sin in not 240   IS 5 ONE 11   2
    / / oil tel duh woil doi sez dooyuh 310   VIVA 2   1
    buncha hardboil guys frum duh A.C. fulla hooch kiddin 332   VIVA 23   1
    hooch kiddin eachudder bout duh clap an talkin big 332   VIVA 23   2
    uh gun on Marcus"-- "duh Swede rolls down tree 332   VIVA 23   8
    begins boxin im on duh koib" --you know alotta 332   VIVA 23   9
    feels so lonely fer duh good ole days we 332   VIVA 23   14
    spent in '18 kickin duh guts outa dem doity 332   VIVA 23   15
    doity frogeaters an humpin duh swell janes on duh 332   VIVA 23   16
    duh swell janes on duh boollevares an wid tears 332   VIVA 23   18
    an offers it tuh duh whole gang accrost duh 332   VIVA 23   20
    duh whole gang accrost duh table-- "fellers have some 332   VIVA 23   21
DULL
    shrill colour, clutched the dull volume of her tumbling . . . 73   T&C SON REAL 4   5
    lice about god's capable dull important head-- by on 85   T&C SON ACTU 4   4
    shivers ofcrin Ging stink. dull, gobular glows and flatchatte 94   & POST IMPR 6   11
    (with the uncouth habitual dull jerk at garters) there . . . 227   IS 5 ONE GERT   9
    has been coarse and dull compared with you, silently 301   IS 5 FOUR 18   8
    which can be as dull as one englishman A: 468   NEW POEMS 6   3
    the godless are the dull and the dull are 499   50 POEMS 13   14
    the dull and the dull are the damned / 499   50 POEMS 13   14
    pinnacle of am though dull were all we taste 521   50 POEMS 34   61
    they come until (over dull all nouns) begins a 557   1 X 1 17   13
    tall) all except the dull ones gus loves all 619   (CHAIRE) 21   14
    / who sharpens every dull here comes the only 624   (CHAIRE) 26   1
    innocence refuted) clumsy some dull cowardice called a world 669   (CHAIRE) 71   12
    timid & loathing for (dull all regular righteous comfortable) 677   95 POEMS 5   6
    kill is astir-- now dull eyes are keen and 769   95 POEMS 95   10
    do is exactly theirs (dull worlds or keen; big 776   73 POEMS 4   11
DULLNESS
    the mystical moment of dullness emphatically are Not To . . . 230   IS 5 ONE 2   22
DULLY
    greyly shall fail and dully disappear-- but the proud 649   (CHAIRE) 51   12
DULUTH
    not enthusiastic cohorts from Duluth God only, gondola knows 256   IS 5 ONE 27   27
DULY
    being of which assertions duly notified threw the 339   VIVA 30   35
DUMB
    tiny troubadours, and (phantom-white) dumb-blooming boughs . 8   T&C OF NICOL   6
    lover stands in the dumb dark svelte and urgent 37   T&C AMORES 2   12
    shores as out of dumb strong hands infinite the 64   T&C POST IMPR 1   5
    your heart pinched from dumb summer? O crazy daddy 80   T&C SON UNRE 5   8

	PAGE	TITLE	LINE

DUMB (CONTINUED)
which lock me seriously. Dumb for a while. my . . . . 133 & SON REAL 4 13
sweetness steal slowly in dumb blossoms of new mingling: . . 139 & SON REAL 10 4
the expensively democratic tyrannically dumb Awake, chaos: we 337 VIVA 28 14
stopped A) with! notgirl'swith? dumb (thewith girl) ness (ish 388 NO THANKS 5 24
me are picked from dumb sleePdeep ness squirmcurl ing . . . . 395 NO THANKS 12 14
deafer than neither was dumb. Skip fred (jump! neddy) . . . . 513 50 POEMS 27 28
fantastic nor pathological but dumb. The number of times . . 514 50 POEMS 28 5
sweet, maggoty minus and dumb death all we inherit, ... 521 50 POEMS 34 63
this is a deaf dumb church and blind with . . . . 647 {CHAIRE} 49 11
who was anything but dumb; since the silence of . . . . 802 73 POEMS 30 26
i) nobody else drive dumb mankind dizzy with haranguing . . . 804 73 POEMS 32 9
+DUMB
FOR CONTEXT, SEE . . . . 268 IS 5 TWO 3 6
FOR CONTEXT, SEE . . . . 342 VIVA 33 24
FOR CONTEXT, SEE . . . . 519 50 POEMS 33 8
DUMB-BLOOMING
tiny troubadours, and (phantom-white) dumb-blooming boughs . 8 T&C OF NICOL 6
DUMBLY
futility" And sit huddling dumbly behind three or two . . . . 354 VIVA 45 18
DUMBNESS
will slowly roam my dumbNess? her other, wet, warm . . . . . 137 & SON REAL 8 6
+DUMBNESS
FOR CONTEXT, SEE . . . . 388 NO THANKS 5 24
DUMBS
sails whose mighty brightness dumbs the utterance of his . . 79 T&C SON UNRE 4 9
DUMDAM
make me glad) dis dumdam slamslum slopp idy wurl . . . . . . 519 50 POEMS 33 8
DUMP
out on the sunny dump of oblivion) a tiny . . . . 197 XLI PORTRAIT 5 22
DUN
the oblivious west's numerous dun magnificence conquers . . . 6 T&C EPITHALAM 127
+DUNCE
FOR CONTEXT, SEE . . . . 763 95 POEMS 90 10
DUNEYED
into the dark so duneyed master enter the sweet . . . . 188 XLI SONGS 10 13
DUNGEON
the yellowsonofabitch into a dungeon, where he died Christ . 339 VIVA 30 37
DUNNO
into the tree? I dunno said the silver dog, ... 125 & SEVEN POEMS 4 15
DURATION
pretend --grim comics of duration: only love immortally . . . 576 1 X 1 36 7
DURING
old etcetera aunt lucy during the recent war could . . . . . 276 IS 5 TWO 10 2
say to Miss Gay during our return voyage, my . . . . 326 VIVA 18 31
/ / & (all during the dropsin king god . . . . 646 {CHAIRE} 48 1
shall be some darkness during which fingers are without . . . 667 {CHAIRE} 69 9
DUSK
but the incurious curtaining dusk be drawn surpassing nets . 5 T&C EPITHALAM 85
mirror and it is dusk on earth a candle . . . . 50 T&C IMPRESS 4 24
for themselves, when passionately dusk brings softly down the 71 T&C SON REAL 2 9
your smiles accuse the dusk with an untimid svelte . . . . . 138 & SON REAL 9 5
pash possibly because . dusk and if it perhaps . . . . 155 & SON ACTU 4 3
the trafficing hum of dusk each street takes of . . . . 168 & SON ACTU 17 3
nerves sumptuously wink ....and little-dusk has his toys to . 169 & SON ACTU 18 9
sticky moon opening in dusk her new wings then . . . . 170 & SON ACTU 19 3
/ / one April dusk the sallow street-lamps were . . . . 194 XLI PORTRAIT 2 1
shalt stand. Nor any dusk but kneelingly believes thy . . . . 351 VIVA 42 13
which are transferred with dusk) wondering why this star . . 428 NO THANKS 45 4
/ / / at dusk just when the Light . . . . 434 NO THANKS 51 1
sunset or thrushes toward dusk among whippoorwills or tree . 512 50 POEMS 26 25
if (as what was dusk becomes darkness) innumerably singular . 741 95 POEMS 69 1
DUSKIEST
man from himself ye duskiest despot's goldenest gal did . . . 552 1 X 1 12 16
DUST
citharede wags in the dust the ghastly warriors amber . . . . 34 T&C ORIENTALE 6 97
one stars flutter into dust but the sea does . . . . 38 T&C AMORES 3 8
formal spasm in the dust this is the passing . . . . 41 T&C AMORES 5 9

		PAGE	TITLE	LINE
DUST (CONTINUED)				
of men to golden dust: she pauses on the	. . . .	75	T&C SON REAL 6	11
fields with the superior dust-of-sleep. wields easily the	. .	163	& SON ACTU 12	4
of oblivion) a tiny dust finely arising at the	. . . . . .	197	XLI PORTRAIT 5	23
just the playthings for dust n'est-ce pas effendi drifts	. .	198	XLI PORTRAIT 6	14
on our ways to dust of your fragility (but	. . . .	293	IS 5 FOUR 10	14
nothing children go of dust / / / /	. . . .	661	{CHAIRE} 63	14
White&Gold daisy in the Dust (trite now and old)	. . . . . .	690	95 POEMS 18	2
/ / plant Magic dust expect hope doubt (wonder	. . . .	780	73 POEMS 8	1
DUST-OF-SLEEP				
fields with the superior dust-of-sleep. wields easily the	. .	163	& SON ACTU 12	4
DUSTILY				
longness of autumn smile dustily to the people, for	. . . . .	190	XLI SONGS 12	20
DUSTY				
into tears, as the dusty new- ness of her	. . . .	148	& SON REAL 19	11
sentiments brings to light dusty heroisms and finally	. . . .	203	XLI LA GUERRE 1	8
DUTY				
father's joy, unto whom duty whispers low "thou must!"	. . .	273	IS 5 TWO 8	4
or must be off duty wanderfuling aft spits) int	. . . .	465	NEW POEMS 3	4
DWELL				
thy fortunate fingers sometime dwell (within a greener shadow		3	T&C EPITHALAM	21
DWELLS				
her voice which always dwells beside the vivid magical	. . .	19	T&C PUELLA MEA	115
thy unimaginable wings, where dwells the breath of all	. . .	40	T&C AMORES 4	46
next door but three dwells; a (ghost) Who screams	. . . . . .	312	VIVA 4	7
DWELT				
heavenly realms of hellas dwelt two very different sons	. . .	799	73 POEMS 27	1
DWINDLED				
unday life's bright less dwindled to a leastful most	. . . .	432	NO THANKS 49	13
DWO				
/ / / Q: dwo we know of anything	. . . .	468	NEW POEMS 6	1
DWRITH				
qu'est-ce que tu veux Dwrith il est trop fort	. . . .	430	NO THANKS 47	19
DYING				
/ the rose is dying the lips of an	. . . .	59	T&C PORTRAIT 7	2
answer modestly i am dying so let us come	. . . .	198	XLI PORTRAIT 6	30
abruptly wholly hugs our dying silent minds, which hand	. . .	305	IS 5 FIVE 4	9
win ter who sit dying thinking huddled behind dir	. . . . . .	354	VIVA 45	4
item i immaculately owe dying one life and will	. . . .	390	NO THANKS 7	13
/ / who before dying demands not rebirth of	. . . .	402	NO THANKS 19	1
weigh a star --dreads dying least; and less, that	. . . . . .	446	NO THANKS 61	8
to succeed in not dying) Is will still occur;	. . . .	452	NO THANKS 67	12
so much greenness only dying makes us grow /	. . . .	491	50 POEMS 5	16
(by a gift called dying born) must grow deep	. . . .	556	1 X 1 16	12
/ / / / dying is fine) but Death	. . . .	604	{CHAIRE} 6	1
to feel of it, dying 's miraculous why? be	. . . .	604	{CHAIRE} 6	10
miraculous why? be cause dying is perfectly natural;	. . . .	604	{CHAIRE} 6	13
thee god almighty for dying (forgive us, o life!	. . . . . .	604	{CHAIRE} 6	24
silent! ly living the dying of glory / /	. . . .	627	{CHAIRE} 29	16
and a time for dying: a night for silence	. . . .	683	95 POEMS 11	11
/ / but also dying (as well as to	. . . .	686	95 POEMS 14	1
life is not worth dying, if (and when) roses	. . . .	744	95 POEMS 72	2
revealed (more than all dying life, all living death)	. . . .	765	95 POEMS 91	7
vanishes with also earth's --"dying" the ghost of you	. . . .	808	73 POEMS 36	14
love, to merely what dying must call life are	. . . .	818	73 POEMS 46	14
heavens for just one dying, i'll give you" silently	. . . . .	837	73 POEMS 65	14
+DYING				
FOR CONTEXT, SEE	. . . .	334	VIVA 25	7
DYING'S				
more black keenest than dying's keener each will kissed	. . .	565	1 X 1 25	11
is more now than dying's when / / /	. . . .	592	1 X 1 52	14
roses will answer" "but dying's meanwhile" (mind murmurs; the		625	{CHAIRE} 27	15
(almost too small for dying's huge because) given much	. . .	735	95 POEMS 63	10
DYINGEST				
all fear --all perfectly dyingest my and foreverless thy?	. .	590	1 X 1 50	23
DYINGS				
all life's busy little dyings may possess) how sincere	. . .	418	NO THANKS 35	4

	PAGE	TITLE	LINE

DYNAMITE
  apart and masturbate with dynamite the boys i mean . . . . . 427 NO THANKS 44   12
  scamper (you bastards throw dynamite) let knowings magic with 452 NO THANKS 67   5
+DYNAMITE
  FOR CONTEXT, SEE . . . . 430 NO THANKS 47   10
E
  Abraham Lincoln and Lydia E. Pinkham, land above all . . . . 230 IS 5 ONE 2   11
  Wouldwoe Washington to Lydia E. McKinley when Buch tooked . . 321 VIVA 13   6
  destructivity to non- entities e. g. the) whis-per it . . . . 391 NO THANKS 8   24
  r-p-o-p-h-e-s-s-a-g-r who a)s w(e loo)k . . . . 396 NO THANKS 13   1
  (mo) b, i; l: e FallleA ps! fl OattumblI . . . . 655 (CHAIRE) 57   2
  trees) dodreamingly phantoms (exchanging) e vero madonna . . 681 95 POEMS 9   6
  dim i nu tiv e this park is e . . . . 696 95 POEMS 24   5
E'ER
  of the flowers --didst e'er depart upon more exquisite   . . .   3 T&C EPITHALAM   20
EACH
  throne twain sphinxes bear each with a writhing youth . . . .   4 T&C EPITHALAM   42
  my body be From each brave eye shall sprout . . . . 16 T&C SONGS 6   2
  lady dead and gone.) Each tapering breast is firm . . . . . . 21 T&C PUELLA MEA 181
  has perfect bliss-- for each breast a blossom is, ... 21 T&C PUELLA MEA 190
  of the world's queen: each is a verb, miraculous . . . . . . 21 T&C PUELLA MEA 209
  might any monarch please.) Each ankle is divinely shy; . . . 21 T&C PUELLA MEA 215
  scimitars like windy torches each is blacker than oblivion . 33 T&C ORIENTALE 6   40
  i have offered up each fragrant night, when all . . . . 39 T&C AMORES 4   30
  heapingandsqueezing tum-bling- scratchingcrowd ingworming . . 100 & POST IMPR 11   14
  ingworming each by screetching Each) on either side the . . . 100 & POST IMPR 11   15
  strolls emitting minute grins each an intaglio. Nothing has . 116 & PORTRAIT 9   7
  her, merrily we became each other humped to tumbling   . . . . 119 & PORTRAIT 11   11
  sit there looking at each other having the fastest . . . . . 126 & SEVEN POEMS 5   6
  pinch assiduously which justgraze each other). As the lady . 150 & SON REAL 21   10
  the sincere stomach of each mill of the ingenious . . . . . . 165 & SON ACTU 14   12
  trafficing hum of dusk each street takes of shadowy . . . . . 168 & SON ACTU 17   4
  that) they look at each other. Nudge. (if they . . . . 171 & SON ACTU 20   10
  Nudge. (if they love each other, who cares?) They . . . . . . 171 & SON ACTU 20   11
  edge. So until light each having each we promised . . . . . . 173 & SON ACTU 22   12
  until light each having each we promised to forget-- . . . . 173 & SON ACTU 22   12
  bodies (eagerly just not each other touch) seeking, some . . 174 & SON ACTU 23   5
  Jumpy Tramp who played each card as if it . . . . 194 XLI PORTRAIT 2   22
  let us now sing each and all fortissimo A- . . . . 230 IS 5 ONE 2   36
  spry concernin questions arty each has his tastes but . . . . 247 IS 5 ONE 18   3
  let us investigate thoroughly each one his optima rerum . . . 261 IS 5 ONE 31   11
  to measure Spring with? each dream nascitur, is not . . . . . 264 IS 5 ONE 33   29
  immaculate unmute antibolshevistic gents (each manufacturing 266 IS 5 TWO 1   10
  worst, of peril heedless, each braver than the other, ... 266 IS 5 TWO 1   19
  braver than the other, each (a typewriter within his . . . . 266 IS 5 TWO 1   19
  me, we smiled to each other, releasing lay, watching . . . . 283 IS 5 THREE 7   21
  white longest hands neatening each crease) will smooth . . . 288 IS 5 FOUR 5   4
  says we are for each other: then laugh, leaning . . . . 290 IS 5 FOUR 7   13
  kiss throw silently things Each at other (if not . . . . . . 312 VIVA 4   13
  found with Holes in each other 's lullaby and . . . . 317 VIVA 9   27
  glass-- are: asking. ? each oth? er rub, ! . . . . 319 VIVA 11   36
  believes thy secret and each morning stoops to blend . . . . 351 VIVA 42   14
  squirms stars Trees, swift each with its Own motion . . . . . 356 VIVA 47   8
  dream if we love each (shyly) other, what clouds . . . . . . 363 VIVA 54   9
  death and forever with each breathing (i do not . . . . 366 VIVA 57   16
  alseep while we were each other disappeared: but i . . . . . . 370 VIVA 61   16
  air) breathe simply my each how my trembling where . . . . . 372 VIVA 63   4
  sharpening life are (behind each no) touching every yes . . . 373 VIVA 64   18
  smooth vigilant perpetual eyes each exact victim, how he . . 386 NO THANKS 3   11
  less with every least most remembering H highest . . . . . . 390 NO THANKS 7   7
  generous) don't All suspect each (nor have i observed . . . . 391 NO THANKS 8   4
  moves remembers is afraid) each hates a Man whom . . . . . . 394 NO THANKS 11   9
  did) who begins stuttering each sentence we both consid . . . 398 NO THANKS 15   10
  bed bed bed) when each other courted both was . . . . 401 NO THANKS 18   4
  famous fatheads find that each and every thing must . . . . . 411 NO THANKS 28   1
  of whose mad skill each world of blood is . . . . 424 NO THANKS 41   13
  discovered be) whose ignorant each breathing dares to hide . 446 NO THANKS 61   11
  magic with bright credos each divisible fool (life imitate . 452 NO THANKS 67   7

EACH (CONTINUED)
    most memory) give entirely each Forever its freedom (Dare . . 453 NO THANKS 68   11
    sprouted by alive green each very lifting & seriously . . . . 480 NEW POEMS 18   24
    this tear jumping from each most least eye of . . . .   502 50 POEMS 16   4
    trembling out of huge each eye look "thank you" . . . . 506 50 POEMS 20   12
    dimension of him whose each foot likes the here . . . . . .   512 50 POEMS 26   6
    haves of give, singing each morning out of each . . . . . .   520 50 POEMS 34   3
    each morning out of each night my father moved . . . . . .   520 50 POEMS 34   3
    theys of we, singing each new leaf out of . . . .   521 50 POEMS 34   50
    new leaf out of each tree (and every child . . . .   521 50 POEMS 34   50
    will whitely yearn from each last shore and home . . . . .   526 50 POEMS 38   8
    unkindest way to kill each of those creatures called . . . . 528 50 POEMS 40   12
    whole uplifting the, of each where all was is . . . .   533 50 POEMS 45   7
    falling both locked in each down a thief by . . . .   533 50 POEMS 45   20
    round as to find. Each why of a leaf . . . .   543 1 X 1 3   7
    a leaf says (floating each how) you're which as . . . . . .   543 1 X 1 3   8
    which as to die (each green of a new) . . . .   543 1 X 1 3   10
    an eternal now welcomes each was of whom among . . . . . .   558 1 X 1 18   5
    this (most common, for each anguish is his grief; . . . . .   562 1 X 1 22   3
    mountains more if than each known allness disappears lovers . 563 1 X 1 23   5
    keenest than dying's keener each will kissed breast awake) .   565 1 X 1 25   12
    wait) buds imitate upward each first flower of two . . . .   573 1 X 1 33   23
    shy wings of because; each why of star (afloat . . . . . .   575 1 X 1 35   18
    / true lovers in each happening of their hearts . . . . . .   576 1 X 1 36   1
    any now and her each here is such an . . . .   576 1 X 1 36   10
    / / we love each other very dearly , ...   577 1 X 1 37   1
    of whens) before each heartbeat which i am . . . .   577 1 X 1 37   20
    dance (and does with each your least your any . . . .   580 1 X 1 40   2
    limb explodes and o each living ablaze greenly thing . . . . 583 1 X 1 43   13
    can count his leaves each herself by opening but . . . . .   591 1 X 1 51   18
    --but beauty is more each than living's all multiplied . . . 592 1 X 1 52   4
    fall (with a shout each around we go all) . . . .   594 1 X 1 54   34
    strolling right through these each illimit able to speak . . 600 (CHAIRE) 2   13
    million many worlds in each least less than particle . . . . 603 (CHAIRE) 5   1
    many fiends and gods each greedier than every) is . . . . .   609 (CHAIRE) 11   2
    unreal in -credible true each new self) smile. Eyes. . . . . 612 (CHAIRE) 14   6
    he's young with mysteries (each truly his more than . . . .   617 (CHAIRE) 19   10
    of mirror lying are each (why do people say . . . .   623 (CHAIRE) 25   5
    life a mere pastime --each joy a deceiver, and . . . . . .   625 (CHAIRE) 27   19
    am. Look at these (each serenely welcoming his only . . . .   626 (CHAIRE) 28   7
    destiny) mountains! how can each" while flame crashed "be . . 626 (CHAIRE) 28   9
    and i and who? each grows" then in a . . . .   626 (CHAIRE) 28   10
    drift hundreds come swimming (Each a keener secret than . . . 630 (CHAIRE) 32   7
    more mostful to arrive each (futuring snowily which sprints . 639 (CHAIRE) 41   11
    laws) laugh, and make each no thy yes: love; . . . .   651 (CHAIRE) 53   10
    in hatred pity fear each more exactly than the . . . . . .   662 (CHAIRE) 64   10
    so right is, all (each thing most lovely) sweet . . . . . .   666 (CHAIRE) 68   2
    have people; and more each particular person is (my . . . .   667 (CHAIRE) 69   3
    are (any more than each leafless) its silent in . . . . . .   667 (CHAIRE) 69   11
    whispershout) laugh matching onceupons each bothing (if) . . 681 95 POEMS 9   9
    silence is becom ing each truebeautifully more-than-thing (& 715 95 POEMS 43   17
    none) boy after girl each brings a world to . . . .   716 95 POEMS 44   11
    someone's heart at your each nearerness) everyone certainly . 717 95 POEMS 45   12
    moment day thankfully become each other) one who feels . . . 720 95 POEMS 48   6
    a (who is neither each both and) Self adventures . . . . .   721 95 POEMS 49   13
    nonillion (& so) nothings each (let's kiss) means home . . . 725 95 POEMS 53   14
    immortal friends the other's each / / / / . . . .   730 95 POEMS 58   6
    to tell me this --each luckiest of lucky days . . . .   734 95 POEMS 62   2
    farthest silence nearer than each our heartbeat--believe that 741 95 POEMS 69   4
    some upward world of each more most prodigious Selves . . .   757 95 POEMS 85   7
    terror) steep not guessable each infinite Oblivions found a . 757 95 POEMS 85   23
    you for me for each leaf newer than can . . . .   760 95 POEMS 87   10
    leaf--here's one more than each creature new (except your . . 762 95 POEMS 89   6
    was playing at birthdays each (a wish no bigger . . . . . .   763 95 POEMS 90   7
    of your treasure blithe each shameless blithe each shameless 763 95 POEMS 90   37
    blithe each shameless blithe each shameless gaiety of blossom 764 95 POEMS 90   37
    --blissfully nonchalant wise and each ignorant . . . . . .   764 95 POEMS 90   40
    fatal --a heart her each petal / / / . . . .   764 95 POEMS 90   54

EACH (CONTINUED)

shadows (quick to seize each nothing which all soulless . . . 765 95 POEMS 91   3
any merry every pretty each bird sings birds sing . . . . . . 773 73 POEMS 1   3
with slender their ladies (Each youngest) in sunlight / . . . 778 73 POEMS 6 24
lovers a chieve oneness) each othering Selves i sit . . . . . 785 73 POEMS 13 14
(as all as can each) they don't and they . . . . 801 73 POEMS 29   8
may) certainly while mute each inch of their murdered . . . . 808 73 POEMS 36 10
certainly earth swims than each my deeper death becomes . . . 810 73 POEMS 38   8
and let her heart's each whisper wear all never . . . . 811 73 POEMS 39   6
a different time, and each most falsely true; or . . . . . . 817 73 POEMS 45   2
under any silence of each bird who dares to . . . . 821 73 POEMS 49   7
fingers numb) with anguished each their me brains of . . . . 822 73 POEMS 50   3
(dreamlike) st makes big each dim inuti ve turns . . . . . . 829 73 POEMS 57   3
endless end of briefer each our bliss-- where seeing . . . . 834 73 POEMS 62 26
you sweet joys for each of them But it . . . . 837 73 POEMS 65   4
mind contrives (but certainly each spirit is) and partially . 842 73 POEMS 70   8
many moments must (amazing each how many centuries) these . . 843 73 POEMS 71   1
of the universe --love. Each believing world denies, whereas 845 73 POEMS 73 11

EACHING

/ / / both eaching come ghostlike (inch) wraithish . . . . . 681 95 POEMS 9   1

EACHNESS

climbi ng i nto eachness begi n dizzily swingthings . . . . . 536 50 POEMS 48   4
reverently share the blessed eachness of all beautiful selves 745 95 POEMS 73 11

EACHS

you turns people into eachs and cowards into grow . . . . . . 537 50 POEMS 49   7

EACHUDDER

went runnin aroun wid eachudder Hell Bent fer election . . . 237 IS 5 ONE 8 18
A.C. fulla hooch kiddin eachudder bout duh clap an . . . . . 332 VIVA 23   2

EAGER

to that fee her eager body's unimmortal flower knew . . . . .   4 T&C EPITHALAM 55
a hurled dream down eager avenues of lifelessness consider . 81 T&C SON UNRE 6   6
of smooth, fruits of eager colours of the little, ... 100 & POST IMPR 11 21
and its chords brittle eager eternal luminous firmly . . . . 110 & PORTRAIT 6 26
to mesh. New and eager. wittily peels the. ploop. . . . . . . 136 & SON REAL 7 13
the jouncing fruit of eager bosoms" Wing Wong / . . . . 341 VIVA 32 21
syllable of the heart's eager dim enormous language loss . . 372 VIVA 63 11
child- man -god one eager souldoll one unsellable not . . . . 524 50 POEMS 36 43
forgivingly a once of eager glory, no more miracle . . . . . 601 (CHAIRE) 3   5
danc ing egghead strutstrolls eager a (twice by Dizzying . . 615 (CHAIRE) 17   5
mender of things with eager fingers (with patient eyes) . . . 660 (CHAIRE) 62   7
whispers that flower murmurs eager this "i will give . . . . 837 73 POEMS 65   7

EAGEREST

voices (whom lure an eagerest strict flame) demand the . . . 362 VIVA 53 10

EAGERLY

luminous stammer of bodies (eagerly just not each other . . . 174 & SON ACTU 23   5
of sudde nly perishing eagerly everyw here shutting . . . . . 646 (CHAIRE) 48 10
dead humblest and proudest eagerly wandering (equally all . . 661 (CHAIRE) 63   5
to imagine quite such eagerly innocent whoms of merciful . . 748 95 POEMS 76 13
kiss me) shy sweet eagerly my most dear (die! . . . . 767 95 POEMS 93   7
faces streets steeples are eagerly tumbl ing through wonder . 835 73 POEMS 63   6
tell you anything" (that eagerly sweet carolling self answers 836 73 POEMS 64   8

EAGLE

the Pheidian soul whose eagle frights creation, in whose . .   3 T&C EPITHALAM 27

EAKSPEASIES

helves surling out of eakspeasies per (reel) hapsingly . . . 330 VIVA 21   1

EAR

feet high behind whose ear sits always a crowned . . . . . . 32 T&C ORIENTALE 6   9
silence (put your smallest ear against yester- day My . . . . 110 & PORTRAIT 6 31
is Nile) put your ear to the ground there . . . . 113 & PORTRAIT 6 113
child. In thy your ear: en amerique on ne . . . . 233 IS 5 ONE 4   5
listen Venezia: incline thine ear you glassworks of Murano; . 256 IS 5 ONE 27   3
who, breathing on the ear of fate, landed a . . . . 266 IS 5 TWO 1 35
whispered again in never's ear (i'm tho thcared giggling . . 316 VIVA 8   5
ing) or it'll disapp ear bangl essly (into sweet . . . . . . 797 73 POEMS 25   8

EARL

the Arrow Ide and Earl & Wilson Collars) of . . . . 230 IS 5 ONE 2   8
AT THE RITZ WEAR earl & wilson COLLARS / . . . . 244 IS 5 ONE 15   5

PAGE   TITLE   LINE

EARLIER
   (but like some passionate earlier flower, the snow will . . . 21 T&C PUELLA MEA 187
EARLIEST
   been forever subject his Earliest word wheeled out on . . . . 197 XLI PORTRAIT 5   21
   be afraid-- here's the earliest star (have you a . . . . . . 357 VIVA 48   2
   love; but at the earliest spear of sun perfectly . . . . 377 VIVA 68   2
EARLY
   / Thy fingers make early flowers of all things. . . . . 13 T&C SONGS 3   1
   (of these two most early stars wincing upon a . . . . 98 & POST IMPR 9   6
   expression began with the early cessation of her skirt. . . . 103 & POST IMPR 13 6
   see by the dawn's early my country 'tis of . . . . 268 IS 5 TWO 3   3
   year: like this most early single star which tugs . . . . . . 305 IS 5 FIVE 4   5
   domains rare with most early soul him shall untouch . . . . . 402 NO THANKS 19   12
   girls) round and round early to better is wiser . . . . 513 50 POEMS 27   10
EARN
   man (who could not earn his bread because he . . . . 473 NEW POEMS 11   2
EARNING
   said "thought you were earning your living or probably . . . 313 VIVA 5   7
EARNS
   be glad; nobody ever earns anything, everything little looks 514 50 POEMS 28   7
EARS
   pearls kingdoms in her ears at the feet of . . . . 33 T&C ORIENTALE 6 68
   microscopic things in my ears scramble faintly tickling . . . 69 T&C POST IMPR 6 29
   of it get out ears dribbles soft right old . . . . 96 & POST IMPR 8   20
   is there anything my ears love it's to go . . . . 100 & POST IMPR 11 33
   of child- ren. my, ears know the fuZZy tune . . . . 100 & POST IMPR 11 36
   wrappedupbody Queerly Has, my, ears, go into Hassan's place . 100 & POST IMPR 11 41
   cuspidor-col ouredRoom and, my ears bend to the little . . . 101 & POST IMPR 11 45
   the blessed while His ears are crammed with the . . . . 117 & PORTRAIT 10   36
   you can see their ears. Ears win- k, funny . . . . 171 & SON ACTU 20   7
   can see their ears. Ears win- k, funny stable. . . . . 171 & SON ACTU 20   7
   a kewpie above the ears (but my uncle Ed . . . . 253 IS 5 ONE 24   10
   above their very tidiyum ears their very tidiyum necks . . . 274 IS 5 TWO 9   14
   poem a (with wee ears and see? tail frisks) . . . . 286 IS 5 FOUR 3   12
   were two glued uncarefully ears in that face a . . . . 355 VIVA 46 .   7
   incredible soft) ness (his ears (eyes / / / . . . . 397 NO THANKS 14   24
   merely (a pair of ears with some lips plus . . . . 501 50 POEMS 15   19
   night where his heartlike ears have flown adorable him . . . 631 (CHAIRE) 33   5
   unimaginable You? (now the ears of my ears awake . . . . . . 663 (CHAIRE) 65   13
   the ears of my ears awake and now the . . . . 663 (CHAIRE) 65   13
   eyes can feel but ears may see there never . . . . 760 95 POEMS 87   5
+EARS
   FOR CONTEXT, SEE . . . . 101 & POST IMPR 11 49
EARTH
   EPITHALAMION Thou aged unreluctant earth who dost with . . .   3 T&C EPITHALAM   1
   significant to the ecstatic earth in token of his . . . . . .   3 T&C EPITHALAM   10
   the eyes of ragged earth who sees them pass) . . . .   4 T&C EPITHALAM   69
   lark and drowns the earth and passes into light . . . .   5 T&C EPITHALAM   80
   we were chaste on earth we ghosts: hark to . . . .   9 T&C SONGS 1   22
   queens of all the earth and the rings upon . . . . 33 T&C ORIENTALE 6 46
   queens of all the earth writhe upon deep rugs . . . . 35 T&C ORIENTALE 6 116
   the world and the earth withers the moon crumbles . . . . . . 38 T&C AMORES 3   5
   also blandly into receptive earth, O let us descend . . . . . 41 T&C AMORES 5   14
   / O sweet spontaneous earth how often have the . . . . 46 T&C LA GUERRE 2 2
   walks scattering poems on earth a candle is extinguished . . 50 T&C IMPRESS 4   4
   it is dusk on earth a candle is lighted . . . . 50 T&C IMPRESS 4   24
   the head of the earth and all the trees . . . . 61 T&C PORTRAIT 9   20
   stop me but first earth , the reckless oral . . . . 67 T&C POST IMPR 4 4
   cold; and how much earth is Madge worth? Inquire . . . . . . 183 XLI SONGS 5   12
   shut eyes the sweet earth where thou liest / . . . . 184 XLI SONGS 6   17
   / / LA GUERRE earth like a tipsy biddy . . . . 203 XLI LA GUERRE 1 1
   mind and sweet uncaring earth by thoughtful war heaped . . . 213 XLI SONNETS 9   3
   resemble, descends into the earth with the year a . . . . . . 300 IS 5 FOUR 17   19
   All) Th (e grEEn ?eartH) N, ew / / . . . . 347 VIVA 38   34
   telling of death love earth dark) and thousand thrusts . . . 356 VIVA 47   5
   one small lady upon earth above; to whom i . . . . 360 VIVA 51   33
   sometimes, to make an earth gladly seem firm for . . . . . . 372 VIVA 63   8
   her spoor) over the earth wandering hunter whom you . . . . . 374 VIVA 65   8

	PAGE	TITLE	LINE
EARTH (CONTINUED)

leaf and, Opening beautiful earth put (only) a Leaf . . . . . 397 NO THANKS 14   15
cancels the childfully diminishing earth --never whose . . . 402 NO THANKS 19   4
where he ends, the earth (whose texture feels of . . . . . . 418 NO THANKS 35   1
place new fragrantly young earth space opening was. Were . . 432 NO THANKS 49   19
could no know: the earth tinily whirls; while daisies . . 451 NO THANKS 66   11
scratchily over which of earth dragged once -ful leaf. . . . 491 50 POEMS 5   2
when what hugs stopping earth than silent is more . . . . . . 502 50 POEMS 16   1
is so near the earth does not open her . . . . 505 50 POEMS 19   11
with voices made of earth and six are in . . . . 507 50 POEMS 21   8
the here of this earth whose both eyes love . . . . 512 50 POEMS 26   8
sleep noone and anyone earth by april wish by . . . . 515 50 POEMS 29   31
octobering flame beckoned) as earth will downward climb, so . 521 50 POEMS 34   42
god who spoke this earth so glad and big . . . . 526 50 POEMS 38   2
silence with a white earth in it you will . . . . 529 50 POEMS 41   2
(out of dark the earth) a procession of wonders . . . . . . 575 1 X 1 35   8
believing) a little gay earth opening is all the . . . . . . 583 1 X 1 43   5
can feel how the earth must fly if a . . . . 587 1 X 1 47   15
the blue heaven green earth neither sea here's more . . . . . 588 1 X 1 48   3
did o no yes earth was in (live live) . . . . 589 1 X 1 49   8
girl on this whirlingest earth? why you're by far . . . . . 590 1 X 1 50   7
larger than sky times earth: a flame beyond soul . . . . . . 599 (CHAIRE) 1   4
even tells) all the earth has turned to sky . . . . 630 (CHAIRE) 32   9
way down to the earth are leapandswooping tinily birds . . . 631 (CHAIRE) 33   11
bombed the by ocean earth bigly shudders) never was . . . . 639 (CHAIRE) 41   4
gay (nothing's false, in earth in air in water . . . . . . 651 (CHAIRE) 53   7
an creature whom than earth hers elf could silent . . . . . 654 (CHAIRE) 56   10
the gift of the earth of the sky knight . . . . 661 (CHAIRE) 63   8
of mad rags strode earth ignorantly blossoming a scarecrow . 662 (CHAIRE) 64   7
gay great happening illimitably earth) how should tasting . . 663 (CHAIRE) 65   8
the sky and the earth and the sea. For . . . . 664 (CHAIRE) 66   23
no bliss of heavenly earth beguiles our spirits, whose . . . 675 95 POEMS 3   2
is true to his earth; so anyone's world does . . . . 676 95 POEMS 4   3
looking (alw ays) while earth and sky grow one . . . . . . 715 95 POEMS 43   9
than anyone on the earth and i like you . . . . 717 95 POEMS 45   2
and tomorrow and the earth) / / / / . . . . 732 95 POEMS 60   16
lover on the ending earth-- and while a (huge . . . . 743 95 POEMS 71   1
us will becauseless ultimate earth accept and primeval . . . 745 95 POEMS 73   6
Star goes under the earth / / / / . . . . 752 95 POEMS 80   8
bouncing up off burned earth but a blind blissfully . . . . 754 95 POEMS 82   3
a gayer he; if earth and sky should break . . . . 760 95 POEMS 87   7
opening, as if an earth was playing at birthdays . . . . . 763 95 POEMS 90   5
know-- brave! brave (the earth and the sky are . . . . . . 767 95 POEMS 93   14
let's do as an earth which can never do . . . . 769 95 POEMS 95   17
green the new the earth more moving (all gay . . . . 778 73 POEMS 6   8
over green the new earth a day of may . . . . 778 73 POEMS 6   18
urba n skyline on earth between whose d owdy . . . . 788 73 POEMS 16   8
essly (into sweet the earth) & nobody (including our . . . . 797 73 POEMS 25   10
a must though the earth in her splendor says . . . . 801 73 POEMS 29   29
less into heaven certainly earth swims than each my . . . . 810 73 POEMS 38   7
(from inexistence moving) sweet earth puts on immortality . . 818 73 POEMS 46   4
Spring --irrevocably; and in earth sky trees : every . . . . 835 73 POEMS 63   22

+EARTH

FOR CONTEXT, SEE . . . . 361 VIVA 52   33

EARTH'S

of heaven combine with earth's madness) --'tis a gate . . . . 21 T&C PUELLA MEA 201
of worlds whereto this earth's a hurled dream down . . . . . 81 T&C SON UNRE 6   5
white idea (Listen drenches: earth's ugly) mind. , Rinsing . 99 & POST IMPR 10   3
A white idea, drenching. earth's brain detaches clottingsand . 99 & POST IMPR 10   20
of autumn do complain earth's ghastlier trees by whom . . . 207 XLI SONNETS 3   2
with his wellfilled pants earth's biggest grafter, nothing . 266 IS 5 TWO 1   33
of Whose compassionate digit, earth's most terrific quadruped 315 VIVA 7   15
learn (nor could all earth's rotting scholars guess that . . 420 NO THANKS 37   8
-ing (mercifully) touch deathful earth's any which Weavingly 557 1 X 1 17   10
celebrate day and welcome earth's arrival with a soul . . . 582 1 X 1 42   4
feel behind this man earth's first sunrise) and his . . . . . 617 (CHAIRE) 19   5
children" nor might any earth's first morning have concealed 626 (CHAIRE) 28   13
this proud nowhere of earth's most prodigious night blossoms 714 95 POEMS 42   2

	PAGE	TITLE	LINE

EARTH'S (CONTINUED)
    prayers are prayers of earth's own clumsily striving (finding 749 95 POEMS 77   6
    nonexistence vanishes with also earth's --"dying" the ghost . 808 73 POEMS 36 13
    twilight voice of deathless earth's innumerable doom: . . . . 821 73 POEMS 49   2
EARTHLESS
    musical? while in an earthless hour my fond soul . . . . . . 12 T&C SONGS 2 41
EARTHLY
    nose upwrinkled into nothing earthly, while the slippery eyes 226 IS 5 ONE MAME   4
EARTHQUAKE
    landscapes made interesting by earTHQuake empty . . . . . . 101 & POST IMPR 11 70
EARTHQUAKES
    not because harm symmetry earthquakes starfish (but because . 452 NO THANKS 67 16
    than cosmic rays war earthquakes famine or the ex . . . . . 475 NEW POEMS 13 19
EARTHS
    ses humble. Over thin earths chatterish strut cuddle & . . . 346 VIVA 37   3
    and and three dancing earths three menandwomen three and . . 507 50 POEMS 21 20
EARWARMERS
    to mention shirts fleaproof earwarmers etcetera wristers . . 276 IS 5 TWO 10 11
EASE
    which fail--look: with what ease that bright how plural . . . 418 NO THANKS 35   9
    at trillionworlded the ecstatic ease with which vast my . . . 517 50 POEMS 31   4
EASIER
    hands "& everything is easier than I had guessed . . . . . . 338 VIVA 29 17
EASILY
    sunset trampling the night easily from the shocked impossible 30 T&C ORIENTALE 4 24
    But first you) press easily at first, it will . . . . 67 T&C POST IMPR 4 18
    memory of Cleopatra while easily tremendously floats in the . 111 & PORTRAIT 6 72
    noise of her eyes easily files my impatience to . . . . 147 & SON REAL 18   8
    accident whose niceness betters easily the intent of genius-- 162 & SON ACTU 11   3
    the superior dust-of-sleep. wields easily the pale club of . 163 & SON ACTU 12   5
    seeking, some street which easily trickles a brittle fuss . . 174 & SON ACTU 23   6
    little while and which easily break in spite of . . . . 264 IS 5 ONE 33 15
    men speaks (among leaves Easily through voices womenlike . . 356 VIVA 47   3
    near your slightest look easily will unclose me though . . . 366 VIVA 57   5
    all that i am easily disappears (leaving no proof . . . . . . 479 NEW POEMS 17 19
    bird can sing as easily creation up all sky . . . . 558 1 X 1 18 13
    perfect nowhere came (as easily as we forget something) . . . 599 (CHAIRE) 1 13
    most of a rose easily (while will be goes . . . . 608 (CHAIRE) 10 10
    is a man (so easily one in another hides; . . . . 609 (CHAIRE) 11   3
    me your scorn of easily hatred of timid & . . . . 677 95 POEMS 5   4
    only love) comprehends huger easily beyonds than timelessly . 741 95 POEMS 69   6
EAST
    are fond of the east side as i lie . . . . 100 & POST IMPR 11   1
    go out into the East side, my mouth goes . . . . 100 & POST IMPR 11 19
    to go into the east Side in a. dark . . . . 100 & POST IMPR 11 34
    goes out into the east side my sex sitting . . . . 101 & POST IMPR 11 59
    repeats eventual perfection while east deserves of dawn. i . 184 XLI SONGS 6 14
    And out of the east toward her a fragile . . . . 284 IS 5 FOUR 1 17
EASTMAN
    If It Isn't An Eastman It Isn't A Kodak . . . . 230 IS 5 ONE 2 34
EAT
    rhythm of precise laziness. Eat the price of an . . . . 162 & SON ACTU 11 15
    in a garret and eat aspirine) but who is . . . . 245 IS 5 ONE 16   5
    thing perhaps is to eat flowers and not to . . . . 264 IS 5 ONE 33 32
    the imaginable, love, and eat sunlight (do you believe . . . 289 IS 5 FOUR 6   8
    why do i weep eat sleep--what does the whole . . . . 295 IS 5 FOUR 12 16
    shit I will not eat" our president, being of . . . . 339 VIVA 30 33
    shape that can but eat and turd ere with . . . . 360 VIVA 51   4
    D drink and E eat of her voice in . . . . 390 NO THANKS 7   4
    die love not Fear eat sleep kill and have . . . . 467 NEW POEMS 5 10
    / If you can't eat you got to smoke . . . . 489 50 POEMS 3   1
    how we drink crawl eat walk die fly do? . . . . 528 50 POEMS 40   4
EATAGE
    fruit is the very eatage of forgetfulness thy lips . . . . . 29 T&C ORIENTALE 3 23
EATEN
    organ is waving moth- eaten tunes. a fattish hand . . . . . . 69 T&C POST IMPR 6   2
    a fleet pillar is eaten by yesterday she was . . . . 110 & PORTRAIT 6   3
    smooth arrow Cleopatra is eaten by yester- day) 0 . . . . . . 111 & PORTRAIT 6 48

EATEN (CONTINUED)
blue hair (all is eaten by yester- day between . . . . 112 & PORTRAIT 6   77
god) Cleopatra you are eaten by yester- day (and . . . . . . 112 & PORTRAIT 6   90
grouped. I have not eaten peppers for a week. . . . . 219 XLI SONNETS 15   2
if he wouldn't have eaten them Yapenese Craps somebody . . . 336 VIVA 27   10
in (thundering) by When eaten spaces grouse rocket know . . . 346 VIVA 37   10
+EATEN
FOR CONTEXT, SEE . . . . 57 T&C PORTRAIT 5   37
FOR CONTEXT, SEE . . . . 101 & POST IMPR 11   46
FOR CONTEXT, SEE . . . . 260 IS 5 ONE 30   2
FOR CONTEXT, SEE . . . . 723 95 POEMS 51   8
EATER
your dead beautiful ladies. Eater of all things lovely--Time! 23 T&C PUELLA MEA   266
the ant, thou ant- eater / / / / . . . . 403 NO THANKS 20   25
+EATERS
FOR CONTEXT, SEE . . . . 332 VIVA 23   16
EATING
world the animals continued eating. And i imagine she, . . . 241 IS 5 ONE 12   6
of iron breathing height eating steepness the ship climbs . . 419 NO THANKS 36   13
EATS
to Strunsky's, Monia's mouth eats tangerines looking at the . 219 XLI SONNETS 15   15
Lord Rothermere. A crocodile eats a native, who in . . . . . 262 IS 5 ONE 32   23
curve of road which eats into a pink cliff . . . . 281 IS 5 THREE 5   8
ful -ly dar kness eats a distance a c . . . . 350 VIVA 41   5
and willbeishfully bursting un- eats wasvino isspaghett (i / 387 NO THANKS 4   18
puts on fur answers eats moves remembers is afraid) . . . . . 394 NO THANKS 11   8
EBONY
ling an ankus of ebony the fountains of the . . . . 32 T&C ORIENTALE 6   14
ECCO
/ / / / ecco a letter starting "dearest . . . . 504 50 POEMS 18   1
+ECCO
FOR CONTEXT, SEE . . . . 788 73 POEMS 16   1
ECHO
goal, at the mere echo of whose shining mirth . . . . 3 T&C EPITHALAM   15
love riding riding the echo down into the silver . . . . . . 14 T&C SONGS 4   12
with the purr of echo pouring in a mesh . . . . 115 & PORTRAIT 8   15
what neither is any echo of dream nor any . . . . 368 VIVA 59   5
any flowering of any echo (but the echo of . . . . 368 VIVA 59   7
any echo (but the echo of the flower of . . . . 368 VIVA 59   7
necessity" (generalissimo e) and echo answers "there is no . 636 (CHAIRE) 38   12
ECKSHUN
idstings yewrety oride lesgo eckshun kemeruh daretoi nig) . 474 NEW POEMS 12   13
ECLATE
pourquoi se promene-t-elle, pourquoi eclate ta voix fragile . 121 & PORTRAIT 12   55
ECLIPSING
not credible the anywhere eclipsing of a spirit's ignorance . 843 73 POEMS 71   10
ECONOMIC
/ / / / economic secu rity" is a . . . . 477 NEW POEMS 15   1
ECSTASIES
of this night amazing ecstasies slowly, in the glutted . . . 36 T&C AMORES 1   23
foolishwise proudhumble citizen of ecstasies more steep than 845 73 POEMS 73   7
ECSTASY
lips are vague with ecstasy my palpitating breasts inhale . . 31 T&C ORIENTALE 5   24
a queer pulp of ecstasy while in the battered . . . . 55 T&C PORTRAIT 3   16
delirious smart of thrilled ecstasy, where sea and sky . . . 79 T&C SON UNRE 4   13
a hoop of grim ecstasy / / / / . . . . 137 & SON REAL 8   18
moon jabbed jerked with ecstasy ....tremble (not knowing how 153 & SON ACTU 2   11
a naming stealth of ecstasy means, like a girl . . . . 168 & SON ACTU 17   9
of horizontal large distinct ecstasy wags and. rages . . . . 202 XLI PORTRAIT 9   36
and same answer, beginning, ecstasy, to dare: prouder than . 351 VIVA 42   5
in breath) have nicknamed ecstasy and And spills smile . . . 358 VIVA 49   9
page) contentment read for ecstasy --for poem prose-- caution 689 95 POEMS 17   5
ECSTATIC
nod significant to the ecstatic earth in token of . . . . . . 3 T&C EPITHALAM   10
which feels the keen ecstatic actual tread (and thereto . . . 19 T&C PUELLA MEA   125
the hair's worm huge, ecstatic, rathe.... yours are the . . . 84 T&C SON ACTU 3   11
floats at trillionworlded the ecstatic ease with which vast . 517 50 POEMS 31   4

	PAGE	TITLE	LINE

ECSTATICALLY
/ / from spiralling ecstatically this proud nowhere of . . . 714 95 POEMS 42   1
ED
ears (but my uncle Ed that's dead from the . . . . 253 IS 5 ONE 24   11
EDDIE
beat it for Chicago. Eddie was waiting for him, ... 145 & SON REAL 16   5
a broad that knew Eddie in Topeka, went clean . . . . 145 & SON REAL 16   7
a shove and asked Eddie did he care to . . . . 145 & SON REAL 16   12
EDDIEANDBILL
far and wee and eddieandbill come running from marbles . . . 24 T&C CHANSONS 1   6
EDGAR
moon over death over edgar the moon over smellings . . . . . 384 NO THANKS 2   7
EDGE
trees are put on edge spring, of the jostle . . . . 61 T&C PORTRAIT 9   21
that (just at the edge of day) i surely . . . . 92 & POST IMPR 4   18
the) pond on whoseswooning edge black trees think (hear . . . 99 & POST IMPR 10   10
my impatience to an edge--my girl's tall and taut, ... 147 & SON REAL 18   9
set my love-tooth on edge. So until light each . . . . 173 & SON ACTU 22   11
bird: the turn ing; edge, of life (inquiry before . . . . . . 712 95 POEMS 40   7
EDGED
the organised hills an edged nothing begins to prune . . . . 160 & SON ACTU 9   9
EDGELESS
clumsy trivi- al acrobatic edgeless gesture of existence, . . 193 XLI PORTRAIT 1   20
push--. deep into the edgeless gloaming gladness hammers . . 202 XLI PORTRAIT 9   37
yes, partly nor some edgeless star could give that . . . . . 414 NO THANKS 31   9
EDGES
/ / / sunset) edges become swiftly corners (Besides . . . . . 345 VIVA 36   1
EDIBLE
can dy lu minous edible spry pinks shy lemons . . . . 179 XLI SONGS 1   6
EDIFICE
notable structure or ideal edifice... situated or established 319 VIVA 11   23
EDITOR
he is persuasive the editor cigarstinking hobgoblin swims . . 259 IS 5 ONE 29   8
EDUCATION
wellcurb simply darling" --O Education: O thos cook & . . . . 257 IS 5 ONE 27   37
it sells hate condoms education snakeoil vac uumcleaners . . 549 1 X 1 9   11
EEL
candy but just (nude eel) now little joe lives . . . . 410 NO THANKS 27   4
EERILY
slop hight evolute my eerily oh gargle to jip . . . . 333 VIVA 24   23
EESEZ
sez dooyuh unnurs tanmih eesez pullih nizmus tash, oi . . . . 310 VIVA 2   2
doot, butoiguttuh braikyooz, datswut eesez tuhmih. (Nowoi . . 310 VIVA 2   5
EET
traipse into the cheeks "eet smeestaire steevensun kum een, . 73 T&C SON REAL 4   12
EEV
less frenziedly have cried eev mahmah hadn chuzd nogged . . . 790 73 POEMS 18   16
EEYEB
artskiDs... with thema Tiss eeyeb Rowspeach es a soft . . . . 318 VIVA 10   20
EFFENDI
for dust n'est-ce pas effendi drifts between tables like . . 198 XLI PORTRAIT 6   15
y play b cries "effendi" "Uh" "coffee" "uh" enter . . . . . . 200 XLI PORTRAIT 8   10
x and y play, effendi approaches, sets down coffee . . . . . 200 XLI PORTRAIT 8   18
+EFFENDI
FOR CONTEXT, SEE . . . . 200 XLI PORTRAIT 8   31
EFFIE
general noise Where is Effie who was dead? --to . . . . 117 & PORTRAIT 10   10
the others i've been Effie who isn't alive just . . . . 117 & PORTRAIT 10   24
EFFIE'S
/ here is little Effie's head whose brains are . . . . 117 & PORTRAIT 10   1
follow me stooping by Effie's little, in (want a . . . . . . 117 & PORTRAIT 10   28
way. here is little Effie's head whose brains are . . . . . . 118 & PORTRAIT 10   43
EFFIGIES
hungering churches (topped with effigies of crowing gold) . . 340 VIVA 31   17
EFFIGY
remain; a shadow phantom effigy or seeming (an almost . . . . 812 73 POEMS 40   3
EFFORT
these prettiest deaths without effort while hungering . . . . 340 VIVA 31   15

                                                   PAGE   TITLE   LINE

+EFFORT
   FOR CONTEXT, SEE . . . . 96 & POST IMPR 8   27
EGG
   a west of robin's egg blue when i entered . . . . 194 XLI PORTRAIT 2   3
EGGED
   much the worse, and egged the firstclassprivates on his . . . 339 VIVA 30   27
EGGHEAD
   topped with danc ing egghead strutstrolls eager a (twice . . 615 (CHAIRE) 17   4
EGGYELLOW
   s 1 ooms an eggyellow smear of wintry sunse . . . . 788 73 POEMS 16   14
EGO
   hugest inherent Trees of Ego, from whose living and . . . . . 195 XLI PORTRAIT 3   19
   eye perceives (as the ego approaches) painfully sterilized . 319 VIVA 11   27
   darling diminutive person jovial ego (& mischievous tenderly 678 95 POEMS 6   5
EGYPT
   strangely fled, who with Egypt went to bed, whom . . . . . . 22 T&C PUELLA MEA   246
   hearty sharp column of Egypt , built like a . . . . 111 & PORTRAIT 6   44
   you whose body is Egypt whose hair is Nile) . . . . 113 & PORTRAIT 6   111
   Troy (N.Y.) to Cairo (Egypt) the luminous dithyrambs of . . . 266 IS 5 TWO 1   7
EGYPT'S
   egyptian day who with Egypt's body lay. Lovely as . . . . . . 18 T&C PUELLA MEA   74
EGYPTIAN
   when swooned the white egyptian day who with Egypt's . . . . 18 T&C PUELLA MEA   73
   there lives a green egyptian noise. ladies with whom . . . . 138 & SON REAL 9   8
EH
   chap hic sum- more eh chuckles skulch.... and i . . . . . . 96 & POST IMPR 8   22
   To Lie In Bed --eh? I'm not. Again. Hush. . . . . 130 & SON REAL 1   14
EHEU
   nerativeness of the stimulus (eheu fu -gaces Postu- me . . . 236 IS 5 ONE 7   17
EIGHT
   a stile he sees eight and twenty ladies in . . . . 15 T&C SONGS 5   3
   babybreasted broad "kitty" twice eight --beer nothing, the . 74 T&C SON REAL 5   12
+EIGHT
   FOR CONTEXT, SEE . . . . 332 VIVA 23   4
EIGHTEEN
   which died it is eighteen hundred years.... exactly under . . 108 & PORTRAIT 4   30
   it self int o eighteen) Don't (for) Please (tnights, ... 343 VIVA 34   14
EIGHTH
   splashes-sink which is west eighth, a star or three . . . . . 169 & SON ACTU 18   2
   bespangled clown standing on eighth street handed me a . . . 802 73 POEMS 30   5
EIGHTY
   his more than some eighty years through which that . . . . . 617 (CHAIRE) 19   11
+EIGHTY
   FOR CONTEXT, SEE . . . . 792 73 POEMS 20   13
EINSTEIN
   (now I've lost the) Einstein expanded Newton's law preserved 315 VIVA 7   5
+EISENHOWER
   FOR CONTEXT, SEE . . . . 636 (CHAIRE) 38   12
EITHER
   of raving colour, on either side the windows are . . . . . . 100 & POST IMPR 11   3
   by screetching Each) on either side the street's . . . . . . 100 & POST IMPR 11   15
   that both precisely beyond either were-- so in darkness . . . 379 VIVA 70   2
   girls) yours is mine either was deafer than neither . . . . . 513 50 POEMS 27   28
   and you are actual either hand is when for . . . . 538 50 POEMS 50   10
   this collective pseudobeast (sans either pain or joy) does . 544 1 X 1 4   6
   the very weather (not either) my treasure, when violets . . . 578 1 X 1 38   6
   worlds have halfsight, seeing either with life's eye (which . 845 73 POEMS 73   1
EITHERING
   (alive twice) and becomes eithering dreams the secret of . . 613 (CHAIRE) 15   11
   shall ever provingly disprove eithering vastnesses of orish . 761 95 POEMS 88   4
EJACULATE
   bath-houses whose opened withins ejaculate. obscenity the . . 94 & POST IMPR 6   4
   his scientifically pressed trousers ejaculate spats a . . . . 259 IS 5 ONE 29   24
EKE
   (ford madox ford) and eke to wit a human . . . . 607 (CHAIRE) 9   14
EKTYOUELLY
   everyone knows, is wut ektyouelly metus. Unbeside which limps 790 73 POEMS 18   14

	PAGE	TITLE	LINE

EL
the old sixth avenue el; in the top of . . . . 553 1 X 1 13   24

+EL
FOR CONTEXT, SEE . . . . 327 VIVA 18   38

+EL'S
FOR CONTEXT, SEE . . . . 101 & POST IMPR 11   48
FOR CONTEXT, SEE . . . . 219 XLI SONNETS 15   5

ELABORATE
and will You with elaborate fingers possibly touch the . . . 58 T&C PORTRAIT 6   16

+ELASTIC
FOR CONTEXT, SEE . . . . 398 NO THANKS 15   17

ELATE
of floating Of ; elate shyly a-live keen parallel . . . . . . 447 NO THANKS 62   2

ELATION
wonder how let's say elation causes the bent eyes . . . . . . 229 IS 5 ONE FRAN   12

ELECTED
behind the emperor ten elected warriors with bodies of . . . 34 T&C ORIENTALE 6   76
return upon the red elected lips scaleless visions) / . . . . 36 T&C AMORES 1   31

ELECTION
eachudder Hell Bent fer election makin believe dey was . . . 237 IS 5 ONE 8   19
tremendous sorrydaze bog triperight election who so thumb . . 333 VIVA 24   15

ELECTRIC
cheap intelligent thighs, the electric trite thighs; the hair 173 & SON ACTU 22   14
shocking fuzz of your electric fur, and what-is-it comes . . 175 & SON ACTU 24   11
which always quivers the electric Distinct face haughtily . . 193 XLI PORTRAIT 1   3
that primeval exposure whose electric solidity remembers some 197 XLI PORTRAIT 5   17
colour of table-cloths, the electric When In Doubt Buy . . . 217 XLI SONNETS 13   4

ELECTRICITY
tell me not how electricity or god was invented . . . . 324 VIVA 16   1

ELECTROMAGNETIC
fond of walls) an electromagnetic (now I've lost the) . . . . 315 VIVA 7   4

ELECTRONS
bigness of his littleness --electrons deify one razorblade . 554 1 X 1 14   5

ELEMENTS
your voice-- beyond these elements remarkably nothing is.... 291 IS 5 FOUR 8   16

ELEPHANT
saffron umbrellas upon an elephant twelve feet high behind . 32 T&C ORIENTALE 6   7
moonlight and the emperor's elephant is a thousand years . . 32 T&C ORIENTALE 6   18
the silently little blue elephant shyly (he was terri . . . . 516 50 POEMS 30   1
through) the little blue elephant at the zoo (jumbled . . . . 516 50 POEMS 30   7
peers at you) has (elephant the blue) put some . . . . 516 50 POEMS 30   9

ELEPHANTANGELCHILD
/ if a cheerfulest Elephantangelchild should sit (holding a . 631 {CHAIRE} 33   1

ELEPHANTINE
cluttered in pursuit pleasantly elephantine while nearby the 56 T&C PORTRAIT 4   8
clenched arms a delicately elephantine face (It is necessary 143 & SON REAL 14   2

ELEPHANTS
and furious and beautiful elephants (mingled in whispering . 95 & POST IMPR 7   14
like laughter and like elephants through our single brain . . 111 & PORTRAIT 6   68

ELEVATE
cow is not to elevate your tool but drop . . . . 500 50 POEMS 14   10

ELEVATING
dancers, whom he considered "elevating--that is, if dancing . 327 VIVA 18   40

+ELEVATING
FOR CONTEXT, SEE . . . . 327 VIVA 18   40

ELEVATOR
smoke who runs the elevator but I bet two . . . . 125 & SEVEN POEMS 4 10
glassworks of Murano; pause elevator nel mezzo del cammin' . 256 IS 5 ONE 27   6

+ELEVATOR
FOR CONTEXT, SEE . . . . 309 VIVA 1   23

ELEVEN
bits come seven come eleven m m make the . . . . 125 & SEVEN POEMS 4 11
elf while) nextto Mesmoked eleven camels ! and i . . . . . . 318 VIVA 10   15

ELF
all about the desertbyIts elf while) nextto Mesmoked eleven . 318 VIVA 10   13
whilepin Kishcam elscasta? netsits Elf allaBout. (chic) -kchi 318 VIVA 10   22
) & it: s; elf, ◇ / / / . . . . 423 NO THANKS 40   36
leavi ng on its elf pro pped uprigh t . . . . 472 NEW POEMS 10   8

PAGE   TITLE   LINE

ELF (CONTINUED)
    s its (ghostsoul sheshape) elf into leasting forever most . . 495 50 POEMS 9   13
    whom than earth hers elf could silent more no . . . . 654 {CHAIRE} 56   11
    who (at her nons- elf 's unself too -thf- . . . . 704 95 POEMS 32   3
ELIENA
    star the most mysterious (eliena, my dear) is this . . . . . 825 73 POEMS 53   4
ELIGIBLE
    of worms. in the eligible day under the unaccountable . . . . 43 T&C AMORES 7   23
+ELIZABETH ARDEN
    FOR CONTEXT, SEE . . . . 726 95 POEMS 54   1
ELLE
    gorge mysterieuse pourquoi se promene-t-elle, pourquoi eclate 121 & PORTRAIT 12   54
+ELLIPSES
    FOR CONTEXT, SEE . . . . 100 & POST IMPR 11   29
ELM
    high gods fled? Speak elm eloquent pandar with thy . . . . . 3 T&C EPITHALAM   9
ELOPING
    ded like a toy eloping to Ire (land must . . . . 320 VIVA 12   12
ELOQUENT
    gods fled? Speak elm eloquent pandar with thy nod . . . . . . 3 T&C EPITHALAM   9
ELSCASTA
    bad me whilepin Kishcam elscasta? netsits Elf allaBout. . . . 318 VIVA 10   21
ELSE
    if this thou catch, else missing. (though love be . . . . . . 13 T&C SONGS 3   19
    think I see someone else there is a lady, ... 102 & POST IMPR 12   23
    says here's luck somebody else says down the hatch . . . . . 108 & PORTRAIT 4   21
    what had been something else carefully slowly fatally turning 283 IS 5 THREE 7   25
    "everything turns into something else, and slips away. . . . . 303 IS 5 FIVE 2   5
    . while some thing else kisses busily a memory, ... 370 VIVA 61   23
    Won derfully is anyone else entirely who doesn't move . . . . 397 NO THANKS 14   3
    human soul and anything else uncanned for everyone carries . 466 NEW POEMS 4   6
    lousy kid that's something else my sweet (i feel . . . . . . 475 NEW POEMS 13   24
    please itself or someone else makes no more difference . . . 549 1 X 1 9   9
    perfectly alone there's nobody else alive (such a sky . . . . 591 1 X 1 51   12
    the dotted line or else an ocean is compelled . . . . 620 {CHAIRE} 22   8
    you dear to what else could a no but . . . . 638 {CHAIRE} 40   4
    no time ago or else a life walking in . . . . 648 {CHAIRE} 50   2
    despairs) Once happened nowhere else imagine Now rapidly this 693 95 POEMS 21   8
    but everybody (i believe) else thought lucinda looked like . 706 95 POEMS 34   4
    you (ne i) nobody else drive dumb mankind dizzy . . . . 804 73 POEMS 32   8
+ELSE
    FOR CONTEXT, SEE . . . . 790 73 POEMS 18   6
+ELSE'S
    FOR CONTEXT, SEE . . . . 782 73 POEMS 10   13
ELSES
    always-so-much-interested-in-everybody-else's-business . . . 250 IS 5 ONE 21   14
    dares un no budy elses un ids dare dare . . . . 519 50 POEMS 33   25
+ELSES
    FOR CONTEXT, SEE . . . . 779 73 POEMS 7   27
ELSEWHERE
    of these <> hurries elsewhere; to blow incredible wampum . . 116 & PORTRAIT 9   16
    awake being not asleep, elsewhere our dreams began which . . 304 IS 5 FIVE 3   7
    more much (as aprils elsewhere stroll) exhumed most . . . . . 546 1 X 1 6   3
    entirely white eyes of elsewhere jabber while (infinite fog . 629 {CHAIRE} 31   4
    called people called sunlight (elsewhere flat the mechanical 658 {CHAIRE} 60   12
+ELSEWHERE
    FOR CONTEXT, SEE . . . . 696 95 POEMS 24   7
ELVES
    eyes which like two elves incredibly amuse themselves) with . 17 T&C PUELLA MEA   39
    box is spilling rancid elves upon neat sunlight into . . . . 69 T&C POST IMPR 6   4
    crank goes round desperate elves and hope- less gnomes . . . 69 T&C POST IMPR 6   21
ELYSIAN
    gof throughof treesOf. (Fields Elysian the like, a) slEEping 104 & POST IMPR 14   6
    the trees Fields slowly Elysian in a firmcool-Ness taxis, . . 104 & POST IMPR 14   14
EMANATES
    minute incessant Was irrevocably emanates a dignity of . . . 111 & PORTRAIT 6   53
EMANATING
    fools the sea(while emanating the triple starred Hotel . . . 319 VIVA 11   20

EMANATION
more only you) most emanation creates creation lovetree! . . 764 95 POEMS 90   47

EMANCIPATED
somewhat more than less emancipated evening had in return . . 258 IS 5 ONE 28   6

EMBARRASSING
watch-chain which would be embarrassing for both parties and 204 XLI LA GUERRE 2 4

EMBLEMS
its cluttered and brittle emblems, or a field (and . . . . . 434 NO THANKS 51   23

EMBOSS
the sun's white hands emboss, betwixt whose absolute feet . . 3 T&C EPITHALAM   29

EMBRACE
her soul burns to embrace--and didst thou know the . . . . . 3 T&C EPITHALAM   12
queen in the inconceivable embrace of whose tremendous hair . 6 T&C EPITHALAM 145
lips me hugely which embrace. as in the hairy . . . . 151 & SON REAL 22   16
these thy lips beautifully embrace nothing and when thy . . . 210 XLI SONNETS 6   12
sliding a little downward, embrace me with your body's . . . 282 IS 5 THREE 6   34

EMBRACES
gate; the prisoner dawn embraces hugely some few most . . . . 376 VIVA 67   10

EMBROIDERED
fleas left the prettily embroidered howdah im- mediately. . . 262 IS 5 ONE 32   28

+EMERALD
FOR CONTEXT, SEE . . . . 747 95 POEMS 75   9

EMERGES
pains appears an if emerges a joy let 's . . . . 425 NO THANKS 42   13

EMERGING
am this blueeyed Finn emerging from a lovehouse who . . . . . 115 & PORTRAIT 8   27
minute pulled the sluice emerging. concrete / / / . . . . . . 119 & PORTRAIT 11   17
in native costume, who emerging from a pissoir enters . . . . 245 IS 5 ONE 16   22
enter a Toy and emerging (believably enlarged) make how . . . 337 VIVA 28   3
gradually (or as these emerging now hills invent the . . . . 372 VIVA 63   2
erect blood finally trembles, emerging to perceive buried in 435 NO THANKS 51   39
smallest joy's a universe emerging from a wish) love . . . . 768 95 POEMS 94   8

EMINENT
but a piece of eminent fragility. Well and when--Does . . . . 141 & SON REAL 12   6

EMIT
allotted sandpile --how silently emit a tiny violetflavoured 231 IS 5 ONE 3   53

EMITS
upward certainly is pouring) emits a pose : to . . . . 95 & POST IMPR 7   10
coming of my love emits a wonderful smell in . . . . 152 & SON ACTU 1   6

EMITTED
her." "The Madam?" I emitted; vaguely watching that . . . . . 228 IS 5 ONE MARJ   11

EMITTING
female indubitably tellurian strolls emitting minute grins . 116 & PORTRAIT 9   6

EMPEROR
/ / / the emperor sleeps in a palace . . . . 32 T&C ORIENTALE 6 1
the harem of the emperor is carpeted with gold . . . . 32 T&C ORIENTALE 6 20
than birds when the emperor is very amorous he . . . . 33 T&C ORIENTALE 6 53
the feet of the emperor a cithern- player squats . . . . . . 34 T&C ORIENTALE 6 70
quiveringgold body behind the emperor ten elected warriors . 34 T&C ORIENTALE 6 75
lust breathe together the emperor, exerting himself among his 34 T&C ORIENTALE 6 99

EMPEROR'S
the fountains of the emperor's palace run sunlight and . . . 32 T&C ORIENTALE 6 15
and moonlight and the emperor's elephant is a thousand . . . 32 T&C ORIENTALE 6 17
the ladies of the emperor's harem are queens of . . . . 33 T&C ORIENTALE 6 44

EMPERORS
(children of) dirtpoor (popes emperors) undeaths through . . 681 95 POEMS 9   12

EMPHATICALLY
mystical moment of dullness emphatically are Not To Be . . . 230 IS 5 ONE 2   22

EMPLOYED
stroke with brushes recently employed anent this muddy . . . 339 VIVA 30   11

EMPLOYS
or write, la moon. Employs a very crazily how . . . . 504 50 POEMS 18   6

EMPTIED
tleora basket of RipeBlackbeRRies emptied suddenl (y down the 101 & POST IMPR 11   54
/ / / / emptied. hills. listen. ,not, alive, ... 416 NO THANKS 33   1

EMPTINESS
(emptying our soul of emptiness) priming at every pore . . . 428 NO THANKS 45   15
house clutch between eyes emptiness toss one at nobody . . . 522 50 POEMS 35   2

		PAGE	TITLE	LINE
EMPTOR				
strawberries democ ra (caveat emptor) cy superfluous hair or	549	1 X 1 9	13
EMPTY				
the harvest whitely peer empty of surprise death's faultless	11	T&C SONGS 2	24
it has lain with empty arms upon the giddy	36	T&C AMORES 1	6
made interesting by earTHQuake empty stomachsClenche Dtothe	101	& POST IMPR 11	70
not live: and the empty twilight cannot grieve nor	165	& SON ACTU 14	8
one butting trolley imposingly empty; snickering shop doors	172	& SON ACTU 21	5
hand's impression in an empty glove, a soon forgotten	360	VIVA 51	8
lost shoulders S the empty spine / / /	414	NO THANKS 31	15
bounceless period unshy the empty house is full O	499	50 POEMS 13	8
+EMPTY				
FOR CONTEXT, SEE	472	NEW POEMS 10	12
FOR CONTEXT, SEE	696	95 POEMS 24	5
EMPTYING				
with clumsily wilted fingers emptying youth colour and what	359	VIVA 50	7
which will forget him (emptying our soul of emptiness)	428	NO THANKS 45	14
EMS				
i (meet) t (touch) ems crouch (lunge)ing	388	NO THANKS 5	3
EN				
odour jigs et tout en face always wiggles the	134	& SON REAL 5	10
i think, her charms en repos.... a fattish leg	143	& SON REAL 14	8
In thy your ear: en amerique on ne boit	233	IS 5 ONE 4	6
ENCHANTED				
instantaneous fern whose scrupulous enchanted fronds toward	19	T&C PUELLA MEA	111
my flesh is an enchanted tree; with her lips'	22	T&C PUELLA MEA	232
/ how this uncouth enchanted person, arising from a	300	IS 5 FOUR 17	1
little fluttering, at the enchanted dike of whose lean	344	VIVA 35	9
ENCHANTING				
drawing into you my enchanting leaves / / /	182	XLI SONGS 4	17
ENCLOSE				
is i. Vast cheeks enclose me. a gigantic uvula	201	XLI PORTRAIT 9	7
gesture are things which enclose me, or which i	366	VIVA 57	3
ENCOMPASS				
nor may truth opening encompass true) while your contriving	373	VIVA 64	16
--nor all their times encompass me and you: when	817	73 POEMS 45	4
ENCORE				
they shat they shat encore he laughed and spat	440	NO THANKS 56	10
ENCOURAGE				
talentgang and water most encourage flame as hatracks into	511	50 POEMS 25	7
END				
a toy on the end of a string /	69	T&C POST IMPR 6	44
l e s asc end-ing inthecarts my, mouth is,	100	& POST IMPR 11	25
round water at one end of the well it's	126	& SEVEN POEMS 5	2
to a less erring end) myself is sculptor of	291	IS 5 FOUR 8	5
fortune (although endlessness should end) / / / /	394	NO THANKS 11	14
thing must have an end (the silly cause of	411	NO THANKS 28	2
less, that death should end) how lucky lovers are	446	NO THANKS 61	8
moon of day predicted end who never began of	527	50 POEMS 39	5
wonderful thing is the end of a string (murmurs	593	1 X 1 53	20
the night at the end of doubleyou 4th) reminds	699	95 POEMS 27	4
begin than love will end; where nothing is to	768	95 POEMS 94	2
but from this endless end of briefer each our	834	73 POEMS 62	25
END-ING				
l e s asc end-ing inthecarts my, mouth is,	100	& POST IMPR 11	25
END'S				
death begins to grow end's ending then these dolls	502	50 POEMS 16	9
ENDBEGI				
lydesc BYS FLUTTERFULLY IF (endbegi ndesginb ecend) tang lesp	421	NO THANKS 38	9
ENDING				
cliff precisely at the Ending of this road, a	435	NO THANKS 51	42
begins to grow end's ending then these dolls of	502	50 POEMS 16	9
your lover on the ending earth-- and while a	743	95 POEMS 71	1
ENDLESS				
dirt but from this endless end of briefer each	834	73 POEMS 62	25
ENDLESSNESS				
spend my fortune (although endlessness should end) / /	394	NO THANKS 11	14

	PAGE	TITLE	LINE

ENDLINGS
now of the sky --endlings of isn't shall never . . . . 512 50 POEMS 26   13
ENDOWED
in return for consciousness endowed him with a changeless . . 258 IS 5 ONE 28   8
ENDS
and single, where he ends, the earth (whose texture . . . . . 418 NO THANKS 35   1
beginnings are his luminous ends who far less lonely . . . . 420 NO THANKS 37   10
a newengland bed these ends of arms which pinch . . . . 506 50 POEMS 20   2
by the star nicked ends next among broken odds . . . . 522 50 POEMS 35   6
as men call him, ends what they call men . . . . 592 1 X 1 52   13
--love! if a world ends more than all worlds . . . . 750 95 POEMS 78   15
/ / here pasture ends-- this girl and boy . . . . 757 95 POEMS 85   1
ENDURE
selfless i can quite endure the absence of that . . . . 812 73 POEMS 40   10
and more by most endure all that you never . . . . 834 73 POEMS 62   11
+ENDWISE
FOR CONTEXT, SEE . . . . 790 73 POEMS 18   16
ENEMIES
loved by his bitterest enemies" is dead the only . . . . . . 336 VIVA 27   2
kind; friends turn to enemies) therefore lament, my dream . . 834 73 POEMS 62   4
ENEMY
yes you're right: my enemy . Love / / . . . . 793 73 POEMS 21   25
ENFOLD
o come, terrible anonymity; enfold phantom me with the . . . 839 73 POEMS 67   9
ENFOLDING
by guest a snowingly enfolding glory is all angry . . . . . . 559 1 X 1 19   2
ENGLAND
dictum of a new england sculptor (well on in . . . . 327 VIVA 18   r39
+ENGLAND
FOR CONTEXT, SEE . . . . 469 NEW POEMS 7   13
FOR CONTEXT, SEE . . . . 506 50 POEMS 20   1
ENGLISH
Beautifully retire through its english the Forwardflung . . . 311 VIVA 3   4
of death and the English / / / / . . . . 357 VIVA 48   14
+ENGLISH
FOR CONTEXT, SEE . . . . 696 95 POEMS 24   8
FOR CONTEXT, SEE . . . . 725 95 POEMS 53   11
FOR CONTEXT, SEE . . . . 787 73 POEMS 15   2
ENGLISHMAN
as dull as one englishman A: to / / . . . . 468 NEW POEMS 6   3
ENGRAVING
heaven's grace, in an engraving belonging to my friend. . . . 158 & SON ACTU 7   8
ENGULF
at look) swirls to engulf (in which in soft) . . . . 613 {CHAIRE} 15   5
ENJOY
friend is particularly to enjoy the composed sudden body . . 193 XLI PORTRAIT 1   2
good kumrads dance) kumrads enjoy s. freud knows whoy . . . . 413 NO THANKS 30   10
ENLARGED
Toy and emerging (believably enlarged) make how many stopped 337 VIVA 28   3
ENLIGHTENED
shoes 'fair friend' we enlightened this stranger 'some people 800 73 POEMS 28   9
ENLIVENING
known suburb the bronx (enlivening an otherwise dead silence 326 VIVA 18   13
ENNI
give all things to enni one bugger thy nabor . . . . 492 50 POEMS 6   11
ENNOBLING
optics know more quite ennobling forsooth? One wondrous fine 254 IS 5 ONE 25   4
ENORMOUS
have seen death's clever enormous voice which hides in . . . 45 T&C LA GUERRE 1   4
the absurd eyelids sulked enormous sobs puckered the foolish 52 T&C PORTRAIT 1   27
futility lived brilliantly the enormous rhythm of absurdity. 103 & POST IMPR 13   11
Caesars borne neatly through enormous twilight surrounded by 111 & PORTRAIT 6   37
until this very frail enormous star (do you see . . . . . . 155 & SON ACTU 4   13
the flower with their enormous fingers unwished / / . . . . . 165 & SON ACTU 14   16
through the thin amorous enormous only lips of the . . . . . 202 XLI PORTRAIT 9   47
of light, against whose enormous curve of flesh exactly . . . 214 XLI SONNETS 10   3
high futile day an enormous stride (and drawing thy . . . . 215 XLI SONNETS 11   15
to a deep lap enormous mindless hands. and no . . . . 225 IS 5 ONE LIZ   9

	PAGE	TITLE	LINE

ENORMOUS (CONTINUED)
hurled downward thousands of enormous dreams / / / . . . . . 301 IS 5 FOUR 18   19
the heart's eager dim enormous language loss or gain . . . . 372 VIVA 63   12
/ / dead every enormous piece of nonsense which . . . . 561 1 X 1 21   1
themselves believing eyes adventuring, enormous nowhere from) 669 (CHAIRE) 71   4
a fatal stillness; while enormous this how patient creature . 674 95 POEMS 2   5
& clearing) gone are enormous near far silent truths . . . . 755 95 POEMS 83   5
+ENORMOUS
FOR CONTEXT, SEE . . . . 157 & SON ACTU 6   12
ENORMOUSLY
sleep they only understand enormously which fail--look: with 418 NO THANKS 35   9
planet grows more and enormously more less: until her-and-his 808 73 POEMS 36   11
ENORMOUSNESS
second implies nonth inkable enormousness by con trast with . 803 73 POEMS 31   11
ENOUGH
if this were not enough (not really enough pulled . . . . . . 154 & SON ACTU 3   6
not enough (not really enough pulled one before one . . . . . 154 & SON ACTU 3   6
◇ "there is not enough of it" their, hands . . . . 255 IS 5 ONE 26   8
never the beginning of enough, is it (i do . . . . 282 IS 5 THREE 6   3
of brightness. (That is enough of life, for you. . . . . . . 282 IS 5 THREE 6   31
for more than just enough dreams to live on) . . . . 298 IS 5 FOUR 15   10
that it's nothing paradoxically enough beyond mere personal . 329 VIVA 20   1
babies aint plenty good enough for i eu can . . . . 476 NEW POEMS 14   9
from mountains made --long enough and just so long . . . . . 511 50 POEMS 25   4
is a fear --long enough and just so long . . . . 511 50 POEMS 25   12
and millstones float --long enough and just so long . . . . 511 50 POEMS 25   20
so long and long enough / / / / . . . . 511 50 POEMS 25   28
too not quite big enough to hold one tiny . . . . 523 50 POEMS 36   31
how much more than enough for both of us . . . . 531 50 POEMS 43   13
and innocently are) seeming's enough for slaves of space . . 745 95 POEMS 73   13
thank heaven somebody's crazy enough to give me a . . . . . . 802 73 POEMS 30   33
me, dear, clocks have enough to do without confusing . . . . 817 73 POEMS 45   7
ENQUIRE
boots of success than enquire whose soul dangles from . . . . 204 XLI LA GUERRE 2   3
ENRAPTURED
yet stand They here enraptured, as among the slow . . . . . . 208 XLI SONNETS 4   12
ENRICH
flame whose myriad tints enrich a visage simple, terse, . . . 254 IS 5 ONE 25   18
ENSCONCED
contemplate her uneyes safely ensconced in thick glass you . 326 VIVA 18   4
contemplate her uneyes safely ensconced in thick glass / . . 327 VIVA 18   46
ENSLAVED
free (for man is enslaved by a dread dizziz . . . . 552 1 X 1 12   3
ENTER
dark so duneyed master enter the sweet gates of . . . . 188 XLI SONGS 10   14
of my body Shall enter fingers of smooth mastery . . . . . . 189 XLI SONGS 11   9
"effendi" "Uh" "coffee" "uh" enter paperboy, c buys . . . . . 200 XLI PORTRAIT 8   11
Snail's On The Thorn enter Morn and God's In . . . . 230 IS 5 ONE 2   28
one function being to enter a Toy and emerging . . . . 337 VIVA 28   2
big sun big moon (enter us) / / / . . . . 393 NO THANKS 10   17
so ancient the houses enter the people are so . . . . 505 50 POEMS 19   6
than now (softlying wisdoms enter guess) childmoon smile to . 518 50 POEMS 32   10
mountains speak the truth) enter a cloverish silence of . . . 745 95 POEMS 73   3
/ / / / enter no (silence is the . . . . 839 73 POEMS 67   1
+ENTER
FOR CONTEXT, SEE . . . . 618 (CHAIRE) 20   1
ENTERED
silence) i without fail entered became and was these . . . . 115 & PORTRAIT 8   21
egg blue when i entered a mad street whose . . . . 194 XLI PORTRAIT 2   4
ENTERS
dimension with a blush enters the becoming garden of . . . . 48 T&C IMPRESS 2   17
emerging from a pissoir enters abruptly Notre Dame (whereas . 245 IS 5 ONE 16   23
al, ways; procession: and Enters this church. toward which . 280 IS 5 THREE 4   29
a truly curving form enters my soul feels all . . . . 419 NO THANKS 36   3
/ / / / enters give whose lost is . . . . 533 50 POEMS 45   1
this great lady's gaze enters a sunset "can grow . . . . . . 626 (CHAIRE) 28   2
ENTERTAIN
her petaled flesh doth entertain the adroit blood's . . . . . 21 T&C PUELLA MEA   185

	PAGE	TITLE	LINE

ENTERTAINED
    four) gentlemen are trinightly entertained by a whore who . . 312 VIVA 4   3
ENTERTAINMENT
    dreamed of the rare entertainment of your eyes, when . . . . 78 T&C SON UNRE 3   2
ENTHUSIASTIC
    thrills the moment of enthusiastic space is a little . . . . 82 T&C SON ACTU 1   12
    Altoona or what not enthusiastic cohorts from Duluth God . . 256 IS 5 ONE 27   27
ENTIRE
    how through the stopped entire day horribly and seriously . . 82 T&C SON ACTU 1   10
    the sensual mysticism of entire vertical being, i am . . . . 201 XLI PORTRAIT 9   23
    your body's suddenly curving entire warm questions / / . . . 282 IS 5 THREE 6   35
    planet (understand) forgets the entire and perpetual sea . . 379 VIVA 70   9
ENTIRELY
    was aware of an entirely dirty circle of habitues . . . . . . 194 XLI PORTRAIT 2   18
    were a kiss) distinct entirely melting sinuous lean... . . . 225 IS 5 ONE LIZ   15
    / FRAN should i entirely ask of god why . . . . 229 IS 5 ONE FRAN   1
    this perfectly clear, it entirely would have been not . . . . 263 IS 5 ONE 32   64
    each crease) will smooth entirely our minds --before leaving 288 IS 5 FOUR 5   5
    dream? oh i mean: entirely having in my careful . . . . . . 295 IS 5 FOUR 12   5
    0 gracefully) a we, entirely whose least breathing may . . . 368 VIVA 59   13
    derfully is anyone else entirely who doesn't move (Moved . . 397 NO THANKS 14   3
    with most memory) give entirely each Forever its freedom . . 453 NO THANKS 68   11
    hurled into young Now entirely arrives gesture past fragrance 456 NO THANKS 71   8
    boygirls need: i can entirely her only love whose . . . . . . 484 NEW POEMS 22   6
    we laugh and shall entirely our doom steer his . . . . . . 528 50 POEMS 40   7
    a sulky gob with entirely white eyes of elsewhere . . . . . 629 {CHAIRE} 31   3
    whisper their joy under entirely the coming . . . . 754 95 POEMS 82   11
ENTIRETY
    every partialness beats one entirety neither may shadow down 425 NO THANKS 42   11
ENTITIES
    Absolute destructivity to non- entities e. g. the) whis-per . 391 NO THANKS 8   24
ENTITLED
    / / / sonnet entitled how to run the . . . . 390 NO THANKS 7   1
    flag that's furled (sestet entitled grass is flesh or . . . . 390 NO THANKS 7   9
    might (publishers note) be entitled a wraith's progress or . 410 NO THANKS 27   10
    are more than not entitled to complain --plunged in . . . . 561 1 X 1 21   8
ENTRAILS
    with, its, little, solemn, entrails / / / / . . . . 94 & POST IMPR 6   29
ENTREAT
    your face and i entreat, by certain foolish perfect . . . . . 42 T&C AMORES 6   15
ENTWHYS
    hadn chuzd nogged id entwhys / / / / . . . . 790 73 POEMS 18   16
ENVISION
    contented fools of fact envision the mystery of freedom? . . 659 {CHAIRE} 61   9
ENVY
    friend and who may envy neither; nor bewail (would . . . . . 394 NO THANKS 11   10
    blind (blow pity to envy and soul to mind) . . . . 560 1 X 1 20   14
EPITHALAMION
    / / / / EPITHALAMION Thou aged unreluctant earth . . . . . . 3 T&C EPITHALAM   T
EPITOME
    perpendicular mammal a grim epitome of chuckling flesh. Weak 151 & SON REAL 22   5
EPOCH
    Christ and Co. the epoch of Mann's righteousness the . . . . 266 IS 5 TWO 1   3
    not die safely whose epoch fits him like a . . . . 394 NO THANKS 11   2
+EPSILON
    FOR CONTEXT, SEE . . . . 431 NO THANKS 48   25
EQUAL
    quilt's pink stops might equal head). Then with the . . . . 506 50 POEMS 20   10
    twice infinity could never equal one) which may your . . . . 510 50 POEMS 24   11
    all matterings of mind equal one violet / / . . . . 736 95 POEMS 64   8
EQUALLING
    soar dip dip soar equalling noise solemn dolls re . . . . . . 384 NO THANKS 2   27
EQUALLY
    and proudest eagerly wandering (equally all alive in . . . . 661 {CHAIRE} 63   6
    pedantic proud or humble, equally they're welcome --as if . . 763 95 POEMS 90   14
EQUALS
    perceive in this world equals the power of your . . . . . . 366 VIVA 57   13
    beware because because because equals (transparent or science 478 NEW POEMS 16   3

	PAGE	TITLE	LINE

EQUALS (CONTINUED)
  in fifty thousand years equals the quote and unquote . . . . 544 1 X 1 4   15
  prove that a hero equals any jerk who was . . . . 636 (CHAIRE) 38   3
  no then of winter equals now of spring; but . . . . 765 95 POEMS 91   11
  (1) we sans love equals mob love being youamiare . . . . . . 803 73 POEMS 31   7
  the ◇ sin cerity equals perspicuity (4) Only The . . . . . . 803 73 POEMS 31   16
+EQUALS
  FOR CONTEXT, SEE . . . . 317 VIVA 9   4
  FOR CONTEXT, SEE . . . . 329 VIVA 20   4
ERE
  of flame half-mute, (haste ere some thrush with silver . . .   6 T&C EPITHALAM   119
  currency of faint cities eternal--ere the sinless taint of .   9 T&C SONGS 1   33
  but eat and turd ere with the dirt death . . . . 360 VIVA 51   5
ERECT
  strong hands infinite the erect deep upon me in . . . . . . 64 T&C POST IMPR 1   6
  in fists hair wood erect cursing hatless who (bent . . . . . 277 IS 5 THREE 1   9
  / if within tonight's erect everywhere of black muscles . . . 299 IS 5 FOUR 16   1
  within me whisper whose erect blood finally trembles, ... 435 NO THANKS 51   38
  wallendas) ready were all erect your yous to cross . . . . . 605 (CHAIRE) 7   12
  become; but growing is" erect her whole life smiled . . . . . 626 (CHAIRE) 28   5
  now is forever: standing erect in the deathless truth . . . . 749 95 POEMS 77   19
+ERECT
  FOR CONTEXT, SEE . . . . 431 NO THANKS 48   10
ERECTING
  impenetrable transparency. the harsh erecting breasts and . . 137 & SON REAL 8   13
ERECTLY
  four tablets of perspiration erectly sitting. --If they knew 73 T&C SON REAL 4   9
ERGO
  w s li psh ergo wnd ow n, r . . . . 445 NO THANKS 60   6
  craft of cost the Ergo perished later all hands . . . . 494 50 POEMS 8   6
+ERGO
  FOR CONTEXT, SEE . . . . 431 NO THANKS 48   23
ERNEST
  / what does little Ernest croon in his death . . . . 409 NO THANKS 26   1
+ERNEST
  FOR CONTEXT, SEE . . . . 409 NO THANKS 26   4
EROTIC
  inclined to be uncouthly erotic more particularly the . . . . 326 VIVA 18   24
ERR
  beauty did in nothing err. If to me there . . . . 21 T&C PUELLA MEA   174
  artificer did most exquisitely err.) When the world was . . . 22 T&C PUELLA MEA   220
  of things like they err / / / / . . . . 552 1 X 1 12   30
  might otherwise forget (to err is human; to forgive . . . . . 636 (CHAIRE) 38   6
  (forgiving not divine, to err inhuman) or any thine . . . . . 798 73 POEMS 26   4
ERRED
  spy (whose aim had erred never) and by that . . . . 360 VIVA 51   15
ERRING
  so and so (an erring child of circumstance whom . . . . 266 IS 5 TWO 1   38
  silences to a less erring end) myself is sculptor . . . . . . 291 IS 5 FOUR 8   5
  most succinctly bred) took erring Olaf soon in hand; . . . . 339 VIVA 30   6
ERRONEOUS
  as it happens quite erroneous impression that he nascitur . . 234 IS 5 ONE 5   5
ERROR
  not to make an error, with twists spontaneously methodical. . 170 & SON ACTU 19   10
ERRORS
  sentence with seven grammatical errors "is dead" beautiful . 336 VIVA 27   5
ESCAPE
  that you thought to escape me and became a . . . . 30 T&C ORIENTALE 4   5
  man can, being all, escape from none) so huge . . . . 609 (CHAIRE) 11   4
ESCAPES
  furious light, and while fire-escapes and roofs and chimneys 62 T&C PORTRAIT 10   15
  and while roofs and fire-escapes and chimneys and while . . . 62 T&C PORTRAIT 10   16
  and while chimneys and fire-escapes and roofs are talking . . 62 T&C PORTRAIT 10   17
  Tail stirs.) And the. fire-escapes-- the night. makes me . . 166 & SON ACTU 15   11
ESCORTED
  by imperishable your glory escorted through infinite . . . . 811 73 POEMS 39   3
ESCORTS
  scattering perfume-gifted wings suddenly escorts with feet . 187 XLI SONGS 9   15

                                                         PAGE   TITLE   LINE

ESCORTS (CONTINUED)
   a so immediate is escorts us home through never's . . . . . . 517 50 POEMS 31   11
ESN7OTHINGISH8S
   trop fort le negre esn7othingish8s c'est fini pRaW, 1T; . . . 430 NO THANKS 47   21
ESPECIALLY
   with whom time feeds especially his immense lips On . . . . . 138 & SON REAL 9   9
   committing nuisances but more especially in your own house . 204 XLI LA GUERRE 2   16
   why birds fly and especially who the moon is. . . . . 368 VIVA 59   21
   say" (and she looked) "especially in winter" (like a . . . . 572 1 X 1 32   5
ESPOUSED
   and hope (by cold espoused unto fear) in dreadful . . . . . . 207 XLI SONNETS 3   7
ESPY
   for fear you would espy the little distinct foot . . . . . . 22 T&C PUELLA MEA   216
ESSENTIAL
   the ignorant most precise essential flame never which waked) 373 VIVA 64   7
ESSENTIALLY
   (or otherwise democratic) but essentially poetic or . . . . . 802 73 POEMS 30   21
EST
   de gustibus non disputandum est my lady is tired . . . . . . 245 IS 5 ONE 16   24
   begins The) now, est hills er dream; new . . . . 350 VIVA 41   12
   on air Harvard Brevis Est for Handkerchief read Papernapkin . 410 NO THANKS 27   5
   yearnswoons; &Isdensekil- ◇ ruptingly) ca-y-est droppe5 . . 430 NO THANKS 47   16
   tu veux Dwrith il est trop fort le negre . . . . 430 NO THANKS 47   20
   turn in to whos est people be come un . . . . 463 NEW POEMS 1   15
   begin to live id est breathe but if such . . . . 510 50 POEMS 24   6
   wednesday next at 1 E.S.T. bring the kiddies let's . . . . . 514 50 POEMS 28   14
   of Black er than est if Im agines more . . . . 759 95 POEMS 86   5
   where a hidi ng) est meta ph or ? . . . . 831 73 POEMS 59   15
ESTABLISH
   kill (make strangely) known (establish new) come, what Being! 422 NO THANKS 39   10
ESTABLISHED
   bald greenish foetal head established It suddenly upon the . 96 & POST IMPR 8   29
   ideal edifice... situated or established ...far from the . . 319 VIVA 11   23
ESTABLISHING
   insensible with a banana, establishing meanwhile a re- . . . 262 IS 5 ONE 32   24
ESTATE
   for murderers of high estate whose mongrel creed is . . . . . 774 73 POEMS 2   10
ET
   les anglais sont gentils et les americains aussi, ils . . . . 120 & PORTRAIT 12   26
   flabby algebraic odour jigs et tout en face always . . . . . 134 & SON REAL 5   10
   intangibility. Personne ne m'aime et j'ai les mains froides. 262 IS 5 ONE 32   26
   in the deep mud et cetera (dreaming, et cetera, ... 276 IS 5 TWO 10   20
   mud et cetera (dreaming, et cetera, of Your smile . . . . . . 276 IS 5 TWO 10   23
+ETA
   FOR CONTEXT, SEE . . . . 431 NO THANKS 48   26
+ETATS-UNIS
   FOR CONTEXT, SEE . . . . 321 VIVA 13   16
ETC
   superc lossal hyperpr digious etc i kn w & . . . . 392 NO THANKS 9   5
   peacemuckers) $ $ $ etc (as the boodle's bent . . . . 635 (CHAIRE) 37   21
ETCETERA
   / my sweet old etcetera aunt lucy during the . . . . 276 IS 5 TWO 10   1
   mention shirts fleaproof earwarmers etcetera wristers . . . . 276 IS 5 TWO 10   12
   fleaproof earwarmers etcetera wristers etcetera, my mother . 276 IS 5 TWO 10   12
   that i would die etcetera bravely of course my . . . . 276 IS 5 TWO 10   14
   could meanwhile my self etcetera lay quietly in the . . . . . 276 IS 5 TWO 10   19
   knees and of your Etcetera) / / / / . . . . 276 IS 5 TWO 10   26
ETERNAL
   its curls of unendured eternal gold over the infinite . . . .   4 T&C EPITHALAM   38
   currency of faint cities eternal--ere the sinless taint of .   9 T&C SONGS 1   33
   have a drink? (the eternal perpetual question) Inside . . . . 97 & POST IMPR 8   42
   its chords brittle eager eternal luminous firmly diminishing 110 & PORTRAIT 6   26
   whose for eheads shone eternal pleasedon't; rising: from the 343 VIVA 34   17
   starhums wherefore & wormSmile eternal; quite perhaps as . . 371 VIVA 62   24
   immortal yonder collidingly absorbs eternal near) day being . 376 VIVA 67   13
   likes it only this eternal mere one bursting soul . . . . . . 414 NO THANKS 31   11
   alive the dear beautiful eternal night / / / . . . . 464 NEW POEMS 2   36
   whereless truth of an eternal now welcomes each was . . . . . 558 1 X 1 18   5

ETERNAL (CONTINUED)
    to complain --plunged in eternal now if who're by . . . . . . 561 1 X 1 21   9
    now disappear night's not eternal terrors like a guess. . . . 582 1 X 1 42   15
    from fragrant mountains of eternal now to frolic in . . . . . 743 95 POEMS 71   12
ETERNALLY
    touches most mere until (eternally) with (now) luminous the . 601 (CHAIRE) 3   15
ETERNITY
    one svelte translation of eternity unto the pale meaning . . 6 T&C EPITHALAM   123
    if in terror of eternity, (or seeming that they . . . . 6 T&C EPITHALAM   139
    and be jerked into eternity. when over my head . . . . 49 T&C IMPRESS 3   22
    i said exhaling into eternity as Nicho' laid before . . . . . 194 XLI PORTRAIT 2   30
    and whittles life to eternity --after which our separating . 297 IS 5 FOUR 14   13
    this steep fragrance of eternity) world by than worlds . . . 450 NO THANKS 65   8
    mountaining roots of mere eternity) stupendous if . . . . . . 517 50 POEMS 31   2
    celestial silence huger than eternity, men will be saviours . 555 1 X 1 15   6
    of perhaps (who knows?) eternity floated a blossoming (while 599 (CHAIRE) 1   8
    like ocean patient) dream's eternity (you feel behind this . 617 (CHAIRE) 19   4
    merely me --traveller from eternity; in a single wish, . . . 651 (CHAIRE) 53   2
    day transcends november's year (eternity being so sans until 765 95 POEMS 91   13
    forever now (hosts of eternity; not guests of seem) . . . . . 817 73 POEMS 45   6
ETERNITY'S
    toc, submit says tic, Eternity's a Five Year Plan: . . . . . 438 NO THANKS 54   6
ETHER
    granted who discovered America ether the movies may claim . . 238 IS 5 ONE 9   14
ETHEREAL
    and perfectly more most ethereal silence through twilight's . 669 (CHAIRE) 71   7
ETHEREALLY
    but essentially poetic or ethereally serious: a fine not . . 802 73 POEMS 30   22
EU
    good enough for i eu can have you rope . . . . 476 NEW POEMS 14   11
EUNUCH
    every door a naked eunuch watches on their heads . . . . . . 33 T&C ORIENTALE 6 36
    opened by the tallest eunuch and the queen of . . . . 33 T&C ORIENTALE 6 63
EUROPE
    a trick of syncopation Europe has --. One day . . . . 135 & SON REAL 6   10
    with faces like Jim Europe / / / / . . . . 241 IS 5 ONE 12   9
+EUROPE
    FOR CONTEXT, SEE . . . . 476 NEW POEMS 14   11
EVANGELIST
    / / / this evangelist buttons with his big . . . . 259 IS 5 ONE 29   1
EVAPORATES
    wine which their nearness evaporates to think is the . . . . 193 XLI PORTRAIT 1 13
EVASIVE
    silence immaculate of god's evasive audible great rose! . . . 5 T&C EPITHALAM   112
EVE
    A Diver on Xmas Eve like Hell Itself which . . . . 239 IS 5 ONE 10   6
    now dis "daughter" uv eve (who aint precisely slim) . . . . . 240 IS 5 ONE 11   1
    wnd ow n, r Eve aling 2 a -sprout . . . . 445 NO THANKS 60   9
EVEN
    utterance of his soul--so even i wholly chained to . . . . . 79 T&C SON UNRE 4   10
    the gods are swallowed even Nile the kind black . . . . 112 & PORTRAIT 6   85
    met before dead's more even than how many ways . . . . 126 & SEVEN POEMS 5 8
    / / / / even a pencil has fear . . . . 141 & SON REAL 12   1
    creature was stirring, not even a mouse. The stockings . . . 142 & SON REAL 13   13
    to make it an even dollar whereupon the Divine . . . . 196 XLI PORTRAIT 4   14
    something like a whisper, "even her." "The Madam?" I . . . . 228 IS 5 ONE MARJ 10
    or three times, and even a few more depending . . . . 236 IS 5 ONE 7   15
    / / / / even if all desires things . . . . 237 IS 5 ONE 8   1
    instigate constructive Horizontal business.... even so, let . 260 IS 5 ONE 30   21
    our attention; to speak even less objectively, i was . . . . 263 IS 5 ONE 32   61
    translated: i say that even after April by God . . . . 264 IS 5 ONE 33   7
    worry in every language even deafanddumb thy sons acclaim . . 268 IS 5 TWO 3   6
    roses who will advise even yourself, lady in the . . . . . . 294 IS 5 FOUR 11   3
    guessed everything would be; even remembering the way who . . 338 VIVA 29   19
    while a transparent blouse even recklessly juggles the . . . 341 VIVA 32   19
    all roses) nobody, not even the rain, has such . . . . 366 VIVA 57   20
    are clever to persuade even silence: therefore wonder opens . 376 VIVA 67   9
    of my books could even be your shelves (that . . . . 386 NO THANKS 3   4

EVEN (CONTINUED)

		PAGE	TITLE	LINE
youknow kindof) aint & even (not having most ever	. . . . . .	412	NO THANKS 29	11
a greedier wand than even death's what beneath breathing	. .	454	NO THANKS 69	4
honour this loneliness of even him who fears and	. . . . . .	456	NO THANKS 71	12
thirsty and supple and even if it's sunday may	. . . .	481	NEW POEMS 19	7
senecktie are gentlemen ppoyds even whose recktie are covered		492	50 POEMS 6	15
so glad and big even a thing all small	. . . .	526	50 POEMS 38	3
liberty my dears-- or even is compelled to fight	. . . . . .	544	1 X 1 4	17
(yes mam) sherman; and even (believe it or not)	. . . .	553	1 X 1 13	13
is such an everywhere, even more true would truest	. . . . .	576	1 X 1 36	11
into a rose and even (we'll adventure the	. . . .	577	1 X 1 37	16
but winter's not forever, even snow melts; and if	. . . . . .	579	1 X 1 39	3
is too small for even me; for me and	. . . .	579	1 X 1 39	7
we're anything brighter than even the sun (we're everything	.	594	1 X 1 54	37
bright word may cry --even the crackling spark of	. . . . . .	605	{CHAIRE} 7	8
makes the suggestion) "or even a daisy-- your thorniest	. . .	625	{CHAIRE} 27	12
keener secret than silence even tells) all the earth	. . . .	630	{CHAIRE} 32	8
little he (having flown even higher) is sunning his	. . . . .	631	{CHAIRE} 33	8
as yet invented by even yankee ingenu ity (out	. . . . . .	644	{CHAIRE} 46	3
some body Dead like even a Poet) could hardly	. . . .	702	95 POEMS 30	7
is a Flop or even to Feel how Everything	. . . .	702	95 POEMS 30	13
/ / yes but even 4 or (& h	. . . .	708	95 POEMS 36	1
this child; nor shall even prevail a million questionings	. .	714	95 POEMS 42	12
birth or death or even than breathing shall blossom	. . . . .	720	95 POEMS 48	13
/ when any mortal (even the most odd) can	. . . .	731	95 POEMS 59	1
much mercy more than even the mercy of perfect	. . . .	735	95 POEMS 63	11
a day (or maybe even less) / / /	. . . .	743	95 POEMS 71	14
so than (how should even omnipotent He feel sorry	. . . . . .	748	95 POEMS 76	9
anybody and fate and even Our whisper it Selves	. . . .	762	95 POEMS 89	12
away we go in even the laziest creature among	. . . .	769	95 POEMS 95	8
(A so wonder pure) even than the green the	. . . .	778	73 POEMS 6	7
instance (or ; why even i suppose one 's	. . . .	779	73 POEMS 7	14
fat pigeons coo) haps even 4 now man's most	. . . .	787	73 POEMS 15	8
now that, more nearest even than your fate and	. . . . . .	809	73 POEMS 37	1
never guessed any thing (even a universe) might be	. . . . .	827	73 POEMS 55	4
than big gest could even begin to be) dream	. . . .	840	73 POEMS 68	16
fear to learn and even fiends: or, if he	. . . .	842	73 POEMS 70	5

+EVEN

		PAGE	TITLE	LINE
FOR CONTEXT, SEE	. . . .	447	NO THANKS 62	14

EVENING

		PAGE	TITLE	LINE
this silver minute of evening. We'll choose the way	. . . .	86	T&C SON ACTU 5	2
more simply upon the evening and a propos such	. . . .	98	& POST IMPR 9	8
in bluishsuspenders half-reading the Evening Something in the		166	& SON ACTU 15	7
only lips of the evening And it is 5	. . . .	202	XLI PORTRAIT 9	48
whom) as the august evening mauls Kneeland, and a	. . . . . .	217	XLI SONNETS 13	7
more than less emancipated evening had in return for	. . . .	258	IS 5 ONE 28	6
and thither through the evening in bruised narrow questioning		275	IS 5 TWO 9	50

EVENSLICING

		PAGE	TITLE	LINE
Babylon slim -ness of evenslicing eyes are chisels scarlet	.	106	& PORTRAIT 2	3

EVENTUAL

		PAGE	TITLE	LINE
language of leaves repeats eventual perfection while east	. .	184	XLI SONGS 6	13

+EVENTUALLY

		PAGE	TITLE	LINE
FOR CONTEXT, SEE	. . . .	49	T&C IMPRESS 3	14

EVER

		PAGE	TITLE	LINE
nimble and complete) than ever to Judea's king were	. . . .	17	T&C PUELLA MEA	27
am wholly dead: nor ever did on such a	. . . .	17	T&C PUELLA MEA	35
or something where who-ever-heard-of-growing and	. . . . . .	127	& SEVEN POEMS 5	43
keen city which nobody's ever visited, where always it's	. .	129	& SEVEN POEMS 7	12
think , did you ever hear a jazz Band?	. . . .	141	& SON REAL 12	16
did something go away ever so quietly when we	. . . .	191	XLI CHANSONS 1	15
/ / Will i ever forget that precarious moment?	. . . .	262	IS 5 ONE 32	1
in the sunlight? down ever so far on the	. . . .	281	IS 5 THREE 5	3
voices rise from down ever so far-- hush. Sunlight,	. . . .	281	IS 5 THREE 5	21
touch) deep things; remembering ever so tinily these, your	.	294	IS 5 FOUR 11	7
whom you do not ever fear, me in your	. . . .	294	IS 5 FOUR 11	17
with moondrool and i'm ever so very little afraid")	. . . . .	303	IS 5 FIVE 2	7
not anything which has ever been invented can spoil	. . . . .	357	VIVA 48	5
than everyone that will Ever love) we 've hidden	. . . . . .	397	NO THANKS 14	10

		PAGE	TITLE	LINE
EVER (CONTINUED)				
even (not having most ever lived people always) don't	412	NO THANKS 29	13
it (rejoice) was and ever shall be nor every	425	NO THANKS 42	11
/ / / (of Ever-Ever Land i speak sweet	466	NEW POEMS 4	1
/ / / (of Ever-Ever Land i speak sweet	466	NEW POEMS 4	1
everyone carries canopeners in Ever-Ever Land (for Ever-Ever	466	NEW POEMS 4	8
everyone carries canopeners in Ever-Ever Land (for Ever-Ever	466	NEW POEMS 4	8
in Ever-Ever Land (for Ever-Ever Land is a place	466	NEW POEMS 4	9
in Ever-Ever Land (for Ever-Ever Land is a place	466	NEW POEMS 4	9
good to us (and Ever-Ever Land is a place	466	NEW POEMS 4	17
good to us (and Ever-Ever Land is a place	466	NEW POEMS 4	17
sameness is normal in Ever-Ever Land for a bad	466	NEW POEMS 4	26
sameness is normal in Ever-Ever Land for a bad	466	NEW POEMS 4	26
time that you should ever think, may god forbid	484	NEW POEMS 22	9
legs or feethands; nobody ever could ever had love	490	50 POEMS 4	17
feethands; nobody ever could ever had love loved whose . . .	490	50 POEMS 4	17
barn be glad; nobody ever earns anything, everything little .	514	50 POEMS 28	7
stone flowers opening for ever these silently lit tle	525	50 POEMS 37	5
are fears only not ever named mountains more if	563	1 X 1 23	4
be you no sunbeam ever lies Bang is the	570	1 X 1 30	5
silverest alive silentness god ever breathed upon beginning)	572	1 X 1 32	9
know) Love only has ever been, is, and will	631	(CHAIRE) 33	14
been, is, and will ever be, So / /	631	(CHAIRE) 33	14
& positive quite n ever & bi g screeching	646	(CHAIRE) 48	15
if not hing had, ever happ ene D /	655	(CHAIRE) 57	13
how how could i ever wear it now when	684	95 POEMS 12	6
me of noone i ever & someone (the others	695	95 POEMS 23	11
cheerfulest goddamned sonofabitch i ever met or hope to . . .	699	95 POEMS 27	14
may be be cause ever ybody wants more (&	727	95 POEMS 55	16
when no am was ever as i then that	752	95 POEMS 80	7
comprehend more than shall ever provingly disprove eithering	761	95 POEMS 88	3
no sub human superstate ever knew (1) we sans	803	73 POEMS 31	6
(no thing) no silence ever told; it has no	819	73 POEMS 47	8
+EVER				
FOR CONTEXT, SEE	127	& SEVEN POEMS 5	45
FOR CONTEXT, SEE	447	NO THANKS 62	13
FOR CONTEXT, SEE	724	95 POEMS 52	23
EVER-EVER				
/ / / (of Ever-Ever Land i speak sweet	466	NEW POEMS 4	1
everyone carries canopeners in Ever-Ever Land (for Ever-Ever	466	NEW POEMS 4	8
in Ever-Ever Land (for Ever-Ever Land is a place	466	NEW POEMS 4	9
good to us (and Ever-Ever Land is a place	466	NEW POEMS 4	17
sameness is normal in Ever-Ever Land for a bad	466	NEW POEMS 4	26
EVERLASTING				
tall boy god of everlasting war received the shuddering . . .	7	T&C EPITHALAM	154
free with the astounding everlasting air-- but if i	212	XLI SONNETS 8	12
EVERY				
mention of desire in every curved and curling thing, ...	5	T&C EPITHALAM	90
beat her heart at every kiss of daisy-cup, and	8	T&C OF NICOL	29
beauteous colour went with every bough that reverently bent .	8	T&C OF NICOL	31
under the stile for every mile the feet go	15	T&C SONGS 5	19
the deep caress of every most shy thing and	19	T&C PUELLA MEA	99
of chalcedony and before every door a naked eunuch	33	T&C ORIENTALE 6	35
take big wobbly foot-steps every goggle cent of it	96	& POST IMPR 8	20
up god knows when every day of their lives	109	& PORTRAIT 5	16
who sews and grows every day paler-paler she sits	125	& SEVEN POEMS 4	4
thick and it loves, every old thing falls in	126	& SEVEN POEMS 5	4
best time tickling away every- body's brain so everybody . .	126	& SEVEN POEMS 5	11
in a putrid window every day almost leans a	144	& SON REAL 15	12
i will bring you every spring handfuls of little	161	& SON ACTU 10	7
i will bring you every year something which is	161	& SON ACTU 10	12
to you to hold every finger shall have its	192	XLI CHANSONS 2	19
biggest bodies lopped of every prettiness you hew form . . .	195	XLI PORTRAIT 3	22
Water And Serve-- from every B.V.D. let freedom ring	230	IS 5 ONE 2	13
created He then, And every beast of the field	267	IS 5 TWO 2	20
we should worry in every language even deafanddumb thy . . .	268	IS 5 TWO 3	6
50 (fifty) flics for every one (I) communist and	274	IS 5 TWO 9	17
begin to spoons dance every- should where say over	287	IS 5 FOUR 4	16

221

EVERY (CONTINUED)

O my lady (and every brittle marvelous breathing thing) . . . 293 IS 5 FOUR 10   13
in: wardly of him (every) who does (where) not . . . . . . 346 VIVA 37   22
and hearts grow brittler every Instant (when of a . . . . . 359 VIVA 50   4
clumsily to cease whom every perfect thing meanwhile doth . . 360 VIVA 51   7
(behind each no) touching every yes / / / . . . . 373 VIVA 64   18
little having less with every least each most remembering . . 390 NO THANKS 7   7
females, well attend! list, every nonelastic male-- uplook, . 398 NO THANKS 15   17
find that each and every thing must have an . . . . 411 NO THANKS 28   2
may mess your pance every kumrad is a bit . . . . 413 NO THANKS 30   13
ought with because with every brain which thinks it . . . . . 424 NO THANKS 41   9
ever shall be nor every partialness beats one entirety . . . 425 NO THANKS 42   11
of emptiness) priming at every pore a deathless life . . . . 428 NO THANKS 45   15
the whole moves; and every part stands still: / . . . . . . 446 NO THANKS 61   14
a (not some not every but any) heart--wholly, ... 480 NEW POEMS 18   3
whose any mystery makes every man's flesh put space . . . . . 484 NEW POEMS 22   7
what immense live without every dancing. singless on- ly . . 491 50 POEMS 5   5
to some dirty window every) twilight i feel (his . . . . . 501 50 POEMS 15   7
than open could that every tree or than all . . . . 502 50 POEMS 16   7
pretty a day (and every fades) is here and . . . . 509 50 POEMS 23   2
of love become while every sun goes round its . . . . 510 50 POEMS 24   14
bald men's hair and every finger is a toe . . . . 511 50 POEMS 25   10
or impossibly 3 individuals every several fat thousand years. 514 50 POEMS 28   2
by his voyage from every to no) who still . . . . 516 50 POEMS 30   3
in the head; if every friend became his foe . . . . 521 50 POEMS 34   47
of each tree (and every child was sure that . . . . 521 50 POEMS 34   51
quick no suit there every -thing nothing i say . . . . . . 523 50 POEMS 36   23
/ love is the every only god who spoke . . . . 526 50 POEMS 38   1
of stern miraculous this every truth--beware of heartless . . 556 1 X 1 16   6
one atomy once, and every cannot stir imagining; while . . . 559 1 X 1 19   10
/ / / dead every enormous piece of nonsense . . . . 561 1 X 1 21   1
than all which and every who; despite what fear . . . . . . 576 1 X 1 36   2
scale to shrillerness per every madge and mabel dick . . . . 579 1 X 1 39   11
fear play host to every isn't that's under the . . . . . . 580 1 X 1 40   5
stars the star (sing! every joy) --wholly now disappear . . . 582 1 X 1 42   14
come love (by yes every new bird no bigger . . . . 583 1 X 1 43   16
if are those eyes every because is murdered twice . . . . . 588 1 X 1 48   8
die or i and every world, before silence begins . . . . . . 601 (CHAIRE) 3   19
scotch was your breakfast every night all day) a . . . . . . 605 (CHAIRE) 7   5
gods each greedier than every) is a man (so . . . . 609 (CHAIRE) 11   2
that memory strolls) and every ours for the mere . . . . . 617 (CHAIRE) 19   12
against old age when every thrush may sing no . . . . 620 (CHAIRE) 22   5
/ / who sharpens every dull here comes the . . . . 624 (CHAIRE) 26   1
thing glimpsed (and on every side swoop mountains flimsying . 634 (CHAIRE) 36   2
why must itself up every of a park anus . . . . 636 (CHAIRE) 38   1
are dancing together) when every leaf opens without any . . . 665 (CHAIRE) 67   8
(my love) alive than every world can understand and . . . . 667 (CHAIRE) 69   4
of the child who's every child (& therefore invisible) . . . 668 (CHAIRE) 70   12
has a doll & every now & then my . . . . 680 95 POEMS 8   22
never (selves any than every more silent ly) heard . . . . 695 95 POEMS 23   16
some that bum who's every one / / / . . . . 698 95 POEMS 26   8
ner the only reason every wo man should go . . . . 700 95 POEMS 28   4
him, eyes --gifted with every keener appetite than mere . . . 714 95 POEMS 42   4
simply which) a marvel every breathing creature feels (but . 735 95 POEMS 63   7
mankind persuades itself that every weed's a rose, roses . . 744 95 POEMS 72   6
thrushsong (and more than every miracle's to breathe) wounded 745 95 POEMS 73   4
merciful ly which is every) un (star rain snow . . . . . . 753 95 POEMS 81   14
sweet such (past can's every can't) immensest mysteries . . . 763 95 POEMS 90   26
joyful your any new (every more only you) most . . . . . . 764 95 POEMS 90   46
a me and an every (who's any who's some) . . . . 769 95 POEMS 95   28
all the any merry every pretty each bird sings . . . . . . 773 73 POEMS 1   3
joy) bird sings love's every truth beyond all since . . . . 783 73 POEMS 11   3
weed a tearose) and every minus plus --fare ill: . . . . . . 798 73 POEMS 26   12
husband of (as happens every now and then upon . . . . 799 73 POEMS 27   9
haranguing --you are deafened every mother's son-- all is . . 804 73 POEMS 32   10
Much better than which, every woman who's (despite the . . . 807 73 POEMS 35   9
i be gay like every lark who lifts his . . . . 815 73 POEMS 43   2
it? it is by every star a different time, ... 817 73 POEMS 45   1

EVERY (CONTINUED)

    leaf twig limb ask every question time can't answer: . . . . 818 73 POEMS 46   10

    spirit. Feeling only (jesus) every (god) where (chr ist) . . 823 73 POEMS 51   16

    earth sky trees : every where a miracle arrives . . . . 835 73 POEMS 63   23

    imagine whose despair when every silence will not make . . . 842 73 POEMS 70   10

    a spirit's ignorance by every wisdom knowledge fears to . . . 843 73 POEMS 71   11

+EVERY

    FOR CONTEXT, SEE . . . . 265 IS 5 ONE 34   2

    FOR CONTEXT, SEE . . . . 493 50 POEMS 7   16

EVERYANYTHING

    we come who) one's everyanything so so world is . . . . 594 1 X 1 54   18

    books might mean) we're everyanything more than believe (with 594 1 X 1 54   41

EVERYBODY

    every- body's brain so everybody just puts out their . . . . 126 & SEVEN POEMS 5 12

    is asleep kid and everybody is." And i hazarded . . . . 228 IS 5 ONE MARJ   5

    born failure and nearly everybody said he should have . . . . 239 IS 5 ONE 10   4

    always-so-much-interested-in-everybody-else's-business . . . 250 IS 5 ONE 21   14

    kilt he was kilt everybody was kilt they called . . . . 271 IS 5 TWO 6   11

    guy drops you know everybody feels sick or when . . . . 272 IS 5 TWO 7   5

    tell you just what everybody was fighting for, my . . . . . . 276 IS 5 TWO 10   5

    creeps the deep thing everybody sometimes calls morning / . . 330 VIVA 21   14

    jam on the shelf everybody guessed was too high . . . . 353 VIVA 44   20

    he she it or everybody gets a bellyful without . . . . 475 NEW POEMS 13   7

    to there's something for everybody it's a" old mr . . . . . . 567 1 X 1 27   16

    neither did you and everybody never breathed quite so . . . . 591 1 X 1 51   15

    with an uppercut but everybody (i believe) else thought . . . 706 95 POEMS 34   3

    / / / / everybody happy? WE-WE-WE & to . . . . 791 73 POEMS 19   1

+EVERYBODY

    FOR CONTEXT, SEE . . . . 727 95 POEMS 55   16

+EVERYBODY'S

    FOR CONTEXT, SEE . . . . 126 & SEVEN POEMS 5 11

    FOR CONTEXT, SEE . . . . 696 95 POEMS 24   6

EVERYBODYELSE'S

    persons (in stead of everybodyelse's) but what's wholly . . . 782 73 POEMS 10   13

+EVERYCHILDFATHERINGONE

    more-than-thing (& falling &) EverychildfatheringOne . . . . 715 95 POEMS 43   21

EVERYONE

    in the window for everyone to see and how . . . . 192 XLI CHANSONS 2   22

    i swear (to noone everyone) constitutes undying; or whatever 264 IS 5 ONE 33   2

    over you all me everyone that's been there knows . . . . . . 272 IS 5 TWO 7   11

    haps) loved (or than everyone that will Ever love) . . . . . 397 NO THANKS 14   10

    anything else uncanned for everyone carries canopeners in . . 466 NEW POEMS 4   7

    an arse upon which everyone has sat except a . . . . 550 1 X 1 10   2

    if that fool called everyone (or you or i) . . . . 603 {CHAIRE} 5   10

    may mean anything which everyone would rather not become; . . 626 {CHAIRE} 28   4

    Someone has been born everyone is noone dance around . . . . 630 {CHAIRE} 32   15

    at your each nearerness) everyone certainly would (my most . 717 95 POEMS 45   13

    vote and politics, as everyone knows, is wut ektyouelly . . . 790 73 POEMS 18   13

+EVERYONE

    FOR CONTEXT, SEE . . . . 698 95 POEMS 26   8

    FOR CONTEXT, SEE . . . . 769 95 POEMS 95   28

EVERYONE'S

    always it's Spring) and everyone's in love and flowers . . . 129 & SEVEN POEMS 7 15

EVERYONES

    her someones married their everyones laughed their cryings . 515 50 POEMS 29   17

EVERYTHING

    in the sky Blue, everything: a bar the bar . . . . 123 & SEVEN POEMS 2   2

    thing here) and changing everything carefully spring is like 124 & SEVEN POEMS 3   9

    gloves and flowers and everything and i remember we . . . . . 239 IS 5 ONE 10   31

    rent's going to and everything and never, never Never . . . 242 IS 5 ONE 13   19

    anyway and it's flutters everything queer; does smells he . . 251 IS 5 ONE 22   4

    we hold lips Eyes everything hands you know what . . . . . 287 IS 5 FOUR 4   18

    / in spite of everything which breathes and moves, ... 288 IS 5 FOUR 5   1

    in his mouth (making everything suddenly old and with . . . 293 IS 5 FOUR 10   27

    its lowest terms with everything cancelled but shadows --what 295 IS 5 FOUR 12   19

    and smiling you answer "everything turns into something else, 303 IS 5 FIVE 2   4

    Reflex you know since Everything is Relative or to . . . . . 315 VIVA 7   8

    the stars for instance everything is planned next to . . . . 322 VIVA 14   3

	PAGE	TITLE	LINE

EVERYTHING (CONTINUED)

with small hands "& everything is easier than I	338	VIVA 29	17
than I had guessed everything would be; even remembering . .	338	VIVA 29	18
More careful Than of everything guard her perhaps only . . .	453	NO THANKS 68	3
all with love and everything perverse or which makes	466	NEW POEMS 4	22
rings are cake & everything is protected by cellophane . . .	470	NEW POEMS 8	18
nobody ever earns anything, everything little looks big in .	514	50 POEMS 28	8
god decided to invent everything he took one breath	566	1 X 1 26	2
than a circustent and everything began when man determined .	566	1 X 1 26	4
worships and (night) then "everything beautiful can grow" my,	572	1 X 1 32	14
than nothing's more than everything) death, as men call . . .	592	1 X 1 52	12
/ / / if everything happens that can't be	594	1 X 1 54	1
one's anything old being everything new (with a what	594	1 X 1 54	14
even the sun (we're everything greater than books might . . .	594	1 X 1 54	38
knows nothing, and feels everything; all around whom is . . .	657	(CHAIRE) 59	3
of sky; and for everything which is natural which	663	(CHAIRE) 65	3
even to Feel how Everything (dreamed & hoped &	702	95 POEMS 30	16
like you better than everything in the sky --sunlight	717	95 POEMS 45	3
than i but always everything which only dies to	718	95 POEMS 46	5
whom the departure of everything real is the arrival	720	95 POEMS 48	10
is the arrival of everything true) and i'm no	720	95 POEMS 48	11
-morrow and yesterday and everything except love / /	762	95 POEMS 89	14

+EVERYTHING

FOR CONTEXT, SEE	411	NO THANKS 28	2
FOR CONTEXT, SEE	523	50 POEMS 36	23
FOR CONTEXT, SEE	618	(CHAIRE) 20	31
FOR CONTEXT, SEE	701	95 POEMS 29	1
FOR CONTEXT, SEE	701	95 POEMS 29	19

EVERYTHING'S

forget to kiss) where everything's nothing --arise, my soul;	834	73 POEMS 62	29

EVERYWHERE

merde which greets one (Everywhere Why) as divine poesy . . .	230	IS 5 ONE 2	17
right all up all everywhere over you all me	272	IS 5 TWO 7	11
shooting his cuffs saluted everywhere saluting reviewing . .	275	IS 5 TWO 9	36
and here reflecting sunlight (everywhere sunlight keen . . .	283	IS 5 THREE 7	14
keen complete silent and everywhere you your kisses your . .	283	IS 5 THREE 7	16
certainly (of what we everywhere do not touch) deep	294	IS 5 FOUR 11	5
if within tonight's erect everywhere of black muscles fools .	299	IS 5 FOUR 16	2
"but I will not everywhere be real to you	338	VIVA 29	13
oceans various and while everywhere beneath thee and about .	351	VIVA 42	8
spatters creasing pillow next everywhere hidinglyseek no o .	358	VIVA 49	4
imagines the snow carefully everywhere descending; nothing .	366	VIVA 57	12
imprisoned, tortured here love everywhere exploding maims and	377	VIVA 68	8
death whenless voices sing everywhere your selves himself . .	450	NO THANKS 65	18
here is such an everywhere, even more true would	576	1 X 1 36	10
and nothing ignoble) everywhere wonder / / /	658	(CHAIRE) 60	26
clown of an angel everywhere welcome (but chiefly at	678	95 POEMS 6	9
although winter may be everywhere with such a silence	717	95 POEMS 45	5
arriving magically here-- an everywhere which you've and i've	741	95 POEMS 69	12
(strolling is there here everywhere fairyair feelable . . .	755	95 POEMS 83	9
shadowy if) swallowing is everywhere beginningless a Magic of	757	95 POEMS 85	13
dear he sings till everywhere is here / /	760	95 POEMS 87	12
marvels "what happened" as everywhere red goes green	800	73 POEMS 28	22
hopes beliefs doubts disappear. Everywhere and joy's perfect	812	73 POEMS 40	14
Now i lay (with everywhere around) me (the great	816	73 POEMS 44	1
creature who's O cean (everywhere nothing but light and . . .	840	73 POEMS 68	22

+EVERYWHERE

FOR CONTEXT, SEE	346	VIVA 37	22
FOR CONTEXT, SEE	646	(CHAIRE) 48	10
FOR CONTEXT, SEE	657	(CHAIRE) 59	7
FOR CONTEXT, SEE	713	95 POEMS 41	7
FOR CONTEXT, SEE	823	73 POEMS 51	16
FOR CONTEXT, SEE	830	73 POEMS 58	5
FOR CONTEXT, SEE	835	73 POEMS 63	23

EVERYWHERE'S

/ / spring! may-- everywhere's here (with a low	767	95 POEMS 93	2

EVERYWHEREING

patience heard above the everywhereing fact of fear; and . .	821	73 POEMS 49	6

		PAGE	TITLE	LINE

EVERYWHERES
    Thickness) points uPDownwardishly find everywheres . . . . . 311 VIVA 3   16
+EVERYWHERES
    FOR CONTEXT, SEE . . . . 416 NO THANKS 33   3
EVIDENT
    / / / of evident invisibles exquisite the hovering . . . . . 54 T&C PORTRAIT 2 1
EVIL
    snowing. Inside snug and evil. the slobbering walls filthily 96 & POST IMPR 8   3
    was like a gas evil to feel. Unwieldy.... the . . . . 135 & SON REAL 6   7
    whose latest Seeds Of Evil sold 69 carloads before . . . . . 245 IS 5 ONE 16   9
    scientific & artificial & evil & legal) we thank . . . . . . 604 (CHAIRE) 6   21
    better; and because no evil is so worse than . . . . 679 95 POEMS 7   11
    cruel fair or blessed evil-- it is you (ne . . . . 804 73 POEMS 32   7
+EVIL
    FOR CONTEXT, SEE . . . . 97 & POST IMPR 8   43
EVILFRINGING
    of darkness: carve an evilfringing flower of madness on . . . 139 & SON REAL 10   8
EVOKE
    toiletbowl, while kindred intellects evoke allegiance per . . 339 VIVA 30   13
EVOLUTE
    so chuck slop hight evolute my eerily oh gargle . . . . 333 VIVA 24   22
EVOLVING
    fact --by their precision evolving vision dreamtree, ... 763 95 POEMS 90   30
EVRY
    me crazy me like evry-ting / / / / . . . . 618 (CHAIRE) 20   31
EVRY-TING
    me crazy me like evry-ting / / / / . . . . 618 (CHAIRE) 20   31
EX
    earthquakes famine or the ex prince of whoses diving . . . . 475 NEW POEMS 13   19
EXACLY
    contras tuh dat not exacly fat "father" (adjustin his . . . . 240 IS 5 ONE 11   3
EXACT
    how behind the doomed exact smile of life's placid . . . . . 43 T&C AMORES 7   30
    the simple ugliness of exact tombs, where a large . . . . . . 86 T&C SON ACTU 5 12
    mind. , Rinsing with exact death the annual brain . . . . . . 99 & POST IMPR 10 4
    Her nose was small, exact, stupid. mouth normal, large, . . . 103 & POST IMPR 13 13
    of an imaginable gesture exact warm unholy / / . . . . 162 & SON ACTU 11   17
    seen frequently fingering the exact beads of a faultless . . 193 XLI PORTRAIT 1   6
    exhales a climbing dark exact walloping human noise of . . . 202 XLI PORTRAIT 9 45
    distinct mouth) do the exact human comely thing? (or . . . . 218 XLI SONNETS 14   8
    vigilant perpetual eyes each exact victim, how he does . . . 386 NO THANKS 3   11
    & & away wanders: exact ly; as if not . . . . 655 (CHAIRE) 57   10
    Noth ing & nothing's exAct ly what any one . . . . 702 95 POEMS 30   2
EXACTES
    toutes les petites femmes exactes qui dansent toujours in . . 121 & PORTRAIT 12 50
EXACTITUDES
    yet, among their loud exactitudes of imprecision, you'll . . 659 (CHAIRE) 61   11
EXACTLY
    husk heaven) you, you exactly paled and curled with . . . . . 71 T&C SON REAL 2 12
    lips begin a smile exactly strange-- this painter should . . 85 T&C SON ACTU 4   8
    ly in to one exactly-mutilated ghost of a chair, ... 96 & POST IMPR 8   34
    sure lyHer eye s exactly sit, ata little roundtable . . . . . 104 & POST IMPR 14 2
    is eighteen hundred years.... exactly under the window under 108 & PORTRAIT 4   32
    ladies more than dead exactly dance in my head, ... 120 & PORTRAIT 12   2
    bien les americains dance exactly in my brain voulez- . . . . 120 & PORTRAIT 12 28
    te ferai Minette, dead exactly dance si vous voulez . . . . . 121 & PORTRAIT 12 39
    her body's doll gay exactly perishing sexual, / / . . . . . . 131 & SON REAL 2   17
    fluffy lust) at six exactly the alarm tore two . . . . 132 & SON REAL 3   11
    to ride her? ....she exactly lay, looking hunks of . . . . . 145 & SON REAL 16   13
    of candlelight (halfstooping to exactly kiss the trite worm . 164 & SON ACTU 13   4
    enormous curve of flesh exactly cubes of tiny fragrance . . . 214 XLI SONNETS 10 4
    anyone hardly should call exactly extraordinary. We refer, of 263 IS 5 ONE 32   36
    / nothing is more exactly terrible than to be . . . . 375 VIVA 66   1
    be saviours --flop grasshopper, exactly nothing's soon; . . . 555 1 X 1 15   8
    than excellent E will exactly do next (our great . . . . . . 650 (CHAIRE) 52   12
    pity fear each more exactly than the other un . . . . 662 (CHAIRE) 64   10
    when to do is exactly theirs (dull worlds or . . . . 776 73 POEMS 4   10

	PAGE	TITLE	LINE
+EXACTLY			
FOR CONTEXT, SEE	104	& POST IMPR 14	20
FOR CONTEXT, SEE	104	& POST IMPR 14	21
FOR CONTEXT, SEE	240	IS 5 ONE 11	3
FOR CONTEXT, SEE	655	(CHAIRE) 57	10
FOR CONTEXT, SEE	676	95 POEMS 4	12
FOR CONTEXT, SEE	702	95 POEMS 30	2
EXACTLY-MUTILATED			
ly in to one exactly-mutilated ghost of a chair, ...	96	& POST IMPR 8	34
EXACTLYGIR			
in little streets while exactlygir lisHlegs; play; ing; nake;	104	& POST IMPR 14	11
EXAGGERATION			
box of newly without exaggeration shot with some difficulty .	263	IS 5 ONE 32	47
EXAMINES			
master's spirit stooping, Crusoelike examines fearingly and .	344	VIVA 35	14
EXAMPLE			
/ / Take for example this: if to the	92	& POST IMPR 4	1
O Life a formula: example, Turn Your Shirttails Into	230	IS 5 ONE 2	33
EXCEEDINGLY			
for me and you, exceedingly too small. Swoop (shrill	579	1 X 1 39	8
EXCELLED			
flesh merely shall be excelled by speaking flower (if	84	T&C SON ACTU 3	4
EXCELLENT			
and nothing less than excellent E will exactly do	650	(CHAIRE) 52	11
EXCELLENTLY			
lover of all things excellently rare; obsolete almost that .	607	(CHAIRE) 9	10
EXCEPT			
absence of any program except last and always and	264	IS 5 ONE 33	18
me to become noone except yourselves r s v	504	50 POEMS 18	5
or joy) does nothing except preexist its hoi in	544	1 X 1 4	7
which everyone has sat except a man / /	550	1 X 1 10	2
/ / / / except in your honour, my	575	1 X 1 35	1
meet for centuries and (except nothing) nothing's won --but .	580	1 X 1 40	18
breathing creature this? nothing except the impossible shall	582	1 X 1 42	12
proud sloppy sleek) all except the cold ones paul	619	(CHAIRE) 21	6
plump tiny tall) all except the dull ones gus	619	(CHAIRE) 21	13
mad moronic maimed) all except the dead ones mike	619	(CHAIRE) 21	20
kind dirty clean) all except the green ones /	619	(CHAIRE) 21	28
closer made of nothing except loneliness / / /	648	(CHAIRE) 50	12
lifetime at the least) except to add an A?	650	(CHAIRE) 52	8
(everyb ody's elsewher e except me 6 e nglish	696	95 POEMS 24	8
(like me like you) except in snow-- a whom	716	95 POEMS 44	4
quite begin to guess (except my life) the true	717	95 POEMS 45	8
whoms of merciful sweetness except Himself?" --"noone unless	748	95 POEMS 76	14
than each creature new (except your fear to whom	762	95 POEMS 89	6
and yesterday and everything except love / / /	762	95 POEMS 89	14
which i've no word except alive --that is, completely	802	73 POEMS 30	14
+EXCEPT			
FOR CONTEXT, SEE	701	95 POEMS 29	1
FOR CONTEXT, SEE	701	95 POEMS 29	5
FOR CONTEXT, SEE	830	73 POEMS 58	11
EXCHANGING			
than trees) dodreamingly phantoms (exchanging) e vero madonna	681	95 POEMS 9	6
again --her murdered selves exchanging swiftly for the . . .	818	73 POEMS 46	5
EXCITATION			
genuine daze of unmarketable excitation, whose careless . . .	150	& SON REAL 21	13
EXCITING			
cruelty of roses. The exciting simplicity of her hipless . .	103	& POST IMPR 13	2
EXCLAMATORY			
the aid of an exclamatory tooth-pick And who may	194	XLI PORTRAIT 2	26
EXCLUDING			
both pale orbs thus excluding a leanderless drowning in . . .	546	1 X 1 6	6
on the few not excluding mr u / /	551	1 X 1 11	4
EXCREMENT			
much Too. originally spontaneous twurls-of-excrement inanely	94	& POST IMPR 6	2
EXCREMENTAL			
with nauseous spiderlegs and excremental hair and the eyes .	55	T&C PORTRAIT 3	11

	PAGE	TITLE	LINE

EXCUSE
hideously cowers-- i do excuse me, love, to Death . . . . . . 207 XLI SONNETS 3   9
beautiful. Let us perhaps excuse me if i repeat . . . . 263 IS 5 ONE 32   59
God there is no excuse for May --bring forth . . . . 264 IS 5 ONE 33   8
an it that stinks Excuse Me whether it's president . . . . . 549 1 X 1 9   1
+EXCUSE
FOR CONTEXT, SEE . . . . 477 NEW POEMS 15   3
EXECUTE
squirms of chrome and execute strides of cobalt nevertheless 199 XLI PORTRAIT 7   6
EXEMPT
....? of Goethe, since exempt from heaven's grace, in . . . . 158 & SON ACTU 7   7
EXERCISE
he's prodded forth to exercise her vote (or made . . . . . . 544 1 X 1 4   10
EXERTING
breathe together the emperor, exerting himself among his . . 34 T&C ORIENTALE 6 99
EXEUNT
at phonograph x wins exeunt ax: by; c, Goo . . . . 200 XLI PORTRAIT 8   30
why) both didn't know exeunt they (not false not . . . . . . 542 1 X 1 2   5
EXHALES
whiter than this world) exhales the hovering high perfume . . 5 T&C EPITHALAM 101
tremendous canyon always only exhales a climbing dark exact . 202 XLI PORTRAIT 9   44
EXHALING
which presently crumpled collapses. exhaling a red soul into 188 XLI SONGS 10   11
that be i said exhaling into eternity as Nicho' . . . . 194 XLI PORTRAIT 2   29
EXHAUSTED
Kitty) arriving in an exhausted condition, i purchased two . 326 VIVA 18   15
EXHUMED
glass box which the exhumed hand of Saint Ignatz . . . . . . 280 IS 5 THREE 4   3
(as aprils elsewhere stroll) exhumed most innocently . . . . 546 1 X 1 6   3
EXHUMES
too frequently) skirt exhumes (which buries again quick- . . 341 VIVA 32   14
EXIST
that petal confutes... to exist being a peculiar form . . . . 264 IS 5 ONE 33   4
isn't that it can't exist (and is that the . . . . 411 NO THANKS 28   11
minds socalled would not exist but if these not . . . . 510 50 POEMS 24   4
some dream of to exist a stranger who is . . . . 559 1 X 1 19   7
rainlife) infinite also ourselves exist sans shallbe or was . 755 95 POEMS 83   14
midnight this hearty fellow'll exist --whereas that delicate 813 73 POEMS 41   6
EXISTENCE
touch the pink hollyhock existence whose pansy eyes look . . 58 T&C PORTRAIT 6   17
froms and whithers of existence, as by shores soundless, . . 79 T&C SON UNRE 4   6
acrobatic edgeless gesture of existence, continually whittles 193 XLI PORTRAIT 1   20
soiled canary-cage of largest existence. (when he would . . . 197 XLI PORTRAIT 5   13
comparable soul which with existence has conversed in vain, . 212 XLI SONNETS 8   2
voice) from some complete existence of to dream into . . . . 559 1 X 1 19   6
aeons of (trivial merely) existence, all when may not . . . . 763 95 POEMS 90   34
EXISTING
but if these not existing minds took life such . . . . 510 50 POEMS 24   5
EXISTING'S
what you didn't lose (existing's tricky: but to live's . . . 807 73 POEMS 35   2
EXISTS
anything (because nothing really exists / / / / . . . . 470 NEW POEMS 8   20
what were motionless move (exists no miracle mightier than . 762 95 POEMS 89   1
EXIT
paperboy, c buys Bawstinamereekin, exit paperboy a finishes . 200 XLI PORTRAIT 8   13
mingle under the mercy. (exit the hors d'oeuvres) / . . . . . 243 IS 5 ONE 14   16
/ / / / exit a kind of unkindness . . . . 389 NO THANKS 6   1
a kind of unkindness exit little mr Big notbusy . . . . 389 NO THANKS 6   1
EXPAND
seeing green armies steadily expand hearing the spear-song of 4 T&C EPITHALAM   71
comes ex -pert- Ly expand: grO w i ? . . . . 471 NEW POEMS 9   8
EXPANDED
I've lost the) Einstein expanded Newton's law preserved . . . 315 VIVA 7   5
+EXPANDING
FOR CONTEXT, SEE . . . . 248 IS 5 ONE 19   30
FOR CONTEXT, SEE . . . . 449 NO THANKS 64   8
EXPANDS
little topples and slightly expands one square foot mired . . 225 IS 5 ONE LIZ   2

227

	PAGE	TITLE	LINE

EXPANDS (CONTINUED)

oh how listens and, expands my somewherealloverme heart my . 251 IS 5 ONE 22   16

EXPECT

/ plant Magic dust expect hope doubt (wonder mistrust) . . . 780 73 POEMS 8   2

EXPECTANT

church. toward which The Expectant stutter (upon artificial . 280 IS 5 THREE 4   33

EXPECTING

that clear candle whose expecting breath exults upon the . . 6 T&C EPITHALAM   117

brittle swoon of centrifugally expecting faces clumsily which 279 IS 5 THREE 3   6

several fat thousand years. Expecting more would be neither . 514 50 POEMS 28   3

EXPECTS

me, whose heart-wholeness overmuch Expects of your hair pale, 12 T&C SONGS 2   39

where <> and nobody expects you to anyway dead . . . . 127 & SEVEN POEMS 5 44

EXPELS

whose pedestal the deep expels (over Selene's car closing . . 4 T&C EPITHALAM   46

+EXPENDING

FOR CONTEXT, SEE . . . . 34 T&C ORIENTALE 6   91

EXPENSIVE

colliding with the most expensive furniture upsets a crucifix 203 XLI LA GUERRE 1 12

EXPENSIVELY

(and such hair) the expensively democratic tyrannically dumb 337 VIVA 28   13

EXPERIENCE

selves merely Continue to experience a neverish subchemistry 361 VIVA 52   27

travelled, gladly beyond any experience, your eyes have their 366 VIVA 57   2

+EXPERIMENTING

FOR CONTEXT, SEE . . . . 201 XLI PORTRAIT 9   24

EXPERTLY

ruglike sentience whose papillae expertly drink the docile . 201 XLI PORTRAIT 9   17

+EXPERTLY

FOR CONTEXT, SEE . . . . 471 NEW POEMS 9   6

+EXPIRING

FOR CONTEXT, SEE . . . . 122 & SEVEN POEMS 1 4

EXPLAIN

snow can begin to explain how children are apt . . . . 515 50 POEMS 29   22

EXPLODE

by it caressed will explode and spill the immediate . . . . . 193 XLI PORTRAIT 1 17

here and here they explode silently into crocuses of . . . . 282 IS 5 THREE 6   30

EXPLODED

through sagging debris of exploded day the hulking . . . . . 151 & SON REAL 22   2

+EXPLODED

FOR CONTEXT, SEE . . . . 320 VIVA 12   11

EXPLODES

nor a first rose explodes but shall increase whole . . . . . 538 50 POEMS 50   13

flame twig or limb explodes and o each living . . . . 583 1 X 1 43   12

EXPLODING

tortured here love everywhere exploding maims and blinds (but 377 VIVA 68   8

pening of (writhing your exploding my) heart before how . . . 480 NEW POEMS 18   15

was are night's total exploding millionminded Who / / . . . . 633 (CHAIRE) 35   16

+EXPLODING

FOR CONTEXT, SEE . . . . 795 73 POEMS 23   24

+EXPLORE

FOR CONTEXT, SEE . . . . 612 (CHAIRE) 14   4

EXPLOSION

es a, fad ed explosion of, pink! stocking w . . . . 94 & POST IMPR 6   5

a sodden fastidious normal explosion; a square mur- mur, . . 201 XLI PORTRAIT 9   12

EXPOSED

my curiously instant appreciation exposed his hibernative . . 197 XLI PORTRAIT 5   9

EXPOSES

mop punching underneath conventions exposes hidden . . . . . 203 XLI LA GUERRE 1   4

EXPOSURE

negative silence that primeval exposure whose electric . . . 197 XLI PORTRAIT 5   17

EXPRESS

bulging in immortal Spring express a cry of How . . . . 255 IS 5 ONE 26   6

a Poet) could hardly express what i Mean is . . . . 702 95 POEMS 30   8

EXPRESSIB

ting with the in -expressib- le num -berlessn- ess . . . . . 739 95 POEMS 67   7

EXPRESSING

deep immediate mask and expressing "as for myself, because . 328 VIVA 19   15

		PAGE	TITLE	LINE

EXPRESSION
stalks the Momentinmyarms your expression my love when most . 94 & POST IMPR 6   23
sharp and impertinently dead. expression began with the early 103 & POST IMPR 13   6
EXQUISE
of (unthinking. c'est l'heure exquise) i remind Me of . . . . 94 & POST IMPR 6   20
EXQUISITE
e'er depart upon more exquisite quest? and did thy . . . . .   3 T&C EPITHALAM   20
stupid sincere youth the exquisite failure uncouth discovers   11 T&C SONGS 2   7
responds) of all things exquisite and dead, all living . . .   19 T&C PUELLA MEA 127
Looked up with impertinently exquisite faces floating hands .   44 T&C AMORES 8   10
/ of evident invisibles exquisite the hovering at the . . . .   54 T&C PORTRAIT 2   2
my spirit with the exquisite froms and whithers of . . . . .   79 T&C SON UNRE 4   5
/ / / inthe, exquisite; morning sure lyHer eye . . . . 104 & POST IMPR 14   1
one the vague tough exquisite flowers, whom hardens richly, . 154 & SON ACTU 3   8
tree leaps a stiffened exquisite i wait the sweet . . . . . . 182 XLI SONGS 2   8
softly are keeping their exquisite dreams--O Love! upon thy . 206 XLI SONNETS 2   10
why (in this most exquisite of cities) all of . . . . 300 IS 5 FOUR 17   11
imitating a few fatally exquisite" (pulling Its shawl . . . . 328 VIVA 19   19
mystery made flesh-- dreamslender exquisite white firstful . 669 (CHAIRE) 71   9
+EXQUISITE
FOR CONTEXT, SEE . . . . 104 & POST IMPR 14   18
FOR CONTEXT, SEE . . . . 536 50 POEMS 48   14
EXQUISITELY
the artificer did most exquisitely err.) When the world . . .   22 T&C PUELLA MEA 220
singular block her, rain-warm-naked exquisitely hashed . . . 133 & SON REAL 4   3
the firm tumult of exquisitely in- secure sharp algebraic . . 201 XLI PORTRAIT 9   19
their guessing fingers did-not-move exquisitely ,like dead . 355 VIVA 46   16
a memory, which how exquisitely flutters in the cornerless . 370 VIVA 61   26
EXROPER
flinger of lariats lean exroper of horned suddenly crashing . 252 IS 5 ONE 23   10
EXTANT
obsolete lips utter their extant smile.... remark a few . . . 260 IS 5 ONE 30   6
EXTEMPORISE
existence. (when he would extemporise the innovation of mus- 197 XLI PORTRAIT 5   14
EXTEND
septembering arms of year extend less humbly wealth to . . . 521 50 POEMS 34   37
into a mountainrange; lenses extend unwish through curving . 554 1 X 1 14   6
EXTENDED
Mary with one lung extended to the pumping Child, ... 142 & SON REAL 13   11
EXTENDING
contours, amiable immensity impeccably extending the courtesy 197 XLI PORTRAIT 5   10
+EXTENDING
FOR CONTEXT, SEE . . . . 416 NO THANKS 33   3
EXTERNALCONTRACTING
on the internalexpanding & externalcontracting brakes . . . 248 IS 5 ONE 19   32
EXTINCT
among pale lips the extinct cigar) at which this . . . . . . 252 IS 5 ONE 23   6
EXTINGUISHED
earth a candle is extinguished the city wakes with . . . . .   50 T&C IMPRESS 4   5
+EXTINGUISHED
FOR CONTEXT, SEE . . . . 267 IS 5 TWO 2   11
EXTINGUISHING
Miggin's harm in is, extinguishing the spittoon by a . . . . 263 IS 5 ONE 32   48
EXTRACT
inherit vacancy) will time extract his inconsiderable doom, . 210 XLI SONNETS 6   11
EXTRACTED
i give you man extracted hate from whispering grass? . . . . 527 50 POEMS 39   9
EXTRAORDINARY
to toy with thy extraordinary lust, (the sinuous rain . . . .   3 T&C EPITHALAM   4
shoul- ders, sprouted the extraordinary arms through an an- .   97 & POST IMPR 8   36
hardly should call exactly extraordinary. We refer, of . . . 263 IS 5 ONE 32   36
EXTREMELY
rile of jovial hair extremely frames the face in . . . . . . 137 & SON REAL 8   17
all of which is extremely unimportant) whereas Life matters . 260 IS 5 ONE 30   11
the way Pay the extremely artistic ◇ fla -me . . . . 267 IS 5 TWO 2   11
with me into the extremely little house of my . . . . 365 VIVA 56   2
with an apish grin (extremely like but quite absurd . . . . . 640 (CHAIRE) 42   7

		PAGE	TITLE	LINE
EXTREMITY				
perching on the sudden extremity of one immense tooth		201	XLI PORTRAIT 9	30
EXUDES				
tomorrowlobs wholeagainst you gringlehow exudes thursday . .		333	VIVA 24	7
EXULTS				
candle whose expecting breath exults upon the tongue of . . .		6	T&C EPITHALAM	118
EYE				
be From each brave eye shall sprout a tree		16	T&C SONGS 6	2
exquisite; morning sure lyHer eye s exactly sit, ata		104	& POST IMPR 14	2
her posture. (As an eye winks). and almost i		131	& SON REAL 2	5
hands. with a little eye that rolled and made		149	& SON REAL 20	6
swig it does who eye sO neatly big /		159	& SON ACTU 8	17
hair. Understanding why his eye laughs, i will bring		161	& SON ACTU 10	11
wonder if i'm alive (eye pries, not open. Tail		166	& SON ACTU 15	10
within his stern blue eye, upon his firm white		273	IS 5 TWO 8	9
of waters) one's eye perceives (as the ego		319	VIVA 11	26
policeman's majestic and buried eye) the almost large he- . .		324	VIVA 16	4
bud plumptumbling hand voices Eye Doangivuh sud- denly . . .		330	VIVA 21	7
sud- denly immense impotently Eye Doancare Eye And How . . .		330	VIVA 21	8
immense impotently Eye Doancare Eye And How replies the . .		330	VIVA 21	8
sum blinked he belowtry eye nowbrow sangsung nee whitermuch .		333	VIVA 24	9
ouch soft-ly me and eye (you leSs) ly		361	VIVA 52	12
it aint no ews eye like the steak all		405	NO THANKS 22	11
steak all ried but eye certainly hate the juse		405	NO THANKS 22	12
not move behind my eye the windmills are silent		434	NO THANKS 51	9
And How much nonexistence eye sed bea yew tea		474	NEW POEMS 12	10
he) with its of eye stuck into a rock		490	50 POEMS 4	3
from each most least eye of star and without		502	50 POEMS 16	4
out of huge each eye look "thank you" nicely		506	50 POEMS 20	12
ids dare dare joy (eye kinely thank yoo) /		519	50 POEMS 33	28
on space? love's murdered eye dissected to mere because . . .		527	50 POEMS 39	13
ectl y crumb ling eye -holes oUt of whe		534	50 POEMS 46	17
old unman who is eye / / / /		602	(CHAIRE) 4	6
mortal) yoo make sno eye kil yoo (friend the		618	(CHAIRE) 20	5
two eyes for an eye four teeth for a		635	(CHAIRE) 37	17
kind with one white eye and one black eye		647	(CHAIRE) 49	17
eye and one black eye and the eyes of		647	(CHAIRE) 49	18
pinafore'd knock out your eye" "well maybe she's up		707	95 POEMS 35	8
measured by his quote eye cue unquote. Much better		807	73 POEMS 35	8
worlds) who's ama zingly Eye / / / /		827	73 POEMS 55	15
seeing either with life's eye (which is if things		845	73 POEMS 73	2
+EYE				
FOR CONTEXT, SEE		797	73 POEMS 25	3
EYEBROW				
you (with one cocked eyebrow) subtracting cliches un by . . .		605	(CHAIRE) 7	2
EYEBROWS				
large bluish face without eyebrows sits in the kitchen . . .		149	& SON REAL 20	1
act of doing her eyebrows. --Marj's laughter smacked me: . .		228	IS 5 ONE MARJ	13
a football with white eyebrows the 3 rd chief		465	NEW POEMS 3	1
+EYEBROWS				
FOR CONTEXT, SEE		318	VIVA 10	20
EYEBROWSMAN				
Mat isse like -with-the-chinese-eyebrowsMan gave me,A, . . .		318	VIVA 10	8
EYED				
/ this little huge -eyed per- son (nea -rly		739	95 POEMS 67	2
+EYED				
FOR CONTEXT, SEE		60	T&C PORTRAIT 8	10
FOR CONTEXT, SEE		105	& PORTRAIT 1	5
FOR CONTEXT, SEE		110	& PORTRAIT 6	36
FOR CONTEXT, SEE		115	& PORTRAIT 8	26
FOR CONTEXT, SEE		188	XLI SONGS 10	13
FOR CONTEXT, SEE		264	IS 5 ONE 33	27
FOR CONTEXT, SEE		339	VIVA 30	23
FOR CONTEXT, SEE		585	1 X 1 45	4
+EYEHOLES				
FOR CONTEXT, SEE		534	50 POEMS 46	17
EYEING				
a bluish cat are eyeing, as with almost melancholy		168	& SON ACTU 17	18

		PAGE	TITLE	LINE

EYELANDS
aling 2 a -sprout eyelands) sin uously&them&twi tching, . . . 445 NO THANKS 60   11

EYELASHES
--a fighter to his eyelashes-- the other, cunning ugly . . . 799 73 POEMS 27   4

EYELESS
last light pours its eyeless miles the chattering sunset . . 64 T&C POST IMPR 1   8

+EYELESSLY
FOR CONTEXT, SEE . . . . 361 VIVA 52   12

EYELIDS
lazy jade and twitching eyelids finger their unquiet spears . 34 T&C ORIENTALE 6   79
purple soul the absurd eyelids sulked enormous sobs puckered 52 T&C PORTRAIT 1   26
mouth and silly purple eyelids of how she was . . . . 56 T&C PORTRAIT 4   15

EYELIDS'
is less than your eyelids' flutter which says we . . . . . . 290 IS 5 FOUR 7   12

EYEPLUMS
a (twice by Dizzying eyeplums pun ctured) moo nface . . . . . 615 (CHAIRE) 17   7

EYES
in whose young chiseled eyes the people saw their . . . . . . 4 T&C EPITHALAM   33
tremulous armor stun the eyes of ragged earth who . . . . . . 4 T&C EPITHALAM   69
mouth flower-faint and undiscovered eyes and dim slow perfect 5 T&C EPITHALAM   98
musics in whose careful eyes are dinned; and the . . . . . . 9 T&C SONGS 1   18
rareness: let thy twain eyes deeply wield a noise . . . . . . 10 T&C SONGS 1   42
of surprise death's faultless eyes (whose hand my folded . . 11 T&C SONGS 2   25
straying. Always thy moist eyes are at kisses playing, . . . 13 T&C SONGS 3   10
his mouth for his eyes are mine. Doll's boy's . . . . 15 T&C SONGS 5   16
at me (with her eyes which like two elves . . . . 17 T&C PUELLA MEA   39
a lady who had eyes which the king's horses . . . . 18 T&C PUELLA MEA   47
Diarmuid looked in Grania's eyes.) But should my lady's . . . 18 T&C PUELLA MEA   60
to undertake Medea's rescuing eyes; nor he when swooned . . . 18 T&C PUELLA MEA   72
doth float, which in eyes and lips consists --always . . . . 20 T&C PUELLA MEA   147
lieth (while within the eyes is dimly heard a . . . . 20 T&C PUELLA MEA   151
glad ladies with lithe eyes and long (when the . . . . 22 T&C PUELLA MEA   225
of Nineveh, in her eyes when day is gone . . . . 23 T&C PUELLA MEA   260
love ladies with crisp eyes and frail, in the . . . . 23 T&C PUELLA MEA   287
itchy mousies with scuttling eyes rustle and run and . . . . 25 T&C CHANSONS 2   14
the field wonderful with eyes a little sorry Another . . . . 26 T&C CHANSONS 3   7
didst not listen thine eyes are as a vase . . . . 27 T&C ORIENTALE 1   11
greentwittering smokes from broken eyes a sound of strangling 28 T&C ORIENTALE 2   5
dilemma of flutes thy eyes are the betrayal of . . . . 29 T&C ORIENTALE 3   32
saw you close your eyes and i came riding . . . . 30 T&C ORIENTALE 4   35
approve these firm unsated eyes which have beheld night's . . 36 T&C AMORES 1   11
petals danced against my eyes and down the singing . . . . . 39 T&C AMORES 4   19
the mischief from her eyes and fold her mouth . . . . 40 T&C AMORES 4   41
flames courtesied before my eyes or twinkling over to . . . . 44 T&C AMORES 8   7
having death in her eyes and it is dawn . . . . 50 T&C IMPRESS 4   8
a song in her eyes the hours descend, putting . . . . 50 T&C IMPRESS 4   30
opening the hard great eyes to noone in particular . . . . . 53 T&C PORTRAIT 1   45
portals of hurt girl eyes sincere with wonder a . . . . 54 T&C PORTRAIT 2   4
excremental hair and the eyes of the mother of . . . . 55 T&C PORTRAIT 3   12
hollyhock existence whose pansy eyes look from morning till . 58 T&C PORTRAIT 6   18
is your mouth your eyes are sticky with dreams . . . . 61 T&C PORTRAIT 9   14
remember me pencil your eyes dear and have a . . . . 71 T&C SON REAL 2   2
dancer with the tightened eyes crisp ogling shoulders and . . 72 T&C SON REAL 3   5
big grin. her sow- eyes clicking mischief from thick . . . . 73 T&C SON REAL 4   7
sweet slow animal bottomless eyes importantly banal, Kitty. a 74 T&C SON REAL 5   7
grey, and silent smileless eyes of Magdalen. The lights . . . 75 T&C SON REAL 6   8
rare entertainment of your eyes, when (being fool to . . . . 78 T&C SON UNRE 3   2
Lady with bright slender eyes (who moves) at sunset . . . . . 91 & POST IMPR 3   2
daintily carrying in her eyes the dangerous first stars) . . 93 & POST IMPR 5   10
gluey grins topple together eyes pout ges- tures stickily . . 96 & POST IMPR 8   17
bells) i say your eyes can take day away . . . . 98 & POST IMPR 9   3
/ / / my eyes are fond of the . . . . 100 & POST IMPR 11   1
i lie asleep my eyes go into Allen street . . . . 100 & POST IMPR 11   2
TUMTITUMTIDDLE if sometimes my eyes stay at home then . . . . 100 & POST IMPR 11   18
scarlet pepper and my eyes were buttoned with pain . . . . . 100 & POST IMPR 11   31
unsuspecting street; THE YELLOW EYES AND --; i Like . . . . . 101 & POST IMPR 11   56
forked in surprisable unliving eyes chopped by a swollen . . 103 & POST IMPR 13   4
among otherlittle roundtables Her, eyes count slow (ly obstre 104 & POST IMPR 14   3

EYES (CONTINUED)

round. tables, Her . eyes / / / /	104	& POST IMPR 14	23
slim -ness of evenslicing eyes are chisels scarlet Goes . . .	106	& PORTRAIT 2	4
teel-ly lugu- bri ous eyes LOOPTHELOOP as fathandsbangrag / .	107	& PORTRAIT 3	12
streets make bright their eyes a blind irisher fiddles . . .	108	& PORTRAIT 4	6
the night with fucking eyes the great black preacher	108	& PORTRAIT 4	26
bags of flesh; became eyes moist lithe shuddering big, . . .	115	& PORTRAIT 8	23
forehead a pair of eyes which mutter thickly (as	116	& PORTRAIT 9	11
the way-- (nervously Whose eyes approve the blessed while . .	117	& PORTRAIT 10	35
silver dog, with ripe eyes and wagged his tail	125	& SEVEN POEMS 4	16
said into his Ripe Eyes and the moon Smiled	125	& SEVEN POEMS 4	27
Not of me. The eyes which biggish loll the	131	& SON REAL 2	13
tickling river in my eyes, the killed world wriggled	135	& SON REAL 6	15
of agony my grunting eyes pin tailored flames Her	137	& SON REAL 8	10
magic while in your eyes there lives a green	138	& SON REAL 9	7
lips and on sprawled eyes squirming with light insane	139	& SON REAL 10	10
of the smile's two eyes.... too, since the world's	141	& SON REAL 12	5
giggling hips and frozen eyes / / / /	143	& SON REAL 14	14
he kept talking about eyes / / / /	145	& SON REAL 16	14
tall with hard long eyes as she stands, with	147	& SON REAL 18	1
weak noise of her eyes easily files my impatience	147	& SON REAL 18	8
see if it could) eyes say the breasts look	150	& SON REAL 21	3
with astute fatuous swallowed eyes smiles, one grin very .	151	& SON REAL 22	13
you the mouth hair eyes, and i mean the	153	& SON ACTU 2	2
with stiffening slow shrill eyes beyond a fit- and-cling . .	155	& SON ACTU 4	8
teasing its lips, absurd eyes, the hair). Creasing its . . .	164	& SON ACTU 13	9
laughter from your preferable, eyes / / / /	166	& SON ACTU 15	16
laughed, and closed his eyes as a girl closes	170	& SON ACTU 19	13
over parting flesh.... And eyes big love-crumbs, and possibly	175	& SON ACTU 24	12
length, breathing with shut eyes the sweet earth where . . .	184	XLI SONGS 6	16
streets of smiles your eyes half- thrush half-angel and . . .	186	XLI SONGS 8	9
air Alive with closed eyes to dash against darkness	189	XLI SONGS 11	6
to shut your big eyes. where did you go?	191	XLI CHANSONS 1	4
little strolling lips and eyes inwardly crisping for my . . .	193	XLI PORTRAIT 1	8
rare unwisdom of thy eyes, and if thy hands	205	XLI SONNETS 1	2
of thy face (whose eyes inherit vacancy) will time	210	XLI SONNETS 6	10
earthly, while the slippery eyes drown in surging flesh). . .	226	IS 5 ONE MAME	4
timidly hinted "novocaine?" the eyes outstart, curl, bloat, .	226	IS 5 ONE MAME	13
elation causes the bent eyes thickly to protrude-- or	229	IS 5 ONE FRAN	13
Girl With The Wrigley Eyes (of you land of	230	IS 5 ONE 2	6
and with upward vacant eyes, painfully perpetually crouched,	231	IS 5 ONE 3	49
doors he's a with eyes and making twice the	251	IS 5 ONE 22	7
thou me cocodrillo-- mine eyes have seen the glory	256	IS 5 ONE 27	10
pinkest vomit out of eyes which noticed nobody he	258	IS 5 ONE 28	14
last with the big eyes i loved like you	271	IS 5 TWO 6	9
the communists have fine Eyes some are young some	274	IS 5 TWO 9	3
Communists have (very) fine eyes (which stroll hither and . .	275	IS 5 TWO 9	48
cetera, of Your smile eyes knees and of your	276	IS 5 TWO 10	26
the sea ...finally your eyes knew me, we smiled	283	IS 5 THREE 7	20
fingers it understood my eyes cheeks mouth its hands	284	IS 5 FOUR 1	4
and twilight) giving your eyes, present me also with	285	IS 5 FOUR 2	15
floor (quietly with bright eyes) drifts (nobody can tell .	286	IS 5 FOUR 3	5
and we hold lips Eyes everything hands you know	287	IS 5 FOUR 4	18
Dear i put my eyes into you but that	289	IS 5 FOUR 6	13
distinct country of your eyes, gifted with green twilight) .	291	IS 5 FOUR 8	27
and with his awkward eyes pushing sleep under and	293	IS 5 FOUR 10	27
tinily these, your crisp eyes actually shall contain new . .	294	IS 5 FOUR 11	9
unsaid gesture lightly my eyes? And send life out	302	IS 5 FIVE 1	6
chiefly which wrong your eyes (frailer than most deep	306	IS 5 FIVE 5	3
think wrists argue) short (eyes do bang hands angle	309	VIVA 1	11
A, (peach a soft eyes syriansang asong tohim self	318	VIVA 10	11
at (now -fed infantile eyes drooling unmind grim yessing . .	337	VIVA 28	6
its indolent lascivious caring eyes watches; truly, curvingly	344	VIVA 35	4
whiteLy are which stumbling eyes which why in (thundering) .	346	VIVA 37	8
over her (silent) with eyes which are really petals	352	VIVA 43	10
box of skin lay eyes like new tools) whence	355	VIVA 46	10
hair falls off and eyes blur And thighs forget	359	VIVA 50	1
good lips stalked or eyes firmly stirred) my mirror	360	VIVA 51	2

	PAGE	TITLE	LINE

EYES (CONTINUED)

	PAGE	TITLE	LINE
but though with wormS eyes writhe amor (Though through . . .	361	VIVA 52	6
beyond any experience, your eyes have their silence: in . . .	366	VIVA 57	2
the voice of your eyes is deeper than all	366	VIVA 57	19
quite who are your eyes (shall any dream come	367	VIVA 58	8
lifted, and (before my eyes sinking) inward, fled; softly . .	369	VIVA 60	8
guessable mirrors which your eyes are You will communicate .	370	VIVA 61	10
my nightmare from his eyes? / / / /	374	VIVA 65	15
/ so standing, our eyes filled with wind, and	378	VIVA 69	1
rabbitsare: swimswim ◇ with eyes and the. m oon	384	NO THANKS 2	32
with smooth vigilant perpetual eyes each exact victim, how .	386	NO THANKS 3	10
& with your wn eyes beh ld The (The	392	NO THANKS 9	11
soft) ness (his ears (eyes / / / /	397	NO THANKS 14	24
by (with hope two eyes a memory this brow	402	NO THANKS 19	6
Two pale slippery small eyes balanced upon one broken	406	NO THANKS 23	9
so new) self whose eyes smell of the sound	424	NO THANKS 41	3
opening was. Were your eyes: lost, believing; hushed with . .	432	NO THANKS 49	20
in dark places paints eyes touches hands with new-	437	NO THANKS 53	5
ea r in gly eyes grip live loop croon	445	NO THANKS 60	24
throbbing prayers whom kneeling eyes (until perfectly their .	450	NO THANKS 65	6
him who fears and eyes lifts lifting hopes and	456	NO THANKS 71	13
is (patiently all the eyes of these with listening	478	NEW POEMS 16	10
map while these not eyes quite try almost their	479	NEW POEMS 17	4
on- ly a child's eyes float silently down more	491	50 POEMS 5	6
i feel (his lousy eyes roaming) wonderful all sky	501	50 POEMS 15	8
does not open her eyes (but the feeble are	505	50 POEMS 19	13
this earth whose both eyes love this now of	512	50 POEMS 26	10
while children climb their eyes to touch his dream	517	50 POEMS 31	14
is firm) under his eyes would stir and squirm	520	50 POEMS 34	8
dead house clutch between eyes emptiness toss one at	522	50 POEMS 35	2
of stone with blossoming eyes know if a lit	525	50 POEMS 37	17
its brightness with your eyes any illimitable star /	526	50 POEMS 38	11
hollow silence has deeper eyes purest than fear's obscener .	565	1 X 1 25	8
two man neral rise eyes "this world's made 'bout	567	1 X 1 27	8
true from a funeral eyes "big thing" / /	567	1 X 1 27	22
of than great more eyes, and what were summer's	573	1 X 1 33	4
was all shall, their eyes would never miss a	576	1 X 1 36	14
make possible mayflowers: quite eyes of air not with	577	1 X 1 37	5
the flowers of his eyes : april's they this	583	1 X 1 43	6
only while your sweet eyes close have disappeared a	588	1 X 1 48	5
opening if are those eyes every because is murdered	588	1 X 1 48	7
some littler bird than eyes can learn look up	592	1 X 1 52	9
more all stars than eyes "only are quite what	603	{CHAIRE} 5	13
each new self) smile. Eyes. & we remember: yes;	612	{CHAIRE} 14	7
tree3ghosts are Is A eyes Strange known Face (whylaughing! .	628	{CHAIRE} 30	9
gob with entirely white eyes of elsewhere jabber while . . .	629	{CHAIRE} 31	4
beast boom boom) two eyes for an eye four	635	{CHAIRE} 37	16
wave-- put out your eyes, and touch the black	639	{CHAIRE} 41	13
black eye and the eyes of his eyes are	647	{CHAIRE} 49	19
the eyes of his eyes are as lost as	647	{CHAIRE} 49	19
eager fingers (with patient eyes) re -new- ing remaking . . .	660	{CHAIRE} 62	10
awake and now the eyes of my eyes are	663	{CHAIRE} 65	14
the eyes of my eyes are opened) / /	663	{CHAIRE} 65	14
a dream (with crazily eyes of window) may be	668	{CHAIRE} 70	4
my not themselves believing eyes adventuring, enormous . . .	669	{CHAIRE} 71	3
spirits, whose miraculously disenchanted eyes live the . . .	675	95 POEMS 3	3
all your more than eyes tell me) there is	683	95 POEMS 11	13
curiosity (and close your eyes) / / / /	689	95 POEMS 17	8
terrors fate hands silence eyes love laughter death (dreams .	693	95 POEMS 21	3
tears are full of eyes) appears. Because only the	697	95 POEMS 25	30
be slime in his eyes and a stone on	707	95 POEMS 35	28
newborn babe: around him, eyes --gifted with every keener . .	714	95 POEMS 42	3
& falling & falling) eyes eyes looking (alw ays)	715	95 POEMS 43	6
falling & falling) eyes eyes looking (alw ays) while	715	95 POEMS 43	6
face with stones for eyes for mind with none)	716	95 POEMS 44	8
their whys stones become eyes locks open keys haven't	716	95 POEMS 44	23
of day for someone's eyes) with silver splendors past	756	95 POEMS 84	4
that singing's always his eyes can feel but ears	760	95 POEMS 87	5

		PAGE	TITLE	LINE

EYES (CONTINUED)

is astir-- now dull eyes are keen and now . . . . 769 95 POEMS 95   10
keen and now keen eyes are keener (for young . . . . 769 95 POEMS 95   10
(with all their minds) eyes blindly stare life herSelf . . . 780 73 POEMS 8   8
brother Fearless by the eyes and did the deed . . . . 799 73 POEMS 27   14
of hope to her eyes, not any longer blinded . . . . 811 73 POEMS 39   5
his loneliness dreaming their eyes have opened to your . . . 812 73 POEMS 40   7
the mercy of your eyes your voice your ways . . . . 819 73 POEMS 47   2
our bliss-- where seeing eyes go blind (where lips . . . . . 834 73 POEMS 62   27
and how crazily houses eyes people smiles faces streets . . . 835 73 POEMS 63   4
faces and cities to eyes) drift bells glide seethe . . . . . 841 73 POEMS 69   21
centuries) these more than eyes restroll and stroll some . . 843 73 POEMS 71   2

+EYES

FOR CONTEXT, SEE . . . . 104 & POST IMPR 14   20
FOR CONTEXT, SEE . . . . 265 IS 5 ONE 34   4
FOR CONTEXT, SEE . . . . 265 IS 5 ONE 34   8
FOR CONTEXT, SEE . . . . 265 IS 5 ONE 34   8
FOR CONTEXT, SEE . . . . 740 95 POEMS 68   4

EYES'

i bite on the eyes' brittle crust (only feeling . . . . . . 132 & SON REAL 3   6
against my mind, the eyes' shuddering burrs of light . . . . 136 & SON REAL 7   6

EYESTHE

girl) ness (ish The eyesthe Is) aRe iS ar . . . . 388 NO THANKS 5   25

EYESUCKS

bea yew tea mis eyesucks unyewkuntel finglestein idstings . . 474 NEW POEMS 12   12

EYESWHICHNEVERSMILE

with his solemn blinky eyeswhichneversmile and after he has . 69 T&C POST IMPR 6   15
you with my solemn eyeswhichneversmile yes, By god. for . . . 69 T&C POST IMPR 6   35

F

! throughwhich! brittlest! whitewhom! f l o a t . . . . . . 416 NO THANKS 33   13
/ / / / F is for foetus (a . . . . 635 (CHAIRE) 37   1

FABLE

feebler than feeble are fable who are less than . . . . . . 505 50 POEMS 19   23

FABRICATE

love's function is to fabricate unknownness (known being . . 446 NO THANKS 61   1

FABULOUS

/ / / / fabulous against , a, fathoming . . . . 159 & SON ACTU 8   1
the lewd guess of fabulous immensity the sky screamed . . . . 419 NO THANKS 36   8
hide more than most fabulous wisdom fears to see . . . . . . 446 NO THANKS 61   12
freedom: star isful beckoningly fabulous crumb / / / . . . . 456 NO THANKS 71   15

FABULOUSLY

thought my golden soul fabulously to glue in a . . . . 9 T&C SONGS 1   30

FACE

the moon a nymphlike face, a form whose snowy . . . . 8 T&C OF NICOL   19
and before your dead face which sleeps, a dream . . . . 11 T&C SONGS 2   29
will touch with her face and all the while . . . . 16 T&C SONGS 6   12
the silence of her face doth immediately make in . . . . . 18 T&C PUELLA MEA   63
the strangeness of her face doth float, which in . . . . . . 20 T&C PUELLA MEA   146
didst not wonder thy face is as a dream . . . . 27 T&C ORIENTALE 1   18
have before a certain face become white perfume only, ... 39 T&C AMORES 4   33
steps to seek your face and i entreat, by . . . . 42 T&C AMORES 6   14
frying curb the quiet face lay which had been . . . . 52 T&C PORTRAIT 1   15
love from her transfigured face a queer pulp of . . . . . . 55 T&C PORTRAIT 3   15
mothermonster with red grumbling face cluttered in pursuit . 56 T&C PORTRAIT 4   1
a narrow thudding timeshaped face plus innocuous winking . . 62 T&C PORTRAIT 10   2
tunes crawl upon my face my hair is lousy . . . . 69 T&C POST IMPR 6   28
a little oldish doll-like face and hairy arms like . . . . . 69 T&C POST IMPR 6   38
volume of her tumbling face scribbled with a big . . . . . . 73 T&C SON REAL 4   5
large lips vivid, the face grey, and silent smileless . . . . 75 T&C SON REAL 6   7
away; if on another's face your sweet hair lay . . . . 76 T&C SON UNRE 1   5
shall i turn my face, and hear one bird . . . . 76 T&C SON UNRE 1   13
wait against the moon's face. / / / / . . . . 80 T&C SON UNRE 5   17
touched me; and to face suddenly the lighted living . . . . 82 T&C SON ACTU 1   14
whose upward lean magnificent face the streets turn young . . 93 & POST IMPR 5   3
Goes with her whitehot face, gashed by hair's blue . . . . . 106 & PORTRAIT 2   8
greenslim purse of whose face opens on a fatgold . . . . . . 114 & PORTRAIT 7   19
peering biggest whey coloured face on which a frown . . . . 117 & PORTRAIT 10   33
lady on her paler-paler face and said never mind, ... 125 & SEVEN POEMS 4   19

	PAGE	TITLE	LINE

FACE (CONTINUED)
jigs et tout en face always wiggles the perfectly . . . . . . 134 & SON REAL 5   10
hair extremely frames the face in a hoop of . . . . 137 & SON REAL 8   18
a frieze of smoking Face Bluish-old and choked pat . . . . . 142 & SON REAL 13   5
arms a delicately elephantine face (It is necessary to . . . 143 & SON REAL 14   2
and to kiss my face and head. / / . . . . 147 & SON REAL 18   14
hand quarried the quartzlike face. his right slapped the . . 148 & SON REAL 19   4
Dick Mid's large bluish face without eyebrows sits in . . . . 149 & SON REAL 20   1
lifts an impertinent puerperal face and with astute fatuous . 151 & SON REAL 22   12
you like the rain's face and the rich improbable . . . . . . 153 & SON ACTU 2   13
hideous gladness, per the face --pinxit, who knows? Who . . . 158 & SON ACTU 7   5
grieve, faint for your face O stay with me . . . . 165 & SON ACTU 14   9
if i am the face of a baby smeared . . . . 166 & SON ACTU 15   13
this window sits a Face (it is twilight) a . . . . 169 & SON ACTU 18   15
(it is twilight) a Face playing on a flute . . . . 169 & SON ACTU 18   16
flashing bacchant. partedpetaled mouth, face delirious. . . . 185 XLI SONGS 7   14
city which is your face your little cheeks the . . . . 186 XLI SONGS 8   6
upon the dark's prodigious face thy voice scattering . . . . 187 XLI SONGS 9   10
quivers the electric Distinct face haughtily vital clinched . 193 XLI PORTRAIT 1   3
the less-than-whiteness of thy face (whose eyes inherit . . . 210 XLI SONNETS 6   9
"Business is rotten" the face yawning said what her . . . . . 225 IS 5 ONE LIZ   12
wobbles an improbably distinct face, and how these wooden . . 229 IS 5 ONE FRAN   3
on (and watching her face grow old and tired . . . . 242 IS 5 ONE 13   14
monkey with a sharp face waddling carefully the length . . . 279 IS 5 THREE 3   9
slate of that nigger's face (but If i should . . . . 287 IS 5 FOUR 4   6
do i prefer this face to another and why . . . . 295 IS 5 FOUR 12   15
staring me in the face a dead yellow small . . . . 296 IS 5 FOUR 13   16
tears streamin down my face i hauls out uh . . . . 332 VIVA 23   19
see nothing with the face of a poet really . . . . 352 VIVA 43   11
flower and not a face with hands which whisper . . . . 352 VIVA 43   12
uncarefully ears in that face a box of skin . . . . 355 VIVA 46   9
budgingly over some numbered face capable of a largest . . . 359 VIVA 50   16
i love god's terrible face, brighter than a spoon, ... 360 VIVA 51   21
i cry, remembering her face, i have never loved . . . . 360 VIVA 51   34
inward, fled; softly your face smile breasts gargled by . . . 369 VIVA 60   9
dreamfuls of despair that face) large one coloured nonthings 402 NO THANKS 19   7
nuts and open your face / / / / . . . . 407 NO THANKS 24   16
was is born: one face who. and hands hold . . . . 479 NEW POEMS 17   14
today? nn-nn went head face goes (if how begins . . . . 506 50 POEMS 20   8
a pillow's green means face or why a quilt's . . . . 506 50 POEMS 20   9
stooped to kiss his face) busy folk buried them . . . . 515 50 POEMS 29   26
/ / denied night's face have shadowless they? i . . . . 527 50 POEMS 39   1
welcomes her dreams his face (her face his dreams . . . . . . 533 50 POEMS 45   10
dreams his face (her face his dreams rejoice rejoice) . . . . 533 50 POEMS 45   11
brave? does mask wear Face? have singings gone to . . . . . . 538 50 POEMS 50   6
A eyes Strange known Face (whylaughing! among: skydiamonds / 628 (CHAIRE) 30   12
never) a kite like face of the child who's . . . . 668 (CHAIRE) 70   10
washed his sweet dirty face & mended his bright . . . . 680 95 POEMS 8   15
smile whose head's his face with stones for eyes . . . . . . 716 95 POEMS 44   7
a grin without a face (a look without an . . . . 797 73 POEMS 25   2
/ / a round face near the top of . . . . 813 73 POEMS 41   1
voice: then a slender face (on the mantelpiece of . . . . . . 813 73 POEMS 41   3
uttering one a third face, away in the sky . . . . 813 73 POEMS 41   9
+FACE
FOR CONTEXT, SEE . . . . 615 (CHAIRE) 17   10
+FACED
FOR CONTEXT, SEE . . . . 196 XLI PORTRAIT 4   2
FOR CONTEXT, SEE . . . . 705 95 POEMS 33   6
FACEFLOWERS
pierced lazily writhe lurch faceflowers stutter treebodies . 436 NO THANKS 52   9
FACENESS
collaps ingly flash a of-faceness stuck thumblike into pie . 330 VIVA 21   5
FACES
feet fearruining and glorygirded faces lead us into the . . . 41 T&C AMORES 5   32
up with impertinently exquisite faces floating hands were . . 44 T&C AMORES 8   10
i see the brutal faces of people contented hideous . . . . . 50 T&C IMPRESS 4   14
of those ladies with faces painteaten and bodies lightly . . 57 T&C PORTRAIT 5   37
mourners move with prose faces and sobbing, garments The . . 59 T&C PORTRAIT 7   8

FACES (CONTINUED)
stand with circular frightened faces glaring at the shabby .   69 T&C POST IMPR 6   7
Poles? perhaps. While permanent faces coyly bandy scandal of   70 T&C SON REAL 1   9
a dignity of papyruscoloured faces superbly limp the . . . . 111 & PORTRAIT 6   54
bash the bragging breasts, puppy-faces to mouth her ugly . . 151 & SON REAL 22   8
doors unlocked by white-grub faces) clothes in delicate . . . 172 & SON ACTU 21   7
circle of habitues their faces like cigarettebutts, chewed . 194 XLI PORTRAIT 2   20
a capable millennium of faces meshing with my curiously . . . 197 XLI PORTRAIT 5   8
the quivering string) invisible faces hauntingly and slow. . 208 XLI SONNETS 4   8
demurely halfsmiling from cool faces, moving purely with . . 211 XLI SONNETS 7   8
a nudging froth of faces clogs Second as Mrs. . . . . 219 XLI SONNETS 15   11
stood sharp angels with faces like Jim Europe / . . . . 241 IS 5 ONE 12   9
in bruised narrow questioning faces) / / / / . . . . 275 IS 5 TWO 9   50
swoon of centrifugally expecting faces clumsily which devours 279 IS 5 THREE 3   7
(upon artificial limbs, with faces like defunct geraniums) / 280 IS 5 THREE 4   34
few windows awaken certain faces busily horribly blunder . . 299 IS 5 FOUR 16   13
asleep with only several faces and a multitude of . . . . . . 312 VIVA 4   6
steeples writhe with rain) faces (at windows) do not . . . . 340 VIVA 31   5
shrink: as through immediately yeswind-faces peer skies; . . 346 VIVA 37   6
todo of murdering uncouth faces which pass rap idly . . . . . 354 VIVA 45   10
/ put off your faces, Death: for day is . . . . 376 VIVA 67   1
Love, put on your faces / / / / . . . . 376 VIVA 67   14
s? bE -ginningly) come-swarm: faces ar; rive go. faces . . . 444 NO THANKS 59   5
faces ar; rive go. faces a (live) sob bel . . . . 444 NO THANKS 59   6
all are three with faces made of cloud dancing . . . . 507 50 POEMS 21   6
tease slim float twitter faces) only stand with me, ... 633 {CHAIRE} 35   5
/ / / when faces called flowers float out . . . . 665 {CHAIRE} 67   1
/ / / joys faces friends feet terrors fate . . . . 693 95 POEMS 21   1
(is? are) who (two faces at a dark window) . . . . 715 95 POEMS 43   2
houses eyes people smiles faces streets steeples are eagerly 835 73 POEMS 63   5
people and streets into faces and cities to eyes) . . . . . . 841 73 POEMS 69   20
+FACES
FOR CONTEXT, SEE . . . . 85 T&C SON ACTU 4   3
FOR CONTEXT, SEE . . . . 388 NO THANKS 5   19
FACT
fails and that's a fact; who threw the bunch . . . . 125 & SEVEN POEMS 4   12
a little different, in fact myself Hereupon helpless i . . . 199 XLI PORTRAIT 7   9
not account for the fact that my Uncle Sol . . . . 239 IS 5 ONE 10   7
the importance of the fact that (in spite of . . . . 323 VIVA 15   21
(in spite of the fact that i and that . . . . 323 VIVA 15   21
thanks to the socalled fact that maost faolks rally . . . . . 331 VIVA 22   3
truth is confused with fact, fish boast of fishing . . . . . 446 NO THANKS 61   4
art-naked: you and the fact that rotgut never was . . . . . . 605 {CHAIRE} 7   3
a bed in it (fact) open this bed, sibyl . . . . 637 {CHAIRE} 39   6
should contented fools of fact envision the mystery of . . . 659 {CHAIRE} 61   9
coax undeath from fancied fact and spaceful time-- no . . . . 664 {CHAIRE} 66   20
a deathful realm of fact --by their precision evolving . . . 763 95 POEMS 90   28
heard above the everywhereing fact of fear; and under . . . . 821 73 POEMS 49   6
FACTS
impeccable feathered with green facts preening solemnity . . 344 VIVA 35   2
soul feels all small facts dissolved by the lewd . . . . . . 419 NO THANKS 36   6
perished have safe small facts of hilltop (barn house . . . . 755 95 POEMS 83   2
here are five simple facts no sub human superstate . . . . . 803 73 POEMS 31   5
FADED
misbutt- oned trouserfly tumbling, faded five or so . . . . . 607 {CHAIRE} 9   6
his brutebeak one fatal faded (pinkish or yellowish maybe) . 697 95 POEMS 25   24
+FADED
FOR CONTEXT, SEE . . . . 94 & POST IMPR 6   5
FADES
a day (and every fades) is here and away . . . . 509 50 POEMS 23   2
FAERIE
with a look of faerie, perhaps a little suddenly . . . . . . 17 T&C PUELLA MEA   41
be, perfect things of faerie, are intense inhabitants; in . . 22 T&C PUELLA MEA   253
FAERIES
actually shall contain new faeries (and if your slim . . . . 294 IS 5 FOUR 11   9
by roamingly stern bright faeries if you love me) . . . . . . 363 VIVA 54   4
FAHRENHEIT
daughter's mother's zero mind fahrenheit) old infrequently . 546 1 X 1 6   2

	PAGE	TITLE	LINE

FAIL
voices pass upon forgetting (fail me not) whose courseless . 9 T&C SONGS 1 2
upon silence) i without fail entered became and was . . . . . 115 & PORTRAIT 8 20
cold (when battling street-lamps fail upon the gold dawn, . . 142 & SON REAL 13 3
failures born who cannot fail having no wealth but . . . . . 394 NO THANKS 11 12
only understand enormously which fail--look: with what ease . 418 NO THANKS 35 9
of rain) thickly i fail slenderly i win (like . . . . 433 NO THANKS 50 10
a fool who could fail pulling all the sky . . . . 481 NEW POEMS 19 11
more frequent than to fail it is most mad . . . . 530 50 POEMS 42 4
he'll spurn rather than fail immeasurable fate) coward, . . . 562 1 X 1 22 8
as fa*te, greyly shall fail and dully disappear-- but . . . . 649 {CHAIRE} 51 12
so skilful) must wither fail and cease --but better . . . . . 742 95 POEMS 70 4

FAILED
my Uncle Sol's farm failed because the chickens ate . . . . . 239 IS 5 ONE 10 15
my mind--if i have failed to snare the glance . . . . 306 IS 5 FIVE 5 5
have tried who have failed who have cried) lie . . . . 393 NO THANKS 10 9
to fool has always failed to fool your heart . . . . 679 95 POEMS 7 8

FAILING
to not forsake a failing year --now, before quite . . . . . . 821 73 POEMS 49 8

FAILS
but that when light fails and this sweet profound . . . . . . 71 T&C SON REAL 2 7
for democracy it never fails and that's a fact; . . . . 125 & SEVEN POEMS 4 12
who flourishes, swiftly which fails but out of serene . . . . 456 NO THANKS 71 6

FAILURE
sincere youth the exquisite failure uncouth discovers a . . . 11 T&C SONGS 2 7
who was a born failure and nearly everybody said . . . . . 239 IS 5 ONE 10 3
clown (should stink of failure more than wars of . . . . . . 414 NO THANKS 31 3
and hands --nourish my failure with thy freedom: star . . . . 456 NO THANKS 71 14

FAILURES
than lend --being through failures born who cannot fail . . . 394 NO THANKS 11 12

FAIN
this frantic heart is fain; try me with thy . . . . 212 XLI SONNETS 8 4

FAINARAIN
sendwisp ben jiffyclaus bug fainarain wee celibate amaranth . 333 VIVA 24 20

FAINT
particoloured peace with mouth flower-faint and undiscovered . 5 T&C EPITHALAM 98
drifting in slow diaphanous faint rout), queen in the . . . . 6 T&C EPITHALAM 144
like the currency of faint cities eternal--ere the sinless . 9 T&C SONGS 1 32
shall know while on faint hills do frailly go . . . . 11 T&C SONGS 2 27
for in the ambiguous faint aspirings the indolent frail . . . 31 T&C ORIENTALE 5 15
close her with intricate faint birds by daisies and . . . . . 65 T&C POST IMPR 2 9
knocked off and a faint piddle-of-drops she says I . . . . . 96 & POST IMPR 8 14
autumn, as i grieve, faint for your face O . . . . 165 & SON ACTU 14 9
intangible commemoration, (from whose faint close as some . . 206 XLI SONNETS 2 12
moon thinner than memory faint -er than all the . . . . 282 IS 5 THREE 6 19

+FAINT
FOR CONTEXT, SEE . . . . 697 95 POEMS 25 11

+FAINTER
FOR CONTEXT, SEE . . . . 282 IS 5 THREE 6 19

FAINTING
smoothness. and mark the fainting murdered petals. with the . 215 XLI SONNETS 11 7

FAINTLY
in my ears scramble faintly tickling putrescent atomies, and 69 T&C POST IMPR 6 29
large lips always clenched faintly, wishes you with all . . . 72 T&C SON REAL 3 7
the alive coolness, very faintly and finally through . . . . 92 & POST IMPR 4 15
above, underdrawers club the faintly sweating air with . . . 144 & SON REAL 15 6
sensuously (the crowd howls faintly blubbering pointing see . 280 IS 5 THREE 4 14
maybe certain nobodies laughing faintly playing moving far . 283 IS 5 THREE 7 8
a (ghost) Who screams Faintly always who Is bluish; . . . . . 312 VIVA 4 8
in the sky finally faintly (higher than high in . . . . 813 73 POEMS 41 10

FAIR
as an opening lily drowsy-fair (when from her couch . . . . . 8 T&C OF NICOL 12
of companions blithe and fair; who to walk with . . . . . . 20 T&C PUELLA MEA 165
with him, which is fair as i judge. / . . . . 171 & SON ACTU 20 14
beyond red rivers of fair perpetual feet the sinuous . . . . 185 XLI SONGS 7 6
proud heart cherished as fair. (The child-head poised with . 207 XLI SONNETS 3 13
his life that his fair city might not die. . . . . 209 XLI SONNETS 5 14
he turned into a fair y! a fair y!! . . . . 401 NO THANKS 18 15

	PAGE	TITLE	LINE

FAIR (CONTINUED)
a fair y! a fair y!! a fair y!!! . . . . 401 NO THANKS 18   16
a fair y!! a fair y!!! but she turned . . . . 401 NO THANKS 18   18
she turned into a fair-y (and it seems to . . . . 401 NO THANKS 18   20
at the recent world's fair was the paytoilet / . . . . 425 NO THANKS 42   16
are and moon come fair come foul he goes . . . . 440 NO THANKS 56   27
liars and the false fair friends and the boths . . . . . . 569 1 X 1 29   10
world) most merry most fair most rare --the livingest . . . . 590 1 X 1 50   4
there & (smoke) a fair y socked flopslump (& . . . . 629 (CHAIRE) 31   11
/ / / / fair ladies tall lovers riding . . . . 778 73 POEMS 6   1
more moving (all gay fair brave tall young come . . . . . . 778 73 POEMS 6   10
out of muchtheworseforwear shoes 'fair friend' we enlightened 800 73 POEMS 28   9
smiles name it cruel fair or blessed evil-- it . . . . . . 804 73 POEMS 32   7
FAIRIE
--the authentic scroll of fairie hands and vanishing with . .   5 T&C EPITHALAM   88
FAIRIES
crank; the box sprouts fairies, out of it sour . . . . . . 69 T&C POST IMPR 6   3
less gnomes and frantic fairies gush clumsily from the . . . 69 T&C POST IMPR 6   22
when Farmer Death (whom fairies hate) shall crumble the . . . 83 T&C SON ACTU 2   11
+FAIRY
FOR CONTEXT, SEE . . . . 317 VIVA 9   4
FOR CONTEXT, SEE . . . . 401 NO THANKS 18   15
FOR CONTEXT, SEE . . . . 401 NO THANKS 18   16
FOR CONTEXT, SEE . . . . 401 NO THANKS 18   20
FOR CONTEXT, SEE . . . . 401 NO THANKS 18   20
FOR CONTEXT, SEE . . . . 629 (CHAIRE) 31   11
FAIRYAIR
is there here everywhere fairyair feelable heavenless warm . 755 95 POEMS 83   9
FAIS
ce (re peat credo fais do do neighbours re . . . . 309 VIVA 1   34
FAIT
non, mon cheri; il fait trop froid"-- they are . . . . . . 304 IS 5 FIVE 3   10
FAITH
not) bang spurting mesh (faith -ful which -ly try . . . . . 388 NO THANKS 5   12
see to stare their faith to how their joy . . . . 580 1 X 1 40   9
/ / ! hope faith! ! life love! bells . . . . 841 73 POEMS 69   2
FAITH'S
above why's first because (faith's last doubt and humbly . . 574 1 X 1 34   10
FAITHFUL
others they have been faithful to many things and . . . . . 43 T&C AMORES 7   8
the obvious they were faithful and which i despise, ... 43 T&C AMORES 7   18
moon, there is something faithful and mad" / / . . . . . . 303 IS 5 FIVE 2   16
FAITHFULLY
LIZ with breathing as (faithfully) her lownecked dress a . . 225 IS 5 ONE LIZ   1
full without fear might faithfully lie down to so . . . . . 418 NO THANKS 35   7
the sun --arriving truly, faithfully who goes (never a . . 756 95 POEMS 84   2
guessed unknowable most joy) faithfully blossoming beyond to 811 73 POEMS 39   8
/ / / / faithfully tinying at twilight voice . . . . 821 73 POEMS 49   1
+FAITHFULLY
FOR CONTEXT, SEE . . . . 388 NO THANKS 5   12
FAKE
little barbarous Greenwich perfumed fake And most, the futile 220 XLI SONNETS 16   10
FAL
ning of (sil ently) fal ling (e ver yw . . . . 713 95 POEMS 41   6
FALL
(phantom-white) dumb-blooming boughs let fall their glorious   8 T&C OF NICOL   6
white hands, who letting fall a thread of lustre . . . . . .   8 T&C OF NICOL   22
their sounds and flowers Fall in a pride of . . . . 11 T&C SONGS 2   32
slipped from immeasurable height, fall, fifty, silent in the 32 T&C ORIENTALE 6   31
of dreaming --and i fall back, quietly amorous of, ... 158 & SON ACTU 7   12
scared i would actually fall off the rail before . . . . . 263 IS 5 ONE 32   62
window she did not fall she went creeping along . . . . . . 284 IS 5 FOUR 1   13
that i do not fall into this street is . . . . 295 IS 5 FOUR 12   25
will maybe (hearing something fall into his hat) go . . . . 298 IS 5 FOUR 15   21
while all the dominoes) fall: down; in, rows / . . . . . . 331 VIVA 22   8
laugh like they would fall apart and masturbate with . . . . 427 NO THANKS 44   11
this star does not fall into his mind feeling . . . . 428 NO THANKS 45   5
down (slowly beneath sight fall ing) fall ing through . . . . 432 NO THANKS 49   7

	PAGE	TITLE	LINE

FALL (CONTINUED)

beneath sight fall ing) fall ing through touch less	432	NO THANKS 49	8
quick who stop damned fall all we go spill	496	50 POEMS 10	14
turn a n d fall which now drop who	536	50 POEMS 48	20
the round (they're gravensteins) fall with kind of a	543	1 X 1 3	28
among) no year will fall this than, a least	573	1 X 1 33	12
that does nothing but fall (with a shout each	594	1 X 1 54	32
above did was always fall (yes but behind yes)	634	(CHAIRE) 36	10
doubt: while all skies fall) and then to slowly	650	(CHAIRE) 52	3
D; while all skies fall at last perfection, now	650	(CHAIRE) 52	16
worse than worst you fall in hate with love	679	95 POEMS 7	12
(and stars moon sun fall rise come go rain	693	95 POEMS 21	19
true) and a climbing fall into far near blue	769	95 POEMS 95	21
sweet) our summer in fall and in winter our	776	73 POEMS 4	30
not numerable leaves are fall i ng) he StandS	826	73 POEMS 54	6
is darkness and to fall (now wrong's the only	834	73 POEMS 62	20

+FALL

| FOR CONTEXT, SEE . . . . | 265 | IS 5 ONE 34 | 6 |
| FOR CONTEXT, SEE . . . . | 449 | NO THANKS 64 | 6 |

FALLEN

/ the glory is fallen out of the sky	41	T&C AMORES 5	1
firmly diminishing have swoopingly fallen svelte sagging gone	110	& PORTRAIT 6	28
a man who had fallen among thieves lay by	258	IS 5 ONE 28	1

FALLING

a noise of petals falling silently through the far-spaced . .	10	T&C SONGS 1	43
/ / light cursed falling in a singular block	133	& SON REAL 4	1
and time's dead which; falling falling both locked in	533	50 POEMS 45	19
time's dead which; falling falling both locked in each . . .	533	50 POEMS 45	19
tery (liftingly caught upon falling) silent! ly living the .	627	(CHAIRE) 29	15
child are watching snowflakes (falling & falling & falling) .	715	95 POEMS 43	5
watching snowflakes (falling & falling & falling) eyes eyes .	715	95 POEMS 43	5
(falling & falling & falling) eyes eyes looking (alw	715	95 POEMS 43	5
each truebeautifully more-than-thing (& falling &) <> / / . .	715	95 POEMS 43	20
motionless under magical foreverfully falling snow. And then	777	73 POEMS 5	13
it takes one very falling most (there: did you	809	73 POEMS 37	11

+FALLING

FOR CONTEXT, SEE	104	& POST IMPR 14	5
FOR CONTEXT, SEE	265	IS 5 ONE 34	5
FOR CONTEXT, SEE	432	NO THANKS 49	7
FOR CONTEXT, SEE	432	NO THANKS 49	8
FOR CONTEXT, SEE	713	95 POEMS 41	6

FALLINGEST

| most him --the climbingly fallingest fool in this trickiest . | 590 | 1 X 1 50 | 14 |

FALLS

loves, every old thing falls in rosebugs and jackknives . . .	126	& SEVEN POEMS 5	5
pass? shallowness of sunlight falls and, cruelly, across the	190	XLI SONGS 12	8
/ / when hair falls off and eyes blur	359	VIVA 50	1

+FALLS

| FOR CONTEXT, SEE . . . . | 673 | 95 POEMS 1 | 4 |

FALSE

know exeunt they (not false not true not you	542	1 X 1 2	6
truthful liars and the false fair friends and the	569	1 X 1 29	10
/ / / nothing false and possible is love	574	1 X 1 34	1
name-- i feel that (false and true are merely	631	(CHAIRE) 33	13
truth is gay (nothing's false, in earth in air	651	(CHAIRE) 53	7
deduction which (be it false or true) disposes me	798	73 POEMS 26	26

FALSELY

| time, and each most falsely true; or so subhuman . . . . . | 817 | 73 POEMS 45 | 2 |

FALSEST

| what hope asserts, what falsest both disprove by proving . . | 576 | 1 X 1 36 | 4 |

FAME

| "and this be my fame, the harder the wind . . . . | 439 | NO THANKS 55 | 26 |

FAMILIAR

| will lie (glued among familiar things newly which are . . . . | 428 | NO THANKS 45 | 3 |
| become one (wholly strange; familiar wholly) dearest more . . | 659 | (CHAIRE) 61 | 7 |

FAMINE

| cosmic rays war earthquakes famine or the ex prince . . . . . | 475 | NEW POEMS 13 | 19 |

	PAGE	TITLE	LINE

FAMISHED
a gold valley the famished arrow sang before. Bow . . . . . . 14 T&C SONGS 4 20
FAMOUS
bedad it is the famous doctor who inserts monkeyglands . . . 245 IS 5 ONE 16 13
/ / / that famous fatheads find that each . . . . 411 NO THANKS 28 1
+FAMOUS
FOR CONTEXT, SEE . . . . 267 IS 5 TWO 2 13
FAN
very (and nellie and fan) some handsomest harry (and . . . . 509 50 POEMS 23 14
+FAN
FOR CONTEXT, SEE . . . . 425 NO THANKS 42 8
FANCIED
may coax undeath from fancied fact and spaceful time-- . . . 664 {CHAIRE} 66 20
FANCY
when (being fool to fancy) i have deemed with . . . . 78 T&C SON UNRE 3 3
superhuman flights of submoronic fancy be more not . . . . . 790 73 POEMS 18 3
things believable) could only fancy we should never know . . 809 73 POEMS 37 7
FAND
the quickness of the fand intrigues the fly) for . . . . . . 425 NO THANKS 42 8
FANG
in the door. a fang of wincing gas showed . . . . 73 T&C SON REAL 4 3
FANTASIES
littler huts with peerless fantasies or the unlovely longness 207 XLI SONNETS 3 4
FANTASTIC
more would be neither fantastic nor pathological but dumb. . 514 50 POEMS 28 4
FAOLKS
socalled fact that maost faolks rally demannd canned saounds) 331 VIVA 22 3
FAR
falling silently through the far-spaced possible nearaway . . 10 T&C SONGS 1 44
little lame balloonman whistles far and wee and eddieandbill 24 T&C CHANSONS 1 5
queer old balloonman whistles far and wee and bettyandisbel . 24 T&C CHANSONS 1 13
the goat-footed balloonMan whistles far and wee / / . . . . . 24 T&C CHANSONS 1 22
when we loved the far- departed mouth sweetly-saluted . . . . 42 T&C AMORES 6 5
mine in time not far away; if on another's . . . . 76 T&C SON UNRE 1 4
of mysteries , life. Far below myself the lunging . . . . . . 202 XLI PORTRAIT 9 35
laughing lightly crowned with far colours, thinking very much 211 XLI SONNETS 7 15
her mouth opens too far and: she attacks her . . . . 243 IS 5 ONE 14 12
only knows that as far as his picture goes . . . . 246 IS 5 ONE 17 10
that gladly (sic) in far lands perished of unheard . . . . . 266 IS 5 TWO 1 14
sunlight? down ever so far on the beach below . . . . 281 IS 5 THREE 5 3
from down ever so far-- hush. Sunlight, there are . . . . . . 281 IS 5 THREE 5 21
laughing faintly playing moving far below us perhaps one . . 283 IS 5 THREE 7 9
edifice... situated or established ...far from the noise of . 319 VIVA 11 24
said he not too far said she what's too . . . . 399 NO THANKS 16 10
said she what's too far said he where you . . . . 399 NO THANKS 16 11
identity) breathes fleet perfectly far from tangible domains 402 NO THANKS 19 11
his luminous ends who far less lonely than a . . . . 420 NO THANKS 37 11
complete miracle of nearest far "i cordially invite me . . . 504 50 POEMS 18 3
/ a peopleshaped toomany-ness far too and will it . . . . . . 528 50 POEMS 40 1
sea of shore so far your nearness reaches a . . . . 537 50 POEMS 49 5
earth? why you're by far the darlingest who (on . . . . 590 1 X 1 50 9
blue took it my far beyond far and high . . . . 593 1 X 1 53 14
it my far beyond far and high beyond high . . . . 593 1 X 1 53 14
the deep is the far o my darling) of . . . . 695 95 POEMS 23 20
a noone's more by far than you're alive or . . . . 716 95 POEMS 44 31
church (no great cathedral) far from the splendor and . . . . 749 95 POEMS 77 2
am a little church (far from the frantic world . . . . 749 95 POEMS 77 13
gone are enormous near far silent truths of mountain . . . . 755 95 POEMS 83 6
a climbing fall into far near blue if beggars . . . . 769 95 POEMS 95 21
any damn thing : far from it; you 're . . . . 793 73 POEMS 21 14
beyond) now and here (far from a grown -up . . . . 832 73 POEMS 60 9
stirring makes a crash --far away (as far as . . . . 839 73 POEMS 67 5
crash --far away (as far as alive) lies april; . . . . 839 73 POEMS 67 5
FAR-SPACED
falling silently through the far-spaced possible nearaway . . 10 T&C SONGS 1 44
FARE
there. yet we scarcely fare much better-- what's become . . . 233 IS 5 ONE 4 9
and every minus plus --fare ill: fare well-- a . . . . 798 73 POEMS 26 13

		PAGE	TITLE	LINE

FARE (CONTINUED)
  minus plus --fare ill: fare well-- a frown would . . . . . . 798 73 POEMS 26   13
+FAREWELL
  FOR CONTEXT, SEE . . . . 798 73 POEMS 26   13
FARM
  added my Uncle Sol's farm failed because the chickens . . . . 239 IS 5 ONE 10   14
  Sol had a chicken farm till the skunks ate . . . . 239 IS 5 ONE 10   18
  Sol had a skunk farm but the skunks caught . . . . 239 IS 5 ONE 10   21
  and started a worm farm) / / / / . . . . 239 IS 5 ONE 10   38
FARMER
  (as i guess) when Farmer Death (whom fairies hate) . . . . . 83 T&C SON ACTU 2   11
FARMERS
  comes the good rain farmers pray for (and no . . . . 754 95 POEMS 82   1
FARMING
  is or to wit farming and be it needlessly . . . . 239 IS 5 ONE 10   11
FART
  do not give a fart for art they kill . . . . 427 NO THANKS 44   15
  have at him they fart they fart full oft . . . . 441 NO THANKS 56   37
  him they fart they fart full oft (with mind . . . . 441 NO THANKS 56   38
  splendor of an angel's fart came one trembling out . . . . . 506 50 POEMS 20   11
FARTHEST
  immeasurable nowhere flames --its farthest silence nearer . . 741 95 POEMS 69   4
  beauty: reoccurs so magically, farthest becomes near (one . . 818 73 POEMS 46   7
FASCINATION
  arms are filled with fascination, when my breast wears . . . 78 T&C SON UNRE 3   10
FASCIST
  (sing down with the fascist beast boom boom) two . . . . . . 635 (CHAIRE) 37   14
FASHION
  that in a lovely fashion doth from my lady's . . . . 21 T&C PUELLA MEA 182
FASHIONABLE
  her limousine oozes in fashionable traffic, just a halfsmile 146 & SON REAL 17   10
FASHIONED
  for all things amorous fashioned very curiously of roses . . 20 T&C PUELLA MEA 137
  ladies in the moon) --fashioned very curiously of roses . . . 22 T&C PUELLA MEA 229
FAST
  shells begin dropping jolly fast you hear the rrmp . . . . . 269 IS 5 TWO 4   4
FASTERISHLY
  Forwardflung backwardSpinning hoop returns fasterishly . . . 311 VIVA 3   5
FASTERS
  you gringlehow exudes thursday fasters by button of whisper . 333 VIVA 24   7
FASTEST
  each other having the fastest time because they've never . . 126 & SEVEN POEMS 5   7
FASTIDIOUS
  meticulous vulgarity: a sodden fastidious normal explosion; a 201 XLI PORTRAIT 9   12
FAT
  with rose the lewd fat bells and a tall . . . . 51 T&C IMPRESS 5   7
  loneliness, and the rather fat man in bluishsuspenders . . . 166 & SON ACTU 15   5
  tuh dat not exacly fat "father" (adjustin his robe) . . . . . 240 IS 5 ONE 11   3
  remarked when surrounded by fat stupid animals the jewess . . 241 IS 5 ONE 11   3
  his black mouth with fat jibing lips, once upon . . . . 277 IS 5 THREE 1   15
  by and by a fat colour reared itself against . . . . 283 IS 5 THREE 7   19
  also; at denfert the fat strongman has put down . . . . . . 384 NO THANKS 2   19
  3 individuals every several fat thousand years. Expecting . . 514 50 POEMS 28   2
  a pool of pink fat screams a hole in . . . . 545 1 X 1 5   7
  all the girls (the fat ones, the lean ones;the . . . . 619 (CHAIRE) 21   24
  (who can and do fat pigeons coo) haps even . . . . 787 73 POEMS 15   7
FATAL
  in lowliness, noting the fatal flight of worlds whereto . . . 81 T&C SON UNRE 6   4
  and chipping with sharp fatal tools in an agony . . . . 199 XLI PORTRAIT 7   4
  the image of one fatal word; so that my . . . . 360 VIVA 51   22
  blood is made (whose fatal songs are moving in . . . . 424 NO THANKS 41   14
  autumnal afternoon: breathing a fatal stillness; while . . . 674 95 POEMS 2   3
  with his brutebeak one fatal faded (pinkish or yellowish . . 697 95 POEMS 25   24
  times, proclaim fate isn't fatal --a heart her each . . . . . 764 95 POEMS 90   53
FATALLY
  something else carefully slowly fatally turning into . . . . 283 IS 5 THREE 7   25
  sensations, imitating a few fatally exquisite" (pulling Its . 328 VIVA 19   18
  which, i note how fatally toward twilight the a . . . . 345 VIVA 36   4

	PAGE	TITLE	LINE

FATALLY (CONTINUED)

tumble climb and mightily fatally i remark how through . . . 434 NO THANKS 51 29

became) and does our fatally unshadowing fate put on . . . . 454 NO THANKS 69 11

FATE

jeer for a hat fate per a somewhat more . . . . 258 IS 5 ONE 28 5

on the ear of fate, landed a seat in . . . . 266 IS 5 TWO 1 35

kisses are a better fate than wisdom lady i . . . . 290 IS 5 FOUR 7 8

true) while your contriving fate, my sharpening life are . . 373 VIVA 64 17

meaningless precision and complete fate (he must deny mind: . 402 NO THANKS 19 14

--open your thighs to fate and (if you can . . . . 420 NO THANKS 37 13

does our fatally unshadowing fate put on one not . . . . . 454 NO THANKS 69 11

is beauty and its fate to grow shall hate . . . . 538 50 POEMS 50 4

rather than fail immeasurable fate) coward, clown, traitor, . 562 1 X 1 22 8

and as green as fate, greyly shall fail and . . . . 649 (CHAIRE) 51 11

faces friends feet terrors fate hands silence eyes love . . . 693 95 POEMS 21 2

alive) above anybody and fate and even Our whisper . . . . . 762 95 POEMS 89 12

nothing) five times, proclaim fate isn't fatal --a heart . . 764 95 POEMS 90 53

darling) i fear no fate (for you are my . . . . 766 95 POEMS 92 6

(for you are my fate, my sweet) i want . . . . 766 95 POEMS 92 6

nearest even than your fate and mine (or any . . . . 809 73 POEMS 37 1

FATES

selves to swarm their fates woke dreamers to their . . . . . 520 50 POEMS 34 11

FATGOLD

face opens on a fatgold grin hooray hoorah for . . . . . . 114 & PORTRAIT 7 20

FATHANDSBANGRAG

ous eyes LOOPTHELOOP as fathandsbangrag / / / / . . . . . . 107 & PORTRAIT 3 15

FATHEADS

/ / that famous fatheads find that each and . . . . 411 NO THANKS 28 1

FATHER

graces and the hours, father of gods and men . . . . 4 T&C EPITHALAM 41

elephantine while nearby the father a thick cheerful man . . 56 T&C PORTRAIT 4 9

dat not exacly fat "father" (adjustin his robe) who . . . . 240 IS 5 ONE 11 4

bravely of course my father used to become hoarse . . . . . 276 IS 5 TWO 10 15

of blackred roses my father will be (deep like . . . . . . 352 VIVA 43 5

with some difficulty one father of one (ask super-) . . . . 398 NO THANKS 15 4

/ / / my father moved through dooms of . . . . 520 50 POEMS 34 1

of each night my father moved through depths of . . . . . . 520 50 POEMS 34 4

of the sea my father moved through griefs of . . . . 520 50 POEMS 34 18

must and shall my father moved through dooms of . . . . . . 520 50 POEMS 34 34

world with snow. My father moved through theys of . . . . . 521 50 POEMS 34 49

when she heard my father sing) then let men . . . . 521 50 POEMS 34 52

men breathe-- because my father lived his soul love . . . . 521 50 POEMS 34 67

aint his daughter her father lays" "black hell upon . . . . 707 95 POEMS 35 20

a dark window) this father and his child are . . . . 715 95 POEMS 43 3

+FATHER

FOR CONTEXT, SEE . . . . 320 VIVA 12 20

FATHER'S

his mother's pride, his father's joy, unto whom duty . . . . 273 IS 5 TWO 8 3

why completely weep my father's fingers brought her sleep: . 520 50 POEMS 34 14

so hugely) stood my father's dream his flesh was . . . . . 520 50 POEMS 34 28

FATHERING

if, with goldenly his fathering (as that himself out . . . . 756 95 POEMS 84 9

+FATHERING

FOR CONTEXT, SEE . . . . 715 95 POEMS 43 21

FATHERLY

kindly lips and body fatherly of a romantic tired . . . . . 57 T&C PORTRAIT 5 31

FATHERS

god of our fathers' fathers bows to a which . . . . 711 95 POEMS 39 3

FATHERS'

the god of our fathers' fathers bows to a . . . . 711 95 POEMS 39 3

FATHOMING

fabulous against , a, fathoming jelly of vital futile . . . . 159 & SON ACTU 8 1

FATTISH

moth- eaten tunes. a fattish hand turns the crank; . . . . . 69 T&C POST IMPR 6 2

from the battered box fattish and mysterious the . . . . . . 69 T&C POST IMPR 6 23

quick to thread the fattish drone of I Want . . . . 140 & SON REAL 11 12

charms en repos.... a fattish leg leaks obscenely from . . . 143 & SON REAL 14 8

	PAGE	TITLE	LINE
FATUOUS			
face and with astute fatuous swallowed eyes smiles, one . . .	151	& SON REAL 22	13
FAULT			
have been not my fault. / / / /	263	IS 5 ONE 32	65
FAULTLESS			
empty of surprise death's faultless eyes (whose hand my . . .	11	T&C SONGS 2	25
exact beads of a faultless languor when invisibly consult . .	193	XLI PORTRAIT 1	6
FAUN			
mouth now droops the faun head now the intimate	54	T&C PORTRAIT 2	9
FAUNA			
some- thing about "*stuffed* fauna" being "very	326	VIVA 18	33
FAVOR			
and why asking no favor but (while down come	783	73 POEMS 11	5
FAVOUR			
and He without Whose favour nothing is (being of	210	XLI SONNETS 6	3
FEAR			
sleepless meadows sweet with fear") then be with me:	9	T&C SONGS 1	27
thin air stooped with fear, across the harvest whitely . . .	11	T&C SONGS 2	22
a day) do not fear, we will go amaying.	13	T&C SONGS 3	7
of immaculate perfume--whereby (with fear aglow) my soul is .	19	T&C PUELLA MEA	108
shy; as if for fear you would espy the	22	T&C PUELLA MEA	216
touch it is the fear of rhyme-- in life's	23	T&C PUELLA MEA	274
is so filled with fear people bells) i say	98	& POST IMPR 9	2
glad flesh of my fear: more neatly ream this	139	& SON REAL 10	7
even a pencil has fear to do the posed	141	& SON REAL 12	1
(by cold espoused unto fear) in dreadful corners hideously .	207	XLI SONNETS 3	7
but imperfect in my fear Or with thy mind	215	XLI SONNETS 11	11
least matter. The big fear Who held us deeply	289	IS 5 FOUR 6	3
but trembling (cowards which fear to miss within your	293	IS 5 FOUR 10	6
you do not ever fear, me in your heart	294	IS 5 FOUR 11	17
(and looking up in fear i see the new	301	IS 5 FOUR 18	4
filling the air with fear and sweetness.... pauses.	304	IS 5 FIVE 3	12
twilight, caught in thickening fear our slightly fingering .	305	IS 5 FIVE 4	6
(at which now O fear turned o Now handspring	343	VIVA 34	10
/ when rain whom fear not children but men	356	VIVA 47	1
breathe with me this fear (which beyond night shall	362	VIVA 53	1
what bird has perfect fear (of suddenly me) like	367	VIVA 58	5
Be bigger than the fear of all hearts never	397	NO THANKS 14	6
a mind full without fear might faithfully lie down	418	NO THANKS 35	7
came a huger than fear a white with madness	432	NO THANKS 49	15
his birth is their fear is their blind fear	439	NO THANKS 55	5
fear is their blind fear --haunts all unsleep this	439	NO THANKS 55	5
can less unminds must fear because and why what	440	NO THANKS 56	5
fool (life imitate gossip fear unlife mean -ness, and . . .	452	NO THANKS 67	8
dream die love not Fear eat sleep kill and	467	NEW POEMS 5	10
any courage is a fear --long enough and just	511	50 POEMS 25	11
kind, a heart to fear, to doubt a mind, ...	521	50 POEMS 34	58
dare whatever dares to fear) i very humbly thank	522	50 POEMS 35	8
upward deepness of less fear much than more climbing	528	50 POEMS 40	8
system universe and bang --fear buries a tomorrow under . . .	531	50 POEMS 43	3
littler th an a: fear no bigger th an	532	50 POEMS 44	14
but breathing yes which fear will never no? measureless . . .	538	50 POEMS 50	2
every who; despite what fear denies, what hope asserts, . . .	576	1 X 1 36	3
or here) let pitiless fear play host to every	580	1 X 1 40	4
under all hate all fear --all perfectly dyingest my	590	1 X 1 50	22
and too wise for fear) of shadowy virtue and	607	(CHAIRE) 9	12
and in fire, but fear-- mind's a coward; lies	651	(CHAIRE) 53	8
countless in hatred pity fear each more exactly than	662	(CHAIRE) 64	9
forevering snow --but never fear (my own, my beautiful . . .	667	(CHAIRE) 69	13
bear is angary we fear for the quo pro	711	95 POEMS 39	20
stars. And (darling) never fear: love, when such marvels . .	741	95 POEMS 69	9
our from hate from fear a which of slim	746	95 POEMS 74	4
creature new (except your fear to whom i give	762	95 POEMS 89	6
doing, my darling) i fear no fate (for you	766	95 POEMS 92	5
has no opposite in fear; the strength so strong	768	95 POEMS 94	10
loves because he cannot fear (you see it in	774	73 POEMS 2	14
(first and last) mostpeople fear most: a mystery for	802	73 POEMS 30	12
the everywhereing fact of fear; and under any silence	821	73 POEMS 49	6

FEAR (CONTINUED)

    five hopes for any fear, but it Must be . . . . 837 73 POEMS 65   9

    precision more than angels fear to learn and even . . . . . . 842 73 POEMS 70   4

+FEAR

    FOR CONTEXT, SEE . . . . 512 50 POEMS 26   2

    FOR CONTEXT, SEE . . . . 586 1 X 1 46   16

FEAR'S

    deeper eyes purest than fear's obscener brightest than hate's 565 1 X 1 25   9

FEARERS

    buried, Satan dead, do fearers worship Much and Quick; . . . 438 NO THANKS 54   2

FEARFUL

    go near because perfectly fearful. meanwhile these speak her 162 & SON ACTU 11   7

FEARINGLY

    spirit stooping, Crusoelike examines fearingly and tenderly a 344 VIVA 35   14

FEARLESS

    his reach) upon his fearless derriere sturdily . . . . 266 IS 5 TWO 1   21

    stroll about hungry and fearless and thirsty and supple . . . 481 NEW POEMS 19   6

    immeasurable anguish pregnant one fearless one good yes . . . 524 50 POEMS 36   38

    / joyful your complete fearless and pure love with . . . . . 761 95 POEMS 88   1

    of pure joyful your fearless and complete love, all . . . . . 761 95 POEMS 88   11

    from wrong, took brother Fearless by the eyes and . . . . . . 799 73 POEMS 27   14

FEARLESSANDBOSOMY

    / / / / fearlessandbosomy this grand: gal who . . . . 792 73 POEMS 20   1

FEARLESSLY

    reeking with stark and fearlessly obscene but really clean . 407 NO THANKS 24   6

FEARRUINING

    but straight glad feet fearruining and glorygirded faces lead 41 T&C AMORES 5   30

FEARS

    was over our mouths fears hearts lungs arms hopes . . . . . . 283 IS 5 THREE 7   2

    i wear your dearest fears beyond their ceaselessness (nor . . 372 VIVA 63   10

    beyond such wheres and fears or any when unwondering . . . . 378 VIVA 69   13

    than most fabulous wisdom fears to see (who laugh . . . . . . 446 NO THANKS 61   12

    of even him who fears and eyes lifts lifting . . . . 456 NO THANKS 71   13

    today can guess or fears to dare whatever dares . . . . 522 50 POEMS 35   8

    steeper than hopes are fears only not ever named . . . . . . 563 1 X 1 23   3

    mindless they higher than fears are hopes lovers are . . . . 563 1 X 1 23   8

    huger than prove our fears were hopes: the moon . . . . 575 1 X 1 35   12

    or was (laws clocks fears hopes beliefs compulsions doubts . 755 95 POEMS 83   16

    joys and hoping's very fears yours is the light . . . . 810 73 POEMS 38   11

    who's your --when all fears hopes beliefs doubts disappear. . 812 73 POEMS 40   13

    by every wisdom knowledge fears to dare, how the . . . . . . 843 73 POEMS 71   11

FEARSOMELY

    time by clever drolls fearsomely who do keep their . . . . 74 T&C SON REAL 5   11

FEAST

    will upon a poet feast) meanwhile this ghost goes . . . . . . 418 NO THANKS 35   11

    selves and lives imperishably feast all timeless souls (the . 456 NO THANKS 71   3

FEATHER

    hat with a big feather is tied under myhis . . . . 69 T&C POST IMPR 6   42

    weightless svelte drifting sexual feather of your shall i . . 140 & SON REAL 11   2

+FEATHER

    FOR CONTEXT, SEE . . . . 653 {CHAIRE} 55   1

FEATHERED

    wholly dies his impeccable feathered with green facts . . . . 344 VIVA 35   2

FEATHERIEST

    with drifted gifts of featheriest slenderness and how . . . . 299 IS 5 FOUR 16   5

FEATHERLY

    the slowly. town, night featherly swifts the Dark on . . . . 89 & POST IMPR 1   3

FEATHERS

    like the rain, (Who feathers frightened fields with the . . . 163 & SON ACTU 12   3

FEATURE

    the daily papers will feature Peace And Good Will, ... 142 & SON REAL 13   9

+FECIT

    FOR CONTEXT, SEE . . . . 388 NO THANKS 5   30

FED

    mouth of time is fed: and if i like . . . . 212 XLI SONNETS 8   8

    minutes past six) the well-fed L's immaculate roar looped . . 219 XLI SONNETS 15   5

    by loving relatives well fed, and fully photographed the . . 273 IS 5 TWO 8   22

    to look at (now -fed infantile eyes drooling unmind . . . . . 337 VIVA 28   6

	PAGE	TITLE	LINE

FED (CONTINUED)
  dreamless knaves on Shadows fed, your Harry's Tom, your . . . 438 NO THANKS 54   9
FEE
  and yielding to that fee her eager body's unimmortal . . . .   4 T&C EPITHALAM   54
  years its of self fee (bly Perpetually coughing And . . . . . 312 VIVA 4   19
FEEBLE
  intellect collywobbling on its feeble stem is believing . . . 329 VIVA 20   3
  the people are so feeble the feeble go to . . . . 505 50 POEMS 19   7
  are so feeble the feeble go to sleep if . . . . 505 50 POEMS 19   7
  her eyes (but the feeble are people the feeble . . . . 505 50 POEMS 19   14
  feeble are people the feeble are so wise the . . . . 505 50 POEMS 19   14
  almost are feebler than feeble are fable who are . . . . . . 505 50 POEMS 19   22
+FEEBLE
  FOR CONTEXT, SEE . . . . 723 95 POEMS 51   1
FEEBLENESS
  strong mere force is feebleness: the truth more first . . . . 768 95 POEMS 94   11
FEEBLER
  are mostly almost are feebler than feeble are fable . . . . . 505 50 POEMS 19   22
FEEBLY
  mess, a star sleepily, feebly, scratches the sore of . . . . 144 & SON REAL 15   9
+FEEBLY
  FOR CONTEXT, SEE . . . . 312 VIVA 4   19
  FOR CONTEXT, SEE . . . . 725 95 POEMS 53   4
  FOR CONTEXT, SEE . . . . 726 95 POEMS 54   15
FEED
  of the fervent dead, feed with felicities me wormperused . . 212 XLI SONNETS 8   7
FEEDS
  ladies with whom time feeds especially his immense lips . . . 138 & SON REAL 9   9
FEEL
  putrescent atomies, and i feel the jerk of the . . . . 69 T&C POST IMPR 6   32
  to a grave astonishment feel in my being the . . . . 79 T&C SON UNRE 4   12
  skilfully modeling silence --to feel how through the stopped 82 T&C SON ACTU 1   10
  midnight) for no reason feel deeply completely conscious of . 92 & POST IMPR 4   10
  the moon, i somehow feel your smile slightly is . . . . 98 & POST IMPR 9   10
  it makes your neck feel pleasant and stoopid and . . . . . . 126 & SEVEN POEMS 5 19
  over again and you, feel all again all over . . . . 127 & SEVEN POEMS 5 36
  you liked made you feel when they touched you . . . . 127 & SEVEN POEMS 5 37
  you so you can feel what you made, men . . . . 127 & SEVEN POEMS 5 39
  what you made, men feel when, you touched, them . . . . . . 127 & SEVEN POEMS 5 39
  a gas evil to feel. Unwieldy.... the bloodbeat in . . . . . 135 & SON REAL 6   7
  understand i love you.... feel your suddenly body reach . . . 157 & SON ACTU 6   6
  after you. I occasionally feel vague how vague i . . . . . . 160 & SON ACTU 9   14
  i who love to feel what it will do . . . . 164 & SON ACTU 13   13
  hows. i like to feel the spine of your . . . . 175 & SON ACTU 24   5
  of cobalt nevertheless i feel that i cleverly am . . . . . . 199 XLI PORTRAIT 7   8
  perhaps it is to feel strike the silver fish . . . . 216 XLI SONNETS 12   1
  a hair) making me feel how myself has been . . . . 301 IS 5 FOUR 18   7
  unsmile or whatever weeds feel and fish think of) . . . . . 359 VIVA 50   18
  then or none let's feel all) mind in mind . . . . 364 VIVA 55   14
  of spring lives F feel opens but shuts understand . . . . . 390 NO THANKS 7   5
  / / may i feel said he (i'll squeal . . . . 399 NO THANKS 16   1
  more swiftness as with (feel) pauseless immeasurably Now . . 402 NO THANKS 19   3
  does not have to feel because he thinks (the . . . . 406 NO THANKS 23   1
  thinks, nor dares to feel (but up with joy; . . . . 424 NO THANKS 41   10
  life adventuring who would feel if spring's least breathing . 450 NO THANKS 65   13
  or which makes some feel more better when all . . . . 466 NEW POEMS 4   23
  when all ought to feel less worse (but only . . . . 466 NEW POEMS 4   24
  else my sweet (i feel that's true) / / . . . . 475 NEW POEMS 13   24
  window every) twilight i feel (his lousy eyes roaming) . . . 501 50 POEMS 15   8
  cry for he could feel the mountains grow. Lifting . . . . . 520 50 POEMS 34   16
  moved through dooms of feel; his anger was as . . . . 520 50 POEMS 34   34
  as perfect hope can feel only despair completely strikes . . 580 1 X 1 40   23
  into flame i can feel how the earth must . . . . 587 1 X 1 47   14
  think) you begin to feel of it, dying 's . . . . 604 (CHAIRE) 6   10
  patient) dream's eternity (you feel behind this man earth's . 617 (CHAIRE) 19   4
  your beautiful name-- i feel that (false and true . . . . . 631 (CHAIRE) 33   13
  prove what heart may feel and soul may touch . . . . 664 (CHAIRE) 66   4
  discover our touch and feel --for love are in . . . . 664 (CHAIRE) 66   15

FEEL (CONTINUED)
    him (by the look feel taste smell & sound . . . . 676 95 POEMS 4   8
    tremendous hug knowing i feel that we & worlds . . . . 680 95 POEMS 8   27
    Flop or even to Feel how Everything (dreamed & . . . . 702 95 POEMS 30   15
    only grin-- dancing to feel nots are their whys . . . . 716 95 POEMS 44   21
    a rose, roses (you feel certain) will only smile . . . . . . 744 95 POEMS 72   7
    should even omnipotent He feel sorry while these were . . . . 748 95 POEMS 76   9
    always his eyes can feel but ears may see . . . . 760 95 POEMS 87   5
    mightier than this: to feel) poor worlds must merely . . . . 762 95 POEMS 89   2
    Is what makes you feel you aren't 6 or . . . . 779 73 POEMS 7   22
    (as think as can feel) they when and they . . . . 801 73 POEMS 29   20
    song of (as mountains feel and lovers) singing is . . . . . . 804 73 POEMS 32   14
    are unimaginably ours to feel-- how should some world . . . . 809 73 POEMS 37   8
    would rather know than feel; mistrusting utterly that . . . . 817 73 POEMS 45   11
FEELABLE
    there here everywhere fairyair feelable heavenless warm sweet 755 95 POEMS 83   10
FEELING
    eyes' brittle crust (only feeling the belly's merry thrust . 132 & SON REAL 3   7
    mixed with your hair; feeling your knees among the   . . . . 169 & SON ACTU 18   6
    is, big horses; light feeling up streets; heels taking   . . 172 & SON ACTU 21   2
    crisping for my friend, feeling is the sacred and . . . . . . 193 XLI PORTRAIT 1   9
    / / / since feeling is first who pays . . . . 290 IS 5 FOUR 7   1
    time (into supreme Now: feeling memory shrink from such . . . 373 VIVA 64   13
    fall into his mind feeling throughout ignorant disappearing . 428 NO THANKS 45   6
    whying) seek than finds feeling (seize) floats (only by . . . 612 {CHAIRE} 14   13
    opened to your morning feeling their stars have risen . . . . 812 73 POEMS 40   8
    steep more than music) feeling that sunlight is (life . . . . 816 73 POEMS 44   6
    not imaginably morethanmostgenerous spirit. Feeling only . . 823 73 POEMS 51   14
    of november sunset (and feeling: that if day has . . . . . . 824 73 POEMS 52   6
+FEELING
    FOR CONTEXT, SEE . . . . 122 & SEVEN POEMS 1 3
FEELS
    vocal fern, always which feels the keen ecstatic actual . . . 19 T&C PUELLA MEA 124
    always worse than naught, feels the tremendous yonder for . . 81 T&C SON UNRE 6   12
    of genius-- painting wholly feels ashamed before this music, 162 & SON ACTU 11   5
    alley, a nigger's voice feels curiously cool (suddenly-Lights 167 & SON ACTU 16   18
    hands what no man feels, no woman understands. / . . . . . . 212 XLI SONNETS 8   14
    drops you know everybody feels sick or when they . . . . . . 272 IS 5 TWO 7   5
    like dat ...suddenly i feels so lonely fer duh . . . . 332 VIVA 23   14
    the earth (whose texture feels of pride and loneliness . . . 418 NO THANKS 35   2
    form enters my soul feels all small facts dissolved . . . . . 419 NO THANKS 36   5
    wandering under weakening stars Feels; if & god said . . . . 479 NEW POEMS 17   11
    spinster's heart my voice feels who inquires is your . . . . 506 50 POEMS 20   7
    an A? henceforth he feels his pride involved (this . . . . . 650 {CHAIRE} 52   9
    he knows nothing, and feels everything; all around whom . . . 657 {CHAIRE} 59   2
    each other) one who feels a world crylaughingly float . . . . 720 95 POEMS 48   7
    marvel every breathing creature feels (but none can think) . 735 95 POEMS 63   7
FEET
    imprint of whose cloven feet the shrieking dryad sought . . .   3 T&C EPITHALAM   13
    emboss, betwixt whose absolute feet anoint with calm of . . .   3 T&C EPITHALAM   30
    to imitate between the feet of awe), thunderer whose . . . .   4 T&C EPITHALAM   36
    gently primeval hands, frivolous feet divine! O singular and   5 T&C EPITHALAM 107
    all white, with shining feet, went forth into the . . . . . .   8 T&C OF NICOL   27
    it shall pass. Our feet tread sleepless meadows sweet . . . .   9 T&C SONGS 1   27
    like flowers at the feet of mowers whose bodies . . . . 11 T&C SONGS 2   33
    go amaying. thy whitest feet crisply are straying. Always . . 13 T&C SONGS 3   8
    for every mile the feet go the heart goes . . . . 15 T&C SONGS 5   19
    uncertain morning, with April feet like sudden flowers and . 17 T&C PUELLA MEA 21
    cunning and withal delirious feet of the Princess Salome . .   17 T&C PUELLA MEA 29
    of thy blood thy feet upon thy ankles are . . . . 29 T&C ORIENTALE 3 29
    upon an elephant twelve feet high behind whose ear . . . . .   32 T&C ORIENTALE 6 8
    her ears at the feet of the emperor a . . . . 34 T&C ORIENTALE 6 69
    soul, but straight glad feet fearruining and glorygirded . . 41 T&C AMORES 5   30
    rose motionless with grieving feet and wings mounts against . 59 T&C PORTRAIT 7 11
    hear your stepping freakish feet feet incorrigible ragging . 61 T&C PORTRAIT 9 35
    your stepping freakish feet feet incorrigible ragging the . . 61 T&C PORTRAIT 9 36
    rub- bercoloured hands and feet filled with quick fingers . . 69 T&C POST IMPR 6 39
    darkling awaiteth her whose feet have trod the silly . . . . 75 T&C SON REAL 6 10

	PAGE	TITLE	LINE

FEET (CONTINUED)

ankles large acute brutal feet propped on irrelevantly . . . 103 & POST IMPR 13	8
window walk the unburied feet of the little ladies . . . . . 108 & PORTRAIT 4	36
her nostrils to her feet she smelled of silence. . . . . . . 135 & SON REAL 6	2
Want a Doll, wispish-agile feet with slid steps parting . . . 140 & SON REAL 11	14
rivers of fair perpetual feet the sinuous riot the . . . . . 185 XLI SONGS 7	7
wings suddenly escorts with feet sun-sheer the smarting . . . 187 XLI SONGS 9	16
from Nicho' settled my feet on the ceiling inhaling . . . . . 194 XLI PORTRAIT 2	13
brittle and small his feet large and fragile his . . . . . 198 XLI PORTRAIT 6	22
shoulders, Thou from whose feet reincarnate song suddenly . . 206 XLI SONNETS 2	7
toll, for whose cool feet this frantic heart is . . . . . . 212 XLI SONNETS 8	4
wonderful, and that my feet have surely known the . . . . . 216 XLI SONNETS 12	13
these wooden big two feet conclude happeningly the unfirm . . 229 IS 5 ONE FRAN	4
attacks her Lobster without feet mingle under the mercy. . . 243 IS 5 ONE 14	14
baby shrapnel or my feet getting dim freezing or . . . . . 272 IS 5 TWO 7	8
begin requiescat this six feet of Breton big good . . . . . 277 IS 5 THREE 1	6
hearts lungs arms hopes feet hands under us the . . . . . . 283 IS 5 THREE 7	2
the sweet small clumsy feet of April came into . . . . . . 306 IS 5 FIVE 5	14
which with dignity square feet turned abruptly Miss Gay . . . 326 VIVA 18	25
& folding hopes, hark; feet (fEEt ◇ / / . . . . 345 VIVA 36	14
folding hopes, hark; feet (fEEt ◇ / / / . . . . 345 VIVA 36	14
these your wrists thighs feet hands poising to again . . . . 369 VIVA 60	13
useless flanks and cringing feet is this (shivering pale . . 374 VIVA 65	12
more than wars of feet all things whose slendering . . . . 414 NO THANKS 31	3
proud dreamhorse moving (whose feet almost walk air). now . . 437 NO THANKS 53	16
lay snares for his feet (who wanders through only . . . . . 439 NO THANKS 55	18
/ / on murdered feet into immense no Where . . . . 479 NEW POEMS 17	2
oflike immens- ely (a feet which is prayer among) . . . . . 482 NEW POEMS 20	4
with its hands and feet (lift and may pitying . . . . 522 50 POEMS 35	11
/ joys faces friends feet terrors fate hands silence . . . . 693 95 POEMS 21	2

+FEET

| FOR CONTEXT, SEE . . . . 345 VIVA 36 | 15 |
| FOR CONTEXT, SEE . . . . 586 1 X 1 46 | 16 |

FEETHANDS

| root like legs or feethands; nobody ever could ever . . . . . 490 50 POEMS 4 | 15 |

FELICITIES

| fervent dead, feed with felicities me wormperused by whom . . 212 XLI SONNETS 8 | 7 |

FELICITOUS

| Schiavoni or in the felicitous vicinity of the de . . . . . . 256 IS 5 ONE 27 | 18 |

FELINE

| MARJ "life? Listen" the feline she with radishred legs . . . 228 IS 5 ONE MARJ | 2 |

FELL

one by one there fell upon the night, like . . . . 8 T&C OF NICOL	10
and smiling my heart fell dead before. / / . . . . 14 T&C SONGS 4	35
a certain gate, rain fell (as it will in . . . . 58 T&C PORTRAIT 6	4
abyss --and wonderfully i fell through the green groove . . . 360 VIVA 51	18
/ / / applaws) "fell ow sit isn'ts" (a . . . . 548 1 X 1 8	2
till into themselves we fell-- how have all time . . . . . . 694 95 POEMS 22	4
his life but he fell for a whore when . . . . 707 95 POEMS 35	18

FELLER

| dribbles soft right old feller belch the chap hic . . . . . . 96 & POST IMPR 8 | 21 |
| on) tangoing (while a feller tries to hold down . . . . . . 242 IS 5 ONE 13 | 7 |

FELLERS

| gang accrost duh table-- "fellers have some on me" . . . . . 332 VIVA 23 | 21 |

FELLERS'

| "my specialty is takin fellers' goils away frum dem" . . . . 332 VIVA 23 | 6 |

FELLOW

crumb said whereupon its fellow five crumbs chuckled as . . . 117 & PORTRAIT 10	13
or less deserved, Young fellow go in peace. which . . . . . . 229 IS 5 ONE FRAN	8
--Here comes a stout fellow in a blouse just . . . . 282 IS 5 THREE 6	24
is altogether a queer fellow as young as he . . . . 296 IS 5 FOUR 13	3
do not make a fellow tall" lily has a . . . . 684 95 POEMS 12	16
moon. Time's a strange fellow; more he gives than . . . . . 750 95 POEMS 78	10
tall strong young finelooking fellow, dressed well but not . 800 73 POEMS 28	4

+FELLOW

| FOR CONTEXT, SEE . . . . 242 IS 5 ONE 13 | 7 |
| FOR CONTEXT, SEE . . . . 548 1 X 1 8 | 2 |

	PAGE	TITLE	LINE

FELLOW'LL
/ / that melancholy fellow'll play his handorgan until . . . 697 95 POEMS 25 — 2
just midnight this hearty fellow'll exist --whereas that . . 813 73 POEMS 41 — 6

FELLOW'S
gurl to be a fellow's twistandtwirl talk about your . . . . . 235 IS 5 ONE 6 — 18

FELLOWMEN
wonder such a monster's fellowmen miscalled are happy should 842 73 POEMS 70 — 13

FELLOWS
flower walking with its fellows in the death of . . . . 214 XLI SONNETS 10 — 2
ask praise of their fellows but i being otherwise . . . . . . 291 IS 5 FOUR 8 — 1

+FELLOWS
FOR CONTEXT, SEE . . . . 332 VIVA 23 — 21

FELT
the glowing throng descend, felt on her flesh the . . . . . . 4 T&C EPITHALAM — 53
came leaping and i felt suddenly dizzy With the . . . . 44 T&C AMORES 8 — 3
--. One day i felt a mountain touch me . . . . 135 & SON REAL 6 — 11
joint tested my gas felt of her radiator made . . . . 248 IS 5 ONE 19 — 7
mouth its hands (slipping) felt of my necktie wandered . . . 284 IS 5 FOUR 1 — 5
Quick; badness not being felt as bad, itself thinks . . . . . 438 NO THANKS 54 — 3

FEMALE
midnight the flyspecked abdominous female indubitably . . . . 116 & PORTRAIT 9 — 3
sharp necessary lips) kid female cracksman of the nifty, . . 140 & SON REAL 11 — 10
thighs a friendless dingy female frenzy bubbles / / . . . . . 151 & SON REAL 22 — 18
people (both male and female created He then, And . . . . . . 267 IS 5 TWO 2 — 18
many stopped millions of female hard for their millions . . . 337 VIVA 28 — 4

FEMALES
Death) concept O hairlesschested females, well attend! list, 398 NO THANKS 15 — 16

+FEMALES
FOR CONTEXT, SEE . . . . 388 NO THANKS 5 — 14

FEMMES
sleep? toutes les petites femmes exactes qui dansent toujours 121 & PORTRAIT 12 — 50

FER
way kiddo but as fer i gimme de good . . . . 237 IS 5 ONE 8 — 12
wid eachudder Hell Bent fer election makin believe dey . . . 237 IS 5 ONE 8 — 19
i feels so lonely fer duh good ole days . . . . 332 VIVA 23 — 14
(day simbully loves id) fer ids dare pain dares . . . . 519 50 POEMS 33 — 21

FERAI
coucher avec moi? te ferai Mimi te ferai Minette, ... 121 & PORTRAIT 12 — 37
te ferai Mimi te ferai Minette, dead exactly dance . . . . . 121 & PORTRAIT 12 — 38

FERN
seriously yearns beyond this fern of sunset frond on . . . . 12 T&C SONGS 2 — 43
know the poignant instantaneous fern whose scrupulous . . . . 19 T&C PUELLA MEA — 110
yearn, the immanent subliminal fern of her delicious voice . 19 T&C PUELLA MEA — 114
her mind) --the vocal fern, always which feels the . . . . . 19 T&C PUELLA MEA — 124

FERNS
shy foot among cool ferns) therefore togethering our . . . . 371 VIVA 62 — 13

FEROCIOUS
feet propped on irrelevantly ferocious heels. Her gasping . . 103 & POST IMPR 13 — 8
taste the accurate demure ferocious rhythm of precise . . . . 162 & SON ACTU 11 — 12
/ / at the ferocious phenomenon of 5 o'clock . . . . 201 XLI PORTRAIT 9 — 1

FEROCITIES
height these various innocent ferocities are superseded by . 202 XLI PORTRAIT 9 — 40

FEROCITY
by the sole prostituted ferocity of silence, it is) . . . . . 202 XLI PORTRAIT 9 — 41

+FERTIG
FOR CONTEXT, SEE . . . . 605 {CHAIRE} 7 — 8

FERVENT
mightier nostrils of the fervent dead, feed with felicities . 212 XLI SONNETS 8 — 6

+FERVENTLY
FOR CONTEXT, SEE . . . . 449 NO THANKS 64 — 9

FETISH
scout the inhuman itarian fetish that man isn't wuman . . . . 492 50 POEMS 6 — 7

FEW
they cleaned up a few times--before she got the . . . . 145 & SON REAL 16 — 5
queerly to do a few gestures to death, the . . . . 225 IS 5 ONE LIZ — 4
times, and even a few more depending on the . . . . 236 IS 5 ONE 7 — 15
extant smile.... remark a few deleted of texture or . . . . . 260 IS 5 ONE 30 — 8
vicinity) invei- gles a few mildly curious rai -ned . . . . . 267 IS 5 TWO 2 — 17

		PAGE	TITLE	LINE
FEW (CONTINUED)				
they throw in a few gas and the oh	272	IS 5 TWO 7	6
/ now that fierce few flowers (stealthily) in the	277	IS 5 THREE 1	1
of their hearts a few philosophers tell me what	281	IS 5 THREE 5	1
we had imagined a few cries drifting through high	283	IS 5 THREE 7	5
well toss him a few thoughts a little love	298	IS 5 FOUR 15	14
of hail (and a few windows awaken certain faces	299	IS 5 FOUR 16	13
you sensations, imitating a few fatally exquisite" (pulling .	328	VIVA 19	18
dawn embraces hugely some few most rare perfectly dear . . .	376	VIVA 67	11
am was. are leaves few this. is these a	491	50 POEMS 5	1
guessed (but only a few and down they forgot	515	50 POEMS 29	9
leaf of ghosts some few creep there here or	541	1 X 1 1	10
the many on the few not excluding mr u	551	1 X 1 11	3
of a jew a few dead dollars and some	644	{CHAIRE} 46	4
of hi llside) a few dim tombstones try to	695	95 POEMS 23	6
/ christ but they're few all (beyond win or	805	73 POEMS 33	1
once world slips from few of sun fingers numb)	822	73 POEMS 50	2
FEWER				
lily could pray and fewer were shyer than doll.	509	50 POEMS 23	23
FEWNESS				
with me in the fewness of these colours; alone	357	VIVA 48	10
FIDDLE				
had been playing a fiddle i had been dancing:	355	VIVA 46	18
FIDDLES				
eyes a blind irisher fiddles a scotch jig in	108	& PORTRAIT 4	8
FIDDLING				
colours like 'cellos keen fiddling colours colours cOOler . .	100	& POST IMPR 11	8
a brittle little person fiddling in the rain (did	498	50 POEMS 12	13
FIELD				
bullying daisies through the field wonderful with eyes a . .	26	T&C CHANSONS 3	6
every beast of the field / / / /	267	IS 5 TWO 2	20
sittin in uh green field watchin four crows drop	332	VIVA 23	31
brittle emblems, or a field (and i pause among	434	NO THANKS 51	24
among whippoorwills or tree field rock hollyhock forest brook	512	50 POEMS 26	26
ain : dreamin g field o ver forest &;	653	{CHAIRE} 55	5
FIELDS				
carved on sharpening air. Fields lying miraculous in violent	86	T&C SON ACTU 5	7
dress, who; touches: the fields (at sunset) / /	91	& POST IMPR 3	20
in gof throughof treesOf. (Fields Elysian the like, a) . . .	104	& POST IMPR 14	6
wait under the trees Fields slowly Elysian in a	104	& POST IMPR 14	14
rain, (Who feathers frightened fields with the superior . . .	163	& SON ACTU 12	3
elingwhiRls) are pouring rush fields drea mf (ull y . . .	423	NO THANKS 40	16
how through deep lifted fields Oxen distinctly move, a . . .	434	NO THANKS 51	31
FIEND				
this cry of one fiend, a thousand dreams thick	439	NO THANKS 55	7
began of god and fiend? i give you man	527	50 POEMS 39	7
seem (blow friend to fiend: blow space to time)	560	1 X 1 20	6
joy, most rare) a fiend, if fiends speak truth;	562	1 X 1 22	5
was --but now that fiend and i are such	730	95 POEMS 58	5
FIENDS				
is the song which fiends and angels sing: all	556	1 X 1 16	9
rare) a fiend, if fiends speak truth; if angels	562	1 X 1 22	5
many selves (so many fiends and gods each greedier	609	{CHAIRE} 11	1
to learn and even fiends: or, if he paints	842	73 POEMS 70	5
FIERCE				
the bloodbeat in her fierce laziness tried to repeat	135	& SON REAL 6	9
/ / now that fierce few flowers (stealthily) in	277	IS 5 THREE 1	1
FIERCELY				
did occur bell beyond fiercely spurting bell a jetted	115	& PORTRAIT 8	18
stink of perfumed noise fiercely mounts from the fireman's .	169	& SON ACTU 18	4
of her youth; whom, fiercely shy and gently brutal, ...	214	XLI SONNETS 10	6
/ what is strictly fiercely and wholly dies his	344	VIVA 35	1
twos or threes which fiercely rapidly pass with their . . .	354	VIVA 45	22
neverish subchemistry of alWays)fiercely live whom on Large	361	VIVA 52	30
such brief selves as fiercely seek findingly new textures . .	373	VIVA 64	14
immensity (upon once whom fiercely by pink mr seized	465	NEW POEMS 3	7
FIERCENESS				
body uses a careful fierceness. Her lips study my	146	& SON REAL 17	3

	PAGE	TITLE	LINE

FIFTEEN
a bloke back in fifteen. Then she came toward . . . . 145 & SON REAL 16   2
FIFTEENGRAND
(having a fortune of fifteengrand f thanks to the . . . . . . 331 VIVA 22   1
FIFTEENTHRATE
his back dressed in fifteenthrate ideas wearing a round . . . 258 IS 5 ONE 28   3
FIFTH
reddish ant travels my fifth finger. a bird chirps . . . . . 281 IS 5 THREE 5   11
nearness reaches a lucky fifth of you turns people . . . . . 537 50 POEMS 49   6
FIFTH'S
i want above fourteenth fifth's deep purring biceps, the . . 220 XLI SONNETS 16   2
FIFTY
timid with nesting incense) fifty marble pillars slipped from 32 T&C ORIENTALE 6   27
from immeasurable height, fall, fifty, silent in the incense 32 T&C ORIENTALE 6   31
the passion of the fifty pillars listening while the . . . . 35 T&C ORIENTALE 6 112
to hold down the fifty bucks per job with . . . . 242 IS 5 ONE 13   8
that there are 50 (fifty) flics for every one . . . . 274 IS 5 TWO 9   17
by priests moving in fifty colours , sensuously (the . . . . 280 IS 5 THREE 4   11
you'll never guess in fifty thousand years equals the . . . . 544 1 X 1 4   14
FIFTYTHREE
prostitute the once -over. fiftythree (and one would see . . 150 & SON REAL 21   2
FIGHT
even is compelled to fight itself from tame to . . . . 544 1 X 1 4   17
+FIGHT
FOR CONTEXT, SEE . . . . 227 IS 5 ONE GERT   14
FIGHTER
born to dare --a fighter to his eyelashes-- the . . . . 799 73 POEMS 27   4
FIGHTING
just what everybody was fighting for, my sister isabel . . . 276 IS 5 TWO 10   5
FILES
of her eyes easily files my impatience to an . . . . 147 & SON REAL 18   8
FILIGREE
smoky laughter into the filigree frame of a microscopic . . . 55 T&C PORTRAIT 3   5
FILL
miraculous in violent silence fill with microscopic . . . . . 86 T&C SON ACTU 5   8
for two dollars i fill her hips with boys . . . . 148 & SON REAL 19   14
FILLED
and all her body filled with May) --moving in . . . . 17 T&C PUELLA MEA   22
is a quick forest filled with sleeping birds thy . . . . . . 29 T&C ORIENTALE 3   6
seen all the silence filled with vivid noiseless boys . . . . 45 T&C LA GUERRE 1   11
bercoloured hands and feet filled with quick fingers and . . 69 T&C POST IMPR 6   39
more illustrious arms are filled with fascination, when my . 78 T&C SON UNRE 3   10
sunset (which is so filled with fear people bells) . . . . . 98 & POST IMPR 9   2
keen city in the sky--filled with pretty people? (and . . . . 129 & SEVEN POEMS 7   3
her long hard body filled with surprise like a . . . . 147 & SON REAL 18   4
hips and her sails filled with dream-- when on . . . . 156 & SON ACTU 5   7
He--and She-- shaped waxworks filled with dead ideas (the . . 250 IS 5 ONE 21   9
separating selves become museums filled with skilfully . . . 297 IS 5 FOUR 14   15
there (like lopsided imaginations) filled with newly murdered 340 VIVA 31   11
(THE ROUND AIR IS FILLED) OPENING / / / . . . . 348 VIVA 39   16
so standing, our eyes filled with wind, and the . . . . 378 VIVA 69   1
when the Light is filled with birds seriously i . . . . 434 NO THANKS 51   3
disappear always who are filled with never are more . . . . . 505 50 POEMS 19   19
+FILLED
FOR CONTEXT, SEE . . . . 266 IS 5 TWO 1   32
FILLING
bringing rain and leaves, filling the air with fear . . . . . 304 IS 5 FIVE 3   12
FILLS
people of perfect darkness fills his mind who will . . . . .   9 T&C SONGS 1   19
A sharp blue day fills with peacefully leaping air . . . . . 62 T&C PORTRAIT 10   8
see! (the new moon fills abruptly with sudden silver . . . . 93 & POST IMPR 5   14
FILTH
unwashed sonorous muscle the filth of a collar hung . . . . . 96 & POST IMPR 8   31
because and why what filth is here unlives do . . . . 440 NO THANKS 56   7
+FILTHIEST
FOR CONTEXT, SEE . . . . 668 (CHAIRE) 70   21
FILTHILY
evil. the slobbering walls filthily push witless creases of . 96 & POST IMPR 8   3

	PAGE	TITLE	LINE
FILTHY			
stricken air which is filthy with agile swarming sonal . . .	69	T&C POST IMPR 6	5
thither and hither in filthy sawdust chucks and rolls	259	IS 5 ONE 29	4
april might make alive filthy some past imagining whowhich .	662	(CHAIRE) 64	5
upon you and all filthy men come annabel darling	707	95 POEMS 35	21
+FILTHY			
FOR CONTEXT, SEE	789	73 POEMS 17	13
FINAL			
followed by gay untimid final flowers (which dressed in . . .	4	T&C EPITHALAM	67
and the sweet strong final bird transcends the sight, ...	7	T&C EPITHALAM	165
applause, and when the final curtain strikes the world . . .	75	T&C SON REAL 6	2
leaf whirling in the final brain of air!) Let	80	T&C SON UNRE 5	11
upon the nude and final silence and shall the	155	& SON ACTU 4	15
silent him into nibbling final worms / / /	277	IS 5 THREE 1	24
herself the sprouting largest final air plunges inward with .	301	IS 5 FOUR 18	16
lazily multitudes out of final towers; captured: in the . . .	345	VIVA 36	7
all distance breathes a final dream of bells; perfectly . . .	750	95 POEMS 78	2
FINALITY			
in this season" think "finality lives up on them	354	VIVA 45	12
FINALLY			
trees and houses and finally, butts into the river	47	T&C IMPRESS 1	10
coolness, very faintly and finally through altogether	92	& POST IMPR 4	16
light dusty heroisms and finally colliding with the most . .	203	XLI LA GUERRE 1	11
sky and the sea ...finally your eyes knew me, ...	283	IS 5 THREE 7	20
piglike big! sorrows always; finally and always, the iflike .	384	NO THANKS 2	12
whisper whose erect blood finally trembles, emerging to . . .	435	NO THANKS 51	38
these those three disappear finally what's left behind is .	501	50 POEMS 15	17
all prehuman history and finally The UN "be quiet	711	95 POEMS 39	16
who strive; and being finally released flee one another . . .	799	73 POEMS 27	30
away in the sky finally faintly (higher than high	813	73 POEMS 41	10
FINANCIAL			
Be- tween its supple financial teeth deliriously sprouting .	201	XLI PORTRAIT 9	3
FINCH			
/ / "o purple finch please tell me why	836	73 POEMS 64	1
FIND			
food its leaves inimitable find beyond the white authentic .	19	T&C PUELLA MEA	119
day comes God will find six crumbs stooping by	117	& PORTRAIT 10	4
said never mind, you'll find But the moon creeped	125	& SEVEN POEMS 4	19
(It is necessary to find Hassan's Place by tiny	143	& SON REAL 14	3
when i turn to find her how my least	152	& SON ACTU 1	8
usual i did not find him in cafes, the	197	XLI PORTRAIT 5	1
of 5 o'clock i find myself gently decomposing in	201	XLI PORTRAIT 9	1
of How do you find the sun, ladies? <>	255	IS 5 ONE 26	7
of Thickness) points uPDownwardishly find everywheres	311	VIVA 3	16
us) to is it find somehow (but O gracefully)	368	VIVA 59	12
doesn't know where to find them (and found a	410	NO THANKS 27	2
who are trying to find their minds (but never	410	NO THANKS 27	8
/ that famous fatheads find that each and every	411	NO THANKS 28	1
shall not for living find the rule) and dark	420	NO THANKS 37	9
as round as to find. Each why of a	543	1 X 1 3	6
year. All lose, whole find / / / /	556	1 X 1 16	15
and there they'll scarcely find us (if they do, ...	579	1 X 1 39	13
/ out of more find than seeks thinking, swim	612	(CHAIRE) 14	1
head, baby & you'll find a heart in it	637	(CHAIRE) 39	2
heart, mabel & you'll find a bed in it	637	(CHAIRE) 39	5
bed, sibyl & you'll find a tart in it	637	(CHAIRE) 39	8
tart, lady & you'll find his mind in it	637	(CHAIRE) 39	11
as lost as you'll find / / / /	647	(CHAIRE) 49	20
it's always ourselves we find in the sea /	682	95 POEMS 10	12
comprehend, remember seek (forgetting find) and in a mystery	688	95 POEMS 16	12
/ / --laughing to find anyone's blind (like me	716	95 POEMS 44	1
in so --laughing to find a noone's more by	716	95 POEMS 44	29
for death's because to find) may, given perfect mercy, . . .	735	95 POEMS 63	2
what seemed myself, i find selves unimaginably mine; beyond .	810	73 POEMS 38	9
+FIND			
FOR CONTEXT, SEE	403	NO THANKS 20	13
FOR CONTEXT, SEE	421	NO THANKS 38	27

		PAGE	TITLE	LINE

FINDETH
Marie and of Maleore findeth of ladies goodly store . . . . . 21 T&C PUELLA MEA 173

FINDING
Rish and Foses) until (finding one's self at some . . . . . . 319 VIVA 11 15
/ / lucky means finding Holes where pockets aren't . . . . . 467 NEW POEMS 5 1
seekingly lips wander a finding whom of girl) dolls . . . . . 565 1 X 1 25 4
was of shall and finding only why smashed it . . . . 566 1 X 1 26 7
earth's own clumsily striving (finding and losing and . . . . 749 95 POEMS 77 7
/ the trick of finding what you didn't lose . . . . 807 73 POEMS 35 1

FINDINGEST
o no O 3rd Findingest whispers understand sobs bigly . . . . 358 VIVA 49 6

FINDINGLY
selves as fiercely seek findingly new textures of actual . . 373 VIVA 64 14
(dark we all findingly Spring the Fragrance unvisible) . . . 482 NEW POEMS 20 8

FINDS
present writing one still finds delighted fingers knitting . 70 T&C SON REAL 1 7
and whying) seek than finds feeling (seize) floats (only . . 612 (CHAIRE) 14 12
all) nor any marvel finds quite disappearance but some . . . 750 95 POEMS 78 12

FINE
for his wrist's too fine the nineteenth says to . . . . . . 15 T&C SONGS 5 12
dance and Whocares dead's fine like hands do you . . . . . . 126 & SEVEN POEMS 5 24
ennobling forsooth? One wondrous fine sonofabitch (to all . . 254 IS 5 ONE 25 5
l'Etoile the communists have fine Eyes some are young . . . . 274 IS 5 TWO 9 3
the Communists have (very) fine eyes (which stroll hither . . 275 IS 5 TWO 9 48
in Dragon st one fine August night, i just . . . . 313 VIVA 5 2
/ / / (one fine day) let's take the . . . . 316 VIVA 8 1
and lithe some very fine mower a tall; tall . . . . . . 509 50 POEMS 23 11
into the sunlight the fine sunlight with a firm . . . . . . 529 50 POEMS 41 7
stones, but never this fine specimen of hypermagical . . . . 554 1 X 1 14 12
/ / dying is fine) but Death ? o . . . . 604 (CHAIRE) 6 1
o pen window this fine morning) fly instead of . . . . . . 724 95 POEMS 52 10
or ethereally serious: a fine not a coarse clown . . . . . 802 73 POEMS 30 23

FINELOOKING
"a tall strong young finelooking fellow, dressed well but . . 800 73 POEMS 28 4

FINELY
oblivion) a tiny dust finely arising at the integration . . . 197 XLI PORTRAIT 5 23

FINGER
beckons with the little finger of his left hand . . . . . . 33 T&C ORIENTALE 6 58
jade and twitching eyelids finger their unquiet spears the . 34 T&C ORIENTALE 6 80
his thumb and first finger (i say "will he . . . . 102 & POST IMPR 12 5
just puts out their finger and they stuff the . . . . 126 & SEVEN POEMS 5 12
wiggles the perfectly dead finger of thitherhithering gas. . 134 & SON REAL 5 12
you to hold every finger shall have its ring . . . . 192 XLI CHANSONS 2 19
ant travels my fifth finger. a bird chirps in . . . . 281 IS 5 THREE 5 11
clock strikes midnight a finger pulls a trigger a . . . . . 338 VIVA 29 23
twirled around your little finger is) what's right about . . 411 NO THANKS 28 7
bellyful without lifting my finger i say to hell . . . . . 475 NEW POEMS 13 9
& seriously voice -like finger of the tree / . . . . 480 NEW POEMS 18 26
men's hair and every finger is a toe and . . . . 511 50 POEMS 25 10
helen) the slimmer the finger the thicker the thumb . . . . 513 50 POEMS 27 6
a jennelman name misder finger isn't important whether it's . 549 1 X 1 9 3
his head by a finger of trunk, and singing . . . . 631 (CHAIRE) 33 3

FINGERED
look look. Skilfully . fingered by (a parenthesis the) . . . 99 & POST IMPR 10 9
perpetual of sleep some silver-fingered fountain steals the . 208 XLI SONNETS 4 14
body the sharp things fingered tinily my heart life . . . . 284 IS 5 FOUR 1 7

FINGERING
mind is seen frequently fingering the exact beads of . . . . 193 XLI PORTRAIT 1 6
thickening fear our slightly fingering spirits starve and . . 305 IS 5 FIVE 4 7

FINGERINGS
syncopate some sunbeam's skilful fingerings; it is utterly to 19 T&C PUELLA MEA 86

+FINGERINGS
FOR CONTEXT, SEE . . . . 463 NEW POEMS 1 7

FINGERS
and did thy fortunate fingers sometime dwell (within a . . . 3 T&C EPITHALAM 21
for blown kisses, condemnatory fingers thinned of pity--so he 9 T&C SONGS 1 13
/ / / Thy fingers make early flowers of . . . . 13 T&C SONGS 3 1
little breasts My strong fingers beneath the snow Into . . . 16 T&C SONGS 6 9

252

		PAGE	TITLE	LINE

FINGERS (CONTINUED)

night when in my fingers drooped your shining body . . . . . 39 T&C AMORES 4   12
often have the doting fingers of prurient philosophers . . . 46 T&C LA GUERRE 2   5
dissonance by the correct fingers of April resolved into . . 47 T&C IMPRESS 1   3
will You with elaborate fingers possibly touch the pink . . . 58 T&C PORTRAIT 6   16
the snow and thy fingers are the rain, and . . . . 61 T&C PORTRAIT 9   30
feet filled with quick fingers and a remarkable tail . . . . 69 T&C POST IMPR 6   39
one still finds delighted fingers knitting for the is . . . . 70 T&C SON REAL 1   8
and your dear strong fingers clutch his heart, as . . . . . . 76 T&C SON UNRE 1   3
things, things obscene (Whose fingers young the caving ages . 77 T&C SON UNRE 2   3
strokable body these men's fingers toss trunks shuffle sacks 114 & PORTRAIT 7   7
thing all full of fingers dead has a smile . . . . 126 & SEVEN POEMS 5   13
indecent stir unclenches into fingers.... she too is tired. . 131 & SON REAL 2   12
decision: burn the terrific fingers which grapple and joke . 146 & SON REAL 17   5
do in my bullying fingers) as for the candle, ... 164 & SON ACTU 13   14
flower with their enormous fingers unwished / / / . . . . . . 165 & SON ACTU 14   16
--and then. My crazy fingers liked your dress ....your . . . 173 & SON ACTU 22   8
my body Shall enter fingers of smooth mastery with . . . . . 189 XLI SONGS 11   9
grieving: from the impressed fingers of sublime Memory, of . 207 XLI SONNETS 3   11
justly touching roses their fingers whitely live by? or . . . 211 XLI SONNETS 7   11
scandal while five other fingers snitch rapidly through mist 259 IS 5 ONE 29   10
this? Do your proud fingers and your arms tremble . . . . . . 279 IS 5 THREE 3   21
fist out of ten fingers voices rise from down . . . . 281 IS 5 THREE 5   20
and with curling infantile fingers it understood my eyes . . 284 IS 5 FOUR 1   4
wandering after it with fingers; till having found what . . . 298 IS 5 FOUR 15   22
slenderly comprehend (clinging as fingers, loving one another 305 IS 5 FIVE 4   2
hands with their guessing fingers did-not-move exquisitely . 355 VIVA 46   15
stands, with clumsily wilted fingers emptying youth colour . 359 VIVA 50   6
have closed myself as fingers, you open always petal . . . . 366 VIVA 57   6
completely weep my father's fingers brought her sleep: vainly 520 50 POEMS 34   14
that spirit her own fingers with and give him . . . . 531 50 POEMS 43   11
(while thumb a plus fingers all with blind him . . . . 546 1 X 1 6   10
of things with eager fingers (with patient eyes) re . . . . . 660 (CHAIRE) 62   8
/ now all the fingers of this tree (darling) . . . . 667 (CHAIRE) 69   1
some darkness during which fingers are without hands; and . . 667 (CHAIRE) 69   10
whose rays five languid fingers were; and molly was . . . . . 682 95 POEMS 10   6
/ why do the fingers of the lit tle . . . . 724 95 POEMS 52   3
from few of sun fingers numb) with anguished each . . . . . . 822 73 POEMS 50   2

+FINGERS

FOR CONTEXT, SEE . . . . 255 IS 5 ONE 26   3

FINGERTIPS

in your hair, (your fingertips the way you move) . . . . . . 291 IS 5 FOUR 8   12

FINGERY

complexly wisdoming friend's --a fingery treesoul onlying . . 517 50 POEMS 31   6

FINGERYHANDS

disappeared. Out of more (fingeryhands me and whying) seek . 612 (CHAIRE) 14   11

FINGLESTEIN

tea mis eyesucks unyewkuntel finglestein idstings yewrety . . 474 NEW POEMS 12   12

FINI

le negre esn7othingish8s c'est fini pRaW, lT; O: allons . . . 430 NO THANKS 47   22

FINISHED

the stars have been finished in the nobler trees . . . . . . 184 XLI SONGS 6   11

FINISHES

Bawstinamereekin, exit paperboy a finishes Helmar lights . . 200 XLI PORTRAIT 8   14

FINISHING

her way of beginningly finishing (and such hair) the . . . . 337 VIVA 28   12

FINKLESTEIN

TOLD $ SEVERAL MILLION FINKLESTEIN (FRITZ) LIVES AT THE . . . 244 IS 5 ONE 15   3

FINLAND

o to be in finland now that russia's here) . . . . 641 (CHAIRE) 43   1

FINN

i am this blueeyed Finn emerging from a lovehouse . . . . . . 115 & PORTRAIT 8   26

FINS

of her nakedness with fins sharply pleasant, my youth . . . . 216 XLI SONNETS 12   3

FIRE

smoke the poppy's pompous fire the pansy's purple patience .   5 T&C EPITHALAM   92
and blazed with snowy fire) unfolding, gave the moon . . . .   8 T&C OF NICOL   18
furious light, and while fire-escapes and roofs and chimneys   62 T&C PORTRAIT 10   15

		PAGE	TITLE	LINE

FIRE (CONTINUED)

and while roofs and fire-escapes and chimneys and while . . . 62 T&C PORTRAIT 10 16
and while chimneys and fire-escapes and roofs are talking . . 62 T&C PORTRAIT 10 17
Tail stirs.) And the. fire-escapes-- the night. makes me . . 166 & SON ACTU 15 11
sings the flinger of fire beyond red rivers of . . . . . . 185 XLI SONGS 7 5
leap through hoops of fire, creating smoothness. People . . . 279 IS 5 THREE 3 16
the very middle of fire all the world becoming . . . . . . 283 IS 5 THREE 7 26
outward into the freezing fire of Thickness) points . . . . . 311 VIVA 3 14
shall increase) open thy fire! for i have had . . . . 360 VIVA 51 32
to know wholly imagining fire) only consider How / . . . . 362 VIVA 53 15
less lonely than a fire is cool took bedfellows . . . . . . 420 NO THANKS 37 11
and all one is fire / / / / . . . . 507 50 POEMS 21 28
icy known swim ignorant fire (adventuring and time's dead . . 533 50 POEMS 45 16
cold to skylessness sticking fire my are your are . . . . . 541 1 X 1 1 4
/ / / / ("fire stop thief help murder . . . . 555 1 X 1 15 1
in water and in fire, but fear-- mind's a . . . . 651 (CHAIRE) 53 8
if the seas catch fire (and live by love . . . . 732 95 POEMS 60 6
through a Dream like fire called flowers over green . . . . . 778 73 POEMS 6 16

FIRE-ESCAPES

furious light, and while fire-escapes and roofs and chimneys 62 T&C PORTRAIT 10 15
and while roofs and fire-escapes and chimneys and while . . . 62 T&C PORTRAIT 10 16
and while chimneys and fire-escapes and roofs are talking . . 62 T&C PORTRAIT 10 17
Tail stirs.) And the. fire-escapes-- the night. makes me . . 166 & SON ACTU 15 11

FIRE'S

gents these (by the fire's ruddy glow united) not . . . . . 254 IS 5 ONE 25 9

FIRED

graze at pause then fired by hypercivic zeal sought . . . . . 258 IS 5 ONE 28 11

FIREMAN'S

fiercely mounts from the fireman's ball, i think and . . . . 169 & SON ACTU 18 4

FIRES

and from those tenuous fires which more and more . . . . . .   6 T&C EPITHALAM 132

FIREWORKS

damn... bring on your fireworks, which are a mixed . . . . . 264 IS 5 ONE 33 21

FIRM

Each tapering breast is firm and smooth that in . . . . . . 21 T&C PUELLA MEA 181
of you, approve these firm unsated eyes which have . . . . . 36 T&C AMORES 1 10
whereas the big and firm legs moving solemnly like . . . . . 95 & POST IMPR 7 13
genie of trunk trickled firm- ly in to one . . . . 96 & POST IMPR 8 33
crooked and it's too firm to be hard but . . . . 126 & SEVEN POEMS 5 3
my height in a firm fragile stinging weather, (breathless . . 140 & SON REAL 11 8
bones, and the trembling -firm-smooth ness and which i . . . 175 & SON ACTU 4 7
supports while devouring the firm tumult of exquisitely in- . 201 XLI PORTRAIT 9 19
stink of rich frail firm asinine life (i pant . . . . 220 XLI SONNETS 16 4
blue eye, upon his firm white lips a smile, ... 273 IS 5 TWO 8 10
are frail) songs less firm than your body's whitest . . . . 306 IS 5 FIVE 5 4
an earth gladly seem firm for you: remember (as . . . . . . 372 VIVA 63 8
swoon & ingly seethe firm swirl hips whirling climb . . . . 445 NO THANKS 60 27
from nowh -ere (! firm!) exp- anding, am a . . . . 449 NO THANKS 64 8
(so timid air is firm) under his eyes would . . . . 520 50 POEMS 34 7
fine sunlight with a firm day in it you . . . . 529 50 POEMS 41 8
(in which in soft) firm who outlift queries of . . . . . . 613 (CHAIRE) 15 7

FIRM-SMOOTH

bones, and the trembling -firm-smooth ness and which i . . . 175 & SON ACTU 24 7

FIRMCOOL

slowly Elysian in a firmcool-Ness taxis, s. QuirM and, . . . 104 & POST IMPR 14 15

FIRMCOOL-NESS

slowly Elysian in a firmcool-Ness taxis, s. QuirM and, . . . 104 & POST IMPR 14 15

FIRMER

means nearer because deeper firmer since darker than little . 126 & SEVEN POEMS 5 2
get another man with firmer lips to take your . . . . 161 & SON ACTU 10 2

FIRMLY

brittle eager eternal luminous firmly diminishing have . . . 110 & PORTRAIT 6 27
/ / irreproachable ladies firmly lewd on dangerous slabs . . 138 & SON REAL 9 1
lips stalked or eyes firmly stirred) my mirror gives . . . . 360 VIVA 51 2
rain (dream hugely) wish firmly. splendidly advancing colour 422 NO THANKS 39 4

+FIRMLY

FOR CONTEXT, SEE . . . . 96 & POST IMPR 8 33

FIRMLYSQUIRMY
    breasts look very good: firmlysquirmy with a slight jounce, . 150 & SON REAL 21   4
FIRST
    smoking song-- as the first star perfects the sensual . . . .   7 T&C EPITHALAM   164
    in a line the first lady says to nine . . . . 15 T&C SONGS 5   5
    shall stop me but first earth , the reckless . . . .   67 T&C POST IMPR 4   3
    and accurate silence.... But first you) press easily at . . . 67 T&C POST IMPR 4   16
    you) press easily at first, it will be leaves . . . . 67 T&C POST IMPR 4   19
    her eyes the dangerous first stars) people move love . . . . 93 & POST IMPR 5   10
    between his thumb and first finger (i say "will . . . . 102 & POST IMPR 12   5
    i am may the first crumb said whereupon its . . . . 117 & PORTRAIT 10   12
    my hips; or, your first twitch of crisp boy . . . . 140 & SON REAL 11   7
    songs for which is first to wither, to pass? . . . . 190 XLI SONGS 12   6
    affords furnished a soft first clue to his innumerable . . . 197 XLI PORTRAIT 5   5
    algebraic music. For the first time in sorting from . . . . . 201 XLI PORTRAIT 9   20
    good (it was the first ride and believe i . . . . 248 IS 5 ONE 19   25
    one his optima rerum first having taken care to . . . . 261 IS 5 ONE 31   11
    me that i had first of all really made . . . . 262 IS 5 ONE 32   5
    last and always and first to live makes unimportant . . . . . 264 IS 5 ONE 33   18
    / / / / first Jock he was kilt . . . . 271 IS 5 TWO 6   1
    i mean when the first guy drops you know . . . . 272 IS 5 TWO 7   4
    moon to squat in first darkness --a little moon . . . . 282 IS 5 THREE 6   16
    / since feeling is first who pays any attention . . . . 290 IS 5 FOUR 7   1
    who grow slowly and first into different deaths Concentric . 311 VIVA 3   8
    S.S. VAN MERDE) having first put right sleuthfully aboard . . 334 VIVA 25   5
    / / / the first president to be loved . . . . 336 VIVA 27   1
    who looked at whom first, anyhow dancing" (a moon . . . . . . 338 VIVA 29   20
    host of overjoyed noncoms (first knocking on the head . . . . 339 VIVA 30   8
    you are afraid "go first" of dreams and little . . . . 353 VIVA 44   26
    a light Out) & first of all foam -like . . . . 358 VIVA 49   2
    (touching skilfully, mysteriously) her first rose or if your 366 VIVA 57   8
    suddenly me) like these first deepest rare quite who . . . . 367 VIVA 58   7
    of shadow, that among first light groping washes my . . . . . 374 VIVA 65   14
    and invisible, with large first new stars knitting the . . . 378 VIVA 69   7
    friend twilight (and a first dream called ocean) and . . . . 424 NO THANKS 41   7
    / / / ondumonde" (first than caref ully; pois . . . . 430 NO THANKS 47   2
    absolute un gulps the first knowledge of death's wandering . 517 50 POEMS 31   13
    unburied which floats the first who, his april touch . . . . 520 50 POEMS 34   10
    we stand nor a first rose explodes but shall . . . . 538 50 POEMS 50   13
    (if all her most first little flowers rise out . . . . 559 1 X 1 19   13
    buds imitate upward each first flower of two / . . . . 573 1 X 1 33   23
    proudly depths above why's first because (faith's last doubt 574 1 X 1 34   9
    air not with twilight's first thrushes may awake more . . . . 577 1 X 1 37   6
    behind this man earth's first sunrise) and his voice . . . . 617 {CHAIRE} 19   5
    nor might any earth's first morning have concealed so . . . . 626 {CHAIRE} 28   13
    younger than young bird first for joy, he's i . . . . 666 {CHAIRE} 68   19
    as much as how (first the arri -v- in . . . . 676 95 POEMS 4   18
    spring she'll be the first to know / / . . . . 718 95 POEMS 46   8
    breathing shall blossom a first star) one / / . . . .   720 95 POEMS 48   14
    / / / / first robin the; you say . . . . 737 95 POEMS 65   1
    not quite undo such first amazement as a leaf--here's . . . . 762 95 POEMS 89   5
    feebleness: the truth more first than sun more last . . . . . 768 95 POEMS 94   12
    / / / the first of all my dreams . . . . 777 73 POEMS 5   1
    among her dollies, dad first ("don't tell your mother") . . . 794 73 POEMS 22   4
    doubt he was whatever (first and last) mostpeople fear . . . 802 73 POEMS 30   11
    / wild (at our first) beasts uttered human words . . . . . . 844 73 POEMS 72   1
FIRSTCLASSPRIVATES
    worse, and egged the firstclassprivates on his rectum . . . . 339 VIVA 30   27
FIRSTFUL
    flesh-- dreamslender exquisite white firstful flame --new . . 669 {CHAIRE} 71   9
FIRSTING
    / / / / thou firsting a hugeness of twi . . . . 349 VIVA 40   2
FIRSTRATE
    holy miraculous difference between firstrate & second implies 803 73 POEMS 31   10
FIRSTS
    a (float through sleeping firsts of wonder) child . . . . . . 757 95 POEMS 85   27
FISH
    rhythms to juggle Kandinsky gold-fish away from the gripping 180 XLI SONGS 2   13

```
                                                          PAGE      TITLE        LINE
FISH (CONTINUED)
  feel strike the silver fish of her nakedness with . . . . . . 216 XLI SONNETS 12    2
  whatever weeds feel and fish think of) / / . . . . . . . . . 359 VIVA 50          18
  is confused with fact, fish boast of fishing and . . . . . . 446 NO THANKS 61      4
  (it dived like a fish but it climbed like . . . . . . . . . . 593 1 X 1 53          9
  fly yes the little fish gambol as glad as . . . . . . . . . . 665 (CHAIRE) 67       6
  he now the little fish quiver so you and . . . . . . . . . . 665 (CHAIRE) 67       13
  sky all the little fish climb through the mind . . . . . . . 665 (CHAIRE) 67       20
  (4) Only The Game Fish Swims Upstream & (5) . . . . . . . . . 803 73 POEMS 31       17
+FISH
  FOR CONTEXT, SEE . . . . . . . . . . . . . . . . . . . . . . 319 VIVA 11           13
+FISH'S
  FOR CONTEXT, SEE . . . . . . . . . . . . . . . . . . . . . . 101 & POST IMPR 11    51
FISHE
  Who? wanted them, stomachslikEDead fishe s s olemnandputrid . 101 & POST IMPR 11    68
FISHERMEN
  might Where live can fisherMen swim and who's myself's . . . 395 NO THANKS 12       8
  with listening hands only fishermen are prevented by . . . . 478 NEW POEMS 16      11
FISHING
  air a sail a fishing boat somebody an invisible . . . . . . . 283 IS 5 THREE 7      7
  fact, fish boast of fishing and men are caught . . . . . . . 446 NO THANKS 61       4
FIST
  unhurried muscled huge chromatic fist skilfully modeling . .  82 T&C SON ACTU 1     9
  breathe). The plump left fist opening "wisdom." Flicker of . 226 IS 5 ONE MAME      7
  in his swivelchair one fist dangling scandal while five . . . 259 IS 5 ONE 29       9
  i suddenly make a fist out of ten fingers . . . . . . . . . . 281 IS 5 THREE 5      19
  us deeply in His fist is no longer, can . . . . . . . . . . . 289 IS 5 FOUR 6       3
  the-seat-of-the pants inani nvisible Fist) drifts a long . .  616 (CHAIRE) 18       10
  but quite absurd gloved fist on hip & the . . . . . . . . . . 640 (CHAIRE) 42       9
  as thick as my fist stuck in the throat . . . . . . . . . . . 709 95 POEMS 37       11
+FIST
  FOR CONTEXT, SEE . . . . . . . . . . . . . . . . . . . . . . 131 & SON REAL 2       8
FISTS
  talkative animals are laid fists of huger silence. I . . . .  45 T&C LA GUERRE 1    9
  how hair, in two fists of shrill colour, clutched . . . . . . 73 T&C SON REAL 4     4
  DarkcOOllonGBody windows, are. clenched. fists of tint. . . . 100 & POST IMPR 11    16
  chuckling flesh. Weak thirsty fists of idiot futures bash . . 151 & SON REAL 22     6
  tent his thick joggling fists he is persuasive the . . . . . 259 IS 5 ONE 29        6
  body, which terminated in fists hair wood erect cursing . . . 277 IS 5 THREE 1      8
  whom assault these whispering fists of hail (and a . . . . . 299 IS 5 FOUR 16      12
FIT
  shrill eyes beyond a fit- and-cling of stuffs the . . . . . . 155 & SON ACTU 4      8
  say the world not fit you) he is not . . . . . . . . . . . . 523 50 POEMS 36       27
+FIT
  FOR CONTEXT, SEE . . . . . . . . . . . . . . . . . . . . . . 726 95 POEMS 54        3
FITE
  lungs "gimme uh swell fite like up ter yknow, . . . . . . . . 227 IS 5 ONE GERT    14
FITS
  me around; my head fits (my head) in your . . . . . . . . . . 123 & SEVEN POEMS 2  12
  die safely whose epoch fits him like a grave) . . . . . . . . 394 NO THANKS 11      2
FIVE
  said whereupon its fellow five crumbs chuckled as if . . . . 117 & PORTRAIT 10     13
  / / / after five times the poem of . . . . . . . . . . . . . 184 XLI SONGS 6        1
  need of just twenty five cents dear friends to . . . . . . . 196 XLI PORTRAIT 4    12
  extending the courtesy of five o'clock became the omen . . . 197 XLI PORTRAIT 5    11
  Goo dnightef feŋdi .... five men in derbies / . . . . . . . . 200 XLI PORTRAIT 8    33
  / / / / FIVE AMERICANS LIZ with breathing . . . . . . . . . . 225 IS 5 ONE LIZ       T
  fist dangling scandal while five other fingers snitch rapidly 259 IS 5 ONE 29       10
  a man, three cats, five white mice, and a . . . . . . . . . . 279 IS 5 THREE 3       8
  along this pole over five squirming mice; or leap . . . . . . 279 IS 5 THREE 3      15
  hinging you --because it's five o'clock and these (i . . . . 282 IS 5 THREE 6       10
  a memory this brow five or three dreamfuls of . . . . . . . . 402 NO THANKS 19       7
  says tic, Eternity's a Five Year Plan: if Joy . . . . . . . . 438 NO THANKS 54       6
  was) assassinating whole grassblades, five ideas can swallow 491 50 POEMS 5        12
  a room's dark around) five (are all dancesing singdance . . . 507 50 POEMS 21        3
  a room's dark around) five (six are in a . . . . . . . . . . 507 50 POEMS 21       10
  all and all around five all around five around) . . . . . . . 507 50 POEMS 21       23
  around five all around five around) five flowers five . . . . 507 50 POEMS 21       24
```

FIVE (CONTINUED)
    all around five around) five flowers five (six are . . . . . 507 50 POEMS 21   25
    five around) five flowers five (six are in a . . . . 507 50 POEMS 21   25
    a room's dark) all five are one flowers five . . . . 507 50 POEMS 21   27
    five are one flowers five flowers and all one . . . . 507 50 POEMS 21   28
    so breathing's to steal-- five wishes are five and . . . . . 543 1 X 1 3   17
    steal-- five wishes are five and one hand is . . . . 543 1 X 1 3   17
    if who're by the five nevers of a lear . . . . 561 1 X 1 21   10
    three: but were it five, i'd still insist that . . . . . . 579 1 X 1 39   6
    oned trouserfly tumbling, faded five or so lightyears of . . 607 {CHAIRE} 9   6
    your mineral general animal (five foot five) neither dead . . 640 {CHAIRE} 42   13
    general animal (five foot five) neither dead nor alive . . . 640 {CHAIRE} 42   13
    stranded star whose rays five languid fingers were; and . . . 682 95 POEMS 10   6
    (to quite become nothing) five times, proclaim fate isn't . . 764 95 POEMS 90   52
    Homer Lea) here are five simple facts no sub . . . . 803 73 POEMS 31   5
    are you, little i (five or six years old) . . . . 824 73 POEMS 52   2
    "i will give you five hopes for any fear, ... 837 73 POEMS 65   8
+FIVE
    FOR CONTEXT, SEE . . . . 60 T&C PORTRAIT 8   6
    FOR CONTEXT, SEE . . . . 725 95 POEMS 53   10
FIXED
    an instant may be fixed so that it will . . . . 264 IS 5 ONE 33   23
FLABBY
    (very occasionally budding a flabby algebraic odour jigs et . 134 & SON REAL 5   8
    couches, weary, upon a flabby mattress of jelly.... than . . 143 & SON REAL 14   12
FLAG
    determined head the sacred flag of truth unfurled, in . . . . 273 IS 5 TWO 8   14
    not kiss your fucking flag" straightway the silver bird . . . 339 VIVA 30   19
    highest fly only the flag that's furled (sestet entitled . . 390 NO THANKS 7   8
    / / red-rag and pink-flag blackshirt and brown strut-mince . 497 50 POEMS 11   1
FLAGS
    into Oblivion wave little flags weeping flatter thoroughly . 391 NO THANKS 8   8
FLAME
    upon the tongue of flame half-mute, (haste ere some . . . . . 6 T&C EPITHALAM   118
    glass turned light to flame and blazed with snowy . . . . . . 8 T&C OF NICOL   18
    flight, a flower, a flame, was a tendril fleetly . . . . . . 23 T&C PUELLA MEA   278
    we on the groaning flame of neat huge trudging . . . . 67 T&C POST IMPR 4   24
    insane chisel the killing flame that dizzily grips. Querying 139 & SON REAL 10   11
    really released, the modern flame of her indomitable body . . 146 & SON REAL 17   2
    workingman (by that bright flame whose myriad tints enrich . 254 IS 5 ONE 25   17
    a willing bulb of flame bubbles) see here and . . . . 282 IS 5 THREE 6   28
    lure an eagerest strict flame) demand the metaphor of . . . . 362 VIVA 53   10
    ignorant most precise essential flame never which waked) & . 373 VIVA 64   7
    a shrine: its puniest flame persists shaken by the . . . . . 435 NO THANKS 51   44
    signalling of singular most flame and surely poets only . . . 456 NO THANKS 71   10
    and water most encourage flame as hatracks into peachtrees . 511 50 POEMS 25   7
    proudly and (by octobering flame beckoned) as earth will . . 521 50 POEMS 34   41
    gives you skilful his flame so is your heart . . . . 575 1 X 1 35   24
    (young trembling any) into flame twig or limb explodes . . . 583 1 X 1 43   10
    until and until into flame i can feel how . . . . 587 1 X 1 47   14
    heart singing like a flame blue took it my . . . . 593 1 X 1 53   12
    sky times earth: a flame beyond soul immemorially forevering 599 {CHAIRE} 1   4
    how can each" while flame crashed "be so am . . . . 626 {CHAIRE} 28   9
    dreamslender exquisite white firstful flame --new moon! as . 669 {CHAIRE} 71   9
    this irre- VocA -ble flame is lives breath es . . . . 719 95 POEMS 47   10
    flaming dream to dreaming flame) united by perfect nothing: . 721 95 POEMS 49   3
    secrecies and his (dreaming flame by flaming dream) merge--at 721 95 POEMS 49   11
+FLAME
    FOR CONTEXT, SEE . . . . 267 IS 5 TWO 2   11
FLAMEFLUNG
    reincarnate song suddenly leaping flameflung, mounts, ... 206 XLI SONNETS 2   8
FLAMES
    flowers wee skipping high-heeled flames courtesied before my 44 T&C AMORES 8   6
    grunting eyes pin tailored flames Her being at this . . . . . 137 & SON REAL 8   10
    singular strictly immeasurable nowhere flames --its farthest 741 95 POEMS 69   3
FLAMING
    some newly remembered dream-- flaming a coolly bell touches . 601 {CHAIRE} 3   13
    life; breathing to breathing flaming dream to dreaming flame) 721 95 POEMS 49   3

		PAGE	TITLE	LINE

FLAMING (CONTINUED)

his (dreaming flame by flaming dream) merge--at not . . . . . 721 95 POEMS 49   11
my sleeping self float flaming symbols of hope, and . . . . . 749 95 POEMS 77   11
now with a million flaming billion kinds of nameless   . . . . 786 73 POEMS 14   15

FLANGING

by inevitable tiredness of flanging shop-girls impersonally . 197 XLI PORTRAIT 5   4

FLANKED

nose pullable and rosy flanked by the scrumptious magdalene . 198 XLI PORTRAIT 6   10

FLANKS

Who with the useless flanks and cringing feet is . . . . . . 374 VIVA 65   12

FLASH

staggerful unstrolls collaps ingly flash a of-faceness stuck 330 VIVA 21   5
e & --cupidoergosum spun= flash omiepsicronlonO-- megaeta? p 431 NO THANKS 48   24

+FLASH

FOR CONTEXT, SEE . . . . 747 95 POEMS 75   11

FLASHING

the sinuous riot the flashing bacchant. partedpetaled mouth, 185 XLI SONGS 7   11
& thingless & before flashing soft neverwheres & sweet   . . . 480 NEW POEMS 18   10

FLASK

i hauls out uh flask an offers it tuh . . . . 332 VIVA 23   20

FLAT

artificial, unpleasantly tremendous. under flat lusts of . . 103 & POST IMPR 13   15
of going soles on flat pavements with icy cries . . . . 142 & SON REAL 13   6
of vol- ume the flat minute gallop of careful . . . . 201 XLI PORTRAIT 9   22
like a ribbon lies flat on the brush / . . . . 231 IS 5 ONE 3   55
now puts on his flat hat / / / . . . . 240 IS 5 ONE 11   4
miggle dim a ram flat hombre sin bangaroom slim . . . . 333 VIVA 24   17
people called sunlight (elsewhere flat the mechanical . . . . 658 {CHAIRE} 60   12

+FLAT

FOR CONTEXT, SEE . . . . 96 & POST IMPR 8   12

FLATCHATTE

dull, gobular glows and flatchatte ringarom a . s . . . . . . 94 & POST IMPR 6   12

FLATFOLK

never welcome spring nor flatfolk prove their world is   . . . 511 50 POEMS 25   17

FLATFOOTING

careens the to collide flatfooting with Wushyuhname a . . . . 330 VIVA 21   10

FLATNESS

the break on ceiling- flatness the Bar. tinking luscious . . 96 & POST IMPR 8   10

FLATTENED

windmills are silent their flattened arms complain steadily . 434 NO THANKS 51   12

+FLATTENED

FOR CONTEXT, SEE . . . . 488 50 POEMS 2   1

FLATTER

wave little flags weeping flatter thoroughly imploring   . . . 391 NO THANKS 8   8

FLATULENCE

mur- mur, a winsome flatulence-- In the soft midst   . . . . . 201 XLI PORTRAIT 9   13

+FLAVOURED

FOR CONTEXT, SEE . . . . 231 IS 5 ONE 3   53

FLAYS

there and here gladness flays hideously hills. It was . . . . 158 & SON ACTU 7   2
of a lean wind flays screaming hills with sleet . . . . 560 1 X 1 20   9

FLEAPROOF

not to mention shirts fleaproof earwarmers etcetera wristers 276 IS 5 TWO 10   11

FLEAS

"peek-a-boo" and thirty tame fleas left the prettily . . . . 262 IS 5 ONE 32   28

FLECKS

gobs the and of flecks of and a chatter . . . . 96 & POST IMPR 8   7

FLED

are the high gods fled? Speak elm eloquent pandar . . . . . . 3 T&C EPITHALAM   8
who with Grania strangely fled, who with Egypt went . . . . . 22 T&C PUELLA MEA   245
my eyes sinking) inward, fled; softly your face smile . . . . 369 VIVA 60   8

FLEE

and being finally released flee one another like the . . . . 799 73 POEMS 27   31
they flock and they flee through a thunder of . . . . 801 73 POEMS 29   15

FLEECE

sheen of full unsheared fleece is mean beside its . . . . . . 11 T&C SONGS 2   12

FLEEING

(whom noone might inter fleeing himself for selves more . . . 394 NO THANKS 11   6

FLEET
   lean lithe deer the fleet flown deer. Four fleet . . . . . .   14 T&C SONGS 4   18
   fleet flown deer. Four fleet does at a gold . . . .   14 T&C SONGS 4   19
   in the glutted heart fleet flowerterrible memories shall . .   36 T&C AMORES 1   25
   shall crumble the mouth-flower fleet He'll not my tower, . .   83 T&C SON ACTU 2   12
   smooth arrow or a fleet pillar is eaten by . . . . 110 & PORTRAIT 6   3
   , built like a fleet pillar or a smooth . . . . 111 & PORTRAIT 6   45
   all birds but more fleet) herself against the air--and . . . 378 VIVA 69   4
   being; suggests identity) breathes fleet perfectly far from . 402 NO THANKS 19   10
   how infinite (deeply immediate fleet and profound this) . . . 763 95 POEMS 90   23
+FLEET&PANELIKE&FRAILTIES
   lings,laced ar:e,by(fleet&panelike&frailties . . . . 416 NO THANKS 33   11
FLEETER
   merry deer ran before. Fleeter be they than dappled . . . . .   14 T&C SONGS 4   6
   the snow only purer fleeter, like the rain only . . . . . .   293 IS 5 FOUR 10   2
FLEETLY
   with numbing forests frolicsome, fleetly mystical, aroam with 19 T&C PUELLA MEA   92
   row between slow glories fleetly go.) Upon a keen . . . . . .   20 T&C PUELLA MEA   144
   flame, was a tendril fleetly curled upon frailness) used . .   23 T&C PUELLA MEA   279
   unhurried clouds of incense fleetly roll) i spill my . . . . 206 XLI SONNETS 2   14
   should this namelessness (completely fleetly) vanish, at the 819 73 POEMS 47   11
FLESH
   wholly renews her pale flesh with delight) --immortally . . .   3 T&C EPITHALAM   7
   descend, felt on her flesh the amorous strain of . . . . . .   4 T&C EPITHALAM   53
   cadence of our gray flesh in the gloom! and . . . .   9 T&C SONGS 1   23
   terror; be thy taut flesh silver, like the currency . . . . .   9 T&C SONGS 1   32
   lily know, her petaled flesh doth entertain the adroit . . .   21 T&C PUELLA MEA   185
   most tiny hinge of flesh, a winsome thing and . . . .   21 T&C PUELLA MEA   194
   appear to me my flesh is an enchanted tree; . . . .   22 T&C PUELLA MEA   232
   passed away-- in her flesh at break of day . . . .   22 T&C PUELLA MEA   258
   her, Recite upon her flesh the rain's pearls . . . .   65 T&C POST IMPR 2 14
   gloats upon Her stunning flesh. Upon the reachings of . . . .   77 T&C SON UNRE 2   1
   the little pushings of flesh, makes my body sorry . . . . . .   82 T&C SON ACTU 1   3
   intent till this our flesh merely shall be excelled . . . . .   84 T&C SON ACTU 3   4
   o u t) flesh stalks the Momentinmyarms your . . . .   94 & POST IMPR 6   22
   an pa) ris her flesh: wakes in little streets . . . .   104 & POST IMPR 14   9
   jolts of lovecrazed abrupt flesh split "Pretty Baby" to . . . 106 & PORTRAIT 2   12
   imminent lisping bags of flesh; became eyes moist lithe . . . 115 & PORTRAIT 8   22
   / / / her flesh Came at meassandca V . . . .   119 & PORTRAIT 11   2
   refrain from jumbling her flesh whose casual mouth's coy . .   131 & SON REAL 2   7
   huge dropping of a flesh from hinging thighs . . . .   133 & SON REAL 4   15
   Hips simply. well fussed flesh does surely to mesh. . . . . . 136 & SON REAL 7   12
   Alice, stinging quips of flesh. Loretta, cut the comedy . . . 138 & SON REAL 9   15
   dream in the glad flesh of my fear: more . . . .   139 & SON REAL 10   7
   twitch of crisp boy flesh dips my height in . . . . 140 & SON REAL 11   7
   wise breasts half-grown, lisping flesh quick to thread the .   140 & SON REAL 11   12
   from whose kind large flesh i turn to the . . . . 142 & SON REAL 13   1
   lazily struts (her thickish flesh superior to the genuine . . 150 & SON REAL 21   12
   grim epitome of chuckling flesh. Weak thirsty fists of . . . 151 & SON REAL 24   2
   worms. Dress deftly your flesh in stupid stuffs, phrase . . . 161 & SON ACTU 10   9
   amid unnaked things, your flesh, a succinct wandlike animal,   170 & SON ACTU 19   7
   brittle flower, and the flesh crisp set my love-tooth . . . . 173 & SON ACTU 22   10
   what-is-it comes over parting flesh.... And eyes big . . . .   175 & SON ACTU 24   12
   sweet annihilation of swift flesh i make me stern . . . . . . 182 XLI SONGS 4   12
   the mystery of my flesh I will rise After . . . . 189 XLI SONGS 11   12
   whose enormous curve of flesh exactly cubes of tiny . . . . . 214 XLI SONNETS 10   3
   as Mrs. Somethingwich (with flesh like an old toy . . . . . . 219 XLI SONNETS 15   12
   eyes drown in surging flesh). A thumblike index down- . . . . 226 IS 5 ONE MAME   5
   you your kisses your flesh mind breathing beside under . . .   283 IS 5 THREE 7   16
   crudities of blood and flesh) Love coins His most . . . . . . 297 IS 5 FOUR 14   11
   poor But TerFLY went (flesh is grass) from Troy, ...   320 VIVA 12   2
   the way of (all flesh is grass) with one . . . .   320 VIVA 12   6
   all) mind in mind flesh In flesh succeeding disappear . . . . 364 VIVA 55   15
   in mind flesh In flesh succeeding disappear / / . . . . 364 VIVA 55   16
   (sestet entitled grass is flesh or swim who can . . . . 390 NO THANKS 7   9
   unprecisely to repass where flesh is heiry montparnasse is .   401 NO THANKS 18   13
   neither may shadow down flesh neither may vibration create .   425 NO THANKS 42   12
   mystery makes every man's flesh put space on; and . . . . . . 484 NEW POEMS 22   8

	PAGE	TITLE	LINE

FLESH (CONTINUED)

my father's dream his flesh was flesh his blood . . . . 520 50 POEMS 34   29
dream his flesh was flesh his blood was blood: . . . . 520 50 POEMS 34   29
share, let blood and flesh be mud and mire, ... 521 50 POEMS 34   54
world of born--pity poor flesh and trees, poor stars . . . . 554 1 X 1 14   10
deep's the mind of flesh and so awake what . . . . 609 (CHAIRE) 11   7
through twilight's mystery made flesh-- dreamslender . . . . 669 (CHAIRE) 71   8
generosities beyond believing (though flesh and blood accuse 683 95 POEMS 11   3
lily brief (rose here&gone) flesh all is If all . . . . . . 690 95 POEMS 18   7
descending put on deathful flesh: are lovers glad? only . . . 768 95 POEMS 94   6
is the blood whose flesh is singing) silence: but . . . . . . 839 73 POEMS 67   1

+FLESH

FOR CONTEXT, SEE . . . . 100 & POST IMPR 11   27
FOR CONTEXT, SEE . . . . 337 VIVA 28   7
FOR CONTEXT, SEE . . . . 615 (CHAIRE) 17   2

FLESHLESS

cessation of her skirt. fleshless melody of the, keenly . . . 103 & POST IMPR 13   6
thing? (or will the fleshless moments go and go . . . . 218 XLI SONNETS 14   9

FLEW

cryingly as the knights flew. / / / / . . . . 302 IS 5 FIVE 1   15
and a dart out flew his wish (it dived . . . . 593 1 X 1 53   8

FLEXION

silkenly brutal a devout flexion / / / / . . . . 68 T&C POST IMPR 5   16

+FLICK

FOR CONTEXT, SEE . . . . 265 IS 5 ONE 34   3

FLICKER

smile the amazed doves flicker upon sunny wings as . . . . 6 T&C EPITHALAM   138
left fist opening "wisdom." Flicker of gold. "Yep. No . . . . 226 IS 5 ONE MAME   8
shy milbrightlions my (hurl flicker handful in) dodging are . 265 IS 5 ONE 34   7

+FLICKER

FOR CONTEXT, SEE . . . . 180 XLI SONGS 2   4
FOR CONTEXT, SEE . . . . 423 NO THANKS 40   28

FLICKER'S

tears, and hark! the flicker's laughing yet, while on . . . . 5 T&C EPITHALAM   75

FLICS

none look alike the flics rush batter the crowd . . . . . . 274 IS 5 TWO 9   5
trampled the kicked by flics rush (the Flics, tidiyum, . . . 274 IS 5 TWO 9   8
by flics rush (the Flics, tidiyum, are very tidiyum . . . . . 274 IS 5 TWO 9   9
there are 50 (fifty) flics for every one (I) . . . . 274 IS 5 TWO 9   17
communist and all the flics are very organically arranged . . 274 IS 5 TWO 9   19

FLIES

writhe like caught. brave: flies; / / / / . . . . 55 T&C PORTRAIT 3   20
of ivory balls.... noting flies, which jerk upon the . . . . 217 XLI SONNETS 13   3
a trigger a bird flies into a mirror) / . . . . 338 VIVA 29   24
are houses people are flies who buzz on) -lar . . . . 436 NO THANKS 52   15

FLIGHT

words, As to a flight of thirty birds shakes . . . . 11 T&C SONGS 2   18
wrists which hint at flight --my lady's very singular . . . . 20 T&C PUELLA MEA   158
of dew, was a flight, a flower, a flame, ... 23 T&C PUELLA MEA   278
thy forehead is a flight of flowers thy head . . . . 29 T&C ORIENTALE 3   4
lowliness, noting the fatal flight of worlds whereto this . . 81 T&C SON UNRE 6   4
pursue curiously a crumbling flight into the absolute stars . 112 & PORTRAIT 6   83
bullet in tickling intuitive flight aches, just, simply, . . 130 & SON REAL 1   10
swallow, that closes a flight in the blue; when . . . . 181 XLI SONGS 3   5
in your no thy flight and make me a . . . . 233 IS 5 ONE 4   3
this time, however, the flight of crows had ceased. . . . . . 263 IS 5 ONE 32   54
carefully (carefully climbing carpeted flight after carpeted 375 VIVA 66   12
carpeted flight after carpeted flight. in stillness, climbing 375 VIVA 66   13

FLIGHTS

of spring chased two flights of squirrel-stairs into a . . . 194 XLI PORTRAIT 2   7
Swede rolls down tree flights an Sam begins boxin . . . . . . 332 VIVA 23   8
nobody could in superhuman flights of submoronic fancy be . . 790 73 POEMS 18   2

FLIMSY

of mind chucks away flimsy which but) always (they're . . . . 501 50 POEMS 15   14

FLIMSYING

every side swoop mountains flimsying become if who'd me . . 634 (CHAIRE) 36   3

FLING

tremulous grace bravely to fling Implacable death's . . . . . 206 XLI SONNETS 2   3

260

	PAGE	TITLE	LINE
FLINGER			
green mountains sings the flinger of fire beyond red	185	XLI SONGS 7	3
at which this (once flinger of lariats lean exroper	252	IS 5 ONE 23	9
FLIPCHUCKING			
ing???? --Out-& steps; which flipchucking . grins gRiNdS d .	445	NO THANKS 60	20
FLITTERCRUMBS			
cruMbshandful, quick-hurl edinwho Is flittercrumbs, ...	265	IS 5 ONE 34	5
+FLITTERING			
FOR CONTEXT, SEE	265	IS 5 ONE 34	2
FOR CONTEXT, SEE	265	IS 5 ONE 34	3
+FLITTERINGISH			
FOR CONTEXT, SEE	265	IS 5 ONE 34	6
FLO'S			
the peacockappareled prodigy of Flo's midnight Frolic dolores	232	IS 5 ONE 3	3
FLOAT			
the very shadowy sheep float free upon terrific pastures . .	9	T&C SONGS 1	8
of her face doth float, which in eyes and . . . . ·	20	T&C PUELLA MEA	146
your drowsy lips where float flowers of kiss and	186	XLI SONGS 8	12
pingness whO perfectly whO flOat newly alOne is dreamest . .	383	NO THANKS 1	6
a-live keen parallel specks float-ing create height, liv- ing	447	NO THANKS 62	3
which is prayer among) float withins he upclimbest And . . .	482	NEW POEMS 20	5
ly a child's eyes float silently down more than	491	50 POEMS 5	6
common's rare and millstones float --long enough and just .	511	50 POEMS 25	19
/ / / a- float on some ? i	571	1 X 1 31	2
if they'll or goldenly float so (dreaming out of	573	1 X 1 33	9
towns (queen poet king float sprout heroes of moonstar . . .	586	1 X 1 46	9
slippery hands tease slim float twitter faces) only stand . .	633	(CHAIRE) 35	5
when faces called flowers float out of the ground	665	(CHAIRE) 67	1
feels a world crylaughingly float away leaving just this . .	720	95 POEMS 48	7
(rouNd er than roUnd) float; who lly & (rOunder	722	95 POEMS 50	6
over my sleeping self float flaming symbols of hope, ...	749	95 POEMS 77	11
lost child and a (float through sleeping firsts of	757	95 POEMS 85	26
+FLOAT			
FOR CONTEXT, SEE	265	IS 5 ONE 34	6
FOR CONTEXT, SEE	416	NO THANKS 33	13
FOR CONTEXT, SEE	431	NO THANKS 48	3
FOR CONTEXT, SEE	431	NO THANKS 48	3
FOR CONTEXT, SEE	495	50 POEMS 9	9
FOR CONTEXT, SEE	655	(CHAIRE) 57	4
FOR CONTEXT, SEE	677	95 POEMS 5	10
FLOAT-ING			
a-live keen parallel specks float-ing create height, liv- ing	447	NO THANKS 62	3
FLOATED			
body with its spirit floated (clothed only in the	369	VIVA 60	19
perhaps (who knows?) eternity floated a blossoming (while . .	599	(CHAIRE) 1	8
FLOATFALLIN			
Is flittercrumbs, fluttercrimbs are floatfallin, g; allwhere:	265	IS 5 ONE 34	5
FLOATFUL			
and the is all floatful and remembering / /	516	50 POEMS 30	18
FLOATI			
un less it were (floati ng through never) a	668	(CHAIRE) 70	7
FLOATING			
with impertinently exquisite faces floating hands were laid .	44	T&C AMORES 8	11
Girl which (like some floating snake upon itself always . . .	95	& POST IMPR 7	9
sinuous problem of colour floating against the clever deadly	112	& PORTRAIT 6	106
moon is like a floating silver hell a song	214	XLI SONNETS 10	13
= an infrafairy of floating ultrawrists who lullabylullaby (I	317	VIVA 9	4
over, the thing of floating Of ; elate shyly	447	NO THANKS 62	1
town (with up so floating many bells down) spring	515	50 POEMS 29	2
remember with up so floating many bells down) one	515	50 POEMS 29	24
of a leaf says (floating each how) you're which	543	1 X 1 3	8
are flying in the floating in the very spirits	591	1 X 1 51	6
shyly tiny winging darting floating merry in the blossoming .	591	1 X 1 51	22
agree) not happened (and floating- ly int o /	652	(CHAIRE) 54	15
+FLOATING			
FOR CONTEXT, SEE	104	& POST IMPR 14	4
FOR CONTEXT, SEE	265	IS 5 ONE 34	6
FOR CONTEXT, SEE	750	95 POEMS 78	9

	PAGE	TITLE	LINE

FLOATINGLY

hollow was young Up floatingly clothes tumbledish olD (with . 534 50 POEMS 46   5
/ / / one (Floatingly) arrive (silent) one by . . . . 557 1 X 1 17   1

+FLOATINGLY

FOR CONTEXT, SEE . . . . 431 NO THANKS 48   4
FOR CONTEXT, SEE . . . . 652 (CHAIRE) 54   15

FLOATS

cries and runs and floats like a toy on . . . . 69 T&C POST IMPR 6   43
Cleopatra while easily tremendously floats in the bright . . 112 & PORTRAIT 6   74
slovenly obscene procession always floats through the thin . 202 XLI PORTRAIT 9   47
grey) white (man) horse floats on 4 3rdtoes P . . . . 408 NO THANKS 25   4
stupendous if discoverably disappearing floats at . . . . . . 517 50 POEMS 31   3
as from unburied which floats the first who, his . . . . . . 520 50 POEMS 34   10
than finds feeling (seize) floats (only by only) a . . . . . 612 (CHAIRE) 14   13
space doom dream while floats the whole perhapsless mystery . 714 95 POEMS 42   7
out of night's almosT Floats a colour (in -to . . . . 719 95 POEMS 47   1
thrush) A hummingbird princess FlOaTs doll-angel-life from . 747 95 POEMS 75   4
most not night as floats a more than day . . . . 818 73 POEMS 46   2

FLOATSCOR

&Isdensekil- ling-whipAlert-floatScor ruptingly) . . . . . . 430 NO THANKS 47   14

FLOATSTANDS

livingly free mysterious dreamsoul floatstands oak by birch . 658 (CHAIRE) 60   17

FLOCK

as can i'm) they flock and they flee through . . . . 801 73 POEMS 29   15

FLOCKS

tipping and tipping, the flocks of pigeons. And the . . . . 166 & SON ACTU 15   4

FLOODED

O. K.)i went right to it flooded-the-carburetor . . . . . . 248 IS 5 ONE 19   9

+FLOODED-THE-CARBURETOR

O. K.)i went right to it flooded-the-carburetor . . . . . . 248 IS 5 ONE 19   9

FLOOR

tipsy tables the abominable floor belches smoky laughter into 55 T&C PORTRAIT 3   4
wearily something from the floor Her hair was mussed, ... 132 & SON REAL 3   17
wonder as over this floor (quietly with bright eyes) . . . . 286 IS 5 FOUR 3   4
does out of the floor quietly Stare a poisoned . . . . . . 784 73 POEMS 12   2

+FLOOZEY

FOR CONTEXT, SEE . . . . 704 95 POEMS 32   9

FLOP

men will be saviours --flop grasshopper, exactly nothing's . 555 1 X 1 15   7
damned) life is a Flop or even to Feel . . . . 702 95 POEMS 30   13

FLOPPED

christ jesus) my heart flopped over and lay still . . . . . 648 (CHAIRE) 50   6

FLOPS

stumbling wings flutters and flops along the grass collides . 47 T&C IMPRESS 1   8
flatfooting with Wushyuhname a girl-flops to the Geddup curb 330 VIVA 21   11

FLOPSLUMP

a fair y socked flopslump (& juke) ing shrieks . . . . . . 629 (CHAIRE) 31   12

FLOTSAM

/ / / / flotsam and jetsam are gentlemen . . . . 492 50 POEMS 6   1

+FLOUNDER

FOR CONTEXT, SEE . . . . 495 50 POEMS 9   ' 4

FLOURISH

wells, which make to flourish the minute spontaneous meadow . 19 T&C PUELLA MEA 122

FLOURISHES

pretty world sweetly who flourishes, swiftly which fails but 456 NO THANKS 71   6

FLOW

steer --souls under whom flow (mountain valley forest) a . . 659 (CHAIRE) 61   5

FLOWER

her eager body's unimmortal flower knew in the darkness . . . 4 T&C EPITHALAM 55
particoloured peace with mouth flower-faint and undiscovered . 5 T&C EPITHALAM 98
of creation, lifts a flower-- whence is the world's . . . . . 6 T&C EPITHALAM 134
o'er the warm long flower of unchastity, imperial Cytherea, . 7 T&C EPITHALAM 160
lay like some gigantic ghost-flower born of night blossoming 8 T&C OF NICOL 2
in tones of stroked flower; let not thy lust . . . . 9 T&C SONGS 1   6
smile, it were a flower of so pure surprise . . . . 18 T&C PUELLA MEA 50
so very new a flower, a flower so frail, ... 18 T&C PUELLA MEA 51
new a flower, a flower so frail, a flower . . . . 18 T&C PUELLA MEA 52
flower so frail, a flower so glad) as trembling . . . . . . 18 T&C PUELLA MEA 52

FLOWER (CONTINUED)
   young and new (a flower such as the world . . . . 18 T&C PUELLA MEA 55
   spoke to Guenever, a flower which most heavy hung . . . . . . 18 T&C PUELLA MEA 58
   smile which like a flower lieth (while within the . . . . . . 20 T&C PUELLA MEA 150
   more silently than a flower, my lady naked in . . . . 21 T&C PUELLA MEA 177
   like some passionate earlier flower, the snow will oft . . . 21 T&C PUELLA MEA 188
   world was like a flower Omar Hafiz and Harun . . . . 22 T&C PUELLA MEA 226
   was a flight, a flower, a flame, was a . . . . 23 T&C PUELLA MEA 278
   inhale the slow supple flower of thy beauty, my . . . . 31 T&C ORIENTALE 5 27
   languorous mouth the thrilling flower) / / / / . . . . 37 T&C AMORES 2 21
   her mouth the new flower with thy unimaginable wings, ... 40 T&C AMORES 4 44
   think that on the flower you gave me when . . . . 42 T&C AMORES 6 3
   head now the intimate flower dreams of parted lips . . . . . 54 T&C PORTRAIT 2 10
   neat sunlight into the flower- stricken air which is . . . . 69 T&C POST IMPR 6 4
   do keep their sunday flower. The babybreasted broad "kitty" . 74 T&C SON REAL 5 11
   counted petals O tremendous flower on whose huge heart . . . 79 T&C SON UNRE 4 3
   hate) shall crumble the mouth-flower fleet He'll not my . . . 83 T&C SON ACTU 2 12
   be excelled by speaking flower (if i have made . . . . 84 T&C SON ACTU 3 5
   / riverly is a flower gone softly by tomb . . . . 90 & POST IMPR 2 1
   (hear little knives of flower stropping sof a. Thick . . . . 99 & POST IMPR 10 12
   Sexis a Lone ly, flower whose secretloveliness hur. ts . . . 101 & POST IMPR 11 73
   a perhaps fraction of flower here placing an inch . . . . . . 124 & SEVEN POEMS 3 17
   darkness: carve an evilfringing flower of madness on gritted 139 & SON REAL 10 9
   swirled justly souls of flower strike the air in . . . . . . 163 & SON ACTU 12 6
   into recent lands the flower with their enormous fingers . . 165 & SON ACTU 14 15
   hushingly bits of downward flower flowing without or cease . 168 & SON ACTU 17 8
   lie a sharp agreeable flower between my amused legs . . . . . 172 & SON ACTU 21 11
   was a distinct brittle flower, and the flesh crisp . . . . . 173 & SON ACTU 22 10
   worth? Inquire of the flower that sways in the . . . . 183 XLI SONGS 5 14
   autumn long; the last flower in whose hair, thy . . . . 190 XLI SONGS 12 3
   love, for the last flower in the hair withers; . . . . 190 XLI SONGS 12 15
   are more like a flower who found you in . . . . 192 XLI CHANSONS 2 4
   blade lie many a flower curled, in other lands . . . . 208 XLI SONNETS 4 10
   you. Yet if not flower, tell me softly who . . . . 211 XLI SONNETS 7 6
   spring utters a striving flower, just where strove the . . . 213 XLI SONNETS 9 7
   her a stealthily frail flower: walking with its fellows . . . 214 XLI SONNETS 10 2
   dark if light should flower: or laughing sparkle from . . . . 292 IS 5 FOUR 9 17
   indolent and with this flower wholly whom you do . . . . . . 294 IS 5 FOUR 11 16
   Nobody wears a yellow flower in his buttonhole he . . . . . . 296 IS 5 FOUR 13 2
   really which is a flower and not a face . . . . 352 VIVA 43 12
   the heart of this flower imagines the snow carefully . . . . 366 VIVA 57 11
   / is there a flower (whom i meet anywhere . . . . 367 VIVA 58 1
   the echo of the flower of Dreaming) somewhere behind . . . . 368 VIVA 59 8
   freedom (Dare until a flower, understanding sizelessly . . . 453 NO THANKS 68 13
   born are maids to flower an hour in all, ... 509 50 POEMS 23 5
   all) o yes to flower until so blithe a . . . . 509 50 POEMS 23 7
   cradling in joy her flower than now (softlying wisdoms . . . 518 50 POEMS 32 8
   their song is a flower of always their flowers . . . . 525 50 POEMS 37 7
   imitate upward each first flower of two / / . . . . 573 1 X 1 33 23
   may grow --childfully serious flower of holiness a pilgrim . 601 (CHAIRE) 3 8
   (and whose brook -bright flower- soft bird -quick voice . . . 660 (CHAIRE) 62 19
   street handed me a flower. Nobody, it's safe to . . . . 802 73 POEMS 30 6
   be your" whispers that flower murmurs eager this "i . . . . . 837 73 POEMS 65 6
FLOWER-FAINT
   particoloured peace with mouth flower-faint and undiscovered 5 T&C EPITHALAM 98
+FLOWERED
   FOR CONTEXT, SEE . . . . 444 NO THANKS 59 29
FLOWERING
   forms delightful with indefinable flowering, the air is deep 31 T&C ORIENTALE 5 10
   of dream nor any flowering of any echo (but . . . . 368 VIVA 59 6
   ArE GLIB SCARCELYEST AMONGS FLOWERING / / / / . . . . 421 NO THANKS 38 31
   your (in my arms flowering so new) self whose . . . . 424 NO THANKS 41 2
   silence silent are more flowering than stars whitely births . 450 NO THANKS 65 5
FLOWERISH
   -pos- sibl y (ShoutflowereD flowerish boom b el Lsb . . . . . 444 NO THANKS 59 30
FLOWERPOTS
   you see that water flowerpots in windows but they . . . . . . 126 & SEVEN POEMS 5 24

	PAGE	TITLE	LINE
FLOWERS			
peaceful theorems of the flowers --didst e'er depart upon	3	T&C EPITHALAM	19
by gay untimid final flowers (which dressed in various	4	T&C EPITHALAM	67
days their sounds and flowers Fall in a pride	11	T&C SONGS 2	31
of petaled hours, like flowers at the feet of	11	T&C SONGS 2	33
Thy fingers make early flowers of all things. thy	13	T&C SONGS 3	1
which girl art thou flowers bringing? To be thy	13	T&C SONGS 3	14
April feet like sudden flowers and all her body	17	T&C PUELLA MEA	21
or two ladies like flowers made, softly used to	23	T&C PUELLA MEA	282
Another comes also picking flowers / / / /	26	T&C CHANSONS 3	9
a tomb softer than flowers Come hither O thou,	27	T&C ORIENTALE 1	26
is a flight of flowers thy head is a	29	T&C ORIENTALE 3	4
upon thy ankles are flowers in vases of silver	29	T&C ORIENTALE 3	29
is deep with desirable flowers i think thou lovest	31	T&C ORIENTALE 5	12
and sunset stars and flowers gold crescendo and silver	39	T&C AMORES 4	7
and shouting of merry flowers wee skipping high-heeled flames	44	T&C AMORES 8	5
freshness as if god's flowers were pulling upon bells	58	T&C PORTRAIT 6	9
smile always the chosen flowers of reminding / /	58	T&C PORTRAIT 6	27
the screech of dissonant flowers, and most of all	61	T&C PORTRAIT 9	33
at moon-cease soon verbal mist-flowers close ghosts on prowl	90	& POST IMPR 2	14
"why do you touch flowers as if they were	91	& POST IMPR 3	8
an old man carrying flowers on his head. young	102	& POST IMPR 12	2
say "will he buy flowers" to you and "Death	102	& POST IMPR 12	6
asleep, on his head flowers, always crying to nobody	102	& POST IMPR 12	15
death, is slender; likes flowers. / / / /	102	& POST IMPR 12	26
everyone's in love and flowers pick themselves / /	129	& SEVEN POEMS 7	16
the vague tough exquisite flowers, whom hardens richly,	154	& SON ACTU 3	9
drowsy lips where float flowers of kiss and there	186	XLI SONGS 8	12
are steeped in burning flowers I will take the	189	XLI SONGS 11	2
a thousand years lipping flowers And set my teeth	189	XLI SONGS 11	16
whittles keen careful futile flowers (isolating with	193	XLI PORTRAIT 1	21
and if thy hands flowers of silence curled upon	205	XLI SONNETS 1	3
in black gloves and flowers and everything and i	239	IS 5 ONE 10	31
May --bring forth your flowers and machinery: sculpture and	264	IS 5 ONE 33	9
machinery: sculpture and prose flowers guess and miss	264	IS 5 ONE 33	10
perhaps is to eat flowers and not to be	264	IS 5 ONE 33	32
now that fierce few flowers (stealthily) in the alive	277	IS 5 THREE 1	2
i swear by all flowers. Don't cry --the best	290	IS 5 FOUR 7	10
frailer you whom certain flowers resemble but trembling	293	IS 5 FOUR 10	5
real: imagine somewhere real flowers, but I can't imagine	338	VIVA 29	7
I can't imagine real flowers for if I could,	338	VIVA 29	8
filled with newly murdered flowers whispering barns bulge a	340	VIVA 31	12
clouds do or Silently Flowers resembles beauty less than	363	VIVA 54	11
how less than least flowers of rain) thickly i	433	NO THANKS 50	9
city screamingly street wonderful flowers And o the Light	437	NO THANKS 53	4
a bouquet of pretend flowers this candy crown with	470	NEW POEMS 8	7
around five around) five flowers five (six are in	507	50 POEMS 21	25
all five are one flowers five flowers and all	507	50 POEMS 21	28
are one flowers five flowers and all one is	507	50 POEMS 21	28
children wound with stone flowers opening for ever these	525	50 POEMS 37	4
flower of always their flowers of stone are silently	525	50 POEMS 37	8
her most first little flowers rise out of tremendous	559	1 X 1 19	13
opening is all the flowers of his eyes :	583	1 X 1 43	6
skies of grin) "my flowers" (the humble man than	585	1 X 1 45	13
certain they're (look again) flowers." "Don't worlds open and	603	(CHAIRE) 5	6
they're possible --but" lifting "flowers" more all stars than	603	(CHAIRE) 5	13
turned to sky are flowers neither why nor how	630	(CHAIRE) 32	10
/ when faces called flowers float out of the	665	(CHAIRE) 67	1
be quite so (when flowers) in credibly (always are	738	95 POEMS 66	14
Dream like fire called flowers over green the new	778	73 POEMS 6	16
writhe o-p-e-n-i-n-g are (leaves; flowers) dreams , come	835	73 POEMS 63	13
+FLOWERS			
FOR CONTEXT, SEE	436	NO THANKS 52	9
FLOWERSTRICKEN			
fattish and mysterious the flowerstricken sun- light is	69	T&C POST IMPR 6	23
FLOWERTERRIBLE			
the glutted heart fleet flowerterrible memories shall rise,	36	T&C AMORES 1	26

	PAGE	TITLE	LINE

FLOWERY
    colours which, are, the, flowery pluckings of a harpsichord . 100 & POST IMPR 11   10
FLOWING
    bits of downward flower flowing without or cease or . . . . . 168 & SON ACTU 17   8
FLOWN
    lithe deer the fleet flown deer. Four fleet does . . . . . . 14 T&C SONGS 4   18
    his heartlike ears have flown adorable him self tail . . . . 631 (CHAIRE) 33   5
    again, little he (having flown even higher) is sunning . . . 631 (CHAIRE) 33   7
FLU
    unheard of maladies including flu) my little darlings, let . 266 IS 5 TWO 1   15
FLUENT
    gloom arise purple pencils fluent spires of fragrance the . . 31 T&C ORIENTALE 5   5
+FLUFF
    FOR CONTEXT, SEE . . . . 127 & SEVEN POEMS 5   41
FLUFFIES
    scritch (while the no-she-yes-he fluffies tittle tattle . . . 773 73 POEMS 1   16
FLUFFY
    proffers its omelet of fluffy lust) at six exactly . . . . . 132 & SON REAL 3   10
    red and gold the fluffy threads, put up your . . . . 192 XLI CHANSONS 2   16
FLUID
    silently perpetuating solids (More fluid Than gas / / . . . . 311 VIVA 3   18
FLUNG
    of Her hunger softly flung over the gasping shores . . . . . 77 T&C SON UNRE 2   5
+FLUNG
    FOR CONTEXT, SEE . . . . 206 XLI SONNETS 2   8
    FOR CONTEXT, SEE . . . . 258 IS 5 ONE 28   18
    FOR CONTEXT, SEE . . . . 311 VIVA 3   5
FLUSH
    drink and when you're flush pride keeps you from . . . . . . 204 XLI LA GUERRE 2   12
FLUTE
    of gloried air... The flute of morning stilled in . . . . . . 12 T&C SONGS 2   46
    Face playing on a flute / / / / . . . . 169 & SON ACTU 18   16
FLUTES
    is the dilemma of flutes thy eyes are the . . . . 29 T&C ORIENTALE 3   31
    do blow upon cool flutes within wide glooms, and . . . . . . 208 XLI SONNETS 4   6
FLUTTER
    the bowl seethes a flutter of stars a turbulence . . . . . . 31 T&C ORIENTALE 5   8
    of thy low hair flutter the level litanies unto . . . . 31 T&C ORIENTALE 5   20
    one by one stars flutter into dust but the . . . . 38 T&C AMORES 3   8
    less than your eyelids' flutter which says we are . . . . . . 290 IS 5 FOUR 7   12
    sprout heroes of moonstar flutter to and swim blossoms . . . 586 1 X 1 46   11
FLUTTERCRIMBS
    quick-hurl edinwho Is flittercrumbs, fluttercrimbs are . . . 265 IS 5 ONE 34   5
FLUTTERFULLY
    sperf ul lydesc BYS FLUTTERFULLY IF (endbegi ndesginb ecend) 421 NO THANKS 38   8
FLUTTERING
    of joy pathetic dress fluttering behind her a mothermonster . 56 T&C PORTRAIT 4   4
    and go, frail azures fluttering from night's outer wing . . . 208 XLI SONNETS 4   2
    any man-- a little fluttering, at the enchanted dike . . . . 344 VIVA 35   9
+FLUTTERING
    FOR CONTEXT, SEE . . . . 122 & SEVEN POEMS 1   11
FLUTTERS
    moth with stumbling wings flutters and flops along the . . . 47 T&C IMPRESS 1   8
    nellie anyway and it's flutters everything queer; does smells 251 IS 5 ONE 22   4
    memory, which how exquisitely flutters in the cornerless . . 370 VIVA 61   27
FLY
    my, love is thatofa fly. pre cisel Yhalf (squashe) . . . . . 94 & POST IMPR 6   27
    1 oo k- pigeons fly ingand whee (:are,SpRiN, k, ... 122 & SEVEN POEMS 1   15
    for many years but fly kites and when the . . . . 253 IS 5 ONE 24   6
    then bite) candy others fly, their; puLLing: bright futures . 314 VIVA 6   14
    song you Know a fly and his reflection walking . . . . 335 VIVA 26   3
    1 what 3 a fly & her his Its . . . . 335 VIVA 26   8
    way) ,which is not fly / / / / . . . . 335 VIVA 26   21
    truth grows why birds fly and especially who the . . . . . . 368 VIVA 59   20
    most remembering H highest fly only the flag that's . . . . . 390 NO THANKS 7   8
    the fand intrigues the fly) for know all men . . . . 425 NO THANKS 42   8
    crawl eat walk die fly do? a notalive undead . . . . 528 50 POEMS 40   4
    how the earth must fly if a truth is . . . . 587 1 X 1 47   15

	PAGE	TITLE	LINE
FLY (CONTINUED)			
down up around again fly) forever was never till	594	1 X 1 54	26
a never in his fly (rub-her-bub) bub? (bubs) where's	642	(CHAIRE) 44	17
as spry as can fly yes the little fish	665	(CHAIRE) 67	5
ingspinson his back mad) fly (ly who all at)	692	95 POEMS 20	5
window this fine morning) fly instead of dancing are . . .	724	95 POEMS 52	10
+FLY			
FOR CONTEXT, SEE	258	IS 5 ONE 28	19
FOR CONTEXT, SEE	607	(CHAIRE) 9	6
FLYING			
merry little birds are flying in the floating in	591	1 X 1 51	6
+FLYING			
FOR CONTEXT, SEE	122	& SEVEN POEMS 1	15
FLYINGLY			
singing ams trample (they flyingly silence / / /	482	NEW POEMS 20	12
FLYNN			
gold. "Yep. No gas. Flynn" the words drizzle untidily	226	IS 5 ONE MAME	8
FLYSPECKED			
motivated by midnight the flyspecked abdominous female . . .	116	& PORTRAIT 9	3
FOAL			
some smooth and awkward foal, whereof young moons begin . . .	11	T&C SONGS 2	3
with you as a foal stands but as the	154	& SON ACTU 3	15
FOAM			
imperial Cytherea, from frail foam sprung with irrevocable .	7	T&C EPITHALAM	161
horse shrieking from splintering foam caught you clutched you	30	T&C ORIENTALE 4	13
where stealing needles of foam in the last light	64	T&C POST IMPR 1	2
taps plus slush of foam knocked off and a	96	& POST IMPR 8	13
& first of all foam -like hair spatters creasing	358	VIVA 49	2
FOCUS			
Plum grinning softly, New focus-of disintegrat i o n	94	& POST IMPR 6	16
FOCUS-OF			
Plum grinning softly, New focus-of disintegrat i o n	94	& POST IMPR 6	16
FOCUSSES			
perfume of whose unrepute focusses in the sweet slow	74	T&C SON REAL 5	6
FOE			
less humbly wealth to foe and friend than he	521	50 POEMS 34	38
every friend became his foe he'd laugh and build	521	50 POEMS 34	47
to borrow) or any foe a friend --cry nay:	798	73 POEMS 26	19
FOES			
around you, friends and foes my tragic tale concludes	799	73 POEMS 27	39
FOETAL			
obscurity a bald greenish foetal head established It suddenly	96	& POST IMPR 8	29
souring sunbeams, of a foetal fragrance to rickety unclosed .	144	& SON REAL 15	2
way knowledge lies, the foetal grave called progress, and . .	484	NEW POEMS 22	11
FOETUS			
/ / ci-git 1 Foetus (unborn to not die	394	NO THANKS 11	1
/ F is for foetus (a punkslapping mobsucking gravypissing . .	635	(CHAIRE) 37	1
FOG			
/ / un der fog 's touch slo ings	463	NEW POEMS 1	2
elsewhere jabber while (infinite fog & puking jukepulse hug)	629	(CHAIRE) 31	6
+FOG			
FOR CONTEXT, SEE	423	NO THANKS 40	14
FOLD			
from her eyes and fold her mouth the new	40	T&C AMORES 4	41
FOLDED			
eyes (whose hand my folded soul shall know while	11	T&C SONGS 2	26
and then our hero folded his umbrella. It seemed	263	IS 5 ONE 32	57
began which now are folded: but the year completes	304	IS 5 FIVE 3	8
world lies: smoothbeautifuL ly folded; a (brea thing and . .	657	(CHAIRE) 59	12
FOLDING			
season of crumbling & folding hopes, hark; feet (fEEt	345	VIVA 36	13
+FOLDING			
FOR CONTEXT, SEE	646	(CHAIRE) 48	11
FOLDISH			
now it's swirly and foldish so only through) the	516	50 POEMS 30	6
FOLDS			
revealed of teasingly transparent folds-- with man's poor . .	5	T&C EPITHALAM	95
word Less) ly (goes folds? folds) cold stones (o-1-d)	417	NO THANKS 34	7

	PAGE	TITLE	LINE

FOLDS (CONTINUED)

Less) ly (goes folds? folds) cold stones (o-l-d) names . . . 417 NO THANKS 34   7
somebody's almost moth er folds (but infinite) gently up . . 629 (CHAIRE) 31   15

FOLIAGE

style of that's the foliage what is it didn't . . . . 257 IS 5 ONE 27   34

FOLIATE

utterly to lull with foliate inscrutable sweetness my soul . 19 T&C PUELLA MEA   88

FOLK

kiss his face) busy folk buried them side by . . . . 515 50 POEMS 29   27
me to shoot dogooding folk on sight / / . . . . 798 73 POEMS 26   28

+FOLK

FOR CONTEXT, SEE . . . . 511 50 POEMS 25   17

FOLKS

of politisions beware of folks with missians to turn . . . . 405 NO THANKS 22   5
s born alive) some folks aint born somes born . . . . 426 NO THANKS 43   10

+FOLKS

FOR CONTEXT, SEE . . . . 331 VIVA 22   3

FOLLOW

almostness which May makes follow soon on the sweet . . . . . 10 T&C SONGS 1   38
watch your step and follow me stooping by Effie's . . . . . . 117 & PORTRAIT 10   27
/ seeker of truth follow no path all paths . . . . 775 73 POEMS 3   2

FOLLOWED

preening upon his hand followed by gay untimid final . . . . 4 T&C EPITHALAM   67

FOLLOWING

in a mesh of following tone: did this and . . . . 115 & PORTRAIT 8   16

FOLLOWS

shall i say body? follows truly through a dribbling . . . . 140 & SON REAL 11   3
moon if you'll notice follows us like a big . . . . 303 IS 5 FIVE 2   10
things are until" "spring follows winter: as clover knows, . 625 (CHAIRE) 27   9

FOND

an earthless hour my fond soul seriously yearns beyond . . . 12 T&C SONGS 2   41
which lives they were fond of the handsome moon . . . . 43 T&C AMORES 7   13
/ my eyes are fond of the east side . . . . 100 & POST IMPR 11   1
inthecarts my, mouth is, fond of tiny plums of . . . . . . 100 & POST IMPR 11   26
there is which isn't fond of walls) an electromagnetic . . . 315 VIVA 7   3

FONDLED

deep, deliberate groping ocean fondled o'er the warm long . . 7 T&C EPITHALAM   159

FOOD

dream; and very secret food its leaves inimitable find . . . 19 T&C PUELLA MEA   118
man but wished him food; no cripple wouldn't creep . . . . . 520 50 POEMS 34   30

+FOOD

FOR CONTEXT, SEE . . . . 511 50 POEMS 25   1

FOOL

your eyes, when (being fool to fancy) i have . . . . 78 T&C SON UNRE 3   3
to me you big fool she says i says . . . . 167 & SON ACTU 16   12
wholly to be a fool while Spring is in . . . . 290 IS 5 FOUR 7   5
things) dream is noone's fool; if this wind who . . . . . . 292 IS 5 FOUR 9   10
i love behold this fool who, in the month . . . . 360 VIVA 51   11
incitions and pity the fool who cright god help . . . . 405 NO THANKS 22   9
i deeply greet this fool and man / / . . . . 441 NO THANKS 56   68
bright credos each divisible fool (life imitate gossip fear . 452 NO THANKS 67   7
been quite such a fool who could fail pulling . . . . 481 NEW POEMS 19   11
ter hate dad hurt fool wurl no gal no . . . . 519 50 POEMS 33   19
must be (the wise fool) if living's to give . . . . 543 1 X 1 3   14
him --the climbingly fallingest fool in this trickiest if? . 590 1 X 1 50   15
(and open) if that fool called everyone (or you . . . . . . 603 (CHAIRE) 5   9
star) --how should a fool that calls him "I" . . . . 609 (CHAIRE) 11   13
meanwhile" (mind murmurs; the fool) "truth would prove . . . 625 (CHAIRE) 27   16
mind should try to fool has always failed to . . . . 679 95 POEMS 7   8
has always failed to fool your heart but most . . . . 679 95 POEMS 7   8
be worse than a fool to have never looked . . . . 707 95 POEMS 35   3

+FOOL

FOR CONTEXT, SEE . . . . 388 NO THANKS 5   9
FOR CONTEXT, SEE . . . . 710 95 POEMS 38   7

FOOLED

thickening fright the sudden fooled light. it is the . . . . 11 T&C SONGS 2   20
of old because you fooled the doctors, i touch . . . . . . 289 IS 5 FOUR 6   15
be fun to be fooled but it's more fun . . . . 410 NO THANKS 27   13

FOOLING
of her riant belly's fooling bore --When The Sun . . . . . . 130 & SON REAL 1   2
how beautifully swims the fooling world in my huge . . . . . 157 & SON ACTU 6   11
And most, the futile fooling labyrinth where noisy colours . 220 XLI SONNETS 16 11
FOOLINGLY
divinely bright; it is foolingly to smite my spirit . . . . . 18 T&C PUELLA MEA 82
FOOLISH .
i entreat, by certain foolish perfect hours dead too, ... 42 T&C AMORES 6   15
enormous sobs puckered the foolish breasts the droll mouth . 52 T&C PORTRAIT 1 28
twitter before him, like foolish butterflies he is the . . . 198 XLI PORTRAIT 6 23
clothes. i am altogether foolish, i suddenly make a . . . . 281 IS 5 THREE 5   19
friend than he to foolish and to wise offered . . . . 521 50 POEMS 34   39
+FOOLISH
FOR CONTEXT, SEE . . . . 100 & POST IMPR 11 43
FOR CONTEXT, SEE . . . . 488 50 POEMS 2   17
FOOLISHWISE
glance an alert clumsily foolishwise (tracking the beast . . 374 VIVA 65   6
(being forever born a foolishwise proudhumble citizen of . . 845 73 POEMS 73   6
FOOLS
everywhere of black muscles fools a weightless slowness . . . 299 IS 5 FOUR 16   2
crooked town) a harbour fools the sea(while emanating . . . 319 VIVA 11   18
dream-- how should contented fools of fact envision the . . . 659 (CHAIRE) 61   9
who illimitably is) making fools understand (like wintry me) 736 95 POEMS 64   5
Whatever sages say and fools, all's well / / . . . . 768 95 POEMS 94   14
FOOT
her brazen breasts, whose foot-stool tells how fought the . . 4 T&C EPITHALAM   43
they must chain his foot for his wrist's too . . . . 15 T&C SONGS 5   11
espy the little distinct foot (if whose very minuteness . . . 22 T&C PUELLA MEA 217
mouths take big wobbly foot-steps every goggle cent of . . . 96 & POST IMPR 8   20
slightly expands one square foot mired in silk wrinkling . . 225 IS 5 ONE LIZ   3
per job with one foot and rock a cradle . . . . 242 IS 5 ONE 13   9
a child 's shy foot among cool ferns) . . . . 371 VIVA 62   13
of him whose each foot likes the here of . . . . 512 50 POEMS 26   7
mineral general animal (five foot five) neither dead nor . . 640 (CHAIRE) 42   13
FOOT-STEPS
mouths take big wobbly foot-steps every goggle cent of . . . 96 & POST IMPR 8   20
FOOT-STOOL
her brazen breasts, whose foot-stool tells how fought the . . 4 T&C EPITHALAM   43
FOOTBALL
/ / / a football with white eyebrows the . . . . 465 NEW POEMS 3   1
FOOTED
it's spring and the goat-footed balloonMan whistles far and . 24 T&C CHANSONS 1 20
+FOOTING
FOR CONTEXT, SEE . . . . 330 VIVA 21   10
FOOTPRINT
and tenderly a recent footprint in the sand of . . . . 344 VIVA 35   15
FOOTSTEP
thou distinctly bring thy footstep, and the rushing of . . . 213 XLI SONNETS 9 11
FOR
WORD DELETED, APPEARED 322 TIMES
FORAGING
grace, goddess, thy crippled thunder-foraging groom or the . 6 T&C EPITHALAM 149
FORBID
ever think, may god forbid and (in his mercy) . . . . 484 NEW POEMS 22   9
conjurers rule? do mannikins forbid the soul? is death . . . 527 50 POEMS 39   20
(sing old age scolds Forbid den Stop Must n't . . . . 729 95 POEMS 57   13
+FORBIDDEN
FOR CONTEXT, SEE . . . . 729 95 POEMS 57   13
FORCE
strength so strong mere force is feebleness: the truth . . . 768 95 POEMS 94   11
FORD
of sunful sin namely (ford madox ford) and eke . . . . . . 607 (CHAIRE) 9   14
sin namely (ford madox ford) and eke to wit . . . . 607 (CHAIRE) 9   14
FORE
y unb uria ble fore (hurry into heads are . . . . 309 VIVA 1   7
(where three dreams live) fore head is stumbling someone . . 785 73 POEMS 13   21
FORE'ER
when's haymow with young fore'er (oh & by the . . . . 316 VIVA 8   17

	PAGE	TITLE	LINE

FOREHEAD
  whereof is darkness thy forehead is a flight of . . . .   29 T&C ORIENTALE 3   4
  her much too white forehead a pair of eyes . . . . 116 & PORTRAIT 9   10
  into a rock of forehead. No body loved big . . . .   490 50 POEMS 4   5
  of joy; praising a forehead called the moon singing . . . . . 520 50 POEMS 34   19
+FOREHEAD
  FOR CONTEXT, SEE . . . . 785 73 POEMS 13   21
FOREHEADS
  and throw backward their foreheads to the barbarous bright .   5 T&C EPITHALAM   77
+FOREHEADS
  FOR CONTEXT, SEE . . . . 343 VIVA 34   15
+FORESHORTENED
  FOR CONTEXT, SEE . . . . 309 VIVA 1   7
FOREST
  head is a quick forest filled with sleeping birds . . . . . .   29 T&C ORIENTALE 3   5
  the way to the forest--no offense to you, white . . . .   86 T&C SON ACTU 5   3
  you in the green forest and were you very . . . . 192 XLI CHANSONS 2   5
  all alone through the forest of wonderful, and that . . . . . 216 XLI SONNETS 12   12
  tree field rock hollyhock forest brook chickadee mountain. . 512 50 POEMS 26   26
  g field o ver forest &; wh o could . . . . 653 (CHAIRE) 55   6
  whom flow (mountain valley forest) a million wheres which . . 659 (CHAIRE) 61   5
  Now rapidly this (a forest has slowly Murdered the . . . . . 693 95 POEMS 21   13
  hilltop (barn house wellsweep forest & clearing) gone are . . 755 95 POEMS 83   4
  / / / this forest pool A so of . . . . 759 95 POEMS 86   2
FORESTS
  my being with numbing forests frolicsome, fleetly mystical, .   19 T&C PUELLA MEA   91
  of thing and stifles forests in white ago? Blow . . . . 560 1 X 1 20   12
  only despair completely strikes forests of mind, mountains of 580 1 X 1 40   25
  angels are mountains rivery forests towerful towns (queen . . 586 1 X 1 46   7
  their trees and by forests with all their mountains) . . . . 754 95 POEMS 82   14
FOREVER
  commendable room has been forever subject his Earliest word . 197 XLI PORTRAIT 5   21
  and because you are forever making poems in the . . . . 204 XLI LA GUERRE 2 23
  (when Rain comes; predicating forever, assuming the laughter 356 VIVA 47   16
  countries, rendering death and forever with each breathing (i 366 VIVA 57   16
  darkness shall quite outmarch forever --and i perceive, . . . 376 VIVA 67   6
  memory) give entirely each Forever its freedom (Dare until . 453 NO THANKS 68   12
  spiralling candy of tiniest forever--crazily from totally . . 480 NEW POEMS 18   23
  sheshape) elf into leasting forever most magical maybes of . 495 50 POEMS 9   13
  us accept (the time forever, and you'll wear your . . . . . . 504 50 POEMS 18   16
  which is built by forever & sunsmell (sometimes a . . . . . . 512 50 POEMS 26   30
  silence these always children forever singing wreathed with . 525 50 POEMS 37   13
  lit tle tree listens forever to always children singing . . . 525 50 POEMS 37   21
  to always children singing forever a song made of . . . . . . 525 50 POEMS 37   21
  is when for sale? forever is to give and . . . . 538 50 POEMS 50   11
  universe in two, peels forever out of his grave . . . . 560 1 X 1 20   19
  most are selves) touch: forever (and so to dark) . . . . . . 564 1 X 1 24   16
  the mind) such a forever is love's any now . . . . 576 1 X 1 36   9
  again: but winter's not forever, even snow melts; and . . . . 579 1 X 1 39   3
  world a piece of forever with summitless younger than . . . . 586 1 X 1 46   4
  up around again fly) forever was never till now . . . . 594 1 X 1 54   27
  till it rolled behind forever, we touched a shy . . . . 612 (CHAIRE) 14   9
  system-- if now than forever could never (by breathless . . . 625 (CHAIRE) 27   21
  into (touch me! love) forever --until is and shall . . . . . 633 (CHAIRE) 35   14
  of the ocean of forever with a never in . . . . 642 (CHAIRE) 44   16
  into the now of forever come riding alive down . . . . 661 (CHAIRE) 63   12
  years & nights & forever) is Less Than Nothing . . . . 702 95 POEMS 30   21
  Whose only now is forever: standing erect in the . . . . . . 749 95 POEMS 77   18
  depths of silence) and forever touch or until she . . . . . . 758 95 POEMS 85   42
  twice i have lived forever in a smile) / . . . . 765 95 POEMS 91   14
  the spring) live! die (forever is now) and dance . . . . . . 767 95 POEMS 93   22
  your returning, spends the forever of his loneliness dreaming 812 73 POEMS 40   6
  are we never, but forever now (hosts of eternity; . . . . . . 817 73 POEMS 45   5
  and dark; but never forever & when) un til . . . . 840 73 POEMS 68   25
  create the whole (being forever born a foolishwise . . . . . 845 73 POEMS 73   6
+FOREVER
  FOR CONTEXT, SEE . . . . 469 NEW POEMS 7   12
  FOR CONTEXT, SEE . . . . 525 50 POEMS 37   4

		PAGE	TITLE	LINE

FOREVER&FOREVER
eagerly everyw here shutting forever&forever fol ding int o . 646 {CHAIRE} 48   11
FOREVER'S
to give and on forever's very now we stand . . . . 538 50 POEMS 50   12
unless by your thinking forever's long let beauty touch . . . 742 95 POEMS 70   12
FOREVERFULLY
my most : locking foreverfully blend we a universe . . . . . 371 VIVA 62   19
doll) motionless under magical foreverfully falling snow. And 777 73 POEMS 5   13
FOREVERING
flame beyond soul immemorially forevering am-- and as . . . . 599 {CHAIRE} 1   5
leafless) its silent in forevering snow --but never fear . . 667 {CHAIRE} 69   12
FOREVERISH
deepening beach locked in foreverish time's tide at poise, . 843 73 POEMS 71   4
FOREVERLESS
perfectly dyingest my and foreverless thy? why our is . . . . 590 1 X 1 50   24
FORGE
Coolitch wiped his valley forge with Sitting Bull's T.P. . . 321 VIVA 13   13
's tears boy Dream's) forge tful: e ver than, ... 447 NO THANKS 62   12
FORGED
with him then Cunning forged a web so subtle . . . . 799 73 POEMS 27   16
FORGET
each we promised to forget-- wherefore is there nothing . . . 173 & SON ACTU 22   12
Perfume? for i do forget.... or mere Music mounting . . . . . 211 XLI SONNETS 7   2
/ Will i ever forget that precarious moment? As . . . . . . 262 IS 5 ONE 32   1
/ Space being (don't forget to remember) Curved (and . . . . 315 VIVA 7   1
eyes blur And thighs forget (when clocks whisper and . . . . 359 VIVA 50   2
(but surely does not forget, perish, sleep cannot be . . . . 377 VIVA 68   9
shuts understand G gladly forget little having less with . . 390 NO THANKS 7   6
important worry) halt stop forget relax wait (little child . 393 NO THANKS 10   5
forgetting all which will forget him (emptying our soul . . . 428 NO THANKS 45   14
children are apt to forget to remember with up . . . . . . 515 50 POEMS 29   23
is more thicker than forget more thinner than recall . . . . 530 50 POEMS 42   1
(as easily as we forget something) livingest the imaginable . 599 {CHAIRE} 1   13
citizens unquote might otherwise forget (to err is human; . . 636 {CHAIRE} 38   6
long as to (yes) forget (and longer dear) our . . . . 686 95 POEMS 14   9
go blind (where lips forget to kiss) where everything's . . . 834 73 POEMS 62   28
FORGETFUL
of height this motionless forgetful where turned at his . . . 520 50 POEMS 34   5
+FORGETFUL
FOR CONTEXT, SEE . . . . 447 NO THANKS 62   12
FORGETFULNESS
Spring assembles beauty from forgetfulness with the wild . . 4 T&C EPITHALAM   58
the very eatage of forgetfulness thy lips are satraps . . . . 29 T&C ORIENTALE 3   23
FORGETS
sea heaving indolent colourless forgets) time Requiescat. . . 277 IS 5 THREE 1   20
as this planet (understand) forgets the entire and perpetual 379 VIVA 70   9
FORGETTING
white voices pass upon forgetting (fail me not) whose . . . . 9 T&C SONGS 1   2
in your pants and forgetting it's there and sitting . . . . . 204 XLI LA GUERRE 2   19
such to murder time (forgetting what's to know wholly . . . . 362 VIVA 53   14
W I elds) un forgetting un. der (theys) the . . . . 417 NO THANKS 34   19
timelessness that heartbeat) mightily forgetting all which . 428 NO THANKS 45   13
living is to grow) forgetting why, remember how in . . . . . 688 95 POEMS 16   3
to dream, remember so (forgetting seem) in time of . . . . . 688 95 POEMS 16   6
and here with paradise) forgetting if, remember yes in . . . 688 95 POEMS 16   9
may comprehend, remember seek (forgetting find) and in a . . 688 95 POEMS 16   12
shall set us free) forgetting me, remember me / . . . . . . 688 95 POEMS 16   15
FORGIVE
afraid perfectly beautiful is, forgive these words which i . 22 T&C PUELLA MEA 242
begin less littler than forgive it is most sane . . . . . . 530 50 POEMS 42   12
god almighty for dying (forgive us, o life! the . . . . 604 {CHAIRE} 6   25
err is human; to forgive divine) that if the . . . . 636 {CHAIRE} 38   6
FORGIVENESS
merrily moving through sweet forgiveness of spring (over the 661 {CHAIRE} 63   7
of me-- who found forgiveness hard because my (as . . . . . . 730 95 POEMS 58   3
FORGIVING
young and death uncommon (forgiving not divine, to err . . . 798 73 POEMS 26   3

		PAGE	TITLE	LINE

FORGIVINGLY
    so (big with innocence) forgivingly a once of eager . . . . . 601 {CHAIRE} 3   4
FORGOT
    when souls which have forgot frivolity in lowliness, noting . 81 T&C SON UNRE 6   3
    go little fourpaws? you forgot to shut your big . . . . 191 XLI CHANSONS 1   3
    few and down they forgot as up they grew . . . . 515 50 POEMS 29   10
FORGOTTEN
    over smooth pages of forgotten joy proving the peaceful . . .   3 T&C EPITHALAM   18
    that i have perhaps forgotten how, always (from these . . . . 297 IS 5 FOUR 14   8
    his life as a forgotten prisoner --"Ici?" --"Ah non, ... 304 IS 5 FIVE 3   9
    empty glove, a soon forgotten tune, a house for . . . . 360 VIVA 51   9
    with his rotten old forgotten full of why (rub-her-bub) . . . 642 {CHAIRE} 44   6
+FORGOTTEN
    FOR CONTEXT, SEE . . . . 232 IS 5 ONE 3   15
FORKED
    of the pretended breasts, forked in surprisable unliving eyes 103 & POST IMPR 13   3
FORLORN
    majestic bulbous lips and forlorn piggish hands joked to . . 56 T&C PORTRAIT 4   12
FORM
    a nymphlike face, a form whose snowy symmetry of . . . . . .   8 T&C OF NICOL   20
    every prettiness you hew form truly / / / . . . . 195 XLI PORTRAIT 3   24
    exist being a peculiar form of sleep what's beyond . . . . . 264 IS 5 ONE 33   4
    into a truly curving form enters my soul feels . . . . 419 NO THANKS 36   2
    this night a mightily form moves whose passenger and . . . . 419 NO THANKS 36   22
    advancing colour strike into form (actually) realness kill . 422 NO THANKS 39   6
    doubt that in whose form less form all goodness . . . . 790 73 POEMS 18   8
    in whose form less form all goodness truth and . . . . 790 73 POEMS 18   9
FORMAL
    the gold year a formal spasm in the dust . . . . 41 T&C AMORES 5   7
FORMED
    fragility of ice newly formed upon an old pool. . . . . 103 & POST IMPR 13   12
FORMER
    again hands again, the former coachman with a pipewrench . . 263 IS 5 ONE 32   45
FORMING
    o Now handspring trans forming it self int o . . . . 343 VIVA 34   12
+FORMLESS
    FOR CONTEXT, SEE . . . . 790 73 POEMS 18   8
FORMS
    stars a turbulence of forms delightful with indefinable . . . 31 T&C ORIENTALE 5   9
    with what huge merciful forms presume / / / . . . . 351 VIVA 42   15
FORMULA
    is wonderful and a formula a bit of tobacco . . . . 68 T&C POST IMPR 5   2
    World O Life a formula: example, Turn Your Shirttails . . . . 230 IS 5 ONE 2   33
FORSAKE
    who dares to not forsake a failing year --now, ... 821 73 POEMS 49   8
FORSOOTH
    know more quite ennobling forsooth? One wondrous fine . . . . 254 IS 5 ONE 25   4
FORT
    Dwrith il est trop fort le negre esn7othingish8s c'est . . . 430 NO THANKS 47   20
FORTH
    of her that brought forth tall Hippolytus, lord on . . . . .   4 T&C EPITHALAM   45
    the wingless thing man forth into bright air, for . . . . . .   4 T&C EPITHALAM   61
    dead. On dappled dawn forth rides the pungent sun . . . . . .   4 T&C EPITHALAM   65
    great rose! Lover, lead forth thy love unto that . . . . . .   6 T&C EPITHALAM   113
    with shining feet, went forth into the dew: right . . . . . .   8 T&C OF NICOL   28
    queen of queens comes forth ankles musical with large . . . . 33 T&C ORIENTALE 6   65
    hands which sent her forth to sleep upon the . . . . 38 T&C AMORES 3   3
    change and she goes forth out of hands and . . . . 38 T&C AMORES 3   11
    dawn the world goes forth to murder dreams.... i . . . . . . 50 T&C IMPRESS 4   11
    excuse for May --bring forth your flowers and machinery: . . 264 IS 5 ONE 33   9
    the pilgrims' and so forth oh say can you . . . . 268 IS 5 TWO 3   2
    son of man goes forth to war with trumpets . . . . 273 IS 5 TWO 8   23
    if sometimes he's prodded forth to exercise her vote . . . . 544 1 X 1 4   9
+FORTH
    FOR CONTEXT, SEE . . . . 230 IS 5 ONE 2   29
FORTISSIMO
    sing each and all fortissimo A- mer i ca, ... 230 IS 5 ONE 2   36

		PAGE	TITLE	LINE
+FORTNIGHTS				
FOR CONTEXT, SEE	343	VIVA 34	15
FORTUNATE				
quest? and did thy fortunate fingers sometime dwell (within .	3	T&C EPITHALAM	21
Never my soul so fortunate is (past the luck	19	T&C PUELLA MEA	102
time time time --how fortunate are you and i, ...	743	95 POEMS 71	10
FORTUNE				
John Unalive (having a fortune of fifteengrand f thanks . . .	331	VIVA 22	1
shall not spend my fortune (although endlessness should end)	394	NO THANKS 11	14
say "i want a fortune" . At which (smiling)	697	95 POEMS 25	5
FORTYEIGHT				
Wong, uninterred at twice fortyeight, succeeded in producing	341	VIVA 32	2
FORUM				
statues of yon motheaten forum be aware notice what	260	IS 5 ONE 30	2
FORWARD				
over the tiller; clattered forward skidding in outrageous . .	277	IS 5 THREE 1	12
FORWARDFLUNG				
through its english the Forwardflung backwardSpinning hoop .	311	VIVA 3	5
FOSES				
dissonance of Rish and Foses) until (finding one's self . . .	319	VIVA 11	13
FOUGHT				
whose foot-stool tells how fought the looser of the	4	T&C EPITHALAM	44
/ my uncle Daniel fought in the civil war	253	IS 5 ONE 24	2
FOUL				
voice if therefore among foul pains appears an if	425	NO THANKS 42	13
moon come fair come foul he goes alone daring	440	NO THANKS 56	27
furnished rooms through whose foul windows absurd clouds . .	442	NO THANKS 57	12
FOUND				
/ / i have found what you are like	163	& SON ACTU 12	1
like a flower who found you in the green	192	XLI CHANSONS 2	5
an angel named Frederick found on a lightning-rod, Boston, .	262	IS 5 ONE 32	30
wine of life and found it sweet-- a tear	273	IS 5 TWO 8	8
a year) ago i found staring me in the	296	IS 5 FOUR 13	15
with fingers; till having found what was thrown away	298	IS 5 FOUR 15	23
road--there's something to be found" and smiling you answer .	303	IS 5 FIVE 2	3
how? down to smoking found Butts / /	314	VIVA 6	32
nothing) 2 boston Dolls; found with Holes in each	317	VIVA 9	25
we both might have found the solution of that	323	VIVA 15	18
busiest city and presently found himself rattling for that .	326	VIVA 18	12
to find them (and found a secondhand set which	410	NO THANKS 27	2
you again. Love (having found) wound up such pretty	451	NO THANKS 66	9
still stands still as found some lost thing (like	516	50 POEMS 30	4
whose lost is his found leading love whose heart	533	50 POEMS 45	2
was lost has been found has been found and	665	(CHAIRE) 67	15
been found has been found and having is giving	665	(CHAIRE) 67	15
out of me-- who found forgiveness hard because my	730	95 POEMS 58	3
& singing &) thing found one old blue wheel	753	95 POEMS 81	20
guessable each infinite Oblivions found a by lost child . . .	757	95 POEMS 85	25
FOUNDCLOWN				
(childlost so; ul) foundclown a -live a , ...	471	NEW POEMS 9	16
FOUNDLOST				
creep (by if) timelessly foundlost glad (children of)	681	95 POEMS 9	10
FOUNDS				
one ness as con founds all itcreating winds /	826	73 POEMS 54	16
FOUNTAIN				
of sleep some silver-fingered fountain steals the world. / .	208	XLI SONNETS 4	14
FOUNTAINING				
(slapsoothed by sundark) brightshadowfully fountaining man's	681	95 POEMS 9	14
FOUNTAINS				
ankus of ebony the fountains of the emperor's palace	32	T&C ORIENTALE 6	15
FOUR				
into the silver dawn. four lean hounds crouched low	14	T&C SONGS 4	4
the red rare deer. Four red roebuck at a	14	T&C SONGS 4	9
into the silver dawn. four lean hounds crouched low	14	T&C SONGS 4	14
the fleet flown deer. Four fleet does at a	14	T&C SONGS 4	19
into the silver dawn. four lean hounds crouched low	14	T&C SONGS 4	24
the tall tense deer. Four tall stags at a	14	T&C SONGS 4	29
into the silver dawn. four lean hounds crouched low	14	T&C SONGS 4	34

		PAGE	TITLE	LINE
FOUR (CONTINUED)				
on which always the four tablets of perspiration erectly	. .	73	T&C SON REAL 4	8
e r s, large four gnarled lips totter Therefore,	. . . . . .	255	IS 5 ONE 26	4
doors. Next door (but four) gentlemen are trininghtly	. . . .	312	VIVA 4	3
uh green field watchin four crows drop into sunset,	. . . . .	332	VIVA 23	31
and (six are in) four are white (three singdance	. . . . . .	507	50 POEMS 21	15
life stands gradually upon four minds (out of some	. . . . .	517	50 POEMS 31	8
eyes for an eye four teeth for a tooth	. . . .	635	(CHAIRE) 37	17
alive must three, must four and (to quite become	. . . . . .	764	95 POEMS 90	51
+FOUR				
FOR CONTEXT, SEE	. . . .	60	T&C PORTRAIT 8	6
FOR CONTEXT, SEE	. . . .	725	95 POEMS 53	10
FOURPAWS				
did you go little fourpaws? you forgot to shut	. . . .	191	XLI CHANSONS 1	2
FOURTEENTH				
god i want above fourteenth fifth's deep purring biceps,	. .	220	XLI SONNETS 16	1
FOURTH				
and very merely my fourth will cure the laziest	. . . . . .	537	50 POEMS 49	2
FOUS				
lezard ladies suddenly j'm'en fous des negres (in the	. . . .	121	& PORTRAIT 12	43
FRACAS				
dishevelling made a pale fracas upon the accurate moon....	.	214	XLI SONNETS 10	9
FRACTION				
carefully moving a perhaps fraction of flower here placing	.	124	& SEVEN POEMS 3	17
am alive this absurd fraction in its lowest terms	. . . . .	295	IS 5 FOUR 12	18
+FRACTION				
FOR CONTEXT, SEE	. . . .	797	73 POEMS 25	16
FRAGILE				
world scarce astir my fragile lady wandering in whose	. . . .	17	T&C PUELLA MEA	13
there trysts curvingly a fragile smile which like a	. . . . .	20	T&C PUELLA MEA	149
rhyme-- in life's very fragile hour (when the world	. . . . .	23	T&C PUELLA MEA	275
take shimmering wind these fragile splendors from us crumple		41	T&C AMORES 5	19
i have made a fragile certain song under the	. . . .	43	T&C AMORES 7	4
Lady swiftly take my fragile certain song that we	. . . . . .	43	T&C AMORES 7	27
you with all her fragile might to not surmise	. . . .	72	T&C SON REAL 3	8
thing most new complete fragile intense, which wholly	. . . .	82	T&C SON ACTU 1	1
slippery house, a strong fragile house (beginning at the	. .	83	T&C SON ACTU 2	3
suddenly lifted in singing--hands fragile whom almost tire	.	85	T&C SON ACTU 4	11
Mimi a la voix fragile qui chatouille Des Italiens	. . . . .	120	& PORTRAIT 12	6
pourquoi eclate ta voix fragile couleur de pivoine?) with	. .	121	& PORTRAIT 12	56
height in a firm fragile stinging weather, (breathless with	.	140	& SON REAL 11	8
/ / before the fragile gradual throne of night	. . . . . .	156	& SON ACTU 5	1
Waiting (always) upon a fragile instant when herself me	. . .	156	& SON ACTU 5	13
a brittle fuss of fragile huge humanity.... Numb thoughts,	.	174	& SON ACTU 23	7
of a vase inexpressibly fragile it is for the	. . . .	193	XLI PORTRAIT 1	15
his feet large and fragile his queer hands twitter	. . . . .	198	XLI PORTRAIT 6	22
a twilight lifting the fragile skill of new leaves'	. . . . .	218	XLI SONNETS 14	4
mountainous worthy in the fragile act of doing her	. . . . .	228	IS 5 ONE MARJ	12
up handle with care fragile and send him home	. . . .	270	IS 5 TWO 5	17
tremble remembering something squirming fragile and which had	279	IS 5 THREE 3	22
east toward her a fragile light bent gatheringly /	. . . . .	284	IS 5 FOUR 1	18
no wisest painter of fragile Marys will understand how	. . .	294	IS 5 FOUR 11	11
the long night a fragile imitation of (perhaps) myself	. . .	300	IS 5 FOUR 17	12
through whose profound and fragile lips the sweet small	. . .	306	IS 5 FIVE 5	13
i am slender and fragile i borrow contact from	. . . .	328	VIVA 19	16
pansy heaven nor a fragile heaven of lilies-of-the-valley but	352	VIVA 43	3
+FRAGILE				
FOR CONTEXT, SEE	. . . .	163	& SON ACTU 12	10
FRAGILITY				
which hides in a fragility of poppies.... i say	. . . . . .	45	T&C LA GUERRE 1	5
in the slow-ly-in creasing fragility --. Dogs bark children	.	63	T&C PORTRAIT 10	31
disguise, appear capable of fragility and indecision --do not	91	& POST IMPR 3	13
skin like the poisonous fragility of ice newly formed	. . . .	103	& POST IMPR 13	12
a piece of eminent fragility. Well and when--Does	. . . . . .	141	& SON REAL 12	6
to dust of your fragility (but chiefly of your	. . . .	293	IS 5 FOUR 10	15
power of your intense fragility: whose texture compels me	. .	366	VIVA 57	14
FRAGMENT				
moon rattles like a fragment of angry candy /	. . . .	70	T&C SON REAL 1	14

FRAGMENT (CONTINUED)

<table>
<tr><td></td><td>PAGE</td><td>TITLE</td><td>LINE</td></tr>
</table>

	PAGE	TITLE	LINE

FRAGMENT (CONTINUED)
thief crook cynic (swimfloatdrifting fragment of heaven) . . 677 95 POEMS 5   11
+FRAGMENT
FOR CONTEXT, SEE . . . . 193 XLI PORTRAIT 1   24
+FRAGMENTS
FOR CONTEXT, SEE . . . . 347 VIVA 38   12
FRAGRANCE
solitude a furtive occult fragrance steals, a gesture of . . 19 T&C PUELLA MEA 106
little while caressed its fragrance makes the lover blest.) . 21 T&C PUELLA MEA 192
dream locked in white fragrance Come hither O thou, ... 27 T&C ORIENTALE 1   19
i was aware of fragrance and i came riding . . . . 30 T&C ORIENTALE 4   9
pencils fluent spires of fragrance the bowl seethes a . . . . 31 T&C ORIENTALE 5   5
sunbeams, of a foetal fragrance to rickety unclosed blinds . 144 & SON REAL 15   2
a moist mistake, whose fragrance hurls me into tears, ... 148 & SON REAL 19   10
jiggled to the jigging fragrance of newness --and then. . . . 173 & SON ACTU 22   7
exactly cubes of tiny fragrance try; i have watched . . . . . 214 XLI SONNETS 10   4
/ / memory believes fragrance of a town (whose . . . . 340 VIVA 31   2
/ / / An (fragrance) Of (Begins) millions Of . . . . 348 VIVA 39   1
gaze climbs this steep fragrance of eternity) world by . . . 450 NO THANKS 65   8
entirely arrives gesture past fragrance fragrant; a than pure 456 NO THANKS 71   9
this new eng land fragrance of pasture and now . . . . 469 NEW POEMS 7   14
all findingly Spring the Fragrance unvisible) ges -tured . . 482 NEW POEMS 20   9
sun light and of fragrance and of Singing) is . . . . 657 {CHAIRE} 59   6
villainy holiness riding in fragrance of sunlight (side by . 661 {CHAIRE} 63   2
darkly a kindness of fragrance opens around them) and . . . . 754 95 POEMS 82   10
in roguish am of fragrance dances a honeydunce; whirling's . 763 95 POEMS 90   9
through the may in fragrance and song wonderingly come . . . 778 73 POEMS 6   12
be sky always (through fragrance and singing) come lovers . . 778 73 POEMS 6   21
cadence may release the fragrance of a freedom which . . . . 842 73 POEMS 70   7
FRAGRANT
precarious bird.) Springing from fragrant shoulders small, . 20 T&C PUELLA MEA 153
have offered up each fragrant night, when all my . . . . . . 39 T&C AMORES 4   30
troubling ship upon the fragrant unspeaking ignorant darkness 112 & PORTRAIT 6   97
/ / / a fragrant sag of fruit distinctly . . . . 219 XLI SONNETS 15   1
arrives gesture past fragrance fragrant; a than pure more . . 456 NO THANKS 71   9
have wandered down from fragrant mountains of eternal now . . 743 95 POEMS 71   12
FRAGRANTLY
all which somewhere is fragrantly, arrive (when Rain comes; . 356 VIVA 47   12
in death's place new fragrantly young earth space opening . . 432 NO THANKS 49   19
FRAID
and s (not a fraid of moon You) ◇ . . . . 469 NEW POEMS 7   19
FRAIL
breathless pearl! O indefinable frail ultimate pose! O . . . 5 T&C EPITHALAM 109
unchastity, imperial Cytherea, from frail foam sprung with . 7 T&C EPITHALAM 161
and fugitive my very frail lady drifting distinctly, moving . 17 T&C PUELLA MEA 18
flower, a flower so frail, a flower so glad) . . . . 18 T&C PUELLA MEA 52
she speak in her frail way, it is wholly . . . . 18 T&C PUELLA MEA 77
things perfect the most frail. (Whoso rideth in the . . . . 20 T&C PUELLA MEA 162
with her lips' most frail parting my body hears . . . . . . 22 T&C PUELLA MEA 233
with crisp eyes and frail, in the city of . . . . 23 T&C PUELLA MEA 287
faint aspirings the indolent frail ascensions, of thy smile . 31 T&C ORIENTALE 5   16
mirror i see a frail man dreaming dreams dreams . . . . . . 50 T&C IMPRESS 4   18
in their houses the frail man is in his . . . . 50 T&C IMPRESS 4   28
stopped hears in the frail anon the shovings and . . . . . . 77 T&C SON UNRE 2   8
building around you, a frail slippery house, a strong . . . . 83 T&C SON ACTU 2   2
lady's body with these frail ladies dangerously respire: . . 85 T&C SON ACTU 4   14
spent day begins to frail (whose grave already three . . . . 115 & PORTRAIT 8   1
in the not too frail lips almost discussed; between . . . . . 146 & SON REAL 17   12
smile, until this very frail enormous star (do you . . . . . 155 & SON ACTU 4   13
like a girl lasciviously frail, peace (dreaming is better) . 168 & SON ACTU 17   10
dreams, love thou art frail --walk the longness of . . . . . 190 XLI SONGS 12   18
pastile-shaped insipid kinesis or frail swooping lozenge. a . 201 XLI PORTRAIT 9   15
colours come and go, frail azures fluttering from night's . . 208 XLI SONNETS 4   2
seen her a stealthily frail flower walking with its . . . . 214 XLI SONNETS 10   1
trivial stink of rich frail firm asinine life (i . . . . . . 220 XLI SONNETS 16   4
most deep dreams are frail) songs less firm than . . . . . . 306 IS 5 FIVE 5   3
silence: in your most frail gesture are things which . . . . 366 VIVA 57   3

		PAGE	TITLE	LINE

FRAILER
of thy heart on frailer ports of costlier commerce . . . . . 79 T&C SON UNRE 4   16
the rain only sweeter frailer you whom certain flowers . . . 293 IS 5 FOUR 10   3
which wrong your eyes (frailer than most deep dreams . . . . 306 IS 5 FIVE 5   3
FRAILEST
Spring, and with their frailest syllable its leaves go . . . 22 T&C PUELLA MEA 235
FRAILLY
doom; but a rain frailly raging whom the hills . . . . 9 T&C SONGS 1   25
on faint hills do frailly go The peaceful terrors . . . . . 11 T&C SONGS 2   27
heart which do so frailly cling....) i who am . . . . 215 XLI SONNETS 11 10
FRAILNESS
tendril fleetly curled upon frailness) used to stroll (very . 23 T&C PUELLA MEA 280
FRAILTIES
hath pondered o'er --and frailties of dimension to occur . . 205 XLI SONNETS 1   12
+FRAILTIES
FOR CONTEXT, SEE . . . . 416 NO THANKS 33   12
FRAILTY
patience and the grave frailty of daisies--by what rare . . . 5 T&C EPITHALAM   94
FRAME
laughter into the filigree frame of a microscopic stage . . . 55 T&C PORTRAIT 3   6
FRAMED
curl.... how Jimmie was framed and got his / . . . . 149 & SON REAL 20   16
/ my naked lady framed in twilight is an . . . . 162 & SON ACTU 11   1
FRAMES
of jovial hair extremely frames the face in a . . . . 137 & SON REAL 8   17
FRAMING
city stilled in the framing twilight of Spring.... and . . . 158 & SON ACTU 7   10
FRAN
cut the comedy kid.... Fran Mag Glad Dorothy / . . . . 138 & SON REAL 9   17
/ / / / FRAN should i entirely ask . . . . 229 IS 5 ONE FRAN   T
Noo York an San Fran dictaphones wireless subways vacuum . . 237 IS 5 ONE 8   8
FRANCE
H.G. Wells, and Anatole France shook hands again and . . . . 263 IS 5 ONE 32   43
FRANK
the devil) my uncle Frank has done nothing for . . . . . . 253 IS 5 ONE 24   5
(or something) my uncle Frank breaks into tears. my . . . . . 253 IS 5 ONE 24   8
the hyenas suppressing my frank qualms in deference to . . . 326 VIVA 18   21
phyllis on the snout frank sank him with an . . . . 706 95 POEMS 34   2
head we call old frank go bluer still as . . . . 754 95 POEMS 82   6
FRANKLY
and which i despise, frankly admitting i have been . . . . . 43 T&C AMORES 7   20
FRANTIC
hope- less gnomes and frantic fairies gush clumsily from . . 69 T&C POST IMPR 6 22
the complete important profane frantic inconsequential . . . 201 XLI PORTRAIT 9 32
whose cool feet this frantic heart is fain; try . . . . . . 212 XLI SONNETS 8   4
this alive secretly i frantic this serene mightily how . . . 415 NO THANKS 32   22
church (far from the frantic world with its rapture . . . . . 749 95 POEMS 77   13
a honeydunce; whirling's a frantic struts a pedantic proud . 763 95 POEMS 90   11
FREAKISH
i hear your stepping freakish feet feet incorrigible ragging 61 T&C PORTRAIT 9 35
FRED
/ (as that named Fred -someBody: hippopotamus, scratch- ing, 252 IS 5 ONE 23   1
neither was dumb. Skip fred (jump! neddy) but under . . . . . 513 50 POEMS 27   30
FREDERICK
of an angel named Frederick found on a lightning-rod, ... 262 IS 5 ONE 32   30
FREE
very shadowy sheep float free upon terrific pastures pale, . 9 T&C SONGS 1   9
spirit with the lithe free twitch of scintillant space, . . . 18 T&C PUELLA MEA 83
planets struggle to be free with the astounding everlasting . 212 XLI SONNETS 8 11
manly heart and conscience free, upon the front steps . . . . 273 IS 5 TWO 8   18
Odysseus Graren't we couldn't free the negro because he . . . 321 VIVA 13   11
these stairs, there's a free room. We almost could . . . . . 365 VIVA 56   7
praise glad things or free truly which live always . . . . . 441 NO THANKS 56   61
paid to make man free (for man is enslaved . . . . 552 1 X 1 12   2
sprawls) here a livingly free mysterious dreamsoul . . . . . 658 (CHAIRE) 60   16
time shall set us free) forgetting me, remember me . . . . . 688 95 POEMS 16   14
that want to be free just trust in the . . . . 711 95 POEMS 39   7
all his years) he's free into the beauty of . . . . 845 73 POEMS 73   9

	PAGE	TITLE	LINE
FREEDOM			
from every B.V.D. let freedom ring amen. i do	230	IS 5 ONE 2	14
pled, their heels for Freedom slaves will click; where . . .	438	NO THANKS 54	18
entirely each Forever its freedom (Dare until a flower, . . .	453	NO THANKS 68	12
my failure with thy freedom: star isful beckoningly fabulous	456	NO THANKS 71	14
now: but we've such freedom such intense digestion so	491	50 POEMS 5	15
/ / / as freedom is a breakfastfood or	511	50 POEMS 25	1
scheming imagine, passion willed, freedom a drug that's . . .	521	50 POEMS 34	56
land of supernod where freedom is compulsory and only	544	1 X 1 4	23
the crowd inclined it's freedom from freedom the common . . .	635	(CHAIRE) 37	24
inclined it's freedom from freedom the common man wants) . .	635	(CHAIRE) 37	24
take your choice. Ain't freedom grand / / /	636	(CHAIRE) 38	14
envision the mystery of freedom? yet, among their loud . . .	659	(CHAIRE) 61	10
and such a sharpening freedom lifts our blood as	675	95 POEMS 3	6
stand soul to soul: freedom to freedom till her	721	95 POEMS 49	9
to soul: freedom to freedom till her utmost secrecies	721	95 POEMS 49	9
now and here of freedom. Come / / /	745	95 POEMS 73	14
Here (only here) is freedom: always here no then	765	95 POEMS 91	10
contrive; imagined, merely know (freedom: what makes a slave)	834	73 POEMS 62	9
the fragrance of a freedom which no mind contrives	842	73 POEMS 70	7
FREEDOM'S			
/ / / what freedom's not some under's mere	538	50 POEMS 50	1
FREEDOMS			
y on (pass the freedoms pappy or uncle shylock	641	(CHAIRE) 43	7
FREEING			
battening gesture prophecies a freeing of ghostly chaos in .	77	T&C SON UNRE 2	12
FREELY			
(this life could dare freely to give as gives	440	NO THANKS 56	13
me for i will freely die" she cried so	711	95 POEMS 39	12
FREEZES			
python over the way freezes a serpent becomes a	384	NO THANKS 2	21
FREEZING			
my feet getting dim freezing or up to your	272	IS 5 TWO 7	8
march outward into the freezing fire of Thickness) points . .	311	VIVA 3	14
FRENZIEDLY			
limps who might less frenziedly have cried eev mahmah	790	73 POEMS 18	15
FRENZY			
a friendless dingy female frenzy bubbles / / /	151	& SON REAL 22	18
FREQUENT			
a kiss) kneeling, your frequent mercy begs, sharply believe .	115	& PORTRAIT 8	8
Nothing, remember love by frequent anguish (imagine Her least	453	NO THANKS 68	8
wave is wet more frequent than to fail it	530	50 POEMS 42	4
FREQUENTLY			
his mind is seen frequently fingering the exact beads	193	XLI PORTRAIT 1	5
swir -ling (not too frequently) skirt exhumes (which	341	VIVA 32	13
FRERE			
wife and nun merchant frere clerk somnour miller and	661	(CHAIRE) 63	10
FRESH			
a jetted music splashing fresh upon silence) i without . . .	115	& PORTRAIT 8	19
for to doom yea (fresh complexions being oke with	552	1 X 1 12	23
/ old mr ly fresh from a fu ruddy	567	1 X 1 27	2
ruddy as a sunrise fresh with blue come true	567	1 X 1 27	19
FRESHLY			
(composed of captains in freshly-creased -uniforms with . . .	274	IS 5 TWO 9	22
FRESHLY-CREASED			
(composed of captains in freshly-creased -uniforms with . . .	274	IS 5 TWO 9	22
FRESHNESS			
from sunny thunder into freshness as if god's flowers	58	T&C PORTRAIT 6	8
FREUD			
a corkscrew) studied with Freud a year or two	236	IS 5 ONE 7	7
or two and when Freud got through with Do-	236	IS 5 ONE 7	8
dance) kumrads enjoy s. freud knows whoy the hope	413	NO THANKS 30	11
no appeal from reason" (freud) --you pays your money	636	(CHAIRE) 38	13
+FREUD			
FOR CONTEXT, SEE	499	50 POEMS 13	3
FREUDIAN			
have mentioned ye olde freudian wish; when i contemplate . .	326	VIVA 18	3

FRIDAY
  a mirror this is friday 1 what 3 a . . . . 335 VIVA 26   6
FRIEND
  engraving belonging to my friend. Whom i salute, by . . . . . 158 & SON ACTU 7   8
  PORTRAITS conversation with my friend is particularly to . . 193 XLI PORTRAIT 1   1
  inwardly crisping for my friend, feeling is the sacred . . . 193 XLI PORTRAIT 1   9
  one, knee with, its, friend observes I pass Mr . . . . 252 IS 5 ONE 23   4
  the vest its wideflung friend clenched weakly dirt while . . 258 IS 5 ONE 28   18
  both would call their friend and who may envy . . . . 394 NO THANKS 11   9
  and to morning's beautiful friend twilight (and a first . . . 424 NO THANKS 41   6
  give as gives a friend not those who slave . . . . 440 NO THANKS 56   14
  wealth to foe and friend than he to foolish . . . . 521 50 POEMS 34   38
  the head; if every friend became his foe he'd . . . . 521 50 POEMS 34   47
  exhumed most innocently undecaying friend hangs at yon gilty 546 1 X 1 6   4
  queen to seem (blow friend to fiend: blow space . . . . 560 1 X 1 20   6
  sno eye kil yoo (friend the laughing grinning) we . . . . . . 618 {CHAIRE} 20   6
  & then my wonderful friend dominic depaola gives me . . . . . 680 95 POEMS 8   24
  by whom (my beautiful friend) the gift to live . . . . 776 73 POEMS 4   18
  you 're wrong, my friend. But what does do, ... 793 73 POEMS 21   16
  or any foe a friend --cry nay: cry yea-- . . . . 798 73 POEMS 26   19
  light (whisper) "was my friend" reme mbering "& friendship . 823 73 POEMS 51   6
FRIEND'
  of muchtheworseforwear shoes 'fair friend' we enlightened . . 800 73 POEMS 28   9
FRIEND'S
  immediate imperceptible content my friend's being, out of the 193 XLI PORTRAIT 1   19
  vast my complexly wisdoming friend's --a fingery treesoul . . 517 50 POEMS 31   5
FRIENDLESS
  of clenched thighs a friendless dingy female frenzy bubbles . 151 & SON REAL 22   18
FRIENDLY
  about thick big this friendly himself of a boulder) . . . . . 658 {CHAIRE} 60   3
FRIENDS
  mean beside its lovelier friends, between your thoughts more   11 T&C SONGS 2   13
  handorgans and April darkness, friends i charge laughing. . .   66 T&C POST IMPR 3   4
  twenty five cents dear friends to make it an . . . . 196 XLI PORTRAIT 4   13
  A Kodak therefore my friends let us now sing . . . . 230 IS 5 ONE 2   35
  believe my most intimate friends would never have gathered. . 262 IS 5 ONE 32   14
  communists pick up themselves friends & their hats legs . . . 275 IS 5 TWO 9   43
  for moons mountains for friends --open your thighs to . . . . 420 NO THANKS 37   12
  and the false fair friends and the boths and . . . . 569 1 X 1 29   10
  / / joys faces friends feet terrors fate hands . . . . 693 95 POEMS 21   1
  i are such immortal friends the other's each / . . . . 730 95 POEMS 58   6
  mate his chicks his friends he loves because he . . . . 774 73 POEMS 2   13
  but look around you, friends and foes my tragic . . . . 799 73 POEMS 27   39
  (cruel now cancels kind; friends turn to enemies) therefore . 834 73 POEMS 62   4
FRIENDSHIP
  friend" reme mbering "& friendship is a miracle" his . . . . 823 73 POEMS 51   8
FRIEZE
  streets mesh in a frieze of smoking Face Bluish-old . . . . . 142 & SON REAL 13   5
FRIGHT
  shakes with a thickening fright the sudden fooled light. . .   11 T&C SONGS 2   19
  writhe captured in brightening fright) / / / / . . . .   77 T&C SON UNRE 2   17
  self perceives with hysterical fright a comic tadpole . . . . 157 & SON ACTU 6   14
FRIGHTENED
  --Children, stand with circular frightened faces glaring at .   69 T&C POST IMPR 6   7
  the rain, (Who feathers frightened fields with the superior . 163 & SON ACTU 12   3
  kiss -ing wishes bodies) squirm-of-frightened shy are whichs 437 NO THANKS 53   7
  swooping whirl over a frightened boy and girl) but . . . . . 777 73 POEMS 5   8
FRIGHTENINGLY
  certain taut precarious holiday frighteningly performed and .   52 T&C PORTRAIT 1   8
FRIGHTENS
  how <> Unvoice (which frightenS a noisy most park's . . . . . 726 95 POEMS 54   7
FRIGHTS
  Pheidian soul whose eagle frights creation, in whose palm . .   3 T&C EPITHALAM   27
FRIGID
  for the brain irrevocably frigid to touch a merest . . . . . 193 XLI PORTRAIT 1   15
+FRINGING
  FOR CONTEXT, SEE . . . . 139 & SON REAL 10   8

+FRISK
    FOR CONTEXT, SEE . . . . 431 NO THANKS 48   6
FRISKS
    ears and see? tail frisks) (gonE) "mouse", We are . . . . . . 286 IS 5 FOUR 3   13
    his white thumbs and frisks down the boulevards without . . . 296 IS 5 FOUR 13   7
FRITZ
    $ SEVERAL MILLION FINKLESTEIN (FRITZ) LIVES AT THE RITZ . . . 244 IS 5 ONE 15   3
FRIVOLITY
    souls which have forgot frivolity in lowliness, noting the . 81 T&C SON UNRE 6   3
FRIVOLOUS
    intimate gently primeval hands, frivolous feet divine! 0 . .   5 T&C EPITHALAM   107
    unwary june-bug and the frivolous angleworm thou dost . . . . 61 T&C PORTRAIT 9   3
    African gesture utters a frivolous intense half of Girl . . . 95 & POST IMPR 7   7
FRO
    window (carefully to and fro moving New and Old . . . . 124 & SEVEN POEMS 3 13
    the gradual of unbeing (fro on stiffening greenly air . . . . 633 {CHAIRE} 35   3
    a to and a fro (and a here there . . . . 769 95 POEMS 95   6
FROCK
    President in a new frock coat (scrambling all up . . . . . . 267 IS 5 TWO 2   3
FROGEATERS
    guts outa dem doity frogeaters an humpin duh swell . . . . . 332 VIVA 23   16
FROID
    cheri; il fait trop froid"-- they are gone: along . . . . . . 304 IS 5 FIVE 3   10
FROIDES
    et j'ai les mains froides. His Royal Highness said . . . . . 262 IS 5 ONE 32   26
+FROING
    FOR CONTEXT, SEE . . . . 747 95 POEMS 75   17
FROISSART
    with heroic breeds; thou, Froissart, for that thou didst . . 209 XLI SONNETS 5   9
FROLIC
    breasts (is it the Frolic or the Century whirl? . . . . 72 T&C SON REAL 3   3
    prodigy of Flo's midnight Frolic dolores small in the . . . . 232 IS 5 ONE 3   4
    yes the pretty birds frolic as spry as can . . . . 665 {CHAIRE} 67   5
    of eternal now to frolic in such mysteries as . . . . 743 95 POEMS 71   13
FROLICSOME
    being with numbing forests frolicsome, fleetly mystical, . . 19 T&C PUELLA MEA   91
    a Jesus sags in frolicsome wooden agony). / / . . . . 134 & SON REAL 5   16
FROM
    WORD DELETED, APPEARED 216 TIMES
FROM-SOFT
    of spreadnessed bE rich from-soft quits (now) ly Comes; . . . 342 VIVA 33   21
FROMS
    spirit with the exquisite froms and whithers of existence, . 79 T&C SON UNRE 4   5
FROND
    this fern of sunset frond on frond opening in . . . . 12 T&C SONGS 2   43
    of sunset frond on frond opening in a rare . . . . 12 T&C SONGS 2   43
FRONDS
    fern whose scrupulous enchanted fronds toward all things . . 19 T&C PUELLA MEA 111
FRONT
    conscience free, upon the front steps of her home . . . . . . 273 IS 5 TWO 8   19
    sunset i perceive in front of our lady a . . . . 279 IS 5 THREE 3   5
    I) "?" quoth the front; and there was yz . . . . 317 VIVA 9   11
FROOD
    let her comma considers frood whom he pronounces young . . . 499 50 POEMS 13   3
FROST
    Time measured is when frost to dance maketh the . . . . 207 XLI SONNETS 3   3
    who said o yes Frost Something there is which . . . . 315 VIVA 7   2
FROTH
    drink coffee covered with froth half-mud and not too . . . . 198 XLI PORTRAIT 6   32
    of Grand. a nudging froth of faces clogs Second . . . . 219 XLI SONNETS 15   10
FROWN
    noun (moreover the delicious frown of the grave great . . . . 21 T&C PUELLA MEA 212
    face on which a frown puzzles, but I know . . . . 117 & PORTRAIT 10   33
    a curse and a frown Amy Lowell got up . . . . 249 IS 5 ONE 20   2
    ill: fare well-- a frown would be a smile . . . . 798 73 POEMS 26   14
FROZEN
    with giggling hips and frozen eyes / / / . . . . 143 & SON REAL 14   14
    because swaddled with a frozen brook of pinkest vomit . . . . 258 IS 5 ONE 28   13

	PAGE	TITLE	LINE
FRUIT			
shall sprout a tree fruit that dangles therefrom the	16	T&C SONGS 6	3
trees of dreaming whose fruit is the very eatage	29	T&C ORIENTALE 3	23
stone of a musical fruit. My lips pleasantly groan	154	& SON ACTU 3	3
a fragrant sag of fruit distinctly grouped. I have	219	XLI SONNETS 15	1
recklessly juggles the jouncing fruit of eager bosoms" Wing .	341	VIVA 32	21
(for he's we) such fruit from what bough that	543	1 X 1 3	22
FRUITS			
the peddlers of smooth, fruits of eager colours of	100	& POST IMPR 11	21
FRUM			
/ buncha hardboil guys frum duh A.C. fulla hooch	332	VIVA 23	1
takin fellers' goils away frum dem" --"somebody hung uh . . .	332	VIVA 23	7
FRYING			
moment because on the frying curb the quiet face	52	T&C PORTRAIT 1	13
FTBLAC			
across! gold's rouNdly) ftblac kl (ness) y ◇	429	NO THANKS 46	4
FUCK			
do not give a fuck for luck they hump	427	NO THANKS 44	3
game and Love's a fuck who dares to call	438	NO THANKS 54	23
FUCKING			
shuffles the night with fucking eyes the great black	108	& PORTRAIT 4	26
will not kiss your fucking flag" straightway the silver . . .	339	VIVA 30	19
+FUCKING			
FOR CONTEXT, SEE	310	VIVA 2	13
+FUGACES			
FOR CONTEXT, SEE	236	IS 5 ONE 7	18
FUGITIVE			
than snow dexterous and fugitive my very frail lady	17	T&C PUELLA MEA	17
FULL			
lamb whose sheen of full unsheared fleece is mean	11	T&C SONGS 2	12
The lily of heaven full of all dreams, draws	65	T&C POST IMPR 2	6
the poor thing all full of fingers dead has	126	& SEVEN POEMS 5	13
bulge: grunting lungs pumped full of sharp thick mind	195	XLI PORTRAIT 3	4
that with his peers full oft hath quaffed the	273	IS 5 TWO 8	7
like (they got pockets full may take a littl	314	VIVA 6	10
/ / / / FULL SPEED ASTERN) m usil	325	VIVA 17	1
man (in a hurry full of an important worry)	393	NO THANKS 10	3
that the g.o.w. is full of) delete / /	411	NO THANKS 28	12
disappearance; as a mind full without fear might faithfully .	418	NO THANKS 35	7
(suddenly announce: hurl) blind full steep love / /	422	NO THANKS 39	16
they fart they fart full oft (with mind with	441	NO THANKS 56	38
scr; a; tch-ing lousy full. of. rain beggars yaw:	442	NO THANKS 57	14
the empty house is full 0 Yes of guk	499	50 POEMS 13	8
his rotten old forgotten full of why (rub-her-bub) bub? . . .	642	{CHAIRE} 44	7
(because my tears are full of eyes) appears. Because	697	95 POEMS 25	30
+FULL			
FOR CONTEXT, SEE	546	1 X 1 6	14
FULLA			
guys frum duh A.C. fulla hooch kiddin eachudder bout	332	VIVA 23	1
+FULLS			
FOR CONTEXT, SEE	646	{CHAIRE} 48	6
FULLY			
relatives well fed, and fully photographed the son of	273	IS 5 TWO 8	22
the most successful b.o. fully speaking concession at the . .	425	NO THANKS 42	15
& meet & swoop fully is are ex quisite	536	50 POEMS 48	14
+FULLY			
FOR CONTEXT, SEE	350	VIVA 41	3
FUN			
once said he) it's fun said she (may i	399	NO THANKS 16	4
and it may be fun to be fooled but	410	NO THANKS 27	13
fooled but it's more fun to be more to	410	NO THANKS 27	14
be more to be fun to be little joe	410	NO THANKS 27	14
kiddies let's all have fun / / / /	514	50 POEMS 28	14
FUNCTION			
and whose vast one function being to enter a	337	VIVA 28	2
/ / / love's function is to fabricate unknownness	446	NO THANKS 61	1
FUNDAMENTAL			
observed how in this fundamental respect the well recognised	261	IS 5 ONE 31	8

                                                    PAGE   TITLE   LINE
FUNERAL
    not to mention splendiferous funeral with tall boys in . . . 239 IS 5 ONE 10   30
    come true from a funeral eyes "big thing" / . . . . 567 1 X 1 27   21
+FUNERAL
    FOR CONTEXT, SEE . . . . 567 1 X 1 27   2
FUNEREALLY
    soul-- by no means funereally hilarious (or otherwise . . . . 802 73 POEMS 30   19
FUNNILY
    pil- lows are noise funnily swallows swallowing revolv- ingly 96 & POST IMPR 8   5
FUNNY
    tried to catch one funny hand opening the hard . . . . 53 T&C PORTRAIT 1   43
    it and the round funny hat with a big . . . . 69 T&C POST IMPR 6   42
    that's played by the Funny hand of the paralyticwhose . . . . 100 & POST IMPR 11   37
    all over, kid how, funny Do tell ....sweat, succeeds . . . . 136 & SON REAL 7   14
    / / it is funny, you will be dead . . . . 153 & SON ACTU 2   1
    nervously obscene need; it's funny. They will all be . . . . 153 & SON ACTU 2   4
    stead. It is a funny, thing. And you will . . . . 153 & SON ACTU 2   9
    ears. Ears win- k, funny stable. In the morning . . . . 171 & SON ACTU 20   8
    was my particular pal funny aint it we was . . . . 270 IS 5 TWO 5   8
FUNNYGRAPHS
    subways vacuum cleaners pianolas funnygraphs skyscrapers an . 237 IS 5 ONE 8   .   10
FUR
    clothed with a luminous fur poilu a Jesus sags . . . . 134 & SON REAL 5   13
    fuzz of your electric fur, and what-is-it comes over . . . . 175 & SON ACTU 24   11
    Muh jax awl gawn. Fur Croi saik ainnoughbudih gutnutntuhplai? 310 VIVA 2   9
    come summer puts on fur answers eats moves remembers . . . . 394 NO THANKS 11   7
FURIOUS
    whose shining mirth the furious hearts of mountains ceased .   3 T&C EPITHALAM   16
    nervous with the soft furious light, and while fire-escapes . 62 T&C PORTRAIT 10   14
    solemnly like careful and furious and beautiful elephants . . 95 & POST IMPR 7   14
    along the whirl- ingPeaceful furious street people drop, . . 100 & POST IMPR 11   39
    platzburg hoppytoad yesmam. the furious taximan p (ee) ps . . 108 & PORTRAIT 4   17
    have surely known the furious ways and the peaceful, ... 216 XLI SONNETS 12   14
    in terror of whose furious beak (as sweetly singing . . . . . 774 73 POEMS 2   5
FURIOUSLY
    roman strength who how furiously plays the hot sweet . . . . 110 & PORTRAIT 6   10
    A swiftlyenormous light --and furiously puzzling through, . . 157 & SON ACTU 6   13
FURLED
    only the flag that's furled (sestet entitled grass is . . . . 390 NO THANKS 7   8
FURNISHED
    ladies who live in furnished souls are unbeautiful and . . . 70 T&C SON REAL 1   1
    flanging shop-girls impersonally affords furnished a soft . . 197 XLI PORTRAIT 5   5
    spittoon by a candle furnished by courtesy of the . . . . . . 263 IS 5 ONE 32   49
    trees) when sunbeams loot furnished rooms through whose foul 442 NO THANKS 57   12
FURNITURE
    discrete lumps of noise.... furniture unsolemnly : bur sting 159 & SON ACTU 8   8
    with the most expensive furniture upsets a crucifix which . . 203 XLI LA GUERRE 1   12
FURTHER
    but that doesn't matter further than of old because . . . . . 289 IS 5 FOUR 6   14
    / come a little further--why be afraid-- here's the . . . . . 357 VIVA 48   1
    always (they're more much further off) further these those . 501 50 POEMS 15   16
    more much further off) further these those three disappear . 501 50 POEMS 15   16
    we'll move away still further: into now / / . . . . 579 1 X 1 39   14
FURTIVE
    her palpable solitude a furtive occult fragrance steals, a . 19 T&C PUELLA MEA   106
FURY
    struggleinweird chords of humorous, fury heapingandsqueezing 100 & POST IMPR 11   13
    goal (in calm and fury: through joy and anguish) . . . . . . 742 95 POEMS 70   7
    girl) but that mere fury soon became silence: in . . . . . . 777 73 POEMS 5   9
FUSION
    crashdis appearing con ter fusion ror collap sing thatthis . 646 {CHAIRE} 48   5
FUSS
    easily trickles a brittle fuss of fragile huge humanity..... 174 & SON ACTU 23   6
    and all the religious fuss infinity pleased our parents . . . 466 NEW POEMS 4   14
FUSSED
    grip Hips simply. well fussed flesh does surely to . . . . . 136 & SON REAL 7   12
FUTILE
    world poises a moment (futile, proud, a costly morsel . . . . 23 T&C PUELLA MEA   268

FUTILE (CONTINUED)
    fathoming jelly of vital futile huge light as she . . . . . . 159 & SON ACTU 8   2
    little strolling with the futile purr of blood; your . . . . 170 & SON ACTU 19   8
    continually whittles keen careful futile flowers (isolating . 193 XLI PORTRAIT 1   21
    through the mysterious high futile day an enormous stride . . 215 XLI SONNETS 11   14
    fake And most, the futile fooling labyrinth where noisy . . . 220 XLI SONNETS 16   11
    hate (travelling in a futile groove god knows why) . . . . . 413 NO THANKS 30   15
FUTILITY
    drab tempo of hasteful futility lived brilliantly the . . . . 103 & POST IMPR 13   11
    a more intensively brutal futility" And sit huddling dumbly . 354 VIVA 45   17
FUTURE
    confuse. Some people 's future is toothsome like (they . . . 314 VIVA 6   8
    these recent memories of future dream these perhaps who . . . 502 50 POEMS 16   10
    from beyond the future's future; and immediate like some . . 601 {CHAIRE} 3   10
    past but welcome the future (and dance your death . . . . . . 732 95 POEMS 60   10
    be more not conceivably future than mrs somethingwitz nay . . 790 73 POEMS 18   5
FUTURE'S
    pilgrim from beyond the future's future; and immediate like . 601 {CHAIRE} 3   10
FUTURES
    thirsty fists of idiot futures bash the bragging breasts, . . 151 & SON REAL 22   6
    fly, their; puLLing: bright futures against the deep sky . . 314 VIVA 6   15
    silence and completely sing? futures are obsolete; pasts are 592 1 X 1 52   11
FUTURING
    mostful to arrive each (futuring snowily which sprints for . 639 {CHAIRE} 41   11
FUZZ
    slowly stroking the, shocking fuzz of your electric fur, . . 175 & SON ACTU 24   10
FUZZILY
    wink bum-nothing and money fuzzily mouths take big wobbly . . 96 & POST IMPR 8   19
FUZZY
    my, ears know the fuZZy tune that's played by . . . . 100 & POST IMPR 11   36
    and stare the gross fuzzy-pash --dead--and the dark gold . . 153 & SON ACTU 2   6
    huge slabs of a fuzzy language with the aid . . . . 194 XLI PORTRAIT 2   25
FUZZY-PASH
    and stare the gross fuzzy-pash --dead--and the dark gold . . 153 & SON ACTU 2   6
G
    / / / / --G O N splashes-sink which . . . . 169 & SON ACTU 18   1
    opens but shuts understand G gladly forget little having . . 390 NO THANKS 7   6
    to non- entities e. g. the) whis-per it (. . . . . 391 NO THANKS 8   25
    a big dove on g w's wig so what . . . . 545 1 X 1 5   12
GAD
    your general yas buy gad) nor asleep booted & . . . . 640 {CHAIRE} 42   3
GADGETS
    Tom is Dick; while Gadgets murder squawk and add, ... 438 NO THANKS 54   11
    cold groan while the gadgets purred and the gangsters . . . . 647 {CHAIRE} 49   9
GAIETY
    tinily birds whose magical gaiety makes your beautiful name-- 631 {CHAIRE} 33   12
    shameless blithe each shameless gaiety of blossom . . . . . . 764 95 POEMS 90   38
GAILY
    dainties which do crowd gaily upon oblivion sweeter than . . 23 T&C PUELLA MEA 272
    smile it sometimes makes gaily go clean through me . . . . . 147 & SON REAL 18   7
    politely refused) set out gaily for the hyenas suppressing . 326 VIVA 18   19
    Really go whirling into gaily white thousands return by . . . 630 {CHAIRE} 32   3
GAIN
    enormous language loss or gain from blame or praise) . . . . 372 VIVA 63   12
    the sun strikes to gain a living wage-- when . . . . 620 {CHAIRE} 22   2
    saint against sinner; put gain over gladness and joy . . . . 769 95 POEMS 95   16
GAINING
    some keener makes losing, gaining --love! if a world . . . . 750 95 POEMS 78   14
GAINSBOROUGH
    and madame something by gainsborough just the playthings for 198 XLI PORTRAIT 6   12
+GAITE
    FOR CONTEXT, SEE . . . . 384 NO THANKS 2   1
GAL
    -mes but gimmie Jimmie's gal. / / / / . . . . 235 IS 5 ONE 6   24
    without why (quite minus gal or pal slightly too . . . . . . 387 NO THANKS 4   4
    alone she's not your gal jack spoke to joe . . . . 496 50 POEMS 10   3
    hurt fool wurl no gal no boy (day simbully . . . . 519 50 POEMS 33   19
    ye duskiest despot's goldenest gal did wring that dragon's . 552 1 X 1 12   16

GAL (CONTINUED)

/ fearlessandbosomy this grand: gal who liked men horses . . 792 73 POEMS 20 3

GALLANT

ship of swank (as gallant as they come) until . . . . 494 50 POEMS 8 2

GALLANTLY

stepped from his cupboard gallantly offering to demonstrate . 326 VIVA 18 11

GALLEON

twilight trembles the imagined galleon of Spring) somewhere . 156 & SON ACTU 5 9

notman (! ye galleon wilts b: e; n, ... 389 NO THANKS 6 8

GALLOP

ume the flat minute gallop of careful hugeness i . . . . . 201 XLI PORTRAIT 9 22

GAMALIEL

"is dead" beautiful Warren Gamaliel Harding "is" dead he's . 336 VIVA 27 6

GAMBOL

yes the little fish gambol as glad as can . . . . 665 {CHAIRE} 67 6

GAME

can: if Hate's a game and Love's a fuck . . . . 438 NO THANKS 54 23

spring should spoil the game, what then? all history's . . . 579 1 X 1 39 4

to beat the noblest game a man can proudly . . . . 679 95 POEMS 7 2

perspicuity (4) Only The Game Fish Swims Upstream & . . . . . 803 73 POEMS 31 17

GAMMON

and smack of back- gammon boards i was aware . . . . 194 XLI PORTRAIT 2 18

GANG

rows over percent. The gang got shot up twice, ... 149 & SON REAL 20 8

it tuh duh whole gang accrost duh table-- "fellers . . . . . 332 VIVA 23 20

+GANG

FOR CONTEXT, SEE . . . . 511 50 POEMS 25 6

GANGSTERS

gadgets purred and the gangsters dined this is a . . . . . . 647 {CHAIRE} 49 10

GAPE

/ / writhe and gape of tortured perspective rasp . . . . . . 48 T&C IMPRESS 2 2

GARBLE

other humped to tumbling garble when a minute pulled . . . . 119 & PORTRAIT 11 13

GARDEN

blush enters the becoming garden of her agony / . . . . 48 T&C IMPRESS 2 18

its life on a garden-wall, and is going to . . . . 147 & SON REAL 18 11

/ this is the garden: colours come and go, ... 208 XLI SONNETS 4 1

snow. This is the garden: pursed lips do blow . . . . 208 XLI SONNETS 4 5

slow. This is the garden. Time shall surely reap . . . . . 208 XLI SONNETS 4 9

bow, & the whole garden will bow) / / . . . . 352 VIVA 43 18

GARDEN-WALL

its life on a garden-wall, and is going to . . . . 147 & SON REAL 18 11

GARDENS

your smile into stupid gardens if this were not . . . . . . 154 & SON ACTU 3 5

moon.... Across the important gardens her body will come . . 214 XLI SONNETS 10 10

down by the Public Gardens i slammed on the . . . . 248 IS 5 ONE 19 28

are gone: along these gardens moves a wind bringing . . . . . 304 IS 5 FIVE 3 11

GARGLE

evolute my eerily oh gargle to jip hug behemoth . . . . . . 333 VIVA 24 23

GARGLED

your face smile breasts gargled by death: drowned only . . . 369 VIVA 60 9

GARGLES

the great black preacher gargles jesus the aesthete indulges 108 & PORTRAIT 4 27

almost melancholy delicacy night gargles windows. / / / . . . 168 & SON ACTU 17 19

GARMENTS

prose faces and sobbing, garments The symbol of the . . . . 59 T&C PORTRAIT 7 8

GARNISHED

prettinesses Pic- abian <> garnished of stark Picasso . . . . 180 XLI SONGS 2 5

GARRET

i live in a garret and eat aspirine) but . . . . 245 IS 5 ONE 16 5

GARTER

the Cluett Shirt Boston Garter and Spearmint Girl With . . . 230 IS 5 ONE 2 5

GARTERS

habitual dull jerk at garters) there 's no sharpest . . . . . 227 IS 5 ONE GERT 10

GAS

a fang of wincing gas showed how hair, in . . . . 73 T&C SON REAL 4 3

dead finger of thitherhithering gas. clothed with a luminous 134 & SON REAL 5 12

hair was like a gas evil to feel. Unwieldy.... . . . . 135 & SON REAL 6 6

	PAGE	TITLE	LINE

GAS (CONTINUED)

of gold. "Yep. No gas. Flynn" the words drizzle . . . . 226 IS 5 ONE MAME 8
universal joint tested my gas felt of her radiator . . . . . 248 IS 5 ONE 19 7
throw in a few gas and the oh baby . . . . 272 IS 5 TWO 7 6
solids (More fluid Than gas / / / / . . . . 311 VIVA 3 18

GASHED

with her whitehot face, gashed by hair's blue cold . . . . . 106 & PORTRAIT 2 8

GASHING

got up with a gashing yellow yawn and tottered . . . . 132 & SON REAL 3 15

GASPED

noone in particular she gasped almost loudly i'm so . . . . . 53 T&C PORTRAIT 1 46

GASPING

of this street a gasping organ is waving moth- . . . . 69 T&C POST IMPR 6 1
softly flung over the gasping shores leaves his smile . . . . 77 T&C SON UNRE 2 6
irrelevantly ferocious heels. Her gasping slippery body moved 103 & POST IMPR 13 9

GASTRONOMIC

important profane frantic inconsequential gastronomic mystery 201 XLI PORTRAIT 9 32

GATE

earth's madness) --'tis a gate unto a palace intricate . . . 21 T&C PUELLA MEA 201
was passing a certain gate, rain fell (as it . . . . 58 T&C PORTRAIT 6 3
partaken softly at whose gate smile always the chosen . . . . 58 T&C PORTRAIT 6 25
therefore wonder opens a gate; the prisoner dawn embraces . . 376 VIVA 67 10

GATES

master enter the sweet gates of my heart and . . . . 188 XLI SONGS 10 15

GATHER

(again love i slowly gather of thy languorous mouth . . . . . 37 T&C AMORES 2 18
all; stories told returned gather the Again: who danc . . . . 89 & POST IMPR 1 8
i speak sweet morons gather roun' who does not . . . . 466 NEW POEMS 4 2

GATHERED

friends would never have gathered. A collarbutton which had . 262 IS 5 ONE 32 15

GATHERING

stealing body ex- pending gathering pouring upon itself . . . 34 T&C ORIENTALE 6 92

+GATHERING

FOR CONTEXT, SEE . . . . 396 NO THANKS 13 4

GATHERINGLY

a fragile light bent gatheringly / / / / . . . . 284 IS 5 FOUR 1 18

GATHERS

round a pale world gathers comfort to her soul, ... 5 T&C EPITHALAM 82
in moan-loll where night gathers morte carved smiles . . . . 90 & POST IMPR 2 10

GAUNT

upon delicious mystery, with gaunt limbs reeking of the . . . 7 T&C EPITHALAM 158

GAVE

which the scared shepherd gave thee for his doom-- . . . . . 6 T&C EPITHALAM 152
with snowy fire) unfolding, gave the moon a nymphlike . `. . . 8 T&C OF NICOL 19
on the flower you gave me when we loved . . . . 42 T&C AMORES 6 3
hocked the diamond he gave her. Bill was put . . . . 145 & SON REAL 16 9
laughed. She came. he gave her a shove and . . . . 145 & SON REAL 16 11
my organ of imperception gave birth to which i . . . . 263 IS 5 ONE 32 33
Mat isse like ◇ gave me, A, (peach a . . . . 318 VIVA 10 9
what God unto him gave) responds, without getting annoyed . . 339 VIVA 30 17
must lay) and she gave him a desdemonial that . . . . 552 1 X 1 12 19
when to me you gave gave darling birds are . . . . 589 1 X 1 49 14
to me you gave gave darling birds are in . . . . 589 1 X 1 49 14
when the boy who gave it to you is . . . . 684 95 POEMS 12 7
suppose" "will's dad never gave me one cent in . . . . 707 95 POEMS 35 17
uprose hungary and she gave a terrible cry "no . . . . 711 95 POEMS 39 10

GAVEST

old trumpets cry; who gavest as one of those . . . . 209 XLI SONNETS 5 13

GAWD

damn ginks like dis Gawd" opening slowlyslowly them--then . . 228 IS 5 ONE MARJ 7

GAWN

Mairsee. Muh jax awl gawn. Fur Croi saik ainnoughbudih . . . 310 VIVA 2 9

GAY

his hand followed by gay untimid final flowers (which . . . . 4 T&C EPITHALAM 67
rigidly her body's doll gay exactly perishing sexual, / . . . 131 & SON REAL 2 17
about Lundun Burlin an gay Paree an some guys . . . . 237 IS 5 ONE 8 5
/ / / / "Gay" is the captivating cognomen . . . . 326 VIVA 18 1
protestations) and offering Miss Gay one (which she politely 326 VIVA 18 19

	PAGE	TITLE	LINE

GAY (CONTINUED)

feet turned abruptly Miss Gay away: "on the whole" . . . . . 326 VIVA 18 — 26
of the demotic) Miss Gay had nothing to say . . . . 326 VIVA 18 — 29
to say to Miss Gay during our return voyage, ... 326 VIVA 18 — 30
Miss (believe it or) Gay is a certain Young . . . . 327 VIVA 18 — 42
than believing) a little gay earth opening is all . . . . . 583 1 X 1 43 — 4
sake of a grave gay brave bright cry of . . . . 587 1 X 1 47 — 21
isn't no! w a gay of a brave and . . . . 606 {CHAIRE} 8 — 6
almost that phenomenon (too gay for malice and too . . . . . 607 {CHAIRE} 9 — 12
despairing to most perfect gay, nowhere to here, never . . . 649 {CHAIRE} 51 — 6
and have. Be thou gay by dark and day: . . . . 651 {CHAIRE} 53 — 5
by dark and day: gay as only truth is . . . . 651 {CHAIRE} 53 — 6
as only truth is gay (nothing's false, in earth . . . . . . 651 {CHAIRE} 53 — 6
--gracious wanderer, be thou gay / / / / . . . . 651 {CHAIRE} 53 — 12
wings: and of the gay great happening illimitably earth) . . 663 {CHAIRE} 65 — 7
and wonders why So gay gay gay and with . . . . 685 95 POEMS 13 — 9
wonders why So gay gay gay and with a . . . . 685 95 POEMS 13 — 9
why So gay gay gay and with a wisdom . . . . 685 95 POEMS 13 — 9
today) my very so gay young love why? how-- . . . . 767 95 POEMS 93 — 15
a great (and a gay and a steep) deep . . . . 769 95 POEMS 95 — 13
bird sings birds sing gay-be-gay because today's today) the . 773 73 POEMS 1 — 5
bird sings birds sing gay-be-gay because today's today) the . 773 73 POEMS 1 — 5
earth more moving (all gay fair brave tall young . . . . . 778 73 POEMS 6 — 9
smile if sorrowful were gay (today tomorrow, doubting . . . 798 73 POEMS 26 — 15
/ may i be gay like every lark who . . . . 815 73 POEMS 43 — 1
this --how anyone so gay possibly could die / . . . . 825 73 POEMS 53 — 5

+GAY

FOR CONTEXT, SEE . . . . 227 IS 5 ONE GERT — 16

GAY-BE-GAY

bird sings birds sing gay-be-gay because today's today) the . 773 73 POEMS 1 — 5

GAYER

higher than high through gayer than gayest someone's heart . 717 95 POEMS 45 — 12
there never lived a gayer he; if earth and . . . . 760 95 POEMS 87 — 6

GAYEST

high through gayer than gayest someone's heart at your . . . 717 95 POEMS 45 — 12

GAYN

where uh guy gets gayn troze uh lobstersalad / . . . . . . 227 IS 5 ONE GERT — 16

GAZE

ness of her obsolete gaze begins to. lean.... a . . . . . . 148 & SON REAL 19 — 12
occasionally three.) and i gaze on the cindercoloured little 217 XLI SONNETS 13 — 14
/ / / come, gaze with me upon this . . . . 273 IS 5 TWO 8 — 1
(until perfectly their imperfect gaze climbs this steep . . . 450 NO THANKS 65 — 7
brook (it through are gaze the unguessed whys by . . . . . 613 {CHAIRE} 15 — 2
autumnal this great lady's gaze enters a sunset "can . . . . 626 {CHAIRE} 28 — 1

GAZING

(or some times vacantly gazing through un washed panes . . 354 VIVA 45 — 8

GEARS

Right- oh and her gears being in A 1 . . . . 248 IS 5 ONE 19 — 17

GEDDUP

a girl-flops to the Geddup curb leans carefully spewing . . . 330 VIVA 21 — 11

GEDUP

sick to rightly die) "gedup" the gentscoon coos gently: . . . 387 NO THANKS 4 — 7

GEE

/ / / / gee i like to think . . . . 126 & SEVEN POEMS 5 — 1
gorry by jingo by gee by gosh by gum . . . . 268 IS 5 TWO 3 — 8

GELDED

you successfully if delicately gelded (or spaded) gentlemen . 231 IS 5 ONE 3 — 44

GEMS

with the little profound gems and the large laughing . . . . 112 & PORTRAIT 6 — 103

GENERAL

surprise bellowing through the general noise Where is Effie . 117 & PORTRAIT 10 — 9
the movies may claim general importance to me to . . . . . 238 IS 5 ONE 9 — 15
Needless To Name and General You know who a . . . . 266 IS 5 TWO 1 — 23
belonging to a retired general) sixteen years of rapid . . . 341 VIVA 32 — 10
and he kissed the general menedjerr and they smoked . . . . 552 1 X 1 12 — 28
certainly told him, and general (yes mam) sherman; and . . . 553 1 X 1 13 — 9
neither awake (there's your general yas buy gad) nor . . . . 640 {CHAIRE} 42 — 2
cannibal) there's your mineral general animal (five foot . . 640 {CHAIRE} 42 — 12

GENERAL (CONTINUED)
/ where's Jack Was General Was the hero of . . . . 642 {CHAIRE} 44   2
GENERALISSIMO
of mil itary necessity" (generalissimo e) and echo answers . 636 {CHAIRE} 38   11
GENEROSITIES
mercy of proportion with generosities beyond believing . . . 683 95 POEMS 11   2
GENEROSITY
immortal jealousy quell divine generosity, thus reason . . . 799 73 POEMS 27   33
GENEROUS
(Wistfully dead seem generous) don't All suspect each . . . 391 NO THANKS 8   3
mind made war being generous this heart could dare) . . . . . 440 NO THANKS 56   2
beautiful or deep or generous what i say is . . . . 475 NEW POEMS 13   14
mindheart one true one generous child- man -god one . . . . . 523 50 POEMS 36   41
burn by their own generous completely light, an angel; . . . 562 1 X 1 22   6
/ for prodigal read generous --for youth read age-- . . . . . 689 95 POEMS 17   1
/ / / how generous is that himself the . . . . 756 95 POEMS 84   1
+GENEROUS
FOR CONTEXT, SEE . . . . 823 73 POEMS 51   13
GENEROUSLY
which her mama had generously provided (despite courte- ous . 326 VIVA 18   17
GENIAL
wheezing bulgily world of genial plac -idity (plus, out . . . 607 {CHAIRE} 9   4
GENIE
A vast wordless nondescript genie of trunk trickled firm- . . 96 & POST IMPR 8   33
GENIUS
easily the intent of genius-- painting wholly feels ashamed . 162 & SON ACTU 11   4
rent of seem and genius please the talentgang and . . . . . . 511 50 POEMS 25   6
+GENTEELLY
FOR CONTEXT, SEE . . . . 107 & PORTRAIT 3   8
GENTILS
dead les anglais sont gentils et les americains aussi, . . . 120 & PORTRAIT 12   26
GENTLE
always sitting in her gentle window like a reminiscence . . . 58 T&C PORTRAIT 6   22
purrs you and the gentle who-horns says-does moo-woo (the . . 773 73 POEMS 1   7
GENTLEMAN
if we are a gentleman not to think of . . . . 326 VIVA 18   5
if you are a gentleman not to sense something . . . . 327 VIVA 18   45
GENTLEMEN
/ / ladies and gentlemen this little girl with . . . . 72 T&C SON REAL 3   1
delicately gelded (or spaded) gentlemen (and ladies) --pretty 231 IS 5 ONE 3   45
Next door (but four) gentlemen are trinightly entertained by 312 VIVA 4   3
flotsam and jetsam are gentlemen poeds urseappeal netsam our 492 50 POEMS 6   2
(neck and senecktie are gentlemen ppoyds even whose recktie . 492 50 POEMS 6   14
+GENTLEMEN
FOR CONTEXT, SEE . . . . 319 VIVA 11   31
FOR CONTEXT, SEE . . . . 549 1 X 1 9   3
GENTLY
untarnished! O small intimate gently primeval hands, ...   5 T&C EPITHALAM 107
peers the sleepy morning) gently draws apart her curtains, .   8 T&C OF NICOL 14
thickening dizzily is reeling gently the street and the . . . 69 T&C POST IMPR 6   24
love hurry in a gently arriving gloom and see! . . . . 93 & POST IMPR 5   11
of a collar hung gently. (spattered) by this instant . . . . 96 & POST IMPR 8   31
o'clock i find myself gently decomposing in the mouth . . . . 201 XLI PORTRAIT 9   2
whom, fiercely shy and gently brutal, the prettiest wrath . . 214 XLI SONNETS 10   7
are to believe these gently O sweetly melancholy trillers . . 230 IS 5 ONE 2   24
new silk lid bounds gently from his baldness a . . . . 259 IS 5 ONE 29   21
up through which sprouting gently, the cathedral leans its . 279 IS 5 THREE 3   3
again utterly disappear; rushing gently swiftly creeping . . 369 VIVA 60   16
twice all that so gently while we were alseep . . . . 370 VIVA 61   14
am seeing something inhaling gently a cigarette (in a . . . . 375 VIVA 66   16
moon over smellings of gently smell of deads (lovers . . . . 384 NO THANKS 2   9
"gedup" the gentscoon coos gently: tug? g (ing intently . . . 387 NO THANKS 4   9
(en ter) nize-aday (most gently herculanean my mortal) yoo . 618 {CHAIRE} 20   3
er folds (but infinite) gently up the with a . . . . 629 {CHAIRE} 31   15
nowhere) and what a gently welcoming darkestness-- now i . . 816 73 POEMS 44   4
what angry skies and gently (very whiteness: absolute peace, 839 73 POEMS 67   13
GENTS
portrait should be included, gents these (by the fire's . . . 254 IS 5 ONE 25   8

		PAGE	TITLE	LINE

GENTS (CONTINUED)

--incalculable bliss! Picture it gents: our hero, Dan who . . 254 IS 5 ONE 25 14

large immaculate unmute antibolshevistic gents (each . . . . 266 IS 5 TWO 1 9

GENTSCOON

rightly die) "gedup" the gentscoon coos gently: tug? g . . . 387 NO THANKS 4 8

GENUINE

glassy darkness holds the genuine apparition of your smile . 78 T&C SON UNRE 3 6

flesh superior to the genuine daze of unmarketable . . . . . 150 & SON REAL 21 12

delirious you know something genuine like a mark in . . . . . 407 NO THANKS 24 12

GENUINELY

normal, large, unclever. hair genuinely artificial, ... 103 & POST IMPR 13 14

GEOFFREY

miller and reve and geoffrey and all) come up . . . . 661 (CHAIRE) 63 11

+GEOMETRICAL

FOR CONTEXT, SEE . . . . 197 XLI PORTRAIT 5 19

GEOMETRIES

into different deaths Concentric geometries of transparency . 311 VIVA 3 9

GEORGE

(as an infantile phenomenon) George Washington almost . . . . 262 IS 5 ONE 32 10

+GEORGE WASHINGTON'

FOR CONTEXT, SEE . . . . 545 1 X 1 5 12

GERANIUMS

with faces like defunct geraniums) / / / / . . . . 280 IS 5 THREE 4 34

+GERMAN

FOR CONTEXT, SEE . . . . 108 & PORTRAIT 4 10

GERT

/ / / / GERT joggle i think will . . . . 227 IS 5 ONE GERT T

you a pound. Turn gert (spin! helen) the slimmer . . . . . 513 50 POEMS 27 3

GESTICULATE

the oblong sins perfectly gesticulate the accurate strenuous 43 T&C AMORES 7 36

GESTICULATES

morsel of sweet tears) gesticulates, and disappears-- of all 23 T&C PUELLA MEA 270

GESTICULATIONS

gigantic uvula with imperceptible gesticulations threatens . 201 XLI PORTRAIT 9 8

GESTURE

occult fragrance steals, a gesture of immaculate . . . . . 19 T&C PUELLA MEA 107

plus little derricks of gesture any skyscraper bulges in . . 68 T&C POST IMPR 5 4

with a small bored gesture that makes the children . . . . 69 T&C POST IMPR 6 19

most old Whose battening gesture prophecies a freeing of . . 77 T&C SON UNRE 2 12

continually with an African gesture utters a frivolous . . . 95 & POST IMPR 7 6

on a green brief gesture of twilight trembles the . . . . . . 156 & SON ACTU 5 8

price of an imaginable gesture exact warm unholy / . . . . . 162 & SON ACTU 11 16

trivi- al acrobatic edgeless gesture of existence, ... 193 XLI PORTRAIT 1 20

Don't cry --the best gesture of my brain is . . . . 290 IS 5 FOUR 7 11

carven thing provoke your gesture possibly or any painting . 291 IS 5 FOUR 8 20

miss within your least gesture the hurting skill which . . . 293 IS 5 FOUR 10 7

coins His most gradual gesture, and whittles life to . . . . 297 IS 5 FOUR 14 12

with a suddenly unsaid gesture lightly my eyes? And . . . . . 302 IS 5 FIVE 1 6

in your most frail gesture are things which enclose . . . . . 366 VIVA 57 3

young Now entirely arrives gesture past fragrance fragrant; a 456 NO THANKS 71 9

GESTURED

us; and by a gestured city stilled in the . . . . 158 & SON ACTU 7 10

+GESTURED

FOR CONTEXT, SEE . . . . 482 NEW POEMS 20 9

GESTURES

finally through altogether delicate gestures of rain a colour 92 & POST IMPR 4 16

to do a few gestures to death, the silent . . . . 225 IS 5 ONE LIZ 5

suggest that certain ideas gestures rhymes, like Gillette . . 230 IS 5 ONE 2 19

traffic this recalls hat gestures bud plumptumbling hand . . 330 VIVA 21 6

vallee and preserved goldfishian gestures) suddenly sally . . 425 NO THANKS 42 3

+GESTURES

FOR CONTEXT, SEE . . . . 96 & POST IMPR 8 17

GESTURING

walls how several smoothly gesturing stars are clever to . . 376 VIVA 67 8

GET

and This, do you get me?) will maybe dance . . . . 72 T&C SON REAL 3 12

goggle cent of it get out ears dribbles soft . . . . 96 & POST IMPR 8 20

dearie? rain wouldn't that get yer goat but we . . . . 109 & PORTRAIT 5 5

GET (CONTINUED)

you and i should get into it, if they . . . . 129 & SEVEN POEMS 7   5
O It's Nice To Get Up In, the slipshod . . . . 130 & SON REAL 1   1
the. ploop. --OOc h get: breath once, all over, ... 136 & SON REAL 7   13
a lady called death get another man with firmer . . . . 161 & SON ACTU 10   2
to bed: i will get in with it, wisely, ... 164 & SON ACTU 13   7
with ◇ (will BigMorning get away with them? j'en . . . . . . 169 & SON ACTU 18   11
His andsoforth do you get me?) according to such . . . . . . 230 IS 5 ONE 2   30
you're married and hands get red washing things and . . . . . 242 IS 5 ONE 13   15
How did the traffic get so jammed? bedad it . . . . 245 IS 5 ONE 16   12
obscene but really clean get what I mean let's . . . . 407 NO THANKS 24   8
say that's not swell (get me) babe not (understand . . . . . 475 NEW POEMS 13   23
cow is not to get yourself a stool but . . . . 500 50 POEMS 14   2
numb can an unworld get? A: number / / . . . . 791 73 POEMS 19   9
change, you're going to get one whole buck' not . . . . 800 73 POEMS 28   12

+GET

FOR CONTEXT, SEE . . . . 330 VIVA 21   11
FOR CONTEXT, SEE . . . . 387 NO THANKS 4   7
FOR CONTEXT, SEE . . . . 547 1 X 1 7   6
FOR CONTEXT, SEE . . . . 547 1 X 1 7   8
FOR CONTEXT, SEE . . . . 567 1 X 1 27   11

+GET-UP

FOR CONTEXT, SEE . . . . 259 IS 5 ONE 29   25

GETS

the poor girls that gets up god knows when . . . . 109 & PORTRAIT 5   15
nite; where uh guy gets gayn troze uh lobstersalad . . . . . 227 IS 5 ONE GERT   16
she it or everybody gets a bellyful without lifting . . . . . 475 NEW POEMS 13   7

GETTING

i think of you, getting mandolin-clink mixed with your . . . 169 & SON ACTU 18   5
shrapnel or my feet getting dim freezing or up . . . . 272 IS 5 TWO 7   8
him gave) responds, without getting annoyed "I will not . . . 339 VIVA 30   18

GETUP

spats a strikingly succulent getup but we knew a . . . . . . 259 IS 5 ONE 29   25

GHASTLIER

autumn do complain earth's ghastlier trees by whom Time . . . 207 XLI SONNETS 3   2

GHASTLY

in the dust the ghastly warriors amber with lust . . . . . . 34 T&C ORIENTALE 6   97

GHIBELLINE

up rose pelf and ghibelline and guelph and ladios . . . . . . 552 1 X 1 12   12

GHOST

lay like some gigantic ghost-flower born of night blossoming   8 T&C OF NICOL   2
in to one exactly-mutilated ghost of a chair, a; . . . . . . 96 & POST IMPR 8   34
balloons move (as her ghost lurks, a Beau Brummell . . . . . 227 IS 5 ONE GERT   4
Kirkland Street the infantile ghost of Professor Royce rolls 232 IS 5 ONE 3   12
morning he is a ghost whom assault these whispering . . . . . 299 IS 5 FOUR 16   11
a cigarette between his ghost-lips gradually) remembering . . 300 IS 5 FOUR 17   20
but three dwells; a (ghost) Who screams Faintly always . . . 312 VIVA 4   7
like) dead) Whoshout (Ghost) atOne (voiceless) O ther . . . 347 VIVA 38   22
will to shave that Ghost is dead (whom noone . . . . 394 NO THANKS 11   5
struck how thin a ghost so deep and he . . . . 414 NO THANKS 31   8
poet feast) meanwhile this ghost goes under, his drowned . . 418 NO THANKS 35   12
now, s tI r ghost ? s tirf lic; . . . . 423 NO THANKS 40   26
surely dream perhaps this ghost) humbly and whom for . . . . 441 NO THANKS 56   50
clownlike that this quickly ghost scribbling from there to . 504 50 POEMS 18   8
cage: then with a ghost 's rainfaint windthin voice-which-is 697 95 POEMS 25   10
see (while a stuttering ghost that maybe had shaved . . . . . 709 95 POEMS 37   7
also earth's --"dying" the ghost of you whispers "is . . . . 808 73 POEMS 36   14
"is very pleasant" my ghost to / / / . . . . 808 73 POEMS 36   15
of cold --open this ghost with millionary knives of . . . . . 839 73 POEMS 67   11

GHOST-FLOWER

lay like some gigantic ghost-flower born of night blossoming   8 T&C OF NICOL   2

GHOST-LIPS

a cigarette between his ghost-lips gradually) remembering . . 300 IS 5 FOUR 17   20

GHOSTLIKE

/ both eaching come ghostlike (inch) wraithish (by inch) . . 681 95 POEMS 9   1

GHOSTLY

prophecies a freeing of ghostly chaos in this dangerous . . . 77 T&C SON UNRE 2   13
stillness (seized among what ghostly nevers of again) silent 432 NO THANKS 49   11

		PAGE	TITLE	LINE

GHOSTLY (CONTINUED)

    woke dreamers to their ghostly roots and should some   . . . . 520 50 POEMS 34   12

    isn't's own isn't go ghostly they doubting can turn . . . . . 580 1 X 1 40   7

    leaving just this strolling ghostly doll of an almost . . . . 720 95 POEMS 48   8

GHOSTS

    transparent company of quivering ghosts-of-love which . . . .   6 T&C EPITHALAM   143

    chaste on earth we ghosts: hark to the sheer . . . .   9 T&C SONGS 1   22

    soon verbal mist-flowers close ghosts on prowl gorge sly . . 90 & POST IMPR 2   15

    DygurdY with thequeer hopping ghosts of child- ren. my, . . . 100 & POST IMPR 11   35

    not speak and are ghosts or huddled in the . . . . 340 VIVA 31   6

    from the window, behold ghosts, a man hugging a . . . . 375 VIVA 66   6

    doom rush (which all ghosts of life became) and . . . . 454 NO THANKS 69   10

    the they leaf of ghosts some few creep there . . . . 541 1 X 1 1   9

    greenly air and to ghosts go drift slippery hands . . . . . . 633 (CHAIRE) 35   4

    clinging with a wraith) ghosts drowning in supreme thunder? . 639 (CHAIRE) 41   2

+GHOSTS

    FOR CONTEXT, SEE . . . . 628 (CHAIRE) 30   8

GHOSTS-OF-LOVE

    transparent company of quivering ghosts-of-love which . . . .   6 T&C EPITHALAM   143

GHOSTSOUL

    ly) tuck. s its (ghostsoul sheshape) elf into leasting . . . 495 50 POEMS 9   12

GHOSTTHINGS

    / hist whist little ghostthings tip-toe twinkle-toe little . 25 T&C CHANSONS 2   2

GIDDY

    empty arms upon the giddy hills to dream of . . . . 36 T&C AMORES 1   7

GIFT

    loaned; we (by a gift called dying born) must . . . . 556 1 X 1 16   12

    (over the under the gift of the earth of . . . . 661 (CHAIRE) 63   8

    a blind blissfully seething gift wandering deeply through . . 754 95 POEMS 82   4

    (my beautiful friend) the gift to live is without . . . . . 776 73 POEMS 4   19

    but to live's a gift) the teachable imposture of . . . . . . 807 73 POEMS 35   2

GIFTED

    impeccable girls in raiment laughter-gifted. / / / / . . . . 85 T&C SON ACTU 4   15

    face thy voice scattering perfume-gifted wings suddenly . . . 187 XLI SONGS 9   13

    country of your eyes, gifted with green twilight) / . . . . . 291 IS 5 FOUR 8   27

    babe: around him, eyes --gifted with every keener appetite . 714 95 POEMS 42   4

    It's we) humble one (gifted with illimitable joy) bird . . . 783 73 POEMS 11   1

    guessed?" "we shall" quoth gifted she: and played the . . . . 807 73 POEMS 35   14

GIFTS

    world's texture with drifted gifts of featheriest slenderness 299 IS 5 FOUR 16   5

GIGANTIC

    castle lay like some gigantic ghost-flower born of night . .   8 T&C OF NICOL   2

    away from the gripping gigantic muscles of Cezanne's logic, . 180 XLI SONGS 2   14

    cheeks enclose me. a gigantic uvula with imperceptible . . . 201 XLI PORTRAIT 9   8

GIGGLING

    she totters, slouches, with giggling hips and frozen eyes . . 143 & SON REAL 14   14

    ear (i'm tho thcared giggling lithped now we muthn't . . . . 316 VIVA 8   7

GIGGLY

    pimply cavaliers and gumchewing giggly girls and not content   61 T&C PORTRAIT 9   7

GILLETTE

    ideas gestures rhymes, like Gillette Razor Blades having been 230 IS 5 ONE 2   20

GILT

    Love's a coach with gilt hopeless wheels mired where . . . . 131 & SON REAL 2   15

GILTY

    friend hangs at yon gilty ceiling per both pale . . . . 546 1 X 1 6   5

GIMME

    leaps from the lungs "gimme uh swell fite like . . . . 227 IS 5 ONE GERT   14

    but as fer i gimme de good ole daze.... . . . . 237 IS 5 ONE 8   12

    likes a certain party gimme the he-man's solid bliss . . . . 247 IS 5 ONE 18   5

GIMMIE

    your Salo -mes but gimmie Jimmie's gal. / / . . . . 235 IS 5 ONE 6   24

+GINGER ALE

    FOR CONTEXT, SEE . . . . 233 IS 5 ONE 4   6

GINGERBREAD

    brains are made of gingerbread when the judgment day . . . . 117 & PORTRAIT 10   2

    brains are made of gingerbread / / / / . . . . 118 & PORTRAIT 10   44

GINKS

    (blushing slightly) --"O damn ginks like dis Gawd" opening . 228 IS 5 ONE MARJ   7

GIRD
    death shall him vastly gird, a coward waiting clumsily . . . 360 VIVA 51   5
+GIRDED
    FOR CONTEXT, SEE . . . .   41 T&C AMORES 5   31
GIRL
    miraculous May! O shining girl of time untarnished! O . . . .   5 T&C EPITHALAM   105
    a day) for which girl art thou flowers bringing? . . . . . .   13 T&C SONGS 3   14
    the Humorous moon dear girl How i was crazy . . . .   44 T&C AMORES 8   18
    dark portals of hurt girl eyes sincere with wonder . . . . .   54 T&C PORTRAIT 2   4
    and gentlemen this little girl with the good teeth . . . . .   72 T&C SON REAL 3   1
    frivolous intense half of Girl which (like some floating . .   95 & POST IMPR 7   8
    wistful in a glib girl i consider her as . . . . 131 & SON REAL 2   2
    poetic carcass of a girl / / / / . . . . 139 & SON REAL 10   14
    on unsuspicious legs of girl. his left hand quarried . . . . 148 & SON REAL 19   3
    with a big toothless girl in Yonkers. Dick Mid's . . . . . . 149 & SON REAL 20   12
    ecstasy means, like a girl lasciviously frail, peace . . . . 168 & SON ACTU 17   10
    his eyes as a girl closes her left hand . . . . 170 & SON ACTU 19   13
    was thinking why the girl-and-bird of you move.... moves.... 174 & SON ACTU 23   12
    as. One opaque big girl jiggles thickly hips to . . . . . . 220 XLI SONNETS 16   15
    Boston Garter and Spearmint Girl With The Wrigley Eyes . . . 230 IS 5 ONE 2   6
    carloads before publication the girl who goes wrong you . . . 245 IS 5 ONE 16   10
    match youse a pretty girl who naked is is . . . . 247 IS 5 ONE 18   7
    high minded pure young girl much kissed, by loving . . . . . 273 IS 5 TWO 8   20
    below me a little girl in white spins, tumbles; . . . . . . 281 IS 5 THREE 5   3
    nowhere and a little girl in white is tumbling . . . . . . 281 IS 5 THREE 5   13
    flatfooting with Wushyuhname a girl-flops to the Geddup curb 330 VIVA 21   11
    hard a hard a girl a girl) sing -ing . . . . 385 NO THANKS 2   51
    hard a girl a girl) sing -ing ing (ing . . . . 385 NO THANKS 2   51
    with! notgirl'swith? dumb (thewith girl) ness (ish The . . . 388 NO THANKS 5   25
    thought are. more (Than girl 's tears boy Dream's) . . . . . 447 NO THANKS 62   10
    (did you kiss a girl with nipples like pink . . . . 498 50 POEMS 12   18
    a finding whom of girl) dolls clutching their dolls . . . . . 565 1 X 1 25   4
    rare --the livingest givingest girl on this whirlingest . . . 590 1 X 1 50   6
    underlined this is a girl who died in her . . . . 647 (CHAIRE) 49   6
    with none) boy after girl each brings a world . . . . 716 95 POEMS 44   10
    here pasture ends-- this girl and boy who're littler . . . . 757 95 POEMS 85   2
    a frightened boy and girl) but that mere fury . . . . 777 73 POEMS 5   8
+GIRL
    FOR CONTEXT, SEE . . . . 235 IS 5 ONE 6   1
    FOR CONTEXT, SEE . . . . 235 IS 5 ONE 6   2
    FOR CONTEXT, SEE . . . . 235 IS 5 ONE 6   3
    FOR CONTEXT, SEE . . . . 235 IS 5 ONE 6   5
    FOR CONTEXT, SEE . . . . 235 IS 5 ONE 6   13
    FOR CONTEXT, SEE . . . . 235 IS 5 ONE 6   14
    FOR CONTEXT, SEE . . . . 235 IS 5 ONE 6   15
    FOR CONTEXT, SEE . . . . 235 IS 5 ONE 6   17
GIRL-AND-BIRD
    was thinking why the girl-and-bird of you move.... moves.... 174 & SON ACTU 23   12
GIRL-FLOPS
    flatfooting with Wushyuhname a girl-flops to the Geddup curb 330 VIVA 21   11
GIRL'S
    / / / my girl's tall with hard long . . . . 147 & SON REAL 18   1
    impatience to an edge--my girl's tall and taut, with . . . . 147 & SON REAL 18   9
+GIRL'S
    FOR CONTEXT, SEE . . . . 388 NO THANKS 5   24
    FOR CONTEXT, SEE . . . . 447 NO THANKS 62   10
GIRLBOYS
    living will yourself become. Girlboys may nothing more than . 484 NEW POEMS 22   5
GIRLEST
    twilight they beyond near) girlest she slender is cradling . 518 50 POEMS 32   6
GIRLGOLD
    is blue (sleep! new girlgold / / / / . . . . 503 50 POEMS 17   12
GIRLHOOD
    as i recollect her girlhood was by the kindly . . . .   57 T&C PORTRAIT 5   30
GIRLISH
    hands joked to a girlish whore with busy rhythmic . . . . . .   56 T&C PORTRAIT 4   13
+GIRLISH
    FOR CONTEXT, SEE . . . . 104 & POST IMPR 14   11

	PAGE	TITLE	LINE
+GIRLISH (CONTINUED)			
FOR CONTEXT, SEE	388	NO THANKS 5	25
GIRLLIKE			
what manshaped whimpered how girllike laughtering blocks when	371	VIVA 62	4
GIRLS			
little peasants for their girls / / / /	30	T&C ORIENTALE 4	42
night utter ripe unspeaking girls. / / / /	45	T&C LA GUERRE 1	15
cavaliers and gumchewing giggly girls and not content Spring,	61	T&C PORTRAIT 9	8
ladies dangerously respire: impeccable girls in raiment . . .	85	T&C SON ACTU 4	15
s,, stomachs of little, girls smoothanduseless i, like, best,	101	& POST IMPR 11	76
stomachs, of the young (girls silky and lewd) like	101	& POST IMPR 11	77
star taps taps. "ready girls". the unspontaneous streets make	108	& PORTRAIT 4	4
for awl the poor girls that gets up god	109	& PORTRAIT 5	14
ships and like young girls and like butterflies and	111	& PORTRAIT 6	65
death most believes, perpetual girls marching to love whose .	138	& SON REAL 9	11
hips with boys and girls / / / /	148	& SON REAL 19	14
mastery with chasteness of sea-girls Will i complete the . .	189	XLI SONGS 11	10
inevitable tiredness of flanging shop-girls impersonally . .	197	XLI PORTRAIT 5	4
pass through the look girls in the style of	257	IS 5 ONE 27	33
refined they go with girls who buck and bite	427	NO THANKS 44	2
refined they come with girls who bite and buck	427	NO THANKS 44	9
grow (and boys and girls have whispered thus and	451	NO THANKS 66	13
thus and so) and girls with boys to bed	451	NO THANKS 66	15
the thumb (it's whirl, girls) round and round early	513	50 POEMS 27	8
be missed (it's in, girls) yours is mine either	513	50 POEMS 27	26
jake hates all the girls (the shy ones, the	619	(CHAIRE) 21	2
paul scorns all the girls (the bright ones, the	619	(CHAIRE) 21	9
gus loves all the girls (the warped ones, the	619	(CHAIRE) 21	16
mike likes all the girls (the fat ones, the	619	(CHAIRE) 21	22
heroes (for god likes girls and tomorrow and the	732	95 POEMS 60	15
+GIRLS			
FOR CONTEXT, SEE	332	VIVA 23	6
FOR CONTEXT, SEE	484	NEW POEMS 22	5
GIRTH			
goes under, his drowned girth are mountains; and beyond . . .	418	NO THANKS 35	12
GIT			
/ / / / ci-git 1 Foetus (unborn to	394	NO THANKS 11	1
abuses it you can git anything you like out	567	1 X 1 27	11
GIVE			
this largeness begins to give you, the dance all	127	& SEVEN POEMS 5	36
would kid Jimmie to give them a kiss but	149	& SON REAL 20	10
/ / twentyseven bums give a prostitute the once	150	& SON REAL 21	1
little arms and i'll give them all to you	192	XLI CHANSONS 2	18
/ / Picasso you give us Things which bulge:	195	XLI PORTRAIT 3	2
teeth the vertical grin give me the Square in	220	XLI SONNETS 16	9
touched the accelerator and give her the juice, good	248	IS 5 ONE 19	22
are leap, which, anyway give rapid lapfulls of idiotic . . .	251	IS 5 ONE 22	22
philosophy does this rose give a damn... bring on	264	IS 5 ONE 33	20
death a marriage) you give me courage so that	293	IS 5 FOUR 10	18
you go away i give roses who will advise	294	IS 5 FOUR 11	2
body will (can you give a) listen to who	314	VIVA 6	22
persons the snow doesn't give a soft white damn	328	VIVA 19	22
make than have and give than lend --being through	394	NO THANKS 11	11
some edgeless star could give that anguish room; but	414	NO THANKS 31	9
he have anything would give a little more than	420	NO THANKS 37	2
bite they do not give a fuck for luck	427	NO THANKS 44	3
behind they do not give a shit for wit	427	NO THANKS 44	7
this they do not give a fart for art	427	NO THANKS 44	15
could dare freely to give as gives a friend	440	NO THANKS 56	13
hips whirling climb to GIVE (yoursmine mineyours yoursmine !	445	NO THANKS 60	28
never with most memory) give entirely each Forever its . . .	453	NO THANKS 68	11
/ reason let others give and realness bring-- ask	454	NO THANKS 69	1
three cheers for labor give all things to enni	492	50 POEMS 6	11
by my throat me give it him good a	496	50 POEMS 10	11
is wiser for worse. Give liz (take! tommy) we	513	50 POEMS 27	11
am through haves of give, singing each morning out	520	50 POEMS 34	2
god and fiend? i give you man extracted hate	527	50 POEMS 39	8
own fingers with and give him nothing (if he	531	50 POEMS 43	12

	PAGE	TITLE	LINE

GIVE (CONTINUED)

/ / / enters give whose lost is his	533	50 POEMS 45	1
sale? forever is to give and on forever's very	538	50 POEMS 50	11
fool) if living's to give so breathing's to steal--	543	1 X 1 3	15
giving as to keeping's give; as yes is to	574	1 X 1 34	3
open your heart: i'll give you a treasure of	586	1 X 1 46	2
/ trees were in (give give) bud when to	589	1 X 1 49	2
trees were in (give give) bud when to me	589	1 X 1 49	3
thy yes: love; and give because the why --gracious	651	{CHAIRE} 53	11
of winter his silence) give me a trillionth part	678	95 POEMS 6	13
of the boys" "he'll give me another if i	684	95 POEMS 12	9
fear to whom i give this little parasol, so	762	95 POEMS 89	7
sky your kingbird doesn't give a damn-- his royal	774	73 POEMS 2	2
crow your kingbird doesn't give a damn for murderers	774	73 POEMS 2	9
somebody's crazy enough to give me a daisy /	802	73 POEMS 30	33
dream called time: and give herself into the mercy	811	73 POEMS 39	10
may name, three i'll give you sweet joys for	837	73 POEMS 65	3
eager this "i will give you five hopes for	837	73 POEMS 65	8
just one dying, i'll give you" silently cries the	837	73 POEMS 65	15

+GIVE

FOR CONTEXT, SEE	227	IS 5 ONE GERT	14
FOR CONTEXT, SEE	235	IS 5 ONE 6	24
FOR CONTEXT, SEE	237	IS 5 ONE 8	12
FOR CONTEXT, SEE	247	IS 5 ONE 18	5
FOR CONTEXT, SEE	310	VIVA 2	3
FOR CONTEXT, SEE	310	VIVA 2	12
FOR CONTEXT, SEE	330	VIVA 21	7
FOR CONTEXT, SEE	445	NO THANKS 60	26

GIVEHURLING

togethering our wholly lives Givehurling with your my most .	371	VIVA 62	16

GIVEN

and never sold and couldn't-be-given-away because	101	& POST IMPR 11	67
watertank but somebody who'd given my Uncle Sol a	239	IS 5 ONE 10	27
hairy Jacqueline who is given a mouse to hold	279	IS 5 THREE 3	19
people socalled were not given hearts how should they	510	50 POEMS 24	1
truth--beware of heartless them (given the scalpel, they . .	556	1 X 1 16	7
because to find) may, given perfect mercy, live a	735	95 POEMS 63	3
for dying's huge because) given much mercy more than	735	95 POEMS 63	11
loaned: whereas night is given (night and death and	816	73 POEMS 44	8
and the rain are given; and given is how	816	73 POEMS 44	9
rain are given; and given is how beautifully snow)	816	73 POEMS 44	9

GIVERS

pa-nt stab are (slopped givers of not) bang spurting	388	NO THANKS 5	11

GIVES

firmly stirred) my mirror gives me, on this afternoon; . . .	360	VIVA 51	3
freely to give as gives a friend not those	440	NO THANKS 56	14
which of a wind gives the truth to summer's	560	1 X 1 20	2
than all of time) gives you skilful his flame	575	1 X 1 35	23
wonderful friend dominic depaola gives me a most tremendous .	680	95 POEMS 8	25
strange fellow; more he gives than takes (and he	750	95 POEMS 78	11

GIVEST

like not what thou givest me to him let	212	XLI SONNETS 8	9

GIVESWOOP

asquirm the dip & giveswoop & swoon & ingly	445	NO THANKS 60	26

GIVING

hinging victim against the giving ropes amid screams of . . .	259	IS 5 ONE 29	17
(between dawn and twilight) giving your eyes, present me . .	285	IS 5 FOUR 2	14
alive like some dream giving more than all life's	418	NO THANKS 35	3
that's bought and sold giving to steal and cruel	521	50 POEMS 34	57
therefore limitless) love's to giving as to keeping's give; .	574	1 X 1 34	3
demanding that lending be giving; it's no good pretending . .	625	{CHAIRE} 27	3
having and having is giving-- but keeping is doting	665	{CHAIRE} 67	9
found and having is giving and giving is living--	665	{CHAIRE} 67	16
having is giving and giving is living-- but keeping	665	{CHAIRE} 67	16
(or whatever kills) a giving who (no taking simply	735	95 POEMS 63	6
proud youngest bud testified "giving (and giving only) is . .	763	95 POEMS 90	17
bud testified "giving (and giving only) is living" worlds . .	763	95 POEMS 90	17

291

GIVINGEST
 most rare --the livingest givingest girl on this whirlingest 590 1 X 1 50 5
GLAD
 frail, a flower so glad) as trembling used to . . . . 18 T&C PUELLA MEA 52
 and to make them glad, when the world was . . . . 20 T&C PUELLA MEA 130
 and to make them glad ladies with lithe eyes . . . . 22 T&C PUELLA MEA 224
 O soul, but straight glad feet fearruining and glorygirded . 41 T&C AMORES 5 30
 i am so very glad that the soul inside . . . . 61 T&C PORTRAIT 9 27
 you are My how glad he winked and hope . . . . 126 & SEVEN POEMS 5 17
 inspired cleat of her glad leg pulled into a . . . . 135 & SON REAL 6 4
 comedy kid.... Fran Mag Glad Dorothy / / / . . . . 138 & SON REAL 9 17
 white dream in the glad flesh of my fear: . . . . 139 & SON REAL 10 7
 do it although the glad monosyllable jounce possibly can . . 227 IS 5 ONE GERT 1
 i sing of Olaf glad and big whose warmest . . . . 339 VIVA 30 1
 blame things under praise glad things or free truly . . . . 441 NO THANKS 56 61
 upfall and Am the glad deep the living from . . . . 449 NO THANKS 64 7
 above all things be glad and young. For if . . . . 484 NEW POEMS 22 1
 and if you are glad whatever's living will yourself . . . . . 484 NEW POEMS 22 3
 in your barn be glad; nobody ever earns anything, ... 514 50 POEMS 28 7
 ar (pleez make me glad) dis dumdam slamslum slopp . . . . . . 519 50 POEMS 33 7
 spoke this earth so glad and big even a . . . . 526 50 POEMS 38 2
 / i am so glad and very merely my . . . . 537 50 POEMS 49 1
 yelps one shi ly glad old unman who is . . . . 602 {CHAIRE} 4 6
 little fish gambol as glad as can be (yes . . . . 665 {CHAIRE} 67 6
 (by if) timelessly foundlost glad (children of) dirtpoor . . 681 95 POEMS 9 11
 deathful flesh: are lovers glad? only their smallest joy's . 768 95 POEMS 94 7
 of hello and goodbye: glad sorry or both (big . . . . 776 73 POEMS 4 39
GLADLY
 new curve of children gladly cricks where a hurdy-gurdy . . . 219 XLI SONNETS 15 7
 (hic) hero dead that gladly (sic) in far lands . . . . . . 266 IS 5 TWO 1 13
 i have never travelled, gladly beyond any experience, your . 366 VIVA 57 1
 to make an earth gladly seem firm for you: . . . . 372 VIVA 63 8
 but shuts understand G gladly forget little having less . . . 390 NO THANKS 7 6
 human curiosity we'll spend (gladly, as lovers must) immortal 675 95 POEMS 3 13
GLADNESS
 bit of tobacco and gladness plus little derricks of . . . . . 68 T&C POST IMPR 5 3
 between there and here gladness flays hideously hills. It . . 158 & SON ACTU 7 2
 i met that hideous gladness, per the face --pinxit, ... 158 & SON ACTU 7 5
 into the edgeless gloaming gladness hammers incessant putrid 202 XLI PORTRAIT 9 38
 my grief or my gladness around me surges . . . . 749 95 POEMS 77 8
 wise and each ignorant gladness--unteaches what despair . . . 764 95 POEMS 90 41
 sinner; put gain over gladness and joy under care-- . . . . . 769 95 POEMS 95 16
GLANCE
 lady will) --at her glance my spirit shies rearing . . . . . 18 T&C PUELLA MEA 45
 (of whose shy delicious glance things which never more . . . 22 T&C PUELLA MEA 251
 failed to snare the glance too shy--if through my . . . . . . 306 IS 5 FIVE 5 6
 his gradual acute lusting glance an alert clumsily . . . . . 374 VIVA 65 5
 where turned at his glance to shining here; that . . . . . . 520 50 POEMS 34 6
+GLANCE
 FOR CONTEXT, SEE . . . . 359 VIVA 50 16
GLAND
 a woman but a gland is only a gland) . . . . 466 NEW POEMS 4 28
 gland is only a gland) / / / / . . . . 466 NEW POEMS 4 28
+GLANDS
 FOR CONTEXT, SEE . . . . 245 IS 5 ONE 16 14
GLARING
 with circular frightened faces glaring at the shabby tiny . . 69 T&C POST IMPR 6 7
GLASS
 tower (which as a glass turned light to flame . . . . 8 T&C OF NICOL 17
 and tottered to a glass bumping things. she picked . . . . . 132 & SON REAL 3 16
 And drank rapidly a glass of water / / . . . . 268 IS 5 TWO 3 14
 dome of many coloured glass, and see his mother's . . . . . . 273 IS 5 TWO 8 2
 and Here Comes a glass box which the exhumed . . . . 280 IS 5 THREE 4 2
 and hErE cOmEs a glass box: surrounded by priests . . . . . . 280 IS 5 THREE 4 9
 It here comes A Glass Box and incense with . . . . 280 IS 5 THREE 4 21
 this window, touching the glass boxes one by one . . . . . . 282 IS 5 THREE 6 25
 within which "ladies&gentlemen" --under glass-- are: asking. 319 VIVA 11 33
 safely ensconced in thick glass you try if we . . . . 326 VIVA 18 4

		PAGE	TITLE	LINE

GLASS (CONTINUED)

safely ensconced in thick glass / / / / . . . . 327 VIVA 18   46

huddled behind dir ty glass mind muddled and cuddled . . . . 354 VIVA 45   6

was into a dirtied glass) Pills for Ills (a . . . . 359 VIVA 50   8

GLASSWORKS

incline thine ear you glassworks of Murano; pause elevator . 256 IS 5 ONE 27   3

GLASSY

at moments when the glassy darkness holds the genuine . . . . 78 T&C SON UNRE 3   5

GLAZED

/ / / a) glazed mind layed in a . . . . 387 NO THANKS 4   1

GLEAM

how much themselves shall gleam, in the poised radiance . . . 81 T&C SON UNRE 6   7

GLIB

becoming wistful in a glib girl i consider her . . . . . . 131 & SON REAL 2   1

f ind) nd ArE GLIB SCARCELYEST AMONGS FLOWERING / . . . . . . 421 NO THANKS 38   31

GLIDE

women-coloured twilight i smilingly glide. I into the big . . 66 T&C POST IMPR 3   10

k ingly ele vator glide pinn) pu (. . . . . 309 VIVA 1   24

stickingly un stride after glide massacre monday did more) . 522 50 POEMS 35   4

to eyes) drift bells glide seethe glow (undering proudly . . 841 73 POEMS 69   22

GLIDED

from the castle wall glided, a drop of radiance, ... 8 T&C OF NICOL   24

GLIDING

spring) ropes of silver gliding from sunny thunder into . . . 58 T&C PORTRAIT 6   7

GLIMPSE

hear such singing (or glimpse such sunlight as will . . . . . 717 95 POEMS 45   10

GLIMPSED

/ possibly thrice we glimpsed-- more likely twice that . . . 607 (CHAIRE) 9   1

the death of thing glimpsed (and on every side . . . . . . 634 (CHAIRE) 36   2

GLINTS

tures stickily point made glints squinting who's a wink . . . 96 & POST IMPR 8   18

+GLITTER

FOR CONTEXT, SEE . . . . 444 NO THANKS 59   22

GLOAM

coming out in the gloam ing together are standing . . . . . 600 (CHAIRE) 2   4

GLOAMING

deep into the edgeless gloaming gladness hammers incessant . 202 XLI PORTRAIT 9   37

+GLOAMING

FOR CONTEXT, SEE . . . . 600 (CHAIRE) 2   4

GLOAT

courseless waters are a gloat of silver; o'er whose . . . . . 9 T&C SONGS 1   3

GLOATS

/ / / god gloats upon Her stunning flesh. . . . . 77 T&C SON UNRE 2   1

rally demannd canned saounds) gloats upon the possession of . 331 VIVA 22   5

GLOBULAR

was a music sinuous globular slippery intense witty huge . . 110 & PORTRAIT 6   23

GLOOM

gray flesh in the gloom! and still to be . . . . 9 T&C SONGS 1   23

the cool writhe of gloom truly which syncopate some . . . . . 19 T&C PUELLA MEA   85

bowl crackles upon the gloom arise purple pencils fluent . . 31 T&C ORIENTALE 5   4

in a gently arriving gloom and see! (the new . . . . 93 & POST IMPR 5   12

and that stumbling in gloom, bad laughters, smiles unbold) . 142 & SON REAL 13   8

man -ufactured harmlessly accurate gloom "I think he might . 464 NEW POEMS 2   20

+GLOOM

FOR CONTEXT, SEE . . . . 251 IS 5 ONE 22   18

GLOOMINESS

humble moving through the gloominess of (try to imagine) . . 324 VIVA 16   13

GLOOMS

cool flutes within wide glooms, and sing (of harps . . . . . 208 XLI SONNETS 4   6

GLORIED

a rare Slowness of gloried air... The flute of . . . . . . 12 T&C SONGS 2   45

GLORIES

a row between slow glories fleetly go.) Upon a . . . . . . 20 T&C PUELLA MEA 144

head-- by on whom glories whisperingly impinge (god's pretty 85 T&C SON ACTU 4   5

for whom the old glories move, the old trumpets . . . . . . 209 XLI SONNETS 5   12

were summer's beside their glories downward if they'll or . . 573 1 X 1 33   6

than timelessly alive all glories we've agreed with nothing . 741 95 POEMS 69   7

of purest poem and glories of sheerest glory a . . . . 748 95 POEMS 76   7

		PAGE	TITLE	LINE

GLORIOUS

boughs let fall their glorious snows, and the unearthly . . .   8 T&C OF NICOL   6

thy sons acclaim your glorious name by gorry by . . . . 268 IS 5 TWO 3   7

GLORY

/ / / the glory is fallen out of . . . .   41 T&C AMORES 5   1

a click of deciding glory inflicted to the negative . . . . . 197 XLI PORTRAIT 5   16

you please) all the glory that or which was . . . . 233 IS 5 ONE 4   11

eyes have seen the glory of the coming of . . . . 256 IS 5 ONE 27   11

guest a snowingly enfolding glory is all angry common . . . . 559 1 X 1 19   2

a once of eager glory, no more miracle may . . . . 601 {CHAIRE} 3   5

living the dying of glory / / / / . . . . 627 {CHAIRE} 29   16

es t sidewalk blossoming glory / / / / . . . . 668 {CHAIRE} 70   25

who've made her, outglory glory the little while they . . . . 742 95 POEMS 70   9

and glories of sheerest glory a little more always . . . . . 748 95 POEMS 76   7

of unceasing birth and glory and death and resurrection: . . 749 95 POEMS 77   10

the moon in her glory says Who the busy . . . . 801 73 POEMS 29   11

may by imperishable your glory escorted through infinite . . 811 73 POEMS 39   3

+GLORY

FOR CONTEXT, SEE . . . . 632 {CHAIRE} 34   12

FOR CONTEXT, SEE . . . . 742 95 POEMS 70   9

GLORYGIRDED

glad feet fearruining and glorygirded faces lead us into . .   41 T&C AMORES 5   31

GLORYING

prodigiously alive most mercifully glorying keen star whom . 808 73 POEMS 36   7

GLOSS

gathers morte carved smiles cloud-gloss is at moon-cease soon   90 & POST IMPR 2   12

GLOVE

impression in an empty glove, a soon forgotten tune, ... 360 VIVA 51   8

collapsing? any was a glove but i'm and you . . . . 538 50 POEMS 50   9

GLOVED

like but quite absurd gloved fist on hip & . . . . 640 {CHAIRE} 42   9

GLOVES

tall boys in black gloves and flowers and everything . . . . 239 IS 5 ONE 10   31

GLOW

(by yon sunset's wintry glow revealed) this tall strong . . . 254 IS 5 ONE 25   1

(by the fire's ruddy glow united) not less than . . . . 254 IS 5 ONE 25   9

his penguinsoul in the glow of a joy which . . . . 631 {CHAIRE} 33   8

locked in gOLd after- gLOw are t ReMbLiN g . . . . 838 73 POEMS 66   8

drift bells glide seethe glow (undering proudly humbly . . . 841 73 POEMS 69   24

+GLOW

FOR CONTEXT, SEE . . . . 750 95 POEMS 78   3

GLOWING

night severed and the glowing throng descend, felt on . . . .   4 T&C EPITHALAM   52

GLOWS

Ging stink. dull, gobular glows and flatchatte ringarom a . .   94 & POST IMPR 6   12

GLUE

golden soul fabulously to glue in a superior terror; . . . .   9 T&C SONGS 1   30

GLUED

his jacket were two glued uncarefully ears in that . . . . . 355 VIVA 46   7

a someone will lie (glued among familiar things newly . . . . 428 NO THANKS 45   2

which are wintry handlebars glued) updives pursued by its . . 585 1 X 1 45   7

GLUEY

smallheaded pearshaped lady in gluey twilight moving, ...   95 & POST IMPR 7   2

who jim him why gluey grins topple together eyes . . . . . .   96 & POST IMPR 8   17

GLUSH

splurging smells waltz the glush of squirting taps plus . . .   96 & POST IMPR 8   12

GLUTTED

ecstasies slowly, in the glutted heart fleet flowerterrible .   36 T&C AMORES 1   24

GLUTTONOUS

one coloured nonthings of gluttonous sky-- nor (as a . . . . 402 NO THANKS 19   8

GNARLED

r s, large four gnarled lips totter Therefore, approaching . 255 IS 5 ONE 26   4

withered and unself her gnarled vomits a rock of . . . . . . 506 50 POEMS 20   4

GNASHING

(i simply understand the gnashing petals of sex which . . . . 133 & SON REAL 4   11

GNOMES

out of it sour gnomes tumble clumsily, the little . . . . . .   69 T&C POST IMPR 6   3

elves and hope- less gnomes and frantic fairies gush . . . .   69 T&C POST IMPR 6   22

GNOMES (CONTINUED)
    carefully luminous with innumerable gnomes Of complete dream 363 VIVA 54   7
GO
    faint hills do frailly go The peaceful terrors of . . . . . .   11 T&C SONGS 2   27
    not fear, we will go amaying. thy whitest feet . . . .   13 T&C SONGS 3   7
    every mile the feet go the heart goes nine . . . .   15 T&C SONGS 5   19
    Into strenuous birds shall go my love walking in . . . . . .   16 T&C SONGS 6   10
    between slow glories fleetly go.) Upon a keen and . . . . . .   20 T&C PUELLA MEA   144
    he that will amaying go with my lord Boccaccio-- . . . . . .   20 T&C PUELLA MEA   169
    frailest syllable its leaves go crisp with miracle. . . . . .   22 T&C PUELLA MEA   236
    word; that i may go unto him, and take . . . .   76 T&C SON UNRE 1   11
    / POST IMPRESSIONS windows go orange in the slowly. . . . . .   89 & POST IMPR 1   1
    lie asleep my eyes go into Allen street the . . . .   100 & POST IMPR 11   2
    then my mouth will go out into the East . . . .   100 & POST IMPR 11   19
    ears love it's to go into the east Side . . . .   100 & POST IMPR 11   34
    Queerly Has, my, ears, go into Hassan's place the . . . . . . 100 & POST IMPR 11   41
    n) 1- ing all go BlacK wh-eel-ing oh ver . . . .   122 & SEVEN POEMS 1   18
    balloon, why then we'd go up higher with all . . . .   129 & SEVEN POEMS 7   8
    and steeples and clouds: go sailing away and away . . . . . . 129 & SEVEN POEMS 7   10
    it sometimes makes gaily go clean through me tickling . . . . 147 & SON REAL 18   7
    die. When we grimly go to bed with these . . . .   147 & SON REAL 18   12
    music, and poetry cannot go near because perfectly fearful. . 162 & SON ACTU 11   7
    her nakedness until it go rapidly to bed: i . . . .   164 & SON ACTU 13   6
    feels curiously cool (suddenly-Lights go! on, by schedule /.   167 & SON ACTU 16   19
    In the morning they go out in pairs: amazingly, ... 171 & SON ACTU 20   8
    INNOCENTES why did you go little fourpaws? you forgot . . . . 191 XLI CHANSONS 1   1
    eyes. where did you go? like little kittens are . . . . 191 XLI CHANSONS 1   5
    or maybe did something go away ever so quietly . . . . 191 XLI CHANSONS 1   14
    garden: colours come and go, frail azures fluttering from . . 208 XLI SONNETS 4   1
    will the fleshless moments go and go across this . . . . . . 218 XLI SONNETS 14   9
    fleshless moments go and go across this dirtied pane . . . . 218 XLI SONNETS 14   9
    less deserved, Young fellow go in peace. which i . . . . . .   229 IS 5 ONE FRAN   8
    of centuries come and go and are no more . . . .   268 IS 5 TWO 3   4
    moon smiled she let go my vest and crept . . . .   284 IS 5 FOUR 1   11
    / / because you go away i give roses . . . .   294 IS 5 FOUR 11   2
    inexcusable, this inexplicable pleasure--you go from several   295 IS 5 FOUR 12   7
    fall into his hat) go wandering after it with . . . .   298 IS 5 FOUR 15   21
    / / / i go to this window just . . . .   301 IS 5 FOUR 18   1
    and night) "let us go a very little beyond . . . .   303 IS 5 FIVE 2   2
    Down, honestly now who go (BANG (BANG / / . . . .   317 VIVA 9   38
    just had let it go at that) that seems . . . .   323 VIVA 15   13
    that you are afraid "go first" of dreams and . . . .   353 VIVA 44   26
    (which beyond night shall go) remembering only dare (Wholly . 362 VIVA 53   2
    room. We almost could go (you and i) into . . . .   365 VIVA 56   8
    a sun which must go sometimes, to make an . . . .   372 VIVA 63   7
    though wish and world go down, one poem yet . . . .   372 VIVA 63   15
    so in darkness ourselves go, mind in mind which . . . . . .   379 VIVA 70   3
    not said she (let's go said he not too . . . .   399 NO THANKS 16   9
    oh no said he) go slow said she (cccome? . . . .   399 NO THANKS 16   28
    / / / / go (perpe) go (tu) to . . . .   403 NO THANKS 20   1
    / / go (perpe) go (tu) to (al adve . . . .   403 NO THANKS 20   1
    ini sterd exte ri) go to (ty) the (om . . . .   403 NO THANKS 20   11
    ingseekfindlosin g motilities are) go to the ant (al . . .   403 NO THANKS 20   15
    ant (al ways alingwaysing) go to the ant thou . . . .   403 NO THANKS 20   21
    to the ant thou go (inging) to the ant, ...   403 NO THANKS 20   21
    what's right about the g.o. world what's wrong with . . . . . 411 NO THANKS 28   8
    are not refined they go with girls who buck . . . .   427 NO THANKS 44   2
    call himself a man? go dreamless knaves on Shadows . . . .   438 NO THANKS 54   9
    hate nor grief can go where goes this whyless . . . .   441 NO THANKS 56   44
    come-swarm: faces ar; rive go. faces a (live) sob . . . . .   444 NO THANKS 59   6
    boys to bed will go, / / / / . . . .   451 NO THANKS 66   16
    quills (asleep who must go things-without-wings / / / . . . . 483 NEW POEMS 21   11
    , le af a:; go e s wh IrlI . . . .   487 50 POEMS 1   15
    come on kid let's go to sleep if you . . . .   489 50 POEMS 3   4
    come on kid let's go to sleep if you . . . .   489 50 POEMS 3   8
    come on kid let's go to sleep if you . . . .   489 50 POEMS 3   12
    (come on kid Let's go to sleep) / / . . . .   489 50 POEMS 3   16
    damned fall all we go spill and chairs tables . . . .   496 50 POEMS 10   14

		PAGE	TITLE	LINE
GO (CONTINUED)				
so feeble the feeble go to sleep if the	505	50 POEMS 19	7
the voice down shall go which and up come	511	50 POEMS 25	23
you will (kiss me) go out into the morning	529	50 POEMS 41	3
(kiss me) you will go on into the sunlight	529	50 POEMS 41	6
in it you will go (kiss me down into	529	50 POEMS 41	9
i) kiss me (will go) / / / /	529	50 POEMS 41	12
our thief goes (you go and i) has pulled	543	1 X 1 3	20
universe next door; let's go / / / /	554	1 X 1 14	15
spook of stop and go) may i achieve another	558	1 X 1 18	9
bigly come crashing into go (all than were nevers	565	1 X 1 25	14
/ / let it go--the smashed word broken open	569	1 X 1 29	1
cracked length wise--let it go it was sworn to	569	1 X 1 29	5
it was sworn to go let them go--the truthful	569	1 X 1 29	7
to go let them go--the truthful liars and the	569	1 X 1 29	8
neithers--you must let them go they were born to	569	1 X 1 29	12
they were born to go let all go--the big	569	1 X 1 29	14
to go let all go--the big small middling tall	569	1 X 1 29	15
and all things--let all go dear so comes love	569	1 X 1 29	19
down isn't's own isn't go ghostly they doubting can	580	1 X 1 40	7
of thingfear) come ships go snowily sailing perfect silence.	586	1 X 1 46	17
in the blossoming) lovers go and lovers come awandering . . .	591	1 X 1 51	9
me why people let go / / / /	593	1 X 1 53	24
run skip around we go yes) there's nothing as	594	1 X 1 54	8
shout each around we go all) there's somebody calling . . .	594	1 X 1 54	35
me you and i'll go strolling right through these	600	(CHAIRE) 2	12
"i'll never let you go until you've made me	622	(CHAIRE) 24	5
g into silenc e go lliw og-dog) life ?	628	(CHAIRE) 30	4
people nimbler than Really go whirling into gaily white . . .	630	(CHAIRE) 32	3
air and to ghosts go drift slippery hands tease	633	(CHAIRE) 35	4
nothing's own nothing children go of dust / /	661	(CHAIRE) 63	14
the roses come and go for kindness and goodness	684	95 POEMS 12	14
sun fall rise come go rain snow) remembers /	693	95 POEMS 21	20
every wo man should go to college is so	700	95 POEMS 28	7
lly & (rOunder than) go : ldenly (Round est)	722	95 POEMS 50	9
we call old frank go bluer still as (shifting	754	95 POEMS 82	6
Magic of green solitude (go marvels come) as littler	757	95 POEMS 85	17
without it (anywhere i go you go, my dear;	766	95 POEMS 92	3
(anywhere i go you go, my dear; and whatever	766	95 POEMS 92	3
where) and away we go in even the laziest	769	95 POEMS 95	7
bed --saints and satyrs, go your way youths and	794	73 POEMS 22	7
my homecoming-- my selves go with you, only i	812	73 POEMS 40	2
bliss-- where seeing eyes go blind (where lips forget	834	73 POEMS 62	27
voyage ? up upup: go ing downdowndown com; ing	840	73 POEMS 68	6
happy should his now go then / / /	842	73 POEMS 70	14
+GO				
FOR CONTEXT, SEE	392	NO THANKS 9	7
FOR CONTEXT, SEE	421	NO THANKS 38	14
FOR CONTEXT, SEE	474	NEW POEMS 12	13
FOR CONTEXT, SEE	710	95 POEMS 38	7
GOAL				
dryad sought her leafy goal, at the mere echo	3	T&C EPITHALAM	14
daffodils (who know the goal of living is to	688	95 POEMS 16	2
beauty knows no their goal (in calm and fury:	742	95 POEMS 70	7
GOAT				
it's spring and the goat-footed balloonMan whistles far and .	24	T&C CHANSONS 1	20
wouldn't that get yer goat but we don't care	109	& PORTRAIT 5	5
and blase a black goat lookingly wanders There is	278	IS 5 THREE 2	16
GOAT-FOOTED				
it's spring and the goat-footed balloonMan whistles far and .	24	T&C CHANSONS 1	20
GOATS				
in the afternoon sky. goats and sheep are driven	281	IS 5 THREE 5	8
GOB				
dis gorge) a sulky gob with entirely white eyes	629	(CHAIRE) 31	3
+GOB				
FOR CONTEXT, SEE	642	(CHAIRE) 44	22
GOBBLEHOBBLE				
defunct king as linotypes gobblehobble our lightheavy twic .	259	IS 5 ONE 29	12

		PAGE	TITLE	LINE
+GOBLIN				
FOR CONTEXT, SEE	259	IS 5 ONE 29	8
GOBLINS				
twitchy witches and tingling goblins hob-a-nob hob-a-nob . .	25	T&C CHANSONS 2	7
GOBS				
but of rapidly goes gobs the and of flecks	96	& POST IMPR 8	7
GOBULAR				
ofcrin Ging stink. dull, gobular glows and flatchatte	94	& POST IMPR 6	12
GOD				
didst thou know the god from but the imprint	3	T&C EPITHALAM	12
charms the tall boy god of everlasting war received	7	T&C EPITHALAM	154
/ / / when god lets my body be	16	T&C SONGS 6	1
the silence a brown god smiles between greentwittering smokes	28	T&C ORIENTALE 2	3
transplendent hand of sombre god i picked you as	30	T&C ORIENTALE 4	40
of the mother of god who spits seeds of	55	T&C PORTRAIT 3	13
solemn eyeswhichneversmile yes, By god. for i am they	69	T&C POST IMPR 6	36
little painted poem of god / / / /	75	T&C SON REAL 6	14
/ / / / god gloats upon Her stunning	77	T&C SON UNRE 2	1
lovings of Her tongue. god Is The Sea. All	77	T&C SON UNRE 2	10
night through moaned space god worships God-- (behold! where	77	T&C SON UNRE 2	15
moaned space god worships God-- (behold! where chaste stars .	77	T&C SON UNRE 2	15
girls that gets up god knows when every day	109	& PORTRAIT 5	15
the kind black great god) Cleopatra you are eaten	112	& PORTRAIT 6	88
the judgment day comes God will find six crumbs	117	& PORTRAIT 10	4
who was dead? --to God in a tiny voice, ...	117	& PORTRAIT 10	11
some shame whispered unto God, my name is must	117	& PORTRAIT 10	22
imagine it I say God amid a monstrous din	117	& PORTRAIT 10	26
I'm not. Again. Hush. God. Please hold. Tight /	130	& SON REAL 1	15
for a while. my god--a patter of kisses, the	133	& SON REAL 4	14
/ / / / god pity me whom (god	140	& SON REAL 11	1
god pity me whom (god distinctly has) the weightless	140	& SON REAL 11	1
/ in making Marjorie god hurried a boy's body	148	& SON REAL 19	1
A cat waiting for god knows makes me wonder	166	& SON ACTU 15	9
not too wide dear god there's a portrait over	198	XLI PORTRAIT 6	6
almost do guess) if god should send the morning;	205	XLI SONNETS 1	9
where strove the droll god-beasts do thou distinctly bring .	213	XLI SONNETS 9	9
/ / / by god i want above fourteenth	220	XLI SONNETS 16	1
is." And i hazarded "god" (blushing slightly) --"O damn . . .	228	IS 5 ONE MARJ	6
i entirely ask of god why on the alert	229	IS 5 ONE FRAN	1
enthusiastic cohorts from Duluth God only, gondola knows . .	256	IS 5 ONE 27	27
even after April by God there is no excuse	264	IS 5 ONE 33	8
"next to of course god america i love you	268	IS 5 TWO 3	1
imagine Harry was o god kilt he was kilt	271	IS 5 TWO 6	11
what i mean a god damned lot of people	272	IS 5 TWO 7	13
do or die for God for country and for	273	IS 5 TWO 8	12
sum it All Up god being Dead (not to	315	VIVA 7	9
not how electricity or god was invented but why	324	VIVA 16	2
i (check undublcheck) babbitt (GOD SAVE THE UNCOMMONWEALTH OF	325	VIVA 17	22
any rag upon what God unto him gave) responds, ...	339	VIVA 30	17
blue slender hands of god / / / /	340	VIVA 31	20
everywhere hidinglyseek no o god dear wait sh please	358	VIVA 49	5
the fool who cright god help me it aint	405	NO THANKS 22	10
in a futile groove god knows why) and so	413	NO THANKS 30	16
man shall which a god sometimes is I the	414	NO THANKS 31	14
let 's thank indecent god p.s. the most successful	425	NO THANKS 42	15
to stroll almost this god this surely dream perhaps	441	NO THANKS 56	48
stars Feels; if & god said & there was	479	NEW POEMS 17	12
should ever think, may god forbid and (in his	484	NEW POEMS 22	9
crashed pal dropped o god alice yells but who	496	50 POEMS 10	7
one generous child- man -god one eager souldoll one	524	50 POEMS 36	43
is the every only god who spoke this earth	526	50 POEMS 38	1
who never began of god and fiend? i give	527	50 POEMS 39	7
and only man is god. Without a heart the	544	1 X 1 4	24
burns cigerr to the god of things like they	552	1 X 1 12	30
can do or be?" god whispered him a snowflake	555	1 X 1 15	14
/ / / when god decided to invent everything	566	1 X 1 26	1
the silverest alive silentness god ever breathed upon	572	1 X 1 32	9
before the moon before God wished Himself into a	577	1 X 1 37	15

		PAGE	TITLE	LINE

GOD (CONTINUED)
    legal) we thank thee god almighty for dying (forgive . . . . 604 {CHAIRE} 6   23
    during the dropsin king god my sic kly a . . . . 646 {CHAIRE} 48   3
    / / / maybe god is a child 's . . . . 652 {CHAIRE} 54   1
    / i thank You God for most this amazing . . . . 663 {CHAIRE} 65   1
    (i sus pect) only god himself & as loveless . . . . 698 95 POEMS 26   2
    world not any un god manufacture might but man . . . . . . 698 95 POEMS 26   4
    Knowing your whole (yes god damned) life is a . . . . 702 95 POEMS 30   12
    by you as the god of our fathers' fathers . . . . 711 95 POEMS 39   3
    ways of man to God i'll think it strange . . . . 731 95 POEMS 59   2
    justify the ways of God to man / / . . . . 731 95 POEMS 59   4
    villains or heroes (for god likes girls and tomorrow . . . . 732 95 POEMS 60   15
    it or don't) by god down this stranger went . . . . 800 73 POEMS 28   15
    good true beautiful things god how he sings the . . . . . . 805 73 POEMS 33   5
    dares; that mountain, any god) while leaf twig limb . . . . 818 73 POEMS 46   9
    Feeling only (jesus) every (god) where (chr ist) what . . . . 823 73 POEMS 51   16
+GOD
    FOR CONTEXT, SEE . . . . 228 IS 5 ONE MARJ   7
    FOR CONTEXT, SEE . . . . 640 {CHAIRE} 42   3
    FOR CONTEXT, SEE . . . . 662 {CHAIRE} 64   8
GOD-BEASTS
    where strove the droll god-beasts do thou distinctly bring . 213 XLI SONNETS 9   9
GOD'S
    intolerable! silence immaculate of god's evasive audible . . 5 T&C EPITHALAM 112
    the sea marvelous from god's hands which sent her . . . . . . 38 T&C AMORES 3   2
    into freshness as if god's flowers were pulling upon . . . . 58 T&C PORTRAIT 6   9
    like bright lice about god's capable dull important head-- . 85 T&C SON ACTU 4   4
    whom glories whisperingly impinge (god's pretty mother) but . 85 T&C SON ACTU 4   6
    his tail that's the god's own and the moon . . . . 125 & SEVEN POEMS 4   17
    Thorn enter Morn and God's In His andsoforth do . . . . . . 230 IS 5 ONE 2   28
    as now i love god's terrible face, brighter than . . . . . . 360 VIVA 51   21
    by un till the god's truth stands art-naked: you . . . . . . 605 {CHAIRE} 7   3
    imagine but please for god's O what the hell . . . . 638 {CHAIRE} 40   9
    die can't quite poison God's sunlight / / / . . . . 708 95 POEMS 36   16
    doubt of impossible ours --God's heaven perhaps comprises . . 748 95 POEMS 76   5
+GODDAMN
    FOR CONTEXT, SEE . . . . 547 1 X 1 7   12
GODDAMNED
    reminds me the cheerfulest goddamned sonofabitch i ever met . 699 95 POEMS 27   12
GODDESS
    whose serious grace one goddess loved too well? . . . . 3 T&C EPITHALAM 24
    roses whose ambrosial grace, goddess, thy crippled . . . . . 6 T&C EPITHALAM 149
    / / spring omnipotent goddess thou dost inveigle into . . . . 61 T&C PORTRAIT 9   1
GODDESSES
    stones (neither awake are goddesses nor sleeping) since he's 617 {CHAIRE} 19   9
GODIVA
    his buggy of lady godiva & that (for no . . . . 699 95 POEMS 27   8
GODLESS
    of) hear ye! the godless are the dull and . . . . 499 50 POEMS 13   14
GODLY
    quintillions of incredible dodderingly godly toothless ◇ ◇ 250 IS 5 ONE 21   12
GODS
    whence are the high gods fled? Speak elm eloquent . . . . . . 3 T&C EPITHALAM   8
    the hours, father of gods and men whose subtle . . . . 4 T&C EPITHALAM   41
    that thou mightest conceive gods (but true to the . . . . . . 46 T&C LA GUERRE 2   18
    softly by tomb rosily gods whiten befall saith rain . . . . . 90 & POST IMPR 2   3
    prowl gorge sly slim gods stare / / / . . . . 90 & POST IMPR 2   16
    the absolute stars the gods are swallowed even Nile . . . . . 112 & PORTRAIT 6   84
    mill of the ingenious gods. (i am punished. They . . . . . . 165 & SON ACTU 14   13
    and large The downlife gods of shut) / . . . . 346 VIVA 37   27
    man, if men are gods; but if gods must . . . . 562 1 X 1 22   1
    are gods; but if gods must be men, the . . . . 562 1 X 1 22   1
    (so many fiends and gods each greedier than every) . . . . . 609 {CHAIRE} 11   1
GODTHANKING
    gift wandering deeply through godthanking ground) bluest whos 754 95 POEMS 82   4
GODTOWN
    brightshadowfully fountaining man's thingfulest godtown . . . 681 95 POEMS 9   15

GOES
    feet go the heart goes nine / / / . . . .   15 T&C SONGS 5   20
    not change and she goes forth out of hands . . . .   38 T&C AMORES 3   11
    is dawn the world goes forth to murder dreams. . . . .   50 T&C IMPRESS 4   11
    whose hand the crank goes desperately, round and round   . . .   69 T&C POST IMPR 6   8
    i don't, the crank goes round desperate elves and . . . . . .   69 T&C POST IMPR 6   21
    Again: who danc ing goes utter ly churning witty, ...   89 & POST IMPR 1   12
    a but of rapidly goes gobs the and of . . . .   96 & POST IMPR 8   7
    East side, my mouth goes to the peddlers, to . . . . 100 & POST IMPR 11   20
    Street For my stomach goes out into the east . . . . 101 & POST IMPR 11   59
    with hisknees huggedtogether it, goes out into the rapid . . 101 & POST IMPR 11   61
    eyes are chisels scarlet Goes with her whitehot face, ... 106 & PORTRAIT 2   5
    in You my stomach goes into your Little Stomach . . . . 123 & SEVEN POEMS 2   9
    clever too like POF goes the alarm off and . . . . 126 & SEVEN POEMS 5   10
    like a thistlefluff-thing which goes land- ing away all . . . 127 & SEVEN POEMS 5   41
    sonnet is A light goes on in the toiletwindow, ... 171 & SON ACTU 20   1
    publication the girl who goes wrong you know (whereas . . . . 245 IS 5 ONE 16   10
    far as his picture goes he's a wet dream . . . . 246 IS 5 ONE 17   11
    the son of man goes forth to war with . . . . 273 IS 5 TWO 8   23
    is look how it goes like a dream (and . . . . 353 VIVA 44   8
    (says. word Less) ly (goes folds? folds) cold stones   . . . . 417 NO THANKS 34   6
    feast) meanwhile this ghost goes under, his drowned girth . . 418 NO THANKS 35   12
    fair come foul he goes alone daring to dare . . . . 440 NO THANKS 56   28
    grief can go where goes this whyless soul a . . . . 441 NO THANKS 56   44
    nn-nn went head face goes (if how begins a . . . . 506 50 POEMS 20   8
    become while every sun goes round its moon / . . . . 510 50 POEMS 24   14
    by a whore dragged goes to meet her why . . . . 533 50 POEMS 45   22
    then over our thief goes (you go and i) . . . . 543 1 X 1 3   19
    easily (while will be goes was) can travel this . . . . 608 {CHAIRE} 10   11
    back and off he goes but we can hear . . . . 624 {CHAIRE} 26   20
    n't Don't &) youth goes right on gr owing . . . . 729 95 POEMS 57   17
    than alive any star goes round --a dream sans . . . . 735 95 POEMS 63   4
    i then that Star goes under the earth / . . . . 752 95 POEMS 80   8
    --arriving truly, faithfully who goes (never a moment ceasing 756 95 POEMS 84   2
    turn woes and right goes wrong (dim worlds or . . . . 776 73 POEMS 4   26
    happened" as everywhere red goes green --groping blank sky . 800 73 POEMS 28   22
+GOES
    FOR CONTEXT, SEE . . . . 487 50 POEMS 1   15
GOETHE
    Some "allemand" ....? of Goethe, since exempt from heaven's . 158 & SON ACTU 7   7
GOGGLE
    big wobbly foot-steps every goggle cent of it get . . . . . .   96 & POST IMPR 8   20
GOIL
    / Jimmie's got a goil goil goil, Jimmie 's . . . . 235 IS 5 ONE 6   1
    Jimmie's got a goil goil goil, Jimmie 's got . . . . 235 IS 5 ONE 6   2
    got a goil goil goil, Jimmie 's got a . . . . 235 IS 5 ONE 6   3
    Jimmie 's got a goil and she coitnly can . . . . 235 IS 5 ONE 6   5
GOILS
    specialty is takin fellers' goils away frum dem" --"somebody 332 VIVA 23   6
GOING
    / / i am going to utter a tree, ...   67 T&C POST IMPR 4   1
    and choked pat of going soles on flat pavements . . . . 142 & SON REAL 13   6
    a garden-wall, and is going to die. When we . . . . 147 & SON REAL 18   12
    de Jingyale. things are going rather kaka over there, ... 233 IS 5 ONE 4   7
    know the dam rent's going to and everything and . . . . 242 IS 5 ONE 13   19
    / you are not going to, dear. You are . . . . 289 IS 5 FOUR 6   1
    dear. You are not going to and i but . . . . 289 IS 5 FOUR 6   1
    i thought you were going to (but that doesn't . . . . 289 IS 5 FOUR 6   19
    you thought you were going to America. Then moving   . . . . . 289 IS 5 FOUR 6   21
    you, you say "let's" going in "take hands" smiling   . . . . . 353 VIVA 44   29
    o man what bubbies going places on such babies . . . . 476 NEW POEMS 14   6
    quite without change, you're going to get one whole . . . . . 800 73 POEMS 28   12
+GOING
    FOR CONTEXT, SEE . . . . 345 VIVA 36   15
    FOR CONTEXT, SEE . . . . 519 50 POEMS 33   16
    FOR CONTEXT, SEE . . . . 547 1 X 1 7   15
    FOR CONTEXT, SEE . . . . 618 {CHAIRE} 20   19
    FOR CONTEXT, SEE . . . . 840 73 POEMS 68   6

GOLD

curls of unendured eternal gold over the infinite breast . .   4 T&C EPITHALAM   38
a great horse of gold into the silver dawn. . . . . 14 T&C SONGS 4   2
fleet does at a gold valley the famished arrow . . . . 14 T&C SONGS 4   19
a great horse of gold into the silver dawn. . . . . 14 T&C SONGS 4   32
emperor is carpeted with gold cloth from the ceiling . . . . 32 T&C ORIENTALE 6 22
weaving insinuating upon the gold cloth incessantly creates . 34 T&C ORIENTALE 6 87
sunset stars and flowers gold crescendo and silver muting . . 39 T&C AMORES 4   8
is dead and the gold year a formal spasm . . . . 41 T&C AMORES 5   5
/ / / stinging gold swarms upon the spires . . . . 51 T&C IMPRESS 5   2
pulling upon bells of gold i looked up and . . . . 58 T&C PORTRAIT 6   11
trumpets blow horses of gold delicately crouching beneath . . 110 & PORTRAIT 6   34
street-lamps fail upon the gold dawn, where teeth of . . . . 142 & SON REAL 13   3
fuzzy-pash --dead--and the dark gold delicately smash. . . . . 153 & SON ACTU 2   7
rhythms to juggle Kandinsky gold-fish away from the gripping 180 XLI SONGS 2   13
of day tortured in gold, which presently crumpled collapses. 188 XLI SONGS 10   8
the chains red and gold the fluffy threads, put . . . . 192 XLI CHANSONS 2 16
3 watch a has gold teeth b pink suspenders . . . . 200 XLI PORTRAIT 8   5
opening "wisdom." Flicker of gold. "Yep. No gas. Flynn" . . . 226 IS 5 ONE MAME   8
with effigies of crowing gold) nuzzle against summer thunder 340 VIVA 31   18
birds (rising through a gold moment) climb: ing i . . . . . . 627 {CHAIRE} 29   2
high window; at the gold of november sunset (and . . . . . . 824 73 POEMS 52   4
leaves (sEe) locked in gOLd after- gLOw are t . . . . 838 73 POEMS 66   6
+GOLD
FOR CONTEXT, SEE . . . . 34 T&C ORIENTALE 6 72
FOR CONTEXT, SEE . . . . 114 & PORTRAIT 7   20
FOR CONTEXT, SEE . . . . 503 50 POEMS 17   12
FOR CONTEXT, SEE . . . . 690 95 POEMS 18   1
GOLD-FISH
rhythms to juggle Kandinsky gold-fish away from the gripping 180 XLI SONGS 2   13
GOLD'S
/ swi (across! gold's rouNdly) ftblac kl . . . . 429 NO THANKS 46   2
GOLDBERG'S
/ / / IKEY (GOLDBERG)'S WORTH I'M TOLD $ . . . . 244 IS 5 ONE 15   1
GOLDBERGER
say human being) one goldberger / / / / . . . . 524 50 POEMS 36   47
GOLDEN
unserious dress ascends the golden crocus from the dead. . .   4 T&C EPITHALAM   64
tickles the air to golden tears, and hark! the . . . .   5 T&C EPITHALAM   74
of thy thought my golden soul fabulously to glue . . . . . .   9 T&C SONGS 1   30
song heard behind a golden door, poet and sage . . . . 22 T&C PUELLA MEA 222
souls of men to golden dust: she pauses on . . . . 75 T&C SON REAL 6 11
lights like baths of golden snow. This is the . . . . 208 XLI SONNETS 4   4
swot to preach the golden rull to vote for . . . . 500 50 POEMS 14   20
again and again; whose golden, crimson dooms conceive an . . 599 {CHAIRE} 1   2
begins to spill such golden blood as makes his . . . . 811 73 POEMS 39   13
GOLDENEST
himself ye duskiest despot's goldenest gal did wring that . . 552 1 X 1 12   16
GOLDENLY
downward if they'll or goldenly float so (dreaming out . . . 573 1 X 1 33   9
a new (silverly rare goldenly so) moon, she is . . . . 666 {CHAIRE} 68   9
not imagined secrecies comprise goldenly huge whole the . . . 750 95 POEMS 78   9
universe-- but if, with goldenly his fathering (as that . . . 756 95 POEMS 84   9
(above nevermoving all nowhere) goldenly whole, prodigiously 808 73 POEMS 36   6
+GOLDENLY
FOR CONTEXT, SEE . . . . 722 95 POEMS 50   9
+GOLDFISH
FOR CONTEXT, SEE . . . . 180 XLI SONGS 2   13
GOLDFISHIAN
la vallee and preserved goldfishian gestures) suddenly sally 425 NO THANKS 42   3
GOLF
see! so long door golf slam bridge train shriek . . . . 309 VIVA 1   18
triple starred Hotel du Golf... that notable structure or . . 319 VIVA 11   22
+GOLLIWOG
FOR CONTEXT, SEE . . . . 628 {CHAIRE} 30   4
+GOLLY
FOR CONTEXT, SEE . . . . 268 IS 5 TWO 3   7

		PAGE	TITLE	LINE

GOLLYWOG
buttons with his big gollywog voice the kingdomofheaven up . 259 IS 5 ONE 29   2
GONDOLA
signore affirm that all gondola signore day below me . . . . 256 IS 5 ONE 27   23
signore day below me gondola signore gondola and above . . . 256 IS 5 ONE 27   24
below me gondola signore gondola and above me pass . . . . . 256 IS 5 ONE 27   24
me pass loudly and gondola rapidly denizens of Omaha . . . . 256 IS 5 ONE 27   25
from Duluth God only, gondola knows Cincingondolanati i . . . 256 IS 5 ONE 27   28
gondola knows Cincingondolanati i gondola don't --the . . . . 256 IS 5 ONE 27   28
GONE
any lady dead and gone.) Each tapering breast is . . . . . . 21 T&C PUELLA MEA 180
eyes when day is gone are the cries of . . . . 23 T&C PUELLA MEA 260
riverly is a flower gone softly by tomb rosily . . . . 90 & POST IMPR 2   2
loved a dinted mug gone Darkness it was so . . . . 97 & POST IMPR 8   40
swoopingly fallen svelte sagging gone into the soaring . . . 110 & PORTRAIT 6   28
said he should have gone into vaudeville perhaps because . . 239 IS 5 ONE 10   4
and see? tail frisks) (gonE) "mouse", We are not . . . . . . 286 IS 5 FOUR 3   14
trop froid"-- they are gone: along these gardens moves . . . 304 IS 5 FIVE 3   11
(we being unwound & gone into the ground) but . . . . 361 VIVA 52   4
--always think i am gone like a sun which . . . . 372 VIVA 63   7
with something) You are gone. there is laughter and . . . . 375 VIVA 66   4
and that noing our gone snow gone yours mine . . . . 491 50 POEMS 5   8
noing our gone snow gone yours mine . We're . . . . 491 50 POEMS 5   8
wear face? have singings gone to say? here youngest . . . . 538 50 POEMS 50   6
our all and one gone away the they leaf . . . . 541 1 X 1 1   7
you (sun or snow) gone into what like all . . . . 568 1 X 1 28   11
now our sun is gone reminding with his bell . . . . 624 (CHAIRE) 26   22
ding int o absolute gone & positive quite n . . . . 646 (CHAIRE) 48   13
(for only me) and gone is who. since becomes . . . . . . 737 95 POEMS 65   4
wellsweep forest & clearing) gone are enormous near far . . . 755 95 POEMS 83   5
a great man is gone. Tall as the truth . . . . 786 73 POEMS 14   4
roaming whylessness-- autumn has gone: will winter never . . 839 73 POEMS 67   8
+GONE
FOR CONTEXT, SEE . . . . 310 VIVA 2   9
FOR CONTEXT, SEE . . . . 690 95 POEMS 18   6
FOR CONTEXT, SEE . . . . 700 95 POEMS 28   15
FOR CONTEXT, SEE . . . . 740 95 POEMS 68   7
GONORRHEA
twelve who hast merely gonorrhea Oldeyed child, to ambitious 105 & PORTRAIT 1   4
GOOD
the striking of a good minstrel between them is . . . . . . 29 T&C ORIENTALE 3 13
dear and have a good time with the tall . . . . 71 T&C SON REAL 2   2
little girl with the good teeth and small important . . . . . 72 T&C SON REAL 3   2
us for we were good; and the last crumb . . . . 117 & PORTRAIT 10   20
supreme sex. In The Good Old Summer Time. My . . . . . . 130 & SON REAL 1   9
will feature Peace And Good Will, and Mary with . . . . . . 142 & SON REAL 13   10
silence on her dress, good for sleeping is her . . . . 147 & SON REAL 18   3
the breasts look very good: firmlysquirmy with a slight . . . 150 & SON REAL 21   3
fer i gimme de good ole daze.... in dem . . . . 237 IS 5 ONE 8   12
give her the juice, good (it was the first . . . . 248 IS 5 ONE 19   23
feet of Breton big good body, which terminated in . . . . . 277 IS 5 THREE 1   6
so lonely fer duh good ole days we spent . . . . 332 VIVA 23   14
a baboon (where once good lips stalked or eyes . . . . . . 360 VIVA 51   2
(mother) child is a good Husband to him (and . . . . . . 398 NO THANKS 15   5
bad which you think good) because he knows, he . . . . . . 406 NO THANKS 23   4
a myth is as good as a smile but . . . . 410 NO THANKS 27   9
death knows whie (all good kumrads you can tell . . . . . . 413 NO THANKS 30   7
altruistic smell moscow pipes good kumrads dance) kumrads . . 413 NO THANKS 30   9
came "I wish you good" the mechanical dawn "morning") . . . . 464 NEW POEMS 2   28
parents one inch looks good to us (and Ever-Ever . . . . . 466 NEW POEMS 4   16
such babies aint plenty good enough for i eu . . . . . . 476 NEW POEMS 14   9
me give it him good a bottle she quick . . . . 496 50 POEMS 10   11
is hands machine no good too quick i know . . . . 523 50 POEMS 36   11
i am born is good but there this cheap . . . . 523 50 POEMS 36   21
pregnant one fearless one good yes completely kind mindheart 524 50 POEMS 36   39
a hell of a good universe next door; let's . . . . 554 1 X 1 14   15
Death if Death were good: for when (instead of . . . . . . 604 (CHAIRE) 6   8
you aren't or are, good luck! aberdeen plato-rabelais peter . 605 (CHAIRE) 7   15

GOOD (CONTINUED)

be giving; it's no good pretending befriending means loving" 625 (CHAIRE) 27　　4
than the other un good people stare for it . . . . 662 (CHAIRE) 64　　11
best is quite so good you don't conceive a . . . . 679 95 POEMS 7　　10
a brother who is good and kind to all" . . . . 684 95 POEMS 12　　12
you are bid a good kind bear is angry . . . . 711 95 POEMS 39　　19
/ now comes the good rain farmers pray for . . . . 754 95 POEMS 82　　1
(beyond win or lose) good true beautiful things god . . . . . 805 73 POEMS 33　　3

+GOOD

FOR CONTEXT, SEE . . . . 200 XLI PORTRAIT 8　　31
FOR CONTEXT, SEE . . . . 411 NO THANKS 28　　8
FOR CONTEXT, SEE . . . . 411 NO THANKS 28　　10
FOR CONTEXT, SEE . . . . 411 NO THANKS 28　　12
FOR CONTEXT, SEE . . . . 618 (CHAIRE) 20　　1
FOR CONTEXT, SEE . . . . 656 (CHAIRE) 58　　11

GOODBY

/ / / / goodby Betty, don't remember me . . . . 71 T&C SON REAL 2　　1

GOODBYE

turns to young (winter goodbye) april hello, / / . . . . . . 737 95 POEMS 65　　7
made of hello and goodbye: glad sorry or both . . . . 776 73 POEMS 4　　38

GOODLY

Maleore findeth of ladies goodly store whose beauty did . . . 21 T&C PUELLA MEA 173
/ it was a goodly co which paid to . . . . 552 1 X 1 12　　1

GOODMORNING

if i should say goodmorning trouble adds up all . . . . . . 287 IS 5 FOUR 4　　2

GOODNESS

as bad, itself thinks goodness what is meek; obey . . . . . . 438 NO THANKS 54　　4
go for kindness and goodness do not make a . . . . 684 95 POEMS 12　　15
form less form all goodness truth and beauty lurk, ... 790 73 POEMS 18　　9

GOODS

yes it delivers the goods, Heaven knows (yet are . . . . . . 264 IS 5 ONE 33　　12

GOOEY

her handless wrists did gooey severe shapes. / / . . . . . . 73 T&C SON REAL 4　　14

GOOSE

sin bangaroom slim guesser goose pin yessir wheel no . . . . 333 VIVA 24　　18

+GOOSEBERRIES

FOR CONTEXT, SEE . . . . 100 & POST IMPR 11　　27

GOOSED

is heiry montparnasse is goosed by raspail). But he . . . . . 401 NO THANKS 18　　14

GORGE

close ghosts on prowl gorge sly slim gods stare . . . . 90 & POST IMPR 2　　15
and apples it will, Gorge indistinct palishflesh of laZilytas 100 & POST IMPR 11　　27
head dis-donc, Paris ta gorge mysterieuse pourquoi se . . . . 121 & PORTRAIT 12　　53
& swallow to dis gorge) a sulky gob with . . . . 629 (CHAIRE) 31　　2

GORGEDIS

carroty youth blonde whis (gorgedis reswal lowing spewnonspew 629 (CHAIRE) 31　　17

GORGEOUS

Old Summer Time. My gorgeous bullet in tickling intuitive . . 130 & SON REAL 1　　10
accurately parsed by this gorgeous rush of upward lips.... . 201 XLI PORTRAIT 9　　27

GORRY

your glorious name by gorry by jingo by gee . . . . 268 IS 5 TWO 3　　7

GOSH

jingo by gee by gosh by gum why talk . . . . 268 IS 5 TWO 3　　8

GOSSIP

divisible fool (life imitate gossip fear unlife mean -ness, . 452 NO THANKS 67　　8

GOT

at least we have got a bulge on death, ... 84 T&C SON ACTU 3　　13
into the tree? you got me said the smoke . . . . 125 & SEVEN POEMS 4　　9
at the dawn. she got up with a gashing . . . . 132 & SON REAL 3　　14
her seen, which has got nothing on something as . . . . . . 141 & SON REAL 12　　14
a few times--before she got the info from a . . . . 145 & SON REAL 16　　6
over percent. The gang got shot up twice, it . . . . 149 & SON REAL 20　　8
Jimmie was framed and got his / / . . . . 149 & SON REAL 20　　16
/ / / Jimmie's got a goil goil goil, ... 235 IS 5 ONE 6　　1
goil goil, Jimmie 's got a goil and she . . . . 235 IS 5 ONE 6　　5
two and when Freud got through with Do- nothing . . . . . . 236 IS 5 ONE 7　　8
mob an accident? somebody got concus- sion of the . . . . . 245 IS 5 ONE 16　　17
clutch (and then somehow got into reverse she kicked . . . . 248 IS 5 ONE 19　　11

GOT (CONTINUED)
    a frown Amy Lowell got up and all the . . . . 249 IS 5 ONE 20   3
    Ruskin says about you got the haven't Marjorie isn't . . . . 257 IS 5 ONE 27   35
    is toothsome like (they got pockets full may take . . . . . . 314 VIVA 6   9
    camels ! and i got a Bad almond chick. . . . . 318 VIVA 10   17
    IN) all those who got athlete's mouth jumping on&off . . . . 404 NO THANKS 21   2
    you can't eat you got to smoke and we . . . . 489 50 POEMS 3   1
    smoke and we aint got nothing to smoke: come . . . . 489 50 POEMS 3   2
    you can't smoke you got to Sing and we . . . . 489 50 POEMS 3   5
    Sing and we aint got nothing to sing; come . . . . 489 50 POEMS 3   6
    you can't sing you got to die and we . . . . 489 50 POEMS 3   9
    die and we aint got Nothing to die, come . . . . 489 50 POEMS 3   10
    you can't die you got to dream and we . . . . 489 50 POEMS 3   13
    dream and we aint got nothing to dream (come . . . . 489 50 POEMS 3   14
    that 's what she's got --ex cept what? why . . . . 701 95 POEMS 29   4
    / / / what Got him was Noth ing . . . . 702 95 POEMS 30   1
    have been Something) what got him was nothing / . . . . 702 95 POEMS 30   23
+GOT
    FOR CONTEXT, SEE . . . . 310 VIVA 2   4
    FOR CONTEXT, SEE . . . . 310 VIVA 2   10
    FOR CONTEXT, SEE . . . . 547 1 X 1 7   1
    FOR CONTEXT, SEE . . . . 547 1 X 1 7   6
    FOR CONTEXT, SEE . . . . 547 1 X 1 7   8
    FOR CONTEXT, SEE . . . . 567 1 X 1 27   14
    FOR CONTEXT, SEE . . . . 726 95 POEMS 54   3
GOTTEN
    that it has for -gotten some- thing ah (my . . . . 232 IS 5 ONE 3   16
GOULD
    / / little joe gould has lost his teeth . . . . 410 NO THANKS 27   1
    set which click) little gould used to amputate his . . . . . 410 NO THANKS 27   3
    of little joe (yankee) gould irketh sundry who are . . . . . 410 NO THANKS 27   7
    to be little joe gould) / / / / . . . . 410 NO THANKS 27   14
    / / as joe gould says in his terrifyingly . . . . 700 95 POEMS 28   1
GOULD'S
    smile but little joe gould's quote oral history unquote . . . 410 NO THANKS 27   9
GOW
    (and is that the g.o.w. is full of) delete . . . . 411 NO THANKS 28   12
GOWER
    to walk with Master Gower in Confessio doth prefer . . . . . 20 T&C PUELLA MEA   166
+GOWN
    FOR CONTEXT, SEE . . . . 445 NO THANKS 60   6
GRAB
    nowbrow sangsung nee whitermuch grab sicksilk soak sulksuck . 333 VIVA 24   10
GRABBED
    between squeals of Nothing grabbed with circular shrieking . 195 XLI PORTRAIT 3   14
    body and almost isn't (grabbed into skies of grin) . . . . . 585 1 X 1 45   11
GRABBING
    but who shot up grabbing had by my throat . . . . 496 50 POEMS 10   9
GRACE
    delicious boy whose serious grace one goddess loved too . . .   3 T&C EPITHALAM   24
    again victorious Pantarkes (whose grace the prince of artists   4 T&C EPITHALAM   35
    perfect roses whose ambrosial grace, goddess, thy crippled .   6 T&C EPITHALAM   148
    whose snowy symmetry of grace haunted the limbs as . . . . .   8 T&C OF NICOL   20
    trust him to your grace, and for in his . . . . 42 T&C AMORES 6   23
    since exempt from heaven's grace, in an engraving belonging . 158 & SON ACTU 7   7
    mouth, face delirious. indivisible grace of dancing / / . . . 185 XLI SONGS 7   16
    taught by thy tremulous grace bravely to fling Implacable . . 206 XLI SONNETS 2   3
    guts and gutted with grace" squeeze your nuts and . . . . . . 407 NO THANKS 24   15
GRACED
    mark in a toilet graced with guts and gutted . . . . 407 NO THANKS 24   14
GRACEFUL
    which distinct disks of graceful oath, upsoarings the break . 96 & POST IMPR 8   9
GRACEFULLY
    find somehow (but O gracefully) a we, entirely whose . . . . 368 VIVA 59   12
    a sunset "can grow (gracefully or otherwise) old. Old . . . . 626 {CHAIRE} 28   2
GRACES
    whose pillow is the graces and the hours, father . . . . . .   4 T&C EPITHALAM   40

		PAGE	TITLE	LINE

GRACIOUS
give because the why --gracious wanderer, be thou gay . . . . 651 (CHAIRE) 53   12
GRADUAL
the amorous strain of gradual hands and yielding to . . . . . 4 T&C EPITHALAM   54
/ before the fragile gradual throne of night slowly . . . . . 156 & SON ACTU 5   1
simply Lustful.... sense a gradual stir of beginning muscle, 157 & SON ACTU 6   3
Love coins His most gradual gesture, and whittles life . . . 297 IS 5 FOUR 14   12
become of with his gradual acute lusting glance an . . . . . 374 VIVA 65   5
from rises army the gradual of unbeing (fro on . . . . 633 (CHAIRE) 35   3
GRADUALLY
featheriest slenderness and how gradually which descending . 299 IS 5 FOUR 16   6
cigarette between his ghost-lips gradually) remembering . . . 300 IS 5 FOUR 17   21
fingers, loving one another gradually into hands) and bend . 305 IS 5 FIVE 4   3
but i slightly smiling, gradually shall reenter the singular 370 VIVA 61   19
unto colour; create me gradually (or as these emerging . . . 372 VIVA 63   2
of space-- life stands gradually upon four minds (out . . . . 517 50 POEMS 31   8
+GRADUALLY
FOR CONTEXT, SEE . . . . 255 IS 5 ONE 26   8
GRADUATE
/ / yonder deadfromtheneckup graduate of a somewhat obscure . 234 IS 5 ONE 5   1
GRAFTER
wellfilled pants earth's biggest grafter, nothing less; the . 266 IS 5 TWO 1   33
GRAIN
was as green as grain septembering arms of year . . . . . . 520 50 POEMS 34   36
GRAMMAR
i'm mistaken chauvesouris-- whose grammar is atrocious; but . 504 50 POEMS 18   10
GRAMMATICAL
declarative sentence with seven grammatical errors "is dead" 336 VIVA 27   4
GRAND
the bumping teem of Grand. a nudging froth of . . . . 219 XLI SONNETS 15   10
in memory of the Grand and Old days: of . . . . 233 IS 5 ONE 4   17
of the de l'Europe Grand and Royal Danielli their . . . . . . 256 IS 5 ONE 27   19
your choice. Ain't freedom grand / / / / . . . . 636 (CHAIRE) 38   14
/ / fearlessandbosomy this grand: gal who liked men . . . . . 792 73 POEMS 20   3
+GRAND
FOR CONTEXT, SEE . . . . 331 VIVA 22   1
+GRANDEUR
FOR CONTEXT, SEE . . . . 233 IS 5 ONE 4   12
GRANDILOQUENT
whole with a distinct grandiloquent deep D; while all . . . . 650 (CHAIRE) 52   15
+GRANDMOTHER
FOR CONTEXT, SEE . . . . 748 95 POEMS 76   6
+GRANDMOTHER'S
FOR CONTEXT, SEE . . . . 748 95 POEMS 76   1
GRANIA
the world! who with Grania strangely fled, who with . . . . . 22 T&C PUELLA MEA   245
GRANIA'S
and Diarmuid looked in Grania's eyes.) But should my . . . . 18 T&C PUELLA MEA   60
+GRANT
FOR CONTEXT, SEE . . . . 321 VIVA 13   10
GRANTED
sir which is why granted who discovered America ether . . . . 238 IS 5 ONE 9   13
/ / / but granted that it's nothing paradoxically . . . . . . 329 VIVA 20   1
/ / / / granted the all saving our . . . . 373 VIVA 64   1
GRAPES
wine than should the grapes of heaven combine with . . . . . 21 T&C PUELLA MEA   200
(swallow s bun chesofnew grapes likeGree n A r . . . . 100 & POST IMPR 11   24
GRAPPLE
the terrific fingers which grapple and joke on my . . . . . . 146 & SON REAL 17   5
GRASP
throbbing neck whereby to grasp the belly's ample vase . . . 21 T&C PUELLA MEA   197
GRASS
spear-song of the marching grass. A silver sudden parody . . 4 T&C EPITHALAM   72
of radiance, to the grass-- shunning the sudden moonbeam's . 8 T&C OF NICOL   24
love walking in the grass their wings will touch . . . . . . 16 T&C SONGS 6   11
and flops along the grass collides with trees and . . . . . 47 T&C IMPRESS 1   9
in your whiskey-voice the grass rises on the head . . . . . . 61 T&C PORTRAIT 9   19
dark gold delicately smash.... grass, and the stars, of . . . 153 & SON ACTU 2   8

GRASS (CONTINUED)
    said, and under the grass lies her head by . . . . 181 XLI SONGS 3   12
    and, cruelly, across the grass Comes the moon love, ... 190 XLI SONGS 12   9
    lay, watching (sprawling, in grass upon a cliff) what . . . . 283 IS 5 THREE 7   23
    TerFLY went (flesh is grass) from Troy, n.y. the . . . . . . 320 VIVA 12   2
    of (all flesh is grass) with one "Paul" a . . . . 320 VIVA 12   6
    my motH) with a grass wid OW er who . . . . 320 VIVA 12   17
    that's furled (sestet entitled grass is flesh or swim . . . . 390 NO THANKS 7   9
    extracted hate from whispering grass? joy in time shut . . . 527 50 POEMS 39   10
    anything under skies over grass until and until into . . . . 587 1 X 1 47   12
GRASSBLADE
    mine) i guess a grassblade Thinks beyond or around . . . . . 364 VIVA 55   6
GRASSBLADES
    (am was) assassinating whole grassblades, five ideas can . . 491 50 POEMS 5   12
GRASSHOPPER
    (com) gi (e) ngly ,grasshopper; / / / / . . . . 396 NO THANKS 13   15
    will be saviours --flop grasshopper, exactly nothing's soon; 555 1 X 1 15   8
+GRASSHOPPER
    FOR CONTEXT, SEE . . . . 396 NO THANKS 13   1
    FOR CONTEXT, SEE . . . . 396 NO THANKS 13   5
    FOR CONTEXT, SEE . . . . 396 NO THANKS 13   13
GRAVE
    purple patience and the grave frailty of daisies--by what . .   5 T&C EPITHALAM   93
    delicious frown of the grave great sensual knees well . . . . 21 T&C PUELLA MEA   213
    wholly chained to a grave astonishment feel in my . . . . . . 79 T&C SON UNRE 4   11
    begins to frail (whose grave already three or two . . . . . . 115 & PORTRAIT 8   2
    faint close as some grave languorous hymn pledged to . . . . 206 XLI SONNETS 2   12
    the silver bird looked grave (departing hurriedly to shave) . 339 VIVA 30   20
    poem huger than the grave? from only Whom shall . . . . 377 VIVA 68   12
    fits him like a grave) with all his toys . . . . 394 NO THANKS 11   2
    knowledge lies, the foetal grave called progress, and . . . . 484 NEW POEMS 22   11
    forever out of his grave and sprinkles nowhere with . . . . . 560 1 X 1 20   19
    collective myth) into thy grave merely to toil the . . . . . 579 1 X 1 39   9
    beautiful sake of a grave gay brave bright cry . . . . 587 1 X 1 47   21
+GRAVE
    FOR CONTEXT, SEE . . . . 342 VIVA 33   19
GRAVENSTEINS
    apples are (yes they're gravensteins) all as red as . . . . . 543 1 X 1 3   4
    and the round (they're gravensteins) fall with kind of . . . 543 1 X 1 3   28
GRAVES
    says! Says over un graves der, speaking (says. word . . . . . 417 NO THANKS 34   3
+GRAVESTONE
    FOR CONTEXT, SEE . . . . 833 73 POEMS 61   11
GRAVEYARD
    a thread invisible) A graveyard dreams through its cluttered 434 NO THANKS 51   22
GRAVYPISSING
    foetus (a punkslapping mobsucking gravypissing poppa but who 635 (CHAIRE) 37   4
GRAY
    sheer cadence of our gray flesh in the gloom! . . . .   9 T&C SONGS 1   23
GRAZE
    tortured perspective rasp and graze of splintered normality . 48 T&C IMPRESS 2   4
    and leal citizens did graze at pause then fired . . . . 258 IS 5 ONE 28   10
+GRAZE
    FOR CONTEXT, SEE . . . . 150 & SON REAL 21   9
GREASEDLIGHTNING
    low through second-in-to-high like greasedlightning) just as 248 IS 5 ONE 19   21
GREAT
    of god's evasive audible great rose! Lover, lead forth . . .   5 T&C EPITHALAM   112
    love riding on a great horse of gold into . . . . 14 T&C SONGS 4   2
    love riding on a great horse of gold into . . . . 14 T&C SONGS 4   32
    in my heart so great a noise, as in . . . . 18 T&C PUELLA MEA   65
    frown of the grave great sensual knees well might . . . . . . 21 T&C PUELLA MEA   213
    the devil ach the great green dancing devil devil . . . . . . 25 T&C CHANSONS 2   24
    me and became a great lily atilt on insolent . . . . 30 T&C ORIENTALE 4   5
    tall marble from a great way i distinguished singing . . . . 30 T&C ORIENTALE 4   21
    chants the litanies the great bells are ringing with . . . . 51 T&C IMPRESS 5   6
    hand opening the hard great eyes to noone in . . . .   53 T&C PORTRAIT 1   44
    smile is the most great common divisor of unequal . . . . . . 74 T&C SON REAL 5   14

GREAT (CONTINUED)

i know, or such great writhing words as, uttering . . . . . . 76 T&C SON UNRE 1   7
with fucking eyes the great black preacher gargles jesus . . 108 & PORTRAIT 4   27
Nile the kind black great god) Cleopatra you are . . . . . . 112 & PORTRAIT 6   88
and the neighing of great steeds moving to war . . . . 209 XLI SONNETS 5   4
not night did the great world (in darkly taking . . . . 432 NO THANKS 49   2
our doom steer his great small wish into upward . . . . . . 528 50 POEMS 40   7
(dear) worlds of than great more eyes, and what . . . . . . 573 1 X 1 33   3
/ noone" autumnal this great lady's gaze enters a . . . . . . 626 (CHAIRE) 28   1
he never tried) the great pink superme diocri ty . . . . . . 635 (CHAIRE) 37   7
exactly do next (our great problem nearly solved we . . . . . 650 (CHAIRE) 52   13
and of the gay great happening illimitably earth) how . . . . 663 (CHAIRE) 65   8
/ / / the great advantage of being alive . . . . 664 (CHAIRE) 66   1
soul may touch --the great (my darling) happens to . . . . . 664 (CHAIRE) 66   5
a little church (no great cathedral) far from the . . . . . . 749 95 POEMS 77   1
the sky: with a great (and a gay and . . . . 769 95 POEMS 95   13
/ / / a great man is gone. Tall . . . . 786 73 POEMS 14   1
everywhere around) me (the great dim deep sound of . . . . . 816 73 POEMS 44   2
+GREAT
FOR CONTEXT, SEE . . . . 209 XLI SONNETS 5   1
GREATER
upon our abdomens for greater privacy and lest punished . . . 261 IS 5 ONE 31   13
the sun (we're everything greater than books might mean) . . 594 1 X 1 54   38
GREATEST
your dead beauties, you greatest lovers in the world! . . . . 22 T&C PUELLA MEA 244
"but why should" the greatest of living magicians (whom . . . 738 95 POEMS 66   3
GREATGRANDMOTHER
comprises poems (my mother's greatgrandmother surely would . 748 95 POEMS 76   6
GREATGRANDMOTHER'S
these from my mother's greatgrandmother's rosebush white . . 748 95 POEMS 76   1
GREATLY
songs it does not greatly matter to the sun, ... 84 T&C SON ACTU 3   7
GREATNESS
and alone only as greatness is alone-- one (above . . . . . . 808 73 POEMS 36   4
GREECE
that or which was Greece all the grandja that . . . . 233 IS 5 ONE 4   11
+GREECE
FOR CONTEXT, SEE . . . . 500 50 POEMS 14   13
GREEDIER
your deepening thighs a greedier wand than even death's . . . 454 NO THANKS 69   4
fiends and gods each greedier than every) is a . . . . 609 (CHAIRE) 11   2
GREEDIEST
and dolls resist Them Greediest Paws of careful time . . . . 260 IS 5 ONE 30   10
GREEDILY
but it swallow) s greedily sugaredellipses it does not . . . 100 & POST IMPR 11   29
GREEDY
/ / / the greedy the people (as if . . . . 801 73 POEMS 29   1
GREEKS
Hassan chuckles seeing the Greeks breathe) / / / . . . . . . 220 XLI SONNETS 16   16
GREEN
kingdom winter cowers, seeing green armies steadily expand . 4 T&C EPITHALAM 71
/ / All in green went my love riding . . . . 14 T&C SONGS 4   1
tall stags at a green mountain the lucky hunter . . . . 14 T&C SONGS 4   29
sang before. All in green went my love riding . . . . 14 T&C SONGS 4   31
devil ach the great green dancing devil devil devil . . . . . 25 T&C CHANSONS 2   25
my soul spoke the green- greeting pale- departing irrevocable 39 T&C AMORES 4   24
doll undressed in unripe green with nauseous spiderlegs and . 55 T&C PORTRAIT 3   9
the reachings of Her green body among unseen things, ... 77 T&C SON UNRE 2   2
with this indubitable and green person "Are You the . . . . . 91 & POST IMPR 3   7
A lady in a green dress, who; touches: the . . . . 91 & POST IMPR 3   19
eyes there lives a green egyptian noise. ladies with . . . . 138 & SON REAL 9   8
in Yonkers. Dick Mid's green large three teeth leak . . . . . 149 & SON REAL 20   14
dream-- when on a green brief gesture of twilight . . . . . . 156 & SON ACTU 5   8
utterable coolness deeds of green thrilling light with . . . 163 & SON ACTU 12   8
/ / / between green mountains sings the flinger . . . . 185 XLI SONGS 7   1
found you in the green forest and were you . . . . 192 XLI CHANSONS 2   5
once noted lifting a Green River (here's to youse) . . . . . 229 IS 5 ONE FRAN   10
your eyes, gifted with green twilight) / / / . . . . 291 IS 5 FOUR 8   27

		PAGE	TITLE	LINE
GREEN (CONTINUED)

askyuh woodundat maik yurarstoin green? Oilsaisough.) --Hool 310 VIVA 2   7
is sittin in uh green field watchin four crows . . . . 332 VIVA 23   30
his impeccable feathered with green facts preening solemnity 344 VIVA 35   2
(ver All) Th (e grEEn ?eartH) N, ew / . . . . 347 VIVA 38   33
i fell through the green groove of twilight, striking . . . . 360 VIVA 51   18
of clover, from the green meadow of time lessness; . . . . . 370 VIVA 61   5
Not more than (if Green invents because where might . . . . . 395 NO THANKS 12   6
yellow violet white orange green- ness o what a . . . . 437 NO THANKS 53   14
by pink mr seized green mrs opening is it . . . . 465 NEW POEMS 3   7
totally sprouted by alive green each very lifting & . . . . . 480 NEW POEMS 18   24
how begins a pillow's green means face or why . . . . 506 50 POEMS 20   9
his pity was as green as grain septembering arms . . . . . . 520 50 POEMS 34   36
into the silence the green silence with a white . . . . 529 50 POEMS 41   1
up comes yesterday most green and young pleasure and . . . . 531 50 POEMS 43   4
as to die (each green of a new) you're . . . . 543 1 X 1 3   10
his pines lifted their green lives and smiled / . . . . 555 1 X 1 15   16
thankfully whole and the green whereless truth of an . . . . 558 1 X 1 18   4
/ / / open green those (dear) worlds of . . . . 573 1 X 1 33   1
all the blue heaven green earth neither sea here's . . . . . 588 1 X 1 48   3
who stood on a green hill and threw his . . . . 593 1 X 1 53   4
/ / if the green opens a little a . . . . 614 {CHAIRE} 16   2
is too if the green robe o p e . . . . 614 {CHAIRE} 16   10
and his voice is green like growing (is miraculous . . . . . 617 {CHAIRE} 19   6
clean) all except the green ones / / / . . . . 619 {CHAIRE} 21   28
as terror and as green as fate, greyly shall . . . . 649 {CHAIRE} 51   11
souls, awakened from summer's green trance, would not . . . . 675 95 POEMS 3   10
beginningless a Magic of green solitude (go marvels come) . . 757 95 POEMS 85   16
in mind) through some green mysterious land until my . . . . 777 73 POEMS 5   4
pure) even than the green the new the earth . . . . 778 73 POEMS 6   7
fire called flowers over green the new earth a . . . . 778 73 POEMS 6   17
went on both knees" green turns red (the roar . . . . 800 73 POEMS 28   17
as everywhere red goes green --groping blank sky with . . . . 800 73 POEMS 28   22
such vivid nothing as green meteors swim signals all . . . . 818 73 POEMS 46   11

+GREEN

FOR CONTEXT, SEE . . . . 100 & POST IMPR 11   24
FOR CONTEXT, SEE . . . . 278 IS 5 THREE 2   6
FOR CONTEXT, SEE . . . . 281 IS 5 THREE 5   9
FOR CONTEXT, SEE . . . . 342 VIVA 33   24
FOR CONTEXT, SEE . . . . 385 NO THANKS 2   43

GREEN'S

/ / / / grEEn's d an cing on . . . . 534 50 POEMS 46   1

GREENER

sometime dwell (within a greener shadow of secret bowers) . .   3 T&C EPITHALAM   22
greenest riding on a greener (o little i) riding . . . . . . 535 50 POEMS 47   6
and a world grows greener minute by second and . . . . 769 95 POEMS 95   1

GREENEST

treetop riding on a greenest riding on a greener . . . . . . 535 50 POEMS 47   5

+GREENEST

FOR CONTEXT, SEE . . . . 581 1 X 1 41   6

GREENISH

bushy obscurity a bald greenish foetal head established It .   96 & POST IMPR 8   29

GREENLY

o each living ablaze greenly thing ; may has . . . . 583 1 X 1 43   13
unbeing (fro on stiffening greenly air and to ghosts . . . . 633 {CHAIRE} 35   4
day: for the leaping greenly spirits of trees and . . . . . 663 {CHAIRE} 65   2
whoing sea leaps to greenly hurl snow suppose we . . . . . . 743 95 POEMS 71   3

GREENNESS

seem by the perusing greenness of thy thought my . . . . . .   9 T&C SONGS 1   29
intense digestion so much greenness only dying makes us . . . 491 50 POEMS 5   16

+GREENNESS

FOR CONTEXT, SEE . . . . 437 NO THANKS 53   14

GREENS

are packed with hardslippery greens and helplessbaby blues . 100 & POST IMPR 11   4
spry pinks shy lemons greens coo 1 choc olate . . . . 179 XLI SONGS 1   10
outer wing strong silent greens serenely lingering, absolute 208 XLI SONNETS 4   3

GREENSLIM

belong to Marj the greenslim purse of whose face . . . . . . 114 & PORTRAIT 7   18

GREENTHATPINK
    ver pinkthisgreen acr) o) greenthatpink) acrobata mong trees 385 NO THANKS 2   43
GREENTWITTERING
    brown god smiles between greentwittering smokes from broken . 28 T&C ORIENTALE 2   4
GREENWICH
    spring, the little barbarous Greenwich perfumed fake And . . 220 XLI SONNETS 16   10
GREET
    by sun i deeply greet this fool and man . . . . 441 NO THANKS 56   67
GREETING
    soul spoke the green- greeting pale- departing irrevocable . 39 T&C AMORES 4   25
GREETS
    lug of love) sincerely greets, with an occult shrug . . . . . 137 & SON REAL 8   4
    otherwise scented merde which greets one (Everywhere Why) as 230 IS 5 ONE 2   17
GREW
    forgot as up they grew autumn winter spring summer) . . . . . 515 50 POEMS 29   10
GREY
    lips vivid, the face grey, and silent smileless eyes . . . . 75 T&C SON REAL 6   7
    where softly preys the grey and perpendicular Always-- or . . 218 XLI SONNETS 14   11
    / / this (that grey) white (man) horse floats . . . . 408 NO THANKS 25   2
    histories plunge? rains a grey snow of mothery same . . . . . 527 50 POEMS 39   28
    and as collapsing that grey mind by wave doom . . . . 599 {CHAIRE} 1   6
    / a like a grey rock wanderin g through . . . . 654 {CHAIRE} 56   2
+GREY
    FOR CONTEXT, SEE . . . . 705 95 POEMS 33   1
GREYLY
    as green as fate, greyly shall fail and dully . . . . 649 {CHAIRE} 51   12
GREYS
    that dizzily grips. Querying greys between mouthed houses . . 139 & SON REAL 10   12
GRIEF
    arose nor hate nor grief can go where goes . . . . 441 NO THANKS 56   43
    dolls of joy and grief these recent memories of . . . . 502 50 POEMS 16   9
    joy she cried his grief bird by snow and . . . . 515 50 POEMS 29   14
    undering joy and overing grief nothing arrives a so . . . . . 517 50 POEMS 31   9
    each anguish is his grief; and, for his joy . . . . 562 1 X 1 22   3
    or joy is my grief or my gladness around . . . . 749 95 POEMS 77   8
GRIEFS
    laugh is a million griefs wide (it shall bury . . . . 439 NO THANKS 55   11
    my father moved through griefs of joy; praising a . . . . . . 520 50 POEMS 34   18
GRIEVE
    the empty twilight cannot grieve nor the autumn, as . . . . . 165 & SON ACTU 14   8
    the autumn, as i grieve, faint for your face . . . . 165 & SON ACTU 14   9
GRIEVING
    the rose motionless with grieving feet and wings mounts . . . 59 T&C PORTRAIT 7   11
    wind's menace and leaf's grieving: from the impressed fingers 207 XLI SONNETS 3   10
GRIM
    in a hoop of grim ecstasy / / / . . . . 137 & SON REAL 8   18
    hulking perpendicular mammal a grim epitome of chuckling . . 151 & SON REAL 22   5
    sits my life; the grim clenched mind of me . . . . 156 & SON ACTU 5   10
    infantile eyes drooling unmind grim yessing childflesh . . . 337 VIVA 28   7
    mere mind's poor pretend --grim comics of duration: only . . 576 1 X 1 36   7
    yet in park this grim most (these one who . . . . 698 95 POEMS 26   5
GRIMLY
    to die. When we grimly go to bed with . . . . 147 & SON REAL 18   12
GRIN
    scribbled with a big grin. her sow- eyes clicking . . . . . . 73 T&C SON REAL 4   6
    opens on a fatgold grin hooray hoorah for the . . . . 114 & PORTRAIT 7   21
    swallowed eyes smiles, one grin very distinctly wobbles from 151 & SON REAL 22   15
    insane teeth the vertical grin give me the Square . . . . . . 220 XLI SONNETS 16   8
    me a mellifluous idiot grin (with what was nose . . . . 226 IS 5 ONE MAME   2
    him with a changeless grin whereon a dozen staunch . . . . . 258 IS 5 ONE 28   8
    rubber) tres (plants how grin ho) cen (tel und . . . . 309 VIVA 1   27
    nicely the lady's small grin said (with more simplicity . . . 506 50 POEMS 20   13
    / you which could grin three smiles into a . . . . 522 50 POEMS 35   1
    thank you which could grin may stern particular Love . . . . 522 50 POEMS 35   9
    a man grinned his grin done his chores laid . . . . 568 1 X 1 28   27
    (seeing something yes) will grin with pain You so&so . . . . 570 1 X 1 30   8
    (grabbed into skies of grin) "my flowers" (the humble . . . . 585 1 X 1 45   12
    spurred with an apish grin (extremely like but quite . . . . 640 {CHAIRE} 42   6

GRIN (CONTINUED)
    (inch) wraithish (by inch) grin ning heshaped two these . . . 681 95 POEMS 9   2
    whom we make (of grin for smile whose head's . . . . 716 95 POEMS 44   6
    to sing an only grin-- dancing to feel nots . . . . 716 95 POEMS 44   20
    / / / a grin without a face (a . . . . 797 73 POEMS 25   1
GRIND
    the next train to grind me into lifeless atoms . . . . 262 IS 5 ONE 32   3
GRINDS
    which flipchucking . grins gRiNdS d is app ea . . . . 445 NO THANKS 60   22
GRINDSTONE
    (s gruntsqueak , while, idling-is-grindstone one; what: of. . 656 (CHAIRE) 58   7
GRINGLEHOW
    scratches tomorrowlobs wholeagainst you gringlehow exudes . . 333 VIVA 24   6
GRINNED
    sam was a man grinned his grin done his . . . . 568 1 X 1 28   27
GRINNING
    dressed like a Plum grinning softly, New focus-of disintegrat   94 & POST IMPR 6   16
    yoo (friend the laughing grinning) we no (smiling) strike . . 618 (CHAIRE) 20   7
+GRINNING
    FOR CONTEXT, SEE . . . . 681 95 POEMS 9   2
GRINS
    jim him why gluey grins topple together eyes pout . . . . . .   96 & POST IMPR 8   17
    tellurian strolls emitting minute grins each an intaglio. . . 116 & PORTRAIT 9   6
    and. rages Laughters jostle grins nudge smiles push--. deep . 202 XLI PORTRAIT 9   36
    steps; which flipchucking . grins gRiNdS d is app . . . . . . 445 NO THANKS 60   21
GRINTGRUNT
    white its stimpstamps) the grintgrunt wugglewiggle . . . . . 773 73 POEMS 1   11
GRIP
    mouth occurs homelessly. While grip Hips simply. well fussed 136 & SON REAL 7   11
    smell of deads (lovers grip sprawl twitch lovers) & . . . . . 384 NO THANKS 2   10
    r in gly eyes grip live loop croon mime . . . . 445 NO THANKS 60   24
GRIPPING
    lips study my head gripping for a decision: burn . . . . . . 146 & SON REAL 17   4
    gold-fish away from the gripping gigantic muscles of . . . . 180 XLI SONGS 2   14
GRIPS
    of Hell) me suddenly grips in chuckles of supreme . . . . . . 130 & SON REAL 1   8
    killing flame that dizzily grips. Querying greys between . . 139 & SON REAL 10   11
GRITTED
    flower of madness on gritted lips and on sprawled . . . . . . 139 & SON REAL 10   9
GROAN
    fruit. My lips pleasantly groan on your taste. Jumped . . . . 154 & SON ACTU 3   3
    and a keen cold groan while the gadgets purred . . . . 647 (CHAIRE) 49   8
GROANING
    last we on the groaning flame of neat huge . . . .   67 T&C POST IMPR 4   24
+GROANING
    FOR CONTEXT, SEE . . . . 656 (CHAIRE) 58   13
+GROANINGISHLY
    FOR CONTEXT, SEE . . . . 656 (CHAIRE) 58   1
GROANS
    instru- ments, waltzing; undigestibly: groans. bounce ! . . . 442 NO THANKS 57   6
GROOM
    goddess, thy crippled thunder-foraging groom or the loud lord   6 T&C EPITHALAM   149
    this little bride & groom are standing) in a . . . . 470 NEW POEMS 8   1
    little bride & little groom in it kind of . . . . 470 NEW POEMS 8   10
GROOVE
    fell through the green groove of twilight, striking into . . 360 VIVA 51   18
    (travelling in a futile groove god knows why) and . . . . . . 413 NO THANKS 30   15
+GROOVING
    FOR CONTEXT, SEE . . . . 286 IS 5 FOUR 3   9
GROPEOFSTRENGTH
    lips comb my mumbling gropeofstrength (staggered by the lug . 137 & SON REAL 8   2
GROPING
    the whispered deep, deliberate groping ocean fondled o'er the   7 T&C EPITHALAM   159
    swallowed, muscle (itch of groping mucous) in my mouth . . . 136 & SON REAL 7   10
    that among first light groping washes my nightmare from . . . 374 VIVA 65   15
    everywhere red goes green --groping blank sky with a . . . . 800 73 POEMS 28   23
+GROPING
    FOR CONTEXT, SEE . . . . 330 VIVA 21   3

+GROPINGNESS
    FOR CONTEXT, SEE . . . . 383 NO THANKS 1   3
GROSS
    / / between nose-red gross walls sprawling with tipsy . . . . 55 T&C PORTRAIT 3   1
    lips and stare the gross fuzzy-pash --dead--and the dark . . 153 & SON ACTU 2   6
    with minute odour these gross days when i think . . . . 165 & SON ACTU 14   5
GROUND
    new mosaic of the ground --let but the incurious . . . . . .   5 T&C EPITHALAM   84
    your ear to the ground there is a music . . . . 113 & PORTRAIT 6   114
    which, considering the back- ground, it is hardly surprising 263 IS 5 ONE 32   35
    & gone into the ground) but though with wormS . . . . 361 VIVA 52   4
    big sound on the ground / / / / . . . . 543 1 X 1 3   30
    float out of the ground and breathing is wishing . . . . . . 665 (CHAIRE) 67   1
    wandering deeply through godthanking ground) bluest whos of . 754 95 POEMS 82   4
GROUPED
    sag of fruit distinctly grouped. I have not eaten . . . . . . 219 XLI SONNETS 15   1
GROUPINGTHE
    (stamens&pistil silent A s groupingThe 6around one darks to . 342 VIVA 33   5
GROUSE
    by When eaten spaces grouse rocket know quite, slightly . . . 346 VIVA 37   11
GROVELLING
    strangling breasts and bestial grovelling hands rasps the . . 28 T&C ORIENTALE 2   8
GROW
    from my lady's body grow; as morning may a . . . . 21 T&C PUELLA MEA 183
    roses of the day grow deep. / / / . . . . 78 T&C SON UNRE 3   14
    which never lets you grow old blinking at the . . . . 96 & POST IMPR 8   24
    the trees, lay, which grow / / / / . . . . 154 & SON ACTU 3   16
    (and watching her face grow old and tired to . . . . 242 IS 5 ONE 13   14
    and their Lives who grow slowly and first into . . . . 311 VIVA 3   8
    minds shrivel and hearts grow brittler every Instant (when . 359 VIVA 50   4
    causeless cloud to purely grow but, never doubt my . . . . . 433 NO THANKS 50   4
    proudly things only which grow and the rain's wings . . . . . 441 NO THANKS 56   54
    tinily whirls; while daisies grow (and boys and girls . . . . 451 NO THANKS 66   12
    money lucky are Breathe grow dream die love not . . . . 467 NEW POEMS 5   8
    only dying makes us grow / / / / . . . . 491 50 POEMS 5   16
    more death begins to grow end's ending then these . . . . . . 502 50 POEMS 16   8
    so dark the mountains grow up from the sky . . . . 505 50 POEMS 19   10
    as hatracks into peachtrees grow or hopes dance best . . . . 511 50 POEMS 25   8
    could feel the mountains grow. Lifting the valleys of . . . . 520 50 POEMS 34   16
    eachs and cowards into grow our can'ts were born . . . . . . 537 50 POEMS 49   8
    and its fate to grow shall hate confound the . . . . 538 50 POEMS 50   4
    you're who as to grow but you're he as . . . . 543 1 X 1 3   11
    called dying born) must grow deep in dark least . . . . 556 1 X 1 16   12
    verbal adventure to illimitably Grow / / / / . . . . 557 1 X 1 17   16
    then "everything beautiful can grow" my, her life marvels . . 572 1 X 1 32   14
    true would truest lovers grow if out of midnight . . . . . . 576 1 X 1 36   11
    but) look: begins to grow more than all real, ... 582 1 X 1 42   8
    better than books don't grow) one's anything old being . . . 594 1 X 1 54   13
    no more miracle may grow --childfully serious flower of . . . 601 (CHAIRE) 3   6
    seeks thinking, swim (opening) grow are (me wander and . . . 612 (CHAIRE) 14   2
    enters a sunset "can grow (gracefully or otherwise) old. . . 626 (CHAIRE) 28   2
    to dream "and poets grow; and (there--see?) children" nor . . 626 (CHAIRE) 28   12
    our doom is to grow (remember this my sweet) . . . . 686 95 POEMS 14   13
    of living is to grow) forgetting why, remember how . . . . . 688 95 POEMS 16   2
    while earth and sky grow one with won der . . . . 715 95 POEMS 43   9
    which only dies to grow can guess and as . . . . 718 95 POEMS 46   6
    houses turning into themselves grow silent upon new perfectly 720 95 POEMS 48   2
    --but better than to grow beauty knows no their . . . . 742 95 POEMS 70   5
    worry if briefer days grow briefest, i am not . . . . 749 95 POEMS 77   3
    worry if longer nights grow longest; i am not . . . . 749 95 POEMS 77   15
    while a star can grow all distance breathes a . . . . 750 95 POEMS 78   1
    is the now to grow it's love by whom . . . . 776 73 POEMS 4   16
    do not conceive--let ocean grow again / / / . . . . 843 73 POEMS 71   14
+GROW
    FOR CONTEXT, SEE . . . . 574 1 X 1 34   12
GROWING
    she sits sewing and growing and that's the truth, ... 125 & SEVEN POEMS 4   5
    roof or something where who-ever-heard-of-growing . . . . . . 127 & SEVEN POEMS 5 43

	PAGE	TITLE	LINE
GROWING (CONTINUED)			
voice is green like growing (is miraculous like tomorrow) . .	617	{CHAIRE} 19	6
of this being are growing stones (neither awake are	617	{CHAIRE} 19	8
rather not become; but growing is" erect her whole	626	{CHAIRE} 28	5
longing --a time for growing and a time for	683	95 POEMS 11	11
+GROWING			
FOR CONTEXT, SEE	471	NEW POEMS 9	8
FOR CONTEXT, SEE	657	{CHAIRE} 59	13
FOR CONTEXT, SEE	729	95 POEMS 57	19
GROWINGEST			
of the wonder (beingest growingest) over all under all . . .	590	1 X 1 50	20
+GROWL			
FOR CONTEXT, SEE	795	73 POEMS 23	5
+GROWLS			
FOR CONTEXT, SEE	705	95 POEMS 33	11
GROWN			
body with wise breasts half-grown, lisping flesh quick to . .	140	& SON REAL 11	11
here (far from a grown -up i&you- ful world	832	73 POEMS 60	9
GROWS			
lady who sews and grows every day paler-paler she	125	& SEVEN POEMS 4	4
Of Tints (and) & (grows) Slowly (slowly) Voyaging tones . . .	348	VIVA 39	6
Nobody knows where truth grows why birds fly and	368	VIVA 59	19
i and who? each grows" then in a whisper, ...	626	{CHAIRE} 28	10
that life (who never grows old) is always beau	724	95 POEMS 52	18
/ if the Lovestar grows most big a voice	752	95 POEMS 80	1
tree called life; which grows higher than soul can	766	95 POEMS 92	12
word; and a world grows greener minute by second	769	95 POEMS 95	1
of their murdered planet grows more and enormously more . . .	808	73 POEMS 36	10
GRREAPSPHOS			
a (r rIvInG . gRrEaPsPhOs) to rea (be) rran	396	NO THANKS 13	12
GRUB			
shop doors unlocked by white-grub faces) clothes in delicate	172	& SON ACTU 21	6
GRUESOME			
the thing. Her voice? gruesome: a trull leaps from	227	IS 5 ONE GERT	13
GRUMBLING			
a mothermonster with red grumbling face cluttered in pursuit	56	T&C PORTRAIT 4	6
+GRUNT			
FOR CONTEXT, SEE	773	73 POEMS 1	11
GRUNTING			
norm of agony my grunting eyes pin tailored flames	137	& SON REAL 8	10
us Things which bulge: grunting lungs pumped full of	195	XLI PORTRAIT 3	4
GRUNTSQUEAK			
ish: ly; come (s gruntsqueak , while, idling-is-grindstone .	656	{CHAIRE} 58	5
GUARD			
careful Than of everything guard her perhaps only A	453	NO THANKS 68	4
/ sentinel robins two guard me and you and	746	95 POEMS 74	2
GUARDIANS			
/ / / white guardians of the universe of	811	73 POEMS 39	1
GUELPH			
pelf and ghibelline and guelph and ladios and laddios	552	1 X 1 12	12
GUENEVER			
and Launcelot spoke to Guenever, a flower which most	18	T&C PUELLA MEA	57
GUERRE			
/ / / LA GUERRE the bigness of cannon	45	T&C LA GUERRE 1	T
dance where danced la guerre. Mimi a la voix	120	& PORTRAIT 12	4
where has danced la guerre j'm'appelle Manon, cinq rue . . .	121	& PORTRAIT 12	34
/ / / LA GUERRE earth like a tipsy	203	XLI LA GUERRE 1	T
both who is la guerre) your me or simplify	577	1 X 1 37	11
GUESS			
magic and (as i guess) when Farmer Death (whom	83	T&C SON ACTU 2	10
there nothing left to guess: the cheap intelligent thighs, .	173	& SON ACTU 22	13
autumn she will never guess. but i know /	183	XLI SONGS 5	15
of life almost do guess) if god should send	205	XLI SONNETS 1	8
sculpture and prose flowers guess and miss machinery is . . .	264	IS 5 ONE 33	10
less; the Honorable Mr. (guess) who, breathing on the	266	IS 5 TWO 1	34
arrived your mind may guess if at sunset it	285	IS 5 FOUR 2	11
your heart will never guess how much my wonderful	292	IS 5 FOUR 9	15
your heart's mine) i guess a grassblade Thinks beyond	364	VIVA 55	6

		PAGE	TITLE	LINE

GUESS (CONTINUED)

trees dance (and i guess though wish and world . . . . 372 VIVA 63   14
more than know means guess) I item i immaculately . . . . . . 390 NO THANKS 7   11
dissolved by the lewd guess of fabulous immensity the . . . . 419 NO THANKS 36   7
all earth's rotting scholars guess that life shall not . . . 420 NO THANKS 37   8
here's to one undiscoverable guess of whose mad skill . . . . 424 NO THANKS 41   12
when) that's yours; i guess you'll have to loan . . . . 451 NO THANKS 66   5
of almost) never shall guess the dimension of him . . . . . . 512 50 POEMS 26   4
day anyone died i guess (and noone stooped to . . . . 515 50 POEMS 29   25
knowledge of death's wandering guess) while children climb . 517 50 POEMS 31   13
now (softlying wisdoms enter guess) childmoon smile to your . 518 50 POEMS 32   10
tomorrow (than today can guess or fears to dare . . . . 522 50 POEMS 35   7
and have is (you guess) perhaps the very unkindest . . . . . 528 50 POEMS 40   10
something as you'll never guess in fifty thousand years . . . 544 1 X 1 4   13
our least begin to guess / / / / . . . . 574 1 X 1 34   14
eternal terrors like a guess. Life's life and strikes . . . . 582 1 X 1 42   15
stupidest teacher will almost guess (with a run skip . . . . 594 1 X 1 54   5
possibly not (at a guess) quite half way down . . . . 631 (CHAIRE) 33   10
a silence who can guess ex- actly what life . . . . 676 95 POEMS 4   11
mindless he begins to guess what no tongue tells . . . . . . 716 95 POEMS 44   16
can quite begin to guess (except my life) the . . . . 717 95 POEMS 45   7
dies to grow can guess and as for spring . . . . 718 95 POEMS 46   7
descend through depths of guess, shadows are substances and . 761 95 POEMS 88   6
alw -ays something is (guess) yes you're right: my . . . . . 793 73 POEMS 21   23
nothing, wanders a little guess (only which is this . . . . . 810 73 POEMS 38   2
mind never may partly guess--thus, my love, to merely . . . . 818 73 POEMS 46   13

GUESSABLE

turning toward me the guessable mirrors which your eyes . . . 370 VIVA 61   10
by terror) steep not guessable each infinite Oblivions found 757 95 POEMS 85   22

GUESSED

Dan who as you've guessed already is the poorbuthonest . . . 254 IS 5 ONE 25   15
easier than I had guessed everything would be; even . . . . . 338 VIVA 29   18
on the shelf everybody guessed was too high look . . . . . . 353 VIVA 44   20
new tools) whence i guessed that he also had . . . . 355 VIVA 46   12
only your less than guessed more than beauty begins . . . . . 450 NO THANKS 65   11
moon stars rain children guessed (but only a few . . . . . . 515 50 POEMS 29   9
have shall we say guessed?" "we shall" quoth gifted . . . . . 807 73 POEMS 35   13
whisper wear all never guessed unknowable most joy) . . . . . 811 73 POEMS 39   7
/ / / i never guessed any thing (even a . . . . 827 73 POEMS 55   3

GUESSER

hombre sin bangaroom slim guesser goose pin yessir wheel . . 333 VIVA 24   18

GUESSING

small hands with their guessing fingers did-not-move . . . . 355 VIVA 46   15

GUESSWHO

her diamond solitaire while guesswho nibbles his ton of . . . 545 1 X 1 5   5
three cents please' --why guesswho nearly leaped out of . . . 800 73 POEMS 28   7

GUEST

plural tide measures her guest (as critics will upon . . . . 418 NO THANKS 35   10
silent, shining host by guest a snowingly enfolding glory . . 559 1 X 1 19   1
/ / / mighty guest of merely me --traveller . . . . 651 (CHAIRE) 53   1
own hope, receive (undaunted guest of dark most downwardness 821 73 POEMS 49   11

GUESTS

nowhere vivid anonymous mythical guests of Is unslowly more . 557 1 X 1 17   6
(hosts of eternity; not guests of seem) believe me, ... 817 73 POEMS 45   6

GUIDING

the momentary wind with guiding smile, lips wisely minced . . 9 T&C SONGS 1   12

GUILTY

hatch mischief) all you guilty scamper (you bastards throw . 452 NO THANKS 67   4

+GUILTY

FOR CONTEXT, SEE . . . . 546 1 X 1 6   5

GUINEA

(hutch) hutchinson says sweet guinea pigs do it it . . . . . 325 VIVA 17   7

GUISE

(if spirits in the guise of things appear) death's: . . . . . 845 73 POEMS 73   3

+GUITAR

FOR CONTEXT, SEE . . . . 519 50 POEMS 33   5

GUITARS

much soundless rubbish of guitars and watches only as . . . . 479 NEW POEMS 17   6

	PAGE	TITLE	LINE

GUK
full O Yes of guk rooms daughter item son . . . . 499 50 POEMS 13   8
GULLS'
we a universe of gulls' drift Of thickly starhums . . . . . . 371 VIVA 62   21
GULPED
of a spark 's gulped by illimitable hell) and . . . . 639 (CHAIRE) 41   8
GULPS
always until absolute un gulps the first knowledge of . . . . 517 50 POEMS 31   13
GUM
on a mountain of gum did something like a . . . . 228 IS 5 ONE MARJ   9
gee by gosh by gum why talk of beauty . . . . 268 IS 5 TWO 3   8
GUMCHEWING
overgrown pimply cavaliers and gumchewing giggly girls and . 61 T&C PORTRAIT 9   7
GUMS
squirming in pretty wrath, gums skidding on slippery udders . 151 & SON REAL 22   10
deliriously sprouting from complacent gums, a morsel prettily 201 XLI PORTRAIT 9   4
GUN
dem" --"somebody hung uh gun on Marcus"-- "duh Swede . . . . 332 VIVA 23   7
the meaning of a gun it is a man . . . . 570 1 X 1 30   6
GUNWALE
"meet again sometime") vanished, gunwale awash. I thereupon . 327 VIVA 18   37
GURDY
gladly cricks where a hurdy-gurdy accurately pants. and . . . 219 XLI SONNETS 15   8
+GURDY
FOR CONTEXT, SEE . . . . 233 IS 5 ONE 4   2
FOR CONTEXT, SEE . . . . 233 IS 5 ONE 4   14
GURDY'S
what is that the hurdy-gurdy's playing / / / . . . . 152 & SON ACTU 1   15
GURGLE
trees winterbrief surly old gurgle a nonsense of sparrows, . 282 IS 5 THREE 6   12
+GURGLING
FOR CONTEXT, SEE . . . . 442 NO THANKS 57   8
GURL
Oh for such a gurl gurl gurl, oh for . . . . 235 IS 5 ONE 6   13
for such a gurl gurl gurl, oh for such . . . . 235 IS 5 ONE 6   14
such a gurl gurl gurl, oh for such a . . . . 235 IS 5 ONE 6   15
oh for such a gurl to be a fellow's . . . . 235 IS 5 ONE 6   17
GUS
except the dull ones gus loves all the girls . . . . 619 (CHAIRE) 21   15
GUSH
gnomes and frantic fairies gush clumsily from the battered . 69 T&C POST IMPR 6   22
find everywheres noisecoloured curvecorners gush silently . . 311 VIVA 3   17
of speeds of trapeze gush somersaults open ing hes . . . . . 536 50 POEMS 48   9
disciple sheep or wolf) gush to it as deity . . . . 804 73 POEMS 32   5
GUSHES
the black unbunged Something gushes vaguely a squeak of . . . 195 XLI PORTRAIT 3   11
GUSHING
neverwheres & sweet nothingly gushing tinsel; silently yes . 480 NEW POEMS 18   11
GUSTIBUS
Notre Dame (whereas de gustibus non disputandum est my . . . 245 IS 5 ONE 16   24
GUTNUTNTUHPLAI
Fur Croi saik ainnoughbudih gutnutntuhplai? HAI ◇ un . . . . 310 VIVA 2   10
GUTS
in '18 kickin duh guts outa dem doity frogeaters . . . . . . 332 VIVA 23   15
a toilet graced with guts and gutted with grace" . . . . . . 407 NO THANKS 24   14
GUTTED
graced with guts and gutted with grace" squeeze your . . . . 407 NO THANKS 24   14
GUY
Toysday nite; where uh guy gets gayn troze uh . . . . 227 IS 5 ONE GERT   16
mean when the first guy drops you know everybody . . . . . . 272 IS 5 TWO 7   4
than i am newspaper guy who refused to shake . . . . 324 VIVA 16   10
GUYS
sont les neiges.... some guys talks big about Lundun . . . . 237 IS 5 ONE 8   4
gay Paree an some guys claims der never was . . . . 237 IS 5 ONE 8   6
never to wonder about guys you used to (and . . . . 242 IS 5 ONE 13   4
/ / buncha hardboil guys frum duh A.C. fulla . . . . 332 VIVA 23   1
GWINE
kum dearie) bud hooz gwine ter hate dad hurt . . . . 519 50 POEMS 33   16

		PAGE	TITLE	LINE
H				
least each most remembering H highest fly only the	. . . . .	390	NO THANKS 7	8
BECAUSE AGAINS emarkable s) h? y & a (from	. . . .	421	NO THANKS 38	24
slowly trust T upon H, and smile could anything	. . . .	650	{CHAIRE} 52	4
HABITS				
way i move my habits laughter i say you	. . . .	285	IS 5 FOUR 2	7
HABITUAL				
itself (with the uncouth habitual dull jerk at garters)	. . .	227	IS 5 ONE GERT	9
HABITUES				
entirely dirty circle of habitues their faces like	. . . . .	194	XLI PORTRAIT 2	19
HAD				
WORD DELETED, APPEARED 53 TIMES				
+HADN'T				
FOR CONTEXT, SEE	. . . .	790	73 POEMS 18	16
HAFIZ				
Harun Omar and Master Hafiz keep your dead beautiful	. . . .	17	T&C PUELLA MEA	1
like a flower Omar Hafiz and Harun loved their	. . . .	22	T&C PUELLA MEA	227
Omar Harun and Master Hafiz, to me your ladies	. . . .	23	T&C PUELLA MEA	263
Harun Omar and Master Hafiz. / / / /	. . . .	23	T&C PUELLA MEA	290
HAIL				
these whispering fists of hail (and a few windows	. . . . . .	299	IS 5 FOUR 16	12
/ / rain or hail sam done the best	. . . .	568	1 X 1 28	1
HAIR				
embrace of whose tremendous hair that blossom stands whereof	6	T&C EPITHALAM	146
yellow wonder of her hair. / / / /	. . . .	8	T&C OF NICOL	32
overmuch Expects of your hair pale, a terror musical?	. . . .	12	T&C SONGS 2	39
of all things. thy hair mostly the hours love:	. . . .	13	T&C SONGS 3	3
lady naked in her hair-- i for those ladies	. . . .	21	T&C PUELLA MEA	178
/ / / / Tumbling-hair picker of buttercups violets	. . . . .	26	T&C CHANSONS 3	1
/ my love thy hair is one kingdom the	. . . .	29	T&C ORIENTALE 3	2
of thy mind the hair of thy head is	. . . .	29	T&C ORIENTALE 3	18
innocent of defeat thy hair upon thy shoulders is	. . . . . .	29	T&C ORIENTALE 3	20
sorrow of thy low hair flutter the level litanies	. . . . . .	31	T&C ORIENTALE 5	20
nauseous spiderlegs and excremental hair and the eyes of	. .	55	T&C PORTRAIT 3	12
is hiding in her hair. The lily of heaven	. . . .	65	T&C POST IMPR 2	2
charge laughing. Into the hair-thin tints of yellow dawn,	. .	66	T&C POST IMPR 3	6
upon my face my hair is lousy with mutilated	. . . .	69	T&C POST IMPR 6	28
wincing gas showed how hair, in two fists of	. . . .	73	T&C SON REAL 4	4
another's face your sweet hair lay in such a	. . . .	76	T&C SON UNRE 1	5
not confuse the clever hair nor rout the young	. . . .	85	T&C SON ACTU 4	7
HerThe delicate-swill tints of hair Whose (the lit-tle	. . .	94	& POST IMPR 6	21
mouth normal, large, unclever. hair genuinely artificial,	. .	103	& POST IMPR 13	14
nakedness with its blue hair (all is eaten by	. . . .	112	& PORTRAIT 6	76
body is Egypt whose hair is Nile) put your	. . . .	113	& PORTRAIT 6	112
your head your unnatural hair has in the morning	. . . . . .	126	& SEVEN POEMS 5	9
from the floor Her hair was mussed, and she	. . . .	132	& SON REAL 3	18
my separate lusts her hair was like a gas	. . . .	135	& SON REAL 6	6
bright rile of jovial hair extremely frames the face	. . . .	137	& SON REAL 8	17
legs pinch, toes choke-- hair-thin strands of magic agony	. .	146	& SON REAL 17	8
sunset of vermouth -colour. Hair. he put between her	. . . .	148	& SON REAL 19	9
was a dude. Dark hair and nice hands. with	. . . .	149	& SON REAL 20	5
By you the mouth hair eyes, and i mean	. . . .	153	& SON ACTU 2	2
immense weapon of your hair. Understanding why his eye	. . .	161	& SON ACTU 10	10
lips, absurd eyes, the hair). Creasing its smoothness--and	.	164	& SON ACTU 13	9
mandolin-clink mixed with your hair; feeling your knees among	169	& SON ACTU 18	6
electric trite thighs; the hair stupidly priceless. / /	. . .	173	& SON ACTU 22	15
with Alice in her hair, (but if you ask	. . . .	183	XLI SONGS 5	4
sweet shy pirouette your hair and then your dancesong	. . . .	186	XLI SONGS 8	15
last flower in whose hair, thy lips are cold	. . . .	190	XLI SONGS 12	3
last flower in the hair withers; thy hair is	. . . .	190	XLI SONGS 12	15
the hair withers; thy hair is acold with dreams,	. . . . . .	190	XLI SONGS 12	16
poised with the serious hair)/ / / / this	. . . .	207	XLI SONNETS 3	14
rushing of thy deep hair and the smiting smile	. . . .	213	XLI SONNETS 9	12
which terminated in fists hair wood erect cursing hatless	. .	277	IS 5 THREE 1	8
lice in the blond hair of nothing / /	. . . .	289	IS 5 FOUR 6	24
a rhythm in your hair, (your fingertips the way	. . . .	291	IS 5 FOUR 8	11
moon thinner than a hair) making me feel how	. . . .	301	IS 5 FOUR 18	6
primeval silence of your hair --let the world say	. . . . . .	306	IS 5 FIVE 5	8

		PAGE	TITLE	LINE

HAIR (CONTINUED)
slowly staring and such hair) the Californian handpicked . . 337 VIVA 28   8
beginningly finishing (and such hair) the expensively . . . . 337 VIVA 28   13
a hand with your hair in my imagination / . . . . 356 VIVA 47   22
of all foam -like hair spatters creasing pillow next . . . . 358 VIVA 49   3
/ / / when hair falls off and eyes . . . . 359 VIVA 50   1
quite softly as your hair what bird has perfect . . . . . . 367 VIVA 58   4
best on bald men's hair and every finger is . . . . 511 50 POEMS 25   9
(caveat emptor) cy superfluous hair or Think We've Met . . . 549 1 X 1 9   13
and a hank of hair) 'd he picked up . . . . 552 1 X 1 12   8
and then a single hair again" marvels "and liars . . . . . . 572 1 X 1 32   16
/ / / / hair your a brook (it . . . . 613 {CHAIRE} 15   1
well miss willy's carroty hair" "it seems like i . . . . . . 707 95 POEMS 35   4
HAIR-THIN
charge laughing. Into the hair-thin tints of yellow dawn, . . 66 T&C POST IMPR 3   6
legs pinch, toes choke-- hair-thin strands of magic agony . . 146 & SON REAL 17   8
HAIR'S
shadows have begun the hair's worm huge, ecstatic, rathe.... 84 T&C SON ACTU 3   11
whitehot face, gashed by hair's blue cold jolts of . . . . . 106 & PORTRAIT 2   9
almost swims into a hair's width: into less? into . . . . . . 633 {CHAIRE} 35   10
+HAIRED
FOR CONTEXT, SEE . . . . 705 95 POEMS 33   2
HAIRLESS
the bothering dear unnecessary hairless o ld / / . . . . . . 250 IS 5 ONE 21   17
HAIRLESSCHESTED
about Death) concept O hairlesschested females, well attend! 398 NO THANKS 15   16
HAIRY
oldish doll-like face and hairy arms like an ogre . . . . . . 69 T&C POST IMPR 6   38
embrace. as in the hairy notching of clenched thighs . . . . 151 & SON REAL 22   17
workingman with hand so hairy-sturdy you may turn O . . . . . 233 IS 5 ONE 4   1
vermilion jacket of nodding hairy Jacqueline who is given . . 279 IS 5 THREE 3   19
HAIRY-STURDY
workingman with hand so hairy-sturdy you may turn O . . . . . 233 IS 5 ONE 4   1
HALF
the tongue of flame half-mute, (haste ere some thrush . . . . 6 T&C EPITHALAM   118
your voice my soul half-beautiful and wholly droll is . . . . 11 T&C SONGS 2   2
utters a frivolous intense half of Girl which (like . . . . . 95 & POST IMPR 7   7
body with wise breasts half-grown, lisping flesh quick to . . 140 & SON REAL 11   11
fat man in bluishsuspenders half-reading the Evening . . . . 166 & SON ACTU 15   6
of smiles your eyes half- thrush half-angel and your . . . . 186 XLI SONGS 8   9
your eyes half- thrush half-angel and your drowsy lips . . . 186 XLI SONGS 8   11
coffee covered with froth half-mud and not too sweet? . . . . 198 XLI PORTRAIT 6   33
del cammin' that means half- way up the Campanile, ... 256 IS 5 ONE 27   7
was wifeless and only half awake, cursed with pimples, . . . 262 IS 5 ONE 32   7
these immaculate thin things half daemon half tree among . . 362 VIVA 53   6
thin things half daemon half tree among sunset dream . . . . 362 VIVA 53   6
quickly signify life's only half (through deep weather then . 364 VIVA 55   12
/ / one's not half two. It's two are . . . . 556 1 X 1 16   1
should april me for half a when, whatever is . . . . 580 1 X 1 40   20
(at a guess) quite half way down to the . . . . 631 {CHAIRE} 33   10
photograph clutched in the half of a hand and . . . . 647 {CHAIRE} 49   3
any world must always half perceive. Only whose vision . . . 845 73 POEMS 73   4
+HALF
FOR CONTEXT, SEE . . . . 94 & POST IMPR 6   27
HALF-ANGEL
your eyes half- thrush half-angel and your drowsy lips . . . 186 XLI SONGS 8   11
HALF-BEAUTIFUL
your voice my soul half-beautiful and wholly droll is . . . . 11 T&C SONGS 2   2
HALF-GROWN
body with wise breasts half-grown, lisping flesh quick to . . 140 & SON REAL 11   11
HALF-MUD
coffee covered with froth half-mud and not too sweet? . . . . 198 XLI PORTRAIT 6   33
HALF-MUTE
the tongue of flame half-mute, (haste ere some thrush . . . . 6 T&C EPITHALAM   118
HALF-READING
fat man in bluishsuspenders half-reading the Evening . . . . 166 & SON ACTU 15   6
HALFGLOOM
somewherealloverme heart my the halfgloom coolish of The what 251 IS 5 ONE 22   18

			PAGE	TITLE	LINE

HALFSIGHT
/ all worlds have halfsight, seeing either with life's . . . 845 73 POEMS 73   1
HALFSINGING
and sweetness.... pauses. (Halfwhispering.... halfsinging . . 304 IS 5 FIVE 3   13
HALFSMILE
fashionable traffic, just a halfsmile (for society's sweet . 146 & SON REAL 17   11
HALFSMILING
of dreams always demurely halfsmiling from cool faces, moving 211 XLI SONNETS 7   8
HALFSTOOPING
nagging button of candlelight (halfstooping to exactly kiss . 164 & SON ACTU 13   4
+HALFWAY
FOR CONTEXT, SEE . . . . 256 IS 5 ONE 27   7
HALFWHISPERING
fear and sweetness.... pauses. (Halfwhispering.... . . . . . 304 IS 5 FIVE 3   13
HALT
of an important worry) halt stop forget relax wait . . . . . 393 NO THANKS 10   5
HALTING
odd occurred" charlie confessed (halting) "a tall strong . . 800 73 POEMS 28   3
HALTS
barn's immense doorway and halts propped on a pitchfork . . . 754 95 POEMS 82   8
HALVES
two. It's two are halves of one: which halves . . . . 556 1 X 1 16   1
halves of one: which halves reintegrating, shall occur no . . 556 1 X 1 16   2
HAMMERING
smoothly onward(amid tinkling-cheering-hammering tables) . . 232 IS 5 ONE 3   9
HAMMERS
the edgeless gloaming gladness hammers incessant putrid . . . 202 XLI PORTRAIT 9   38
HAND
day preening upon his hand followed by gay untimid . . . . .   4 T&C EPITHALAM   66
death's faultless eyes (whose hand my folded soul shall . . . 11 T&C SONGS 2   26
strange; apt in my hand warmly to lie it . . . . 21 T&C PUELLA MEA   195
moon from the transplendent hand of sombre god i . . . . . . 30 T&C ORIENTALE 4   40
finger of his left hand then the <> door . . . . 33 T&C ORIENTALE 6   59
to catch one funny hand opening the hard great . . . . 53 T&C PORTRAIT 1   44
eaten tunes. a fattish hand turns the crank; the . . . . . . 69 T&C POST IMPR 6   2
smiling, man in whose hand the crank goes desperately, . . . 69 T&C POST IMPR 6   8
in his little toylike hand) and then he will . . . . 69 T&C POST IMPR 6   18
played by the Funny hand of the paralyticwhose dod . . . . . 100 & POST IMPR 11   37
Beard rests. onthetopwhose silly, Hand revolves, per- fectly, 101 & POST IMPR 11   47
is like a perhaps hand (which comes carefully out . . . . . . 124 & SEVEN POEMS 3   1
is like a perhaps Hand in a window (carefully . . . . 124 & SEVEN POEMS 3   11
creeped into the pink hand of the smoke that . . . . 125 & SEVEN POEMS 4   21
of girl. his left hand quarried the quartzlike face. . . . . 148 & SON REAL 19   3
girl closes her left hand upon a mirror. / . . . . 170 & SON ACTU 19   14
/ / workingman with hand so hairy-sturdy you may . . . . . . 233 IS 5 ONE 4   1
(whereas, upon the other hand, myself) but let us . . . . . . 245 IS 5 ONE 16   15
care to rise one hand did nothing on the . . . . 258 IS 5 ONE 28   17
hurl my yes, crumbles hand (ful released conarefetti) ev . . 265 IS 5 ONE 34   2
box which the exhumed hand of Saint Ignatz miraculously . . . 280 IS 5 THREE 4   4
dying silent minds, which hand in hand at some . . . . 305 IS 5 FIVE 4   9
minds, which hand in hand at some window try . . . . 305 IS 5 FIVE 4   9
hat gestures bud plumptumbling hand voices Eye Doangivuh sud- 330 VIVA 21   7
erring Olaf soon in hand; but--though an host of . . . . . . 339 VIVA 30   6
or What does a hand with your hair in . . . . 356 VIVA 47   21
in rubbery one somewhat hand the paper destinies of . . . . . 499 50 POEMS 13   5
you are actual either hand is when for sale? . . . . 538 50 POEMS 50   10
are five and one hand is a mind then . . . . 543 1 X 1 3   18
mountain's heartbeat in his hand / / / / . . . . 562 1 X 1 22   14
nigger caught in his hand a little star no . . . . 622 {CHAIRE} 24   2
the world's best one hand snatch / / / . . . . 645 {CHAIRE} 47   4
the half of a hand and the word love . . . . 647 {CHAIRE} 49   4
is a child 's hand) very carefully bring -ing . . . . 652 {CHAIRE} 54   3
+HAND
FOR CONTEXT, SEE . . . . 410 NO THANKS 27   2
+HAND ORGAN
FOR CONTEXT, SEE . . . . 442 NO THANKS 57   7
HAND'S
meanwhile doth miss; a hand's impression in an empty . . . . 360 VIVA 51   8

316

		PAGE	TITLE	LINE

HANDBAG
    rescue miss nobody's probably handbag) because i say that's . 475 NEW POEMS 13   22
HANDED
    standing on eighth street handed me a flower. Nobody, ... 802 73 POEMS 30   6
HANDFUL
    milbrightlions my (hurl flicker handful in) dodging are . . . 265 IS 5 ONE 34   7
    punks or just a handful absolutely doesn't matter and . . . . 549 1 X 1 9   5
+HANDFUL
    FOR CONTEXT, SEE . . . . 265 IS 5 ONE 34   2
    FOR CONTEXT, SEE . . . . 265 IS 5 ONE 34   4
HANDFULS
    bring you every spring handfuls of little normal worms. . . . 161 & SON ACTU 10   8
HANDIWORK
    host to scrutinize his handiwork: they (summoned by that . . 799 73 POEMS 27   25
HANDKERCHIEF
    Harvard Brevis Est for Handkerchief read Papernapkin no . . . 410 NO THANKS 27   5
HANDLE
    per- fectly, slowlywith, the handle ofa crankin It The . . . 101 & POST IMPR 11   48
    tenderly this side up handle with care fragile and . . . . . 270 IS 5 TWO 5   15
HANDLEBARS
    (on which are wintry handlebars glued) updives pursued by . . 585 1 X 1 45   6
HANDLESS
    dee beeg wun" her handless wrists did gooey severe . . . . . 73 T&C SON REAL 4   14
    this whole tear. By handless hints do conjurers rule? . . . . 527 50 POEMS 39   17
HANDMIRROR
    she puts down the handmirror. "Look at" arranging before . . 226 IS 5 ONE MAME   1
HANDORGAN
    to the little silent handorgan prop- ping the curve . . . . . 101 & POST IMPR 11   45
    Something, we heard a handorgan in twilight playing like . . 174 & SON ACTU 23   15
    melancholy fellow'll play his handorgan until you say "i . . 697 95 POEMS 25   3
HANDORGANS
    the strenuous briefness Life: handorgans and April darkness, 66 T&C POST IMPR 3   3
HANDPICKED
    such hair) the Californian handpicked thrill mechanically . . 337 VIVA 28   9
HANDS
    robe the sun's white hands emboss, betwixt whose absolute . . 3 T&C EPITHALAM   29
    amorous strain of gradual hands and yielding to that . . . . 4 T&C EPITHALAM   54
    authentic scroll of fairie hands and vanishing with dawn). . 5 T&C EPITHALAM   88
    small intimate gently primeval hands, frivolous feet divine! 5 T&C EPITHALAM   107
    bed prepared by whitest hands of waiting years, curtained . . 6 T&C EPITHALAM   114
    Discordia's apple in thy hands, which the scared shepherd . . 6 T&C EPITHALAM   151
    a creature of white hands, who letting fall a . . . . 8 T&C OF NICOL   22
    very singular and slenderest hands moreover are (which as . . 20 T&C PUELLA MEA 160
    breasts and bestial grovelling hands rasps the purple dark- . 28 T&C ORIENTALE 2   9
    hundred colours in their hands scimitars like windy torches . 33 T&C ORIENTALE 6   39
    the rings upon their hands are from mines a . . . . 33 T&C ORIENTALE 6   47
    streaming from playful immortal hands the bursting of the . . 36 T&C AMORES 1   18
    sea marvelous from god's hands which sent her forth . . . . . 38 T&C AMORES 3   3
    goes forth out of hands and she returns into . . . . 38 T&C AMORES 3   11
    and she returns into hands and is with sleep.... . . . . . 38 T&C AMORES 3   12
    impertinently exquisite faces floating hands were laid upon . 44 T&C AMORES 8   11
    lips and forlorn piggish hands joked to a girlish . . . . . . 56 T&C PORTRAIT 4   12
    delivered into both my hands herself to always keep" . . . . 57 T&C PORTRAIT 5   19
    thou comest and your hands are the snow and . . . . 61 T&C PORTRAIT 9   28
    face plus innocuous winking hands, carefully inhabits number 62 T&C PORTRAIT 10   3
    out of dumb strong hands infinite the erect deep . . . . . . 64 T&C POST IMPR 1   5
    ogre and rub- bercoloured hands and feet filled with . . . . 69 T&C POST IMPR 6   39
    him, and take his hands, saying, Accept all happiness . . . . 76 T&C SON UNRE 1   11
    little suddenly lifted in singing--hands fragile whom almost 85 T&C SON ACTU 4   11
    know only that your hands move more simply upon . . . . . . 98 & POST IMPR 9   7
    hung ugly. , the hands sharp and impertinently dead. . . . . 103 & POST IMPR 13   5
    world has these men's hands but their bodies big . . . . . . 114 & PORTRAIT 7   14
    of Her- ....kIss her: hands will play on, mE . . . . 122 & SEVEN POEMS 1   9
    Whocares dead's fine like hands do you see that . . . . . . 126 & SEVEN POEMS 5   24
    with her long hard hands keeping silence on her . . . . . . 147 & SON REAL 18   2
    Dark hair and nice hands. with a little eye . . . . 149 & SON REAL 20   5
    and the rich improbable hands of the Wind) / . . . . 153 & SON ACTU 2   14
    vacancy when, Thy patters? hands.... is swig it does . . . . 159 & SON ACTU 8   16

		PAGE	TITLE	LINE
HANDS				
with neat obscure obvious hands Time stuff the sincere	. . .	165	& SON ACTU 14	11
perfect is With killing hands / / / /		188	XLI SONGS 10	22
and i will take hands and looking up at		192	XLI CHANSONS 2	25
and fragile his queer hands twitter before him, like	. . . .	198	XLI PORTRAIT 6	23
eyes, and if thy hands flowers of silence curled	. . . . . .	205	XLI SONNETS 1	3
and when thy bashful hands assume silence beyond the	. . . .	210	XLI SONNETS 6	14
i'll take between thy hands what no man feels,	. . . .	212	XLI SONNETS 8	13
deep lap enormous mindless hands. and no one knows	. . . .	225	IS 5 ONE LIZ	9
which you're married and hands get red washing things	. . . .	242	IS 5 ONE 13	15
lapfulls of idiotic big hands / / / /		251	IS 5 ONE 22	23
enough of it" their, hands minutely answered / /	. . . . . .	255	IS 5 ONE 26	9
and Anatole France shook hands again and yet again	. . . .	263	IS 5 ONE 32	44
yet again shook again hands again, the former coachman	. . .	263	IS 5 ONE 32	44
ceased. I withdrew my hands from the tennisracket. All	. . .	263	IS 5 ONE 32	55
dirt coats smile looking hands spit blood teeth the	. . . .	275	IS 5 TWO 9	46
deftly propping on smallest hands the slim hinging you	. . .	282	IS 5 THREE 6	7
lungs arms hopes feet hands under us the unspeaking	. . . . .	283	IS 5 THREE 7	2
me with its small hands and with curling infantile	. . . . .	284	IS 5 FOUR 1	2
eyes cheeks mouth its hands (slipping) felt of my	. . . . .	284	IS 5 FOUR 1	5
heart life the little hands withdrew, jerkily, themselves	. .	284	IS 5 FOUR 1	8
them) knowing my lips hands the way i move	. . . .	285	IS 5 FOUR 2	6
picks strawberries with beringed hands) but if i Should	. . .	287	IS 5 FOUR 4	9
hold lips Eyes everything hands you know what happens)	. . .	287	IS 5 FOUR 4	19
Doom (with white longest hands neatening each crease) will	.	288	IS 5 FOUR 5	3
your body smile brain hands merely to become the	. . . . .	295	IS 5 FOUR 12	3
in both pockets curled hands moves) why then toward	. . . .	299	IS 5 FOUR 16	10
one another gradually into hands) and bend into the	. . . .	305	IS 5 FIVE 4	3
short (eyes do bang hands angle scoot bulbs marry	. . . . .	309	VIVA 1	12
who refused to shake hands with ludendorff and your	. . . .	324	VIVA 16	11
is blond with small hands "& everything is easier	. . . . .	338	VIVA 29	16
only such blue slender hands of god / /		340	VIVA 31	20
not a face with hands which whisper This is		352	VIVA 43	13
"let's" going in "take hands" smiling "coming up these	. . .	353	VIVA 44	31
his white sincere small hands with their guessing fingers	. .	355	VIVA 46	15
then (then the only hands so to speak are		359	VIVA 50	14
rain, has such small hands / / / /		366	VIVA 57	20
your wrists thighs feet hands poising to again utterly	. . .	369	VIVA 60	13
suppose possibly are certain hands, terse and invisible, with		378	VIVA 69	6
places paints eyes touches hands with new- ness and	. . . .	437	NO THANKS 53	5
day) : you; smile, hands (an- onymo -Us /		449	NO THANKS 64	15
lifts lifting hopes and hands --nourish my failure with	. . .	456	NO THANKS 71	13
of these with listening hands only fishermen are prevented	.	478	NEW POEMS 16	11
one face who. and hands hold his whose unlife		479	NEW POEMS 17	15
Ergo perished later all hands (you may recall) being	. . . .	494	50 POEMS 8	7
purple book between what hands had been before they	. . . .	506	50 POEMS 20	3
terrible selfhood with its hands and feet (lift and	. . . .	522	50 POEMS 35	11
sing all here is hands machine no good too	. . . .	523	50 POEMS 36	10
no vacation here is hands is work since i		523	50 POEMS 36	20
ships than dreams more hands are offering jonquils) down	. .	585	1 X 1 45	16
keen pure silence) such hands can build a (who	. . . . .	617	(CHAIRE) 19	2
ghosts go drift slippery hands tease slim float twitter	. . .	633	(CHAIRE) 35	5
this tree (darling) have hands, and all the hands	. . . . .	667	(CHAIRE) 69	2
hands, and all the hands have people; and more	. . . . . .	667	(CHAIRE) 69	2
which fingers are without hands; and i have no	. . . . . .	667	(CHAIRE) 69	10
friends feet terrors fate hands silence eyes love laughter	.	693	95 POEMS 21	3
+HANDS				
FOR CONTEXT, SEE	. . . .	107	& PORTRAIT 3	15
FOR CONTEXT, SEE	. . . .	490	50 POEMS 4	15
FOR CONTEXT, SEE	. . . .	612	(CHAIRE) 14	11
HANDS'				
which biggish loll the hands' will tumbling into shall	. . .	131	& SON REAL 2	14
HANDSOME				
were fond of the handsome moon never spoke ill	. . . . . .	43	T&C AMORES 7	13
Jesus he was a handsome man and what i	. . . .	60	T&C PORTRAIT 8	8
he was kilt a handsome man and James and	. . . .	271	IS 5 TWO 6	2
/ / / / handsome and clever and he	. . . .	709	95 POEMS 37	1
sons of zeus: one, handsome strong and born to	. . . . . .	799	73 POEMS 27	3

	PAGE	TITLE	LINE
HANDSOMELY			
gestures) suddenly sally rand handsomely who did because she	425	NO THANKS 42	5
HANDSOMEST			
nellie and fan) some handsomest harry (and sally and	509	50 POEMS 23	15
HANDSPRING			
fear turned o Now handspring trans forming it self	343	VIVA 34	11
HANG			
ribbled lonely truth (from hang from droop w ar	415	NO THANKS 32	11
Joy with Pain shall hang in hock who dares	438	NO THANKS 54	7
HANGED			
new wings then decently hanged himself, one afternoon. The .	170	& SON ACTU 19	4
/ / / / hanged if n y in	476	NEW POEMS 14	1
time) --when skies are hanged and oceans drowned, the	560	1 X 1 20	7
HANGEST			
Spring, with this thou hangest canary-birds in parlor windows	61	T&C PORTRAIT 9	10
HANGING			
was made of brass hangIng from strings (or) someThing	123	& SEVEN POEMS 2	3
with sticking out breasts hanging clothes. On the line. . . .	167	& SON ACTU 16	1
Bishop Taylor who needs hanging that marriage is a	167	& SON ACTU 16	4
of common sunset is hanging, snow speaks slowly /	202	XLI PORTRAIT 9	51
HANGS			
where the surrounded smile hangs breathless / / /	83	T&C SON ACTU 2	16
times a night one hangs a hat upon her	427	NO THANKS 44	5
most innocently undecaying friend hangs at yon gilty ceiling	546	1 X 1 6	5
+HANGS			
FOR CONTEXT, SEE	723	95 POEMS 51	12
HANK			
a bone and a hank of hair) 'd he	552	1 X 1 12	8
HAPPEN			
can'ts were born to happen our mosts have died	537	50 POEMS 49	9
mystery which will never happen again, a miracle which . . .	667	(CHAIRE) 69	6
HAPPENED			
August night, i just happened to meet "how do	313	VIVA 5	4
they couldn't agree) not happened (and floating- ly int . . .	652	(CHAIRE) 54	15
miracle which has never happened before-- and shining this .	667	(CHAIRE) 69	7
(dreams hopes despairs) Once happened nowhere else imagine .	693	95 POEMS 21	7
because my (as it happened) self he was --but	730	95 POEMS 58	4
my voice marvels "what happened" as everywhere red goes . . .	800	73 POEMS 28	21
+HAPPENED			
FOR CONTEXT, SEE	655	(CHAIRE) 57	13
HAPPENING			
true lovers in each happening of their hearts live	576	1 X 1 36	1
of the gay great happening illimitably earth) how should . .	663	(CHAIRE) 65	8
HAPPENINGLY			
big two feet conclude happeningly the unfirm drooping bloated	229	IS 5 ONE FRAN	5
HAPPENLESS			
and shall be immeasurable happenless unnow shuts more than .	502	50 POEMS 16	6
HAPPENS			
rapidly all together there happens Something, and They cease	62	T&C PORTRAIT 10	18
under the as it happens quite erroneous impression that . . .	234	IS 5 ONE 5	4
sleep what's beyond logic happens beneath will; nor can . . .	264	IS 5 ONE 33	5
hands you know what happens) but if i should, ...	287	IS 5 FOUR 4	20
Love Spring thirsty for happens only and beautiful there . .	437	NO THANKS 53	8
Only to have smelled Happens--skip dance kids hop point . . .	437	NO THANKS 53	13
/ / if everything happens that can't be done	594	1 X 1 54	1
--the great (my darling) happens to be that love	664	(CHAIRE) 66	5
the husband of (as happens every now and then	799	73 POEMS 27	9
HAPPIER			
that your valentine makes happier me than i but	718	95 POEMS 46	4
HAPPINESS			
hands, saying, Accept all happiness from me. Then shall . . .	76	T&C SON UNRE 1	12
substance; all heartless spectres, happiness) lovers alone .	765	95 POEMS 91	4
HAPPY			
hob-a-nob hob-a-nob little hoppy happy toad in tweeds tweeds	25	T&C CHANSONS 2	9
contented hideous hopeless cruel happy and it is day, ...	50	T&C IMPRESS 4	15
don't want to dead's happy like the way underclothes	126	& SEVEN POEMS 5	27
believe i we was happy to see how nice	248	IS 5 ONE 19	26
iful than these heroic happy dead who rushed like	268	IS 5 TWO 3	10

HAPPY (CONTINUED)

/ / / everybody happy? WE-WE-WE & to hell . . . . 791 73 POEMS 19   1

monster's fellowmen miscalled are happy should his now go . . 842 73 POEMS 70   14

HAPSINGLY

of eakspeasies per (reel) hapsingly proregress heandshe-ingly 330 VIVA 21   1

HARANGUING

dumb mankind dizzy with haranguing --you are deafened every . 804 73 POEMS 32   9

HARBOUR

the crooked town) a harbour fools the sea(while . . . . . . 319 VIVA 11   18

HARBOURING

snare she sought the harbouring dark, and (catching up . . . 8 T&C OF NICOL   26

HARD

funny hand opening the hard great eyes to noone . . . . 53 T&C PORTRAIT 1   44

out into the rapid hard wo- men and intotheslow . . . . 101 & POST IMPR 11   61

oo-oo. dearie not so hard dear you're killing me . . . . . . 109 & PORTRAIT 5   22

too firm to be hard but it's sharp and . . . . 126 & SEVEN POEMS 5   4

my girl's tall with hard long eyes as she . . . . 147 & SON REAL 18   1

stands, with her long hard hands keeping silence on . . . . . 147 & SON REAL 18   2

sleeping is her long hard body filled with surprise . . . . . 147 & SON REAL 18   4

when she smiles a hard long smile it sometimes . . . . 147 & SON REAL 18   6

you because when you're hard up you pawn your . . . . 204 XLI LA GUERRE 2   10

(bent by wind) slammed hard- over the tiller; clattered . . . 277 IS 5 THREE 1   10

stopped millions of female hard for their millions of . . . . 337 VIVA 28   4

pstareth oseings over (a hard a hard a girl . . . . 385 NO THANKS 2   50

over (a hard a hard a girl a girl) . . . . 385 NO THANKS 2   51

notSoft soft one are hard one notHard) not boys . . . . 388 NO THANKS 5   22

it no matter how hard he never tried) the . . . . 635 {CHAIRE} 37   6

me-- who found forgiveness hard because my (as it . . . . . . 730 95 POEMS 58   3

+HARD

FOR CONTEXT, SEE . . . . 388 NO THANKS 5   22

HARDBOIL

/ / / buncha hardboil guys frum duh A.C. . . . . 332 VIVA 23   1

HARDENS

tough exquisite flowers, whom hardens richly, darkness. On . 154 & SON ACTU 3   9

HARDER

leaves and a little harder for roses only a . . . . 67 T&C POST IMPR 4   20

roses only a little harder last we on the . . . . 67 T&C POST IMPR 4   22

stick on my brain harder than can twitch its . . . . 136 & SON REAL 7   7

be my fame, the harder the wind blows the . . . . 439 NO THANKS 55   27

/ / / / harder perhaps than a newengland . . . . 506 50 POEMS 20   1

HARDING

dead" beautiful Warren Gamaliel Harding "is" dead he's "dead" 336 VIVA 27   6

HARDLY

back- ground, it is hardly surprising if anyone hardly . . . 263 IS 5 ONE 32   35

hardly surprising if anyone hardly should call exactly . . . 263 IS 5 ONE 32   35

Yapenese Craps somebody might hardly never not have been . . 336 VIVA 27   11

even a Poet) could hardly express what i Mean . . . . 702 95 POEMS 30   8

HARDSLIPPERY

windows are packed with hardslippery greens and helplessbaby 100 & POST IMPR 11   4

HAREM

thousand years old the harem of the emperor is . . . . 32 T&C ORIENTALE 6   19

ladies of the emperor's harem are queens of all . . . . 33 T&C ORIENTALE 6   45

HAREMINA

six divine inches of Haremina in the thick of . . . . 194 XLI PORTRAIT 2   15

HARK

to golden tears, and hark! the flicker's laughing yet, . . . 5 T&C EPITHALAM   74

on earth we ghosts: hark to the sheer cadence . . . . 9 T&C SONGS 1   22

crumbling & folding hopes, hark; feet (fEEt ◇ / . . . . . . 345 VIVA 36   14

who of life's life (hark! what silence)?" "Worlds? o . . . . 603 {CHAIRE} 5   4

so alive: chaos so (hark --that screech of space) . . . . . . 639 {CHAIRE} 41   5

deepens with wind (and hark begins to Rain) a . . . . 785 73 POEMS 13   6

these all these thankful (hark) birds singing wholly are . . 819 73 POEMS 47   20

HARM

Wiggin took Wrs. Miggin's harm in is, extinguishing the . . . 263 IS 5 ONE 32   48

compose poems not because harm symmetry earthquakes starfish 452 NO THANKS 67   15

HARMLESS

otherwise dead silence with harmless quips, out of Briggs . . 326 VIVA 18   13

HARMLESSLY
ling through man -ufactured harmlessly accurate gloom "I . . 464 NEW POEMS 2   19
HARMONICA
sunset, playin uh busted harmonica / / / / . . . . 332 VIVA 23   32
HARMONIOUSLY
of paper sailors--argonauta argo harmoniously being with his 326 VIVA 18   7
HARNESS
cowards will scheme to harness: let all unfools of . . . . . 439 NO THANKS 55   15
+HARNESS
FOR CONTEXT, SEE . . . . 342 VIVA 33   14
HARPS
colours colours cOOler than harps colours p r i . . . . 100 & POST IMPR 11   8
glooms, and sing (of harps celestial to the quivering . . . . 208 XLI SONNETS 4   7
HARPSICHORD
flowery pluckings of a harpsichord colours of Pure percussion 100 & POST IMPR 11   11
HARRY
wilted and not old, harry, a woman in the . . . . 53 T&C PORTRAIT 1   33
like you can't imagine Harry was o god kilt . . . . 271 IS 5 TWO 6   10
and fan) some handsomest harry (and sally and nan . . . . . . 509 50 POEMS 23   15
HARRY'S
on Shadows fed, your Harry's Tom, your Tom is . . . . 438 NO THANKS 54   10
HARSH
an impenetrable transparency. the harsh erecting breasts and 137 & SON REAL 8   13
HARUN
/ / PUELLA MEA Harun Omar and Master Hafiz . . . . 17 T&C PUELLA MEA   1
flower Omar Hafiz and Harun loved their ladies in . . . . . . 22 T&C PUELLA MEA   227
Paris and Solomon, Omar Harun and Master Hafiz, to . . . . . 23 T&C PUELLA MEA   263
your dead beautiful ladies Harun Omar and Master Hafiz. . . . 23 T&C PUELLA MEA   290
HARVARD
with one "Paul" a harvard boy alas! (who simply . . . . 320 VIVA 12   7
joe lives on air Harvard Brevis Est for Handkerchief . . . . 410 NO THANKS 27   5
HARVEST
with fear, across the harvest whitely peer empty of . . . . . 11 T&C SONGS 2   23
HAS
WORD DELETED, APPEARED 75 TIMES
HASHED
block her, rain-warm-naked exquisitely hashed (little careful 133 & SON REAL 4   3
HASN'T
something as one one hasn't a why or because . . . . 594 1 X 1 54   10
HASSAN
to the kanoon but Hassan chuckles seeing the Greeks . . . . . 220 XLI SONNETS 16   16
HASSAN'S
my, ears, go into Hassan's place the canounchir p . . . . . . 100 & POST IMPR 11   41
is necessary to find Hassan's Place by tiny streets . . . . . 143 & SON REAL 14   3
HAST
/ / when thou hast taken thy last applause, ... 75 T&C SON REAL 6   1
PORTRAITS being twelve who hast merely gonorrhea Oldeyed . . 105 & PORTRAIT 1   3
who standest as thou hast stood and thou shalt . . . . 351 VIVA 42   12
HASTE
tongue of flame half-mute, (haste ere some thrush with . . . 6 T&C EPITHALAM   119
one threaded moment lose: haste) the very shadowy sheep . . . 9 T&C SONGS 1   8
your charming strength O haste annihilator drawing into you . 182 XLI SONGS 4   15
so, let us make haste --consider well this ruined . . . . . 260 IS 5 ONE 30   21
a which) replies in haste I must be you . . . . 570 1 X 1 30   4
HASTEFUL
her drab tempo of hasteful futility lived brilliantly the . . 103 & POST IMPR 13   10
HASTEN
moved myriads wonderfully loved, (hasten, it is the moment . 9 T&C SONGS 1   16
HAT
shove my round red hat back on my head . . . . 69 T&C POST IMPR 6   34
and the round funny hat with a big feather . . . . 69 T&C POST IMPR 6   42
swollen inanity of picture hat. the arms hung ugly. . . . . . 103 & POST IMPR 13   4
puts on his flat hat / / / / . . . . 240 IS 5 ONE 11   4
round jeer for a hat fate per a somewhat . . . . 258 IS 5 ONE 28   4
without his coat and hat --(and i wonder just . . . . 296 IS 5 FOUR 13   8
something fall into his hat) go wandering after it . . . . . 298 IS 5 FOUR 15   21
is traffic this recalls hat gestures bud plumptumbling hand . 330 VIVA 21   6
night one hangs a hat upon her tit one . . . . 427 NO THANKS 44   5

HAT (CONTINUED)
Death should take his hat off to this dame: . . . . 790 73 POEMS 18   6
HATCH
else says down the hatch the nigger smiles the . . . . . . 108 & PORTRAIT 4   21
(all you mischief- hatchers hatch mischief) all you guilty . 452 NO THANKS 67   2
HATCHERS
come (all you mischief- hatchers hatch mischief) all you . . 452 NO THANKS 67   2
HATE
Farmer Death (whom fairies hate) shall crumble the . . . . . 83 T&C SON ACTU 2   11
of death Humanity i hate you / / / . . . . 204 XLI LA GUERRE 2   25
human rind-- when over hate has triumphed darkly love . . . . 213 XLI SONNETS 9   5
ourselves against the worms hate laugh shimmy / / . . . . . . 238 IS 5 ONE 9   21
the reason that i hate people and lean out . . . . 295 IS 5 FOUR 12   23
ried but eye certainly hate the juse / / . . . . 405 NO THANKS 22   12
bit of quite unmitigated hate (travelling in a futile . . . . 413 NO THANKS 30   14
this poet arose nor hate nor grief can go . . . . 441 NO THANKS 56   43
bud hooz gwine ter hate dad hurt fool wurl . . . . 519 50 POEMS 33   17
truth --i say though hate were why men breathe-- . . . . . . 521 50 POEMS 34   66
give you man extracted hate from whispering grass? joy . . . 527 50 POEMS 39   9
/ / / / hate blows a bubble of . . . . 531 50 POEMS 43   1
fate to grow shall hate confound the wise? doubt . . . . . . 538 50 POEMS 50   5
than if it sells hate condoms education snakeoil vac . . . . 549 1 X 1 9   11
makes love armies (than hate itself and no meanness . . . . . 580 1 X 1 40   15
over all under all hate all fear --all perfectly . . . . . . 590 1 X 1 50   22
worst you fall in hate with love --human one . . . . 679 95 POEMS 7   12
house this our from hate from fear a which . . . . 746 95 POEMS 74   4
blundering proud hugenesses of hate sometimes called world) . 783 73 POEMS 11   7
HATE'S
Minds nothing can: if Hate's a game and Love's . . . . 438 NO THANKS 54   23
fear's obscener brightest than hate's more black keenest than 565 1 X 1 25   10
HATES
remembers is afraid) each hates a Man whom both . . . . 394 NO THANKS 11   9
/ / / jake hates all the girls (the . . . . 619 (CHAIRE) 21   1
HATH
thoughtful trees whom night hath pondered o'er --and . . . . 205 XLI SONNETS 1   11
be aware notice what hath remained --the stone cringes . . . 260 IS 5 ONE 30   3
his peers full oft hath quaffed the wine of . . . . 273 IS 5 TWO 8   7
HATHOLE
hit the whigh shaped hathole thangew yelps one shi . . . . . 602 (CHAIRE) 4   5
HATLESS
hair wood erect cursing hatless who (bent by wind) . . . . . 277 IS 5 THREE 1   9
talking individual, mysterious witty hatless. Cats which move 279 IS 5 THREE 3   12
HATRACKS
most encourage flame as hatracks into peachtrees grow or . . 511 50 POEMS 25   8
HATRED
scarecrow demongod countless in hatred pity fear each more . 662 (CHAIRE) 64   9
your scorn of easily hatred of timid & loathing . . . . . . 677 95 POEMS 5   5
HATS
themselves friends & their hats legs & arms brush . . . . . 275 IS 5 TWO 9   44
+HATS
FOR CONTEXT, SEE . . . . 245 IS 5 ONE 16   1
HAUGHTILY
the electric Distinct face haughtily vital clinched in a . . 193 XLI PORTRAIT 1   3
HAULS
down my face i hauls out uh flask an . . . . 332 VIVA 23   19
HAUNTED
snowy symmetry of grace haunted the limbs as music . . . . . 8 T&C OF NICOL   21
miles of perishing air, haunted with huddling infinite . . . 305 IS 5 FIVE 4   12
and i are thoroughly haunted by what neither is . . . . . . 368 VIVA 59   3
HAUNTERS
softly who be these haunters of dreams always demurely . . . 211 XLI SONNETS 7   7
HAUNTINGLY
quivering string) invisible faces hauntingly and slow. This . 208 XLI SONNETS 4   8
HAUNTS
the limbs as music haunts the lyre, a creature . . . . 8 T&C OF NICOL   21
is their blind fear --haunts all unsleep this cry . . . . . 439 NO THANKS 55   6
HAVE
WORD DELETED, APPEARED 192 TIMES

322

	PAGE	TITLE	LINE
HAVEN'T			
about you got the haven't Marjorie isn't this wellcurb . . .	257	IS 5 ONE 27	35
eyes locks open keys haven't is have doubt and	716	95 POEMS 44	25
HAVES			
sames of am through haves of give, singing each	520	50 POEMS 34	2
HAVING			
of skipping maenads knows,-- having Discordia's apple in thy	6	T&C EPITHALAM	151
song upon her mouth having death in her eyes	50	T&C IMPRESS 4	8
death upon her mouth having a song in her	50	T&C IMPRESS 4	30
looking at each other having the fastest time because	126	& SEVEN POEMS 5	6
and the little striker having the best time tickling	126	& SEVEN POEMS 5	11
her wonderful But i (having in my arms caught	162	& SON ACTU 11	9
So until light each having each we promised to	173	& SON ACTU 22	12
as (HO PARTHENON) and having ordered yaoorti from Nicho' . .	194	XLI PORTRAIT 2	10
and coquettishly- cocked bonnet having ceased the captain . .	196	XLI PORTRAIT 4	6
like Gillette Razor Blades having been used and reused . . .	230	IS 5 ONE 2	21
the wellknown parvenu who (having dreamed of a corkscrew) . .	236	IS 5 ONE 7	6
careful of her and (having thoroughly oiled the universal . .	248	IS 5 ONE 19	5
his optima rerum first having taken care to lie	261	IS 5 ONE 31	12
astonishment much impressed by having once noticed (as an . .	262	IS 5 ONE 32	9
oh i mean: entirely having in my careful how	295	IS 5 FOUR 12	5
it with fingers; till having found what was thrown	298	IS 5 FOUR 15	22
/ Lord John Unalive (having a fortune of fifteengrand	331	VIVA 22	1
name S.S. VAN MERDE) having first put right sleuthfully . . .	334	VIVA 25	5
to undeath) salute. and having worshipped for my doom	358	VIVA 49	14
the month of June, having of certain stars and	360	VIVA 51	12
G gladly forget little having less with every least	390	NO THANKS 7	6
born who cannot fail having no wealth but love, ...	394	NO THANKS 11	13
aint & even (not having most ever lived people	412	NO THANKS 29	12
/ / / death (having lost) put on his	451	NO THANKS 66	1
see you again. Love (having found) wound up such	451	NO THANKS 66	9
most despair? all knowing's having and have is (you	528	50 POEMS 40	10
as any (men's hells having wrestled with) man drops	558	1 X 1 18	1
accuse their mountains of having altitude--and march	620	{CHAIRE} 22	11
meet again, little he (having flown even higher) is	631	{CHAIRE} 33	7
wishing and wishing is having-- but keeping is downward . . .	665	{CHAIRE} 67	2
sound and wishing is having and having is giving--	665	{CHAIRE} 67	9
wishing is having and having is giving-- but keeping	665	{CHAIRE} 67	9
has been found and having is giving and giving	665	{CHAIRE} 67	16
HAVINGEST			
very (in sad this havingest world) most merry most	590	1 X 1 50	2
HAWK			
cringes the hugest heartless hawk and veers the vast	774	73 POEMS 2	7
HAWKED			
your honest redskin toma hawked and scalped his victim . . .	643	{CHAIRE} 45	2
HAY			
shoulders him doll self) hay completely thus or that	516	50 POEMS 30	12
you in the newmown hay and he telling you	707	95 POEMS 35	26
HAYMOW			
made sense in when's haymow with young fore'er (oh	316	VIVA 8	16
HAYMOWS			
as long as there's haymows you never can tell"	707	95 POEMS 35	10
HAZARDED			
everybody is." And i hazarded "god" (blushing slightly) --"O	228	IS 5 ONE MARJ	5
HE			
WORD DELETED, APPEARED 227 TIMES			
HE-IN-HER			
the She-in-him with the He-in-her (& both all hopped	317	VIVA 9	32
HE-MAN'S			
certain party gimme the he-man's solid bliss for youse . . .	247	IS 5 ONE 18	5
HE-SHE			
crumbs things? Its noyesiyou he-she (Weres / / /	417	NO THANKS 34	24
HE'D			
on to the bulls he'd bumped a bloke back	145	& SON REAL 16	2
friend became his foe he'd laugh and build a	521	50 POEMS 34	48
should break in two he'd make them one (his	760	95 POEMS 87	8
HE'LL			
crumble the mouth-flower fleet He'll not my tower, laborious,	83	T&C SON ACTU 2	13

HE'LL (CONTINUED)
    he winked and hope he'll do it again or . . . . 126 & SEVEN POEMS 5   17
    you ask the rain he'll not tell where.) beauty . . . . 183 XLI SONGS 5   6
    or (as various worlds he'll spurn rather than fail . . . . . 562 1 X 1 22   7
    tallest of the boys" "he'll give me another if . . . . 684 95 POEMS 12   9
    meet no matter how he'll try to try) So . . . . 685 95 POEMS 13   4
    than still) and what he'll sing and sing to . . . . 752 95 POEMS 80   4
HE'S
    hopping sawdust you kiddo he's a palping wreaths of . . . . . 96 & POST IMPR 8   16
    as his picture goes he's a wet dream by . . . . 246 IS 5 ONE 17   12
    like Out of doors he's a with eyes and . . . . 251 IS 5 ONE 22   6
    minions <> "allezcirculez") --my he's brave.... the . . . . . 275 IS 5 TWO 9   40
    Gamaliel Harding "is" dead he's "dead" if he wouldn't . . . . 336 IS 5 TWO 8   8
    i) has pulled (for he's we) such fruit from . . . . 543 1 X 1 3   21
    polloi and if sometimes he's prodded forth to exercise   . . . 544 1 X 1 4   9
    goddesses nor sleeping) since he's young with mysteries (each 617 (CHAIRE) 19   9
    loving" (sighs mind: and he's clever) "for all, yes . . . . . 625 (CHAIRE) 27   6
    the Battle of Because he's squatting in the middle . . . . . 642 (CHAIRE) 44   4
    Navy of the Moon he's swooning at the bottom . . . . 642 (CHAIRE) 44   14
    bird first for joy, he's i he's i / . . . . 666 (CHAIRE) 68   20
    for joy, he's i he's i / / / . . . . 666 (CHAIRE) 68   20
    but more, the older he's the younger she's / . . . . 742 95 POEMS 70   17
    is I AM and he's the soul of chivalry . . . . 774 73 POEMS 2   4
    will dance! and when he's plucked such mysteries as . . . . . 843 73 POEMS 71   13
    with all his years) he's free into the beauty . . . . 845 73 POEMS 73   9
HEAD
    certain altar at whose head stands that clear candle . . . .   6 T&C EPITHALAM   116
    a little turn her head i know that i . . . . 17 T&C PUELLA MEA   33
    ivory. The immaculate crisp head is such as only . . . . . . 20 T&C PUELLA MEA   139
    flight of flowers thy head is a quick forest . . . . 29 T&C ORIENTALE 3   5
    song my love thy head is a casket of . . . . 29 T&C ORIENTALE 3   16
    the hair of thy head is one warrior innocent . . . . 29 T&C ORIENTALE 3   18
    eternity. when over my head a shooting star Bur . . . . 49 T&C IMPRESS 3   22
    horror of her toylike head and vainly tried to . . . . 53 T&C PORTRAIT 1   41
    now droops the faun head now the intimate flower . . . . . . 54 T&C PORTRAIT 2   9
    grass rises on the head of the earth and . . . . 61 T&C PORTRAIT 9   20
    / / at the head of this street a . . . . 69 T&C POST IMPR 6   1
    hat back on my head i sit up and . . . . 69 T&C POST IMPR 6   34
    god's capable dull important head-- by on whom glories   . . . 85 T&C SON ACTU 4   4
    a bald greenish foetal head established It suddenly upon . . 96 & POST IMPR 8   29
    carrying flowers on his head. young death sits in . . . . . . 102 & POST IMPR 12   2
    thirds asleep, on his head flowers, always crying to . . . . 102 & POST IMPR 12   14
    here is little Effie's head whose brains are made . . . . . . 117 & PORTRAIT 10   1
    here is little Effie's head whose brains are made . . . . . . 118 & PORTRAIT 10   43
    exactly dance in my head, precisely dance where danced . . . 120 & PORTRAIT 12   3
    dansent toujours in my head dis-donc, Paris ta gorge . . . . 121 & PORTRAIT 12   52
    precisely dance in my head ladies carefully dead / . . . . . 121 & PORTRAIT 12   60
    under me around; my head fits (my head) in . . . . 123 & SEVEN POEMS 2   11
    my head fits (my head) in your Brain--my, head's . . . . . . 123 & SEVEN POEMS 2   12
    laughing) with your head. all big / / . . . . 123 & SEVEN POEMS 2   15
    of sitting on your head your unnatural hair has . . . . 126 & SEVEN POEMS 5   9
    shoveling her small manure-shaped head one sheet on which . . 134 & SON REAL 5   3
    Her lips study my head gripping for a decision: . . . . 146 & SON REAL 17   4
    kiss my face and head. / / / / . . . . 147 & SON REAL 18   14
    the grass lies her head by oaks and roses . . . . 181 XLI SONGS 3   13
    of men his peaked head smoulders like a new . . . . 198 XLI PORTRAIT 6   19
    cherished as fair. (The child-head poised with the serious . 207 XLI SONNETS 3   14
    dolores small in the head keen chassised like a . . . . 232 IS 5 ONE 3   5
    above his blond determined head the sacred flag of . . . . . 273 IS 5 TWO 8   13
    (first knocking on the head him) do through icy . . . . 339 VIVA 30   8
    would not sell his head) squads right impatiently replied . . 473 NEW POEMS 11   3
    know (a he of head comes to some dirty . . . . 501 50 POEMS 15   6
    behind is (just a head of he is) merely . . . . 501 50 POEMS 15   18
    better today? nn-nn went head face goes (if how . . . . 506 50 POEMS 20   8
    pink stops might equal head). Then with the splendor . . . . 506 50 POEMS 20   10
    the (on his quiet head his magical shoulders him . . . . . . 516 50 POEMS 30   11
    looked him in the head; if every friend became . . . . 521 50 POEMS 34   46
    the top of his head: to tell him / . . . . 553 1 X 1 13   24

		PAGE	TITLE	LINE
HEAD (CONTINUED)				
red candle over his head by a finger of		631	{CHAIRE} 33	2
/ / open his head, baby & you'll find		637	{CHAIRE} 39	1
whos of this snowy head we call old frank		754	95 POEMS 82	5
three dreams live) fore head is stumbling someone (named . .		785	73 POEMS 13	22
+HEAD				
FOR CONTEXT, SEE		101	& POST IMPR 11	51
FOR CONTEXT, SEE		479	NEW POEMS 17	10
HEAD'S				
head) in your Brain--my, head's big she (said laughing . . .		123	& SEVEN POEMS 2	12
grin for smile whose head's his face with stones		716	95 POEMS 44	7
HEADACHES				
houses, clouds. kisses, lice; headaches: ifs.) yet shall . .		361	VIVA 52	20
+HEADED				
FOR CONTEXT, SEE		95	& POST IMPR 7	1
HEADS				
eunuch watches on their heads turbans of a hundred		33	T&C ORIENTALE 6	37
pillow, dear where our heads lived and were. /		288	IS 5 FOUR 5	10
ble fore (hurry into heads are legs think wrists		309	VIVA 1	9
HEADWAITERS				
young man to whom headwaiters bow so? hush--the author . . .		245	IS 5 ONE 16	7
HEALING				
and primeval whyless sky; healing our by immeasurable night .		745	95 POEMS 73	7
HEANDSHE				
per (reel) hapsingly proregress heandshe-ingly people trickle		330	VIVA 21	2
HEANDSHE-INGLY				
per (reel) hapsingly proregress heandshe-ingly people trickle		330	VIVA 21	2
HEAP				
and thrown on the ash-heap where lies what was		203	XLI LA GUERRE 1	16
HEAPED				
earth by thoughtful war heaped wholly with high wilt		213	XLI SONNETS 9	4
HEAPINGANDSQUEEZING				
chords of humorous, fury heapingandsqueezing tum-bling- . . .		100	& POST IMPR 11	13
HEAR				
will their hungering whispers hear with weepings soundless, .		9	T&C SONGS 1	20
the rain, and i hear the screech of dissonant		61	T&C PORTRAIT 9	31
most of all i hear your stepping freakish feet		61	T&C PORTRAIT 9	34
sunset ludicrously dies, i hear only tidewings in the		64	T&C POST IMPR 1	10
turn my face, and hear one bird sing terribly		76	T&C SON UNRE 1	13
edge black trees think (hear little knives of flower		99	& POST IMPR 10	12
buy? Les belles bottes--oh hear ,pas cheres") and my		102	& POST IMPR 12	20
yester- day My Lady hear the purple trumpets blow		110	& PORTRAIT 6	32
succeeds breathings stopped to hear, in darkness, water the .		136	& SON REAL 7	17
, did you ever hear a jazz Band? or		141	& SON REAL 12	16
against my mind, to hear nearing our hearts' irrevocable . .		215	XLI SONNETS 11	12
children and you shall hear the true story of		236	IS 5 ONE 7	2
dropping jolly fast you hear the rrmp and then		269	IS 5 TWO 4	5
if men should not hear them men are old		481	NEW POEMS 19	4
liked the king of) hear ye! the godless are		499	50 POEMS 13	13
goes but we can hear him still if now		624	{CHAIRE} 26	21
have the luck to hear such singing (or glimpse		717	95 POEMS 45	10
5 a m i hear eng (which cannot sing)		787	73 POEMS 15	2
HEARD				
the eyes is dimly heard a wistful and precarious		20	T&C PUELLA MEA	151
was like a song heard behind a golden door, ...		22	T&C PUELLA MEA	222
i cried when i heard over time and tide		44	T&C AMORES 8	19
roof or something where who-ever-heard-of-growing		127	& SEVEN POEMS 5	43
Nothing and Something, we heard a handorgan in twilight . . .		174	& SON ACTU 23	14
i imagine she, and heard them slobber and in		241	IS 5 ONE 12	7
certain stars and planets heard, rose very slowly in		360	VIVA 51	12
never saw so much heard so much smelled so		474	NEW POEMS 12	6
spring danced when she heard my father sing) then		521	50 POEMS 34	52
yes (always we have heard them sing the dark		582	1 X 1 42	6
/ until and i heard a certain a bird		587	1 X 1 47	1
every more silent ly) heard (& how look at		695	95 POEMS 23	17
seems like i just heard your annabel screech have		707	95 POEMS 35	5
cried so high thermopylae heard her and marathon and		711	95 POEMS 39	14
bird. Mostpeople have been heard screaming for international		802	73 POEMS 30	29

HEARD (CONTINUED)
```
pure truth of patience heard above the everywhereing fact . .  821  73 POEMS 49       5
```
HEARING
```
green armies steadily expand hearing the spear-song of the   .    4  T&C EPITHALAM    72
taste and smell and hearing and sight keep hitting  . . . .  199  XLI PORTRAIT 7    3
then he will maybe (hearing something fall into his . . . .  298  IS 5 FOUR 15     20
understand) slightly i am hearing somebody coming up stairs, 375  VIVA 66          10
maid says Who and (hearing not a which) replies . . . . . .  570  1 X 1 30          3
how should tasting touching hearing seeing breathing  . . .  663  (CHAIRE) 65       9
othering Selves i sit (hearing the rain) un til . . . . . .  785  73 POEMS 13      18
```
HEARS
```
frail parting my body hears the cry of Spring, . . . . . .   22  T&C PUELLA MEA  234
and his blood stopped hears in the frail anon . . . . . . .   77  T&C SON UNRE 2    8
youth. And if somebody hears what i say--let him . . . . .   216  XLI SONNETS 12    9
Santa Claus a criminal (hears Darwin; asks about Death) . .  398  NO THANKS 15     14
```
HEARSE
```
pain to take the hearse, see you again. Love  . . . . . . .  451  NO THANKS 66      7
```
HEART
```
upward from the troubled heart of May; a Winged . . . . . .    8  T&C OF NICOL      8
lays bare her trembling heart, with beads of dew  . . . . .    8  T&C OF NICOL     15
right wildly beat her heart at every kiss of  . . . . . . .    8  T&C OF NICOL     29
is sorrowful: but my heart smote in trembling thirds  . . .   11  T&C SONGS 2      16
simply touch me, whose heart-wholeness overmuch Expects of .  12  T&C SONGS 2      38
low and smiling my heart fell dead before. /  . . . . . . .   14  T&C SONGS 4      35
drink water but his heart drinks wine the tenth . . . . . .   15  T&C SONGS 5       8
the feet go the heart goes nine / / . . . . . . . . . . . .   15  T&C SONGS 5      20
the while shall my heart be With the bulge  . . . . . . . .   16  T&C SONGS 6      13
immediately make in my heart so great a noise, . . . . . .    18  T&C PUELLA MEA   65
of thy beauty, my heart discovers thee unto whom  . . . . .   31  T&C ORIENTALE 5  28
slowly, in the glutted heart fleet flowerterrible memories .  36  T&C AMORES 1     25
shining body when my heart sang between your perfect  . . .   39  T&C AMORES 4     14
lintel of defeat, her heart breaks in a smile--and  . . . .   75  T&C SON REAL 6   13
strong fingers clutch this heart, as mine in time . . . . .   76  T&C SON UNRE 1    4
be-- you of my heart, send me a little  . . . . . . . . . .   76  T&C SON UNRE 1   10
your peculiar mouth my heart made wise; at moments  . . . .   78  T&C SON UNRE 3    4
flower on whose huge heart prospecting darkness roams torture 79  T&C SON UNRE 4    4
white ship of thy heart on frailer ports of . . . . . . . .   79  T&C SON UNRE 4   15
of somewhere in your heart pinched from dumb summer? . . . .  80  T&C SON UNRE 5    7
her how my least heart-beat becomes less. And then . . . . . 152  & SON ACTU 1      9
sweet gates of my heart and take the rose, . . . . . . . . . 188  XLI SONGS 10     16
known, scarcely to sing (heart, could we bear the . . . . .  205  XLI SONNETS 1    15
the image my proud heart cherished as fair. (The  . . . . .  207  XLI SONNETS 3    13
cool feet this frantic heart is fain; try me  . . . . . . .  212  XLI SONNETS 8     4
them round the hurt heart which do so frailly . . . . . . .  215  XLI SONNETS 11   10
and, expands my somewherealloverme heart my the halfgloom .  251  IS 5 ONE 22      17
their mother, of his heart the queen --incalculable bliss!   254  IS 5 ONE 25      12
the world: with manly heart and conscience free, upon . . .  273  IS 5 TWO 8       18
things fingered tinily my heart life the little hands . . .  284  IS 5 FOUR 1       7
normal corners of your heart will never guess how . . . . .  292  IS 5 FOUR 9      14
fear, me in your heart softly; not all but  . . . . . . . .  294  IS 5 FOUR 11     18
so long since my heart has been with yours  . . . . . . . .  297  IS 5 FOUR 14      1
living rhythm of your Heart possibly will understand; or  .  300  IS 5 FOUR 17      8
of memory comes my heart, singing like an idiot,  . . . . .  304  IS 5 FIVE 3       2
and big whose warmest heart recoiled at war: a . . . . . . . 339  VIVA 30           2
suddenly, as when the heart of this flower imagines . . . .  366  VIVA 57          11
if i am not heart, because at least i . . . . . . . . . . .  372  VIVA 63           6
only by you my heart always moves / / . . . . . . . . . . .  379  VIVA 70          14
love! soul clings and heart conceives and mind leaps  . . .  386  NO THANKS 3      12
among the vines (my heart pursues against the little  . . .  434  NO THANKS 51     16
set traps for his heart, lay snares for his . . . . . . . .  439  NO THANKS 55     17
war being generous this heart could dare) unhearts can . . . 440  NO THANKS 56      3
oft (with mind with heart he spat and laughed . . . . . . .  441  NO THANKS 56     39
not every but any) heart--wholly, idiotically--before such . 480  NEW POEMS 18      4
(writhing your exploding my) heart before how worlds delicate 480  NEW POEMS 18     15
/ / may my heart always be open to  . . . . . . . . . . . .  481  NEW POEMS 19      1
darker than a spinster's heart my voice feels who . . . . .  506  50 POEMS 20       6
joy so pure a heart of star by him . . . . . . . . . . . .   520  50 POEMS 34      22
and cruel kind, a heart to fear, to doubt . . . . . . . . .  521  50 POEMS 34      58
```

	PAGE	TITLE	LINE

HEART (CONTINUED)

found leading love whose heart is her mind) supremely . . . . 533 50 POEMS 45   4
an imal without a heart. Huge this collective pseudobeast . . 544 1 X 1 4   4
is god. Without a heart the animal is very . . . . 544 1 X 1 4   25
him sings a whippoorwill; heart was big as the . . . . . . 568 1 X 1 28   16
flame so is your heart alert, of languages there's . . . . 575 1 X 1 35   25
/ / open your heart: i'll give you a . . . . 586 1 X 1 46   1
dream) throbbing like a heart singing like a flame . . . . 593 1 X 1 53   11
Life; whose brother married Heart, now Mrs Death. Poor . . . 621 (CHAIRE) 23   3
as clover knows, maybe" (heart makes the suggestion) "or . . 625 (CHAIRE) 27   11
& you'll find a heart in it (cracked) open . . . . 637 (CHAIRE) 39   2
it (cracked) open that heart, mabel & you'll find . . . . . 637 (CHAIRE) 39   4
met christ jesus) my heart flopped over and lay . . . . . . 648 (CHAIRE) 50   5
were so dark of heart they might not speak, ... 649 (CHAIRE) 51   1
disprove than prove what heart may feel and soul . . . . . 664 (CHAIRE) 66   4
and spaceful time-- no heart can leap, no soul . . . . . . 664 (CHAIRE) 66   21
birds dive to the heart of the sky all . . . . 665 (CHAIRE) 67   19
/ / this man's heart is true to his . . . . 676 95 POEMS 4   1
failed to fool your heart but most (without the . . . . . . 679 95 POEMS 7   8
gayer than gayest someone's heart at your each nearerness) . 717 95 POEMS 45   12
is wind) trust your heart if the seas catch . . . . 732 95 POEMS 60   5
fate isn't fatal --a heart her each petal / . . . . 764 95 POEMS 90   54
/ i carry my heart with me (i carry . . . . 766 95 POEMS 92   1
carry it in my heart) i am never without . . . . 766 95 POEMS 92   2
apart i carry your heart (i carry it in . . . . 766 95 POEMS 92   15
carry it in my heart) / / / / . . . . 766 95 POEMS 92   15
a mind and a heart but unquestionably a soul-- . . . . . . 802 73 POEMS 30   17
all) therefore despair, my heart and die into the . . . . . 834 73 POEMS 62   23

+HEART

FOR CONTEXT, SEE . . . . 524 50 POEMS 36   41
FOR CONTEXT, SEE . . . . 605 (CHAIRE) 7   6

HEART-BEAT

her how my least heart-beat becomes less. And then . . . . 152 & SON ACTU 1   9

HEART-WHOLENESS

simply touch me, whose heart-wholeness overmuch Expects of . 12 T&C SONGS 2   38

HEART'S

my seeing blood, her heart's chatter riveted a weeping . . . 132 & SON REAL 3   3
dreaming becomes if your heart's mine) i guess a . . . . . . 364 VIVA 55   5
a syllable of the heart's eager dim enormous language . . . . 372 VIVA 63   11
world; and let her heart's each whisper wear all . . . . . . 811 73 POEMS 39   6

HEARTBEAT

divides by timelessness that heartbeat) mightily forgetting . 428 NO THANKS 45   12
to hold a mountain's heartbeat in his hand / . . . . 562 1 X 1 22   14
whens) before each heartbeat which i am alive . . . . . . 577 1 X 1 37   20
his longest life's a heartbeat of some sun; his . . . . . . 609 1 X 1 11   11
stars but not one heartbeat of this child; nor . . . . 714 95 POEMS 42   11
nearer than each our heartbeat--believe that love (and only . 741 95 POEMS 69   5
silent pasture, all a heartbeat dares; that mountain, any . . 818 73 POEMS 46   8

HEARTBEATS

than (day disappears) their heartbeats dare some upward world 757 95 POEMS 85   5

HEARTED-NUJOLNEEDING-THERE'S-A-REASON

pretty littleliverpill- hearted-Nujolneeding-There's-A-Reason 231 IS 5 ONE 3   47

HEARTLESS

this every truth--beware of heartless them (given the . . . . 556 1 X 1 16   6
wraiths proclaim substance; all heartless spectres, ... 765 95 POEMS 91   4
know) cringes the hugest heartless hawk and veers the . . . . 774 73 POEMS 2   7

HEARTLIKE

high night where his heartlike ears have flown adorable . . . 631 (CHAIRE) 33   5

HEARTS

shining mirth the furious hearts of mountains ceased to . . . 3 T&C EPITHALAM   16
to whom belong the hearts of lovers! --I beseech . . . . . . 7 T&C EPITHALAM   167
the kindness of their hearts a few philosophers tell . . . . 281 IS 5 THREE 5   1
over our mouths fears hearts lungs arms hopes feet . . . . . 283 IS 5 THREE 7   2
/ / our touching hearts slenderly comprehend (clinging as . 305 IS 5 FIVE 4   1
(somewhere between our unlighted hearts lust lurks slovenly . 322 VIVA 14   10
When minds shrivel and hearts grow brittler every Instant . . 359 VIVA 50   4
amor (Though through our hearts hugely squirm roots) us . . . 361 VIVA 52   8
the fear of all hearts never which have (Per . . . . 397 NO THANKS 14   7

HEARTS (CONTINUED)
    naLOVEme crazily ships bulge hearts by darts pierced lazily . 436 NO THANKS 52   7
    when Souls are outlawed, Hearts are sick, Hearts being   . . . 438 NO THANKS 54   21
    outlawed, Hearts are sick, Hearts being sick, Minds nothing . 438 NO THANKS 54   22
    socalled were not given hearts how should they be?   . . . . . 510 50 POEMS 24   1
    they be? their socalled hearts would think these socalled . . 510 50 POEMS 24   2
    soul to mind) --whose hearts are mountains, roots are . . . . 560 1 X 1 20   15
    each happening of their hearts live longer than all . . . . . 576 1 X 1 36   1
    these (or many thousand hearts which don't and dream   . . . . 743 95 POEMS 71   6
    day it's brains without hearts have set saint against . . . . 769 95 POEMS 95   15
    to sing if broken hearts were whole and cowards . . . . 798 73 POEMS 26   8
HEARTS'
    to hear nearing our hearts' irrevocable play-- through the . 215 XLI SONNETS 11   13
HEARTY
    destroyed hero clamps the hearty sharp column of Egypt   . . . 111 & PORTRAIT 6   42
    arse with all his hearty soul aglow) his nightly   . . . . . . 254 IS 5 ONE 25   21
    at just midnight this hearty fellow'll exist --whereas that . 813 73 POEMS 41   6
HEAT
    / PORTRAITS the nimble heat had long on a . . . . 52 T&C PORTRAIT 1   3
    bayonets roasted hot with heat-- Olaf (upon what were . . . . 339 VIVA 30   30
HEAVE
    legs she begins to heave and twine about me, ... 147 & SON REAL 18   13
HEAVEN
    the pale meaning of heaven clings, (whose million leaves . .   6 T&C EPITHALAM   124
    should the grapes of heaven combine with earth's madness) . . 21 T&C PUELLA MEA   200
    in the kingdom of heaven through day and space   . . . . . . 30 T&C ORIENTALE 4   33
    with silence the undulous heaven yearns where in tense   . . . 37 T&C AMORES 2   8
    hair. The lily of heaven full of all dreams, ... 65 T&C POST IMPR 2   5
    stars begin to husk heaven) you, you exactly paled   . . . . . 71 T&C SON REAL 2   12
    against the clever deadly heaven i salute you whose . . . . . 112 & PORTRAIT 6   108
    unto the stars of Heaven.... i do signore affirm   . . . . . . 256 IS 5 ONE 27   21
    it delivers the goods, Heaven knows (yet are we . . . . 264 IS 5 ONE 33   12
    not be a pansy heaven nor a fragile heaven   . . . . 352 VIVA 43   2
    heaven nor a fragile heaven of lilies-of-the-valley but it . 352 VIVA 43   3
    it will be a heaven of blackred roses my . . . . 352 VIVA 43   4
    down with hell and heaven and all the religious . . . . 466 NEW POEMS 4   13
    unimagined sky deeper than heaven is hell / / . . . . 563 1 X 1 23   12
    climb all the blue heaven green earth neither sea . . . . . . 588 1 X 1 48   3
    cynic (swimfloatdrifting fragment of heaven) trickstervillain 677 95 POEMS 5   11
    of impossible ours --God's heaven perhaps comprises poems (my 748 95 POEMS 76   5
    love? why then to heaven with hell. Whatever sages . . . . . 768 95 POEMS 94   13
    lose or win (come heaven, come hell) precisely ours . . . . . 776 73 POEMS 4   14
    a world born deaf) "heaven or hell" / / . . . . 787 73 POEMS 15   16
    the sun in his heaven says Now the timid . . . . 801 73 POEMS 29   23
    hell rational --i thank heaven somebody's crazy enough to . . 802 73 POEMS 30   32
    are dreams, less into heaven certainly earth swims than . . . 810 73 POEMS 38   7
+HEAVEN
    FOR CONTEXT, SEE . . . . 259 IS 5 ONE 29   3
    FOR CONTEXT, SEE . . . . 320 VIVA 12   13
HEAVEN'S
    magnificence conquers magnificence. In heaven's intolerable .   6 T&C EPITHALAM   129
    Goethe, since exempt from heaven's grace, in an engraving . . 158 & SON ACTU 7   7
HEAVENLESS
    here everywhere fairyair feelable heavenless warm sweet . . . 755 95 POEMS 83   10
    / / unlove's the heavenless hell and homeless home . . . . . 765 95 POEMS 91   1
HEAVENLY
    never mind consider rather heavenly things and but the . . . 322 VIVA 14   2
    thing: no bliss of heavenly earth beguiles our spirits, . . . 675 95 POEMS 3   2
    / / / in heavenly realms of hellas dwelt . . . . 799 73 POEMS 27   1
HEAVENS
    if there are any heavens my mother will (all . . . . 352 VIVA 43   1
    of a bliss "seven heavens for just one dying, ... 837 73 POEMS 65   13
HEAVILY
    an old toy balloon) heavily swims to Strunsky's, Monia's . . 219 XLI SONNETS 15   13
HEAVING
    over: and the sea heaving indolent colourless forgets) time . 277 IS 5 THREE 1   19
HEAVY
    a flower which most heavy hung with silence when . . . . . . 18 T&C PUELLA MEA   58

	PAGE	TITLE	LINE

+HEAVY
FOR CONTEXT, SEE . . . . 259 IS 5 ONE 29   13
HECTOCOTYLIFEROUSLY
of somebody who was hectocotyliferously propagated when Miss 326 VIVA 18   9
HEED
sky yield to and heed the mauve of twilight . . . . 93 & POST IMPR 5   7
HEEDLESS
the worst, of peril heedless, each braver than the . . . . . 266 IS 5 TWO 1   18
HEELED
merry flowers wee skipping high-heeled flames courtesied . . 44 T&C AMORES 8   6
HEELS
soon on the sweet heels of passed afterday, clothe . . . . . 10 T&C SONGS 1   39
propped on irrelevantly ferocious heels. Her gasping slippery 103 & POST IMPR 13   8
light feeling up streets; heels taking derbies (where?) a . . 172 & SON ACTU 21   3
have liars pled, their heels for Freedom slaves will . . . . 438 NO THANKS 54   18
HEIGHT
pillars slipped from immeasurable height, fall, fifty, silent 32 T&C ORIENTALE 6 31
boy flesh dips my height in a firm fragile . . . . 140 & SON REAL 11   8
of madness (at Myself's height these various innocent . . . . 202 XLI PORTRAIT 9   40
seas of iron breathing height eating steepness the ship . . . 419 NO THANKS 36   13
parallel specks float-ing create height, liv- ing ly who: . . 447 NO THANKS 62   4
moved through depths of height this motionless forgetful . . 520 50 POEMS 34   4
+HEIGHT
FOR CONTEXT, SEE . . . . 333 VIVA 24   22
HEIGHTS
never has plumbed the heights of prowst but respects . . . . 499 50 POEMS 13   11
last doubt and humbly heights below) kneeling, we--true . . . 574 1 X 1 34   10
+HEINOUS
FOR CONTEXT, SEE . . . . 267 IS 5 TWO 2   15
HEIRY
repass where flesh is heiry montparnasse is goosed by . . . . 401 NO THANKS 18   13
HELD
a piece of money held between his thumb and . . . . 102 & POST IMPR 12   4
The big fear Who held us deeply in His . . . . 289 IS 5 FOUR 6   3
HELEN
among my and your skyscrapers--Helen & Cleopatra were Just . 230 IS 5 ONE 2   27
in life) re the helen molle dancers, whom he . . . . 327 VIVA 18   r39
pound. Turn gert (spin! helen) the slimmer the finger . . . . 513 50 POEMS 27   5
HELEN'S
all the Troys of Helen's beauty: never did Lord . . . . 18 T&C PUELLA MEA   68
HELIOS
car closing uncouth) of Helios the sweet wheels tremulous-- . 4 T&C EPITHALAM   48
HELL
the skilful mystery of Hell) me suddenly grips in . . . . . . 130 & SON REAL 1   7
in twilight playing like hell / / / / . . . . 174 & SON ACTU 23   15
like a floating silver hell a song of adolescent . . . . . . 214 XLI SONNETS 10   13
runnin aroun wid eachudder Hell Bent fer election makin . . . 237 IS 5 ONE 8   18
on Xmas Eve like Hell Itself which may or . . . . 239 IS 5 ONE 10   6
she kicked what the hell) next minute i was . . . . 248 IS 5 ONE 19   13
made...) why then to Hell with that: the other; . . . . 264 IS 5 ONE 33   30
as now i love. Hell (by most humble me . . . . 360 VIVA 51   31
1 wife in impossibly hell Memo 1 son in . . . . 389 NO THANKS 6   20
start a magazine to hell with literature we want . . . . . . 407 NO THANKS 24   2
like we) down with hell and heaven and all . . . . 466 NEW POEMS 4   13
from i say to hell with that that doesn't . . . . 475 NEW POEMS 13   5
finger i say to hell with that i say . . . . 475 NEW POEMS 13   9
if they don't to hell with them) is hows . . . . 500 50 POEMS 14   23
case if--listen: there's a hell of a good universe . . . . . 554 1 X 1 14   14
deeper than heaven is hell / / / / . . . . 563 1 X 1 23   12
god's O what the hell yes it's true that . . . . 638 (CHAIRE) 40   10
's gulped by illimitable hell) and never have breathed . . . 639 (CHAIRE) 41   8
gainst one immense deep hell -o of keen moon) . . . . 687 95 POEMS 15   7
her father lays" "black hell upon you and all . . . . 707 95 POEMS 35   21
be as thankful as hell and bury the statue . . . . 711 95 POEMS 39   26
still More) what the hell are we all morticians? . . . . . . 727 95 POEMS 55   21
day knocked living the hell out of me-- who . . . . 730 95 POEMS 58   2
/ unlove's the heavenless hell and homeless home of . . . . . 765 95 POEMS 91   1
then to heaven with hell. Whatever sages say and . . . . . . 768 95 POEMS 94   13

HELL (CONTINUED)

win (come heaven, come hell) precisely ours is the . . . . . 776 73 POEMS 4   14

born deaf) "heaven or hell" / / / / . . . . 787 73 POEMS 15   16

happy? WE-WE-WE & to hell with the chappy who . . . . 791 73 POEMS 19   3

international measures that render hell rational --i thank . 802 73 POEMS 30   31

HELLAS

smooth coffee tasting of hellas, i drink, or sometimes . . . 217 XLI SONNETS 13   11

in heavenly realms of hellas dwelt two very different . . . . 799 73 POEMS 27   1

HELLENIKON

the cindercoloured little {MEGA} {HELLENIKON KSENODOCHEION . 217 XLI SONNETS 13   15

HELLO

made of roses & hello: (of solongs and, ashes) . . . . 66 T&C POST IMPR 3   16

it's they shall cry hello to the spring what . . . . 560 1 X 1 20   16

/ / / / Hello is what a mirror . . . . 570 1 X 1 30   1

young (winter goodbye) april hello, / / / / . . . . 737 95 POEMS 65   8

(big with unthings) tosses hello whirling whose rhyme . . . . 751 95 POEMS 79   4

worlds are made of hello and goodbye: glad sorry . . . . . . 776 73 POEMS 4   38

+HELLO

FOR CONTEXT, SEE . . . . 687 95 POEMS 15   7

HELLS

/ as any (men's hells having wrestled with) man . . . . 558 1 X 1 18   1

HELMAR

/ 5 ◇ smoke Helmar cigarettes 2 play backgammon, ... 200 XLI PORTRAIT 8   2

exit paperboy a finishes Helmar lights another x and . . . . 200 XLI PORTRAIT 8   15

HELP

fool who cright god help me it aint no . . . . 405 NO THANKS 22   10

/ ("fire stop thief help murder save the world" . . . . 555 1 X 1 15   1

but who just couldn't help it no matter how . . . . 635 {CHAIRE} 37   5

HELPLESS

in fact myself Hereupon helpless i utter lilac shrieks . . . 199 XLI PORTRAIT 7   11

HELPLESSBABY

with hardslippery greens and helplessbaby blues and stic-ky . 100 & POST IMPR 11   5

HELPLESSLY

as, uttering overmuch, stand helplessly before the spirit at 76 T&C SON UNRE 1   8

HELPLESSNESS

icy waters roll that helplessness which others stroke with . 339 VIVA 30   10

HELVES

/ / / / helves surling out of eakspeasies . . . . 330 VIVA 21   1

HEMLOCK

by maple pine by hemlock spruce by tamarack (. . . . . 658 {CHAIRE} 60   20

HENARUB

ardensteil-henarub-izabeth) this noN allgotupfittokill . . . 726 95 POEMS 54   1

HENCE

is what particularly matters hence in a little sunlight . . . 238 IS 5 ONE 9   18

HENCEFORTH

to add an A? henceforth he feels his pride . . . . 650 {CHAIRE} 52   9

HENRI

j'm'appelle Manon, cinq rue Henri Mounier voulez-vous coucher 121 & PORTRAIT 12   35

queenly legs cinq rue Henri Mounier a little love . . . . . . 121 & PORTRAIT 12   46

HENRY

low's small negro son, Henry Wadsworth Bryant. By this . . . 263 IS 5 ONE 32   53

HER

WORD DELETED, APPEARED 289 TIMES

HER-AND-HIS

enormously more less: until her-and-his nonexistence vanishes 808 73 POEMS 36   12

HERALD

still the mad magnificent herald Spring assembles beauty from 4 T&C EPITHALAM   57

HERCULANEAN

ter) nize-aday (most gently herculanean my mortal) yoo make . 618 {CHAIRE} 20   3

HERE

most of her (this here and This, do you . . . . 72 T&C SON REAL 3   12

known; and man, whose here is always worse than . . . . 81 T&C SON UNRE 6   11

colour) while there and here the lithe indolent prostitute . 93 & POST IMPR 5   16

he is there and here, or that, or this . . . . 102 & POST IMPR 12   11

/ / / / here is little Effie's head . . . . 117 & PORTRAIT 10   1

up and down the here we are now judgment . . . . 118 & PORTRAIT 10   40

back in this way. here is little Effie's head . . . . 118 & PORTRAIT 10   43

and a known thing here) and changing everything carefully . . 124 & SEVEN POEMS 3   8

		PAGE	TITLE	LINE

HERE (CONTINUED)

	PAGE	TITLE	LINE
perhaps fraction of flower here placing an inch of	124	& SEVEN POEMS 3	17
that between there and here gladness flays hideously hills. .	158	& SON ACTU 7	1
sung; yet stand They here enraptured, as among the	208	XLI SONNETS 4	12
mounting unsurely twilight but here were something more . . .	211	XLI SONNETS 7	4
Maeterlinck now that April's here? (ask the man who	233	IS 5 ONE 4	22
metope now that triglyph's here) / / / /	257	IS 5 ONE 27	40
/ / candles and Here Comes a glass box	280	IS 5 THREE 4	2
begin crossing people) and hErE cOmEs a glass box:	280	IS 5 THREE 4	9
pointing see yes) It here comes A Glass Box	280	IS 5 THREE 4	19
bridegrooms Naked and luminous (here the absurd I; life, . .	281	IS 5 THREE 5	18
between your naked shoulderblades. --Here comes a stout . . .	282	IS 5 THREE 6	23
of flame bubbles) see here and here they explode	282	IS 5 THREE 6	30
bubbles) see here and here they explode silently into	282	IS 5 THREE 6	30
kite in the trees, here and here reflecting sunlight	283	IS 5 THREE 7	11
the trees, here and here reflecting sunlight (everywhere . .	283	IS 5 THREE 7	12
knows, or why jerks Here &, here, gr(oo	286	IS 5 FOUR 3	8
why jerks Here &, here, gr(oo)ving the	286	IS 5 FOUR 3	8
in Paris we met here / / / /	304	IS 5 FIVE 3	15
people drink smile if here there (like lopsided imaginations)	340	VIVA 31	9
also there: and being here imprisoned, tortured here love . .	377	VIVA 68	7
being here imprisoned, tortured here love everywhere	377	VIVA 68	7
/ / / / here is the ocean, this	379	VIVA 70	1
al-down) most whis per (here) ingc r O wing;	423	NO THANKS 40	8
the little moon a here and there lark who;	434	NO THANKS 51	18
why what filth is here unlives do cry on	440	NO THANKS 56	7
joy) what stink is here unpoets do cry unfools	440	NO THANKS 56	31
/ / birds (here, inven ting air U	448	NO THANKS 63	2
/ there is a here and that here was	505	50 POEMS 19	1
a here and that here was a town (and	505	50 POEMS 19	2
(and every fades) is here and away (but born	509	50 POEMS 23	3
each foot likes the here of this earth whose	512	50 POEMS 26	8
why (it's now, boys) here we come / /	513	50 POEMS 27	36
this what that a here and there a peers	516	50 POEMS 30	8
his glance to shining here; that if (so timid	520	50 POEMS 34	6
began to sing all here is hands machine no	523	50 POEMS 36	10
any never no vacation here is hands is work	523	50 POEMS 36	19
of the coin comes here a man would have	531	50 POEMS 43	9
singings gone to say? here youngest selves yet younger . . .	538	50 POEMS 50	7
some few creep there here or on unearth /	541	1 X 1 1	11
unslowly more who (and here who there who) descend	557	1 X 1 17	8
now and her each here is such an everywhere, ...	576	1 X 1 36	10
very amazing now or here) let pitiless fear play	580	1 X 1 40	4
obsolete; pasts are unborn (here less than nothing's more . .	592	1 X 1 52	12
books tell how) so here is away and so	594	1 X 1 54	23
who sharpens every dull here comes the only man	624	(CHAIRE) 26	2
his copious whichwhat skilfully here & (simply infinite) . .	629	(CHAIRE) 31	9
finland now that russia's here) swing low sweet ca	641	(CHAIRE) 43	2
nly perishing eagerly everyw here shutting forever&forever .	646	(CHAIRE) 48	11
perfect gay, nowhere to here, never to beautiful: a	649	(CHAIRE) 51	7
last perfection, now and here --but look: not sunlight? . . .	650	(CHAIRE) 52	17
sickness of mind sprawls) here a livingly free mysterious . .	658	(CHAIRE) 60	15
are in we and here is a secret they	664	(CHAIRE) 66	7
its way to now -here / / / /	676	95 POEMS 4	26
amaze our now and here with paradise) forgetting if, ...	688	95 POEMS 16	8
married his wife and here is a riddle for	707	95 POEMS 35	19
and they whistle (now here is a job to	709	95 POEMS 37	10
ling (e ver yw here) s Now / /	713	95 POEMS 41	10
--there by arriving magically here-- an everywhere which . .	741	95 POEMS 69	11
is the now and here of freedom. Come /	745	95 POEMS 73	14
slim of blue of here will who straight up	746	95 POEMS 74	6
hills (not where not here but neither's blue most	750	95 POEMS 78	5
the coming quitenotimaginable silenceofsound (here is that .	754	95 POEMS 82	13
mountain (strolling is there here everywhere fairyair	755	95 POEMS 83	8
/ / / / here pasture ends-- this girl	757	95 POEMS 85	1
sings till everywhere is here / / / /	760	95 POEMS 87	12
mind --nothing believable inhabits here: overs of known . . .	761	95 POEMS 88	5
lovers are the song. Here (only here) is freedom:	765	95 POEMS 91	10

	PAGE	TITLE	LINE

HERE (CONTINUED)
the song. Here (only here) is freedom: always here	765	95 POEMS 91	10
here) is freedom: always here no then of winter	765	95 POEMS 91	10
always sing is you here is the deepest secret	766	95 POEMS 92	10
deepest secret nobody knows (here is the root of	766	95 POEMS 92	11
/ spring! may-- everywhere's here (with a low high	767	95 POEMS 93	2
a fro (and a here there where) and away	769	95 POEMS 95	7
lead where truth is here / / / /	775	73 POEMS 3	4
/ / / "right here the other night something	800	73 POEMS 28	1
of kings" Homer Lea) here are five simple facts	803	73 POEMS 31	5
selves they put on here again --to livingest one	819	73 POEMS 47	16
a there of a) here of a rubythroat's home	827	73 POEMS 55	8
nce e very w here noon e is exc	830	73 POEMS 58	8
when beyond) now and here (far from a grown	832	73 POEMS 60	8
un til one strict here of amazing most now, ...	840	73 POEMS 68	28

+HERE
FOR CONTEXT, SEE	353	VIVA 44	23
FOR CONTEXT, SEE	398	NO THANKS 15	20
FOR CONTEXT, SEE	519	50 POEMS 33	14

HERE&GONE
| most lily brief (rose here&gone) flesh all is If . . . . . . | 690 | 95 POEMS 18 | 6 |

HERE'LL
| my, her life marvels "here'll be a canoe and . . . . | 572 | 1 X 1 32 | 15 |

HERE'S
his whistle somebody says here's luck somebody else says . .	108	& PORTRAIT 4	20
to the Odour. (and here's what WhoEver will know	154	& SON ACTU 3	13
lifting a Green River (here's to youse) "a bloke	229	IS 5 ONE FRAN	10
/ / / / here's a little mouse) and	286	IS 5 FOUR 3	1
you and i, since here's a little he or	286	IS 5 FOUR 3	17
/ / / well) here's looking at ourselves two	323	VIVA 15	1
has little wings and here's my hotel this is	353	VIVA 44	11
little further--why be afraid-- here's the earliest star . .	357	VIVA 48	2
sure that's) but listen here's (correct you said it	400	NO THANKS 17	11
/ / / / here's to opening and upward, ...	424	NO THANKS 41	1
sound of rain and here's to silent certainly mountains; . . .	424	NO THANKS 41	4
with laughing and drunkenness) here's to one undiscoverable .	424	NO THANKS 41	12
yet younger selves conceive here's music's music and the . .	538	50 POEMS 50	8
green earth neither sea here's more than room for	588	1 X 1 48	4
was really a dream-- here's, wherever you aren't or	605	{CHAIRE} 7	15
/ / / / here's s omething round (&	753	95 POEMS 81	1
first amazement as a leaf--here's one more than each	762	95 POEMS 89	5

HEREANYNOEVERY
| mare som e w hereanynoevery ing (danc) ing wills&weres . . . | 493 | 50 POEMS 7 | 16 |

HERELESS
| of poor how colding hereless. air theres what immense . . . . | 491 | 50 POEMS 5 | 4 |

HEREUPON
| different, in fact myself Hereupon helpless i utter lilac . . | 199 | XLI PORTRAIT 7 | 11 |

HEREWITH
| my tragic tale concludes herewith: soldier, beware of mrs . . | 799 | 73 POEMS 27 | 40 |

HERO
how the dainty destroyed hero clamps the hearty sharp	111	& PORTRAIT 6	42
Picture it gents: our hero, Dan who as you've	254	IS 5 ONE 25	14
octopus, and then our hero folded his umbrella. It	263	IS 5 ONE 32	56
blurb anent the (hic) hero dead that gladly (sic)	266	IS 5 TWO 1	13
teem) still doth our hero contemplate in raptures of	544	1 X 1 4	19
to prove that a hero equals any jerk who	636	{CHAIRE} 38	3
Was General Was the hero of the Battle of	642	{CHAIRE} 44	3
the luck; since our hero is quite without change, ...	800	73 POEMS 28	11

HERO'S
| nakedness (table but three) hero's carnivorous (smile by . . | 546 | 1 X 1 6 | 8 |

HEROD'S
| in the noise of Herod's silence, long ago. If . . . . | 17 | T&C PUELLA MEA | 32 |

HEROES
deeds of history her heroes, sounds the tread of	209	XLI SONNETS 5	2
will do more than heroes beautifully in shrill armour	302	IS 5 FIVE 1	12
as villains strive and heroes through the mere mind's	576	1 X 1 36	6
poet king float sprout heroes of moonstar flutter to	586	1 X 1 46	10
with its villains or heroes (for god likes girls	732	95 POEMS 60	14

		PAGE	TITLE	LINE

HEROES (CONTINUED)
    were whole and cowards heroes (the popular the wise, ... 798 73 POEMS 26   9
HEROIC
    to valor, battle with heroic breeds; thou, Froissart, for . . 209 XLI SONNETS 5   8
    beaut- iful than these heroic happy dead who rushed . . . . . 268 IS 5 TWO 3   10
HEROISMS
    brings to light dusty heroisms and finally colliding with . . 203 XLI LA GUERRE 1   9
HERR
    stem is believing science=(2b)-n herr professor m / / . . . . 329 VIVA 20   4
HERS
    creature whom than earth hers elf could silent more . . . . . 654 {CHAIRE} 56   10
HERSELF
    into both my hands herself to always keep" always? . . . . . . 57 T&C PORTRAIT 5   19
    / / life boosts herself rapidly at me through . . . . 151 & SON REAL 22   1
    silence (slenderly wholly rising, herself uprearing wholly . 156 & SON ACTU 5   6
    a fragile instant when herself me (slowly, wholly me) . . . . 156 & SON ACTU 5   14
    hither my soul repairs herself with prisms of sharp . . . . . 180 XLI SONGS 2   10
    mounts, inimitably to lose herself where the wet stars . . . 206 XLI SONNETS 2   9
    knowing --and all about herself the sprouting largest final . 301 IS 5 FOUR 18   15
    mother will (all by herself) have one. It will . . . . 352 VIVA 43   1
    birds but more fleet) herself against the air--and whose . . 378 VIVA 69   5
    love's secret supremely clothes herself with day) i mean, . . 379 VIVA 70   5
    quite is nothing but herself, and than this (mere . . . . . . 573 1 X 1 33   17
    count his leaves each herself by opening but shining . . . . 591 1 X 1 51   18
    truth of yes (only herself and who illimitably is) . . . . . 736 95 POEMS 64   3
    eyes blindly stare life herSelf stands / / / . . . . 780 73 POEMS 8   9
    called time: and give herself into the mercy of . . . . 811 73 POEMS 39   11
    delicate creature is most herself while uttering one a . . . 813 73 POEMS 41   8
    still ness which really's herself (and to think that . . . . 827 73 POEMS 55   10
+HERSELF
    FOR CONTEXT, SEE . . . . 317 VIVA 9   12
    FOR CONTEXT, SEE . . . . 654 {CHAIRE} 56   10
+HERSELVES
    FOR CONTEXT, SEE . . . . 739 95 POEMS 67   11
HES
    gush somersaults open ing hes shes & meet & . . . . 536 50 POEMS 48   11
HESHAPED
    (by inch) grin ning heshaped two these (stroll more . . . . 681 95 POEMS 9   3
HESITATE
    / to start, to hesitate; to stop (kneeling in . . . . 650 {CHAIRE} 52   1
HETERONOMOUSLY
    than (that by doDreaming heteronomously metameric me are . . 395 NO THANKS 12   12
HEURES
    / / / 16 heures l'Etoile the communists have . . . . 274 IS 5 TWO 9   1
HEUREUX
    to die nous sommes heureux my soul a limp . . . . 133 & SON REAL 4   18
HEW
    of every prettiness you hew form truly / / . . . . 195 XLI PORTRAIT 3   24
HEWN
    of silence into joists hewn from hugest colour (and . . . . . 378 VIVA 69   10
+HEY
    FOR CONTEXT, SEE . . . . 310 VIVA 2   11
    FOR CONTEXT, SEE . . . . 310 VIVA 2   11
HEYDAY
    unfurled, in the bright heyday of his youth the . . . . 273 IS 5 TWO 8   15
HG
    tea regressed. Kipling again H.G. Wells, and Anatole France . 263 IS 5 ONE 32   43
HIBERNATIVE
    instant appreciation exposed his hibernative contours, . . . 197 XLI PORTRAIT 5   9
HIC
    feller belch the chap hic sum- more eh chuckles . . . . . . 96 & POST IMPR 8   21
    -technic blurb anent the (hic) hero dead that gladly . . . . 266 IS 5 TWO 1   12
HID
    a little bird and hid in a tree of . . . . 30 T&C ORIENTALE 4 19
    The whole truth not hid by matter; not by . . . . 765 95 POEMS 91   6
HIDDEN
    punching underneath conventions exposes hidden obscenities . 203 XLI LA GUERRE 1   5
    Ever love) we 've hidden him in A leaf . . . . 397 NO THANKS 14   12

333

		PAGE	TITLE	LINE

HIDE
from us crumple them hide them in thy breath . . . . 41 T&C AMORES 5 20
black bod ies leaves hide / / / / . . . . 354 VIVA 45 29
each breathing dares to hide more than most fabulous . . . . 446 NO THANKS 61 11
hope or mind can hide) and this is the . . . . 766 95 POEMS 92 13
that you never were hide, poor dishonoured mind who . . . . . 834 73 POEMS 62 13
HIDEHIDEHIDE
rustle and run and hidehidehide whisk whisk look out . . . . 25 T&C CHANSONS 2 15
HIDEOUS
faces of people contented hideous hopeless cruel happy and . 50 T&C IMPRESS 4 15
quake before this its hideous Work most old Whose . . . . . . 77 T&C SON UNRE 2 11
stomachsofold pe o pleLike hideous vegetaBles weasOned . . . 101 & POST IMPR 11 65
body moved with the hideous spontane- ity of a . . . . 103 & POST IMPR 13 9
te rin g from Hideous trees or Maybe Mandolins . . . . 122 & SEVEN POEMS 1 12
window-sills) i met that hideous gladness, per the face . . . 158 & SON ACTU 7 5
+HIDEOUS
FOR CONTEXT, SEE . . . . 789 73 POEMS 17 17
HIDEOUSLY
trudging kiss moistly climbing hideously with large minute . 67 T&C POST IMPR 4 25
and here gladness flays hideously hills. It was in . . . . 158 & SON ACTU 7 2
a personal radiance sits hideously upon the trafficing hum . 168 & SON ACTU 17 2
fear) in dreadful corners hideously cowers-- i do excuse . . 207 XLI SONNETS 3 8
HIDES
clever enormous voice which hides in a fragility of . . . . . 45 T&C LA GUERRE 1 5
easily one in another hides; yet man can, being . . . . 609 {CHAIRE} 11 3
HIDING
/ the moon is hiding in her hair. The . . . . 65 T&C POST IMPR 2 1
the oval shove of hiding pleasure. Alice, stinging quips . . 138 & SON REAL 9 14
(one itself showing, itself hiding one) life's only and . . . 531 50 POEMS 43 6
+HIDING
FOR CONTEXT, SEE . . . . 831 73 POEMS 59 14
HIDINGLYSEEK
creasing pillow next everywhere hidinglyseek no o god dear . 358 VIVA 49 4
HIEROGLYPHS
smiles the liontamer nearby hieroglyphs soar dip dip soar . . 384 NO THANKS 2 24
HIGH
--immortally whence are the high gods fled? Speak elm . . . . 3 T&C EPITHALAM 8
world) exhales the hovering high perfume curious of that . . 5 T&C EPITHALAM 102
the sun, so one high shining tower (which as . . . . 8 T&C OF NICOL 17
an elephant twelve feet high behind whose ear sits . . . . . 32 T&C ORIENTALE 6 8
merry flowers wee skipping high-heeled flames courtesied . . 44 T&C AMORES 8 6
my lust like a high troubling ship upon the . . . . 112 & PORTRAIT 6 96
-pole is climbing people high, up-in tenements talk. in . . . 128 & SEVEN POEMS 6 4
war heaped wholly with high wilt of human rind-- . . . . . . 213 XLI SONNETS 9 4
play-- through the mysterious high futile day an enormous . . 215 XLI SONNETS 11 14
passed from low through second-in-to-high like . . . . 248 IS 5 ONE 19 20
her home by the high minded pure young girl . . . . 273 IS 5 TWO 8 20
few cries drifting through high air a sail a . . . . 283 IS 5 THREE 7 6
erd) oma insCol Lide.! high n , o ; . . . . 347 VIVA 38 15
everybody guessed was too high look (it's back again . . . . 353 VIVA 44 21
and a hundred joys high are such shoulders as . . . . 439 NO THANKS 55 13
far beyond far and high beyond high bluer took . . . . 593 1 X 1 53 15
far and high beyond high bluer took it your . . . . 593 1 X 1 53 15
and deep in the high that does nothing but . . . . 594 1 X 1 54 32
cloud in a white high night where his heartlike . . . . 631 {CHAIRE} 33 4
it blue is the high is the deep is . . . . 695 95 POEMS 23 19
jack's white horse (up high in the night at . . . . 699 95 POEMS 27 2
i have hunted her high and that pretty pink . . . . 707 95 POEMS 35 7
die" she cried so high thermopylae heard her and . . . . . . 711 95 POEMS 39 13
will leap higher than high through gayer than gayest . . . . 717 95 POEMS 45 11
dance, i and you; high (are become more than . . . . 762 95 POEMS 89 11
here (with a low high low and the bird . . . . 767 95 POEMS 93 3
we know (with a high low high in the . . . . 767 95 POEMS 93 19
(with a high low high in the may in . . . . 767 95 POEMS 93 19
damn for murderers of high estate whose mongrel creed . . . . 774 73 POEMS 2 10
finally faintly (higher than high in the rain in . . . . . . 813 73 POEMS 41 10
old) peering from some high window; at the gold . . . . 824 73 POEMS 52 3

<table>
<thead>
<tr><th></th><th>PAGE</th><th>TITLE</th><th>LINE</th></tr>
</thead>
<tbody>
</tbody>
</table>

HIGH-HEELED
    merry flowers wee skipping high-heeled flames courtesied . . 44 T&C AMORES 8   6
HIGHER
    windows but they live higher in their house than . . . . . . 126 & SEVEN POEMS 5   25
    then we'd go up higher with all the pretty . . . . 129 & SEVEN POEMS 7   8
    sky which only is higher than the sky / . . . . 530 50 POEMS 42   16
    lovers are mindless they higher than fears are hopes . . . . 563 1 X 1 23   8
    is life than lose: higher than have --but beauty . . . . . . 592 1 X 1 52   3
    he (having flown even higher) is sunning his penguinsoul . . 631 (CHAIRE) 33   8
    sunlight as will leap higher than high through gayer . . . . 717 95 POEMS 45   11
    called life; which grows higher than soul can hope . . . . . 766 95 POEMS 92   13
    the sky finally faintly (higher than high in the . . . . . . 813 73 POEMS 41   10
HIGHEST
    each most remembering H highest fly only the flag . . . . . . 390 NO THANKS 7   8
HIGHFALOOTIN
    all to use a highfalootin phrase luxuries that is . . . . . . 239 IS 5 ONE 10   9
HIGHLY
    slyly crept into my highly sexed mind. It seemed . . . . .   262 IS 5 ONE 32   4
HIGHNESS
    mains froides. His Royal Highness said "peek-a-boo" and . . . 262 IS 5 ONE 32   27
HIGHT
    owch so chuck slop hight evolute my eerily oh . . . . 333 VIVA 24   22
HILARIOUS
    by no means funereally hilarious (or otherwise democratic) . 802 73 POEMS 30   19
HILL
    plunge skilfully into the hill. / / / / . . . . 155 & SON ACTU 4   17
    on top of this hill at Calchidas, in the . . . . 281 IS 5 THREE 5   2
    to climb the best hill, driven by black wine. . . . . 434 NO THANKS 51   6
    stood on a green hill and threw his wish . . . . 593 1 X 1 53   5
    little you-i as the hill becomes nil) and will . . . . 593 1 X 1 53   22
HILLS
    yet, while on the hills the pines deepen to . . . .   5 T&C EPITHALAM   75
    fraily raging whom the hills sink into and their . . . . . .   9 T&C SONGS 1   25
    new wine from steep hills by darkness softly brought-- . . .   9 T&C SONGS 1   36
    know while on faint hills do frailly go The . . . .   11 T&C SONGS 2   27
    arms upon the giddy hills to dream of you, ...   36 T&C AMORES 1   7
    suddenly the lighted living hills / / / / . . . .   82 T&C SON ACTU 1   15
    at sunset and who--touches--the hills without any reason (i .   91 & POST IMPR 3   5
    here gladness flays hideously hills. It was in the . . . . . 158 & SON ACTU 7   2
    skin of the organised hills an edged nothing begins . . . . . 160 & SON ACTU 9   8
    / / the hills like poets put on . . . . 188 XLI SONGS 10   1
    which and quite silently hills made of blueandgreen paper . . 278 IS 5 THREE 2   5
    The) now, est hills er dream; new . . . . 350 VIVA 41   12
    as these emerging now hills invent the air) breathe . . . . . 372 VIVA 63   3
    / / / emptied. hills. listen. ,not, alive, trees, ... 416 NO THANKS 33   1
    lean wind flays screaming hills with sleet and snow: . . . . 560 1 X 1 20   10
    death is killed dead. Hills jump with brooks: trees . . . . . 580 1 X 1 40   27
    / / / / (hills chime with thrush) A . . . . 747 95 POEMS 75   1
    amazing the and peaceful hills (not where not here . . . . . 750 95 POEMS 78   4
    threeing alive pasture and hills / / / / . . . . 751 95 POEMS 79   8
+HILLS
    FOR CONTEXT, SEE . . . . 511 50 POEMS 25   3
+HILLSIDE
    FOR CONTEXT, SEE . . . . 695 95 POEMS 23   4
HILLTOP
    safe small facts of hilltop (barn house wellsweep forest . . 755 95 POEMS 83   2
HIM
    WORD DELETED, APPEARED 97 TIMES
HIMSELF
    together the emperor, exerting himself among his pillows . .   34 T&C ORIENTALE 6 100
    ing away all by himself on somebody's roof or . . . . 127 & SEVEN POEMS 5   42
    wings then decently hanged himself, one afternoon. The last . 170 & SON ACTU 19   4
    undeniable disease of Life, himself occasionally contrives an 193 XLI PORTRAIT 1   23
    manner or by drowning himself in the watertank but . . . . . 239 IS 5 ONE 10   26
    me if i repeat himself: these, or nearly these, ... 263 IS 5 ONE 32   59
    the in spite of himself fa -mous soldier minus . . . . 267 IS 5 TWO 2   13
    what was thrown away himself taptaptaps out of your . . . . . 298 IS 5 FOUR 15   25
    city and presently found himself rattling for that well . . . 326 VIVA 18   12

HIMSELF (CONTINUED)

noone might inter fleeing himself for selves more strangely . 394 NO THANKS 11   6
who dares to call himself a man? go dreamless . . . . 438 NO THANKS 54   8
who dares to call himself a man? loudly for . . . . 438 NO THANKS 54 16
who dares to call himself a man? King Christ, ... 438 NO THANKS 54 24
Who dares to call Himself a man. / / . . . . 438 NO THANKS 54 28
sing everywhere your selves himself recognize) / / / . . . . 450 NO THANKS 65 18
did save man from himself ye duskiest despot's goldenest . . 552 1 X 1 12 15
man determined to destroy himself he picked the was . . . . . 566 1 X 1 26   6
moon before God wished Himself into a rose and . . . . 577 1 X 1 37 15
shall occur --see! now himself uplifts of stars the . . . . . 582 1 X 1 42 13
the shadow of love himself: who's we --nor can . . . . 601 {CHAIRE} 3 17
the proud power of himself death immense is not . . . . 649 {CHAIRE} 51 13
thick big this friendly himself of a boulder) nothing . . . . 658 {CHAIRE} 60   4
dead and hoping death himself will do the same . . . . 679 95 POEMS 7   4
sus pect) only god himself & as loveless some . . . . 698 95 POEMS 26   2
million whos (while only himself was him) two were . . . . . 709 95 POEMS 37   4
of merciful sweetness except Himself?" --"noone unless it's a 748 95 POEMS 76 14
(and smiled) "who holds Himself as the little white . . . . . 748 95 POEMS 76 17
how generous is that himself the sun --arriving truly, . . . 756 95 POEMS 84   1
his fathering (as that himself out of all silence . . . . . . 756 95 POEMS 84 10
one spirit serenely truly himself; and alone only as . . . . 808 73 POEMS 36   3

+HIMSELF

FOR CONTEXT, SEE . . . . 317 VIVA 9 14
FOR CONTEXT, SEE . . . . 318 VIVA 10 11
FOR CONTEXT, SEE . . . . 631 {CHAIRE} 33   5

HIMSELF'S

nothing seem --we are himself's own self; his very . . . . . 756 95 POEMS 84 14

HINGE

is a most tiny hinge of flesh, a winsome . . . . 21 T&C PUELLA MEA 193

HINGING

of a flesh from hinging thighs .... merci.... i . . . . 133 & SON REAL 4 16
up suddenly his bunged hinging victim against the giving . . 259 IS 5 ONE 29 15
smallest hands the slim hinging you --because it's five . . . 282 IS 5 THREE 6   8

HINT

in skilful wrists which hint at flight --my lady's . . . . . 20 T&C PUELLA MEA 158

HINTED

and when i timidly hinted "novocaine?" the eyes outstart, . . 226 IS 5 ONE MAME 12

HINTS

how timidly, throb; which hints being; suggests identity) . . 402 NO THANKS 19 10
whole tear. By handless hints do conjurers rule? do . . . . . 527 50 POEMS 39 17

HIP

sang before. Horn at hip went my love riding . . . . 14 T&C SONGS 4 11
ta ppin g toe hip popot amus Back gen . . . . 107 & PORTRAIT 3   5
absurd gloved fist on hip & the scowl of . . . . 640 {CHAIRE} 42   9

HIPLESS

exciting simplicity of her hipless body, pausing to invent . 103 & POST IMPR 13 2

HIPPOLYTUS

that brought forth tall Hippolytus, lord on whose pedestal . 4 T&C EPITHALAM 45

HIPPOPOTAMUS

that named Fred -someBody: hippopotamus, scratch- ing, one, . 252 IS 5 ONE 23 2

+HIPPOPOTAMUS

FOR CONTEXT, SEE . . . . 107 & PORTRAIT 3 5

HIPS

hideously with large minute hips, O press worms rushing . . . 67 T&C POST IMPR 4 28
and how between her hips India is / / . . . . 95 & POST IMPR 7 19
occurs homelessly. While grip Hips simply. well fussed flesh 136 & SON REAL 7 11
the keenness of my hips; or, your first twitch . . . . 140 & SON REAL 11 6
totters, slouches, with giggling hips and frozen eyes / . . . 143 & SON REAL 14 14
dollars i fill her hips with boys and girls . . . . 148 & SON REAL 19 14
in threedimensional distress these hips were made for . . . . 150 & SON REAL 21 7
slowly, lean in the hips and her sails filled . . . . 156 & SON ACTU 5 7
mouth in his teeth (hips pumping pleasure into hips). . . . . 161 & SON ACTU 10 4
(hips pumping pleasure into hips). Seeing how the limp . . . 161 & SON ACTU 10 4
big girl jiggles thickly hips to the kanoon but . . . . 220 XLI SONNETS 16 15
ingly seethe firm swirl hips whirling climb to GIVE . . . . . 445 NO THANKS 60 27

HIS

WORD DELETED, APPEARED 321 TIMES

		PAGE	TITLE	LINE

+HIS
   FOR CONTEXT, SEE . . . . 263 IS 5 ONE 32   48
   FOR CONTEXT, SEE . . . . 310 VIVA 2   2
HIST
   / / / / hist whist little ghostthings tip-toe . . . . 25 T&C CHANSONS 2   1
HISTORIES
   unstrange synthetic now true histories plunge? rains a grey . 527 50 POEMS 39   27
HISTORY
   shine the deeds of history her heroes, sounds the . . . . . . 209 XLI SONNETS 5   2
   joe gould's quote oral history unquote might (publishers . . 410 NO THANKS 27   10
   his breath away all history oped her teeming womb . . . . . . 552 1 X 1 12   21
   still insist that all history is too small for . . . . . . 579 1 X 1 39   7
   marathon and all prehuman history and finally The UN . . . . 711 95 POEMS 39   15
   blue most both) and history immeasurably is wealthier by . . 750 95 POEMS 78   6
HISTORY'S
   game, what then? all history's a winter sport or . . . . . 579 1 X 1 39   5
HIT
   they come) until she hit a mine and sank . . . . 494 50 POEMS 8   3
   and some six cents hit the whigh shaped hathole . . . . . . 602 (CHAIRE) 4   4
HITHER
   of crimson music Come hither O thou, is life . . . . 27 T&C ORIENTALE 1   6
   of divine silence Come hither O thou, is life . . . . 27 T&C ORIENTALE 1   13
   in white fragrance Come hither O thou, is life . . . . . . 27 T&C ORIENTALE 1   20
   softer than flowers Come hither O thou, is love . . . . . 27 T&C ORIENTALE 1   27
   stark Picasso throttling trees hither my soul repairs herself 180 XLI SONGS 2   8
   crazily skating thither and hither in filthy sawdust chucks . 259 IS 5 ONE 29   4
   fine eyes (which stroll hither and thither through the . . . 275 IS 5 TWO 9   49
   connivance accurately thither and hither myself struts . . . 299 IS 5 FOUR 16   8
   (a long ruined streets hither and) softly thither between . . 319 VIVA 11   5
   more openly than usual hither, thither who briskly busily . . 354 VIVA 45   14
   roots) us ly; though hither nosing lymoles cru. Ising . . . . 361 VIVA 52   11
+HITHERING
   FOR CONTEXT, SEE . . . . 134 & SON REAL 5   12
HITLER
   be unlucky and the hitler lies down with the . . . . 466 NEW POEMS 4   20
HITLER'S
   a stalinist arse in hitler's window on wednesday next . . . . 514 50 POEMS 28   13
HITTING
   hearing and sight keep hitting and chipping with sharp . . . 199 XLI PORTRAIT 7   3
HO
   which is known as (HO PARTHENON) and having ordered . . . . 194 XLI PORTRAIT 2   9
   tres (plants how grin ho) cen (tel und ead . . . . 309 VIVA 1   28
HOARSE
   father used to become hoarse talking about how it . . . . . . 276 IS 5 TWO 10   16
HOAX
   a most stares colossal hoax of clocks and calendars . . . . . 659 (CHAIRE) 61   14
HOB
   witches and tingling goblins hob-a-nob hob-a-nob little hoppy 25 T&C CHANSONS 2   8
   and tingling goblins hob-a-nob hob-a-nob little hoppy happy . 25 T&C CHANSONS 2   8
HOB-A-NOB
   witches and tingling goblins hob-a-nob hob-a-nob little hoppy 25 T&C CHANSONS 2   8
   and tingling goblins hob-a-nob hob-a-nob little hoppy happy . 25 T&C CHANSONS 2   8
+HOBBLE
   FOR CONTEXT, SEE . . . . 259 IS 5 ONE 29   12
HOBBY
   a woopsing queer colon hobby photography never has plumbed . 499 50 POEMS 13   10
HOBGOBLIN
   persuasive the editor cigarstinking hobgoblin swims upward in 259 IS 5 ONE 29   8
HOCK
   Pain shall hang in hock who dares to call . . . . 438 NO THANKS 54   7
HOCKED
   which was very silly hocked the diamond he gave . . . . 145 & SON REAL 16   8
HOE
   Him self in the hoe tell days are teased: . . . . 317 VIVA 9   15
HOI
   nothing except preexist its hoi in its polloi and . . . . . . 544 1 X 1 4   8
HOISTING
   tightens caught in the hoisting light any woman is . . . . . 68 T&C POST IMPR 5   12

HOISTING (CONTINUED)
But look: up- raising, hoisting, a little perhaps that . . . 282 IS 5 THREE 6   5
HOISTS
colour (and which night hoists miraculously above the always 378 VIVA 69   11
HOLD
Again. Hush. God. Please hold. Tight / / / . . . . 130 & SON REAL 1   15
all to you to hold every finger shall have . . . . 192 XLI CHANSONS 2   18
a feller tries to hold down the fifty bucks . . . . 242 IS 5 ONE 13   8
given a mouse to hold lovingly, our lady what . . . . 279 IS 5 THREE 3   20
damned table and we hold lips Eyes everything hands . . . . . 287 IS 5 FOUR 4   18
face who. and hands hold his whose unlife bursts . . . . . . 479 NEW POEMS 17   15
say no world can hold a you shall see . . . . 523 50 POEMS 36   2
quite big enough to hold one tiny this with . . . . 523 50 POEMS 36   32
jungles of despair to hold a mountain's heartbeat in . . . . 562 1 X 1 22   14
HOLDING
with his, mouth carefully holding, it, in his little . . . . 69 T&C POST IMPR 6 17
cheerfulest Elephantangelchild should sit (holding a red . . 631 {CHAIRE} 33   2
HOLDS
and curling thing, yet holds continuous intercourse--through   5 T&C EPITHALAM   90
when the glassy darkness holds the genuine apparition of . . 78 T&C SON UNRE 3   5
"someone" (and smiled) "who holds Himself as the little . . . 748 95 POEMS 76   17
HOLE
sam (down! alice) a hole in the ocean will . . . . 513 50 POEMS 27   24
pink fat screams a hole in it that birth . . . . 545 1 X 1 5   8
till they digged his hole : sam was a . . . . 568 1 X 1 28   4
(of petals of silence) hole bigger than never to . . . . . 634 {CHAIRE} 36   7
its soul and a hole in its life where . . . . 647 {CHAIRE} 49   13
diminutive world with a hole in it out of . . . . 652 {CHAIRE} 54   11
slowly Murdered the House) hole swallows it self while . . . 693 95 POEMS 21   15
+HOLE
FOR CONTEXT, SEE . . . . 602 {CHAIRE} 4   5
FOR CONTEXT, SEE . . . . 707 95 POEMS 35   2
FOR CONTEXT, SEE . . . . 707 95 POEMS 35   27
HOLES
boston Dolls; found with Holes in each other 's . . . . . . 317 VIVA 9   27
by Them opens sharp holes in dark places paints . . . . . . 437 NO THANKS 53   5
/ lucky means finding Holes where pockets aren't lucky . . . 467 NEW POEMS 5   2
plus a couple of) holes probably that's what (mr . . . . . 501 50 POEMS 15   20
y crumb ling eye -holes oUt of whe reful . . . . 534 50 POEMS 46   18
HOLIDAY
a certain taut precarious holiday frighteningly performed and 52 T&C PORTRAIT 1   7
HOLINESS
--childfully serious flower of holiness a pilgrim from beyond 601 {CHAIRE} 3   8
/ honour corruption villainy holiness riding in fragrance of 661 {CHAIRE} 63   1
HOLLERS
the soul inside me Hollers for thou comest and . . . . . . 61 T&C PORTRAIT 9   27
HOLLOW
d an cing on hollow was young Up floatingly . . . . 534 50 POEMS 46   3
(than are all unworlds hollow silence has deeper eyes . . . 565 1 X 1 25   7
HOLLYHOCK
possibly touch the pink hollyhock existence whose pansy eyes 58 T&C PORTRAIT 6   17
or tree field rock hollyhock forest brook chickadee mountain. 512 50 POEMS 26   26
HOLY
kings thy wrists are holy which are the keepers . . . . . . 29 T&C ORIENTALE 3 27
think of you the holy city which is your . . . . 186 XLI SONGS 8   5
click; where Boobs are holy, poets mad, illustrious punks . . 438 NO THANKS 54   19
calm (Bright) calm st?? holy (soft briGht deep) yeS . . . . . 455 NO THANKS 70   6
deep ????Ht ?????T) Who (holy alone) holy (alone holy) . . . 455 NO THANKS 70   15
?????T) Who (holy alone) holy (alone holy) alone / . . . . . 455 NO THANKS 70   15
(holy alone) holy (alone holy) alone / / / . . . . 455 NO THANKS 70   15
being youamiare (2) the holy miraculous difference between . 803 73 POEMS 31   9
+HOLY
FOR CONTEXT, SEE . . . . 332 VIVA 23   5
FOR CONTEXT, SEE . . . . 605 {CHAIRE} 7   10
FOR CONTEXT, SEE . . . . 635 {CHAIRE} 37   19
HOMBRE
dim a ram flat hombre sin bangaroom slim guesser . . . . . 333 VIVA 24   17

		PAGE	TITLE	LINE

HOME
of dead song about home and love from her . . . . 55 T&C PORTRAIT 3 14
my eyes stay at home then my mouth will . . . . 100 & POST IMPR 11 18
containing the words country home and mother when sung . . . 204 XLI LA GUERRE 2 7
fragile and send him home to his old mother . . . . 270 IS 5 TWO 5 18
front steps of her home by the high minded . . . . 273 IS 5 TWO 8 19
suddenly so huge a home (only more than immeasurable . . . . 454 NO THANKS 69 6
immediate is escorts us home through never's always until . . 517 50 POEMS 31 11
each last shore and home come young so truly . . . . 526 50 POEMS 38 8
nothing's only our hugest home; the most who die, ... 560 1 X 1 20 23
perfectly beautiful bow "my home ionian isles / / . . . . . . 585 1 X 1 45 21
welcome (but chiefly at home in snowily nowheres of . . . . . 678 95 POEMS 6 10
course dominic took him home & mrs dominic washed . . . . . . 680 95 POEMS 8 12
bubbles: and may came home with a smooth round . . . . 682 95 POEMS 10 9
one two came hurrying home to the dearest little . . . . . . 709 95 POEMS 37 13
/ / / / home means that when the . . . . 728 95 POEMS 56 1
leaks it 's our (home means if any moon . . . . 728 95 POEMS 56 4
each (let's kiss) means home / / / . . . . 728 95 POEMS 56 16
you and i, whose home is timelessness: we who . . . . 743 95 POEMS 71 10
heavenless hell and homeless home of knowledgeable shadows . 765 95 POEMS 91 1
bring this beautiful wanderer home to a dream called . . . . 811 73 POEMS 39 10
here of a rubythroat's home with its still ness . . . . 827 73 POEMS 55 9

+HOME
FOR CONTEXT, SEE . . . . 333 VIVA 24 4

HOMECOMING
/ / / your homecoming will be my homecoming-- . . . . 812 73 POEMS 40 1
homecoming will be my homecoming-- my selves go with . . . . 812 73 POEMS 40 1

HOMELESS
lust lurks slovenly and homeless and when a kiss . . . . . . 322 VIVA 14 11
the heavenless hell and homeless home of knowledgeable . . . 765 95 POEMS 91 1

HOMELESSLY
in my mouth occurs homelessly. While grip Hips simply. . . . 136 & SON REAL 7 11

HOMER
divine right of kings" Homer Lea) here are five . . . . 803 73 POEMS 31 4

HOMES
day with the sonorous homes of light swiftly sink . . . . . . 79 T&C SON UNRE 4 1

HOMING
own secret) we, like homing through welcoming sweet miracles 659 (CHAIRE) 61 1

HOMONOMOUSLY
sleePdeep ness squirmcurl ing homonomously metameric You / / 395 NO THANKS 12 16

HONEST
suddenly without thinking under honest trees, a stream does. 160 & SON ACTU 9 2
i discreetly (masturbates one honest breadcrumb) say "i . . . 546 1 X 1 6 12
/ / when your honest redskin toma hawked and . . . . 643 (CHAIRE) 45 1

+HONEST
FOR CONTEXT, SEE . . . . 254 IS 5 ONE 25 16

HONESTLY
which did lie Down, honestly now who go (BANG . . . . 317 VIVA 9 37

HONESTY
eyes live the magnificent honesty of space. Mountains are . . 675 95 POEMS 3 4

HONEY
the common man wants) honey swoRkey mollypants / / . . . . . 635 (CHAIRE) 37 26

HONEYCAKE
waiter cleverly lugs indigestible honeycake to men ....one . 217 XLI SONNETS 13 9

HONEYDUNCE
of fragrance dances a honeydunce; whirling's a frantic struts 763 95 POEMS 90 10

+HONI
FOR CONTEXT, SEE . . . . 635 (CHAIRE) 37 26

HONORABLE
grafter, nothing less; the Honorable Mr. (guess) who, ... 266 IS 5 TWO 1 34

HONOUR
surely poets only understands) honour this loneliness of even 456 NO THANKS 71 12
/ except in your honour, my loveliest, nothing may . . . . . 575 1 X 1 35 2
(and rest, my love) honour / / / / . . . . 575 1 X 1 35 42
/ / / / honour corruption villainy holiness riding . . . . . 661 (CHAIRE) 63 1
the stars walk backward) honour the past but welcome . . . . 732 95 POEMS 60 9

HOOCH
frum duh A.C. fulla hooch kiddin eachudder bout duh . . . . . 332 VIVA 23 2

	PAGE	TITLE	LINE
HOODED			
the pungent sun with hooded day preening upon his	4	T&C EPITHALAM	66
HOOP			
the face in a hoop of grim ecstasy /	137	& SON REAL 8	18
english the Forwardflung backwardSpinning hoop returns . . .	311	VIVA 3	5
HOOPS			
mice; or leap through hoops of fire, creating smoothness. . .	279	IS 5 THREE 3	16
HOORAH			
a fatgold grin hooray hoorah for the large men	114	& PORTRAIT 7	23
HOORAY			
on a fatgold grin hooray hoorah for the large	114	& PORTRAIT 7	22
+HOOVER			
FOR CONTEXT, SEE	325	VIVA 17	16
HOP			
bettyandisbel come dancing from hop-scotch and jump-rope and	24	T&C CHANSONS 1	15
smelled Happens--skip dance kids hop point at red blue . . .	437	NO THANKS 53	13
HOP-SCOTCH			
bettyandisbel come dancing from hop-scotch and jump-rope and	24	T&C CHANSONS 1	15
HOPE			
comfort to her soul, hope richly scattered by the	5	T&C EPITHALAM	83
round desperate elves and hope- less gnomes and frantic . . .	69	T&C POST IMPR 6	21
glad he winked and hope he'll do it again	126	& SEVEN POEMS 5	17
the narrowing hours and hope (by cold espoused unto	207	XLI SONNETS 3	7
swallowed is by (with hope two eyes a memory	402	NO THANKS 19	6
freud knows whoy the hope that you may mess	413	NO THANKS 30	12
unselves to lend for hope of hope must coo	440	NO THANKS 56	17
lend for hope of hope must coo or boo	440	NO THANKS 56	17
their dance (sleep wake hope and then) they said	515	50 POEMS 29	19
much than more climbing hope meets most despair? all	528	50 POEMS 40	9
bigger th an a hope) is st anding st	532	50 POEMS 44	17
in white ago? Blow hope to terror; blow seeing	560	1 X 1 20	13
what fear denies, what hope asserts, what falsest both . . .	576	1 X 1 36	3
(though such as perfect hope can feel only despair	580	1 X 1 40	23
pitiless a massacre the hope most innocent (so deep's	609	(CHAIRE) 11	6
i ever met or hope to meet in the	699	95 POEMS 27	15
float flaming symbols of hope, and i wake to	749	95 POEMS 77	12
higher than soul can hope or mind can hide)	766	95 POEMS 92	13
under all silences, the hope which has no opposite	768	95 POEMS 94	10
plant Magic dust expect hope doubt (wonder mistrust) despair	780	73 POEMS 8	2
the very secret of hope to her eyes, not	811	73 POEMS 39	4
from my hope's own hope, receive (undaunted guest of	821	73 POEMS 49	10
/ / / ! hope faith! ! life love!	841	73 POEMS 69	1
HOPE'S			
is subtracted from my hope's own hope, receive (undaunted . .	821	73 POEMS 49	10
HOPED			
wristers etcetera, my mother hoped that i would die	276	IS 5 TWO 10	13
and (stating that she hoped we might "meet again	326	VIVA 18	36
how Everything (dreamed & hoped & prayed for months	702	95 POEMS 30	17
HOPEFEAR			
of ifbut offspring of hopefear sons of unless and	512	50 POEMS 26	2
HOPELESS			
of people contented hideous hopeless cruel happy and it . . .	50	T&C IMPRESS 4	15
a coach with gilt hopeless wheels mired where sits	131	& SON REAL 2	15
We doctors know a hopeless case if--listen: there's a	554	1 X 1 14	14
+HOPELESS			
FOR CONTEXT, SEE	69	T&C POST IMPR 6	21
HOPES			
chimney with care in hopes that Saint Nicholas" /	142	& SON REAL 13	14
fears hearts lungs arms hopes feet hands under us	283	IS 5 THREE 7	2
i touch you with hopes and words and with	289	IS 5 FOUR 6	15
out of your brain, hopes, life to (carefully turning	298	IS 5 FOUR 15	26
more ponderous wishes or hopes less tall than mine"	328	VIVA 19	9
of crumbling & folding hopes, hark; feet (fEEt ◇	345	VIVA 36	14
wheels; wonders: murders. cries: hopes; houses, clouds. . . .	361	VIVA 52	18
and eyes lifts lifting hopes and hands --nourish my	456	NO THANKS 71	13
into peachtrees grow or hopes dance best on bald	511	50 POEMS 25	9
who've climbed steeper than hopes are fears only not	563	1 X 1 23	3
higher than fears are hopes lovers are those who	563	1 X 1 23	8

	PAGE	TITLE	LINE

HOPES (CONTINUED)
  prove our fears were hopes: the moon open for . . . . 575 1 X 1 35   13
  love laughter death (dreams hopes despairs) Once happened . . 693 95 POEMS 21   5
  was (laws clocks fears hopes beliefs compulsions doubts & . . 755 95 POEMS 83   16
  your --when all fears hopes beliefs doubts disappear. . . . . 812 73 POEMS 40   13
  will give you five hopes for any fear, but . . . . 837 73 POEMS 65   9
HOPING
  about thyself a small hoping insect, humanity, achieves . . . 351 VIVA 42   10
  or playing dead and hoping death himself will do . . . . . 679 95 POEMS 7   4
  time for crying-- for hoping for despair for peace . . . . . 683 95 POEMS 11   10
HOPING'S
  sorrow's own joys and hoping's very fears yours is . . . . . 810 73 POEMS 38   11
HOPPED
  He-in-her (& both all hopped up) prettily then which . . . . 317 VIVA 9   33
HOPPING
  kid in no sir hopping sawdust you kiddo he's . . . . 96 & POST IMPR 8   15
  hur- DygurdY with thequeer hopping ghosts of child- ren. . . 100 & POST IMPR 11   35
  twilight, a little puppy hopping between skipping children . 167 & SON ACTU 16   8
HOPPY
  goblins hob-a-nob hob-a-nob little hoppy happy toad in tweeds 25 T&C CHANSONS 2   9
HOPPYTOAD
  intones: bloo-moo-n sirkusricky platzburg hoppytoad yesmam. . 108 & PORTRAIT 4   16
HORDES
  and suddenly by shining hordes in sweet unserious dress . . .   4 T&C EPITHALAM   63
HORIZON
  when unwondering immense directionless horizon) --do you . . 378 VIVA 69   15
HORIZONTAL
  hips were made for Horizontal Business (set on big . . . . . 150 & SON REAL 21   7
  the lunging leer of horizontal large distinct ecstasy wags . 202 XLI PORTRAIT 9   35
  partnership (to instigate constructive Horizontal . . . . . . 260 IS 5 ONE 30   20
HORN
  cruel bugle sang before. Horn at hip went my . . . . 14 T&C SONGS 4   11
HORNED
  lariats lean exroper of horned suddenly crashing things) man 252 IS 5 ONE 23   11
HORNETS
  all things pure and hornets wail by children stung . . . . . 511 50 POEMS 25   14
HORNS
  you and the gentle who-horns says-does moo-woo (the prance . 773 73 POEMS 1   8
HORRIBLE
  plays the hot sweet horrible stops of her body . . . . 110 & PORTRAIT 6   11
  was chased by a horrible thing which raced sideways . . . . . 682 95 POEMS 10   7
HORRIBLY
  the stopped entire day horribly and seriously thrills the . . 82 T&C SON ACTU 1   11
  day away more softly horribly suddenly; (of these two . . . . 98 & POST IMPR 9   4
  less objectively, i was horribly scared i would actually . . 263 IS 5 ONE 32   62
  awaken certain faces busily horribly blunder through new . . 299 IS 5 FOUR 16   14
  mrs opening is it horribly smith spouts cornucopiously not . 465 NEW POEMS 3   9
HORROR
  i was lifting the horror of her toylike head . . . . 53 T&C PORTRAIT 1   39
  solve the depths of horror to defend a sunbeam's . . . . . . 562 1 X 1 22   11
  THANKSGIVING (1956) a monstering horror swallows this unworld 711 95 POEMS 39   1
HORRORS
  through spontaneous deft strictly horrors which stars may not 386 NO THANKS 3   7
HORS
  the mercy. (exit the hors d'oeuvres) / / / . . . . 243 IS 5 ONE 14   16
HORSE
  riding on a great horse of gold into the . . . . 14 T&C SONGS 4   2
  riding on a great horse of gold into the . . . . 14 T&C SONGS 4   32
  came riding upon a horse of porphyry into the . . . . 30 T&C ORIENTALE 4 10
  rode down the red horse shrieking from splintering foam . . . 30 T&C ORIENTALE 4 12
  (that grey) white (man) horse floats on 4 3rdtoes . . . . . . 408 NO THANKS 25   3
  too busy sitting the horse / / / / . . . . 545 1 X 1 5   15
  / / the little horse is newlY Born) he . . . . 657 (CHAIRE) 59   1
  / / jack's white horse (up high in the . . . . 699 95 POEMS 27   1
+HORSE
  FOR CONTEXT, SEE . . . . 437 NO THANKS 53   1
  FOR CONTEXT, SEE . . . . 437 NO THANKS 53   16

	PAGE	TITLE	LINE
HORSES			
eyes which the king's horses might not kill.) But	18	T&C PUELLA MEA	48
thy thighs are white horses yoked to a chariot	29	T&C ORIENTALE 3	11
the purple trumpets blow horses of gold delicately crouching	110	& PORTRAIT 6	34
man's tiny racket. The horses sleep upstairs. And you	171	& SON ACTU 20	6
morning (that is, big horses; light feeling up streets;	172	& SON ACTU 21	2
/ after all white horses are in bed will	302	IS 5 FIVE 1	1
colliding on huge blue horses, and the poets looked	302	IS 5 FIVE 1	13
KEY LENGTH EXCEEDED: painted-with-horses-with-painted-	384	NO THANKS 2	31
gal who liked men horses roses & $ (in	792	73 POEMS 20	5
HOST			
in hand; but--though an host of overjoyed noncoms (first	339	VIVA 30	7
you are silent, shining host by guest a snowingly	559	1 X 1 19	1
let pitiless fear play host to every isn't that's	580	1 X 1 40	4
scientist petitions the celestial host to scrutinize his	799	73 POEMS 27	24
HOSTESS			
she: and played the hostess to my morethanme /	807	73 POEMS 35	15
HOSTS			
never, but forever now (hosts of eternity; not guests	817	73 POEMS 45	6
HOT			
wo- men and intotheslow hot women my Stomach ruBSiTSElf	101	& POST IMPR 11	62
how furiously plays the hot sweet horrible stops of	110	& PORTRAIT 6	10
the old men and hot men se promenent doucement	120	& PORTRAIT 12	22
the old men and hot men precisely dance in	121	& PORTRAIT 12	59
on and I was hot all Hot and the	123	& SEVEN POEMS 2	5
I was hot all Hot and the bar was	123	& SEVEN POEMS 2	5
a phrasing crease of hot subliminal lips, as if	130	& SON REAL 1	4
drool softly, in the hot alley, a nigger's voice	167	& SON ACTU 16	17
were a thunderbolt red- hot peeling off huge slabs	194	XLI PORTRAIT 2	24
all of Just Add Hot Water And Serve-- from	230	IS 5 ONE 2	12
to (and them slim hot queens with dam next	242	IS 5 ONE 13	5
pop weird up her hot ow you hurt tho	316	VIVA 8	10
skilfully applied bayonets roasted hot with heat-- Olaf (upon	339	VIVA 30	30
i'm thick in a hot young queen with a	469	NEW POEMS 7	3
y in a real hot spell with o man	476	NEW POEMS 14	3
+HOT			
FOR CONTEXT, SEE	106	& PORTRAIT 2	7
FOR CONTEXT, SEE	193	XLI PORTRAIT 1	11
HOTEL			
their limousine inhabit the Hotel Meurice (whereas i live	245	IS 5 ONE 16	4
emanating the triple starred Hotel du Golf... that notable	319	VIVA 11	22
wings and here's my hotel this is the door	353	VIVA 44	12
+HOTEL			
FOR CONTEXT, SEE	309	VIVA 1	28
FOR CONTEXT, SEE	317	VIVA 9	15
HOTLY			
and we will confuse hotly our moreover irrevocable bodies	111	& PORTRAIT 6	61
HOUNDS			
silver dawn. four lean hounds crouched low and smiling	14	T&C SONGS 4	4
silver dawn. four lean hounds crouched low and smiling	14	T&C SONGS 4	14
silver dawn. four lean hounds crouched low and smiling	14	T&C SONGS 4	24
silver dawn. four lean hounds crouched low and smiling	14	T&C SONGS 4	34
HOUR			
wife the sky and hour by hour wholly renews	3	T&C EPITHALAM	6
sky and hour by hour wholly renews her pale	3	T&C EPITHALAM	6
length her soft intrinsic hour, and from those tenuous	6	T&C EPITHALAM	131
dimness in the unshapeful hour making dear moan in	9	T&C SONGS 1	5
while in an earthless hour my fond soul seriously	12	T&C SONGS 2	41
in life's very fragile hour (when the world was	23	T&C PUELLA MEA	275
sink in the sorrowful hour, thy counted petals O	79	T&C SON UNRE 4	2
cringing air) the largest hour push deep his din	115	& PORTRAIT 8	12
consummation of day, the hour) she says to me	167	& SON ACTU 16	12
maids to flower an hour in all, all) o	509	50 POEMS 23	5
afternoon (at the magical hour when is becomes if)	802	73 POEMS 30	2
+HOUR			
FOR CONTEXT, SEE	346	VIVA 37	14
HOURS			
the graces and the hours, father of gods and	4	T&C EPITHALAM	40

	PAGE	TITLE	LINE
HOURS (CONTINUED)			
a pride of petaled hours, like flowers at the	11	T&C SONGS 2	32
thy hair mostly the hours love: a smoothness which	13	T&C SONGS 3	3
the young and awkward hours my lady perfectly moving, ...	17	T&C PUELLA MEA	10
by certain foolish perfect hours dead too, if that	42	T&C AMORES 6	16
/ / / the hours rise up putting off	50	T&C IMPRESS 4	1
in her eyes the hours descend, putting on stars.	50	T&C IMPRESS 4	31
the nibbling timid teethful hours wilts the stern texture . .	112	& PORTRAIT 6	79
where you danced simple hours and you take all	127	& SEVEN POEMS 5	32
dead athwart the narrowing hours and hope (by cold	207	XLI SONNETS 3	6
HOUSE			
who in Thy very house silently sits looking beyond	57	T&C PORTRAIT 5	7
you, a frail slippery house, a strong fragile house	83	T&C SON ACTU 2	3
house, a strong fragile house (beginning at the singular . .	83	T&C SON ACTU 2	3
live higher in their house than you so that's	126	& SEVEN POEMS 5	25
when all through the house not a creature was	142	& SON REAL 13	12
especially in your own house Humanity i love you	204	XLI LA GUERRE 2	16
striking in a dark house / / / /	229	IS 5 ONE FRAN	15
they are building a house down there by the	281	IS 5 THREE 5	10
thrilled you are a house around which i am	292	IS 5 FOUR 9	3
prowls carefully around this house of you love being	292	IS 5 FOUR 9	12
sparkle from the shut house (around and around which	292	IS 5 FOUR 9	19
soon forgotten tune, a house for lease. I have	360	VIVA 51	9
into the extremely little house of my mind. Clocks	365	VIVA 56	2
be alone in the house, with somebody and with	375	VIVA 66	2
period unshy the empty house is full O Yes	499	50 POEMS 13	8
smiles into a dead house clutch between eyes emptiness . . .	522	50 POEMS 35	2
has slowly Murdered the House) hole swallows it self	693	95 POEMS 21	14
and you and little house this our from hate	746	95 POEMS 74	3
facts of hilltop (barn house wellsweep forest & clearing) . .	755	95 POEMS 83	3
begins to Rain) a house like shape stirs through	785	73 POEMS 13	9
+HOUSE			
FOR CONTEXT, SEE	115	& PORTRAIT 8	27
FOR CONTEXT, SEE	479	NEW POEMS 17	1
HOUSELESS			
dare. Will take the houseless wisping rune of road	86	T&C SON ACTU 5	5
+HOUSELIKE			
FOR CONTEXT, SEE	785	73 POEMS 13	9
HOUSES			
collides with trees and houses and finally, butts into . . .	47	T&C IMPRESS 1	10
people are in their houses the frail man is	50	T&C IMPRESS 4	27
the lean and definite houses are troubled. A sharp	62	T&C PORTRAIT 10	6
The lean and definite houses are troubled. in the	62	T&C PORTRAIT 10	11
Night, argues with certain houses / / / /	93	& POST IMPR 5	18
jolts of delapida- tion bath-houses whose opened withins . .	94	& POST IMPR 6	4
anything save that these houses bulge like memories in . .	98	& POST IMPR 9	16
the pretty people than houses and steeples and clouds: . . .	129	& SEVEN POEMS 7	9
Querying greys between mouthed houses curl thirstily. Dead .	139	& SON REAL 10	12
On this street the houses immensely speak (it is	219	XLI SONNETS 15	3
windows of thousands of houses--Lisboa. Like the crackle of .	281	IS 5 THREE 5	6
along the air over houses roofs And out of	284	IS 5 FOUR 1	15
thither between (tumb ling) houses (as the kno wing	319	VIVA 11	8
a dream (and between houses, really a kind of	353	VIVA 44	9
wonders: murders. cries: hopes; houses, clouds. kisses, lice;	361	VIVA 52	19
sing- u (cities are houses people are flies who	436	NO THANKS 52	14
(windows called sidewalks of houses called cities) spring . .	436	NO THANKS 52	17
singular- ly (cities are houses are) is (are owned	436	NO THANKS 52	19
are so ancient the houses enter the people are	505	50 POEMS 19	6
sun and out of houses pour maids mothers widows	624	(CHAIRE) 26	5
a town (if its houses turning into themselves grow	720	95 POEMS 48	2
barks and how crazily houses eyes people smiles faces	835	73 POEMS 63	3
this whenworld squirm turns houses to people and streets . .	841	73 POEMS 69	18
+HOUSES			
FOR CONTEXT, SEE	346	VIVA 37	1
FOR CONTEXT, SEE	788	73 POEMS 16	10
HOVER			
now the pretty birds hover so she and so	665	(CHAIRE) 67	12

HOVERING
    this world) exhales the hovering high perfume curious of . .   5 T&C EPITHALAM 102
    evident invisibles exquisite the hovering at the dark portals 54 T&C PORTRAIT 2 2
HOVERS
    of whose lean lips, hovers how slenderly the illustrious . . 344 VIVA 35   10
HOW
    breasts, whose foot-stool tells how fought the looser of . .   4 T&C EPITHALAM 44
    we may watch together how behind the doomed exact . . . . . . 43 T&C AMORES 7 29
    Humorous moon dear girl How i was crazy how . . . . 44 T&C AMORES 8 19
    How i was crazy how i cried when i . . . . 44 T&C AMORES 8 19
    O sweet spontaneous earth how often have the doting . . . . 46 T&C LA GUERRE 2 2
    prodded thy beauty . how often have religions taken . . . . . 46 T&C LA GUERRE 2 13
    / i was considering how within night's loose sack . . . . . . 49 T&C IMPRESS 3 1
    silly purple eyelids of how she was with child . . . . 56 T&C PORTRAIT 4 16
    want to know is how do you like your . . . . 60 T&C PORTRAIT 8 10
    of wincing gas showed how hair, in two fists . . . . 73 T&C SON REAL 4 3
    of lifelessness consider for how much themselves shall gleam, 81 T&C SON UNRE 6 7
    modeling silence --to feel how through the stopped entire . . 82 T&C SON ACTU 1 10
    me of Woman and how between her hips India . . . . 95 & POST IMPR 7 18
    perfumed roman strength who how furiously plays the hot . . . 110 & PORTRAIT 6 9
    triumphs and listen well how the dainty destroyed hero . . . 111 & PORTRAIT 6 41
    dead's more even than how many ways of sitting . . . . . . 126 & SEVEN POEMS 5 8
    and you are My how glad he winked and . . . . 126 & SEVEN POEMS 5 16
    necks just to see how always squirms the skilful . . . . . 130 & SON REAL 1 6
    once, all over, kid how, funny Do tell ....sweat, ... 136 & SON REAL 7 14
    pink big lips curl.... how Jimmie was framed and . . . . 149 & SON REAL 20 16
    turn to find her how my least heart-beat becomes . . . . . 152 & SON ACTU 1 9
    ecstasy ....tremble (not knowing how much better than me . . 153 & SON ACTU 2 12
    of perfect hunger Yes) how beautifully swims the fooling . . 157 & SON ACTU 6 10
    I occasionally feel vague how vague i don't know . . . . 160 & SON ACTU 9 14
    pleasure into hips). Seeing how the limp huddling string . . 161 & SON ACTU 10 5
    our blood, miss by how terrible inches speech--it made . . . 174 & SON ACTU 23 10
    wind and cold; and how much earth is Madge . . . . 183 XLI SONGS 5 12
    everyone to see and how they'll stare! oh but . . . . 192 XLI CHANSONS 2 23
    night whisperless to mark, how that asleep whitely she . . . 205 XLI SONNETS 1 7
    much on looks but dat baby ached." and . . . . 226 IS 5 ONE MAME 11
    possibly can tell better how the balloons move (as . . . . 227 IS 5 ONE GERT 3
    improbably distinct face, and how these wooden big two . . . 229 IS 5 ONE FRAN 4
    try to not wonder how let's say elation causes . . . . . 229 IS 5 ONE FRAN 12
    the sternly allotted sandpile --how silently emit a tiny . . 231 IS 5 ONE 3 52
    her shake a shimmie how you wish that you . . . . 235 IS 5 ONE 6 12
    smell of babies and how you know the dam . . . . . . 242 IS 5 ONE 13 18
    i cough too much). How did the traffic get . . . . 245 IS 5 ONE 16 12
    was happy to see how nice she acted right . . . . 248 IS 5 ONE 19 26
    dear oh) the iceman how, luminously oh how listens . . . . 251 IS 5 ONE 22 15
    iceman how, luminously oh how listens and, expands my . . . 251 IS 5 ONE 22 16
    express a cry of How do you find the . . . . 255 IS 5 ONE 26 7
    clinging to the stone, how obsolete lips utter their . . . . 260 IS 5 ONE 30 5
    ourselves to be observed how in this fundamental respect . . 261 IS 5 ONE 31 8
    us now passionately remember how-- braving the worst, of . . 266 IS 5 TWO 1 17
    become hoarse talking about how it was a privilege . . . . 276 IS 5 TWO 10 16
    you will comprehend. and how this has arrived your . . . . 285 IS 5 FOUR 2 10
    walls will not reckon how strangely my life is . . . . . 292 IS 5 FOUR 9 5
    heart will never guess how much my wonderful jealousy . . . 292 IS 5 FOUR 9 15
    fragile Marys will understand how smiling may be made . . . 294 IS 5 FOUR 11 13
    having in my careful how careful arms created this . . . . 295 IS 5 FOUR 12 5
    ask "life, the question how do i drink dream . . . . 295 IS 5 FOUR 12 14
    drink dream smile and how do i prefer this . . . . 295 IS 5 FOUR 12 15
    i have perhaps forgotten how, always (from these hurrying . . 297 IS 5 FOUR 14 9
    of featheriest slenderness and how gradually which descending 299 IS 5 FOUR 16 6
    / / / / how this uncouth enchanted person, ... 300 IS 5 FOUR 17 1
    hair) making me feel how myself has been coarse . . . . . 301 IS 5 FOUR 18 8
    to rubber) tres (plants how grin ho) cen (tel . . . . 309 VIVA 1 27
    just happened to meet "how do you do" she . . . . 313 VIVA 5 5
    may you be any how? down to smoking found . . . . 314 VIVA 6 28
    breath of brud breathe how is aunt death did . . . . . . 316 VIVA 8 21
    / tell me not how electricity or god was . . . . 324 VIVA 16 1
    Eye Doancare Eye And How replies the upsquirtingly careens . 330 VIVA 21 9

HOW (CONTINUED)

clap an talkin big how dey could kill sixereight . . . . . . 332 VIVA 23   3
emerging (believably enlarged) make how many stopped millions 337 VIVA 28   3
whose lean lips, hovers how slenderly the illustrious unknown 344 VIVA 35   10
(Besides which, i note how fatally toward twilight the . . . 345 VIVA 36   3
/ / / / how ses humble. Over thin . . . . 346 VIVA 37   1
know quite, slightly or how at the yearhour tree- . . . . . 346 VIVA 37   14
n (o) w the how dis (appeared cleverly) world . . . . 347 VIVA 38   3
there one is look how it goes like a . . . . 353 VIVA 44   8
only dare (Wholly consider how these immaculate thin things . 362 VIVA 53   4
imagining fire) only consider How / / / / . . . . 362 VIVA 53   16
knows the meaning; or how dreaming becomes if your . . . . . 364 VIVA 55   3
busily a memory, which how exquisitely flutters in the . . . 370 VIVA 61   26
of what manshaped whimpered how girllike laughtering blocks . 371 VIVA 62   3
breathe simply my each how my trembling where my . . . . . . 372 VIVA 63   4
perceive, within transparent walls how several smoothly . . . 376 VIVA 67   8
implore you to notice how the keen ship lifts . . . . 378 VIVA 69   3
consider wonderful that your (how luminous) life toward . . . 379 VIVA 70   11
eyes each exact victim, how he does not stir) . . . . 386 NO THANKS 3   11
/ / sonnet entitled how to run the world) . . . . 390 NO THANKS 7   1
/ / why why How many winds make wonderful . . . . 395 NO THANKS 12   2
i touch said he how much said she a . . . . 399 NO THANKS 16   6
nor (as a blind, how timidly, throb; which hints . . . . . . 402 NO THANKS 19   9
if any anguish struck how thin a ghost so . . . . 414 NO THANKS 31   8
frantic this serene mightily how rooted who of iron . . . . . 415 NO THANKS 32   23
/ / / / how dark and single, where . . . . 418 NO THANKS 35   1
little dyings may possess) how sincere large distinct and . . 418 NO THANKS 35   5
what ease that bright how plural tide measures her . . . . . 418 NO THANKS 35   10
strength (less than these how less than least flowers . . . . 433 NO THANKS 50   8
mightily fatally i remark how through deep lifted fields . . 434 NO THANKS 51   30
that death should end) how lucky lovers are (whose . . . . . 446 NO THANKS 61   9
trifle less (merely beyond how very) closely than Nothing, . 453 NO THANKS 68   6
selves transported are into how suddenly so huge a . . . . . 454 NO THANKS 69   6
o ther w ise how e mpty park bundl . . . . 472 NEW POEMS 10   12
touched quite so And How much nonexistence eye sed . . . . . 474 NEW POEMS 12   9
exploding my) heart before how worlds delicate of . . . . . 480 NEW POEMS 18   16
learn from one bird how to sing than teach . . . . 484 NEW POEMS 22   13
teach ten thousand stars how not to dance / . . . . 484 NEW POEMS 22   14
clutch an of poor how colding hereless. air theres . . . . . 491 50 POEMS 5   4
man) don't ask me how i know (a he . . . . 501 50 POEMS 15   6
(can't keep up with how big very them) now . . . . 501 50 POEMS 15   10
Employs a very crazily how clownlike that this quickly . . . 504 50 POEMS 18   7
head face goes (if how begins a pillow's green . . . . 506 50 POEMS 20   9
were not given hearts how should they be? their . . . . . . 510 50 POEMS 24   2
to begin to imagine how (only are shall be . . . . 512 50 POEMS 26   17
lived in a pretty how town (with up so . . . . 515 50 POEMS 29   1
can begin to explain how children are apt to . . . . 515 50 POEMS 29   23
/ / not time's how (anchored in what mountaining . . . . . . 517 50 POEMS 31   1
Love surround your trite how terrible selfhood with its . . . 522 50 POEMS 35   11
time's more than most how immeasurable anguish pregnant one . 523 50 POEMS 36   35
will it tell us how we drink crawl eat . . . . 528 50 POEMS 40   4
he should not sing) how much more than enough . . . . 531 50 POEMS 43   13
leaf says (floating each how) you're which as to . . . . . . 543 1 X 1 3   8
undream that strictly (and how) scienti fic land of . . . . . 544 1 X 1 4   21
achieve another steepest thing-- how more than sleep . . . . 558 1 X 1 18   11
bear slickern a weazel how be you (sun or . . . . 568 1 X 1 28   9
stare their faith to how their joy to why . . . . 580 1 X 1 40   9
/ / / / how tinily of squir (two . . . . 581 1 X 1 41   1
flame i can feel how the earth must fly . . . . 587 1 X 1 47   15
sweeter than books tell how) so here is away . . . . 594 1 X 1 54   22
particle of perfect dark-- how should a loudness called . . . 603 {CHAIRE} 5   3
roams the youngest star) --how should a fool that . . . . . 609 {CHAIRE} 11   13
illimitably his destiny) mountains! how can each" while flame 626 {CHAIRE} 28   9
flowers neither why nor how when is now and . . . . 630 {CHAIRE} 32   10
no atom couldn't die (how and am quick i . . . . 634 {CHAIRE} 36   14
help it no matter how hard he never tried) . . . . 635 {CHAIRE} 37   6
of more than dream-- how should contented fools of . . . . . 659 {CHAIRE} 61   9
great happening illimitably earth) how should tasting . . . . 663 {CHAIRE} 65   9

	PAGE	TITLE	LINE
HOW (CONTINUED)			
stillness; while enormous this how patient creature (who's .	674	95 POEMS 2	5
nothing as much as how (first the arri -v-	676	95 POEMS 4	18
stride (instead of scheming how to beat the noblest	679	95 POEMS 7	2
& so that 's how dominic has a doll	680	95 POEMS 8	21
may take mine" "o how how how could i	684	95 POEMS 12	5
take mine" "o how how how could i ever	684	95 POEMS 12	5
mine" "o how how how could i ever wear	684	95 POEMS 12	5
to meet no matter how he'll try to try)	685	95 POEMS 13	4
grow) forgetting why, remember how in time of lilacs	688	95 POEMS 16	3
into themselves we fell-- how have all time and	694	95 POEMS 22	5
silent ly) heard (& how look at it blue	695	95 POEMS 23	17
or even to Feel how Everything (dreamed & hoped	702	95 POEMS 30	15
b ut for chreyesake how ca n i s	703	95 POEMS 31	16
could have showed billy how" "your bastard boy must	707	95 POEMS 35	14
pink shoulders you know how and he twitches a	711	95 POEMS 39	22
! o (rounD) moon, how do you (rouNd er	722	95 POEMS 50	2
She with the & how <> Unvoice (which frightenS	726	95 POEMS 54	5
time time time time --how fortunate are you and	743	95 POEMS 71	10
less believably so than (how should even omnipotent He . . .	748	95 POEMS 76	9
some dreaming tree (and how i'll stand more still	752	95 POEMS 80	3
a lmost) dis appearing how patiently be coming some	753	95 POEMS 81	10
/ / / / how generous is that himself	756	95 POEMS 84	1
beyond is brief that how infinite (deeply immediate fleet . .	763	95 POEMS 90	21
bird on the bough) how? why --we never we	767	95 POEMS 93	5
gay young love why? how-- we never we know	767	95 POEMS 93	17
a dream of spring --how you and i are	777	73 POEMS 5	16
wore his (mountains understand how) life like a (now	786	73 POEMS 14	9
oxen is science) Q: how numb can an unworld	791	73 POEMS 19	9
mo ment) where what how when who why which	797	73 POEMS 25	20
they when and they how and they live for	801	73 POEMS 29	21
true beautiful things god how he sings the robin	805	73 POEMS 33	5
unimaginably ours to feel-- how should some world (we	809	73 POEMS 37	9
your skies: so, in how merciful love's own name, ...	812	73 POEMS 40	9
given; and given is how beautifully snow) now i	816	73 POEMS 44	9
most my shining love) how more than dark i	819	73 POEMS 47	5
my dear) is this --how anyone so gay possibly	825	73 POEMS 53	5
a dog barks and how crazily houses eyes people	835	73 POEMS 63	3
In spectral such hugest how hush, one dead leaf	839	73 POEMS 67	3
/ / pity his how illimitable plight who dies	842	73 POEMS 70	1
/ / / / how many moments must (amazing	843	73 POEMS 71	1
moments must (amazing each how many centuries) these more . .	843	73 POEMS 71	2
knowledge fears to dare, how the (myself's own self	843	73 POEMS 71	12
+HOW			
FOR CONTEXT, SEE	333	VIVA 24	6
FOR CONTEXT, SEE	708	95 POEMS 36	3
HOWARD			
sung at the old howard Humanity i love you	204	XLI LA GUERRE 2	8
HOWDAH			
the air in a howdah of jasper beneath saffron	32	T&C ORIENTALE 6	4
left the prettily embroidered howdah im- mediately.	262	IS 5 ONE 32	28
HOWEVER			
sentience whose whitehot lips however suddenly ap- proached .	193	XLI PORTRAIT 1	11
a merest shape which however slenderly by it caressed	193	XLI PORTRAIT 1	16
ring amen. i do however protest, anent the un	230	IS 5 ONE 2	15
Bryant. By this time, however, the flight of crows	263	IS 5 ONE 32	54
days are teased: let (however) us Walk very (therefore . . .	317	VIVA 9	17
HOWISH			
whose (if loud most howish time derange the silent	420	NO THANKS 37	5
HOWJEDOOZE			
kelly in response to howjedooze the candidate's new silk . .	259	IS 5 ONE 29	20
HOWLESSLY			
layed in a urinal howlessly and without why (quite	387	NO THANKS 4	3
HOWLING			
by the inspired sister's howling moves off will anyone . . .	196	XLI PORTRAIT 4	18
HOWLS			
, sensuously (the crowd howls faintly blubbering pointing see	280	IS 5 THREE 4	14
and all the world howls stadesmen beware of politisions . . .	405	NO THANKS 22	3

HOWPALE

to 7th s o howpale) bluedmufFletomben outerly jeT ting . . . 342 VIVA 33   8

HOWS

does, i like its hows. i like to feel . . . . 175 & SON ACTU 24   5

and (i understand) is hows to hump a cows . . . . 500 50 POEMS 14   8

at uncle toms) is hows to hump a cows . . . . 500 50 POEMS 14   16

hell with them) is hows to hump a cows . . . . 500 50 POEMS 14   24

a writewho room) as hows of whi ne climbscr . . . . 795 73 POEMS 23   18

HT

near deep calm deep ????Ht ?????T) Who (holy alone) . . . . 455 NO THANKS 70   14

HUBBUB

faces) clothes in delicate hubbub as you stood thinking . . . 172 & SON ACTU 21   7

HUDDLED

and are ghosts or huddled in the darkness of . . . . 340 VIVA 31   7

who sit dying thinking huddled behind dir ty glass . . . . . 354 VIVA 45   5

HUDDLING

colours of the little, huddling nuts and the bad . . . . . . 100 & POST IMPR 11   21

Seeing how the limp huddling string of your smile . . . . . 161 & SON ACTU 10   5

perishing air, haunted with huddling infinite wishless . . . 305 IS 5 FIVE 4   13

brutal futility" And sit huddling dumbly behind three or . . 354 VIVA 45   18

round with cold three (huddling a- gainst one immense . . . . 687 95 POEMS 15   5

HUES

be- tween taxis swirl hues crowds mov -ing ing . . . . 384 NO THANKS 2   4

HUG

uttering tits punish my hug presto! the bright rile . . . . . 137 & SON REAL 8   14

your cool bark and hug you safe and tight . . . . 192 XLI CHANSONS 2   10

oh gargle to jip hug behemoth truly pseudo yours . . . . . . 333 VIVA 24   24

ing) al most fe (hug) males (one-t wo-l oop-l . . . . 388 NO THANKS 5   14

fog & puking jukepulse hug) large less than more . . . . . . 629 {CHAIRE} 31   6

me a most tremendous hug knowing i feel that . . . . 680 95 POEMS 8   25

HUGE

far-spaced possible nearaway from huge trees drenched by a . 10 T&C SONGS 1   45

groaning flame of neat huge trudging kiss moistly climbing . 67 T&C POST IMPR 4   24

tremendous flower on whose huge heart prospecting darkness . 79 T&C SON UNRE 4   4

utters one unhurried muscled huge chromatic fist skilfully . 82 T&C SON ACTU 1   8

begun the hair's worm huge, ecstatic, rathe.... yours are . . 84 T&C SON ACTU 3   11

It suddenly upon the huge neck around whose unwashed . . . . 96 & POST IMPR 8   30

globular slippery intense witty huge and its chords brittle . 110 & PORTRAIT 6   24

merry thrust Boost my huge passion like a business . . . . . 132 & SON REAL 3   8

stump of a mouth, huge dropping of a flesh . . . . 133 & SON REAL 4   15

fooling world in my huge blood, cracking brains A . . . . . . 157 & SON ACTU 6   11

jelly of vital futile huge light as she does . . . . 159 & SON ACTU 8   2

brittle fuss of fragile huge humanity.... Numb thoughts, . . 174 & SON ACTU 23   7

red- hot peeling off huge slabs of a fuzzy . . . . 194 XLI PORTRAIT 2   25

shrill armour colliding on huge blue horses, and the . . . . 302 IS 5 FIVE 1   13

and bend into the huge disaster of the year: . . . . 305 IS 5 FIVE 4   4

her star with what huge merciful forms presume / . . . . . . 351 VIVA 42   15

mOOn whisper less creature huge grO pingness whO perfectly . 383 NO THANKS 1   3

into how suddenly so huge a home (only more . . . . 454 NO THANKS 69   6

one trembling out of huge each eye look "thank . . . . 506 50 POEMS 20   12

imal without a heart. Huge this collective pseudobeast (sans 544 1 X 1 4   5

escape from none) so huge a tumult is the . . . . 609 {CHAIRE} 11   5

too small for dying's huge because) given much mercy . . . . 735 95 POEMS 63   10

/ / this little huge -eyed per- son (nea . . . . 739 95 POEMS 67   1

earth-- and while a (huge which by which huger . . . . 743 95 POEMS 71   2

by which huger than huge) whoing sea leaps to . . . . 743 95 POEMS 71   3

imagined secrecies comprise goldenly huge whole the . . . . . 750 95 POEMS 78   9

wonder) child unbreathingly share (huge Perhaps by hugest) . 757 95 POEMS 85   30

HUGELY

with love through meadows hugely move. yet what am . . . . . 11 T&C SONGS 2   35

the thinning lips me hugely which embrace. as in . . . . . . 151 & SON REAL 22   16

(Though through our hearts hugely squirm roots) us ly; . . . 361 VIVA 52   8

molecules) nakedest (aiming for hugely the ignorant most . . 373 VIVA 64   6

the prisoner dawn embraces hugely some few most rare . . . . 376 VIVA 67   11

move deeply, rain (dream hugely) wish firmly. splendidly . . 422 NO THANKS 39   3

(over utmost him so hugely) stood my father's dream . . . . . 520 50 POEMS 34   28

and from all selfsubtracting hugely doom treasures of reeking 843 73 POEMS 71   7

	PAGE	TITLE	LINE

HUGENESS
anything have (almost when hugeness will shut quietly) . . . 163 & SON ACTU 12   20
minute gallop of careful hugeness i am conjugated by . . . . 201 XLI PORTRAIT 9   22
leap from the mute hugeness of depriving deep, with . . . . . 210 XLI SONNETS 6   5
/ thou firsting a hugeness of twi -light pale . . . . 349 VIVA 40   2
bubble of despair into hugeness world system universe and . . 531 50 POEMS 43   2
HUGENESSES
down come blundering proud hugenesses of hate sometimes . . . 783 73 POEMS 11   7
HUGER
are laid fists of huger silence. I have seen . . . . 45 T&C LA GUERRE 1   9
--Who wields a poem huger than the grave? from . . . . 377 VIVA 68   12
sheer nothing) came a huger than fear a white . . . . 432 NO THANKS 49   15
threads of celestial silence huger than eternity, men will . 555 1 X 1 15   5
a procession of wonders huger than prove our fears . . . . . 575 1 X 1 35   11
(and only love) comprehends huger easily beyonds than . . . . 741 95 POEMS 69   6
(huge which by which huger than huge) whoing sea . . . . . . 743 95 POEMS 71   2
soon became silence: in huger always whom two tiny . . . . . 777 73 POEMS 5   10
HUGEST
brain's axe only chops hugest inherent Trees of Ego, ... 195 XLI PORTRAIT 3   18
train shriek chewing whistles hugest to morrow from smiles . 309 VIVA 1   19
into joists hewn from hugest colour (and which night . . . . 378 VIVA 69   10
self of weary the hugest sea of shore so . . . . 537 50 POEMS 49   4
--all nothing's only our hugest home; the most who . . . . . 560 1 X 1 20   23
soul) quite at the hugest which of his who . . . . 580 1 X 1 40   26
share (huge Perhaps by hugest) dooms of miracle drift . . . . 757 95 POEMS 85   31
creatures know) cringes the hugest heartless hawk and veers . 774 73 POEMS 2   7
star to disappear, that hugest whole creation may be . . . . 809 73 POEMS 37   13
unsinging. In spectral such hugest how hush, one dead . . . . 839 73 POEMS 67   3
HUGGEDTOGETHER
A billiken with hisknees huggedtogether it, goes out into . . 101 & POST IMPR 11   61
HUGGING
Is (not- quite trees hugging with the rash, coherent . . . . 155 & SON ACTU 4   5
behold ghosts, a man hugging a woman in a . . . . 375 VIVA 66   8
HUGS
Of (but a roof hugs whom) as the august . . . . 217 XLI SONNETS 13   5
until autumn abruptly wholly hugs our dying silent minds, . . 305 IS 5 FIVE 4   8
/) when what hugs stopping earth than silent . . . . 502 50 POEMS 16   1
HUH
worry about the rain huh dearie? yknow i'm sorry . . . . . . 109 & PORTRAIT 5   9
HULKING
of exploded day the hulking perpendicular mammal a grim . . . 151 & SON REAL 22   3
HUM
hideously upon the trafficing hum of dusk each street . . . . 168 & SON ACTU 17   2
/ / , mean- hum a) now (nit y . . . . 309 VIVA 1   2
HUMAN
climbing dark exact walloping human noise of digestible mill- 202 XLI PORTRAIT 9   45
with high wilt of human rind-- when over hate . . . . 213 XLI SONNETS 9   4
mouth) do the exact human comely thing? (or will . . . . . 218 XLI SONNETS 14   8
youth, what sight shall human optics know more quite . . . . 254 IS 5 ONE 25   3
down) down with the human soul and anything else . . . . . . 466 NEW POEMS 4   5
alive one i say human being) one goldberger / . . . . 524 50 POEMS 36   46
eke to wit a human being --let's remember that . . . . . . 607 (CHAIRE) 9   15
forget (to err is human; to forgive divine) that . . . . . 636 (CHAIRE) 38   6
is a rubbish of human rind with a photograph . . . . 647 (CHAIRE) 49   1
to nowhere from arrive human the most catastrophe april . . . 662 (CHAIRE) 64   3
the no of all nothing--human merely being doubt unimaginable 663 (CHAIRE) 65   11
white sleep wherein all human curiosity we'll spend (gladly, 675 95 POEMS 3   12
in hate with love --human one mortally immortal i . . . . . 679 95 POEMS 7   13
mind, these immeasurable mysteries (human one; and one . . . 721 95 POEMS 49   8
then upon a merely human plane) someone completely beautiful 799 73 POEMS 27   10
simple facts no sub human superstate ever knew (1) . . . . 803 73 POEMS 31   6
our first) beasts uttered human words --our second coming . . 844 73 POEMS 72   1
+HUMAN
FOR CONTEXT, SEE . . . . 700 95 POEMS 28   2
FOR CONTEXT, SEE . . . . 790 73 POEMS 18   2
HUMANITY
fuss of fragile huge humanity.... Numb thoughts, kicking in . 174 & SON ACTU 23   7
/ / / / Humanity i love you because . . . . 204 XLI LA GUERRE 2   1

HUMANITY (CONTINUED)
    at the old howard Humanity i love you because . . . . 204 XLI LA GUERRE 2   9
    in your own house Humanity i love you because . . . . 204 XLI LA GUERRE 2   17
    the lap of death Humanity i hate you / . . . . 204 XLI LA GUERRE 2   24
    a small hoping insect, humanity, achieves (moult beyond . . . 351 VIVA 42   10
+HUMANITY
    FOR CONTEXT, SEE . . . . 309 VIVA 1   2
HUMANUSETTS
    SAVE THE UNCOMMONWEALTH OF HUMANUSETTS / / / / . . . . 325 VIVA 17   22
HUMBLE
    with ludendorff and your humble moving through the gloominess 324 VIVA 16   12
    / / how ses humble. Over thin earths chatterish . . . . . . 346 VIVA 37   2
    love. Hell (by most humble me which shall increase) . . . . . 360 VIVA 51   31
    youful larger of smallish) Humble a rosily , nimblest; . . . 503 50 POEMS 17   4
    grin) "my flowers" (the humble man than sunlight older . . . 585 1 X 1 45   13
    part of inquisitive merrily humble your livingest courage / . 678 95 POEMS 6   15
    a pedantic proud or humble, equally they're welcome --as . . 763 95 POEMS 90   13
    welcome --as if the humble proud youngest bud testified . . . 763 95 POEMS 90   15
    us e It's we) humble one (gifted with illimitable . . . . . . 783 73 POEMS 11   1
+HUMBLE
    FOR CONTEXT, SEE . . . . 845 73 POEMS 73   7
HUMBLEST
    death should be dead humblest and proudest eagerly wandering 661 {CHAIRE} 63   5
HUMBLY
    dream perhaps this ghost) humbly and whom for worst . . . . . 441 NO THANKS 56   51
    of year extend less humbly wealth to foe and . . . . 521 50 POEMS 34   38
    to fear) i very humbly thank you which could . . . . 522 50 POEMS 35   9
    (faith's last doubt and humbly heights below) kneeling, . . . 574 1 X 1 34   10
    unmiracle can quite appease-- humbly in their imagined bodies 714 95 POEMS 42   6
    of His presence (welcoming humbly His light and proudly . . . 749 95 POEMS 77   20
    seethe glow (undering proudly humbly overing) all bright all 841 73 POEMS 69   26
HUMMINGBIRD
    chime with thrush) A hummingbird princess FlOaTs . . . . . . 747 95 POEMS 75   3
HUMOROUS
    important stars and the Humorous moon dear girl How . . . . . 44 T&C AMORES 8   16
    they, struggleinweird chords of humorous, fury . . . . 100 & POST IMPR 11   13
HUMP
    fuck for luck they hump them thirteen times a . . . . 427 NO THANKS 44   4
    / the way to hump a cow is not . . . . 500 50 POEMS 14   1
    understand) is hows to hump a cows the way . . . . 500 50 POEMS 14   8
    cows the way to hump a cow is not . . . . 500 50 POEMS 14   9
    toms) is hows to hump a cows the way . . . . 500 50 POEMS 14   16
    cows the way to hump a cow is not . . . . 500 50 POEMS 14   17
    them) is hows to hump a cows / / . . . . 500 50 POEMS 14   24
HUMPED
    we became each other humped to tumbling garble when . . . . . 119 & PORTRAIT 11   12
HUMPIN
    dem doity frogeaters an humpin duh swell janes on . . . . . . 332 VIVA 23   16
+HUMS
    FOR CONTEXT, SEE . . . . 371 VIVA 62   23
HUNCH
    thirteen pants have a hunch admit in threedimensional . . . . 150 & SON REAL 21   5
HUNCHED
    (where?) a pup hurriedly hunched over swill; one butting . . 172 & SON ACTU 21   4
+HUNCHED
    FOR CONTEXT, SEE . . . . 153 & SON ACTU 2   5
HUNDRED
    cool moon there are thrice-three-hundred doors carven of . . 33 T&C ORIENTALE 6   33
    heads turbans of a hundred colours in their hands . . . . . . 33 T&C ORIENTALE 6   37
    died it is eighteen hundred years.... exactly under the . . . 108 & PORTRAIT 4   30
    it operated in the hundred ands All the chips . . . . 149 & SON REAL 20   9
    more than certain a hundred these sounds crowds odours . . . 238 IS 5 ONE 9   2
    much stench) and a hundred joys high are such . . . . 439 NO THANKS 55   13
    me, some thousand million hundred more bright worlds than . . 580 1 X 1 40   12
    dream two were a hundred million whos (while only . . . . . . 709 95 POEMS 37   3
    miracles a million thousand hundred nothing seem --we are . . 756 95 POEMS 84   13
+HUNDRED
    FOR CONTEXT, SEE . . . . 231 IS 5 ONE 3   42

	PAGE	TITLE	LINE
+HUNDRED (CONTINUED)			
FOR CONTEXT, SEE	354	VIVA 45	20
FOR CONTEXT, SEE	803	73 POEMS 31	15
HUNDREDS			
my sister isabel created hundreds (and hundreds) of socks . .	276	IS 5 TWO 10	8
isabel created hundreds (and hundreds) of socks not to . .	276	IS 5 TWO 10	10
parts but all these hundreds upon thousands of people	510	50 POEMS 24	9
millions and dreaming drift hundreds come swimming (Each a .	630	(CHAIRE) 32	6
with what thousands of (hundreds of) millions of	840	73 POEMS 68	30
HUNDREDTH			
KEY LENGTH EXCEEDED: thrice-three-hundredth	33	T&C ORIENTALE 6	61
HUNG			
flower which most heavy hung with silence when the	18	T&C PUELLA MEA	58
filth of a collar hung gently. (spattered) by this	96	& POST IMPR 8	31
picture hat. the arms hung ugly. , the hands	103	& POST IMPR 13	5
mouse. The stockings were hung by the chimney with	142	& SON REAL 13	13
away frum dem" --"somebody hung uh gun on Marcus"--	332	VIVA 23	7
and some like it hung and some like it	497	50 POEMS 11	6
the crackling spark of (hung in a) "fert ig"	605	(CHAIRE) 7	8
HUNGARY			
s a" suddenly uprose hungary and she gave a	711	95 POEMS 39	9
UN "be quiet little hungary and do as you	711	95 POEMS 39	17
HUNGER			
/ / lean candles hunger in the silence a	28	T&C ORIENTALE 2	1
one marvel seeing the hunger of my lips for	42	T&C AMORES 6	9
the lunge of Her hunger softly flung over the	77	T&C SON UNRE 2	5
simple instant of perfect hunger Yes) how beautifully swims .	157	& SON ACTU 6	8
(the not whose spiral hunger may appease what merely	456	NO THANKS 71	4
+HUNGER			
FOR CONTEXT, SEE	101	& POST IMPR 11	71
HUNGERING			
mind who will their hungering whispers hear with weepings . .	9	T&C SONGS 1	20
after ages, and of hungering days for whom the	209	XLI SONNETS 5	11
with thunder of those hungering wings of His, into	210	XLI SONNETS 6	6
wormperused by whom the hungering mouth of time is	212	XLI SONNETS 8	8
deaths without effort while hungering churches (topped with .	340	VIVA 31	16
HUNGRILY			
rebirth of such than hungrily more swiftness as with	402	NO THANKS 19	2
HUNGRY			
ly devours darkness the hungry star which will e	49	T&C IMPRESS 3	12
are whichs small its hungry for Is for Love	437	NO THANKS 53	8
my mind stroll about hungry and fearless and thirsty	481	NEW POEMS 19	5
blood was blood: no hungry man but wished him	520	50 POEMS 34	30
HUNK			
mind is a big hunk of irrevocable nothing which	199	XLI PORTRAIT 7	2
HUNKS			
exquisitely hashed (little careful hunks-of-lilac laughter .	133	& SON REAL 4	4
....she exactly lay, looking hunks of love in The	145	& SON REAL 16	13
HUNKS-OF-LILAC			
exquisitely hashed (little careful hunks-of-lilac laughter .	133	& SON REAL 4	4
HUNTED			
sees them pass) while hunted from his kingdom winter	4	T&C EPITHALAM	70
through musical shadows while hunted by daemons seethe . . .	586	1 X 1 46	13
annabel screech have you hunted her round by the	707	95 POEMS 35	6
the rasberrypatch" i have hunted her low i have	707	95 POEMS 35	7
her low i have hunted her high and that	707	95 POEMS 35	7
HUNTER			
green mountain the lucky hunter sang before. All in	14	T&C SONGS 4	30
over the earth wandering hunter whom you knew once?	374	VIVA 65	8
+HUNTER			
FOR CONTEXT, SEE	259	IS 5 ONE 29	27
HUNTING			
/ / "so you're hunting for ann well i'm	707	95 POEMS 35	1
HURDY			
what is that the hurdy-gurdy's playing / / /	152	& SON ACTU 1	15
gladly cricks where a hurdy-gurdy accurately pants. and . . .	219	XLI SONNETS 15	8
+HURDY GURDY			
FOR CONTEXT, SEE	100	& POST IMPR 11	34

		PAGE	TITLE	LINE

HURDY-GURDY
    gladly cricks where a hurdy-gurdy accurately pants. and . . . 219 XLI SONNETS 15   8
+HURDY-GURDY
    FOR CONTEXT, SEE . . . . 442 NO THANKS 57   7
HURDY-GURDY'S
    what is that the hurdy-gurdy's playing / / / . . . . 152 & SON ACTU 1   15
HURDYSTURDYGURDY
    O turn that airy hurdysturdygurdy but when will turn . . . . 233 IS 5 ONE 4   2
HURDYSTURDYGURDYMAN
    me a child, stout hurdysturdygurdyman waiter, make me a . . . 233 IS 5 ONE 4   14
HURL
    / / / life hurl my yes, crumbles hand . . . . 265 IS 5 ONE 34   1
    litter ing brightmillion ofS hurl; edindodg: ing whom areEyes 265 IS 5 ONE 34   3
    shy-dodge is bright cruMbshandful, quick-hurl edinwho Is . . 265 IS 5 ONE 34   4
    mil, shy milbrightlions my (hurl flicker handful in) dodging 265 IS 5 ONE 34   7
    selves. create (suddenly announce: hurl) blind full steep . . 422 NO THANKS 39   15
    loop croon mime nakedly hurl asquirm the dip & . . . . 445 NO THANKS 60   25
    eold almos tladyf eebly hurl ing cr u mb . . . . 725 95 POEMS 53   5
    sea leaps to greenly hurl snow suppose we could . . . . 743 95 POEMS 71   3
HURLED
    whereto this earth's a hurled dream down eager avenues . . . 81 T&C SON UNRE 6   5
    air plunges inward with hurled downward thousands of enormous 301 IS 5 FOUR 18   18
    of serene perfectly Nothing hurled into young Now entirely . 456 NO THANKS 71   7
+HURLED
    FOR CONTEXT, SEE . . . . 265 IS 5 ONE 34   3
HURLING
    throughout ignorant disappearing me hurling vastness of love 428 NO THANKS 45   8
+HURLING
    FOR CONTEXT, SEE . . . . 330 VIVA 21   1
    FOR CONTEXT, SEE . . . . 371 VIVA 62   16
    FOR CONTEXT, SEE . . . . 444 NO THANKS 59   13
HURLS
    moist mistake, whose fragrance hurls me into tears, as . . . 148 & SON REAL 19   10
HURRIED
    in making Marjorie god hurried a boy's body on . . . . 148 & SON REAL 19   1
HURRIEDLY
    derbies (where?) a pup hurriedly hunched over swill; one . . 172 & SON ACTU 21   4
    several pieces and is hurriedly picked up and thrown . . . . 203 XLI LA GUERRE 1   15
    bird looked grave (departing hurriedly to shave) but--though 339 VIVA 30   21
HURRIES
    authenticity of these ◇ hurries elsewhere; to blow . . . . . 116 & PORTRAIT 9   15
+HURRIES
    FOR CONTEXT, SEE . . . . 724 95 POEMS 52   24
HURRY
    stars) people move love hurry in a gently arriving . . . . . 93 & POST IMPR 5   11
    arms caught the picture) hurry it slowly to my . . . . 162 & SON ACTU 11   10
    it is in a hurry beyond that any this . . . . 238 IS 5 ONE 9   4
    unb uria ble fore (hurry into heads are legs . . . . 309 VIVA 1   7
    little man (in a hurry full of an important . . . . 393 NO THANKS 10   2
    and i may not hurry it with a thousand . . . . 835 73 POEMS 63   27
HURRYING
    how, always (from these hurrying crudities of blood and . . . 297 IS 5 FOUR 14   10
    a hun dred doomed hurrying brains (by twos or . . . . 354 VIVA 45   21
    of one two came hurrying home to the dearest . . . . 709 95 POEMS 37   13
    splendor and squalor of hurrying cities --i do not . . . . . 749 95 POEMS 77   2
HURT
    the dark portals of hurt girl eyes sincere with . . . . 54 T&C PORTRAIT 2   4
    of them round the hurt heart which do so . . . . 215 XLI SONNETS 11   10
    (so as not to hurt the perspective of the . . . . 267 IS 5 TWO 2   15
    her hot ow you hurt tho nithe steered his . . . . 316 VIVA 8   11
    mountains; and beyond all hurt of praise the unimaginable . . 418 NO THANKS 35   13
    what man can 't hurt any more h u . . . . 472 NEW POEMS 10   15
    gwine ter hate dad hurt fool wurl no gal . . . . 519 50 POEMS 33   18
    she asked would it hurt too much and 'twas . . . . 707 95 POEMS 35   24
+HURT
    FOR CONTEXT, SEE . . . . 262 IS 5 ONE 32   16
    FOR CONTEXT, SEE . . . . 388 NO THANKS 5   17

	PAGE	TITLE	LINE

+HURTFUL
   FOR CONTEXT, SEE . . . . 519 50 POEMS 33   18
HURTING
   toward me with its hurting sexual smell of lilies. . . . . . . 214 XLI SONNETS 10   11
   your least gesture the hurting skill which lives) and . . . . 293 IS 5 FOUR 10   7
   (but now don't you're hurting o Me please you're . . . . . . 343 VIVA 34   5
HURTS
   / POEM, OR BEAUTY HURTS MR. VINAL take it . . . . 230 IS 5 ONE 2   T
+HURTS
   FOR CONTEXT, SEE . . . . 101 & POST IMPR 11   74
HUSBAND
   child is a good Husband to him (and whose . . . . 398 NO THANKS 15   6
   now Ugly was the husband of (as happens every . . . . 799 73 POEMS 27   8
HUSH
   man murder the petals hush mysteriously invisible mourners . 59 T&C PORTRAIT 7   5
   stirring. (Must be summer. Hush. Worms.) But It's Nicer . . . 130 & SON REAL 1   12
   --eh? I'm not. Again. Hush. God. Please hold. Tight . . . . . 130 & SON REAL 1   15
   whom headwaiters bow so? hush--the author of Women By . . . 245 IS 5 ONE 16   8
   down ever so far-- hush. Sunlight, there are old . . . . . . 281 IS 5 THREE 5   22
   blunder through new light hush we are made of . . . . 299 IS 5 FOUR 16   15
   wheres: ex: tend: ing: hush) andDark IshbusY ing-roundly-dis 416 NO THANKS 33   3
   / / / / hush) noones are coming out . . . . 600 (CHAIRE) 2   1
   lous citi zens of (hush / / / / . . . . 600 (CHAIRE) 2   19
   spectral such hugest how hush, one dead leaf stirring . . . . 839 73 POEMS 67   3
+HUSH
   FOR CONTEXT, SEE . . . . 472 NEW POEMS 10   15
HUSHED
   anguish of dream-send is hushed in moan-loll where night . . 90 & POST IMPR 2   7
   your eyes: lost, believing; hushed with when / / . . . . . . 432 NO THANKS 49   20
+HUSHED
   FOR CONTEXT, SEE . . . . 844 73 POEMS 72   3
HUSHINGLY
   do not speak) tumbled hushingly bits of downward flower . . . 168 & SON ACTU 17   7
HUSK
   smaller stars begin to husk heaven) you, you exactly . . . . 71 T&C SON REAL 2   11
HUTCH
   tuh de mans l (hutch) hutchinson says sweet guinea . . . . . 325 VIVA 17   7
HUTCHINSON
   de mans l (hutch) hutchinson says sweet guinea pigs . . . . . 325 VIVA 17   7
HUTS
   sagest pane of littler huts with peerless fantasies or . . . 207 XLI SONNETS 3   4
HYENAS
   out gaily for the hyenas suppressing my frank qualms . . . . 326 VIVA 18   20
HYMN
   as some grave languorous hymn pledged to illimitable . . . . 206 XLI SONNETS 2   12
HYPERCIVIC
   pause then fired by hypercivic zeal sought newer pastures . . 258 IS 5 ONE 28   11
HYPERLUXURIOUS
   an launch we a Hyperluxurious Supersieve (which Ultima Thule 334 VIVA 25   2
HYPERMAGICAL
   this fine specimen of hypermagical ultraomnipotence. We . . . 554 1 X 1 14   12
+HYPERPRODIGIOUS
   FOR CONTEXT, SEE . . . . 392 NO THANKS 9   4
HYPNOTISM
   the soothings of plastic hypnotism . i am accurately . . . . 201 XLI PORTRAIT 9   26
HYPNOU
   little {MEGA} {HELLENIKON KSENODOCHEION HYPNOU} / / / / . . . 217 XLI SONNETS 13   15
+HYPOCRITICAL
   FOR CONTEXT, SEE . . . . 635 (CHAIRE) 37   11
HYSTERICAL
   chattering self perceives with hysterical fright a comic . . 157 & SON ACTU 6   14
I
   the hearts of lovers! --I beseech thee bless thy . . . . . . 7 T&C EPITHALAM 167
   / SONGS (thee will i praise between those rivers . . . . . . 9 T&C SONGS 1   1
   move. yet what am i that such and such . . . . 12 T&C SONGS 2   36
   and small. Death, Thee i call rich beyond wishing . . . . . . 13 T&C SONGS 3   17
   little turn her head i know that i am . . . . 17 T&C PUELLA MEA   34
   head i know that i am wholly dead: nor . . . . 17 T&C PUELLA MEA   34

I (CONTINUED)

	PAGE	TITLE	LINE
naked in her hair-- i for those ladies nothing	21	T&C PUELLA MEA	179
forgive these words which i have made. And never	22	T&C PUELLA MEA	242
/ / / ORIENTALE i spoke to thee with	27	T&C ORIENTALE 1	1
life not a smile? i spoke to thee with	27	T&C ORIENTALE 1	8
life not a song? i spoke to thee with	27	T&C ORIENTALE 1	15
is life not love? i speak to thee with	27	T&C ORIENTALE 1	22
/ / listen beloved i dreamed it appeared that	30	T&C ORIENTALE 4	3
on insolent waters but i was aware of fragrance	30	T&C ORIENTALE 4	8
aware of fragrance and i came riding upon a	30	T&C ORIENTALE 4	9
porphyry into the waters i rode down the red	30	T&C ORIENTALE 4	11
my mouth listen beloved i dreamed in my dream	30	T&C ORIENTALE 4	17
from a great way i distinguished singing and i	30	T&C ORIENTALE 4	21
i distinguished singing and i came riding upon a	30	T&C ORIENTALE 4	22
the shocked impossible tower i caught you strained you . . .	30	T&C ORIENTALE 4	26
my blood listen beloved i dreamed i thought you	30	T&C ORIENTALE 4	30
listen beloved i dreamed i thought you would have	30	T&C ORIENTALE 4	31
through day and space i saw you close your	30	T&C ORIENTALE 4	34
close your eyes and i came riding upon a	30	T&C ORIENTALE 4	35
years arched with agony i reined them in tottering	30	T&C ORIENTALE 4	37
hand of sombre god i picked you as an	30	T&C ORIENTALE 4	41
/ / unto thee i burn incense the bowl	31	T&C ORIENTALE 5	1
deep with desirable flowers i think thou lovest incense . . .	31	T&C ORIENTALE 5	13
level litanies unto thee i burn incense, over the	31	T&C ORIENTALE 5	21
discovers thee unto whom i burn olbanum / /	31	T&C ORIENTALE 5	30
and urgent (again love i slowly gather of thy	37	T&C AMORES 2	17
/ / / if i believe in death be	39	T&C AMORES 4	1
silver muting of seatides i trusted not, one night	39	T&C AMORES 4	10
pale- departing irrevocable sea i knew thee death. and . . .	39	T&C AMORES 4	28
thee death. and when i have offered up each	39	T&C AMORES 4	30
/ / / / i like to think that	42	T&C AMORES 6	1
for a dead thing, i shall instruct him silently	42	T&C AMORES 6	11
seek your face and i entreat, by certain foolish	42	T&C AMORES 6	14
sumptuously being kind because i trust him to your	42	T&C AMORES 6	22
my unkempt adoration if i have made a fragile	43	T&C AMORES 7	3
things and which die i have been sometimes true	43	T&C AMORES 7	11
were faithful and which i despise, frankly admitting i . . .	43	T&C AMORES 7	19
i despise, frankly admitting i have been true only	43	T&C AMORES 7	21
wires came leaping and i felt suddenly dizzy With	44	T&C AMORES 8	3
were laid upon me I was whirled and tossed	44	T&C AMORES 8	12
moon dear girl How i was crazy how i	44	T&C AMORES 8	19
i was crazy how i cried when i heard	44	T&C AMORES 8	19
how i cried when i heard over time and	44	T&C AMORES 8	19
cannon is skilful, but i have seen death's clever	45	T&C LA GUERRE 1	3
a fragility of poppies.... i say that sometimes on	45	T&C LA GUERRE 1	7
fists of huger silence. I have seen all the	45	T&C LA GUERRE 1	10
noiseless boys at Roupy i have seen between barrages, ...	45	T&C LA GUERRE 1	13
/ / / / i was considering how within	49	T&C IMPRESS 3	1
star's nibbling in- fin -i- tes- i -mal- ly	49	T&C IMPRESS 3	6
in- fin -i- tes- i -mal- ly devours darkness	49	T&C IMPRESS 3	8
forth to murder dreams.... i see in the street	50	T&C IMPRESS 4	12
are digging bread and i see the brutal faces	50	T&C IMPRESS 4	14
day, in the mirror i see a frail man	50	T&C IMPRESS 4	18
at tremont and bromfield i paused a moment because	52	T&C PORTRAIT 1	11
the wagon but as i was lifting the horror	53	T&C PORTRAIT 1	38
/ / / / i walked the boulevard i	56	T&C PORTRAIT 4	1
i walked the boulevard i saw a dirty child	56	T&C PORTRAIT 4	2
is short it was i think yourself delivered into	57	T&C PORTRAIT 5	18
Death said "then as i recollect her girlhood was	57	T&C PORTRAIT 5	29
but the other day i was passing a certain	58	T&C PORTRAIT 6	2
upon bells of gold i looked up and thought	58	T&C PORTRAIT 6	11
handsome man and what i want to know is	60	T&C PORTRAIT 8	9
slobber of your thighs i am so very glad	61	T&C PORTRAIT 9	26
are the rain, and i hear the screech of	61	T&C PORTRAIT 9	31
and most of all i hear your stepping freakish	61	T&C PORTRAIT 9	34
the brittle towns asleep i look where stealing needles . . .	64	T&C POST IMPR 1	2
chattering sunset ludicrously dies, i hear only tidewings in	64	T&C POST IMPR 1	10
and April darkness, friends i charge laughing. Into the . . .	66	T&C POST IMPR 3	5

	PAGE	TITLE	LINE

I (CONTINUED)

into the women-coloured twilight i smilingly glide. I into . 66 T&C POST IMPR 3 9
twilight i smilingly glide. I into the big vermilion . . . . 66 T&C POST IMPR 3 10
(Do you think?) the i do, world is probably . . . . 66 T&C POST IMPR 3 14
/ / / / i am going to utter . . . . 67 T&C POST IMPR 4 1
raging with thin impulse i will have a dream . . . . 67 T&C POST IMPR 4 6
will have a dream i think it shall be . . . . 67 T&C POST IMPR 4 9
the children laugh. But i don't, the crank goes . . . . . . 69 T&C POST IMPR 6 21
tickling putrescent atomies, and i feel the jerk of . . . . 69 T&C POST IMPR 6 32
yelling over the music i understand him i shove . . . . . . 69 T&C POST IMPR 6 33
music i understand him i shove my round red . . . . 69 T&C POST IMPR 6 34
back on my head i sit up and blink . . . . 69 T&C POST IMPR 6 34
yes, By god. for i am they are pointing . . . . 69 T&C POST IMPR 6 37
little red coat with i have a real pocket . . . . 69 T&C POST IMPR 6 41
roses darling, it's all i ask of you-- but . . . . 71 T&C SON REAL 2 6
lips take twilight where i know: proving to Death . . . . . 71 T&C SON REAL 2 13
lingering a little while i see thee then ponder . . . . . . 75 T&C SON REAL 6 5
they let thee play; i see the large lips . . . . 75 T&C SON REAL 6 7
always be so; and i say that if your . . . . 76 T&C SON UNRE 1 1
if your lips, which i have loved, should touch . . . . . . 76 T&C SON UNRE 1 2
such a silence as i know, or such great . . . . 76 T&C SON UNRE 1 6
if this should be, i say if this should . . . . 76 T&C SON UNRE 1 9
a little word; that i may go unto him, ... 76 T&C SON UNRE 1 11
from me. Then shall i turn my face, and . . . . 76 T&C SON UNRE 1 13
is at moments after i have dreamed of the . . . . 78 T&C SON UNRE 3 1
(being fool to fancy) i have deemed with your . . . . 78 T&C SON UNRE 3 3
tremendous lie of sleep i watch the roses of . . . . 78 T&C SON UNRE 3 14
of his soul--so even i wholly chained to a . . . . 79 T&C SON UNRE 4 10
and the trees stand. I think i too have . . . . 80 T&C SON UNRE 5 3
trees stand. I think i too have known autumn . . . . 80 T&C SON UNRE 5 3
of magic and (as i guess) when Farmer Death . . . . 83 T&C SON ACTU 2 10
by speaking flower (if i have made songs it . . . . 84 T&C SON ACTU 3 6
yours are the poems i do not write. In . . . . 84 T&C SON ACTU 3 12
hills without any reason (i have spoken with this . . . . . 91 & POST IMPR 3 6
mountains different from the i am who wanders imminently . . 91 & POST IMPR 3 17
occurs deeply, beautifully and i (being at a window . . . . 92 & POST IMPR 4 8
the edge of day) i surely make a millionth . . . . 92 & POST IMPR 4 18
miss you; or if i certainly create, lady, one . . . . 92 & POST IMPR 4 20
/ / / / I remark this beach has . . . . 94 & POST IMPR 6 1
softly, New focus-of disintegrat i o n ? my . . . . 94 & POST IMPR 6 16
(unthinking. c'est l'heure exquise) i remind Me of HerThe . 94 & POST IMPR 6 20
/ / / / i was sitting in mcsorley's. . . . . 96 & POST IMPR 8 1
faint piddle-of-drops she says I ploc spittle what the . . . 96 & POST IMPR 8 14
eh chuckles skulch.... and i was sitting in the . . . . . . 96 & POST IMPR 8 23
so near to me, i ask of shad- ow . . . . 97 & POST IMPR 8 40
perpetual question) Inside snugandevil. i was sitting in . . 97 & POST IMPR 8 43
with fear people bells) i say your eyes can . . . . 98 & POST IMPR 9 2
upon a single colour, i know only that your . . . . 98 & POST IMPR 9 7
as means the moon, i somehow feel your smile . . . . 98 & POST IMPR 9 10
clumsy dark threatens (and i do not speak nor . . . . 98 & POST IMPR 9 13
the east side as i lie asleep my eyes . . . . 100 & POST IMPR 11 2
harps colours p r i c k i n . . . . 100 & POST IMPR 11 9
r i c k i n glike piccolos thumPing . . . . 100 & POST IMPR 11 9
YELLOW EYES AND --; i Like to Lie On . . . . 101 & POST IMPR 11 57
of little, girls smoothanduseless i, like, best, the, . . . 101 & POST IMPR 11 76
thumb and first finger (i say "will he buy . . . . 102 & POST IMPR 12 6
life has a beard" i say to you who . . . . 102 & POST IMPR 12 9
my love slowly answered I think so. But I . . . . 102 & POST IMPR 12 22
I think so. But I think I see someone . . . . 102 & POST IMPR 12 23
so. But I think I see someone else there . . . . 102 & POST IMPR 12 23
by yester- day) O i tell you out of . . . . 111 & PORTRAIT 6 51
the clever deadly heaven i salute you whose body . . . . . . 112 & PORTRAIT 6 108
silver dig) by beauty i declare to you if . . . . 115 & PORTRAIT 8 4
to you if what i am at one o'clock . . . . 115 & PORTRAIT 8 5
splashing fresh upon silence) i without fail entered became . 115 & PORTRAIT 8 20
twenty minutes to one, i am this blueeyed Finn . . . . . . 115 & PORTRAIT 8 26
in a tiny voice, i am may the first . . . . 117 & PORTRAIT 10 12
cried the third crumb, i am should and this . . . . 117 & PORTRAIT 10 17

		PAGE	TITLE	LINE

I (CONTINUED)

	PAGE	TITLE	LINE
alive just imagine it I say God amid a	117 & PORTRAIT 10	25
a frown puzzles, but I know the way-- (nervously	117 & PORTRAIT 10	34
V ingint oA chute i had cement for her, ...	119 & PORTRAIT 11	9
/ &: SEVEN POEMS i will be M o	122 & SEVEN POEMS 1	1
lovely; muscles-sinke x p i r i n g	122 & SEVEN POEMS 1	4
x p i r i n g S uddenl	122 & SEVEN POEMS 1	4
tell you a dream i had once i was	123 & SEVEN POEMS 2	1
dream i had once i was away up in	123 & SEVEN POEMS 2	1
from strings (or) someThing i was lying on the	123 & SEVEN POEMS 2	3
bar it was cOOl i didn't have anything on	123 & SEVEN POEMS 2	4
have anything on and I was hot all Hot	123 & SEVEN POEMS 2	4
up into the tree? I didn't said the little	125 & SEVEN POEMS 4	3
runs the elevator but I bet two bits come	125 & SEVEN POEMS 4	10
violets into the tree? I dunno said the silver	125 & SEVEN POEMS 4	15
/ / / gee i like to think of	126 & SEVEN POEMS 5	1
if dead says may i have this one and	126 & SEVEN POEMS 5	20
you you say for i like kittens i do	127 & SEVEN POEMS 5	49
for i like kittens i do and jackknives i	127 & SEVEN POEMS 5	50
i do and jackknives i do and pennies i	127 & SEVEN POEMS 5	50
i do and pennies i do and rosebugs i	127 & SEVEN POEMS 5	50
i do and rosebugs i do / / /	127 & SEVEN POEMS 5	51
(and if you and i should get into it, ...	129 & SEVEN POEMS 7	4
in a glib girl i consider her as a	131 & SON REAL 2	2
eye winks). and almost i refrain from jumbling her	131 & SON REAL 2	6
weeping skyscraper in me i bite on the eyes'	132 & SON REAL 3	6
do you? and always (i simply understand the gnashing . . .	133 & SON REAL 4	10
hinging thighs .... merci.... i want to die nous	133 & SON REAL 4	17
lymph she kissed and i .... cheri.... nous sommes	133 & SON REAL 4	22
has --. One day i felt a mountain touch	135 & SON REAL 6	11
mountain touch me where i stood (maybe nine miles	135 & SON REAL 6	12
feather of your shall i say body? follows truly	140 & SON REAL 11	3
the fattish drone of I Want a Doll, wispish-agile	140 & SON REAL 11	13
nothing on something as i think , did you	141 & SON REAL 12	15
whose kind large flesh i turn to the cruel-littleness . . .	142 & SON REAL 13	2
always. More interesting, as i think, her charms en	143 & SON REAL 14	7
sore of morning. But i am interested more intricately . . .	144 & SON REAL 15	10
when for two dollars i fill her hips with	148 & SON REAL 19	14
you should see when i turn to find her	152 & SON ACTU 1	8
--and then we are I and She.... what is	152 & SON ACTU 1	14
mouth hair eyes, and i mean the unique and	153 & SON ACTU 2	2
you will be and i and all the days	153 & SON ACTU 2	10
/ / / / i have loved, let us	154 & SON ACTU 3	1
the whole possibly have i loved....? you) sheath before . . .	154 & SON ACTU 3	11
you as bite teeth; i stood with you as	154 & SON ACTU 3	15
/ utterly and amusingly i am pash possibly because	155 & SON ACTU 4	1
silence and shall the (i do but touch you)	155 & SON ACTU 4	16
/ / / when i have thought of you	157 & SON ACTU 6	1
me before shutting.... understand i love you.... feel your .	157 & SON ACTU 6	6
wines women and window-sills) i met that hideous gladness, .	158 & SON ACTU 7	5
to my friend. Whom i salute, by what is	158 & SON ACTU 7	9
dream of dreaming --and i fall back, quietly amorous	158 & SON ACTU 7	12
love, and after you. I occasionally feel vague how	160 & SON ACTU 9	14
feel vague how vague i don't know tenuous Now-	160 & SON ACTU 9	15
/ / / if i should sleep with a	161 & SON ACTU 10	1
his body squirms kissingly, i will bring you every	161 & SON ACTU 10	7
why his eye laughs, i will bring you every	161 & SON ACTU 10	12
speak her wonderful But i (having in my arms	162 & SON ACTU 11	9
/ / / / i have found what you	163 & SON ACTU 12	1
between my arms; but i should rather than anything	163 & SON ACTU 12	19
upon the room's silence, i will sew a nagging	164 & SON ACTU 13	2
go rapidly to bed: i will get in with	164 & SON ACTU 13	7
(this white worm and i who love to feel	164 & SON ACTU 13	12
these gross days when i think of you and	165 & SON ACTU 14	7
nor the autumn, as i grieve, faint for your	165 & SON ACTU 14	9
of the ingenious gods. (i am punished. They have	165 & SON ACTU 14	13
me wonder if, if i am the face of	166 & SON ACTU 15	12
big fool she says i says to her i	167 & SON ACTU 16	13

I (CONTINUED)

i says to her i says Sally i says . . . . 167 & SON ACTU 16   13
her i says Sally i says the mmmoon, begins . . . . 167 & SON ACTU 16   14
from the fireman's ball, i think and also i . . . . 169 & SON ACTU 18   4
i think and also i think of you, getting . . . . 169 & SON ACTU 18   5
out of the night. I am living with a . . . . 171 & SON ACTU 20   13
which is fair as i judge. / / / . . . . 171 & SON ACTU 20   14
maybe the world.... But i have wondered since isn't . . . . 172 & SON ACTU 21   9
breasts tickle, laughing when i wilt and wince / . . . . . 172 & SON ACTU 21   15
the world's smell (but i was thinking why the . . . . 174 & SON ACTU 23   12
/ / / / i like my body when . . . . 175 & SON ACTU 24   1
better and nerves more. i like your body. i . . . . 175 & SON ACTU 24   4
i like your body. i like what it does, ... 175 & SON ACTU 24   4
like what it does, i like its hows. i . . . . 175 & SON ACTU 24   5
i like its hows. i like to feel the . . . . 175 & SON ACTU 24   5
-firm-smooth ness and which i will again and again . . . . 175 & SON ACTU 24   7
again and again kiss, i like kissing this and . . . . 175 & SON ACTU 24   9
and that of you, i like, slowly stroking the, ... 175 & SON ACTU 24   10
big love-crumbs, and possibly i like the thrill of . . . . 175 & SON ACTU 24   13
leaps a stiffened exquisite i wait the sweet annihilation . . 182 XLI SONGS 4   9
annihilation of swift flesh i make me stern against . . . . . 182 XLI SONGS 4   13
will never guess. but i know / / / . . . . 183 XLI SONGS 5   16
east deserves of dawn. i lie at length, breathing . . . . . . 184 XLI SONGS 6   15
the sunset being sheathed i sit and think of . . . . 186 XLI SONGS 8   3
star is uttered, and i think of you / . . . . 186 XLI SONGS 8   20
/ / / / i will wade out till . . . . 189 XLI SONGS 11   1
steeped in burning flowers I will take the sun . . . . . . 189 XLI SONGS 11   3
chasteness of sea-girls Will i complete the mystery of . . . 189 XLI SONGS 11   11
mystery of my flesh I will rise After a . . . . 189 XLI SONGS 11   13
to come away? see i will comfort you because . . . . 192 XLI CHANSONS 2   7
you smell so sweetly i will kiss your cool . . . . 192 XLI CHANSONS 2   9
my little sister and i will take hands and . . . . 192 XLI CHANSONS 2   25
robin's egg blue when i entered a mad street . . . . 194 XLI PORTRAIT 2   4
of back- gammon boards i was aware of an . . . . 194 XLI PORTRAIT 2   18
who may that be i said exhaling into eternity . . . . 194 XLI PORTRAIT 2   29
/ / as usual i did not find him . . . . 197 XLI PORTRAIT 5   1
integration of my soul i coughed , naturally / . . . . . . 197 XLI PORTRAIT 5   24
buddha or answer modestly i am dying so let . . . . 198 XLI PORTRAIT 6   30
agony of sensual chisels i perform squirms of chrome . . . 199 XLI PORTRAIT 7   5
strides of cobalt nevertheless i feel that i cleverly . . . . 199 XLI PORTRAIT 7   7
nevertheless i feel that i cleverly am being altered . . . 199 XLI PORTRAIT 7   8
am being altered that i slightly am becoming something . . . 199 XLI PORTRAIT 7   8
fact myself Hereupon helpless i utter lilac shrieks and . . . 199 XLI PORTRAIT 7   11
phenomenon of 5 o'clock i find myself gently decomposing . . 201 XLI PORTRAIT 9   1
the mor- sel is i. Vast cheeks enclose me. . . . . 201 XLI PORTRAIT 9   6
gallop of careful hugeness i am conjugated by the . . . . . 201 XLI PORTRAIT 9   22
of entire vertical being, i am skilfully construed by . . . . 201 XLI PORTRAIT 9   24
of plastic hypnotism . i am accurately parsed by . . . . . . 201 XLI PORTRAIT 9   26
is) still 5 o'clock I stare only always into . . . . 202 XLI PORTRAIT 9   43
/ / / Humanity i love you because you . . . . 204 XLI LA GUERRE 2   1
the old howard Humanity i love you because when . . . . . . 204 XLI LA GUERRE 2   9
your own house Humanity i love you because you . . . . . . 204 XLI LA GUERRE 2   17
lap of death Humanity i hate you / / . . . . 204 XLI LA GUERRE 2   25
of incense fleetly roll) i spill my bright incalculable . . . 206 XLI SONNETS 2   15
dreadful corners hideously cowers-- i do excuse me, love, . . 207 XLI SONNETS 3   9
lucent and large signories --i shall not smile beloved; . . . 210 XLI SONNETS 6   8
shall not smile beloved; i shall not weep: when . . . . . . 210 XLI SONNETS 6   8
were roses. Perfume? for i do forget.... or mere . . . . . 211 XLI SONNETS 7   1
is fed: and if i like not what thou . . . . 212 XLI SONNETS 8   9
everlasting air-- but if i like, i'll take between . . . . . 212 XLI SONNETS 8   13
/ / / / I have seen her a . . . . 214 XLI SONNETS 10   1
of tiny fragrance try; i have watched certain petals . . . . 214 XLI SONNETS 10   5
of him utterly afraid, i love of thee (beloved) . . . . . . 215 XLI SONNETS 11   3
(beloved) this and truly i would be near when . . . . 215 XLI SONNETS 11   5
of all most would i be one of them . . . . 215 XLI SONNETS 11   9
do so frailly cling....) i who am but imperfect . . . . . . 215 XLI SONNETS 11   11
to my mind that i am come by little . . . . 216 XLI SONNETS 12   6
if somebody hears what i say--let him be pitiful: . . . . . 216 XLI SONNETS 12   10

PAGE TITLE LINE

I (CONTINUED)
/ / / when i am in Boston, i . . . . 217 XLI SONNETS 13 1
i am in Boston, i do not speak. and . . . . 217 XLI SONNETS 13 1
do not speak. and i sit in the click . . . . 217 XLI SONNETS 13 2
coffee tasting of hellas, i drink, or sometimes two . . . . 217 XLI SONNETS 13 11
(Very occasionally three.) and i gaze on the cindercoloured . 217 XLI SONNETS 13 14
of fruit distinctly grouped. I have not eaten peppers . . . . 219 XLI SONNETS 15 2
/ / by god i want above fourteenth fifth's . . . . 220 XLI SONNETS 16 1
frail firm asinine life (i pant for what's below. . . . . . 220 XLI SONNETS 16 5
below. the singer. Wall. i want the perpendicular lips . . . 220 XLI SONNETS 16 6
Baboon sniggering insipidities while. i sit, sipping singular 220 XLI SONNETS 16 13
no one knows what (i am sure of this) . . . . 225 IS 5 ONE LIZ 10
yanks back skin "see" (i, seeing, ceased to breathe). . . . . 226 IS 5 ONE MAME 6
baby ached." and when i timidly hinted "novocaine?" the . . . 226 IS 5 ONE MAME 12
/ / GERT joggle i think will do it . . . . 227 IS 5 ONE GERT 1
and everybody is." And i hazarded "god" (blushing slightly) . 228 IS 5 ONE MARJ 5
"even her." "The Madam?" I emitted; vaguely watching that . . 228 IS 5 ONE MARJ 11
drooped to a purr... i left her permanently smiling . . . . . 228 IS 5 ONE MARJ 15
/ / FRAN should i entirely ask of god . . . . 229 IS 5 ONE FRAN 1
unfirm drooping bloated calves i would receive the answer . . 229 IS 5 ONE FRAN 7
go in peace. which i do, being as Dick . . . . 229 IS 5 ONE FRAN 9
Wilson Collars) of you i sing: land of Abraham . . . . 230 IS 5 ONE 2 10
let freedom ring amen. i do however protest, anent . . . . . 230 IS 5 ONE 2 15
this radically defunct periodical. i would suggest that . . . 230 IS 5 ONE 2 18
all fortissimo A- mer i ca, I love, You. . . . . 230 IS 5 ONE 2 38
A- mer i ca, I love, You. And there're . . . . 231 IS 5 ONE 3 39
So this is Paris. i will sit in the . . . . 233 IS 5 ONE 4 16
nothing which you and i are accustomed to accomplish . . . . 236 IS 5 ONE 7 13
kiddo but as fer i gimme de good ole . . . . 237 IS 5 ONE 8 12
sumpn youse knows wot i refers ter Satter Nailyuh . . . . . . 237 IS 5 ONE 8 15
loses all the time i had an uncle named . . . . 239 IS 5 ONE 10 2
flowers and everything and i remember we all cried . . . . . 239 IS 5 ONE 10 32
/ / / (and i imagine never mind Joe . . . . 241 IS 5 ONE 12 1
animals continued eating. And i imagine she, and heard . . . 241 IS 5 ONE 12 6
never, never really wonder i mean about the smell . . . . . . 242 IS 5 ONE 13 16
at no window because i can't sleep (smoking sawdust . . . . . 242 IS 5 ONE 13 21
the Hotel Meurice (whereas i live in a garret . . . . 245 IS 5 ONE 16 5
you know (whereas when i lie down i cough . . . . 245 IS 5 ONE 16 11
when i lie down i cough too much). How . . . . 245 IS 5 ONE 16 11
me as for me i only knows that as . . . . 246 IS 5 ONE 17 9
tastes but as for i i likes a certain . . . . 247 IS 5 ONE 18 3
but as for i i likes a certain party . . . . 247 IS 5 ONE 18 4
consequently a little stiff i was careful of her . . . . . . 248 IS 5 ONE 19 4
springs were O. K.) i went right to it . . . . 248 IS 5 ONE 19 9
the hell) next minute i was back in neutral . . . . 248 IS 5 ONE 19 14
corner of Divinity avenue i touched the accelerator and . . . 248 IS 5 ONE 19 22
first ride and believe i we was happy to . . . . 248 IS 5 ONE 19 25
by the Public Gardens i slammed on the internalexpanding . . 248 IS 5 ONE 19 28
but and her a I mean me a Irish, ... 251 IS 5 ONE 22 10
with, its, friend observes I pass Mr Tom Larsen . . . . 252 IS 5 ONE 23 4
with-ered unspea-king: tWeNtY, f i n g e r . . . . 255 IS 5 ONE 26 3
the stars of Heaven.... i do signore affirm that . . . . . 256 IS 5 ONE 27 22
only, gondola knows Cincingondolanati i gondola don't --the . 256 IS 5 ONE 27 28
whom the stiffened puke i put him all into . . . . 258 IS 5 ONE 28 22
of deeply bulging thousands i too omit one kelly . . . . . . 259 IS 5 ONE 29 19
/ / / Will i ever forget that precarious . . . . 262 IS 5 ONE 32 1
that precarious moment? As i was standing on the . . . . . . 262 IS 5 ONE 32 2
seemed to me that i had first of all . . . . 262 IS 5 ONE 32 5
all born, seeing that i was wifeless and only . . . . 262 IS 5 ONE 32 6
if you understand that i mean what i say . . . . 262 IS 5 ONE 32 13
that i mean what i say i believe my . . . . 262 IS 5 ONE 32 13
mean what i say i believe my most intimate . . . . 262 IS 5 ONE 32 13
gave birth to which i should or- dinarily have . . . . 263 IS 5 ONE 32 33
all concerned than that i am not a policeman. . . . . 263 IS 5 ONE 32 41
of crows had ceased. I withdrew my hands from . . . . 263 IS 5 ONE 32 55
perhaps excuse me if i repeat himself: these, or . . . . . . 263 IS 5 ONE 32 59
speak even less objectively, i was horribly scared i . . . . 263 IS 5 ONE 32 62
i was horribly scared i would actually fall off . . . . 263 IS 5 ONE 32 62

			PAGE	TITLE	LINE

I (CONTINUED)

	PAGE	TITLE	LINE
after all arrived. If i should have made this	263	IS 5 ONE 32	64
voices, lip to lip i swear (to noone everyone)	264	IS 5 ONE 33	2
these moments be translated: i say that even after	264	IS 5 ONE 33	6
of the best overseeing) i mean that the blond	264	IS 5 ONE 33	17
live makes unimportant what i and you believe; not	264	IS 5 ONE 33	19
pastel. (While you and i have lips and voices	264	IS 5 ONE 33	25
of course god america i love you land of	268	IS 5 TWO 3	1
& we're NOT (oh-- --i say that's jolly odd	269	IS 5 TWO 4	13
it we was buddies i used to know him	270	IS 5 TWO 5	11
with the big eyes i loved like you can't	271	IS 5 TWO 6	9
-ten you know what i mean when the first	272	IS 5 TWO 7	3
been there knows what i mean a god damned	272	IS 5 TWO 7	13
must!" and who replies "I can!" --yon clean upstanding . . .	273	IS 5 TWO 8	5
flics for every one (I) communist and all the	274	IS 5 TWO 9	18
my mother hoped that i would die etcetera bravely	276	IS 5 TWO 10	14
anguish (clim b) ing s-p-i-r-a- l and, disappear) Satanic . .	278	IS 5 THREE 2	12
spine against thick sunset i perceive in front of	279	IS 5 THREE 3	5
tell me what am i doing on top of	281	IS 5 THREE 5	2
luminous (here the absurd I; life, to peer and	281	IS 5 THREE 5	18
peer and wear clothes. i am altogether foolish, i	281	IS 5 THREE 5	19
i am altogether foolish, i suddenly make a fist	281	IS 5 THREE 5	19
old men behind me I tell you; several, incredible, ...	281	IS 5 THREE 5	24
of enough, is it (i do not pretend to	282	IS 5 THREE 6	3
five o'clock and these (i notice) trees winterbrief surly . .	282	IS 5 THREE 6	11
of life, for you. I understand. Once again....) sliding . . .	282	IS 5 THREE 6	32
lips hands the way i move my habits laughter	285	IS 5 FOUR 2	6
move my habits laughter i say you will perhaps	285	IS 5 FOUR 2	8
does he think about, i wonder as over this	286	IS 5 FOUR 3	2
the same you and i, since here's a little	286	IS 5 FOUR 3	17
/ / but if i should say goodmorning trouble	287	IS 5 FOUR 4	1
nigger's face (but If i should say thankyouverymuch mr . . .	287	IS 5 FOUR 4	7
beringed hands) but if i Should say solong my	287	IS 5 FOUR 4	10
a dream (but if i should say Now the	287	IS 5 FOUR 4	13
what happens) but if i should, Say, / /	287	IS 5 FOUR 4	20
--before leaving my room i turn, and (stooping through . . .	288	IS 5 FOUR 5	7
not going to and i but that doesn't in	289	IS 5 FOUR 6	2
can you imagine it i can't which doesn't matter	289	IS 5 FOUR 6	5
(do you believe it? i begin to and that	289	IS 5 FOUR 6	9
that doesn't matter) which i suggest teach us a	289	IS 5 FOUR 6	10
we consider life. Dear i put my eyes into	289	IS 5 FOUR 6	13
you fooled the doctors, i touch you with hopes	289	IS 5 FOUR 6	15
as we, you and i, used to move when	289	IS 5 FOUR 6	19
used to move when i thought you were going	289	IS 5 FOUR 6	19
fate than wisdom lady i swear by all flowers.	290	IS 5 FOUR 7	10
a paragraph And death i think is no parenthesis	290	IS 5 FOUR 7	16
of their fellows but i being otherwise made compose	291	IS 5 FOUR 8	2
is.... therefore, lady am i content should any by	291	IS 5 FOUR 8	18
/ / / supposing i dreamed this) only imagine, ...	292	IS 5 FOUR 9	1
a house around which i am a wind-- your	292	IS 5 FOUR 9	4
if this wind who i am prowls carefully around	292	IS 5 FOUR 9	11
marvelous breathing thing) since i and you are on	293	IS 5 FOUR 10	14
in vain: Nor am i afraid that this, which	293	IS 5 FOUR 10	22
because you go away i give roses who will	294	IS 5 FOUR 11	2
asks in love, am i separated from your body	295	IS 5 FOUR 12	3
of a dream? oh i mean: entirely having in	295	IS 5 FOUR 12	4
that strangers arrive when i have kissed you into	295	IS 5 FOUR 12	9
the question how do i drink dream smile and	295	IS 5 FOUR 12	14
smile and how do i prefer this face to	295	IS 5 FOUR 12	15
another and why do i weep eat sleep--what does	295	IS 5 FOUR 12	16
"to be, being, that i am alive this absurd	295	IS 5 FOUR 12	17
if you like and i like, for the reason	295	IS 5 FOUR 12	22
for the reason that i hate people and lean	295	IS 5 FOUR 12	22
and the reason that i laugh and breathe is	295	IS 5 FOUR 12	24
and the reason that i do not fall into	295	IS 5 FOUR 12	25
coat and hat --(and i wonder just why that	296	IS 5 FOUR 13	9
should please him or i wonder what he does)	296	IS 5 FOUR 13	10
perhaps a year) ago i found staring me in	296	IS 5 FOUR 13	15

358

		PAGE	TITLE	LINE

I (CONTINUED)

of a town-- that i have perhaps forgotten how, ...	297 IS 5 FOUR 14	8
/ / / / i am a beggar always	298 IS 5 FOUR 15	1
his breast BLIND) yes i am this person of	298 IS 5 FOUR 15	6
/ / / / i go to this window	301 IS 5 FOUR 18	1
looking up in fear i see the new moon	301 IS 5 FOUR 18	5
and becomes crisper until i smile with knowing --and	301 IS 5 FOUR 18	13
/ / touching you i say (it being Spring	303 IS 5 FIVE 2	1
so very little afraid") i say "along this particular	303 IS 5 FIVE 2	8
/ / / if i have made, my lady, ...	306 IS 5 FIVE 5	1
song upon my mind--if i have failed to snare	306 IS 5 FIVE 5	5
(l'on parle de repapering; i don't think so. maybe:	312 VIVA 4	23
one fine August night, i just happened to meet	313 VIVA 5	3
floating ultrawrists who lullabylullaby (I could have been .	317 VIVA 9	7
You might have been I) "?" quoth the front;	317 VIVA 9	9
eleven camels ! and i got a Bad almond	318 VIVA 10	17
what time is it i wonder never mind consider	322 VIVA 14	1
of the fact that i and that you had	323 VIVA 15	22
what you and what i (of course) carefully had	323 VIVA 15	28
over this younger than i am newspaper guy who	324 VIVA 16	10
in big cumbine wid i (check undublcheck) babbitt (GOD	325 VIVA 17	18
olde freudian wish; when i contemplate her uneyes safely . .	326 VIVA 18	4
in an exhausted condition, i purchased two bags of	326 VIVA 18	15
sometime") vanished, gunwale awash. I thereupon loosened my .	327 VIVA 18	37
radcliffe college, cambridge, mass. i try if you are	327 VIVA 18	45
/ / / / i will cultivate within me	328 VIVA 19	1
"as for myself, because i am slender and fragile	328 VIVA 19	15
am slender and fragile i borrow contact from that	328 VIVA 19	17
carefully around it) "things i mean the Rain is	328 VIVA 19	20
could kill sixeight cops-- "I sidesteps im an draws	332 VIVA 23	4
bull like dat ...suddenly i feels so lonely fer	332 VIVA 23	14
streamin down my face i hauls out uh flask	332 VIVA 23	19
down my spine like i was dead er sumpn:	332 VIVA 23	28
dead er sumpn: next i knows me (er somebody	332 VIVA 23	28
You know Separated what i Mean (oweld song by	335 VIVA 26	17
; neither you nor i and by the way)	335 VIVA 26	19
somewhere real flowers, but I can't imagine real flowers . .	338 VIVA 29	8
real flowers for if I could, they would somehow	338 VIVA 29	8
he smiles smiling) "but I will not everywhere be	338 VIVA 29	12
everything is easier than I had guessed everything would . .	338 VIVA 29	18
/ / / / i sing of Olaf glad	339 VIVA 30	1
responds, without getting annoyed "I will not kiss your . . .	339 VIVA 30	19
"there is some shit I will not eat" our	339 VIVA 30	33
(of His mercy infinite) i pray to see; and	339 VIVA 30	39
untrue, the best mouth i have seen on any	344 VIVA 35	8
swiftly corners (Besides which, i note how fatally toward . .	345 VIVA 36	3
a nd O impercept i bl / / /	350 VIVA 41	17
think "wonder if" if i were a child "we	353 VIVA 44	3
the door (opening it i think things which were	353 VIVA 44	13
again there therehere And) i say "won't you" (remembering) .	353 VIVA 44	24
ly "toc tic" as i have seen trees (in	354 VIVA 45	25
/ / / / i met a man under	355 VIVA 46	1
like new tools) whence i guessed that he also	355 VIVA 46	12
been playing a fiddle i had been dancing: which	355 VIVA 46	18
the laughter of afterwards-- i spirally understand What . . .	356 VIVA 47	18
thing possibly more intricate) i (breath in breath) have . .	358 VIVA 49	8
me, on this afternoon; i am a shape that	360 VIVA 51	4
a house for lease. I have never loved you	360 VIVA 51	10
you dear as now i love behold this fool	360 VIVA 51	10
the abyss --and wonderfully i fell through the green	360 VIVA 51	18
into many a piece. I have never loved you	360 VIVA 51	20
you dear as now i love god's terrible face, ...	360 VIVA 51	20
that has not occurred: i am a birdcage without	360 VIVA 51	25
who, living, noone is. I have never loved you	360 VIVA 51	30
you dear as now i love. Hell (by most	360 VIVA 51	30
open thy fire! for i have had some bliss	360 VIVA 51	32
earth above; to whom i cry, remembering her face, ...	360 VIVA 51	34
cry, remembering her face, i have never loved you	360 VIVA 51	35

359

	PAGE	TITLE	LINE
I (CONTINUED)			
you dear as now i love / / /	360	VIVA 51	35
/ / / if i love You (thickness means	363	VIVA 54	1
if your heart's mine) i guess a grassblade Thinks	364	VIVA 55	5
you see and really i have no servants. We	365	VIVA 56	5
could go (you and i) into a together whitely	365	VIVA 56	9
so or so slowly i opened the window a	365	VIVA 56	11
/ / / somewhere i have never travelled, gladly	366	VIVA 57	1
enclose me, or which i cannot touch because they	366	VIVA 57	4
will unclose me though i have closed myself as	366	VIVA 57	6
be to close me, i and my life will	366	VIVA 57	9
forever with each breathing (i do not know what	366	VIVA 57	17
there a flower (whom i meet anywhere able to	367	VIVA 58	2
darling since you and i are thoroughly haunted by	368	VIVA 59	3
/ / / because i love you) last night	369	VIVA 60	1
/ if you and i awakening discover that (somehow	370	VIVA 61	1
each other disappeared: but i slightly smiling, gradually . .	370	VIVA 61	16
unvisible when. Wait if i am not heart, because	372	VIVA 63	6
heart, because at least i beat --always think i	372	VIVA 63	6
i beat --always think i am gone like a	372	VIVA 63	7
than surround this throat) i wear your dearest fears . . .	372	VIVA 63	10
and trees dance (and i guess though wish and	372	VIVA 63	14
despair impersonates a street i lean from the window, ...	375	VIVA 66	6
lest we understand) slightly i am hearing somebody coming . .	375	VIVA 66	10
of terror) and continually i am seeing something inhaling . .	375	VIVA 66	15
quite outmarch forever --and i perceive, within transparent .	376	VIVA 67	7
whining rigging over us, i implore you to notice	378	VIVA 69	2
clothes herself with day) i mean, should any curious . . .	379	VIVA 70	6
reintegrate beckon through me, i think it is less	379	VIVA 70	13
a softishsongly v o i c e o ver	385	NO THANKS 2	56
un- eats wasvino isspaghett (i / / / /	387	NO THANKS 4	18
/ / / / i (meet) t (touch) ems	388	NO THANKS 5	1
jeff dick son fec i (m c) t (m	388	NO THANKS 5	31
x x x ii) I / / / /	388	NO THANKS 5	40
b: e; n, d i ng like like, like	389	NO THANKS 6	12
than know means guess) I item i immaculately owe	390	NO THANKS 7	12
means guess) I item i immaculately owe dying one	390	NO THANKS 7	12
suspect each (nor have i observed some chucking some	391	NO THANKS 8	5
lossal hyperpr digious etc i kn w & if	392	NO THANKS 9	5
supp sedly thr w i n g a b	392	NO THANKS 9	22
/ / / may i feel said he (i'll	399	NO THANKS 16	1
fun said she (may i touch said he how	399	NO THANKS 16	5
are said she) may i stay said he (which	399	NO THANKS 16	13
kiss said she may i move said he is	399	NO THANKS 16	17
(no but Rully yes i know) but what it	400	NO THANKS 17	4
you don't have to i mean Reely) but (no	400	NO THANKS 17	7
be sil why sure) i mean the (o well	400	NO THANKS 17	8
course yeh well naturally i und certain i o	400	NO THANKS 17	10
naturally i und certain i o posi but i	400	NO THANKS 17	10
i o posi but i know sure that's) but	400	NO THANKS 17	11
Rilly yeh ughhuh yuh) i know (o sure i	400	NO THANKS 17	14
i know (o sure i know yes of course)	400	NO THANKS 17	15
of course) but what i mean is Nobody Understands	400	NO THANKS 17	18
really clean get what I mean let's not spoil	407	NO THANKS 24	8
why) and so do i (because they are afraid	413	NO THANKS 30	17
a god sometimes is I the lost shoulders 'S	414	NO THANKS 31	15
yes this alive secretly i frantic this serene mightily . . .	415	NO THANKS 32	21
o; w (says W I elds) un forgetting un.	417	NO THANKS 34	16
if a mys teriouSly ("i am alive") brave	423	NO THANKS 40	3
: ke (c. l i, m ! b)	423	NO THANKS 40	32
do because they can't i mean move yes sir	425	NO THANKS 42	6
/ / the boys i mean are not refined	427	NO THANKS 44	1
for wit the boys i mean are not refined	427	NO THANKS 44	8
with dynamite the boys i mean are not refined	427	NO THANKS 44	13
their pants the boys i mean are not refined	427	NO THANKS 44	19
be unknown most secret i will breathe such crude	428	NO THANKS 45	10
/ / / much i cannot) tear up the	433	NO THANKS 50	1
flowers of rain) thickly i fail slenderly i win	433	NO THANKS 50	10

I (CONTINUED)

thickly i fail slenderly i win (like touch all . . . . . . 433 NO THANKS 50   10
filled with birds seriously i begin to climb the . . . . . . 434 NO THANKS 51   5
Clock dimly cries nine, i stride among the vines . . . . . . 434 NO THANKS 51   15
or a field (and i pause among the smell . . . . 434 NO THANKS 51   24
climb and mightily fatally i remark how through deep . . . . 434 NO THANKS 51   30
wind blows the taller i am" / / / . . . . 439 NO THANKS 55   28
may never have) do i salute (by moon by . . . . 441 NO THANKS 56   65
(by moon by sun i deeply greet this fool . . . . 441 NO THANKS 56   67
(yoursmine mineyours yoursmine ! i ( ) t) / . . . . 445 NO THANKS 60   31
Do. omful relaxing -ly) i downrise outwrithein- ing upfall . 449 NO THANKS 64   4
cause a colour and i do not know him . . . . 450 NO THANKS 65   15
of when) that's yours; i guess you'll have to . . . . 451 NO THANKS 66   5
all those & that "I may say professor" asleep . . . . 464 NEW POEMS 2   10
-ufactured harmlessly accurate gloom "I think he might now . 464 NEW POEMS 2   20
unto canned swoonsong came "I wish you good" the . . . . . . 464 NEW POEMS 2   28
& that those you i St ep into the . . . . 464 NEW POEMS 2   31
/ (of Ever-Ever Land i speak sweet morons gather . . . . . . 466 NEW POEMS 4   1
lucky luck- ier luck -I- est / / / . . . . 467 NEW POEMS 5   15
Ly expand: grO w i ? n g Is . . . . 471 NEW POEMS 9   10
/ The Mind's (i never you never he . . . . 474 NEW POEMS 12   2
/ / / if i or anybody don't know . . . . 475 NEW POEMS 13   1
next meal's coming from i say to hell with . . . . 475 NEW POEMS 13   5
without lifting my finger i say to hell with . . . . 475 NEW POEMS 13   9
to hell with that i say that doesn't matter) . . . . 475 NEW POEMS 13   10
deep or generous what i say is whistle that . . . . 475 NEW POEMS 13   15
nobody's probably handbag) because i say that's not swell . . 475 NEW POEMS 13   22
something else my sweet (i feel that's true) / . . . . . . 475 NEW POEMS 13   24
plenty good enough for i eu can have you . . . . 476 NEW POEMS 14   10
of love, all that i am easily disappears (leaving . . . . . 479 NEW POEMS 17   18
if it's sunday may i be wrong for whenever . . . . 481 NEW POEMS 19   7
more than boygirls need: i can entirely her only . . . . . 484 NEW POEMS 22   6
s wa it sp i t) (t he s . . . . 488 50 POEMS 2   12
warped this perhapsy stumbl i Ngflounderpirouettin g : seized 495 50 POEMS 9   3
jesus what blood darling i said / / / . . . . 496 50 POEMS 10   20
nows and adding and (i understand) is hows to . . . . 500 50 POEMS 14   7
don't ask me how i know (a he of . . . . 501 50 POEMS 15   6
dirty window every) twilight i feel (his lousy eyes . . . . 501 50 POEMS 15   7
miracle of nearest far "i cordially invite me to . . . . . 504 50 POEMS 18   4
is the sky and i am for you just . . . . 511 50 POEMS 25   27
one day anyone died i guess (and noone stooped . . . . . . 515 50 POEMS 29   25
so least as truth --i say though hate were . . . . 521 50 POEMS 34   66
whatever dares to fear) i very humbly thank you . . . . . . 522 50 POEMS 35   9
/ / / / i say no world can . . . . 523 50 POEMS 36   1
no good too quick i know this suit you . . . . 523 50 POEMS 36   11
o much cheap me i work i know i . . . . 523 50 POEMS 36   16
cheap me i work i know i say i . . . . 523 50 POEMS 36   16
i work i know i say i have not . . . . 523 50 POEMS 36   16
i know i say i have not any never . . . . 523 50 POEMS 36   16
hands is work since i am born is good . . . . 523 50 POEMS 36   20
there every -thing nothing i say the world not . . . . . . 523 50 POEMS 36   25
you) he is not (i say the world yes . . . . 523 50 POEMS 36   29
not buyable alive one i say human being) one . . . . 524 50 POEMS 36   46
face have shadowless they? i bring you peace the . . . . . 527 50 POEMS 39   3
of god and fiend? i give you man extracted . . . . 527 50 POEMS 39   8
same rotting keen dream? i rise which am the . . . . 527 50 POEMS 39   31
we'll not have (but i imagine that yes is . . . . 528 50 POEMS 40   13
a memory and memory i) kiss me (will go) . . . . 529 50 POEMS 41   12
us darling. And if i sing you are my . . . . 531 50 POEMS 43   14
a greener (o little i) riding on a leaf . . . . 535 50 POEMS 47   7
/ mortals) climbi ng i nto eachness begi n . . . . 536 50 POEMS 48   3
/ / / / i am so glad and . . . . 537 50 POEMS 49   1
cannot be so sunful i am through you so . . . . 537 50 POEMS 49   16
am through you so i / / / / . . . . 537 50 POEMS 49   16
true not you not i) it comes so who . . . . 542 1 X 1 2   7
goes (you go and i) has pulled (for he's . . . . 543 1 X 1 3   20
impart one stands supreme i mean the an imal . . . . 544 1 X 1 4   3
blind him of who) i discreetly (masturbates one honest . . . 546 1 X 1 6   11

		PAGE	TITLE	LINE

I (CONTINUED)

one honest breadcrumb) say "i understand quite what you . . .	546	1 X 1 6	12
not) you told him: i told him; we told	553	1 X 1 13	17
stop and go) may i achieve another steepest thing--	558	1 X 1 18	10
breathing for me while i am away?) / /	558	1 X 1 18	15
a stranger who is i awakening am. Living no	559	1 X 1 19	8
nor cruel (only complete) i not not you not	564	1 X 1 24	9
which) replies in haste I must be you no	570	1 X 1 30	4
float on some ? i call twilight you 'll	571	1 X 1 31	4
before each heartbeat which i am alive to kiss	577	1 X 1 37	20
are we? surely not i not you behold nor	582	1 X 1 42	10
voice more leastfully than i am you , we	583	1 X 1 43	20
/ / / / i think you like" a	585	1 X 1 45	1
/ / until and i heard a certain a	587	1 X 1 47	1
a certain a bird i dreamed i could sing	587	1 X 1 47	3
a bird i dreamed i could sing but like	587	1 X 1 47	3
and until into flame i can feel how the	587	1 X 1 47	14
of a soul until i awoke for the beautiful	587	1 X 1 47	19
and such a sun i never knew and neither	591	1 X 1 51	14
has anybody seen little you-i who stood on a	593	1 X 1 53	3
a string (murmurs little you-i as the hill becomes	593	1 X 1 53	21
never till now now i love you and you	594	1 X 1 54	28
can you die or i and every world, before	601	(CHAIRE) 3	18
everyone (or you or i) were wise." "You mean	603	(CHAIRE) 5	10
"Or worse! poor worlds; i mean they're possible --but" . . .	603	(CHAIRE) 5	12
Death ? o baby i wouldn't like Death if	604	(CHAIRE) 6	4
have r olle d i nt o n o	606	(CHAIRE) 8	12
can travel this or i and you / /	608	(CHAIRE) 10	13
fool that calls him "I" presume to comprehend not	609	(CHAIRE) 11	13
nob odyknowswhos esh ? i rt) n't / /	611	(CHAIRE) 13	11
never part: Soul was (i understand) seduced by Life;	621	(CHAIRE) 23	2
will always remain: who i am. Look at these	626	(CHAIRE) 28	6
"be so am and i and who? each grows"	626	(CHAIRE) 28	10
gold moment) climb: ing i -nto wintry twi- light	627	(CHAIRE) 29	3
which is Who and i am you are i	630	(CHAIRE) 32	12
i am you are i am we (pretty twinkle	630	(CHAIRE) 32	12
makes your beautiful name-- i feel that (false and	631	(CHAIRE) 33	13
way X -mas) ter- i -ous wisp A of	632	(CHAIRE) 34	11
you are and until i am dreams until comes	633	(CHAIRE) 35	7
/ / / quick i the death of thing	634	(CHAIRE) 36	1
(how and am quick i they'll all not conceive	634	(CHAIRE) 36	14
don't seem to realize i can't make it clearer	638	(CHAIRE) 40	7
must understand why because i am dead / /	638	(CHAIRE) 40	16
and jerked 300 lbs) i mean observe his these	645	(CHAIRE) 47	2
itfulls o f cringewiltdroolery i mean really th underscream .	646	(CHAIRE) 48	7
walking in the dark i met christ jesus) my	648	(CHAIRE) 50	4
his pride involved (this i who's also you) and	650	(CHAIRE) 52	10
single wish, receive all i am and dream and	651	(CHAIRE) 53	4
(im) c-a-t (mo) b, i; l: e FallleA ps!	655	(CHAIRE) 57	2
/ / / / i thank You God for	663	(CHAIRE) 65	1
infinite which is yes (i who have died am	663	(CHAIRE) 65	5
in we am in i are in you) this	664	(CHAIRE) 66	12
for you are and i am and we are	664	(CHAIRE) 66	17
in you am in i are in we /	664	(CHAIRE) 66	24
so you and so i (now the mountains are	665	(CHAIRE) 67	13
first for joy, he's i he's i / /	666	(CHAIRE) 68	20
joy, he's i he's i / / / /	666	(CHAIRE) 68	20
now you are and i am now and we're	667	(CHAIRE) 69	5
are without hands; and i have no you: and	667	(CHAIRE) 69	10
carefully o ver (& i) some newer than life	668	(CHAIRE) 70	17
voltaire you beautiful anarchist (i salute thee / /	677	95 POEMS 5	16
--human one mortally immortal i can turn immense all	679	95 POEMS 7	13
most tremendous hug knowing i feel that we &	680	95 POEMS 8	27
lily has a rose (i have none) "don't cry	684	95 POEMS 12	2
how how how could i ever wear it now	684	95 POEMS 12	6
give me another if i let him kiss me	684	95 POEMS 12	10
the wisest man am i) So young young young	685	95 POEMS 13	12
something you have and i 've been doing as	686	95 POEMS 14	6

	PAGE	TITLE	LINE
I (CONTINUED)			
did you and did i climb (crazily kissing) till	694	95 POEMS 22	2
mind me of noone i ever & someone (the	695	95 POEMS 23	11
long ago laid them) i never (selves any than	695	95 POEMS 23	14
/ / / dim i nu tiv e this	696	95 POEMS 24	2
handorgan until you say "i want a fortune"	697	95 POEMS 25	5
so moon could dream (i sus pect) only god	698	95 POEMS 26	1
the cheerfulest goddamned sonofabitch i ever met or hope . .	699	95 POEMS 27	14
wer) say o if i 'd OH n lygawntueco	700	95 POEMS 28	11
(just as well as i do) what it takes;	701	95 POEMS 29	11
what it takes; & i don't mean It-- &	701	95 POEMS 29	13
don't mean It-- & i don't mean any thing	701	95 POEMS 29	15
could hardly express what i Mean is what knocked	702	95 POEMS 30	9
chreyesake how ca n i s ell drunk if	703	95 POEMS 31	18
s ell drunk if i be pencils / /	703	95 POEMS 31	19
an uppercut but everybody (i believe) else thought lucinda .	706	95 POEMS 34	3
hair" "it seems like i just heard your annabel	707	95 POEMS 35	5
round by the rasberrypatch" "i have hunted her low	707	95 POEMS 35	7
have hunted her low i have hunted her high	707	95 POEMS 35	7
slut of a mother i rather suppose" "will's dad	707	95 POEMS 35	16
c ollapse d . i: ns; unli, gh; t:	710	95 POEMS 38	5
shall murder me for i will freely die" she	711	95 POEMS 39	12
/ / / / i love you much (most	717	95 POEMS 45	1
on the earth and i like you better than	717	95 POEMS 45	2
makes happier me than i but always everything which	718	95 POEMS 46	4
/ / / someone i am wandering a town	720	95 POEMS 48	1
upon new perfectly blue) i am any (while around	720	95 POEMS 48	4
running away from them (i wonder) or isn't she	724	95 POEMS 52	15
least timorous pigeons) squ -I- nts (while showe ring . . .	726	95 POEMS 54	11
Amingfeeblyoff s, p; r: i; n, g / /	726	95 POEMS 54	16
men tion least) & i ob serve no body	727	95 POEMS 55	6
now that fiend and i are such immortal friends	730	95 POEMS 58	5
magicians (whom you and i some times call april)	738	95 POEMS 66	6
fortunate are you and i, whose home is timelessness:	743	95 POEMS 71	10
/ / / / i shall imagine life is	744	95 POEMS 72	1
call life, you and i may reverently share the	745	95 POEMS 73	10
chino ise r (!) i (?) e (.) s	747	95 POEMS 75	19
of roses-- "and who" i asked my love "	748	95 POEMS 76	12
/ / / / i am a little church	749	95 POEMS 77	1
squalor of hurrying cities --i do not worry if	749	95 POEMS 77	3
briefer days grow briefest, i am not sorry when	749	95 POEMS 77	4
symbols of hope, and i wake to a perfect	749	95 POEMS 77	12
perfect patience of mountains i am a little church	749	95 POEMS 77	13
at peace with nature --i do not worry if	749	95 POEMS 77	15
longer nights grow longest; i am not sorry when	749	95 POEMS 77	16
singing winter by spring, i lift my diminutive spire	749	95 POEMS 77	17
am was ever as i then that Star goes	752	95 POEMS 80	7
your fear to whom i give this little parasol, ...	762	95 POEMS 89	7
less than dead) dance, i and you; high (are	762	95 POEMS 89	10
so sans until twice i have lived forever in	765	95 POEMS 91	14
/ / / / i carry your heart with	766	95 POEMS 92	1
your heart with me (i carry it in my	766	95 POEMS 92	1
it in my heart) i am never without it	766	95 POEMS 92	2
never without it (anywhere i go you go, my	766	95 POEMS 92	3
your doing, my darling) i fear no fate (for	766	95 POEMS 92	5
my fate, my sweet) i want no world (for	766	95 POEMS 92	6
keeping the stars apart i carry your heart (i	766	95 POEMS 92	15
i carry your heart (i carry it in my	766	95 POEMS 92	15
today) the romp cries i and the me purrs	773	73 POEMS 1	6
his royal warcry is I AM and he's the	774	73 POEMS 2	3
--his royal warcry is I AM true to his	774	73 POEMS 2	12
are in love and i am) to sing, my	776	73 POEMS 4	3
spring --how you and i are blossoming / /	777	73 POEMS 5	16
(or ; why even i suppose one 's wife)	779	73 POEMS 7	15
is that you & i are more than you	782	73 POEMS 10	18
more than you & i (be ca us e	782	73 POEMS 10	19
is asking What have i done that You wouldn't	784	73 POEMS 12	7
darkness (in whom always i do nothing) deepens with	785	73 POEMS 13	4

I (CONTINUED)

oneness) each othering Selves i sit (hearing the rain) . . . 785 73 POEMS 13 16
just 5 a m i hear eng (which cannot . . . . 787 73 POEMS 15 2
(a look without an i) be care ful (touch . . . . 797 73 POEMS 25 3
--come such perfection-- another i and you, is a . . . . . . 798 73 POEMS 26 24
blind stare, he whispers "i ran" / / / . . . . 800 73 POEMS 28 24
that render hell rational --i thank heaven somebody's crazy . 802 73 POEMS 30 32
it is you (ne i) nobody else drive dumb . . . . 804 73 POEMS 32 8
you never left (and i refer to thinking) rests . . . . . . 807 73 POEMS 35 5
and all mysteries which i or you (blinded by . . . . 809 73 POEMS 37 5
you what seemed myself, i find selves unimaginably mine; . . 810 73 POEMS 38 9
go with you, only i remain; a shadow phantom . . . . 812 73 POEMS 40 2
no more than selfless i can quite endure the . . . . 812 73 POEMS 40 10
the dark) whispers. And i and my love are . . . . 813 73 POEMS 41 12
/ / / may i be gay like every . . . . 815 73 POEMS 43 1
/ / / Now i lay (with everywhere around) . . . . 816 73 POEMS 44 1
gently welcoming darkestness-- now i lay me down (in . . . . 816 73 POEMS 44 5
how beautifully snow) now i lay me down to . . . . 816 73 POEMS 44 10
to dream of (nothing i or any somebody or . . . . 816 73 POEMS 44 11
nobody may keep. now i lay me down to . . . . 816 73 POEMS 44 14
how more than dark i am, no song (no . . . . 819 73 POEMS 47 5
/ / but he" i staring into winter twi . . . . 823 73 POEMS 51 2
who are you, little i (five or six years . . . . 824 73 POEMS 52 1
numerable leaves are fall i ng) he StandS lift . . . . . . 826 73 POEMS 54 7
/ / / / i never guessed any thing . . . . 827 73 POEMS 55 1
/ / "could that" i marvelled "be you?" and . . . . 828 73 POEMS 56 1
--look-- selves, stir: writhe o-p-e-n-i-n-g are (leaves; . . 835 73 POEMS 63 12
arrives (yes) you and i may not hurry it . . . . 835 73 POEMS 63 26
world (and you and i who love so much . . . . 836 73 POEMS 64 3
live) must die" "if i should tell you anything" . . . . . . 836 73 POEMS 64 6
carolling self answers me) "i could not sing" / . . . . . . 836 73 POEMS 64 10
flower murmurs eager this "i will give you five . . . . . . 837 73 POEMS 65 8
alive) lies april; and i ◇ some perpetually roaming . . . . 839 73 POEMS 67 6
+I
FOR CONTEXT, SEE . . . . 310 VIVA 2 1
FOR CONTEXT, SEE . . . . 310 VIVA 2 2
FOR CONTEXT, SEE . . . . 310 VIVA 2 3
FOR CONTEXT, SEE . . . . 310 VIVA 2 4
FOR CONTEXT, SEE . . . . 310 VIVA 2 4
FOR CONTEXT, SEE . . . . 310 VIVA 2 5
FOR CONTEXT, SEE . . . . 330 VIVA 21 7
FOR CONTEXT, SEE . . . . 330 VIVA 21 8
FOR CONTEXT, SEE . . . . 330 VIVA 21 8
FOR CONTEXT, SEE . . . . 398 NO THANKS 15 20
FOR CONTEXT, SEE . . . . 398 NO THANKS 15 23
FOR CONTEXT, SEE . . . . 405 NO THANKS 22 11
FOR CONTEXT, SEE . . . . 405 NO THANKS 22 12
FOR CONTEXT, SEE . . . . 417 NO THANKS 34 23
FOR CONTEXT, SEE . . . . 474 NEW POEMS 12 10
FOR CONTEXT, SEE . . . . 519 50 POEMS 33 28
FOR CONTEXT, SEE . . . . 602 {CHAIRE} 4 6
FOR CONTEXT, SEE . . . . 618 {CHAIRE} 20 5
FOR CONTEXT, SEE . . . . 705 95 POEMS 33 13
FOR CONTEXT, SEE . . . . 803 73 POEMS 31 8
FOR CONTEXT, SEE . . . . 827 73 POEMS 55 15
+I.Q.
FOR CONTEXT, SEE . . . . 807 73 POEMS 35 8
I&YOU
from a grown -up i&you- ful world of known) . . . . 832 73 POEMS 60 10
I'D
/ / / / i'd think "wonder if" if . . . . 353 VIVA 44 1
and negation's dead undoom. I'd rather learn from one . . . . 484 NEW POEMS 22 13
but were it five, i'd still insist that all . . . . 579 1 X 1 39 6
by the old swimminghole" "i'd be worse than a . . . . 707 95 POEMS 35 3
may that you and i'd be quite --come such . . . . 798 73 POEMS 26 22
+I'D
FOR CONTEXT, SEE . . . . 700 95 POEMS 28 11

I'LL

	PAGE	TITLE	LINE
rushing through loam. (afterward i'll climb by tall careful .	67	T&C POST IMPR 4	13
/ / / / i'll tell you a dream	123	& SEVEN POEMS 2	1
say (like that) sure i'll come with you you	127	& SEVEN POEMS 5	49
move.... moves.... and also, i'll admit--) till, at the . . .	174	& SON ACTU 23	13
your little arms and i'll give them all to	192	XLI CHANSONS 2	18
but if i like, i'll take between thy hands	212	XLI SONNETS 8	13
untidily from released cheeks "I'll tell duh woild; some . .	226	IS 5 ONE MAME	10
but once er year) i'll tell de woild one	237	IS 5 ONE 8	16
bliss for youse ideas i'll match youse a pretty	247	IS 5 ONE 18	6
i feel said he (i'll squeal said she just	399	NO THANKS 16	2
me an ounce and i'll sell you a pound.	513	50 POEMS 27	1
distorting than socalled civilization i'll kiss a stalinist .	514	50 POEMS 28	12
/ open your heart: i'll give you a treasure	586	1 X 1 46	2
lieve me you and i'll go strolling right through	600	(CHAIRE) 2	12
than not to understand "i'll never let you go	622	(CHAIRE) 24	5
you'll (silently alighting) and i'll sing while at us	659	(CHAIRE) 61	12
of man to God i'll think it strange that	731	95 POEMS 59	3
dreaming tree (and how i'll stand more still than	752	95 POEMS 80	3
you suddenly blossoming tree --i'll sing / / /	767	95 POEMS 93	24
tongue may name, three i'll give you sweet joys	837	73 POEMS 65	3
for just one dying, i'll give you" silently cries	837	73 POEMS 65	14
understands: only for whom i'll keep my tryst until	843	73 POEMS 71	6

+I'LL

	PAGE	TITLE	LINE
FOR CONTEXT, SEE	310	VIVA 2	1
FOR CONTEXT, SEE	310	VIVA 2	7

I'M

	PAGE	TITLE	LINE
she gasped almost loudly i'm so drunG k, dear	53	T&C PORTRAIT 1	48
rain huh dearie? yknow i'm sorry for awl the	109	& PORTRAIT 5	12
up the song, might i'm called and did no	117	& PORTRAIT 10	16
Lie In Bed --eh? I'm not. Again. Hush. God.	130	& SON REAL 1	14
makes me wonder if i'm alive (eye pries, not	166	& SON ACTU 15	10
said (crossing them slowly) "I'm asleep. Yep. Youse is . .	228	IS 5 ONE MARJ	3
/ IKEY (GOLDBERG)'S WORTH I'M TOLD $ SEVERAL MILLION	244	IS 5 ONE 15	1
Thingish with moondrool and i'm ever so very little	303	IS 5 FIVE 2	7
again in never's ear (i'm tho thcared giggling lithped . . .	316	VIVA 8	6
thin bums dream ing i'm thick in a hot	469	NEW POEMS 7	3
to where --name unless i'm mistaken chauvesouris-- whose . .	504	50 POEMS 18	9
was a glove but i'm and you are actual	538	50 POEMS 50	10
me you leap and i'm born we 're sunlight	589	1 X 1 49	19
this trickiest if? why i'm by much the luckiest	590	1 X 1 50	17
silence)?" "Worlds? o no: i'm certain they're (look again) .	603	(CHAIRE) 5	5
/ / / / i'm asking you dear to	638	(CHAIRE) 40	1
passed (as close as i'm to you yes closer	648	(CHAIRE) 50	9
hunting for ann well i'm looking for will" "did	707	95 POEMS 35	1
who but your daughter i'm asking yes who but	707	95 POEMS 35	13
liberal titty and lisps "i'm busy right now" so	711	95 POEMS 39	24
than you're alive or i'm-- crying to lose (as	716	95 POEMS 44	32
of everything true) and i'm no (if deeply less	720	95 POEMS 48	11
unbig a why as i'm (almost too small for	735	95 POEMS 63	1
precisely as unbig as i'm a why (almost too	735	95 POEMS 63	9
dear) as living as i'm and as you're --let's	769	95 POEMS 95	25
(as you're as can i'm) they flock and they	801	73 POEMS 29	14

I'VE

	PAGE	TITLE	LINE
and with the others i've been Effie who isn't	117	& PORTRAIT 10	23
him be pitiful: because i've travelled all alone through . .	216	XLI SONNETS 12	11
walls) an electromagnetic (now I've lost the) Einstein . . .	315	VIVA 7	4
to decline to admit i've died) seeing your bald	329	VIVA 20	2
/ / / / i've come to ask you	572	1 X 1 32	1
you have known and i've only we our least	574	1 X 1 34	13
a rose no rose i've and losing's less than	684	95 POEMS 12	18
luckiest of lucky days i've loved, shall love, do	734	95 POEMS 62	3
everywhere which you've and i've agreed and we've (with . . .	741	95 POEMS 69	12
a mystery for which i've no word except alive	802	73 POEMS 30	13

+I'VE

	PAGE	TITLE	LINE
FOR CONTEXT, SEE	686	95 POEMS 14	6

ICE

	PAGE	TITLE	LINE
the poisonous fragility of ice newly formed upon an	103	& POST IMPR 13	12

		PAGE	TITLE	LINE
ICE (CONTINUED)				
care so what yoo-gointa-doo? (ice coal wood man) nic		618	{CHAIRE} 20	19
ICECAKES				
surrounded by well- drawn icecakes beheld being too strong, .		262	IS 5 ONE 32	12
ICECOALWOOD				
of his ZOOM DOOM icecoalwood truck a wistful little		680	95 POEMS 8	5
ICEMAN				
dark dear oh) the iceman how, luminously oh how		251	IS 5 ONE 22	14
ICI				
as a forgotten prisoner --"Ici?" --"Ah non, mon cheri; . . .		304	IS 5 FIVE 3	10
ICY				
on flat pavements with icy cries of this and		142	& SON REAL 13	7
head him) do through icy waters roll that helplessness . . .		339	VIVA 30	9
who music wear burst icy known swim ignorant fire		533	50 POEMS 45	15
ID				
; tee-die uM-tuM tidl -id umptyumpty (OO-- ! ting		426	NO THANKS 43	23
not begin to live id est breathe but if		510	50 POEMS 24	6
wurl sho am wick id id ar (now heer		519	50 POEMS 33	12
sho am wick id id ar (now heer we		519	50 POEMS 33	12
boy (day simbully loves id) fer ids dare pain		519	50 POEMS 33	21
mahmah hadn chuzd nogged id entwhys / / /		790	73 POEMS 18	16
moangrowl-&-thin g stirs (m id) a life whats wh		795	73 POEMS 23	7
IDE				
land of the Arrow Ide and Earl & Wilson		230	IS 5 ONE 2	7
IDEA				
/ SNO a white idea (Listen drenches: earth's ugly)		99	& POST IMPR 10	2
don't speak A white idea, drenching. earth's brain detaches .		99	& POST IMPR 10	19
in millionaires a cute idea n'est-ce pas? (whereas, upon . .		245	IS 5 ONE 16	14
IDEAL				
that notable structure or ideal edifice... situated or . . .		319	VIVA 11	23
IDEALISTS				
(alarm ing notion for idealists? so what) all politicians . .		790	73 POEMS 18	11
IDEAS				
as if They were ideas?" "because, sir things which		91	& POST IMPR 3	10
would suggest that certain ideas gestures rhymes, like . . .		230	IS 5 ONE 2	19
solid bliss for youse ideas i'll match youse a		247	IS 5 ONE 18	6
waxworks filled with dead ideas (the oh quintillions of . . .		250	IS 5 ONE 21	10
back dressed in fifteenthrate ideas wearing a round jeer . .		258	IS 5 ONE 28	3
being dollars toenails or ideas thoroughly's stolen		322	VIVA 14	8
assassinating whole grassblades, five ideas can swallow a . .		491	50 POEMS 5	13
IDENTITY				
which hints being; suggests identity) breathes fleet		402	NO THANKS 19	10
IDIOM				
with keen creatures of idiom (beings alert and innocent . . .		19	T&C PUELLA MEA	93
sculptor of your body's idiom: the musician of your		291	IS 5 FOUR 8	7
IDIOT				
Weak thirsty fists of idiot futures bash the bragging		151	& SON REAL 22	6
before me a mellifluous idiot grin (with what was		226	IS 5 ONE MAME	2
heart, singing like an idiot, whispering like a drunken . . .		304	IS 5 FIVE 3	3
fate) coward, clown, traitor, idiot, dreamer, beast-- such .		562	1 X 1 22	9
IDIOTIC				
give rapid lapfulls of idiotic big hands / /		251	IS 5 ONE 22	23
IDIOTICALLY				
every but any) heart--wholly, idiotically--before such . . .		480	NEW POEMS 18	4
IDLE				
when the your-and my- idle vertical worthless self unite . .		260	IS 5 ONE 30	15
IDLENESS				
of shall we say: Idleness, while meaning its opposite? . . .		263	IS 5 ONE 32	39
IDLING				
(s gruntsqueak , while, idling-is-grindstone one; what: of. .		656	{CHAIRE} 58	7
+IDLING-IS-GRINDSTON				
(s gruntsqueak , while, idling-is-grindstone one; what: of. .		656	{CHAIRE} 58	7
IDLY				
faces which pass rap idly with their breaths.) "people . . .		354	VIVA 45	11
e lurche s viv idly from ti (& d		703	95 POEMS 31	8
IF				
upon sunny wings as if in terror of eternity, ...		6	T&C EPITHALAM	139
call rich beyond wishing if this thou catch, else		13	T&C SONGS 3	18

IF (CONTINUED)

	PAGE	TITLE	LINE
Herod's silence, long ago. If she a little turn	17	T&C PUELLA MEA	33
whose leman was. And if my lady look at	17	T&C PUELLA MEA	38
a little lovelier. And if she speak in her	18	T&C PUELLA MEA	77
did in nothing err. If to me there shall	21	T&C PUELLA MEA	175
is divinely shy; as if for fear you would	22	T&C PUELLA MEA	216
the little distinct foot (if whose very minuteness doth . . .	22	T&C PUELLA MEA	217
roses and of ivory if naked she appear to	22	T&C PUELLA MEA	231
/ / / / if i believe in death	39	T&C AMORES 4	1
departed mouth sweetly-saluted lingers. if one marvel seeing	42	T&C AMORES 6	8
perfect hours dead too, if that he come receive	42	T&C AMORES 6	18
of my unkempt adoration if i have made a	43	T&C AMORES 7	3
thunder into freshness as if god's flowers were pulling . . .	58	T&C PORTRAIT 6	9
to the queer monkey (if you toss him a	69	T&C POST IMPR 6	10
not care, above Cambridge if sometimes in its box	70	T&C SON REAL 1	12
of perspiration erectly sitting. --If they knew you at . . .	73	T&C SON REAL 4	10
and i say that if your lips, which i	76	T&C SON UNRE 1	2
time not far away; if on another's face your	76	T&C SON UNRE 1	5
the spirit at bay; if this should be, i	76	T&C SON UNRE 1	9
should be, i say if this should be-- you	76	T&C SON UNRE 1	9
quick of twilight ....or if sunset utters one unhurried . . .	82	T&C SON ACTU 1	7
excelled by speaking flower (if i have made songs	84	T&C SON ACTU 3	6
you touch flowers as if they were unalive, as	91	& POST IMPR 3	9
they were unalive, as if They were ideas?" "because, ...	91	& POST IMPR 3	10
Take for example this: if to the colour of	92	& POST IMPR 4	2
possible and beautiful sound: if a (perhaps) clock strikes, .	92	& POST IMPR 4	14
wholly miss you; or if i certainly create, lady, ...	92	& POST IMPR 4	20
fists of tint. TUMTITUMTIDDLE if sometimes my eyes stay . . .	100	& POST IMPR 11	18
nice concupiscence appeared rounded. if she were alive, death	103	& POST IMPR 13	17
i declare to you if what i am at	115	& PORTRAIT 8	5
five crumbs chuckled as if they were alive and	117	& PORTRAIT 10	14
do it again or if it talks about you	126	& SEVEN POEMS 5	18
pleasant and stoopid and if dead says may i	126	& SEVEN POEMS 5	19
drunkard passes who knows if the moon's a balloon, ...	129	& SEVEN POEMS 7	1
with pretty people? (and if you and i should	129	& SEVEN POEMS 7	4
should get into it, if they should take me	129	& SEVEN POEMS 7	5
hot subliminal lips, as if a score of youngest	130	& SON REAL 1	4
(and one would see if it could) eyes say	150	& SON REAL 21	2
loved, let us see if that's all. Bit into	154	& SON ACTU 3	1
smile into stupid gardens if this were not enough	154	& SON ACTU 3	6
because . dusk and if it perhaps drea-mingly Is	155	& SON ACTU 4	3
/ / / / if i should sleep with	161	& SON ACTU 10	1
knows makes me wonder if i'm alive (eye pries, ...	166	& SON ACTU 15	10
night. makes me wonder if, if i am the	166	& SON ACTU 15	12
makes me wonder if, if i am the face	166	& SON ACTU 15	12
at each other. Nudge. (if they love each other, ...	171	& SON ACTU 20	11
in her hair, (but if you ask the rain	183	XLI SONGS 5	5
played each card as if it were a thunderbolt	194	XLI PORTRAIT 2	23
/ / / SONNETS if learned darkness from our	205	XLI SONNETS 1	1
of thy eyes, and if thy hands flowers of	205	XLI SONNETS 1	3
life almost do guess) if god should send the	205	XLI SONNETS 1	9
almost than you. Yet if not flower, tell me	211	XLI SONNETS 7	6
time is fed: and if i like not what	212	XLI SONNETS 8	9
astounding everlasting air-- but if i like, i'll take . . .	212	XLI SONNETS 8	13
of her youth. And if somebody hears what i	216	XLI SONNETS 12	9
her mouth thinks of (if it were a kiss)	225	IS 5 ONE LIZ	14
rings the bell. But if her tall corpsecoloured body	227	IS 5 ONE GERT	8
Resharpened. (Case in point if we are to believe	230	IS 5 ONE 2	24
Shirttails Into Drawers and If It Isn't An Eastman	230	IS 5 ONE 2	34
all of you successfully if delicately gelded (or spaded) . .	231	IS 5 ONE 3	43
better-- what's become of (if you please) all the	233	IS 5 ONE 4	10
/ / / even if all desires things moments	237	IS 5 ONE 8	1
(and me and you if we're not very careful)	250	IS 5 ONE 21	4
nobody he looked as if he did not care	258	IS 5 ONE 28	16
unimportant) whereas Life matters if or when the your-and . .	260	IS 5 ONE 30	13
brief : an American, if you understand that i	262	IS 5 ONE 32	13
it is hardly surprising if anyone hardly should call	263	IS 5 ONE 32	35
us perhaps excuse me if i repeat himself: these, ...	263	IS 5 ONE 32	59

		PAGE	TITLE	LINE

IF (CONTINUED)

	PAGE	TITLE	LINE
train after all arrived. If i should have made	263	IS 5 ONE 32	63
sing with who cares if some oneeyed son of	264	IS 5 ONE 33	27
is crum bs (alll) if, ey Es / /	265	IS 5 ONE 34	8
was a privilege and if only he could meanwhile	276	IS 5 TWO 10	17
/ / / / if being mortised with a	285	IS 5 FOUR 2	1
your mind may guess if at sunset it should, ...	285	IS 5 FOUR 2	12
/ / / but if i should say goodmorning	287	IS 5 FOUR 4	1
that nigger's face (but If i should say thankyouverymuch . .	287	IS 5 FOUR 4	7
with beringed hands) but if i Should say solong	287	IS 5 FOUR 4	9
in a dream (but if i should say Now	287	IS 5 FOUR 4	13
all saucers but cups if begin to spoons dance	287	IS 5 FOUR 4	16
know what happens) but if i should, Say, /	287	IS 5 FOUR 4	20
one least smile (shyly if a poem should lift	291	IS 5 FOUR 8	25
dream is noone's fool; if this wind who i	292	IS 5 FOUR 9	11
wonderful jealousy is dark if light should flower: or	292	IS 5 FOUR 9	17
contain new faeries (and if your slim lips are	294	IS 5 FOUR 11	10
seriously --that since and if you disappear solemnly myselves	295	IS 5 FOUR 12	11
down to? love? Love if you like and i	295	IS 5 FOUR 12	22
/ / / / if within tonight's erect everywhere	299	IS 5 FOUR 16	1
me, my very lady, if scarcely the somewhat city	302	IS 5 FIVE 1	3
particular road the moon if you'll notice follows us	303	IS 5 FIVE 2	9
/ / / / if i have made, my	306	IS 5 FIVE 5	1
whitest song upon my mind--if i have failed to	306	IS 5 FIVE 5	5
snare the glance too shy--if through my singing slips	306	IS 5 FIVE 5	6
things Each at other (if not quarrelling in a	312	VIVA 4	13
By invisibilities spattered (or if it may be socalled) . . .	317	VIVA 9	20
thick glass you try if we are a gentleman	326	VIVA 18	5
not deem it miraculous if their (so to speak)	326	VIVA 18	8
away: "on the whole" (if you will permit a	326	VIVA 18	27
he considered "elevating--that is, if dancing CAN be ele- . .	327	VIVA 18	40
cambridge, mass. i try if you are a gentleman	327	VIVA 18	45
soak sulksuck whim poke if inch dimmer twist on	333	VIVA 24	12
"is" dead he's "dead" if he wouldn't have eaten	336	VIVA 27	10
imagine real flowers for if I could, they would	338	VIVA 29	8
cafes people drink smile if here there (like lopsided	340	VIVA 31	9
dream; new . oh if when: & a nd	350	VIVA 41	13
/ / / / if there are any heavens	352	VIVA 43	1
/ i'd think "wonder if" if i were a	353	VIVA 44	2
i'd think "wonder if" if i were a child	353	VIVA 44	2
exquisitely ,like dead children (if he had been playing . . .	355	VIVA 46	18
/ / / / if i love You (thickness	363	VIVA 54	1
roamingly stern bright faeries if you love me) distance . . .	363	VIVA 54	5
gnomes Of complete dream if we love each (shyly)	363	VIVA 54	9
or how dreaming becomes if your heart's mine) i	364	VIVA 55	5
big there is but if so or so slowly	365	VIVA 56	10
her first rose or if your wish be to	366	VIVA 57	9
/ / / / if you and i awakening	370	VIVA 61	1
still unvisible when. Wait if i am not heart, ...	372	VIVA 63	6
you knew once? what if (merely suppose) mine should	374	VIVA 65	10
/ / / but if a living dance upon	377	VIVA 68	1
and perpetual sea --but if yourself consider wonderful that .	379	VIVA 70	10
not when or unless if or to prove, imperfectly	386	NO THANKS 3	6
i kn w & if you d n't why	392	NO THANKS 9	6
are Not more than (if Green invents because where	395	NO THANKS 12	6
like this said he if you kiss said she	399	NO THANKS 16	16
it love said she) if you're willing said he	399	NO THANKS 16	19
touched renown) suddenly themselves if all dreams unmake . .	414	NO THANKS 31	5
he which knows not if any anguish struck how	414	NO THANKS 31	7
november's may) from whose (if loud most howish time	420	NO THANKS 37	5
thighs to fate and (if you can withholding nothing)	420	NO THANKS 37	13
ul lydesc BYS FLUTTERFULLY IF (endbegi ndesginb ecend) tang .	421	NO THANKS 38	8
/ / / as if as if a mys	423	NO THANKS 40	1
/ as if as if a mys teriouSly ("i	423	NO THANKS 40	2
and let must or if be damned with whomever's	424	NO THANKS 41	8
may vibration create voice if therefore among foul pains . .	425	NO THANKS 42	13
foul pains appears an if emerges a joy let	425	NO THANKS 42	13
rises, and; droops as if upon a thread invisible)	434	NO THANKS 51	21

IF (CONTINUED)

a Five Year Plan: if Joy with Pain shall . . . . 438 NO THANKS 54   7
to kiss the mike if Jew turn kike who . . . . 438 NO THANKS 54   15
sick, Minds nothing can: if Hate's a game and . . . . 438 NO THANKS 54   23
(love may not care if time totters, light droops, ... 446 NO THANKS 61   6
measures bend nor marvel if a thought should weigh . . . . . 446 NO THANKS 61   7
/ / / / if night's mostness (and whom . . . . 450 NO THANKS 65   1
merely day close) opens if more than silence silent . . . . 450 NO THANKS 65   4
whitely births of mind if air is throbbing prayers . . . . . 450 NO THANKS 65   6
adventuring who would feel if spring's least breathing should 450 NO THANKS 65   13
/ / / / if i or anybody don't . . . . 475 NEW POEMS 13   1
that doesn't matter (and if he she it or . . . . 475 NEW POEMS 13   6
that doesn't matter) but if somebody or you are . . . . . . 475 NEW POEMS 13   12
/ / / hanged if n y in a . . . . 476 NEW POEMS 14   2
under weakening stars Feels; if & god said & . . . . 479 NEW POEMS 17   11
bursts only so; only if you should turn the . . . . 479 NEW POEMS 17   17
of beauty; before keen if dim quiveringly spangle & . . . . 480 NEW POEMS 18   7
than to know and if men should not hear . . . . 481 NEW POEMS 19   4
and supple and even if it's sunday may i . . . . 481 NEW POEMS 19   7
glad and young. For if you're young, whatever life . . . . . 484 NEW POEMS 22   2
will become you; and if you are glad whatever's . . . . . . 484 NEW POEMS 22   3
/ / / / If you can't eat you . . . . 489 50 POEMS 3   1
let's go to sleep if you can't smoke you . . . . 489 50 POEMS 3   5
let's go to sleep if you can't sing you . . . . 489 50 POEMS 3   9
let's go to sleep if you can't die you . . . . 489 50 POEMS 3   13
prowst but respects artists if they are sincere proud . . . . 499 50 POEMS 13   11
wonens will allows which if they don't to hell . . . . 500 50 POEMS 14   23
star and without was if minus and shall be . . . . 502 50 POEMS 16   5
have lost their shadows if which did not do . . . . 502 50 POEMS 16   11
feeble go to sleep if the people sit down) . . . . 505 50 POEMS 19   8
being born) when and if nothing disappears they will . . . . 505 50 POEMS 19   18
went head face goes (if how begins a pillow's . . . . 506 50 POEMS 20   9
have no minds but if they had their minds . . . . 510 50 POEMS 24   3
would not exist but if these not existing minds . . . . . . 510 50 POEMS 24   5
id est breathe but if such life could its . . . . 510 50 POEMS 24   7
thousands of people socalled if multiplied by twice infinity 510 50 POEMS 24   10
doesn't determine its roundness: if swallows tryst in your . 514 50 POEMS 28   6
in a mist and if (by Him Whose blood . . . . 514 50 POEMS 28   9
wish by spirit and if by yes. Women and . . . . 515 50 POEMS 29   32
of mere eternity) stupendous if discoverably disappearing . . 517 50 POEMS 31   2
to shining here; that if (so timid air is . . . . 520 50 POEMS 34   7
him in the head; if every friend became his . . . . 521 50 POEMS 34   47
with blossoming eyes know if a lit tle tree . . . . 525 50 POEMS 37   18
and give him nothing (if he should not sing) . . . . 531 50 POEMS 43   12
of us darling. And if i sing you are . . . . 531 50 POEMS 43   14
be (the wise fool) if living's to give so . . . . 543 1 X 1 3   15
in its polloi and if sometimes he's prodded forth . . . . . 544 1 X 1 4   9
no more difference than if it sells hate condoms . . . . . 549 1 X 1 9   10
know a hopeless case if--listen: there's a hell of . . . . 554 1 X 1 14   14
ye screamers, till your if is up and vanish . . . . 555 1 X 1 15   9
mystery miracle peace: or (if begin the colours of . . . . 559 1 X 1 19   5
april than the year (if all her most first . . . . 559 1 X 1 19   13
/ / / what if a much of a . . . . 560 1 X 1 20   1
still be man what if a keen of a . . . . 560 1 X 1 20   9
to the spring what if a dawn of a . . . . 560 1 X 1 20   17
--plunged in eternal now if who're by the five . . . . . . 561 1 X 1 21   9
/ / no man, if men are gods; but . . . . 562 1 X 1 22   1
men are gods; but if gods must be men, ... 562 1 X 1 22   1
most rare) a fiend, if fiends speak truth; if . . . . 562 1 X 1 22   5
if fiends speak truth; if angels burn by their . . . . . . 562 1 X 1 22   5
ever named mountains more if than each known allness . . . . 563 1 X 1 23   5
(once like a spark) if strangers meet life begins-- . . . . 564 1 X 1 24   2
only truthful --truthfully, once if strangers (who deep our . 564 1 X 1 24   13
like out of it if you gut a mind . . . . 567 1 X 1 27   13
in -ch of an if & who is the . . . . 571 1 X 1 31   8
come to ask you if there isn't a new . . . . 572 1 X 1 32   1
outside your window saying if that's all, just if" . . . . . 572 1 X 1 32   2
if that's all, just if" "that's all there is . . . . 572 1 X 1 32   3

		PAGE	TITLE	LINE
IF (CONTINUED)				
beside their glories downward if they'll or goldenly float	.	573	1 X 1 33	7
as yes is to if, love is to yes		574	1 X 1 34	4
outgrow all whose mosts if you have known and		574	1 X 1 34	13
would truest lovers grow if out of midnight dropped		576	1 X 1 36	12
than are (yes; and if time should ask into		576	1 X 1 36	13
more secretly than our (if disappear should some world) . . .		577	1 X 1 37	7
even snow melts; and if spring should spoil the		579	1 X 1 39	4
they'll scarcely find us (if they do, we'll move		579	1 X 1 39	13
under the spring --but if a look should april		580	1 X 1 40	6
limp and prove --but if a look should april		580	1 X 1 40	11
nothing) nothing's won --but if a look should april		580	1 X 1 40	19
begins to yes but if a look should april		580	1 X 1 40	22
/ / / / if (among silent skies bluer		583	1 X 1 43	1
: april's they this if now or this (young		583	1 X 1 43	8
the earth must fly if a truth is a		587	1 X 1 47	16
littlest why, it into if shall climb all the		588	1 X 1 48	2
million whys; but opening if are those eyes every		588	1 X 1 48	7
fool in this trickiest if? why i'm by much		590	1 X 1 50	16
multiplied with infinity sans if the mightiest meditations of		592	1 X 1 52	5
/ / / / if everything happens that can't		594	1 X 1 54	1
very magically smiling and if we are not perfectly		600	{CHAIRE} 2	10
but differently; or as if worlds wanted us to		603	{CHAIRE} 5	8
never close (and open) if that fool called everyone		603	{CHAIRE} 5	9
i wouldn't like Death if Death were good: for		604	{CHAIRE} 6	6
stare are still wondering if the stunt was really		605	{CHAIRE} 7	14
/ / / / if the green opens a		614	{CHAIRE} 16	1
and much is too if the green robe o		614	{CHAIRE} 16	9
worshipping (as calmly as if aristide maillols occurred with		617	{CHAIRE} 19	13
no new moon in if all screech-owls have not		620	{CHAIRE} 22	6
can hear him still if now our sun is		624	{CHAIRE} 26	22
and sorrow a system-- if now than forever could		625	{CHAIRE} 27	21
/ / / / if a cheerfulest Elephantangelchild should		631	{CHAIRE} 33	1
red christmas bow) --and if, when we meet again, ...		631	{CHAIRE} 33	7
swoop mountains flimsying become if who'd) me under a		634	{CHAIRE} 36	4
to forgive divine) that if the quote state unquote		636	{CHAIRE} 38	7
absolute (my soul tastes If as some world of		639	{CHAIRE} 41	7
and blind with an if in its soul and		647	{CHAIRE} 49	12
wings would be streaming if something had (maybe they		652	{CHAIRE} 54	13
wanders: exact ly; as if not hing had, ever		655	{CHAIRE} 57	11
/ / / / if (touched by love's own		659	{CHAIRE} 61	1
mountains) in april (but if he should Smile) comes		660	{CHAIRE} 62	25
be they'll some or if where shall breathe a		666	{CHAIRE} 68	6
dare be beautiful one if should sing (at yes		666	{CHAIRE} 68	16
lifts our blood as if whole supreme this complete		675	95 POEMS 3	7
made --yes; or as if our souls, awakened from		675	95 POEMS 3	9
torn trousers (quite as if he were really her		680	95 POEMS 8	17
matching onceupons each bothing (if) creep (by if) timelessly		681	95 POEMS 9	9
bothing (if) creep (by if) timelessly foundlost glad		681	95 POEMS 9	10
"he'll give me another if i let him kiss		684	95 POEMS 12	10
here with paradise) forgetting if, remember yes in time . . .		688	95 POEMS 16	9
here&gone) flesh all is If all blood And When		690	95 POEMS 18	7
bowed to immortal us if in one little bed		694	95 POEMS 22	7
po wer) say o if i 'd OH n		700	95 POEMS 28	11
shru gg ing as if to say b ut		703	95 POEMS 31	15
i s ell drunk if i be pencils /		703	95 POEMS 31	19
time of year-- and if what calls itself a		717	95 POEMS 45	9
am wandering a town (if its houses turning into		720	95 POEMS 48	1
true) and i'm no (if deeply less conceivable than		720	95 POEMS 48	12
's our (home means if any moon or possibly		728	95 POEMS 56	5
wind) trust your heart if the seas catch fire		732	95 POEMS 60	6
/ / over us if (as what was dusk		741	95 POEMS 69	1
is not worth dying, if (and when) roses complain		744	95 POEMS 72	2
--i do not worry if briefer days grow briefest, ...		749	95 POEMS 77	3
--i do not worry if longer nights grow longest;		749	95 POEMS 77	15
makes losing, gaining --love! if a world ends more		750	95 POEMS 78	15
/ / / / if the Lovestar grows most		752	95 POEMS 80	1
who comforts his children, if he disappears; till of		756	95 POEMS 84	6

	PAGE	TITLE	LINE

IF (CONTINUED)

not a universe-- but if, with goldenly his fathering . . . . 756 95 POEMS 84   9
now alive creatures (bright if by shadowy if) swallowing . . 757 95 POEMS 85   10
(bright if by shadowy if) swallowing is everywhere . . . . . 757 95 POEMS 85   12
Black er than est if Im agines more than . . . . 759 95 POEMS 86   6
lived a gayer he; if earth and sky should . . . . 760 95 POEMS 87   7
poems are opening, as if an earth was playing . . . . 763 95 POEMS 90   5
equally they're welcome --as if the humble proud youngest . . 763 95 POEMS 90   15
/ / / / if up's the word; and . . . . 769 95 POEMS 95   1
and most by more-- if death is the loser . . . . 769 95 POEMS 95   3
into far near blue if beggars are rich (and . . . . 769 95 POEMS 95   22
chappy who doesn't agree (if you can't dentham comma . . . . 791 73 POEMS 19   5
/ / / / if seventy were young and . . . . 798 73 POEMS 26   1
would be to sing if broken hearts were whole . . . . 798 73 POEMS 26   8
would be a smile if sorrowful were gay (today . . . . 798 73 POEMS 26   15
greedy the people (as if as can yes) they . . . . 801 73 POEMS 29   2
hour when is becomes if) a bespangled clown standing . . . . 802 73 POEMS 30   3
/ / / / if in beginning twilight of . . . . 808 73 POEMS 36   1
/ / / silently if, out of not knowable . . . . 810 73 POEMS 38   1
your smile sings or if (spiralling as luminous they . . . . 810 73 POEMS 38   5
mercy of that star, if out of climbing whom . . . . 811 73 POEMS 39   12
because and sings an if of day to yes . . . . 815 73 POEMS 43   7
sunset (and feeling: that if day has to become . . . . . . 824 73 POEMS 52   6
lf a shy (an if a whis per a . . . . 831 73 POEMS 59   11
concerning no and yes: if they've become the same . . . . . 834 73 POEMS 62   17
to live) must die" "if i should tell you . . . . 836 73 POEMS 64   6
and even fiends: or, if he paints with sound, ... 842 73 POEMS 70   5
a dream speak; or if to no millionth metaphor . . . . 842 73 POEMS 70   11
life's eye (which is if things seem spirits) or . . . . . . 845 73 POEMS 73   2
things seem spirits) or (if spirits in the guise . . . . . 845 73 POEMS 73   3

+IF

FOR CONTEXT, SEE . . . . 790 73 POEMS 18   16

IF'S

is a pleasant country: if's wintry (my lovely) let's . . . . 578 1 X 1 38   2

IFBUT

wherelings whenlings (daughters of ifbut offspring of . . . . 512 50 POEMS 26   2

IFLESS

& through slowquickly opening ifless this irre- VocA -ble . . 719 95 POEMS 47   7

IFLIKE

finally and always, the iflike moon over moving me--the . . . 384 NO THANKS 2   12

IFS

clouds. kisses, lice; headaches: ifs.) yet shall our . . . . 361 VIVA 52   20
stars; climbing silence for ifs diving under because) only . 439 NO THANKS 55   23
keen star whom she-and-he-like ifs of am perceive (but . . . 808 73 POEMS 36   8

+IFS

FOR CONTEXT, SEE . . . . 445 NO THANKS 60   3

IGNATZ

exhumed hand of Saint Ignatz miraculously inhabits. (people . 280 IS 5 THREE 4   4

IGNOBLE

puny impatient and nothing ignoble) everywhere wonder / . . 658 {CHAIRE} 60   25

IGNOBLEST

the of an it ignoblest he to nowhere from . . . . 662 {CHAIRE} 64   1

IGNORANCE

/ / / all ignorance toboggans into know and . . . . 579 1 X 1 39   1
and trudges up to ignorance again: but winter's not . . . . 579 1 X 1 39   2
love with one least ignorance may comprehend more than . . . 761 95 POEMS 88   2
eclipsing of a spirit's ignorance by every wisdom knowledge . 843 73 POEMS 71   10

IGNORANT

upon the fragrant unspeaking ignorant darkness of New Lady . 112 & PORTRAIT 6   98
(aiming for hugely the ignorant most precise essential flame 373 VIVA 64   7
his mind feeling throughout ignorant disappearing me hurling 428 NO THANKS 45   7
shall discovered be) whose ignorant each breathing dares to . 446 NO THANKS 61   11
burst icy known swim ignorant fire (adventuring and time's . 533 50 POEMS 45   16
the actual more minds ignorant of stern miraculous this . . . 556 1 X 1 16   5
nonchalant wise and each ignorant gladness--unteaches what . 764 95 POEMS 90   40

IGNORANTLY

for my doom pass ignorantly into sleep's bright land . . . . 358 VIVA 49   15
mad rags strode earth ignorantly blossoming a scarecrow . . . 662 {CHAIRE} 64   7

IGNORING
     green facts preening solemnity ignoring, through its indolent 344 VIVA 35   3
II
     (m x x x ii) I / / /   . . . . 388 NO THANKS 5   39
IKEY
     / / / / IKEY (GOLDBERG)'S WORTH I'M TOLD   . . . . 244 IS 5 ONE 15   1
IL
     into this noth ing il treno per Roma si-gnori?   . . . . 278 IS 5 THREE 2   19
     --"Ah non, mon cheri; il fait trop froid"-- they   . . . . . . 304 IS 5 FIVE 3   10
     que tu veux Dwrith il est trop fort le   . . . . 430 NO THANKS 47   20
ILL
     handsome moon never spoke ill of the pretty stars . . . . . . 43 T&C AMORES 7   14
     at which (shal) lpounceupcrackw (ill) jumps of THuNdeRB . . . 347 VIVA 38   8
     every minus plus --fare ill: fare well-- a frown   . . . . . . 798 73 POEMS 26   13
ILLEGITIMATE
     right of majorities, that illegitimate offspring of the . . . 803 73 POEMS 31   3
ILLIMITABLE
     languorous hymn pledged to illimitable dissipation unhurried 206 XLI SONNETS 2   13
     with your eyes any illimitable star / / /. . . . . 526 50 POEMS 38   12
     spark 's gulped by illimitable hell) and never have . . . . . 639 (CHAIRE) 41   8
     also me the keen illimitable secret of begin /   . . . . 669 (CHAIRE) 71   14
     night spirits and with illimitable day (shrived of that . . . 745 95 POEMS 73   8
     humble one (gifted with illimitable joy) bird sings love's . 783 73 POEMS 11   2
     / pity his how illimitable plight who dies to . . . . 842 73 POEMS 70   1
+ILLIMITABLE
     FOR CONTEXT, SEE   . . . . 600 (CHAIRE) 2   13
ILLIMITABLY
     joy: quietly & before illimitably spiralling candy of tiniest 480 NEW POEMS 18   21
     whole verbal adventure to illimitably Grow / / /   . . . . . . 557 1 X 1 17   16
     how more than sleep illimitably my --being so very   . . . . . 558 1 X 1 18   11
     welcoming his only and illimitably his destiny) mountains! . 626 (CHAIRE) 28   8
     the gay great happening illimitably earth) how should tasting 663 (CHAIRE) 65   8
     (only herself and who illimitably is) making fools understand 736 95 POEMS 64   4
     that this and tree illimitably try to seize the . . . . 822 73 POEMS 50   5
ILLS
     dirtied glass) Pills for Ills (a recipe against Laughing . . 359 VIVA 50   8
ILLUSION
     departed is youth's indispensable illusion" / / / / . . . . . 57 T&C PORTRAIT 5   41
ILLUSTRIOUS
     when my once more illustrious arms are filled with   . . . . . 78 T&C SON UNRE 3   9
     LIVE that Upwardlooking Serene Illustrious and Beatific Lord 315 VIVA 7   12
     hovers how slenderly the illustrious unknown (warily as their 344 VIVA 35   11
     are holy, poets mad, illustrious punks of Progress shriek; . 438 NO THANKS 54   20
     implacable unthing next, our illustrious scientist petitions 799 73 POEMS 27   23
ILS
     et les americains aussi, ils payent bien les americains . . . 120 & PORTRAIT 12   27
IMAGE
     consult with some delicious image the a little strolling . . 193 XLI PORTRAIT 1   7
     that loveliness receiving the image my proud heart cherished 207 XLI SONNETS 3   13
     & her his Its image strutting (very jerkily) not   . . . . . . 335 VIVA 26   10
     a spoon, collects the image of one fatal word;   . . . . 360 VIVA 51   22
IMAGINABLE
     the price of an imaginable gesture exact warm unholy   . . . . 162 & SON ACTU 11   16
     once more with the imaginable, love, and eat sunlight . . . . 289 IS 5 FOUR 6   8
     put on one not imaginable star : then a . . . . 454 NO THANKS 69   12
     forget something) livingest the imaginable moon / / / . . . . 599 (CHAIRE) 1   14
     (beyond death and life) imaginable mysteries / / / . . . . . 674 95 POEMS 2   13
     flaming dream) merge--at not imaginable which instant born, a 721 95 POEMS 49   12
     whiteness: absolute peace, never imaginable mystery) descend 839 73 POEMS 67   15
+IMAGINABLE
     FOR CONTEXT, SEE   . . . . 754 95 POEMS 82   12
IMAGINABLY
     miracle" his always not imaginably morethanmostgenerous . . . 823 73 POEMS 51   12
IMAGINATION
     never to have no imagination) or never never to . . . . 242 IS 5 ONE 13   3
     your hair in my imagination / / / / . . . . 356 VIVA 47   23
     a leastful most under imagination. When (out of sheer . . . . 432 NO THANKS 49   14
     of an angel named imagination / / / / . . . . 639 (CHAIRE) 41   14

	PAGE	TITLE	LINE

+IMAGINATION
    FOR CONTEXT, SEE . . . . 397 NO THANKS 14   22
IMAGINATIONS
    here there (like lopsided imaginations) filled with newly . . 340 VIVA 31   10
IMAGINE
    other somethings did-- you imagine His surprise bellowing . . 117 & PORTRAIT 10   8
    who isn't alive just imagine it I say God . . . . 117 & PORTRAIT 10   25
    / / (and i imagine never mind Joe agreeably . . . . 241 IS 5 ONE 12   1
    continued eating. And i imagine she, and heard them . . . . 241 IS 5 ONE 12   6
    loved like you can't imagine Harry was o god . . . . 271 IS 5 TWO 6   10
    no longer, can you imagine it i can't which . . . . 289 IS 5 FOUR 6   4
    i dreamed this) only imagine, when day has thrilled . . . . 292 IS 5 FOUR 9   2
    gloominess of (try to imagine) whispering of a named . . . . 324 VIVA 16   14
    people are in real: imagine somewhere real flowers, but . . . 338 VIVA 29   6
    flowers, but I can't imagine real flowers for if . . . . . . 338 VIVA 29   8
    without love separate, smileless--merely imagine your sorrow 374 VIVA 65   2
    love by frequent anguish (imagine Her least never with . . . 453 NO THANKS 68   9
    begin to begin to imagine how (only are shall . . . . 512 50 POEMS 26   17
    mud and mire, scheming imagine, passion willed, freedom a . . 521 50 POEMS 34   55
    not have (but i imagine that yes is the . . . . 528 50 POEMS 40   13
    become more am than imagine / / / / . . . . 571 1 X 1 31   17
    just isn't what we imagine but please for god's . . . . . . 638 (CHAIRE) 40   9
    Once happened nowhere else imagine Now rapidly this (a . . . 693 95 POEMS 21   9
    could not love, dear; imagine ourselves like living neither . 743 95 POEMS 71   4
    / / i shall imagine life is not worth . . . . 744 95 POEMS 72   1
    " could begin to imagine quite such eagerly innocent . . . . 748 95 POEMS 76   13
    of 8 ysomethi ng (imagine) with, pansies / / . . . . 792 73 POEMS 20   16
    begin to begin to imagine) something which nobody may . . . . 816 73 POEMS 44   12
    poets, lovers tell- measure imagine, mystery, a kiss --not . 817 73 POEMS 45   10
    spirit is) and partially imagine whose despair when every . . 842 73 POEMS 70   9
+IMAGINE
    FOR CONTEXT, SEE . . . . 704 95 POEMS 32   13
    FOR CONTEXT, SEE . . . . 779 73 POEMS 7   29
IMAGINED
    of twilight trembles the imagined galleon of Spring) . . . . 156 & SON ACTU 5   9
    bluer than we had imagined a few cries drifting . . . . . . 283 IS 5 THREE 7   4
    begins the most not imagined life adventuring who would . . . 450 NO THANKS 65   12
    possible is love (who's imagined, therefore limitless) love's 574 1 X 1 34   2
    appease-- humbly in their imagined bodies kneel (over time . 714 95 POEMS 42   6
    day's death: as not imagined secrecies comprise goldenly huge 750 95 POEMS 78   8
    create is now contrive; imagined, merely know (freedom: what 834 73 POEMS 62   8
IMAGINES
    heart of this flower imagines the snow carefully everywhere . 366 VIVA 57   11
+IMAGINES
    FOR CONTEXT, SEE . . . . 759 95 POEMS 86   7
IMAGINING
    what's to know wholly imagining fire) only consider How . . . 362 VIVA 53   15
    and upon the beyond imagining spasm rise we you-with-me . . . 442 NO THANKS 57   21
    and every cannot stir imagining; while you are motionless-- . 559 1 X 1 19   11
    than all real, all imagining; and we who are . . . . 582 1 X 1 42   9
    alive filthy some past imagining whowhich of mad rags . . . . 662 (CHAIRE) 64   5
IMITATE
    made him bold to imitate between the feet of . . . . 4 T&C EPITHALAM   36
    not stroll living spawn imitate) ce (re peat credo . . . . . 309 VIVA 1   32
    each divisible fool (life imitate gossip fear unlife mean . . 452 NO THANKS 67   8
    do not wait) buds imitate upward each first flower . . . . . 573 1 X 1 33   22
IMITATED
    so my Uncle Sol imitated the skunks in a . . . . 239 IS 5 ONE 10   24
IMITATING
    from this you sensations, imitating a few fatally exquisite" 328 VIVA 19   18
IMITATION
    long night a fragile imitation of (perhaps) myself carefully 300 IS 5 FOUR 17   12
    this person and this imitation resemble, descends into the . 300 IS 5 FOUR 17   18
IMMACULATE
    sweet sweet intolerable! silence immaculate of god's evasive   5 T&C EPITHALAM   111
    steals, a gesture of immaculate perfume--whereby (with fear . 19 T&C PUELLA MEA   107
    and of ivory. The immaculate crisp head is such . . . . . . 20 T&C PUELLA MEA   139
    thy smile rises the immaculate sorrow of thy low . . . . . . 31 T&C ORIENTALE 5   17

IMMACULATE (CONTINUED)
    opening one beyond one immaculate curving cool treasures of . 156 & SON ACTU 5   3
    six) the well-fed L's immaculate roar looped straightens, . . 219 XLI SONNETS 15   5
    luminous dithyrambs of large immaculate unmute . . . . 266 IS 5 TWO 1   8
    (Wholly consider how these immaculate thin things half daemon 362 VIVA 53   5
IMMACULATELY
    (hei -nous thought) otherwise immaculately tabulated . . . . 267 IS 5 TWO 2   16
    guess) I item i immaculately owe dying one life . . . . 390 NO THANKS 7   12
IMMANENT
    things intrinsic yearn, the immanent subliminal fern of her . 19 T&C PUELLA MEA   113
IMMATERIAL
    lonjewray or shrouds is immaterial it stinks a salesman . . . 549 1 X 1 9   7
IMMEASURABLE
    marble pillars slipped from immeasurable height, fall, fifty, 32 T&C ORIENTALE 6   30
    home (only more than immeasurable dream wherelessly . . . . . 454 NO THANKS 69   7
    into the not merely immeasurable into the mightily alive . . 464 NEW POEMS 2   34
    minus and shall be immeasurable happenless unnow shuts more . 502 50 POEMS 16   6
    and to wise offered immeasurable is proudly and (by . . . . . 521 50 POEMS 34   40
    more than most how immeasurable anguish pregnant one fearless 523 50 POEMS 36   36
    spurn rather than fail immeasurable fate) coward, clown, . . 562 1 X 1 22   8
    the unimmortal mind, these immeasurable mysteries (human one; 721 95 POEMS 49   7
    darkness) innumerably singular strictly immeasurable nowhere 741 95 POEMS 69   3
    sky; healing our by immeasurable night spirits and with . . . 745 95 POEMS 73   7
IMMEASURABLY
    as with (feel) pauseless immeasurably Now cancels the . . . . 402 NO THANKS 19   3
    try almost their mind immeasurably roots among much soundless 479 NEW POEMS 17   5
    most both) and history immeasurably is wealthier by a . . . . 750 95 POEMS 78   6
IMMEDIACY
    from) querying affirmation; virginal immediacy of precision: 669 {CHAIRE} 71   6
IMMEDIATE
    explode and spill the immediate imperceptible content my . . 193 XLI PORTRAIT 1   17
    the street) this deep immediate mask and expressing "as . . . 328 VIVA 19   14
    / / / serene immediate silliest and whose vast . . . . 337 VIVA 28   1
    prodigious am a so immediate is escorts us home . . . . 517 50 POEMS 31   11
    increase whole truthful infinite immediate us / / / . . . . . 538 50 POEMS 50   14
    the future's future; and immediate like some newly remembered 601 {CHAIRE} 3   11
    that how infinite (deeply immediate fleet and profound this) 763 95 POEMS 90   22
IMMEDIATELY
    of her face doth immediately make in my heart . . . . 18 T&C PUELLA MEA   64
    & shrink: as through immediately yeswind-faces peer skies; . 346 VIVA 37   5
+IMMEDIATELY
    FOR CONTEXT, SEE . . . . 262 IS 5 ONE 32   28
IMMEMORIAL
    adventure the into most immemorial of whens) before . . . . 577 1 X 1 37   18
IMMEMORIALLY
    a flame beyond soul immemorially forevering am-- and as . . . 599 {CHAIRE} 1   5
IMMENSE
    table. and, whose distended immense Both paws slowly loved . 97 & POST IMPR 8   38
    time feeds especially his immense lips On whose deep . . . . 138 & SON REAL 9   9
    stupid stuffs, phrase the immense weapon of your hair. . . . 161 & SON ACTU 10   10
    sudden extremity of one immense tooth myself surveys safely . 201 XLI PORTRAIT 9   30
    lilies.... beyond night's silken immense swoon the moon is . 214 XLI SONNETS 10   12
    Eye Doangivuh sud- denly immense impotently Eye Doancare Eye 330 VIVA 21   8
    or any when unwondering immense directionless horizon) --do . 378 VIVA 69   14
    on murdered feet into immense no Where which to . . . . 479 NEW POEMS 17   2
    hereless. air theres what immense live without every dancing. 491 50 POEMS 5   4
    once man (clutched by immense the-seat-of-the pants inani . . 616 {CHAIRE} 18   6
    power of himself death immense is not so as . . . . 649 {CHAIRE} 51   13
    immortal i can turn immense all time's because to . . . . . . 679 95 POEMS 7   14
    (huddling a- gainst one immense deep hell -o of . . . . 687 95 POEMS 15   6
    he reaches the barn's immense doorway and halts propped . . . 754 95 POEMS 82   7
IMMENSELY
    this street the houses immensely speak (it is nine . . . . . 219 XLI SONNETS 15   3
    meanness unsmaller) armies can immensely meet for centuries . 580 1 X 1 40   17
+IMMENSELY
    FOR CONTEXT, SEE . . . . 482 NEW POEMS 20   3
IMMENSER
    world by than worlds immenser world will pray so . . . . . . 450 NO THANKS 65   9

		PAGE	TITLE	LINE

IMMENSEST
(past can's every can't) immensest mysteries contradict a . . 763 95 POEMS 90   26
IMMENSITY
his hibernative contours, amiable immensity impeccably . . . 197 XLI PORTRAIT 5   10
lewd guess of fabulous immensity the sky screamed the . . . . 419 NO THANKS 36   8
aft spits) int o immensity (upon once whom fiercely . . . . . 465 NEW POEMS 3   6
IMMINENT
and was these twin imminent lisping bags of flesh; . . . . . 115 & PORTRAIT 8   22
IMMINENTLY
i am who wanders imminently across the renewed world" . . . . 91 & POST IMPR 3   18
+IMMOBILE
FOR CONTEXT, SEE . . . . 655 (CHAIRE) 57   1
IMMORTAL
and still to be immortal is our doom; but . . . . 9 T&C SONGS 1   24
meteors streaming from playful immortal hands the bursting of 36 T&C AMORES 1   18
the sky the last immortal leaf is dead and . . . . 41 T&C AMORES 5   2
as one of those immortal men his life that . . . . 209 XLI SONNETS 5   13
twentysix selves bulging in immortal Spring express a cry . . 255 IS 5 ONE 26   6
worlds whirl beyond worlds: immortal yonder collidingly . . . 376 VIVA 67   12
, then it's Spring immortal Always & lewd shy . . . . 442 NO THANKS 57   20
climb, so naked for immortal work his shoulders marched . . . 521 50 POEMS 34   43
the sun and yanks immortal stars awry? Blow king . . . . . . 560 1 X 1 20   4
his life: and carve immortal jungles of despair to . . . . . 562 1 X 1 22   13
(gladly, as lovers must) immortal and the courage to . . . . 675 95 POEMS 3   13
love --human one mortally immortal i can turn immense . . . . 679 95 POEMS 7   13
and space bowed to immortal us if in one . . . . 694 95 POEMS 22   6
and i are such immortal friends the other's each . . . . . . 730 95 POEMS 58   6
the pest thus did immortal jealousy quell divine generosity, 799 73 POEMS 27   32
IMMORTALITY
sweet earth puts on immortality again --her murdered selves . 818 73 POEMS 46   4
IMMORTALLY
pale flesh with delight) --immortally whence are the high . . 3 T&C EPITHALAM   8
of duration: only love immortally occurs beyond the mind) . . 576 1 X 1 36   8
+IMMORTALS
FOR CONTEXT, SEE . . . . 536 50 POEMS 48   21
IMPACT
that we may resume impact with the inutile collide . . . . . 289 IS 5 FOUR 6   7
IMPALED
whose cool incorrigible arms impaled upon delicious mystery, 7 T&C EPITHALAM   157
IMPART
man kind progress doth impart one stands supreme i . . . . . 544 1 X 1 4   2
IMPATIENCE
eyes easily files my impatience to an edge--my girl's . . . . 147 & SON REAL 18   9
IMPATIENT
(nothing pampered puny impatient and nothing ignoble) . . . 658 (CHAIRE) 60   23
IMPATIENTLY
his head) squads right impatiently replied two billion pubic 473 NEW POEMS 11   4
IMPECCABLE
frail ladies dangerously respire: impeccable girls in raiment 85 T&C SON ACTU 4   15
and wholly dies his impeccable feathered with green facts . . 344 VIVA 35   2
+IMPECCABLE
FOR CONTEXT, SEE . . . . 274 IS 5 TWO 9   33
IMPECCABLY
hibernative contours, amiable immensity impeccably extending 197 XLI PORTRAIT 5   10
IMPENETRABLE
this instant commits an impenetrable transparency. the harsh 137 & SON REAL 8   12
IMPERCEPTIBLE
and spill the immediate imperceptible content my friend's . . 193 XLI PORTRAIT 1   17
a gigantic uvula with imperceptible gesticulations threatens 201 XLI PORTRAIT 9   8
+IMPERCEPTIBLE
FOR CONTEXT, SEE . . . . 103 & POST IMPR 13   2
FOR CONTEXT, SEE . . . . 350 VIVA 41   17
IMPERCEPTION
which my organ of imperception gave birth to which . . . . . 263 IS 5 ONE 32   33
IMPERFECT
i who am but imperfect in my fear Or . . . . 215 XLI SONNETS 11   11
made, my lady, intricate imperfect various things chiefly . . 306 IS 5 FIVE 5   2
eyes (until perfectly their imperfect gaze climbs this steep 450 NO THANKS 65   7

	PAGE	TITLE	LINE

IMPERFECTLY
if or to prove, imperfectly or since but through . . . . . . 386 NO THANKS 3   6
+IMPERFECTNESS
FOR CONTEXT, SEE . . . . 197 XLI PORTRAIT 5   2
IMPERIAL
long flower of unchastity, imperial Cytherea, from frail foam   7 T&C EPITHALAM   161
IMPERISHABLE
amethyst. Lady at whose imperishable smile the amazed doves .   6 T&C EPITHALAM   137
sleep safely may by imperishable your glory escorted through 811 73 POEMS 39   2
IMPERISHABLY
whose selves and lives imperishably feast all timeless souls 456 NO THANKS 71   3
IMPERSONALLY
tiredness of flanging shop-girls impersonally affords . . . . 197 XLI PORTRAIT 5   5
IMPERSONATES
is laughter and despair impersonates a street i lean . . . . 375 VIVA 66   5
IMPERTINENT
udders she lifts an impertinent puerperal face and with . . . 151 & SON REAL 22   12
IMPERTINENTLY
side Looked up with impertinently exquisite faces floating .   44 T&C AMORES 8   10
the hands sharp and impertinently dead. expression began with 103 & POST IMPR 13   5
IMPETUOUS
beside the vivid magical impetuous and utter ponds of . . . .   19 T&C PUELLA MEA 117
desire of a doomed impetuous acute sentience whose whitehot . 193 XLI PORTRAIT 1   10
IMPINGE
upon which indolent miracles impinge) --it is distinctly to .   19 T&C PUELLA MEA   96
on whom glories whisperingly impinge (god's pretty mother) .   85 T&C SON ACTU 4   5
IMPLACABLE
in noon-- noon the implacable bassoon-- now Twilight seeks .   12 T&C SONGS 2   47
grace bravely to fling Implacable death's mysteriously sable 206 XLI SONNETS 2   4
over them- selves this implacable unthing next, our . . . . . 799 73 POEMS 27   22
IMPLIES
between firstrate & second implies nonth inkable enormousness 803 73 POEMS 31   10
IMPLORE
rigging over us, i implore you to notice how . . . . 378 VIVA 69   2
IMPLORING
flags weeping flatter thoroughly imploring threaten) the . . 391 NO THANKS 8   9
IMPLY
Well and when--Does susceptibility imply perspicuity, or? . . 141 & SON REAL 12   8
IMPORTANCE
movies may claim general importance to me to you . . . . . . 238 IS 5 ONE 9   15
of that in the importance of the fact that . . . . 323 VIVA 15   20
IMPORTANT
Up with the pale important stars and the Humorous . . . . . .   44 T&C AMORES 8   15
good teeth and small important breasts (is it the . . . . . .   72 T&C SON REAL 3   2
about god's capable dull important head-- by on whom . . . .   85 T&C SON ACTU 4   4
surveys safely the complete important profane frantic . . . . 201 XLI PORTRAIT 9   31
accurate moon.... Across the important gardens her body will 214 XLI SONNETS 10   10
at that) that seems important doesn't it and doesn't . . . . 323 VIVA 15   15
hurry full of an important worry) halt stop forget . . . . . 393 NO THANKS 10   4
name misder finger isn't important whether it's millions of . 549 1 X 1 9   4
IMPORTANTLY
slow animal bottomless eyes importantly banal, Kitty. a . . .   74 T&C SON REAL 5   7
IMPORTING
was a suspicious madder, importing the cruelty of roses. . . 103 & POST IMPR 13   1
IMPOSINGLY
swill; one butting trolley imposingly empty; snickering shop 172 & SON ACTU 21   5
IMPOSSIBLE
did Lord Jason (in impossible things victorious impossibly) .   18 T&C PUELLA MEA   69
easily from the shocked impossible tower i caught you . . . .   30 T&C ORIENTALE 4 25
bring-- ask the always impossible of me and shall . . . . . . 454 NO THANKS 69   2
this? nothing except the impossible shall occur --see! now . 582 1 X 1 42   12
without any doubt of impossible ours --God's heaven perhaps . 748 95 POEMS 76   4
IMPOSSIBLY
(in impossible things victorious impossibly) so wholly burn,   18 T&C PUELLA MEA   70
/ / / / impossibly motivated by midnight the . . . . 116 & PORTRAIT 9   1
Memo 1 wife in impossibly hell Memo 1 son . . . . 389 NO THANKS 6   19
possibly 2 1/2 or impossibly 3 individuals every several . . 514 50 POEMS 28   1

		PAGE	TITLE	LINE

+IMPOSSIBLY
  FOR CONTEXT, SEE . . . . 347 VIVA 38   23
  FOR CONTEXT, SEE . . . . 444 NO THANKS 59   25
IMPOSTURE
  a gift) the teachable imposture of always arriving at . . . . 807 73 POEMS 35   3
IMPOTENCE
  timelessness, outtowering this noisy impotence of not and . . 351 VIVA 42   4
IMPOTENTLY
  Doangivuh sud- denly immense impotently Eye Doancare Eye And 330 VIVA 21   8
IMPRECISION
  their loud exactitudes of imprecision, you'll (silently . . . 659 (CHAIRE) 61 11
IMPREGNABLE
  because separated by an impregnable Because (amount of inter 335 VIVA 26   13
IMPRESSED
  leaf's grieving: from the impressed fingers of sublime . . . 207 XLI SONNETS 3 11
  to my astonishment much impressed by having once noticed . . 262 IS 5 ONE 32   9
IMPRESSION
  it happens quite erroneous impression that he nascitur / . . 234 IS 5 ONE 5   5
  doth miss; a hand's impression in an empty glove, ... 360 VIVA 51   8
IMPRESSIONS
  / / / / IMPRESSIONS the sky a silver . . . . 47 T&C IMPRESS 1   T
  / / / POST IMPRESSIONS beyond the brittle towns . . . . 64 T&C POST IMPR 1 T
  / / / POST IMPRESSIONS windows go orange in . . . . 89 & POST IMPR 1   T
IMPRINT
  god from but the imprint of whose cloven feet . . . .   3 T&C EPITHALAM 13
+IMPRISON
  FOR CONTEXT, SEE . . . . 491 50 POEMS 5   13
IMPRISONED
  there: and being here imprisoned, tortured here love . . . . 377 VIVA 68   7
IMPROBABLE
  suddenly (as sometimes the improbable beauty of my lady . . . 18 T&C PUELLA MEA 43
  face and the rich improbable hands of the Wind) . . . . 153 & SON ACTU 2 14
  probable roses of her improbable world and without any . . . 748 95 POEMS 76   3
IMPROBABLY
  whore delicately wobbles an improbably distinct face, and how 229 IS 5 ONE FRAN 3
  Memo 1 son in improbably yale / / / . . . . 389 NO THANKS 6   22
+IMPROBABLY
  FOR CONTEXT, SEE . . . . 728 95 POEMS 56   9
IMPULSE
  darkness raging with thin impulse i will have a . . . . 67 T&C POST IMPR 4 5
IMPURE
  so long will the impure think all things pure . . . . 511 50 POEMS 25 13
IN
  WORD DELETED, APPEARED 824 TIMES
INANE
  Dead stars stink. dawn. Inane, the poetic carcass of . . . . 139 & SON REAL 10 13
INANELY
  Too. originally spontaneous twurls-of-excrement inanely . . . 94 & POST IMPR 6   2
INANITY
  chopped by a swollen inanity of picture hat. the . . . . . . 103 & POST IMPR 13 4
INCALCULABLE
  i spill my bright incalculable soul. / / / . . . . 206 XLI SONNETS 2 15
  his heart the queen --incalculable bliss! Picture it gents: . 254 IS 5 ONE 25 13
  creation may be less incalculable than a single kiss . . . . 809 73 POEMS 37 14
INCAPABLE
  my position. A bachelor incapable of occupation, he had . . . 263 IS 5 ONE 32 37
INCENSE
  of bells comprehended through incense / / / / . . . . 29 T&C ORIENTALE 3 33
  unto thee i burn incense the bowl crackles upon . . . . 31 T&C ORIENTALE 5 2
  i think thou lovest incense for in the ambiguous . . . . . . 31 T&C ORIENTALE 5 14
  unto thee i burn incense, over the dim smoke . . . . 31 T&C ORIENTALE 5 22
  diamond timid with nesting incense) fifty marble pillars . . 32 T&C ORIENTALE 6 26
  fifty, silent in the incense is tangled a cool . . . . 32 T&C ORIENTALE 6 32
  like boys and like incense and like sunlight and . . . . . . 111 & PORTRAIT 6 64
  dissipation unhurried clouds of incense fleetly roll) i spill 206 XLI SONNETS 2 14
  A Glass Box and incense with and oh sunlight-- . . . . 280 IS 5 THREE 4 22
INCESSANT
  out of the minute incessant Was irrevocably emanates a . . . 111 & PORTRAIT 6 52

377

INCESSANT (CONTINUED)
    edgeless gloaming gladness hammers incessant putrid spikes of 202 XLI PORTRAIT 9   38
INCESSANTLY
    upon the gold cloth incessantly creates patterns of sudden .   34 T&C ORIENTALE 6   88
INCH
    notice the convulsed orange inch of moon perching on . . . .   86 T&C SON ACTU 5   1
    flower here placing an inch of air there) and . . . . 124 & SEVEN POEMS 3   18
    worth the whole, an inch of nothing for your . . . . 161 & SON ACTU 10   14
    sulksuck whim poke if inch dimmer twist on permament . . . . 333 VIVA 24   12
    pleased our parents one inch looks good to us . . . . 466 NEW POEMS 4   16
    both eaching come ghostlike (inch) wraithish (by inch) grin . 681 95 POEMS 9   2
    ghostlike (inch) wraithish (by inch) grin ning heshaped two . 681 95 POEMS 9   2
    certainly while mute each inch of their murdered planet . . . 808 73 POEMS 36   10
+INCH
    FOR CONTEXT, SEE . . . . 100 & POST IMPR 11   38
    FOR CONTEXT, SEE . . . . 100 & POST IMPR 11   38
    FOR CONTEXT, SEE . . . . 571 1 X 1 31   6
INCHES
    miss by how terrible inches speech--it made you a . . . . . . 174 & SON ACTU 23   10
    ceiling inhaling six divine inches of Haremina in the . . . . 194 XLI PORTRAIT 2   14
+INCISIONS
    FOR CONTEXT, SEE . . . . 405 NO THANKS 22   8
INCISIVE
    themselves with a more incisive simplicity a more intensively 354 VIVA 45   16
INCITIONS
    who tend to make incitions and pity the fool . . . . 405 NO THANKS 22   8
INCLINE
    look & listen Venezia: incline thine ear you glassworks . . . 256 IS 5 ONE 27   2
INCLINED
    zoo were that day inclined to be uncouthly erotic . . . . . . 326 VIVA 18   23
    he might now be inclined to describe it rather . . . . . . 464 NEW POEMS 2   21
    bent is the crowd inclined it's freedom from freedom . . . . 635 (CHAIRE) 37   23
INCLUDE
    such marvels vanish, will include --there by arriving . . . . 741 95 POEMS 69   10
INCLUDED
    rich portrait should be included, gents these (by the . . . . 254 IS 5 ONE 25   8
INCLUDING
    of unheard of maladies including flu) my little darlings, . . 266 IS 5 TWO 1   15
    may recall) being lost including captain Pater / / . . . . . 494 50 POEMS 8   8
    the earth) & nobody (including our selves) will reme . . . . 797 73 POEMS 25   12
INCOGNIZABLE
    insufferable clay clothed with incognizable amethyst. Lady at   6 T&C EPITHALAM   136
INCOMPARABLE
    (but true to the incomparable couch of death thy . . . . . . 46 T&C LA GUERRE 2   21
INCOMPLETELY
    phenomenon) George Washington almost incompletely surrounded 262 IS 5 ONE 32   11
INCONCEIVABLE
    rout), queen in the inconceivable embrace of whose tremendous   6 T&C EPITHALAM   145
INCONSEQUENTIAL
    complete important profane frantic inconsequential . . . . . 201 XLI PORTRAIT 9   32
INCONSIDERABLE
    will time extract his inconsiderable doom, when these thy . . 210 XLI SONNETS 6   11
INCORRIGIBLE
    sleep, betwixt whose cool incorrigible arms impaled upon . .   7 T&C EPITHALAM   156
    stepping freakish feet feet incorrigible ragging the world, / 61 T&C PORTRAIT 9   36
INCORRUPTIBLE
    accurate strenuous lips of incorruptible Nothing under the . 43 T&C AMORES 7   37
INCREASE
    new lights begin and increase, since your mind has . . . . . 297 IS 5 FOUR 14   4
    humble me which shall increase) open thy fire! for . . . . . 360 VIVA 51   31
    rose explodes but shall increase whole truthful infinite . . 538 50 POEMS 50   13
+INCREASING
    FOR CONTEXT, SEE . . . . 63 T&C PORTRAIT 10   31
INCREDIBLE
    hurries elsewhere; to blow incredible wampum / / / . . . . . 116 & PORTRAIT 9   17
    (the oh quintillions of incredible dodderingly godly . . . . 250 IS 5 ONE 21   11
    I tell you; several, incredible, sleepy / / / . . . . 281 IS 5 THREE 5   24
    one name control more incredible splendor than our merely . . 377 VIVA 68   5

INCREDIBLE (CONTINUED)

and propaganda (it is incredible But others don't scream . . 391 NO THANKS 8   12

(silent: madeofimagination ; the incredible soft) ness (his . 397 NO THANKS 14   23

we'll believe in that incredible unanimal mankind (and not . 620 {CHAIRE} 22   13

this aflame with dreams incredible is) / / / . . . . 832 73 POEMS 60   16

+INCREDIBLE

FOR CONTEXT, SEE . . . . 612 {CHAIRE} 14   5

INCREDIBLY

which like two elves incredibly amuse themselves) with a . .   17 T&C PUELLA MEA   40

+INCREDIBLY

FOR CONTEXT, SEE . . . . 738 95 POEMS 66   14

INCURIOUS

ground --let but the incurious curtaining dusk be drawn . . .   5 T&C EPITHALAM   85

INDECENT

thighs, with a sharp indecent stir unclenches into . . . . . 131 & SON REAL 2   10

joy let 's thank indecent god p.s. the most . . . . 425 NO THANKS 42   14

INDECISION

capable of fragility and indecision --do not suppose these .   91 & POST IMPR 3   13

INDEED

of the (very prettily indeed) arra- nged souvenir of . . . . 267 IS 5 TWO 2   12

+INDEED

FOR CONTEXT, SEE . . . . 793 73 POEMS 21   6

INDEFINABLE

and breathless pearl! O indefinable frail ultimate pose! O .   5 T&C EPITHALAM   109

of forms delightful with indefinable flowering, the air is .   31 T&C ORIENTALE 5   10

INDESTRUCTIBLE

is comparatively crude; an indestructible occult supersnare . 799 73 POEMS 27   18

INDEX

surging flesh). A thumblike index down- dragging yanks back . 226 IS 5 ONE MAME   5

INDIA

how between her hips India is / / / . . . .   95 & POST IMPR 7   19

INDIANS

likes People preferring Negroes Indians Youse n.b. ye twang . 410 NO THANKS 27   6

INDIGENOUS

according to such supposedly indigenous throstles Art is O . 230 IS 5 ONE 2   31

INDIGESTIBLE

a waiter cleverly lugs indigestible honeycake to men ....one 217 XLI SONNETS 13   9

INDIGESTION

mark who suffers from indigestion question mark is a . . . . 246 IS 5 ONE 17   4

a water- melon causes indigestion to William Cullen Longfel- 263 IS 5 ONE 32   52

INDIGNANT

and swaggering cookies of indignant light / / / . . . . 226 IS 5 ONE MAME   14

with angry seasalt and indignant clover marrying to . . . . . 376 VIVA 67   4

INDIGNANTLY

Century whirl? one's memory indignantly protests) this little   72 T&C SON REAL 3   4

INDISPENSABLE

wherefrom departed is youth's indispensable illusion" / / / .   57 T&C PORTRAIT 5   40

INDISPUTABLY

of, through the autumn indisputably roaming death's big . . . 158 & SON ACTU 7   13

INDISTINCT

apples it will, Gorge indistinct palishflesh of laZilytas . . 100 & POST IMPR 11   27

INDIVIDUAL

to this always talking individual, mysterious witty hatless. 279 IS 5 THREE 3   12

pitying terrible some alive individual ten centuries of . . . 561 1 X 1 21   5

INDIVIDUALS

1/2 or impossibly 3 individuals every several fat thousand . 514 50 POEMS 28   2

INDIVISIBLE

partedpetaled mouth, face delirious. indivisible grace of . . 185 XLI SONGS 7   15

INDOLENCE

million leaves in winsome indolence simmer upon thinking . .   6 T&C EPITHALAM   125

INDOLENT

very deftly upon which indolent miracles impinge) --it is . .   19 T&C PUELLA MEA   96

ambiguous faint aspirings the indolent frail ascensions, of .   31 T&C ORIENTALE 5   16

and here the lithe indolent prostitute Night, argues with . .   93 & POST IMPR 5   16

oddly to strut my indolent priceless smile, until this . . . 155 & SON ACTU 4   11

and the sea heaving indolent colourless forgets) time . . . . 277 IS 5 THREE 1   20

carry also, with that indolent and with this flower . . . . . 294 IS 5 FOUR 11   15

solemnity ignoring, through its indolent lascivious caring . 344 VIVA 35   4

		PAGE	TITLE	LINE

INDOLENTLY
you must shake well) indolently dreaming puzzling over that . 323 VIVA 15   6
INDOMITABLE
modern flame of her indomitable body uses a careful . . . . . 146 & SON REAL 17   2
INDUBITABLE
have spoken with this indubitable and green person "Are . . . 91 & POST IMPR 3   7
INDUBITABLY
the flyspecked abdominous female indubitably tellurian . . . 116 & PORTRAIT 9   4
INDULGED
that my Uncle Sol indulged in that possibly most . . . . . . 239 IS 5 ONE 10   8
INDULGES
gargles jesus the aesthete indulges his soul for certain . . 108 & PORTRAIT 4   28
INDUSTRY
the murderous saliva of industry. the mor- sel is . . . . . . 201 XLI PORTRAIT 9   5
INERT
confessed a button solemnly inert. Brushing from whom the . . 258 IS 5 ONE 28   20
INEVITABLE
twilight spon- taneously by inevitable tiredness of flanging 197 XLI PORTRAIT 5   4
INEXACTLY
(may be seen to inexactly pass and unprecisely to . . . . . . 401 NO THANKS 18   11
INEXCUSABLE
in that possibly most inexcusable of all to use . . . . 239 IS 5 ONE 10   8
created this at length inexcusable, this inexplicable . . . . 295 IS 5 FOUR 12   7
INEXISTENCE
moon, and our (from inexistence moving) sweet earth puts . . 818 73 POEMS 46   3
INEXPLICABLE
at length inexcusable, this inexplicable pleasure--you go . . 295 IS 5 FOUR 12   7
seemed sweet deep and inexplicable not being dollars toenails 322 VIVA 14   7
INEXPRESSIBLE
will not rise yesterday. Inexpressible itchings to be . . . . 262 IS 5 ONE 32   20
+INEXPRESSIBLE
FOR CONTEXT, SEE . . . . 739 95 POEMS 67   6
INEXPRESSIBLY
contours of a vase inexpressibly fragile it is for . . . . . 193 XLI PORTRAIT 1   14
INEXTINGUISHABLE
spring offers her lily inextinguishable, taught by thy . . . 206 XLI SONNETS 2   2
INFANTILE
along Kirkland Street the infantile ghost of Professor Royce 232 IS 5 ONE 3   12
once noticed (as an infantile phenomenon) George Washington . 262 IS 5 ONE 32   10
hands and with curling infantile fingers it understood my . . 284 IS 5 FOUR 1   3
look at (now -fed infantile eyes drooling unmind grim . . . . 337 VIVA 28   6
INFINITE
eternal gold over the infinite breast in bright degrees, . . 4 T&C EPITHALAM   39
of dumb strong hands infinite the erect deep upon . . . . . . 64 T&C POST IMPR 1   5
irrevocable bodies while the infinite processions move like . 111 & PORTRAIT 6   62
air, haunted with huddling infinite wishless melancholy, . . 305 IS 5 FIVE 4   13
Christ (of His mercy infinite) i pray to see; . . . . 339 VIVA 30   38
you should turn the infinite corner of love, all . . . . . . 479 NEW POEMS 17   18
(leas tly) smiles the infinite nothing of M an . . . . 534 50 POEMS 46   22
shall increase whole truthful infinite immediate us / / . . . 538 50 POEMS 50   14
called mankind unteach whole infinite the who of life's . . . 603 {CHAIRE} 5   4
/ / / / infinite jukethrob smoke & swallow . . . . 629 {CHAIRE} 31   1
of elsewhere jabber while (infinite fog & puking jukepulse . 629 {CHAIRE} 31   5
skilfully here & (simply infinite) there & (smoke) a . . . . 629 {CHAIRE} 31   10
moth er folds (but infinite) gently up the with . . . . . . 629 {CHAIRE} 31   15
wing resuming) selves, into infinite tomorrow steer --souls . 659 {CHAIRE} 61   4
is natural which is infinite which is yes (i . . . . 663 {CHAIRE} 65   4
sweet mistfully whispering rainlife) infinite also ourselves 755 95 POEMS 83   13
steep not guessable each infinite Oblivions found a by . . . 757 95 POEMS 85   23
is brief that how infinite (deeply immediate fleet and . . . 763 95 POEMS 90   21
your glory escorted through infinite countries be my darling 811 73 POEMS 39   3
life and my (and infinite our) merely to undie . . . . 817 73 POEMS 45   14
fleetly) vanish, at the infinite precise thrill of your . . . 819 73 POEMS 47   12
+INFINITE
FOR CONTEXT, SEE . . . . 629 {CHAIRE} 31   21
+INFINITESIMALLY
FOR CONTEXT, SEE . . . . 49 T&C IMPRESS 3   4

                                                        PAGE   TITLE   LINE

INFINITY
  / a connotation of infinity sharpens the temporal splendor . 81 T&C SON UNRE 6   1
  all the religious fuss infinity pleased our parents one . . . 466 NEW POEMS 4   15
  if multiplied by twice infinity could never equal one) . . . 510 50 POEMS 24   11
  living's all multiplied with infinity sans if the mightiest . 592 1 X 1 52   5
INFLECTED
  is a verb, miraculous inflected oral devious, beneath the . . 21 T&C PUELLA MEA 210
INFLICTED
  click of deciding glory inflicted to the negative silence . . 197 XLI PORTRAIT 5 16
INFO
  times--before she got the info from a broad that . . . . . . 145 & SON REAL 16   6
INFRAFAIRY
  & z = an infrafairy of floating ultrawrists who . . . . 317 VIVA 9   4
INFRAWORLD
  ultramachinations of some loveless infraworld) a woman knows; 807 73 POEMS 35   11
INFREQUENTLY
  zero mind fahrenheit) old infrequently more and more much . . 546 1 X 1 6   2
INGENIOUS
  each mill of the ingenious gods. (i am punished. . . . . . . 165 & SON ACTU 14 13
+INGENUITY
  FOR CONTEXT, SEE . . . . 644 {CHAIRE} 46   3
INGING
  the ant thou go (inging) to the ant, thou . . . . 403 NO THANKS 20 22
INHABIT
  alighting from their limousine inhabit the Hotel Meurice . . 245 IS 5 ONE 16   4
  suggesting that our souls inhabit whatever is between them) . 285 IS 5 FOUR 2   5
INHABITANTS
  of faerie, are intense inhabitants; in whose warm superlative 22 T&C PUELLA MEA 254
INHABITED
  You (thickness means worlds inhabited by roamingly stern . . 363 VIVA 54   3
INHABITS
  innocuous winking hands, carefully inhabits number 1 on . . . 62 T&C PORTRAIT 10 4
  of Saint Ignatz miraculously inhabits. (people tumble down. . 280 IS 5 THREE 4 5
  orish mind --nothing believable inhabits here: overs of known 761 95 POEMS 88   5
INHALE
  ecstasy my palpitating breasts inhale the slow supple flower 31 T&C ORIENTALE 5 24
INHALING
  feet on the ceiling inhaling six divine inches of . . . . . . 194 XLI PORTRAIT 2 14
  i am seeing something inhaling gently a cigarette (in . . . . 375 VIVA 66   16
INHERENT
  axe only chops hugest inherent Trees of Ego, from . . . . . . 195 XLI PORTRAIT 3 18
INHERIT
  thy face (whose eyes inherit vacancy) will time extract . . . 210 XLI SONNETS 6 10
  dumb death all we inherit, all bequeath and nothing . . . . 521 50 POEMS 34   64
INHIBIT
  bloodshed and kindred questions inhibit unprepared . . . . . 266 IS 5 TWO 1   30
INHUMAN
  bretish they scout the inhuman itarian fetish that man . . . 492 50 POEMS 6   6
  not divine, to err inhuman) or any thine a . . . . 798 73 POEMS 26   4
+INHUMANITARIAN
  FOR CONTEXT, SEE . . . . 492 50 POEMS 6   6
INIMITABLE
  secret food its leaves inimitable find beyond the white . . . 19 T&C PUELLA MEA 119
  within me scrupulously the Inimitable which is loneliness, . 328 VIVA 19   2
INIMITABLY
  In heaven's intolerable athanor inimitably tortured the base   6 T&C EPITHALAM 130
  suddenly leaping flameflung, mounts, inimitably to lose . . . 206 XLI SONNETS 2   8
INJUSTICE
  remarked Robinson Jefferson to Injustice Taughed your story . 321 VIVA 13   2
INLEY
  tucks it up back inley clamored Clever Rusefelt to . . . . . 321 VIVA 13   8
INNERLY
  / / / / innerly UningstrolL (stamens&pistil silent A . . . . 342 VIVA 33   1
INNOCENCE
  whisper so (big with innocence) forgivingly a once of . . . . 601 {CHAIRE} 3   3
  not speak, a little innocence will make them sing; . . . . . 649 {CHAIRE} 51 2
  to beautiful: a little innocence creates a day. And . . . . 649 {CHAIRE} 51 8
  wished without a little innocence, although it were as . . . 649 {CHAIRE} 51 10

			PAGE	TITLE	LINE

INNOCENCE (CONTINUED)

so as a little innocence / / / / . . . . 649 (CHAIRE) 51   14

miracle of your sweet innocence refuted) clumsy some dull . . 669 (CHAIRE) 71   11

doom treasures of reeking innocence are born. Then, with . . 843 73 POEMS 71   8

INNOCENT

idiom (beings alert and innocent very deftly upon which . . . 19 T&C PUELLA MEA   94

head is one warrior innocent of defeat thy hair . . . . . . 29 T&C ORIENTALE 3   19

Myself's height these various innocent ferocities are . . . . 202 XLI PORTRAIT 9   40

massacre the hope most innocent (so deep's the mind . . . . . 609 (CHAIRE) 11   7

imagine quite such eagerly innocent whoms of merciful . . . . 748 95 POEMS 76   13

INNOCENTES

/ / / CHANSONS INNOCENTES in Just- spring when . . . . . . 24 T&C CHANSONS 1   T

/ / / CHANSONS INNOCENTES why did you go . . . . 191 XLI CHANSONS 1   T

INNOCENTLY

to wickedly comprehend the innocently Doomed brief all which 356 VIVA 47   10

elsewhere stroll) exhumed most innocently undecaying friend . 546 1 X 1 6   4

selves wholly which and innocently are) seeming's enough for 745 95 POEMS 73   12

INNOCUOUS

thudding timeshaped face plus innocuous winking hands, . . . 62 T&C PORTRAIT 10   3

INNOVATION

he would extemporise the innovation of mus- cularity upon . . 197 XLI PORTRAIT 5   14

INNUMERABLE

strenuous music of the innumerable capering damned) --staring 118 & PORTRAIT 10   38

first clue to his innumerable whereabouts violet logic of . . 197 XLI PORTRAIT 5   6

together with what keen innumerable lives he has not . . . . 285 IS 5 FOUR 2   22

mind carefully luminous with innumerable gnomes Of complete . 363 VIVA 54   7

amoral morality sort-of-aliveing by innumerable . . . . . . 410 NO THANKS 27   12

voice of deathless earth's innumerable doom: againing (yes by 821 73 POEMS 49   2

INNUMERABLY

was dusk becomes darkness) innumerably singular strictly . . 741 95 POEMS 69   2

INOBVIOUS

deference to her not inobvious perturba- tions unhappily, the 326 VIVA 18   21

INQUIRE

earth is Madge worth? Inquire of the flower that . . . . . . 183 XLI SONGS 5   14

INQUIRES

my voice feels who inquires is your cough better . . . . . . 506 50 POEMS 20   7

INQUIRY

ing; edge, of life (inquiry before snow / / . . . . 712 95 POEMS 40   9

INQUISITIVE

a trillionth part of inquisitive merrily humble your . . . . 678 95 POEMS 6   14

INSANE

eyes squirming with light insane chisel the killing flame . . 139 & SON REAL 10   10

the perpendicular lips the insane teeth the vertical grin . . 220 XLI SONNETS 16   7

INSCRUTABLE

to lull with foliate inscrutable sweetness my soul obedient; 19 T&C PUELLA MEA   88

INSECT

thyself a small hoping insect, humanity, achieves (moult . . 351 VIVA 42   10

INSECTS

is it themselves these insects mean? when microscopic . . . . 555 1 X 1 15   3

+INSECURE

FOR CONTEXT, SEE . . . . 201 XLI PORTRAIT 9   19

INSENSIBLE

in revenge beats it insensible with a banana, establishing . 262 IS 5 ONE 32   24

INSERTS

the famous doctor who inserts monkeyglands in millionaires a 245 IS 5 ONE 16   13

INSIDE

glad that the soul inside me Hollers for thou . . . . 61 T&C PORTRAIT 9   27

York and beautifully snowing. Inside snug and evil. the . . . 96 & POST IMPR 8   3

(the eternal perpetual question) Inside snugandevil. i was . 97 & POST IMPR 8   43

coming with his kid inside her. He laughed. She . . . . 145 & SON REAL 16   10

just like a coffin's inside when you die, pretentious . . . . 198 XLI PORTRAIT 6   2

two billion pubic lice inside one pair of trousers . . . . . 473 NEW POEMS 11   5

INSIGNIFICANTLY

unswift mouths of snow insignificantly whisper.... / / / . . 218 XLI SONNETS 14   15

INSINUATING

her subtle body weaving insinuating upon the gold cloth . . . 34 T&C ORIENTALE 6   87

INSIPID

building a serene pastile-shaped insipid kinesis or frail . . 201 XLI PORTRAIT 9   15

382

INSIPIDITIES
    and the Baboon sniggering insipidities while. i sit, sipping 220 XLI SONNETS 16 13
INSIST
    it five, i'd still insist that all history is . . . . 579 1 X 1 39   6
INSLANTS
    to rickety unclosed blinds inslants peregrinate, a cigar-stub 144 & SON REAL 15   3
INSOLENT
    great lily atilt on insolent waters but i was . . . . 30 T&C ORIENTALE 4 7
INSPIRED
    smelled of silence. The inspired cleat of her glad . . . . . 135 & SON REAL 6   3
    was attracted by the inspired sister's howling moves off . . 196 XLI PORTRAIT 4 17
INSTANCE
    on other people: for instance a plugged promise-- then . . . 298 IS 5 FOUR 15   18
    but the stars for instance everything is planned next . . . . 322 VIVA 14   3
    him over Wasn't (for instance) the Knowing your whole . . . . 702 95 POEMS 30   11
    your oldest pal for instance (or ; why even . . . . 779 73 POEMS 7   12
INSTANT
    gently. (spattered) by this instant of semiluminous nausea A 96 & POST IMPR 8 32
    merely terricolous American an instant doubts the . . . . . . 116 & PORTRAIT 9   12
    Her being at this instant commits an impenetrable . . . . . . 137 & SON REAL 8   11
    (always) upon a fragile instant when herself me (slowly, . . 156 & SON ACTU 5   13
    white speech (the simple instant of perfect hunger Yes) . . . 157 & SON ACTU 6   8
    meshing with my curiously instant appreciation exposed his . 197 XLI PORTRAIT 5   9
    very well provided an instant may be fixed so . . . . 264 IS 5 ONE 33   23
    lingers beyond a little instant, along with rhyme and . . . . 293 IS 5 FOUR 10   10
    philosphy" strictly at which instant (leaped into the street) 328 VIVA 19   12
    spoil this or this instant) kiss me a little: . . . . 357 VIVA 48   6
    hearts grow brittler every Instant (when of a morning . . . . 359 VIVA 50   5
    merge--at not imaginable which instant born, a (who is . . . 721 95 POEMS 49   13
+INSTANT
    FOR CONTEXT, SEE . . . . 122 & SEVEN POEMS 1 16
INSTANTANEOUS
    to know the poignant instantaneous fern whose scrupulous . .   19 T&C PUELLA MEA 110
INSTEAD
    to think they died instead then shall the voice . . . . 268 IS 5 TWO 3   12
    were good: for when (instead of stopping to think) . . . . . 604 {CHAIRE} 6   9
    advantage of being alive (instead of undying) is not . . . . 664 {CHAIRE} 66   2
    life in your stride (instead of scheming how to . . . . 679 95 POEMS 7   1
    this fine morning) fly instead of dancing are they . . . . . 724 95 POEMS 52   11
+INSTEAD
    FOR CONTEXT, SEE . . . . 153 & SON ACTU 2   8
    FOR CONTEXT, SEE . . . . 611 {CHAIRE} 13   2
    FOR CONTEXT, SEE . . . . 782 73 POEMS 10   11
INSTIGATE
    peculiarly momentary partnership (to instigate constructive . 260 IS 5 ONE 30   18
INSTINCT
    generosity, thus reason vanquished instinct and matter became 799 73 POEMS 27   34
INSTINCTIVE
    springs, beyond the sweet instinctive wells, which make to .   19 T&C PUELLA MEA 121
INSTRUCT
    dead thing, i shall instruct him silently with becoming . . .   42 T&C AMORES 6   11
INSTRUCTION
    pursuing a course of instruction at radcliffe college, . . . 327 VIVA 18   44
INSTRUMENT
    the music for no instrument yours the preposterous colour . .   84 T&C SON ACTU 3   1
    a bitch invents an instrument to measure Spring with? . . . . 264 IS 5 ONE 33   28
INSTRUMENTS
    evoke allegiance per blunt instruments-- Olaf (being to all . 339 VIVA 30   14
    all the chic; by instruments, both span and spic, ... 438 NO THANKS 54   13
+INSTRUMENTS
    FOR CONTEXT, SEE . . . . 442 NO THANKS 57   5
INSUFFERABLE
    whence is the world's insufferable clay clothed with . . . .   6 T&C EPITHALAM 135
INSUFFICIENT
    ample sun, under the insufficient day under the noise . . . .   43 T&C AMORES 7   39
+INSUFFICIENTLY
    FOR CONTEXT, SEE . . . . 398 NO THANKS 15   1

		PAGE	TITLE	LINE

INSULATED
from ancient greath on insulated brows (while tossing boms . 500 50 POEMS 14   14
INSURED
alarm and rainbows are insured against old age when . . . . . 620 (CHAIRE) 22   4
INTAGLIO
minute grins each an intaglio. Nothing has also carved . . . 116 & PORTRAIT 9   7
INTANGIBILITY
cult based on consubstantial intangibility. Personne ne . . . 262 IS 5 ONE 32   25
INTANGIBLE
thy dim shrine of intangible commemoration, (from whose faint 206 XLI SONNETS 2   11
INTEGRATION
have seen see doom's integration........ a wind has blown . 80 T&C SON UNRE 5   13
finely arising at the integration of my soul i . . . . 197 XLI PORTRAIT 5   23
INTELLECT
died) seeing your bald intellect collywobbling on its feeble 329 VIVA 20   3
INTELLECTS
muddy toiletbowl, while kindred intellects evoke allegiance . 339 VIVA 30   13
INTELLIGENCE
up you pawn your intelligence to buy a drink . . . . 204 XLI LA GUERRE 2   11
INTELLIGENT
to guess: the cheap intelligent thighs, the electric trite . 173 & SON ACTU 22   14
INTEND
sleep--what does the whole intend" they wonder. oh and . . . 295 IS 5 FOUR 12   16
INTENSE
twinge of all living intense things. Never my soul . . . . . 19 T&C PUELLA MEA   101
things of faerie, are intense inhabitants; in whose warm . . 22 T&C PUELLA MEA   254
most new complete fragile intense, which wholly trembling . . 82 T&C SON ACTU 1   1
gesture utters a frivolous intense half of Girl which . . . . 95 & POST IMPR 7   7
music sinuous globular slippery intense witty huge and its . 110 & PORTRAIT 6   24
the power of your intense fragility: whose texture compels . 366 VIVA 57   14
we've such freedom such intense digestion so much greenness . 491 50 POEMS 5   15
INTENSIVELY
incisive simplicity a more intensively brutal futility" And . 354 VIVA 45   17
INTENT
anoint with calm of intent stars circling the acerb . . . . . 3 T&C EPITHALAM   31
--mine the unbought contemptuous intent till this our flesh . 84 T&C SON ACTU 3   3
niceness betters easily the intent of genius-- painting . . . 162 & SON ACTU 11   3
INTENTLY
gently: tug? g (ing intently it refuses. to refuse; . . . . . 387 NO THANKS 4   9
INTENTS
(to all purposes and intents) in which distinct and . . . . . 254 IS 5 ONE 25   6
Olaf (being to all intents a corpse and wanting . . . . 339 VIVA 30   15
INTER
impregnable Because (amount of inter -vening) anyway You know 335 VIVA 26   14
dead (whom noone might inter fleeing himself for selves . . . 394 NO THANKS 11   5
INTERCOURSE
thing, yet holds continuous intercourse--through skies and . 5 T&C EPITHALAM   91
INTEREST
anyone's world does -n't interest him (by the look . . . . . 676 95 POEMS 4   6
INTERESTED
both dead, are invariably interested in so many things-- . . 70 T&C SON REAL 1   6
morning. But i am interested more intricately in the . . . . 144 & SON REAL 15   10
godly toothless always-so-much-interested-in-everybody- . . . 250 IS 5 ONE 21   13
your story is so interested but you make me . . . . 321 VIVA 13   3
or uncle shylock not interested / / / / . . . . 641 (CHAIRE) 43   8
INTERESTING
like uninteresting- landscapes made interesting by earTHQuake 101 & POST IMPR 11   70
of scarlet. always. More interesting, as i think, her . . . . 143 & SON REAL 14   7
"stuffed fauna" being "very interesting"... we also . . . . . 326 VIVA 18   33
INTERMINABLE
pout And affectionate leer interminable pyramidal, napkins . 243 IS 5 ONE 14   6
INTERNALEXPANDING
i slammed on the internalexpanding & externalcontracting . . 248 IS 5 ONE 19   30
INTERNATIONAL
been heard screaming for international measures that render . 802 73 POEMS 30   30
INTERRED
Dead (not to mention inTerred) LONG LIVE that Upwardlooking . 315 VIVA 7   10

	PAGE	TITLE	LINE

INTERRUPT
   and lest punished bottoms interrupt philosophy / / / . . . . 261 IS 5 ONE 31   14
INTERSECT
   and a chatter sobbings intersect with which distinct disks . 96 & POST IMPR 8   8
INTERVAL
   a chair, a; domeshaped interval of complete plasticity, . . . 97 & POST IMPR 8   35
+INTERVENING
   FOR CONTEXT, SEE . . . . 335 VIVA 26   14
INTI
   differ- ently solemn and inti and sitting on one . . . . . . 126 & SEVEN POEMS 5 28
INTIMATE
   time untarnished! O small intimate gently primeval hands, . .   5 T&C EPITHALAM ° 106
   faun head now the intimate flower dreams of parted . . . . . 54 T&C PORTRAIT 2   10
   i believe my most intimate friends would never have . . . . 262 IS 5 ONE 32   14
   Slowly (slowly) Voyaging tones intimate tumult (Into) bangs . 348 VIVA 39   7
INTO
   WORD DELETED, APPEARED 222 TIMES
INTOLERABLE
   visible beatitude sweet sweet intolerable! silence immaculate   5 T&C EPITHALAM 111
   conquers magnificence. In heaven's intolerable athanor . . .   6 T&C EPITHALAM 129
INTOLERANT
   my breast wears the intolerant brightness of your charms: . . 78 T&C SON UNRE 3 11
INTONES
   a turk a waiter intones: bloo-moo-n sirkusricky platzburg . . 108 & PORTRAIT 4   13
INTOTHESLOW
   hard wo- men and intotheslow hot women my Stomach . . . . . . 101 & POST IMPR 11 62
INTRICATE
   gate unto a palace intricate (whereof the luscious pillars . 21 T&C PUELLA MEA 202
   singing close her with intricate faint birds by daisies . . . 65 T&C POST IMPR 2 9
   have made, my lady, intricate imperfect various things . . . 306 IS 5 FIVE 5   1
   some- thing possibly more intricate) i (breath in breath) . . 358 VIVA 49   8
INTRICATELY
   i am interested more intricately in the delicate scorn . . . 144 & SON REAL 15   11
   minute clumsy smelloftheworld. We intricately alive, cleaving 174 & SON ACTU 23   3
INTRIGUES
   quickness of the fand intrigues the fly) for know . . . . . . 425 NO THANKS 42   8
INTRINSIC
   at length her soft intrinsic hour, and from those . . . . . .   6 T&C EPITHALAM 131
   fronds toward all things intrinsic yearn, the immanent . . . 19 T&C PUELLA MEA 112
   contrives an unreal precise intrinsic frag- ment of . . . . . 193 XLI PORTRAIT 1   24
INTRO
   one and was never intro- duced you say Yes . . . . 126 & SEVEN POEMS 5 20
+INTRODUCED
   FOR CONTEXT, SEE . . . . 126 & SEVEN POEMS 5 20
INTUITIVE
   gorgeous bullet in tickling intuitive flight aches, just, . . 130 & SON REAL 1   10
INUNDERSTOOD
   / / one nonsufficiently inunderstood re with some difficulty 398 NO THANKS 15   1
INUTILE
   resume impact with the inutile collide once more with . . . . 289 IS 5 FOUR 6   7
INVADES
   by the abundant sun invades the new mosaic of . . . .   5 T&C EPITHALAM   84
INVARIABLY
   Longfellow, both dead, are invariably interested in so many . 70 T&C SON REAL 1   6
   rical putrescence whereto my invariably commendable room has 197 XLI PORTRAIT 5   20
INVEIGLE
   omnipotent goddess thou dost inveigle into crossing sidewalks 61 T&C PORTRAIT 9   2
+INVEIGLES
   FOR CONTEXT, SEE . . . . 267 IS 5 TWO 2   16
INVENT
   hipless body, pausing to invent im- perceptible bulgings of . 103 & POST IMPR 13   2
   these emerging now hills invent the air) breathe simply . . . 372 VIVA 63   3
   when god decided to invent everything he took one . . . . . . 566 1 X 1 26   1
INVENTED
   electricity or god was invented but why (captured by . . . . 324 VIVA 16   2
   which has ever been invented can spoil this or . . . . 357 VIVA 48   6
   dangerous machine as yet invented by even yankee ingenu . . . 644 {CHAIRE} 46   2

385

	PAGE	TITLE	LINE

+INVENTING
    FOR CONTEXT, SEE . . . . 448 NO THANKS 63   2
INVENTS
    son of a bitch invents an instrument to measure . . . . . . 264 IS 5 ONE 33   28
    more than (if Green invents because where might Where . . . . 395 NO THANKS 12   6
INVERNO
    the narrow light of inverno) this is the season . . . . 345 VIVA 36   11
INVESTIGATE
    in dreams let us investigate thoroughly each one his . . . . 261 IS 5 ONE 31   10
INVESTIGATOR
    (sh) the world renowned investigator of paper . . . . 326 VIVA 18   6
INVINCIBLE
    beautiful jam or my invincible Nearness rapes laughter from . 166 & SON ACTU 15   15
    am upward deep most invincible unthing --stern sexual . . . . 351 VIVA 42   2
+INVINCIBLE
    FOR CONTEXT, SEE . . . . 349 VIVA 40   13
INVISIBILITIES
    along perhaps the By invisibilities spattered (or if it . . . 317 VIVA 9   20
INVISIBLE
    the petals hush mysteriously invisible mourners move with . . 59 T&C PORTRAIT 7   7
    to the quivering string) invisible faces hauntingly and slow. 208 XLI SONNETS 4   8
    fishing boat somebody an invisible spectator, maybe certain . 283 IS 5 THREE 7   7
    certain hands, terse and invisible, with large first new . . 378 VIVA 69   7
    if upon a thread invisible) A graveyard dreams through . . . 434 NO THANKS 51   21
    every child (& therefore invisible) anyhow you 've (whoever . 668 {CHAIRE} 70   14
    as perfect this (almost invisible where of a there . . . . . 827 73 POEMS 55   8
+INVISIBLE
    FOR CONTEXT, SEE . . . . 616 {CHAIRE} 18   9
INVISIBLES
    / / of evident invisibles exquisite the hovering at . . . . . 54 T&C PORTRAIT 2   1
INVISIBLY
    men and loving) as invisibly when upon her palpable . . . . . 19 T&C PUELLA MEA 104
    a faultless languor when invisibly consult with some . . . . 193 XLI PORTRAIT 1   7
    the very swift and invisibly living rhythm of your . . . . . 300 IS 5 FOUR 17   7
    blocks when builds its invisibly skil ful toyTown which . . . 371 VIVA 62   7
+INVISIBLY
    FOR CONTEXT, SEE . . . . 347 VIVA 38   11
INVITATION
    why her tiniest whispered invitation is like a clock . . . . 229 IS 5 ONE FRAN   14
INVITE
    with quivering continual thighs invite the thrilling rain the 3 T&C EPITHALAM   2
    nearest far "i cordially invite me to become noone . . . . . 504 50 POEMS 18   4
INVOLVE
    whose irrefutable spiral antics involve me with the soothings 201 XLI PORTRAIT 9   25
INVOLVED
    he feels his pride involved (this i who's also . . . . . . 650 {CHAIRE} 52   9
INVOLVES
    lady whose still-born smile involves the comedy of decay, . . 144 & SON REAL 15   14
INWARD
    from this vast nonchalant inward walk of vol- ume . . . . . . 201 XLI PORTRAIT 9   21
    largest final air plunges inward with hurled downward . . . . 301 IS 5 FOUR 18   18
    (before my eyes sinking) inward, fled; softly your face . . . 369 VIVA 60   8
INWARDLY
    strolling lips and eyes inwardly crisping for my friend, . . 193 XLI PORTRAIT 1   8
+INWARDLY
    FOR CONTEXT, SEE . . . . 346 VIVA 37   21
INWARDLYNESS
    through algebras of proud inwardlyness to collide spirally . 311 VIVA 3   11
IONIAN
    beautiful bow "my home ionian isles / / / . . . . 585 1 X 1 45   21
+IRELAND
    FOR CONTEXT, SEE . . . . 320 VIVA 12   12
IRISH
    I mean me a Irish, cook but well oh . . . . 251 IS 5 ONE 22   11
IRISHER
    their eyes a blind irisher fiddles a scotch jig . . . . . . 108 & PORTRAIT 4   8
IRKETH
    little joe (yankee) gould irketh sundry who are trying . . . 410 NO THANKS 27   7

386

		PAGE	TITLE	LINE

IRON
  permitted me for twenty iron men her common purple . . . . . 52 T&C PORTRAIT 1 22
  to collide spirally with iron arithmethics and mesh witH . . 311 VIVA 3 11
  how rooted who of iron / / / . . . . 415 NO THANKS 32 24
  lifts on seas of iron breathing height eating steepness . . . 419 NO THANKS 36 12
IRONIN
  trifl e w hile ironin g! nob odyknowswhos esh . . . . 611 {CHAIRE} 13 8
IRREFUTABLE
  experi- menting colossus whose irrefutable spiral antics . . 201 XLI PORTRAIT 9 25
  / / / weazened Irrefutable unastonished two, countenances . . 255 IS 5 ONE 26 1
IRRELEVANTLY
  brutal feet propped on irrelevantly ferocious heels. Her . . 103 & POST IMPR 13 8
IRREPROACHABLE
  / / / / irreproachable ladies firmly lewd on . . . . 138 & SON REAL 9 1
IRRESPONSIBLE
  suddenly and softly into irresponsible toys.) when this man . 62 T&C PORTRAIT 10 22
  around and around the irresponsible toys circle wildly in . . 63 T&C PORTRAIT 10 30
IRREVOCABLE
  frail foam sprung with irrevocable nakedness to strike the . 7 T&C EPITHALAM 162
  green- greeting pale- departing irrevocable sea i knew thee . 39 T&C AMORES 4 26
  confuse hotly our moreover irrevocable bodies while the . . . 111 & PORTRAIT 6 61
  a big hunk of irrevocable nothing which touch and . . . . . 199 XLI PORTRAIT 7 2
  hear nearing our hearts' irrevocable play-- through the . . . 215 XLI SONNETS 11 13
  microscopic yes) acceptance of irrevocable time particular . 821 73 POEMS 49 4
+IRREVOCABLE
  FOR CONTEXT, SEE . . . . 719 95 POEMS 47 8
IRREVOCABLY
  the minute incessant Was irrevocably emanates a dignity of . 111 & PORTRAIT 6 52
  is for the brain irrevocably frigid to touch a . . . . 193 XLI PORTRAIT 1 15
  sing) for it's Spring --irrevocably; and in earth sky . . . . 835 73 POEMS 63 20
IS
WORD DELETED, APPEARED 836 TIMES
+ISAACS
  FOR CONTEXT, SEE . . . . 474 NEW POEMS 12 12
ISABEL
  fighting for, my sister isabel created hundreds (and . . . . 276 IS 5 TWO 10 8
+ISBEL
  FOR CONTEXT, SEE . . . . 24 T&C CHANSONS 1 14
ISFUL
  with thy freedom: star isful beckoningly fabulous crumb / . . 456 NO THANKS 71 15
ISLAND
  posolutely dead, like Coney Island in winter / / . . . . . . 72 T&C SON REAL 3 15
+ISLANDS
  FOR CONTEXT, SEE . . . . 445 NO THANKS 60 11
ISLES
  bow "my home ionian isles / / / / . . . . 585 1 X 1 45 21
ISN'T
  i've been Effie who isn't alive just imagine it . . . . 117 & PORTRAIT 10 24
  i have wondered since isn't it odd of you . . . . 172 & SON ACTU 21 10
  Drawers and If It Isn't An Eastman It Isn't . . . . 230 IS 5 ONE 2 34
  Isn't An Eastman It Isn't A Kodak therefore my . . . . 230 IS 5 ONE 2 34
  nightly supper sups it isn't snowing snow you know . . . . . 254 IS 5 ONE 25 23
  got the haven't Marjorie isn't this wellcurb simply darling" 257 IS 5 ONE 27 36
  odd, jolly jolly odd isn't it jolly odd. / . . . . 269 IS 5 TWO 4 17
  move. It's different too isn't it different dear from . . . . 289 IS 5 FOUR 6 17
  Something there is which isn't fond of walls) an . . . . . . 315 VIVA 7 3
  texture of their p-ss) isn't (and that it mayn't . . . . . . 411 NO THANKS 28 6
  the g--d -ld w. isn't that it can't exist . . . . 411 NO THANKS 28 10
  itarian fetish that man isn't wuman vive the millenni . . . . 492 50 POEMS 6 8
  the sky --endlings of isn't shall never begin to . . . . . . 512 50 POEMS 26 13
  all they sowed their isn't they reaped their same . . . . . 515 50 POEMS 29 7
  jennelman name misder finger isn't important whether it's . . 549 1 X 1 9 3
  twice (blow life to isn't: blow death to was) . . . . 560 1 X 1 20 22
  ask you if there isn't a new moon outside . . . . 572 1 X 1 32 1
  play host to every isn't that's under the spring . . . . . 580 1 X 1 40 5
  me, down isn't's own isn't go ghostly they doubting . . . . 580 1 X 1 40 7
  whisperful body and almost isn't (grabbed into skies of . . . 585 1 X 1 45 11
  / / / so isn't small one littlest why, ... 588 1 X 1 48 1

ISN'T (CONTINUED)

man we loved so isn't no! w a gay . . . . 606 (CHAIRE) 8   4
(1y infin) It's Snowing Isn't That Perfectly Wonderful / . . 629 (CHAIRE) 31   22
joy which wasn't and isn't and won't be words . . . . 631 (CHAIRE) 33   9
it clearer war just isn't what we imagine but . . . . 638 (CHAIRE) 40   8
me but that me isn't me can't you see . . . . 638 (CHAIRE) 40   11
them (i wonder) or isn't she a ware that . . . . 724 95 POEMS 52   16
five times, proclaim fate isn't fatal --a heart her . . . . 764 95 POEMS 90   53
Upstream & (5) unbeingdead isn't beingalive / / . . . . . . 803 73 POEMS 31   18
/ / all which isn't singing is mere talking . . . . 804 73 POEMS 32   1
is merely talk which isn't singing and all talking's . . . . 804 73 POEMS 32   11

+ISN'T

FOR CONTEXT, SEE . . . . 321 VIVA 13   12
FOR CONTEXT, SEE . . . . 646 (CHAIRE) 48   16

ISN'T'S

should april me, down isn't's own isn't go ghostly . . . . 580 1 X 1 40   7

ISN'TS

in black light dancing isn'ts on why, digging bridges . . . 439 NO THANKS 55 21
applaws) "fell ow sit isn'ts" (a paw s / . . . . 548 1 X 1 8   5

ISOLATING

keen careful futile flowers (isolating with perpetually . . . 193 XLI PORTRAIT 1 22

ISOUD

slowly dote, La beale Isoud whose leman was. And . . . . . . 17 T&C PUELLA MEA 37

ISWAS

of certainly never the iswas teetertiptotterish sp- . . . . . 495 50 POEMS 9   15

IT

WORD DELETED, APPEARED 339 TIMES

IT'LL

as for the candle, it'll turn into a little . . . . 164 & SON ACTU 13   15
(touch noth ing) or it'll disapp ear bangl essly . . . . . . 797 73 POEMS 25   7

IT'S

WORD DELETED, APPEARED 67 TIMES

ITALIENS

fragile qui chatouille Des Italiens the putain with the . . . 120 & PORTRAIT 12   8

ITCH

the, mouth's, swallowed, muscle (itch of groping mucous) in . 136 & SON REAL 7   9

ITCHINGS

not rise yesterday. Inexpressible itchings to be photographed 262 IS 5 ONE 32   20

ITCHY

in tweeds tweeds little itchy mousies with scuttling eyes . . 25 T&C CHANSONS 2 12

ITCREATING

as con founds all itcreating winds / / / . . . . 826 73 POEMS 54   17

ITEM

/ / / / ITEM this man is o . . . . 243 IS 5 ONE 14   T
upright but not piano item: a water- melon causes . . . . . 263 IS 5 ONE 32   51
/ / / / item: is Clumsily with of . . . . 371 VIVA 62   1
know means guess) I item i immaculately owe dying . . . . . 390 NO THANKS 7   12
destinies of nations sic item a bounceless period unshy . . . 499 50 POEMS 13   7
of guk rooms daughter item son a woopsing queer . . . . . . 499 50 POEMS 13   9

+ITEMS

FOR CONTEXT, SEE . . . . 388 NO THANKS 5   1

ITFULLS

thatthis is whichwhat yell itfulls o f cringewiltdroolery i . 646 (CHAIRE) 48   6

ITLIKE

With a cleverjeRk in itlike the motionofa Sharp Knife-sN . . 101 & POST IMPR 11 50

ITMAKING

(elsewhere flat the mechanical itmaking sickness of mind . . 658 (CHAIRE) 60   13

ITS

WORD DELETED, APPEARED 87 TIMES

ITSELF

pending gathering pouring upon itself stiffenS to a white . . 34 T&C ORIENTALE 6 92
some floating snake upon itself always and slowly which . . . 95 & POST IMPR 7   9
bright knives, it stains itself, with currants and cherries . 100 & POST IMPR 11 23
like a billiard-cue chalking itself, as not to make . . . . . 170 & SON ACTU 19   10
occasionally from which detaching itself bumps clumsily into 201 XLI PORTRAIT 9 10
tall corpsecoloured body seat itself (with the uncouth . . . 227 IS 5 ONE GERT   9
Xmas Eve like Hell Itself which may or may . . . . 239 IS 5 ONE 10   6
a door opens by itself woman.) they so to . . . . 243 IS 5 ONE 14   8

ITSELF (CONTINUED)
    a fat colour reared itself against the sky and . . . . 283 IS 5 THREE 7   19
    an crawled up into itself, an awful big light . . . . 332 VIVA 23   26
    being felt as bad, itself thinks goodness what is . . . . . . 438 NO THANKS 54   4
    are merely surfaces (one itself showing, itself hiding one) . 531 50 POEMS 43   6
    surfaces (one itself showing, itself hiding one) life's only 531 50 POEMS 43   6
    is compelled to fight itself from tame to teem) . . . . 544 1 X 1 4   18
    but whether to please itself or someone else makes . . . . . 549 1 X 1 9   9
    piece of nonsense which itself must call a state . . . . . . 561 1 X 1 21   2
    love armies (than hate itself and no meanness unsmaller) . . 580 1 X 1 40   15
    this out of within itself moo ving lump of . . . . 602 {CHAIRE} 4   1
    / / why must itself up every of a . . . . 636 {CHAIRE} 38   1
    and if what calls itself a world should have . . . . 717 95 POEMS 45   9
    we die to breathe, itself becomes her wonder --and . . . . . 742 95 POEMS 70   15
    but though mankind persuades itself that every weed's a . . . 744 95 POEMS 72   6
+ITSELF
    FOR CONTEXT, SEE . . . . 69 T&C POST IMPR 6   40
    FOR CONTEXT, SEE . . . . 101 & POST IMPR 11   63
    FOR CONTEXT, SEE . . . . 101 & POST IMPR 11   74
    FOR CONTEXT, SEE . . . . 318 VIVA 10   13
    FOR CONTEXT, SEE . . . . 318 VIVA 10   21
    FOR CONTEXT, SEE . . . . 341 VIVA 32   16
    FOR CONTEXT, SEE . . . . 343 VIVA 34   13
    FOR CONTEXT, SEE . . . . 423 NO THANKS 40   36
    FOR CONTEXT, SEE . . . . 472 NEW POEMS 10   7
    FOR CONTEXT, SEE . . . . 495 50 POEMS 9   12
    FOR CONTEXT, SEE . . . . 693 95 POEMS 21   15
    FOR CONTEXT, SEE . . . . 710 95 POEMS 38   9
ITSTERS
    this world (as timorous itsters all to call their . . . . . . 664 {CHAIRE} 66   13
IVORIES
    smoke that shook the ivories and she said said . . . . 125 & SEVEN POEMS 4 22
IVORY
    of roses and of ivory. The immaculate crisp head . . . . . . 20 T&C PUELLA MEA 138
    of roses and of ivory if naked she appear . . . . 22 T&C PUELLA MEA 230
    the putain with the ivory throat Marie Louise Lallemand . . . 120 & SON ACTU 14   9
    / / / the ivory performing rose of you, ... 165 & SON ACTU 14   1
    a song of adolescent ivory. / / / / . . . . 214 XLI SONNETS 10   14
    in the click of ivory balls.... noting flies, which . . . . . 217 XLI SONNETS 13   2
IYOU
    you-with-me around (me) you IYou / / / / . . . . 442 NO THANKS 57   25
IZABETH
    ardensteil-henarub-izabeth) this noN allgotupfittokill . . . 726 95 POEMS 54   1
+J.E. HOOVER
    FOR CONTEXT, SEE . . . . 325 VIVA 17   14
+J.P. MORGAN
    FOR CONTEXT, SEE . . . . 325 VIVA 17   12
J'AI
    Personne ne m'aime et j'ai les mains froides. His . . . . . . 262 IS 5 ONE 32   26
J'EN
    get away with them? j'en doute,) cherie, j'en doute. . . . . 169 & SON ACTU 18   12
    them? j'en doute,) cherie, j'en doute. the accurate key . . . 169 & SON ACTU 18   13
J'M'APPELLE
    has danced la guerre j'm'appelle Manon, cinq rue Henri . . . 121 & PORTRAIT 12   34
J'M'EN
    mon lezard ladies suddenly j'm'en fous des negres (in . . . . 121 & PORTRAIT 12   43
JAB
    it is, like the, Jab: of a dark tool. . . . . 101 & POST IMPR 11   49
JABBED
    knocked by sun moon jabbed jerked with ecstasy ....tremble . 153 & SON ACTU 2   11
JABBER
    white eyes of elsewhere jabber while (infinite fog & . . . . 629 {CHAIRE} 31   5
JACK
    medals drew (while messrs jack james john and jim . . . . . . 266 IS 5 TWO 1   25
    / spoke joe to jack leave her alone she's . . . . 496 50 POEMS 10   1
    she's not your gal jack spoke to joe 's . . . . 496 50 POEMS 10   4
    / we miss you, jack--tactfully you (with one cocked . . . . . 605 {CHAIRE} 7   1
    luck! aberdeen plato-rabelais peter jack / / / / . . . . . . 605 {CHAIRE} 7   16

		PAGE	TITLE	LINE
JACK (CONTINUED)				
/ / / where's Jack Was General Was the	. . . .	642	(CHAIRE) 44	1
+JACK				
FOR CONTEXT, SEE	. . . .	398	NO THANKS 15	21
JACK'S				
/ / / / jack's white horse (up high	. . . .	699	95 POEMS 27	1
+JACK'S				
FOR CONTEXT, SEE	. . . .	310	VIVA 2	9
JACKET				
out of the vermilion jacket of nodding hairy Jacqueline	. . .	279	IS 5 THREE 3	19
dirty collar of his jacket were two glued uncarefully	. . . .	355	VIVA 46	7
JACKKNIFE				
the penny and the jackknife and the rosebug and	. . . . . .	127	& SEVEN POEMS 5	47
JACKKNIVES				
falls in rosebugs and jackknives and kittens and pennies	. .	126	& SEVEN POEMS 5	5
kittens i do and jackknives i do and pennies	. . . .	127	& SEVEN POEMS 5	50
JACQUELINE				
jacket of nodding hairy Jacqueline who is given a	. . . . .	279	IS 5 THREE 3	19
JADE				
with bodies of lazy jade and twitching eyelids finger	. . . .	34	T&C ORIENTALE 6	77
JAKE				
/ / / / jake hates all the girls	. . . .	619	(CHAIRE) 21	1
JAM				
baby smeared with beautiful jam or my invincible Nearness	. .	166	& SON ACTU 15	13
, they are like jam on the shelf everybody	. . . .	353	VIVA 44	20
JAMES				
drew (while messrs jack james john and jim in	. . . .	266	IS 5 TWO 1	25
a handsome man and James and next let me	. . . .	271	IS 5 TWO 6	3
JAMMED				
the traffic get so jammed? bedad it is the	. . . .	245	IS 5 ONE 16	12
JANES				
an humpin duh swell janes on duh boollevares an	. . . . . .	332	VIVA 23	17
JANUARY				
warm air turning into January darkness up through which	. . .	279	IS 5 THREE 3	2
+JAPANESE				
FOR CONTEXT, SEE	. . . .	336	VIVA 27	10
JASON				
beauty: never did Lord Jason (in impossible things victorious	18	T&C PUELLA MEA	69
JASPER				
in a howdah of jasper beneath saffron umbrellas upon	. . . .	32	T&C ORIENTALE 6	5
JAY				
/ / / crazy jay blue) demon laughshriek ing	. . . .	677	95 POEMS 5	1
JAZZ				
a dribbling moan of jazz whose arched occasional steep	. . .	140	& SON REAL 11	4
you ever hear a jazz Band? or unnoise men	. . . .	141	& SON REAL 12	16
cornered always moist mouth) --jazz, for whose twitching	. .	227	IS 5 ONE GERT	5
JE				
Lallemand n'est-ce pas que je suis belle cheri? les	. . . . .	120	& PORTRAIT 12	11
by innumerable kind-of-deaths (Amerique Je T'Aime and it may	410	NO THANKS 27	13
JEALOUSY				
how much my wonderful jealousy is dark if light	. . . . . .	292	IS 5 FOUR 9	16
pest thus did immortal jealousy quell divine generosity, thus	799	73 POEMS 27	32
JEER				
ideas wearing a round jeer for a hat fate	. . . .	258	IS 5 ONE 28	4
JEEZUS				
an draws back huly jeezus" --an-- "my specialty is	. . . . .	332	VIVA 23	5
JEFF				
(wit (hprettyw) ith) mr jeff dick son fec i	. . . .	388	NO THANKS 5	29
JEFFERSON				
/ / remarked Robinson Jefferson to Injustice Taughed your	. .	321	VIVA 13	1
JEHOVAH				
/ / / / Jehovah buried, Satan dead, do	. . . .	438	NO THANKS 54	1
JELLY				
a flabby mattress of jelly.... than when to the	. . . . . .	143	& SON REAL 14	12
against , a, fathoming jelly of vital futile huge	. . . . . .	159	& SON ACTU 8	1
JENNELMAN				
were say or a jennelman name misder finger isn't	. . . . . .	549	1 X 1 9	3

		PAGE	TITLE	LINE

JERK
over the music and jerk the little string and . . . . 69 T&C POST IMPR 6   13
and i feel the jerk of the little string! . . . . 69 T&C POST IMPR 6   32
balls.... noting flies, which jerk upon the weak colour . . . 217 XLI SONNETS 13   3
the uncouth habitual dull jerk at garters) there 's . . . . . 227 IS 5 ONE GERT   10
treno per Roma si-gnori? jerk. ilyr, ushes / / . . . . 278 IS 5 THREE 2   21
a hero equals any jerk who was afraid to . . . . 636 (CHAIRE) 38   3

+JERK
FOR CONTEXT, SEE . . . . 101 & POST IMPR 11   50

JERKED
of dawn and be jerked into eternity. when over . . . . 49 T&C IMPRESS 3   20
by sun moon jabbed jerked with ecstasy ....tremble (not . . . 153 & SON ACTU 2   11
universe (who clean and jerked 300 lbs) i mean . . . . 645 (CHAIRE) 47   2

JERKILY
the little hands withdrew, jerkily, themselves quietly they . 284 IS 5 FOUR 1   8
Its image strutting (very jerkily) not toucH- ing because . . 335 VIVA 26   12

+JERKILY
FOR CONTEXT, SEE . . . . 278 IS 5 THREE 2   21

JERKS
Nobody knows, or why jerks Here &, here, gr(. . . . . . . 286 IS 5 FOUR 3   8

JERRY
a tall; tall some jerry so very (and nellie . . . . 509 50 POEMS 23   13

JES
move yes sir she jes was which the radio . . . . 425 NO THANKS 42   7
is ? niggers) Not jes livin not Jes alive . . . . 426 NO THANKS 43   4
Not jes livin not Jes alive But So alive . . . . 426 NO THANKS 43   6

JESUS
and break onetwothreefourfive pigeonsjustlikethat Jesus he . 60 T&C PORTRAIT 8   7
great black preacher gargles jesus the aesthete indulges his 108 & PORTRAIT 4   27
luminous fur poilu a Jesus sags in frolicsome wooden . . . 134 & SON REAL 5   15
the coming of Christ Jesus ? ?? ??? ! . . . . 196 XLI PORTRAIT 4   21
dear sh not yet jesus what blood darling i . . . . 496 50 POEMS 10   19
he couldn't believe it (jesus told him; he wouldn't . . . . 553 1 X 1 13   3
dark i met christ jesus) my heart flopped over . . . . . . 648 (CHAIRE) 50   5
morethanmostgenerous spirit. Feeling only (jesus) every (god) 823 73 POEMS 51   16

+JESUS
FOR CONTEXT, SEE . . . . 332 VIVA 23   5

JET
o howpale) bluedmuffFletomben outerly jeT ting lip ssixs ting 342 VIVA 33   11

JETSAM
/ / flotsam and jetsam are gentlemen poeds urseappeal . . . . 492 50 POEMS 6   1

JETTED
fiercely spurting bell a jetted music splashing fresh upon . 115 & PORTRAIT 8   19

JEW
the nigger smiles the jew stands beside his teddy-bears . . . 108 & PORTRAIT 4   23
kiss the mike if Jew turn kike who dares . . . . 438 NO THANKS 54   15
De Big Boss (crying) jew wop rich poor (sing . . . . 618 (CHAIRE) 20   11
ity (out of a jew a few dead dollars . . . . 644 (CHAIRE) 46   4

JEWEL
casket of the cool jewel of thy mind the . . . . 29 T&C ORIENTALE 3   17

JEWELS
beads of dew made jewels by the sun, so . . . . 8 T&C OF NICOL   16
among his pillows throws jewels at the queen of . . . . . . 34 T&C ORIENTALE 6 101
a clutter of trite jewels now like a moth . . . . 47 T&C IMPRESS 1   6

JEWESS
fat stupid animals the jewess shrieked the messiah tumbled . 241 IS 5 ONE 12   4

JEWISH
three castles He looks jewish , next door but . . . . 312 VIVA 4   16

JEWS
pants. and pompous ancient jews obscurely twitch through the 219 XLI SONNETS 15   9
is old as the jews are a moon is . . . . 436 NO THANKS 52   24

+JEWS
FOR CONTEXT, SEE . . . . 405 NO THANKS 22   12

JIBING
black mouth with fat jibing lips, once upon a . . . . 277 IS 5 THREE 1   15

JIFFYCLAUS
wheel no sendwisp ben jiffyclaus bug fainarain wee celibate . 333 VIVA 24   19

		PAGE	TITLE	LINE

JIG
    irisher fiddles a scotch jig in a stinking joyman . . . . . . 108 & PORTRAIT 4   9
JIGAJIG
    of the Art of Jigajig sitting pretty on the . . . . 642 {CHAIRE} 44   23
JIGGING
    leaves jiggled to the jigging fragrance of newness --and . . 173 & SON ACTU 22   7
JIGGLE
    -ven tu- al -ly jiggle the bait of dawn . . . . 49 T&C IMPRESS 3   18
JIGGLED
    as rapidly upon the jiggled norm of agony my . . . . 137 & SON REAL 8   9
    by stuttering pearl, leaves jiggled to the jigging fragrance 173 & SON ACTU 22   6
JIGGLES
    One opaque big girl jiggles thickly hips to the . . . . . . 220 XLI SONNETS 16   15
JIGS
    the Bar. tinking luscious jigs dint of ripe silver . . . . 96 & POST IMPR 8   11
    a flabby algebraic odour jigs et tout en face . . . . 134 & SON REAL 5   9
JILL
    the and bitch whispers jill mopping too bad dear . . . . . 496 50 POEMS 10   16
JIM
    badly Yep cigars who jim him why gluey grins . . . . 96 & POST IMPR 8   16
    angels with faces like Jim Europe / / / . . . . 241 IS 5 ONE 12   9
    jack james john and jim in token of their . . . . 266 IS 5 TWO 1   25
    j & ji & jim, jimm ; jimmy s: . . . . 471 NEW POEMS 9   23
    (rub-her-bub) bub? (bubs) where's Jim Soon Admiral Soon the . 642 {CHAIRE} 44   11
    little women alive (but jim stood still for a . . . . 709 95 POEMS 37   15
JIMMIE
    to pull his joint. Jimmie was a dude. Dark . . . . 149 & SON REAL 20   5
    the chips would kid Jimmie to give them a . . . . 149 & SON REAL 20   10
    them a kiss but Jimmie lived regular. stewed three . . . . . 149 & SON REAL 20   11
    big lips curl.... how Jimmie was framed and got . . . . . . 149 & SON REAL 20   16
    a goil goil goil, Jimmie 's got a goil . . . . 235 IS 5 ONE 6   4
    wish that you was Jimmie. Oh for such a . . . . 235 IS 5 ONE 6   12
JIMMIE'S
    and made its point Jimmie's sister worked for Dick. . . . . 149 & SON REAL 20   7
    / / / / Jimmie's got a goil goil . . . . 235 IS 5 ONE 6   1
    Salo -mes but gimmie Jimmie's gal. / / / . . . . 235 IS 5 ONE 6   24
JIMMY
    & jim, jimm ; jimmy s: A V o . . . . 471 NEW POEMS 9   24
JINGO
    name by gorry by jingo by gee by gosh . . . . 268 IS 5 TWO 3   8
JIP
    eerily oh gargle to jip hug behemoth truly pseudo . . . . . 333 VIVA 24   24
JIPPYMUGUN
    o (peemuvdepipl) marx okays jippymugun roomur j e (wut) . . . 325 VIVA 17   12
JOB
    the fifty bucks per job with one foot and . . . . 242 IS 5 ONE 13   9
    / squints a blond job at her diamond solitaire . . . . . . 545 1 X 1 5   2
    (now here is a job to be done) while . . . . 709 95 POEMS 37   10
JOCK
    / / / first Jock he was kilt a . . . . 271 IS 5 TWO 6   1
JOE
    i imagine never mind Joe agreeably cheerfully remarked when . 241 IS 5 ONE 12   2
    / / / little joe gould has lost his . . . . 410 NO THANKS 27   1
    (nude eel) now little joe lives on air Harvard . . . . . . 410 NO THANKS 27   4
    ye twang of little joe (yankee) gould irketh sundry . . . . . 410 NO THANKS 27   7
    a smile but little joe gould's quote oral history . . . . . 410 NO THANKS 27   9
    fun to be little joe gould) / / / . . . . 410 NO THANKS 27   14
    / / / spoke joe to jack leave her . . . . 496 50 POEMS 10   1
    gal jack spoke to joe 's left crashed pal . . . . 496 50 POEMS 10   4
    / / / as joe gould says in his . . . . 700 95 POEMS 28   1
+JOE'S
    FOR CONTEXT, SEE . . . . 496 50 POEMS 10   4
+JOG
    FOR CONTEXT, SEE . . . . 629 {CHAIRE} 31   19
JOGGLE
    / / / GERT joggle i think will do . . . . 227 IS 5 ONE GERT   1
JOGGLED
    geometries of transparency slightly joggled sink through . . 311 VIVA 3   10

		PAGE	TITLE	LINE
JOGGLING				
the tent his thick joggling fists he is persuasive	. . . . .	259	IS 5 ONE 29	6
JOHN				
(while messrs jack james john and jim in token	. . . .	266	IS 5 TWO 1	25
/ / / Lord John Unalive (having a fortune	. . . .	331	VIVA 22	1
(rub-her-bub) bub? (bubs) where's John Big Doughgob Big	. . .	642	{CHAIRE} 44	21
JOINING				
lips of spring simply joining with the wonderless city's	. .	218	XLI SONNETS 14	6
JOINT				
bulls to pull his joint. Jimmie was a dude.	. . . .	149	& SON REAL 20	4
thoroughly oiled the universal joint tested my gas felt	. . .	248	IS 5 ONE 19	7
JOISTS				
spikes of silence into joists hewn from hugest colour	. . . .	378	VIVA 69	9
JOKE				
fingers which grapple and joke on my passionate anatomy	. . .	146	& SON REAL 17	5
JOKED				
and forlorn piggish hands joked to a girlish whore	. . . .	56	T&C PORTRAIT 4	13
JOLLY				
/ / / it's jolly odd what pops into	. . . .	269	IS 5 TWO 4	1
what pops into your jolly tete when the jolly	. . . .	269	IS 5 TWO 4	3
jolly tete when the jolly shells begin dropping jolly	. . . .	269	IS 5 TWO 4	4
jolly shells begin dropping jolly fast you hear the	. . . . .	269	IS 5 TWO 4	4
(oh-- --i say that's jolly odd old thing, jolly	. . . . . .	269	IS 5 TWO 4	14
jolly odd old thing, jolly odd, jolly jolly odd	. . . .	269	IS 5 TWO 4	15
old thing, jolly odd, jolly jolly odd isn't it	. . . . . .	269	IS 5 TWO 4	16
thing, jolly odd, jolly jolly odd isn't it jolly	. . . . . .	269	IS 5 TWO 4	17
jolly odd isn't it jolly odd. / / /	. . . .	269	IS 5 TWO 4	18
JOLTS				
codified with superb sunlight, jolts of delapida- tion	. . .	94	& POST IMPR 6	3
by hair's blue cold jolts of lovecrazed abrupt flesh	. . . .	106	& PORTRAIT 2	10
JONAH				
soothe psychotic myths like Jonah And The Whale :	. . . . . .	398	NO THANKS 15	19
JONES				
or probably dead" so Jones was murdered by a	. . . .	313	VIVA 5	9
he cannot understand (why Jones don't pay me what	. . . . . .	406	NO THANKS 23	6
JONQUILS				
more hands are offering jonquils) down again who but	. . . .	585	1 X 1 45	17
JOSTLE				
edge spring, of the jostle of thy breasts and	. . . .	61	T&C PORTRAIT 9	23
wags and. rages Laughters jostle grins nudge smiles push--.	.	202	XLI PORTRAIT 9	36
JOSTLING				
suddenly dizzy With the jostling and shouting of merry	. . .	44	T&C AMORES 8	5
JOUJOUX				
like une boite a joujoux, want nice sleep? toutes	. . . . . .	121	& PORTRAIT 12	49
JOUNCE				
firmlysquirmy with a slight jounce, thirteen pants have a	. .	150	& SON REAL 21	4
although the glad monosyllable jounce possibly can tell	. . .	227	IS 5 ONE GERT	2
JOUNCING				
a microscopic stage whose jouncing curtain. , rises upon	. .	55	T&C PORTRAIT 3	7
even recklessly juggles the jouncing fruit of eager bosoms"	.	341	VIVA 32	20
JOVIAL				
the bright rile of jovial hair extremely frames the	. . . . .	137	& SON REAL 8	17
you darling diminutive person jovial ego (& mischievous	. . .	678	95 POEMS 6	5
JOY				
smooth pages of forgotten joy proving the peaceful theorems	.	3	T&C EPITHALAM	18
on noisy wheels of joy pathetic dress fluttering behind	. . .	56	T&C PORTRAIT 4	3
mother's pride, his father's joy, unto whom duty whispers	. .	273	IS 5 TWO 8	3
made (wears pain at joy, come summer puts on	. . . .	394	NO THANKS 11	7
feel (but up with joy; and up with laughing	. . . .	424	NO THANKS 41	11
an if emerges a joy let 's thank indecent	. . . .	425	NO THANKS 42	13
Five Year Plan: if Joy with Pain shall hang	. . . .	438	NO THANKS 54	7
daring to dare for joy of joy) what stink	. . . .	440	NO THANKS 56	30
dare for joy of joy) what stink is here	. . . .	440	NO THANKS 56	30
dimensionless new alls of joy: quietly & before illimitably	.	480	NEW POEMS 18	21
then these dolls of joy and grief these recent	. . . .	502	50 POEMS 16	9
leaf she laughed his joy she cried his grief	. . . .	515	50 POEMS 29	14
(out of some undering joy and overing grief nothing	. . . .	517	50 POEMS 31	9
slender is cradling in joy her flower than now	. . . . . .	518	50 POEMS 32	7

		PAGE	TITLE	LINE
JOY (CONTINUED)				
un ids dare dare joy (eye kinely thank yoo)		519	50 POEMS 33	27
moved through griefs of joy; praising a forehead called . . .		520	50 POEMS 34	18
singing desire into begin joy was his song and		520	50 POEMS 34	21
was his song and joy so pure a heart		520	50 POEMS 34	21
hate from whispering grass? joy in time shut and		527	50 POEMS 39	11
small thing dance little joy (shine most prayer) /		535	50 POEMS 47	11
(sans either pain or joy) does nothing except preexist . . .		544	1 X 1 4	6
grief; and, for his joy is more than joy, ...		562	1 X 1 22	4
joy is more than joy, most rare) a fiend, ...		562	1 X 1 22	4
faith to how their joy to why their stride		580	1 X 1 40	9
the star (sing! every joy) --wholly now disappear night's . .		582	1 X 1 42	14
snowing ly upward with Joy, no where (no) when		584	1 X 1 44	13
a mere pastime --each joy a deceiver, and sorrow		625	{CHAIRE} 27	19
the glow of a joy which wasn't and isn't		631	{CHAIRE} 33	9
young bird first for joy, he's i he's i		666	{CHAIRE} 68	19
yes for) white ly (joy! joy! joy) and whiteliest		715	95 POEMS 43	15
for) white ly (joy! joy! joy) and whiteliest all		715	95 POEMS 43	15
white ly (joy! joy! joy) and whiteliest all wonderings . . .		715	95 POEMS 43	15
calm and fury: through joy and anguish) who've made		742	95 POEMS 70	8
whose any sadness or joy is my grief or		749	95 POEMS 77	8
them) and whisper their joy under entirely the coming		754	95 POEMS 82	11
gain over gladness and joy under care-- let's do		769	95 POEMS 95	16
one (gifted with illimitable joy) bird sings love's every . .		783	73 POEMS 11	2
did the deed of joy with him then Cunning		799	73 POEMS 27	15
never guessed unknowable most joy) faithfully blossoming . .		811	73 POEMS 39	7
of oneness dream! ! joy truth! ! soul /		841	73 POEMS 69	38
JOY'S				
are the words but joy's the voice down shall		511	50 POEMS 25	22
glad? only their smallest joy's a universe emerging from . .		768	95 POEMS 94	7
doubts disappear. Everywhere and joy's perfect wholeness . .		812	73 POEMS 40	14
JOYBEGOTTEN				
nonelastic male-- uplook, all joybegotten whelps whom soothe		398	NO THANKS 15	18
JOYFUL				
in the blossoming always joyful selves are singing) "sweet .		591	1 X 1 51	24
/ / / / joyful your complete fearless and		761	95 POEMS 88	1
the coming of pure joyful your fearless and complete		761	95 POEMS 88	10
people of a person; joyful your any new (every		764	95 POEMS 90	45
JOYFULLY				
miracles of air (and joyfully all truths of wing		659	{CHAIRE} 61	3
JOYMAN				
jig in a stinking joyman bar a cockney is		108	& PORTRAIT 4	10
JOYS				
stench) and a hundred joys high are such shoulders		439	NO THANKS 55	13
like nothing are the joys of his voice until		587	1 X 1 47	5
/ / / / joys faces friends feet terrors		693	95 POEMS 21	1
trick to seem their joys turn woes and right		776	73 POEMS 4	25
mine; beyond sorrow's own joys and hoping's very fears . . .		810	73 POEMS 38	11
i'll give you sweet joys for each of them		837	73 POEMS 65	4
JUBILEE				
dreamtree, truthtree tree of jubilee: with aeons of (trivial		763	95 POEMS 90	32
JUDEA'S				
complete) than ever to Judea's king were the shapely		17	T&C PUELLA MEA	27
JUDGE				
is fair as i judge. / / / /		171	& SON ACTU 20	14
JUDGMENT				
of gingerbread when the judgment day comes God will		117	& PORTRAIT 10	3
here we are now judgment day cross the threshold		118	& PORTRAIT 10	40
JUDICE				
/ / ADHUC SUB JUDICE LIS when mack smacked		706	95 POEMS 34	T
JUGGLE				
and Matisse rhythms to juggle Kandinsky gold-fish away from .		180	XLI SONGS 2	13
JUGGLES				
transparent blouse even recklessly juggles the jouncing fruit		341	VIVA 32	20
JUICE				
and give her the juice, good (it was the		248	IS 5 ONE 19	23
JUILLET				
the. m oon over juillet moon over s -unday		384	NO THANKS 2	33

		PAGE	TITLE	LINE
JUKE				
y socked flopslump (& juke) ing shrieks Yew May		629	{CHAIRE} 31	12
JUKEJOG				
pers again & again (jukejog mist & strict) &		629	{CHAIRE} 31	19
JUKEPULSE				
(infinite fog & puking jukepulse hug) large less than		629	{CHAIRE} 31	6
JUKETHROB				
/ / / infinite jukethrob smoke & swallow to		629	{CHAIRE} 31	1
JULY				
Pudd 's 4th of July oration, with a curse		249	IS 5 ONE 20	2
JUMBLED				
elephant at the zoo (jumbled to queer this what		516	50 POEMS 30	7
JUMBLING				
almost i refrain from jumbling her flesh whose casual		131	& SON REAL 2	6
JUMP				
dancing from hop-scotch and jump-rope and it's spring and . .		24	T&C CHANSONS 1	15
was dumb. Skip fred (jump! neddy) but under the		513	50 POEMS 27	31
is killed dead. Hills jump with brooks: trees tumble		580	1 X 1 40	27
run with me now jump shout (laugh dance cry		835	73 POEMS 63	17
JUMP-ROPE				
dancing from hop-scotch and jump-rope and it's spring and . .		24	T&C CHANSONS 1	15
JUMPED				
groan on your taste. Jumped the quick wall of		154	& SON ACTU 3	4
JUMPING				
merely to become the jumping puppets of a dream?		295	IS 5 FOUR 12	4
who got athlete's mouth jumping on&off bandwaggons (MEMORIAM		404	NO THANKS 21	3
than any this tear jumping from each most least		502	50 POEMS 16	4
JUMPS				
which (shal) lpounceupcrackw (ill) jumps of THuNdeRB		347	VIVA 38	8
JUMPY				
disdain, led by a Jumpy Tramp who played each		194	XLI PORTRAIT 2	21
JUNE				
crossing sidewalks the unwary june-bug and the frivolous . .		61	T&C PORTRAIT 9	3
in the month of June, having of certain stars		360	VIVA 51	11
JUNE-BUG				
crossing sidewalks the unwary june-bug and the frivolous . .		61	T&C PORTRAIT 9	3
+JUNG				
FOR CONTEXT, SEE		499	50 POEMS 13	4
JUNGLES				
life: and carve immortal jungles of despair to hold		562	1 X 1 22	13
JUST				
/ CHANSONS INNOCENTES in Just- spring when the world		24	T&C CHANSONS 1	1
of the world (and just as smaller stars begin		71	T&C SON REAL 2	11
do not wonder that (just at the edge of		92	& POST IMPR 4	18
Effie who isn't alive just imagine it I say		117	& PORTRAIT 10	25
O My lover, there's just room for me in		123	& SEVEN POEMS 2	8
body's brain so everybody just puts out their finger		126	& SEVEN POEMS 5	12
should stretch neat necks just to see how always		130	& SON REAL 1	6
tickling intuitive flight aches, just, simply, into, her. . .		130	& SON REAL 1	11
of her kiss have just throttled my seeing blood, ...		132	& SON REAL 3	1
oozes in fashionable traffic, just a halfsmile (for society's		146	& SON REAL 17	10
taut, with thin legs just like a vine that's		147	& SON REAL 18	10
to see me it's just a little like music, ...		152	& SON ACTU 1	2
stammer of bodies (eagerly just not each other touch)		174	& SON ACTU 23	5
you safe and tight just as your mother would, ...		192	XLI CHANSONS 2	11
there is need of just twenty five cents dear		196	XLI PORTRAIT 4	12
/ / / it's just like a coffin's inside		198	XLI PORTRAIT 6	1
madame something by gainsborough just the playthings for dust		198	XLI PORTRAIT 6	13
utters a striving flower, just where strove the droll		213	XLI SONNETS 9	8
land above all of Just Add Hot Water And		230	IS 5 ONE 2	12
skyscrapers--Helen & Cleopatra were Just Too Lovely, The . .		230	IS 5 ONE 2	27
through second-in-to-high like greasedlightning) just as we .		248	IS 5 ONE 19	21
very tidiyum chins, and just above their very tidiyum		274	IS 5 TWO 9	13
in freshly-creased -uniforms with only-just- shined buttons .		274	IS 5 TWO 9	23
more did tell you just what everybody was fighting		276	IS 5 TWO 10	4
fellow in a blouse just outside this window, touching		282	IS 5 THREE 6	25
hat --(and i wonder just why that should please		296	IS 5 FOUR 13	9
ask for more than just enough dreams to live		298	IS 5 FOUR 15	10

	PAGE	TITLE	LINE
JUST (CONTINUED)			
go to this window just as day dissolves when	301	IS 5 FOUR 18	2
fine August night, i just happened to meet "how	313	VIVA 5	3
of Course life being just a Reflex you know	315	VIVA 7	7
over that one oh just thinking it over (at	323	VIVA 15	8
it over (at that just supposing we had met	323	VIVA 15	9
we had met and just but you know supposing	323	VIVA 15	10
you know supposing we just had let it go	323	VIVA 15	13
luck (1) ing of just bells (touch) ing ?	350	VIVA 41	8
nothing he smiled (but just by the dirty collar	355	VIVA 46	6
it refuses. to refuse; just, look) ing dead but	387	NO THANKS 4	12
(i'll squeal said she just once said he) it's	399	NO THANKS 16	3
bad brittle candy but just (nude eel) now little	410	NO THANKS 27	4
/ / at dusk just when the Light is	434	NO THANKS 51	2
/ / nor woman (just as it be gan	472	NEW POEMS 10	2
a mine and sank just off the coast of	494	50 POEMS 8	4
what's left behind is (just a head of he	501	50 POEMS 15	18
made --long enough and just so long will being	511	50 POEMS 25	4
fear --long enough and just so long will the	511	50 POEMS 25	12
float --long enough and just so long tomorrow will	511	50 POEMS 25	20
i am for you just so long and long	511	50 POEMS 25	28
the blue) put some just a now and now	516	50 POEMS 30	9
it's over a (see just over this) wall the	543	1 X 1 3	1
But over a (see just over this) wall the	543	1 X 1 3	25
of other punks or just a handful absolutely doesn't	549	1 X 1 9	5
a little child who's just as small as me	555	1 X 1 15	13
saying if that's all, just if" "that's all there	572	1 X 1 32	3
gravypissing poppa but who just couldn't help it no	635	(CHAIRE) 37	5
make it clearer war just isn't what we imagine	638	(CHAIRE) 40	8
Takes. now you know (just as well as i	701	95 POEMS 29	10
"it seems like i just heard your annabel screech	707	95 POEMS 35	5
want to be free just trust in the u	711	95 POEMS 39	8
crylaughingly float away leaving just this strolling ghostly	720	95 POEMS 48	8
/ / / at just 5 a m i	787	73 POEMS 15	1
unjust man complained "is just" ("or un-" the just	806	73 POEMS 34	2
just" ("or un-" the just rejoined / / /	806	73 POEMS 34	2
(we marvel) doubt, for just sweet terrifying the particular .	809	73 POEMS 37	9
croon more particularly at just midnight this hearty	813	73 POEMS 41	5
bliss "seven heavens for just one dying, i'll give	837	73 POEMS 65	14
+JUST			
FOR CONTEXT, SEE	60	T&C PORTRAIT 8	6
FOR CONTEXT, SEE	237	IS 5 ONE 8	19
FOR CONTEXT, SEE	425	NO THANKS 42	7
FOR CONTEXT, SEE	426	NO THANKS 43	4
FOR CONTEXT, SEE	426	NO THANKS 43	6
FOR CONTEXT, SEE	790	73 POEMS 18	16
JUSTGRAZE			
to pinch assiduously which justgraze each other). As the . .	150	& SON REAL 21	9
JUSTIFY			
the most odd) can justify the ways of man	731	95 POEMS 59	2
normal mortals can not justify the ways of God	731	95 POEMS 59	4
JUSTLY			
the wind and swirled justly souls of flower strike	163	& SON ACTU 12	6
ladies of my dreams justly touching roses their fingers . . .	211	XLI SONNETS 7	11
span and spic, are justly measured Spic and Span:	438	NO THANKS 54	14
K			
her springs were O. K.) i went right to	248	IS 5 ONE 19	9
uh cupl un wait k (relijinisde) o (peemuvdepipl) marx	325	VIVA 17	10
KAKA			
things are going rather kaka over there, over there.	233	IS 5 ONE 4	7
KANDINSKY			
Matisse rhythms to juggle Kandinsky gold-fish away from the .	180	XLI SONGS 2	13
KANOON			
than when to the kanoon she totters, slouches, with	143	& SON REAL 14	13
thickly hips to the kanoon but Hassan chuckles seeing	220	XLI SONNETS 16	15
KEEN			
fleetly mystical, aroam with keen creatures of idiom (beings	19	T&C PUELLA MEA	93
always which feels the keen ecstatic actual tread (and . . .	19	T&C PUELLA MEA	125

	PAGE	TITLE	LINE

KEEN (CONTINUED)
```
  fleetly go.) Upon a keen and lovely throat the  . . . . . . .   20 T&C PUELLA MEA   145
  dark colours like 'cellos keen fiddling colours colours . . .  100 & POST IMPR 11     7
  deep beasts coming with keen ridiculous silks coming with . .  112 & PORTRAIT 6     101
  coming out of a keen city in the sky--filled . . . . . . . .   129 & SEVEN POEMS 7    2
  away sailing into a keen city which nobody's ever . . . . . .  129 & SEVEN POEMS 7   11
  phonograph's voice like a keen spider skipping quickly over .  166 & SON ACTU 15      1
  of existence, continually whittles keen careful futile  . . . 193 XLI PORTRAIT 1    21
  small in the head keen chassised like a Rolls . . . . . . . .  232 IS 5 ONE 3         5
  reflecting sunlight (everywhere sunlight keen complete silent  283 IS 5 THREE 7      14
  lady: together with what keen innumerable lives he has  . . .  285 IS 5 FOUR 2       21
  of your smile the keen primeval silence of your . . . . . . .  306 IS 5 FIVE 5        8
  to notice how the keen ship lifts (skilfully like . . . . . . 378 VIVA 69            3
  ; elate shyly a-live keen parallel specks float-ing create  . 447 NO THANKS 62       3
  underwish of beauty; before keen if dim quiveringly spangle .  480 NEW POEMS 18       7
  of twilight would rejoice keen as midsummer's keen beyond . .  520 50 POEMS 34       25
  rejoice keen as midsummer's keen beyond conceiving mind of  .  520 50 POEMS 34       25
  of mothery same rotting keen dream? i rise which  . . . . . .  527 50 POEMS 39       30
  man what if a keen of a lean wind . . . . . . . . . . . . . .  560 1 X 1 20           9
  his soul comes a keen pure silence) such hands  . . . . . . .  617 (CHAIRE) 19        2
  when their lives are keen he throws the world . . . . . . . .  624 (CHAIRE) 26       17
  thick scream and a keen cold groan while the  . . . . . . . .  647 (CHAIRE) 49        8
  disappearing also me the keen illimitable secret of begin . . 669 (CHAIRE) 71       13
  deep hell -o of keen moon) dream unthings silent  . . . . . . 687 95 POEMS 15         8
  now dull eyes are keen and now keen eyes . . . . . . . . . .   769 95 POEMS 95       10
  are keen and now keen eyes are keener (for . . . . . . . . .   769 95 POEMS 95       10
  theirs (dull worlds or keen; big little and all) . . . . . .   776 73 POEMS 4        11
  alive most mercifully glorying keen star whom she-and-he-like  808 73 POEMS 36        7
```
KEENER
```
  black keenest than dying's keener each will kissed breast . .  565 1 X 1 25          11
  come swimming (Each a keener secret than silence even . . . .  630 (CHAIRE) 32        7
  eyes --gifted with every keener appetite than mere unmiracle   714 95 POEMS 42        4
  quite disappearance but some keener makes losing, gaining . .  750 95 POEMS 78       13
  now keen eyes are keener (for young is the . . . . . . . . .   769 95 POEMS 95       10
```
KEENEST
```
  than hate's more black keenest than dying's keener each . . .  565 1 X 1 25          11
  two were the cleanest keenest bravest killers you'd care  . .  709 95 POEMS 37        5
```
KEENLY
```
  death, silence, and the keenly musical light of sudden  . . .   84 T&C SON ACTU 3    14
  fleshless melody of the, keenly lascivious legs. painful  . .  103 & POST IMPR 13     7
  blood now accurately wan) keenly, to dreamings more than  . .  344 VIVA 35            7
```
KEENNESS
```
  youth swallows curvingly the keenness of my hips; or, . . . .  140 & SON REAL 11      6
```
KEEP
```
  Omar and Master Hafiz keep your dead beautiful ladies.  . . .   17 T&C PUELLA MEA     2
  ladies are all one-- keep your dead beautiful ladies. . . . .   23 T&C PUELLA MEA   265
  the city of Bagdad.) Keep your dead beautiful ladies  . . . .   23 T&C PUELLA MEA   289
  hands herself to always keep" always? the young man . . . . .   57 T&C PORTRAIT 5    20
  boys at Tabari' s, keep your teeth snowy, stick . . . . . . .   71 T&C SON REAL 2     4
  drolls fearsomely who do keep their sunday flower. The  . . .   74 T&C SON REAL 5    11
  and hearing and sight keep hitting and chipping with  . . . .  199 XLI PORTRAIT 7     3
  shall time no refuge keep though all the weird  . . . . . . .  377 VIVA 68           13
  little mouth) stumbling (can't keep up with how big . . . . .  501 50 POEMS 15       10
  old age sticks up Keep Off signs) & youth . . . . . . . . . .  729 95 POEMS 57        2
  something which nobody may keep. now i lay me . . . . . . . .  816 73 POEMS 44       13
  only for whom i'll keep my tryst until that . . . . . . . . .  843 73 POEMS 71        6
```
KEEPERS
```
  holy which are the keepers of the keys of . . . . . . . . . .   29 T&C ORIENTALE 3   28
```
KEEPING
```
  her long hard hands keeping silence on her dress, . . . . . .  147 & SON REAL 18      2
  wet stars softly are keeping their exquisite dreams--O Love!   206 XLI SONNETS 2      9
  a matter of not keeping still; we were two . . . . . . . . .   289 IS 5 FOUR 6       23
  wishing is having-- but keeping is downward and doubting . .   665 (CHAIRE) 67        3
  having is giving-- but keeping is doting and nothing  . . . .  665 (CHAIRE) 67       10
  giving is living-- but keeping is darkness and winter . . . .  665 (CHAIRE) 67       17
  is the wonder that's keeping the stars apart i . . . . . . .   766 95 POEMS 92       14
```
KEEPING'S
```
  to giving as to keeping's give; as yes is . . . . . . . . .   574 1 X 1 34           3
```

		PAGE	TITLE	LINE
KEEPS				
when you're flush pride keeps you from the pawn		204	XLI LA GUERRE 2	12
KEGS				
trunks shuffle sacks spin kegs they curl loving around . . .		114	& PORTRAIT 7	8
KELLY				
i too omit one kelly in response to howjedooze		259	IS 5 ONE 29	19
KELTYER				
the possession of quotes keltyer close " " aureally		331	VIVA 22	6
KEMERUH				
yewrety oride lesgo eckshun kemeruh daretoi nig) Ah, ...		474	NEW POEMS 12	14
KEPT				
in The Chair he kept talking about eyes /		145	& SON REAL 16	14
been a man and kept a date and played		479	NEW POEMS 17	9
+KERPLUNK				
FOR CONTEXT, SEE		519	50 POEMS 33	4
KEW				
women my Stomach ruBSiTSElf kew-ri-ous-ly a mong Them (among		101	& POST IMPR 11	63
rose bishop budge from kew a anglican was who		552	1 X 1 12	6
KEW-RI-OUS-LY				
women my Stomach ruBSiTSElf kew-ri-ous-ly a mong Them (among		101	& POST IMPR 11	63
KEWPIE				
knits and is a kewpie above the ears (but		253	IS 5 ONE 24	10
KEY				
j'en doute. the accurate key to a palace --You, ...		169	& SON ACTU 18	14
+KEY				
FOR CONTEXT, SEE		349	VIVA 40	16
KEYS				
the keepers of the keys of thy blood thy		29	T&C ORIENTALE 3	28
become eyes locks open keys haven't is have doubt		716	95 POEMS 44	24
KICK				
their passive prey did kick and curse until for		339	VIVA 30	24
KICKED				
got into reverse she kicked what the hell) next		248	IS 5 ONE 19	12
knocked down trampled the kicked by flics rush (the		274	IS 5 TWO 9	7
KICKIN				
we spent in '18 kickin duh guts outa dem		332	VIVA 23	15
KICKING				
huge humanity.... Numb thoughts, kicking in the rivers of . .		174	& SON ACTU 23	9
KID				
the lands thaz me kid in no sir hopping		96	& POST IMPR 8	15
breath once, all over, kid how, funny Do tell		136	& SON REAL 7	14
Loretta, cut the comedy kid.... Fran Mag Glad Dorothy		138	& SON REAL 9	16
with sharp necessary lips) kid female cracksman of the . . .		140	& SON REAL 11	9
was coming with his kid inside her. He laughed.		145	& SON REAL 16	10
All the chips would kid Jimmie to give them		149	& SON REAL 20	10
?? ??? ! nix, kid / / / /		196	XLI PORTRAIT 4	26
Yep. Youse is asleep kid and everybody is." And		228	IS 5 ONE MARJ	4
daze.... in dem daze kid Christmas meant sumpn youse		237	IS 5 ONE 8	13
he said to us Kid. daze nutn like it.		259	IS 5 ONE 29	27
live on) after all, kid you might as well		298	IS 5 FOUR 15	12
scream murmur wink at kid anaesthetize marry bump off		391	NO THANKS 8	15
notbre- notbrea-k . The kid) er Santa Claus a		398	NO THANKS 15	13
not (understand me) lousy kid that's something else my . . .		475	NEW POEMS 13	24
to smoke: come on kid let's go to sleep		489	50 POEMS 3	3
to sing; come on kid let's go to sleep		489	50 POEMS 3	7
to die, come on kid let's go to sleep		489	50 POEMS 3	11
to dream (come on kid Let's go to sleep)		489	50 POEMS 3	15
+KID				
FOR CONTEXT, SEE		310	VIVA 2	8
KIDDIES				
1 E.S.T. bring the kiddies let's all have fun		514	50 POEMS 28	14
KIDDIN				
duh A.C. fulla hooch kiddin eachudder bout duh clap		332	VIVA 23	2
KIDDING				
believed would they no kidding this was my particular		270	IS 5 TWO 5	6
KIDDO				
sir hopping sawdust you kiddo he's a palping wreaths		96	& POST IMPR 8	15
take it from me kiddo believe me my country, ...		230	IS 5 ONE 2	1

		PAGE	TITLE	LINE

KIDDO (CONTINUED)
    right in its way kiddo but as fer i . . . . 237 IS 5 ONE 8   11
KIDS
    have smelled Happens--skip dance kids hop point at red   . . . 437 NO THANKS 53   13
KIKE
    mike if Jew turn kike who dares to call . . . . 438 NO THANKS 54   15
    / / / a kike is the most dangerous . . . . 644 (CHAIRE) 46   1
KILL
    king's horses might not kill.) But should my lady . . . . . .   18 T&C PUELLA MEA   48
    winter, whom Spring shall kill / / / / . . . . 293 IS 5 FOUR 10   31
    big how dey could kill sixereight cops-- "I sidesteps . . . . 332 VIVA 23   3
    into form (actually) realness kill (make strangely) known . . 422 NO THANKS 39   8
    fart for art they kill like you would take . . . . 427 NO THANKS 44   16
    who dream, create and kill while the whole moves; . . . . . . 446 NO THANKS 61   13
    not Fear eat sleep kill and have you am . . . . 467 NEW POEMS 5   10
    sing) then let men kill which cannot share, let . . . . 521 50 POEMS 34   53
    very unkindest way to kill each of those creatures . . . . . 528 50 POEMS 40   11
    again" marvels "and liars kill their kind but" her, ... 572 1 X 1 32   17
    quote state unquote says "kill" killing is an act . . . . . . 636 (CHAIRE) 38   8
    murdered we whom cannot kill more mostful to arrive . . . . . 639 (CHAIRE) 41   10
    wisdom no knowledge can kill is astir-- now dull . . . . . . 769 95 POEMS 95   9
+KILL
    FOR CONTEXT, SEE . . . . 618 (CHAIRE) 20   5
    FOR CONTEXT, SEE . . . . 726 95 POEMS 54   3
KILLED
    in my eyes, the killed world wriggled like a . . . . 135 & SON REAL 6   16
    was yz SHOT AND KILLED her (in his arms) . . . . 317 VIVA 9   12
    his who death is killed dead. Hills jump with . . . . 580 1 X 1 40   27
    dooms of miracle drift killed swim born a dream . . . . . . 757 95 POEMS 85   33
+KILLED
    FOR CONTEXT, SEE . . . . 271 IS 5 TWO 6   2
    FOR CONTEXT, SEE . . . . 271 IS 5 TWO 6   7
    FOR CONTEXT, SEE . . . . 271 IS 5 TWO 6   8
    FOR CONTEXT, SEE . . . . 271 IS 5 TWO 6   11
    FOR CONTEXT, SEE . . . . 271 IS 5 TWO 6   11
    FOR CONTEXT, SEE . . . . 271 IS 5 TWO 6   11
KILLERS
    the cleanest keenest bravest killers you'd care to see   . . . 709 95 POEMS 37   6
KILLING
    so hard dear you're killing me / / / . . . . 109 & PORTRAIT 5   23
    light insane chisel the killing flame that dizzily grips. . . 139 & SON REAL 10   11
    which perfect is With killing hands / / / . . . . 188 XLI SONGS 10   22
    o Me please you're killing) death is like now . . . . 343 VIVA 34   6
    said he (but you're killing said she but it's . . . . 399 NO THANKS 16   20
    state unquote says "kill" killing is an act of . . . . . . 636 (CHAIRE) 38   8
+KILLING
    FOR CONTEXT, SEE . . . . 430 NO THANKS 47   13
KILLS
    like the light that kills and let's as silence, ... 160 & SON ACTU 9   10
    sans meaning (or whatever kills) a giving who (no . . . . . . 735 95 POEMS 63   5
KILT
    first Jock he was kilt a handsome man and . . . . 271 IS 5 TWO 6   2
    was cleverest he was kilt and my youngest boy . . . . 271 IS 5 TWO 6   7
    my youngest boy was kilt last with the big . . . . 271 IS 5 TWO 6   8
    Harry was o god kilt he was kilt everybody . . . . 271 IS 5 TWO 6   11
    god kilt he was kilt everybody was kilt they . . . . 271 IS 5 TWO 6   11
    was kilt everybody was kilt they called them the . . . . . 271 IS 5 TWO 6   11
KILTIES
    they called them the kilties / / / / . . . . 271 IS 5 TWO 6   12
KIN
    done the best he kin till they digged his . . . . 568 1 X 1 28   3
KIND
    your lover sumptuously being kind because i trust him . . . .   42 T&C AMORES 6   21
    swallowed even Nile the kind black great god) Cleopatra . . . 112 & PORTRAIT 6   88
    unnoticed woman from whose kind large flesh i turn . . . . . 142 & SON REAL 13   1
    the a week you kind of, know (kind well . . . . 251 IS 5 ONE 22   8
    you kind of, know (kind well of A sort . . . . 251 IS 5 ONE 22   8
    between houses, really a kind of mouse) but he . . . . . . 353 VIVA 44   9

	PAGE	TITLE	LINE

KIND (CONTINUED)
```
/ / exit a kind of unkindness exit little . . . . . . . . . .  389  NO THANKS 6        1
morality sort-of-aliveing by innumerable kind-of-deaths . . .  410  NO THANKS 27      12
/ / / / kind) YM& WC (of sort . . . . . . . . . . . . . . .    464  NEW POEMS 2        1
are standing) in a kind of crown he dressed . . . . . . . . .  470  NEW POEMS 8        2
little groom in it kind of stands on a . . . . . . . . . .     470  NEW POEMS 8       10
across the way are kind of afraid) afraid of . . . . . . .     501  50 POEMS 15        2
sort of really really kind of afraid of) these . . . . . . .   501  50 POEMS 15       23
to steal and cruel kind, a heart to fear, . . . . . . . . .    521  50 POEMS 34       57
one good yes completely kind mindheart one true one . . . . .  524  50 POEMS 36       40
(they're gravensteins) fall with kind of a blind big . . . .  543  1 X 1 3           29
blessings which to man kind progress doth impart one . . . .  544  1 X 1 4            2
animal is very very kind so kind it wouldn't . . . . . . . .   544  1 X 1 4           26
very very kind so kind it wouldn't like a . . . . . . . . .    544  1 X 1 4           27
not rich (only aware) kind neither nor cruel (only . . . . .  564  1 X 1 24           6
"and liars kill their kind but" her, my "love . . . . . . . .  572  1 X 1 32          17
the lean ones;the mean kind dirty clean) all except . . . . .  619  (CHAIRE) 21      26
dog of no known kind with one white eye . . . . . . . . . . .  647  (CHAIRE) 49      16
who is good and kind to all" "o no . . . . . . . . . . . . .   684  95 POEMS 12       12
manufacture might but man kind yet in park this . . . . . . .  698  95 POEMS 26        5
are bid a good kind bear is angary we . . . . . . . . . . . .  711  95 POEMS 39       19
Young m oon: be kind to olde r this . . . . . . . . . . . . .  733  95 POEMS 61        2
stairs speaks in his kind sweet big voice: then . . . . . . .  813  73 POEMS 41        2
nothingness (cruel now cancels kind; friends turn to enemies) 834  73 POEMS 62        3
```
KIND-OF-DEATHS
```
morality sort-of-aliveing by innumerable kind-of-deaths . . .  410  NO THANKS 27      12
```
KINDER
```
much more big & kinder of ring & which . . . . . . . . . .    470  NEW POEMS 8       13
of ring & which kinder of stands on a . . . . . . . . . . .   470  NEW POEMS 8       14
```
KINDEST
```
biggest & thickest & kindest of ring & all . . . . . . . .    470  NEW POEMS 8       16
```
KINDLY
```
girlhood was by the kindly lips and body fatherly . . . . . .  57  T&C PORTRAIT 5    30
```
+KINDLY
```
FOR CONTEXT, SEE . . . . . . . . . . . . . . . . . . . . . .  519  50 POEMS 33       28
```
KINDNESS
```
will out of the kindness of their hearts a . . . . . . . . .  281  IS 5 THREE 5       1
come and go for kindness and goodness do not . . . . . . . .  684  95 POEMS 12       15
(while looming darkly a kindness of fragrance opens around .  754  95 POEMS 82       10
and profound this) beautiful kindness sweet such (past can's  763  95 POEMS 90       24
```
KINDOF
```
(sortof people well youknow kindof) aint & even (not . . . .  412  NO THANKS 29       8
```
KINDRED
```
--or, since bloodshed and kindred questions inhibit . . . . .  266  IS 5 TWO 1        29
this muddy toiletbowl, while kindred intellects evoke . . . .  339  VIVA 30           13
```
KINDS
```
to shave) but--though all kinds of officers (a yearning . . .  339  VIVA 30           22
breathed quite so many kinds of yes) not a . . . . . . . . .  591  1 X 1 51          16
a million flaming billion kinds of nameless silence) sky; . .  786  73 POEMS 14       15
```
KINELY
```
dare dare joy (eye kinely thank yoo) / / . . . . . . . . . .  519  50 POEMS 33       28
```
KINESIS
```
a serene pastile-shaped insipid kinesis or frail swooping . .  201  XLI PORTRAIT 9    15
```
KING
```
crisp Sheba with her king in the morning wandering. . . . . .  17  T&C PUELLA MEA     8
than ever to Judea's king were the shapely sharp . . . . . .   17  T&C PUELLA MEA    27
and beautiful. (Caliph and king their ladies had to . . . .   20  T&C PUELLA MEA   129
is one kingdom the king whereof is darkness thy . . . . . .    29  T&C ORIENTALE 3    3
sits always a crowned king twir- ling an ankus . . . . . . .   32  T&C ORIENTALE 6   11
their hets off? the king & queen alighting from . . . . . .   245  IS 5 ONE 16        2
terse, seated like any king or prince upon his . . . . . . .  254  IS 5 ONE 25       19
in arranging; sunlight with-ered unspea-king: tWeNtY, f i n .  255  IS 5 ONE 26        3
through mist a defunct king as linotypes gobblehobble our . .  259  IS 5 ONE 29       11
call himself a man? King Christ, this world is . . . . . . .  438  NO THANKS 54      25
attitude and liked the king of) hear ye! the . . . . . . .   499  50 POEMS 13       13
immortal stars awry? Blow king to beggar and queen . . . . .  560  1 X 1 20           5
towerful towns (queen poet king float sprout heroes of . . .  586  1 X 1 46           9
(all during the dropsin king god my sic kly . . . . . . . .   646  (CHAIRE) 48        3
```

		PAGE	TITLE	LINE

KING (CONTINUED)
HE of a zagflash king poUnc es buzzsqueaking th . . . . 747 95 POEMS 75   11
KING'S
had eyes which the king's horses might not kill.) . . . . . . 18 T&C PUELLA MEA   48
KINGBIRD
of the sky your kingbird doesn't give a damn-- . . . . 774 73 POEMS 2   2
most crafty crow your kingbird doesn't give a damn . . . . . 774 73 POEMS 2   9
KINGDOM
while hunted from his kingdom winter cowers, seeing green . .   4 T&C EPITHALAM   70
trembling bliss of a kingdom wholly is. Beneath her . . . . . 21 T&C PUELLA MEA 206
thy hair is one kingdom the king whereof is . . . . 29 T&C ORIENTALE 3   2
a star in the kingdom of heaven through day . . . . 30 T&C ORIENTALE 4 32
shall reenter the singular kingdom (sleep) . while some . . . 370 VIVA 61   20
with a twitch like kingdom come (moon The sq . . . . 469 NEW POEMS 7   4
KINGDOMOFHEAVEN
big gollywog voice the kingdomofheaven up behind and crazily 259 IS 5 ONE 29   3
KINGDOMS
musical with large pearls kingdoms in her ears at . . . . . . 33 T&C ORIENTALE 6 68
KINGS
tremulous-- are there no kings in Argos, that the . . . . . .   4 T&C EPITHALAM   49
to a chariot of kings they are the striking . . . . 29 T&C ORIENTALE 3 12
is the combining of kings thy wrists are holy . . . . 29 T&C ORIENTALE 3 25
what like all them kings you read about and . . . . 568 1 X 1 28   12
the divine right of kings" Homer Lea) here are . . . . 803 73 POEMS 31   4
KIPLING
Meanwhile the tea regressed. Kipling again H.G. Wells, and . 263 IS 5 ONE 32   43
KIRKLAND
tables) while softly along Kirkland Street the infantile . . 232 IS 5 ONE 3   11
KISHCAM
smoked bad me whilepin Kishcam elscasta? netsits Elf . . . . 318 VIVA 10   21
KISS
her heart at every kiss of daisy-cup, and from . . . .   8 T&C OF NICOL   29
her mouth to wholly kiss-- never boast your dead . . . . . . 22 T&C PUELLA MEA 248
in scarlet in whose kiss is the combining of . . . . 29 T&C ORIENTALE 3 25
of neat huge trudging kiss moistly climbing hideously with . 67 T&C POST IMPR 4 25
trembling memory undertakes --your kiss, the little pushings 82 T&C SON ACTU 1   3
Then you will slowly kiss me / / / . . . . 86 T&C SON ACTU 5   14
of New Lady whose kiss is a procession of . . . . 112 & PORTRAIT 6   99
whose displeasure lives a kiss) kneeling, your frequent mercy 115 & PORTRAIT 8   7
the curvedship of Her- ....kIss her: hands will play . . . . 122 & SEVEN POEMS 1   9
In, the slipshod mucous kiss of her riant belly's . . . . . 130 & SON REAL 1   1
dirty colours of her kiss have just throttled my . . . . . . 132 & SON REAL 3   1
to love whose bodies kiss me with the square . . . . 138 & SON REAL 9   12
about me, and to kiss my face and head. . . . . 147 & SON REAL 18   14
to give them a kiss but Jimmie lived regular. . . . . 149 & SON REAL 20   10
death's big rotten particular kiss. / / / / . . . . 158 & SON ACTU 7   14
shut quietly) almost, your kiss / / / / . . . . 163 & SON ACTU 12   22
candlelight (halfstooping to exactly kiss the trite worm of . 164 & SON ACTU 13   4
liked your dress ....your kiss, your kiss was a . . . . . . 173 & SON ACTU 22   9
dress ....your kiss, your kiss was a distinct brittle . . . . 173 & SON ACTU 22   9
and again and again kiss, i like kissing this . . . . 175 & SON ACTU 24   9
where float flowers of kiss and there is the . . . . 186 XLI SONGS 8   12
so sweetly i will kiss your cool bark and . . . . 192 XLI CHANSONS 2   9
(if it were a kiss) distinct entirely melting sinuous . . . . 225 IS 5 ONE LIZ   14
the mirror)? therefore we'll kiss; for maybe what was . . . 286 IS 5 FOUR 3   21
(stooping through the morning) kiss this pillow, dear where . 288 IS 5 FOUR 5   8
are together, we will kiss or smile or move. . . . . 289 IS 5 FOUR 6   17
things will never wholly kiss you; wholly to be . . . . . . 290 IS 5 FOUR 7   4
has walked into my kiss as a stranger into . . . . 297 IS 5 FOUR 14   6
very young noisily who kiss throw silently things Each . . . 312 VIVA 4   12
homeless and when a kiss departs our lips are . . . . 322 VIVA 14   12
annoyed "I will not kiss your fucking flag" straightway . . . 339 VIVA 30   19
this or this instant) kiss me a little: the . . . . 357 VIVA 48   7
for a dog, a kiss without lips; a prayer . . . . 360 VIVA 51   26
all saving our young kiss only must unexist, solemnly . . . . 373 VIVA 64   2
said he if you kiss said she may i . . . . 399 NO THANKS 16   16
a (piercing clothes thoughts kiss -ing wishes bodies) . . . . 437 NO THANKS 53   6
Spic and Span: to kiss the mike if Jew . . . . 438 NO THANKS 54   15

	PAGE	TITLE	LINE

KISS (CONTINUED)

the rain (did you kiss a girl with nipples . . . . 498 50 POEMS 12   17
than socalled civilization i'll kiss a stalinist arse in . . 514 50 POEMS 28   12
(and noone stooped to kiss his face) busy folk . . . . 515 50 POEMS 29   26
in it you will (kiss me) go out into . . . . 529 50 POEMS 41   3
warm world in it (kiss me) you will go . . . . 529 50 POEMS 41   6
it you will go (kiss me down into your . . . . 529 50 POEMS 41   9
memory and memory i) kiss me (will go) / . . . . 529 50 POEMS 41   12
scalpel, they dissect a kiss; or, sold the reason, ... 556 1 X 1 16   7
i am alive to kiss / / / / . . . . 577 1 X 1 37   20
her? darling, did you (kiss me) quickly count to . . . . . 599 {CHAIRE} 1   10
throws the world a kiss and slings his wheel . . . . 624 {CHAIRE} 26   18
we're alive, dear: it's (kiss me now) spring! now . . . . . 665 {CHAIRE} 67   11
you aren't afraid to kiss the dirt (and consequently . . . 679 95 POEMS 7   5
if i let him kiss me twice but my . . . . 684 95 POEMS 12   10
are) lovers cling & kiss neither beholding a nor . . . . . 698 95 POEMS 26   6
so) nothings each (let's kiss) means home / / . . . . 728 95 POEMS 56   15
one last more than kiss) to call most the . . . . 741 95 POEMS 69   13
never we know (so kiss me) shy sweet eagerly . . . . 767 95 POEMS 93   7
incalculable than a single kiss / / / / . . . . 809 73 POEMS 37   14
deeper death becomes your kiss losing through you what . . . 810 73 POEMS 38   8
measure imagine, mystery, a kiss --not though mankind would . 817 73 POEMS 45   10
(where lips forget to kiss) where everything's nothing . . . 834 73 POEMS 62   28

KISSED

la bocca mia "he kissed wholly trembling" or so . . . . . . 84 T&C SON ACTU 3 16
own and the moon kissed the little lady on . . . . 125 & SEVEN POEMS 4 18
lump of lymph she kissed and i .... cheri............ 133 & SON REAL 4   21
solidity which a. , kissed with is nearness. (peers: . . . . 159 & SON ACTU 8   10
pure young girl much kissed, by loving relatives well . . . . 273 IS 5 TWO 8   21
arrive when i have kissed you into a memory . . . . 295 IS 5 FOUR 12   9
remembering badly, softly your kissed thrice suddenly smile / 300 IS 5 FOUR 17   24
nothing says) and he kissed the general menedjerr and . . . 552 1 X 1 12   28
dying's keener each will kissed breast awake) slow tottering 565 1 X 1 25   12
fountaining man's thingfulest godtown (kissed bigly by bells) 681 95 POEMS 9   16

KISSES

wisely minced for blown kisses, condemnatory fingers thinned   9 T&C SONGS 1   13
moist eyes are at kisses playing, whose strangeness much . . 13 T&C SONGS 3   10
my god--a patter of kisses, the chewed stump of . . . . . . 133 & SON REAL 4   14
and everywhere you your kisses your flesh mind breathing . . 283 IS 5 THREE 7   16
my blood approves, and kisses are a better fate . . . . . . 290 IS 5 FOUR 7   8
cries: hopes; houses, clouds. kisses, lice; headaches: ifs.) 361 VIVA 52   19
while some thing else kisses busily a memory, which . . . . 370 VIVA 61   24

KISSING

it shall not stop kissing). / / / / . . . . 13 T&C SONGS 3   21
sits looking beyond the kissing and the striving of . . . . 57 T&C PORTRAIT 5   9
between my amused legs kissing with little dints of . . . . 172 & SON ACTU 21   13
again kiss, i like kissing this and that of . . . . 175 & SON ACTU 24   9
voices which are for kissing and to sing with . . . . 264 IS 5 ONE 33   26
did i climb (crazily kissing) till into themselves we . . . 694 95 POEMS 22   3

KISSINGLY

over his body squirms kissingly, i will bring you . . . . . 161 & SON ACTU 10   7

KITCHEN

eyebrows sits in the kitchen nights and chews a . . . . . . 149 & SON REAL 20   2

KITCHENETTE

(once crammed into someone's kitchenette) wheezing bulgily . 607 {CHAIRE} 9   3

KITE

like pieces of a kite in the trees, here . . . . 283 IS 5 THREE 7   11
ng through never) a kite like face of the . . . . 668 {CHAIRE} 70   9

+KITELIKE

FOR CONTEXT, SEE . . . . 668 {CHAIRE} 70   9

KITES

many years but fly kites and when the string . . . . 253 IS 5 ONE 24   6

KITTEN

well and see the kitten and the penny and . . . . 127 & SEVEN POEMS 5 46

KITTENS

rosebugs and jackknives and kittens and pennies they all . . 126 & SEVEN POEMS 5   5
say for i like kittens i do and jackknives . . . . 127 & SEVEN POEMS 5 50
you go? like little kittens are all the leaves . . . . 191 XLI CHANSONS 1   6

KITTENS (CONTINUED)
in the rain. little kittens who are called spring, ... 191 XLI CHANSONS 1   9
KITTY
/ / / / "kitty". sixteen, 5' 1", white, ... 74 T&C SON REAL 5   1
bottomless eyes importantly banal, Kitty. a whore. Sixteen . 74 T&C SON REAL 5   8
flower. The babybreasted broad "kitty" twice eight --beer . . 74 T&C SON REAL 5   12
out of Briggs by Kitty) arriving in an exhausted . . . . . . 326 VIVA 18   14
KNAVES
a man? go dreamless knaves on Shadows fed, your . . . . 438 NO THANKS 54   9
KNEAD
will all be dead knead of lustfulhunched deeplytoplay lips . 153 & SON ACTU 2   5
KNEE
hippopotamus, scratch- ing, one, knee with, its, friend . . . 252 IS 5 ONE 23   3
KNEEL
lovers are those who kneel lovers are these whose . . . . . . 563 1 X 1 23   9
in their imagined bodies kneel (over time space doom . . . . 714 95 POEMS 42   6
KNEELAND
the august evening mauls Kneeland, and a waiter cleverly . . 217 XLI SONNETS 13   8
KNEELING
displeasure lives a kiss) kneeling, your frequent mercy begs, 115 & PORTRAIT 8   8
wherein silently always are kneeling the various deaths which 285 IS 5 FOUR 2   20
is throbbing prayers whom kneeling eyes (until perfectly . . 450 NO THANKS 65   6
and humbly heights below) kneeling, we--true lovers--pray . 574 1 X 1 34   11
to hesitate; to stop (kneeling in doubt: while all . . . . . 650 {CHAIRE} 52   2
KNEELINGLY
Nor any dusk but kneelingly believes thy secret and . . . . . 351 VIVA 42   13
KNEES
the grave great sensual knees well might any monarch . . . . 21 T&C PUELLA MEA 213
thee upon their scraggy knees squeezing and buffeting thee . 46 T&C LA GUERRE 2   15
toward him on her knees across the locked room. . . . . 145 & SON REAL 16   3
your hair; feeling your knees among the supercilious . . . . 169 & SON ACTU 18   6
of Your smile eyes knees and of your Etcetera) . . . . 276 IS 5 TWO 10   26
people crumble to their knees. people begin crossing people) 280 IS 5 THREE 4   7
(upon what were once knees) does almost ceaselessly repeat . 339 VIVA 30   31
a prayer lacking any knees but something beats within . . . . 360 VIVA 51   27
stranger went on both knees" green turns red (the . . . . . . 800 73 POEMS 28   16
+KNEES
FOR CONTEXT, SEE . . . . 101 & POST IMPR 11   60
KNEW
eager body's unimmortal flower knew in the darkness a . . . . 4 T&C EPITHALAM   56
departing irrevocable sea i knew thee death. and when . . . . 39 T&C AMORES 4   28
/ / / somebody knew Lincoln somebody Xerxes this . . . . . . 62 T&C PORTRAIT 10   1
erectly sitting. --If they knew you at Dick Mid's . . . . . . 73 T&C SON REAL 4   10
from a broad that knew Eddie in Topeka, went . . . . 145 & SON REAL 16   7
succulent getup but we knew a muffhunter and he . . . . 259 IS 5 ONE 29   27
sea ...finally your eyes knew me, we smiled to . . . . 283 IS 5 THREE 7   20
wandering hunter whom you knew once? what if (merely . . . . 374 VIVA 65   9
a sun i never knew and neither did you . . . . 591 1 X 1 51   14
sub human superstate ever knew (1) we sans love . . . . 803 73 POEMS 31   6
+KNEW
FOR CONTEXT, SEE . . . . 602 {CHAIRE} 4   3
KNIFE
itlike the motionofa Sharp Knife-sN ap-ingof fadeadf ish' . . 101 & POST IMPR 11   51
KNIGHT
earth of the sky knight and ploughman pardoner wife . . . . . 661 {CHAIRE} 63   9
KNIGHTS
light cryingly as the knights flew. / / / . . . . 302 IS 5 FIVE 1   15
KNITS
tears. my uncle Tom knits and is a kewpie . . . . 253 IS 5 ONE 24   10
KNITTING
still finds delighted fingers knitting for the is it . . . . 70 T&C SON REAL 1   8
large first new stars knitting the structure of distinct . . 378 VIVA 69   8
KNIVES
trees think (hear little knives of flower stropping sof . . . 99 & POST IMPR 10   12
melons slitted with bright knives, it stains itself, with . . 100 & POST IMPR 11   23
this ghost with millionary knives of wind-- scatter his . . . 839 73 POEMS 67   11
KNOCK
was brewed which could knock you down (while scotch . . . . . 605 {CHAIRE} 7   4

```
                                                    PAGE      TITLE       LINE
KNOCK (CONTINUED)
    that pretty pink pinafore'd knock out your eye" "well  . . . .  707  95 POEMS 35        8
KNOCKED
    plus slush of foam knocked off and a faint  . . . . . . . .   96  & POST IMPR 8     13
    the locked room. he knocked her cold and beat . . . . . . .  145  & SON REAL 16      4
    and nights that matter knocked by sun moon jabbed . . . . .  153  & SON ACTU 2      11
    crowd sprawls collapses singing knocked down trampled the . .  274  IS 5 TWO 9       7
    i Mean is what knocked him over Wasn't (for . . . . . . . .  702  95 POEMS 30       10
    stranger one black day knocked living the hell out  . . . . .  730  95 POEMS 58       2
+KNOCKED
    FOR CONTEXT, SEE  . . . . . . . . . . . . . . . . . . . . .  790  73 POEMS 18       16
KNOCKETH
    my lord Boccaccio-- whoso knocketh at the door of . . . . . .   20  T&C PUELLA MEA   171
KNOCKING
    of overjoyed noncoms (first knocking on the head him) . . . .  339  VIVA 30           8
KNOW
    to embrace--and didst thou know the god from but  . . . . . .    3  T&C EPITHALAM    12
    my folded soul shall know while on faint hills . . . . . . .   11  T&C SONGS 2       26
    turn her head i know that i am wholly . . . . . . . . . . . .   17  T&C PUELLA MEA    34
    is wont wholly to know the poignant instantaneous fern  . . .   19  T&C PUELLA MEA   109
    morning may a lily know, her petaled flesh doth . . . . . . .   21  T&C PUELLA MEA   184
    what i want to know is how do you . . . . . . . . . . . . . .   60  T&C PORTRAIT 8     9
    take twilight where i know: proving to Death that . . . . . .   71  T&C SON REAL 2    13
    stage which shall not know thy smile again, lingering . . . .   75  T&C SON REAL 6     4
    a silence as i know, or such great writhing . . . . . . . .   76  T&C SON UNRE 1     6
    and sky marry-- to know the white ship of . . . . . . . . .   79  T&C SON UNRE 4    15
    a single colour, i know only that your hands . . . . . . . .   98  & POST IMPR 9      7
    child- ren. my, ears know the fuZZy tune that's . . . . . .  100  & POST IMPR 11    36
    frown puzzles, but I know the way-- (nervously Whose  . . . .  117  & PORTRAIT 10     34
    say Yes because you know you want it to . . . . . . . . . .  126  & SEVEN POEMS 5   21
    who can but you know you never can and  . . . . . . . . . .  126  & SEVEN POEMS 5   31
    here's what WhoEver will know Had you as bite . . . . . . .  154  & SON ACTU 3      13
    how vague i don't know tenuous Now- spears and  . . . . . .  160  & SON ACTU 9      15
    is white (but you know that) they look at . . . . . . . . .  171  & SON ACTU 20     10
    never guess. but i know / / / / . . . . . . . . . . . . . .  183  XLI SONGS 5       16
    maybe asleep? do you know? or maybe did something . . . . .  191  XLI CHANSONS 1    13
    slim) sim ply don't know duh meanin uv duh . . . . . . . .  240  IS 5 ONE 11        2
    babies and how you know the dam rent's going  . . . . . . .  242  IS 5 ONE 13       19
    who goes wrong you know (whereas when i lie . . . . . . . .  245  IS 5 ONE 16       11
    Brand -new; and you know consequently a little stiff  . . . .  248  IS 5 ONE 19        3
    week you kind of, know (kind well of A  . . . . . . . . . .  251  IS 5 ONE 22        8
    sight shall human optics know more quite ennobling forsooth?  254  IS 5 ONE 25        3
    and of course you know their mother, of his . . . . . . . .  254  IS 5 ONE 25       11
    isn't snowing snow you know it's snowing buttercups / . . . .  254  IS 5 ONE 25       23
    Name and General You know who a string of . . . . . . . . .  266  IS 5 TWO 1        23
    buddies i used to know him lift the poor . . . . . . . . .  270  IS 5 TWO 5        12
    / lis -ten you know what i mean when  . . . . . . . . . . .  272  IS 5 TWO 7         3
    first guy drops you know everybody feels sick or  . . . . . .  272  IS 5 TWO 7         4
    up to your you know what in water or . . . . . . . . . . .  272  IS 5 TWO 7         9
    and never never will know, they don't want to . . . . . . .  272  IS 5 TWO 7        16
    do not pretend to know the reason any more  . . . . . . . .  282  IS 5 THREE 6       4
    Eyes everything hands you know what happens) but if . . . . .  287  IS 5 FOUR 4       19
    just a Reflex you know since Everything is Relative . . . . .  315  VIVA 7            8
    and just but you know supposing we just had . . . . . . . .  323  VIVA 15           11
    on duh koib" --you know alotta sweet bull like . . . . . .  332  VIVA 23           11
    / ohld song you Know a fly and his  . . . . . . . . . . . .  335  VIVA 26            2
    inter -vening) anyway You know Separated what i Mean . . . .  335  VIVA 26           16
    eaten spaces grouse rocket know quite, slightly or how  . . .  346  VIVA 37           11
    time (forgetting what's to know wholly imagining fire) only .  362  VIVA 53           14
    breathing (i do not know what it is about . . . . . . . . .  366  VIVA 57           17
    horizon) --do you perhaps know these workmen? / / . . . . .  378  VIVA 69           16
    sleep as more than know means guess) I item . . . . . . . .  390  NO THANKS 7       11
    but Rully yes i know) but what it comes . . . . . . . . . .  400  NO THANKS 17       5
    o posi but i know sure that's) but listen . . . . . . . . .  400  NO THANKS 17      11
    yeh ughhuh yuh) i know (o sure i know . . . . . . . . . . .  400  NO THANKS 17      14
    know (o sure i know yes of course) but  . . . . . . . . . .  400  NO THANKS 17      16
    authentic and delirious you know something genuine like a . .  407  NO THANKS 24      12
    his teeth and doesn't know where to find them . . . . . . .  410  NO THANKS 27       1
```

404

	PAGE	TITLE	LINE

KNOW (CONTINUED)

intrigues the fly) for know all men ((CHAIRETE)) as	425	NO THANKS 42	9
and i do not know him (and while behind	450	NO THANKS 65	15
as themselves could not know: the earth tinily whirls;	451	NO THANKS 66	10
/ Q: dwo we know of anything which can	468	NEW POEMS 6	2
i or anybody don't know where it her his	475	NEW POEMS 13	3
is better than to know and if men should	481	NEW POEMS 19	3
ask me how i know (a he of head	501	50 POEMS 15	6
what princess selene doesn't know a thing who's much	504	50 POEMS 18	11
good too quick i know this suit you pay	523	50 POEMS 36	11
me i work i know i say i have	523	50 POEMS 36	16
stone with blossoming eyes know if a lit tle	525	50 POEMS 37	18
not why) both didn't know exeunt they (not false	542	1 X 1 2	4
hypermagical ultraomnipotence. We doctors know a hopeless	554	1 X 1 14	13
clover clover clover (nobody'll know) sam was a man	568	1 X 1 28	25
all ignorance toboggans into know and trudges up to	579	1 X 1 39	1
or although (and buds know better than books don't	594	1 X 1 54	11
true are merely to know) Love only has ever	631	(CHAIRE) 33	13
should Smile) comes nobody'll know / / / /	660	(CHAIRE) 62	27
time of daffodils (who know the goal of living	688	95 POEMS 16	1
it Takes. now you know (just as well as	701	95 POEMS 29	10
pretty pink shoulders you know how and he twitches	711	95 POEMS 39	22
be the first to know / / / /	718	95 POEMS 46	8
mother's greatgrandmother surely would know) of purest poem	748	95 POEMS 76	6
must die to merely Know / / / /	759	95 POEMS 86	12
why --we never we know (so kiss me) shy	767	95 POEMS 93	6
have --we never we know-- brave! brave (the earth	767	95 POEMS 93	12
how-- we never we know (with a high low	767	95 POEMS 93	18
(as sweetly singing creatures know) cringes the hugest	774	73 POEMS 2	6
fancy we should never know are unimaginably ours to	809	73 POEMS 37	7
though mankind would rather know than feel; mistrusting	817	73 POEMS 45	11
now contrive; imagined, merely know (freedom: what makes a	834	73 POEMS 62	8

+KNOW

FOR CONTEXT, SEE	109	& PORTRAIT 5	11
FOR CONTEXT, SEE	227	IS 5 ONE GERT	15
FOR CONTEXT, SEE	272	IS 5 TWO 7	19
FOR CONTEXT, SEE	392	NO THANKS 9	5
FOR CONTEXT, SEE	412	NO THANKS 29	8
FOR CONTEXT, SEE	538	50 POEMS 50	2

KNOWABLE

| if, out of not knowable night's utmost nothing, wanders | 810 | 73 POEMS 38 | 1 |

KNOWETH

| the tale of Chaucer knoweth many a pair of | 20 | T&C PUELLA MEA | 164 |

KNOWING

with ecstasy ....tremble (not knowing how much better than	153	& SON ACTU 2	12
whatever is between them) knowing my lips hands the	285	IS 5 FOUR 2	6
until i smile with knowing --and all about herself	301	IS 5 FOUR 18	13
say "won't you" (remembering) knowing that you are afraid	353	VIVA 44	25
a most tremendous hug knowing i feel that we	680	95 POEMS 8	26
Wasn't (for instance) the Knowing your whole (yes god	702	95 POEMS 30	11

+KNOWING

| FOR CONTEXT, SEE | 319 | VIVA 11 | 9 |

KNOWING'S

| meets most despair? all knowing's having and have is | 528 | 50 POEMS 40 | 10 |

KNOWINGS

| bastards throw dynamite) let knowings magic with bright | 452 | NO THANKS 67 | 6 |

KNOWLEDGE

spare: for that way knowledge lies, the foetal grave	484	NEW POEMS 22	11
un gulps the first knowledge of death's wandering guess)	517	50 POEMS 31	13
us a wisdom no knowledge can kill is astir--	769	95 POEMS 95	9
ignorance by every wisdom knowledge fears to dare, how	843	73 POEMS 71	11

+KNOWLEDGE

| FOR CONTEXT, SEE | 700 | 95 POEMS 28 | 8 |

KNOWLEDGEABLE

| and homeless home of knowledgeable shadows (quick to seize | 765 | 95 POEMS 91 | 2 |

KNOWN

| learn, scents of not known musics in whose careful | 9 | T&C SONGS 1 | 17 |
| a rose more sweetly known, more silently than a | 21 | T&C PUELLA MEA | 176 |

KNOWN (CONTINUED)
    think i too have known autumn too long (and . . . .   80 T&C SON UNRE 5   3
    woman amorous to be known; and man, whose here . . . .   81 T&C SON UNRE 6   10
    stomachs which have not, known other stomachs and their . . . 101 & POST IMPR 11   72
    strange thing and a known thing here) and changing . . . . . 124 & SEVEN POEMS 3   8
    mid-victorian attic which is known as {HO PARTHENON} and . . 194 XLI PORTRAIT 2   8
    about us and birds known, scarcely to sing (heart, ... 205 XLI SONNETS 1   14
    my feet have surely known the furious ways and . . . . 216 XLI SONNETS 12   13
    things moments be murdered known photographed, ourselves . . 237 IS 5 ONE 8   2
    y is a WELL KNOWn ATHLETE'S BRIDE (lullaby) & . . . . 317 VIVA 9   1
    rattling for that well known suburb the bronx (enlivening . . 326 VIVA 18   12
    the unimaginable night not known / / / / . . . . 418 NO THANKS 35   14
    realness kill (make strangely) known (establish new) come, . 422 NO THANKS 39   10
    tasted Beautiful to have known Only to have smelled . . . . . 437 NO THANKS 53   12
    is to fabricate unknownness (known being wishless; but love, 446 NO THANKS 61   2
    measured and safe and known where it's lucky to . . . . 466 NEW POEMS 4   18
    music wear burst icy known swim ignorant fire (adventuring . 533 50 POEMS 45   15
    more if than each known allness disappears lovers are . . . . 563 1 X 1 23   6
    mosts if you have known and i've only we . . . . 574 1 X 1 34   13
    sweet this creative never known complexity was born before . 577 1 X 1 37   13
    Is A eyes Strange known Face (whylaughing! among: skydiamonds 628 {CHAIRE} 30   11
    a dog of no known kind with one white . . . . 647 {CHAIRE} 49   16
    inhabits here: overs of known descend through depths of . . . 761 95 POEMS 88   6
    sky (silently all then known things or dreamed become . . . . 822 73 POEMS 50   7
    i&you- ful world of known) who and who (2 . . . . 832 73 POEMS 60   11
+KNOWN
    FOR CONTEXT, SEE . . . . 236 IS 5 ONE 7   4
    FOR CONTEXT, SEE . . . . 508 50 POEMS 22   12
KNOWS
    lord of skipping maenads knows,-- having Discordia's apple in   6 T&C EPITHALAM   150
    do to yer nobody knows for she knows the . . . .   25 T&C CHANSONS 2   20
    nobody knows for she knows the devil ooch the . . . .   25 T&C CHANSONS 2   21
    in sun-light THE nobody (knows and WhoEver would)? dance . . 101 & POST IMPR 11   80
    that gets up god knows when every day of . . . . 109 & PORTRAIT 5   16
    whispering drunkard passes who knows if the moon's a . . . . 129 & SEVEN POEMS 7   1
    the face --pinxit, who knows? Who knows? Some "allemand" . . 158 & SON ACTU 7   6
    --pinxit, who knows? Who knows? Some "allemand" . . . .? of . 158 & SON ACTU 7   6
    cat waiting for god knows makes me wonder if . . . . 166 & SON ACTU 15   9
    warmth (after dream who knows?) a blackish cat and . . . . . 168 & SON ACTU 17   16
    hands. and no one knows what (i am sure . . . . 225 IS 5 ONE LIZ   10
    one ask Dad, He knows). / / / / . . . . 233 IS 5 ONE 4   24
    Christmas meant sumpn youse knows wot i refers ter . . . . . 237 IS 5 ONE 8   14
    for me i only knows that as far as . . . . 246 IS 5 ONE 17   9
    Duluth God only, gondola knows Cincingondolanati i gondola . 256 IS 5 ONE 27   28
    delivers the goods, Heaven knows (yet are we mindful, ... 264 IS 5 ONE 33   12
    everyone that's been there knows what i mean a . . . . 272 IS 5 TWO 7   12
    can tell because Nobody knows, or why jerks Here . . . . . . 286 IS 5 FOUR 3   7
    be owned by who knows) only turn a little . . . . 303 IS 5 FIVE 2   14
    er sumpn: next i knows me (er somebody is . . . . 332 VIVA 23   29
    love (of which Who knows the meaning; or how . . . . 364 VIVA 55   2
    darling (for only Nobody knows where truth grows why . . . . 368 VIVA 59   18
    to think because he knows (that anything is bad . . . . 406 NO THANKS 23   3
    think good) because he knows, he cannot understand (why . . . 406 NO THANKS 23   5
    pay me what he knows he owes) because he . . . . 406 NO THANKS 23   6
    in life) and death knows whie (all good kumrads . . . . 413 NO THANKS 30   6
    kumrads enjoy s. freud knows whoy the hope that . . . . 413 NO THANKS 30   11
    a futile groove god knows why) and so do . . . . 413 NO THANKS 30   16
    stands unslain he which knows not if any anguish . . . . . . 414 NO THANKS 31   7
    none but well she knows; and can perfectly speak . . . . . . 575 1 X 1 35   29
    out of perhaps (who knows?) eternity floated a blossoming . . 599 {CHAIRE} 1   7
    follows winter: as clover knows, maybe" (heart makes the . . 625 {CHAIRE} 27   10
    is newlY Born) he knows nothing, and feels everything; . . . 657 {CHAIRE} 59   2
    have learned what he knows from his slut of . . . . 707 95 POEMS 35   15
    see what no mind knows a mindless he begins . . . . 716 95 POEMS 44   14
    than to grow beauty knows no their goal (in . . . . 742 95 POEMS 70   6
    the deepest secret nobody knows (here is the root . . . . . . 766 95 POEMS 92   10
    and politics, as everyone knows, is wut ektyouelly metus. . . 790 73 POEMS 18   13
    loveless infraworld) a woman knows; and certain men quite . . 807 73 POEMS 35   11

	PAGE	TITLE	LINE

+KNOWS
    FOR CONTEXT, SEE . . . . 611 {CHAIRE} 13   10
KNUCKLING
    a polite uproar of knuckling silent planes a nudging . . . . 68 T&C POST IMPR 5 14
    (my loveFist in her knuckling thighs, with a sharp . . . . . 131 & SON REAL 2   8
KODAK
    Eastman It Isn't A Kodak therefore my friends let . . . . . . 230 IS 5 ONE 2   35
KODAKS
    voices Baedekers Mothers and kodaks --by night upon the . . . 256 IS 5 ONE 27   16
KOIB
    boxin im on duh koib" --you know alotta sweet . . . . 332 VIVA 23   10
KOW
    his death at afternoon? (kow dow r 2 bul . . . . 409 NO THANKS 26   3
KRASSIN
    whispering of a named Krassin / / / / . . . . 324 VIVA 16   16
KSENODOCHEION
    cindercoloured little {MEGA} {HELLENIKON KSENODOCHEION . . . 217 XLI SONNETS 13 15
KUM
    cheeks "eet smeestaire steevensun kum een, dare ease Bet, . . 73 T&C SON REAL 4 13
    ar (now heer we kum dearie) bud hooz gwine . . . . 519 50 POEMS 33   14
KUMRAD
    mess your pance every kumrad is a bit of . . . . 413 NO THANKS 30   13
KUMRADS
    / / / / kumrads die because they're told) . . . . 413 NO THANKS 30   1
    die because they're told) kumrads die before they're old . . 413 NO THANKS 30   2
    die before they're old (kumrads aren't afraid to die . . . . 413 NO THANKS 30   3
    aren't afraid to die kumrads don't and kumrads won't . . . . 413 NO THANKS 30   4
    die kumrads don't and kumrads won't believe in life) . . . . 413 NO THANKS 30   5
    knows whie (all good kumrads you can tell by . . . . 413 NO THANKS 30   7
    smell moscow pipes good kumrads dance) kumrads enjoy s. . . . 413 NO THANKS 30   9
    pipes good kumrads dance) kumrads enjoy s. freud knows . . . 413 NO THANKS 30   10
KYKERPLUNG
    coon wid a plon kykerplung guit ar (pleez make . . . . . . 519 50 POEMS 33   4
L
    sticks tuh de mans l (hutch) hutchinson says sweet . . . . . 325 VIVA 17   6
    dove for the nearest l; surreptitiously cogitating the dictum 327 VIVA 18   38
    ,males await she patiently l) littlecrownGrave whose . . . . 342 VIVA 33   18
L'ECHELLE
    man (rue d e l'echelle) die can't quite poison . . . . . . 708 95 POEMS 36   14
+L'ECHELLE
    FOR CONTEXT, SEE . . . . 708 95 POEMS 36   14
L'ETOILE
    / / 16 heures l'Etoile the communists have fine . . . . . . 274 IS 5 TWO 9   2
L'EUROPE
    vicinity of the de l'Europe Grand and Royal Danielli . . . . 256 IS 5 ONE 27   18
L'HEURE
    Slivers of (unthinking. c'est l'heure exquise) i remind Me . 94 & POST IMPR 6   19
+L'HOTEL
    FOR CONTEXT, SEE . . . . 708 95 POEMS 36   11
L'ON
    to live at present (l'on parle de repapering; i . . . . . . 312 VIVA 4   22
L'S
    ofa crankin It The L's roar tortures-pleasantly myears it . . 101 & POST IMPR 11 48
    past six) the well-fed L's immaculate roar looped . . . . . 219 XLI SONNETS 15 5
LA
    of Tristram slowly dote, La beale Isoud whose leman . . . . 17 T&C PUELLA MEA 37
    / / / / / LA GUERRE the bigness of . . . . 45 T&C LA GUERRE 1 T
    light of sudden nothing.... la bocca mia "he kissed . . . . 84 T&C SON ACTU 3 15
    precisely croons dance where danced la guerre. Mimi a la . . 120 & PORTRAIT 12 4
    la guerre. Mimi a la voix fragile qui chatouille . . . . . 120 & PORTRAIT 12 6
    dance where has danced la guerre j'm'appelle Manon, cinq . . 121 & PORTRAIT 12 33
    / / / / LA GUERRE earth like a . . . . 203 XLI LA GUERRE 1 T
    (of croons canned a la vallee and preserved goldfishian . . . 425 NO THANKS 42   3
    vertiginously absorbed which a la / / / / . . . . 465 NEW POEMS 3   12
    cannot read or write, la moon. Employs a very . . . . 504 50 POEMS 18   6
    nor both who is la guerre) your me or . . . . 577 1 X 1 37   11
    tle once beau ti ful la dy (sitting sew ing . . . . 724 95 POEMS 52   6
    meta ph or ? la lune / / / . . . . 831 73 POEMS 59   19

	PAGE	TITLE	LINE

LABELLING
measured; disdains the trivial labelling of punctual . . . . 377 VIVA 68 11
LABOR
um three cheers for labor give all things to . . . . 492 50 POEMS 6 10
LABORIOUS
He'll not my tower, laborious, casual where the surrounded . 83 T&C SON ACTU 2 14
LABYRINTH
most, the futile fooling labyrinth where noisy colours . . . 220 XLI SONNETS 16 11
+LACE
FOR CONTEXT, SEE . . . . 369 VIVA 60 2
LACED
ing-roundly-dis tinct; chuck lings, laced ar: e, by (. . . . 416 NO THANKS 33 9
LACK
doth prefer shall not lack for beauty there, nor . . . . . . 20 T&C PUELLA MEA 168
LACKING
without lips; a prayer lacking any knees but something . . . 360 VIVA 51 27
LADDIOS
guelph and ladios and laddios (on radios and raddios) . . . . 552 1 X 1 12 13
LADIES
sees eight and twenty ladies in a line the . . . . 15 T&C SONGS 5 4
lady says to nine ladies his lips drink water . . . . 15 T&C SONGS 5 6
lady says to nine ladies they must chain his . . . . 15 T&C SONGS 5 10
nineteenth says to nine ladies you take his mouth . . . . . . 15 T&C SONGS 5 14
keep your dead beautiful ladies. Mine is a little . . . . . . 17 T&C PUELLA MEA 2
than any of your ladies were. In her perfectest . . . . 17 T&C PUELLA MEA 4
lay. Lovely as those ladies were mine is a . . . . 18 T&C PUELLA MEA 75
(Caliph and king their ladies had to love them . . . . 20 T&C PUELLA MEA 129
than any of those ladies were.) Her body is . . . . 20 T&C PUELLA MEA 134
of Maleore findeth of ladies goodly store whose beauty . . . 21 T&C PUELLA MEA 173
hair-- i for those ladies nothing care nor any . . . . 21 T&C PUELLA MEA 179
to make them glad ladies with lithe eyes and . . . . 22 T&C PUELLA MEA 225
and Harun loved their ladies in the moon) --fashioned . . . . 22 T&C PUELLA MEA 228
Hafiz, to me your ladies are all one-- keep . . . . 23 T&C PUELLA MEA 264
keep your dead beautiful ladies. Eater of all things . . . . 23 T&C PUELLA MEA 265
slowly) one or two ladies like flowers made, softly . . . . . 23 T&C PUELLA MEA 282
to wholly move slender ladies made of dream (in . . . . 23 T&C PUELLA MEA 284
to laugh and love ladies with crisp eyes and . . . . 23 T&C PUELLA MEA 287
Keep your dead beautiful ladies Harun Omar and Master . . . . 23 T&C PUELLA MEA 289
blacker than oblivion the ladies of the emperor's harem . . . 33 T&C ORIENTALE 6 43
the company of those ladies with faces painteaten and . . . . 57 T&C PORTRAIT 5 37
/ SONNETS--REALITIES the Cambridge ladies who live in . . . . 70 T&C SON REAL 1 1
Professor D ....the Cambridge ladies do not care, above . . . 70 T&C SON REAL 1 11
/ / / / ladies and gentlemen this little . . . . 72 T&C SON REAL 3 1
body with these frail ladies dangerously respire: impeccable 85 T&C SON ACTU 4 14
bigtwittering zither-and the mealy, ladies dancing . . . . . 100 & POST IMPR 11 42
feet of the little ladies more than dead / . . . . 108 & PORTRAIT 4 37
My Lady Lady Of Ladies you who move beautifully . . . . 112 & PORTRAIT 6 94
/ / / little ladies more than dead exactly . . . . 120 & PORTRAIT 12 1
promenent doucement le soir (ladies accurately dead les . . . 120 & PORTRAIT 12 24
avec moi? Non? pourquoi?) ladies skilfully dead precisely . . 121 & PORTRAIT 12 31
voulez chatouiller mon lezard ladies suddenly j'm'en fous des 121 & PORTRAIT 12 42
dance in my head ladies carefully dead / / . . . . 121 & PORTRAIT 12 61
/ / / irreproachable ladies firmly lewd on dangerous . . . . 138 & SON REAL 9 1
a green egyptian noise. ladies with whom time feeds . . . . . 138 & SON REAL 9 8
too-- are they not ladies, ladies of my dreams . . . . 211 XLI SONNETS 7 10
are they not ladies, ladies of my dreams justly . . . . 211 XLI SONNETS 7 10
(or spaded) gentlemen (and ladies) --pretty littleliverpill- 231 IS 5 ONE 3 45
you find the sun, ladies? ◇ "there is not . . . . 255 IS 5 ONE 26 7
"as long as there's ladies my annie is one . . . . 707 95 POEMS 35 11
/ / / fair ladies tall lovers riding are . . . . 778 73 POEMS 6 1
lovers with slender their ladies (Each youngest) in sunlight 778 73 POEMS 6 23
+LADIES
FOR CONTEXT, SEE . . . . 552 1 X 1 12 13
LADIES&GENTLEMEN
sterilized contours; within which "ladies&gentlemen" --under 319 VIVA 11 31
LADIOS
ghibelline and guelph and ladios and laddios (on radios . . . 552 1 X 1 12 13

+LADS

FOR CONTEXT, SEE . . . . 552 1 X 1 12   14

LADY

	PAGE	TITLE	LINE
clothed with incognizable amethyst. Lady at whose	6	T&C EPITHALAM	137
a line the first lady says to nine ladies	15	T&C SONGS 5	5
drinks wine the tenth lady says to nine ladies	15	T&C SONGS 5	9
her perfectest array my lady, moving in the day, ...	17	T&C PUELLA MEA	6
and awkward hours my lady perfectly moving, through the . . .	17	T&C PUELLA MEA	11
scarce astir my fragile lady wandering in whose perishable .	17	T&C PUELLA MEA	13
fugitive my very frail lady drifting distinctly, moving like	17	T&C PUELLA MEA	18
the unskilful day my lady utterly alive, to me	17	T&C PUELLA MEA	24
was. And if my lady look at me (with	17	T&C PUELLA MEA	38
improbable beauty of my lady will) --at her glance	18	T&C PUELLA MEA	44
the miracle of a lady who had eyes which	18	T&C PUELLA MEA	47
kill.) But should my lady smile, it were a	18	T&C PUELLA MEA	49
than a flower, my lady naked in her hair--	21	T&C PUELLA MEA	178
nothing care nor any lady dead and gone.) Each	21	T&C PUELLA MEA	180
miracle. Love!--maker of my lady, in that always beyond . . .	22	T&C PUELLA MEA	237
/ / O Distinct Lady of my unkempt adoration	43	T&C AMORES 7	2
the unaccountable sun) Distinct Lady swiftly take my fragile	43	T&C AMORES 7	25
unchangingly the always old lady always sitting in her . . .	58	T&C PORTRAIT 6	21
persuade to serenade his lady the musical tom-cat, thou . . .	61	T&C PORTRAIT 9	5
or so thought the lady. / / /	84	T&C SON ACTU 3	17
should have loved my lady. And by this throat	85	T&C SON ACTU 4	9
the wind is a Lady with bright slender eyes	91	& POST IMPR 3	1
the) wind being A lady in a green dress, ...	91	& POST IMPR 3	19
if i certainly create, lady, one of the thousand	92	& POST IMPR 4	20
/ my smallheaded pearshaped lady in gluey twilight moving, .	95	& POST IMPR 7	2
a more minute adventure) lady. The clumsy dark threatens . .	98	& POST IMPR 9	13
else there is a lady, whose name is Afterwards	102	& POST IMPR 12	24
against yester- day My Lady hear the purple trumpets	110	& PORTRAIT 6	32
day (and O My Lady Lady Of Ladies you	112	& PORTRAIT 6	93
(and O My Lady Lady Of Ladies you who	112	& PORTRAIT 6	93
ignorant darkness of New Lady whose kiss is a	112	& PORTRAIT 6	99
there is a music Lady the noiseless truth of	113	& PORTRAIT 6	116
didn't said the little lady who sews and grows	125	& SEVEN POEMS 4	4
moon kissed the little lady on her paler-paler face	125	& SEVEN POEMS 4	18
day almost leans a lady whose still-born smile involves . . .	144	& SON REAL 15	13
agony ....by day this lady in her limousine oozes	146	& SON REAL 17	9
each other). As the lady lazily struts (her thickish	150	& SON REAL 21	10
should sleep with a lady called death get another	161	& SON ACTU 10	1
/ / my naked lady framed in twilight is	162	& SON ACTU 11	1
/ / / / Lady of Silence from the	187	XLI SONGS 9	1
sinuous lean... whereof this lady in some book had	225	IS 5 ONE LIZ	16
non disputandum est my lady is tired of That	245	IS 5 ONE 16	25
well this ruined aqueduct lady, which used to lead	260	IS 5 ONE 30	23
in front of our lady a ring of people	279	IS 5 THREE 3	5
to hold lovingly, our lady what do you think	279	IS 5 THREE 3	21
which are your lover lady: together with what keen	285	IS 5 FOUR 2	21
better fate than wisdom lady i swear by all	290	IS 5 FOUR 7	10
remarkably nothing is.... therefore, lady am i content should	291	IS 5 FOUR 8	17
with laughter O my lady (and every brittle marvelous	293	IS 5 FOUR 10	12
will advise even yourself, lady in the most certainly	294	IS 5 FOUR 11	3
beside me, my very lady, if scarcely the somewhat	302	IS 5 FIVE 1	2
i have made, my lady, intricate imperfect various things . .	306	IS 5 FIVE 5	1
perfectly alive) my shame: lady through whose profound and .	306	IS 5 FIVE 5	13
bliss of one small lady upon earth above; to	360	VIVA 51	33
/ / / / lady will you come with	365	VIVA 56	1
(wed) open the tart, lady & you'll find his	637	{CHAIRE} 39	10
of his buggy of lady godiva & that (for	699	95 POEMS 27	8

+LADY

FOR CONTEXT, SEE . . . . 724 95 POEMS 52   6
FOR CONTEXT, SEE . . . . 725 95 POEMS 53   4

LADY'LL

	PAGE	TITLE	LINE
eight --beer nothing, the lady'll have a whiskey-sour-- whose	74	T&C SON REAL 5	13

LADY'S

	PAGE	TITLE	LINE
eyes.) But should my lady's beauty play at not	18	T&C PUELLA MEA	61
hint at flight --my lady's very singular and slenderest . . .	20	T&C PUELLA MEA	159

LADY'S (CONTINUED)

fashion doth from my lady's body grow; as morning . . . . . . 21 T&C PUELLA MEA 183
sleepshaped lilies-- should my lady's body with these frail . 85 T&C SON ACTU 4 13
"thank you" nicely the lady's small grin said (with . . . . . 506 50 POEMS 20 13
noone" autumnal this great lady's gaze enters a sunset . . . 626 (CHAIRE) 28 1

LAFT

but you make me laft welates Wouldwoe Washington to . . . . . 321 VIVA 13 4

LAID

faces floating hands were laid upon me I was . . . . 44 T&C AMORES 8 11
long talkative animals are laid fists of huger silence. . . . 45 T&C LA GUERRE 1 9
into eternity as Nicho' laid before me bread more . . . . . . 194 XLI PORTRAIT 2 30
grin done his chores laid him down. Sleep well . . . . 568 1 X 1 28 29
others have long ago laid them) i never (selves . . . . 695 95 POEMS 23 13

LAIN

body. for it has lain with empty arms upon . . . . 36 T&C AMORES 1 5

LALLEMAND

ivory throat Marie Louise Lallemand n'est-ce pas que je . . . 120 & PORTRAIT 12 10

LAMB

or as a single lamb whose sheen of full . . . . 11 T&C SONGS 2 11

LAMBS

season 'tis, my lovely lambs, of Sumner Volstead Christ . . . 266 IS 5 TWO 1 1

LAME

mud- luscious the little lame balloonman whistles far and . . 24 T&C CHANSONS 1 4
these torn pockets of lame and begging colour) while . . . . 93 & POST IMPR 5 15
the other, cunning ugly lame; but as you'll shortly . . . . . 799 73 POEMS 27 5

LAMED

(the warped ones, the lamed ones; the mad moronic . . . . . . 619 (CHAIRE) 21 17

LAMENT

turn to enemies) therefore lament, my dream and don . . . . . 834 73 POEMS 62 5

LAMP

retchings of a worthless lamp. when With a minute . . . . . . 96 & POST IMPR 8 26

LAMPS

of cold (when battling street-lamps fail upon the gold . . . 142 & SON REAL 13 3
April dusk the sallow street-lamps were turning snowy against 194 XLI PORTRAIT 2 2
bread more downy than street-lamps upon an almostclean plate 194 XLI PORTRAIT 2 32

LAND

for in his own land he is called death. . . . . 42 T&C AMORES 6 24
a thistlefluff-thing which goes land- ing away all by . . . . 127 & SEVEN POEMS 5 41
country, 'tis of you, land of the Cluett Shirt . . . . 230 IS 5 ONE 2 4
Wrigley Eyes (of you land of the Arrow Ide . . . . 230 IS 5 ONE 2 7
of you i sing: land of Abraham Lincoln and . . . . 230 IS 5 ONE 2 11
and Lydia E. Pinkham, land above all of Just . . . . 230 IS 5 ONE 2 12
america i love you land of the pilgrims' and . . . . 268 IS 5 TWO 3 2
toy eloping to Ire (land must be heav en . . . . 320 VIVA 12 12
ignorantly into sleep's bright land / / / / . . . . 358 VIVA 49 15
/ / (of Ever-Ever Land i speak sweet morons . . . . 466 NEW POEMS 4 1
carries canopeners in Ever-Ever Land (for Ever-Ever Land is . 466 NEW POEMS 4 8
Ever-Ever Land (for Ever-Ever Land is a place that's . . . . 466 NEW POEMS 4 9
to us (and Ever-Ever Land is a place that's . . . . 466 NEW POEMS 4 17
is normal in Ever-Ever Land for a bad cigar . . . . 466 NEW POEMS 4 26
over this new eng land fragrance of pasture and . . . . 469 NEW POEMS 7 14
(and how) scienti fic land of supernod where freedom . . . . 544 1 X 1 4 22
the ocean and the land (do lovers suffer? all . . . . 768 95 POEMS 94 4
through some green mysterious land until my second dream . . 777 73 POEMS 5 4

LANDED

the ear of fate, landed a seat in the . . . . 266 IS 5 TWO 1 36

LANDING

twic twoc ingly attacks landing a onetwo which doubles . . . 259 IS 5 ONE 29 14

LANDS

afar in the lost lands. / / / / . . . . 76 T&C SON UNRE 1 14
ploc spittle what the lands thaz me kid in . . . . 96 & POST IMPR 8 15
have stolen into recent lands the flower with their . . . . . 165 & SON ACTU 14 14
flower curled, in other lands where other songs be . . . . . 208 XLI SONNETS 4 11
gladly (sic) in far lands perished of unheard of . . . . . . 266 IS 5 TWO 1 14

LANDSCAPES

and cHuckling like uninteresting- landscapes made interesting 101 & POST IMPR 11 70

LANGUAGE

nobler trees and the language of leaves repeats eventual . . 184 XLI SONGS 6 12

		PAGE	TITLE	LINE
LANGUAGE (CONTINUED)				
slabs of a fuzzy language with the aid of		194	XLI PORTRAIT 2	26
should worry in every language even deafanddumb thy sons . .		268	IS 5 TWO 3	6
skidding in outrageous sabots language trickling pried his .		277	IS 5 THREE 1	13
heart's eager dim enormous language loss or gain from		372	VIVA 63	12
LANGUAGES				
a luxury of telescoped languages) she smokes three castles .		312	VIVA 4	15
your heart alert, of languages there's none but well		575	1 X 1 35	27
LANGUID				
silks coming with sharp languid perfumes coming with the . .		112	& PORTRAIT 6	102
star whose rays five languid fingers were; and molly		682	95 POEMS 10	6
LANGUOR				
beads of a faultless languor when invisibly consult with . .		193	XLI PORTRAIT 1	6
LANGUOROUS				
slowly gather of thy languorous mouth the thrilling flower) .		37	T&C AMORES 2	19
close as some grave languorous hymn pledged to illimitable .		206	XLI SONNETS 2	12
+LAOTSZE				
FOR CONTEXT, SEE		553	1 X 1 13	6
LAP				
making poems in the lap of death Humanity i		204	XLI LA GUERRE 2	23
promptly to a deep lap enormous mindless hands. and		225	IS 5 ONE LIZ	9
LAPFULLS				
which, anyway give rapid lapfulls of idiotic big hands . . .		251	IS 5 ONE 22	22
LARGE				
rise which are her large and shapely thighs) in		21	T&C PUELLA MEA	204
forth ankles musical with large pearls kingdoms in her . . .		33	T&C ORIENTALE 6	67
moistly climbing hideously with large minute hips, O press .		67	T&C POST IMPR 4	26
the ripe quite too large lips always clenched faintly, . . .		72	T&C SON REAL 3	7
play; i see the large lips vivid, the face		75	T&C SON REAL 6	7
exact tombs, where a large road crosses and all		86	T&C SON ACTU 5	12
lascivious legs. painful ankles large acute brutal feet . . .		103	& POST IMPR 13	7
exact, stupid. mouth normal, large, unclever. hair genuinely		103	& POST IMPR 13	13
profound gems and the large laughing stones a sinuous		112	& PORTRAIT 6	104
of bestial Marj lie large men who praise Marj's		114	& PORTRAIT 7	3
hooray hoorah for the large men who lie between		114	& PORTRAIT 7	23
woman from whose kind large flesh i turn to		142	& SON REAL 13	1
passionate anatomy oh yes! Large legs pinch, toes choke-- . .		146	& SON REAL 17	7
LARGENESS				
still as anything in largeness and this largeness begins . .		127	& SEVEN POEMS 5	35
in largeness and this largeness begins to give you, ...		127	& SEVEN POEMS 5	35
that's not all) because largeness tells you so you		127	& SEVEN POEMS 5	38
LARGER				
/ / / youful larger of smallish) Humble a		503	50 POEMS 17	2
abyss of orange dream larger than sky times earth:		599	(CHAIRE) 1	4
mercy, live a dream larger than alive any star		735	95 POEMS 63	4
LARGEST				
of cringing air) the largest hour push deep his		115	& PORTRAIT 8	12
the soiled canary-cage of largest existence. (when he would .		197	XLI PORTRAIT 5	13
about herself the sprouting largest final air plunges inward		301	IS 5 FOUR 18	16
face capable of a largest nonglance the least unsmile		359	VIVA 50	16
LARGO				
speak) offspring has that largo appearance of somebody who .		326	VIVA 18	8
LARIATS				
this (once flinger of lariats lean exroper of horned		252	IS 5 ONE 23	10
LARK				
thrills the unimaginable upward lark and drowns the earth . .		5	T&C EPITHALAM	79
a here and there lark who; rises, and; droops		434	NO THANKS 51	18
be gay like every lark who lifts his life		815	73 POEMS 43	2
LARSEN				
I pass Mr Tom Larsen twirls among pale lips		252	IS 5 ONE 23	5
LASCIVIOUS				
young tree, her slim lascivious arms alight in skilful . . .		20	T&C PUELLA MEA	157
melody of the, keenly lascivious legs. painful ankles large .		103	& POST IMPR 13	7
ignoring, through its indolent lascivious caring eyes		344	VIVA 35	4
LASCIVIOUSLY				
means, like a girl lasciviously frail, peace (dreaming is . .		168	& SON ACTU 17	10
LAST				
of the sky the last immortal leaf is dead		41	T&C AMORES 5	2

LAST (CONTINUED)

of foam in the last light thread the creeping	64	T&C POST IMPR 1	3
upon me in the last light pours its eyeless	64	T&C POST IMPR 1	7
only tidewings in the last light twitching at the	64	T&C POST IMPR 1	11
only a little harder last we on the groaning	67	T&C POST IMPR 4	23
thou hast taken thy last applause, and when the	75	T&C SON REAL 6	1
lights have laughed their last; without, the street darkling	75	T&C SON REAL 6	9
us and start the last leaf whirling in the	80	T&C SON UNRE 5	11
were good; and the last crumb with some shame	117	& PORTRAIT 10	21
himself, one afternoon. The last thing he saw was	170	& SON ACTU 19	5
the autumn long; the last flower in whose hair, ...	190	XLI SONGS 12	3
autumn love, for the last flower in the hair	190	XLI SONGS 12	14
right up to the last minute coming back down	248	IS 5 ONE 19	27
of any program except last and always and first	264	IS 5 ONE 33	18
youngest boy was kilt last with the big eyes	271	IS 5 TWO 6	8
very little beyond the last road--there's something to be . .	303	IS 5 FIVE 2	3
because i love you) last night clothed in sealace	369	VIVA 60	1
creeping through my dreams last night, all of your	369	VIVA 60	17
whitely yearn from each last shore and home come	526	50 POEMS 38	8
why's first because (faith's last doubt and humbly heights	574	1 X 1 34	10
vast dark until sink last things (least all turns	633	{CHAIRE} 35	8
all skies fall at last perfection, now and here	650	{CHAIRE} 52	17
and we've (with one last more than kiss) to	741	95 POEMS 6	13
are done; and whose last doing shall not quite	762	95 POEMS 89	4
first than sun more last than star --do lovers	768	95 POEMS 94	12
was whatever (first and last) mostpeople fear most: a	802	73 POEMS 30	11

LATE

| will not be too late worms are the words . . . . | 511 | 50 POEMS 25 | 21 |

LATER

| cost the Ergo perished later all hands (you may . . . . | 494 | 50 POEMS 8 | 6 |

LATEST

| Women By Night whose latest Seeds Of Evil sold . . . . . . | 245 | IS 5 ONE 16 | 8 |

LATTER

| pipewrench of the again latter then opening a box . . . . . . | 263 | IS 5 ONE 32 | 46 |

LAUGH

new sweetly used to laugh and love ladies with	23	T&C PUELLA MEA	286
that makes the children laugh. But i don't, the	69	T&C POST IMPR 6	20
against the worms hate laugh shimmy / / /	238	IS 5 ONE 9	21
for each other: then laugh, leaning back in my	290	IS 5 FOUR 7	14
the reason that i laugh and breathe is oh	295	IS 5 FOUR 12	24
the cognoscenti bingbongwhom chewchoo laugh dingle nails . .	333	VIVA 24	3
it. this caress that laugh both quickly signify life's . . .	364	VIVA 55	10
and cannot write who laugh like they would fall	427	NO THANKS 44	11
breeding they wince) his laugh is a million griefs	439	NO THANKS 55	11
fears to see (who laugh and cry) who dream, ...	446	NO THANKS 61	13
became his foe he'd laugh and build a world	521	50 POEMS 34	48
cry and shall we laugh and shall entirely our	528	50 POEMS 40	6
coward; lies are laws) laugh, and make each no	651	{CHAIRE} 53	10
vero madonna (nudge whispershout) laugh matching onceupons .	681	95 POEMS 9	8
realms of regions dark) laugh long at Beautiful and	799	73 POEMS 27	28
me now jump shout (laugh dance cry sing) for	835	73 POEMS 63	17

+LAUGH

| FOR CONTEXT, SEE . . . . | 330 | VIVA 21 | 3 |

LAUGHED

Magdalen. The lights have laughed their last; without, the .	75	T&C SON REAL 6	9
kid inside her. He laughed. She came. he gave	145	& SON REAL 16	11
windows and roses he laughed, and closed his eyes	170	& SON ACTU 19	13
they shat encore he laughed and spat (this life	440	NO THANKS 56	11
heart he spat and laughed with self with life	441	NO THANKS 56	40
tree by leaf she laughed his joy she cried	515	50 POEMS 29	14
someones married their everyones laughed their cryings and .	515	50 POEMS 29	18

+LAUGHED

| FOR CONTEXT, SEE . . . . | 321 | VIVA 13 | 4 |

LAUGHING

and hark! the flicker's laughing yet, while on the	5	T&C EPITHALAM	75
darkness, friends i charge laughing. Into the hair-thin tints	66	T&C POST IMPR 3	5
gems and the large laughing stones a sinuous problem	112	& PORTRAIT 6	104
head's big she (said laughing) with your head.	123	& SEVEN POEMS 2	14

LAUGHING (CONTINUED)
of the nifty, ruffian-rogue, laughing body with wise breasts 140 & SON REAL 11 11
obscene shy breasts tickle, laughing when i wilt and . . . . 172 & SON ACTU 21 15
or better, queens, queens laughing lightly crowned with far . 211 XLI SONNETS 7 14
spectator, maybe certain nobodies laughing faintly playing . 283 IS 5 THREE 7 8
light should flower: or laughing sparkle from the shut . . . 292 IS 5 FOUR 9 18
Ills (a recipe against Laughing Virginity Death) then dearest 359 VIVA 50 9
joy; and up with laughing and drunkenness) here's to . . . . 424 NO THANKS 41 11
thousandth why and discover laughing) / / / / . . . . 453 NO THANKS 68 16
kil yoo (friend the laughing grinning) we no (smiling) . . . 618 {CHAIRE} 20 6
moment there's time for laughing and there's time for . . . . 683 95 POEMS 11 9
/ / / / --laughing to find anyone's blind . . . . 716 95 POEMS 44 1
you) vanish in so --laughing to find a noone's . . . . 716 95 POEMS 44 29
(finding and losing and laughing and crying) children whose . 749 95 POEMS 77 7
+LAUGHING
FOR CONTEXT, SEE . . . . 628 {CHAIRE} 30 13
+LAUGHINGLY
FOR CONTEXT, SEE . . . . 720 95 POEMS 48 7
LAUGHS
Understanding why his eye laughs, i will bring you . . . . . 161 & SON ACTU 10 11
Tres) & (pas) youth laughs (sing old age scolds . . . . 729 95 POEMS 57 10
LAUGHSHRIEK
crazy jay blue) demon laughshriek ing at me your . . . . . . 677 95 POEMS 5 2
LAUGHSIN
n ? my mind laughsin- to Slivers of (unthinking. . . . . . . 94 & POST IMPR 6 18
LAUGHTER
a tale made of laughter and of dew, was . . . . 23 T&C PUELLA MEA 277
abominable floor belches smoky laughter into the filigree . . 55 T&C PORTRAIT 3 5
impeccable girls in raiment laughter-gifted. / / / / . . . . 85 T&C SON ACTU 4 15
like money and like laughter and like elephants through . . . 111 & PORTRAIT 6 67
shuddering big, the luminous laughter, and the legs whereas, 115 & PORTRAIT 8 24
hashed (little careful hunks-of-lilac laughter splashed from 133 & SON REAL 4 4
my invincible Nearness rapes laughter from your preferable. 166 & SON ACTU 15 16
doing her eyebrows. --Marj's laughter smacked me: pummeling . 228 IS 5 ONE MARJ 13
i move my habits laughter i say you will . . . . 285 IS 5 FOUR 2 7
with rhyme with and laughter O my lady (and . . . . 293 IS 5 FOUR 10 11
predicating forever, assuming the laughter of afterwards-- i 356 VIVA 47 17
are gone. there is laughter and despair impersonates a . . . 375 VIVA 66 4
lucky 's to spend laughter not money lucky are . . . . 467 NEW POEMS 5 5
hands silence eyes love laughter death (dreams hopes . . . . 693 95 POEMS 21 4
LAUGHTER-GIFTED
impeccable girls in raiment laughter-gifted. / / / / . . . . 85 T&C SON ACTU 4 15
LAUGHTERING
manshaped whimpered how girllike laughtering blocks when . . 371 VIVA 62 5
LAUGHTERS
stumbling in gloom, bad laughters, smiles unbold) also, . . . 142 & SON REAL 13 8
ecstasy wags and. rages Laughters jostle grins nudge smiles . 202 XLI PORTRAIT 9 36
LAUNCELOT
world was mad and Launcelot spoke to Guenever, a . . . . . . 18 T&C PUELLA MEA 57
LAUNCH
in midmost o.c. an launch we a Hyperluxurious Supersieve . . 334 VIVA 25 2
LAUNDRY
Handkerchief read Papernapkin no laundry bills likes People . 410 NO THANKS 27 5
LAVENDER
its box of sky lavender and cornerless, the moon . . . . . 70 T&C SON REAL 1 13
LAW
the) Einstein expanded Newton's law preserved conTinuum (but 315 VIVA 7 5
comma bentham; or 1 law for the lions & . . . . 791 73 POEMS 19 7
LAWS
or science must bait laws with stars to catch . . . . 478 NEW POEMS 16 5
dollars and some twisted laws) it comes both prigged . . . . 644 {CHAIRE} 46 5
a coward; lies are laws) laugh, and make each . . . . 651 {CHAIRE} 53 9
sans shallbe or was (laws clocks fears hopes beliefs . . . . 755 95 POEMS 83 16
LAY
marble all the castle lay like some gigantic ghost-flower . . 8 T&C OF NICOL 1
whom passion wastes will lay between their little breasts . . 16 T&C SONGS 6 8
who with Egypt's body lay. Lovely as those ladies . . . . . . 18 T&C PUELLA MEA 74
curb the quiet face lay which had been dorothy . . . . 52 T&C PORTRAIT 1 16

LAY (CONTINUED)

face your sweet hair lay in such a silence . . . . 76 T&C SON UNRE 1 5
ride her? ....she exactly lay, looking hunks of love . . . . 145 & SON REAL 16 13
but as the trees, lay, which grow / / . . . . 154 & SON ACTU 3 16
had fallen among thieves lay by the roadside on . . . . . . 258 IS 5 ONE 28 2
meanwhile my self etcetera lay quietly in the deep . . . . . 276 IS 5 TWO 10 19
to each other, releasing lay, watching (sprawling, in grass . 283 IS 5 THREE 7 21
a box of skin lay eyes like new tools) . . . . 355 VIVA 46 10
traps for his heart, lay snares for his feet . . . . 439 NO THANKS 55 18
like a bool to lay a wreath from ancient . . . . 500 50 POEMS 14 13
loaf and women must lay) and she gave him . . . . 552 1 X 1 12 18
heart flopped over and lay still while he passed . . . . . . 648 (CHAIRE) 50 7
thousand years and then lay down with a smile) . . . . 709 95 POEMS 37 16
was there such a lay-- whom, among her dollies, ... 794 73 POEMS 22 2
/ / Now i lay (with everywhere around) me . . . . 816 73 POEMS 44 1
welcoming darkestness-- now i lay me down (in a . . . . 816 73 POEMS 44 5
beautifully snow) now i lay me down to dream . . . . 816 73 POEMS 44 10
may keep. now i lay me down to dream . . . . 816 73 POEMS 44 14
LAYED
/ a) glazed mind layed in a urinal howlessly . . . . 387 NO THANKS 4 1
LAYS
apart her curtains, and lays bare her trembling heart, . . . 8 T&C OF NICOL 15
and the duckbilled platitude lays & lays and Lays . . . . . . 321 VIVA 13 15
duckbilled platitude lays & lays and Lays aytash unee . . . . 321 VIVA 13 15
lays & lays and Lays aytash unee / / . . . . 321 VIVA 13 16
his daughter her father lays" "black hell upon you . . . . . 707 95 POEMS 35 20
LAZIEST
fourth will cure the laziest self of weary the . . . . . . 537 50 POEMS 49 3
go in even the laziest creature among us a . . . . 769 95 POEMS 95 8
LAZILY
wisping rune of road lazily carved on sharpening air. . . . . 86 T&C SON ACTU 5 6
other). As the lady lazily struts (her thickish flesh . . . . 150 & SON REAL 21 10
little tilted streets spill lazily multitudes out of final . 345 VIVA 36 6
hearts by darts pierced lazily writhe lurch faceflowers . . . 436 NO THANKS 52 8
LAZILYTAS
Gorge indistinct palishflesh of laZilytas tingg OO seberries, 100 & POST IMPR 11 27
LAZINESS
bloodbeat in her fierce laziness tried to repeat a . . . . . 135 & SON REAL 6 9
ferocious rhythm of precise laziness. Eat the price of . . . 162 & SON ACTU 11 15
LAZY
of dream (in the lazy world and new sweetly . . . . 23 T&C PUELLA MEA 285
warriors with bodies of lazy jade and twitching eyelids . . . 34 T&C ORIENTALE 6 77
LBS
clean and jerked 300 lbs) i mean observe his . . . . 645 (CHAIRE) 47 2
LDS
wor (magi c ally) lds / / / / . . . . 829 73 POEMS 57 17
LE
ecend) tang lesp ang le s ofC omeg o . . . . 421 NO THANKS 38 12
il est trop fort le negre esn7othingish8s c'est fini . . . . 430 NO THANKS 47 20
LEA
right of kings" Homer Lea) here are five simple . . . . . . 803 73 POEMS 31 4
LEAD
audible great rose! Lover, lead forth thy love unto . . . . . 6 T&C EPITHALAM 113
fearruining and glorygirded faces lead us into the serious . 41 T&C AMORES 5 33
the neck up is lead all over Brattle Street . . . . 253 IS 5 ONE 24 14
lady, which used to lead something into somewhere) / . . . . 260 IS 5 ONE 30 24
no path all paths lead where truth is here . . . . 775 73 POEMS 3 3
's A pril Lives lead their own persons (in . . . . 782 73 POEMS 10 10
LEADING
lost is his found leading love whose heart is . . . . 533 50 POEMS 45 3
LEAF
sky the last immortal leaf is dead and the . . . . 41 T&C AMORES 5 3
and start the last leaf whirling in the final . . . . 80 T&C SON UNRE 5 11
consider her as a leaf thinks of the sky, ... 131 & SON REAL 2 2
tables like an old leaf between toadstools he is . . . . . . 198 XLI PORTRAIT 6 16
acute from root to leaf) but should voices (whom . . . . . . 362 VIVA 53 8
hidden him in A leaf and, Opening beautiful earth . . . . . 397 NO THANKS 14 12
earth put (only) a Leaf among dark ness. sunlight's . . . . . 397 NO THANKS 14 16

			PAGE	TITLE	LINE

LEAF (CONTINUED)

opening and upward, to leaf and to sap and . . . . 424 NO THANKS 41   1
earth dragged once -ful leaf. & were who skies . . . . . . 491 50 POEMS 5   3
tree (this life one leaf) but love is the . . . . 511 50 POEMS 25   26
now and tree by leaf she laughed his joy . . . . 515 50 POEMS 29   13
we, singing each new leaf out of each tree . . . . 521 50 POEMS 34   50
i) riding on a leaf o least who sing . . . . 535 50 POEMS 47   8
gone away the they leaf of ghosts some few . . . . 541 1 X 1 1   9
Each why of a leaf says (floating each how) . . . . 543 1 X 1 3   7
in winter" (like a leaf opening) as we stood, ... 572 1 X 1 32   5
bigger than to sing) leaf is wing and tree . . . . 583 1 X 1 43   18
by one merely opening leaf (beyond whose nearness there . . . 592 1 X 1 52   7
so world is a leaf so tree is a . . . . 594 1 X 1 54   19
dancing together) when every leaf opens without any sound . . 665 {CHAIRE} 67   8
moon dream wing tree leaf bird sun & singing . . . . 753 95 POEMS 81   17
dream until No least leaf almost stirs as never . . . . . . 758 95 POEMS 85   38
for me for each leaf newer than can be: . . . . 760 95 POEMS 87   10
first amazement as a leaf--here's one more than each . . . . 762 95 POEMS 89   5
mountain, any god) while leaf twig limb ask every . . . . . 818 73 POEMS 46   9
whose universe a single leaf may be) the more . . . . 821 73 POEMS 49   13
how hush, one dead leaf stirring makes a crash . . . . . . 839 73 POEMS 67   4

+LEAF

FOR CONTEXT, SEE . . . . 346 VIVA 37   27
FOR CONTEXT, SEE . . . . 487 50 POEMS 1   13
FOR CONTEXT, SEE . . . . 673 95 POEMS 1   2

LEAF'S

cold, wind's menace and leaf's grieving: from the impressed . 207 XLI SONNETS 3   10

LEAFLESS

(any more than each leafless) its silent in forevering . . . 667 {CHAIRE} 69   12

LEAFY

shrieking dryad sought her leafy goal, at the mere . . . . . 3 T&C EPITHALAM   14

LEAK

green large three teeth leak smoke: remembering, two pink . . 149 & SON REAL 20   14
and speeches sawdust perpetually leak rather is it between . 261 IS 5 ONE 31   5

LEAKS

repos.... a fattish leg leaks obscenely from the dress. . . . 143 & SON REAL 14   8
when the certainly roof leaks it 's our (home . . . . 728 95 POEMS 56   3

LEAL

a dozen staunch and leal citizens did graze at . . . . . . 258 IS 5 ONE 28   9

LEAN

the silver dawn. four lean hounds crouched low and . . . . 14 T&C SONGS 4   4
the silver dawn. four lean hounds crouched low and . . . . 14 T&C SONGS 4   14
than slippered sleep the lean lithe deer the fleet . . . . 14 T&C SONGS 4   17
the silver dawn. four lean hounds crouched low and . . . . 14 T&C SONGS 4   24
the silver dawn. four lean hounds crouched low and . . . . 14 T&C SONGS 4   34
/ / / / lean candles hunger in the . . . . 28 T&C ORIENTALE 2   1
street Spring comes the lean and definite houses are . . . . 62 T&C PORTRAIT 10   6
of the world. The lean and definite houses are . . . . . . 62 T&C PORTRAIT 10   10
cathedral before whose upward lean magnificent face the . . . 93 & POST IMPR 5   3
obsolete gaze begins to. lean.... a little against me, . . . 148 & SON REAL 19   12
herself uprearing wholly slowly, lean in the hips and . . . . 156 & SON ACTU 5   7
distinct entirely melting sinuous lean... whereof this lady . 225 IS 5 ONE LIZ   15
(once flinger of lariats lean exroper of horned suddenly . . 252 IS 5 ONE 23   10
i hate people and lean out of this window . . . . 295 IS 5 FOUR 12   23
enchanted dike of whose lean lips, hovers how slenderly . . . 344 VIVA 35   10
impersonates a street i lean from the window, behold . . . . 375 VIVA 66   6
a keen of a lean wind flays screaming hills . . . . 560 1 X 1 20   9
(the fat ones, the lean ones;the mean kind dirty . . . . . . 619 {CHAIRE} 21   24

LEANDERLESS

orbs thus excluding a leanderless drowning in sub (at . . . . 546 1 X 1 6   6

LEANEYED

beneath silver youths the leaneyed Caesars borne neatly . . . 110 & PORTRAIT 6   36

LEANING

cliff back and up leaning out of yellowgreen water. . . . . . 281 IS 5 THREE 5   9
at sunset it should, leaning against me, smile; or . . . . . 285 IS 5 FOUR 2   13
each other: then laugh, leaning back in my arms . . . . . . 290 IS 5 FOUR 7   14

LEANS

window every day almost leans a lady whose still-born . . . . 144 & SON REAL 15   13

	PAGE	TITLE	LINE

LEANS (CONTINUED)
   was nutn like Nooer Leans Shikahgo Sain Looey Noo . . . . . . 237 IS 5 ONE 8   7
   sprouting gently, the cathedral leans its dreamy spine . . . 279 IS 5 THREE 3   4
   to the Geddup curb leans carefully spewing into her . . . . . 330 VIVA 21   11
LEAP
   in my mouth and leap into the ripe air . . . . 189 XLI SONGS 11   4
   called Love) upward doth leap from the mute hugeness . . . . 210 XLI SONNETS 6   4
   / will suddenly trees leap from winter and will . . . . . . 218 XLI SONNETS 14   1
   wiggle yes has are leap, which, anyway give rapid . . . . . 251 IS 5 ONE 22   21
   five squirming mice; or leap through hoops of fire, ... 279 IS 5 THREE 3 16
   U n: starT birDs (lEAp) Openi ng t hing . . . . 347 VIVA 38   30
   when to me you leap and i'm born we . . . . 589 1 X 1 49   19
   believe (with a spin leap alive we're alive) we're . . . . 594 1 X 1 54   43
   time-- no heart can leap, no soul can breathe . . . . 664 {CHAIRE} 66   21
   such sunlight as will leap higher than high through . . . . 717 95 POEMS 45   11
   my life does not leap than with the mystery . . . . 810 73 POEMS 38   4
LEAPANDSWOOPING
   to the earth are leapandswooping tinily birds whose magical . 631 {CHAIRE} 33   11
LEAPED
   strictly at which instant (leaped into the street) this . . . 328 VIVA 19   12
   please' --why guesswho nearly leaped out of . . . . 800 73 POEMS 28   7
LEAPING
   Over the wires came leaping and i felt suddenly . . . . . . 44 T&C AMORES 8   2
   and tide and death leaping Sweetly your voice / . . . . . . 44 T&C AMORES 8   22
   day fills with peacefully leaping air the minute mind . . . . 62 T&C PORTRAIT 10 8
   feet reincarnate song suddenly leaping flameflung, mounts, . 206 XLI SONNETS 2   7
   amazing day: for the leaping greenly spirits of trees . . . . 663 {CHAIRE} 65   2
   slowly swoop wholly up leaping through merciful sunlight) to 841 73 POEMS 69   32
LEAPS
   for now the red leaps in the maple's cheek, ... 4 T&C EPITHALAM   62
   blend ing the tree leaps a stiffened exquisite i . . . . . 182 XLI SONGS 4   7
   voice? gruesome: a trull leaps from the lungs "gimme . . . . 227 IS 5 ONE GERT 14
   fasterishly whipped the top leaps bounding upon other tops . 311 VIVA 3   6
   heart conceives and mind leaps (and that which we . . . . . 386 NO THANKS 3   13
   which of one street leaps quick squirmthicklying lu minous . 493 50 POEMS 7   11
   than huge) whoing sea leaps to greenly hurl snow . . . . . . 743 95 POEMS 71   3
   stands and looks and leaps upon the air) / . . . . 774 73 POEMS 2   16
+LEAPS
   FOR CONTEXT, SEE . . . . 396 NO THANKS 13   7
   FOR CONTEXT, SEE . . . . 655 {CHAIRE} 57   3
LEAR
   five nevers of a lear / / / / . . . . 561 1 X 1 21   10
LEARN
   all blossoms that do learn, scents of not known . . . . . . 9 T&C SONGS 1   17
   no patient mind unstrange learn (nor could all earth's . . . 420 NO THANKS 37   8
   dead undoom. I'd rather learn from one bird how . . . . . . 484 NEW POEMS 22   13
   nay but lucy could learn and lily could pray . . . . 509 50 POEMS 23   21
   bird than eyes can learn look up to silence . . . . 592 1 X 1 52   9
   see who could not learn to look --from the . . . . 649 {CHAIRE} 51   3
   than angels fear to learn and even fiends: or, ... 842 73 POEMS 70   4
LEARNED
   / / SONNETS if learned darkness from our searched . . . . . 205 XLI SONNETS 1   1
   bastard boy must have learned what he knows from . . . . . 707 95 POEMS 35   15
LEARNING
   none can think) a learning under teach-- precisely as . . . . 735 95 POEMS 63   8
LEASE
   tune, a house for lease. I have never loved . . . . 360 VIVA 51   9
LEAST
   have a whiskey-sour-- whose least amazing smile is the . . . 74 T&C SON REAL 5 14
   write. In this at least we have got a . . . . 84 T&C SON ACTU 3 13
   find her how my least heart-beat becomes less. And . . . . . 152 & SON ACTU 1   9
   that doesn't in the least matter. The big fear . . . . . . 289 IS 5 FOUR 6   2
   slenderly should create one least smile (shyly if a . . . . 291 IS 5 FOUR 8   23
   to miss within your least gesture the hurting skill . . . . 293 IS 5 FOUR 10   7
   Creation, MAN: at a least crooking of Whose compassionate . . 315 VIVA 7   14
   a largest nonglance the least unsmile or whatever weeds . . . 359 VIVA 50   17
   a we, entirely whose least breathing may surprise ourselves . 368 VIVA 59   13
   not heart, because at least i beat --always think . . . . . 372 VIVA 63   6

	PAGE	TITLE	LINE

LEAST (CONTINUED)

which is the thrilling least of all (for love's . . . . 379 VIVA 70 4
having less with every least each most remembering H . . . . 390 NO THANKS 7 7
these how less than least flowers of rain) thickly . . . . . 433 NO THANKS 50 9
a star --dreads dying least; and less, that death . . . . . 446 NO THANKS 61 8
would feel if spring's least breathing should cause a . . . . 450 NO THANKS 65 13
frequent anguish (imagine Her least never with most memory) . 453 NO THANKS 68 10
no proof not the least shadow of a. Not . . . . 479 NEW POEMS 17 20
jumping from each most least eye of star and . . . . 502 50 POEMS 16 4
less than these are least is who are am . . . . 505 50 POEMS 19 23
and nothing quite so least as truth --i say . . . . 521 50 POEMS 34 65
less bigger than the least begin less littler than . . . . 530 50 POEMS 42 11
on a leaf o least who sing small thing . . . . 535 50 POEMS 47 9
grow deep in dark least ourselves remembering love only . . . 556 1 X 1 16 13
fall this than, a least dare of snow less . . . . 573 1 X 1 33 13
i've only we our least begin to guess / . . . . 574 1 X 1 34 14
does with each your least your any most very . . . . 580 1 X 1 40 2
many worlds in each least less than particle of . . . . . . 603 {CHAIRE} 5 2
of some sun; his least unmotion roams the youngest . . . . . 609 {CHAIRE} 11 12
is dirtiest any city's least street) of mirror lying . . . . 623 {CHAIRE} 25 3
until sink last things (least all turns almost now; . . . . . 633 {CHAIRE} 35 9
a lifetime at the least) except to add an . . . . 650 {CHAIRE} 52 7
a noisy most park's least timorous pigeons) squ -I- . . . . . 726 95 POEMS 54 10
(not to men tion least) & i ob serve . . . . 727 95 POEMS 55 6
roses are probably the least probable roses of her . . . . 748 95 POEMS 76 2
conceiving) dream until No least leaf almost stirs as . . . . 758 95 POEMS 85 37
pure love with one least ignorance may comprehend more . . . 761 95 POEMS 88 2
emanation creates creation lovetree! least the rose alive . . 764 95 POEMS 90 49

LEASTFUL

less dwindled to a leastful most under imagination. When . . 432 NO THANKS 49 13

LEASTFULLY

tree is voice more leastfully than i am you . . . . 583 1 X 1 43 20

LEASTING

(ghostsoul sheshape) elf into leasting forever most magical . 495 50 POEMS 9 13

+LEASTLY

FOR CONTEXT, SEE . . . . 534 50 POEMS 46 19

LEATHERFACED

skinny voice of the leatherfaced woman with the crimson . . . 196 XLI PORTRAIT 4 2

LEAVE

hair). Creasing its smoothness--and leave the bed agrin with 164 & SON ACTU 13 10
spoke joe to jack leave her alone she's not . . . . 496 50 POEMS 10 2

LEAVES

heaven clings, (whose million leaves in winsome indolence . . 6 T&C EPITHALAM 125
very secret food its leaves inimitable find beyond the . . . 19 T&C PUELLA MEA 119
their frailest syllable its leaves go crisp with miracle. . . 22 T&C PUELLA MEA 236
first, it will be leaves and a little harder . . . . 67 T&C POST IMPR 4 19
over the gasping shores leaves his smile wan, and . . . . . . 77 T&C SON UNRE 2 7
away and all the leaves away, and the trees . . . . 80 T&C SON UNRE 5 2
rain away and the leaves and the sky and . . . . 80 T&C SON UNRE 5 14
tunes OR s-cra p-y leaVes flut te rin g . . . . 122 & SEVEN POEMS 1 11
battered by stuttering pearl, leaves jiggled to the jigging . 173 & SON ACTU 22 6
quite through with and leaves say alas, much is . . . . . . 181 XLI SONGS 3 2
into you my enchanting leaves / / / . . . . 182 XLI SONGS 4 18
and the language of leaves repeats eventual perfection while 184 XLI SONGS 6 12
kittens are all the leaves which open in the . . . . 191 XLI CHANSONS 1 7
before my doubting window leaves softly to stir, of . . . . 205 XLI SONNETS 1 10
and slips away.... (these leaves are Thingish with moondrool 303 IS 5 FIVE 2 6
wind bringing rain and leaves, filling the air with . . . . 304 IS 5 FIVE 3 12
whose black bod ies leaves hide / / / . . . . 354 VIVA 45 28
but men speaks (among leaves Easily through voices womenlike 356 VIVA 47 3
way trees are Made leaves open Clouds take sun . . . . . . 359 VIVA 50 11
/ am was. are leaves few this. is these . . . . 491 50 POEMS 5 1
lie; bloodies with dizzying leaves the sun and yanks . . . . 560 1 X 1 20 3
tree can count his leaves each herself by opening . . . . . 591 1 X 1 51 17
that rain awaited by leaves with all their trees . . . . . . 754 95 POEMS 82 13
sky is wild with leaves; which dance and dancing . . . . . . 777 73 POEMS 5 6
and whose not numerable leaves are fall i ng) . . . . 826 73 POEMS 54 5
stir: writhe o-p-e-n-i-n-g are (leaves; flowers) dreams , . . 835 73 POEMS 63 13

	PAGE	TITLE	LINE

LEAVES (CONTINUED)
/ / / D-re-A-mi-N-gl-Y leaves (sEe) locked in gOLd . . . . . 838 73 POEMS 66   2
+LEAVES
FOR CONTEXT, SEE . . . . 342 VIVA 33   25
LEAVES'
fragile skill of new leaves' voices, and sharp lips . . . . . 218 XLI SONNETS 14   5
LEAVING
strikes the world away, leaving to shadowy silence and . . . 75 T&C SON REAL 6   3
entirely our minds --before leaving my room i turn, ... 288 IS 5 FOUR 5   6
i am easily disappears (leaving no proof not the . . . . . . 479 NEW POEMS 17   19
among not numerable ams (leaving a perfectly distinct unhe; . 558 1 X 1 18   7
world crylaughingly float away leaving just this strolling . 720 95 POEMS 48   8
+LEAVING
FOR CONTEXT, SEE . . . . 472 NEW POEMS 10   6
LED
cigarettebutts, chewed with disdain, led by a Jumpy Tramp . . 194 XLI PORTRAIT 2   21
LEELEE
dare ease Bet, an Leelee, an dee beeg wun" . . . . 73 T&C SON REAL 4   13
LEER
below myself the lunging leer of horizontal large distinct . 202 XLI PORTRAIT 9   35
the pout And affectionate leer interminable pyramidal, . . . 243 IS 5 ONE 14   5
+LEERING
FOR CONTEXT, SEE . . . . 704 95 POEMS 32   6
LEFT
little finger of his left hand then the ◇ . . . . 33 T&C ORIENTALE 6   58
legs of girl. his left hand quarried the quartzlike . . . . . 148 & SON REAL 19   3
a girl closes her left hand upon a mirror. . . . . 170 & SON ACTU 19   14
wherefore is there nothing left to guess: the cheap . . . . . 173 & SON ACTU 22   13
to breathe). The plump left fist opening "wisdom." Flicker . 226 IS 5 ONE MAME   7
to a purr... i left her permanently smiling / . . . . 228 IS 5 ONE MARJ   15
and thirty tame fleas left the prettily embroidered howdah . 262 IS 5 ONE 32   28
wanders There is nothing left of the world but . . . . 278 IS 5 THREE 2   17
spoke to joe 's left crashed pal dropped o . . . . 496 50 POEMS 10   5
three disappear finally what's left behind is (just a . . . . 501 50 POEMS 15   17
order) is wHISpEr it left; at the age of . . . . 792 73 POEMS 20   11
the place you never left (and i refer to . . . . 807 73 POEMS 35   4
+LEFTS
FOR CONTEXT, SEE . . . . 388 NO THANKS 5   15
LEC
cleat of her glad leg pulled into a sole . . . . 135 & SON REAL 6   4
en repos.... a fattish leg leaks obscenely from the . . . . . 143 & SON REAL 14   8
LEGAL
artificial & evil & legal) we thank thee god . . . . 604 (CHAIRE) 6   21
LEGALLY
observed some chucking some legally into Oblivion wave little 391 NO THANKS 8   7
+LEGISLATURE
FOR CONTEXT, SEE . . . . 266 IS 5 TWO 1   36
LEGS
Beneath her thighs such legs are seen as were . . . . 21 T&C PUELLA MEA   207
and with trumpets thy legs are the trees of . . . . 29 T&C ORIENTALE 3   22
seasons you have dirty legs and a muddy petticoat, ... 61 T&C PORTRAIT 9   12
man with the brittle legs winces swiflty out of . . . . . . 62 T&C PORTRAIT 10   24
the big and firm legs moving solemnly like careful . . . . . 95 & POST IMPR 7   13
of the, keenly lascivious legs. painful ankles large acute . 103 & POST IMPR 13   7
lust whose arms and legs like white squirming pipes . . . . . 110 & PORTRAIT 6   6
who sleep between the legs of Lil / / . . . . 114 & PORTRAIT 7   29
luminous laughter, and the legs whereas, at twenty minutes . 115 & PORTRAIT 8   24
Marie Louise with queenly legs cinq rue Henri Mounier . . . . 121 & PORTRAIT 12   46
your Little Stomach My legs are in your legs . . . . 123 & SEVEN POEMS 2   9
legs are in your legs Your arms under me . . . . 123 & SEVEN POEMS 2   10
and the Y her legs panting as they press . . . . 132 & SON REAL 3   9
anatomy oh yes! Large legs pinch, toes choke-- hair-thin . 146 & SON REAL 17   7
and taut, with thin legs just like a vine . . . . 147 & SON REAL 18   10
to bed with these legs she begins to heave . . . . 147 & SON REAL 18   13
boy's body on unsuspicious legs of girl. his left . . . . . 148 & SON REAL 19   3
Business (set on big legs nice to pinch assiduously . . . . 150 & SON REAL 21   8
flower between my amused legs kissing with little dints . . . 172 & SON ACTU 21   12
turd in April his legs are brittle and small . . . . 198 XLI PORTRAIT 6   21

```
                                                         PAGE     TITLE        LINE
LEGS (CONTINUED)
    feline she with radishred legs said (crossing them slowly)  . 228 IS 5 ONE MARJ     3
    is armed with large legs rancid voices Baedekers Mothers  . . 256 IS 5 ONE 27       15
    friends & their hats legs & arms brush dirt . . . . . . . . . 275 IS 5 TWO 9        44
    (hurry into heads are legs think wrists argue) short   . . . . 309 VIVA 1           10
    voice these root like legs or feethands; nobody ever   . . . . 490 50 POEMS 4       13
    absolute courage with its legs and arms / / . . . . . . . . . 522 50 POEMS 35       14
+LEGS
    FOR CONTEXT, SEE  . . . . . . . . . . . . . . . . . . . . . .  55 T&C PORTRAIT 3    10
    FOR CONTEXT, SEE  . . . . . . . . . . . . . . . . . . . . . . 104 & POST IMPR 14    11
    FOR CONTEXT, SEE  . . . . . . . . . . . . . . . . . . . . . . 616 {CHAIRE} 18       16
LEGTHELESSNE
    ver (whi! tethatr? apidly legthelessne sssuc kedt oward  . . . 385 NO THANKS 2      61
LEMAN
    La beale Isoud whose leman was. And if my . . . . . . . . . .  17 T&C PUELLA MEA    37
LEMONS
    stic-ky chromes and pretty- lemons and virginal pinks and . . 100 & POST IMPR 11     6
    edible spry pinks shy lemons greens coo l choc  . . . . . . . 179 XLI SONGS 1        9
LENA
    lovers like rej and lena smile (while looming darkly  . . . . 754 95 POEMS 82        9
LEND
    have and give than lend --being through failures born . . . . 394 NO THANKS 11      11
    who slave unselves to lend for hope of hope . . . . . . . . . 440 NO THANKS 56      16
    doubting believing and to lend to borrow) or any  . . . . . . 798 73 POEMS 26       18
LENDING
    no use demanding that lending be giving; it's no  . . . . . . 625 {CHAIRE} 27        3
LENGTH
    year dies, risen at length from palpitating veils. O  . . . .   5 T&C EPITHALAM    104
    base day utters at length her soft intrinsic hour,  . . . . .   6 T&C EPITHALAM    131
    dawn. i lie at length, breathing with shut eyes . . . . . . . 184 XLI SONGS 6       15
    face waddling carefully the length of this padded pole; . . . 279 IS 5 THREE 3      10
    arms created this at length inexcusable, this inexplicable  . 295 IS 5 FOUR 12       6
    or the oath cracked length wise--let it go it . . . . . . . . 569 1 X 1 29           4
LENSES
    razorblade into a mountainrange; lenses extend unwish through 554 1 X 1 14           6
LEOPARDS
    upwardcringing swiftness plunge these leopards of white dream 139 & SON REAL 10      6
    by daemons seethe luminous leopards (on wingfeet of . . . . . 586 1 X 1 46          16
LES
    to nobody something about les roses les bluets yes, . . . . . 102 & POST IMPR 12    16
    something about les roses les bluets yes, will He . . . . . . 102 & POST IMPR 12    17
    yes, will He buy? Les belles bottes--oh hear ,pas . . . . . . 102 & POST IMPR 12    20
    je suis belle cheri? les anglais m'aiment tous, les . . . . . 120 & PORTRAIT 12     12
    les anglais m'aiment tous, les americains aussi.... "bon dos, 120 & PORTRAIT 12     13
    soir (ladies accurately dead les anglais sont gentils et  . . 120 & PORTRAIT 12     25
    anglais sont gentils et les americains aussi, ils payent  . . 120 & PORTRAIT 12     26
    aussi, ils payent bien les americains dance exactly in  . . . 120 & PORTRAIT 12     27
    want nice sleep? toutes les petites femmes exactes qui  . . . 121 & PORTRAIT 12     50
    ask ourselves ou sont les neiges.... some guys talks  . . . . 237 IS 5 ONE 8         3
    ne m'aime et j'ai les mains froides. His Royal  . . . . . . . 262 IS 5 ONE 32       26
LESCHIN
    yours podia of radarw leschin / / / / . . . . . . . . . . . . 333 VIVA 24           26
LESGO
    finglestein idstings yewrety oride lesgo eckshun kemeruh  . . 474 NEW POEMS 12      13
LESS
    is most desire, yet less than those twain perfect . . . . . .   6 T&C EPITHALAM    147
    desperate elves and hope- less gnomes and frantic fairies . .  69 T&C POST IMPR 6   22
    my least heart-beat becomes less. And then all her  . . . . . 152 & SON ACTU 1       9
    weep: when from the less-than-whiteness of thy face (whose  . 210 XLI SONNETS 6      9
    the answer more or less deserved, Young fellow go . . . . . . 229 IS 5 ONE FRAN      8
    a little sunlight and less moonlight ourselves against the  . 238 IS 5 ONE 9        19
    ruddy glow united) not less than sixteen children and . . . . 254 IS 5 ONE 25       10
    a somewhat more than less emancipated evening had in  . . . . 258 IS 5 ONE 28        5
    attention; to speak even less objectively, i was horribly . . 263 IS 5 ONE 32       61
    earth's biggest grafter, nothing less; the Honorable Mr.  . . 266 IS 5 TWO 1        33
    of my brain is less than your eyelids' flutter . . . . . . . 290 IS 5 FOUR 7        11
    or silences to a less erring end) myself is . . . . . . . . . 291 IS 5 FOUR 8        5
    dreams are frail) songs less firm than your body's  . . . . . 306 IS 5 FIVE 5        4
```

LESS (CONTINUED)

	PAGE	TITLE	LINE
(without more ado about less than nothing) 2 boston	317	VIVA 9	22
ponderous wishes or hopes less tall than mine" (opening	328	VIVA 19	9
me and eye (you leSs) ly (un der	361	VIVA 52	13
Silently Flowers resembles beauty less than our breathing /	363	VIVA 54	12
i think it is less wonderful than this only	379	VIVA 70	13
Over tOwns mOOn whisper less creature huge grO pingness	383	NO THANKS 1	3
more a part are (less who are aware) than	386	NO THANKS 3	3
gladly forget little having less with every least each	390	NO THANKS 7	6
carry weapons) are not Less than (that by doDreaming	395	NO THANKS 12	11
this death named Smith less strange? Married and lies	406	NO THANKS 23	13
der, speaking (says. word Less) ly (goes folds? folds)	417	NO THANKS 34	6
luminous ends who far less lonely than a fire	420	NO THANKS 37	11
kl (ness) y ◇ Less? thE (against is)	429	NO THANKS 46	7
fall ing through touch less stillness (seized among what	432	NO THANKS 49	10
silently unday life's bright less dwindled to a leastful	432	NO THANKS 49	13
more than most strength (less than these how less	433	NO THANKS 50	8
(less than these how less than least flowers of	433	NO THANKS 50	9
could dare) unhearts can less unminds must fear because	440	NO THANKS 56	4
--dreads dying least; and less, that death should end)	446	NO THANKS 61	8
(unlove disappearing) only your less than guessed more than	450	NO THANKS 65	11
perhaps only A trifle less (merely beyond how very)	453	NO THANKS 68	5
of) A soursweet bedtime -less un- (wonderful) story	464	NEW POEMS 2	5
all ought to feel less worse (but only sameness	466	NEW POEMS 4	24
stands on a much less thin very much more	470	NEW POEMS 8	12
are fable who are less than these are least	505	50 POEMS 19	23
arms of year extend less humbly wealth to foe	521	50 POEMS 34	38
into upward deepness of less fear much than more	528	50 POEMS 40	8
mad and moonly and less it shall unbe than	530	50 POEMS 42	6
the sea love is less always than to win	530	50 POEMS 42	9
always than to win less never than alive less	530	50 POEMS 42	10
less never than alive less bigger than the least	530	50 POEMS 42	11
than the least begin less littler than forgive it	530	50 POEMS 42	12
least dare of snow less quite is nothing but	573	1 X 1 33	15
(afloat on not quite less than all of time)	575	1 X 1 35	21
a when, whatever is less alive than never begins	580	1 X 1 40	20
pasts are unborn (here less than nothing's more than	592	1 X 1 52	12
worlds in each least less than particle of perfect	603	{CHAIRE} 5	2
puking jukepulse hug) large less than more magnetic pink	629	{CHAIRE} 31	6
a hair's width: into less? into not) love, stand	633	{CHAIRE} 35	10
they'll all not conceive less who than love) /	634	{CHAIRE} 36	16
also you) and nothing less than excellent E will	650	{CHAIRE} 52	11
for whom create is less than have or one	664	{CHAIRE} 66	8
window) may be un less it were (floati ng	668	{CHAIRE} 70	6
we & worlds are less alive than dolls &	680	95 POEMS 8	31
rose i've and losing's less than winning (but love	684	95 POEMS 12	19
nights & forever) is Less Than Nothing (which would	702	95 POEMS 30	21
i'm no (if deeply less conceivable than birth or	720	95 POEMS 48	12
tice nobod y wants Less (not to men tion	727	95 POEMS 55	5
day (or maybe even less) / / / /	743	95 POEMS 71	14
a little more always less believably so than (how	748	95 POEMS 76	8
we'll (for what were less than dead) dance, i	762	95 POEMS 89	10
more than machine turns less than beast at 6	787	73 POEMS 15	12
that in whose form less form all goodness truth	790	73 POEMS 18	9
which limps who might less frenziedly have cried eev	790	73 POEMS 18	15
more and enormously more less: until her-and-his nonexistence	808	73 POEMS 36	11
whole creation may be less incalculable than a single	809	73 POEMS 37	13
voices who are dreams, less into heaven certainly earth	810	73 POEMS 38	7

+LESS

	PAGE	TITLE	LINE
FOR CONTEXT, SEE	719	95 POEMS 47	7

LESS-THAN-WHITENESS

	PAGE	TITLE	LINE
weep: when from the less-than-whiteness of thy face (whose	210	XLI SONNETS 6	9

LESSNESS

	PAGE	TITLE	LINE
green meadow of time lessness; quietly turning toward me	370	VIVA 61	7
the chasm of time lessness; but two dim disks	605	{CHAIRE} 7	13

+LESSNESS

	PAGE	TITLE	LINE
FOR CONTEXT, SEE	385	NO THANKS 2	61

		PAGE	TITLE	LINE
+LESSON				
FOR CONTEXT, SEE	126	& SEVEN POEMS 5	29
LEST				
for greater privacy and lest punished bottoms interrupt . . .	261	IS 5 ONE 31	13
and slightly (why? or lest we understand) slightly i	375	VIVA 66	9
LET				
mosaic of the ground --let but the incurious curtaining . . .	5	T&C EPITHALAM	85
and (phantom-white) dumb-blooming boughs let fall their . . .	8	T&C OF NICOL	6
tones of stroked flower; let not thy lust one	9	T&C SONGS 1	7
musically revealed in rareness: let thy twain eyes deeply . .	10	T&C SONGS 1	42
into receptive earth, O let us descend take shimmering . . .	41	T&C AMORES 5	14
the tinsel part they let thee play; i see	75	T&C SON REAL 6	6
final brain of air!) Let us as we have	80	T&C SON UNRE 5	12
the ostensible centuries therefore let us be a little	111	& PORTRAIT 6	56
started when Bill's chip let on to the bulls	145	& SON REAL 16	1
/ i have loved, let us see if that's	154	& SON ACTU 3	1
/ / / / let us tremble) a personal	168	& SON ACTU 17	1
i am dying so let us come in together	198	XLI PORTRAIT 6	31
givest me to him let me complain, whose seat	212	XLI SONNETS 8	10
somebody hears what i say--let him be pitiful: because . . .	216	XLI SONNETS 12	10
Serve-- from every B.V.D. let freedom ring amen. i	230	IS 5 ONE 2	14
Kodak therefore my friends let us now sing each	230	IS 5 ONE 2	35
other hand, myself) but let us next demand wherefore	245	IS 5 ONE 16	15
Horizontal business.... even so, let us make haste --consider	260	IS 5 ONE 30	21
to sleep by dolls let us not be continually	261	IS 5 ONE 31	2
reversed meantime in dreams let us investigate thoroughly . .	261	IS 5 ONE 31	10
It seemed too beautiful. Let us perhaps excuse me	263	IS 5 ONE 32	59
flu) my little darlings, let us now passionately remember . .	266	IS 5 TWO 1	16
inhibit unprepared digestions, come: let us mildly	266	IS 5 TWO 1	31
and James and next let me see yes Will	271	IS 5 TWO 6	4
very tidiyum necks begin) let us add that there	274	IS 5 TWO 9	16
the moon smiled she let go my vest and	284	IS 5 FOUR 1	11
being Spring and night) "let us go a very	303	IS 5 FIVE 2	2
silence of your hair --let the world say "his	306	IS 5 FIVE 5	9
tell days are teased: let (however) us Walk very	317	VIVA 9	17
supposing we just had let it go at that)	323	VIVA 15	13
most brilliant pupil mated, let us not deem it	326	VIVA 18	8
dream called ocean) and let must or if be	424	NO THANKS 41	8
if emerges a joy let 's thank indecent god	425	NO THANKS 42	13
will scheme to harness: let all unfools of unbeing	439	NO THANKS 55	15
(you bastards throw dynamite) let knowings magic with bright	452	NO THANKS 67	6
/ / / reason let others give and realness	454	NO THANKS 69	1
but the doctors won't let her comma considers frood	499	50 POEMS 13	3
The place is now let us accept (the time	504	50 POEMS 18	14
my father sing) then let men kill which cannot	521	50 POEMS 34	53
kill which cannot share, let blood and flesh be	521	50 POEMS 34	54
mortals told make two. Let liars wilt, repaying life	556	1 X 1 16	11
/ / / / let it go--the smashed word	569	1 X 1 29	1
the oath cracked length wise--let it go it was	569	1 X 1 29	5
was sworn to go let them go--the truthful liars	569	1 X 1 29	8
boths and neithers--you must let them go they were	569	1 X 1 29	12
were born to go let all go--the big small	569	1 X 1 29	15
the biggest and all things--let all go dear so	569	1 X 1 29	19
amazing now or here) let pitiless fear play host	580	1 X 1 40	4
tell me why people let go / / /	593	1 X 1 53	24
to understand "i'll never let you go until you've	622	(CHAIRE) 24	5
me another if i let him kiss me twice	684	95 POEMS 12	10
"o no no no let the roses come and	684	95 POEMS 12	14
your thinking forever's long let beauty touch a blunder . . .	742	95 POEMS 70	13
way youths and maidens: let us pray / /	794	73 POEMS 22	8
with a world; and let her heart's each whisper	811	73 POEMS 39	6
as men do not conceive--let ocean grow again /	843	73 POEMS 71	14
LET'S				
/ / / / let's live suddenly without thinking	160	& SON ACTU 9	1
nothing begins to prune let's live like the light	160	& SON ACTU 9	10
light that kills and let's as silence, because Whirl's . . .	160	& SON ACTU 9	11
to not wonder how let's say elation causes the	229	IS 5 ONE FRAN	12
/ (one fine day) let's take the train for	316	VIVA 8	2

		PAGE	TITLE	LINE

LET'S (CONTINUED)

(and you, you say "let's" going in "take hands" . . . . 353 VIVA 44 — 29
weather then or none let's feel all) mind in . . . . 364 VIVA 55 — 14
breathing may surprise ourselves --let's then despise what is 368 VIVA 59 — 16
why not said she (let's go said he not . . . . 399 NO THANKS 16 — 9
/ / / / "let's start a magazine to . . . . 407 NO THANKS 24 — 1
get what I mean let's not spoil it let's . . . . 407 NO THANKS 24 — 9
let's not spoil it let's make it serious something . . . . . 407 NO THANKS 24 — 10
smoke: come on kid let's go to sleep if . . . . 489 50 POEMS 3 — 4
sing; come on kid let's go to sleep if . . . . 489 50 POEMS 3 — 8
die, come on kid let's go to sleep if . . . . 489 50 POEMS 3 — 12
dream (come on kid Let's go to sleep) / . . . . 489 50 POEMS 3 — 16
E.S.T. bring the kiddies let's all have fun / . . . . 514 50 POEMS 28 — 14
good universe next door; let's go / / / . . . . 554 1 X 1 14 — 15
if's wintry (my lovely) let's open the year both . . . . 578 1 X 1 38 — 4
/ / / this (let's remember) day died again . . . . 599 (CHAIRE) 1 — 1
wit a human being --let's remember that / / . . . . 607 (CHAIRE) 9 — 16
now" so rah-rah-rah democracy let's all be as thankful . . . 711 95 POEMS 39 — 26
(& so) nothings each (let's kiss) means home / . . . . . . 725 95 POEMS 53 — 14
/ / / / let's, from some loud unworld's . . . . 745 95 POEMS 73 — 1
but misers are poor) --let's touch the sky: with . . . . . . 769 95 POEMS 95 — 5
young is the year) --let's touch the sky: with . . . . 769 95 POEMS 95 — 12
and joy under care-- let's do as an earth . . . . 769 95 POEMS 95 — 17
and most by more) --let's touch the sky: with . . . . 769 95 POEMS 95 — 19
but misers are poor-- let's love until noone could . . . . . 769 95 POEMS 95 — 24
i'm and as you're --let's touch the sky: with . . . . 769 95 POEMS 95 — 26

+LET'S

FOR CONTEXT, SEE . . . . 425 NO THANKS 42 — 13
FOR CONTEXT, SEE . . . . 474 NEW POEMS 12 — 13

LETS

/ / when god lets my body be From . . . . 16 T&C SONGS 6 — 1
the ale, which never lets you grow old blinking . . . . . . 96 & POST IMPR 8 — 24

LETTER

/ / ecco a letter starting "dearest we" unsigned: . . . . . 504 50 POEMS 18 — 1

LETTING

of white hands, who letting fall a thread of . . . . 8 T&C OF NICOL — 22
pain their crazy meal letting thy tigers of smooth . . . . 139 & SON REAL 10 — 3

LEVEL

low and smiling the level meadows ran before. Softer . . . . 14 T&C SONGS 4 — 15
low hair flutter the level litanies unto thee i . . . . . . 31 T&C ORIENTALE 5 — 20

+LEVER

FOR CONTEXT, SEE . . . . 248 IS 5 ONE 19 — 16

LEVIATHAN

we sailed on the Leviathan / / / / . . . . 313 VIVA 5 — 12

LEWD

ringing with rose the lewd fat bells and a . . . . 51 T&C IMPRESS 5 — 7
young (girls silky and lewd) like corn s l . . . . 101 & POST IMPR 11 — 77
and WhoEver would)? dance lewd dollies pretty and putrid . . 101 & POST IMPR 11 — 80
/ irreproachable ladies firmly lewd on dangerous slabs of . 138 & SON REAL 9 — 1
but touch you) timid lewd moon plunge skilfully into . . . . 155 & SON ACTU 4 — 16
facts dissolved by the lewd guess of fabulous immensity . . . 419 NO THANKS 36 — 7
Spring immortal Always & lewd shy New and upon . . . . 442 NO THANKS 57 — 20

LEWDLY

was Spring.... us drew lewdly the murmurous minute clumsy . . 174 & SON ACTU 23 — 2

LEZARD

vous voulez chatouiller mon lezard ladies suddenly j'm'en . . 121 & PORTRAIT 12 — 42

LIAR

true as bread: no liar looked him in the . . . . 521 50 POEMS 34 — 46

LIARS

loudly for Truth have liars pled, their heels for . . . . . 438 NO THANKS 54 — 17
told make two. Let liars wilt, repaying life they're . . . . 556 1 X 1 16 — 11
let them go--the truthful liars and the false fair . . . . 569 1 X 1 29 — 9
hair again" marvels "and liars kill their kind but" . . . . . 572 1 X 1 32 — 17

LIBERAL

and he twitches a liberal titty and lisps "i'm . . . . . . 711 95 POEMS 39 — 23

LIBERTY

shall the voice of liberty be mute?" He. spoke. . . . . . . 268 IS 5 TWO 3 — 13
and unquote loss of liberty my dears-- or even . . . . . . 544 1 X 1 4 — 16

	PAGE	TITLE	LINE
LIBERTY (CONTINUED)			
bury the statue of liberty (because it begins to	711	95 POEMS 39	27
LIBIDO			
Woman unacquainted with the libido and pursuing a course . .	327	VIVA 18	43
LICE			
angelfaces clustered like bright lice about god's capable . .	85	T&C SON ACTU 4	3
we were two alert lice in the blond hair	289	IS 5 FOUR 6	24
hopes; houses, clouds. kisses, lice; headaches: ifs.) yet .	361	VIVA 52	20
replied two billion pubic lice inside one pair of	473	NEW POEMS 11	5
LID			
the candidate's new silk lid bounds gently from his	259	IS 5 ONE 29	21
+LID			
FOR CONTEXT, SEE	117	& PORTRAIT 10	5
LIDL			
LISN dem gud am lidl yelluh bas tuds weer	547	1 X 1 7	14
LIDS			
clicking mischief from thick lids. the chunklike nose on . .	73	T&C SON REAL 4	7
LIE			
my hand warmly to lie it is a throbbing	21	T&C PUELLA MEA	195
--turning from the tremendous lie of sleep i watch	78	T&C SON UNRE 3	13
east side as i lie asleep my eyes go	100	& POST IMPR 11	2
--; i Like to Lie On My Couch at	101	& POST IMPR 11	58
breasts of bestial Marj lie large men who praise	114	& PORTRAIT 7	3
the large men who lie between the breasts of	114	& PORTRAIT 7	4
one word and you lie still as anything in	127	& SEVEN POEMS 5	34
But It's Nicer To Lie In Bed --eh? I'm	130	& SON REAL 1	13
of you really to lie a sharp agreeable flower	172	& SON ACTU 21	10
deserves of dawn. i lie at length, breathing with	184	XLI SONGS 6	15
and on Death's blade lie many a flower curled, ...	208	XLI SONNETS 4	10
know (whereas when i lie down i cough too	245	IS 5 ONE 16	11
having taken care to lie upon our abdomens for	261	IS 5 ONE 31	12
prettily then which did lie Down, honestly now who	317	VIVA 9	36
preponderatingly because unless statistics lie he was more .	339	VIVA 30	41
failed who have cried) lie bravely down sleep big	393	NO THANKS 10	11
without fear might faithfully lie down to so much	418	NO THANKS 35	7
Spring a someone will lie (glued among familiar things . . .	428	NO THANKS 45	2
the truth to summer's lie; bloodies with dizzying leaves . .	560	1 X 1 20	2
(trite now and old) lie we so must most	690	95 POEMS 18	4
bed she and he lie (undead) / / /	694	95 POEMS 22	8
/ out of the lie of no rises a	736	95 POEMS 64	1
slave) therefore, my life, lie down and more by	834	73 POEMS 62	10
LIES			
a breathing a , lies (slo wlythe wom an	104	& POST IMPR 14	7
and under the grass lies her head by oaks	181	XLI SONGS 3	13
on the ash-heap where lies what was once the	203	XLI LA GUERRE 1	18
out like a ribbon lies flat on the brush	231	IS 5 ONE 3	55
less strange? Married and lies afraid; aggressive and: . . .	406	NO THANKS 23	14
unlucky and the hitler lies down with the cohn)	466	NEW POEMS 4	20
for that way knowledge lies, the foetal grave called	484	NEW POEMS 22	11
angels sing: all murdering lies by mortals told make	556	1 X 1 16	10
you no sunbeam ever lies Bang is the meaning	570	1 X 1 30	5
fear-- mind's a coward; lies are laws) laugh, and	651	{CHAIRE} 53	9
and in this world lies: smoothbeautifuL ly folded; a	657	{CHAIRE} 59	11
(as far as alive) lies april; and i ◇	839	73 POEMS 67	5
LIEST			
sweet earth where thou liest / / / /	184	XLI SONGS 6	17
LIETH			
which like a flower lieth (while within the eyes	20	T&C PUELLA MEA	150
LIFE			
be a day and life be nothing, it shall	13	T&C SONGS 3	21
hither O thou, is life not a smile? i	27	T&C ORIENTALE 1	7
hither O thou, is life not a song? i	27	T&C ORIENTALE 1	14
hither O thou, is life not love? i speak	27	T&C ORIENTALE 1	21
into the strenuous briefness Life: handorgans and April . . .	66	T&C POST IMPR 3	2
of-love-and-of-death dollies of perfect life, dollies of . .	101	& POST IMPR 11	82
/ / / suppose Life is an old man	102	& POST IMPR 12	2
and "Death is young life wears velour trousers life	102	& POST IMPR 12	8
life wears velour trousers life totters, life has a	102	& POST IMPR 12	9

423

		PAGE	TITLE	LINE

LIFE (CONTINUED)

	PAGE	TITLE	LINE
velour trousers life totters, life has a beard" i	102	& POST IMPR 12	9
silent. --"Do you see Life? he is there and	102	& POST IMPR 12	11
the square crime of life.... Cecile, the oval shove	138	& SON REAL 9	13
spent all of its life on a garden-wall, and	147	& SON REAL 18	11
/ / / / life boosts herself rapidly at	151	& SON REAL 22	1
somewhere unspeaking sits my life; the grim clenched mind . .	156	& SON ACTU 5	10
/ / / when life is quite through with	181	XLI SONGS 3	1
large undeniable disease of Life, himself occasionally . . .	193	XLI PORTRAIT 1	23
mystery of mysteries , life. Far below myself the	201	XLI PORTRAIT 9	34
putting the secret of life in your pants and	204	XLI LA GUERRE 2	19
lips the whole of life almost do guess) if	205	XLI SONNETS 1	8
those immortal men his life that his fair city	209	XLI SONNETS 5	14
rich frail firm asinine life (i pant for what's	220	XLI SONNETS 16	4
/ / / MARJ "life? Listen" the feline she	228	IS 5 ONE MARJ	1
is O World O Life a formula: example, Turn	230	IS 5 ONE 2	32
is extremely unimportant) whereas Life matters if or when . .	260	IS 5 ONE 30	12
/ / / / life hurl my yes, crumbles	265	IS 5 ONE 34	1
quaffed the wine of life and found it sweet--	273	IS 5 TWO 8	8
(here the absurd I; life, to peer and wear	281	IS 5 THREE 5	18
(That is enough of life, for you. I understand.	282	IS 5 THREE 6	32
fingered tinily my heart life the little hands withdrew, . .	284	IS 5 FOUR 1	7
these things we consider life. Dear i put my	289	IS 5 FOUR 6	12
reckon how strangely my life is curved since the	292	IS 5 FOUR 9	6
disappear solemnly myselves ask "life, the question how do .	295	IS 5 FOUR 12	14
gradual gesture, and whittles life to eternity --after which	297	IS 5 FOUR 14	13
of your brain, hopes, life to (carefully turning a	298	IS 5 FOUR 15	26
my eyes? And send life out of me and	302	IS 5 FIVE 1	7
the year completes his life as a forgotten prisoner	304	IS 5 FIVE 3	9
that beFore) of Course life being just a Reflex	315	VIVA 7	7
sculptor (well on in life) re the helen molle	327	VIVA 18	r39
please my musn't broke) life Is like that please	343	VIVA 34	2
word; so that my life (which liked the sun	360	VIVA 51	23
me, i and my life will shut very beautifully, ...	366	VIVA 57	10
as sternly much not life nor stop as a	371	VIVA 62	26
contriving fate, my sharpening life are (behind each no) . .	373	VIVA 64	17
that your (how luminous) life toward twilight will dissolve .	379	VIVA 70	11
immaculately owe dying one life and will my rest	390	NO THANKS 7	13
luck The skeleton of life or did anybody Open	395	NO THANKS 12	3
said she but it's life said he but your	399	NO THANKS 16	21
earth --never whose proudly life swallowed is by (with . . .	402	NO THANKS 19	5
which and out of) Life, dost Thou contain a	406	NO THANKS 23	12
kumrads won't believe in life) and death knows whie	413	NO THANKS 30	6
rotting scholars guess that life shall not for living	420	NO THANKS 37	9
every pore a deathless life with magic until peace	428	NO THANKS 45	16
laughed and spat (this life could dare freely to	440	NO THANKS 56	12
laughed with self with life this poet arose nor	441	NO THANKS 56	41
the most not imagined life adventuring who would feel	450	NO THANKS 65	12
credos each divisible fool (life imitate gossip fear unlife .	452	NO THANKS 67	8
(which all ghosts of life became) and does our	454	NO THANKS 69	10
if you're young, whatever life you wear it will	484	NEW POEMS 22	2
tree or than all life more death begins to	502	50 POEMS 16	8
rock of mindscream into life; possibly darker than a	506	50 POEMS 20	5
not existing minds took life such life could not	510	50 POEMS 24	5
minds took life such life could not begin to	510	50 POEMS 24	6
breathe but if such life could its breath would	510	50 POEMS 24	7
is a tree (this life one leaf) but love	511	50 POEMS 25	26
suspected selves of space-- life stands gradually upon four .	517	50 POEMS 31	8
birth was wicked and life is worse squats a	545	1 X 1 5	10
your victim (death and life safely beyond) plays with	554	1 X 1 14	3
Let liars wilt, repaying life they're loaned; we (by . . .	556	1 X 1 16	11
never to twice (blow life to isn't: blow death	560	1 X 1 20	22
sunbeam's architecture with his life: and carve immortal . .	562	1 X 1 22	12
spark) if strangers meet life begins-- not poor not	564	1 X 1 24	3
most beautiful" her, my life worships and (night) then . . .	572	1 X 1 32	12
can grow" my, her life marvels "here'll be a	572	1 X 1 32	15
like a guess. Life's life and strikes my your	582	1 X 1 42	16
/ / / / life is more true than	592	1 X 1 52	1

	PAGE	TITLE	LINE

LIFE (CONTINUED)

did reveal) deeper is life than lose: higher than . . . . . . 592 1 X 1 52 — 3
the who of life's life (hark! what silence)?" "Worlds? . . . 603 (CHAIRE) 5 — 4
dying (forgive us, o life! the sin of Death . . . . 604 (CHAIRE) 6 — 25
(i understand) seduced by Life; whose brother married Heart, 621 (CHAIRE) 23 — 3
would prove truthless and life a mere pastime --each . . . . 625 (CHAIRE) 27 — 18
is" erect her whole life smiled "was and will . . . . 626 (CHAIRE) 28 — 5
/ snow means that life is a black cannonadin . . . . 628 (CHAIRE) 30 — 2
e go lliw og-dog) life ? tree3ghosts are Is . . . . 628 (CHAIRE) 30 — 6
a hole in its life where the young bell . . . . 647 (CHAIRE) 49 — 13
ago or else a life walking in the dark . . . . 648 (CHAIRE) 50 — 2
the birth day of life and of love and . . . . 663 (CHAIRE) 65 — 7
i) some newer than life (or than death) is . . . . 668 (CHAIRE) 70 — 19
not (beyond death and life) imaginable mysteries / / . . . . 674 95 POEMS 2 — 13
guess ex- actly what life will do) loves nothing . . . . . . 676 95 POEMS 4 — 14
/ because you take life in your stride (instead . . . . 679 95 POEMS 7 — 1
three like your my life and our / / . . . . 687 95 POEMS 15 — 12
diversified (putting it quietly) life was a blindman / . . . 699 95 POEMS 27 — 21
whole (yes god damned) life is a Flop or . . . . 702 95 POEMS 30 — 13
one cent in his life but he fell for . . . . 707 95 POEMS 35 — 17
three times in its life made three) brawny and . . . . 709 95 POEMS 37 — 8
turn ing; edge, of life (inquiry before snow / . . . . 712 95 POEMS 40 — 8
to guess (except my life) the true time of . . . . 717 95 POEMS 45 — 8
stand, am to am (life to life; breathing to . . . . 721 95 POEMS 49 — 2
to am (life to life; breathing to breathing flaming . . . . . 721 95 POEMS 49 — 2
they possibly afraid that life is running away from . . . . . 724 95 POEMS 52 — 13
she a ware that life (who never grows old) . . . . 724 95 POEMS 52 — 17
touch a blunder (called life) we die to breathe, ... 742 95 POEMS 70 — 14
/ i shall imagine life is not worth dying, ... 744 95 POEMS 72 — 1
that nonexistence millions call life, you and i may . . . . . 745 95 POEMS 73 — 10
A hummingbird princess FlOaTs doll-angel-life from Bet: To; . 747 95 POEMS 75 — 5
rain make april my life is the life of . . . . 749 95 POEMS 77 — 5
my life is the life of the reaper and . . . . 749 95 POEMS 77 — 5
still as (shifting his life from which to which) . . . . . . 754 95 POEMS 82 — 6
Im agines more than life must die to merely . . . . 759 95 POEMS 86 — 9
(more than all dying life, all living death) and . . . . . . 765 95 POEMS 91 — 7
of a tree called life; which grows higher than . . . . 766 95 POEMS 92 — 12
is the loser and life is the winner (and . . . . 769 95 POEMS 95 — 3
minds) eyes blindly stare life herSelf stands / / . . . . . . 780 73 POEMS 8 — 9
his (mountains understand how) life like a (now with . . . . 786 73 POEMS 14 — 9
stirs (m id) a life whats wh (un) ich . . . . 795 73 POEMS 23 — 8
ugliness and logic thwarted life: and thus-- but look . . . . 799 73 POEMS 27 — 38
this world) more my life does not leap than . . . . 810 73 POEMS 38 — 3
his arms my very life who's your --when all . . . . 812 73 POEMS 40 — 12
lark who lifts his life from all the dark . . . . 815 73 POEMS 43 — 3
feeling that sunlight is (life and day are) only . . . . . . 816 73 POEMS 44 — 7
would make your whole life and my (and infinite . . . . 817 73 POEMS 45 — 13
what dying must call life are you / / . . . . 818 73 POEMS 46 — 14
a slave) therefore, my life, lie down and more . . . . 834 73 POEMS 62 — 10
! hope faith! ! life love! bells cry bells . . . . 841 73 POEMS 69 — 3
lover (looking through both life and death) timelessly . . . 845 73 POEMS 73 — 12

+LIFE

FOR CONTEXT, SEE . . . . 346 VIVA 37 — 27
FOR CONTEXT, SEE . . . . 755 95 POEMS 83 — 12

LIFE'S

into light (slowly in life's serene perpetual round a . . . . — 5 T&C EPITHALAM — 81
fear of rhyme-- in life's very fragile hour (when . . . . . . — 23 T&C PUELLA MEA — 275
doomed exact smile of life's placid obscure palpable carnival — 43 T&C AMORES 7 — 30
in my arms for life's not a paragraph And . . . . 290 IS 5 FOUR 7 — 15
laugh both quickly signify life's only half (through deep . . 364 VIVA 55 — 12
clover marrying to themselves Life's animals) but not . . . . 376 VIVA 67 — 5
giving more than all life's busy little dyings may . . . . . 418 NO THANKS 35 — 4
night by silently unday life's bright less dwindled to . . . 432 NO THANKS 49 — 13
all of wishing) though life's lived wrongsideout, sameness . 446 NO THANKS 61 — 3
death a whore with life's disease which quacks will . . . . . 527 50 POEMS 39 — 22
showing, itself hiding one) life's only and true value . . . 531 50 POEMS 43 — 7
the month of may: life's the deathboard where all . . . . . . 574 1 X 1 34 — 6
terrors like a guess. Life's life and strikes my . . . . . . 582 1 X 1 42 — 16

LIFE'S (CONTINUED)

infinite the who of life's life (hark! what silence)?" . . . 603 {CHAIRE} 5   4
planet's year, his longest life's a heartbeat of some . . . . 609 {CHAIRE} 11   11
halfsight, seeing either with life's eye (which is if . . . . 845 73 POEMS 73   2

LIFELESS

to grind me into lifeless atoms various ab- surd . . . . . . 262 IS 5 ONE 32   3

LIFELESSNESS

down eager avenues of lifelessness consider for how much . . 81 T&C SON UNRE 6   6

LIFELUMP

did more) ask a lifelump buried by the star . . . . 522 50 POEMS 35   5

LIFEPRESERVERS

is all aleak; and lifepreservers there are none: and . . . . 438 NO THANKS 54   26

LIFETIME

day which seems a lifetime at the least) except . . . . . . 650 {CHAIRE} 52   7

LIFT

threshold have no dread lift the sheet back in . . . . . . 118 & PORTRAIT 10   42
used to know him lift the poor cuss tenderly . . . . 270 IS 5 TWO 5   13
if a poem should lift to me the distinct . . . . 291 IS 5 FOUR 8   25
its hands and feet (lift and may pitying Who . . . . 522 50 POEMS 35   12
all nothing will actually lift a luminous whole; turn . . . 649 {CHAIRE} 51   5
winter by spring, i lift my diminutive spire to . . . . . . 749 95 POEMS 77   17
i ng) he StandS lift ing against the shrieking . . . . . . 826 73 POEMS 54   10

+LIFT

FOR CONTEXT, SEE . . . . 613 {CHAIRE} 15   7

LIFTED

collision collapse As peacefully, lifted into the awful . . . 48 T&C IMPRESS 2   12
throat a little suddenly lifted in singing--hands fragile . . 85 T&C SON ACTU 4   10
weed coral and stones; lifted, and (before my eyes . . . . 369 VIVA 60   7
remark how through deep lifted fields Oxen distinctly move, . 434 NO THANKS 51   30
slept while his pines lifted their green lives and . . . . 555 1 X 1 15   16
touching hearing seeing breathing any--lifted from the no of 663 {CHAIRE} 65   10

LIFTING

but as i was lifting the horror of her . . . . 53 T&C PORTRAIT 1   39
bothness (say a twilight lifting the fragile skill of . . . 218 XLI SONNETS 14   4
Dick Mid once noted lifting a Green River (here's . . . . . 229 IS 5 ONE FRAN   10
fears and eyes lifts lifting hopes and hands --nourish . . . 456 NO THANKS 71   13
gets a bellyful without lifting my finger i say . . . . . . 475 NEW POEMS 13   9
alive green each very lifting & seriously voice -like . . . . 480 NEW POEMS 18   24
feel the mountains grow. Lifting the valleys of the . . . . 520 50 POEMS 34   17
mean they're possible --but" lifting "flowers" more all stars 603 {CHAIRE} 5   13

LIFTINGLY

a single mys- tery (liftingly caught upon falling) silent! . 627 {CHAIRE} 29   14

LIFTS

the magus of creation, lifts a flower-- whence is . . . . . . 6 T&C EPITHALAM   134
whose tall mysterious shepherd lifts a cheek teartroubled to . 9 T&C SONGS 1   10
on slippery udders she lifts an impertinent puerperal face . 151 & SON REAL 22   12
how the keen ship lifts (skilfully like some bird . . . . . 378 VIVA 69   3
sun died) the ship lifts on seas of iron . . . . 419 NO THANKS 36   11
who fears and eyes lifts lifting hopes and hands . . . . . . 456 NO THANKS 71   13
such a sharpening freedom lifts our blood as if . . . . . . 675 95 POEMS 3   6
like every lark who lifts his life from all . . . . 815 73 POEMS 43   3

LIGHT

earth and passes into light (slowly in life's serene . . . . 5 T&C EPITHALAM   80
as a glass turned light to flame and blazed . . . . 8 T&C OF NICOL   18
fright the sudden fooled light. it is the autumn . . . . . . 11 T&C SONGS 2   20
street of the sky light walks scattering poems on . . . . . 50 T&C IMPRESS 4   3
with the soft furious light, and while fire-escapes and . . . 62 T&C PORTRAIT 10   15
foam in the last light thread the creeping shores . . . . . . 64 T&C POST IMPR 1   3
me in the last light pours its eyeless miles . . . . 64 T&C POST IMPR 1   7
tidewings in the last light twitching at the world . . . . 64 T&C POST IMPR 1   11
caught in the hoisting light any woman is smooth . . . . . . 68 T&C POST IMPR 5   12
mysterious the flowerstricken sun- light is thickening . . . 69 T&C POST IMPR 6   24
you-- but that when light fails and this sweet . . . . . . 71 T&C SON REAL 2   7
the sonorous homes of light swiftly sink in the . . . . . . 79 T&C SON UNRE 4   2
and the keenly musical light of sudden nothing.... la . . . 84 T&C SON ACTU 3   14
tread the serene nervous light of paradise-- by angelfaces . 85 T&C SON ACTU 4   2
dirty squeal of soiling light yanKing from bushy obscurity . 96 & POST IMPR 8   28
and a propos such light and shape as means . . . . 98 & POST IMPR 9   9

LIGHT (CONTINUED)
    derl y tottering in sun-light THE nobody (knows and . . . . . 101 & POST IMPR 11   78
    under flat lusts of light her nice concupiscence appeared . . 103 & POST IMPR 13   15
    / / / / light cursed falling in a . . . . 133 & SON REAL 4   1
    eyes' shuddering burrs of light stick on my brain . . . . . . 136 & SON REAL 7   7
    sprawled eyes squirming with light insane chisel the killing   139 & SON REAL 10   10
    with the rash, coherent light) only to trace . . . . 155 & SON ACTU 4   6
    cracking brains A swiftlyenormous light --and furiously . . . 157 & SON ACTU 6   12
    of vital futile huge light as she does not . . . .   159 & SON ACTU 8   2
    let's live like the light that kills and let's . . . .   160 & SON ACTU 9   10
    deeds of green thrilling light with thinned newfragile . . . 163 & SON ACTU 12   8
    street takes of shadowy light the droll snowing delirium . .   168 & SON ACTU 17   5
    my sonnet is A light goes on in the . . . .   171 & SON ACTU 20   1
    (that is, big horses; light feeling up streets; heels . . .   172 & SON ACTU 21   7
    on edge. So until light each having each we . . . .   173 & SON ACTU 22   11
    neglected sentiments brings to light dusty heroisms and . . . 203 XLI LA GUERRE 1   8
    in the death of light, against whose enormous curve . . . . . 214 XLI SONNETS 10   3
    swaggering cookies of indignant light / / / / . . . . 226 IS 5 ONE MAME   14
    toward her a fragile light bent gatheringly / / . . . . 284 IS 5 FOUR 1   18
    jealousy is dark if light should flower: or laughing . . . . 292 IS 5 FOUR 9   17
    horribly blunder through new light hush we are made . . . . . 299 IS 5 FOUR 16   14
    or moves --climbing (past light after light) to turn, ... 300 IS 5 FOUR 17   4
    --climbing (past light after light) to turn, disappears the . 300 IS 5 FOUR 17   5
    verses, through the sharp light cryingly as the knights . . . 302 IS 5 FIVE 1   15
    itself, an awful big light squoits down my spine . . . . . . 332 VIVA 23   27
    captured: in the narrow light of inverno) this is . . . . . . 345 VIVA 36   9
    a hugeness of twi -light pale beyond soft- liness . . . . . . 349 VIVA 40   3
    / / twi- is -Light bird ful -ly dar . . . .   350 VIVA 41   2
    / / / a light Out) & first of . . . .   358 VIVA 49   1
    shadow, that among first light groping washes my nightmare .   374 VIVA 65   14
    dusk just when the Light is filled with birds . . . .   434 NO THANKS 51   3
    flowers And o the Light thrown by Them opens . . . .   437 NO THANKS 53   4
    who moves in black light dancing isn'ts on why, ...   439 NO THANKS 55   20
    care if time totters, light droops, all measures bend . . . . 446 NO THANKS 61   6
    the awful mystery of light / / / / . . . .   454 NO THANKS 69   14
    sit down) and this light is so dark the . . . .   505 50 POEMS 19   9
    their own generous completely light, an angel; or (as . . . . 562 1 X 1 22   6
    i -nto wintry twi- light (all together a manying . . . . . .   627 {CHAIRE} 29   7
    strange ness Of sun light and of fragrance and . . . . . .   657 {CHAIRE} 59   6
    presence (welcoming humbly His light and proudly His . . . . 749 95 POEMS 77   20
    fears yours is the light by which my spirit's . . . . 810 73 POEMS 38   12
    staring into winter twi light (whisper) "was my friend" . . . 823 73 POEMS 51   5
    cean (everywhere nothing but light and dark; but never . . . 840 73 POEMS 68   24
+LIGHT
    FOR CONTEXT, SEE . . . .   719 95 POEMS 47   2
LIGHT'S
    / / / / light's lives lurch a once . . . .   633 {CHAIRE} 35   1
LIGHTED
    earth a candle is lighted and it is dark. . . . .   50 T&C IMPRESS 4   25
    to face suddenly the lighted living hills / / . . . .   82 T&C SON ACTU 1   15
LIGHTHEAVY
    as linotypes gobblehobble our lightheavy twic twoc ingly . . 259 IS 5 ONE 29   13
LIGHTLY
    faces painteaten and bodies lightly desperate certainly . . .   57 T&C PORTRAIT 5   38
    better, queens, queens laughing lightly crowned with far . . 211 XLI SONNETS 7   14
    a suddenly unsaid gesture lightly my eyes? And send . . . . . 302 IS 5 FIVE 1   6
LIGHTNING
    Frederick found on a lightning-rod, Boston, Mass. such were . 262 IS 5 ONE 32   31
    world iS Slapped: with; liGhtninG ! at which (shal) . . . . . 347 VIVA 38   5
+LIGHTNING
    FOR CONTEXT, SEE . . . .   248 IS 5 ONE 19   21
LIGHTNING-ROD
    Frederick found on a lightning-rod, Boston, Mass. such were . 262 IS 5 ONE 32   31
LIGHTS
    eyes of Magdalen. The lights have laughed their last; . . . .   75 T&C SON REAL 6   9
    voice feels curiously cool (suddenly-Lights go! on, by . . . 167 & SON ACTU 16   19
    paperboy a finishes Helmar lights another x and y . . . . . . 200 XLI PORTRAIT 8   15
    greens serenely lingering, absolute lights like baths of . . 208 XLI SONNETS 4   4

	PAGE	TITLE	LINE
LIGHTS (CONTINUED)			
a darkness where new lights begin and increase, since	297	IS 5 FOUR 14	3
LIGHTYEARS			
faded five or so lightyears of pyjamastring) a (vastly . . .	607	{CHAIRE} 9	7
LIKE			
all the castle lay like some gigantic ghost-flower born . . .	8	T&C OF NICOL	2
fell upon the night, like angel's tears, the syllables . . .	8	T&C OF NICOL	10
thy taut flesh silver, like the currency of faint	9	T&C SONGS 1	32
pride of petaled hours, like flowers at the feet	11	T&C SONGS 2	33
lady drifting distinctly, moving like a myth in the	17	T&C PUELLA MEA	19
morning, with April feet like sudden flowers and all	17	T&C PUELLA MEA	21
(with her eyes which like two elves incredibly amuse	17	T&C PUELLA MEA	39
a fragile smile which like a flower lieth (while	20	T&C PUELLA MEA	150
blood's mysterious skein (but like some passionate earlier .	21	T&C PUELLA MEA	187
When the world was like a song heard behind	22	T&C PUELLA MEA	221
(when the world was like a flower Omar Hafiz	22	T&C PUELLA MEA	226
(when the world was like a tale made of	23	T&C PUELLA MEA	276
one or two ladies like flowers made, softly used	23	T&C PUELLA MEA	282
in their hands scimitars like windy torches each is	33	T&C ORIENTALE 6	39
/ / / i like to think that on	42	T&C AMORES 6	1
soul it is not like any songs (the singers	43	T&C AMORES 7	6
of trite jewels now like a moth with stumbling	47	T&C IMPRESS 1	7
into a stale shriek like an alarm-clock) / /	49	T&C IMPRESS 3	28
struggle slowly and writhe like caught. brave: flies; / . . .	55	T&C PORTRAIT 3	20
in her gentle window like a reminiscence partaken softly . .	58	T&C PORTRAIT 6	22
is how do you like your blueeyed boy Mister	60	T&C PORTRAIT 8	10
with a little oldish doll-like face and hairy arms	69	T&C POST IMPR 6	38
face and hairy arms like an ogre and rub-	69	T&C POST IMPR 6	38
and runs and floats like a toy on the	69	T&C POST IMPR 6	43
cornerless, the moon rattles like a fragment of angry	70	T&C SON REAL 1	14
be absitively posolutely dead, like Coney Island in winter .	72	T&C SON REAL 3	15
beyond doomed thought is like a woman amorous to	81	T&C SON UNRE 6	10
paradise-- by angelfaces clustered like bright lice about . .	85	T&C SON ACTU 4	3
waddles toward, me, dressed like a Plum grinning softly, . .	94	& POST IMPR 6	15
half of Girl which (like some floating snake upon	95	& POST IMPR 7	8
firm legs moving solemnly like careful and furious and . . .	95	& POST IMPR 7	14
that these houses bulge like memories in one crooked	98	& POST IMPR 9	17
and breathless-scarlet, dark colours like 'cellos keen . . .	100	& POST IMPR 11	7
glike piccolos thumPing colours like a bangofpiano colours .	100	& POST IMPR 11	9
of Pure percussion colours- like-trumpets they (writhe they,	100	& POST IMPR 11	12
tortures-pleasantly myears it is, like the, Jab: of a	101	& POST IMPR 11	49
EYES AND --; i Like to Lie On My	101	& POST IMPR 11	57
right on the stomach like A billiken with hisknees	101	& POST IMPR 11	60
stomachs bLurting and cHuckling like uninteresting-	101	& POST IMPR 11	69
little, girls smoothanduseless i, like, best, the, stomachs,	101	& POST IMPR 11	76
(girls silky and lewd) like corn s l e	101	& POST IMPR 11	77
rhythm of absurdity. skin like the poisonous fragility of . .	103	& POST IMPR 13	12
treesOf. (Fields Elysian the like, a) slEEping neck a	104	& POST IMPR 14	7
/ / Cleopatra built like a smooth arrow or	110	& PORTRAIT 6	2
whose arms and legs like white squirming pipes wiggle	110	& PORTRAIT 6	7
slim warm moist built like an organ and it	110	& PORTRAIT 6	18
of Egypt , built like a fleet pillar or	111	& PORTRAIT 6	45
the infinite processions move like moths and like boys . . .	111	& PORTRAIT 6	63
move like moths and like boys and like incense	111	& PORTRAIT 6	63
and like boys and like incense and like sunlight	111	& PORTRAIT 6	64
and like incense and like sunlight and like ships	111	& PORTRAIT 6	64
and like sunlight and like ships and like young	111	& PORTRAIT 6	65
and like ships and like young girls and like	111	& PORTRAIT 6	65
like young girls and like butterflies and like money	111	& PORTRAIT 6	65
and like butterflies and like money and like laughter	111	& PORTRAIT 6	66
and like money and like laughter and like elephants	111	& PORTRAIT 6	67
and like laughter and like elephants through our single . . .	111	& PORTRAIT 6	68
winds of my lust like a high troubling ship	112	& PORTRAIT 6	96
six subjunctive crumbs twitch like mutilated thumbs: picture	117	& PORTRAIT 10	31
Mimi with the body like une boite a joujoux, ...	121	& PORTRAIT 12	49
/ / Spring is like a perhaps hand (which	124	& SEVEN POEMS 3	1
everything carefully spring is like a perhaps Hand in	124	& SEVEN POEMS 3	10
/ / gee i like to think of dead	126	& SEVEN POEMS 5	1

LIKE (CONTINUED)

morning dead's clever too like POF goes the alarm . . . . . . 126 & SEVEN POEMS 5   10
dead has a smile like the nicest man you've . . . . 126 & SEVEN POEMS 5   14
and Whocares dead's fine like hands do you see . . . . . . 126 & SEVEN POEMS 5   24
want to dead's happy like the way underclothes All . . . . . 126 & SEVEN POEMS 5   27
your musiclesson and you like music and to have . . . . . . 126 & SEVEN POEMS 5   30
have to? dead's nice like a dance where you . . . . 127 & SEVEN POEMS 5   32
touched, them dead's sorry like a thistlefluff-thing which . 127 & SEVEN POEMS 5   41
say Sure you say (like that) sure i'll come . . . . 127 & SEVEN POEMS 5   49
you say for i like kittens i do and . . . . 127 & SEVEN POEMS 5   50
Boost my huge passion like a business and the . . . . 132 & SON REAL 3   8
lusts her hair was like a gas evil to . . . . 135 & SON REAL 6   6
the killed world wriggled like a twitched string. / . . . . . 135 & SON REAL 6   17
body filled with surprise like a white shocking wire, ... 147 & SON REAL 18   5
with thin legs just like a vine that's spent . . . . 147 & SON REAL 18   10
it's just a little like music, a little more . . . . 152 & SON ACTU 1   2
music, a little more like curving colour (say orange) . . . . 152 & SON ACTU 1   3
than me will you like the rain's face and . . . . 153 & SON ACTU 2   13
to prune let's live like the light that kills . . . . 160 & SON ACTU 9   10
found what you are like the rain, (Who feathers . . . . . . 163 & SON ACTU 12   1
/ (the phonograph's voice like a keen spider skipping . . . . 166 & SON ACTU 15   1
stealth of ecstasy means, like a girl lasciviously frail, . . 168 & SON ACTU 17   10
blood; your sex squeaked like a billiard-cue chalking itself, 170 & SON ACTU 19   9
handorgan in twilight playing like hell / / / . . . . 174 & SON ACTU 23   15
/ / / i like my body when it . . . . 175 & SON ACTU 24   1
and nerves more. i like your body. i like . . . . 175 & SON ACTU 24   4
like your body. i like what it does, i . . . . 175 & SON ACTU 24   4
what it does, i like its hows. i like . . . . 175 & SON ACTU 24   5
like its hows. i like to feel the spine . . . . 175 & SON ACTU 24   5
and again kiss, i like kissing this and that . . . . 175 & SON ACTU 24   9
that of you, i like, slowly stroking the, shocking . . . . . 175 & SON ACTU 24   10
love-crumbs, and possibly i like the thrill of under . . . . 175 & SON ACTU 24   13
/ / the hills like poets put on purple . . . . 188 XLI SONGS 10   2
where did you go? like little kittens are all . . . . 191 XLI CHANSONS 1   6
little you are more like a flower who found . . . . 192 XLI CHANSONS 2   4
of habitues their faces like cigarettebutts, chewed with . . 194 XLI PORTRAIT 2   20
/ / it's just like a coffin's inside when . . . . 198 XLI PORTRAIT 6   1
effendi drifts between tables like an old leaf between . . . 198 XLI PORTRAIT 6   16
his peaked head smoulders like a new turd in . . . . 198 XLI PORTRAIT 6   20
hands twitter before him, like foolish butterflies he is . . 198 XLI PORTRAIT 6   23
repapered he will nod like buddha or answer modestly . . . . 198 XLI PORTRAIT 6   28
/ LA GUERRE earth like a tipsy biddy with . . . . 203 XLI LA GUERRE 1   1
serenely lingering, absolute lights like baths of golden . . 208 XLI SONNETS 4   4
fed: and if i like not what thou givest . . . . 212 XLI SONNETS 8   9
air-- but if i like, i'll take between thy . . . . 212 XLI SONNETS 8   13
swoon the moon is like a floating silver hell . . . . 214 XLI SONNETS 10   13
to snare the timid like of her mind to . . . . 216 XLI SONNETS 12   5
Mrs. Somethingwich (with flesh like an old toy balloon) . . . 219 XLI SONNETS 15   12
"gimme uh swell fite like up ter yknow, Rektuz, ... 227 IS 5 ONE GERT   15
slightly) --"O damn ginks like dis Gawd" opening slowlyslowly 228 IS 5 ONE MARJ   7
of gum did something like a whisper, "even her." . . . . . . 228 IS 5 ONE MARJ   10
tiniest whispered invitation is like a clock striking in . . 229 IS 5 ONE FRAN   15
certain ideas gestures rhymes, like Gillette Razor Blades . . 230 IS 5 ONE 2   20
And there're a <> like all of you successfully . . . . 231 IS 5 ONE 3   42
Odor? ono. comes out like a ribbon lies flat . . . . 231 IS 5 ONE 3   55
the head keen chassised like a Rolls Royce swoops . . . . . . 232 IS 5 ONE 3   5
der never was nutn like Nooer Leans Shikahgo Sain . . . . . . 237 IS 5 ONE 8   7
Diver on Xmas Eve like Hell Itself which may . . . . 239 IS 5 ONE 10   6
remember we all cried like the Missouri when my . . . . 239 IS 5 ONE 10   32
sharp angels with faces like Jim Europe / / . . . . 241 IS 5 ONE 12   9
from low through second-in-to-high like greasedlightning) . . 248 IS 5 ONE 19   20
smells he smiles is like Out of doors he's . . . . 251 IS 5 ONE 22   6
can play the triangle like the devil) my uncle . . . . 253 IS 5 ONE 24   4
visage simple, terse, seated like any king or prince . . . . 254 IS 5 ONE 25   19
Danielli their numbers are like unto the stars of . . . . . . 256 IS 5 ONE 27   21
us Kid. daze nutn like it. / / / . . . . 259 IS 5 ONE 29   28
it will not rub, like any other pastel. (While . . . . . . 264 IS 5 ONE 33   24
happy dead who rushed like lions to the roaring . . . . . . 268 IS 5 TWO 3   11

	PAGE	TITLE	LINE

LIKE (CONTINUED)

	PAGE	TITLE	LINE
big eyes i loved like you can't imagine Harry	271	IS 5 TWO 6	9
artificial limbs, with faces like defunct geraniums) / / . .	280	IS 5 THREE 4	34
of thousands of houses--Lisboa. Like the crackle of a	281	IS 5 THREE 5	6
Clouds over me are like bridegrooms Naked and luminous . . .	281	IS 5 THREE 5	16
perhaps one villa caught like pieces of a kite	283	IS 5 THREE 7	10
the room's Silence) this like a littlest poem a	286	IS 5 FOUR 3	9
solong my tailor chuckles like a woman in a	287	IS 5 FOUR 4	13
/ / you are like the snow only purer	293	IS 5 FOUR 10	1
snow only purer fleeter, like the rain only sweeter	293	IS 5 FOUR 10	2
love? Love if you like and i like, for	295	IS 5 FOUR 12	22
you like and i like, for the reason that	295	IS 5 FOUR 12	22
you'll notice follows us like a big yellow dog.	303	IS 5 FIVE 2	10
comes my heart, singing like an idiot, whispering like . . .	304	IS 5 FIVE 3	2
like an idiot, whispering like a drunken man who	304	IS 5 FIVE 3	3
disaster of the year: like this most early single	305	IS 5 FIVE 4	5
's future is toothsome like (they got pockets full	314	VIVA 6	8
but: that Mat isse like ◇ gave me, A, ...	318	VIVA 10	7
seven years expl0 ded like a toy eloping to	320	VIVA 12	12
who smelt rath er like her fath er who	320	VIVA 12	20
cathedral ought to look like) it doesn't look at	323	VIVA 15	25
doesn't look at all like what you and what	323	VIVA 15	27
know alotta sweet bull like dat ...suddenly i feels	332	VIVA 23	12
squoits down my spine like i was dead er	332	VIVA 23	27
smile if here there (like lopsided imaginations) filled with	340	VIVA 31	9
musn't broke) life Is like that please stroke for	343	VIVA 34	3
you're killing) death is like now That please squirtnowing .	343	VIVA 34	7
drownInsound(& (we (are like) dead) Whoshout (Ghost) . . .	347	VIVA 38	21
father will be (deep like a rose tall like	352	VIVA 43	5
like a rose tall like a rose) standing near	352	VIVA 43	6
look how it goes like a dream (and between	353	VIVA 44	8
reach , they are like jam on the shelf	353	VIVA 44	19
of skin lay eyes like new tools) whence i	355	VIVA 46	10
guessing fingers did-not-move exquisitely ,like dead children	355	VIVA 46	17
first of all foam -like hair spatters creasing pillow	358	VIVA 49	3
fear (of suddenly me) like these first deepest rare	367	VIVA 58	6
world has been Picked, like a piece of clover, ...	370	VIVA 61	4
think i am gone like a sun which must	372	VIVA 63	7
keen ship lifts (skilfully like some bird which is	378	VIVA 69	4
n, d i ng like like, like bad, like	389	NO THANKS 6	14
d i ng like like, like bad, like candy:	389	NO THANKS 6	14
i ng like like, like bad, like candy: &	389	NO THANKS 6	14
like like, like bad, like candy: & you are	389	NO THANKS 6	14
whose epoch fits him like a grave) with all	394	NO THANKS 11	2
whom soothe psychotic myths like Jonah And The Whale	398	NO THANKS 15	19
(which way said she like this said he if	399	NO THANKS 16	15
aint no ews eye like the steak all ried	405	NO THANKS 22	11
you know something genuine like a mark in a	407	NO THANKS 24	12
pride and loneliness alive like some dream giving more . . .	418	NO THANKS 35	3
cannot write who laugh like they would fall apart	427	NO THANKS 44	11
for art they kill like you would take a	427	NO THANKS 44	16
fail slenderly i win (like touch all stars or	433	NO THANKS 50	11
and yawned: it looks like rain (they've played for	451	NO THANKS 66	2
purpose by simple people like we) down with hell	466	NEW POEMS 4	12
/ / ◇ tosses like thin bums dream ing	469	NEW POEMS 7	2
twot with a twitch like kingdom come (moon The	469	NEW POEMS 7	4
lifting & seriously voice -like finger of the tree	480	NEW POEMS 18	26
than dreams are round like a spoon are both	483	NEW POEMS 21	4
a voice these root like legs or feethands; nobody	490	50 POEMS 4	13
come to town some like it shot and some	497	50 POEMS 11	5
it shot and some like it hung and some	497	50 POEMS 11	6
it hung and some like it in the twot	497	50 POEMS 11	7
a girl with nipples like pink thimbles) ask him	498	50 POEMS 12	19
the slot and bellow like a bool to lay	500	50 POEMS 14	12
found some lost thing (like a curtain on which	516	50 POEMS 30	4
so kind it wouldn't like a soul and couldn't	544	1 X 1 4	27
the god of things like they err / /	552	1 X 1 12	30
/ / / (once like a spark) if strangers	564	1 X 1 24	1

430

		PAGE	TITLE	LINE
LIKE (CONTINUED)				
can git anything you like out of it if	567	1 X 1 27	12
snow) gone into what like all them kings you	568	1 X 1 28	12
looked) "especially in winter" (like a leaf opening) as . . .	572	1 X 1 32	5
night's not eternal terrors like a guess. Life's life	582	1 X 1 42	15
/ i think you like" a strawberry bang this	585	1 X 1 45	1
i could sing but like nothing are the joys	587	1 X 1 47	4
came with a song like a dream of a	587	1 X 1 47	8
bird with a song like not anything under skies	587	1 X 1 47	10
alive with a trill like until / / /	587	1 X 1 47	24
his wish (it dived like a fish but it	593	1 X 1 53	9
fish but it climbed like a dream) throbbing like	593	1 X 1 53	10
like a dream) throbbing like a heart singing like	593	1 X 1 53	11
like a heart singing like a flame blue took	593	1 X 1 53	12
future's future; and immediate like some newly remembered . .	601	(CHAIRE) 3	11
squirts a two ne like nothing verdi slightly knu	602	(CHAIRE) 4	3
o baby i wouldn't like Death if Death were	604	(CHAIRE) 6	5
build a (who are like ocean patient) dream's eternity	617	(CHAIRE) 19	3
his voice is green like growing (is miraculous like	617	(CHAIRE) 19	6
like growing (is miraculous like tomorrow) all around the . .	617	(CHAIRE) 19	6
wood man) nic he like wint-air nic like ot-am	618	(CHAIRE) 20	22
he like wint-air nic like ot-am sum-air (young old	618	(CHAIRE) 20	24
sum-air (young old nic) like spring yoo un-air-stan? me . . .	618	(CHAIRE) 20	27
un-air-stan? me crazy me like evry-ting / / /	618	(CHAIRE) 20	30
an apish grin (extremely like but quite absurd gloved	640	(CHAIRE) 42	7
/ / / a like a grey rock wanderin	654	(CHAIRE) 56	1
love's own secret) we, like homing through welcoming sweet .	659	(CHAIRE) 61	1
through never) a kite like face of the child	668	(CHAIRE) 70	10
For whatever we lose (like a you or a	682	95 POEMS 10	11
dream unthings silent three like your my life and	687	95 POEMS 15	10
(or some body Dead like even a Poet) could	702	95 POEMS 30	6
else thought lucinda looked like steve / / /	706	95 POEMS 34	4
carroty hair" "it seems like i just heard your	707	95 POEMS 35	5
a which that walks like a who but the	711	95 POEMS 39	4
to find anyone's blind (like me like you) except	716	95 POEMS 44	3
anyone's blind (like me like you) except in snow--	716	95 POEMS 44	3
have doubt and believe (like me like you) vanish	716	95 POEMS 44	27
and believe (like me like you) vanish in so	716	95 POEMS 44	27
the earth and i like you better than everything	717	95 POEMS 45	3
will blossom: will sing (like april's own april and	735	95 POEMS 63	13
is) making fools understand (like wintry me) that not	736	95 POEMS 64	6
love, dear; imagine ourselves like living neither nor dead .	743	95 POEMS 71	5
lost) & som ething like a mind with out	753	95 POEMS 81	4
a pitchfork (breathing) lovers like rej and lena smile . . .	754	95 POEMS 82	9
world disappear all and (like any these my) words	761	95 POEMS 88	13
riding through a Dream like fire called flowers over	778	73 POEMS 6	16
to Rain) a house like shape stirs through (not	785	73 POEMS 13	10
(mountains understand how) life like a (now with one	786	73 POEMS 14	10
so what) all politicians like the sight of vote	790	73 POEMS 18	12
released flee one another like the pest thus did	799	73 POEMS 27	31
of him self sang like a bird. Mostpeople have	802	73 POEMS 30	28
glorying keen star whom she-and-he-like ifs of am perceive .	808	73 POEMS 36	8
may i be gay like every lark who lifts	815	73 POEMS 43	2
coming made stones sing like birds-- but o the	844	73 POEMS 72	2
+LIKE				
FOR CONTEXT, SEE	8	T&C OF NICOL	19
FOR CONTEXT, SEE	53	T&C PORTRAIT 1	40
FOR CONTEXT, SEE	60	T&C PORTRAIT 8	6
FOR CONTEXT, SEE	69	T&C POST IMPR 6	18
FOR CONTEXT, SEE	73	T&C SON REAL 4	8
FOR CONTEXT, SEE	100	& POST IMPR 11	9
FOR CONTEXT, SEE	101	& POST IMPR 11	50
FOR CONTEXT, SEE	101	& POST IMPR 11	65
FOR CONTEXT, SEE	101	& POST IMPR 11	68
FOR CONTEXT, SEE	148	& SON REAL 19	4
FOR CONTEXT, SEE	159	& SON ACTU 8	14
FOR CONTEXT, SEE	170	& SON ACTU 19	7
FOR CONTEXT, SEE	201	XLI PORTRAIT 9	16

		PAGE	TITLE	LINE

+LIKE (CONTINUED)

FOR CONTEXT, SEE . . . . 226 IS 5 ONE MAME 5
FOR CONTEXT, SEE . . . . 330 VIVA 21 5
FOR CONTEXT, SEE . . . . 344 VIVA 35 13
FOR CONTEXT, SEE . . . . 349 VIVA 40 17
FOR CONTEXT, SEE . . . . 356 VIVA 47 4
FOR CONTEXT, SEE . . . . 371 VIVA 62 4
FOR CONTEXT, SEE . . . . 384 NO THANKS 2 11
FOR CONTEXT, SEE . . . . 384 NO THANKS 2 12
FOR CONTEXT, SEE . . . . 397 NO THANKS 14 18
FOR CONTEXT, SEE . . . . 482 NEW POEMS 20 3
FOR CONTEXT, SEE . . . . 631 {CHAIRE} 33 5
FOR CONTEXT, SEE . . . . 681 95 POEMS 9 1
FOR CONTEXT, SEE . . . . 829 73 POEMS 57 1

LIKED
the way men you liked made you feel when . . . . 127 & SEVEN POEMS 5 37
then. My crazy fingers liked your dress ....your kiss, . . . 173 & SON ACTU 22 8
that my life (which liked the sun and the . . . . 360 VIVA 51 23
his scientific attitude and liked the prince of wales . . . . 499 50 POEMS 13 2
scientif ic attitude and liked the king of) hear . . . . . . 499 50 POEMS 13 13
this grand: gal who liked men horses roses & . . . . 792 73 POEMS 20 5

LIKEGREE
s bun chesofnew grapes likeGree n A r e . . . . 100 & POST IMPR 11 24

LIKELY
thrice we glimpsed-- more likely twice that (once crammed . . 607 {CHAIRE} 9 2

LIKES
young death, is slender; likes flowers. / / / . . . . 102 & POST IMPR 12 26
as for i i likes a certain party gimme . . . . 247 IS 5 ONE 18 4
Papernapkin no laundry bills likes People preferring Negroes 410 NO THANKS 27 6
that anguish room; but likes it only this eternal . . . . . . 414 NO THANKS 31 10
him whose each foot likes the here of this . . . . 512 50 POEMS 26 7
the dead ones mike likes all the girls (the . . . . 619 {CHAIRE} 21 22
be seen with the likes of your son" "and . . . . 707 95 POEMS 35 12
or heroes (for god likes girls and tomorrow and . . . . . . 732 95 POEMS 60 15

LIL
between the legs of Lil / / / / . . . . 114 & PORTRAIT 7 29
wus de woids uf lil Oinis / / / . . . . 409 NO THANKS 26 4

LILAC
exquisitely hashed (little careful hunks-of-lilac laughter . 133 & SON REAL 4 4
Hereupon helpless i utter lilac shrieks and scarlet . . . . . 199 XLI PORTRAIT 7 11

LILAC'S
skies and trees the lilac's smoke the poppy's pompous . . . . 5 T&C EPITHALAM 92

LILACS
tac-tic. tac-toc. Time and lilacs.... minutes and love.... do 133 & SON REAL 4 8
how in time of lilacs who proclaim the aim . . . . 688 95 POEMS 16 4

LILIED
sweetest to man, whose lilied robe the sun's white . . . . . 3 T&C EPITHALAM 29

LILIES
body amorous (whiter than lilies which are born and . . . . 5 T&C EPITHALAM 100
moreover are (which as lilies smile and quail) of . . . . . . 20 T&C PUELLA MEA 161
almost tire the sleepshaped lilies-- should my lady's body . 85 T&C SON ACTU 4 12
hurting sexual smell of lilies.... beyond night's silken . . 214 XLI SONNETS 10 12
a fragile heaven of lilies-of-the-valley but it will be . . . 352 VIVA 43 3

+LILIES-OF-THE-VALLE
a fragile heaven of lilies-of-the-valley but it will be . . . 352 VIVA 43 3

LILT
omeg o CRINGE WITHS lilt (-ing- lyful of) . . . . 421 NO THANKS 38 16

LILY
and as an opening lily drowsy-fair (when from her . . . . . . 8 T&C OF NICOL 12
as morning may a lily know, her petaled flesh . . . . 21 T&C PUELLA MEA 184
and became a great lily atilt on insolent waters . . . . . . 30 T&C ORIENTALE 4 6
in her hair. The lily of heaven full of . . . . 65 T&C POST IMPR 2 4
white spring offers her lily inextinguishable, taught by thy 206 XLI SONNETS 2 2
lucy could learn and lily could pray and fewer . . . . 509 50 POEMS 23 22
/ / / / lily has a rose (i . . . . 684 95 POEMS 12 1
make a fellow tall" lily has a rose no . . . . 684 95 POEMS 12 17
we so must most lily brief (rose here&gone) flesh . . . . . . 690 95 POEMS 18 5

+LILY
    FOR CONTEXT, SEE . . . . 73 T&C SON REAL 4   13
LIMB
    The Artificial Arm and Limb) --or, since bloodshed and . . . 266 IS 5 TWO 1   28
    into flame twig or limb explodes and o each . . . . 583 1 X 1 43   11
    god) while leaf twig limb ask every question time . . . . . . 818 73 POEMS 46   9
LIMBER
    doer a wooer some limber and lithe some very . . . . 509 50 POEMS 23   10
LIMBS
    delicious mystery, with gaunt limbs reeking of the whispered   7 T&C EPITHALAM 158
    of grace haunted the limbs as music haunts the . . . . 8 T&C OF NICOL   21
    take not thy tingling limbs from me: make my . . . . 139 & SON REAL 10   2
    Expectant stutter (upon artificial limbs, with faces like . . 280 IS 5 THREE 4   33
LIME
    stick to beer and lime, wear dark, and where . . . . 71 T&C SON REAL 2   4
LIMITLESS
    love (who's imagined, therefore limitless) love's to giving . 574 1 X 1 34   2
LIMOUSINE
    this lady in her limousine oozes in fashionable traffic, . . 146 & SON REAL 17   9
    queen alighting from their limousine inhabit the Hotel . . . 245 IS 5 ONE 16   3
LIMP
    of papyruscoloured faces superbly limp the ostensible . . . . 111 & PORTRAIT 6   54
    heureux my soul a limp lump of lymph she . . . . 133 & SON REAL 4   19
    other, wet, warm lips limp, across my bruising smile; . . . . 137 & SON REAL 8   8
    hips). Seeing how the limp huddling string of your . . . . . 161 & SON ACTU 10   5
    stride and breathing to limp and prove --but if . . . . 580 1 X 1 40   10
LIMPS
    ragged beside the who limps man crying silence upward . . . . 437 NO THANKS 53   10
    ektyouelly metus. Unbeside which limps who might less . . . . 790 73 POEMS 18   15
LINCOLN
    / / somebody knew Lincoln somebody Xerxes this man: . . . . . 62 aughter   1
LIONS
    1 law for the lions & oxen is science) . . . . 791 73 POEMS 19   7
LIONTAMER
    a rod smiles the liontamer nearby hieroglyphs soar dip . . . 384 NO THANKS 2   24
LIP
    / voices to voices, lip to lip i swear . . . . 264 IS 5 ONE 33   1
    to voices, lip to lip i swear (to noone . . . . 264 IS 5 ONE 33   1
    bluedmufFletomben outerly jeT ting lip ssixs ting sWervesca . 342 VIVA 33   12
LIPPING
    After a thousand years lipping flowers And set my . . . . . . 189 XLI SONGS 11   15
LIPS
    wind with guiding smile, lips wisely minced for blown . . . .   9 T&C SONGS 1   12
    bringing? To be thy lips is a sweet thing . . . . 13 T&C SONGS 3   15
    to nine ladies his lips drink water but his . . . . 15 T&C SONGS 5   7
    dance upon Between my lips which did sing a . . . . 16 T&C SONGS 6   5
    such a throat the lips of Tristram slowly dote, ... 17 T&C PUELLA MEA 36
    which in ee instant,   IS 5 . . 20   147
LINK
    play: withs of star link clauses of warmth (after . . . . . . 168 & SON ACTU 17   15
LINOTYPES
    a defunct king as linotypes gobblehobble our lightheavy twic 259 IS 5 ONE 29   12
LINTEL
    she pauses on the lintel of defeat, her heart . . . . 75 T&C SON REAL 6 12
LIONS
    dead who rushed like lions to the roaring slaughter . . . . . 268 IS 5 TWO 3   11
    1 law for the lions & oxen is science) . . . . 791 73 POEMS 19   7
LIONTAMER
    a rod smiles the liontamer nearby hieroglyphs soar dip . . . 384 NO THANKS 2   24
LIP
    / voices to voices, lip to lip i swear . . . . 264 IS 5 ONE 33   1
    to voices, lip to lip i swear (to noone . . . . 264 IS 5 ONE 33   1
    bluedmufFletomben outerly jeT ting lip ssixs ting sWervesca . 342 VIVA 33   12
LIPPING
    After a thousand years lipping flowers And set my . . . . . . 189 XLI SONGS 11   15
LIPS
    wind with guiding smile, lips wisely minced for blown . . . .   9 T&C SONGS 1   12
    bringing? To be thy lips is a sweet thing . . . . 13 T&C SONGS 3   15

	PAGE	TITLE	LINE
LIPS (CONTINUED)			
to nine ladies his lips drink water but his	15	T&C SONGS 5	7
dance upon Between my lips which did sing a	16	T&C SONGS 6	5
such a throat the lips of Tristram slowly dote, ...	17	T&C PUELLA MEA	36
which in eyes and lips consists --always upon the	20	T&C PUELLA MEA	147
lovely--Time! upon whose watering lips the world poises a . .	23	T&C PUELLA MEA	267
eatage of forgetfulness thy lips are satraps in scarlet . . .	29	T&C ORIENTALE 3	24
dim smoke straining my lips are vague with ecstasy	31	T&C ORIENTALE 5	23
upon the red elected lips scaleless visions) / /	36	T&C AMORES 1	31
your soul upon my lips / / / /	38	T&C AMORES 3	19
the hunger of my lips for a dead thing, ...	42	T&C AMORES 6	10
gesticulate the accurate strenuous lips of incorruptible . .	43	T&C AMORES 7	37
flower dreams of parted lips dim upon the syrinx	54	T&C PORTRAIT 2	11
man with majestic bulbous lips and forlorn piggish hands . .	56	T&C PORTRAIT 4	11
was by the kindly lips and body fatherly of	57	T&C PORTRAIT 5	31
rose is dying the lips of an old man	59	T&C PORTRAIT 7	3
stallion sweetness , the lips of an old man	59	T&C PORTRAIT 7	16
and curled with mystic lips take twilight where i	71	T&C SON REAL 2	13
ripe quite too large lips always clenched faintly, wishes . .	72	T&C SON REAL 3	7
i see the large lips vivid, the face grey, ...	75	T&C SON REAL 6	7
say that if your lips, which i have loved, ...	76	T&C SON UNRE 1	2
the young mouth whose lips begin a smile exactly	85	T&C SON ACTU 4	8
one o'clock to little lips (which have not sinned	115	& PORTRAIT 8	6
Nous) with the long lips of Lucienne which dangle	120	& PORTRAIT 12	20
pivoine?) with the long lips of Lucienne which dangle	121	& PORTRAIT 12	58
crease of hot subliminal lips, as if a score	130	& SON REAL 1	4
in darkness, water the lips of death / /	136	& SON REAL 7	17
distinct sex whose sharp lips comb my mumbling	137	& SON REAL 8	1
her other, wet, warm lips limp, across my bruising	137	& SON REAL 8	8
feeds especially his immense lips On whose deep nakedness . .	138	& SON REAL 9	9
of madness on gritted lips and on sprawled eyes	139	& SON REAL 10	9
(breathless with sharp necessary lips) kid female cracksman . .	140	& SON REAL 11	9
a careful fierceness. Her lips study my head gripping	146	& SON REAL 17	3
the not too frail lips almost discussed; between her	146	& SON REAL 17	12
he put between her lips a moist mistake, whose	148	& SON REAL 19	10
remembering, two pink big lips curl.... how Jimmie was . . .	149	& SON REAL 20	15
wobbles from the thinning lips me hugely which embrace. . . .	151	& SON REAL 22	16
a vise whose stilling lips murder suddenly me, but	152	& SON ACTU 1	11
knead of lustfulhunched deeplytoplay lips and stare the gross	153	& SON ACTU 2	6
a musical fruit. My lips pleasantly groan on your	154	& SON ACTU 3	3
press in the young lips unearthly slenderness / /	156	& SON ACTU 5	15
another man with firmer lips to take your new	161	& SON ACTU 10	2
pester skilfully, teasing its lips, absurd eyes, the hair). .	164	& SON ACTU 13	9
half-angel and your drowsy lips where float flowers of . . .	186	XLI SONGS 8	12
in whose hair, thy lips are cold with songs	190	XLI SONGS 12	4
the a little strolling lips and eyes inwardly crisping . . .	193	XLI PORTRAIT 1	8
acute sentience whose whitehot lips however suddenly ap- . .	193	XLI PORTRAIT 1	11
gorgeous rush of upward lips.... cleverly perching on the . .	201	XLI PORTRAIT 9	28
thin amorous enormous only lips of the evening And	202	XLI PORTRAIT 9	47
whitely she seems whose lips the whole of life	205	XLI SONNETS 1	8
is the garden: pursed lips do blow upon cool	208	XLI SONNETS 4	5
doom, when these thy lips beautifully embrace nothing and . .	210	XLI SONNETS 6	12
leaves' voices, and sharp lips of spring simply joining . . .	218	XLI SONNETS 14	5
i want the perpendicular lips the insane teeth the	220	XLI SONNETS 16	7
--jazz, for whose twitching lips, between you and me	227	IS 5 ONE GERT	6
Larsen twirls among pale lips the extinct cigar) at	252	IS 5 ONE 23	6
s, large four gnarled lips totter Therefore, approaching my .	255	IS 5 ONE 26	4
the stone, how obsolete lips utter their extant smile...... .	260	IS 5 ONE 30	6
you and i have lips and voices which are	264	IS 5 ONE 33	25
upon his firm white lips a smile, one thought	273	IS 5 TWO 8	10
mouth with fat jibing lips, once upon a (that	277	IS 5 THREE 1	16
between them) knowing my lips hands the way i	285	IS 5 FOUR 2	6
table and we hold lips Eyes everything hands you	287	IS 5 FOUR 4	18
own reason) in your lips slenderly should create one	291	IS 5 FOUR 8	22
(and if your slim lips are amused, no wisest	294	IS 5 FOUR 11	10
a cigarette between his ghost-lips gradually) remembering . .	300	IS 5 FOUR 17	20
whose profound and fragile lips the sweet small clumsy . . .	306	IS 5 FIVE 5	13
a kiss departs our lips are made of thing	322	VIVA 14	12

LIPS (CONTINUED)

	PAGE	TITLE	LINE
dike of whose lean lips, hovers how slenderly the	344	VIVA 35	10
baboon (where once good lips stalked or eyes firmly	360	VIVA 51	2
dog, a kiss without lips; a prayer lacking any	360	VIVA 51	27
of ears with some lips plus a couple of)	501	50 POEMS 15	20
lovers are these whose lips smash unimagined sky deeper . . .	563	1 X 1 23	10
phantoms curl (mouth seekingly lips wander a finding whom . .	565	1 X 1 25	3
eyes go blind (where lips forget to kiss) where	834	73 POEMS 62	28

LIPS'

enchanted tree; with her lips' most frail parting my	22	T&C PUELLA MEA	233

LIPSHITS

then up rose mr lipshits pres (who always nothing	552	1 X 1 12	26

LIPSTICK

hero's carnivorous (smile by lipstick smell by matchabelli) .	546	1 X 1 6	9

LISBOA

windows of thousands of houses--Lisboa. Like the crackle of .	281	IS 5 THREE 5	6

LIS

/ ADHUC SUB JUDICE LIS when mack smacked phyllis	706	95 POEMS 34	T

+LISPED

FOR CONTEXT, SEE	316	VIVA 8	7

LISPING

was these twin imminent lisping bags of flesh; became	115	& PORTRAIT 8	22
with wise breasts half-grown, lisping flesh quick to thread .	140	& SON REAL 11	12

+LISPINGLY

FOR CONTEXT, SEE	431	NO THANKS 48	7

LISPS

a liberal titty and lisps "i'm busy right now"	711	95 POEMS 39	24

LIST

hairlesschested females, well attend! list, every nonelastic	398	NO THANKS 15	17

LISTEN

and thou didst not listen thine eyes are as	27	T&C ORIENTALE 1	10
/ / / / listen beloved i dreamed it	30	T&C ORIENTALE 4	1
you upon my mouth listen beloved i dreamed in	30	T&C ORIENTALE 4	15
you upon my blood listen beloved i dreamed i	30	T&C ORIENTALE 4	29
SNO a white idea (Listen drenches: earth's ugly) mind. . . .	99	& POST IMPR 10	2
by their triumphs and listen well how the dainty	111	& PORTRAIT 6	40
/ / MARJ "life? Listen" the feline she with	228	IS 5 ONE MARJ	2
/ / / / listen my children and you	236	IS 5 ONE 7	1
MEMORABILIA stop look & listen Venezia: incline thine ear . .	256	IS 5 ONE 27	2
peer through windows, unobserved --listen, for (out of all .	292	IS 5 FOUR 9	9
mr can you maybe listen there's me & some	314	VIVA 6	1
(can you give a) listen to who may you	314	VIVA 6	23
what it comes to (listen you don't have to	400	NO THANKS 17	6
mean Reely) but (no listen don't be sil why	400	NO THANKS 17	7
know sure that's) but listen here's (correct you said	400	NO THANKS 17	11
said it yeah) but listen but (it's Rilly yeh	400	NO THANKS 17	13
/ / emptied. hills. listen. ,not, alive, trees, dream(. . .	416	NO THANKS 33	1
know a hopeless case if--listen: there's a hell of	554	1 X 1 14	14
/ / / / (listen) this a dog barks	835	73 POEMS 63	1

+LISTEN

FOR CONTEXT, SEE	272	IS 5 TWO 7	1
FOR CONTEXT, SEE	547	1 X 1 7	10
FOR CONTEXT, SEE	547	1 X 1 7	10

LISTENING

of the fifty pillars listening while the queens of	35	T&C ORIENTALE 6	114
eyes of these with listening hands only fishermen are	478	NEW POEMS 16	10

LISTENS

how, luminously oh how listens and, expands my	251	IS 5 ONE 22	16
a lit tle tree listens forever to always children	525	50 POEMS 37	20

LITANIES

hair flutter the level litanies unto thee i burn	31	T&C ORIENTALE 5	20
spires silver chants the litanies the great bells are	51	T&C IMPRESS 5	5

LITERALLY

distinctly confine their omnipotent literally their putting .	391	NO THANKS 8	21

LITERATURE

magazine to hell with literature we want something redblooded	407	NO THANKS 24	2
a weakness for living literature "loyaltea" / / /	546	1 X 1 6	15

		PAGE	TITLE	LINE
LITHE				
	slippered sleep the lean lithe deer the fleet flown	14	T&C SONGS 4	17
	my spirit with the lithe free twitch of scintillant	18	T&C PUELLA MEA	83
	them glad ladies with lithe eyes and long (when	22	T&C PUELLA MEA	225
	there and here the lithe indolent prostitute Night, argues .	93	& POST IMPR 5	16
	flesh; became eyes moist lithe shuddering big, the luminous .	115	& PORTRAIT 8	23
	wooer some limber and lithe some very fine mower	509	50 POEMS 23	10
LITHPED				
	(i'm tho thcared giggling lithped now we muthn't pleathe . .	316	VIVA 8	7
LITTER				
	mil (lions of aflickf) litter ing brightmillion ofS hurl; . .	265	IS 5 ONE 34	3
LITTLE				
	will lay between their little breasts My strong fingers . . .	16	T&C SONGS 6	8
	ladies. Mine is a little lovelier than any of	17	T&C PUELLA MEA	3
	the day, is a little stranger thing than crisp	17	T&C PUELLA MEA	7
	ago. If she a little turn her head i	17	T&C PUELLA MEA	33
	of faerie, perhaps a little suddenly (as sometimes the . . .	18	T&C PUELLA MEA	42
	were mine is a little lovelier. And if she	18	T&C PUELLA MEA	76
	Bagdad-- mine is a little lovelier than any of	20	T&C PUELLA MEA	133
	is, which being a little while caressed its fragrance	21	T&C PUELLA MEA	191
	you would espy the little distinct foot (if whose	22	T&C PUELLA MEA	217
	is mud- luscious the little lame balloonman whistles far . .	24	T&C CHANSONS 1	3
	/ / hist whist little ghostthings tip-toe twinkle-toe little	25	T&C CHANSONS 2	2
	little ghostthings tip-toe twinkle-toe little twitchy witches	25	T&C CHANSONS 2	5
	tingling goblins hob-a-nob hob-a-nob little hoppy happy toad	25	T&C CHANSONS 2	9
	toad in tweeds tweeds little itchy mousies with scuttling . .	25	T&C CHANSONS 2	12
	wonderful with eyes a little sorry Another comes also	26	T&C CHANSONS 3	7
	me and became a little bird and hid in	30	T&C ORIENTALE 4	19
	is picked by the little peasants for their girls	30	T&C ORIENTALE 4	42
	and beckons with the little finger of his left	33	T&C ORIENTALE 6	57
	/ / / your little voice Over the wires	44	T&C AMORES 8	1
	be leaves and a little harder for roses only	67	T&C POST IMPR 4	20
	for roses only a little harder last we on	67	T&C POST IMPR 4	22
	tobacco and gladness plus little derricks of gesture any . .	68	T&C POST IMPR 5	4
	gnomes tumble clumsily, the little box is spilling rancid . .	69	T&C POST IMPR 6	3
	music and jerk the little string and the monkey	69	T&C POST IMPR 6	13
	holding, it, in his little toylike hand) and then	69	T&C POST IMPR 6	18
	the jerk of the little string! the tiny smiling	69	T&C POST IMPR 6	32
	queer monkey with a little oldish doll-like face and	69	T&C POST IMPR 6	37
	(and he has a little red coat with i	69	T&C POST IMPR 6	41
	ladies and gentlemen this little girl with the good	72	T&C SON REAL 3	1
	memory indignantly protests) this little dancer with the . .	72	T&C SON REAL 3	5
	smile again, lingering a little while i see thee	75	T&C SON REAL 6	5
	is Lust.... mine also, little painted poem of god	75	T&C SON REAL 6	14
	heart, send me a little word; that i may	76	T&C SON UNRE 1	10
	as was mine a little while; moments when my	78	T&C SON UNRE 3	8
	undertakes --your kiss, the little pushings of flesh, makes .	82	T&C SON ACTU 1	3
	enthusiastic space is a little wonderful, and say Perhaps . .	82	T&C SON ACTU 1	13
	/ / / by little accurate saints thickly which	85	T&C SON ACTU 4	1
	by this throat a little suddenly lifted in singing--hands . .	85	T&C SON ACTU 4	10
	(squashe) d with, its, little, solemn, entrails / /	94	& POST IMPR 6	29
	black trees think (hear little knives of flower stropping . .	99	& POST IMPR 10	12
	eager colours of the little, huddling nuts and the	100	& POST IMPR 11	21
	ears bend to the little silent handorgan prop- ping	101	& POST IMPR 11	45
	carry-tadpole! s,, stomachs of little, girls smoothanduseless	101	& POST IMPR 11	75
	s exactly sit, ata little roundtable among otherlittle . . .	104	& POST IMPR 14	2
	her flesh: wakes in little streets while exactlygir lisHlegs;	104	& POST IMPR 14	10
	her sitsat a surely! little, roundtable amongother;	104	& POST IMPR 14	20
	unburied feet of the little ladies more than dead	108	& PORTRAIT 4	37
	let us be a little uncouth and amorous in	111	& PORTRAIT 6	57
	perfumes coming with the little profound gems and the	112	& PORTRAIT 6	103
	at one o'clock to little lips (which have not	115	& PORTRAIT 8	6
	/ / here is little Effie's head whose brains	117	& PORTRAIT 10	1
	and this is my little sister could with our	117	& PORTRAIT 10	18
	me stooping by Effie's little, in (want a match	117	& PORTRAIT 10	28
	this way. here is little Effie's head whose brains	118	& PORTRAIT 10	43
	/ / / / little ladies more than dead	120	& PORTRAIT 12	1
	rue Henri Mounier a little love begs, Mimi with	121	& PORTRAIT 12	47

LITTLE (CONTINUED)

	PAGE	TITLE	LINE
stomach goes into your Little Stomach My legs are	123	& SEVEN POEMS 2	9
I didn't said the little lady who sews and	125	& SEVEN POEMS 4	4
the moon kissed the little lady on her paler-paler	125	& SEVEN POEMS 4	18
firmer since darker than little round water at one	126	& SEVEN POEMS 5	2
alarm off and the little striker having the best	126	& SEVEN POEMS 5	11
her, rain-warm-naked exquisitely hashed (little careful . . .	133	& SON REAL 4	4
begins to. lean.... a little against me, when for	148	& SON REAL 19	13
nice hands. with a little eye that rolled and	149	& SON REAL 20	6
me it's just a little like music, a little	152	& SON ACTU 1	2
little like music, a little more like curving colour	152	& SON ACTU 1	3
every spring handfuls of little normal worms. Dress deftly .	161	& SON ACTU 10	8
it'll turn into a little curse of wax. Something, ...	164	& SON ACTU 13	16
--this is twilight, a little puppy hopping between skipping .	167	& SON ACTU 16	8
nerves sumptuously wink ....and little-dusk has his toys to .	169	& SON ACTU 18	9
succinct wandlike animal, a little strolling with the futile	170	& SON ACTU 19	8
amused legs kissing with little dints of april, making . . .	172	& SON ACTU 21	13
it was raining a little, and the spring; a	173	& SON ACTU 22	1
stumbled above the square, little amorous-tadpole people . .	173	& SON ACTU 22	4
speech--it made you a little dizzy did the world's	174	& SON ACTU 23	11
is your face your little cheeks the streets of	186	XLI SONGS 8	7
why did you go little fourpaws? you forgot to	191	XLI CHANSONS 1	2
did you go? like little kittens are all the	191	XLI CHANSONS 1	6
open in the rain. little kittens who are called	191	XLI CHANSONS 1	9
/ / / / little tree little silent Christmas	192	XLI CHANSONS 2	1
/ / little tree little silent Christmas tree you	192	XLI CHANSONS 2	2
tree you are so little you are more like	192	XLI CHANSONS 2	3
threads, put up your little arms and i'll give	192	XLI CHANSONS 2	17
very proud and my little sister and i will	192	XLI CHANSONS 2	25
delicious image the a little strolling lips and eyes	193	XLI PORTRAIT 1	7
am becoming something a little different, in fact myself . .	199	XLI PORTRAIT 7	9
i am come by little countries to the yes	216	XLI SONNETS 12	7
gaze on the cindercoloured little (MEGA) (HELLENIKON	217	XLI SONNETS 13	14
Square in spring, the little barbarous Greenwich perfumed . .	220	XLI SONNETS 16	10
her lownecked dress a little topples and slightly expands . .	225	IS 5 ONE LIZ	2
pretty dribbling child, a little child. In thy your	233	IS 5 ONE 4	4
matters hence in a little sunlight and less moonlight	238	IS 5 ONE 9	19
you know consequently a little stiff i was careful	248	IS 5 ONE 19	4
up and all the little schoolchildren sat down /	249	IS 5 ONE 20	4
cling, being for a little while and which easily	264	IS 5 ONE 33	15
maladies including flu) my little darlings, let us now . . .	266	IS 5 TWO 1	16
beach below me a little girl in white spins, ...	281	IS 5 THREE 5	3
somewhere nowhere and a little girl in white is	281	IS 5 THREE 5	13
up- raising, hoisting, a little perhaps that and this, . . .	282	IS 5 THREE 6	5
in first darkness --a little moon thinner than memory	282	IS 5 THREE 6	17
Once again....) sliding a little downward, embrace me with .	282	IS 5 THREE 6	34
world becoming bright and little melted. / / /	283	IS 5 THREE 7	27
my heart life the little hands withdrew, jerkily, themselves	284	IS 5 FOUR 1	8
/ / here's a little mouse) and what does	286	IS 5 FOUR 3	1
i, since here's a little he or is it	286	IS 5 FOUR 3	17
nothing lingers beyond a little instant, along with rhyme . .	293	IS 5 FOUR 10	10
a few thoughts a little love preferably, anything which . . .	298	IS 5 FOUR 15	15
us go a very little beyond the last road--there's	303	IS 5 FIVE 2	2
i'm ever so very little afraid") i say "along	303	IS 5 FIVE 2	7
knows) only turn a little your. so. And there's	303	IS 5 FIVE 2	15
on any man-- a little fluttering, at the enchanted	344	VIVA 35	9
toward twilight the a little tilted streets spill lazily . .	345	VIVA 36	5
mouse) but he has little wings and here's my	353	VIVA 44	10
first" of dreams and little bats & mice (and	353	VIVA 44	26
up on them a little more openly than usual	354	VIVA 45	13
/ / come a little further--why be afraid-- here's	357	VIVA 48	1
instant) kiss me a little: the air darkens and	357	VIVA 48	7
never) and by that little trick or this he	360	VIVA 51	16
me into the extremely little house of my mind.	365	VIVA 56	2
You will communicate a little more than twice all	370	VIVA 61	11
kind of unkindness exit little mr Big notbusy Busi	389	NO THANKS 6	2
understand G gladly forget little having less with every . .	390	NO THANKS 7	6
legally into Oblivion wave little flags weeping flatter . . .	391	NO THANKS 8	7

	PAGE	TITLE	LINE

LITTLE (CONTINUED)

	PAGE	TITLE		LINE
/ / / / little man (in a hurry	393	NO THANKS	10	1
stop forget relax wait (little child who have tried	393	NO THANKS	10	7
/ / / this little pair had a little	401	NO THANKS	18	1
little pair had a little scare right in the	401	NO THANKS	18	2
/ / what does little Ernest croon in his	409	NO THANKS	26	1
/ / / / little joe gould has lost	410	NO THANKS	27	1
secondhand set which click) little gould used to amputate . .	410	NO THANKS	27	2
just (nude eel) now little joe lives on air	410	NO THANKS	27	4
n.b. ye twang of little joe (yankee) gould irketh	410	NO THANKS	27	7
as a smile but little joe gould's quote oral	410	NO THANKS	27	9
be fun to be little joe gould) / /	410	NO THANKS	27	14
be twirled around your little finger is) what's right	411	NO THANKS	28	7
than all life's busy little dyings may possess) how	418	NO THANKS	35	4
anything would give a little more than it away	420	NO THANKS	37	2
heart pursues against the little moon a here and	434	NO THANKS	51	17
be of love (a little) More careful Than of	453	NO THANKS	68	1
/ / / this little bride & groom are	470	NEW POEMS	8	1
crown with this candy little bride & little groom	470	NEW POEMS	8	9
candy little bride & little groom in it kind	470	NEW POEMS	8	9
/ / / so little he is so. Little	471	NEW POEMS	9	1
little he is so. Little ness be (ing) comes	471	NEW POEMS	9	3
always be open to little birds who are the	481	NEW POEMS	19	1
and) ask a brittle little person fiddling in the	498	50 POEMS	12	12
wonderful all sky (a little mouth) stumbling (can't keep . .	501	50 POEMS	15	9
ever earns anything, everything little looks big in a	514	50 POEMS	28	8
Women and men (both little and small) cared for	515	50 POEMS	29	5
them side by side little by little and was	515	50 POEMS	29	28
by side little by little and was by was	515	50 POEMS	29	28
/ / the silently little blue elephant shyly (he	516	50 POEMS	30	1
so only through) the little blue elephant at the	516	50 POEMS	30	7
a now and now little the (on his quiet	516	50 POEMS	30	10
silence of stone these little children wound with stone . . .	525	50 POEMS	37	3
is love makes the little thickness of the coin	531	50 POEMS	43	8
on a greener (o little i) riding on a	535	50 POEMS	47	7
sing small thing dance little joy (shine most prayer)	535	50 POEMS	47	11
blood, asked "something a little child who's just as	555	1 X 1	15	12
all her most first little flowers rise out of	559	1 X 1	19	13
bluer than believing) a little gay earth opening is	583	1 X 1	43	4
love" (all the merry little birds are flying in	591	1 X 1	51	5
by has anybody seen little you-i who stood on	593	1 X 1	53	3
of a string (murmurs little you-i as the hill	593	1 X 1	53	21
/ o the round little man we loved so	606	{CHAIRE}	8	3
the green opens a little a little was much	614	{CHAIRE}	16	4
opens a little a little was much and much	614	{CHAIRE}	16	5
in his hand a little star no bigger than	622	{CHAIRE}	24	3
when we meet again, little he (having flown even	631	{CHAIRE}	33	7
might not speak, a little innocence will make them	649	{CHAIRE}	51	2
never to beautiful: a little innocence creates a day.	649	{CHAIRE}	51	8
or wished without a little innocence, although it were . .	649	{CHAIRE}	51	10
not so as a little innocence / / /	649	{CHAIRE}	51	14
pleasanter (some big dark little day which seems a	650	{CHAIRE}	52	6
/ / / the little horse is newlY Born)	657	{CHAIRE}	59	1
can fly yes the little fish gambol as glad	665	{CHAIRE}	67	6
so he now the little fish quiver so you	665	{CHAIRE}	67	13
the sky all the little fish climb through the	665	{CHAIRE}	67	20
icecoalwood truck a wistful little clown whom somebody buried	680	95 POEMS	8	6
us if in one little bed she and he	694	95 POEMS	22	7
who but that sly little bitch could have showed	707	95 POEMS	35	14
home to the dearest little women alive (but jim	709	95 POEMS	37	14
& day "all poor little peoples that want to	711	95 POEMS	39	7
The UN "be quiet little hungary and do as	711	95 POEMS	39	17
bigger much than biggest (little is) now (dancing yes	715	95 POEMS	43	14
/ / / this little huge -eyed per- son	739	95 POEMS	67	1
her, outglory glory the little while they live-- unless . . .	742	95 POEMS	70	10
me and you and little house this our from	746	95 POEMS	74	3
of sheerest glory a little more always less believably . .	748	95 POEMS	76	8
holds Himself as the little white rose of a	748	95 POEMS	76	17

	PAGE	TITLE	LINE

LITTLE (CONTINUED)

/ i am a little church (no great cathedral) . . . . 749 95 POEMS 77   1
mountains i am a little church (far from the . . . . 749 95 POEMS 77   13
whom i give this little parasol, so she may . . . . 762 95 POEMS 89   7
worlds and young (big little and all worlds) merely . . . . 776 73 POEMS 4   6
worlds or keen; big little and all) but lose . . . . 776 73 POEMS 4   12
but pitiful they've (big little and all) no power . . . . . 776 73 POEMS 4   22
worlds or bright; big little and all) whereas (my . . . . . 776 73 POEMS 4   28
sorry or both (big little and all) / / . . . . 776 73 POEMS 4   40
utmost nothing, wanders a little guess (only which is . . . . 810 73 POEMS 38   2
/ who are you, little i (five or six . . . . 824 73 POEMS 52   1
/ / / 2 little whos (he and she) . . . . 832 73 POEMS 60   1
who and who (2 little ams and over them . . . . 832 73 POEMS 60   13

+LITTLE

FOR CONTEXT, SEE . . . . 94 & POST IMPR 6   21
FOR CONTEXT, SEE . . . . 101 & POST IMPR 11   53
FOR CONTEXT, SEE . . . . 104 & POST IMPR 14   3
FOR CONTEXT, SEE . . . . 122 & SEVEN POEMS 1 21
FOR CONTEXT, SEE . . . . 314 VIVA 6   10
FOR CONTEXT, SEE . . . . 409 NO THANKS 26   4
FOR CONTEXT, SEE . . . . 525 50 POEMS 37   5
FOR CONTEXT, SEE . . . . 525 50 POEMS 37   19
FOR CONTEXT, SEE . . . . 547 1 X 1 7   14
FOR CONTEXT, SEE . . . . 724 95 POEMS 52   4

LITTLE-DUSK

nerves sumptuously wink ....and little-dusk has his toys to . 169 & SON ACTU 18   9

LITTLECROWNGRAVE

she patiently 1) littlecrownGrave whose whorlclown of . . . 342 VIVA 33   19

LITTLEEXACTLY

surely! little, roundtable amongother; littleexactly round. . 104 & POST IMPR 14 21

LITTLELIVERPILL

gentlemen (and ladies) --pretty littleliverpill- ◇ americans 231 IS 5 ONE 3   46

LITTLENESS

i turn to the cruel-littleness of cold (when battling . . . . 142 & SON REAL 13   2
the bigness of his littleness --electrons deify one . . . . . 554 1 X 1 14   4

+LITTLENESS

FOR CONTEXT, SEE . . . . 471 NEW POEMS 9   3

LITTLER

the sagest pane of littler huts with peerless fantasies . . . 207 XLI SONNETS 3   4
the least begin less littler than forgive it is . . . . 530 50 POEMS 42   12
& th (is no littler th an a: fear . . . . 532 50 POEMS 44   11
beyond) or does some littler bird than eyes can . . . . 592 1 X 1 52   9
girl and boy who're littler than (day disappears) their . . . 757 95 POEMS 85   3
(go marvels come) as littler much than littlest they . . . . 757 95 POEMS 85   18

LITTLEST

slippery body is Death's littlest pal, skilled in quick . . . 74 T&C SON REAL 5 3
Silence) this like a littlest poem a (with wee . . . . 286 IS 5 FOUR 3   10
so isn't small one littlest why, it into if . . . . 588 1 X 1 48   1
/ / / on littlest this the of twig . . . . 687 95 POEMS 15   1
as littler much than littlest they adventure (wish by . . . . 757 95 POEMS 85   19

LITTLETIN

drop, coppers into, the littletin-cup His wrappedupbody . . . 100 & POST IMPR 11 40

LITTLETIN-CUP

drop, coppers into, the littletin-cup His wrappedupbody . . . 100 & POST IMPR 11 40

LIVE

superlative body do distinctly live all sweet cities passed . 22 T&C PUELLA MEA 256
the Cambridge ladies who live in furnished souls are . . . . 70 T&C SON REAL 1   1
Black People, cherie, who live under stones.) Don't be . . . 86 T&C SON ACTU 5 10
in windows but they live higher in their house . . . . 126 & SEVEN POEMS 5 25
/ / / let's live suddenly without thinking under . . . . . . 160 & SON ACTU 9   1
begins to prune let's live like the light that . . . . 160 & SON ACTU 9   10
you and do not live: and the empty twilight . . . . 165 & SON ACTU 14   7
roses their fingers whitely live by? or better, queens, . . . 211 XLI SONNETS 7 12
Hotel Meurice (whereas i live in a garret and . . . . 245 IS 5 ONE 16   5
always and first to live makes unimportant what i . . . . . . 264 IS 5 ONE 33   18
just enough dreams to live on) after all, kid . . . . 298 IS 5 FOUR 15   11
door nobody seems to live at present (l'on parle . . . . . . 312 VIVA 4   22
to mention inTerred) LONG LIVE that Upwardlooking Serene . . 315 VIVA 7   11

	PAGE	TITLE	LINE
LIVE (CONTINUED)			
they are dine to live / / / /	334	VIVA 25	7
and is alive-- o live with me in the	357	VIVA 48	10
subchemistry of alWays)fiercely live whom on Large Darkness	361	VIVA 52	30
servants. We could almost live at the top of	365	VIVA 56	6
as that which we live for dies) / /	386	NO THANKS 3	14
because where might Where live can fisherMen swim and	395	NO THANKS 12	7
deep and he might live) yes, partly nor some	414	NO THANKS 31	8
all stars or to live in the moon a	433	NO THANKS 50	12
unfools unfree undeaths who live nor shall they be	440	NO THANKS 56	34
or free truly which live always shall be may	441	NO THANKS 56	62
this world of yes live (skilfully curled) all worlds	443	NO THANKS 58	8
rive go. faces a (live) sob bel ls (pour	444	NO THANKS 59	6
in gly eyes grip live loop croon mime nakedly	445	NO THANKS 60	24
ul) foundclown a -live a , bird !	471	NEW POEMS 9	17
air theres what immense live without every dancing. singless	491	50 POEMS 5	5
teach a wretch to live straighter than a needle)	498	50 POEMS 12	2
could not begin to live id est breathe but	510	50 POEMS 24	6
breakfastfood or truth can live with right and wrong	511	50 POEMS 25	2
comes or (a) new (live) now ; & th	532	50 POEMS 44	7
o ver and) a- live wanders remembe r ing	534	50 POEMS 46	9
die, the more we live / / / /	560	1 X 1 20	24
happening of their hearts live longer than all which	576	1 X 1 36	2
yes earth was in (live live) spring with all	589	1 X 1 49	9
earth was in (live live) spring with all beautiful	589	1 X 1 49	10
a (vastly and particulary) live that undeluded notselfpitying	607	{CHAIRE} 9	8
whose miraculously disenchanted eyes live the magnificent . .	675	95 POEMS 3	4
seas catch fire (and live by love though the	732	95 POEMS 60	7
may, given perfect mercy, live a dream larger than	735	95 POEMS 63	3
the little while they live-- unless by your thinking	742	95 POEMS 70	10
my most dear (die! live) the new is the	767	95 POEMS 93	9
may in the spring) live! die (forever is now)	767	95 POEMS 93	21
friend) the gift to live is without until: but	776	73 POEMS 4	19
my (where three dreams live) fore head is stumbling	785	73 POEMS 13	21
they how and they live for until though the	801	73 POEMS 29	22
love so much to live) must die" "if i	836	73 POEMS 64	4
LIVE'S			
(existing's tricky: but to live's a gift) the teachable . . .	807	73 POEMS 35	2
LIVED			
tempo of hasteful futility lived brilliantly the enormous . .	103	& POST IMPR 13	11
a kiss but Jimmie lived regular. stewed three times	149	& SON REAL 20	11
and records while he lived presented to him upon	239	IS 5 ONE 10	28
lives he has not lived. / / / /	285	IS 5 FOUR 2	22
dear where our heads lived and were. / /	288	IS 5 FOUR 5	10
(not having most ever lived people always) don't die	412	NO THANKS 29	13
of wishing) though life's lived wrongsideout, sameness chokes	446	NO THANKS 61	3
/ / / anyone lived in a pretty how	515	50 POEMS 29	1
breathe-- because my father lived his soul love is	521	50 POEMS 34	67
may see there never lived a gayer he; if	760	95 POEMS 87	6
until twice i have lived forever in a smile)	765	95 POEMS 91	14
LIVELY			
perfectly putting it mildly lively (but Death is strictly . .	604	{CHAIRE} 6	16
+LIVER			
FOR CONTEXT, SEE	231	IS 5 ONE 3	46
LIVES			
to Nothing and which lives they were fond of	43	T&C AMORES 7	12
every day of their lives aint you, oo-oo. dearie	109	& PORTRAIT 5	18
sinned in whose displeasure lives a kiss) kneeling, your . .	115	& PORTRAIT 8	7
in your eyes there lives a green egyptian noise.	138	& SON REAL 9	7
SEVERAL MILLION FINKLESTEIN (FRITZ) LIVES AT THE RITZ WEAR .	244	IS 5 ONE 15	3
with what keen innumerable lives he has not lived.	285	IS 5 FOUR 2	22
the hurting skill which lives) and since nothing lingers . .	293	IS 5 FOUR 10	8
Its own and their Lives who grow slowly and	311	VIVA 3	7
this season" think "finality lives up on them a	354	VIVA 45	12
therefore togethering our wholly lives Givehurling with your	371	VIVA 62	16
which we die for lives (may never cease views	386	NO THANKS 3	9
which we die for lives as wholly as that	386	NO THANKS 3	13
the music of spring lives F feel opens but	390	NO THANKS 7	5

440

	PAGE	TITLE	LINE
LIVES (CONTINUED)			
eel) now little joe lives on air Harvard Brevis	410	NO THANKS 27	4
smell of minute mown lives) oh my spirit you	434	NO THANKS 51	25
luminous whose selves and lives imperishably feast all . . .	456	NO THANKS 71	2
pines lifted their green lives and smiled / /	555	1 X 1 15	16
alone (his briefest breathing lives some planet's year, his .	609	(CHAIRE) 11	10
visitor their very oldest lives one pays him with	624	(CHAIRE) 26	8
wrong and when their lives are keen he throws	624	(CHAIRE) 26	17
/ / / light's lives lurch a once world	633	(CHAIRE) 35	1
could anyone who simply lives to die dream that	718	95 POEMS 46	2
VocA -ble flame is lives breath es (over- ing	719	95 POEMS 47	12
it 's A pril Lives lead their own persons	782	73 POEMS 10	10
+LIVES			
FOR CONTEXT, SEE	417	NO THANKS 34	10
LIVIN			
? niggers) Not jes livin not Jes alive But	426	NO THANKS 43	5
LIVING			
the twinge of all living intense things. Never my	19	T&C PUELLA MEA	101
exquisite and dead, all living things and beautiful. (Caliph	19	T&C PUELLA MEA	128
face suddenly the lighted living hills / / /	82	T&C SON ACTU 1	15
the night. I am living with a mouse who	171	& SON ACTU 20	13
of Ego, from whose living and biggest bodies lopped	195	XLI PORTRAIT 3	20
very swift and invisibly living rhythm of your Heart	300	IS 5 FOUR 17	7
ead the not stroll living spawn imitate) ce (re	309	VIVA 1	32
you were earning your living or probably dead" so	313	VIVA 5	7
he is undead who, living, noone is. I have	360	VIVA 51	29
/ but if a living dance upon dead minds	377	VIVA 68	1
the) whis-per it (Living / / / /	391	NO THANKS 8	28
life shall not for living find the rule) and	420	NO THANKS 37	9
the glad deep the living from nowh -ere (!	449	NO THANKS 64	7
/ my specialty is living said a man (who	473	NEW POEMS 11	1
are the secrets of living whatever they sing is	481	NEW POEMS 19	2
you are glad whatever's living will yourself become. Girlboys	484	NEW POEMS 22	4
yes is the only living thing) and we'll make	528	50 POEMS 40	14
no? measureless our pure living complete love whose doom . .	538	50 POEMS 50	3
with a weakness for living literature "loyaltea" / /	546	1 X 1 6	15
is i awakening am. Living no single thing dares	559	1 X 1 19	9
explodes and o each living ablaze greenly thing ;	583	1 X 1 43	13
strikes to gain a living wage-- when thorns regard	620	(CHAIRE) 22	2
upon falling) silent! ly living the dying of glory	627	(CHAIRE) 29	16
giving and giving is living-- but keeping is darkness	665	(CHAIRE) 67	16
know the goal of living is to grow) forgetting	688	95 POEMS 16	2
ly what any one Living (or some body Dead	702	95 POEMS 30	4
one black day knocked living the hell out of	730	95 POEMS 58	2
should" the greatest of living magicians (whom you and . . .	738	95 POEMS 66	5
dear; imagine ourselves like living neither nor dead these .	743	95 POEMS 71	5
(and giving only) is living" worlds of prose mind	763	95 POEMS 90	18
all dying life, all living death) and never which	765	95 POEMS 91	7
the year, dear) as living as i'm and as	769	95 POEMS 95	25
+LIVING			
FOR CONTEXT, SEE	426	NO THANKS 43	5
LIVING'S			
(the wise fool) if living's to give so breathing's	543	1 X 1 3	15
is more each than living's all multiplied with infinity . . .	592	1 X 1 52	4
LIVINGEST			
fair most rare --the livingest givingest girl on this	590	1 X 1 50	5
as we forget something) livingest the imaginable moon / . . .	599	(CHAIRE) 1	14
inquisitive merrily humble your livingest courage / / / . . .	678	95 POEMS 6	16
on here again --to livingest one star as small	819	73 POEMS 47	17
LIVINGLY			
mind sprawls) here a livingly free mysterious dreamsoul . . .	658	(CHAIRE) 60	16
+LIVINGLY			
FOR CONTEXT, SEE	447	NO THANKS 62	5
LIZ			
/ / FIVE AMERICANS LIZ with breathing as (faithfully)	225	IS 5 ONE LIZ	T
wiser for worse. Give liz (take! tommy) we order	513	50 POEMS 27	12
LLOYD'S			
recktie are covered by lloyd's / / / /	492	50 POEMS 6	16

		PAGE	TITLE	LINE

LOAF
tail (for men must loaf and women must lay) . . . . 552 1 X 1 12   18

LOAM
her worms rushing through loam. (afterward i'll climb by . . 67 T&C POST IMPR 4   12
worms rushing slowly through loam / / / / . . . . 67 T&C POST IMPR 4   30

LOAMHOME
dingle nails personally bung loamhome picpac obviously . . . 333 VIVA 24   4

LOAN
guess you'll have to loan me pain to take . . . . 451 NO THANKS 66   6

LOANED
wilt, repaying life they're loaned; we (by a gift . . . . . . 556 1 X 1 16   11
and day are) only loaned: whereas night is given . . . . . . 816 73 POEMS 44   7

LOATHING
hatred of timid & loathing for (dull all regular . . . . . 677 95 POEMS 5   6

+LOBS
FOR CONTEXT, SEE . . . . 333 VIVA 24   5

LOBSTER
and: she attacks her Lobster without feet mingle under . . . 243 IS 5 ONE 14   13

LOBSTERSALAD
gets gayn troze uh lobstersalad / / / / . . . . 227 IS 5 ONE GERT   16

LOCK
petals of sex which lock me seriously. Dumb for . . . . 133 & SON REAL 4   11

LOCKED
is as a dream locked in white fragrance Come . . . . 27 T&C ORIENTALE 1   18
her knees across the locked room. he knocked her . . . . . . 145 & SON REAL 16   3
which; falling falling both locked in each down a . . . . . . 533 50 POEMS 45   20
/ D-re-A-mi-N-gl-Y leaves (sEe) locked in gOLd after- gLOw . 838 73 POEMS 66   4
some never deepening beach locked in foreverish time's tide . 843 73 POEMS 71   4

LOCKING
your my most : locking foreverfully blend we a . . . . 371 VIVA 62   18

LOCKS
whys stones become eyes locks open keys haven't is . . . . . 716 95 POEMS 44   24

+LOCOMOTIVE
FOR CONTEXT, SEE . . . . 179 XLI SONGS 1   14

LOGGIA
dollarbringing virgins "from the Loggia where are we angels . 257 IS 5 ONE 27   30

LOGIC
gigantic muscles of Cezanne's logic, oho. a street there . . 180 XLI SONGS 2   16
his innumerable whereabouts violet logic of annihi- lation . 197 XLI PORTRAIT 5   6
of sleep what's beyond logic happens beneath will; nor . . . 264 IS 5 ONE 33   5
bowed to ugliness and logic thwarted life: and thus-- . . . . 799 73 POEMS 27   38

LOLL
dream-send is hushed in moan-loll where night gathers morte . 90 & POST IMPR 2   9
The eyes which biggish loll the hands' will tumbling . . . . 131 & SON REAL 2   13

LOLLS
prostrate within twitching shadow lolls sobbing with lust / . 28 T&C ORIENTALE 2   15

+LONDON
FOR CONTEXT, SEE . . . . 237 IS 5 ONE 8   5

LONELIEST
this whyless soul a loneliest road who dares to . . . . . . 441 NO THANKS 56   46

LONELINESS
And the skil- ful loneliness, and the rather fat . . . . . . 166 & SON ACTU 15   5
the Inimitable which is loneliness, these unique dreams never 328 VIVA 19   3
feels of pride and loneliness alive like some dream . . . . . 418 NO THANKS 35   2
only understands) honour this loneliness of even him who . . 456 NO THANKS 71   12
made of nothing except loneliness / / / / . . . . 648 {CHAIRE} 50   12
the forever of his loneliness dreaming their eyes have . . . 812 73 POEMS 40   6

+LONELINESS
FOR CONTEXT, SEE . . . . 673 95 POEMS 1   1

LONELY
...suddenly i feels so lonely fer duh good ole . . . . 332 VIVA 23   14
apparelling its soullessness by lonely antics of ridiculous . 373 VIVA 64   4
win ter sc ribbled lonely truth (from hang from . . . . . . 415 NO THANKS 32   10
ends who far less lonely than a fire is . . . . 420 NO THANKS 37   11
so never is most lonely man alone (his briefest . . . . . . 609 {CHAIRE} 11   9

+LONELY
FOR CONTEXT, SEE . . . . 101 & POST IMPR 11   73

		PAGE	TITLE	LINE

LONG
fondled o'er the warm long flower of unchastity, imperial . . 7 T&C EPITHALAM 160
sinless taint of thy long sinful arms about me . . . . 9 T&C SONGS 1 34
noise of Herod's silence, long ago. If she a . . . . 17 T&C PUELLA MEA 32
with lithe eyes and long (when the world was . . . . 22 T&C PUELLA MEA 225
that sometimes on these long talkative animals are laid . . . 45 T&C LA GUERRE 1 8
the nimble heat had long on a certain taut . . . . 52 T&C PORTRAIT 1 5
have known autumn too long (and what have you . . . . 80 T&C SON UNRE 5 4
Allen street the dark long cool tunnel of raving . . . . . . 100 & POST IMPR 11 3
hideous vegetaBles weasOned with-be- ing-put-too-long in . . 101 & POST IMPR 11 66
Pour Nous) with the long lips of Lucienne which . . . . . . 120 & PORTRAIT 12 20
de pivoine?) with the long lips of Lucienne which . . . . . . 121 & PORTRAIT 12 58
girl's tall with hard long eyes as she stands, ... 147 & SON REAL 18 1
she stands, with her long hard hands keeping silence . . . . 147 & SON REAL 18 2
for sleeping is her long hard body filled with . . . . 147 & SON REAL 18 4
she smiles a hard long smile it sometimes makes . . . . . . 147 & SON REAL 18 6
beautiful prisoner. Mine looked long at the sticky moon . . . 170 & SON ACTU 19 2
love walk the autumn long; the last flower in . . . . 190 XLI SONGS 12 2
of occupation, he had long suppressed the desire to . . . . 263 IS 5 ONE 32 38
/ it is so long since my heart has . . . . 297 IS 5 FOUR 14 1
cities) all of the long night a fragile imitation . . . . . 300 IS 5 FOUR 17 12
(to is see! so long door golf slam bridge . . . . 309 VIVA 1 17
(not to mention inTerred) LONG LIVE that Upwardlooking Serene 315 VIVA 7 11
crum bling people (a long ruined streets hither and) . . . . 319 VIVA 11 4
are from mountains made --long enough and just so . . . . . . 511 50 POEMS 25 4
enough and just so long will being pay the . . . . 511 50 POEMS 25 4
courage is a fear --long enough and just so . . . . 511 50 POEMS 25 12
enough and just so long will the impure think . . . . 511 50 POEMS 25 12
rare and millstones float --long enough and just so . . . . . 511 50 POEMS 25 20
enough and just so long tomorrow will not be . . . . 511 50 POEMS 25 20
for you just so long and long enough / . . . . 511 50 POEMS 25 28
just so long and long enough / / / . . . . 511 50 POEMS 25 28
nvisible Fist) drifts a long conway 's unstreet with . . . . 616 (CHAIRE) 18 12
've been doing as long as to (yes) forget . . . . 686 95 POEMS 14 8
someone (the others have long ago laid them) i . . . . 695 95 POEMS 23 13
with my bill as long as there's haymows you . . . . 707 95 POEMS 35 10
never can tell" "as long as there's ladies my . . . . 707 95 POEMS 35 11
by your thinking forever's long let beauty touch a . . . . . 742 95 POEMS 70 12
of regions dark) laugh long at Beautiful and Brave . . . . . 799 73 POEMS 27 28
(by name myself) one long ago who had died . . . . 828 73 POEMS 56 6
+LONG
FOR CONTEXT, SEE . . . . 100 & POST IMPR 11 15
FOR CONTEXT, SEE . . . . 287 IS 5 FOUR 4 10
LONGER
His fist is no longer, can you imagine it . . . . 289 IS 5 FOUR 6 4
of their hearts live longer than all which and . . . . . . 576 1 X 1 36 2
to (yes) forget (and longer dear) our birth's the . . . . . 686 95 POEMS 14 9
do not worry if longer nights grow longest; i . . . . 749 95 POEMS 77 15
her eyes, not any longer blinded with a world; . . . . 811 73 POEMS 39 5
LONGEST
since Doom (with white longest hands neatening each crease) . 288 IS 5 FOUR 5 3
some planet's year, his longest life's a heartbeat of . . . . 609 (CHAIRE) 11 11
if longer nights grow longest; i am not sorry . . . . 749 95 POEMS 77 15
LONGFELLOW
believe in Christ and Longfellow, both dead, are invariably . 70 T&C SON REAL 1 5
+LONGFELLOW'S
FOR CONTEXT, SEE . . . . 263 IS 5 ONE 32 52
LONGING
despair for peace for longing --a time for growing . . . . . 683 95 POEMS 11 10
LONGNESS
art frail --walk the longness of autumn smile dustily . . . . 190 XLI SONGS 12 19
fantasies or the unlovely longness of the year droops . . . . 207 XLI SONNETS 3 5
+LONGS
FOR CONTEXT, SEE . . . . 66 T&C POST IMPR 3 17
LONJEWRAY
and whether it's in lonjewray or shrouds is immaterial . . . 549 1 X 1 9 6
LOOEY
Nooer Leans Shikahgo Sain Looey Noo York an San . . . . 237 IS 5 ONE 8 8

```
                                                        PAGE      TITLE       LINE
LOOK
  And if my lady look at me (with her . . . . . . . . . . . .   17 T&C PUELLA MEA    38
  amuse themselves) with a look of faerie, perhaps a  . . . . .  17 T&C PUELLA MEA    41
  and hidehidehide whisk whisk look out for the old . . . . . .  25 T&C CHANSONS 2    17
  existence whose pansy eyes look from morning till night  . . .  58 T&C PORTRAIT 6    18
  brittle towns asleep i look where stealing needles of . . . .  64 T&C POST IMPR 1    2
  will sit, up, and look at, you with his . . . . . . . . . . .  69 T&C POST IMPR 6   14
  clotted with loosely voices look look. Skilfully . fingered .  99 & POST IMPR 10    7
  with loosely voices look look. Skilfully . fingered by  . . .  99 & POST IMPR 10    8
  window, into which people look (while people stare arranging  124 & SEVEN POEMS 3    4
  eyes say the breasts look very good: firmlysquirmy with . . . 150 & SON REAL 21     3
  you know that) they look at each other. Nudge. . . . . . . .  171 & SON ACTU 20    10
  only don't be afraid look the spangles that sleep . . . . . .  192 XLI CHANSONS 2   13
  puts down the handmirror. "Look at" arranging before me . . . 226 IS 5 ONE MAME     1
  / / MEMORABILIA stop look & listen Venezia: incline . . . . . 256 IS 5 ONE 27       1
  now pass through the look girls in the style  . . . . . . . . 257 IS 5 ONE 27      32
  / / / / look at this) a 75  . . . . . . . . . . . . . . . . . 270 IS 5 TWO 5        1
  young some old none look alike the flics rush . . . . . . . . 274 IS 5 TWO 9        5
  any more than.) But look: up- raising, hoisting, a  . . . . . 282 IS 5 THREE 6      4
  Disappeared into ourselves who (look) . , startled /  . . . . 286 IS 5 FOUR 3      24
  dog. You don't believe? look back. (Along the sand  . . . . . 303 IS 5 FIVE 2      11
  this cathedral ought to look like) it doesn't look  . . . . . 323 VIVA 15          25
  look like) it doesn't look at all like what . . . . . . . . . 323 VIVA 15          25
  of stopped male to look at (now -fed infantile  . . . . . . . 337 VIVA 28           5
  twilight") there one is look how it goes like . . . . . . . . 353 VIVA 44           7
  guessed was too high look (it's back again there  . . . . . . 353 VIVA 44          22
  too near your slightest look easily will unclose me . . . . . 366 VIVA 57           5
  (and only where remembers look, this was of a . . . . . . . . 371 VIVA 62          11
  refuses. to refuse; just, look) ing dead but not  . . . . . . 387 NO THANKS 4      12
  -ly not (not as look men who are turned . . . . . . . . . . . 387 NO THANKS 4      13
  only understand enormously which fail--look: with what ease . 418 NO THANKS 35      9
  ( vast ness. Be) look now (come soul; & . . . . . . . . . . . 448 NO THANKS 63     13
  of huge each eye look "thank you" nicely the  . . . . . . . . 506 50 POEMS 20      12
  spring --but if a look should april me, down  . . . . . . . . 580 1 X 1 40          6
  prove --but if a look should april me, some  . . . . . . . . . 580 1 X 1 40         11
  won --but if a look should april me for . . . . . . . . . . . 580 1 X 1 40         19
  yes but if a look should april me (though . . . . . . . . . . 580 1 X 1 40         22
  the dark alive but) look: begins to grow more . . . . . . . . 582 1 X 1 42          8
  than eyes can learn look up to silence and  . . . . . . . . . 592 1 X 1 52         10
  no: i'm certain they're (look again) flowers." "Don't worlds  603 {CHAIRE} 5        6
  whys by me at look) swirls to engulf (in  . . . . . . . . . . 613 {CHAIRE} 15       4
  remain: who i am. Look at these (each serenely . . . . . . . 626 {CHAIRE} 28       7
  could not learn to look --from the reality of . . . . . . . . 649 {CHAIRE} 51       3
  now and here --but look: not sunlight? yes! and . . . . . . . 650 {CHAIRE} 52      18
  interest him (by the look feel taste smell & . . . . . . . . 676 95 POEMS 4        7
  shy (and with a look the very boldest man . . . . . . . . . . 685 95 POEMS 13       2
  ly) heard (& how look at it blue is . . . . . . . . . . . . . 695 95 POEMS 23      18
  for will" "did you look for him down by . . . . . . . . . . . 707 95 POEMS 35       2
  telling you no" "than look you down through the . . . . . . . 707 95 POEMS 35      27
  / the (oo) is l00k (aliv e) e yes . . . . . . . . . . . . . . 740 95 POEMS 68       2
  with almost breathing me) --look up: and we'll (for . . . . . 762 95 POEMS 89       9
  it Selves but don't look down and to -morrow . . . . . . . . 762 95 POEMS 89      13
  without a face (a look without an i) be . . . . . . . . . . . 797 73 POEMS 25       2
  life: and thus-- but look around you, friends and . . . . . . 799 73 POEMS 27      39
  through wonder ful sunlight --look-- selves, stir: writhe . . 835 73 POEMS 63      10
+LOOK
  FOR CONTEXT, SEE  . . . . . . . . . . . . . . . . . . . . . . 122 & SEVEN POEMS 1   14
  FOR CONTEXT, SEE  . . . . . . . . . . . . . . . . . . . . . . 347 VIVA 38           27
  FOR CONTEXT, SEE  . . . . . . . . . . . . . . . . . . . . . . 396 NO THANKS 13       3
  FOR CONTEXT, SEE  . . . . . . . . . . . . . . . . . . . . . . 398 NO THANKS 15      18
  FOR CONTEXT, SEE  . . . . . . . . . . . . . . . . . . . . . . 610 {CHAIRE} 12       14
LOOKED
  was young and Diarmuid looked in Grania's eyes.) But  . . . .  18 T&C PUELLA MEA    60
  over to my side Looked up with impertinently exquisite  . . .  44 T&C AMORES 8       9
  bells of gold i looked up and thought to . . . . . . . . . .  58 T&C PORTRAIT 6    11
  own beautiful prisoner. Mine looked long at the sticky . . . 170 & SON ACTU 19      2
  which noticed nobody he looked as if he did . . . . . . . . . 258 IS 5 ONE 28       15
  / / the moon looked into my window it . . . . . . . . . . . . 284 IS 5 FOUR 1        1
```

LOOKED (CONTINUED)

horses, and the poets looked at them, and made	302	IS 5 FIVE 1	14
remembering the way who looked at whom first, anyhow	338	VIVA 29	20
straightway the silver bird looked grave (departing hurriedly	339	VIVA 30	20
as bread: no liar looked him in the head;	521	50 POEMS 34	46
to say" (and she looked) "especially in winter" (like	572	1 X 1 32	5
believe" else thought lucinda looked like steve / /	706	95 POEMS 34	4
fool to have never looked there" "and you couldn't	707	95 POEMS 35	3
and 'twas me that looked up at my willy	707	95 POEMS 35	25

LOOKING

very house silently sits looking beyond the kissing and . . .	57	T&C PORTRAIT 5	8
they all sit there looking at each other having	126	& SEVEN POEMS 5	6
her? ....she exactly lay, looking hunks of love in	145	& SON REAL 16	13
quietly when we weren't looking. / / / /	191	XLI CHANSONS 1	16
will take hands and looking up at our beautiful	192	XLI CHANSONS 2	26
Monia's mouth eats tangerines looking at the moon-- /	219	XLI SONNETS 15	15
university spends her time looking picturesque under the as .	234	IS 5 ONE 5	3
brush dirt coats smile looking hands spit blood teeth	275	IS 5 TWO 9	46
it is twilight (and looking up in fear i	301	IS 5 FOUR 18	4
/ / well) here's looking at ourselves two solids	323	VIVA 15	1
any bird, a collar looking for a dog, a	360	VIVA 51	26
for ann well i'm looking for will" "did you	707	95 POEMS 35	1
silence . is a looking bird: the turn ing;	712	95 POEMS 40	4
& falling) eyes eyes looking (alw ays) while earth	715	95 POEMS 43	7
denies, whereas your lover (looking through both life and . .	845	73 POEMS 73	12

+LOOKING

FOR CONTEXT, SEE	315	VIVA 7	11
FOR CONTEXT, SEE	800	73 POEMS 28	4

LOOKINGLY

blase a black goat lookingly wanders There is nothing	278	IS 5 THREE 2	16

LOOKS

right. Aint much on looks but how dat baby	226	IS 5 ONE MAME	11
arising from a restaurant, looks breathes or moves --climbing	300	IS 5 FOUR 17	3
smokes three castles He looks jewish , next door	312	VIVA 4	16
universe and yawned: it looks like rain (they've played . . .	451	NO THANKS 66	2
our parents one inch looks good to us (and	466	NEW POEMS 4	16
earns anything, everything little looks big in a mist	514	50 POEMS 28	8
dream ing own soul looks and the is all	516	50 POEMS 30	16
way he stands and looks and leaps upon the	774	73 POEMS 2	16
--does doesn't unsays says looks smiles or simply Is	779	73 POEMS 7	19

+LOOM

FOR CONTEXT, SEE	388	NO THANKS 5	19

LOOMING

infinite wishless melancholy, suddenly looming) accurate . .	305	IS 5 FIVE 4	14
and lena smile (while looming darkly a kindness of	754	95 POEMS 82	9

+LOOMINGLY

FOR CONTEXT, SEE	437	NO THANKS 53	1

+LOOMS

FOR CONTEXT, SEE	788	73 POEMS 16	13

LOOP

gly eyes grip live loop croon mime nakedly hurl	445	NO THANKS 60	24

+LOOP

FOR CONTEXT, SEE	107	& PORTRAIT 3	13
FOR CONTEXT, SEE	388	NO THANKS 5	15

LOOPED

well-fed L's immaculate roar looped straightens, into neatest	219	XLI SONNETS 15	5

LOOPTHELOOP

lugu- bri ous eyes LOOPTHELOOP as fathandsbangrag / /	107	& PORTRAIT 3	13

LOOSE

considering how within night's loose sack a star's nibbling .	49	T&C IMPRESS 3	2

LOOSELY

annual brain clotted with loosely voices look look. Skilfully	99	& POST IMPR 10	6
wending putrescence. a. of, loosely ; voices / /	99	& POST IMPR 10	23

LOOSENED

gunwale awash. I thereupon loosened my collar and dove . . .	327	VIVA 18	37

LOOSENESS

skyscraper bulges in the looseness of morning but in	68	T&C POST IMPR 5	6

	PAGE	TITLE	LINE

LOOSER
tells how fought the looser of the warlike zone . . . . . .   4 T&C EPITHALAM   44
LOOT
these trees) when sunbeams loot furnished rooms through whose 442 NO THANKS 57   11
LOPPED
living and biggest bodies lopped of every prettiness you . . 195 XLI PORTRAIT 3   21
LOPSIDED
if here there (like lopsided imaginations) filled with newly 340 VIVA 31   9
LORD
brought forth tall Hippolytus, lord on whose pedestal the . .   4 T&C EPITHALAM   46
groom or the loud lord of skipping maenads knows,-- . . . . .   6 T&C EPITHALAM 150
Helen's beauty: never did Lord Jason (in impossible things . 18 T&C PUELLA MEA 69
amaying go with my lord Boccaccio-- whoso knocketh at . . . . 20 T&C PUELLA MEA 170
to be photographed with Lord Rothermere playing with Lord . . 262 IS 5 ONE 32   20
Lord Rothermere playing with Lord Rothermere billiards very . 262 IS 5 ONE 32   21
well by moonlight with Lord Rothermere. A crocodile eats . . 262 IS 5 ONE 32   22
Serene Illustrious and Beatific Lord of Creation, MAN: at . . 315 VIVA 7   13
/ / / / Lord John Unalive (having a . . . . 331 VIVA 22   1
LORETTA
stinging quips of flesh. Loretta, cut the comedy kid.... . . 138 & SON REAL 9   15
LOSE
lust one threaded moment lose: haste) the very shadowy . . .   9 T&C SONGS 1   7
flameflung, mounts, inimitably to lose herself where the wet 206 XLI SONNETS 2   8
never had any to lose) and a myth is . . . . 410 NO THANKS 27   8
as red as to lose and as round as . . . . 543 1 X 1 3   5
rides his year. All lose, whole find / / . . . . 556 1 X 1 16   15
deeper is life than lose: higher than have --but . . . . . 592 1 X 1 52   3
a man can proudly lose, or playing dead and . . . . 679 95 POEMS 7   3
alone. For whatever we lose (like a you or . . . . 682 95 POEMS 10   11
or i'm-- crying to lose (as down someone who's . . . . . . 716 95 POEMS 44   33
the true and to lose is to have --we . . . . 767 95 POEMS 93   11
little and all) but lose or win (come heaven, ... 776 73 POEMS 4   13
all (beyond win or lose) good true beautiful things . . . . 805 73 POEMS 33   3
finding what you didn't lose (existing's tricky: but to . . . 807 73 POEMS 35   1
LOSER
if death is the loser and life is the . . . . 769 95 POEMS 95   3
LOSES
/ / / nobody loses all the time i . . . . 239 IS 5 ONE 10   1
LOSING
did not do the losing spectres mime until out . . . . 502 50 POEMS 16   12
clumsily striving (finding and losing and laughing and . . . 749 95 POEMS 77   7
but some keener makes losing, gaining --love! if a . . . . 750 95 POEMS 78   14
death becomes your kiss losing through you what seemed . . . 810 73 POEMS 38   9
+LOSING
FOR CONTEXT, SEE . . . . 403 NO THANKS 20   13
LOSING'S
no rose i've and losing's less than winning (but . . . . . 684 95 POEMS 12   19
LOSS
eager dim enormous language loss or gain from blame . . . . . 372 VIVA 63   12
the quote and unquote loss of liberty my dears-- . . . . . 544 1 X 1 4   15
LOST
more sink and are lost the divine alchemist, the . . . . .   6 T&C EPITHALAM 133
terribly afar in the lost lands. / / / . . . . 76 T&C SON UNRE 1   14
my mouth, steer our lost bodies carefully downward) / . . . . 215 XLI SONNETS 11   17
an electromagnetic (now I've lost the) Einstein expanded . . 315 VIVA 7   4
little joe gould has lost his teeth and doesn't . . . . . . 410 NO THANKS 27   1
sometimes is I the lost shoulders S the empty . . . . 414 NO THANKS 31   15
was. Were your eyes: lost, believing; hushed with when . . . 432 NO THANKS 49   20
/ / death (having lost) put on his universe . . . . 451 NO THANKS 66   1
(you may recall) being lost including captain Pater / . . . . 494 50 POEMS 8   7
these perhaps who have lost their shadows if which . . . . . 502 50 POEMS 16   11
still as found some lost thing (like a curtain . . . . 516 50 POEMS 30   4
/ enters give whose lost is his found leading . . . . 533 50 POEMS 45   2
his eyes are as lost as you'll find / . . . . 647 (CHAIRE) 49   20
when more than was lost has been found has . . . . 665 (CHAIRE) 67   15
/ / / albutnotquitemost lost (in this br am . . . . 695 95 POEMS 23   2
round (& so mething lost) & som ething like . . . . 753 95 POEMS 81   3
Oblivions found a by lost child and a (float . . . . 757 95 POEMS 85   25

		PAGE	TITLE	LINE

LOST (CONTINUED)
  your beauty, then my lost my dazed my whereful . . . . 819 73 POEMS 47   14
+LOST
  FOR CONTEXT, SEE . . . . 471 NEW POEMS 9   14
  FOR CONTEXT, SEE . . . . 681 95 POEMS 9   10
LOT
  softly in the vacant lot of his physiognomy his . . . . . . 259 IS 5 ONE 29   23
  mean a god damned lot of people don't and . . . . 272 IS 5 TWO 7   13
  much said she a lot said he) why not . . . . 399 NO THANKS 16   7
+LOT
  FOR CONTEXT, SEE . . . . 332 VIVA 23   12
LOTH
  mired in silk wrinkling loth stocking begins queerly to . . . 225 IS 5 ONE LIZ   3
LOUD
  thunder-foraging groom or the loud lord of skipping maenads .   6 T&C EPITHALAM   150
  may) from whose (if loud most howish time derange . . . . . . 420 NO THANKS 37   5
  freedom? yet, among their loud exactitudes of imprecision, . 659 {CHAIRE} 61   11
  / let's, from some loud unworld's most rightful wrong . . . . 745 95 POEMS 73   1
LOUDLY
  particular she gasped almost loudly i'm so drunG k, ... 53 T&C PORTRAIT 1   47
  and above me pass loudly and gondola rapidly denizens . . . . 256 IS 5 ONE 27   25
  call himself a man? loudly for Truth have liars . . . . 438 NO THANKS 54   17
LOUDNESS
  dark-- how should a loudness called mankind unteach whole . . 603 {CHAIRE} 5   3
LOUISE
  the ivory throat Marie Louise Lallemand n'est-ce pas que . . 120 & PORTRAIT 12   10
  twilight of Paris Marie Louise with queenly legs cinq . . . . 121 & PORTRAIT 12   45
LOUSY
  face my hair is lousy with mutilated singing microscopic . . 69 T&C POST IMPR 6 28
  we want something redblooded lousy with pure reeking with . . 407 NO THANKS 24   4
  nd scr; a; tch-ing lousy full. of. rain beggars . . . . 442 NO THANKS 57   14
  babe not (understand me) lousy kid that's something else . . 475 NEW POEMS 13   23
  twilight i feel (his lousy eyes roaming) wonderful all . . . 501 50 POEMS 15   8
LOVE
  Lover, lead forth thy love unto that bed prepared . . . . . .   6 T&C EPITHALAM   113
  transparent company of quivering ghosts-of-love which . . . .   6 T&C EPITHALAM   143
  me dream shall my love wholly taste thee as . . . .   9 T&C SONGS 1   35
  whose bodies strong with love through meadows hugely move. . 11 T&C SONGS 2   34
  hair mostly the hours love: a smoothness which sings, ... 13 T&C SONGS 3   3
  which sings, saying (though love be a day) do . . . . 13 T&C SONGS 3   6
  much says; singing (though love be a day) for . . . . 13 T&C SONGS 3   13
  catch, else missing. (though love be a day and . . . . 13 T&C SONGS 3   20
  in green went my love riding on a great . . . . 14 T&C SONGS 4   1
  at hip went my love riding riding the echo . . . . 14 T&C SONGS 4   11
  at belt went my love riding riding the mountain . . . . 14 T&C SONGS 4   21
  in green went my love riding on a great . . . . 14 T&C SONGS 4   31
  birds shall go my love walking in the grass . . . . 16 T&C SONGS 6   11
  their ladies had to love them and to make . . . . 20 T&C PUELLA MEA 130
  dead and careful painters love to use for their . . . . 20 T&C PUELLA MEA 141
  and caliph had to love them and to make . . . . 22 T&C PUELLA MEA 224
  go crisp with miracle. Love!--maker of my lady, in . . . . . 22 T&C PUELLA MEA 237
  used to laugh and love ladies with crisp eyes . . . . 23 T&C PUELLA MEA 286
  thou, is life not love? i speak to thee . . . . 27 T&C ORIENTALE 1 21
  hither O thou, is love not death? / / . . . . 27 T&C ORIENTALE 1 28
  / / / my love thy hair is one . . . . 29 T&C ORIENTALE 3 1
  a pleasant song my love thy head is a . . . . 29 T&C ORIENTALE 3 15
  svelte and urgent (again love i slowly gather of . . . . . . 37 T&C AMORES 2   17
  and is with sleep.... love, the breaking of your . . . . . . 38 T&C AMORES 3   14
  song about home and love from her transfigured face . . . . . 55 T&C PORTRAIT 3 14
  proving to Death that Love is so and so. . . . . 71 T&C SON REAL 2 14
  wind wind wind--did you love somebody and have you . . . . . 80 T&C SON UNRE 5   6
  / / / my love is building a building . . . . 83 T&C SON ACTU 2   1
  of your mouth) my love is building a magic, ... 83 T&C SON ACTU 2   9
  first stars) people move love hurry in a gently . . . . 93 & POST IMPR 5   11
  Momentinmyarms your expression my love when most passionate. 94 & POST IMPR 6   24
  most passionate. , my, love is thatofa fly. pre . . . . 94 & POST IMPR 6   26
  there anything my ears love it's to go into . . . . 100 & POST IMPR 11 33
  pretty and putrid dollies of-love-and-of-death dollies of . . 101 & POST IMPR 11 81

447

LOVE (CONTINUED)

	PAGE	TITLE	LINE
,pas cheres") and my love slowly answered I think	102	& POST IMPR 12	22
Henri Mounier a little love begs, Mimi with the	121	& PORTRAIT 12	47
Spring) and everyone's in love and flowers pick themselves .	129	& SEVEN POEMS 7	16
and lilacs.... minutes and love.... do you? and always . . .	133	& SON REAL 4	8
by the lug of love) sincerely greets, with an	137	& SON REAL 8	3
perpetual girls marching to love whose bodies kiss me	138	& SON REAL 9	11
lay, looking hunks of love in The Chair he	145	& SON REAL 16	13
/ SONNETS--ACTUALITIES when my love comes to see me	152	& SON ACTU 1	1
the coming of my love emits a wonderful smell	152	& SON ACTU 1	6
before shutting.... understand i love you.... feel your . . .	157	& SON ACTU 6	6
after all: (after me) love, and after you. I	160	& SON ACTU 9	13
worm and i who love to feel what it	164	& SON ACTU 13	13
other. Nudge. (if they love each other, who cares?)	171	& SON ACTU 20	11
flesh crisp set my love-tooth on edge. So until	173	& SON ACTU 22	11
flesh.... And eyes big love-crumbs, and possibly i like . . .	175	& SON ACTU 24	12
/ / / cruelly, love walk the autumn long;	190	XLI SONGS 12	1
grass Comes the moon love, walk the autumn love, ...	190	XLI SONGS 12	12
love, walk the autumn love, for the last flower	190	XLI SONGS 12	14
is acold with dreams, love thou art frail --walk	190	XLI SONGS 12	18
/ / Humanity i love you because you would	204	XLI LA GUERRE 2	1
old howard Humanity i love you because when you're	204	XLI LA GUERRE 2	9
own house Humanity i love you because you are	204	XLI LA GUERRE 2	17
keeping their exquisite dreams--O Love! upon thy dim shrine .	206	XLI SONNETS 2	10
i do excuse me, love, to Death and Time	207	XLI SONNETS 3	9
for that thou didst love the pen while others	209	XLI SONNETS 5	9
(being of men called Love) upward doth leap from	210	XLI SONNETS 6	4
hate has triumphed darkly love and the small spiritual . . .	213	XLI SONNETS 9	5
the smiting smile didst love to use in other	213	XLI SONNETS 9	12
him utterly afraid, i love of thee (beloved) this	215	XLI SONNETS 11	3
mer i ca, I love, You. And there're a	231	IS 5 ONE 3	40
to speak were in Love once? now her mouth	243	IS 5 ONE 14	10
token of their country's love received my dears the	266	IS 5 TWO 1	26
course god america i love you land of the	268	IS 5 TWO 3	2
more with the imaginable, love, and eat sunlight (do	289	IS 5 FOUR 6	8
this house of you love being such, or such, ...	292	IS 5 FOUR 9	13
suddenly which is of love and death a marriage)	293	IS 5 FOUR 10	18
/ you being in love will tell who softly	295	IS 5 FOUR 12	1
who softly asks in love, am i separated from	295	IS 5 FOUR 12	2
all come down to? love? Love if you like	295	IS 5 FOUR 12	21
come down to? love? Love if you like and	295	IS 5 FOUR 12	21
of this window is love, love and the reason	295	IS 5 FOUR 12	23
this window is love, love and the reason that	295	IS 5 FOUR 12	23
and breathe is oh love and the reason that	295	IS 5 FOUR 12	24
into this street is love." / / / /	295	IS 5 FOUR 12	25
of blood and flesh) Love coins His most gradual	297	IS 5 FOUR 14	11
few thoughts a little love preferably, anything which you . .	298	IS 5 FOUR 15	15
womenlike telling of death love earth dark) and thousand . .	356	VIVA 47	5
sobs bigly climb what (love being some- thing possibly . . .	358	VIVA 49	7
dear as now i love behold this fool who, ...	360	VIVA 51	10
dear as now i love god's terrible face, brighter	360	VIVA 51	20
dear as now i love. Hell (by most humble	360	VIVA 51	30
dear as now i love / / / /	360	VIVA 51	35
/ / if i love You (thickness means worlds	363	VIVA 54	1
bright faeries if you love me) distance is mind	363	VIVA 54	5
complete dream if we love each (shyly) other, what	363	VIVA 54	9
/ / speaking of love (of which Who knows	364	VIVA 55	1
/ / because i love you) last night clothed	369	VIVA 60	1
/ / be unto love as rain is unto	372	VIVA 63	1
being not amazing: without love separate, smileless--merely .	374	VIVA 65	1
near) day being come, Love, put on your faces	376	VIVA 67	14
minds why, it is love; but at the earliest	377	VIVA 68	2
here imprisoned, tortured here love everywhere exploding . .	377	VIVA 68	8
must be opened?) Love / / / /	377	VIVA 68	15
does not stir) O love, my love! soul clings	386	NO THANKS 3	12
stir) O love, my love! soul clings and heart	386	NO THANKS 3	12
having no wealth but love, who shall not spend	394	NO THANKS 11	13
everyone that will Ever love) we 've hidden him	397	NO THANKS 14	10

		PAGE	TITLE	LINE

LOVE (CONTINUED)

	PAGE	TITLE	LINE
he conceives to be Love did <> did) who	398	NO THANKS 15	6
said he is it love said she) if you're	399	NO THANKS 16	18
they are afraid to love / / /	413	NO THANKS 30	18
hurl) blind full steep love / / / /	422	NO THANKS 39	16
me hurling vastness of love (sometimes in Spring somewhere .	428	NO THANKS 45	8
hungry for Is for Love Spring thirsty for happens	437	NO THANKS 53	8
awn) then, o my love , then it's Spring	442	NO THANKS 57	17
/ / / / love is a place &	443	NO THANKS 58	1
through this place of love move (with brightness of	443	NO THANKS 58	3
(known being wishless; but love, all of wishing) though . . .	446	NO THANKS 61	2
are caught by worms (love may not care if	446	NO THANKS 61	5
hearse, see you again. Love (having found) wound up	451	NO THANKS 66	9
/ / be of love (a little) More careful	453	NO THANKS 68	1
closely than Nothing, remember love by frequent anguish . . .	453	NO THANKS 68	8
down above all with love and everything perverse or	466	NEW POEMS 4	21
Breathe grow dream die love not Fear eat sleep	467	NEW POEMS 5	9
the infinite corner of love, all that i am	479	NEW POEMS 17	18
do nothing usefully and love yourself so more than	481	NEW POEMS 19	10
can entirely her only love whose any mystery makes	484	NEW POEMS 22	6
ever could ever had love loved whose his climbing	490	50 POEMS 4	18
the only mystery of love become while every sun	510	50 POEMS 24	13
life one leaf) but love is the sky and	511	50 POEMS 25	27
earth whose both eyes love this now of the	512	50 POEMS 26	11
moved through dooms of love through sames of am	520	50 POEMS 34	1
father lived his soul love is the whole and	521	50 POEMS 34	68
grin may stern particular Love surround your trite how . . .	522	50 POEMS 35	10
/ / / / love is the every only	526	50 POEMS 38	1
mighty briefness dig for love beginning means return seas . .	526	50 POEMS 38	5
the skies by merciful love whispered were, completes its . .	526	50 POEMS 38	10
/ / / / love is more thicker than	530	50 POEMS 42	1
deeper than the sea love is less always than	530	50 POEMS 42	9
true value neither is love makes the little thickness	531	50 POEMS 43	8
is his found leading love whose heart is her	533	50 POEMS 45	3
our pure living complete love whose doom is beauty	538	50 POEMS 50	3
dark least ourselves remembering love only rides his year. .	556	1 X 1 16	14
/ / / / love is a spring at	563	1 X 1 23	1
go dear so comes love / / / /	569	1 X 1 29	21
kind but" her, my "love creates love only" our	572	1 X 1 32	18
her, my "love creates love only" our / /	572	1 X 1 32	18
false and possible is love (who's imagined, therefore	574	1 X 1 34	1
yes is to if, love is to yes must's	574	1 X 1 34	4
your (and rest, my love) honour / / /	575	1 X 1 35	41
comics of duration: only love immortally occurs beyond the .	576	1 X 1 36	7
/ / / we love each other very dearly	577	1 X 1 37	1
treasure, when violets appear love is a deeper season	578	1 X 1 38	9
darkly themselves unmade makes love armies (than hate itself	580	1 X 1 40	14
; may has come love (by yes every new	583	1 X 1 43	15
you made for by love love said did o	589	1 X 1 49	5
made for by love love said did o no	589	1 X 1 49	6
thy? why our is love and neverless / /	590	1 X 1 50	27
lovetime and viva sweet love" (all the merry little	591	1 X 1 51	4
lovetime and viva sweet love" / / / /	591	1 X 1 51	28
till now now i love you and you love	594	1 X 1 54	28
love you and you love me (and books are	594	1 X 1 54	28
luminous the shadow of love himself: who's we --nor	601	(CHAIRE) 3	17
are merely to know) Love only has ever been, ...	631	(CHAIRE) 33	14
only stand with me, love! against these its until	633	(CHAIRE) 35	6
into less? into not) love, stand with me while	633	(CHAIRE) 35	12
never into (touch me! love) forever --until is and	633	(CHAIRE) 35	14
conceive less who than love) / / / /	634	(CHAIRE) 36	16
an act of christian love. "Nothing" in 1944 A	636	(CHAIRE) 38	8
hand and the word love underlined this is a	647	(CHAIRE) 49	5
each no thy yes: love; and give because the	651	(CHAIRE) 53	11
of life and of love and wings: and of	663	(CHAIRE) 65	7
happens to be that love are in we, that	664	(CHAIRE) 66	6
are in we, that love are in we and	664	(CHAIRE) 66	6
that we are in love, that we are in	664	(CHAIRE) 66	10

                                       PAGE   TITLE   LINE

LOVE (CONTINUED)

	PAGE	TITLE	LINE
that we are in love: with us they've nothing	664	(CHAIRE) 66	10
nothing to do (for love are in we am	664	(CHAIRE) 66	12
touch and feel --for love are in we are	664	(CHAIRE) 66	16
in we are in love are in we; for	664	(CHAIRE) 66	16
all possible worlds) in love a billion brains may	664	(CHAIRE) 66	18
and the sea. For love are in you am	664	(CHAIRE) 66	24
/ / / / love our so right is,	666	(CHAIRE) 68	1
particular person is (my love) alive than every world	667	(CHAIRE) 69	3
fall in hate with love --human one mortally immortal	679	95 POEMS 7	12
less than winning (but love is more than love)	684	95 POEMS 12	20
love is more than love) / / / / .	684	95 POEMS 12	20
cry and sing, my love and wonder) is something	686	95 POEMS 14	4
fate hands silence eyes love laughter death (dreams hopes	693	95 POEMS 21	4
/ / / i love you much (most beautiful	717	95 POEMS 45	1
believe in nothing but love / / / / .	717	95 POEMS 45	14
fire (and live by love though the stars walk	732	95 POEMS 60	7
days i've loved, shall love, do love you, was	734	95 POEMS 62	3
loved, shall love, do love you, was and will	734	95 POEMS 62	3
each our heartbeat--believe that love (and only love)	741	95 POEMS 69	5
that love (and only love) comprehends huger easily beyonds	741	95 POEMS 69	5
And (darling) never fear: love, when such marvels vanish,	741	95 POEMS 69	10
suppose we could not love, dear; imagine ourselves like	743	95 POEMS 71	4
rightful wrong climbing, my love (till mountains speak the	745	95 POEMS 73	2
who" i asked my love " could begin to	748	95 POEMS 76	12
keener makes losing, gaining --love! if a world ends	750	95 POEMS 78	15
for his own (his love) his dear he sings	760	95 POEMS 87	11
complete fearless and pure love with one least ignorance	761	95 POEMS 88	1
your fearless and complete love, all safely small big	761	95 POEMS 88	11
yesterday and everything except love / / / /	762	95 POEMS 89	14
very so gay young love why? how-- we never	767	95 POEMS 93	16
as it's to time, love did no more begin	768	95 POEMS 94	2
no more begin than love will end; where nothing	768	95 POEMS 94	2
to stroll to swim love is the air the	768	95 POEMS 94	4
emerging from a wish) love is the voice under	768	95 POEMS 94	9
than star --do lovers love? why then to heaven	768	95 POEMS 94	13
misers are poor-- let's love until noone could quite	769	95 POEMS 95	24
(for you are in love and i am) to	776	73 POEMS 4	2
now to grow it's love by whom (my beautiful	776	73 POEMS 4	17
the yes of yes love was and shall be	776	73 POEMS 4	33
lover and his only love, strolling slowly (mind in	777	73 POEMS 5	2
right: my enemy . Love / / / /	793	73 POEMS 21	26
knew (1) we sans love equals mob love being	803	73 POEMS 31	7
sans love equals mob love being youamiare (2) the	803	73 POEMS 31	8
And i and my love are alone / /	813	73 POEMS 41	12
may partly guess--thus, my love, to merely what dying	818	73 POEMS 46	13
very most my shining love) how more than dark	819	73 POEMS 47	4
you and i who love so much to live)	836	73 POEMS 64	4
hope faith! ! life love! bells cry bells (the	841	73 POEMS 69	4
time's tide at poise, love alone understands: only for	843	73 POEMS 71	5
axis of the universe --love. Each believing world denies,	845	73 POEMS 73	11

+LOVE

	PAGE	TITLE	LINE
FOR CONTEXT, SEE	436	NO THANKS 52	4
FOR CONTEXT, SEE	480	NEW POEMS 18	6
FOR CONTEXT, SEE	495	50 POEMS 9	24
FOR CONTEXT, SEE	719	95 POEMS 47	20

LOVE-CRUMBS

	PAGE	TITLE	LINE
flesh.... And eyes big love-crumbs, and possibly i like	175	& SON ACTU 24	12

LOVE-TOOTH

	PAGE	TITLE	LINE
flesh crisp set my love-tooth on edge. So until	173	& SON ACTU 22	11

LOVE'S

	PAGE	TITLE	LINE
tumbling into shall --and Love's a coach with gilt	131	& SON REAL 2	15
in the blue; when love's had his tears out,	181	XLI SONGS 3	6
than our merely universe, love's also there: and being	377	VIVA 68	6
least of all (for love's secret supremely clothes herself	379	VIVA 70	4
Hate's a game and Love's a fuck who dares	438	NO THANKS 54	23
/ / / / love's function is to fabricate	446	NO THANKS 61	1
and starved on space? love's murdered eye dissected to	527	50 POEMS 39	13

		PAGE	TITLE	LINE

LOVE'S (CONTINUED)
(who's imagined, therefore limitless) love's to giving as to . 574 1 X 1 34   3
all now turns when (love's a universe beyond obey . . . . . . 574 1 X 1 34   7
such a forever is love's any now and her . . . . 576 1 X 1 36   9
/ if (touched by love's own secret) we, like . . . . 659 {CHAIRE} 61   1
illimitable joy) bird sings love's every truth beyond all . . 783 73 POEMS 11   3
so, in how merciful love's own name, linger no . . . . 812 73 POEMS 40   9

LOVECRAZED
blue cold jolts of lovecrazed abrupt flesh split "Pretty . . 106 & PORTRAIT 2   11

LOVED
serious grace one goddess loved too well? Chryselephantine . 3 T&C EPITHALAM   24
the moved myriads wonderfully loved, (hasten, it is the . . . 9 T&C SONGS 1   15
Omar Hafiz and Harun loved their ladies in the . . . . 22 T&C PUELLA MEA   228
is because you have loved me, moon and sunset . . . . 39 T&C AMORES 4   5
gave me when we loved the far- departed mouth . . . . 42 T&C AMORES 6   4
lips, which i have loved, should touch another's, and . . . . 76 T&C SON UNRE 1   2
this painter should have loved my lady. And by . . . . 85 T&C SON ACTU 4   9
immense Both paws slowly loved a dinted mug gone . . . . . . 97 & POST IMPR 8   39
an organ and it loved he was a roman . . . . 110 & PORTRAIT 6   20
/ / i have loved, let us see if . . . . 154 & SON ACTU 3   1
whole possibly have i loved....? you) sheath before sheath . 154 & SON ACTU 3   11
the big eyes i loved like you can't imagine . . . . 271 IS 5 TWO 6   9
first president to be loved by his bitterest enemies" . . . . 336 VIVA 27   1
lease. I have never loved you dear as now . . . . 360 VIVA 51   10
piece. I have never loved you dear as now . . . . 360 VIVA 51   20
is. I have never loved you dear as now . . . . 360 VIVA 51   30
face, i have never loved you dear as now . . . . 360 VIVA 51   35
which have (Per haps) loved (or than everyone that . . . . 397 NO THANKS 14   9
/ / / nobody loved this he) with its . . . . 490 50 POEMS 4   1
of forehead. No body loved big that quick sharp . . . . . . 490 50 POEMS 4   7
could ever had love loved whose his climbing shoulders . . . 490 50 POEMS 4   18
spring summer) that noone loved him more by more . . . . . . 515 50 POEMS 29   12
round little man we loved so isn't no! w . . . . 606 {CHAIRE} 8   4
of lucky days i've loved, shall love, do love . . . . 734 95 POEMS 62   3

LOVEFIST
rooting dies also. (my loveFist in her knuckling thighs, . . 131 & SON REAL 2   8

LOVEFLESH
a pillar of youngly loveflesh topped with danc ing . . . . . 615 {CHAIRE} 17   2

LOVEHOUSE
Finn emerging from a lovehouse who buttons his coat . . . . . 115 & PORTRAIT 8   27

LOVELESS
panes which by some loveless trick sepa rate one . . . . . . 354 VIVA 45   19
god himself & as loveless some world not any . . . . 698 95 POEMS 26   3
the ultramachinations of some loveless infraworld) a woman . 807 73 POEMS 35   11

LOVELIER
is mean beside its lovelier friends, between your thoughts . 11 T&C SONGS 2   13
Mine is a little lovelier than any of your . . . . 17 T&C PUELLA MEA   3
mine is a little lovelier. And if she speak . . . . 18 T&C PUELLA MEA   76
mine is a little lovelier than any of those . . . . 20 T&C PUELLA MEA   133

LOVELIEST
in your honour, my loveliest, nothing may move may . . . . . 575 1 X 1 35   3

LOVELINESS
and his worms, when loveliness says sweetly Yes to . . . . 183 XLI SONGS 5   9
sublime Memory, of that loveliness receiving the image my . . 207 XLI SONNETS 3   12

+LOVELINESS
FOR CONTEXT, SEE . . . . 101 & POST IMPR 11   74

LOVELY
with Egypt's body lay. Lovely as those ladies were . . . . 18 T&C PUELLA MEA   75
Upon a keen and lovely throat the strangeness of . . . . . . 20 T&C PUELLA MEA   145
smooth that in a lovely fashion doth from my . . . . 21 T&C PUELLA MEA   182
Eater of all things lovely--Time! upon whose watering lips . 23 T&C PUELLA MEA   266
undMe the traffic of lovely; muscles-sinke x p i . . . . . . 122 & SEVEN POEMS 1   4
Cleopatra were Just Too Lovely, The Snail's On The . . . . . 230 IS 5 ONE 2   27
the season 'tis, my lovely lambs, of Sumner Volstead . . . . 266 IS 5 TWO 1   1
country: if's wintry (my lovely) let's open the year . . . . 578 1 X 1 38   3
all (each thing most lovely) sweet things cannot spring . . . 666 {CHAIRE} 68   3

LOVER
evasive audible great rose! Lover, lead forth thy love . . . 6 T&C EPITHALAM   113

LOVER (CONTINUED)

its fragrance makes the lover blest.) Her waist is . . . . . 21 T&C PUELLA MEA 192
with ardor the yellow lover stands in the dumb . . . . . . 37 T&C AMORES 2 11
receive him as your lover sumptuously being kind because . . 42 T&C AMORES 6 19
of death thy rhythmic lover thou answerest them only . . . . 46 T&C LA GUERRE 2 24
was COOl O My lover, there's just room for . . . . 123 & SEVEN POEMS 2 7
deaths which are your lover lady: together with what . . . . 285 IS 5 FOUR 2 21
his mercy) your true lover spare: for that way . . . . . . 484 NEW POEMS 22 10
live that undeluded notselfpitying lover of all things . . . 607 (CHAIRE) 9 10
me twice but my lover has a brother who . . . . 684 95 POEMS 12 11
/ stand with your lover on the ending earth-- . . . . 743 95 POEMS 71 1
dreams was of a lover and his only love, ... 777 73 POEMS 5 2
world denies, whereas your lover (looking through both life . 845 73 POEMS 73 12

LOVERS

belong the hearts of lovers! --I beseech thee bless . . . . . 7 T&C EPITHALAM 167
dead beauties, you greatest lovers in the world! who . . . . 22 T&C PUELLA MEA 244
profound Paris moves with lovers, two and two bound . . . . 71 T&C SON REAL 2 8
gently smell of deads (lovers grip sprawl twitch lovers) . . 384 NO THANKS 2 10
(lovers grip sprawl twitch lovers) & one dog? piglike . . . . 384 NO THANKS 2 10
should end) how lucky lovers are (whose selves abide . . . . 446 NO THANKS 61 9
each known allness disappears lovers are mindless they higher 563 1 X 1 23 7
than fears are hopes lovers are those who kneel . . . . 563 1 X 1 23 9
are those who kneel lovers are these whose lips . . . . . 563 1 X 1 23 10
heights below) kneeling, we--true lovers--pray that us will . 574 1 X 1 34 11
/ / / true lovers in each happening of . . . . 576 1 X 1 36 1
more true would truest lovers grow if out of . . . . 576 1 X 1 36 11
winging in the blossoming) lovers go and lovers come . . . . 591 1 X 1 51 9
blossoming) lovers go and lovers come awandering awondering . 591 1 X 1 51 9
we'll spend (gladly, as lovers must) immortal and the . . . . 675 95 POEMS 3 13
(these one who are) lovers cling & kiss neither . . . . . . 698 95 POEMS 26 6
on a pitchfork (breathing) lovers like rej and lena . . . . 754 95 POEMS 82 9
all heartless spectres, happiness) lovers alone wear . . . 765 95 POEMS 91 5
told sings only--and all lovers are the song. Here . . . . . 765 95 POEMS 91 9
and the land (do lovers suffer? all divinities proudly . . . 768 95 POEMS 94 5
on deathful flesh: are lovers glad? only their smallest . . . 768 95 POEMS 94 7
last than star --do lovers love? why then to . . . . 768 95 POEMS 94 13
/ fair ladies tall lovers riding are through the . . . . . . 778 73 POEMS 6 1
fragrance and singing) come lovers with slender their ladies 778 73 POEMS 6 22
(not numerably or as lovers a chieve oneness) each . . . . 785 73 POEMS 13 13
(as mountains feel and lovers) singing is silence / . . . . . 804 73 POEMS 32 14
Time cannot children, poets, lovers tell- measure imagine, . 817 73 POEMS 45 9

LOVES

bad candies my, mouth loves melons slitted with bright . . . 100 & POST IMPR 11 22
tingg OO seberries, it, loves these better than, ... 100 & POST IMPR 11 28
and thick and it loves, every old thing falls . . . . 126 & SEVEN POEMS 5 4
nothing and whom dawn loves most to touch wishing . . . . . 211 XLI SONNETS 7 17
no boy (day simbully loves id) fer ids dare . . . . 519 50 POEMS 33 21
the dull ones gus loves all the girls (the . . . . 619 (CHAIRE) 21 15
soft bird -quick voice loves children and sunlight and . . . 660 (CHAIRE) 62 21
what life will do) loves nothing as much as . . . . 676 95 POEMS 4 15
chicks his friends he loves because he cannot fear . . . . . 774 73 POEMS 2 14

LOVEST

flowers i think thou lovest incense for in the . . . . . . 31 T&C ORIENTALE 5 14

LOVESTAR

/ / if the Lovestar grows most big a . . . . 752 95 POEMS 80 1

LOVETIME

time for springtime is lovetime and viva sweet love" . . . . 591 1 X 1 51 3
time for springtime is lovetime and viva sweet love" . . . . 591 1 X 1 51 27

LOVETREE

most emanation creates creation lovetree! least the rose . . 764 95 POEMS 90 49

LOVING

all dead men and loving) as invisibly when upon . . . . . . 19 T&C PUELLA MEA 104
spin kegs they curl loving around beers the world . . . . . 114 & PORTRAIT 7 10
girl much kissed, by loving relatives well fed, and . . . . . 273 IS 5 TWO 8 21
comprehend (clinging as fingers, loving one another gradually 305 IS 5 FIVE 4 2
good pretending befriending means loving" (sighs mind: and . 625 (CHAIRE) 27 5

LOVINGLY

a mouse to hold lovingly, our lady what do . . . . 279 IS 5 THREE 3 20

		PAGE	TITLE	LINE

LOVINGS
the shovings and the lovings of Her tongue. god . . . . 77 T&C SON UNRE 2   9
LOW
four lean hounds crouched low and smiling the merry . . . . . 14 T&C SONGS 4   4
four lean hounds crouched low and smiling the level . . . . . 14 T&C SONGS 4   14
four lean hounds crouched low and smiling the sheer . . . . . 14 T&C SONGS 4   24
four lean hounds crouched low and smiling my heart . . . . . 14 T&C SONGS 4   34
immaculate sorrow of thy low hair flutter the level . . . . . 31 T&C ORIENTALE 5 19
old blinking at the low ceiling my being pleasantly . . . . . 96 & POST IMPR 8   24
1 shape passed from low through second-in-to-high like . . . 248 IS 5 ONE 19   19
unto whom duty whispers low "thou must!" and who . . . . . . 273 IS 5 TWO 8   4
that russia's here) swing low sweet ca rr y . . . . 641 (CHAIRE) 43   3
"i have hunted her low i have hunted her . . . . 707 95 POEMS 35   7
everywhere's here (with a low high low and the . . . . 767 95 POEMS 93   3
(with a low high low and the bird on . . . . 767 95 POEMS 93   3
know (with a high low high in the may . . . . 767 95 POEMS 93   19
LOWELL
and a frown Amy Lowell got up and all . . . . 249 IS 5 ONE 20   3
LOWEST
absurd fraction in its lowest terms with everything cancelled 295 IS 5 FOUR 12   18
LOWLINESS
have forgot frivolity in lowliness, noting the fatal flight . 81 T&C SON UNRE 6   4
LOWNECKED
breathing as (faithfully) her lownecked dress a little . . . 225 IS 5 ONE LIZ   1
+LOYALTY
FOR CONTEXT, SEE . . . . 546 1 X 1 6   16
LOZENGE
kinesis or frail swooping lozenge. a ruglike sentience whose 201 XLI PORTRAIT 9   16
LUCENT
of His, into the lucent and large signories --i . . . . 210 XLI SONNETS 6   7
LUCIENNE
the long lips of Lucienne which dangle the old . . . . 120 & PORTRAIT 12   21
the long lips of Lucienne which dangle the old . . . . 121 & PORTRAIT 12   58
LUCINDA
(i believe) else thought lucinda looked like steve / . . . . 706 95 POEMS 34   4
LUCK
fortunate is (past the luck of all dead men . . . . 19 T&C PUELLA MEA 103
whistle somebody says here's luck somebody else says down . . 108 & PORTRAIT 4   20
distance a c (h) luck (l) ing of just . . . . 350 VIVA 41   7
make wonderful and is luck The skeleton of life . . . . 395 NO THANKS 12   3
give a fuck for luck they hump them thirteen . . . . 427 NO THANKS 44   3
and have you am luck -y is we lucky . . . . 467 NEW POEMS 5   11
-y is we lucky luck- ier luck -I- est . . . . 467 NEW POEMS 5   12
we lucky luck- ier luck -I- est / / . . . . 467 NEW POEMS 5   14
worlds may have better luck, some day?" "Or worse! . . . . . 603 (CHAIRE) 5   11
aren't or are, good luck! aberdeen plato-rabelais peter jack 605 (CHAIRE) 7   15
world should have the luck to hear such singing . . . . 717 95 POEMS 45   10
people have all the luck; since our hero is . . . . 800 73 POEMS 28   10
+LUCKIER
FOR CONTEXT, SEE . . . . 467 NEW POEMS 5   12
LUCKIEST
i'm by much the luckiest what of the wonder . . . . 590 1 X 1 50   18
tell me this --each luckiest of lucky days i've . . . . 734 95 POEMS 62   2
+LUCKIEST
FOR CONTEXT, SEE . . . . 467 NEW POEMS 5   13
LUCKIH
green? Oilsaisough.) --Hool spairruh luckih? Thangzkeed. . . 310 VIVA 2   8
LUCKILY
do the posed body luckily made a pen is . . . . 141 & SON REAL 12   2
LUCKY
a green mountain the lucky hunter sang before. All . . . . . 14 T&C SONGS 4   30
death should end) how lucky lovers are (whose selves . . . . 446 NO THANKS 61   9
and known where it's lucky to be unlucky and . . . . 466 NEW POEMS 4   19
/ / / lucky means finding Holes where . . . . 467 NEW POEMS 5   1
Holes where pockets aren't lucky 's to spend laughter . . . . 467 NEW POEMS 5   3
spend laughter not money lucky are Breathe grow dream . . . . 467 NEW POEMS 5   6
luck -y is we lucky luck- ier luck -I- . . . . 467 NEW POEMS 5   12
your nearness reaches a lucky fifth of you turns . . . . . . 537 50 POEMS 49   6

453

	PAGE	TITLE	LINE

LUCKY (CONTINUED)
    people say it's un lucky to break one) whole . . . . 623 {CHAIRE} 25   7
    this --each luckiest of lucky days i've loved, shall . . . . 734 95 POEMS 62   2
+LUCKY
    FOR CONTEXT, SEE . . . . 310 VIVA 2   8
    FOR CONTEXT, SEE . . . . 467 NEW POEMS 5   11
+LUCKY'S
    FOR CONTEXT, SEE . . . . 467 NEW POEMS 5   3
LUCY
    sweet old etcetera aunt lucy during the recent war . . . . . 276 IS 5 TWO 10   2
    never say nay but lucy could learn and lily . . . . 509 50 POEMS 23   21
LUDENDORFF
    to shake hands with ludendorff and your humble moving . . . . 324 VIVA 16   12
LUDICROUS
    sting the skinfull of Ludicrous, solidity which a. , ... 159 & SON ACTU 8   10
LUDICROUSLY
    miles the chattering sunset ludicrously dies, i hear only . . 64 T&C POST IMPR 1   9
LUFFED
    c. a. she suddenly luffed --thanking me; and (stating . . . . 326 VIVA 18   35
LUG
    gropeofstrength (staggered by the lug of love) sincerely . . 137 & SON REAL 8   2
LUGBRIN
    the (om nivorou salways lugbrin g ingseekfindlosin g . . . . 403 NO THANKS 20   12
LUGS
    and a waiter cleverly lugs indigestible honeycake to men . . 217 XLI SONNETS 13   8
    unwhores a wai ter lugs his copious whichwhat skilfully . . . 629 {CHAIRE} 31   9
+LUGUBRIOUS
    FOR CONTEXT, SEE . . . . 107 & PORTRAIT 3   10
LUKEWARM
    purchased two bags of lukewarm peanuts with the dime . . . . 326 VIVA 18   15
LULL
    it is utterly to lull with foliate inscrutable sweetness . . 19 T&C PUELLA MEA   87
LULLA
    's lullaby and other lulla wise by UnBroken LULLAlullabyBY . 317 VIVA 9   29
LULLABY
    WELL KNOWn ATHLETE'S BRIDE (lullaby) & z = an . . . . 317 VIVA 9   2
    in each other 's lullaby and other lulla wise . . . . 317 VIVA 9   28
LULLABYLULLABY
    of floating ultrawrists who lullabylullaby (I could have been 317 VIVA 9   6
LULLALULLABYBY
    lulla wise by UnBroken LULLAlullabyBY the She-in-him with the 317 VIVA 9   30
LUMBERMAN
    tightness solid screams whisper.) Lumberman of The Distinct . 195 XLI PORTRAIT 3   16
LUMINOSITY
    toys in unsmooth sexual luminosity spree. --dear) the . . . . 159 & SON ACTU 8   13
LUMINOUS
    chords brittle eager eternal luminous firmly diminishing have 110 & PORTRAIT 6   26
    lithe shuddering big, the luminous laughter, and the legs . . 115 & PORTRAIT 8   24
    gas. clothed with a luminous fur poilu a Jesus . . . . 134 & SON REAL 5   13
    smile makes something suddenly luminous and precise --and . . 152 & SON ACTU 1   13
    intricately alive, cleaving the luminous stammer of bodies . 174 & SON ACTU 23   4
    to Cairo (Egypt) the luminous dithyrambs of large immaculate 266 IS 5 TWO 1   7
    like bridegrooms Naked and luminous (here the absurd I; . . . 281 IS 5 THREE 5   17
    distance is mind carefully luminous with innumerable gnomes . 363 VIVA 54   7
    wonderful that your (how luminous) life toward twilight will 379 VIVA 70   11
    dark beginnings are his luminous ends who far less . . . . . 420 NO THANKS 37   10
    and meaningless secret on luminous whose selves and lives . . 456 NO THANKS 71   2
    hunted by daemons seethe luminous leopards (on wingfeet of . 586 1 X 1 46   15
    until (eternally) with (now) luminous the shadow of love . . 601 {CHAIRE} 3   16
    will actually lift a luminous whole; turn sheer despairing . 649 {CHAIRE} 51   5
    / / / / luminous tendril of celestial wish . . . . 669 {CHAIRE} 71   1
    or if (spiralling as luminous they climb oblivion) voices . . 810 73 POEMS 38   5
    the o f her luminous se lf a shy . . . . 831 73 POEMS 59   7
+LUMINOUS
    FOR CONTEXT, SEE . . . . 96 & POST IMPR 8   32
    FOR CONTEXT, SEE . . . . 179 XLI SONGS 1   4
    FOR CONTEXT, SEE . . . . 493 50 POEMS 7   12

		PAGE	TITLE	LINE
LUMINOUSLY				
oh) the iceman how, luminously oh how listens and, ...		251	IS 5 ONE 22	15
LUMP				
my soul a limp lump of lymph she kissed		133	& SON REAL 4	19
within itself moo ving lump of twilight squirts a		602	(CHAIRE) 4	2
+LUMP				
FOR CONTEXT, SEE		522	50 POEMS 35	5
LUMPS				
thing silent spits discrete lumps of noise.... furniture . .		159	& SON ACTU 8	7
LUNDUN				
guys talks big about Lundun Burlin an gay Paree		237	IS 5 ONE 8	5
LUNE				
ph or ? la lune / / / /		831	73 POEMS 59	19
LUNG				
and Mary with one lung extended to the pumping		142	& SON REAL 13	10
LUNGE				
curiously con) --but the lunge of Her hunger softly		77	T&C SON UNRE 2	5
(touch) ems crouch (lunge)ing bruiseD Suddenly by		388	NO THANKS 5	4
LUNGING				
Far below myself the lunging leer of horizontal large		202	XLI PORTRAIT 9	35
+LUNGING				
FOR CONTEXT, SEE		705	95 POEMS 33	8
LUNGS				
Things which bulge: grunting lungs pumped full of sharp . . .		195	XLI PORTRAIT 3	4
trull leaps from the lungs "gimme uh swell fite		227	IS 5 ONE GERT	14
our mouths fears hearts lungs arms hopes feet hands		283	IS 5 THREE 7	2
LURCH				
with thinned newfragile yellows lurch and. press --in the . .		163	& SON ACTU 12	11
whycol our ed shy lurch small invin cible nod		349	VIVA 40	14
darts pierced lazily writhe lurch faceflowers stutter		436	NO THANKS 52	9
and which under burst lurch things phantoms curl (mouth . . .		565	1 X 1 25	2
/ / light's lives lurch a once world quickly		633	(CHAIRE) 35	1
+LURCH				
FOR CONTEXT, SEE		388	NO THANKS 5	17
LURCHE				
l of peopl e lurche s viv idly from		703	95 POEMS 31	6
LURCHED				
my Uncle Sol's coffin lurched because somebody pressed a . .		239	IS 5 ONE 10	33
LURE				
but should voices (whom lure an eagerest strict flame) . . .		362	VIVA 53	9
LURK				
all the whys which lurk between your naked shoulderblades. .		282	IS 5 THREE 6	22
goodness truth and beauty lurk, simply to her does		790	73 POEMS 18	9
LURKS				
move (as her ghost lurks, a Beau Brummell sticking		227	IS 5 ONE GERT	4
our unlighted hearts lust lurks slovenly and homeless and . .		322	VIVA 14	10
LUSCIOUS				
palace intricate (whereof the luscious pillars rise which are		21	T&C PUELLA MEA	203
the world is mud- luscious the little lame balloonman		24	T&C CHANSONS 1	3
flatness the Bar. tinking luscious jigs dint of ripe		96	& POST IMPR 8	11
+LUSHLY				
FOR CONTEXT, SEE		342	VIVA 33	23
LUST				
toy with thy extraordinary lust, (the sinuous rain which . .		3	T&C EPITHALAM	4
flower; let not thy lust one threaded moment lose:		9	T&C SONGS 1	7
shadow lolls sobbing with lust / / / /		28	T&C ORIENTALE 2	17
creates patterns of sudden lust her stealing body ex-		34	T&C ORIENTALE 6	89
ghastly warriors amber with lust breathe together the		34	T&C ORIENTALE 6	98
a smile--and she is Lust.... mine also, little painted . . .		75	T&C SON REAL 6	13
silver tube of wise lust whose arms and legs		110	& PORTRAIT 6	6
the winds of my lust like a high troubling		112	& PORTRAIT 6	96
its omelet of fluffy lust) at six exactly the		132	& SON REAL 3	10
between our unlighted hearts lust lurks slovenly and homeless		322	VIVA 14	10
LUSTFUL				
become perfectly and simply Lustful.... sense a gradual stir		157	& SON ACTU 6	3
LUSTFULHUNCHED				
be dead knead of lustfulhunched deeplytoplay lips and stare .		153	& SON ACTU 2	5

	PAGE	TITLE	LINE

LUSTING
with his gradual acute lusting glance an alert clumsily . . . 374 VIVA 65   5
LUSTRE
fall a thread of lustre from the castle wall . . . . 8 T&C OF NICOL   23
LUSTS
unpleasantly tremendous. under flat lusts of light her nice . 103 & POST IMPR 13   15
sole mass my separate lusts her hair was like . . . . 135 & SON REAL 6   5
LUXURIES
use a highfalootin phrase luxuries that is or to . . . . . . 239 IS 5 ONE 10   10
+LUXURIOUS
FOR CONTEXT, SEE . . . . 334 VIVA 25   2
LUXURY
not quarrelling in a luxury of telescoped languages) she . . 312 VIVA 4   14
LYDIA
of Abraham Lincoln and Lydia E. Pinkham, land above . . . . 230 IS 5 ONE 2   11
welates Wouldwoe Washington to Lydia E. McKinley when Buch . 321 VIVA 13   6
LYING
on sharpening air. Fields lying miraculous in violent silence 86 T&C SON ACTU 5   7
(or) someThing i was lying on the bar it . . . . 123 & SEVEN POEMS 2   3
nothing, he murmurs carefully lying down) / / / . . . . 299 IS 5 FOUR 16   16
sit may take it lying down) down with the . . . . 466 NEW POEMS 4   4
least street) of mirror lying are each (why do . . . . 623 {CHAIRE} 25   5
LYMAN
it's a" old mr lyman ruddy as a sunrise . . . . 567 1 X 1 27   17
+LYMAN
FOR CONTEXT, SEE . . . . 567 1 X 1 27   1
LYMOLES
ly; though hither nosing lymoles cru. Ising thither: t, . . . 361 VIVA 52   11
LYMPH
a limp lump of lymph she kissed and i . . . . 133 & SON REAL 4   20
LYRE
as music haunts the lyre, a creature of white . . . . 8 T&C OF NICOL   21
M
believing science=(2b)-n herr professor m / / / / . . . . . . 329 VIVA 20   4
dick son fec i (m c) t (m x . . . . 388 NO THANKS 5   32
i (m c) t (m x x x ii) . . . . 388 NO THANKS 5   35
n than in the m / / / / . . . . 488 50 POEMS 2   25
o w (A) a (M) s / / / . . . . 740 95 POEMS 68   11
M'AIME
consubstantial intangibility. Personne ne m'aime et j'ai les 262 IS 5 ONE 32   26
M'AIMENT
belle cheri? les anglais m'aiment tous, les americains . . . 120 & PORTRAIT 12   12
+MA'AM
FOR CONTEXT, SEE . . . . 108 & PORTRAIT 4   16
FOR CONTEXT, SEE . . . . 553 1 X 1 13   11
MABEL
per every madge and mabel dick and dave --tomorrow . . . . 579 1 X 1 39   11
(cracked) open that heart, mabel & you'll find a . . . . . . 637 {CHAIRE} 39   4
+MACHINATIONS
FOR CONTEXT, SEE . . . . 807 73 POEMS 35   10
MACHINE
all here is hands machine no good too quick . . . . 523 50 POEMS 36   10
is the most dangerous machine as yet invented by . . . . . . 644 {CHAIRE} 46   2
by brain) more than machine turns less than beast . . . . . 787 73 POEMS 15   11
MACHINERY
forth your flowers and machinery: sculpture and prose flowers 264 IS 5 ONE 33   9
flowers guess and miss machinery is the more accurate, . . . 264 IS 5 ONE 33   11
MACK
SUB JUDICE LIS when mack smacked phyllis on the . . . . . . 706 95 POEMS 34   1
MAD
rain? And still the mad magnificent herald Spring assembles . 4 T&C EPITHALAM   57
when the world was mad and Launcelot spoke to . . . . 18 T&C PUELLA MEA   56
world was young and mad, in the city of . . . . 20 T&C PUELLA MEA   131
when i entered a mad street whose mouth dripped . . . . . . 194 XLI PORTRAIT 2   4
is something faithful and mad" / / / / . . . . 303 IS 5 FIVE 2   16
undiscoverable guess of whose mad skill each world of . . . . 424 NO THANKS 41   13
Boobs are holy, poets mad, illustrious punks of Progress . . 438 NO THANKS 54   19
fail it is most mad and moonly and less . . . . 530 50 POEMS 42   5

MAD (CONTINUED)
the lamed ones; the mad moronic maimed) all except . . . . . 619 {CHAIRE} 21   18
past imagining whowhich of mad rags strode earth ignorantly . 662 {CHAIRE} 64   6
(dropp ingspinson his back mad) fly (ly who all . . . . 692 95 POEMS 20   5
had; making annie slightly mad but very wonderful in . . . . 794 73 POEMS 22   5
MADAM
Dick Mid's Place the madam was a bulb stuck . . . . 73 T&C SON REAL 4   2
/ / the waddling madam star taps taps. "ready . . . . 108 & PORTRAIT 4   2
whisper, "even her." "The Madam?" I emitted; vaguely watching 228 IS 5 ONE MARJ   11
MADAM'S
/ / on the Madam's best april the twenty . . . . 251 IS 5 ONE 22   1
MADAME
magdalene of whoisit and madame something by gainsborough . . 198 XLI PORTRAIT 6   11
man would have from madame death neverless now and . . . . . 531 50 POEMS 43   9
MADDER
dress was a suspicious madder, importing the cruelty of . . . 103 & POST IMPR 13   1
MADE
the prince of artists made him bold to imitate . . . .   4 T&C EPITHALAM   35
with beads of dew made jewels by the sun, ...   8 T&C OF NICOL   16
words which i have made. And never boast your . . . . 22 T&C PUELLA MEA 242
was like a tale made of laughter and of . . . . 23 T&C PUELLA MEA 277
two ladies like flowers made, softly used to wholly . . . . . 23 T&C PUELLA MEA 282
wholly move slender ladies made of dream (in the . . . . . . 23 T&C PUELLA MEA 284
adoration if i have made a fragile certain song . . . . 43 T&C AMORES 7   3
do, world is probably made of roses & hello: . . . . 66 T&C POST IMPR 3 15
peculiar mouth my heart made wise; at moments when . . . . . 78 T&C SON UNRE 3   4
flower (if i have made songs it does not . . . . 84 T&C SON ACTU 3   6
ges- tures stickily point made glints squinting who's a . . . 96 & POST IMPR 8   18
cHuckling like uninteresting- landscapes made interesting by 101 & POST IMPR 11   70
head whose brains are made of gingerbread when the . . . . . 117 & PORTRAIT 10   2
head whose brains are made of gingerbread / / . . . . 118 & PORTRAIT 10   44
bar the bar was made of brass hangIng from . . . . 123 & SEVEN POEMS 2   2
way men you liked made you feel when they . . . . 127 & SEVEN POEMS 5 37
can feel what you made, men feel when, you . . . . 127 & SEVEN POEMS 5 39
the posed body luckily made a pen is dreadfully . . . . 141 & SON REAL 12   2
eye that rolled and made its point Jimmie's sister . . . . . 149 & SON REAL 20   6
distress these hips were made for Horizontal Business (set . 150 & SON REAL 21   7
how terrible inches speech--it made you a little dizzy . . . 174 & SON REAL 23   11
wrath of blossoms dishevelling made a pale fracas upon . . . 214 XLI SONNETS 10   8
felt of her radiator made sure her springs were . . . . . . 248 IS 5 ONE 19   8
first of all really made quite a mistake in . . . . 262 IS 5 ONE 32   5
If i should have made this perfectly clear, it . . . . 263 IS 5 ONE 32   64
dream nascitur, is not made...) why then to Hell . . . . . . 264 IS 5 ONE 33   29
and quite silently hills made of blueandgreen paper . . . . 278 IS 5 THREE 2   6
but i being otherwise made compose curves and yellows, . . . 291 IS 5 FOUR 8   3
how smiling may be made as skilfully.) But carry . . . . . . 294 IS 5 FOUR 11   13
light hush we are made of the same thing . . . . 299 IS 5 FOUR 16   15
looked at them, and made verses, through the sharp . . . . . 302 IS 5 FIVE 1   14
/ if i have made, my lady, intricate imperfect . . . . 306 IS 5 FIVE 5   1
a vow but both made sense in when's haymow . . . . 316 VIVA 8   15
departs our lips are made of thing in beginning . . . . . . 322 VIVA 14   12
the way trees are Made leaves open Clouds take . . . . 359 VIVA 50   11
around (as poems are made) Our picking it. this . . . . . . 364 VIVA 55   9
for selves more strangely made (wears pain at joy, ... 394 NO THANKS 11   6
world of blood is made (whose fatal songs are . . . . 424 NO THANKS 41   13
/ / this mind made war being generous this . . . . 440 NO THANKS 56   1
their names (this poet made war whose naught and . . . . . . 440 NO THANKS 56   24
are both making silence two-made-of-one & nothing tells . . . 483 NEW POEMS 21   6
are three with faces made of cloud dancing and . . . . 507 50 POEMS 21   6
three singing with voices made of earth and six . . . . . . 507 50 POEMS 21   8
molehills are from mountains made --long enough and just . . 511 50 POEMS 25   3
singing forever a song made of silent as stone . . . . 525 50 POEMS 37   22
that someone called they made him pay with his . . . . 543 1 X 1 3   24
exercise her vote (or made by threats of something . . . . . 544 1 X 1 4   11
unself. A world of made is not a world . . . . 554 1 X 1 14   9
rise eyes "this world's made 'bout right it's the . . . . . . 567 1 X 1 27   9
when to me you made for by love love . . . . 589 1 X 1 49   5
only) a silence only made of, bird / / . . . . 612 {CHAIRE} 14   14

MADE (CONTINUED)

you go until you've made me white" so she . . . . 622 (CHAIRE) 24   6
his that (sh) who made the world's best one . . . . 645 (CHAIRE) 47   4
to you yes closer made of nothing except loneliness . . . . . 648 (CHAIRE) 50   11
silence through twilight's mystery made flesh-- dreamslender 669 (CHAIRE) 71   8
(and we alone had) made --yes; or as if . . . . 675 95 POEMS 3   8
times in its life made three) brawny and brainy . . . . . . 709 95 POEMS 37   8
joy and anguish) who've made her, outglory glory the . . . . 742 95 POEMS 70   9
die) but worlds are made of hello and goodbye: . . . . 776 73 POEMS 4   37
words --our second coming made stones sing like birds-- . . . 844 73 POEMS 72   2

MADEMOISELLE

is this dai nty mademoiselle the o f her . . . . 831 73 POEMS 59   4

MADEOFIMAGINATION

Disappears some thing (silent: madeofimagination ; the . . . 397 NO THANKS 14   22

MADGE

/ / / Where's Madge then, Madge and her . . . . 183 XLI SONGS 5   1
/ Where's Madge then, Madge and her men? buried . . . . . . 183 XLI SONGS 5   2
how much earth is Madge worth? Inquire of the . . . . 183 XLI SONGS 5   13
to shrillerness per every madge and mabel dick and . . . . . 579 1 X 1 39   11

+MADLY

FOR CONTEXT, SEE . . . . 692 95 POEMS 20   5

MADNESS

heaven combine with earth's madness) --'tis a gate unto . . . 21 T&C PUELLA MEA 201
an evilfringing flower of madness on gritted lips and . . . . 139 & SON REAL 10   9
incessant putrid spikes of madness (at Myself's height these 202 XLI PORTRAIT 9   38
fear a white with madness wind and broke oceans . . . . . . 432 NO THANKS 49   16
doing shall undo (nor madness nor mere death nor . . . . . . 577 1 X 1 37   10
(more secret or than madness did reveal) deeper is . . . . . 592 1 X 1 52   2

MADONNA

phantoms (exchanging) e vero madonna (nudge whispershout) . . 681 95 POEMS 9   7

MADOX

sunful sin namely (ford madox ford) and eke to . . . . . . 607 (CHAIRE) 9   14

MAENADS

loud lord of skipping maenads knows,-- having Discordia's . . 6 T&C EPITHALAM 150

MAETERLINCK

drinks what's become of Maeterlinck now that April's here? . 233 IS 5 ONE 4   21

MAG

the comedy kid.... Fran Mag Glad Dorothy / / . . . . 138 & SON REAL 9   17

MAGAZINE

/ "let's start a magazine to hell with literature . . . . . 407 NO THANKS 24   1

MAGDALEN

silent smileless eyes of Magdalen. The lights have laughed . 75 T&C SON REAL 6   8

MAGDALENE

flanked by the scrumptious magdalene of whoisit and madame . 198 XLI PORTRAIT 6   10

MAGGIE

/ / / / maggie and milly and molly . . . . 682 95 POEMS 10   1
play one day) and maggie discovered a shell that . . . . . . 682 95 POEMS 10   3

MAGGOTY

all utterly things sweet, maggoty minus and dumb death . . . 521 50 POEMS 34   63

MAGIC

Thus, Around the reckless magic of your mouth) my . . . . . . 83 T&C SON ACTU 2   8
love is building a magic, a discrete tower of . . . . 83 T&C SON ACTU 2   9
a discrete tower of magic and (as i guess) . . . . 83 T&C SON ACTU 2   10
an untimid svelte subdued magic while in your eyes . . . . . 138 & SON REAL 9   6
choke-- hair-thin strands of magic agony ....by day this . . 146 & SON REAL 17   8
by one with his magic stick (in which a . . . . 282 IS 5 THREE 6   26
should disappear moon's utmost magic, or stones speak or . . 377 VIVA 68   4
a deathless life with magic until peace outthunders silence. 428 NO THANKS 45   16
throw dynamite) let knowings magic with bright credos each . 452 NO THANKS 67   6
he a moon a magic out of the black . . . . 493 50 POEMS 7   9
adventure soon a deeper magic: that white sleep wherein . . . 675 95 POEMS 3   11
is everywhere beginningless a Magic of green solitude (go . . 757 95 POEMS 85   15
/ / / plant Magic dust expect hope doubt . . . . 780 73 POEMS 8   1

MAGICAL

dwells beside the vivid magical impetuous and utter ponds . . 19 T&C PUELLA MEA 116
into leasting forever most magical maybes of certainly never 495 50 POEMS 9   14
his quiet head his magical shoulders him doll self) . . . . . 516 50 POEMS 30   11
leapandswooping tinily birds whose magical gaiety makes your 631 (CHAIRE) 33   12

		PAGE	TITLE	LINE

MAGICAL (CONTINUED)
    pick ing up a magical stick t, a, p, ... 697 95 POEMS 25   8
    by doll) motionless under magical foreverfully falling snow. 777 73 POEMS 5   12
    winter afternoon (at the magical hour when is becomes . . . . 802 73 POEMS 30   2
+MAGICAL
    FOR CONTEXT, SEE . . . . 554 1 X 1 14   12
MAGICALLY
    slowly all together very magically smiling and if we . . . . 600 (CHAIRE) 2   10
    include --there by arriving magically here-- an everywhere . 741 95 POEMS 69   11
    who's beauty: reoccurs so magically, farthest becomes near . 818 73 POEMS 46   7
+MAGICALLY
    FOR CONTEXT, SEE . . . . 829 73 POEMS 57   14
MAGICIANS
    the greatest of living magicians (whom you and i . . . . . . 738 95 POEMS 66   5
MAGNETIC
    large less than more magnetic pink unwhores a wai . . . . . . 629 (CHAIRE) 31   7
MAGNIFICENCE
    oblivious west's numerous dun magnificence conquers . . . . . 6 T&C EPITHALAM 128
    numerous dun magnificence conquers magnificence. In heaven's 6 T&C EPITHALAM 128
MAGNIFICENT
    And still the mad magnificent herald Spring assembles beauty 4 T&C EPITHALAM 57
    before whose upward lean magnificent face the streets turn . 93 & POST IMPR 5   3
    purple thought against the magnificent clamor of day tortured 188 XLI SONGS 10   5
    disenchanted eyes live the magnificent honesty of space. . . 675 95 POEMS 3   4
    prodigious a now of magnificent sound (which makes this . . . 841 73 POEMS 69   12
MAGUS
    the divine alchemist, the magus of creation, lifts a . . . . 6 T&C EPITHALAM 134
MAID
    says it is a maid says Who and (hearing . . . . 570 1 X 1 30   2
MAIDENS
    beget the spring that maidens whom passion wastes will . . . 16 T&C SONGS 6   7
    your way youths and maidens: let us pray / . . . . 794 73 POEMS 22   8
MAIDS
    away (but born are maids to flower an hour . . . . 509 50 POEMS 23   4
    out of houses pour maids mothers widows wives bringing . . . 624 (CHAIRE) 26   6
MAILLOLS
    calmly as if aristide maillols occurred with any ticking . . 617 (CHAIRE) 19   13
MAIMED
    ones; the mad moronic maimed) all except the dead . . . . . . 619 (CHAIRE) 21   19
MAIMS
    here love everywhere exploding maims and blinds (but surely . 377 VIVA 68   8
MAINLY
    a wraith's progress or mainly awash while chiefly submerged . 410 NO THANKS 27   11
MAINS
    m'aime et j'ai les mains froides. His Royal Highness . . . . 262 IS 5 ONE 32   26
MAJESTIC
    thick cheerful man with majestic bulbous lips and forlorn . . 56 T&C PORTRAIT 4   11
    (captured by a policeman's majestic and buried eye) the . . . 324 VIVA 16   4
MAJORITIES
    "the divine right of majorities, that illegitimate offspring 803 73 POEMS 31   2
MAKE
    / / Thy fingers make early flowers of all . . . . 13 T&C SONGS 3   1
    her face doth immediately make in my heart so . . . . 18 T&C PUELLA MEA 64
    sweet instinctive wells, which make to flourish the minute . 19 T&C PUELLA MEA 122
    love them and to make them glad, when the . . . . 20 T&C PUELLA MEA 130
    love them and to make them glad ladies with . . . . 22 T&C PUELLA MEA 224
    and streets skilfully to make a possible and beautiful . . . 92 & POST IMPR 4   12
    of day) i surely make a millionth poem which . . . . 92 & POST IMPR 4   19
    girls". the unspontaneous streets make bright their eyes a . 108 & PORTRAIT 4   6
    come eleven m m make the world safe for . . . . 125 & SEVEN POEMS 4 11
    tingling limbs from me: make my pain their crazy . . . . . . 139 & SON REAL 10   2
    or unnoise men don't make soup who drink. / . . . . 141 & SON REAL 18   18
    of body, which will make oddly to strut my . . . . 155 & SON ACTU 4   10
    itself, as not to make an error, with twists . . . . 170 & SON ACTU 19   10
    of swift flesh i make me stern against your . . . . 182 XLI SONGS 4   13
    sharp thick mind you make us shrill presents always . . . . . 195 XLI PORTRAIT 3   5
    cents dear friends to make it an even dollar . . . . 196 XLI PORTRAIT 4   14
    no thy flight and make me a child, a . . . . 233 IS 5 ONE 4   4

MAKE (CONTINUED)

grandja that was dada? make me a child, stout . . . . 233 IS 5 ONE 4   14
child, stout hurdysturdygurdyman waiter, make me a child. So 233 IS 5 ONE 4   15
even so, let us make haste --consider well this . . . . 260 IS 5 ONE 30   21
altogether foolish, i suddenly make a fist out of . . . . . . 281 IS 5 THREE 5   19
so interested but you make me laft welates Wouldwoe . . . . . 321 VIVA 13   4
and emerging (believably enlarged) make how many stopped . . 337 VIVA 28   3
must go sometimes, to make an earth gladly seem . . . . 372 VIVA 63   8
nor bewail (would rather make than have and give . . . . . . 394 NO THANKS 11   11
why How many winds make wonderful and is luck . . . . 395 NO THANKS 12   2
ammunicions who tend to make incitions and pity the . . . . . 405 NO THANKS 22   8
not spoil it let's make it serious something authentic . . . 407 NO THANKS 24   10
form (actually) realness kill (make strangely) known . . . . 422 NO THANKS 39   9
dare not share) such make their names (this poet . . . . . . 440 NO THANKS 56   23
kykerplung guit ar (pleez make me glad) dis dumdam . . . . . 519 50 POEMS 33   7
of the birch to make an acorn--valleys accuse their . . . . . 520 50 POEMS 34   10
living thing) and we'll make yes / / / . . . . 528 50 POEMS 40   14
co which paid to make man free (for man . . . . 552 1 X 1 12   2
lies by mortals told make two. Let liars wilt, ... 556 1 X 1 16   10
of original soon or make it ten times ten . . . . 561 1 X 1 21   7
need sunbeams or snowflakes make possible mayflowers: quite . 577 1 X 1 37   3
herculanean my mortal) yoo make sno eye kil yoo . . . . 618 (CHAIRE) 20   5
to realize i can't make it clearer war just . . . . 638 (CHAIRE) 40   7
a little innocence will make them sing; teach them . . . . . 649 (CHAIRE) 51   2
are laws) laugh, and make each no thy yes: . . . . 651 (CHAIRE) 53   10
most catastrophe april might make alive filthy some past . . 662 (CHAIRE) 64   4
and goodness do not make a fellow tall" lily . . . . 684 95 POEMS 12   16
snow-- a whom we make (of grin for smile . . . . 716 95 POEMS 44   5
when sun and rain make april my life is . . . . 749 95 POEMS 77   4
break in two he'd make them one (his song's . . . . 760 95 POEMS 87   8
timelessness whose absence would make your whole life and . . 817 73 POEMS 45   13
every silence will not make a dream speak; or . . . . 842 73 POEMS 70   10

+MAKE

FOR CONTEXT, SEE . . . . 310 VIVA 2   6

MAKER

go crisp with miracle. Love!--maker of my lady, in . . . . . 22 T&C PUELLA MEA 237

MAKES

of almostness which May makes follow soon on the . . . . . . 10 T&C SONGS 1   38
while caressed its fragrance makes the lover blest.) Her . . 21 T&C PUELLA MEA 192
small bored gesture that makes the children laugh. But . . . 69 T&C POST IMPR 6   19
little pushings of flesh, makes my body sorry when . . . . . 82 T&C SON ACTU 1   3
behind your back it makes your neck feel pleasant . . . . . . 126 & SEVEN POEMS 5   19
long smile it sometimes makes gaily go clean through . . . . 147 & SON REAL 18   6
the tool her smile makes something suddenly luminous and . . 152 & SON ACTU 1   12
waiting for god knows makes me wonder if i'm . . . . 166 & SON ACTU 15   9
the. fire-escapes-- the night. makes me wonder if, if . . . . 166 & SON ACTU 15   12
not tell where.) beauty makes terms with time and . . . . . 183 XLI SONGS 5   7
well oh don't you makes burst want to dear . . . . 251 IS 5 ONE 22   12
and first to live makes unimportant what i and . . . . 264 IS 5 ONE 33   19
never doubt my weakness makes more than most strength . . . . 433 NO THANKS 50   7
everything perverse or which makes some feel more better . . 466 NEW POEMS 4   23
love whose any mystery makes every man's flesh put . . . . . 484 NEW POEMS 22   7
much greenness only dying makes us grow / / . . . . 491 50 POEMS 5   16
(with more simplicity than makes a world) / / . . . . 506 50 POEMS 20   14
value neither is love makes the little thickness of . . . . . 531 50 POEMS 43   8
itself or someone else makes no more difference than . . . . 549 1 X 1 9   10
have darkly themselves unmade makes love armies (than hate . 580 1 X 1 40   14
clover knows, maybe" (heart makes the suggestion) "or even . 625 (CHAIRE) 27   11
birds whose magical gaiety makes your beautiful name-- i . . 631 (CHAIRE) 33   12
and with a something makes the oldest man (whoever . . . . . 685 95 POEMS 13   14
dream that your valentine makes happier me than i . . . . . . 718 95 POEMS 46   4
disappearance but some keener makes losing, gaining --love! . 750 95 POEMS 78   13
mongrel creed is Might Makes Right --his royal warcry . . . . 774 73 POEMS 2   11
or simply Is what makes you feel you aren't . . . . 779 73 POEMS 7   21
such golden blood as makes his moon alive sing . . . . 811 73 POEMS 39   13
/ mi (dreamlike) st makes big each dim inuti . . . . 829 73 POEMS 57   2
merely know (freedom: what makes a slave) therefore, my . . . 834 73 POEMS 62   9
one dead leaf stirring makes a crash --far away . . . . 839 73 POEMS 67   4

MAKES (CONTINUED)

of magnificent sound (which makes this whenworld squirm turns 841 73 POEMS 69   14

+MAKES

FOR CONTEXT, SEE . . . . 423 NO THANKS 40   37

MAKETH

when frost to dance maketh the sagest pane of . . . . 207 XLI SONNETS 3   3

MAKIN

Hell Bent fer election makin believe dey was chust . . . . . 237 IS 5 ONE 8   19

MAKING

in the unshapeful hour making dear moan in tones . . . . . .   9 T&C SONGS 1   6

/ / / in making Marjorie god hurried a . . . . 148 & SON REAL 19   1

spears and The Then-arrows making do our mouths something . . 160 & SON ACTU 9   16

little dints of april, making the obscene shy breasts . . . . 172 & SON ACTU 21   14

because you are forever making poems in the lap . . . . 204 XLI LA GUERRE 2   23

a with eyes and making twice the a week . . . . 251 IS 5 ONE 22   7

smile in his mouth (making everything suddenly old and . . . 293 IS 5 FOUR 10   26

thinner than a hair) making me feel how myself . . . . 301 IS 5 FOUR 18   7

a spoon are both making silence two-made-of-one & nothing . . 483 NEW POEMS 21   5

and who illimitably is) making fools understand (like wintry 736 95 POEMS 64   5

tell your mother") had; making annie slightly mad but . . . . 794 73 POEMS 22   5

+MAKING

FOR CONTEXT, SEE . . . . 658 {CHAIRE} 60   13

MALADIES

perished of unheard of maladies including flu) my little . . 266 IS 5 TWO 1   15

MALE

his din of wallowing male (shock beyond shock blurted) . . . 115 & PORTRAIT 8   13

-ned on people (both male and female created He . . . . 267 IS 5 TWO 2   18

their millions of stopped male to look at (now . . . . 337 VIVA 28   5

attend! list, every nonelastic male-- uplook, all joybegotten 398 NO THANKS 15   17

MALEORE

of Marie and of Maleore findeth of ladies goodly . . . . . . 21 T&C PUELLA MEA 172

MALES

Ingharness Of curvish (,males await she patiently 1 . . . . 342 VIVA 33   17

al most fe (hug) males (one-t wo-1 oop-1 eftsthrowr . . . . . 388 NO THANKS 5   14

MALICE

phenomenon (too gay for malice and too wise for . . . . 607 {CHAIRE} 9   12

MAM

him, and general (yes mam) sherman; and even (believe . . . . 553 1 X 1 13   11

MAMA

the dime which her mama had generously provided (despite . . 326 VIVA 18   17

+MAMA

FOR CONTEXT, SEE . . . . 790 73 POEMS 18   16

MAME

/ / / / MAME she puts down the . . . . 226 IS 5 ONE MAME   T

MAMMAL

day the hulking perpendicular mammal a grim epitome of . . . 151 & SON REAL 22   3

MAN

the crown sweetest to man, whose lilied robe the . . . . . .   3 T&C EPITHALAM   28

drives the wingless thing man forth into bright air, ...   4 T&C EPITHALAM   61

i see a frail man dreaming dreams dreams in . . . . 50 T&C IMPRESS 4   19

their houses the frail man is in his bed . . . . 50 T&C IMPRESS 4   28

crowd whinnied and a man squeezing her waist said . . . . . . 53 T&C PORTRAIT 1   35

father a thick cheerful man with majestic bulbous lips . . . 56 T&C PORTRAIT 4   10

/ / the young man sitting in Dick Mid's . . . . 57 T&C PORTRAIT 5   2

striving of that old man who at her redstone . . . . 57 T&C PORTRAIT 5   10

keep" always? the young man sitting in Dick Mid's . . . . . . 57 T&C PORTRAIT 5   23

a romantic tired business man somewhat tweaked and dinted . . 57 T&C PORTRAIT 5   32

lips of an old man murder the petals hush . . . . 59 T&C PORTRAIT 7   3

lips of an old man murder the petals. / . . . . 59 T&C PORTRAIT 7   16

he was a handsome man and what i want . . . . 60 T&C PORTRAIT 8   8

Lincoln somebody Xerxes this man: a narrow thudding . . . . . 62 T&C PORTRAIT 10   2

irresponsible toys.) when this man with the brittle legs . . 62 T&C PORTRAIT 10   23

/ / / any man is wonderful and a . . . . 68 T&C POST IMPR 5   1

the shabby tiny smiling, man in whose hand the . . . . 69 T&C POST IMPR 6   8

the monkeyandtheorgan and the man are dancing slowly are . . 69 T&C POST IMPR 6   25

the tiny smiling shabby man is yelling over the . . . . 69 T&C POST IMPR 6   33

to be known; and man, whose here is always . . . . 81 T&C SON UNRE 6   11

Life is an old man carrying flowers on his . . . . 102 & POST IMPR 12   2

		PAGE	TITLE	LINE
MAN (CONTINUED)

nothing or an old man 3 thirds asleep, on	102	& POST IMPR 12	13
smile like the nicest man you've never met who	126	& SEVEN POEMS 5	14
called death get another man with firmer lips to	161	& SON ACTU 10	2
and the rather fat man in bluishsuspenders half-reading the .	166	& SON ACTU 15	6
thy hands what no man feels, no woman understands.	212	XLI SONNETS 8	14
April's here? (ask the man who owns one ask	233	IS 5 ONE 4	23
/ / ITEM this man is o so Waiter	243	IS 5 ONE 14	1
interminable pyramidal, napkins (this man is oh so tired . .	243	IS 5 ONE 14	7
softish almost round young man to whom headwaiters bow . . .	245	IS 5 ONE 16	7
this young question mark man question mark who suffers . . .	246	IS 5 ONE 17	1
horned suddenly crashing things) man spits quickly into the .	252	IS 5 ONE 23	11
/ / / a man who had fallen among	258	IS 5 ONE 28	1
was kilt a handsome man and James and next	271	IS 5 TWO 6	3
photographed the son of man goes forth to war	273	IS 5 TWO 8	23
clumsily which devours a man, three cats, five white	279	IS 5 THREE 3	7
whispering like a drunken man who (at a certain	304	IS 5 FIVE 3	3
but two occupy a man and his wife: Both	312	VIVA 4	10
was murdered by a man named Smith and we	313	VIVA 5	10
Beatific Lord of Creation, MAN: at a least crooking	315	VIVA 7	13
aboard all to--mendaciously speaking--a man wrongers who . .	334	VIVA 25	6
is dead the only man woman or child who	336	VIVA 27	3
have seen on any man-- a little fluttering, at	344	VIVA 35	8
/ i met a man under the moon on	355	VIVA 46	1
window, behold ghosts, a man hugging a woman in	375	VIVA 66	7
/ / / little man (in a hurry full	393	NO THANKS 10	1
afraid) each hates a Man whom both would call	394	NO THANKS 11	9
this (that grey) white (man) horse floats on 4	408	NO THANKS 25	3
always men while a man shall which a god	414	NO THANKS 31	14
/ / conceive a man, should he have anything	420	NO THANKS 37	1
nothing) World, conceive a man / / / /	420	NO THANKS 37	14
beside the who limps man crying silence upward --to	437	NO THANKS 53	11
to call himself a man? go dreamless knaves on	438	NO THANKS 54	8
to call himself a man? loudly for Truth have	438	NO THANKS 54	16
to call himself a man? King Christ, this world	438	NO THANKS 54	24
to call Himself a man. / / / /	438	NO THANKS 54	28
greet this fool and man / / / /	441	NO THANKS 56	68
nonvisibly smi- ling through man -ufactured harmlessly . . .	464	NEW POEMS 2	18
bundl e of what man can 't hurt any	472	NEW POEMS 10	14
is living said a man (who could not earn	473	NEW POEMS 11	2
hot spell with o man what bubbies going places	476	NEW POEMS 14	5
might have been a man and kept a date	479	NEW POEMS 17	9
ideas can swallow a man; three words im -prison	491	50 POEMS 5	13
inhuman itarian fetish that man isn't wuman vive the	492	50 POEMS 6	8
what (of a crazy man) don't ask me how	501	50 POEMS 15	5
the moon in the man. Up sam (down! alice)	513	50 POEMS 27	19
was blood: no hungry man but wished him food;	520	50 POEMS 34	30
true one generous child- man -god one eager souldoll	524	50 POEMS 36	42
all small and sad man, may his mighty briefness	526	50 POEMS 38	4
fiend? i give you man extracted hate from whispering . . .	527	50 POEMS 39	8
coin comes here a man would have from madame	531	50 POEMS 43	9
the blessings which to man kind progress doth impart . . .	544	1 X 1 4	1
is compulsory and only man is god. Without a	544	1 X 1 4	24
has sat except a man / / / /	550	1 X 1 10	2
which paid to make man free (for man is	552	1 X 1 12	2
make man free (for man is enslaved by a	552	1 X 1 12	3
and raddios) did save man from himself ye duskiest	552	1 X 1 12	15
hells having wrestled with) man drops into his own	558	1 X 1 18	2
secret will still be man what if a keen	560	1 X 1 20	8
/ / / no man, if men are gods;	562	1 X 1 22	1
men, the sometimes only man is this (most common, ...	562	1 X 1 22	2
and everything began when man determined to destroy himself .	566	1 X 1 26	5
with blue true two man neral rise eyes "this	567	1 X 1 27	5
: sam was a man stout as a bridge	568	1 X 1 28	5
know) sam was a man grinned his grin done	568	1 X 1 28	26
gun it is a man means No and (seeing	570	1 X 1 30	7
"my flowers" (the humble man than sunlight older with . . .	585	1 X 1 45	14
o the round little man we loved so isn't	606	(CHAIRE) 8	3

462

	PAGE	TITLE	LINE

MAN (CONTINUED)

than every) is a man (so easily one in . . . . 609 (CHAIRE) 11   2
in another hides; yet man can, being all, escape . . . . . . 609 (CHAIRE) 11   4
never is most lonely man alone (his briefest breathing . . . 609 (CHAIRE) 11   9
tless puppet of once man (clutched by immense the-seat-of-the 616 (CHAIRE) 18   5
(you feel behind this man earth's first sunrise) and . . . . 617 (CHAIRE) 19   4
yoo-gointa-doo? (ice coal wood man) nic he like wint-air . . 618 (CHAIRE) 20 21
here comes the only man reminding with his bell . . . . . . 624 (CHAIRE) 26   2
from freedom the common man wants) honey swoRkey mollypants . 635 (CHAIRE) 37 25
the noblest game a man can proudly lose, or . . . . 679 95 POEMS 7   3
look the very boldest man can scarcely dare to . . . . . . 685 95 POEMS 13   2
at which the rightest man remembers there is such . . . . . 685 95 POEMS 13   6
wisdom not the wisest man will partly understand (although . 685 95 POEMS 13 10
understand (although the wisest man am i) So young . . . . . 685 95 POEMS 13 12
something makes the oldest man (whoever he may be) . . . . . 685 95 POEMS 13 14
may be) the only man who'll never die / . . . . 685 95 POEMS 13 16
god manufacture might but man kind yet in park . . . . 698 95 POEMS 26   4
in his terrifyingly hu man man ner the only . . . . 700 95 POEMS 28   3
his terrifyingly hu man man ner the only reason . . . . . . 700 95 POEMS 28   3
only reason every wo man should go to college . . . . 700 95 POEMS 28   5
in l'ho tel nor man (rue d e l'echelle) . . . . 708 95 POEMS 36 13
justify the ways of man to God i'll think . . . . 731 95 POEMS 59   2
ways of God to man / / / / . . . . 731 95 POEMS 59   4
/ / a great man is gone. Tall as . . . . 786 73 POEMS 14   2
/ "nothing" the unjust man complained "is just" ("or . . . . 806 73 POEMS 34   1
nor angel called a man is measured by his . . . . 807 73 POEMS 35   7

+MAN

FOR CONTEXT, SEE . . . . 24 T&C CHANSONS 1   4
FOR CONTEXT, SEE . . . . 24 T&C CHANSONS 1 12
FOR CONTEXT, SEE . . . . 24 T&C CHANSONS 1 21
FOR CONTEXT, SEE . . . . 108 & PORTRAIT 4 17
FOR CONTEXT, SEE . . . . 140 & SON REAL 11 10
FOR CONTEXT, SEE . . . . 233 IS 5 ONE 4   1
FOR CONTEXT, SEE . . . . 233 IS 5 ONE 4 14
FOR CONTEXT, SEE . . . . 251 IS 5 ONE 22 14
FOR CONTEXT, SEE . . . . 254 IS 5 ONE 25 16
FOR CONTEXT, SEE . . . . 263 IS 5 ONE 32 45
FOR CONTEXT, SEE . . . . 318 VIVA 10   8
FOR CONTEXT, SEE . . . . 384 NO THANKS 2 19
FOR CONTEXT, SEE . . . . 390 NO THANKS 7 14
FOR CONTEXT, SEE . . . . 534 50 POEMS 46 24
FOR CONTEXT, SEE . . . . 602 (CHAIRE) 4   6
FOR CONTEXT, SEE . . . . 699 95 POEMS 27 21
FOR CONTEXT, SEE . . . . 710 95 POEMS 38   1

MAN'S

teasingly transparent folds-- with man's poor soul . . . . 5 T&C EPITHALAM 96
quite outdoes the mandolin- man's tiny racket. The horses . . 171 & SON ACTU 20   6
certain party gimme the he-man's solid bliss for youse . . . 247 IS 5 ONE 18   5
any mystery makes every man's flesh put space on; . . . . . . 484 NEW POEMS 22   7
/ / / this man's heart is true to . . . . 676 95 POEMS 4   1
by sundark) brightshadowfully fountaining man's thingfulest . 681 95 POEMS 9 15
haps even 4 now man's most vast (unmind by . . . . 787 73 POEMS 15   9

MANAGEMENT

by courtesy of the management on Thursdays, opposite which . 263 IS 5 ONE 32 50

+MANAGER

FOR CONTEXT, SEE . . . . 552 1 X 1 12 28

MANDOLIN

think of you, getting mandolin-clink mixed with your hair; . 169 & SON ACTU 18   5
which quite outdoes the mandolin- man's tiny racket. The . . 171 & SON ACTU 20   5

MANDOLIN-CLINK

think of you, getting mandolin-clink mixed with your hair; . 169 & SON ACTU 18   5

MANDOLINS

Hideous trees or Maybe Mandolins l oo k- pigeons . . . . . . 122 & SEVEN POEMS 1 13

MANGLING

sun-stirring. sweetly to the mangling air muchness of buds . 135 & SON REAL 6 13

MANGY

a on Dirty bed Mangy from person Porous sits . . . . 312 VIVA 4 18

		PAGE	TITLE	LINE

+MANIKINS
FOR CONTEXT, SEE . . . . 527 50 POEMS 39 19
MANKIND
us spilled) than all mankind something more small occurs . . 514 50 POEMS 28 10
the mightiest meditations of mankind cancelled are by one . . 592 1 X 1 52 6
should a loudness called mankind unteach whole infinite the . 603 (CHAIRE) 5 3
in that incredible unanimal mankind (and not until) / . . . . 620 (CHAIRE) 22 14
in vain but though mankind persuades itself that every . . . 744 95 POEMS 72 5
nobody else drive dumb mankind dizzy with haranguing --you . 804 73 POEMS 32 9
a kiss --not though mankind would rather know than . . . . . 817 73 POEMS 45 11
+MANKIND
FOR CONTEXT, SEE . . . . 554 1 X 1 14 1
FOR CONTEXT, SEE . . . . 698 95 POEMS 26 4
MANLY
before the world: with manly heart and conscience free, . . . 273 IS 5 TWO 8 18
MANN'S
Co. the epoch of Mann's righteousness the age of . . . . . . 266 IS 5 TWO 1 3
MANNER
skunks in a subtle manner or by drowning himself . . . . . . 239 IS 5 ONE 10 25
+MANNER
FOR CONTEXT, SEE . . . . 700 95 POEMS 28 4
MANNIKINS
do conjurers rule? do mannikins forbid the soul? is . . . . . 527 50 POEMS 39 19
MANON
danced la guerre j'm'appelle Manon, cinq rue Henri Mounier . 121 & PORTRAIT 12 35
MANS
ini sticks tuh de mans 1 (hutch) hutchinson says . . . . . . 325 VIVA 17 5
MANSHAPED
Clumsily with of what manshaped whimpered how girllike . . . 371 VIVA 62 3
MANTELPIECE
slender face (on the mantelpiece of a bedroom) begins . . . . 813 73 POEMS 41 3
MANUFACTURE
not any un god manufacture might but man kind . . . . 698 95 POEMS 26 4
+MANUFACTURED
FOR CONTEXT, SEE . . . . 464 NEW POEMS 2 18
MANUFACTURING
unmute antibolshevistic gents (each manufacturing word by . . 266 IS 5 TWO 1 10
MANUNKIND
pity this busy monster, manunkind, not. Progress is a . . . . 554 1 X 1 14 1
MANURE
pillow shoveling her small manure-shaped head one sheet on . 134 & SON REAL 5 3
MANURE-SHAPED
pillow shoveling her small manure-shaped head one sheet on . 134 & SON REAL 5 3
MANWHOSE
the tiny motheaten old manwhose Beard rests. onthetopwhose . 101 & POST IMPR 11 46
MANY
tale of Chaucer knoweth many a pair of companions . . . . . . 20 T&C PUELLA MEA 164
have been faithful to many things and which die . . . . 43 T&C AMORES 7 9
invariably interested in so many things-- at the present . . 70 T&C SON REAL 1 6
more even than how many ways of sitting on . . . . 126 & SEVEN POEMS 5 8
on Death's blade lie many a flower curled, in . . . . 208 XLI SONNETS 4 10
has done nothing for many years but fly kites . . . . 253 IS 5 ONE 24 5
upon this dome of many coloured glass, and see . . . . 273 IS 5 TWO 8 2
thither to thence swore many a vow but both . . . . 316 VIVA 8 14
(believably enlarged) make how many stopped millions of . . . 337 VIVA 28 4
of twilight, striking into many a piece. I have . . . . 360 VIVA 51 19
blame or praise) but many a thought shall die . . . . 372 VIVA 63 13
/ why why How many winds make wonderful and . . . . 395 NO THANKS 12 2
(with up so floating many bells down) spring summer . . . . . 515 50 POEMS 29 2
with up so floating many bells down) one day . . . . 515 50 POEMS 29 24
an anthologist sold the many on the few not . . . . 551 1 X 1 11 3
never breathed quite so many kinds of yes) not . . . . 591 1 X 1 51 16
swim so now million many worlds in each least . . . . 603 (CHAIRE) 5 1
/ / / so many selves (so many fiends . . . . 609 (CHAIRE) 11 1
so many selves (so many fiends and gods each . . . . 609 (CHAIRE) 11 1
nor dead these (or many thousand hearts which don't . . . . . 743 95 POEMS 71 6
don't and dream or many million minds which sleep . . . . . . 743 95 POEMS 71 7
/ / / how many moments must (amazing each . . . . 843 73 POEMS 71 1

	PAGE	TITLE	LINE

MANY (CONTINUED)
    must (amazing each how many centuries) these more than . . . 843 73 POEMS 71   2
MANYING
    light (all together a manying one -ness) nine souls . . . . . 627 (CHAIRE) 29   9
+MANYNESS
    FOR CONTEXT, SEE . . . . 528 50 POEMS 40   1
MAP
    no Where which to map while these not eyes . . . . 479 NEW POEMS 17   4
MAPLE
    oak by birch by maple pine by hemlock spruce . . . . 658 (CHAIRE) 60   18
MAPLE'S
    red leaps in the maple's cheek, and suddenly by . . . .   4 T&C EPITHALAM   62
MAPLES
    the mountain, while his maples wept air to blood, ... 555 1 X 1 15   11
MARATHON
    thermopylae heard her and marathon and all prehuman history . 711 95 POEMS 39   14
MARBLE
    OF NICOLETTE dreaming in marble all the castle lay . . . . .   8 T&C OF NICOL   1
    a tree of tall marble from a great way . . . . 30 T&C ORIENTALE 4 20
    with nesting incense) fifty marble pillars slipped from . . . 32 T&C ORIENTALE 6 28
MARBLES
    eddieandbill come running from marbles and piracies and it's 24 T&C CHANSONS 1   7
MARCH
    witH Which when both march outward into the freezing . . . . 311 VIVA 3   14
    mountains of having altitude--and march denounces april as a 620 (CHAIRE) 22   11
+MARCH
    FOR CONTEXT, SEE . . . . 376 VIVA 67   6
MARCHED
    the poem her belly marched through me as one . . . . 135 & SON REAL 6   1
    immortal work his shoulders marched against the dark his . . 521 50 POEMS 34   44
MARCHING
    the spear-song of the marching grass. A silver sudden . . . .   4 T&C EPITHALAM   72
    most believes, perpetual girls marching to love whose bodies 138 & SON REAL 9   11
    vast armies of the marching dead, with standards and . . . . 209 XLI SONNETS 5   3
MARCUS
    hung uh gun on Marcus"-- "duh Swede rolls down . . . . . . 332 VIVA 23   8
MARGINS
    wings mounts against the margins of steep song a . . . . . . 59 T&C PORTRAIT 7   14
MARIE
    at the door of Marie and of Maleore findeth . . . . 21 T&C PUELLA MEA 172
    with the ivory throat Marie Louise Lallemand n'est-ce pas . . 120 & PORTRAIT 12   10
    bon cul de Paris" (Marie Vierge Priez Pour Nous) . . . . . . 120 & PORTRAIT 12   14
    the twilight of Paris Marie Louise with queenly legs . . . . 121 & PORTRAIT 12   45
MARJ
    the breasts of bestial Marj lie large men who . . . . 114 & PORTRAIT 7   3
    and boozing belong to Marj the greenslim purse of . . . . . 114 & PORTRAIT 7   17
    the breasts of bestial Marj for the strong men . . . . 114 & PORTRAIT 7   26
    / / / / MARJ "life? Listen" the feline . . . . 228 IS 5 ONE MARJ   T
MARJ'S
    large men who praise Marj's cleancornered strokable body . . 114 & PORTRAIT 7   5
    of doing her eyebrows. --Marj's laughter smacked me: . . . . 228 IS 5 ONE MARJ   13
MARJORIE
    / / in making Marjorie god hurried a boy's . . . . 148 & SON REAL 19   1
    you got the haven't Marjorie isn't this wellcurb simply . . . 257 IS 5 ONE 27   35
MARK
    perfect night whisperless to mark, how that asleep whitely . 205 XLI SONNETS 1   7
    of thy smoothness. and mark the fainting murdered petals. . . 215 XLI SONNETS 11   7
    / this young question mark man question mark who . . . . . . 246 IS 5 ONE 17   1
    question mark man question mark who suffers from indigestion 246 IS 5 ONE 17   2
    suffers from indigestion question mark is a remarkably . . . 246 IS 5 ONE 17   5
    something genuine like a mark in a toilet graced . . . . . . 407 NO THANKS 24   12
MARRIAGE
    who needs hanging that marriage is a sure cure . . . . 167 & SON ACTU 16   5
    love and death a marriage) you give me courage . . . . 293 IS 5 FOUR 10   18
MARRIAGEABLE
    particularly the brand of marriageable nymph which is armed . 256 IS 5 ONE 27   14
MARRIED
    tired to which you're married and hands get red . . . . . . 242 IS 5 ONE 13   15

465

	PAGE	TITLE	LINE
MARRIED (CONTINUED)			
named Smith less strange? Married and lies afraid; aggressive	406	NO THANKS 23	14
all to her someones married their everyones laughed their . .	515	50 POEMS 29	17
by Life; whose brother married Heart, now Mrs Death.	621	{CHAIRE} 23	3
a whore when he married his wife and here	707	95 POEMS 35	18
MARRY			
where sea and sky marry-- to know the white	79	T&C SON UNRE 4	14
hands angle scoot bulbs marry a become) ened (to	309	VIVA 1	13
wink at kid anaesthetize marry bump off or otherwise	391	NO THANKS 8	15
MARRYING			
seasalt and indignant clover marrying to themselves Life's .	376	VIVA 67	5
MARVEL			
sweetly-saluted lingers. if one marvel seeing the hunger of .	42	T&C AMORES 6	8
could we bear the marvel of this thing?) /	205	XLI SONNETS 1	15
dost Thou contain a marvel than this death named	406	NO THANKS 23	12
all measures bend nor marvel if a thought should	446	NO THANKS 61	7
taking simply which) a marvel every breathing creature feels	735	95 POEMS 63	7
takes all) nor any marvel finds quite disappearance but . . .	750	95 POEMS 78	12
should some world (we marvel) doubt, for just sweet	809	73 POEMS 37	9
MARVELLED			
/ "could that" i marvelled "be you?" and a	828	73 POEMS 56	1
MARVELLING			
a certain reckoning demands... marvelling And what may have .	374	VIVA 65	4
MARVELLOUS			
everybodyelse's) but what's wholly marvellous my Darling is .	782	73 POEMS 10	15
you'll shortly comprehend a marvellous artificer now Ugly was	799	73 POEMS 27	7
MARVELLOUSLY			
dark most downwardness and marvellously self diminutive whose	821	73 POEMS 49	12
MARVELOUS			
as is the sea marvelous from god's hands which	38	T&C AMORES 3	1
lady (and every brittle marvelous breathing thing) since i .	293	IS 5 FOUR 10	13
MARVELS			
grow" my, her life marvels "here'll be a canoe	572	1 X 1 32	15
a single hair again" marvels "and liars kill their	572	1 X 1 32	17
fear: love, when such marvels vanish, will include --there .	741	95 POEMS 69	10
of green solitude (go marvels come) as littler much	757	95 POEMS 85	17
avenue) "then" my voice marvels "what happened" as everywhere	800	73 POEMS 28	21
MARX			
k (relijinisde) o (peemuvdepipl) marx okays jippymugun roomur	325	VIVA 17	12
MARY			
And Good Will, and Mary with one lung extended	142	& SON REAL 13	10
dead dead dead) whereupon mary quite contrary didn't die . .	401	NO THANKS 18	8
MARYS			
wisest painter of fragile Marys will understand how smiling .	294	IS 5 FOUR 11	12
MASK			
street) this deep immediate mask and expressing "as for . . .	328	VIVA 19	14
blind the brave? does mask wear face? have singings	538	50 POEMS 50	6
MASS			
pulled into a sole mass my separate lusts her	135	& SON REAL 6	4
on a lightning-rod, Boston, Mass. such were the not	262	IS 5 ONE 32	31
Young Woman of cambridge, mass. to whom nobody seems	326	VIVA 18	2
at radcliffe college, cambridge, mass. i try if you	327	VIVA 18	44
MASSACRE			
un stride after glide massacre monday did more) ask	522	50 POEMS 35	4
wish: so pitiless a massacre the hope most innocent	609	{CHAIRE} 11	6
MASTER			
MEA Harun Omar and Master Hafiz keep your dead	17	T&C PUELLA MEA	1
who to walk with Master Gower in Confessio doth	20	T&C PUELLA MEA	166
Solomon, Omar Harun and Master Hafiz, to me your	23	T&C PUELLA MEA	263
ladies Harun Omar and Master Hafiz. / / /	23	T&C PUELLA MEA	290
money and then his master will yell at him	69	T&C POST IMPR 6	12
the dark so duneyed master enter the sweet gates	188	XLI SONGS 10	13
be sought or seeking master or disciple sheep or	804	73 POEMS 32	4
+MASTER			
FOR CONTEXT, SEE	642	{CHAIRE} 44	23
MASTER'S			
unknown (warily as their master's spirit stooping, Crusoelike	344	VIVA 35	13

MASTERPIECE
    up) we spill our masterpiece / / / / . . . . 650 {CHAIRE} 52   20
MASTERY
    enter fingers of smooth mastery with chasteness of sea-girls   189 XLI SONGS 11   9
MASTURBATE
    would fall apart and masturbate with dynamite the boys . . . 427 NO THANKS 44   12
MASTURBATES
    his baldness a smile masturbates softly in the vacant . . . . 259 IS 5 ONE 29   22
    of who) i discreetly (masturbates one honest breadcrumb) say 546 1 X 1 6   11
MASTURBATION
    a sure cure for masturbation). A dirty wind, twitches . . . . 167 & SON ACTU 16   5
MATCH
    little, in (want a match or can you see?) . . . . 117 & PORTRAIT 10   29
    for youse ideas i'll match youse a pretty girl . . . . 247 IS 5 ONE 18   6
MATCHABELLI
    by lipstick smell by matchabelli) tits as (while thumb . . . 546 1 X 1 6   9
MATCHING
    madonna (nudge whispershout) laugh matching onceupons each . 681 95 POEMS 9   8
MATE
    AM true to his mate his chicks his friends . . . . 774 73 POEMS 2   13
MATED
    probably most brilliant pupil mated, let us not deem . . . . 326 VIVA 18   7
MATISSE
    of sharp mind and Matisse rhythms to juggle Kandinsky . . . . 180 XLI SONGS 2   12
+MATISSE
    FOR CONTEXT, SEE . . . . 318 VIVA 10   7
    FOR CONTEXT, SEE . . . . 318 VIVA 10   20
MATTER
    it does not greatly matter to the sun, nor . . . .   84 T&C SON ACTU 3   7
    days and nights that matter knocked by sun moon . . . . 153 & SON ACTU 2   10
    doesn't in the least matter. The big fear Who . . . . 289 IS 5 FOUR 6   2
    i can't which doesn't matter and what does is . . . . 289 IS 5 FOUR 6   5
    to and that doesn't matter) which i suggest teach . . . . . . 289 IS 5 FOUR 6   9
    you but that doesn't matter further than of old . . . . 289 IS 5 FOUR 6   13
    to (but that doesn't matter) when you thought you . . . . . . 289 IS 5 FOUR 6   20
    Then moving was a matter of not keeping still; . . . . 289 IS 5 FOUR 6   23
    with that that doesn't matter (and if he she . . . . 475 NEW POEMS 13   6
    i say that doesn't matter) but if somebody or . . . . 475 NEW POEMS 13   11
    a handful absolutely doesn't matter and whether it's in . . . 549 1 X 1 9   6
    couldn't help it no matter how hard he never . . . . 635 {CHAIRE} 37   6
    dare to meet no matter how he'll try to . . . . 685 95 POEMS 13   3
    truth not hid by matter; not by mind revealed . . . . 765 95 POEMS 91   6
    when Anybody-- yes; no matter who, some total (preferably . . 779 73 POEMS 7   4
    reason vanquished instinct and matter became the slave of . . 799 73 POEMS 27   35
+MATTER
    FOR CONTEXT, SEE . . . . 103 & POST IMPR 13   1
MATTERED
    air muchness of buds mattered. a valley spilled its . . . . . 135 & SON REAL 6   14
MATTERINGS
    me) that not all matterings of mind equal one . . . . 736 95 POEMS 64   7
MATTERS
    nothing is what particularly matters hence in a little . . . 238 IS 5 ONE 9   18
    extremely unimportant) whereas Life matters if or when the . 260 IS 5 ONE 30   13
    oceans do Not sleep matters nothing; then (then the . . . . . 359 VIVA 50   13
+MATTERS
    FOR CONTEXT, SEE . . . . 790 73 POEMS 18   14
MATTRESS
    weary, upon a flabby mattress of jelly.... than when . . . . 143 & SON REAL 14   12
MATURELY
    here were something more maturely childish, more beautiful . 211 XLI SONNETS 7   4
MAULS
    as the august evening mauls Kneeland, and a waiter . . . . . 217 XLI SONNETS 13   7
MAUVE
    to and heed the mauve of twilight (who slenderly . . . . . .   93 & POST IMPR 5   8
MAXIMS
    succeeded in producing sixtyfour maxims whose) centripetal . 341 VIVA 32   3
MAY
    veils. O still miraculous May! O shining girl of . . . . . .   5 T&C EPITHALAM   105

MAY (CONTINUED)

	PAGE	TITLE	LINE
the troubled heart of May; a Winged Passion woke	8	T&C OF NICOL	8
witchery of almostness which May makes follow soon on	10	T&C SONGS 1	38
her body filled with May) --moving in the unskilful	17	T&C PUELLA MEA	22
body grow; as morning may a lily know, her	21	T&C PUELLA MEA	184
certain song that we may watch together how behind	43	T&C AMORES 7	28
/ / SONNETS--UNREALITIES it may not always be so;	76	T&C SON UNRE 1	1
little word. that i may go unto him, and	76	T&C SON UNRE 1	11
(god's pretty mother) but may not confuse the clever	85	T&C SON ACTU 4	6
tiny voice, i am may the first crumb said	117	& PORTRAIT 10	12
and if dead says may i have this one	126	& SEVEN POEMS 5	20
however suddenly ap- proached may never quite taste the . . .	193	XLI PORTRAIT 1	12
exclamatory tooth-pick And who may that be i said	194	XLI PORTRAIT 2	28
hand so hairy-sturdy you may turn O turn that	233	IS 5 ONE 4	2
America ether the movies may claim general importance to . .	238	IS 5 ONE 9	15
like Hell Itself which may or may not account	239	IS 5 ONE 10	7
Itself which may or may not account for the	239	IS 5 ONE 10	7
is no excuse for May --bring forth your flowers	264	IS 5 ONE 33	8
well provided an instant may be fixed so that	264	IS 5 ONE 33	23
has arrived your mind may guess if at sunset	285	IS 5 FOUR 2	11
this dear, that we may resume impact with the	289	IS 5 FOUR 6	6
will understand how smiling may be made as skilfully.) . . .	294	IS 5 FOUR 11	13
big red dog that may be owned by who	303	IS 5 FIVE 2	13
(they got pockets full may take a littl e	314	VIVA 6	10
the deep sky in May mine's tou ching this	314	VIVA 6	17
a) listen to who may you be any how?	314	VIVA 6	24
spattered (or if it may be socalled) memory Of	317	VIVA 9	21
entirely whose least breathing may surprise ourselves --let's	368	VIVA 59	14
cool stupendous is nor may truth opening encompass true) . .	373	VIVA 64	16
demands... marvelling And what may have become of with . . .	374	VIVA 65	4
strictly horrors which stars may not observe; while roses . .	386	NO THANKS 3	8
we die for lives (may never cease views with	386	NO THANKS 3	9
their friend and who may envy neither; nor bewail	394	NO THANKS 11	10
than) whose tiniest smile? may Be bigger than the	397	NO THANKS 14	5
/ / / / may i feel said he	399	NO THANKS 16	1
it's fun said she (may i touch said he	399	NO THANKS 16	5
you are said she) may i stay said he	399	NO THANKS 16	13
you kiss said she may i move said he	399	NO THANKS 16	17
quite contrary didn't die (may be seen to inexactly	401	NO THANKS 18	11
(he must deny mind: may believe in brains. /	402	NO THANKS 19	15
Je T'Aime and it may be fun to be	410	NO THANKS 27	13
the hope that you may mess your pance every	413	NO THANKS 30	12
life's busy little dyings may possess) how sincere large . .	418	NO THANKS 35	4
by standing in november's may) from whose (if loud	420	NO THANKS 37	4
beats one entirety neither may shadow down flesh neither . .	425	NO THANKS 42	12
shadow down flesh neither may vibration create voice if . . .	425	NO THANKS 42	12
what is and what may be unknown most secret	428	NO THANKS 45	9
waves which only He may walk Who dares to . . . . ,	438	NO THANKS 54	27
must coo or boo may strut or creep ungenerous	440	NO THANKS 56	19
live always shall be may never have) do i	441	NO THANKS 56	64
caught by worms (love may not care if time	446	NO THANKS 61	5
not whose spiral hunger may appease what merely riches . . .	456	NO THANKS 71	4
those & that "I may say professor" asleep wop	464	NEW POEMS 2	10
to stand or sit may take it lying down)	466	NEW POEMS 4	4
/ / / / may my heart always be	481	NEW POEMS 19	1
them men are old may my mind stroll about	481	NEW POEMS 19	5
even if it's sunday may i be wrong for	481	NEW POEMS 19	7
are not young and may myself do nothing usefully	481	NEW POEMS 19	9
will yourself become. Girlboys may nothing more than boygirls	484	NEW POEMS 22	5
you should ever think, may god forbid and (in	484	NEW POEMS 22	9
and shall be: cities may overflow (am was) assassinating . .	491	50 POEMS 5	11
later all hands (you may recall) being lost including . . .	494	50 POEMS 8	7
never equal one) which may your million selves and	510	50 POEMS 24	12
you which could grin may stern particular Love surround . . .	522	50 POEMS 35	10
and feet (lift and may pitying Who from sharp	522	50 POEMS 35	12
small and sad man, may his mighty briefness dig	526	50 POEMS 38	4
will cure when pimps may please? must through unstrange . . .	527	50 POEMS 39	24
a snowflake "yes: you may sleep now, my mountain"	555	1 X 1 15	14

		PAGE	TITLE	LINE

MAY (CONTINUED)

of stop and go) may i achieve another steepest	558	1 X 1 18	10
too yes, sir what may be better or what	568	1 X 1 28	21
be better or what may be worse and what	568	1 X 1 28	22
be worse and what may be clover clover clover	568	1 X 1 28	23
in the month of may: life's the deathboard where	574	1 X 1 34	5
honour, my loveliest, nothing may move may rest --you	575	1 X 1 35	5
loveliest, nothing may move may rest --you bring (out	575	1 X 1 35	5
with twilight's first thrushes may awake more secretly than .	577	1 X 1 37	6
ablaze greenly thing ; may has come love (by	583	1 X 1 43	14
no where (no) when may breathe so sky so	584	1 X 1 44	16
glory, no more miracle may grow --childfully serious flower .	601	(CHAIRE) 3	6
wise." "You mean worlds may have better luck, some	603	(CHAIRE) 5	11
than any bright word may cry --even the crackling	605	(CHAIRE) 7	7
age when every thrush may sing no new moon	620	(CHAIRE) 22	5
or otherwise) old. Old may mean anything which everyone . . .	626	(CHAIRE) 28	3
juke) ing shrieks Yew May n't Dew Thiz Tew	629	(CHAIRE) 31	12
million wheres which never may become one (wholly strange; .	659	(CHAIRE) 61	6
than prove what heart may feel and soul may	664	(CHAIRE) 66	4
may feel and soul may touch --the great (my	664	(CHAIRE) 66	4
love a billion brains may coax undeath from fancied	664	(CHAIRE) 66	19
she is you nothing may, quite your my (my	666	(CHAIRE) 68	11
crazily eyes of window) may be un less it	668	(CHAIRE) 70	4
milly and molly and may went down to the	682	95 POEMS 10	1
while blowing bubbles: and may came home with a	682	95 POEMS 10	9
cry dear violet you may take mine" "o how	684	95 POEMS 12	4
oldest man (whoever he may be) the only man	685	95 POEMS 13	15
things beyond whatever mind may comprehend, remember seek . .	688	95 POEMS 16	11
paradise) mind without soul may blast some universe to . . .	714	95 POEMS 42	9
your coming although winter may be everywhere with such . . .	717	95 POEMS 45	5
putting it mildly much) may be be cause ever	727	95 POEMS 55	13
dreams or a slogan may topple you (trees are	732	95 POEMS 60	2
death's because to find) may, given perfect mercy, live . . .	735	95 POEMS 63	3
life, you and i may reverently share the blessed	745	95 POEMS 73	10
can feel but ears may see there never lived	760	95 POEMS 87	5
with one least ignorance may comprehend more than shall . . .	761	95 POEMS 88	2
little parasol, so she may above people walk in	762	95 POEMS 89	8
merely) existence, all when may not measure a now	763	95 POEMS 90	35
/ / / spring! may-- everywhere's here (with a	767	95 POEMS 93	1
low high in the may in the spring) live!	767	95 POEMS 93	20
SONG but we've the may (for you are in	776	73 POEMS 4	1
colours all into singing) may wonder a with deep	778	73 POEMS 6	4
come they) through the may in fragrance and song	778	73 POEMS 6	11
earth a day of may under more a blue	778	73 POEMS 6	18
yea-- november would be may that you and i'd	798	73 POEMS 26	21
in her splendor says May / / / /	801	73 POEMS 29	30
certain men quite possibly may have shall we say	807	73 POEMS 35	12
perceive (but believe scarcely may) certainly while mute each	808	73 POEMS 36	9
that hugest whole creation may be less incalculable than . .	809	73 POEMS 37	13
universe of sleep safely may by imperishable your glory . . .	811	73 POEMS 39	2
/ / / / may i be gay like	815	73 POEMS 43	1
imagine) something which nobody may keep. now i lay	816	73 POEMS 44	13
world's millionary mind never may partly guess--thus, my . .	818	73 POEMS 46	13
universe a single leaf may be) the more than	821	73 POEMS 49	13
(yes) you and i may not hurry it with	835	73 POEMS 63	26
sorrows not any tongue may name, three i'll give	837	73 POEMS 65	2
newly one moving cadence may release the fragrance of	842	73 POEMS 70	6
wonder no world deny may or believe / /	845	73 POEMS 73	14

MAYBE

dreamed one afternoon ....or maybe read? of a time	72	T&C SON REAL 3	10
you get me?) will maybe dance and maybe sing	72	T&C SON REAL 3	13
will maybe dance and maybe sing and be absitively	72	T&C SON REAL 3	13
from Hideous trees or Maybe Mandolins l oo k-	122	& SEVEN POEMS 1	13
you've never met who maybe winks at you in	126	& SEVEN POEMS 5	15
me where i stood (maybe nine miles off). It	135	& SON REAL 6	12
stood thinking of anything, maybe the world.... But i	172	& SON ACTU 21	9
is what we stroke maybe asleep? do you know?	191	XLI CHANSONS 1	12
do you know? or maybe did something go away	191	XLI CHANSONS 1	13

	PAGE	TITLE	LINE

MAYBE (CONTINUED)

somebody an invisible spectator, maybe certain nobodies . . .	283	IS 5 THREE 7	8
therefore we'll kiss; for maybe what was Disappeared into . .	286	IS 5 FOUR 3	21
promise-- then he will maybe (hearing something fall into . .	298	IS 5 FOUR 15	20
i don't think so. maybe: somebody?) or, bedbugs /	312	VIVA 4	24
but mr can you maybe listen there's me &	314	VIVA 6	1
winter: as clover knows, maybe" (heart makes the suggestion)	625	{CHAIRE} 27	10
/ / / / maybe god is a child	652	{CHAIRE} 54	1
streaming if something had (maybe they couldn't agree) not .	652	{CHAIRE} 54	14
faded (pinkish or yellowish maybe) piece of pitiful paper-- .	697	95 POEMS 25	25
out your eye" "well maybe she's up to some	707	95 POEMS 35	9
a stuttering ghost that maybe had shaved three times	709	95 POEMS 37	7
death a day (or maybe even less) / /	743	95 POEMS 71	14

+MAYBE

| FOR CONTEXT, SEE . . . . | 727 | 95 POEMS 55 | 13 |
| FOR CONTEXT, SEE . . . . | 789 | 73 POEMS 17 | 19 |

MAYBES

| leasting forever most magical maybes of certainly never the . | 495 | 50 POEMS 9 | 14 |

MAYFLOWERS

| or snowflakes make possible mayflowers: quite eyes of air . . | 577 | 1 X 1 37 | 4 |

+MAYING

| FOR CONTEXT, SEE . . . . | 13 | T&C SONGS 3 | 7 |
| FOR CONTEXT, SEE . . . . | 20 | T&C PUELLA MEA | 169 |

MAYN'T

| isn't (and that it mayn't be twirled around your . . . . . . | 411 | NO THANKS 28 | 6 |

+MAYN'T

| FOR CONTEXT, SEE . . . . | 629 | {CHAIRE} 31 | 12 |

MAZURKAS

| his tiny cane and, mazurkas about tweak- ing his . . . . . . | 274 | IS 5 TWO 9 | 32 |

MCCANN

| Uncle Sol could sing McCann He Was A Diver . . . . | 239 | IS 5 ONE 10 | 6 |

MCKINLEY

| Washington to Lydia E. McKinley when Buch tooked out . . . . | 321 | VIVA 13 | 6 |

MCSORLEY'S

| i was sitting in mcsorley's. outside it was New . . . . . . | 96 | & POST IMPR 8 | 1 |
| i was sitting in mcsorley's It, did not answer. . . . . . . | 97 | & POST IMPR 8 | 43 |

ME

pass upon forgetting (fail me not) whose courseless waters .	9	T&C SONGS 1	3
fear") then be with me: unseriously seem by the	9	T&C SONGS 1	28
long sinful arms about me dream shall my love	9	T&C SONGS 1	34
softly brought-- (be with me in the sacred witchery	10	T&C SONGS 1	37
mysteries very simply touch me, whose heart-wholeness	12	T&C SONGS 2	38
lady utterly alive, to me is a more curious	17	T&C PUELLA MEA	25
my lady look at me (with her eyes which	17	T&C PUELLA MEA	38
it is to quell me with the twinge of	19	T&C PUELLA MEA	100
nothing err. If to me there shall appear than	21	T&C PUELLA MEA	175
naked she appear to me my flesh is an	22	T&C PUELLA MEA	231
beauties, mine being unto me sweeter (of whose shy	22	T&C PUELLA MEA	250
and Master Hafiz, to me your ladies are all	23	T&C PUELLA MEA	264
body thy body to me is April in whose	29	T&C ORIENTALE 3	9
you thought to escape me and became a great	30	T&C ORIENTALE 4	5
had desire to thwart me and became a little	30	T&C ORIENTALE 4	18
you would have deceived me and became a star	30	T&C ORIENTALE 4	32
because you have loved me, moon and sunset stars	39	T&C AMORES 4	5
the flower you gave me when we loved the	42	T&C AMORES 6	3
hands were laid upon me I was whirled and	44	T&C AMORES 8	11
dorothy and once permitted me for twenty iron men	52	T&C PORTRAIT 1	20
said to Death teach me of her Thy yonder	57	T&C PORTRAIT 5	5
that the soul inside me Hollers for thou comest	61	T&C PORTRAIT 9	27
the erect deep upon me in the last light	64	T&C POST IMPR 1	6
tree, Nobody shall stop me but first earth , ...	67	T&C POST IMPR 4	2
goodby Betty, don't remember me pencil your eyes dear	71	T&C SON REAL 2	1
This, do you get me?) will maybe dance and	72	T&C SON REAL 3	12
of my heart, send me a little word; that	76	T&C SON UNRE 1	10
Accept all happiness from me. Then shall i turn	76	T&C SON UNRE 1	12
Perhaps her body touched me; and to face suddenly	82	T&C SON ACTU 1	14
you will slowly kiss me / / / /	86	T&C SON ACTU 5	14
the renewed world" to me said the) wind being	91	& POST IMPR 3	19

ME (CONTINUED)

booming smell waddles toward, me, dressed like a Plum . . . . 94 & POST IMPR 6 15
l'heure exquise) i remind Me of HerThe delicate-swill tints . 94 & POST IMPR 6 20
smooth thighs thinkingly) remind me of Woman and how . . . . 95 & POST IMPR 7 17
what the lands thaz me kid in no sir . . . . 96 & POST IMPR 8 15
was so near to me, i ask of shad- . . . . 97 & POST IMPR 8 40
hard dear you're killing me / / / / . . . . 109 & PORTRAIT 5 23
mercy begs, sharply believe me, wholly, well --did (wisely . 115 & PORTRAIT 8 9
your step and follow me stooping by Effie's little, ... 117 & PORTRAIT 10 27
hands will play on, mE as dea d tunes . . . . 122 & SEVEN POEMS 1 10
there's just room for me in You my stomach . . . . 123 & SEVEN POEMS 2 8
legs Your arms under me around; my head fits . . . . 123 & SEVEN POEMS 2 11
the tree? you got me said the smoke who . . . . 125 & SEVEN POEMS 4 9
dead says come with me he says (andwhyevernot) into . . . . . 127 & SEVEN POEMS 5 45
if they should take me and take you into . . . . 129 & SEVEN POEMS 7 6
skilful mystery of Hell) me suddenly grips in chuckles . . . 130 & SON REAL 1 7
is tired. Not of me. The eyes which biggish . . . . 131 & SON REAL 2 13
a weeping skyscraper in me i bite on the . . . . 132 & SON REAL 3 5
of sex which lock me seriously. Dumb for a . . . . 133 & SON REAL 4 12
her belly marched through me as one army. From . . . . 135 & SON REAL 6 1
felt a mountain touch me where i stood (maybe . . . . 135 & SON REAL 6 11
love whose bodies kiss me with the square crime . . . . 138 & SON REAL 9 12
thy tingling limbs from me: make my pain their . . . . 139 & SON REAL 10 2
/ / god pity me whom (god distinctly has) . . . . 140 & SON REAL 11 1
gaily go clean through me tickling aches, and the . . . . . . 147 & SON REAL 18 7
heave and twine about me, and to kiss my . . . . 147 & SON REAL 18 14
mistake, whose fragrance hurls me into tears, as the . . . . 148 & SON REAL 19 11
lean.... a little against me, when for two dollars . . . . . 148 & SON REAL 19 13
boosts herself rapidly at me through sagging debris of . . . 151 & SON REAL 22 1
from the thinning lips me hugely which embrace. as . . . . . 151 & SON REAL 22 16
love comes to see me it's just a little . . . . 152 & SON ACTU 1 1
stilling lips murder suddenly me, but of my corpse . . . . . 152 & SON ACTU 1 11
how much better than me will you like the . . . . 153 & SON ACTU 2 13
grim clenched mind of me somewhere begins again, shares . . . 156 & SON ACTU 5 11
fragile instant when herself me (slowly, wholly me) will . . 156 & SON ACTU 5 14
herself me (slowly, wholly me) will press in the . . . . . . 156 & SON ACTU 5 14
it will do to me before shutting.... understand i . . . . . 157 & SON ACTU 6 5
suddenly body reach for me with a speed of . . . . 157 & SON ACTU 6 7
Whirl's after all: (after me) love, and after you. . . . . . 160 & SON ACTU 9 13
face O stay with me slightly. or until with . . . . 165 & SON ACTU 14 10
for god knows makes me wonder if i'm alive . . . . 166 & SON ACTU 15 9
fire-escapes-- the night. makes me wonder if, if i . . . . . 166 & SON ACTU 15 12
hour) she says to me you big fool she . . . . 167 & SON ACTU 16 12
star or three annoys me, but the stink of . . . . 169 & SON ACTU 18 3
/ / you asked me to come: it was . . . . 173 & SON ACTU 22 1
the thrill of under me you so quite new . . . . 175 & SON ACTU 24 14
swift flesh i make me stern against your charming . . . . . . 182 XLI SONGS 4 13
as Nicho' laid before me bread more downy than . . . . 194 XLI PORTRAIT 2 31
i. Vast cheeks enclose me. a gigantic uvula with . . . . . . 201 XLI PORTRAIT 9 7
irrefutable spiral antics involve me with the soothings of . 201 XLI PORTRAIT 9 26
cowers-- i do excuse me, love, to Death and . . . . 207 XLI SONNETS 3 9
if not flower, tell me softly who be these . . . . 211 XLI SONNETS 7 6
heart is fain; try me with thy perfumes which . . . . 212 XLI SONNETS 8 5
dead, feed with felicities me wormperused by whom the . . . . 212 XLI SONNETS 8 7
not what thou givest me to him let me . . . . 212 XLI SONNETS 8 9
me to him let me complain, whose seat is . . . . 212 XLI SONNETS 8 10
to thee perchance to me deeper. / / / . . . . 213 XLI SONNETS 9 17
body will come toward me with its hurting sexual . . . . . . 214 XLI SONNETS 10 11
the vertical grin give me the Square in spring, ... 220 XLI SONNETS 16 9
"Look at" arranging before me a mellifluous idiot grin . . . 226 IS 5 ONE MAME 2
lips, between you and me almost succeeds while toddle . . . . 227 IS 5 ONE GERT 6
eyebrows. --Marj's laughter smacked me: pummeling the . . . . 228 IS 5 ONE MARJ 14
VINAL take it from me kiddo believe me my . . . . 230 IS 5 ONE 2 1
from me kiddo believe me my country, 'tis of . . . . 230 IS 5 ONE 2 2
andsoforth do you get me?) according to such supposedly . . . 230 IS 5 ONE 2 30
thy flight and make me a child, a pretty . . . . 233 IS 5 ONE 4 4
that was dada? make me a child, stout hurdysturdygurdyman . . 233 IS 5 ONE 4 14
stout hurdysturdygurdyman waiter, make me a child. So this . 233 IS 5 ONE 4 15

	PAGE	TITLE	LINE
ME (CONTINUED)			
(eheu fu -gaces Postu- me boo who) / /	236	IS 5 ONE 7	20
claim general importance to me to you nothing is	238	IS 5 ONE 9	16
person personally they tell me as for me i	246	IS 5 ONE 17	8
tell me as for me i only knows that	246	IS 5 ONE 17	8
rule this world (and me and you if we're	250	IS 5 ONE 21	3
her a I mean me a Irish, cook but	251	IS 5 ONE 22	10
the Campanile, believe thou me cocodrillo-- mine eyes have .	256	IS 5 ONE 27	9
gondola signore day below me gondola signore gondola and . .	256	IS 5 ONE 27	24
signore gondola and above me pass loudly and gondola	256	IS 5 ONE 27	25
next train to grind me into lifeless atoms various	262	IS 5 ONE 32	3
mind. It seemed to me that i had first	262	IS 5 ONE 32	5
had always not nothurt me not much and in	262	IS 5 ONE 32	16
Let us perhaps excuse me if i repeat himself:	263	IS 5 ONE 32	59
extremely artistic ◇ fla -me of the (very prettily	267	IS 5 TWO 2	12
soldier minus his na- me (so as not to	267	IS 5 TWO 2	15
James and next let me see yes Will that	271	IS 5 TWO 6	4
everywhere over you all me everyone that's been there	272	IS 5 TWO 7	11
/ come, gaze with me upon this dome of	273	IS 5 TWO 8	1
a few philosophers tell me what am i doing	281	IS 5 THREE 5	1
on the beach below me a little girl in	281	IS 5 THREE 5	3
in sand Clouds over me are like bridegrooms Naked	281	IS 5 THREE 5	16
are old men behind me I tell you; several, ...	281	IS 5 THREE 6	24
a little downward, embrace me with your body's suddenly . . .	282	IS 5 THREE 6	34
...finally your eyes knew me, we smiled to each	283	IS 5 THREE 7	21
my window it touched me with its small hands	284	IS 5 FOUR 1	2
it should, leaning against me, smile; or (between dawn . . .	285	IS 5 FOUR 2	13
giving your eyes, present me also with the terror	285	IS 5 FOUR 2	15
content should any by me carven thing provoke your	291	IS 5 FOUR 8	19
poem should lift to me the distinct country of	291	IS 5 FOUR 8	26
a marriage) you give me courage so that against	293	IS 5 FOUR 10	18
do not ever fear, me in your heart softly;	294	IS 5 FOUR 11	18
from several persons: believe me that strangers arrive when .	295	IS 5 FOUR 12	8
ago i found staring me in the face a	296	IS 5 FOUR 13	16
than a hair) making me feel how myself has	301	IS 5 FOUR 18	7
will you walking beside me, my very lady, if	302	IS 5 FIVE 1	2
send life out of me and the night absolutely	302	IS 5 FIVE 1	7
the night absolutely into me.... a wise and puerile	302	IS 5 FIVE 1	8
you maybe listen there's me & some people and	314	VIVA 6	2
Curved (and that reminds me who said o yes	315	VIVA 7	2
isse like ◇ gave me, A, (peach a soft	318	VIVA 10	9
soft desert smoked bad me whilepin Kishcam elscasta? netsits .	318	VIVA 10	21
interested but you make me laft welates Wouldwoe Washington .	321	VIVA 13	4
/ / / tell me not how electricity or	324	VIVA 16	1
she suddenly luffed --thanking me; and (stating that she . .	326	VIVA 18	36
i will cultivate within me scrupulously the Inimitable which	328	VIVA 19	2
which tends to compel me to decline to admit	329	VIVA 20	2
"fellers have some on me" --dey was petrified. De	332	VIVA 23	24
sumpn: next i knows me (er somebody is sittin	332	VIVA 23	29
was more brave than me: more blond than you.	339	VIVA 30	42
don't you're hurting o Me please you're killing) death . . .	343	VIVA 34	6
is why something about me reminded him of ourselves) . . .	355	VIVA 46	20
you a wish?) touch me, before we perish (believe	357	VIVA 48	3
or this instant) kiss me a little: the air	357	VIVA 48	7
alive-- o live with me in the fewness of	357	VIVA 48	10
stirred) my mirror gives me, on this afternoon; i	360	VIVA 51	3
Hell (by most humble me which shall increase) open	360	VIVA 51	31
thither: t, ouch soft-ly me and eye (you leSs	361	VIVA 52	12
/ / breathe with me this fear (which beyond	362	VIVA 53	1
faeries if you love me) distance is mind carefully	363	VIVA 54	6
will you come with me into the extremely little	365	VIVA 56	1
are things which enclose me, or which i cannot	366	VIVA 57	3
look easily will unclose me though i have closed	366	VIVA 57	5
wish be to close me, i and my life	366	VIVA 57	9
fragility: whose texture compels me with the colour of . . .	366	VIVA 57	15
opens; only something in me understands the voice of	366	VIVA 57	18
perfect fear (of suddenly me) like these first deepest . . .	367	VIVA 58	6
in sealace appeared to me your mind drifting with	369	VIVA 60	3

472

	PAGE	TITLE	LINE

ME (CONTINUED)

	PAGE	TITLE	LINE
lessness; quietly turning toward me the guessable mirrors . .	370	VIVA 61	9
is unto colour; create me gradually (or as these	372	VIVA 63	2
dissolve reintegrate beckon through me, i think it is	379	VIVA 70	12
iflike moon over moving me--the moon m ov--in g	384	NO THANKS 2	13
by doDreaming heteronomously metameric me are picked from . .	395	NO THANKS 12	13
who cright god help me it aint no ews	405	NO THANKS 22	10
(why Jones don't pay me what he knows he	406	NO THANKS 23	6
what's wrong with (between me and we) the g--d	411	NO THANKS 28	9
feeling throughout ignorant disappearing me hurling vastness	428	NO THANKS 45	7
upon sunset, crickets within me whisper whose erect blood . .	435	NO THANKS 51	37
imagining spasm rise we you-with-me around (me) you IYou . .	442	NO THANKS 57	23
rise we you-with-me around (me) you IYou / /	442	NO THANKS 57	24
you'll have to loan me pain to take the	451	NO THANKS 66	6
the always impossible of me and shall who wave	454	NO THANKS 69	2
a -rithmetic o- ver me you & all those	464	NEW POEMS 2	9
that's not swell (get me) babe not (understand me)	475	NEW POEMS 13	23
me) babe not (understand me) lousy kid that's something . . .	475	NEW POEMS 13	23
apes <> ng with me n more o n	488	50 POEMS 2	22
had by my throat me give it him good	496	50 POEMS 10	10
rull to vote for me (all decent mem and	500	50 POEMS 14	21
crazy man) don't ask me how i know (a	501	50 POEMS 15	6
far "i cordially invite me to become noone except	504	50 POEMS 18	4
/ / / buy me an ounce and i'll	513	50 POEMS 27	1
mine is yours ask me the name of the	513	50 POEMS 27	19
guit ar (pleez make me glad) dis dumdam slamslum	519	50 POEMS 33	7
much o much cheap me i work i know	523	50 POEMS 36	16
it you will (kiss me) go out into the	529	50 POEMS 41	3
world in it (kiss me) you will go on	529	50 POEMS 41	6
you will go (kiss me down into your memory	529	50 POEMS 41	9
and memory i) kiss me (will go) / /	529	50 POEMS 41	12
it that stinks Excuse Me whether it's president of	549	1 X 1 9	2
to biz don't ask me what it's pliz) then	552	1 X 1 12	5
just as small as me can do or be?"	555	1 X 1 15	13
do the breathing for me while i am away?)	558	1 X 1 18	15
and sprinkles nowhere with me and you? Blow soon	560	1 X 1 20	20
is la guerre) your me or simplify my you	577	1 X 1 37	11
too small for even me; for me and you, ...	579	1 X 1 39	7
for even me; for me and you, exceedingly too	579	1 X 1 39	8
a look should april me, down isn't's own isn't	580	1 X 1 40	6
a look should april me, some thousand million hundred	580	1 X 1 40	11
a look should april me for half a when, ...	580	1 X 1 40	19
a look should april me (though such as perfect	580	1 X 1 40	22
room for three of me and only while your	588	1 X 1 48	4
give) bud when to me you made for by	589	1 X 1 49	3
beautiful things when to me you gave gave darling	589	1 X 1 49	13
in) song when to me you leap and i'm	589	1 X 1 49	18
and will somebody tell me why people let go	593	1 X 1 53	24
you and you love me (and books are shuter	594	1 X 1 54	28
darling, did you (kiss me) quickly count to never?	599	(CHAIRE) 1	11
perfectly careful be lieve me you and i'll go	600	(CHAIRE) 2	12
mo re) time me n sit (1 oo	610	(CHAIRE) 12	12
swim (opening) grow are (me wander and nows to	612	(CHAIRE) 14	3
Out of more (fingeryhands me and whying) seek than	612	(CHAIRE) 14	12
the unguessed whys by me at look) swirls to	613	(CHAIRE) 15	4
like spring yoo un-air-stan? me crazy me like evry-ting . . .	618	(CHAIRE) 20	28
yoo un-air-stan? me crazy me like evry-ting / /	618	(CHAIRE) 20	30
go until you've made me white" so she did	622	(CHAIRE) 24	6
faces) only stand with me, love! against these its	633	(CHAIRE) 35	6
not) love, stand with me while silence sings not	633	(CHAIRE) 35	12
and never into (touch me! love) forever --until is	633	(CHAIRE) 35	14
flimsying become if who'd) me under a opens (of	634	(CHAIRE) 36	5
it's true that was me but that me isn't	638	(CHAIRE) 40	11
was me but that me isn't me can't you	638	(CHAIRE) 40	11
but that me isn't me can't you see now	638	(CHAIRE) 40	11
(over you reels and me a moon; beneath, bombed	639	(CHAIRE) 41	3
mighty guest of merely me --traveller from eternity; in . . .	651	(CHAIRE) 53	1
to you and to me (and quite with out	652	(CHAIRE) 54	7

473

	PAGE	TITLE	LINE

ME (CONTINUED)

	PAGE	TITLE	LINE
alive, dear: it's (kiss me now) spring! now the	665	(CHAIRE) 67	11
vanishes, teach disappearing also me the keen illimitable . .	669	(CHAIRE) 71	13
demon laughshriek ing at me your scorn of easily	677	95 POEMS 5	3
winter his silence) give me a trillionth part of	678	95 POEMS 6	13
friend dominic depaola gives me a most tremendous hug	680	95 POEMS 8	25
a you or a me) it's always ourselves we	682	95 POEMS 10	11
more than eyes tell me) there is a time	683	95 POEMS 11	14
the boys" "he'll give me another if i let	684	95 POEMS 12	9
i let him kiss me twice but my lover	684	95 POEMS 12	10
set us free) forgetting me, remember me / /	688	95 POEMS 16	15
free) forgetting me, remember me / / / /	688	95 POEMS 16	15
ing drun kenly) mind me of noone i ever	695	95 POEMS 23	11
ody's elsewher e except me 6 e nglish sparrow	696	95 POEMS 24	8
of doubleyou 4th) reminds me in spite of his	699	95 POEMS 27	6
reason at all) reminds me the cheerfulest goddamned	699	95 POEMS 27	11
m e to ti me shru gg ing as	703	95 POEMS 31	13
"will's dad never gave me one cent in his	707	95 POEMS 35	17
the rasberrypatch and 'twas me that she asked would	707	95 POEMS 35	24
too much and 'twas me that looked up at	707	95 POEMS 35	25
b usiness soca lled me n dis cussing "parity"	708	95 POEMS 36	9
gh; t: "ah gwonyuhdoanfool me" toitselfw. hispering / / . . .	710	95 POEMS 38	8
horror swallows this unworld me by you as the	711	95 POEMS 39	2
slave's unlife shall murder me for i will freely	711	95 POEMS 39	11
find anyone's blind (like me like you) except in	716	95 POEMS 44	3
doubt and believe (like me like you) vanish in	716	95 POEMS 44	27
your valentine makes happier me than i but always	718	95 POEMS 46	4
of an almost vanished me (for whom the departure	720	95 POEMS 48	9
the hell out of me-- who found forgiveness hard	730	95 POEMS 58	2
birthday comes to tell me this --each luckiest of	734	95 POEMS 62	1
fools understand (like wintry me) that not all matterings . .	736	95 POEMS 64	6
say something (for only me) and gone is who.	737	95 POEMS 65	3
my o -nl- y me / / / /	739	95 POEMS 67	17
sentinel robins two guard me and you and little	746	95 POEMS 74	2
a smiling" she told me "someone" (and smiled) "who	748	95 POEMS 76	16
or my gladness around me surges a miracle of	749	95 POEMS 77	9
sing and sing to me and while this dream	752	95 POEMS 80	4
us for you for me for each leaf newer	760	95 POEMS 87	9
air with almost breathing me) --look up: and we'll	762	95 POEMS 89	9
carry your heart with me (i carry it in	766	95 POEMS 92	1
is done by only me is your doing, my	766	95 POEMS 92	4
we know (so kiss me) shy sweet eagerly my	767	95 POEMS 93	7
a you and a me and an every (who's	769	95 POEMS 95	27
cries i and the me purrs you and the	773	73 POEMS 1	6
/ / / / Me up at does out	784	73 POEMS 12	1
false or true) disposes me to shoot dogooding folk	798	73 POEMS 26	27
but not over, stopped me by 'could you spare	800	73 POEMS 28	6
on eighth street handed me a flower. Nobody, it's	802	73 POEMS 30	6
crazy enough to give me a daisy / /	802	73 POEMS 30	33
lay (with everywhere around) me (the great dim deep	816	73 POEMS 44	2
darkestness-- now i lay me down (in a most	816	73 POEMS 44	5
snow) now i lay me down to dream of	816	73 POEMS 44	10
keep. now i lay me down to dream of	816	73 POEMS 44	14
all their times encompass me and you: when are	817	73 POEMS 45	4
guests of seem) believe me, dear, clocks have enough	817	73 POEMS 45	7
thanks of always merest me / / / /	821	73 POEMS 49	14
with anguished each their me brains of that this	822	73 POEMS 50	3
the world, but to me some (by name myself)	828	73 POEMS 56	4
come run run with me now jump shout (laugh	835	73 POEMS 63	16
purple finch please tell me why this summer world	836	73 POEMS 64	2
sweet carolling self answers me) "i could not sing"	836	73 POEMS 64	9
terrible anonymity; enfold phantom me with the murdering . .	839	73 POEMS 67	10

+ME

	PAGE	TITLE	LINE
FOR CONTEXT, SEE	122	& SEVEN POEMS 1	3
FOR CONTEXT, SEE	227	IS 5 ONE GERT	14
FOR CONTEXT, SEE	235	IS 5 ONE 6	24
FOR CONTEXT, SEE	237	IS 5 ONE 8	12
FOR CONTEXT, SEE	247	IS 5 ONE 18	5

		PAGE	TITLE	LINE

+ME (CONTINUED)

FOR CONTEXT, SEE	251 IS 5 ONE 22	17
FOR CONTEXT, SEE	310 VIVA 2	2
FOR CONTEXT, SEE	310 VIVA 2	5
FOR CONTEXT, SEE	629 (CHAIRE) 31	13
FOR CONTEXT, SEE	807 73 POEMS 35	15

MEA

| / / / PUELLA MEA Harun Omar and Master . . . . | 17 T&C PUELLA MEA | T |

MEADOW

flourish the minute spontaneous meadow of her mind) --the . .	19 T&C PUELLA MEA	123
came into the ragged meadow of my soul. /	306 IS 5 FIVE 5	15
clover, from the green meadow of time lessness; quietly . . .	370 VIVA 61	5

MEADOWS

Our feet tread sleepless meadows sweet with fear") then . . .	9 T&C SONGS 1	27
strong with love through meadows hugely move. yet what . . .	11 T&C SONGS 2	35
and smiling the level meadows ran before. Softer be	14 T&C SONGS 4	15

MEADS

| war across the smiling meads; thou by whose page . . . . . . | 209 XLI SONNETS 5 | 5 |

MEAL

| my pain their crazy meal letting thy tigers of . . . . | 139 & SON REAL 10 | 2 |

MEAL'S

| her his my next meal's coming from i say . . . . | 475 NEW POEMS 13 | 4 |

MEALS

| mouse who shares my meals with him, which is . . . . | 171 & SON ACTU 20 | 14 |

MEALY

| the bigtwittering zither-and the mealy, ladies dancing . . . | 100 & POST IMPR 11 | 42 |

MEAN

full unsheared fleece is mean beside its lovelier friends, .	11 T&C SONGS 2	12
hair eyes, and i mean the unique and nervously	153 & SON ACTU 2	2
never really wonder i mean about the smell of	242 IS 5 ONE 13	17
and her a I mean me a Irish, cook	251 IS 5 ONE 22	10
you understand that i mean what i say i	262 IS 5 ONE 32	13
the best overseeing) i mean that the blond absence.	264 IS 5 ONE 33	17
you know what i mean when the first guy	272 IS 5 TWO 7	3
there knows what i mean a god damned lot	272 IS 5 TWO 7	13
a dream? oh i mean: entirely having in my	295 IS 5 FOUR 12	4
/ / / , mean- hum a) now (nit	309 VIVA 1	1
around it) "things i mean the Rain is no	328 VIVA 19	20
know Separated what i Mean (oweld song by ;	335 VIVA 26	17
herself with day) i mean, should any curious dawn	379 VIVA 70	6
don't have to i mean Reely) but (no listen	400 NO THANKS 17	7
sil why sure) i mean the (o well ughhuh	400 NO THANKS 17	8
course) but what i mean is Nobody Understands Her	400 NO THANKS 17	18
clean get what I mean let's not spoil it	407 NO THANKS 24	8
because they can't i mean move yes sir she	425 NO THANKS 42	6
/ the boys i mean are not refined they	427 NO THANKS 44	1
wit the boys i mean are not refined they	427 NO THANKS 44	8
dynamite the boys i mean are not refined they	427 NO THANKS 44	13
pants the boys i mean are not refined they	427 NO THANKS 44	19
imitate gossip fear unlife mean -ness, and to succeed	452 NO THANKS 67	9
one stands supreme i mean the an imal without	544 1 X 1 4	3
understand quite what you mean by" sold! to the	546 1 X 1 6	13
it themselves these insects mean? when microscopic shriekings	555 1 X 1 15	3
shining who by thousands mean only one amazing thing	591 1 X 1 51	19
greater than books might mean) we're everyanything more than	594 1 X 1 54	40
i) were wise." "You mean worlds may have better	603 (CHAIRE) 5	11
worse! poor worlds; i mean they're possible --but" lifting .	603 (CHAIRE) 5	12
ones, the lean ones;the mean kind dirty clean) all	619 (CHAIRE) 21	25
otherwise) old. Old may mean anything which everyone would .	626 (CHAIRE) 28	3
jerked 300 lbs) i mean observe his these regard	645 (CHAIRE) 47	2
o f cringewiltdroolery i mean really th underscream of . . .	646 (CHAIRE) 48	8
of a boulder) nothing mean in tenderly whoms of	658 (CHAIRE) 60	6
takes; & i don't mean It-- & i don't	701 95 POEMS 29	13
It-- & i don't mean any thing real Ly	701 95 POEMS 29	16
hardly express what i Mean is what knocked him	702 95 POEMS 30	9

MEANDER

| window; yes women sturdily meander in my mind, woven . . . . | 435 NO THANKS 51 | 34 |

		PAGE	TITLE	LINE

MEANIN
ply don't know duh meanin uv duh woid sin . . . . 240 IS 5 ONE 11   2
MEANING
eternity unto the pale meaning of heaven clings, (whose . . .   6 T&C EPITHALAM   124
deleted of texture or meaning monuments and dolls resist   . . 260 IS 5 ONE 30   9
we say: Idleness, while meaning its opposite? Nothing could . 263 IS 5 ONE 32   39
which Who knows the meaning; or how dreaming becomes   . . . . 364 VIVA 55   3
lies Bang is the meaning of a gun it . . . .   570 1 X 1 30   6
bowing Cockatoo proffers the meaning of the stars 14th   . . . 697 95 POEMS 25   28
round --a dream sans meaning (or whatever kills) a . . . . . 735 95 POEMS 63   5
MEANINGLESS
soul him shall untouch meaningless precision and complete . . 402 NO THANKS 19   14
/ morsel miraculous and meaningless secret on luminous whose 456 NO THANKS 71   1
+MEANINGLESSNESS
FOR CONTEXT, SEE . . . . 347 VIVA 38   13
MEANNESS
hate itself and no meanness unsmaller) armies can immensely . 580 1 X 1 40   16
+MEANNESS
FOR CONTEXT, SEE . . . . 452 NO THANKS 67   9
MEANS
light and shape as means the moon, i somehow . . . .   98 & POST IMPR 9   9
think of dead it means nearer because deeper firmer . . . . . 126 & SEVEN POEMS 5 1
naming stealth of ecstasy means, like a girl lasciviously . . 168 & SON ACTU 17 10
mezzo del cammin' that means half- way up the . . . . 256 IS 5 ONE 27   7
wickedly to tease by means of skilfully applied bayonets   . . 339 VIVA 30   29
spirally understand What touching means or What does a   . . . 356 VIVA 47   20
i love You (thickness means worlds inhabited by roamingly . . 363 VIVA 54   2
must or any dream means more than sleep as   . . . . 390 NO THANKS 7   11
as more than know means guess) I item i . . . . 390 NO THANKS 7   11
/ / / lucky means finding Holes where pockets . . . . 467 NEW POEMS 5   1
begins a pillow's green means face or why a . . . . 506 50 POEMS 20   9
dig for love beginning means return seas who could   . . . . 526 50 POEMS 38   5
it is a man means No and (seeing something . . . . 570 1 X 1 30   7
no good pretending befriending means loving" (sighs mind: and 625 (CHAIRE) 27   5
/ / / snow means that life is a . . . . 628 (CHAIRE) 30   1
wand) a by no means almost white morethanPerson; who   . . . . 697 95 POEMS 25   18
/ / / home means that when the certainly . . . . 728 95 POEMS 56   1
it 's our (home means if any moon or . . . . 728 95 POEMS 56   5
nothings each (let's kiss) means home / / / . . . . 728 95 POEMS 56   15
a soul-- by no means funereally hilarious (or otherwise . . . 802 73 POEMS 30   19
MEANT
dem daze kid Christmas meant sumpn youse knows wot . . . . . 237 IS 5 ONE 8   14
a moon has always meant and whatever a sun   . . . . 766 95 POEMS 92   8
MEANTIME
of childhood is reversed meantime in dreams let us . . . . . 261 IS 5 ONE 31   10
MEANWHILE
near because perfectly fearful. meanwhile these speak her . . 162 & SON ACTU 11   8
with a banana, establishing meanwhile a re- ligious cult   . . 262 IS 5 ONE 32   24
am not a policeman. Meanwhile the tea regressed. Kipling   . . 263 IS 5 ONE 32   42
if only he could meanwhile my self etcetera lay . . . . . . 276 IS 5 TWO 10   18
whom every perfect thing meanwhile doth miss; a hand's   . . . 360 VIVA 51   7
upon a poet feast) meanwhile this ghost goes under, ... 418 NO THANKS 35   12
will answer" "but dying's meanwhile" (mind murmurs; the fool) 625 (CHAIRE) 27   15
+MEANWHILE
FOR CONTEXT, SEE . . . . 309 VIVA 1   1
MEASSANDCA
her flesh Came at meassandca V ingint oA chute . . . . 119 & PORTRAIT 11   5
MEASURE
invents an instrument to measure Spring with? each dream   . . 264 IS 5 ONE 33   28
all when may not measure a now of your . . . . 763 95 POEMS 90   35
children, poets, lovers tell- measure imagine, mystery, a . . 817 73 POEMS 45   10
MEASURED
trees by whom Time measured is when frost to   . . . . 207 XLI SONNETS 3   2
sleep cannot be photographed, measured; disdains the trivial 377 VIVA 68   10
and spic, are justly measured Spic and Span: to . . . . . . 438 NO THANKS 54   14
is a place that's measured and safe and known . . . . 466 NEW POEMS 4   18
called a man is measured by his quote eye . . . . 807 73 POEMS 35   8

MEASURELESS
    fear will never no? measureless our pure living complete . . 538 50 POEMS 50   3
MEASURES
    bright how plural tide measures her guest (as critics . . . . 418 NO THANKS 35   10
    totters, light droops, all measures bend nor marvel if . . . 446 NO THANKS 61   6
    heard screaming for international measures that render hell . 802 73 POEMS 30   31
MECHANICAL
    wish you good" the mechanical dawn "morning") & that . . . . 464 NEW POEMS 2   28
    sunlight (elsewhere flat the mechanical itmaking sickness of   658 {CHAIRE} 60   12
MECHANICALLY
    the Californian handpicked thrill mechanically packed and . . 337 VIVA 28   9
MECHANISM
    ity of a solemn mechanism. beneath her drab tempo . . . . . . 103 & POST IMPR 13   10
MEDALS
    a string of pretty medals drew (while messrs jack . . . . . . 266 IS 5 TWO 1   24
MEDEA'S
    wholly burn, to undertake Medea's rescuing eyes; nor he . . .   18 T&C PUELLA MEA   72
+MEDIOCRITY
    FOR CONTEXT, SEE . . . .   635 {CHAIRE} 37   8
MEDITATIONS
    sans if the mightiest meditations of mankind cancelled are . 592 1 X 1 52   6
MEDITERRANEAN
    under us the unspeaking Mediterranean bluer than we had . . . 283 IS 5 THREE 7   3
MEEAH
    remarking cries of paklavah meeah. (Very occasionally three.) 217 XLI SONNETS 13   12
MEEK
    thinks goodness what is meek; obey says toc, submit . . . . . 438 NO THANKS 54   4
    the bold ones; the meek proud sloppy sleek) all . . . . 619 {CHAIRE} 21   4
MEET
    i just happened to meet "how do you do" . . . . 313 VIVA 5   4
    she hoped we might "meet again sometime") vanished, gunwale . 326 VIVA 18   36
    a flower (whom i meet anywhere able to be . . . . 367 VIVA 58   2
    / / / i (meet) t (touch) ems crouch . . . . 388 NO THANKS 5   2
    whore dragged goes to meet her why she his . . . .   533 50 POEMS 45   23
    ing hes shes & meet & swoop fully is . . . . 536 50 POEMS 48   12
    a spark) if strangers meet life begins-- not poor . . . . . . 564 1 X 1 24   2
    unsmaller) armies can immensely meet for centuries and . . .   580 1 X 1 40   17
    --and if, when we meet again, little he (having . . . . 631 {CHAIRE} 33   7
    / / / / meet mr universe (who clean . . . . 645 {CHAIRE} 47   1
    can scarcely dare to meet no matter how he'll . . . . 685 95 POEMS 13   3
    met or hope to meet in the course of . . . . 699 95 POEMS 27   15
MEETING
    dark, and where your meeting breasts are round have . . . . .   71 T&C SON REAL 2   5
MEETS
    a certain corner, suddenly) meets the tall policeman of . . . 304 IS 5 FIVE 3   4
    than more climbing hope meets most despair? all knowing's . . 528 50 POEMS 40   9
MEGA
    on the cindercoloured little {MEGA} {HELLENIKON KSENODOCHEION 217 XLI SONNETS 13   14
MEGAETA
    --cupidoergosum spun= flash omiepsicronlonO-- megaeta? p aul   431 NO THANKS 48   26
MELANCHOLY
    eyeing, as with almost melancholy delicacy night gargles . . 168 & SON ACTU 17   18
    these gently O sweetly melancholy trillers amid the thrillers 230 IS 5 ONE 2   25
    with huddling infinite wishless melancholy, suddenly looming) 305 IS 5 FIVE 4   13
    / / / that melancholy fellow'll play his handorgan . . . . .   697 95 POEMS 25   1
MELLIFLUOUS
    arranging before me a mellifluous idiot grin (with what . . . 226 IS 5 ONE MAME   2
MELODY
    where to a normal melody of probable violins dance . . . . .   43 T&C AMORES 7   33
    trembly mist of atrocious melody.... tiniest dead tunes crawl   69 T&C POST IMPR 6 27
    of her skirt. fleshless melody of the, keenly lascivious . . 103 & POST IMPR 13   7
MELON
    who threw the ripe melon into the tree? you . . . . 125 & SEVEN POEMS 4   8
    piano item: a water- melon causes indigestion to William . . 263 IS 5 ONE 32   52
MELONS
    candies my, mouth loves melons slitted with bright knives, . 100 & POST IMPR 11   22
MELTED
    becoming bright and little melted. / / / / . . . . 283 IS 5 THREE 7   27

		PAGE	TITLE	LINE

MELTING
a kiss) distinct entirely melting sinuous lean... whereof . . 225 IS 5 ONE LIZ 15
MELTS
not forever, even snow melts; and if spring should . . . . . 579 1 X 1 39 4
MEM
for me (all decent mem and wonens will allows . . . . 500 50 POEMS 14 21
MEMO
are dead you captain) Memo 1 wife in impossibly . . . . . . 389 NO THANKS 6 18
wife in impossibly hell Memo 1 son in improbably . . . . . . 389 NO THANKS 6 20
MEMORABILIA
/ / / / MEMORABILIA stop look & listen . . . . 256 IS 5 ONE 27 T
MEMORIAM
mouth jumping on&off bandwaggons (MEMORIAM / / / / . . . . . 404 NO THANKS 21 5
MEMORIES
glutted heart fleet flowerterrible memories shall rise, . . . 36 T&C AMORES 1 27
these houses bulge like memories in one crooked street . . . 98 & POST IMPR 9 17
the bed agrin with memories (this white worm and . . . . . . 164 & SON ACTU 13 11
filled with skilfully stuffed memories / / / / . . . . 297 IS 5 FOUR 14 15
and grief these recent memories of future dream these . . . . 502 50 POEMS 16 10
MEMORY
the Century whirl? one's memory indignantly protests) this . 72 T&C SON REAL 3 4
intense, which wholly trembling memory undertakes --your . . 82 T&C SON ACTU 1 2
uncouth and amorous in memory of Cleopatra and of . . . . . . 111 & PORTRAIT 6 58
our single brain in memory of Cleopatra while easily . . . . 111 & PORTRAIT 6 71
impressed fingers of sublime Memory, of that loveliness . . . 207 XLI SONNETS 3 12
and think drinks, in memory of the Grand and . . . . 233 IS 5 ONE 4 17
little moon thinner than memory faint -er than all . . . . . 282 IS 5 THREE 6 18
kissed you into a memory slowly, oh seriously --that . . . . 295 IS 5 FOUR 12 9
treacherous bright streets of memory comes my heart, singing 304 IS 5 FIVE 3 2
softly among one's own memory (but) along perhaps the . . . . 317 VIVA 9 19
it may be socalled) memory Of (without more ado . . . . . . 317 VIVA 9 21
/ / / / memory believes fragrance of a . . . . 340 VIVA 31 1
(when of a morning Memory stands, with clumsily wilted . . . 359 VIVA 50 5
else kisses busily a memory, which how exquisitely flutters . 370 VIVA 61 26
(into supreme Now: feeling memory shrink from such brief . . 373 VIVA 64 13
hope two eyes a memory this brow five or . . . . 402 NO THANKS 19 6
least never with most memory) give entirely each Forever . . 453 NO THANKS 68 11
me down into your memory and a memory and . . . . 529 50 POEMS 41 10
your memory and a memory and memory i) kiss . . . . 529 50 POEMS 41 11
and a memory and memory i) kiss me (will . . . . 529 50 POEMS 41 11
years through which that memory strolls) and every ours . . . 617 (CHAIRE) 19 11
+MEMORY
FOR CONTEXT, SEE . . . . 447 NO THANKS 62 18
MEN
father of gods and men whose subtle throne twain . . . . . . 4 T&C EPITHALAM 41
luck of all dead men and loving) as invisibly . . . . 19 T&C PUELLA MEA 103
the street where strong men are digging bread and . . . . . . 50 T&C IMPRESS 4 13
me for twenty iron men her common purple soul . . . . 52 T&C PORTRAIT 1 23
the silly souls of men to golden dust: she . . . . 75 T&C SON REAL 6 11
the rapid hard wo- men and intotheslow hot women . . . . . . 101 & POST IMPR 1 62
bestial Marj lie large men who praise Marj's cleancornered . 114 & PORTRAIT 7 4
hoorah for the large men who lie between the . . . . 114 & PORTRAIT 7 24
Marj for the strong men who sleep between the . . . . 114 & PORTRAIT 7 27
which dangle the old men and hot men se . . . . 120 & PORTRAIT 12 22
old men and hot men se promenent doucement le . . . . 120 & PORTRAIT 12 23
which dangle the old men and hot men precisely . . . . 121 & PORTRAIT 12 59
old men and hot men precisely dance in my . . . . 121 & PORTRAIT 12 59
all over the way men you liked made you . . . . 127 & SEVEN POEMS 5 37
feel what you made, men feel when, you touched, ... 127 & SEVEN POEMS 5 39
jazz Band? or unnoise men don't make soup who . . . . 141 & SON REAL 12 18
then, Madge and her men? buried with Alice in . . . . 183 XLI SONGS 5 2
is the cheerfulest of men his peaked head smoulders . . . . . 198 XLI PORTRAIT 6 18
the most courteous of men should you remark the . . . . 198 XLI PORTRAIT 6 25
5 derbies-with-men-in-them smoke Helmar . . . . 200 XLI PORTRAIT 8 2
dnightef fendi .... five men in derbies / / . . . . 200 XLI PORTRAIT 8 33
one of those immortal men his life that his . . . . 209 XLI SONNETS 5 13
nothing is (being of men called Love) upward doth . . . . . 210 XLI SONNETS 6 4
lugs indigestible honeycake to men ....one perfectly smooth . 217 XLI SONNETS 13 9

MEN (CONTINUED)
Sunlight, there are old men behind me I tell . . . . 281 IS 5 THREE 5   24
fear not children but men speaks (among leaves Easily . . . . 356 VIVA 47   2
not (not as look men who are turned to . . . . 387 NO THANKS 4   13
all his toys (money men motors "my" yachts wolfhounds . . . . 394 NO THANKS 11   3
then comes peace unto men who are always men . . . . 414 NO THANKS 31   13
men who are always men while a man shall . . . . 414 NO THANKS 31   13
fly) for know all men ({CHAIRETE}) as it was . . . . 425 NO THANKS 42   9
ls (pour wo (things) men selves-them inghurl) bangbells . . . 444 NO THANKS 59   11
boast of fishing and men are caught by worms . . . . 446 NO THANKS 61   5
to know and if men should not hear them . . . . 481 NEW POEMS 19   4
should not hear them men are old may my . . . . 481 NEW POEMS 19   4
be wrong for whenever men are right they are . . . . 481 NEW POEMS 19   8
his did. Women and men (both little and small) . . . . 515 50 POEMS 29   5
by yes. Women and men (both dong and ding) . . . . 515 50 POEMS 29   33
father sing) then let men kill which cannot share, ... 521 50 POEMS 34   53
though hate were why men breathe-- because my father . . . . 521 50 POEMS 34   66
that dragon's tail (for men must loaf and women . . . . 552 1 X 1 12   18
silence huger than eternity, men will be saviours --flop . . 555 1 X 1 15   6
/ no man, if men are gods; but if . . . . 562 1 X 1 22   1
if gods must be men, the sometimes only man . . . . 562 1 X 1 22   2
than everything) death, as men call him, ends what . . . . . 592 1 X 1 52   13
ends what they call men --but beauty is more . . . . 592 1 X 1 52   13
you and all filthy men come annabel darling come . . . . . . 707 95 POEMS 35   21
wants Less (not to men tion least) & i . . . . 727 95 POEMS 55   5
grand: gal who liked men horses roses & $ . . . . 792 73 POEMS 20   5
woman knows; and certain men quite possibly may have . . . . 807 73 POEMS 35   12
plucked such mysteries as men do not conceive--let ocean . . 843 73 POEMS 71   13
+MEN
FOR CONTEXT, SEE . . . . 488 50 POEMS 2   22
FOR CONTEXT, SEE . . . . 500 50 POEMS 14   21
FOR CONTEXT, SEE . . . . 610 {CHAIRE} 12   12
FOR CONTEXT, SEE . . . . 708 95 POEMS 36   9
FOR CONTEXT, SEE . . . . 842 73 POEMS 70   13
MEN'S
cleancornered strokable body these men's fingers toss trunks 114 & PORTRAIT 7   6
the world has these men's hands but their bodies . . . . . . 114 & PORTRAIT 7   14
dance best on bald men's hair and every finger . . . . 511 50 POEMS 25   9
/ / as any (men's hells having wrestled with) . . . . 558 1 X 1 18   1
they doubting can turn men's see to stare their . . . . 580 1 X 1 40   8
MENACE
and rough cold, wind's menace and leaf's grieving: from . . . 207 XLI SONNETS 3   10
MENANDWOMEN
three dancing earths three menandwomen three and all around . 507 50 POEMS 21   21
MENDACIOUSLY
right sleuthfully aboard all to--mendaciously speaking--a man 334 VIVA 25   6
MENDED
sweet dirty face & mended his bright torn trousers . . . . . 680 95 POEMS 8   15
MENDER
asks his name) a mender of things with eager . . . . 660 {CHAIRE} 62   5
MENTION
Spring, that omits no mention of desire in every . . . . . . 5 T&C EPITHALAM   89
a scrumptious not to mention splendiferous funeral with tall 239 IS 5 ONE 10   30
of socks not to mention shirts fleaproof earwarmers etcetera 276 IS 5 TWO 10   11
being Dead (not to mention inTerred) LONG LIVE that . . . . . 315 VIVA 7   10
+MENTION
FOR CONTEXT, SEE . . . . 727 95 POEMS 55   5
MENTIONED
nobody seems to have mentioned ye olde freudian wish; . . . . 326 VIVA 18   3
MERCHANT
pardoner wife and nun merchant frere clerk somnour miller . . 661 {CHAIRE} 63   10
MERCI
from hinging thighs .... merci.... i want to die . . . . . . 133 & SON REAL 4   17
+MERCI
FOR CONTEXT, SEE . . . . 310 VIVA 2   8
MERCIFUL
star with what huge merciful forms presume / / . . . . 351 VIVA 42   15
perfectly the skies by merciful love whispered were, ... 526 50 POEMS 38   10

	PAGE	TITLE	LINE
MERCIFUL (CONTINUED)			
they beautifully wandering in merciful miracles wonderingly .	582	1 X 1 42	2
eagerly innocent whoms of merciful sweetness except Himself?"	748	95 POEMS 76	14
my diminutive spire to merciful Him Whose only now	749	95 POEMS 77	18
be coming some (& merciful ly which is every)	753	95 POEMS 81	12
skies: so, in how merciful love's own name, linger	812	73 POEMS 40	9
wholly up leaping through merciful sunlight) to burst in . .	841	73 POEMS 69	32
death) timelessly celebrates the merciful wonder no world . .	845	73 POEMS 73	13
MERCIFULLY			
there who) descend -ing (mercifully) touch deathful earth's .	557	1 X 1 17	9
whole, prodigiously alive most mercifully glorying keen star	808	73 POEMS 36	7
+MERCIFULLY			
FOR CONTEXT, SEE	753	95 POEMS 81	12
MERCY			
kiss) kneeling, your frequent mercy begs, sharply believe me,	115	& PORTRAIT 8	8
feet mingle under the mercy. (exit the hors d'oeuvres) . . .	243	IS 5 ONE 14	15
died Christ (of His mercy infinite) i pray to	339	VIVA 30	38
forbid and (in his mercy) your true lover spare:	484	NEW POEMS 22	10
in time's a noble mercy of proportion with generosities . . .	683	95 POEMS 11	1
find) may, given perfect mercy, live a dream larger	735	95 POEMS 63	3
huge because) given much mercy more than even the	735	95 POEMS 63	11
more than even the mercy of perfect sunlight after	735	95 POEMS 63	12
sands, at pitiless the mercy of time time time	743	95 POEMS 71	8
give herself into the mercy of that star, if	811	73 POEMS 39	11
/ / without the mercy of your eyes your	819	73 POEMS 47	1
MERDE			
-spontaneous and otherwise scented merde which greets one . .	230	IS 5 ONE 2	16
philophilic name S.S. VAN MERDE) having first put right . . .	334	VIVA 25	4
he smote the monster merde then up rose pride	552	1 X 1 12	10
MERE			
leafy goal, at the mere echo of whose shining	3	T&C EPITHALAM	15
i do forget.... or mere Music mounting unsurely twilight . .	211	XLI SONNETS 7	2
nothing paradoxically enough beyond mere personal pride which	329	VIVA 20	1
it only this eternal mere one bursting soul why, ...	414	NO THANKS 31	11
a fraid of moon You) not-mere-ly-won-der-ing-&	469	NEW POEMS 7	20
what mountaining roots of mere eternity) stupendous if . . .	517	50 POEMS 31	2
murdered eye dissected to mere because and why? take	527	50 POEMS 39	14
freedom's not some under's mere above but breathing yes . .	538	50 POEMS 50	1
phantom by prodigious time's mere brain contrived: a spook .	558	1 X 1 18	9
herself, and than this (mere most) breast spring's million .	573	1 X 1 33	17
and heroes through the mere mind's poor pretend --grim . . .	576	1 X 1 36	6
undo (nor madness nor mere death nor both who	577	1 X 1 37	10
coolly bell touches most mere until (eternally) with (now) .	601	(CHAIRE) 3	14
from beautiful obvious to Mere but one small most	608	(CHAIRE) 10	8
every ours for the mere worshipping (as calmly as	617	(CHAIRE) 19	12
truthless and life a mere pastime --each joy a	625	(CHAIRE) 27	18
read for sheer wonder mere surprise (then turn the	689	95 POEMS 17	3
every keener appetite than mere unmiracle can quite appease--	714	95 POEMS 42	5
the strength so strong mere force is feebleness: the	768	95 POEMS 94	11
and girl) but that mere fury soon became silence:	777	73 POEMS 5	9
which isn't singing is mere talking and all talking's	804	73 POEMS 32	1
MERELY			
clothe thy soul's coming merely, with a croon of	10	T&C SONGS 1	40
till this our flesh merely shall be excelled by	84	T&C SON ACTU 3	4
being twelve who hast merely gonorrhea Oldeyed child, to . .	105	& PORTRAIT 1	3
mutter thickly (as one merely terricolous American an instant	116	& PORTRAIT 9	11
of it, my dears merely the prime minister of	245	IS 5 ONE 16	19
body smile brain hands merely to become the jumping	295	IS 5 FOUR 12	3
to be deciphered selves merely Continue to experience a . . .	361	VIVA 52	27
amazing: without love separate, smileless--merely imagine . .	374	VIVA 65	2
knew once? what if (merely suppose) mine should overhear . .	374	VIVA 65	10
incredible splendor than our merely universe, love's also . .	377	VIVA 68	6
mostness (and whom did merely day close) opens if	450	NO THANKS 65	1
only A trifle less (merely beyond how very) closely	453	NO THANKS 68	6
hunger may appease what merely riches of our pretty	456	NO THANKS 71	5
ep into the not merely immeasurable into the mightily	464	NEW POEMS 2	34
head of he is) merely (a pair of ears	501	50 POEMS 15	19
mime until out of merely not nothing comes only	502	50 POEMS 16	13

		PAGE	TITLE	LINE

MERELY (CONTINUED)

pleasure and pain are merely surfaces (one itself showing, . 531 50 POEMS 43   5
so glad and very merely my fourth will cure . . . . 537 50 POEMS 49   2
myth) into thy grave merely to toil the scale . . . . 579 1 X 1 39   10
more bright worlds than merely by doubting have darkly . . . 580 1 X 1 40   13
cancelled are by one merely opening leaf (beyond whose . . . 592 1 X 1 52   7
are quite what worlds merely might be / / . . . . 603 (CHAIRE) 5   14
(false and true are merely to know) Love only . . . . 631 (CHAIRE) 33   13
/ mighty guest of merely me --traveller from eternity; . . . 651 (CHAIRE) 53   1
no of all nothing--human merely being doubt unimaginable You? 663 (CHAIRE) 65   11
/ / / whatever's merely wilful, and not miraculous . . . . . 742 95 POEMS 70   1
life must die to merely Know / / / . . . . 759 95 POEMS 86   11
feel) poor worlds must merely do, which than are . . . . . . 762 95 POEMS 89   3
with aeons of (trivial merely) existence, all when may . . . 763 95 POEMS 90   34
little and all worlds) merely have the must to . . . . 776 73 POEMS 4   7
and then upon a merely human plane) someone completely . . . 799 73 POEMS 27   10
miraculously whole; with not merely a mind and a . . . . . . 802 73 POEMS 30   17
mother's son-- all is merely talk which isn't singing . . . . 804 73 POEMS 32   11
or you (blinded by merely things believable) could only . . . 809 73 POEMS 37   6
my (and infinite our) merely to undie / / . . . . 817 73 POEMS 45   14
guess--thus, my love, to merely what dying must call . . . . 818 73 POEMS 46   14
/ timeless ly this (merely and whose not numerable . . . . . 826 73 POEMS 54   3
is now contrive; imagined, merely know (freedom: what makes . 834 73 POEMS 62   8

+MERELY

FOR CONTEXT, SEE . . . . 469 NEW POEMS 7   20

MEREST

frigid to touch a merest shape which however slenderly . . . 193 XLI PORTRAIT 1   16
than thanks of always merest me / / / . . . . 821 73 POEMS 49   14

MERGE

flame by flaming dream) merge--at not imaginable which . . . 721 95 POEMS 49   12

MERRILY

had cement for her, merrily we became each other . . . . . . 119 & PORTRAIT 11   10
alive in miraculous day) merrily moving through sweet . . . . 661 (CHAIRE) 63   7
trillionth part of inquisitive merrily humble your livingest 678 95 POEMS 6   15

MERRY

low and smiling the merry deer ran before. Fleeter . . . . . 14 T&C SONGS 4   5
jostling and shouting of merry flowers wee skipping . . . . . 44 T&C AMORES 8   5
(only feeling the belly's merry thrust Boost my huge . . . . 132 & SON REAL 3   7
this havingest world) most merry most fair most rare . . . . 590 1 X 1 50   3
sweet love" (all the merry little birds are flying . . . . . 591 1 X 1 51   5
tiny winging darting floating merry in the blossoming always 591 1 X 1 51   23
am we (pretty twinkle merry bells) Someone has been . . . . . 630 (CHAIRE) 32   13
(the all the any merry every pretty each bird . . . . 773 73 POEMS 1   3

MES

other days (drawing my Mes from sleep whose stranger . . . . 213 XLI SONNETS 9   13
talk about your Salo -mes but gimmie Jimmie's gal. . . . . . 235 IS 5 ONE 6   24

MESH

echo pouring in a mesh of following tone: did . . . . 115 & PORTRAIT 8   15
flesh does surely to mesh. New and eager. wittily . . . . . . 136 & SON REAL 7   12
teeth of slowturning streets mesh in a frieze of . . . . . . 142 & SON REAL 13   4
with iron arithmethics and mesh witH Which when both . . . . 311 VIVA 3   12
of not) bang spurting mesh (faith -ful which -ly . . . . . . 388 NO THANKS 5   12

MESHING

capable millennium of faces meshing with my curiously instant 197 XLI PORTRAIT 5   8

MESMOKED

desertbyIts elf while) nextto Mesmoked eleven camels ! and . 318 VIVA 10   15

MESS

painstakingly utters a slippery mess, a star sleepily, . . . 144 & SON REAL 15   8
hope that you may mess your pance every kumrad . . . . 413 NO THANKS 30   12

MESSIAH

the jewess shrieked the messiah tumbled successfully into the 241 IS 5 ONE 12   5

MESSRS

pretty medals drew (while messrs jack james john and . . . . 266 IS 5 TWO 1   25

MET

time because they've never met before dead's more even . . . 126 & SEVEN POEMS 5   7
nicest man you've never met who maybe winks at . . . . 126 & SEVEN POEMS 5   14
women and window-sills) i met that hideous gladness, per . . 158 & SON ACTU 7   5
were in Paris we met here / / / . . . . 304 IS 5 FIVE 3   15

481

MET (CONTINUED)
   just supposing we had met and just but you . . . . 323 VIVA 15   10
   / / / i met a man under the . . . . 355 VIVA 46   1
   hair or Think We've Met subhuman rights Before / . . . . . . 549 1 X 1 9   14
   in the dark i met christ jesus) my heart . . . . 648 (CHAIRE) 50   4
   goddamned sonofabitch i ever met or hope to meet . . . . . . 699 95 POEMS 27   14
META
   a hidi ng) est meta ph or ? la . . . . 831 73 POEMS 59   16
METAL
   occult supersnare of resistless metal: and (stealing toward . 799 73 POEMS 27   19
METAMERIC
   (that by doDreaming heteronomously metameric me are picked . 395 NO THANKS 12   13
   ness squirmcurl ing homonomously metameric You / / / . . . . 395 NO THANKS 12   16
METAPHOR
   you will permit a metaphor savouring slightly of the . . . . 326 VIVA 18   27
   strict flame) demand the metaphor of our projectile am . . . 362 VIVA 53   11
   if to no millionth metaphor opens the simple agony . . . . . 842 73 POEMS 70   11
+METAPHOR
   FOR CONTEXT, SEE . . . . 831 73 POEMS 59   16
METEORS
   of the dark with meteors streaming from playful immortal . . 36 T&C AMORES 1   16
   vivid nothing as green meteors swim signals all some . . . . 818 73 POEMS 46   11
METHODICAL
   error, with twists spontaneously methodical. He suddenly . . 170 & SON ACTU 19   11
METICULOUS
   flowers (isolating with perpetually meticulous concupiscence 193 XLI PORTRAIT 1   22
   into the throat A meticulous vulgarity: a sodden fastidious . 201 XLI PORTRAIT 9   11
METOPE
   (O to be a metope now that triglyph's here) . . . . 257 IS 5 ONE 27   39
METUS
   knows, is wut ektyouelly metus. Unbeside which limps who . . 790 73 POEMS 18   14
MEURICE
   limousine inhabit the Hotel Meurice (whereas i live in . . . 245 IS 5 ONE 16   4
MEZZO
   Murano; pause elevator nel mezzo del cammin' that means . . . 256 IS 5 ONE 27   7
MIA
   sudden nothing.... la bocca mia "he kissed wholly trembling" 84 T&C SON ACTU 3   15
MICE
   three cats, five white mice, and a baboon. O . . . . 279 IS 5 THREE 3   8
   pole over five squirming mice; or leap through hoops . . . . 279 IS 5 THREE 3   16
   and little bats & mice (and you, you say . . . . 353 VIVA 44   27
MICROSCOPIC
   filigree frame of a microscopic stage whose jouncing curtain. 55 T&C PORTRAIT 3   6
   lousy with mutilated singing microscopic things in my ears . 69 T&C POST IMPR 6 28
   violent silence fill with microscopic whithering ...(that's . 86 T&C SON ACTU 5   8
   chambers close quotes the microscopic pithecoid President in 267 IS 5 TWO 2   2
   these insects mean? when microscopic shriekings shall have . 555 1 X 1 15   4
   doom: againing (yes by microscopic yes) acceptance of . . . . 821 73 POEMS 49   3
+MICROSCOPIC
   FOR CONTEXT, SEE . . . . 361 VIVA 52   15
MID
   of squirrel-stairs into a mid-victorian attic which is known 194 XLI PORTRAIT 2   8
   do, being as Dick Mid once noted lifting a . . . . 229 IS 5 ONE FRAN   9
+MID
   FOR CONTEXT, SEE . . . . 795 73 POEMS 23   6
MID-VICTORIAN
   of squirrel-stairs into a mid-victorian attic which is known 194 XLI PORTRAIT 2   8
MID'S
   man sitting in Dick Mid's Place said to Death . . . . 57 T&C PORTRAIT 5   3
   man sitting in Dick Mid's Place asked "always" Death . . . . 57 T&C PORTRAIT 5   23
   you rang at Dick Mid's Place the madam was . . . . 73 T&C SON REAL 4   1
   knew you at Dick Mid's the three trickling chins . . . . . . 73 T&C SON REAL 4   10
   / / / Dick Mid's large bluish face without . . . . 149 & SON REAL 20   1
   girl in Yonkers. Dick Mid's green large three teeth . . . . . 149 & SON REAL 20   14
MIDDLE
   sawdust cigarettes in the middle of the night / . . . . 242 IS 5 ONE 13   23
   / slightly before the middle of Congressman Pudd 's . . . . . 249 IS 5 ONE 20   1
   while in the very middle of fire all the . . . . 283 IS 5 THREE 7   26

MIDDLE (CONTINUED)
     / / in a middle of a room stands . . . . 338 VIVA 29   1
     Large Darkness And The Middle Of The E a . . . . 361 VIVA 52   31
     scare right in the middle of a bed bed . . . . 401 NO THANKS 18   3
     he's squatting in the middle of remember with his . . . . . . 642 (CHAIRE) 44   5
MIDDLING
     all go--the big small middling tall bigger really the . . . . 569 1 X 1 29   16
MIDMOST
     / / murderfully in midmost o.c. an launch we . . . . 334 VIVA 25   1
MIDNIGHT
     to the colour of midnight to a more than . . . . 92 & POST IMPR 4   2
     a window in this midnight) for no reason feel . . . . 92 & POST IMPR 4   9
     and this spire strike midnight (and did occur bell . . . . . 115 & PORTRAIT 8   17
     / impossibly motivated by midnight the flyspecked abdominous 116 & PORTRAIT 9   2
     of the shore. By midnight, a moon scratches the . . . . . . 160 & SON ACTU 9   6
     peacockappareled prodigy of Flo's midnight Frolic dolores . . 232 IS 5 ONE 3   3
     cloud a clock strikes midnight a finger pulls a . . . . . . 338 VIVA 29   22
     grow if out of midnight dropped more suns than . . . . 576 1 X 1 36   12
     more particularly at just midnight this hearty fellow'll . . 813 73 POEMS 41   6
+MIDNITE
     FOR CONTEXT, SEE . . . . 795 73 POEMS 23   12
MIDST
     flatulence-- In the soft midst of the tongue sits . . . . . . 201 XLI PORTRAIT 9   14
MIDSUMMER'S
     would rejoice keen as midsummer's keen beyond conceiving mind 520 50 POEMS 34   25
     / / out of midsummer's blazing most not night . . . . 818 73 POEMS 46   1
MIGGIN'S
     Mr. Wiggin took Wrs. Miggin's harm in is, extinguishing . . . 263 IS 5 ONE 32   48
MIGGLE
     so thumb o'clock asters miggle dim a ram flat . . . . 333 VIVA 24   16
MIGHT
     which the king's horses might not kill.) But should . . . . . 18 T&C PUELLA MEA   48
     great sensual knees well might any monarch please.) Each . . 21 T&C PUELLA MEA   214
     with all her fragile might to not surmise she . . . . 72 T&C SON REAL 3   8
     took up the song, might i'm called and did . . . . 117 & PORTRAIT 10   16
     that his fair city might not die. / / . . . . 209 XLI SONNETS 5   14
     after all, kid you might as well toss him . . . . 298 IS 5 FOUR 15   13
     have been You, You might have been I) "?" . . . . 317 VIVA 9   9
     chair but not Cassiopeia's might those be stockings dribbling 322 VIVA 14   6
     puzzling but we both might have found the solution . . . . . 323 VIVA 15   18
     that she hoped we might "meet again sometime") vanished, . . 326 VIVA 18   36
     them Yapenese Craps somebody might hardly never not have . . 336 VIVA 27   11
     is dead (whom noone might inter fleeing himself for . . . . . 394 NO THANKS 11   5
     Green invents because where might Where live can fisherMen . 395 NO THANKS 12   7
     quote oral history unquote might (publishers note) be . . . . 410 NO THANKS 27   10
     so deep and he might live) yes, partly nor . . . . 414 NO THANKS 31   8
     mind full without fear might faithfully lie down to . . . . . 418 NO THANKS 35   7
     such a deathlessness) remembrance might no patient mind . . . 420 NO THANKS 37   7
     gloom "I think he might now be inclined to . . . . 464 NEW POEMS 2   21
     only as this (which might have been a man . . . . 479 NEW POEMS 17   8
     a quilt's pink stops might equal head). Then with . . . . . . 506 50 POEMS 20   10
     vainly no smallest voice might cry for he could . . . . 520 50 POEMS 34   15
     / / / / might these be thrushes climbing . . . . 582 1 X 1 42   1
     everything greater than books might mean) we're everyanything 594 1 X 1 54   40
     a blossoming (while anyone might slowly count to soon) . . . 599 (CHAIRE) 1   9
     quite what worlds merely might be / / / . . . . 603 (CHAIRE) 5   14
     and (there--see?) children" nor might any earth's first . . . 626 (CHAIRE) 28   13
     "no"? quote citizens unquote might otherwise forget (to err . 636 (CHAIRE) 38   5
     dark of heart they might not speak, a little . . . . 649 (CHAIRE) 51   1
     the most catastrophe april might make alive filthy some . . . 662 (CHAIRE) 64   4
     any un god manufacture might but man kind yet . . . . 698 95 POEMS 26   4
     blast some universe to might have been, and stop . . . . . . 714 95 POEMS 42   10
     whose mongrel creed is Might Makes Right --his royal . . . . 774 73 POEMS 2   11
     Unbeside which limps who might less frenziedly have cried . . 790 73 POEMS 18   15
     thing (even a universe) might be so not quite . . . . 827 73 POEMS 55   5
MIGHTEST
     buffeting thee that thou mightest conceive gods (but true . . 46 T&C LA GUERRE 2   17

MIGHTIER
    which have seduced the mightier nostrils of the fervent . . . 212 XLI SONNETS 8   6
    move (exists no miracle mightier than this: to feel) . . . . 762 95 POEMS 89   2
MIGHTIEST
    infinity sans if the mightiest meditations of mankind . . . . 592 1 X 1 52   6
    courage to receive time's mightiest dream / / / . . . . 675 95 POEMS 3   14
MIGHTILY
    i frantic this serene mightily how rooted who of . . . . . . 415 NO THANKS 32   23
    only this night a mightily form moves whose passenger . . . . 419 NO THANKS 36   22
    by timelessness that heartbeat) mightily forgetting all which 428 NO THANKS 45   13
    you tumble climb and mightily fatally i remark how . . . . . 434 NO THANKS 51   29
    merely immeasurable into the mightily alive the dear . . . . 464 NEW POEMS 2   35
MIGHTY
    adores perceived sails whose mighty brightness dumbs the . . 79 T&C SON UNRE 4   9
    which rise slim curving mighty children while a python . . . 384 NO THANKS 2   20
    sad man, may his mighty briefness dig for love . . . . 526 50 POEMS 38   4
    / / / / mighty guest of merely me . . . . 651 (CHAIRE) 53   1
MIKE
    Span: to kiss the mike if Jew turn kike . . . . 438 NO THANKS 54   15
    except the dead ones mike likes all the girls . . . . 619 (CHAIRE) 21   22
MIL
    And they're a hun-dred-mil-lion-oth-ers, like . . . . 231 IS 5 ONE 3   42
    ev eryflitter, inga. where mil (lions of aflickf) litter . . 265 IS 5 ONE 34   3
    crimbflitteringish is arefloatsis ingfallall! mil, shy . . . 265 IS 5 ONE 34   6
    against the argument of mil itary necessity" (generalissimo . 636 (CHAIRE) 38   10
MILBRIGHTLIONS
    arefloatsis ingfallall! mil, shy milbrightlions my (hurl . . 265 IS 5 ONE 34   6
MILDLY
    digestions, come: let us mildly contemplate beginning with . 266 IS 5 TWO 1   31
    invei- gles a few mildly curious rai -ned on . . . . 267 IS 5 TWO 2   17
    putting it more than mildly Absolute destructivity to non- . 391 NO THANKS 8   22
    natural; perfectly putting it mildly lively (but Death is . . 604 (CHAIRE) 6   16
    Most (not putting it mildly much) may be be . . . . 727 95 POEMS 55   11
MILE
    the stile for every mile the feet go the . . . . 15 T&C SONGS 5   19
    are from mines a mile deep but the body . . . . 33 T&C ORIENTALE 6   48
    come a more millionth mile shyly to its doom . . . . 367 VIVA 58   10
    is darker than a mile. / / / / . . . . 371 VIVA 62   27
    cripple wouldn't creep one mile uphill to only see . . . . . 520 50 POEMS 34   31
MILES
    light pours its eyeless miles the chattering sunset . . . . . 64 T&C POST IMPR 1   8
    sea through her blind miles of crumbling silence seriously . 81 T&C SON UNRE 6   13
    rose coiled within cobalt miles of sky yield to . . . . 93 & POST IMPR 5   6
    i stood (maybe nine miles off). It was spring . . . . 135 & SON REAL 6   12
    understand the (through pale miles of perishing air, haunted 305 IS 5 FIVE 4   12
+MILITARY
    FOR CONTEXT, SEE . . . . 636 (CHAIRE) 38   11
MILKY
    d an O of milky tranceworld writhes in twi . . . . 615 (CHAIRE) 17   17
MILL
    sincere stomach of each mill of the ingenious gods. . . . . . 165 & SON ACTU 14   12
    human noise of digestible mill- ions whose rich slovenly . . 202 XLI PORTRAIT 9   45
MILLENNI
    isn't wuman vive the millenni um three cheers for . . . . . . 492 50 POEMS 6   9
MILLENNIUM
    woolworthian pinnacle a capable millennium of faces meshing . 197 XLI PORTRAIT 5   8
+MILLENNIUM
    FOR CONTEXT, SEE . . . . 492 50 POEMS 6   9
MILLER
    merchant frere clerk somnour miller and reve and geoffrey . . 661 (CHAIRE) 63   10
MILLION
    of heaven clings, (whose million leaves in winsome indolence . 6 T&C EPITHALAM   125
    porphyry which was a million years building he takes . . . . 32 T&C ORIENTALE 6   3
    perhaps shall pass a million years (while a bee . . . . 181 XLI SONGS 3   8
    I'M TOLD $ SEVERAL MILLION FINKLESTEIN (FRITZ) LIVES AT . . . 244 IS 5 ONE 15   2
    is is worth a million statues / / / . . . . 247 IS 5 ONE 18   8
    with terror through a million billion trillion stars / . . . 258 IS 5 ONE 28   24
    starings rinsed with thoroughly million yells they f-oo-l . . 388 NO THANKS 5   8

MILLION (CONTINUED)
    his laugh is a million griefs wide (it shall . . . . 439 NO THANKS 55   11
    : then a small million of dark voices sing . . . . 454 NO THANKS 69   13
    one) which may your million selves and my suffice . . . . . . 510 50 POEMS 24   12
    (mere most) breast spring's million (who are and do . . . . . 573 1 X 1 33   19
    april me, some thousand million hundred more bright worlds . 580 1 X 1 40   12
    close have disappeared a million whys; but opening if . . . . 588 1 X 1 48   6
    / swim so now million many worlds in each . . . . 603 (CHAIRE) 5   1
    (mountain valley forest) a million wheres which never may . . 659 (CHAIRE) 61   6
    two were a hundred million whos (while only himself . . . . . 709 95 POEMS 37   3
    shall even prevail a million questionings against the silence 714 95 POEMS 42   12
    and dream or many million minds which sleep and . . . . 743 95 POEMS 71   7
    and our night's thousand million miracles a million thousand 756 95 POEMS 84   12
    thousand million miracles a million thousand hundred nothing 756 95 POEMS 84   13
    it, now with a million flaming billion kinds of . . . . 786 73 POEMS 14   14
+MILLION
    FOR CONTEXT, SEE . . . . 231 IS 5 ONE 3   42
    FOR CONTEXT, SEE . . . . 779 73 POEMS 7   26
MILLIONAIRES
    who inserts monkeyglands in millionaires a cute idea n'est-ce 245 IS 5 ONE 16   14
MILLIONARY
    united by perfect nothing: millionary wherewhens distant, as 721 95 POEMS 49   5
    signals all some world's millionary mind never may partly . . 818 73 POEMS 46   12
    --open this ghost with millionary knives of wind-- scatter . 839 73 POEMS 67   11
MILLIONMINDED
    are night's total exploding millionminded Who / / / . . . . . 633 (CHAIRE) 35   16
MILLIONS
    whites shoving, the dotting millions of windows of thousands 281 IS 5 THREE 5   6
    make how many stopped millions of female hard for . . . . . . 337 VIVA 28   4
    female hard for their millions of stopped male to . . . . . . 337 VIVA 28   5
    An (fragrance) Of (Begins) millions Of Tints (and) & . . . . 348 VIVA 39   3
    isn't important whether it's millions of other punks or . . . 549 1 X 1 9   4
    white thousands return by millions and dreaming drift . . . . 630 (CHAIRE) 32   5
    (shrived of that nonexistence millions call life, you and . . 745 95 POEMS 73   9
    Who the busy the millions (as you're as can . . . . 801 73 POEMS 29   13
    thousands of (hundreds of) millions of CriesWhichAreWings / / 840 73 POEMS 68   31
+MILLIONS
    FOR CONTEXT, SEE . . . . 202 XLI PORTRAIT 9   45
    FOR CONTEXT, SEE . . . . 265 IS 5 ONE 34   3
    FOR CONTEXT, SEE . . . . 265 IS 5 ONE 34   3
    FOR CONTEXT, SEE . . . . 265 IS 5 ONE 34   6
MILLIONTH
    i surely make a millionth poem which will not . . . . 92 & POST IMPR 4   19
    dream come a more millionth mile shyly to its . . . . 367 VIVA 58   10
    or if to no millionth metaphor opens the simple . . . . 842 73 POEMS 70   11
MILLS
    &-moon-He-be-hind-a-mills tosses like thin bums . . . . 469 NEW POEMS 7   1
MILLSTONES
    and common's rare and millstones float --long enough and . . 511 50 POEMS 25   19
MILLY
    / / maggie and milly and molly and may . . . . 682 95 POEMS 10   1
    remember her troubles, and milly befriended a stranded star . 682 95 POEMS 10   5
MIME
    grip live loop croon mime nakedly hurl asquirm the . . . . . 445 NO THANKS 60   24
    do the losing spectres mime until out of merely . . . . 502 50 POEMS 16   12
MIMI
    where danced la guerre. Mimi a la voix fragile . . . . 120 & PORTRAIT 12   5
    avec moi? te ferai Mimi te ferai Minette, dead . . . . 121 & PORTRAIT 12   37
    a little love begs, Mimi with the body like . . . . 121 & PORTRAIT 12   48
MIMICRY
    watched unhands describe what mimicry, with angry seasalt and 376 VIVA 67   3
MINCE
    pink-flag blackshirt and brown strut-mince and stink-brag . . 497 50 POEMS 11   3
MINCED
    guiding smile, lips wisely minced for blown kisses, ...   9 T&C SONGS 1   12
MIND
    perfect darkness fills his mind who will their hungering . .   9 T&C SONGS 1   20
    spontaneous meadow of her mind) --the vocal fern, always . . 19 T&C PUELLA MEA 123

LINE
MIND (CONTINUED)

cool jewel of thy mind the hair of thy . . . . 29 T&C ORIENTALE 3 17
leaping air the minute mind of the world. The . . . . 62 T&C PORTRAIT 10 9
things which in my mind blossom will stumble beneath . . . . 91 & POST IMPR 3 11
o n ? my mind laughsin- to Slivers of . . . . 94 & POST IMPR 6 18
crooked street of a mind peacefully and skilfully which . . . 98 & POST IMPR 9 18
(Listen drenches: earth's ugly) mind. , Rinsing with exact . 99 & POST IMPR 10 3
nnual (ugliness of) rinsed mind slowly: from! the: A . . . . 99 & POST IMPR 10 22
face and said never mind, you'll find But the . . . . 125 & SEVEN POEMS 4 19
of the sky, my mind takes to nib -bling, ... 131 & SON REAL 2 4
the village of her mind bodily which ravelling, to . . . . . 136 & SON REAL 7 2
systole purrs against my mind, the eyes' shuddering burrs . . 136 & SON REAL 7 6
wonderful smell in my mind, you should see when . . . . . . 152 & SON ACTU 1 7
life; the grim clenched mind of me somewhere begins . . . . . 156 & SON ACTU 5 11
you, worn upon my mind all night, quitting only . . . . . . 165 & SON ACTU 14 2
/ / / the mind is its own beautiful . . . . 170 & SON ACTU 19 1
with prisms of sharp mind and Matisse rhythms to . . . . . . 180 XLI SONGS 2 11
a sadistic modesty his mind is seen frequently fingering . . 193 XLI PORTRAIT 1 5
full of sharp thick mind you make us shrill . . . . 195 XLI PORTRAIT 3 4
/ / / my mind is a big hunk . . . . 199 XLI PORTRAIT 7 1
unjoyously bullied of vilest mind and sweet uncaring earth . 213 XLI SONNETS 9 2
fear Or with thy mind against my mind, to . . . . 215 XLI SONNETS 11 12
thy mind against my mind, to hear nearing our . . . . 215 XLI SONNETS 11 12
timid like of her mind to my mind that . . . . 216 XLI SONNETS 12 6
her mind to my mind that i am come . . . . 216 XLI SONNETS 12 6
(and i imagine never mind Joe agreeably cheerfully remarked . 241 IS 5 ONE 12 2
into my highly sexed mind. It seemed to me . . . . 262 IS 5 ONE 32 4
your kisses your flesh mind breathing beside under around . . 283 IS 5 THREE 7 16
this has arrived your mind may guess if at . . . . 285 IS 5 FOUR 2 11
and increase, since your mind has walked into my . . . . . . 297 IS 5 FOUR 14 5
who begs in your mind (slightly smiling, patient, unspeaking 298 IS 5 FOUR 15 2
and cling to my mind always But now she . . . . 301 IS 5 FOUR 18 11
tall policeman of my mind. awake being not asleep, ... 304 IS 5 FIVE 3 5
whitest song upon my mind--if i have failed to . . . . . . 306 IS 5 FIVE 5 5
it i wonder never mind consider rather heavenly things . . . 322 VIVA 14 1
bells (touch) ing ? mind (moon begins The) . . . . 350 VIVA 41 9
behind dir ty glass mind muddled and cuddled by . . . . . . 354 VIVA 45 6
rate one stilled unmoving mind from a hun dred . . . . . . 354 VIVA 45 20
love me) distance is mind carefully luminous with innumerable 363 VIVA 54 6
none let's feel all) mind in mind flesh In . . . . 364 VIVA 55 15
feel all) mind in mind flesh In flesh succeeding . . . . . . 364 VIVA 55 15
little house of my mind. Clocks strike. The moon's . . . . 365 VIVA 56 3
appeared to me your mind drifting with chuckling rubbish . . 369 VIVA 60 4
in darkness ourselves go, mind in mind which is . . . . . . 379 VIVA 70 3
ourselves go, mind in mind which is the thrilling . . . . . 379 VIVA 70 3
and heart conceives and mind leaps (and that which . . . . . 386 NO THANKS 3 13
/ / a) glazed mind layed in a urinal . . . . 387 NO THANKS 4 1
fate (he must deny mind: may believe in brains. . . . . . . 402 NO THANKS 19 15
his disappearance; as a mind full without fear might . . . . 418 NO THANKS 35 6
remembrance might no patient mind unstrange learn (nor could 420 NO THANKS 37 7
speak whatever's on their mind they do whatever's in . . . . 427 NO THANKS 44 17
not fall into his mind feeling throughout ignorant . . . . . 428 NO THANKS 45 5
sturdily meander in my mind, woven by always upon . . . . . 435 NO THANKS 51 35
/ / / this mind made war being generous . . . . 440 NO THANKS 56 1
fart full oft (with mind with heart he spat . . . . 441 NO THANKS 56 39
stars whitely births of mind if air is throbbing . . . . . 450 NO THANKS 65 5
quite try almost their mind immeasurably roots among much . . 479 NEW POEMS 17 5
are old may my mind stroll about hungry and . . . . 481 NEW POEMS 19 5
space on; and his mind take off time that . . . . 484 NEW POEMS 22 8
off rag its of mind chucks away flimsy which . . . . 501 50 POEMS 15 14
midsummer's keen beyond conceiving mind of sun will stand, . 520 50 POEMS 34 26
fear, to doubt a mind, to differ a disease . . . . 521 50 POEMS 34 58
whose heart is her mind) supremely whole uplifting the, . . . 533 50 POEMS 45 4
one hand is a mind then over our thief . . . . 543 1 X 1 3 18
and couldn't use a mind / / / / . . . . 544 1 X 1 4 28
from daughter's mother's zero mind fahrenheit) old . . . . . 546 1 X 1 6 1
envy and soul to mind) --whose hearts are mountains, ... 560 1 X 1 20 14
if you gut a mind to there's something for . . . . 567 1 X 1 27 14

MIND (CONTINUED)
    speak (snowflake and rainbow mind and soul november and . . . 575 1 X 1 35   33
    immortally occurs beyond the mind) such a forever is . . . . 576 1 X 1 36   8
    completely strikes forests of mind, mountains of soul) quite 580 1 X 1 40   25
    as collapsing that grey mind by wave doom disappeared, . . . 599 (CHAIRE) 1   6
    innocent (so deep's the mind of flesh and so . . . . 609 (CHAIRE) 11   7
    now Mrs Death. Poor Mind / / / / . . . . 621 (CHAIRE) 23   4
    befriending means loving" (sighs mind: and he's clever) "for 625 (CHAIRE) 27   6
    answer" "but dying's meanwhile" (mind murmurs; the fool) . . 625 (CHAIRE) 27   16
    & you'll find his mind in it (dead) / . . . . 637 (CHAIRE) 39   11
    who died in her mind with a warm thick . . . . 647 (CHAIRE) 49   6
    mechanical itmaking sickness of mind sprawls) here a livingly 658 (CHAIRE) 60   14
    not so much that mind no more can disprove . . . . 664 (CHAIRE) 66   3
    fish climb through the mind of the sea (all . . . . 665 (CHAIRE) 67   20
    the sky) because a mind no other mind should . . . . 679 95 POEMS 7   7
    a mind no other mind should try to fool . . . . 679 95 POEMS 7   7
    him of coercion or mind and soul convict him . . . . 683 95 POEMS 11   4
    sweet things beyond whatever mind may comprehend, remember . 688 95 POEMS 16   11
    slant ing drun kenly) mind me of noone i . . . . 695 95 POEMS 23   10
    perhapsless mystery of paradise) mind without soul may blast 714 95 POEMS 42   9
    stones for eyes for mind with none) boy after . . . . 716 95 POEMS 44   9
    to see what no mind knows a mindless he . . . . 716 95 POEMS 44   14
    reckoned by the unimmortal mind, these immeasurable mysteries 721 95 POEMS 49   6
    at this wedding) never mind a world with its . . . . 732 95 POEMS 60   13
    not all matterings of mind equal one violet / . . . . 736 95 POEMS 64   7
    som ething like a mind with out a body . . . . 753 95 POEMS 81   5
    eithering vastnesses of orish mind --nothing believable . . . 761 95 POEMS 88   4
    living" worlds of prose mind utterly beyond is brief . . . . 763 95 POEMS 90   19
    by matter; not by mind revealed (more than all . . . . . . 765 95 POEMS 91   6
    soul can hope or mind can hide) and this . . . . 766 95 POEMS 92   13
    only love, strolling slowly (mind in mind) through some . . . 777 73 POEMS 5   3
    strolling slowly (mind in mind) through some green mysterious 777 73 POEMS 5   3
    became the slave of mind; thus virtue triumphed over . . . . 799 73 POEMS 27   35
    with not merely a mind and a heart but . . . . 802 73 POEMS 30   17
    all some world's millionary mind never may partly . . . . . . 818 73 POEMS 46   12
    were hide, poor dishonoured mind who thought yourself so . . 834 73 POEMS 62   13
    a freedom which no mind contrives (but certainly each . . . . 842 73 POEMS 70   7
MIND'S
    / / / The Mind's (i never you . . . . 474 NEW POEMS 12   1
    heroes through the mere mind's poor pretend --grim comics . . 576 1 X 1 36   6
    in fire, but fear-- mind's a coward; lies are . . . . 651 (CHAIRE) 53   9
MINDED
    home by the high minded pure young girl much . . . . 273 IS 5 TWO 8   20
+MINDED
    FOR CONTEXT, SEE . . . . 633 (CHAIRE) 35   16
MINDFUL
    knows (yet are we mindful, though not as yet . . . . 264 IS 5 ONE 33   13
MINDHEART
    good yes completely kind mindheart one true one generous . . 523 50 POEMS 36   41
MINDLESS
    a deep lap enormous mindless hands. and no one . . . . . . 225 IS 5 ONE LIZ   9
    O, the darling benevolent mindless He--and She-- shaped . . . 250 IS 5 ONE 21   7
    allness disappears lovers are mindless they higher than fears 563 1 X 1 23   7
    no mind knows a mindless he begins to guess . . . . 716 95 POEMS 44   15
MINDS
    unbeautiful and have comfortable minds (also, with the . . .   70 T&C SON REAL 1   2
    will smooth entirely our minds --before leaving my room . . . 288 IS 5 FOUR 5   5
    hugs our dying silent minds, which hand in hand . . . . . . 305 IS 5 FIVE 4   9
    intimate tumult (Into) bangs minds into dream (An) quickly . 348 VIVA 39   9
    and night shouts) When minds shrivel and hearts grow . . . . 359 VIVA 50   3
    living dance upon dead minds why, it is love; . . . . 377 VIVA 68   1
    trying to find their minds (but never had any . . . . 410 NO THANKS 27   8
    sick, Hearts being sick, Minds nothing can: if Hate's . . . . 438 NO THANKS 54   22
    socalled people have no minds but if they had . . . . 510 50 POEMS 24   3
    if they had their minds socalled would not exist . . . . . 510 50 POEMS 24   4
    if these not existing minds took life such life . . . . . . 510 50 POEMS 24   5
    stands gradually upon four minds (out of some undering . . . 517 50 POEMS 31   8
    mosts the actual more minds ignorant of stern miraculous . . 556 1 X 1 16   5

		PAGE	TITLE	LINE

MINDS (CONTINUED)
nothing deeper than our minds to call the stars. . . . . . . 741 95 POEMS 69   8
dream or many million minds which sleep and move) . . . . . . 743 95 POEMS 71   7
our (with all their minds) eyes blindly stare life . . . . . 780 73 POEMS 8   7
all things swim climb minds (down slowly swoop wholly . . . . 841 73 POEMS 69   28
+MINDS
FOR CONTEXT, SEE . . . . 817 73 POEMS 45   3
MINDSCREAM
vomits a rock of mindscream into life; possibly darker . . . 506 50 POEMS 20   5
MINE
for his eyes are mine. Doll's boy's asleep under . . . . . . 15 T&C SONGS 5   16
your dead beautiful ladies. Mine is a little lovelier . . . . 17 T&C PUELLA MEA   3
as those ladies were mine is a little lovelier. . . . . . .   18 T&C PUELLA MEA   76
the city of Bagdad-- mine is a little lovelier . . . . 20 T&C PUELLA MEA   133
boast your dead beauties, mine being unto me sweeter . . . . 22 T&C PUELLA MEA   250
smile--and she is Lust.... mine also, little painted poem . . 75 T&C SON REAL 6   14
clutch his heart, as mine in time not far . . . . 76 T&C SON UNRE 1   4
such strangeness as was mine a little while; moments . . . . 78 T&C SON UNRE 3   8
the preposterous colour unbeheld --mine the unbought . . . . 84 T&C SON ACTU 3   3
its own beautiful prisoner. Mine looked long at the . . . . . 170 & SON ACTU 19   3
believe thou me cocodrillo-- mine eyes have seen the . . . . 256 IS 5 ONE 27   10
hopes less tall than mine" (opening the windows) "and . . . . 328 VIVA 19   10
becomes if your heart's mine) i guess a grassblade . . . . . 364 VIVA 55   5
what if (merely suppose) mine should overhear and answer . . 374 VIVA 65   11
said he (you are Mine said she) / / . . . . 399 NO THANKS 16   32
gone snow gone yours mine . We're alive and . . . . 491 50 POEMS 5   9
until she hit a mine and sank just off . . . . 494 50 POEMS 8   3
pie (it's try, boys) mine is yours ask me . . . . 513 50 POEMS 27   18
in, girls) yours is mine either was deafer than . . . . . . 513 50 POEMS 27   27
violet you may take mine" "o how how how . . . . 684 95 POEMS 12   4
or any thine a mine --dingdong: dongding-- to say . . . . . 798 73 POEMS 26   5
than your fate and mine (or any truth beyond . . . . 809 73 POEMS 37   2
i find selves unimaginably mine; beyond sorrow's own joys . . 810 73 POEMS 38   10
+MINE
FOR CONTEXT, SEE . . . . 445 NO THANKS 60   29
FOR CONTEXT, SEE . . . . 445 NO THANKS 60   29
MINE'S
deep sky in May mine's tou ching this crump . . . . 314 VIVA 6   17
MINERAL
a cannibal) there's your mineral general animal (five foot . 640 (CHAIRE) 42   11
MINES
their hands are from mines a mile deep but . . . . 33 T&C ORIENTALE 6   47
MINETTE
ferai Mimi te ferai Minette, dead exactly dance si . . . . . 121 & PORTRAIT 12   38
MINEYOURS
climb to GIVE (yoursmine mineyours yoursmine ! i (. . . . . 445 NO THANKS 60   29
MINGLE
her Lobster without feet mingle under the mercy. (exit . . . 243 IS 5 ONE 14   14
MINGLED
furious and beautiful elephants (mingled in whispering . . . 95 & POST IMPR 7   15
MINGLING
with a croon of mingling robes musically revealed in . . . . 10 T&C SONGS 1   41
dumb blossoms of new mingling: deeper: blood of my . . . . . 139 & SON REAL 10   4
yours shut by our mingling arms through a darkness . . . . . 297 IS 5 FOUR 14   2
curious dawn discuss our mingling spirits, you would . . . . 379 VIVA 70   7
MINIONS
saluting reviewing processions of minions ◇ "allezcirculez") 275 IS 5 TWO 9   37
MINISTER
dears merely the prime minister of Siam in native . . . . . 245 IS 5 ONE 16   20
MINSTREL
striking of a good minstrel between them is always . . . . 29 T&C ORIENTALE 3   13
MINUS
himself fa -mous soldier minus his na- me (so . . . . 267 IS 5 TWO 2   14
and without why (quite minus gal or pal slightly . . . . . . 387 NO THANKS 4   4
you directly perceive or minus news alimony blackmail . . . . 391 NO THANKS 8   10
and without was if minus and shall be immeasurable . . . . . 502 50 POEMS 16   5
utterly things sweet, maggoty minus and dumb death all . . . 521 50 POEMS 34   63
a tearose) and every minus plus --fare ill: fare . . . . . . 798 73 POEMS 26   12

	PAGE	TITLE	LINE

MINUS (CONTINUED)
me with the murdering minus of cold --open this . . . . 839 73 POEMS 67   10
MINUTE
make to flourish the minute spontaneous meadow of her . . . . 19 T&C PUELLA MEA 122
peacefully leaping air the minute mind of the world. . . . . 62 T&C PORTRAIT 10   9
climbing hideously with large minute hips, O press worms . . 67 T&C POST IMPR 4   27
it seriously in, his minute pocket) Sometimes he does . . . . 69 T&C POST IMPR 6   11
body sorry when the minute moon is a remarkable . . . . 82 T&C SON ACTU 1   4
perching on this silver minute of evening. We'll choose . . . 86 T&C SON ACTU 5   2
is three animals. The minute waist continually with an . . . 95 & POST IMPR 7   5
lamp. when With a minute terrif iceffort one dirty . . . . . 96 & POST IMPR 8   27
slightly is a more minute adventure) lady. The clumsy . . . . 98 & POST IMPR 9   12
you out of the minute incessant Was irrevocably emanates . . 111 & PORTRAIT 6   52
indubitably tellurian strolls emitting minute grins each an . 116 & PORTRAIT 9   6
tumbling garble when a minute pulled the sluice emerging. . . 119 & PORTRAIT 11   15
muscle amorous pricks with minute odour these gross days . . 165 & SON ACTU 14   5
drew lewdly the murmurous minute clumsy smelloftheworld. We . 174 & SON ACTU 23   2
vol- ume the flat minute gallop of careful hugeness . . . . . 201 XLI PORTRAIT 9   22
what the hell) next minute i was back in . . . . 248 IS 5 ONE 19   14
up to the last minute coming back down by . . . . 248 IS 5 ONE 19   27
among the smell of minute mown lives) oh my . . . . 434 NO THANKS 51   25
never do wrong does (minute by second and most . . . . 469 NEW POEMS 7   18
a world grows greener minute by second and most . . . . 769 95 POEMS 95   2
MINUTELY
all the people are minutely dead. Then you will . . . . 86 T&C SON ACTU 5   13
of it" their, hands minutely answered / / / . . . . 255 IS 5 ONE 26   10
MINUTENESS
foot (if whose very minuteness doth abuse reason, why . . . . 22 T&C PUELLA MEA 218
MINUTES
legs whereas, at twenty minutes to one, i am . . . . 115 & PORTRAIT 8   25
tac-toc. Time and lilacs.... minutes and love.... do you? . . 133 & SON REAL 4   8
speak (it is nine minutes past six) the well-fed . . . . . . 219 XLI SONNETS 15   4
MIRACLE
rearing (as in the miracle of a lady who . . . . 18 T&C PUELLA MEA 46
leaves go crisp with miracle. Love!--maker of my lady, . . . 22 T&C PUELLA MEA 236
but covering one complete miracle of nearest far "i . . . . . 504 50 POEMS 18   3
disappear causing through mystery miracle peace: or (if begin 559 1 X 1 19   4
eager glory, no more miracle may grow --childfully serious . . 601 (CHAIRE) 3   6
never have breathed such miracle murdered we whom cannot . . 639 (CHAIRE) 41   9
never happen again, a miracle which has never happened . . . 667 (CHAIRE) 69   7
moon! as (by the miracle of your sweet innocence . . . . . . 669 (CHAIRE) 71   10
call most the amazing miracle of all / / . . . . 741 95 POEMS 69   14
around me surges a miracle of unceasing birth and . . . . . . 749 95 POEMS 77   9
by hugest) dooms of miracle drift killed swim born . . . . . 757 95 POEMS 85   32
of darlings! by that miracle which is the coming . . . . . . 761 95 POEMS 88   9
motionless move (exists no miracle mightier than this: to . . 762 95 POEMS 89   2
beyond perceive) quivers this miracle of summer night her . . 809 73 POEMS 37   3
"& friendship is a miracle" his always not imaginably . . . . 823 73 POEMS 51   10
: every where a miracle arrives (yes) you and . . . . 835 73 POEMS 63   24
MIRACLE'S
(and more than every miracle's to breathe) wounded us . . . . 745 95 POEMS 73   4
MIRACLES
deftly upon which indolent miracles impinge) --it is . . . . 19 T&C PUELLA MEA 96
beautifully wandering in merciful miracles wonderingly . . . 582 1 X 1 42   3
homing through welcoming sweet miracles of air (and joyfully 659 (CHAIRE) 61   2
our night's thousand million miracles a million thousand . . 756 95 POEMS 84   12
MIRACULOUS
palpitating veils. O still miraculous May! O shining girl . .   5 T&C EPITHALAM 105
each is a verb, miraculous inflected oral devious, beneath .   21 T&C PUELLA MEA 209
sharpening air. Fields lying miraculous in violent silence .   86 T&C SON ACTU 5   7
us not deem it miraculous if their (so to . . . . 326 VIVA 18   8
/ / / structure, miraculous challenge, devout am upward . . . 351 VIVA 42   1
/ / / morsel miraculous and meaningless secret on . . . . . . 456 NO THANKS 71   1
minds ignorant of stern miraculous this every truth--beware . 556 1 X 1 16   5
of it, dying 's miraculous why? be cause dying . . . . 604 (CHAIRE) 6   11
green like growing (is miraculous like tomorrow) all around . 617 (CHAIRE) 19   6
(equally all alive in miraculous day) merrily moving through 661 (CHAIRE) 63   6
merely wilful, and not miraculous (be never it so . . . . . . 742 95 POEMS 70   2

	PAGE	TITLE	LINE

MIRACULOUS (CONTINUED)
youamiare (2) the holy miraculous difference between . . . . 803 73 POEMS 31 9
+MIRACULOUS
FOR CONTEXT, SEE . . . . 600 (CHAIRE) 2 16
MIRACULOUSLY
hand of Saint Ignatz miraculously inhabits. (people tumble . 280 IS 5 THREE 4 4
(and which night hoists miraculously above the always beyond 378 VIVA 69 12
beguiles our spirits, whose miraculously disenchanted eyes . 675 95 POEMS 3 3
is, completely alert and miraculously whole; with not merely 802 73 POEMS 30 16
MIRE
flesh be mud and mire, scheming imagine, passion willed, . . 521 50 POEMS 34 54
MIRED
with gilt hopeless wheels mired where sits rigidly her . . . 131 & SON REAL 2 15
expands one square foot mired in silk wrinkling loth . . . . 225 IS 5 ONE LIZ 3
MIRROR
is day, in the mirror i see a frail . . . . 50 T&C IMPRESS 4 17
dreams dreams in the mirror and it is dusk . . . . 50 T&C IMPRESS 4 22
left hand upon a mirror. / / / / . . . . 170 & SON ACTU 19 14
we saw in the mirror)? therefore we'll kiss; for . . . . . . 286 IS 5 FOUR 3 20
reflection walking upon a mirror this is friday 1 . . . . . . 335 VIVA 26 5
bird flies into a mirror) / / / / . . . . 338 VIVA 29 24
eyes firmly stirred) my mirror gives me, on this . . . . . . 360 VIVA 51 3
a cigarette (in a mirror / / / / . . . . 375 VIVA 66 16
Hello is what a mirror says it is a . . . . 570 1 X 1 30 1
city's least street) of mirror lying are each (why . . . . . 623 (CHAIRE) 25 4
+MIRROR
FOR CONTEXT, SEE . . . . 226 IS 5 ONE MAME 1
MIRRORS
toward me the guessable mirrors which your eyes are . . . . . 370 VIVA 61 10
alive in spite of mirrors (have died beyond the . . . . 386 NO THANKS 3 1
why, digging bridges with mirrors from whispers to stars; . . 439 NO THANKS 55 21
solidities, unwinding dizzily & mirrors; sprung dimensionless 480 NEW POEMS 18 20
MIRTH
echo of whose shining mirth the furious hearts of . . . . . . 3 T&C EPITHALAM 15
MIS
sed bea yew tea mis eyesucks unyewkuntel finglestein idstings 474 NEW POEMS 12 11
+MISBUTTONED
FOR CONTEXT, SEE . . . . 607 (CHAIRE) 9 5
MISCALLED
such a monster's fellowmen miscalled are happy should his . . 842 73 POEMS 70 14
MISCHIEF
her and brush the mischief from her eyes and . . . . 40 T&C AMORES 4 41
her sow- eyes clicking mischief from thick lids. the . . . . 73 T&C SON REAL 4 7
/ come (all you mischief- hatchers hatch mischief) all . . . 452 NO THANKS 67 1
you mischief- hatchers hatch mischief) all you guilty scamper 452 NO THANKS 67 3
MISCHIEVOUS
person jovial ego (& mischievous tenderly phoebeing alter) . 678 95 POEMS 6 6
MISCONCEPTION
rests upon a dismal misconception; namely that some neither . 807 73 POEMS 35 6
MISERS
beggars are rich but misers are poor) --let's touch . . . . . 769 95 POEMS 95 4
robin a song) but misers are poor-- let's love . . . . . . 769 95 POEMS 95 23
MISS
which will not wholly miss you; or if i . . . . 92 & POST IMPR 4 20
rivers of our blood, miss by how terrible inches . . . . . 174 & SON ACTU 23 9
prose flowers guess and miss machinery is the more . . . . . 264 IS 5 ONE 33 10
(cowards which fear to miss within your least gesture . . . . 293 IS 5 FOUR 10 7
was hectocotyliferously propagated when Miss G touched n.y. . 326 VIVA 18 10
ous protestations) and offering Miss Gay one (which she . . . 326 VIVA 18 19
square feet turned abruptly Miss Gay away: "on the . . . . . 326 VIVA 18 26
slightly of the demotic) Miss Gay had nothing to . . . . . . 326 VIVA 18 29
nothing to say to Miss Gay during our return . . . . 326 VIVA 18 30
CAN be ele- vating" Miss (believe it or) Gay . . . . 327 VIVA 18 42
perfect thing meanwhile doth miss; a hand's impression in . . 360 VIVA 51 7
a whatses to rescue miss nobody's probably handbag) because . 475 NEW POEMS 13 21
their eyes would never miss a yes) / / . . . . 576 1 X 1 36 14
/ / / we miss you, jack--tactfully you (with . . . . 605 (CHAIRE) 7 1
a circusheart and we miss them more than any . . . . 605 (CHAIRE) 7 7

		PAGE	TITLE	LINE
MISS (CONTINUED)				
"and you couldn't well miss willy's carroty hair" "it	707	95 POEMS 35	4
+MISS				
FOR CONTEXT, SEE	474	NEW POEMS 12	11
MISSED				
ocean will never be missed (it's in, girls) yours	513	50 POEMS 27	24
u will not be missed who as an anthologist	551	1 X 1 11	1
MISSING				
this thou catch, else missing. (though love be a	13	T&C SONGS 3	19
+MISSING				
FOR CONTEXT, SEE	388	NO THANKS 5	16
+MISSIONS				
FOR CONTEXT, SEE	405	NO THANKS 22	5
MISSOURI				
all cried like the Missouri when my Uncle Sol's	239	IS 5 ONE 10	32
MIST				
down in a trembly mist of atrocious melody.... tiniest . . .	69	T&C POST IMPR 6	26
at moon-cease soon verbal mist-flowers close ghosts on prowl	90	& POST IMPR 2	14
fingers snitch rapidly through mist a defunct king as	259	IS 5 ONE 29	11
looks big in a mist and if (by Him	514	50 POEMS 28	8
again & again (jukejog mist & strict) & again	629	{CHAIRE} 31	19
+MIST				
FOR CONTEXT, SEE	829	73 POEMS 57	1
MIST-FLOWERS				
at moon-cease soon verbal mist-flowers close ghosts on prowl	90	& POST IMPR 2	14
MISTAKE				
her lips a moist mistake, whose fragrance hurls me	148	& SON REAL 19	10
really made quite a mistake in being at all	262	IS 5 ONE 32	6
MISTAKEN				
whom he pronounces young mistaken and cradles in rubbery . .	499	50 POEMS 13	4
where --name unless i'm mistaken chauvesouris-- whose grammar	504	50 POEMS 18	9
MISTER				
like your blueeyed boy Mister Death / / /	60	T&C PORTRAIT 8	11
+MISTER				
FOR CONTEXT, SEE	73	T&C SON REAL 4	12
FOR CONTEXT, SEE	247	IS 5 ONE 18	1
FOR CONTEXT, SEE	549	1 X 1 9	3
MISTFULLY				
feelable heavenless warm sweet mistfully whispering rainlife)	755	95 POEMS 83	11
MISTRANSLATE				
is afraid only to mistranslate a rhythm in your	291	IS 5 FOUR 8	10
MISTRUST				
seeming that they would mistrust a while the moving	6	T&C EPITHALAM	140
expect hope doubt (wonder mistrust) despair and right where .	780	73 POEMS 8	3
MISTRUSTING				
rather know than feel; mistrusting utterly that timelessness	817	73 POEMS 45	12
MIXED				
of you, getting mandolin-clink mixed with your hair; feeling	169	& SON ACTU 18	6
fireworks, which are a mixed splendor of piston and	264	IS 5 ONE 33	21
+MMAMAKMAKEMAKESWWOWORWORLWORLD				
i, m ! b)&it:s;elf, mmamakmakemakesWwOwoRworLworlD	423	NO THANKS 40	37
MOAN				
unshapeful hour making dear moan in tones of stroked	9	T&C SONGS 1	6
dream-send is hushed in moan-loll where night gathers morte .	90	& POST IMPR 2	9
truly through a dribbling moan of jazz whose arched	140	& SON REAL 11	4
/ / / / moan (is) ing the she	493	50 POEMS 7	1
MOAN-LOLL				
dream-send is hushed in moan-loll where night gathers morte .	90	& POST IMPR 2	9
MOANED				
this dangerous night through moaned space god worships God--	77	T&C SON UNRE 2	15
MOANGROWL				
nite) thatthis crou ched moangrowl-&-thin g stirs (m id) . .	795	73 POEMS 23	5
MOANGROWL-&-THIN				
nite) thatthis crou ched moangrowl-&-thin g stirs (m id) . .	795	73 POEMS 23	5
MOB				
next demand wherefore yon mob an accident? somebody got . . .	245	IS 5 ONE 16	16
a coarse clown (no mob, but a person) and	802	73 POEMS 30	24
we sans love equals mob love being youamiare (2)	803	73 POEMS 31	7

	PAGE	TITLE	LINE

MOBSUCKING
for foetus (a punkslapping mobsucking gravypissing poppa but 635 {CHAIRE} 37   3
MOCK
the world prettily upward, mock us....) and there was . . . . 133 & SON REAL 4   5
MODELING
huge chromatic fist skilfully modeling silence --to feel how   82 T&C SON ACTU 1   9
MODERN
dark really released, the modern flame of her indomitable . . 146 & SON REAL 17   1
MODESTLY
like buddha or answer modestly i am dying so . . . . 198 XLI PORTRAIT 6   29
MODESTY
synopsis despite a sadistic modesty his mind is seen . . . . 193 XLI PORTRAIT 1   5
MOI
voulez- vous coucher avec moi? Non? pourquoi?) ladies . . . . 120 & PORTRAIT 12   30
Mounier voulez-vous coucher avec moi? te ferai Mimi te . . . 121 & PORTRAIT 12   36
MOIST
are straying. Always thy moist eyes are at kisses . . . . . . 13 T&C SONGS 3   10
was thick slim warm moist built like an organ . . . . 110 & PORTRAIT 6   17
of flesh; became eyes moist lithe shuddering big, the . . . . 115 & PORTRAIT 8   23
between her lips a moist mistake, whose fragrance hurls . . . 148 & SON REAL 19   10
its three- cornered always moist mouth) --jazz, for whose . . 227 IS 5 ONE GERT   5
MOISTLY
neat huge trudging kiss moistly climbing hideously with large 67 T&C POST IMPR 4 25
MOLECULES
lonely antics of ridiculous molecules) nakedest (aiming for . 373 VIVA 64   5
MOLEHILLS
right and wrong or molehills are from mountains made . . . . 511 50 POEMS 25   3
+MOLES
FOR CONTEXT, SEE . . . . 361 VIVA 52   11
MOLLE
life) re the helen molle dancers, whom he considered . . . . 327 VIVA 18   r39
MOLLY
maggie and milly and molly and may went down . . . . 682 95 POEMS 10   1
languid fingers were; and molly was chased by a . . . . 682 95 POEMS 10   7
MOLLYPANTS
man wants) honey swoRkey mollypants / / / / . . . . 635 {CHAIRE} 37   26
MOMENT
thy lust one threaded moment lose: haste) the very . . . . .   9 T&C SONGS 1   7
(hasten, it is the moment which shall seek all . . . .   9 T&C SONGS 1   16
the world poises a moment (futile, proud, a costly . . . . . 23 T&C PUELLA MEA 268
rises she stands a moment in the passion of . . . . 35 T&C ORIENTALE 6 111
bromfield i paused a moment because on the frying . . . . . . 52 T&C PORTRAIT 1   12
your charms: one pierced moment whiter than the rest . . . . 78 T&C SON UNRE 3   12
and seriously thrills the moment of enthusiastic space is . . 82 T&C SON ACTU 1   12
reused to the mystical moment of dullness emphatically are . 230 IS 5 ONE 2   22
ever forget that precarious moment? As i was standing . . . . 262 IS 5 ONE 32   1
dirty collars) only a moment (or was it perhaps . . . . 296 IS 5 FOUR 13   13
to you in a moment" The is blond with . . . . 338 VIVA 29   14
did anybody Open a moment are Not more than . . . . 395 NO THANKS 12   4
(rising through a gold moment) climb: ing i -nto . . . . . . 627 {CHAIRE} 29   2
smaller than a rose's moment there's time for laughing . . . 683 95 POEMS 11   8
around him streets taking moment off by moment day . . . . . 720 95 POEMS 48   5
taking moment off by moment day thankfully become each . . . 720 95 POEMS 48   5
who goes, (never a moment ceasing to begin the . . . . 756 95 POEMS 84   3
sweet terrifying the particular moment it takes one very . . 809 73 POEMS 37   11
the absence of that moment when a stranger takes . . . . . . 812 73 POEMS 40   11
to be at any moment born-- some for whom . . . . 842 73 POEMS 70   2
+MOMENT
FOR CONTEXT, SEE . . . . 797 73 POEMS 25   18
MOMENTARY
cheek teartroubled to the momentary wind with guiding smile,   9 T&C SONGS 1   11
unite in a peculiarly momentary partnership (to instigate . . 260 IS 5 ONE 30   17
MOMENTINMYARMS
) flesh stalks the Momentinmyarms your expression my love . . 94 & POST IMPR 6   22
MOMENTLY
simmer upon thinking twilight momently) as down the oblivious   6 T&C EPITHALAM 126
+MOMENTOUS
FOR CONTEXT, SEE . . . . 392 NO THANKS 9   2

		PAGE	TITLE	LINE

MOMENTS
/ it is at moments after i have dreamed . . . . 78 T&C SON UNRE 3   1
heart made wise; at moments when the glassy darkness . . . . 78 T&C SON UNRE 3   5
mine a little while; moments when my once more . . . . 78 T&C SON UNRE 3   9
/ when my sensational moments are no more unjoyously . . . . 213 XLI SONNETS 9   1
(or will the fleshless moments go and go across . . . . 218 XLI SONNETS 14   9
if all desires things moments be murdered known photographed, 237 IS 5 ONE 8   1
will; nor can these moments be translated: i say . . . . . . 264 IS 5 ONE 33   6
/ / how many moments must (amazing each how . . . . 843 73 POEMS 71   1
MON
si vous voulez chatouiller mon lezard ladies suddenly j'm'en 121 & PORTRAIT 12   42
prisoner --"Ici?" --"Ah non, mon cheri; il fait trop . . . . 304 IS 5 FIVE 3   10
MONARCH
knees well might any monarch please.) Each ankle is . . . . . 21 T&C PUELLA MEA 214
MONDAY
stride after glide massacre monday did more) ask a . . . . . 522 50 POEMS 35   4
+MONDE
FOR CONTEXT, SEE . . . . 430 NO THANKS 47   1
MONEY
of queens and white money upon her nakedness he . . . . 34 T&C ORIENTALE 6 102
catch a piece of money and then his master . . . . 69 T&C POST IMPR 6 12
a wink bum-nothing and money fuzzily mouths take big . . . . 96 & POST IMPR 8   19
smiling, a piece of money held between his thumb . . . . . . 102 & POST IMPR 12   4
like butterflies and like money and like laughter and . . . . 111 & POST IMPR 6   66
with all his toys (money men motors "my" yachts . . . . 394 NO THANKS 11   3
to spend laughter not money lucky are Breathe grow . . . . . 467 NEW POEMS 5   6
(freud) --you pays your money and you doesn't take . . . . . 636 (CHAIRE) 38   13
o no in- deed; money can't do (never did . . . . 793 73 POEMS 21   8
+MONEY
FOR CONTEXT, SEE . . . . 346 VIVA 37   16
MONGREL
of high estate whose mongrel creed is Might Makes . . . . . . 774 73 POEMS 2   11
MONIA'S
heavily swims to Strunsky's, Monia's mouth eats tangerines . 219 XLI SONNETS 15   14
MONKEY
pointing to the queer monkey (if you toss him . . . . 69 T&C POST IMPR 6   9
little string and the monkey will sit, up, and . . . . 69 T&C POST IMPR 6 14
pointing at the queer monkey with a little oldish . . . . . . 69 T&C POST IMPR 6 37
a baboon. O a monkey with a sharp face . . . . 279 IS 5 THREE 3   9
this padded pole; a monkey attached by a chain . . . . 279 IS 5 THREE 3   10
MONKEYANDTHEORGAN
the children and the monkeyandtheorgan and the man are . . . 69 T&C POST IMPR 6 25
MONKEYGLANDS
famous doctor who inserts monkeyglands in millionaires a cute 245 IS 5 ONE 16   14
MONOSYLLABLE
it although the glad monosyllable jounce possibly can tell . 227 IS 5 ONE GERT   2
MONSTER
and he smote the monster merde then up rose . . . . 552 1 X 1 12   10
/ pity this busy monster, manunkind, not. Progress is . . . . 554 1 X 1 14   1
+MONSTER
FOR CONTEXT, SEE . . . . 56 T&C PORTRAIT 4   5
MONSTER'S
--small wonder such a monster's fellowmen miscalled are happy 842 73 POEMS 70   13
MONSTERING
/ THANKSGIVING (1956) a monstering horror swallows this . . . 711 95 POEMS 39   1
MONSTROUS
say God amid a monstrous din watch your step . . . . 117 & PORTRAIT 10   26
MONTH
curious of that one month for whom the whole . . . .   5 T&C EPITHALAM   103
fool who, in the month of June, having of . . . . 360 VIVA 51   11
a schoolroom in the month of may: life's the . . . . 574 1 X 1 34   5
MONTHS
at 33rd) pulled six months for selling snow / . . . . 266 IS 5 TWO 1   40
in the twot nine months young / / / . . . . 497 50 POEMS 11   8
hoped & prayed for months & weeks & days . . . . 702 95 POEMS 30   19
MONTPARNASSE
where flesh is heiry montparnasse is goosed by raspail). . . 401 NO THANKS 18   13

	PAGE	TITLE	LINE

MONUMENTS
of texture or meaning monuments and dolls resist Them . . . . 260 IS 5 ONE 30   9
MOO
turk a waiter intones: bloo-moo-n sirkusricky platzburg . . . 108 & PORTRAIT 4   13
out of within itself moo ving lump of twilight . . . . . . 602 {CHAIRE} 4   1
Dizzying eyeplums pun ctured) moo nface swimming ly . . . . 615 {CHAIRE} 17   9
the gentle who-horns says-does moo-woo (the prance with the . 773 73 POEMS 1   8
MOO-WOO
the gentle who-horns says-does moo-woo (the prance with the . 773 73 POEMS 1   8
MOON
white towers to the moon, soft sighed the passionate . . . .   8 T&C OF NICOL   3
fire) unfolding, gave the moon a nymphlike face, a . . . . .   8 T&C OF NICOL   19
drenched by a rounding moon) / / / / . . . .   10 T&C SONGS 1   45
seeks the thrill of moon, washed with a wild . . . .   12 T&C SONGS 2   48
their ladies in the moon) --fashioned very curiously of . . .   22 T&C PUELLA MEA 228
shied at the automaton moon from the transplendent hand . . .   30 T&C ORIENTALE 4 39
is tangled a cool moon there are thrice-three-hundred doors .   32 T&C ORIENTALE 6 32
/ there is a moon sole in the blue . . . . ,   37 T&C AMORES 2   2
the earth withers the moon crumbles one by one . . . .   38 T&C AMORES 3   6
you have loved me, moon and sunset stars and . . . .   39 T&C AMORES 4   6
fond of the handsome moon never spoke ill of . . . .   43 T&C AMORES 7   14
stars and the Humorous moon dear girl How i . . . .   44 T&C AMORES 8   17
/ / / the moon is hiding in her . . . .   65 T&C POST IMPR 2 1
lavender and cornerless, the moon rattles like a fragment . .   70 T&C SON REAL 1 14
sorry when the minute moon is a remarkable splinter . . . . .   82 T&C SON ACTU 1   4
convulsed orange inch of moon perching on this silver . . . .   86 T&C SON ACTU 5   1
a parenthesis! said the moon) / / / . . . .   89 & POST IMPR 1   17
smiles cloud-gloss is at moon-cease soon verbal mist-flowers   90 & POST IMPR 2   12
and see! (the new moon fills abruptly with sudden . . . . .   93 & POST IMPR 5   13
shape as means the moon, i somehow feel your . . . .   98 & POST IMPR 9   10
god's own and the moon kissed the little lady . . . . 125 & SEVEN POEMS 4 18
you'll find But the moon creeped into the pink . . . . 125 & SEVEN POEMS 4 20
be sorry And The Moon came! along-along to the . . . . 125 & SEVEN POEMS 4 24
silver dog and the moon came and the Moon . . . . 125 & SEVEN POEMS 4 26
moon came and the Moon said into his Ripe . . . . 125 & SEVEN POEMS 4 27
Ripe Eyes and the moon Smiled ,so / / . . . . 125 & SEVEN POEMS 4 28
matter knocked by sun moon jabbed jerked with ecstasy . . . . 153 & SON ACTU 2   11
touch you) timid lewd moon plunge skilfully into the . . . . 155 & SON ACTU 4   17
shore. By midnight, a moon scratches the skin of . . . . . . 160 & SON ACTU 9   7
long at the sticky moon opening in dusk her . . . . 170 & SON ACTU 19   2
the silver of the moon / / / / . . . . 189 XLI SONGS 11   17
the grass Comes the moon love, walk the autumn . . . . 190 XLI SONGS 12   11
fracas upon the accurate moon.... Across the important . . . 214 XLI SONNETS 10   9
silken immense swoon the moon is like a floating . . . . . . 214 XLI SONNETS 10   13
tangerines looking at the moon-- / / / / . . . . 219 XLI SONNETS 15   15
it is winter a moon in the afternoon and . . . . 279 IS 5 THREE 3   1
tone now for a moon to squat in first . . . . 282 IS 5 THREE 6   15
first darkness --a little moon thinner than memory faint . . 282 IS 5 THREE 6   17
/ / / the moon looked into my window . . . . 284 IS 5 FOUR 1   1
with a button the moon smiled she let go . . . . 284 IS 5 FOUR 1   10
i see the new moon thinner than a hair) . . . . 301 IS 5 FOUR 18   5
this particular road the moon if you'll notice follows . . . 303 IS 5 FIVE 2   9
so. And there's the moon, there is something faithful . . . . 303 IS 5 FIVE 2   16
smirks and there's the moon, thinner than a watchspring . . . 322 VIVA 14   14
first, anyhow dancing" (a moon swims out of a . . . . 338 VIVA 29   21
(touch) ing ? mind (moon begins The) now, ... 350 VIVA 41   10
a man under the moon on Sunday. by way . . . . 355 VIVA 46   1
the sun and the moon) resembles something that has . . . . . 360 VIVA 51   23
a most tinyness, the moon (with white wig and . . . . 365 VIVA 56   12
and especially who the moon is. / / / . . . . 368 VIVA 59   21
/ / / / mOOn Over tOwns mOOn whisper . . . . 383 NO THANKS 1   1
/ mOOn Over tOwns mOOn whisper less creature huge . . . . . . 383 NO THANKS 1   1
is dreamest oNLY THE MooN o VER ToWNS SLoWLY . . . . 383 NO THANKS 1   9
/ / / / moon over gai -te. a . . . . 384 NO THANKS 2   1
dream & : the moon over death over edgar . . . . 384 NO THANKS 2   7
death over edgar the moon over smellings of gently . . . . . 384 NO THANKS 2   8
and always, the iflike moon over moving me--the moon . . . . 384 NO THANKS 2   12
moon over moving me--the moon m ov--in g over . . . . 384 NO THANKS 2   14

494

MOON (CONTINUED)

m oon over juillet moon over s -unday O: . . . . 384 NO THANKS 2   33
snow big sun big moon (enter us) / / . . . . 393 NO THANKS 10   16
are moving in the moon / / / / . . . . 424 NO THANKS 41   14
to live in the moon a while) and shall . . . . 433 NO THANKS 50   12
pursues against the little moon a here and there . . . . . . 434 NO THANKS 51   17
the jews are a moon is as round as) . . . . 436 NO THANKS 52   24
all sun are and moon come fair come foul . . . . 440 NO THANKS 56   26
do i salute (by moon by sun i deeply . . . . 441 NO THANKS 56   66
nobody can sell the Moon to The) moon / . . . . 452 NO THANKS 67   18
the Moon to The) moon / / / / . . . . 452 NO THANKS 67   18
&-moon-He-be-hind-a-mills tosses like thin bums . . . . . . 469 NEW POEMS 7   1
twitch like kingdom come (moon The sq uirmwri th-ing . . . . 469 NEW POEMS 7   5
a ndn ooneandfor e-ver) moon She over this new . . . . . . 469 NEW POEMS 7   13
(not a fraid of moon You) <> / / . . . . 469 NEW POEMS 7   19
porkie sit into a moon) blacker than dreams are . . . . . . 483 NEW POEMS 21   2
who a he a moon a magic out of . . . . 493 50 POEMS 7   8
read or write, la moon. Employs a very crazily . . . . . . 504 50 POEMS 18   6
sun goes round its moon / / / / . . . . 510 50 POEMS 24   14
rain -bow & a moon 's whis- per in . . . . 512 50 POEMS 26   21
the name of the moon in the man. Up . . . . 513 50 POEMS 27   19
reaped their same sun moon stars rain children guessed . . . 515 50 POEMS 29   8
dream stars rain sun moon (and only the snow . . . . 515 50 POEMS 29   21
went their came sun moon stars rain / / . . . . 515 50 POEMS 29   36
silence (both an only moon the with star one . . . . 518 50 POEMS 32   3
a forehead called the moon singing desire into begin . . . . 520 50 POEMS 34   19
bring you peace the moon of day predicted end . . . . 527 50 POEMS 39   4
there isn't a new moon outside your window saying . . . . . 572 1 X 1 32   2
fears were hopes: the moon open for you and . . . . 575 1 X 1 35   13
was born before the moon before God wished Himself . . . . 577 1 X 1 37   14
something) livingest the imaginable moon / / / . . . . . . 599 (CHAIRE) 1   14
may sing no new moon in if all screech-owls . . . . 620 (CHAIRE) 22   5
bell to reappear a moon / / / / . . . . 624 (CHAIRE) 26   24
reels and me a moon; beneath, bombed the by . . . . 639 (CHAIRE) 41   3
the Navy of the Moon he's swooning at the . . . . 642 (CHAIRE) 44   13
(silverly rare goldenly so) moon, she is you nothing . . . . 666 (CHAIRE) 68   10
white firstful flame --new moon! as (by the miracle . . . . 669 (CHAIRE) 71   10
the stars and the moon are we're; but also . . . . 686 95 POEMS 14   18
hell -o of keen moon) dream unthings silent three . . . . . 687 95 POEMS 15   9
while nobody (and stars moon sun fall rise come . . . . . . 693 95 POEMS 21   18
/ round a so moon could dream (i sus . . . . 698 95 POEMS 26   1
/ ! o (rounD) moon, how do you (rouNd . . . . 722 95 POEMS 50   2
(home means if any moon or possibly sun shines . . . . . . 728 95 POEMS 56   5
huge whole the upfloating moon. Time's a strange fellow; . . 750 95 POEMS 78   9
un (star rain snow moon dream wing tree leaf . . . . 753 95 POEMS 81   15
you are whatever a moon has always meant and . . . . 766 95 POEMS 92   8
a which though the moon in her glory says . . . . 801 73 POEMS 29   11
be silent in a moon or two) / / . . . . 805 73 POEMS 33   8
are my sun, my moon, and all my stars . . . . 810 73 POEMS 38   14
blood as makes his moon alive sing more will . . . . 811 73 POEMS 39   13
day whose sun is moon, and our (from inexistence . . . . . 818 73 POEMS 46   2
a the o f moon / / / / . . . . 820 73 POEMS 48   13
won der ful sun moon stars the all, & . . . . 840 73 POEMS 68   12

+MOON

FOR CONTEXT, SEE . . . . 108 & PORTRAIT 4   13
FOR CONTEXT, SEE . . . . 122 & SEVEN POEMS 1   27
FOR CONTEXT, SEE . . . . 167 & SON ACTU 16   16
FOR CONTEXT, SEE . . . . 384 NO THANKS 2   32
FOR CONTEXT, SEE . . . . 385 NO THANKS 2   36
FOR CONTEXT, SEE . . . . 436 NO THANKS 52   20
FOR CONTEXT, SEE . . . . 518 50 POEMS 32   11
FOR CONTEXT, SEE . . . . 615 (CHAIRE) 17   9
FOR CONTEXT, SEE . . . . 723 95 POEMS 51   5
FOR CONTEXT, SEE . . . . 733 95 POEMS 61   1

MOON-CEASE

smiles cloud-gloss is at moon-cease soon verbal mist-flowers   90 & POST IMPR 2   12

MOON'S

suddenly wait against the moon's face. / / / . . . . 80 T&C SON UNRE 5   17

	PAGE	TITLE	LINE

MOON'S (CONTINUED)
```
    who knows if the moon's a balloon, coming out . . . . . . . .  129  & SEVEN POEMS 7      1
    suddenly looming) accurate undaunted moon's bright third  . .  305  IS 5 FIVE 4        15
    mind. Clocks strike. The moon's round, through the window . .  365  VIVA 56            4
    sun perfectly should disappear moon's utmost magic, or stones 377  VIVA 68            4
    ly and (th e moon's al-down) most whis per  . . . . . . . .    423  NO THANKS 40       7
+MOON'S
    FOR CONTEXT, SEE . . . . . . . . . . . . . . . . . . . . . .    94  & POST IMPR 6     21
MOONBEAM'S
    grass-- shunning the sudden moonbeam's treacherous snare she    8  T&C OF NICOL       25
MOONDAY
    / / whippoorwill this moonday into (big with unthings)  . . .  751  95 POEMS 79        2
MOONDROOL
    leaves are Thingish with moondrool and i'm ever so  . . . . .  303  IS 5 FIVE 2        6
MOONLIGHT
    palace run sunlight and moonlight and the emperor's elephant   32  T&C ORIENTALE 6   17
    little sunlight and less moonlight ourselves against the  . .  238  IS 5 ONE 9        20
    billiards very well by moonlight with Lord Rothermere. A  . .  262  IS 5 ONE 32       22
    the ocean, this is moonlight: say that both precisely . . . .  379  VIVA 70            1
MOONLY
    is most mad and moonly and less it shall  . . . . . . . . .    530  50 POEMS 42        5
MOONS
    awkward foal, whereof young moons begin the newness of  . . .  11  T&C SONGS 2         4
    cool took bedfellows for moons mountains for friends --open .  420  NO THANKS 37      12
MOONSTAR
    float sprout heroes of moonstar flutter to and swim . . . . .  586  1 X 1 46          10
MOP
    biddy with an old mop punching underneath conventions exposes 203  XLI LA GUERRE 1    2
MOPPING
    and bitch whispers jill mopping too bad dear sh . . . . . . .  496  50 POEMS 10       17
MORALITY
    submerged or an amoral morality sort-of-aliveing by . . . . .  410  NO THANKS 27      12
MORE
    --didst e'er depart upon more exquisite quest? and did  . . .   3  T&C EPITHALAM      20
    in the darkness a more burning rain? And still  . . . . . . .   4  T&C EPITHALAM      56
    those tenuous fires which more and more sink and  . . . . . .   6  T&C EPITHALAM     132
    fires which more and more sink and are lost . . . . . . . . .   6  T&C EPITHALAM     132
    friends, between your thoughts more white than wool My  . . .  11  T&C SONGS 2        14
    Spring (with her beauty more than snow dexterous and  . . . .  17  T&C PUELLA MEA    16
    to me is a more curious thing (a thing  . . . . . . . . . . .  17  T&C PUELLA MEA    25
    curious thing (a thing more nimble and complete) than . . . .  17  T&C PUELLA MEA    26
    appear than a rose more sweetly known, more silently  . . . .  21  T&C PUELLA MEA   176
    rose more sweetly known, more silently than a flower, . . . .  21  T&C PUELLA MEA   177
    glance things which never more shall be, perfect things . . .  22  T&C PUELLA MEA   252
    queen of queens is more transparent than water, she . . . . .  33  T&C ORIENTALE 6   51
    moments when my once more illustrious arms are filled . . . .  78  T&C SON UNRE 3     9
    of midnight to a more than darkness (which is . . . . . . . .  92  & POST IMPR 4      3
    the chap hic sum- more eh chuckles skulch.... and . . . . . .  96  & POST IMPR 8     22
    can take day away more softly horribly suddenly; (of  . . . .  98  & POST IMPR 9      4
    that your hands move more simply upon the evening . . . . . .  98  & POST IMPR 9      8
    smile slightly is a more minute adventure) lady. The  . . . .  98  & POST IMPR 9     11
    of the little ladies more than dead / / . . . . . . . . . . . 108  & PORTRAIT 4      37
    / / little ladies more than dead exactly dance . . . . . . . 120  & PORTRAIT 12      1
    never met before dead's more even than how many . . . . . . . 126  & SEVEN POEMS 5    8
    flesh of my fear: more neatly ream this pith . . . . . . . . 139  & SON REAL 10       7
    thud of scarlet. always. More interesting, as i think,  . . . 143  & SON REAL 14      6
    But i am interested more intricately in the delicate  . . . . 144  & SON REAL 15     10
    like music, a little more like curving colour (say  . . . . . 152  & SON ACTU 1       3
    Muscles better and nerves more. i like your body. . . . . . . 175  & SON ACTU 24      3
    so little you are more like a flower who  . . . . . . . . . . 192  XLI CHANSONS 2     4
    laid before me bread more downy than street-lamps upon  . . . 194  XLI PORTRAIT 2    32
    him in cafes, the more dissolute atmosphere of a  . . . . . . 197  XLI PORTRAIT 5     1
    continually committing nuisances but more especially in your 204  XLI LA GUERRE 2    15
    but here were something more maturely childish, more  . . . . 211  XLI SONNETS 7      4
    something more maturely childish, more beautiful almost than 211  XLI SONNETS 7      5
    sensational moments are no more unjoyously bullied of vilest 213  XLI SONNETS 9      1
    would receive the answer more or less deserved, Young . . . . 229  IS 5 ONE FRAN      7
    and even a few more depending on the remu-  . . . . . . . . . 236  IS 5 ONE 7        16
```

		PAGE	TITLE	LINE

MORE (CONTINUED)

	PAGE	TITLE	LINE
/ / death is more than certain a hundred	238	IS 5 ONE 9	1
shall human optics know more quite ennobling forsooth? One .	254	IS 5 ONE 25	4
fate per a somewhat more than less emancipated evening . . .	258	IS 5 ONE 28	5
miss machinery is the more accurate, yes it delivers	264	IS 5 ONE 33	11
go and are no more what of it we	268	IS 5 TWO 3	5
beauty what could be more beaut- iful than these	268	IS 5 TWO 3	9
could and what is more did tell you just	276	IS 5 TWO 10	4
know the reason any more than.) But look: up-	282	IS 5 THREE 6	4
the inutile collide once more with the imaginable, love, . .	289	IS 5 FOUR 6	8
does not ask for more than just enough dreams	298	IS 5 FOUR 15	9
never bother you any more. / / / /	298	IS 5 FOUR 15	28
suddenly that will do more than heroes beautifully in	302	IS 5 FIVE 1	12
gush silently perpetuating solids (More fluid Than gas / . .	311	VIVA 3	17
socalled) memory Of (without more ado about less than	317	VIVA 9	22
to be uncouthly erotic more particularly the primates--from .	326	VIVA 18	25
a conduct worthy of more ponderous wishes or hopes	328	VIVA 19	7
statistics lie he was more brave than me: more	339	VIVA 30	42
more brave than me: more blond than you. /	339	VIVA 30	42
wan) keenly, to dreamings more than truth untrue, the	344	VIVA 35	7
soft- liness than dream more sing (buoyant & who	349	VIVA 40	6
prouder than all mountains, more than all oceans various . .	351	VIVA 42	6
on them a little more openly than usual hither, ...	354	VIVA 45	13
of themselves with a more incisive simplicity a more	354	VIVA 45	16
more incisive simplicity a more intensively brutal futility"	354	VIVA 45	17
being some- thing possibly more intricate) i (breath in . . .	358	VIVA 49	8
any dream come a more millionth mile shyly to	367	VIVA 58	10
will communicate a little more than twice all that	370	VIVA 61	12
remember (as those pearls more than surround this throat) . .	372	VIVA 63	9
/ / nothing is more exactly terrible than to	375	VIVA 66	1
or one name control more incredible splendor than our	377	VIVA 68	5
is all birds but more fleet) herself against the	378	VIVA 69	4
we, of ourselves who more a part are (less	386	NO THANKS 3	3
or any dream means more than sleep as more	390	NO THANKS 7	11
more than sleep as more than know means guess)	390	NO THANKS 7	11
literally their putting it more than mildly Absolute	391	NO THANKS 8	22
fleeing himself for selves more strangely made (wears pain .	394	NO THANKS 11	6
a moment are Not more than (if Green invents	395	NO THANKS 12	6
who doesn't move (Moved more suddenly than) whose tiniest . .	397	NO THANKS 14	4
of such than hungrily more swiftness as with (feel)	402	NO THANKS 19	2
be fooled but it's more fun to be more	410	NO THANKS 27	14
more fun to be more to be fun to	410	NO THANKS 27	14
(should stink of failure more than wars of feet	414	NO THANKS 31	3
like some dream giving more than all life's busy	418	NO THANKS 35	3
would give a little more than it away (his	420	NO THANKS 37	2
doubt my weakness makes more than most strength (less	433	NO THANKS 50	7
breathing dares to hide more than most fabulous wisdom . . .	446	NO THANKS 61	12
be, yond! thought are. more (Than girl 's tears	447	NO THANKS 62	10
day close) opens if more than silence silent are	450	NO THANKS 65	4
than silence silent are more flowering than stars whitely . .	450	NO THANKS 65	4
your less than guessed more than beauty begins the	450	NO THANKS 65	11
of love (a little) More careful Than of everything	453	NO THANKS 68	2
huge a home (only more than immeasurable dream wherelessly .	454	NO THANKS 69	7
fragrant; a than pure more signalling of singular most . . .	456	NO THANKS 71	10
which makes some feel more better when all ought	466	NEW POEMS 4	23
second and most by more) --let's touch the sky:	469	NEW POEMS 7	18
less thin very much more big & kinder of	470	NEW POEMS 8	12
stands on a much more than very much biggest	470	NEW POEMS 8	15
can 't hurt any more h u sh nor	472	NEW POEMS 10	15
curvings upon a mostless more of star o- pening	480	NEW POEMS 18	13
and love yourself so more than truly there's never	481	NEW POEMS 19	10
become. Girlboys may nothing more than boygirls need: i . . .	484	NEW POEMS 22	5
ng with me n more o n than in	488	50 POEMS 2	23
eyes float silently down more than two those that	491	50 POEMS 5	7
which but) always (they're more much further off) further . .	501	50 POEMS 15	16
earth than silent is more silent than more than	502	50 POEMS 16	2
is more silent than more than much more is	502	50 POEMS 16	2
than more than much more is or total sun	502	50 POEMS 16	2

MORE (CONTINUED)

immeasurable happenless unnow shuts more than open could that	502	50 POEMS 16	7
or than all life more death begins to grow	502	50 POEMS 16	8
filled with never are more than more is are	505	50 POEMS 19	20
never are more than more is are mostly almost	505	50 POEMS 19	21
small grin said (with more simplicity than makes a	506	50 POEMS 20	14
fat thousand years. Expecting more would be neither fantastic	514	50 POEMS 28	3
than all mankind something more small occurs or something . .	514	50 POEMS 28	10
small occurs or something more distorting than socalled . . .	514	50 POEMS 28	11
that noone loved him more by more when by	515	50 POEMS 29	12
loved him more by more when by now and	515	50 POEMS 29	12
deep by deep and more by more they dream	515	50 POEMS 29	30
deep and more by more they dream their sleep	515	50 POEMS 29	30
is the whole and more than all / /	521	50 POEMS 34	68
glide massacre monday did more) ask a lifelump buried	522	50 POEMS 35	5
tiny this with time's more than most how immeasurable	523	50 POEMS 36	34
silently singing a song more silent than silence these . . .	525	50 POEMS 37	11
less fear much than more climbing hope meets most	528	50 POEMS 40	9
/ / love is more thicker than forget more	530	50 POEMS 42	1
more thicker than forget more thinner than recall more . . .	530	50 POEMS 42	2
more thinner than recall more seldom than a wave	530	50 POEMS 42	3
a wave is wet more frequent than to fail	530	50 POEMS 42	4
sane and sunly and more it cannot die than	530	50 POEMS 42	14
not sing) how much more than enough for both	531	50 POEMS 43	13
mosts have died in more our twentieth will open	537	50 POEMS 49	10
mind fahrenheit) old infrequently more and more much (as . .	546	1 X 1 6	2
old infrequently more and more much (as aprils elsewhere . .	546	1 X 1 6	3
someone else makes no more difference than if it	549	1 X 1 9	10
numerable mosts the actual more minds ignorant of stern . . .	556	1 X 1 16	4
guests of Is unslowly more who (and here who	557	1 X 1 17	7
another steepest thing-- how more than sleep illimitably my .	558	1 X 1 18	11
motionless-- whose moving is more april than the year	559	1 X 1 19	12
most who die, the more we live / /	560	1 X 1 20	24
ten times ten are more than not entitled to	561	1 X 1 21	7
for his joy is more than joy, most rare)	562	1 X 1 22	4
not ever named mountains more if than each known	563	1 X 1 23	5
obscener brightest than hate's more black keenest than . . .	565	1 X 1 25	10
who is the) more dream than become more	571	1 X 1 31	14
more dream than become more am than imagine /	571	1 X 1 31	16
worlds of than great more eyes, and what were	573	1 X 1 33	4
such an everywhere, even more true would truest lovers . . .	576	1 X 1 36	11
out of midnight dropped more suns than are (yes;	576	1 X 1 36	12
other very dearly , more than raindrops need sunbeams	577	1 X 1 37	2
first thrushes may awake more secretly than our (if	577	1 X 1 37	7
some thousand million hundred more bright worlds than merely	580	1 X 1 40	12
look: begins to grow more than all real, all	582	1 X 1 42	9
and tree is voice more leastfully than i am	583	1 X 1 43	20
with ships than dreams more hands are offering jonquils) . .	585	1 X 1 45	16
earth neither sea here's more than room for three	588	1 X 1 48	4
/ / life is more true than reason will	592	1 X 1 52	1
than reason will deceive (more secret or than madness	592	1 X 1 52	2
have --but beauty is more each than living's all	592	1 X 1 52	4
(here less than nothing's more than everything) death, as . .	592	1 X 1 52	12
men --but beauty is more now than dying's when	592	1 X 1 52	14
might mean) we're everyanything more than believe (with a . .	594	1 X 1 54	41
of eager glory, no more miracle may grow --childfully . . .	601	(CHAIRE) 3	6
possible --but" lifting "flowers" more all stars than eyes .	603	(CHAIRE) 5	13
and we miss them more than any bright word	605	(CHAIRE) 7	7
possibly thrice we glimpsed-- more likely twice that (once .	607	(CHAIRE) 9	2
who) The distance is more much than all of	608	(CHAIRE) 10	3
/ / out of more find than seeks thinking, ...	612	(CHAIRE) 14	1
she disappeared. Out of more (fingeryhands me and whying) . .	612	(CHAIRE) 14	11
mysteries (each truly his more than some eighty years	617	(CHAIRE) 19	10
one breathing) be" soul "more" cries: with a smile	625	(CHAIRE) 27	24
hug) large less than more magnetic pink unwhores a	629	(CHAIRE) 31	7
we whom cannot kill more mostful to arrive each	639	(CHAIRE) 41	10
hers elf could silent more no be / /	654	(CHAIRE) 56	13
strange; familiar wholly) dearest more than reality of more .	659	(CHAIRE) 61	8

MORE (CONTINUED)

    more than reality of more than dream-- how should . . . . . . 659 (CHAIRE) 61   8
    hatred pity fear each more exactly than the other . . . . . . 662 (CHAIRE) 64   10
    much that mind no more can disprove than prove . . . . 664 (CHAIRE) 66   3
    dancing, the mountains) when more than was lost has . . . . . 665 (CHAIRE) 67   15
    hands have people; and more each particular person is . . . . 667 (CHAIRE) 69   3
    all trees are (any more than each leafless) its . . . . 667 (CHAIRE) 69   11
    virginal immediacy of precision: more and perfectly more most 669 (CHAIRE) 71   6
    precision: more and perfectly more most ethereal silence . . 669 (CHAIRE) 71   7
    heshaped two these (stroll more slowly than trees) . . . . . 681 95 POEMS 9   4
    day for singing but more than all (as all . . . . 683 95 POEMS 11   13
    all (as all your more than eyes tell me) . . . . 683 95 POEMS 11   13
    winning (but love is more than love) / / . . . . 684 95 POEMS 12   20
    (selves any than every more silent ly) heard (& . . . . 695 95 POEMS 23   16
    becoming each truebeautifully more-than-thing (& falling &) 715 95 POEMS 43   19
    to find a noone's more by far than you're . . . . 716 95 POEMS 44   30
    much (most beautiful darling) more than anyone on the . . . . 717 95 POEMS 45   2
    cause ever ybody wants more (& more & still . . . . 727 95 POEMS 55   18
    ybody wants more (& more & still More) what . . . . 727 95 POEMS 55   19
    (& more & still More) what the hell are . . . . 727 95 POEMS 55   20
    because) given much mercy more than even the mercy . . . . . 735 95 POEMS 63   11
    we've (with one last more than kiss) to call . . . . 741 95 POEMS 69   13
    wonderful is death; but more, the older he's the . . . . . . 742 95 POEMS 70   17
    silence of thrushsong (and more than every miracle's to . . . 745 95 POEMS 73   4
    sheerest glory a little more always less believably so . . . 748 95 POEMS 76   8
    Time's a strange fellow; more he gives than takes . . . . . . 750 95 POEMS 78   11
    if a world ends more than all worlds begin . . . . 750 95 POEMS 78   16
    (and how i'll stand more still than still) and . . . . 752 95 POEMS 80   3
    (until his voice is more than bird) and when . . . . 752 95 POEMS 80   6
    he disappears; till of more much than dark most . . . . 756 95 POEMS 84   7
    upward world of each more most prodigious Selves both . . . . 757 95 POEMS 85   7
    est if Im agines more than life must die . . . . 759 95 POEMS 86   9
    / / / now (more near ourselves than we) . . . . 760 95 POEMS 87   1
    least ignorance may comprehend more than shall ever provingly 761 95 POEMS 88   3
    as a leaf--here's one more than each creature new . . . . . . 762 95 POEMS 89   6
    you; high (are become more than alive) above anybody . . . . 762 95 POEMS 89   11
    your any new (every more only you) most emanation . . . . . . 764 95 POEMS 90   46
    not by mind revealed (more than all dying life, ... 765 95 POEMS 91   7
    time, love did no more begin than love will . . . . 768 95 POEMS 94   2
    is feebleness: the truth more first than sun more . . . . . . 768 95 POEMS 94   12
    more first than sun more last than star --do . . . . 768 95 POEMS 94   12
    second and most by more-- if death is the . . . . 769 95 POEMS 95   2
    the new the earth more moving (all gay fair . . . . 778 73 POEMS 6   8
    day of may under more a blue than blue . . . . 778 73 POEMS 6   19
    you & i are more than you & i . . . . 782 73 POEMS 10   18
    vast (unmind by brain) more than machine turns less . . . . . 787 73 POEMS 15   11
    of submoronic fancy be more not conceivably future than . . . 790 73 POEMS 18   4
    their murdered planet grows more and enormously more less: . 808 73 POEMS 36   11
    grows more and enormously more less: until her-and-his . . . 808 73 POEMS 36   11
    / / now that, more nearest even than your . . . . 809 73 POEMS 37   1
    which is this world) more my life does not . . . . 810 73 POEMS 38   3
    his moon alive sing more will wonderfully birds than . . . . 811 73 POEMS 39   14
    own name, linger no more than selfless i can . . . . 812 73 POEMS 40   10
    bedroom) begins to croon more particularly at just midnight . 813 73 POEMS 41   5
    (in a most steep more than music) feeling that . . . . 816 73 POEMS 44   6
    night as floats a more than day whose sun . . . . 818 73 POEMS 46   2
    my shining love) how more than dark i am, ... 819 73 POEMS 47   5
    leaf may be) the more than thanks of always . . . . 821 73 POEMS 49   14
    life, lie down and more by most endure all . . . . 834 73 POEMS 62   11
    colour can create precision more than angels fear to . . . . 842 73 POEMS 70   4
    how many centuries) these more than eyes restroll and . . . . 843 73 POEMS 71   2
    proudhumble citizen of ecstasies more steep than climb can . 845 73 POEMS 73   8

+MORE

    FOR CONTEXT, SEE . . . . 423 NO THANKS 40   14
    FOR CONTEXT, SEE . . . . 423 NO THANKS 40   14
    FOR CONTEXT, SEE . . . . 610 (CHAIRE) 12   9
    FOR CONTEXT, SEE . . . . 618 (CHAIRE) 20   1

MORE-THAN-THING
  becom ing each truebeautifully more-than-thing (& falling &) 715 95 POEMS 43   19
MOREOVER
  singular and slenderest hands moreover are (which as lilies . 20 T&C PUELLA MEA 160
  the body's breathing noun (moreover the delicious frown of . 21 T&C PUELLA MEA 212
  will confuse hotly our moreover irrevocable bodies while the 111 & PORTRAIT 6   61
MORETHANME
  the hostess to my morethanme / / / / . . . . 807 73 POEMS 35   15
+MORETHANMOSTGENEROU
  his always not imaginably morethanmostgenerous spirit. . . . 823 73 POEMS 51   13
MORETHANPERSON
  no means almost white morethanPerson; who (riding through . . 697 95 POEMS 25   19
+MORGAN
  FOR CONTEXT, SEE . . . . 325 VIVA 17   12
MORN
  On The Thorn enter Morn and God's In His . . . . 230 IS 5 ONE 2   28
MORNING
  petals peers the sleepy morning) gently draws apart her . . . 8 T&C OF NICOL   14
  air... The flute of morning stilled in noon-- noon . . . . . 12 T&C SONGS 2   46
  her king in the morning wandering. Through the young . . . . 17 T&C PUELLA MEA   9
  myth in the uncertain morning, with April feet like . . . . . 17 T&C PUELLA MEA   20
  lady's body grow; as morning may a lily know, ... 21 T&C PUELLA MEA 184
  pansy eyes look from morning till night into the . . . . . . 58 T&C PORTRAIT 6   18
  in the looseness of morning but in twilight becomes . . . . . 68 T&C POST IMPR 5   6
  colour comes, which is morning, O do not wonder . . . . 92 & POST IMPR 4   17
  / / inthe, exquisite; morning sure lyHer eye s . . . . 104 & POST IMPR 14   2
  In theex qui site morning, her sureLyeye s sit-ex . . . . . . 104 & POST IMPR 14   19
  hair has in the morning dead's clever too like . . . . 126 & SEVEN POEMS 5   9
  scratches the sore of morning. But i am interested . . . . . 144 & SON REAL 15   10
  funny stable. In the morning they go out in . . . . 171 & SON ACTU 20   8
  cares?) They pull the morning out of the night. . . . . 171 & SON ACTU 20   12
  went away it was morning (that is, big horses; . . . . 172 & SON ACTU 21   1
  god should send the morning; and before my doubting . . . . . 205 XLI SONNETS 1   9
  and (stooping through the morning) kiss this pillow, dear . . 288 IS 5 FOUR 5   8
  moves) why then toward morning he is a ghost . . . . 299 IS 5 FOUR 16   11
  thing everybody sometimes calls morning / / / / . . . . 330 VIVA 21   14
  thy secret and each morning stoops to blend her . . . . 351 VIVA 42   14
  Instant (when of a morning Memory stands, with clumsily . . . 359 VIVA 50   5
  always, snow and to morning; and to morning's beautiful . . . 424 NO THANKS 41   6
  good" the mechanical dawn "morning") & that those you . . . . 464 NEW POEMS 2   30
  of give, singing each morning out of each night . . . . 520 50 POEMS 34   3
  go out into the morning the young morning with . . . . 529 50 POEMS 41   4
  the morning the young morning with a warm world . . . . 529 50 POEMS 41   5
  might any earth's first morning have concealed so . . . . . . 626 {CHAIRE} 28   13
  pen window this fine morning) fly instead of dancing . . . . 724 95 POEMS 52   10
  is stumbling someone (named Morning) / / / / . . . . 785 73 POEMS 13   24
  have opened to your morning feeling their stars have . . . . 812 73 POEMS 40   7
+MORNING
  FOR CONTEXT, SEE . . . . 169 & SON ACTU 18   11
  FOR CONTEXT, SEE . . . . 287 IS 5 FOUR 4   2
  FOR CONTEXT, SEE . . . . 618 {CHAIRE} 20   1
  FOR CONTEXT, SEE . . . . 723 95 POEMS 51   16
MORNING'S
  to morning; and to morning's beautiful friend twilight (and . 424 NO THANKS 41   6
MORONIC
  lamed ones; the mad moronic maimed) all except the . . . . . 619 {CHAIRE} 21   19
+MORONIC
  FOR CONTEXT, SEE . . . . 790 73 POEMS 18   3
MORONS
  Land i speak sweet morons gather roun' who does . . . . 466 NEW POEMS 4   2
MORROW
  look down and to -morrow and yesterday and everything . . . . 762 95 POEMS 89   14
MORSEL
  (futile, proud, a costly morsel of sweet tears) gesticulates, 23 T&C PUELLA MEA 269
  from complacent gums, a morsel prettily wanders buoyed on . . 201 XLI PORTRAIT 9   4
  / / / / morsel miraculous and meaningless secret . . . . . . 456 NO THANKS 71   1
+MORSEL
  FOR CONTEXT, SEE . . . . 201 XLI PORTRAIT 9   5

		PAGE	TITLE	LINE

MORTAL

(most gently herculanean my mortal) yoo make sno eye . . . . 618 {CHAIRE} 20   4

/ / when any mortal (even the most odd) . . . . 731 95 POEMS 59   1

MORTALLY

with love --human one mortally immortal i can turn . . . . . 679 95 POEMS 7   13

MORTALS

/ / / / mortals) climbi ng i nto . . . . 536 50 POEMS 48   1

all murdering lies by mortals told make two. Let . . . . . . 556 1 X 1 16   10

it strange that normal mortals can not justify the . . . . . 731 95 POEMS 59   3

MORTE

moan-loll where night gathers morte carved smiles cloud-gloss 90 & POST IMPR 2   11

MORTICIANS

hell are we all morticians? / / / / . . . . 727 95 POEMS 55   21

MORTISED

/ / if being mortised with a dream myself . . . . 285 IS 5 FOUR 2   1

MOSAIC

sun invades the new mosaic of the ground --let . . . . 5 T&C EPITHALAM   84

MOSCOW

by their altruistic smell moscow pipes good kumrads dance) . 413 NO THANKS 30   9

MOST

blossom stands whereof is most desire, yet less than . . . . 6 T&C EPITHALAM 147

Guenever, a flower which most heavy hung with silence . . . . 18 T&C PUELLA MEA   58

smallest thought with a most swift radiance wherein slowly . 18 T&C PUELLA MEA   79

deep caress of every most shy thing and mute, ... 19 T&C PUELLA MEA   99

were.) Her body is most beauteous, being for all . . . . . . 20 T&C PUELLA MEA 135

all things perfect the most frail. (Whoso rideth in . . . . 20 T&C PUELLA MEA 162

Her waist is a most tiny hinge of flesh, ... 21 T&C PUELLA MEA 193

then the artificer did most exquisitely err.) When the . . . 22 T&C PUELLA MEA 220

tree; with her lips' most frail parting my body . . . . . . 22 T&C PUELLA MEA 233

of dissonant flowers, and most of all i hear . . . . 61 T&C PORTRAIT 9   33

time when the beautiful most of her (this here . . . . 72 T&C SON REAL 3   11

amazing smile is the most great common divisor of . . . . . 74 T&C SON REAL 5   14

this its hideous Work most old Whose battening gesture . . . 77 T&C SON UNRE 2   11

/ SONNETS--ACTUALITIES a thing most new complete fragile . . 82 T&C SON ACTU 1   1

expression my love when most passionate. , my, love . . . . 94 & POST IMPR 6   25

suddenly; (of these two most early stars wincing upon . . . . 98 & POST IMPR 9   5

whose deep nakedness death most believes, perpetual girls . . 138 & SON REAL 9   10

mus- cularity upon the most crimson assistance of my . . . . 197 XLI PORTRAIT 5   15

butterflies he is the most courteous of men should . . . . . 198 XLI PORTRAIT 6   25

finally colliding with the most expensive furniture upsets a 203 XLI LA GUERRE 1   11

and whom dawn loves most to touch wishing by . . . . 211 XLI SONNETS 7   17

/ / / who's most afraid of death? thou . . . . 215 XLI SONNETS 11   1

stem. But of all most would i be one . . . . 215 XLI SONNETS 11   9

Greenwich perfumed fake And most, the futile fooling . . . . 220 XLI SONNETS 16   11

indulged in that possibly most inexcusable of all to . . . . 239 IS 5 ONE 10   8

say i believe my most intimate friends would never . . . . . 262 IS 5 ONE 32   14

chiefly of your smile, most suddenly which is of . . . . . . 293 IS 5 FOUR 10   17

yourself, lady in the most certainly (of what we . . . . . . 294 IS 5 FOUR 11   4

flesh) Love coins His most gradual gesture, and whittles . . 297 IS 5 FOUR 14   12

or why (in this most exquisite of cities) all . . . . 300 IS 5 FOUR 17   11

the year: like this most early single star which . . . . . . 305 IS 5 FIVE 4   5

your eyes (frailer than most deep dreams are frail) . . . . . 306 IS 5 FIVE 5   3

the world say "his most wise music stole nothing . . . . . . 306 IS 5 FIVE 5   9

Whose compassionate digit, earth's most terrific quadruped . 315 VIVA 7   15

being with his probably most brilliant pupil mated, let . . . 326 VIVA 18   7

wellbeloved colonel (trig westpointer most succinctly bred) . 339 VIVA 30   5

devout am upward deep most invincible unthing --stern sexual 351 VIVA 42   2

i love. Hell (by most humble me which shall . . . . 360 VIVA 51   31

opened the window a most tinyness, the moon (with . . . . . . 365 VIVA 56   12

their silence: in your most frail gesture are things . . . . 366 VIVA 57   3

Givehurling with your my most : locking foreverfully blend . 371 VIVA 62   17

for hugely the ignorant most precise essential flame never . 373 VIVA 64   7

embraces hugely some few most rare perfectly dear (and . . . 376 VIVA 67   11

try are ing) al most fe (hug) males (one-t . . . . 388 NO THANKS 5   14

with every least each most remembering H highest fly . . . . 390 NO THANKS 7   7

tangible domains rare with most early soul him shall . . . . 402 NO THANKS 19   12

/ / / / most (people simply can't) won't . . . . 412 NO THANKS 29   1

(people simply can't) won't (most parent people mustn't . . . 412 NO THANKS 29   4

MOST (CONTINUED)

    parent people mustn't shouldn't) most daren't (sortof people 412 NO THANKS 29   6
    & even (not having most ever lived people always) . . . . . . 412 NO THANKS 29   13
    always) don't die (becoming most buried unbecomingly very by   412 NO THANKS 29   15
    buried unbecomingly very by most) people / / / . . . .   412 NO THANKS 29   19
    unmake (when in a most smashed unworld stands unslain . . . . 414 NO THANKS 31   6
    from whose (if loud most howish time derange the . . . . . .   420 NO THANKS 37   5
    (th e moon's al-down) most whis per (here) ingc . . . . 423 NO THANKS 40   7
    indecent god p.s. the most successful b.o. fully speaking . . 425 NO THANKS 42   15
    what may be unknown most secret i will breathe . . . .   428 NO THANKS 45   10
    dwindled to a leastful most under imagination. When (out . . 432 NO THANKS 49   13
    weakness makes more than most strength (less than these . . . 433 NO THANKS 50   7
    (side walks are) is most (windows where blaze naLOVEme . . . 436 NO THANKS 52   3
    houses called cities) spring most singular- ly (cities are . 436 NO THANKS 52   18
    to hide more than most fabulous wisdom fears to . . . . 446 NO THANKS 61   12
    than beauty begins the most not imagined life adventuring . . 450 NO THANKS 65   12
    Her least never with most memory) give entirely each . . . . 453 NO THANKS 68   10
    more signalling of singular most flame and surely poets . . . 456 NO THANKS 71   10
    (minute by second and most by more) --let's touch . . . . .   469 NEW POEMS 7   18
    elf into leasting forever most magical maybes of certainly . 495 50 POEMS 9   13
    tear jumping from each most least eye of star . . . .   502 50 POEMS 16   4
    the talentgang and water most encourage flame as hatracks . . 511 50 POEMS 25   7
    with time's more than most how immeasurable anguish pregnant   523 50 POEMS 36   35
    more climbing hope meets most despair? all knowing's having . 528 50 POEMS 40   9
    to fail it is most mad and moonly and . . . .   530 50 POEMS 42   5
    than forgive it is most sane and sunly and . . . .   530 50 POEMS 42   13
    and up comes yesterday most green and young pleasure . . . .   531 50 POEMS 43   4
    dance little joy (shine most prayer) / / / . . . .   535 50 POEMS 47   12
    aprils elsewhere stroll) exhumed most innocently undecaying . 546 1 X 1 6   4
    year (if all her most first little flowers rise . . . . . .   559 1 X 1 19   13
    our hugest home; the most who die, the more . . . .   560 1 X 1 20   24
    only man is this (most common, for each anguish . . . . . .   562 1 X 1 22   3
    is more than joy, most rare) a fiend, if . . . .   562 1 X 1 22   4
    strangers (who deep our most are selves) touch: forever . . . 564 1 X 1 24   14
    were nevers ugly beautiful most is now) / / . . . .   565 1 X 1 25   16
    upon beginning) "beautiful o most beautiful" her, my life . . 572 1 X 1 32   11
    and than this (mere most) breast spring's million (who . . . 573 1 X 1 33   18
    we'll adventure the into most immemorial of whens) . . . . . 577 1 X 1 37   18
    your least your any most very amazing now or . . . .   580 1 X 1 40   3
    sad this havingest world) most merry most fair most . . . . . 590 1 X 1 50   3
    havingest world) most merry most fair most rare --the . . . . 590 1 X 1 50   4
    most merry most fair most rare --the livingest givingest . . 590 1 X 1 50   4
    's the dizzily he most him --the climbingly fallingest . . . 590 1 X 1 50   13
    a coolly bell touches most mere until (eternally) with . . . 601 {CHAIRE} 3   14
    Mere but one small most of a rose easily . . . .   608 {CHAIRE} 10   9
    a massacre the hope most innocent (so deep's the . . . . .   609 {CHAIRE} 11   7
    asleep) so never is most lonely man alone (his . . . . . .   609 {CHAIRE} 11   9
    goo-dmore-ning (en ter) nize-aday (most gently herculanean my 618 {CHAIRE} 20   2
    a kike is the most dangerous machine as yet . . . .   644 {CHAIRE} 46   1
    turn sheer despairing to most perfect gay, nowhere to . . . . 649 {CHAIRE} 51   6
    us very deafly a most stares colossal hoax of . . . .   659 {CHAIRE} 61   13
    crylessly drifting through vast most nothing's own nothing . 661 {CHAIRE} 63   13
    from arrive human the most catastrophe april might make . . . 662 {CHAIRE} 64   3
    thank You God for most this amazing day: for . . . .   663 {CHAIRE} 65   1
    is, all (each thing most lovely) sweet things cannot . . . . 666 {CHAIRE} 68   3
    more and perfectly more most ethereal silence through . . . . 669 {CHAIRE} 71   7
    fool your heart but most (without the smallest doubt) . . . . 679 95 POEMS 7   9
    depaola gives me a most tremendous hug knowing i . . . . . .   680 95 POEMS 8   25
    lie we so must most lily brief (rose here&gone) . . . . 690 95 POEMS 18   5
    in park this grim most (these one who are) . . . .   698 95 POEMS 26   5
    proud nowhere of earth's most prodigious night blossoms a . . 714 95 POEMS 42   2
    i love you much (most beautiful darling) more than . . . . . 717 95 POEMS 45   1
    everyone certainly would (my most beautiful darling) believe   717 95 POEMS 45   14
    (which frightenS a noisy most park's least timorous pigeons)   726 95 POEMS 54   8
    serve no body wants Most (not putting it mildly . . . . . .   727 95 POEMS 55   9
    any mortal (even the most odd) can justify the . . . .   731 95 POEMS 59   1
    must often have wondered "most people be quite so . . . . .   738 95 POEMS 66   12
    than kiss) to call most the amazing miracle of . . . . 741 95 POEMS 69   14

		PAGE	TITLE	LINE
MOST (CONTINUED)

from some loud unworld's most rightful wrong climbing, my . . 745 95 POEMS 73   1
here but neither's blue most both) and history immeasurably . 750 95 POEMS 78   5
if the Lovestar grows most big a voice comes . . . . 752 95 POEMS 80   1
more much than dark most nowhere no particle is . . . . . . 756 95 POEMS 84   7
world of each more most prodigious Selves both now . . . . . 757 95 POEMS 85   7
(every more only you) most emanation creates creation . . . . 764 95 POEMS 90   47
shy sweet eagerly my most dear (die! live) the . . . . 767 95 POEMS 93   8
minute by second and most by more-- if death . . . . 769 95 POEMS 95   2
and veers the vast most crafty crow your kingbird . . . . . . 774 73 POEMS 2   8
even 4 now man's most vast (unmind by brain) . . . . 787 73 POEMS 15   9
and last) mostpeople fear most: a mystery for which . . . . . 802 73 POEMS 30   12
goldenly whole, prodigiously alive most mercifully glorying . 808 73 POEMS 36   7
takes one very falling most (there: did you see . . . . . . 809 73 POEMS 37   11
all never guessed unknowable most joy) faithfully blossoming 811 73 POEMS 39   7
that delicate creature is most herself while uttering one . . 813 73 POEMS 41   7
me down (in a most steep more than music) . . . . 816 73 POEMS 44   5
different time, and each most falsely true; or so . . . . . 817 73 POEMS 45   2
out of midsummer's blazing most not night as floats . . . . 818 73 POEMS 46   1
your ways (o very most my shining love) how . . . . 819 73 POEMS 47   4
(undaunted guest of dark most downwardness and marvellously . 821 73 POEMS 49   11
than blondest star the most mysterious (eliena, my dear) . . 825 73 POEMS 53   3
down and more by most endure all that you . . . . 834 73 POEMS 62   11
strict here of amazing most now, with what thousands . . . . 840 73 POEMS 68   28

+MOST

FOR CONTEXT, SEE . . . . 331 VIVA 22   3
FOR CONTEXT, SEE . . . . 334 VIVA 25   1
FOR CONTEXT, SEE . . . . 733 95 POEMS 61   4
FOR CONTEXT, SEE . . . . 823 73 POEMS 51   13

MOSTFUL

whom cannot kill more mostful to arrive each (futuring . . . 639 {CHAIRE} 41   10

MOSTLESS

angel curvings upon a mostless more of star o- . . . . . . 480 NEW POEMS 18   12

MOSTLY

all things. thy hair mostly the hours love: a . . . . 13 T&C SONGS 3   3
than more is are mostly almost are feebler than . . . . . . 505 50 POEMS 19   21

MOSTNESS

/ / if night's mostness (and whom did merely . . . . 450 NO THANKS 65   1

MOSTPEOPLE

whatever (first and last) mostpeople fear most: a mystery . . 802 73 POEMS 30   12
sang like a bird. Mostpeople have been heard screaming . . . 802 73 POEMS 30   29

MOSTS

born to happen our mosts have died in more . . . . 537 50 POEMS 49   10
but than all numerable mosts the actual more minds . . . . . 556 1 X 1 16   4
to outgrow all whose mosts if you have known . . . . 574 1 X 1 34   13

+MOSTS

FOR CONTEXT, SEE . . . . 342 VIVA 33   25

MOTH

jewels now like a moth with stumbling wings flutters . . . . 47 T&C IMPRESS 1   7
gasping organ is waving moth-eaten tunes. a fattish . . . . 69 T&C POST IMPR 6   1
heav en FoR my motH) with a grass wid . . . . 320 VIVA 12   17
Mee as somebody's almost moth er folds (but infinite) . . . . 629 {CHAIRE} 31   14

MOTHEATEN

curve of the tiny motheaten old manwhose Beard rests. . . . . 101 & POST IMPR 11   46
busted statues of yon motheaten forum be aware notice . . . . 260 IS 5 ONE 30   2

MOTHER

the eyes of the mother of god who spits . . . . 55 T&C PORTRAIT 3   12
whisperingly impinge (god's pretty mother) but may not . . . 85 T&C SON ACTU 4   6
so old for the mother of twelve undershirts (we . . . . . . 167 & SON ACTU 16   3
tight just as your mother would, only don't be . . . . 192 XLI CHANSONS 2   11
words country home and mother when sung at the . . . . 204 XLI LA GUERRE 2   8
course you know their mother, of his heart the . . . . 254 IS 5 ONE 25   12
home to his old mother in a new nice . . . . 270 IS 5 TWO 5   19
etcetera wristers etcetera, my mother hoped that i would . . 276 IS 5 TWO 10   13
are any heavens my mother will (all by herself) . . . . . . 352 VIVA 43   1
one (ask super-) wonderful (mother) child is a good . . . . . 398 NO THANKS 15   5
his slut of a mother i rather suppose" "will's . . . . 707 95 POEMS 35   16
first ("don't tell your mother") had; making annie slightly . 794 73 POEMS 22   4

		PAGE	TITLE	LINE

+MOTHER
    FOR CONTEXT, SEE . . . . 320 VIVA 12   17
    FOR CONTEXT, SEE . . . . 629 (CHAIRE) 31   14
MOTHER'S
    glass, and see his mother's pride, his father's joy, ... 273 IS 5 TWO 8   3
    my (his from daughter's mother's zero mind fahrenheit) old . 546 1 X 1 6   1
    the silence of his mother's smile --whose only secret . . . . 714 95 POEMS 42   13
    / these from my mother's greatgrandmother's rosebush white . 748 95 POEMS 76   1
    perhaps comprises poems (my mother's greatgrandmother surely 748 95 POEMS 76   6
    --you are deafened every mother's son-- all is merely . . . . 804 73 POEMS 32   10
MOTHERMONSTER
    fluttering behind her a mothermonster with red grumbling face 56 T&C PORTRAIT 4   5
MOTHERS
    legs rancid voices Baedekers Mothers and kodaks --by night . 256 IS 5 ONE 27   16
    of houses pour maids mothers widows wives bringing this . . . 624 (CHAIRE) 26   6
MOTHERY
    a grey snow of mothery same rotting keen dream? . . . . 527 50 POEMS 39   29
MOTHS
    infinite processions move like moths and like boys and . . . 111 & PORTRAIT 6   63
MOTIF
    / the surely Cued motif smites truly to Beautifully . . . . . 311 VIVA 3   3
MOTILITIES
    lugbrin g ingseekfindlosin g motilities are) go to the . . . 403 NO THANKS 20   14
MOTION
    each with its Own motion deeply to wickedly comprehend . . . 356 VIVA 47   9
    rouNdly)ftblac kl(ness)y a-motion-upo-nmotio-n . . . . 429 NO THANKS 46   6
MOTIONLESS
    symbol of the rose motionless with grieving feet and . . . . 59 T&C PORTRAIT 7   10
    depths of height this motionless forgetful where turned at . 520 50 POEMS 34   5
    imagining; while you are motionless-- whose moving is more . 559 1 X 1 19   11
    / now what were motionless move (exists no miracle . . . . . 762 95 POEMS 89   1
    sleep (doll by doll) motionless under magical foreverfully . 777 73 POEMS 5   12
+MOTIONLESS
    FOR CONTEXT, SEE . . . . 429 NO THANKS 46   6
MOTIONOFA
    cleverjeRk in itlike the motionofa Sharp Knife-sN ap-ingof . 101 & POST IMPR 11 50
MOTIVATED
    / / / impossibly motivated by midnight the flyspecked . . . . 116 & PORTRAIT 9   2
MOTORS
    his toys (money men motors "my" yachts wolfhounds women) . . 394 NO THANKS 11   3
MOTTLE
    pompous a the swallowed mottle with smooth or a . . . . 96 & POST IMPR 8   6
MOULDS
    tears always) and silence moulds such strangeness as was . . 78 T&C SON UNRE 3   7
MOULT
    hoping insect, humanity, achieves (moult beyond difficult . . 351 VIVA 42   11
    achieves (moult beyond difficult moult) amazing doom who . . 351 VIVA 42   11
MOUNIER
    Manon, cinq rue Henri Mounier voulez-vous coucher avec moi? . 121 & PORTRAIT 12 35
    legs cinq rue Henri Mounier a little love begs, ... 121 & PORTRAIT 12 47
MOUNT
    (Sl0 wLy) steps (to mount the wand) a by . . . . 697 95 POEMS 25   17
MOUNTAIN
    love riding riding the mountain down into the silver . . . . 14 T&C SONGS 4   22
    stags at a green mountain the lucky hunter sang . . . . 14 T&C SONGS 4   29
    day i felt a mountain touch me where i . . . . 135 & SON REAL 6   11
    voice squatting on a mountain of gum did something . . . . . 228 IS 5 ONE MARJ   9
    hollyhock forest brook chickadee mountain. Mountain) . . . . 512 50 POEMS 26   27
    forest brook chickadee mountain. Mountain) whycoloured worlds 512 50 POEMS 26   27
    un) "have you" the mountain, while his maples wept . . . . . 555 1 X 1 15   11
    may sleep now, my mountain" and this mountain slept . . . . . 555 1 X 1 15   15
    my mountain" and this mountain slept while his pines . . . . 555 1 X 1 15   15
    / out of the mountain of his soul comes . . . . 617 (CHAIRE) 19   1
    --souls under whom flow (mountain valley forest) a million . 659 (CHAIRE) 61   5
    far silent truths of mountain (strolling is there here . . . 755 95 POEMS 83   7
    a heartbeat dares; that mountain, any god) while leaf . . . . 818 73 POEMS 46   9
MOUNTAIN'S
    despair to hold a mountain's heartbeat in his hand . . . . . 562 1 X 1 22   14

	PAGE	TITLE	LINE

MOUNTAINING
how (anchored in what mountaining roots of mere eternity) . . 517 50 POEMS 31   1
MOUNTAINOUS
emitted; vaguely watching that mountainous worthy in the   . . 228 IS 5 ONE MARJ   12
MOUNTAINRANGE
one razorblade into a mountainrange; lenses extend unwish . . 554 1 X 1 14   6
MOUNTAINS
the furious hearts of mountains ceased to beat? Wind . . . .   3 T&C EPITHALAM   16
and otherwise roses and mountains different from the i . . . 91 & POST IMPR 3   16
/ / between green mountains sings the flinger of . . . . . . 185 XLI SONGS 7   2
dare: prouder than all mountains, more than all oceans . . . 351 VIVA 42   6
open Clouds take sun mountains stand And oceans do . . . . . 359 VIVA 50   12
his drowned girth are mountains; and beyond all hurt . . . . 418 NO THANKS 35   13
ship climbs murmuring silver mountains which disappear (and . 419 NO THANKS 36   16
took bedfellows for moons mountains for friends --open your . 420 NO THANKS 37   12
here's to silent certainly mountains; and to a disappearing . 424 NO THANKS 41   4
refined they shake the mountains when they dance / . . . . . 427 NO THANKS 44   20
broke oceans and tore mountains from their sockets and . . . 432 NO THANKS 49   17
is so dark the mountains grow up from the . . . . 505 50 POEMS 19   9
or molehills are from mountains made --long enough and . . . 511 50 POEMS 25   3
he could feel the mountains grow. Lifting the valleys . . . . 520 50 POEMS 34   16
mind) --whose hearts are mountains, roots are trees, it's . . 560 1 X 1 20   15
only not ever named mountains more if than each . . . . 563 1 X 1 23   5
strikes forests of mind, mountains of soul) quite at . . . . 580 1 X 1 40   25
younger than angels are mountains rivery forests towerful . . 586 1 X 1 46   6
an acorn--valleys accuse their mountains of having . . . . . 620 (CHAIRE) 22   11
and illimitably his destiny) mountains! how can each" while . 626 (CHAIRE) 28   9
on every side swoop mountains flimsying become if who'd) . . 634 (CHAIRE) 36   3
children and sunlight and mountains) in april (but if . . . . 660 (CHAIRE) 62   24
can be (yes the mountains are dancing together) when . . . . 665 (CHAIRE) 67   7
so i (now the mountains are dancing, the mountains) . . . . . 665 (CHAIRE) 67   14
mountains are dancing, the mountains) when more than was . . 665 (CHAIRE) 67   14
the sea (all the mountains are dancing; are dancing) . . . . 665 (CHAIRE) 67   21
magnificent honesty of space. Mountains are mountains now; . 675 95 POEMS 3   5
of space. Mountains are mountains now; skies now are . . . . 675 95 POEMS 3   5
wandered down from fragrant mountains of eternal now to . . . 743 95 POEMS 71   12
climbing, my love (till mountains speak the truth) enter . . 745 95 POEMS 73   2
a perfect patience of mountains i am a little . . . . 749 95 POEMS 77   12
forests with all their mountains) / / / / . . . . 754 95 POEMS 82   14
who: and wore his (mountains understand how) life like . . . 786 73 POEMS 14   7
very song of (as mountains feel and lovers) singing . . . . . 804 73 POEMS 32   13
MOUNTING
forget.... or mere Music mounting unsurely twilight but here 211 XLI SONNETS 7   2
MOUNTS
grieving feet and wings mounts against the margins of . . . . 59 T&C PORTRAIT 7   13
of perfumed noise fiercely mounts from the fireman's ball, . 169 & SON ACTU 18   4
song suddenly leaping flameflung, mounts, inimitably to lose 206 XLI SONNETS 2   8
MOURNERS
petals hush mysteriously invisible mourners move with prose . 59 T&C PORTRAIT 7   7
MOUSE
stirring, not even a mouse. The stockings were hung . . . . . 142 & SON REAL 13   13
am living with a mouse who shares my meals . . . . 171 & SON ACTU 20   13
who is given a mouse to hold lovingly, our . . . . 279 IS 5 THREE 3   19
/ here's a little mouse) and what does he . . . . 286 IS 5 FOUR 3   1
see? tail frisks) (gonE) "mouse", We are not the . . . . . . 286 IS 5 FOUR 3   15
really a kind of mouse) but he has little . . . . 353 VIVA 44   10
/ / / / mouse) Won derfully is anyone . . . . 397 NO THANKS 14   1
quietly Stare a poisoned mouse still who alive is . . . . . . 784 73 POEMS 12   4
MOUSIES
tweeds tweeds little itchy mousies with scuttling eyes rustle 25 T&C CHANSONS 2   12
MOUTH
of particoloured peace with mouth flower-faint and . . . . .   5 T&C EPITHALAM   98
ladies you take his mouth for his eyes are . . . . 15 T&C SONGS 5   15
consists --always upon the mouth there trysts curvingly a . . 20 T&C PUELLA MEA 148
Semiramis put up her mouth to wholly kiss-- never . . . . . . 22 T&C PUELLA MEA 248
didst not answer thy mouth is as a chord . . . . 27 T&C ORIENTALE 1   4
clutched you upon my mouth listen beloved i dreamed . . . . . 30 T&C ORIENTALE 4   14
gather of thy languorous mouth the thrilling flower) / . . . 37 T&C AMORES 2   19

		PAGE	TITLE	LINE

MOUTH (CONTINUED)

stars was on my mouth petals danced against my . . . . 39 T&C AMORES 4 18
eyes and fold her mouth the new flower with . . . . 40 T&C AMORES 4 43
loved the far- departed mouth sweetly-saluted lingers. if one 42 T&C AMORES 6 6
a song upon her mouth having death in her . . . . 50 T&C IMPRESS 4 8
with death upon her mouth having a song in . . . . 50 T&C IMPRESS 4 30
foolish breasts the droll mouth wilted and not old, ... 52 T&C PORTRAIT 1 31
suppression the accurate boy mouth now droops the faun . . . 54 T&C PORTRAIT 2 8
whore with busy rhythmic mouth and silly purple eyelids . . . 56 T&C PORTRAIT 4 14
who at her redstone mouth renews his childhood and . . . . . 57 T&C PORTRAIT 5 11
petticoat, drowsy is your mouth your eyes are sticky . . . . 61 T&C PORTRAIT 9 14
open skilfully with his, mouth carefully holding, it, in . . 69 T&C POST IMPR 6 17
deemed with your peculiar mouth my heart made wise; . . . . . 78 T&C SON UNRE 3 4
reckless magic of your mouth) my love is building . . . . . . 83 T&C SON ACTU 2 8
hate) shall crumble the mouth-flower fleet He'll not my . . . 83 T&C SON ACTU 2 12
nor rout the young mouth whose lips begin a . . . . 85 T&C SON ACTU 4 7
at home then my mouth will go out into . . . . 100 & POST IMPR 11 19
the East side, my mouth goes to the peddlers, ... 100 & POST IMPR 11 20
the bad candies my, mouth loves melons slitted with . . . . . 100 & POST IMPR 11 22
asc end-ing inthecarts my, mouth is, fond of tiny . . . . . . 100 & POST IMPR 11 25
was small, exact, stupid. mouth normal, large, unclever. hair 103 & POST IMPR 13 13
chewed stump of a mouth, huge dropping of a . . . . 133 & SON REAL 4 15
groping mucous) in my mouth occurs homelessly. While grip . . 136 & SON REAL 7 10
shrugging with colour) the mouth who sits between her . . . . 143 & SON REAL 14 5
vicious vegetable of her mouth. Upon the whole he . . . . . . 148 & SON REAL 19 6
bragging breasts, puppy-faces to mouth her ugly nipples . . . 151 & SON REAL 22 8
day. By you the mouth hair eyes, and i . . . . 153 & SON ACTU 2 2
to take your new mouth in his teeth (hips . . . . 161 & SON ACTU 10 3
it slowly to my mouth, taste the accurate demure . . . . . . 162 & SON ACTU 11 11
the flashing bacchant. partedpetaled mouth, face delirious. . 185 XLI SONGS 7 14
the sun in my mouth and leap into the . . . . 189 XLI SONGS 11 3
a mad street whose mouth dripped with slavver of . . . . . . 194 XLI PORTRAIT 2 5
gently decomposing in the mouth of New York. Be- . . . . . . 201 XLI PORTRAIT 9 2
by whom the hungering mouth of time is fed: . . . . 212 XLI SONNETS 8 8
stride (and drawing thy mouth toward my mouth, steer . . . . 215 XLI SONNETS 11 16
thy mouth toward my mouth, steer our lost bodies . . . . . . 215 XLI SONNETS 11 17
city's sublime cheap distinct mouth) do the exact human . . . 218 XLI SONNETS 14 7
swims to Strunsky's, Monia's mouth eats tangerines looking at 219 XLI SONNETS 15 14
yawning said what her mouth thinks of (if it . . . . 225 IS 5 ONE LIZ 13
three- cornered always moist mouth) --jazz, for whose . . . . 227 IS 5 ONE GERT 5
Love once? now her mouth opens too far and: . . . . 243 IS 5 ONE 14 12
trickling pried his black mouth with fat jibing lips, ... 277 IS 5 THREE 1 15
understood my eyes cheeks mouth its hands (slipping) felt . . 284 IS 5 FOUR 1 4
careful smile in his mouth (making everything suddenly old . 293 IS 5 FOUR 10 26
truth untrue, the best mouth i have seen on . . . . 344 VIVA 35 8
those who got athlete's mouth jumping on&off bandwaggons . . 404 NO THANKS 21 3
all sky (a little mouth) stumbling (can't keep up . . . . . . 501 50 POEMS 15 9
lurch things phantoms curl (mouth seekingly lips wander a . . 565 1 X 1 25 3

MOUTH-FLOWER

hate) shall crumble the mouth-flower fleet He'll not my . . . 83 T&C SON ACTU 2 12

MOUTH'S

her flesh whose casual mouth's coy rooting dies also. . . . . 131 & SON REAL 2 7
twitch its terrors; the, mouth's, swallowed, muscle (itch of 136 & SON REAL 7 9

MOUTHED

grips. Querying greys between mouthed houses curl thirstily. 139 & SON REAL 10 12

+MOUTHED

FOR CONTEXT, SEE . . . . 337 VIVA 28 12

MOUTHS

moving of beauteous dead mouths throughout that very proud . 6 T&C EPITHALAM 141
bum-nothing and money fuzzily mouths take big wobbly . . . . 96 & POST IMPR 8 19
of tilting din whose mouths distinctly walk your smiles . . . 138 & SON REAL 9 3
Then-arrows making do our mouths something red, something . . 160 & SON ACTU 9 17
of paleness; the unswift mouths of snow insignificantly . . . 218 XLI SONNETS 14 14
sunlight was over our mouths fears hearts lungs arms . . . . 283 IS 5 THREE 7 2

MOV

taxis swirl hues crowds mov -ing ing ing among . . . . 384 NO THANKS 2 4

MOVE

love through meadows hugely move. yet what am i . . . . 11 T&C SONGS 2 35

MOVE (CONTINUED)

softly used to wholly move slender ladies made of . . . . . . 23 T&C PUELLA MEA 283
hush mysteriously invisible mourners move with prose faces . 59 T&C PORTRAIT 7 7
dangerous first stars) people move love hurry in a . . . . . 93 & POST IMPR 5 11
only that your hands move more simply upon the . . . . 98 & POST IMPR 9 8
while the infinite processions move like moths and like . . . 111 & PORTRAIT 6 63
Of Ladies you who move beautifully in the winds . . . . 112 & PORTRAIT 6 95
the girl-and-bird of you move.... moves.... and also, i'll . 174 & SON ACTU 23 13
whom the old glories move, the old trumpets cry; . . . . . . 209 XLI SONNETS 5 12
better how the balloons move (as her ghost lurks, ... 227 IS 5 ONE GERT 3
witty hatless. Cats which move smoothly from neck to . . . . 279 IS 5 THREE 3 13
hands the way i move my habits laughter i . . . . 285 IS 5 FOUR 2 6
kiss or smile or move. It's different too isn't . . . . 289 IS 5 FOUR 6 17
and i, used to move when i thought you . . . . 289 IS 5 FOUR 6 19
fingertips the way you move) the painter of your . . . . . . 291 IS 5 FOUR 8 13
who does (where) not move ; is .crowned the . . . . 346 VIVA 37 24
with their guessing fingers did-not-move exquisitely ,like . 355 VIVA 46 16
else entirely who doesn't move (Moved more suddenly than) . . 397 NO THANKS 14 4
said she may i move said he is it . . . . 399 NO THANKS 16 17
/ / / / move deeply, rain (dream hugely) . . . . 422 NO THANKS 39 1
they can't i mean move yes sir she jes . . . . 425 NO THANKS 42 6
a village does not move behind my eye the . . . . 434 NO THANKS 51 8
lifted fields Oxen distinctly move, a yellowandbluish cat . . 434 NO THANKS 51 31
this place of love move (with brightness of peace) . . . . . 443 NO THANKS 58 3
people who rain (are move as) proces -sion Its . . . . 482 NEW POEMS 20 2
my loveliest, nothing may move may rest --you bring . . . . 575 1 X 1 35 5
begin are, the worlds move in your (and rest, ... 575 1 X 1 35 39
(if they do, we'll move away still further: into . . . . . . 579 1 X 1 39 14
minds which sleep and move) blind sands, at pitiless . . . 743 95 POEMS 71 7
now what were motionless move (exists no miracle mightier . . 762 95 POEMS 89 1
april;and i breathe-move-and-seem some perpetually . . . . 839 73 POEMS 67 6

+MOVE

FOR CONTEXT, SEE . . . . 444 NO THANKS 59 24

MOVED

he stands counting the moved myriads wonderfully loved, . . . 9 T&C SONGS 1 14
Her gasping slippery body moved with the hideous spontane- . 103 & POST IMPR 13 9
entirely who doesn't move (Moved more suddenly than) whose . 397 NO THANKS 14 4
being summer's spring who moved by standing in november's . . 420 NO THANKS 37 4
/ / my father moved through dooms of love . . . . 520 50 POEMS 34 1
each night my father moved through depths of height . . . . 520 50 POEMS 34 4
the sea my father moved through griefs of joy; . . . . 520 50 POEMS 34 18
and shall my father moved through dooms of feel; . . . . . . 520 50 POEMS 34 34
with snow. My father moved through theys of we, ... 521 50 POEMS 34 49

MOVEMENTS

unmarketable excitation, whose careless movements carefully . 150 & SON REAL 21 14

MOVES

this sweet profound Paris moves with lovers, two and . . . . 71 T&C SON REAL 2 8
bright slender eyes (who moves) at sunset and . . . . 91 & POST IMPR 3 3
girl-and-bird of you move.... moves.... and also, i'll . . . 174 & SON ACTU 23 13
the inspired sister's howling moves off will anyone tell . . 196 XLI PORTRAIT 4 18
everything which breathes and moves, since Doom (with white . 288 IS 5 FOUR 5 2
both pockets curled hands moves) why then toward morning . . 299 IS 5 FOUR 16 10
restaurant, looks breathes or moves --climbing (past light . 300 IS 5 FOUR 17 3
gone: along these gardens moves a wind bringing rain . . . . 304 IS 5 FIVE 3 11
you my heart always moves / / / / . . . . 379 VIVA 70 14
on fur answers eats moves remembers is afraid) each . . . . 394 NO THANKS 11 8
night a mightily form moves whose passenger and whose . . . . 419 NO THANKS 36 22
only white darkness who moves in black light dancing . . . . 439 NO THANKS 55 20
kill while the whole moves; and every part stands . . . . . . 446 NO THANKS 61 14

MOVIES

discovered America ether the movies may claim general . . . . 238 IS 5 ONE 9 14
she could what the movies try to do because . . . . 425 NO THANKS 42 5

MOVING

mistrust a while the moving of beauteous dead mouths . . . . 6 T&C EPITHALAM 141
perfectest array my lady, moving in the day, is . . . . 17 T&C PUELLA MEA 6
hours my lady perfectly moving, through the new world . . . . 17 T&C PUELLA MEA 11
frail lady drifting distinctly, moving like a myth in . . . . 17 T&C PUELLA MEA 19
body filled with May) --moving in the unskilful day . . . . . 17 T&C PUELLA MEA 23

MOVING (CONTINUED)
  lady in gluey twilight moving, suddenly is three animals. . .   95 & POST IMPR 7   3
  big and firm legs moving solemnly like careful and . . . . .   95 & POST IMPR 7   13
  (carefully to and fro moving New and Old things, ... 124 & SEVEN POEMS 3 13
  while people stare carefully moving a perhaps fraction of . . 124 & SEVEN POEMS 3 16
  neighing of great steeds moving to war across the . . . . . . 209 XLI SONNETS 5   5
  halfsmiling from cool faces, moving purely with muted step, . 211 XLI SONNETS 7   8
  box: surrounded by priests moving in fifty colours , ... 280 IS 5 THREE 4   11
  nobodies laughing faintly playing moving far below us perhaps 283 IS 5 THREE 7   9
  it different dear from moving as we, you and . . . .   289 IS 5 FOUR 6   18
  going to America. Then moving was a matter of . . . .   289 IS 5 FOUR 6   23
  a wise and puerile moving of your arm will . . . . 302 IS 5 FIVE 1   9
  ludendorff and your humble moving through the gloominess of . 324 VIVA 16   12
  the iflike moon over moving me--the moon m ov--in . . . . . . 384 NO THANKS 2   12
  m ov--in g over (moving) you beautifully also; at . . . . . . 384 NO THANKS 2   18
  (whose fatal songs are moving in the moon / . . . .   424 NO THANKS 41   14
  what a proud dreamhorse moving (whose feet almost walk   . . . 437 NO THANKS 53   16
  the with star one moving are twilight they beyond . . . . . . 518 50 POEMS 32   4
  you are motionless-- whose moving is more april than . . . . 559 1 X 1 19   12
  in miraculous day) merrily moving through sweet forgiveness . 661 {CHAIRE} 63   7
  new the earth more moving (all gay fair brave . . . . 778 73 POEMS 6   9
  and our (from inexistence moving) sweet earth puts on . . . . 818 73 POEMS 46   3
  with sound, newly one moving cadence may release the   . . . . 842 73 POEMS 70   6
+MOVING
  FOR CONTEXT, SEE . . . . 122 & SEVEN POEMS 1   2
  FOR CONTEXT, SEE . . . . 384 NO THANKS 2   4
  FOR CONTEXT, SEE . . . . 384 NO THANKS 2   15
  FOR CONTEXT, SEE . . . . 602 {CHAIRE} 4   1
  FOR CONTEXT, SEE . . . . 808 73 POEMS 36   5
MOWER
  lithe some very fine mower a tall; tall some . . . .   509 50 POEMS 23   11
MOWERS
  at the feet of mowers whose bodies strong with . . . . . .   11 T&C SONGS 2   33
MOWN
  the smell of minute mown lives) oh my spirit . . . .   434 NO THANKS 51   25
+MOWN
  FOR CONTEXT, SEE . . . . 707 95 POEMS 35   26
MR
  POEM, OR BEAUTY HURTS MR. VINAL take it from . . . .   230 IS 5 ONE 2   T
  the true story of Mr Do -nothing the wellknown . . . . . .   236 IS 5 ONE 7   3
  / / / / mr youse needn't be so . . . .   247 IS 5 ONE 18   1
  friend observes I pass Mr Tom Larsen twirls among . . . . .   252 IS 5 ONE 23   5
  with some difficulty sardines. Mr. Wiggin took Wrs. Miggin's 263 IS 5 ONE 32   47
  nothing less; the Honorable Mr. (guess) who, breathing on . . 266 IS 5 TWO 1   34
  i should say thankyouverymuch mr rosenbloom picks . . . . . . 287 IS 5 FOUR 4   8
  / / / but mr can you maybe listen . . . .   314 VIVA 6   1
  lt (wit (hprettyw) ith) mr jeff dick son fec . . . .   388 NO THANKS 5   28
  of unkindness exit little mr Big notbusy Busi ness . . . .   389 NO THANKS 6   3
  whom fiercely by pink mr seized green mrs opening . . . . . . 465 NEW POEMS 3   7
  / / mrs & mr across the way are . . . .   501 50 POEMS 15   2
  holes probably that's what (mr & mrs are sort . . . .   501 50 POEMS 15   21
  / / / / mr u will not be . . . .   551 1 X 1 11   1
  the few not excluding mr u / / / . . . .   551 1 X 1 11   4
  tomb then up rose mr lipshits pres (who always . . . . . .   552 1 X 1 12   26
  / / / old mr ly fresh from a . . . .   567 1 X 1 27   1
  everybody it's a" old mr lyman ruddy as a . . . .   567 1 X 1 27   17
  / / / meet mr universe (who clean and . . . .   645 {CHAIRE} 47   1
  paper-- but now, as Mr bowing Cockatoo proffers the . . . . . 697 95 POEMS 25   27
MRS
  coyly bandy scandal of Mrs. N and Professor D . . . .   70 T&C SON REAL 1   10
  faces clogs Second as Mrs. Somethingwich (with flesh like . . 219 XLI SONNETS 15   11
  pink mr seized green mrs opening is it horribly . . . . . .   465 NEW POEMS 3   8
  / / / / mrs & mr across the . . . .   501 50 POEMS 15   1
  that's what (mr & mrs are sort of really . . . .   501 50 POEMS 15   21
  brother married Heart, now Mrs Death. Poor Mind / . . . . .   621 {CHAIRE} 23   4
  took him home & mrs dominic washed his sweet . . . .   680 95 POEMS 8   13
  not conceivably future than mrs somethingwitz nay . . . . .   790 73 POEMS 18   5
  herewith: soldier, beware of mrs smith / / / . . . .   799 73 POEMS 27   41

+MRS.
  FOR CONTEXT, SEE . . . . 263 IS 5 ONE 32   48
MUCH
  kisses playing, whose strangeness much says; singing (though   13 T&C SONGS 3   11
  lifelessness consider for how much themselves shall gleam, in   81 T&C SON UNRE 6   7
  has been used too. much Too. originally spontaneous . . . . .   94 & POST IMPR 6   1
  also carved upon her much too white forehead a . . . . 116 & PORTRAIT 9   9
  or to nothing as much as being by her . . . . 141 & SON REAL 12   13
  ....tremble (not knowing how much better than me will . . . . 153 & SON ACTU 2   12
  of you somewhat too much and am become perfectly . . . . . . 157 & SON ACTU 6   2
  and leaves say alas, much is to do for . . . . 181 XLI SONGS 3   3
  and cold; and how much earth is Madge worth? . . . . 183 XLI SONGS 5   12
  far colours, thinking very much of nothing and whom . . . . . 211 XLI SONNETS 7   16
  noive all right. Aint much on looks but how . . . . 226 IS 5 ONE MAME   11
  yet we scarcely fare much better-- what's become of . . . . . 233 IS 5 ONE 4   9
  down i cough too much). How did the traffic . . . . 245 IS 5 ONE 16   12
  always-so-much-interested-in-everybody-else's business . . . 250 IS 5 ONE 21   13
  above the nombril, and much to my astonishment much . . . . . 262 IS 5 ONE 32   9
  much to my astonishment much impressed by having once . . . . 262 IS 5 ONE 32   9
  not nothurt me not much and in the same . . . . 262 IS 5 ONE 32   17
  minded pure young girl much kissed, by loving relatives . . . 273 IS 5 TWO 8   21
  will never guess how much my wonderful jealousy is . . . . . 292 IS 5 FOUR 9   15
  voices and boots were much the worse, and egged . . . . 339 VIVA 30   26
  quite perhaps as sternly much not life nor stop . . . . 371 VIVA 62   26
  touch said he how much said she a lot . . . . 399 NO THANKS 16   6
  lie down to so much sleep they only understand . . . . 418 NO THANKS 35   8
  / / / / much i cannot) tear up . . . . 433 NO THANKS 50   1
  dead, do fearers worship Much and Quick; badness not . . . . 438 NO THANKS 54   2
  wide (it shall bury much stench) and a hundred . . . . 439 NO THANKS 55   12
  which stands on a much less thin very much . . . . 470 NEW POEMS 8   11
  much less thin very much more big & kinder . . . . 470 NEW POEMS 8   12
  of stands on a much more than very much . . . . 470 NEW POEMS 8   15
  much more than very much biggest & thickest & . . . . 470 NEW POEMS 8   15
  they never saw so much heard so much smelled . . . . 474 NEW POEMS 12   6
  so much heard so much smelled so much tasted . . . . 474 NEW POEMS 12   6
  so much smelled so much tasted plus touched quite . . . . . . 474 NEW POEMS 12   6
  quite so And How much nonexistence eye sed bea . . . . 474 NEW POEMS 12   9
  mind immeasurably roots among much soundless rubbish of . . 479 NEW POEMS 17   6
  such intense digestion so much greenness only dying makes . . 491 50 POEMS 5   16
  but) always (they're more much further off) further these . . 501 50 POEMS 15   16
  silent than more much more is or total . . . . 502 50 POEMS 16   2
  know a thing who's much too busy being her . . . . 504 50 POEMS 18   12
  this world into bigger much some out of (not . . . . 516 50 POEMS 30   15
  pay a store too much yes what too much . . . . 523 50 POEMS 36   14
  much yes what too much o much cheap me . . . . 523 50 POEMS 36   15
  what too much o much cheap me i work . . . . 523 50 POEMS 36   15
  yes any world is much too not quite big . . . . 523 50 POEMS 36   30
  deepness of less fear much than more climbing hope . . . . . 528 50 POEMS 40   9
  should not sing) how much more than enough for . . . . 531 50 POEMS 43   13
  so what he is much too busy sitting the . . . . 545 1 X 1 5   15
  infrequently more and more much (as aprils elsewhere stroll) 546 1 X 1 6   3
  / what if a much of a which of . . . . 560 1 X 1 20   1
  if? why i'm by much the luckiest what of . . . . 590 1 X 1 50   18
  -idity (plus, out of much its misbutt- oned trouserfly . . . 607 {CHAIRE} 9   5
  The distance is more much than all of timely . . . . 608 {CHAIRE} 10   3
  little a little was much and much is too . . . . 614 {CHAIRE} 16   7
  little was much and much is too if the . . . . 614 {CHAIRE} 16   7
  undying) is not so much that mind no more . . . . 664 {CHAIRE} 66   2
  do) loves nothing as much as how (first the . . . . 676 95 POEMS 4   17
  would it hurt too much and 'twas me that . . . . 707 95 POEMS 35   24
  the) with the bigger much than biggest (little is) . . . . . 715 95 POEMS 43   13
  / i love you much (most beautiful darling) more . . . . . . 717 95 POEMS 45   1
  (not putting it mildly much) may be be cause . . . . 727 95 POEMS 55   12
  dying's huge because) given much mercy more than even . . . 735 95 POEMS 63   11
  disappears; till of more much than dark most nowhere . . . . 756 95 POEMS 84   7
  marvels come) as littler much than littlest they adventure . 757 95 POEMS 85   18
  quote eye cue unquote. Much better than which, every . . . . 807 73 POEMS 35   9
  yourself so wise; and much could understand concerning no . . 834 73 POEMS 62   15

	PAGE	TITLE	LINE

MUCH (CONTINUED)
i who love so much to live) must die" . . . . 836 73 POEMS 64   4
+MUCH
FOR CONTEXT, SEE   . . . . 12 T&C SONGS 2   3
FOR CONTEXT, SEE   . . . . 287 IS 5 FOUR 4   7
FOR CONTEXT, SEE   . . . . 333 VIVA 24   10
FOR CONTEXT, SEE   . . . . 789 73 POEMS 17   12
MUCHMOUTHED
world (the pertly papped muchmouthed) her way of beginningly 337 VIVA 28   12
MUCHNESS
to the mangling air muchness of buds mattered. a . . . . . 135 & SON REAL 6   14
MUCHTHEWORSEFORWEAR
nearly leaped out of muchtheworseforwear shoes 'fair friend' 800 73 POEMS 28   8
+MUCILAGE
FOR CONTEXT, SEE   . . . . 325 VIVA 17   2
MUCKERS
/ / / when muckers pimps and tratesmen delivered . . . . . 405 NO THANKS 22   1
MUCOUS
Up In, the slipshod mucous kiss of her riant . . . . 130 & SON REAL 1   1
muscle (itch of groping mucous) in my mouth occurs . . . . 136 & SON REAL 7   10
MUD
when the world is mud- luscious the little lame . . . . 24 T&C CHANSONS 1   2
tadpole wriggling in delicious mud / / / / . . . . 157 & SON REAL 6   15
coffee covered with froth half-mud and not too sweet? . . . . 198 XLI PORTRAIT 6   33
quietly in the deep mud et cetera (dreaming, et . . . . 276 IS 5 TWO 10   20
blood and flesh be mud and mire, scheming imagine, ... 521 50 POEMS 34   54
+MUDDIED
FOR CONTEXT, SEE   . . . . 656 {CHAIRE} 58   9
MUDDLED
dir ty glass mind muddled and cuddled by dreams . . . . 354 VIVA 45   6
MUDDY
dirty legs and a muddy petticoat, drowsy is your . . . . . . 61 T&C PORTRAIT 9   12
recently employed anent this muddy toiletbowl, while kindred 339 VIVA 30   12
MUFFHUNTER
but we knew a muffhunter and he said to . . . . 259 IS 5 ONE 29   27
+MUFFLE
FOR CONTEXT, SEE   . . . . 342 VIVA 33   9
MUG
slowly loved a dinted mug gone Darkness it was . . . . 97 & POST TMPR 8   39
MUH
spairruh luckih? Thangzkeed. Mairsee. Muh jax awl gawn. Fur . 310 VIVA 2   9
MULTIPLIED
of people socalled if multiplied by twice infinity could . . 510 50 POEMS 24   10
each than living's all multiplied with infinity sans if . . . 592 1 X 1 52   5
MULTIPLY
call it beautifool to multiply because and why dividing . . . 500 50 POEMS 14   5
MULTITUDE
several faces and a multitude of chins: next door . . . . . . 312 VIVA 4   6
MULTITUDES
tilted streets spill lazily multitudes out of final towers; . 345 VIVA 36   7
MUMBLE
this crump led cap mumble some thing to oh . . . . 314 VIVA 6   19
MUMBLING
sharp lips comb my mumbling gropeofstrength (staggered by the 137 & SON REAL 8   2
MURANO
ear you glassworks of Murano; pause elevator nel mezzo . . . 256 IS 5 ONE 27   4
MURDER
world goes forth to murder dreams.... i see in . . . . 50 T&C IMPRESS 4   11
of an old man murder the petals hush mysteriously . . . . . . 59 T&C PORTRAIT 7   3
of an old man murder the petals. / / . . . . 59 T&C PORTRAIT 7   16
vise whose stilling lips murder suddenly me, but of . . . . . 152 & SON ACTU 1   11
am tell such to murder time (forgetting what's to . . . . . . 362 VIVA 53   13
is Dick; while Gadgets murder squawk and add, the . . . . . . 438 NO THANKS 54   11
("fire stop thief help murder save the world" what . . . . . 555 1 X 1 15   1
"no slave's unlife shall murder me for i will . . . . 711 95 POEMS 39   11
MURDERED
and mark the fainting murdered petals. with the caving . . . 215 XLI SONNETS 11   8
desires things moments be murdered known photographed, . . . 237 IS 5 ONE 8   2

	PAGE	TITLE	LINE

MURDERED (CONTINUED)
    dead" so Jones was murdered by a man named . . . . 313 VIVA 5   9
    imaginations) filled with newly murdered flowers whispering . 340 VIVA 31   11
    / / / on murdered feet into immense no . . . . 479 NEW POEMS 17   2
    starved on space? love's murdered eye dissected to mere . . . 527 50 POEMS 39   13
    eyes every because is murdered twice / / / . . . . 588 1 X 1 48   8
    have breathed such miracle murdered we whom cannot kill . . . 639 {CHAIRE} 41   9
    (a forest has slowly Murdered the House) hole swallows . . . 693 95 POEMS 21   14
    each inch of their murdered planet grows more and . . . . . . 808 73 POEMS 36   10
    on immortality again --her murdered selves exchanging swiftly 818 73 POEMS 46   5
MURDERERS
    give a damn for murderers of high estate whose . . . . 774 73 POEMS 2   10
MURDERFULLY
    / / / / murderfully in midmost o.c. an . . . . 334 VIVA 25   1
MURDERING
    peace (dreaming is better) murdering coolness slowly in . . . 168 & SON ACTU 17   13
    a crisp todo of murdering uncouth faces which pass . . . . . 354 VIVA 45   10
    and angels sing: all murdering lies by mortals told . . . . . 556 1 X 1 16   10
    phantom me with the murdering minus of cold --open . . . . . 839 73 POEMS 67   10
MURDEROUS
    wanders buoyed on the murderous saliva of industry. the . . . 201 XLI PORTRAIT 9   5
MURDERS
    world's whens, wheels; wonders: murders. cries: hopes; . . . 361 VIVA 52   18
MURMUR
    the tide's acute weaving murmur / / / / . . . . 369 VIVA 60   21
    But others don't scream murmur wink at kid anaesthetize . . . 391 NO THANKS 8   14
+MURMUR
    FOR CONTEXT, SEE . . . . 201 XLI PORTRAIT 9   12
MURMURING
    steepness the ship climbs murmuring silver mountains which . 419 NO THANKS 36   16
MURMUROUS
    radiance wherein slowly drift murmurous things divinely . . . 18 T&C PUELLA MEA 81
    us drew lewdly the murmurous minute clumsy smelloftheworld. . 174 & SON ACTU 23   2
MURMURS
    as perhaps nothing, he murmurs carefully lying down) / . . . 299 IS 5 FOUR 16   16
    end of a string (murmurs little you-i as the . . . . 593 1 X 1 53   21
    "but dying's meanwhile" (mind murmurs; the fool) "truth would 625 {CHAIRE} 27   16
    your" whispers that flower murmurs eager this "i will . . . . 837 73 POEMS 65   7
MUSCLE
    around whose unwashed sonorous muscle the filth of a . . . . 96 & POST IMPR 8   30
    terrors; the, mouth's, swallowed, muscle (itch of groping . . 136 & SON REAL 7   9
    gradual stir of beginning muscle, and what it will . . . . . 157 & SON ACTU 6   4
    the unkind dawn its muscle amorous pricks with minute . . . . 165 & SON ACTU 14   4
MUSCLED
    sunset utters one unhurried muscled huge chromatic fist . . . 82 T&C SON ACTU 1   8
MUSCLES
    climb by tall careful muscles into nervous and accurate . . . 67 T&C POST IMPR 4 15
    the traffic of lovely; muscles-sinke x p i r . . . . 122 & SEVEN POEMS 1   4
    quite new a thing. Muscles better and nerves more. . . . . . 175 & SON ACTU 24   3
    from the gripping gigantic muscles of Cezanne's logic, oho. . 180 XLI SONGS 2   15
    erect everywhere of black muscles fools a weightless slowness 299 IS 5 FOUR 16   2
MUSCLES-SINKE
    the traffic of lovely; muscles-sinke x p i r . . . . 122 & SEVEN POEMS 1   4
+MUSCULARITY
    FOR CONTEXT, SEE . . . . 197 XLI PORTRAIT 5   14
MUSEUMS
    our separating selves become museums filled with skilfully . 297 IS 5 FOUR 14   14
MUSIC
    haunted the limbs as music haunts the lyre, a . . . . 8 T&C OF NICOL   21
    a chord of crimson music Come hither O thou, ... 27 T&C ORIENTALE 1   5
    at him over the music and jerk the little . . . . 69 T&C POST IMPR 6 13
    is yelling over the music i understand him i . . . . 69 T&C POST IMPR 6 33
    / yours is the music for no instrument yours . . . . 84 T&C SON ACTU 3   1
    roman theirs was a music sinuous globular slippery intense . 110 & PORTRAIT 6   23
    ground there is a music Lady the noiseless truth . . . . . . 113 & PORTRAIT 6   115
    spurting bell a jetted music splashing fresh upon silence) . 115 & PORTRAIT 8   19
    crammed with the strenuous music of the innumerable capering 118 & PORTRAIT 10   37
    musiclesson and you like music and to have somebody . . . . . 126 & SEVEN POEMS 5 30

MUSIC (CONTINUED)

just a little like music, a little more like . . . . 152 & SON ACTU 1   2
feels ashamed before this music, and poetry cannot go . . . . 162 & SON ACTU 11   6
in- secure sharp algebraic music. For the first time . . . . 201 XLI PORTRAIT 9   20
do forget.... or mere Music mounting unsurely twilight but . 211 XLI SONNETS 7   2
and will the stabbing music of your white youth . . . . . . 218 XLI SONNETS 14   2
say "his most wise music stole nothing from death"-- . . . . 306 IS 5 FIVE 5   9
in whose silence the music of spring lives F . . . . 390 NO THANKS 7   4
--opens the sun: who music wear burst icy known . . . . . . 533 50 POEMS 45   14
selves conceive here's music's music and the day of . . . . 538 50 POEMS 50   8
most steep more than music) feeling that sunlight is . . . . 816 73 POEMS 44   6

MUSIC'S
younger selves conceive here's music's music and the day . . 538 50 POEMS 50   8

MUSICAL
hair pale, a terror musical? while in an earthless . . . . 12 T&C SONGS 2   40
queens comes forth ankles musical with large pearls kingdoms 33 T&C ORIENTALE 6   67
serenade his lady the musical tom-cat, thou stuffest the . . 61 T&C PORTRAIT 9   5
silence, and the keenly musical light of sudden nothing.... . 84 T&C SON ACTU 3   14
the stone of a musical fruit. My lips pleasantly . . . . . . 154 & SON ACTU 3   3
Thou to whom the musical white spring offers her . . . . . . 206 XLI SONNETS 2   1
blossoms of person) through musical shadows while hunted by . 586 1 X 1 46   13

MUSICALLY
croon of mingling robes musically revealed in rareness: let . 10 T&C SONGS 1   41
allons 9 & . (musically-who? pivoting) SmileS "ahlbrhoon / . 430 NO THANKS 47   28

MUSICALLY-WHO
allons 9 & . (musically-who? pivoting) SmileS "ahlbrhoon / . 430 NO THANKS 47   28

MUSICIAN
your body's idiom: the musician of your wrists; the . . . . 291 IS 5 FOUR 8   8

MUSICLESSON
dear, Time for your musiclesson and you like music . . . . . 126 & SEVEN POEMS 5   29

MUSICS
scents of not known musics in whose careful eyes . . . . . . 9 T&C SONGS 1   18

MUSN'T
cries to please my musn't broke) life Is like . . . . 343 VIVA 34   2

+MUSN'T
FOR CONTEXT, SEE . . . . 316 VIVA 8   8

MUSSED
floor Her hair was mussed, and she coughed while . . . . . . 132 & SON REAL 3   18

+MUSSOLINI
FOR CONTEXT, SEE . . . . 325 VIVA 17   2

MUST
to nine ladies they must chain his foot for . . . . 15 T&C SONGS 5   11
always the touch of must and shall, whose slippery . . . . . 74 T&C SON REAL 5   2
God, my name is must and with the others . . . . 117 & PORTRAIT 10   23
into, her. Thirsty stirring. (Must be summer. Hush. Worms.) . 130 & SON REAL 1   12
stranger dreams thy strangeness must abuse....) Time being . 213 XLI SONNETS 9   14
/ / it really must be Nice, never to . . . . 242 IS 5 ONE 13   1
with the other) it Must be nice never to . . . . 242 IS 5 ONE 13   10
duty whispers low "thou must!" and who replies "I . . . . . 273 IS 5 TWO 8   5
eloping to Ire (land must be heav en FoR . . . . 320 VIVA 12   12
solution (of course you must shake well) indolently dreaming 323 VIVA 15   5
like a sun which must go sometimes, to make . . . . 372 VIVA 63   7
our young kiss only must unexist, solemnly and per . . . . 373 VIVA 64   3
such a day as must remember he who watched . . . . 376 VIVA 67   2
all the weird worlds must be opened?) Love . . . . 377 VIVA 68   14
can and bathe who must or any dream means . . . . 390 NO THANKS 7   10
and complete fate (he must deny mind: may believe . . . . . 402 NO THANKS 19   15
each and every thing must have an end (the . . . . 411 NO THANKS 28   2
called ocean) and let must or if be damned . . . . 424 NO THANKS 41   8
unhearts can less unminds must fear because and why . . . . 440 NO THANKS 56   5
for hope of hope must coo or boo may . . . . 440 NO THANKS 56   18
shall they be and must they have at him . . . . 440 NO THANKS 56   36
rd chief something or must be off duty wanderfuling . . . . 465 NEW POEMS 3   3
equals (transparent or science must bait laws with stars . . 478 NEW POEMS 16   4
/ / / / must being shall one only . . . . 480 NEW POEMS 18   1
shall one only thing must: the opening of a . . . . 480 NEW POEMS 18   2
of quills (asleep who must go things-without-wings / / . . . 483 NEW POEMS 21   11
Scorning the pomp of must and shall my father . . . . 520 50 POEMS 34   33

		PAGE	TITLE	LINE
MUST (CONTINUED)				
when pimps may please? must through unstrange synthetic now .		527	50 POEMS 39	25
as to do what must (whispers) be must be		543	1 X 1 3	13
what must (whispers) be must be (the wise fool)		543	1 X 1 3	13
dragon's tail (for men must loaf and women must		552	1 X 1 12	18
must loaf and women must lay) and she gave		552	1 X 1 12	18
gift called dying born) must grow deep in dark		556	1 X 1 16	12
of nonsense which itself must call a state submicroscopic . .		561	1 X 1 21	2
gods; but if gods must be men, the sometimes		562	1 X 1 22	1
the boths and neithers--you must let them go they		569	1 X 1 29	12
replies in haste I must be you no sunbeam		570	1 X 1 30	4
feel how the earth must fly if a truth		587	1 X 1 47	15
/ / / why must itself up every of		636	{CHAIRE} 38	1
any christ but you must understand why because i		638	{CHAIRE} 40	14
shining this our now must come to then our		667	{CHAIRE} 69	8
spend (gladly, as lovers must) immortal and the courage . . .		675	95 POEMS 3	13
old) lie we so must most lily brief (rose		690	95 POEMS 18	4
how" "your bastard boy must have learned what he		707	95 POEMS 35	15
scolds Forbid den Stop Must n't Don't &) youth		729	95 POEMS 57	15
some times call april) must often have wondered "most		738	95 POEMS 66	9
never it so skilful) must wither fail and cease		742	95 POEMS 70	4
agines more than life must die to merely Know		759	95 POEMS 86	10
to feel) poor worlds must merely do, which than		762	95 POEMS 89	3
least the rose alive must three, must four and		764	95 POEMS 90	50
rose alive must three, must four and (to quite		764	95 POEMS 90	50
worlds) merely have the must to say and the		776	73 POEMS 4	8
they bow to a must though the earth in		801	73 POEMS 29	28
to merely what dying must call life are you		818	73 POEMS 46	14
so much to live) must die" "if i should		836	73 POEMS 64	5
of them But it must be your" whispers that		837	73 POEMS 65	5
any fear, but it Must be your" perfectly alive		837	73 POEMS 65	10
a) mystery "but it must be Your" / /		837	73 POEMS 65	18
/ how many moments must (amazing each how many		843	73 POEMS 71	1
appear) death's: any world must always half perceive. Only .		845	73 POEMS 73	4
MUST'S				
love is to yes must's a schoolroom in the		574	1 X 1 34	5
+MUSTACHE				
FOR CONTEXT, SEE		310	VIVA 2	2
MUSTACHES				
all have very tidiyum mustaches, and very tidiyum chins, . .		274	IS 5 TWO 9	12
MUSTN'T				
won't (most parent people mustn't shouldn't) most daren't . .		412	NO THANKS 29	5
+MUSTN'T				
FOR CONTEXT, SEE		729	95 POEMS 57	15
MUTE				
the tongue of flame half-mute, (haste ere some thrush		6	T&C EPITHALAM	118
most shy thing and mute, it is to quell		19	T&C PUELLA MEA	99
doth leap from the mute hugeness of depriving deep, ...		210	XLI SONNETS 6	5
weakly dirt while the mute trouserfly confessed a button . .		258	IS 5 ONE 28	19
voice of liberty be mute?" He. spoke. And drank		268	IS 5 TWO 3	13
scarcely may) certainly while mute each inch of their		808	73 POEMS 36	10
MUTED				
faces, moving purely with muted step, yet somewhat proudly .		211	XLI SONNETS 7	9
MUTENESS				
shrug asking Through her Muteness will slowly roam my		137	& SON REAL 8	5
MUTHN'T				
giggling lithped now we muthn't pleathe don't as pop		316	VIVA 8	8
MUTILATED				
hair is lousy with mutilated singing microscopic things in .		69	T&C POST IMPR 6	28
ly in to one exactly-mutilated ghost of a chair, ...		96	& POST IMPR 8	34
subjunctive crumbs twitch like mutilated thumbs: picture His		117	& PORTRAIT 10	31
MUTING				
gold crescendo and silver muting of seatides i trusted . . .		39	T&C AMORES 4	8
a weightless slowness (deftly muting the world's texture with		299	IS 5 FOUR 16	4
MUTTER				
pair of eyes which mutter thickly (as one merely		116	& PORTRAIT 9	11
+MUTTERING				
FOR CONTEXT, SEE		705	95 POEMS 33	3

		PAGE	TITLE	LINE

MUTTERINGS
        among who dreams whom mutterings dream & : the . . . . 384 NO THANKS 2   6
MY
        greenness of thy thought my golden soul fabulously to . . . .   9 T&C SONGS 1   30
        about me dream shall my love wholly taste thee . . . .   9 T&C SONGS 1   35
        Always before your voice my soul half-beautiful and wholly . 11 T&C SONGS 2   1
        his skin, so of my stupid sincere youth the . . . . 11 T&C SONGS 2   6
        more white than wool My thought is sorrowful: but . . . . . . 11 T&C SONGS 2   15
        thought is sorrowful: but my heart smote in trembling . . . . 11 T&C SONGS 2   16
        faultless eyes (whose hand my folded soul shall know . . . . 11 T&C SONGS 2   26
        shall pass) and these my days their sounds and . . . . 11 T&C SONGS 2   31
        in an earthless hour my fond soul seriously yearns . . . . . 12 T&C SONGS 2   41
        All in green went my love riding on a . . . . 14 T&C SONGS 4   1
        Horn at hip went my love riding riding the . . . . 14 T&C SONGS 4   11
        Bow at belt went my love riding riding the . . . . 14 T&C SONGS 4   21
        All in green went my love riding on a . . . . 14 T&C SONGS 4   31
        crouched low and smiling my heart fell dead before. . . . . . 14 T&C SONGS 4   35
        / when god lets my body be From each . . . .   16 T&C SONGS 6   1
        will dance upon Between my lips which did sing . . . . 16 T&C SONGS 6   5
        between their little breasts My strong fingers beneath the . 16 T&C SONGS 6   9
        strenuous birds shall go my love walking in the . . . . 16 T&C SONGS 6   11
        all the while shall my heart be With the . . . . 16 T&C SONGS 6   13
        In her perfectest array my lady, moving in the . . . . 17 T&C PUELLA MEA   6
        young and awkward hours my lady perfectly moving, through . . 17 T&C PUELLA MEA   11
        new world scarce astir my fragile lady wandering in . . . . . 17 T&C PUELLA MEA   13
        snow dexterous and fugitive my very frail lady drifting . . . 17 T&C PUELLA MEA   18
        in the unskilful day my lady utterly alive, to . . . . 17 T&C PUELLA MEA   24
        leman was. And if my lady look at me . . . . 17 T&C PUELLA MEA   38
        the improbable beauty of my lady will) --at her . . . . 18 T&C PUELLA MEA   44
        will) --at her glance my spirit shies rearing (as . . . . . . 18 T&C PUELLA MEA   45
        not kill.) But should my lady smile, it were . . . . 18 T&C PUELLA MEA   49
        Grania's eyes.) But should my lady's beauty play at . . . . . 18 T&C PUELLA MEA   61
        doth immediately make in my heart so great a . . . . 18 T&C PUELLA MEA   65
        is wholly to bewitch my smallest thought with a . . . . 18 T&C PUELLA MEA   79
        is foolingly to smite my spirit with the lithe . . . . 18 T&C PUELLA MEA   83
        with foliate inscrutable sweetness my soul obedient; it is . 19 T&C PUELLA MEA   89
        it is to stroke my being with numbing forests . . . . 19 T&C PUELLA MEA   90
        is distinctly to confute my reason with the deep . . . . . . 19 T&C PUELLA MEA   98
        living intense things. Never my soul so fortunate is . . . . 19 T&C PUELLA MEA 102
        perfume--whereby (with fear aglow) my soul is wont wholly . . 19 T&C PUELLA MEA 109
        which hint at flight --my lady's very singular and . . . . . 20 T&C PUELLA MEA 159
        will amaying go with my lord Boccaccio-- whoso knocketh . . . 20 T&C PUELLA MEA 170
        silently than a flower, my lady naked in her . . . . 21 T&C PUELLA MEA 178
        lovely fashion doth from my lady's body grow; as . . . . . . 21 T&C PUELLA MEA 183
        and strange; apt in my hand warmly to lie . . . . 21 T&C PUELLA MEA 195
        she appear to me my flesh is an enchanted . . . . 22 T&C PUELLA MEA 232
        lips' most frail parting my body hears the cry . . . . 22 T&C PUELLA MEA 234
        with miracle. Love!--maker of my lady, in that always . . . . 22 T&C PUELLA MEA 237
        / / / / my love thy hair is . . . . 29 T&C ORIENTALE 3   1
        always a pleasant song my love thy head is . . . .   29 T&C ORIENTALE 3   15
        you clutched you upon my mouth listen beloved i . . . . 30 T&C ORIENTALE 4   13
        beloved i dreamed in my dream you had desire . . . . 30 T&C ORIENTALE 4   17
        you broke you upon my blood listen beloved i . . . . 30 T&C ORIENTALE 4   28
        the dim smoke scraining my lips are vague with . . . . 31 T&C ORIENTALE 5   23
        are vague with ecstasy my palpitating breasts inhale the . . 31 T&C ORIENTALE 5   24
        flower of thy beauty, my heart discovers thee unto . . . . . 31 T&C ORIENTALE 5   28
        consider O woman this my body. for it has . . . . 36 T&C AMORES 1   3
        of your soul upon my lips / / / . . . . 38 T&C AMORES 3   19
        one night when in my fingers drooped your shining . . . . . . 39 T&C AMORES 4   12
        your shining body when my heart sang between your . . . . . . 39 T&C AMORES 4   14
        of stars was on my mouth petals danced against . . . . 39 T&C AMORES 4   18
        mouth petals danced against my eyes and down the . . . . . . 39 T&C AMORES 4   19
        the singing reaches of my soul spoke the green- . . . . 39 T&C AMORES 4   22
        fragrant night, when all my days shall have before . . . . . 39 T&C AMORES 4   31
        seeing the hunger of my lips for a dead . . . . 42 T&C AMORES 6   9
        O Distinct Lady of my unkempt adoration if i . . . .   43 T&C AMORES 7   2
        Distinct Lady swiftly take my fragile certain song that . . . 43 T&C AMORES 7   27
        high-heeled flames courtesied before my eyes or twinkling . . 44 T&C AMORES 8   7

514

		PAGE	TITLE	LINE

MY (CONTINUED)

	PAGE	TITLE	LINE
or twinkling over to my side Looked up with	44	T&C AMORES 8	8
into eternity. when over my head a shooting star	49	T&C IMPRESS 3	22
yourself delivered into both my hands herself to always . . .	57	T&C PORTRAIT 5	19
and dinted then did my servant become of the	57	T&C PORTRAIT 5	35
dead tunes crawl upon my face my hair is	69	T&C POST IMPR 6	27
crawl upon my face my hair is lousy with	69	T&C POST IMPR 6	28
singing microscopic things in my ears scramble faintly . . .	69	T&C POST IMPR 6	29
understand him i shove my round red hat back	69	T&C POST IMPR 6	34
red hat back on my head i sit up	69	T&C POST IMPR 6	34
blink at you with my solemn eyeswhichneversmile yes, By . . .	69	T&C POST IMPR 6	35
should be-- you of my heart, send me a	76	T&C SON UNRE 1	10
Then shall i turn my face, and hear one	76	T&C SON UNRE 1	13
with your peculiar mouth my heart made wise; at	78	T&C SON UNRE 3	4
little while; moments when my once more illustrious arms . .	78	T&C SON UNRE 3	9
filled with fascination, when my breast wears the intolerant	78	T&C SON UNRE 3	10
prospecting darkness roams torture my spirit with the	79	T&C SON UNRE 4	5
grave astonishment feel in my being the delirious smart . . .	79	T&C SON UNRE 4	12
pushings of flesh, makes my body sorry when the	82	T&C SON ACTU 1	4
/ / / / my love is building a	83	T&C SON ACTU 2	1
magic of your mouth) my love is building a	83	T&C SON ACTU 2	9
mouth-flower fleet He'll not my tower, laborious, casual . .	83	T&C SON ACTU 2	13
painter should have loved my lady. And by this	85	T&C SON ACTU 4	9
the sleepshaped lilies-- should my lady's body with these . .	85	T&C SON ACTU 4	13
sir things which in my mind blossom will stumble	91	& POST IMPR 3	11
(brea) K ing my Nose puts on sharp	94	& POST IMPR 6	9
i o n ? my mind laughsin- to Slivers	94	& POST IMPR 6	17
the Momentinmyarms your expression my love when most . . .	94	& POST IMPR 6	24
when most passionate. , my, love is thatofa fly.	94	& POST IMPR 6	26
/ / / / my smallheaded pearshaped lady in	95	& POST IMPR 7	1
at the low ceiling my being pleasantly was punctuated	96	& POST IMPR 8	25
/ / / / my eyes are fond of	100	& POST IMPR 11	1
as i lie asleep my eyes go into Allen	100	& POST IMPR 11	2
tint. TUMTITUMTIDDLE if sometimes my eyes stay at home . . .	100	& POST IMPR 11	18
stay at home then my mouth will go out	100	& POST IMPR 11	19
into the East side, my mouth goes to the	100	& POST IMPR 11	19
and the bad candies my, mouth loves melons slitted	100	& POST IMPR 11	22
s asc end-ing inthecarts my, mouth is, fond of	100	& POST IMPR 11	25
a scarlet pepper and my eyes were buttoned with	100	& POST IMPR 11	31
WITH is there anything my ears love it's to	100	& POST IMPR 11	33
ghosts of child- ren. my, ears know the fuZZy	100	& POST IMPR 11	36
His wrappedupbody Queerly Has, my, ears, go into Hassan's . .	100	& POST IMPR 11	41
the cuspidor-col ouredRoom and, my ears bend to the	101	& POST IMPR 11	45
Like to Lie On My Couch at Christopher Street	101	& POST IMPR 11	58
at Christopher Street For my stomach goes out into	101	& POST IMPR 11	58
into the east side my sex sitting up- right	101	& POST IMPR 11	59
and intotheslow hot women my Stomach ruBSiTSElf kew-ri-ous-ly	101	& POST IMPR 11	62
hear ,pas cheres") and my love slowly answered I	102	& POST IMPR 12	22
ear against yester- day My Lady hear the purple	110	& PORTRAIT 6	32
yester- day (and O My Lady Lady Of Ladies	112	& PORTRAIT 6	93
in the winds of my lust like a high	112	& PORTRAIT 6	96
should and this is my little sister could with	117	& PORTRAIT 10	18
shame whispered unto God, my name is must and	117	& PORTRAIT 10	22
dead exactly dance in my head, precisely dance where . . .	120	& PORTRAIT 12	3
americains dance exactly in my brain voulez- vous coucher . .	120	& PORTRAIT 12	28
qui dansent toujours in my head dis-donc, Paris ta	121	& PORTRAIT 12	51
men precisely dance in my head ladies carefully dead	121	& PORTRAIT 12	60
bar was COOl O My lover, there's just room	123	& SEVEN POEMS 2	7
for me in You you my stomach goes into your	123	& SEVEN POEMS 2	9
into your Little Stomach My legs are in your	123	& SEVEN POEMS 2	9
arms under me around; my head fits (my head)	123	& SEVEN POEMS 2	11
around; my head fits (my head) in your Brain--my, ...	123	& SEVEN POEMS 2	12
(my head) in your Brain--my, head's big she (said	123	& SEVEN POEMS 2	12
see and you are My how glad he winked	126	& SEVEN POEMS 5	16
string dead never says my dear, Time for your	126	& SEVEN POEMS 5	29
Good Old Summer Time. My gorgeous bullet in tickling	130	& SON REAL 1	10
/ / / / my strength becoming wistful in	131	& SON REAL 2	1
thinks of the sky, my mind takes to nib	131	& SON REAL 2	4

		PAGE	TITLE	LINE

MY (CONTINUED)

	PAGE	TITLE	LINE
coy rooting dies also. (my loveFist in her knuckling	131	& SON REAL 2	8
kiss have just throttled my seeing blood, her heart's	132	& SON REAL 3	3
belly's merry thrust Boost my huge passion like a	132	& SON REAL 3	8
Dumb for a while. my god--a patter of kisses, ...	133	& SON REAL 4	13
die nous sommes heureux my soul a limp lump	133	& SON REAL 4	19
into a sole mass my separate lusts her hair	135	& SON REAL 6	5
its tickling river in my eyes, the killed world	135	& SON REAL 6	15
unmitigated systole purrs against my mind, the eyes'	136	& SON REAL 7	6
of light stick on my brain harder than can	136	& SON REAL 7	7
of groping mucous) in my mouth occurs homelessly. While . . .	136	& SON REAL 7	10
whose sharp lips comb my mumbling gropeofstrength (staggered	137	& SON REAL 8	2
Muteness will slowly roam my dumbNess? her other, wet, . . .	137	& SON REAL 8	6
warm lips limp, across my bruising smile; as rapidly	137	& SON REAL 8	8
jiggled norm of agony my grunting eyes pin tailored	137	& SON REAL 8	10
and uttering tits punish my hug presto! the bright	137	& SON REAL 8	14
/ nearer: breath of my breath: take not thy	139	& SON REAL 10	1
limbs from me: make my pain their crazy meal	139	& SON REAL 10	2
mingling: deeper: blood of my blood: with upwardcringing . .	139	& SON REAL 10	5
the glad flesh of my fear: more neatly ream	139	& SON REAL 10	7
curvingly the keenness of my hips; or, your first	140	& SON REAL 11	6
crisp boy flesh dips my height in a firm	140	& SON REAL 11	8
fierceness. Her lips study my head gripping for a	146	& SON REAL 17	4
grapple and joke on my passionate anatomy oh yes!	146	& SON REAL 17	6
/ / / / my girl's tall with hard	147	& SON REAL 18	1
her eyes easily files my impatience to an edge--my	147	& SON REAL 18	9
my impatience to an edge--my girl's tall and taut, ...	147	& SON REAL 18	9
me, and to kiss my face and head. /	147	& SON REAL 18	14
/ / SONNETS--ACTUALITIES when my love comes to see	152	& SON ACTU 1	1
darkness.... the coming of my love emits a wonderful	152	& SON ACTU 1	6
a wonderful smell in my mind, you should see	152	& SON ACTU 1	7
to find her how my least heart-beat becomes less.	152	& SON ACTU 1	9
suddenly me, but of my corpse the tool her	152	& SON ACTU 1	12
and the stars, of my shoulder in stead. It	153	& SON ACTU 2	8
of a musical fruit. My lips pleasantly groan on	154	& SON ACTU 3	3
make oddly to strut my indolent priceless smile, until . . .	155	& SON ACTU 4	11
Spring) somewhere unspeaking sits my life; the grim clenched	156	& SON ACTU 5	10
the fooling world in my huge blood, cracking brains	157	& SON ACTU 6	11
an engraving belonging to my friend. Whom i salute, ...	158	& SON ACTU 7	8
/ / / / my naked lady framed in	162	& SON ACTU 11	1
But i (having in my arms caught the picture)	162	& SON ACTU 11	9
hurry it slowly to my mouth, taste the accurate	162	& SON ACTU 11	11
smile is stirringofbirds between my arms; but i should . . .	163	& SON ACTU 12	18
it will do in my bullying fingers) as for	164	& SON ACTU 13	14
of you, worn upon my mind all night, quitting	165	& SON ACTU 14	2
with beautiful jam or my invincible Nearness rapes laughter .	166	& SON ACTU 15	15
among the supercilious chimneys, my nerves sumptuously wink .	169	& SON ACTU 18	8
/ / / / my sonnet is A light	171	& SON ACTU 20	1
toiletwindow, that's straightacross from my window, night air	171	& SON ACTU 20	3
a mouse who shares my meals with him, which	171	& SON ACTU 20	14
sharp agreeable flower between my amused legs kissing with .	172	& SON ACTU 21	11
of newness --and then. My crazy fingers liked your	173	& SON ACTU 22	8
the flesh crisp set my love-tooth on edge. So	173	& SON ACTU 22	11
/ / i like my body when it is	175	& SON ACTU 24	1
/ / / of my soul a street is:	180	XLI SONGS 2	1
Picasso throttling trees hither my soul repairs herself with	180	XLI SONGS 2	9
annihilator drawing into you my enchanting leaves / /	182	XLI SONGS 4	17
ways cloaked with renewal my body turns toward thee	184	XLI SONGS 6	8
the sweet gates of my heart and take the	188	XLI SONGS 10	16
will wade out till my thighs are steeped in	189	XLI SONGS 11	2
take the sun in my mouth and leap into	189	XLI SONGS 11	3
the sleeping curves of my body Shall enter fingers	189	XLI SONGS 11	8
complete the mystery of my flesh I will rise	189	XLI SONGS 11	12
lipping flowers And set my teeth in the silver	189	XLI SONGS 11	17
be very proud and my little sister and i	192	XLI CHANSONS 2	25
/ PORTRAITS conversation with my friend is particularly to .	193	XLI PORTRAIT 1	1
eyes inwardly crisping for my friend, feeling is the	193	XLI PORTRAIT 1	9
the immediate imperceptible content my friend's being, out of	193	XLI PORTRAIT 1	19

	PAGE	TITLE	LINE

MY (CONTINUED)

yaoorti from Nicho' settled my feet on the ceiling	194	XLI PORTRAIT 2	13
of faces meshing with my curiously instant appreciation . . .	197	XLI PORTRAIT 5	8
most crimson assistance of my com- forter a click	197	XLI PORTRAIT 5	15
geomet- rical putrescence whereto my invariably commendable .	197	XLI PORTRAIT 5	20
at the integration of my soul i coughed , ...	197	XLI PORTRAIT 5	23
/ / / / my mind is a big	199	XLI PORTRAIT 7	1
to rapture should surprise my soul slowly which on	205	XLI SONNETS 1	5
the morning; and before my doubting window leaves softly . .	205	XLI SONNETS 1	10
fleetly roll) i spill my bright incalculable soul. /	206	XLI SONNETS 2	15
loveliness receiving the image my proud heart cherished as .	207	XLI SONNETS 3	13
not ladies, ladies of my dreams justly touching roses	211	XLI SONNETS 7	10
/ come nothing to my comparable soul which with	212	XLI SONNETS 8	1
/ / / when my sensational moments are no	213	XLI SONNETS 9	1
in other days (drawing my Mes from sleep whose	213	XLI SONNETS 9	13
am but imperfect in my fear Or with thy	215	XLI SONNETS 11	11
with thy mind against my mind, to hear nearing	215	XLI SONNETS 11	12
drawing thy mouth toward my mouth, steer our lost	215	XLI SONNETS 11	17
with fins sharply pleasant, my youth has travelled toward . .	216	XLI SONNETS 12	3
of her mind to my mind that i am	216	XLI SONNETS 12	6
of wonderful, and that my feet have surely known	216	XLI SONNETS 12	13
white youth wounded by my arms' bothness (say a	218	XLI SONNETS 14	3
me kiddo believe me my country, 'tis of you, ...	230	IS 5 ONE 2	3
these crepuscular violinists among my and your	230	IS 5 ONE 2	26
Isn't A Kodak therefore my friends let us now	230	IS 5 ONE 2	35
-gotten some- thing ah (my necktie / / /	232	IS 5 ONE 3	18
/ / / listen my children and you shall	236	IS 5 ONE 7	1
into vaudeville perhaps because my Uncle Sol could sing . . .	239	IS 5 ONE 10	5
for the fact that my Uncle Sol indulged in	239	IS 5 ONE 10	7
be it needlessly added my Uncle Sol's farm failed	239	IS 5 ONE 10	14
ate the vegetables so my Uncle Sol had a	239	IS 5 ONE 10	17
ate the chickens when my Uncle Sol had a	239	IS 5 ONE 10	20
and died and so my Uncle Sol imitated the	239	IS 5 ONE 10	24
but somebody who'd given my Uncle Sol a Victor	239	IS 5 ONE 10	27
like the Missouri when my Uncle Sol's coffin lurched	239	IS 5 ONE 10	33
button (and down went my Uncle Sol and started	239	IS 5 ONE 10	36
a bit of it, my dears merely the prime	245	IS 5 ONE 16	19
gustibus non disputandum est my lady is tired of	245	IS 5 ONE 16	25
the universal joint tested my gas felt of her	248	IS 5 ONE 19	7
bare, ly nudg. ing (my lev-er Right- oh and	248	IS 5 ONE 19	15
how listens and, expands my somewherealloverme heart my the .	251	IS 5 ONE 22	17
expands my somewherealloverme heart my the halfgloom coolish	251	IS 5 ONE 22	17
/ / / / my uncle Daniel fought in	253	IS 5 ONE 24	1
triangle like the devil) my uncle Frank has done	253	IS 5 ONE 24	4
string breaks (or something) my uncle Frank breaks into . . .	253	IS 5 ONE 24	8
Frank breaks into tears. my uncle Tom knits and	253	IS 5 ONE 24	9
above the ears (but my uncle Ed that's dead	253	IS 5 ONE 24	11
lips totter Therefore, approaching my twentysix selves . . .	255	IS 5 ONE 26	5
put him all into my arms and staggered banged	258	IS 5 ONE 28	22
or when the your-and my- idle vertical worthless self	260	IS 5 ONE 30	14
thoughts slyly crept into my highly sexed mind. It	262	IS 5 ONE 32	4
nombril, and much to my astonishment much impressed by . . .	262	IS 5 ONE 32	9
i say i believe my most intimate friends would	262	IS 5 ONE 32	14
unhurried reflections to which my organ of imperception gave	263	IS 5 ONE 32	32
refer, of course, to my position. A bachelor incapable . . .	263	IS 5 ONE 32	36
had ceased. I withdrew my hands from the tennisracket. . . .	263	IS 5 ONE 32	55
would have been not my fault. / / /	263	IS 5 ONE 32	65
/ / life hurl my yes, crumbles hand (ful	265	IS 5 ONE 34	1
ingfallall! mil, shy milbrightlions my (hurl flicker handful	265	IS 5 ONE 34	7
/ the season 'tis, my lovely lambs, of Sumner	266	IS 5 TWO 1	1
of maladies including flu) my little darlings, let us	266	IS 5 TWO 1	16
their country's love received my dears the order of	266	IS 5 TWO 1	27
by the dawn's early my country 'tis of centuries	268	IS 5 TWO 3	3
no kidding this was my particular pal funny aint	270	IS 5 TWO 5	6
he was kilt and my youngest boy was kilt	271	IS 5 TWO 6	7
oh baby shrapnel or my feet getting dim freezing	272	IS 5 TWO 7	8
of minions ◇ "allezcirculez") --my he's brave.... the . . .	275	IS 5 TWO 9	40
/ / / / my sweet old etcetera aunt	276	IS 5 TWO 10	1

MY (CONTINUED)

	PAGE	TITLE	LINE
everybody was fighting for, my sister isabel created hundreds	276	IS 5 TWO 10	7
earwarmers etcetera wristers etcetera, my mother hoped that i	276	IS 5 TWO 10	12
etcetera bravely of course my father used to become	276	IS 5 TWO 10	15
only he could meanwhile my self etcetera lay quietly	276	IS 5 TWO 10	18
a reddish ant travels my fifth finger. a bird	281	IS 5 THREE 5	11
the moon looked into my window it touched me	284	IS 5 FOUR 1	1
infantile fingers it understood my eyes cheeks mouth its . .	284	IS 5 FOUR 1	4
hands (slipping) felt of my necktie wandered against my . . .	284	IS 5 FOUR 1	5
my necktie wandered against my shirt and into my	284	IS 5 FOUR 1	6
my shirt and into my body the sharp things	284	IS 5 FOUR 1	6
sharp things fingered tinily my heart life the little	284	IS 5 FOUR 1	7
smiled she let go my vest and crept through	284	IS 5 FOUR 1	11
is between them) knowing my lips hands the way	285	IS 5 FOUR 2	6
the way i move my habits laughter i say	285	IS 5 FOUR 2	7
i Should say solong my tailor chuckles like a	287	IS 5 FOUR 4	10
our minds --before leaving my room i turn, and	288	IS 5 FOUR 5	6
life. Dear i put my eyes into you but	289	IS 5 FOUR 6	13
is in the world my blood approves, and kisses	290	IS 5 FOUR 7	7
--the best gesture of my brain is less than	290	IS 5 FOUR 7	11
laugh, leaning back in my arms for life's not	290	IS 5 FOUR 7	14
not reckon how strangely my life is curved since	292	IS 5 FOUR 9	6
never guess how much my wonderful jealousy is dark	292	IS 5 FOUR 9	16
and with laughter O my lady (and every brittle	293	IS 5 FOUR 10	12
mean: entirely having in my careful how careful arms	295	IS 5 FOUR 12	5
is so long since my heart has been with	297	IS 5 FOUR 14	1
mind has walked into my kiss as a stranger	297	IS 5 FOUR 14	6
are and cling to my mind always But now	301	IS 5 FOUR 18	11
you walking beside me, my very lady, if scarcely	302	IS 5 FIVE 1	2
suddenly unsaid gesture lightly my eyes? And send life . . .	302	IS 5 FIVE 1	6
streets of memory comes my heart, singing like an	304	IS 5 FIVE 3	2
the tall policeman of my mind. awake being not	304	IS 5 FIVE 3	5
if i have made, my lady, intricate imperfect various	306	IS 5 FIVE 5	1
body's whitest song upon my mind--if i have failed	306	IS 5 FIVE 5	5
glance too shy--if through my singing slips the very	306	IS 5 FIVE 5	6
are so perfectly alive) my shame: lady through whose	306	IS 5 FIVE 5	12
the ragged meadow of my soul. / / /	306	IS 5 FIVE 5	15
be heav en FoR my motH) with a grass	320	VIVA 12	16
for the hyenas suppressing my frank qualms in deference . . .	326	VIVA 18	21
during our return voyage, my pensive companion dimly remarked	326	VIVA 18	31
awash. I thereupon loosened my collar and dove for	327	VIVA 18	37
back huly jeezus" --an-- "my specialty is takin fellers' . .	332	VIVA 23	5
wid tears streamin down my face i hauls out	332	VIVA 23	19
big light squoits down my spine like i was	332	VIVA 23	27
chuck slop hight evolute my eerily oh gargle to	333	VIVA 24	23
don't cries to please my musn't broke) life Is	343	VIVA 34	1
there are any heavens my mother will (all by	352	VIVA 43	1
heaven of blackred roses my father will be (deep	352	VIVA 43	5
a rose) standing near my swaying over her (silent)	352	VIVA 43	7
which whisper This is my beloved my (suddenly in	352	VIVA 43	15
This is my beloved my (suddenly in sunlight he	352	VIVA 43	15
little wings and here's my hotel this is the	353	VIVA 44	11
to be out of my reach , they are	353	VIVA 44	17
with your hair in my imagination / / /	356	VIVA 47	23
and having worshipped for my doom pass ignorantly into . . .	358	VIVA 49	14
or eyes firmly stirred) my mirror gives me, on	360	VIVA 51	3
fatal word; so that my life (which liked the	360	VIVA 51	23
but something beats within my shirt to prove he	360	VIVA 51	28
extremely little house of my mind. Clocks strike. The	365	VIVA 56	3
close me, i and my life will shut very	366	VIVA 57	10
/ / / / my darling since you and	368	VIVA 59	1
what is not courage my darling (for only Nobody	368	VIVA 59	17
stones; lifted, and (before my eyes sinking) inward, fled; .	369	VIVA 60	7
gently swiftly creeping through my dreams last night, all . .	369	VIVA 60	17
lives Givehurling with your my most : locking foreverfully .	371	VIVA 62	17
the air) breathe simply my each how my trembling	372	VIVA 63	4
simply my each how my trembling where my still	372	VIVA 63	5
how my trembling where my still unvisible when. Wait	372	VIVA 63	5

	PAGE	TITLE	LINE
MY (CONTINUED)			
while your contriving fate, my sharpening life are (behind .	373	VIVA 64	17
first light groping washes my nightmare from his eyes? . . .	374	VIVA 65	15
this only by you my heart always moves /	379	VIVA 70	14
are aware) than of my books could even be	386	NO THANKS 3	4
not stir) O love, my love! soul clings and	386	NO THANKS 3	12
one life and will my rest to these children	390	NO THANKS 7	13
toys (money men motors "my" yachts wolfhounds women) and . .	394	NO THANKS 11	3
who shall not spend my fortune (although endlessness should .	394	NO THANKS 11	14
truly curving form enters my soul feels all small	419	NO THANKS 36	3
passenger and whose pilot my spirit is / /	419	NO THANKS 36	24
and to your (in my arms flowering so new)	424	NO THANKS 41	2
grow but, never doubt my weakness makes more than	433	NO THANKS 50	6
does not move behind my eye the windmills are	434	NO THANKS 51	9
stride among the vines (my heart pursues against the	434	NO THANKS 51	16
minute mown lives) oh my spirit you tumble climb	434	NO THANKS 51	26
women sturdily meander in my mind, woven by always	435	NO THANKS 51	34
say "and this be my fame, the harder the	439	NO THANKS 55	26
nstretchy: awn) then, o my love , then it's	442	NO THANKS 57	17
hopes and hands --nourish my failure with thy freedom: . . .	456	NO THANKS 71	14
/ / / / my specialty is living said	473	NEW POEMS 11	1
where it her his my next meal's coming from	475	NEW POEMS 13	4
a bellyful without lifting my finger i say to	475	NEW POEMS 13	9
kid that's something else my sweet (i feel that's	475	NEW POEMS 13	24
of (writhing your exploding my) heart before how worlds . . .	480	NEW POEMS 18	15
/ / / may my heart always be open	481	NEW POEMS 19	1
men are old may my mind stroll about hungry	481	NEW POEMS 19	5
up grabbing had by my throat me give it	496	50 POEMS 10	10
than a spinster's heart my voice feels who inquires	506	50 POEMS 20	7
your million selves and my suffice to through the	510	50 POEMS 24	12
ease with which vast my complexly wisdoming friend's --a . .	517	50 POEMS 31	5
/ / / / my father moved through dooms	520	50 POEMS 34	1
out of each night my father moved through depths	520	50 POEMS 34	4
some why completely weep my father's fingers brought her .	520	50 POEMS 34	14
valleys of the sea my father moved through griefs	520	50 POEMS 34	18
him so hugely) stood my father's dream his flesh	520	50 POEMS 34	28
of must and shall my father moved through dooms	520	50 POEMS 34	34
a world with snow. My father moved through theys	521	50 POEMS 34	49
danced when she heard my father sing) then let	521	50 POEMS 34	52
why men breathe-- because my father lived his soul	521	50 POEMS 34	67
i sing you are my voice, / / /	531	50 POEMS 43	14
glad and very merely my fourth will cure the	537	50 POEMS 49	2
to skylessness sticking fire my are your are birds	541	1 X 1 1	5
unquote loss of liberty my dears-- or even is	544	1 X 1 4	16
/ / / / my (his from daughter's mother's	546	1 X 1 6	1
you may sleep now, my mountain" and this mountain	555	1 X 1 15	15
more than sleep illimitably my --being so very born	558	1 X 1 18	11
o most beautiful" her, my life worships and (night)	572	1 X 1 32	12
"everything beautiful can grow" my, her life marvels "here'll	572	1 X 1 32	15
their kind but" her, my "love creates love only"	572	1 X 1 32	18
except in your honour, my loveliest, nothing may move	575	1 X 1 35	3
in your (and rest, my love) honour / /	575	1 X 1 35	41
your me or simplify my you , darling sweet	577	1 X 1 37	11
pleasant country: if's wintry (my lovely) let's open the . .	578	1 X 1 38	3
very weather (not either) my treasure, when violets appear .	578	1 X 1 38	7
deeper season than reason; my sweet one (and april's . . .	578	1 X 1 38	11
/ / darling! because my blood can sing and	580	1 X 1 40	1
Life's life and strikes my your our blossoming sphere	582	1 X 1 42	16
into skies of grin) "my flowers" (the humble man	585	1 X 1 45	12
one perfectly beautiful bow "my home ionian isles /	585	1 X 1 45	21
fear --all perfectly dyingest my and foreverless thy? why . .	590	1 X 1 50	24
is your time is my time is our time	591	1 X 1 51	2
is your time is my time is our time	591	1 X 1 51	26
flame blue took it my far beyond far and	593	1 X 1 53	13
so your is a my (with a down up	594	1 X 1 54	23
blueness) whos (ex- plore my unreal in -credible true	612	(CHAIRE) 14	5
nize-aday (most gently herculanean my mortal) yoo make sno .	618	(CHAIRE) 20	4
daisy-- your thorniest question my roses will answer" "but .	625	(CHAIRE) 27	14

		PAGE	TITLE	LINE

MY (CONTINUED)

	PAGE	TITLE	LINE
screech of space) absolute (my soul tastes If as	639	(CHAIRE) 41	6
the dropsin king god my sic kly a thingish	646	(CHAIRE) 48	3
i met christ jesus) my heart flopped over and	648	(CHAIRE) 50	5
(now the ears of my ears awake and now	663	(CHAIRE) 65	13
now the eyes of my eyes are opened) /	663	(CHAIRE) 65	14
may touch --the great (my darling) happens to be	664	(CHAIRE) 66	5
--it's april (yes, april; my darling) it's spring! yes . . .	665	(CHAIRE) 67	4
nothing may, quite your my (my your and) self	666	(CHAIRE) 68	12
may, quite your my (my your and) self without, ...	666	(CHAIRE) 68	12
each particular person is (my love) alive than every	667	(CHAIRE) 69	3
snow --but never fear (my own, my beautiful my	667	(CHAIRE) 69	13
never fear (my own, my beautiful my blossoming) for	667	(CHAIRE) 69	13
(my own, my beautiful my blossoming) for also then's	667	(CHAIRE) 69	14
bright deathlessness to these my not themselves believing . .	669	(CHAIRE) 71	3
every now & then my wonderful friend dominic depaola	680	95 POEMS 8	22
kiss me twice but my lover has a brother	684	95 POEMS 12	11
to cry and sing, my love and wonder) is	686	95 POEMS 14	4
to grow (remember this my sweet) not only wherever	686	95 POEMS 14	14
silent three like your my life and our /	687	95 POEMS 15	11
is the far o my darling) of (down /	695	95 POEMS 23	20
14th st dis (because my tears are full of	697	95 POEMS 25	29
to some tricks with my bill as long as	707	95 POEMS 35	9
long as there's ladies my annie is one nor	707	95 POEMS 35	11
that looked up at my willy and you in	707	95 POEMS 35	25
why as thick as my fist stuck in the	709	95 POEMS 37	11
begin to guess (except my life) the true time	717	95 POEMS 45	8
nearerness) everyone certainly would (my most beautiful . . .	717	95 POEMS 45	13
they are our also my darling) but should some	728	95 POEMS 56	8
found forgiveness hard because my (as it happened) self . . .	730	95 POEMS 58	4
and will be and my birthday is / /	734	95 POEMS 62	4
can't u -nderstan- d my o -nl- y me	739	95 POEMS 67	15
most rightful wrong climbing, my love (till mountains speak .	745	95 POEMS 73	2
/ / these from my mother's greatgrandmother's rosebush white	748	95 POEMS 76	1
heaven perhaps comprises poems (my mother's greatgrandmother	748	95 POEMS 76	6
"and who" i asked my love " could begin	748	95 POEMS 76	12
and rain make april my life is the life	749	95 POEMS 77	5
reaper and the sower; my prayers are prayers of	749	95 POEMS 77	6
sadness or joy is my grief or my gladness	749	95 POEMS 77	8
is my grief or my gladness around me surges	749	95 POEMS 77	8
death and resurrection: over my sleeping self float flaming .	749	95 POEMS 77	11
by spring, i lift my diminutive spire to merciful	749	95 POEMS 77	17
and (like any these my) words of words turn	761	95 POEMS 88	13
(i carry it in my heart) i am never	766	95 POEMS 92	2
i go you go, my dear; and whatever is	766	95 POEMS 92	3
me is your doing, my darling) i fear no	766	95 POEMS 92	4
fate (for you are my fate, my sweet) i	766	95 POEMS 92	6
you are my fate, my sweet) i want no	766	95 POEMS 92	6
(for beautiful you are my world, my true) and	766	95 POEMS 92	7
you are my world, my true) and it's you	766	95 POEMS 92	7
(i carry it in my heart) / / /	766	95 POEMS 92	15
me) shy sweet eagerly my most dear (die! live)	767	95 POEMS 93	7
sky are one today) my very so gay young	767	95 POEMS 93	15
i am) to sing, my darling: while old worlds	776	73 POEMS 4	4
it's love by whom (my beautiful friend) the gift	776	73 POEMS 4	18
little and all) whereas (my sweet) our summer in	776	73 POEMS 4	29
the first of all my dreams was of a	777	73 POEMS 5	1
green mysterious land until my second dream begins-- the . .	777	73 POEMS 5	5
but what's wholly marvellous my Darling is that you	782	73 POEMS 10	15
rain) un til against my (where three dreams live)	785	73 POEMS 13	20
it; you 're wrong, my friend. But what does	793	73 POEMS 21	16
(guess) yes you're right: my enemy . Love /	793	73 POEMS 21	25
you, friends and foes my tragic tale concludes herewith: . .	799	73 POEMS 27	40
into sixth avenue) "then" my voice marvels "what happened" .	800	73 POEMS 28	21
played the hostess to my morethanme / / /	807	73 POEMS 35	15
whispers "is very pleasant" my ghost to / /	808	73 POEMS 36	15
is this world) more my life does not leap	810	73 POEMS 38	3
earth swims than each my deeper death becomes your	810	73 POEMS 38	8

MY (CONTINUED)

the light by which my spirit's born: yours is . . . . 810 73 POEMS 38   12
is the darkness of my soul's return --you are . . . . 810 73 POEMS 38   13
soul's return --you are my sun, my moon, and . . . . 810 73 POEMS 38   14
--you are my sun, my moon, and all my . . . . 810 73 POEMS 38   14
my moon, and all my stars / / / . . . . 810 73 POEMS 38   14
through infinite countries be my darling (open the very . . . 811 73 POEMS 39   4
your homecoming will be my homecoming-- my selves go . . . . 812 73 POEMS 40   1
will be my homecoming-- my selves go with you, ... 812 73 POEMS 40   2
takes in his arms my very life who's your . . . . 812 73 POEMS 40   12
whispers. And i and my love are alone / . . . . 813 73 POEMS 41   12
your whole life and my (and infinite our) merely . . . . . . 817 73 POEMS 45   13
never may partly guess--thus, my love, to merely what . . . . 818 73 POEMS 46   13
ways (o very most my shining love) how more . . . . 819 73 POEMS 47   4
of your beauty, then my lost my dazed my . . . . 819 73 POEMS 47   14
beauty, then my lost my dazed my whereful selves . . . . . . 819 73 POEMS 47   14
my lost my dazed my whereful selves they put . . . . 819 73 POEMS 47   15
whisper is subtracted from my hope's own hope, receive . . . 821 73 POEMS 49   10
twi light (whisper) "was my friend" reme mbering "& . . . . . 823 73 POEMS 51   6
the most mysterious (eliena, my dear) is this --how . . . . 825 73 POEMS 53   4
to enemies) therefore lament, my dream and don a . . . . . . 834 73 POEMS 62   5
makes a slave) therefore, my life, lie down and . . . . . . 834 73 POEMS 62   10
cowards all) therefore despair, my heart and die into . . . . 834 73 POEMS 62   23
where everything's nothing --arise, my soul; and sing / . . . 834 73 POEMS 62   30
with a thousand poems my darling but nobody will . . . . . 835 73 POEMS 63   29
for whom i'll keep my tryst until that tide . . . . 843 73 POEMS 71   6

+MY
FOR CONTEXT, SEE . . . . 94 & POST IMPR 6   22
FOR CONTEXT, SEE . . . . 310 VIVA 2   9
FOR CONTEXT, SEE . . . . 398 NO THANKS 15   20

MYEARS
The L's roar tortures-pleasantly myears it is, like the, . . 101 & POST IMPR 11   49

MYHIS
feather is tied under myhis chin.) that climbs and . . . . 69 T&C POST IMPR 6   42

MYRIAD
that bright flame whose myriad tints enrich a visage . . . 254 IS 5 ONE 25   17
gladness--unteaches what despair preaches myriad wonder . . . 764 95 POEMS 90   43

MYRIADS
stands counting the moved myriads wonderfully loved, (hasten, 9 T&C SONGS 1   15

MYRON
the discobolus of one Myron / / / / / . . . . 203 XLI LA GUERRE 1   21

MYSELF
up and thought to myself Death and will You . . . . 58 T&C PORTRAIT 6   14
than darkness (which is myself and Paris and all . . . . . 92 & POST IMPR 4   4
little different, in fact myself Hereupon helpless i utter . 199 XLI PORTRAIT 7   10
5 o'clock i find myself gently decomposing in the . . . . . 201 XLI PORTRAIT 9   1
of one immense tooth myself surveys safely the complete . . . 201 XLI PORTRAIT 9   31
, life. Far below myself the lunging leer of . . . . 202 XLI PORTRAIT 9   35
upon the other hand, myself) but let us next . . . . 245 IS 5 ONE 16   15
breathing beside under around myself) by and by a . . . . . 283 IS 5 THREE 7   17
mortised with a dream myself speaks (whispering, suggesting . 285 IS 5 FOUR 2   2
a less erring end) myself is sculptor of your . . . . 291 IS 5 FOUR 8   6
courage so that against myself the sharp days slobber . . . . 293 IS 5 FOUR 10   20
but the beginning of mySelf / / / / . . . . 294 IS 5 FOUR 11   21
accurately thither and hither myself struts unremembered . . 299 IS 5 FOUR 16   8
fragile imitation of (perhaps) myself carefully wanders . . . 300 IS 5 FOUR 17   13
making me feel how myself has been coarse and . . . . 301 IS 5 FOUR 18   8
/ / / / myself, walking in Dragon st . . . . 313 VIVA 5   1
and expressing "as for myself, because i am slender . . . . . 328 VIVA 19   15
though i have closed myself as fingers, you open . . . . . 366 VIVA 57   6
always petal by petal myself as Spring opens (touching . . 366 VIVA 57   7
not young and may myself do nothing usefully and . . . . 481 NEW POEMS 19   9
say, observed him but myself; and why? because without . . . 802 73 POEMS 30   9
through you what seemed myself, i find selves unimaginably . 810 73 POEMS 38   9
me some (by name myself) one long ago who . . . . 828 73 POEMS 56   6

+MYSELF
FOR CONTEXT, SEE . . . . 666 {CHAIRE} 68   12
FOR CONTEXT, SEE . . . . 730 95 POEMS 58   7

	PAGE	TITLE	LINE

MYSELF'S
spikes of madness (at Myself's height these various innocent 202 XLI PORTRAIT 9 40
fisherMen swim and who's myself's Antimere Should words carry 395 NO THANKS 12 9
to dare, how the (myself's own self who's) child . . . . . . 843 73 POEMS 71 12

MYSELVES
if you disappear solemnly myselves ask "life, the question . 295 IS 5 FOUR 12 13

MYSTERIES
that such and such mysteries very simply touch me, ... 12 T&C SONGS 2 37
inconsequential gastronomic mystery of mysteries , life. Far 201 XLI PORTRAIT 9 33
since he's young with mysteries (each truly his more . . . . 617 (CHAIRE) 19 10
death and life) imaginable mysteries / / / . . . . 674 95 POEMS 2 13
unimmortal mind, these immeasurable mysteries (human one; and 721 95 POEMS 49 7
to frolic in such mysteries as birth and death . . . . . . 743 95 POEMS 71 13
can's every can't) immensest mysteries contradict a deathful 763 95 POEMS 90 27
alive --while and all mysteries which i or you . . . . 809 73 POEMS 37 5
when he's plucked such mysteries as men do not . . . . . . 843 73 POEMS 71 13

MYSTERIEUSE
dis-donc, Paris ta gorge mysterieuse pourquoi se . . . . . . 121 & PORTRAIT 12 53

MYSTERIOUS
the syllables of that mysterious prayer, and as an . . . . . 8 T&C OF NICOL 11
pastures pale, whose tall mysterious shepherd lifts a cheek . 9 T&C SONGS 1 10
entertain the adroit blood's mysterious skein (but like some 21 T&C PUELLA MEA 186
battered box fattish and mysterious the flowerstricken sun- . 69 T&C POST IMPR 6 23
irrevocable play-- through the mysterious high futile day an 215 XLI SONNETS 11 14
this always talking individual, mysterious witty hatless. . . 279 IS 5 THREE 3 12
b ecome s whi (mysterious ly) te one t . . . . 581 1 X 1 41 11
here a livingly free mysterious dreamsoul floatstands oak by 658 (CHAIRE) 60 16
mind) through some green mysterious land until my second . . 777 73 POEMS 5 4
blondest star the most mysterious (eliena, my dear) is . . . 825 73 POEMS 53 3

+MYSTERIOUS
FOR CONTEXT, SEE . . . . 632 (CHAIRE) 34 6

MYSTERIOUSLY
murder the petals hush mysteriously invisible mourners move . 59 T&C PORTRAIT 7 6
to fling Implacable death's mysteriously sable robe from her 206 XLI SONNETS 2 4
Spring opens (touching skilfully, mysteriously) her first . . 366 VIVA 57 8

+MYSTERIOUSLY
FOR CONTEXT, SEE . . . . 423 NO THANKS 40 2
FOR CONTEXT, SEE . . . . 581 1 X 1 41 11

MYSTERY
arms impaled upon delicious mystery, with gaunt limbs reeking 7 T&C EPITHALAM 157
perishable poise is the mystery of Spring (with her . . . . . 17 T&C PUELLA MEA 15
always squirms the skilful mystery of Hell) me suddenly . . . 130 & SON REAL 1 7
Will i complete the mystery of my flesh I . . . . 189 XLI SONGS 11 11
profane frantic inconsequential gastronomic mystery of . . . 201 XLI PORTRAIT 9 32
assume silence beyond the mystery of rhyme / / . . . . . . 210 XLI SONNETS 6 15
unto you by a mystery? ...the cathedral recedes into . . . . 279 IS 5 THREE 3 23
sing against the awful mystery of light / / . . . . 454 NO THANKS 69 14
only love whose any mystery makes every man's flesh . . . . 484 NEW POEMS 22 7
to through the only mystery of love become while . . . . . . 510 50 POEMS 24 13
to disappear causing through mystery miracle peace: or (if . 559 1 X 1 19 4
of fact envision the mystery of freedom? yet, among . . . . . 659 (CHAIRE) 61 10
now and we're a mystery which will never happen . . . . . . 667 (CHAIRE) 69 6
ethereal silence through twilight's mystery made flesh-- . . 669 (CHAIRE) 71 8
find) and in a mystery to be (when time . . . . 688 95 POEMS 16 13
floats the whole perhapsless mystery of paradise) mind . . . 714 95 POEMS 42 8
ceasing to begin the mystery of day for someone's . . . . . 756 95 POEMS 84 4
mostpeople fear most: a mystery for which i've no . . . . . 802 73 POEMS 30 13
leap than with the mystery your smile sings or . . . . 810 73 POEMS 38 4
lovers tell- measure imagine, mystery, a kiss --not though . 817 73 POEMS 45 10
we call rose a) mystery "but it must be . . . . 837 73 POEMS 65 17
absolute peace, never imaginable mystery) descend / / / . . . 839 73 POEMS 67 15

+MYSTERY
FOR CONTEXT, SEE . . . . 627 (CHAIRE) 29 13
FOR CONTEXT, SEE . . . . 814 73 POEMS 42 8

MYSTIC
paled and curled with mystic lips take twilight where . . . . 71 T&C SON REAL 2 13
deep purring biceps, the mystic screech of Broadway, the . . 220 XLI SONNETS 16 2

MYSTICAL
    numbing forests frolicsome, fleetly mystical, aroam with keen   19 T&C PUELLA MEA   92
    and reused to the mystical moment of dullness emphatically   . 230 IS 5 ONE 2   22
MYSTICISM
    conjugated by the sensual mysticism of entire vertical being, 201 XLI PORTRAIT 9   23
MYTH
    distinctly, moving like a myth in the uncertain morning,   . . 17 T&C PUELLA MEA   19
    stuffs the alert willing myth of body, which will . . . . . . 155 & SON ACTU 4   9
    to lose) and a myth is as good as . . . . 410 NO THANKS 27   9
    small. Swoop (shrill collective myth) into thy grave merely . 579 1 X 1 39   9
MYTHICAL
    perfectly) nowhere vivid anonymous mythical guests of Is   . . 557 1 X 1 17   6
MYTHS
    whelps whom soothe psychotic myths like Jonah And The . . . . 398 NO THANKS 15   19
MYVERYLITTLE
    BlacK wh-eel-ing oh ver mYveRylitTle street where you will   . 122 & SEVEN POEMS 1   21
N
    bandy scandal of Mrs. N and Professor D ....the . . . .   70 T&C SON REAL 1   10
    / / --G O N splashes-sink which is west . . . . 169 & SON ACTU 18   1
    feeble stem is believing science=(2b)-n herr professor m / . 329 VIVA 20   4
    / / hanged if n y in a real . . . .   476 NEW POEMS 14   2
+N.B.
    FOR CONTEXT, SEE . . . .   410 NO THANKS 27   7
N-SAINT
    ddaanncciinn (GlY) a nda n-saint dance! Dan Sai ntd . . . . . 431 NO THANKS 48   19
N'EST
    throat Marie Louise Lallemand n'est-ce pas que je suis   . . . 120 & PORTRAIT 12   11
    the playthings for dust n'est-ce pas effendi drifts between . 198 XLI PORTRAIT 6   14
    millionaires a cute idea n'est-ce pas? (whereas, upon che . . 245 IS 5 ONE 16   14
N'EST-CE
    throat Marie Louise Lallemand n'est-ce pas que je suis   . . . 120 & PORTRAIT 12   11
    the playthings for dust n'est-ce pas effendi drifts between . 198 XLI PORTRAIT 6   14
    millionaires a cute idea n'est-ce pas? (whereas, upon the . . 245 IS 5 ONE 16   14
NABBED
    circumstance whom the bulls nabbed at 33rd) pulled six   . . . 266 IS 5 TWO 1   39
NAGGING
    i will sew a nagging button of candlelight (halfstooping   . . 164 & SON ACTU 13   3
NAILS
    bingbongwhom chewchoo laugh dingle nails personally bung   . . 333 VIVA 24   3
NAILYUH
    i refers ter Satter Nailyuh (comes but once er   . . . . . . 237 IS 5 ONE 8   15
NAKED
    a flower, my lady naked in her hair-- i . . . .   21 T&C PUELLA MEA   178
    and of ivory if naked she appear to me   . . . .   22 T&C PUELLA MEA   231
    before every door a naked eunuch watches on their   . . . .   33 T&C ORIENTALE 6   35
    a singular block her, rain-warm-naked exquisitely hashed   . . 133 & SON REAL 4   2
    / / / my naked lady framed in twilight   . . . . 162 & SON ACTU 11   1
    he saw was you naked amid unnaked things, your   . . . . . . 170 & SON ACTU 19   6
    a pretty girl who naked is is worth a . . . .   247 IS 5 ONE 18   7
    me are like bridegrooms Naked and luminous (here the   . . . 281 IS 5 THREE 5   17
    which lurk between your naked shoulderblades. --Here comes a 282 IS 5 THREE 6   23
    is this (shivering pale naked very poor) creature of   . . . 374 VIVA 65   13
    will downward climb, so naked for immortal work his . . . . 521 50 POEMS 34   43
    the god's truth stands art-naked: you and the fact   . . . . 605 (CHAIRE) 7   3
+NAKED
    FOR CONTEXT, SEE   . . . . 104 & POST IMPR 14   11
NAKEDEST
    antics of ridiculous molecules) nakedest (aiming for hugely . 373 VIVA 64   6
NAKEDLY
    live loop croon mime nakedly hurl asquirm the dip . . . . . . 445 NO THANKS 60   25
NAKEDNESS
    foam sprung with irrevocable nakedness to strike the young .   7 T&C EPITHALAM   162
    white money upon her nakedness he nods and all   . . . . . .   34 T&C ORIENTALE 6 102
    street of time her nakedness with its blue hair . . . . 112 & PORTRAIT 6   76
    lips On whose deep nakedness death most believes, perpetual . 138 & SON REAL 9   10
    trite worm of her nakedness until it go rapidly . . . . 164 & SON ACTU 13   5
    silver fish of her nakedness with fins sharply pleasant,   . . 216 XLI SONNETS 12   2
    sub (at the next) nakedness (table but three) hero's   . . . 546 1 X 1 6   7

NALOVEME
    most (windows where blaze naLOVEme crazily ships bulge hearts 436 NO THANKS 52   4
NAME
    is a lady, whose name is Afterwards she is . . . . 102 & POST IMPR 12   24
    whispered unto God, my name is must and with . . . . 117 & PORTRAIT 10   22
    sturdily seated--Colonel Needless To Name and General You . . 266 IS 5 TWO 1   23
    sons acclaim your glorious name by gorry by jingo . . . . . 268 IS 5 TWO 3   7
    shall receive the philophilic name S.S. VAN MERDE) having . . 334 VIVA 25   4
    stones speak or one name control more incredible splendor . . 377 VIVA 68   5
    of snow things without name beyond because things over . . . 441 NO THANKS 56   57
    from there to where --name unless i'm mistaken chauvesouris-- 504 50 POEMS 18   9
    yours ask me the name of the moon in . . . . 513 50 POEMS 27   19
    say or a jennelman name misder finger isn't important . . . . 549 1 X 1 9   3
    gaiety makes your beautiful name-- i feel that (false . . . . 631 (CHAIRE) 33   12
    (no- one asks his name) a mender of things . . . . 660 (CHAIRE) 62   4
    reasons threats and smiles name it cruel fair or . . . . . 804 73 POEMS 32   7
    how merciful love's own name, linger no more than . . . . . 812 73 POEMS 40   9
    told; it has no name-- but should this namelessness . . . . 819 73 POEMS 47   8
    to me some (by name myself) one long ago . . . . 828 73 POEMS 56   5
    not any tongue may name, three i'll give you . . . . 837 73 POEMS 65   2
+NAME
    FOR CONTEXT, SEE . . . . 267 IS 5 TWO 2   14
    FOR CONTEXT, SEE . . . . 267 IS 5 TWO 2   14
    FOR CONTEXT, SEE . . . . 330 VIVA 21   10
    FOR CONTEXT, SEE . . . . 436 NO THANKS 52   4
NAMED
    i had an uncle named Sol who was a . . . . 239 IS 5 ONE 10   2
    / / (as that named Fred -someBody: hippopotamus, scratch- . . 252 IS 5 ONE 23   1
    Thumbprints of an angel named Frederick found on a . . . . 262 IS 5 ONE 32   30
    murdered by a man named Smith and we sailed . . . . 313 VIVA 5   10
    imagine) whispering of a named Krassin / / / . . . . 324 VIVA 16   15
    marvel than this death named Smith less strange? Married . . 406 NO THANKS 23   13
    fears only not ever named mountains more if than . . . . . 563 1 X 1 23   4
    skin of an angel named imagination / / / . . . . 639 (CHAIRE) 41   14
    head is stumbling someone (named Morning) / / / . . . . . . 785 73 POEMS 13   23
NAMELESS
    flaming billion kinds of nameless silence) sky; / / . . . . 786 73 POEMS 14   16
NAMELESSNESS
    name-- but should this namelessness (completely fleetly) . . 819 73 POEMS 47   9
NAMELY
    and of sunful sin namely (ford madox ford) and . . . . . . 607 (CHAIRE) 9   14
    upon a dismal misconception; namely that some neither ape . . 807 73 POEMS 35   6
NAMES
    folds) cold stones (o-1-d) names aren'ts) L iv . . . . . . 417 NO THANKS 34   8
    share) such make their names (this poet made war . . . . . 440 NO THANKS 56   23
    (and we speak our names / / / / . . . . 502 50 POEMS 16   14
NAMING
    cease or time; a naming stealth of ecstasy means, ... 168 & SON ACTU 17   9
NAN
    harry (and sally and nan they tremble and cower . . . . . . 509 50 POEMS 23   16
+NAPKIN
    FOR CONTEXT, SEE . . . . 410 NO THANKS 27   5
NAPKINS
    affectionate leer interminable pyramidal, napkins (this man . 243 IS 5 ONE 14   6
NAPOLEON
    of twilight and somebody Napoleon / / / / . . . . 63 T&C PORTRAIT 10 39
NAPPED
    Awake, chaos: we have napped. / / / / . . . . 337 VIVA 28   15
NARROW
    Xerxes this man: a narrow thudding timeshaped face plus . . . 62 T&C PORTRAIT 10 2
    the evening in bruised narrow questioning faces) / / . . . . 275 IS 5 TWO 9   50
    towers; captured: in the narrow light of inverno) this . . . 345 VIVA 36   9
NARROWING
    things dead athwart the narrowing hours and hope (by . . . . 207 XLI SONNETS 3   6
NASCITUR
    erroneous impression that he nascitur / / / / . . . . 234 IS 5 ONE 5   6
    Spring with? each dream nascitur, is not made...) why . . . . 264 IS 5 ONE 33   29

	PAGE	TITLE	LINE

NATION'S
of officers (a yearning nation's blueeyed pride) their . . . 339 VIVA 30 23

NATIONS
the paper destinies of nations sic item a bounceless . . . . 499 50 POEMS 13 6

NATIVE
minister of Siam in native costume, who emerging from . . . . 245 IS 5 ONE 16 20
A crocodile eats a native, who in revenge beats . . . . 262 IS 5 ONE 32 23

NATURAL
sincere large distinct and natural he comes to his . . . . . 418 NO THANKS 35 5
cause dying is perfectly natural; perfectly putting it mildly 604 {CHAIRE} 6 14
for everything which is natural which is infinite which . . . 663 {CHAIRE} 65 4

NATURALLY
soul i coughed , naturally / / / / . . . . 197 XLI PORTRAIT 5 25
yuh course yeh well naturally i und certain i . . . . 400 NO THANKS 17 10

NATURE
anguish) at peace with nature --i do not worry . . . . . . 749 95 POEMS 77 14

NAUGHT
is always worse than naught, feels the tremendous yonder . . 81 T&C SON UNRE 6 11
poet made war whose naught and all sun are . . . . 440 NO THANKS 56 25

NAUGHTY
poked thee ,has the naughty thumb of science prodded . . . . 46 T&C LA GUERRE 2 10

NAUSEA
this instant of semiluminous nausea A vast wordless . . . . . 96 & POST IMPR 8 32

NAUSEOUS
in unripe green with nauseous spiderlegs and excremental hair 55 T&C PORTRAIT 3 10

NAVY
the saviour of the Navy of the Moon he's . . . . 642 {CHAIRE} 44 13

NAY
born to never say nay but lucy could learn . . . . 509 50 POEMS 23 20
future than mrs somethingwitz nay somethingelsestein. Death . 790 73 POEMS 18 6
foe a friend --cry nay: cry yea-- november would . . . . . 798 73 POEMS 26 20

NB
preferring Negroes Indians Youse n.b. ye twang of little . . 410 NO THANKS 27 7

NE
ear: en amerique on ne boit que de Jingyale. . . . . 233 IS 5 ONE 4 6
on consubstantial intangibility. Personne ne m'aime et j'ai . 262 IS 5 ONE 32 26
twilight squirts a two ne like nothing verdi slightly . . . . 602 {CHAIRE} 4 3
te r? n oo ne) / / / / . . . . 653 {CHAIRE} 55 15
and wh (g o ne) o w (A) a . . . . 740 95 POEMS 68 9
as hows of whi ne climbscr e AM e . . . . 795 73 POEMS 23 20
eup ona tim e ne wsp aper / / . . . . 796 73 POEMS 24 11
evil-- it is you (ne i) nobody else drive . . . . 804 73 POEMS 32 8

NEAR
Darkness it was so near to me, i ask . . . . 97 & POST IMPR 8 40
and poetry cannot go near because perfectly fearful. . . . . 162 & SON ACTU 11 7
truly i would be near when his scythe takes . . . . 215 XLI SONNETS 11 6
world wanders with a near and careful smile in . . . . 293 IS 5 FOUR 10 25
like a rose) standing near my swaying over her . . . . 352 VIVA 43 7
because they are too near your slightest look easily . . . . 366 VIVA 57 4
yonder collidingly absorbs eternal near) day being come, . . 376 VIVA 67 13
s??? big (soft) soft near calm (Bright) calm st?? . . . . . . 455 NO THANKS 70 4
(soft briGht deep) yeS near sta? calm star big . . . . 455 NO THANKS 70 8
yEs alone (wHo Yes near deep whO big alone . . . . 455 NO THANKS 70 12
whO big alone soft near deep calm deep ????Ht . . . . 455 NO THANKS 70 12
the sky is so near the earth does not . . . . 505 50 POEMS 19 11
are twilight they beyond near) girlest she slender is . . . . 518 50 POEMS 32 5
clearing) gone are enormous near far silent truths of . . . . 755 95 POEMS 83 6
/ / now (more near ourselves than we) is . . . . 760 95 POEMS 87 1
climbing fall into far near blue if beggars are . . . . 769 95 POEMS 95 21
/ a round face near the top of the . . . . 813 73 POEMS 41 1
so magically, farthest becomes near (one silent pasture, all 818 73 POEMS 46 7

NEARAWAY
through the far-spaced possible nearaway from huge trees . . 10 T&C SONGS 1 44

NEARBY
pursuit pleasantly elephantine while nearby the father a . . 56 T&C PORTRAIT 4 9
rod smiles the liontamer nearby hieroglyphs soar dip dip . . 384 NO THANKS 2 24

NEARER
of dead it means nearer because deeper firmer since . . . . . 126 & SEVEN POEMS 5 1

	PAGE	TITLE	LINE
NEARER (CONTINUED)			
/ / / / nearer: breath of my breath:	139	& SON REAL 10	1
flames --its farthest silence nearer than each our	741	95 POEMS 69	4
+NEARERANDNEARERANDNEARER			
hear the rrmp and then nearerandnearerandNEARER and before .	269	IS 5 TWO 4	6
NEARERNESS			
heart at your each nearerness) everyone certainly would (my .	717	95 POEMS 45	13
NEAREST			
and dove for the nearest 1; surreptitiously cogitating the .	327	VIVA 18	38
one complete miracle of nearest far "i cordially invite . . .	504	50 POEMS 18	3
/ now that, more nearest even than your fate	809	73 POEMS 37	1
NEARING			
my mind, to hear nearing our hearts' irrevocable play-- . . .	215	XLI SONNETS 11	13
NEARISHNESS			
do? a notalive undead too-nearishness and shall we cry . . .	528	50 POEMS 40	5
NEARLY			
her and ourselves a nearly-opaque perfume disinterestedly . .	146	& SON REAL 17	13
a born failure and nearly everybody said he should	239	IS 5 ONE 10	4
repeat himself: these, or nearly these, were the not	263	IS 5 ONE 32	60
next (our great problem nearly solved we dare adorn	650	(CHAIRE) 52	13
cents please' --why guesswho nearly leaped out of	800	73 POEMS 28	7
+NEARLY			
FOR CONTEXT, SEE	739	95 POEMS 67	3
NEARLY-OPAQUE			
her and ourselves a nearly-opaque perfume disinterestedly . .	146	& SON REAL 17	13
NEARNESS			
, kissed with is nearness. (peers: body of aching	159	& SON ACTU 8	11
jam or my invincible Nearness rapes laughter from your . . .	166	& SON ACTU 15	15
the wine which their nearness evaporates to think is	193	XLI PORTRAIT 1	13
shore so far your nearness reaches a lucky fifth	537	50 POEMS 49	5
opening leaf (beyond whose nearness there is no beyond) . . .	592	1 X 1 52	8
/ / / all nearness pauses, while a star	750	95 POEMS 78	1
of all silence strolls) nearness awakened, any bird should .	756	95 POEMS 84	11
NEAT			
the groaning flame of neat huge trudging kiss moistly	67	T&C POST IMPR 4	24
spilling rancid elves upon neat sunlight into the flower- . .	69	T&C POST IMPR 6	4
angels suddenly should stretch neat necks just to see	130	& SON REAL 1	5
slightly. or until with neat obscure obvious hands Time . . .	165	& SON ACTU 14	11
there 's no sharpest neat word for the thing.	227	IS 5 ONE GERT	10
NEATENING			
(with white longest hands neatening each crease) will smooth	288	IS 5 FOUR 5	4
NEATEST			
roar looped straightens, into neatest distance.... A new . .	219	XLI SONNETS 15	6
NEATLY			
the leaneyed Caesars borne neatly through enormous twilight .	111	& PORTRAIT 6	37
of my fear: more neatly ream this pith of	139	& SON REAL 10	7
does who eye sO neatly big / / /	159	& SON ACTU 8	17
NECESSARY			
weather, (breathless with sharp necessary lips) kid female .	140	& SON REAL 11	9
elephantine face (It is necessary to find Hassan's Place . .	143	& SON REAL 14	3
and buy things so necessary as is death and	238	IS 5 ONE 9	8
NECESSITY			
argument of mil itary necessity" (generalissimo e) and echo .	636	(CHAIRE) 38	11
NECK			
it is a throbbing neck whereby to grasp the	21	T&C PUELLA MEA	196
of desire the taut neck of the citharede wags	34	T&C ORIENTALE 6	96
suddenly upon the huge neck around whose unwashed sonorous .	96	& POST IMPR 8	30
the like, a) slEEping neck a breathing a , ...	104	& POST IMPR 14	7
back it makes your neck feel pleasant and stoopid	126	& SEVEN POEMS 5	19
why on the alert neck of this brittle whore	229	IS 5 ONE FRAN	2
that's dead from the neck up is lead all	253	IS 5 ONE 24	13
which move smoothly from neck to neck of bottles, ...	279	IS 5 THREE 3	13
smoothly from neck to neck of bottles, cats smoothly	279	IS 5 THREE 3	13
one bugger thy nabor (neck and senecktie are gentlemen . . .	492	50 POEMS 6	13
+NECK			
FOR CONTEXT, SEE	234	IS 5 ONE 5	1
+NECKED			
FOR CONTEXT, SEE	225	IS 5 ONE LIZ	1

	PAGE	TITLE	LINE

NECKLESS
    weary twig of a neckless nudity (very occasionally budding . 134 & SON REAL 5   6
NECKS
    suddenly should stretch neat necks just to see how . . . . . 130 & SON REAL 1   5
    ears their very tidiyum necks begin) let us add . . . . 274 IS 5 TWO 9   15
NECKTIE
    some- thing ah (my necktie / / / / . . . . 232 IS 5 ONE 3   19
    (slipping) felt of my necktie wandered against my shirt . . . 284 IS 5 FOUR 1   5
+NECKTIE
    FOR CONTEXT, SEE . . . . 492 50 POEMS 6   13
NECKTIES
    death and unlike shirts neckties trousers we cannot wear . . 238 IS 5 ONE 9   10
NED
    few mildly curious rai -ned on people (both male . . . . . 267 IS 5 TWO 2   18
NEDDY
    dumb. Skip fred (jump! neddy) but under the wonder . . . . . 513 50 POEMS 27   32
NEE
    belowtry eye nowbrow sangsung nee whitermuch grab sicksilk . 333 VIVA 24   10
NEED
    unique and nervously obscene need; it's funny. They will . . 153 & SON ACTU 2   4
    the drum there is need of just twenty five . . . . 196 XLI PORTRAIT 4   11
    nothing more than boygirls need: i can entirely her . . . . 484 NEW POEMS 22   5
    , more than raindrops need sunbeams or snowflakes make . . . 577 1 X 1 37   3
+NEEDING
    FOR CONTEXT, SEE . . . . 231 IS 5 ONE 3   47
NEEDLE
    live straighter than a needle) ask her ask when . . . . 498 50 POEMS 12   3
NEEDLES
    i look where stealing needles of foam in the . . . . 64 T&C POST IMPR 1   2
NEEDLESS
    fearless derriere sturdily seated--Colonel Needless To Name . 266 IS 5 TWO 1   22
NEEDLESSLY
    farming and be it needlessly added my Uncle Sol's . . . . . 239 IS 5 ONE 10   12
NEEDN'T
    / / mr youse needn't be so spry concernin . . . . 247 IS 5 ONE 18   1
NEEDS
    it Bishop Taylor who needs hanging that marriage is . . . . . 167 & SON ACTU 16   4
NEGANT
    States Of America unde negant redire quemquam supp sedly . . 392 NO THANKS 9   19
NEGATION'S
    grave called progress, and negation's dead undoom. I'd rather 484 NEW POEMS 22   12
NEGATIVE
    glory inflicted to the negative silence that primeval . . . . 197 XLI PORTRAIT 5   16
NEGLECTED
    hidden obscenities nudging into neglected sentiments brings . 203 XLI LA GUERRE 1 7
NEGRE
    est trop fort le negre esn7othingish8s c'est fini pRaW, . . . 430 NO THANKS 47   20
NEGRES
    suddenly j'm'en fous des negres (in the twilight of . . . . . 121 & PORTRAIT 12   43
NEGRESS
    over patriotic swill. The, negress, in the, rocker by . . . . 166 & SON ACTU 15   3
NEGRO
    Cullen Longfel- low's small negro son, Henry Wadsworth . . . 263 IS 5 ONE 32   53
    we couldn't free the negro because he ant but . . . . 321 VIVA 13   11
NEGROES
    bills likes People preferring Negroes Indians Youse n.b. ye . 410 NO THANKS 27   6
NEIGES
    ourselves ou sont les neiges.... some guys talks big . . . . 237 IS 5 ONE 8   3
+NEIGHBOR
    FOR CONTEXT, SEE . . . . 492 50 POEMS 6   12
NEIGHBOURS
    credo fais do do neighbours re babies while; / . . . . 309 VIVA 1   35
NEIGHING
    with standards and the neighing of great steeds moving . . . 209 XLI SONNETS 5   4
NEITHER
    (oweld song by ; neither you nor i and . . . . 335 VIVA 26   19
    thoroughly haunted by what neither is any echo of . . . . . . 368 VIVA 59   4
    and who may envy neither; nor bewail (would rather . . . . . 394 NO THANKS 11   10

NEITHER (CONTINUED)

	PAGE	TITLE	LINE
partialness beats one entirety neither may shadow down flesh	425	NO THANKS 42	12
may shadow down flesh neither may vibration create voice . .	425	NO THANKS 42	12
either was deafer than neither was dumb. Skip fred	513	50 POEMS 27	28
Expecting more would be neither fantastic nor pathological .	514	50 POEMS 28	4
only and true value neither is love makes the	531	50 POEMS 43	7
/ / / / neither could say (it comes	542	1 X 1 2	1
rich (only aware) kind neither nor cruel (only complete) . .	564	1 X 1 24	6
blue heaven green earth neither sea here's more than	588	1 X 1 48	3
i never knew and neither did you and everybody	591	1 X 1 51	14
being are growing stones (neither awake are goddesses nor . .	617	{CHAIRE} 19	8
to sky are flowers neither why nor how when	630	{CHAIRE} 32	10
/ / / / neither awake (there's your general	640	{CHAIRE} 42	1
animal (five foot five) neither dead nor alive (in	640	{CHAIRE} 42	14
deceiving) whose ways are neither reasoned nor unreasoned, .	683	95 POEMS 11	5
lovers cling & kiss neither beholding a nor seen	698	95 POEMS 26	7
born, a (who is neither each both and) Self	721	95 POEMS 49	13
imagine ourselves like living neither nor dead these (or . .	743	95 POEMS 71	5
misconception; namely that some neither ape nor angel called	807	73 POEMS 35	7

NEITHER'S

where not here but neither's blue most both) and	750	95 POEMS 78	5

NEITHERS

and the boths and neithers--you must let them go	569	1 X 1 29	12

NEL

of Murano; pause elevator nel mezzo del cammin' that	256	IS 5 ONE 27	6

NELLIE

best april the twenty nellie anyway and it's flutters	251	IS 5 ONE 22	2
jerry so very (and nellie and fan) some handsomest	509	50 POEMS 23	14

NERAL

blue true two man neral rise eyes "this world's	567	1 X 1 27	6

+NERVE

FOR CONTEXT, SEE	226	IS 5 ONE MAME	10

NERVES

the supercilious chimneys, my nerves sumptuously wink . . . .and	169	& SON ACTU 18	8
thing. Muscles better and nerves more. i like your	175	& SON ACTU 24	3

NERVOUS

angrily, their roofs are nervous with the soft furious . . .	62	T&C PORTRAIT 10	14
tall careful muscles into nervous and accurate silence.	67	T&C POST IMPR 4	16
which tread the serene nervous light of paradise-- by	85	T&C SON ACTU 4	2

NERVOUSLY

I know the way-- (nervously Whose eyes approve the	117	& PORTRAIT 10	35
mean the unique and nervously obscene need; it's funny. . . .	153	& SON ACTU 2	3

NESTING

(one diamond timid with nesting incense) fifty marble pillars	32	T&C ORIENTALE 6	26

NETS

dusk be drawn surpassing nets are sedulously spun to	5	T&C EPITHALAM	86

NETSAM

are gentlemen poeds urseappeal netsam our spinsters and . . .	492	50 POEMS 6	3

NETSITS

me whilepin Kishcam elscasta? netsits Elf allaBout. (chic) .	318	VIVA 10	21

NEUTRAL

i was back in neutral tried and again slo-wly;	248	IS 5 ONE 19	14

NEVER

Troys of Helen's beauty: never did Lord Jason (in	18	T&C PUELLA MEA	68
all living intense things. Never my soul so fortunate	19	T&C PUELLA MEA	102
i have made. And never boast your dead beauties, ...	22	T&C PUELLA MEA	243
mouth to wholly kiss-- never boast your dead beauties, . . .	22	T&C PUELLA MEA	249
delicious glance things which never more shall be, perfect .	22	T&C PUELLA MEA	252
of the handsome moon never spoke ill of the	43	T&C AMORES 7	14
drinking the ale, which never lets you grow old	96	& POST IMPR 8	24
ing-put-too-long in windows and never sold and <> because . .	101	& POST IMPR 11	66
safe for democracy it never fails and that's a	125	& SEVEN POEMS 4	12
paler-paler face and said never mind, you'll find But	125	& SEVEN POEMS 4	19
fastest time because they've never met before dead's more . .	126	& SEVEN POEMS 5	7
the nicest man you've never met who maybe winks	126	& SEVEN POEMS 5	14
this one and was never intro- duced you say	126	& SEVEN POEMS 5	20
on one string dead never says my dear, Time	126	& SEVEN POEMS 5	29
but you know you never can and why have	126	& SEVEN POEMS 5	31

NEVER (CONTINUED)
    the autumn she will never guess. but i know . . . . 183 XLI SONGS 5   15
    suddenly ap- proached may never quite taste the wine   . . . . 193 XLI PORTRAIT 1   12
    some guys claims der never was nutn like Nooer . . . . 237 IS 5 ONE 8   6
    / (and i imagine never mind Joe agreeably cheerfully . . . . 241 IS 5 ONE 12   2
    really must be Nice, never to have no imagination) . . . . . 242 IS 5 ONE 13   2
    have no imagination) or never never to wonder about . . . . . 242 IS 5 ONE 13   3
    no imagination) or never never to wonder about guys . . . . . 242 IS 5 ONE 13   4
    it Must be nice never to have no doubts . . . . 242 IS 5 ONE 13   11
    and dishes) and to never, never really wonder i . . . . . . 242 IS 5 ONE 13   16
    dishes) and to never, never really wonder i mean   . . . . . . 242 IS 5 ONE 13   16
    to and everything and never, never Never to stand . . . . . 242 IS 5 ONE 13   19
    and everything and never, never Never to stand at . . . . . 242 IS 5 ONE 13   19
    everything and never, never Never to stand at no . . . . . 242 IS 5 ONE 13   20
    most intimate friends would never have gathered. A   . . . . . 262 IS 5 ONE 32   14
    of people don't and never never will know, they . . . . . . 272 IS 5 TWO 7   14
    people don't and never never will know, they don't . . . . 272 IS 5 TWO 7   15
    observe; although once is never the beginning of enough, . . 282 IS 5 THREE 6   2
    syntax of things will never wholly kiss you; wholly . . . . . 290 IS 5 FOUR 7   4
    of your heart will never guess how much my . . . . 292 IS 5 FOUR 9   15
    whom somehow you are never wholly rid (and who . . . . . . 298 IS 5 FOUR 15   8
    (carefully turning a corner) never bother you any more. . . . 298 IS 5 FOUR 15   28
    is it i wonder never mind consider rather heavenly . . . . . 322 VIVA 14   1
    loneliness, these unique dreams never shall soil their   . . . 328 VIVA 19   4
    Craps somebody might hardly never not have been unsorry, . . 336 VIVA 27   11
    for lease. I have never loved you dear as . . . . 360 VIVA 51   10
    (whose aim had erred never) and by that little . . . . . . 360 VIVA 51   16
    a piece. I have never loved you dear as . . . . 360 VIVA 51   20
    noone is. I have never loved you dear as . . . . 360 VIVA 51   30
    her face, i have never loved you dear as . . . . 360 VIVA 51   35
    / somewhere i have never travelled, gladly beyond any . . . . 366 VIVA 57   1
    most precise essential flame never which waked) & . . . . . . 373 VIVA 64   8
    die for lives (may never cease views with smooth   . . . . . . 386 NO THANKS 3   9
    fear of all hearts never which have (Per haps) . . . . 397 NO THANKS 14   7
    the childfully diminishing earth --never whose proudly life . 402 NO THANKS 19   5
    find their minds (but never had any to lose) . . . . 410 NO THANKS 27   8
    to purely grow but, never doubt my weakness makes . . . . . 433 NO THANKS 50   5
    always shall be may never have) do i salute . . . . 441 NO THANKS 56   64
    sidewalk out of (blown never quite to -gether by   . . . . . 442 NO THANKS 57   3
    anguish (imagine Her least never with most memory) give . . . 453 NO THANKS 68   10
    The Mind's (i never you never he she . . . . 474 NEW POEMS 12   2
    (i never you never he she or it . . . . 474 NEW POEMS 12   2
    he she or it never we you and they . . . . 474 NEW POEMS 12   4
    we you and they never saw so much heard . . . . 474 NEW POEMS 12   4
    more than truly there's never been quite such a . . . . . 481 NEW POEMS 19   11
    shoulders queerly twilight : never, no (body. Nothing / . . . 490 50 POEMS 4   20
    magical maybes of certainly never the iswas . . . . 495 50 POEMS 9   15
    queer colon hobby photography never has plumbed the heights . 499 50 POEMS 13   10
    who are filled with never are more than more . . . . 505 50 POEMS 19   20
    betty was born to never say nay but lucy . . . . 509 50 POEMS 23   20
    by twice infinity could never equal one) which may . . . . . 510 50 POEMS 24   11
    the blind and robins never welcome spring nor flatfolk . . . 511 50 POEMS 25   16
    and children of almost) never shall guess the dimension . . . 512 50 POEMS 26   4
    --endlings of isn't shall never begin to begin to . . . . . 512 50 POEMS 26   14
    in the ocean will never be missed (it's in, ... 513 50 POEMS 27   24
    i have not any never no vacation here is . . . . 523 50 POEMS 36   18
    day predicted end who never began of god and . . . . 527 50 POEMS 39   6
    than to win less never than alive less bigger . . . . . . 530 50 POEMS 42   10
    yes which fear will never no? measureless our pure   . . . . . 538 50 POEMS 50   2
    --which something as you'll never guess in fifty thousand . . 544 1 X 1 4   13
    stars and stones, but never this fine specimen of . . . . . 554 1 X 1 14   11
    you? Blow soon to never and never to twice . . . . 560 1 X 1 20   21
    soon to never and never to twice (blow life . . . . 560 1 X 1 20   21
    so&so true wars are never won / / / . . . . 570 1 X 1 30   10
    shall, their eyes would never miss a yes) / . . . . 576 1 X 1 36   14
    darling sweet this creative never known complexity was born . 577 1 X 1 37   13
    is less alive than never begins to yes but . . . . 580 1 X 1 40   21
    such a sun i never knew and neither did . . . . 591 1 X 1 51   14

		PAGE	TITLE	LINE
NEVER (CONTINUED)				
did you and everybody never breathed quite so many	. . . . .	591	1 X 1 51	15
again fly) forever was never till now now i	. . . .	594	1 X 1 54	27
me) quickly count to never? you were wrong --then	. . . . .	599	(CHAIRE) 1	11
us to understand they'd never close (and open) if	. . . . .	603	(CHAIRE) 5	9
the fact that rotgut never was brewed which could	. . . .	605	(CHAIRE) 7	4
waking calls asleep) so never is most lonely man	. . . . . .	609	(CHAIRE) 11	9
wealthy sisters swore they'd never part: Soul was (i	. . . .	621	(CHAIRE) 23	1
not to understand "i'll never let you go until	. . . . . .	622	(CHAIRE) 24	5
pay at all he never seems to care he	. . . .	624	(CHAIRE) 26	12
now than forever could never (by breathless one breathing)	.	625	(CHAIRE) 27	22
nothing and nothing into never and never into (touch	. . . .	633	(CHAIRE) 35	13
nothing into never and never into (touch me! love)	. . . . .	633	(CHAIRE) 35	14
silence) hole bigger than never to have been what	. . . . .	634	(CHAIRE) 36	8
matter how hard he never tried) the great pink	. . . . . .	635	(CHAIRE) 37	6
ocean earth bigly shudders) never was death so alive:	. . . .	639	(CHAIRE) 41	5
by illimitable hell) and never have breathed such miracle	. .	639	(CHAIRE) 41	9
of forever with a never in his fly (rub-her-bub)	. . . . . .	642	(CHAIRE) 44	16
gay, nowhere to here, never to beautiful: a little	. . . . .	649	(CHAIRE) 51	7
a million wheres which never may become one (wholly	. . . .	659	(CHAIRE) 61	6
come up from the never of when come into	. . . .	661	(CHAIRE) 63	11
is a secret they never will share for whom	. . . .	664	(CHAIRE) 66	7
cowardice quite agree) shall never discover our touch and	. .	664	(CHAIRE) 66	15
downward and doubting and never --it's april (yes, april;	. .	665	(CHAIRE) 67	3
a mystery which will never happen again, a miracle	. . . .	667	(CHAIRE) 69	6
a miracle which has never happened before-- and shining	. . .	667	(CHAIRE) 69	7
in forevering snow --but never fear (my own, my	. . . . . .	667	(CHAIRE) 69	13
were (floati ng through never) a kite like face	. . . . .	668	(CHAIRE) 70	9
how patient creature (who's never by never robbed of	. . . .	674	95 POEMS 2	7
creature (who's never by never robbed of day) puts	. . . .	674	95 POEMS 2	7
the only man who'll never die / / /	. . . .	685	95 POEMS 13	16
ago laid them) i never (selves any than every	. . . . . .	695	95 POEMS 23	14
is so that she never can (kno wledge is	. . . .	700	95 POEMS 28	8
a fool to have never looked there" "and you	. . . .	707	95 POEMS 35	3
as there's haymows you never can tell" "as long	. . . . . .	707	95 POEMS 35	10
rather suppose" "will's dad never gave me one cent	. . . . .	707	95 POEMS 35	17
/ / / / never could anyone who simply	. . . .	718	95 POEMS 46	1
ware that life (who never grows old) is always	. . . . . .	724	95 POEMS 52	18
away at this wedding) never mind a world with	. . . . . .	732	95 POEMS 60	13
the stars. And (darling) never fear: love, when such	. . . .	741	95 POEMS 69	9
and not miraculous (be never it so skilful) must	. . . . .	742	95 POEMS 70	3
truly, faithfully who goes (never a moment ceasing to	. . . .	756	95 POEMS 84	3
leaf almost stirs as never (in againless depths of	. . . . .	758	95 POEMS 85	39
in a tree, who never sings the same thing	. . . .	760	95 POEMS 87	3
ears may see there never lived a gayer he;	. . . .	760	95 POEMS 87	6
all living death) and never which has been or	. . . . . .	765	95 POEMS 91	8
my heart) i am never without it (anywhere i	. . . .	766	95 POEMS 92	2
bough) how? why --we never we know (so kiss	. . . .	767	95 POEMS 93	6
is to have --we never we know-- brave! brave	. . . .	767	95 POEMS 93	12
love why? how-- we never we know (with a	. . . .	767	95 POEMS 93	18
an earth which can never do wrong does (minute	. . . . . .	769	95 POEMS 95	17
deed; money can't do (never did & never will)	. . . .	793	73 POEMS 21	9
do (never did & never will) any damn thing	. . . .	793	73 POEMS 21	11
died the other day never was there such a	. . . .	794	73 POEMS 22	2
(truth to sing) could never quite tell right from	. . . . .	799	73 POEMS 27	13
a person) and while never saying a word who	. . . .	802	73 POEMS 30	25
at the place you never left (and i refer	. . . .	807	73 POEMS 35	4
only fancy we should never know are unimaginably ours	. . . .	809	73 POEMS 37	7
each whisper wear all never guessed unknowable most joy)	. .	811	73 POEMS 39	7
you: when are we never, but forever now (hosts	. . . . . .	817	73 POEMS 45	5
some world's millionary mind never may partly guess--thus, my		818	73 POEMS 46	13
/ / / i never guessed any thing (even	. . . .	827	73 POEMS 55	2
endure all that you never were hide, poor dishonoured	. . . .	834	73 POEMS 62	12
has gone: will winter never come? o come, terrible	. . . . .	839	73 POEMS 67	8
(very whiteness: absolute peace, never imaginable mystery)	.	839	73 POEMS 67	15
light and dark; but never forever & when) un	. . . .	840	73 POEMS 68	25
restroll and stroll some never deepening beach locked in	. .	843	73 POEMS 71	3

	PAGE	TITLE	LINE

+NEVER
   FOR CONTEXT, SEE . . . . 69 T&C POST IMPR 6 15
   FOR CONTEXT, SEE . . . . 69 T&C POST IMPR 6 35
   FOR CONTEXT, SEE . . . . 646 (CHAIRE) 48 14
NEVER'S
   dear whispered again in never's ear (i'm tho thcared . . . . 316 VIVA 8 5
   escorts us home through never's always until absolute un . . 517 50 POEMS 31 12
NEVERISH
   Continue to experience a neverish subchemistry of alWays . . 361 VIVA 52 28
NEVERLESS
   have from madame death neverless now and without winter . . . 531 50 POEMS 43 10
   our is love and neverless / / / / . . . . 590 1 X 1 50 27
NEVERMOVING
   is alone-- one (above nevermoving all nowhere) goldenly . . . 808 73 POEMS 36 5
NEVERS
   (seized among what ghostly nevers of again) silent not . . . 432 NO THANKS 49 11
   then) they said their nevers they slept their dream . . . . . 515 50 POEMS 29 20
   who're by the five nevers of a lear / . . . . 561 1 X 1 21 10
   go (all than were nevers ugly beautiful most is . . . . . . 565 1 X 1 25 15
NEVERTHELESS
   execute strides of cobalt nevertheless i feel that i . . . . 199 XLI PORTRAIT 7 7
+NEVERTOBEEXTINGUISHED
   extremely artistic nevertobeextinguished fla -me of the(very 267 IS 5 TWO 2 11
NEVERWHERES
   & before flashing soft neverwheres & sweet nothingly gushing 480 NEW POEMS 18 10
NEW
   abundant sun invades the new mosaic of the ground . . . . . . 5 T&C EPITHALAM 84
   taste thee as a new wine from steep hills . . . . 9 T&C SONGS 1 35
   perfectly moving, through the new world scarce astir my . . . 17 T&C PUELLA MEA 12
   (it were so very new a flower, a flower . . . . 18 T&C PUELLA MEA 51
   world was young and new (a flower such as . . . . 18 T&C PUELLA MEA 54
   the lazy world and new sweetly used to laugh . . . . 23 T&C PUELLA MEA 285
   fold her mouth the new flower with thy unimaginable . . . . . 40 T&C AMORES 4 43
   SONNETS--ACTUALITIES a thing most new complete fragile . . . 82 T&C SON ACTU 1 1
   gloom and see! (the new moon fills abruptly with . . . . . . 93 & POST IMPR 5 13
   a Plum grinning softly, New focus-of disintegrat i o . . . . 94 & POST IMPR 6 16
   mcsorley's. outside it was New York and beautifully snowing. 96 & POST IMPR 8 1
   answer. outside. (it was New York and beautifully, ... 97 & POST IMPR 8 45
   unspeaking ignorant darkness of New Lady whose kiss is . . . 112 & PORTRAIT 6 98
   to and fro moving New and Old things, while . . . . 124 & SEVEN POEMS 3 13
   does surely to mesh. New and eager. wittily peels . . . . . . 136 & SON REAL 7 12
   in dumb blossoms of new mingling: deeper: blood of . . . . . 139 & SON REAL 10 4
   tears, as the dusty new- ness of her obsolete . . . . 148 & SON REAL 19 11
   lips to take your new mouth in his teeth . . . . 161 & SON ACTU 10 3
   opening in dusk her new wings then decently hanged . . . . . 170 & SON ACTU 19 3
   It is so quite new a thing. Muscles better . . . . 175 & SON ACTU 24 2
   me you so quite new / / / / . . . . 175 & SON ACTU 24 14
   head smoulders like a new turd in April his . . . . 198 XLI PORTRAIT 6 20
   in the mouth of New York. Be- tween its . . . . 201 XLI PORTRAIT 9 2
   the fragile skill of new leaves' voices, and sharp . . . . . 218 XLI SONNETS 14 5
   into neatest distance.... A new curve of children gladly . . 219 XLI SONNETS 15 7
   / she being Brand -new; and you know consequently . . . . . . 248 IS 5 ONE 19 2
   to howjedooze the candidate's new silk lid bounds gently . . 259 IS 5 ONE 29 20
   pithecoid President in a new frock coat (scrambling all . . . 267 IS 5 TWO 2 3
   old mother in a new nice pine box (collect . . . . 270 IS 5 TWO 5 20
   suggest teach us a new terror always which shall . . . . . . 289 IS 5 FOUR 6 10
   eyes actually shall contain new faeries (and if your . . . . 294 IS 5 FOUR 11 9
   through a darkness where new lights begin and increase, . . . 297 IS 5 FOUR 14 3
   busily horribly blunder through new light hush we are . . . . 299 IS 5 FOUR 16 14
   fear i see the new moon thinner than a . . . . 301 IS 5 FOUR 18 5
   the dictum of a new england sculptor (well on . . . . 327 VIVA 18 r39
   est hills er dream; new . oh if when: . . . . 350 VIVA 41 12
   skin lay eyes like new tools) whence i guessed . . . . 355 VIVA 46 11
   as fiercely seek findingly new textures of actual cool . . . 373 VIVA 64 14
   invisible, with large first new stars knitting the structure 378 VIVA 69 7
   (make strangely) known (establish new) come, what Being! open 422 NO THANKS 39 11
   my arms flowering so new) self whose eyes smell . . . . 424 NO THANKS 41 2
   skies--and in death's place new fragrantly young earth space 432 NO THANKS 49 19

NEW (CONTINUED)

eyes touches hands with new- ness and these startled . . . . 437 NO THANKS 53   5
Always & lewd shy New and upon the beyond . . . . 442 NO THANKS 57   20
moon She over this new eng land fragrance of . . . . 469 NEW POEMS 7   13
& mirrors; sprung dimensionless new alls of joy: quietly . . 480 NEW POEMS 18   21
(sky she) open new (dark we all . . . . 482 NEW POEMS 20   7
Silent is blue (sleep! new girlgold / / / . . . . 503 50 POEMS 17   11
of we, singing each new leaf out of each . . . . 521 50 POEMS 34   50
be comes or (a) new (live) now ; & . . . . 532 50 POEMS 44   6
(each green of a new) you're who as to . . . . 543 1 X 1 3   10
if there isn't a new moon outside your window . . . . 572 1 X 1 32   2
love (by yes every new bird no bigger than . . . . 583 1 X 1 43   16
anything old being everything new (with a what which . . . 594 1 X 1 54   14
in -credible true each new self) smile. Eyes. & . . . . 612 (CHAIRE) 14   6
thrush may sing no new moon in if all . . . . 620 (CHAIRE) 22   5
& bi g screeching new black perfectly isn 't) . . . . 646 (CHAIRE) 48   16
(with patient eyes) re -new- ing remaking what other . . . . 660 (CHAIRE) 62   11
where shall breathe a new (silverly rare goldenly so) . . . . 666 (CHAIRE) 68   7
exquisite white firstful flame --new moon! as (by the . . . . 669 (CHAIRE) 71   10
themselves grow silent upon new perfectly blue) i am . . . . 720 95 POEMS 48   3
more than each creature new (except your fear to . . . . . . 762 95 POEMS 89   6
person; joyful your any new (every more only you) . . . . . 764 95 POEMS 90   45
dear; (die! live) the new is the true and . . . . 767 95 POEMS 93   10
than the green the new the earth more moving . . . . 778 73 POEMS 6   8
flowers over green the new earth a day of . . . . 778 73 POEMS 6   17
+NEW
   FOR CONTEXT, SEE . . . . 100 & POST IMPR 11   24
   FOR CONTEXT, SEE . . . . 342 VIVA 33   24
   FOR CONTEXT, SEE . . . . 347 VIVA 38   34
+NEW DEAL
   FOR CONTEXT, SEE . . . . 410 NO THANKS 27   4
+NEW ORLEANS
   FOR CONTEXT, SEE . . . . 237 IS 5 ONE 8   7
+NEW YORK
   FOR CONTEXT, SEE . . . . 237 IS 5 ONE 8   8
   FOR CONTEXT, SEE . . . . 476 NEW POEMS 14   2
NEWBORN
   prodigious night blossoms a newborn babe: around him, eyes . 714 95 POEMS 42   3
NEWENGLAND
   harder perhaps than a newengland bed these ends of . . . . . 506 50 POEMS 20   1
NEWER
   by hypercivic zeal sought newer pastures or because swaddled 258 IS 5 ONE 28   12
   ver (& i) some newer than life (or than . . . . 668 (CHAIRE) 70   18
   me for each leaf newer than can be: and . . . . 760 95 POEMS 87   10
NEWFRAGILE
   thrilling light with thinned newfragile yellows lurch and. . 163 & SON ACTU 12   10
NEWLY
   poisonous fragility of ice newly formed upon an old . . . . . 103 & POST IMPR 13   12
   outstart, curl, bloat, are newly baked and swaggering cookies 226 IS 5 ONE MAME   13
   opening a box of newly without exaggeration shot with . . . 263 IS 5 ONE 32   46
   lopsided imaginations) filled with newly murdered flowers . . 340 VIVA 31   11
   whO perfectly whO flOat newly alOne is dreamest oNLY . . . . 383 NO THANKS 1   7
   (glued among familiar things newly which are transferred with 428 NO THANKS 45   3
   would stir and squirm newly as from unburied which . . . . . 520 50 POEMS 34   9
   and immediate like some newly remembered dream-- flaming a . 601 (CHAIRE) 3   12
   the little horse is newlY Born) he knows nothing, ... 657 (CHAIRE) 59   1
   he paints with sound, newly one moving cadence may . . . . . 842 73 POEMS 70   6
NEWLYS
   / / / / newlys of silence (both an . . . . 518 50 POEMS 32   1
NEWMOWN
   and you in the newmown hay and he telling . . . . 707 95 POEMS 35   26
NEWNESS
   young moons begin the newness of his skin, so . . . . 11 T&C SONGS 2   5
   the jigging fragrance of newness --and then. My crazy . . . . 173 & SON ACTU 22   7
+NEWNESS
   FOR CONTEXT, SEE . . . . 148 & SON REAL 19   11
   FOR CONTEXT, SEE . . . . 437 NO THANKS 53   5

		PAGE	TITLE	LINE

NEWS
a and c discuss news in turkish x and . . . . 200 XLI PORTRAIT 8   20
directly perceive or minus news alimony blackmail whathavewe 391 NO THANKS 8   11

NEWSPAPER
younger than i am newspaper guy who refused to . . . . 324 VIVA 16   10

+NEWSPAPER
FOR CONTEXT, SEE . . . . 796 73 POEMS 24   11

NEWSREEL
to yonder s called newsreel s called theatre & . . . . 392 NO THANKS 9   9

NEWTON'S
lost the) Einstein expanded Newton's law preserved conTinuum 315 VIVA 7   5

NEXT
hot queens with dam next to nothing on) tangoing . . . . . . 242 IS 5 ONE 13   5
myself) but let us next demand wherefore yon mob . . . . . . 245 IS 5 ONE 13   15
kicked what the hell) next minute i was back . . . . 248 IS 5 ONE 19   13
rail waiting for the next train to grind me . . . . 262 IS 5 ONE 32   3
/ / / / "next to of course god . . . . 268 IS 5 TWO 3   1
man and James and next let me see yes . . . . 271 IS 5 TWO 6   4
there are 6 doors. Next door (but four) gentlemen . . . . . . 312 VIVA 4   2
a multitude of chins: next door but three dwells; . . . . . . 312 VIVA 4   6
always who Is bluish; next Door but two occupy . . . . 312 VIVA 4   9
He looks jewish , next door but One a . . . . 312 VIVA 4   17
thickly spi) tting But next door nobody seems to . . . . . . 312 VIVA 4   21
instance everything is planned next to that patch of . . . . 322 VIVA 14   4
was dead er sumpn: next i knows me (er . . . . 332 VIVA 23   28
hair spatters creasing pillow next everywhere hidinglyseek no 358 VIVA 49   4
would run down the next day. / / / . . . . 365 VIVA 56   14
it her his my next meal's coming from i . . . . 475 NEW POEMS 13   4
hitler's window on wednesday next at 1 E.S.T. bring . . . . . 514 50 POEMS 28   13
the star nicked ends next among broken odds of . . . . 522 50 POEMS 35   6
in sub (at the next) nakedness (table but three) . . . . . . 546 1 X 1 6   7
of a good universe next door; let's go / . . . . 554 1 X 1 14   15
E will exactly do next (our great problem nearly . . . . . . 650 {CHAIRE} 52   13
selves this implacable unthing next, our illustrious . . . . 799 73 POEMS 27   23

NEXTTO
the desertbyIts elf while) nextto Mesmoked eleven camels ! . 318 VIVA 10   14

NIBBLE
take a littl e nibble now And then bite) . . . . 314 VIVA 6   11

NIBBLES
belly whose deep squirm nibbles. another couches, weary, upon 143 & SON REAL 14   11
diamond solitaire while guesswho nibbles his ton of torse . . 545 1 X 1 5   5

NIBBLING
loose sack a star's nibbling in- fin -i- tes- . . . . 49 T&C IMPRESS 3   4
yester- day between the nibbling timid teethful hours wilts . 112 & PORTRAIT 6   79
large silent him into nibbling final worms / / . . . . 277 IS 5 THREE 1   24

+NIBBLING
FOR CONTEXT, SEE . . . . 131 & SON REAL 2   4

NIC
(ice coal wood man) nic he like wint-air nic . . . . 618 {CHAIRE} 20   21
nic he like wint-air nic like ot-am sum-air (young . . . . . 618 {CHAIRE} 20   24
ot-am sum-air (young old nic) like spring yoo un-air-stan? . 618 {CHAIRE} 20   26

NICE
lusts of light her nice concupiscence appeared rounded. if . 103 & POST IMPR 13   15
boite a joujoux, want nice sleep? toutes les petites . . . . 121 & PORTRAIT 12   49
why have to? dead's nice like a dance where . . . . 127 & SEVEN POEMS 5   32
/ SONNETS--REALITIES O It's Nice To Get Up In, ... 130 & SON REAL 1   1
dude. Dark hair and nice hands. with a little . . . . 149 & SON REAL 20   5
(set on big legs nice to pinch assiduously which . . . . . . 150 & SON REAL 21   8
it really must be Nice, never to have no . . . . 242 IS 5 ONE 13   2
other) it Must be nice never to have no . . . . 242 IS 5 ONE 13   11
happy to see how nice she acted right up . . . . 248 IS 5 ONE 19   26
mother in a new nice pine box (collect / . . . . 270 IS 5 TWO 5   20

+NICE
FOR CONTEXT, SEE . . . . 316 VIVA 8   11
FOR CONTEXT, SEE . . . . 618 {CHAIRE} 20   2

NICELY
seems to be doing nicely / / / / . . . . 401 NO THANKS 18   21
eye look "thank you" nicely the lady's small grin . . . . . 506 50 POEMS 20   13

	PAGE	TITLE	LINE

+NICELY
FOR CONTEXT, SEE . . . . 94 & POST IMPR 6   14
NICELYBITS
for. putrescence is Cubical sliced-nicelybits Of, shivers . . 94 & POST IMPR 6   11
NICENESS
is an accident whose niceness betters easily the intent . . . 162 & SON ACTU 11   3
NICER
Hush. Worms.) But It's Nicer To Lie In Bed . . . . 130 & SON REAL 1   13
NICEST
a smile like the nicest man you've never met . . . . 126 & SEVEN POEMS 5   14
NICHO'
having ordered yaoorti from Nicho' settled my feet on . . . . 194 XLI PORTRAIT 2   12
exhaling into eternity as Nicho' laid before me bread . . . . 194 XLI PORTRAIT 2   30
almostclean plate "Achilles" said Nicho' "and did you perhaps 194 XLI PORTRAIT 2   37
NICHOLAS
in hopes that Saint Nicholas" / / / / . . . . 142 & SON REAL 13   14
+NICK
FOR CONTEXT, SEE . . . . 618 (CHAIRE) 20   21
FOR CONTEXT, SEE . . . . 618 (CHAIRE) 20   24
FOR CONTEXT, SEE . . . . 618 (CHAIRE) 20   26
NICKED
buried by the star nicked ends next among broken . . . . . . 522 50 POEMS 35   6
NICKELS
as three dimes seven nickels and ten pennies have . . . . . . 196 XLI PORTRAIT 4   9
NICKNAMED
(breath in breath) have nicknamed ecstasy and And spills . . 358 VIVA 49   9
NICOLETTE
/ / / OF NICOLETTE dreaming in marble all . . . . 8 T&C OF NICOL   T
NIFTY
female cracksman of the nifty, ruffian-rogue, laughing body . 140 & SON REAL 11   10
NIG
lesgo eckshun kemeruh daretoi nig) Ah, Soul / . . . . 474 NEW POEMS 12   15
NIGGER
down the hatch the nigger smiles the jew stands . . . . 108 & PORTRAIT 4   22
/ one day a nigger caught in his hand . . . . 622 (CHAIRE) 24   1
NIGGER'S
the hot alley, a nigger's voice feels curiously cool . . . . 167 & SON ACTU 16   18
the slate of that nigger's face (but If i . . . . 287 IS 5 FOUR 4   5
NIGGERS
alive (who is ? niggers) Not jes livin not . . . . 426 NO THANKS 43   3
somes born alive (but niggers is all born so . . . . 426 NO THANKS 43   13
NIGHT
strictness Danae saw the night severed and the glowing . . . 4 T&C EPITHALAM   52
gigantic ghost-flower born of night blossoming in white . . . 8 T&C OF NICOL   2
there fell upon the night, like angel's tears, the . . . . . 8 T&C OF NICOL   10
of silver; o'er whose night three willows wail, a . . . . . 9 T&C SONGS 1   4
scarlet sunset trampling the night easily from the shocked . 30 T&C ORIENTALE 4   24
shall remember of this night amazing ecstasies slowly, in . . 36 T&C AMORES 1   22
sole in the blue night amorous of waters tremulous, ... 37 T&C AMORES 2   4
i trusted not, one night when in my fingers . . . . 39 T&C AMORES 4   11
offered up each fragrant night, when all my days . . . . . . 39 T&C AMORES 4   31
seen between barrages, the night utter ripe unspeaking girls. 45 T&C LA GUERRE 1   15
street of the sky night walks scattering poems / . . . . . . 50 T&C IMPRESS 4   33
look from morning till night into the street unchangingly . . 58 T&C PORTRAIT 3   19
chaos in this dangerous night through moaned space god . . . 77 T&C SON UNRE 2   14
temporal splendor of this night when souls which have . . . . 81 T&C SON UNRE 6   2
own-- on such a night the sea through her . . . . 81 T&C SON UNRE 6   13
in the slowly. town, night featherly swifts the Dark . . . . 89 & POST IMPR 1   2
hushed in moan-loll where night gathers morte carved smiles . 90 & POST IMPR 2   10
the lithe indolent prostitute Night, argues with certain . . 93 & POST IMPR 5   17
the sailor shuffles the night with fucking eyes the . . . . . 108 & PORTRAIT 4   26
Child, and "'Twas the night before Christmas when all . . . . 142 & SON REAL 13   12
fragile gradual throne of night slowly when several stars . . 156 & SON ACTU 5   1
upon my mind all night, quitting only in the . . . . 165 & SON ACTU 14   3
And the. fire-escapes-- the night. makes me wonder if, . . . 166 & SON ACTU 15   12
with almost melancholy delicacy night gargles windows. / / . 168 & SON ACTU 17   19
straightacross from my window, night air bothered with a . . 171 & SON ACTU 20   3
morning out of the night. I am living with . . . . 171 & SON ACTU 20   12

		PAGE	TITLE	LINE

NIGHT (CONTINUED)
rose through the sensible night a quick bird (tenderly . . . 187 XLI SONGS 9   6
through the cold perfect night whisperless to mark, how . . . 205 XLI SONNETS 1   6
of thoughtful trees whom night hath pondered o'er --and . . . 205 XLI SONNETS 1   11
the middle of the night / / / / . . . . 242 IS 5 ONE 13   23
author of Women By Night whose latest Seeds Of . . . . 245 IS 5 ONE 16   8
Mothers and kodaks --by night upon the Riva Schiavoni . . . . 256 IS 5 ONE 27   17
all of the long night a fragile imitation of . . . . 300 IS 5 FOUR 17   12
of me and the night absolutely into me.... a . . . . 302 IS 5 FIVE 1   7
(it being Spring and night) "let us go a . . . . 303 IS 5 FIVE 2   2
st one fine August night, i just happened to . . . . 313 VIVA 5   3
(when clocks whisper and night shouts) When minds shrivel . . 359 VIVA 50   3
this fear (which beyond night shall go) remembering only . . 362 VIVA 53   2
i love you) last night clothed in sealace appeared . . . . . 369 VIVA 60   1
through my dreams last night, all of your body . . . . 369 VIVA 60   18
hugest colour (and which night hoists miraculously above the 378 VIVA 69   11
of praise the unimaginable night not known / / . . . . 418 NO THANKS 35   14
disappear (and only was night and through only this . . . . 419 NO THANKS 36   20
and through only this night a mightily form moves . . . . . . 419 NO THANKS 36   21
them thirteen times a night one hangs a hat . . . . 427 NO THANKS 44   4
peace outthunders silence. And (night climbs the air / . . . 428 NO THANKS 45   18
unday by silently not night did the great world . . . . . . 432 NO THANKS 49   1
of again) silent not night by silently unday life's . . . . . 432 NO THANKS 49   12
the dear beautiful eternal night / / / / . . . . 464 NEW POEMS 2   36
quick squirmthicklying lu minous night mare som e w . . . . . 493 50 POEMS 7   13
morning out of each night my father moved through . . . . . 520 50 POEMS 34   3
so both and oneful night cannot be so sky . . . . 537 50 POEMS 49   14
my life worships and (night) then "everything beautiful can . 572 1 X 1 32   13
was your breakfast every night all day) a 3ringbrain . . . . 605 (CHAIRE) 7   5
now stars shine at night / / / / . . . . 622 (CHAIRE) 24   8
in a white high night where his heartlike ears . . . . 631 (CHAIRE) 33   4
--it's spring (all our night becomes day) o, it's . . . . . 665 (CHAIRE) 67   18
time for dying: a night for silence and a . . . . 683 95 POEMS 11   12
(up high in the night at the end of . . . . 699 95 POEMS 27   3
voice-with-a-smile of democracy announces night & day "all . 711 95 POEMS 39   6
of earth's most prodigious night blossoms a newborn babe: . . 714 95 POEMS 42   2
healing our by immeasurable night spirits and with . . . . . 745 95 POEMS 73   7
"right here the other night something odd occurred" charlie . 800 73 POEMS 28   1
this miracle of summer night her trillion secrets touchably . 809 73 POEMS 37   3
breathe suns of the night, bring this beautiful wanderer . . 811 73 POEMS 39   9
are) only loaned: whereas night is given (night and . . . .. 816 73 POEMS 44   8
whereas night is given (night and death and the . . . . . . 816 73 POEMS 44   8
midsummer's blazing most not night as floats a more . . . . 818 73 POEMS 46   1
day has to become night this is a beautiful . . . . 824 73 POEMS 52   7

+NIGHT
FOR CONTEXT, SEE . . . . 200 XLI PORTRAIT 8   31
FOR CONTEXT, SEE . . . . 227 IS 5 ONE GERT   15
FOR CONTEXT, SEE . . . . 795 73 POEMS 23   1

NIGHT'S
eyes which have beheld night's speechless carnival the . . . 36 T&C AMORES 1   13
was considering how within night's loose sack a star's . . . 49 T&C IMPRESS 3   2
frail azures fluttering from night's outer wing strong silent 208 XLI SONNETS 4   2
smell of lilies.... beyond night's silken immense swoon the . 214 XLI SONNETS 10   12
/ / / if night's mostness (and whom did . . . . 450 NO THANKS 65   1
/ / / denied night's face have shadowless they? . . . . . . 527 50 POEMS 39   1
joy) --wholly now disappear night's not eternal terrors like 582 1 X 1 42   15
be and was are night's total exploding millionminded Who . . 633 (CHAIRE) 35   15
/ / out of night's almosT Floats a colour . . . . 719 95 POEMS 47   1
should sing: and our night's thousand million miracles a . . 756 95 POEMS 84   12
out of not knowable night's utmost nothing, wanders a . . . . 810 73 POEMS 38   2

NIGHTFALL
to appreciate rome at nightfall; and because against this . . 355 VIVA 46   13

NIGHTLY
hearty soul aglow) his nightly supper sups it isn't . . . . . 254 IS 5 ONE 25   22

+NIGHTLY
FOR CONTEXT, SEE . . . . 312 VIVA 4   3

NIGHTMARE
light groping washes my nightmare from his eyes? / . . . . . 374 VIVA 65   15

535

		PAGE	TITLE	LINE

+NIGHTMARE
FOR CONTEXT, SEE . . . . 493 50 POEMS 7   13

NIGHTS
sits in the kitchen nights and chews a two-bit . . . . 149 & SON REAL 20   2
all the days and nights that matter knocked by . . . . 153 & SON ACTU 2   10
/ / when unto nights of autumn do complain . . . . 207 XLI SONNETS 3   1
days & years & nights & forever) is Less . . . . 702 95 POEMS 30   20
not worry if longer nights grow longest; i am . . . . 749 95 POEMS 77   15

NIKE
creation, in whose palm Nike presents the crown sweetest . .   3 T&C EPITHALAM   28

NIL
as the hill becomes nil) and will somebody tell . . . . . . 593 1 X 1 53   22

NILE
gods are swallowed even Nile the kind black great . . . . . 112 & PORTRAIT 6   86
Egypt whose hair is Nile) put your ear to . . . . 113 & PORTRAIT 6   112

NIMBLE
thing (a thing more nimble and complete) than ever . . . . .   17 T&C PUELLA MEA   26
/ / PORTRAITS the nimble heat had long on . . . .   52 T&C PORTRAIT 1   2

NIMBLER
/ blossoming are people nimbler than Really go whirling . . . 630 (CHAIRE) 32   2

NIMBLEST
Humble a rosily , nimblest; c-urlin-g noworld Silent is . . . 503 50 POEMS 17   6

NINE
first lady says to nine ladies his lips drink . . . .   15 T&C SONGS 5   6
tenth lady says to nine ladies they must chain . . . .   15 T&C SONGS 5   10
the nineteenth says to nine ladies you take his . . . .   15 T&C SONGS 5   14
go the heart goes nine / / / / . . . .   15 T&C SONGS 5   20
where i stood (maybe nine miles off). It was . . . . 135 & SON REAL 6   12
immensely speak (it is nine minutes past six) the . . . . . . 219 XLI SONNETS 15   4
one Clock dimly cries nine, i stride among the . . . . 434 NO THANKS 51   15
it in the twot nine months young / / . . . . 497 50 POEMS 11   8
/ / / / nine birds (rising through a . . . . 627 (CHAIRE) 29   1
a manying one -ness) nine souls only alive with . . . . 627 (CHAIRE) 29   11

NINETEENTH
wrist's too fine the nineteenth says to nine ladies . . . . .   15 T&C SONGS 5   13

NINEVEH
are the smells of Nineveh, in her eyes when . . . .   23 T&C PUELLA MEA 259

NINTH
traffic collapses: through west ninth slowly cars pour into . 800 73 POEMS 28   19

NIPPLE
from the dress. one nipple tries. playfully to peek . . . . . 143 & SON REAL 14   9

NIPPLES
to mouth her ugly nipples squirming in pretty wrath, ... 151 & SON REAL 22   9
kiss a girl with nipples like pink thimbles) ask . . . . . . 498 50 POEMS 12   18

NIPPONIZED
sir) it took a nipponized bit of the old . . . . 553 1 X 1 13   21

NIT
mean- hum a) now (nit y unb uria ble . . . . 309 VIVA 1   4

NITE
ter yknow, Rektuz, Toysday nite; where uh guy gets . . . . . 227 IS 5 ONE GERT   15
/ / / / nite) thatthis crou ched moangrowl-&-thin . . . . . . 795 73 POEMS 23   1

NIX
? ?? ??? ! nix, kid / / / . . . . 196 XLI PORTRAIT 4   26

NIZMUS
unnurs tanmih eesez pullih nizmus tash, oi dough un . . . . . 310 VIVA 2   2

NN
your cough better today? nn-nn went head face goes . . . . . 506 50 POEMS 20   8
your cough better today? nn-nn went head face goes . . . . . 506 50 POEMS 20   8

NN-NN
your cough better today? nn-nn went head face goes . . . . . 506 50 POEMS 20   8

NO
WORD DELETED, APPEARED 167 TIMES

+NO ONE
FOR CONTEXT, SEE . . . . 469 NEW POEMS 7   11
FOR CONTEXT, SEE . . . . 653 (CHAIRE) 55   13
FOR CONTEXT, SEE . . . . 660 (CHAIRE) 62   2
FOR CONTEXT, SEE . . . . 705 95 POEMS 33   16
FOR CONTEXT, SEE . . . . 720 95 POEMS 48   12

		PAGE	TITLE	LINE

+NO (CONTINUED)
    FOR CONTEXT, SEE . . . . 830 73 POEMS 58   9
NO-SHE-YES-HE
    and scritch (while the no-she-yes-he fluffies tittle tattle . 773 73 POEMS 1   16
NO-VOICE
    's rainfaint windthin voice-which-is no-voice sobcries "paw? 697 95 POEMS 25   13
NOBLE
    / in time's a noble mercy of proportion with . . . . 683 95 POEMS 11   1
NOBLER
    been finished in the nobler trees and the language . . . . . 184 XLI SONGS 6   11
NOBLEST
    how to beat the noblest game a man can . . . . 679 95 POEMS 7   2
NOBLY
    windows absurd clouds cruise nobly ridiculous skies (the; . . 442 NO THANKS 57   13
NOBODIES
    invisible spectator, maybe certain nobodies laughing faintly 283 IS 5 THREE 7   8
NOBODY
    she'll do to yer nobody knows for she knows . . . . 25 T&C CHANSONS 2   20
    to utter a tree, Nobody shall stop me but . . . . 67 T&C POST IMPR 4   1
    tottering in sun-light THE nobody (knows and WhoEver would)? 101 & POST IMPR 11   80
    flowers, always crying to nobody something about les roses . 102 & POST IMPR 12   16
    thing where <> and nobody expects you to anyway . . . . 127 & SEVEN POEMS 5   43
    swell bangup time wen nobody wore no cloze an . . . . 237 IS 5 ONE 8   17
    / / / / nobody loses all the time . . . . 239 IS 5 ONE 10   1
    of eyes which noticed nobody he looked as if . . . . 258 IS 5 ONE 28   15
    a 75 done this nobody would have believed would . . . . 270 IS 5 TWO 5   3
    with bright eyes) drifts (nobody can tell because Nobody . . 286 IS 5 FOUR 3   5
    (nobody can tell because Nobody knows, or why jerks . . . . . 286 IS 5 FOUR 3   7
    / / / / Nobody wears a yellow flower . . . . 296 IS 5 FOUR 13   1
    tting But next door nobody seems to live at . . . . 312 VIVA 4   21
    cambridge, mass. to whom nobody seems to have mentioned . . . 326 VIVA 18   3
    him of ourselves) as Nobody came slowly over the . . . . . . 355 VIVA 46   21
    deeper than all roses) nobody, not even the rain, ... 366 VIVA 57   20
    my darling (for only Nobody knows where truth grows . . . . 368 VIVA 59   18
    / o sure) but nobody unders (no but Rully . . . . 400 NO THANKS 17   3
    what i mean is Nobody Understands Her RERLY / . . . . 400 NO THANKS 17   18
    earthquakes starfish (but because nobody can sell the Moon . 452 NO THANKS 67   17
    / / / / nobody loved this he) with . . . . 490 50 POEMS 4   1
    like legs or feethands; nobody ever could ever had . . . . . 490 50 POEMS 4   16
    your barn be glad; nobody ever earns anything, everything . . 514 50 POEMS 28   7
    emptiness toss one at nobody shoulder and thick stickingly . 522 50 POEMS 35   3
    are perfectly alone there's nobody else alive (such a . . . . 591 1 X 1 51   12
    swallows it self while nobody (and stars moon sun . . . . . . 693 95 POEMS 21   17
    is the deepest secret nobody knows (here is the . . . . 766 95 POEMS 92   10
    / / / / nobody could in superhuman flights . . . . 790 73 POEMS 18   1
    sweet the earth) & nobody (including our selves) will . . . . 797 73 POEMS 25   11
    handed me a flower. Nobody, it's safe to say, ... 802 73 POEMS 30   7
    is you (ne i) nobody else drive dumb mankind . . . . 804 73 POEMS 32   8
    to imagine) something which nobody may keep. now i . . . . . 816 73 POEMS 44   13
    poems my darling but nobody will stop it With . . . . 835 73 POEMS 63   30
+NOBODY
    FOR CONTEXT, SEE . . . . 310 VIVA 2   10
    FOR CONTEXT, SEE . . . . 314 VIVA 6   20
    FOR CONTEXT, SEE . . . . 490 50 POEMS 4   5
    FOR CONTEXT, SEE . . . . 490 50 POEMS 4   20
    FOR CONTEXT, SEE . . . . 519 50 POEMS 33   24
    FOR CONTEXT, SEE . . . . 611 {CHAIRE} 13   10
    FOR CONTEXT, SEE . . . . 724 95 POEMS 52   21
    FOR CONTEXT, SEE . . . . 727 95 POEMS 55   3
    FOR CONTEXT, SEE . . . . 727 95 POEMS 55   8
NOBODY'LL
    be clover clover clover (nobody'll know) sam was a . . . . . 568 1 X 1 28   25
    he should Smile) comes nobody'll know / / / . . . . 660 {CHAIRE} 62   27
NOBODY'S
    a keen city which nobody's ever visited, where always . . . . 129 & SEVEN POEMS 7   12
    whatses to rescue miss nobody's probably handbag) because i . 475 NEW POEMS 13   21
NOD
    eloquent pandar with thy nod significant to the ecstatic . .   3 T&C EPITHALAM   9

NOD (CONTINUED)
    been repapered he will nod like buddha or answer . . . . . . 198 XLI PORTRAIT 6   27
    lurch small invin cible nod oc cul t ke . . . . 349 VIVA 40   15
+NOD
    FOR CONTEXT, SEE . . . . 544 1 X 1 4   22
NODDING
    the vermilion jacket of nodding hairy Jacqueline who is . . . 279 IS 5 THREE 3   19
NODS
    upon her nakedness he nods and all depart through . . . . . .   34 T&C ORIENTALE 6 104
NOEL
    we'll dance and sing "Noel Noel" / / / . . . . 192 XLI CHANSONS 2   28
    dance and sing "Noel Noel" / / / / . . . . 192 XLI CHANSONS 2   28
NOGGED
    eev mahmah hadn chuzd nogged id entwhys / / . . . . 790 73 POEMS 18   16
NOING
    those that and that noing our gone snow gone . . . . 491 50 POEMS 5   7
NOISE
    eyes deeply wield a noise of petals falling silently . . . .   10 T&C SONGS 1   43
    carefully dancing in the noise of Herod's silence, long . . .   17 T&C PUELLA MEA   31
    heart so great a noise, as in the sharp . . . .   18 T&C PUELLA MEA   65
    true only to the noise of worms. in the . . . .   43 T&C AMORES 7   22
    insufficient day under the noise of worms / / . . . .   43 T&C AMORES 7   40
    chuck pil- lows are noise funnily swallows swallowing revolv-   96 & POST IMPR 8   5
    bellowing through the general noise Where is Effie who . . . 117 & PORTRAIT 10   9
    lives a green egyptian noise. ladies with whom time . . . . . 138 & SON REAL 9   8
    aches, and the weak noise of her eyes easily . . . . 147 & SON REAL 18   8
    spits discrete lumps of noise.... furniture unsolemnly : bur   159 & SON ACTU 8   7
    the stink of perfumed noise fiercely mounts from the . . . . 169 & SON ACTU 18   3
    dark exact walloping human noise of digestible mill- ions . . 202 XLI PORTRAIT 9   45
    established ...far from the noise of waters) one's . . . . . 319 VIVA 11   24
    dip dip soar equalling noise solemn dolls re -volve . . . . . 384 NO THANKS 2   27
NOISECOLOURED
    points uPDownwardishly find everywheres noisecoloured . . . . 311 VIVA 3   16
NOISELESS
    silence filled with vivid noiseless boys at Roupy i . . . . .   45 T&C LA GUERRE 1 11
    a music Lady the noiseless truth of swirling worms . . . . . 113 & PORTRAIT 6   117
NOISES
    sizeless a silence by noises called people called sunlight . 658 (CHAIRE) 60   9
NOISILY
    wife: Both very young noisily who kiss throw silently . . . . 312 VIVA 4   11
NOISY
    dirty child skating on noisy wheels of joy pathetic . . . . .   56 T&C PORTRAIT 4   3
    futile fooling labyrinth where noisy colours stroll.... and . 220 XLI SONNETS 16   12
    sexual timelessness, outtowering this noisy impotence of not   351 VIVA 42   4
    Unvoice (which frightenS a noisy most park's least timorous . 726 95 POEMS 54   8
+NOISY
    FOR CONTEXT, SEE . . . . 417 NO THANKS 34   23
NOMBRIL
    dressed, cleanshaven above the nombril, and much to my . . . 262 IS 5 ONE 32   8
NON
    vous coucher avec moi? Non? pourquoi?) ladies skilfully dead   120 & PORTRAIT 12   30
    Dame (whereas de gustibus non disputandum est my lady . . . . 245 IS 5 ONE 16   24
    forgotten prisoner --"Ici?" --"Ah non, mon cheri; il fait . . 304 IS 5 FIVE 3   10
    / / ◇ this noN allgotupfittokill She with the . . . . 726 95 POEMS 54   2
NONCHALANT
    sorting from this vast nonchalant inward walk of vol- . . . . 201 XLI PORTRAIT 9   21
    gaiety of blossom --blissfully nonchalant wise and each . . . 764 95 POEMS 90   39
NONCOMS
    an host of overjoyed noncoms (first knocking on the . . . . . 339 VIVA 30   8
NONDESCRIPT
    nausea A vast wordless nondescript genie of trunk trickled .   96 & POST IMPR 8   33
NONE
    are young some old none look alike the flics . . . . 274 IS 5 TWO 9   4
    deep weather then or none let's feel all) mind . . . . 364 VIVA 55   14
    and lifepreservers there are none: and waves which only . . . 438 NO THANKS 54   26
    alert, of languages there's none but well she knows; . . . . 575 1 X 1 35   28
    being all, escape from none) so huge a tumult . . . . 609 (CHAIRE) 11   4
    a rose (i have none) "don't cry dear violet . . . . 684 95 POEMS 12   2

	PAGE	TITLE	LINE

NONE (CONTINUED)
    eyes for mind with none) boy after girl each . . . . 716 95 POEMS 44   9
    breathing creature feels (but none can think) a learning . . 735 95 POEMS 63   8
NONELASTIC
    well attend! list, every nonelastic male-- uplook, all . . . 398 NO THANKS 15   17
+NONENTITIES
    FOR CONTEXT, SEE . . . . 391 NO THANKS 8   23
NONEXISTENCE
    so And How much nonexistence eye sed bea yew . . . . 474 NEW POEMS 12   9
    day (shrived of that nonexistence millions call life, you . . 745 95 POEMS 73   9
    more less: until her-and-his nonexistence vanishes with also 808 73 POEMS 36   12
NONGLANCE
    capable of a largest nonglance the least unsmile or . . . . . 359 VIVA 50   16
NONILLION
    unworld crash to 1 nonillion (& so) nothings each . . . . . 728 95 POEMS 56   13
NONLEAF
    .crowned the with shrill Nonleaf daemons and large The . . . 346 VIVA 37   27
NONLEGS
    's unstreet with treadwatering nonlegs (strictly) smiling / / 616 {CHAIRE} 18   16
NONS
    nouns wan wan too nons too and and nuns . . . . 508 50 POEMS 22   4
    / who (at her nons- elf 's unself too . . . . 704 95 POEMS 32   2
+NONSELF'S
    FOR CONTEXT, SEE . . . . 704 95 POEMS 32   2
NONSENSE
    Are in the beautiful nonsense of twilight and somebody . . . 63 T&C PORTRAIT 10   38
    surly old gurgle a nonsense of sparrows, the cathedral . . . 282 IS 5 THREE 6   12
    any) heart--wholly, idiotically--before such nonsense which . 480 NEW POEMS 18   5
    every enormous piece of nonsense which itself must call . . . 561 1 X 1 21   2
    doting and nothing and nonsense --alive; we're alive, dear: . 665 {CHAIRE} 67   10
NONSUFFICIENTLY
    / / / one nonsufficiently inunderstood re with some . . . . . 398 NO THANKS 15   1
NONSUN
    / / / / nonsun blob a cold to . . . . 541 1 X 1 1   1
NONTHINGS
    face) large one coloured nonthings of gluttonous sky-- nor . 402 NO THANKS 19   8
+NONTHINKABLE
    FOR CONTEXT, SEE . . . . 803 73 POEMS 31   10
NONVISIBLY
    uh" pause "Cookie but" nonvisibly smi- ling through man . . . 464 NEW POEMS 2   17
NOON
    of morning stilled in noon-- noon the implacable bassoon-- . 12 T&C SONGS 2   46
    morning stilled in noon-- noon the implacable bassoon-- now . 12 T&C SONGS 2   47
    e very w here noon e is exc ep . . . . 830 73 POEMS 58   9
NOONE
    hard great eyes to noone in particular she gasped . . . . . . 53 T&C PORTRAIT 1   45
    lip i swear (to noone everyone) constitutes undying; or . . . 264 IS 5 ONE 33   2
    terror of shrines which noone has suspected (but wherein . . 285 IS 5 FOUR 2   17
    is undead who, living, noone is. I have never . . . . 360 VIVA 51   29
    Ghost is dead (whom noone might inter fleeing himself . . . . 394 NO THANKS 11   5
    invite me to become noone except yourselves r s . . . . 504 50 POEMS 18   5
    winter spring summer) that noone loved him more by . . . . . 515 50 POEMS 29   12
    died i guess (and noone stooped to kiss his . . . . 515 50 POEMS 29   26
    they dream their sleep noone and anyone earth by . . . . . . 515 50 POEMS 29   31
    / / / / noone" autumnal this great lady's . . . . 626 {CHAIRE} 28   1
    been born everyone is noone dance around the snowman . . . . 630 {CHAIRE} 32   15
    kenly) mind me of noone i ever & someone . . . . 695 95 POEMS 23   11
    and such a darkness noone can quite begin to . . . . 717 95 POEMS 45   7
    / / / / noone and a star stand, ... 721 95 POEMS 49   1
    merciful sweetness except Himself?" --"noone unless it's a . 748 95 POEMS 76   15
    poor-- let's love until noone could quite be (and . . . . . . 769 95 POEMS 95   24
    almost someone always who's noone) a noone who, till . . . . 812 73 POEMS 40   4
    always who's noone) a noone who, till their and . . . . . . 812 73 POEMS 40   5
NOONE'S
    all things) dream is noone's fool; if this wind . . . . . . 292 IS 5 FOUR 9   10
    --laughing to find a noone's more by far than . . . . 716 95 POEMS 44   30
NOONES
    / / / hush) noones are coming out in . . . . 600 {CHAIRE} 2   2

	PAGE	TITLE	LINE
NOR			
i am wholly dead: nor ever did on such	17	T&C PUELLA MEA	35
undertake Medea's rescuing eyes; nor he when swooned the . .	18	T&C PUELLA MEA	72
lack for beauty there, nor he that will amaying	20	T&C PUELLA MEA	169
those ladies nothing care nor any lady dead and	21	T&C PUELLA MEA	180
matter to the sun, nor will rain care cautiously	84	T&C SON ACTU 3	8
confuse the clever hair nor rout the young mouth	85	T&C SON ACTU 4	7
i do not speak nor think nor am aware	98	& POST IMPR 9	14
not speak nor think nor am aware of anything	98	& POST IMPR 9	14
empty twilight cannot grieve nor the autumn, as i	165	& SON ACTU 14	9
logic happens beneath will; nor can these moments be	264	IS 5 ONE 33	6
days slobber in vain: Nor am i afraid that	293	IS 5 FOUR 10	22
by ; neither you nor i and by the	335	VIVA 26	19
and thou shalt stand. Nor any dusk but kneelingly	351	VIVA 42	13
be a pansy heaven nor a fragile heaven of	352	VIVA 43	2
any echo of dream nor any flowering of any	368	VIVA 59	5
sternly much not life nor stop as a tear	371	VIVA 62	26
fears beyond their ceaselessness (nor has a syllable of . . .	372	VIVA 63	11
actual cool stupendous is nor may truth opening encompass . .	373	VIVA 64	16
don't All suspect each (nor have i observed some	391	NO THANKS 8	4
who may envy neither; nor bewail (would rather make	394	NO THANKS 11	10
nonthings of gluttonous sky-- nor (as a blind, how	402	NO THANKS 19	9
might live) yes, partly nor some edgeless star could	414	NO THANKS 31	9
patient mind unstrange learn (nor could all earth's rotting .	420	NO THANKS 37	8
which thinks it thinks, nor dares to feel (but	424	NO THANKS 41	10
and ever shall be nor every partialness beats one	425	NO THANKS 42	11
unfree undeaths who live nor shall they be and	440	NO THANKS 56	35
life this poet arose nor hate nor grief can	441	NO THANKS 56	43
poet arose nor hate nor grief can go where	441	NO THANKS 56	43
droops, all measures bend nor marvel if a thought	446	NO THANKS 61	7
/ / / / nor woman (just as it	472	NEW POEMS 10	1
more h u sh nor child) / / /	472	NEW POEMS 10	18
robins never welcome spring nor flatfolk prove their world .	511	50 POEMS 25	17
their world is round nor dingsters die at break	511	50 POEMS 25	18
would be neither fantastic nor pathological but dumb. The . .	514	50 POEMS 28	4
very now we stand nor a first rose explodes	538	50 POEMS 50	13
(only aware) kind neither nor cruel (only complete) i	564	1 X 1 24	7
No doing shall undo (nor madness nor mere death	577	1 X 1 37	10
shall undo (nor madness nor mere death nor both	577	1 X 1 37	10
madness nor mere death nor both who is la	577	1 X 1 37	10
i not you behold nor any breathing creature this?	582	1 X 1 42	11
love himself: who's we --nor can you die or	601	{CHAIRE} 3	18
(neither awake are goddesses nor sleeping) since he's young .	617	{CHAIRE} 19	9
grow; and (there--see?) children" nor might any earth's first	626	{CHAIRE} 28	12
are flowers neither why nor how when is now	630	{CHAIRE} 32	10
general yas buy gad) nor asleep booted & spurred	640	{CHAIRE} 42	4
foot five) neither dead nor alive (in real the	640	{CHAIRE} 42	15
ways are neither reasoned nor unreasoned, his wisdom cancels	683	95 POEMS 11	5
kiss neither beholding a nor seen by some that	698	95 POEMS 26	7
my annie is one nor she wouldn't be seen	707	95 POEMS 35	12
"parity" in l'ho tel nor man (rue d e	708	95 POEMS 36	12
heartbeat of this child; nor shall even prevail a	714	95 POEMS 42	11
ourselves like living neither nor dead these (or many	743	95 POEMS 71	5
(and he takes all) nor any marvel finds quite	750	95 POEMS 78	12
that some neither ape nor angel called a man	807	73 POEMS 35	7
so subhuman superminds declare --nor all their times	817	73 POEMS 45	4
NORM			
rapidly upon the jiggled norm of agony my grunting	137	& SON REAL 8	9
NORMAL			
carnival where to a normal melody of probable violins	43	T&C AMORES 7	32
small, exact, stupid. mouth normal, large, unclever. hair .	103	& POST IMPR 13	13
spring handfuls of little normal worms. Dress deftly your . .	161	& SON ACTU 10	8
Evening Something in the normal window. and a cat.	166	& SON ACTU 15	8
vulgarity: a sodden fastidious normal explosion; a square . .	201	XLI PORTRAIT 9	12
such, or such, the normal corners of your heart	292	IS 5 FOUR 9	14
(but only sameness is normal in Ever-Ever Land for	466	NEW POEMS 4	25
think it strange that normal mortals can not justify	731	95 POEMS 59	3

NORMALITY
    and graze of splintered normality crackle and sag of . . . . 48 T&C IMPRESS 2   5
+NORMANDY
    FOR CONTEXT, SEE . . . . 708 95 POEMS 36   12
NORTH
    wild roses sometimes) with north over the barn / . . . . . . 512 50 POEMS 26   34
NOSE
    the wart on her nose what she'll do to . . . . 25 T&C CHANSONS 2   18
    / / / between nose-red gross walls sprawling with . . . . . . 55 T&C PORTRAIT 3   1
    thick lids. the chunklike nose on which always the . . . . . 73 T&C SON REAL 4   8
) K ing my Nose puts on sharp robes . . . . 94 & POST IMPR 6   9
    an old pool. Her nose was small, exact, stupid. . . . . 103 & POST IMPR 13   13
    woman with the crimson nose and coquettishly- cocked bonnet . 196 XLI PORTRAIT 4   4
    notable of the sultan's nose pullable and rosy flanked . . . 198 XLI PORTRAIT 6   9
    grin (with what was nose upwrinkled into nothing earthly, . . 226 IS 5 ONE MAME   3
    wing spirit prowls, its nose winces before a dissonance . . . 319 VIVA 11   11
NOSE-RED
    / / / between nose-red gross walls sprawling with . . . . . . 55 T&C PORTRAIT 3   1
NOSING
    us ly; though hither nosing lymoles cru. Ising thither: . . . 361 VIVA 52   11
NOSTER
    / / / the Noster was a ship of . . . . 494 50 POEMS 8   1
NOSTRILS
    one army. From her nostrils to her feet she . . . . 135 & SON REAL 6   2
    have seduced the mightier nostrils of the fervent dead, . . . 212 XLI SONNETS 8   6
NOT
    WORD DELETED, APPEARED 363 TIMES
+NOT-MERE-LY-WON-DER-ING-&
    s(not a fraid of moon You)not-mere-ly-won-der-ing-& . . . . 469 NEW POEMS 7   20
NOTABLE
    over the door very notable of the sultan's nose . . . . 198 XLI PORTRAIT 6   8
    Hotel du Golf... that notable structure or ideal edifice... . 319 VIVA 11   22
NOTALIVE
    die fly do? a notalive undead too-nearishness and shall . . . 528 50 POEMS 40   5
NOTB
    sentence we both consid (notb- notbr- notbre- notbrea-k . . . 398 NO THANKS 15   12
NOTBR
    we both consid (notb- notbr- notbre- notbrea-k . The . . . . 398 NO THANKS 15   12
NOTBRE
    both consid (notb- notbr- notbre- notbrea-k . The kid) . . . 398 NO THANKS 15   12
NOTBREA
    consid (notb- notbr- notbre- notbrea-k . The kid) er . . . . 398 NO THANKS 15   12
NOTBREA-K
    consid (notb- notbr- notbre- notbrea-k . The kid) er . . . . 398 NO THANKS 15   12
NOTBUSY
    exit little mr Big notbusy Busi ness notman (. . . . . . . 389 NO THANKS 6   4
NOTCHING
    as in the hairy notching of clenched thighs a . . . . 151 & SON REAL 22   17
NOTE
    corners (Besides which, i note how fatally toward twilight . 345 VIVA 36   3
    history unquote might (publishers note) be entitled a . . . . 410 NO THANKS 27   10
+NOTE
    FOR CONTEXT, SEE . . . . 725 95 POEMS 53   1
NOTED
    as Dick Mid once noted lifting a Green River . . . . 229 IS 5 ONE FRAN   9
NOTGIRL'SWITH
    (a stopped A) with! notgirl'swith? dumb (thewith girl) ness . 388 NO THANKS 5   24
NOTHARD
    one are hard one notHard) not boys boy- ish . . . . 388 NO THANKS 5   22
NOTHING
    day and life be nothing, it shall not stop . . . . 13 T&C SONGS 3   21
    whose beauty did in nothing err. If to me . . . . 21 T&C PUELLA MEA 174
    i for those ladies nothing care nor any lady . . . . 21 T&C PUELLA MEA 179
    been sometimes true to Nothing and which lives they . . . . . 43 T&C AMORES 7   12
    strenuous lips of incorruptible Nothing under the ample sun, . 43 T&C AMORES 7   38
    "kitty" twice eight --beer nothing, the lady'll have a . . . 74 T&C SON REAL 5   13
    musical light of sudden nothing.... la bocca mia "he . . . . 84 T&C SON ACTU 3   15
    squinting who's a wink bum-nothing and money fuzzily mouths . 96 & POST IMPR 8   19

NOTHING (CONTINUED)

	PAGE	TITLE	LINE
that, or this or nothing or an old man	102	& POST IMPR 12	13
grins each an intaglio. Nothing has also carved upon	116	& PORTRAIT 9	8
to something or to nothing as much as being	141	& SON REAL 12	13
seen, which has got nothing on something as i	141	& SON REAL 12	15
organised hills an edged nothing begins to prune let's . . .	160	& SON ACTU 9	9
whole, an inch of nothing for your soul. /	161	& SON ACTU 10	14
forget-- wherefore is there nothing left to guess: the . . .	173	& SON ACTU 22	13
at the corner of Nothing and Something, we heard	174	& SON ACTU 23	14
or between squeals of Nothing grabbed with circular shrieking	195	XLI PORTRAIT 7	14
big hunk of irrevocable nothing which touch and taste	199	XLI PORTRAIT 7	2
He without Whose favour nothing is (being of men	210	XLI SONNETS 6	3
thy lips beautifully embrace nothing and when thy bashful . .	210	XLI SONNETS 6	13
thinking very much of nothing and whom dawn loves	211	XLI SONNETS 7	17
/ / / come nothing to my comparable soul	212	XLI SONNETS 8	1
was nose upwrinkled into nothing earthly, while the slippery	226	IS 5 ONE MAME	3
story of Mr Do -nothing the wellknown parvenu who	236	IS 5 ONE 7	4
got through with Do- nothing Do -nothing could do	236	IS 5 ONE 7	10
with Do- nothing Do -nothing could do nothing which	236	IS 5 ONE 7	11
Do -nothing could do nothing which you and i	236	IS 5 ONE 7	12
to me to you nothing is what particularly matters	238	IS 5 ONE 9	16
with dam next to nothing on) tangoing (while a	242	IS 5 ONE 13	5
uncle Frank has done nothing for many years but	253	IS 5 ONE 24	5
rise one hand did nothing on the vest its	258	IS 5 ONE 28	17
while meaning its opposite? Nothing could be clearer to . . .	263	IS 5 ONE 32	40
pants earth's biggest grafter, nothing less; the Honorable .	266	IS 5 TWO 1	33
lookingly wanders There is nothing left of the world	278	IS 5 THREE 2	17
the blond hair of nothing / / / /	289	IS 5 FOUR 6	24
beyond these elements remarkably nothing is.... therefore,	291	IS 5 FOUR 8	17
which lives) and since nothing lingers beyond a little . . .	293	IS 5 FOUR 10	9
same thing as perhaps nothing, he murmurs carefully lying . .	299	IS 5 FOUR 16	16
most wise music stole nothing from death"-- you only	306	IS 5 FIVE 5	10
ado about less than nothing) 2 boston Dolls; found	317	VIVA 9	23
demotic) Miss Gay had nothing to say to the	326	VIVA 18	29
and the animals had nothing to say to Miss	326	VIVA 18	29
but granted that it's nothing paradoxically enough beyond . .	329	VIVA 20	1
really petals and see nothing with the face of	352	VIVA 43	11
by way of saying nothing he smiled (but just	355	VIVA 46	4
do Not sleep matters nothing; then (then the only	359	VIVA 50	14
snow carefully everywhere descending; nothing which we are to	366	VIVA 57	13
/ / / nothing is more exactly terrible	375	VIVA 66	1
(if you can withholding nothing) World, conceive a man . . .	420	NO THANKS 37	14
When (out of sheer nothing) came a huger than	432	NO THANKS 49	15
Hearts being sick, Minds nothing can: if Hate's a	438	NO THANKS 54	22
how very) closely than Nothing, remember love by frequent . .	453	NO THANKS 68	8
out of serene perfectly Nothing hurled into young Now	456	NO THANKS 71	7
cellophane against anything (because nothing really exists /	470	NEW POEMS 8	20
and may myself do nothing usefully and love yourself	481	NEW POEMS 19	9
making silence two-made-of-one & nothing tells anywhere "snow	483	NEW POEMS 21	7
yourself become. Girlboys may nothing more than boygirls . .	484	NEW POEMS 22	5
and we aint got nothing to smoke: come on	489	50 POEMS 3	3
and we aint got nothing to sing; come on	489	50 POEMS 3	7
and we aint got Nothing to die, come on	489	50 POEMS 3	11
and we aint got nothing to dream (come on	489	50 POEMS 3	15
: never, no (body. Nothing / / / /	490	50 POEMS 4	22
out of merely not nothing comes only one snowflake	502	50 POEMS 16	13
born) when and if nothing disappears they will disappear . .	505	50 POEMS 19	18
joy and overing grief nothing arrives a so prodigious	517	50 POEMS 31	10
inherit, all bequeath and nothing quite so least as	521	50 POEMS 34	65
suit there every -thing nothing i say the world	523	50 POEMS 36	25
with and give him nothing (if he should not	531	50 POEMS 43	12
tly) smiles the infinite nothing of M an /	534	50 POEMS 46	22
pain or joy) does nothing except preexist its hoi	544	1 X 1 4	7
lipshits pres (who always nothing says) and he kissed	552	1 X 1 12	27
snow less quite is nothing but herself, and than	573	1 X 1 33	16
/ / / / / nothing false and possible is	574	1 X 1 34	1
your honour, my loveliest, nothing may move may rest	575	1 X 1 35	4
for centuries and (except nothing) nothing's won --but if . .	580	1 X 1 40	18

NOTHING (CONTINUED)

any breathing creature this? nothing except the impossible .	582	1 X 1 42	12
these (whom; pretends blue nothing) are built of soon	584	1 X 1 44	2
could sing but like nothing are the joys of	587	1 X 1 47	4
we go yes) there's nothing as something as one	594	1 X 1 54	9
the high that does nothing but fall (with a	594	1 X 1 54	32
a two ne like nothing verdi slightly knu as	602	(CHAIRE) 4	3
silence sings not into nothing and nothing into never	633	(CHAIRE) 35	13
not into nothing and nothing into never and never	633	(CHAIRE) 35	13
act of christian love. "Nothing" in 1944 A D	636	(CHAIRE) 38	9
yes closer made of nothing except loneliness / /	648	(CHAIRE) 50	11
the reality of all nothing will actually lift a	649	(CHAIRE) 51	4
who's also you) and nothing less than excellent E	650	(CHAIRE) 52	11
newlY Born) he knows nothing, and feels everything; all . . .	657	(CHAIRE) 59	2
/ / / / (nothing whichful about thick big	658	(CHAIRE) 60	1
himself of a boulder) nothing mean in tenderly whoms	658	(CHAIRE) 60	5
spruce by tamarack (nothing pampered puny impatient and . .	658	(CHAIRE) 60	22
pampered puny impatient and nothing ignoble) everywhere . .	658	(CHAIRE) 60	24
vast most nothing's own nothing children go of dust	661	(CHAIRE) 63	14
the no of all nothing--human merely being doubt unimaginable	663	(CHAIRE) 65	11
love: with us they've nothing times nothing to do	664	(CHAIRE) 66	11
us they've nothing times nothing to do (for love	664	(CHAIRE) 66	11
keeping is doting and nothing and nonsense --alive; we're . .	665	(CHAIRE) 67	10
moon, she is you nothing may, quite your my	666	(CHAIRE) 68	11
life will do) loves nothing as much as how	676	95 POEMS 4	16
(& daunted by always nothing) you darling diminutive person .	678	95 POEMS 6	3
forever) is Less Than Nothing (which would have been	702	95 POEMS 30	22
what got him was nothing / / /	702	95 POEMS 30	23
beautiful darling) believe in nothing but love / /	717	95 POEMS 45	14
flame) united by perfect nothing: millionary wherewhens . . .	721	95 POEMS 49	4
glories we've agreed with nothing deeper than our minds . . .	741	95 POEMS 69	8
a million thousand hundred nothing seem --we are himself's .	756	95 POEMS 84	13
vastnesses of orish mind --nothing believable inhabits here:	761	95 POEMS 88	5
and (to quite become nothing) five times, proclaim fate . . .	764	95 POEMS 90	52
(quick to seize each nothing which all soulless wraiths . . .	765	95 POEMS 91	3
love will end; where nothing is to breathe to	768	95 POEMS 94	3
whom always i do nothing) deepens with wind (and	785	73 POEMS 13	5
/ / / / "nothing" the unjust man complained	806	73 POEMS 34	1
not knowable night's utmost nothing, wanders a little guess .	810	73 POEMS 38	2
down to dream of (nothing i or any somebody	816	73 POEMS 44	10
answer: and such vivid nothing as green meteors swim	818	73 POEMS 46	11
(chr ist) what absolute nothing / / / /	823	73 POEMS 51	20
to kiss) where everything's nothing --arise, my soul; and . .	834	73 POEMS 62	29
of wind-- scatter his nothing all over what angry	839	73 POEMS 67	12
who's O cean (everywhere nothing but light and dark;	840	73 POEMS 68	23

+NOTHING

FOR CONTEXT, SEE	101	& POST IMPR 11	74
FOR CONTEXT, SEE	237	IS 5 ONE 8	7
FOR CONTEXT, SEE	259	IS 5 ONE 29	28
FOR CONTEXT, SEE	278	IS 5 THREE 2	18
FOR CONTEXT, SEE	310	VIVA 2	10
FOR CONTEXT, SEE	430	NO THANKS 47	21
FOR CONTEXT, SEE	547	1 X 1 7	9
FOR CONTEXT, SEE	655	(CHAIRE) 57	12
FOR CONTEXT, SEE	702	95 POEMS 30	1
FOR CONTEXT, SEE	797	73 POEMS 25	5
FOR CONTEXT, SEE	814	73 POEMS 42	1
FOR CONTEXT, SEE	819	73 POEMS 47	6

NOTHING'S

saviours --flop grasshopper, exactly nothing's soon; scream,	555	1 X 1 15	8
death to was) --all nothing's only our hugest home;	560	1 X 1 20	23
centuries and (except nothing) nothing's won --but if a . . .	580	1 X 1 40	18
unborn (here less than nothing's more than everything) death,	592	1 X 1 52	12
only truth is gay (nothing's false, in earth in	651	(CHAIRE) 53	7
drifting through vast most nothing's own nothing children go	661	(CHAIRE) 63	14
was Noth ing & nothing's exAct ly what any	702	95 POEMS 30	2

NOTHINGLY

soft neverwheres & sweet nothingly gushing tinsel; silently .	480	NEW POEMS 18	11

	PAGE	TITLE	LINE

NOTHINGNESS
breath drive them in nothingness for we would sleep . . . . . 41 T&C AMORES 5   22
descend the path to nothingness (cruel now cancels kind; . . 834 73 POEMS 62   2
NOTHINGS
1 nonillion (& so) nothings each (let's kiss) means . . . . . 728 95 POEMS 56   13
+NOTHINGS
FOR CONTEXT, SEE . . . . 442 NO THANKS 57   7
NOTHURT
which had always not nothurt me not much and . . . . 262 IS 5 ONE 32   16
NOTICE
/ / / / notice the convulsed orange inch . . . . 86 T&C SON ACTU 5   1
motheaten forum be aware notice what hath remained --the . . 260 IS 5 ONE 30   3
o'clock and these (i notice) trees winterbrief surly old . . 282 IS 5 THREE 6   11
the moon if you'll notice follows us like a . . . . 303 IS 5 FIVE 2   10
i implore you to notice how the keen ship . . . . 378 VIVA 69   3
+NOTICE
FOR CONTEXT, SEE . . . . 727 95 POEMS 55   1
NOTICED
out of eyes which noticed nobody he looked as . . . . 258 IS 5 ONE 28   15
impressed by having once noticed (as an infantile phenomenon) 262 IS 5 ONE 32   10
NOTIFIED
of which assertions duly notified threw the yellowsonofabitch 339 VIVA 30   35
NOTING
forgot frivolity in lowliness, noting the fatal flight of . . 81 T&C SON UNRE 6   4
click of ivory balls.... noting flies, which jerk upon . . . 217 XLI SONNETS 13   3
NOTION
not occur (alarm ing notion for idealists? so what) . . . . . 790 73 POEMS 18   11
NOTMAN
Big notbusy Busi ness notman (! ye galleon . . . . 389 NO THANKS 6   6
NOTRE
a pissoir enters abruptly Notre Dame (whereas de gustibus . . 245 IS 5 ONE 16   23
NOTS
grin-- dancing to feel nots are their whys stones . . . . . 716 95 POEMS 44   22
NOTSELFPITYING
particulary) live that undeluded notselfpitying lover of all 607 {CHAIRE} 9   9
NOTSOFT
diskface, es (are two notSoft soft one are hard . . . . . . 388 NO THANKS 5   21
NOTWITHSTANDING
on the top of notwithstanding with his censored up . . . . 642 {CHAIRE} 44   25
NOUN
beneath the body's breathing noun (moreover the delicious . . 21 T&C PUELLA MEA 211
NOUNS
/ / / / nouns to nouns wan wan . . . . 508 50 POEMS 22   1
/ / nouns to nouns wan wan too nons . . . . 508 50 POEMS 22   1
until (over dull all nouns) begins a whole verbal . . . . . 557 1 X 1 17   14
NOURISH
lifting hopes and hands --nourish my failure with thy . . . . 456 NO THANKS 71   14
NOUS
(Marie Vierge Priez Pour Nous) with the long lips . . . . . . 120 & PORTRAIT 12   18
i want to die nous sommes heureux my soul . . . . 133 & SON REAL 4   18
and i .... cheri.... nous sommes / / / . . . . 133 & SON REAL 4   23
perspective of the (hei -nous thought) otherwise immaculately 267 IS 5 TWO 2   16
NOVEMBER
rainbow mind and soul november and april) who younger . . . . 575 1 X 1 35   35
--cry nay: cry yea-- november would be may that . . . . . . 798 73 POEMS 26   21
at the gold of november sunset (and feeling: that . . . . . 824 73 POEMS 52   5
NOVEMBER'S
moved by standing in november's may) from whose (if . . . . . 420 NO THANKS 37   4
but april's day transcends november's year (eternity being so 765 95 POEMS 91   12
NOVOCAINE
when i timidly hinted "novocaine?" the eyes outstart, curl, . 226 IS 5 ONE MAME   12
NOW
into bright air, for now the red leaps in . . . . 4 T&C EPITHALAM   61
perfumed paraphrase of death). Now is the time when . . . . . 6 T&C EPITHALAM   121
noon the implacable bassoon-- now Twilight seeks the thrill . 12 T&C SONGS 2   48
clutter of trite jewels now like a moth with . . . . 47 T&C IMPRESS 1   7
the accurate boy mouth now droops the faun head . . . . . . 54 T&C PORTRAIT 2   9
droops the faun head now the intimate flower dreams . . . . . 54 T&C PORTRAIT 2   10

NOW (CONTINUED)

the stern texture of Now the arrow and the	112	& PORTRAIT 6	80
the here we are now judgment day cross the	118	& PORTRAIT 10	40
i don't know tenuous Now- spears and The Then-arrows	160	& SON ACTU 9	15
my friends let us now sing each and all	230	IS 5 ONE 2	36
what's become of Maeterlinck now that April's here? (ask . .	233	IS 5 ONE 4	22
/ / / / now dis "daughter" uv eve	240	IS 5 ONE 11	1
(adjustin his robe) who now puts on his flat	240	IS 5 ONE 11	4
were in Love once? now her mouth opens too	243	IS 5 ONE 14	11
dear somehow quickyes when (now, dark dear oh) the	251	IS 5 ONE 22	13
O yes beautiful we now pass through the look	257	IS 5 ONE 27	32
to be a metope now that triglyph's here) /	257	IS 5 ONE 27	40
little darlings, let us now passionately remember how-- . . .	266	IS 5 TWO 1	16
/ / / / now that fierce few flowers	277	IS 5 THREE 1	1
is washed with tone now for a moon to	282	IS 5 THREE 6	15
if i should say Now the all saucers but	287	IS 5 FOUR 4	15
my mind always But now she sharpens and becomes	301	IS 5 FOUR 18	12
in considerable twilight touch (now) with a suddenly unsaid .	302	IS 5 FIVE 1	5
big yellow dog that's.... now it's red a big	303	IS 5 FIVE 2	12
our dreams began which now are folded: but the	304	IS 5 FIVE 3	8
, mean- hum a) now (nit y unb uria	309	VIVA 1	3
a littl e nibble now And then bite) candy	314	VIVA 6	11
of walls) an electromagnetic (now I've lost the) Einstein . .	315	VIVA 7	4
tho thcared giggling lithped now we muthn't pleathe don't . .	316	VIVA 8	7
did lie Down, honestly now who go (BANG (BANG	317	VIVA 9	38
male to look at (now -fed infantile eyes drooling	337	VIVA 28	5
bE rich from-soft quits (now) ly Comes; : lush	342	VIVA 33	21
that please stroke for now stroke answers (but now	343	VIVA 34	4
now stroke answers (but now don't you're hurting o	343	VIVA 34	5
killing) death is like now That please squirtnowing for . . .	343	VIVA 34	7
we're replies (at which now O fear turned o	343	VIVA 34	10
O fear turned o Now handspring trans forming it	343	VIVA 34	10
curvingly while reacts (sharp now with blood now accurately .	344	VIVA 35	6
(sharp now with blood now accurately wan) keenly, to	344	VIVA 35	6
deathmoney into spiralS and Now (comes un, season of	346	VIVA 37	19
(moon begins The) now, est hills er dream;	350	VIVA 41	12
loved you dear as now i love behold this	360	VIVA 51	10
loved you dear as now i love god's terrible	360	VIVA 51	20
loved you dear as now i love. Hell (by	360	VIVA 51	30
loved you dear as now i love / /	360	VIVA 51	35
(or as these emerging now hills invent the air)	372	VIVA 63	2
tinying time (into supreme Now: feeling memory shrink from .	373	VIVA 64	12
dark ness. sunlight's thenlike? now Disappears some thing . .	397	NO THANKS 14	18
your wife said she now said he) ow said	399	NO THANKS 16	23
with (feel) pauseless immeasurably Now cancels the childfully	402	NO THANKS 19	3
but just (nude eel) now little joe lives on	410	NO THANKS 27	4
are.) & som ewhereishbudofshape now, s tI r ghost	423	NO THANKS 40	23
feet almost walk air). now who stops. Smiles. he	437	NO THANKS 53	17
vast ness. Be) look now (come soul; & :	448	NO THANKS 63	14
Nothing hurled into young Now entirely arrives gesture past .	456	NO THANKS 71	8
"I think he might now be inclined to describe	464	NEW POEMS 2	21
fragrance of pasture and now ti p toe ingt	469	NEW POEMS 7	14
woman for all her now: but we've such freedom	491	50 POEMS 5	14
how big very them) now (it tears off rag	501	50 POEMS 15	11
yes. The place is now let us accept (the	504	50 POEMS 18	13
before they died squirming: now withered and unself her . . .	506	50 POEMS 20	4
both eyes love this now of the sky --endlings	512	50 POEMS 26	12
over the why (it's now, boys) here we come	513	50 POEMS 27	34
by more when by now and tree by leaf	515	50 POEMS 29	13
round blue but quite now it's swirly and foldish	516	50 POEMS 30	6
put some just a now and now little the	516	50 POEMS 30	10
just a now and now little the (on his	516	50 POEMS 30	10
joy her flower than now (softlying wisdoms enter guess) . . .	518	50 POEMS 32	8
wick id id ar (now heer we kum dearie)	519	50 POEMS 33	14
steer and pure so now and now so yes	520	50 POEMS 34	23
pure so now and now so yes the wrists	520	50 POEMS 34	23
must through unstrange synthetic now true histories plunge? .	527	50 POEMS 39	26
from madame death neverless now and without winter spring? .	531	50 POEMS 43	10

	PAGE	TITLE	LINE

NOW (CONTINUED)

	PAGE	TITLE	LINE
or (a) new (live) now ; & th (is	532	50 POEMS 44	8
n d fall which now drop who all dreamlike	536	50 POEMS 48	20
and on forever's very now we stand nor a	538	50 POEMS 50	12
him pay with his now. But over a (see	543	1 X 1 3	24
"yes: you may sleep now, my mountain" and this	555	1 X 1 15	15
earth's any which Weavingly now one by wonder (on	557	1 X 1 17	11
truth of an eternal now welcomes each was of	558	1 X 1 18	5
complain --plunged in eternal now if who're by the	561	1 X 1 21	9
ugly beautiful most is now) / / / /	565	1 X 1 25	16
the deathboard where all now turns when (love's a	574	1 X 1 34	6
forever is love's any now and her each here	576	1 X 1 36	9
away still further: into now / / / /	579	1 X 1 39	14
any most very amazing now or here) let pitiless	580	1 X 1 40	3
impossible shall occur --see! now himself uplifts of stars .	582	1 X 1 42	13
(sing! every joy) --wholly now disappear night's not eternal	582	1 X 1 42	14
april's they this if now or this (young trembling	583	1 X 1 43	8
--but beauty is more now than dying's when /	592	1 X 1 52	14
forever was never till now now i love you	594	1 X 1 54	27
was never till now now i love you and	594	1 X 1 54	28
mere until (eternally) with (now) luminous the shadow of . .	601	(CHAIRE) 3	15
/ / swim so now million many worlds in	603	(CHAIRE) 5	1
whose brother married Heart, now Mrs Death. Poor Mind	621	(CHAIRE) 23	4
so she did and now stars shine at night	622	(CHAIRE) 24	7
hear him still if now our sun is gone	624	(CHAIRE) 26	22
sorrow a system-- if now than forever could never	625	(CHAIRE) 27	21
nor how when is now and which is Who	630	(CHAIRE) 32	11
(least all turns almost now; now almost swims into	633	(CHAIRE) 35	9
all turns almost now; now almost swims into a	633	(CHAIRE) 35	9
me can't you see now no not any christ	638	(CHAIRE) 40	12
the crumb of our Now) twiceuponatime wave-- put out	639	(CHAIRE) 41	12
to be in finland now that russia's here) swing	641	(CHAIRE) 43	2
fall at last perfection, now and here --but look:	650	(CHAIRE) 52	17
when come into the now of forever come riding	661	(CHAIRE) 63	12
being doubt unimaginable You? (now the ears of my	663	(CHAIRE) 65	13
my ears awake and now the eyes of my	663	(CHAIRE) 65	14
dear: it's (kiss me now) spring! now the pretty	665	(CHAIRE) 67	11
(kiss me now) spring! now the pretty birds hover	665	(CHAIRE) 67	12
she and so he now the little fish quiver	665	(CHAIRE) 67	13
you and so i (now the mountains are dancing, ...	665	(CHAIRE) 67	14
/ / / / now all the fingers of	667	(CHAIRE) 69	1
world can understand and now you are and i	667	(CHAIRE) 69	5
are and i am now and we're a mystery	667	(CHAIRE) 69	5
and shining this our now must come to then	667	(CHAIRE) 69	8
/ / / / now air is air and	675	95 POEMS 3	1
space. Mountains are mountains now; skies now are skies-- . .	675	95 POEMS 3	5
are mountains now; skies now are skies-- and such	675	95 POEMS 3	5
on its way to now -here / / /	676	95 POEMS 4	25
a doll & every now & then my wonderful	680	95 POEMS 8	22
i ever wear it now when the boy who	684	95 POEMS 12	6
roses (who amaze our now and here with paradise)	688	95 POEMS 16	8
in the Dust (trite now and old) lie we	690	95 POEMS 18	3
happened nowhere else imagine Now rapidly this (a forest . .	693	95 POEMS 21	10
of pitiful paper-- but now, as Mr bowing Cockatoo	697	95 POEMS 25	27
, what it Takes. now you know (just as	701	95 POEMS 29	9
ann" "she's coming right now in the rasberrypatch and	707	95 POEMS 35	23
sing and they whistle (now here is a job	709	95 POEMS 37	10
lisps "i'm busy right now" so rah-rah-rah democracy let's . .	711	95 POEMS 39	24
ver yw here) s Now / / / /	713	95 POEMS 41	11
than biggest (little is) now (dancing yes for) white	715	95 POEMS 43	14
self he was --but now that fiend and i	730	95 POEMS 58	5
fragrant mountains of eternal now to frolic in such	743	95 POEMS 71	12
time --ours is the now and here of freedom.	745	95 POEMS 73	14
merciful Him Whose only now is forever: standing erect . . .	749	95 POEMS 77	18
/ / / / now comes the good rain	754	95 POEMS 82	1
worlds are to dream now dreams are to breathe	755	95 POEMS 83	19
most prodigious Selves both now alive creatures (bright if .	757	95 POEMS 85	9
/ / / / now (more near ourselves than	760	95 POEMS 87	1

	PAGE	TITLE	LINE

NOW (CONTINUED)

/ / / / now what were motionless move	762	95 POEMS 89	1
may not measure a now of your treasure blithe	763	95 POEMS 90	36
then of winter equals now of spring; but april's	765	95 POEMS 91	11
live! die (forever is now) and dance you suddenly	767	95 POEMS 93	22
can kill is astir-- now dull eyes are keen	769	95 POEMS 95	10
eyes are keen and now keen eyes are keener	769	95 POEMS 95	10
precisely ours is the now to grow it's love	776	73 POEMS 4	16
/ / / / now is a ship which	781	73 POEMS 9	1
how) life like a (now with one sweet sun	786	73 POEMS 14	10
sweet sun in it, now with a million flaming	786	73 POEMS 14	13
coo) haps even 4 now man's most vast (unmind	787	73 POEMS 15	9
comprehend a marvellous artificer now Ugly was the husband .	799	73 POEMS 27	8
of (as happens every now and then upon a	799	73 POEMS 27	9
in his heaven says Now the timid the tender	801	73 POEMS 29	24
begin ning it is now and always will be	803	73 POEMS 31	14
/ / / / now that, more nearest even	809	73 POEMS 37	1
/ / / / Now i lay (with everywhere	816	73 POEMS 44	1
a gently welcoming darkestness-- now i lay me down	816	73 POEMS 44	5
is how beautifully snow) now i lay me down	816	73 POEMS 44	10
which nobody may keep. now i lay me down	816	73 POEMS 44	14
we never, but forever now (hosts of eternity; not	817	73 POEMS 45	5
e: s are silent now . in silverly notqu	820	73 POEMS 48	4
forsake a failing year --now, before quite your whisper's . .	821	73 POEMS 49	9
where and when beyond) now and here (far from	832	73 POEMS 60	8
/ / / / now does our world descend	834	73 POEMS 62	1
path to nothingness (cruel now cancels kind; friends turn . .	834	73 POEMS 62	3
doer's doom create is now contrive; imagined, merely know . .	834	73 POEMS 62	7
darkness and to fall (now wrong's the only right	834	73 POEMS 62	21
run run with me now jump shout (laugh dance	835	73 POEMS 63	16
here of amazing most now, with what thousands of	840	73 POEMS 68	29
drowned by prodigious a now of magnificent sound (which . . .	841	73 POEMS 69	12
are happy should his now go then / /	842	73 POEMS 70	14

+NOW

FOR CONTEXT, SEE	310	VIVA 2	5
FOR CONTEXT, SEE	347	VIVA 38	1
FOR CONTEXT, SEE	347	VIVA 38	16
FOR CONTEXT, SEE	385	NO THANKS 2	41
FOR CONTEXT, SEE	396	NO THANKS 13	4
FOR CONTEXT, SEE	398	NO THANKS 15	20
FOR CONTEXT, SEE	430	NO THANKS 47	4
FOR CONTEXT, SEE	445	NO THANKS 60	5
FOR CONTEXT, SEE	606	{CHAIRE} 8	5

NOWBROW

| blinked he belowtry eye nowbrow sangsung nee whitermuch grab | 333 | VIVA 24 | 9 |

NOWHERE

comes carefully out of Nowhere) arranging a window, into . .	124	& SEVEN POEMS 3	3
in a tree, somewhere nowhere and a little girl	281	IS 5 THREE 5	12
as (out from behind Nowhere) creeps the deep thing	330	VIVA 21	13
(into disappear and perfectly) nowhere vivid anonymous . . .	557	1 X 1 17	4
his grave and sprinkles nowhere with me and you?	560	1 X 1 20	20
who (on this busily nowhere rollingest it) 's the	590	1 X 1 50	11
the way from perfect nowhere came (as easily as	599	{CHAIRE} 1	12
to most perfect gay, nowhere to here, never to	649	{CHAIRE} 51	7
it ignoblest he to nowhere from arrive human the	662	{CHAIRE} 64	2
believing eyes adventuring, enormous nowhere from) querying .	669	{CHAIRE} 71	4
are we're; but also nowhere / / / /	686	95 POEMS 14	21
hopes despairs) Once happened nowhere else imagine Now . .	693	95 POEMS 21	8
spiralling ecstatically this proud nowhere of earth's most .	714	95 POEMS 42	2
innumerably singular strictly immeasurable nowhere flames . .	741	95 POEMS 69	3
much than dark most nowhere no particle is not	756	95 POEMS 84	7
the very quick of nowhere) we --While one thrush	758	95 POEMS 85	47
one (above nevermoving all nowhere) goldenly whole, ...	808	73 POEMS 36	5
of always and of nowhere) and what a gently	816	73 POEMS 44	3

+NOWHERE

FOR CONTEXT, SEE	421	NO THANKS 38	26
FOR CONTEXT, SEE	449	NO THANKS 64	7
FOR CONTEXT, SEE	479	NEW POEMS 17	2

	PAGE	TITLE	LINE

+NOWHERE (CONTINUED)
FOR CONTEXT, SEE . . . . 584 1 X 1 44   14
FOR CONTEXT, SEE . . . . 606 (CHAIRE) 8   15
FOR CONTEXT, SEE . . . . 676 95 POEMS 4   25
NOWHEREGOINGALWAYS
f-e-e-t-noWheregoingaLwaYS . . . . 345 VIVA 36   15
NOWHERES
at home in snowily nowheres of winter his silence) . . . . . 678 95 POEMS 6   11
NOWORLD
rosily , nimblest; c-urlin-g noworld Silent is blue (sleep! . 503 50 POEMS 17   8
NOWS
why dividing thens by nows and adding and (i . . . . 500 50 POEMS 14   6
are (me wander and nows to the power of . . . . 612 (CHAIRE) 14   3
NOYESIYOU
se! crumbs things? Its noyesiyou he-she (Weres / / . . . . . 417 NO THANKS 34   23
NUCLEOLUS
and behind) has a nucleolus: the Prefect of Police . . . . . 274 IS 5 TWO 9   26
NUCLEUS
organically arranged and their nucleus (composed of captains 274 IS 5 TWO 9   21
NUDE
shall dance upon the nude and final silence and . . . . . . 155 & SON ACTU 4   14
brittle candy but just (nude eel) now little joe . . . . . . 410 NO THANKS 27   4
NUDGE
look at each other. Nudge. (if they love each . . . . 171 & SON ACTU 20   10
rages Laughters jostle grins nudge smiles push--. deep into . 202 XLI PORTRAIT 9   37
(exchanging) e vero madonna (nudge whispershout) laugh . . . 681 95 POEMS 9   7
NUDGING
knuckling silent planes a nudging bulb silkenly brutal a . . 68 T&C POST IMPR 5   15
conventions exposes hidden obscenities nudging into neglected 203 XLI LA GUERRE 1   6
teem of Grand. a nudging froth of faces clogs . . . . 219 XLI SONNETS 15   10
+NUDGING
FOR CONTEXT, SEE . . . . 248 IS 5 ONE 19   15
NUDITY
twig of a neckless nudity (very occasionally budding a . . . 134 & SON REAL 5   6
NUISANCE
emit a tiny violetflavoured nuisance: Odor? ono. comes out . 231 IS 5 ONE 3   53
NUISANCES
you are continually committing nuisances but more especially 204 XLI LA GUERRE 2   15
NUJOLNEEDING-
littleliverpill- hearted-Nujolneeding-There's-A-Reason . . . 231 IS 5 ONE 3   47
NUMB
split "Pretty Baby" to numb rhythm before christ / . . . . . 106 & PORTRAIT 2   15
of fragile huge humanity.... Numb thoughts, kicking in the . 174 & SON ACTU 23   8
/ / / / numb (and that was and . . . . 415 NO THANKS 32   1
is science) Q: how numb can an unworld get? . . . . 791 73 POEMS 19   9
few of sun fingers numb) with anguished each their . . . . . 822 73 POEMS 50   2
+NUMB
FOR CONTEXT, SEE . . . . 789 73 POEMS 17   1
NUMBER
winking hands, carefully inhabits number 1 on something . . . 62 T&C PORTRAIT 10   4
winces swiflty out of number 1 someThing street and . . . . . 62 T&C PORTRAIT 10   25
they were alive and number two took up the . . . . 117 & PORTRAIT 10   15
pathological but dumb. The number of times a wheel . . . . . 514 50 POEMS 28   5
an unworld get? A· number / / / / . . . . 791 73 POEMS 19   10
NUMBERED
creep budgingly over some numbered face capable of a . . . . 359 VIVA 50   16
+NUMBERLESSNESS
FOR CONTEXT, SEE . . . . 739 95 POEMS 67   9
NUMBERS
and Royal Danielli their numbers are like unto the . . . . . 256 IS 5 ONE 27   20
NUMBING
stroke my being with numbing forests frolicsome, fleetly . . 19 T&C PUELLA MEA   91
a street superimposing a numbing im- perfectness upon such . 197 XLI PORTRAIT 5   2
NUMERABLE
quantity; but than all numerable mosts the actual more . . . 556 1 X 1 16   4
of whom among not numerable ams (leaving a perfectly . . . . 558 1 X 1 18   6
presume to comprehend not numerable whom? / / / . . . . . . 609 (CHAIRE) 11   14
(merely and whose not numerable leaves are fall i . . . . . 826 73 POEMS 54   5

		PAGE	TITLE	LINE

NUMERABLY
shape stirs through (not numerably or as lovers a . . . . . . 785 73 POEMS 13   12
NUMEROUS
down the oblivious west's numerous dun magnificence conquers   6 T&C EPITHALAM   127
NUN
ploughman pardoner wife and nun merchant frere clerk somnour   661 {CHAIRE} 63   9
NUNS
nons too and and nuns two nuns w an . . . . 508 50 POEMS 22   7
and and nuns two nuns w an d ering . . . . 508 50 POEMS 22   7
NUTS
of the little, huddling nuts and the bad candies . . . . . . 100 & POST IMPR 11   21
with grace" squeeze your nuts and open your face . . . . . . 407 NO THANKS 24   16
NUZZLE
With the bulge and nuzzle of the sea / . . . . 16 T&C SONGS 6   14
effigies of crowing gold) nuzzle against summer thunder . . . 340 VIVA 31   18
NY
as prove from Troy (N.Y.) to Cairo (Egypt) the . . . . 266 IS 5 TWO 1   6
is grass) from Troy, n.y. the way of (all . . . . 320 VIVA 12   4
when Miss G touched n.y. our skeleton stepped from . . . . . 326 VIVA 18   10
NYMPH
the brand of marriageable nymph which is armed with . . . . . 256 IS 5 ONE 27   14
NYMPHLIKE
gave the moon a nymphlike face, a form whose . . . .   8 T&C OF NICOL   19
O
length from palpitating veils. O still miraculous May! O . .   5 T&C EPITHALAM   105
O still miraculous May! O shining girl of time . . . .   5 T&C EPITHALAM   105
girl of time untarnished! O small intimate gently primeval .   5 T&C EPITHALAM   106
hands, frivolous feet divine! O singular and breathless . . .   5 T&C EPITHALAM   108
singular and breathless pearl! O indefinable frail ultimate .   5 T&C EPITHALAM   109
indefinable frail ultimate pose! O visible beatitude sweet .   5 T&C EPITHALAM   110
thee for his doom-- O thou within the chancel . . . .   7 T&C EPITHALAM   153
bird transcends the sight, O thou to whom belong . . . . . .   7 T&C EPITHALAM   166
crimson music Come hither O thou, is life not . . . . 27 T&C ORIENTALE 1   7
divine silence Come hither O thou, is life not . . . . 27 T&C ORIENTALE 1   14
white fragrance Come hither O thou, is life not . . . . 27 T&C ORIENTALE 1   21
than flowers Come hither O thou, is love not . . . . 27 T&C ORIENTALE 1   28
/ / AMORES consider O woman this my body. . . . . 36 T&C AMORES 1   1
blandly into receptive earth, O let us descend take . . . . . 41 T&C AMORES 5   14
wondering be unto us O soul, but straight glad . . . . 41 T&C AMORES 5   28
/ / / / O Distinct Lady of my . . . . 43 T&C AMORES 7   1
/ / / / O sweet spontaneous earth how . . . . 46 T&C LA GUERRE 2   1
with large minute hips, O press worms rushing slowly . . . . 67 T&C POST IMPR 4   28
hour, thy counted petals O tremendous flower on whose . . . . 79 T&C SON UNRE 4   3
pinched from dumb summer? O crazy daddy of death . . . . . . 80 T&C SON UNRE 5   9
comes, which is morning, O do not wonder that . . . . 92 & POST IMPR 4   17
eaten by yester- day) O i tell you out . . . . 111 & PORTRAIT 6   51
by yester- day (and O My Lady Lady Of . . . . 112 & PORTRAIT 6   93
the bar was COOl O My lover, there's just . . . . 123 & SEVEN POEMS 2   7
/ / / SONNETS--REALITIES O It's Nice To Get . . . . 130 & SON REAL 1   1
faint for your face O stay with me slightly. . . . . 165 & SON ACTU 14   10
/ / / --G O N splashes-sink which is . . . . 169 & SON ACTU 18   1
against your charming strength O haste annihilator drawing . 182 XLI SONGS 4   15
/ / / / O Thou to whom the . . . . 206 XLI SONNETS 2   1
are keeping their exquisite dreams--O Love! upon thy dim . . 206 XLI SONNETS 2   10
has conversed in vain, O scrupulously take thy trivial . . . 212 XLI SONNETS 8   3
hazarded "god" (blushing slightly) --"O damn ginks like dis . 228 IS 5 ONE MARJ   6
to believe these gently O sweetly melancholy trillers amid . 230 IS 5 ONE 2   24
indigenous throstles Art is O World O Life a . . . . 230 IS 5 ONE 2   32
Art is O World O Life a formula: example, ... 230 IS 5 ONE 2   32
hairy-sturdy you may turn O turn that airy hurdysturdygurdy . 233 IS 5 ONE 4   2
when will turn backward O backward Time in your . . . . . . 233 IS 5 ONE 4   3
ITEM this man is o so Waiter this; woman . . . . 243 IS 5 ONE 14   1
sure her springs were O. K.) i went right . . . . 248 IS 5 ONE 19   8
/ / / oDE o the sweet & aged . . . . 250 IS 5 ONE 21   1
we're not very careful) O), the darling benevolent mindless . 250 IS 5 ONE 21   6
are we angels by O yes beautiful we now . . . . 257 IS 5 ONE 27   31
this wellcurb simply darling" --O Education: O thos cook . . 257 IS 5 ONE 27   37
simply darling" --O Education: O thos cook & son . . . . . 257 IS 5 ONE 27   37

O (CONTINUED)

thos cook & son (O to be a metope . . . . 257 IS 5 ONE 27 39
can't imagine Harry was o god kilt he was . . . . 271 IS 5 TWO 6 10
mice, and a baboon. O a monkey with a . . . . 279 IS 5 THREE 3 9
rhyme and with laughter O my lady (and every . . . . 293 IS 5 FOUR 10 12
reminds me who said o yes Frost Something there . . . . . . 315 VIVA 7 2
now don't you're hurting o Me please you're killing) . . . . 343 VIVA 34 5
That please squirtnowing for o squirting we're replies (at . 343 VIVA 34 9
replies (at which now O fear turned o Now . . . . 343 VIVA 34 10
now O fear turned o Now handspring trans forming . . . . . . 343 VIVA 34 10
; w : theraIncomIng o all the roofs roar . . . . 347 VIVA 38 18
when: & a nd O impercept i bl / . . . . 350 VIVA 41 17
darkens and is alive-- o live with me in . . . . 357 VIVA 48 10
next everywhere hidinglyseek no o god dear wait sh . . . . . 358 VIVA 49 5
dear wait sh please o no O 3rd Findingest . . . . 358 VIVA 49 5
sh please o no O 3rd Findingest whispers understand . . . . 358 VIVA 49 5
it find somehow (but O gracefully) a we, entirely . . . . . . 368 VIVA 59 12
moon over s -unday O: m o o n . . . . 385 NO THANKS 2 35
he does not stir) O love, my love! soul . . . . 386 NO THANKS 3 12
/ / / / o pr gress verily thou . . . . 392 NO THANKS 9 1
asks about Death) concept O hairlesschested females, well . . 398 NO THANKS 15 16
/ / / / o sure) but nobody unders . . . . 400 NO THANKS 17 1
sure) i mean the (o well ughhuh sure why . . . . 400 NO THANKS 17 8
ughhuh yuh) i know (o sure i know yes . . . . 400 NO THANKS 17 15
c'est fini pRaW, lT; O: allons 9 & . . . . 430 NO THANKS 47 23
street wonderful flowers And o the Light thrown by . . . . . 437 NO THANKS 53 4
white orange green- ness o what a proud dreamhorse . . . . . 437 NO THANKS 53 16
undigestibly: groans. bounce ! o-ras-ourh an-dorg-an . . . . 442 NO THANKS 57 7
yaw: nstretchy: awn) then, o my love , then . . . . 442 NO THANKS 57 17
colours; are: m, ove o im -pos- sibl y . . . . 444 NO THANKS 59 25
a , bird ! O & j & ji . - - - . . . . 471 NEW POEMS 9 19
jimmy s: A V o (. : ; . . . . 471 NEW POEMS 9 28
real hot spell with o man what bubbies going . . . . 476 NEW POEMS 14 4
left crashed pal dropped o god alice yells but . . . . . . 496 50 POEMS 10 7
empty house is full O Yes of guk rooms . . . . 499 50 POEMS 13 8
hour in all, all) o yes to flower until . . . . 509 50 POEMS 23 7
yes what too much o much cheap me i . . . . 523 50 POEMS 36 15
(sitting in a tree-) o small you sitting in . . . . 535 50 POEMS 47 2
riding on a greener (o little i) riding on . . . . 535 50 POEMS 47 7
riding on a leaf o least who sing small . . . . 535 50 POEMS 47 9
ygUDuh ydoan yunnuhstan ydoan o yunnuhstan dem yguduh ged . . 547 1 X 1 7 4
yguduh ged riduh ydoan o nudn LISN bud LISN . . . . 547 1 X 1 7 9
breathed upon beginning) "beautiful o most beautiful" her, my 572 1 X 1 32 11
or limb explodes and o each living ablaze greenly . . . . . 583 1 X 1 43 12
love love said did o no yes earth was . . . . 589 1 X 1 49 7
/ / / / o by the by has . . . . 593 1 X 1 53 1
(hark! what silence)?" "Worlds? o no: i'm certain they're . . 603 {CHAIRE} 5 5
fine) but Death ? o baby i wouldn't like . . . . 604 {CHAIRE} 6 2
for dying (forgive us, o life! the sin of . . . . 604 {CHAIRE} 6 25
/ / / / o the round little man . . . . 606 {CHAIRE} 8 1
dreamseems (vivi d an O of milky tranceworld writhes . . . . 615 {CHAIRE} 17 15
but please for god's O what the hell yes . . . . 638 {CHAIRE} 40 9
/ / / / o to be in finland . . . . 641 {CHAIRE} 43 1
sic kly a thingish o crashdis appearing con ter . . . . . . 646 {CHAIRE} 48 4
our night becomes day) o, it's spring! all the . . . . . . 665 {CHAIRE} 67 18
you may take mine" "o how how how could . . . . 684 95 POEMS 12 5
and kind to all" "o no no no let . . . . 684 95 POEMS 12 13
one immense deep hell -o of keen moon) dream . . . . 687 95 POEMS 15 8
deep is the far o my darling) of (down . . . . 695 95 POEMS 23 20
is po wer) say o if i 'd OH . . . . 700 95 POEMS 28 10
/ / / ! o (rounD) moon, how do . . . . 722 95 POEMS 50 2
/ / / / O the sun comes up-up-up . . . . 773 73 POEMS 1 1
be sil ly , o no in- deed; money . . . . 793 73 POEMS 21 6
your voice your ways (o very most my shining . . . . 819 73 POEMS 47 4
/ / / / "o purple finch please tell . . . . 836 73 POEMS 64 1
will winter never come? o come, terrible anonymity; enfold . 839 73 POEMS 67 9
sing like birds-- but o the starhushed silence which . . . . 844 73 POEMS 72 3

                                                        PAGE   TITLE   LINE
O'CLOCK
    i am at one o'clock to little lips (which . . . . 115 & PORTRAIT 8   5
    the courtesy of five o'clock became the omen of . . . . . . 197 XLI PORTRAIT 5   11
    ferocious phenomenon of 5 o'clock i find myself gently   . . . 201 XLI PORTRAIT 9   1
    it is) still 5 o'clock I stare only always . . . . 202 XLI PORTRAIT 9   42
    And it is 5 o'clock in the oblong air, ... 202 XLI PORTRAIT 9   49
    you --because it's five o'clock and these (i notice) . . . . 282 IS 5 THREE 6   10
    election who so thumb o'clock asters miggle dim a . . . . . . 333 VIVA 24   15
O'ER
    deliberate groping ocean fondled o'er the warm long flower .   7 T&C EPITHALAM   159
    a gloat of silver; o'er whose night three willows . . . . . .   9 T&C SONGS 1   4
    whom night hath pondered o'er --and frailties of dimension . 205 XLI SONNETS 1   11
OAK
    to close when the oak begs permission of the . . . . 620 {CHAIRE} 22   9
    free mysterious dreamsoul floatstands oak by birch by maple . 658 {CHAIRE} 60   18
OAKS
    lies her head by oaks and roses deliberated.) / . . . . 181 XLI SONGS 3   14
OATH
    distinct disks of graceful oath, upsoarings the break on . . 96 & POST IMPR 8   9
    open vow or the oath cracked length wise--let it . . . . . . 569 1 X 1 29   4
OBEDIENT
    inscrutable sweetness my soul obedient; it is to stroke . . . 19 T&C PUELLA MEA   89
OBEY
    goodness what is meek; obey says toc, submit says . . . . . . 438 NO THANKS 54   5
    (love's a universe beyond obey or command, reality or . . . . 574 1 X 1 34   7
OBJECT
    almost large he- shaped object vomits cleverly against a . . 324 VIVA 16   6
    at war: a conscientious object-or his wellbeloved colonel . . 339 VIVA 30   3
OBJECTED
    should or- dinarily have objected to which, considering the . 263 IS 5 ONE 32   34
OBJECTIVELY
    to speak even less objectively, i was horribly scared . . . . 263 IS 5 ONE 32   62
+OBJECTOR
    FOR CONTEXT, SEE . . . . 339 VIVA 30   3
OBLIVION
    do crowd gaily upon oblivion sweeter than any there . . . . . 23 T&C PUELLA MEA 272
    each is blacker than oblivion the ladies of the . . . . 33 T&C ORIENTALE 6 42
    the sunny dump of oblivion) a tiny dust finely . . . . 197 XLI PORTRAIT 5   22
    chucking some legally into Oblivion wave little flags weeping 391 NO THANKS 8   7
    as luminous they climb oblivion) voices who are dreams, . . . 810 73 POEMS 38   6
OBLIVIONS
    not guessable each infinite Oblivions found a by lost . . . . 757 95 POEMS 85   24
OBLIVIOUS
    momently) as down the oblivious west's numerous dun . . . . .   6 T&C EPITHALAM   127
OBLONG
    square virtues and the oblong sins perfectly gesticulate the 43 T&C AMORES 7   34
    5 o'clock in the oblong air, from which a . . . . 202 XLI PORTRAIT 9   50
OBSCENE
    among unseen things, things obscene (Whose fingers young the   77 T&C SON UNRE 2   3
    a nearly-opaque perfume disinterestedly obscene. / / / / . . 146 & SON REAL 17   14
    the unique and nervously obscene need; it's funny. They . . . 153 & SON ACTU 2   3
    of april, making the obscene shy breasts tickle, laughing . . 172 & SON ACTU 21   14
    ions whose rich slovenly obscene procession always floats . . 202 XLI PORTRAIT 9   46
    with stark and fearlessly obscene but really clean get . . . 407 NO THANKS 24   6
OBSCENELY
    a fattish leg leaks obscenely from the dress. one . . . . . . 143 & SON REAL 14   9
OBSCENER
    eyes purest than fear's obscener brightest than hate's more . 565 1 X 1 25   9
OBSCENITIES
    underneath conventions exposes hidden obscenities nudging . . 203 XLI LA GUERRE 1   5
OBSCENITY
    whose opened withins ejaculate. obscenity the tide Did dl . . 94 & POST IMPR 6   5
OBSCURE
    smile of life's placid obscure palpable carnival where to . . 43 T&C AMORES 7   31
    or until with neat obscure obvious hands Time stuff . . . . . 165 & SON ACTU 14   11
    graduate of a somewhat obscure to be sure university . . . . 234 IS 5 ONE 5   2
OBSCURELY
    and pompous ancient jews obscurely twitch through the bumping 219 XLI SONNETS 15   9

551

	PAGE	TITLE	LINE

OBSCURITY
light yanKing from bushy obscurity a bald greenish foetal . . 96 & POST IMPR 8   28
OBSERVE
/ / / but observe; although once is never . . . . 282 IS 5 THREE 6   1
which stars may not observe; while roses wince) that . . . . 386 NO THANKS 3   8
300 lbs) i mean observe his these regard his . . . . 645 (CHAIRE) 47   3
+OBSERVE
FOR CONTEXT, SEE . . . . 727 95 POEMS 55   7
OBSERVED
of ourselves to be observed how in this fundamental . . . . . 261 IS 5 ONE 31   7
each (nor have i observed some chucking some legally . . . . 391 NO THANKS 8   5
it's safe to say, observed him but myself; and . . . . 802 73 POEMS 30   8
OBSERVES
knee with, its, friend observes I pass Mr Tom . . . . 252 IS 5 ONE 23   4
OBSOLETE
new- ness of her obsolete gaze begins to. lean.... . . . . . 148 & SON REAL 19   12
to the stone, how obsolete lips utter their extant . . . . . 260 IS 5 ONE 30   5
completely sing? futures are obsolete; pasts are unborn (here 592 1 X 1 52   11
all things excellently rare; obsolete almost that phenomenon 607 (CHAIRE) 9   11
+OBSTREPEROUS
FOR CONTEXT, SEE . . . . 104 & POST IMPR 14   4
OBVIOUS
the complicated and the obvious they were faithful and . . . 43 T&C AMORES 7   17
until with neat obscure obvious hands Time stuff the . . . . 165 & SON ACTU 14   11
be will) from beautiful obvious to Mere but one . . . . 608 (CHAIRE) 10   7
+OBVIOUS
FOR CONTEXT, SEE . . . . 829 73 POEMS 57   5
OBVIOUSLY
personally bung loamhome picpac obviously scratches . . . . . 333 VIVA 24   5
OCCASION
him upon the auspicious occasion of his decease a . . . . . . 239 IS 5 ONE 10   29
OCCASIONAL
the time when all occasional things close into silence, . . . 6 T&C EPITHALAM 121
of jazz whose arched occasional steep youth swallows . . . . 140 & SON REAL 11   5
OCCASIONALLY
a neckless nudity (very occasionally budding a flabby . . . . 134 & SON REAL 5   7
and after you. I occasionally feel vague how vague . . . . . 160 & SON ACTU 9   14
disease of Life, himself occasionally contrives an unreal . . 193 XLI PORTRAIT 1   24
the tubular downward blackness occasionally from which . . . 201 XLI PORTRAIT 9   9
of paklavah meeah. (Very occasionally three.) and i gaze . . 217 XLI SONNETS 13   13
OCCULT
palpable solitude a furtive occult fragrance steals, a . . . 19 T&C PUELLA MEA 106
sincerely greets, with an occult shrug asking Through her . . 137 & SON REAL 8   4
comparatively crude; an indestructible occult supersnare of . 799 73 POEMS 27   18
+OCCULT
FOR CONTEXT, SEE . . . . 349 VIVA 40   14
OCCUPATION
A bachelor incapable of occupation, he had long suppressed . 263 IS 5 ONE 32   37
OCCUPIED
not unpainful thoughts which occupied the subject of our . . 263 IS 5 ONE 32   61
OCCUPY
next Door but two occupy a man and his . . . . 312 VIVA 4   10
OCCUR
strike midnight (and did occur bell beyond fiercely spurting 115 & PORTRAIT 8   17
frailties of dimension to occur about us and birds . . . . . 205 XLI SONNETS 1   12
dying) Is will still occur; birds disappear becomingly: a . . 452 NO THANKS 67   13
which halves reintegrating, shall occur no death and any . . 556 1 X 1 16   2
except the impossible shall occur --see! now himself uplifts 582 1 X 1 42   12
to her does not occur (alarm ing notion for . . . . 790 73 POEMS 18   10
OCCURRED
something that has not occurred: i am a birdcage . . . . . . 360 VIVA 51   24
as if aristide maillols occurred with any ticking of . . . . 617 (CHAIRE) 19   14
other night something odd occurred" charlie confessed . . . . 800 73 POEMS 28   2
OCCURS
things) the bright rain occurs deeply, beautifully and i . . 92 & POST IMPR 4   7
mucous) in my mouth occurs homelessly. While grip Hips . . . 136 & SON REAL 7   10
mankind something more small occurs or something more . . . . 514 50 POEMS 28   10
duration: only love immortally occurs beyond the mind) such . 576 1 X 1 36   8

OCEAN

whispered deep, deliberate groping ocean fondled o'er the . . 7 T&C EPITHALAM 159
/ here is the ocean, this is moonlight: say . . . . 379 VIVA 70 1
a first dream called ocean) and let must or . . . . 424 NO THANKS 41 7
of wonderful thunder! of? ocean. a ndn ooneandfor e-ver) . . 469 NEW POEMS 7 10
is so aged the ocean wanders the streets are . . . . 505 50 POEMS 19 4
a hole in the ocean will never be missed . . . . 513 50 POEMS 27 24
sailing perfect silence. Absolute ocean / / / / . . . . . . 586 1 X 1 46 20
a (who are like ocean patient) dream's eternity (you . . . . 617 {CHAIRE} 19 3
line or else an ocean is compelled to close . . . . 620 {CHAIRE} 22 8
beneath, bombed the by ocean earth bigly shudders) never . . 639 {CHAIRE} 41 4
the bottom of the ocean of forever with a . . . . 642 {CHAIRE} 44 15
is the air the ocean and the land (do . . . . 768 95 POEMS 94 4
men do not conceive--let ocean grow again / / . . . . 843 73 POEMS 71 14
+OCEAN

FOR CONTEXT, SEE . . . . 334 VIVA 25 1
FOR CONTEXT, SEE . . . . 840 73 POEMS 68 20
OCEANING

is or total sun oceaning than any this tear . . . . 502 50 POEMS 16 3
crimson dooms conceive an oceaning abyss of orange dream . . 599 {CHAIRE} 1 3
OCEANS

mountains, more than all oceans various and while everywhere 351 VIVA 42 7
sun mountains stand And oceans do Not sleep matters . . . . . 359 VIVA 50 13
madness wind and broke oceans and tore mountains from . . . . 432 NO THANKS 49 16
skies are hanged and oceans drowned, the single secret . . . 560 1 X 1 20 7
OCTOBERING

is proudly and (by octobering flame beckoned) as earth . . . 521 50 POEMS 34 41
OCTOPUS

over. One brief convulsive octopus, and then our hero . . . . 263 IS 5 ONE 32 56
ODD

the battered bodies the odd unlovely souls struggle slowly . 55 T&C PORTRAIT 3 18
wondered since isn't it odd of you really to . . . . 172 & SON ACTU 21 10
/ / it's jolly odd what pops into your . . . . 269 IS 5 TWO 4 2
--i say that's jolly odd old thing, jolly odd, ... 269 IS 5 TWO 4 14
odd old thing, jolly odd, jolly jolly odd isn't . . . . . . 269 IS 5 TWO 4 16
jolly odd, jolly jolly odd isn't it jolly odd. . . . . 269 IS 5 TWO 4 17
odd isn't it jolly odd. / / / / . . . . 269 IS 5 TWO 4 18
mortal (even the most odd) can justify the ways . . . . 731 95 POEMS 59 1
the other night something odd occurred" charlie confessed . . 800 73 POEMS 28 2
ODDLY

body, which will make oddly to strut my indolent . . . . . . 155 & SON ACTU 4 10
ODDS

ends next among broken odds of yes terday's tomorrow . . . . 522 50 POEMS 35 6
ODE

/ / / / oDE o the sweet & . . . . 250 IS 5 ONE 21 T
ODOR

a tiny violetflavoured nuisance: Odor? ono. comes out like . 231 IS 5 ONE 3 53
ODOUR

witchery of sound and odour drives the wingless thing . . . . 4 T&C EPITHALAM 60
sharp robes of uncouth odour, for an onion! for . . . . 94 & POST IMPR 6 9
budding a flabby algebraic odour jigs et tout en . . . . . . 134 & SON REAL 5 8
sheath stripped to the Odour. (and here's what WhoEver . . . 154 & SON ACTU 3 13
amorous pricks with minute odour these gross days when . . . 165 & SON ACTU 14 5
ODOURS

hundred these sounds crowds odours it is in a . . . . 238 IS 5 ONE 9 3
ODYSSEUS

Clever Rusefelt to Theodore Odysseus Graren't we couldn't . . 321 VIVA 13 10
OF

WORD DELETED, APPEARED 1959 TIMES
OF-FACENESS

collaps ingly flash a of-faceness stuck thumblike into pie . 330 VIVA 21 5
+OF-LOVE-AND-OF-DEAT

pretty and putrid dollies of-love-and-of-death dollies of . . 101 & POST IMPR 11 81
OFA

fectly, slowlywith, the handle ofa crankin It The L's . . . . 101 & POST IMPR 11 48
OFF

the young city putting off dimension with a blush . . . . . . 48 T&C IMPRESS 2 16
hours rise up putting off stars and it is . . . . 50 T&C IMPRESS 4 1

	PAGE	TITLE	LINE

OFF (CONTINUED)
slush of foam knocked off and a faint piddle-of-drops . . . . 96 & POST IMPR 8   13
POF goes the alarm off and the little striker . . . . 126 & SEVEN POEMS 5   10
take all your prickley-clothes off and squeeze- . . . . 127 & SEVEN POEMS 5   33
stood (maybe nine miles off). It was spring sun-stirring. . . 135 & SON REAL 6   12
thunderbolt red- hot peeling off huge slabs of a . . . . . . 194 XLI PORTRAIT 2   25
inspired sister's howling moves off will anyone tell him . . 196 XLI PORTRAIT 4   19
pipples taking their hets off? the king & queen . . . . 245 IS 5 ONE 16   1
i would actually fall off the rail before the . . . . 263 IS 5 ONE 32   63
which you can't pass off on other people: for . . . . 298 IS 5 FOUR 15   17
other tops to caroming off persist displacing Its own . . . . 311 VIVA 3   7
/ when hair falls off and eyes blur And . . . . 359 VIVA 50   1
/ / / put off your faces, Death: for . . . . 376 VIVA 67   1
kid anaesthetize marry bump off or otherwise amplify others) 391 NO THANKS 8   15
something or must be off duty wanderfuling aft spits) . . . . 465 NEW POEMS 3   3
and his mind take off time that you should . . . . 484 NEW POEMS 22   8
mine and sank just off the coast of Sum . . . . 494 50 POEMS 8   4
them) now (it tears off rag its of mind . . . . 501 50 POEMS 15   12
(they're more much further off) further these those three . . 501 50 POEMS 15   16
upon his back and off he goes but we . . . . 624 (CHAIRE) 26   20
/ / / / off a pane) the (dropp . . . . 692 95 POEMS 20   1
him streets taking moment off by moment day thankfully . . . 720 95 POEMS 48   5
age sticks up Keep Off signs) & youth yanks . . . . 729 95 POEMS 57   3
shrill shower bouncing up off burned earth but a . . . . . . 754 95 POEMS 82   2
should take his hat off to this dame: he . . . . 790 73 POEMS 18   7
+OFF
FOR CONTEXT, SEE . . . . 101 & POST IMPR 11   51
FOR CONTEXT, SEE . . . . 404 NO THANKS 21   4
OFFENSE
way to the forest--no offense to you, white town . . . . . . 86 T&C SON ACTU 5   3
OFFERED
and when i have offered up each fragrant night, ... 39 T&C AMORES 4   30
foolish and to wise offered immeasurable is proudly and . . . 521 50 POEMS 34   40
OFFERING
from his cupboard gallantly offering to demonstrate the . . . 326 VIVA 18   11
courte- ous protestations) and offering Miss Gay one (which . 326 VIVA 18   19
dreams more hands are offering jonquils) down again who . . . 585 1 X 1 45   17
OFFERS
the musical white spring offers her lily inextinguishable, . 206 XLI SONNETS 2   2
out uh flask an offers it tuh duh whole . . . . 332 VIVA 23   20
OFFICERS
but--though all kinds of officers (a yearning nation's . . . 339 VIVA 30   22
OFFSPRING
their (so to speak) offspring has that largo appearance . . . 326 VIVA 18   8
whenlings (daughters of ifbut offspring of hopefear sons of . 512 50 POEMS 26   2
of majorities, that illegitimate offspring of the divine . . 803 73 POEMS 31   3
+OFFSPRING
FOR CONTEXT, SEE . . . . 726 95 POEMS 54   15
OFLIKE
as) proces -sion Its oflike immens- ely (a feet . . . . 482 NEW POEMS 20   3
OFOF
oat iNg, the ofpieces ofof sunligh tof fa 1 . . . . 104 & POST IMPR 14   5
OFPIECES
surElyfl) oat iNg, the ofpieces ofof sunligh tof fa . . . . . 104 & POST IMPR 14   5
OFS
aflickf) litter ing brightmillion ofS hurl; edindodg: ing . . 265 IS 5 ONE 34   3
OFT
flower, the snow will oft utter, whereof the year . . . . . . 21 T&C PUELLA MEA   188
with his peers full oft hath quaffed the wine . . . . 273 IS 5 TWO 8   7
fart they fart full oft (with mind with heart . . . . 441 NO THANKS 56   38
OFTEN
sweet spontaneous earth how often have the doting fingers . . 46 T&C LA GUERRE 2   2
thy beauty . how often have religions taken thee . . . . . . 46 T&C LA GUERRE 2   14
times call april) must often have wondered "most people . . . 738 95 POEMS 66   9
OGLING
the tightened eyes crisp ogling shoulders and the ripe . . . 72 T&C SON REAL 3   6
OGRE
hairy arms like an ogre and rub- bercoloured hands . . . . . 69 T&C POST IMPR 6   38

	PAGE	TITLE	LINE
OH			
He buy? Les belles bottes--oh hear ,pas cheres") and	102	& POST IMPR 12	20
all go BlacK wh-eel-ing oh ver mYveRylitTle street where . .	122	& SEVEN POEMS 1	19
on my passionate anatomy oh yes! Large legs pinch, ...	146	& SON REAL 17	7
and how they'll stare! oh but you'll be very	192	XLI CHANSONS 2	24
that you was Jimmie. Oh for such a gurl	235	IS 5 ONE 6	13
a gurl gurl gurl, oh for such a gurl	235	IS 5 ONE 6	16
napkins (this man is oh so tired of this	243	IS 5 ONE 14	7
ing (my lev-er Right- oh and her gears being	248	IS 5 ONE 19	17
with dead ideas (the oh quintillions of incredible	250	IS 5 ONE 21	10
toothless <> <> bipeds) OH the bothering dear unnecessary . .	250	IS 5 ONE 21	15
Irish, cook but well oh don't you makes burst	251	IS 5 ONE 22	11
when (now, dark dear oh) the iceman how, luminously	251	IS 5 ONE 22	13
the iceman how, luminously oh how listens and, expands . . .	251	IS 5 ONE 22	16
pilgrims' and so forth oh say can you see	268	IS 5 TWO 3	2
! & we're NOT (oh-- --i say that's jolly	269	IS 5 TWO 4	12
few gas and the oh baby shrapnel or my	272	IS 5 TWO 7	7
and incense with and oh sunlight-- the crash of	280	IS 5 THREE 4	23
the colours (of the oh silently striding) priests-and- . . .	280	IS 5 THREE 4	25
puppets of a dream? oh i mean: entirely having	295	IS 5 FOUR 12	4
into a memory slowly, oh seriously --that since and	295	IS 5 FOUR 12	10
whole intend" they wonder. oh and they cry "to	295	IS 5 FOUR 12	17
laugh and breathe is oh love and the reason	295	IS 5 FOUR 12	24
mumble some thing to oh no body will (can	314	VIVA 6	20
haymow with young fore'er (oh & by the way	316	VIVA 8	18
a what is it oh yes chair but not	322	VIVA 14	5
puzzling over that one oh just thinking it over	323	VIVA 15	8
course) carefully had decided oh no (but / /	323	VIVA 15	29
hight evolute my eerily oh gargle to jip hug	333	VIVA 24	23
er dream; new . oh if when: & a	350	VIVA 41	13
don't stop said she oh no said he) go	399	NO THANKS 16	27
of minute mown lives) oh my spirit you tumble	434	NO THANKS 51	25
o if i 'd OH n lygawntueco llege /	700	95 POEMS 28	13
+OH			
FOR CONTEXT, SEE	331	VIVA 22	8
OHO			
muscles of Cezanne's logic, oho. a street there is	180	XLI SONGS 2	17
OI			
eesez pullih nizmus tash, oi dough un giv uh	310	VIVA 2	2
un giv uh shid oi sez. Tom oidoughwuntuh doot, ...	310	VIVA 2	3
Vury Sin Silly : oi / / / /	398	NO THANKS 15	23
OIDOUGHWUNTUH			
shid oi sez. Tom oidoughwuntuh doot, butoiguttuh braikyooz, .	310	VIVA 2	4
OIL			
/ / / / oil tel duh woil doi	310	VIVA 2	1
+OIL			
FOR CONTEXT, SEE	549	1 X 1 9	11
OILED			
her and (having thoroughly oiled the universal joint tested .	248	IS 5 ONE 19	6
OILSAISOUGH			
woodundat maik yurarstoin green? Oilsaisough.) --Hool	310	VIVA 2	7
OINIS			
de woids uf lil Oinis / / / /	409	NO THANKS 26	4
OIWUN			
And The Whale : oiwun uhsoi roitee runow dutmoi	398	NO THANKS 15	20
+OK			
FOR CONTEXT, SEE	248	IS 5 ONE 19	8
+OKAY			
FOR CONTEXT, SEE	552	1 X 1 12	23
OKAYED			
all screech-owls have not okayed his voice --and any	620	{CHAIRE} 22	6
OKAYS			
(relijinisde) o (peemuvdepipl) marx okays jippymugun roomur j	325	VIVA 17	12
OLAF			
/ i sing of Olaf glad and big whose	339	VIVA 30	1
succinctly bred) took erring Olaf soon in hand; but--though .	339	VIVA 30	6
allegiance per blunt instruments-- Olaf (being to all intents	339	VIVA 30	15
roasted hot with heat-- Olaf (upon what were once	339	VIVA 30	31

		PAGE	TITLE	LINE
OLAF (CONTINUED)				
pray to see; and Olaf, too preponderatingly because unless	.	339	VIVA 30	39
OLBANUM				
unto whom i burn olbanum / / / /		31	T&C ORIENTALE 5	32
OLD				
is puddle-wonderful the queer old balloonman whistles far and		24	T&C CHANSONS 1	12
look out for the old woman with the wart		25	T&C CHANSONS 2	17
is a thousand years old the harem of the		32	T&C ORIENTALE 6	18
mouth wilted and not old, harry, a woman in		53	T&C PORTRAIT 1	33
the striving of that old man who at her		57	T&C PORTRAIT 5	10
street unchangingly the always old lady always sitting in . .		58	T&C PORTRAIT 6	21
the lips of an old man murder the petals		59	T&C PORTRAIT 7	3
the lips of an old man murder the petals.		59	T&C PORTRAIT 7	16
its hideous Work most old Whose battening gesture prophecies		77	T&C SON UNRE 2	11
ears dribbles soft right old feller belch the chap		96	& POST IMPR 8	21
never lets you grow old blinking at the low		96	& POST IMPR 8	24
of the tiny motheaten old manwhose Beard rests. onthetopwhose		101	& POST IMPR 11	46
suppose Life is an old man carrying flowers on		102	& POST IMPR 12	2
or nothing or an old man 3 thirds asleep, ...		102	& POST IMPR 12	13
newly formed upon an old pool. Her nose was		103	& POST IMPR 13	13
Lucienne which dangle the old men and hot men		120	& PORTRAIT 12	22
Lucienne which dangle the old men and hot men		121	& PORTRAIT 12	59
fro moving New and Old things, while people stare		124	& SEVEN POEMS 3	14
and it loves, every old thing falls in rosebugs		126	& SEVEN POEMS 5	5
sex. In The Good Old Summer Time. My gorgeous		130	& SON REAL 1	9
frieze of smoking Face Bluish-old and choked pat of		142	& SON REAL 13	5
the line. not so old for the mother of		167	& SON ACTU 16	2
between tables like an old leaf between toadstools he		198	XLI PORTRAIT 6	16
tipsy biddy with an old mop punching underneath conventions .		203	XLI LA GUERRE 1	2
when sung at the old howard Humanity i love		204	XLI LA GUERRE 2	8
days for whom the old glories move, the old		209	XLI SONNETS 5	12
old glories move, the old trumpets cry; who gavest		209	XLI SONNETS 5	12
(with flesh like an old toy balloon) heavily swims		219	XLI SONNETS 15	12
of the Grand and Old days: of Amy Sandburg		233	IS 5 ONE 4	17
watching her face grow old and tired to which		242	IS 5 ONE 13	14
say that's jolly odd old thing, jolly odd, jolly		269	IS 5 TWO 4	15
him home to his old mother in a new		270	IS 5 TWO 5	19
some are young some old none look alike the		274	IS 5 TWO 9	4
/ / my sweet old etcetera aunt lucy during		276	IS 5 TWO 10	1
hush. Sunlight, there are old men behind me I		281	IS 5 THREE 5	24
notice) trees winterbrief surly old gurgle a nonsense of . .		282	IS 5 THREE 6	11
matter further than of old because you fooled the		289	IS 5 FOUR 6	14
mouth (making everything suddenly old and with his awkward .		293	IS 5 FOUR 10	27
young as he is old when autumn comes, who		296	IS 5 FOUR 13	4
kumrads die before they're old (kumrads aren't afraid to . .		413	NO THANKS 30	2
by a -oo- is old as the jews are		436	NO THANKS 52	23
hear them men are old may my mind stroll		481	NEW POEMS 19	4
Up floatingly clothes tumbledish olD (with sprouts o ver . .		534	50 POEMS 46	6
mother's zero mind fahrenheit) old infrequently more and more		546	1 X 1 6	2
nipponized bit of the old sixth avenue el; in		553	1 X 1 13	22
/ / / / old mr ly fresh from		567	1 X 1 27	1
for everybody it's a" old mr lyman ruddy as		567	1 X 1 27	17
don't grow) one's anything old being everything new (with . .		594	1 X 1 54	14
one shi ly glad old unman who is eye		602	(CHAIRE) 4	6
like ot-am sum-air (young old nic) like spring yoo		618	(CHAIRE) 20	26
rainbows are insured against old age when every thrush . . .		620	(CHAIRE) 22	4
grow (gracefully or otherwise) old. Old may mean anything . .		626	(CHAIRE) 28	3
(gracefully or otherwise) old. Old may mean anything which .		626	(CHAIRE) 28	3
remember with his rotten old forgotten full of why		642	(CHAIRE) 44	6
bell tolled and the old vine twined this is		647	(CHAIRE) 49	15
Dust (trite now and old) lie we so must		690	95 POEMS 18	3
him down by the old swimminghole" "i'd be worse		707	95 POEMS 35	2
you down through the old swimminghole there'll be slime . . .		707	95 POEMS 35	27
life (who never grows old) is always beau tiful		724	95 POEMS 52	18
/ / / / old age sticks up Keep		729	95 POEMS 57	1
youth yanks them down (old age cries No Tres)		729	95 POEMS 57	6
(pas) youth laughs (sing old age scolds Forbid den		729	95 POEMS 57	12
right on gr owing old / / / /		729	95 POEMS 57	20

OLD (CONTINUED)

who. since becomes why: old turns to young (winter . . . . . 737 95 POEMS 65   6
&) thing found one old blue wheel in a . . . . 753 95 POEMS 81   21
snowy head we call old frank go bluer still . . . . 754 95 POEMS 82   6
sing, my darling: while old worlds and young (big . . . . . . 776 73 POEMS 4   5
(five or six years old) peering from some high . . . . 824 73 POEMS 52   2

+OLD

FOR CONTEXT, SEE . . . . 101 & POST IMPR 11   64
FOR CONTEXT, SEE . . . . 104 & POST IMPR 14   16
FOR CONTEXT, SEE . . . . 237 IS 5 ONE 8   12
FOR CONTEXT, SEE . . . . 250 IS 5 ONE 21   18
FOR CONTEXT, SEE . . . . 335 VIVA 26   1
FOR CONTEXT, SEE . . . . 335 VIVA 26   18
FOR CONTEXT, SEE . . . . 411 NO THANKS 28   8
FOR CONTEXT, SEE . . . . 411 NO THANKS 28   10
FOR CONTEXT, SEE . . . . 411 NO THANKS 28   12
FOR CONTEXT, SEE . . . . 417 NO THANKS 34   8
FOR CONTEXT, SEE . . . . 610 {CHAIRE} 12   2
FOR CONTEXT, SEE . . . . 703 95 POEMS 31   1
FOR CONTEXT, SEE . . . . 725 95 POEMS 53   3
FOR CONTEXT, SEE . . . . 733 95 POEMS 61   5

OLDE

to have mentioned ye olde freudian wish; when i . . . . 326 VIVA 18   3

OLDER

humble man than sunlight older with ships than dreams . . . . 585 1 X 1 45   15
death; but more, the older he's the younger she's . . . . . . 742 95 POEMS 70   17

+OLDER

FOR CONTEXT, SEE . . . . 733 95 POEMS 61   2

OLDEST

this visitor their very oldest lives one pays him . . . . . . 624 {CHAIRE} 26   8
a something makes the oldest man (whoever he may . . . . . . 685 95 POEMS 13   14
the other well your oldest pal for instance (or . . . . 779 73 POEMS 7   10

OLDEYED

who hast merely gonorrhea Oldeyed child, to ambitious weeness 105 & PORTRAIT 1   5

OLDISH

monkey with a little oldish doll-like face and hairy . . . . 69 T&C POST IMPR 6   38

OLYMPIAN

too well? Chryselephantine Zeus Olympian sceptred colossus of 3 T&C EPITHALAM   25

OMAHA

gondola rapidly denizens of Omaha Altoona or what not . . . . 256 IS 5 ONE 27   26

OMAR

/ PUELLA MEA Harun Omar and Master Hafiz keep . . . . 17 T&C PUELLA MEA   1
was like a flower Omar Hafiz and Harun loved . . . . 22 T&C PUELLA MEA   227
Diarmuid Paris and Solomon, Omar Harun and Master Hafiz, . . 23 T&C PUELLA MEA   263
dead beautiful ladies Harun Omar and Master Hafiz. / . . . . 23 T&C PUELLA MEA   290

+OMEGA

FOR CONTEXT, SEE . . . . 431 NO THANKS 48   25

OMELET

they press proffers its omelet of fluffy lust) at . . . . . . 132 & SON REAL 3   10

OMEN

five o'clock became the omen of his presence it . . . . 197 XLI PORTRAIT 5   11

+OMICRON

FOR CONTEXT, SEE . . . . 431 NO THANKS 48   25

OMIEPSICRONLONO

& --cupidoergosum spun= flash omiepsicronlonO-- megaeta? p . 431 NO THANKS 48   25

OMIT

bulging thousands i too omit one kelly in response . . . . . 259 IS 5 ONE 29   19

OMITS

with dawn). Spring, that omits no mention of desire . . . . . 5 T&C EPITHALAM   89

+OMNIPOTENCE

FOR CONTEXT, SEE . . . . 554 1 X 1 14   13

OMNIPOTENT

of awe), thunderer whose omnipotent brow showers its curls . 4 T&C EPITHALAM   37
/ / / spring omnipotent goddess thou dost inveigle . . . . . 61 T&C PORTRAIT 9   1
Very distinctly confine their omnipotent literally their . . 391 NO THANKS 8   21
than (how should even omnipotent He feel sorry while . . . . 748 95 POEMS 76   9

+OMNIVOROUS

FOR CONTEXT, SEE . . . . 403 NO THANKS 20   11

ON
    WORD DELETED, APPEARED 235 TIMES
ON&OFF
    got athlete's mouth jumping on&off bandwaggons (MEMORIAM / / 404 NO THANKS 21   4
ONCE
    the people saw their once again victorious Pantarkes (whose .   4 T&C EPITHALAM   34
    had been dorothy and once permitted me for twenty . . . . . . 52 T&C PORTRAIT 1   18
    while; moments when my once more illustrous arms are . . . . 78 T&C SON UNRE 3   9
    does not disdain picKles, once, it, ate a scarlet . . . . . . 100 & POST IMPR 11   30
    a dream i had once i was away up . . . . 123 & SEVEN POEMS 2   1
    --OOc h get: breath once, all over, kid how, ... 136 & SON REAL 7   14
    give a prostitute the once -over. fiftythree (and one . . . . 150 & SON REAL 21   1
    where lies what was once the discobolus of one . . . . 203 XLI LA GUERRE 1 19
    being as Dick Mid once noted lifting a Green . . . . 229 IS 5 ONE FRAN   9
    Satter Nailyuh (comes but once er year) i'll tell . . . . . . 237 IS 5 ONE 8   15
    speak were in Love once? now her mouth opens . . . . 243 IS 5 ONE 14   10
    cigar) at which this (once flinger of lariats lean . . . . . 252 IS 5 ONE 23   9
    much impressed by having once noticed (as an infantile . . . 262 IS 5 ONE 32   10
    with fat jibing lips, once upon a (that is . . . . 277 IS 5 THREE 1   17
    / but observe; although once is never the beginning . . . . . 282 IS 5 THREE 6   2
    for you. I understand. Once again....) sliding a little . . . 282 IS 5 THREE 6   32
    with the inutile collide once more with the imaginable, . . . 289 IS 5 FOUR 6   8
    who after not coming once in seven years exp10 . . . . 320 VIVA 12   11
    Olaf (upon what were once knees) does almost ceaselessly . . 339 VIVA 30   31
    thick --who therefore Thee (once and once only, Queen . . . . 358 VIVA 49   11
    therefore Thee (once and once only, Queen among centuries . . 358 VIVA 49   11
    of a baboon (where once good lips stalked or . . . . 360 VIVA 51   2
    hunter whom you knew once? what if (merely suppose) . . . . . 374 VIVA 65   9
    squeal said she just once said he) it's fun . . . . 399 NO THANKS 16   3
    int o immensity (upon once whom fiercely by pink . . . . . . 465 NEW POEMS 3   6
    which of earth dragged once -ful leaf. & were . . . . 491 50 POEMS 5   2
    partly seem one atomy once, and every cannot stir . . . . . . 559 1 X 1 19   10
    / / / / (once like a spark) if . . . . 564 1 X 1 24   1
    possible; only truthful --truthfully, once if strangers (who 564 1 X 1 24   12
    with innocence) forgivingly a once of eager glory, no . . . . 601 (CHAIRE) 3   4
    more likely twice that (once crammed into someone's . . . . . 607 (CHAIRE) 9   3
    weigh tless puppet of once man (clutched by immense . . . . . 616 (CHAIRE) 18   4
    light's lives lurch a once world quickly from rises . . . . . 633 (CHAIRE) 35   2
    / / / / once White&Gold daisy in the . . . . 690 95 POEMS 18   1
    who all at) stops (once / / / / . . . . 692 95 POEMS 20   8
    death (dreams hopes despairs) Once happened nowhere else . . 693 95 POEMS 21   6
    of the lit tle once beau tiful la dy . . . . 724 95 POEMS 52   5
    000,000 anybodyelses-- but for once (imag -ine) You / . . . . 779 73 POEMS 7   28
    / / while a once world slips from few . . . . 822 73 POEMS 50   1
+ONCE
    FOR CONTEXT, SEE . . . . 248 IS 5 ONE 19   33
    FOR CONTEXT, SEE . . . . 610 (CHAIRE) 12   4
    FOR CONTEXT, SEE . . . . 710 95 POEMS 38   1
    FOR CONTEXT, SEE . . . . 789 73 POEMS 17   21
    FOR CONTEXT, SEE . . . . 796 73 POEMS 24   7
ONCEUPONS
    (nudge whispershout) laugh matching onceupons each bothing . 681 95 POEMS 9   8
ONDUMONDE
    / / / / ondumonde" (first than caref ully; . . . . 430 NO THANKS 47   1
ONE
    boy whose serious grace one goddess loved too well? . . . . .   3 T&C EPITHALAM   24
    perfume curious of that one month for whom the . . . .   5 T&C EPITHALAM   103
    close into silence, only one tree, one svelte translation . .   6 T&C EPITHALAM   122
    silence, only one tree, one svelte translation of eternity .   6 T&C EPITHALAM   122
    Winged Passion woke and one by one there fell . . . .   8 T&C OF NICOL   9
    woke and one by one there fell upon the . . . .   8 T&C OF NICOL   9
    by the sun, so one high shining tower (which . . . .   8 T&C OF NICOL   17
    let not thy lust one threaded moment lose: haste) . . . . . .   9 T&C SONGS 1   7
    your ladies are all one-- keep your dead beautiful . . . . . 23 T&C PUELLA MEA 264
    than any there is one; to touch it is . . . . 23 T&C PUELLA MEA 273
    to stroll (very slowly) one or two ladies like . . . . 23 T&C PUELLA MEA. 281
    love thy hair is one kingdom the king whereof . . . . 29 T&C ORIENTALE 3 2
    of thy head is one warrior innocent of defeat . . . . 29 T&C ORIENTALE 3 18

ONE (CONTINUED)
cloth from the ceiling (one diamond timid with nesting . . . 32 T&C ORIENTALE 6 24
withers the moon crumbles one by one stars flutter . . . . . 38 T&C AMORES 3   7
moon crumbles one by one stars flutter into dust . . . . . . 38 T&C AMORES 3   7
seatides i trusted not, one night when in my . . . . 39 T&C AMORES 4   11
mouth sweetly-saluted lingers. if one marvel seeing the . . . 42 T&C AMORES 6   8
vainly tried to catch one funny hand opening the . . . . . . 53 T&C PORTRAIT 1   43
curtain. , rises upon one startling doll undressed in . . . . 55 T&C PORTRAIT 3   8
and They cease (and one by one are turned . . . . 62 T&C PORTRAIT 10 21
cease (and one by one are turned suddenly and . . . . 62 T&C PORTRAIT 10 21
at the present writing one still finds delighted fingers . . 70 T&C SON REAL 1   7
not surmise she dreamed one afternoon ....or maybe read? . . 72 T&C SON REAL 3   9
my face, and hear one bird sing terribly afar . . . . 76 T&C SON UNRE 1   13
brightness of your charms: one pierced moment whiter than . . 78 T&C SON UNRE 3   12
....or if sunset utters one unhurried muscled huge chromatic 82 T&C SON ACTU 1   7
i certainly create, lady, one of the thousand selves . . . . 92 & POST IMPR 4   21
for an onion! for one--onion for. putrescence is Cubical . . 94 & POST IMPR 6   10
a minute terrif iceffort one dirty squeal of soiling . . . . 96 & POST IMPR 8   27
firm- ly in to one exactly-mutilated ghost of a . . . . 96 & POST IMPR 8   34
bulge like memories in one crooked street of a . . . . . . 98 & POST IMPR 9   17
what i am at one o'clock to little lips . . . . 115 & PORTRAIT 8   5
at twenty minutes to one, i am this blueeyed . . . . 115 & PORTRAIT 8   26
which mutter thickly (as one merely terricolous American an . 116 & PORTRAIT 9   11
little round water at one end of the well . . . . 126 & SEVEN POEMS 5 2
may i have this one and was never intro- . . . . 126 & SEVEN POEMS 5 20
inti and sitting on one string dead never says . . . . 126 & SEVEN POEMS 5 28
and squeeze- into-largeness without one word and you lie . . 127 & SEVEN POEMS 5 34
/ / / / (one!) the wisti-twisti barber -pole . . . . 128 & SEVEN POEMS 6 1
her small manure-shaped head one sheet on which distinctly . 134 & SON REAL 5   4
marched through me as one army. From her nostrils . . . . . . 135 & SON REAL 6   2
syncopation Europe has --. One day i felt a . . . . 135 & SON REAL 6   11
Will, and Mary with one lung extended to the . . . . 142 & SON REAL 13   10
obscenely from the dress. one nipple tries. playfully to . . 143 & SON REAL 14   9
sweating air with pinkness, one pale dog behind a . . . . . . 144 & SON REAL 15   7
once -over. fiftythree (and one would see if it . . . . 150 & SON REAL 21   2
fatuous swallowed eyes smiles, one grin very distinctly . . . 151 & SON REAL 22   15
(not really enough pulled one before one the vague . . . . . 154 & SON ACTU 3   7
enough pulled one before one the vague tough exquisite . . . 154 & SON ACTU 3   7
several stars are opening one beyond one immaculate curving . 156 & SON ACTU 5   3
are opening one beyond one immaculate curving cool treasures 156 & SON ACTU 5   3
then decently hanged himself, one afternoon. The last thing . 170 & SON ACTU 19   4
out in pairs: amazingly, one pair is white (but . . . . 171 & SON ACTU 20   9
hurriedly hunched over swill; one butting trolley imposingly 172 & SON ACTU 21   4
/ / / / one April dusk the sallow . . . . 194 XLI PORTRAIT 2   1
the sudden extremity of one immense tooth myself surveys . . 201 XLI PORTRAIT 9   30
once the discobolus of one Myron / / / . . . . 203 XLI LA GUERRE 1 20
cry; who gavest as one of those immortal men . . . . 209 XLI SONNETS 5   13
most would i be one of them round the . . . . 215 XLI SONNETS 11   9
indigestible honeycake to men ....one perfectly smooth coffee 217 XLI SONNETS 13 10
sipping singular anisettes as. One opaque big girl jiggles . 220 XLI SONNETS 16 14
topples and slightly expands one square foot mired in . . . . 225 IS 5 ONE LIZ   3
mindless hands. and no one knows what (i am . . . . 225 IS 5 ONE LIZ   10
scented merde which greets one (Everywhere Why) as divine . 230 IS 5 ONE 2   17
the man who owns one ask Dad, He knows). . . . . 233 IS 5 ONE 4   23
i'll tell de woild one swell bangup time wen . . . . 237 IS 5 ONE 8   16
bucks per job with one foot and rock a . . . . 242 ⌐S 5 ONE 13   9
-someBody: hippopotamus, scratch- ing, one, knee with, its, . 252 IS 5 ONE 23   3
more quite ennobling forsooth? One wondrous fine sonofabitch 254 IS 5 ONE 25   5
not care to rise one hand did nothing on . . . . 258 IS 5 ONE 28   17
upward in his swivelchair one fist dangling scandal while . . 259 IS 5 ONE 29   9
thousands i too omit one kelly in response to . . . . 259 IS 5 ONE 29   19
us investigate thoroughly each one his optima rerum first . . 261 IS 5 ONE 31   11
tennisracket. All was over. One brief convulsive octopus, and 263 IS 5 ONE 32   56
white lips a smile, one thought alone: to do . . . . 273 IS 5 TWO 8   11
(fifty) flics for every one (I) communist and all . . . . . . 274 IS 5 TWO 9   18
touching the glass boxes one by one with his . . . . 282 IS 5 THREE 6   26
glass boxes one by one with his magic stick . . . . 282 IS 5 THREE 6   26
far below us perhaps one villa caught like pieces . . . . . . 283 IS 5 THREE 7   10

ONE (CONTINUED)

lips slenderly should create one least smile (shyly if . . .	291	IS 5 FOUR 8	23
(clinging as fingers, loving one another gradually into . . .	305	IS 5 FIVE 4	2
, next door but One a on Dirty bed	312	VIVA 4	17
walking in Dragon st one fine August night, i	313	VIVA 5	2
/ / / / (one fine day) let's take	316	VIVA 8	1
flesh is grass) with one "Paul" a harvard boy	320	VIVA 12	6
two solids in (all one it) solution (of course	323	VIVA 15	3
dreaming puzzling over that one oh just thinking it	323	VIVA 15	7
and offering Miss Gay one (which she politely refused) . . .	326	VIVA 18	19
silliest and whose vast one function being to enter	337	VIVA 28	2
A s groupingThe 6around one darks to 7th s	342	VIVA 33	6
(all by herself) have one. It will not be	352	VIVA 43	2
in this twilight") there one is look how it	353	VIVA 44	6
loveless trick sepa rate one stilled unmoving mind from . . .	354	VIVA 45	20
collects the image of one fatal word; so that	360	VIVA 51	22
had some bliss of one small lady upon earth	360	VIVA 51	33
and world go down, one poem yet shall swim	372	VIVA 63	15
or stones speak or one name control more incredible	377	VIVA 68	4
sprawl twitch lovers) & one dog? piglike big! sorrows	384	NO THANKS 2	11
most fe (hug) males (one-t wo-l oop-l eftsthrowr ightsm . . .	388	NO THANKS 5	14
(are two notSoft soft one are hard one notHard)	388	NO THANKS 5	21
soft one are hard one notHard) not boys boy-	388	NO THANKS 5	22
i immaculately owe dying one life and will my	390	NO THANKS 7	13
/ / / / one nonsufficiently inunderstood re with	398	NO THANKS 15	1
re with some difficulty one father of one (ask	398	NO THANKS 15	4
difficulty one father of one (ask super-) wonderful (mother)	398	NO THANKS 15	5
despair that face) large one coloured nonthings of gluttonous	402	NO THANKS 19	8
small eyes balanced upon one broken babypout (pretty teeth .	406	NO THANKS 23	10
only this eternal mere one bursting soul why, then	414	NO THANKS 31	11
and drunkenness) here's to one undiscoverable guess of whose	424	NO THANKS 41	12
nor every partialness beats one entirety neither may shadow .	425	NO THANKS 42	11
thirteen times a night one hangs a hat upon	427	NO THANKS 44	5
hat upon her tit one carves a cross in	427	NO THANKS 44	6
it away; or cause one causeless cloud to purely	433	NO THANKS 50	4
what's death come (in one bed. / /	433	NO THANKS 50	16
steadily against the west one Clock dimly cries nine, ...	434	NO THANKS 51	14
unsleep this cry of one fiend, a thousand dreams	439	NO THANKS 55	7
unshadowing fate put on one not imaginable star :	454	NO THANKS 69	12
infinity pleased our parents one inch looks good to	466	NEW POEMS 4	16
be as dull as one englishman A: to /	468	NEW POEMS 6	3
of ring & all one two three rings are	470	NEW POEMS 8	17
billion pubic lice inside one pair of trousers (which	473	NEW POEMS 11	6
there was is born: one face who. and hands	479	NEW POEMS 17	14
shadow of a. Not one smallest dream) / /	479	NEW POEMS 17	20
/ must being shall one only thing must: the	480	NEW POEMS 18	2
sky over him with one smile / / /	481	NEW POEMS 19	12
are both making silence two-made-of-one & nothing tells . . .	483	NEW POEMS 21	6
I'd rather learn from one bird how to sing	484	NEW POEMS 22	13
all things to enni one bugger thy nabor (neck	492	50 POEMS 6	12
black this which of one street leaps quick squirmthicklying .	493	50 POEMS 7	11
and cradles in rubbery one somewhat hand the paper	499	50 POEMS 13	5
not nothing comes only one snowflake (and we speak	502	50 POEMS 16	14
remarkably brief but covering one complete miracle of nearest	504	50 POEMS 18	3
an angel's fart came one trembling out of huge	506	50 POEMS 20	12
are in a room's) one is red and (six	507	50 POEMS 21	12
dark) all five are one flowers five flowers and	507	50 POEMS 21	27
five flowers and all one is fire / /	507	50 POEMS 21	28
infinity could never equal one) which may your million . . .	510	50 POEMS 24	11
a tree (this life one leaf) but love is	511	50 POEMS 25	26
floating many bells down) one day anyone died i	515	50 POEMS 29	25
moon the with star one moving are twilight they	518	50 POEMS 32	4
/ / / / one slipslouch twi tterstamp coon	519	50 POEMS 33	1
no cripple wouldn't creep one mile uphill to only	520	50 POEMS 34	31
between eyes emptiness toss one at nobody shoulder and . . .	522	50 POEMS 35	2
big enough to hold one tiny this with time's	523	50 POEMS 36	32
yes completely kind mindheart one true one generous child- .	523	50 POEMS 36	41
kind mindheart one true one generous child- man -god	523	50 POEMS 36	41

ONE (CONTINUED)

how immeasurable anguish pregnant one fearless one good yes .	524	50 POEMS 36	38
anguish pregnant one fearless one good yes completely kind .	524	50 POEMS 36	39
generous child- man -god one eager souldoll one unsellable .	524	50 POEMS 36	43
-god one eager souldoll one unsellable not buyable alive . .	524	50 POEMS 36	44
unsellable not buyable alive one i say human being)	524	50 POEMS 36	46
i say human being) one goldberger / / /	524	50 POEMS 36	46
so deep and strong one queerying wave will whitely	526	50 POEMS 38	7
pain are merely surfaces (one itself showing, itself hiding .	531	50 POEMS 43	6
itself showing, itself hiding one) life's only and true . . .	531	50 POEMS 43	6
birds our all and one gone away the they	541	1 X 1 1	7
wishes are five and one hand is a mind	543	1 X 1 3	18
kind progress doth impart one stands supreme i mean	544	1 X 1 4	3
who) i discreetly (masturbates one honest breadcrumb) say "i	546	1 X 1 6	12
being oke with him) one william shakespeare broke the	552	1 X 1 12	24
his littleness --electrons deify one razorblade into a . . .	554	1 X 1 14	5
two are halves of one: which halves reintegrating, shall . .	556	1 X 1 16	1
they undream a dream) one is the song which	556	1 X 1 16	9
/ / / / one (Floatingly) arrive (silent) one	557	1 X 1 17	1
one (Floatingly) arrive (silent) one by (alive) from (into .	557	1 X 1 17	2
any which Weavingly now one by wonder (on twilight)	557	1 X 1 17	11
thing dares partly seem one atomy once, and every	559	1 X 1 19	10
invent everything he took one breath bigger than a	566	1 X 1 26	2
opening) as we stood, one (truthed by wisping tinily) . . .	572	1 X 1 32	7
than reason; my sweet one (and april's where we're)	578	1 X 1 38	11
whi (mysterious ly) te one t hou / /	581	1 X 1 41	13
to born of be One : petals him starrily	584	1 X 1 44	7
who but zooms through one perfectly beautiful bow "my	585	1 X 1 45	20
/ so isn't small one littlest why, it into	588	1 X 1 48	1
by thousands mean only one amazing thing (secretly adoring .	591	1 X 1 51	20
mankind cancelled are by one merely opening leaf (beyond . .	592	1 X 1 52	7
nothing as something as one one hasn't a why	594	1 X 1 54	9
as something as one one hasn't a why or	594	1 X 1 54	10
we're alive) we're wonderful one times one / /	594	1 X 1 54	45
we're wonderful one times one / / / /	594	1 X 1 54	45
shaped hathole thangew yelps one shi ly glad old	602	(CHAIRE) 4	5
you, jack--tactfully you (with one cocked eyebrow)	605	(CHAIRE) 7	1
obvious to Mere but one small most of a	608	(CHAIRE) 10	8
a man (so easily one in another hides; yet	609	(CHAIRE) 11	3
/ / / / one day a nigger caught	622	(CHAIRE) 24	1
un lucky to break one) whole with sky /	623	(CHAIRE) 25	7
their very oldest lives one pays him with a	624	(CHAIRE) 26	9
could never (by breathless one breathing) be" soul "more" . .	625	(CHAIRE) 27	23
(all together a manying one -ness) nine souls only	627	(CHAIRE) 29	10
made the world's best one hand snatch / /	645	(CHAIRE) 47	4
black perfectly isn 't) one rose opened / /	646	(CHAIRE) 48	17
no known kind with one white eye and one	647	(CHAIRE) 49	17
one white eye and one black eye and the	647	(CHAIRE) 49	18
gruntsqueak , while, idling-is-grindstone one; what: of. . .	656	(CHAIRE) 58	8
silence, who; is: somE oNe. / / / /	657	(CHAIRE) 59	16
which never may become one (wholly strange; familiar wholly)	659	(CHAIRE) 61	7
in Spring comes (no- one asks his name) a	660	(CHAIRE) 62	3
it or he is one / / / /	662	(CHAIRE) 64	12
less than have or one times one than when	664	(CHAIRE) 66	9
have or one times one than when times where--	664	(CHAIRE) 66	9
completely dare be beautiful one if should sing (at	666	(CHAIRE) 68	16
af fa ll s) one l iness / /	673	95 POEMS 1	7
hate with love --human one mortally immortal i can	679	95 POEMS 7	13
the beach (to play one day) and maggie discovered	682	95 POEMS 10	2
three (huddling a- gainst one immense deep hell -o	687	95 POEMS 15	6
immortal us if in one little bed she and	694	95 POEMS 22	7
S with his brutebeak one fatal faded (pinkish or	697	95 POEMS 25	24
this grim most (these one who are) lovers cling	698	95 POEMS 26	6
that bum who's every one / / / /	698	95 POEMS 26	8
exAct ly what any one Living (or some body	702	95 POEMS 30	4
ladies my annie is one nor she wouldn't be	707	95 POEMS 35	11
dad never gave me one cent in his life	707	95 POEMS 35	17
in the throat of one two came hurrying home	709	95 POEMS 37	12

ONE (CONTINUED)
    thousand stars but not one heartbeat of this child; . . . . . 714 95 POEMS 42   11
    earth and sky grow one with won der until . . . . 715 95 POEMS 43   10
    thankfully become each other) one who feels a world . . . . 720 95 POEMS 48   6
    blossom a first star) one / / / / . . . . 720 95 POEMS 48   14
    these immeasurable mysteries (human one; and one celestial) . 721 95 POEMS 49   8
    mysteries (human one; and one celestial) stand soul to . . . 721 95 POEMS 49   8
    / a total stranger one black day knocked living . . . . 730 95 POEMS 58   1
    matterings of mind equal one violet / / / . . . . 736 95 POEMS 64   8
    agreed and we've (with one last more than kiss) . . . . 741 95 POEMS 69   13
    singing &) thing found one old blue wheel in . . . . 753 95 POEMS 81   21
    of nowhere) we --While one thrush sings / / . . . . 758 95 POEMS 85   48
    two he'd make them one (his song's so true) . . . . 760 95 POEMS 87   8
    and pure love with one least ignorance may comprehend . . . . 761 95 POEMS 88   2
    amazement as a leaf--here's one more than each creature . . . 762 95 POEMS 89   5
    and the sky are one today) my very so . . . . 767 95 POEMS 93   15
    (who's any who's some) one who's we / / . . . . 769 95 POEMS 95   28
    why even i suppose one 's wife) --does doesn't . . . . 779 73 POEMS 7   17
    e It's we) humble one (gifted with illimitable joy) . . . . . 783 73 POEMS 11   1
    like a (now with one sweet sun in it, ... 786 73 POEMS 14   12
    different sons of zeus: one, handsome strong and born . . . . 799 73 POEMS 27   3
    being finally released flee one another like the pest . . . . 799 73 POEMS 27   31
    you're going to get one whole buck' not a . . . . 800 73 POEMS 28   12
    stranger replied-- but as one whole buck became his . . . . . 800 73 POEMS 28   14
    / / / / one winter afternoon (at the . . . . 802 73 POEMS 30   1
    a snowstopped silent world) one spirit serenely truly . . . . 808 73 POEMS 36   2
    as greatness is alone-- one (above nevermoving all nowhere) . 808 73 POEMS 36   5
    particular moment it takes one very falling most (there: . . 809 73 POEMS 37   11
    most herself while uttering one a third face, away . . . . . 813 73 POEMS 41   8
    magically, farthest becomes near (one silent pasture, all a . 818 73 POEMS 46   8
    here again --to livingest one star as small these . . . . . . 819 73 POEMS 47   17
    the shrieking sky such one ness as con founds . . . . 826 73 POEMS 54   13
    some (by name myself) one long ago who had . . . . 828 73 POEMS 56   6
    / / / / one t hi s snowflake . . . . 833 73 POEMS 61   1
    gra v es t one / / / / . . . . 833 73 POEMS 61   15
    "seven heavens for just one dying, i'll give you" . . . . . . 837 73 POEMS 65   14
    such hugest how hush, one dead leaf stirring makes . . . . . 839 73 POEMS 67   3
    & when) un til one strict here of amazing . . . . 840 73 POEMS 68   27
    paints with sound, newly one moving cadence may release . . . 842 73 POEMS 70   6
+ONE
    FOR CONTEXT, SEE . . . . 73 T&C SON REAL 4   13
    FOR CONTEXT, SEE . . . . 347 VIVA 38   22
    FOR CONTEXT, SEE . . . . 360 VIVA 51   29
    FOR CONTEXT, SEE . . . . 394 NO THANKS 11   5
    FOR CONTEXT, SEE . . . . 469 NEW POEMS 7   11
    FOR CONTEXT, SEE . . . . 605 {CHAIRE) 7   2
    FOR CONTEXT, SEE . . . . 605 {CHAIRE) 7   2
    FOR CONTEXT, SEE . . . . 653 {CHAIRE) 55   13
    FOR CONTEXT, SEE . . . . 660 {CHAIRE) 62   2
    FOR CONTEXT, SEE . . . . 705 95 POEMS 33   16
    FOR CONTEXT, SEE . . . . 715 95 POEMS 43   21
    FOR CONTEXT, SEE . . . . 720 95 POEMS 48   12
    FOR CONTEXT, SEE . . . . 725 50 POEMS 53   8
    FOR CONTEXT, SEE . . . . 725 95 POEMS 53   8
    FOR CONTEXT, SEE . . . . 830 73 POEMS 58   9
ONE'S
    or the Century whirl? one's memory indignantly protests) this 72 T&C SON REAL 3   4
    (therefore and) softly among one's own memory (but) along . . 317 VIVA 9   18
    and Foses) until (finding one's self at some distance . . . . 319 VIVA 11   15
    noise of waters) one's eye perceives (as the . . . . 319 VIVA 11   25
    of those creatures called one's self so we'll not . . . . . . 528 50 POEMS 40   12
    / / / / one's not half two. It's . . . . 556 1 X 1 16   1
    than books don't grow) one's anything old being everything . 594 1 X 1 54   14
    around we come who) one's everyanything so so world . . . . 594 1 X 1 54   18
+ONE'S
    FOR CONTEXT, SEE . . . . 779 73 POEMS 7   17
ONEEYED
    who cares if some oneeyed son of a bitch . . . . 264 IS 5 ONE 33   27

		PAGE	TITLE	LINE

ONEFUL
are so both and oneful night cannot be so . . . . 537 50 POEMS 49   13
+ONEHUNDREDPERCENTORIGINAL
always will be or the onehundredpercentoriginal sin . . . . . 803 73 POEMS 31   15
ONENESS
lived wrongsideout, sameness chokes oneness truth is confused 446 NO THANKS 61   3
we 're sunlight of oneness / / / / . . . . 589 1 X 1 49   21
as lovers a chieve oneness) each othering Selves i . . . . . 785 73 POEMS 13   14
in a thunder of oneness dream! ! joy truth! . . . . 841 73 POEMS 69   36
+ONENESS
FOR CONTEXT, SEE . . . . 627 (CHAIRE) 29   10
FOR CONTEXT, SEE . . . . 826 73 POEMS 54   13
ONES
the girls (the shy ones, the bold ones; the . . . . 619 (CHAIRE) 21   3
shy ones, the bold ones; the meek proud sloppy . . . . 619 (CHAIRE) 21   4
all except the cold ones paul scorns all the . . . . 619 (CHAIRE) 21   7
the girls (the bright ones, the dim ones; the . . . . 619 (CHAIRE) 21   10
bright ones, the dim ones; the slim plump tiny . . . . 619 (CHAIRE) 21   11
all except the dull ones gus loves all the . . . . 619 (CHAIRE) 21   14
the girls (the warped ones, the lamed ones; the . . . . 619 (CHAIRE) 21   17
warped ones, the lamed ones; the mad moronic maimed) . . . . 619 (CHAIRE) 21   18
all except the dead ones mike likes all the . . . . 619 (CHAIRE) 21   21
the girls (the fat ones, the lean ones;the mean . . . . 619 (CHAIRE) 21   24
all except the green ones / / / / . . . . 619 (CHAIRE) 21   28
ONESELF
all talking's talking to oneself (whether that oneself be . . 804 73 POEMS 32   2
to oneself (whether that oneself be sought or seeking . . . . 804 73 POEMS 32   3
and all talking's to oneself alone but the very . . . . 804 73 POEMS 32   12
ONETWO
ingly attacks landing a onetwo which doubles up suddenly . . 259 IS 5 ONE 29   14
ONETWOTHREEFOURFIVE
watersmooth-silver stallion and break onetwothreefourfive . . 60 T&C PORTRAIT 8   6
ONION
uncouth odour, for an onion! for one--onion for. putrescence 94 & POST IMPR 6   10
for an onion! for one--onion for. putrescence is Cubical . . 94 & POST IMPR 6   10
ONLY
things close into silence, only one tree, one svelte . . . . 6 T&C EPITHALAM   122
head is such as only certain dead and careful . . . . 20 T&C PUELLA MEA   140
face become white perfume only, from the ashes then . . . . . 39 T&C AMORES 4   36
i have been true only to the noise of . . . . 43 T&C AMORES 7   22
lover thou answerest them only with spring) / / . . . . 46 T&C LA GUERRE 2   26
ludicrously dies, i hear only tidewings in the last . . . . . 64 T&C POST IMPR 1   10
little harder for roses only a little harder last . . . . . . 67 T&C POST IMPR 4   22
single colour, i know only that your hands move . . . . 98 & POST IMPR 9   7
the eyes' brittle crust (only feeling the belly's merry . . . 132 & SON REAL 3   7
rash, coherent light) only to trace with stiffening . . . . 155 & SON ACTU 4   7
mind all night, quitting only in the unkind dawn . . . . . . 165 & SON ACTU 14   3
as your mother would, only don't be afraid look . . . . 192 XLI CHANSONS 2   12
Distinct your brain's axe only chops hugest inherent Trees . 195 XLI PORTRAIT 3   18
5 o'clock I stare only always into the tremendous . . . . . 202 XLI PORTRAIT 9   43
, tremendous canyon always only exhales a climbing dark . . . 202 XLI PORTRAIT 9   44
the thin amorous enormous only lips of the evening . . . . . 202 XLI PORTRAIT 9   47
as for me i only knows that as far . . . . 246 IS 5 ONE 17   9
cohorts from Duluth God only, gondola knows Cincingondolanati 256 IS 5 ONE 27   27
i was wifeless and only half awake, cursed with . . . . 262 IS 5 ONE 32   7
in freshly-creased -uniforms with only-just- shined buttons . 274 IS 5 TWO 9   23
a privilege and if only he could meanwhile my . . . . 276 IS 5 TWO 10   17
poet who is afraid only to mistranslate a rhythm . . . . . . 291 IS 5 FOUR 8   10
supposing i dreamed this) only imagine, when day has . . . . 292 IS 5 FOUR 9   2
are like the snow only purer fleeter, like the . . . . 293 IS 5 FOUR 10   1
fleeter, like the rain only sweeter frailer you whom . . . . 293 IS 5 FOUR 10   3
under some dirty collars) only a moment (or was . . . . 296 IS 5 FOUR 13   12
owned by who knows) only turn a little your. . . . . 303 IS 5 FIVE 2   15
nothing from death"-- you only will create (who are . . . . . 306 IS 5 FIVE 5   11
who is asleep with only several faces and a . . . . 312 VIVA 4   5
enemies" is dead the only man woman or child . . . . 336 VIVA 27   3
summer thunder (together) smell only such blue slender hands 340 VIVA 31   19
Thee (once and once only, Queen among centuries universes . . 358 VIVA 49   11

		PAGE	TITLE	LINE

ONLY (CONTINUED)

	PAGE	TITLE	LINE
nothing; then (then the only hands so to speak	359	VIVA 50	14
night shall go) remembering only dare (Wholly consider how .	362	VIVA 53	3
know wholly imagining fire) only consider How / /	362	VIVA 53	16
both quickly signify life's only half (through deep weather .	364	VIVA 55	12
that closes and opens; only something in me understands . . .	366	VIVA 57	18
courage my darling (for only Nobody knows where truth	368	VIVA 59	18
gargled by death: drowned only again carefully through . . .	369	VIVA 60	10
its spirit floated (clothed only in the tide's acute	369	VIVA 60	20
upups to dowNdown (and only where remembers look, this . . .	371	VIVA 62	10
saving our young kiss only must unexist, solemnly and	373	VIVA 64	2
than the grave? from only Whom shall time no	377	VIVA 68	13
less wonderful than this only by you my heart	379	VIVA 70	14
newly alOne is dreamest oNLY THE MooN o VER	383	NO THANKS 1	9
remembering H highest fly only the flag that's furled	390	NO THANKS 7	8
Opening beautiful earth put (only) a Leaf among dark	397	NO THANKS 14	16
room; but likes it only this eternal mere one	414	NO THANKS 31	10
so much sleep they only understand enormously which	418	NO THANKS 35	8
mountains which disappear (and only was night and through . .	419	NO THANKS 36	19
was night and through only this night a mightily	419	NO THANKS 36	21
Spring thirsty for happens only and beautiful there is . . .	437	NO THANKS 53	9
Beautiful to have known Only to have smelled Happens--skip .	437	NO THANKS 53	13
none: and waves which only He may walk Who	438	NO THANKS 54	27
feet (who wanders through only white darkness who moves . . .	439	NO THANKS 55	19
ifs diving under because) only who'll say "and this	439	NO THANKS 55	25
best (and proudly things only which grow and the	441	NO THANKS 56	54
pray so (unlove disappearing) only your less than guessed . .	450	NO THANKS 65	10
everything guard her perhaps only A trifle less (merely . . .	453	NO THANKS 68	4
so huge a home (only more than immeasurable dream	454	NO THANKS 69	7
flame and surely poets only understands) honour this	456	NO THANKS 71	11
feel less worse (but only sameness is normal in	466	NEW POEMS 4	25
but a gland is only a gland) / /	466	NEW POEMS 4	28
these with listening hands only fishermen are prevented by .	478	NEW POEMS 16	11
of guitars and watches only as this (which might	479	NEW POEMS 17	8
his whose unlife bursts only so; only if you	479	NEW POEMS 17	17
unlife bursts only so; only if you should turn	479	NEW POEMS 17	17
must being shall one only thing must: the opening	480	NEW POEMS 18	2
i can entirely her only love whose any mystery	484	NEW POEMS 22	6
digestion so much greenness only dying makes us grow	491	50 POEMS 5	16
merely not nothing comes only one snowflake (and we	502	50 POEMS 16	14
suffice to through the only mystery of love become	510	50 POEMS 24	13
begin to imagine how (only are shall be were	512	50 POEMS 26	17
rain children guessed (but only a few and down	515	50 POEMS 29	9
rain sun moon (and only the snow can begin	515	50 POEMS 29	22
swirly and foldish so only through) the little blue	516	50 POEMS 30	6
visible to us) whom only his dream ing own	516	50 POEMS 30	15
of silence (both an only moon the with star	518	50 POEMS 32	2
one mile uphill to only see him smile. Scorning	520	50 POEMS 34	32
love is the every only god who spoke this	526	50 POEMS 38	1
that yes is the only living thing) and we'll	528	50 POEMS 40	14
all the sea which only is deeper than the	530	50 POEMS 42	7
all the sky which only is higher than the	530	50 POEMS 42	15
itself hiding one) life's only and true value neither	531	50 POEMS 43	7
freedom is compulsory and only man is god. Without	544	1 X 1 4	24
least ourselves remembering love only rides his year. All . .	556	1 X 1 16	14
to was) --all nothing's only our hugest home; the	560	1 X 1 20	23
be men, the sometimes only man is this (most	562	1 X 1 22	2
than hopes are fears only not ever named mountains	563	1 X 1 23	4
not poor not rich (only aware) kind neither nor	564	1 X 1 24	5
kind neither nor cruel (only complete) i not not	564	1 X 1 24	8
not you not possible; only truthful --truthfully, once if . .	564	1 X 1 24	11
of shall and finding only why smashed it into	566	1 X 1 26	7
my "love creates love only" our / / /	572	1 X 1 32	18
have known and i've only we our least begin	574	1 X 1 34	14
--grim comics of duration: only love immortally occurs beyond	576	1 X 1 36	7
perfect hope can feel only despair completely strikes forests	580	1 X 1 40	24
three of me and only while your sweet eyes	588	1 X 1 48	5
who by thousands mean only one amazing thing (secretly . . .	591	1 X 1 51	20

ONLY (CONTINUED)
all stars than eyes "only are quite what worlds . . . . 603 (CHAIRE) 5   14
finds feeling (seize) floats (only by only) a silence . . . . 612 (CHAIRE) 14   13
(seize) floats (only by only) a silence only made . . . . . . 612 (CHAIRE) 14   14
by only) a silence only made of, bird / . . . . 612 (CHAIRE) 14   14
dull here comes the only man reminding with his . . . . 624 (CHAIRE) 26   2
(each serenely welcoming his only and illimitably his . . . . 626 (CHAIRE) 28   8
one -ness) nine souls only alive with a single . . . . 627 (CHAIRE) 29   13
merely to know) Love only has ever been, is, ... 631 (CHAIRE) 33   14
slim float twitter faces) only stand with me, love! . . . . . 633 (CHAIRE) 35   6
and day: gay as only truth is gay (nothing's . . . . 651 (CHAIRE) 53   6
he may be) the only man who'll never die . . . . 685 95 POEMS 13   15
this my sweet) not only wherever the sun and . . . . 686 95 POEMS 14   15
of eyes) appears. Because only the truest things always . . . 697 95 POEMS 25   31
dream (i sus pect) only god himself & as . . . . 698 95 POEMS 26   2
man man ner the only reason every wo man . . . . 700 95 POEMS 28   4
hundred million whos (while only himself was him) two . . . . 709 95 POEMS 37   4
his mother's smile --whose only secret all creation sings . . 714 95 POEMS 42   14
begins to sing an only grin-- dancing to feel . . . . 716 95 POEMS 44   20
but always everything which only dies to grow can . . . . . . 718 95 POEMS 46   6
a truth of yes (only herself and who illimitably . . . . . . 736 95 POEMS 64   3
you say something (for only me) and gone is . . . . 737 95 POEMS 65   3
heartbeat--believe that love (and only love) comprehends . . 741 95 POEMS 69   5
(you feel certain) will only smile / / / . . . . 744 95 POEMS 72   8
to merciful Him Whose only now is forever: standing . . . . . 749 95 POEMS 77   18
testified "giving (and giving only) is living" worlds of . . 763 95 POEMS 90   18
any new (every more only you) most emanation creates . . . . 764 95 POEMS 90   46
will be told sings only--and all lovers are the . . . . 765 95 POEMS 91   9
are the song. Here (only here) is freedom: always . . . . . . 765 95 POEMS 91   10
whatever is done by only me is your doing, ... 766 95 POEMS 92   4
flesh: are lovers glad? only their smallest joy's a . . . . . 768 95 POEMS 94   7
and shall be this only truth (a dream of . . . . 776 73 POEMS 4   34
a lover and his only love, strolling slowly (mind . . . . . . 777 73 POEMS 5   2
cerity equals perspicuity (4) Only The Game Fish Swims . . . 803 73 POEMS 31   17
truly himself; and alone only as greatness is alone-- . . . . 808 73 POEMS 36   4
merely things believable) could only fancy we should never . 809 73 POEMS 37   7
wanders a little guess (only which is this world) . . . . . . 810 73 POEMS 38   3
selves go with you, only i remain; a shadow . . . . 812 73 POEMS 40   2
(life and day are) only loaned: whereas night is . . . . . . 816 73 POEMS 44   7
imaginably morethanmostgenerous spirit. Feeling only (jesus) 823 73 POEMS 51   15
fall (now wrong's the only right since brave are . . . . . . 834 73 POEMS 62   21
poise, love alone understands: only for whom i'll keep . . . 843 73 POEMS 71   5
must always half perceive. Only whose vision can create . . . 845 73 POEMS 73   5
+ONLY
FOR CONTEXT, SEE . . . . 491 50 POEMS 5   5
FOR CONTEXT, SEE . . . . 691 95 POEMS 19   5
FOR CONTEXT, SEE . . . . 700 95 POEMS 28   13
FOR CONTEXT, SEE . . . . 739 95 POEMS 67   15
FOR CONTEXT, SEE . . . . 785 73 POEMS 13   1
ONLY-JUST
in freshly-creased -uniforms with only-just- shined buttons . 274 IS 5 TWO 9   23
ONLYING
friend's --a fingery treesoul onlying from serene whom . . . 517 50 POEMS 31   6
day's bloodlight climbs the onlying world) whose silence are 719 95 POEMS 47   2
ONO
tiny violetflavoured nuisance: Odor? ono. comes out like a . 231 IS 5 ONE 3   54
dbut sth epoutin (gWh. ono: w s li psh . . . . 445 NO THANKS 60   5
ONTHETOPWHOSE
old manwhose Beard rests. onthetopwhose silly, Hand revolves, 101 & POST IMPR 11 47
OO-OO
their lives aint you, oo-oo. dearie not so hard . . . . 109 & PORTRAIT 5   20
OOC
wittily peels the. ploop. --OOc h get: breath once, ... 136 & SON REAL 7   13
OOCH
she knows the devil ooch the devil ouch the . . . . 25 T&C CHANSONS 2   21
OOZES
lady in her limousine oozes in fashionable traffic, just . . 146 & SON REAL 17   10

OPAQUE
    her and ourselves a nearly-opaque perfume disinterestedly . . 146 & SON REAL 17   13
    singular anisettes as. One opaque big girl jiggles thickly . 220 XLI SONNETS 16   14
OPED
    breath away all history oped her teeming womb said . . . . . 552 1 X 1 12   21
OPEN
    peanut (which he will open skilfully with his, mouth . . . .   69 T&C POST IMPR 6   17
    alive (eye pries, not open. Tail stirs.) And the. . . . . . . 166 & SON ACTU 15   11
    all the leaves which open in the rain. little . . . . 191 XLI CHANSONS 1   8
    trees are Made leaves open Clouds take sun mountains . . . . 359 VIVA 50   12
    me which shall increase) open thy fire! for i . . . . 360 VIVA 51   32
    myself as fingers, you open always petal by petal . . . . . . 366 VIVA 57   7
    life or did anybody Open a moment are Not . . . . 395 NO THANKS 12   4
    squeeze your nuts and open your face / / . . . .   407 NO THANKS 24   16
    moons mountains for friends --open your thighs to fate . . . 420 NO THANKS 37   13
    new) come, what Being! open us open our selves. . . . . 422 NO THANKS 39   12
    what Being! open us open our selves. create (suddenly . . . . 422 NO THANKS 39   12
    flower, understanding sizelessly sunlight Open what . . . . . 453 NO THANKS 68   15
    my heart always be open to little birds who . . . . 481 NEW POEMS 19   1
    And (sky she) open new (dark we . . . . 482 NEW POEMS 20   7
    unnow shuts more than open could that every tree . . . . . . 502 50 POEMS 16   7
    the earth does not open her eyes (but the . . . . 505 50 POEMS 19   12
    of trapeze gush somersaults open ing hes shes & . . . . 536 50 POEMS 48   10
    more our twentieth will open wide a wide open . . . . 537 50 POEMS 49   11
    open wide a wide open door we are so . . . . 537 50 POEMS 49   12
    go--the smashed word broken open vow or the oath . . . . . .   569 1 X 1 29   3
    / / / / open green those (dear) worlds . . . .   573 1 X 1 33   1
    were hopes: the moon open for you and close . . . . 575 1 X 1 35   14
    wintry (my lovely) let's open the year both is . . . . 578 1 X 1 38   4
    / / / / open your heart: i'll give . . . . 586 1 X 1 46   1
    again) flowers." "Don't worlds open and worlds close?" . . . 603 {CHAIRE} 5   6
    they'd never close (and open) if that fool called . . . . . . 603 {CHAIRE} 5   9
    (and the wholly babble open at blessed are the . . . . 635 {CHAIRE} 37   19
    / / / / open his head, baby & . . . . 637 {CHAIRE} 39   1
    heart in it (cracked) open that heart, mabel & . . . .   637 {CHAIRE} 39   4
    bed in it (fact) open this bed, sibyl & . . . . 637 {CHAIRE} 39   7
    tart in it (wed) open the tart, lady & . . . .   637 {CHAIRE} 39   10
    stones become eyes locks open keys haven't is have . . . . . 716 95 POEMS 44   24
    countries be my darling (open the very secret of . . . . . . 811 73 POEMS 39   4
    murdering minus of cold --open this ghost with millionary . . 839 73 POEMS 67   11
+OPEN
    FOR CONTEXT, SEE . . . .   724 95 POEMS 52   8
OPENED
    the <> door is opened by the tallest eunuch . . . .   33 T&C ORIENTALE 6   62
    delapida- tion bath-houses whose opened withins ejaculate. .   94 & POST IMPR 6   4
    or so slowly i opened the window a most . . . . 365 VIVA 56   11
    weird worlds must be opened?) Love / / . . . . 377 VIVA 68   14
    isn 't) one rose opened / / / / . . . . 646 {CHAIRE} 48   17
    of my eyes are opened) / / / / . . . .   663 {CHAIRE} 65   14
    space to diminutive this opened drawer) tweak S with . . . . 697 95 POEMS 25   22
    dreaming their eyes have opened to your morning feeling . . . 812 73 POEMS 40   7
+OPENERS
    FOR CONTEXT, SEE . . . .   466 NEW POEMS 4   7
OPENI
    n: starT birDs (lEAp) Openi ng t hing ; . . . . 347 VIVA 38   30
OPENING
    prayer, and as an opening lily drowsy-fair (when from . . . .   8 T&C OF NICOL   12
    sunset frond on frond opening in a rare Slowness . . . . . .   12 T&C SONGS 2   44
    catch one funny hand opening the hard great eyes . . . . . .   53 T&C PORTRAIT 1   44
    when several stars are opening one beyond one immaculate . .   156 & SON ACTU 5   2
    at the sticky moon opening in dusk her new . . . .   170 & SON ACTU 19   3
    The plump left fist opening "wisdom." Flicker of gold. . . . 226 IS 5 ONE MAME   7
    ginks like dis Gawd" opening slowlyslowly them--then . . . .   228 IS 5 ONE MARJ   7
    the again latter then opening a box of newly . . . .   263 IS 5 ONE 32   46
    / / / / opening of the chambers close . . . .   267 IS 5 TWO 2   1
    less tall than mine" (opening the windows) "and there . . . . 328 VIVA 19   10
    ROUND AIR IS FILLED) OPENING / / / / . . . . 348 VIVA 39   16
    this is the door (opening it i think things . . . . 353 VIVA 44   13

		PAGE	TITLE	LINE
OPENING (CONTINUED)				
is nor may truth opening encompass true) while your	. . . . .	373	VIVA 64	16
in A leaf and, Opening beautiful earth put (only)	. . . . . .	397	NO THANKS 14	14
/ / here's to opening and upward, to leaf	. . . .	424	NO THANKS 41	1
fragrantly young earth space opening was. Were your eyes:	. .	432	NO THANKS 49	19
sky and through this opening universe will wraiths of	. . . .	454	NO THANKS 69	9
mr seized green mrs opening is it horribly smith	. . . . . .	465	NEW POEMS 3	9
only thing must: the opening of a (not some	. . . .	480	NEW POEMS 18	2
wound with stone flowers opening for ever these silently	. .	525	50 POEMS 37	4
winter" (like a leaf opening) as we stood, one	. . . . . .	572	1 X 1 32	6
a little gay earth opening is all the flowers	. . . .	583	1 X 1 43	5
a million whys; but opening if are those eyes	. . . .	588	1 X 1 48	7
leaves each herself by opening but shining who by	. . . . . .	591	1 X 1 51	18
are by one merely opening leaf (beyond whose nearness	. . .	592	1 X 1 52	7
than seeks thinking, swim (opening) grow are (me wander	. . .	612	{CHAIRE} 14	2
dreams & through slowquickly opening ifless this irre- VocA	.	719	95 POEMS 47	7
to sing) poems are opening, as if an earth	. . . .	763	95 POEMS 90	4
comes up-up-up in the opening sky (the all the	. . . . . .	773	73 POEMS 1	1
+OPENING				
FOR CONTEXT, SEE	. . . .	480	NEW POEMS 18	14
FOR CONTEXT, SEE	. . . .	835	73 POEMS 63	12
OPENLY				
them a little more openly than usual hither, thither	. . . .	354	VIVA 45	13
OPENS				
purse of whose face opens on a fatgold grin	. . . .	114	& PORTRAIT 7	19
of this a door opens by itself woman.) they	. . . .	243	IS 5 ONE 14	8
once? now her mouth opens too far and: she	. . . .	243	IS 5 ONE 14	12
petal myself as Spring opens (touching skilfully,	. . . . . .	366	VIVA 57	7
you that closes and opens; only something in me	. . . . . .	366	VIVA 57	18
even silence: therefore wonder opens a gate; the prisoner	. .	376	VIVA 67	10
spring lives F feel opens but shuts understand G	. . . . . .	390	NO THANKS 7	5
Light thrown by Them opens sharp holes in dark	. . . . . .	437	NO THANKS 53	4
did merely day close) opens if more than silence	. . . . . .	450	NO THANKS 65	3
his dreams rejoice rejoice) --opens the sun: who music	. . .	533	50 POEMS 45	13
/ if the green opens a little a little	. . . .	614	{CHAIRE} 16	3
who'd) me under a opens (of petals of silence)	. . . . . .	634	{CHAIRE} 36	5
together) when every leaf opens without any sound and	. . . .	665	{CHAIRE} 67	8
a kindness of fragrance opens around them) and whisper	. . .	754	95 POEMS 82	10
to no millionth metaphor opens the simple agony of	. . . . .	842	73 POEMS 70	12
+OPENS				
FOR CONTEXT, SEE	. . . .	614	{CHAIRE} 16	11
OPERATED				
shot up twice, it operated in the hundred ands	. . . .	149	& SON REAL 20	9
+OPIUM				
FOR CONTEXT, SEE	. . . .	325	VIVA 17	11
OPPOSITE				
Idleness, while meaning its opposite? Nothing could be	. . .	263	IS 5 ONE 32	40
the management on Thursdays, opposite which a church stood	.	263	IS 5 ONE 32	50
hope which has no opposite in fear; the strength	. . . . . .	768	95 POEMS 94	10
OPTICS				
what sight shall human optics know more quite ennobling	. . .	254	IS 5 ONE 25	3
OPTIMA				
thoroughly each one his optima rerum first having taken	. . .	261	IS 5 ONE 31	11
OR				
WORD DELETED, APPEARED 315 TIMES				
ORAL				
a verb, miraculous inflected oral devious, beneath the body's		21	T&C PUELLA MEA	210
earth , the reckless oral darkness raging with thin	. . . . .	67	T&C POST IMPR 4	4
little joe gould's quote oral history unquote might	. . . . .	410	NO THANKS 27	9
ORANGE				
/ notice the convulsed orange inch of moon perching	. . . .	86	T&C SON ACTU 5	1
POST IMPRESSIONS windows go orange in the slowly. town,	. . .	89	& POST IMPR 1	1
like curving colour (say orange) against silence, or	. . . .	152	& SON ACTU 1	4
blue yellow violet white orange green- ness o what	. . . . .	437	NO THANKS 53	14
an oceaning abyss of orange dream larger than sky	. . . . . .	599	{CHAIRE} 1	3
ORARANCIDHURD				
o-ras-ourh an-dorg-an ble-at-ssw-ee-t-noth ings orarancidhurd	442	hO THANKS 57	7

	PAGE	TITLE	LINE

ORATION
  's 4th of July oration, with a curse and . . . . 249 IS 5 ONE 20   2
ORBS
  ceiling per both pale orbs thus excluding a leanderless . . . 546 1 X 1 6   6
ORCHID
  ment of actuality), an orchid whose velocity is sculptural . 193 XLI PORTRAIT 1   26
ORDER
  received my dears the order of The Artificial Arm . . . . . . 266 IS 5 TWO 1   27
  liz (take! tommy) we order a steak and they . . . . 513 50 POEMS 27   15
  & $ (in that order) is wHISpEr it left; . . . . 792 73 POEMS 20   8
ORDERED
  (HO PARTHENON) and having ordered yaoorti from Nicho' settled 194 XLI PORTRAIT 2   10
+ORDINARILY
  FOR CONTEXT, SEE . . . . 263 IS 5 ONE 32   33
+ORDINARY
  FOR CONTEXT, SEE . . . . 708 95 POEMS 36   2
ORGAN
  this street a gasping organ is waving moth- eaten . . . . . . 69 T&C POST IMPR 6   1
  moist built like an organ and it loved he . . . . 110 & PORTRAIT 6   18
  reflections to which my organ of imperception gave birth . . 263 IS 5 ONE 32   33
+ORGAN
  FOR CONTEXT, SEE . . . . 69 T&C POST IMPR 6   25
  FOR CONTEXT, SEE . . . . 101 & POST IMPR 11   45
  FOR CONTEXT, SEE . . . . 174 & SON ACTU 23   15
  FOR CONTEXT, SEE . . . . 442 NO THANKS 57   7
  FOR CONTEXT, SEE . . . . 697 95 POEMS 25   3
ORGANICALLY
  the flics are very organically arranged and their nucleus . . 274 IS 5 TWO 9   19
ORGANISED
  the skin of the organised hills an edged nothing . . . . . . 160 & SON ACTU 9   8
+ORGANS
  FOR CONTEXT, SEE . . . . 66 T&C POST IMPR 3   3
ORIDE
  unyewkuntel finglestein idstings yewrety oride lesgo eckshun 474 NEW POEMS 12   13
ORIENTALE
  / / / ORIENTALE i spoke to thee . . . . 27 T&C ORIENTALE 1   T
ORIGINAL
  individual ten centuries of original soon or make it . . . . 561 1 X 1 21   6
+ORIGINAL
  FOR CONTEXT, SEE . . . . 803 73 POEMS 31   15
ORIGINALLY
  used too. much Too. originally spontaneous . . . . 94 & POST IMPR 6   2
ORISH
  disprove eithering vastnesses of orish mind --nothing . . . . 761 95 POEMS 88   4
OSTENSIBLE
  faces superbly limp the ostensible centuries therefore let us 111 & PORTRAIT 6   55
OT
  like wint-air nic like ot-am sum-air (young old nic) . . . . 618 (CHAIRE) 20   24
OTHER
  / / but the other day i was passing . . . . 58 T&C PORTRAIT 6   1
  which have not, known other stomachs and their Sexis . . . . 101 & POST IMPR 11   72
  to rise as the other somethings did-- you imagine . . . . . . 117 & PORTRAIT 10   7
  merrily we became each other humped to tumbling garble . . . 119 & PORTRAIT 11   12
  there looking at each other having the fastest time . . . . . 126 & SEVEN POEMS 5   6
  roam my dumbNess? her other, wet, warm lips limp, ... 137 & SON REAL 8   7
  assiduously which justgraze each other). As the lady lazily . 150 & SON REAL 21   10
  they look at each other. Nudge. (if they love . . . . 171 & SON ACTU 20   10
  (if they love each other, who cares?) They pull . . . . 171 & SON ACTU 20   11
  (eagerly just not each other touch) seeking, some street . . 174 & SON ACTU 23   5
  a flower curled, in other lands where other songs . . . . . . 208 XLI SONNETS 4   11
  in other lands where other songs be sung; yet . . . . 208 XLI SONNETS 4   11
  love to use in other days (drawing my Mes . . . . 213 XLI SONNETS 9   13
  a cradle with the other) it Must be nice . . . . 242 IS 5 ONE 13   10
  pas? (whereas, upon the other hand, myself) but let . . . . . 245 IS 5 ONE 16   15
  dangling scandal while five other fingers snitch rapidly . . 259 IS 5 ONE 29   10
  not rub, like any other pastel. (While you and . . . . 264 IS 5 ONE 33   24
  Hell with that: the other; this, since the thing . . . . . . 264 IS 5 ONE 33   30
  each braver than the other, each (a typewriter within . . . . 266 IS 5 TWO 1   19

	PAGE	TITLE	LINE
OTHER			
we smiled to each other, releasing lay, watching (sprawling,	283	IS 5 THREE 7	21
we are for each other: then laugh, leaning back	290	IS 5 FOUR 7	13
can't pass off on other people: for instance a	298	IS 5 FOUR 15	17
top leaps bounding upon other tops to caroming off	311	VIVA 3	6
silently things Each at other (if not quarrelling in	312	VIVA 4	13
with Holes in each other 's lullaby and other	317	VIVA 9	27
other 's lullaby and other lulla wise by UnBroken	317	VIVA 9	29
we love each (shyly) other, what clouds do or	363	VIVA 54	10
while we were each other disappeared: but i slightly	370	VIVA 61	16
bed bed) when each other courted both was very	401	NO THANKS 18	4
whether it's millions of other punks or just a	549	1 X 1 9	4
/ we love each other very dearly , more	577	1 X 1 37	1
-new- ing remaking what other -wise we should have	660	{CHAIRE} 62	13
more exactly than the other un good people stare	662	{CHAIRE} 64	11
because a mind no other mind should try to	679	95 POEMS 7	7
day thankfully become each other) one who feels a	720	95 POEMS 48	6
course) or on the other well your oldest pal	779	73 POEMS 7	8
people (& not the other way round) because it	782	73 POEMS 10	6
/ annie died the other day never was there	794	73 POEMS 22	1
to his eyelashes-- the other, cunning ugly lame; but	799	73 POEMS 27	5
/ "right here the other night something odd occurred"	800	73 POEMS 28	1
+OTHER			
FOR CONTEXT, SEE	104	& POST IMPR 14	21
FOR CONTEXT, SEE	237	IS 5 ONE 8	18
FOR CONTEXT, SEE	310	VIVA 2	12
FOR CONTEXT, SEE	319	VIVA 11	37
FOR CONTEXT, SEE	332	VIVA 23	2
FOR CONTEXT, SEE	347	VIVA 38	22
OTHER'S			
such immortal friends the other's each / / /	730	95 POEMS 58	6
OTHERING			
a chieve oneness) each othering Selves i sit (hearing	785	73 POEMS 13	15
OTHERLITTLE			
ata little roundtable among otherlittle roundtables Her, eyes	104	& POST IMPR 14	3
OTHERS			
songs (the singers the others they have been faithful	43	T&C AMORES 7	7
must and with the others i've been Effie who	117	& PORTRAIT 10	23
love the pen while others wrote in steel, accept	209	XLI SONNETS 5	10
& some people and others please don't confuse. Some	314	VIVA 6	4
And then bite) candy others fly, their; puLLing: bright . . .	314	VIVA 6	13
roll that helplessness which others stroke with brushes . . .	339	VIVA 30	10
(it is incredible But others don't scream murmur wink	391	NO THANKS 8	13
off or otherwise amplify others) the so to speak	391	NO THANKS 8	16
thinks (the thoughts of others, be it understood) he	406	NO THANKS 23	2
/ / reason let others give and realness bring--	454	NO THANKS 69	1
ever & someone (the others have long ago laid	695	95 POEMS 23	12
+OTHERS			
FOR CONTEXT, SEE	231	IS 5 ONE 3	42
OTHERWISE			
without any reason and otherwise roses and mountains	91	& POST IMPR 3	15
the un -spontaneous and otherwise scented merde which greets	230	IS 5 ONE 2	16
the (hei -nous thought) otherwise immaculately tabulated . .	267	IS 5 TWO 2	16
fellows but i being otherwise made compose curves and	291	IS 5 FOUR 8	2
the bronx (enlivening an otherwise dead silence with harmless	326	VIVA 18	13
marry bump off or otherwise amplify others) the so	391	NO THANKS 8	16
"can grow (gracefully or otherwise) old. Old may mean	626	{CHAIRE} 28	3
quote citizens unquote might otherwise forget (to err is . .	636	{CHAIRE} 38	5
means funereally hilarious (or otherwise democratic) but . .	802	73 POEMS 30	20
+OTHERWISE			
FOR CONTEXT, SEE	472	NEW POEMS 10	10
FOR CONTEXT, SEE	660	{CHAIRE} 62	13
OU			
yawning will ask ourselves ou sont les neiges.... some . . .	237	IS 5 ONE 8	3
OUCH			
devil ooch the devil ouch the devil ach the	25	T&C CHANSONS 2	22
cru. Ising thither: t, ouch soft-ly me and eye	361	VIVA 52	12

OUGHT
   decided what this cathedral ought to look like) it . . . . . 323 VIVA 15 24
   whomever's afraid down with ought with because with every . . 424 NO THANKS 41 9
   more better when all ought to feel less worse . . . . 466 NEW POEMS 4 24
OUNCE
   / buy me an ounce and i'll sell you . . . . 513 50 POEMS 27 1
OUR
   the sheer cadence of our gray flesh in the . . . . 9 T&C SONGS 1 23
   to be immortal is our doom; but a rain . . . . 9 T&C SONGS 1 24
   sunsets, it shall pass. Our feet tread sleepless meadows . . 9 T&C SONGS 1 27
   contemptuous intent till this our flesh merely shall be . . . 84 T&C SON ACTU 3 4
   churning witty, twitters upon Our (ta-te-ta in a parenthesis! 89 & POST IMPR 1 15
   we will confuse hotly our moreover irrevocable bodies while . 111 & PORTRAIT 6 61
   and like elephants through our single brain in memory . . . . 111 & PORTRAIT 6 69
   little sister could with our big brother who is . . . . . . 117 & PORTRAIT 10 19
   The Then-arrows making do our mouths something red, something 160 & SON ACTU 9 17
   in the rivers of our blood, miss by how . . . . 174 & SON ACTU 23 9
   and looking up at our beautiful tree we'll dance . . . . . 192 XLI CHANSONS 2 26
   if learned darkness from our searched world should wrest . 205 XLI SONNETS 1 1
   sleep bereaves us of our slow tranquillities and He . . . . 210 XLI SONNETS 6 2
   mind, to hear nearing our hearts' irrevocable play-- through 215 XLI SONNETS 11 13
   toward my mouth, steer our lost bodies carefully downward) . 215 XLI SONNETS 11 17
   bliss! Picture it gents: our hero, Dan who as . . . . 254 IS 5 ONE 25 14
   king as linotypes gobblehobble our lightheavy twic twoc ingly 259 IS 5 ONE 29 13
   care to lie upon our abdomens for greater privacy . . . . . 261 IS 5 ONE 31 12
   convulsive octopus, and then our hero folded his umbrella. . 263 IS 5 ONE 32 56
   occupied the subject of our attention; to speak even . . . . 263 IS 5 ONE 32 61
   perceive in front of our lady a ring of . . . . 279 IS 5 THREE 3 5
   mouse to hold lovingly, our lady what do you . . . . 279 IS 5 THREE 3 21
   / sunlight was over our mouths fears hearts lungs . . . . . 283 IS 5 THREE 7 2
   speaks (whispering, suggesting that our souls inhabit . . . . 285 IS 5 FOUR 2 4
   crease) will smooth entirely our minds --before leaving my . 288 IS 5 FOUR 5 5
   this pillow, dear where our heads lived and were. . . . . . 288 IS 5 FOUR 5 10
   and you are on our ways to dust of . . . . 293 IS 5 FOUR 10 14
   with yours shut by our mingling arms through a . . . . . . 297 IS 5 FOUR 14 2
   to eternity --after which our separating selves become . . . 297 IS 5 FOUR 14 14
   being not asleep, elsewhere our dreams began which now . . . 304 IS 5 FIVE 3 7
   / / / / our touching hearts slenderly comprehend . . . . . 305 IS 5 FIVE 4 1
   caught in thickening fear our slightly fingering spirits . . 305 IS 5 FIVE 4 7
   autumn abruptly wholly hugs our dying silent minds, which . . 305 IS 5 FIVE 4 9
   thoroughly's stolen (somewhere between our unlighted hearts . 322 VIVA 14 10
   when a kiss departs our lips are made of . . . . 322 VIVA 14 12
   Miss G touched n.y. our skeleton stepped from his . . . . . 326 VIVA 18 10
   to Miss Gay during our return voyage, my pensive . . . . . 326 VIVA 18 31
   I will not eat" our president, being of which . . . . 339 VIVA 30 34
   (ppear ah! Star whycol our ed shy lurch small . . . . 349 VIVA 40 12
   writhe amor (Though through our hearts hugely squirm roots) . 361 VIVA 52 8
   ifs.) yet shall our Not to be deciphered . . . . 361 VIVA 52 23
   demand the metaphor of our projectile am tell such . . . . . 362 VIVA 53 12
   resembles beauty less than our breathing / / / . . . . . . 363 VIVA 54 12
   (as poems are made) Our picking it. this caress . . . . . . 364 VIVA 55 9
   ferns) therefore togethering our wholly lives Givehurling . 371 VIVA 62 15
   granted the all saving our young kiss only must . . . . . . 373 VIVA 64 2
   more incredible splendor than our merely universe, love's . 377 VIVA 68 6
   / / so standing, our eyes filled with wind, ... 378 VIVA 69 1
   any curious dawn discuss our mingling spirits, you would . . 379 VIVA 70 7
   Being! open us open our selves. create (suddenly announce: . 422 NO THANKS 39 13
   will forget him (emptying our soul of emptiness) priming . . 428 NO THANKS 45 14
   life became) and does our fatally unshadowing fate put . . . 454 NO THANKS 69 11
   what merely riches of our pretty world sweetly who . . . . . 456 NO THANKS 71 5
   religious fuss infinity pleased our parents one inch looks . 466 NEW POEMS 4 15
   that and that noing our gone snow gone yours . . . . 491 50 POEMS 5 7
   gentlemen poeds urseappeal netsam our spinsters and coeds) . 492 50 POEMS 6 4
   snowflake (and we speak our names / / / . . . . 502 50 POEMS 16 14
   laugh and shall entirely our doom steer his great . . . . . 528 50 POEMS 40 7
   and cowards into grow our can'ts were born to . . . . 537 50 POEMS 49 9
   were born to happen our mosts have died in . . . . 537 50 POEMS 49 10
   have died in more our twentieth will open wide . . . . . . 537 50 POEMS 49 11

OUR (CONTINUED)

	PAGE	TITLE	LINE
will never no? measureless our pure living complete love . .	538	50 POEMS 50	3
are your are birds our all and one gone	541	1 X 1 1	6
a mind then over our thief goes (you go	543	1 X 1 3	19
to teem) still doth our hero contemplate in raptures	544	1 X 1 4	19
was) --all nothing's only our hugest home; the most	560	1 X 1 20	23
if strangers (who deep our most are selves) touch:	564	1 X 1 24	14
"love creates love only" our / / / /	572	1 X 1 32	18
and i've only we our least begin to guess	574	1 X 1 34	14
wonders huger than prove our fears were hopes: the	575	1 X 1 35	12
awake more secretly than our (if disappear should some . . .	577	1 X 1 37	7
and dave --tomorrow is our permanent address and there . . .	579	1 X 1 39	12
and strikes my your our blossoming sphere / /	582	1 X 1 42	16
and foreverless thy? why our is love and neverless	590	1 X 1 50	26
is my time is our time for springtime is	591	1 X 1 51	2
is my time is our time for springtime is	591	1 X 1 51	26
but bluest took it our away beyond where what	593	1 X 1 53	17
him still if now our sun is gone reminding	624	(CHAIRE) 26	22
for the crumb of our Now) twiceuponatime wave-- put	639	(CHAIRE) 41	12
will exactly do next (our great problem nearly solved	650	(CHAIRE) 52	13
rapturously up) we spill our masterpiece / / /	650	(CHAIRE) 52	20
agree) shall never discover our touch and feel --for	664	(CHAIRE) 66	15
cringing --it's spring (all our night becomes day) o, ...	665	(CHAIRE) 67	18
/ / / love our so right is, all	666	(CHAIRE) 68	1
before-- and shining this our now must come to	667	(CHAIRE) 69	8
must come to then our then shall be some	667	(CHAIRE) 69	9
of heavenly earth beguiles our spirits, whose miraculously .	675	95 POEMS 3	2
a sharpening freedom lifts our blood as if whole	675	95 POEMS 3	6
--yes; or as if our souls, awakened from summer's	675	95 POEMS 3	9
forget (and longer dear) our birth's the because of	686	95 POEMS 14	10
of a why but our doom is to grow	686	95 POEMS 14	12
your my life and our / / / /	687	95 POEMS 15	.12
of roses (who amaze our now and here with	688	95 POEMS 16	8
as the god of our fathers' fathers bows to	711	95 POEMS 39	3
a world to build our clown --shouting to see	716	95 POEMS 44	12
roof leaks it 's our (home means if any	728	95 POEMS 56	4
sun shines they are our also my darling) but	728	95 POEMS 56	8
silence nearer than each our heartbeat--believe that love . .	741	95 POEMS 69	4
with nothing deeper than our minds to call the	741	95 POEMS 69	8
primeval whyless sky; healing our by immeasurable night . . .	745	95 POEMS 73	7
and little house this our from hate from fear	746	95 POEMS 74	3
bird should sing: and our night's thousand million miracles .	756	95 POEMS 84	12
and fate and even Our whisper it Selves but	762	95 POEMS 89	12
fall and in winter our spring is the yes	766	95 POEMS 92	31
all) whereas (my sweet) our summer in fall and	776	73 POEMS 4	30
and right where soulless our (with all their minds)	780	73 POEMS 8	6
earth) & nobody (including our selves) will reme mber	797	73 POEMS 25	12
this implacable unthing next, our illustrious scientist . . .	799	73 POEMS 27	23
all the luck; since our hero is quite without	800	73 POEMS 28	11
and my (and infinite our) merely to undie /	817	73 POEMS 45	14
sun is moon, and our (from inexistence moving) sweet	818	73 POEMS 46	3
of all things under our blonder than blondest star	825	73 POEMS 53	1
/ / now does our world descend the path	834	73 POEMS 62	1
end of briefer each our bliss-- where seeing eyes	834	73 POEMS 62	26
/ / wild (at our first) beasts uttered human	844	73 POEMS 72	1
beasts uttered human words --our second coming made stones .	844	73 POEMS 72	2
the starhushed silence which our third's / / /	844	73 POEMS 72	3

OURS

	PAGE	TITLE	LINE
memory strolls) and every ours for the mere worshipping . . .	617	(CHAIRE) 19	12
drowning in supreme thunder? ours (over you reels and	639	(CHAIRE) 41	2
of space and time --ours is the now and	745	95 POEMS 73	14
any doubt of impossible ours --God's heaven perhaps comprises	748	95 POEMS 76	4
heaven, come hell) precisely ours is the now to	776	73 POEMS 4	15
never know are unimaginably ours to feel-- how should	809	73 POEMS 37	8

OURSELVES

	PAGE	TITLE	LINE
discussed; between her and ourselves a nearly-opaque perfume	146	& SON REAL 17	13
be murdered known photographed, ourselves yawning will ask .	237	IS 5 ONE 8	2
ourselves yawning will ask ourselves ou sont les neiges..... .	237	IS 5 ONE 8	2

	PAGE	TITLE	LINE
OURSELVES (CONTINUED)			
sunlight and less moonlight ourselves against the worms hate	238	IS 5 ONE 9	20
beddings and bumpings of ourselves to be observed how	261	IS 5 ONE 31	7
as yet awake, of ourselves which shout and cling, ...	264	IS 5 ONE 33	14
slowly fatally turning into ourselves... while in the very .	283	IS 5 THREE 7	25
what was Disappeared into ourselves who (look) . , ...	286	IS 5 FOUR 3	23
well) here's looking at ourselves two solids in (all	323	VIVA 15	1
that you had carefully ourselves decided what this cathedral	323	VIVA 15	24
me reminded him of ourselves) as Nobody came slowly	355	VIVA 46	20
least breathing may surprise ourselves --let's then despise .	368	VIVA 59	15
were-- so in darkness ourselves go, mind in mind	379	VIVA 70	3
the clock) we, of ourselves who more a part	386	NO THANKS 3	2
deep in dark least ourselves remembering love only rides . .	556	1 X 1 16	13
lovers--pray that us will ourselves continue to outgrow all .	574	1 X 1 34	12
a me) it's always ourselves we find in the	682	95 POEMS 10	12
tongue tells (such as ourselves) begins to sing an	716	95 POEMS 44	18
not love, dear; imagine ourselves like living neither nor . .	743	95 POEMS 71	5
whispering rainlife) infinite also ourselves exist sans . . .	755	95 POEMS 83	14
/ now (more near ourselves than we) is a	760	95 POEMS 87	1
+OURSELVES			
FOR CONTEXT, SEE	422	NO THANKS 39	13
FOR CONTEXT, SEE	577	1 X 1 37	7
FOR CONTEXT, SEE	829	73 POEMS 57	10
OUT			
hidehidehide whisk whisk look out for the old woman	25	T&C CHANSONS 2	17
and she goes forth out of hands and she	38	T&C AMORES 3	11
the glory is fallen out of the sky the	41	T&C AMORES 5	1
brittle legs winces swiflty out of number 1 someThing	62	T&C PORTRAIT 10	25
the creeping shores as out of dumb strong hands	64	T&C POST IMPR 1	5
the box sprouts fairies, out of it sour gnomes	69	T&C POST IMPR 6	3
cent of it get out ears dribbles soft right	96	& POST IMPR 8	20
my mouth will go out into the East side, ...	100	& POST IMPR 11	19
For my stomach goes out into the east side	101	& POST IMPR 11	59
hisknees huggedtogether it, goes out into the rapid hard . .	101	& POST IMPR 11	61
O i tell you out of the minute incessant	111	& PORTRAIT 6	51
hand (which comes carefully out of Nowhere) arranging a . . .	124	& SEVEN POEMS 3	3
so everybody just puts out their finger and they	126	& SEVEN POEMS 5	12
moon's a balloon, coming out of a keen city	129	& SEVEN POEMS 7	2
blue woman with sticking out breasts hanging clothes. On . .	167	& SON ACTU 16	1
the morning they go out in pairs: amazingly, one	171	& SON ACTU 20	8
They pull the morning out of the night. I	171	& SON ACTU 20	12
love's had his tears out, perhaps shall pass a	181	XLI SONGS 3	6
/ i will wade out till my thighs are	189	XLI SONGS 11	1
dreaming of being taken out and allowed to shine, ...	192	XLI CHANSONS 2	15
content my friend's being, out of the spontaneous clumsy . .	193	XLI PORTRAIT 1	19
sumptuous screech of simplicity (out of the black unbunged .	195	XLI PORTRAIT 3	9
his Earliest word wheeled out on the sunny dump	197	XLI PORTRAIT 5	22
nuisance: Odor? ono. comes out like a ribbon lies	231	IS 5 ONE 3	55
we cannot wear it out no sir which is	238	IS 5 ONE 9	11
he smiles is like Out of doors he's a	251	IS 5 ONE 22	6
brook of pinkest vomit out of eyes which noticed	258	IS 5 ONE 28	14
bottles, cats smoothly willowing out and in between bottles,	279	IS 5 THREE 3	14
twilight takes the sting out of the vermilion jacket	279	IS 5 THREE 3	18
/ / / will out of the kindness of	281	IS 5 THREE 5	1
back and up leaning out of yellowgreen water. they	281	IS 5 THREE 5	9
suddenly make a fist out of ten fingers voices	281	IS 5 THREE 5	20
over houses roofs And out of the east toward	284	IS 5 FOUR 1	17
windows, unobserved --listen, for (out of all things) dream .	292	IS 5 FOUR 9	9
hate people and lean out of this window is	295	IS 5 FOUR 12	23
thrown away himself taptaptaps out of your brain, hopes, . .	298	IS 5 FOUR 15	26
eyes? And send life out of me and the	302	IS 5 FIVE 1	7
McKinley when Buch tooked out his C.O.D. Abe tucks	321	VIVA 13	7
silence with harmless quips, out of Briggs by Kitty)	326	VIVA 18	13
she politely refused) set out gaily for the hyenas	326	VIVA 18	19
/ / helves surling out of eakspeasies per (reel)	330	VIVA 21	1
own Shush Shame as (out from behind Nowhere) creeps	330	VIVA 21	13
my face i hauls out uh flask an offers	332	VIVA 23	20
dancing" (a moon swims out of a cloud a	338	VIVA 29	21

	PAGE	TITLE	LINE

OUT (CONTINUED)

	PAGE	TITLE	LINE
streets spill lazily multitudes out of final towers;	345	VIVA 36	7
were supposed to be out of my reach ,	353	VIVA 44	17
/ / a light Out) & first of all	358	VIVA 49	1
centuries universes between Who out of deeplyness rose to	358	VIVA 49	13
& perfectingly We dive out of tinying time (into	373	VIVA 64	10
children building this rainman out of snow / /	390	NO THANKS 7	14
wander into which and out of) Life, dost Thou	406	NO THANKS 23	11
/ / / / out of a supermetamathical subpreincestures	425	NO THANKS 42	1
most under imagination. When (out of sheer nothing) came	432	NO THANKS 49	14
when from a sidewalk out of (blown never quite	442	NO THANKS 57	3
by large sorry) creatures out of (clumsily shining out	442	NO THANKS 57	4
out of (clumsily shining out of) instru- ments, waltzing;	442	NO THANKS 57	5
unununun? butbutbut?? tonton??? ing???? --Out-& steps; which	445	NO THANKS 60	18
swiftly which fails but out of serene perfectly Nothing	456	NO THANKS 71	7
The sq uirmwri th-ing out of wonderful thunder! of?	469	NEW POEMS 7	9
yell that spell that out big (bigger than cosmic	475	NEW POEMS 13	18
a moon a magic out of the black this	493	50 POEMS 7	9
losing spectres mime until out of merely not nothing	502	50 POEMS 16	13
fart came one trembling out of huge each eye	506	50 POEMS 20	12
into bigger much some out of (not visible to	516	50 POEMS 30	15
gradually upon four minds (out of some undering joy	517	50 POEMS 31	9
give, singing each morning out of each night my	520	50 POEMS 34	3
singing each new leaf out of each tree (and	521	50 POEMS 34	50
of spiralling why and out of black because your	522	50 POEMS 35	13
will (kiss me) go out into the morning the	529	50 POEMS 41	4
crumb ling eye -holes oUt of whe reful whom	534	50 POEMS 46	18
first little flowers rise out of tremendous darkness into	559	1 X 1 19	14
in two, peels forever out of his grave and	560	1 X 1 20	19
git anything you like out of it if you	567	1 X 1 27	12
goldenly float so (dreaming out of dreams among) no	573	1 X 1 33	10
may rest --you bring (out of dark the earth)	575	1 X 1 35	7
truest lovers grow if out of midnight dropped more	576	1 X 1 36	12
with brooks: trees tumble out of twigs and sticks;	580	1 X 1 40	28
swoop and a dart out flew his wish (it	593	1 X 1 53	8
by wave doom disappeared, out of perhaps (who knows?)	599	(CHAIRE) 1	7
hush) noones are coming out in the gloam ing	600	(CHAIRE) 2	4
/ / / this out of within itself moo	602	(CHAIRE) 4	1
genial plac -idity (plus, out of much its misbutt-	607	(CHAIRE) 9	5
/ / / / out of more find than	612	(CHAIRE) 14	1
where and she disappeared. Out of more (fingeryhands me	612	(CHAIRE) 14	11
/ / / / out of the mountain of	617	(CHAIRE) 19	1
disappear a sun and out of houses pour maids	624	(CHAIRE) 26	5
of trunk, and singing out of a red book)	631	(CHAIRE) 33	3
Now) twiceuponatime wave-- put out your eyes, and touch	639	(CHAIRE) 41	13
even yankee ingenu ity (out of a jew a	644	(CHAIRE) 46	4
me (and quite with out crushing) the papery weightless	652	(CHAIRE) 54	8
a hole in it out of which demons with	652	(CHAIRE) 54	12
faces called flowers float out of the ground and	665	(CHAIRE) 67	1
sobcries "paw? lee" --whereupon out (Sl0 wLy) steps (to	697	95 POEMS 25	15
pretty pink pinafore'd knock out your eye" "well maybe	707	95 POEMS 35	8
/ / / / out of night's almosT Floats	719	95 POEMS 47	1
knocked living the hell out of me-- who found	730	95 POEMS 58	2
/ / / / out of the lie of	736	95 POEMS 64	1
big a voice comes out of some dreaming tree	752	95 POEMS 80	2
like a mind with out a body (turn ing	753	95 POEMS 81	6
fathering (as that himself out of all silence strolls)	756	95 POEMS 84	10
which captain am sails out of sleep steering for	781	73 POEMS 9	3
Me up at does out of the floor quietly	784	73 POEMS 12	2
dame: he won't be out of work while she	790	73 POEMS 18	7
--why guesswho nearly leaped out of muchtheworseforwear shoes	800	73 POEMS 28	8
/ / silently if, out of not knowable night's	810	73 POEMS 38	1
of that star, if out of climbing whom begins	811	73 POEMS 39	12
/ / / / out of midsummer's blazing most	818	73 POEMS 46	1

+OUT

	PAGE	TITLE	LINE
FOR CONTEXT, SEE	94	& POST IMPR 6	21
FOR CONTEXT, SEE	423	NO THANKS 40	14
FOR CONTEXT, SEE	446	NO THANKS 61	3

		PAGE	TITLE	LINE
OUT-&				
unununun? butbutbut?? tonton??? ing???? --Out-& steps; which		445	NO THANKS 60	18
OUTA				
'18 kickin duh guts outa dem doity frogeaters an		332	VIVA 23	15
OUTDOES				
sublimated tom-tom which quite outdoes the mandolin- man's	.	171	& SON ACTU 20	5
OUTER				
azures fluttering from night's outer wing strong silent . . .		208	XLI SONNETS 4	2
OUTERLY				
s o howpale) bluedmufFletomben outerly jeT ting lip ssixs . .		342	VIVA 33	10
OUTGLORY				
anguish) who've made her, outglory glory the little while . .		742	95 POEMS 70	9
OUTGROW				
will ourselves continue to outgrow all whose mosts if		574	1 X 1 34	12
OUTLAWED				
shriek; when Souls are outlawed, Hearts are sick, Hearts	. .	438	NO THANKS 54	21
OUTLIFT				
in soft) firm who outlift queries of self pouring		613	{CHAIRE} 15	7
OUTLINED				
dream of bells; perfectly outlined against afterglow are all		750	95 POEMS 78	3
OUTMARCH				
not darkness shall quite outmarch forever --and i perceive,	.	376	VIVA 67	6
OUTRAGEOUS				
clattered forward skidding in outrageous sabots language	. .	277	IS 5 THREE 1	12
OUTSIDE				
was sitting in mcsorley's. outside it was New York		96	& POST IMPR 8	1
It, did not answer. outside. (it was New York		97	& POST IMPR 8	45
in a blouse just outside this window, touching the		282	IS 5 THREE 6	25
isn't a new moon outside your window saying if		572	1 X 1 32	2
OUTSTART				
hinted "novocaine?" the eyes outstart, curl, bloat, are newly		226	IS 5 ONE MAME	13
OUTTHUNDERS				
with magic until peace outthunders silence. And (night climbs		428	NO THANKS 45	17
OUTTOWERING				
unthing --stern sexual timelessness, outtowering this noisy	.	351	VIVA 42	3
OUTWARD				
Rolls Royce swoops smoothly outward (amid ◇ tables) while	.	232	IS 5 ONE 3	8
Which when both march outward into the freezing fire		311	VIVA 3	14
OUTWRITHEIN				
relaxing -ly) i downrise outwrithein- ing upfall and Am . . .		449	NO THANKS 64	5
OVAL				
of life.... Cecile, the oval shove of hiding pleasure. . . .		138	& SON REAL 9	13
+OVALS				
FOR CONTEXT, SEE		100	& POST IMPR 11	28
OVER				
Wind beautifully who wanderest over smooth pages of forgotten		3	T&C EPITHALAM	18
of unendured eternal gold over the infinite breast in		4	T&C EPITHALAM	39
pedestal the deep expels (over Selene's car closing uncouth)		4	T&C EPITHALAM	47
thee i burn incense, over the dim smoke straining		31	T&C ORIENTALE 5	22
/ your little voice Over the wires came leaping		44	T&C AMORES 8	2
my eyes or twinkling over to my side Looked		44	T&C AMORES 8	8
cried when i heard over time and tide and		44	T&C AMORES 8	20
jerked into eternity. when over my head a shooting		49	T&C IMPRESS 3	22
will yell at him over the music and jerk		69	T&C POST IMPR 6	13
shabby man is yelling over the music i understand		69	T&C POST IMPR 6	33
Her hunger softly flung over the gasping shores leaves . . .		77	T&C SON UNRE 2	6
you, the dance all over again and you, feel		127	& SEVEN POEMS 5	36
feel all again all over the way men you		127	& SEVEN POEMS 5	37
get: breath once, all over, kid how, funny Do		136	& SON REAL 7	14
And had some rows over percent. The gang got		149	& SON REAL 20	8
a prostitute the once -over. fiftythree (and one would . . .		150	& SON REAL 21	2
string of your smile over his body squirms kissingly, ...		161	& SON ACTU 10	6
keen spider skipping quickly over patriotic swill. The, . . .		166	& SON ACTU 15	2
a pup hurriedly hunched over swill; one butting trolley . . .		172	& SON ACTU 21	4
fur, and what-is-it comes over parting flesh.... And eyes . .		175	& SON ACTU 24	12
god there's a portrait over the door very notable		198	XLI PORTRAIT 6	8
of human rind-- when over hate has triumphed darkly		213	XLI SONNETS 9	5
are going rather kaka over there, over there. yet		233	IS 5 ONE 4	8

574

OVER (CONTINUED)

rather kaka over there, over there. yet we scarcely	233 IS 5 ONE 4	8
up is lead all over Brattle Street by a	253 IS 5 ONE 24	14
the tennisracket. All was over. One brief convulsive octopus,	263 IS 5 ONE 32	56
coat (scrambling all up over the tribune dances crazily	267 IS 5 TWO 2	5
all up all everywhere over you all me everyone	272 IS 5 TWO 7	11
by wind) slammed hard- over the tiller; clattered forward	277 IS 5 THREE 1	11
upon a (that is over: and the sea heaving	277 IS 5 THREE 1	19
rapidly along this pole over five squirming mice; or	279 IS 5 THREE 3	15
tumbling in sand Clouds over me are like bridegrooms	281 IS 5 THREE 5	15
/ / sunlight was over our mouths fears hearts	283 IS 5 THREE 7	1
creeping along the air over houses roofs And out	284 IS 5 FOUR 1	15
about, i wonder as over this floor (quietly with	286 IS 5 FOUR 3	3
every- should where say over the damned table and	287 IS 5 FOUR 4	17
autumn, cleverly dies and over the ripe world wanders	293 IS 5 FOUR 10	24
well) indolently dreaming puzzling over that one oh just	323 VIVA 15	7
oh just thinking it over (at that just supposing	323 VIVA 15	8
spray -ing threecoloured puke over this younger than i	324 VIVA 16	8
/ how ses humble. Over thin earths chatterish strut	346 VIVA 37	3
standing near my swaying over her (silent) with eyes	352 VIVA 43	8
as Nobody came slowly over the town / /	355 VIVA 46	21
always which creep budgingly over some numbered face capable	359 VIVA 50	15
Tomorrow by her spoor) over the earth wandering hunter	374 VIVA 65	8
Death: for day is over (and such a day	376 VIVA 67	1
and the whining rigging over us, i implore you	378 VIVA 69	2
/ / / mOOn Over tOwns mOOn whisper less	383 NO THANKS 1	1
/ / / moon over gai -te. a sharp	384 NO THANKS 2	1
& : the moon over death over edgar the	384 NO THANKS 2	7
the moon over death over edgar the moon over	384 NO THANKS 2	7
over edgar the moon over smellings of gently smell	384 NO THANKS 2	9
always, the iflike moon over moving me--the moon m	384 NO THANKS 2	12
moon m ov--in g over (moving) you beautifully also;	384 NO THANKS 2	18
children while a python over the way freezes a	384 NO THANKS 2	21
and the. m oon over juillet moon over s	384 NO THANKS 2	33
oon over juillet moon over s -unday O: m	384 NO THANKS 2	33
airso vertheseu pstareth oseings over (a hard a hard	385 NO THANKS 2	49
/ snow) says! Says over un graves der, speaking	417 NO THANKS 34	2
name beyond because things over blame things under praise	441 NO THANKS 56	59
/ / we) under) over, the thing of floating	447 NO THANKS 62	1
ooneandfor e-ver) moon She over this new eng land	469 NEW POEMS 7	13
pulling all the sky over him with one smile	481 NEW POEMS 19	12
these a or scratchily over which of earth dragged	491 50 POEMS 5	2
roses sometimes) with north over the barn / /	512 50 POEMS 26	35
under the wonder is over the why (it's now,	513 50 POEMS 27	33
will stand, so strictly (over utmost him so hugely)	520 50 POEMS 34	27
/ / / it's over a (see just over	543 1 X 1 3	1
over a (see just over this) wall the apples	543 1 X 1 3	2
is a mind then over our thief goes (you	543 1 X 1 3	19
with his now. But over a (see just over	543 1 X 1 3	25
over a (see just over this) wall the red	543 1 X 1 3	26
and the sooner it's over the sooner to biz	552 1 X 1 12	4
twilight) they come until (over dull all nouns) begins	557 1 X 1 17	13
/ / / what over and which under burst	565 1 X 1 25	1
not anything under skies over grass until and until	587 1 X 1 47	12
the wonder (beingest growingest) over all under all hate	590 1 X 1 50	21
/ / "summer is over --it's no use demanding	625 {CHAIRE} 27	1
(holding a red candle over his head by a	631 {CHAIRE} 33	2
in supreme thunder? ours (over you reels and me	639 {CHAIRE} 41	3
jesus) my heart flopped over and lay still while	648 {CHAIRE} 50	6
sweet forgiveness of spring (over the under the gift	661 {CHAIRE} 63	8
is what knocked him over Wasn't (for instance) the	702 95 POEMS 30	10
their imagined bodies kneel (over time space doom dream	714 95 POEMS 42	7
is lives breath es (over- ing un -derfully &	719 95 POEMS 47	14
/ / / / over us if (as what	741 95 POEMS 69	1
and death and resurrection: over my sleeping self float	749 95 POEMS 77	11
against sinner; put gain over gladness and joy under	769 95 POEMS 95	16
swoop (and swooping whirl over a frightened boy and	777 73 POEMS 5	8
like fire called flowers over green the new earth	778 73 POEMS 6	17

	PAGE	TITLE	LINE

OVER (CONTINUED)

blissful pair) skilfully wafted over them- selves this   . . .   799 73 POEMS 27   21
mind; thus virtue triumphed over vice and beauty bowed   . . .   799 73 POEMS 27   36
dressed well but not over, stopped me by 'could . . . .   800 73 POEMS 28   5
of winter will stand (over a snowstopped silent world)   . . .   808 73 POEMS 36   2
(2 little ams and over them this aflame with . . . .   832 73 POEMS 60   14
scatter his nothing all over what angry skies and . . . . . .   839 73 POEMS 67   12

+OVER

FOR CONTEXT, SEE   . . . .   122 & SEVEN POEMS 1   19
FOR CONTEXT, SEE   . . . .   251 IS 5 ONE 22   17
FOR CONTEXT, SEE   . . . .   347 VIVA 38   14
FOR CONTEXT, SEE   . . . .   347 VIVA 38   33
FOR CONTEXT, SEE   . . . .   383 NO THANKS 1   9
FOR CONTEXT, SEE   . . . .   385 NO THANKS 2   40
FOR CONTEXT, SEE   . . . .   385 NO THANKS 2   41
FOR CONTEXT, SEE   . . . .   385 NO THANKS 2   42
FOR CONTEXT, SEE   . . . .   385 NO THANKS 2   42
FOR CONTEXT, SEE   . . . .   385 NO THANKS 2   48
FOR CONTEXT, SEE   . . . .   385 NO THANKS 2   58
FOR CONTEXT, SEE   . . . .   464 NEW POEMS 2   8
FOR CONTEXT, SEE   . . . .   534 50 POEMS 46   7
FOR CONTEXT, SEE   . . . .   653 {CHAIRE} 55   5
FOR CONTEXT, SEE   . . . .   668 {CHAIRE} 70   16
FOR CONTEXT, SEE   . . . .   726 95 POEMS 54   13
FOR CONTEXT, SEE   . . . .   796 73 POEMS 24   2

OVERFLOW

shall be: cities may overflow (am was) assassinating whole .   491 50 POEMS 5   11

OVERGROWN

stuffest the parks with overgrown pimply cavaliers and   . . .   61 T&C PORTRAIT 9   6

OVERHEAR

(merely suppose) mine should overhear and answer Who with . .   374 VIVA 65   11

OVERING

some undering joy and overing grief nothing arrives a . . . .   517 50 POEMS 31   9
glow (undering proudly humbly overing) all bright all things   841 73 POEMS 69   26

+OVERING

FOR CONTEXT, SEE   . . . .   719 95 POEMS 47   14
FOR CONTEXT, SEE   . . . .   796 73 POEMS 24   4

OVERJOYED

but--though an host of overjoyed noncoms (first knocking on .   339 VIVA 30   7

OVERLOVE

nonsense which is the overlove & underwish of beauty; . . . .   480 NEW POEMS 18   6

OVERMUCH

touch me, whose heart-wholeness overmuch Expects of your hair   12 T&C SONGS 2   38
writhing words as, uttering overmuch, stand helplessly before   76 T&C SON UNRE 1   7

OVERS

--nothing believable inhabits here: overs of known descend .   761 95 POEMS 88   6

OVERSEEING

spite of the best overseeing) i mean that the . . . .   264 IS 5 ONE 33   16

OW

weird up her hot ow you hurt tho nithe   . . . .   316 VIVA 8   10
she now said he) ow said she (tiptop said . . . .   399 NO THANKS 16   24

OWCH

wee celibate amaranth clutch owch so chuck slop hight . . . .   333 VIVA 24   21

OWE

I item i immaculately owe dying one life and   . . . .   390 NO THANKS 7   12

+OWE

FOR CONTEXT, SEE   . . . .   547 1 X 1 7   4
FOR CONTEXT, SEE   . . . .   547 1 X 1 7   9

OWES

what he knows he owes) because he cannot understand, ...   406 NO THANKS 23   6

OWLS

moon in if all screech-owls have not okayed his . . . . . .   620 {CHAIRE} 22   6

OWN

and for in his own land he is called   . . . .   42 T&C AMORES 6   24
tremendous yonder for his own-- on such a night . . . . . .   81 T&C SON UNRE 6   12
tail that's the god's own and the moon kissed . . . .   125 & SEVEN POEMS 4   17
the mind is its own beautiful prisoner. Mine looked . . . . .   170 & SON ACTU 19   1
more especially in your own house Humanity i love . . . . . .   204 XLI LA GUERRE 2   16

OWN (CONTINUED)
    word by word his own unrivalled brand of pyro . . . . 266 IS 5 TWO 1   11
    any painting (for its own reason) in your lips . . . . 291 IS 5 FOUR 8   21
    off persist displacing Its own and their Lives who . . . . . 311 VIVA 3   7
    and) softly among one's own memory (but) along perhaps . . . 317 VIVA 9   18
    carefully spewing into her own Shush Shame as (out . . . . . 330 VIVA 21   12
    swift each with its Own motion deeply to wickedly . . . . . . 356 VIVA 47   9
    only his dream ing own soul looks and the . . . . 516 50 POEMS 30   16
    spin that spirit her own fingers with and give . . . . 531 50 POEMS 43   11
    man drops into his own paradise thankfully whole and . . . . 558 1 X 1 18   2
    angels burn by their own generous completely light, an . . . 562 1 X 1 22   6
    april me, down isn't's own isn't go ghostly they . . . . . . 580 1 X 1 40   7
    if (touched by love's own secret) we, like homing . . . . . . 659 (CHAIRE) 61   1
    through vast most nothing's own nothing children go of . . . 661 (CHAIRE) 63   14
    --but never fear (my own, my beautiful my blossoming) . . . . 667 (CHAIRE) 69   13
    will sing (like april's own april and awake's awake) . . . . 735 95 POEMS 63   14
    are prayers of earth's own clumsily striving (finding and . . 749 95 POEMS 77   6
    seem --we are himself's own self; his very him . . . . 756 95 POEMS 84   14
    be: and for his own (his love) his dear . . . . 760 95 POEMS 87   11
    pril Lives lead their own persons (in stead of . . . . 782 73 POEMS 10   10
    unimaginably mine; beyond sorrow's own joys and hoping's very 810 73 POEMS 38   11
    in how merciful love's own name, linger no more . . . . 812 73 POEMS 40   9
    subtracted from my hope's own hope, receive (undaunted guest 821 73 POEMS 49   10
    dare, how the (myself's own self who's) child will . . . . . 843 73 POEMS 71   12
+OWN
    FOR CONTEXT, SEE . . . . 392 NO THANKS 9   11
OWNED
    dog that may be owned by who knows) only . . . . 303 IS 5 FIVE 2   13
    houses are) is (are owned by a m- by . . . . 436 NO THANKS 52   19
OWNS
    (ask the man who owns one ask Dad, He . . . . 233 IS 5 ONE 4   23
OXEN
    through deep lifted fields Oxen distinctly move, a . . . . . 434 NO THANKS 51   31
    for the lions & oxen is science) Q: how . . . . 791 73 POEMS 19   8
+P.S.
    FOR CONTEXT, SEE . . . . 425 NO THANKS 42   15
PACKED
    side the windows are packed with hardslippery greens and . . 100 & POST IMPR 11   4
    Californian handpicked thrill mechanically packed and . . . . 337 VIVA 28   10
PADDED
    the length of this padded pole; a monkey attached . . . . . . 279 IS 5 THREE 3   10
PAGE
    meads; thou by whose page we break the precious . . . . 209 XLI SONNETS 5   6
    surprise (then turn the page) contentment read for ecstasy . 689 95 POEMS 17   4
PAGES
    who wanderest over smooth pages of forgotten joy proving . .   3 T&C EPITHALAM   18
PAID
    a goodly co which paid to make man free . . . . 552 1 X 1 12   2
PAIN
    eyes were buttoned with pain THE BLACK CAT WITH . . . . 100 & POST IMPR 11   31
    from me: make my pain their crazy meal letting . . . . 139 & SON REAL 10   2
    more strangely made (wears pain at joy, come summer . . . . . 394 NO THANKS 11   7
    Plan: if Joy with Pain shall hang in hock . . . . 438 NO THANKS 54   7
    have to loan me pain to take the hearse, ... 451 NO THANKS 66   6
    id) fer ids dare pain dares un no budy . . . . 519 50 POEMS 33   23
    and young pleasure and pain are merely surfaces (one . . . . 531 50 POEMS 43   5
    collective pseudobeast (sans either pain or joy) does nothing 544 1 X 1 4   6
    yes) will grin with pain You so&so true wars . . . . 570 1 X 1 30   9
PAINFUL
    the, keenly lascivious legs. painful ankles large acute . . . 103 & POST IMPR 13   7
PAINFULLY
    with upward vacant eyes, painfully perpetually crouched, . . 231 IS 5 ONE 3   49
    (as the ego approaches) painfully sterilized contours; within 319 VIVA 11   28
PAINS
    if therefore among foul pains appears an if emerges . . . . . 425 NO THANKS 42   13
PAINSTAKINGLY
    behind a slopcaked shrub painstakingly utters a slippery . . 144 & SON REAL 15   8

PAINTEATEN
   those ladies with faces painteaten and bodies lightly . . . . 57 T&C PORTRAIT 5   37
PAINTED
   Lust.... mine also, little painted poem of god / . . . . . . 75 T&C SON REAL 6   14
   swimswam painted-with-horses-with-painted-with eyes and . . . 384 NO THANKS 2   31
   painted-with-horses-with-painted-with eyes and the.m . . . . 384 NO THANKS 2   31
   which tiny the was painted in round blue but . . . . 516 50 POEMS 30   5
+PAINTED-WITH-HORSES-WITH-PAINTED-WITH
   swimswam painted-with-horses-with-painted-with eyes and . . . 384 NO THANKS 2   31
PAINTER
   smile exactly strange-- this painter should have loved my . . 85 T&C SON ACTU 4   9
   way you move) the painter of your voice-- beyond . . . . . . 291 IS 5 FOUR 8   15
   are amused, no wisest painter of fragile Marys will . . . . . 294 IS 5 FOUR 11   11
PAINTERS
   certain dead and careful painters love to use for . . . . . . 20 T&C PUELLA MEA   141
PAINTING
   night's speechless carnival the painting of the dark with . . 36 T&C AMORES 1   14
   the intent of genius-- painting wholly feels ashamed before . 162 & SON ACTU 11   5
   gesture possibly or any painting (for its own reason) . . . . 291 IS 5 FOUR 8   21
PAINTS
   holes in dark places paints eyes touches hands with . . . . . 437 NO THANKS 53   5
   fiends: or, if he paints with sound, newly one . . . . 842 73 POEMS 70   5
PAIR
   Chaucer knoweth many a pair of companions blithe and . . . . 20 T&C PUELLA MEA   164
   too white forehead a pair of eyes which mutter . . . . 116 & PORTRAIT 9   10
   in pairs: amazingly, one pair is white (but you . . . . 171 & SON ACTU 20   9
   / / this little pair had a little scare . . . . 401 NO THANKS 18   2
   pubic lice inside one pair of trousers (which had . . . . . . 473 NEW POEMS 11   6
   he is) merely (a pair of ears with some . . . . 501 50 POEMS 15   19
   (stealing toward the blissful pair) skilfully wafted over . . 799 73 POEMS 27   20
PAIRS
   they go out in pairs: amazingly, one pair is . . . . 171 & SON ACTU 20   8
PAKLAVAH
   two remarking cries of paklavah meeah. (Very occasionally . . 217 XLI SONNETS 13   12
PAL
   body is Death's littlest pal, skilled in quick softness. . . 74 T&C SON REAL 5   3
   this was my particular pal funny aint it we . . . . 270 IS 5 TWO 5   7
   (quite minus gal or pal slightly too sick to . . . . 387 NO THANKS 4   5
   joe 's left crashed pal dropped o god alice . . . . 496 50 POEMS 10   6
   other well your oldest pal for instance (or ; . . . . 779 73 POEMS 7   11
PALACE
   a gate unto a palace intricate (whereof the luscious . . . . 21 T&C PUELLA MEA   202
   emperor sleeps in a palace of porphyry which was . . . . . . 32 T&C ORIENTALE 6   2
   fountains of the emperor's palace run sunlight and moonlight   32 T&C ORIENTALE 6   16
   accurate key to a palace --You, --in this window . . . . . . 169 & SON ACTU 18   14
PALE
   hour wholly renews her pale flesh with delight) --immortally   3 T&C EPITHALAM   7
   serene perpetual round a pale world gathers comfort to . . .   5 T&C EPITHALAM   82
   of eternity unto the pale meaning of heaven clings, ...   6 T&C EPITHALAM   124
   free upon terrific pastures pale, whose tall mysterious . . .   9 T&C SONGS 1   9
   Expects of your hair pale, a terror musical? while . . . . .   12 T&C SONGS 2   39
   spoke the green- greeting pale- departing irrevocable sea i . 39 T&C AMORES 4   25
   up Up with the pale important stars and the . . . . 44 T&C AMORES 8   15
   air with pinkness, one pale dog behind a slopcaked . . . . . 144 & SON REAL 15   7
   dust-of-sleep. wields easily the pale club of the wind . . . 163 & SON ACTU 12   5
   blossoms dishevelling made a pale fracas upon the accurate . 214 XLI SONNETS 10   8
   but who is this pale softish almost round young . . . . 245 IS 5 ONE 16   6
   Tom Larsen twirls among pale lips (the extinct cigar) . . . . 252 IS 5 ONE 23   6
   to understand the (through pale miles of perishing air, . . . 305 IS 5 FIVE 4   12
   hugeness of twi -light pale beyond soft- liness than . . . . 349 VIVA 40   4
   feet is this (shivering pale naked very poor) creature . . . 374 VIVA 65   13
   not bald. (Coughs.) Two pale slippery small eyes balanced . . 406 NO THANKS 23   9
   tremble and cower so pale: pale) for betty was . . . . 509 50 POEMS 23   18
   and cower so pale: pale) for betty was born . . . . 509 50 POEMS 23   18
   gilty ceiling per both pale orbs thus excluding a . . . . . . 546 1 X 1 6   5
+PALE
   FOR CONTEXT, SEE . . . . 342 VIVA 33   8

PALED
    heaven) you, you exactly paled and curled with mystic . . . .   71 T&C SON REAL 2   12
PALENESS
    a pulseless blur of paleness; the unswift mouths of . . . . . 218 XLI SONNETS 14   13
PALER
    sheer peaks ran before. Paler be they than daunting . . . . .   14 T&C SONGS 4   26
    and grows every day paler-paler she sits sewing and . . . . . 125 & SEVEN POEMS 4   5
    and grows every day paler-paler she sits sewing and . . . . . 125 & SEVEN POEMS 4   5
    little lady on her paler-paler face and said never . . . . .   125 & SEVEN POEMS 4 18
    little lady on her paler-paler face and said never . . . . .   125 & SEVEN POEMS 4 18
PALISHFLESH
    it will, Gorge indistinct palishflesh of laZilytas tingg OO . 100 & POST IMPR 11   27
PALM
    frights creation, in whose palm Nike presents the crown . . .   3 T&C EPITHALAM   27
PALMIST
    the rod quoth the palmist. / / / / . . . .   643 {CHAIRE} 45   6
PALPABLE
    invisibly when upon her palpable solitude a furtive occult .   19 T&C PUELLA MEA 105
    of life's placid obscure palpable carnival where to a . . . .   43 T&C AMORES 7   31
PALPING
    you kiddo he's a palping wreaths of badly Yep . . . .   96 & POST IMPR 8   16
PALPITATING
    risen at length from palpitating veils. 0 still miraculous .   5 T&C EPITHALAM   104
    vague with ecstasy my palpitating breasts inhale the slow . .   31 T&C ORIENTALE 5 24
PAMPERED
    by tamarack (nothing pampered puny impatient and nothing . . 658 {CHAIRE} 60   22
PANDAR
    fled? Speak elm eloquent pandar with thy nod significant . .   3 T&C EPITHALAM   9
PANE
    dance maketh the sagest pane of littler huts with . . . . . . 207 XLI SONNETS 3   3
    go across this dirtied pane where softly preys the . . . . .   218 XLI SONNETS 14   10
    / / off a pane) the (dropp ingspinson his . . . . 692 95 POEMS 20   1
+PANELIKE
    FOR CONTEXT, SEE . . . .   416 NO THANKS 33   11
PANES
    gazing through un washed panes into a crisp todo . . . . . .   354 VIVA 45   9
    two partly tran sparent panes which by some loveless . . . .   354 VIVA 45   19
PANSIES
    ysomethi ng (imagine) with, pansies / / / / . . . . 792 73 POEMS 20   17
PANSY
    pink hollyhock existence whose pansy eyes look from morning .   58 T&C PORTRAIT 6   18
    will not be a pansy heaven nor a fragile . . . .   352 VIVA 43   2
PANSY'S
    poppy's pompous fire the pansy's purple patience and the . .   5 T&C EPITHALAM   93
PANT
    firm asinine life (i pant for what's below. the . . . . 220 XLI SONNETS 16   5
+PANT
    FOR CONTEXT, SEE . . . .   388 NO THANKS 5   9
PANTARKES
    their once again victorious Pantarkes (whose grace the prince   4 T&C EPITHALAM   34
PANTING
    the Y her legs panting as they press proffers . . . .   132 & SON REAL 3   9
PANTS
    a slight jounce, thirteen pants have a hunch admit . . . . .   150 & SON REAL 21   5
    of life in your pants and forgetting it's there . . . . 204 XLI LA GUERRE 2 19
    where a hurdy-gurdy accurately pants. and pompous ancient . . 219 XLI SONNETS 15   8
    beginning with his wellfilled pants earth's biggest grafter,   266 IS 5 TWO 1   32
    do whatever's in their pants the boys i mean . . . .   427 NO THANKS 44   18
    (clutched by immense the-seat-of-the pants inani nvisible . . 616 {CHAIRE} 18   8
+PANTS
    FOR CONTEXT, SEE . . . .   413 NO THANKS 30   12
    FOR CONTEXT, SEE . . . .   635 {CHAIRE} 37   26
PAPER
    Why according to tomorrow's paper the proletariat will not .   262 IS 5 ONE 32   18
    hills made of blueandgreen paper scorchbend ingthem -selves-U 278 IS 5 THREE 2   6
    world renowned investigator of paper sailors--argonauta argo   326 VIVA 18   6
    a suicide sniffing a Paper rose smiling to a . . . .   338 VIVA 29   3
    one somewhat hand the paper destinies of nations sic . . . .   499 50 POEMS 13   6

		PAGE	TITLE	LINE

PAPER (CONTINUED)

maybe) piece of pitiful paper-- but now, as Mr . . . . 697 95 POEMS 25   26

PAPERBOY

"Uh" "coffee" "uh" enter paperboy, c buys Bawstinamereekin, . 200 XLI PORTRAIT 8   12

c buys Bawstinamereekin, exit paperboy a finishes Helmar . . 200 XLI PORTRAIT 8   14

PAPERNAPKIN

Est for Handkerchief read Papernapkin no laundry bills likes 410 NO THANKS 27   5

PAPERS

also, tomorrow the daily papers will feature Peace And . . . 142 & SON REAL 13   9

PAPERY

dre ams whichful sarcasms papery deathfuls) awaits yes this . 415 NO THANKS 32   19

how worlds delicate of bombast--papery what & vast . . . . . 480 NEW POEMS 18   17

with out crushing) the papery weightless diminutive world . . 652 (CHAIRE) 54   9

PAPILLAE

a ruglike sentience whose papillae expertly drink the docile 201 XLI PORTRAIT 9   16

PAPPED

ughhuh world (the pertly papped muchmouthed) her way of . . . 337 VIVA 28   11

PAPPY

on (pass the freedoms pappy or uncle shylock not . . . . . . 641 (CHAIRE) 43   7

PAPYRUSCOLOURED

emanates a dignity of papyruscoloured faces superbly limp the 111 & PORTRAIT 6   53

PARADISE

serene nervous light of paradise-- by angelfaces clustered . 85 T&C SON ACTU 4   2

drops into his own paradise thankfully whole and the . . . . 558 1 X 1 18   2

now and here with paradise) forgetting if, remember yes . . . 688 95 POEMS 16   8

whole perhapsless mystery of paradise) mind without soul may 714 95 POEMS 42   8

PARADOXICALLY

granted that it's nothing paradoxically enough beyond mere . 329 VIVA 20   1

PARAGRAPH

for life's not a paragraph And death i think . . . . 290 IS 5 FOUR 7   15

PARALLEL

elate shyly a-live keen parallel specks float-ing create . . 447 NO THANKS 62   3

PARALYTICWHOSE

Funny hand of the paralyticwhose dod d e rin . . . . 100 & POST IMPR 11   37

PARAMOUR

thrilling rain the slender paramour to toy with thy . . . . . 3 T&C EPITHALAM   3

PARAPHRASE

tears complete the perfumed paraphrase of death). Now is . . 6 T&C EPITHALAM 120

PARASOL

i give this little parasol, so she may above . . . . 762 95 POEMS 89   7

PARDON

say you will perhaps pardon, possibly you will comprehend. . 285 IS 5 FOUR 2   9

PARDONER

sky knight and ploughman pardoner wife and nun merchant . . . 661 (CHAIRE) 63   9

PARENT

simply can't) won't (most parent people mustn't shouldn't) . 412 NO THANKS 29   5

PARENTHESIS

Our (ta-te-ta in a parenthesis! said the moon) . . . . . . 89 & POST IMPR 1   17

. fingered by (a parenthesis the) pond on whoseswooning . . . 99 & POST IMPR 10   9

i think is no parenthesis / / / / . . . . 290 IS 5 FOUR 7   16

PARENTS

fuss infinity pleased our parents one inch looks good . . . . 466 NEW POEMS 4   15

PARIS

and thirsty blood of Paris would not all the . . . . 18 T&C PUELLA MEA 67

cries of Babylon.) Diarmuid Paris and Solomon, Omar Harun . . 23 T&C PUELLA MEA 262

and this sweet profound Paris moves with lovers, two . . . . 71 T&C SON REAL 2   8

(which is myself and Paris and all things) the . . . . 92 & POST IMPR 4   4

/ / / / Paris; this April sunset completely . . . . 93 & POST IMPR 5   1

dos, bon cul de Paris" (Marie Vierge Priez Pour . . . . 120 & PORTRAIT 12   14

(in the twilight of Paris Marie Louise with queenly . . . . . 121 & PORTRAIT 12   44

in my head dis-donc, Paris ta gorge mysterieuse pourquoi . . 121 & PORTRAIT 12   52

child. So this is Paris. i will sit in . . . . 233 IS 5 ONE 4   15

when you were in Paris we met here / . . . . 304 IS 5 FIVE 3   15

+PARIS

FOR CONTEXT, SEE . . . . 104 & POST IMPR 14   8

FOR CONTEXT, SEE . . . . 237 IS 5 ONE 8   5

PARITY

me n dis cussing "parity" in l'ho tel nor . . . . 708 95 POEMS 36   11

PARK
    trickles carefully into the park sits Down. pigeons circle .   62 T&C PORTRAIT 10 26
    a woman in a park. Complete. and slightly (why? . . . . 375 VIVA 66 8
    ise how e mpty park bundl e of what . . . . 472 NEW POEMS 10 13
    up every of a park anus stick some quote . . . . 636 {CHAIRE} 38 1
    nu tiv e this park is e mpty (everyb . . . . 696 95 POEMS 24 5
    man kind yet in park this grim most (these . . . . 698 95 POEMS 26 5
PARK'S
    frightenS a noisy most park's least timorous pigeons) squ . . 726 95 POEMS 54 9
PARKS
    tom-cat, thou stuffest the parks with overgrown pimply . . . 61 T&C PORTRAIT 9 6
    of The what are parks for wiggle yes has . . . . 251 IS 5 ONE 22 20
PARLE
    live at present (l'on parle de repapering; i don't . . . . . 312 VIVA 4 23
PARLOR
    thou hangest canary-birds in parlor windows spring slattern . 61 T&C PORTRAIT 9 10
PARODY
    grass. A silver sudden parody of snow tickles the . . . . . . 5 T&C EPITHALAM 73
PARSED
    . i am accurately parsed by this gorgeous rush . . . . 201 XLI PORTRAIT 9 27
PART
    then ponder the tinsel part they let thee play; . . . . 75 T&C SON REAL 6 6
    / / / curtains part) the peacockappareled prodigy of . . . . 232 IS 5 ONE 3 1
    ourselves who more a part are (less who are . . . . 386 NO THANKS 3 3
    whole moves; and every part stands still: / / . . . . 446 NO THANKS 61 14
    sisters swore they'd never part: Soul was (i understand) . . 621 {CHAIRE} 23 1
    give me a trillionth part of inquisitive merrily humble . . . 678 95 POEMS 6 14
PARTAKEN
    window like a reminiscence partaken softly at whose gate . . 58 T&C PORTRAIT 6 24
PARTED
    intimate flower dreams of parted lips dim upon the . . . . . 54 T&C PORTRAIT 2 11
PARTEDPETALED
    riot the flashing bacchant. partedpetaled mouth, face . . . . 185 XLI SONGS 7 13
PARTHENON
    is known as (HO PARTHENON) and having ordered yaoorti . . . . 194 XLI PORTRAIT 2 9
PARTIALLY
    each spirit is) and partially imagine whose despair when . . 842 73 POEMS 70 9
PARTIALNESS
    shall be nor every partialness beats one entirety neither . . 425 NO THANKS 42 11
PARTICLE
    each least less than particle of perfect dark-- how . . . . 603 {CHAIRE} 5 2
    dark most nowhere no particle is not a universe-- . . . . . . 756 95 POEMS 84 8
+PARTICLES
    FOR CONTEXT, SEE . . . . 403 NO THANKS 20 5
PARTICOLOURED
    Surely from robes of particoloured peace with mouth . . . . . 5 T&C EPITHALAM 97
PARTICULAR
    eyes to noone in particular she gasped almost loudly . . . . 53 T&C PORTRAIT 1 45
    roaming death's big rotten particular kiss. / / / . . . . . . 158 & SON ACTU 7 14
    kidding this was my particular pal funny aint it . . . . . . 270 IS 5 TWO 5 6
    i say "along this particular road the moon if . . . . 303 IS 5 FIVE 2 9
    could grin may stern particular Love surround your trite . . 522 50 POEMS 35 10
    together un der a particular tree are all breathing . . . . 600 {CHAIRE} 2 7
    people; and more each particular person is (my love) . . . . 667 {CHAIRE} 69 3
    just sweet terrifying the particular moment it takes one . . 809 73 POEMS 37 10
    acceptance of irrevocable time particular pure truth of . . . 821 73 POEMS 49 5
PARTICULARLY
    with my friend is particularly to enjoy the composed . . . . 193 XLI PORTRAIT 1 1
    you nothing is what particularly matters hence in a . . . . 238 IS 5 ONE 9 17
    coming of the Americans particularly the brand of . . . . . 256 IS 5 ONE 27 13
    be uncouthly erotic more particularly the primates--from . . 326 VIVA 18 25
    refuted by these (particularly belonging to a retired . . . 341 VIVA 32 7
    begins to croon more particularly at just midnight this . . . 813 73 POEMS 41 5
PARTICULARY
    pyjamastring) a (vastly and particulary) live that undeluded 607 {CHAIRE} 9 8
PARTIES
    be embarrassing for both parties and because you . . . . . . 204 XLI LA GUERRE 2 5

		PAGE	TITLE	LINE

PARTING
her lips' most frail parting my body hears the . . . . 22 T&C PUELLA MEA 233
feet with slid steps parting the tousle of saxophonic . . . . 140 & SON REAL 11 15
and what-is-it comes over parting flesh.... And eyes big . . 175 & SON ACTU 24 12
PARTLY
behind three or two partly tran sparent panes which . . . . . 354 VIVA 45 18
he might live) yes, partly nor some edgeless star . . . . . . 414 NO THANKS 31 9
no single thing dares partly seem one atomy once, ... 559 1 X 1 19 9
the wisest man will partly understand (although the wisest . 685 95 POEMS 13 11
millionary mind never may partly guess--thus, my love, to . . 818 73 POEMS 46 13
PARTNER
d e r in g partner whEEl shi min chb . . . . 100 & POST IMPR 11 38
PARTNERSHIP
in a peculiarly momentary partnership (to instigate . . . . . 260 IS 5 ONE 30 18
PARTS
souls are wholes not parts but all these hundreds . . . . . . 510 50 POEMS 24 8
PARTY
i likes a certain party gimme the he-man's solid . . . . . . 247 IS 5 ONE 18 4
PARVENU
Do -nothing the wellknown parvenu who (having dreamed of . . 236 IS 5 ONE 7 4
PAS
Les belles bottes--oh hear ,pas cheres") and my love . . . . 102 & POST IMPR 12 21
Marie Louise Lallemand n'est-ce pas que je suis belle . . . . 120 & PORTRAIT 12 11
playthings for dust n'est-ce pas effendi drifts between . . . 198 XLI PORTRAIT 6 14
a cute idea n'est-ce pas? (whereas, upon the other . . . . . 245 IS 5 ONE 16 14
cries No Tres) & (pas) youth laughs (sing old . . . . 729 95 POEMS 57 9
PASH
and stare the gross fuzzy-pash --dead--and the dark gold . . 153 & SON ACTU 2 6
and amusingly i am pash possibly because . dusk . . . . 155 & SON ACTU 4 1
PASS
earth who sees them pass) while hunted from his . . . . 4 T&C EPITHALAM 69
rivers whose white voices pass upon forgetting (fail me . . . 9 T&C SONGS 1 2
their sunsets, it shall pass. Our feet tread sleepless . . . 9 T&C SONGS 1 26
sleeps, a dream shall pass) and these my days . . . . 11 T&C SONGS 2 30
afraid and we will pass the simple ugliness of . . . . 86 T&C SON ACTU 5 11
tears out, perhaps shall pass a million years (while . . . . 181 XLI SONGS 3 7
first to wither, to pass? shallowness of sunlight falls . . . 190 XLI SONGS 12 6
its, friend observes I pass Mr Tom Larsen twirls . . . . . . 252 IS 5 ONE 23 5
gondola and above me pass loudly and gondola rapidly . . . . 256 IS 5 ONE 27 25
yes beautiful we now pass through the look girls . . . . . . 257 IS 5 ONE 27 32
anything which you can't pass off on other people: . . . . . 298 IS 5 FOUR 15 17
murdering uncouth faces which pass rap idly with their . . . 354 VIVA 45 10
threes which fiercely rapidly pass with their breaths) in . . 354 VIVA 45 23
worshipped for my doom pass ignorantly into sleep's bright . 358 VIVA 49 15
be seen to inexactly pass and unprecisely to repass . . . . . 401 NO THANKS 18 11
ca rr y on (pass the freedoms pappy or . . . . 641 (CHAIRE) 43 7
PASSED
the sweet heels of passed afterday, clothe thy soul's . . . . 10 T&C SONGS 1 39
live all sweet cities passed away-- in her flesh . . . . . . 22 T&C PUELLA MEA 257
in A 1 shape passed from low through second-in-to-high . . . 248 IS 5 ONE 19 18
lay still while he passed (as close as i'm . . . . 648 (CHAIRE) 50 8
PASSENGER
mightily form moves whose passenger and whose pilot my . . . 419 NO THANKS 36 23
PASSES
drowns the earth and passes into light (slowly in . . . . . . 5 T&C EPITHALAM 80
Voices a: whispering drunkard passes who knows if the . . . . 128 & SEVEN POEMS 6 6
PASSING
dust this is the passing of all shining things . . . . 41 T&C AMORES 5 10
sleep this is the passing of all shining things . . . . 41 T&C AMORES 5 25
other day i was passing a certain gate, rain . . . . 58 T&C PORTRAIT 6 2
PASSION
of May; a Winged Passion woke and one by . . . . 8 T&C OF NICOL 9
spring that maidens whom passion wastes will lay between . . 16 T&C SONGS 6 7
a moment in the passion of the fifty pillars . . . . 35 T&C ORIENTALE 6 112
thrust Boost my huge passion like a business and . . . . . . 132 & SON REAL 3 8
and mire, scheming imagine, passion willed, freedom a drug . 521 50 POEMS 34 55
PASSIONATE
moon, soft sighed the passionate darkness to the tune . . . . 8 T&C OF NICOL 4

PASSIONATE (CONTINUED)
  skein (but like some passionate earlier flower, the snow . .   21 T&C PUELLA MEA 187
  my love when most passionate. , my, love is . . . .   94 & POST IMPR 6   25
  and joke on my passionate anatomy oh yes! Large . . . . 146 & SON REAL 17   6
PASSIONATELY
  bound for themselves, when passionately dusk brings softly .   71 T&C SON REAL 2   9
  darlings, let us now passionately remember how-- braving the 266 IS 5 TWO 1   17
PASSIVE
  nation's blueeyed pride) their passive prey did kick and . . 339 VIVA 30   24
PAST
  soul so fortunate is (past the luck of all . . . .   19 T&C PUELLA MEA 103
  dear communion with the past, and wed to valor, ... 209 XLI SONNETS 5   7
  (it is nine minutes past six) the well-fed L's . . . . 219 XLI SONNETS 15   4
  breathes or moves --climbing (past light after light) to . . 300 IS 5 FOUR 17   4
  Now entirely arrives gesture past fragrance fragrant; a than   456 NO THANKS 71   9
  make alive filthy some past imagining whowhich of mad . . . . 662 (CHAIRE) 64   5
  walk backward) honour the past but welcome the future . . . . 732 95 POEMS 60   9
  eyes) with silver splendors past conceiving who comforts his   756 95 POEMS 84   5
  beautiful kindness sweet such (past can's every can't) . . . 763 95 POEMS 90   25
PASTEL
  rub, like any other pastel. (While you and i . . . . 264 IS 5 ONE 33   24
PASTILE
  Woolworth building a serene pastile-shaped insipid kinesis or 201 XLI PORTRAIT 9 15
PASTILE-SHAPED
  Woolworth building a serene pastile-shaped insipid kinesis or 201 XLI PORTRAIT 9 15
PASTIME
  and life a mere pastime --each joy a deceiver, ... 625 (CHAIRE) 27   18
PASTMASTER
  John Big Doughgob Big pastmaster of the Art of . . . . 642 (CHAIRE) 44   23
PASTS
  sing? futures are obsolete; pasts are unborn (here less . . . 592 1 X 1 52   11
PASTURE
  eng land fragrance of pasture and now ti p . . . . 469 NEW POEMS 7   14
  rock wanderin g through pasture wom an creature whom . . . . 654 (CHAIRE) 56   6
  his rings) threeing alive pasture and hills / / . . . . 751 95 POEMS 79   8
  blue wheel in a pasture / / / / . . . . 753 95 POEMS 81   21
  / / / here pasture ends-- this girl and . . . . 757 95 POEMS 85   1
  becomes near (one silent pasture, all a heartbeat dares; . . 818 73 POEMS 46   8
PASTURES
  float free upon terrific pastures pale, whose tall mysterious   9 T&C SONGS 1   9
  hypercivic zeal sought newer pastures or because swaddled . . 258 IS 5 ONE 28   12
PAT
  Face Bluish-old and choked pat of going soles on . . . . . .   142 & SON REAL 13   6
PATCH
  planned next to that patch of darkness there's a . . . . . .   322 VIVA 14   4
+PATCH
  FOR CONTEXT, SEE . . . .   707 95 POEMS 35   6
  FOR CONTEXT, SEE . . . .   707 95 POEMS 35   23
PATER
  being lost including captain Pater / / / / / . . . .   494 50 POEMS 8   8
PATH
  of truth follow no path all paths lead where . . . .   775 73 POEMS 3   2
  our world descend the path to nothingness (cruel now . . .   834 73 POEMS 62   2
PATHETIC
  noisy wheels of joy pathetic dress fluttering behind her . .   56 T&C PORTRAIT 4   4
PATHOLOGICAL
  be neither fantastic nor pathological but dumb. The number . 514 50 POEMS 28   4
PATHS
  follow no path all paths lead where truth is . . . .   775 73 POEMS 3   3
PATIENCE
  fire the pansy's purple patience and the grave frailty . . .   5 T&C EPITHALAM   93
) why. Being is patience is patient is (patiently . . . . . . 478 NEW POEMS 16   9
  wake to a perfect patience of mountains i am . . . .   749 95 POEMS 77   12
  particular pure truth of patience heard above the . . . . . . 821 73 POEMS 49   5
PATIENT
  your mind (slightly smiling, patient, unspeaking with a sign   298 IS 5 FOUR 15   3
  deathlessness) remembrance might no patient mind unstrange . 420 NO THANKS 37   7
  Being is patience is patient is (patiently all the . . . . . 478 NEW POEMS 16   9

583

	PAGE	TITLE	LINE
PATIENT (CONTINUED)			
(who are like ocean patient) dream's eternity (you feel . . .	617	{CHAIRE} 19	3
with eager fingers (with patient eyes) re -new- ing	660	{CHAIRE} 62	9
while enormous this how patient creature (who's never by . .	674	95 POEMS 2	6
PATIENTLY			
(,males await she patiently 1) littlecrownGrave whose . . .	342	VIVA 33	18
patience is patient is (patiently all the eyes of	478	NEW POEMS 16	9
lmost) dis appearing how patiently be coming some (&	753	95 POEMS 81	10
PATRIOTIC			
spider skipping quickly over patriotic swill. The, negress, .	166	& SON ACTU 15	2
PATTER			
a while. my god--a patter of kisses, the chewed	133	& SON REAL 4	14
PATTERNS			
gold cloth incessantly creates patterns of sudden lust her .	34	T&C ORIENTALE 6	88
PATTERS			
pollenizing vacancy when, Thy patters? hands.... is swig it .	159	& SON ACTU 8	16
PAUL			
is grass) with one "Paul" a harvard boy alas!	320	VIVA 12	6
except the cold ones paul scorns all the girls	619	{CHAIRE} 21	8
+PAUL			
FOR CONTEXT, SEE	431	NO THANKS 48	27
PAUSE			
you glassworks of Murano; pause elevator nel mezzo del . . .	256	IS 5 ONE 27	5
citizens did graze at pause then fired by hypercivic	258	IS 5 ONE 28	10
a field (and i pause among the smell of	434	NO THANKS 51	24
universe to a uh" pause "Cookie but" nonvisibly smi-	464	NEW POEMS 2	15
it rather as a" pause "uh" cough "Biscuit" (&	464	NEW POEMS 2	23
+PAUSE			
FOR CONTEXT, SEE	548	1 X 1 8	6
PAUSED			
tremont and bromfield i paused a moment because on	52	T&C PORTRAIT 1	12
PAUSELESS			
swiftness as with (feel) pauseless immeasurably Now cancels .	402	NO THANKS 19	3
PAUSES			
to golden dust: she pauses on the lintel of	75	T&C SON REAL 6	12
with fear and sweetness.... pauses. (Halfwhispering.... . . .	304	IS 5 FIVE 3	13
/ / all nearness pauses, while a star can	750	95 POEMS 78	1
PAUSING			
of her hipless body, pausing to invent im- perceptible . . .	103	& POST IMPR 13	2
PAVEMENTS			
going soles on flat pavements with icy cries of	142	& SON REAL 13	7
PAW			
windthin voice-which-is no-voice sobcries "paw? lee"	697	95 POEMS 25	14
PAWN			
you're hard up you pawn your intelligence to buy	204	XLI LA GUERRE 2	10
keeps you from the pawn shop and because you	204	XLI LA GUERRE 2	13
PAWS			
whose distended immense Both paws slowly loved a dinted . . .	97	& POST IMPR 8	38
dolls resist Them Greediest Paws of careful time all	260	IS 5 ONE 30	10
+PAWS			
FOR CONTEXT, SEE	191	XLI CHANSONS 1	2
PAY			
pronounced by the way Pay the extremely artistic ◇	267	IS 5 TWO 2	10
understand (why Jones don't pay me what he knows	406	NO THANKS 23	6
so long will being pay the rent of seem	511	50 POEMS 25	5
know this suit you pay a store too much	523	50 POEMS 36	12
called they made him pay with his now. But	543	1 X 1 3	24
a tear some cannot pay at all he never	624	{CHAIRE} 26	11
PAYENT			
les americains aussi, ils payent bien les americains dance .	120	& PORTRAIT 12	27
PAYS			
feeling is first who pays any attention to the	290	IS 5 FOUR 7	2
very oldest lives one pays him with a smile	624	{CHAIRE} 26	9
from reason" (freud) --you pays your money and you	636	{CHAIRE} 38	13
PAYTOILET			
world's fair was the paytoilet / / / /	425	NO THANKS 42	16
PEACE			
from robes of particoloured peace with mouth flower-faint and	5	T&C EPITHALAM	97

PEACE (CONTINUED)
    daily papers will feature Peace And Good Will, and . . . . . 142 & SON REAL 13   10
    a girl lasciviously frail, peace (dreaming is better) . . . . 168 & SON ACTU 17   11
    Young fellow go in peace. which i do, being . . . . 229 IS 5 ONE FRAN   8
    soul why, then comes peace unto men who are . . . . 414 NO THANKS 31   13
    life with magic until peace outthunders silence. And (night . 428 NO THANKS 45   16
    move (with brightness of peace) all places yes is . . . . . . 443 NO THANKS 58   4
    they? i bring you peace the moon of day . . . . 527 50 POEMS 39   3
    causing through mystery miracle peace: or (if begin the . . . 559 1 X 1 19   4
    hoping for despair for peace for longing --a time . . . . . . 683 95 POEMS 11   10
    rapture and anguish) at peace with nature --i do . . . . . . 749 95 POEMS 77   14
    gently (very whiteness: absolute peace, never imaginable . . 839 73 POEMS 67   14
PEACEFUL
    forgotten joy proving the peaceful theorems of the flowers .   3 T&C EPITHALAM   19
    do frailly go The peaceful terrors of the snow, ... 11 T&C SONGS 2   28
    furious ways and the peaceful, and because she is . . . . . . 216 XLI SONNETS 12   14
    all amazing the and peaceful hills (not where not . . . . . . 750 95 POEMS 78   4
+PEACEFUL
    FOR CONTEXT, SEE . . . . 100 & POST IMPR 11   39
PEACEFULLY
    of collision collapse As peacefully, lifted into the awful . 48 T&C IMPRESS 2   11
    blue day fills with peacefully leaping air the minute . . . . 62 T&C PORTRAIT 10   8
    street of a mind peacefully and skilfully which is . . . . . 98 & POST IMPR 9   18
+PEACEMAKERS
    FOR CONTEXT, SEE . . . . 635 (CHAIRE) 37   20
PEACEMUCKERS
    at blessed are the peacemuckers) $ $ $ etc . . . . 635 (CHAIRE) 37   20
PEACEPEACEPEACE
) & chatters about Peacepeacepeace (to droppingly descend . . 267 IS 5 TWO 2   7
PEACH
    <> gave me, A, (peach a soft eyes syriansang . . . . 318 VIVA 10   10
+PEACHES
    FOR CONTEXT, SEE . . . . 318 VIVA 10   20
PEACHTREES
    flame as hatracks into peachtrees grow or hopes dance . . . . 511 50 POEMS 25   8
PEACOCKAPPARELED
    / curtains part) the peacockappareled prodigy of Flo's . . . 232 IS 5 ONE 3   2
PEAKED
    cheerfulest of men his peaked head smoulders like a . . . . . 198 XLI PORTRAIT 6   19
PEAKS
    and smiling the sheer peaks ran before. Paler be . . . . . . 14 T&C SONGS 4   25
PEANUT
    will be thrown a peanut (which he will open . . . . 69 T&C POST IMPR 6   16
PEANUTS
    two bags of lukewarm peanuts with the dime which . . . . . . 326 VIVA 18   16
PEARL
    O singular and breathless pearl! O indefinable frail ultimate   5 T&C EPITHALAM   108
    wiggled battered by stuttering pearl, leaves jiggled to the . 173 & SON ACTU 22   5
    with chuckling rubbish of pearl weed coral and stones; . . . 369 VIVA 60   6
PEARLS
    ankles musical with large pearls kingdoms in her ears . . . . 33 T&C ORIENTALE 6   67
    bruised air aflutter with pearls they are alone he . . . . . 34 T&C ORIENTALE 6 106
    her flesh the rain's pearls singly-whispering. / / / . . . . 65 T&C POST IMPR 2   16
    you: remember (as those pearls more than surround this . . . 372 VIVA 63   9
PEARSHAPED
    / / / my smallheaded pearshaped lady in gluey twilight . . . . 95 & POST IMPR 7   1
PEASANTS
    picked by the little peasants for their girls / . . . . 30 T&C ORIENTALE 4   42
PECKING
    ing his wing collar pecking at his im -peccable . . . . 274 IS 5 TWO 9   33
PECULIAR
    have deemed with your peculiar mouth my heart made . . . . . 78 T&C SON UNRE 3   4
    to exist being a peculiar form of sleep what's . . . . 264 IS 5 ONE 33   4
PECULIARLY
    self unite in a peculiarly momentary partnership (to . . . . 260 IS 5 ONE 30   16
PEDANTIC
    a frantic struts a pedantic proud or humble, equally . . . . 763 95 POEMS 90   12

PEDDLERS

mouth goes to the peddlers, to the peddlers of . . . . 100 & POST IMPR 11 20

the peddlers, to the peddlers of smooth, fruits of . . . . . 100 & POST IMPR 11 20

PEDESTAL

Hippolytus, lord on whose pedestal the deep expels (over . . 4 T&C EPITHALAM 46

PEEK

nipple tries. playfully to peek into the belly whose . . . . 143 & SON REAL 14 10

PEEK-A-BOO

His Royal Highness said "peek-a-boo" and thirty tame fleas . 262 IS 5 ONE 32 27

PEELING

a thunderbolt red- hot peeling off huge slabs of . . . . . . 194 XLI PORTRAIT 2 24

PEELS

New and eager. wittily peels the. ploop. --OOc h . . . . . . 136 & SON REAL 7 13

this universe in two, peels forever out of his . . . . 560 1 X 1 20 19

+PEEPS

FOR CONTEXT, SEE . . . . 108 & PORTRAIT 4 18

PEER

across the harvest whitely peer empty of surprise death's . . 11 T&C SONGS 2 23

absurd I; life, to peer and wear clothes. i . . . . 281 IS 5 THREE 5 18

can do is to peer through windows, unobserved --listen, . . . 292 IS 5 FOUR 9 8

as through immediately yeswind-faces peer skies; whiteLy are 346 VIVA 37 6

PEERED

her cheeks. A brain peered at the dawn. she . . . . 132 & SON REAL 3 13

PEERING

mutilated thumbs: picture His peering biggest whey coloured . 117 & PORTRAIT 10 32

or six years old) peering from some high window; . . . . . . 824 73 POEMS 52 3

PEERLESS

of littler huts with peerless fantasies or the unlovely . . . 207 XLI SONNETS 3 4

PEERS

couch of poppy petals peers the sleepy morning) gently . . . 8 T&C OF NICOL 13

kissed with is nearness. (peers: body of aching toys . . . . 159 & SON ACTU 8 11

boy that with his peers full oft hath quaffed . . . . 273 IS 5 TWO 8 7

here and there a peers at you) has (elephant . . . . 516 50 POEMS 30 9

PELF

pride and up rose pelf and ghibelline and guelph . . . . . . 552 1 X 1 12 11

PEN

body luckily made a pen is dreadfully afraid of . . . . . . 141 & SON REAL 12 3

thou didst love the pen while others wrote in . . . . 209 XLI SONNETS 5 9

PENCIL

Betty, don't remember me pencil your eyes dear and . . . . . 71 T&C SON REAL 2 2

/ / even a pencil has fear to do . . . . 141 & SON REAL 12 1

PENCILS

the gloom arise purple pencils fluent spires of fragrance . . 31 T&C ORIENTALE 5 4

drunk if i be pencils / / / / . . . . 703 95 POEMS 31 20

PENGUINSOUL

higher) is sunning his penguinsoul in the glow of . . . . . 631 (CHAIRE) 33 8

PENING

more of star o- pening of (writhing your exploding . . . . 480 NEW POEMS 18 15

PENNIES

a, penny or three, pennies he will be thrown . . . . 69 T&C POST IMPR 6 16

jackknives and kittens and pennies they all sit there . . . . 126 & SEVEN POEMS 5 6

jackknives i do and pennies i do and rosebugs . . . . 127 & SEVEN POEMS 5 50

seven nickels and ten pennies have been deposited upon . . . 196 XLI PORTRAIT 4 10

PENNY

he has caught a, penny or three, pennies he . . . . 69 T&C POST IMPR 6 15

the kitten and the penny and the jackknife and . . . . . . 127 & SEVEN POEMS 5 46

tool but drop a penny in the slot and . . . . 500 50 POEMS 14 11

+PENSE

FOR CONTEXT, SEE . . . . 635 (CHAIRE) 37 26

PENSIVE

our return voyage, my pensive companion dimly remarked some- 326 VIVA 18 31

PEOPLE

young chiseled eyes the people saw their once again . . . . . 4 T&C EPITHALAM 33

are dinned; and the people of perfect darkness fills . . . . 9 T&C SONGS 1 19

the brutal faces of people contented hideous hopeless cruel . 50 T&C IMPRESS 4 15

it is dark. the people are in their houses . . . . 50 T&C IMPRESS 4 27

whithering ...(that's the Black People, cherie, who live . . 86 T&C SON ACTU 5 9

crosses and all the people are minutely dead. Then . . . . . 86 T&C SON ACTU 5 13

PEOPLE (CONTINUED)

	PAGE	TITLE	LINE
the dangerous first stars) people move love hurry in	93	& POST IMPR 5	11
so filled with fear people bells) i say your	98	& POST IMPR 9	2
whirl- ingPeaceful furious street people drop, coppers into,	100	& POST IMPR 11	39
a window, into which people look (while people stare	124	& SEVEN POEMS 3	4
which people look (while people stare arranging and changing	124	& SEVEN POEMS 3	5
and Old things, while people stare carefully moving a	124	& SEVEN POEMS 3	15
barber -pole is climbing people high, up-in tenements talk..	128	& SEVEN POEMS 6	4
the sky--filled with pretty people? (and if you and	129	& SEVEN POEMS 7	3
with all the pretty people than houses and steeples	129	& SEVEN POEMS 7	8
the square, little amorous-tadpole people wiggled battered by	173	& SON ACTU 22	4
smile dustily to the people, for winter who crookedly	190	XLI SONGS 12	20
the sweet & aged people who rule this world	250	IS 5 ONE 21	2
curious rai -ned on people (both male and female	267	IS 5 TWO 2	18
god damned lot of people don't and never never	272	IS 5 TWO 7	14
lady a ring of people a brittle swoon of	279	IS 5 THREE 3	5
of fire, creating smoothness. People stare, the drunker . . .	279	IS 5 THREE 3	17
Saint Ignatz miraculously inhabits. (people tumble down. . .	280	IS 5 THREE 4	5
inhabits. (people tumble down. people crumble to their knees.	280	IS 5 THREE 4	6
crumble to their knees. people begin crossing people) and . .	280	IS 5 THREE 4	7
knees. people begin crossing people) and hErE cOmEs a	280	IS 5 THREE 4	8
reason that i hate people and lean out of	295	IS 5 FOUR 12	23
pass off on other people: for instance a plugged	298	IS 5 FOUR 15	17
there's me & some people and others please don't	314	VIVA 6	3
please don't confuse. Some people 's future is toothsome . .	314	VIVA 6	7
a mong crum bling people (a long ruined streets	319	VIVA 11	3
(reel) hapsingly proregress heandshe-ingly people trickle . .	330	VIVA 21	2
is Spring and sometimes people are in real: imagine	338	VIVA 29	6
the darkness of cafes people drink smile if here	340	VIVA 31	8
idly with their breaths.) "people are walking deaths in . . .	354	VIVA 45	11
no laundry bills likes People preferring Negroes Indians . .	410	NO THANKS 27	6
/ / / most (people simply can't) won't (most	412	NO THANKS 29	1
can't) won't (most parent people mustn't shouldn't) most . .	412	NO THANKS 29	5
shouldn't) most daren't (sortof people well youknow kindof) .	412	NO THANKS 29	7
having most ever lived people always) don't die (becoming . .	412	NO THANKS 29	14
unbecomingly very by most) people / / / /	412	NO THANKS 29	19
u (cities are houses people are flies who buzz	436	NO THANKS 52	15
inghurl) bangbells (yawnchurches suck people) reel (dark- ly)	444	NO THANKS 59	14
in to whos est people be come un /	463	NEW POEMS 1	16
on purpose by simple people like we) down with	466	NEW POEMS 4	12
/ / / the people who rain (are move	482	NEW POEMS 20	1
the houses enter the people are so feeble the	505	50 POEMS 19	7
to sleep if the people sit down) and this	505	50 POEMS 19	8
(but the feeble are people the feeble are so	505	50 POEMS 19	14
are so wise the people remember being born) when	505	50 POEMS 19	15
/ / / these people socalled were not given	510	50 POEMS 24	1
would think these socalled people have no minds but	510	50 POEMS 24	3
hundreds upon thousands of people socalled if multiplied by .	510	50 POEMS 24	10
fifth of you turns people into eachs and cowards	537	50 POEMS 49	7
'bout right it's the people that abuses it you	567	1 X 1 27	10
somebody tell me why people let go / /	593	1 X 1 53	24
are each (why do people say it's un lucky	623	{CHAIRE} 25	6
/ / blossoming are people nimbler than Really go	630	{CHAIRE} 32	1
silence by noises called people called sunlight (elsewhere .	658	{CHAIRE} 60	10
the other un good people stare for it or	662	{CHAIRE} 64	11
all the hands have people; and more each particular	667	{CHAIRE} 69	2
often have wondered "most people be quite so (when	738	95 POEMS 66	13
so she may above people walk in the air	762	95 POEMS 89	8
despair preaches myriad wonder people of a person; joyful . .	764	95 POEMS 90	44
thingS dare to do people (& not the other	782	73 POEMS 10	4
enlightened this stranger 'some people have all the luck; . .	800	73 POEMS 28	10
/ the greedy the people (as if as can	801	73 POEMS 29	1
how crazily houses eyes people smiles faces streets steeples	835	73 POEMS 63	4
squirm turns houses to people and streets into faces	841	73 POEMS 69	19

+PEOPLE

	PAGE	TITLE	LINE
FOR CONTEXT, SEE	101	& POST IMPR 11	65
FOR CONTEXT, SEE	245	IS 5 ONE 16	1
FOR CONTEXT, SEE	275	IS 5 TWO 9	38

+PEOPLE (CONTINUED)
    FOR CONTEXT, SEE . . . . 325 VIVA 17   11
    FOR CONTEXT, SEE . . . . 703 95 POEMS 31   5
    FOR CONTEXT, SEE . . . . 802 73 POEMS 30   12
    FOR CONTEXT, SEE . . . . 802 73 POEMS 30   29
PEOPLES
    day "all poor little peoples that want to be . . . . 711 95 POEMS 39   7
PEOPLESHAPED
    / / / a peopleshaped toomany-ness far too and . . . . 528 50 POEMS 40   1
PEOPLING
    murdering coolness slowly in peopling places seeks play: . . 168 & SON ACTU 17   14
PEPPER
    it, ate a scarlet pepper and my eyes were . . . . 100 & POST IMPR 11   30
PEPPERS
    I have not eaten peppers for a week. On . . . . 219 XLI SONNETS 15   2
PER
    met that hideous gladness, per the face --pinxit, who . . . . 158 & SON ACTU 7   5
    Why) as divine poesy per that and this radically . . . . . . 230 IS 5 ONE 2   17
    down the fifty bucks per job with one foot . . . . 242 IS 5 ONE 13   8
    for a hat fate per a somewhat more than . . . . 258 IS 5 ONE 28   5
    noth ing il treno per Roma si-gnori? jerk. ilyr, ... 278 IS 5 THREE 2   19
    kindred intellects evoke allegiance per blunt instruments-- . 339 VIVA 30   14
    must unexist, solemnly and per rules apparelling its . . . . 373 VIVA 64   3
    at yon gilty ceiling per both pale orbs thus . . . . 546 1 X 1 6   5
    the scale to shrillerness per every madge and mabel . . . . . 579 1 X 1 39   11
PERCEIVE
    against thick sunset i perceive in front of our . . . . . . 279 IS 5 THREE 3   5
    which we are to perceive in this world equals . . . . 366 VIVA 57   13
    outmarch forever --and i perceive, within transparent walls . 376 VIVA 67   7
    wistFully dead you directly perceive or minus news alimony . 391 NO THANKS 8   10
    finally trembles, emerging to perceive buried in cliff . . . 435 NO THANKS 51   39
    she-and-he-like ifs of am perceive (but believe scarcely may) 808 73 POEMS 36   8
    (or any truth beyond perceive) quivers this miracle of . . . 809 73 POEMS 37   2
    world must always half perceive. Only whose vision can . . . 845 73 POEMS 73   4
PERCEIVED
    unspeaking watcher who adores perceived sails whose mighty . 79 T&C SON UNRE 4 9
PERCEIVES
    whims, the chattering self perceives with hysterical fright a 157 & SON ACTU 6   14
    waters) one's eye perceives (as the ego approaches) . . . . 319 VIVA 11   26
PERCENT
    had some rows over percent. The gang got shot . . . . 149 & SON REAL 20   8
+PERCENT
    FOR CONTEXT, SEE . . . . 803 73 POEMS 31   15
PERCEPTIBLE
    pausing to invent im- perceptible bulgings of the pretended . 103 & POST IMPR 13 3
PERCHANCE
    were sweeter to thee perchance to me deeper. / . . . . 213 XLI SONNETS 9   17
PERCHED
    move, a yellowandbluish cat (perched why Curvingly at this) . 434 NO THANKS 51   32
PERCHING
    orange inch of moon perching on this silver minute . . . . . 86 T&C SON ACTU 5 2
    of upward lips.... cleverly perching on the sudden extremity 201 XLI PORTRAIT 9 30
PERCUSSION
    harpsichord colours of Pure percussion colours- like-trumpets 100 & POST IMPR 11 11
PEREGRINATE
    rickety unclosed blinds inslants peregrinate, a cigar-stub . 144 & SON REAL 15   4
PEREGRINATIONS
    im- perfectness upon such peregrinations as twilight spon- . 197 XLI PORTRAIT 5 3
PERFECT
    eyes and dim slow perfect body amorous (whiter than . . . . .   5 T&C EPITHALAM 99
    less than those twain perfect roses whose ambrosial grace, .   6 T&C EPITHALAM 148
    and the people of perfect darkness fills his mind . . . . . .   9 T&C SONGS 1   19
    quail) of all things perfect the most frail. (Whoso . . . . . 20 T&C PUELLA MEA 162
    whereof the year has perfect bliss-- for each breast . . . . 21 T&C PUELLA MEA 189
    never more shall be, perfect things of faerie, are . . . . . 22 T&C PUELLA MEA 253
    heart sang between your perfect breasts darkness and beauty . 39 T&C AMORES 4   15
    entreat, by certain foolish perfect hours dead too, if . . . 42 T&C AMORES 6   15
    dollies of-love-and-of-death dollies of perfect life, dollies 101 & POST IMPR 11 82

PERFECT (CONTINUED)

again, shares the year's perfect agony. Waiting (always) upon 156 & SON ACTU 5   12
(the simple instant of perfect hunger Yes) how beautifully . 157 & SON ACTU 6   8
take the rose, which perfect is With killing hands . . . . 188 XLI SONGS 10   20
(proud through the cold perfect night whisperless to mark, . 205 XLI SONNETS 1   6
to cease whom every perfect thing meanwhile doth miss; . . . 360 VIVA 51   7
hair what bird has perfect fear (of suddenly me) . . . . . . 367 VIVA 58   5
say according to his perfect satisfaction vanishing from a . 516 50 POEMS 30   13
me (though such as perfect hope can feel only . . . . 580 1 X 1 40   23
ships go snowily sailing perfect silence. Absolute ocean / . 586 1 X 1 46   19
all the way from perfect nowhere came (as easily . . . . . . 599 (CHAIRE) 1   12
less than particle of perfect dark-- how should a . . . . . 603 (CHAIRE) 5   2
sheer despairing to most perfectly gay, nowhere to here, . . . 649 (CHAIRE) 51   6
dreaming flame) united by perfect nothing: millionary . . . . 721 95 POEMS 49   4
to find) may, given perfect mercy, live a dream . . . . 735 95 POEMS 63   3
even the mercy of perfect sunlight after days of . . . . . . 735 95 POEMS 63   12
i wake to a perfect patience of mountains i . . . . 749 95 POEMS 77   12
disappear. Everywhere and joy's perfect wholeness we're / / . 812 73 POEMS 40   14
believab ly smallest as perfect this (almost invisible where 827 73 POEMS 55   7

PERFECTEST
ladies were. In her perfectest array my lady, moving . . . . 17 T&C PUELLA MEA   5

PERFECTINGLY
never which waked) & perfectingly We dive out of . . . . . . 373 VIVA 64   8

PERFECTION
of leaves repeats eventual perfection while east deserves of 184 XLI SONGS 6   13
/ / does yesterday's perfection seem not quite so . . . . . . 414 NO THANKS 31   1
will breathe such crude perfection as divides by timelessness 428 NO THANKS 45   11
skies fall at last perfection, now and here --but . . . . . . 650 (CHAIRE) 52   17
be quite --come such perfection-- another i and you, ... 798 73 POEMS 26   23

PERFECTLY
awkard hours my lady perfectly moving, through the new . . . 17 T&C PUELLA MEA   11
actual tread (and thereto perfectly responds) of all things . 19 T&C PUELLA MEA   126
shoulders small, ardent, and perfectly withal smooth to . . . 20 T&C PUELLA MEA   154
body words are afraid perfectly beautiful is, forgive these . 22 T&C PUELLA MEA   241
and the oblong sins perfectly gesticulate the accurate . . . 43 T&C AMORES 7   35
face always wiggles the perfectly dead finger of . . . . . . 134 & SON REAL 5   11
much and am become perfectly and simply Lustful.... sense . . 157 & SON ACTU 6   2
cannot go near because perfectly fearful. meanwhile these . . 162 & SON ACTU 11   7
honeycake to men ....one perfectly smooth coffee tasting of . 217 XLI SONNETS 13   10
which a church stood perfectly upright but not piano . . . . 263 IS 5 ONE 32   51
should have made this perfectly clear, it entirely would . . 263 IS 5 ONE 32   64
create (who are so perfectly alive) my shame: lady . . . . . 306 IS 5 FIVE 5   12
some few most rare perfectly dear (and worlds whirl . . . . . 376 VIVA 67   11
earliest spear of sun perfectly should disappear moon's . . . 377 VIVA 68   3
huge grO pingness whO perfectly whO flOat newly alOne . . . . 383 NO THANKS 1   5
suggests identity) breathes fleet perfectly far from tangible 402 NO THANKS 19   11
whom kneeling eyes (until perfectly their imperfect gaze . . 450 NO THANKS 65   7
but out of serene perfectly Nothing hurled into young . . . . 456 NO THANKS 71   7
come young so truly perfectly the skies by merciful . . . . . 526 50 POEMS 38   9
from (into disappear and perfectly) nowhere vivid anonymous . 557 1 X 1 17   4
numerable ams (leaving a perfectly distinct unhe; a ticking . 558 1 X 1 18   7
she knows; and can perfectly speak (snowflake and rainbow . . 575 1 X 1 35   31
but zooms through one perfectly beautiful bow "my home . . . 585 1 X 1 45   20
hate all fear --all perfectly dyingest my and foreverless . . 590 1 X 1 50   23
but any two are perfectly alone there's nobody else . . . . . 591 1 X 1 51   11
if we are not perfectly careful be lieve me . . . . 600 (CHAIRE) 2   11
be cause dying is perfectly natural; perfectly putting it . . 604 (CHAIRE) 6   14
dying is perfectly natural; perfectly putting it mildly . . . 604 (CHAIRE) 6   14
It's Snowing Isn't That Perfectly Wonderful / / / . . . . . . 629 (CHAIRE) 31   22
g screeching new black perfectly isn 't) one rose . . . . . . 646 (CHAIRE) 48   16
all around whom is perfectly a strange ness Of . . . . 657 (CHAIRE) 59   4
of precision: more and perfectly more most ethereal silence . 669 (CHAIRE) 71   7
grow silent upon new perfectly blue) i am any . . . . 720 95 POEMS 48   3
final dream of bells; perfectly outlined against afterglow . 750 95 POEMS 78   3
it Must be your" perfectly alive blossom of a . . . . 837 73 POEMS 65   11

+PERFECTLY
FOR CONTEXT, SEE . . . . 101 & POST IMPR 11   47
FOR CONTEXT, SEE . . . . 534 50 POEMS 46   12

		PAGE	TITLE	LINE

+PERFECTLY (CONTINUED)

FOR CONTEXT, SEE . . . . 726 95 POEMS 54   6

PERFECTNESS

superimposing a numbing im- perfectness upon such . . . . . . 197 XLI PORTRAIT 5   3

PERFECTS

as the first star perfects the sensual dome of . . . .   7 T&C EPITHALAM   164

PERFORM

of sensual chisels i perform squirms of chrome and . . . . . 199 XLI PORTRAIT 7   5

PERFORMED

taut precarious holiday frighteningly performed and at . . . 52 T&C PORTRAIT 1   9

PERFORMING

/ / the ivory performing rose of you, worn . . . . 165 & SON ACTU 14   1

PERFORMS

stand-ing. unsits her (wrist performs a thundering trivial) . 159 & SON ACTU 8   5

PERFUME

exhales the hovering high perfume curious of that one . . . .   5 T&C EPITHALAM   102
a gesture of immaculate perfume--whereby (with fear aglow) my 19 T&C PUELLA MEA 108
certain face become white perfume only, from the ashes . . . 39 T&C AMORES 4   35
brings softly down the perfume of the world (and . . . . . . 71 T&C SON REAL 2   10
Unspontaneous. cute. the signal perfume of whose unrepute . . 74 T&C SON REAL 5   5
and ourselves a nearly-opaque perfume disinterestedly . . . . 146 & SON REAL 17   14
face thy voice scattering perfume-gifted wings suddenly . . . 187 XLI SONGS 9   13
and what were roses. Perfume? for i do forget.... . . . . . . 211 XLI SONNETS 7   1

PERFUME-GIFTED

face thy voice scattering perfume-gifted wings suddenly . . . 187 XLI SONGS 9   13

PERFUMED

several tears complete the perfumed paraphrase of death). Now   6 T&C EPITHALAM   120
pipes wiggle upon the perfumed roman strength who how . . . . 110 & PORTRAIT 6   8
but the stink of perfumed noise fiercely mounts from . . . . 169 & SON ACTU 18   3
the little barbarous Greenwich perfumed fake And most, the . 220 XLI SONNETS 16   10

PERFUMES

coming with sharp languid perfumes coming with the little . . 112 & PORTRAIT 6   102
try me with thy perfumes which have seduced the . . . . 212 XLI SONNETS 8   5

PERHAPS

a look of faerie, perhaps a little suddenly (as . . . . 18 T&C PUELLA MEA   42
the is it Poles? perhaps. While permanent faces coyly . . . . 70 T&C SON REAL 1   9
little wonderful, and say Perhaps her body touched me; . . . 82 T&C SON ACTU 1   14
beautiful sound: if a (perhaps) clock strikes, in the . . . . 92 & POST IMPR 4   14
Spring is like a perhaps hand (which comes carefully . . . . 124 & SEVEN POEMS 3   1
spring is like a perhaps Hand in a window . . . . 124 & SEVEN POEMS 3 10
stare carefully moving a perhaps fraction of flower here . . 124 & SEVEN POEMS 3 16
dusk and if it perhaps drea-mingly Is (not- quite . . . . . . 155 & SON ACTU 4   4
had his tears out, perhaps shall pass a million . . . . 181 XLI SONGS 3   7
Nicho' "and did you perhaps wish also shishkabob?" / . . . . 194 XLI PORTRAIT 2   38
/ / / / perhaps it is to feel . . . . 216 XLI SONNETS 12   1
have gone into vaudeville perhaps because my Uncle Sol . . . 239 IS 5 ONE 10   5
too beautiful. Let us perhaps excuse me if i . . . . 263 IS 5 ONE 32   59
this, since the thing perhaps is to eat flowers . . . . 264 IS 5 ONE 33   31
raising, hoisting, a little perhaps that and this, deftly . . 282 IS 5 THREE 6   6
moving far below us perhaps one villa caught like . . . . . . 283 IS 5 THREE 7   10
i say you will perhaps pardon, possibly you will . . . . . . 285 IS 5 FOUR 2   9
moment (or was it perhaps a year) ago i . . . . 296 IS 5 FOUR 13   15
town-- i have perhaps forgotten how, always (from . . . 297 IS 5 FOUR 14   8
the same thing as perhaps nothing, he murmurs carefully . . . 299 IS 5 FOUR 16   15
a fragile imitation of (perhaps) myself carefully wanders . . 300 IS 5 FOUR 17   13
own memory (but) along perhaps the By invisibilities . . . . 317 VIVA 9   19
not have been unsorry, perhaps / / / / . . . . 336 VIVA 27   11
& wormSmile eternal; quite perhaps as sternly much not . . . 371 VIVA 62   25
directionless horizon) --do you perhaps know these workmen? / 378 VIVA 69   16
god this surely dream perhaps this ghost) humbly and . . . . 441 NO THANKS 56   50
of everything guard her perhaps only A trifle less . . . . . 453 NO THANKS 68   4
of future dream these perhaps who have lost their . . . . . . 502 50 POEMS 16   11
/ / / harder perhaps than a newengland bed . . . . 506 50 POEMS 20   1
have is (you guess) perhaps the very unkindest way . . . . . 528 50 POEMS 40   11
unreal world, will you perhaps do the breathing for . . . . . 558 1 X 1 18   14
doom disappeared, out of perhaps (who knows?) eternity . . . 599 {CHAIRE} 1   7
impossible ours --God's heaven perhaps comprises poems (my . 748 95 POEMS 76   5
child unbreathingly share (huge Perhaps by hugest) dooms of . 757 95 POEMS 85   30

+PERHAPS
  FOR CONTEXT, SEE . . . . 330 VIVA 21   1
  FOR CONTEXT, SEE . . . . 397 NO THANKS 14   8
  FOR CONTEXT, SEE . . . . 787 73 POEMS 15   5

PERHAPSLESS
  while floats the whole perhapsless mystery of paradise) mind 714 95 POEMS 42   8

PERHAPSY
  / / warped this perhapsy stumbl i NgflounderpirouettiN g . . 495 50 POEMS 9   1

PERIL
  braving the worst, of peril heedless, each braver than . . . 266 IS 5 TWO 1   18

PERIOD
  sic item a bounceless period unshy the empty house . . . . . 499 50 POEMS 13   7

PERIODICAL
  and this radically defunct periodical. i would suggest that . 230 IS 5 ONE 2   18

PERISH
  touch me, before we perish (believe that not anything . . . . 357 VIVA 48   4
  surely does not forget, perish, sleep cannot be photographed, 377 VIVA 68   9

PERISHABLE
  lady wandering in whose perishable poise is the mystery . . . 17 T&C PUELLA MEA   14

PERISHED
  (sic) in far lands perished of unheard of maladies . . . . . 266 IS 5 TWO 1   14
  of cost the Ergo perished later all hands (you . . . . 494 50 POEMS 8   6
  / / / / perished have safe small facts . . . . 755 95 POEMS 83   1

PERISHING
  body's doll gay exactly perishing sexual, / / / . . . . 131 & SON REAL 2   17
  (through pale miles of perishing air, haunted with huddling . 305 IS 5 FIVE 4   12
  underscream of sudde nly perishing eagerly everyw here . . . 646 {CHAIRE} 48   10

PERMAMENT
  inch dimmer twist on permament and slap tremendous sorrydaze 333 VIVA 24   13

PERMANENT
  it Poles? perhaps. While permanent faces coyly bandy scandal 70 T&C SON REAL 1   9
  dave --tomorrow is our permanent address and there they'll . 579 1 X 1 39   12

+PERMANENT
  FOR CONTEXT, SEE . . . . 310 VIVA 2   12
  FOR CONTEXT, SEE . . . . 333 VIVA 24   13

PERMANENTLY
  purr... i left her permanently smiling / / / . . . . 228 IS 5 ONE MARJ   15

PERMISSION
  when the oak begs permission of the birch to . . . . 620 {CHAIRE} 22   9

PERMIT
  whole" (if you will permit a metaphor savouring slightly . . 326 VIVA 18   27

PERMITTED
  been dorothy and once permitted me for twenty iron . . . . . 52 T&C PORTRAIT 1   19

PERPENDICULAR
  exploded day the hulking perpendicular mammal a grim epitome 151 & SON REAL 22   3
  expertly drink the docile perpendicular taste of this . . . . 201 XLI PORTRAIT 9   17
  preys the grey and perpendicular Always-- or possibly there . 218 XLI SONNETS 14   11
  Wall. i want the perpendicular lips the insane teeth . . . . 220 XLI SONNETS 16   7

PERPETUAL
  (slowly in life's serene perpetual round a pale world . . . . 5 T&C EPITHALAM   81
  a drink? (the eternal perpetual question) Inside snugandevil. 97 & POST IMPR 8   42
  nakedness death most believes, perpetual girls marching to . 138 & SON REAL 9   11
  red rivers of fair perpetual feet the sinuous riot . . . . . 185 XLI SONGS 7   6
  the slow deep trees perpetual of sleep some silver-fingered . 208 XLI SONNETS 4   13
  forgets the entire and perpetual sea --but if yourself . . . 379 VIVA 70   9
  views with smooth vigilant perpetual eyes each exact victim, 386 NO THANKS 3   10

+PERPETUAL
  FOR CONTEXT, SEE . . . . 403 NO THANKS 20   1

PERPETUALLY
  futile flowers (isolating with perpetually meticulous . . . . 193 XLI PORTRAIT 1   22
  you because you are perpetually putting the secret of . . . . 204 XLI LA GUERRE 2   18
  upward vacant eyes, painfully perpetually crouched, ... 231 IS 5 ONE 3   50
  actions and speeches sawdust perpetually leak rather is it . 261 IS 5 ONE 31   5
  of self fee (bly Perpetually coughing And thickly spi) . . . 312 VIVA 4   20
  unmind grim yessing childflesh perpetually acruise and her . 337 VIVA 28   7
  and .i <> some perpetually roaming whylessness-- autumn has . 839 73 POEMS 67   7

PERPETUALNESS
  the poised radiance of perpetualness. When what's in velvet . 81 T&C SON UNRE 6   8

		PAGE	TITLE	LINE
PERPETUATING				
noisecoloured curvecorners gush silently perpetuating solids		311	VIVA 3	17
PERSIAN				
stopS. b swears in persian at phonograph x wins		200	XLI PORTRAIT 8	29
PERSIST				
tops to caroming off persist displacing Its own and		311	VIVA 3	7
PERSISTING				
the breath of all persisting stars / / /		40	T&C AMORES 4	47
PERSISTS				
shrine: its puniest flame persists shaken by the sea		435	NO THANKS 51	44
PERSON				
this indubitable and green person "Are You the wind?"		91	& POST IMPR 3	7
is a remarkably charming person personally they tell me . . .		246	IS 5 ONE 17	6
yes i am this person of whom somehow you		298	IS 5 FOUR 15	7
how this uncouth enchanted person, arising from a restaurant,		300	IS 5 FOUR 17	2
whom or cautiously this person and this imitation resemble, .		300	IS 5 FOUR 17	17
Dirty bed Mangy from person Porous sits years its		312	VIVA 4	18
ask a brittle little person fiddling in the rain		498	50 POEMS 12	13
and swim blossoms of person) through musical shadows while .		586	1 X 1 46	12
and more each particular person is (my love) alive		667	(CHAIRE) 69	3
nothing) you darling diminutive person jovial ego (&		678	95 POEMS 6	4
wonder people of a person; joyful your any new		764	95 POEMS 90	44
(no mob, but a person) and while never saying		802	73 POEMS 30	24
+PERSON				
FOR CONTEXT, SEE		697	95 POEMS 25	19
FOR CONTEXT, SEE		739	95 POEMS 67	2
PERSONAL				
let us tremble) a personal radiance sits hideously upon . . .		168	& SON ACTU 17	1
paradoxically enough beyond mere personal pride which tends .		329	VIVA 20	1
PERSONALLY				
a remarkably charming person personally they tell me as . . .		246	IS 5 ONE 17	7
chewchoo laugh dingle nails personally bung loamhome picpac .		333	VIVA 24	3
PERSONNE				
based on consubstantial intangibility. Personne ne m'aime et		262	IS 5 ONE 32	26
PERSONS				
pleasure--you go from several persons: believe me that . . .		295	IS 5 FOUR 12	8
is no respecter of persons the snow doesn't give		328	VIVA 19	21
Lives lead their own persons (in stead of everybodyelse's) .		782	73 POEMS 10	11
PERSPECTIVE				
and gape of tortured perspective rasp and graze of		48	T&C IMPRESS 2	3
not to hurt the perspective of the (hei -nous		267	IS 5 TWO 2	15
PERSPICUITY				
and when--Does susceptibility imply perspicuity, or? shut up.		141	& SON REAL 12	8
◇ sin cerity equals perspicuity (4) Only The Game		803	73 POEMS 31	16
PERSPIRATION				
the four tablets of perspiration erectly sitting. --If they .		73	T&C SON REAL 4	9
PERSUADE				
frivolous angleworm thou dost persuade to serenade his lady .		61	T&C PORTRAIT 9	4
stars are clever to persuade even silence: therefore wonder .		376	VIVA 67	9
PERSUADES				
vain but though mankind persuades itself that every weed's .		744	95 POEMS 72	5
PERSUASIVE				
joggling fists he is persuasive the editor cigarstinking . .		259	IS 5 ONE 29	7
PERTLY				
vicarious ughhuh world (the pertly papped muchmouthed) her .		337	VIVA 28	11
+PERTURBATIONS				
FOR CONTEXT, SEE		326	VIVA 18	21
+PERUSED				
FOR CONTEXT, SEE		212	XLI SONNETS 8	7
PERUSING				
unseriously seem by the perusing greenness of thy thought . .		9	T&C SONGS 1	29
PERVERSE				
with love and everything perverse or which makes some		466	NEW POEMS 4	22
PEST				
one another like the pest thus did immortal jealousy		799	73 POEMS 27	31
PESTER				
in with it, wisely, pester skilfully, teasing its lips, . . .		164	& SON ACTU 13	8

PETAL
    and have you the petal of somewhere in your . . . . 80 T&C SON UNRE 5   7
    whatever this and that petal confutes... to exist being . . . 264 IS 5 ONE 33   3
    fingers, you open always petal by petal myself as . . . . . . 366 VIVA 57   7
    open always petal by petal myself as Spring opens . . . . . . 366 VIVA 57   7
    --a heart her each petal / / / / . . . . 764 95 POEMS 90   54
PETALED
    in a pride of petaled hours, like flowers at . . . . 11 T&C SONGS 2   32
    a lily know, her petaled flesh doth entertain the . . . . . . 21 T&C PUELLA MEA 185
+PETALED
    FOR CONTEXT, SEE . . . . 185 XLI SONGS 7   13
PETALS
    her couch of poppy petals peers the sleepy morning) . . . . . 8 T&C OF NICOL   13
    wield a noise of petals falling silently through the . . . . 10 T&C SONGS 1   43
    was on my mouth petals danced against my eyes . . . . 39 T&C AMORES 4   18
    old man murder the petals hush mysteriously invisible . . . . 59 T&C PORTRAIT 7   4
    old man murder the petals. / / / / . . . . 59 T&C PORTRAIT 7   17
    sorrowful hour, thy counted petals O tremendous flower on . . 79 T&C SON UNRE 4   3
    simply understand the gnashing petals of sex which lock . . . 133 & SON REAL 4   11
    i have watched certain petals rapidly wish in the . . . . . . 214 XLI SONNETS 10   5
    mark the fainting murdered petals. with the caving stem. . . 215 XLI SONNETS 11   8
    eyes which are really petals and see nothing with . . . . . . 352 VIVA 43   10
    lit tle children are petals their song is a . . . . 525 50 POEMS 37   6
    of be One : petals him starrily her and . . . . 584 1 X 1 44   8
    under a opens (of petals of silence) hole bigger . . . . . . 634 {CHAIRE} 36   6
PETER
    good luck! aberdeen plato-rabelais peter jack / / / . . . . . 605 {CHAIRE} 7   16
PETITES
    nice sleep? toutes les petites femmes exactes qui dansent . . 121 & PORTRAIT 12   50
PETITIONS
    next, our illustrious scientist petitions the celestial host 799 73 POEMS 27   24
PETRIFIED
    on me" --dey was petrified. De room swung roun . . . . 332 VIVA 23   24
PETTICOAT
    legs and a muddy petticoat, drowsy is your mouth . . . . . . 61 T&C PORTRAIT 9   13
PHANTOM
    of tiny troubadours, and (phantom-white) dumb-blooming boughs 8 T&C OF NICOL   5
    distinct unhe; a ticking phantom by prodigious time's mere . 558 1 X 1 18   8
    i remain; a shadow phantom effigy or seeming (an . . . . . . 812 73 POEMS 40   3
    come, terrible anonymity; enfold phantom me with the . . . . 839 73 POEMS 67   10
PHANTOM-WHITE
    of tiny troubadours, and (phantom-white) dumb-blooming boughs 8 T&C OF NICOL   5
PHANTOMS
    under burst lurch things phantoms curl (mouth seekingly lips 565 1 X 1 25   2
    slowly than trees) dodreamingly phantoms (exchanging) e vero 681 95 POEMS 9   5
+PHANTOMS
    FOR CONTEXT, SEE . . . . 795 73 POEMS 23   14
PHEIDIAN
    sceptred colossus of the Pheidian soul whose eagle frights . 3 T&C EPITHALAM   26
PHENOMENA
    soil their raiment with phenomena: such being a conduct . . . 328 VIVA 19   5
PHENOMENON
    / at the ferocious phenomenon of 5 o'clock i . . . . 201 XLI PORTRAIT 9   1
    noticed (as an infantile phenomenon) George Washington almost 262 IS 5 ONE 32   10
    rare; obsolete almost that phenomenon (too gay for malice . . 607 {CHAIRE} 9   11
PHILOPHILIC
    Plumbing shall receive the philophilic name S.S. VAN MERDE) . 334 VIVA 25   4
PHILOSOPHERS
    doting fingers of prurient philosophers pinched and poked . . 46 T&C LA GUERRE 2   6
    their hearts a few philosophers tell me what am . . . . 281 IS 5 THREE 5   1
PHILOSOPHY
    lest punished bottoms interrupt philosophy / / / / . . . . . 261 IS 5 ONE 31   14
    you believe; not for philosophy does this rose give . . . . . 264 IS 5 ONE 33   20
PHILOSPHY
    "and there is a philosphy" strictly at which instant . . . . 328 VIVA 19   11
PHOEBEING
    ego (& mischievous tenderly phoebeing alter) clown of an . . 678 95 POEMS 6   7

PAGE   TITLE   LINE

PHONOGRAPH
  ingd o w, n phonograph stopS. b swears in . . . . 200 XLI PORTRAIT 8   27
  swears in persian at phonograph x wins exeunt ax: . . . . . . 200 XLI PORTRAIT 8   29
+PHONOGRAPH
  FOR CONTEXT, SEE . . . . 200 XLI PORTRAIT 8   25
PHONOGRAPH'S
  / / / (the phonograph's voice like a keen . . . . 166 & SON ACTU 15   1
+PHONOGRAPHS
  FOR CONTEXT, SEE . . . . 237 IS 5 ONE 8   10
PHOTOGRAPH
  human rind with a photograph clutched in the half . . . . . . 647 (CHAIRE) 49   2
PHOTOGRAPHED
  moments be murdered known photographed, ourselves yawning . . 237 IS 5 ONE 8   2
  Inexpressible itchings to be photographed with Lord . . . . . 262 IS 5 ONE 32   20
  well fed, and fully photographed the son of man . . . . 273 IS 5 TWO 8   22
  perish, sleep cannot be photographed, measured; disdains the 377 VIVA 68   10
PHOTOGRAPHY
  woopsing queer colon hobby photography never has plumbed the 499 50 POEMS 13   10
PHRASE
  flesh in stupid stuffs, phrase the immense weapon of . . . . 161 & SON ACTU 10   10
  to use a highfalootin phrase luxuries that is or . . . . . . 239 IS 5 ONE 10   9
PHRASING
  Begins To (with a phrasing crease of hot subliminal . . . . . 130 & SON REAL 1   3
PHYLLIS
  LIS when mack smacked phyllis on the snout frank . . . . . . 706 95 POEMS 34   1
PHYSIOGNOMY
  vacant lot of his physiognomy his scientifically pressed . . 259 IS 5 ONE 29   23
PIANO
  perfectly upright but not piano item: a water- melon . . . . 263 IS 5 ONE 32   51
+PIANO
  FOR CONTEXT, SEE . . . . 100 & POST IMPR 11   10
PIANOLAS
  wireless subways vacuum cleaners pianolas funnygraphs . . . . 237 IS 5 ONE 8   10
+PICABIAN
  FOR CONTEXT, SEE . . . . 180 XLI SONGS 2   3
PICASSO
  <> garnished of stark Picasso throttling trees hither my . . 180 XLI SONGS 2   6
  / / / / Picasso you give us Things . . . . 195 XLI PORTRAIT 3   1
PICCOLOS
  k i n glike piccolos thumPing colours like a . . . . 100 & POST IMPR 11   9
PICK
  a coin he will pick it cleverly from, the . . . . 69 T&C POST IMPR 6   10
  in love and flowers pick themselves / / / . . . . 129 & SEVEN POEMS 7   16
  aid of an exclamatory tooth-pick And who may that . . . . . 194 XLI PORTRAIT 2   27
  he's brave.... the communists pick up themselves friends & . 275 IS 5 TWO 9   42
  (smiling) he stops: & pick ing up a magical . . . . 697 95 POEMS 25   7
PICKED
  of sombre god i picked you as an apple . . . . 30 T&C ORIENTALE 4   41
  as an apple is picked by the little peasants . . . . 30 T&C ORIENTALE 4   42
  glass bumping things. she picked wearily something from the . 132 & SON REAL 3   17
  pieces and is hurriedly picked up and thrown on . . . . 203 XLI LA GUERRE 1   15
  this world has been Picked, like a piece of . . . . 370 VIVA 61   4
  heteronomously metameric me are picked from dumb sleePdeep . 395 NO THANKS 12   13
  of hair) 'd he picked up a thousand pounds . . . . 552 1 X 1 12   9
  to destroy himself he picked the was of shall . . . . 566 1 X 1 26   6
+PICKED
  FOR CONTEXT, SEE . . . . 337 VIVA 28   9
PICKER
  / / / Tumbling-hair picker of buttercups violets dandelions . 26 T&C CHANSONS 3   2
PICKING
  sorry Another comes also picking flowers / / / . . . . . . 26 T&C CHANSONS 3   9
  poems are made) Our picking it. this caress that . . . . . . 364 VIVA 55   9
+PICKING
  FOR CONTEXT, SEE . . . . 697 95 POEMS 25   7
PICKLES
  it does not disdain picKles, once, it, ate a . . . . 100 & POST IMPR 11   30
PICKS
  say thankyouverymuch mr rosenbloom picks strawberries with . 287 IS 5 FOUR 4   8

PICPAC
    nails personally bung loamhome picpac obviously scratches . . 333 VIVA 24   4
PICTURE
    a swollen inanity of picture hat. the arms hung . . . . . . 103 & POST IMPR 13   4
    twitch like mutilated thumbs: picture His peering biggest . . 117 & PORTRAIT 10   32
    my arms caught the picture) hurry it slowly to . . . . . . 162 & SON ACTU 11   10
    as far as his picture goes he's a wet . . . . 246 IS 5 ONE 17   11
    the queen --incalculable bliss! Picture it gents: our hero, . 254 IS 5 ONE 25   14
PICTURESQUE
    spends her time looking picturesque under the as it . . . . . 234 IS 5 ONE 5   3
PIDDLE
    off and a faint piddle-of-drops she says I ploc . . . . 96 & POST IMPR 8   14
PIDDLE-OF-DROPS
    off and a faint piddle-of-drops she says I ploc . . . . 96 & POST IMPR 8   14
PIE
    of-faceness stuck thumblike into pie is traffic this recalls 330 VIVA 21   5
    they send us a pie (it's try, boys) mine . . . . 513 50 POEMS 27   15
PIECE
    does not catch a piece of money and then . . . . 69 T&C POST IMPR 6 12
    a cafe smiling, a piece of money held between . . . . 102 & POST IMPR 12   4
    the world's but a piece of eminent fragility. Well . . . . . 141 & SON REAL 12   6
    striking into many a piece. I have never loved . . . . 360 VIVA 51   19
    been Picked, like a piece of clover, from the . . . . 370 VIVA 61   4
    / dead every enormous piece of nonsense which itself . . . . 561 1 X 1 21   1
    of tiniest world a piece of forever with summitless . . . . . 586 1 X 1 46   4
    we played with a piece of when till it . . . . 612 {CHAIRE} 14   8
    (pinkish or yellowish maybe) piece of pitiful paper-- but . . 697 95 POEMS 25   25
+PIECE
    FOR CONTEXT, SEE . . . . 813 73 POEMS 41   3
PIECES
    which smashes into several pieces and is hurriedly picked . . 203 XLI LA GUERRE 1 15
    / Among these red pieces of day (against which . . . . 278 IS 5 THREE 2   3
    one villa caught like pieces of a kite in . . . . 283 IS 5 THREE 7   10
    / / / / pieces (in darker than small . . . . 623 {CHAIRE} 25   1
+PIECES
    FOR CONTEXT, SEE . . . . 104 & POST IMPR 14   5
PIERCED
    of your charms: one pierced moment whiter than the . . . . . 78 T&C SON UNRE 3 12
    bulge hearts by darts pierced lazily writhe lurch faceflowers 436 NO THANKS 52   8
PIERCING
    startled whats are a (piercing clothes thoughts- kiss -ing . . 437 NO THANKS 53   6
PIGEONS
    the park sits Down. pigeons circle around and around . . . . 62 T&C PORTRAIT 10 28
    Mandolins l oo k- pigeons fly ingand whee (:are,SpRiN, . . . 122 & SEVEN POEMS 1 15
    tipping, the flocks of pigeons. And the skil- ful . . . . . . 166 & SON ACTU 15   4
    most park's least timorous pigeons) squ -I- nts (while . . . 726 95 POEMS 54   10
    can and do fat pigeons coo) haps even 4 . . . . 787 73 POEMS 15   7
PIGEONSJUSTLIKETHAT
    stallion and break onetwothreefourfive pigeonsjustlikethat . 60 T&C PORTRAIT 8   6
PIGGISH
    bulbous lips and forlorn piggish hands joked to a . . . . . . 56 T&C PORTRAIT 4   12
PIGLIKE
    lovers) & one dog? piglike big! sorrows always; finally . . . 384 NO THANKS 2   11
PIGS
    hutchinson says sweet guinea pigs do it it buy . . . . 325 VIVA 17   8
PIL
    of screaming warmth chuck pil- lows are noise funnily . . . . 96 & POST IMPR 8   4
+PILE
    FOR CONTEXT, SEE . . . . 231 IS 5 ONE 3   51
PILGRIM
    flower of holiness a pilgrim from beyond the future's . . . . 601 {CHAIRE} 3   9
PILGRIMS'
    you land of the pilgrims' and so forth oh . . . . 268 IS 5 TWO 3   2
+PILL
    FOR CONTEXT, SEE . . . . 231 IS 5 ONE 3   46
PILLAR
    arrow or a fleet pillar is eaten by yesterday . . . . 110 & PORTRAIT 6   3
    built like a fleet pillar or a smooth arrow . . . . 111 & PORTRAIT 6   46

		PAGE	TITLE	LINE

PILLAR (CONTINUED)

the arrow and the pillar pursue curiously a crumbling . . . . 112 & PORTRAIT 6   82
/ / (swooning) a pillar of youngly loveflesh topped . . . . . 615 (CHAIRE) 17   1

+PILLAR

FOR CONTEXT, SEE . . . . 385 NO THANKS 2   48

PILLARS

intricate (whereof the luscious pillars rise which are her . 21 T&C PUELLA MEA 203
nesting incense) fifty marble pillars slipped from . . . . . 32 T&C ORIENTALE 6   29
passion of the fifty pillars listening while the queens . . . 35 T&C ORIENTALE 6 113

PILLOW

in bright degrees, whose pillow is the graces and . . . . . . 4 T&C EPITHALAM   40
very big a sufficient pillow shoveling her small . . . . . . 134 & SON REAL 5   2
the morning) kiss this pillow, dear where our heads . . . . 288 IS 5 FOUR 5   9
-like hair spatters creasing pillow next everywhere . . . . . 358 VIVA 49   3

PILLOW'S

(if how begins a pillow's green means face or . . . . 506 50 POEMS 20   9

PILLOWS

exerting himself among his pillows throws jewels at the . . . 34 T&C ORIENTALE 6 100

+PILLOWS

FOR CONTEXT, SEE . . . . 96 & POST IMPR 8   4

PILLS

into a dirtied glass) Pills for Ills (a recipe . . . . . . 359 VIVA 50   8

PILOT

whose passenger and whose pilot my spirit is / . . . . . . 419 NO THANKS 36   24

PIMPLES

half awake, cursed with pimples, correctly dressed, ... 262 IS 5 ONE 32   7

PIMPLY

the parks with overgrown pimply cavaliers and gumchewing . . 61 T&C PORTRAIT 9   6

PIMPS

/ / when muckers pimps and tratesmen delivered are . . . . . 405 NO THANKS 22   1
quacks will cure when pimps may please? must through . . . . 527 50 POEMS 39   24

PIN

agony my grunting eyes pin tailored flames Her being . . . . 137 & SON REAL 8   10
bangaroom slim guesser goose pin yessir wheel no sendwisp . . 333 VIVA 24   18

PINAFORE'D

and that pretty pink pinafore'd knock out your eye" . . . . 707 95 POEMS 35   8

PINCH

oh yes! Large legs pinch, toes choke-- hair-thin strands . . 146 & SON REAL 17   7
big legs nice to pinch assiduously which justgraze each . . . 150 & SON REAL 21   8
ends of arms which pinch that purple book between . . . . . . 506 50 POEMS 20   2

PINCHED

fingers of prurient philosophers pinched and poked thee ,has 46 T&C LA GUERRE 2   6
somewhere in your heart pinched from dumb summer? O . . . . . 80 T&C SON UNRE 5   8

PINCIAN

also had climbed the pincian to appreciate rome at . . . . . 355 VIVA 46   12

PINE

in a new nice pine box (collect / / . . . . 270 IS 5 TWO 5   20
by birch by maple pine by hemlock spruce by . . . . 658 (CHAIRE) 60   19

PINES

on the hills the pines deepen to whispers primeval . . . . . 5 T&C EPITHALAM   76
mountain slept while his pines lifted their green lives . . . 555 1 X 1 15   16

PINK

fingers possibly touch the pink hollyhock existence whose . . 58 T&C PORTRAIT 6   17
fad ed explosion of, pink! stocking w h e . . . . 94 & POST IMPR 6   6
moon creeped into the pink hand of the smoke . . . . 125 & SEVEN POEMS 4   21
leak smoke: remembering, two pink big lips curl.... how . . . 149 & SON REAL 20   15
careless movements carefully scatter pink propaganda of . . . 150 & SON REAL 21   15
has gold teeth b pink suspenders c reads Atlantis . . . . . . 200 XLI PORTRAIT 8   6
which eats into a pink cliff back and up . . . . 281 IS 5 THREE 5   9
/ / thethe the pink Tartskids with thecas-tanets in . . . . . 318 VIVA 10   2
once whom fiercely by pink mr seized green mrs . . . . 465 NEW POEMS 3   7
/ / red-rag and pink-flag blackshirt and brown strut-mince . 497 50 POEMS 11   1
girl with nipples like pink thimbles) ask him ask . . . . . . 498 50 POEMS 12   19
or why a quilt's pink stops might equal head). . . . . 506 50 POEMS 20   10
squirms a pool of pink fat screams a hole . . . . 545 1 X 1 5   7
less than more magnetic pink unwhores a wai ter . . . . 629 (CHAIRE) 31   7
never tried) the great pink superme diocri ty of . . . . . . 635 (CHAIRE) 37   7
high and that pretty pink pinafore'd knock out your . . . . . 707 95 POEMS 35   8

PINK (CONTINUED)
    sam shrugs his pretty pink shoulders you know how . . . . . . 711 95 POEMS 39   22
+PINK
    FOR CONTEXT, SEE . . . . 385 NO THANKS 2   43
PINK-FLAG
    / / red-rag and pink-flag blackshirt and brown strut-mince . 497 50 POEMS 11   1
PINKEST
    a frozen brook of pinkest vomit out of eyes . . . . 258 IS 5 ONE 28   14
PINKHAM
    Lincoln and Lydia E. Pinkham, land above all of . . . . . . 230 IS 5 ONE 2   11
PINKISH
    are both slowly with pinkish ponderous arms bedecked whose . 225 IS 5 ONE LIZ   7
    brutebeak one fatal faded (pinkish or yellowish maybe) piece 697 95 POEMS 25   24
+PINKISH
    FOR CONTEXT, SEE . . . . 318 VIVA 10   19
    FOR CONTEXT, SEE . . . . 318 VIVA 10   21
PINKNESS
    faintly sweating air with pinkness, one pale dog behind . . . 144 & SON REAL 15   6
PINKS
    pretty- lemons and virginal pinks and wealthy vermilion and . 100 & POST IMPR 11   6
    lu minous edible spry pinks shy lemons greens coo . . . . . . 179 XLI SONGS 1   8
PINKTHISGREEN
    (r all; o ver pinkthisgreen acr) o) greenthatpink) acrobata . 385 NO THANKS 2   43
PINNACLE
    lation demonstrating from woolworthian pinnacle a capable . . 197 XLI PORTRAIT 5   7
    of same, conform the pinnacle of am though dull . . . . . . 521 50 POEMS 34   60
+PINNACLE
    FOR CONTEXT, SEE . . . . 309 VIVA 1   24
+PINWHEELING
    FOR CONTEXT, SEE . . . . 495 50 POEMS 9   18
PINXIT
    gladness, per the face --pinxit, who knows? Who knows? . . . 158 & SON ACTU 7   6
PIPES
    legs like white squirming pipes wiggle upon the perfumed . . 110 & PORTRAIT 6   7
    their altruistic smell moscow pipes good kumrads dance) . . . 413 NO THANKS 30   9
PIPEWRENCH
    former coachman with a pipewrench of the again latter . . . . 263 IS 5 ONE 32   45
PIPPLES
    / why are these pipples taking their hets off? . . . . 245 IS 5 ONE 16   1
PIRACIES
    running from marbles and piracies and it's spring when . . . 24 T&C CHANSONS 1   8
PIROUETTE
    is the sweet shy pirouette your hair and then . . . . 186 XLI SONGS 8   14
+PIROUETTING
    FOR CONTEXT, SEE . . . . 495 50 POEMS 9   4
PISS
    you would take a piss they speak whatever's on . . . . 427 NO THANKS 44   16
+PISS
    FOR CONTEXT, SEE . . . . 411 NO THANKS 28   5
+PISSING
    FOR CONTEXT, SEE . . . . 635 {CHAIRE} 37   4
PISSOIR
    who emerging from a pissoir enters abruptly Notre Dame . . . 245 IS 5 ONE 16   22
PISTIL
    of piston and of pistil; very well provided an . . . . 264 IS 5 ONE 33   22
+PISTIL
    FOR CONTEXT, SEE . . . . 342 VIVA 33   3
PISTON
    a mixed splendor of piston and of pistil; very . . . . 264 IS 5 ONE 33   22
PITCHFORK
    halts propped on a pitchfork (breathing) lovers like rej . . 754 95 POEMS 82   8
PITH
    more neatly ream this pith of darkness: carve an . . . . . . 139 & SON REAL 10   8
PITHECOID
    close quotes the microscopic pithecoid President in a new . . 267 IS 5 TWO 2   2
PITIFUL
    i say--let him be pitiful: because i've travelled all . . . . 216 XLI SONNETS 12   10
    yellowish maybe) piece of pitiful paper-- but now, as . . . . 697 95 POEMS 25   26

PITIFUL (CONTINUED)
    is without until: but pitiful they've (big little and . . . . 776 73 POEMS 4   21
PITILESS
    now or here) let pitiless fear play host to . . . . 580 1 X 1 40   4
    the simplest wish: so pitiless a massacre the hope . . . . . 609 (CHAIRE) 11   6
    move) blind sands, at pitiless the mercy of time . . . . . . 743 95 POEMS 71   8
PITY
    condemnatory fingers thinned of pity--so he stands counting .   9 T&C SONGS 1   14
    / / / god pity me whom (god distinctly . . . . 140 & SON REAL 11   1
    to make incitions and pity the fool who cright . . . . 405 NO THANKS 22   9
    right as rain his pity was as green as . . . . 520 50 POEMS 34   36
    / / / / pity this busy monster, manunkind, ... 554 1 X 1 14   1
    not a world of born--pity poor flesh and trees, ... 554 1 X 1 14   10
    seeing to blind (blow pity to envy and soul . . . . 560 1 X 1 20   14
    demongod countless in hatred pity fear each more exactly . . 662 (CHAIRE) 64   9
    / / / / pity his how illimitable plight . . . . 842 73 POEMS 70   1
PITYING
    feet (lift and may pitying Who from sharp soft . . . . 522 50 POEMS 35   12
    submicroscopic is-- compared with pitying terrible some alive 561 1 X 1 21   4
+PITYING
    FOR CONTEXT, SEE . . . . 607 (CHAIRE) 9   9
PIVOINE
    voix fragile couleur de pivoine?) with the long lips . . . . 121 & PORTRAIT 12   56
PIVOTING
    9 & . (musically-who? pivoting) SmileS "ahlbrhoon / / . . . . 430 NO THANKS 47   29
PLACE
    sitting in Dick Mid's Place said to Death teach . . . . 57 T&C PORTRAIT 5   3
    sitting in Dick Mid's Place asked "always" Death said . . . . 57 T&C PORTRAIT 5   24
    rang at Dick Mid's Place the madam was a . . . . 73 T&C SON REAL 4   1
    ears, go into Hassan's place the canounchir p ing . . . . . . 100 & POST IMPR 11   41
    necessary to find Hassan's Place by tiny streets shrugging . 143 & SON REAL 14   3
    won't be a single place dark or unhappy then . . . . 192 XLI CHANSONS 2   20
    and in the same place. Why according to tomorrow's . . . . . 262 IS 5 ONE 32   17
    alive skies--and in death's place new fragrantly young earth 432 NO THANKS 49   18
    / love is a place & through this place . . . . 443 NO THANKS 58   1
    place & through this place of love move (with . . . . 443 NO THANKS 58   2
    Ever-Ever Land is a place that's as simple as . . . . 466 NEW POEMS 4   9
    Ever-Ever Land is a place that's measured and safe . . . . . 466 NEW POEMS 4   17
    her beautiful yes. The place is now let us . . . . 504 50 POEMS 18   13
    always arriving at the place you never left (and . . . . . . 807 73 POEMS 35   4
PLACES
    coolness slowly in peopling places seeks play: withs of . . . 168 & SON ACTU 17   14
    sharp holes in dark places paints eyes touches hands . . . . 437 NO THANKS 53   5
    brightness of peace) all places yes is a world . . . . 443 NO THANKS 58   5
    man what bubbies going places on such babies aint . . . . . . 476 NEW POEMS 14   7
PLACID
    exact smile of life's placid obscure palpable carnival where 43 T&C AMORES 7   31
+PLACIDITY
    FOR CONTEXT, SEE . . . . 607 (CHAIRE) 9   4
PLACING
    stare arranging and changing placing carefully there a . . . 124 & SEVEN POEMS 3   6
    fraction of flower here placing an inch of air . . . . 124 & SEVEN POEMS 3   17
PLAN
    Eternity's a Five Year Plan: if Joy with Pain . . . . 438 NO THANKS 54   6
    righter than books could plan) the stupidest teacher will . . 594 1 X 1 54   4
PLANE
    upon a merely human plane) someone completely beautiful; and 799 73 POEMS 27   10
PLANES
    crackle and sag of planes clamors of collision collapse . . . 48 T&C IMPRESS 2   8
    uproar of knuckling silent planes a nudging bulb silkenly . . 68 T&C POST IMPR 5   14
    vaguely a squeak of planes or between squeals of . . . . . . 195 XLI PORTRAIT 3   11
PLANET
    disappear unreally; as this planet (understand) forgets the . 379 VIVA 70   8
    inch of their murdered planet grows more and enormously . . . 808 73 POEMS 36   10
PLANET'S
    briefest breathing lives some planet's year, his longest . . 609 (CHAIRE) 11   10
PLANETS
    seat is where revolving planets struggle to be free . . . . . 212 XLI SONNETS 8   11

		PAGE	TITLE	LINE
PLANETS (CONTINUED)				
of certain stars and planets heard, rose very slowly		360	VIVA 51	12
PLANNED				
for instance everything is planned next to that patch		322	VIVA 14	3
PLANT				
/ / / / plant Magic dust expect hope		780	73 POEMS 8	1
PLANTS				
acle to rubber) tres (plants how grin ho) cen		309	VIVA 1	27
PLASTIC				
with the soothings of plastic hypnotism . i am		201	XLI PORTRAIT 9	26
PLASTICITY				
domeshaped interval of complete plasticity, shoul- ders, . .		97	& POST IMPR 8	35
PLATE				
street-lamps upon an almostclean plate "Achilles" said Nicho'		194	XLI PORTRAIT 2	34
+PLATINUM				
FOR CONTEXT, SEE		704	95 POEMS 32	8
PLATITUDE				
T.P. and the duckbilled platitude lays & lays and		321	VIVA 13	15
PLATO				
/ / / / plato told him: he couldn't		553	1 X 1 13	1
are, good luck! aberdeen plato-rabelais peter jack / / . . .		605	{CHAIRE} 7	16
PLATO-RABELAIS				
are, good luck! aberdeen plato-rabelais peter jack / / . . .		605	{CHAIRE} 7	16
PLATZBURG				
waiter intones: bloo-moo-n sirkusricky platzburg hoppytoad .		108	& PORTRAIT 4	15
PLAY				
should my lady's beauty play at not speaking (sometimes . . .		18	T&C PUELLA MEA	61
--. Dogs bark children play -ing Are in the		63	T&C PORTRAIT 10	35
part they let thee play; i see the large		75	T&C SON REAL 6	6
streets while exactlygir lisHlegs; play; ing; nake; D and . .		104	& POST IMPR 14	11
....kIss her: hands will play on, mE as dea		122	& SEVEN POEMS 1	10
and to have somebody play who can but you		126	& SEVEN POEMS 5	30
in peopling places seeks play: withs of star link		168	& SON ACTU 17	14
has his toys to play with ◇ (will BigMorning		169	& SON ACTU 18	9
smoke Helmar cigarettes 2 play backgammon, 3 watch a		200	XLI PORTRAIT 8	4
Atlantis x and y play b cries "effendi" "Uh"		200	XLI PORTRAIT 8	9
another x and y play, effendi approaches, sets down		200	XLI PORTRAIT 8	18
turkish x and y play b spits x and		200	XLI PORTRAIT 8	21
spits x and y play, b starts armenian record		200	XLI PORTRAIT 8	24
nearing our hearts' irrevocable play-- through the mysterious		215	XLI SONNETS 11	13
war band and can play the triangle like the		253	IS 5 ONE 24	3
here) let pitiless fear play host to every isn't		580	1 X 1 40	4
to the beach (to play one day) and maggie		682	95 POEMS 10	2
/ that melancholy fellow'll play his handorgan until you . .		697	95 POEMS 25	2
+PLAY				
FOR CONTEXT, SEE		153	& SON ACTU 2	5
FOR CONTEXT, SEE		310	VIVA 2	10
PLAYED				
the fuZZy tune that's played by the Funny hand		100	& POST IMPR 11	36
a Jumpy Tramp who played each card as if		194	XLI PORTRAIT 2	22
looks like rain (they've played for timelessness with chips .		451	NO THANKS 66	3
kept a date and played a tune) death's dollhead		479	NEW POEMS 17	9
we remember: yes; we played with a piece of		612	{CHAIRE} 14	8
quoth gifted she: and played the hostess to my		807	73 POEMS 35	15
PLAYER				
the emperor a cithern- player squats with quiveringgold body		34	T&C ORIENTALE 6	71
PLAYFUL				
with meteors streaming from playful immortal hands the . . .		36	T&C AMORES 1	17
PLAYFULLY				
dress. one nipple tries. playfully to peek into the		143	& SON REAL 14	10
PLAYIN				
crows drop into sunset, playin uh busted harmonica /		332	VIVA 23	32
PLAYING				
eyes are at kisses playing, whose strangeness much says; . .		13	T&C SONGS 3	10
is that the hurdy-gurdy's playing / / / /		152	& SON ACTU 1	15
is twilight) a Face playing on a flute /		169	& SON ACTU 18	16
a handorgan in twilight playing like hell / /		174	& SON ACTU 23	15
photographed with Lord Rothermere playing with Lord		262	IS 5 ONE 32	21

	PAGE	TITLE	LINE

PLAYING (CONTINUED)

certain nobodies laughing faintly playing moving far below us 283 IS 5 THREE 7 9
themselves quietly they began playing with a button the . . . 284 IS 5 FOUR 1 9
(if he had been playing a fiddle i had . . . . 355 VIVA 46 18
their dolls wallow toys playing writhe with toys (than . . . 565 1 X 1 25 6
can proudly lose, or playing dead and hoping death . . . . . 679 95 POEMS 7 3
if an earth was playing at birthdays each (a . . . . 763 95 POEMS 90 6

PLAYS

strength who how furiously plays the hot sweet horrible . . . 110 & PORTRAIT 6 10
and life safely beyond) plays with the bigness of . . . . . . 554 1 X 1 14 4

PLAYTHINGS

by gainsborough just the playthings for dust n'est-ce pas . . 198 XLI PORTRAIT 6 13

PLEASANT

them is always a pleasant song my love thy . . . . 29 T&C ORIENTALE 3 14
makes your neck feel pleasant and stoopid and if . . . . . . 126 & SEVEN POEMS 5 19
nakedness with fins sharply pleasant, my youth has travelled 216 XLI SONNETS 12 3
/ yes is a pleasant country: if's wintry (my . . . . 578 1 X 1 38 1
you whispers "is very pleasant" my ghost to / . . . . 808 73 POEMS 36 15

PLEASANTER

smile could anything be pleasanter (some big dark little . . 650 (CHAIRE) 52 5

PLEASANTLY

face cluttered in pursuit pleasantly elephantine while nearby 56 T&C PORTRAIT 4 8
low ceiling my being pleasantly was punctuated by the . . . . 96 & POST IMPR 8 25
It The L's roar tortures-pleasantly myears it is, like . . . 101 & POST IMPR 11 49
musical fruit. My lips pleasantly groan on your taste. . . . 154 & SON ACTU 3 3

PLEASE

well might any monarch please.) Each ankle is divinely . . . 21 T&C PUELLA MEA 214
not. Again. Hush. God. Please hold. Tight / / . . . . 130 & SON REAL 1 15
become of (if you please) all the glory that . . . . 233 IS 5 ONE 4 10
Waiter this; woman is please shut that the pout . . . . . . 243 IS 5 ONE 14 4
just why that should please him or i wonder . . . . 296 IS 5 FOUR 13 10
some people and others please don't confuse. Some people . . 314 VIVA 6 4
/ don't cries to please my musn't broke) life . . . . 343 VIVA 34 1
life Is like that please stroke for now stroke . . . . 343 VIVA 34 3
you're hurting o Me please you're killing) death is . . . . . 343 VIVA 34 6
is like now That please squirtnowing for o squirting . . . . 343 VIVA 34 7
o eighteen) Don't (for) Please (tnights, on whose for . . . . 343 VIVA 34 15
god dear wait sh please o no O 3rd . . . . 358 VIVA 49 5
of seem and genius please the talentgang and water . . . . . 511 50 POEMS 25 6
cure when pimps may please? must through unstrange synthetic 527 50 POEMS 39 24
it that stinks to please but whether to please . . . . 549 1 X 1 9 8
please but whether to please itself or someone else . . . . . 549 1 X 1 9 9
what we imagine but please for god's O what . . . . 638 (CHAIRE) 40 9
/ "o purple finch please tell me why this . . . . 836 73 POEMS 64 2

+PLEASE

FOR CONTEXT, SEE . . . . 316 VIVA 8 8
FOR CONTEXT, SEE . . . . 519 50 POEMS 33 7
FOR CONTEXT, SEE . . . . 552 1 X 1 12 5

PLEASE'

you spare three cents please' --why guesswho nearly leaped . 800 73 POEMS 28 6

PLEASED

the religious fuss infinity pleased our parents one inch . . 466 NEW POEMS 4 15

PLEASEDON'T

for eheads shone eternal pleasedon't; rising: from the Shall. 343 VIVA 34 17

PLEASURE

oval shove of hiding pleasure. Alice, stinging quips of . . . 138 & SON REAL 9 14
his teeth (hips pumping pleasure into hips). Seeing how . . . 161 & SON ACTU 10 4
length inexcusable, this inexplicable pleasure--you go from . 295 IS 5 FOUR 12 7
most green and young pleasure and pain are merely . . . . . . 531 50 POEMS 43 5

PLED

for Truth have liars pled, their heels for Freedom . . . . . 438 NO THANKS 54 17

PLEDGED

some grave languorous hymn pledged to illimitable dissipation 206 XLI SONNETS 2 13

PLENTY

on such babies aint plenty good enough for i . . . . 476 NEW POEMS 14 8

PLIGHT

pity his how illimitable plight who dies to be . . . . 842 73 POEMS 70 1

PLOC
    piddle-of-drops she says I ploc spittle what the lands   . . .   96 & POST IMPR 8   14
PLOOP
    eager. wittily peels the. ploop. --OOc h get: breath   . . . . 136 & SON REAL 7   13
PLOUGHMAN
    the sky knight and ploughman pardoner wife and nun   . . . . . 661 {CHAIRE} 63   9
PLUCKED
    dance! and when he's plucked such mysteries as men   . . . . . 843 73 POEMS 71   13
PLUCKINGS
    which, are, the, flowery pluckings of a harpsichord colours . 100 & POST IMPR 11   10
PLUGGED
    people: for instance a plugged promise-- then he will . . . . 298 IS 5 FOUR 15   19
PLUM
    me, dressed like a Plum grinning softly, New focus-of . . . .   94 & POST IMPR 6   16
PLUMBED
    hobby photography never has plumbed the heights of prowst . . 499 50 POEMS 13   10
PLUMBING
    (which Ultima Thule Of Plumbing shall receive the philophilic 334 VIVA 25   3
PLUMP
    ceased to breathe). The plump left fist opening "wisdom." . . 226 IS 5 ONE MAME   7
    dim ones; the slim plump tiny tall) all except . . . . 619 {CHAIRE} 21   12
PLUMPTUMBLING
    recalls hat gestures bud plumptumbling hand voices Eye   . . . 330 VIVA 21   7
PLUMS
    is, fond of tiny plums of tangerines and apples . . . . 100 & POST IMPR 11   26
+PLUMS
    FOR CONTEXT, SEE . . . . 615 {CHAIRE} 17   7
PLUNGE
    blood: with upwardcringing swiftness plunge these leopards of 139 & SON REAL 10   6
    you) timid lewd moon plunge skilfully into the hill. . . . . 155 & SON ACTU 4   17
    synthetic now true histories plunge? rains a grey snow   . . . 527 50 POEMS 39   27
PLUNGED
    not entitled to complain --plunged in eternal now if   . . . . 561 1 X 1 21   9
PLUNGES
    sprouting largest final air plunges inward with hurled   . . . 301 IS 5 FOUR 18   17
PLUNGING
    not sunlight? yes! and (plunging rapturously up) we spill . . 650 {CHAIRE} 52   19
+PLUNKY
    FOR CONTEXT, SEE . . . . 519 50 POEMS 33   3
PLURAL
    ease that bright how plural tide measures her guest . . . . . 418 NO THANKS 35   10
PLUS
    narrow thudding timeshaped face plus innocuous winking hands,   62 T&C PORTRAIT 10   3
    of tobacco and gladness plus little derricks of gesture . . .   68 T&C POST IMPR 5   4
    glush of squirting taps plus slush of foam knocked   . . . . .   96 & POST IMPR 8   13
    smelled so much tasted plus touched quite so And   . . . . 474 NEW POEMS 12   8
    ears with some lips plus a couple of) holes   . . . . 501 50 POEMS 15   20
    as (while thumb a plus fingers all with blind . . . . 546 1 X 1 6   10
    of genial plac -idity (plus, out of much its   . . . . 607 {CHAIRE} 9   5
    tearose) and every minus plus --fare ill: fare well-- . . . . 798 73 POEMS 26   12
POCKET
    seriously in, his minute pocket) Sometimes he does not   . . .   69 T&C POST IMPR 6   11
    i have a real pocket in it and the   . . . .   69 T&C POST IMPR 6   41
POCKETS
    sudden silver these torn pockets of lame and begging   . . . .   93 & POST IMPR 5   15
    (rememberingly with in both pockets curled hands moves) why . 299 IS 5 FOUR 16   10
    toothsome like (they got pockets full may take a   . . . . . . 314 VIVA 6   10
    means finding Holes where pockets aren't lucky 's to   . . . . 467 NEW POEMS 5   3
POCO
    to sense something un poco putrido when we contemplate   . . . 327 VIVA 18   45
PODIA
    behemoth truly pseudo yours podia of radarw leschin / . . . . 333 VIVA 24   25
POEM
    that always beyond this poem or any poem she   . . . .   22 T&C PUELLA MEA 239
    this poem or any poem she of whose body . . . .   22 T&C PUELLA MEA 239
    mine also, little painted poem of god / / . . . .   75 T&C SON REAL 6   14
    surely make a millionth poem which will not wholly   . . . .   92 & POST IMPR 4   19
    / / / the poem her belly marched through   . . . . 135 & SON REAL 6   1

	PAGE	TITLE	LINE

POEM (CONTINUED)

after five times the poem of thy remembrance surprises . . . 184 XLI SONGS 6 — 2
/ / / / POEM, OR BEAUTY HURTS MR. . . . . 230 IS 5 ONE 2 — T
this like a littlest poem a (with wee ears . . . . 286 IS 5 FOUR 3 — 11
smile (shyly if a poem should lift to me . . . . 291 IS 5 FOUR 8 — 25
world go down, one poem yet shall swim / . . . . 372 VIVA 63 — 15
brains... --Who wields a poem huger than the grave? . . . . . 377 VIVA 68 — 12
read for ecstasy --for poem prose-- caution for curiosity . . 689 95 POEMS 17 — 6
would know) of purest poem and glories of sheerest . . . . . 748 95 POEMS 76 — 7
/ / / / POEM (or "the divine right . . . . 803 73 POEMS 31 — 1

POEMS

sky light walks scattering poems on earth a candle . . . . . 50 T&C IMPRESS 4 — 3
sky night walks scattering poems / / / / . . . . 50 T&C IMPRESS 4 — 33
rathe.... yours are the poems i do not write. . . . . 84 T&C SON ACTU 3 — 12
/ / &: SEVEN POEMS i will be M . . . . 122 & SEVEN POEMS 1 — T
you are forever making poems in the lap of . . . . 204 XLI LA GUERRE 2 — 23
beyond or around (as poems are made) Our picking . . . . . . 364 VIVA 55 — 8
becomingly: a thunderbolt compose poems not because harm . . 452 NO THANKS 67 — 14
whose silence are cries poems children dreams & through . . . 719 95 POEMS 47 — 6
--God's heaven perhaps comprises poems (my mother's . . . . . 748 95 POEMS 76 — 6
a sight to sing) poems are opening, as if . . . . 763 95 POEMS 90 — 4
it with a thousand poems my darling but nobody . . . . 835 73 POEMS 63 — 28

POESY

(Everywhere Why) as divine poesy per that and this . . . . . 230 IS 5 ONE 2 — 17

POET

behind a golden door, poet and sage and caliph . . . . 22 T&C PUELLA MEA — 223
of your wrists; the poet who is afraid only . . . . 291 IS 5 FOUR 8 — 9
the face of a poet really which is a . . . . 352 VIVA 43 — 11
critics will upon a poet feast) meanwhile this ghost . . . . 418 NO THANKS 35 — 11
and to a disappearing poet of always, snow and . . . . . . 424 NO THANKS 41 — 5
make their names (this poet made war whose naught . . . . . 440 NO THANKS 56 — 24
self with life this poet arose nor hate nor . . . . 441 NO THANKS 56 — 42
? n g Is poet iS (childlost so; ul . . . . 471 NEW POEMS 9 — 13
beast-- such was a poet and shall be and . . . . 562 1 X 1 22 — 10
forests towerful towns (queen poet king float sprout heroes . 586 1 X 1 46 — 9
Dead like even a Poet) could hardly express what . . . . . . 702 95 POEMS 30 — 7

POETIC

stink. dawn. Inane, the poetic carcass of a girl . . . . . . 139 & SON REAL 10 — 14
otherwise democratic) but essentially poetic or ethereally . 802 73 POEMS 30 — 21

POETRY

before this music, and poetry cannot go near because . . . . 162 & SON ACTU 11 — 6

POETS

/ the hills like poets put on purple thought . . . . 188 XLI SONGS 10 — 2
/ / / / poets yeggs and thirsties since . . . . 261 IS 5 ONE 31 — 1
blue horses, and the poets looked at them, and . . . . . . 302 IS 5 FIVE 1 — 14
where Boobs are holy, poets mad, illustrious punks of . . . 438 NO THANKS 54 — 19
most flame and surely poets only understands) honour this . . 456 NO THANKS 71 — 11
turned to dream "and poets grow; and (there--see?) children" 626 {CHAIRE} 28 — 12
time. Time cannot children, poets, lovers tell- measure . . . 817 73 POEMS 45 — 9

+POETS

FOR CONTEXT, SEE . . . . 492 50 POEMS 6 — 2
FOR CONTEXT, SEE . . . . 492 50 POEMS 6 — 14

POF

dead's clever too like POF goes the alarm off . . . . 126 & SEVEN POEMS 5 — 10

POIGNANT

wholly to know the poignant instantaneous fern whose . . . . 19 T&C PUELLA MEA — 110

POILU

with a luminous fur poilu a Jesus sags in . . . . 134 & SON REAL 5 — 14

POINT

pout ges- tures stickily point made glints squinting who's . 96 & POST IMPR 8 — 18
rolled and made its point Jimmie's sister worked for . . . . 149 & SON REAL 20 — 6
Be Resharpened. (Case in point if we are to . . . . 230 IS 5 ONE 2 — 23
Happens--skip dance kids hop point at red blue yellow . . . . 437 NO THANKS 53 — 13

POINTING

desperately, round and round pointing to the queer monkey . . 69 T&C POST IMPR 6 — 9
i am they are pointing at the queer monkey . . . . 69 T&C POST IMPR 6 — 37
crowd howls faintly blubbering pointing see yes) It here . . 280 IS 5 THREE 4 — 15

	PAGE	TITLE	LINE

POINTS
  freezing fire of Thickness) points uPDownwardishly find . . . 311 VIVA 3   14
POISE
  wandering in whose perishable poise is the mystery of . . . . 17 T&C PUELLA MEA   14
  sincere with wonder a poise a wounding a beautiful . . . . . 54 T&C PORTRAIT 2   6
  foreverish time's tide at poise, love alone understands: only 843 73 POEMS 71   4
POISED
  shall gleam, in the poised radiance of perpetualness. When . 81 T&C SON UNRE 6   8
  as fair. (The child-head poised with the serious hair)/ . . . 207 XLI SONNETS 3   14
+POISED
  FOR CONTEXT, SEE . . . . 430 NO THANKS 47   3
POISES
  circling the acerb pole poises, smiling, the diadumenos in .   3 T&C EPITHALAM   32
  watering lips the world poises a moment (futile, proud, . . . 23 T&C PUELLA MEA   268
POISING
  wrists thighs feet hands poising to again utterly disappear; 369 VIVA 60   14
POISON
  / when the proficient poison of sure sleep bereaves . . . . . 210 XLI SONNETS 6   1
  l'echelle) die can't quite poison God's sunlight / / . . . . 708 95 POEMS 36   16
POISONED
  floor quietly Stare a poisoned mouse still who alive . . . . 784 73 POEMS 12   4
POISONOUS
  absurdity. skin like the poisonous fragility of ice newly . . 103 & POST IMPR 13   12
POKE
  sicksilk soak sulksuck whim poke if inch dimmer twist . . . . 333 VIVA 24   12
POKED
  prurient philosophers pinched and poked thee ,has the naughty 46 T&C LA GUERRE 2   8
POLE
  stars circling the acerb pole poises, smiling, the diadumenos   3 T&C EPITHALAM   31
  (one!) the wisti-twisti barber -pole is climbing people high, 128 & SEVEN POEMS 6   3
  length of this padded pole; a monkey attached by . . . . . . 279 IS 5 THREE 3   10
  and rapidly along this pole over five squirming mice; . . . . 279 IS 5 THREE 3   15
POLES
  for the is it Poles? perhaps. While permanent faces . . . . . 70 T&C SON REAL 1   8
POLICE
  nucleolus: the Prefect of Police (a dapper derbied creature, 274 IS 5 TWO 9   27
POLICEMAN
  i am not a policeman. Meanwhile the tea regressed. . . . . . 263 IS 5 ONE 32   41
  suddenly) meets the tall policeman of my mind. awake . . . . 304 IS 5 FIVE 3   5
POLICEMAN'S
  why (captured by a policeman's majestic and buried eye) . . . 324 VIVA 16   4
POLICEMEN
  it With All The Policemen In The World / . . . . 835 73 POEMS 63   31
POLISHED
  (with white wig and polished buttons) would take you . . . . 365 VIVA 56   13
POLITE
  smooth and ridiculous a polite uproar of knuckling silent . . 68 T&C POST IMPR 5   14
POLITELY
  Gay one (which she politely refused) set out gaily . . . . . 326 VIVA 18   19
POLITICIAN
  / / / a politician is an arse upon . . . . 550 1 X 1 10   1
POLITICIANS
  idealists? so what) all politicians like the sight of . . . . 790 73 POEMS 18   12
+POLITICIANS
  FOR CONTEXT, SEE . . . . 405 NO THANKS 22   4
POLITICS
  sight of vote and politics, as everyone knows, is . . . . . . 790 73 POEMS 18   13
POLLENIZING
  Her. thuglike stare the pollenizing vacancy when, Thy . . . . 159 & SON ACTU 8   15
POLLOI
  its hoi in its polloi and if sometimes he's . . . . 544 1 X 1 4   8
+POLLY
  FOR CONTEXT, SEE . . . . 697 95 POEMS 25   14
POMP
  him smile. Scorning the pomp of must and shall . . . . 520 50 POEMS 34   33
POMPOUS
  lilac's smoke the poppy's pompous fire the pansy's purple . .   5 T&C EPITHALAM   92
  swallows swallowing revolv- ingly pompous a the swallowed . . 96 & POST IMPR 8   6

603

		PAGE	TITLE	LINE

POMPOUS (CONTINUED)

hurdy-gurdy accurately pants. and pompous ancient jews . . . 219 XLI SONNETS 15   9

POND

by (a parenthesis the) pond on whoseswooning edge black . . . 99 & POST IMPR 10   10

PONDER

i see thee then ponder the tinsel part they . . . . 75 T&C SON REAL 6   6

/ / / / (ponder, darling, these busted statues . . . . 260 IS 5 ONE 30   1

PONDERED

trees whom night hath pondered o'er --and frailties of . . . 205 XLI SONNETS 1   11

PONDEROUS

both slowly with pinkish ponderous arms bedecked whose white 225 IS 5 ONE LIZ   7

conduct worthy of more ponderous wishes or hopes less . . . . 328 VIVA 19   7

PONDS

magical impetuous and utter ponds of dream; and very . . . . 19 T&C PUELLA MEA   117

POOL

formed upon an old pool. Her nose was small, ... 103 & POST IMPR 13   13

of torse squirms a pool of pink fat screams . . . . 545 1 X 1 5   6

/ / this forest pool A so of Black . . . . 759 95 POEMS 86   2

POOPED

of a supermetamathical subpreincestures pooped universe (of . 425 NO THANKS 42   2

POOR

transparent folds-- with man's poor soul superlatively brave. 5 T&C EPITHALAM   96

sorry for awl the poor girls that gets up . . . . 109 & PORTRAIT 5   14

and they stuff the poor thing all full of . . . . 126 & SEVEN POEMS 5   13

know him lift the poor cuss tenderly this side . . . . . . 270 IS 5 TWO 5   14

and around which a poor wind will roam / . . . . 292 IS 5 FOUR 9   20

/ / / / poor But TerFLY went (flesh . . . . 320 VIVA 12   1

(shivering pale naked very poor) creature of shadow, that . . 374 VIVA 65   13

skies clutch an of poor how colding hereless. air . . . . . 491 50 POEMS 5   3

a world of born--pity poor flesh and trees, poor . . . . . . 554 1 X 1 14   10

poor flesh and trees, poor stars and stones, but . . . . . . 554 1 X 1 14   11

meet life begins-- not poor not rich (only aware) . . . . . 564 1 X 1 24   4

through the mere mind's poor pretend --grim comics of . . . . 576 1 X 1 36   6

some day?" "Or worse! poor worlds; i mean they're . . . . . 603 {CHAIRE} 5   12

(crying) jew wop rich poor (sing ing) He no . . . . 618 {CHAIRE} 20   12

Heart, now Mrs Death. Poor Mind / / / . . . . 621 {CHAIRE} 23   4

night & day "all poor little peoples that want . . . . . . 711 95 POEMS 39   7

m oo n (poor shadoweaten was of is . . . . 723 95 POEMS 51   8

than this: to feel) poor worlds must merely do, ... 762 95 POEMS 89   3

rich but misers are poor) --let's touch the sky: . . . . . . 769 95 POEMS 95   4

song) but misers are poor-- let's love until noone . . . . 769 95 POEMS 95   23

you never were hide, poor dishonoured mind who thought . . . 834 73 POEMS 62   13

+POOR

FOR CONTEXT, SEE . . . . 681 95 POEMS 9   11

POORBUTHONEST

guessed already is the poorbuthonest workingman (by that . . 254 IS 5 ONE 25   16

POP

muthn't pleathe don't as pop weird up her hot . . . . 316 VIVA 8   9

POPES

glad (children of) dirtpoor (popes emperors) undeaths through 681 95 POEMS 9   12

POPPA

(a punkslapping mobsucking gravypissing poppa but who just . 635 {CHAIRE} 37   4

POPPIES

in a fragility of poppies.... i say that sometimes . . . . . 45 T&C LA GUERRE 1   6

bee dozes on the poppies, the dears; when all's . . . . . . 181 XLI SONGS 3   10

POPPY

from her couch of poppy petals peers the sleepy . . . . . . 8 T&C OF NICOL   13

POPPY'S

the lilac's smoke the poppy's pompous fire the pansy's . . . 5 T&C EPITHALAM   92

POPS

it's jolly odd what pops into your jolly tete . . . . 269 IS 5 TWO 4   2

POPULAR

and cowards heroes (the popular the wise, a weed . . . . . . 798 73 POEMS 26   10

PORE

emptiness) priming at every pore a deathless life with . . . 428 NO THANKS 45   15

PORKIE

/ / porky & porkie sit into a moon) . . . . 483 NEW POEMS 21   1

		PAGE	TITLE	LINE
PORKY				
/ / / / porky & porkie sit into		483	NEW POEMS 21	1
POROUS				
bed Mangy from person Porous sits years its of		312	VIVA 4	18
PORPHYRY				
upon a horse of porphyry into the waters i		30	T&C ORIENTALE 4	10
in a palace of porphyry which was a million		32	T&C ORIENTALE 6	2
PORTALS				
hovering at the dark portals of hurt girl eyes		54	T&C PORTRAIT 2	3
PORTRAIT				
dear god there's a portrait over the door very		198	XLI PORTRAIT 6	7
which distinct and rich portrait should be included, gents .		254	IS 5 ONE 25	8
PORTRAITS				
/ / / / PORTRAITS the nimble heat had		52	T&C PORTRAIT 1	T
/ / / / PORTRAITS being twelve who hast		105	& PORTRAIT 1	T
/ / / / PORTRAITS conversation with my friend		193	XLI PORTRAIT 1	T
PORTS				
thy heart on frailer ports of costlier commerce bent		79	T&C SON UNRE 4	16
POSE				
O indefinable frail ultimate pose! O visible beatitude sweet		5	T&C EPITHALAM	109
is pouring) emits a pose : to twitter wickedly		95	& POST IMPR 7	11
POSED				
fear to do the posed body luckily made a		141	& SON REAL 12	2
POSITION				
of course, to my position. A bachelor incapable of		263	IS 5 ONE 32	37
POSITIVE				
o absolute gone & positive quite n ever &		646	{CHAIRE} 48	14
+POSITIVELY				
FOR CONTEXT, SEE		72	T&C SON REAL 3	14
FOR CONTEXT, SEE		400	NO THANKS 17	10
POSOLUTELY				
sing and be absitively posolutely dead, like Coney Island . .		72	T&C SON REAL 3	14
POSSESS				
busy little dyings may possess) how sincere large distinct .		418	NO THANKS 35	4
POSSESSION				
saounds) gloats upon the possession of quotes keltyer close .		331	VIVA 22	6
POSSIBLE				
silently through the far-spaced possible nearaway from huge .		10	T&C SONGS 1	44
skilfully to make a possible and beautiful sound: if		92	& POST IMPR 4	13
not not you not possible; only truthful --truthfully, once .		564	1 X 1 24	10
/ nothing false and possible is love (who's imagined, ...		574	1 X 1 34	1
sunbeams or snowflakes make possible mayflowers: quite eyes .		577	1 X 1 37	4
worlds; i mean they're possible --but" lifting "flowers" more		603	{CHAIRE} 5	12
(above and under all possible worlds) in love a		664	{CHAIRE} 66	18
POSSIBLLITY				
we also discussed the possiblility of rain... in distant . .		326	VIVA 18	33
POSSIBLY				
You with elaborate fingers possibly touch the pink hollyhock		58	T&C PORTRAIT 6	16
darkness. On the whole possibly have i loved....? you) . . .		154	& SON ACTU 3	11
amusingly i am pash possibly because . dusk and		155	& SON ACTU 4	2
eyes big love-crumbs, and possibly i like the thrill		175	& SON ACTU 24	13
and perpendicular Always-- or possibly there drift a		218	XLI SONNETS 14	12
the glad monosyllable jounce possibly can tell better how . .		227	IS 5 ONE GERT	2
Sol indulged in that possibly most inexcusable of all		239	IS 5 ONE 10	8
you will perhaps pardon, possibly you will comprehend. and .		285	IS 5 FOUR 2	10
and what does is possibly this dear, that we		289	IS 5 FOUR 6	6
thing provoke your gesture possibly or any painting (for . .		291	IS 5 FOUR 8	20
rhythm of your Heart possibly will understand; or why		300	IS 5 FOUR 17	8
(love being some- thing possibly more intricate) i (breath .		358	VIVA 49	8
whose do you suppose possibly are certain hands, terse . . .		378	VIVA 69	6
of mindscream into life; possibly darker than a spinster's .		506	50 POEMS 20	6
/ / there are possibly 2 1/2 or impossibly		514	50 POEMS 28	1
/ / / / possibly thrice we glimpsed-- more		607	{CHAIRE} 9	1
won't be words while possibly not (at a guess)		631	{CHAIRE} 33	10
of dancing are they possibly afraid that life is		724	95 POEMS 52	12
if any moon or possibly sun shines they are		728	95 POEMS 56	6
and certain men quite possibly may have shall we		807	73 POEMS 35	12
--how anyone so gay possibly could die / /		825	73 POEMS 53	6

		PAGE	TITLE	LINE

POST
/ / / / POST IMPRESSIONS beyond the brittle . . . . 64 T&C POST IMPR 1   T
/ / / / POST IMPRESSIONS windows go orange . . . . 89 & POST IMPR 1   T
+POSTUME
FOR CONTEXT, SEE . . . . 236 IS 5 ONE 7   19
POSTURE
nib -bling, of her posture. (As an eye winks). . . . . . . 131 & SON REAL 2   5
+POTS
FOR CONTEXT, SEE . . . . 126 & SEVEN POEMS 5   24
+POUNCE
FOR CONTEXT, SEE . . . . 347 VIVA 38   8
+POUNCES
FOR CONTEXT, SEE . . . . 747 95 POEMS 75   12
POUND
i'll sell you a pound. Turn gert (spin! helen) . . . . . . 513 50 POEMS 27   1
POUNDS
picked up a thousand pounds or two and he . . . . 552 1 X 1 12   9

a fortune of fifteengrand thanks to the socalled fact . . . 331 VIVA 22   2
POUR
Paris" (Marie Vierge Priez Pour Nous) with the long . . . . . 120 & PORTRAIT 12   17
(live) sob bel ls (pour wo (things) men selves-them . . . . . 444 NO THANKS 59   9
and out of houses pour maids mothers widows wives . . . . . . 624 {CHAIRE} 26   5
west ninth slowly cars pour into sixth avenue) "then" . . . . 800 73 POEMS 28   19
POURING
body ex- pending gathering pouring upon itself stiffenS to . 34 T&C ORIENTALE 6   92
which upward certainly is pouring) emits a pose : . . . . . . 95 & POST IMPR 7   10
the purr of echo pouring in a mesh of . . . . 115 & PORTRAIT 8   15
r e elingwhiRls) are pouring rush fields drea mf . . . . . . 423 NO THANKS 40   16
outlift queries of self pouring (alive twice) and becomes . . 613 {CHAIRE} 15   9
POURQUOI
coucher avec moi? Non? pourquoi?) ladies skilfully dead . . . 120 & PORTRAIT 12   30
Paris ta gorge mysterieuse pourquoi se promene-t-elle, . . . 121 & PORTRAIT 12   54
mysterieuse pourquoi se promene-t-elle, pourquoi eclate ta . 121 & PORTRAIT 12   54
POURS
in the last light pours its eyeless miles the . . . . 64 T&C POST IMPR 1   8
POUT
grins topple together eyes pout ges- tures stickily point . . 96 & POST IMPR 8   17
please shut that the pout And affectionate leer interminable 243 IS 5 ONE 14   5
+POUT
FOR CONTEXT, SEE . . . . 406 NO THANKS 23   10
+POUTING
FOR CONTEXT, SEE . . . . 445 NO THANKS 60   5
POWER
this world equals the power of your intense fragility: . . . 366 VIVA 57   14
and nows to the power of blueness) whos (ex- . . . . 612 {CHAIRE} 14   4
disappear-- but the proud power of himself death immense . . 649 {CHAIRE} 51   13
little and all) no power beyond the trick to . . . . 766 95 POEMS 92   23
+POWER
FOR CONTEXT, SEE . . . . 700 95 POEMS 28   9
PPEGORHRASS
(e loo) k upnowgath PPEGORHRASS eringint (o- aThe) : . . . . 396 NO THANKS 13   5
PPOYDS
and senecktie are gentlemen ppoyds even whose recktie are . . 492 50 POEMS 6   14
PRACTICING
then to pull but practicing the art of swot . . . . 500 50 POEMS 14   19
PRAISE
SONGS (thee will i praise between those rivers whose . . . . 9 T&C SONGS 1   1
lie large men who praise Marj's cleancornered strokable body 114 & PORTRAIT 7   4
in steel, accept all praise of after ages, and . . . . . . 209 XLI SONNETS 5   10
/ / some ask praise of their fellows but . . . . 291 IS 5 FOUR 8   1
gain from blame or praise) but many a thought . . . . 372 VIVA 63   12
beyond all hurt of praise the unimaginable night not . . . . 418 NO THANKS 35   13
over blame things under praise glad things or free . . . . . 441 NO THANKS 56   60
PRAISING
their youngest angels (whose praising bodies in a row . . . . 20 T&C PUELLA MEA 143
through griefs of joy; praising a forehead called the . . . . 520 50 POEMS 34   19

PRANCE
who-horns says-does moo-woo (the prance with the three white 773 73 POEMS 1   9
PRATFALL
so clever as the pratfall of a clown (should . . . . 414 NO THANKS 31   2
PRAW
negre esn7othingish8s c'est fini pRaW, 1T; O: allons 9 . . . 430 NO THANKS 47   23
PRAY
His mercy infinite) i pray to see; and Olaf, ... 339 VIVA 30   39
worlds immenser world will pray so (unlove disappearing) only 450 NO THANKS 65   9
learn and lily could pray and fewer were shyer . . . . . . 509 50 POEMS 23   22
heights below) kneeling, we--true lovers--pray that us will . 574 1 X 1 34   11
the good rain farmers pray for (and no sharp . . . . 754 95 POEMS 82   1
and maidens: let us pray / / / / . . . . 794 73 POEMS 22   8
they work and they pray and they bow to . . . . 801 73 POEMS 29   27
PRAYED
(dreamed & hoped & prayed for months & weeks . . . . 702 95 POEMS 30   18
PRAYER
syllables of that mysterious prayer, and as an opening . . .   8 T&C OF NICOL   11
kiss without lips; a prayer lacking any knees but . . . . . 360 VIVA 51   27
(a feet which is prayer among) float withins he . . . . . . 482 NEW POEMS 20   4
little joy (shine most prayer) / / / / . . . . 535 50 POEMS 47   12
PRAYERS
if air is throbbing prayers whom kneeling eyes (until . . . 450 NO THANKS 65   6
and the sower; my prayers are prayers of earth's . . . . . 749 95 POEMS 77   6
sower; my prayers are prayers of earth's own clumsily . . . 749 95 POEMS 77   6
wonderingly come (brighter than prayers) riding through a . . 778 73 POEMS 6   14
PREACH
art of swot to preach the golden rull to . . . . 500 50 POEMS 14   20
PREACHER
eyes the great black preacher gargles jesus the aesthete . . 108 & PORTRAIT 4   27
PREACHES
ignorant gladness--unteaches what despair preaches myriad . . 764 95 POEMS 90   42
PRECARIOUS
heard a wistful and precarious bird.) Springing from fragrant 20 T&C PUELLA MEA   152
on a certain taut precarious holiday frighteningly performed 52 T&C PORTRAIT 1   6
i ever forget that precarious moment? As i was . . . . . . 262 IS 5 ONE 32   1
PRECIOUS
page we break the precious bread of dear communion . . . . . 209 XLI SONNETS 5   6
PRECISE
skilful uncouth prison, a precise clumsy prison (building . . 83 T&C SON ACTU 2   6
something suddenly luminous and precise --and then we are . . 152 & SON ACTU 1   13
demure ferocious rhythm of precise laziness. Eat the price . 162 & SON ACTU 11   14
occasionally contrives an unreal precise intrinsic frag- ment 193 XLI PORTRAIT 1   24
hugely the ignorant most precise essential flame never which 373 VIVA 64   7
vanish, at the infinite precise thrill of your beauty, . . . 819 73 POEMS 47   12
PRECISELY
dance in my head, precisely dance where danced la . . . . . 120 & PORTRAIT 12   3
pourquoi?) ladies skilfully dead precisely dance where has . 121 & PORTRAIT 12   32
men and hot men precisely dance in my head . . . . 121 & PORTRAIT 12   60
uv eve (who aint precisely slim) sim ply don't . . . . . . 240 IS 5 ONE 11   1
moonlight: say that both precisely beyond either were-- so . 379 VIVA 70   2
perceive buried in cliff precisely at the Ending of . . . . 435 NO THANKS 51   41
the coast of Sum precisely where a craft of . . . . 494 50 POEMS 8   5
/ / / / precisely as unbig a why . . . . 735 95 POEMS 63   1
a learning under teach-- precisely as unbig as i'm . . . . . 735 95 POEMS 63   9
(come heaven, come hell) precisely ours is the now . . . . . 776 73 POEMS 4   15
+PRECISELY
FOR CONTEXT, SEE . . . . 94 & POST IMPR 6   27
FOR CONTEXT, SEE . . . . 430 NO THANKS 47   10
PRECISION
him shall untouch meaningless precision and complete fate (he 402 NO THANKS 19   14
affirmation; virginal immediacy of precision: more and . . . 669 {CHAIRE} 71   6
of fact --by their precision evolving vision dreamtree, . . . 763 95 POEMS 90   29
of colour can create precision more than angels fear . . . . 842 73 POEMS 70   4
PREDICATING
arrive (when Rain comes; predicating forever, assuming the . 356 VIVA 47   16
PREDICTED
the moon of day predicted end who never began . . . . 527 50 POEMS 39   5

		PAGE	TITLE	LINE

PREENING
sun with hooded day preening upon his hand followed . . . . . 4 T&C EPITHALAM 66
feathered with green facts preening solemnity ignoring, . . . 344 VIVA 35 3
PREEXIST
joy) does nothing except preexist its hoi in its . . . . . . 544 1 X 1 4 7
PREFECT
has a nucleolus: the Prefect of Police (a dapper . . . . . . 274 IS 5 TWO 9 27
PREFER
Gower in Confessio doth prefer shall not lack for . . . . . . 20 T&C PUELLA MEA 167
and how do i prefer this face to another . . . . 295 IS 5 FOUR 12 15
PREFERABLE
rapes laughter from your preferable, eyes / / / . . . . 166 & SON ACTU 15 16
PREFERABLY
thoughts a little love preferably, anything which you can't . 298 IS 5 FOUR 15 15
matter who, some total (preferably blonde of course) or . . . 779 73 POEMS 7 5
PREFERRING
laundry bills likes People preferring Negroes Indians Youse . 410 NO THANKS 27 6
PREGNANT
most how immeasurable anguish pregnant one fearless one good 524 50 POEMS 36 38
PREHUMAN
and marathon and all prehuman history and finally The . . . . 711 95 POEMS 39 15
PREPARED
love unto that bed prepared by whitest hands of . . . . 6 T&C EPITHALAM 114
PREPONDERATINGLY
see; and Olaf, too preponderatingly because unless statistics 339 VIVA 30 40
PREPOSTEROUS
no instrument yours the preposterous colour unbeheld --mine . 84 T&C SON ACTU 3 2
PRES
up rose mr lipshits pres (who always nothing says) . . . . . 552 1 X 1 12 26
PRESENCE
the omen of his presence it was spring by . . . . 197 XLI PORTRAIT 5 11
deathless truth of His presence (welcoming humbly His light . 749 95 POEMS 77 19
PRESENT
many things-- at the present writing one still finds . . . . 70 T&C SON REAL 1 7
twilight) giving your eyes, present me also with the . . . . 285 IS 5 FOUR 2 15
seems to live at present (l'on parle de repapering; . . . . . 312 VIVA 4 22
PRESENTED
records while he lived presented to him upon the . . . . . . 239 IS 5 ONE 10 28
and which had been presented unto you by a . . . . 279 IS 5 THREE 3 23
PRESENTLY
tortured in gold, which presently crumpled collapses. . . . . 188 XLI SONGS 10 8
best busiest city and presently found himself rattling for . 326 VIVA 18 12
PRESENTS
in whose palm Nike presents the crown sweetest to . . . . . . 3 T&C EPITHALAM 28
you make us shrill presents always shut in the . . . . 195 XLI PORTRAIT 3 6
PRESERVED
Einstein expanded Newton's law preserved conTinuum (but we . 315 VIVA 7 5
a la vallee and preserved goldfishian gestures) suddenly . . 425 NO THANKS 42 3
+PRESERVERS
FOR CONTEXT, SEE . . . . 438 NO THANKS 54 26
PRESIDENT
quotes the microscopic pithecoid President in a new frock . . 267 IS 5 TWO 2 2
/ / the first president to be loved by . . . . 336 VIVA 27 1
will not eat" our president, being of which assertions . . . 339 VIVA 30 34
beh ld The (The president The president of The . . . . 392 NO THANKS 9 13
The (The president The president of The president of . . . . 392 NO THANKS 9 14
The president of The president of the The) president . . . . 392 NO THANKS 9 14
president of the The) president of the (united The . . . . . 392 NO THANKS 9 15
of the (united The president of the united states . . . . . . 392 NO THANKS 9 16
the united states The president of the united states . . . . 392 NO THANKS 9 17
united states of The President Of The) United States . . . . 392 NO THANKS 9 18
Excuse Me whether it's president of the you were . . . . . . 549 1 X 1 9 2
+PRESIDENT
FOR CONTEXT, SEE . . . . 552 1 X 1 12 26
PRESS
silence.... But first you) press easily at first, it . . . . 67 T&C POST IMPR 4 18
large minute hips, O press worms rushing slowly through . . . 67 T&C POST IMPR 4 29
legs panting as they press proffers its omelet of . . . . . . 132 & SON REAL 3 9

	PAGE	TITLE	LINE

PRESS (CONTINUED)
    (slowly, wholly me) will press in the young lips . . . . . . 156 & SON ACTU 5   14
    newfragile yellows lurch and. press --in the woods which . . 163 & SON ACTU 12   11
PRESSED
    coffin lurched because somebody pressed a button (and down . 239 IS 5 ONE 10   34
    his physiognomy his scientifically pressed trousers ejaculate 259 IS 5 ONE 29   24
PRESTO
    tits punish my hug presto! the bright rile of . . . . 137 & SON REAL 8   15
PRESUME
    what huge merciful forms presume / / / / . . . . 351 VIVA 42   15
    that calls him "I" presume to comprehend not numerable . . . 609 (CHAIRE) 11   13
PRETEND
    a streetcar and you pretend you don't but really . . . . . . 126 & SEVEN POEMS 5 15
    it (i do not pretend to know the reason . . . . 282 IS 5 THREE 6   3
    carrying a bouquet of pretend flowers this candy crown . . . 470 NEW POEMS 8   7
    the mere mind's poor pretend --grim comics of duration: . . . 576 1 X 1 36   6
PRETENDED
    perceptible bulgings of the pretended breasts, forked in . . 103 & POST IMPR 13   3
PRETENDING
    will come soon" & pretending they're birds sit creatures . . 483 NEW POEMS 21   9
    giving; it's no good pretending befriending means loving" . . 625 (CHAIRE) 27   4
PRETENDS
    / / these (whom; pretends blue nothing) are built . . . . . . 584 1 X 1 44   1
PRETENTIOUS
    inside when you die, pretentious and shiny and not . . . . . 198 XLI PORTRAIT 6   3
PRETTIEST
    and gently brutal, the prettiest wrath of blossoms . . . . . 214 XLI SONNETS 10   7
    or three contains these prettiest deaths without effort while 340 VIVA 31   14
PRETTILY
    splashed from the world prettily upward, mock us....) and . . 133 & SON REAL 4   5
    complacent gums, a morsel prettily wanders buoyed on the . . 201 XLI PORTRAIT 9   4
    tame fleas left the prettily embroidered howdah im- . . . . . 262 IS 5 ONE 32   28
    -me of the (very prettily indeed) arra- nged souvenir . . . . 267 IS 5 TWO 2   12
    both all hopped up) prettily then which did lie . . . . 317 VIVA 9   34
+PRETTILY
    FOR CONTEXT, SEE . . . . 632 (CHAIRE) 34   13
PRETTINESS
    bodies lopped of every prettiness you hew form truly . . . . 195 XLI PORTRAIT 3   23
PRETTINESSES
    soul a street is: prettinesses Pic- abian <> garnished . . . 180 XLI SONGS 2   3
PRETTY
    spoke ill of the pretty stars and to the . . . . 43 T&C AMORES 7   15
    glories whisperingly impinge (god's pretty mother) but may . 85 T&C SON ACTU 4   6
    and stic-ky chromes and pretty- lemons and virginal pinks . . 100 & POST IMPR 11   5
    would)? dance lewd dollies pretty and putrid dollies . . . . 101 & POST IMPR 11   81
    lovecrazed abrupt flesh split "Pretty Baby" to numb rhythm . 106 & PORTRAIT 2   12
    in the sky--filled with pretty people? (and if you . . . . . 129 & SEVEN POEMS 7   3
    higher with all the pretty people than houses and . . . . . . 129 & SEVEN POEMS 7 8
    ugly nipples squirming in pretty wrath, gums skidding on . . 151 & SON REAL 22   9
    spaded) gentlemen (and ladies) --pretty littleliverpill- <> . 231 IS 5 ONE 3   45
    me a child, a pretty dribbling child, a little . . . . 233 IS 5 ONE 4   4
    i'll match youse a pretty girl who naked is . . . . 247 IS 5 ONE 18   7
    who a string of pretty medals drew (while messrs . . . . . . 266 IS 5 TWO 1   24
    upon one broken babypout (pretty teeth wander into which . . 406 NO THANKS 23   11
    found) wound up such pretty toys as themselves could . . . . 451 NO THANKS 66   9
    merely riches of our pretty world sweetly who flourishes, . . 456 NO THANKS 71   5
    / / / a pretty a day (and every . . . . 509 50 POEMS 23   1
    anyone lived in a pretty how town (with up . . . . 515 50 POEMS 29   1
    are i am we (pretty twinkle merry bells) Someone . . . . . . 630 (CHAIRE) 32   13
    Art of Jigajig sitting pretty on the top of . . . . 642 (CHAIRE) 44   24
    it's spring! yes the pretty birds frolic as spry . . . . . . 665 (CHAIRE) 67   5
    now) spring! now the pretty birds hover so she . . . . 665 (CHAIRE) 67   12
    it's spring! all the pretty birds dive to the . . . . 665 (CHAIRE) 67   19
    her high and that pretty pink pinafore'd knock out . . . . . 707 95 POEMS 35   8
    uncle sam shrugs his pretty pink shoulders you know . . . . . 711 95 POEMS 39   21
    the any merry every pretty each bird sings birds . . . . . . 773 73 POEMS 1   3
+PRETTY
    FOR CONTEXT, SEE . . . . 388 NO THANKS 5   28

		PAGE	TITLE	LINE

+PRETTY (CONTINUED)
FOR CONTEXT, SEE . . . . 656 (CHAIRE) 58   11
PREVAIL
    child; nor shall even prevail a million questionings against 714 95 POEMS 42   12
PREVENTED
    hands only fishermen are prevented by cathedrals / / . . . . 478 NEW POEMS 16   12
PREY
    blueeyed pride) their passive prey did kick and curse . . . . 339 VIVA 30   24
PREYS
    dirtied pane where softly preys the grey and perpendicular . 218 XLI SONNETS 14   10
PRICE
    precise laziness. Eat the price of an imaginable gesture . . 162 & SON ACTU 11   15
PRICELESS
    to strut my indolent priceless smile, until this very . . . . 155 & SON ACTU 4   11
    thighs; the hair stupidly priceless. / / / / . . . . 173 & SON ACTU 22   15
+PRICKING
FOR CONTEXT, SEE . . . . 100 & POST IMPR 11   9
PRICKLEY
    you take all your prickley-clothes off and squeeze- . . . . . 127 & SEVEN POEMS 5   33
PRICKLEY-CLOTHES
    you take all your prickley-clothes off and squeeze- . . . . . 127 & SEVEN POEMS 5   33
PRICKS
    dawn its muscle amorous pricks with minute odour these . . . 165 & SON ACTU 14   5
PRIDE
    flowers Fall in a pride of petaled hours, like . . . . 11 T&C SONGS 2   32
    seen as were the pride of the world's queen: . . . . 21 T&C PUELLA MEA 208
    and when you're flush pride keeps you from the . . . . 204 XLI LA GUERRE 2   12
    and see his mother's pride, his father's joy, unto . . . . . 273 IS 5 TWO 8   3
    enough beyond mere personal pride which tends to compel . . . 329 VIVA 20   2
    (a yearning nation's blueeyed pride) their passive prey did . 339 VIVA 30   23
    (whose texture feels of pride and loneliness alive like . . . 418 NO THANKS 35   2
    merde then up rose pride and up rose pelf . . . . 552 1 X 1 12   11
    henceforth he feels his pride involved (this i who's . . . . 650 (CHAIRE) 52   9
PRIED
    outrageous sabots language trickling pried his black mouth . 277 IS 5 THREE 1   14
PRIES
    if i'm alive (eye pries, not open. Tail stirs.) . . . . . . 166 & SON ACTU 15   10
PRIESTS
    glass box: surrounded by priests moving in fifty colours . . 280 IS 5 THREE 4   10
    the oh silently striding) priests-and- slowly, al, ways; . . 280 IS 5 THREE 4   27
PRIESTS-AND
    the oh silently striding) priests-and- slowly, al, ways; . . 280 IS 5 THREE 4   27
PRIEZ
    de Paris" (Marie Vierge Priez Pour Nous) with the . . . . . . 120 & PORTRAIT 12   16
PRIGGED
    laws) it comes both prigged and canted / / . . . . 644 (CHAIRE) 46   6
PRIMATES
    erotic more particularly the primates--from which with . . . 326 VIVA 18   25
PRIME
    my dears merely the prime minister of Siam in . . . . 245 IS 5 ONE 16   19
PRIMEVAL
    pines deepen to whispers primeval and throw backward their . 5 T&C EPITHALAM   76
    O small intimate gently primeval hands, frivolous feet . . . 5 T&C EPITHALAM   107
    the negative silence that primeval exposure whose electric . 197 XLI PORTRAIT 5   17
    your smile the keen primeval silence of your hair . . . . . 306 IS 5 FIVE 5   8
    ultimate earth accept and primeval whyless sky; healing our . 745 95 POEMS 73   6
PRIMING
    our soul of emptiness) priming at every pore a . . . . 428 NO THANKS 45   15
PRINCE
    Pantarkes (whose grace the prince of artists made him . . . . 4 T&C EPITHALAM   35
    like any king or prince upon his uncorrupted arse . . . . . 254 IS 5 ONE 25   19
    famine or the ex prince of whoses diving into . . . . 475 NEW POEMS 13   20
    attitude and liked the prince of wales wife wants . . . . . 499 50 POEMS 13   2
PRINCESS
    delirious feet of the Princess Salome carefully dancing in . 17 T&C PUELLA MEA   30
    atrocious; but so what princess selene doesn't know a . . . . 504 50 POEMS 18   11
    with thrush) A hummingbird princess FlOaTs doll-angel-life . 747 95 POEMS 75   3

	PAGE	TITLE	LINE

PRISMATIC
--and furiously puzzling through, prismatic, whims, the . . . 157 & SON ACTU 6   13

PRISMS
soul repairs herself with prisms of sharp mind and . . . . . 180 XLI SONGS 2   11

PRISON
smile) a skilful uncouth prison, a precise clumsy prison . .   83 T&C SON ACTU 2   6
prison, a precise clumsy prison (building thatandthis into .   83 T&C SON ACTU 2   7
man; three words im -prison a woman for all . . . . 491 50 POEMS 5   14

PRISONER
is its own beautiful prisoner. Mine looked long at . . . . . 170 & SON ACTU 19   1
life as a forgotten prisoner --"Ici?" --"Ah non, mon . . . . 304 IS 5 FIVE 3   9
opens a gate; the prisoner dawn embraces hugely some . . . . 376 VIVA 67   10

PRIVACY
our abdomens for greater privacy and lest punished bottoms . 261 IS 5 ONE 31   13

+PRIVATES
FOR CONTEXT, SEE . . . . 339 VIVA 30   27

PRIVILEGE
how it was a privilege and if only he . . . . 276 IS 5 TWO 10   17

PRO
fear for the quo pro quid" uncle sam shrugs . . . . 711 95 POEMS 39   20

PROBABLE
a normal melody of probable violins dance the square . . . .   43 T&C AMORES 7   33
are probably the least probable roses of her improbable . . . 748 95 POEMS 76   2

PROBABLY
i do, world is probably made of roses & . . . .   66 T&C POST IMPR 3   15
earning your living or probably dead" so Jones was . . . . . 313 VIVA 5   8
harmoniously being with his probably most brilliant pupil . . 326 VIVA 18   7
to rescue miss nobody's probably handbag) because i say . . . 475 NEW POEMS 13   22
a couple of) holes probably that's what (mr & . . . . 501 50 POEMS 15   20
but should some im probably unworld crash to 1 . . . . 728 95 POEMS 56   10
rosebush white roses are probably the least probable roses . 748 95 POEMS 76   2

PROBLEM
laughing stones a sinuous problem of colour floating against 112 & PORTRAIT 6   105
do next (our great problem nearly solved we dare . . . . . . 650 {CHAIRE} 52   13

PROCESSION
whose kiss is a procession of deep beasts coming . . . . . . 112 & PORTRAIT 6   100
whose rich slovenly obscene procession always floats through 202 XLI PORTRAIT 9   46
priests-and- slowly, al, ways; procession: and Enters this . 280 IS 5 THREE 4   28
dark the earth) a procession of wonders huger than . . . . . 575 1 X 1 35   9

+PROCESSION
FOR CONTEXT, SEE . . . . 482 NEW POEMS 20   2

PROCESSIONS
bodies while the infinite processions move like moths and . . 111 & PORTRAIT 6   62
saluted everywhere saluting reviewing processions of minions 275 IS 5 TWO 9   37

PROCLAIM
time of lilacs who proclaim the aim of waking . . . . 688 95 POEMS 16   4
become nothing) five times, proclaim fate isn't fatal --a . . 764 95 POEMS 90   52
which all soulless wraiths proclaim substance; all heartless 765 95 POEMS 91   3

PRODDED
naughty thumb of science prodded thy beauty . how . . . . .   46 T&C LA GUERRE 2   11
and if sometimes he's prodded forth to exercise her . . . . . 544 1 X 1 4   9

PRODIGAL
/ / / for prodigal read generous --for youth . . . . 689 95 POEMS 17   1

PRODIGIES
up and vanish under prodigies of un) "have you" . . . . . . 555 1 X 1 15   10

PRODIGIOUS
(tenderly upon the dark's prodigious face thy voice . . . . . 187 XLI SONGS 9   10
nothing arrives a so prodigious am a so immediate . . . . . . 517 50 POEMS 31   10
a ticking phantom by prodigious time's mere brain contrived: 558 1 X 1 18   8
nowhere of earth's most prodigious night blossoms a newborn . 714 95 POEMS 42   2
of each more most prodigious Selves both now alive . . . . . 757 95 POEMS 85   8
was are drowned by prodigious a now of magnificent . . . . . 841 73 POEMS 69   11

PRODIGIOUSLY
all nowhere) goldenly whole, prodigiously alive most . . . . 808 73 POEMS 36   6

PRODIGY
curtains part) the peacockappareled prodigy of Flo's midnight 232 IS 5 ONE 3   3

PRODUCING
twice fortyeight, succeeded in producing sixtyfour maxims . . 341 VIVA 32   2

PROFANE
safely the complete important profane frantic inconsequential 201 XLI PORTRAIT 9   32
PROFESSOR
of Mrs. N and Professor D ....the Cambridge ladies . . . . . 70 T&C SON REAL 1   10
the infantile ghost of Professor Royce rolls remembering that 232 IS 5 ONE 3   12
is believing science=(2b)-n herr professor m / / / . . . . . 329 VIVA 20   4
that "I may say professor" asleep wop "shapley has . . . . . 464 NEW POEMS 2   10
PROFFERS
panting as they press proffers its omelet of fluffy . . . . . 132 & SON REAL 3   10
as Mr bowing Cockatoo proffers the meaning of the . . . . . . 697 95 POEMS 25   28
PROFICIENT
/ / when the proficient poison of sure sleep . . . . 210 XLI SONNETS 6   1
PROFOUND
fails and this sweet profound Paris moves with lovers, . . . 71 T&C SON REAL 2   7
coming with the little profound gems and the large . . . . . 112 & PORTRAIT 6   103
shame: lady through whose profound and fragile lips the . . . 306 IS 5 FIVE 5   13
(deeply immediate fleet and profound this) beautiful kindness 763 95 POEMS 90   23
PROFUSE
solidity remembers some accurately profuse scratchings in a . 197 XLI PORTRAIT 5   18
PROGRAM
blond absence of any program except last and always . . . . . 264 IS 5 ONE 33   17
PROGRESS
be entitled a wraith's progress or mainly awash while . . . . 410 NO THANKS 27   11
mad, illustrous punks of Progress shriek; when Souls are . . 438 NO THANKS 54   20
the foetal grave called progress, and negation's dead undoom. 484 NEW POEMS 22   12
which to man kind progress doth impart one stands . . . . . . 544 1 X 1 4   2
busy monster, manunkind, not. Progress is a comfortable . . . 554 1 X 1 14   2
+PROGRESS
FOR CONTEXT, SEE . . . . 330 VIVA 21   2
FOR CONTEXT, SEE . . . . 392 NO THANKS 9   1
PROJECTILE
the metaphor of our projectile am tell such to . . . . 362 VIVA 53   12
PROLETARIAT
to tomorrow's paper the proletariat will not rise yesterday. 262 IS 5 ONE 32   18
PROLONGS
rain care cautiously who prolongs unserious twilight) shadows 84 T&C SON ACTU 3   9
PROMENE
gorge mysterieuse pourquoi se promene-t-elle, pourquoi eclate 121 & PORTRAIT 12   54
PROMENE-T-ELLE
gorge mysterieuse pourquoi se promene-t-elle, pourquoi eclate 121 & PORTRAIT 12   54
PROMENENT
and hot men se promenent doucement le soir (ladies . . . . . 120 & PORTRAIT 12   23
PROMISE
for instance a plugged promise-- then he will maybe . . . . . 298 IS 5 FOUR 15   19
PROMISED
each having each we promised to forget-- wherefore is . . . . 173 & SON ACTU 22   12
PROMPTLY
white thick wrists deliver promptly to a deep lap . . . . . . 225 IS 5 ONE LIZ   8
PRONOUNCED
amid thunderous anthropoid applause) pronounced by the way . 267 IS 5 TWO 2   9
PRONOUNCES
considers frood whom he pronounces young mistaken and cradles 499 50 POEMS 13   4
PROOF
easily disappears (leaving no proof not the least shadow . . 479 NEW POEMS 17   19
+PROOF
FOR CONTEXT, SEE . . . . 276 IS 5 TWO 10   11
PROP
the little silent handorgan prop- ping the curve of . . . . . 101 & POST IMPR 11   45
PROPAGANDA
movements carefully scatter pink propaganda of annihilation / 150 & SON REAL 21   15
alimony blackmail whathavewe and propaganda (it is incredible 391 NO THANKS 8   12
PROPAGATED
somebody who was hectocotyliferously propagated when Miss G . 326 VIVA 18   9
PROPHECIES
old Whose battening gesture prophecies a freeing of ghostly . 77 T&C SON UNRE 2   12
PROPORTION
a noble mercy of proportion with generosities beyond . . . . 683 95 POEMS 11   1

		PAGE	TITLE	LINE

PROPOS
the evening and a propos such light and shape . . . . 98 & POST IMPR 9   9
PROPPED
large acute brutal feet propped on irrelevantly ferocious . . 103 & POST IMPR 13   8
immense doorway and halts propped on a pitchfork (breathing) 754 95 POEMS 82   8
+PROPPED
FOR CONTEXT, SEE . . . . 472 NEW POEMS 10   8
PROPPING
that and this, deftly propping on smallest hands the   . . . . 282 IS 5 THREE 6   7
POREGRESS
eakspeasies per (reel) hapsingly proregress heandshe-ingly . 330 VIVA 21   2
PROSE
invisible mourners move with prose faces and sobbing, ... 59 T&C PORTRAIT 7   8
and machinery: sculpture and prose flowers guess and miss . . 264 IS 5 ONE 33   9
for ecstasy --for poem prose-- caution for curiosity (and . . 689 95 POEMS 17   6
is living" worlds of prose mind utterly beyond is . . . . . . 763 95 POEMS 90   19
PROSPECTING
on whose huge heart prospecting darkness roams torture my . . 79 T&C SON UNRE 4   4
PROSTITUTE
sixteen, 5' 1", white, prostitute. ducking always the touch . 74 T&C SON REAL 5   1
here the lithe indolent prostitute Night, argues with certain 93 & POST IMPR 5   16
twentyseven bums give a prostitute the once -over. fiftythree 150 & SON REAL 21   1
PROSTITUTED
superseded by the sole prostituted ferocity of silence, it . 202 XLI PORTRAIT 9   41
PROSTRATE
dark- ness a worshipper prostrate within twitching shadow . . 28 T&C ORIENTALE 2   14
PROTECTED
cake'& everything is protected by cellophane against anything 470 NEW POEMS 8   18
PROTEST
amen. i do however protest, anent the un -spontaneous . . . . 230 IS 5 ONE 2   15
PROTESTANT
(also, with the church's protestant blessings daughters, . . 70 T&C SON REAL 1   3
PROTESTATIONS
provided (despite courte- ous protestations) and offering . . 326 VIVA 18   18
PROTESTS
whirl? one's memory indignantly protests) this little dancer 72 T&C SON REAL 3   4
PROTRUDE
bent eyes thickly to protrude-- or why her tiniest . . . . . 229 IS 5 ONE FRAN   13
PROTUBERANT
thundering trivial) it. y protuberant through the room's . . 159 & SON ACTU 8   6
PROUD
mouths throughout that very proud transparent company of . .   6 T&C EPITHALAM   142
poises a moment (futile, proud, a costly morsel of . . . . . 23 T&C PUELLA MEA   268
which ravelling, to a proud continual stitch of the . . . . . 136 & SON REAL 7   3
but you'll be very proud and my little sister . . . . 192 XLI CHANSONS 2   24
on thy beauty dreams (proud through the cold perfect . . . . 205 XLI SONNETS 1   6
receiving the image my proud heart cherished as fair. . . . . 207 XLI SONNETS 3   13
of this? Do your proud fingers and your arms . . . . 279 IS 5 THREE 3   21
sink through algebras of proud inwardlyness to collide . . . 311 VIVA 3   10
/ / what a proud dreamhorse pulling (smoothloomingly) through 437 NO THANKS 53   1
ness o what a proud dreamhorse moving (whose feet . . . . . . 437 NO THANKS 53   16
/ / / / proud of his scientific attitude . . . . 499 50 POEMS 13   1
if they are sincere proud of his scientif ic . . . . 499 50 POEMS 13   12
bold ones; the meek proud sloppy sleek) all except . . . . . 619 {CHAIRE} 21   5
red book) on a proud round cloud in a . . . . 631 {CHAIRE} 33   4
dully disappear-- but the proud power of himself death . . . 649 {CHAIRE} 51   13
from spiralling ecstatically this proud nowhere of earth's . 714 95 POEMS 42   2
frantic struts a pedantic proud or humble, equally they're . 763 95 POEMS 90   13
--as if the humble proud youngest bud testified "giving . . . 763 95 POEMS 90   15
(while down come blundering proud hugenesses of hate . . . . 783 73 POEMS 11   7
PROUDER
beginning, ecstasy, to dare: prouder than all mountains, more 351 VIVA 42   6
PROUDEST
be dead humblest and proudest eagerly wandering (equally all 661 {CHAIRE} 63   5
+PROUDESTLY
FOR CONTEXT, SEE . . . . 408 NO THANKS 25   7
PROUDHUMBLE
forever born a foolishwise proudhumble citizen of ecstasies . 845 73 POEMS 73   7

	PAGE	TITLE	LINE

PROUDLY

muted step, yet somewhat proudly too-- are they not . . . . . 211 XLI SONNETS 7   9
diminishing earth --never whose proudly life swallowed is by 402 NO THANKS 19   5
worst or best (and proudly things only which grow . . . . . . 441 NO THANKS 56   53
wise offered immeasurable is proudly and (by octobering flame 521 50 POEMS 34   41
command, reality or un-) proudly depths above why's first . . 574 1 X 1 34   9
game a man can proudly lose, or playing dead . . . . 679 95 POEMS 7   3
humbly His light and proudly His darkness) / / . . . . 749 95 POEMS 77   20
lovers suffer? all divinities proudly descending put on . . . 768 95 POEMS 94   6
glide seethe glow (undering proudly humbly overing) all . . . 841 73 POEMS 69   25

+PROUST

FOR CONTEXT, SEE . . . . 499 50 POEMS 13   11

PROVE

quite beyond dispute as prove from Troy (N.Y.) to . . . . . . 266 IS 5 TWO 1   6
within my shirt to prove he is undead who, ... 360 VIVA 51   28
unless if or to prove, imperfectly or since but . . . . 386 NO THANKS 3   6
welcome spring nor flatfolk prove their world is round . . . 511 50 POEMS 25   17
of wonders huger than prove our fears were hopes: . . . . . . 575 1 X 1 35   11
breathing to limp and prove --but if a look . . . . 580 1 X 1 40   10
the fool) "truth would prove truthless and life a . . . . . . 625 {CHAIRE} 27   17
quote statue unquote to prove that a hero equals . . . . . . 636 {CHAIRE} 38   3
more can disprove than prove what heart may feel . . . . . . 664 {CHAIRE} 66   3

PROVIDED

of pistil; very well provided an instant may be . . . . . . 264 IS 5 ONE 33   23
her mama had generously provided (despite courte- ous . . . . 326 VIVA 18   17

PROVING

pages of forgotten joy proving the peaceful theorems of . . . 3 T&C EPITHALAM   19
twilight where i know: proving to Death that Love . . . . . . 71 T&C SON REAL 2   14
falsest both disprove by proving true (all doubts, all . . . 576 1 X 1 36   4

+PROVING

FOR CONTEXT, SEE . . . . 425 NO THANKS 42   7

PROVINGLY

more than shall ever provingly disprove eithering vastnesses 761 95 POEMS 88   3

PROVOKE

by me carven thing provoke your gesture possibly or . . . . . 291 IS 5 FOUR 8   19

PROWL

mist-flowers close ghosts on prowl gorge sly slim gods . . . 90 & POST IMPR 2   15

PROWLS

wind who i am prowls carefully around this house . . . . . . 292 IS 5 FOUR 9   11
the kno wing spirit prowls, its nose winces before . . . . . 319 VIVA 11   10

PROXIMITY

the sacred and agonizing proximity to its desire of . . . . . 193 XLI PORTRAIT 1   10
of rain... in distant proximity to a Y. W. . . . . 326 VIVA 18   35

PRUNE

edged nothing begins to prune let's live like the . . . . . . 160 & SON ACTU 9   9

PRURIENT

the doting fingers of prurient philosophers pinched and poked 46 T&C LA GUERRE 2   6

PS

furious taximan p (ee) ps on his whistle somebody . . . . . . 108 & PORTRAIT 4   18
's thank indecent god p.s. the most successful b.o. . . . . . 425 NO THANKS 42   15

+PSALMIST

FOR CONTEXT, SEE . . . . 643 {CHAIRE} 45   6

PSEUDO

jip hug behemoth truly pseudo yours podia of radarw . . . . . 333 VIVA 24   25

PSEUDOBEAST

heart. Huge this collective pseudobeast (sans either pain or 544 1 X 1 4   5

PSYCHOTIC

joybegotten whelps whom soothe psychotic myths like Jonah And 398 NO THANKS 15   19

PUBIC

impatiently replied two billion pubic lice inside one pair . 473 NEW POEMS 11   5

PUBLIC

back down by the Public Gardens i slammed on . . . . 248 IS 5 ONE 19   27

PUBLICATION

sold 69 carloads before publication the girl who goes . . . . 245 IS 5 ONE 16   10

PUBLISHERS

oral history unquote might (publishers note) be entitled a . 410 NO THANKS 27   10

PUCKERED

eyelids sulked enormous sobs puckered the foolish breasts the 52 T&C PORTRAIT 1   28

PUD
    a) mu) ddied bushscytheblade "pud-dih-gud") S creang roami . 656 {CHAIRE} 58   11
PUD-DIH-GUD
    a) mu) ddied bushscytheblade "pud-dih-gud") S creang roami . 656 {CHAIRE} 58   11
PUDD
    the middle of Congressman Pudd 's 4th of July . . . . 249 IS 5 ONE 20   1
PUDDLE
    when the world is puddle-wonderful the queer old balloonman . 24 T&C CHANSONS 1   10
PUDDLE-WONDERFUL
    when the world is puddle-wonderful the queer old balloonman . 24 T&C CHANSONS 1   10
PUELLA
    / / / / PUELLA MEA Harun Omar and . . . . 17 T&C PUELLA MEA   T
PUERILE
    me.... a wise and puerile moving of your arm . . . . 302 IS 5 FIVE 1   9
PUERPERAL
    she lifts an impertinent puerperal face and with astute . . . 151 & SON REAL 22   12
PUKE
    from whom the stiffened puke i put him all . . . . 258 IS 5 ONE 28   21
    almost spray -ing threecoloured puke over this younger than . 324 VIVA 16   8
PUKING
    while (infinite fog & puking jukepulse hug) large less . . . 629 {CHAIRE} 31   6
PULL
    for the bulls to pull his joint. jimmie was . . . . 149 & SON REAL 20   4
    other, who cares?) They pull the morning out of . . . . . . 171 & SON ACTU 20   12
    push and then to pull but practicing the art . . . . 500 50 POEMS 14   18
    afraid of) these (down pull & who'll shades / . . . . 501 50 POEMS 15   24
PULLABLE
    of the sultan's nose pullable and rosy flanked by . . . . . . 198 XLI PORTRAIT 6   9
PULLED
    garble when a minute pulled the sluice emerging. concrete . . 119 & PORTRAIT 11   16
    of her glad leg pulled into a sole mass . . . . 135 & SON REAL 6   4
    enough (not really enough pulled one before one the . . . . . 154 & SON ACTU 3   7
    bulls nabbed at 33rd) pulled six months for selling . . . . . 266 IS 5 TWO 1   40
    go and i) has pulled (for he's we) such . . . . 543 1 X 1 3   21
PULLING
    if god's flowers were pulling upon bells of gold . . . . . . 58 T&C PORTRAIT 6   10
    candy others fly, their; puLLing: bright futures against the 314 VIVA 6   14
    a few fatally exquisite" (pulling Its shawl carefully around 328 VIVA 19   19
    what a proud dreamhorse pulling (smoothloomingly) through . . 437 NO THANKS 53   1
    fool who could fail pulling all the sky over . . . . 481 NEW POEMS 19   12
+PULLING
    FOR CONTEXT, SEE . . . . 310 VIVA 2   2
PULLS
    strikes midnight a finger pulls a trigger a bird . . . . . . 338 VIVA 29   23
PULP
    transfigured face a queer pulp of ecstasy while in . . . . . 55 T&C PORTRAIT 3   16
+PULSE
    FOR CONTEXT, SEE . . . . 629 {CHAIRE} 31   6
PULSELESS
    possibly there drift a pulseless blur of paleness; the . . . 218 XLI SONNETS 14   12
PUMMELING
    --Marj's laughter smacked me: pummeling the curtains, drooped 228 IS 5 ONE MARJ   14
PUMPED
    which bulge: grunting lungs pumped full of sharp thick . . . 195 XLI PORTRAIT 3   4
PUMPING
    lung extended to the pumping Child, and "'Twas the . . . . . 142 & SON REAL 13   11
    in his teeth (hips pumping pleasure into hips). Seeing . . . 161 & SON ACTU 10   4
PUNCHING
    with an old mop punching underneath conventions exposes . . . 203 XLI LA GUERRE 1   2
PUNCTUAL
    the trivial labelling of punctual brains... --Who wields a . 377 VIVA 68   11
PUNCTUATED
    my being pleasantly was punctuated by the al- ways . . . . . 96 & POST IMPR 8   25
+PUNCTURED
    FOR CONTEXT, SEE . . . . 615 {CHAIRE} 17   8
PUNGENT
    dawn forth rides the pungent sun with hooded day . . . . . . 4 T&C EPITHALAM   65

	PAGE	TITLE	LINE
PUNIEST			
in a shrine: its puniest flame persists shaken by	435	NO THANKS 51	44
PUNISH			
who is would don't punish us for we were	117	& PORTRAIT 10	20
breasts and uttering tits punish my hug presto! the	137	& SON REAL 8	14
PUNISHED			
ingenious gods. (i am punished. They have stolen into	165	& SON ACTU 14	13
greater privacy and lest punished bottoms interrupt	261	IS 5 ONE 31	14
PUNKS			
holy, poets mad, illustrious punks of Progress shriek; when .	438	NO THANKS 54	20
it's millions of other punks or just a handful	549	1 X 1 9	4
+PUNKS			
FOR CONTEXT, SEE	477	NEW POEMS 15	7
PUNKSLAPPING			
is for foetus (a punkslapping mobsucking gravypissing poppa .	635	(CHAIRE) 37	2
PUNY			
tamarack (nothing pampered puny impatient and nothing . . .	658	(CHAIRE) 60	22
PUP			
taking derbies (where?) a pup hurriedly hunched over swill; .	172	& SON ACTU 21	3
Street by a castrated pup / / / /	253	IS 5 ONE 24	15
PUPIL			
his probably most brilliant pupil mated, let us not	326	VIVA 18	7
PUPPET			
(ncient) a weigh tless puppet of once man (clutched	616	(CHAIRE) 18	4
PUPPETS			
to become the jumping puppets of a dream? oh	295	IS 5 FOUR 12	4
PUPPY			
bash the bragging breasts, puppy-faces to mouth her ugly . .	151	& SON REAL 22	8
is twilight, a little puppy hopping between skipping children	167	& SON ACTU 16	8
PUPPY-FACES			
bash the bragging breasts, puppy-faces to mouth her ugly . .	151	& SON REAL 22	8
PURCHASED			
an exhausted condition, i purchased two bags of lukewarm . .	326	VIVA 18	15
PURE			
a flower of so pure surprise (it were so	18	T&C PUELLA MEA	50
a harpsichord colours of Pure percussion colours-	100	& POST IMPR 11	11
by the high minded pure young girl much kissed, ...	273	IS 5 TWO 8	20
something redblooded lousy with pure reeking with stark and .	407	NO THANKS 24	4
fragrance fragrant; a than pure more signalling of singular .	456	NO THANKS 71	9
impure think all things pure and hornets wail by	511	50 POEMS 25	13
song and joy so pure a heart of star	520	50 POEMS 34	21
him could steer and pure so now and now	520	50 POEMS 34	23
never no? measureless our pure living complete love whose . .	538	50 POEMS 50	3
/ purer than purest pure whisper of a whisper	601	(CHAIRE) 3	1
soul comes a keen pure silence) such hands can	617	(CHAIRE) 19	2
your complete fearless and pure love with one least	761	95 POEMS 88	1
is the coming of pure joyful your fearless and	761	95 POEMS 88	10
deep (A so wonder pure) even than the green	778	73 POEMS 6	6
of irrevocable time particular pure truth of patience heard .	821	73 POEMS 49	5
PURELY			
from cool faces, moving purely with muted step, yet	211	XLI SONNETS 7	8
one causeless cloud to purely grow but, never doubt	433	NO THANKS 50	4
PURER			
like the snow only purer fleeter, like the rain	293	IS 5 FOUR 10	2
/ / / / purer than purest pure whisper	601	(CHAIRE) 3	1
PUREST			
silence has deeper eyes purest than fear's obscener brightest	565	1 X 1 25	9
/ / purer than purest pure whisper of a	601	(CHAIRE) 3	1
surely would know) of purest poem and glories of	748	95 POEMS 76	7
PURPLE			
pompous fire the pansy's purple patience and the grave . . .	5	T&C EPITHALAM	93
grovelling hands rasps the purple dark- ness a worshipper . .	28	T&C ORIENTALE 2	9
upon the gloom arise purple pencils fluent spires of	31	T&C ORIENTALE 5	4
iron men her common purple soul the absurd eyelids	52	T&C PORTRAIT 1	24
rhythmic mouth and silly purple eyelids of how she	56	T&C PORTRAIT 4	15
My Lady hear the purple trumpets blow horses of	110	& PORTRAIT 6	33
like poets put on purple thought against the magnificent . .	188	XLI SONGS 10	3
being not for us, purple roses were sweeter to	213	XLI SONNETS 9	15

PURPLE (CONTINUED)
   arms which pinch that purple book between what hands . . . . 506 50 POEMS 20   2
   / / / "o purple finch please tell me . . . . 836 73 POEMS 64   1
PURPLED
   that dangles therefrom the purpled world will dance upon . . 16 T&C SONGS 6   4
PURPOSE
   built that way on purpose by simple people like . . . . . . 466 NEW POEMS 4   11
PURPOSES
   fine sonofabitch (to all purposes and intents) in which . . . 254 IS 5 ONE 25   6
+PURPOSIVE
   FOR CONTEXT, SEE . . . . 477 NEW POEMS 15   6
PURR
   strokes, vibrant with the purr of echo pouring in . . . . . . 115 & PORTRAIT 8   14
   strolling with the futile purr of blood; your sex . . . . . . 170 & SON ACTU 19   8
   is where strange birds purr / / / / . . . . 180 XLI SONGS 2   20
   curtains, drooped to a purr....i left her permanently . . . . 228 IS 5 ONE MARJ   14
PURRED
   groan while the gadgets purred and the gangsters dined . . . 647 {CHAIRE} 49   9
PURRING
   above fourteenth fifth's deep purring biceps, the mystic . . 220 XLI SONNETS 16   2
PURRS
   of the unmitigated systole purrs against my mind, the . . . . 136 & SON REAL 7   5
   i and the me purrs you and the gentle . . . . 773 73 POEMS 1   6
PURSE
   to Marj the greenslim purse of whose face opens . . . . . . 114 & PORTRAIT 7   18
PURSED
   This is the garden: pursed lips do blow upon . . . . 208 XLI SONNETS 4   5
PURSUE
   arrow and the pillar pursue curiously a crumbling flight . . 112 & PORTRAIT 6   82
PURSUED
   wintry handlebars glued) updives pursued by its wigglesome . 585 1 X 1 45   7
PURSUES
   brain of cleverly-crinkling -water pursues the angry dream of 160 & SON ACTU 9   5
   the vines (my heart pursues against the little moon . . . . . 434 NO THANKS 51   16
PURSUING
   with the libido and pursuing a course of instruction . . . . 327 VIVA 18   44
PURSUIT
   grumbling face cluttered in pursuit pleasantly elephantine . 56 T&C PORTRAIT 4   7
PUSH
   the slobbering walls filthily push witless creases of . . . . 96 & POST IMPR 8   4
   air) the largest hour push deep his din of . . . . 115 & PORTRAIT 8   12
   jostle grins nudge smiles push--. deep into the edgeless . . 202 XLI PORTRAIT 9   37
   cow is not to push and then to pull . . . . 500 50 POEMS 14   18
PUSHING
   with his awkward eyes pushing sleep under and thoroughly . . 293 IS 5 FOUR 10   28
PUSHINGS
   --your kiss, the little pushings of flesh, makes my . . . . . 82 T&C SON ACTU 1   3
PUT
   bed, whom white-thighed Semiramis put up her mouth to . . . . 22 T&C PUELLA MEA 248
   all the trees are put on edge spring, of . . . . 61 T&C PORTRAIT 9   21
   hideous vegetaBles weasOned with-be- ing-put-too-long in . . 101 & POST IMPR 11   66
   into the soaring silence (put your smallest ear against . . . 110 & PORTRAIT 6   29
   whose hair is Nile) put your ear to the . . . . 113 & PORTRAIT 6   113
   gave her. Bill was put wise that she was . . . . 145 & SON REAL 16   9
   vermouth -colour. Hair. he put between her lips a . . . . . 148 & SON REAL 19   9
   the hills like poets put on purple thought against . . . . . 188 XLI SONGS 10   2
   gold the fluffy threads, put up your little arms . . . . . . 192 XLI CHANSONS 2   17
   doubts about why you put the ring on (and . . . . 242 IS 5 ONE 13   12
   the stiffened puke i put him all into my . . . . 258 IS 5 ONE 28   22
   we are spanked and put to sleep by dolls . . . . 261 IS 5 ONE 31   2
   consider life. Dear i put my eyes into you . . . . 289 IS 5 FOUR 6   13
   VAN MERDE) having first put right sleuthfully aboard all . . 334 VIVA 25   5
   / / / / put off your faces, Death: . . . . 376 VIVA 67   1
   day being come, Love, put on your faces / . . . . 376 VIVA 67   14
   the fat strongman has put down his carpet from . . . . 384 NO THANKS 2   19
   and, Opening beautiful earth put (only) a Leaf among . . . . 397 NO THANKS 14   16
   / death (having lost) put on his universe and . . . . 451 NO THANKS 66   1
   our fatally unshadowing fate put on one not imaginable . . . 454 NO THANKS 69   12

PUT (CONTINUED)
makes every man's flesh put space on; and his . . . . 484 NEW POEMS 22   8
has (elephant the blue) put some just a now . . . . 516 50 POEMS 30   9
our Now) twiceuponatime wave-- put out your eyes, and . . . . 639 (CHAIRE) 41   13
all divinities proudly descending put on deathful flesh: are 768 95 POEMS 94   6
set saint against sinner; put gain over gladness and . . . . 769 95 POEMS 95   16
my whereful selves they put on here again --to . . . . 819 73 POEMS 47   16
PUTAIN
chatouille Des Italiens the putain with the ivory throat . . 120 & PORTRAIT 12   9
PUTRESCENCE
onion! for one--onion for. putrescence is Cubical . . . . . 94 & POST IMPR 6   10
from! the: A wending putrescence. a. of, loosely ; . . . . . 99 & POST IMPR 10   23
/ / an amiable putrescence carpenters the village of . . . . 136 & SON REAL 7   1
carouse of geomet- rical putrescence whereto my invariably . 197 XLI PORTRAIT 5   20
+PUTRESCENCE
FOR CONTEXT, SEE . . . . 309 VIVA 1   25
PUTRESCENT
ears scramble faintly tickling putrescent atomies, and i feel 69 T&C POST IMPR 6   29
PUTRID
lewd dollies pretty and putrid dollies of-love-and-of-death . 101 & POST IMPR 11   81
with which in a putrid window every day almost . . . . 144 & SON REAL 15   12
gloaming gladness hammers incessant putrid spikes of madness 202 XLI PORTRAIT 9   38
+PUTRID
FOR CONTEXT, SEE . . . . 101 & POST IMPR 11   68
PUTRIDO
sense something un poco putrido when we contemplate her . . . 327 VIVA 18   45
PUTS
K ing my Nose puts on sharp robes of . . . . 94 & POST IMPR 6   9
brain so everybody just puts out their finger and . . . . . 126 & SEVEN POEMS 5   12
/ / MAME she puts down the handmirror. "Look . . . . 226 IS 5 ONE MAME   1
his robe) who now puts on his flat hat . . . . 240 IS 5 ONE 11   4
at joy, come summer puts on fur answers eats . . . . 394 NO THANKS 11   7
never robbed of day) puts always on by always . . . . 674 95 POEMS 2   8
inexistence moving) sweet earth puts on immortality again . . 818 73 POEMS 46   4
PUTTING
sunset the young city putting off dimension with a . . . . . 48 T&C IMPRESS 2   16
the hours rise up putting off stars and it . . . . 50 T&C IMPRESS 4   1
eyes the hours descend, putting on stars.... in the . . . . . 50 T&C IMPRESS 4   32
because you are perpetually putting the secret of life . . . 204 XLI LA GUERRE 2   18
their omnipotent literally their putting it more than mildly 391 NO THANKS 8   22
is perfectly natural; perfectly putting it mildly lively (but 604 (CHAIRE) 6   15
we say somewhat diversified (putting it quietly) life was . . 699 95 POEMS 27   18
body wants Most (not putting it mildly much) may . . . . . . 727 95 POEMS 55   11
+PUTTING
FOR CONTEXT, SEE . . . . 477 NEW POEMS 15   8
PUZZLES
on which a frown puzzles, but I know the . . . . 117 & PORTRAIT 10   34
PUZZLING
swiftlyenormous light --and furiously puzzling through, . . . 157 & SON ACTU 6   13
shake well) indolently dreaming puzzling over that one oh . . 323 VIVA 15   6
and doesn't that seem puzzling but we both might . . . . . . 323 VIVA 15   18
PYJAMASTRING
or so lightyears of pyjamastring) a (vastly and particulary) 607 (CHAIRE) 9   7
PYRAMIDAL
And affectionate leer interminable pyramidal, napkins (this . 243 IS 5 ONE 14   6
+PYROTECHNIC
FOR CONTEXT, SEE . . . . 266 IS 5 TWO 1   11
PYTHON
mighty children while a python over the way freezes . . . . . 384 NO THANKS 2   21
Q
/ / / / Q: dwo we know of . . . . 468 NEW POEMS 6   1
& oxen is science) Q: how numb can an . . . . 791 73 POEMS 19   9
QU'EST
◇ ruptingly) ca-y-est droppe5 qu'est-ce que tu veux Dwrith . 430 NO THANKS 47   18
QU'EST-CE
◇ ruptingly) ca-y-est droppe5 qu'est-ce que tu veux Dwrith . 430 NO THANKS 47   18
QUACKS
with life's disease which quacks will cure when pimps . . . . 527 50 POEMS 39   23

	PAGE	TITLE	LINE

QUADRUPED
digit, earth's most terrific quadruped swoons into . . . . . 315 VIVA 7 16
QUAFFED
peers full oft hath quaffed the wine of life . . . . 273 IS 5 TWO 8 7
QUAI
vomits cleverly against a quai wall almost spray -ing . . . . 324 VIVA 16 7
QUAIL
as lilies smile and quail) of all things perfect . . . . . . 20 T&C PUELLA MEA 161
QUAKE
terrors of his being quake before this its hideous . . . . . 77 T&C SON UNRE 2 11
QUALMS
hyenas suppressing my frank qualms in deference to her . . . 326 VIVA 18 21
QUANTITY
no death and any quantity; but than all numerable . . . . . . 556 1 X 1 16 3
QUARRELLING
at other (if not quarrelling in a luxury of . . . . 312 VIVA 4 14
QUARRIED
girl. his left hand quarried the quartzlike face. his . . . . 148 & SON REAL 19 3
QUARTZLIKE
left hand quarried the quartzlike face. his right slapped . . 148 & SON REAL 19 4
QUE
Louise Lallemand n'est-ce pas que je suis belle cheri? . . . 120 & PORTRAIT 12 11
amerique on ne boit que de Jingyale. things are . . . . 233 IS 5 ONE 4 6
ruptingly) ca-y-est droppe5 qu'est-ce que tu veux Dwrith il . 430 NO THANKS 47 18
QUEEN
slow diaphanous faint rout), queen in the inconceivable . . . 6 T&C EPITHALAM 145
pride of the world's queen: each is a verb, ... 21 T&C PUELLA MEA 208
the body of the queen of queens is more . . . . 33 T&C ORIENTALE 6 50
tallest eunuch and the queen of queens comes forth . . . . . 33 T&C ORIENTALE 6 63
their unquiet spears the queen of queens is dancing . . . . . 34 T&C ORIENTALE 6 84
throws jewels at the queen of queens and white . . . . 34 T&C ORIENTALE 6 101
off? the king & queen alighting from their limousine . . . . 245 IS 5 ONE 16 2
of his heart the queen --incalculable bliss! Picture it . . . 254 IS 5 ONE 25 12
(once and once only, Queen among centuries universes between 358 VIVA 49 11
in a hot young queen with a twot with . . . . 469 NEW POEMS 7 3
king to beggar and queen to seem (blow friend . . . . 560 1 X 1 20 5
rivery forests towerful towns (queen poet king float sprout . 586 1 X 1 46 8
QUEENLY
Paris Marie Louise with queenly legs cinq rue Henri . . . . . 121 & PORTRAIT 12 45
QUEENS
the emperor's harem are queens of all the earth . . . . 33 T&C ORIENTALE 6 45
of the queen of queens is more transparent than . . . . 33 T&C ORIENTALE 6 50
and the queen of queens comes forth ankles musical . . . . . 33 T&C ORIENTALE 6 64
spears the queen of queens is dancing her subtle . . . . . . 34 T&C ORIENTALE 6 84
at the queen of queens and white money upon . . . . 34 T&C ORIENTALE 6 101
pillars listening while the queens of all the earth . . . . . 35 T&C ORIENTALE 6 115
live by? or better, queens, queens laughing lightly crowned . 211 XLI SONNETS 7 14
by? or better, queens, queens laughing lightly crowned with . 211 XLI SONNETS 7 14
(and them slim hot queens with dam next to . . . . 242 IS 5 ONE 13 5
QUEER
world is puddle-wonderful the queer old balloonman whistles . 24 T&C CHANSONS 1 11
her transfigured face a queer pulp of ecstasy while . . . . . 55 T&C PORTRAIT 3 15
round pointing to the queer monkey (if you toss . . . . 69 T&C POST IMPR 6 9
are pointing at the queer monkey with a little . . . . 69 T&C POST IMPR 6 37
large and fragile his queer hands twitter before him, ... 198 XLI PORTRAIT 6 23
and it's flutters everything queer; does smells he smiles . . 251 IS 5 ONE 22 5
he is altogether a queer fellow as young as . . . . 296 IS 5 FOUR 13 3
item son a woopsing queer colon hobby photography never . . . 499 50 POEMS 13 9
the zoo (jumbled to queer this what that a . . . . 516 50 POEMS 30 8
+QUEER
FOR CONTEXT, SEE . . . . 100 & POST IMPR 11 35
QUEERLY
the littletin-cup His wrappedupbody Queerly Has, my, ears, go 100 & POST IMPR 11 40
wrinkling loth stocking begins queerly to do a few . . . . . 225 IS 5 ONE LIZ 4
whose his climbing shoulders queerly twilight : never, no . . 490 50 POEMS 4 19
QUEERYING
deep and strong one queerying wave will whitely yearn . . . . 526 50 POEMS 38 7

	PAGE	TITLE	LINE

QUELL
mute, it is to quell me with the twinge . . . . 19 T&C PUELLA MEA 100
thus did immortal jealousy quell divine generosity, thus . . 799 73 POEMS 27   33
QUEMQUAM
America unde negant redire quemquam supp sedly thr w . . . . 392 NO THANKS 9   19
QUERIES
onlying from serene whom queries not suspected selves of . . 517 50 POEMS 31   7
soft) firm who outlift queries of self pouring (alive . . . . 613 (CHAIRE) 15   8
QUERYING
flame that dizzily grips. Querying greys between mouthed . . 139 & SON REAL 10   12
adventuring, enormous nowhere from) querying affirmation; . . 669 (CHAIRE) 71   5
+QUERYING
FOR CONTEXT, SEE . . . . 526 50 POEMS 38   7
QUEST
depart upon more exquisite quest? and did thy fortunate . . .   3 T&C EPITHALAM   20
QUESTION
drink? (the eternal perpetual question) Inside snugandevil. i 97 & POST IMPR 8 42
/ / this young question mark man question mark . . . . 246 IS 5 ONE 17   1
young question mark man question mark who suffers from . . . 246 IS 5 ONE 17   2
who suffers from indigestion question mark is a remarkably . 246 IS 5 ONE 17   4
myselves ask "life, the question how do i drink . . . . 295 IS 5 FOUR 12   14
a daisy-- your thorniest question my roses will answer" . . . 625 (CHAIRE) 27   13
twig limb ask every question time can't answer: and . . . . . 818 73 POEMS 46   10
+QUESTION
FOR CONTEXT, SEE . . . . 468 NEW POEMS 6   1
QUESTIONING
evening in bruised narrow questioning faces) / / / . . . . . 275 IS 5 TWO 9   50
QUESTIONINGS
even prevail a million questionings against the silence of . 714 95 POEMS 42   12
QUESTIONS
be so spry concernin questions arty each has his . . . . . . 247 IS 5 ONE 18   2
since bloodshed and kindred questions inhibit unprepared . . 266 IS 5 TWO 1   29
suddenly curving entire warm questions / / / / . . . . 282 IS 5 THREE 6   35
+QUESTIONS
FOR CONTEXT, SEE . . . . 319 VIVA 11   40
QUI
a la voix fragile qui chatouille Des Italiens the . . . . . . 120 & PORTRAIT 12   7
les petites femmes exactes qui dansent toujours in my . . . . 121 & PORTRAIT 12 51
+QUI
FOR CONTEXT, SEE . . . . 635 (CHAIRE) 37   26
QUICK
thy head is a quick forest filled with sleeping . . . . 29 T&C ORIENTALE 3 5
and feet filled with quick fingers and a remarkable . . . . . 69 T&C POST IMPR 6 39
littlest pal, skilled in quick softness. Unspontaneous. cute. 74 T&C SON REAL 5 4
remarkable splinter in the quick of twilight ....or if . . .   82 T&C SON ACTU 1 5
breasts half-grown, lisping flesh quick to thread the fattish 140 & SON REAL 11 12
your taste. Jumped the quick wall of your smile . . . . 154 & SON ACTU 3   4
the sensible night a quick bird (tenderly upon the . . . . . 187 XLI SONGS 9   8
shy-dodge is bright cruMbshandful, quick-hurl edinwho Is . . 265 IS 5 ONE 34   4
perpetually acruise and her quick way of slowly staring . . . 337 VIVA 28   8
exhumes (which buries again quick- ly its self in) . . . . . 341 VIVA 32   15
fearers worship Much and Quick; badness not being felt . . . 438 NO THANKS 54   2
body loved big that quick sharp thick snake of . . . . 490 50 POEMS 4   8
of one street leaps quick squirmthicklying lu minous night . 493 50 POEMS 7   11
good a bottle she quick who stop damned fall . . . . 496 50 POEMS 10   13
machine no good too quick i know this suit . . . . 523 50 POEMS 36   11
cheap this suit too quick no suit there every . . . . 523 50 POEMS 36   23
/ / / / quick i the death of . . . . 634 (CHAIRE) 36   1
die (how and am quick i they'll all not . . . . 634 (CHAIRE) 36   14
-bright flower- soft bird -quick voice loves children and . . 660 (CHAIRE) 62   21
tiptoe at the very quick of nowhere) we --While . . . . 758 95 POEMS 85   46
home of knowledgeable shadows (quick to seize each nothing . 765 95 POEMS 91   2
QUICK-HURL
shy-dodge is bright cruMbshandful, quick-hurl edinwho Is . . 265 IS 5 ONE 34   4
QUICKLY
a keen spider skipping quickly over patriotic swill. The, . . 166 & SON ACTU 15   2
crashing things) man spits quickly into the very bright . . . 252 IS 5 ONE 23   12
up all sorts of quickly things on the slate . . . . 287 IS 5 FOUR 4   3

| | PAGE | TITLE | LINE |

QUICKLY (CONTINUED)
    minds into dream (An) quickly Not un deux trois . . . . 348 VIVA 39   10
    caress that laugh both quickly signify life's only half . . . 364 VIVA 55   11
    how clownlike that this quickly ghost scribbling from there . 504 50 POEMS 18   8
    did you (kiss me) quickly count to never? you . . . . 599 (CHAIRE) 1   11
    lurch a once world quickly from rises army the . . . . 633 (CHAIRE) 35   2
    wept: and so she quickly dreamed a dream of . . . . 777 73 POEMS 5   15
    flowers) dreams , come quickly come run run with . . . . . . 835 73 POEMS 63   14
+QUICKLY
    FOR CONTEXT, SEE . . . . 341 VIVA 32   15
    FOR CONTEXT, SEE . . . . 719 95 POEMS 47   7
QUICKNESS
    (proov -ing that the quickness of the fand intrigues . . . . 425 NO THANKS 42   8
QUICKYES
    want to dear somehow quickyes when (now, dark dear . . . . . 251 IS 5 ONE 22   13
QUID
    for the quo pro quid" uncle sam shrugs his . . . . 711 95 POEMS 39   20
QUIET
    the frying curb the quiet face lay which had . . . . 52 T&C PORTRAIT 1   15
    little the (on his quiet head his magical shoulders . . . . . 516 50 POEMS 30   10
    finally The UN "be quiet little hungary and do . . . . . . 711 95 POEMS 39   17
QUIETLY
    --and i fall back, quietly amorous of, through the . . . . . 158 & SON ACTU 7   12
    when hugeness will shut quietly) almost, your kiss / . . . . 163 & SON ACTU 12   21
    go away ever so quietly when we weren't looking. . . . . . . 191 XLI CHANSONS 1   15
    my self etcetera lay quietly in the deep mud . . . . 276 IS 5 TWO 10   19
    hands withdrew, jerkily, themselves quietly they began . . . 284 IS 5 FOUR 1   9
    as over this floor (quietly with bright eyes) drifts . . . . 286 IS 5 FOUR 3   4
    meadow of time lessness; quietly turning toward me the . . . 370 VIVA 61   7
    new alls of joy: quietly & before illimitably spiralling . . 480 NEW POEMS 18   21
    somewhat diversified (putting it quietly) life was a blindman 699 95 POEMS 27   20
    out of the floor quietly Stare a poisoned mouse . . . . . . 784 73 POEMS 12   3
QUILLS
    birds sit creatures of quills (asleep who must go . . . . . 483 NEW POEMS 21   10
QUILT'S
    face or why a quilt's pink stops might equal . . . . 506 50 POEMS 20   10
QUINTILLIONS
    dead ideas (the oh quintillions of incredible dodderingly . . 250 IS 5 ONE 21   11
QUIPS
    hiding pleasure. Alice, stinging quips of flesh. Loretta, cut 138 & SON REAL 9   14
    dead silence with harmless quips, out of Briggs by . . . . 326 VIVA 18   13
QUITE
    shoulders and the ripe quite too large lips always . . . . . 72 T&C SON REAL 3   6
    perhaps drea-mingly Is (not- quite trees hugging with the . . 155 & SON ACTU 4   5
    of sublimated tom-tom which quite outdoes the mandolin- man's 171 & SON ACTU 20   5
    body. It is so quite new a thing. Muscles . . . . 175 & SON ACTU 24   2
    under me you so quite new / / / . . . . 175 & SON ACTU 24   14
    / when life is quite through with and leaves . . . . 181 XLI SONGS 3   1
    unhappy then when you're quite dressed you'll stand in . . . 192 XLI CHANSONS 2   21
    ap- proached may never quite taste the wine which . . . . . 193 XLI PORTRAIT 1   12
    the as it happens quite erroneous impression that he . . . . 234 IS 5 ONE 5   4
    human optics know more quite ennobling forsooth? One wondrous 254 IS 5 ONE 25   4
    of all really made quite a mistake in being . . . . 262 IS 5 ONE 32   6
    no sense. Which being quite beyond dispute as prove . . . . 266 IS 5 TWO 1   5
    day (against which and quite silently hills made of . . . . 278 IS 5 THREE 2   5
    spaces grouse rocket know quite, slightly or how at . . . . 346 VIVA 37   12
    be and seem so quite softly as your hair . . . . 367 VIVA 58   4
    these first deepest rare quite who are your eyes . . . . . . 367 VIVA 58   8
    wherefore & wormSmile eternal; quite perhaps as sternly much 371 VIVA 62   24
    but not darkness shall quite outmarch forever --and i . . . . 376 VIVA 67   6
    howlessly and without why (quite minus gal or pal . . . . . 387 NO THANKS 4   4
    dead dead) whereupon mary quite contrary didn't die (may . . 401 NO THANKS 18   9
    is a bit of quite unmitigated hate (travelling in . . . . . 413 NO THANKS 30   14
    yesterday's perfection seem not quite so clever as the . . . 414 NO THANKS 31   1
    out of (blown never quite to -gether by large . . . . 442 NO THANKS 57   3
    much tasted plus touched quite so And How much . . . . 474 NEW POEMS 12   8
    while these not eyes quite try almost their mind . . . . . . 479 NEW POEMS 17   4
    truly there's never been quite such a fool who . . . . 481 NEW POEMS 19   11

		PAGE	TITLE	LINE

QUITE (CONTINUED)

in round blue but quite now it's swirly and . . . . 516 50 POEMS 30   6
all bequeath and nothing quite so least as truth . . . . . 521 50 POEMS 34   65
is much too not quite big enough to hold . . . . 523 50 POEMS 36   31
breadcrumb) say "i understand quite what you mean by" . . . 546 1 X 1 6   13
dare of snow less quite is nothing but herself, ... 573 1 X 1 33   15
star (afloat on not quite less than all of . . . . 575 1 X 1 35   21
snowflakes make possible mayflowers: quite eyes of air not . 577 1 X 1 37   5
mind, mountains of soul) quite at the hugest which . . . . . 580 1 X 1 40   26
and everybody never breathed quite so many kinds of . . . . 591 1 X 1 51   16
than eyes "only are quite what worlds merely might . . . . . 603 (CHAIRE) 5   14
not (at a guess) quite half way down to . . . . 631 (CHAIRE) 33   10
grin (extremely like but quite absurd gloved fist on . . . . 640 (CHAIRE) 42   8
absolute gone & positive quite n ever & bi . . . . 646 (CHAIRE) 48   14
and to me (and quite with out crushing) the . . . . 652 (CHAIRE) 54   7
to call their cowardice quite agree) shall never discover . . 664 (CHAIRE) 66   14
is you nothing may, quite your my (my your . . . . 666 (CHAIRE) 68   11
because no best is quite so good you don't . . . . 679 95 POEMS 7   10
his bright torn trousers (quite as if he were . . . . 680 95 POEMS 8   16
e l'echelle) die can't quite poison God's sunlight / . . . . 708 95 POEMS 36   16
than mere unmiracle can quite appease-- humbly in their . . . 714 95 POEMS 42   5
a darkness noone can quite begin to guess (except . . . . . 717 95 POEMS 45   7
wondered "most people be quite so (when flowers) in . . . . 738 95 POEMS 66   13
could begin to imagine quite such eagerly innocent whoms . . 748 95 POEMS 76   13
nor any marvel finds quite disappearance but some keener . . 750 95 POEMS 78   13
last doing shall not quite undo such first amazement . . . . 762 95 POEMS 89   4
must four and (to quite become nothing) five times, ... 764 95 POEMS 90   51
love until noone could quite be (and young is . . . . 769 95 POEMS 95   24
you and i'd be quite --come such perfection-- another . . . . 798 73 POEMS 26   22
to sing) could never quite tell right from wrong, ... 799 73 POEMS 27   13
since our hero is quite without change, you're going . . . 800 73 POEMS 28   11
knows; and certain men quite possibly may have shall . . . . 807 73 POEMS 35   12
than selfless i can quite endure the absence of . . . . . . 812 73 POEMS 40   10
failing year --now, before quite your whisper's whisper is . 821 73 POEMS 49   9
might be so not quite believab ly smallest as . . . . 827 73 POEMS 55   6

+QUITE

FOR CONTEXT, SEE . . . . 695 95 POEMS 23   1

+QUITENESS

FOR CONTEXT, SEE . . . . 820 73 POEMS 48   6

QUITENOTIMAGINABLE

under entirely the coming quitenotimaginable silenceofsound . 754 95 POEMS 82   12

QUITS

spreadnessed bE rich from-soft quits (now) ly Comes; : . . . 342 VIVA 33   21

QUITTING

my mind all night, quitting only in the unkind . . . . . . 165 & SON ACTU 14   3

QUIVER

now the little fish quiver so you and so . . . . 665 (CHAIRE) 67   13

QUIVERING

earth who dost with quivering continual thighs invite the . . 3 T&C EPITHALAM   2
proud transparent company of quivering ghosts-of-love which . 6 T&C EPITHALAM   143
harps celestial to the quivering string) invisible faces . . 208 XLI SONNETS 4   7
eyes, painfully perpetually crouched, quivering, upon the . . 231 IS 5 ONE 3   50

QUIVERINGGOLD

cithern- player squats with quiveringgold body behind the . . 34 T&C ORIENTALE 6   72

QUIVERINGLY

before keen if dim quiveringly spangle & thingless & . . . . 480 NEW POEMS 18   8

QUIVERS

trembling thirds of anguish quivers to your words, As . . . . 11 T&C SONGS 2   17
body atop which always quivers the electric Distinct face . . 193 XLI PORTRAIT 1   3
any truth beyond perceive) quivers this miracle of summer . . 809 73 POEMS 37   3

QUO

we fear for the quo pro quid" uncle sam . . . . 711 95 POEMS 39   20

QUOTE

but little joe gould's quote oral history unquote might . . . 410 NO THANKS 27   9
thousand years equals the quote and unquote loss of . . . . 544 1 X 1 4   15
park anus stick some quote statue unquote to prove . . . . . 636 (CHAIRE) 38   2
dare to answer "no"? quote citizens unquote might otherwise . 636 (CHAIRE) 38   5
divine) that if the quote state unquote says "kill" . . . . . 636 (CHAIRE) 38   7

	PAGE	TITLE	LINE

QUOTE (CONTINUED)
   is measured by his quote eye cue unquote. Much . . . . 807 73 POEMS 35   8
QUOTES
   of the chambers close quotes the microscopic pithecoid . . . 267 IS 5 TWO 2   2
   upon the possession of quotes keltyer close " " . . . . 331 VIVA 22   6
QUOTH
   have been I) "?" quoth the front; and there . . . . 317 VIVA 9   10
   and spoil the rod quoth the palmist. / / . . . . 643 (CHAIRE) 45   6
   say guessed?" "we shall" quoth gifted she: and played . . . . 807 73 POEMS 35   14
R
   at afternoon? (kow dow r 2 bul retoinis wus . . . . 409 NO THANKS 26   3
+R.S.V.P.
   FOR CONTEXT, SEE . . . . 504 50 POEMS 18   5
RABBITSARE
   dolls re -volve whirlswans rabbitsare: swimswim ◇ with eyes 384 NO THANKS 2   29
RABELAIS
   are, good luck! aberdeen plato-rabelais peter jack / / . . . 605 (CHAIRE) 7   16
RACED
   a horrible thing which raced sideways while blowing bubbles: 682 95 POEMS 10   8
RACKET
   the mandolin- man's tiny racket. The horses sleep upstairs. . 171 & SON ACTU 20   6
+RACKET
   FOR CONTEXT, SEE . . . . 263 IS 5 ONE 32   55
+RACKS
   FOR CONTEXT, SEE . . . . 511 50 POEMS 25   8
RADARW
   pseudo yours podia of radarw leschin / / / . . . . 333 VIVA 24   26
RADCLIFFE
   course of instruction at radcliffe college, cambridge, mass. 327 VIVA 18   44
RADDIOS
   laddios (on radios and raddios) did save man from . . . . . . 552 1 X 1 12   14
RADIANCE
   glided, a drop of radiance, to the grass-- shunning . . . . .   8 T&C OF NICOL   24
   with a most swift radiance wherein slowly drift murmurous . .   18 T&C PUELLA MEA   80
   gleam, in the poised radiance of perpetualness. When what's .   81 T&C SON UNRE 6   8
   us tremble) a personal radiance sits hideously upon the . . . 168 & SON ACTU 17   1
RADIATOR
   gas felt of her radiator made sure her springs . . . . 248 IS 5 ONE 19   8
   doll wired to the radiator of his ZOOM DOOM . . . . 680 95 POEMS 8   3
RADICALLY
   per that and this radically defunct periodical. i would . . . 230 IS 5 ONE 2   18
RADIO
   jes was which the radio aint (proov -ing that . . . . 425 NO THANKS 42   7
RADIOS
   ladios and laddios (on radios and raddios) did save . . . . . 552 1 X 1 12   14
RADISHRED
   the feline she with radishred legs said (crossing them . . . 228 IS 5 ONE MARJ   2
RAG
   corpse and wanting any rag upon what God unto . . . . 339 VIVA 30   16
   / / / / red-rag and pink-flag blackshirt and . . . . 497 50 POEMS 11   1
   now (it tears off rag its of mind chucks . . . . 501 50 POEMS 15   12
   was who (with a rag and a bone and . . . . 552 1 X 1 12   8
+RAG
   FOR CONTEXT, SEE . . . . 107 & PORTRAIT 3   15
RAGE
   and Brave --wildly who rage, vainly who strive; and . . . . . 799 73 POEMS 27   29
RAGES
   distinct ecstasy wags and. rages Laughters jostle grins nudge 202 XLI PORTRAIT 9   36
RAGGED
   stun the eyes of ragged earth who sees them . . . .   4 T&C EPITHALAM   69
   April came into the ragged meadow of my soul. . . . . 306 IS 5 FIVE 5   15
   beautiful there is a ragged beside the who limps . . . . . . 437 NO THANKS 53   10
RAGGING
   freakish feet feet incorrigible ragging the world, / / . . .   61 T&C PORTRAIT 9   37
RAGING
   but a rain frailly raging whom the hills sink . . . .   9 T&C SONGS 1   25
   the reckless oral darkness raging with thin impulse i . . . .   67 T&C POST IMPR 4   5

		PAGE	TITLE	LINE
RAGS				
imagining whowhich of mad rags strode earth ignorantly . . .	662	(CHAIRE) 64	6
RAH				
busy right now" so rah-rah-rah democracy let's all be	711	95 POEMS 39	25
busy right now" so rah-rah-rah democracy let's all be	711	95 POEMS 39	25
busy right now" so rah-rah-rah democracy let's all be	711	95 POEMS 39	25
RAH-RAH-RAH				
busy right now" so rah-rah-rah democracy let's all be	711	95 POEMS 39	25
RAIL				
standing on the third rail waiting for the next	262	IS 5 ONE 32	2
actually fall off the rail before the really train	263	IS 5 ONE 32	63
RAIMENT				
respire: impeccable girls in raiment laughter-gifted. / / / .	85	T&C SON ACTU 4	15
never shall soil their raiment with phenomena: such being . .	328	VIVA 19	4
RAIN				
thighs invite the thrilling rain the slender paramour to . .	3	T&C EPITHALAM	3
extraordinary lust, (the sinuous rain which rising from thy .	3	T&C EPITHALAM	5
darkness a more burning rain? And still the mad	4	T&C EPITHALAM	56
our doom; but a rain frailly raging whom the	9	T&C SONGS 1	25
passing a certain gate, rain fell (as it will	58	T&C PORTRAIT 6	3
thy fingers are the rain, and i hear the	61	T&C PORTRAIT 9	30
wind has blown the rain away and blown the	80	T&C SON UNRE 5	1
wind has blown the rain away and the leaves	80	T&C SON UNRE 5	13
the sun, nor will rain care cautiously who prolongs	84	T&C SON ACTU 3	8
gods whiten befall saith rain anguish of dream-send is . . .	90	& POST IMPR 2	4
all things) the bright rain occurs deeply, beautifully and .	92	& POST IMPR 4	6
completely conscious of the rain or rather Somebody who . . .	92	& POST IMPR 4	11
altogether delicate gestures of rain a colour comes, which .	92	& POST IMPR 4	16
streets turn young with rain, spiral acres of bloated	93	& POST IMPR 5	4
shade will youse dearie? rain wouldn't that get yer	109	& PORTRAIT 5	3
should worry about the rain huh dearie? yknow i'm	109	& PORTRAIT 5	8
a singular block her, rain-warm-naked exquisitely hashed . .	133	& SON REAL 4	2
you are like the rain, (Who feathers frightened fields . . .	163	& SON ACTU 12	2
if you ask the rain he'll not tell where.)	183	XLI SONGS 5	5
/ / in the rain- darkness, the sunset being	186	XLI SONGS 8	1
which open in the rain. little kittens who are	191	XLI CHANSONS 1	8
purer fleeter, like the rain only sweeter frailer you	293	IS 5 FOUR 10	2
dark and, deep with rain.... (he, slightly whom or	300	IS 5 FOUR 17	15
moves a wind bringing rain and leaves, filling the	304	IS 5 FIVE 3	12
discussed the possiblility of rain... in distant proximity to	326	VIVA 18	34
"things i mean the Rain is no respecter of	328	VIVA 19	21
the steeples writhe with rain) faces (at windows) do	340	VIVA 31	5
/ / / when rain whom fear not children	356	VIVA 47	1
is fragrantly, arrive (when Rain comes; predicating forever,	356	VIVA 47	15
nobody, not even the rain, has such small hands	366	VIVA 57	20
be unto love as rain is unto colour; create	372	VIVA 63	1
bravely down sleep big rain big snow big sun	393	NO THANKS 10	13
/ / move deeply, rain (dream hugely) wish firmly.	422	NO THANKS 39	2
of the sound of rain and here's to silent	424	NO THANKS 41	3
world (in darkly taking rain) drown, beyond sound down . . .	432	NO THANKS 49	2
than least flowers of rain) thickly i fail slenderly . . .	433	NO THANKS 50	9
tch-ing lousy full. of. rain beggars yaw: nstretchy: awn) . .	442	NO THANKS 57	14
yawned: it looks like rain (they've played for timelessness .	451	NO THANKS 66	2
/ the people who rain (are move as) proces	482	NEW POEMS 20	2
person fiddling in the rain (did you kiss a	498	50 POEMS 12	16
be were dawn dark rain snow rain -bow &	512	50 POEMS 26	18
dawn dark rain snow rain -bow & a moon	512	50 POEMS 26	18
same sun moon stars rain children guessed (but only	515	50 POEMS 29	8
slept their dream stars rain sun moon (and only	515	50 POEMS 29	21
came sun moon stars rain / / / /	515	50 POEMS 29	36
was as right as rain his pity was as	520	50 POEMS 34	35
/ / / / rain or hail sam done	568	1 X 1 28	1
alive (in real the rain) / / / /	640	(CHAIRE) 42	16
fall rise come go rain snow) remembers / /	693	95 POEMS 21	20
a dream in the rain / / / /	716	95 POEMS 44	36
sorry when sun and rain make april my life	749	95 POEMS 77	4
is every) un (star rain snow moon dream wing	753	95 POEMS 81	15
now comes the good rain farmers pray for (and	754	95 POEMS 82	1

	PAGE	TITLE	LINE

RAIN (CONTINUED)
    silenceofsound (here is that rain awaited by leaves with . . 754 95 POEMS 82   13
    (and hark begins to Rain) a house like shape . . . . 785 73 POEMS 13   8
    i sit (hearing the rain) un til against my . . . . 785 73 POEMS 13   19
    than high in the rain in the wind in . . . . 813 73 POEMS 41   11
    dim deep sound of rain; and of always and . . . . 816 73 POEMS 44   3
    and death and the rain are given; and given . . . . 816 73 POEMS 44   8
+RAIN
    FOR CONTEXT, SEE . . . . 333 VIVA 24   20
    FOR CONTEXT, SEE . . . . 347 VIVA 38   17
    FOR CONTEXT, SEE . . . . 653 (CHAIRE) 55   2
    FOR CONTEXT, SEE . . . . 696 95 POEMS 24   12
RAIN-WARM-NAKED
    a singular block her, rain-warm-naked exquisitely hashed . . 133 & SON REAL 4   2
RAIN'S
    upon her flesh the rain's pearls singly-whispering. // . . . 65 T&C POST IMPR 2   15
    will you like the rain's face and the rich . . . . 153 & SON ACTU 2   13
    which grow and the rain's wings the birds of . . . . 441 NO THANKS 56   55
RAINBOW
    perfectly speak (snowflake and rainbow mind and soul november 575 1 X 1 35   33
+RAINBOW
    FOR CONTEXT, SEE . . . . 512 50 POEMS 26   18
RAINBOWS
    roses with alarm and rainbows are insured against old . . . . 620 (CHAIRE) 22   4
RAINDROPS
    dearly , more than raindrops need sunbeams or snowflakes . . 577 1 X 1 37   3
+RAINED
    FOR CONTEXT, SEE . . . . 267 IS 5 TWO 2   17
RAINFAINT
    with a ghost 's rainfaint windthin voice-which-is no-voice . 697 95 POEMS 25   11
RAINING
    to come: it was raining a little, and the . . . . 173 & SON ACTU 22   1
RAINLIFE
    warm sweet mistfully whispering rainlife) infinite also . . . 755 95 POEMS 83   12
RAINMAN
    these children building this rainman out of snow / . . . . . 390 NO THANKS 7   14
RAINS
    now true histories plunge? rains a grey snow of . . . . . . 527 50 POEMS 39   28
RAINTHERAIN
    rai n th e raintherain / / / / . . . . 696 95 POEMS 24   16
RAISE
    / / / / raise the shade will youse . . . . 109 & PORTRAIT 5   1
RAISING
    than.) But look: up- raising, hoisting, a little perhaps . . 282 IS 5 THREE 6   5
RAM
    asters miggle dim a ram flat hombre sin bangaroom . . . . . . 333 VIVA 24   16
RAN
    smiling the merry deer ran before. Fleeter be they . . . . . 14 T&C SONGS 4   5
    smiling the level meadows ran before. Softer be they . . . . 14 T&C SONGS 4   15
    smiling the sheer peaks ran before. Paler be they . . . . . . 14 T&C SONGS 4   25
    stare, he whispers "i ran" / / / / . . . . 800 73 POEMS 28   24
RANCID
    little box is spilling rancid elves upon neat sunlight . . . 69 T&C POST IMPR 6   4
    armed with large legs rancid voices Baedekers Mothers and . . 256 IS 5 ONE 27   15
+RANCID
    FOR CONTEXT, SEE . . . . 442 NO THANKS 57   7
RAND
    goldfishian gestures) suddenly sally rand handsomely who did 425 NO THANKS 42   4
RANG
    / / when you rang at Dick Mid's Place . . . . 73 T&C SON REAL 4   1
+RANGE
    FOR CONTEXT, SEE . . . . 554 1 X 1 14   6
RAPES
    or my invincible Nearness rapes laughter from your . . . . . 166 & SON ACTU 15   15
RAPID
    goes out into the rapid hard wo- men and . . . . 101 & POST IMPR 11   61
    leap, which, anyway give rapid lapfulls of idiotic big . . . 251 IS 5 ONE 22   22
    general) sixteen years of rapid animal whose swir -ling . . . 341 VIVA 32   11

		PAGE	TITLE	LINE

RAPIDLY
and roofs are talking rapidly all together there happens . . 62 T&C PORTRAIT 10 18
or a but of rapidly goes gobs the and . . . . 96 & POST IMPR 8 7
my bruising smile; as rapidly upon the jiggled norm . . . . . 137 & SON REAL 8 9
/ life boosts herself rapidly at me through sagging . . . . . 151 & SON REAL 22 1
nakedness until it go rapidly to bed: i will . . . . 164 & SON ACTU 13 7
have watched certain petals rapidly wish in the corners . . . 214 XLI SONNETS 10 5
pass loudly and gondola rapidly denizens of Omaha Altoona . . 256 IS 5 ONE 27 26
five other fingers snitch rapidly through mist a defunct . . 259 IS 5 ONE 29 11
He. spoke. And drank rapidly a glass of water . . . . 268 IS 5 TWO 3 14
who step smoothly and rapidly along this pole over . . . . . 279 IS 5 THREE 3 15
sea, in the afternoon. rapidly a reddish ant travels . . . . 281 IS 5 THREE 5 11
or threes which fiercely rapidly pass with their breaths) . . 354 VIVA 45 22
nowhere else imagine Now rapidly this (a forest has . . . . . 693 95 POEMS 21 11
+RAPIDLY
FOR CONTEXT, SEE . . . . 354 VIVA 45 10
FOR CONTEXT, SEE . . . . 385 NO THANKS 2 60
RAPTURE
upon a wish, to rapture should surprise my soul . . . . 205 XLI SONNETS 1 4
frantic world with its rapture and anguish) at peace . . . . 749 95 POEMS 77 14
RAPTURES
our hero contemplate in raptures of undream that strictly . . 544 1 X 1 4 20
RAPTUROUSLY
sunlight? yes! and (plunging rapturously up) we spill our . . 650 {CHAIRE} 52 19
RARE
frailty of daisies--by what rare unease revealed of teasingly 5 T&C EPITHALAM 94
frond opening in a rare Slowness of gloried air... . . . . . 12 T&C SONGS 2 44
sweet deer the red rare deer. Four red roebuck . . . . 14 T&C SONGS 4 8
have dreamed of the rare entertainment of your eyes, ... 78 T&C SON UNRE 3 2
world should wrest the rare unwisdom of thy eyes, ... 205 XLI SONNETS 1 2
like these first deepest rare quite who are your . . . . . . 367 VIVA 58 7
hugely some few most rare perfectly dear (and worlds . . . . 376 VIVA 67 11
far from tangible domains rare with most early soul . . . . . 402 NO THANKS 19 12
of dong and common's rare and millstones float --long . . . . 511 50 POEMS 25 19
more than joy, most rare) a fiend, if fiends . . . . 562 1 X 1 22 4
merry most fair more rare --the livingest givingest girl . . 590 1 X 1 50 4
of all things excellently rare; obsolete almost that . . . . 607 {CHAIRE} 9 10
breathe a new (silverly rare goldenly so) moon, she . . . . . 666 {CHAIRE} 68 8
RARELY
then your dancesong soul. rarely-beloved a single star is . . 186 XLI SONGS 8 18
RARELY-BELOVED
then your dancesong soul. rarely-beloved a single star is . . 186 XLI SONGS 8 18
RARENESS
robes musically revealed in rareness: let thy twain eyes . . 10 T&C SONGS 1 42
RASBERRYPATCH
her round by the rasberrypatch" "i have hunted her . . . . . 707 95 POEMS 35 6
right now in the rasberrypatch and 'twas me that . . . . . . 707 95 POEMS 35 23
RASH
trees hugging with the rash, coherent light) only . . . . . 155 & SON ACTU 4 5
RASP
gape of tortured perspective rasp and graze of splintered . . 48 T&C IMPRESS 2 4
RASPAIL
montparnasse is goosed by raspail). But he turned into . . . 401 NO THANKS 18 14
RASPS
and bestial grovelling hands rasps the purple dark- ness . . 28 T&C ORIENTALE 2 9
RATE
some loveless trick sepa rate one stilled unmoving mind . . . 354 VIVA 45 20
from second to tenth rate (3) as it was . . . . 803 73 POEMS 31 13
+RATE
FOR CONTEXT, SEE . . . . 258 IS 5 ONE 28 3
FOR CONTEXT, SEE . . . . 803 73 POEMS 31 10
RATHE
hair's worm huge, ecstatic, rathe.... yours are the poems . . 84 T&C SON ACTU 3 11
RATHER
of the rain or rather Somebody who uses roofs . . . . 92 & POST IMPR 4 11
arms; but i should rather than anything have (almost . . . . 163 & SON ACTU 12 19
ful loneliness, and the rather fat man in bluishsuspenders . 166 & SON ACTU 15 5
you because you would rather black the boots of . . . . 204 XLI LA GUERRE 2 2

RATHER (CONTINUED)
    Jingyale. things are going rather kaka over there, over . . . 233 IS 5 ONE 4   7
    speeches sawdust perpetually leak rather is it between such . 261 IS 5 ONE 31   6
    wonder never mind consider rather heavenly things and but . . 322 VIVA 14   2
    neither; nor bewail (would rather make than have and . . . . 394 NO THANKS 11   11
    inclined to describe it rather as a" pause "uh" . . . . 464 NEW POEMS 2   22
    negation's dead undoom. I'd rather learn from one bird . . . 484 NEW POEMS 22   13
    various worlds he'll spurn rather than fail immeasurable . . 562 1 X 1 22   8
    anything which everyone would rather not become; but growing 626 (CHAIRE) 28   4
    of a mother i rather suppose" "will's dad never . . . . 707 95 POEMS 35   16
    --not though mankind would rather know than feel; mistrusting 817 73 POEMS 45   11
+RATHER
    FOR CONTEXT, SEE . . . . 84 T&C SON ACTU 3   11
    FOR CONTEXT, SEE . . . . 320 VIVA 12   17
    FOR CONTEXT, SEE . . . . 320 VIVA 12   21
RATIONAL
    measures that render hell rational --i thank heaven . . . . . 802 73 POEMS 30   31
RATTLES
    and cornerless, the moon rattles like a fragment of . . . . . 70 T&C SON REAL 1   14
RATTLING
    and presently found himself rattling for that well known . . 326 VIVA 18   12
RAUCOUS
    fragment of heaven) trickstervillain raucous rogue & vivid . 677 95 POEMS 5   13
RAVELLING
    her mind bodily which ravelling, to a proud continual . . . . 136 & SON REAL 7   3
RAVING
    long cool funnel of raving colour, on either side . . . . . . 100 & POST IMPR 11   3
    crazily seething of this raving city screamingly street . . . 437 NO THANKS 53   3
RAWROO
    rye roh rowster shouts rawrOO / / / / . . . . 773 73 POEMS 1   20
RAY
    did-he-does-she) & the ree ray rye roh rowster shouts . . . . 773 73 POEMS 1   18
RAYS
    big (bigger than cosmic rays war earthquakes famine or . . . 475 NEW POEMS 13   19
    a stranded star whose rays five languid fingers were; . . . . 682 95 POEMS 10   6
RAZOR
    gestures rhymes, like Gillette Razor Blades having been used 230 IS 5 ONE 2   20
RAZORBLADE
    littleness --electrons deify one razorblade into a . . . . . 554 1 X 1 14   5
+RAZORS
    FOR CONTEXT, SEE . . . . 237 IS 5 ONE 8   10
RD
    white eyebrows the 3 rd chief something or must . . . . 465 NEW POEMS 3   3
RE
    fais do do neighbours re babies while; / / . . . . 309 VIVA 1   35
    (well on in life) re the helen molle dancers, ... 327 VIVA 18   r39
    / one nonsufficiently inunderstood re with some difficulty . 398 NO THANKS 15   2
REACH
    feel your suddenly body reach for me with a . . . . 157 & SON ACTU 6   6
    (a typewriter within his reach) upon his fearless derriere . 266 IS 5 TWO 1   20
    be out of my reach , they are like . . . . 353 VIVA 44   18
    always are beyond the reach of death and the . . . . 357 VIVA 48   13
REACHES
    and down the singing reaches of my soul spoke . . . . 39 T&C AMORES 4   21
    so far your nearness reaches a lucky fifth of . . . . 537 50 POEMS 49   5
    which to which) he reaches the barn's immense doorway . . . . 754 95 POEMS 82   7
REACHINGS
    stunning flesh. Upon the reachings of Her green body . . . . 77 T&C SON UNRE 2   2
REACTS
    watches; truly, curvingly while reacts (sharp now with blood 344 VIVA 35   5
READ
    one afternoon ....or maybe read? of a time when . . . . 72 T&C SON REAL 3   10
    in some book had read / / / / . . . . 225 IS 5 ONE LIZ   16
    preserved conTinuum (but we read that beFore) of Course . . . 315 VIVA 7   6
    Brevis Est for Handkerchief read Papernapkin no laundry bills 410 NO THANKS 27   5
    and buck who cannot read and cannot write who . . . . 427 NO THANKS 44   10
    v p" she cannot read or write, la moon. . . . . 504 50 POEMS 18   6
    all them kings you read about and on him . . . . 568 1 X 1 28   13

	PAGE	TITLE	LINE
READ (CONTINUED)			
/ / for prodigal read generous --for youth read	689	95 POEMS 17	1
read generous --for youth read age-- read for sheer	689	95 POEMS 17	2
--for youth read age-- read for sheer wonder mere	689	95 POEMS 17	3
turn the page) contentment read for ecstasy --for poem . . .	689	95 POEMS 17	5
READING			
fat man in bluishsuspenders half-reading the Evening	166	& SON ACTU 15	6
READS			
b pink suspenders c reads Atlantis x and y	200	XLI PORTRAIT 8	8
READY			
madam star taps taps. "ready girls". the unspontaneous . . .	108	& PORTRAIT 4	4
ig" (tent-sky wholly wallendas) ready were all erect your . .	605	{CHAIRE} 7	11
+READY			
FOR CONTEXT, SEE	474	NEW POEMS 12	13
REAL			
with i have a real pocket in it and	69	T&C POST IMPR 6	41
sometimes people are in real: imagine somewhere real flowers,	338	VIVA 29	6
in real: imagine somewhere real flowers, but I can't	338	VIVA 29	7
but I can't imagine real flowers for if I	338	VIVA 29	8
would somehow not Be real" (so he smiles smiling)	338	VIVA 29	10
will not everywhere be real to you in a	338	VIVA 29	13
n y in a real hot spell with o	476	NEW POEMS 14	3
grow more than all real, all imagining; and we	582	1 X 1 42	9
dead nor alive (in real the rain) / /	640	{CHAIRE} 42	16
don't mean any thing real Ly what ; or	701	95 POEMS 29	17
the departure of everything real is the arrival of	720	95 POEMS 48	10
REALITIES			
/ / / / SONNETS--REALITIES the Cambridge ladies who	70	T&C SON REAL 1	T
/ / / / SONNETS--REALITIES O It's Nice To	130	& SON REAL 1	T
REALITY			
beyond obey or command, reality or un-) proudly depths . . .	574	1 X 1 34	8
to look --from the reality of all nothing will	649	{CHAIRE} 51	4
wholly) dearest more than reality of more than dream-- . . .	659	{CHAIRE} 61	8
REALIZE			
you don't seem to realize i can't make it	638	{CHAIRE} 40	7
REALLY			
pretend you don't but really you do see and	126	& SEVEN POEMS 5	16
/ whereas by dark really released, the modern flame	146	& SON REAL 17	1
were not enough (not really enough pulled one before	154	& SON ACTU 3	6
it odd of you really to lie a sharp	172	& SON ACTU 21	10
/ / / it really must be Nice, never	242	IS 5 ONE 13	1
and to never, never really wonder i mean about	242	IS 5 ONE 13	16
had first of all really made quite a mistake	262	IS 5 ONE 32	5
the rail before the really train after all arrived.	263	IS 5 ONE 32	63
with eyes which are really petals and see nothing	352	VIVA 43	10
face of a poet really which is a flower	352	VIVA 43	11
dream (and between houses, really a kind of mouse)	353	VIVA 44	9
as you see and really i have no servants.	365	VIVA 56	5
and fearlessly obscene but really clean get what I	407	NO THANKS 24	7
against anything (because nothing really exists / / /	470	NEW POEMS 8	20
mrs are sort of really really kind of afraid	501	50 POEMS 15	22
are sort of really really kind of afraid of)	501	50 POEMS 15	23
creation up all sky (really unreal world, will you	558	1 X 1 18	14
small middling tall bigger really the biggest and all	569	1 X 1 29	17
if the stunt was really a dream-- here's, wherever	605	{CHAIRE} 7	14
are people nimbler than Really go whirling into gaily	630	{CHAIRE} 32	2
f cringewiltdroolery i mean really th underscream of sudde .	646	{CHAIRE} 48	8
as if he were really her & she but)	680	95 POEMS 8	17
were blossoming) roses which really are dreams of roses-- . .	748	95 POEMS 76	10
+REALLY			
FOR CONTEXT, SEE	331	VIVA 22	3
FOR CONTEXT, SEE	331	VIVA 22	8
FOR CONTEXT, SEE	400	NO THANKS 17	4
FOR CONTEXT, SEE	400	NO THANKS 17	7
FOR CONTEXT, SEE	400	NO THANKS 17	13
FOR CONTEXT, SEE	400	NO THANKS 17	18
FOR CONTEXT, SEE	701	95 POEMS 29	17

		PAGE	TITLE	LINE

REALLY'S
its still ness which really's herself (and to think . . . . . 827 73 POEMS 55   10

REALM
mysteries contradict a deathful realm of fact --by their . . 763 95 POEMS 90   28

REALMS
/ / in heavenly realms of hellas dwelt two . . . . 799 73 POEMS 27   1
savage yell from shining realms of regions dark) laugh . . . 799 73 POEMS 27   27
tree smiling stand (all realms of where and when . . . . . 832 73 POEMS 60   6

REALNESS
strike into form (actually) realness kill (make strangely) . 422 NO THANKS 39   7
let others give and realness bring-- ask the always . . . . . 454 NO THANKS 69   1

REAM
my fear: more neatly ream this pith of darkness: . . . . . . 139 & SON REAL 10   7

REAP
garden. Time shall surely reap and on Death's blade . . . . . 208 XLI SONNETS 4   9

REAPED
sowed their isn't they reaped their same sun moon . . . . . . 515 50 POEMS 29   7
summer autumn winter spring reaped their sowing and went . . 515 50 POEMS 29   35

REAPER
the life of the reaper and the sower; my . . . . 749 95 POEMS 77   5

REAPPEAR
with his bell to reappear a moon / / . . . . 624 {CHAIRE} 26   24

+REAPPEAR
FOR CONTEXT, SEE . . . . 349 VIVA 40   7

REARED
by a fat colour reared itself against the sky . . . . 283 IS 5 THREE 7   19

REARING
glance my spirit shies rearing (as in the miracle . . . . . 18 T&C PUELLA MEA   46

+REARRANGINGLY
FOR CONTEXT, SEE . . . . 396 NO THANKS 13   15

REASON
littleliverpill-hearted-Nujolneeding-There's-A-Reason . . . . 231 IS 5 ONE 3   47
distinctly to confute my reason with the deep caress . . . . 19 T&C PUELLA MEA   98
very minuteness doth abuse reason, why then the artificer . . 22 T&C PUELLA MEA   219
who--touches--the hills without any reason (i have spoken . . 91 & POST IMPR 3   5
suppose these without any reason and otherwise roses and . . 91 & POST IMPR 3   15
this midnight) for no reason feel deeply completely conscious 92 & POST IMPR 4   10
pretend to know the reason any more than.) But . . . . 282 IS 5 THREE 6   4
painting (for its own reason) in your lips slenderly . . . . 291 IS 5 FOUR 8   22
i like, for the reason that i hate people . . . . 295 IS 5 FOUR 12   22
love, love and the reason that i laugh and . . . . 295 IS 5 FOUR 12   24
oh love and the reason that i do not . . . . 295 IS 5 FOUR 12   24
/ / / / reason let others give and . . . . 454 NO THANKS 69   1
kiss; or, sold the reason, they undream a dream) . . . . . . 556 1 X 1 16   8
a deeper season than reason; my sweet one (and . . . . 578 1 X 1 38   10
is more true than reason will deceive (more secret . . . . . 592 1 X 1 52   1
is no appeal from reason" (freud) --you pays your . . . . . . 636 {CHAIRE} 38   13
& that (for no reason at all) reminds me . . . . 699 95 POEMS 27   9
man ner the only reason every wo man should . . . . 700 95 POEMS 28   4
quell divine generosity, thus reason vanquished instinct and 799 73 POEMS 27   34

REASONED
whose ways are neither reasoned nor unreasoned, his wisdom . 683 95 POEMS 11   5

+REASONED
FOR CONTEXT, SEE . . . . 255 IS 5 ONE 26   1

REASONS
--toss in sobs and reasons threats and smiles name . . . . . 804 73 POEMS 32   6

REASSURINGLY
tidiyum, are very tidiyum reassuringly similar, they all have 274 IS 5 TWO 9   10

REBIRTH
before dying demands not rebirth of such than hungrily . . . 402 NO THANKS 19   1

RECALL
all hands (you may recall) being lost including captain . . . 494 50 POEMS 8   7
forget more thinner than recall more seldom than a . . . . . 530 50 POEMS 42   2

RECALLS
pie is traffic this recalls hat gestures bud plumptumbling . 330 VIVA 21   6

RECEDES
a mystery? ...the cathedral recedes into weather without . . 279 IS 5 THREE 3   24

		PAGE	TITLE	LINE

RECEIVE
if that he come receive him as your lover . . . . 42 T&C AMORES 6 18
bloated calves i would receive the answer more or . . . . . . 229 IS 5 ONE FRAN 7
Thule Of Plumbing shall receive the philophilic name S.S. . . . 334 VIVA 25 3
in a single wish, receive all i am and . . . . 651 (CHAIRE) 53 3
and the courage to receive time's mightiest dream / . . . . . 675 95 POEMS 3 14
my hope's own hope, receive (undaunted guest of dark . . . . 821 73 POEMS 49 10
RECEIVED
god of everlasting war received the shuddering sacrament of . 7 T&C EPITHALAM 155
of their country's love received my dears the order . . . . . 266 IS 5 TWO 1 27
which descending are suddenly received) or by doomful . . . . 299 IS 5 FOUR 16 7
RECEIVING
Memory, of that loveliness receiving the image my proud . . . 207 XLI SONNETS 3 12
RECENT
They have stolen into recent lands the flower with . . . . . 165 & SON ACTU 14 14
aunt lucy during the recent war could and what . . . . 276 IS 5 TWO 10 2
fearingly and tenderly a recent footprint in the sand . . . . 344 VIVA 35 15
speaking concession at the recent world's fair was the . . . 425 NO THANKS 42 15
joy and grief these recent memories of future dream . . . . . 502 50 POEMS 16 10
RECENTLY
profuse scratchings in a recently discovered cave, the . . . 197 XLI PORTRAIT 5 19
others stroke with brushes recently employed anent this muddy 339 VIVA 30 11
RECEPTIVE
we also blandly into receptive earth, O let us . . . . 41 T&C AMORES 5 13
RECIPE
Pills for Ills (a recipe against Laughing Virginity Death) . 359 VIVA 50 9
RECITE
and twilights Deepen her, Recite upon her flesh the . . . . . 65 T&C POST IMPR 2 12
RECKLESS
first earth , the reckless oral darkness raging with . . . . 67 T&C POST IMPR 4 4
into Thus, Around the reckless magic of your mouth) . . . . . 83 T&C SON ACTU 2 8
RECKLESSLY
a transparent blouse even recklessly juggles the jouncing . . 341 VIVA 32 19
RECKON
your walls will not reckon how strangely my life . . . . . . 292 IS 5 FOUR 9 5
RECKONED
millionary wherewhens distant, as reckoned by the unimmortal 721 95 POEMS 49 6
RECKONING
your sorrow a certain reckoning demands... marvelling And . . 374 VIVA 65 3
RECKTIE
gentlemen ppoyds even whose recktie are covered by lloyd's . 492 50 POEMS 6 15
RECLINES
is very amorous he reclines upon the couch of . . . . 33 T&C ORIENTALE 6 54
RECOGNISED
fundamental respect the well recognised regime of childhood . 261 IS 5 ONE 31 9
RECOGNIZE
everywhere your selves himself recognize) / / / / . . . . . . 450 NO THANKS 65 18
+RECOIL
FOR CONTEXT, SEE . . . . 388 NO THANKS 5 17
RECOILED
big whose warmest heart recoiled at war: a conscientious . . 339 VIVA 30 2
RECOLLECT
said "then as i recollect her girlhood was by . . . . 57 T&C PORTRAIT 5 29
RECORD
play, b starts armenian record pho nographisrunn ingd o . . . 200 XLI PORTRAIT 8 24
RECORDS
a Victor Victrola and records while he lived presented . . . 239 IS 5 ONE 10 28
+RECTOR'S
FOR CONTEXT, SEE . . . . 227 IS 5 ONE GERT 15
RECTUM
the firstclassprivates on his rectum wickedly to tease by . . 339 VIVA 30 28
+RECTUMS
FOR CONTEXT, SEE . . . . 492 50 POEMS 6 15
RED
air, for now the red leaps in the maple's . . . . 4 T&C EPITHALAM 61
swift sweet deer the red rare deer. Four red . . . . 14 T&C SONGS 4 8
red rare deer. Four red roebuck at a white . . . . 14 T&C SONGS 4 9
i rode down the red horse shrieking from splintering . . . . 30 T&C ORIENTALE 4 11

RED (CONTINUED)
    slowly return upon the red elected lips scaleless visions) .   36 T&C AMORES 1   31
    / / / between nose-red gross walls sprawling with . . . . . .   55 T&C PORTRAIT 3   1
    her a mothermonster with red grumbling face cluttered in . .   56 T&C PORTRAIT 4   6
    i shove my round red hat back on my . . . .   69 T&C POST IMPR 6   34
    he has a little red coat with i have . . . .   69 T&C POST IMPR 6   41
    do our mouths something red, something tall / / . . . .   160 & SON ACTU 9   17
    flinger of fire beyond red rivers of fair perpetual . . . . .   185 XLI SONGS 7   5
    crumpled collapses. exhaling a red soul into the dark . . . .   188 XLI SONGS 10   11
    the balls the chains red and gold the fluffy . . . .   192 XLI CHANSONS 2   16
    it were a thunderbolt red- hot peeling off huge . . . .   194 XLI PORTRAIT 2   23
    married and hands get red washing things and dishes) . . . .   242 IS 5 ONE 13   15
    / / Among these red pieces of day (against . . . .   278 IS 5 THREE 2   3
    dog that's.... now it's red a big red dog . . . .   303 IS 5 FIVE 2   12
    it's red a big red dog that may be . . . .   303 IS 5 FIVE 2   13
    kids hop point at red blue yellow violet white . . . .   437 NO THANKS 53   14
    / / / / red-rag and pink-flag blackshirt and . . . .   497 50 POEMS 11   1
    a room's) one is red and (six are in) . . . .   507 50 POEMS 21   13
    they're gravensteins) all as red as to lose and . . . . . .   543 1 X 1 3   5
    over this) wall the red and the round (they're . . . . . .   543 1 X 1 3   27
    should sit (holding a red candle over his head . . . .   631 (CHAIRE) 33   2
    singing out of a red book) on a proud . . . .   631 (CHAIRE) 33   3
    all (and his tail's red christmas bow) --and if, ...   631 (CHAIRE) 33   6
    although it were as red as terror and as . . . .   649 (CHAIRE) 51   11
    a riddle for you red says it aint his . . . .   707 95 POEMS 35   19
    both knees" green turns red (the roar of traffic . . . . . .   800 73 POEMS 28   17
    "what happened" as everywhere red goes green --groping blank   800 73 POEMS 28   22
+RED
    FOR CONTEXT, SEE . . . .   228 IS 5 ONE MARJ   2
    FOR CONTEXT, SEE . . . .   352 VIVA 43   4
RED-RAG
    / / / / red-rag and pink-flag blackshirt and . . . .   497 50 POEMS 11   1
REDBLOODED
    literature we want something redblooded lousy with pure . . .   407 NO THANKS 24   3
REDDISH
    the afternoon. rapidly a reddish ant travels my fifth . . . .   281 IS 5 THREE 5   11
REDIRE
    Of America unde negant redire quemquam supp sedly thr . . . .   392 NO THANKS 9   19
REDOLENT
    sable robe from her redolent shoulders, Thou from whose . . .   206 XLI SONNETS 2   5
REDSKIN
    / when your honest redskin toma hawked and scalped . . . . .   643 (CHAIRE) 45   1
REDSTONE
    man who at her redstone mouth renews his childhood . . . . .   57 T&C PORTRAIT 5   11
REE
    tattle did-he-does-she) & the ree ray rye roh rowster . . . .   773 73 POEMS 1   18
REEKING
    mystery, with gaunt limbs reeking of the whispered deep, . .   7 T&C EPITHALAM   158
    redblooded lousy with pure reeking with stark and fearlessly   407 NO THANKS 24   5
    hugely doom treasures of reeking innocence are born. Then, .   843 73 POEMS 71   8
REEL
    out of eakspeasies per (reel) hapsingly proregress . . . . .   330 VIVA 21   1
    bangbells (yawnchurches suck people) reel (dark- ly) whirling 444 NO THANKS 59   14
REELING
    is thickening dizzily is reeling gently the street and . . .   69 T&C POST IMPR 6   24
+REELING
    FOR CONTEXT, SEE . . . .   423 NO THANKS 40   14
REELS
    thunder? ours (over you reels and me a moon; . . . .   639 (CHAIRE) 41   3
REENTER
    slightly smiling, gradually shall reenter the singular . . .   370 VIVA 61   19
REFER
    call exactly extraordinary. We refer, of course, to my . . .   263 IS 5 ONE 32   36
    never left (and i refer to thinking) rests upon . . . . . .   807 73 POEMS 35   5
REFERS
    youse knows wot i refers ter Satter Nailyuh (comes . . . . .   237 IS 5 ONE 8   15
REFINED
    i mean are not refined they go with girls . . . .   427 NO THANKS 44   1

		PAGE	TITLE	LINE
REFINED (CONTINUED)				
i mean are not refined they come with girls		427	NO THANKS 44	8
i mean are not refined they cannot chat of		427	NO THANKS 44	13
i mean are not refined they shake the mountains		427	NO THANKS 44	19
REFLECTING				
trees, here and here reflecting sunlight (everywhere sunlight		283	IS 5 THREE 7	12
REFLECTION				
a fly and his reflection walking upon a mirror		335	VIVA 26	4
REFLECTIONS				
were the not unhurried reflections to which my organ		263	IS 5 ONE 32	32
REFLEX				
life being just a Reflex you know since Everything		315	VIVA 7	7
REFRAIN				
winks). and almost i refrain from jumbling her flesh		131	& SON REAL 2	6
thy remembrance surprises with refrain of unreasoning summer		184	XLI SONGS 6	4
REFUGE				
Whom shall time no refuge keep though all the		377	VIVA 68	13
REFUSE				
intently it refuses. to refuse; just, look) ing dead		387	NO THANKS 4	11
REFUSED				
am newspaper guy who refused to shake hands with		324	VIVA 16	10
one (which she politely refused) set out gaily for		326	VIVA 18	19
REFUSES				
g (ing intently it refuses. to refuse; just, look)		387	NO THANKS 4	10
REFUTED				
thirtytwo seconds centrifugally is refuted by these (. . . .		341	VIVA 32	6
of your sweet innocence refuted) clumsy some dull cowardice .		669	(CHAIRE) 71	11
REGARD				
living wage-- when thorns regard their roses with alarm . . .		620	(CHAIRE) 22	3
mean observe his these regard his that (sh) who		645	(CHAIRE) 47	3
REGIME				
respect the well recognised regime of childhood is reversed .		261	IS 5 ONE 31	9
REGIONS				
from shining realms of regions dark) laugh long at		799	73 POEMS 27	27
+REGRESS				
FOR CONTEXT, SEE		330	VIVA 21	2
REGRESSED				
policeman. Meanwhile the tea regressed. Kipling again H.G. .		263	IS 5 ONE 32	42
REGULAR				
kiss but Jimmie lived regular. stewed three times a		149	& SON REAL 20	11
loathing for (dull all regular righteous comfortable)		677	95 POEMS 5	7
REINCARNATE				
Thou from whose feet reincarnate song suddenly leaping . . .		206	XLI SONNETS 2	7
REINED				
arched with agony i reined them in tottering before		30	T&C ORIENTALE 4	37
REINTEGRATE				
toward twilight will dissolve reintegrate beckon through me,		379	VIVA 70	12
REINTEGRATING				
of one: which halves reintegrating, shall occur no death . .		556	1 X 1 16	2
REJ				
pitchfork (breathing) lovers like rej and lena smile (while .		754	95 POEMS 82	9
REJOICE				
in the beginning it (rejoice) was and ever shall		425	NO THANKS 42	10
wrists of twilight would rejoice keen as midsummer's keen . .		520	50 POEMS 34	24
(her face his dreams rejoice rejoice) --opens the sun: . . .		533	50 POEMS 45	12
face his dreams rejoice rejoice) --opens the sun: who		533	50 POEMS 45	12
REJOINED				
("or un-" the just rejoined / / / /		806	73 POEMS 34	2
REKTUZ				
like up ter yknow, Rektuz, Toysday nite; where uh		227	IS 5 ONE GERT	15
+RELATES				
FOR CONTEXT, SEE		321	VIVA 13	5
RELATIVE				
know since Everything is Relative or to sum it		315	VIVA 7	8
RELATIVELY				
wistfulLy dead are not relatively speaking uncultured (who .		391	NO THANKS 8	18
RELATIVES				
much kissed, by loving relatives well fed, and fully		273	IS 5 TWO 8	21

632

RELAX
    worry) halt stop forget relax wait (little child who . . . . 393 NO THANKS 10   5
RELAXING
    of these antiquities--antiquities--relaxing hurries . . . . . 116 & PORTRAIT 9   14
    / / Do. omful relaxing -ly) i downrise outwrithein- . . . . . 449 NO THANKS 64   3
RELEASE
    one moving cadence may release the fragrance of a . . . . . . 842 73 POEMS 70   6
RELEASED
    whereas by dark really released, the modern flame of . . . . 146 & SON REAL 17   1
    words drizzle untidily from released cheeks "I'll tell duh . 226 IS 5 ONE MAME   9
    yes, crumbles hand (ful released conarefetti) ev eryflitter, 265 IS 5 ONE 34   2
    thrill mechanically packed and released for all this very . . 337 VIVA 28   10
    strive; and being finally released flee one another like . . 799 73 POEMS 27   30
RELEASING
    smiled to each other, releasing lay, watching (sprawling, in 283 IS 5 THREE 7   21
+RELIGION
    FOR CONTEXT, SEE . . . . 325 VIVA 17   11
RELIGIONS
    . how often have religions taken thee upon their . . . . . . 46 T&C LA GUERRE 2 14
RELIGIOUS
    heaven and all the religious fuss infinity pleased our . . . 466 NEW POEMS 4   14
+RELIGIOUS
    FOR CONTEXT, SEE . . . . 262 IS 5 ONE 32   24
REMAIN
    "was and will always remain: who i am. Look . . . . 626 {CHAIRE} 28   6
    with you, only i remain; a shadow phantom effigy . . . . . . 812 73 POEMS 40   2
REMAINED
    aware notice what hath remained --the stone cringes clinging 260 IS 5 ONE 30   3
REMAKING
    eyes) re -new- ing remaking what other -wise we . . . . 660 {CHAIRE} 62   12
REMARK
    / / / I remark this beach has been . . . . 94 & POST IMPR 6   1
    of men should you remark the walls have been . . . . 198 XLI PORTRAIT 6 26
    utter their extant smile.... remark a few deleted of . . . . 260 IS 5 ONE 30   7
    and mightily fatally i remark how through deep lifted . . . . 434 NO THANKS 51   30
REMARKABLE
    quick fingers and a remarkable tail which is allbyitself . . 69 T&C POST IMPR 6 40
    minute moon is a remarkable splinter in the quick . . . . . . 82 T&C SON ACTU 1   5
+REMARKABLE
    FOR CONTEXT, SEE . . . . 421 NO THANKS 38   21
REMARKABLY
    question mark is a remarkably charming person personally they 246 IS 5 ONE 17   5
    voice-- beyond these elements remarkably nothing is.... . . . 291 IS 5 FOUR 8   17
    starting "dearest we" unsigned: remarkably brief but covering 504 50 POEMS 18   2
REMARKED
    mind Joe agreeably cheerfully remarked when surrounded by fat 241 IS 5 ONE 12   2
    / / / / remarked Robinson Jefferson to Injustice . . . . . . 321 VIVA 13   1
    my pensive companion dimly remarked some- thing about . . . . 326 VIVA 18   31
REMARKING
    drink, or sometimes two remarking cries of paklavah meeah. . 217 XLI SONNETS 13 12
REMEMBER
    to come you shall remember of this night amazing . . . . . . 36 T&C AMORES 1   22
    / goodby Betty, don't remember me pencil your eyes . . . . . 71 T&C SON REAL 2   1
    and everything and i remember we all cried like . . . . 239 IS 5 ONE 10   32
    let us now passionately remember how-- braving the worst, . . 266 IS 5 TWO 1   17
    being (don't forget to remember) Curved (and that reminds . . 315 VIVA 7   1
    seem firm for you: remember (as those pearls more . . . . . . 372 VIVA 63   9
    a day as must remember he who watched unhands . . . . 376 VIVA 67   2
    very) closely than Nothing, remember love by frequent anguish 453 NO THANKS 68   8
    so wise the people remember being born) when and . . . . . . 505 50 POEMS 19   16
    apt to forget to remember with up so floating . . . . 515 50 POEMS 29   23
    / / this (let's remember) day died again and . . . . 599 {CHAIRE} 1   1
    a human being --let's remember that / / / . . . . 607 {CHAIRE} 9   16
    smile. Eyes. & we remember: yes; we played with . . . . 612 {CHAIRE} 14   8
    in the middle of remember with his rotten old . . . . 642 {CHAIRE} 44   5
    so sweetly she couldn't remember her troubles, and milly . . 682 95 POEMS 10   4
    doom is to grow (remember this my sweet) not . . . . 686 95 POEMS 14   13
    to grow) forgetting why, remember how in time of . . . . . . 688 95 POEMS 16   3

		PAGE	TITLE	LINE

REMEMBER (CONTINUED)
waking is to dream, remember so (forgetting seem) in . . . . 688 95 POEMS 16   6
with paradise) forgetting if, remember yes in time of . . . . 688 95 POEMS 16   9
whatever mind may comprehend, remember seek (forgetting find) 688 95 POEMS 16   12
us free) forgetting me, remember me / / / . . . . 688 95 POEMS 16   15
+REMEMBER
FOR CONTEXT, SEE . . . . 797 73 POEMS 25   14
REMEMBERED
immediate like some newly remembered dream-- flaming a coolly 601 (CHAIRE) 3   12
REMEMBERING
three teeth leak smoke: remembering, two pink big lips . . . 149 & SON REAL 20   15
of Professor Royce rolls remembering that it has for . . . . 232 IS 5 ONE 3   14
and your arms tremble remembering something squirming fragile 279 IS 5 THREE 3   22
not touch) deep things; remembering ever so tinily these, . . 294 IS 5 FOUR 11   7
between his ghost-lips gradually) remembering badly, softly . 300 IS 5 FOUR 17   22
everything would be; even remembering the way who looked . . 338 VIVA 29   19
i say "won't you" (remembering) knowing that you are . . . . 353 VIVA 44   24
to whom i cry, remembering her face, i have . . . . 360 VIVA 51   34
beyond night shall go) remembering only dare (Wholly consider 362 VIVA 53   3
every least each most remembering H highest fly only . . . . 390 NO THANKS 7   7
is all floatful and remembering / / / / . . . . 516 50 POEMS 30   18
in dark least ourselves remembering love only rides his . . . 556 1 X 1 16   13
+REMEMBERING
FOR CONTEXT, SEE . . . . 534 50 POEMS 46   10
FOR CONTEXT, SEE . . . . 823 73 POEMS 51   6
REMEMBERINGLY
hither myself struts unremembered (rememberingly with in both 299 IS 5 FOUR 16   9
REMEMBERS
exposure whose electric solidity remembers some accurately . 197 XLI PORTRAIT 5   18
dowNdown (and only where remembers look, this was of . . . . 371 VIVA 62   10
fur answers eats moves remembers is afraid) each hates . . . 394 NO THANKS 11   8
which the rightest man remembers there is such a . . . . . . 685 95 POEMS 13   7
come go rain snow) remembers / / / / . . . . 693 95 POEMS 21   21
REMEMBRANCE
the poem of thy remembrance surprises with refrain of . . . . 184 XLI SONGS 6   3
of such a deathlessness) remembrance might no patient mind . 420 NO THANKS 37   7
REMIND
c'est l'heure exquise) i remind Me of HerThe delicate-swill . 94 & POST IMPR 6   20
thickly smooth thighs thinkingly) remind me of Woman and . . 95 & POST IMPR 7   17
+REMIND
FOR CONTEXT, SEE . . . . 695 95 POEMS 23   7
REMINDED
why something about me reminded him of ourselves) as . . . . 355 VIVA 46   20
REMINDING
the chosen flowers of reminding / / / / . . . . 58 T&C PORTRAIT 6   27
comes the only man reminding with his bell to . . . . 624 (CHAIRE) 26   3
our sun is gone reminding with his bell to . . . . 624 (CHAIRE) 26   23
REMINDS
remember) Curved (and that reminds me who said o . . . . . . 315 VIVA 7   2
end of doubleyou 4th) reminds me in spite of . . . . 699 95 POEMS 27   6
no reason at all) reminds me the cheerfulest goddamned . . . 699 95 POEMS 27   10
REMINISCENCE
gentle window like a reminiscence partaken softly at whose . 58 T&C PORTRAIT 6   23
+REMUNERATIVENESS
FOR CONTEXT, SEE . . . . 236 IS 5 ONE 7   16
RENDER
for international measures that render hell rational --i . . 802 73 POEMS 30   31
RENDERING
colour of its countries, rendering death and forever with . . 366 VIVA 57   16
RENEWAL
responding ways cloaked with renewal my body turns toward . . 184 XLI SONGS 6   7
RENEWED
wanders imminently across the renewed world" to me said . . . 91 & POST IMPR 3   18
+RENEWING
FOR CONTEXT, SEE . . . . 660 (CHAIRE) 62   10
RENEWS
hour by hour wholly renews her pale flesh with . . . . 3 T&C EPITHALAM   7
at her redstone mouth renews his childhood and He . . . . . . 57 T&C PORTRAIT 5   11

RENOWN
   whose slendering sweetness touched renown) suddenly . . . . . 414 NO THANKS 31   4
RENOWNED
   of (sh) the world renowned investigator of paper . . . . . . 326 VIVA 18   6
RENT
   will being pay the rent of seem and genius . . . . 511 50 POEMS 25   5
RENT'S
   you know the dam rent's going to and everything . . . . . . 242 IS 5 ONE 13   19
REOCCURS
   the deathlessness who's beauty: reoccurs so magically, . . . 818 73 POEMS 46   6
REPAIRS
   trees hither my soul repairs herself with prisms of . . . . . 180 XLI SONGS 2   10
REPAPERED
   the walls have been repapered he will nod like . . . . 198 XLI PORTRAIT 6   26
REPAPERING
   present (l'on parle de repapering; i don't think so. . . . . 312 VIVA 4   23
REPASS
   pass and unprecisely to repass where flesh is heiry . . . . . 401 NO THANKS 18   12
REPAYING
   two. Let liars wilt, repaying life they're loaned; we . . . . 556 1 X 1 16   11
REPEAT
   fierce laziness tried to repeat a trick of syncopation . . . 135 & SON REAL 6   9
   excuse me if i repeat himself: these, or nearly . . . . 263 IS 5 ONE 32   59
   knees) does almost ceaselessly repeat "there is some shit . . 339 VIVA 30   32
+REPEAT
   FOR CONTEXT, SEE . . . . 309 VIVA 1   32
REPEATS
   the language of leaves repeats eventual perfection while east 184 XLI SONGS 6   12
REPLIED
   head) squads right impatiently replied two billion pubic lice 473 NEW POEMS 11   4
   a word this stranger replied-- but as one whole . . . . 800 73 POEMS 28   13
   who had died , replied / / / / . . . . 828 73 POEMS 56   8
REPLIES
   "thou must!" and who replies "I can!" --yon clean . . . . . . 273 IS 5 TWO 8   5
   Doancare Eye And How replies the upsquirtingly careens the . 330 VIVA 21   9
   for o squirting we're replies (at which now O . . . . 343 VIVA 34   9
   (hearing not a which) replies in haste I must . . . . 570 1 X 1 30   3
REPOS
   think, her charms en repos.... a fattish leg leaks . . . . . 143 & SON REAL 14   8
REQUIESCAT
   the alive west begin requiescat this six feet of . . . . . . 277 IS 5 THREE 1   5
   indolent colourless forgets) time Requiescat. carry carefully 277 IS 5 THREE 1   21
RERUM
   each one his optima rerum first having taken care . . . . . 261 IS 5 ONE 31   11
RESCUE
   into a whatses to rescue miss nobody's probably handbag) . . 475 NEW POEMS 13   21
RESCUING
   burn, to undertake Medea's rescuing eyes; nor he when . . . . 18 T&C PUELLA MEA 72
RESEMBLE
   you whom certain flowers resemble but trembling (cowards . . 293 IS 5 FOUR 10   5
   person and this imitation resemble, descends into the earth . 300 IS 5 FOUR 17   18
RESEMBLES
   sun and the moon) resembles something that has not . . . . . 360 VIVA 51   24
   do or Silently Flowers resembles beauty less than our . . . . 363 VIVA 54   11
RESHARPENED
   are Not To Be Resharpened. (Case in point if . . . . 230 IS 5 ONE 2   23
RESIST
   meaning monuments and dolls resist Them Greediest Paws of . . 260 IS 5 ONE 30   10
RESISTLESS
   indestructible occult supersnare of resistless metal: and . . 799 73 POEMS 27   19
RESOLVED
   correct fingers of April resolved into a clutter of . . . . . 47 T&C IMPRESS 1   4
RESPECT
   how in this fundamental respect the well recognised regime . 261 IS 5 ONE 31   8
RESPECTER
   the Rain is no respecter of persons the snow . . . . 328 VIVA 19   21
RESPECTS
   heights of prowst but respects artists if they are . . . . . 499 50 POEMS 13   11

RESPIRE
    these frail ladies dangerously respire: impeccable girls in . 85 T&C SON ACTU 4   14
RESPONDING
    unreasoning summer that by responding ways cloaked with . . . 184 XLI SONGS 6   6
RESPONDS
    tread (and thereto perfectly responds) of all things . . . . 19 T&C PUELLA MEA 126
    God unto him gave) responds, without getting annoyed "I . . . 339 VIVA 30   18
RESPONSE
    omit one kelly in response to howjedooze the candidate's . . 259 IS 5 ONE 29   20
REST
    moment whiter than the rest --turning from the tremendous . . 78 T&C SON UNRE 3   12
    life and will my rest to these children building . . . . . . 390 NO THANKS 7   13
    nothing may move may rest --you bring (out of . . . . 575 1 X 1 35   5
    move in your (and rest, my love) honour / . . . . 575 1 X 1 35   41
RESTAURANT
    person, arising from a restaurant, looks breathes or moves . 300 IS 5 FOUR 17   3
RESTROLL
    these more than eyes restroll and stroll some never . . . . . 843 73 POEMS 71   3
RESTS
    motheaten old manwhose Beard rests. onthetopwhose silly, Hand 101 & POST IMPR 11   47
    i refer to thinking) rests upon a dismal misconception; . . . 807 73 POEMS 35   5
RESUME
    dear, that we may resume impact with the inutile . . . . . . 289 IS 5 FOUR 6   6
RESUMING
    all truths of wing resuming) selves, into infinite tomorrow . 659 (CHAIRE) 61   3
RESURRECTION
    glory and death and resurrection: over my sleeping self . . . 749 95 POEMS 77   10
+RESWALLOWING
    FOR CONTEXT, SEE . . . . 629 (CHAIRE) 31   17
RETCHINGS
    by the al- ways retchings of a worthless lamp. . . . . 96 & POST IMPR 8   26
RETIRE
    smites truly to Beautifully retire through its english the . 311 VIVA 3   4
RETIRED
    particularly belonging to a retired general) sixteen years of 341 VIVA 32   9
RETURN
    memories shall rise, slowly return upon the red elected . . . 36 T&C AMORES 1   30
    emancipated evening had in return for consciousness endowed . 258 IS 5 ONE 28   7
    Miss Gay during our return voyage, my pensive companion . . . 326 VIVA 18   31
    for love beginning means return seas who could sing . . . . . 526 50 POEMS 38   5
    into gaily white thousands return by millions and dreaming . 630 (CHAIRE) 32   4
    darkness of my soul's return --you are my sun, ... 810 73 POEMS 38   13
+RETURN
    FOR CONTEXT, SEE . . . . 536 50 POEMS 48   15
RETURNED
    us all; stories told returned gather the Again: who . . . . . 89 & POST IMPR 1   7
+RETURNEST
    FOR CONTEXT, SEE . . . . 409 NO THANKS 26   3
RETURNING
    till their and your returning, spends the forever of . . . . 812 73 POEMS 40   5
RETURNS
    of hands and she returns into hands and is . . . . 38 T&C AMORES 3   12
    the Forwardflung backwardSpinning hoop returns fasterishly . 311 VIVA 3   5
    curving wherewhen till unwish returns on its unself. A . . . 554 1 X 1 14   8
REUSED
    having been used and reused to the mystical moment . . . . . 230 IS 5 ONE 2   21
REVE
    clerk somnour miller and reve and geoffrey and all) . . . . . 661 (CHAIRE) 63   10
REVEAL
    or than madness did reveal) deeper is life than . . . . . . 592 1 X 1 52   2
REVEALED
    daisies--by what rare unease revealed of teasingly . . . . . 5 T&C EPITHALAM   95
    of mingling robes musically revealed in rareness: let thy . . 10 T&C SONGS 1   41
    yon sunset's wintry glow revealed) this tall strong stalwart 254 IS 5 ONE 25   2
    matter; not by mind revealed (more than all dying . . . . . . 765 95 POEMS 91   6
+REVEALING
    FOR CONTEXT, SEE . . . . 445 NO THANKS 60   8

		PAGE	TITLE	LINE

REVENGE
    a native, who in revenge beats it insensible with . . . . . . 262 IS 5 ONE 32   23
REVERENTLY
    with every bough that reverently bent to touch the . . . . . 8 T&C OF NICOL   31
    you and i may reverently share the blessed eachness . . . . . 745 95 POEMS 73   10
REVERSE
    then somehow got into reverse she kicked what the . . . . . . 248 IS 5 ONE 19   11
REVERSED
    regime of childhood is reversed meantime in dreams let . . . 261 IS 5 ONE 31   9
REVIEWING
    cuffs saluted everywhere saluting reviewing processions of . 275 IS 5 TWO 9   37
+REVOLVE
    FOR CONTEXT, SEE . . . . 384 NO THANKS 2   28
REVOLVES
    rests. onthetopwhose silly, Hand revolves, per- fectly, . . . 101 & POST IMPR 11   47
REVOLVING
    whose seat is where revolving planets struggle to be . . . . 212 XLI SONNETS 8   11
+REVOLVINGLY
    FOR CONTEXT, SEE . . . . 96 & POST IMPR 8   5
RHYME
    is the fear of rhyme-- in life's very fragile . . . . 23 T&C PUELLA MEA   274
    beyond the mystery of rhyme / / / / . . . . 210 XLI SONNETS 6   15
    little instant, along with rhyme and with laughter O . . . . 293 IS 5 FOUR 10   11
    tosses hello whirling whose rhyme (spilling his rings) . . . 751 95 POEMS 79   5
RHYMES
    that certain ideas gestures rhymes, like Gillette Razor . . . 230 IS 5 ONE 2   20
RHYTHM
    lived brilliantly the enormous rhythm of absurdity. skin like 103 & POST IMPR 13   11
    "Pretty Baby" to numb rhythm before christ / / . . . . 106 & PORTRAIT 2   15
    the accurate demure ferocious rhythm of precise laziness. Eat 162 & SON ACTU 11   13
    only to mistranslate a rhythm in your hair, (your . . . . . . 291 IS 5 FOUR 8   11
    swift and invisibly living rhythm of your Heart possibly . . 300 IS 5 FOUR 17   8
RHYTHMIC
    couch of death thy rhythmic lover thou answerest them . . . . 46 T&C LA GUERRE 2 23
    girlish whore with busy rhythmic mouth and silly purple . . . 56 T&C PORTRAIT 4 14
RHYTHMS
    sharp mind and Matisse rhythms to juggle Kandinsky gold-fish 180 XLI SONGS 2   12
+RHYTHMS
    FOR CONTEXT, SEE . . . . 416 NO THANKS 33   15
RIANT
    mucous kiss of her riant belly's fooling bore --When . . . . 130 & SON REAL 1   2
RIBBON
    from which a singular ribbon of common sunset is . . . . . . 202 XLI PORTRAIT 9 50
    comes out like a ribbon lies flat on the . . . . 231 IS 5 ONE 3   55
RICH
    Death, Thee i call rich beyond wishing if this . . . . 13 T&C SONGS 3   17
    rain's face and the rich improbable hands of the . . . . . . 153 & SON ACTU 2   14
    digestible mill- ions whose rich slovenly obscene procession 202 XLI PORTRAIT 9 46
    the trivial stink of rich frail firm asinine life . . . . . . 220 XLI SONNETS 16 3
    in which distinct and rich portrait should be included, . . . 254 IS 5 ONE 25   7
    whorlclown of spreadnessed bE rich from-soft quits (now) ly . 342 VIVA 33   21
    begins-- not poor not rich (only aware) kind neither . . . . 564 1 X 1 24   4
    Boss (crying) jew wop rich poor (sing ing) He . . . . 618 {CHAIRE} 20   12
    winner (and beggars are rich but misers are poor) . . . . . . 769 95 POEMS 95   4
    blue if beggars are rich (and a robin will . . . . 769 95 POEMS 95   22
RICHES
    may appease what merely riches of our pretty world . . . . . 456 NO THANKS 71   5
RICHLY
    to her soul, hope richly scattered by the abundant . . . . . 5 T&C EPITHALAM   83
    exquisite flowers, whom hardens richly, darkness. On the . . 154 & SON ACTU 3   10
RICKETY
    a foetal fragrance to rickety unclosed blinds inslants . . . 144 & SON REAL 15   3
RID
    you are never wholly rid (and who does not . . . . 298 IS 5 FOUR 15   8
+RID
    FOR CONTEXT, SEE . . . . 547 1 X 1 7   8
RIDDLE
    and here is a riddle for you red says . . . . 707 95 POEMS 35   19

		PAGE	TITLE	LINE

RIDE
defunct who used to ride a watersmooth-silver stallion and . 60 T&C PORTRAIT 8 4
did he care to ride her? ....she exactly lay, ... 145 & SON REAL 16 12
(it was the first ride and believe i we . . . . 248 IS 5 ONE 19 25
RIDES
On dappled dawn forth rides the pungent sun with . . . . . 4 T&C EPITHALAM 65
ourselves remembering love only rides his year. All lose, . . 556 1 X 1 16 14
+RIDES
FOR CONTEXT, SEE . . . . 398 NO THANKS 15 21
RIDETH
the most frail. (Whoso rideth in the tale of . . . . 20 T&C PUELLA MEA 163
RIDICULOUS
woman is smooth and ridiculous a polite uproar of . . . . . . 68 T&C POST IMPR 5 13
an an- gle of ridiculous velocity commenting upon an . . . . 97 & POST IMPR 8 37
beasts coming with keen ridiculous silks coming with sharp . 112 & PORTRAIT 6 101
by lonely antics of ridiculous molecules) nakedest (aiming . 373 VIVA 64 5
absurd clouds cruise nobly ridiculous skies (the; mselve; s . 442 NO THANKS 57 13
RIDING
green went my love riding on a great horse . . . . 14 T&C SONGS 4 1
hip went my love riding riding the echo down . . . . 14 T&C SONGS 4 11
went my love riding riding the echo down into . . . . 14 T&C SONGS 4 12
belt went my love riding riding the mountain down . . . . . 14 T&C SONGS 4 21
went my love riding riding the mountain down into . . . . . 14 T&C SONGS 4 22
green went my love riding on a great horse . . . . 14 T&C SONGS 4 31
fragrance and i came riding upon a horse of . . . . 30 T&C ORIENTALE 4 9
singing and i came riding upon a scarlet sunset . . . . . . 30 T&C ORIENTALE 4 23
eyes and i came riding upon a thousand crimson . . . . . . 30 T&C ORIENTALE 4 35
sitting in a treetop riding on a greenest riding . . . . . 535 50 POEMS 47 5
riding on a greenest riding on a greener (o . . . . 535 50 POEMS 47 6
greener (o little i) riding on a leaf o . . . . 535 50 POEMS 47 8
honour corruption villainy holiness riding in fragrance of . 661 (CHAIRE) 63 2
wonder of blossoming yes riding) to him who died . . . . . 661 (CHAIRE) 63 4
now of forever come riding alive down while crylessly . . . 661 (CHAIRE) 63 12
almost white morethanPerson; who (riding through space to . 697 95 POEMS 25 20
fair ladies tall lovers riding are through the (with . . . 778 73 POEMS 6 2
come (brighter than prayers) riding through a Dream like . . 778 73 POEMS 6 15
RIED
like the steak all ried but eye certainly hate . . . . . . 405 NO THANKS 22 11
RIGGING
wind, and the whining rigging over us, i implore . . . . . 378 VIVA 69 2
RIGHT
forth into the dew: right wildly beat her heart . . . . . . 8 T&C OF NICOL 28
out ears dribbles soft right old feller belch the . . . . . 96 & POST IMPR 8 21
my sex sitting up- right on the stomach like . . . . 101 & POST IMPR 11 60
the quartzlike face. his right slapped the amusing big . . . 148 & SON REAL 19 4
woild; some noive all right. Aint much on looks . . . . . . 226 IS 5 ONE MAME 10
skyscrapers an safetyrazors sall right in its way kiddo . . . 237 IS 5 ONE 8 11
O. K.) i went right to it <> cranked . . . . 248 IS 5 ONE 19 9
nudg. ing (my lev-er Right- oh and her gears . . . . 248 IS 5 ONE 19 16
how nice she acted right up to the last . . . . 248 IS 5 ONE 19 26
with the bugs crawling right all up all everywhere . . . . . 272 IS 5 TWO 7 10
MERDE) having first put right sleuthfully aboard all . . . . 334 VIVA 25 5
had a little scare right in the middle of . . . . 401 NO THANKS 18 3
little finger is) what's right about the g.o. world . . . . . 411 NO THANKS 28 8
sell his head) squads right impatiently replied two billion . 473 NEW POEMS 11 4
for whenever men are right they are not young . . . . 481 NEW POEMS 19 8
truth can live with right and wrong or molehills . . . . . 511 50 POEMS 25 2
his anger was as right as rain his pity . . . . 520 50 POEMS 34 35
"this world's made 'bout right it's the people that . . . . 567 1 X 1 27 10
and i'll go strolling right through these each illimit . . . 600 (CHAIRE) 2 13
serpents bargain for the right to squirm and the . . . . . 620 (CHAIRE) 22 1
cut your thumb so right he sharpens wrong and . . . . 624 (CHAIRE) 26 16
/ love our so right is, all (each thing . . . . 666 (CHAIRE) 68 1
come ann" "she's coming right now in the rasberrypatch . . . 707 95 POEMS 35 23
and lisps "i'm busy right now" so rah-rah-rah democracy . . . 711 95 POEMS 39 24
Don't &) youth goes right on gr owing old . . . . 729 95 POEMS 57 18
creed is Might Makes Right --his royal warcry is . . . . . . 774 73 POEMS 2 11
joys turn woes and right goes wrong (dim worlds . . . . . . 776 73 POEMS 4 26

RIGHT (CONTINUED)
    (wonder mistrust) despair and right where soulless our (with 780 73 POEMS 8   5
    is (guess) yes you're right: my enemy . Love . . . . 793 73 POEMS 21   25
    could never quite tell right from wrong, took brother . . . . 799 73 POEMS 27   13
    / / / / "right here the other night . . . . 800 73 POEMS 28   1
    POEM (or "the divine right of majorities, that illegitimate . 803 73 POEMS 31   2
    offspring of the divine right of kings" Homer Lea) . . . . .   803 73 POEMS 31   4
    (now wrong's the only right since brave are cowards . . . . . 834 73 POEMS 62   21
+RIGHT
    FOR CONTEXT, SEE . . . . 333 VIVA 24   14
    FOR CONTEXT, SEE . . . . 398 NO THANKS 15   20
    FOR CONTEXT, SEE . . . . 405 NO THANKS 22   11
    FOR CONTEXT, SEE . . . . 474 NEW POEMS 12   13
RIGHTEOUS
    for (dull all regular righteous comfortable) unworlds thief . 677 95 POEMS 5   7
RIGHTEOUSNESS
    the epoch of Mann's righteousness the age of dollars . . . .   266 IS 5 TWO 1   3
RIGHTER
    be done (and anything's righter than books could plan) . . .   594 1 X 1 54   2
RIGHTEST
    smile at which the rightest man remembers there is . . . . .   685 95 POEMS 13   6
RIGHTFUL
    some loud unworld's most rightful wrong climbing, my love . . 745 95 POEMS 73   1
RIGHTLY
    slightly too sick to rightly die) "gedup" the gentscoon . . . 387 NO THANKS 4   6
RIGHTS
    Think We've Met subhuman rights Before / / / . . . .   549 1 X 1 9   14
+RIGHTS
    FOR CONTEXT, SEE . . . . 388 NO THANKS 5   16
RIGIDLY
    wheels mired where sits rigidly her body's doll gay . . . . . 131 & SON REAL 2   16
RILE
    hug presto! the bright rile of jovial hair extremely . . . .   137 & SON REAL 8   16
RIND
    high wilt of human rind-- when over hate has . . . .   213 XLI SONNETS 9   4
    a rubbish of human rind with a photograph clutched . . . . .   647 {CHAIRE} 49   1
RING
    finger shall have its ring and there won't be . . . . 192 XLI CHANSONS 2 19
    every B.V.D. let freedom ring amen. i do however . . . . . .   230 IS 5 ONE 2   14
    why you put the ring on (and watching her . . . . 242 IS 5 ONE 13   12
    of our lady a ring of people a brittle . . . .   279 IS 5 THREE 3   5
    stands on a thin ring which stands on a . . . . 470 NEW POEMS 8   11
    big & kinder of ring & which kinder of . . . .   470 NEW POEMS 8   13
    thickest & kindest of ring & all one two . . . .   470 NEW POEMS 8   17
    -I- nts (while showe ring cigaretteash O ver that . . . . . . 726 95 POEMS 54   13
+RING
    FOR CONTEXT, SEE . . . . 605 {CHAIRE} 7   6
RINGAROM
    gobular glows and flatchatte ringarom a . s --w . . . .   94 & POST IMPR 6   12
RINGING
    the great bells are ringing with rose the lewd . . . .   51 T&C IMPRESS 5   6
RINGS
    the earth and the rings upon their hands are . . . .   33 T&C ORIENTALE 6 46
    almost succeeds while toddle rings the bell. But if . . . . . 227 IS 5 ONE GERT   7
    all one two three rings are cake & everything . . . . 470 NEW POEMS 8   17
    whose rhyme (spilling his rings) threeing alive pasture and . 751 95 POEMS 79   6
RINSED
    a nnual (ugliness of) rinsed mind slowly: from! the: . . . .   99 & POST IMPR 10 22
    Suddenly by thousand starings rinsed with thoroughly million 388 NO THANKS 5   7
RINSING
    earth's ugly) mind. , Rinsing with exact death the . . . . .   99 & POST IMPR 10   4
RIOT
    perpetual feet the sinuous riot the flashing bacchant. . . .   185 XLI SONGS 7   9
RIPE
    barrages, the night utter ripe unspeaking girls. / / . . . .   45 T&C LA GUERRE 1 15
    ogling shoulders and the ripe quite too large lips . . . . .   72 T&C SON REAL 3   6
    luscious jigs dint of ripe silver with warmlyish wetflat . .   96 & POST IMPR 8   11
    truth, who threw the ripe melon into the tree? . . . .   125 & SEVEN POEMS 4 8

		PAGE	TITLE	LINE

RIPE (CONTINUED)

the silver dog, with ripe eyes and wagged his . . . . 125 & SEVEN POEMS 4   16
Moon said into his Ripe Eyes and the moon . . . . 125 & SEVEN POEMS 4   27
and leap into the ripe air Alive with closed . . . . 189 XLI SONGS 11   4
dies and over the ripe world wanders with a . . . . 293 IS 5 FOUR 10   24

RIPEBLACKBERRIES

lit. tleora basket of RipeBlackbeRRies emptied suddenl (y . . 101 & POST IMPR 11   53

RISE

(whereof the luscious pillars rise which are her large . . . 21 T&C PUELLA MEA 203
fleet flowerterrible memories shall rise, slowly return upon   36 T&C AMORES 1   29
ashes then thou wilt rise and thou wilt come . . . . 40 T&C AMORES 4   39
/ / the hours rise up putting off stars . . . . 50 T&C IMPRESS 4   1
waiting for something to rise as the other somethings . . . . 117 & PORTRAIT 10   6
my flesh I will rise After a thousand years . . . . 189 XLI SONGS 11   13
did not care to rise one hand did nothing . . . . 258 IS 5 ONE 28   16
the proletariat will not rise yesterday. Inexpressible . . . 262 IS 5 ONE 32   19
of ten fingers voices rise from down ever so . . . . 281 IS 5 THREE 5   21
carefully through deepness to rise these your wrists thighs . 369 VIVA 60   11
his carpet from which rise slim curving mighty children . . . 384 NO THANKS 2   20
the beyond imagining spasm rise we you-with-me around (me) . 442 NO THANKS 57   21
rotting keen dream? i rise which am the sun . . . . 527 50 POEMS 39   31
most first little flowers rise out of tremendous darkness . . 559 1 X 1 19   13
true two man neral rise eyes "this world's made . . . . 567 1 X 1 27   7
stars moon sun fall rise come go rain snow) . . . . 693 95 POEMS 21   19

RISEN

the whole year dies, risen at length from palpitating . . . .   5 T&C EPITHALAM 104
feeling their stars have risen through your skies: so, . . . 812 73 POEMS 40   8

RISES

ascensions, of thy smile rises the immaculate sorrow of . . . 31 T&C ORIENTALE 5   17
alone he beckons, she rises she stands a moment . . . . 35 T&C ORIENTALE 6 109
whose jouncing curtain. , rises upon one startling doll . . . 55 T&C PORTRAIT 3   7
your whiskey-voice the grass rises on the head of . . . . . . 61 T&C PORTRAIT 9   20
and there lark who; rises, and; droops as if . . . . 434 NO THANKS 51   19
once world quickly from rises army the gradual of . . . . . . 633 {CHAIRE} 35   2
the lie of no rises a truth of yes . . . . 736 95 POEMS 64   2

RISH

before a dissonance of Rish and Foses) until (finding . . . . 319 VIVA 11   13

RISING

(the sinuous rain which rising from thy bed steals . . . . .   3 T&C EPITHALAM   5
of silence (slenderly wholly rising, herself uprearing wholly 156 & SON ACTU 5   6
eheads shone eternal pleasedon't; rising: from the Shall. / . 343 VIVA 34   18
/ / nine birds (rising through a gold moment) . . . . 627 {CHAIRE} 29   1

RISSIONS

to turn us into rissions and blokes with ammunicions . . . . 405 NO THANKS 22   6

RITZ

(FRITZ) LIVES AT THE RITZ WEAR earl & wilson . . . . 244 IS 5 ONE 15   4

RIVA

--by night upon the Riva Schiavoni or in the . . . . 256 IS 5 ONE 27   17

RIVER

finally, butts into the river / / / / . . . . 47 T&C IMPRESS 1   11
valley spilled its tickling river in my eyes, the . . . . . . 135 & SON REAL 6   15
noted lifting a Green River (here's to youse) "a . . . . . . 229 IS 5 ONE FRAN   10

RIVERLY

/ / / / riverly is a flower gone . . . . 90 & POST IMPR 2   1

RIVERS

i praise between those rivers whose white voices pass . . . .   9 T&C SONGS 1   1
thoughts, kicking in the rivers of our blood, miss . . . . . 174 & SON ACTU 23   9
of fire beyond red rivers of fair perpetual feet . . . . . . 185 XLI SONGS 7   5

RIVERY

than angels are mountains rivery forests towerful towns . . . 586 1 X 1 46   7

RIVETED

blood, her heart's chatter riveted a weeping skyscraper in . 132 & SON REAL 3   4

ROAD

houseless wisping rune of road lazily carved on sharpening . 86 T&C SON ACTU 5   6
tombs, where a large road crosses and all the . . . . 86 T&C SON ACTU 5   12
along a curve of road which eats into a . . . . 281 IS 5 THREE 5   8
little beyond the last road--there's something to be found" . 303 IS 5 FIVE 2   3
say "along this particular road the moon if you'll . . . . . 303 IS 5 FIVE 2   9

		PAGE	TITLE	LINE

ROAD (CONTINUED)
the Ending of this road, a candle in a . . . . 435 NO THANKS 51   42
whyless soul a loneliest road who dares to stroll . . . . . . 441 NO THANKS 56   46
ROADSIDE
thieves lay by the roadside on his back dressed . . . . 258 IS 5 ONE 28   2
ROAM
her Muteness will slowly roam my dumbNess? her other, ... 137 & SON REAL 8   5
a poor wind will roam / / / / . . . . 292 IS 5 FOUR 9   20
ROAMING
through the autumn indisputably roaming death's big rotten . 158 & SON ACTU 7   13
feel (his lousy eyes roaming) wonderful all sky (a . . . . . 501 50 POEMS 15   8
i <> some perpetually roaming whylessness-- autumn has gone: 839 73 POEMS 67   7
ROAMINGLY
means worlds inhabited by roamingly stern bright faeries if . 363 VIVA 54   3
ROAMS
huge heart prospecting darkness roams torture my spirit with   79 T&C SON UNRE 4   4
sun; his least unmotion roams the youngest star) --how . . . 609 {CHAIRE} 11   12
ROAR
crankin It The L's roar tortures-pleasantly myears it is, . . 101 & POST IMPR 11   49
the well-fed L's immaculate roar looped straightens, into . . 219 XLI SONNETS 15   5
o all the roofs roar drownInsound(& (we (are . . . . 347 VIVA 38   18
green turns red (the roar of traffic collapses: through . . . 800 73 POEMS 28   17
ROARING
like lions to the roaring slaughter they did not . . . . . . 268 IS 5 TWO 3   11
+ROARING
FOR CONTEXT, SEE . . . . 388 NO THANKS 5   19
ROASTED
of skilfully applied bayonets roasted hot with heat-- Olaf . 339 VIVA 30   30
ROBBED
(who's never by never robbed of day) puts always . . . . . . 674 95 POEMS 2   7
ROBE
to man, whose lilied robe the sun's white hands . . . .   3 T&C EPITHALAM   29
Implacable death's mysteriously sable robe from her redolent 206 XLI SONNETS 2   5
fat "father" (adjustin his robe) who now puts on . . . . . . 240 IS 5 ONE 11   4
too if the green robe o p e n . . . . 614 {CHAIRE} 16   10
ROBERT
and they smoked a robert burns cigerr to the . . . . 552 1 X 1 12   29
ROBES
superlatively brave. Surely from robes of particoloured peace   5 T&C EPITHALAM   97
a croon of mingling robes musically revealed in rareness: . .   10 T&C SONGS 1   41
Nose puts on sharp robes of uncouth odour, for . . . .   94 & POST IMPR 6   9
ROBIN
/ / / first robin the; you say something . . . . 737 95 POEMS 65   1
are rich (and a robin will sing his robin . . . . 769 95 POEMS 95   22
robin will sing his robin a song) but misers . . . . 769 95 POEMS 95   23
how he sings the robin (who 'll be silent . . . . 805 73 POEMS 33   6
ROBIN'S
against a west of robin's egg blue when i . . . . 194 XLI PORTRAIT 2   3
ROBINS
are the blind and robins never welcome spring nor . . . . . . 511 50 POEMS 25   16
/ / / sentinel robins two guard me and . . . . 746 95 POEMS 74   1
ROBINSON
/ / / remarked Robinson Jefferson to Injustice Taughed . . . 321 VIVA 13   1
ROCK
with one foot and rock a cradle with the . . . . 242 IS 5 ONE 13   9
-gness Am root air rock day) : you; smile, ... 449 NO THANKS 64   13
eye stuck into a rock of forehead. No body . . . . 490 50 POEMS 4   4
her gnarled vomits a rock of mindscream into life; . . . . . 506 50 POEMS 20   5
whippoorwills or tree field rock hollyhock forest brook . . . 512 50 POEMS 26   26
censored up a wench's rock-a-bye (rub-her-bub) bub? (bubs) / 642 {CHAIRE} 44   27
a like a grey rock wanderin g through pasture . . . . 654 {CHAIRE} 56   3
ROCK-A-BYE
censored up a wench's rock-a-bye (rub-her-bub) bub? (bubs) / 642 {CHAIRE} 44   27
ROCKER
The, negress, in the, rocker by the, curb, tipping . . . . . 166 & SON ACTU 15   3
ROCKET
When eaten spaces grouse rocket know quite, slightly or . . . 346 VIVA 37   11

		PAGE	TITLE	LINE

ROD
   Frederick found on a lightning-rod, Boston, Mass. such were . 262 IS 5 ONE 32   31
   a serpent becomes a rod smiles the liontamer nearby . . . . 384 NO THANKS 2   23
   child and spoil the rod quoth the palmist. / . . . . 643 (CHAIRE) 45   5
RODE
   into the waters i rode down the red horse . . . . 30 T&C ORIENTALE 4 11
ROEBUCK
   rare deer. Four red roebuck at a white water . . . . 14 T&C SONGS 4   9
ROGUE
   cracksman of the nifty, ruffian-rogue, laughing body with . . 140 & SON REAL 11 10
   of heaven) trickstervillain raucous rogue & vivid voltaire . 677 95 POEMS 5 13
ROGUISH
   no bigger than) in roguish am of fragrance dances . . . . . 763 95 POEMS 90   8
ROH
   the ree ray rye roh rowster shouts rawrOO / . . . . 773 73 POEMS 1 18
ROLL
   clouds of incense fleetly roll) i spill my bright . . . . . 206 XLI SONNETS 2 14
   do through icy waters roll that helplessness which others . . 339 VIVA 30   9
ROLLED
   a little eye that rolled and made its point . . . . 149 & SON REAL 20   6
   of when till it rolled behind forever, we touched . . . . . 612 (CHAIRE) 14   9
+ROLLED
   FOR CONTEXT, SEE . . . . 606 (CHAIRE) 8 10
ROLLING
   in white spins, tumbles; rolling in sand. across this . . . . 281 IS 5 THREE 5   4
ROLLINGEST
   (on this busily nowhere rollingest it) 's the dizzily . . . . 590 1 X 1 50 11
ROLLS
   keen chassised like a Rolls Royce swoops smoothly outward . . 232 IS 5 ONE 3   5
   ghost of Professor Royce rolls remembering that it has . . . 232 IS 5 ONE 3 13
   filthy sawdust chucks and rolls against the tent his . . . . 259 IS 5 ONE 29   5
   on Marcus"-- "duh Swede rolls down tree flights an . . . . . 332 VIVA 23   8
ROLYPOLY
   slowlyslowly them--then carefully the rolypoly voice . . . . 228 IS 5 ONE MARJ   8
ROMA
   ing il treno per Roma si-gnori? jerk. ilyr, ushes . . . . . . 278 IS 5 THREE 2 20
ROMAN
   wiggle upon the perfumed roman strength who how furiously . . 110 & PORTRAIT 6   8
   loved he was a roman theirs was a music . . . . 110 & PORTRAIT 6 22
ROMANTIC
   body fatherly of a romantic tired business man somewhat . . . 57 T&C PORTRAIT 5 32
ROME
   the pincian to appreciate rome at nightfall; and because . . 355 VIVA 46 13
ROMP
   because today's today) the romp cries i and the . . . . . . 773 73 POEMS 1   6
ROOF
   by himself on somebody's roof or some- thing where . . . . . 127 & SEVEN POEMS 5 42
   Buy Of (but a roof hugs whom) as the . . . . 217 XLI SONNETS 13   5
   that when the certainly roof leaks it 's our . . . . 728 95 POEMS 56   3
ROOFS
   chimneys converse angrily, their roofs are nervous with the . 62 T&C PORTRAIT 10 14
   and while fire-escapes and roofs and chimneys and while . . . 62 T&C PORTRAIT 10 16
   and chimneys and while roofs and fire-escapes and chimneys . 62 T&C PORTRAIT 10 16
   chimneys and fire-escapes and roofs are talking rapidly all . 62 T&C PORTRAIT 10 18
   rather Somebody who uses roofs and streets skilfully to . . . 92 & POST IMPR 4 12
   the air over houses roofs And out of the . . . . 284 IS 5 FOUR 1 16
   theraIncomIng o all the roofs roar drownInsound(& (we . . . 347 VIVA 38 18
ROOM
   My lover, there's just room for me in You . . . . 123 & SEVEN POEMS 2   8
   knees across the locked room. he knocked her cold . . . . . 145 & SON REAL 16   4
   whereto my invariably commendable room has been forever . . . 197 XLI PORTRAIT 5 21
   minds --before leaving my room i turn, and (stooping . . . . 288 IS 5 FOUR 5   6
   --dey was petrified. De room swung roun an crawled . . . . 332 VIVA 23 25
   a middle of a room stands a suicide sniffing . . . . 338 VIVA 29   1
   stairs, there's a free room. We almost could go . . . . . . 365 VIVA 56   8
   could give that anguish room; but likes it only . . . . . . 414 NO THANKS 31 10
   world aint square with room for the devil and . . . . 568 1 X 1 28 18
   sea here's more than room for three of me . . . . 588 1 X 1 48   4

ROOM (CONTINUED)
ed in a writhewho room) as hows of whi . . . . 795 73 POEMS 23   17
+ROOM
    FOR CONTEXT, SEE . . . . 101 & POST IMPR 11   44
    FOR CONTEXT, SEE . . . . 333 VIVA 24   17
ROOM'S
    y protuberant through the room's skilful of thing silent . . 159 & SON ACTU 8   6
    / / upon the room's silence, i will sew . . . . 164 & SON ACTU 13   1
    gr(oo)ving the room's Silence) this like a . . . . 286 IS 5 FOUR 3   9
    six are in a room's dark around) five (are . . . . 507 50 POEMS 21   2
    six are in a room's dark around) five (six . . . . 507 50 POEMS 21   9
    (six are in a room's) one is red and . . . . 507 50 POEMS 21   11
    (six are in a room's dark) all five are . . . . 507 50 POEMS 21   26
ROOMS
    when sunbeams loot furnished rooms through whose foul windows 442 NO THANKS 57   12
    0 Yes of guk rooms daughter item son a . . . . 499 50 POEMS 13   9
+ROOSEVELT
    FOR CONTEXT, SEE . . . . 321 VIVA 13   9
+ROOSTER
    FOR CONTEXT, SEE . . . . 773 73 POEMS 1   19
ROOT
    sunset dream acute from root to leaf) but should . . . . . 362 VIVA 53   8
    (susta- inin -gness Am root air rock day) : . . . . 449 NO THANKS 64   13
    of a voice these root like legs or feethands; . . . . 490 50 POEMS 4   12
    knows (here is the root of the root and . . . . 766 95 POEMS 92   11
    the root of the root and the bud of . . . . 766 95 POEMS 92   11
ROOTED
    this serene mightily how rooted who of iron / . . . . 415 NO THANKS 32   23
ROOTING
    whose casual mouth's coy rooting dies also. (my loveFist . . 131 & SON REAL 2   7
ROOTS
    our hearts hugely squirm roots) us ly; though hither . . . . 361 VIVA 52   9
    almost their mind immeasurably roots among much soundless . . 479 NEW POEMS 17   5
    (anchored in what mountaining roots of mere eternity) . . . . 517 50 POEMS 31   1
    dreamers to their ghostly roots and should some why . . . . 520 50 POEMS 34   12
    --whose hearts are mountains, roots are trees, it's they . . 560 1 X 1 20   15
    you (trees are their roots and wind is wind) . . . . 732 95 POEMS 60   3
ROPE
    dancing from hop-scotch and jump-rope and it's spring and . . 24 T&C CHANSONS 1 15
    eu can have you rope / / / / . . . . 476 NEW POEMS 14   14
+ROPER
    FOR CONTEXT, SEE . . . . 252 IS 5 ONE 23   10
ROPES
    it will in spring) ropes of silver gliding from . . . . . . 58 T&C PORTRAIT 6   6
    victim against the giving ropes amid screams of deeply . . . 259 IS 5 ONE 29   17
    snow: strangles valleys by ropes of thing and stifles . . . . 560 1 X 1 20   11
ROR
    appearing con ter fusion ror collap sing thatthis is . . . . 646 {CHAIRE} 48   5
ROSE
    god's evasive audible great rose! Lover, lead forth thy . . . 5 T&C EPITHALAM   112
    unearthly sweetness of a rose swam upward from the . . . . . 8 T&C OF NICOL   7
    which did sing a rose shall beget the spring . . . . 16 T&C SONGS 6   6
    shall appear than a rose more sweetly known, more . . . . . 21 T&C PUELLA MEA   176
    bells are ringing with rose the lewd fat bells . . . . 51 T&C IMPRESS 5   6
    / / / the rose is dying the lips . . . . 59 T&C PORTRAIT 7   1
    The symbol of the rose motionless with grieving feet . . . . 59 T&C PORTRAIT 7   9
    spiral acres of bloated rose coiled within cobalt miles . . . 93 & POST IMPR 5   5
    / the ivory performing rose of you, worn upon . . . . 165 & SON ACTU 14   1
    cage of thy body rose through the sensible night . . . . . . 187 XLI SONGS 9   4
    heart and take the rose, which perfect is With . . . . 188 XLI SONGS 10   19
    for philosophy does this rose give a damn... bring . . . . . 264 IS 5 ONE 33   20
    a dead yellow small rose / / / / . . . . 296 IS 5 FOUR 13   16
    suicide sniffing a Paper rose smiling to a self . . . . 338 VIVA 29   3
    be (deep like a rose tall like a rose) . . . . 352 VIVA 43   5
    rose tall like a rose) standing near my swaying . . . . . . 352 VIVA 43   6
    Who out of deeplyness rose to undeath) salute. and . . . . . 358 VIVA 49   13
    stars and planets heard, rose very slowly in a . . . . 360 VIVA 51   13
    skilfully, mysteriously) her first rose or if your wish . . . 366 VIVA 57   8

	PAGE	TITLE	LINE
ROSE (CONTINUED)			
stand nor a first rose explodes but shall increase	538	50 POEMS 50	13
it's pliz) then up rose bishop budge from kew	552	1 X 1 12	6
monster merde then up rose pride and up rose	552	1 X 1 12	11
rose pride and up rose pelf and ghibelline and	552	1 X 1 12	11
the tomb then up rose mr lipshits pres (who	552	1 X 1 12	26
wished Himself into a rose and even (we'll	577	1 X 1 37	15
slowly count to soon) rose--did you see her? darling, ...	599	(CHAIRE) 1	10
small most of a rose easily (while will be	608	(CHAIRE) 10	9
perfectly isn 't) one rose opened / / /	646	(CHAIRE) 48	17
/ lily has a rose (i have none) "don't	684	95 POEMS 12	1
tall" lily has a rose no rose i've and	684	95 POEMS 12	17
has a rose no rose i've and losing's less	684	95 POEMS 12	18
must most lily brief (rose here&gone) flesh all is	690	95 POEMS 18	6
you (o nly) asl (rose) eep / / /	691	95 POEMS 19	7
that every weed's a rose, roses (you feel certain)	744	95 POEMS 72	7
as the little white rose of a child" /	748	95 POEMS 76	17
creation lovetree! least the rose alive must three, must . .	764	95 POEMS 90	50
the (whom we call rose a) mystery "but it	837	73 POEMS 65	17
+ROSE			
FOR CONTEXT, SEE	711	95 POEMS 39	9
FOR CONTEXT, SEE	798	73 POEMS 26	11
ROSE'S			
are smaller than a rose's moment there's time for	683	95 POEMS 11	8
ROSEBUG			
the jackknife and the rosebug and you say Sure	127	& SEVEN POEMS 5	47
ROSEBUGS			
old thing falls in rosebugs and jackknives and kittens . . .	126	& SEVEN POEMS 5	5
pennies i do and rosebugs i do / /	127	& SEVEN POEMS 5	51
ROSEBUSH			
from my mother's greatgrandmother's rosebush white roses are	748	95 POEMS 76	1
ROSENBLOOM			
should say thankyouverymuch mr rosenbloom picks strawberries	287	IS 5 FOUR 4	8
ROSES			
than those twain perfect roses whose ambrosial grace, ...	6	T&C EPITHALAM	148
fashioned very curiously of roses and of ivory. The	20	T&C PUELLA MEA	138
--fashioned very curiously of roses and of ivory if	22	T&C PUELLA MEA	230
is probably made of roses & hello: (of solongs	66	T&C POST IMPR 3	16
think it shall be roses and spring will bring	67	T&C POST IMPR 4	10
a little harder for roses only a little harder	67	T&C POST IMPR 4	21
breasts are round have roses darling, it's all i	71	T&C SON REAL 2	6
sleep i watch the roses of the day grow	78	T&C SON UNRE 3	14
any reason and otherwise roses and mountains different from .	91	& POST IMPR 3	16
nobody something about les roses les bluets yes, will	102	& POST IMPR 12	17
importing the cruelty of roses. The exciting simplicity of .	103	& POST IMPR 13	1
tasted worms windows and roses he laughed, and closed	170	& SON ACTU 19	12
head by oaks and roses deliberated.) / / /	181	XLI SONGS 3	14
/ and what were roses. Perfume? for i do	211	XLI SONNETS 7	1
my dreams justly touching roses their fingers whitely live .	211	XLI SONNETS 7	11
not for us, purple roses were sweeter to thee	213	XLI SONNETS 9	15
go away i give roses who will advise even	294	IS 5 FOUR 11	2
a heaven of blackred roses my father will be	352	VIVA 43	4
is deeper than all roses) nobody, not even the	366	VIVA 57	19
may not observe; while roses wince) that which we	386	NO THANKS 3	8
a wonder of wild roses sometimes) with north over	512	50 POEMS 26	32
when thorns regard their roses with alarm and rainbows . . .	620	(CHAIRE) 22	3
your thorniest question my roses will answer" "but dying's .	625	(CHAIRE) 27	14
no no let the roses come and go for	684	95 POEMS 12	14
seem) in time of roses (who amaze our now	688	95 POEMS 16	7
dying, if (and when) roses complain their beauties are . . .	744	95 POEMS 72	3
every weed's a rose, roses (you feel certain) will	744	95 POEMS 72	7
mother's greatgrandmother's rosebush white roses are probably	748	95 POEMS 76	2
probably the least probable roses of her improbable world . .	748	95 POEMS 76	2
while these were blossoming) roses which really are dreams .	748	95 POEMS 76	10
really are dreams of roses-- "and who" i asked	748	95 POEMS 76	11
who liked men horses roses & $ (in that	792	73 POEMS 20	5
+ROSES			
FOR CONTEXT, SEE	319	VIVA 11	13

ROSETREE
/ / / / rosetree, rosetree --you're a song . . . . 763 95 POEMS 90   1
/ / / rosetree, rosetree --you're a song to . . . . 763 95 POEMS 90   1
ROSILY
gone softly by tomb rosily gods whiten befall saith . . . . . 90 & POST IMPR 2   3
of smallish) Humble a rosily , nimblest; c-urlin-g noworld . 503 50 POEMS 17   5
ROSY
sultan's nose pullable and rosy flanked by the scrumptious . 198 XLI PORTRAIT 6   9
ROTGUT
and the fact that rotgut never was brewed which . . . . . . 605 {CHAIRE} 7   4
ROTHERMERE
be photographed with Lord Rothermere playing with Lord . . . 262 IS 5 ONE 32   21
Rothermere playing with Lord Rothermere billiards very well . 262 IS 5 ONE 32   21
by moonlight with Lord Rothermere. A crocodile eats a . . . . 262 IS 5 ONE 32   22
ROTTEN
indisputably roaming death's big rotten particular kiss. / / 158 & SON ACTU 7   14
big unkeen "Business is rotten" the face yawning said . . . . 225 IS 5 ONE LIZ   12
of remember with his rotten old forgotten full of . . . . . . 642 {CHAIRE} 44   6
ROTTING
(nor could all earth's rotting scholars guess that life . . . 420 NO THANKS 37   8
snow of mothery same rotting keen dream? i rise . . . . 527 50 POEMS 39   30
ROUGH
and Time storms and rough cold, wind's menace and . . . . . . 207 XLI SONNETS 3   10
ROUN
petrified. De room swung roun an crawled up into . . . . . . 332 VIVA 23   25
ROUN'
speak sweet morons gather roun' who does not dare . . . . . . 466 NEW POEMS 4   2
ROUND
in life's serene perpetual round a pale world gathers . . . .   5 T&C EPITHALAM   81
the crank goes desperately, round and round pointing to . . . 69 T&C POST IMPR 6   9
goes desperately, round and round pointing to the queer . . . 69 T&C POST IMPR 6   9
don't, the crank goes desperate elves and hope- . . . . . 69 T&C POST IMPR 6   21
him i shove my round red hat back on . . . . 69 T&C POST IMPR 6   34
in it and the round funny hat with a . . . . 69 T&C POST IMPR 6   41
your meeting breasts are round have roses darling, it's . . . 71 T&C SON REAL 2   5
little, roundtable amongother; littleexactly round. tables, . 104 & POST IMPR 14   21
since darker than little round water at one end . . . . 126 & SEVEN POEMS 5   2
says (andwhyevernot) into the round well and see the . . . . 127 & SEVEN POEMS 5   46
be one of them round the hurt heart which . . . . 215 XLI SONNETS 11   10
this pale softish almost round young man to whom . . . . . . 245 IS 5 ONE 16   6
fifteenthrate ideas wearing a round jeer for a hat . . . . . 258 IS 5 ONE 28   4
Stood (apparition.) WITH (THE ROUND AIR IS FILLED) OPENING . 348 VIVA 39   16
Clocks strike. The moon's round, through the window as . . . 365 VIVA 56   4
oward black, this) roUnd ingrOundIngly rouNdar (round) . . . 385 NO THANKS 2   63
) roUnd ingrOundIngly rouNdar (round) ounDing ; ball balll . 385 NO THANKS 2   63
a moon is as round as) Death / / . . . . 436 NO THANKS 52   25
blacker than dreams are round like a spoon are . . . . . . 483 NEW POEMS 21   4
while every sun goes round its moon / / . . . . 510 50 POEMS 24   14
prove their world is round nor dingsters die at . . . . . . 511 50 POEMS 25   17
thumb (it's whirl, girls) round and round early to . . . . . 513 50 POEMS 27   9
whirl, girls) round and round early to better is . . . . . . 513 50 POEMS 27   9
the was painted in round blue but quite now . . . . 516 50 POEMS 30   5
to lose and as round as to find. Each . . . . 543 1 X 1 3   6
the red and the round (they're gravensteins) fall with . . . 543 1 X 1 3   27
/ / o the round little man we loved . . . . 606 {CHAIRE} 8   2
book) on a proud round cloud in a white . . . . 631 {CHAIRE} 33   4
home with a smooth round stone as small as . . . . 682 95 POEMS 10   9
twig three souls sit round with cold three (huddling . . . . 687 95 POEMS 15   4
/ / / / round a so moon could . . . . 698 95 POEMS 26   1
have you hunted her round by the rasberrypatch" "i . . . . . 707 95 POEMS 35   6
/ / ! o (rounD) moon, how do you . . . . 722 95 POEMS 50   2
moon, how do you (rouNd er than roUnd) float; . . . . 722 95 POEMS 50   4
you (rouNd er than roUnd) float; who lly & . . . . 722 95 POEMS 50   6
than) go : ldenly (Round est) ? / / . . . . 722 95 POEMS 50   10
alive any star goes round --a dream sans meaning . . . . . . 735 95 POEMS 63   4
/ here's s omething round (& so mething lost) . . . . 753 95 POEMS 81   2
not the other way round) because it 's A . . . . 782 73 POEMS 10   7
/ / / a round face near the top . . . . 813 73 POEMS 41   1

+ROUND
   FOR CONTEXT, SEE . . . . 466 NEW POEMS 4   2
ROUNDAR
   this) roUnd ingrOundIngly rouNdar (round) ounDing ; ball . . 385 NO THANKS 2   63
ROUNDED
   her nice concupiscence appeared rounded. if she were alive, . 103 & POST IMPR 13 16
ROUNDER
   float; who lly & (rOunder than) go : ldenly . . . . 722 95 POEMS 50   8
+ROUNDER
   FOR CONTEXT, SEE . . . . 722 95 POEMS 50   4
+ROUNDEST
   FOR CONTEXT, SEE . . . . 722 95 POEMS 50   10
ROUNDING
   trees drenched by a rounding moon) / / / . . . . 10 T&C SONGS 1   45
   un -derfully & a- rounding death) L o v . . . . 719 95 POEMS 47   18
+ROUNDINGLY
   FOR CONTEXT, SEE . . . . 385 NO THANKS 2   63
ROUNDLY
   hush) andDark IshbusY ing-roundly-dis tinct; chuck lings, . 416 NO THANKS 33   7
   swi (across! gold's rouNdly) ftblac kl (ness) . . . . . . 429 NO THANKS 46   3
ROUNDNESS
   turns doesn't determine its roundness: if swallows tryst in . 514 50 POEMS 28   6
ROUNDTABLE
   exactly sit, ata little roundtable among otherlittle . . . . 104 & POST IMPR 14 2
   sitsat a surely! little, roundtable amongother; littleexactly 104 & POST IMPR 14 21
ROUNDTABLES
   little roundtable among otherlittle roundtables Her, eyes . . 104 & POST IMPR 14 3
ROUPY
   vivid noiseless boys at Roupy i have seen between . . . . . . 45 T&C LA GUERRE 1 12
ROUT
   in slow diaphanous faint rout), queen in the inconceivable . 6 T&C EPITHALAM 144
   the clever hair nor rout the young mouth whose . . . . 85 T&C SON ACTU 4   7
ROW
   praising bodies in a row between slow glories fleetly . . . . 20 T&C PUELLA MEA 143
ROWS
   Dick. And had some rows over percent. The gang . . . . 149 & SON REAL 20   7
   dominoes) fall: down; in, rows / / / / . . . . 331 VIVA 22   8
ROWSPEACH
   with thema Tiss eeyeb Rowspeach es a soft desert . . . . . . 318 VIVA 10   20
ROYAL
   de l'Europe Grand and Royal Danielli their numbers are . . . 256 IS 5 ONE 27   19
   les mains froides. His Royal Highness said "peek-a-boo" and . 262 IS 5 ONE 32   27
   give a damn-- his royal warcry is I AM . . . . 774 73 POEMS 2   3
   Might Makes Right --his royal warcry is I AM . . . . 774 73 POEMS 2   12
ROYCE
   chassised like a Rolls Royce swoops smoothly outward (amid . 232 IS 5 ONE 3   6
   infantile ghost of Professor Royce rolls remembering that it 232 IS 5 ONE 3   13
RRMP
   fast you hear the rrmp and then ◇ and . . . . 269 IS 5 TWO 4   5
RUB
   that it will not rub, like any other pastel. . . . . 264 IS 5 ONE 33   24
   ? each oth? er rub, ! berq; : uestions . . . . 319 VIVA 11   39
   forgotten full of why (rub-her-bub) bub? (bubs) where's Jim . 642 {CHAIRE} 44   8
   never in his fly (rub-her-bub) bub? (bubs) where's John . . . 642 {CHAIRE} 44 18
   up a wench's rock-a-bye (rub-her-bub) bub? (bubs) / / . . . . 642 {CHAIRE} 44 28
RUB-HER-BUB
   forgotten full of why (rub-her-bub) bub? (bubs) where's Jim . 642 {CHAIRE} 44   8
   never in his fly (rub-her-bub) bub? (bubs) where's John . . . 642 {CHAIRE} 44 18
   up a wench's rock-a-bye (rub-her-bub) bub? (bubs) / / . . . . 642 {CHAIRE} 44 28
RUBBER
   pu (acle to rubber) tres (plants how grin . . . . 309 VIVA 1   27
+RUBBER
   FOR CONTEXT, SEE . . . . 69 T&C POST IMPR 6 38
   FOR CONTEXT, SEE . . . . 319 VIVA 11   39
RUBBERY
   mistaken and cradles in rubbery one somewhat hand the . . . . 499 50 POEMS 13   5
RUBBISH
   mind drifting with chuckling rubbish of pearl weed coral . . 369 VIVA 60   5

RUBBISH (CONTINUED)

roots among much soundless rubbish of guitars and watches . . 479 NEW POEMS 17 6

/ this is a rubbish of human rind with . . . . 647 (CHAIRE) 49 1

RUBSITSELF

hot women my Stomach ruBSiTSElf kew-ri-ous-ly a mong Them . . 101 & POST IMPR 11 63

RUBY&EMERALD

To; Bouncing, Bet the ruby&emerald zigging HE of a . . . . . 747 95 POEMS 75 9

RUBYTHROAT'S

a) here of a rubythroat's home with its still . . . . 827 73 POEMS 55 9

RUDDY

these (by the fire's ruddy glow united) not less . . . . . . 254 IS 5 ONE 25 9

fresh from a fu ruddy as a sun with . . . . 567 1 X 1 27 3

a" old mr lyman ruddy as a sunrise fresh . . . . 567 1 X 1 27 18

RUE

guerre j'm'appelle Manon, cinq rue Henri Mounier voulez-vous 121 & PORTRAIT 12 35

with queenly legs cinq rue Henri Mounier a little . . . . . . 121 & PORTRAIT 12 46

l'ho tel nor man (rue d e l'echelle) die . . . . 708 95 POEMS 36 13

RUFFIAN

cracksman of the nifty, ruffian-rogue, laughing body with . . 140 & SON REAL 11 10

/ / for any ruffian of the sky your . . . . 774 73 POEMS 2 1

RUFFIAN-ROGUE

cracksman of the nifty, ruffian-rogue, laughing body with . . 140 & SON REAL 11 10

RUGGED

stout as a bridge rugged as a bear slickern . . . . 568 1 X 1 28 7

RUGLIKE

frail swooping lozenge. a ruglike sentience whose papillae . 201 XLI PORTRAIT 9 16

RUGS

earth writhe upon deep rugs / / / / . . . . 35 T&C ORIENTALE 6 116

RUINED

haste --consider well this ruined aqueduct lady, which used . 260 IS 5 ONE 30 22

bling people (a long ruined streets hither and) softly . . . 319 VIVA 11 4

+RUINING

FOR CONTEXT, SEE . . . . 41 T&C AMORES 5 30

RULE

& aged people who rule this world (and me . . . . 250 IS 5 ONE 21 3

for living find the rule) and dark beginnings are . . . . . . 420 NO THANKS 37 9

handless hints do conjurers rule? do mannikins forbid the . . 527 50 POEMS 39 18

+RULE

FOR CONTEXT, SEE . . . . 500 50 POEMS 14 20

RULES

unexist, solemnly and per rules apparelling its soullessness 373 VIVA 64 3

+RUMOR

FOR CONTEXT, SEE . . . . 325 VIVA 17 13

RUN

scuttling eyes rustle and run and hidehidehide whisk whisk . 25 T&C CHANSONS 2 14

of the emperor's palace run sunlight and moonlight and . . . 32 T&C ORIENTALE 6 16

all the clocks would run down the next day. . . . . 365 VIVA 56 14

sonnet entitled how to run the world) A always . . . . 390 NO THANKS 7 1

almost guess (with a run skip around we go . . . . 594 1 X 1 54 6

, come quickly come run run with me now . . . . 835 73 POEMS 63 15

come quickly come run run with me now jump . . . . 835 73 POEMS 63 15

RUNE

take the houseless wisping rune of road lazily carved . . . . 86 T&C SON ACTU 5 5

RUNG

waist said the cop's rung for the wagon but . . . . 53 T&C PORTRAIT 1 37

RUNNIN

no cloze an went runnin aroun wid eachudder Hell . . . . . . 237 IS 5 ONE 8 18

RUNNING

wee and eddieandbill come running from marbles and piracies . 24 T&C CHANSONS 1 7

afraid that life is running away from them (i . . . . 724 95 POEMS 52 14

+RUNNING

FOR CONTEXT, SEE . . . . 200 XLI PORTRAIT 8 26

RUNS

climbs and cries and runs and floats like a . . . . 69 T&C POST IMPR 6 43

said the smoke who runs the elevator but I . . . . 125 & SEVEN POEMS 4 10

RUPTINGLY

: yearnswoons; &Isdensekil- <> ruptingly) ca-y-est droppe5 . 430 NO THANKS 47 15

```
RUSEFELT
   back inley clamored Clever Rusefelt to Theodore Odysseus  . . 321 VIVA 13          9
RUSH
   parsed by this gorgeous rush of upward lips.... cleverly  . . 201 XLI PORTRAIT 9  27
   look alike the flics rush batter the crowd sprawls  . . . . . 274 IS 5 TWO 9       5
   the kicked by flics rush (the Flics, tidiyum, are . . . . . . 274 IS 5 TWO 9       8
   e elingwhiRls) are pouring rush fields drea mf (ull . . . . . 423 NO THANKS 40    16
   will wraiths of doom rush (which all ghosts of  . . . . . . . 454 NO THANKS 69    10
   and a steep) deep rush through amazing day it's . . . . . . . 769 95 POEMS 95     14
RUSHED
   heroic happy dead who rushed like lions to the  . . . . . . . 268 IS 5 TWO 3      11
+RUSHES
   FOR CONTEXT, SEE  . . . . . . . . . . . . . . . . . . . . . . 278 IS 5 THREE 2    22
RUSHING
   will bring her worms rushing through loam. (afterward i'll  .  67 T&C POST IMPR 4 12
   hips, O press worms rushing slowly through loam / . . . . . .  67 T&C POST IMPR 4 30
   thy footstep, and the rushing of thy deep hair . . . . . . . 213 XLI SONNETS 9    11
   to again utterly disappear; rushing gently swiftly creeping . 369 VIVA 60         16
RUSKIN
   what is it didn't Ruskin says about you got . . . . . . . . . 257 IS 5 ONE 27     34
RUSSIA'S
   in finland now that russia's here) swing low sweet  . . . . . 641 (CHAIRE) 43      2
+RUSSIANS
   FOR CONTEXT, SEE  . . . . . . . . . . . . . . . . . . . . . . 405 NO THANKS 22     6
RUSTLE
   mousies with scuttling eyes rustle and run and hidehidehide .  25 T&C CHANSONS 2  14
RUSTLING
   air bothered with a rustling din sort of sublimated . . . . . 171 & SON ACTU 20    3
RYE
   & the ree ray rye roh rowster shouts rawrOO . . . . . . . . . 773 73 POEMS 1      18
S
   kumrads dance) kumrads enjoy s. freud knows whoy the  . . . . 413 NO THANKS 30    11
   I the lost shoulders S the empty spine / . . . . . . . . . . 414 NO THANKS 31     15
   -ing- lyful of) ! (s r BIRDS BECAUSE AGAINS . . . . . . . . . 421 NO THANKS 38    20
SABLE
   fling Implacable death's mysteriously sable robe from her . . 206 XLI SONNETS 2    4
SABOTEUR
   denounces april as a saboteur then we'll believe in . . . . . 620 (CHAIRE) 22     12
SABOTS
   forward skidding in outrageous sabots language trickling  . . 277 IS 5 THREE 1    13
SACK
   how within night's loose sack a star's nibbling in- . . . . .  49 T&C IMPRESS 3    3
SACKS
   fingers toss trunks shuffle sacks spin kegs they curl . . . . 114 & PORTRAIT 7     8
SACRAMENT
   war received the shuddering sacrament of sleep, betwixt whose   7 T&C EPITHALAM  155
SACRED
   with me in the sacred witchery of almostness which  . . . . .  10 T&C SONGS 1     37
   friend, feeling is the sacred and agonizing proximity to  . . 193 XLI PORTRAIT 1   9
   blond determined head the sacred flag of truth unfurled,  . . 273 IS 5 TWO 8      14
SAD
   thing all small and sad man, may his mighty . . . . . . . . . 526 50 POEMS 38      3
   is the very (in sad this havingest world) most  . . . . . . . 590 1 X 1 50         2
SADISTIC
   of synopsis despite a sadistic modesty his mind is  . . . . . 193 XLI PORTRAIT 1   5
SADNESS
   crying) children whose any sadness or joy is my . . . . . . . 749 95 POEMS 77      8
SAFE
   m make the world safe for democracy it never  . . . . . . . . 125 & SEVEN POEMS 4 11
   bark and hug you safe and tight just as . . . . . . . . . . . 192 XLI CHANSONS 2  10
   place that's measured and safe and known where it's . . . . . 466 NEW POEMS 4     18
   into the where so safe we are / / . . . . . . . . . . . . . . 746 95 POEMS 74      8
   / / perished have safe small facts of hilltop . . . . . . . . 755 95 POEMS 83      1
   a flower. Nobody, it's safe to say, observed him  . . . . . . 802 73 POEMS 30      7
SAFELY
   immense tooth myself surveys safely the complete important  . 201 XLI PORTRAIT 9  31
   i contemplate her uneyes safely ensconced in thick glass  . . 326 VIVA 18          4
   we contemplate her uneyes safely ensconced in thick glass . . 327 VIVA 18         46
```

	PAGE	TITLE	LINE

SAFELY (CONTINUED)

    (unborn to not die safely whose epoch fits him . . . . 394 NO THANKS 11   2
    victim (death and life safely beyond) plays with the . . . . 554 1 X 1 14   3
    and complete love, all safely small big wickedly worlds . . . 761 95 POEMS 88   11
    the universe of sleep safely may by imperishable your . . . . 811 73 POEMS 39   2

SAFETYRAZORS

    pianolas funnygraphs skyscrapers an safetyrazors sall right . 237 IS 5 ONE 8   10

SAFFRON

    howdah of jasper beneath saffron umbrellas upon an elephant . 32 T&C ORIENTALE 6   5

SAG

    splintered normality crackle and sag of planes clamors of . . 48 T&C IMPRESS 2   7
    / / a fragrant sag of fruit distinctly grouped. . . . . 219 XLI SONNETS 15   1

SAGE

    golden door, poet and sage and caliph had to . . . . 22 T&C PUELLA MEA 223

SAGES

    heaven with hell. Whatever sages say and fools, all's . . . . 768 95 POEMS 94   14

SAGEST

    to dance maketh the sagest pane of littler huts . . . . 207 XLI SONNETS 3   3

SAGGING

    have swoopingly fallen svelte sagging gone into the soaring . 110 & PORTRAIT 6   28
    rapidly at me through sagging debris of exploded day . . . . 151 & SON REAL 22   2

SAGS

    fur poilu a Jesus sags in frolicsome wooden agony). . . . . . 134 & SON REAL 5   15

SAHARAS

    cancels conflict and agreement --saharas have their . . . . . 683 95 POEMS 11   7

SAID

    man squeezing her waist said the cop's rung for . . . . 53 T&C PORTRAIT 1   36
    in Dick Mid's Place said to Death teach me . . . . 57 T&C PORTRAIT 5   4
    his childhood and He said "willingly for the tale . . . . . . 57 T&C PORTRAIT 5   14
    Place asked "always" Death said "then as i recollect . . . . 57 T&C PORTRAIT 5   28
    (ta-te-ta in a parenthesis! said the moon) / . . . . 89 & POST IMPR 1   17
    renewed world" to me said the) wind being A . . . . 91 & POST IMPR 3   19
    may the first crumb said whereupon its fellow five . . . . . 117 & PORTRAIT 10   12
    Brain--my, head's big she (said laughing) with your . . . . 123 & SEVEN POEMS 2 14
    the tree? I didn't said the little lady who . . . . 125 & SEVEN POEMS 4   4
    tree? you got me said the smoke who runs . . . . 125 & SEVEN POEMS 4 10
    the tree? I dunno said the silver dog, with . . . . 125 & SEVEN POEMS 4 15
    her paler-paler face and said never mind, you'll find . . . . 125 & SEVEN POEMS 4 19
    the ivories and she said said She Win and . . . . 125 & SEVEN POEMS 4 23
    ivories and she said said She Win and you . . . . 125 & SEVEN POEMS 4 23
    came and the Moon said into his Ripe Eyes . . . . 125 & SEVEN POEMS 4 27
    when all's done and said, and under the grass . . . . 181 XLI SONGS 3   11
    may that be i said exhaling into eternity as . . . . 194 XLI PORTRAIT 2   29
    an almostclean plate "Achilles" said Nicho' "and did you . . 194 XLI PORTRAIT 2   36
    rotten" the face yawning said what her mouth thinks . . . . . 225 IS 5 ONE LIZ   12
    she with radishred legs said (crossing them slowly) "I'm . . 228 IS 5 ONE MARJ   3
    failure and nearly everybody said he should have gone . . . . 239 IS 5 ONE 10   4
    a muffhunter and he said to us Kid. daze . . . . 259 IS 5 ONE 29   27
    froides. His Royal Highness said "peek-a-boo" and thirty tame 262 IS 5 ONE 32   27
    you do" she smiling said "thought you were earning . . . . . 313 VIVA 5   6
    that reminds me who said o yes Frost Something . . . . 315 VIVA 7   2
    / may i feel said he (i'll squeal said . . . . 399 NO THANKS 16   1
    said he (i'll squeal said she just once said . . . . 399 NO THANKS 16   2
    said she just once said he) it's fun said . . . . 399 NO THANKS 16   3
    said he) it's fun said she (may i touch . . . . 399 NO THANKS 16   4
    she (may i touch said he how much said . . . . 399 NO THANKS 16   5
    said he how much said she a lot said . . . . 399 NO THANKS 16   6
    said she a lot said he) why not said . . . . 399 NO THANKS 16   7
    said he) why not said she (let's go said . . . . 399 NO THANKS 16   8
    said she (let's go said he not too far . . . . 399 NO THANKS 16   9
    he not too far said she what's too far . . . . 399 NO THANKS 16   10
    she what's too far said he where you are . . . . 399 NO THANKS 16   11
    he where you are said she) may i stay . . . . 399 NO THANKS 16   12
    she) may i stay said he (which way said . . . . 399 NO THANKS 16   13
    said he (which way said she like this said . . . . 399 NO THANKS 16   14
    said she like this said he if you kiss . . . . 399 NO THANKS 16   15
    he if you kiss said she may i move . . . . 399 NO THANKS 16   16
    she may i move said he is it love . . . . 399 NO THANKS 16   17

	PAGE	TITLE	LINE

SAID (CONTINUED)
he is it love said she) if you're willing . . . . 399 NO THANKS 16   18
she) if you're willing said he (but you're killing . . . . . 399 NO THANKS 16   19
he (but you're killing said she but it's life . . . . 399 NO THANKS 16   20
she but it's life said he but your wife . . . . 399 NO THANKS 16   21
he but your wife said she now said he) . . . . 399 NO THANKS 16   22
wife said she now said he) ow said she . . . . 399 NO THANKS 16   23
now said he) ow said she (tiptop said he . . . . 399 NO THANKS 16   24
ow said she (tiptop said he don't stop said . . . . 399 NO THANKS 16   25
said he don't stop said she oh no said . . . . 399 NO THANKS 16   26
said she oh no said he) go slow said . . . . 399 NO THANKS 16   27
said he) go slow said she (cccome? said he . . . . 399 NO THANKS 16   28
slow said she (cccome? said he ummm said she) . . . . . . 399 NO THANKS 16   29
(cccome? said he ummm said she) you're divine! said . . . . 399 NO THANKS 16   30
said she) you're divine! said he (you are Mine . . . . . . 399 NO THANKS 16   31
he (you are Mine said she) / / / . . . . 399 NO THANKS 16   32
listen here's (correct you said it yeah) but listen . . . . . 400 NO THANKS 17   12
my specialty is living said a man (who could . . . . 473 NEW POEMS 11   1
Feels; if & god said & there was is . . . . 479 NEW POEMS 17   12
what blood darling i said / / / / . . . . 496 50 POEMS 10   20
the lady's small grin said (with more simplicity than . . . . 506 50 POEMS 20   13
hope and then) they said their nevers they slept . . . . . . 515 50 POEMS 29   20
oped her teeming womb said demon for to doom . . . . 552 1 X 1 12   22
for by love love said did o no yes . . . . 589 1 X 1 49   6
+SAID
FOR CONTEXT, SEE . . . . 474 NEW POEMS 12   10
SAIL
through high air a sail a fishing boat somebody . . . . 283 IS 5 THREE 7   7
SAILED
named Smith and we sailed on the Leviathan / . . . . 313 VIVA 5   11
SAILING
steeples and clouds: go sailing away and away sailing . . . . 129 & SEVEN POEMS 7   10
sailing away and away sailing into a keen city . . . . 129 & SEVEN POEMS 7   11
come ships go snowily sailing perfect silence. Absolute ocean 586 1 X 1 46   18
SAILOR
beside his teddy-bears the sailor shuffles the night with . . 108 & PORTRAIT 4   25
SAILORS
renowned investigator of paper sailors--argonauta argo   . . . 326 VIVA 18   6
SAILS
watcher who adores perceived sails whose mighty brightness . 79 T&C SON UNRE 4   9
the hips and her sails filled with dream-- when . . . . 156 & SON ACTU 5   7
ship which captain am sails out of sleep steering . . . . . . 781 73 POEMS 9   3
SAIN
like Nooer Leans Shikahgo Sain Looey Noo York an . . . . . . 237 IS 5 ONE 8   7
SAINT
care in hopes that Saint Nicholas" / / / . . . . 142 & SON REAL 13   14
the exhumed hand of Saint Ignatz miraculously inhabits. . . . 280 IS 5 THREE 4   4
without hearts have set saint against sinner; put gain   . . . 769 95 POEMS 95   15
+SAINT
FOR CONTEXT, SEE . . . . 431 NO THANKS 48   21
SAINTS
/ by little accurate saints thickly which tread the . . . . . 85 T&C SON ACTU 4   1
very wonderful in bed --saints and satyrs, go your . . . . . 794 73 POEMS 22   7
SAITH
rosily gods whiten befall saith rain anguish of dream-send . 90 & POST IMPR 2   4
SAKE
halfsmile (for society's sweet sake) in the not too . . . . . 146 & SON REAL 17   11
awoke for the beautiful sake of a grave gay . . . . 587 1 X 1 47   20
+SAKE
FOR CONTEXT, SEE . . . . 310 VIVA 2   9
FOR CONTEXT, SEE . . . . 703 95 POEMS 31   16
+SALAD
FOR CONTEXT, SEE . . . . 227 IS 5 ONE GERT   16
SALE
hand is when for sale? forever is to give . . . . 538 50 POEMS 50   11
SALESMAN
/ / / a salesman is an it that . . . . 549 1 X 1 9   1
immaterial it stinks a salesman is an it that . . . . 549 1 X 1 9   8

	PAGE	TITLE	LINE

SALIVA
    buoyed on the murderous saliva of industry. the mor- . . . . 201 XLI PORTRAIT 9   5
SALLOW
    one April dusk the sallow street-lamps were turning snowy . . 194 XLI PORTRAIT 2   2
SALLY
    to her i says Sally i says the mmmoon, ... 167 & SON ACTU 16   13
    preserved goldfishian gestures) suddenly sally rand . . . . . 425 NO THANKS 42   4
    some handsomest harry (and sally and nan they tremble . . . . 509 50 POEMS 23   16
SALOME
    feet of the Princess Salome carefully dancing in the   . . . . 17 T&C PUELLA MEA   30
+SALOMES
    FOR CONTEXT, SEE . . . . 235 IS 5 ONE 6   23
+SALT
    FOR CONTEXT, SEE . . . . 376 VIVA 67   4
SALUTE
    clever deadly heaven i salute you whose body is . . . . 112 & PORTRAIT 6   108
    my friend. Whom i salute, by what is dear . . . . 158 & SON ACTU 7   9
    deeplyness rose to undeath) salute. and having worshipped for 358 VIVA 49   14
    never have) do i salute (by moon by sun . . . . 441 NO THANKS 56   65
    you beautiful anarchist (i salute thee / / / . . . . 677 95 POEMS 5   16
SALUTED
    the far- departed mouth sweetly-saluted lingers. if one . . . 42 T&C AMORES 6   6
    being shooting his cuffs saluted everywhere saluting . . . . 275 IS 5 TWO 9   36
SALUTING
    his cuffs saluted everywhere saluting reviewing processions . 275 IS 5 TWO 9   36
SAM
    down tree flights an Sam begins boxin im on . . . . 332 VIVA 23   8
    in the man. Up sam (down! alice) a hole . . . . 513 50 POEMS 27   21
    / rain or hail sam done the best he . . . . 568 1 X 1 28   2
    digged his hole : sam was a man stout . . . . 568 1 X 1 28   5
    clover clover (nobody'll know) sam was a man grinned . . . . 568 1 X 1 28   26
    quo pro quid" uncle sam shrugs his pretty pink . . . . 711 95 POEMS 39   21
SAME
    much and in the same place. Why according to . . . . 262 IS 5 ONE 32   17
    We are not the same you and i, since . . . . 286 IS 5 FOUR 3   16
    are made of the same thing as perhaps nothing, ... 299 IS 5 FOUR 16   15
    impotence of not and same answer, beginning, ecstasy, to . . 351 VIVA 42   4
    add, the cult of Same is all the chic; . . . . 438 NO THANKS 54   12
    / / / worshipping Same they squirm and they . . . . 439 NO THANKS 55   1
    isn't they reaped their same sun moon stars rain . . . . . . 515 50 POEMS 29   7
    differ a disease of same, conform the pinnacle of . . . . . . 521 50 POEMS 34   59
    grey snow of mothery same rotting keen dream? i . . . . 527 50 POEMS 39   29
    himself will do the same because you aren't afraid . . . . . 679 95 POEMS 7   4
    who never sings the same thing twice and still . . . . 760 95 POEMS 87   3
    if they've become the same it's time you unbecame . . . . . . 834 73 POEMS 62   17
SAMENESS
    though life's lived wrongsideout, sameness chokes oneness . . 446 NO THANKS 61   3
    less worse (but only sameness is normal in Ever-Ever . . . . 466 NEW POEMS 4   25
SAMES
    dooms of love through sames of am through haves . . . . 520 50 POEMS 34   2
+SAN FRANCISCO
    FOR CONTEXT, SEE . . . . 237 IS 5 ONE 8   8
SAND
    spins, tumbles; rolling in sand. across this water, crowding 281 IS 5 THREE 5   4
    white is tumbling in sand Clouds over me are . . . . 281 IS 5 THREE 5   14
    look back. (Along the sand behind us, a big . . . . 303 IS 5 FIVE 2   11
    recent footprint in the sand of was) / / . . . . 344 VIVA 35   15
+SAND
    FOR CONTEXT, SEE . . . . 99 & POST IMPR 10   21
    FOR CONTEXT, SEE . . . . 119 & PORTRAIT 11   5
SANDBURG
    Old days: of Amy Sandburg of Algernon Carl Swinburned. . . . 233 IS 5 ONE 4   18
SANDPILE
    upon the sternly allotted sandpile --how silently emit a . . 231 IS 5 ONE 3   51
SANDS
    sleep and move) blind sands, at pitiless the mercy . . . . . 743 95 POEMS 71   8
SANE
    forgive it is most sane and sunly and more . . . . 530 50 POEMS 42   13

		PAGE	TITLE	LINE

SANG
water the cruel bugle sang before. Horn at hip . . . . 14 T&C SONGS 4 — 10
valley the famished arrow sang before. Bow at belt . . . . . 14 T&C SONGS 4 — 20
mountain the lucky hunter sang before. All in green . . . . . 14 T&C SONGS 4 — 30
body when my heart sang between your perfect breasts . . . . 39 T&C AMORES 4 — 15
summer autumn winter he sang his didn't he danced . . . . . 515 50 POEMS 29 — 4
discovered a shell that sang so sweetly she couldn't . . . . 682 95 POEMS 10 — 3
silence of him self sang like a bird. Mostpeople . . . . . . 802 73 POEMS 30 — 28

+SANG
FOR CONTEXT, SEE . . . . 318 VIVA 10 — 11

SANGSUNG
he belowtry eye nowbrow sangsung nee whitermuch grab sicksilk 333 VIVA 24 — 10

SANK
hit a mine and sank just off the coast . . . . 494 50 POEMS 8 — 3
on the snout frank sank him with an uppercut . . . . 706 95 POEMS 34 — 2

SANS
Huge this collective pseudobeast (sans either pain or joy) . 544 1 X 1 4 — 6
all multiplied with infinity sans if the mightiest . . . . 592 1 X 1 52 — 5
goes round --a dream sans meaning (or whatever kills) . . . . 735 95 POEMS 63 — 5
infinite also ourselves exist sans shallbe or was (laws . . . 755 95 POEMS 83 — 14
year (eternity being so sans until twice i have . . . . . . 765 95 POEMS 91 — 13
ever knew (1) we sans love equals mob love . . . . 803 73 POEMS 31 — 7

SANTA
. The kid) er Santa Claus a criminal (hears . . . . 398 NO THANKS 15 — 14

SAP
to leaf and to sap and to your (in . . . . 424 NO THANKS 41 — 1

SARCASMS
g dre ams whichful sarcasms papery deathfuls) awaits yes . . 415 NO THANKS 32 — 18

SARDINES
shot with some difficulty sardines. Mr. Wiggin took Wrs. . . 263 IS 5 ONE 32 — 47

SAT
all the little schoolchildren sat down / / / . . . . 249 IS 5 ONE 20 — 4
upon which everyone has sat except a man / . . . . 550 1 X 1 10 — 2

SATAN
/ / Jehovah buried, Satan dead, do fearers worship . . . . . 438 NO THANKS 54 — 1

SATANIC
s-p-i-r-a- l and, disappear) Satanic and blase a black . . . 278 IS 5 THREE 2 — 15

SATISFACTION
according to his perfect satisfaction vanishing from a this . 516 50 POEMS 30 — 14

SATRAPS
forgetfulness thy lips are satraps in scarlet in whose . . . 29 T&C ORIENTALE 3 — 24

SATTER
wot i refers ter Satter Nailyuh (comes but once . . . . . . 237 IS 5 ONE 8 — 15

+SATURNALIA
FOR CONTEXT, SEE . . . . 237 IS 5 ONE 8 — 15

SATYRS
in bed --saints and satyrs, go your way youths . . . . 794 73 POEMS 22 — 7

SAUCERS
say Now the all saucers but cups if begin . . . . 287 IS 5 FOUR 4 — 15

SAVAGE
they (summoned by that savage yell from shining realms . . . 799 73 POEMS 27 — 26

SAVE
am aware of anything save that these houses bulge . . . . . . 98 & POST IMPR 9 — 16
(check undublcheck) babbitt (GOD SAVE THE UNCOMMONWEALTH OF . 325 VIVA 17 — 22
radios and raddios) did save man from himself ye . . . . . 552 1 X 1 12 — 15
stop thief help murder save the world" what world? . . . . . 555 1 X 1 15 — 1
victim , not to save a world for stalin . . . . 643 {CHAIRE} 45 — 3

SAVING
/ granted the all saving our young kiss only . . . . 373 VIVA 64 — 2

SAVIOUR
Soon Admiral Soon the saviour of the Navy of . . . . 642 {CHAIRE} 44 — 13

SAVIOURS
eternity, men will be saviours --flop grasshopper, exactly . 555 1 X 1 15 — 6

+SAVO
FOR CONTEXT, SEE . . . . 471 NEW POEMS 9 — 25

SAVOURING
will permit a metaphor savouring slightly of the demotic) . . 326 VIVA 18 — 27

SAW

chiseled eyes the people saw their once again victorious . . 4 T&C EPITHALAM 33
whose brightening strictness Danae saw the night severed and 4 T&C EPITHALAM 52
day and space i saw you close your eyes . . . . 30 T&C ORIENTALE 4 34
walked the boulevard i saw a dirty child skating . . . . . . 56 T&C PORTRAIT 4 2
The last thing he saw was you naked amid . . . . 170 & SON ACTU 19 5
(or was something we saw in the mirror)? therefore . . . . . 286 IS 5 FOUR 3 20
you and they never saw so much heard so . . . . 474 NEW POEMS 12 5

SAWDUST

in no sir hopping sawdust you kiddo he's a . . . . 96 & POST IMPR 8 15
up-in tenements talk. in sawdust Voices a: whispering . . . . 128 & SEVEN POEMS 6 5
i can't sleep (smoking sawdust cigarettes in the middle . . . 242 IS 5 ONE 13 21
and hither in filthy sawdust chucks and rolls against . . . . 259 IS 5 ONE 29 4
their actions and speeches sawdust perpetually leak rather is 261 IS 5 ONE 31 5

SAXOPHONIC

parting the tousle of saxophonic brogue. / / / . . . . 140 & SON REAL 11 15

SAY

fragility of poppies.... i say that sometimes on these . . . 45 T&C LA GUERRE 1 7
be so; and i say that if your lips, ... 76 T&C SON UNRE 1 1
this should be, i say if this should be-- . . . . 76 T&C SON UNRE 1 9
what have you to say, wind wind wind--did you . . . . 80 T&C SON UNRE 5 5
a little wonderful, and say Perhaps her body touched . . . . 82 T&C SON ACTU 1 13
fear people bells) i say your eyes can take . . . . 98 & POST IMPR 9 3
and first finger (i say "will he buy flowers" . . . . 102 & POST IMPR 12 6
has a beard" i say to you who are . . . . 102 & POST IMPR 12 10
just imagine it I say God amid a monstrous . . . . 117 & PORTRAIT 10 25
never intro- duced you say Yes because you know . . . . 126 & SEVEN POEMS 5 21
the rosebug and you say Sure you say (like . . . . 127 & SEVEN POEMS 5 48
you say Sure you say (like that) sure i'll . . . . 127 & SEVEN POEMS 5 49
come with you you say for i like kittens . . . . 127 & SEVEN POEMS 5 49
of your shall i say body? follows truly through . . . . . . 140 & SON REAL 11 3
if it could) eyes say the breasts look very . . . . 150 & SON REAL 21 3
more like curving colour (say orange) against silence, or . . 152 & SON ACTU 1 3
through with and leaves say alas, much is to . . . . 181 XLI SONGS 3 2
somebody hears what i say--let him be pitiful: because . . . 216 XLI SONNETS 12 10
by my arms' bothness (say a twilight lifting the . . . . . . 218 XLI SONNETS 14 4
not wonder how let's say elation causes the bent . . . . . . 229 IS 5 ONE FRAN 12
i mean what i say i believe my most . . . . 262 IS 5 ONE 32 13
desire of shall we say: Idleness, while meaning its . . . . . 263 IS 5 ONE 32 39
moments be translated: i say that even after April . . . . 264 IS 5 ONE 33 6
and so forth oh say can you see by . . . . 268 IS 5 TWO 3 3
we're NOT (oh-- --i say that's jolly odd old . . . . 269 IS 5 TWO 4 13
my habits laughter i say you will perhaps pardon, ... 285 IS 5 FOUR 2 8
but if i should say goodmorning trouble adds up . . . . . . 287 IS 5 FOUR 4 1
(but If i should say thankyouverymuch mr rosenbloom picks . . 287 IS 5 FOUR 4 7
but if i Should say solong my tailor chuckles . . . . 287 IS 5 FOUR 4 10
(but if i should say Now the all saucers . . . . 287 IS 5 FOUR 4 14
dance every- should where say over the damned table . . . . . 287 IS 5 FOUR 4 17
but if i should, Say, / / / / . . . . 287 IS 5 FOUR 4 21
/ touching you i say (it being Spring and . . . . 303 IS 5 FIVE 2 1
very little afraid") i say "along this particular road . . . 303 IS 5 FIVE 2 8
hair --let the world say "his most wise music . . . . 306 IS 5 FIVE 5 9
Gay had nothing to say to the animals and . . . . 326 VIVA 18 29
animals had nothing to say to Miss Gay during . . . . 326 VIVA 18 30
there therehere And) i say "won't you" (remembering) knowing 353 VIVA 44 24
mice (and you, you say "let's" going in "take . . . . 353 VIVA 44 29
ocean, this is moonlight: say that both precisely beyond . . 379 VIVA 70 1
under because) only who'll say "and this be my . . . . 439 NO THANKS 55 25
& that "I may say professor" asleep wop "shapley . . . . . . 464 NEW POEMS 2 10
meal's coming from i say to hell with that . . . . 475 NEW POEMS 13 5
lifting my finger i say to hell with that . . . . 475 NEW POEMS 13 9
hell with that i say that doesn't matter) but . . . . 475 NEW POEMS 13 11
or generous what i say is whistle that sing . . . . 475 NEW POEMS 13 15
probably handbag) because i say that's not swell (get . . . . 475 NEW POEMS 13 22
was born to never say nay but lucy could . . . . 509 50 POEMS 23 20
that wispily is to say according to his perfect . . . . 516 50 POEMS 30 13
least as truth --i say though hate were why . . . . 521 50 POEMS 34 66
/ / / i say no world can hold . . . . 523 50 POEMS 36 1

	PAGE	TITLE	LINE

SAY (CONTINUED)

work i know i say i have not any . . . . 523 50 POEMS 36   16
every -thing nothing i say the world not fit . . . . 523 50 POEMS 36   26
he is not (i say the world yes any . . . . 523 50 POEMS 36   29
buyable alive one i say human being) one goldberger . . . . . 524 50 POEMS 36   46
have singings gone to say? here youngest selves yet . . . . . 538 50 POEMS 50   6
/ / neither could say (it comes so slow . . . . 542 1 X 1 2   1
(masturbates one honest breadcrumb) say "i understand quite . 546 1 X 1 6   12
of the you were say or a jennelman name . . . . 549 1 X 1 9   2
all there is to say" (and she looked) "especially . . . . . . 572 1 X 1 32   4
each (why do people say it's un lucky to . . . . 623 (CHAIRE) 25   6
to am he sharpens say to sing you'd almost . . . . 624 (CHAIRE) 26   14
his handorgan until you say "i want a fortune" . . . . . . 697 95 POEMS 25   4
of a shall we say somewhat diversified (putting it . . . . 699 95 POEMS 27   16
wledge is po wer) say o if i 'd . . . . 700 95 POEMS 28   10
ing as if to say b ut for chreyesake . . . . 703 95 POEMS 31   15
first robin the; you say something (for only me) . . . . . 737 95 POEMS 65   2
with hell. Whatever sages say and fools, all's well . . . . 768 95 POEMS 94   14
have the must to say and the when to . . . . 776 73 POEMS 4   8
cannot sing) lish sparrows say then 2 or per . . . . 787 73 POEMS 15   4
mine --dingdong: dongding-- to say would be to sing . . . . 798 73 POEMS 26   7
stars in their silence say Be the cunning the . . . . 801 73 POEMS 29   18
Nobody, it's safe to say, observed him but myself; . . . . 802 73 POEMS 30   8
may have shall we say guessed?" "we shall" quoth . . . . . 807 73 POEMS 35   13

+SAY

FOR CONTEXT, SEE . . . . 310 VIVA 2   7
FOR CONTEXT, SEE . . . . 398 NO THANKS 15   20

SAYING

hear with weepings soundless, saying of "alas we were . . . . 9 T&C SONGS 1   21
a smoothness which sings, saying (though love be a . . . . . 13 T&C SONGS 3   5
and take his hands, saying, Accept all happiness from . . . . 76 T&C SON UNRE 1   12
Sunday. by way of saying nothing he smiled (but . . . . 355 VIVA 46   3
moon outside your window saying if that's all, just . . . . . 572 1 X 1 32   2
person) and while never saying a word who was . . . . 802 73 POEMS 30   25

SAYINGLY

big vermilion departure swim, sayingly; (Do you think?) the . 66 T&C POST IMPR 3   12

SAYS

playing, whose strangeness much says; singing (though love be 13 T&C SONGS 3   12
line the first lady says to nine ladies his . . . . 15 T&C SONGS 5   6
wine the tenth lady says to nine ladies they . . . . . . 15 T&C SONGS 5   10
too fine the nineteenth says to nine ladies you . . . . . 15 T&C SONGS 5   14
a faint piddle-of-drops she says I ploc spittle what . . . . 96 & POST IMPR 8   14
on his whistle somebody says here's luck somebody else . . . 108 & PORTRAIT 4   20
here's luck somebody else says down the hatch the . . . . . 108 & PORTRAIT 4   21
stoopid and if dead says may i have this . . . . 126 & SEVEN POEMS 5   20
one string dead never says my dear, Time for . . . . 126 & SEVEN POEMS 5   29
you to anyway dead says come with me he . . . . 127 & SEVEN POEMS 5   45
come with me he says (andwhyevernot) into the round . . . . 127 & SEVEN POEMS 5   45
day, the hour) she says to me you big . . . . 167 & SON ACTU 16   12
you big fool she says i says to her . . . . 167 & SON ACTU 16   13
fool she says i says to her i says . . . . 167 & SON ACTU 16   13
says to her i says Sally i says the . . . . 167 & SON ACTU 16   13
i says Sally i says the mmmoon, begins to, ... 167 & SON ACTU 16   14
his worms, when loveliness says sweetly Yes to wind . . . . 183 XLI SONGS 5   10
is it didn't Ruskin says about you got the . . . . 257 IS 5 ONE 27   35
your eyelids' flutter which says we are for each . . . . . 290 IS 5 FOUR 7   12
mans 1 (hutch) hutchinson says sweet guinea pigs do . . . . 325 VIVA 17   7
/ / / snow) says! Says over un graves . . . . 417 NO THANKS 34   1
/ / snow) says! Says over un graves der, ... 417 NO THANKS 34   1
un graves der, speaking (says. word Less) ly (goes . . . . 417 NO THANKS 34   5
iv es (c omeS says) s; n; o; w . . . . 417 NO THANKS 34   14
s; n; o; w (says W I elds) un . . . . 417 NO THANKS 34   14
what is meek; obey says toc, submit says tic, ... 438 NO THANKS 54   5
obey says toc, submit says tic, Eternity's a Five . . . . . 438 NO THANKS 54   5
why of a leaf says (floating each how) you're . . . . 543 1 X 1 3   7
pres (who always nothing says) and he kissed the . . . . . 552 1 X 1 12   27
is what a mirror says it is a maid . . . . 570 1 X 1 30   1
it is a maid says Who and (hearing not . . . . 570 1 X 1 30   2

654

SAYS (CONTINUED)

the quote state unquote says "kill" killing is an . . . . . . 636 (CHAIRE) 38   7
/ as joe gould says in his terrifyingly hu . . . . 700 95 POEMS 28   1
riddle for you red says it aint his daughter . . . . 707 95 POEMS 35   19
and the gentle who-horns says-does moo-woo (the prance with . 773 73 POEMS 1   8
wife) --does doesn't unsays says looks smiles or simply . . . 779 73 POEMS 7   19
bell in the steeple says Why the chary the . . . . 801 73 POEMS 29   6
moon in her glory says Who the busy the . . . . 801 73 POEMS 29   12
sun in his heaven says Now the timid the . . . . 801 73 POEMS 29   24
earth in her splendor says May / / / . . . . 801 73 POEMS 29   30

+SAYS

FOR CONTEXT, SEE . . . . 94 & POST IMPR 6   14
FOR CONTEXT, SEE . . . . 310 VIVA 2   1
FOR CONTEXT, SEE . . . . 310 VIVA 2   2
FOR CONTEXT, SEE . . . . 310 VIVA 2   3
FOR CONTEXT, SEE . . . . 310 VIVA 2   5

SAYS-DOES

and the gentle who-horns says-does moo-woo (the prance with . 773 73 POEMS 1   8

SAYSTHESEA

w h e e saysthesea-brE aking-b Re akin g . . . . 94 & POST IMPR 6   7

SCALE

merely to toil the scale to shrillerness per every . . . . . 579 1 X 1 39   10

SCALELESS

the red elected lips scaleless visions) / / / . . . . 36 T&C AMORES 1   32

SCALPED

redskin toma hawked and scalped his victim , not . . . . . . 643 (CHAIRE) 45   2

SCALPEL

heartless them (given the scalpel, they dissect a kiss; . . . 556 1 X 1 16   7

SCAMPER

mischief) all you guilty scamper (you bastards throw . . . . 452 NO THANKS 67   5

SCANDAL

permanent faces coyly bandy scandal of Mrs. N and . . . . . . 70 T&C SON REAL 1   10
swivelchair one fist dangling scandal while five other . . . 259 IS 5 ONE 29   9

SCARCE

through the new world scarce astir my fragile lady . . . . . 17 T&C PUELLA MEA   12

SCARCELY

of quivering ghosts-of-love which scarcely sings drifting in   6 T&C EPITHALAM   143
us and birds known, scarcely to sing (heart, could . . . . . 205 XLI SONNETS 1   14
over there. yet we scarcely fare much better-- what's . . . . 233 IS 5 ONE 4   9
my very lady, if scarcely the somewhat city wiggles . . . . . 302 IS 5 FIVE 1   3
address and there they'll scarcely find us (if they . . . . . 579 1 X 1 39   13
very boldest man can scarcely dare to meet no . . . . 685 95 POEMS 13   3
am perceive (but believe scarcely may) certainly while mute . 808 73 POEMS 36   9

SCARCELYEST

ind) nd ArE GLIB SCARCELYEST AMONGS FLOWERING / / . . . . . . 421 NO THANKS 38   31

SCARE

pair had a little scare right in the middle . . . . 401 NO THANKS 18   2

SCARECROW

earth ignorantly blossoming a scarecrow demongod countless in 662 (CHAIRE) 64   8

SCARED

thy hands, which the scared shepherd gave thee for . . . . .   6 T&C EPITHALAM   152
objectively, i was horribly scared i would actually fall . . 263 IS 5 ONE 32   62

+SCARED

FOR CONTEXT, SEE . . . . 316 VIVA 8   6

SCARLET

lips are satraps in scarlet in whose kiss is . . . . 29 T&C ORIENTALE 3   24
came riding upon a scarlet sunset trampling the night . . . . 30 T&C ORIENTALE 4   23
and wealthy vermilion and breathless-scarlet, dark colours . 100 & POST IMPR 11   7
once, it, ate a scarlet pepper and my eyes . . . . 100 & POST IMPR 11   30
evenslicing eyes are chisels scarlet Goes with her whitehot . 106 & PORTRAIT 2   5
utters a thud of scarlet. always. More interesting, as . . . 143 & SON REAL 14   6
utter lilac shrieks and scarlet bellowings. / / / . . . . . . 199 XLI PORTRAIT 7   11
in twi nn ingly scarlet woundsmile) / / / . . . . 615 (CHAIRE) 17   21

+SCARLETLY

FOR CONTEXT, SEE . . . . 342 VIVA 33   13

SCATTER

whose careless movements carefully scatter pink propaganda of 150 & SON REAL 21   14
millionary knives of wind-- scatter his nothing all over . . 839 73 POEMS 67   12

	PAGE	TITLE	LINE

SCATTERED
her soul, hope richly scattered by the abundant sun . . . . . 5 T&C EPITHALAM 83
SCATTERING
the sky light walks scattering poems on earth a . . . . 50 T&C IMPRESS 4 3
the sky night walks scattering poems / / / . . . . 50 T&C IMPRESS 4 33
prodigious face thy voice scattering perfume-gifted wings . . 187 XLI SONGS 9 13
SCENTED
un -spontaneous and otherwise scented merde which greets one 230 IS 5 ONE 2 16
SCENTS
blossoms that do learn, scents of not known musics . . . . . 9 T&C SONGS 1 17
SCEPTRED
well? Chryselephantine Zeus Olympian sceptred colossus of the 3 T&C EPITHALAM 26
SCHEDULE
(suddenly-Lights go! on, by schedule / / / / . . . . 167 & SON ACTU 16 19
SCHEME
shoulders as cowards will scheme to harness: let all . . . . 439 NO THANKS 55 14
SCHEMING
be mud and mire, scheming imagine, passion willed, freedom . 521 50 POEMS 34 55
your stride (instead of scheming how to beat the . . . . . . 679 95 POEMS 7 2
SCHIAVONI
night upon the Riva Schiavoni or in the felicitous . . . . . 256 IS 5 ONE 27 17
SCHOLARS
could all earth's rotting scholars guess that life shall . . 420 NO THANKS 37 8
SCHOOLCHILDREN
and all the little schoolchildren sat down / / . . . . 249 IS 5 ONE 20 4
SCHOOLROOM
to yes must's a schoolroom in the month of . . . . 574 1 X 1 34 5
SCIENCE
the naughty thumb of science prodded thy beauty . . . . 46 T&C LA GUERRE 2 11
because equals (transparent or science must bait laws with . 478 NEW POEMS 16 4
lions & oxen is science) Q: how numb can . . . . 791 73 POEMS 19 8
SCIENTIFIC
/ proud of his scientific attitude and liked the . . . . . . 499 50 POEMS 13 1
(but Death is strictly scientific & artificial & evil . . . . 604 (CHAIRE) 6 19
+SCIENTIFIC
FOR CONTEXT, SEE . . . . 499 50 POEMS 13 12
FOR CONTEXT, SEE . . . . 544 1 X 1 4 21
SCIENTIFICALLY
of his physiognomy his scientifically pressed trousers . . . 259 IS 5 ONE 29 24
SCIENTIST
unthing next, our illustrious scientist petitions the . . . . 799 73 POEMS 27 23
SCIMITARS
colours in their hands scimitars like windy torches each . . 33 T&C ORIENTALE 6 39
SCINTILLANT
lithe free twitch of scintillant space, with the cool . . . . 18 T&C PUELLA MEA 84
SCOLDS
laughs (sing old age scolds Forbid den Stop Must . . . . . . 729 95 POEMS 57 13
SCOOT
do bang hands angle scoot bulbs marry a become) . . . . 309 VIVA 1 13
SCORCHBEND
made of blueandgreen paper scorchbend ingthem -selves-U pcurv 278 IS 5 THREE 2 7
SCORE
lips, as if a score of youngest angels suddenly . . . . 130 & SON REAL 1 4
SCORN
intricately in the delicate scorn with which in a . . . . . . 144 & SON REAL 15 11
ing at me your scorn of easily hatred of . . . . 677 95 POEMS 5 4
SCORNING
only see him smile. Scorning the pomp of must . . . . 520 50 POEMS 34 33
SCORNS
the cold ones paul scorns all the girls (the . . . . 619 (CHAIRE) 21 8
SCOTCH
bettyandisbel come dancing from hop-scotch and jump-rope and 24 T&C CHANSONS 1 15
blind irisher fiddles a scotch jig in a stinking . . . . . . 108 & PORTRAIT 4 9
knock you down (while scotch was your breakfast every . . . . 605 (CHAIRE) 7 5
SCOUT
coeds) thoroughly bretish they scout the inhuman itarian . . 492 50 POEMS 6 6
SCOWL
on hip & the scowl of a cannibal) there's . . . . 640 (CHAIRE) 42 10

| | | PAGE | TITLE | LINE |

SCRAGGY
    taken thee upon their scraggy knees squeezing and buffeting . 46 T&C LA GUERRE 2 15
SCRAMBLE
    things in my ears scramble faintly tickling putrescent . . . 69 T&C POST IMPR 6 29
SCRAMBLING
    a new frock coat (scrambling all up over the . . . . 267 IS 5 TWO 2   4
+SCRAPY
    FOR CONTEXT, SEE . . . . 122 & SEVEN POEMS 1 11
SCRATCH
    named Fred -someBody: hippopotamus, scratch- ing, one, knee . 252 IS 5 ONE 23   2
    begins to scretch and scratch-scrutch and scritch (while the 773 73 POEMS 1   14
SCRATCH-SCRUTCH
    begins to scretch and scratch-scrutch and scritch (while the 773 73 POEMS 1   14
SCRATCHES
    a star sleepily, feebly, scratches the sore of morning. . . . 144 & SON REAL 15   9
    By midnight, a moon scratches the skin of the . . . . 160 & SON ACTU 9   8
    bung loamhome picpac obviously scratches tomorrowlobs . . . . 333 VIVA 24   5
SCRATCHILY
    is these a or scratchily over which of earth . . . . 491 50 POEMS 5   2
+SCRATCHING
    FOR CONTEXT, SEE . . . . 442 NO THANKS 57   14
SCRATCHINGCROWD
    humorous, fury heapingandsqueezing tum-bling- scratchingcrowd 100 & POST IMPR 11 14
SCRATCHINGS
    remembers some accurately profuse scratchings in a recently . 197 XLI PORTRAIT 5 18
SCREAM
    incredible But others don't scream murmur wink at kid . . . . 391 NO THANKS 8   14
    grasshopper, exactly nothing's soon; scream, all ye . . . . . 555 1 X 1 15   9
    with a warm thick scream and a keen cold . . . . 647 (CHAIRE) 49   7
+SCREAM
    FOR CONTEXT, SEE . . . . 506 50 POEMS 20   5
    FOR CONTEXT, SEE . . . . 646 (CHAIRE) 48   9
    FOR CONTEXT, SEE . . . . 656 (CHAIRE) 58   12
    FOR CONTEXT, SEE . . . . 795 73 POEMS 23   21
SCREAMED
    fabulous immensity the sky screamed the sun died) the . . . . 419 NO THANKS 36   9
SCREAMERS
    soon; scream, all ye screamers, till your if is . . . . 555 1 X 1 15   9
SCREAMGROA
    / / / after screamgroa ning. ish: ly; come . . . . 656 (CHAIRE) 58   1
SCREAMING
    push witless creases of screaming warmth chuck pil- lows . . 96 & POST IMPR 8   4
    a lean wind flays screaming hills with sleet and . . . . . . 560 1 X 1 20   10
    Mostpeople have been heard screaming for international . . . 802 73 POEMS 30   30
+SCREAMING
    FOR CONTEXT, SEE . . . . 726 95 POEMS 54   14
SCREAMINGLY
    of this raving city screamingly street wonderful flowers And 437 NO THANKS 53   3
SCREAMS
    circular shrieking tightness solid screams whisper.) . . . . 195 XLI PORTRAIT 3 15
    the giving ropes amid screams of deeply bulging thousands . . 259 IS 5 ONE 29   18
    dwells; a (ghost) Who screams Faintly always who Is . . . . . 312 VIVA 4   8
    pool of pink fat screams a hole in it . . . . 545 1 X 1 5   8
SCREECH
    and i hear the screech of dissonant flowers, and . . . . . . 61 T&C PORTRAIT 9 32
    shut in the sumptuous screech of simplicity (out of . . . . . 195 XLI PORTRAIT 3 7
    purring biceps, the mystic screech of Broadway, the trivial . 220 XLI SONNETS 16 2
    moon in if all screech-owls have not okayed his . . . . 620 (CHAIRE) 22   6
    chaos so (hark --that screech of space) absolute (my . . . . 639 (CHAIRE) 41   6
    just heard your annabel screech have you hunted her . . . . . 707 95 POEMS 35   5
SCREECH-OWLS
    moon in if all screech-owls have not okayed his . . . . 620 (CHAIRE) 22   6
SCREECHING
    ever & bi g screeching new black perfectly isn . . . . 646 (CHAIRE) 48   16
SCREETCHING
    scratchingcrowd ingworming each by screetching Each) on . . . 100 & POST IMPR 11 14
SCRETCH
    speckled strut begins to scretch and scratch-scrutch and . . 773 73 POEMS 1   13

SCRIBBLED
   of her tumbling face scribbled with a big grin. . . . . 73 T&C SON REAL 4   6
+SCRIBBLED
   FOR CONTEXT, SEE . . . . 415 NO THANKS 32   8
SCRIBBLING
   that this quickly ghost scribbling from there to where   . . . 504 50 POEMS 18   8
SCRITCH
   scretch and scratch-scrutch and scritch (while the . . . . . 773 73 POEMS 1   15
SCROLL
   brutal dew, --the authentic scroll of fairie hands and . . .   5 T&C EPITHALAM   87
SCRUMPTIOUS
   rosy flanked by the scrumptious magdalene of whoisit and . . 198 XLI PORTRAIT 6   10
   of his decease a scrumptious not to mention splendiferous . . 239 IS 5 ONE 10   30
SCRUPULOUS
   poignant instantaneous fern whose scrupulous enchanted fronds 19 T&C PUELLA MEA   111
SCRUPULOUSLY
   conversed in vain, O scrupulously take thy trivial toll, . . 212 XLI SONNETS 8   3
   will cultivate within me scrupulously the Inimitable which is 328 VIVA 19   2
SCRUTCH
   begins to scretch and scratch-scrutch and scritch (while the 773 73 POEMS 1   14
SCRUTINIZE
   the celestial host to scrutinize his handiwork: they . . . . 799 73 POEMS 27   25
SCULPTOR
   erring end) myself is sculptor of your body's idiom: . . . . 291 IS 5 FOUR 8   6
   of a new england sculptor (well on in life) . . . . 327 VIVA 18   r39
SCULPTURAL
   orchid whose velocity is sculptural / / / / . . . . 193 XLI PORTRAIT 1   26
SCULPTURE
   your flowers and machinery: sculpture and prose flowers guess 264 IS 5 ONE 33   9
SCUTTLING
   little itchy mousies with scuttling eyes rustle and run . . . 25 T&C CHANSONS 2   13
SCYTHE
   be near when his scythe takes crisply the whim . . . . 215 XLI SONNETS 11   6
+SCYTHE
   FOR CONTEXT, SEE . . . . 656 {CHAIRE} 58   10
SE
   men and hot men se promenent doucement le soir . . . . 120 & PORTRAIT 12   23
   ta gorge mysterieuse pourquoi se promene-t-elle, pourquoi . . 121 & PORTRAIT 12   54
SEA
   and nuzzle of the sea / / / / . . . . 16 T&C SONGS 6   14
   / as is the sea marvelous from god's hands . . . . 38 T&C AMORES 3   1
   into dust but the sea does not change and . . . . 38 T&C AMORES 3   9
   greeting pale- departing irrevocable sea i knew thee death. . 39 T&C AMORES 4   27
   wind is dragging the sea with dream -S / . . . . 51 T&C IMPRESS 5   12
   tongue. god Is The Sea. All terrors of his . . . . 77 T&C SON UNRE 2   10
   of thrilled ecstasy, where sea and sky marry-- to . . . . . . 79 T&C SON UNRE 4   13
   such a night the sea through her blind miles . . . . 81 T&C SON UNRE 6   13
   mastery with chasteness of sea-girls Will i complete the . . 189 XLI SONGS 11   10
   is over: and the sea heaving indolent colourless forgets) . . 277 IS 5 THREE 1   19
   down there by the sea, in the afternoon. rapidly . . . . . . 281 IS 5 THREE 5   10
   the sky and the sea ...finally your eyes knew . . . . 283 IS 5 THREE 7   19
   a harbour fools the sea(while emanating the triple . . . . . 319 VIVA 11   18
   the entire and perpetual sea --but if yourself consider . . . 379 VIVA 70   9
   persists shaken by the sea / / / / . . . . 435 NO THANKS 51   45
   the she of the sea un der a who . . . . 493 50 POEMS 7   5
   the valleys of the sea my father moved through . . . . 520 50 POEMS 34   17
   unbe than all the sea which only is deeper . . . . 530 50 POEMS 42   7
   is deeper than the sea love is less always . . . . 530 50 POEMS 42   8
   of weary the hugest sea of shore so far . . . . 537 50 POEMS 49   4
   heaven green earth neither sea here's more than room . . . . 588 1 X 1 48   3
   the earth and the sea. For love are in . . . . 664 {CHAIRE} 66   23
   the mind of the sea (all the mountains are . . . . 665 {CHAIRE} 67   20
   we find in the sea / / / / . . . . 682 95 POEMS 10   12
   huger than huge) whoing sea leaps to greenly hurl . . . . . . 743 95 POEMS 71   3
   bells cry bells (the sea of the sky is . . . . 841 73 POEMS 69   6
+SEA
   FOR CONTEXT, SEE . . . . 94 & POST IMPR 6   7

SEA-GIRLS
   mastery with chasteness of sea-girls Will i complete the . . 189 XLI SONGS 11   10
+SEA'S
   FOR CONTEXT, SEE . . . . 447 NO THANKS 62   16
SEALACE
   last night clothed in sealace appeared to me your . . . . . . 369 VIVA 60   2
SEARCHED
   learned darkness from our searched world should wrest the . . 205 XLI SONNETS 1   1
SEAS
   the ship lifts on seas of iron breathing height . . . . 419 NO THANKS 36   12
   love beginning means return seas who could sing so . . . . . 526 50 POEMS 38   6
   your heart if the seas catch fire (and live . . . . 732 95 POEMS 60   6
SEASALT
   what mimicry, with angry seasalt and indignant clover . . . . 376 VIVA 67   4
SEASAYS
   s --w hee e; seasays. Break snice-Ly in-twin K . . . . 94 & POST IMPR 6   14
SEASON
   / / / the season 'tis, my lovely lambs, ... 266 IS 5 TWO 1   1
   inverno) this is the season of crumbling & folding . . . . . 345 VIVA 36   12
   and Now (comes un, season of in: wardly of . . . . 346 VIVA 37   21
   walking deaths in this season" think "finality lives up . . . 354 VIVA 45   12
   love is a deeper season than reason; my sweet . . . . 578 1 X 1 38   9
SEASONS
   windows spring slattern of seasons you have dirty legs . . . 61 T&C PORTRAIT 9   11
SEAT
   let me complain, whose seat is where revolving planets . . . 212 XLI SONNETS 8   10
   her tall corpsecoloured body seat itself (with the uncouth . 227 IS 5 ONE GERT   8
   of fate, landed a seat in the legislat- ure . . . . 266 IS 5 TWO 1   36
   man (clutched by immense the-seat-of-the pants inani nvisible 616 (CHAIRE) 18   7
SEATED
   a visage simple, terse, seated like any king or . . . . 254 IS 5 ONE 25   19
   Irrefutable unastonished two, countenances seated in . . . . 255 IS 5 ONE 26   2
   his fearless derriere sturdily seated--Colonel Needless To . 266 IS 5 TWO 1   22
SEATIDES
   and silver muting of seatides i trusted not, one . . . . . . 39 T&C AMORES 4   9
SECOND
   froth of faces clogs Second as Mrs. Somethingwich (with . . . 219 XLI SONNETS 15   11
   passed from low through second-in-to-high like . . . . 248 IS 5 ONE 19   20
   wrong does (minute by second and most by more) . . . . 469 NEW POEMS 7   18
   grows greener minute by second and most by more-- . . . . . . 769 95 POEMS 95   2
   mysterious land until my second dream begins-- the sky . . . 777 73 POEMS 5   5
   difference between firstrate & second implies nonth inkable . 803 73 POEMS 31   10
   the tiny stumble from second to tenth rate (3) . . . . 803 73 POEMS 31   12
   uttered human words --our second coming made stones sing . . 844 73 POEMS 72   2
SECOND-IN-TO-HIGH
   passed from low through second-in-to-high like . . . . 248 IS 5 ONE 19   20
SECONDHAND
   them (and found a secondhand set which click) little . . . . 410 NO THANKS 27   2
SECONDS
   centripetal wisdom in thirtytwo seconds centrifugally is . . 341 VIVA 32   5
SECRECIES
   freedom till her utmost secrecies and his (dreaming flame . . 721 95 POEMS 49   10
   death: as not imagined secrecies comprise goldenly huge whole 750 95 POEMS 78   8
SECRET
   a greener shadow of secret bowers) among the curves . . . . . 3 T&C EPITHALAM   22
   of dream; and very secret food its leaves inimitable . . . . 19 T&C PUELLA MEA   118
   are perpetually putting the secret of life in your . . . . . 204 XLI LA GUERRE 2   18
   but kneelingly believes thy secret and each morning stoops . 351 VIVA 42   14
   of all (for love's secret supremely clothes herself with . . 379 VIVA 70   5
   may be unknown most secret i will breathe such . . . . 428 NO THANKS 45   10
   morsel miraculous and meaningless secret on luminous whose . 456 NO THANKS 71   2
   oceans drowned, the single secret will still be man . . . . . 560 1 X 1 20   8
   reason will deceive (more secret or than madness did . . . . 592 1 X 1 52   2
   becomes eithering dreams the secret of / / / . . . . 613 (CHAIRE) 15   12
   swimming (Each a keener secret than silence even tells) . . . 630 (CHAIRE) 32   7
   (touched by love's own secret) we, like homing through . . . 659 (CHAIRE) 61   1
   and here is a secret they never will share . . . . 664 (CHAIRE) 66   7
   me the keen illimitable secret of begin / / . . . . 669 (CHAIRE) 71   14

	PAGE	TITLE	LINE

SECRET (CONTINUED)
mother's smile --whose only secret all creation sings / . . . 714 95 POEMS 42   14
here is the deepest secret nobody knows (here is . . . . . . 766 95 POEMS 92   10
darling (open the very secret of hope to her . . . . 811 73 POEMS 39   4
SECRETLOVELINESS
Lone ly, flower whose secretloveliness hur. ts itse; l. . . . 101 & POST IMPR 11   74
SECRETLY
awaits yes this alive secretly i frantic this serene . . . . 415 NO THANKS 32   21
thrushes may awake more secretly than our (if disappear . . . 577 1 X 1 37   7
only one amazing thing (secretly adoring shyly tiny winging . 591 1 X 1 51   21
SECRETS
birds who are the secrets of living whatever they . . . . . . 481 NEW POEMS 19   2
summer night her trillion secrets touchably alive --while and 809 73 POEMS 37   4
SECURE
tumult of exquisitely in- secure sharp algebraic music. For . 201 XLI PORTRAIT 9   20
SECURELY
attached by a chain securely to this always talking . . . . . 279 IS 5 THREE 3   11
+SECURITY
FOR CONTEXT, SEE . . . . 477 NEW POEMS 15   1
SEDUCED
thy perfumes which have seduced the mightier nostrils of . . 212 XLI SONNETS 8   5
Soul was (i understand) seduced by Life; whose brother . . . 621 {CHAIRE} 23   3
SEDULOUSLY
drawn surpassing nets are sedulously spun to snare the . . .   5 T&C EPITHALAM   86
SEE
stroke and sweet to see as a supple and . . . . 20 T&C PUELLA MEA 155
to murder dreams.... i see in the street where . . . . 50 T&C IMPRESS 4   12
digging bread and i see the brutal faces of . . . .   50 T&C IMPRESS 4   14
in the mirror i see a frail man dreaming . . . . 50 T&C IMPRESS 4   18
a little while i see thee then ponder the . . . .   75 T&C SON REAL 6   5
let thee play; i see the large lips vivid, ... 75 T&C SON REAL 6   7
as we have seen see doom's integration........ a wind . . . 80 T&C SON UNRE 5 12
gently arriving gloom and see! (the new moon fills . . . . . 93 & POST IMPR 5   13
are silent. --"Do you see Life? he is there . . . . 102 & POST IMPR 12 10
But I think I see someone else there is . . . . 102 & POST IMPR 12 23
match or can you see?) which the six subjunctive . . . . . . 117 & PORTRAIT 10   29
but really you do see and you are My . . . . 126 & SEVEN POEMS 5 16
like hands do you see that water flowerpots in . . . . 126 & SEVEN POEMS 5 24
so that's all you see but you don't want . . . . 126 & SEVEN POEMS 5 26
the round well and see the kitten and the . . . . 127 & SEVEN POEMS 5 46
neat necks just to see how always squirms the . . . . 130 & SON REAL 1   6
fiftythree (and one would see if it could) eyes . . . . . . 150 & SON REAL 21   2
my love comes to see me it's just a . . . . 152 & SON ACTU 1   1
my mind, you should see when i turn to . . . . 152 & SON ACTU 1   8
have loved, let us see if that's all. Bit . . . . 154 & SON ACTU 3   1
enormous star (do you see it?) and this shall . . . . 155 & SON ACTU 4   13
upstairs. And you can see their ears. Ears win- . . . . . . 171 & SON ACTU 20   7
sorry to come away? see i will comfort you . . . . 192 XLI CHANSONS 2 7
window for everyone to see and how they'll stare! . . . . . 192 XLI CHANSONS 2 22
dragging yanks back skin "see" (i, seeing, ceased to . . . . 226 IS 5 ONE MAME   6
can shimmie when you see her shake shake shake, ... 235 IS 5 ONE 6   7
shake shake, when you see her shake a shimmie . . . . 235 IS 5 ONE 6   11
we was happy to see how nice she acted . . . . 248 IS 5 ONE 19   26
oh say can you see by the dawn's early . . . . 268 IS 5 TWO 3   3
and next let me see yes Will that was . . . . 271 IS 5 TWO 6   5
many coloured glass, and see his mother's pride, his . . . . 273 IS 5 TWO 8   2
howls faintly blubbering pointing see yes) It here comes . . 280 IS 5 THREE 4   16
bulb of flame bubbles) see here and here they . . . . 282 IS 5 THREE 6   29
(with wee ears and see? tail frisks) (gonE) "mouse", ... 286 IS 5 FOUR 3   12
up in fear i see the new moon thinner . . . . 301 IS 5 FOUR 18   5
become) ened (to is see! so long door golf . . . . 309 VIVA 1   16
infinite) i pray to see; and Olaf, too preponderatingly . . 339 VIVA 30   39
are aLl (cry alL See) o (ver All) Th . . . . 347 VIVA 38   33
are really petals and see nothing with the face . . . . . . 352 VIVA 43   10
a child "we can see a bat in this . . . . 353 VIVA 44   4
the window as you see and really i have . . . . 365 VIVA 56   5
fabulous wisdom fears to see (who laugh and cry) . . . . . . 446 NO THANKS 61   12
to take the hearse, see you again. Love (having . . . . . . 451 NO THANKS 66   8

	PAGE	TITLE	LINE
SEE (CONTINUED)			
mile uphill to only see him smile. Scorning the	520	50 POEMS 34	32
hold a you shall see the not because and	523	50 POEMS 36	3
/ it's over a (see just over this) wall	543	1 X 1 3	1
now. But over a (see just over this) wall	543	1 X 1 3	25
call twilight you 'll see an in -ch of	571	1 X 1 31	5
doubting can turn men's see to stare their faith	580	1 X 1 40	8
the impossible shall occur --see! now himself uplifts of . .	582	1 X 1 42	13
to soon) rose--did you see her? darling, did you	599	(CHAIRE) 1	10
"and poets grow; and (there--see?) children" nor might any .	626	(CHAIRE) 28	12
isn't me can't you see now no not any	638	(CHAIRE) 40	12
sing; teach them to see who could not learn	649	(CHAIRE) 51	3
killers you'd care to see (while a stuttering ghost	709	95 POEMS 37	6
with won der until (see the) with the bigger	715	95 POEMS 43	11
our clown --shouting to see what no mind knows	716	95 POEMS 44	13
all worlds begin to (see?) begin / / /	750	95 POEMS 78	16
feel but ears may see there never lived a	760	95 POEMS 87	5
--you're a song to see: whose all (you're a	763	95 POEMS 90	2
he cannot fear (you see it in the way	774	73 POEMS 2	15
most (there: did you see it?) star to disappear, ...	809	73 POEMS 37	12
/ / D-re-A-mi-N-gl-Y leaves (sEe) locked in gOLd after- . . .	838	73 POEMS 66	3
SEEDS			
of god who spits seeds of dead song about	55	T&C PORTRAIT 3	13
By Night whose latest Seeds Of Evil sold 69	245	IS 5 ONE 16	8
SEEING			
his kingdom winter cowers, seeing green armies steadily . . .	4	T&C EPITHALAM	71
lingers. if one marvel seeing the hunger of my	42	T&C AMORES 6	9
have just throttled my seeing blood, her heart's chatter . .	132	& SON REAL 3	3
perspicuity, or? shut up. Seeing seeing her is not	141	& SON REAL 12	11
or? shut up. Seeing seeing her is not to	141	& SON REAL 12	12
pumping pleasure into hips). Seeing how the limp huddling . .	161	& SON ACTU 10	5
kanoon but Hassan chuckles seeing the Greeks breathe) / . . .	220	XLI SONNETS 16	16
back skin "see" (i, seeing, ceased to breathe). The	226	IS 5 ONE MAME	6
being at all born, seeing that i was wifeless	262	IS 5 ONE 32	6
to admit i've died) seeing your bald intellect collywobbling	329	VIVA 20	3
and continually i am seeing something inhaling gently a . . .	375	VIVA 66	15
stung or as the seeing are the blind and	511	50 POEMS 25	15
hope to terror; blow seeing to blind (blow pity	560	1 X 1 20	13
man means No and (seeing something yes) will grin	570	1 X 1 30	8
should tasting touching hearing seeing breathing any--lifted	663	(CHAIRE) 65	9
each our bliss-- where seeing eyes go blind (where	834	73 POEMS 62	27
all worlds have halfsight, seeing either with life's eye . .	845	73 POEMS 73	1
SEEK			
the moment which shall seek all blossoms that do	9	T&C SONGS 1	16
with becoming steps to seek your face and i	42	T&C AMORES 6	13
brief selves as fiercely seek findingly new textures of . . .	373	VIVA 64	14
(fingeryhands me and whying) seek than finds feeling (seize)	612	(CHAIRE) 14	12
mind may comprehend, remember seek (forgetting find) and in .	688	95 POEMS 16	12
+SEEK			
FOR CONTEXT, SEE	358	VIVA 49	4
FOR CONTEXT, SEE	403	NO THANKS 20	13
SEEKER			
/ / / / seeker of truth follow no	775	73 POEMS 3	1
SEEKING			
not each other touch) seeking, some street which easily . . .	174	& SON ACTU 23	5
oneself be sought or seeking master or disciple sheep	804	73 POEMS 32	3
SEEKINGLY			
things phantoms curl (mouth seekingly lips wander a finding .	565	1 X 1 25	3
SEEKS			
implacable bassoon-- now Twilight seeks the thrill of moon, .	12	T&C SONGS 2	48
slowly in peopling places seeks play: withs of star	168	& SON ACTU 17	14
of more find than seeks thinking, swim (opening) grow	612	(CHAIRE) 14	1
SEEM			
be with me: unseriously seem by the perusing greenness . . .	9	T&C SONGS 1	28
it and doesn't that seem puzzling but we both	323	VIVA 15	17
able to be and seem so quite softly as	367	VIVA 58	3
make an earth gladly seem firm for you: remember	372	VIVA 63	8
who are turned to seem) "stetti" and willbeishfully bursting	387	NO THANKS 4	14

	PAGE	TITLE	LINE
SEEM (CONTINUED)			
the (Wistfully dead seem generous) don't All suspect	391	NO THANKS 8	3
/ does yesterday's perfection seem not quite so clever . . .	414	NO THANKS 31	1
pay the rent of seem and genius please the	511	50 POEMS 25	5
single thing dares partly seem one atomy once, and	559	1 X 1 19	9
beggar and queen to seem (blow friend to fiend:	560	1 X 1 20	5
course but you don't seem to realize i can't	638	{CHAIRE} 40	6
dream, remember so (forgetting seem) in time of roses	688	95 POEMS 16	6
million thousand hundred nothing seem --we are himself's own	756	95 POEMS 84	13
beyond the trick to seem their joys turn woes	776	73 POEMS 4	24
through a thunder of seem though the stars in	801	73 POEMS 29	16
eternity; not guests of seem) believe me, dear, clocks . . .	817	73 POEMS 45	6
april;and i breathe-move-and-seem some perpetually	839	73 POEMS 67	6
(which is if things seem spirits) or (if spirits	845	73 POEMS 73	2
SEEMED			
highly sexed mind. It seemed to me that i	262	IS 5 ONE 32	5
folded his umbrella. It seemed too beautiful. Let us	263	IS 5 ONE 32	58
the table all which seemed sweet deep and inexplicable . . .	322	VIVA 14	7
losing through you what seemed myself, i find selves	810	73 POEMS 38	9
SEEMING			
terror of eternity, (or seeming that they would mistrust . .	6	T&C EPITHALAM	140
shadow phantom effigy or seeming (an almost someone always .	812	73 POEMS 40	3
SEEMING'S			
which and innocently are) seeming's enough for slaves of . .	745	95 POEMS 73	13
SEEMS			
that asleep whitely she seems whose lips the whole	205	XLI SONNETS 1	7
But next door nobody seems to live at present	312	VIVA 4	22
go at that) that seems important doesn't it and	323	VIVA 15	15
mass. to whom nobody seems to have mentioned ye	326	VIVA 18	3
a fair-y (and it seems to be doing nicely	401	NO THANKS 18	21
at all he never seems to care he sharpens	624	{CHAIRE} 26	12
dark little day which seems a lifetime at the	650	{CHAIRE} 52	7
willy's carroty hair" "it seems like i just heard	707	95 POEMS 35	5
+SEEMS			
FOR CONTEXT, SEE	615	{CHAIRE} 17	12
SEEMSWOOP			
liv- ing ly who: seemSwoop (whir -ling be, yond!	447	NO THANKS 62	7
SEEN			
thighs such legs are seen as were the pride	21	T&C PUELLA MEA	207
skilful, but i have seen death's clever enormous voice . . .	45	T&C LA GUERRE 1	3
huger silence. I have seen all the silence filled	45	T&C LA GUERRE 1	10
at Roupy i have seen between barrages, the night	45	T&C LA GUERRE 1	13
us as we have seen see doom's integration........ a	80	T&C SON UNRE 5	12
as being by her seen, which has got nothing	141	& SON REAL 12	14
modesty his mind is seen frequently fingering the exact . . .	193	XLI PORTRAIT 1	5
/ / I have seen her a stealthily frail	214	XLI SONNETS 10	1
cocodrillo-- mine eyes have seen the glory of the	256	IS 5 ONE 27	10
best mouth i have seen on any man-- a	344	VIVA 35	8
tic" as i have seen trees (in whose black	354	VIVA 45	26
didn't die (may be seen to inexactly pass and	401	NO THANKS 18	11
the by has anybody seen little you-i who stood	593	1 X 1 53	2
neither beholding a nor seen by some that bum	698	95 POEMS 26	7
nor she wouldn't be seen with the likes of	707	95 POEMS 35	12
SEES			
of ragged earth who sees them pass) while hunted	4	T&C EPITHALAM	69
under a stile he sees eight and twenty ladies	15	T&C SONGS 5	3
SEETHE			
& swoon & ingly seethe firm swirl hips whirling	445	NO THANKS 60	27
while hunted by daemons seethe luminous leopards (on wingfeet	586	1 X 1 46	15
eyes) drift bells glide seethe glow (undering proudly humbly	841	73 POEMS 69	23
SEETHES			
of fragrance the bowl seethes a flutter of stars	31	T&C ORIENTALE 5	7
SEETHING			
(stepp) this (ing) crazily seething of this raving city . . .	437	NO THANKS 53	2
but a blind blissfully seething gift wandering deeply through	754	95 POEMS 82	3
SEIZE			
seek than finds feeling (seize) floats (only by only)	612	{CHAIRE} 14	13
knowledgeable shadows (quick to seize each nothing which all	765	95 POEMS 91	2

		PAGE	TITLE	LINE

SEIZE (CONTINUED)
    tree illimitably try to seize the doom of sky . . . . 822 73 POEMS 50   6
SEIZED
    through touch less stillness (seized among what ghostly . . . 432 NO THANKS 49   10
    fiercely by pink mr seized green mrs opening is . . . . 465 NEW POEMS 3   7
    i NgflounderpirouettiN g : seized (tatterdemalion dow . . . 495 50 POEMS 9   6
SELDOM
    thinner than recall more seldom than a wave is . . . . 530 50 POEMS 42   3
SELENE
    but so what princess selene doesn't know a thing . . . . . . 504 50 POEMS 18   11
SELENE'S
    the deep expels (over Selene's car closing uncouth) of . . .   4 T&C EPITHALAM   47
SELF
    prismatic, whims, the chattering self perceives with . . . . 157 & SON ACTU 6   14
    my- idle vertical worthless self unite in a peculiarly . . . 260 IS 5 ONE 30   16
    he could meanwhile my self etcetera lay quietly in . . . . . 276 IS 5 TWO 10   19
    sits years its of self fee (bly Perpetually coughing . . . . 312 VIVA 4   19
    her (in his arms) Self & Him self in . . . . 317 VIVA 9   13
    arms) Self & Him self in the hoe tell . . . . 317 VIVA 9   15
    eyes syriansang asong tohim self all about the desertbyIts . 318 VIVA 10   11
    Foses) until (finding one's self at some distance from . . . 319 VIVA 11   15
    rose smiling to a self "somewhere it is Spring . . . . 338 VIVA 29   4
    again quick- ly its self in) while a transparent . . . . . . 341 VIVA 32   17
    handspring trans forming it self int o eighteen) Don't . . . 343 VIVA 34   13
    arms flowering so new) self whose eyes smell of . . . . 424 NO THANKS 41   3
    spat and laughed with self with life this poet . . . . 441 NO THANKS 56   41
    magical shoulders him doll self) hay completely thus or . . . 516 50 POEMS 30   12
    those creatures called one's self so we'll not have . . . . . 528 50 POEMS 40   12
    will cure the laziest self of weary the hugest . . . . 537 50 POEMS 49   3
    -credible true each new self) smile. Eyes. & we . . . . 612 (CHAIRE) 14   7
    who outlift queries of self pouring (alive twice) and . . . . 613 (CHAIRE) 15   8
    tomorrow) all around the self of this being are . . . . 617 (CHAIRE) 19   7
    have flown adorable him self tail and all (and . . . . 631 (CHAIRE) 33   6
    my (my your and) self without, completely dare be . . . . . . 666 (CHAIRE) 68   13
    House) hole swallows it self while nobody (and stars . . . . 693 95 POEMS 21   16
    neither each both and) Self adventures deathlessness / / . . 721 95 POEMS 49   14
    my (as it happened) self he was --but now . . . . 730 95 POEMS 58   4
    resurrection: over my sleeping self float flaming symbols of 749 95 POEMS 77   11
    --we are himself's own self; his very him / . . . . 756 95 POEMS 84   14
    the silence of him self sang like a bird. . . . . 802 73 POEMS 30   28
    most downwardness and marvellously self diminutive whose . . 821 73 POEMS 49   12
    (that eagerly sweet carolling self answers me) "i could . . . 836 73 POEMS 64   9
    how the (myself's own self who's) child will dance! . . . . . 843 73 POEMS 71   12
+SELF
    FOR CONTEXT, SEE . . . . 607 (CHAIRE) 9   9
    FOR CONTEXT, SEE . . . . 831 73 POEMS 59   8
SELFHOOD
    your trite how terrible selfhood with its hands and . . . . . 522 50 POEMS 35   11
SELFLESS
    linger no more than selfless i can quite endure . . . . 812 73 POEMS 40   10
SELFSUBTRACTING
    turn; and from all selfsubtracting hugely doom treasures of . 843 73 POEMS 71   7
SELL
    angle we do not sell and buy things so . . . . 238 IS 5 ONE 9   7
    (but because nobody can sell the Moon to The) . . . . 452 NO THANKS 67   18
    because he would not sell his head) squads right . . . . . . 473 NEW POEMS 11   3
    an ounce and i'll sell you a pound. Turn . . . . 513 50 POEMS 27   1
    as can yes) they sell and they buy and . . . . 801 73 POEMS 29   3
+SELL
    FOR CONTEXT, SEE . . . . 703 95 POEMS 31   18
SELLING
    pulled six months for selling snow / / / . . . . 266 IS 5 TWO 1   40
+SELLING
    FOR CONTEXT, SEE . . . . 104 & POST IMPR 14   17
SELLS
    difference than if it sۥlls hate condoms education snakeoil . 549 1 X ۥ 9   10
SELVES-THEM
    (pour wo (things) men selves-them inghurl) bangbells . . . . 444 NO THANKS 59   12

	PAGE	TITLE	LINE

SELVES-U
    blueandgreen paper scorchbend ingthem -selves-U pcurv E, . . 278 IS 5 THREE 2   8
SEMILUMINOUS
    by this instant of semiluminous nausea A vast wordless . . . 96 & POST IMPR 8   32
SEMIRAMIS
    to bed, whom white-thighed Semiramis put up her mouth . . . . 22 T&C PUELLA MEA 247
SEND
    you of my heart, send me a little word; . . . . 76 T&C SON UNRE 1   10
    saith rain anguish of dream-send is hushed in moan-loll . . . 90 & POST IMPR 2   6
    guess) if god should send the morning; and before . . . . . . 205 XLI SONNETS 1   9
    with care fragile and send him home to his . . . . 270 IS 5 TWO 5   18
    lightly my eyes? And send life out of me . . . . 302 IS 5 FIVE 1   7
    a steak and they send us a pie (it's . . . . 513 50 POEMS 27   15
SENDWISP
    pin yessir wheel no sendwisp ben jiffyclaus bug fainarain . . 333 VIVA 24   19
SENECKTIE
    thy nabor (neck and senecktie are gentlemen ppoyds even . . . 492 50 POEMS 6   13
SENSATIONAL
    / / when my sensational moments are no more . . . . 213 XLI SONNETS 9   1
SENSATIONS
    and from this you sensations, imitating a few fatally . . . . 328 VIVA 19   18
SENSE
    perfectly and simply Lustful.... sense a gradual stir of . . 157 & SON ACTU 6   3
    of dollars and no sense. Which being quite beyond . . . . . . 266 IS 5 TWO 1   4
    vow but both made sense in when's haymow with . . . . 316 VIVA 8   15
    a gentleman not to sense something un poco putrido . . . . . 327 VIVA 18   45
+SENSE
    FOR CONTEXT, SEE . . . . 602 {CHAIRE} 4   4
SENSIBLE
    body rose through the sensible night a quick bird . . . . . . 187 XLI SONGS 9   5
SENSUAL
    first star perfects the sensual dome of darkness, and . . . . 7 T&C EPITHALAM 164
    of the grave great sensual knees well might any . . . . 21 T&C PUELLA MEA 213
    in an agony of sensual chisels i perform squirms . . . . . . 199 XLI PORTRAIT 7   5
    am conjugated by the sensual mysticism of entire vertical . . 201 XLI PORTRAIT 9   23
SENSUOUSLY
    in fifty colours , sensuously (the crowd howls faintly . . . 280 IS 5 THREE 4   12
SENT
    from god's hands which sent her forth to sleep . . . . 38 T&C AMORES 3   3
SENTENCE
    wrote a simple declarative sentence with seven grammatical . 336 VIVA 27   4
    who begins stuttering each sentence we both consid (notb- . . 398 NO THANKS 15   10
SENTIENCE
    a doomed impetuous acute sentience whose whitehot lips . . . 193 XLI PORTRAIT 1   11
    swooping lozenge. a ruglike sentience whose papillae expertly 201 XLI PORTRAIT 9   16
SENTIMENTS
    obscenities nudging into neglected sentiments brings to light 203 XLI LA GUERRE 1   7
SENTINEL
    / / / / sentinel robins two guard me . . . . 746 95 POEMS 74   1
SEPARATE
    a sole mass my separate lusts her hair was . . . . 135 & SON REAL 6   5
    not amazing: without love separate, smileless--merely imagine 374 VIVA 65   2
+SEPARATE
    FOR CONTEXT, SEE . . . . 354 VIVA 45   19
SEPARATED
    in love, am i separated from your body smile . . . . 295 IS 5 FOUR 12   3
    not toucH- ing because separated by an impregnable Because . 335 VIVA 26   13
    -vening) anyway You know Separated what i Mean (oweld . . . . 335 VIVA 26   16
SEPARATING
    eternity --after which our separating selves become museums . 297 IS 5 FOUR 14   14
SEPTEMBERING
    as green as grain septembering arms of year extend . . . . . 521 50 POEMS 34   37
SERENADE
    thou dost persuade to serenade his lady the musical . . . . . 61 T&C PORTRAIT 9   4
SERENE
    light (slowly in life's serene perpetual round a pale . . . . 5 T&C EPITHALAM 81
    stars and to the serene the complicated and the . . . . 43 T&C AMORES 7   16
    thickly which tread the serene nervous light of paradise-- . 85 T&C SON ACTU 4   2

SERENE (CONTINUED)
the Woolworth building a serene pastile-shaped insipid . . . 201 XLI PORTRAIT 9   15
LONG LIVE that Upwardlooking Serene Illustrious and Beatific 315 VIVA 7   12
/ / / / serene immediate silliest and whose . . . . 337 VIVA 28   1
secretly i frantic this serene mightily how rooted who . . . 415 NO THANKS 32   22
fails but out of serene perfectly Nothing hurled into . . . . 456 NO THANKS 71   7
fingery treesoul onlying from serene whom queries not . . . . 517 50 POEMS 31   6
SERENELY
sunset completely utters utters serenely silently a cathedral 93 & POST IMPR 5   2
wing strong silent greens serenely lingering, absolute lights 208 XLI SONNETS 4   3
Look at these (each serenely welcoming his only and . . . . . 626 (CHAIRE) 28   7
silent world) one spirit serenely truly himself; and alone . 808 73 POEMS 36   3
SERIOUS
that delicious boy whose serious grace one goddess loved . .   3 T&C EPITHALAM   24
lead us into the serious steep darkness / / . . . .   41 T&C AMORES 5   35
child-head poised with the serious hair)/ / / / . . . . 207 XLI SONNETS 3   14
it let's make it serious something authentic and delirious . 407 NO THANKS 24   10
miracle may grow --childfully serious flower of holiness a . 601 (CHAIRE) 3   7
essentially poetic or ethereally serious: a fine not a . . . 802 73 POEMS 30   22
SERIOUSLY
hour my fond soul seriously yearns beyond this fern . . . . .   12 T&C SONGS 2   42
air and stuff it seriously in, his minute pocket) . . . . . .   69 T&C POST IMPR 6   11
miles of crumbling silence seriously smiles / / / . . . . . .   81 T&C SON UNRE 6   14
entire day horribly and seriously thrills the moment of . . .   82 T&C SON ACTU 1   11
sex which lock me seriously. Dumb for a while. . . . .   133 & SON REAL 4   12
a memory slowly, oh seriously --that since and if . . . . . . 295 IS 5 FOUR 12   10
is filled with birds seriously i begin to climb . . . . 434 NO THANKS 51   4
each very lifting & seriously voice -like finger of . . . . . 480 NEW POEMS 18   25
SERPENT
the way freezes a serpent becomes a rod smiles . . . . 384 NO THANKS 2   22
SERPENTS
/ / / when serpents bargain for the right . . . . 620 (CHAIRE) 22   1
SERVANT
of her Thy yonder servant who in Thy very . . . .   57 T&C PORTRAIT 5   6
dinted then did my servant become of the company . . . . . .   57 T&C PORTRAIT 5   35
SERVANTS
really i have no servants. We could almost live . . . . 365 VIVA 56   6
SERVE
Add Hot Water And Serve-- from every B.V.D. let . . . . 230 IS 5 ONE 2   12
least) & i ob serve no body wants Most . . . . 727 95 POEMS 55   8
SES
/ / / how ses humble. Over thin earths . . . . 346 VIVA 37   2
SESTET
the flag that's furled (sestet entitled grass is flesh . . . 390 NO THANKS 7   9
SET
made for Horizontal Business (set on big legs nice . . . . . 150 & SON REAL 21   8
and the flesh crisp set my love-tooth on edge. . . . . 173 & SON ACTU 22   10
years lipping flowers And set my teeth in the . . . . 189 XLI SONGS 11   17
(which she politely refused) set out gaily for the . . . . . 326 VIVA 18   19
(and found a secondhand set which click) little gould . . . . 410 NO THANKS 27   2
all unfools of unbeing set traps for his heart, ... 439 NO THANKS 55   17
time from time shall set us free) forgetting me, ... 688 95 POEMS 16   14
brains without hearts have set saint against sinner; put . . 769 95 POEMS 95   15
SETS
y play, effendi approaches, sets down coffee withdraws a . . 200 XLI PORTRAIT 8   18
SETTLED
ordered yaoorti from Nicho' settled my feet on the . . . . . 194 XLI PORTRAIT 2   13
SEVEN
/ / / &: SEVEN POEMS i will be . . . . 122 & SEVEN POEMS 1   T
bet two bits come seven come eleven m m . . . . 125 & SEVEN POEMS 4   11
that as three dimes seven nickels and ten pennies . . . . . . 196 XLI PORTRAIT 4   9
not coming once in seven years exp10 ded like . . . . 320 VIVA 12   11
simple declarative sentence with seven grammatical errors "is 336 VIVA 27   4
blossom of a bliss "seven heavens for just one . . . . 837 73 POEMS 65   13
SEVENTY
/ / / if seventy were young and death . . . . 798 73 POEMS 26   1
SEVERAL
some thrush with silver several tears complete the perfumed .   6 T&C EPITHALAM   119

	PAGE	TITLE	LINE

SEVERAL (CONTINUED)
of night slowly when several stars are opening one . . . . . 156 & SON ACTU 5 2
crucifix which smashes into several pieces and is hurriedly . 203 XLI LA GUERRE 1 14
WORTH I'M TOLD $ SEVERAL MILLION FINKLESTEIN (FRITZ) LIVES . 244 IS 5 ONE 15 2
me I tell you; several, incredible, sleepy / / . . . . 281 IS 5 THREE 5 24
inexplicable pleasure--you go from several persons: believe . 295 IS 5 FOUR 12 7
is asleep with only several faces and a multitude . . . . . . 312 VIVA 4 5
within transparent walls how several smoothly gesturing stars 376 VIVA 67 8
impossibly 3 individuals every several fat thousand years. . 514 50 POEMS 28 2
SEVERE
handless wrists did gooey severe shapes. / / / . . . . 73 T&C SON REAL 4 14
SEVERED
Danae saw the night severed and the glowing throng . . . . . 4 T&C EPITHALAM 52
SEW
room's silence, i will sew a nagging button of . . . . . . 164 & SON ACTU 13 2
tiful la dy (sitting sew ing at an o . . . . 724 95 POEMS 52 7
SEWING
day paler-paler she sits sewing and growing and that's . . . 125 & SEVEN POEMS 4 5
SEWS
the little lady who sews and grows every day . . . . 125 & SEVEN POEMS 4 4
SEX
the east side my sex sitting up- right on . . . . 101 & POST IMPR 11 59
in chuckles of supreme sex. In The Good Old . . . . 130 & SON REAL 1 8
the gnashing petals of sex which lock me seriously. . . . . . 133 & SON REAL 4 11
/ her careful distinct sex whose sharp lips comb . . . . . . 137 & SON REAL 8 1
purr of blood; your sex squeaked like a billiard-cue . . . . 170 & SON ACTU 19 9
SEXED
crept into my highly sexed mind. It seemed to . . . . 262 IS 5 ONE 32 4
SEXES
(among their stomachs andtheir sexes) stomachsofold pe o . . 101 & POST IMPR 11 64
SEXIS
other stomachs and their Sexis a Lone ly, flower . . . . . 101 & POST IMPR 11 73
SEXUAL
doll gay exactly perishing sexual, / / / / . . . . 131 & SON REAL 2 17
the weightless svelte drifting sexual feather of your shall . 140 & SON REAL 11 2
aching toys in unsmooth sexual luminosity spree. --dear) the 159 & SON ACTU 8 13
me with its hurting sexual smell of lilies.... beyond . . . . 214 XLI SONNETS 10 11
most invincible unthing --stern sexual timelessness, ... 351 VIVA 42 3
SH
not to think of (sh) the world renowned investigator . . . . 326 VIVA 18 5
o god dear wait sh please o no O . . . . 358 VIVA 49 5
mopping too bad dear sh not yet jesus what . . . . 496 50 POEMS 10 18
these regard his that (sh) who made the world's . . . . . . 645 (CHAIRE) 47 3
SHABBY
faces glaring at the shabby tiny smiling, man in . . . . . . 69 T&C POST IMPR 6 8
string! the tiny smiling shabby man is yelling over . . . . . 69 T&C POST IMPR 6 33
SHADE
/ / raise the shade will youse dearie? rain . . . . 109 & PORTRAIT 5 1
SHADES
(down pull & who'll shades / / / / . . . . 501 50 POEMS 15 25
SHADOW
dwell (within a greener shadow of secret bowers) among . . . 3 T&C EPITHALAM 22
worshipper prostrate within twitching shadow lolls sobbing . 28 T&C ORIENTALE 2 14
very poor) creature of shadow, that among first light . . . . 374 VIVA 65 14
C can't casts no shadow D drink and E . . . . 390 NO THANKS 7 3
one entirety neither may shadow down flesh neither may . . . 425 NO THANKS 42 12
proof not the least shadow of a. Not one . . . . 479 NEW POEMS 17 20
with (now) luminous the shadow of love himself: who's . . . . 601 (CHAIRE) 3 16
only i remain; a shadow phantom effigy or seeming . . . . . . 812 73 POEMS 40 3
+SHADOW
FOR CONTEXT, SEE . . . . 97 & POST IMPR 8 40
SHADOWEATEN
oo n (poor shadoweaten was of is and . . . . 723 95 POEMS 51 8
+SHADOWFULLY
FOR CONTEXT, SEE . . . . 681 95 POEMS 9 14
SHADOWLESS
denied night's face have shadowless they? i bring you . . . . 527 50 POEMS 39 2

666

SHADOWS
     who prolongs unserious twilight) shadows have begun the . . . 84 T&C SON ACTU 3   10
     with everything cancelled but shadows --what does it all . . 295 IS 5 FOUR 12   20
     go dreamless knaves on Shadows fed, your Harry's Tom, ... 438 NO THANKS 54   9
     who have lost their shadows if which did not . . . . 502 50 POEMS 16   11
     of person) through musical shadows while hunted by daemons . 586 1 X 1 46   13
     through depths of guess, shadows are substances and wings . . 761 95 POEMS 88   7
     homeless home of knowledgeable shadows (quick to seize each . 765 95 POEMS 91   2
SHADOWY
     lose: haste) the very shadowy sheep float free upon . . . . .   9 T&C SONGS 1   8
     world away, leaving to shadowy silence and dismay that . . . 75 T&C SON REAL 6   3
     each street takes of shadowy light the droll snowing . . . . 168 & SON ACTU 17   4
     wise for fear) of shadowy virtue and of sunful . . . . 607 {CHAIRE} 9   13
     creatures (bright if by shadowy if) swallowing is everywhere 757 95 POEMS 85   11
SHAKE
     when you see her shake shake shake, when you . . . . 235 IS 5 ONE 6   7
     you see her shake shake shake, when you see . . . . 235 IS 5 ONE 6   8
     see her shake shake shake, when you see her . . . . 235 IS 5 ONE 6   9
     when you see her shake a shimmie how you . . . . 235 IS 5 ONE 6   11
     (of course you must shake well) indolently dreaming puzzling 323 VIVA 15   5
     guy who refused to shake hands with ludendorff and . . . . . 324 VIVA 16   11
     are not refined they shake the mountains when they . . . . . 427 NO THANKS 44   20
SHAKEN
     its puniest flame persists shaken by the sea / . . . . 435 NO THANKS 51   45
SHAKES
     flight of thirty birds shakes with a thickening fright . . . 11 T&C SONGS 2   19
SHAKESPEARE
     with him) one william shakespeare broke the silence of . . . 552 1 X 1 12   24
SHALL
     is the moment which shall seek all blossoms that . . . . . .   9 T&C SONGS 1   16
     and their sunsets, it shall pass. Our feet tread . . . . . .   9 T&C SONGS 1   26
     arms about me dream shall my love wholly taste . . . .   9 T&C SONGS 1   35
     hand my folded soul shall know while on faint . . . . 11 T&C SONGS 2   26
     which sleeps, a dream shall pass) and these my . . . . 11 T&C SONGS 2   30
     life be nothing, it shall not stop kissing). / . . . . 13 T&C SONGS 3   21
     From each brave eye shall sprout a tree fruit . . . . 16 T&C SONGS 6   2
     did sing a rose shall beget the spring that . . . . 16 T&C SONGS 6   6
     snow Into strenuous birds shall go my love walking . . . . . 16 T&C SONGS 6   10
     and all the while shall my heart be With . . . . 16 T&C SONGS 6   13
     in Confessio doth prefer shall not lack for beauty . . . . . 20 T&C PUELLA MEA 168
     If to me there shall appear than a rose . . . . 21 T&C PUELLA MEA 175
     things which never more shall be, perfect things of . . . . . 22 T&C PUELLA MEA 252
     time to come you shall remember of this night . . . . 36 T&C AMORES 1   21
     heart fleet flowerterrible memories shall rise, slowly return 36 T&C AMORES 1   28
     when all my days shall have before a certain . . . . 39 T&C AMORES 4   32
     a dead thing, i shall instruct him silently with . . . . . . 42 T&C AMORES 6   11
     utter a tree, Nobody shall stop me but first . . . . 67 T&C POST IMPR 4   2
     dream i think it shall be roses and spring . . . . 67 T&C POST IMPR 4   10
     touch of must and shall, whose slippery body is . . . . 74 T&C SON REAL 5   2
     dismay that stage which shall not know thy smile . . . . . . 75 T&C SON REAL 6   4
     happiness from me. Then shall i turn my face, ... 76 T&C SON UNRE 1   13
     for how much themselves shall gleam, in the poised . . . . . 81 T&C SON UNRE 6   7
     Death (whom fairies hate) shall crumble the mouth-flower . . 83 T&C SON ACTU 2   11
     this our flesh merely shall be excelled by speaking . . . . . 84 T&C SON ACTU 3   4
     tiny add death what shall? / / / / . . . . 105 & PORTRAIT 1   13
     hands' will tumbling into shall --and Love's a coach . . . . 131 & SON REAL 2   14
     sexual feather of your shall i say body? follows . . . . . . 140 & SON REAL 11   3
     see it?) and this shall dance upon the nude . . . . 155 & SON ACTU 4   14
     and final silence and shall the (i do but . . . . 155 & SON ACTU 4   15
     his tears out, perhaps shall pass a million years . . . . . . 181 XLI SONGS 3   7
     curves of my body Shall enter fingers of smooth . . . . . . 189 XLI SONGS 11   9
     to hold every finger shall have its ring and . . . . 192 XLI CHANSONS 2   19
     is the garden. Time shall surely reap and on . . . . 208 XLI SONNETS 4   9
     and large signories --i shall not smile beloved; i . . . . . 210 XLI SONNETS 6   8
     not smile beloved; i shall not weep: when from . . . . 210 XLI SONNETS 6   8
     my children and you shall hear the true story . . . . 236 IS 5 ONE 7   2
     stalwart youth, what sight shall human optics know more . . . 254 IS 5 ONE 25   3
     the suppressed desire of shall we say: Idleness, while . . . 263 IS 5 ONE 32   39

SHALL (CONTINUED)

they died instead then shall the voice of liberty . . . . . 268 IS 5 TWO 3   13
new terror always which shall brighten carefully these things 289 IS 5 FOUR 6   11
things) winter, whom Spring shall kill / / / . . . . 293 IS 5 FOUR 10   31
your crisp eyes actually shall contain new faeries (and . . . 294 IS 5 FOUR 11   9
these unique dreams never shall soil their raiment with . . . 328 VIVA 19   4
Ultima Thule Of Plumbing shall receive the philophilic name . 334 VIVA 25   3
pleasedon't; rising: from the Shall. / / / / . . . . 343 VIVA 34   18
(buoyant & who silently shall to rea- disa) ular, ... 349 VIVA 40   8
with the dirt death shall him vastly gird, a . . . . 360 VIVA 51   5
most humble me which shall increase) open thy fire! . . . . . 360 VIVA 51   31
headaches: ifs.) yet shall our Not to be . . . . 361 VIVA 52   22
fear (which beyond night shall go) remembering only dare . . 362 VIVA 53   2
who are your eyes (shall any dream come a . . . . 367 VIVA 58   9
i slightly smiling, gradually shall reenter the singular . . 370 VIVA 61   19
but many a thought shall die which was not . . . . 372 VIVA 63   13
down, one poem yet shall swim / / / . . . . 372 VIVA 63   15
animals) but not darkness shall quite outmarch forever --and 376 VIVA 67   6
grave? from only Whom shall time no refuge keep . . . . 377 VIVA 68   13
wealth but love, who shall not spend my fortune . . . . 394 NO THANKS 11   13
most early soul him shall untouch meaningless precision and . 402 NO THANKS 19   13
men while a man shall which a god sometimes . . . . 414 NO THANKS 31   14
scholars guess that life shall not for living find . . . . . 420 NO THANKS 37   9
(rejoice) was and ever shall be nor every partialness . . . . 425 NO THANKS 42   11
moon a while) and shall carve time so we'll . . . . 433 NO THANKS 50   13
if Joy with Pain shall hang in hock who . . . . 438 NO THANKS 54   7
million griefs wide (it shall bury much stench) and . . . . . 439 NO THANKS 55   12
undeaths who live nor shall they be and must . . . . 440 NO THANKS 56   35
truly which live always shall be may never have) . . . . . . 441 NO THANKS 56   63
selves abide under whatever shall discovered be) whose . . . 446 NO THANKS 61   10
impossible of me and shall who wave among your . . . . 454 NO THANKS 69   3
/ / must being shall one only thing must: . . . . 480 NEW POEMS 18   1
/ / / you shall above all things be . . . . 484 NEW POEMS 22   1
. We're alive and shall be: cities may overflow . . . . 491 50 POEMS 5   11
was if minus and shall be immeasurable happenless unnow . . . 502 50 POEMS 16   5
joy's the voice down shall go which and up . . . . 511 50 POEMS 25   23
children of almost) never shall guess the dimension of . . . 512 50 POEMS 26   4
sky --endlings of isn't shall never begin to begin . . . . . 512 50 POEMS 26   14
imagine how (only are shall be were dawn dark . . . . 512 50 POEMS 26   17
pomp of must and shall my father moved through . . . . 520 50 POEMS 34   33
can hold a you shall see the not because . . . . 523 50 POEMS 36   3
notalive undead too-nearishness and shall we cry and shall . 528 50 POEMS 40   6
shall we cry and shall we laugh and shall . . . . 528 50 POEMS 40   6
shall we laugh and shall entirely our doom steer . . . . . . 528 50 POEMS 40   6
moonly and less it shall unbe than all the . . . . 530 50 POEMS 42   6
its fate to grow shall hate confound the wise? . . . . 538 50 POEMS 50   5
first rose explodes but shall increase whole truthful . . . . 538 50 POEMS 50   13
mean? when microscopic shriekings shall have snarled threads 555 1 X 1 15   4
one: which halves reintegrating, shall occur no death and . . 556 1 X 1 16   2
are trees, it's they shall cry hello to the . . . . 560 1 X 1 20   16
was a poet and shall be and is --who'll . . . . 562 1 X 1 22   10
picked the was of shall and finding only why . . . . 566 1 X 1 26   7
into his was all shall, their eyes would never . . . . 576 1 X 1 36   14
selves . No doing shall undo (nor madness nor . . . . 577 1 X 1 37   9
nothing except the impossible shall occur --see! now himself 582 1 X 1 42   12
why, it into it shall climb all the blue . . . . 588 1 X 1 48   2
forever --until is and shall be and was are . . . . 633 (CHAIRE) 35   15
green as fate, greyly shall fail and dully disappear-- . . . 649 (CHAIRE) 51   12
their cowardice quite agree) shall never discover our touch . 664 (CHAIRE) 66   15
some or if where shall breathe a new (silverly . . . . 666 (CHAIRE) 68   7
to then our then shall be some darkness during . . . . 667 (CHAIRE) 69   9
(when time from time shall set us free) forgetting . . . . . 688 95 POEMS 16   14
the course of a shall we say somewhat diversified . . . . . . 699 95 POEMS 27   16
cry "no slave's unlife shall murder me for i . . . . 711 95 POEMS 39   11
of this child; nor shall even prevail a million . . . . 714 95 POEMS 42   11
or even than breathing shall blossom a first star) . . . . . 720 95 POEMS 48   13
lucky days i've loved, shall love, do love you, ... 734 95 POEMS 62   3
/ / / i shall imagine life is not . . . . 744 95 POEMS 72   1

SHALL (CONTINUED)

may comprehend more than shall ever provingly disprove . . . 761 95 POEMS 88   3
and whose last doing shall not quite undo such . . . . 762 95 POEMS 89   4
yes love was and shall be this only truth . . . . 776 73 POEMS 4   33
quite possibly may have shall we say guessed?" "we . . . . . 807 73 POEMS 35   13
we say guessed?" "we shall" quoth gifted she: and . . . . . . 807 73 POEMS 35   14
tryst until that tide shall turn; and from all . . . . 843 73 POEMS 71   6

+SHALL

FOR CONTEXT, SEE . . . . 347 VIVA 38   8

SHALLBE

also ourselves exist sans shallbe or was (laws clocks . . . . 755 95 POEMS 83   15
with their voices) all shallbe and was are drowned . . . . . 841 73 POEMS 69   9

SHALLOWNESS

to wither, to pass? shallowness of sunlight falls and, . . . 190 XLI SONGS 12   7

SHALT

hast stood and thou shalt stand. Nor any dusk . . . . 351 VIVA 42   12

SHAME

last crumb with some shame whispered unto God, my . . . . . . 117 & PORTRAIT 10   21
so perfectly alive) my shame: lady through whose profound . . 306 IS 5 FIVE 5   12
into her own Shush Shame as (out from behind . . . . 330 VIVA 21   12

SHAMELESS

your treasure blithe each shameless blithe each shameless . . 763 95 POEMS 90   37
each shameless blithe each shameless gaiety of blossom . . . 764 95 POEMS 90   37

SHAPE

propos such light and shape as means the moon, ... 98 & POST IMPR 9   9
to touch a merest shape which however slenderly by . . . . . 193 XLI PORTRAIT 1   16
being in A 1 shape passed from low through . . . . 248 IS 5 ONE 19   18
afternoon; i am a shape that can but eat . . . . 360 VIVA 51   4
Rain) a house like shape stirs through (not numerably . . . . 785 73 POEMS 13   10

+SHAPE

FOR CONTEXT, SEE . . . . 423 NO THANKS 40   22
FOR CONTEXT, SEE . . . . 495 50 POEMS 9   12

SHAPED

pillow shoveling her small manure-shaped head one sheet on . 134 & SON REAL 5   3
Woolworth building a serene pastile-shaped insipid kinesis or 201 XLI PORTRAIT 9   15
benevolent mindless He--and She-- shaped waxworks filled with 250 IS 5 ONE 21   9
the almost large he- shaped object vomits cleverly against . 324 VIVA 16   6
cents hit the whigh shaped hathole thangew yelps one . . . . 602 (CHAIRE) 4   5

+SHAPED

FOR CONTEXT, SEE . . . . 62 T&C PORTRAIT 10   2
FOR CONTEXT, SEE . . . . 85 T&C SON ACTU 4   12
FOR CONTEXT, SEE . . . . 95 & POST IMPR 7   1
FOR CONTEXT, SEE . . . . 97 & POST IMPR 8   35
FOR CONTEXT, SEE . . . . 371 VIVA 62   3
FOR CONTEXT, SEE . . . . 528 50 POEMS 40   1
FOR CONTEXT, SEE . . . . 681 95 POEMS 9   3

SHAPELESS

protestant blessings daughters, unscented shapeless spirited) 70 T&C SON REAL 1   4

SHAPELY

Judea's king were the shapely sharp cunning and withal . . . 17 T&C PUELLA MEA   28
are her large and shapely thighs) in whose dome . . . . 21 T&C PUELLA MEA   204

SHAPES

wrists did gooey severe shapes. / / / / . . . . 73 T&C SON REAL 4   14

+SHAPES

FOR CONTEXT, SEE . . . . 488 50 POEMS 2   19

SHAPLEY

say professor" asleep wop "shapley has compared the universe 464 NEW POEMS 2   12

SHARE

aims they dare not share) such make their names . . . . 440 NO THANKS 56   22
men kill which cannot share, let blood and flesh . . . . . . 521 50 POEMS 34   53
secret they never will share for whom create is . . . . 664 (CHAIRE) 66   7
and i may reverently share the blessed eachness of . . . . . 745 95 POEMS 73   10
of wonder) child unbreathingly share (huge Perhaps by hugest) 757 95 POEMS 85   30

SHARES

me somewhere begins again, shares the year's perfect agony. . 156 & SON ACTU 5   12
with a mouse who shares my meals with him, ... 171 & SON ACTU 20   13

SHARP

king were the shapely sharp cunning and withal delirious . . 17 T&C PUELLA MEA   28

	PAGE	TITLE	LINE

SHARP (CONTINUED)

noise, as in the sharp and thirsty blood of . . . . 18 T&C PUELLA MEA 66
houses are troubled. A sharp blue day fills with . . . . . . 62 T&C PORTRAIT 10 7
my Nose puts on sharp robes of uncouth odour, ... 94 & POST IMPR 6 9
in itlike the motionofa Sharp Knife-sN ap-ingof fadeadf ish' 101 & POST IMPR 11 51
ugly. , the hands sharp and impertinently dead. expression . 103 & POST IMPR 13 5
hero clamps the hearty sharp column of Egypt , ... 111 & PORTRAIT 6 42
ridiculous silks coming with sharp languid perfumes coming . 112 & PORTRAIT 6 102
be hard but it's sharp and thick and it . . . . 126 & SEVEN POEMS 5 4
knuckling thighs, with a sharp indecent stir unclenches into 131 & SON REAL 2 10
careful distinct sex whose sharp lips comb my mumbling . . . 137 & SON REAL 8 1
stinging weather, (breathless with sharp necessary lips) kid 140 & SON REAL 11 9
really to lie a sharp agreeable flower between my . . . . . . 172 & SON ACTU 21 11
herself with prisms of sharp mind and Matisse rhythms . . . . 180 XLI SONGS 2 11
lungs pumped full of sharp thick mind you make . . . . 195 XLI PORTRAIT 3 4
hitting and chipping with sharp fatal tools in an . . . . . . 199 XLI PORTRAIT 7 4
of exquisitely in- secure sharp algebraic music. For the . . 201 XLI PORTRAIT 9 20
new leaves' voices, and sharp lips of spring simply . . . . . 218 XLI SONNETS 14 5
in the darkness) stood sharp angels with faces like . . . . . 241 IS 5 ONE 12 9
a monkey with a sharp face waddling carefully the . . . . . . 279 IS 5 THREE 3 9
into my body the sharp things fingered tinily my . . . . . . 284 IS 5 FOUR 1 7
that against myself the sharp days slobber in vain: . . . . . 293 IS 5 FOUR 10 21
made verses, through the sharp light cryingly as the . . . . 302 IS 5 FIVE 1 15
truly, curvingly while reacts (sharp now with blood now . . . 344 VIVA 35 6
over gai -te. a sharp crone dodders be- tween . . . . 384 NO THANKS 2 3
thrown by Them opens sharp holes in dark places . . . . 437 NO THANKS 53 5
loved big that quick sharp thick snake of a . . . . 490 50 POEMS 4 9
may pitying Who from sharp soft worms of spiralling . . . . . 522 50 POEMS 35 12
pray for (and no sharp shrill shower bouncing up . . . . . . 754 95 POEMS 82 2

SHARPEN

silence) blacktreesthink tiny, angels sharpen: themselves (on 99 & POST IMPR 10 15

SHARPENING

road lazily carved on sharpening air. Fields lying miraculous 86 T&C SON ACTU 5 6
your contriving fate, my sharpening life are (behind each . . 373 VIVA 64 17
skies-- and such a sharpening freedom lifts our blood . . . . 675 95 POEMS 3 6

SHARPENS

a connotation of infinity sharpens the temporal splendor of . 81 T&C SON UNRE 6 2
always But now she sharpens and becomes crisper until . . . . 301 IS 5 FOUR 18 12
/ / / who sharpens every dull here comes . . . . 624 (CHAIRE) 26 1
seems to care he sharpens is to am he . . . . 624 (CHAIRE) 26 13
is to am he sharpens say to sing you'd . . . . 624 (CHAIRE) 26 14
thumb so right he sharpens wrong and when their . . . . 624 (CHAIRE) 26 16

SHARPEST

garters) there 's no sharpest neat word for the . . . . 227 IS 5 ONE GERT 10

SHARPLY

your frequent mercy begs, sharply believe me, wholly, well . 115 & PORTRAIT 8 9
her nakedness with fins sharply pleasant, my youth has . . . 216 XLI SONNETS 12 3

SHAT

cry on him they shat they shat encore he . . . . 440 NO THANKS 56 9
him they shat they shat encore he laughed and . . . . 440 NO THANKS 56 10

SHAVE

grave (departing hurriedly to shave) but--though all kinds of 339 VIVA 30 21
and the will to shave that Ghost is dead . . . . 394 NO THANKS 11 4

SHAVED

ghost that maybe had shaved three times in its . . . . 709 95 POEMS 37 7

+SHAVEN

FOR CONTEXT, SEE . . . . 262 IS 5 ONE 32 8

SHAWL

fatally exquisite" (pulling Its shawl carefully around it) . 328 VIVA 19 19

SHE

WORD DELETED, APPEARED 130 TIMES

SHE-AND-HE-LIKE

glorying keen star whom she-and-he-like ifs of am perceive . 808 73 POEMS 36 8

SHE-IN-HIM

by UnBroken LULLAlullabyBY the She-in-him with the He-in-her 317 VIVA 9 31

SHE'LL

on her nose what she'll do to yer nobody . . . . 25 T&C CHANSONS 2 19
and without winter spring? she'll spin that spirit her . . . 531 50 POEMS 43 11

	PAGE	TITLE	LINE

SHE'LL (CONTINUED)
and as for spring she'll be the first to . . . . 718 95 POEMS 46   8
SHE'S
jack leave her alone she's not your gal jack . . . . 496 50 POEMS 10   3
Cept: that 's what she's got --ex cept what? . . . . 701 95 POEMS 29   3
your eye" "well maybe she's up to some tricks . . . . 707 95 POEMS 35   9
come annie come ann" "she's coming right now in . . . . . . 707 95 POEMS 35   23
older he's the younger she's / / / / . . . . 742 95 POEMS 70   18
(and to think that she's warming three worlds) who's . . . . 827 73 POEMS 55   11
SHEA
sold! to the dollarfull shea with a weakness for . . . . . . 546 1 X 1 6   14
SHEATH
have i loved....? you) sheath before sheath stripped to . . . 154 & SON ACTU 3   12
loved....? you) sheath before sheath stripped to the Odour. . 154 & SON ACTU 3   12
SHEATHED
darkness, the sunset being sheathed i sit and think . . . . . 186 XLI SONGS 8   3
SHEBA
stranger thing than crisp Sheba with her king in . . . . . . 17 T&C PUELLA MEA   8
SHEEN
a single lamb whose sheen of full unsheared fleece . . . . . 11 T&C SONGS 2   11
SHEEP
haste) the very shadowy sheep float free upon terrific . . . 9 T&C SONGS 1   8
afternoon sky. goats and sheep are driven by somebody . . . . 281 IS 5 THREE 5   8
seeking master or disciple sheep or wolf) gush to . . . . . . 804 73 POEMS 32   4
SHEER
ghosts: hark to the sheer cadence of our gray . . . . 9 T&C SONGS 1   22
low and smiling the sheer peaks ran before. Paler . . . . . . 14 T&C SONGS 4   25
suddenly escorts with feet sun-sheer the smarting beauty of . 187 XLI SONGS 9   17
imagination. When (out of sheer nothing) came a huger . . . . 432 NO THANKS 49   14
a luminous whole; turn sheer despairing to most perfect . . . 649 (CHAIRE) 51   6
read age-- read for sheer wonder mere surprise (then . . . . 689 95 POEMS 17   3
SHEEREST
poem and glories of sheerest glory a little more . . . . . . 748 95 POEMS 76   7
SHEET
no dread lift the sheet back in this way. . . . . 118 & PORTRAIT 10   42
small manure-shaped head one sheet on which distinctly wags . 134 & SON REAL 5   4
SHELF
like jam on the shelf everybody guessed was too . . . . 353 VIVA 44   20
SHELL
will stiff-ly throw the shell away with a small . . . . 69 T&C POST IMPR 6   18
and maggie discovered a shell that sang so sweetly . . . . . 682 95 POEMS 10   3
SHELLS
tete when the jolly shells begin dropping jolly fast . . . . 269 IS 5 TWO 4   4
SHELVES
could even be your shelves (that which we die . . . . 386 NO THANKS 3   4
SHEPHERD
hands, which the scared shepherd gave thee for his . . . . . 6 T&C EPITHALAM 152
pale, whose tall mysterious shepherd lifts a cheek . . . . . 9 T&C SONGS 1   10
SHERMAN
and general (yes mam) sherman; and even (believe it . . . . . 553 1 X 1 13   12
SHES
somersaults open ing hes shes & meet & swoop . . . . 536 50 POEMS 48   11
SHESHAPE
tuck. s its (ghostsoul sheshape) elf into leasting forever . 495 50 POEMS 9   12
SHIED
throne and as they shied at the automaton moon . . . . 30 T&C ORIENTALE 4   39
SHIES
her glance my spirit shies rearing (as in the . . . . 18 T&C PUELLA MEA   45
SHIFTING
go bluer still as (shifting his life from which . . . . 754 95 POEMS 82   6
SHIKAHGO
nutn like Nooer Leans Shikahgo Sain Looey Noo York . . . . . 237 IS 5 ONE 8   7
SHIMMERING
let us descend take shimmering wind these fragile splendors . 41 T&C AMORES 5   18
SHIMMIE
and she coitnly can shimmie when you see her . . . . 235 IS 5 ONE 6   6
see her shake a shimmie how you wish that . . . . 235 IS 5 ONE 6   12

	PAGE	TITLE	LINE

SHIMMY

the worms hate laugh shimmy / / / / . . . . 238 IS 5 ONE 9   21

SHINE

out and allowed to shine, the balls the chains . . . . 192 XLI CHANSONS 2   15

in whose swordgreat story shine the deeds of history . . . . 209 XLI SONNETS 5   1

thing dance little joy (shine most prayer) / / . . . . 535 50 POEMS 47   12

did and now stars shine at night / / . . . . 622 {CHAIRE} 24   8

SHINED

freshly-creased -uniforms with only-just- shined buttons . . 274 IS 5 TWO 9   24

SHINES

moon or possibly sun shines they are our also . . . . 728 95 POEMS 56   7

SHINING

mere echo of whose shining mirth the furious hearts . . . . . 3 T&C EPITHALAM   15

cheek, and suddenly by shining hordes in sweet unserious . . 4 T&C EPITHALAM   63

still miraculous May! O shining girl of time untarnished! . . 5 T&C EPITHALAM   105

sun, so one high shining tower (which as a . . . . 8 T&C OF NICOL   17

silk) all white, with shining feet, went forth into . . . . . 8 T&C OF NICOL   27

my fingers drooped your shining body when my heart . . . . . 39 T&C AMORES 4   13

the passing of all shining things therefore we also . . . . . 41 T&C AMORES 5   10

the passing of all shining things no lingering no . . . . . 41 T&C AMORES 5   25

creatures out of (clumsily shining out of) instru- ments, . . 442 NO THANKS 57   5

at his glance to shining here; that if (so . . . . 520 50 POEMS 34   6

when you are silent, shining host by guest a . . . . 559 1 X 1 19   1

herself by opening but shining who by thousands mean . . . . 591 1 X 1 51   19

never happened before-- and shining this our now must . . . 667 {CHAIRE} 69   8

that savage yell from shining realms of regions dark) . . . . 799 73 POEMS 27   27

(o very most my shining love) how more than . . . . 819 73 POEMS 47   4

SHINY

you die, pretentious and shiny and not too wide . . . . . . 198 XLI PORTRAIT 6   4

SHIP

to know the white ship of thy heart on . . . . 79 T&C SON UNRE 4   15

like a high troubling ship upon the fragrant unspeaking . . . 112 & PORTRAIT 6   97

notice how the keen ship lifts (skilfully like some . . . . . 378 VIVA 69   3

the sun died) the ship lifts on seas of . . . . 419 NO THANKS 36   11

height eating steepness the ship climbs murmuring silver . . 419 NO THANKS 36   15

the Noster was a ship of swank (as gallant . . . . 494 50 POEMS 8   1

/ now is a ship which captain am sails . . . . 781 73 POEMS 9   1

+SHIP

FOR CONTEXT, SEE . . . . 122 & SEVEN POEMS 1   7

SHIPPED

alas! (who simply wor shipped her) who after not . . . . . 320 VIVA 12   10

SHIPS

like sunlight and like ships and like young girls . . . . . . 111 & PORTRAIT 6   65

where blaze naLOVEme crazily ships bulge hearts by darts . . 436 NO THANKS 52   6

than sunlight older with ships than dreams more hands . . . . 585 1 X 1 45   15

wingfeet of thingfear) come ships go snowily sailing perfect 586 1 X 1 46   17

SHIRT

land of the Cluett Shirt Boston Garter and Spearmint . . . . 230 IS 5 ONE 2   5

necktie wandered against my shirt and into my body . . . . . 284 IS 5 FOUR 1   6

something beats within my shirt to prove he is . . . . 360 VIVA 51   28

+SHIRT

FOR CONTEXT, SEE . . . . 497 50 POEMS 11   2

FOR CONTEXT, SEE . . . . 611 {CHAIRE} 13   10

SHIRTS

is death and unlike shirts neckties trousers we cannot . . . 238 IS 5 ONE 9   9

socks not to mention shirts fleaproof earwarmers etcetera . . 276 IS 5 TWO 10   11

SHIRTTAILS

formula: example, Turn Your Shirttails Into Drawers and If . 230 IS 5 ONE 2   33

SHISHKABOB

you perhaps wish also shishkabob?" / / / / . . . . 194 XLI PORTRAIT 2   38

SHIT

repeat "there is some shit I will not eat" . . . . 339 VIVA 30   33

do not give a shit for wit the boys . . . . 427 NO THANKS 44   7

+SHIT

FOR CONTEXT, SEE . . . . 310 VIVA 2   3

FOR CONTEXT, SEE . . . . 789 73 POEMS 17   11

+SHITS

FOR CONTEXT, SEE . . . . 552 1 X 1 12   26

SHIVERING
  cringing feet is this (shivering pale naked very poor) . . . 374 VIVA 65   13
SHIVERS
  is Cubical sliced-nicelybits Of, shivers ofcrin Ging stink. . 94 & POST IMPR 6   11
SHOCK
  din of wallowing male (shock beyond shock blurted) strokes, . 115 & PORTRAIT 8   13
  wallowing male (shock beyond shock blurted) strokes, vibrant 115 & PORTRAIT 8   13
SHOCKED
  night easily from the shocked impossible tower i caught . . . 30 T&C ORIENTALE 4   25
SHOCKING
  surprise like a white shocking wire, when she smiles . . . . 147 & SON REAL 18   5
  like, slowly stroking the, shocking fuzz of your electric . . 175 & SON ACTU 24   10
SHOES
  you'll wear your silver shoes / / / / . . . . 504 50 POEMS 18   16
  leaped out of muchtheworseforwear shoes 'fair friend' we . . 800 73 POEMS 28   8
SHONE
  on whose for eheads shone eternal pleasedon't; rising: from . 343 VIVA 34   16
SHOOK
  of the smoke that shook the ivories and she . . . . 125 & SEVEN POEMS 4   21
  Wells, and Anatole France shook hands again and yet . . . . . 263 IS 5 ONE 32   44
  again and yet again shook again hands again, the . . . . . . 263 IS 5 ONE 32   44
SHOOT
  true) disposes me to shoot dogooding folk on sight . . . . . 798 73 POEMS 26   27
SHOOTING
  over my head a shooting star Bur s (t . . . . 49 T&C IMPRESS 3   23
  -peccable cravat directing being shooting his cuffs saluted . 275 IS 5 TWO 9   35
SHOP
  trolley imposingly empty; snickering shop doors unlocked by . 172 & SON ACTU 21   6
  inevitable tiredness of flanging shop-girls impersonally . . 197 XLI PORTRAIT 5   4
  you from the pawn shop and because you are . . . . 204 XLI LA GUERRE 2   13
SHOP-GIRLS
  inevitable tiredness of flanging shop-girls impersonally . . 197 XLI PORTRAIT 5   4
SHORE
  angry dream of the shore. By midnight, a moon . . . . 160 & SON ACTU 9   6
  yearn from each last shore and home come young . . . . 526 50 POEMS 38   8
  the hugest sea of shore so far your nearness . . . . 537 50 POEMS 49   4
SHORES
  light thread the creeping shores as out of dumb . . . . 64 T&C POST IMPR 1   4
  flung over the gasping shores leaves his smile wan, ... 77 T&C SON UNRE 2   6
  of existence, as by shores soundless, the unspeaking watcher 79 T&C SON UNRE 4   7
SHORT
  for the tale is short it was i think . . . . 57 T&C PORTRAIT 5   16
  legs think wrists argue) short (eyes do bang hands . . . . . 309 VIVA 1   11
SHORTLY
  lame; but as you'll shortly comprehend a marvellous artificer 799 73 POEMS 27   6
SHOT
  percent. The gang got shot up twice, it operated . . . . . . 149 & SON REAL 20   8
  of newly without exaggeration shot with some difficulty . . . 263 IS 5 ONE 32   47
  and there was yz SHOT AND KILLED her (in . . . . 317 VIVA 9   12
  trick or this he shot the aeronaut down, into . . . . 360 VIVA 51   17
  alice yells but who shot up grabbing had by . . . . 496 50 POEMS 10   8
  town some like it shot and some like it . . . . 497 50 POEMS 11   5
SHOULD
  might not kill.) But should my lady smile, it . . . . 18 T&C PUELLA MEA   49
  in Grania's eyes.) But should my lady's beauty play . . . . . 18 T&C PUELLA MEA   61
  a dizzier wine than should the grapes of heaven . . . . 21 T&C PUELLA MEA   200
  which i have loved, should touch another's, and your . . . . 76 T&C SON UNRE 1   2
  at bay; if this should be, i say if . . . . 76 T&C SON UNRE 1   9
  i say if this should be-- you of my . . . . 76 T&C SON UNRE 1   9
  exactly strange-- this painter should have loved my lady. . . 85 T&C SON ACTU 4   9
  tire the sleepshaped lilies-- should my lady's body with . . 85 T&C SON ACTU 4   13
  do we dearie we should worry about the rain . . . . 109 & PORTRAIT 5   7
  third crumb, i am should and this is my . . . . 117 & PORTRAIT 10   17
  if you and i should get into it, if . . . . 129 & SEVEN POEMS 7   4
  into it, if they should take me and take . . . . 129 & SEVEN POEMS 7   6
  of youngest angels suddenly should stretch neat necks just . 130 & SON REAL 1   5
  in my mind, you should see when i turn . . . . 152 & SON ACTU 1   8
  / / if i should sleep with a lady . . . . 161 & SON ACTU 10   1

SHOULD (CONTINUED)

my arms; but i should rather than anything have . . . . 163 & SON ACTU 12   19
tell him why he should blow two bits for . . . . 196 XLI PORTRAIT 4   20
most courteous of men should you remark the walls . . . . . . 198 XLI PORTRAIT 6   26
from our searched world should wrest the rare unwisdom   . . . 205 XLI SONNETS 1   2
a wish, to rapture should surprise my soul slowly . . . . . . 205 XLI SONNETS 1   4
do guess) if god should send the morning; and . . . . 205 XLI SONNETS 1   9
/ / / FRAN should i entirely ask of . . . . 229 IS 5 ONE FRAN   1
nearly everybody said he should have gone into vaudeville . . 239 IS 5 ONE 10   4
distinct and rich portrait should be included, gents these . 254 IS 5 ONE 25   8
not be continually astonished should from their actions and . 261 IS 5 ONE 31   3
birth to which i should or- dinarily have objected . . . . . 263 IS 5 ONE 32   33
surprising if anyone hardly should call exactly . . . . 263 IS 5 ONE 32   35
all arrived. If i should have made this perfectly . . . . . . 263 IS 5 ONE 32   64
what of it we should worry in every language . . . . 268 IS 5 TWO 3   5
if at sunset it should, leaning against me, smile; . . . . . 285 IS 5 FOUR 2   13
/ but if i should say goodmorning trouble adds . . . . 287 IS 5 FOUR 4   1
face (but If i should say thankyouverymuch mr rosenbloom . . 287 IS 5 FOUR 4   7
hands) but if i Should say solong my tailor . . . . 287 IS 5 FOUR 4   10
dream (but if i should say Now the all . . . . 287 IS 5 FOUR 4   14
to spoons dance every- should where say over the . . . . . . 287 IS 5 FOUR 4   17
happens) but if i should, Say, / / / . . . . 287 IS 5 FOUR 4   20
lady am i content should any by me carven . . . . 291 IS 5 FOUR 8   18
in your lips slenderly should create one least smile . . . . 291 IS 5 FOUR 8   23
(shyly if a poem should lift to me the . . . . 291 IS 5 FOUR 8   25
is dark if light should flower: or laughing sparkle . . . . . 292 IS 5 FOUR 9   17
wonder just why that should please him or i . . . . 296 IS 5 FOUR 13   10
root to leaf) but should voices (whom lure an . . . . 362 VIVA 53   9
if (merely suppose) mine should overhear and answer Who . . . 374 VIVA 65   11
spear of sun perfectly should disappear moon's utmost magic, . 377 VIVA 68   3
with day) i mean, should any curious dawn discuss . . . . . . 379 VIVA 70   6
my fortune (although endlessness should end) / / / . . . . . 394 NO THANKS 11   14
and who's myself's Antimere Should words carry weapons) are . 395 NO THANKS 12   10
pratfall of a clown (should stink of failure more . . . . . . 414 NO THANKS 31   3
/ conceive a man, should he have anything would . . . . 420 NO THANKS 37   1
marvel if a thought should weigh a star --dreads . . . . . . 446 NO THANKS 61   7
and less, that death should end) how lucky lovers . . . . . . 446 NO THANKS 61   8
if spring's least breathing should cause a colour and . . . . 450 NO THANKS 65   13
so; only if you should turn the infinite corner . . . . 479 NEW POEMS 17   17
know and if men should not hear them men . . . . 481 NEW POEMS 19   4
off time that you should ever think, may god . . . . 484 NEW POEMS 22   9
not given hearts how should they be? their socalled . . . . . 510 50 POEMS 24   2
their ghostly roots and should some why completely weep . . . 520 50 POEMS 34   13
him nothing (if he should not sing) how much . . . . 531 50 POEMS 43   12
(yes; and if time should ask into his was . . . . 576 1 X 1 36   13
than our (if disappear should some world) selves . . . . . . 577 1 X 1 37   8
melts; and if spring should spoil the game, what . . . . . . 579 1 X 1 39   4
--but if a look should april me, down isn't's . . . . 580 1 X 1 40   6
--but if a look should april me, some thousand . . . . 580 1 X 1 40   11
--but if a look should april me for half . . . . 580 1 X 1 40   19
but if a look should april me (though such . . . . 580 1 X 1 40   22
of perfect dark-- how should a loudness called mankind . . . 603 (CHAIRE) 5   3
the youngest star) --how should a fool that calls . . . . . . 609 (CHAIRE) 11   13
if a cheerfulest Elephantangelchild should sit (holding a red 631 (CHAIRE) 33   1
more than dream-- how should contented fools of fact . . . . 659 (CHAIRE) 61   9
what other -wise we should have thrown a- way . . . . 660 (CHAIRE) 62   14
april (but if he should Smile) comes nobody'll know . . . . . 660 (CHAIRE) 62   25
who died that death should be dead humblest and . . . . 661 (CHAIRE) 63   4
happening illimitably earth) how should tasting touching . . 663 (CHAIRE) 65   9
be beautiful one if should sing (at yes of . . . . 666 (CHAIRE) 68   16
mind no other mind should try to fool has . . . . 679 95 POEMS 7   7
reason every wo man should go to college is . . . . 700 95 POEMS 28   6
calls itself a world should have the luck to . . . . 717 95 POEMS 45   9
also my darling) but should some im probably unworld . . . . 728 95 POEMS 56   9
/ / "but why should" the greatest of living . . . . 738 95 POEMS 66   1
believably so than (how should even omnipotent He feel . . . 748 95 POEMS 76   9
nearness awakened, any bird should sing: and our night's . . 756 95 POEMS 84   11
if earth and sky should break in two he'd . . . . 760 95 POEMS 87   7

SHOULD (CONTINUED)

somethingwitz nay somethingelsestein. Death should take his . 790 73 POEMS 18   6

could only fancy we should never know are unimaginably . . . 809 73 POEMS 37   7

ours to feel-- how should some world (we marvel) . . . . . . 809 73 POEMS 37   9

has no name-- but should this namelessness (completely . . . 819 73 POEMS 47   9

must die" "if i should tell you anything" (that . . . . 836 73 POEMS 64   7

fellowmen miscalled are happy should his now go then . . . . 842 73 POEMS 70   14

SHOULDER

the stars, of my shoulder in stead. It is . . . . 153 & SON ACTU 2   8

toss one at nobody shoulder and thick stickingly un . . . . . 522 50 POEMS 35   3

SHOULDERBLADES

lurk between your naked shoulderblades. --Here comes a stout 282 IS 5 THREE 6   23

SHOULDERS

bird.) Springing from fragrant shoulders small, ardent, and . 20 T&C PUELLA MEA 153

thy hair upon thy shoulders is an army with . . . . 29 T&C ORIENTALE 3 20

tightened eyes crisp ogling shoulders and the ripe quite . . 72 T&C SON REAL 3   6

robe from her redolent shoulders, Thou from whose feet . . . 206 XLI SONNETS 2   5

to death, the silent shoulders are both slowly with . . . . . 225 IS 5 ONE LIZ   6

is I the lost shoulders S the empty spine . . . . 414 NO THANKS 31 15

joys high are such shoulders as cowards will scheme . . . . . 439 NO THANKS 55 13

loved whose his climbing shoulders queerly twilight : never, 490 50 POEMS 4   19

quiet head his magical shoulders him doll self) hay . . . . . 516 50 POEMS 30 11

for immortal work his shoulders marched against the dark . . 521 50 POEMS 34 44

shrugs his pretty pink shoulders you know how and . . . . . . 711 95 POEMS 39 22

+SHOULDERS

FOR CONTEXT, SEE . . . . 97 & POST IMPR 8 35

SHOULDN'T

(most parent people mustn't shouldn't) most daren't (sortof . 412 NO THANKS 29   6

SHOUT

awake, of ourselves which shout and cling, being for . . . . 264 IS 5 ONE 33 14

the yearhour tree- spires shout appalling deathmoney into . . 346 VIVA 37 15

but fall (with a shout each around we go . . . . 594 1 X 1 54 33

with me now jump shout (laugh dance cry sing) . . . . 835 73 POEMS 63 17

+SHOUT

FOR CONTEXT, SEE . . . . 347 VIVA 38 22

FOR CONTEXT, SEE . . . . 681 95 POEMS 9   7

SHOUTFLOWERED

im -pos- sibl y (ShoutflowereD flowerish boom b el . . . . . 444 NO THANKS 59 29

SHOUTING

With the jostling and shouting of merry flowers wee . . . . . 44 T&C AMORES 8   5

floats in the bright shouting street of time her . . . . . . 112 & PORTRAIT 6 75

to build our clown --shouting to see what no . . . . 716 95 POEMS 44 13

SHOUTS

clocks whisper and night shouts) When minds shrivel and . . . 359 VIVA 50   3

ray rye roh rowster shouts rawrOO / / / . . . . 773 73 POEMS 1 19

SHOVE

i understand him i shove my round red hat . . . . 69 T&C POST IMPR 6 34

life.... Cecile, the oval shove of hiding pleasure. Alice, . 138 & SON REAL 9 13

he gave her a shove and asked Eddie did . . . . 145 & SON REAL 16 11

SHOVELING

big a sufficient pillow shoveling her small manure-shaped . . 134 & SON REAL 5   2

SHOVING

tints: browns and whites shoving, the dotting millions of . . 281 IS 5 THREE 5   5

SHOVINGS

the frail anon the shovings and the lovings of . . . . 77 T&C SON UNRE 2   9

SHOWED

fang of wincing gas showed how hair, in two . . . . 73 T&C SON REAL 4   3

little bitch could have showed billy how" "your bastard . . . 707 95 POEMS 35 14

SHOWER

(and no sharp shrill shower bouncing up off burned . . . . . 754 95 POEMS 82   2

+SHOWERING

FOR CONTEXT, SEE . . . . 726 95 POEMS 54 12

SHOWERS

thunderer whose omnipotent brow showers its curls of . . . .   4 T&C EPITHALAM 37

SHOWING

merely surfaces (one itself showing, itself hiding one) . . . 531 50 POEMS 43   6

SHRAPNEL

and the oh baby shrapnel or my feet getting . . . . 272 IS 5 TWO 7   7

		PAGE	TITLE	LINE

SHRIEK
   (t into a stale shriek like an alarm-clock) / . . . . 49 T&C IMPRESS 3   27
   golf slam bridge train shriek chewing whistles hugest to . . 309 VIVA 1   18
   illustrious punks of Progress shriek; when Souls are . . . . 438 NO THANKS 54   20
SHRIEKED
   stupid animals the jewess shrieked the messiah tumbled . . . 241 IS 5 ONE 12   4
SHRIEKING
   whose cloven feet the shrieking dryad sought her leafy . . . 3 T&C EPITHALAM   14
   down the red horse shrieking from splintering foam caught . . 30 T&C ORIENTALE 4   12
   Nothing grabbed with circular shrieking tightness solid . . . 195 XLI PORTRAIT 3   14
   lift ing against the shrieking sky such one ness . . . . . . 826 73 POEMS 54   12
+SHRIEKING
   FOR CONTEXT, SEE . . . . 677 95 POEMS 5   2
SHRIEKINGS
   insects mean? when microscopic shriekings shall have snarled 555 1 X 1 15   4
SHRIEKS
   helpless i utter lilac shrieks and scarlet bellowings. / . . 199 XLI PORTRAIT 7   11
   heandshe-ingly people trickle curselaughgroping shrieks . . . 330 VIVA 21   3
   flopslump (& juke) ing shrieks Yew May n't Dew . . . . . . 629 (CHAIRE) 31   12
SHRILL
   in two fists of shrill colour, clutched the dull . . . . . 73 T&C SON REAL 4   4
   trace with stiffening slow shrill eyes beyond a fit- . . . . 155 & SON ACTU 4   8
   mind you make us shrill presents always shut in . . . . . . 195 XLI PORTRAIT 3   5
   than heroes beautifully in shrill armour colliding on huge . 302 IS 5 FIVE 1   12
   is .crowned the with shrill Nonleaf daemons and large . . . . 346 VIVA 37   26
   exceedingly too small. Swoop (shrill collective myth) into . 579 1 X 1 39   9
   for (and no sharp shrill shower bouncing up off . . . . . . 754 95 POEMS 82   2
SHRILLERNESS
   toil the scale to shrillerness per every madge and . . . . . 579 1 X 1 39   10
SHRINE
   Love! upon thy dim shrine of intangible commemoration, (from 206 XLI SONNETS 2   11
   a candle in a shrine: its puniest flame persists . . . . . . 435 NO THANKS 51   43
SHRINES
   with the terror of shrines which noone has suspected . . . . 285 IS 5 FOUR 2   16
SHRINK
   chatterish strut cuddle & shrink: as through immediately . . 346 VIVA 37   4
   supreme Now: feeling memory shrink from such brief selves . . 373 VIVA 64   13
SHRIVED
   and with illimitable day (shrived of that nonexistence . . . 745 95 POEMS 73   9
SHRIVEL
   night shouts) When minds shrivel and hearts grow brittler . . 359 VIVA 50   4
SHROUDS
   it's in lonjewray or shrouds is immaterial it stinks . . . . 549 1 X 1 9   7
SHRUB
   dog behind a slopcaked shrub painstakingly utters a slippery 144 & SON REAL 15   7
SHRUG
   greets, with an occult shrug asking Through her Muteness . . 137 & SON REAL 8   4
SHRUGGING
   Place by tiny streets shrugging with colour) the mouth . . . 143 & SON REAL 14   4
+SHRUGGING
   FOR CONTEXT, SEE . . . . 703 95 POEMS 31   13
SHRUGS
   pro quid" uncle sam shrugs his pretty pink shoulders . . . . 711 95 POEMS 39   21
SHUDDERING
   everlasting war received the shuddering sacrament of sleep, . 7 T&C EPITHALAM   155
   became eyes moist lithe shuddering big, the luminous . . . . 115 & PORTRAIT 8   23
   my mind, the eyes' shuddering burrs of light stick . . . . . 136 & SON REAL 7   6
SHUDDERS
   of sparrows, the cathedral shudders blackening; the sky is . 282 IS 5 THREE 6   13
   by ocean earth bigly shudders) never was death so . . . . . 639 (CHAIRE) 41   4
SHUFFLE
   men's fingers toss trunks shuffle sacks spin kegs they . . . 114 & PORTRAIT 7   8
SHUFFLES
   his teddy-bears the sailor shuffles the night with fucking . 108 & PORTRAIT 4   25
SHUNNING
   radiance, to the grass-- shunning the sudden moonbeam's . . . 8 T&C OF NICOL   25
SHUSH
   spewing into her own Shush Shame as (out from . . . . 330 VIVA 21   12

SHUT
    susceptibility imply perspicuity, or? shut up. Seeing seeing   141 & SON REAL 12   9
    (almost when hugeness will shut quietly) almost, your kiss .   163 & SON ACTU 12   20
    at length, breathing with shut eyes the sweet earth . . . . . 184 XLI SONGS 6   16
    fourpaws? you forgot to shut your big eyes. where . . . . . . 191 XLI CHANSONS 1   3
    us shrill presents always shut in the sumptuous screech . . . 195 XLI PORTRAIT 3   7
    this; woman is please shut that the pout And . . . .   243 IS 5 ONE 14   4
    laughing sparkle from the shut house (around and around . . . 292 IS 5 FOUR 9   19
    has been with yours shut by our mingling arms . . . .   297 IS 5 FOUR 14   2
    The downlife gods of shut) / / / . . . . 346 VIVA 37   28
    and my life will shut very beautifully, suddenly, as . . . . 366 VIVA 57   10
    grass? joy in time shut and starved on space? . . . .   527 50 POEMS 39   11
SHUTER
    me (and books are shuter than books can be) . . . .   594 1 X 1 54   29
SHUTS
    F feel opens but shuts understand G gladly forget . . . . . . 390 NO THANKS 7   5
    be immeasurable happenless unnow shuts more than open could . 502 50 POEMS 16   7
SHUTTING
    do to me before shutting.... understand i love you.... . . .   157 & SON ACTU 6   5
    perishing eagerly everyw here shutting forever&forever fol . 646 {CHAIRE} 48   11
SHY
    caress of every most shy thing and mute, it . . . .   19 T&C PUELLA MEA   99
    Each ankle is divinely shy; as if for fear . . . .   21 T&C PUELLA MEA   215
    me sweeter (of whose shy delicious glance things which . . .   22 T&C PUELLA MEA   251
    april, making the obscene shy breasts tickle, laughing when . 172 & SON ACTU 21   14
    minous edible spry pinks shy lemons greens coo 1 . . . . . .   179 XLI SONGS 1   8
    there is the sweet shy pirouette your hair and . . . . 186 XLI SONGS 8   14
    her youth; whom, fiercely shy and gently brutal, the . . . . 214 XLI SONNETS 10   6
    edindodg: ing whom areEyes shy-dodge is bright cruMbshandful, 265 IS 5 ONE 34   4
    is arefloatsis ingfallall! mil, shy milbrightlions my (hurl . 265 IS 5 ONE 34   6
    snare the glance too shy--if through my singing slips . . . . 306 IS 5 FIVE 5   6
    Star whycol our ed shy lurch small invin cible . . . . 349 VIVA 40   14
    of a child 's shy foot among cool ferns . . . . 371 VIVA 62   13
    -ing wishes bodies) squirm-of-frightened shy are whichs small 437 NO THANKS 53   7
    immortal Always & lewd shy New and upon the . . . .   442 NO THANKS 57   20
    you and close will shy wings of because; each . . . .   575 1 X 1 35   16
    forever, we touched a shy animal called where and . . . . .   612 {CHAIRE} 14   9
    all the girls (the shy ones, the bold ones; . . . .   619 {CHAIRE} 21   3
    / / / So shy shy shy (and with . . . .   685 95 POEMS 13   1
    / / So shy shy shy (and with a . . . .   685 95 POEMS 13   1
    / So shy shy shy (and with a look . . . .   685 95 POEMS 13   1
    know (so kiss me) shy sweet eagerly my most . . . .   767 95 POEMS 93   7
    luminous se lf a shy (an if a whis . . . .   831 73 POEMS 59   10
+SHY
    FOR CONTEXT, SEE . . . .   421 NO THANKS 38   24
SHY-DODGE
    edindodg: ing whom areEyes shy-dodge is bright cruMbshandful, 265 IS 5 ONE 34   4
SHYBRIGHTEYES
    handful in) dodging are shybrigHteyes is crum bs (alll) . . . 265 IS 5 ONE 34   8
SHYER
    pray and fewer were shyer than doll. doll / . . . .   509 50 POEMS 23   23
+SHYEST
    FOR CONTEXT, SEE . . . .   831 73 POEMS 59   9
SHYLOCK
    freedoms pappy or uncle shylock not interested / / . . . . . 641 {CHAIRE} 43   8
SHYLY
    create one least smile (shyly if a poem should . . . . . .   291 IS 5 FOUR 8   24
    if we love each (shyly) other, what clouds do . . . .   363 VIVA 54   9
    a more millionth mile shyly to its doom mean . . . .   367 VIVA 58   11
    floating Of ; elate shyly a-live keen parallel specks . . . 447 NO THANKS 62   3
    silently little blue elephant shyly (he was terri bly . . .   516 50 POEMS 30   1
    amazing thing (secretly adoring shyly tiny winging darting . 591 1 X 1 51   21
+SHYLY
    FOR CONTEXT, SEE . . . .   602 {CHAIRE} 4   5
SI
    Minette, dead exactly dance si vous voulez chatouiller mon .   121 & PORTRAIT 12   40
    il treno per Roma si-gnori? jerk. ilyr, ushes / . . . . . .   278 IS 5 THREE 2   20

		PAGE	TITLE	LINE

SI-GNORI
il treno per Roma si-gnori? jerk. ilyr, ushes / . . . . 278 IS 5 THREE 2   20
SIAM
the prime minister of Siam in native costume, who . . . . . . 245 IS 5 ONE 16   20
SIBYL
(fact) open this bed, sibyl & you'll find a . . . . 637 (CHAIRE) 39   7
SIC
hero dead that gladly (sic) in far lands perished . . . . . 266 IS 5 TWO 1   13
paper destinies of nations sic item a bounceless period . . . 499 50 POEMS 13   6
dropsin king god my sic kly a thingish o . . . . 646 (CHAIRE) 48   3
SICK
you know everybody feels sick or when they throw . . . . . . 272 IS 5 TWO 7   5
or pal slightly too sick to rightly die) "gedup" . . . . . . 387 NO THANKS 4   6
are outlawed, Hearts are sick, Hearts being sick, Minds . . . 438 NO THANKS 54   21
are sick, Hearts being sick, Minds nothing can: if . . . . . 438 NO THANKS 54   22
+SICKLY
FOR CONTEXT, SEE . . . . 646 (CHAIRE) 48   3
SICKNESS
flat the mechanical itmaking sickness of mind sprawls) here . 658 (CHAIRE) 60   14
SICKSILK
sangsung nee whitermuch grab sicksilk soak sulksuck whim poke 333 VIVA 24   11
SIDE
twinkling over to my side Looked up with impertinently . . . 44 T&C AMORES 8   8
fond of the east side as i lie asleep . . . . 100 & POST IMPR 11   1
raving colour, on either side the windows are packed . . . . 100 & POST IMPR 11   3
screetching Each) on either side the street's . . . . 100 & POST IMPR 11   15
out into the East side, my mouth goes to . . . . 100 & POST IMPR 11   19
go into the east Side in a. dark street . . . . 100 & POST IMPR 11   34
out into the east side my sex sitting up- . . . . 101 & POST IMPR 11   59
poor cuss tenderly this side up handle with care . . . . . . 270 IS 5 TWO 5   15
/ / / Spring (side walks are) is most . . . . 436 NO THANKS 52   1
busy folk buried them side by side little by . . . . 515 50 POEMS 29   27
buried them side by side little by little and . . . . 515 50 POEMS 29   27
glimpsed (and on every side swoop mountains flimsying become 634 (CHAIRE) 36   2
in fragrance of sunlight (side by side all in . . . . 661 (CHAIRE) 63   2
of sunlight (side by side all in a singing . . . . 661 (CHAIRE) 63   2
+SIDE
FOR CONTEXT, SEE . . . . 446 NO THANKS 61   3
SIDESTEPS
kill sixeight cops-- "I sidesteps im an draws back . . . . 332 VIVA 23   4
SIDEWALK
/ when from a sidewalk out of (blown never . . . . 442 NO THANKS 57   2
f ilthi es t sidewalk blossoming glory / / . . . . 668 (CHAIRE) 70   25
SIDEWALKS
dost inveigle into crossing sidewalks the unwary june-bug and 61 T&C PORTRAIT 9   2
on) -lar (windows called sidewalks of houses called cities) . 436 NO THANKS 52   16
+SIDEWALKS
FOR CONTEXT, SEE . . . . 436 NO THANKS 52   1
SIDEWAYS
horrible thing which raced sideways while blowing bubbles: . 682 95 POEMS 10   8
+SIEVE
FOR CONTEXT, SEE . . . . 334 VIVA 25   2
SIGHED
to the moon, soft sighed the passionate darkness to . . . . .   8 T&C OF NICOL   4
SIGHS
pretending befriending means loving" (sighs mind: and he's . 625 (CHAIRE) 27   6
SIGHT
final bird transcends the sight, O thou to whom . . . .   7 T&C EPITHALAM   166
smell and hearing and sight keep hitting and chipping . . . . 199 XLI PORTRAIT 7   3
strong stalwart youth, what sight shall human optics know . . 254 IS 5 ONE 25   3
sound down (slowly beneath sight fall ing) fall ing . . . . . 432 NO THANKS 49   6
whose all (you're a sight to sing) poems are . . . . 763 95 POEMS 90   3
all politicians like the sight of vote and politics, ... 790 73 POEMS 18   12
shoot dogooding folk on sight / / / / / . . . . 798 73 POEMS 26   28
+SIGHT
FOR CONTEXT, SEE . . . . 845 73 POEMS 73   1
SIGN
patient, unspeaking with a sign on his breast BLIND) . . . . 298 IS 5 FOUR 15   4

	PAGE	TITLE	LINE

SIGNAL
softness. Unspontaneous. cute. the signal perfume of whose . 74 T&C SON REAL 5 5
SIGNALLING
a than pure more signalling of singular most flame . . . . . 456 NO THANKS 71 10
SIGNALS
as green meteors swim signals all some world's millionary . . 818 73 POEMS 46 12
SIGNIFICANT
pandar with thy nod significant to the ecstatic earth . . . . 3 T&C EPITHALAM 10
+SIGNIFICANT
FOR CONTEXT, SEE . . . . 101 & POST IMPR 11 74
SIGNIFY
that laugh both quickly signify life's only half (through . . 364 VIVA 55 11
SIGNORE
of Heaven.... i do signore affirm that all gondola . . . . . 256 IS 5 ONE 27 22
affirm that all gondola signore day below me gondola . . . . 256 IS 5 ONE 27 23
day below me gondola signore gondola and above me . . . . . . 256 IS 5 ONE 27 24
+SIGNORI
FOR CONTEXT, SEE . . . . 278 IS 5 THREE 2 20
SIGNORIES
the lucent and large signories --i shall not smile . . . . . 210 XLI SONNETS 6 7
SIGNS
voice --and any wave signs on the dotted line . . . . 620 {CHAIRE} 22 7
sticks up Keep Off signs) & youth yanks them . . . . 729 95 POEMS 57 4
SIL
(no listen don't be sil why sure) i mean . . . . 400 NO THANKS 17 8
SILENCE
beatitude sweet sweet intolerable! silence immaculate of . . 5 T&C EPITHALAM 111
occasional things close into silence, only one tree, one . . 6 T&C EPITHALAM 122
the noise of Herod's silence, long ago. If she . . . . 17 T&C PUELLA MEA 32
most heavy hung with silence when the world was . . . . . . 18 T&C PUELLA MEA 59
as it will) the silence of her face doth . . . . 18 T&C PUELLA MEA 63
a vase of divine silence Come hither O thou, ... 27 T&C ORIENTALE 1 12
candles hunger in the silence a brown god smiles . . . . . . 28 T&C ORIENTALE 2 2
waters tremulous, blinded with silence the undulous heaven . 37 T&C AMORES 2 7
laid fists of huger silence. I have seen all . . . . 45 T&C LA GUERRE 1 9
have seen all the silence filled with vivid noiseless . . . 45 T&C LA GUERRE 1 10
into nervous and accurate silence.... But first you) press . 67 T&C POST IMPR 4 16
away, leaving to shadowy silence and dismay that stage . . . 75 T&C SON REAL 6 3
lay in such a silence as i know, or . . . . 76 T&C SON UNRE 1 6
through tears always) and silence moulds such strangeness as 78 T&C SON UNRE 3 7
blind miles of crumbling silence seriously smiles / / . . . . 81 T&C SON UNRE 6 14
chromatic fist skilfully modeling silence --to feel how . . . 82 T&C SON ACTU 1 9
a bulge on death, silence, and the keenly musical . . . . . 84 T&C SON ACTU 3 14
lying miraculous in violent silence fill with microscopic . . 86 T&C SON ACTU 5 7
stropping sof a. Thick silence) blacktreesthink tiny, angels 99 & POST IMPR 10 13
gone into the soaring silence (put your smallest ear . . . . 110 & PORTRAIT 6 28
music splashing fresh upon silence) i without fail entered . 115 & PORTRAIT 8 20
feet she smelled of silence. The inspired cleat of . . . . . 135 & SON REAL 6 3
long hard hands keeping silence on her dress, good . . . . 147 & SON REAL 18 3
colour (say orange) against silence, or darkness.... the . . 152 & SON ACTU 1 5
the nude and final silence and shall the (i . . . . 155 & SON ACTU 4 15
curving cool treasures of silence (slenderly wholly rising, . 156 & SON ACTU 5 4
kills and let's as silence, because Whirl's after all: . . . 160 & SON ACTU 9 11
/ upon the room's silence, i will sew a . . . . 164 & SON ACTU 13 2
/ / Lady of Silence from the winsome cage . . . . 187 XLI SONGS 9 1
inflicted to the negative silence that primeval exposure . . 197 XLI PORTRAIT 5 17
squirming cube of undimishied silence, supports while . . . . 201 XLI PORTRAIT 9 18
sole prostituted ferocity of silence, it is) still 5 . . . . 202 XLI PORTRAIT 9 41
thy hands flowers of silence curled upon a wish, ... 205 XLI SONNETS 1 3
thy bashful hands assume silence beyond the mystery of . . . 210 XLI SONNETS 6 15
oo)ving the room's Silence) this like a littlest . . . . . . 286 IS 5 FOUR 3 9
smile the keen primeval silence of your hair --let . . . . . 306 IS 5 FIVE 5 8
(enlivening an otherwise dead silence with harmless quips, . 326 VIVA 18 13
your eyes have their silence: in your most frail . . . . . . 366 VIVA 57 2
clever to persuade even silence: therefore wonder opens a . . 376 VIVA 67 9
driving white spikes of silence into joists hewn from . . . . 378 VIVA 69 9
her voice in whose silence the music of spring . . . . . . 390 NO THANKS 7 4
magic until peace outthunders silence. And (night climbs the 428 NO THANKS 45 17

	PAGE	TITLE	LINE
SILENCE (CONTINUED)			
who limps man crying silence upward --to have tasted	437	NO THANKS 53	11
whispers to stars; climbing silence for ifs diving under . .	439	NO THANKS 55	23
opens if more than silence silent are more flowering	450	NO THANKS 65	4
ams trample (they flyingly silence / / / /	482	NEW POEMS 20	12
spoon are both making silence two-made-of-one & nothing tells	483	NEW POEMS 21	5
/ / newlys of silence (both an only moon	518	50 POEMS 32	1
singing in stone a silence of stone these little	525	50 POEMS 37	2
song more silent than silence these always children forever .	525	50 POEMS 37	12
of silent as stone silence of song / /	525	50 POEMS 37	23
/ up into the silence the green silence with	529	50 POEMS 41	1
the silence the green silence with a white earth	529	50 POEMS 41	2
william shakespeare broke the silence of the tomb then . . .	552	1 X 1 12	25
snarled threads of celestial silence huger than eternity, men	555	1 X 1 15	5
are all unworlds hollow silence has deeper eyes purest . . .	565	1 X 1 25	8
go snowily sailing perfect silence. Absolute ocean / / . . .	586	1 X 1 46	19
learn look up to silence and completely sing? futures	592	1 X 1 52	10
and every world, before silence begins a star /	601	(CHAIRE) 3	20
life's life (hark! what silence)?" "Worlds? o no: i'm	603	(CHAIRE) 5	5
(only by only) a silence only made of, bird	612	(CHAIRE) 14	14
comes a keen pure silence) such hands can build	617	(CHAIRE) 19	2
a keener secret than silence even tells) all the	630	(CHAIRE) 32	8
stand with me while silence sings not into nothing	633	(CHAIRE) 35	12
opens (of petals of silence) hole bigger than never	634	(CHAIRE) 36	6
and a gro Wing) silence, who; is: somE oNe.	657	(CHAIRE) 59	14
whoms of sizeless a silence by noises called people	658	(CHAIRE) 60	9
perfectly more most ethereal silence through twilight's . . .	669	(CHAIRE) 71	8
& sound of a silence who can guess ex-	676	95 POEMS 4	10
nowheres of winter his silence) give me a trillionth	678	95 POEMS 6	12
dying: a night for silence and a day for	683	95 POEMS 11	12
feet terrors fate hands silence eyes love laughter death . .	693	95 POEMS 21	3
/ / / / silence . is a looking	712	95 POEMS 40	1
million questionings against the silence of his mother's . .	714	95 POEMS 42	13
whiteliest all wonderings are silence is becom ing each . . .	715	95 POEMS 43	16
everywhere with such a silence and such a darkness	717	95 POEMS 45	6
the onlying world) whose silence are cries poems children . .	719	95 POEMS 47	5
nowhere flames --its farthest silence nearer than each our .	741	95 POEMS 69	4
truth) enter a cloverish silence of thrushsong (and more . .	745	95 POEMS 73	3
am not sorry when silence becomes singing winter by	749	95 POEMS 77	16
himself out of all silence strolls) nearness awakened, any .	756	95 POEMS 84	10
(in againless depths of silence) and forever touch or	758	95 POEMS 85	41
words turn to a silence who's the voice of	761	95 POEMS 88	14
mere fury soon became silence: in huger always whom	777	73 POEMS 5	10
billion kinds of nameless silence) sky; / / /	786	73 POEMS 14	17
the stars in their silence say Be the cunning	801	73 POEMS 29	17
but dumb; since the silence of him self sang	802	73 POEMS 30	27
and lovers) singing is silence / / / /	804	73 POEMS 32	14
song (no thing) no silence ever told; it has	819	73 POEMS 47	8
fear; and under any silence of each bird who	821	73 POEMS 49	7
/ / enter no (silence is the blood whose	839	73 POEMS 67	1
whose flesh is singing) silence: but unsinging. In spectral .	839	73 POEMS 67	2
whose despair when every silence will not make a	842	73 POEMS 70	10
but o the starhushed silence which our third's /	844	73 POEMS 72	3
+SILENCE			
FOR CONTEXT, SEE	628	(CHAIRE) 30	3
FOR CONTEXT, SEE	830	73 POEMS 58	2
SILENCEOFSOUND			
entirely the coming quitenotimaginable silenceofsound (here .	754	95 POEMS 82	12
SILENCES			
Unstrength, against the strong silences of your song; or . .	11	T&C SONGS 2	10
and yellows, angles or silences to a less erring	291	IS 5 FOUR 8	4
the voice under all silences, the hope which has	768	95 POEMS 94	9
SILENT			
that the song is silent, of the steep unspeaking	4	T&C EPITHALAM	50
sword and thou art silent thy breast is as	27	T&C ORIENTALE 1	24
immeasurable height, fall, fifty, silent in the incense is .	32	T&C ORIENTALE 6	31
polite uproar of knuckling silent planes a nudging bulb . . .	68	T&C POST IMPR 5	14
the face grey, and silent smileless eyes of Magdalen.	75	T&C SON REAL 6	8

SILENT (CONTINUED)

	PAGE	TITLE	LINE
bend to the little silent handorgan prop- ping the	101	& POST IMPR 11	45
to you who are silent. --"Do you see Life?	102	& POST IMPR 12	10
room's skilful of thing silent spits discrete lumps of . . .	159	& SON ACTU 8	7
/ little tree little silent Christmas tree you are	192	XLI CHANSONS 2	2
night's outer wing strong silent greens serenely lingering, .	208	XLI SONNETS 4	3
gestures to death, the silent shoulders are both slowly . . .	225	IS 5 ONE LIZ	6
carefully the blessed large silent him into nibbling final .	277	IS 5 THREE 1	23
(everywhere sunlight keen complete silent and everywhere you	283	IS 5 THREE 7	15
wholly hugs our dying silent minds, which hand in	305	IS 5 FIVE 4	9
/ innerly UningstrolL (stamens&pistil silent A s groupingThe	342	VIVA 33	4
my swaying over her (silent) with eyes which are	352	VIVA 43	9
now Disappears some thing (silent: madeofimagination ; the .	397	NO THANKS 14	21
howish time derange the silent whys of such a	420	NO THANKS 37	6
rain and here's to silent certainly mountains; and to	424	NO THANKS 41	4
/ / / silent unday by silently not	432	NO THANKS 49	1
ghostly nevers of again) silent not night by silently	432	NO THANKS 49	12
eye the windmills are silent their flattened arms complain .	434	NO THANKS 51	11
if more than silence silent are more flowering than	450	NO THANKS 65	4
hugs stopping earth than silent is more silent than	502	50 POEMS 16	1
than silent is more silent than more than much	502	50 POEMS 16	2
, nimblest; c-urlin-g noworld Silent is blue (sleep! new . .	503	50 POEMS 17	9
singing a song more silent than silence these always	525	50 POEMS 37	11
a song made of silent as stone silence of	525	50 POEMS 37	23
/ one (Floatingly) arrive (silent) one by (alive) from . . .	557	1 X 1 17	2
/ when you are silent, shining host by guest	559	1 X 1 19	1
/ / if (among silent skies bluer than believing)	583	1 X 1 43	2
(liftingly caught upon falling) silent! ly living the dying .	627	{CHAIRE} 29	15
earth hers elf could silent more no be /	654	{CHAIRE} 56	13
than each leafless) its silent in forevering snow --but . . .	667	{CHAIRE} 69	12
keen moon) dream unthings silent three like your my	687	95 POEMS 15	10
any than every more silent ly) heard (& how	695	95 POEMS 23	16
turning into themselves grow silent upon new perfectly blue)	720	95 POEMS 48	3
are enormous near far silent truths of mountain (strolling .	755	95 POEMS 83	6
robin (who 'll be silent in a moon or	805	73 POEMS 33	7
stand (over a snowstopped silent world) one spirit serenely .	808	73 POEMS 36	2
farthest becomes near (one silent pasture, all a heartbeat .	818	73 POEMS 46	8
h; e: s are silent now . in silverly	820	73 POEMS 48	3

SILENTLY

	PAGE	TITLE	LINE
noise of petals falling silently through the far-spaced . . .	10	T&C SONGS 1	43
more sweetly known, more silently than a flower, my	21	T&C PUELLA MEA	177
i shall instruct him silently with becoming steps to	42	T&C AMORES 6	12
in Thy very house silently sits looking beyond the	57	T&C PORTRAIT 5	7
completely utters utters serenely silently a cathedral before	93	& POST IMPR 5	2
sternly allotted sandpile --how silently emit a tiny	231	IS 5 ONE 3	52
(against which and quite silently hills made of blueandgreen	278	IS 5 THREE 2	5
colours (of the oh silently striding) priests-and- slowly, .	280	IS 5 THREE 4	26
and here they explode silently into crocuses of brightness. .	282	IS 5 THREE 6	31
has suspected (but wherein silently always are kneeling the .	285	IS 5 FOUR 2	18
dull compared with you, silently who are and cling	301	IS 5 FOUR 18	9
everywheres noisecoloured curvecorners gush silently	311	VIVA 3	17
noisily who kiss throw silently things Each at other	312	VIVA 4	12
sing (buoyant & who silently shall to rea- disa)	349	VIVA 40	8
what clouds do or Silently Flowers resembles beauty less . .	363	VIVA 54	10
/ silent unday by silently not night did the	432	NO THANKS 49	1
silent not night by silently unday life's bright less . . .	432	NO THANKS 49	12
sweet nothingly gushing tinsel; silently yes before angel . .	480	NEW POEMS 18	11
a child's eyes float silently down more than two	491	50 POEMS 5	6
/ / / the silently little blue elephant shyly	516	50 POEMS 30	1
opening for ever these silently lit tle children are	525	50 POEMS 37	5
flowers of stone are silently singing a song more	525	50 POEMS 37	10
exactitudes of imprecision, you'll (silently alighting) and .	659	{CHAIRE} 61	12
a body (turn ing silently to a lmost) dis	753	95 POEMS 81	7
/ / / / silently if, out of not	810	73 POEMS 38	1
the doom of sky (silently all then known things	822	73 POEMS 50	7
dying, i'll give you" silently cries the (whom we	837	73 POEMS 65	15

+SILENTLY

	PAGE	TITLE	LINE
FOR CONTEXT, SEE	627	{CHAIRE} 29	15

	PAGE	TITLE	LINE
+SILENTLY (CONTINUED)			
FOR CONTEXT, SEE	695	95 POEMS 23	16
FOR CONTEXT, SEE	713	95 POEMS 41	5
FOR CONTEXT, SEE	795	73 POEMS 23	10
SILENTNESS			
tinily the silverest alive silentness god ever breathed upon	572	1 X 1 32	9
SILK			
(catching up her delicate silk) all white, with shining . . .	8	T&C OF NICOL	27
square foot mired in silk wrinkling loth stocking begins . .	225	IS 5 ONE LIZ	3
howjedooze the candidate's new silk lid bounds gently from .	259	IS 5 ONE 29	20
+SILK			
FOR CONTEXT, SEE	333	VIVA 24	11
SILKEN			
of lilies.... beyond night's silken immense swoon the moon .	214	XLI SONNETS 10	12
SILKENLY			
planes a nudging bulb silkenly brutal a devout flexion . . .	68	T&C POST IMPR 5	15
SILKS			
coming with keen ridiculous silks coming with sharp languid .	112	& PORTRAIT 6	102
SILKY			
of the young (girls silky and lewd) like corn	101	& POST IMPR 11	77
SILLIEST			
/ / serene immediate silliest and whose vast one	337	VIVA 28	1
SILLS			
of wines women and window-sills) i met that hideous	158	& SON ACTU 7	4
SILLY			
busy rhythmic mouth and silly purple eyelids of how	56	T&C PORTRAIT 4	15
feet have trod the silly souls of men to	75	T&C SON REAL 6	11
manwhose Beard rests. onthetopwhose silly, Hand revolves, . .	101	& POST IMPR 11	47
and which was very silly hocked the diamond he	145	& SON REAL 16	8
wid yooze Vury Sin Silly : oi / /	398	NO THANKS 15	22
have an end (the silly cause of trivial which	411	NO THANKS 28	3
+SILLY			
FOR CONTEXT, SEE	104	& POST IMPR 14	16
FOR CONTEXT, SEE	400	NO THANKS 17	8
FOR CONTEXT, SEE	793	73 POEMS 21	4
SILVER			
the marching grass. A silver sudden parody of snow	5	T&C EPITHALAM	73
ere some thrush with silver several tears complete the . . .	6	T&C EPITHALAM	119
are a gloat of silver; o'er whose night three	9	T&C SONGS 1	4
be thy taut flesh silver, like the currency of	9	T&C SONGS 1	32
of gold into the silver dawn. four lean hounds	14	T&C SONGS 4	3
echo down into the silver dawn. four lean hounds	14	T&C SONGS 4	13
mountain down into the silver dawn. four lean hounds	14	T&C SONGS 4	23
of gold into the silver dawn. four lean hounds	14	T&C SONGS 4	33
flowers in vases of silver in thy beauty is	29	T&C ORIENTALE 3	30
flowers gold crescendo and silver muting of seatides i . . .	39	T&C AMORES 4	8
IMPRESSIONS the sky a silver dissonance by the correct . . .	47	T&C IMPRESS 1	1
swarms upon the spires silver chants the litanies the	51	T&C IMPRESS 5	4
in spring) ropes of silver gliding from sunny thunder	58	T&C PORTRAIT 6	7
used to ride a watersmooth-silver stallion and break	60	T&C PORTRAIT 8	4
moon perching on this silver minute of evening. We'll	86	T&C SON ACTU 5	2
fills abruptly with sudden silver these torn pockets of . . .	93	& POST IMPR 5	14
jigs dint of ripe silver with warmlyish wetflat splurging . .	96	& POST IMPR 8	11
yesterday she was a silver tube of wise lust	110	& PORTRAIT 6	5
gold delicately crouching beneath silver youths the leaneyed	110	& PORTRAIT 6	35
stars with spades of silver dig) by beauty i	115	& PORTRAIT 8	3
/ Who threw the silver dollar up into the	125	& SEVEN POEMS 4	2
I dunno said the silver dog, with ripe eyes	125	& SEVEN POEMS 4	15
along-along to the waggy silver dog and the moon	125	& SEVEN POEMS 4	25
my teeth in the silver of the moon /	189	XLI SONGS 11	17
perpetual of sleep some silver-fingered fountain steals the .	208	XLI SONNETS 4	14
is like a floating silver hell a song of	214	XLI SONNETS 10	13
to feel strike the silver fish of her nakedness	216	XLI SONNETS 12	2
fucking flag" straightway the silver bird looked grave . . .	339	VIVA 30	20
the ship climbs murmuring silver mountains which disappear .	419	NO THANKS 36	16
and you'll wear your silver shoes / / /	504	50 POEMS 18	16
for someone's eyes) with silver splendors past conceiving who	756	95 POEMS 84	5

		PAGE	TITLE	LINE

SILVER-FINGERED
perpetual of sleep some silver-fingered fountain steals the . 208 XLI SONNETS 4   14

SILVEREST
by wisping tinily the silverest alive silentness god ever . . 572 1 X 1 32   8

SILVERLY
shall breathe a new (silverly rare goldenly so) moon, ... 666 {CHAIRE} 68   8
silent now . in silverly notqu -it- eness dre . . . . 820 73 POEMS 48   5

+SILVERY
FOR CONTEXT, SEE . . . . 632 {CHAIRE} 34   4

SIMILAR
are very tidiyum reassuringly similar, they all have very . . 274 IS 5 TWO 9   10

SIMMER
leaves in winsome indolence simmer upon thinking twilight . . 6 T&C EPITHALAM 126

SIMPLE
we will pass the simple ugliness of exact tombs, ... 86 T&C SON ACTU 5   11
dance where you danced simple hours and you take . . . . . . 127 & SEVEN POEMS 5   32
of white speech (the simple instant of perfect hunger . . . . 157 & SON ACTU 6   8
tints enrich a visage simple, terse, seated like any . . . . 254 IS 5 ONE 25   18
child who wrote a simple declarative sentence with seven . . 336 VIVA 27   4
a place that's as simple as simple can be . . . . 466 NEW POEMS 4   10
that's as simple as simple can be and was . . . . 466 NEW POEMS 4   10
way on purpose by simple people like we) down . . . . 466 NEW POEMS 4   12
ago and) ask a simple crazy thing singing in . . . . 498 50 POEMS 12   28
Lea) here are five simple facts no sub human . . . . 803 73 POEMS 31   5
millionth metaphor opens the simple agony of time --small . . 842 73 POEMS 70   12

SIMPLEST
a tumult is the simplest wish: so pitiless a . . . . 609 {CHAIRE} 11   5

SIMPLICITY
of roses. The exciting simplicity of her hipless body, . . . 103 & POST IMPR 13   2
the sumptuous screech of simplicity (out of the black . . . . 195 XLI PORTRAIT 3   8
with a more incisive simplicity a more intensively brutal . . 354 VIVA 45   16
grin said (with more simplicity than makes a world) . . . . . 506 50 POEMS 20   14

SIMPLIFY
guerre) your me or simplify my you , darling . . . . 577 1 X 1 37   11

SIMPLY
and such mysteries very simply touch me, whose . . . . 12 T&C SONGS 2   37
your hands move more simply upon the evening and . . . . . . 98 & POST IMPR 9   8
intuitive flight aches, just, simply, into, her. Thirsty . . 130 & SON REAL 1   11
you? and always (i simply understand the gnashing petals . . 133 & SON REAL 4   10
homelessly. While grip Hips simply. well fussed flesh does . 136 & SON REAL 7   11
am become perfectly and simply Lustful.... sense a gradual . 157 & SON ACTU 6   3
sharp lips of spring simply joining with the wonderless . . . 218 XLI SONNETS 14   6
Marjorie isn't this wellcurb simply darling" --O Education: O 257 IS 5 ONE 27   36
harvard boy alas! (who simply wor shipped her) who . . . . . 320 VIVA 12   9
invent the air) breathe simply my each how my . . . . 372 VIVA 63   4
/ / most (people simply can't) won't (most parent . . . . . 412 NO THANKS 29   2
whichwhat skilfully here & (simply infinite) there & (smoke) 629 {CHAIRE} 31   10
never could anyone who simply lives to die dream . . . . . . 718 95 POEMS 46   2
giving who (no taking simply which) a marvel every . . . . . 735 95 POEMS 63   6
says looks smiles or simply Is what makes you . . . . 779 73 POEMS 7   20
truth and beauty lurk, simply to her does not . . . . 790 73 POEMS 18   10

+SIMPLY
FOR CONTEXT, SEE . . . . 240 IS 5 ONE 11   1
FOR CONTEXT, SEE . . . . 519 50 POEMS 33   21

SIN
meanin uv duh woid sin in not disagreeable contras . . . . . 240 IS 5 ONE 11   2
a ram flat hombre sin bangaroom slim guesser goose . . . . . 333 VIVA 24   17
us, o life! the sin of Death / / . . . . 604 {CHAIRE} 6   25
virtue and of sunful sin namely (ford madox ford) . . . . . . 607 {CHAIRE} 9   13

SINCE
nearer because deeper firmer since darker than little round . 126 & SEVEN POEMS 5   2
smile's two eyes.... too, since the world's but a . . . . . . 141 & SON REAL 12   5
"allemand" ....? of Goethe, since exempt from heaven's grace, 158 & SON ACTU 7   7
But i have wondered since isn't it odd of . . . . 172 & SON ACTU 21   9
poets yeggs and thirsties since we are spanked and . . . . . 261 IS 5 ONE 31   2
that: the other; this, since the thing perhaps is . . . . . . 264 IS 5 ONE 33   31
Arm and Limb) --or, since bloodshed and kindred questions . . 266 IS 5 TWO 1   29
same you and i, since here's a little he . . . . 286 IS 5 FOUR 3   17

	PAGE	TITLE	LINE

SINCE (CONTINUED)

which breathes and moves, since Doom (with white longest	288	IS 5 FOUR 5	2
/ / / / since feeling is first who	290	IS 5 FOUR 7	1
my life is curved since the best he can	292	IS 5 FOUR 9	7
skill which lives) and since nothing lingers beyond a	293	IS 5 FOUR 10	8
brittle marvelous breathing thing) since i and you are	293	IS 5 FOUR 10	14
slowly, oh seriously --that since and if you disappear	295	IS 5 FOUR 12	11
it is so long since my heart has been	297	IS 5 FOUR 14	1
lights begin and increase, since your mind has walked	297	IS 5 FOUR 14	5
a Reflex you know since Everything is Relative or	315	VIVA 7	8
/ / my darling since you and i are	368	VIVA 59	1
to prove, imperfectly or since but through spontaneous deft	386	NO THANKS 3	6
is hands work since i am born is	523	50 POEMS 36	20
comes so slow not since not why) both didn't	542	1 X 1 2	3
are goddesses nor sleeping) since he's young with mysteries	617	{CHAIRE} 19	9
and gone is who. since becomes why: old turns	737	95 POEMS 65	5
every truth beyond all since and why asking no	783	73 POEMS 11	4
have all the luck; since our hero is quite	800	73 POEMS 28	11
was anything but dumb; since the silence of him	802	73 POEMS 30	27
wrong's the only right since brave are cowards all)	834	73 POEMS 62	22

SINCERE

so of my stupid sincere youth the exquisite failure	11	T&C SONGS 2	6
of hurt girl eyes sincere with wonder a poise	54	T&C PORTRAIT 2	5
hands Time stuff the sincere stomach of each mill	165	& SON ACTU 14	12
this wall his white sincere small hands with their	355	VIVA 46	14
dyings may possess) how sincere large distinct and natural	418	NO THANKS 35	5
artists if they are sincere proud of his scientif	499	50 POEMS 13	12

SINCERELY

the lug of love) sincerely greets, with an occult	137	& SON REAL 8	4

+SINCERELY

FOR CONTEXT, SEE	398	NO THANKS 15	22

+SINCERITY

FOR CONTEXT, SEE	803	73 POEMS 31	15

SINFUL

taint of thy long sinful arms about me dream	9	T&C SONGS 1	34

SING

my lips which did sing a rose shall beget	16	T&C SONGS 6	5
of crocuses When you sing in your whiskey-voice the	61	T&C PORTRAIT 9	18
maybe dance and maybe sing and be absitively posolutely	72	T&C SON REAL 3	13
and hear one bird sing terribly afar in the	76	T&C SON UNRE 1	14
woods which stutter and sing And the coolness of	163	& SON ACTU 12	16
tree we'll dance and sing "Noel Noel" / /	192	XLI CHANSONS 2	27
birds known, scarcely to sing (heart, could we bear	205	XLI SONNETS 1	14
within wide glooms, and sing (of harps celestial to	208	XLI SONNETS 4	6
Collars) of you i sing: land of Abraham Lincoln	230	IS 5 ONE 2	11
friends let us now sing each and all fortissimo	230	IS 5 ONE 2	36
my Uncle Sol could sing McCann He Was A	239	IS 5 ONE 10	6
for kissing and to sing with who cares if	264	IS 5 ONE 33	26
/ / i sing of Olaf glad and	339	VIVA 30	1
hing ; s (--sing)all are aLl (cry	347	VIVA 38	32
liness than dream more sing (buoyant & who silently	349	VIVA 40	6
a girl a girl) sing -ing ing (ing sing)	385	NO THANKS 2	51
sing -ing ing (ing sing) ing a soft a	385	NO THANKS 2	53
wobbly- ing thing -birds) sing- u (cities are houses	436	NO THANKS 52	12
ting air U) sing tw iligH (t's	448	NO THANKS 63	5
death's death whenless voices sing everywhere your selves	450	NO THANKS 65	17
million of dark voices sing against the awful mystery	454	NO THANKS 69	13
say is whistle that sing that yell that spell	475	NEW POEMS 13	17
of living whatever they sing is better than to	481	NEW POEMS 19	3
one bird how to sing than teach ten thousand	484	NEW POEMS 22	13
smoke you got to Sing and we aint got	489	50 POEMS 3	6
aint got nothing to sing; come on kid let's	489	50 POEMS 3	7
sleep if you can't sing you got to die	489	50 POEMS 3	9
she heard my father sing) then let men kill	521	50 POEMS 34	52
ginning and began to sing all here is hands	523	50 POEMS 36	9
return seas who could sing so deep and strong	526	50 POEMS 38	6
(if he should not sing) how much more than	531	50 POEMS 43	12
darling. And if i sing you are my voice,	531	50 POEMS 43	14

		PAGE	TITLE	LINE

SING (CONTINUED)

leaf o least who sing small thing dance little . . . . 535 50 POEMS 47 10
which fiends and angels sing: all murdering lies by . . . . . 556 1 X 1 16 9
born no bird can sing as easily creation up . . . . 558 1 X 1 18 12
because my blood can sing and dance (and does . . . . 580 1 X 1 40 1
we have heard them sing the dark alive but) . . . . 582 1 X 1 42 6
of stars the star (sing! every joy) --wholly now . . . . . . 582 1 X 1 42 14
no bigger than to sing) leaf is wing and . . . . 583 1 X 1 43 17
i dreamed i could sing but like nothing are . . . . 587 1 X 1 47 3
to silence and completely sing? futures are obsolete; pasts . 592 1 X 1 52 10
a bough (and birds sing sweeter than books tell . . . . . . 594 1 X 1 54 20
/ / / chas sing does (who , ins . . . . 611 (CHAIRE) 13 1
jew wop rich poor (sing ing) He no care . . . . 618 (CHAIRE) 20 12
when every thrush may sing no new moon in . . . . 620 (CHAIRE) 22 5
he sharpens say to sing you'd almost cut your . . . . 624 (CHAIRE) 26 14
ty of mocra c (sing down with the fascist . . . . 635 (CHAIRE) 37 13
ter fusion ror collap sing thatthis is whichwhat yell . . . 646 (CHAIRE) 48 6
innocence will make them sing; teach them to see . . . . . 649 (CHAIRE) 51 2
(silently alighting) and i'll sing while at us very . . . . 659 (CHAIRE) 61 12
beautiful one if should sing (at yes of day) . . . . 666 (CHAIRE) 68 16
as to cry and sing, my love and wonder) . . . . 686 95 POEMS 14 3
brawny and brainy they sing and they whistle (now . . . . . 709 95 POEMS 37 9
as ourselves) begins to sing an only grin-- dancing . . . . 716 95 POEMS 44 19
& (pas) youth laughs (sing old age scolds Forbid . . . . . 729 95 POEMS 57 11
climb; will blossom: will sing (like april's own april . . . 735 95 POEMS 63 13
still) and what he'll sing and sing to me . . . . 752 95 POEMS 80 4
what he'll sing and sing to me and while . . . . 752 95 POEMS 80 4
awakened, any bird should sing: and our night's thousand . . 756 95 POEMS 84 11
(you're a sight to sing) poems are opening, as . . . . . . 763 95 POEMS 90 3
a sun will always sing is you here is . . . . 766 95 POEMS 92 9
suddenly blossoming tree --i'll sing / / / / . . . . 767 95 POEMS 93 24
(and a robin will sing his robin a song) . . . . 769 95 POEMS 95 22
each bird sings birds sing gay-be-gay because today's today) 773 73 POEMS 1 4
and i am) to sing, my darling: while old . . . . 776 73 POEMS 4 3
sometimes called world) to sing / / / / . . . . 783 73 POEMS 11 8
hear eng (which cannot sing) lish sparrows say then . . . . 787 73 POEMS 15 3
say would be to sing if broken hearts were . . . . 798 73 POEMS 26 7
Beautiful, who (truth to sing) could never quite tell . . . 799 73 POEMS 27 12
makes his moon alive sing more will wonderfully birds . . . 811 73 POEMS 39 14
--arise, my soul; and sing / / / / . . . . 834 73 POEMS 62 30
shout (laugh dance cry sing) for it's Spring --irrevocably; . 835 73 POEMS 63 19
me) "i could not sing" / / / / . . . . 836 73 POEMS 64 10
second coming made stones sing like birds-- but o . . . . . 844 73 POEMS 72 2

+SING

FOR CONTEXT, SEE . . . . 507 50 POEMS 21 4
FOR CONTEXT, SEE . . . . 507 50 POEMS 21 17

SINGDANCE

five (are all dancesing singdance all are three with . . . . 507 50 POEMS 21 4
four are white (three singdance six dancesing three all . . . 507 50 POEMS 21 17

SINGER

thee bless thy suppliant singer and his wandering word. . . . 7 T&C EPITHALAM 168
for what's below. the singer. Wall. i want the . . . . . . 220 XLI SONNETS 16 6

SINGERS

like any songs (the singers the others they have . . . . . . 43 T&C AMORES 7 7

SINGING

whose strangeness much says; singing (though love be a . . . 13 T&C SONGS 3 12
great way i distinguished singing and i came riding . . . . . 30 T&C ORIENTALE 4 22
eyes and down the singing reaches of my soul . . . . 39 T&C AMORES 4 21
cover her briefness in singing close her with intricate . . . 65 T&C POST IMPR 2 8
is lousy with mutilated singing microscopic things in my . . 69 T&C POST IMPR 6 28
little suddenly lifted in singing--hands fragile whom almost 85 T&C SON ACTU 4 11
the crowd sprawls collapses singing knocked down trampled the 274 IS 5 TWO 9 7
memory comes my heart, singing like an idiot, whispering . . 304 IS 5 FIVE 3 2
too shy--if through my singing slips the very skilful . . . 306 IS 5 FIVE 5 6
ges -tured together- ly singing ams trample (they flyingly . 482 NEW POEMS 20 11
a simple crazy thing singing in the snow / . . . . 498 50 POEMS 12 31
cloud dancing and three singing with voices made of . . . . 507 50 POEMS 21 8
around around all clouds singing three and and three . . . . 507 50 POEMS 21 19

		PAGE	TITLE	LINE

SINGING (CONTINUED)

through haves of give, singing each morning out of . . . . . 520 50 POEMS 34 3
forehead called the moon singing desire into begin joy . . . 520 50 POEMS 34 20
through theys of we, singing each new leaf out . . . . 521 50 POEMS 34 50
/ / these children singing in stone a silence . . . . 525 50 POEMS 37 1
of stone are silently singing a song more silent . . . . . . 525 50 POEMS 37 10
these always children forever singing wreathed with singing . 525 50 POEMS 37 14
forever singing wreathed with singing blossoms children of . 525 50 POEMS 37 14
forever to always children singing forever a song made . . . 525 50 POEMS 37 21
in the very spirits singing in are winging in . . . . 591 1 X 1 51 7
always joyful selves are singing) "sweet spring is your . . . 591 1 X 1 51 24
throbbing like a heart singing like a flame blue . . . . . . 593 1 X 1 53 12
finger of trunk, and singing out of a red . . . . 631 (CHAIRE) 33 3
of fragrance and of Singing) is ev erywhere (a . . . . 657 (CHAIRE) 59 7
side all in a singing wonder of blossoming yes . . . . 661 (CHAIRE) 63 3
and a day for singing but more than all . . . . 683 95 POEMS 11 12
the sky --sunlight and singing welcome your coming although . 717 95 POEMS 45 4
luck to hear such singing (or glimpse such sunlight . . . . . 717 95 POEMS 45 10
sorry when silence becomes singing winter by spring, i . . . 749 95 POEMS 77 16
leaf bird sun & singing &) thing found one . . . . 753 95 POEMS 81 19
we) is a bird singing in a tree, who . . . . 760 95 POEMS 87 2
furious beak (as sweetly singing creatures know) cringes the 774 73 POEMS 2 6
into colours all into singing) may wonder a with . . . . . 778 73 POEMS 6 4
always (through fragrance and singing) come lovers with . . . 778 73 POEMS 6 22
/ all which isn't singing is mere talking and . . . . 804 73 POEMS 32 1
merely talk which isn't singing and all talking's to . . . . 804 73 POEMS 32 11
mountains feel and lovers) singing is silence / / . . . . . 804 73 POEMS 32 14
these thankful (hark) birds singing wholly are / / . . . . 819 73 POEMS 47 20
blood whose flesh is singing) silence: but unsinging. In . . 839 73 POEMS 67 2

+SINGING

FOR CONTEXT, SEE . . . . 304 IS 5 FIVE 3 13
FOR CONTEXT, SEE . . . . 403 NO THANKS 20 20

SINGING'S

twice and still that singing's always his eyes can . . . . . 760 95 POEMS 87 4

SINGINGS

mask wear face? have singings gone to say? here . . . . . . 538 50 POEMS 50 6

SINGLE

song; or as a single lamb whose sheen of . . . . 11 T&C SONGS 2 11
stars wincing upon a single colour, i know only . . . . . . 98 & POST IMPR 9 6
like elephants through our single brain in memory of . . . . 111 & PORTRAIT 6 70
dancesong soul. rarely-beloved a single star is uttered, and 186 XLI SONGS 8 19
there won't be a single place dark or unhappy . . . . 192 XLI CHANSONS 2 20
like this most early single star which tugs weakly . . . . 305 IS 5 FIVE 4 5
/ how dark and single, where he ends, the . . . . 418 NO THANKS 35 1
awakening am. Living no single thing dares partly seem . . . 559 1 X 1 19 9
and oceans drowned, the single secret will still be . . . . 560 1 X 1 20 8
world and then a single hair again" marvels "and . . . . . 572 1 X 1 32 16
only alive with a single mys- tery (liftingly caught . . . . 627 (CHAIRE) 29 13
from eternity; in a single wish, receive all i . . . . . . 651 (CHAIRE) 53 3
is wealthier by a single sweet day's death: as . . . . . . 750 95 POEMS 78 7
less incalculable than a single kiss / / / . . . . 809 73 POEMS 37 14
diminutive whose universe a single leaf may be) the . . . . 821 73 POEMS 49 13

SINGLESS

live without every dancing. singless on- ly a child's . . . 491 50 POEMS 5 5

SINGLY

flesh the rain's pearls singly-whispering. / / / / . . . . 65 T&C POST IMPR 2 16

SINGLY-WHISPERING

flesh the rain's pearls singly-whispering. / / / / . . . . 65 T&C POST IMPR 2 16

SINGS

quivering ghosts-of-love which scarcely sings drifting in . . 6 T&C EPITHALAM 143
love: a smoothness which sings, saying (though love be . . . 13 T&C SONGS 3 5
/ between green mountains sings the flinger of fire . . . . 185 XLI SONGS 7 3
about and on him sings a whippoorwill; heart was . . . . . 568 1 X 1 28 14
with me while silence sings not into nothing and . . . . . 633 (CHAIRE) 35 12
only secret all creation sings / / / / . . . . 714 95 POEMS 42 14
we --While one thrush sings / / / / . . . . 758 95 POEMS 85 48
a tree, who never sings the same thing twice . . . . 760 95 POEMS 87 3
song's so true) who sings for us for you . . . . 760 95 POEMS 87 9

	PAGE	TITLE	LINE

SINGS (CONTINUED)
love) his dear he sings till everywhere is here . . . . 760 95 POEMS 87   12
or will be told sings only--and all lovers are . . . . 765 95 POEMS 91   9
every pretty each bird sings birds sing gay-be-gay because . 773 73 POEMS 1   4
with illimitable joy) bird sings love's every truth beyond . 783 73 POEMS 11   3
things god how he sings the robin (who '11 . . . . 805 73 POEMS 33   5
the mystery your smile sings or if (spiralling as . . . . . 810 73 POEMS 38   5
why beyond because and sings an if of day . . . . 815 73 POEMS 43   7
SINGULAR
frivolous feet divine! O singular and breathless pearl! O . . 5 T&C EPITHALAM   108
flight --my lady's very singular and slenderest hands . . . . 20 T&C PUELLA MEA   159
house (beginning at the singular beginning of your smile) . . 83 T&C SON ACTU 2   4
cursed falling in a singular block her, rain-warm-naked . . . 133 & SON REAL 4   1
air, from which a singular ribbon of common sunset . . . . . 202 XLI PORTRAIT 9   50
while. i sit, sipping singular anisettes as. One opaque . . . 220 XLI SONNETS 16   14
gradually shall reenter the singular kingdom (sleep) . while 370 VIVA 61   20
called cities) spring most singular- ly (cities are houses . 436 NO THANKS 52   18
pure more signalling of singular most flame and surely . . . 456 NO THANKS 71   10
dusk becomes darkness) innumerably singular strictly . . . . 741 95 POEMS 69   2
+SINGULAR
FOR CONTEXT, SEE . . . . 349 VIVA 40   5
FOR CONTEXT, SEE . . . . 436 NO THANKS 52   12
FOR CONTEXT, SEE . . . . 508 50 POEMS 22   10
+SINGULARLY
FOR CONTEXT, SEE . . . . 436 NO THANKS 52   18
+SINISTER
FOR CONTEXT, SEE . . . . 403 NO THANKS 20   7
SINK
which more and more sink and are lost the . . . . 6 T&C EPITHALAM   133
raging whom the hills sink into and their sunsets, ... 9 T&C SONGS 1   26
homes of light swiftly sink in the sorrowful hour, ... 79 T&C SON UNRE 4   2
/ --G O N splashes-sink which is west eighth, ... 169 & SON ACTU 18   1
of transparency slightly joggled sink through algebras of . . 311 VIVA 3   10
comes vast dark until sink last things (least all . . . . . 633 {CHAIRE} 35   8
SINKING
and (before my eyes sinking) inward, fled; softly your . . . 369 VIVA 60   8
+SINKING
FOR CONTEXT, SEE . . . . 646 {CHAIRE} 48   2
+SINKINGLY
FOR CONTEXT, SEE . . . . 309 VIVA 1   21
SINLESS
faint cities eternal--ere the sinless taint of thy long . . . 9 T&C SONGS 1   33
SINNED
lips (which have not sinned in whose displeasure lives . . . 115 & PORTRAIT 8   6
SINNER
have set saint against sinner; put gain over gladness . . . . 769 95 POEMS 95   15
SINS
virtues and the oblong sins perfectly gesticulate the . . . . 43 T&C AMORES 7   34
SINUOUS
thy extraordinary lust, (the sinuous rain which rising from . 3 T&C EPITHALAM   5
theirs was a music sinuous globular slippery intense witty . 110 & PORTRAIT 6   23
large laughing stones a sinuous problem of colour floating . 112 & PORTRAIT 6   105
fair perpetual feet the sinuous riot the flashing bacchant. . 185 XLI SONGS 7   8
kiss) distinct entirely melting sinuous lean... whereof this 225 IS 5 ONE LIZ   15
+SINUOUSLY
FOR CONTEXT, SEE . . . . 445 NO THANKS 60   11
SIPPING
insipidities while. i sit, sipping singular anisettes as. One 220 XLI SONNETS 16   13
SIR
They were ideas?" "because, sir things which in my . . . . 91 & POST IMPR 3   10
me kid in no sir hopping sawdust you kiddo . . . . 96 & POST IMPR 8   15
wear it out no sir which is why granted . . . . 238 IS 5 ONE 9   12
i mean move yes sir she jes was which . . . . 425 NO THANKS 42   7
didn't believe it, no sir) it took a nipponized . . . . . . 553 1 X 1 13   20
his angels too yes, sir what may be better . . . . 568 1 X 1 28   20
+SIR
FOR CONTEXT, SEE . . . . 333 VIVA 24   18

SIRKUSRICKY
a waiter intones: bloo-moo-n sirkusricky platzburg hoppytoad 108 & PORTRAIT 4   14
SIS
by the way asked sis breath of brud breathe . . . . 316 VIVA 8   19
SISTER
this is my little sister could with our big . . . . 117 & PORTRAIT 10   18
made its point Jimmie's sister worked for Dick. And . . . . 149 & SON REAL 20   7
proud and my little sister and i will take . . . . 192 XLI CHANSONS 2   25
was fighting for, my sister isabel created hundreds (and . . 276 IS 5 TWO 10   7
SISTER'S
attracted by the inspired sister's howling moves off will . . 196 XLI PORTRAIT 4   18
SISTERS
/ / three wealthy sisters swore they'd never part: . . . . . 621 (CHAIRE) 23   1
SIT
and the monkey will sit, up, and look at, ... 69 T&C POST IMPR 6   14
on my head i sit up and blink at . . . . 69 T&C POST IMPR 6   34
lyHer eye s exactly sit, ata little roundtable among . . . 104 & POST IMPR 14   2
morning, her sureLyeye s sit-ex actly her sitsat a . . . . . 104 & POST IMPR 14   20
and pennies they all sit there looking at each . . . . 126 & SEVEN POEMS 5   6
sunset being sheathed i sit and think of you . . . . 186 XLI SONGS 8   3
not speak. and i sit in the click of . . . . 217 XLI SONNETS 13   2
sniggering insipidities while. i sit, sipping singular . . . 220 XLI SONNETS 16   13
is Paris. i will sit in the corner and . . . . 233 IS 5 ONE 4   16
in win ter who sit dying thinking huddled behind . . . . . 354 VIVA 45   3
intensively brutal futility" And sit huddling dumbly behind . 354 VIVA 45   17
dare to stand or sit may take it lying . . . . 466 NEW POEMS 4   3
/ porky & porkie sit into a moon) blacker . . . . 483 NEW POEMS 21   2
& pretending they're birds sit creatures of quills (asleep . 483 NEW POEMS 21   9
sleep if the people sit down) and this light . . . . 505 50 POEMS 19   8
/ applaws) "fell ow sit isn'ts" (a paw s . . . . 548 1 X 1 8   4
) time me n sit (1 oo k) dre . . . . 610 (CHAIRE) 12   14
a cheerfulest Elephantangelchild should sit (holding a red . 631 (CHAIRE) 33   1
of twig three souls sit round with cold three . . . . 687 95 POEMS 15   3
each othering Selves i sit (hearing the rain) un . . . . . . 785 73 POEMS 13   17
SITS
high behind whose ear sits always a crowned king . . . . . 32 T&C ORIENTALE 6   10
Thy very house silently sits looking beyond the kissing . . . 57 T&C PORTRAIT 5   8
carefully into the park sits Down. pigeons circle around . . 62 T&C PORTRAIT 10   27
his head. young death sits in a cafe smiling, ... 102 & POST IMPR 12   3
every day paler-paler she sits sewing and growing and . . . . 125 & SEVEN POEMS 4   5
hopeless wheels mired where sits rigidly her body's doll . . 131 & SON REAL 2   16
/ / / she sits dropping on a caret . . . . 143 & SON REAL 14   1
colour) the mouth who sits between her cheeks utters . . . . 143 & SON REAL 14   5
bluish face without eyebrows sits in the kitchen nights . . . 149 & SON REAL 20   2
of Spring) somewhere unspeaking sits my life; the grim . . . 156 & SON ACTU 10   10
tremble) a personal radiance sits hideously upon the . . . . 168 & SON ACTU 17   1
--You, --in this window sits a Face (it is . . . . 169 & SON ACTU 18   15
midst of the tongue sits the Woolworth building a . . . . . . 201 XLI PORTRAIT 9   14
Mangy from person Porous sits years its of self . . . . 312 VIVA 4   19
+SITS
FOR CONTEXT, SEE . . . . 104 & POST IMPR 14   20
SITSAT
s sit-ex actly her sitsat a surely! little, roundtable . . . 104 & POST IMPR 14   20
SITTIN
me (er somebody is sittin in uh green field . . . . 332 VIVA 23   30
SITTING
/ the young man sitting in Dick Mid's Place . . . . 57 T&C PORTRAIT 5   2
always? the young man sitting in Dick Mid's Place . . . . . . 57 T&C PORTRAIT 5   23
always old lady always sitting in her gentle window . . . . . 58 T&C PORTRAIT 6   21
tablets of perspiration erectly sitting. --If they knew you . 73 T&C SON REAL 4   9
/ / i was sitting in mcsorley's. outside it . . . . 96 & POST IMPR 8   1
skulch.... and i was sitting in the din thinking . . . . . . 96 & POST IMPR 8   23
Inside snugandevil. i was sitting in mcsorley's It, did . . . 97 & POST IMPR 8   43
east side my sex sitting up- right on the . . . . 101 & POST IMPR 11   59
is Afterwards she is sitting beside young death, is . . . . . 102 & POST IMPR 12   25
how many ways of sitting on your head your . . . . 126 & SEVEN POEMS 5   8
solemn and inti and sitting on one string dead . . . . 126 & SEVEN POEMS 5   28
forgetting it's there and sitting down on it and . . . . . . 204 XLI LA GUERRE 2   20

688

SITTING (CONTINUED)

   his valley forge with Sitting Bull's T.P. and the . . . . . . 321 VIVA 13   14
   / / / / (sitting in a tree-) o . . . . 535 50 POEMS 47   1
   tree-) o small you sitting in a tree- sitting . . . . 535 50 POEMS 47   3
   sitting in a tree- sitting in a treetop riding . . . . . . 535 50 POEMS 47   4
   is much too busy sitting the horse / / . . . . 545 1 X 1 5   15
   the Art of Jigajig sitting pretty on the top . . . . 642 (CHAIRE) 44   24
   beau tiful la dy (sitting sew ing at an . . . . 724 95 POEMS 52   7
SITUATED
   structure or ideal edifice... situated or established ...far 319 VIVA 11   23
SIX
   comes God will find six crumbs stooping by the . . . . 117 & PORTRAIT 10   4
   you see?) which the six subjunctive crumbs twitch like . . . 117 & PORTRAIT 10   30
   of fluffy lust) at six exactly the alarm tore . . . . 132 & SON REAL 3   11
   on the ceiling inhaling six divine inches of Haremina . . . . 194 XLI PORTRAIT 2 14
   is nine minutes past six) the well-fed L's immaculate . . . . 219 XLI SONNETS 15 4
   nabbed at 33rd) pulled six months for selling snow . . . . . 266 IS 5 TWO 1   40
   west begin requiescat this six feet of Breton big . . . . . . 277 IS 5 THREE 1   5
   / / / / six are in a room's . . . . 507 50 POEMS 21   1
   made of earth and six are in a room's . . . . 507 50 POEMS 21   9
   room's dark around) five (six are in a room's) . . . . 507 50 POEMS 21   11
   one is red and (six are in) four are . . . . 507 50 POEMS 21   14
   are white (three singdance six dancesing three all around . . 507 50 POEMS 21   17
   around) five flowers five (six are in a room's . . . . . . 507 50 POEMS 21   26
   knu as and some six cents hit the whigh . . . . 602 (CHAIRE) 4   4
   little i (five or six years old) peering from . . . . 824 73 POEMS 52   2
+SIX
   FOR CONTEXT, SEE . . . . 342 VIVA 33   12
   FOR CONTEXT, SEE . . . . 725 95 POEMS 53   10
SIXEREIGHT
   how dey could kill sixereight cops-- "I sidesteps im . . . . 332 VIVA 23   4
SIXTEEN
   / / / "kitty". sixteen, 5' 1", white, prostitute. . . . . . . 74 T&C SON REAL 5 1
   banal, Kitty. a whore. Sixteen you corking brute amused . . . 74 T&C SON REAL 5 8
   united) not less than sixteen children and of course . . . . 254 IS 5 ONE 25   10
   to a retired general) sixteen years of rapid animal . . . . . 341 VIVA 32   10
+SIXTEEN
   FOR CONTEXT, SEE . . . . 779 73 POEMS 7   24
SIXTH
   bit of the old sixth avenue el; in the . . . . 553 1 X 1 13   22
   slowly cars pour into sixth avenue) "then" my voice . . . . . 800 73 POEMS 28   20
+SIXTH
   FOR CONTEXT, SEE . . . . 602 (CHAIRE) 4   4
SIXTY
   or 6 teen or sixty 000,000 anybodyelses-- but for . . . . . . 779 73 POEMS 7   25
SIXTYFOUR
   fortyeight, succeeded in producing sixtyfour maxims whose) . 341 VIVA 32   3
SIZELESS
   in tenderly whoms of sizeless a silence by noises . . . . . . 658 (CHAIRE) 60   8
   breathe but by the sizeless truth of a dream . . . . 664 (CHAIRE) 66 22
SIZELESSLY
   until a flower, understanding sizelessly sunlight Open what . 453 NO THANKS 68 14
SKATING
   saw a dirty child skating on noisy wheels of . . . . 56 T&C PORTRAIT 4 3
   up behind and crazily skating thither and hither in . . . . . 259 IS 5 ONE 29   4
SKEIN
   the adroit blood's mysterious skein (but like some passionate 21 T&C PUELLA MEA 186
SKELETON
   G touched n.y. our skeleton stepped from his cupboard . . . . 326 VIVA 18   10
   and is luck The skeleton of life or did . . . . 395 NO THANKS 12   3
SKELETONS
   s wince among those skeletons of these trees) when . . . . . 442 NO THANKS 57   9
SKIDDING
   in pretty wrath, gums skidding on slippery udders she . . . . 151 & SON REAL 22 10
   the tiller; clattered forward skidding in outrageous sabots . 277 IS 5 THREE 1   12
+SKIDS
   FOR CONTEXT, SEE . . . . 318 VIVA 10   3
   FOR CONTEXT, SEE . . . . 318 VIVA 10   19

SKIES
      yet holds continuous intercourse--through skies and trees the   5 T&C EPITHALAM   91
      through immediately yeswind-faces peer skies; whiteLy are . .   346 VIVA 37   7
      air with writhing alive skies--and in death's place new . . .   432 NO THANKS 49   18
      clouds cruise nobly ridiculous skies (the; mselve; s a; . . .   442 NO THANKS 57   13
      leaf. & were who skies clutch an of poor . . . .   491 50 POEMS 5   3
      so truly perfectly the skies by merciful love whispered . . .   526 50 POEMS 38   9
      space to time) --when skies are hanged and oceans . . . . . .   560 1 X 1 20   7
      / if (among silent skies bluer than believing) a . . . . . .   583 1 X 1 43   2
      almost isn't (grabbed into skies of grin) "my flowers" . . .   585 1 X 1 45   11
      like not anything under skies over grass until and . . . . .   587 1 X 1 47   11
      in doubt: while all skies fall) and then to . . . .   650 (CHAIRE) 52   3
      deep D; while all skies fall at last perfection, ...   650 (CHAIRE) 52   16
      Mountains are mountains now; skies now are skies-- and . . .   675 95 POEMS 3   5
      now; skies now are skies-- and such a sharpening . . . . . .   675 95 POEMS 3   5
      dream adventure truths of skies-- darling of darlings! by . .   761 95 POEMS 88   8
      have risen through your skies: so, in how merciful . . . .   812 73 POEMS 40   8
      all over what angry skies and gently (very whiteness: . . . .   839 73 POEMS 67   12
SKILFUL
      which syncopate some sunbeam's skilful fingerings; it is . .   19 T&C PUELLA MEA   86
      lascivious arms alight in skilful wrists which hint at . . .   20 T&C PUELLA MEA 158
      bigness of cannon is skilful, but i have seen . . . .   45 T&C LA GUERRE 1   2
      of your smile) a skilful uncouth prison, a precise . . . . .   83 T&C SON ACTU 2   5
      how always squirms the skilful mystery of Hell) me . . . . .   130 & SON REAL 1   7
      protuberant through the room's skilful of thing silent spits   159 & SON ACTU 8   6
      singing slips the very skilful strangeness of your smile . .   306 IS 5 FIVE 5   7
      of time) gives you skilful his flame so is . . . .   575 1 X 1 35   23
      (be never it so skilful) must wither fail and . . . .   742 95 POEMS 70   3
+SKILFUL
      FOR CONTEXT, SEE . . . .   166 & SON ACTU 15   4
      FOR CONTEXT, SEE . . . .   371 VIVA 62   7
SKILFULLY
      (which he will open skilfully with his, mouth carefully . . .   69 T&C POST IMPR 6 17
      muscled huge chromatic fist skilfully modeling silence --to .   82 T&C SON ACTU 1   9
      uses roofs and streets skilfully to make a possible . . . . .   92 & POST IMPR 4   12
      a mind peacefully and skilfully which is disappearing / . . .   98 & POST IMPR 9   18
      loosely voices look look. Skilfully . fingered by (a . . . .   99 & POST IMPR 10   8
      moi? Non? pourquoi?) ladies skilfully dead precisely dance .   121 & PORTRAIT 12   31
      timid lewd moon plunge skilfully into the hill. / . . . . . .   155 & SON ACTU 4   17
      with it, wisely, pester skilfully, teasing its lips, absurd .   164 & SON ACTU 13   8
      vertical being, i am skilfully construed by a delicately . .   201 XLI PORTRAIT 9   24
      may be made as skilfully.) But carry also, with . . . . . .   294 IS 5 FOUR 11   14
      become museums filled with skilfully stuffed memories / / . .   297 IS 5 FOUR 14   15
      tease by means of skilfully applied bayonets roasted hot . .   339 VIVA 30   29
      as Spring opens (touching skilfully, mysteriously) her first   366 VIVA 57   8
      the keen ship lifts (skilfully like some bird which . . . . .   378 VIVA 69   3
      world of yes live (skilfully curled) all worlds / . . . . . .   443 NO THANKS 58   9
      lugs his copious whichwhat skilfully here & (simply infinite)   629 (CHAIRE) 31   9
      toward the blissful pair) skilfully wafted over them- selves   799 73 POEMS 27   21
SKILL
      twilight lifting the fragile skill of new leaves' voices, . .   218 XLI SONNETS 14   4
      least gesture the hurting skill which lives) and since . . .   293 IS 5 FOUR 10   8
      guess of whose mad skill each world of blood . . . .   424 NO THANKS 41   13
SKILLED
      is Death's littlest pal, skilled in quick softness. . . . . .   74 T&C SON REAL 5   4
SKIN
      the newness of his skin, so of my stupid . . . .   11 T&C SONGS 2   5
      enormous rhythm of absurdity. skin like the poisonous . . . .   103 & POST IMPR 13   12
      a moon scratches the skin of the organised hills . . . . . .   160 & SON ACTU 9   8
      down- dragging yanks back skin "see" (i, seeing, ceased . . .   226 IS 5 ONE MAME   6
      face a box of skin lay eyes like new . . . .   355 VIVA 46   10
      and touch the black skin of an angel named . . . .   639 (CHAIRE) 41   13
+SKIN
      FOR CONTEXT, SEE . . . .   643 (CHAIRE) 45   1
SKINFULL
      : bur sting the skinfull of Ludicrous, solidity which . . . .   159 & SON ACTU 8   10
SKINNY
      / / / the skinny voice of the leatherfaced . . . .   196 XLI PORTRAIT 4   1

	PAGE	TITLE	LINE

SKIP
Only to have smelled Happens--skip dance kids hop point . . . 437 NO THANKS 53   13
than neither was dumb. Skip fred (jump! neddy) but . . . . . 513 50 POEMS 27   29
guess (with a run skip around we go yes) . . . . 594 1 X 1 54   7
SKIPPING
the loud lord of skipping maenads knows,-- having Discordia's   6 T&C EPITHALAM   150
of merry flowers wee skipping high-heeled flames courtesied .   44 T&C AMORES 8   6
like a keen spider skipping quickly over patriotic swill. . . 166 & SON ACTU 15   1
little puppy hopping between skipping children (It is the . . 167 & SON ACTU 16   9
SKIRT
early cessation of her skirt. fleshless melody of the, . . . 103 & POST IMPR 13   6
(not too frequently) skirt exhumes (which buries again . . . 341 VIVA 32   14
SKULCH
sum- more eh chuckles skulch.... and i was sitting . . . . . 96 & POST IMPR 8   22
SKULL
clown's smirk in the skull of a baboon (where . . . . 360 VIVA 51   1
SKUNK
Uncle Sol had a skunk farm but the skunks . . . . 239 IS 5 ONE 10   21
SKUNKS
chicken farm till the skunks ate the chickens when . . . . . 239 IS 5 ONE 10   19
skunk farm but the skunks caught cold and died . . . . 239 IS 5 ONE 10   22
Uncle Sol imitated the skunks in a subtle manner . . . . . . 239 IS 5 ONE 10   25
SKY
to his wife the sky and hour by hour . . . .   3 T&C EPITHALAM   6
to the barbarous bright sky, and suddenly from the . . . . .   5 T&C EPITHALAM   78
fallen out of the sky the last immortal leaf . . . . 41 T&C AMORES 5   2
/ / IMPRESSIONS the sky a silver dissonance by . . . . 47 T&C IMPRESS 1   1
the street of the sky light walks scattering poems . . . . . 50 T&C IMPRESS 4   3
the street of the sky night walks scattering poems . . . . . 50 T&C IMPRESS 4   33
in its box of sky lavender and cornerless, the . . . . 70 T&C SON REAL 1   13
ecstasy, where sea and sky marry-- to know the . . . . 79 T&C SON UNRE 4   13
away and blown the sky away and all the . . . . 80 T&C SON UNRE 5   2
the leaves and the sky and the trees stand: . . . . 80 T&C SON UNRE 5   14
within cobalt miles of sky yield to and heed . . . . 93 & POST IMPR 5   6
away up in the sky Blue, everything: a bar . . . . 123 & SEVEN POEMS 2   2
keen city in the sky--filled with pretty people? (and . . . 129 & SEVEN POEMS 7   3
leaf thinks of the sky, my mind takes to . . . . 131 & SON REAL 2   4
/ / SONGS the sky was can dy lu . . . . 179 XLI SONGS 1   2
/ into the smiting sky tense with blend ing . . . . 182 XLI SONGS 4   2
typewriter, in the afternoon sky. goats and sheep are . . . 281 IS 5 THREE 5   7
cathedral shudders blackening; the sky is washed with tone . 282 IS 5 THREE 6   14
reared itself against the sky and the sea ...finally . . . . 283 IS 5 THREE 7   19
futures against the deep sky in May mine's tou . . . . 314 VIVA 6   16
coloured nonthings of gluttonous sky-- nor (as a blind, . . . 402 NO THANKS 19   8
of fabulous immensity the sky screamed the sun died) . . . . 419 NO THANKS 36   9
wherelessly spiralling) beyond time's sky and through this . 454 NO THANKS 69   8
fail pulling all the sky over him with one . . . . 481 NEW POEMS 19   12
withins he upclimbest And (sky she) open new . . . . 482 NEW POEMS 20   6
agains t (whi) te sky ? t rees whic . . . . 487 50 POEMS 1   6
eyes roaming) wonderful all sky (a little mouth) stumbling . 501 50 POEMS 15   9
grow up from the sky is so near the . . . . 505 50 POEMS 19   11
but love is the sky and i am for . . . . 511 50 POEMS 25   27
this now of the sky --endlings of isn't shall . . . . 512 50 POEMS 26   12
die than all the sky which only is higher . . . . 530 50 POEMS 42   15
is higher than the sky / / / / . . . . 530 50 POEMS 42   16
night cannot be so sky sky cannot be so . . . . 537 50 POEMS 49   14
cannot be so sky sky cannot be so sunful . . . . 537 50 POEMS 49   15
easily creation up all sky (really unreal world, will . . . 558 1 X 1 18   13
whose lips smash unimagined sky deeper than heaven is . . . 563 1 X 1 23   11
when may breathe so sky so . wish / . . . . 584 1 X 1 44   18
else alive (such a sky and such a sun . . . . 591 1 X 1 51   13
orange dream larger than sky times earth: a flame . . . . . 599 (CHAIRE) 1   4
in a) "fert ig" (tent-sky wholly wallendas) ready were . . . 605 (CHAIRE) 7   10
break one) whole with sky / / / / . . . . 623 (CHAIRE) 25   8
earth has turned to sky are flowers neither why . . . . . . 630 (CHAIRE) 32   9
the earth of the sky knight and ploughman pardoner . . . . . 661 (CHAIRE) 63   8
blue true dream of sky; and for everything which . . . . . . 663 (CHAIRE) 65   3
whose sleep is the sky and the earth and . . . . 664 (CHAIRE) 66   23

691

SKY (CONTINUED)
    the heart of the sky all the little fish . . . . 665 (CHAIRE) 67   19
    dare to climb the sky) because a mind no . . . . 679 95 POEMS 7   6
    ays) while earth and sky grow one with won . . . . 715 95 POEMS 43   9
    than everything in the sky --sunlight and singing welcome . . 717 95 POEMS 45   3
    accept and primeval whyless sky; healing our by immeasurable 745 95 POEMS 73   6
    this dream is climbing sky (until his voice is . . . . 752 95 POEMS 80   5
    he; if earth and sky should break in two . . . . 760 95 POEMS 87   7
    the bud and the sky of the sky of . . . . 766 95 POEMS 92   12
    the sky of the sky of a tree called . . . . 766 95 POEMS 92   12
    (the earth and the sky are one today) my . . . . 767 95 POEMS 93   14
    poor) --let's touch the sky: with a to and . . . . 769 95 POEMS 95   5
    year) --let's touch the sky: with a great (and . . . . 769 95 POEMS 95   12
    more) --let's touch the sky: with a strange (and . . . . . . 769 95 POEMS 95   19
    you're --let's touch the sky: with a you and . . . . 769 95 POEMS 95   26
    up-up-up in the opening sky (the all the any . . . . 773 73 POEMS 1   2
    any ruffian of the sky your kingbird doesn't give . . . . . . 774 73 POEMS 2   1
    second dream begins-- the sky is wild with leaves; . . . . . 777 73 POEMS 5   6
    than blue can be sky always (through fragrance and . . . . . 778 73 POEMS 6   20
    kinds of nameless silence) sky; / / / / . . . . 786 73 POEMS 14   17
    goes green --groping blank sky with a blind stare, ... 800 73 POEMS 28   23
    face, away in the sky finally faintly (higher than . . . . . 813 73 POEMS 41   9
    seize the doom of sky (silently all then known . . . . 822 73 POEMS 50   6
    ing against the shrieking sky such one ness as . . . . 826 73 POEMS 54   13
    --irrevocably; and in earth sky trees : every where . . . . . 835 73 POEMS 63   22
    (the sea of the sky is ablaze with their . . . . 841 73 POEMS 69   6
+SKY
    FOR CONTEXT, SEE . . . . 347 VIVA 38   13
    FOR CONTEXT, SEE . . . . 423 NO THANKS 40   12
SKYDIAMONDS
    known Face (whylaughing! among: skydiamonds / / / / . . . . . 628 (CHAIRE) 30   13
SKYLESSNESS
    blob a cold to skylessness sticking fire my are . . . . . . 541 1 X 1 1   3
SKYLINE
    ub sub urba n skyline on earth between whose . . . . 788 73 POEMS 16   8
SKYSCRAPER
    derricks of gesture any skyscraper bulges in the looseness . 68 T&C POST IMPR 5   5
    chatter riveted a weeping skyscraper in me i bite . . . . . . 132 & SON REAL 3   4
SKYSCRAPERS
    among my and your skyscrapers--Helen & Cleopatra were Just . 230 IS 5 ONE 2   27
    vacuum cleaners pianolas funnygraphs skyscrapers an . . . . . 237 IS 5 ONE 8   10
SLABS
    firmly lewd on dangerous slabs of tilting din whose . . . . . 138 & SON REAL 9   2
    hot peeling off huge slabs of a fuzzy language . . . . 194 XLI PORTRAIT 2   25
SLAM
    so long door golf slam bridge train shriek chewing . . . . . 309 VIVA 1   18
SLAMMED
    the Public Gardens i slammed on the internalexpanding & . . . 248 IS 5 ONE 19   28
    who (bent by wind) slammed hard- over the tiller; . . . . . . 277 IS 5 THREE 1   10
SLAMSLUM
    me glad) dis dumdam slamslum slopp idy wurl sho . . . . . . 519 50 POEMS 33   8
SLANT
    (still u ntumbled but slant ing drun kenly) mind . . . . . . 695 95 POEMS 23   8
+SLANTS
    FOR CONTEXT, SEE . . . . 144 & SON REAL 15   3
SLAP
    twist on permament and slap tremendous sorrydaze bog . . . . 333 VIVA 24   13
SLAPPED
    quartzlike face. his right slapped the amusing big vital . . 148 & SON REAL 19   4
    (appeared cleverly) world iS Slapped: with; liGhtninG ! at . 347 VIVA 38   5
+SLAPPING
    FOR CONTEXT, SEE . . . . 635 (CHAIRE) 37   2
SLAPSOOTHED
    (popes emperors) undeaths through (slapsoothed by sundark) . 681 95 POEMS 9   13
SLATE
    quickly things on the slate of that nigger's face . . . . . 287 IS 5 FOUR 4   4
SLATTERN
    in parlor windows spring slattern of seasons you have . . . . 61 T&C PORTRAIT 9   11

	PAGE	TITLE	LINE
SLAUGHTER			
lions to the roaring slaughter they did not stop	268	IS 5 TWO 3	11
SLAVE			
friend not those who slave unselves to lend for	440	NO THANKS 56	15
and matter became the slave of mind; thus virtue	799	73 POEMS 27	35
(freedom: what makes a slave) therefore, my life, lie	834	73 POEMS 62	9
SLAVE'S			
a terrible cry "no slave's unlife shall murder me	711	95 POEMS 39	11
SLAVES			
their heels for Freedom slaves will click; where Boobs . . .	438	NO THANKS 54	18
are) seeming's enough for slaves of space and time	745	95 POEMS 73	13
SLAVVER			
whose mouth dripped with slavver of spring chased two	194	XLI PORTRAIT 2	5
SLEEK			
than daunting death the sleek slim deer the tall	14	T&C SONGS 4	27
the meek proud sloppy sleek) all except the cold	619	(CHAIRE) 21	5
SLEEP			
the shuddering sacrament of sleep, betwixt whose cool	7	T&C EPITHALAM	155
be they than slippered sleep the lean lithe deer	14	T&C SONGS 4	16
sent her forth to sleep upon the world and	38	T&C AMORES 3	4
hands and is with sleep.... love, the breaking of	38	T&C AMORES 3	13
nothingness for we would sleep this is the passing	41	T&C AMORES 5	24
the tremendous lie of sleep i watch the roses	78	T&C SON UNRE 3	13
the strong men who sleep between the legs of	114	& PORTRAIT 7	29
a joujoux, want nice sleep? toutes les petites femmes	121	& PORTRAIT 12	49
/ if i should sleep with a lady called	161	& SON ACTU 10	1
fields with the superior dust-of-sleep. wields easily the . .	163	& SON ACTU 12	4
tiny racket. The horses sleep upstairs. And you can	171	& SON ACTU 20	6
look the spangles that sleep all the year in	192	XLI CHANSONS 2	14
deep trees perpetual of sleep some silver-fingered fountain .	208	XLI SONNETS 4	13
proficient poison of sure sleep bereaves us of our	210	XLI SONNETS 6	1
(drawing my Mes from sleep whose stranger dreams thy	213	XLI SONNETS 9	13
window because i can't sleep (smoking sawdust cigarettes in .	242	IS 5 ONE 13	21
spanked and put to sleep by dolls let us	261	IS 5 ONE 31	2
a peculiar form of sleep what's beyond logic happens	264	IS 5 ONE 33	4
his awkward eyes pushing sleep under and thoroughly into . .	293	IS 5 FOUR 10	29
do i weep eat sleep--what does the whole intend"	295	IS 5 FOUR 12	16
And oceans do Not sleep matters nothing; then (then	359	VIVA 50	13
reenter the singular kingdom (sleep) . while some thing . . .	370	VIVA 61	21
does not forget, perish, sleep cannot be photographed, . . .	377	VIVA 68	9
dream means more than sleep as more than know	390	NO THANKS 7	11
cried) lie bravely down sleep big rain big snow	393	NO THANKS 10	12
down to so much sleep they only understand enormously	418	NO THANKS 35	8
love not Fear eat sleep kill and have you	467	NEW POEMS 5	10
kid let's go to sleep if you can't smoke	489	50 POEMS 3	4
kid let's go to sleep if you can't sing	489	50 POEMS 3	8
kid let's go to sleep if you can't die	489	50 POEMS 3	12
kid Let's go to sleep) / / / /	489	50 POEMS 3	16
noworld Silent is blue (sleep! new girlgold / /	503	50 POEMS 17	11
the feeble go to sleep if the people sit	505	50 POEMS 19	8
and did their dance (sleep wake hope and then)	515	50 POEMS 29	19
more they dream their sleep noone and anyone earth	515	50 POEMS 29	30
father's fingers brought her sleep: vainly no smallest voice	520	50 POEMS 34	14
snowlflake "yes: you may sleep now, my mountain" and	555	1 X 1 15	15
thing-- how more than sleep illimitably my --being so	558	1 X 1 18	11
chores laid him down. Sleep well / / /	568	1 X 1 28	30
of a dream whose sleep is the sky and	664	(CHAIRE) 66	23
deeper magic: that white sleep wherein all human curiosity .	675	95 POEMS 3	11
ol d than (a sleep) whom and tipto e	733	95 POEMS 61	7
many million minds which sleep and move) blind sands, ...	743	95 POEMS 71	7
whom two tiny selves sleep (doll by doll) motionless	777	73 POEMS 5	11
am sails out of sleep steering for dream /	781	73 POEMS 9	3
of the universe of sleep safely may by imperishable	811	73 POEMS 39	1
SLEEP'S			
doom pass ignorantly into sleep's bright land / /	358	VIVA 49	15
SLEEPDEEP			
are picked from dumb sleePdeep ness squirmcurl ing	395	NO THANKS 12	14

		PAGE	TITLE	LINE

SLEEPILY
slippery mess, a star sleepily, feebly, scratches the sore . 144 & SON REAL 15   9
SLEEPING
quick forest filled with sleeping birds thy breasts are . . . 29 T&C ORIENTALE 3   6
Elysian the like, a) slEEping neck a breathing a . . . . . . 104 & POST IMPR 14   7
her dress, good for sleeping is her long hard . . . . 147 & SON REAL 18   3
against darkness in the sleeping curves of my body . . . . . 189 XLI SONGS 11   8
his april touch drove sleeping selves to swarm their . . . . 520 50 POEMS 34   11
awake are goddesses nor sleeping) since he's young with . . . 617 (CHAIRE) 19   9
and resurrection: over my sleeping self float flaming symbols 749 95 POEMS 77   11
and a (float through sleeping firsts of wonder) child . . . . 757 95 POEMS 85   27
SLEEPLESS
pass. Our feet tread sleepless meadows sweet with fear") . .   9 T&C SONGS 1   27
SLEEPS
your dead face which sleeps, a dream shall pass) . . . . . . 11 T&C SONGS 2   30
/ / the emperor sleeps in a palace of . . . . 32 T&C ORIENTALE 6   2
his bed the city sleeps with death upon her . . . . 50 T&C IMPRESS 4   30
SLEEPSHAPED
whom almost tire the sleepshaped lilies-- should my lady's . 85 T&C SON ACTU 4   12
SLEEPY
poppy petals peers the sleepy morning) gently draws apart . .   8 T&C OF NICOL   14
tell you; several, incredible, sleepy / / / / . . . . 281 IS 5 THREE 5   25
SLEET
flays screaming hills with sleet and snow: strangles valleys 560 1 X 1 20   10
SLENDER
the thrilling rain the slender paramour to toy with . . . . .   3 T&C EPITHALAM   3
three willows wail, a slender dimness in the unshapeful . . .   9 T&C SONGS 1   5
used to wholly move slender ladies made of dream . . . . . . 23 T&C PUELLA MEA 284
a Lady with bright slender eyes (who moves) at . . . . 91 & POST IMPR 3   2
beside young death, is slender; likes flowers. / / . . . . . 102 & POST IMPR 12   25
myself, because i am slender and fragile i borrow . . . . . . 328 VIVA 19   16
smell only such blue slender hands of god / . . . . 340 VIVA 31   20
beyond near) girlest she slender is cradling in joy . . . . . 518 50 POEMS 32   6
singing) come lovers with slender their ladies (Each . . . . 778 73 POEMS 6   23
big voice: then a slender face (on the mantelpiece . . . . . 813 73 POEMS 41   3
+SLENDER
FOR CONTEXT, SEE . . . . 669 (CHAIRE) 71   9
SLENDEREST
lady's very singular and slenderest hands moreover are (which 20 T&C PUELLA MEA 160
SLENDERING
feet all things whose slendering sweetness touched renown) . 414 NO THANKS 31   4
SLENDERLY
mauve of twilight (who slenderly descends, daintily carrying 93 & POST IMPR 5   9
cool treasures of silence (slenderly wholly rising, herself . 156 & SON ACTU 5   5
merest shape which however slenderly by it caressed will . . 193 XLI PORTRAIT 1   16
reason) in your lips slenderly should create one least . . . 291 IS 5 FOUR 8   23
/ our touching hearts slenderly comprehend (clinging as . . . 305 IS 5 FIVE 4   1
lean lips, hovers how slenderly the illustrious unknown . . . 344 VIVA 35   10
rain) thickly i fail slenderly i win (like touch . . . . . . 433 NO THANKS 50   10
+SLENDERLY
FOR CONTEXT, SEE . . . . 101 & POST IMPR 11   77
SLENDERNESS
the young lips unearthly slenderness / / / / . . . . 156 & SON ACTU 5   15
drifted gifts of featheriest slenderness and how gradually . 299 IS 5 FOUR 16   5
SLEPT
times a week. and slept twice a week with . . . . 149 & SON REAL 20   12
said their nevers they slept their dream stars rain . . . . . 515 50 POEMS 29   20
mountain" and this mountain slept while his pines lifted . . 555 1 X 1 15   15
SLEUTHFULLY
having first put right sleuthfully aboard all . . . . 334 VIVA 25   5
SLICED
for. putrescence is Cubical sliced-nicelybits Of, shivers . . 94 & POST IMPR 6   11
+SLICING
FOR CONTEXT, SEE . . . . 106 & PORTRAIT 2   3
SLICKERN
rugged as a bear slickern a weazel how be . . . . 568 1 X 1 28   8
SLID
Doll, wispish-agile feet with slid steps parting the tousle . 140 & SON REAL 11   14

SLIDING
    I understand. Once again....) sliding a little downward, . . 282 IS 5 THREE 6   33
SLIGHT
    good: firmlysquirmy with a slight jounce, thirteen pants have 150 & SON REAL 21   4
SLIGHTEST
    are too near your slightest look easily will unclose . . . . 366 VIVA 57   5
SLIGHTLY
    somehow feel your smile slightly is a more minute . . . . . . 98 & POST IMPR 9   11
    O stay with me slightly. or until with neat . . . . 165 & SON ACTU 14   10
    being altered that i slightly am becoming something a . . . . 199 XLI PORTRAIT 7   8
    a little topples and slightly expands one square foot . . . . 225 IS 5 ONE LIZ   2
    i hazarded "god" (blushing slightly) --"O damn ginks like . . 228 IS 5 ONE MARJ   6
    / / / / slightly before the middle of . . . . 249 IS 5 ONE 20   1
    begs in your mind (slightly smiling, patient, unspeaking with 298 IS 5 FOUR 15   3
    deep with rain.... (he, slightly whom or cautiously this . . 300 IS 5 FOUR 17   16
    in thickening fear our slightly fingering spirits starve and 305 IS 5 FIVE 4   7
    Concentric geometries of transparency slightly joggled sink . 311 VIVA 3   9
    permit a metaphor savouring slightly of the demotic) Miss . . 326 VIVA 18   27
    grouse rocket know quite, slightly or how at the . . . . . . 346 VIVA 37   13
    these colours; alone who slightly always are beyond the . . . 357 VIVA 48   12
    other disappeared: but i slightly smiling, gradually shall . 370 VIVA 61   17
    a park. Complete. and slightly (why? or lest we . . . . 375 VIVA 66   9
    or lest we understand) slightly i am hearing somebody . . . . 375 VIVA 66   10
    minus gal or pal slightly too sick to rightly . . . . 387 NO THANKS 4   6
    ne like nothing verdi slightly knu as and some . . . . 602 (CHAIRE) 4   3
    mother") had; making annie slightly mad but very wonderful . 794 73 POEMS 22   5
SLIM
    daunting death the sleek slim deer the tall tense . . . . . . 14 T&C SONGS 4   27
    and young tree, her slim lascivious arms alight in . . . . . 20 T&C PUELLA MEA 157
    on prowl gorge sly slim gods stare / / . . . .   90 & POST IMPR 2   16
    / / / Babylon slim -ness of evenslicing eyes . . . . 106 & PORTRAIT 2   1
    body it was thick slim warm moist built like . . . . 110 & PORTRAIT 6   17
    eve (who aint precisely slim) sim ply don't know . . . . . . 240 IS 5 ONE 11   1
    used to (and them slim hot queens with dam . . . . 242 IS 5 ONE 13   5
    on smallest hands the slim hinging you --because it's . . . . 282 IS 5 THREE 6   8
    faeries (and if your slim lips are amused, no . . . . 294 IS 5 FOUR 11   10
    flat hombre sin bangaroom slim guesser goose pin yessir . . . 333 VIVA 24   18
    carpet from which rise slim curving mighty children while . . 384 NO THANKS 2   20
    the dim ones; the slim plump tiny tall) all . . . . 619 (CHAIRE) 21   11
    drift slippery hands tease slim float twitter faces) only . . 633 (CHAIRE) 35   5
    fear a which of slim of blue of here . . . . 746 95 POEMS 74   5
+SLIM
    FOR CONTEXT, SEE . . . . 114 & PORTRAIT 7   18
SLIME
    old swimminghole there'll be slime in his eyes and . . . . . 707 95 POEMS 35   28
SLIMMER
    gert (spin! helen) the slimmer the finger the thicker . . . . 513 50 POEMS 27   6
+SLIMNESS
    FOR CONTEXT, SEE . . . . 106 & PORTRAIT 2   1
SLINGS
    world a kiss and slings his wheel upon his . . . . 624 (CHAIRE) 26   19
+SLINKILY
    FOR CONTEXT, SEE . . . . 430 NO THANKS 47   7
SLIPPED
    incense) fifty marble pillars slipped from immeasurable . . . 32 T&C ORIENTALE 6 30
    <> cranked her up, slipped the clutch (and then . . . . 248 IS 5 ONE 19   10
SLIPPERED
    Softer be they than slippered sleep the lean lithe . . . . . 14 T&C SONGS 4   16
SLIPPERY
    must and shall, whose slippery body is Death's littlest . . . 74 T&C SON REAL 5   3
    around you, a frail slippery house, a strong fragile . . . . 83 T&C SON ACTU 2   2
    ferocious heels. Her gasping slippery body moved with the . . 103 & POST IMPR 13   9
    a music sinuous globular slippery intense witty huge and . . 110 & PORTRAIT 6   24
    shrub painstakingly utters a slippery mess, a star sleepily, 144 & SON REAL 15   8
    wrath, gums skidding on slippery udders she lifts an . . . . 151 & SON REAL 22   10
    to think is the slippery contours of a vase . . . . 193 XLI PORTRAIT 1 14
    nothing earthly, while the slippery eyes drown in surging . . 226 IS 5 ONE MAME   4
    bald. (Coughs.) Two pale slippery small eyes balanced upon . 406 NO THANKS 23   9

| | | PAGE | TITLE | LINE |

SLIPPERY (CONTINUED)
to ghosts go drift slippery hands tease slim float . . . . . 633 {CHAIRE} 35   5
+SLIPPERY
FOR CONTEXT, SEE . . . . 100 & POST IMPR 11   4
SLIPPING
cheeks mouth its hands (slipping) felt of my necktie . . . . 284 IS 5 FOUR 1   5
SLIPS
into something else, and slips away.... (these leaves are . . 303 IS 5 FIVE 2   5
shy--if through my singing slips the very skilful strangeness 306 IS 5 FIVE 5   6
while a once world slips from few of sun . . . . 822 73 POEMS 50   1
+SLIPS
FOR CONTEXT, SEE . . . . 445 NO THANKS 60   6
SLIPSHOD
Get Up In, the slipshod mucous kiss of her . . . . 130 & SON REAL 1   1
SLIPSLOUCH
/ / / one slipslouch twi tterstamp coon wid . . . . 519 50 POEMS 33   1
SLITS
the alarm tore two slits in her cheeks. A . . . . 132 & SON REAL 3   13
SLITTED
my, mouth loves melons slitted with bright knives, it . . . . 100 & POST IMPR 11 22
SLIVERS
my mind laughsin- to Slivers of (unthinking. c'est l'heure . 94 & POST IMPR 6   18
SLO-WLY
neutral tried and again slo-wly; bare, ly nudg. ing . . . . . 248 IS 5 ONE 19   15
SLOBBER
thy breasts and the slobber of your thighs i . . . . 61 T&C PORTRAIT 9   24
she, and heard them slobber and in the darkness) . . . . . . 241 IS 5 ONE 12   7
myself the sharp days slobber in vain: Nor am . . . . 293 IS 5 FOUR 10   21
SLOBBERING
snug and evil. the slobbering walls filthily push witless . . 96 & POST IMPR 8   3
SLOGAN
for dreams or a slogan may topple you (trees . . . . 732 95 POEMS 60   2
SLOP
clutch owch so chuck slop hight evolute my eerily . . . . . . 333 VIVA 24   22
SLOPCAKED
pale dog behind a slopcaked shrub painstakingly utters a . . 144 & SON REAL 15   7
SLOPPED
blood) pa-nt stab are (slopped givers of not) bang . . . . . 388 NO THANKS 5   11
+SLOPPIDY
FOR CONTEXT, SEE . . . . 519 50 POEMS 33   8
SLOPPY
and you have a sloppy body from being brought . . . . 61 T&C PORTRAIT 9   16
ones; the meek proud sloppy sleek) all except the . . . . . . 619 {CHAIRE} 21   5
SLOT
a penny in the slot and bellow like a . . . . 500 50 POEMS 14   11
+SLOUCH
FOR CONTEXT, SEE . . . . 519 50 POEMS 33   1
SLOUCHES
the kanoon she totters, slouches, with giggling hips and . . 143 & SON REAL 14   13
SLOVENLY
mill- ions whose rich slovenly obscene procession always . . 202 XLI PORTRAIT 9   46
unlighted hearts lust lurks slovenly and homeless and when . 322 VIVA 14   11
SLOW
undiscovered eyes and dim slow perfect body amorous (whiter . 5 T&C EPITHALAM   99
scarcely sings drifting in slow diaphanous faint rout), queen 6 T&C EPITHALAM   144
in a row between slow glories fleetly go.) Upon . . . . 20 T&C PUELLA MEA   144
palpitating breasts inhale the slow supple flower of thy . . 31 T&C ORIENTALE 5   25
circle wildly in the slow-ly-in creasing fragility --. Dogs . 63 T&C PORTRAIT 10 31
focusses in the sweet slow animal bottomless eyes importantly 74 T&C SON REAL 5   6
roundtables Her, eyes count slow (ly obstre peroustimidi ties 104 & POST IMPR 14   3
to trace with stiffening slow shrill eyes beyond a . . . . . 155 & SON ACTU 4   8
invisible faces hauntingly and slow. This is the garden. . . 208 XLI SONNETS 4   8
enraptured, as among the slow deep trees perpetual of . . . . 208 XLI SONNETS 4   13
bereaves us of our slow tranquillities and He without . . . . 210 XLI SONNETS 6   2
ter you think, die slow ly "toc tic" as . . . . 354 VIVA 45   24
no said he) go slow said she (cccome? said . . . . 399 NO THANKS 16   28
say (it comes so slow not since not why) . . . . 542 1 X 1 2   2
will kissed breast awake) slow tottering visions bigly come . 565 1 X 1 25   13

	PAGE	TITLE	LINE
+SLOW			
FOR CONTEXT, SEE	101	& POST IMPR 11	62
SLOW-LY-IN			
circle wildly in the slow-ly-in creasing fragility --. Dogs .	63	T&C PORTRAIT 10	31
+SLOWLIEST			
FOR CONTEXT, SEE	463	NEW POEMS 1	5
SLOWLY			
and passes into light (slowly in life's serene perpetual . .	5	T&C EPITHALAM	81
the lips of Tristram slowly dote, La beale Isoud	17	T&C PUELLA MEA	36
most swift radiance wherein slowly drift murmurous things . .	18	T&C PUELLA MEA	80
used to stroll (very slowly) one or two ladies	23	T&C PUELLA MEA	281
this night amazing ecstasies slowly, in the glutted heart . .	36	T&C AMORES 1	23
flowerterrible memories shall rise, slowly return upon the .	36	T&C AMORES 1	29
urgent (again love i slowly gather of thy languorous	37	T&C AMORES 2	17
odd unlovely souls struggle slowly and writhe like caught. .	55	T&C PORTRAIT 3	19
O press worms rushing slowly through loam / /	67	T&C POST IMPR 4	30
the man are dancing slowly are tottering up and	69	T&C POST IMPR 6	26
dead. Then you will slowly kiss me / /	86	T&C SON ACTU 5	14
go orange in the slowly. town, night featherly swifts	89	& POST IMPR 1	1
upon itself always and slowly which upward certainly is . . .	95	& POST IMPR 7	10
distended immense Both paws slowly loved a dinted mug	97	& POST IMPR 8	39
(ugliness of) rinsed mind slowly: from! the: A wending . . .	99	& POST IMPR 10	22
cheres") and my love slowly answered I think so.	102	& POST IMPR 12	22
under the trees Fields slowly Elysian in a firmcool-Ness . .	104	& POST IMPR 14	14
Through her Muteness will slowly roam my dumbNess? her .	137	& SON REAL 8	5
of smooth sweetness steal slowly in dumb blossoms of	139	& SON REAL 10	4
gradual throne of night slowly when several stars are	156	& SON ACTU 5	2
rising, herself uprearing wholly slowly, lean in the hips . .	156	& SON ACTU 5	6
instant when herself me (slowly, wholly me) will press . . .	156	& SON ACTU 5	14
the picture) hurry it slowly to my mouth, taste	162	& SON ACTU 11	10
is better) murdering coolness slowly in peopling places seeks	168	& SON ACTU 17	13
of you, i like, slowly stroking the, shocking fuzz	175	& SON ACTU 24	10
is hanging, snow speaks slowly / / / /	202	XLI PORTRAIT 9	52
should surprise my soul slowly which on thy beauty	205	XLI SONNETS 1	5
silent shoulders are both slowly with pinkish ponderous arms	225	IS 5 ONE LIZ	7
legs said (crossing them slowly) "I'm asleep. Yep. Youse . .	228	IS 5 ONE MARJ	3
oh silently striding) priests-and- slowly, al, ways;	280	IS 5 THREE 7	28
been something else carefully slowly fatally turning into . .	283	IS 5 THREE 7	25
you into a memory slowly, oh seriously --that since	295	IS 5 FOUR 12	10
moon's bright third tumbling slowly / / / /	305	IS 5 FIVE 4	15
their Lives who grow slowly and first into different	311	VIVA 3	8
her quick way of slowly staring and such hair)	337	VIVA 28	8
Tints (and) & (grows) Slowly (slowly) Voyaging tones intimate	348	VIVA 39	6
(and) & (grows) Slowly (slowly) Voyaging tones intimate . . .	348	VIVA 39	6
ourselves) as Nobody came slowly over the town /	355	VIVA 46	21
planets heard, rose very slowly in a tight balloon	360	VIVA 51	13
if so or so slowly i opened the window	365	VIVA 56	11
MooN o VER ToWNS SLoWLY SPRoUTING SPIR IT /	383	NO THANKS 1	11
drown, beyond sound down (slowly beneath sight fall ing) . .	432	NO THANKS 49	4
blossoming (while anyone might slowly count to soon)	599	(CHAIRE) 1	9
darkness to gether are slowly all together very magically . .	600	(CHAIRE) 2	9
fall) and then to slowly trust T upon H, ...	650	(CHAIRE) 52	3
two these (stroll more slowly than trees) dodreamingly . . .	681	95 POEMS 9	4
this (a forest has slowly Murdered the House) hole	693	95 POEMS 21	13
his only love, strolling slowly (mind in mind) through . . .	777	73 POEMS 5	3
collapses: through west ninth slowly cars pour into sixth . .	800	73 POEMS 28	19
swim climb minds (down slowly swoop wholly up leaping	841	73 POEMS 69	30
+SLOWLY			
FOR CONTEXT, SEE	63	T&C PORTRAIT 10	31
FOR CONTEXT, SEE	104	& POST IMPR 14	3
FOR CONTEXT, SEE	104	& POST IMPR 14	8
FOR CONTEXT, SEE	248	IS 5 ONE 19	15
FOR CONTEXT, SEE	354	VIVA 45	24
FOR CONTEXT, SEE	697	95 POEMS 25	15
SLOWLYSLOWLY			
like dis Gawd" opening slowlyslowly them--then carefully the	228	IS 5 ONE MARJ	7
SLOWLYWITH			
Hand revolves, per- fectly, slowlywith, the handle ofa . . .	101	& POST IMPR 11	48

		PAGE	TITLE	LINE

SLOWNESS
    opening in a rare Slowness of gloried air... The . . . . . . 12 T&C SONGS 2   45
    muscles fools a weightless slowness (deftly muting the . . . 299 IS 5 FOUR 16   3
SLOWQUICKLY
    children dreams & through slowquickly opening ifless this . . 719 95 POEMS 47   7
SLOWTURNING
    dawn, where teeth of slowturning streets mesh in a . . . . . 142 & SON REAL 13   4
SLUICE
    a minute pulled the sluice emerging. concrete / / . . . . . . 119 & PORTRAIT 11   16
+SLUM
    FOR CONTEXT, SEE . . . . 519 50 POEMS 33   8
+SLUMPING
    FOR CONTEXT, SEE . . . . 629 (CHAIRE) 31   12
SLUSH
    of squirting taps plus slush of foam knocked off . . . . . . 96 & POST IMPR 8   13
+SLUSH
    FOR CONTEXT, SEE . . . . 789 73 POEMS 17   16
SLUT
    he knows from his slut of a mother i . . . . 707 95 POEMS 35   16
SLY
    ghosts on prowl gorge sly slim gods stare / . . . . 90 & POST IMPR 2   16
    yes who but that sly little bitch could have . . . . 707 95 POEMS 35   14
+SLY
    FOR CONTEXT, SEE . . . . 495 50 POEMS 9   12
SLYLY
    various ab- surd thoughts slyly crept into my highly . . . . 262 IS 5 ONE 32   4
SMACK
    er of cards and smack of back- gammon boards . . . . 194 XLI PORTRAIT 2   17
SMACKED
    her eyebrows. --Marj's laughter smacked me: pummeling the . . 228 IS 5 ONE MARJ   13
    JUDICE LIS when mack smacked phyllis on the snout . . . . . . 706 95 POEMS 34   1
SMALL
    of time untarnished! O small intimate gently primeval hands,   5 T&C EPITHALAM   106
    a sweet thing and small. Death, Thee i call . . . . 13 T&C SONGS 3   16
    Springing from fragrant shoulders small, ardent, and . . . . 20 T&C PUELLA MEA 153
    shell away with a small bored gesture that makes . . . . . . 69 T&C POST IMPR 6 19
    the good teeth and small important breasts (is it . . . . . . 72 T&C SON REAL 3   2
    pool. Her nose was small, exact, stupid. mouth normal, . . . 103 & POST IMPR 13   13
    sufficient pillow shoveling her small manure-shaped head one 134 & SON REAL 5   3
    legs are brittle and small his feet large and . . . . 198 XLI PORTRAIT 6   21
    darkly love and the small spiritual cry of spring . . . . . . 213 XLI SONNETS 9   6
    Flo's midnight Frolic dolores small in the head keen . . . . 232 IS 5 ONE 3   5
    William Cullen Longfel- low's small negro son, Henry . . . . 263 IS 5 ONE 32   53
    touched me with its small hands and with curling . . . . . . 284 IS 5 FOUR 1   2
    face a dead yellow small rose / / / . . . . 296 IS 5 FOUR 13   16
    fragile lips the sweet small clumsy feet of April . . . . . . 306 IS 5 FIVE 5   14
    The is blond with small hands "& everything is . . . . 338 VIVA 29   16
    our ed shy lurch small invin cible nod oc . . . . 349 VIVA 40   14
    and about thyself a small hoping insect, humanity, achieves . 351 VIVA 42   9
    wall his white sincere small hands with their guessing . . . 355 VIVA 46   14
    some bliss of one small lady upon earth above; . . . . 360 VIVA 51   33
    the rain, has such small hands / / / . . . . 366 VIVA 57   20
    (Coughs.) Two pale slippery small eyes balanced upon one . . 406 NO THANKS 23   9
    my soul feels all small facts dissolved by the . . . . 419 NO THANKS 36   5
    squirm-of-frightened shy are whichs small its hungry for Is . 437 NO THANKS 53   7
    star : then a small million of dark voices . . . . 454 NO THANKS 69   13
    you" nicely the lady's small grin said (with more . . . . . 506 50 POEMS 20   13
    all mankind something more small occurs or something more . . 514 50 POEMS 28   10
    men (both little and small) cared for anyone not . . . . . . 515 50 POEMS 29   5
    even a thing all small and sad man, may . . . . 526 50 POEMS 38   3
    doom steer his great small wish into upward deepness . . . . 528 50 POEMS 40   7
    in a tree-) o small you sitting in a . . . . 535 50 POEMS 47   2
    o least who sing small thing dance little joy . . . . 535 50 POEMS 47   10
    child who's just as small as me can do . . . . 555 1 X 1 15   13
    let all go--the big small middling tall bigger really . . . . 569 1 X 1 29   16
    all history is too small for even me; for . . . . 579 1 X 1 39   7
    and you, exceedingly too small. Swoop (shrill collective . . 579 1 X 1 39   8
    / / so isn't small one littlest why, it . . . . 588 1 X 1 48   1

	PAGE	TITLE	LINE

SMALL (CONTINUED)
    to Mere but one small most of a rose . . . . 608 (CHAIRE) 10   8
    pieces (in darker than small is dirtiest any city's . . . . . 623 (CHAIRE) 25   2
    smooth round stone as small as a world and . . . . 682 95 POEMS 10   10
    as i'm (almost too small for death's because to . . . . 735 95 POEMS 63   2
    a why (almost too small for dying's huge because) . . . . . . 735 95 POEMS 63   10
    / perished have safe small facts of hilltop (barn . . . . . . 755 95 POEMS 83   1
    complete love, all safely small big wickedly worlds of . . . 761 95 POEMS 88   11
    livingest one star as small these all these thankful . . . . 819 73 POEMS 47   18
    simple agony of time --small wonder such a monster's . . . . 842 73 POEMS 70   13
SMALLENING
    tight balloon until the smallening world became absurd; him . 360 VIVA 51   14
SMALLER
    world (and just as smaller stars begin to husk . . . . 71 T&C SON REAL 2   11
    thousand of which are smaller than a rose's moment . . . . . 683 95 POEMS 11   8
SMALLEST
    wholly to bewitch my smallest thought with a most . . . . . . 18 T&C PUELLA MEA   79
    soaring silence (put your smallest ear against yester- day . 110 & PORTRAIT 6   30
    this, deftly propping on smallest hands the slim hinging . . 282 IS 5 THREE 6   7
    of a. Not one smallest dream) / / / . . . . 479 NEW POEMS 17   20
    her sleep: vainly no smallest voice might cry for . . . . . 520 50 POEMS 34   15
    but most (without the smallest doubt) because no best . . . . 679 95 POEMS 7   9
    lovers glad? only their smallest joy's a universe emerging . 768 95 POEMS 94   7
    not quite believab ly smallest as perfect this (almost . . . 827 73 POEMS 55   7
SMALLHEADED
    / / / my smallheaded pearshaped lady in gluey . . . . 95 & POST IMPR 7   1
SMALLISH
    / youful larger of smallish) Humble a rosily , ... 503 50 POEMS 17   3
SMART
    my being the delirious smart of thrilled ecstasy, where . . . 79 T&C SON UNRE 4   12
SMARTING
    with feet sun-sheer the smarting beauty of dawn) / . . . . . 187 XLI SONGS 9   18
SMASH
    the dark gold delicately smash.... grass, and the stars, . . 153 & SON ACTU 2   7
    are these whose lips smash unimagined sky deeper than . . . . 563 1 X 1 23   11
SMASHED
    (when in a most smashed unworld stands unslain he . . . . . . 414 NO THANKS 31   6
    and finding only why smashed it into because / . . . . 566 1 X 1 26   8
    / let it go--the smashed word broken open vow . . . . 569 1 X 1 29   2
SMASHES
    upsets a crucifix which smashes into several pieces and . . . 203 XLI LA GUERRE 1 14
SMEAR
    1 ooms an eggyellow smear of wintry sunse t . . . . 788 73 POEMS 16   14
SMEARED
    face of a baby smeared with beautiful jam or . . . . 166 & SON ACTU 15   13
SMELL
    Of, CleaN a booming smell waddles toward, me, dressed . . . . 94 & POST IMPR 6   15
    love emits a wonderful smell in my mind, you . . . . 152 & SON ACTU 1   7
    dizzy did the world's smell (but i was thinking . . . . . . 174 & SON ACTU 23   11
    comfort you because you smell so sweetly i will . . . . 192 XLI CHANSONS 2   8
    touch and taste and smell and hearing and sight . . . . . . 199 XLI PORTRAIT 7   3
    with its hurting sexual smell of lilies.... beyond night's . 214 XLI SONNETS 10   11
    i mean about the smell of babies and how . . . . 242 IS 5 ONE 13   17
    against summer thunder (together) smell only such blue . . . 340 VIVA 31   19
    over smellings of gently smell of deads (lovers grip . . . . 384 NO THANKS 2   9
    tell by their altruistic smell moscow pipes good kumrads . . 413 NO THANKS 30   8
    new) self whose eyes smell of the sound of . . . . 424 NO THANKS 41   3
    i pause among the smell of minute mown lives) . . . . 434 NO THANKS 51   25
    carnivorous (smile by lipstick smell by matchabelli) tits as 546 1 X 1 6   9
    the look feel taste smell & sound of a . . . . 676 95 POEMS 4   8
    (because it begins to smell) / / / / . . . . 711 95 POEMS 39   28
+SMELL
    FOR CONTEXT, SEE . . . . 512 50 POEMS 26   30
SMELLED
    to her feet she smelled of silence. The inspired . . . . . . 135 & SON REAL 6   3
    known Only to have smelled Happens--skip dance kids hop . . . 437 NO THANKS 53   13
    much heard so much smelled so much tasted plus . . . . 474 NEW POEMS 12   6

		PAGE	TITLE	LINE

SMELLINGS
   edgar the moon over smellings of gently smell of . . . . . . 384 NO THANKS 2   9
SMELLOFTHEWORLD
   the murmurous minute clumsy smelloftheworld. We intricately . 174 & SON ACTU 23   3
SMELLS
   of day are the smells of Nineveh, in her . . . . 23 T&C PUELLA MEA   259
   with warmlyish wetflat splurging smells waltz the glush of . 96 & POST IMPR 8   12
   flutters everything queer; does smells he smiles is like . . 251 IS 5 ONE 22   5
SMELT
   wid OW er who smelt rath er like her . . . . 320 VIVA 12   19
   her fath er who smelt rath er (Er camef . . . . 320 VIVA 12   21
SMILE
   Lady at whose imperishable smile the amazed doves flicker . .   6 T&C EPITHALAM   137
   momentary wind with guiding smile, lips wisely minced for . .   9 T&C SONGS 1   12
   But should my lady smile, it were a flower . . . . 18 T&C PUELLA MEA   49
   trysts curvingly a fragile smile which like a flower . . . . 20 T&C PUELLA MEA   149
   are (which as lilies smile and quail) of all . . . . 20 T&C PUELLA MEA   161
   to thee with a smile and thou didst not . . . . 27 T&C ORIENTALE 1   2
   is life not a smile? i spoke to thee . . . . 27 T&C ORIENTALE 1   7
   frail ascensions, of thy smile rises the immaculate sorrow . 31 T&C ORIENTALE 5   17
   behind the doomed exact smile of life's placid obscure . . . 43 T&C AMORES 7   30
   softly at whose gate smile always the chosen flowers . . . . 58 T&C PORTRAIT 6   25
   whiskey-sour-- whose least amazing smile is the most great . 74 T&C SON REAL 5   14
   shall not know thy smile again, lingering a little . . . . . 75 T&C SON REAL 6   4
   heart breaks in a smile--and she is Lust.... mine . . . . . . 75 T&C SON REAL 6   13
   gasping shores leaves his smile wan, and his blood . . . . . 77 T&C SON UNRE 2   7
   genuine apparition of your smile (it was through tears . . . 78 T&C SON UNRE 3   6
   singular beginning of your smile) a skilful uncouth prison, . 83 T&C SON ACTU 2   5
   casual where the surrounded smile hangs breathless / / . . . 83 T&C SON ACTU 2   15
   whose lips begin a smile exactly strange-- this painter . . . 85 T&C SON ACTU 4   8
   selves who are your smile. / / / / . . . . 92 & POST IMPR 4   21
   i somehow feel your smile slightly is a more . . . . 98 & POST IMPR 9   11
   fingers dead has a smile like the nicest man . . . . 126 & SEVEN POEMS 5   14
   limp, across my bruising smile; as rapidly upon the . . . . . 137 & SON REAL 8   8
   a lady whose still-born smile involves the comedy of . . . . 144 & SON REAL 15   14
   smiles a hard long smile it sometimes makes gaily . . . . . . 147 & SON REAL 18   6
   corpse the tool her smile makes something suddenly luminous . 152 & SON ACTU 1   12
   quick wall of your smile into stupid gardens if . . . . 154 & SON ACTU 3   5
   strut my indolent priceless smile, until this very frail . . 155 & SON ACTU 4   11
   huddling string of your smile over his body squirms . . . . . 161 & SON ACTU 10   6
   the coolness of your smile is stirringofbirds between my . . 163 & SON ACTU 12   17
   the longness of autumn smile dustily to the people, ... 190 XLI SONGS 12   20
   signories --i shall not smile beloved; i shall not . . . . . 210 XLI SONNETS 6   8
   hair and the smiting smile didst love to use . . . . 213 XLI SONNETS 9   12
   that any this taxi smile or angle we do . . . . 238 IS 5 ONE 9   6
   of the way he smile) but and her a . . . . 251 IS 5 ONE 22   9
   from his baldness a smile masturbates softly in the . . . . . 259 IS 5 ONE 29   22
   lips utter their extant smile.... remark a few deleted . . . 260 IS 5 ONE 30   6
   firm white lips a smile, one thought alone: to . . . . 273 IS 5 TWO 8   10
   arms brush dirt coats smile looking hands spit blood . . . . 275 IS 5 TWO 9   46
   et cetera, of Your smiles knees and of . . . . 276 IS 5 TWO 10   25
   should, leaning against me, smile; or (between dawn and . . . 285 IS 5 FOUR 2   13
   we will kiss or smile or move. It's different . . . . 289 IS 5 FOUR 6   17
   should create one least smile (shyly if a poem . . . . 291 IS 5 FOUR 8   23
   (but chiefly of your smile, most suddenly which is . . . . . 293 IS 5 FOUR 10   16
   a near and careful smile in his mouth (making . . . . 293 IS 5 FOUR 10   26
   separated from your body smile brain hands merely to . . . . 295 IS 5 FOUR 12   3
   do i drink dream smile and how do i . . . . 295 IS 5 FOUR 12   14
   your kissed thrice suddenly smile / / / / . . . . 300 IS 5 FOUR 17   24
   becomes crisper until i smile with knowing --and all . . . . 301 IS 5 FOUR 18   13
   skilful strangeness of your smile the keen primeval silence . 306 IS 5 FIVE 5   7
   of cafes people drink smile if here there (like . . . . 340 VIVA 31   9
   ecstasy and And spills smile cheaply thick --who therefore . 358 VIVA 49   10
   doom than you will smile) / / / / . . . . 367 VIVA 58   12
   fled; softly your face smile breasts gargled by death: . . . 369 VIVA 60   9
   suddenly than) whose tiniest smile? may Be bigger than . . . 397 NO THANKS 14   5
   as good as a smile but little joe gould's . . . . 410 NO THANKS 27   9
   rock day) : you; smile, hands (an- onymo -Us . . . . 449 NO THANKS 64   15

SMILE (CONTINUED)

over him with one smile / / / /	481	NEW POEMS 19	12
wisdoms enter guess) childmoon smile to your breathing doll .	518	50 POEMS 32	11
to only see him smile. Scorning the pomp of	520	50 POEMS 34	32
but three) hero's carnivorous (smile by lipstick smell by . .	546	1 X 1 6	8
true each new self) smile. Eyes. & we remember:	612	(CHAIRE) 14	7
pays him with a smile another with a tear	624	(CHAIRE) 26	9
"more" cries: with a smile / / / /	625	(CHAIRE) 27	24
T upon H, and smile could anything be pleasanter	650	(CHAIRE) 52	4
(but if he should Smile) comes nobody'll know /	660	(CHAIRE) 62	26
wrong) and with a smile at which the rightest	685	95 POEMS 13	6
lay down with a smile) / / / /	709	95 POEMS 37	16
a who but the voice-with-a-smile of democracy announces night	711	95 POEMS 39	5
silence of his mother's smile --whose only secret all	714	95 POEMS 42	13
make (of grin for smile whose head's his face	716	95 POEMS 44	6
feel certain) will only smile / / / /	744	95 POEMS 72	8
like rej and lena smile (while looming darkly a	754	95 POEMS 82	9
lived forever in a smile) / / / /	765	95 POEMS 91	14
frown would be a smile if sorrowful were gay	798	73 POEMS 26	14
with the mystery your smile sings or if (spiralling	810	73 POEMS 38	4

+SMILE

FOR CONTEXT, SEE	69	T&C POST IMPR 6	15
FOR CONTEXT, SEE	69	T&C POST IMPR 6	35
FOR CONTEXT, SEE	146	& SON REAL 17	11
FOR CONTEXT, SEE	371	VIVA 62	24
FOR CONTEXT, SEE	615	(CHAIRE) 17	21

SMILE'S

| of this of the smile's two eyes.... too, since . . . . | 141 | & SON REAL 12 | 4 |

SMILED

Eyes and the moon Smiled ,so / / /	125	& SEVEN POEMS 4	29
eyes knew me, we smiled to each other, releasing	283	IS 5 THREE 7	21
a button the moon smiled she let go my	284	IS 5 FOUR 1	10
of saying nothing he smiled (but just by the	355	VIVA 46	5
their green lives and smiled / / / /	555	1 X 1 15	16
erect her whole life smiled "was and will always	626	(CHAIRE) 28	5
told me "someone" (and smiled) "who holds Himself as	748	95 POEMS 76	16

SMILELESS

| face grey, and silent smileless eyes of Magdalen. The . . . . | 75 | T&C SON REAL 6 | 8 |
| amazing: without love separate, smileless--merely imagine . . | 374 | VIVA 65 | 2 |

SMILES

silence a brown god smiles between greentwittering smokes . .	28	T&C ORIENTALE 2	4
of crumbling silence seriously smiles / / / /	81	T&C SON UNRE 6	14
night gathers morte carved smiles cloud-gloss is at	90	& POST IMPR 2	11
the hatch the nigger smiles the jew stands beside	108	& PORTRAIT 4	22
mouths distinctly walk your smiles accuse the dusk with . . .	138	& SON REAL 9	4
in gloom, bad laughters, smiles unbold) also, tomorrow the .	142	& SON REAL 13	8
shocking wire, when she smiles a hard long smile	147	& SON REAL 18	5
astute fatuous swallowed eyes smiles, one grin very	151	& SON REAL 22	14
cheeks the streets of smiles your eyes half- thrush	186	XLI SONGS 8	8
Laughters jostle grins nudge smiles push--. deep into the . .	202	XLI PORTRAIT 9	37
queer; does smells he smiles is like Out of	251	IS 5 ONE 22	5
hugest to morrow from smiles sin k ingly ele	309	VIVA 1	21
Be real" (so he smiles smiling) "but I will	338	VIVA 29	11
serpent becomes a rod smiles the liontamer nearby hieroglyphs	384	NO THANKS 2	23
& . (musically-who? pivoting) SmileS "ahlbrhoon / / /	430	NO THANKS 47	30
air). now who stops. Smiles. he stamps / /	437	NO THANKS 53	17
which could grin three smiles into a dead house	522	50 POEMS 35	1
reful whom (leas tly) smiles the infinite nothing of	534	50 POEMS 46	21
(who , ins tead, smiles alw ays a trifl	611	(CHAIRE) 13	4
doesn't unsays says looks smiles or simply Is what	779	73 POEMS 7	19
and reasons threats and smiles name it cruel fair	804	73 POEMS 32	6
crazily houses eyes people smiles faces streets steeples are	835	73 POEMS 63	4

SMILING

the acerb pole poises, smiling, the diadumenos in whose . . .	3	T&C EPITHALAM	32
hounds crouched low and smiling the merry deer ran	14	T&C SONGS 4	4
hounds crouched low and smiling the level meadows ran	14	T&C SONGS 4	14
hounds crouched low and smiling the sheer peaks ran	14	T&C SONGS 4	24
hounds crouched low and smiling my heart fell dead	14	T&C SONGS 4	34

		PAGE	TITLE	LINE

SMILING (CONTINUED)
at the shabby tiny smiling, man in whose hand . . . . 69 T&C POST IMPR 6   8
little string! the tiny smiling shabby man is yelling . . . . 69 T&C POST IMPR 6 33
sits in a cafe smiling, a piece of money . . . . 102 & POST IMPR 12   4
to war across the smiling meads; thou by whose . . . . 209 XLI SONNETS 5   5
i left her permanently smiling / / / / . . . . 228 IS 5 ONE MARJ 15
Marys will understand how smiling may be made as . . . . . . 294 IS 5 FOUR 11   13
in your mind (slightly smiling, patient, unspeaking with a . 298 IS 5 FOUR 15   3
to be found" and smiling you answer "everything turns . . . . 303 IS 5 FIVE 2   4
halfsinging stirs the always smiling chevaux de bois) when . 304 IS 5 FIVE 3   14
do you do" she smiling said "thought you were . . . . 313 VIVA 5   5
sniffing a Paper rose smiling to a self "somewhere . . . . . 338 VIVA 29   4
real" (so he smiles smiling) "but I will not . . . . 338 VIVA 29   12
going in "take hands" smiling "coming up these dark . . . . . 353 VIVA 44   31
disappeared: but i slightly smiling, gradually shall reenter 370 VIVA 61   18
all together very magically smiling and if we are . . . . . . 600 (CHAIRE) 2   10
with treadwatering nonlegs (strictly) smiling / / / / . . . . 616 (CHAIRE) 18   16
laughing grinning) we no (smiling) strike agains De Big . . . 618 (CHAIRE) 20   8
fortune" . At which (smiling) he stops: & pick . . . . 697 95 POEMS 25   6
--"noone unless it's a smiling" she told me "someone" . . . . 748 95 POEMS 76   16
are this wonderful tree smiling stand (all realms of . . . . 832 73 POEMS 60   5
+SMILING
FOR CONTEXT, SEE . . . . 211 XLI SONNETS 7   8
FOR CONTEXT, SEE . . . . 464 NEW POEMS 2   17
SMILINGLY
the women-coloured twilight i smilingly glide. I into the . . 66 T&C POST IMPR 3 9
SMIRK
/ / a clown's smirk in the skull of . . . . 360 VIVA 51   1
SMIRKS
in beginning corners dawn smirks and there's the moon, . . . 322 VIVA 14   13
SMITE
it is foolingly to smite my spirit with the . . . . 18 T&C PUELLA MEA 82
SMITES
the surely Cued motif smites truly to Beautifully retire . . 311 VIVA 3   3
SMITH
by a man named Smith and we sailed on . . . . 313 VIVA 5   10
than this death named Smith less strange? Married and . . . 406 NO THANKS 23   13
opening is it horribly smith spouts cornucopiously not . . . 465 NEW POEMS 3   9
soldier, beware of mrs smith / / / / . . . . 799 73 POEMS 27   41
SMITING
/ / into the smiting sky tense with blend . . . . 182 XLI SONGS 4   1
deep hair and the smiting smile didst love to . . . . 213 XLI SONNETS 9   12
SMOKE
and trees the lilac's smoke the poppy's pompous fire . . . . 5 T&C EPITHALAM   92
incense, over the dim smoke straining my lips are . . . . . . 31 T&C ORIENTALE 5 22
got me said the smoke who runs the elevator . . . . 125 & SEVEN POEMS 4 10
pink hand of the smoke that shook the ivories . . . . 125 & SEVEN POEMS 4 21
large three teeth leak smoke: remembering, two pink big . . . 149 & SON REAL 20 15
/ / 5 ◇ smoke Helmar cigarettes 2 play . . . . 200 XLI PORTRAIT 8   2
eat you got to smoke and we aint got . . . . 489 50 POEMS 3   2
aint got nothing to smoke: come on kid let's . . . . 489 50 POEMS 3   3
sleep if you can't smoke you got to Sing . . . . 489 50 POEMS 3   5
/ / infinite jukethrob smoke & swallow to dis . . . . 629 (CHAIRE) 31   1
(simply infinite) there & (smoke) a fair y socked . . . . . 629 (CHAIRE) 31   11
+SMOKE
FOR CONTEXT, SEE . . . . 423 NO THANKS 40   29
SMOKED
es a soft desert smoked bad me whilepin Kishcam . . . . 318 VIVA 10   21
general menedjerr and they smoked a robert burns cigerr . . . 552 1 X 1 12   29
+SMOKED
FOR CONTEXT, SEE . . . . 318 VIVA 10   15
SMOKES
god smiles between greentwittering smokes from broken eyes a 28 T&C ORIENTALE 2 5
of telescoped languages) she smokes three castles He looks . 312 VIVA 4   15
SMOKING
the young world into smoking song-- as the first . . . . . . 7 T&C EPITHALAM 163
in a frieze of smoking Face Bluish-old and choked . . . . . 142 & SON REAL 13   5
because i can't sleep (smoking sawdust cigarettes in the . . 242 IS 5 ONE 13   21

SMOKING (CONTINUED)
    any how? down to smoking found Butts / / . . . . 314 VIVA 6   31
SMOKY
    the abominable floor belches smoky laughter into the filigree 55 T&C PORTRAIT 3   4
SMOOTH
    beautifully who wanderest over smooth pages of forgotten joy   3 T&C EPITHALAM   18
    droll is as some smooth and awkward foal, whereof . . . . . . 11 T&C SONGS 2   3
    discovers a trembling and smooth Unstrength, against the . . 11 T&C SONGS 2   8
    ardent, and perfectly withal smooth to stroke and sweet . . . 20 T&C PUELLA MEA 155
    breast is firm and smooth that in a lovely . . . . 21 T&C PUELLA MEA 181
    light any woman is smooth and ridiculous a polite . . . . . 68 T&C POST IMPR 5 13
    (mingled in whispering thickly smooth thighs thinkingly) . . 95 & POST IMPR 7 15
    the swallowed mottle with smooth or a but of . . . . 96 & POST IMPR 8   6
    to the peddlers of smooth, fruits of eager colours . . . . 100 & POST IMPR 11 20
    Cleopatra built like a smooth arrow or a fleet . . . . . . 110 & PORTRAIT 6   2
    fleet pillar or a smooth arrow Cleopatra is eaten . . . . . 111 & PORTRAIT 6   46
    letting thy tigers of smooth sweetness steal slowly in . . . 139 & SON REAL 10   3
    bones, and the trembling -firm-smooth ness and which i . . . 175 & SON ACTU 24   7
    Shall enter fingers of smooth mastery with chasteness of . . 189 XLI SONGS 11   9
    to men ....one perfectly smooth coffee tasting of hellas, . . 217 XLI SONNETS 13 10
    neatening each crease) will smooth entirely our minds . . . . 288 IS 5 FOUR 5   5
    never cease views with smooth vigilant perpetual eyes each . 386 NO THANKS 3   10
    came home with a smooth round stone as small . . . . 682 95 POEMS 10   9
+SMOOTH
    FOR CONTEXT, SEE . . . . 60 T&C PORTRAIT 8   4
SMOOTHANDUSELESS
    stomachs of little, girls smoothanduseless i, like, best, . . 101 & POST IMPR 11 76
SMOOTHBEAUTIFUL
    in this world lies: smoothbeautifuL ly folded; a (brea . . . 657 (CHAIRE) 59   11
SMOOTHDUMB
    ly Comes; : lush ly-smootHdumb droopnew-gree N. . . . . . . 342 VIVA 33   24
SMOOTHLOOMINGLY
    a proud dreamhorse pulling (smoothloomingly) through (stepp) 437 NO THANKS 53   1
SMOOTHLY
    a Rolls Royce swoops smoothly outward (amid ◇ tables) . . . 232 IS 5 ONE 3   7
    hatless. Cats which move smoothly from neck to neck . . . . . 279 IS 5 THREE 3   13
    neck of bottles, cats smoothly willowing out and in . . . . . 279 IS 5 THREE 3   14
    between bottles, who step smoothly and rapidly along this . . 279 IS 5 THREE 3   14
    transparent walls how several smoothly gesturing stars are . 376 VIVA 67   8
SMOOTHNESS
    the hours love: a smoothness which sings, saying (though . . 13 T&C SONGS 3   4
    the hair). Creasing its smoothness--and leave the bed agrin . 164 & SON ACTU 13 10
    the whim of thy smoothness. and mark the fainting . . . . . 215 XLI SONNETS 11   7
    hoops of fire, creating smoothness. People stare, the drunker 279 IS 5 THREE 3   16
+SMOOTHNESS
    FOR CONTEXT, SEE . . . . 175 & SON ACTU 24   7
SMOTE
    sorrowful: but my heart smote in trembling thirds of . . . . 11 T&C SONGS 2   16
    or two and he smote the monster merde then . . . . 552 1 X 1 12   10
SMOTHER
    fingering spirits starve and smother; until autumn abruptly . 305 IS 5 FIVE 4   7
SMOULDERS
    men his peaked head smoulders like a new turd . . . . 198 XLI PORTRAIT 6 19
SNAIL'S
    Just Too Lovely, The Snail's On The Thorn enter . . . . . . 230 IS 5 ONE 2   28
SNAKE
    which (like some floating snake upon itself always and . . . 95 & POST IMPR 7   9
    that quick sharp thick snake of a voice these . . . . 490 50 POEMS 4   10
+SNAKE
    FOR CONTEXT, SEE . . . . 101 & POST IMPR 11 52
SNAKEOIL
    sells hate condoms education snakeoil vac uumcleaners terror 549 1 X 1 9   11
+SNAPPING
    FOR CONTEXT, SEE . . . . 101 & POST IMPR 11 51
SNARE
    are sedulously spun to snare the brutal dew, --the . . . . .   5 T&C EPITHALAM 87
    the sudden moonbeam's treacherous snare she sought the . . .   8 T&C OF NICOL 25
    these years or to snare the timid like of . . . . 216 XLI SONNETS 12   5

	PAGE	TITLE	LINE

SNARE (CONTINUED)

i have failed to snare the glance too shy--if . . . . 306 IS 5 FIVE 5   5

+SNARE

FOR CONTEXT, SEE . . . . 799 73 POEMS 27   19

SNARES

for his heart, lay snares for his feet (who . . . . 439 NO THANKS 55   18

SNARLED

microscopic shriekings shall have snarled threads of . . . . 555 1 X 1 15   4

SNATCH

world's best one hand snatch / / / / . . . . 645 {CHAIRE} 47   4

+SNICKER

FOR CONTEXT, SEE . . . . 194 XLI PORTRAIT 2   16

SNICKERING

butting trolley imposingly empty; snickering shop doors . . . 172 & SON ACTU 21   5

SNIFFING

room stands a suicide sniffing a Paper rose smiling . . . . . 338 VIVA 29   3

SNIGGERING

stroll.... and the Baboon sniggering insipidities while. i . 220 XLI SONNETS 16   13

SNITCH

while five other fingers snitch rapidly through mist a . . . 259 IS 5 ONE 29   10

SNORE

(whose dormers choke and snore the steeples writhe with . . . 340 VIVA 31   4

SNOUT

smacked phyllis on the snout frank sank him with . . . . . . 706 95 POEMS 34   1

SNOW

silver sudden parody of snow tickles the air to . . . .   5 T&C EPITHALAM   73

peaceful terrors of the snow, and before your dead . . . . . 11 T&C SONGS 2   28

strong fingers beneath the snow Into strenuous birds shall . 16 T&C SONGS 6   9

her beauty more than snow dexterous and fugitive my . . . . . 17 T&C PUELLA MEA   16

passionate earlier flower, the snow will oft utter, whereof . 21 T&C PUELLA MEA   188

your hands are the snow and thy fingers are . . . . 61 T&C PORTRAIT 9   29

common sunset is hanging, snow speaks slowly / / . . . . . . 202 XLI PORTRAIT 9   52

like baths of golden snow. This is the garden: . . . . 208 XLI SONNETS 4   4

the unswift mouths of snow insignificantly whisper.... / / . 218 XLI SONNETS 14   14

sups it isn't snowing snow you know it's snowing . . . . . . 254 IS 5 ONE 25   23

six months for selling snow / / / / . . . . 266 IS 5 TWO 1   40

you are like the snow only purer fleeter, like . . . . 293 IS 5 FOUR 10   1

respecter of persons the snow doesn't give a soft . . . . . . 328 VIVA 19   22

this flower imagines the snow carefully everywhere . . . . . 366 VIVA 57   12

this rainman out of snow / / / / . . . . 390 NO THANKS 7   14

sleep big rain big snow big sun big moon . . . . 393 NO THANKS 10   14

/ / / / snow) says! Says over un . . . . 417 NO THANKS 34   1

/ / / / SNOW cru is ingw Hi . . . . 421 NO THANKS 38   1

disappearing poet of always, snow and to morning; and . . . . 424 NO THANKS 41   5

wings the birds of snow things without name beyond . . . . . 441 NO THANKS 56   56

it be gan to snow he dis a ppeare . . . . 472 NEW POEMS 10   3

& nothing tells anywhere "snow will come soon" & . . . . . . 483 NEW POEMS 21   8

that noing our gone snow gone yours mine . . . . 491 50 POEMS 5   8

thing singing in the snow / / / / . . . . 498 50 POEMS 12   32

were dawn dark rain snow rain -bow & a . . . . 512 50 POEMS 26   18

his grief bird by snow and stir by still . . . . 515 50 POEMS 29   15

moon (and only the snow can begin to explain . . . . 515 50 POEMS 29   22

build a world with snow. My father moved through . . . . . . 521 50 POEMS 34   48

plunge? rains a grey snow of mothery same rotting . . . . . . 527 50 POEMS 39   28

hills with sleet and snow: strangles valleys by ropes . . . . 560 1 X 1 20   10

be you (sun or snow) gone into what like . . . . 568 1 X 1 28   10

a least dare of snow less quite is nothing . . . . 573 1 X 1 33   15

winter's not forever, even snow melts; and if spring . . . . 579 1 X 1 39   3

/ / / / snow means that life is . . . . 628 {CHAIRE} 30   1

its silent in forevering snow --but never fear (my . . . . . 667 {CHAIRE} 69   12

rise come go rain snow) remembers / / / . . . . 693 95 POEMS 21   20

of life (inquiry before snow / / / / . . . . 712 95 POEMS 40   9

like you) except in snow-- a whom we make . . . . 716 95 POEMS 44   4

leaps to greenly hurl snow suppose we could not . . . . 743 95 POEMS 71   3

every) un (star rain snow moon dream wing tree . . . . 753 95 POEMS 81   15

under magical foreverfully falling snow. And then this . . . 777 73 POEMS 5   13

given is how beautifully snow) now i lay me . . . . 816 73 POEMS 44   9

		PAGE	TITLE	LINE

+SNOW
FOR CONTEXT, SEE . . . . 99 & POST IMPR 10   1
FOR CONTEXT, SEE . . . . 417 NO THANKS 34   14
FOR CONTEXT, SEE . . . . 618 (CHAIRE) 20   5
FOR CONTEXT, SEE . . . . 713 95 POEMS 41   10

SNOWFLAKE
nothing comes only one snowflake (and we speak our . . . . . 502 50 POEMS 16   14
and can perfectly speak (snowflake and rainbow mind and . . . 575 1 X 1 35   32
-v- in -g) a snowflake twi- sts , on . . . . 676 95 POEMS 4   22
one t hi s snowflake (a li ght in . . . . 833 73 POEMS 61   5

SNOWFLAKES
raindrops need sunbeams or snowflakes make possible . . . . . 577 1 X 1 37   3
his child are watching snowflakes (falling & falling & . . . 715 95 POEMS 43   4

SNOWILY
thingfear) come ships go snowily sailing perfect silence. . . 586 1 X 1 46   18
to arrive each (futuring snowily which sprints for the . . . 639 (CHAIRE) 41   11
chiefly at home in snowily nowheres of winter his . . . . . . 678 95 POEMS 6   11

SNOWING
New York and beautifully snowing. Inside snug and evil. . . . 96 & POST IMPR 8   2
New York and beautifully, snowing.... / / / / . . . . 97 & POST IMPR 8   45
shadowy light the droll snowing delirium (we do not . . . . . 168 & SON ACTU 17   5
supper sups it isn't snowing snow you know it's . . . . 254 IS 5 ONE 25   23
snow you know it's snowing buttercups / / / . . . . 254 IS 5 ONE 25   24
and around ing swim snowing ly upward with Joy, ... 584 1 X 1 44   12
again (ly infin) It's Snowing Isn't That Perfectly Wonderful 629 (CHAIRE) 31   22

SNOWINGLY
host by guest a snowingly enfolding glory is all . . . . . . 559 1 X 1 19   2

+SNOWINGLY
FOR CONTEXT, SEE . . . . 584 1 X 1 44   12

SNOWLFLAKE
god whispered him a snowlflake "yes: you may sleep . . . . . 555 1 X 1 15   14

SNOWMAN
noone dance around the snowman / / / / . . . . 630 (CHAIRE) 32   16

SNOWS
let fall their glorious snows, and the unearthly sweetness .   8 T&C OF NICOL   6

SNOWSTOPPED
will stand (over a snowstopped silent world) one spirit . . . 808 73 POEMS 36   2

SNOWY
flame and blazed with snowy fire) unfolding, gave the . . . .   8 T&C OF NICOL   18
face, a form whose snowy symmetry of grace haunted . . . . .   8 T&C OF NICOL   20
s, keep your teeth snowy, stick to beer and . . . . 71 T&C SON REAL 2   4
sallow street-lamps were turning snowy against a west of . . 194 XLI PORTRAIT 2   3
bluest whos of this snowy head we call old . . . . 754 95 POEMS 82   5

SNUG
and beautifully snowing. Inside snug and evil. the slobbering 96 & POST IMPR 8   3

SNUGANDEVIL
eternal perpetual question) Inside snugandevil. i was sitting 97 & POST IMPR 8   43

SO
WORD DELETED, APPEARED 238 TIMES

SO&SO
grin with pain You so&so true wars are never . . . . 570 1 X 1 30   9

SOAK
nee whitermuch grab sicksilk soak sulksuck whim poke if . . . 333 VIVA 24   11

SOAR
the liontamer nearby hieroglyphs soar dip dip soar equalling 384 NO THANKS 2   25
hieroglyphs soar dip dip soar equalling noise solemn dolls . 384 NO THANKS 2   27

SOARING
sagging gone into the soaring silence (put your smallest . . 110 & PORTRAIT 6   28

+SOARINGS
FOR CONTEXT, SEE . . . . 96 & POST IMPR 8   9

SOB
go. faces a (live) sob bel ls (pour wo . . . . 444 NO THANKS 59   7

SOBBING
within twitching shadow lolls sobbing with lust / / . . . . . 28 T&C ORIENTALE 2   16
with prose faces and sobbing, garments The symbol of . . . . 59 T&C PORTRAIT 7   8

SOBBINGS
of and a chatter sobbings intersect with which distinct . . . 96 & POST IMPR 8   8

SOBCRIES
    rainfaint windthin voice-which-is no-voice sobcries "paw? . . 697 95 POEMS 25   13
SOBS
    absurd eyelids sulked enormous sobs puckered the foolish . . 52 T&C PORTRAIT 1   28
    3rd Findingest whispers understand sobs bigly climb what . . 358 VIVA 49   7
    or devil --toss in sobs and reasons threats and . . . . . . 804 73 POEMS 32   6
SOCALLED
    if it may be socalled) memory Of (without more . . . . 317 VIVA 9   21
    pounds thanks to the socalled fact that maost faolks . . . . 331 VIVA 22   3
    / / these people socalled were not given hearts . . . . 510 50 POEMS 24   1
    should they be? their socalled hearts would think these . . . 510 50 POEMS 24   2
    hearts would think these socalled people have no minds . . . 510 50 POEMS 24   3
    they had their minds socalled would not exist but . . . . . 510 50 POEMS 24   4
    upon thousands of people socalled if multiplied by twice . . 510 50 POEMS 24   10
    something more distorting than socalled civilization i'll . . 514 50 POEMS 28   11
+SOCALLED
    FOR CONTEXT, SEE . . . . 392 NO THANKS 9   8
    FOR CONTEXT, SEE . . . . 392 NO THANKS 9   9
    FOR CONTEXT, SEE . . . . 708 95 POEMS 36   8
SOCIETY'S
    just a halfsmile (for society's sweet sake) in the . . . . . 146 & SON REAL 17   11
SOCKED
    (smoke) a fair y socked flopslump (& juke) ing . . . . . . 629 {CHAIRE} 31   12
SOCKETS
    tore mountains from their sockets and strewed the black . . . 432 NO THANKS 49   17
SOCKS
    hundreds (and hundreds) of socks not to mention shirts . . . 276 IS 5 TWO 10   10
SODDEN
    A meticulous vulgarity: a sodden fastidious normal explosion; 201 XLI PORTRAIT 9   12
SOFT
    utters at length her soft intrinsic hour, and from . . . . .   6 T&C EPITHALAM   131
    towers to the moon, soft sighed the passionate darkness . . .   8 T&C OF NICOL   4
    are nervous with the soft furious light, and while . . . . . 62 T&C PORTRAIT 10 14
    get out ears dribbles soft right old feller belch . . . . . . 96 & POST IMPR 8   21
    impersonally affords furnished a soft first clue to his . . . 197 XLI PORTRAIT 5   5
    winsome flatulence-- In the verb midst of the tongue . . . . 201 XLI PORTRAIT 9   14
    me, A, (peach a soft eyes syriansang asong tohim . . . . . . 318 VIVA 10   11
    eeyeb Rowspeach es a soft desert smoked bad me . . . . . . 318 VIVA 10   21
    snow doesn't give a soft white damn Whom it . . . . 328 VIVA 19   22
    of spreadnessed bE rich from-soft quits (now) ly Comes; . . . 342 VIVA 33   21
    twi -light pale beyond soft- liness than dream more . . . . . 349 VIVA 40   5
    Ising thither: t, ouch soft-ly me and eye (you . . . . 361 VIVA 52   12
    (ing sing) ing a soft a song a softishsongly . . . . 385 NO THANKS 2   53
    es (are two notSoft soft one are hard one . . . . 388 NO THANKS 5   21
    madeofimagination ; the incredible soft) ness (his ears (eyes 397 NO THANKS 14   23
    brIght bRight s??? big (soft) soft near calm (Bright) . . . . 455 NO THANKS 70   3
    bRight s??? big (soft) soft near calm (Bright) calm . . . . 455 NO THANKS 70   4
    (Bright) calm st?? holy (soft briGht deep) yeS near . . . . . 455 NO THANKS 70   7
    deep whO big alone soft near deep calm deep . . . . 455 NO THANKS 70   12
    thingless & before flashing soft neverwheres & sweet . . . . 480 NEW POEMS 18   10
    pitying Who from sharp soft worms of spiralling why . . . . . 522 50 POEMS 35   12
    engulf (in which in soft) firm who outlift queries . . . . . 613 {CHAIRE} 15   6
    whose brook -bright flower- soft bird -quick voice loves . . 660 {CHAIRE} 62   20
+SOFT
    FOR CONTEXT, SEE . . . . 388 NO THANKS 5   21
SOFT-LY
    Ising thither: t, ouch soft-ly me and eye (you . . . . 361 VIVA 52   12
SOFTER
    level meadows ran before. Softer be they than slippered . . . 14 T&C SONGS 4   16
    is as a tomb softer than flowers Come hither . . . . 27 T&C ORIENTALE 1 26
    than water, she is softer than birds when the . . . . 33 T&C ORIENTALE 6 52
+SOFTER
    FOR CONTEXT, SEE . . . . 653 {CHAIRE} 55   16
SOFTISH
    who is this pale softish almost round young man . . . . 245 IS 5 ONE 16   6
SOFTISHSONGLY
    soft a song a softishsongly v o i c . . . . 385 NO THANKS 2   53

	PAGE	TITLE	LINE

+SOFTLINESS
    FOR CONTEXT, SEE . . . . 349 VIVA 40   5

SOFTLY
    steep hills by darkness softly brought-- (be with me . . . .   9 T&C SONGS 1   36
    ladies like flowers made, softly used to wholly move . . . .   23 T&C PUELLA MEA   283
    like a reminiscence partaken softly at whose gate smile . . .   58 T&C PORTRAIT 6   25
    are turned suddenly and softly into irresponsible toys.) when   62 T&C PORTRAIT 10   21
    when passionately dusk brings softly down the perfume of . .   71 T&C SON REAL 2   10
    lunge of Her hunger softly flung over the gasping . . . . . .   77 T&C SON UNRE 2   5
    white town whose spires softly dare. Will take the . . . . .   86 T&C SON ACTU 5   4
    is a flower gone softly by tomb rosily gods . . . .   90 & POST IMPR 2   2
    like a Plum grinning softly, New focus-of disintegrat i . . .   94 & POST IMPR 6   16
    take day away more softly horribly suddenly; (of these . . .   98 & POST IMPR 9   4
    mmmoon, begins to, drool softly, in the hot alley, ... 167 & SON ACTU 16   17
    my doubting window leaves softly to stir, of thoughtful . . . 205 XLI SONNETS 1   10
    where the wet stars softly are keeping their exquisite . . . 206 XLI SONNETS 2   9
    not flower, tell me softly who be these haunters . . . . . . 211 XLI SONNETS 7   6
    this dirtied pane where softly preys the grey and . . . . . 218 XLI SONNETS 14   10
    (amid <> tables) while softly along Kirkland Street the . . . 232 IS 5 ONE 3   11
    baldness a smile masturbates softly in the vacant lot . . . . 259 IS 5 ONE 29   22
    me in your heart softly; not all but the . . . . 294 IS 5 FOUR 11   19
    love will tell who softly asks in love, am . . . . 295 IS 5 FOUR 12   2
    ghost-lips gradually) remembering badly, softly your kissed . 300 IS 5 FOUR 17   22
    Walk very (therefore and) softly among one's own memory . . . 317 VIVA 9   18
    ruined streets hither and) softly thither between (tumb ling) 319 VIVA 11   5
    and seem so quite softly as your hair what . . . . 367 VIVA 58   4
    eyes sinking) inward, fled; softly your face smile breasts . 369 VIVA 60   8
    able to speak very softly altogeth er miracu lous . . . . . . 600 (CHAIRE) 2   15

+SOFTLY
    FOR CONTEXT, SEE . . . . 361 VIVA 52   12

SOFTLYING
    her flower than now (softlying wisdoms enter guess) childmoon 518 50 POEMS 32   9

SOFTNESS
    pal, skilled in quick softness. Unspontaneous. cute. the . .   74 T&C SON REAL 5   4

+SOFTNESS
    FOR CONTEXT, SEE . . . . 397 NO THANKS 14   23

SOIL
    unique dreams never shall soil their raiment with phenomena: 328 VIVA 19   4

SOILED
    the way in the soiled canary-cage of largest existence. . . . 197 XLI PORTRAIT 5   12

SOILING
    one dirty squeal of soiling light yanKing from bushy . . . .   96 & POST IMPR 8   28

SOIR
    se promenent doucement le soir (ladies accurately dead les . 120 & PORTRAIT 12   24

+SOIT
    FOR CONTEXT, SEE . . . . 635 (CHAIRE) 37   26

SOL
    had an uncle named Sol who was a born . . . . 239 IS 5 ONE 10   3
    perhaps because my Uncle Sol could sing McCann He . . . . . . 239 IS 5 ONE 10   5
    fact that my Uncle Sol indulged in that possibly . . . . . . 239 IS 5 ONE 10   8
    vegetables so my Uncle Sol had a chicken farm . . . . 239 IS 5 ONE 10   17
    chickens when my Uncle Sol had a skunk farm . . . . 239 IS 5 ONE 10   20
    and so my Uncle Sol imitated the skunks in . . . . 239 IS 5 ONE 10   24
    who'd given my Uncle Sol a Victor Victrola and . . . . 239 IS 5 ONE 10   27
    down went my Uncle Sol and started a worm . . . . 239 IS 5 ONE 10   37

SOL'S
    needlessly added my Uncle Sol's farm failed because the . . . 239 IS 5 ONE 10   14
    Missouri when my Uncle Sol's coffin lurched because somebody 239 IS 5 ONE 10   33

SOLD
    in windows and never sold and <> because Who? . . . . 101 & POST IMPR 11   66
    latest Seeds Of Evil sold 69 carloads before publication . . 245 IS 5 ONE 16   9
    drug that's bought and sold giving to steal and . . . . . . 521 50 POEMS 34   56
    what you mean by" sold! to the dollarfull shea . . . . 546 1 X 1 6   14
    who as an anthologist sold the many on the . . . . 551 1 X 1 11   3
    dissect a kiss; or, sold the reason, they undream . . . . . 556 1 X 1 16   8

SOLDIER
    of himself fa -mous soldier minus his na- me . . . . 267 IS 5 TWO 2   14
    tragic tale concludes herewith: soldier, beware of mrs smith 799 73 POEMS 27   41

	PAGE	TITLE	LINE
SOLE			
there is a moon sole in the blue night	37	T&C AMORES 2	2
leg pulled into a sole mass my separate lusts	135	& SON REAL 6	4
are superseded by the sole prostituted ferocity of silence, .	202	XLI PORTRAIT 9	41
SOLEMN			
at, you with his solemn blinky eyeswhichneversmile and after	69	T&C POST IMPR 6	14
at you with my solemn eyeswhichneversmile yes, By god. . . .	69	T&C POST IMPR 6	35
d with, its, little, solemn, entrails / / /	94	& POST IMPR 6	29
spontane- ity of a solemn mechanism. beneath her drab	103	& POST IMPR 13	10
All so differ- ently solemn and inti and sitting	126	& SEVEN POEMS 5	28
dip soar equalling noise solemn dolls re -volve whirlswans .	384	NO THANKS 2	27
+SOLEMN			
FOR CONTEXT, SEE	101	& POST IMPR 11	68
SOLEMNITY			
with green facts preening solemnity ignoring, through its . .	344	VIVA 35	3
SOLEMNLY			
and firm legs moving solemnly like careful and furious . . .	95	& POST IMPR 7	13
trouserfly confessed a button solemnly inert. Brushing from .	258	IS 5 ONE 28	20
and if you disappear solemnly myselves ask "life, the	295	IS 5 FOUR 12	12
kiss only must unexist, solemnly and per rules apparelling .	373	VIVA 64	3
SOLES			
choked pat of going soles on flat pavements with	142	& SON REAL 13	6
SOLID			
with circular shrieking tightness solid screams whisper.) . .	195	XLI PORTRAIT 3	15
party gimme the he-man's solid bliss for youse ideas	247	IS 5 ONE 18	5
SOLIDITIES			
bombast--papery what & vast solidities, unwinding dizzily & .	480	NEW POEMS 18	18
SOLIDITY			
the skinfull of Ludicrous, solidity which a. , kissed	159	& SON ACTU 8	10
primeval exposure whose electric solidity remembers some . .	197	XLI PORTRAIT 5	17
SOLIDS			
curvecorners gush silently perpetuating solids (More fluid .	311	VIVA 3	17
looking at ourselves two solids in (all one it)	323	VIVA 15	2
SOLITAIRE			
job at her diamond solitaire while guesswho nibbles his . . .	545	1 X 1 5	4
SOLITUDE			
when upon her palpable solitude a furtive occult fragrance .	19	T&C PUELLA MEA	105
a Magic of green solitude (go marvels come) as	757	95 POEMS 85	16
SOLOMON			
Babylon.) Diarmuid Paris and Solomon, Omar Harun and Master .	23	T&C PUELLA MEA	262
SOLONG			
if i Should say solong my tailor chuckles like	287	IS 5 FOUR 4	10
SOLONGS			
roses & hello: (of solongs and, ashes) / /	66	T&C POST IMPR 3	17
SOLUTION			
in (all one it) solution (of course you must	323	VIVA 15	4
might have found the solution of that in the	323	VIVA 15	18
SOLVE			
be and is --who'll solve the depths of horror	562	1 X 1 22	11
SOLVED			
(our great problem nearly solved we dare adorn the	650	(CHAIRE) 52	13
SOMBRE			
the transplendent hand of sombre god i picked you	30	T&C ORIENTALE 4	40
SOME			
flame half-mute, (haste ere some thrush with silver several .	6	T&C EPITHALAM	119
the castle lay like some gigantic ghost-flower born of . . .	8	T&C OF NICOL	2
wholly droll is as some smooth and awkward foal, ...	11	T&C SONGS 2	3
gloom truly which syncopate some sunbeam's skilful	19	T&C PUELLA MEA	86
mysterious skein (but like some passionate earlier flower, .	21	T&C PUELLA MEA	187
of Girl which (like some floating snake upon itself	95	& POST IMPR 7	8
the last crumb with some shame whispered unto God, ...	117	& PORTRAIT 10	21
on somebody's roof or some- thing where ◇ and	127	& SEVEN POEMS 5	42
for Dick. And had some rows over percent. The	149	& SON REAL 20	7
you will be dead some day. By you the	153	& SON ACTU 2	1
who knows? Who knows? Some "allemand" ....? of Goethe, . . .	158	& SON ACTU 7	6
each other touch) seeking, some street which easily trickles	174	& SON ACTU 23	5
when invisibly consult with some delicious image the a . . .	193	XLI PORTRAIT 1	7
whose electric solidity remembers some accurately profuse . .	197	XLI PORTRAIT 5	18

SOME (CONTINUED)
whose faint close as some grave languorous hymn pledged . . . 206 XLI SONNETS 2   12
trees perpetual of sleep some silver-fingered fountain steals 208 XLI SONNETS 4   14
whereof this lady in some book had read / . . . . 225 IS 5 ONE LIZ   16
"I'll tell duh woild; some noive all right. Aint . . . . . . 226 IS 5 ONE MAME   10
it has for -gotten some- thing ah (my necktie . . . . 232 IS 5 ONE 3   16
ou sont les neiges.... some guys talks big about . . . . . . 237 IS 5 ONE 8.   3
an gay Paree an some guys claims der never . . . . 237 IS 5 ONE 8   6
without exaggeration shot with some difficulty sardines. Mr. 263 IS 5 ONE 32   47
with who cares if some oneeyed son of a . . . . 264 IS 5 ONE 33   27
communists have fine Eyes some are young some old . . . . . . 274 IS 5 TWO 9   4
Eyes some are young some old none look alike . . . . 274 IS 5 TWO 9   4
/ / / / some ask praise of their . . . . 291 IS 5 FOUR 8   1
of this trunk, under some dirty collars) only a . . . . 296 IS 5 FOUR 13   12
hand in hand at some window try to understand . . . . 305 IS 5 FIVE 4   10
listen there's me & some people and others please . . . . . . 314 VIVA 6   3
others please don't confuse. Some people 's future is . . . . 314 VIVA 6   6
crump led cap mumble some thing to oh no . . . . 314 VIVA 6   19
(finding one's self at some distance from the crooked . . . . 319 VIVA 11   16
pensive companion dimly remarked some- thing about . . . . . 326 VIVA 18   31
duh table-- "fellers have some on me" --dey was . . . . 332 VIVA 23   22
ceaselessly repeat "there is some shit I will not . . . . . . 339 VIVA 30   33
cuddled by dreams (or some times vacantly gazing through . . 354 VIVA 45   7
sparent panes which by some loveless trick sepa rate . . . . 354 VIVA 45   19
climb what (love being some- thing possibly more intricate) . 358 VIVA 49   7
which creep budgingly over some numbered face capable of . . 359 VIVA 50   15
for i have had some bliss of one small . . . . 360 VIVA 51   32
kingdom (sleep) . while some thing else kisses busily . . . . 370 VIVA 61   22
prisoner dawn embraces hugely some few most rare perfectly . 376 VIVA 67   11
ship lifts (skilfully like some bird which is all . . . . . . 378 VIVA 69   4
(nor have i observed some chucking some legally into . . . . 391 NO THANKS 8   6
i observed some chucking some legally into Oblivion wave . . 391 NO THANKS 8   6
sunlight's thenlike? now Disappears some thing (silent: . . . 397 NO THANKS 14   20
nonsufficiently inunderstood re with some difficulty one . . 398 NO THANKS 15   3
live) yes, partly nor some edgeless star could give . . . . . 414 NO THANKS 31   9
and loneliness alive like some dream giving more than . . . . 418 NO THANKS 35   3
(they s born alive) some folks aint born somes . . . . 426 NO THANKS 43   10
perverse or which makes some feel more better when . . . . . 466 NEW POEMS 4   23
opening of a (not some not every but any) . . . . 480 NEW POEMS 18   3
all come to town some like it shot and . . . . 497 50 POEMS 11   5
like it shot and some like it hung and . . . . 497 50 POEMS 11   6
like it hung and some like it in the . . . . 497 50 POEMS 11   7
of head comes to some dirty window every) twilight . . . . . 501 50 POEMS 15   7
pair of ears with some lips plus a couple . . . . 501 50 POEMS 15   19
a doer a wooer some limber and lithe some . . . . 509 50 POEMS 23   10
some limber and lithe some very fine mower a . . . . 509 50 POEMS 23   11
mower a tall; tall some jerry so very (and . . . . 509 50 POEMS 23   13
(and nellie and fan) some handsomest harry (and sally . . . . 509 50 POEMS 23   15
stands still as found some lost thing (like a . . . . 516 50 POEMS 30   4
(elephant the blue) put some just a now and . . . . 516 50 POEMS 30   9
world into bigger much some out of (not visible . . . . 516 50 POEMS 30   15
four minds (out of some undering joy and overing . . . . . . 517 50 POEMS 31   9
ghostly roots and should some why completely weep my . . . . 520 50 POEMS 34   13
/ what freedom's not some under's mere above but . . . . . . 538 50 POEMS 50   1
they leaf of ghosts some few creep there here . . . . 541 1 X 1 1   9
of your voice) from some complete existence of to . . . . . . 559 1 X 1 19   6
to dream into complete some dream of to exist . . . . 559 1 X 1 19   7
compared with pitying terrible some alive individual ten . . 561 1 X 1 21   5
/ a- float on some one ? i call twilight . . . . 571 1 X 1 31   2
our (if disappear should some world) selves . No . . . . . . 577 1 X 1 37   8
look should april me, some thousand million hundred more . . 580 1 X 1 40   12
no beyond) or does some littler bird than eyes . . . . 592 1 X 1 52   9
future; and immediate like some newly remembered dream-- . . 601 (CHAIRE) 3   11
slightly knu as and some six cents hit the . . . . 602 (CHAIRE) 4   4
may have better luck, some day?" "Or worse! poor . . . . . . 603 (CHAIRE) 5   11
(his briefest breathing lives some planet's year, his longest 609 (CHAIRE) 11   10
life's a heartbeat of some sun; his least unmotion . . . . . 609 (CHAIRE) 11   11
truly his more than some eighty years through which . . . . . 617 (CHAIRE) 19   11

		PAGE	TITLE	LINE
SOME (CONTINUED)

another with a tear some cannot pay at all . . . . 624 {CHAIRE} 26 11
a -way It with some- thing sil -very ; . . . . 632 {CHAIRE} 34 3
a park anus stick some quote statue unquote to . . . . 636 {CHAIRE} 38 2
soul tastes If as some world of a spark . . . . 639 {CHAIRE} 41 7
few dead dollars and some twisted laws) it comes . . . . . 644 {CHAIRE} 46 5
could anything be pleasanter (some big dark little day . . . 650 {CHAIRE} 52 6
Wing) silence, who; is: somE oNe. / / / . . . . 657 {CHAIRE} 59 15
might make alive filthy some past imagining whowhich of . . . 662 {CHAIRE} 64 5
but we be they'll some or if where shall . . . . 666 {CHAIRE} 68 6
our then shall be some darkness during which fingers . . . . 667 {CHAIRE} 69 9
o ver (& i) some newer than life (or . . . . 668 {CHAIRE} 70 17
sweet innocence refuted) clumsy some dull cowardice called a 669 {CHAIRE} 71 11
to stand (alone) in some autumnal afternoon: breathing a . . 674 95 POEMS 2 1
himself & as loveless some world not any un . . . . 698 95 POEMS 26 3
a nor seen by some that bum who's every . . . . 698 95 POEMS 26 8
any one Living (or some body Dead like even . . . . 702 95 POEMS 30 4
stag geri ng up some streetfu l of peopl . . . . 703 95 POEMS 31 4
maybe she's up to some tricks with my bill . . . . 707 95 POEMS 35 9
without soul may blast some universe to might have . . . . 714 95 POEMS 42 9
my darling) but should some im probably unworld crash . . . . 728 95 POEMS 56 9
(whom you and i some times call april) must . . . . 738 95 POEMS 66 7
/ / let's, from some loud unworld's most rightful . . . . . 745 95 POEMS 73 1
finds quite disappearance but some keener makes losing, . . . 750 95 POEMS 78 13
voice comes out of some dreaming tree (and how . . . . 752 95 POEMS 80 2
how patiently be coming some (& merciful ly which . . . . . 753 95 POEMS 81 11
disappears) their heartbeats dare some upward world of each . 757 95 POEMS 85 6
every (who's any who's some) one who's we / . . . . 769 95 POEMS 95 28
(mind in mind) through some green mysterious land until . . 777 73 POEMS 5 4
yes; no matter who, some total (preferably blonde of . . . . 779 73 POEMS 7 4
we enlightened this stranger 'some people have all the . . . 800 73 POEMS 28 10
dismal misconception; namely that some neither ape nor angel 807 73 POEMS 35 7
(despite the ultramachinations of some loveless infraworld) a 807 73 POEMS 35 11
to feel-- how should some world (we marvel) doubt, ... 809 73 POEMS 37 9
meteors swim signals all some world's millionary mind never . 818 73 POEMS 46 12
years old) peering from some high window; at the . . . . . 824 73 POEMS 52 3
world, but to me some (by name myself) one . . . . 828 73 POEMS 56 4
april; and i <> some perpetually roaming whylessness-- autumn 839 73 POEMS 67 6
at any moment born-- some for whom crumbs of . . . . 842 73 POEMS 70 3
eyes restroll and stroll some never deepening beach locked . 843 73 POEMS 71 3
+SOME

FOR CONTEXT, SEE . . . . 96 & POST IMPR 8 21
SOMEBODY

/ / / / somebody knew Lincoln somebody Xerxes . . . . 62 T&C PORTRAIT 10 1
/ somebody knew Lincoln somebody Xerxes this man: a . . . . . 62 T&C PORTRAIT 10 1
nonsense of twilight and somebody Napoleon / / . . . . 63 T&C PORTRAIT 10 39
wind wind--did you love somebody and have you the . . . . . 80 T&C SON UNRE 5 6
the rain or rather Somebody who uses roofs and . . . . 92 & POST IMPR 4 12
ps on his whistle somebody says here's luck somebody . . . . 108 & PORTRAIT 4 19
somebody says here's luck somebody else says down the . . . . 108 & PORTRAIT 4 21
music and to have somebody play who can but . . . . 126 & SEVEN POEMS 5 30
her youth. And if somebody hears what i say--let . . . . . . 216 XLI SONNETS 12 9
in the watertank but somebody who'd given my Uncle . . . . . 239 IS 5 ONE 10 27
Sol's coffin lurched because somebody pressed a button (and . 239 IS 5 ONE 10 34
yon mob an accident? somebody got concus- sion of . . . . . 245 IS 5 ONE 16 17
(as that named Fred -someBody: hippopotamus, scratch- ing, . 252 IS 5 ONE 23 2
sheep are driven by somebody along a curve of . . . . 281 IS 5 THREE 5 8
sail a fishing boat somebody an invisible spectator, maybe . 283 IS 5 THREE 7 7
don't think so. maybe: somebody?) or, bedbugs / / . . . . . 312 VIVA 4 24
that largo appearance of somebody who was hectocotyliferously 326 VIVA 18 9
goils away frum dem" --"somebody hung uh gun on . . . . . . 332 VIVA 23 7
i knows me (er somebody is sittin in uh . . . . 332 VIVA 23 30
eaten them Yapenese Craps somebody might hardly never not . . 336 VIVA 27 11
in the house, with somebody and with something) You . . . . 375 VIVA 66 2
slightly i am hearing somebody coming up stairs, carefully . 375 VIVA 66 10
doesn't matter) but if somebody or you are beautiful . . . . 475 NEW POEMS 13 12
becomes nil) and will somebody tell me why people . . . . . 593 1 X 1 53 23
we go all) there's somebody calling who's we we're . . . . . 594 1 X 1 54 36

710

		PAGE	TITLE	LINE

SOMEBODY (CONTINUED)
wistful little clown whom somebody buried upsidedown in an . 680 95 POEMS 8   8
(nothing i or any somebody or you can begin . . . . 816 73 POEMS 44   11
+SOMEBODY
FOR CONTEXT, SEE . . . . 702 95 POEMS 30   4
SOMEBODY'S
all by himself on somebody's roof or some- thing . . . . . . 127 & SEVEN POEMS 5   42
Thiz Tew Mee as somebody's almost moth er folds . . . . 629 (CHAIRE) 31   14
rational --i thank heaven somebody's crazy enough to give . . 802 73 POEMS 30   32
SOMEHOW
means the moon, i somehow feel your smile slightly . . . . . 98 & POST IMPR 9   10
the clutch (and then somehow got into reverse she . . . . . . 248 IS 5 ONE 19   11
burst want to dear somehow quickyes when (now, dark . . . . . 251 IS 5 ONE 22   12
this person of whom somehow you are never wholly . . . . . . 298 IS 5 FOUR 15   7
I could, they would somehow not Be real" (so . . . . 338 VIVA 29   9
to is it find somehow (but O gracefully) a . . . . 368 VIVA 59   12
i awakening discover that (somehow in the dark) this . . . . 370 VIVA 61   2
SOMEONE
I think I see someone else there is a . . . . 102 & POST IMPR 12   23
sometimes in) Spring a someone will lie (glued among . . . . 428 NO THANKS 45   2
from what bough that someone called they made him . . . . . . 543 1 X 1 3   23
to please itself or someone else makes no more . . . . 549 1 X 1 9   9
(pretty twinkle merry bells) Someone has been born everyone . 630 (CHAIRE) 32   14
noone i ever & someone (the others have long . . . . 695 95 POEMS 23   12
to lose (as down someone who's we ungrows) a . . . . 716 95 POEMS 44   34
/ / / / someone i am wandering a . . . . 720 95 POEMS 48   1
smiling" she told me "someone" (and smiled) "who holds . . . 748 95 POEMS 76   16
fore head is stumbling someone (named Morning) / / . . . . . 785 73 POEMS 13   23
a merely human plane) someone completely beautiful; and . . . 799 73 POEMS 27   11
or seeming (an almost someone always who's noone) a . . . . . 812 73 POEMS 40   4
+SOMEONE
FOR CONTEXT, SEE . . . . 657 (CHAIRE) 59   15
FOR CONTEXT, SEE . . . . 828 73 POEMS 56   4
SOMEONE'S
that (once crammed into someone's kitchenette) wheezing . . . 607 (CHAIRE) 9   3
through gayer than gayest someone's heart at your each . . . 717 95 POEMS 45   12
mystery of day for someone's eyes) with silver splendors . . 756 95 POEMS 84   4
SOMEONES
was all to her someones married their everyones laughed . . . 515 50 POEMS 29   17
SOMERSAULTS
speeds of trapeze gush somersaults open ing hes shes . . . . 536 50 POEMS 48   9
SOMES
some folks aint born somes born dead an somes . . . . 426 NO THANKS 43   11
somes born dead an somes born alive (but niggers . . . . . . 426 NO THANKS 43   12
SOMETHING
inhabits number 1 on something street Spring comes the . . . 62 T&C PORTRAIT 10   4
all together there happens Something, and They cease (and . . 62 T&C PORTRAIT 10   19
out of number 1 someThing street and trickles carefully . . . 62 T&C PORTRAIT 10   25
always crying to nobody something about les roses les . . . . 102 & POST IMPR 12   16
the coffinlid waiting for something to rise as the . . . . . 117 & PORTRAIT 10   6
hangIng from strings (or) someThing i was lying on . . . . . 123 & SEVEN POEMS 2   3
things. she picked wearily something from the floor Her . . . 132 & SON REAL 3   17
her is not to something or to nothing as . . . . 141 & SON REAL 12   13
has got nothing on something as i think , ... 141 & SON REAL 12   15
tool her smile makes something suddenly luminous and precise 152 & SON ACTU 1   12
making do our mouths something red, something tall / . . . . 160 & SON ACTU 9   17
our mouths something red, something tall / / / . . . . 160 & SON ACTU 9   17
bring you every year something which is worth the . . . . . . 161 & SON ACTU 10   13
little curse of wax. Something, distinct and. Amusing, . . . 164 & SON ACTU 13   17
bluishsuspenders half-reading the Evening Something in the . 166 & SON ACTU 15   7
corner of Nothing and Something, we heard a handorgan . . . . 174 & SON ACTU 23   14
know? or maybe did something go away ever so . . . . 191 XLI CHANSONS 1   14
of the black unbunged Something gushes vaguely a squeak . . . 195 XLI PORTRAIT 3   11
of whoisit and madame something by gainsborough just the . . 198 XLI PORTRAIT 6   12
i slightly am becoming something a little different, in . . . 199 XLI PORTRAIT 7   9
twilight but here were something more maturely childish, more 211 XLI SONNETS 7   4
mountain of gum did something like a whisper, "even . . . . . 228 IS 5 ONE MARJ   10
the string breaks (or something) my uncle Frank breaks . . . 253 IS 5 ONE 24   8

SOMETHING (CONTINUED)
   which used to lead something into somewhere) / / . . . . . . 260 IS 5 ONE 30   24
   your arms tremble remembering something squirming fragile and 279 IS 5 THREE 3   22
   cliff) what had been something else carefully slowly fatally 283 IS 5 THREE 7   24
   It ? (or was something we saw in the . . . . 286 IS 5 FOUR 3   20
   he will maybe (hearing something fall into his hat) . . . . . 298 IS 5 FOUR 15   20
   beyond the last road--there's something to be found" and . . 303 IS 5 FIVE 2   3
   answer "everything turns into something else, and slips . . . 303 IS 5 FIVE 2   5
   the moon, there is something faithful and mad" / . . . . . . 303 IS 5 FIVE 2   16
   said o yes Frost Something there is which isn't . . . . 315 VIVA 7   3
   gentleman not to sense something un poco putrido when . . . . 327 VIVA 18   45
   dancing: which is why something about me reminded him . . . . 355 VIVA 46   20
   and the moon) resembles something that has not occurred: . . 360 VIVA 51   24
   lacking any knees but something beats within my shirt . . . . 360 VIVA 51   28
   closes and opens; only something in me understands the . . . 366 VIVA 57   18
   with somebody and with something) You are gone. there . . . . 375 VIVA 66   3
   continually i am seeing something inhaling gently a cigarette 375 VIVA 66   15
   with literature we want something redblooded lousy with pure 407 NO THANKS 24   3
   let's make it serious something authentic and delirious you . 407 NO THANKS 24   11
   and delirious you know something genuine like a mark . . . . 407 NO THANKS 24   12
   the 3 rd chief something or must be off . . . . 465 NEW POEMS 3   3
   me) lousy kid that's something else my sweet (i . . . . 475 NEW POEMS 13   24
   spilled) than all mankind something more small occurs or . . 514 50 POEMS 28   10
   more small occurs or something more distorting than socalled 514 50 POEMS 28   11
   made by threats of something worth than death to . . . . . . 544 1 X 1 4   11
   change their coat --which something as you'll never guess . . 544 1 X 1 4   13
   air to blood, asked "something a little child who's . . . . . 555 1 X 1 15   12
   a mind to there's something for everybody it's a" . . . . . . 567 1 X 1 27   15
   means No and (seeing something yes) will grin with . . . . . 570 1 X 1 30   8
   yes) there's nothing as something as one one hasn't . . . . . 594 1 X 1 54   9
   easily as we forget something) livingest the imaginable moon 599 (CHAIRE) 1   13
   creates a day. And something thought or done or . . . . 649 (CHAIRE) 51   9
   would be streaming if something had (maybe they couldn't . . 652 (CHAIRE) 54   14
   young and with a something makes the oldest man . . . . 685 95 POEMS 13   14
   love and wonder) is something you have and i . . . . 686 95 POEMS 14   5
   (which would have been Something) what got him was . . . . . 702 95 POEMS 30   23
   robin the; you say something (for only me) and . . . . 737 95 POEMS 65   2
   will do alw -ays something is (guess) yes you're . . . . . . 793 73 POEMS 21   22
   here the other night something odd occurred" charlie . . . . 800 73 POEMS 28   1
   to begin to imagine) something which nobody may keep. . . . . 816 73 POEMS 44   13
+SOMETHING
   FOR CONTEXT, SEE . . . . 127 & SEVEN POEMS 5   42
   FOR CONTEXT, SEE . . . . 232 IS 5 ONE 3   16
   FOR CONTEXT, SEE . . . . 237 IS 5 ONE 8   14
   FOR CONTEXT, SEE . . . . 310 VIVA 2   12
   FOR CONTEXT, SEE . . . . 314 VIVA 6   19
   FOR CONTEXT, SEE . . . . 326 VIVA 18   31
   FOR CONTEXT, SEE . . . . 332 VIVA 23   28
   FOR CONTEXT, SEE . . . . 358 VIVA 49   7
   FOR CONTEXT, SEE . . . . 370 VIVA 61   22
   FOR CONTEXT, SEE . . . . 397 NO THANKS 14   20
   FOR CONTEXT, SEE . . . . 495 50 POEMS 9   23
   FOR CONTEXT, SEE . . . . 632 (CHAIRE) 34   3
   FOR CONTEXT, SEE . . . . 701 95 POEMS 29   22
   FOR CONTEXT, SEE . . . . 753 95 POEMS 81   1
   FOR CONTEXT, SEE . . . . 753 95 POEMS 81   2
   FOR CONTEXT, SEE . . . . 753 95 POEMS 81   3
   FOR CONTEXT, SEE . . . . 753 95 POEMS 81   11
   FOR CONTEXT, SEE . . . . 792 73 POEMS 20   14
SOMETHINGELSESTEIN
   than mrs somethingwitz nay somethingelsestein. Death should . 790 73 POEMS 18   6
SOMETHINGS
   rise as the other somethings did-- you imagine His . . . . 117 & PORTRAIT 10   7
+SOMETHINGS
   FOR CONTEXT, SEE . . . . 442 NO THANKS 57   8
SOMETHINGWICH
   clogs Second as Mrs. Somethingwich (with flesh like an . . . 219 XLI SONNETS 15   11

SOMETHINGWITZ
conceivably future than mrs somethingwitz nay . . . . 790 73 POEMS 18   5
SOMETIME
did thy fortunate fingers sometime dwell (within a greener .   3 T&C EPITHALAM   21
we might "meet again sometime") vanished, gunwale awash. I . 327 VIVA 18   37
SOMETIMES
a little suddenly (as sometimes the improbable beauty of . .   18 T&C PUELLA MEA   43
play at not speaking (sometimes as it will) the . . . .   18 T&C PUELLA MEA   62
die i have been sometimes true to Nothing and . . . .   43 T&C AMORES 7   11
poppies.... i say that sometimes on these long talkative . .   45 T&C LA GUERRE 1   7
in, his minute pocket) Sometimes he does not catch . . . . .   69 T&C POST IMPR 6 11
care, above Cambridge if sometimes in its box of . . . . . .   70 T&C SON REAL 1   12
of tint. TUMTITUMTIDDLE if sometimes my eyes stay at . . . . 100 & POST IMPR 11   18
hard long smile it sometimes makes gaily go clean . . . . . . 147 & SON REAL 18   6
hellas, i drink, or sometimes two remarking cries of . . . . 217 XLI SONNETS 13   11
the deep thing everybody sometimes calls morning / / . . . . 330 VIVA 21   14
it is Spring and sometimes people are in real: . . . . 338 VIVA 29   5
us always trying (or sometimes trying under us) to . . . . . 368 VIVA 59   10
sun which must go sometimes, to make an earth . . . . 372 VIVA 63   8
shall which a god sometimes is I the lost . . . . 414 NO THANKS 31   14
/ / / / sometimes in) Spring a someone . . . . 428 NO THANKS 45   1
hurling vastness of love (sometimes in Spring somewhere . . . 428 NO THANKS 45   8
by forever & sunsmell (sometimes a wonder of wild . . . . . . 512 50 POEMS 26   31
wonder of wild roses sometimes) with north over the . . . . . 512 50 POEMS 26   33
its polloi and if sometimes he's prodded forth to . . . . . . 544 1 X 1 4   9
must be men, the sometimes only man is this . . . . 562 1 X 1 22   2
proud hugenesses of hate sometimes called world) to sing . . 783 73 POEMS 11   8
+SOMETIMES
FOR CONTEXT, SEE . . . . 354 VIVA 45   7
FOR CONTEXT, SEE . . . . 738 95 POEMS 66   7
SOMEWHAT
romantic tired business man somewhat tweaked and dinted then   57 T&C PORTRAIT 5   33
have thought of you somewhat too much and am . . . .   157 & SON ACTU 6   1
with muted step, yet somewhat proudly too-- are they . . . . 211 XLI SONNETS 7   9
deadfromtheneckup graduate of a somewhat obscure to be sure . 234 IS 5 ONE 5   2
hat fate per a somewhat more than less emancipated . . . . . 258 IS 5 ONE 28   5
lady, if scarcely the somewhat city wiggles in considerable . 302 IS 5 FIVE 1   3
cradles in rubbery one somewhat hand the paper destinies . . 499 50 POEMS 13   5
a shall we say somewhat diversified (putting it quietly) . . 699 95 POEMS 27   16
SOMEWHERE
you the petal of somewhere in your heart pinched . . . . . .   80 T&C SON UNRE 5   7
it talks about you somewhere behind your back it . . . . . . 126 & SEVEN POEMS 5 18
imagined galleon of Spring) somewhere unspeaking sits my . . 156 & SON ACTU 5   10
clenched mind of me somewhere begins again, shares the . . . 156 & SON ACTU 5   11
to lead something into somewhere) / / / / . . . .   260 IS 5 ONE 30   24
chirps in a tree, somewhere nowhere and a little . . . . . . 281 IS 5 THREE 5   12
or ideas thoroughly's stolen (somewhere between our unlighted 322 VIVA 14   9
smiling to a self "somewhere it is Spring and . . . . 338 VIVA 29   5
are in real: imagine somewhere real flowers, but I . . . . . 338 VIVA 29   7
Doomed brief all which somewhere is fragrantly, arrive (when   356 VIVA 47   11
/ / / / somewhere i have never travelled, ... 366 VIVA 57   1
the flower of Dreaming) somewhere behind us always trying . . 368 VIVA 59   9
love (sometimes in Spring somewhere between what is and . . . 428 NO THANKS 45   9
+SOMEWHERE
FOR CONTEXT, SEE . . . . 423 NO THANKS 40   21
FOR CONTEXT, SEE . . . . 493 50 POEMS 7   14
SOMEWHEREALLOVERME
listens and, expands my somewhereallloverme heart my the . . . 251 IS 5 ONE 22   17
SOMMES
want to die nous sommes heureux my soul a . . . . 133 & SON REAL 4   18
i .... cheri.... nous sommes / / / / . . . . 133 & SON REAL 4   23
SOMNOUR
nun merchant frere clerk somnour miller and reve and . . . . 661 {CHAIRE} 63   10
SON
O thos cook & son (O to be a . . . . 257 IS 5 ONE 27   38
Longfel- low's small negro son, Henry Wadsworth Bryant. By . 263 IS 5 ONE 32   53
cares if some oneeyed son of a bitch invents . . . . 264 IS 5 ONE 33   27
and fully photographed the son of man goes forth . . . . . .   273 IS 5 TWO 8   23

		PAGE	TITLE	LINE

SON (CONTINUED)

ith) mr jeff dick son fec i (m c) . . . . 388 NO THANKS 5   30
impossibly hell Memo 1 son in improbably yale / . . . . 389 NO THANKS 6   21
guk rooms daughter item son a woopsing queer colon . . . . . 499 50 POEMS 13   9
the likes of your son" "and who but your . . . . 707 95 POEMS 35   12
ing cr u mb son ebyo neatt wothre efourfi . . . . 725 95 POEMS 53   8
little huge -eyed per- son (nea -rly burs- ting . . . . 739 95 POEMS 67   3
are deafened every mother's son-- all is merely talk . . . . 804 73 POEMS 32   10

+SON

FOR CONTEXT, SEE . . . . 339 VIVA 30   36

SONAL

filthy with agile swarming sonal crea- tures --Children, . . 69 T&C POST IMPR 6   5

SONG

in Argos, that the song is silent, of the . . . . 4 T&C EPITHALAM   49
steadily expand hearing the spear-song of the marching grass. 4 T&C EPITHALAM   72
young world into smoking song-- as the first star . . . . . . 7 T&C EPITHALAM   163
strong silences of your song; or as a single . . . . 11 T&C SONGS 2   10
world was like a song heard behind a golden . . . . 22 T&C PUELLA MEA   221
to thee with a song and thou didst not . . . . 27 T&C ORIENTALE 1   9
is life not a song? i spoke to thee . . . . 27 T&C ORIENTALE 1   14
is always a pleasant song my love thy head . . . . 29 T&C ORIENTALE 3   14
made a fragile certain song under the window of . . . . 43 T&C AMORES 7   5
take my fragile certain song that we may watch . . . . 43 T&C AMORES 7   27
city wakes with a song upon her mouth having . . . . 50 T&C IMPRESS 4   7
her mouth having a song in her eyes the . . . . 50 T&C IMPRESS 4   30
spits seeds of dead song about home and love . . . . 55 T&C PORTRAIT 3   14
the margins of steep song a stallion sweetness , ... 59 T&C PORTRAIT 7   14
two took up the song, might i'm called and . . . . 117 & PORTRAIT 10   15
from whose feet reincarnate song suddenly leaping flameflung, 206 XLI SONNETS 2   7
floating silver hell a song of adolescent ivory. / . . . . . 214 XLI SONNETS 10   14
than your body's whitest song upon my mind--if i . . . . . . 306 IS 5 FIVE 5   4
/ / / ohld song you Know a fly . . . . 335 VIVA 26   1
what i Mean (oweld song by ; neither you . . . . 335 VIVA 26   18
ing a soft a song a softishsongly v o . . . . 385 NO THANKS 2   53
begin joy was his song and joy so pure . . . . 520 50 POEMS 34   21
children are petals their song is a flower of . . . . 525 50 POEMS 37   7
are silently singing a song more silent than silence . . . . 525 50 POEMS 37   11
children singing forever a song made of silent as . . . . . . 525 50 POEMS 37   22
as stone silence of song / / / / . . . . 525 50 POEMS 37   24
dream) one is the song which fiends and angels . . . . 556 1 X 1 16   9
who came with a song like a dream of . . . . 587 1 X 1 47   8
a bird with a song like not anything under . . . . 587 1 X 1 47   9
in (trees are in) song when to me you . . . . 589 1 X 1 49   17
rosetree, rosetree --you're a song to see: whose all . . . . 763 95 POEMS 90   2
all lovers are the song. Here (only here) is . . . . 765 95 POEMS 91   9
sing his robin a song) but misers are poor-- . . . . 769 95 POEMS 95   23
/ / / / SONG but we've the may . . . . 776 73 POEMS 4   T
may in fragrance and song wonderingly come (brighter than . . 778 73 POEMS 6   12
alone but the very song of (as mountains feel . . . . 804 73 POEMS 32   13
dark i am, no song (no thing) no silence . . . . 819 73 POEMS 47   6

+SONG

FOR CONTEXT, SEE . . . . 186 XLI SONGS 8   17
FOR CONTEXT, SEE . . . . 318 VIVA 10   11
FOR CONTEXT, SEE . . . . 385 NO THANKS 2   53
FOR CONTEXT, SEE . . . . 464 NEW POEMS 2   27
FOR CONTEXT, SEE . . . . 745 95 POEMS 73   3

SONG'S

make them one (his song's so true) who sings . . . . 760 95 POEMS 87   8

SONGS

/ / / / SONGS (thee will i praise . . . . 9 T&C SONGS 1   T
is not like any songs (the singers the others . . . . 43 T&C AMORES 7   6
(if i have made songs it does not greatly . . . . 84 T&C SON ACTU 3   6
the violin spitting squeaky songs into the cuspidor-col . . . 101 & POST IMPR 11   44
/ / / / SONGS the sky was can . . . . 179 XLI SONGS 1   T
lips are cold with songs for which is first . . . . 190 XLI SONGS 12   4
you unflinchingly applaud all songs containing the words . . 204 XLI LA GUERRE 2   7
other lands where other songs be sung; yet stand . . . . . . 208 XLI SONNETS 4   11
deep dreams are frail) songs less firm than your . . . . . . 306 IS 5 FIVE 5   4

SONGS (CONTINUED)
   is made (whose fatal songs are moving in the . . . . 424 NO THANKS 41   14
SONNET
   / / / my sonnet is A light goes . . . . 171 & SON ACTU 20   1
   / / / / sonnet entitled how to run . . . . 390 NO THANKS 7   1
SONNETS
   / / / / SONNETS--REALITIES the Cambridge ladies who . . . . . 70 T&C SON REAL 1   T
   / / / / SONNETS--UNREALITIES it may not always . . . . 76 T&C SON UNRE 1   T
   / / / / SONNETS--ACTUALITIES a thing most new . . . . 82 T&C SON ACTU 1   T
   / / / / SONNETS--REALITIES O It's Nice To . . . . 130 & SON REAL 1   T
   / / / / SONNETS--ACTUALITIES when my love comes . . . . 152 & SON ACTU 1   T
   / / / / SONNETS if learned darkness from . . . . 205 XLI SONNETS 1   T
SONOFABITCH
   forsooth? One wondrous fine sonofabitch (to all purposes and 254 IS 5 ONE 25   5
   me the cheerfulest goddamned sonofabitch i ever met or . . . 699 95 POEMS 27   13
SONOROUS
   citied day with the sonorous homes of light swiftly . . . . . 79 T&C SON UNRE 4   1
   neck around whose unwashed sonorous muscle the filth of . . . 96 & POST IMPR 8   30
SONS
   language even deafanddumb thy sons acclaim your glorious name 268 IS 5 TWO 3   7
   ifbut offspring of hopefear sons of unless and children . . . 512 50 POEMS 26   3
   dwelt two very different sons of zeus: one, handsome . . . . 799 73 POEMS 27   2
SONT
   accurately dead les anglais sont gentils et les americains . 120 & PORTRAIT 12   26
   will ask ourselves ou sont les neiges.... some guys . . . . . 237 IS 5 ONE 8   3
SOON
   which May makes follow soon on the sweet heels . . . . 10 T&C SONGS 1   38
   cloud-gloss is at moon-cease soon verbal mist-flowers close . 90 & POST IMPR 2   13
   bred) took erring Olaf soon in hand; but--though an . . . . . 339 VIVA 30   6
   an empty glove, a soon forgotten tune, a house . . . . 360 VIVA 51   9
   anywhere "snow will come soon" & pretending they're birds . . 483 NEW POEMS 21   8
   --flop grasshopper, exactly nothing's soon; scream, all ye . 555 1 X 1 15   8
   me and you? Blow soon to never and never . . . . 560 1 X 1 20   21
   ten centuries of original soon or make it ten . . . . 561 1 X 1 21   6
   nothing) are built of soon carved of to born . . . . 584 1 X 1 44   4
   might slowly count to soon) rose--did you see her? . . . . . 599 {CHAIRE} 1   9
   bub? (bubs) where's Jim Soon Admiral Soon the saviour . . . . 642 {CHAIRE} 44   11
   where's Jim Soon Admiral Soon the saviour of the . . . . . . 642 {CHAIRE} 44   12
   trance, would not adventure soon a deeper magic: that . . . . 675 95 POEMS 3   10
   but that mere fury soon became silence: in huger . . . . . . 777 73 POEMS 5   9
+SOON
   FOR CONTEXT, SEE . . . . 122 & SEVEN POEMS 1   26
SOONER
   dread dizziz and the sooner it's over the sooner . . . . . . 552 1 X 1 12   4
   sooner it's over the sooner to biz don't ask . . . . 552 1 X 1 12   4
SOOTHE
   all joybegotten whelps whom soothe psychotic myths like Jonah 398 NO THANKS 15   18
+SOOTHED
   FOR CONTEXT, SEE . . . . 681 95 POEMS 9   13
SOOTHINGS
   involve me with the soothings of plastic hypnotism . . . . . 201 XLI PORTRAIT 9   26
SORE
   sleepily, feebly, scratches the sore of morning. But i . . . 144 & SON REAL 15   9
SORROW
   smile rises the immaculate sorrow of thy low hair . . . . . . 31 T&C ORIENTALE 5   18
   separate, smileless--merely imagine your sorrow a certain . . 374 VIVA 65   3
   against the dark his sorrow was as true as . . . . 521 50 POEMS 34   45
   joy a deceiver, and sorrow a system-- if now . . . . 625 {CHAIRE} 27   20
SORROW'S
   selves unimaginably mine; beyond sorrow's own joys and . . . 810 73 POEMS 38   11
SORROWFUL
   wool My thought is sorrowful: but my heart smote . . . . . . 11 T&C SONGS 2   15
   swiftly sink in the sorrowful hour, thy counted petals . . . 79 T&C SON UNRE 4   2
   be a smile if sorrowful were gay (today tomorrow, ... 798 73 POEMS 26   15
SORROWS
   one dog? piglike big! sorrows always; finally and always, . . 384 NO THANKS 2   11
   / / "though your sorrows not any tongue may . . . . 837 73 POEMS 65   1

SORRY
    with eyes a little sorry Another comes also picking . . . . . 26 T&C CHANSONS 3   7
    flesh, makes my body sorry when the minute moon . . . . 82 T&C SON ACTU 1   4
    huh dearie? yknow i'm sorry for awl the poor . . . . 109 & PORTRAIT 5   13
    and you won't be sorry And The Moon came! . . . . 125 & SEVEN POEMS 4 24
    you touched, them dead's sorry like a thistlefluff-thing . . 127 & SEVEN POEMS 5 41
    and were you very sorry to come away? see . . . . 192 XLI CHANSONS 2   6
    to -gether by large sorry) creatures out of (clumsily . . . . 442 NO THANKS 57   4
    even omnipotent He feel sorry while these were blossoming) . 748 95 POEMS 76   9
    briefest, i am not sorry when sun and rain . . . . 749 95 POEMS 77   4
    longest; i am not sorry when silence becomes singing . . . . 749 95 POEMS 77 16
    hello and goodbye: glad sorry or both (big little . . . . . . 776 73 POEMS 4   39
SORRYDAZE
    permanent and slap tremendous sorrydaze bog triperight . . . 333 VIVA 24   14
SORT
    with a rustling din sort of sublimated tom-tom which . . . . 171 & SON ACTU 20   4
    is tired of That sort of thing / / . . . . 245 IS 5 ONE 16   25
    (kind well of A sort of the way he . . . . 251 IS 5 ONE 22   9
    or an amoral morality sort-of-aliveing by innumerable . . . . 410 NO THANKS 27 12
    kind) YM& WC (of sort of) A soursweet bedtime . . . . 464 NEW POEMS 2   3
    (mr & mrs are sort of really really kind . . . . 501 50 POEMS 15   22
SORT-OF-ALIVEING
    or an amoral morality sort-of-aliveing by innumerable . . . . 410 NO THANKS 27 12
SORTING
    the first time in sorting from this vast nonchalant . . . . . 201 XLI PORTRAIT 9 21
SORTOF
    mustn't shouldn't) most daren't (sortof people well youknow . 412 NO THANKS 29   7
SORTS
    trouble adds up all sorts of quickly things on . . . . 287 IS 5 FOUR 4   3
SOUGHT
    feet the shrieking dryad sought her leafy goal, at . . . . . 3 T&C EPITHALAM 14
    moonbeam's treacherous snare she sought the harbouring dark, 8 T&C OF NICOL   26
    fired by hypercivic zeal sought newer pastures or because . . 258 IS 5 ONE 28   12
    (whether that oneself be sought or seeking master or . . . . 804 73 POEMS 32   3
SOUL
    his coming whom her soul burns to embrace--and didst . . . . 3 T&C EPITHALAM 11
    colossus of the Pheidian soul whose eagle frights creation, . 3 T&C EPITHALAM 26
    gathers comfort to her soul, hope richly scattered by . . . . 5 T&C EPITHALAM 82
    folds-- with man's poor soul superlatively brave. Surely from 5 T&C EPITHALAM 96
    thy thought my golden soul fabulously to glue in . . . . . . 9 T&C SONGS 1   30
    before your voice my soul half-beautiful and wholly droll . . 11 T&C SONGS 2   1
    (whose hand my folded soul shall know while on . . . . 11 T&C SONGS 2   26
    earthless hour my fond soul seriously yearns beyond this . . 12 T&C SONGS 2   42
    foliate inscrutable sweetness my soul obedient; it is to . . 19 T&C PUELLA MEA 89
    intense things. Never my soul so fortunate is (past . . . . . 19 T&C PUELLA MEA 102
    (with fear aglow) my soul is wont wholly to . . . . 19 T&C PUELLA MEA 109
    to thee with a soul and thou didst not . . . . 27 T&C ORIENTALE 1 16
    the breaking of your soul upon my lips / . . . . 38 T&C AMORES 3   17
    singing reaches of my soul spoke the green- greeting . . . . 39 T&C AMORES 4   22
    be unto us O soul, but straight glad feet . . . . 41 T&C AMORES 5   29
    the window of your soul it is not like . . . . 43 T&C AMORES 7   5
    men her common purple soul the absurd eyelids sulked . . . . 52 T&C PORTRAIT 1 25
    very glad that the soul inside me Hollers for . . . . 61 T&C PORTRAIT 9 27
    the utterance of his soul--so even i wholly chained . . . . 79 T&C SON UNRE 4 10
    the aesthete indulges his soul for certain things which . . . 108 & PORTRAIT 4 29
    nous sommes heureux my soul a limp lump of . . . . 133 & SON REAL 4 19
    of nothing for your soul. / / / / . . . . 161 & SON ACTU 10 14
    / / of my soul a street is: prettinesses . . . . 180 XLI SONGS 2   2
    throttling trees hither my soul repairs herself with prisms . 180 XLI SONGS 2   9
    and then your dancesong soul. rarely-beloved a single star . 186 XLI SONGS 8   18
    collapses. exhaling a red soul into the dark so . . . . 188 XLI SONGS 10 11
    the integration of my soul i coughed , naturally . . . . . . 197 XLI PORTRAIT 5 23
    success than enquire whose soul dangles from his watch-chain 204 XLI LA GUERRE 2 3
    rapture should surprise my soul slowly which on thy . . . . . 205 XLI SONNETS 1   5
    spill my bright incalculable soul. / / / / . . . . 206 XLI SONNETS 2 15
    nothing to my comparable soul which with existence has . . . 212 XLI SONNETS 8   1
    with all his hearty soul aglow) his nightly supper . . . . . 254 IS 5 ONE 25   21
    ragged meadow of my soul. / / / / . . . . 306 IS 5 FIVE 5   15

SOUL (CONTINUED)

O love, my love! soul clings and heart conceives . . . . . . 386 NO THANKS 3 12
rare with most early soul him shall untouch meaningless . . . 402 NO THANKS 19 12
eternal mere one bursting soul why, then comes peace . . . . 414 NO THANKS 31 11
curving form enters my soul feels all small facts . . . . . . 419 NO THANKS 36 4
forget him (emptying our soul of emptiness) priming at . . . 428 NO THANKS 45 14
where goes this whyless soul a loneliest road who . . . . . . 441 NO THANKS 56 45
Be) look now (come soul; & : and who . . . . 448 NO THANKS 63 16
down with the human soul and anything else uncanned . . . . . 466 NEW POEMS 4 5
daretoi nig) Ah, Soul / / / / . . . . 474 NEW POEMS 12 16
his dream ing own soul looks and the is . . . . 516 50 POEMS 30 16
my father lived his soul love is the whole . . . . 521 50 POEMS 34 67
do mannikins forbid the soul? is death a whore . . . . 527 50 POEMS 39 20
it wouldn't like a soul and couldn't use a . . . . 544 1 X 1 4 27
pity to envy and soul to mind) --whose hearts . . . . . . 560 1 X 1 20 14
and rainbow mind and soul november and april) who . . . . . 575 1 X 1 35 34
of mind, mountains of soul) quite at the hugest . . . . . . 580 1 X 1 40 25
earth's arrival with a soul sunlight? yes (always we . . . . 582 1 X 1 42 4
a whole of a soul until i awoke for . . . . 587 1 X 1 47 18
earth: a flame beyond soul immemorially forevering am-- and . 599 (CHAIRE) 1 5
the mountain of his soul comes a keen pure . . . . 617 (CHAIRE) 19 1
swore they'd never part: Soul was (i understand) seduced . . 621 (CHAIRE) 23 2
breathless one breathing) be" soul "more" cries: with a . . . 625 (CHAIRE) 27 23
of space) absolute (my soul tastes If as some . . . . 639 (CHAIRE) 41 6
an if in its soul and a hole in . . . . 647 (CHAIRE) 49 12
heart may feel and soul may touch --the great . . . . 664 (CHAIRE) 66 4
heart can leap, no soul can breathe but by . . . . 664 (CHAIRE) 66 21
coercion or mind and soul convict him of deceiving) . . . . . 683 95 POEMS 11 4
a stone on his soul" / / / / . . . . 707 95 POEMS 35 28
of paradise) mind without soul may blast some universe . . . 714 95 POEMS 42 9
and one celestial) stand soul to soul: freedom to . . . . . . 721 95 POEMS 49 9
celestial) stand soul to soul: freedom to freedom till . . . 721 95 POEMS 49 9
which grows higher than soul can hope or mind . . . . 766 95 POEMS 92 13
AM and he's the soul of chivalry in terror . . . . 774 73 POEMS 2 4
heart but unquestionably a soul-- by no means funereally . . 802 73 POEMS 30 18
everything's nothing --arise, my soul; and sing / / . . . . . 834 73 POEMS 62 30
! joy truth! ! soul / / / / . . . . 841 73 POEMS 69 40
+SOUL
FOR CONTEXT, SEE . . . . 471 NEW POEMS 9 15
FOR CONTEXT, SEE . . . . 495 50 POEMS 9 12
FOR CONTEXT, SEE . . . . 517 50 POEMS 31 6
FOR CONTEXT, SEE . . . . 631 (CHAIRE) 33 8
FOR CONTEXT, SEE . . . . 658 (CHAIRE) 60 17
SOUL'S
passed afterday, clothe thy soul's coming merely, with a . . 10 T&C SONGS 1 40
the darkness of my soul's return --you are my . . . . 810 73 POEMS 38 13
SOULDOLL
man -god one eager souldoll one unsellable not buyable . . . 524 50 POEMS 36 44
SOULLESS
each nothing which all soulless wraiths proclaim substance; . 765 95 POEMS 91 3
despair and right where soulless our (with all their . . . . 780 73 POEMS 8 6
SOULLESSNESS
per rules apparelling its soullessness by lonely antics of . 373 VIVA 64 4
SOULS
bodies the odd unlovely souls struggle slowly and writhe . . 55 T&C PORTRAIT 3 19
who live in furnished souls are unbeautiful and have . . . . 70 T&C SON REAL 1 1
common divisor of unequal souls. / / / / . . . . 74 T&C SON REAL 5 15
have trod the silly souls of men to golden . . . . 75 T&C SON REAL 6 11
of this night when souls which have forgot frivolity . . . . 81 T&C SON UNRE 6 3
wind and swirled justly souls of flower strike the . . . . 163 & SON ACTU 12 6
(whispering, suggesting that our souls inhabit whatever is . 285 IS 5 FOUR 2 4
of Progress shriek; when Souls are outlawed, Hearts are . . . 438 NO THANKS 54 21
imperishably feast all timeless souls (the not whose spiral . 456 NO THANKS 71 3
stink and as for souls why souls are wholes . . . . 510 50 POEMS 24 8
as for souls why souls are wholes not parts . . . . 510 50 POEMS 24 8
manying one -ness) nine souls only alive with a . . . . . . 627 (CHAIRE) 29 12
into infinite tomorrow steer --souls under whom flow . . . . 659 (CHAIRE) 61 5
or as if our souls, awakened from summer's green . . . . . . 675 95 POEMS 3 9

	PAGE	TITLE	LINE

SOULS (CONTINUED)
the of twig three souls sit round with cold . . . . 687 95 POEMS 15   3
SOUND
of April: witchery of sound and odour drives the . . . . . .   4 T&C EPITHALAM   60
from broken eyes a sound of strangling breasts and . . . . . 28 T&C ORIENTALE 2   6
a possible and beautiful sound: if a (perhaps) clock . . . . 92 & POST IMPR 4   13
eyes smell of the sound of rain and here's . . . . 424 NO THANKS 41   3
taking rain) drown, beyond sound down (slowly beneath sight . 432 NO THANKS 49   3
of a blind big sound on the ground / . . . . 543 1 X 1 3   30
leaf opens without any sound and wishing is having . . . . . 665 (CHAIRE) 67   8
feel taste smell & sound of a silence who . . . . 676 95 POEMS 4   9
(the great dim deep sound of rain; and of . . . . 816 73 POEMS 44   2
a now of magnificent sound (which makes this whenworld . . . 841 73 POEMS 69   13
if he paints with sound, newly one moving cadence . . . . . 842 73 POEMS 70   5
+SOUND
FOR CONTEXT, SEE . . . . 347 VIVA 38   19
FOR CONTEXT, SEE . . . . 754 95 POEMS 82   12
SOUNDLESS
whispers hear with weepings soundless, saying of "alas we . .   9 T&C SONGS 1   21
existence, as by shores soundless, the unspeaking watcher who 79 T&C SON UNRE 4   8
immeasurably roots among much soundless rubbish of guitars . 479 NEW POEMS 17   6
SOUNDS
these my days their sounds and flowers Fall in . . . . 11 T&C SONGS 2   31
of history her heroes, sounds the tread of those . . . . . . 209 XLI SONNETS 5   2
certain a hundred these sounds crowds odours it is . . . . . 238 IS 5 ONE 9   3
+SOUNDS
FOR CONTEXT, SEE . . . . 331 VIVA 22   4
SOUP
unnoise men don't make soup who drink. // . . . . 141 & SON REAL 12   18
SOUR
fairies, out of it sour gnomes tumble clumsily, the . . . . 69 T&C POST IMPR 6   3
the lady'll have a whiskey-sour-- whose least amazing smile . 74 T&C SON REAL 5   13
+SOUR
FOR CONTEXT, SEE . . . . 442 NO THANKS 57   7
SOURING
wall the colour drub souring sunbeams, of a foetal . . . . 144 & SON REAL 15   2
SOURSWEET
(of sort of) A soursweet bedtime -less un- (wonderful) . . . 464 NEW POEMS 2   4
SOUVENIR
prettily indeed) arra- nged souvenir of the in spite . . . . 267 IS 5 TWO 2   13
SOW
a big grin. her sow- eyes clicking mischief from . . . . . . 73 T&C SON REAL 4   6
SOWED
not at all they sowed their isn't they reaped . . . . 515 50 POEMS 29   7
SOWER
the reaper and the sower; my prayers are prayers . . . . . . 749 95 POEMS 77   5
SOWING
winter spring reaped their sowing and went their came . . . . 515 50 POEMS 29   35
SPACE
free twitch of scintillant space, with the cool writhe . . . 18 T&C PUELLA MEA   84
heaven through day and space i saw you close . . . . 30 T&C ORIENTALE 4   34
dangerous night through moaned space god worships God-- . . . 77 T&C SON UNRE 2   15
the moment of enthusiastic space is a little wonderful, . . . 82 T&C SON ACTU 1   12
/ / / / Space being (don't forget to . . . . 315 VIVA 7   1
new fragrantly young earth space opening was. Were your . . . 432 NO THANKS 49   19
every man's flesh put space on; and his mind . . . . 484 NEW POEMS 22   8
not suspected selves of space-- life stands gradually upon . 517 50 POEMS 31   7
shut and starved on space? love's murdered eye dissected . . 527 50 POEMS 39   12
friend to fiend: blow space to time) --when skies . . . . . . 560 1 X 1 20   6
than all of timely space (was and be will) . . . . 608 (CHAIRE) 10   4
(hark --that screech of space) absolute (my soul tastes . . . 639 (CHAIRE) 41   6
the magnificent honesty of space. Mountains are mountains . . 675 95 POEMS 3   4
have all time and space bowed to immortal us . . . . 694 95 POEMS 22   5
morethanPerson; who (riding through space to diminutive this 697 95 POEMS 25   20
bodies kneel (over time space doom dream while floats . . . . 714 95 POEMS 42   7
enough for slaves of space and time --ours is . . . . 745 95 POEMS 73   13
SPACED
falling silently through the far-spaced possible nearaway . . 10 T&C SONGS 1   44

	PAGE	TITLE	LINE

SPACEFUL
from fancied fact and spaceful time-- no heart can . . . . . 664 {CHAIRE} 66   20
SPACES
(thundering) by When eaten spaces grouse rocket know quite, . 346 VIVA 37   11
SPADED
if delicately gelded (or spaded) gentlemen (and ladies) . . . 231 IS 5 ONE 3   44
SPADES
two young stars with spades of silver dig) by . . . . 115 & PORTRAIT 8   3
+SPAGHETTI
FOR CONTEXT, SEE . . . . 387 NO THANKS 4   18
SPAN
chic; by instruments, both span and spic, are justly . . . . 438 NO THANKS 54   13
justly measured Spic and Span: to kiss the mike . . . . 438 NO THANKS 54   14
SPANGLE
keen if dim quiveringly spangle & thingless & before . . . . 480 NEW POEMS 18   9
SPANGLES
be afraid look the spangles that sleep all the . . . . 192 XLI CHANSONS 2   13
+SPANGLES
FOR CONTEXT, SEE . . . . 421 NO THANKS 38   10
SPANKED
thirsties since we are spanked and put to sleep . . . . 261 IS 5 ONE 31   2
stly (stuck in a spanked behind / / / . . . . 408 NO THANKS 25   16
SPARE
mercy) your true lover spare: for that way knowledge . . . . 484 NEW POEMS 22   10
was he aiming ; spare the child and spoil . . . . 643 {CHAIRE} 45   5
me by 'could you spare three cents please' --why . . . . . . 800 73 POEMS 28   6
+SPARE
FOR CONTEXT, SEE . . . . 310 VIVA 2   8
FOR CONTEXT, SEE . . . . 310 VIVA 2   8
SPARK
/ (once like a spark) if strangers meet life . . . . 564 1 X 1 24   1
cry --even the crackling spark of (hung in a) . . . . 605 {CHAIRE} 7   8
some world of a spark 's gulped by illimitable . . . . 639 {CHAIRE} 41   7
SPARKLE
should flower: or laughing sparkle from the shut house . . . 292 IS 5 FOUR 9   18
SPARROW
me 6 e nglish sparrow s) a utumn & . . . . 696 95 POEMS 24   9
SPARROWS
gurgle a nonsense of sparrows, the cathedral shudders . . . . 282 IS 5 THREE 6   12
(which cannot sing) lish sparrows say then 2 or . . . . 787 73 POEMS 15   4
+SPARROWS
FOR CONTEXT, SEE . . . . 442 NO THANKS 57   8
FOR CONTEXT, SEE . . . . 725 95 POEMS 53   11
SPASM
gold year a formal spasm in the dust this . . . . 41 T&C AMORES 5   7
upon the beyond imagining spasm rise we you-with-me around . 442 NO THANKS 57   21
SPAT
encore he laughed and spat (this life could dare . . . . . . 440 NO THANKS 56   11
mind with heart he spat and laughed with self . . . . 441 NO THANKS 56   40
SPATS
scientifically pressed trousers ejaculate spats a strikingly 259 IS 5 ONE 29   24
SPATTERED
a collar hung gently. (spattered) by this instant of . . . . 96 & POST IMPR 8   32
perhaps the By invisibilities spattered (or if it may . . . . 317 VIVA 9   20
SPATTERS
all foam -like hair spatters creasing pillow next everywhere 358 VIVA 49   3
SPAWN
the not stroll living spawn imitate) ce (re peat . . . . . . 309 VIVA 1   32
they squirm and they spawn and a world is . . . . 439 NO THANKS 55   2
SPEAK
the high gods fled? Speak elm eloquent pandar with . . . . .   3 T&C EPITHALAM   9
lovelier. And if she speak in her frail way, ... 18 T&C PUELLA MEA   77
life not love? i speak to thee with a . . . . 27 T&C ORIENTALE 1   22
(and i do not speak nor think nor am . . . . 98 & POST IMPR 9   14
themselves (on air) don't speak A white idea, drenching. . . 99 & POST IMPR 10   18
perfectly fearful. meanwhile these speak her wonderful But i 162 & SON ACTU 11   8
delirium (we do not speak) tumbled hushingly bits of . . . . 168 & SON ACTU 17   6
Boston, i do not speak. and i sit in . . . . 217 XLI SONNETS 13   1

SPEAK (CONTINUED)

street the houses immensely speak (it is nine minutes . . . . 219 XLI SONNETS 15   3
woman.) they so to speak were in Love once? . . . . 243 IS 5 ONE 14   9
of our attention; to speak even less objectively, i . . . . . 263 IS 5 ONE 32   61
if their (so to speak) offspring has that largo . . . . 326 VIVA 18   8
(at windows) do not speak and are ghosts or . . . . 340 VIVA 31   6
only hands so to speak are they always which . . . . 359 VIVA 50   14
utmost magic, or stones speak or one name control . . . . . . 377 VIVA 68   4
others) the so to speak wistfulLy dead are not . . . . . . 391 NO THANKS 8   17
take a piss they speak whatever's on their mind . . . . 427 NO THANKS 44   17
(of Ever-Ever Land i speak sweet morons gather roun' . . . . 466 NEW POEMS 4   1
one snowflake (and we speak our names / / . . . . 502 50 POEMS 16   14
a fiend, if fiends speak truth; if angels burn . . . . . . 562 1 X 1 22   5
knows; and can perfectly speak (snowflake and rainbow mind . 575 1 X 1 35   31
each illimit able to speak very softly altogeth er . . . . . 600 (CHAIRE) 2   14
heart they might not speak, a little innocence will . . . . . 649 (CHAIRE) 51   1
my love (till mountains speak the truth) enter a . . . . . . 745 95 POEMS 73   2
not make a dream speak; or if to no . . . . 842 73 POEMS 70   11

+SPEAKEASIES

FOR CONTEXT, SEE . . . . 330 VIVA 21   1

SPEAKING

beauty play at not speaking (sometimes as it will) . . . . . 18 T&C PUELLA MEA   62
shall be excelled by speaking flower (if i have . . . . 84 T&C SON ACTU 3   5
sleuthfully aboard all to--mendaciously speaking--a man . . . 334 VIVA 25   6
/ / / / speaking of love (of which . . . . 364 VIVA 55   1
dead are not relatively speaking uncultured (who Very . . . . 391 NO THANKS 8   19
over un graves der, speaking (says. word Less) ly . . . . . . 417 NO THANKS 34   4
most successful b.o. fully speaking concession at the recent 425 NO THANKS 42   15

SPEAKS

sunset is hanging, snow speaks slowly / / / . . . . 202 XLI PORTRAIT 9   52
with a dream myself speaks (whispering, suggesting that our . 285 IS 5 FOUR 2   2
not children but men speaks (among leaves Easily through . . 356 VIVA 47   3
top of the stairs speaks in his kind sweet . . . . 813 73 POEMS 41   2

SPEAR

steadily expand hearing the spear-song of the marching grass.   4 T&C EPITHALAM   72
but at the earliest spear of sun perfectly should . . . . . 377 VIVA 68   2

SPEAR-SONG

steadily expand hearing the spear-song of the marching grass.   4 T&C EPITHALAM   72

SPEARMINT

Shirt Boston Garter and Spearmint Girl With The Wrigley . . . 230 IS 5 ONE 2   5

SPEARS

eyelids finger their unquiet spears the queen of queens . . . 34 T&C ORIENTALE 6   83
don't know tenuous Now- spears and The Then-arrows making . . 160 & SON ACTU 9   16

SPECIALTY

huly jeezus" --an-- "my specialty is takin fellers' goils . . 332 VIVA 23   6
/ / / my specialty is living said a . . . . 473 NEW POEMS 11   1

SPECIMEN

but never this fine specimen of hypermagical . . . . 554 1 X 1 14   12

+SPECKED

FOR CONTEXT, SEE . . . . 116 & PORTRAIT 9   3

SPECKLED

wugglewiggle champychumpchomps yes the speckled strut begins 773 73 POEMS 1   13

SPECKS

shyly a-live keen parallel specks float-ing create height, . 447 NO THANKS 62   3

SPECTATOR

boat somebody an invisible spectator, maybe certain nobodies 283 IS 5 THREE 7   7

SPECTRAL

silence: but unsinging. In spectral such hugest how hush, . . 839 73 POEMS 67   3

SPECTRES

not do the losing spectres mime until out of . . . . 502 50 POEMS 16   12
proclaim substance; all heartless spectres, happiness) lovers 765 95 POEMS 91   4

SPEECH

a speed of white speech (the simple instant of . . . . . . 157 & SON ACTU 6   7
by how terrible inches speech--it made you a little . . . . . 174 & SON ACTU 23   10

SPEECHES

from their actions and speeches sawdust perpetually leak . . 261 IS 5 ONE 31   4

SPEECHLESS

which have beheld night's speechless carnival the painting of 36 T&C AMORES 1   13

		PAGE	TITLE	LINE

SPEED
for me with a speed of white speech (the . . . . 157 & SON ACTU 6   7
/ / / FULL SPEED ASTERN) m usil (age) . . . . 325 VIVA 17   1
SPEEDS
n dizzily swingthings of speeds of trapeze gush somersaults . 536 50 POEMS 48   8
SPELL
sing that yell that spell that out big (bigger . . . . . . 475 NEW POEMS 13   17
in a real hot spell with o man what . . . . 476 NEW POEMS 14   3
SPEND
love, who shall not spend my fortune (although endlessness . 394 NO THANKS 11   13
aren't lucky 's to spend laughter not money lucky . . . . . . 467 NEW POEMS 5   4
all human curiosity we'll spend (gladly, as lovers must) . . 675 95 POEMS 3   12
SPENDS
to be sure university spends her time looking picturesque . . 234 IS 5 ONE 5   2
their and your returning, spends the forever of his . . . . . 812 73 POEMS 40   6
SPENT
/ / when the spent day begins to frail . . . . 115 & PORTRAIT 8   1
like a vine that's spent all of its life . . . . 147 & SON REAL 18   11
good ole days we spent in '18 kickin duh . . . . 332 VIVA 23   15
+SPEW
FOR CONTEXT, SEE . . . . 629 (CHAIRE) 31   18
SPEWING
Geddup curb leans carefully spewing into her own Shush . . . 330 VIVA 21   12
SPEWNONSPEW
whis (gorgedis reswal lowing spewnonspew clutch) pers again & 629 (CHAIRE) 31   18
SPHERE
my your our blossoming sphere / / / / / . . . . 582 1 X 1 42   16
SPHINXES
whose subtle throne twain sphinxes bear each with a . . . . . 4 T&C EPITHALAM   42
SPIC
instruments, both span and spic, are justly measured Spic . . 438 NO THANKS 54   13
spic, are justly measured Spic and Span: to kiss . . . . . . 438 NO THANKS 54   14
SPIDER
voice like a keen spider skipping quickly over patriotic . . 166 & SON ACTU 15   1
SPIDERLEGS
unripe green with nauseous spiderlegs and excremental hair . 55 T&C PORTRAIT 3   10
SPIKES
gladness hammers incessant putrid spikes of madness (at . . . 202 XLI PORTRAIT 9   38
distinct sunset driving white spikes of silence into joists . 378 VIVA 69   9
SPILL
caressed will explode and spill the immediate imperceptible . 193 XLI PORTRAIT 1   17
incense fleetly roll) i spill my bright incalculable soul. . 206 XLI SONNETS 2   15
a little tilted streets spill lazily multitudes out of . . . 345 VIVA 36   6
fall all we go spill and chairs tables the . . . . 496 50 POEMS 10   14
(plunging rapturously up) we spill our masterpiece / / . . . 650 (CHAIRE) 52   20
climbing whom begins to spill such golden blood as . . . . . 811 73 POEMS 39   12
SPILLED
buds mattered. a valley spilled its tickling river in . . . . 135 & SON REAL 6   14
blood was for us spilled) than all mankind something . . . . 514 50 POEMS 28   9
SPILLING
the little box is spilling rancid elves upon neat . . . . . . 69 T&C POST IMPR 6   4
hello whirling whose rhyme (spilling his rings) threeing . . 751 95 POEMS 79   6
SPILLS
nicknamed ecstasy and And spills smile cheaply thick --who . 358 VIVA 49   10
SPIN
toss trunks shuffle sacks spin kegs they curl loving . . . . 114 & PORTRAIT 7   8
a pound. Turn gert (spin! helen) the slimmer the . . . . . . 513 50 POEMS 27   4
without winter spring? she'll spin that spirit her own . . . 531 50 POEMS 43   11
than believe (with a spin leap alive we're alive) . . . . . . 594 1 X 1 54   42
+SPIN
FOR CONTEXT, SEE . . . . 495 50 POEMS 9   17
SPINE
(y down the squirming sPine of the) unsuspecting street; . . 101 & POST IMPR 11   54
like to feel the spine of your body and . . . . 175 & SON ACTU 24   5
cathedral leans its dreamy spine against thick sunset i . . . 279 IS 5 THREE 3   4
light squoits down my spine like i was dead . . . . 332 VIVA 23   27
shoulders S the empty spine / / / / . . . . 414 NO THANKS 31   15

721

	PAGE	TITLE	LINE

+SPINNING
    FOR CONTEXT, SEE . . . . 311 VIVA 3   5
SPINS
    little girl in white spins, tumbles; rolling in sand. . . . . 281 IS 5 THREE 5   3
+SPINS
    FOR CONTEXT, SEE . . . . 692 95 POEMS 20   3
SPINSTER'S
    possibly darker than a spinster's heart my voice feels . . . 506 50 POEMS 20   6
SPINSTERS
    poeds urseappeal netsam our spinsters and coeds) thoroughly . 492 50 POEMS 6   4
SPIRAL
    turn young with rain, spiral acres of bloated rose . . . . . 93 & POST IMPR 5   5
    menting colossus whose irrefutable spiral antics involve me . 201 XLI PORTRAIT 9   25
    souls (the not whose spiral hunger may appease what . . . . . 456 NO THANKS 71   4
+SPIRAL
    FOR CONTEXT, SEE . . . . 278 IS 5 THREE 2   12
SPIRALLING
    than immeasurable dream wherelessly spiralling) beyond time's 454 NO THANKS 69   8
    quietly & before illimitably spiralling candy of tiniest . . 480 NEW POEMS 18   22
    sharp soft worms of spiralling why and out of . . . . 522 50 POEMS 35   13
    / / / from spiralling ecstatically this proud nowhere . . . . 714 95 POEMS 42   1
    smile sings or if (spiralling as luminous they climb . . . . 810 73 POEMS 38   5
SPIRALLY
    proud inwardlyness to collide spirally with iron arithmethics 311 VIVA 3   11
    laughter of afterwards-- i spirally understand What touching 356 VIVA 47   18
SPIRALS
    shout appalling deathmoney into spiralS and Now (comes un, . 346 VIVA 37   17
SPIRE
    did this and this spire strike midnight (and did . . . . . . 115 & PORTRAIT 8   17
    i lift my diminutive spire to merciful Him Whose . . . . . . 749 95 POEMS 77   17
SPIRES
    arise purple pencils fluent spires of fragrance the bowl . . 31 T&C ORIENTALE 5   5
    gold swarms upon the spires silver chants the litanies . . . 51 T&C IMPRESS 5   3
    you, white town whose spires softly dare. Will take . . . . 86 T&C SON ACTU 5   4
    at the yearhour tree- spires shout appalling deathmoney into 346 VIVA 37   15
SPIRIT
    --at her glance my spirit shies rearing (as in . . . . 18 T&C PUELLA MEA   45
    foolingly to smite my spirit with the lithe free . . . . . . 18 T&C PUELLA MEA   83
    stand helplessly before the spirit at bay; if this . . . . . 76 T&C SON UNRE 1   8
    darkness roams torture my spirit with the exquisite froms . . 79 T&C SON UNRE 4   5
    (as the kno wing spirit prowls, its nose winces . . . . 319 VIVA 11   10
    (warily as their master's spirit stooping, Crusoelike . . . . 344 VIVA 35   13
    your body with its spirit floated (clothed only in . . . . . 369 VIVA 60   19
    and whose pilot my spirit is / / / . . . . 419 NO THANKS 36   24
    mown lives) oh my spirit you tumble climb and . . . . 434 NO THANKS 51   26
    by april wish by spirit and if by yes. . . . . 515 50 POEMS 29   32
    spring? she'll spin that spirit her own fingers with . . . . 531 50 POEMS 43   11
    / / / / spirit colossal (& daunted by . . . . 678 95 POEMS 6   1
    snowstopped silent world) one spirit serenely truly himself; 808 73 POEMS 36   3
    always not imaginably morethanmostgenerous spirit. Feeling . 823 73 POEMS 51   14
    contrives (but certainly each spirit is) and partially . . . 842 73 POEMS 70   8
+SPIRIT
    FOR CONTEXT, SEE . . . . 383 NO THANKS 1   11
SPIRIT'S
    light by which my spirit's born: yours is the . . . . 810 73 POEMS 38   12
    anywhere eclipsing of a spirit's ignorance by every wisdom . 843 73 POEMS 71   10
SPIRITED
    blessings daughters, unscented shapeless spirited) they . . . 70 T&C SON REAL 1   4
SPIRITS
    fear our slightly fingering spirits starve and smother; until 305 IS 5 FIVE 4   7
    dawn discuss our mingling spirits, you would disappear . . . 379 VIVA 70   7
    floating in the very spirits singing in are winging . . . . . 591 1 X 1 51   7
    for the leaping greenly spirits of trees and a . . . . 663 (CHAIRE) 65   2
    heavenly earth beguiles our spirits, whose miraculously . . . 675 95 POEMS 3   2
    our by immeasurable night spirits and with illimitable day . 745 95 POEMS 73   8
    is if things seem spirits) or (if spirits in . . . . 845 73 POEMS 73   2
    seem spirits) or (if spirits in the guise of . . . . 845 73 POEMS 73   3

		PAGE	TITLE	LINE

SPIRITUAL
love and the small spiritual cry of spring utters . . . . . . 213 XLI SONNETS 9   6
SPIT
coats smile looking hands spit blood teeth the Communists . . 275 IS 5 TWO 9   47
+SPIT
FOR CONTEXT, SEE . . . . 488 50 POEMS 2   11
SPITE
which easily break in spite of the best overseeing) . . . . . 264 IS 5 ONE 33   16
souvenir of the in spite of himself fa -mous . . . . 267 IS 5 TWO 2   13
/ / / in spite of everything which breathes . . . . 288 IS 5 FOUR 5   1
the fact that (in spite of the fact that . . . . 323 VIVA 15   21
we who're alive in spite of mirrors (have died . . . . 386 NO THANKS 3   1
4th) reminds me in spite of his buggy of . . . . 699 95 POEMS 27   7
SPITS
mother of god who spits seeds of dead song . . . . 55 T&C PORTRAIT 3   13
skilful of thing silent spits discrete lumps of noise..... . 159 & SON ACTU 8   7
and y play b spits x and y play, ... 200 XLI PORTRAIT 8   21
suddenly crashing things) man spits quickly into the very . . 252 IS 5 ONE 23   11
off duty wanderfuling aft spits) int o immensity (upon   . . . 465 NEW POEMS 3   4
SPITTING
s And the violin spitting squeaky songs into the . . . . . . 101 & POST IMPR 11   44
+SPITTING
FOR CONTEXT, SEE . . . . 312 VIVA 4   20
SPITTLE
she says I ploc spittle what the lands thaz . . . . 96 & POST IMPR 8   14
SPITTOON
into the very bright spittoon / / / / . . . . 252 IS 5 ONE 23   12
in is, extinguishing the spittoon by a candle furnished . . . 263 IS 5 ONE 32   49
SPLASHED
(little careful hunks-of-lilac laughter splashed from the . . 133 & SON REAL 4   4
SPLASHES
/ --G O N splashes-sink which is west eighth, ... 169 & SON ACTU 18   1
SPLASHES-SINK
/ --G O N splashes-sink which is west eighth, ... 169 & SON ACTU 18   1
SPLASHING
bell a jetted music splashing fresh upon silence) i . . . . . 115 & PORTRAIT 8   19
SPLENDIDLY
(dream hugely) wish firmly. splendidly advancing colour . . . 422 NO THANKS 39   4
SPLENDIFEROUS
scrumptious not to mention splendiferous funeral with tall . 239 IS 5 ONE 10   30
SPLENDOR
infinity sharpens the temporal splendor of this night when . 81 T&C SON UNRE 6   2
which are a mixed splendor of piston and of . . . . 264 IS 5 ONE 33   22
name control more incredible splendor than our merely . . . . 377 VIVA 68   5
head). Then with the splendor of an angel's fart . . . . . . 506 50 POEMS 20   11
cathedral) far from the splendor and squalor of hurrying . . 749 95 POEMS 77   2
the earth in her splendor says May / / . . . . 801 73 POEMS 29   29
SPLENDORS
shimmering wind these fragile splendors from us crumple them 41 T&C AMORES 5   19
someone's eyes) with silver splendors past conceiving who . . 756 95 POEMS 84   5
SPLINTER
moon is a remarkable splinter in the quick of . . . . 82 T&C SON ACTU 1   5
SPLINTERED
rasp and graze of splintered normality crackle and sag   . . . 48 T&C IMPRESS 2   4
SPLINTERING
red horse shrieking from splintering foam caught you clutched 30 T&C ORIENTALE 4   12
SPLIT
of lovecrazed abrupt flesh split "Pretty Baby" to numb   . . . 106 & PORTRAIT 2   12
SPLURGING
silver with warmlyish wetflat splurging smells waltz the . . 96 & POST IMPR 8   12
SPOIL
ever been invented can spoil this or this instant) . . . . . 357 VIVA 48   6
I mean let's not spoil it let's make it . . . . 407 NO THANKS 24   9
and if spring should spoil the game, what then? . . . . 579 1 X 1 39   4
spare the child and spoil the rod quoth the . . . . 643 {CHAIRE} 45   5
SPOKE
was mad and Launcelot spoke to Guenever, a flower . . . . . . 18 T&C PUELLA MEA   57
/ / ORIENTALE i spoke to thee with a . . . . 27 T&C ORIENTALE 1   1

SPOKE (CONTINUED)

not a smile? i spoke to thee with a . . . . 27 T&C ORIENTALE 1   8
not a song? i spoke to thee with a . . . . 27 T&C ORIENTALE 1   15
reaches of my soul spoke the green- greeting pale- . . . . . 39 T&C AMORES 4   23
the handsome moon never spoke ill of the pretty . . . . 43 T&C AMORES 7   14
liberty be mute?" He. spoke. And drank rapidly a . . . . . . 268 IS 5 TWO 3   14
/ / / / spoke joe to jack leave . . . . 496 50 POEMS 10   1
not your gal jack spoke to joe 's left . . . . 496 50 POEMS 10   4
every only god who spoke this earth so glad . . . . 526 50 POEMS 38   2

SPOKEN

any reason (i have spoken with this indubitable and . . . . . 91 & POST IMPR 3   6

SPONTANE

moved with the hideous spontane- ity of a solemn . . . . . . 103 & POST IMPR 13   9

+SPONTANEITY

FOR CONTEXT, SEE . . . . 103 & POST IMPR 13   9

SPONTANEOUS

to flourish the minute spontaneous meadow of her mind) . . . 19 T&C PUELLA MEA   123
/ / O sweet spontaneous earth how often have . . . . 46 T&C LA GUERRE 2   1
too. much Too. originally spontaneous twurls-of-excrement . . 94 & POST IMPR 6   2
being, out of the spontaneous clumsy trivi- al acrobatic . . 193 XLI PORTRAIT 1   19
protest, anent the un -spontaneous and otherwise scented . . 230 IS 5 ONE 2   16
the as tonishing & spontaneous & difficult ugliness of . . . 354 VIVA 45   15
or since but through spontaneous deft strictly horrors which 386 NO THANKS 3   7

SPONTANEOUSLY

an error, with twists spontaneously methodical. He suddenly . 170 & SON ACTU 19   11

+SPONTANEOUSLY

FOR CONTEXT, SEE . . . . 197 XLI PORTRAIT 5   3

SPOOK

mere brain contrived: a spook of stop and go) . . . . 558 1 X 1 18   9

SPOON

face, brighter than a spoon, collects the image of . . . . . 360 VIVA 51   21
are round like a spoon are both making silence . . . . 483 NEW POEMS 21   4

SPOONS

cups if begin to spoons dance every- should where . . . . . . 287 IS 5 FOUR 4   16

SPOOR

beast Tomorrow by her spoor) over the earth wandering . . . . 374 VIVA 65   7

SPORT

all history's a winter sport or three: but were . . . . 579 1 X 1 39   5

SPOT

a line around the spot and call it beautifool . . . . 500 50 POEMS 14   3

+SPOUTING

FOR CONTEXT, SEE . . . . 179 XLI SONGS 1   17

SPOUTS

is it horribly smith spouts cornucopiously not unrecognizable 465 NEW POEMS 3   9

SPRAWL

of deads (lovers grip sprawl twitch lovers) & one . . . . . . 384 NO THANKS 2   10

+SPRAWL

FOR CONTEXT, SEE . . . . 430 NO THANKS 47   21

SPRAWLED

gritted lips and on sprawled eyes squirming with light . . . 139 & SON REAL 10   10

SPRAWLING

between nose-red gross walls sprawling with tipsy tables the 55 T&C PORTRAIT 3   2
other, releasing lay, watching (sprawling, in grass upon a . 283 IS 5 THREE 7   22

SPRAWLS

rush batter the crowd sprawls collapses singing knocked down 274 IS 5 TWO 9   6
itmaking sickness of mind sprawls) here a livingly free . . . 658 {CHAIRE} 60   14

SPRAY

a quai wall almost spray -ing threecoloured puke over . . . . 324 VIVA 16   7

SPREADNESSED

littlecrownGrave whose whorlclown of spreadnessed bE rich . . 342 VIVA 33   20

SPREE

in unsmooth sexual luminosity spree. --dear) the uncouthly . 159 & SON ACTU 8   13

SPRING

the mad magnificent herald Spring assembles beauty from . . .   4 T&C EPITHALAM   57
and vanishing with dawn). Spring, that omits no mention . . .   5 T&C EPITHALAM   89
rose shall beget the spring that maidens whom passion . . . . 16 T&C SONGS 6   6
is the mystery of Spring (with her beauty more . . . . 17 T&C PUELLA MEA   15
hears the cry of Spring, and with their frailest . . . . . . 22 T&C PUELLA MEA   234

SPRING (CONTINUED)
  CHANSONS INNOCENTES in Just- spring when the world is . . . .   24 T&C CHANSONS 1   2
  and piracies and it's spring when the world is . . . .   24 T&C CHANSONS 1   9
  and jump-rope and it's spring and the goat-footed balloonMan   24 T&C CHANSONS 1   17
  is the approach of spring thy thighs are white . . . .   29 T&C ORIENTALE 3 10
  answerest them only with spring) / / / / . . . .   46 T&C LA GUERRE 2 27
  (as it will in spring) ropes of silver gliding . . . .   58 T&C PORTRAIT 6   5
  / / / / spring omnipotent goddess thou dost . . . .   61 T&C PORTRAIT 9   1
  girls and not content Spring, with this thou hangest . . . .   61 T&C PORTRAIT 9   9
  canary-birds in parlor windows spring slattern of seasons you   61 T&C PORTRAIT 9   11
  are put on edge spring, of the jostle of . . . .   61 T&C PORTRAIT 9   22
  1 on something street Spring comes the lean and . . . .   62 T&C PORTRAIT 10   5
  shall be roses and spring will bring her worms . . . .   67 T&C POST IMPR 4 11
  / / / / Spring is like a perhaps . . . .   124 & SEVEN POEMS 3   1
  and changing everything carefully spring is like a perhaps . 124 & SEVEN POEMS 3   10
  visited, where always it's Spring) and everyone's in love .   129 & SEVEN POEMS 7   15
  miles off). It was spring sun-stirring. sweetly to the . . . 135 & SON REAL 6   12
  the imagined galleon of Spring) somewhere unspeaking sits my   156 & SON ACTU 5   9
  It was in the spring of this very year . . . .   158 & SON ACTU 7   3
  this very year (a spring of wines women and . . . . 158 & SON ACTU 7   4
  the framing twilight of Spring.... and the dream of . . . . . 158 & SON ACTU 7   11
  will bring you every spring handfuls of little normal . . . . 161 & SON ACTU 10   7
  a little, and the spring; a clumsy brightness of . . . . . . 173 & SON ACTU 22   2
  this day it was Spring.... us drew lewdly the . . . . 174 & SON ACTU 23   1
  kittens who are called spring, is what we stroke . . . . . . 191 XLI CHANSONS 1   10
  dripped with slavver of spring chased two flights of . . . . 194 XLI PORTRAIT 2   6
  his presence it was spring by the way in . . . . 197 XLI PORTRAIT 5   12
  whom the musical white spring offers her lily . . . . 206 XLI SONNETS 2   1
  small spiritual cry of spring utters a striving flower, . . . 213 XLI SONNETS 9   6
  and sharp lips of spring simply joining with the . . . . . . 218 XLI SONNETS 14   5
  me the Square in spring, the little barbarous Greenwich . . . 220 XLI SONNETS 16   9
  selves bulging in immortal Spring express a cry of . . . . . 255 IS 5 ONE 26   6
  an instrument to measure Spring with? each dream nascitur, . 264 IS 5 ONE 33   28
  be a fool while Spring is in the world . . . . 290 IS 5 FOUR 7   6
  beautiful things) winter, whom Spring shall kill / / . . . . 293 IS 5 FOUR 10   31
  i say (it being Spring and night) "let us . . . .   303 IS 5 FIVE 2   1
  self "somewhere it is Spring and sometimes people are . . . . 338 VIVA 29   5
  by petal myself as Spring opens (touching skilfully, ... 366 VIVA 57   7
  silence the music of spring lives F feel opens . . . . 390 NO THANKS 7   4
  autumn's winter being summer's spring who moved by standing . 420 NO THANKS 37   3
  / / sometimes in) Spring a someone will lie . . . . 428 NO THANKS 45   2
  of love (sometimes in Spring somewhere between what is . . . 428 NO THANKS 45   8
  / / / / Spring (side walks are) is . . . . 436 NO THANKS 52   1
  of houses called cities) spring most singular- ly (cities . . 436 NO THANKS 52   17
  for Is for Love Spring thirsty for happens only . . . . 437 NO THANKS 53   8
  love , then it's Spring immortal Always & lewd . . . . 442 NO THANKS 57   19
  dark we all findingly Spring the Fragrance unvisible) ges . . 482 NEW POEMS 20   8
  and robins never welcome spring nor flatfolk prove their . . 511 50 POEMS 25   16
  floating many bells down) spring summer autumn winter he . . 515 50 POEMS 29   3
  they grew autumn winter spring summer) that noone loved . . . 515 50 POEMS 29   11
  ding) summer autumn winter spring reaped their sowing and . . 515 50 POEMS 29   34
  child was sure that spring danced when she heard . . . . . . 521 50 POEMS 34   51
  now and without winter spring? she'll spin that spirit . . . 531 50 POEMS 43   10
  cry hello to the spring what if a dawn . . . . 560 1 X 1 20   16
  / love is a spring at which crazy they . . . . 563 1 X 1 23   1
  snow melts; and if spring should spoil the game, ... 579 1 X 1 39   4
  isn't that's under the spring --but if a look . . . . 580 1 X 1 40   5
  you , we are spring / / / / . . . . 583 1 X 1 43   21
  was in (live live) spring with all beautiful things . . . . . 589 1 X 1 49   10
  / / / "sweet spring is your time is . . . . 591 1 X 1 51   1
  selves are singing) "sweet spring is your time is . . . . . . 591 1 X 1 51   25
  (young old nic) like spring yoo un-air-stan? me crazy . . . . 618 (CHAIRE) 20   27
  sweet things are until" "spring follows winter: as clover . . 625 (CHAIRE) 27   9
  / / / in Spring comes (no- one asks . . . . 660 (CHAIRE) 62   2
  through sweet forgiveness of spring (over the under the . . . 661 (CHAIRE) 63   7
  april; my darling) it's spring! yes the pretty birds . . . . 665 (CHAIRE) 67   4
  it's (kiss me now) spring! now the pretty birds . . . . 665 (CHAIRE) 67   11
  winter and cringing --it's spring (all our night becomes . . 665 (CHAIRE) 67   18

	PAGE	TITLE	LINE
SPRING (CONTINUED)			
becomes day) o, it's spring! all the pretty birds	665	(CHAIRE) 67	18
lovely) sweet things cannot spring but we be they'll	666	(CHAIRE) 68	4
such a thing as spring and wonders why So	685	95 POEMS 13	8
guess and as for spring she'll be the first	718	95 POEMS 46	7
becomes singing winter by spring, i lift my diminutive . . .	749	95 POEMS 77	17
winter equals now of spring; but april's day transcends . . .	765	95 POEMS 91	11
and in winter our spring is the yes of	766	95 POEMS 92	31
/ / / / spring! may-- everywhere's here (with	767	95 POEMS 93	1
the may in the spring) live! die (forever is	767	95 POEMS 93	20
dreamed a dream of spring --how you and i	777	73 POEMS 5	15
/ / because it's Spring thingS dare to do	782	73 POEMS 10	2
down to dream of Spring / / / /	816	73 POEMS 44	14
cry sing) for it's Spring --irrevocably; and in earth	835	73 POEMS 63	19
+SPRING			
FOR CONTEXT, SEE	322	VIVA 14	14
FOR CONTEXT, SEE	508	50 POEMS 22	12
SPRING'S			
who would feel if spring's least breathing should cause . . .	450	NO THANKS 65	13
this (mere most) breast spring's million (who are and	573	1 X 1 33	19
SPRINGING			
wistful and precarious bird.) Springing from fragrant	20	T&C PUELLA MEA	153
SPRINGS			
beyond the white authentic springs, beyond the sweet	19	T&C PUELLA MEA	120
radiator made sure her springs were O. K.) i	248	IS 5 ONE 19	8
SPRINGTIME			
the world had in Springtime when the world was	18	T&C PUELLA MEA	56
is our time for springtime is lovetime and viva	591	1 X 1 51	3
is our time for springtime is lovetime and viva	591	1 X 1 51	27
SPRINKLES			
of his grave and sprinkles nowhere with me and	560	1 X 1 20	20
+SPRINKLING			
FOR CONTEXT, SEE	122	& SEVEN POEMS 1	16
SPRINTS			
each (futuring snowily which sprints for the crumb of	639	(CHAIRE) 41	11
SPROUT			
each brave eye shall sprout a tree fruit that	16	T&C SONGS 6	2
Eve aling 2 a -sprout eyelands) sin uously&them&twi tching, .	445	NO THANKS 60	11
(queen poet king float sprout heroes of moonstar flutter . .	586	1 X 1 46	10
SPROUTED			
complete plasticity, shoul- ders, sprouted the extraordinary	97	& POST IMPR 8	36
tiniest forever--crazily from totally sprouted by alive green	480	NEW POEMS 18	23
SPROUTING			
supple financial teeth deliriously sprouting from complacent	201	XLI PORTRAIT 9	3
darkness up through which sprouting gently, the cathedral . .	279	IS 5 THREE 3	3
all about herself the sprouting largest final air plunges . .	301	IS 5 FOUR 18	16
o VER ToWNS SLoWLY SPRoUTING SPIR IT / /	383	NO THANKS 1	11
SPROUTS			
the crank; the box sprouts fairies, out of it	69	T&C POST IMPR 6	2
clothes tumbledish olD (with sprouts o ver and) a-	534	50 POEMS 46	7
SPRUCE			
maple pine by hemlock spruce by tamarack (nothing	658	(CHAIRE) 60	20
SPRUNG			
Cytherea, from frail foam sprung with irrevocable nakedness .	7	T&C EPITHALAM	162
unwinding dizzily & mirrors; sprung dimensionless new alls of	480	NEW POEMS 18	20
SPRY			
dy lu minous edible spry pinks shy lemons greens	179	XLI SONGS 1	7
youse needn't be so spry concernin questions arty each . . .	247	IS 5 ONE 18	1
pretty birds frolic as spry as can fly yes	665	(CHAIRE) 67	5
SPUN			
surpassing nets are sedulously spun to snare the brutal . . .	5	T&C EPITHALAM	86
& e & --cupidoergosum spun= flash omiepsicronlonO-- megaeta?	431	NO THANKS 48	24
SPURN			
(as various worlds he'll spurn rather than fail immeasurable	562	1 X 1 22	7
SPURRED			
nor asleep booted & spurred with an apish grin	640	(CHAIRE) 42	5
SPURTING			
occur bell beyond fiercely spurting bell a jetted music . . .	115	& PORTRAIT 8	18

	PAGE	TITLE	LINE

SPURTING (CONTINUED)
  givers of not) bang spurting mesh (faith -ful which . . . . . 388 NO THANKS 5   12
SPY
  him did an archer spy (whose aim had erred . . . . 360 VIVA 51   15
SQUADS
  not sell his head) squads right impatiently replied two . . . 473 NEW POEMS 11   4
SQUALOR
  from the splendor and squalor of hurrying cities --i . . . . 749 95 POEMS 77   2
SQUARE
  probable violins dance the square virtues and the oblong . . 43 T&C AMORES 7   34
  kiss me with the square crime of life.... Cecile, ... 138 & SON REAL 9   12
  wonderfully stumbled above the square, little amorous-tadpole 173 & SON ACTU 22   3
  fastidious normal explosion; a square mur- mur, a winsome . . 201 XLI PORTRAIT 9   12
  grin give me the Square in spring, the little . . . . 220 XLI SONNETS 16   9
  and slightly expands one square foot mired in silk . . . . . 225 IS 5 ONE LIZ   3
  primates--from which with dignity square feet turned abruptly 326 VIVA 18   25
  as the world aint square with room for the . . . . 568 1 X 1 28   17
SQUASHE
  fly. pre cisel Yhalf (squashe) d with, its, little, ... 94 & POST IMPR 6   28
SQUAT
  for a moon to squat in first darkness --a . . . . 282 IS 5 THREE 6   16
SQUATS
  emperor a cithern- player squats with quiveringgold body . . 34 T&C ORIENTALE 6   71
  and life is worse squats a big dove on . . . . 545 1 X 1 5   11
SQUATTING
  carefully the rolypoly voice squatting on a mountain of . . . 228 IS 5 ONE MARJ   9
  Battle of Because he's squatting in the middle of . . . . . 642 {CHAIRE} 44   4
SQUAWK
  Dick; while Gadgets murder squawk and add, the cult . . . . 438 NO THANKS 54   11
SQUEAK
  Something gushes vaguely a squeak of planes or between . . . 195 XLI PORTRAIT 3   11
+SQUEAK
  FOR CONTEXT, SEE . . . . 656 {CHAIRE} 58   5
SQUEAKED
  of blood; your sex squeaked like a billiard-cue chalking . . 170 & SON ACTU 19   9
+SQUEAKING
  FOR CONTEXT, SEE . . . . 747 95 POEMS 75   13
SQUEAKY
  And the violin spitting squeaky songs into the cuspidor-col . 101 & POST IMPR 11   44
SQUEAL
  terrif iceffort one dirty squeal of soiling light yanKing . . 96 & POST IMPR 8   27
  feel said he (i'll squeal said she just once . . . . 399 NO THANKS 16   2
SQUEALS
  of planes or between squeals of Nothing grabbed with . . . . 195 XLI PORTRAIT 3   13
SQUEEZE
  your prickley-clothes off and squeeze- into-largeness without 127 & SEVEN POEMS 5   33
  and gutted with grace" squeeze your nuts and open . . . . . 407 NO THANKS 24   16
SQUEEZING
  upon their scraggy knees squeezing and buffeting thee that . 46 T&C LA GUERRE 2   16
  whinnied and a man squeezing her waist said the . . . . . . 53 T&C PORTRAIT 1   35
+SQUEEZING
  FOR CONTEXT, SEE . . . . 100 & POST IMPR 11   13
SQUINTING
  stickily point made glints squinting who's a wink bum-nothing 96 & POST IMPR 8   18
SQUINTS
  / / / / squints a blond job at . . . . 545 1 X 1 5   1
+SQUINTS
  FOR CONTEXT, SEE . . . . 726 95 POEMS 54   10
SQUIRM
  the belly whose deep squirm nibbles. another couches, weary, 143 & SON REAL 14   11
  through our hearts hugely squirm roots) us ly; though . . . . 361 VIVA 52   8
  kiss -ing wishes bodies) squirm-of-frightened shy are whichs 437 NO THANKS 53   7
  / worshipping Same they squirm and they spawn and . . . . . 439 NO THANKS 55   2
  eyes would stir and squirm newly as from unburied . . . . . 520 50 POEMS 34   8
  for the right to squirm and the sun strikes . . . . 620 {CHAIRE} 22   1
  (which makes this whenworld squirm turns houses to people . . 841 73 POEMS 69   16
+SQUIRM
  FOR CONTEXT, SEE . . . . 104 & POST IMPR 14   15

	PAGE	TITLE	LINE

+SQUIRM (CONTINUED)
    FOR CONTEXT, SEE . . . . 469 NEW POEMS 7   7
+SQUIRM-OF-FRIGHTENE
    kiss -ing wishes bodies) squirm-of-frightened shy are whichs 437 NO THANKS 53   7
SQUIRMCURL
    from dumb sleePdeep ness squirmcurl ing homonomously . . . . 395 NO THANKS 12   15
SQUIRMING
    suddenl (y down the squirming sPine of the) unsuspecting . . 101 & POST IMPR 11   54
    and legs like white squirming pipes wiggle upon the . . . . . 110 & PORTRAIT 6   7
    and on sprawled eyes squirming with light insane chisel . . . 139 & SON REAL 10   10
    mouth her ugly nipples squirming in pretty wrath, gums . . . 151 & SON REAL 22   9
    perpendicular taste of this squirming cube of undimishied . . 201 XLI PORTRAIT 9   18
    this pole over five squirming mice; or leap through . . . . . 279 IS 5 THREE 3   15
    arms tremble remembering something squirming fragile and . . 279 IS 5 THREE 3   22
    been before they died squirming: now withered and unself . . 506 50 POEMS 20   4
+SQUIRMING
    FOR CONTEXT, SEE . . . . 493 50 POEMS 7   12
    FOR CONTEXT, SEE . . . . 581 1 X 1 41   4
SQUIRMS
    to see how always squirms the skilful mystery of . . . . . . 130 & SON REAL 1   6
    smile over his body squirms kissingly, i will bring . . . . . 161 & SON ACTU 10   6
    sensual chisels i perform squirms of chrome and execute . . . 199 XLI PORTRAIT 7   5
    dark) and thousand thrusts squirms stars Trees, swift each . 356 VIVA 47   7
    his ton of torse squirms a pool of pink . . . . 545 1 X 1 5   6
SQUIRMTHICKLYING
    one street leaps quick squirmthicklying lu minous night mare 493 50 POEMS 7   12
SQUIRMWRITHED
    trickle curselaughgroping shrieks bubble squirmwrithed . . . 330 VIVA 21   4
+SQUIRMY
    FOR CONTEXT, SEE . . . . 150 & SON REAL 21   4
SQUIRREL
    chased two flights of squirrel-stairs into a mid-victorian . 194 XLI PORTRAIT 2   7
SQUIRREL-STAIRS
    chased two flights of squirrel-stairs into a mid-victorian . 194 XLI PORTRAIT 2   7
SQUIRTING
    waltz the glush of squirting taps plus slush of . . . . 96 & POST IMPR 8   13
    please squirtnowing for o squirting we're replies (at which . 343 VIVA 34   9
+SQUIRTINGLY
    FOR CONTEXT, SEE . . . . 330 VIVA 21   9
SQUIRTNOWING
    like now That please squirtnowing for o squirting we're . . . 343 VIVA 34   8
SQUIRTS
    ving lump of twilight squirts a two ne like . . . . 602 (CHAIRE) 4   2
+SQUIRTS
    FOR CONTEXT, SEE . . . . 332 VIVA 23   27
SS
    receive the philophilic name S.S. VAN MERDE) having first . . 334 VIVA 25   4
ST
    near calm (Bright) calm st?? holy (soft briGht deep) . . . . 455 NO THANKS 70   6
    of the stars 14th st dis (because my tears . . . . 697 95 POEMS 25   29
+ST LOUIS
    FOR CONTEXT, SEE . . . . 237 IS 5 ONE 8   7
STA
    briGht deep) yeS near sta? calm star big yEs . . . . 455 NO THANKS 70   8
STAB
    (whom, blinds; blood) pa-nt stab are (slopped givers of . . . 388 NO THANKS 5   10
STABBING
    winter and will the stabbing music of your white . . . . . . 218 XLI SONNETS 14   2
STABLE
    Ears win- k, funny stable. In the morning they . . . . 171 & SON ACTU 20   8
STAG
    o ld as who stag geri ng up some . . . . 703 95 POEMS 31   2
STAGE
    frame of a microscopic stage whose jouncing curtain. , . . . 55 T&C PORTRAIT 3   7
    silence and dismay that stage which shall not know . . . . . 75 T&C SON REAL 6   4
STAGGERED
    comb my mumbling gropeofstrength (staggered by the lug of . . 137 & SON REAL 8   2
    into my arms and staggered banged with terror through . . . . 258 IS 5 ONE 28   23

		PAGE	TITLE	LINE

STAGGERFUL
curselaughgroping shrieks bubble squirmwrithed staggerful . . 330 VIVA 21   4
+STAGGERING
FOR CONTEXT, SEE . . . . 703 95 POEMS 31   2
STAGS
tense deer. Four tall stags at a green mountain . . . . . . 14 T&C SONGS 4 29
STAINS
with bright knives, it stains itself, with currants and . . . 100 & POST IMPR 11 23
STAIRS
chased two flights of squirrel-stairs into a mid-victorian . 194 XLI PORTRAIT 2   7
"coming up these dark stairs. / / / / . . . . 353 VIVA 44 32
the top of these stairs, there's a free room. . . . . 365 VIVA 56   7
hearing somebody coming up stairs, carefully (carefully . . . 375 VIVA 66 11
stillness, climbing the carpeted stairs of terror) and . . . 375 VIVA 66 14
the top of the stairs speaks in his kind . . . . 813 73 POEMS 41   1
STALE
s (t into a stale shriek like an alarm-clock) . . . . 49 T&C IMPRESS 3 27
STALIN
save a world for stalin was he aiming ; . . . . 643 (CHAIRE) 45   3
STALINIST
civilization i'll kiss a stalinist arse in hitler's window . 514 50 POEMS 28 12
STALKED
(where once good lips stalked or eyes firmly stirred) . . . . 360 VIVA 51   2
STALKS
u t) flesh stalks the Momentinmyarms your expression . . . . 94 & POST IMPR 6 22
STALLION
of steep song a stallion sweetness , the lips . . . . 59 T&C PORTRAIT 7 15
to ride a watersmooth-silver stallion and break . . . . 60 T&C PORTRAIT 8   5
STALWART
revealed) this tall strong stalwart youth, what sight shall . 254 IS 5 ONE 25   2
STAMENS&PISTIL
/ / innerly UningstrolL (stamens&pistil silent A s . . . . . 342 VIVA 33   3
STAMMER
alive, cleaving the luminous stammer of bodies (eagerly just 174 & SON ACTU 23   4
+STAMP
FOR CONTEXT, SEE . . . . 519 50 POEMS 33   2
STAMPS
who stops. Smiles. he stamps / / / / . . . . 437 NO THANKS 53 18
+STAMPS
FOR CONTEXT, SEE . . . . 773 73 POEMS 1 11
STAND
sonal crea- tures --Children, stand with circular frightened 69 T&C POST IMPR 6   7
words as, uttering overmuch, stand helplessly before the . . 76 T&C SON UNRE 1   8
away, and the trees stand. I think i too . . . . 80 T&C SON UNRE 5   3
sky and the trees stand: the trees stand. The . . . . 80 T&C SON UNRE 5 15
trees stand: the trees stand. The trees, suddenly wait . . . 80 T&C SON UNRE 5 16
as she does not stand-ing. unsits her (wrist performs . . . . 159 & SON ACTU 8   3
you're quite dressed you'll stand in the window for . . . . 192 XLI CHANSONS 2 22
songs be sung; yet stand They here enraptured, as . . . . . 208 XLI SONNETS 4 12
never, never Never to stand at no window because . . . . . . 242 IS 5 ONE 13 20
-ling to a: dead. stand- ; Still) / / . . . . 248 IS 5 ONE 19 37
stood and thou shalt stand. Nor any dusk but . . . . 351 VIVA 42 12
Clouds take sun mountains stand And oceans do Not . . . . . . 359 VIVA 50 13
does not dare to stand or sit may take . . . . 466 NEW POEMS 4   3
of because do not stand against yes which is . . . . 512 50 POEMS 26 29
mind of sun will stand, so strictly (over utmost . . . . . . 520 50 POEMS 34 26
forever's very now we stand nor a first rose . . . . 538 50 POEMS 50 12
float twitter faces) only stand with me, love! against . . . 633 (CHAIRE) 35   6
less? into not) love, stand with me while silence . . . . . 633 (CHAIRE) 35 12
1944 A D "can stand against the argument of . . . . 636 (CHAIRE) 38 10
/ / / to stand (alone) in some autumnal . . . . 674 95 POEMS 2   1
noone and a star stand, am to am (life . . . . 721 95 POEMS 49   1
one; and one celestial) stand soul to soul: freedom . . . . 721 95 POEMS 49   8
/ / / / stand with your lover on . . . . 743 95 POEMS 71   1
tree (and how i'll stand more still than still) . . . . . . 752 95 POEMS 80   3
twilight of winter will stand (over a snowstopped silent . . 808 73 POEMS 36   1
this wonderful tree smiling stand (all realms of where . . . 832 73 POEMS 60   5

STAND-ING
    as she does not stand-ing. unsits her (wrist performs . . . . 159 & SON ACTU 8   3
STANDARDS
    the marching dead, with standards and the neighing of . . . . 209 XLI SONNETS 5   4
STANDEST
    moult) amazing doom who standest as thou hast stood . . . . . 351 VIVA 42   12
STANDING
    moment? As i was standing on the third rail . . . . 262 IS 5 ONE 32   2
    tall like a rose) standing near my swaying over . . . . 352 VIVA 43   7
    / / / so standing, our eyes filled with . . . . 378 VIVA 69   1
    spring who moved by standing in november's may) from . . . . 420 NO THANKS 37   4
    bride & groom are standing) in a kind of . . . . 470 NEW POEMS 8   2
    gloam ing together are standing together un der a . . . . . . 600 (CHAIRE) 2   6
    only now is forever: standing erect in the deathless . . . . 749 95 POEMS 77   19
    if) a bespangled clown standing on eighth street handed . . . 802 73 POEMS 30   5
+STANDING
    FOR CONTEXT, SEE . . . . 532 50 POEMS 44   18
STANDS
    altar at whose head stands that clear candle whose . . . . . 6 T&C EPITHALAM 117
    tremendous hair that blossom stands whereof is most desire, . 6 T&C EPITHALAM 146
    thinned of pity--so he stands counting the moved myriads . . 9 T&C SONGS 1   14
    beckons, she rises she stands a moment in the . . . . 35 T&C ORIENTALE 6 110
    ardor the yellow lover stands in the dumb dark . . . . 37 T&C AMORES 2   12
    nigger smiles the jew stands beside his teddy-bears the . . . 108 & PORTRAIT 4   23
    long eyes as she stands, with her long hard . . . . 147 & SON REAL 18   2
    you as a foal stands but as the trees, ... 154 & SON ACTU 3   16
    upper class American unsullied stands, before the world: with 273 IS 5 TWO 8   17
    middle of a room stands a suicide sniffing a . . . . 338 VIVA 29   2
    of a morning Memory stands, with clumsily wilted fingers . . 359 VIVA 50   5
    a most smashed unworld stands unslain he which knows . . . . 414 NO THANKS 31   6
    moves; and every part stands still: / / / . . . . 446 NO THANKS 61   14
    in it kind of stands on a thin ring . . . . 470 NEW POEMS 8   10
    a thin ring which stands on a much less . . . . 470 NEW POEMS 8   11
    & which kinder of stands on a much more . . . . 470 NEW POEMS 8   14
    to no) who still stands still as found some . . . . 516 50 POEMS 30   4
    selves of space-- life stands gradually upon four minds . . . 517 50 POEMS 31   8
    progress doth impart one stands supreme i mean the . . . . . 544 1 X 1 4   3
    till the god's truth stands art-naked: you and the . . . . . 605 (CHAIRE) 7   3
    in the way he stands and looks and leaps . . . . 774 73 POEMS 2   15
    blindly stare life herSelf stands / / / / . . . . 780 73 POEMS 8   9
    fall i ng) he StandS lift ing against the . . . . 826 73 POEMS 54   9
+STANDS
    FOR CONTEXT, SEE . . . . 469 NEW POEMS 7   16
    FOR CONTEXT, SEE . . . . 658 (CHAIRE) 60   17
+STANDSTILL
    FOR CONTEXT, SEE . . . . 248 IS 5 ONE 19   37
STAR
    song-- as the first star perfects the sensual dome . . . . . 7 T&C EPITHALAM 164
    me and became a star in the kingdom of . . . . 30 T&C ORIENTALE 4 32
    devours darkness the hungry star which will e -ven . . . . . 49 T&C IMPRESS 3   12
    my head a shooting star Bur s (t into . . . . 49 T&C IMPRESS 3   24
    / the waddling madam star taps taps. "ready girls". . . . . . 108 & PORTRAIT 4   2
    a slippery mess, a star sleepily, feebly, scratches the . . . 144 & SON REAL 15   9
    this very frail enormous star (do you see it?) . . . . 155 & SON ACTU 4   13
    seeks play: withs of star link clauses of warmth . . . . . . 168 & SON ACTU 17   14
    is west eighth, a star or three annoys me, ... 169 & SON ACTU 18   2
    soul. rarely-beloved a single star is uttered, and i . . . . 186 XLI SONGS 8   19
    this most early single star which tugs weakly at . . . . . . 305 IS 5 FIVE 4   5
    disa) ular, (ppear ah! Star whycol our ed shy . . . . 349 VIVA 40   10
    stoops to blend her star with what huge merciful . . . . . . 351 VIVA 42   15
    afraid-- here's the earliest star (have you a wish?) . . . . 357 VIVA 48   2
    partly nor some edgeless star could give that anguish . . . . 414 NO THANKS 31   9
    dusk) wondering why this star does not fall into . . . . . . 428 NO THANKS 45   4
    thought should weigh a star --dreads dying least; and . . . . 446 NO THANKS 61   7
    on one not imaginable star : then a small . . . . 454 NO THANKS 69   12
    yeS near sta? calm star big yEs alone (wHo . . . . 455 NO THANKS 70   8
    failure with thy freedom: star isful beckoningly fabulous . . 456 NO THANKS 71   14
    a mostless more of star o- pening of (writhing . . . . . . 480 NEW POEMS 18   13

		PAGE	TITLE	LINE

STAR (CONTINUED)
most least eye of star and without was if . . . . 502 50 POEMS 16   4
only moon the with star one moving are twilight . . . . 518 50 POEMS 32   3
pure a heart of star by him could steer . . . . 520 50 POEMS 34   22
lifelump buried by the star nicked ends next among . . . . . 522 50 POEMS 35   5
your eyes any illimitable star / / / / . . . . 526 50 POEMS 38   12
because; each why of star (afloat on not quite . . . . 575 1 X 1 35   19
uplifts of stars the star (sing! every joy) --wholly . . . . 582 1 X 1 42   13
before silence begins a star / / / / . . . . 601 (CHAIRE) 3   20
unmotion roams the youngest star) --how should a fool . . . . 609 (CHAIRE) 11   12
his hand a little star no bigger than not . . . . 622 (CHAIRE) 24   3
so unimaginably young a star / / / / . . . . 626 (CHAIRE) 28   14
milly befriended a stranded star whose rays five languid . . 682 95 POEMS 10   5
shall blossom a first star) one / / / . . . . 720 95 POEMS 48   14
/ noone a star stand, am to am . . . . 721 95 POEMS 49   1
dream; dancin g you Star / / / / . . . . 733 95 POEMS 61   12
larger than alive any star goes round --a dream . . . . 735 95 POEMS 63   4
nearness pauses, while a star can grow all distance . . . . . 750 95 POEMS 78   1
as i then that Star goes under the earth . . . . 752 95 POEMS 80   8
which is every) un (star rain snow moon dream . . . . 753 95 POEMS 81   14
sun more last than star --do lovers love? why . . . . 768 95 POEMS 94   12
most mercifully glorying keen star whom she-and-he-like ifs . 808 73 POEMS 36   7
did you see it?) star to disappear, that hugest . . . . 809 73 POEMS 37   12
the mercy of that star, if out of climbing . . . . 811 73 POEMS 39   11
it is by every star a different time, and . . . . 817 73 POEMS 45   1
again --to livingest one star as small these all . . . . . . 819 73 POEMS 47   17
our blonder than blondest star the most mysterious (eliena, . 825 73 POEMS 53   2
+STAR
FOR CONTEXT, SEE . . . . 455 NO THANKS 70   2
FOR CONTEXT, SEE . . . . 455 NO THANKS 70   6
FOR CONTEXT, SEE . . . . 455 NO THANKS 70   8
FOR CONTEXT, SEE . . . . 532 50 POEMS 44   20
FOR CONTEXT, SEE . . . . 586 1 X 1 46   10
FOR CONTEXT, SEE . . . . 752 95 POEMS 80   1
STAR'S
night's loose sack a star's nibbling in- fin -i- . . . . . . 49 T&C IMPRESS 3   3
STARE
gorge sly slim gods stare / / / / . . . . 90 & POST IMPR 2   16
people look (while people stare arranging and changing . . . 124 & SEVEN POEMS 3   5
Old things, while people stare carefully moving a perhaps . . 124 & SEVEN POEMS 3   15
lustfulhunched deeplytoplay lips and stare the gross . . . . 153 & SON ACTU 6   6
the uncouthly Her. thuglike stare the pollenizing vacancy . . 159 & SON ACTU 8   14
see and how they'll stare! oh but you'll be . . . . 192 XLI CHANSONS 2   23
still 5 o'clock I stare only always into the . . . . 202 XLI PORTRAIT 9   43
fire, creating smoothness. People stare, the drunker applaud 279 IS 5 THREE 3   17
turn men's sea to stare their faith to how . . . . 580 1 X 1 40   8
two dim disks of stare are still wondering if . . . . 605 (CHAIRE) 7   13
other un good people stare for it or he . . . . 662 (CHAIRE) 64   11
their minds) eyes blindly stare life herSelf stands / . . . . 780 73 POEMS 8   8
of the floor quietly Stare a poisoned mouse still . . . . . . 784 73 POEMS 12   3
sky with a blind stare, he whispers "i ran" . . . . 800 73 POEMS 28   24
STARES
very deafly a most stares colossal hoax of clocks . . . . . . 659 (CHAIRE) 61   13
STARFISH
because harm symmetry earthquakes starfish (but because . . . 452 NO THANKS 67   16
STARHUMS
gulls' drift Of thickly starhums wherefore & wormSmile . . . 371 VIVA 62   23
STARHUSHED
birds-- but o the starhushed silence which our third's . . . 844 73 POEMS 72   3
STARING
the innumerable capering damned) --staring wildly up and down 118 & PORTRAIT 10   39
year) ago i found staring me in the face . . . . 296 IS 5 FOUR 13   15
quick way of slowly staring and such hair) the . . . . 337 VIVA 28   8
/ but he" i staring into winter twi light . . . . 823 73 POEMS 51   3
STARINGS
bruiseD Suddenly by thousand starings rinsed with thoroughly 388 NO THANKS 5   7
STARK
abian <> garnished of stark Picasso throttling trees hither . 180 XLI SONGS 2   6

STARK (CONTINUED)
with pure reeking with stark and fearlessly obscene but . . . 407 NO THANKS 24   5
STARLESSNESS
yearns where in tense starlessness anoint with ardor the . . 37 T&C AMORES 2   9
STARRED
while emanating the triple starred Hotel du Golf... that . . 319 VIVA 11   21
STARRILY
One : petals him starrily her and around ing . . . . 584 1 X 1 44   9
STARS
with calm of intent stars circling the acerb pole . . . . . . 3 T&C EPITHALAM   31
seethes a flutter of stars a turbulence of forms . . . . . . 31 T&C ORIENTALE 5   8
bursting of the wafted stars (in time to come . . . . 36 T&C AMORES 1   20
crumbles one by one stars flutter into dust but . . . . . . 38 T&C AMORES 3   8
me, moon and sunset stars and flowers gold crescendo . . . . 39 T&C AMORES 4   7
darkness and beauty of stars was on my mouth . . . . 39 T&C AMORES 4   17
breath of all persisting stars / / / / . . . . 40 T&C AMORES 4   47
ill of the pretty stars and to the serene . . . . 43 T&C AMORES 7   15
with the pale important stars and the Humorous moon . . . . . 44 T&C AMORES 8   16
rise up putting off stars and it is dawn . . . . 50 T&C IMPRESS 4   1
hours descend, putting on stars.... in the street of . . . . 50 T&C IMPRESS 4   32
(and just as smaller stars begin to husk heaven) . . . . . . 71 T&C SON REAL 2   11
God-- (behold! where chaste stars writhe captured in . . . . 77 T&C SON UNRE 2   17
eyes the dangerous first stars) people move love hurry . . . 93 & POST IMPR 5   10
these two most early stars wincing upon a single . . . . . . 98 & POST IMPR 9   6
flight into the absolute stars the gods are swallowed . . . . 112 & PORTRAIT 6   83
three or two young stars with spades of silver . . . . . . 115 & PORTRAIT 8   3
houses curl thirstily. Dead stars stink. dawn. Inane, the . . 139 & SON REAL 10   13
smash.... grass, and the stars, of my shoulder in . . . . . . 153 & SON ACTU 2   8
night slowly when several stars are opening one beyond . . . 156 & SON ACTU 5   2
thee again for the stars have been finished in . . . . 184 XLI SONGS 6   10
herself where the wet stars softly are keeping their . . . . 206 XLI SONNETS 2   9
are like unto the stars of Heaven.... i do . . . . 256 IS 5 ONE 27   21
a million billion trillion stars / / / / . . . . 258 IS 5 ONE 28   24
things and but the stars for instance everything is . . . . 322 VIVA 14   3
and thousand thrusts squirms stars Trees, swift each with . . 356 VIVA 47   7
June, having of certain stars and planets heard, rose . . . . 360 VIVA 51   12
how several smoothly gesturing stars are clever to persuade . 376 VIVA 67   8
with large first new stars knitting the structure of . . . . 378 VIVA 69   7
deft strictly horrors which stars may not observe; while . . 386 NO THANKS 3   8
win (like touch all stars or to live in . . . . 433 NO THANKS 50   11
mirrors from whispers to stars; climbing silence for ifs . . 439 NO THANKS 55   22
are more flowering than stars whitely births of mind . . . . 450 NO THANKS 65   5
must bait laws with stars to catch telescopes) . . . . . . 478 NEW POEMS 16   6
dollhead wandering under weakening stars Feels; if & god . . 479 NEW POEMS 17   10
than teach ten thousand stars how not to dance . . . . . . 484 NEW POEMS 22   14
their same sun moon stars rain children guessed (but . . . . 515 50 POEMS 29   8
they slept their dream stars rain sun moon (and . . . . . . 515 50 POEMS 29   21
their came sun moon stars rain / / / . . . . 515 50 POEMS 29   36
flesh and trees, poor stars and stones, but never . . . . . 554 1 X 1 14   11
sun and yanks immortal stars awry? Blow king to . . . . . . 560 1 X 1 20   4
now himself uplifts of stars the star (sing! every . . . . . 582 1 X 1 42   13
lifting "flowers" more all stars than eyes "only are . . . . 603 {CHAIRE} 5   13
she did and now stars shine at night / . . . . 622 {CHAIRE} 24   8
the sun and the stars and the moon are . . . . 686 95 POEMS 14   16
self while nobody (and stars moon sun fall rise . . . . . . 693 95 POEMS 21   18
the meaning of the stars 14th st dis (because . . . . 697 95 POEMS 25   28
and stop ten thousand stars but not one heartbeat . . . . . 714 95 POEMS 42   10
by love though the stars walk backward) honour the . . . . . 732 95 POEMS 60   8
minds to call the stars. And (darling) never fear: . . . . . 741 95 POEMS 69   9
wonder that's keeping the stars apart i carry your . . . . . 766 95 POEMS 92   14
of seem though the stars in their silence say . . . . 801 73 POEMS 29   17
moon, and all my stars / / / / . . . . 810 73 POEMS 38   14
your morning feeling their stars have risen through your . . 812 73 POEMS 40   8
der ful sun moon stars the all, & a . . . . 840 73 POEMS 68   12
START
cruelly for us and start the last leaf whirling . . . . . . 80 T&C SON UNRE 5   10
ook-- s U n: starT birDs (1EAp) Openi ng . . . . 347 VIVA 38   30
/ / / "let's start a magazine to hell . . . . 407 NO THANKS 24   1

START (CONTINUED)
/ / / to start, to hesitate; to stop . . . . 650 {CHAIRE} 52   1
+START
FOR CONTEXT, SEE . . . . 226 IS 5 ONE MAME 13
STARTED
/ / / it started when Bill's chip let . . . . 145 & SON REAL 16 1
my Uncle Sol and started a worm farm) / . . . . 239 IS 5 ONE 10 38
STARTING
/ ecco a letter starting "dearest we" unsigned: remarkably . 504 50 POEMS 18 1
STARTLED
who (look) . , startled / / / / . . . . 286 IS 5 FOUR 3 24
new- ness and these startled whats are a (piercing . . . . . 437 NO THANKS 53 6
STARTLING
, rises upon one startling doll undressed in unripe . . . . . 55 T&C PORTRAIT 3 8
STARTS
and y play, b starts armenian record pho nographisrunn . . . 200 XLI PORTRAIT 8 24
STARVE
our slightly fingering spirits starve and smother; until . . 305 IS 5 FIVE 4 7
STARVED
in time shut and starved on space? love's murdered . . . . . 527 50 POEMS 39 12
STATE
itself must call a state submicroscopic is-- compared with . 561 1 X 1 21 3
that if the quote state unquote says "kill" killing . . . . . 636 {CHAIRE} 38 7
+STATE
FOR CONTEXT, SEE . . . . 803 73 POEMS 31 6
STATES
president of the united states The president of the . . . . . 392 NO THANKS 9 17
president of the united states of The President Of . . . . . 392 NO THANKS 9 18
President Of The) United States Of America unde negant . . . 392 NO THANKS 9 18
+STATESMEN
FOR CONTEXT, SEE . . . . 405 NO THANKS 22 3
STATING
luffed --thanking me; and (stating that she hoped we . . . . 326 VIVA 18 36
STATISTICS
too preponderatingly because unless statistics lie he was . . 339 VIVA 30 41
STATUE
anus stick some quote statue unquote to prove that . . . . . 636 {CHAIRE} 38 2
hell and bury the statue of liberty (because it . . . . 711 95 POEMS 39 27
STATUES
is worth a million statues / / / / . . . . 247 IS 5 ONE 18 8
(ponder, darling, these busted statues of yon motheaten forum 260 IS 5 ONE 30 1
STAUNCH
grin whereon a dozen staunch and leal citizens did . . . . . 258 IS 5 ONE 28 9
STAY
if sometimes my eyes stay at home then my . . . . 100 & POST IMPR 11 18
for your face O stay with me slightly. or . . . . 165 & SON ACTU 14 10
said she) may i stay said he (which way . . . . 399 NO THANKS 16 13
STEAD
of my shoulder in stead. It is a funny, ... 153 & SON ACTU 2 8
their own persons (in stead of everybodyelse's) but what's . 782 73 POEMS 10 12
STEADILY
cowers, seeing green armies steadily expand hearing the . . .   4 T&C EPITHALAM 71
their flattened arms complain steadily against the west one . 434 NO THANKS 51 13
+STEADY
FOR CONTEXT, SEE . . . . 387 NO THANKS 4 15
STEAK
ews eye like the steak all ried but eye . . . . 405 NO THANKS 22 11
tommy) we order a steak and they send us . . . . 513 50 POEMS 27 15
STEAL
tigers of smooth sweetness steal slowly in dumb blossoms . . 139 & SON REAL 10 3
and sold giving to steal and cruel kind, a . . . . 521 50 POEMS 34 57
give so breathing's to steal-- five wishes are five . . . . . 543 1 X 1 3 16
STEALING
of sudden lust her stealing body ex- pending gathering . . . 34 T&C ORIENTALE 6 91
asleep i look where stealing needles of foam in . . . . 64 T&C POST IMPR 1 2
of resistless metal: and (stealing toward the blissful pair) 799 73 POEMS 27 20
STEALS
rising from thy bed steals to his wife the . . . .   3 T&C EPITHALAM 6

	PAGE	TITLE	LINE

STEALS (CONTINUED)
a furtive occult fragrance steals, a gesture of immaculate . 19 T&C PUELLA MEA 106
sleep some silver-fingered fountain steals the world. / / . . 208 XLI SONNETS 4   14
STEALTH
or time; a naming stealth of ecstasy means, like . . . . . . 168 & SON ACTU 17   9
STEALTHILY
have seen her a stealthily frail flower walking with . . . . 214 XLI SONNETS 10   1
that fierce few flowers (stealthily) in the alive west . . . 277 IS 5 THREE 1   2
STEAM
(who stood within his steam be- ginning and began . . . . . . 523 50 POEMS 36   7
STEEDS
the neighing of great steeds moving to war across . . . . . . 209 XLI SONNETS 5   4
STEEL
while others wrote in steel, accept all praise of . . . . . . 209 XLI SONNETS 5   10
STEEP
is silent, of the steep unspeaking tower within whose . . . .   4 T&C EPITHALAM 50
a new wine from steep hills by darkness softly . . . .   9 T&C SONGS 1   36
us into the serious steep darkness / / / . . . . 41 T&C AMORES 5   36
against the margins of steep song a stallion sweetness . . . 59 T&C PORTRAIT 7 14
jazz whose arched occasional steep youth swallows curvingly . 140 & SON REAL 11   5
announce: hurl) blind full steep love / / / . . . . 422 NO THANKS 39   16
imperfect gaze climbs this steep fragrance of eternity) world 450 NO THANKS 65   8
adventure (wish by terror) steep not guessable each infinite 757 95 POEMS 85   21
a gay and a steep) deep rush through amazing . . . . 769 95 POEMS 95   14
down (in a most steep more than music) feeling . . . . 816 73 POEMS 44   5
citizen of ecstasies more steep than climb can time . . . . . 845 73 POEMS 73   8
STEEPED
till my thighs are steeped in burning flowers I . . . . 189 XLI SONGS 11   2
STEEPER
they drink who've climbed steeper than hopes are fears . . . 563 1 X 1 23   3
STEEPEST
may i achieve another steepest thing-- how more than . . . . 558 1 X 1 18   10
STEEPLE
the bell in the steeple says Why the chary . . . . 801 73 POEMS 29   5
STEEPLES
people than houses and steeples and clouds: go sailing . . . 129 & SEVEN POEMS 7 9
choke and snore the steeples writhe with rain) faces . . . . 340 VIVA 31   4
people smiles faces streets steeples are eagerly tumbl ing . 835 73 POEMS 63   6
STEEPNESS
iron breathing height eating steepness the ship climbs . . . 419 NO THANKS 36   14
STEER
mouth toward my mouth, steer our lost bodies carefully . . . 215 XLI SONNETS 11 17
star by him could steer and pure so now . . . . 520 50 POEMS 34   22
shall entirely our doom steer his great small wish . . . . . 528 50 POEMS 40   7
selves, into infinite tomorrow steer --souls under whom flow 659 (CHAIRE) 61   4
STEERED
you hurt tho nithe steered his big was) thither . . . . 316 VIVA 8   12
STEERING
sails out of sleep steering for dream / / . . . . 781 73 POEMS 9   4
STEM
petals. with the caving stem. But of all most . . . . 215 XLI SONNETS 11 8
collywobbling on its feeble stem is believing science=(2b)-n 329 VIVA 20   3
STENCH
(it shall bury much stench) and a hundred joys . . . . 439 NO THANKS 55   12
STEP
monstrous din watch your step and follow me stooping . . . . 117 & PORTRAIT 10 27
moving purely with muted step, yet somewhat proudly too-- . . 211 XLI SONNETS 7 9
in between bottles, who step smoothly and rapidly along . . . 279 IS 5 THREE 3   14
+STEP
FOR CONTEXT, SEE . . . . 464 NEW POEMS 2   31
STEPP
dreamhorse pulling (smoothloomingly) through (stepp) this . . 437 NO THANKS 53   2
STEPPED
touched n.y. our skeleton stepped from his cupboard gallantly 326 VIVA 18   10
've (whoever we are) stepped carefully o ver (& . . . . 668 (CHAIRE) 70   16
STEPPING
all i hear your stepping freakish feet feet incorrigible . . 61 T&C PORTRAIT 9 34

		PAGE	TITLE	LINE

STEPS
him silently with becoming steps to seek your face . . . . . 42 T&C AMORES 6   13
mouths take big wobbly foot-steps every goggle cent of . . . 96 & POST IMPR 8   20
wispish-agile feet with slid steps parting the tousle of . . 140 & SON REAL 11   15
free, upon the front steps of her home by . . . . 273 IS 5 TWO 8   19
butbutbut?? tonton??? ing???? --Out-& steps; which . . . . . 445 NO THANKS 60   19
--whereupon out (SlO wLy) steps (to mount the wand) . . . . . 697 95 POEMS 25   16
STERILIZED
the ego approaches) painfully sterilized contours; within . . 319 VIVA 11   28
STERN
teethful hours wilts the stern texture of Now the . . . . . . 112 & PORTRAIT 6   80
flesh i make me stern against your charming strength . . . . 182 XLI SONGS 4   13
a tear within his stern blue eye, upon his . . . . 273 IS 5 TWO 8   9
deep most invincible unthing --stern sexual timelessness, . . 351 VIVA 42   3
worlds inhabited by roamingly stern bright faeries if you . . 363 VIVA 54   4
which could grin may stern particular Love surround your . . 522 50 POEMS 35   10
more minds ignorant of stern miraculous this every . . . . . 556 1 X 1 16   5
STERNLY
crouched, quivering, upon the sternly allotted sandpile --how 231 IS 5 ONE 3   51
eternal; quite perhaps as sternly much not life nor . . . . . 371 VIVA 62   25
STETTI
are turned to seem) "stetti" and willbeishfully bursting un- 387 NO THANKS 4   15
STEVE
thought lucinda looked like steve / / / / . . . . 706 95 POEMS 34   4
+STEVENSON
FOR CONTEXT, SEE . . . . 73 T&C SON REAL 4   12
STEWED
but Jimmie lived regular. stewed three times a week. . . . . 149 & SON REAL 20   11
STIC-KY
and helplessbaby blues and stic-ky chromes and pretty- lemons 100 & POST IMPR 11   5
STICK
keep your teeth snowy, stick to beer and lime, ... 71 T&C SON REAL 2   4
shuddering burrs of light stick on my brain harder . . . . . 136 & SON REAL 7   7
one with his magic stick (in which a willing . . . . 282 IS 5 THREE 6   27
of a park anus stick some quote statue unquote . . . . 636 (CHAIRE) 38   2
ing up a magical stick t, a, p, s . . . . 697 95 POEMS 25   8
STICKILY
eyes pout ges- tures stickily point made glints squinting . . 96 & POST IMPR 8   18
STICKING
a blue woman with sticking out breasts hanging clothes. . . . 167 & SON ACTU 16   1
lurks, a Beau Brummell sticking in its three- cornered . . . 227 IS 5 ONE GERT   4
a cold to skylessness sticking fire my are your . . . . 541 1 X 1 1   4
STICKINGLY
nobody shoulder and thick stickingly un stride after glide . 522 50 POEMS 35   3
STICKS
m usil (age) ini sticks tuh de mans 1 . . . . 325 VIVA 17   4
out of twigs and sticks; / / / / . . . . 580 1 X 1 40   28
/ / old age sticks up Keep Off signs) . . . . 729 95 POEMS 57   1
STICKY
mouth your eyes are sticky with dreams and you . . . . 61 T&C PORTRAIT 9   14
looked long at the sticky moon opening in dusk . . . . 170 & SON ACTU 19   2
+STICKY
FOR CONTEXT, SEE . . . . 100 & POST IMPR 11   5
STIFF
and then he will stiff-ly throw the shell away . . . . 69 T&C POST IMPR 6   18
know consequently a little stiff i was careful of . . . . . . 248 IS 5 ONE 19   4
STIFF-LY
and then he will stiff-ly throw the shell away . . . . 69 T&C POST IMPR 6   18
STIFFENED
the tree leaps a stiffened exquisite i wait the . . . . 182 XLI SONGS 4   8
Brushing from whom the stiffened puke i put him . . . . 258 IS 5 ONE 28   21
STIFFENING
only to trace with stiffening slow shrill eyes beyond . . . . 155 & SON ACTU 4   8
of unbeing (fro on stiffening greenly air and to . . . . . . 633 (CHAIRE) 35   4
STIFFENS
gathering pouring upon itself stiffenS to a white thorn . . . 34 T&C ORIENTALE 6   92
+STIFFLY
FOR CONTEXT, SEE . . . . 69 T&C POST IMPR 6   18

		PAGE	TITLE	LINE

+STIFFLY (CONTINUED)

FOR CONTEXT, SEE . . . . 445 NO THANKS 60   1

STIFLES

ropes of thing and stifles forests in white ago? . . . . . . 560 1 X 1 20   12

STILE

boy's asleep under a stile he sees eight and . . . . 15 T&C SONGS 5   2
boy's asleep under the stile for every mile the . . . . . . 15 T&C SONGS 5   18

STILL

more burning rain? And still the mad magnificent herald . . . 4 T&C EPITHALAM   57
from palpitating veils. O still miraculous May! O shining . . 5 T&C EPITHALAM   105
in the gloom! and still to be immortal is . . . . 9 T&C SONGS 1   24
the present writing one still finds delighted fingers . . . . 70 T&C SON REAL 1   7
word and you lie still as anything in largeness . . . . . . 127 & SEVEN POEMS 5   34
leans a lady whose still-born smile involves the comedy . . . 144 & SON REAL 15   13
of silence, it is) still 5 o'clock I stare . . . . 202 XLI PORTRAIT 9   42
a: dead. stand- ; Still) / / / / . . . . 248 IS 5 ONE 19   38
matter of not keeping still; we were two alert . . . . . . 289 IS 5 FOUR 6   23
my trembling where my still unvisible when. Wait if . . . . . 372 VIVA 63   5
and every part stands still: / / / / . . . . 446 NO THANKS 61   14
not dying) Is will still occur; birds disappear becomingly: . 452 NO THANKS 67   13
snow and stir by still anyone's any was all . . . . 515 50 POEMS 29   15
every to no) who still stands still as found . . . . 516 50 POEMS 30   4
no) who still stands still as found some lost . . . . 516 50 POEMS 30   4
from tame to teem) still doth our hero contemplate . . . . 544 1 X 1 4   19
the single secret will still be man what if . . . . 560 1 X 1 20   8
were it five, i'd still insist that all history . . . . . . 579 1 X 1 39   6
do, we'll move away still further: into now / . . . . 579 1 X 1 39   14
disks of stare are still wondering if the stunt . . . . . . 605 (CHAIRE) 7   13
we can hear him still if now our sun . . . . 624 (CHAIRE) 26   21
flopped over and lay still while he passed (as . . . . . . 648 (CHAIRE) 50   7
tombstones try to re (still u ntumbled but slant . . . . . 695 95 POEMS 23   7
alive (but jim stood still for a thousand years . . . . . . 709 95 POEMS 37   15
more (& more & still More) what the hell . . . . 727 95 POEMS 55   20
how i'll stand more still than still) and what . . . . . . 752 95 POEMS 80   3
stand more still than still) and what he'll sing . . . . . 752 95 POEMS 80   3
old frank go bluer still as (shifting his life . . . . . . 754 95 POEMS 82   6
same thing twice and still that singing's always his . . . . 760 95 POEMS 87   4
Stare a poisoned mouse still who alive is asking . . . . . . 784 73 POEMS 12   5
rubythroat's home with its still ness which really's herself 827 73 POEMS 55   9

STILL-BORN

leans a lady whose still-born smile involves the comedy . . . 144 & SON REAL 15   13

STILLED

The flute of morning stilled in noon-- noon the . . . . . . 12 T&C SONGS 2   46
by a gestured city stilled in the framing twilight . . . . . 158 & SON ACTU 7   10
trick sepa rate one stilled unmoving mind from a . . . . . . 354 VIVA 45   20

STILLING

is a vise whose stilling lips murder suddenly me, ... 152 & SON ACTU 1   11

STILLNESS

after carpeted flight. in stillness, climbing the carpeted . 375 VIVA 66   13
ing through touch less stillness (seized among what ghostly . 432 NO THANKS 49   10
afternoon: breathing a fatal stillness; while enormous this . 674 95 POEMS 2   4
a dream and (through stillness beyond conceiving) dream until 757 95 POEMS 85   35

+STILLNESS

FOR CONTEXT, SEE . . . . 814 73 POEMS 42   13
FOR CONTEXT, SEE . . . . 827 73 POEMS 55   9

STIMPSTAMPS

the three white its stimpstamps) the grintgrunt wugglewiggle 773 73 POEMS 1   10

STIMULUS

remu- nerativeness of the stimulus (eheu fu -gaces Postu- . . 236 IS 5 ONE 7   17

STING

furniture unsolemnly : bur sting the skinfull of Ludicrous, . 159 & SON ACTU 8   9
while twilight takes the sting out of the vermilion . . . . . 279 IS 5 THREE 3   18

+STING

FOR CONTEXT, SEE . . . . 342 VIVA 33   12

STINGING

/ / / / stinging gold swarms upon the . . . . 51 T&C IMPRESS 5   1
of hiding pleasure. Alice, stinging quips of flesh. Loretta, 138 & SON REAL 9   14
in a firm fragile stinging weather, (breathless with sharp . 140 & SON REAL 11   8

	PAGE	TITLE	LINE

STINK
Of, shivers ofcrin Ging stink. dull, gobular glows and . . . 94 & POST IMPR 6 11
curl thirstily. Dead stars stink. dawn. Inane, the poetic . . 139 & SON REAL 10 13
annoys me, but the stink of perfumed noise fiercely . . . . . 169 & SON ACTU 18 3
of Broadway, the trivial stink of rich frail firm . . . . . . 220 XLI SONNETS 16 3
of a clown (should stink of failure more than . . . . 414 NO THANKS 31 3
joy of joy) what stink is here unpoets do . . . . 440 NO THANKS 56 31
and brown strut-mince and stink-brag have all come to . . . . 497 50 POEMS 11 3
could its breath would stink and as for souls . . . . 510 50 POEMS 24 7

STINK-BRAG
and brown strut-mince and stink-brag have all come to . . . . 497 50 POEMS 11 3

STINKING
scotch jig in a stinking joyman bar a cockney . . . . 108 & PORTRAIT 4 9

+STINKING
FOR CONTEXT, SEE . . . . 259 IS 5 ONE 29 8

STINKS
is an it that stinks Excuse Me whether it's . . . . 549 1 X 1 9 1
shrouds is immaterial it stinks a salesman is an . . . . . 549 1 X 1 9 7
is an it that stinks to please but whether . . . . 549 1 X 1 9 8

+STINKS
FOR CONTEXT, SEE . . . . 474 NEW POEMS 12 12

STIR
with a sharp indecent stir unclenches into fingers.... she . 131 & SON REAL 2 10
Lustful.... sense a gradual stir of beginning muscle, and . . 157 & SON ACTU 6 3
window leaves softly to stir, of thoughtful trees whom . . . 205 XLI SONNETS 1 10
how he does not stir) O love, my love! . . . . 386 NO THANKS 3 11
bird by snow and stir by still anyone's any . . . . 515 50 POEMS 29 15
under his eyes would stir and squirm newly as . . . . 520 50 POEMS 34 8
once, and every cannot stir imagining; while you are . . . . 559 1 X 1 19 10
ful sunlight --look-- selves, stir: writhe o-p-e-n-i-n-g are 835 73 POEMS 63 11

+STIR
FOR CONTEXT, SEE . . . . 423 NO THANKS 40 23
FOR CONTEXT, SEE . . . . 423 NO THANKS 40 27

STIRRED
stalked or eyes firmly stirred) my mirror gives me, ... 360 VIVA 51 2

STIRRING
simply, into, her. Thirsty stirring. (Must be summer. Hush. . 130 & SON REAL 1 12
off). It was spring sun-stirring. sweetly to the mangling . . 135 & SON REAL 6 13
not a creature was stirring, not even a mouse. . . . . 142 & SON REAL 13 13
hush, one dead leaf stirring makes a crash --far . . . . . . 839 73 POEMS 67 4

STIRRINGOFBIRDS
of your smile is stirringofbirds between my arms; but . . . . 163 & SON ACTU 12 18

STIRS
pries, not open. Tail stirs.) And the. fire-escapes-- the . . 166 & SON ACTU 15 11
sweetness.... pauses. (Halfwhispering.... halfsinging stirs . 304 IS 5 FIVE 3 14
No least leaf almost stirs as never (in againless . . . . . 758 95 POEMS 85 38
a house like shape stirs through (not numerably or . . . . . 785 73 POEMS 13 11
crou ched moangrowl-&-thin g stirs (m id) a life . . . . . . 795 73 POEMS 23 6

+STIRS
FOR CONTEXT, SEE . . . . 710 95 POEMS 38 1

STITCH
to a proud continual stitch of the unmitigated systole . . . 136 & SON REAL 7 3

STOCKING
ed explosion of, pink! stocking w h e e . . . . 94 & POST IMPR 6 6
in silk wrinkling loth stocking begins queerly to do . . . . 225 IS 5 ONE LIZ 4

STOCKINGS
even a mouse. The stockings were hung by the . . . . 142 & SON REAL 13 13
Cassiopeia's might those be stockings dribbling from the . . 322 VIVA 14 6

STOLE
"his most wise music stole nothing from death"-- you . . . . 306 IS 5 FIVE 5 9

STOLEN
am punished. They have stolen into recent lands the . . . . 165 & SON ACTU 14 14
toenails or ideas thoroughly's stolen (somewhere between our 322 VIVA 14 9

STOMACH
Christopher Street For my stomach goes out into the . . . . . 101 & POST IMPR 11 59
up- right on the stomach like A billiken with . . . . 101 & POST IMPR 11 60
intotheslow hot women my Stomach ruBSiTSElf kew-ri-ous-ly a . 101 & POST IMPR 11 62
me in You my stomach goes into your Little . . . . 123 & SEVEN POEMS 2 9

STOMACH (CONTINUED)
    goes into your Little Stomach My legs are in . . . . 123 & SEVEN POEMS 2   9
    Time stuff the sincere stomach of each mill of . . . . . . 165 & SON ACTU 14   12
STOMACHS
    mong Them (among their stomachs andtheir sexes) . . . . . . 101 & POST IMPR 11   64
    s s olemnandputrid vast, stomachs bLurting and cHuckling like 101 & POST IMPR 11   69
    stomachsClenche Dtothe <> cHuBbY stomachs which have not, . . 101 & POST IMPR 11   72
    have not, known other stomachs and their Sexis a . . . . . . 101 & POST IMPR 11   73
    to no-thing signifi- cant stomachs: Who carry-tadpole! s,, . 101 & POST IMPR 11   75
    stomachs: Who carry-tadpole! s,, stomachs of little, girls . 101 & POST IMPR 11   75
    i, like, best, the, stomachs, of the young (girls . . . . . 101 & POST IMPR 11   76
STOMACHSCLENCHE
    interesting by earTHQuake empty stomachsClenche Dtothe <> . . 101 & POST IMPR 11   71
STOMACHSLIKEDEAD
    because Who? wanted them, stomachslikEDead fishe s s . . . . 101 & POST IMPR 11   68
STOMACHSOFOLD
    stomachs andtheir sexes) stomachsofold pe o pleLike hideous 101 & POST IMPR 11   64
STONE
    as teeth, in the stone of a musical fruit. . . . . 154 & SON ACTU 3   2
    what hath remained --the stone cringes clinging to the . . . 260 IS 5 ONE 30   4
    cringes clinging to the stone, how obsolete lips utter . . . 260 IS 5 ONE 30   5
    these children singing in stone a silence of stone . . . . . 525 50 POEMS 37   1
    stone a silence of stone these little children wound . . . . 525 50 POEMS 37   2
    little children wound with stone flowers opening for ever . . 525 50 POEMS 37   3
    always their flowers of stone are silently singing a . . . . 525 50 POEMS 37   9
    singing blossoms children of stone with blossoming eyes know 525 50 POEMS 37   16
    made of silent as stone silence of song / . . . . 525 50 POEMS 37   23
    with a smooth round stone as small as a . . . . 682 95 POEMS 10   9
    his eyes and a stone on his soul" / . . . . 707 95 POEMS 35   28
+STONE
    FOR CONTEXT, SEE . . . . 57 T&C PORTRAIT 5   11
STONES
    cherie, who live under stones.) Don't be afraid and . . . . 86 T&C SON ACTU 5   10
    and the large laughing stones a sinuous problem of . . . . . 112 & PORTRAIT 6   104
    pearl weed coral and stones; lifted, and (before my . . . . 369 VIVA 60   6
    moon's utmost magic, or stones speak or one name . . . . . . 377 VIVA 68   4
    (goes folds? folds) cold stones (o-l-d) names aren'ts) . . . 417 NO THANKS 34   8
    trees, poor stars and stones, but never this fine . . . . . 554 1 X 1 14   11
    this being are growing stones (neither awake are goddesses . 617 (CHAIRE) 19   8
    head's his face with stones for eyes for mind . . . . 716 95 POEMS 44   8
    nots are their whys stones become eyes locks open . . . . . 716 95 POEMS 44   23
    --our second coming made stones sing like birds-- but . . . 844 73 POEMS 72   2
+STONES
    FOR CONTEXT, SEE . . . . 511 50 POEMS 25   19
    FOR CONTEXT, SEE . . . . 581 1 X 1 41   5
STOOD
    touch me where i stood (maybe nine miles off). . . . . 135 & SON REAL 6   12
    as bite teeth; i stood with you as a . . . . 154 & SON ACTU 3   15
    delicate hubbub as you stood thinking of anything, maybe . . 172 & SON ACTU 21   8
    and in the darkness) stood sharp angels with faces . . . . . 241 IS 5 ONE 12   9
    opposite which a church stood perfectly upright but not . . . 263 IS 5 ONE 32   51
    deux trois der die Stood (apparition.) WITH (THE ROUND . . . 348 VIVA 39   15
    standest as thou hast stood and thou shalt stand. . . . . . 351 VIVA 42   12
    utmost him so hugely) stood my father's dream his . . . . . 520 50 POEMS 34   28
    and why but (who stood within his steam be- . . . . 523 50 POEMS 36   7
    leaf opening) as we stood, one (truthed by wisping . . . . . 572 1 X 1 32   7
    seen little you-i who stood on a green hill . . . . 593 1 X 1 53   4
    women alive (but jim stood still for a thousand . . . . . . 709 95 POEMS 37   15
STOOL
    her brazen breasts, whose foot-stool tells how fought the . .   4 T&C EPITHALAM   43
    to get yourself a stool but draw a line . . . . 500 50 POEMS 14   2
STOOPED
    through the thin air stooped with fear, across the . . . . 11 T&C SONGS 2   22
    i guess (and noone stooped to kiss his face) . . . . 515 50 POEMS 29   26
STOOPING
    will find six crumbs stooping by the coffinlid waiting . . . 117 & PORTRAIT 10   5
    step and follow me stooping by Effie's little, in . . . . . 117 & PORTRAIT 10   28
    room i turn, and (stooping through the morning) kiss . . . . 288 IS 5 FOUR 5   7

		PAGE	TITLE	LINE
STOOPING (CONTINUED)				
as their master's spirit stooping, Crusoelike examines	. . .	344	VIVA 35	13
+STOOPING				
FOR CONTEXT, SEE	. . . .	164	& SON ACTU 13	4
STOOPS				
secret and each morning stoops to blend her star	. . . . . .	351	VIVA 42	14
STOP				
nothing, it shall not stop kissing). / / /	. . . .	13	T&C SONGS 3	21
a tree, Nobody shall stop me but first earth	. . . .	67	T&C POST IMPR 4	2
/ / / MEMORABILIA stop look & listen Venezia:	. . . .	256	IS 5 ONE 27	1
slaughter they did not stop to think they died	. . . .	268	IS 5 TWO 3	12
much not life nor stop as a tear is	. . . .	371	VIVA 62	26
an important worry) halt stop forget relax wait (little	. . .	393	NO THANKS 10	5
(tiptop said he don't stop said she oh no	. . . .	399	NO THANKS 16	26
bottle she quick who stop damned fall all we	. . . .	496	50 POEMS 10	13
/ / / ("fire stop thief help murder save	. . . .	555	1 X 1 15	1
contrived: a spook of stop and go) may i	. . . .	558	1 X 1 18	9
start, to hesitate; to stop (kneeling in doubt: while	. . . .	650	(CHAIRE) 52	1
might have been, and stop ten thousand stars but	. . . . . .	714	95 POEMS 42	10
age scolds Forbid den Stop Must n't Don't &)	. . . .	729	95 POEMS 57	14
darling but nobody will stop it With All The	. . . .	835	73 POEMS 63	30
STOPPED				
wan, and his blood stopped hears in the frail	. . . .	77	T&C SON UNRE 2	8
feel how through the stopped entire day horribly and	. . . .	82	T&C SON ACTU 1	10
tell ....sweat, succeeds breathings stopped to hear, in	. . .	136	& SON REAL 7	15
enlarged) make how many stopped millions of female hard	. . .	337	VIVA 28	4
for their millions of stopped male to look at	. . . .	337	VIVA 28	5
boys boy- ish (a stopped A) with! notgirl'swith? dumb	. . . .	388	NO THANKS 5	24
well but not over, stopped me by 'could you	. . . .	800	73 POEMS 28	5
+STOPPED				
FOR CONTEXT, SEE	. . . .	808	73 POEMS 36	2
STOPPING				
) when what hugs stopping earth than silent is	. . . .	502	50 POEMS 16	1
for when (instead of stopping to think) you begin	. . . . . .	604	(CHAIRE) 6	9
STOPS				
the hot sweet horrible stops of her body Cleopatra	. . . .	110	& PORTRAIT 6	11
o w, n phonograph stopS. b swears in persian	. . . .	200	XLI PORTRAIT 8	28
walk air). now who stops. Smiles. he stamps /	. . . .	437	NO THANKS 53	17
why a quilt's pink stops might equal head). Then	. . . . . .	506	50 POEMS 20	10
(ly who all at) stops (once / / /	. . . .	692	95 POEMS 20	7
At which (smiling) he stops: & pick ing up	. . . .	697	95 POEMS 25	6
STORE				
findeth of ladies goodly store whose beauty did in	. . . .	21	T&C PUELLA MEA	173
suit you pay a store too much yes what	. . . .	523	50 POEMS 36	13
STORIES				
Dark on us all; stories told returned gather the	. . . . . .	89	& POST IMPR 1	7
STORMS				
to Death and Time storms and rough cold, wind's	. . . . . .	207	XLI SONNETS 3	10
STORY				
Thou in whose swordgreat story shine the deeds of	. . . . . .	209	XLI SONNETS 5	1
shall hear the true story of Mr Do -nothing	. . . .	236	IS 5 ONE 7	3
to Injustice Taughed your story is so interested but	. . . .	321	VIVA 13	3
bedtime -less un- (wonderful) story atrickling a -rithmetic	.	464	NEW POEMS 2	7
STOUT				
make me a child, stout hurdysturdygurdyman waiter, make me	.	233	IS 5 ONE 4	14
shoulderblades. --Here comes a stout fellow in a blouse	. . .	282	IS 5 THREE 6	24
sam was a man stout as a bridge rugged	. . . .	568	1 X 1 28	6
STRAIGHT				
us O soul, but straight glad feet fearruining and	. . . . . .	41	T&C AMORES 5	29
of here will who straight up into the where	. . . .	746	95 POEMS 74	7
STRAIGHTACROSS				
in the toiletwindow, that's straightacross from my window,	.	171	& SON ACTU 20	2
STRAIGHTENS				
L's immaculate roar looped straightens, into neatest	. . . .	219	XLI SONNETS 15	6
STRAIGHTER				
a wretch to live straighter than a needle) ask	. . . .	498	50 POEMS 12	3
STRAIGHTWAY				
kiss your fucking flag" straightway the silver bird looked	.	339	VIVA 30	20

<table>
<thead>
<tr><th></th><th>PAGE</th><th>TITLE</th><th>LINE</th></tr>
</thead>
</table>

STRAIN
    her flesh the amorous strain of gradual hands and . . . . . . 4 T&C EPITHALAM 53
STRAINED
    tower i caught you strained you broke you upon . . . . 30 T&C ORIENTALE 4 27
STRAINING
    over the dim smoke straining my lips are vague . . . . 31 T&C ORIENTALE 5 23
STRANDED
    and milly befriended a stranded star whose rays five . . . . 682 95 POEMS 10 5
STRANDS
    pinch, toes choke-- hair-thin strands of magic agony . . . .by . 146 & SON REAL 17 8
STRANGE
    a winsome thing and strange; apt in my hand . . . . 21 T&C PUELLA MEA 194
    begin a smile exactly strange-- this painter should have . . 85 T&C SON ACTU 4 8
    placing carefully there a strange thing and a known . . . . . 124 & SEVEN POEMS 3 7
    street there is where strange birds purr / / . . . . 180 XLI SONGS 2 20
    death named Smith less strange? Married and lies afraid; . . 406 NO THANKS 23 13
    are Is A eyes Strange known Face (whylaughing! among: . . . . 628 {CHAIRE} 30 10
    whom is perfectly a strange ness Of sun light . . . . 657 {CHAIRE} 59 4
    may become one (wholly strange; familiar wholly) dearest more 659 {CHAIRE} 61 7
    God i'll think it strange that normal mortals can . . . . . . 731 95 POEMS 59 3
    upfloating moon. Time's a strange fellow; more he gives . . . 750 95 POEMS 78 10
    the sky: with a strange (and a true) and . . . . 769 95 POEMS 95 20
+STRANGE
    FOR CONTEXT, SEE . . . . 829 73 POEMS 57 7
STRANGELY
    world! who with Grania strangely fled, who with Egypt . . . . 22 T&C PUELLA MEA 245
    will not reckon how strangely my life is curved . . . . 292 IS 5 FOUR 9 6
    himself for selves more strangely made (wears pain at . . . . 394 NO THANKS 11 6
    (actually) realness kill (make strangely) known (establish . 422 NO THANKS 39 10
STRANGENESS
    at kisses playing, whose strangeness much says; singing . . . 13 T&C SONGS 3 11
    and lovely throat the strangeness of her face doth . . . . . 20 T&C PUELLA MEA 146
    and silence moulds such strangeness as was mine a . . . . . . 78 T&C SON UNRE 3 8
    whose stranger dreams thy strangeness must abuse....) Time . 213 XLI SONNETS 9 14
    slips the very skilful strangeness of your smile the . . . . 306 IS 5 FIVE 5 7
+STRANGENESS
    FOR CONTEXT, SEE . . . . 657 {CHAIRE} 59 4
STRANGER
    day, is a little stranger thing than crisp Sheba . . . . . . 17 T&C PUELLA MEA 7
    Mes from sleep whose stranger dreams thy strangeness must . . 213 XLI SONNETS 9 14
    my kiss as a stranger into the streets and . . . . 297 IS 5 FOUR 14 6
    of to exist a stranger who is i awakening . . . . 559 1 X 1 19 8
    / / a total stranger one black day knocked . . . . 730 95 POEMS 58 1
    friend' we enlightened this stranger 'some people have all . 800 73 POEMS 28 9
    not a word this stranger replied-- but as one . . . . 800 73 POEMS 28 13
    by god down this stranger went on both knees" . . . . 800 73 POEMS 28 16
    that moment when a stranger takes in his arms . . . . 812 73 POEMS 40 11
STRANGERS
    persons: believe me that strangers arrive when i have . . . . 295 IS 5 FOUR 12 8
    like a spark) if strangers meet life begins-- not . . . . . . 564 1 X 1 24 2
    truthful --truthfully, once if strangers (who deep our most . 564 1 X 1 24 13
STRANGLES
    with sleet and snow: strangles valleys by ropes of . . . . . 560 1 X 1 20 11
STRANGLING
    eyes a sound of strangling breasts and bestial grovelling . . 28 T&C ORIENTALE 2 7
STRAWBERRIES
    thankyouverymuch mr rosenbloom picks strawberries with . . . 287 IS 5 FOUR 4 8
    snakeoil vac uumcleaners terror strawberries democ ra (caveat 549 1 X 1 9 12
+STRAWBERRIES
    FOR CONTEXT, SEE . . . . 614 {CHAIRE} 16 11
STRAWBERRY
    think you like" a strawberry bang this blueeyed world . . . . 585 1 X 1 45 2
STRAYING
    whitest feet crisply are straying. Always thy moist eyes . . 13 T&C SONGS 3 8
STREAM
    under honest trees, a stream does. the brain of . . . . 160 & SON ACTU 9 3
STREAMIN
    boollevares an wid tears streamin down my face i . . . . . . 332 VIVA 23 19

		PAGE	TITLE	LINE

STREAMING
the dark with meteors streaming from playful immortal hands . 36 T&C AMORES 1   17
with wings would be streaming if something had (maybe . . . . 652 (CHAIRE) 54   13
STREAMS
by willows, bending upon streams? / / / / . . . . 211 XLI SONNETS 7   18
STREET
is dawn into the street of the sky light . . . . 50 T&C IMPRESS 4   3
i see in the street where strong men are . . . . 50 T&C IMPRESS 4   12
on stars.... in the street of the sky night . . . . 50 T&C IMPRESS 4   33
till night into the street unchangingly the always old . . . 58 T&C PORTRAIT 6   19
number 1 on something street Spring comes the lean . . . . . 62 T&C PORTRAIT 10   4
of number 1 someThing street and trickles carefully into . . 62 T&C PORTRAIT 10   26
the head of this street a gasping organ is . . . . 69 T&C POST IMPR 6   1
is reeling gently the street and the children and . . . . . . 69 T&C POST IMPR 6   24
their last; without, the street darkling awaiteth her whose . 75 T&C SON REAL 6   9
memories in one crooked street of a mind peacefully . . . . . 98 & POST IMPR 9   17
eyes go into Allen street the dark long cool . . . . 100 & POST IMPR 11   2
Side in a. dark street a hur- DygurdY with . . . . 100 & POST IMPR 11   34
the whirl- ingPeaceful furious street people drop, coppers . 100 & POST IMPR 11   39
sPine of the) unsuspecting street; THE YELLOW EYES AND . . . 101 & POST IMPR 11   55
My Couch at Christopher Street For my stomach goes . . . . . 101 & POST IMPR 11   58
in the bright shouting street of time her nakedness . . . . . 112 & PORTRAIT 6   75
o ving in the Street of her bodyfee l . . . . 122 & SEVEN POEMS 1   2
wh-eel-ing oh ver mYveRylitTle street where you will come, . 122 & SEVEN POEMS 1   22
of cold (when battling street-lamps fail upon the gold . . . 142 & SON REAL 13   3
hum of dusk each street takes of shadowy light . . . . 168 & SON ACTU 17   4
other touch) seeking, some street which easily trickles a . . 174 & SON ACTU 23   6
of my soul a street is: prettinesses Pic- abian . . . . 180 XLI SONGS 2   2
Cezanne's logic, oho. a street there is where strange . . . . 180 XLI SONGS 2   18
April dusk the sallow street-lamps were turning snowy against 194 XLI PORTRAIT 2   2
i entered a mad street whose mouth dripped with . . . . 194 XLI PORTRAIT 2   4
bread more downy than street-lamps upon an almostclean plate 194 XLI PORTRAIT 2   32
dissolute atmosphere of a street superimposing a numbing im- 197 XLI PORTRAIT 5   2
a week. On this street the houses immensely speak . . . . . . 219 XLI SONNETS 15   3
while softly along Kirkland Street the infantile ghost of . . 232 IS 5 ONE 3   11
lead all over Brattle Street by a castrated pup . . . . 253 IS 5 ONE 24   15
not fall into this street is love." / / . . . . 295 IS 5 FOUR 12   25
instant (leaped into the street) this deep immediate mask . . 328 VIVA 19   14
barns bulge a tiniest street or three contains these . . . . 340 VIVA 31   13
and despair impersonates a street i lean from the . . . . . . 375 VIVA 66   5
this raving city screamingly street wonderful flowers And o . 437 NO THANKS 53   3
this which of one street leaps quick squirmthicklying lu . . 493 50 POEMS 7   11
dirtiest any city's least street) of mirror lying are . . . . 623 (CHAIRE) 25   4
clown standing on eighth street handed me a flower. . . . . . 802 73 POEMS 30   5
+STREET
FOR CONTEXT, SEE . . . . 697 95 POEMS 25   29
STREET-LAMPS
of cold (when battling street-lamps fail upon the gold . . . 142 & SON REAL 13   3
April dusk the sallow street-lamps were turning snowy against 194 XLI PORTRAIT 2   2
bread more downy than street-lamps upon an almostclean plate 194 XLI PORTRAIT 2   32
STREET'S
on either side the street's DarkcOOllonGBody windows, are. . 100 & POST IMPR 11   15
+STREET'S
FOR CONTEXT, SEE . . . . 789 73 POEMS 17   3
STREETCAR
at you in a streetcar and you pretend you . . . . 126 & SEVEN POEMS 5   15
STREETFU
geri ng up some streetfu l of peopl e . . . . 703 95 POEMS 31   4
STREETS
who uses roofs and streets skilfully to make a . . . . 92 & POST IMPR 4   12
lean magnificent face the streets turn young with rain, . . . 93 & POST IMPR 5   4
flesh: wakes in little streets while exactlygir lisHlegs; . . 104 & POST IMPR 14   10
"ready girls". the unspontaneous streets make bright their . 108 & PORTRAIT 4   5
where teeth of slowturning streets mesh in a frieze . . . . . 142 & SON REAL 13   4
Hassan's Place by tiny streets shrugging with colour) the . . 143 & SON REAL 14   4
horses; light feeling up streets; heels taking derbies . . . 172 & SON ACTU 21   3
your little cheeks the streets of smiles your eyes . . . . . 186 XLI SONGS 8   7
a stranger into the streets and colours of a . . . . 297 IS 5 FOUR 14   7

741

	PAGE	TITLE	LINE

STREETS (CONTINUED)

(perhaps) myself carefully wanders streets dark and, deep . . 300 IS 5 FOUR 17 14
the brittle treacherous bright streets of memory comes my . . 304 IS 5 FIVE 3 1
people (a long ruined streets hither and) softly thither . . 319 VIVA 11 4
the a little tilted streets spill lazily multitudes out . . . 345 VIVA 36 6
Ls) -to sun (crash). Streets glit ter a, strut: . . . . . . 444 NO THANKS 59 21
the ocean wanders the streets are so ancient the . . . . . . 505 50 POEMS 19 5
any (while around him streets taking moment off by . . . . 720 95 POEMS 48 4
eyes people smiles faces streets steeples are eagerly tumbl . 835 73 POEMS 63 5
houses to people and streets into faces and cities . . . . . 841 73 POEMS 69 19

STRENGTH

upon the perfumed roman strength who how furiously plays . . 110 & PORTRAIT 6 9
/ / / my strength becoming wistful in a . . . . 131 & SON REAL 2 1
stern against your charming strength O haste annihilator . . 182 XLI SONGS 4 14
makes more than most strength (less than these how . . . . . 433 NO THANKS 50 8
opposite in fear; the strength so strong mere force . . . . . 768 95 POEMS 94 11

+STRENGTH

FOR CONTEXT, SEE . . . . 137 & SON REAL 8 2

STRENUOUS

beneath the snow Into strenuous birds shall go my . . . . . 16 T&C SONGS 6 10
perfectly gesticulate the accurate strenuous lips of . . . . 43 T&C AMORES 7 37
/ / into the strenuous briefness Life: handorgans and . . . . 66 T&C POST IMPR 3 1
are crammed with the strenuous music of the innumerable . . . 118 & PORTRAIT 10 37

STRETCH

youngest angels suddenly should stretch neat necks just to . 130 & SON REAL 1 5

+STRETCH

FOR CONTEXT, SEE . . . . 442 NO THANKS 57 15

+STRETCHANDSTRETCHANDSTRETCHANDSTRETCHAND

did stretchandstretchandstretchandstretchand did . . . . . . 398 NO THANKS 15 8

STREWED

from their sockets and strewed the black air with . . . . . . 432 NO THANKS 49 17

STRICKEN

sunlight into the flower- stricken air which is filthy . . . 69 T&C POST IMPR 6 5

+STRICKEN

FOR CONTEXT, SEE . . . . 69 T&C POST IMPR 6 23

STRICT

(whom lure an eagerest strict flame) demand the metaphor . . 362 VIVA 53 10
again (jukejog mist & strict) & again (ly infin) . . . . . . 629 {CHAIRE} 31 19
when) un til one strict here of amazing most . . . . 840 73 POEMS 68 27

STRICTLY

there is a philosphy" strictly at which instant (leaped . . . 328 VIVA 19 11
/ / what is strictly fiercely and wholly dies . . . . 344 VIVA 35 1
but through spontaneous deft strictly horrors which stars may 386 NO THANKS 3 7
sun will stand, so strictly (over utmost him so . . . . . . 520 50 POEMS 34 27
raptures of undream that strictly (and how) scienti fic . . . 544 1 X 1 4 21
lively (but Death is strictly scientific & artificial & . . . 604 {CHAIRE} 6 18
unstreet with treadwatering nonlegs (strictly) smiling / / / 616 {CHAIRE} 18 16
becomes darkness) innumerably singular strictly immeasurable 741 95 POEMS 69 3

+STRICTLY

FOR CONTEXT, SEE . . . . 629 {CHAIRE} 31 19

STRICTNESS

tower within whose brightening strictness Danae saw the night 4 T&C EPITHALAM 51

STRIDE

futile day an enormous stride (and drawing thy mouth . . . . 215 XLI SONNETS 11 15
dimly cries nine, i stride among the vines (my . . . . . . 434 NO THANKS 51 15
and thick stickingly un stride after glide massacre monday . 522 50 POEMS 35 4
joy to why their stride and breathing to limp . . . . 580 1 X 1 40 10
take life in your stride (instead of scheming how . . . . . 679 95 POEMS 7 1

STRIDES

of chrome and execute strides of cobalt nevertheless i . . . 199 XLI PORTRAIT 7 6

STRIDING

(of the oh silently striding) priests-and- slowly, al, ways; 280 IS 5 THREE 4 27

STRIKE

with irrevocable nakedness to strike the young world into . . 7 T&C EPITHALAM 163
this and this spire strike midnight (and did occur . . . . . 115 & PORTRAIT 8 17
justly souls of flower strike the air in utterable . . . . . 163 & SON ACTU 12 6
it is to feel strike the silver fish of . . . . 216 XLI SONNETS 12 1
of my mind. Clocks strike. The moon's round, through . . . . 365 VIVA 56 3

	PAGE	TITLE	LINE

STRIKE (CONTINUED)
    firmly. splendidly advancing colour strike into form . . . . 422 NO THANKS 39   5
    grinning) we no (smiling) strike agains De Big Boss . . . . . 618 {CHAIRE} 20   8
STRIKER
    off and the little striker having the best time . . . . 126 & SEVEN POEMS 5   11
STRIKES
    when the final curtain strikes the world away, leaving . . . 75 T&C SON REAL 6   2
    if a (perhaps) clock strikes, in the alive coolness, ... 92 & POST IMPR 4   14
    a cloud a clock strikes midnight a finger pulls . . . . 338 VIVA 29   22
    feel only despair completely strikes forests of mind, ... 580 1 X 1 40   24
    guess. Life's life and strikes my your our blossoming . . . . 582 1 X 1 42   16
    squirm and the sun strikes to gain a living . . . . 620 {CHAIRE} 22   2
STRIKING
    kings they are the striking of a good minstrel . . . . 29 T&C ORIENTALE 3   13
    is like a clock striking in a dark house . . . . 229 IS 5 ONE FRAN   15
    green groove of twilight, striking into many a piece. . . . . 360 VIVA 51   19
STRIKINGLY
    trousers ejaculate spats a strikingly succulent getup but we 259 IS 5 ONE 29   25
STRING
    and jerk the little string and the monkey will . . . . 69 T&C POST IMPR 6   13
    jerk of the little string! the tiny smiling shabby . . . . . 69 T&C POST IMPR 6   32
    the end of a string / / / / . . . . 69 T&C POST IMPR 6   44
    and sitting on one string dead never says my . . . . 126 & SEVEN POEMS 5   28
    wriggled like a twitched string. / / / / . . . . 135 & SON REAL 6   17
    how the limp huddling string of your smile over . . . . 161 & SON ACTU 10   5
    celestial to the quivering string) invisible faces hauntingly 208 XLI SONNETS 4   7
    kites and when the string breaks (or something) my . . . . . 253 IS 5 ONE 24   8
    You know who a string of pretty medals drew . . . . 266 IS 5 TWO 1   24
    the end of a string (murmurs little you-i as . . . . 593 1 X 1 53   20
+STRING
    FOR CONTEXT, SEE . . . . 607 {CHAIRE} 9   7
STRINGS
    of brass hangIng from strings (or) someThing i was . . . . . 123 & SEVEN POEMS 2   3
    she coughed while tying strings / / / / . . . . 132 & SON REAL 3   18
STRIPPED
    you) sheath before sheath stripped to the Odour. (and . . . . 154 & SON ACTU 3   13
STRIVE
    all certainties, as villains strive and heroes through the . 576 1 X 1 36   5
    who rage, vainly who strive; and being finally released . . . 799 73 POEMS 27   29
STRIVING
    the kissing and the striving of that old man . . . . 57 T&C PORTRAIT 5   9
    of spring utters a striving flower, just where strove . . . . 213 XLI SONNETS 9   7
    of earth's own clumsily striving (finding and losing and . . 749 95 POEMS 77   6
STRODE
    whowhich of mad rags strode earth ignorantly blossoming a . . 662 {CHAIRE} 64   6
STROKABLE
    who praise Marj's cleancornered strokable body these men's . 114 & PORTRAIT 7   5
STROKE
    obedient; it is to stroke my being with numbing . . . . 19 T&C PUELLA MEA   90
    perfectly withal smooth to stroke and sweet to see . . . . . 20 T&C PUELLA MEA   155
    spring, is what we stroke maybe asleep? do you . . . . 191 XLI CHANSONS 1   11
    that helplessness which others stroke with brushes recently . 339 VIVA 30   10
    Is like that please stroke for now stroke answers . . . . . . 343 VIVA 34   3
    please stroke for now stroke answers (but now don't . . . . . 343 VIVA 34   4
STROKED
    moan in tones of stroked flower; let not thy . . . .   9 T&C SONGS 1   6
STROKES
    (shock beyond shock blurted) strokes, vibrant with the purr . 115 & PORTRAIT 8   14
STROKING
    you, i like, slowly stroking the, shocking fuzz of . . . . . 175 & SON ACTU 24   10
STROLL
    upon frailness) used to stroll (very slowly) one or . . . . . 23 T&C PUELLA MEA   280
    labyrinth where noisy colours stroll.... and the Baboon . . . 220 XLI SONNETS 16   12
    (very) fine eyes (which stroll hither and thither through . . 275 IS 5 TWO 9   49
    und ead the not stroll living spawn imitate) ce . . . . 309 VIVA 1   31
    road who dares to stroll almost this god this . . . . 441 NO THANKS 56   47
    old may my mind stroll about hungry and fearless . . . . . . 481 NEW POEMS 19   5
    much (as aprils elsewhere stroll) exhumed most innocently . . 546 1 X 1 6   3

STROLL (CONTINUED)
ning heshaped two these (stroll more slowly than trees) . . . 681 95 POEMS 9   3
is to breathe to stroll to swim love is . . . . 768 95 POEMS 94   3
than eyes restroll and stroll some never deepening beach . . 843 73 POEMS 71   3
STROLLING
wandlike animal, a little strolling with the futile purr . . 170 & SON ACTU 19   8
image the a little strolling lips and eyes inwardly . . . . 193 XLI PORTRAIT 1   8
you and i'll go strolling right through these each . . . . . 600 (CHAIRE) 2   12
away leaving just this strolling ghostly doll of an . . . . . 720 95 POEMS 48   8
silent truths of mountain (strolling is there here everywhere 755 95 POEMS 83   8
and his only love, strolling slowly (mind in mind) . . . . . 777 73 POEMS 5   3
+STROLLING
FOR CONTEXT, SEE . . . . 342 VIVA 33   2
FOR CONTEXT, SEE . . . . 430 NO THANKS 47   10
STROLLS
abdominous female indubitably tellurian strolls emitting . . 116 & PORTRAIT 9   5
through which that memory strolls) and every ours for . . . . 617 (CHAIRE) 19   11
out of all silence strolls) nearness awakened, any bird . . . 756 95 POEMS 84   10
of the truth; and strolls the axis of the . . . . 845 73 POEMS 73   10
+STROLLS
FOR CONTEXT, SEE . . . . 347 VIVA 38   14
FOR CONTEXT, SEE . . . . 615 (CHAIRE) 17   4
STRONG
darkness, and the sweet strong final bird transcends the . .   7 T&C EPITHALAM 165
smooth Unstrength, against the strong silences of your song;   11 T&C SONGS 2   9
of mowers whose bodies strong with love through meadows . . .   11 T&C SONGS 2   34
their little breasts My strong fingers beneath the snow . . .   16 T&C SONGS 6   9
in the street where strong men are digging bread . . . . . .   50 T&C IMPRESS 4   12
as out of dumb strong hands infinite the erect . . . .   64 T&C POST IMPR 1   5
another's, and your dear strong fingers clutch his heart, . .   76 T&C SON UNRE 1   3
frail slippery house, a strong fragile house (beginning at .   83 T&C SON ACTU 2   3
bestial Marj for the strong men who sleep between . . . . . . 114 & PORTRAIT 7   27
from night's outer wing strong silent greens serenely . . . 208 XLI SONNETS 4   3
glow revealed) this tall strong stalwart youth, what sight . 254 IS 5 ONE 25   2
icecakes beheld being too strong, in brief : an . . . . 262 IS 5 ONE 32   12
sing so deep and strong one queerying wave will . . . . 526 50 POEMS 38   6
fear; the strength so strong mere force is feebleness: . . . 768 95 POEMS 94   11
of zeus: one, handsome strong and born to dare . . . . 799 73 POEMS 27   3
confessed (halting) "a tall strong young finelooking fellow, 800 73 POEMS 28   3
STRONGMAN
at denfert the fat strongman has put down his . . . . 384 NO THANKS 2   19
STROPPING
little knives of flower stropping sof a. Thick silence) . . .   99 & POST IMPR 10   13
STROVE
striving flower, just where strove the droll god-beasts do . 213 XLI SONNETS 9   8
STRUCK
not if any anguish struck how thin a ghost . . . . 414 NO THANKS 31   7
STRUCTURE
du Golf... that notable structure or ideal edifice... . . . 319 VIVA 11   22
/ / / / structure, miraculous challenge, devout am . . . . . 351 VIVA 42   1
new stars knitting the structure of distinct sunset driving . 378 VIVA 69   8
STRUGGLE
the odd unlovely souls struggle slowly and writhe like . . .   55 T&C PORTRAIT 3   19
is where revolving planets struggle to be free with . . . . . 212 XLI SONNETS 8   11
STRUGGLEINWEIRD
like-trumpets they (writhe they, struggleinweird chords of . 100 & POST IMPR 11   12
STRUNSKY'S
balloon) heavily swims to Strunsky's, Monia's mouth eats . . 219 XLI SONNETS 15   13
STRUT
will make oddly to strut my indolent priceless smile, ... 155 & SON ACTU 4   10
Over thin earths chatterish strut cuddle & shrink: as . . . . 346 VIVA 37   4
coo or boo may strut or creep ungenerous who . . . . 440 NO THANKS 56   19
Streets glit ter a, strut: do; colours; are: m, ... 444 NO THANKS 59   24
pink-flag blackshirt and brown strut-mince and stink-brag . . 497 50 POEMS 11   3
champychumpchomps yes the speckled strut begins to scretch . 773 73 POEMS 1   13
STRUT-MINCE
pink-flag blackshirt and brown strut-mince and stink-brag . . 497 50 POEMS 11   3

STRUTS
As the lady lazily struts (her thickish flesh superior . . . 150 & SON REAL 21 10
thither and hither myself struts unremembered (rememberingly 299 IS 5 FOUR 16 9
honeydunce; whirling's a frantic struts a pedantic proud or . 763 95 POEMS 90 12
+STRUTS
FOR CONTEXT, SEE . . . . 445 NO THANKS 60 2
STRUTSTROLLS
with danc ing egghead strutstrolls eager a (twice by . . . . 615 (CHAIRE) 17 4
STRUTTING
her his Its image strutting (very jerkily) not toucH- . . . . 335 VIVA 26 11
STUB
blinds inslants peregrinate, a cigar-stub disintegrates, . . 144 & SON REAL 15 4
STUCK
madam was a bulb stuck in the door. a . . . . 73 T&C SON REAL 4 2
ingly flash a of-faceness stuck thumblike into pie is . . . . 330 VIVA 21 5
s) ro ude stly (stuck in a spanked behind . . . . 408 NO THANKS 25 16
with its of eye stuck into a rock of . . . . 490 50 POEMS 4 3
thick as my fist stuck in the throat of . . . . 709 95 POEMS 37 12
STUDIED
dreamed of a corkscrew) studied with Freud a year . . . . . . 236 IS 5 ONE 7 7
STUDY
careful fierceness. Her lips study my head gripping for . . . 146 & SON REAL 17 3
STUFF
from, the air and stuff it seriously in, his . . . . 69 T&C POST IMPR 6 11
their finger and they stuff the poor thing all . . . . 126 & SEVEN POEMS 5 13
obscure obvious hands Time stuff the sincere stomach of . . . 165 & SON ACTU 14 12
STUFFED
museums filled with skilfully stuffed memories / / / . . . . 297 IS 5 FOUR 14 15
remarked some- thing about "*stuffed* fauna" being . . . . . . .326 VIVA 18 32
STUFFEST
the musical tom-cat, thou stuffest the parks with overgrown . 61 T&C PORTRAIT 9 5
STUFFS
a fit- and-cling of stuffs the alert willing myth . . . . . . 155 & SON ACTU 4 9
your flesh in stupid stuffs, phrase the immense weapon . . . 161 & SON ACTU 10 9
STUMBLE
my mind blossom will stumble beneath a clumsiest disguise, . 91 & POST IMPR 3 12
trast with the tiny stumble from second to tenth . . . . . . 803 73 POEMS 31 12
STUMBLED
brightness of air wonderfully stumbled above the square, . . 173 & SON ACTU 22 3
STUMBLING
like a moth with stumbling wings flutters and flops . . . . . 47 T&C IMPRESS 1 7
of this and that stumbling in gloom, bad laughters, ... 142 & SON REAL 13 8
skies; whiteLy are which stumbling eyes which why in . . . . 346 VIVA 37 8
sky (a little mouth) stumbling (can't keep up with . . . . . 501 50 POEMS 15 9
live) fore head is stumbling someone (named Morning) / . . . 785 73 POEMS 13 22
+STUMBLING
FOR CONTEXT, SEE . . . . 495 50 POEMS 9 2
STUMP
of kisses, the chewed stump of a mouth, huge . . . . 133 & SON REAL 4 14
STUN
in various tremulous armor stun the eyes of ragged . . . . . 4 T&C EPITHALAM 68
STUNG
hornets wail by children stung or as the seeing . . . . 511 50 POEMS 25 14
STUNNING
god gloats upon Her stunning flesh. Upon the reachings . . . 77 T&C SON UNRE 2 1
STUNT
still wondering if the stunt was really a dream-- . . . . . . 605 (CHAIRE) 7 14
STUPENDOUS
textures of actual cool stupendous is nor may truth . . . . . 373 VIVA 64 15
roots of mere eternity) stupendous if discoverably . . . . . 517 50 POEMS 31 2
STUPID
skin, so of my stupid sincere youth the exquisite . . . . . . 11 T&C SONGS 2 6
nose was small, exact, stupid. mouth normal, large, unclever. 103 & POST IMPR 13 13
of your smile into stupid gardens if this were . . . . 154 & SON ACTU 3 5
deftly your flesh in stupid stuffs, phrase the immense . . . 161 & SON ACTU 10 9
when surrounded by fat stupid animals the jewess shrieked . . 241 IS 5 ONE 12 3

	PAGE	TITLE	LINE

+STUPID
    FOR CONTEXT, SEE . . . . 126 & SEVEN POEMS 5 19
STUPIDEST
    books could plan) the stupidest teacher will almost guess . . 594 1 X 1 54   5
STUPIDLY
    trite thighs; the hair stupidly priceless. / / / . . . . . . 173 & SON ACTU 22   15
STURDILY
    upon his fearless derriere sturdily seated--Colonel Needless 266 IS 5 TWO 1   22
    this) window; yes women sturdily meander in my mind, ... 435 NO THANKS 51   34
STURDY
    workingman with hand so hairy-sturdy you may turn O . . . . . 233 IS 5 ONE 4   1
+STURDY
    FOR CONTEXT, SEE . . . . 233 IS 5 ONE 4   2
    FOR CONTEXT, SEE . . . . 233 IS 5 ONE 4   14
STUTTER
    --in the woods which stutter and sing And the . . . . 163 & SON ACTU 12   14
    toward which The Expectant stutter (upon artificial limbs, . 280 IS 5 THREE 4   33
    lazily writhe lurch faceflowers stutter treebodies wobbly- . 436 NO THANKS 52   9
STUTTERING
    people wiggled battered by stuttering pearl, leaves jiggled . 173 & SON ACTU 22   5
    <> did) who begins stuttering each sentence we both . . . . . 398 NO THANKS 15   10
    to see (while a stuttering ghost that maybe had . . . . . . 709 95 POEMS 37   7
+STUTTERS
    FOR CONTEXT, SEE . . . . 656 (CHAIRE) 58   9
STYLE
    look girls in the style of that's the foliage . . . . 257 IS 5 ONE 27   33
SUB
    a leanderless drowning in sub (at the next) nakedness . . . . 546 1 X 1 6   7
    / / / ADHUC SUB JUDICE LIS when mack . . . . 706 95 POEMS 34   T
    uglies t s ub sub urba n skyline on . . . . 788 73 POEMS 16   6
    five simple facts no sub human superstate ever knew . . . . . 803 73 POEMS 31   5
+SUB
    FOR CONTEXT, SEE . . . . 788 73 POEMS 16   4
SUBCHEMISTRY
    to experience a neverish subchemistry of alWays)fiercely . . 361 VIVA 52   28
SUBDUED
    with an untimid svelte subdued magic while in your . . . . . 138 & SON REAL 9   5
SUBHUMAN
    or Think We've Met subhuman rights Before / / . . . . 549 1 X 1 9   14
    falsely true; or so subhuman superminds declare --nor all . . 817 73 POEMS 45   3
+SUBHUMAN
    FOR CONTEXT, SEE . . . . 803 73 POEMS 31   5
SUBJECT
    room has been forever subject his Earliest word wheeled . . . 197 XLI PORTRAIT 5 21
    thoughts which occupied the subject of our attention; to . . 263 IS 5 ONE 32   61
SUBJUNCTIVE
    see?) which the six subjunctive crumbs twitch like mutilated 117 & PORTRAIT 10 30
SUBLIMATED
    rustling din sort of sublimated tom-tom which quite outdoes . 171 & SON ACTU 20   4
SUBLIME
    the impressed fingers of sublime Memory, of that loveliness . 207 XLI SONNETS 3 11
    with the wonderless city's sublime cheap distinct mouth) do . 218 XLI SONNETS 14 7
SUBLIMINAL
    intrinsic yearn, the immanent subliminal fern of her . . . . 19 T&C PUELLA MEA 113
    phrasing crease of hot subliminal lips, as if a . . . . . . 130 & SON REAL 1   4
SUBMERGED
    mainly awash while chiefly submerged or an amoral morality . 410 NO THANKS 27   11
SUBMICROSCOPIC
    must call a state submicroscopic is-- compared with pitying . 561 1 X 1 21   3
SUBMIT
    meek; obey says toc, submit says tic, Eternity's a . . . . . 438 NO THANKS 54   5
SUBMORONIC
    in superhuman flights of submoronic fancy be more not . . . . 790 73 POEMS 18   3
SUBPREINCESTURES
    out of a supermetamathical subpreincestures pooped universe . 425 NO THANKS 42   1
SUBSTANCE
    all soulless wraiths proclaim substance; all heartless . . . 765 95 POEMS 91   4

		PAGE	TITLE	LINE

SUBSTANCES
   of guess, shadows are substances and wings are birds; . . . . 761 95 POEMS 88   7
SUBSTANTIAL
   i gondola don't --the substantial dollarbringing virgins . . 256 IS 5 ONE 27   29
SUBTLE
   gods and men whose subtle throne twain sphinxes bear . . . . 4 T&C EPITHALAM   41
   queens is dancing her subtle body weaving insinuating upon . 34 T&C ORIENTALE 6   85
   the skunks in a subtle manner or by drowning . . . . 239 IS 5 ONE 10   25
   forged a web so subtle air is comparatively crude; . . . . . 799 73 POEMS 27   16
SUBTRACTED
   your whisper's whisper is subtracted from my hope's own . . . 821 73 POEMS 49   10
SUBTRACTING
   (with one cocked eyebrow) subtracting cliches un by un . . . 605 {CHAIRE} 7   2
+SUBTRACTING
   FOR CONTEXT, SEE . . . . 843 73 POEMS 71   7
SUBURB
   for that well known suburb the bronx (enlivening an . . . . . 326 VIVA 18   12
+SUBURBAN
   FOR CONTEXT, SEE . . . . 788 73 POEMS 16   6
SUBWAYS
   San Fran dictaphones wireless subways vacuum cleaners . . . . 237 IS 5 ONE 8   9
SUCCEED
   mean -ness, and to succeed in not dying) Is . . . . 452 NO THANKS 67   11
SUCCEEDED
   uninterred at twice fortyeight, succeeded in producing . . . 341 VIVA 32   2
SUCCEEDING
   mind flesh In flesh succeeding disappear / / / . . . . 364 VIVA 55   16
SUCCEEDS
   funny Do tell ....sweat, succeeds breathings stopped to hear, 136 & SON REAL 7   15
   you and me almost succeeds while toddle rings the . . . . . 227 IS 5 ONE GERT   7
SUCCESS
   black the boots of success than enquire whose soul . . . . 204 XLI LA GUERRE 2   3
SUCCESSFUL
   god p.s. the most successful b.o. fully speaking concession . 425 NO THANKS 42   15
SUCCESSFULLY
   like all of you successfully if delicately gelded (or . . . . 231 IS 5 ONE 3   43
   shrieked the messiah tumbled successfully into the world the 241 IS 5 ONE 12   5
SUCCINCT
   things, your flesh, a succinct wandlike animal, a little . . 170 & SON ACTU 19   7
SUCCINCTLY
   colonel (trig westpointer most succinctly bred) took erring . 339 VIVA 30   5
SUCCULENT
   ejaculate spats a strikingly succulent getup but we knew . . 259 IS 5 ONE 29   25
SUCH
   what am i that such and such mysteries very . . . . 12 T&C SONGS 2   36
   i that such and such mysteries very simply touch . . . . . . 12 T&C SONGS 2   36
   nor ever did on such a throat the lips . . . . 17 T&C PUELLA MEA   35
   and new (a flower such as the world had . . . . 18 T&C PUELLA MEA   55
   immaculate crisp head is such as only certain dead . . . . . 20 T&C PUELLA MEA   140
   is. Beneath her thighs such legs are seen as . . . . 21 T&C PUELLA MEA   207
   sweet hair lay in such a silence as i . . . . 76 T&C SON UNRE 1   6
   as i know, or such great writhing words as, ... 76 T&C SON UNRE 1   6
   always) and silence moulds such strangeness as was mine . . . 78 T&C SON UNRE 3   8
   for his own-- on such a night the sea . . . . 81 T&C SON UNRE 6   13
   evening and a propos such light and shape as . . . . 98 & POST IMPR 9   9
   numbing im- perfectness upon such peregrinations as twilight 197 XLI PORTRAIT 5   3
   get me?) according to such supposedly indigenous throstles . 230 IS 5 ONE 2   31
   was Jimmie. Oh for such a gurl gurl gurl, ... 235 IS 5 ONE 6   13
   gurl gurl, oh for such a gurl to be . . . . 235 IS 5 ONE 6   17
   rather is it between such beddings and bumpings of . . . . . 261 IS 5 ONE 31   6
   a lightning-rod, Boston, Mass. such were the not unhurried . 263 IS 5 ONE 32   32
   of you love being such, or such, the normal . . . . 292 IS 5 FOUR 9   13
   love being such, oh for such, the normal corners of . . . . . 292 IS 5 FOUR 9   13
   their raiment with phenomena: such being a conduct worthy . . 328 VIVA 19   5
   of slowly staring and such hair) the Californian handpicked . 337 VIVA 28   8
   of beginningly finishing (and such hair) the expensively . . 337 VIVA 28   13
   thunder (together) smell only such blue slender hands of . . 340 VIVA 31   20
   our projectile am tell such to murder time (forgetting . . . 362 VIVA 53   13

747

	PAGE	TITLE	LINE

SUCH (CONTINUED)

even the rain, has such small hands / /	366 VIVA 57	20
feeling memory shrink from such brief selves as fiercely . .	373 VIVA 64	13
day is over (and such a day as must	376 VIVA 67	2
above the always beyond such wheres and fears or	378 VIVA 69	13
there B being no such thing for C can't	390 NO THANKS 7	2
demands not rebirth of such than hungrily more swiftness . .	402 NO THANKS 19	2
the silent whys of such a deathlessness) remembrance might .	420 NO THANKS 37	6
secret i will breathe such crude perfection as divides . . .	428 NO THANKS 45	10
hundred joys high are such shoulders as cowards will	439 NO THANKS 55	13
they dare not share) such make their names (this	440 NO THANKS 56	23
(having found) wound up such pretty toys as themselves . . .	451 NO THANKS 66	9
bubbies going places on such babies aint plenty good	476 NEW POEMS 14	7
but any) heart--wholly, idiotically--before such nonsense . .	480 NEW POEMS 18	5
there's never been quite such a fool who could	481 NEW POEMS 19	11
her now: but we've such freedom such intense digestion . . .	491 50 POEMS 5	15
but we've such freedom such intense digestion so much	491 50 POEMS 5	15
existing minds took life such life could not begin	510 50 POEMS 24	6
est breathe but if such life could its breath	510 50 POEMS 24	7
pulled (for he's we) such fruit from what bough	543 1 X 1 3	22
traitor, idiot, dreamer, beast-- such was a poet and	562 1 X 1 22	10
occurs beyond the mind) such a forever is love's	576 1 X 1 36	9
her each here is such an everywhere, even more	576 1 X 1 36	10
should april me (though such as perfect hope can	580 1 X 1 40	23
there's nobody else alive (such a sky and such	591 1 X 1 51	13
(such a sky and such a sun i never	591 1 X 1 51	13
a keen pure silence) such hands can build a	617 (CHAIRE) 19	2
and never have breathed such miracle murdered we whom	639 (CHAIRE) 41	9
now are skies-- and such a sharpening freedom lifts	675 95 POEMS 3	6
man remembers there is such a thing as spring	685 95 POEMS 13	7
what no tongue tells (such as ourselves) begins to	716 95 POEMS 44	18
may be everywhere with such a silence and such	717 95 POEMS 45	6
such a silence and such a darkness noone can	717 95 POEMS 45	6
the luck to hear such singing (or glimpse such	717 95 POEMS 45	10
such singing (or glimpse such sunlight as will leap	717 95 POEMS 45	10
fiend and i are such immortal friends the other's	730 95 POEMS 58	5
never fear: love, when such marvels vanish, will include .	741 95 POEMS 69	10
now to frolic in such mysteries as birth and	743 95 POEMS 71	13
begin to imagine quite such eagerly innocent whoms of	748 95 POEMS 76	13
shall not quite undo such first amazement as a	762 95 POEMS 89	5
this) beautiful kindness sweet such (past can's every can't)	763 95 POEMS 90	25
day never was there such a lay-- whom, among	794 73 POEMS 22	2
i'd be quite --come such perfection-- another i and	798 73 POEMS 26	23
whom begins to spill such golden blood as makes	811 73 POEMS 39	13
time can't answer: and such vivid nothing as green	818 73 POEMS 46	11
against the shrieking sky such one ness as con	826 73 POEMS 54	13
but unsinging. In spectral such hugest how hush, one	839 73 POEMS 67	3
of time --small wonder such a monster's fellowmen miscalled .	842 73 POEMS 70	13
and when he's plucked such mysteries as men do	843 73 POEMS 71	13

SUCK

| selves-them inghurl) bangbells (yawnchurches suck people) . . | 444 NO THANKS 59 | 14 |

+SUCK

| FOR CONTEXT, SEE . . . . | 333 VIVA 24 | 11 |

+SUCKED

| FOR CONTEXT, SEE . . . . | 385 NO THANKS 2 | 61 |

+SUCKING

| FOR CONTEXT, SEE . . . . | 635 (CHAIRE) 37 | 3 |

+SUCKS

| FOR CONTEXT, SEE . . . . | 474 NEW POEMS 12 | 12 |

SUDDEN

marching grass. A silver sudden parody of snow tickles . . .	5 T&C EPITHALAM	73
the grass-- shunning the sudden moonbeam's treacherous snare	8 T&C OF NICOL	25
a thickening fright the sudden fooled light. it is	11 T&C SONGS 2	20
with April feet like sudden flowers and all her	17 T&C PUELLA MEA	21
incessantly creates patterns of sudden lust her stealing body	34 T&C ORIENTALE 6	88
keenly musical light of sudden nothing.... la bocca mia . . .	84 T&C SON ACTU 3	15
moon fills abruptly with sudden silver these torn pockets . .	93 & POST IMPR 5	14
to enjoy the composed sudden body atop which always	193 XLI PORTRAIT 1	2

SUDDEN (CONTINUED)
    cleverly perching on the sudden extremity of one immense   . . 201 XLI PORTRAIT 9   30
SUDDENLY
    the maple's cheek, and suddenly by shining hordes in   . . . .   4 T&C EPITHALAM   62
    barbarous bright sky, and suddenly from the valley thrills .   5 T&C EPITHALAM   78
    faerie, perhaps a little suddenly (as sometimes the . . . . .   18 T&C PUELLA MEA   42
    leaping and i felt suddenly dizzy With the jostling . . . . .   44 T&C AMORES 8   3
    by one are turned suddenly and softly into irresponsible   . .   62 T&C PORTRAIT 10   21
    trees stand. The trees, suddenly wait against the moon's   . .   80 T&C SON UNRE 5   17
    me; and to face suddenly the lighted living hills . . . . . .   82 T&C SON ACTU 1   15
    this throat a little suddenly lifted in singing--hands   . . .   85 T&C SON ACTU 4   10
    in gluey twilight moving, suddenly is three animals. The   . .   95 & POST IMPR 7   3
    foetal head established It suddenly upon the huge neck   . . .   96 & POST IMPR 8   29
    away more softly horribly suddenly; (of these two most   . . .   98 & POST IMPR 9   4
    wholly, well --did (wisely suddenly into a dangerous womb .   115 & PORTRAIT 8   10
    chatouiller mon lezard ladies suddenly j'm'en fous des negres 121 & PORTRAIT 12   42
    score of youngest angels suddenly should stretch neat necks . 130 & SON REAL 1   5
    mystery of Hell) me suddenly grips in chuckles of . . . . . .   130 & SON REAL 1   7
    Upon the whole he suddenly clapped a tiny sunset . . . . . .   148 & SON REAL 19   7
    whose stilling lips murder suddenly me, but of my . . . . . .   152 & SON ACTU 1   11
    her smile makes something suddenly luminous and precise --and 152 & SON ACTU 1   13
    love you.... feel your suddenly body reach for me . . . . . .   157 & SON ACTU 6   6
    / / let's live suddenly without thinking under honest . . . .   160 & SON ACTU 9   1
    voice feels curiously cool (suddenly-Lights go! on, by   . . . 167 & SON ACTU 16   19
    twists spontaneously methodical. He suddenly tasted worms . . 170 & SON ACTU 19   12
    voice scattering perfume-gifted wings suddenly escorts with . 187 XLI SONGS 9   15
    whose whitehot lips however suddenly ap- proached may never . 193 XLI PORTRAIT 1   11
    whose feet reincarnate song suddenly leaping flameflung,   . . 206 XLI SONNETS 2   7
    / / / will suddenly trees leap from winter . . . . 218 XLI SONNETS 14   1
    lean exroper of horned suddenly crashing things) man spits . 252 IS 5 ONE 23   11
    onetwo which doubles up suddenly his bunged hinging victim . 259 IS 5 ONE 29   15
    am altogether foolish, i suddenly make a fist out . . . . . .   281 IS 5 THREE 5   19
    me with your body's suddenly curving entire warm questions . 282 IS 5 THREE 6   34
    of your smile, most suddenly which is of love . . . .   293 IS 5 FOUR 10   17
    his mouth (making everything suddenly old and with his   . . . 293 IS 5 FOUR 10   27
    gradually which descending are suddenly received) or by . . . 299 IS 5 FOUR 16   6
    softly your kissed thrice suddenly smile / / . . . .   300 IS 5 FOUR 17   24
    touch (now) with a suddenly unsaid gesture lightly my . . . .   302 IS 5 FIVE 1   5
    your arm will do suddenly that will do more . . . .   302 IS 5 FIVE 1   10
    (at a certain corner, suddenly) meets the tall policeman   . . 304 IS 5 FIVE 3   4
    huddling infinite wishless melancholy, suddenly looming)   . . 305 IS 5 FIVE 4   14
    W. c. a. she suddenly luffed --thanking me; and . . . .   326 VIVA 18   35
    sweet bull like dat ...suddenly i feels so lonely . . . . . .   332 VIVA 23   13
    is my beloved my (suddenly in sunlight he will . . . .   352 VIVA 43   16
    will shut very beautifully, suddenly, as when the heart . . .   366 VIVA 57   10
    has perfect fear (of suddenly me) like these first . . . . .   367 VIVA 58   6
    (lunge)ing bruiseD Suddenly by thousand starings rinsed . . 388 NO THANKS 5   6
    doesn't move (Moved more suddenly than) whose tiniest smile? 397 NO THANKS 14   4
    slendering sweetness touched renown) suddenly themselves if . 414 NO THANKS 31   5
    open our selves. create (suddenly announce: hurl) blind full 422 NO THANKS 39   15
    and preserved goldfishian gestures) suddenly sally rand . . . 425 NO THANKS 42   4
    transported are into how suddenly so huge a home . . . . . .   454 NO THANKS 69   6
    the u s a" suddenly uprose hungary and she . . . .   711 95 POEMS 39   9
    now) and dance you suddenly blossoming tree --i'll sing . . .   767 95 POEMS 93   23
+SUDDENLY
    FOR CONTEXT, SEE . . . .   101 & POST IMPR 11   52
    FOR CONTEXT, SEE . . . .   101 & POST IMPR 11   54
    FOR CONTEXT, SEE . . . .   122 & SEVEN POEMS 1   4
    FOR CONTEXT, SEE . . . .   330 VIVA 21   7
    FOR CONTEXT, SEE . . . .   646 (CHAIRE) 48   9
SUDDENLY-LIGHTS
    voice feels curiously cool (suddenly-Lights go! on, by . . .   167 & SON ACTU 16   19
SUFFER
    the land (do lovers suffer? all divinities proudly descending 768 95 POEMS 94   5
SUFFERS
    man question mark who suffers from indigestion question mark   246 IS 5 ONE 17   3
SUFFICE
    million selves and my suffice to through the only . . . . . .   510 50 POEMS 24   12

	PAGE	TITLE	LINE

SUFFICIENT
    not very big a sufficient pillow shoveling her small . . . . 134 & SON REAL 5   2
SUGAREDELLIPSES
    it swallow) s greedily sugaredellipses it does not disdain . 100 & POST IMPR 11   29
SUGGEST
    defunct periodical. i would suggest that certain ideas . . . 230 IS 5 ONE 2   19
    doesn't matter) which i suggest teach us a new . . . . 289 IS 5 FOUR 6   10
SUGGESTING
    dream myself speaks (whispering, suggesting that our souls . 285 IS 5 FOUR 2   4
SUGGESTION
    maybe" (heart makes the suggestion) "or even a daisy-- . . . 625 {CHAIRE} 27   ·11
SUGGESTS
    throb; which hints being; suggests identity) breathes fleet . 402 NO THANKS 19   10
SUICIDE
    a room stands a suicide sniffing a Paper rose . . . . 338 VIVA 29   2
SUIS
    n'est-ce pas que je suis belle cheri? les anglais . . . . . . 120 & PORTRAIT 12   11
SUIT
    quick i know this suit you pay a store . . . . 523 50 POEMS 36   12
    there this cheap this suit too quick no suit . . . . 523 50 POEMS 36   22
    suit too quick no suit there every -thing nothing . . . . . . 523 50 POEMS 36   23
SULKED
    soul the absurd eyelids sulked enormous sobs puckered the . . 52 T&C PORTRAIT 1   26
SULKSUCK
    whitermuch grab sicksilk soak sulksuck whim poke if inch . . 333 VIVA 24   11
SULKY
    to dis gorge) a sulky gob with entirely white . . . . 629 {CHAIRE} 31   3
SULTAN'S
    very notable of the sultan's nose pullable and rosy . . . . . 198 XLI PORTRAIT 6   9
SUM
    belch the chap hic sum- more eh chuckles skulch. . . . .°. 96 & POST IMPR 8   21
    is Relative or to sum it All Up god . . . . 315 VIVA 7   9
    by button of whisper sum blinked he belowtry eye . . . . . . 333 VIVA 24   8
    off the coast of Sum precisely where a craft . . . . 494 50 POEMS 8   4
    wint-air nic like ot-am sum-air (young old nic) like . . . . 618 {CHAIRE} 20   25
+SUM
    FOR CONTEXT, SEE . . . . 431 NO THANKS 48   23
SUM-AIR
    wint-air nic like ot-am sum-air (young old nic) like . . . . 618 {CHAIRE} 20   25
SUMMER
    heart pinched from dumb summer? O crazy daddy of . . . . . . 80 T&C SON UNRE 5   8
    In The Good Old Summer Time. My gorgeous bullet . . . . 130 & SON REAL 1   9
    Thirsty stirring. (Must be summer. Hush. Worms.) But It's . . 130 & SON REAL 1   12
    with refrain of unreasoning summer that by responding ways . 184 XLI SONGS 6   5
    crowing gold) nuzzle against summer thunder (together) smell 340 VIVA 31   18
    pain at joy, come summer puts on fur answers . . . . 394 NO THANKS 11   7
    many bells down) spring summer autumn winter he sang . . . . 515 50 POEMS 29   3
    grew autumn winter spring summer) that noone loved him . . . 515 50 POEMS 29   11
    (both dong and ding) summer autumn winter spring reaped . . . 515 50 POEMS 29   34
    / / / / "summer is over --it's no . . . . 625 {CHAIRE} 27   1
    whereas (my sweet) our summer in fall and in . . . . 776 73 POEMS 4   30
    quivers this miracle of summer night her trillion secrets . . 809 73 POEMS 37   3
    tell me why this summer world (and you and . . . . 836 73 POEMS 64   3
+SUMMER
    FOR CONTEXT, SEE . . . . 618 {CHAIRE} 20   25
SUMMER'S
    (his autumn's winter being summer's spring who moved by . . . 420 NO THANKS 37   3
    gives the truth to summer's lie; bloodies with dizzying . . . 560 1 X 1 20   2
    eyes, and what were summer's beside their glories downward . 573 1 X 1 33   5
    our souls, awakened from summer's green trance, would not . . 675 95 POEMS 3   10
SUMMITLESS
    piece of forever with summitless younger than angels are . . 586 1 X 1 46   5
SUMMONED
    scrutinize his handiwork: they (summoned by that savage yell 799 73 POEMS 27   26
SUMNER
    my lovely lambs, of Sumner Volstead Christ and Co. . . . . . 266 IS 5 TWO 1   2
SUMPTUOUS
    always shut in the sumptuous screech of simplicity (out . . . 195 XLI PORTRAIT 3   7

	PAGE	TITLE	LINE

SUMPTUOUSLY
    him as your lover sumptuously being kind because i . . . . . 42 T&C AMORES 6   19
    supercilious chimneys, my nerves sumptuously wink ....and . . 169 & SON ACTU 18   8
SUN
    forth rides the pungent sun with hooded day preening . . . . 4 T&C EPITHALAM   65
    scattered by the abundant sun invades the new mosaic . . . . 5 T&C EPITHALAM   83
    made jewels by the sun, so one high shining . . . . 8 T&C OF NICOL   16
    day under the unaccountable sun) Distinct Lady swiftly take . 43 T&C AMORES 7   24
    Nothing under the ample sun, under the insufficient day . . . 43 T&C AMORES 7   39
    and mysterious the flowerstricken sun- light is thickening . 69 T&C POST IMPR 6   23
    greatly matter to the sun, nor will rain care . . . . 84 T&C SON ACTU 3   7
    derl y tottering in sun-light THE nobody (knows and . . . . 101 & POST IMPR 11   78
    fooling bore --When The Sun Begins To (with a . . . . 130 & SON REAL 1   3
    off). It was spring sun-stirring. sweetly to the mangling . . 135 & SON REAL 6   13
    that matter knocked by sun moon jabbed jerked with . . . . . 153 & SON ACTU 2   11
    suddenly escorts with feet sun-sheer the smarting beauty of . 187 XLI SONGS 9   17
    I will take the sun in my mouth and . . . . 189 XLI SONGS 11   3
    do you find the sun, ladies? <> "there is . . . . 255 IS 5 ONE 26   7
    leaves open Clouds take sun mountains stand And oceans . . 359 VIVA 50   12
    life (which liked the sun and the moon) resembles . . . . . 360 VIVA 51   23
    am gone like a sun which must go sometimes, ... 372 VIVA 63   7
    the earliest spear of sun perfectly should disappear moon's . 377 VIVA 68   3
    rain big snow big sun big moon (enter us) . . . . 393 NO THANKS 10   15
    the sky screamed the sun died) the ship lifts . . . . 419 NO THANKS 36   10
    whose naught and all sun are and moon come . . . . 440 NO THANKS 56   26
    salute (by moon by sun i deeply greet this . . . . 441 NO THANKS 56   66
    ellSB el Ls) -to sun (crash). Streets glit ter . . . . . . 444 NO THANKS 59   21
    more is or total sun oceaning than any this . . . . 502 50 POEMS 16   3
    love become while every sun goes round its moon . . . . . . 510 50 POEMS 24   14
    they reaped their same sun moon stars rain children . . . . 515 50 POEMS 29   8
    their dream stars rain sun moon (and only the . . . . 515 50 POEMS 29   21
    and went their came sun moon stars rain / . . . . 515 50 POEMS 29   36
    beyond conceiving mind of sun will stand, so strictly . . . 520 50 POEMS 34   26
    rise which am the sun of whom // . . . . 527 50 POEMS 39   32
    rejoice rejoice) --opens the sun: who music wear burst . . . 533 50 POEMS 45   13
    with dizzying leaves the sun and yanks immortal stars . . . 560 1 X 1 20   3
    fu ruddy as a sun with blue true two . . . . 567 1 X 1 27   3
    weazel how be you (sun or snow) gone into . . . . 568 1 X 1 28   10
    sky and such a sun i never knew and . . . . 591 1 X 1 51   13
    brighter than even the sun (we're everything greater than . . 594 1 X 1 54   37
    a heartbeat of some sun; his least unmotion roams . . . . . 609 {CHAIRE} 11   11
    to squirm and the sun strikes to gain a . . . . 620 {CHAIRE} 22   2
    bell to disappear a sun and out of houses . . . . 624 {CHAIRE} 26   4
    still if now our sun is gone reminding with . . . . 624 {CHAIRE} 26   22
    a strange ness Of sun light and of fragrance . . . . 657 {CHAIRE} 59   5
    not only wherever the sun and the stars and . . . . 686 95 POEMS 14   16
    nobody (and stars moon sun fall rise come go . . . . 693 95 POEMS 21   19
    any moon or possibly sun shines they are our . . . . 728 95 POEMS 56   7
    am not sorry when sun and rain make april . . . . 749 95 POEMS 77   4
    wing tree leaf bird sun & singing &) thing . . . . 753 95 POEMS 81   18
    is that himself the sun --arriving truly, faithfully who . . 756 95 POEMS 84   1
    meant and whatever a sun will always sing is . . . . 766 95 POEMS 92   9
    truth more first than sun more last than star . . . . 768 95 POEMS 94   12
    / / 0 the sun comes up-up-up in the . . . . 773 73 POEMS 1   1
    (now with one sweet sun in it, now with . . . . 786 73 POEMS 14   12
    for until though the sun in his heaven says . . . . 801 73 POEMS 29   23
    return --you are my sun, my moon, and all . . . . 810 73 POEMS 38   14
    more than day whose sun is moon, and our . . . . 818 73 POEMS 46   2
    slips from few of sun fingers numb) with anguished . . . . 822 73 POEMS 50   2
    / / / & sun & sil e nce . . . . 830 73 POEMS 58   1
    ing won der ful sun moon stars the all, ... 840 73 POEMS 68   11
+SUN
    FOR CONTEXT, SEE . . . . 347 VIVA 38   28
    FOR CONTEXT, SEE . . . . 541 1 X 1 1   1
SUN-LIGHT
    derl y tottering in sun-light THE nobody (knows and . . . . 101 & POST IMPR 11   78
SUN-SHEER
    suddenly escorts with feet sun-sheer the smarting beauty of . 187 XLI SONGS 9   17

SUN-STIRRING
    off). It was spring sun-stirring. sweetly to the mangling . . 135 & SON REAL 6   13
SUN'S
    whose lilied robe the sun's white hands emboss, betwixt . . .   3 T&C EPITHALAM   29
    and this is the sun's birthday; this is the . . . . 663 {CHAIRE) 65   6
SUNBEAM
    must be you no sunbeam ever lies Bang is . . . . 570 1 X 1 30   5
SUNBEAM'S
    truly which syncopate some sunbeam's skilful fingerings; it . 19 T&C PUELLA MEA   86
    horror to defend a sunbeam's architecture with his life: . . 562 1 X 1 22   12
SUNBEAMS
    the colour drub souring sunbeams, of a foetal fragrance . . . 144 & SON REAL 15   2
    of these trees) when sunbeams loot furnished rooms through . 442 NO THANKS 57   11
    more than raindrops need sunbeams or snowflakes make possible 577 1 X 1 37   3
SUNDARK
    undeaths through (slapsoothed by sundark) brightshadowfully . 681 95 POEMS 9   13
SUNDAY
    who do keep their sunday flower. The babybreasted broad . . . 74 T&C SON REAL 5   11
    under the moon on Sunday. by way of saying . . . . 355 VIVA 46   2
    and even if it's sunday may i be wrong . . . . 481 NEW POEMS 19   7
+SUNDAY
    FOR CONTEXT, SEE . . . . 384 NO THANKS 2   33
SUNDRY
    joe (yankee) gould irketh sundry who are trying to . . . . 410 NO THANKS 27   7
SUNFUL
    sky cannot be so sunful i am through you . . . . 537 50 POEMS 49   15
    shadowy virtue and of sunful sin namely (ford madox . . . . 607 {CHAIRE) 9   13
SUNG
 ' home and mother when sung at the old howard . . . . 204 XLI LA GUERRE 2   8
    where other songs be sung; yet stand They here . . . . . . 208 XLI SONNETS 4   11
+SUNG
    FOR CONTEXT, SEE . . . . 333 VIVA 24   10
SUNLIGHT
    the emperor's palace run sunlight and moonlight and the . . . 32 T&C ORIENTALE 6 16
    rancid elves upon neat sunlight into the flower- stricken . . 69 T&C POST IMPR 6 4
    inanely codified with superb sunlight, jolts of delapida- . . 94 & POST IMPR 6 3
    like incense and like sunlight and like ships and . . . . . 111 & PORTRAIT 6   64
    LiNg an in-stant with sunLight t h e n) . . . . 122 & SEVEN POEMS 1 16
    to pass? shallowness of sunlight falls and, cruelly, across . 190 XLI SONGS 12   7
    hence in a little sunlight and less moonlight ourselves . . . 238 IS 5 ONE 9   19
    countenances seated in arranging; sunlight with-ered . . . . 255 IS 5 ONE 26   2
    incense with and oh sunlight-- the crash of the . . . . . . 280 IS 5 THREE 4   23
    at Calchidas, in the sunlight? down ever so far . . . . . . 281 IS 5 THREE 5   2
    ever so far-- hush. Sunlight, there are old men . . . . . . 281 IS 5 THREE 5   23
    / / / / sunlight was over our mouths . . . . 283 IS 5 THREE 7   1
    here and here reflecting sunlight (everywhere sunlight keen . 283 IS 5 THREE 7   13
    here reflecting sunlight (everywhere sunlight keen complete . 283 IS 5 THREE 7   14
    imaginable, love, and eat sunlight (do you believe it? . . . 289 IS 5 FOUR 6   8
    beloved my (suddenly in sunlight he will bow, & . . . . . . 352 VIVA 43   16
    a flower, understanding sizelessly sunlight Open what . . . . 453 NO THANKS 68   14
    go on into the sunlight the fine sunlight with . . . . . . 529 50 POEMS 41   7
    the sunlight the fine sunlight with a firm day . . . . . . 529 50 POEMS 41   8
    arrival with a soul sunlight? yes (always we have . . . . . 582 1 X 1 42   5
    (the humble man than sunlight older with ships than . . . . 585 1 X 1 45   14
    i'm born we 're sunlight of oneness / / . . . . 589 1 X 1 49   20
    here --but look: not sunlight? yes! and (plunging rapturously 650 {CHAIRE) 52   18
    noises called people called sunlight (elsewhere flat the . . 658 {CHAIRE) 60   11
    voice loves children and sunlight and mountains) in april . . 660 {CHAIRE) 62   23
    riding in fragrance of sunlight (side by side all . . . . . 661 {CHAIRE) 63   2
    can't quite poison God's sunlight / / / / . . . . 708 95 POEMS 36   16
    everything in the sky --sunlight and singing welcome your . . 717 95 POEMS 45   4
    singing (or glimpse such sunlight as will leap higher . . . . 717 95 POEMS 45   11
    the mercy of perfect sunlight after days of dark, ... 735 95 POEMS 63   12
    happiness) lovers alone wear sunlight. The whole truth not . 765 95 POEMS 91   5
    ladies (Each youngest) in sunlight / / / / . . . . 778 73 POEMS 6   24
    than music) feeling that sunlight is (life and day . . . . . 816 73 POEMS 44   6
    ing through wonder ful sunlight --look-- selves, stir: writhe 835 73 POEMS 63   9
    up leaping through merciful sunlight) to burst in a . . . . . 841 73 POEMS 69   33

		PAGE	TITLE	LINE
+SUNLIGHT				
FOR CONTEXT, SEE	. . . .	69	T&C POST IMPR 6	23
FOR CONTEXT, SEE	. . . .	101	& POST IMPR 11	78
FOR CONTEXT, SEE	. . . .	104	& POST IMPR 14	5
FOR CONTEXT, SEE	. . . .	657	(CHAIRE) 59	5
FOR CONTEXT, SEE	. . . .	710	95 POEMS 38	5
FOR CONTEXT, SEE	. . . .	796	73 POEMS 24	1
SUNLIGHT'S				
Leaf among dark ness. sunlight's thenlike? now Disappears . .	397	NO THANKS 14	17
SUNLY				
is most sane and sunly and more it cannot	530	50 POEMS 42	13
SUNNING				
flown even higher) is sunning his penguinsoul in the	631	(CHAIRE) 33	8
SUNNY				
amazed doves flicker upon sunny wings as if in	6	T&C EPITHALAM	138
of silver gliding from sunny thunder into freshness as . . .	58	T&C PORTRAIT 6	7
wheeled out on the sunny dump of oblivion) a	197	XLI PORTRAIT 5	22
SUNRISE				
lyman ruddy as a sunrise fresh with blue come	567	1 X 1 27	18
this man earth's first sunrise) and his voice is	617	(CHAIRE) 19	5
+SUNRISE				
FOR CONTEXT, SEE	567	1 X 1 27	3
SUNS				
of midnight dropped more suns than are (yes; and	576	1 X 1 36	12
blossoming beyond to breathe suns of the night, bring	811	73 POEMS 39	9
SUNSET				
beyond this fern of sunset frond on frond opening	12	T&C SONGS 2	43
riding upon a scarlet sunset trampling the night easily . . .	30	T&C ORIENTALE 4	23
loved me, moon and sunset stars and flowers gold	39	T&C AMORES 4	6
the awful beauty of sunset the young city putting	48	T&C IMPRESS 2	14
are troubled. in the sunset their chimneys converse angrily,	62	T&C PORTRAIT 10	12
eyeless miles the chattering sunset ludicrously dies, i hear	64	T&C POST IMPR 1	9
of twilight ....or if sunset utters one unhurried muscled . .	82	T&C SON ACTU 1	7
eyes (who moves) at sunset and who--touches--the hills . . .	91	& POST IMPR 3	3
touches: the fields (at sunset) / / / /	91	& POST IMPR 3	21
/ Paris; this April sunset completely utters utters serenely	93	& POST IMPR 5	1
/ / of this sunset (which is so filled	98	& POST IMPR 9	1
suddenly clapped a tiny sunset of vermouth -colour. Hair. . .	148	& SON REAL 19	8
the rain- darkness, the sunset being sheathed i sit	186	XLI SONGS 8	2
singular ribbon of common sunset is hanging, snow speaks . .	202	XLI PORTRAIT 9	51
dreamy spine against thick sunset i perceive in front	279	IS 5 THREE 3	4
may guess if at sunset it should, leaning against	285	IS 5 FOUR 2	12
four crows drop into sunset, playin uh busted harmonica . . .	332	VIVA 23	32
/ / / / sunset) edges become swiftly corners	345	VIVA 36	1
daemon half tree among sunset dream acute from root	362	VIVA 53	7
the structure of distinct sunset driving white spikes of . .	378	VIVA 69	8
woven by always upon sunset, crickets within me whisper . . .	435	NO THANKS 51	36
's whis- per in sunset or thrushes toward dusk	512	50 POEMS 26	24
lady's gaze enters a sunset "can grow (gracefully or	626	(CHAIRE) 28	2
the gold of november sunset (and feeling: that if	824	73 POEMS 52	5
+SUNSET				
FOR CONTEXT, SEE	788	73 POEMS 16	14
SUNSET'S				
/ than (by yon sunset's wintry glow revealed) this	254	IS 5 ONE 25	1
SUNSETS				
sink into and their sunsets, it shall pass. Our	9	T&C SONGS 1	26
SUNSMELL				
built by forever & sunsmell (sometimes a wonder of	512	50 POEMS 26	30
SUPER				
father of one (ask super-) wonderful (mother) child is . . .	398	NO THANKS 15	5
SUPERB				
twurls-of-excrement inanely codified with superb sunlight, .	94	& POST IMPR 6	3
SUPERBLY				
dignity of papyruscoloured faces superbly limp the ostensible	111	& PORTRAIT 6	54
SUPERCILIOUS				
your knees among the supercilious chimneys, my nerves	169	& SON ACTU 18	7
+SUPERCOLOSSAL				
FOR CONTEXT, SEE	392	NO THANKS 9	3

		PAGE	TITLE	LINE

SUPERFLUOUS
ra (caveat emptor) cy superfluous hair or Think We've . . . . 549 1 X 1 9   13
SUPERHUMAN
/ nobody could in superhuman flights of submoronic fancy . . 790 73 POEMS 18   2
SUPERIMPOSING
atmosphere of a street superimposing a numbing im- . . . . . 197 XLI PORTRAIT 5   2
SUPERIOR
to glue in a superior terror; be thy taut . . . .   9 T&C SONGS 1   31
struts (her thickish flesh superior to the genuine daze . . . 150 & SON REAL 21   12
frightened fields with the superior dust-of-sleep. wields . . 163 & SON ACTU 12   4
SUPERLATIVE
inhabitants; in whose warm superlative body do distinctly . . 22 T&C PUELLA MEA   255
SUPERLATIVELY
with man's poor soul superlatively brave. Surely from robes .   5 T&C EPITHALAM   96
SUPERME
tried) the great pink superme diocri ty of mocra . . . . . . 635 {CHAIRE} 37   8
SUPERMETAMATHICAL
/ out of a supermetamathical subpreincestures pooped universe 425 NO THANKS 42   1
SUPERMINDS
true; or so subhuman superminds declare --nor all their . . . 817 73 POEMS 45   3
SUPERNOD
scienti fic land of supernod where freedom is compulsory . . 544 1 X 1 4   22
SUPERSEDED
various innocent ferocities are superseded by the sole . . . 202 XLI PORTRAIT 9   41
SUPERSIEVE
launch we a Hyperluxurious Supersieve (which Ultima Thule Of 334 VIVA 25   2
SUPERSNARE
crude; an indestructible occult supersnare of resistless . . 799 73 POEMS 27   19
SUPERSTATE
facts no sub human superstate ever knew (1) we . . . . 803 73 POEMS 31   6
SUPPER
soul aglow) his nightly supper sups it isn't snowing . . . . 254 IS 5 ONE 25   22
SUPPLE
to see as a supple and young tree, her . . . . 20 T&C PUELLA MEA   156
breasts inhale the slow supple flower of thy beauty, ... 31 T&C ORIENTALE 5   26
York. Be- tween its supple financial teeth deliriously . . . 201 XLI PORTRAIT 9   3
fearless and thirsty and supple and even if it's . . . . . . 481 NEW POEMS 19   6
SUPPLIANT
beseech thee bless thy suppliant singer and his wandering . .   7 T&C EPITHALAM   168
+SUPPORT
FOR CONTEXT, SEE . . . . 408 NO THANKS 25   9
SUPPORTS
cube of undimishied silence, supports while devouring the . . 201 XLI PORTRAIT 9   18
SUPPOSE
and indecision --do not suppose these without any reason . . 91 & POST IMPR 3   14
/ / / / suppose Life is an old . . . . 102 & POST IMPR 12   1
once? what if (merely suppose) mine should overhear and . . . 374 VIVA 65   10
air--and whose do you suppose possibly are certain hands, . . 378 VIVA 69   6
a mother i rather suppose" "will's dad never gave . . . . . . 707 95 POEMS 35   16
to greenly hurl snow suppose we could not love, ... 743 95 POEMS 71   4
; why even i suppose one 's wife) --does . . . . 779 73 POEMS 7   16
SUPPOSED
think things which were supposed to be out of . . . . 353 VIVA 44   16
SUPPOSEDLY
me?) according to such supposedly indigenous throstles Art is 230 IS 5 ONE 2   31
+SUPPOSEDLY
FOR CONTEXT, SEE . . . . 392 NO THANKS 9   19
SUPPOSING
/ / / / supposing i dreamed this) only . . . . 292 IS 5 FOUR 9   1
over (at that just supposing we had met and . . . . 323 VIVA 15   9
just but you know supposing we just had let . . . . 323 VIVA 15   12
SUPPRESS
suppressed the desire to suppress the suppressed desire of . 263 IS 5 ONE 32   38
SUPPRESSED
occupation, he had long suppressed the desire to suppress . . 263 IS 5 ONE 32   38
desire to suppress the suppressed desire of shall we . . . . 263 IS 5 ONE 32   38
SUPPRESSING
gaily for the hyenas suppressing my frank qualms in . . . . . 326 VIVA 18   21

	PAGE	TITLE	LINE
SUPPRESSION			
a wounding a beautiful suppression the accurate boy mouth . .	54	T&C PORTRAIT 2	7
SUPREME			
grips in chuckles of supreme sex. In The Good	130	& SON REAL 1	8
of tinying time (into supreme Now: feeling memory shrink . .	373	VIVA 64	11
doth impart one stands supreme i mean the an	544	1 X 1 4	3
wraith) ghosts drowning in supreme thunder? ours (over you .	639	{CHAIRE} 41	2
blood as if whole supreme this complete doubtless universe .	675	95 POEMS 3	7
SUPREMELY			
all (for love's secret supremely clothes herself with day) .	379	VIVA 70	5
heart is her mind) supremely whole uplifting the, of	533	50 POEMS 45	5
SUPS			
aglow) his nightly supper sups it isn't snowing snow	254	IS 5 ONE 25	22
SURE			
believe in death be sure of this it is	39	T&C AMORES 4	2
/ inthe, exquisite; morning sure lyHer eye s exactly	104	& POST IMPR 14	2
rosebug and you say Sure you say (like that)	127	& SEVEN POEMS 5	48
you say (like that) sure i'll come with you	127	& SEVEN POEMS 5	49
that marriage is a sure cure for masturbation). A	167	& SON ACTU 16	5
the proficient poison of sure sleep bereaves us of	210	XLI SONNETS 6	1
knows what (i am sure of this) her blunt	225	IS 5 ONE LIZ	10
somewhat obscure to be sure university spends her time . . .	234	IS 5 ONE 5	2
of her radiator made sure her springs were O.	248	IS 5 ONE 19	8
/ / / o sure) but nobody unders (no	400	NO THANKS 17	2
don't be sil why sure) i mean the (o	400	NO THANKS 17	8
the (o well ughhuh sure why not yuh course	400	NO THANKS 17	9
posi but i know sure that's) but listen here's	400	NO THANKS 17	11
yuh) i know (o sure i know yes of	400	NO THANKS 17	15
(and every child was sure that spring danced when	521	50 POEMS 34	51
+SURE			
FOR CONTEXT, SEE	519	50 POEMS 33	9
SURELY			
poor soul superlatively brave. Surely from robes of	5	T&C EPITHALAM	97
edge of day) i surely make a millionth poem	92	& POST IMPR 4	18
actly her sitsat a surely! little, roundtable amongother; .	104	& POST IMPR 14	20
well fussed flesh does surely to mesh. New and	136	& SON REAL 7	12
the garden. Time shall surely reap and on Death's	208	XLI SONNETS 4	9
that my feet have surely known the furious ways	216	XLI SONNETS 12	13
/ / / the surely Cued motif smites truly	311	VIVA 3	1
maims and blinds (but surely does not forget, perish, ...	377	VIVA 68	9
almost this god this surely dream perhaps this ghost) . . .	441	NO THANKS 56	49
singular most flame and surely poets only understands) honour	456	NO THANKS 71	11
we who are we? surely not i not you	582	1 X 1 42	10
poems (my mother's greatgrandmother surely would know) of . .	748	95 POEMS 76	6
+SURELY			
FOR CONTEXT, SEE	104	& POST IMPR 14	2
SURELYEYE			
qui site morning, her sureLyeye s sit-ex actly her	104	& POST IMPR 14	20
SURFACES			
and pain are merely surfaces (one itself showing, itself . .	531	50 POEMS 43	5
SURGES			
my gladness around me surges a miracle of unceasing	749	95 POEMS 77	9
SURGING			
slippery eyes drown in surging flesh). A thumblike index . .	226	IS 5 ONE MAME	5
SURLING			
/ / / helves surling out of eakspeasies per	330	VIVA 21	1
SURLY			
(i notice) trees winterbrief surly old gurgle a nonsense . .	282	IS 5 THREE 6	11
SURMISE			
fragile might to not surmise she dreamed one afternoon . . .	72	T&C SON REAL 3	8
+SURPASS			
FOR CONTEXT, SEE	814	73 POEMS 42	5
SURPASSING			
curtaining dusk be drawn surpàssing nets are sedulously spun	5	T&C EPITHALAM	86
SURPRISABLE			
pretended breasts, forked in surprisable unliving eyes . . .	103	& POST IMPR 13	3
SURPRISE			
whitely peer empty of surprise death's faultless eyes (whose	11	T&C SONGS 2	24

SURPRISE (CONTINUED)
    flower of so pure surprise (it were so very . . . . 18 T&C PUELLA MEA 50
    did-- you imagine His surprise bellowing through the general 117 & PORTRAIT 10   8
    hard body filled with surprise like a white shocking . . . . 147 & SON REAL 18   4
    wish, to rapture should surprise my soul slowly which . . . . 205 XLI SONNETS 1   4
    whose least breathing may surprise ourselves --let's then . . 368 VIVA 59   14
    for sheer wonder mere surprise (then turn the page) . . . . . 689 95 POEMS 17   3
SURPRISES
    poem of thy remembrance surprises with refrain of unreasoning 184 XLI SONGS 6   4
SURPRISING
    ground, it is hardly surprising if anyone hardly should . . . 263 IS 5 ONE 32   35
SURREPTITIOUSLY
    for the nearest 1; surreptitiously cogitating the dictum of . 327 VIVA 18   38
SURROUND
    those pearls more than surround this throat) i wear . . . . . 372 VIVA 63   9
    may stern particular Love surround your trite how terrible . 522 50 POEMS 35   10
SURROUNDED
    laborious, casual where the surrounded smile hangs breathless 83 T&C SON ACTU 2 15
    neatly through enormous twilight surrounded by their triumphs 111 & PORTRAIT 6   38
    agreeably cheerfully remarked when surrounded by fat stupid . 241 IS 5 ONE 12   3
    George Washington almost incompletely surrounded by well- . . 262 IS 5 ONE 32   11
    cOmEs a glass box: surrounded by priests moving in . . . . . 280 IS 5 THREE 4   10
SURVEYS
    one immense tooth myself surveys safely the complete . . . . 201 XLI PORTRAIT 9 31
SUSCEPTIBILITY
    fragility. Well and when--Does susceptibility imply . . . . . 141 & SON REAL 12   7
SUSPECT
    seem generous) don't All suspect each (nor have i . . . . . . 391 NO THANKS 8   4
+SUSPECT
    FOR CONTEXT, SEE . . . . 698 95 POEMS 26   1
SUSPECTED
    shrines which noone has suspected (but wherein silently . . . 285 IS 5 FOUR 2   17
    serene whom queries not suspected selves of space-- life . . 517 50 POEMS 31   7
SUSPENDERS
    gold teeth b pink suspenders c reads Atlantis x . . . . 200 XLI PORTRAIT 8   7
+SUSPENDERS
    FOR CONTEXT, SEE . . . . 166 & SON ACTU 15   6
SUSPICIOUS
    the dress was a suspicious madder, importing the cruelty . . 103 & POST IMPR 13 1
+SUSTAININGNESS
    FOR CONTEXT, SEE . . . . 449 NO THANKS 64   10
SVELTE
    only one tree, one svelte translation of eternity unto . . .   6 T&C EPITHALAM 123
    in the dumb dark svelte and urgent (again love . . . . 37 T&C AMORES 2   13
    diminishing have swoopingly fallen svelte sagging gone into . 110 & PORTRAIT 6   28
    dusk with an untimid svelte subdued magic while in . . . . . 138 & SON REAL 9   5
    distinctly has) the weightless svelte drifting sexual feather 140 & SON REAL 11   2
SWADDLED
    newer pastures or because swaddled with a frozen brook . . . 258 IS 5 ONE 28   13
SWAGGERING
    are newly baked and swaggering cookies of indignant light . . 226 IS 5 ONE MAME 14
SWAGGERS
    (a dapper derbied creature, swaggers daintily twiddling his . 274 IS 5 TWO 9   29
SWALLOW
    currants and cherries it (swallow s bun chesofnew grapes . . 100 & POST IMPR 11 24
    cubesandovalsof sweetness but it swallow) s greedily . . . . 100 & POST IMPR 11 29
    to do for the swallow, that closes a flight . . . . 181 XLI SONGS 3   4
    grassblades, five ideas can swallow a man; three words . . . 491 50 POEMS 5   13
    infinite jukethrob smoke & swallow to dis gorge) a . . . . . 629 {CHAIRE} 31   1
SWALLOWED
    ingly pompous a the swallowed mottle with smooth or . . . . . 96 & POST IMPR 8   6
    stars the gods are swallowed even Nile the kind . . . . 112 & PORTRAIT 6   84
    its terrors; the, mouth's, swallowed, muscle (itch of groping 136 & SON REAL 7   9
    and with astute fatuous swallowed eyes smiles, one grin . . . 151 & SON REAL 22   13
    --never whose proudly life swallowed is by (with hope . . . . 402 NO THANKS 19   5
SWALLOWING
    are noise funnily swallows swallowing revolv- ingly pompous a 96 & POST IMPR 8   5
    if by shadowy if) swallowing is everywhere beginningless a . 757 95 POEMS 85   12

```
                                                            PAGE      TITLE       LINE
SWALLOWS
  lows are noise funnily swallows swallowing revolv- ingly  . .  96 & POST IMPR 8    5
  arched occasional steep youth swallows curvingly the keenness 140 & SON REAL 11    5
  determine its roundness: if swallows tryst in your barn  . . . 514 50 POEMS 28     6
  Murdered the House) hole swallows it self while nobody  . . . 693 95 POEMS 21     15
  (1956) a monstering horror swallows this unworld me by  . . . 711 95 POEMS 39      1
SWAM
  sweetness of a rose swam upward from the troubled . . . . . .   8 T&C OF NICOL     8
SWANK
  was a ship of swank (as gallant as they . . . . . . . . . . 494 50 POEMS 8        1
+SWANS
  FOR CONTEXT, SEE  . . . . . . . . . . . . . . . . . . . . . 384 NO THANKS 2      29
SWARM
  eLl s? bE -ginningly) come-swarm: faces ar; rive go. . . . . 444 NO THANKS 59     5
  drove sleeping selves to swarm their fates woke dreamers  . . 520 50 POEMS 34     11
  work while she can swarm. To doubt that in . . . . . . . . 790 73 POEMS 18        8
SWARMING
  is filthy with agile swarming sonal crea- tures --Children, .  69 T&C POST IMPR 6  5
SWARMS
  birds thy breasts are swarms of white bees upon . . . . . . .  29 T&C ORIENTALE 3  7
  / / stinging gold swarms upon the spires silver . . . . . . .  51 T&C IMPRESS 5    2
+SWAT
  FOR CONTEXT, SEE  . . . . . . . . . . . . . . . . . . . . . 500 50 POEMS 14      19
SWAYING
  rose) standing near my swaying over her (silent) with . . . . 352 VIVA 43         8
SWAYS
  of the flower that sways in the autumn she  . . . . . . . . 183 XLI SONGS 5      14
SWEAR
  lip to lip i swear (to noone everyone) constitutes  . . . . 264 IS 5 ONE 33       2
  than wisdom lady i swear by all flowers. Don't  . . . . . . 290 IS 5 FOUR 7      10
SWEARS
  n phonograph stopS. b swears in persian at phonograph . . . . 200 XLI PORTRAIT 8 29
SWEAT
  how, funny Do tell ....sweat, succeeds breathings stopped to 136 & SON REAL 7     15
SWEATING
  underdrawers club the faintly sweating air with pinkness, one 144 & SON REAL 15    6
SWEDE
  gun on Marcus"-- "duh Swede rolls down tree flights . . . . . 332 VIVA 23         8
+SWEEP
  FOR CONTEXT, SEE  . . . . . . . . . . . . . . . . . . . . . 755 95 POEMS 83       3
SWEET
  uncouth) of Helios the sweet wheels tremulous-- are there . .   4 T&C EPITHALAM   48
  by shining hordes in sweet unserious dress ascends the  . . .  4 T&C EPITHALAM   63
  pose! O visible beatitude sweet sweet intolerable! silence  .   5 T&C EPITHALAM  110
  O visible beatitude sweet sweet intolerable! silence . . . .    5 T&C EPITHALAM  110
  of darkness, and the sweet strong final bird transcends . . .   7 T&C EPITHALAM  165
  feet tread sleepless meadows sweet with fear") then be  . . .   9 T&C SONGS 1     27
  follow soon on the sweet heels of passed afterday, . . . . .   10 T&C SONGS 1     39
  thy lips is a sweet thing and small. Death, . . . . . . . . .  13 T&C SONGS 3     15
  dappled dreams the swift sweet deer the red rare . . . . . .   14 T&C SONGS 4      7
  authentic springs, beyond the sweet instinctive wells, which   19 T&C PUELLA MEA 121
  smooth to stroke and sweet to see as a . . . . . . . . . . .   20 T&C PUELLA MEA 155
  do distinctly live all sweet cities passed away-- in  . . . .  22 T&C PUELLA MEA 257
  a costly morsel of sweet tears) gesticulates, and . . . . . .  23 T&C PUELLA MEA 269
  / / / O sweet spontaneous earth how often . . . . . . . . . .  46 T&C LA GUERRE 2   1
  light fails and this sweet profound Paris moves with  . . . .  71 T&C SON REAL 2    7
  unrepute focusses in the sweet slow animal bottomless eyes  .  74 T&C SON REAL 5    6
  on another's face your sweet hair lay in such . . . . . . . .  76 T&C SON UNRE 1    5
  furiously plays the hot sweet horrible stops of her . . . . . 110 & PORTRAIT 6    11
  a halfsmile (for society's sweet sake) in the not . . . . . . 146 & SON REAL 17   11
  exquisite i wait the sweet annihilation of swift flesh  . . . 182 XLI SONGS 4     10
  with shut eyes the sweet earth where thou liest . . . . . . . 184 XLI SONGS 6     17
  and there is the sweet shy pirouette your hair  . . . . . . . 186 XLI SONGS 8     14
  duneyed master enter the sweet gates of my heart  . . . . . . 188 XLI SONGS 10    15
  half-mud and not too sweet? / / / / . . . . . . . . . . . . . 198 XLI PORTRAIT 6  35
  of vilest mind and sweet uncaring earth by thoughtful . . . . 213 XLI SONNETS 9    3
  / oDE o the sweet & aged people who . . . . . . . . . . . . . 250 IS 5 ONE 21      2
  life and found it sweet-- a tear within his . . . . . . . . . 273 IS 5 TWO 8       8
```

SWEET (CONTINUED)

/ / / my sweet old etcetera aunt lucy . . . . 276 IS 5 TWO 10 1
and fragile lips the sweet small clumsy feet of . . . . . . 306 IS 5 FIVE 5 14
table all which seemed sweet deep and inexplicable not . . . 322 VIVA 14 7
1 (hutch) hutchinson says sweet guinea pigs do it . . . . . 325 VIVA 17 7
koib" --you know alotta sweet bull like dat ...suddenly . . . 332 VIVA 23 12
Ever-Ever Land i speak sweet morons gather roun' who . . . . 466 NEW POEMS 4 2
that's something else my sweet (i feel that's true) . . . . . 475 NEW POEMS 13 24
flashing soft neverwheres & sweet nothingly gushing tinsel; . 480 NEW POEMS 18 11
bitter all utterly things sweet, maggoty minus and dumb . . . 521 50 POEMS 34 62
my you , darling sweet this creative never known . . . . . . 577 1 X 1 37 13
season than reason; my sweet one (and april's where . . . . . 578 1 X 1 38 11
and only while your sweet eyes close have disappeared . . . . 588 1 X 1 48 5
/ / / / "sweet spring is your time . . . . 591 1 X 1 51 1
is lovetime and viva sweet love" (all the merry . . . . . . 591 1 X 1 51 4
joyful selves are singing) "sweet spring is your time . . . . 591 1 X 1 51 25
is lovetime and viva sweet love" / / / . . . . 591 1 X 1 51 28
all, yes for all sweet things are until" "spring . . . . . . 625 (CHAIRE) 27 8
russia's here) swing low sweet ca rr y on . . . . 641 (CHAIRE) 43 4
like homing through welcoming sweet miracles of air (and . . 659 (CHAIRE) 61 2
day) merrily moving through sweet forgiveness of spring (over 661 (CHAIRE) 63 7
(each thing most lovely) sweet things cannot spring but . . . 666 (CHAIRE) 68 3
the miracle of your sweet innocence refuted) clumsy some . . 669 (CHAIRE) 71 11
mrs dominic washed his sweet dirty face & mended . . . . . . 680 95 POEMS 8 13
grow (remember this my sweet) not only wherever the . . . . . 686 95 POEMS 14 14
in time of all sweet things beyond whatever mind . . . . . . 688 95 POEMS 16 10
wealthier by a single sweet day's death: as not . . . . . . 750 95 POEMS 78 7
fairyair feelable heavenless warm sweet mistfully whispering 755 95 POEMS 83 11
profound this) beautiful kindness sweet such (past can's . . 763 95 POEMS 90 25
are my fate, my sweet) i want no world . . . . 766 95 POEMS 92 6
(so kiss me) shy sweet eagerly my most dear . . . . 767 95 POEMS 93 7
and all) whereas (my sweet) our summer in fall . . . . . . 776 73 POEMS 4 29
/ it's so damn sweet when Anybody-- yes; no . . . . 779 73 POEMS 7 2
a (now with one sweet sun in it, now . . . . 786 73 POEMS 14 12
ear bangl essly (into sweet the earth) & nobody . . . . . . 797 73 POEMS 25 9
marvel) doubt, for just sweet terrifying the particular . . . 809 73 POEMS 37 10
speaks in his kind sweet big voice: then a . . . . 813 73 POEMS 41 2
our (from inexistence moving) sweet earth puts on immortality 818 73 POEMS 46 3
you anything" (that eagerly sweet carolling self answers me) 836 73 POEMS 64 8
three i'll give you sweet joys for each of . . . . 837 73 POEMS 65 3

+SWEET

FOR CONTEXT, SEE . . . . 442 NO THANKS 57 7
FOR CONTEXT, SEE . . . . 464 NEW POEMS 2 4

SWEETER

mine being unto me sweeter (of whose shy delicious . . . . . 22 T&C PUELLA MEA 250
crowd gaily upon oblivion sweeter than any there is . . . . . 23 T&C PUELLA MEA 273
us, purple roses were sweeter to thee perchance to . . . . . 213 XLI SONNETS 9 16
like the rain only sweeter frailer you whom certain . . . . . 293 IS 5 FOUR 10 3
bough (and birds sing sweeter than books tell how) . . . . . 594 1 X 1 54 20

SWEETEST

Nike presents the crown sweetest to man, whose lilied . . . . 3 T&C EPITHALAM 28

SWEETLY

than a rose more sweetly known, more silently than . . . . . 21 T&C PUELLA MEA 176
lazy world and new sweetly used to laugh and . . . . 23 T&C PUELLA MEA 286
the far- departed mouth sweetly-saluted lingers. if one . . . 42 T&C AMORES 6 6
tide and death leaping Sweetly your voice / / . . . . 44 T&C AMORES 8 23
It was spring sun-stirring. sweetly to the mangling air . . . 135 & SON REAL 6 13
worms, when loveliness says sweetly Yes to wind and . . . . 183 XLI SONGS 5 10
because you smell so sweetly i will kiss your . . . . 192 XLI CHANSONS 2 8
believe these gently O sweetly melancholy trillers amid the . 230 IS 5 ONE 2 24
of our pretty world sweetly who flourishes, swiftly which . . 456 NO THANKS 71 6
shell that sang so sweetly she couldn't remember her . . . 682 95 POEMS 10 4
whose furious beak (as sweetly singing creatures know) . . . 774 73 POEMS 2 6

SWEETLY-SALUTED

the far- departed mouth sweetly-saluted lingers. if one . . . 42 T&C AMORES 6 6

SWEETNESS

snows, and the unearthly sweetness of a rose swam . . . . . . 8 T&C OF NICOL 7
lull with foliate inscrutable sweetness my soul obedient; it 19 T&C PUELLA MEA 89

		PAGE	TITLE	LINE

SWEETNESS (CONTINUED)
    steep song a stallion sweetness , the lips of . . . . 59 T&C PORTRAIT 7   15
    these better than, cubesandovalsof sweetness but it swallow) 100 & POST IMPR 11   29
    thy tigers of smooth sweetness steal slowly in dumb . . . . . 139 & SON REAL 10   3
    air with fear and sweetness.... pauses. (Halfwhispering.... . 304 IS 5 FIVE 3   13
    all things whose slendering sweetness touched renown) . . . . 414 NO THANKS 31   4
    innocent whoms of merciful sweetness except Himself?" . . . . 748 95 POEMS 76   14
SWELL
    the lungs "gimme uh swell fite like up ter . . . . 227 IS 5 ONE GERT   14
    tell de woild one swell bangup time wen nobody . . . . 237 IS 5 ONE 8   16
    frogeaters an humpin duh swell janes on duh boollevares . . . 332 VIVA 23   17
    i say that's not swell (get me) babe not . . . . 475 NEW POEMS 13   23
SWERVESCA
    ting lip ssixs ting sWervesca rletlycaR v Ingharness Of . . . 342 VIVA 33   13
SWIFLTY
    the brittle legs winces swiflty out of number 1 . . . . 62 T&C PORTRAIT 10   25
SWIFT
    than dappled dreams the swift sweet deer the red . . . . . . 14 T&C SONGS 4   7
    thought with a most swift radiance wherein slowly drift . . . 18 T&C PUELLA MEA   79
    the sweet annihilation of swift flesh i make me . . . . 182 XLI SONGS 4   11
    turn, disappears the very swift and invisibly living rhythm . 300 IS 5 FOUR 17   6
    thrusts squirms stars Trees, swift each with its Own . . . . 356 VIVA 47   8
SWIFTLY
    unaccountable sun) Distinct Lady swiftly take my fragile . . 43 T&C AMORES 7   26
    sonorous homes of light swiftly sink in the sorrowful . . . . 79 T&C SON UNRE 4   2
    / sunset) edges become swiftly corners (Besides which, i . . 345 VIVA 36   1
    utterly disappear; rushing gently swiftly creeping through my 369 VIVA 60   16
    world sweetly who flourishes, swiftly which fails but out . . 456 NO THANKS 71   6
    --her murdered selves exchanging swiftly for the . . . . . . 818 73 POEMS 46   5
+SWIFTLY
    FOR CONTEXT, SEE . . . . 429 NO THANKS 46   1
SWIFTLYENORMOUS
    blood, cracking brains A swiftlyenormous light --and . . . . 157 & SON ACTU 6   12
SWIFTNESS
    my blood: with upwardcringing swiftness plunge these leopards 139 & SON REAL 10   6
    such than hungrily more swiftness as with (feel) pauseless . 402 NO THANKS 19   2
SWIFTS
    slowly. town, night featherly swifts the Dark on us . . . . . 89 & POST IMPR 1   3
SWIG
    Thy patters? hands.... is swig it does who eye . . . . 159 & SON ACTU 8   16
SWILL
    remind Me of HerThe delicate-swill tints of hair Whose . . . 94 & POST IMPR 6   20
    skipping quickly over patriotic swill. The, negress, in the, 166 & SON ACTU 15   2
    pup hurriedly hunched over swill; one butting trolley . . . . 172 & SON ACTU 21   4
SWIM
    the big vermilion departure swim, sayingly; (Do you think?) . 66 T&C POST IMPR 3   12
    one poem yet shall swim / / / / . . . . 372 VIVA 63   15
    grass is flesh or swim who can and bathe . . . . 390 NO THANKS 7   9
    Where live can fisherMen swim and who's myself's Antimere . . 395 NO THANKS 12   8
    wear burst icy known swim ignorant fire (adventuring and . . 533 50 POEMS 45   16
    her and around ing swim snowing ly upward with . . . . 584 1 X 1 44   11
    moonstar flutter to and swim blossoms of person) through . . 586 1 X 1 46   12
    / / / / swim so now million many . . . . 603 {CHAIRE} 5   1
    find than seeks thinking, swim (opening) grow are (me . . . . 612 {CHAIRE} 14   2
    of miracle drift killed swim born a dream and . . . . 757 95 POEMS 85   33
    breathe to stroll to swim love is the air . . . . 768 95 POEMS 94   3
    nothing as green meteors swim signals all some world's . . . 818 73 POEMS 46   11
    all bright all things swim climb minds (down slowly . . . . . 841 73 POEMS 69   28
SWIMFLOATDRIFTING
    unworlds thief crook cynic (swimfloatdrifting fragment of . . 677 95 POEMS 5   10
SWIMMING
    pun ctured) moo nface swimming ly dreamseems (vivi d . . . . 615 {CHAIRE} 17   10
    dreaming drift hundreds come swimming (Each a keener secret . 630 {CHAIRE} 32   6
+SWIMMING
    FOR CONTEXT, SEE . . . . 429 NO THANKS 46   11
SWIMMINGHOLE
    down by the old swimminghole" "i'd be worse than . . . . . . 707 95 POEMS 35   2
    down through the old swimminghole there'll be slime in . . . 707 95 POEMS 35   27

	PAGE	TITLE	LINE

+SWIMMINGLY
FOR CONTEXT, SEE . . . . 615 {CHAIRE} 17   10

SWIMS
hunger Yes) how beautifully swims the fooling world in . . . 157 & SON ACTU 6   10
old toy balloon) heavily swims to Strunsky's, Monia's mouth . 219 XLI SONNETS 15   13
the editor cigarstinking hobgoblin swims upward in his . . . 259 IS 5 ONE 29   8
anyhow dancing" (a moon swims out of a cloud . . . . 338 VIVA 29   21
almost now; now almost swims into a hair's width: . . . . . . 633 {CHAIRE} 35   9
Only The Game Fish Swims Upstream & (5) unbeingdead . . . . . 803 73 POEMS 31   17
into heaven certainly earth swims than each my deeper . . . . 810 73 POEMS 38   7

SWIMSWIM
re -volve whirlswans rabbitsare: swimswim ◇ with eyes and . 384 NO THANKS 2   30

SWINBURNED
Sandburg of Algernon Carl Swinburned. Waiter a drink waiter . 233 IS 5 ONE 4   19

SWING
now that russia's here) swing low sweet ca rr . . . . 641 {CHAIRE} 43   3

SWINGTHINGS
eachness begi n dizzily swingthings of speeds of trapeze . . 536 50 POEMS 48   7

SWIRL
dodders be- tween taxis swirl hues crowds mov -ing . . . . . 384 NO THANKS 2   4
& ingly seethe firm swirl hips whirling climb to . . . . . 445 NO THANKS 60   27

SWIRLED
of the wind and swirled justly souls of flower . . . . . . 163 & SON ACTU 12   6

SWIRLING
the noiseless truth of swirling worms is tomorrow / . . . . . 113 & PORTRAIT 6   117

+SWIRLING
FOR CONTEXT, SEE . . . . 341 VIVA 32   12

SWIRLS
by me at look) swirls to engulf (in which . . . . 613 {CHAIRE} 15   5

SWIRLY
but quite now it's swirly and foldish so only . . . . 516 50 POEMS 30   6

SWIVELCHAIR
swims upward in his swivelchair one fist dangling scandal . . 259 IS 5 ONE 29   9

SWOLLEN
eyes chopped by a swollen inanity of picture hat. . . . . . . 103 & POST IMPR 13   4

SWOON
vital clinched in a swoon of synopsis despite a . . . . . . 193 XLI PORTRAIT 1   4
beyond night's silken immense swoon the moon is like . . . . 214 XLI SONNETS 10   12
of people a brittle swoon of centrifugally expecting faces . 279 IS 5 THREE 3   6
hhurt-re coil charge &) swooN Crowdloomroar: ing; diskface, . 388 NO THANKS 5   18
dip & giveswoop & swoon & ingly seethe firm . . . . 445 NO THANKS 60   26

SWOONED
eyes; nor he when swooned the white egyptian day . . . . . . 18 T&C PUELLA MEA   73

SWOONING
/ / / / (swooning) a pillar of youngly . . . . 615 {CHAIRE} 17   1
of the Moon he's swooning at the bottom of . . . . 642 {CHAIRE} 44   14

+SWOONING
FOR CONTEXT, SEE . . . . 99 & POST IMPR 10   10
FOR CONTEXT, SEE . . . . 495 50 POEMS 9   9

+SWOONINGLY
FOR CONTEXT, SEE . . . . 445 NO THANKS 60   26

SWOONS
earth's most terrific quadruped swoons into billiardBalls! / 315 VIVA 7   16

+SWOONS
FOR CONTEXT, SEE . . . . 430 NO THANKS 47   12

SWOONSONG
& so unto canned swoonsong came "I wish you . . . . 464 NEW POEMS 2   27

SWOOP
shes & meet & swoop fully is are ex . . . . 536 50 POEMS 48   13
you, exceedingly too small. Swoop (shrill collective myth) . 579 1 X 1 39   9
at blue with a swoop and a dart out . . . . 593 1 X 1 53   7
(and on every side swoop mountains flimsying become if . . . 634 {CHAIRE} 36   3
which dance and dancing swoop (and swooping whirl over . . . 777 73 POEMS 5   7
climb minds (down slowly swoop wholly up leaping through . . 841 73 POEMS 69   30

+SWOOP
FOR CONTEXT, SEE . . . . 445 NO THANKS 60   26
FOR CONTEXT, SEE . . . . 447 NO THANKS 62   7

	PAGE	TITLE	LINE

SWOOPING
insipid kinesis or frail swooping lozenge. a ruglike . . . . 201 XLI PORTRAIT 9   16
and dancing swoop (and swooping whirl over a frightened . . . 777 73 POEMS 5   7

+SWOOPING
FOR CONTEXT, SEE . . . . 631 (CHAIRE) 33   11

SWOOPINGLY
luminous firmly diminishing have swoopingly fallen svelte . . 110 & PORTRAIT 6   27

SWOOPS
like a Rolls Royce swoops smoothly outward (amid ◇ . . . . . 232 IS 5 ONE 3   7

SWORD
to thee with a sword and thou art silent . . . . 27 T&C ORIENTALE 1   23

SWORDGREAT
/ Thou in whose swordgreat story shine the deeds . . . . . . 209 XLI SONNETS 5   1

SWORE
was) thither to thence swore many a vow but . . . . 316 VIVA 8   14
/ three wealthy sisters swore they'd never part: Soul . . . . 621 (CHAIRE) 23   1

SWORKEY
common man wants) honey swoRkey mollypants / / / . . . . . . 635 (CHAIRE) 37   26

SWORN
it go it was sworn to go let them . . . . 569 1 X 1 29   6

SWOT
practicing the art of swot to preach the golden . . . . . . 500 50 POEMS 14   19

SWUNG
was petrified. De room swung roun an crawled up . . . . . . 332 VIVA 23   25

SYLLABLE
and with their frailest syllable its leaves go crisp . . . . 22 T&C PUELLA MEA 235
ceaselessness (nor has a syllable of the heart's eager . . . 372 VIVA 63   11

SYLLABLES
like angel's tears, the syllables of that mysterious prayer,   8 T&C OF NICOL   11

SYMBOL
and sobbing, garments The symbol of the rose motionless . . . 59 T&C PORTRAIT 7   9

SYMBOLS
sleeping self float flaming symbols of hope, and i . . . . . 749 95 POEMS 77   11

SYMMETRY
a form whose snowy symmetry of grace haunted the . . . . . .   8 T&C OF NICOL   20
poems not because harm symmetry earthquakes starfish (but . . 452 NO THANKS 67   15

SYNCOPATE
of gloom truly which syncopate some sunbeam's skilful . . . . 19 T&C PUELLA MEA   85

SYNCOPATION
repeat a trick of syncopation Europe has --. One . . . . . . 135 & SON REAL 6   10

SYNOPSIS
in a swoon of synopsis despite a sadistic modesty . . . . . . 193 XLI PORTRAIT 1   4

SYNTAX
any attention to the syntax of things will never . . . . . . 290 IS 5 FOUR 7   3

SYNTHETIC
please? must through unstrange synthetic now true histories . 527 50 POEMS 39   26

SYPHILIS
with trumpets clap and syphilis / / / / . . . . 273 IS 5 TWO 8   24

SYRIANSANG
(peach a soft eyes syriansang asong tohim self all . . . . . 318 VIVA 10   11

SYRINX
lips dim upon the syrinx / / / / . . . . 54 T&C PORTRAIT 2   12

SYSTEM
despair into hugeness world system universe and bang --fear . 531 50 POEMS 43   2
deceiver, and sorrow a system-- if now than forever . . . . . 625 (CHAIRE) 27   20

SYSTOLE
stitch of the unmitigated systole purrs against my mind, . . 136 & SON REAL 7   4

T'AIME
innumerable kind-of-deaths (Amerique Je T'Aime and it may be 410 NO THANKS 27   13

TA
my head dis-donc, Paris ta gorge mysterieuse pourquoi se . . 121 & PORTRAIT 12   53
se promene-t-elle, pourquoi eclate ta voix fragile couleur de 121 & PORTRAIT 12   55

TA-TE-TA
witty, twitters upon Our (ta-te-ta in a parenthesis! said . . 89 & POST IMPR 1   16

TABARI'
tall tight boys at Tabari' s, keep your teeth . . . . 71 T&C SON REAL 2   3

TABLE
upon an un- clean table. and, whose distended immense . . . . 97 & POST IMPR 8   38

	PAGE	TITLE	LINE
TABLE (CONTINUED)			
the weak colour of table-cloths, the electric When In	217	XLI SONNETS 13	4
say over the damned table and we hold lips	287	IS 5 FOUR 4	17
stockings dribbling from the table all which seemed sweet . .	322	VIVA 14	6
whole gang accrost duh table-- "fellers have some on	332	VIVA 23	21
(at the next) nakedness (table but three) hero's carnivorous	546	1 X 1 6	8
+TABLE			
FOR CONTEXT, SEE	104	& POST IMPR 14	2
FOR CONTEXT, SEE	104	& POST IMPR 14	21
TABLE-CLOTHS			
the weak colour of table-cloths, the electric When In	217	XLI SONNETS 13	4
TABLES			
walls sprawling with tipsy tables the abominable floor . . .	55	T&C PORTRAIT 3	3
roundtable amongother; littleexactly round. tables, Her . . .	104	& POST IMPR 14	21
pas effendi drifts between tables like an old leaf	198	IS 5 ONE 6	16
smoothly outward (amid ◇ tables) while softly along Kirkland	232	IS 5 ONE 3	10
go spill and chairs tables the and bitch whispers	496	50 POEMS 10	15
+TABLES			
FOR CONTEXT, SEE	104	& POST IMPR 14	3
TABLETS			
which always the four tablets of perspiration erectly	73	T&C SON REAL 4	9
TABULATED			
-nous thought) otherwise immaculately tabulated vicinity) . .	267	IS 5 TWO 2	16
TAC			
there was a clock. tac-tic. tac-toc. Time and lilacs.... . .	133	& SON REAL 4	7
was a clock. tac-tic. tac-toc. Time and lilacs.... minutes .	133	& SON REAL 4	7
TAC-TIC			
there was a clock. tac-tic. tac-toc. Time and lilacs.... . .	133	& SON REAL 4	7
TAC-TOC			
was a clock. tac-tic. tac-toc. Time and lilacs.... minutes .	133	& SON REAL 4	7
TACTFULLY			
/ we miss you, jack--tactfully you (with one cocked	605	{CHAIRE} 7	1
TADPOLE			
signifi- cant stomachs: Who carry-tadpole! s,, stomachs of .	101	& POST IMPR 11	75
hysterical fright a comic tadpole wriggling in delicious mud	157	& SON ACTU 6	15
above the square, little amorous-tadpole people wiggled . . .	173	& SON ACTU 22	4
+TAFT			
FOR CONTEXT, SEE	321	VIVA 13	2
TAIL			
fingers and a remarkable tail which is allbyitself alive. . .	69	T&C POST IMPR 6	40
eyes and wagged his tail that's the god's own	125	& SEVEN POEMS 4	16
(eye pries, not open. Tail stirs.) And the. fire-escapes-- .	166	& SON ACTU 15	11
wee ears and see? tail frisks) (gonE) "mouse", We	286	IS 5 FOUR 3	13
did wring that dragon's tail (for men must loaf	552	1 X 1 12	17
flown adorable him self tail and all (and his	631	{CHAIRE} 33	6
TAIL'S			
and all (and his tail's red christmas bow) --and	631	{CHAIRE} 33	6
TAILOR			
Should say solong my tailor chuckles like a woman	287	IS 5 FOUR 4	11
TAILORED			
my grunting eyes pin tailored flames Her being at	137	& SON REAL 8	10
+TAILS			
FOR CONTEXT, SEE	230	IS 5 ONE 2	33
TAINT			
cities eternal--ere the sinless taint of thy long sinful . .	9	T&C SONGS 1	33
TAKE			
to nine ladies you take his mouth for his	15	T&C SONGS 5	15
O let us descend take shimmering wind these fragile	41	T&C AMORES 5	17
sun) Distinct Lady swiftly take my fragile certain song . . .	43	T&C AMORES 7	26
curled with mystic lips take big twilight where i know:	71	T&C SON REAL 2	13
go unto him, and take his hands, saying, Accept	76	T&C SON UNRE 1	11
spires softly dare. Will take the houseless wisping rune . .	86	T&C SON ACTU 5	5
/ / / / Take for example this: if	92	& POST IMPR 4	1
and money fuzzily mouths take big wobbly foot-steps every . .	96	& POST IMPR 8	19
say your eyes can take day away more softly	98	& POST IMPR 9	3
simple hours and you take all your prickley-clothes off . . .	127	& SEVEN POEMS 5	33
it, if they should take me and take you	129	& SEVEN POEMS 7	6
should take me and take you into their balloon, ...	129	& SEVEN POEMS 7	6

TAKE (CONTINUED)
   breath of my breath: take not thy tingling limbs . . . . . . 139 & SON REAL 10   1
   with firmer lips to take your new mouth in . . . . 161 & SON ACTU 10   3
   of my heart and take the rose, which perfect . . . . 188 XLI SONGS 10   17
   burning flowers I will take the sun in my . . . . 189 XLI SONGS 11   3
   sister and i will take hands and looking up . . . . 192 XLI CHANSONS 2   25
   in vain, O scrupulously take thy trivial toll, for . . . . . 212 XLI SONNETS 8   3
   if i like, i'll take between thy hands what . . . . 212 XLI SONNETS 8   13
   BEAUTY HURTS MR. VINAL take it from me kiddo . . . . 230 IS 5 ONE 2   1
   got pockets full may take a littl e nibble . . . . 314 VIVA 6   10
   (one fine day) let's take the train for because . . . . . . 316 VIVA 8   2
   say "let's" going in "take hands" smiling "coming up . . . . 353 VIVA 44   30
   Made leaves open Clouds take sun mountains stand And . . . . 359 VIVA 50   12
   and polished buttons) would take you away --and all . . . . 365 VIVA 56   13
   kill like you would take a piss they speak . . . . 427 NO THANKS 44   16
   loan me pain to take the hearse, see you . . . . 451 NO THANKS 66   7
   stand or sit may take it lying down) down . . . . 466 NEW POEMS 4   4
   on; and his mind take off time that you . . . . 484 NEW POEMS 22   8
   for worse. Give liz (take! tommy) we order a . . . . 513 50 POEMS 27   13
   mere because and why? take this whole tear. By . . . . . . 527 50 POEMS 39   16
   money and you doesn't take your choice. Ain't freedom . . . 636 (CHAIRE) 38   14
   / / because you take life in your stride . . . . 679 95 POEMS 7   1
   dear violet you may take mine" "o how how . . . . 684 95 POEMS 12   4
   nay somethingelsestein. Death should take his hat off to . . 790 73 POEMS 18   6
TAKEN
   how often have religions taken thee upon their scraggy . . . 46 T&C LA GUERRE 2 14
   / when thou hast taken thy last applause, and . . . . 75 T&C SON REAL 6   1
   box dreaming of being taken out and allowed to . . . . 192 XLI CHANSONS 2   15
   optima rerum first having taken care to lie upon . . . . . 261 IS 5 ONE 31   12
TAKES
   million years building he takes the air in a . . . . 32 T&C ORIENTALE 6   4
   the sky, my mind takes to nib -bling, of . . . . 131 & SON REAL 2   4
   of dusk each street takes of shadowy light the . . . . 168 & SON ACTU 17   4
   near when his scythe takes crisply the whim of . . . . . . 215 XLI SONNETS 11   6
   drunker applaud while twilight takes the sting out of . . . . 279 IS 5 THREE 3   18
   why , what it Takes. now you know (just . . . . 701 95 POEMS 29   9
   i do) what it takes; & i don't mean . . . . 701 95 POEMS 29   13
   more he gives than takes (and he takes all) . . . . 750 95 POEMS 78   11
   than takes (and he takes all) nor any marvel . . . . 750 95 POEMS 78   12
   the particular moment it takes one very falling most . . . . 809 73 POEMS 37   11
   moment when a stranger takes in his arms my . . . . 812 73 POEMS 40   12
TAKIN
   --an-- "my specialty is takin fellers' goils away frum . . . 332 VIVA 23   6
TAKING
   feeling up streets; heels taking derbies (where?) a pup . . . 172 & SON ACTU 21   3
   why are these pipples taking their hets off? the . . . . . . 245 IS 5 ONE 16   1
   great world (in darkly taking rain) drown, beyond sound . . . 432 NO THANKS 49   2
   (while around him streets taking moment off by moment . . . . 720 95 POEMS 48   5
   a giving who (no taking simply which) a marvel . . . . . . 735 95 POEMS 63   6
TALE
   (Whoso rideth in the tale of Chaucer knoweth many . . . . . . 20 T&C PUELLA MEA 163
   world was like a tale made of laughter and . . . . 23 T&C PUELLA MEA 276
   said "willingly for the tale is short it was . . . . 57 T&C PORTRAIT 5   16
   and foes my tragic tale concludes herewith: soldier, beware . 799 73 POEMS 27   40
TALENTGANG
   and genius please the talentgang and water most encourage . . 511 50 POEMS 25   6
TALK
   people high, up-in tenements talk. in sawdust Voices a: . . . 128 & SEVEN POEMS 6   5
   be a fellow's twistandtwirl talk about your Sal- Sal- . . . 235 IS 5 ONE 6   19
   your Sal- Sal- Sal-, talk about your Salo -mes . . . . . . 235 IS 5 ONE 6   22
   gosh by gum why talk of beauty what could . . . . 268 IS 5 TWO 3   9
   son-- all is merely talk which isn't singing and . . . . . 804 73 POEMS 32   11
TALKATIVE
   sometimes on these long talkative animals are laid fists . . 45 T&C LA GUERRE 1   8
TALKIN
   bout duh clap an talkin big how dey could . . . . 332 VIVA 23   3
TALKING
   fire-escapes and roofs are talking rapidly all together there 62 T&C PORTRAIT 10 18

	PAGE	TITLE	LINE

TALKING (CONTINUED)
The Chair he kept talking about eyes / / . . . . 145 & SON REAL 16   14
used to become hoarse talking about how it was . . . . 276 IS 5 TWO 10   16
securely to this always talking individual, mysterious witty . 279 IS 5 THREE 3   11
isn't singing is mere talking and all talking's talking . . . 804 73 POEMS 32   1
talking and all talking's talking to oneself (whether that . 804 73 POEMS 32   2
TALKING'S
mere talking and all talking's talking to oneself (whether . 804 73 POEMS 32   2
isn't singing and all talking's to oneself alone but . . . . 804 73 POEMS 32   12
TALKS
again or if it talks about you somewhere behind . . . . . . 126 & SEVEN POEMS 5   18
les neiges.... some guys talks big about Lundun Burlin . . . 237 IS 5 ONE 8   4
by a whore who Talks in the daytime, when . . . . 312 VIVA 4   4
TALL
her that brought forth tall Hippolytus, lord on whose . . . . 4 T&C EPITHALAM   45
of whose charms the tall boy god of everlasting . . . . 7 T&C EPITHALAM   154
terrific pastures pale, whose tall mysterious shepherd lifts . 9 T&C SONGS 1   10
sleek slim deer the tall tense deer. Four tall . . . . 14 T&C SONGS 4   28
tall tense deer. Four tall stags at a green . . . . 14 T&C SONGS 4   29
in a tree of tall marble from a great . . . . 30 T&C ORIENTALE 4   20
fat bells and a tall wind is dragging the . . . . 51 T&C IMPRESS 5   8
(afterward i'll climb by tall careful muscles into nervous . 67 T&C POST IMPR 4   15
good time with the tall tight boys at Tabari' . . . . 71 T&C SON REAL 2   3
/ / my girl's tall with hard long eyes . . . . 147 & SON REAL 18   1
to an edge--my girl's tall and taut, with thin . . . . 147 & SON REAL 18   9
mouths something red, something tall / / / / . . . . 160 & SON ACTU 9   17
bell. But if her tall corpsecoloured body seat itself . . . . 227 IS 5 ONE GERT   8
mention splendiferous funeral with tall boys in black gloves 239 IS 5 ONE 10   31
wintry glow revealed) this tall strong stalwart youth, what . 254 IS 5 ONE 25   2
corner, suddenly) meets the tall policeman of my mind. . . . 304 IS 5 FIVE 3   5
wishes or hopes less tall than mine" (opening the . . . . . . 328 VIVA 19   10
(deep like a rose tall like a rose) standing . . . . 352 VIVA 43   6
very fine mower a tall; tall some jerry so . . . . 509 50 POEMS 23   12
fine mower a tall; tall some jerry so very . . . . 509 50 POEMS 23   12
go--the big small middling tall bigger really the biggest . . 569 1 X 1 29   17
the slim plump tiny tall) all except the dull . . . . 619 {CHAIRE} 21   12
not make a fellow tall" lily has a rose . . . . 684 95 POEMS 12   16
/ / fair ladies tall lovers riding are through . . . . 778 73 POEMS 6   1
(all gay fair brave tall young come they) through . . . . . . 778 73 POEMS 6   10
great man is gone. Tall as the truth was . . . . 786 73 POEMS 14   5
charlie confessed (halting) "a tall strong young finelooking 800 73 POEMS 28   3
TALLER
the wind blows the taller i am" / / . . . . 439 NO THANKS 55   28
TALLEST
is opened by the tallest eunuch and the queen . . . . 33 T&C ORIENTALE 6   62
to you is the tallest of the boys" "he'll . . . . 684 95 POEMS 12   8
TAMARACK
by hemlock spruce by tamarack (nothing pampered puny . . . . 658 {CHAIRE} 60   21
+TAMBOURINES
FOR CONTEXT, SEE . . . . 100 & POST IMPR 11   43
TAME
said "peek-a-boo" and thirty tame fleas left the prettily . . 262 IS 5 ONE 32   28
to fight itself from tame to teem) still doth . . . . 544 1 X 1 4   18
+TAMER
FOR CONTEXT, SEE . . . . 384 NO THANKS 2   24
TANGERINES
of tiny plums of tangerines and apples it will, ... 100 & POST IMPR 11   26
Strunsky's, Monia's mouth eats tangerines looking at the . . 219 XLI SONNETS 15   15
TANGIBLE
fleet perfectly far from tangible domains rare with most . . 402 NO THANKS 19   11
TANGLE
this br am bliest tangle of hi llside) a . . . . 695 95 POEMS 23   4
es buzzsqueaking th ey tangle in twitter y t . . . . 747 95 POEMS 75   15
+TANGLE
FOR CONTEXT, SEE . . . . 421 NO THANKS 38   9
TANGLED
in the incense is tangled a cool moon there . . . . 32 T&C ORIENTALE 6   32

TANGOING
next to nothing on) tangoing (while a feller tries . . . . . 242 IS 5 ONE 13   6
+TANK
FOR CONTEXT, SEE . . . . 239 IS 5 ONE 10   26
TAPERING
dead and gone.) Each tapering breast is firm and . . . . . . 21 T&C PUELLA MEA 181
+TAPPING
FOR CONTEXT, SEE . . . . 107 & PORTRAIT 3   1
+TAPPINGPEOPLEONTHEBACK
of minions tappingpeopleontheback "allezcirculez") . . . . . 275 IS 5 TWO 9   38
TAPS
the glush of squirting taps plus slush of foam . . . . 96 & POST IMPR 8   13
the waddling madam star taps taps. "ready girls". the . . . . 108 & PORTRAIT 4   3
waddling madam star taps taps. "ready girls". the . . . . . . 108 & PORTRAIT 4   4
+TAPS
FOR CONTEXT, SEE . . . . 697 95 POEMS 25   9
TAPTAPTAPS
was thrown away himself taptaptaps out of your brain, ... 298 IS 5 FOUR 15   26
TART
& you'll find a tart in it (wed) open . . . . 637 (CHAIRE) 39   8
it (wed) open the tart, lady & you'll find . . . . 637 (CHAIRE) 39   10
+TART
FOR CONTEXT, SEE . . . . 318 VIVA 10   19
TARTSKIDS
/ thethe the pink Tartskids with thecas-tanets in 5/4; . . . 318 VIVA 10   3
TASTE
shall my love wholly taste thee as a new . . . .   9 T&C SONGS 1   35
pleasantly groan on your taste. Jumped the quick wall . . . . 154 & SON ACTU 3   4
slowly to my mouth, taste the accurate demure ferocious . . . 162 & SON ACTU 11   11
proached may never quite taste the wine which their . . . . 193 XLI PORTRAIT 1   12
nothing which touch and taste and smell and hearing . . . . . 199 XLI PORTRAIT 7   3
drink the docile perpendicular taste of this squirming cube . 201 XLI PORTRAIT 9   17
dull were all we taste as bright, bitter all . . . . 521 50 POEMS 34   61
always dream, is to taste not (beyond death and . . . . . . 674 95 POEMS 2   10
(by the look feel taste smell & sound of . . . . 676 95 POEMS 4   8
TASTED
spontaneously methodical. He suddenly tasted worms windows . 170 & SON ACTU 19   12
silence upward --to have tasted Beautiful to have known . . . 437 NO THANKS 53   12
much smelled so much tasted plus touched quite so . . . . . 474 NEW POEMS 12   7
TASTES
arty each has his tastes but as for i . . . . 247 IS 5 ONE 18   3
space) absolute (my soul tastes If as some world . . . . . . 639 (CHAIRE) 41   7
TASTING
....one perfectly smooth coffee tasting of hellas, i drink, . 217 XLI SONNETS 13 11
illimitably earth) how should tasting touching hearing seeing 663 (CHAIRE) 65   9
+TASTING
FOR CONTEXT, SEE . . . . 100 & POST IMPR 11   27
TATTERDEMALION
g : seized (tatterdemalion dow nupfloatsw oon InG . . . . . 495 50 POEMS 9   7
TATTLE
the no-she-yes-he fluffies tittle tattle did-he-does-she) & . 773 73 POEMS 1   17
TAUGHED
Robinson Jefferson to Injustice Taughed your story is so . . 321 VIVA 13   2
TAUGHT
offers her lily inextinguishable, taught by thy tremulous . . 206 XLI SONNETS 2   3
TAUT
superior terror; be thy taut flesh silver, like the . . . . .   9 T&C SONGS 1   31
thorn of desire the taut neck of the citharede . . . . 34 T&C ORIENTALE 6 96
long on a certain taut precarious holiday frighteningly . . . 52 T&C PORTRAIT 1   6
edge--my girl's tall and taut, with thin legs just . . . . . 147 & SON REAL 18   10
TAXI
beyond that any this taxi smile or angle we . . . . 238 IS 5 ONE 9   6
TAXIMAN
hoppytoad yesmam. the furious taximan p (ee) ps on . . . . . 108 & PORTRAIT 4   17
TAXIS
Elysian in a firmcool-Ness taxis, s. QuirM and, b . . . . . 104 & POST IMPR 14   15
crone dodders be- tween taxis swirl hues crowds mov . . . . . 384 NO THANKS 2   4

		PAGE	TITLE	LINE

TAYLOR
by is it Bishop Taylor who needs hanging that . . . . 167 & SON ACTU 16   4

TE
witty, twitters upon Our (ta-te-ta in a parenthesis! said . . 89 & POST IMPR 1 16
voulez-vous coucher avec moi? te ferai Mimi te ferai . . . . 121 & PORTRAIT 12 37
moi? te ferai Mimi te ferai Minette, dead exactly . . . . . . 121 & PORTRAIT 12 38

TEA
a policeman. Meanwhile the tea regressed. Kipling again H.G. 263 IS 5 ONE 32 42
eye sed bea yew tea mis eyesucks unyewkuntel finglestein . . 474 NEW POEMS 12 11

TEACH
Place said to Death teach me of her Thy . . . . 57 T&C PORTRAIT 5   5
matter) which i suggest teach us a new terror . . . . 289 IS 5 FOUR 6 10
how to sing than teach ten thousand stars how . . . . 484 NEW POEMS 22 14
/ / (will you teach a wretch to live . . . . 498 50 POEMS 12   1
will make them sing; teach them to see who . . . . 649 (CHAIRE) 51   3
called a world vanishes, teach disappearing also me the . . . 669 (CHAIRE) 71 13
think) a learning under teach-- precisely as unbig as . . . . 735 95 POEMS 63   8

TEACHABLE
live's a gift) the teachable imposture of always arriving . . 807 73 POEMS 35   3

TEACHER
could plan) the stupidest teacher will almost guess (with . . 594 1 X 1 54   5

TEAR
found it sweet-- a tear within his stern blue . . . . 273 IS 5 TWO 8   9
nor stop as a tear is darker than a . . . . 371 VIVA 62 27
/ much i cannot) tear up the world: & . . . . 433 NO THANKS 50   2
oceaning than any this tear jumping from each most . . . . . 502 50 POEMS 16   4
why? take this whole tear. By handless hints do . . . . 527 50 POEMS 39 16
smile another with a tear some cannot pay at . . . . 624 (CHAIRE) 26 10

TEAROSE
wise, a weed a tearose) and every minus plus . . . . 798 73 POEMS 26 11

TEARS
the air to golden tears, and hark! the flicker's . . . . . .   5 T&C EPITHALAM 74
thrush with silver several tears complete the perfumed . . .   6 T&C EPITHALAM 119
the night, like angel's tears, the syllables of that . . . .   8 T&C OF NICOL 10
costly morsel of sweet tears) gesticulates, and disappears-- 23 T&C PUELLA MEA 269
smile (it was through tears always) and silence moulds . . . 78 T&C SON UNRE 3   7
fragrance hurls me into tears, as the dusty new- . . . . . . 148 & SON REAL 19 11
when love's had his tears out, perhaps shall pass . . . . . . 181 XLI SONGS 3   6
uncle Frank breaks into tears. my uncle Tom knits . . . . . . 253 IS 5 ONE 24   9
duh boollevares an wid tears streamin down my face . . . . . 332 VIVA 23 18
more (Than girl 's tears boy Dream's) forge tful: . . . . . . 447 NO THANKS 62 12
very them) now (it tears off rag its of . . . . 501 50 POEMS 15 11
st dis (because my tears are full of eyes) . . . . 697 95 POEMS 25 29

TEARTROUBLED
shepherd lifts a cheek teartroubled to the momentary wind . .   9 T&C SONGS 1 11

TEASE
his rectum wickedly to tease by means of skilfully . . . . . 339 VIVA 30 28
go drift slippery hands tease slim float twitter faces) . . . 633 (CHAIRE) 35   5

+TEASE
FOR CONTEXT, SEE . . . . 316 VIVA 8 22

TEASED
hoe tell days are teased: let (however) us Walk . . . . 317 VIVA 9 16

TEASING
it, wisely, pester skilfully, teasing its lips, absurd eyes, 164 & SON ACTU 13   8

TEASINGLY
rare unease revealed of teasingly transparent folds-- with .   5 T&C EPITHALAM 95

TECHNIC
unrivalled brand of pyro -technic blurb anent the (hic) . . . 266 IS 5 TWO 1 12

TEDDY
jew stands beside his teddy-bears the sailor shuffles the . . 108 & PORTRAIT 4 24

TEDDY-BEARS
jew stands beside his teddy-bears the sailor shuffles the . . 108 & PORTRAIT 4 24

TEE
so Alive) ump-A-tum ; tee-die uM-tuM tidl -id umptyumpty . . 426 NO THANKS 43 20

TEE-DIE
so Alive) ump-A-tum ; tee-die uM-tuM tidl -id umptyumpty . . 426 NO THANKS 43 20

TEEM
twitch through the bumping teem of Grand. a nudging . . . . . 219 XLI SONNETS 15 10

766

	PAGE	TITLE	LINE

TEEM (CONTINUED)
    itself from tame to teem) still doth our hero . . . . 544 1 X 1 4   18
TEEMING
    all history oped her teeming womb said demon for . . . . . . 552 1 X 1 12   21
TEEN
    aren't 6 or 6 teen or sixty 000,000 anybodyelses-- . . . . . 779 73 POEMS 7   25
TEETERTIPTOTTERISH
    certainly never the iswas teetertiptotterish sp- inwhirlpin . 495 50 POEMS 9   16
TEETH
    Tabari' s, keep your teeth snowy, stick to beer . . . . 71 T&C SON REAL 2   4
    girl with the good teeth and small important breasts . . . . 72 T&C SON REAL 3   2
    the gold dawn, where teeth of slowturning streets mesh . . . 142 & SON REAL 13   4
    Mid's green large three teeth leak smoke: remembering, two . 149 & SON REAL 20   14
    Bit into you as teeth, in the stone of . . . . 154 & SON ACTU 3   2
    Had you as bite teeth; i stood with you . . . . 154 & SON ACTU 3   14
    new mouth in his teeth (hips pumping pleasure into . . . . . 161 & SON ACTU 10   3
    flowers And set my teeth in the silver of . . . . 189 XLI SONGS 11   17
    watch a has gold teeth b pink suspenders c . . . . 200 XLI PORTRAIT 8   6
    tween its supple financial teeth deliriously sprouting from . 201 XLI PORTRAIT 9   3
    perpendicular lips the insane teeth the vertical grin give . 220 XLI SONNETS 16   7
    looking hands spit blood teeth the Communists have (very) . . 275 IS 5 TWO 9   47
    one broken babypout (pretty teeth wander into which and . . . 406 NO THANKS 23   11
    gould has lost his teeth and doesn't know where . . . . . . 410 NO THANKS 27   1
    for an eye four teeth for a tooth (and . . . . 635 (CHAIRE) 37   18
TEETHE
    aunt death did always teethe / / / / . . . . 316 VIVA 8   22
TEETHFUL
    between the nibbling timid teethful hours wilts the stern . . 112 & PORTRAIT 6   79
TELESCOPED
    in a luxury of telescoped languages) she smokes three . . . . 312 VIVA 4   14
TELESCOPES
    with stars to catch telescopes) why. Being is . . . . . . 478 NEW POEMS 16   6
TELL
    yester- day) O i tell you out of the . . . . 111 & PORTRAIT 6   51
    / / / i'll tell you a dream i . . . . 123 & SEVEN POEMS 2 1
    kid how, funny Do tell ....sweat, succeeds breathings stopped 136 & SON REAL 7   14
    the rain he'll not tell where.) beauty makes terms . . . . . 183 XLI SONGS 5   6
    moves off will anyone tell him why he should . . . . 196 XLI PORTRAIT 4   20
    Yet if not flower, tell me softly who be . . . . 211 XLI SONNETS 7   6
    from released cheeks "I'll tell duh woild; some noive . . . . 226 IS 5 ONE MAME   10
    monosyllable jounce possibly can tell better how the balloons 227 IS 5 ONE GERT   2
    once er year) i'll tell de woild one swell . . . . 237 IS 5 ONE 8   16
    charming person personally they tell me as for me . . . . . . 246 IS 5 ONE 17   7
    what is more did tell you just what everybody . . . . 276 IS 5 TWO 10   4
    hearts a few philosophers tell me what am i . . . . 281 IS 5 THREE 5   1
    men behind me I tell you; several, incredible, sleepy . . . . 281 IS 5 THREE 5   24
    eyes) drifts (nobody can tell because Nobody knows, or . . . 286 IS 5 FOUR 3   6
    being in love will tell who softly asks in . . . . 295 IS 5 FOUR 12   2
    self in the hoe tell days are teased: let . . . . 317 VIVA 9   15
    / / / / tell me not how electricity . . . . 324 VIVA 16   1
    of our projectile am tell such to murder time . . . . 362 VIVA 53   13
    good kumrads you can tell by their altruistic smell . . . . . 413 NO THANKS 30   7
    too and will it tell us who we are . . . . 528 50 POEMS 40   2
    are and will it tell us why we dream . . . . 528 50 POEMS 40   3
    dream and will it tell us how we drink . . . . 528 50 POEMS 40   3
    of his head: to tell him / / / . . . . 553 1 X 1 13   24
    nil) and will somebody tell me why people let . . . . 593 1 X 1 53   23
    sing sweeter than books tell how) so here is . . . . 594 1 X 1 54   22
    your more than eyes tell me) there is a . . . . 683 95 POEMS 11   14
    haymows you never can tell" "as long as there's . . . . . . 707 95 POEMS 35   10
    your birthday comes to tell me this --each luckiest . . . . . 734 95 POEMS 62   1
    dollies, dad first ("don't tell your mother") had; making . . 794 73 POEMS 22   4
    sing) could never quite tell right from wrong, took . . . . . 799 73 POEMS 27   13
    cannot children, poets, lovers tell- measure imagine, ... 817 73 POEMS 45   9
    "o purple finch please tell me why this summer . . . . 836 73 POEMS 64   2
    die" "if i should tell you anything" (that eagerly . . . . . 836 73 POEMS 64   7
+TELL
    FOR CONTEXT, SEE . . . . 310 VIVA 2   1

+TELL (CONTINUED)

FOR CONTEXT, SEE . . . . 474 NEW POEMS 12   12

TELLING

Easily through voices womenlike telling of death love earth . 356 VIVA 47   4
newmown hay and he telling you no" "than look . . . . 707 95 POEMS 35   26

TELLS

brazen breasts, whose foot-stool tells how fought the looser   4 T&C EPITHALAM   43
not all) because largeness tells you so you can . . . . . . 127 & SEVEN POEMS 5   38
silence two-made-of-one & nothing tells anywhere "snow will . 483 NEW POEMS 21   7
secret than silence even tells) all the earth has . . . . . 630 {CHAIRE} 32   8
guess what no tongue tells (such as ourselves) begins . . . 716 95 POEMS 44   17

TELLURIAN

flyspecked abdominous female indubitably tellurian strolls . 116 & PORTRAIT 9   4

TEMPO

mechanism. beneath her drab tempo of hasteful futility lived 103 & POST IMPR 13   10

TEMPORAL

of infinity sharpens the temporal splendor of this night . . 81 T&C SON UNRE 6   2

TEN

body behind the emperor ten elected warriors with bodies . . 34 T&C ORIENTALE 6   75
dimes seven nickels and ten pennies have been deposited . . . 196 XLI PORTRAIT 4   9
/ / / lis -ten you know what i . . . . 272 IS 5 TWO 7   2
a fist out of ten fingers voices rise from . . . . 281 IS 5 THREE 5   20
to sing than teach ten thousand stars how not . . . . 484 NEW POEMS 22   14
terrible some alive individual ten centuries of original soon 561 1 X 1 21   6
soon or make it ten times ten are more . . . . 561 1 X 1 21   7
make it ten times ten are more than not . . . . 561 1 X 1 21   7
--saharas have their centuries; ten thousand of which are . . 683 95 POEMS 11   7
have been, and stop ten thousand stars but not . . . . 714 95 POEMS 42   10

TEND

blokes with ammunicions who tend to make incitions and . . . 405 NO THANKS 22   8
ev: ery: wheres: ex: tend: ing: hush) andDark . . . . 416 NO THANKS 33   3

TENDER

Now the timid the tender (as doubt as can . . . . 801 73 POEMS 29   25

TENDERLY

night a quick bird (tenderly upon the dark's prodigious . . . 187 XLI SONGS 9   9
lift the poor cuss tenderly this side up handle . . . . . . 270 IS 5 TWO 5   15
Crusoelike examines fearingly and tenderly a recent footprint 344 VIVA 35   14
boulder) nothing mean in tenderly whoms of sizeless a . . . 658 {CHAIRE} 60   6
jovial ego (& mischievous tenderly phoebeing alter) clown of 678 95 POEMS 6   6

+TENDONED

FOR CONTEXT, SEE . . . . 231 IS 5 ONE 3   48

TENDRIL

a flame, was a tendril fleetly curled upon frailness) . . . . 23 T&C PUELLA MEA   279
/ / / luminous tendril of celestial wish (whying . . . . . . 669 {CHAIRE} 71   1

TENDS

mere personal pride which tends to compel me to . . . . . . 329 VIVA 20   2

TENEMENTS

climbing people high, up-in tenements talk. in sawdust Voices 128 & SEVEN POEMS 6   5

TENNISRACKET

my hands from the tennisracket. All was over. One . . . . . 263 IS 5 ONE 32   55

TENSE

slim deer the tall tense deer. Four tall stags . . . . 14 T&C SONGS 4   28
heaven yearns where in tense starlessness anoint with ardor . 37 T&C AMORES 2   9
into the smiting sky tense with blend ing the . . . . 182 XLI SONGS 4   2

TENSETENDONED

littleliverpill- ◇ americans (who tensetendoned and with . . 231 IS 5 ONE 3   48

TENT

and rolls against the tent his thick joggling fists . . . . . 259 IS 5 ONE 29   6
in a) "fert ig" (tent-sky wholly wallendas) ready were . . . 605 {CHAIRE} 7   10

+TENT

FOR CONTEXT, SEE . . . . 566 1 X 1 26   3

TENT-SKY

in a) "fert ig" (tent-sky wholly wallendas) ready were . . . 605 {CHAIRE} 7   10

TENTH

heart drinks wine the tenth lady says to nine . . . . 15 T&C SONGS 5   9
stumble from second to tenth rate (3) as it . . . . 803 73 POEMS 31   12

TENUOUS

hour, and from those tenuous fires which more and . . . . . .   6 T&C EPITHALAM   132

TENUOUS (CONTINUED)
    vague i don't know tenuous Now- spears and The . . . . 160 & SON ACTU 9   15
TERMINATED
    big good body, which terminated in fists hair wood . . . . . 277 IS 5 THREE 1   7
TERMS
    tell where.) beauty makes terms with time and his . . . . . . 183 XLI SONGS 5   7
    fraction in its lowest terms with everything cancelled but . 295 IS 5 FOUR 12   18
TERRIBLE
    blood, miss by how terrible inches speech--it made you . . . 174 & SON ACTU 23   10
    now i love god's terrible face, brighter than a . . . . 360 VIVA 51   21
    nothing is more exactly terrible than to be alone . . . . . . 375 VIVA 66   1
    surround your trite how terrible selfhood with its hands . . 522 50 POEMS 35   11
    is-- compared with pitying terrible some alive individual ten 561 1 X 1 21   4
    and she gave a terrible cry "no slave's unlife . . . . 711 95 POEMS 39   10
    never come? o come, terrible anonymity; enfold phantom me . . 839 73 POEMS 67   9
+TERRIBLE
    FOR CONTEXT, SEE . . . . 36 T&C AMORES 1   26
TERRIBLY
    hear one bird sing terribly afar in the lost . . . . 76 T&C SON UNRE 1   14
+TERRIBLY
    FOR CONTEXT, SEE . . . . 516 50 POEMS 30   1
TERRICOLOUS
    thickly (as one merely terricolous American an instant doubts 116 & PORTRAIT 9   12
TERRIFIC
    sheep float free upon terrific pastures pale, whose tall . . 9 T&C SONGS 1   9
    a decision: burn the terrific fingers which grapple and . . . 146 & SON REAL 17   5
    compassionate digit, earth's most terrific quadruped swoons . 315 VIVA 7   15
+TERRIFIC
    FOR CONTEXT, SEE . . . . 96 & POST IMPR 8   27
TERRIFYING
    doubt, for just sweet terrifying the particular moment it . . 809 73 POEMS 37   10
TERRIFYINGLY
    gould says in his terrifyingly hu man man ner . . . . 700 95 POEMS 28   2
TERROR
    wings as if in terror of eternity, (or seeming . . . . 6 T&C EPITHALAM   139
    glue in a superior terror; be thy taut flesh . . . . 9 T&C SONGS 1   31
    your hair pale, a terror musical? while in an . . . . 12 T&C SONGS 2   40
    and staggered banged with terror through a million billion . 258 IS 5 ONE 28   23
    me also with the terror of shrines which noone . . . . 285 IS 5 FOUR 2   16
    teach us a new terror always which shall brighten . . . . . . 289 IS 5 FOUR 6   10
    the carpeted stairs of terror) and continually i am . . . . . 375 VIVA 66   14
    education snakeoil vac uumcleaners terror strawberries democ 549 1 X 1 9   12
    ago? Blow hope to terror; blow seeing to blind . . . . 560 1 X 1 20   13
    were as red as terror and as green as . . . . 649 (CHAIRE) 51   11
    they adventure (wish by terror) steep not guessable each . . 757 95 POEMS 85   21
    soul of chivalry in terror of whose furious beak . . . . . . 774 73 POEMS 2   5
+TERROR
    FOR CONTEXT, SEE . . . . 646 (CHAIRE) 48   5
TERRORS
    frailly go The peaceful terrors of the snow, and . . . . . . 11 T&C SONGS 2   28
    Is The Sea. All terrors of his being quake . . . . 77 T&C SON UNRE 2   10
    than can twitch its terrors; the, mouth's, swallowed, muscle 136 & SON REAL 7   8
    disappear night's not eternal terrors like a guess. Life's . 582 1 X 1 42   15
    joys faces friends feet terrors fate hands silence eyes . . . 693 95 POEMS 21   2
TERSE
    enrich a visage simple, terse, seated like any king . . . . . 254 IS 5 ONE 25   18
    possibly are certain hands, terse and invisible, with large . 378 VIVA 69   6
TESTED
    oiled the universal joint tested my gas felt of . . . . 248 IS 5 ONE 19   7
TESTIFIED
    humble proud youngest bud testified "giving (and giving only) 763 95 POEMS 90   16
+TESTIMONIAL
    FOR CONTEXT, SEE . . . . 552 1 X 1 12   19
TETE
    pops into your jolly tete when the jolly shells . . . . 269 IS 5 TWO 4   3
TEXTURE
    hours wilts the stern texture of Now the arrow . . . . 112 & PORTRAIT 6   80
    a few deleted of texture or meaning monuments and . . . . . . 260 IS 5 ONE 30   8

		PAGE	TITLE	LINE

TEXTURE (CONTINUED)
(deftly muting the world's texture with drifted gifts of . . 299 IS 5 FOUR 16   4
your intense fragility: whose texture compels me with the . . 366 VIVA 57   14
doth depend upon the texture of their p-ss) isn't . . . . . . 411 NO THANKS 28   5
ends, the earth (whose texture feels of pride and . . . . . . 418 NO THANKS 35   2
TEXTURES
fiercely seek findingly new textures of actual cool . . . . . 373 VIVA 64   15
THAN
WORD DELETED, APPEARED 338 TIMES
THANK
a joy let 's thank indecent god p.s. the . . . . 425 NO THANKS 42   14
huge each eye look "thank you" nicely the lady's . . . . . . 506 50 POEMS 20   13
dare joy (eye kinely thank yoo) / / / . . . . 519 50 POEMS 33   28
fear) i very humbly thank you which could grin . . . . 522 50 POEMS 35   9
evil & legal) we thank thee god almighty for . . . . 604 (CHAIRE) 6   22
/ / / i thank You God for most . . . . 663 (CHAIRE) 65   1
render hell rational --i thank heaven somebody's crazy enough 802 73 POEMS 30   32
+THANK
FOR CONTEXT, SEE . . . . 602 (CHAIRE) 4   5
THANKFUL
let's all be as thankful as hell and bury . . . . 711 95 POEMS 39   26
small these all these thankful (hark) birds singing wholly . 819 73 POEMS 47   20
THANKFULLY
into his own paradise thankfully whole and the green . . . . 558 1 X 1 18   3
off by moment day thankfully become each other) one . . . . . 720 95 POEMS 48   6
THANKING
a. she suddenly luffed --thanking me; and (stating that . . . 326 VIVA 18   36
+THANKING
FOR CONTEXT, SEE . . . . 754 95 POEMS 82   4
THANKS
fortune of fifteengrand pounds thanks to the socalled fact . 331 VIVA 22   3
be) the more than thanks of always merest me . . . . 821 73 POEMS 49   14
+THANKS
FOR CONTEXT, SEE . . . . 310 VIVA 2   8
THANKSGIVING
/ / / THANKSGIVING (1956) a monstering horror . . . . 711 95 POEMS 39   T
THANKYOUVERYMUCH
If i should say thankyouverymuch mr rosenbloom picks . . . . 287 IS 5 FOUR 4   7
THAT
WORD DELETED, APPEARED 338 TIMES
THAT'S
WORD DELETED, APPEARED 29 TIMES
THATANDTHIS
precise clumsy prison (building thatandthis into Thus, Around 83 T&C SON ACTU 2   7
+THATCH
FOR CONTEXT, SEE . . . . 645 (CHAIRE) 47   3
THATOFA
, my, love is thatofa fly. pre cisel Yhalf . . . .   94 & POST IMPR 6   27
THATTHIS
fusion ror collap sing thatthis is whichwhat yell itfulls . . 646 (CHAIRE) 48   6
/ / / nite) thatthis crou ched moangrowl-&-thin g . . . . . . 795 73 POEMS 23   2
THAZ
spittle what the lands thaz me kid in no . . . .   96 & POST IMPR 8   15
THCARED
never's ear (i'm tho thcared giggling lithped now we . . . . 316 VIVA 8   6
THE
WORD DELETED, APPEARED 2740 TIMES
THE-SEAT-OF-THE
man (clutched by immense the-seat-of-the pants inani nvisible 616 (CHAIRE) 18   7
THEATRE
called newsreel s called theatre & with your wn . . . . 392 NO THANKS 9   10
THEE
the scared shepherd gave thee for his doom-- O . . . .   6 T&C EPITHALAM   152
of lovers! --I beseech thee bless thy suppliant singer . . .   7 T&C EPITHALAM   167
/ / / SONGS (thee will i praise between . . . .   9 T&C SONGS 1   1
my love wholly taste thee as a new wine . . . .   9 T&C SONGS 1   35
thing and small. Death, Thee i call rich beyond . . . .   13 T&C SONGS 3   17
ORIENTALE i spoke to thee with a smile and . . . .   27 T&C ORIENTALE 1   1

THEE (CONTINUED)

smile? i spoke to thee with a song and	27 T&C ORIENTALE 1	8
song? i spoke to thee with a soul and	27 T&C ORIENTALE 1	16
love? i speak to thee with a sword and	27 T&C ORIENTALE 1	23
/ / / unto thee i burn incense the	31 T&C ORIENTALE 5	1
the level litanies unto thee i burn incense, over	31 T&C ORIENTALE 5	21
beauty, my heart discovers thee unto whom i burn	31 T&C ORIENTALE 5	28
irrevocable sea i knew thee death. and when i	39 T&C AMORES 4	28
philosophers pinched and poked thee ,has the naughty thumb	46 T&C LA GUERRE 2	9
often have religions taken thee upon their scraggy knees	46 T&C LA GUERRE 2	15
knees squeezing and buffeting thee that thou mightest	46 T&C LA GUERRE 2	17
little while i see thee then ponder the tinsel	75 T&C SON REAL 6	5
tinsel part they let thee play; i see the	75 T&C SON REAL 6	6
my body turns toward thee again for the stars	184 XLI SONGS 6	9
roses were sweeter to thee perchance to me deeper.	213 XLI SONNETS 9	16
afraid, i love of thee (beloved) this and truly	215 XLI SONNETS 11	3
and while everywhere beneath thee and about thyself a	351 VIVA 42	9
cheaply thick --who therefore Thee (once and once only,	358 VIVA 49	11
& legal) we thank thee god almighty for dying	604 (CHAIRE) 6	22
beautiful anarchist (i salute thee / / / /	677 95 POEMS 5	16

THEIR
WORD DELETED, APPEARED 143 TIMES
+THEIR

| FOR CONTEXT, SEE | 519 50 POEMS 33 | 22 |
| FOR CONTEXT, SEE | 519 50 POEMS 33 | 26 |

THEIRS

| he was a roman theirs was a music sinuous | 110 & PORTRAIT 6 | 22 |
| to do is exactly theirs (dull worlds or keen; | 776 73 POEMS 4 | 10 |

+THEIRS

| FOR CONTEXT, SEE | 519 50 POEMS 33 | 23 |

THEM
WORD DELETED, APPEARED 55 TIMES
THEMSELVES

two elves incredibly amuse themselves) with a look of	17 T&C PUELLA MEA	40
and two bound for themselves, when passionately dusk brings	71 T&C SON REAL 2	9
consider for how much themselves shall gleam, in the	81 T&C SON UNRE 6	7
blacktreesthink tiny, angels sharpen: themselves (on air)	99 & POST IMPR 10	15
love and flowers pick themselves / / / /	129 & SEVEN POEMS 7	16
the communists pick up themselves friends & their hats	275 IS 5 TWO 9	43
little hands withdrew, jerkily, themselves quietly they began	284 IS 5 FOUR 1	8
& difficult ugliness of themselves with a more incisive	354 VIVA 45	16
indignant clover marrying to themselves Life's animals) but	376 VIVA 67	5
sweetness touched renown) suddenly themselves if all dreams	414 NO THANKS 31	5
such pretty toys as themselves could not know: the	451 NO THANKS 66	10
what world? is it themselves these insects mean? when	555 1 X 1 15	3
by doubting have darkly themselves unmade makes love armies	580 1 X 1 40	14
to these my not themselves believing eyes adventuring,	669 (CHAIRE) 71	3
(crazily kissing) till into themselves we fell-- how have	694 95 POEMS 22	4
its houses turning into themselves grow silent upon new	720 95 POEMS 48	2

+THEMSELVES

FOR CONTEXT, SEE	278 IS 5 THREE 2	7
FOR CONTEXT, SEE	442 NO THANKS 57	14
FOR CONTEXT, SEE	444 NO THANKS 59	12
FOR CONTEXT, SEE	695 95 POEMS 23	14
FOR CONTEXT, SEE	799 73 POEMS 27	21

THEN

meadows sweet with fear") then be with me: unseriously	9 T&C SONGS 1	28
doth abuse reason, why then the artificer did most	22 T&C PUELLA MEA	219
of his left hand then the ◇ door is	33 T&C ORIENTALE 6	60
only, from the ashes then thou wilt rise and	40 T&C AMORES 4	38
asked "always" Death said "then as i recollect her	57 T&C PORTRAIT 5	29
somewhat tweaked and dinted then did my servant become	57 T&C PORTRAIT 5	34
piece of money and then his master will yell	69 T&C POST IMPR 6	12
little toylike hand) and then he will stiff-ly throw	69 T&C POST IMPR 6	18
while i see thee then ponder the tinsel part	75 T&C SON REAL 6	5
all happiness from me. Then shall i turn my	76 T&C SON UNRE 1	13
people are minutely dead. Then you will slowly kiss	86 T&C SON ACTU 5	14
eyes stay at home then my mouth will go	100 & POST IMPR 11	19

	PAGE	TITLE	LINE
THEN (CONTINUED)			
into their balloon, why then we'd go up higher	129	& SEVEN POEMS 7	7
bloke back in fifteen. Then she came toward him	145	& SON REAL 16	3
heart-beat becomes less. And then all her beauty is	152	& SON ACTU 1	10
luminous and precise --and then we are I and	152	& SON ACTU 1	14
Now- spears and The Then-arrows making do our mouths	160	& SON ACTU 9	16
dusk her new wings then decently hanged himself, one	170	& SON ACTU 19	4
fragrance of newness --and then. My crazy fingers liked	173	& SON ACTU 22	8
/ / Where's Madge then, Madge and her men?	183	XLI SONGS 5	1
pirouette your hair and then your dancesong soul.	186	XLI SONGS 8	16
place dark or unhappy then when you're quite dressed	192	XLI CHANSONS 2	21
dis Gawd" opening slowlyslowly them--then carefully the	228	IS 5 ONE MARJ	8
slipped the clutch (and then somehow got into reverse	248	IS 5 ONE 19	11
did graze at pause then fired by hypercivic zeal	258	IS 5 ONE 28	11
of the again latter then opening a box of	263	IS 5 ONE 32	46
brief convulsive octopus, and then our hero folded his	263	IS 5 ONE 32	56
is not made...) why then to Hell with that:	264	IS 5 ONE 33	30
and female created He then, And every beast of	267	IS 5 TWO 2	20
think they died instead then shall the voice of	268	IS 5 TWO 3	13
hear the rrmp and then <> and before you	269	IS 5 TWO 4	6
were going to America. Then moving was a matter	289	IS 5 FOUR 6	22
are for each other: then laugh, leaning back in	290	IS 5 FOUR 7	13
instance a plugged promise-- then he will maybe (hearing	298	IS 5 FOUR 15	20
curled hands moves) why then toward morning he is	299	IS 5 FOUR 16	11
e nibble now And then bite) candy others fly,	314	VIVA 6	11
all hopped up) prettily then which did lie Down,	317	VIVA 9	35
against Laughing Virginity Death) then dearest the way trees	359	VIVA 50	10
Not sleep matters nothing; then (then the only hands	359	VIVA 50	14
sleep matters nothing; then (then the only hands so	359	VIVA 50	14
half (through deep weather then or none let's feel	364	VIVA 55	13
may surprise ourselves --let's then despise what is not	368	VIVA 59	16
one bursting soul why, then comes peace unto men	414	NO THANKS 31	12
beggars yaw: nstretchy: awn) then, o my love ,	442	NO THANKS 57	16
o my love , then it's Spring immortal Always	442	NO THANKS 57	18
not imaginable star : then a small million of	454	NO THANKS 69	13
not to push and then to pull but practicing	500	50 POEMS 14	18
to grow end's ending then these dolls of joy	502	50 POEMS 16	9
stops might equal head). Then with the splendor of	506	50 POEMS 20	11
(sleep wake hope and then) they said their nevers	515	50 POEMS 29	19
heard my father sing) then let men kill which	521	50 POEMS 34	53
hand is a mind then over our thief goes	543	1 X 1 3	19
me what it's pliz) then up rose bishop budge	552	1 X 1 12	6
smote the monster merde then up rose pride and	552	1 X 1 12	11
silence of the tomb then up rose mr lipshits	552	1 X 1 12	26
life worships and (night) then "everything beautiful can	572	1 X 1 32	14
a whole world and then a single hair again"	572	1 X 1 32	16
spoil the game, what then? all history's a winter	579	1 X 1 39	4
never? you were wrong --then all the way from	599	(CHAIRE) 1	12
april as a saboteur then we'll believe in that	620	(CHAIRE) 22	13
and who? each grows" then in a whisper, as	626	(CHAIRE) 28	11
all skies fall) and then to slowly trust T	650	(CHAIRE) 52	3
now must come to then our then shall be	667	(CHAIRE) 69	8
come to then our then shall be some darkness	667	(CHAIRE) 69	9
& every now & then my wonderful friend dominic	680	95 POEMS 8	22
sheer wonder mere surprise (then turn the page) contentment	689	95 POEMS 17	4
s this dingy cage: then with a ghost 's	697	95 POEMS 25	10
a thousand years and then lay down with a	709	95 POEMS 37	16
was ever as i then that Star goes under	752	95 POEMS 80	8
freedom: always here no then of winter equals now	765	95 POEMS 91	11
--do lovers love? why then to heaven with hell.	768	95 POEMS 94	13
foreverfully falling snow. And then this dreamer wept: and	777	73 POEMS 5	14
sing) lish sparrows say then 2 or per (who	787	73 POEMS 15	5
happens every now and then upon a merely human	799	73 POEMS 27	9
of joy with him then Cunning forged a web	799	73 POEMS 27	16
pour into sixth avenue) "then" my voice marvels "what	800	73 POEMS 28	21
kind sweet big voice: then a slender face (on	813	73 POEMS 41	3
thrill of your beauty, then my lost my dazed	819	73 POEMS 47	13
of sky (silently all then known things or dreamed	822	73 POEMS 50	7

THEN (CONTINUED)
    should his now go then / / / / . . . . 842 73 POEMS 70   14
    reeking innocence are born. Then, with not credible the . . . 843 73 POEMS 71   9
+THEN
    FOR CONTEXT, SEE . . . . 122 & SEVEN POEMS 1 17
    FOR CONTEXT, SEE . . . . 430 NO THANKS 47   4
THEN-ARROWS
    Now- spears and The Then-arrows making do our mouths . . . . 160 & SON ACTU 9   16
THEN'S
    my blossoming) for also then's until / / / . . . . 667 {CHAIRE} 69   14
THENCE
    big was) thither to thence swore many a vow . . . . 316 VIVA 8   13
THENLIKE
    among dark ness. sunlight's thenlike? now Disappears some . . 397 NO THANKS 14   18
THENS
    because and why dividing thens by nows and adding . . . . . . 500 50 POEMS 14   6
THEODORE
    clamored Clever Rusefelt to Theodore Odysseus Graren't we . . 321 VIVA 13   10
THEOREMS
    joy proving the peaceful theorems of the flowers --didst . . 3 T&C EPITHALAM   19
THERAINCOMING
    o ; w : theraIncomIng o all the roofs . . . . 347 VIVA 38   17
THERE
    sweet wheels tremulous-- are there no kings in Argos, ... 4 T&C EPITHALAM   49
    and one by one there fell upon the night, ... 8 T&C OF NICOL   10
    --always upon the mouth there trysts curvingly a fragile . . 20 T&C PUELLA MEA   148
    not lack for beauty there, nor he that will . . . . 20 T&C PUELLA MEA   168
    err. If to me there shall appear than a . . . . 21 T&C PUELLA MEA   175
    oblivion sweeter than any there is one; to touch . . . . . 23 T&C PUELLA MEA   273
    tangled a cool moon there are thrice-three-hundred doors . . 33 T&C ORIENTALE 6 33
    / / / / there is a moon sole . . . . 37 T&C AMORES 2   1
    talking rapidly all together there happens Something, and . . 62 T&C PORTRAIT 10 18
    and begging colour) while there and here the lithe . . . . . 93 & POST IMPR 5   16
    BLACK CAT WITH is there anything my ears love . . . . 100 & POST IMPR 11   33
    see Life? he is there and here, or that, ... 102 & POST IMPR 12   11
    I see someone else there is a lady, whose . . . . 102 & POST IMPR 12   24
    ear to the ground there is a music Lady . . . . 113 & PORTRAIT 6   115
    and changing placing carefully there a strange thing and . . 124 & SEVEN POEMS 3   7
    an inch of air there) and without breaking anything. . . . . 124 & SEVEN POEMS 3 18
    pennies they all sit there looking at each other . . . . . . 126 & SEVEN POEMS 5   6
    upward, mock us....) and there was a clock. tac-tic. . . . . 133 & SON REAL 4   7
    while in your eyes there lives a green egyptian . . . . 138 & SON REAL 9   7
    autumn is: that between there and here gladness flays . . . 158 & SON ACTU 7   1
    to forget-- wherefore is there nothing left to guess: . . . . 173 & SON ACTU 22   13
    logic, oho. a street there is where strange birds . . . . . . 180 XLI SONGS 2   19
    flowers of kiss and there is the sweet shy . . . . 186 XLI SONGS 8   14
    have its ring and there won't be a single . . . . 192 XLI CHANSONS 2   20
    deposited upon the drum there is need of just . . . . 196 XLI PORTRAIT 4   11
    pants and forgetting it's there and sitting down on . . . . . 204 XLI LA GUERRE 2 20
    perpendicular Always-- or possibly there drift a pulseless . 218 XLI SONNETS 14   12
    dull jerk at garters) there 's no sharpest neat . . . . 227 IS 5 ONE GERT   10
    going rather kaka over there, over there. yet we . . . . . . 233 IS 5 ONE 4   8
    kaka over there, over there. yet we scarcely fare . . . . . . 233 IS 5 ONE 4   8
    the sun, ladies? <> "there is not enough of . . . . 255 IS 5 ONE 26   8
    after April by God there is no excuse for . . . . 264 IS 5 ONE 33   8
    me everyone that's been there knows what i mean . . . . 272 IS 5 TWO 7   12
    let us add that there are 50 (fifty) flics . . . . 274 IS 5 TWO 9   17
    black goat lookingly wanders There is nothing left of . . . . 278 IS 5 THREE 2   17
    building a house down there by the sea, in . . . . 281 IS 5 THREE 5   10
    so far-- hush. Sunlight, there are old men behind . . . . . . 281 IS 5 THREE 5   24
    And there's the moon, there is something faithful and . . . . 303 IS 5 FIVE 2   16
    / / / / there are 6 doors. Next . . . . 312 VIVA 4   1
    o yes Frost Something there is which isn't fond . . . . 315 VIVA 7   3
    quoth the front; and there was yz SHOT AND . . . . 317 VIVA 9   11
    (opening the windows) "and there is a philosphy" strictly . . 328 VIVA 19   11
    does almost ceaselessly repeat "there is some shit I . . . . 339 VIVA 30   33
    drink smile if here there (like lopsided imaginations) filled 340 VIVA 31   9
    / / / if there are any heavens my . . . . 352 VIVA 43   1

	PAGE	TITLE	LINE

THERE (CONTINUED)

bat in this twilight") there one is look how . . . . 353 VIVA 44 — 6
look (it's back again there therehere And) i say . . . . . . 353 VIVA 44 — 23
a together whitely big there is but if so . . . . 365 VIVA 56 — 10
/ / / is there a flower (whom i . . . . 367 VIVA 58 — 1
something) You are gone. there is laughter and despair . . . 375 VIVA 66 — 4
merely universe, love's also there: and being here . . . . . 377 VIVA 68 — 6
world) A always don't there B being no such . . . . 390 NO THANKS 7 — 2
moon a here and there lark who; rises, and; . . . . 434 NO THANKS 51 — 18
happens only and beautiful there is a ragged beside . . . . . 437 NO THANKS 53 — 10
all aleak; and lifepreservers there are none: and waves . . . 438 NO THANKS 54 — 26
& god said & there was is born: one . . . . 479 NEW POEMS 17 — 12
quickly ghost scribbling from there to where --name unless . 504 50 POEMS 18 — 8
/ / / / there is a here and . . . . 505 50 POEMS 19 — 1
/ / / / there are possibly 2 1/2 : . . . . 514 50 POEMS 28 — 1
that a here and there a peers at you) . . . . 516 50 POEMS 30 — 9
born is good but there this cheap this suit . . . . 523 50 POEMS 36 — 22
too quick no suit there every -thing nothing i . . . . . . 523 50 POEMS 36 — 23
ghosts some few creep there here or on unearth . . . . . . 541 1 X 1 1 — 10
who (and here who there who) descend -ing (mercifully) . . . 557 1 X 1 17 — 8
to ask you if there isn't a new moon . . . . 572 1 X 1 32 — 1
just if" "that's all there is to say" (and . . . . 572 1 X 1 32 — 4
our permanent address and there they'll scarcely find us . . 579 1 X 1 39 — 13
leaf (beyond whose nearness there is no beyond) or . . . . . 592 1 X 1 52 — 8
"and poets grow; and (there--see?) children" nor might any . 626 (CHAIRE) 28 — 12
here & (simply infinite) there & (smoke) a fair . . . . . . 629 (CHAIRE) 31 — 10
e) and echo answers "there is no appeal from . . . . 636 (CHAIRE) 38 — 12
than eyes tell me) there is a time for . . . . 683 95 POEMS 11 — 14
the rightest man remembers there is such a thing . . . . . 685 95 POEMS 13 — 7
to have never looked there" "and you couldn't well . . . . 707 95 POEMS 35 — 3
marvels vanish, will include --there by arriving magically . 741 95 POEMS 69 — 11
of mountain (strolling is there here everywhere fairyair . . 755 95 POEMS 83 — 8
but ears may see there never lived a gayer . . . . 760 95 POEMS 87 — 6
fro (and a here there where) and away we . . . . 769 95 POEMS 95 — 7
other day never was there such a lay-- whom, ... 794 73 POEMS 22 — 2
one very falling most (there: did you see it?) . . . . . . 809 73 POEMS 37 — 12
invisible where of a there of a) here of . . . . 827 73 POEMS 55 — 8

+THERE

FOR CONTEXT, SEE . . . . 73 T&C SON REAL 4 — 13
FOR CONTEXT, SEE . . . . 237 IS 5 ONE 8 — 6
FOR CONTEXT, SEE . . . . 320 VIVA 12 — 24
FOR CONTEXT, SEE . . . . 519 50 POEMS 33 — 26

THERE'LL

through the old swimminghole there'll be slime in his . . . . 707 95 POEMS 35 — 28

THERE'RE

I love, You. And there're a ◇ like all . . . . 231 IS 5 ONE 3 — 41

THERE'S

ght s (oon & there's a m oo)n. . . . . 122 & SEVEN POEMS 1 — 26
COO1 0 My lover, there's just room for me . . . . 123 & SEVEN POEMS 2 — 8
too wide dear god there's a portrait over the . . . . 198 XLI PORTRAIT 6 — 7
little beyond the last road--there's something to be found" . 303 IS 5 FIVE 2 — 3
little your. so. And there's the moon, there is . . . . . . 303 IS 5 FIVE 2 — 16
can you maybe listen there's me & some people . . . . . . 314 VIVA 6 — 1
that patch of darkness there's a what is it . . . . 322 VIVA 14 — 4
corners dawn smirks and there's the moon, thinner than . . . 322 VIVA 14 — 14
top of these stairs, there's a free room. We . . . . 365 VIVA 56 — 7
so more than truly there's never been quite such . . . . . 481 NEW POEMS 19 — 11
a hopeless case if--listen: there's a hell of a . . . . . . 554 1 X 1 14 — 14
gut a mind to there's something for everybody it's . . . . 567 1 X 1 27 — 15
heart alert, of languages there's none but well she . . . . 575 1 X 1 35 — 28
two are perfectly alone there's nobody else alive (such . . . 591 1 X 1 51 — 12
around we go yes) there's nothing as something as . . . . . 594 1 X 1 54 — 9
around we go all) there's somebody calling who's we . . . . 594 1 X 1 54 — 36
/ / neither awake (there's your general yas buy . . . . . . 640 (CHAIRE) 42 — 2
scowl of a cannibal) there's your mineral general animal . . 640 (CHAIRE) 42 — 11
than a rose's moment there's time for laughing and . . . . 683 95 POEMS 11 — 9
time for laughing and there's time for crying-- for . . . . 683 95 POEMS 11 — 9
bill as long as there's haymows you never can . . . . 707 95 POEMS 35 — 10

THERE'S (CONTINUED)
   tell" "as long as there's ladies my annie is . . . . 707 95 POEMS 35   11
+THERE'S
   FOR CONTEXT, SEE . . . . 259 IS 5 ONE 29   28
THEREFORE
   of all shining things therefore we also blandly into . . . .   41 T&C AMORES 5   11
   limp the ostensible centuries therefore let us be a . . . . . 111 & PORTRAIT 6   56
   It Isn't A Kodak therefore my friends let us . . . . 230 IS 5 ONE 2   35
   four gnarled lips totter Therefore, approaching my twentysix 255 IS 5 ONE 26   5
   saw in the mirror)? therefore we'll kiss; for maybe . . . . . 286 IS 5 FOUR 3   21
   elements remarkably nothing is.... therefore, lady am i . . . 291 IS 5 FOUR 8   17
   (however) us Walk very (therefore and) softly among one's . . 317 VIVA 9   18
   smile cheaply thick --who therefore Thee (once and once . . . 358 VIVA 49   11
   among cool ferns) therefore togethering our wholly lives . . 371 VIVA 62   15
   to persuade even silence: therefore wonder opens a gate; . . 376 VIVA 67   9
   vibration create voice if therefore among foul pains appears 425 NO THANKS 42   13
   is love (who's imagined, therefore limitless) love's to . . . 574 1 X 1 34   2
   who's every child (& therefore invisible) anyhow you 've . . 668 {CHAIRE} 70   14
   friends turn to enemies) therefore lament, my dream and . . . 834 73 POEMS 62   5
   what makes a slave) therefore, my life, lie down . . . . . . 834 73 POEMS 62   10
   brave are cowards all) therefore despair, my heart and . . . 834 73 POEMS 62   23
THEREFROM
   tree fruit that dangles therefrom the purpled world will . .   16 T&C SONGS 6   3
THEREHERE
   (it's back again there therehere And) i say "won't . . . . . 353 VIVA 44   23
THERES
   hearted-Nujolneeding-There's-A-Reason americans(who . . . . . 231 IS 5 ONE 3   47
   how colding hereless. air theres what immense live without . 491 50 POEMS 5   4
THERETO
   ecstatic actual tread (and thereto perfectly responds) of all   19 T&C PUELLA MEA 126
THEREUPON
   vanished, gunwale awash. I thereupon loosened my collar and . 327 VIVA 18   37
THERMOPYLAE
   she cried so high thermopylae heard her and marathon . . . . 711 95 POEMS 39   13
THESE
   WORD DELETED, APPEARED 98 TIMES
THESILLYOLD
   st ott er s thesillyold WomanSellingBalloonS In theex qui . . 104 & POST IMPR 14   16
THETHE
   / / / / thethe the pink Tartskids with . . . . 318 VIVA 10   1
THEWITH
   A) with! notgirl'swith? dumb (thewith girl) ness (ish The . . 388 NO THANKS 5   25
THEY
   WORD DELETED, APPEARED 156 TIMES
THEY'D
   wanted us to understand they'd never close (and open) . . . . 603 {CHAIRE} 5   9
   three wealthy sisters swore they'd never part: Soul was . . . 621 {CHAIRE} 23   1
THEY'LL
   to see and how they'll stare! oh but you'll . . . . 192 XLI CHANSONS 2   23
   their glories downward if they'll or goldenly float so . . . 573 1 X 1 33   7
   permanent address and there they'll scarcely find us (if . . 579 1 X 1 39   13
   and am quick i they'll all not conceive less . . . . 634 {CHAIRE} 36   15
   spring but we be they'll some or if where . . . . 666 {CHAIRE} 68   5
THEY'RE
   / kumrads die because they're told) kumrads die before . . . 413 NO THANKS 30   1
   told) kumrads die before they're old (kumrads aren't afraid . 413 NO THANKS 30   2
   come soon" & pretending they're birds sit creatures of . . . 483 NEW POEMS 21   9
   flimsy which but) always (they're more much further off) . . 501 50 POEMS 15   15
   the apples are (yes they're gravensteins) all as red . . . . 543 1 X 1 3   4
   red and the round (they're gravensteins) fall with kind . . . 543 1 X 1 3   28
   liars wilt, repaying life they're loaned; we (by a . . . . . 556 1 X 1 16   11
   o no: i'm certain they're (look again) flowers." "Don't . . . 603 {CHAIRE} 5   5
   poor worlds; i mean they're possible --but" lifting "flowers" 603 {CHAIRE} 5   12
   proud or humble, equally they're welcome --as if the . . . . 763 95 POEMS 90   14
   / / christ but they're few all (beyond win . . . . 805 73 POEMS 33   1
+THEY'RE
   FOR CONTEXT, SEE . . . . 474 NEW POEMS 12   14

	PAGE	TITLE	LINE

THEY'VE

the fastest time because they've never met before dead's . . 126 & SEVEN POEMS 5   7
it looks like rain (they've played for timelessness with . . 451 NO THANKS 66   3
in love: with us they've nothing times nothing to . . . . . . 664 (CHAIRE) 66 11
without until: but pitiful they've (big little and all) . . . 776 73 POEMS 4 21
no and yes: if they've become the same it's . . . . 834 73 POEMS 62 17

THEYS

un forgetting un. der (theys) the : se! crumbs . . . . . . 417 NO THANKS 34 21
/ / / / theys s0 alive (who is . . . . 426 NO THANKS 43   1
My father moved through theys of we, singing each . . . . . 521 50 POEMS 34 49
is are ex quisite theys of re turn a . . . . 536 50 POEMS 48 15

THICK

nearby the father a thick cheerful man with majestic . . . . 56 T&C PORTRAIT 4 10
eyes clicking mischief from thick lids. the chunklike nose . 73 T&C SON REAL 4   7
flower stropping sof a. Thick silence) blacktreesthink tiny, 99 & POST IMPR 10 13
a body it was thick slim warm moist built . . . . 110 & PORTRAIT 6 17
but it's sharp and thick and it loves, every . . . . 126 & SEVEN POEMS 5   4
of Haremina in the thick of the snick- er . . . . 194 XLI PORTRAIT 2 16
pumped full of sharp thick mind you make us . . . . 195 XLI PORTRAIT 3   4
arms bedecked whose white thick wrists deliver promptly to . 225 IS 5 ONE LIZ   8
against the tent his thick joggling fists he is . . . . . . 259 IS 5 ONE 29   6
its dreamy spine against thick sunset i perceive in . . . . . 279 IS 5 THREE 3   4
uneyes safely ensconced in thick glass you try if . . . . . 326 VIVA 18   4
uneyes safely ensconced in thick glass / / . . . . 327 VIVA 18 46
And spills smile cheaply thick --who therefore Thee (once . . 358 VIVA 49 10
fiend, a thousand dreams thick (cringing they brood breeding 439 NO THANKS 55   8
bums dream ing i'm thick in a hot young . . . . 469 NEW POEMS 7   3
big that quick sharp thick snake of a voice . . . . 490 50 POEMS 4 10
at nobody shoulder and thick stickingly un stride after . . . 522 50 POEMS 35   3
mind with a warm thick scream and a keen . . . . 647 (CHAIRE) 49   7
/ (nothing whichful about thick big this friendly himself . . 658 (CHAIRE) 60   2
wisp of why as thick as my fist stuck . . . . 709 95 POEMS 37 11

THICKENING

birds shakes with a thickening fright the sudden fooled . . . 11 T&C SONGS 2 19
flowerstricken sun- light is thickening dizzily is reeling . 69 T&C POST IMPR 6 24
at twilight, caught in thickening fear our slightly fingering 305 IS 5 FIVE 4   6

THICKER

slimmer the finger the thicker the thumb (it's whirl, ... 513 50 POEMS 27   6
/ love is more thicker than forget more thinner . . . . . . 530 50 POEMS 42   1

THICKEST

very much biggest & thickest & kindest of ring . . . . . . 470 NEW POEMS 8 16

THICKISH

lady lazily struts (her thickish flesh superior to the . . . 150 & SON REAL 21 12

THICKLY

by little accurate saints thickly which tread the serene . . 85 T&C SON ACTU 4   1
elephants (mingled in whispering thickly smooth thighs . . . 95 & POST IMPR 7 15
of eyes which mutter thickly (as one merely terricolous . . . 116 & PORTRAIT 9 11
opaque big girl jiggles thickly hips to the kanoon . . . . 220 XLI SONNETS 16 15
causes the bent eyes thickly to protrude-- or why . . . . . 229 IS 5 ONE FRAN 13
(bly Perpetually coughing And thickly spi) tting But next . . 312 VIVA 4 20
of gulls' drift Of thickly starhums wherefore & wormSmile . . 371 VIVA 62 22
least flowers of rain) thickly i fail slenderly i . . . . . 433 NO THANKS 50   9

+THICKLY

FOR CONTEXT, SEE . . . . 493 50 POEMS 7 12

THICKLYFOOLISH

the mealy, ladies dancing thicklyfoolish, with, the, tam, . . 100 & POST IMPR 11 43

THICKNESS

the freezing fire of Thickness) points uPDownwardishly find . 311 VIVA 3 14
if i love You (thickness means worlds inhabited by . . . . 363 VIVA 54   2
love makes the little thickness of the coin comes . . . . . 531 50 POEMS 43   8

THIEF

in each down a thief by a whore dragged . . . . 533 50 POEMS 45 21
mind then over our thief goes (you go and . . . . 543 1 X 1 3 19
/ / ("fire stop thief help murder save the . . . . 555 1 X 1 15   1
regular righteous comfortable) unworlds thief crook cynic . . 677 95 POEMS 5   9

THIEVES

who had fallen among thieves lay by the roadside . . . . . . 258 IS 5 ONE 28   1

776

	PAGE	TITLE	LINE
THIGHED			
went to bed, whom white-thighed Semiramis put up her	22	T&C PUELLA MEA	247
THIGHS			
dost with quivering continual thighs invite the thrilling . .	3	T&C EPITHALAM	2
her large and shapely thighs) in whose dome the	21	T&C PUELLA MEA	204
wholly is. Beneath her thighs such legs are seen	21	T&C PUELLA MEA	207
approach of spring thy thighs are white horses yoked	29	T&C ORIENTALE 3	11
the slobber of your thighs i am so very	61	T&C PORTRAIT 9	25
in whispering thickly smooth thighs thinkingly) remind me of	95	& POST IMPR 7	15
loveFist in her knuckling thighs, with a sharp indecent . . .	131	& SON REAL 2	9
a flesh from hinging thighs .... merci.... i want	133	& SON REAL 4	16
hairy notching of clenched thighs a friendless dingy female .	151	& SON REAL 22	17
guess: the cheap intelligent thighs, the electric trite . . .	173	& SON ACTU 22	14
thighs, the electric trite thighs; the hair stupidly	173	& SON ACTU 22	15
wade out till my thighs are steeped in burning	189	XLI SONGS 11	2
and eyes blur And thighs forget (when clocks whisper	359	VIVA 50	2
rise these your wrists thighs feet hands poising to	369	VIVA 60	13
for friends --open your thighs to fate and (if	420	NO THANKS 37	13
wave among your deepening thighs a greedier wand than	454	NO THANKS 69	4
breasts will be breasts thighs will be thighs deeds	511	50 POEMS 25	24
breasts thighs will be thighs deeds cannot dream what	511	50 POEMS 25	24
THIMBLES			
with nipples like pink thimbles) ask him ask who	498	50 POEMS 12	19
THIN			
year: When through the thin air stooped with fear, ...	11	T&C SONGS 2	22
with a wild and thin despair of violin /	12	T&C SONGS 2	49
charge laughing. Into the hair-thin tints of yellow dawn, . .	66	T&C POST IMPR 3	6
oral darkness raging with thin impulse i will have	67	T&C POST IMPR 4	5
legs pinch, toes choke-- hair-thin strands of magic agony . .	146	& SON REAL 17	8
tall and taut, with thin legs just like a	147	& SON REAL 18	10
always floats through the thin amorous enormous only lips . .	202	XLI PORTRAIT 9	47
how ses humble. Over thin earths chatterish strut cuddle . .	346	VIVA 37	3
consider how these immaculate thin things half daemon half .	362	VIVA 53	5
any anguish struck how thin a ghost so deep	414	NO THANKS 31	8
/ ◇ tosses like thin bums dream ing i'm	469	NEW POEMS 7	2
of stands on a thin ring which stands on	470	NEW POEMS 8	11
on a much less thin very much more big	470	NEW POEMS 8	12
nite) thatthis crou ched moangrowl-&-thin g stirs (m id) . .	795	73 POEMS 23	5
+THIN			
FOR CONTEXT, SEE	697	95 POEMS 25	11
THINE			
thou didst not listen thine eyes are as a	27	T&C ORIENTALE 1	11
& listen Venezia: incline thine ear you glassworks of	256	IS 5 ONE 27	2
err inhuman) or any thine a mine --dingdong: dongding-- . . .	798	73 POEMS 26	5
THING			
odour drives the wingless thing man forth into bright	4	T&C EPITHALAM	60
every curved and curling thing, yet holds continuous	5	T&C EPITHALAM	90
lips is a sweet thing and small. Death, Thee	13	T&C SONGS 3	15
is a little stranger thing than crisp Sheba with	17	T&C PUELLA MEA	7
is a more curious thing (a thing more nimble	17	T&C PUELLA MEA	25
more curious thing (a thing more nimble and complete)	17	T&C PUELLA MEA	26
of every most shy thing and mute, it is	19	T&C PUELLA MEA	99
of flesh, a winsome thing and strange; apt in	21	T&C PUELLA MEA	194
lips for a dead thing, i shall instruct him	42	T&C AMORES 6	10
becomes unutterably crisp a thing, which tightens caught in .	68	T&C POST IMPR 5	9
/ / SONNETS--ACTUALITIES a thing most new complete fragile .	82	T&C SON REAL 1	1
itse; 1. f to no-thing signifi- cant stomachs: Who	101	& POST IMPR 11	74
carefully there a strange thing and a known thing	124	& SEVEN POEMS 3	8
thing and a known thing here) and changing everything	124	& SEVEN POEMS 3	8
it loves, every old thing falls in rosebugs and	126	& SEVEN POEMS 5	5
they stuff the poor thing all full of fingers	126	& SEVEN POEMS 5	13
dead's sorry like a thistlefluff-thing which goes land- ing .	127	& SEVEN POEMS 5	41
somebody's roof or some- thing where ◇ and nobody	127	& SEVEN POEMS 5	43
It is a funny, thing. And you will be	153	& SON ACTU 2	9
the room's skilful of thing silent spits discrete lumps . . .	159	& SON ACTU 8	6
one afternoon. The last thing he saw was you	170	& SON ACTU 19	5
so quite new a thing. Muscles better and nerves	175	& SON ACTU 24	2
the marvel of this thing?) / / / /	205	XLI SONNETS 1	15

THING (CONTINUED)

the exact human comely thing? (or will the fleshless . . . . 218 XLI SONNETS 14 8
neat word for the thing. Her voice? gruesome: a . . . . 227 IS 5 ONE GERT 11
has for -gotten some- thing ah (my necktie / . . . . 232 IS 5 ONE 3 17
of That sort of thing / / / / . . . . 245 IS 5 ONE 16 25
other; this, since the thing perhaps is to eat . . . . 264 IS 5 ONE 33 31
that's jolly odd old thing, jolly odd, jolly jolly . . . . . 269 IS 5 TWO 4 15
any by me carven thing provoke your gesture possibly . . . . 291 IS 5 FOUR 8 19
every brittle marvelous breathing thing) since i and you . . 293 IS 5 FOUR 10 13
made of the same thing as perhaps nothing, he . . . . 299 IS 5 FOUR 16 15
led cap mumble some thing to oh no body . . . . 314 VIVA 6 20
lips are made of thing in beginning corners dawn . . . . . . 322 VIVA 14 12
companion dimly remarked some- thing about "stuffed . . . . . 326 VIVA 18 32
Nowhere) creeps the deep thing everybody sometimes calls . . 330 VIVA 21 13
ylike writhe of brea Thing / / / / . . . . 349 VIVA 40 19
what (love being some- thing possibly more intricate) i . . . 358 VIVA 49 8
cease whom every perfect thing meanwhile doth miss; a . . . . 360 VIVA 51 7
(sleep) . while some thing else kisses busily a . . . . 370 VIVA 61 23
B being no such thing for C can't casts . . . . 390 NO THANKS 7 2
thenlike? now Disappears some thing (silent: . . . . 397 NO THANKS 14 21
that each and every thing must have an end . . . . 411 NO THANKS 28 2
stutter treebodies wobbly- ing thing -birds) sing- u (cities 436 NO THANKS 52 11
we) under) over, the thing of floating Of ; . . . . 447 NO THANKS 62 1
being shall one only thing must: the opening of . . . . 480 NEW POEMS 18 2
ask a simple crazy thing singing in the snow . . . . 498 50 POEMS 12 30
selene doesn't know a thing who's much too busy . . . . 504 50 POEMS 18 11
as found some lost thing (like a curtain on . . . . 516 50 POEMS 30 4
no suit there every -thing nothing i say the . . . . 523 50 POEMS 36 24
and big even a thing all small and sad . . . . 526 50 POEMS 38 3
is the only living thing) and we'll make yes . . . . 528 50 POEMS 40 14
least who sing small thing dance little joy (shine . . . . . 535 50 POEMS 47 10
i achieve another steepest thing-- how more than sleep . . . 558 1 X 1 18 10
am. Living no single thing dares partly seem one . . . . . . 559 1 X 1 19 9
valleys by ropes of thing and stifles forests in . . . . . . 560 1 X 1 20 11
a funeral eyes "big thing" / / / / . . . . 567 1 X 1 27 24
each living ablaze greenly thing ; may has come . . . . 583 1 X 1 43 13
mean only one amazing thing (secretly adoring shyly tiny . . 591 1 X 1 51 20
where what a wonderful thing is the end of . . . . 593 1 X 1 53 19
-way It with some- thing sil -very ; bright, ... 632 (CHAIRE) 34 4
i the death of thing glimpsed (and on every . . . . 634 (CHAIRE) 36 1
ly folded; a (brea thing and a gro Wing) . . . . 657 (CHAIRE) 59 13
right is, all (each thing most lovely) sweet things . . . . . 666 (CHAIRE) 68 2
air is air and thing is thing: no bliss . . . . 675 95 POEMS 3 1
air and thing is thing: no bliss of heavenly . . . . 675 95 POEMS 3 1
chased by a horrible thing which raced sideways while . . . . 682 95 POEMS 10 7
there is such a thing as spring and wonders . . . . 685 95 POEMS 13 7
i don't mean any thing real Ly what ; . . . . 701 95 POEMS 29 17
becom ing each truebeautifully more-than-thing (& falling &) 715 95 POEMS 43 19
sun & singing &) thing found one old blue . . . . 753 95 POEMS 81 20
never sings the same thing : twice and still that . . . . . . 760 95 POEMS 87 3
never will) any damn thing : far from it; . . . . 793 73 POEMS 21 13
am, no song (no thing) no silence ever told; . . . . 819 73 POEMS 47 7
i never guessed any thing (even a universe) might . . . . . . 827 73 POEMS 55 4
be) dream of; a thing: of a creature who's . . . . 840 73 POEMS 68 18

+THING

FOR CONTEXT, SEE . . . . 310 VIVA 2 13
FOR CONTEXT, SEE . . . . 795 73 POEMS 23 5

THINGFEAR

leopards (on wingfeet of thingfear) come ships go snowily . . 586 1 X 1 46 16

THINGFULEST

sundark) brightshadowfully fountaining man's thingfulest . . 681 95 POEMS 9 15

THINGISH

away.... (these leaves are Thingish with moondrool and i'm . 303 IS 5 FIVE 2 6
my sic kly a thingish o crashdis appearing con . . . . 646 (CHAIRE) 48 4

THINGLESS

dim quiveringly spangle & thingless & before flashing soft . 480 NEW POEMS 18 9

THINGS

time when all occasional things close into silence, only . . 6 T&C EPITHALAM 121

		PAGE	TITLE	LINE

THINGS (CONTINUED)

	PAGE	TITLE	LINE
early flowers of all things. thy hair mostly the	13	T&C SONGS 3	2
Lord Jason (in impossible things victorious impossibly) so .	18	T&C PUELLA MEA	69
wherein slowly drift murmurous things divinely bright; it is	18	T&C PUELLA MEA	81
of all living intense things. Never my soul so	19	T&C PUELLA MEA	101
enchanted fronds toward all things intrinsic yearn, the . . .	19	T&C PUELLA MEA	112
perfectly responds) of all things exquisite and dead, all .	19	T&C PUELLA MEA	127
and dead, all living things and beautiful. (Caliph and . . .	19	T&C PUELLA MEA	128
beauteous, being for all things amorous fashioned very . . .	20	T&C PUELLA MEA	136
and quail) of all things perfect the most frail.	20	T&C PUELLA MEA	162
whose shy delicious glance things which never more shall . .	22	T&C PUELLA MEA	252
more shall be, perfect things of faerie, are intense	22	T&C PUELLA MEA	253
ladies. Eater of all things lovely--Time! upon whose watering	23	T&C PUELLA MEA	266
passing of all shining things therefore we also blandly . . .	41	T&C AMORES 5	10
passing of all shining things no lingering no backward- . . .	41	T&C AMORES 5	25
been faithful to many things and which die i	43	T&C AMORES 7	9
with mutilated singing microscopic things in my ears scramble	69	T&C POST IMPR 6	29
interested in so many things-- at the present writing	70	T&C SON REAL 1	6
green body among unseen things, things obscene (Whose fingers	77	T&C SON UNRE 2	3
body among unseen things, things obscene (Whose fingers young	77	T&C SON UNRE 2	3
were ideas?" "because, sir things which in my mind	91	& POST IMPR 3	11
and Paris and all things) the bright rain occurs	92	& POST IMPR 4	5
his soul for certain things which died it is	108	& PORTRAIT 4	29
moving New and Old things, while people stare carefully . . .	124	& SEVEN POEMS 3	14
to a glass bumping things. she picked wearily something . . .	132	& SON REAL 3	16
you naked amid unnaked things, your flesh, a succinct	170	& SON ACTU 19	6
Picasso you give us Things which bulge: grunting lungs . . .	195	XLI PORTRAIT 3	2
the year droops with things dead athwart the narrowing . . .	207	XLI SONNETS 3	6
boit que de Jingyale. things are going rather kaka	233	IS 5 ONE 4	7
even if all desires things moments be murdered known	237	IS 5 ONE 8	1
not sell and buy things so necessary as is	238	IS 5 ONE 9	8
hands get red washing things and dishes) and to	242	IS 5 ONE 13	16
of horned suddenly crashing things) man spits quickly into .	252	IS 5 ONE 23	11
my body the sharp things fingered tinily my heart	284	IS 5 FOUR 1	7
all sorts of quickly things on the slate of	287	IS 5 FOUR 4	4
shall brighten carefully these things we consider life. Dear	289	IS 5 FOUR 6	12
to the syntax of things will never wholly kiss	290	IS 5 FOUR 7	3
for (out of all things) dream is noone's fool;	292	IS 5 FOUR 9	10
thoroughly into all beautiful things) winter, whom Spring . .	293	IS 5 FOUR 10	30
do not touch) deep things; remembering ever so tinily	294	IS 5 FOUR 11	6
lady, intricate imperfect various things chiefly which wrong	306	IS 5 FIVE 5	2
who kiss throw silently things Each at other (if	312	VIVA 4	12
mind consider rather heavenly things and but the stars . . .	322	VIVA 14	2
shawl carefully around it) "things i mean the Rain	328	VIVA 19	20
(opening it i think things which were supposed to	353	VIVA 44	14
how these immaculate thin things half daemon half tree . . .	362	VIVA 53	6
most frail gesture are things which enclose me, or	366	VIVA 57	3
wars of feet all things whose slendering sweetness touched .	414	NO THANKS 31	4
the : se! crumbs things? Its noyesiyou he-she (Weres	417	NO THANKS 34	22
lie (glued among familiar things newly which are transferred	428	NO THANKS 45	3
or best (and proudly things only which grow and	441	NO THANKS 56	53
the birds of snow things without name beyond because	441	NO THANKS 56	57
without name beyond because things over blame things under .	441	NO THANKS 56	59
because things over blame things under praise glad things . .	441	NO THANKS 56	60
things under praise glad things or free truly which	441	NO THANKS 56	61
bel ls (pour wo (things) men selves-them inghurl) bangbells .	444	NO THANKS 59	10
(asleep who must go things-without-wings / / / /	483	NEW POEMS 21	12
you shall above all things be glad and young.	484	NEW POEMS 22	1
for labor give all things to enni one bugger	492	50 POEMS 6	11
the impure think all things pure and hornets wail	511	50 POEMS 25	13
bright, bitter all utterly things sweet, maggoty minus and .	521	50 POEMS 34	62
to the god of things like they err /	552	1 X 1 12	30
is all angry common things to disappear causing through . . .	559	1 X 1 19	3
which under burst lurch things phantoms curl (mouth seekingly	565	1 X 1 25	2
the biggest and all things--let all go dear so	569	1 X 1 29	19
spring with all beautiful things when to me you	589	1 X 1 49	12
notselfpitying lover of all things excellently rare; obsolete	607	(CHAIRE) 9	10
yes for all sweet things are until" "spring follows	625	(CHAIRE) 27	8

779

	PAGE	TITLE		LINE
THINGS (CONTINUED)				
dark until sink last things (least all turns almost	633	{CHAIRE}	35	8
name) a mender of things with eager fingers (with	660	{CHAIRE}	62	6
thing most lovely) sweet things cannot spring but we	666	{CHAIRE}	68	4
time of all sweet things beyond whatever mind may	688	95 POEMS	16	10
Because only the truest things always are true because . . .	697	95 POEMS	25	31
/ because it's Spring thingS dare to do people	782	73 POEMS	10	3
lose) good true beautiful things god how he sings	805	73 POEMS	33	4
you (blinded by merely things believable) could only fancy .	809	73 POEMS	37	6
(silently all then known things or dreamed become un-	822	73 POEMS	50	8
/ / of all things under our blonder than	825	73 POEMS	53	1
overing) all bright all things swim climb minds (down	841	73 POEMS	69	28
eye (which is if things seem spirits) or (if	845	73 POEMS	73	2
in the guise of things appear) death's: any world	845	73 POEMS	73	3
+THINGS				
FOR CONTEXT, SEE	25	T&C CHANSONS	2	2
FOR CONTEXT, SEE	347	VIVA	38	31
FOR CONTEXT, SEE	536	50 POEMS	48	7
+THINGS-WITHOUT-WING				
(asleep who must go things-without-wings / / / /	483	NEW POEMS	21	12
THINK				
with desirable flowers i think thou lovest incense for . . .	31	T&C ORIENTALE	5	13
/ i like to think that on the flower	42	T&C AMORES	6	2
short it was i think yourself delivered into both	57	T&C PORTRAIT	5	18
swim, sayingly; (Do you think?) the i do, world	66	T&C POST IMPR	3	13
have a dream i think it shall be roses	67	T&C POST IMPR	4	10
the trees stand. I think i too have known	80	T&C SON UNRE	5	3
do not speak nor think nor am aware of	98	& POST IMPR	9	14
whoseswooning edge black trees think (hear little knives of .	99	& POST IMPR	10	11
love slowly answered I think so. But I think	102	& POST IMPR	12	22
think so. But I think I see someone else	102	& POST IMPR	12	23
gee i like to think of dead it means	126	& SEVEN POEMS	5	1
on something as i think , did you ever	141	& SON REAL	12	15
More interesting, as i think, her charms en repos...	143	& SON REAL	14	7
gross days when i think of you and do	165	& SON ACTU	14	7
the fireman's ball, i think and also i think	169	& SON ACTU	18	4
think and also i think of you, getting mandolin-clink	169	& SON ACTU	18	5
sheathed i sit and think of you the holy	186	XLI SONGS	8	4
is uttered, and i think of you / /	186	XLI SONGS	8	21
their nearness evaporates to think is the slippery contours .	193	XLI PORTRAIT	1	14
/ GERT joggle i think will do it although	227	IS 5 ONE GERT		1
and drink thinks and think drinks, in memory of	233	IS 5 ONE	4	16
did not stop to think they died instead then	268	IS 5 TWO	3	12
lady what do you think of this? Do your	279	IS 5 THREE	3	21
and what does he think about, i wonder as	286	IS 5 FOUR	3	2
paragraph And death i think is no parenthesis /	290	IS 5 FOUR	7	16
into heads are legs think wrists argue) short (eyes	309	VIVA	1	10
de repapering; i don't think so. maybe: somebody?) or, . . .	312	VIVA	4	24
a gentleman not to think of (sh) the world	326	VIVA	18	5
/ / / i'd think "wonder if" if i	353	VIVA	44	1
door (opening it i think things which were supposed	353	VIVA	44	14
deaths in this season" think "finality lives up on	354	VIVA	45	12
in win ter you think, die slow ly "toc	354	VIVA	45	24
weeds feel and fish think of) / / /	359	VIVA	50	18
least i beat --always think i am gone like	372	VIVA	63	7
beckon through me, i think it is less wonderful	379	VIVA	70	13
does not have to think because he knows (that	406	NO THANKS	23	3
is bad which you think good) because he knows, ...	406	NO THANKS	23	4
harmlessly accurate gloom "I think he might now be	464	NEW POEMS	2	21
that you should ever think, may god forbid and	484	NEW POEMS	22	9
their socalled hearts would think these socalled people have	510	50 POEMS	24	2
long will the impure think all things pure and	511	50 POEMS	25	13
cy superfluous hair or Think We've Met subhuman rights . . .	549	1 X 1	9	14
/ / / i think you like" a strawberry	585	1 X 1	45	1
(instead of stopping to think) you begin to feel	604	{CHAIRE}	6	9
man to God i'll think it strange that normal	731	95 POEMS	59	3
feels (but none can think) a learning under teach--	735	95 POEMS	63	8
cunning the craven (as think as can feel) they	801	73 POEMS	29	20

THINK (CONTINUED)
  really's herself (and to think that she's warming three . . . 827 73 POEMS 55   11
+THINK
  FOR CONTEXT, SEE . . . . 99 & POST IMPR 10   14
THINKING
  winsome indolence simmer upon thinking twilight momently) as   6 T&C EPITHALAM   126
  sitting in the din thinking drinking the ale, which . . . . . 96 & POST IMPR 8   23
  let's live suddenly without thinking under honest trees, a . 160 & SON ACTU 9   1
  hubbub as you stood thinking of anything, maybe the . . . . . 172 & SON ACTU 21   8
  smell (but i was thinking why the girl-and-bird of . . . . . 174 & SON ACTU 23   12
  crowned with far colours, thinking very much of nothing . . . 211 XLI SONNETS 7   16
  that one oh just thinking it over (at that . . . . 323 VIVA 15   8
  ter who sit dying thinking huddled behind dir ty . . . . . . 354 VIVA 45   4
  more find than seeks thinking, swim (opening) grow are . . . 612 (CHAIRE) 14   2
  live-- unless by your thinking forever's long let beauty . . 742 95 POEMS 70   11
  (and i refer to thinking) rests upon a dismal . . . . 807 73 POEMS 35   5
THINKINGLY
  whispering thickly smooth thighs thinkingly) remind me of . . 95 & POST IMPR 7   16
THINKLESS
  cause of trivial which thinkless unwishing doth depend upon . 411 NO THANKS 28   4
THINKS
  her as a leaf thinks of the sky, my . . . . 131 & SON REAL 2   3
  said what her mouth thinks of (if it were . . . . 225 IS 5 ONE LIZ   13
  the corner and drink thinks and think drinks, in . . . . . . 233 IS 5 ONE 4   16
  i guess a grassblade Thinks beyond or around (as . . . . . 364 VIVA 55   7
  to feel because he thinks (the thoughts of others, ... 406 NO THANKS 23   1
  with every brain which thinks it thinks, nor dares . . . . . 424 NO THANKS 41   10
  brain which thinks it thinks, nor dares to feel . . . . . . 424 NO THANKS 41   10
  felt as bad, itself thinks goodness what is meek; . . . . . . 438 NO THANKS 54   4
THINNED
  blown kisses, condemnatory fingers thinned of pity--so he . .   9 T&C SONGS 1   13
  green thrilling light with thinned newfragile yellows lurch . 163 & SON ACTU 12   9
THINNER
  darkness --a little moon thinner than memory faint -er . . . 282 IS 5 THREE 6   17
  see the new moon thinner than a hair) making . . . . 301 IS 5 FOUR 18   6
  and there's the moon, thinner than a watchspring / . . . . . 322 VIVA 14   14
  thicker than forget more thinner than recall more seldom . . 530 50 POEMS 42   2
THINNING
  distinctly wobbles from the thinning lips me hugely which . . 151 & SON REAL 22´   16
THIRD
  no wrong cried the third crumb, i am should . . . . 117 & PORTRAIT 10   17
  was standing on the third rail waiting for the . . . . 262 IS 5 ONE 32   2
  accurate undaunted moon's bright third tumbling slowly / / . 305 IS 5 FIVE 4   15
  while uttering one a third face, away in the . . . . 813 73 POEMS 41   9
THIRD'S
  starhushed silence which our third's / / / / . . . . 844 73 POEMS 72   3
THIRDS
  heart smote in trembling thirds of anguish quivers to . . . .   11 T&C SONGS 2   16
  an old man 3 thirds asleep, on his head . . . . 102 & POST IMPR 12   13
THIRSTIES
  / poets yeggs and thirsties since we are spanked . . . . . . 261 IS 5 ONE 31   1
THIRSTILY
  between mouthed houses curl thirstily. Dead stars stink. . . 139 & SON REAL 10   13
THIRSTY
  in the sharp and thirsty blood of Paris would . . . .   18 T&C PUELLA MEA   66
  just, simply, into, her. Thirsty stirring. (Must be summer. . 130 & SON REAL 1   11
  of chuckling flesh. Weak thirsty fists of idiot futures . . . 151 & SON REAL 22   6
  Is for Love Spring thirsty for happens only and . . . . . . 437 NO THANKS 53   8
  hungry and fearless and thirsty and supple and even . . . . . 481 NEW POEMS 19   6
THIRTEEN
  with a slight jounce, thirteen pants have a hunch . . . . . 150 & SON REAL 21   5
  luck they hump them thirteen times a night one . . . . . . 427 NO THANKS 44   4
THIRTY
  to a flight of thirty birds shakes with a . . . .   11 T&C SONGS 2   18
  Highness said "peek-a-boo" and thirty tame fleas left the . . 262 IS 5 ONE 32   27
THIRTYTWO
  whose) centripetal wisdom in thirtytwo seconds centrifugally 341 VIVA 32   5

THIS
  WORD DELETED, APPEARED 335 TIMES
THISTLEFLUFF
  dead's sorry like a thistlefluff-thing which goes land- ing . 127 & SEVEN POEMS 5   41
THISTLEFLUFF-THING
  dead's sorry like a thistlefluff-thing which goes land- ing . 127 & SEVEN POEMS 5   41
THITHER
  behind and crazily skating thither and hither in filthy . . . 259 IS 5 ONE 29   4
  (which stroll hither and thither through the evening in . . . 275 IS 5 TWO 9   49
  by doomful connivance accurately thither and hither myself . 299 IS 5 FOUR 16   8
  steered his big was) thither to thence swore many . . . . . . 316 VIVA 8   13
  streets hither and) softly thither between (tumb ling) houses 319 VIVA 11   6
  openly than usual hither, thither who briskly busily carry . 354 VIVA 45   14
  nosing lymoles cru. Ising thither: t, ouch soft-ly me . . . . 361 VIVA 52   12
THITHERHITHERING
  perfectly dead finger of thitherhithering gas. clothed with a 134 & SON REAL 5   12
+THOMAS
  FOR CONTEXT, SEE . . . . 257 IS 5 ONE 27   38
THORN
  stiffenS to a white thorn of desire the taut . . . . 34 T&C ORIENTALE 6 94
  The Snail's On The Thorn enter Morn and God's . . . . 230 IS 5 ONE 2   28
THORNIEST
  even a daisy-- your thorniest question my roses will . . . . 625 (CHAIRE) 27   13
THORNS
  a living wage-- when thorns regard their roses with . . . . . 620 (CHAIRE) 22   3
THOROUGHLY
  of her and (having thoroughly oiled the universal joint . . . 248 IS 5 ONE 19   6
  dreams let us investigate thoroughly each one his optima . . 261 IS 5 ONE 31   11
  pushing sleep under and thoroughly into all beautiful things) 293 IS 5 FOUR 10   29
  you and i are thoroughly haunted by what neither . . . . . . 368 VIVA 59   3
  thousand starings rinsed with thoroughly million yells they . 388 NO THANKS 5   8
  little flags weeping flatter thoroughly imploring threaten) . 391 NO THANKS 8   9
  our spinsters and coeds) thoroughly bretish they scout the . 492 50 POEMS 6   5
THOROUGHLY'S
  dollars toenails or ideas thoroughly's stolen (somewhere . . 322 VIVA 14   9
THOS
  darling" --O Education: O thos cook & son (O . . . . 257 IS 5 ONE 27   38
THOSE
  intrinsic hour, and from those tenuous fires which more . . .   6 T&C EPITHALAM 132
  desire, yet less than those twain perfect roses whose . . . .   6 T&C EPITHALAM 147
  will i praise between those rivers whose white voices . . . .   9 T&C SONGS 1   1
  body lay. Lovely as those ladies were mine is . . . . 18 T&C PUELLA MEA 75
  lovelier than any of those ladies were.) Her body . . . . . . 20 T&C PUELLA MEA 134
  her hair-- i for those ladies nothing care nor . . . . 21 T&C PUELLA MEA 179
  of the company of those ladies with faces painteaten . . . . 57 T&C PORTRAIT 5   36
  sounds the tread of those vast armies of the . . . . 209 XLI SONNETS 5   3
  gavest as one of those immortal men his life . . . . 209 XLI SONNETS 5   13
  deep, with thunder of those hungering wings of His, ... 210 XLI SONNETS 6   6
  but not Cassiopeia's might those be stockings dribbling from 322 VIVA 14   6
  for you: remember (as those pearls more than surround . . . . 372 VIVA 63   9
  / / IN) all those who got athlete's mouth . . . . 404 NO THANKS 21   2
  gives a friend not those who slave unselves to . . . . 440 NO THANKS 56   15
  arrow, s wince among those skeletons of these trees) . . . . 442 NO THANKS 57   9
  me you & all those & that "I may . . . . 464 NEW POEMS 2   9
  dawn "morning") & that those you i St ep . . . . 464 NEW POEMS 2   30
  down more than two those that and that noing . . . . 491 50 POEMS 5   7
  further off) further these those three disappear finally . . 501 50 POEMS 15   17
  to kill each of those creatures called one's self . . . . . . 528 50 POEMS 40   12
  are hopes lovers are those who kneel lovers are . . . . 563 1 X 1 23   9
  / / open green those (dear) worlds of than . . . . 573 1 X 1 33   1
  but opening if are those eyes every because is . . . . 588 1 X 1 48   7
+THOSE
  FOR CONTEXT, SEE . . . . 385 NO THANKS 2   48
THOU
  / / / EPITHALAMION Thou aged unreluctant earth who . . . . .   3 T&C EPITHALAM   1
  burns to embrace--and didst thou know the god from . . . . .   3 T&C EPITHALAM   12
  for his doom-- O thou within the chancel of . . . .   7 T&C EPITHALAM 153
  transcends the sight, O thou to whom belong the . . . .   7 T&C EPITHALAM 166

THOU (CONTINUED)

for which girl art thou flowers bringing? To be . . . . 13 T&C SONGS 3 14
beyond wishing if this thou catch, else missing. (though . . 13 T&C SONGS 3 18
with a smile and thou didst not answer thy . . . . 27 T&C ORIENTALE 1 2
music Come hither O thou, is life not a . . . . 27 T&C ORIENTALE 1 7
with a song and thou didst not listen thine . . . . 27 T&C ORIENTALE 1 9
silence Come hither O thou, is life not a . . . . 27 T&C ORIENTALE 1 14
with a soul and thou didst not wonder thy . . . . 27 T&C ORIENTALE 1 17
fragrance Come hither O thou, is life not love? . . . . . . 27 T&C ORIENTALE 1 21
with a sword and thou art silent thy breast . . . . 27 T&C ORIENTALE 1 24
flowers Come hither O thou, is love not death? . . . . . . 27 T&C ORIENTALE 1 28
desirable flowers i think thou lovest incense for in . . . . 31 T&C ORIENTALE 5 14
from the ashes then thou wilt rise and thou . . . . 40 T&C AMORES 4 39
thou wilt rise and thou wilt come to her . . . . 40 T&C AMORES 4 39
and buffeting thee that thou mightest conceive gods (but . . 46 T&C LA GUERRE 2 17
death thy rhythmic lover thou answerest them only with . . . 46 T&C LA GUERRE 2 25
/ spring omnipotent goddess thou dost inveigle into crossing 61 T&C PORTRAIT 9 1
and the frivolous angleworm thou dost persuade to serenade . 61 T&C PORTRAIT 9 4
lady the musical tom-cat, thou stuffest the parks with . . . 61 T&C PORTRAIT 9 5
content Spring, with this thou hangest canary-birds in parlor 61 T&C PORTRAIT 9 10
inside me Hollers for thou comest and your hands . . . . . . 61 T&C PORTRAIT 9 28
/ / / when thou hast taken thy last . . . . 75 T&C SON REAL 6 1
the sweet earth where thou liest / / / . . . . 184 XLI SONGS 6 17
acold with dreams, love thou art frail --walk the . . . . . 190 XLI SONGS 12 18
/ / / O Thou to whom the musical . . . . 206 XLI SONNETS 2 1
from her redolent shoulders, Thou from whose feet reincarnate 206 XLI SONNETS 2 6
/ / / / Thou in whose swordgreat story . . . . 209 XLI SONNETS 5 1
across the smiling meads; thou by whose page we . . . . . . 209 XLI SONNETS 5 6
battle with heroic breeds; thou, Froissart, for that thou . . 209 XLI SONNETS 5 9
thou, Froissart, for that thou didst love the pen . . . . . 209 XLI SONNETS 5 9
i like not what thou givest me to him . . . . 212 XLI SONNETS 8 9
the droll god-beasts do thou distinctly bring thy footstep, . 213 XLI SONNETS 9 10
most afraid of death? thou art of him utterly . . . . 215 XLI SONNETS 11 1
up the Campanile, believe thou me cocodrillo-- mine eyes . . 256 IS 5 ONE 27 9
whom duty whispers low "thou must!" and who replies . . . . 273 IS 5 TWO 8 5
/ / / / thou firsting a hugeness of . . . . 349 VIVA 40 1
doom who standest as thou hast stood and thou . . . . 351 VIVA 42 12
thou hast stood and thou shalt stand. Nor any . . . . 351 VIVA 42 12
o pr gress verily thou art m mentous superc . . . . 392 NO THANKS 9 2
go to the ant thou go (inging) to the . . . . 403 NO THANKS 20 21
(inging) to the ant, thou ant- eater / / . . . . 403 NO THANKS 20 24
out of) Life, dost Thou contain a marvel than . . . . 406 NO THANKS 23 12
dream and have. Be thou gay by dark and . . . . 651 {CHAIRE} 53 5
why --gracious wanderer, be thou gay / / / . . . . 651 {CHAIRE} 53 12

+THOU

FOR CONTEXT, SEE . . . . 409 NO THANKS 26 3
FOR CONTEXT, SEE . . . . 581 1 X 1 41 14

THOUGH

smoothness which sings, saying (though love be a day) . . . . 13 T&C SONGS 3 6
strangeness much says; singing (though love be a day) . . . . 13 T&C SONGS 3 13
thou catch, else missing. (though love be a day . . . . . . 13 T&C SONGS 3 20
(yet are we mindful, though not as yet awake, ... 264 IS 5 ONE 33 13
Olaf soon in hand; but--though an host of overjoyed . . . . 339 VIVA 30 7
(departing hurriedly to shave) but--though all kinds of . . . 339 VIVA 30 22
into the ground) but though with wormS eyes writhe . . . . 361 VIVA 52 5
wormS eyes writhe amor (Though through our hearts hugely . . 361 VIVA 52 7
squirm roots) us ly; though hither nosing lymoles cru. . . . 361 VIVA 52 10
easily will unclose me though i have closed myself . . . . . 366 VIVA 57 6
dance (and i guess though wish and world go . . . . 372 VIVA 63 15
time no refuge keep though all the weird worlds . . . . . . 377 VIVA 68 14
love, all of wishing) though life's lived wrongsideout, . . . 446 NO THANKS 61 3
the pinnacle of am though dull were all we . . . . 521 50 POEMS 34 61
as truth --i say though hate were why men . . . . 521 50 POEMS 34 66
look should april me (though such as perfect hope . . . . . 580 1 X 1 40 23
with generosities beyond believing (though flesh and blood . 683 95 POEMS 11 3
(and live by love though the stars walk backward) . . . . . 732 95 POEMS 60 8
are in vain but though mankind persuades itself that . . . . 744 95 POEMS 72 5
they die for because though the bell in the . . . . 801 73 POEMS 29 5

THOUGH (CONTINUED)

turn to a which though the moon in her . . . . 801 73 POEMS 29   11
a thunder of seem though the stars in their . . . . 801 73 POEMS 29   17
they live for until though the sun in his . . . . 801 73 POEMS 29   23
bow to a must though the earth in her . . . . 801 73 POEMS 29   29
mystery, a kiss --not though mankind would rather know . . . 817 73 POEMS 45   11
/ / / / "though your sorrows not any . . . . 837 73 POEMS 65   1

THOUGHT

perusing greenness of thy thought my golden soul fabulously .   9 T&C SONGS 1   29
white than wool My thought is sorrowful: but my . . . . 11 T&C SONGS 2   15
to bewitch my smallest thought with a most swift . . . . . . 18 T&C PUELLA MEA 79
it appeared that you thought to escape me and . . . . 30 T&C ORIENTALE 4   4
beloved i dreamed i thought you would have deceived . . . . . 30 T&C ORIENTALE 4 31
i looked up and thought to myself Death and . . . . 58 T&C PORTRAIT 6   14
in velvet beyond doomed thought is like a woman . . . . 81 T&C SON UNRE 6   9
wholly trembling" or so thought the lady. / / . . . . 84 T&C SON ACTU 3   17
/ when i have thought of you somewhat too . . . . 157 & SON ACTU 6   1
poets put on purple thought against the magnificent clamor . 188 XLI SONGS 10   3
of the (hei -nous thought) otherwise immaculately tabulated . 267 IS 5 TWO 2   16
lips a smile, one thought alone: to do or . . . . 273 IS 5 TWO 8   11
to move when i thought you were going to . . . . 289 IS 5 FOUR 6   19
doesn't matter) when you thought you were going to . . . . . 289 IS 5 FOUR 6   21
do" she smiling said "thought you were earning your . . . . . 313 VIVA 5   6
praise) but many a thought shall die which was . . . . 372 VIVA 63   13
nor marvel if a thought should weigh a star . . . . 446 NO THANKS 61   7
(whir -ling be, yond! thought are. more (Than girl . . . . . 447 NO THANKS 62   9
a day. And something thought or done or wished . . . . 649 (CHAIRE) 51   9
everybody (i believe) else thought lucinda looked like steve 706 95 POEMS 34   4
poor dishonoured mind who thought yourself so wise; and . . . 834 73 POEMS 62   14

THOUGHTFUL

softly to stir, of thoughtful trees whom night hath . . . . 205 XLI SONNETS 1   11
sweet uncaring earth by thoughtful war heaped wholly with . . 213 XLI SONNETS 9   3

THOUGHTS

lovelier friends, between your thoughts more white than wool 11 T&C SONGS 2   14
fragile huge humanity.... Numb thoughts, kicking in the . . . 174 & SON ACTU 23   9
atoms various ab- surd thoughts slyly crept into my . . . . . 262 IS 5 ONE 32   4
were the not unpainful thoughts which occupied the subject . 263 IS 5 ONE 32   60
toss him a few thoughts a little love preferably, ... 298 IS 5 FOUR 15   14
because he thinks (the thoughts of others, be it . . . . . . 406 NO THANKS 23   2
are a (piercing clothes thoughts kiss -ing wishes bodies) . . 437 NO THANKS 53   6

THOUSAND

came riding upon a thousand crimson years arched with . . . . 30 T&C ORIENTALE 4 36
emperor's elephant is a thousand years old the harem . . . . 32 T&C ORIENTALE 6 18
lady, one of the thousand selves who are your . . . . 92 & POST IMPR 4   21
will rise After a thousand years lipping flowers And . . . . 189 XLI SONGS 11   14
love earth dark) and thousand thrusts squirms stars Trees, . 356 VIVA 47   6
)ing bruiseD Suddenly by thousand starings rinsed with . . . 388 NO THANKS 5   6
of one fiend, a thousand dreams thick (cringing they . . . . 439 NO THANKS 55   8
sing than teach ten thousand stars how not to . . . . 484 NEW POEMS 22   14
individuals every several fat thousand years. Expecting more 514 50 POEMS 28   3
never guess in fifty thousand years equals the quote . . . . 544 1 X 1 4   14
he picked up a thousand pounds or two and . . . . 552 1 X 1 12   9
should april me, some thousand million hundred more bright . 580 1 X 1 40   12
have their centuries; ten thousand of which are smaller . . . 683 95 POEMS 11   7
stood still for a thousand years and then lay . . . . 709 95 POEMS 37   15
been, and stop ten thousand stars but not one . . . . 714 95 POEMS 42   10
dead these (or many thousand hearts which don't and . . . . 743 95 POEMS 71   6
sing: and our night's thousand million miracles a million . 756 95 POEMS 84   12
million miracles a million thousand hundred nothing seem --we 756 95 POEMS 84   13
hurry it with a thousand poems my darling but . . . . 835 73 POEMS 63   28

THOUSANDS

screams of deeply bulging thousands i too omit one . . . . . 259 IS 5 ONE 29   18
millions of windows of thousands of houses--Lisboa. Like the 281 IS 5 THREE 5   6
inward with hurled downward thousands of enormous dreams / . 301 IS 5 FOUR 18   19
all these hundreds upon thousands of people socalled if . . . 510 50 POEMS 24   9
but shining who by thousands mean only one amazing . . . . . 591 1 X 1 51   19
whirling into gaily white thousands return by millions and . 630 (CHAIRE) 32   4
most now, with what thousands of (hundreds of) millions . . . 840 73 POEMS 68   30

THOUSANDTH
sizelessly sunlight Open what thousandth why and discover . . 453 NO THANKS 68 15
THREAD
who letting fall a thread of lustre from the . . . . 8 T&C OF NICOL 23
in the last light thread the creeping shores as . . . . 64 T&C POST IMPR 1 4
lisping flesh quick to thread the fattish drone of . . . . . 140 & SON REAL 11 12
as if upon a thread invisible) A graveyard dreams . . . . . . 434 NO THANKS 51 21
THREADED
not thy lust one threaded moment lose: haste) the . . . . . . 9 T&C SONGS 1 7
THREADS
and gold the fluffy threads, put up your little . . . . 192 XLI CHANSONS 2 16
shriekings shall have snarled threads of celestial silence . 555 1 X 1 15 5
THREATEN
weeping flatter thoroughly imploring threaten) the wistFully 391 NO THANKS 8 9
THREATENS
lady. The clumsy dark threatens (and i do not . . . . 98 & POST IMPR 9 13
uvula with imperceptible gesticulations threatens the tubular 201 XLI PORTRAIT 9 9
THREATS
vote (or made by threats of something worth than . . . . . . 544 1 X 1 4 11
in sobs and reasons threats and smiles name it . . . . 804 73 POEMS 32 6
THREE
silver; o'er whose night three willows wail, a slender . . . 9 T&C SONGS 1 4
cool moon there are thrice-three-hundred doors carven of . . 33 T&C ORIENTALE 6 33
there are thrice-three-hundredth doors carven of . . . . . . 33 T&C ORIENTALE 6 61
caught a, penny or three, pennies he will be . . . . 69 T&C POST IMPR 6 16
at Dick Mid's the three trickling chins began to . . . . . . 73 T&C SON REAL 4 11
twilight moving, suddenly is three animals. The minute waist 95 & POST IMPR 7 4
frail (whose grave already three or two young stars . . . . 115 & PORTRAIT 8 2
Jimmie lived regular. stewed three times a week. and . . . . 149 & SON REAL 20 11
Dick Mid's green large three teeth leak smoke: remembering, . 149 & SON REAL 20 14
eighth, a star or three annoys me, but the . . . . 169 & SON ACTU 18 2
captain announces that as three dimes seven nickels and . . 196 XLI PORTRAIT 4 8
paklavah meeah. (Very occasionally three.) and i gaze on . . 217 XLI SONNETS 13 13
Brummell sticking in its three- cornered always moist mouth) 227 IS 5 ONE GERT 4
drink waiter two or three drinks what's become of . . . . . 233 IS 5 ONE 4 20
to accomplish two or three times, and even a . . . . 236 IS 5 ONE 7 15
which devours a man, three cats, five white mice, ... 279 IS 5 THREE 3 7
chins: next door but three dwells; a (ghost) Who . . . . . . 312 VIVA 4 7
telescoped languages) she smokes three castles He looks . . . 312 VIVA 4 15
a tiniest street or three contains these prettiest deaths . . 340 VIVA 31 14
sit huddling dumbly behind three or two partly tran . . . . 354 VIVA 45 18
this brow five or three dreamfuls of despair that . . . . . . 402 NO THANKS 19 7
& all one two three rings are cake & . . . . 470 NEW POEMS 8 17
can swallow a man; three words im -prison a . . . . 491 50 POEMS 5 13
vive the millenni um three cheers for labor give . . . . . . 492 50 POEMS 6 10
off) further these those three disappear finally what's left 501 50 POEMS 15 17
dancesing singdance all are three with faces made of . . . . 507 50 POEMS 21 5
of cloud dancing and three singing with voices made . . . . 507 50 POEMS 21 7
in) four are white (three singdance six dancesing three . . . 507 50 POEMS 21 17
(three singdance six dancesing three all around around all . 507 50 POEMS 21 17
around all clouds singing three and and three dancing . . . . 507 50 POEMS 21 19
singing three and and three dancing earths three menandwomen 507 50 POEMS 21 20
and three dancing earths three menandwomen three and all . . 507 50 POEMS 21 21
dancing earths three menandwomen three and all around all . 507 50 POEMS 21 21
you which could grin three smiles into a dead . . . . 522 50 POEMS 35 1
next) nakedness (table but three) hero's carnivorous (smile . 546 1 X 1 6 8
a winter sport or three: but were it five, ... 579 1 X 1 39 5
more than room for three of me and only . . . . 588 1 X 1 48 4
/ / / / three wealthy sisters swore they'd . . . . 621 (CHAIRE) 23 1
this the of twig three souls sit round with . . . . 687 95 POEMS 15 2
sit round with cold three (huddling a- gainst one . . . . . 687 95 POEMS 15 5
moon) dream unthings silent three like your my life . . . . 687 95 POEMS 15 10
that maybe had shaved three times in its life . . . . 709 95 POEMS 37 8
in its life made three) brawny and brainy they . . . . 709 95 POEMS 37 8
the rose alive must three, must four and (to . . . . 764 95 POEMS 90 50
(the prance with the three white its stimpstamps) the . . . . 773 73 POEMS 1 10
til against my (where three dreams live) fore head . . . . . 785 73 POEMS 13 21
by 'could you spare three cents please' --why guesswho . . . 800 73 POEMS 28 6

THREE (CONTINUED)
    think that she's warming three worlds) who's ama zingly . . . 827 73 POEMS 55   12
    any tongue may name, three i'll give you sweet . . . . 837 73 POEMS 65   3
+THREE
    FOR CONTEXT, SEE . . . . 60 T&C PORTRAIT 8   6
    FOR CONTEXT, SEE . . . . 332 VIVA 23   8
    FOR CONTEXT, SEE . . . . 725 95 POEMS 53   9
THREECOLOURED
    wall almost spray -ing threecoloured puke over this younger . 324 VIVA 16   8
THREEDIMENSIONAL
    a hunch admit in threedimensional distress these hips were . 150 & SON REAL 21   6
THREEING
    rhyme (spilling his rings) threeing alive pasture and hills . 751 95 POEMS 79   7
THREES
    brains (by twos or threes which fiercely rapidly pass . . . . 354 VIVA 45   22
THRESHOLD
    judgment day cross the threshold have no dread lift . . . . .. 118 & PORTRAIT 10   41
THREW
    / / / Who threw the silver dollar up . . . . 125 & SEVEN POEMS 4   2
    that's the truth, who threw the ripe melon into . . . . 125 & SEVEN POEMS 4   7
    that's a fact; who threw the bunch of violets . . . . 125 & SEVEN POEMS 4   13
    which assertions duly notified threw the yellowsonofabitch . 339 VIVA 30   36
    a green hill and threw his wish at blue . . . . 593 1 X 1 53   5
THRICE
    cool moon there are thrice-three-hundred doors carven of . . 33 T&C ORIENTALE 6 33
    there are thrice-three-hundredth doors carven of . . . . . . 33 T&C ORIENTALE 6 61
    badly, softly your kissed thrice suddenly smile / / . . . . . 300 IS 5 FOUR 17   24
    / / / possibly thrice we glimpsed-- more likely . . . . 607 (CHAIRE) 9   1
+THRICE-THREE-HUNDRED
    cool moon there are thrice-three-hundred doors carven of . . 33 T&C ORIENTALE 6 33
+THRICE-THREE-HUNDREDTH
    then the thrice-three-hundredth door is open . . . . 33 T&C ORIENTALE 6 61
THRILL
    now Twilight seeks the thrill of moon, washed with . . . . . 12 T&C SONGS 2   48
    possibly i like the thrill of under me you . . . . 175 & SON ACTU 24   13
    hair) the Californian handpicked thrill mechanically packed . 337 VIVA 28   9
    at the infinite precise thrill of your beauty, then . . . . . 819 73 POEMS 47   13
THRILLED
    the delirious smart of thrilled ecstasy, where sea and . . . 79 T&C SON UNRE 4   13
    imagine, when day has thrilled you are a house . . . . 292 IS 5 FOUR 9   2
THRILLERS
    melancholy trillers amid the thrillers these crepuscular . . 230 IS 5 ONE 2   25
THRILLING
    continual thighs invite the thrilling rain the slender . . .   3 T&C EPITHALAM   3
    thy languorous mouth the thrilling flower) / / / . . . . . . 37 T&C AMORES 2   20
    coolness deeds of green thrilling light with thinned . . . . 163 & SON ACTU 12   8
    mind which is the thrilling least of all (for . . . . 379 VIVA 70   4
THRILLS
    suddenly from the valley thrills the unimaginable upward lark   5 T&C EPITHALAM   78
    day horribly and seriously thrills the moment of enthusiastic 82 T&C SON ACTU 1   11
THROAT
    did on such a throat the lips of Tristram . . . . 17 T&C PUELLA MEA   35
    a keen and lovely throat the strangeness of her . . . . 20 T&C PUELLA MEA 145
    lady. And by this throat a little suddenly lifted . . . . . . 85 T&C SON ACTU 4   10
    putain with the ivory throat Marie Louise Lallemand n'est-ce 120 & PORTRAIT 12   9
    bumps clumsily into the throat A meticulous vulgarity: a . . 201 XLI PORTRAIT 9   11
    more than surround this throat) i wear your dearest . . . . . 372 VIVA 63   9
    grabbing had by my throat me give it him . . . . 496 50 POEMS 10   10
    fist stuck in the throat of one two came . . . . 709 95 POEMS 37   12
+THROAT'S
    FOR CONTEXT, SEE . . . . 827 73 POEMS 55   9
THROB
    a blind, how timidly, throb; which hints being; suggests . . 402 NO THANKS 19   9
+THROB
    FOR CONTEXT, SEE . . . . 629 (CHAIRE) 31   1
THROBBING
    lie it is a throbbing neck whereby to grasp . . . . 21 T&C PUELLA MEA 196
    mind if air is throbbing prayers whom kneeling eyes . . . . . 450 NO THANKS 65   6

	PAGE	TITLE	LINE
THROBBING (CONTINUED)			
climbed like a dream) throbbing like a heart singing	593	1 X 1 53	11
THRONE			
and men whose subtle throne twain sphinxes bear each	4	T&C EPITHALAM	41
in tottering before the throne and as they shied	30	T&C ORIENTALE 4	38
before the fragile gradual throne of night slowly when . . .	156	& SON ACTU 5	1
THRONG			
severed and the glowing throng descend, felt on her	4	T&C EPITHALAM	52
THROSTLES			
to such supposedly indigenous throstles Art is O World . . .	230	IS 5 ONE 2	32
THROTTLED			
her kiss have just throttled my seeing blood, her	132	& SON REAL 3	2
THROTTLING			
garnished of stark Picasso throttling trees hither my soul .	180	XLI SONGS 2	7
THROUGH			
thing, yet holds continuous intercourse--through skies and .	5	T&C EPITHALAM	91
of petals falling silently through the far-spaced possible .	10	T&C SONGS 1	44
of a year: When through the thin air stooped	11	T&C SONGS 2	22
bodies strong with love through meadows hugely move. yet . .	11	T&C SONGS 2	35
in the morning wandering. Through the young and awkward . . .	17	T&C PUELLA MEA	10
my lady perfectly moving, through the new world scarce . . .	17	T&C PUELLA MEA	12
the big bullying daisies through the field wonderful with . .	26	T&C ORIENTALE 3	6
betrayal of bells comprehended through incense / / /	29	T&C ORIENTALE 3	33
the kingdom of heaven through day and space i	30	T&C ORIENTALE 4	34
nods and all depart through the bruised air aflutter	34	T&C ORIENTALE 6	106
bring her worms rushing through loam. (afterward i'll climb .	67	T&C POST IMPR 4	12
press worms rushing slowly through loam / / /	67	T&C POST IMPR 4	30
in this dangerous night through moaned space god worships . .	77	T&C SON UNRE 2	15
your smile (it was through tears always) and silence	78	T&C SON UNRE 3	7
a night the sea through her blind miles of	81	T&C SON UNRE 6	13
silence --to feel how through the stopped entire day . . .	82	T&C SON ACTU 1	10
very faintly and finally through altogether delicate gestures	92	& POST IMPR 4	16
sprouted the extraordinary arms through an an- gle of	97	& POST IMPR 8	36
leaneyed Caesars borne neatly through enormous twilight . . .	111	& PORTRAIT 6	37
laughter and like elephants through our single brain in . . .	111	& PORTRAIT 6	69
imagine His surprise bellowing through the general noise . .	117	& PORTRAIT 10	9
poem her belly marched through me as one army.	135	& SON REAL 6	1
an occult shrug asking Through her Muteness will slowly . . .	137	& SON REAL 8	5
say body? follows truly through a dribbling moan of	140	& SON REAL 11	4
before Christmas when all through the house not a	142	& SON REAL 13	12
makes gaily go clean through me tickling aches, and	147	& SON REAL 18	7
herself rapidly at me through sagging debris of exploded . .	151	& SON REAL 22	2
light --and furiously puzzling through, prismatic, whims, the	157	& SON ACTU 6	13
back, quietly amorous of, through the autumn indisputably . .	158	& SON ACTU 7	13
trivial) it. y protuberant through the room's skilful of . .	159	& SON ACTU 8	6
when life is quite through with and leaves say	181	XLI SONGS 3	1
of thy body rose through the sensible night a	187	XLI SONGS 9	5
obscene procession always floats through the thin amorous . .	202	XLI PORTRAIT 9	47
thy beauty dreams (proud through the cold perfect night . . .	205	XLI SONNETS 1	6
our hearts' irrevocable play-- through the mysterious high .	215	XLI SONNETS 11	14
i've travelled all alone through the forest of wonderful,. .	216	XLI SONNETS 12	12
ancient jews obscurely twitch through the bumping teem of . .	219	XLI SONNETS 15	10
and when Freud got through with Do- nothing Do	236	IS 5 ONE 7	8
shape passed from low through second-in-to-high like	248	IS 5 ONE 19	19
beautiful we now pass through the look girls in	257	IS 5 ONE 27	32
staggered banged with terror through a million billion . . .	258	IS 5 ONE 28	23
other fingers snitch rapidly through mist a defunct king .	259	IS 5 ONE 29	11
stroll hither and thither through the evening in bruised . .	275	IS 5 TWO 9	49
into January darkness up through which sprouting gently, the	279	IS 5 THREE 3	3
squirming mice; or leap through hoops of fire, creating . . .	279	IS 5 THREE 3	16
a few cries drifting through high air a sail	283	IS 5 THREE 7	5
my vest and crept through the window she did	284	IS 5 FOUR 1	12
i turn, and (stooping through the morning) kiss this	288	IS 5 FOUR 5	8
do is to peer through windows, unobserved --listen, for . . .	292	IS 5 FOUR 9	8
by our mingling arms through a darkness where new	297	IS 5 FOUR 14	2
faces busily horribly blunder through new light hush we . . .	299	IS 5 FOUR 16	14
them, and made verses, through the sharp light cryingly . . .	302	IS 5 FIVE 1	15
try to understand the (through pale miles of perishing . . .	305	IS 5 FIVE 4	12

	PAGE	TITLE	LINE

THROUGH (CONTINUED)

the glance too shy--if through my singing slips the . . . . . 306 IS 5 FIVE 5   6
alive) my shame: lady through whose profound and fragile . . 306 IS 5 FIVE 5   13
truly to Beautifully retire through its english the . . . . . 311 VIVA 3   4
transparency slightly joggled sink through algebras of proud 311 VIVA 3   10
and your humble moving through the gloominess of (try . . . . 324 VIVA 16   12
the head him) do through icy waters roll that . . . . 339 VIVA 30   9
facts preening solemnity ignoring, through its indolent . . . 344 VIVA 35   3
cuddle & shrink: as through immediately yeswind-faces peer . 346 VIVA 37   5
some times vacantly gazing through un washed panes into . . . 354 VIVA 45   8
speaks (among leaves Easily through voices womenlike telling 356 VIVA 47   4
--and wonderfully i fell through the green groove of . . . . 360 VIVA 51   18
eyes writhe amor (Though through our hearts hugely squirm . . 361 VIVA 52   7
signify life's only half (through deep weather then or . . . 364 VIVA 55   12
strike. The moon's round, through the window as you . . . . . 365 VIVA 56   4
drowned only again carefully through deepness to rise these . 369 VIVA 60   11
rushing gently swiftly creeping through my dreams last night, 369 VIVA 60   17
will dissolve reintegrate beckon through me, i think it . . . 379 VIVA 70   12
imperfectly or since but through spontaneous deft strictly . 386 NO THANKS 3   7
give than lend --being through failures born who cannot . . . 394 NO THANKS 11   12
only was night and through only this night a . . . . 419 NO THANKS 36   21
fall ing) fall ing through touch less stillness (seized . . . 432 NO THANKS 49   9
invisible) A graveyard dreams through its cluttered and . . . 434 NO THANKS 51   22
fatally i remark how through deep lifted fields Oxen . . . . 434 NO THANKS 51   30
proud dreamhorse pulling (smoothloomingly) through (stepp) . 437 NO THANKS 53   1
his feet (who wanders through only white darkness who . . . . 439 NO THANKS 55   19
sunbeams loot furnished rooms through whose foul windows . . 442 NO THANKS 57   12
is a place & through this place of love . . . . 443 NO THANKS 58   2
beyond time's sky and through this opening universe will . . 454 NO THANKS 69   9
but" nonvisibly smi- ling through man -ufactured harmlessly . 464 NEW POEMS 2   18
and my suffice to through the only mystery of . . . . 510 50 POEMS 24   13
and foldish so only through) the little blue elephant . . . . 516 50 POEMS 30   6
is escorts us home through never's always until absolute . . 517 50 POEMS 31   12
/ my father moved through dooms of love through . . . . . . 520 50 POEMS 34   1
through dooms of love through sames of am through . . . . . . 520 50 POEMS 34   2
through sames of am through haves of give, singing . . . . . 520 50 POEMS 34   2
night my father moved through depths of height this . . . . . 520 50 POEMS 34   4
sea my father moved through griefs of joy; praising . . . . . 520 50 POEMS 34   18
shall my father moved through dooms of feel; his . . . . . . 520 50 POEMS 34   34
snow. My father moved through theys of we, singing . . . . . 521 50 POEMS 34   49
pimps may please? must through unstrange synthetic now true . 527 50 POEMS 39   25
so sunful i am through you so i / . . . . 537 50 POEMS 49   16
mountainrange; lenses extend unwish through curving wherewhen 554 1 X 1 14   7
things to disappear causing through mystery miracle peace: or 559 1 X 1 19   4
villains strive and heroes through the mere mind's poor . . . 576 1 X 1 36   6
these be thrushes climbing through almost (do they . . . . . 582 1 X 1 42   1
again who but zooms through one perfectly beautiful bow . . . 585 1 X 1 45   19
swim blossoms of person) through musical shadows while hunted 586 1 X 1 46   12
i'll go strolling right through these each illimit able . . . 600 (CHAIRE) 2   13
your a brook (it through are gaze the unguessed . . . . 613 (CHAIRE) 15   2
than some eighty years through which that memory strolls) . . 617 (CHAIRE) 19   11
/ nine birds (rising through a gold moment) climb: . . . . . 627 (CHAIRE) 29   2
grey rock wanderin g through pasture wom an creature . . . . 654 (CHAIRE) 56   5
secret) we, like homing through welcoming sweet miracles of . 659 (CHAIRE) 61   2
miraculous day) merrily moving through sweet forgiveness of . 661 (CHAIRE) 63   7
down while crylessly drifting through vast most nothing's own 661 (CHAIRE) 63   13
the little fish climb through the mind of the . . . . 665 (CHAIRE) 67   20
it were (floati ng through never) a kite like . . . . 668 (CHAIRE) 70   8
more most ethereal silence through twilight's mystery made . 669 (CHAIRE) 71   8
dirtpoor (popes emperors) undeaths through (slapsoothed by . 681 95 POEMS 9   13
white morethanPerson; who (riding through space to diminutive 697 95 POEMS 25   20
"than look you down through the old swimminghole there'll . . 707 95 POEMS 35   27
leap higher than high through gayer than gayest someone's . . 717 95 POEMS 45   12
poems children dreams & through slowquickly opening ifless . 719 95 POEMS 47   7
(in calm and fury: through joy and anguish) who've . . . . . 742 95 POEMS 70   8
seething gift wandering deeply through godthanking ground) . 754 95 POEMS 82   4
child and a (float through sleeping firsts of wonder) . . . . 757 95 POEMS 85   27
born a dream and (through stillness beyond conceiving) dream 757 95 POEMS 85   34

		PAGE	TITLE	LINE

THROUGH (CONTINUED)

		PAGE	TITLE	LINE
overs of known descend through depths of guess, shadows	. . .	761	95 POEMS 88	6
a steep) deep rush through amazing day it's brains	. . . . .	769	95 POEMS 95	14
slowly (mind in mind) through some green mysterious land	. .	777	73 POEMS 5	4
tall lovers riding are through the (with wonder into	. . . .	778	73 POEMS 6	2
tall young come they) through the may in fragrance	. . . . .	778	73 POEMS 6	11
(brighter than prayers) riding through a Dream like fire	. .	778	73 POEMS 6	15
can be sky always (through fragrance and singing) come	. . .	778	73 POEMS 6	21
house like shape stirs through (not numerably or as	. . . . .	785	73 POEMS 13	11
roar of traffic collapses: through west ninth slowly cars	. .	800	73 POEMS 28	18
flock and they flee through a thunder of seem	. . . .	801	73 POEMS 29	16
becomes your kiss losing through you what seemed myself,	. .	810	73 POEMS 38	9
imperishable your glory escorted through infinite countries	.	811	73 POEMS 39	3
their stars have risen through your skies: so, in	. . . . .	812	73 POEMS 40	8
are eagerly tumbl ing through wonder ful sunlight --look--	.	835	73 POEMS 63	8
swoop wholly up leaping through merciful sunlight) to burst	.	841	73 POEMS 69	32
whereas your lover (looking through both life and death)	. .	845	73 POEMS 73	12

+THROUGH

		PAGE	TITLE	LINE
FOR CONTEXT, SEE	. . . .	733	95 POEMS 61	8

THROUGHOF

		PAGE	TITLE	LINE
l l in gof throughof treesOf. (Fields Elysian the	. . . . . .	104	& POST IMPR 14	5

THROUGHOUT

		PAGE	TITLE	LINE
of beauteous dead mouths throughout that very proud	. . . . .	6	T&C EPITHALAM	141
into his mind feeling throughout ignorant disappearing me	. .	428	NO THANKS 45	7

THROUGHWHICH

		PAGE	TITLE	LINE
by (◇ ! throughwhich! brittlest! whitewhom! f l	. . . . . .	416	NO THANKS 33	12

THROW

		PAGE	TITLE	LINE
to whispers primeval and throw backward their foreheads to	.	5	T&C EPITHALAM	76
then he will stiff-ly throw the shell away with	. . . .	69	T&C POST IMPR 6	18
sick or when they throw in a few gas	. . . .	272	IS 5 TWO 7	6
young noisily who kiss throw silently things Each at	. . . .	312	VIVA 4	12
guilty scamper (you bastards throw dynamite) let knowings	. .	452	NO THANKS 67	5

+THROW

		PAGE	TITLE	LINE
FOR CONTEXT, SEE	. . . .	388	NO THANKS 5	16

+THROWING

		PAGE	TITLE	LINE
FOR CONTEXT, SEE	. . . .	392	NO THANKS 9	20

THROWN

		PAGE	TITLE	LINE
pennies he will be thrown a peanut (which he	. . . .	69	T&C POST IMPR 6	16
hurriedly picked up and thrown on the ash-heap where	. . . .	203	XLI LA GUERRE 1	16
having found what was thrown away himself taptaptaps out	. .	298	IS 5 FOUR 15	24
And o the Light thrown by Them opens sharp	. . . .	437	NO THANKS 53	4
/ / / a thrown a -way It with	. . . .	632	(CHAIRE) 34	1
&: mys (a thrown a- way X -mas)	. . . .	632	(CHAIRE) 34	7
-wise we should have thrown a- way (and whose	. . . .	660	(CHAIRE) 62	16

THROWS

		PAGE	TITLE	LINE
himself among his pillows throws jewels at the queen	. . . .	34	T&C ORIENTALE 6	100
lives are keen he throws the world a kiss	. . . .	624	(CHAIRE) 26	18

+THROWS

		PAGE	TITLE	LINE
FOR CONTEXT, SEE	. . . .	227	IS 5 ONE GERT	16

THRUSH

		PAGE	TITLE	LINE
half-mute, (haste ere some thrush with silver several tears	.	6	T&C EPITHALAM	119
smiles your eyes half- thrush half-angel and your drowsy	. .	186	XLI SONGS 8	10
old age when every thrush may sing no new	. . . .	620	(CHAIRE) 22	5
/ (hills chime with thrush) A hummingbird princess FlOaTs	. .	747	95 POEMS 75	1
nowhere) we --While one thrush sings / / /	. . . .	758	95 POEMS 85	48

THRUSHES

		PAGE	TITLE	LINE
per in sunset or thrushes toward dusk among whippoorwills	. .	512	50 POEMS 26	25
not with twilight's first thrushes may awake more secretly	.	577	1 X 1 37	6
/ might these be thrushes climbing through almost (do	. . . .	582	1 X 1 42	1

+THRUSHES

		PAGE	TITLE	LINE
FOR CONTEXT, SEE	. . . .	820	73 POEMS 48	1

THRUSHSONG

		PAGE	TITLE	LINE
a cloverish silence of thrushsong (and more than every	. . .	745	95 POEMS 73	3

THRUST

		PAGE	TITLE	LINE
feeling the belly's merry thrust Boost my huge passion	. . .	132	& SON REAL 3	7

THRUSTS

		PAGE	TITLE	LINE
earth dark) and thousand thrusts squirms stars Trees, swift	.	356	VIVA 47	7

	PAGE	TITLE	LINE

THUD
her cheeks utters a thud of scarlet. always. More . . . . . . 143 & SON REAL 14   6
THUDDING
this man: a narrow thudding timeshaped face plus innocuous . 62 T&C PORTRAIT 10   2
THUGLIKE
--dear) the uncouthly Her. thuglike stare the pollenizing . . 159 & SON ACTU 8   14
THULE
Hyperluxurious Supersieve (which Ultima Thule Of Plumbing . . 334 VIVA 25   3
THUMB
thee ,has the naughty thumb of science prodded thy . . . . . 46 T&C LA GUERRE 2   10
money held between his thumb and first finger (i . . . . . . 102 & POST IMPR 12   5
triperight election who so thumb o'clock asters miggle dim . 333 VIVA 24   15
finger the thicker the thumb (it's whirl, girls) round . . . 513 50 POEMS 27   6
matchabelli) tits as (while thumb a plus fingers all . . . . 546 1 X 1 6   10
you'd almost cut your thumb so right he sharpens . . . . . . 624 (CHAIRE) 26   15
idling-is-grindstone one; what: of. thumb stutt (er (s . . . 656 (CHAIRE) 58   8
THUMBLIKE
in surging flesh). A thumblike index down- dragging yanks . . 226 IS 5 ONE MAME   5
flash a of-faceness stuck thumblike into pie is traffic . . . 330 VIVA 21   5
THUMBPRINTS
embroidered howdah im- mediately. Thumbprints of an angel . . 262 IS 5 ONE 32   30
THUMBS
crumbs twitch like mutilated thumbs: picture His peering . . 117 & PORTRAIT 10   31
who twiddles his white thumbs and frisks down the . . . . . 296 IS 5 FOUR 13   6
THUMPING
i n glike piccolos thumPing colours like a bangofpiano . . . 100 & POST IMPR 11   9
+THUMPS
FOR CONTEXT, SEE . . . . 442 NO THANKS 57   8
THUNDER
grace, goddess, thy crippled thunder-foraging groom or the . 6 T&C EPITHALAM 149
silver gliding from sunny thunder into freshness as if . . . 58 T&C PORTRAIT 6   8
of depriving deep, with thunder of those hungering wings . . 210 XLI SONNETS 6   6
gold) nuzzle against summer thunder (together) smell only . . 340 VIVA 31   19
th-ing out of wonderful thunder! of? ocean. a ndn . . . . . 469 NEW POEMS 7   10
ghosts drowning in supreme thunder? ours (over you reels . . 639 (CHAIRE) 41   2
they flee through a thunder of seem though the . . . . . . 801 73 POEMS 29   16
to burst in a thunder of oneness dream! ! . . . . 841 73 POEMS 69   36
+THUNDER
FOR CONTEXT, SEE . . . . 646 (CHAIRE) 48   8
THUNDER-FORAGING
grace, goddess, thy crippled thunder-foraging groom or the . 6 T&C EPITHALAM 149
THUNDERB
lpounceupcrackw (ill) jumps of THuNdeRB loSSo!MiN -visiblya . 347 VIVA 38   10
THUNDERBOLT
if it were a thunderbolt red- hot peeling off . . . . 194 XLI PORTRAIT 2   23
birds disappear becomingly: a thunderbolt compose poems not . 452 NO THANKS 67   14
THUNDERER
the feet of awe), thunderer whose omnipotent brow showers . . 4 T&C EPITHALAM 37
THUNDERING
her (wrist performs a thundering trivial) it. y protuberant . 159 & SON ACTU 8   5
eyes which why in (thundering) by When eaten spaces . . . . . 346 VIVA 37   9
THUNDEROUS
(to droppingly descend amid thunderous anthropoid applause) . 267 IS 5 TWO 2   9
+THUNDERS
FOR CONTEXT, SEE . . . . 428 NO THANKS 45   17
THURSDAY
wholeagainst you gringlehow exudes thursday fasters by button 333 VIVA 24   7
+THURSDAY
FOR CONTEXT, SEE . . . . 227 IS 5 ONE GERT   15
THURSDAYS
of the management on Thursdays, opposite which a church . . . 263 IS 5 ONE 32   50
THUS
prison (building thatandthis into Thus, Around the reckless . 83 T&C SON ACTU 2   7
and girls have whispered thus and so) and girls . . . . . . 451 NO THANKS 66   14
doll self) hay completely thus or that wispily is . . . . . 516 50 POEMS 30   12
per both pale orbs thus excluding a leanderless drowning . . 546 1 X 1 6   6
another like the pest thus did immortal jealousy quell . . . 799 73 POEMS 27   32
jealousy quell divine generosity, thus reason vanquished . . 799 73 POEMS 27   34

THUS (CONTINUED)
the slave of mind; thus virtue triumphed over vice . . . . . 799 73 POEMS 27   36
logic thwarted life: and thus-- but look around you, ... 799 73 POEMS 27   38
mind never may partly guess--thus, my love, to merely . . . . 818 73 POEMS 46   13
THWART
you had desire to thwart me and became a . . . . 30 T&C ORIENTALE 4   18
THWARTED
both was very very thwarted) and when which was . . . . 401 NO THANKS 18   5
to ugliness and logic thwarted life: and thus-- but . . . . . 799 73 POEMS 27   38
THY
paramour to toy with thy extraordinary lust, (the sinuous . .   3 T&C EPITHALAM   4
rain which rising from thy bed steals to his . . . .   3 T&C EPITHALAM   5
elm eloquent pandar with thy nod significant to the . . . . .   3 T&C EPITHALAM   9
exquisite quest? and did thy fortunate fingers sometime dwell   3 T&C EPITHALAM   21
rose! Lover, lead forth thy love unto that bed . . . .   6 T&C EPITHALAM   113
whose ambrosial grace, goddess, thy crippled thunder-foraging   6 T&C EPITHALAM   149
having Discordia's apple in thy hands, which the scared . . .   6 T&C EPITHALAM   151
--I beseech thee bless thy suppliant singer and his . . . . .   7 T&C EPITHALAM   168
stroked flower; let not thy lust one threaded moment . . . .   9 T&C SONGS 1   7
the perusing greenness of thy thought my golden soul . . . .   9 T&C SONGS 1   29
a superior terror; be thy taut flesh silver, like . . . . . .   9 T&C SONGS 1   31
the sinless taint of thy long sinful arms about . . . .   9 T&C SONGS 1   34
of passed afterday, clothe thy soul's coming merely, with . . 10 T&C SONGS 1   40
revealed in rareness: let thy twain eyes deeply wield . . . . 10 T&C SONGS 1   42
/ / / / Thy fingers make early flowers . . . . 13 T&C SONGS 3   1
flowers of all things. thy hair mostly the hours . . . . . . 13 T&C SONGS 3   3
we will go amaying. thy whitest feet crisply are . . . . . . 13 T&C SONGS 3   8
crisply are straying. Always thy moist eyes are at . . . . . 13 T&C SONGS 3   10
flowers bringing? To be thy lips is a sweet . . . . 13 T&C SONGS 3   15
thou didst not answer thy mouth is as a . . . . 27 T&C ORIENTALE 1   4
thou didst not wonder thy face is as a . . . . 27 T&C ORIENTALE 1   18
and thou art silent thy breast is as a . . . . 27 T&C ORIENTALE 1   25
/ / my love thy hair is one kingdom . . . . 29 T&C ORIENTALE 3   2
king whereof is darkness thy forehead is a flight . . . . . . 29 T&C ORIENTALE 3   4
a flight of flowers thy head is a quick . . . . 29 T&C ORIENTALE 3   5
filled with sleeping birds thy breasts are swarms of . . . . 29 T&C ORIENTALE 3   7
upon the bough of thy body thy body to . . . . 29 T&C ORIENTALE 3   8
bough of thy body thy body to me is . . . . 29 T&C ORIENTALE 3   9
the approach of spring thy thighs are white horses . . . . . 29 T&C ORIENTALE 3   11
pleasant song my love thy head is a casket . . . . 29 T&C ORIENTALE 3   16
the cool jewel of thy mind the hair of . . . . 29 T&C ORIENTALE 3   17
mind the hair of thy head is one warrior . . . . 29 T&C ORIENTALE 3   18
warrior innocent of defeat thy hair upon thy shoulders . . . 29 T&C ORIENTALE 3   20
defeat thy hair upon thy shoulders is an army . . . . 29 T&C ORIENTALE 3   20
victory and with trumpets thy legs are the trees . . . . . . 29 T&C ORIENTALE 3   22
very eatage of forgetfulness thy lips are satraps in . . . . 29 T&C ORIENTALE 3   24
the combining of kings thy wrists are holy which . . . . . . 29 T&C ORIENTALE 3   26
of the keys of thy blood thy feet upon . . . . 29 T&C ORIENTALE 3   28
keys of thy blood thy feet upon thy ankles . . . . 29 T&C ORIENTALE 3   29
blood thy feet upon thy ankles are flowers in . . . . 29 T&C ORIENTALE 3   29
vases of silver in thy beauty is the dilemma . . . . 29 T&C ORIENTALE 3   31
the dilemma of flutes thy eyes are the betrayal . . . . 29 T&C ORIENTALE 3   32
indolent frail ascensions, of thy smile rises the immaculate 31 T&C ORIENTALE 5   17
the immaculate sorrow of thy low hair flutter the . . . . . . 31 T&C ORIENTALE 5   19
slow supple flower of thy beauty, my heart discovers . . . . 31 T&C ORIENTALE 5   28
i slowly gather of thy languorous mouth the thrilling . . . . 37 T&C AMORES 2   19
the new flower with thy unimaginable wings, where dwells . . 40 T&C AMORES 4   45
them hide them in thy breath drive them in . . . . 41 T&C AMORES 5   21
thumb of science prodded thy beauty . how often . . . . 46 T&C LA GUERRE 2   12
incomparable couch of death thy rhythmic lover thou answerest 46 T&C LA GUERRE 2   22
teach me of her Thy yonder servant who in . . . . 57 T&C PORTRAIT 5   6
yonder servant who in Thy very house silently sits . . . . . 57 T&C PORTRAIT 5   7
of the jostle of thy breasts and the slobber . . . . 61 T&C PORTRAIT 9   24
are the snow and thy fingers are the rain, ... 61 T&C PORTRAIT 9   30
when thou hast taken thy last applause, and when . . . . . . 75 T&C SON REAL 6   1
which shall not know thy smile again, lingering a . . . . . . 75 T&C SON REAL 6   4
in the sorrowful hour, thy counted petals O tremendous . . . 79 T&C SON UNRE 4   3
the white ship of thy heart on frailer ports . . . . 79 T&C SON UNRE 4   15

		PAGE	TITLE	LINE

THY (CONTINUED)

my breath: take not thy tingling limbs from me: . . . . 139 & SON REAL 10   1
their crazy meal letting thy tigers of smooth sweetness . . . 139 & SON REAL 10   3
the pollenizing vacancy when, Thy patters? hands.... is swig 159 & SON ACTU 8   16
times the poem of thy remembrance surprises with refrain . . 184 XLI SONGS 6   3
the winsome cage of thy body rose through the . . . . 187 XLI SONGS 9   3
the dark's prodigious face thy voice scattering . . . . 187 XLI SONGS 9   11
flower in whose hair, thy lips are cold with . . . . 190 XLI SONGS 12   4
in the hair withers; thy hair is acold with . . . . 190 XLI SONGS 12   16
the rare unwisdom of thy eyes, and if thy . . . . 205 XLI SONNETS 1   2
thy eyes, and if thy hands flowers of silence . . . . 205 XLI SONNETS 1   3
soul slowly which on thy beauty dreams (proud through . . . . 205 XLI SONNETS 1   5
lily inextinguishable, taught by thy tremulous grace bravely 206 XLI SONNETS 2   3
exquisite dreams--O Love! upon thy dim shrine of intangible . 206 XLI SONNETS 2   10
from the less-than-whiteness of thy face (whose eyes inherit 210 XLI SONNETS 6   9
inconsiderable doom, when these thy lips beautifully embrace 210 XLI SONNETS 6   12
embrace nothing and when thy bashful hands assume silence . . 210 XLI SONNETS 6   14
vain, O scrupulously take thy trivial toll, for whose . . . . 212 XLI SONNETS 8   3
fain; try me with thy perfumes which have seduced . . . . . . 212 XLI SONNETS 8   5
like, i'll take between thy hands what no man . . . . 212 XLI SONNETS 8   13
do thou distinctly bring thy footstep, and the rushing . . . 213 XLI SONNETS 9   11
and the rushing of thy deep hair and the . . . . 213 XLI SONNETS 9   11
sleep whose stranger dreams thy strangeness must abuse....) . 213 XLI SONNETS 9   14
crisply the whim of thy smoothness. and mark the . . . . . . 215 XLI SONNETS 11   7
my fear Or with thy mind against my mind, ... 215 XLI SONNETS 11   12
enormous stride (and drawing thy mouth toward my mouth, . . . 215 XLI SONNETS 11   16
Time in your no thy flight and make me . . . . 233 IS 5 ONE 4   3
a little child. In thy your ear: en amerique . . . . 233 IS 5 ONE 4   5
every language even deafanddumb thy sons acclaim your . . . . 268 IS 5 TWO 3   7
dusk but kneelingly believes thy secret and each morning . . 351 VIVA 42   14
which shall increase) open thy fire! for i have . . . . . . 360 VIVA 51   32
--nourish my failure with thy freedom: star isful beckoningly 456 NO THANKS 71   14
to enni one bugger thy nabor (neck and senecktie . . . . . . 492 50 POEMS 6   12
(shrill collective myth) into thy grave merely to toil . . . 579 1 X 1 39   9
dyingest my and foreverless thy? why our is love . . . . . 590 1 X 1 50   25
and make each no thy yes: love; and give . . . . 651 (CHAIRE) 53   10

THYSELF

beneath thee and about thyself a small hoping insect, ... 351 VIVA 42   9

TIC

there was a clock. tac-tic. tac-toc. Time and lilacs.... . . 133 & SON REAL 4   7
die slow ly "toc tic" as i have seen . . . . 354 VIVA 45   25
says toc, submit says tic, Eternity's a Five Year . . . . . . 438 NO THANKS 54   5

TICKING

perfectly distinct unhe; a ticking phantom by prodigious . . 558 1 X 1 18   8
maillols occurred with any ticking of a clock / . . . . 617 (CHAIRE) 19   14

TICKLE

the obscene shy breasts tickle, laughing when i wilt . . . . 172 & SON ACTU 21   15

TICKLES

sudden parody of snow tickles the air to golden . . . .   5 T&C EPITHALAM   74

TICKLING

my ears scramble faintly tickling putrescent atomies, and i . 69 T&C POST IMPR 6   29
having the best time tickling away every- body's brain . . . 126 & SEVEN POEMS 5   11
My gorgeous bullet in tickling intuitive flight aches, just, 130 & SON REAL 1   10
a valley spilled its tickling river in my eyes, ... 135 & SON REAL 6   15
go clean through me tickling aches, and the weak . . . . . . 147 & SON REAL 18   7

TIDE

heard over time and tide and death leaping Sweetly . . . . . 44 T&C AMORES 8   21
withins ejaculate. obscenity the tide Did dl es a, ... 94 & POST IMPR 6   5
that bright how plural tide measures her guest (as . . . . . 418 NO THANKS 35   10
locked in foreverish time's tide at poise, love alone . . . . 843 73 POEMS 71   4
my tryst until that tide shall turn; and from . . . . 843 73 POEMS 71   6

TIDE'S

(clothed only in the tide's acute weaving murmur / . . . . . 369 VIVA 60   21

+TIDES

FOR CONTEXT, SEE . . . . 39 T&C AMORES 4   9

TIDEWINGS

dies, i hear only tidewings in the last light . . . . 64 T&C POST IMPR 1   10

	PAGE	TITLE	LINE
TIDIYUM			
flics rush (the Flics, tidiyum, are very tidiyum reassuringly	274	IS 5 TWO 9	9
Flics, tidiyum, are very tidiyum reassuringly similar, they .	274	IS 5 TWO 9	10
they all have very tidiyum mustaches, and very tidiyum . . .	274	IS 5 TWO 9	11
tidiyum mustaches, and very tidiyum chins, and just above . .	274	IS 5 TWO 9	13
just above their very tidiyum ears their very tidiyum	274	IS 5 TWO 9	14
tidiyum ears their very tidiyum necks begin) let us	274	IS 5 TWO 9	15
with only-just- shined buttons tidiyum before and behind) has	274	IS 5 TWO 9	25
TIDL			
ump-A-tum ; tee-die uM-tuM tidl -id umptyumpty (OO-- ! . . .	426	NO THANKS 43	22
TIED			
a big feather is tied under myhis chin.) that	69	T&C POST IMPR 6	42
TIES			
slow (ly obstre peroustimidi ties surElyfl) oat iNg, the . .	104	& POST IMPR 14	4
TIGERS			
crazy meal letting thy tigers of smooth sweetness steal . . .	139	& SON REAL 10	3
TIGHT			
time with the tall tight boys at Tabari' s, ...	71	T&C SON REAL 2	3
Hush. God. Please hold. Tight / / / /	130	& SON REAL 1	15
hug you safe and tight just as your mother	192	XLI CHANSONS 2	10
very slowly in a tight balloon until the smallening	360	VIVA 51	13
TIGHTENED			
little dancer with the tightened eyes crisp ogling shoulders	72	T&C SON REAL 3	5
TIGHTENS			
crisp a thing, which tightens caught in the hoisting	68	T&C POST IMPR 5	10
TIGHTNESS			
grabbed with circular shrieking tightness solid screams . . .	195	XLI PORTRAIT 3	14
TILL			
eyes look from morning till night into the street	58	T&C PORTRAIT 6	18
the unbought contemptuous intent till this our flesh merely .	84	T&C SON ACTU 3	4
and also, i'll admit--) till, at the corner of	174	& SON ACTU 23	14
i will wade out till my thighs are steeped	189	XLI SONGS 11	2
had a chicken farm till the skunks ate the	239	IS 5 ONE 10	18
after it with fingers; till having found what was	298	IS 5 FOUR 15	22
unwish through curving wherewhen till unwish returns on its .	554	1 X 1 14	7
scream, all ye screamers, till your if is up	555	1 X 1 15	9
the best he kin till they digged his hole	568	1 X 1 28	4
fly) forever was never till now now i love	594	1 X 1 54	27
cliches un by un till the god's truth stands	605	(CHAIRE) 7	3
a piece of when till it rolled behind forever, ...	612	(CHAIRE) 14	9
i climb (crazily kissing) till into themselves we fell-- . .	694	95 POEMS 22	3
soul: freedom to freedom till her utmost secrecies and . . .	721	95 POEMS 49	10
wrong climbing, my love (till mountains speak the truth) . .	745	95 POEMS 73	2
children, if he disappears; till of more much than	756	95 POEMS 84	7
his dear he sings till everywhere is here /	760	95 POEMS 87	12
noone) a noone who, till their and your returning, ...	812	73 POEMS 40	5
TILLER			
slammed hard- over the tiller; clattered forward skidding in	277	IS 5 THREE 1	11
TILTED			
twilight the a little tilted streets spill lazily multitudes	345	VIVA 36	6
TILTING			
on dangerous slabs of tilting din whose mouths distinctly . .	138	& SON REAL 9	2
TIME			
O shining girl of time untarnished! O small intimate	5	T&C EPITHALAM	106
death). Now is the time when all occasional things	6	T&C EPITHALAM	121
Eater of all things lovely--Time! upon whose watering lips .	23	T&C PUELLA MEA	266
the wafted stars (in time to come you shall	36	T&C AMORES 1	21
when i heard over time and tide and death	44	T&C AMORES 8	20
and have a good time with the tall tight	71	T&C SON REAL 2	2
maybe read? of a time when the beautiful most	72	T&C SON REAL 3	11
corking brute amused from time to time by clever	74	T&C SON REAL 5	10
amused from time to time by clever drolls fearsomely	74	T&C SON REAL 5	10
heart, as mine in time not far away; if	76	T&C SON UNRE 1	4
bright shouting street of time her nakedness with its	112	& PORTRAIT 6	75
other having the fastest time because they've never met . . .	126	& SEVEN POEMS 5	7
striker having the best time tickling away every- body's . .	126	& SEVEN POEMS 5	11
never says my dear, Time for your musiclesson and	126	& SEVEN POEMS 5	29
The Good Old Summer Time. My gorgeous bullet in	130	& SON REAL 1	9

	PAGE	TITLE	LINE

TIME (CONTINUED)

	PAGE	TITLE	LINE
a clock. tac-tic. tac-toc. Time and lilacs.... minutes and	133	& SON REAL 4	8
noise. ladies with whom time feeds especially his immense	138	& SON REAL 9	8
neat obscure obvious hands Time stuff the sincere stomach	165	& SON ACTU 14	12
without or cease or time; a naming stealth of	168	& SON ACTU 17	9
beauty makes terms with time and his worms, when	183	XLI SONGS 5	8
music. For the first time in sorting from this	201	XLI PORTRAIT 9	20
ghastlier trees by whom Time measured is when frost	207	XLI SONNETS 3	2
love, to Death and Time storms and rough cold,	207	XLI SONNETS 3	9
This is the garden. Time shall surely reap and	208	XLI SONNETS 4	9
eyes inherit vacancy) will time extract his inconsiderable	210	XLI SONNETS 6	10
the hungering mouth of time is fed: and if	212	XLI SONNETS 8	8
thy strangeness must abuse....) Time being not for us,	213	XLI SONNETS 9	15
turn backward O backward Time in your no thy	233	IS 5 ONE 4	3
sure university spends her time looking picturesque under the	234	IS 5 ONE 5	3
woild one swell bangup time wen nobody wore no	237	IS 5 ONE 8	17
nobody loses all the time i had an uncle	239	IS 5 ONE 10	1
Greediest Paws of careful time all of which is	260	IS 5 ONE 30	11
Wadsworth Bryant. By this time, however, the flight of	263	IS 5 ONE 32	54
heaving indolent colourless forgets) time Requiescat. carry	277	IS 5 THREE 1	20
with thecas-tanets in 5/4; Time chick. chick but: that	318	VIVA 10	5
/ / / what time is it i wonder	322	VIVA 14	1
tell such to murder time (forgetting what's to know	362	VIVA 53	13
the green meadow of time lessness; quietly turning toward	370	VIVA 61	6
dive out of tinying time (into supreme Now: feeling	373	VIVA 64	10
from only Whom shall time no refuge keep though	377	VIVA 68	13
(if loud most howish time derange the silent whys	420	NO THANKS 37	5
while) and shall carve time so we'll before what's	433	NO THANKS 50	14
may not care if time totters, light droops, all	446	NO THANKS 61	6
his mind take off time that you should ever	484	NEW POEMS 22	8
let us accept (the time forever, and you'll wear	504	50 POEMS 18	15
what dreams can do --time is a tree (this	511	50 POEMS 25	26
whispering grass? joy in time shut and starved on	527	50 POEMS 39	11
fiend: blow space to time) --when skies are hanged	560	1 X 1 20	6
less than all of time) gives you skilful his	575	1 X 1 35	22
are (yes; and if time should ask into his	576	1 X 1 36	13
"sweet spring is your time is my time is	591	1 X 1 51	2
your time is my time is our time for	591	1 X 1 51	2
my time is our time for springtime is lovetime	591	1 X 1 51	3
"sweet spring is your time is my time is	591	1 X 1 51	26
your time is my time is our time for	591	1 X 1 51	26
my time is our time for springtime is lovetime	591	1 X 1 51	27
cross the chasm of time lessness; but two dim	605	(CHAIRE) 7	12
o mo re) time me n sit (1	610	(CHAIRE) 12	11
in a whisper, as time turned to dream "and	626	(CHAIRE) 28	11
/ / / no time ago or else a	648	(CHAIRE) 50	1
fancied fact and spaceful time-- no heart can leap,	664	(CHAIRE) 66	20
a rose's moment there's time for laughing and there's	683	95 POEMS 11	9
for laughing and there's time for crying-- for hoping	683	95 POEMS 11	9
peace for longing --a time for growing and a	683	95 POEMS 11	11
for growing and a time for dying: a night	683	95 POEMS 11	11
me) there is a time for timelessness / /	683	95 POEMS 11	14
/ / / in time of daffodils (who know	688	95 POEMS 16	1
why, remember how in time of lilacs who proclaim	688	95 POEMS 16	4
so (forgetting seem) in time of roses (who amaze	688	95 POEMS 16	7
if, remember yes in time of all sweet things	688	95 POEMS 16	10
mystery to be (when time from time shall set	688	95 POEMS 16	14
be (when time from time shall set us free)	688	95 POEMS 16	14
fell-- how have all time and space bowed to	694	95 POEMS 22	5
imagined bodies kneel (over time space doom dream while	714	95 POEMS 42	7
my life) the true time of year-- and if	717	95 POEMS 45	8
pitiless the mercy of time time time time time	743	95 POEMS 71	9
the mercy of time time time time time --how	743	95 POEMS 71	9
mercy of time time time time time --how fortunate	743	95 POEMS 71	9
of time time time time time --how fortunate are	743	95 POEMS 71	9
time time time time time --how fortunate are you	743	95 POEMS 71	9
slaves of space and time --ours is the now	745	95 POEMS 73	13
timelessness as it's to time, love did no more	768	95 POEMS 94	1

TIME (CONTINUED)
    to a dream called time: and give herself into . . . . 811 73 POEMS 39   10
    / / / what time is it? it is . . . . 817 73 POEMS 45   1
    every star a different time, and each most falsely . . . . . 817 73 POEMS 45   2
    without confusing timelessness and time. Time cannot . . . . 817 73 POEMS 45   8
    confusing timelessness and time. Time cannot children, poets, 817 73 POEMS 45   9
    limb ask every question time can't answer: and such . . . . 818 73 POEMS 46   10
    yes) acceptance of irrevocable time particular pure truth of 821 73 POEMS 49   4
    become the same it's time you unbecame where climbing . . . . 834 73 POEMS 62   18
    the simple agony of time --small wonder such a . . . . 842 73 POEMS 70   12
    steep than climb can time with all his years) . . . . 845 73 POEMS 73   8
+TIME
    FOR CONTEXT, SEE . . . . 591 1 X 1 51   3
    FOR CONTEXT, SEE . . . . 591 1 X 1 51   27
    FOR CONTEXT, SEE . . . . 639 (CHAIRE) 41   12
    FOR CONTEXT, SEE . . . . 650 (CHAIRE) 52   7
    FOR CONTEXT, SEE . . . . 703 95 POEMS 31   9
    FOR CONTEXT, SEE . . . . 703 95 POEMS 31   12
    FOR CONTEXT, SEE . . . . 796 73 POEMS 24   10
TIME'S
    dream wherelessly spiralling) beyond time's sky and through . 454 NO THANKS 69   8
    / / / not time's how (anchored in what . . . . 517 50 POEMS 31   1
    one tiny this with time's more than most how . . . . 523 50 POEMS 36   33
    ignorant fire (adventuring and time's dead which; falling . . 533 50 POEMS 45   18
    ticking phantom by prodigious time's mere brain contrived: a 558 1 X 1 18   8
    the courage to receive time's mightiest dream / / . . . . . . 675 95 POEMS 3   14
    can turn immense all time's because to why / . . . . 679 95 POEMS 7   14
    / / / in time's a noble mercy of . . . . 683 95 POEMS 11   1
    whole the upfloating moon. Time's a strange fellow; more . . 750 95 POEMS 78   10
    beach locked in foreverish time's tide at poise, love . . . . 843 73 POEMS 71   4
TIMELESS
    lives imperishably feast all timeless souls (the not whose . 456 NO THANKS 71   3
    / / / / timeless ly this (merely and . . . . 826 73 POEMS 54   1
+TIMELESS
    FOR CONTEXT, SEE . . . . 464 NEW POEMS 2   4
TIMELESSLY
    (if) creep (by if) timelessly foundlost glad (children of) . 681 95 POEMS 9   10
    huger easily beyonds than timelessly alive all glories we've 741 95 POEMS 69   7
    both life and death) timelessly celebrates the merciful . . . 845 73 POEMS 73   13
+TIMELESSLY
    FOR CONTEXT, SEE . . . . 826 73 POEMS 54   1
TIMELESSNESS
    invincible unthing --stern sexual timelessness, outtowering . 351 VIVA 42   3
    perfection as divides by timelessness that heartbeat) . . . . 428 NO THANKS 45   11
    rain (they've played for timelessness with chips of when) . . 451 NO THANKS 66   3
    is a time for timelessness / / / / . . . . 683 95 POEMS 11   14
    i, whose home is timelessness: we who have wandered . . . . . 743 95 POEMS 71   11
    / / being to timelessness as it's to time, ... 768 95 POEMS 94   1
    to do without confusing timelessness and time. Time cannot . 817 73 POEMS 45   8
    feel; mistrusting utterly that timelessness whose absence . . 817 73 POEMS 45   12
+TIMELESSNESS
    FOR CONTEXT, SEE . . . . 370 VIVA 61   6
    FOR CONTEXT, SEE . . . . 605 (CHAIRE) 7   12
TIMELY
    much than all of timely space (was and be . . . . 608 (CHAIRE) 10   4
TIMES
    which distinctly wags at times the weary twig of . . . . . . 134 & SON REAL 5   5
    cleaned up a few times--before she got the info . . . . 145 & SON REAL 16   6
    lived regular. stewed three times a week. and slept . . . . . 149 & SON REAL 20   11
    / / after five times the poem of thy . . . . 184 XLI SONGS 6   2
    accomplish two or three times, and even a few . . . . 236 IS 5 ONE 7   15
    by dreams (or some times vacantly gazing through un . . . . . 354 VIVA 45   8
    they hump them thirteen times a night one hangs . . . . 427 NO THANKS 44   4
    dumb. The number of times a wheel turns doesn't . . . . 514 50 POEMS 28   5
    or make it ten times ten are more than . . . . 561 1 X 1 21   7
    alive) we're wonderful one times one / / / . . . . 594 1 X 1 54   45
    dream larger than sky times earth: a flame beyond . . . . . . 599 (CHAIRE) 1   4
    than have or one times one than when times . . . . 664 (CHAIRE) 66   9

TIMES (CONTINUED)
  times one than when times where-- that we are . . . . 664 {CHAIRE} 66   9
  with us they've nothing times nothing to do (for . . . . . . 664 {CHAIRE} 66   11
  maybe had shaved three times in its life made . . . . 709 95 POEMS 37   8
  you and i some times call april) must often . . . . 738 95 POEMS 66   8
  quite become nothing) five times, proclaim fate isn't fatal . 764 95 POEMS 90   52
  declare --nor all their times encompass me and you: . . . . . 817 73 POEMS 45   4
TIMESHAPED
  man: a narrow thudding timeshaped face plus innocuous winking 62 T&C PORTRAIT 10   2
TIMID
  the ceiling (one diamond timid with nesting incense) fifty . 32 T&C ORIENTALE 6 25
  day between the nibbling timid teethful hours wilts the . . . 112 & PORTRAIT 6   79
  do but touch you) timid lewd moon plunge skilfully . . . . . 155 & SON ACTU 4   16
  or to snare the timid like of her mind . . . . 216 XLI SONNETS 12   5
  here; that if (so timid air is firm) under . . . . 520 50 POEMS 34   7
  of easily hatred of timid & loathing for (dull . . . . 677 95 POEMS 5   5
  heaven says Now the timid the tender (as doubt . . . . 801 73 POEMS 29   25
+TIMIDITIES
  FOR CONTEXT, SEE . . . . 104 & POST IMPR 14   4
TIMIDLY
  ached." and when i timidly hinted "novocaine?" the eyes . . . 226 IS 5 ONE MAME   12
  (as a blind, how timidly, throb; which hints being; . . . . . 402 NO THANKS 19   9
TIMOROUS
  you) this world (as timorous itsters all to call . . . . . 664 {CHAIRE} 66   13
  noisy most park's least timorous pigeons) squ -I- nts . . . . 726 95 POEMS 54   10
+TIN
  FOR CONTEXT, SEE . . . . 100 & POST IMPR 11   40
TING
  -id umptyumpty (OO-- ! ting Bam- : do) , ... 426 NO THANKS 43   26
TINGLING
  little twitchy witches and tingling goblins hob-a-nob . . . . 25 T&C CHANSONS 2   6
  breath: take not thy tingling limbs from me: make . . . . . . 139 & SON REAL 10   1
TINIEST
  mist of atrocious melody.... tiniest dead tunes crawl upon . 69 T&C POST IMPR 6 27
  protrude-- or why her tiniest whispered invitation is like . 229 IS 5 ONE FRAN   14
  whispering barns bulge a tiniest street or three contains . . 340 VIVA 31   13
  more suddenly than) whose tiniest smile? may Be bigger . . . 397 NO THANKS 14   5
  illimitably spiralling candy of tiniest forever--crazily from 480 NEW POEMS 18   22
  you a treasure of tiniest world a piece of . . . . 586 1 X 1 46   3
TINILY
  the sharp things fingered tinily my heart life the . . . . 284 IS 5 FOUR 1   7
  things; remembering ever so tinily these, your crisp eyes . . 294 IS 5 FOUR 11   8
  not know: the earth tinily whirls; while daisies grow . . . . 451 NO THANKS 66   11
  one (truthed by wisping tinily the silverest alive silentness 572 1 X 1 32   8
  / / / how tinily of squir (two be . . . . 581 1 X 1 41   2
  the earth are leapandswooping tinily birds whose magical . . 631 {CHAIRE} 33   11
TINKING
  ceiling- flatness the Bar. tinking luscious jigs dint of . . 96 & POST IMPR 8   11
TINKLING
  outward(amid tinkling-cheering-hammering tables) . . . . . . 232 IS 5 ONE 3   9
+TINKLING-CHEERING-HAMMERING
  outward(amid tinkling-cheering-hammering tables) . . . . . . 232 IS 5 ONE 3   9
TINSEL
  thee then ponder the tinsel part they let thee . . . . 75 T&C SON REAL 6   6
  & sweet nothingly gushing tinsel; silently yes before angel . 480 NEW POEMS 18   11
TINT
  are. clenched. fists of tint. TUMTITUMTIDDLE if sometimes my 100 & POST IMPR 11   16
TINTS
  laughing. Into the hair-thin tints of yellow dawn, into . . . 66 T&C POST IMPR 3   6
  Me of HerThe delicate-swill tints of hair Whose (the . . . . 94 & POST IMPR 6   21
  bright flame whose myriad tints enrich a visage simple, . . . 254 IS 5 ONE 25   17
  across this water, crowding tints: browns and whites shoving, 281 IS 5 THREE 5   5
  Of (Begins) millions Of Tints (and) & (grows) Slowly . . . . 348 VIVA 39   4
TINY
  to the tune of tiny troubadours, and (phantom-white) . . . .   8 T&C OF NICOL   5
  waist is a most tiny hinge of flesh, a . . . . 21 T&C PUELLA MEA   193
  glaring at the shabby tiny smiling, man in whose . . . . . . 69 T&C POST IMPR 6   8
  the little string! the tiny smiling shabby man is . . . . . . 69 T&C POST IMPR 6   32

TINY (CONTINUED)

<table>
<thead>
<tr><th></th><th>PAGE</th><th>TITLE</th><th>LINE</th></tr>
</thead>
<tbody>
<tr><td>a. Thick silence) blacktreesthink tiny, angels sharpen: . . .</td><td>99</td><td>& POST IMPR 10</td><td>15</td></tr>
<tr><td>mouth is, fond of tiny plums of tangerines and . . . .</td><td>100</td><td>& POST IMPR 11</td><td>26</td></tr>
<tr><td>the curve of the tiny motheaten old manwhose Beard . . . . .</td><td>101</td><td>& POST IMPR 11</td><td>46</td></tr>
<tr><td>ambitious weeness of boots tiny add death what shall? . . . .</td><td>105</td><td>& PORTRAIT 1</td><td>9</td></tr>
<tr><td>--to God in a tiny voice, i am may . . . .</td><td>117</td><td>& PORTRAIT 10</td><td>11</td></tr>
<tr><td>find Hassan's Place by tiny streets shrugging with colour)</td><td>143</td><td>& SON REAL 14</td><td>4</td></tr>
<tr><td>he suddenly clapped a tiny sunset of vermouth -colour. . . .</td><td>148</td><td>& SON REAL 19</td><td>8</td></tr>
<tr><td>outdoes the mandolin- man's tiny racket. The horses sleep . .</td><td>171</td><td>& SON ACTU 20</td><td>6</td></tr>
<tr><td>dump of oblivion) a tiny dust finely arising at . . . .</td><td>197</td><td>XLI PORTRAIT 5</td><td>23</td></tr>
<tr><td>flesh exactly cubes of tiny fragrance try; i have . . . . . .</td><td>214</td><td>XLI SONNETS 10</td><td>4</td></tr>
<tr><td>--how silently emit a tiny violetflavoured nuisance: Odor?</td><td>231</td><td>IS 5 ONE 3</td><td>53</td></tr>
<tr><td>swaggers daintily twiddling his tiny cane and, mazurkas about</td><td>374</td><td>VIVA 65</td><td>31</td></tr>
<tr><td>a curtain on which tiny the was painted in . . . .</td><td>516</td><td>50 POEMS 30</td><td>5</td></tr>
<tr><td>enough to hold one tiny this with time's more . . . .</td><td>523</td><td>50 POEMS 36</td><td>32</td></tr>
<tr><td>thing (secretly adoring shyly tiny winging darting floating .</td><td>591</td><td>1 X 1 51</td><td>22</td></tr>
<tr><td>ones; the slim plump tiny tall) all except the . . . .</td><td>619</td><td>{CHAIRE} 21</td><td>12</td></tr>
<tr><td>huger always whom two tiny selves sleep (doll by . . . . . .</td><td>777</td><td>73 POEMS 5</td><td>11</td></tr>
<tr><td>con trast with the tiny stumble from second to . . . .</td><td>803</td><td>73 POEMS 31</td><td>12</td></tr>
</tbody>
</table>

TINYING

<table>
<tbody>
<tr><td>We dive out of tinying time (into supreme Now: . . . .</td><td>373</td><td>VIVA 64</td><td>10</td></tr>
<tr><td>/ / / faithfully tinying at twilight voice of . . . .</td><td>821</td><td>73 POEMS 49</td><td>1</td></tr>
</tbody>
</table>

TINYNESS

<table>
<tbody>
<tr><td>the window a most tinyness, the moon (with white . . . . . .</td><td>365</td><td>VIVA 56</td><td>12</td></tr>
</tbody>
</table>

TIP

<table>
<tbody>
<tr><td>hist whist little ghostthings tip-toe twinkle-toe little . .</td><td>25</td><td>T&C CHANSONS 2</td><td>3</td></tr>
<tr><td>omiepsicronlonO-- megaeta? p aul D-as-in-tip-toe r apeR / / .</td><td>431</td><td>NO THANKS 48</td><td>28</td></tr>
</tbody>
</table>

+TIP

<table>
<tbody>
<tr><td>FOR CONTEXT, SEE . . . .</td><td>495</td><td>50 POEMS 9</td><td>16</td></tr>
</tbody>
</table>

TIP-TOE

<table>
<tbody>
<tr><td>hist whist little ghostthings tip-toe twinkle-toe little . .</td><td>25</td><td>T&C CHANSONS 2</td><td>3</td></tr>
</tbody>
</table>

TIPPING

<table>
<tbody>
<tr><td>rocker by the, curb, tipping and tipping, the flocks . . . .</td><td>166</td><td>& SON ACTU 15</td><td>3</td></tr>
<tr><td>the, curb, tipping and tipping, the flocks of pigeons. . . .</td><td>166</td><td>& SON ACTU 15</td><td>4</td></tr>
</tbody>
</table>

TIPSY

<table>
<tbody>
<tr><td>gross walls sprawling with tipsy tables the abominable floor</td><td>55</td><td>T&C PORTRAIT 3</td><td>2</td></tr>
<tr><td>GUERRE earth like a tipsy biddy with an old . . . .</td><td>203</td><td>XLI LA GUERRE 1</td><td>1</td></tr>
</tbody>
</table>

TIPTOE

<table>
<tbody>
<tr><td>and he become (on tiptoe at the very quick . . . .</td><td>758</td><td>95 POEMS 85</td><td>45</td></tr>
</tbody>
</table>

+TIPTOE

<table>
<tbody>
<tr><td>FOR CONTEXT, SEE . . . .</td><td>733</td><td>95 POEMS 61</td><td>7</td></tr>
</tbody>
</table>

+TIPTOEING

<table>
<tbody>
<tr><td>FOR CONTEXT, SEE . . . .</td><td>469</td><td>NEW POEMS 7</td><td>14</td></tr>
</tbody>
</table>

TIPTOP

<table>
<tbody>
<tr><td>he) ow said she (tiptop said he don't stop . . . .</td><td>399</td><td>NO THANKS 16</td><td>25</td></tr>
</tbody>
</table>

TIRE

<table>
<tbody>
<tr><td>singing--hands fragile whom almost tire the sleepshaped . . .</td><td>85</td><td>T&C SON ACTU 4</td><td>11</td></tr>
</tbody>
</table>

TIRED

<table>
<tbody>
<tr><td>fatherly of a romantic tired business man somewhat tweaked .</td><td>57</td><td>T&C PORTRAIT 5</td><td>32</td></tr>
<tr><td>fingers.... she too is tired. Not of me. The . . . .</td><td>131</td><td>& SON REAL 2</td><td>12</td></tr>
<tr><td>face grow old and tired to which you're married . . . .</td><td>242</td><td>IS 5 ONE 13</td><td>14</td></tr>
<tr><td>man is oh so tired of this a door . . . .</td><td>243</td><td>IS 5 ONE 14</td><td>7</td></tr>
<tr><td>est my lady is tired of That sort of . . . .</td><td>245</td><td>IS 5 ONE 16</td><td>25</td></tr>
</tbody>
</table>

TIREDNESS

<table>
<tbody>
<tr><td>spon- taneously by inevitable tiredness of flanging . . . . .</td><td>197</td><td>XLI PORTRAIT 5</td><td>4</td></tr>
</tbody>
</table>

TIS

<table>
<tbody>
<tr><td>believe me my country, 'tis of you, land of . . . .</td><td>230</td><td>IS 5 ONE 2</td><td>3</td></tr>
<tr><td>/ / the season 'tis, my lovely lambs, of . . . .</td><td>266</td><td>IS 5 TWO 1</td><td>1</td></tr>
<tr><td>dawn's early my country 'tis of centuries come and . . . . .</td><td>268</td><td>IS 5 TWO 3</td><td>4</td></tr>
</tbody>
</table>

TIT

<table>
<tbody>
<tr><td>a hat upon her tit one carves a cross . . . .</td><td>427</td><td>NO THANKS 44</td><td>5</td></tr>
</tbody>
</table>

TITS

<table>
<tbody>
<tr><td>erecting breasts and uttering tits punish my hug presto! . .</td><td>137</td><td>& SON REAL 8</td><td>13</td></tr>
<tr><td>lipstick smell by matchabelli) tits as (while thumb a . . . .</td><td>546</td><td>1 X 1 6</td><td>9</td></tr>
</tbody>
</table>

TITTLE

<table>
<tbody>
<tr><td>(while the no-she-yes-he fluffies tittle tattle . . . .</td><td>773</td><td>73 POEMS 1</td><td>16</td></tr>
</tbody>
</table>

TITTY

<table>
<tbody>
<tr><td>he twitches a liberal titty and lisps "i'm busy . . . .</td><td>711</td><td>95 POEMS 39</td><td>23</td></tr>
</tbody>
</table>

TIV
/ dim i nu tiv e this park is . . . . 696 95 POEMS 24   4

TO
WORD DELETED, APPEARED 996 TIMES

TOAD
hob-a-nob little hoppy happy toad in tweeds tweeds little . . 25 T&C CHANSONS 2   10

+TOAD
FOR CONTEXT, SEE . . . . 108 & PORTRAIT 4   16

TOADSTOOLS
an old leaf between toadstools he is the cheerfulest . . . . 198 XLI PORTRAIT 6   17

TOBACCO
formula a bit of tobacco and gladness plus little . . . . . . 68 T&C POST IMPR 5   3

TOBOGGANS
/ / all ignorance toboggans into know and trudges . . . . . 579 1 X 1 39   1

TOC
was a clock. tac-tic. tac-toc. Time and lilacs.... minutes . 133 & SON REAL 4   7
think, die slow ly "toc tic" as i have . . . . 354 VIVA 45   25
is meek; obey says toc, submit says tic, Eternity's . . . . . 438 NO THANKS 54   5

TODAY
is your cough better today? nn-nn went head face . . . . . 506 50 POEMS 20   8
yes terday's tomorrow (than today can guess or fears . . . . 522 50 POEMS 35   7
died am alive again today, and this is the . . . . 663 (CHAIRE) 65   5
the sky are one today) my very so gay . . . . 767 95 POEMS 93   15
sing gay-be-gay because today's today) the romp cries i . . . 773 73 POEMS 1   5
if sorrowful were gay (today tomorrow, doubting believing and 798 73 POEMS 26   16

TODAY'S
birds sing gay-be-gay because today's today) the romp cries . 773 73 POEMS 1   5

TODDLE
me almost succeeds while toddle rings the bell. But . . . . . 227 IS 5 ONE GERT   7

TODO
panes into a crisp todo of murdering uncouth faces . . . . . 354 VIVA 45   9

TOE
hist whist little ghostthings tip-toe twinkle-toe little . . 25 T&C CHANSONS 2   3
whist little ghostthings tip-toe twinkle-toe little twitchy . 25 T&C CHANSONS 2   4
/ ta ppin g toe hip popot amus Back . . . . 107 & PORTRAIT 3   4
omiepsicronlonO-- megaeta? p aul D-as-in-tip-toe r apeR / / . 431 NO THANKS 48   28
and now ti p toe ingt o a child . . . . 469 NEW POEMS 7   15
every finger is a toe and any courage is . . . . 511 50 POEMS 25   10

TOENAILS
inexplicable not being dollars toenails or ideas thoroughly's 322 VIVA 14   8

TOES
yes! Large legs pinch, toes choke-- hair-thin strands of . . 146 & SON REAL 17   7

+TOES
FOR CONTEXT, SEE . . . . 408 NO THANKS 25   6

TOGETHER
amber with lust breathe together the emperor, exerting . . . 34 T&C ORIENTALE 6   99
that we may watch together how behind the doomed . . . . . . 43 T&C AMORES 7   28
are talking rapidly all together there happens Something, and 62 T&C PORTRAIT 10   18
why gluey grins topple together eyes pout ges- tures . . . . 96 & POST IMPR 8   17
let us come in together and drink coffee covered . . . . . . 198 XLI PORTRAIT 6   31
are your lover lady: together with what keen innumerable . . 285 IS 5 FOUR 2   21
and so: we are together, we will kiss or . . . . 289 IS 5 FOUR 6   16
nuzzle against summer thunder (together) smell only such blue 340 VIVA 31   19
and i) into a together whitely big there is . . . . 365 VIVA 56   9
Fragrance unvisible) ges -tured together- ly singing ams . . 482 NEW POEMS 20   10
in the gloam ing together are standing together un . . . . . 600 (CHAIRE) 2   5
ing together are standing together un der a particular . . . 600 (CHAIRE) 2   6
gether are slowly all together very magically smiling and . . 600 (CHAIRE) 2   9
wintry twi- light (all together a manying one -ness) . . . . 627 (CHAIRE) 29   8
the mountains are dancing together) when every leaf opens . . 665 (CHAIRE) 67   7

+TOGETHER
FOR CONTEXT, SEE . . . . 101 & POST IMPR 11   61
FOR CONTEXT, SEE . . . . 442 NO THANKS 57   3
FOR CONTEXT, SEE . . . . 600 (CHAIRE) 2   8

TOGETHERING
cool ferns) therefore togethering our wholly lives . . . . . 371 VIVA 62   15

+TOGETHERLY
FOR CONTEXT, SEE . . . . 482 NEW POEMS 20   10

		PAGE	TITLE	LINE

TOHIM
    soft eyes syriansang asong tohim self all about the . . . . . 318 VIVA 10   11
TOIL
    thy grave merely to toil the scale to shrillerness . . . . . 579 1 X 1 39   10
TOILET
    a mark in a toilet graced with guts and . . . . 407 NO THANKS 24   13
+TOILET
    FOR CONTEXT, SEE . . . . 425 NO THANKS 42   16
+TOILET PAPER
    FOR CONTEXT, SEE . . . . 321 VIVA 13   14
TOILETBOWL
    employed anent this muddy toiletbowl, while kindred . . . . . 339 VIVA 30   12
TOILETWINDOW
    goes on in the toiletwindow, that's straightacross from my . 171 & SON ACTU 20   2
TOITSELFW
    t: "ah gwonyuhdoanfool me" toitselfw. hispering / / / . . . . 710 95 POEMS 38   9
TOKEN
    the ecstatic earth in token of his coming whom . . . . 3 T&C EPITHALAM   11
    john and jim in token of their country's love . . . . 266 IS 5 TWO 1   26
TOLD
    on us all; stories told returned gather the Again: . . . . . 89 & POST IMPR 1   7
    twelve undershirts (we are told by is it Bishop . . . . 167 & SON ACTU 16   3
    IKEY (GOLDBERG)'S WORTH I'M TOLD $ SEVERAL MILLION . . . . . 244 IS 5 ONE 15   2
    kumrads die because they're told) kumrads die before they're 413 NO THANKS 30   1
    / / / plato told him: he couldn't believe . . . . 553 1 X 1 13   1
    couldn't believe it (jesus told him; he wouldn't believe . . 553 1 X 1 13   4
    it) lao tsze certainly told him, and general (yes . . . . . 553 1 X 1 13   8
    it or not) you told him: i told him; . . . . 553 1 X 1 13   17
    you told him: i told him; we told him . . . . 553 1 X 1 13   17
    i told him; we told him (he didn't believe . . . . 553 1 X 1 13   18
    murdering lies by mortals told make two. Let liars . . . . 556 1 X 1 16   10
    it's a smiling" she told me "someone" (and smiled) . . . . 748 95 POEMS 76   16
    been or will be told sings only--and all lovers . . . . . . 765 95 POEMS 91   8
    thing) no silence ever told; it has no name-- . . . . 819 73 POEMS 47   8
TOLL
    scrupulously take thy trivial toll, for whose cool feet . . . 212 XLI SONNETS 8   3
TOLLED
    where the young bell tolled and the old vine . . . . 647 {CHAIRE} 49   14
TOM
    his lady the musical tom-cat, thou stuffest the parks . . . . 61 T&C PORTRAIT 9   5
    din sort of sublimated tom-tom which quite outdoes the . . . 171 & SON ACTU 20   4
    din sort of sublimated tom-tom which quite outdoes the . . . 171 & SON ACTU 20   4
    observes I pass Mr Tom Larsen twirls among pale . . . . 252 IS 5 ONE 23   5
    into tears. my uncle Tom knits and is a . . . . 253 IS 5 ONE 24   9
    uh shid oi sez. Tom oidoughwuntuh doot, butoiguttuh . . . . 310 VIVA 2   3
    Shadows fed, your Harry's Tom, your Tom is Dick; . . . . . . 438 NO THANKS 54   10
    your Harry's Tom, your Tom is Dick; while Gadgets . . . . . 438 NO THANKS 54   10
+TOM
    FOR CONTEXT, SEE . . . . 342 VIVA 33   9
TOM-CAT
    his lady the musical tom-cat, thou stuffest the parks . . . . 61 T&C PORTRAIT 9   5
TOM-TOM
    din sort of sublimated tom-tom which quite outdoes the . . . 171 & SON ACTU 20   4
+TOMAHAWKED
    FOR CONTEXT, SEE . . . . 643 {CHAIRE} 45   1
TOMB
    breast is as a tomb softer than flowers Come . . . . 27 T&C ORIENTALE 1 25
    flower gone softly by tomb rosily gods whiten befall . . . . 90 & POST IMPR 2   2
    the silence of the tomb then up rose mr . . . . 552 1 X 1 12   25
TOMBS
    simple ugliness of exact tombs, where a large road . . . . . 86 T&C SON ACTU 5 12
TOMBSTONES
    llside) a few dim tombstones try to re (still . . . . 695 95 POEMS 23   6
TOMMY
    the legislat- ure whereas tommy so and so (an . . . . 266 IS 5 TWO 1   37
    worse. Give liz (take! tommy) we order a steak . . . . . . 513 50 POEMS 27   14
TOMORROW
    of swirling worms is tomorrow / / / / . . . . 113 & PORTRAIT 6 120

		PAGE	TITLE	LINE

TOMORROW (CONTINUED)

laughters, smiles unbold) also, tomorrow the daily papers . . 142 & SON REAL 13   9

flutters in the cornerless tomorrow / / / / . . . . 370 VIVA 61   28

foolishwise (tracking the beast Tomorrow by her spoor) over . 374 VIVA 65   7

and just so long tomorrow will not be too . . . . 511 50 POEMS 25   21

odds of yes terday's tomorrow (than today can guess . . . . . 522 50 POEMS 35   7

bang --fear buries a tomorrow under woe and up . . . . . . 531 50 POEMS 43   3

mabel dick and dave --tomorrow is our permanent address . . . 579 1 X 1 39   12

growing (is miraculous like tomorrow) all around the self . . 617 (CHAIRE) 19   7

resuming) selves, into infinite tomorrow steer --souls under 659 (CHAIRE) 61   4

god likes girls and tomorrow and the earth) / . . . . 732 95 POEMS 60   16

sorrowful were gay (today tomorrow, doubting believing and to 798 73 POEMS 26   16

+TOMORROW

FOR CONTEXT, SEE . . . . 309 VIVA 1   20

FOR CONTEXT, SEE . . . . 762 95 POEMS 89   13

TOMORROW'S

place. Why according to tomorrow's paper the proletariat will 262 IS 5 ONE 32   18

TOMORROWLOBS

loamhome picpac obviously scratches tomorrowlobs wholeagainst 333 VIVA 24   5

TOMS

tossing boms at uncle toms) is hows to hump . . . . 500 50 POEMS 14   15

TON

while guesswho nibbles his ton of torse squirms a . . . . . 545 1 X 1 5   5

TONE

a mesh of following tone: did this and this . . . . 115 & PORTRAIT 8   16

sky is washed with tone now for a moon . . . . 282 IS 5 THREE 6   14

TONES

making dear moan in tones of stroked flower; let . . . . . . 9 T&C SONGS 1   6

(grows) Slowly (slowly) Voyaging tones intimate tumult (Into) 348 VIVA 39   7

TONGUE

breath exults upon the tongue of flame half-mute, (haste . . 6 T&C EPITHALAM   118

the lovings of Her tongue. god Is The Sea. . . . . 77 T&C SON UNRE 2   9

soft midst of the tongue sits the Woolworth building . . . . 201 XLI PORTRAIT 9   14

to guess what no tongue tells (such as ourselves) . . . . . 716 95 POEMS 44   17

your sorrows not any tongue may name, three i'll . . . . . 837 73 POEMS 65   2

TONIGHT'S

/ / if within tonight's erect everywhere of black . . . . . 299 IS 5 FOUR 16   1

TOO

grace one goddess loved too well? Chryselephantine Zeus . . . 3 T&C EPITHALAM   24

foot for his wrist's too fine the nineteenth says . . . . . 15 T&C SONGS 5   12

foolish perfect hours dead too, if that he come . . . . . . 42 T&C AMORES 6   17

and the ripe quite too large lips always clenched . . . . . 72 T&C SON REAL 3   6

stand. I think i too have known autumn too . . . . 80 T&C SON UNRE 5   3

too have known autumn too long (and what have . . . . 80 T&C SON UNRE 5   4

beach has been used too. much Too. originally spontaneous . . 94 & POST IMPR 6   1

been used too. much Too. originally spontaneous . . . . . . 94 & POST IMPR 6   1

hideous vegetaBles weasOned with-be- ing-put-too-long in . . 101 & POST IMPR 11   66

carved upon her much too white forehead a pair . . . . . . 116 & PORTRAIT 9   10

of the well it's too cool to be crooked . . . . 126 & SEVEN POEMS 5   3

be crooked and it's too firm to be hard . . . . 126 & SEVEN POEMS 5   3

the morning dead's clever too like POF goes the . . . . . . 126 & SEVEN POEMS 5   10

unclenches into fingers.... she too is tired. Not of . . . . 131 & SON REAL 2   12

the smile's two eyes.... too, since the world's but . . . . 141 & SON REAL 12   5

sake) in the not too frail lips almost discussed; . . . . . 146 & SON REAL 17   12

thought of you somewhat too much and am become . . . . . . 157 & SON ACTU 6   1

and shiny and not too wide dear god there's . . . . 198 XLI PORTRAIT 6   5

froth half-mud and not too sweet? / / / . . . . 198 XLI PORTRAIT 6   34

step, yet somewhat proudly too-- are they not ladies, ... 211 XLI SONNETS 7   9

& Cleopatra were Just Too Lovely, The Snail's On . . . . . . 230 IS 5 ONE 2   27

now her mouth opens too far and: she attacks . . . . 243 IS 5 ONE 14   12

lie down i cough too much). How did the . . . . 245 IS 5 ONE 16   11

deeply bulging thousands i too omit one kelly in . . . . . . 259 IS 5 ONE 29   19

drawn icecakes beheld being too strong, in brief : . . . . . 262 IS 5 ONE 32   12

his umbrella. It seemed too beautiful. Let us perhaps . . . 263 IS 5 ONE 32   58

or move. It's different too isn't it different dear . . . . 289 IS 5 FOUR 6   17

to snare the glance too shy--if through my singing . . . . . 306 IS 5 FIVE 5   6

to see; and Olaf, too preponderatingly because unless . . . . 339 VIVA 30   39

whose swir -ling (not too frequently) skirt exhumes . . . . 341 VIVA 32   13

		PAGE	TITLE	LINE

TOO (CONTINUED)
shelf everybody guessed was too high look (it's back   . . . . 353 VIVA 44   21
touch because they are too near your slightest look . . . . . 366 VIVA 57   4
gal or pal slightly too sick to rightly die)   . . . . 387 NO THANKS 4   6
go said he not too far said she what's   . . . . 399 NO THANKS 16   10
far said she what's too far said he where . . . . 399 NO THANKS 16   11
bitch whispers jill mopping too bad dear sh not . . . . 496 50 POEMS 10   17
a thing who's much too busy being her beautiful . . . . 504 50 POEMS 18   12
to nouns wan wan too nons too and and . . . . 508 50 POEMS 22   4
wan wan too nons too and and nuns two . . . . 508 50 POEMS 22   4
tomorrow will not be too late worms are the . . . . 511 50 POEMS 25   21
hands machine no good too quick i know this . . . . 523 50 POEMS 36   11
you pay a store too much yes what too . . . . 523 50 POEMS 36   13
too much yes what too much o much cheap . . . . 523 50 POEMS 36   15
this cheap this suit too quick no suit there   . . . . 523 50 POEMS 36   22
any world is much too not quite big enough   . . . . 523 50 POEMS 36   31
a peopleshaped toomany-ness far too and will it tell   . . . . 528 50 POEMS 40   1
do? a notalive undead too-nearishness and shall we cry   . . . 528 50 POEMS 40   5
what he is much too busy sitting the horse   . . . . 545 1 X 1 5   15
devil and his angels too yes, sir what may   . . . . 568 1 X 1 28   19
that all history is too small for even me;   . . . . 579 1 X 1 39   7
me and you, exceedingly too small. Swoop (shrill collective . 579 1 X 1 39   8
obsolete almost that phenomenon (too gay for malice and   . . . 607 (CHAIRE) 9   12
gay for malice and too wise for fear) of   . . . . 607 (CHAIRE) 9   12
much and much is too if the green robe   . . . . 614 (CHAIRE) 16   9
nons- elf 's unself too -thf- ully lee -r-   . . . . 704 95 POEMS 32   4
asked would it hurt too much and 'twas me . . . .°. . 707 95 POEMS 35   24
why as i'm (almost too small for death's because   . . . . . . 735 95 POEMS 63   2
i'm a why (almost too small for dying's huge   . . . . 735 95 POEMS 63   10
+TOO
FOR CONTEXT, SEE   . . . . 465 NEW POEMS 3   11
TOO-NEARISHNESS
do? a notalive undead too-nearishness and shall we cry   . . . 528 50 POEMS 40   5
TOOK
alive and number two took up the song, might   . . . . 117 & PORTRAIT 10   15
difficulty sardines. Mr. Wiggin took Wrs. Miggin's harm in . 263 IS 5 ONE 32   48
westpointer most succinctly bred) took erring Olaf soon in . 339 VIVA 30   6
a fire is cool took bedfellows for moons mountains   . . . . . 420 NO THANKS 37   12
these not existing minds took life such life could . . . . . 510 50 POEMS 24   5
him a desdemonial that took his breath away all . . . . 552 1 X 1 12   20
it, no sir) it took a nipponized bit of . . . . 553 1 X 1 13   20
to invent everything he took one breath bigger than . . . . . 566 1 X 1 26   2
like a flame blue took it my far beyond . . . . 593 1 X 1 53   13
high beyond high bluer took it your but bluest   . . . . 593 1 X 1 53   16
it your but bluest took it our away beyond   . . . . 593 1 X 1 53   17
so of course dominic took him home & mrs   . . . . 680 95 POEMS 8   11
tell right from wrong, took brother Fearless by the . . . . . 799 73 POEMS 27   14
TOOKED
E. McKinley when Buch tooked out his C.O.D. Abe . . . . 321 VIVA 13   7
TOOL
Jab: of a dark tool. With a cleverjeRk in . . . . 101 & POST IMPR 11   50
of my corpse the tool her smile makes something . . . . 152 & SON ACTU 1   12
not to elevate your tool but drop a penny . . . . 500 50 POEMS 14   10
TOOLS
chipping with sharp fatal tools in an agony of   . . . . 199 XLI PORTRAIT 7   4
lay eyes like new tools) whence i guessed that   . . . . 355 VIVA 46   11
TOOMANY
/ / a peopleshaped toomany-ness far too and will   . . . . . . 528 50 POEMS 40   1
TOOMANY-NESS
/ / a peopleshaped toomany-ness far too and will   . . . . . . 528 50 POEMS 40   1
TOOTH
flesh crisp set my love-tooth on edge. So until . . . . 173 & SON ACTU 22   11
aid of an exclamatory tooth-pick And who may that . . . . . . 194 XLI PORTRAIT 2   27
extremity of one immense tooth myself surveys safely the   . . 201 XLI PORTRAIT 9   31
four teeth for a tooth (and the wholly babble . . . . 635 (CHAIRE) 37   18
TOOTH-PICK
aid of an exclamatory tooth-pick And who may that . . . . . . 194 XLI PORTRAIT 2   27

	PAGE	TITLE	LINE

+TOOTHFULLY
  FOR CONTEXT, SEE . . . . 704 95 POEMS 32   4
TOOTHLESS
  week with a big toothless girl in Yonkers. Dick . . . . 149 & SON REAL 20   12
  of incredible dodderingly godly toothless ◇ ◇ bipeds) OH . 250 IS 5 ONE 21   12
TOOTHPICK
  ort 2 be nt toothpick s) ro ude stly . . . . 408 NO THANKS 25   12
TOOTHSOME
  people 's future is toothsome like (they got pockets . . . . 314 VIVA 6   8
TOP
  am i doing on top of this hill at . . . . 281 IS 5 THREE 5   2
  returns fasterishly whipped the top leaps bounding upon other 311 VIVA 3   6
  almost live at the top of these stairs, there's . . . . 365 VIVA 56   7
  avenue el; in the top of his head: to . . . . 553 1 X 1 13   24
  sitting pretty on the top of notwithstanding with his . . . . 642 {CHAIRE} 44   25
  round face near the top of the stairs speaks . . . . 813 73 POEMS 41   1
+TOP
  FOR CONTEXT, SEE . . . . 101 & POST IMPR 11   47
  FOR CONTEXT, SEE . . . . 399 NO THANKS 16   25
TOPEKA
  that knew Eddie in Topeka, went clean daffy, and . . . . . . 145 & SON REAL 16   7
TOPPED
  effort while hungering churches (topped with effigies of . . 340 VIVA 31   16
  pillar of youngly loveflesh topped with danc ing egghead . . 615 {CHAIRE} 17   2
TOPPLE
  him why gluey grins topple together eyes pout ges- . . . . . 96 & POST IMPR 8   17
  or a slogan may topple you*(trees are their . . . . 732 95 POEMS 60   2
TOPPLES
  lownecked dress a little topples and slightly expands one . . 225 IS 5 ONE LIZ   2
TOPS
  leaps bounding upon other tops to caroming off persist . . . 311 VIVA 3   6
TORCHES
  hands scimitars like windy torches each is blacker than . . . 33 T&C ORIENTALE 6   39
TORE
  six exactly the alarm tore two slits in her . . . . 132 & SON REAL 3   12
  and broke oceans and tore mountains from their sockets . . . 432 NO THANKS 49   16
TORN
  with sudden silver these torn pockets of lame and . . . . . . 93 & POST IMPR 5   15
  uto f) mor e torn (f og r e . . . . 423 NO THANKS 40   14
  & mended his bright torn trousers (quite as if . . . . . . 680 95 POEMS 8   16
TORSE
  the arse before the torse / / / / . . . . 477 NEW POEMS 15   10
  nibbles his ton of torse squirms a pool of . . . . 545 1 X 1 5   5
+TORSO
  FOR CONTEXT, SEE . . . . 477 NEW POEMS 15   10
TORTURE
  heart prospecting darkness roams torture my spirit with the . 79 T&C SON UNRE 4   5
TORTURED
  heaven's intolerable athanor inimitably tortured the base day   6 T&C EPITHALAM   130
  writhe and gape of tortured perspective rasp and graze . . . 48 T&C IMPRESS 2   2
  magnificent clamor of day tortured in gold, which presently . 188 XLI SONGS 10   7
  and being here imprisoned, tortured here love everywhere . . 377 VIVA 68   7
TORTURES
  It The L's roar tortures-pleasantly myears it is, like . . . 101 & POST IMPR 11   49
TORTURES-PLEASANTLY
  It The L's roar tortures-pleasantly myears it is, like . . . 101 & POST IMPR 11   49
TOSS
  queer monkey (if you toss him a coin he . . . . 69 T&C POST IMPR 6   10
  body these men's fingers toss trunks shuffle sacks spin . . . 114 & PORTRAIT 7   7
  you might as well toss him a few thoughts . . . . 298 IS 5 FOUR 15   14
  up the world: & toss it away; or cause . . . . 433 NO THANKS 50   2
  clutch between eyes emptiness toss one at nobody shoulder . . 522 50 POEMS 35   2
  as deity or devil --toss in sobs and reasons . . . . 804 73 POEMS 32   6
TOSSED
  I was whirled and tossed into delicious dancing up . . . . . 44 T&C AMORES 8   12
TOSSES
  / / / ◇ tosses like thin bums dream . . . . 469 NEW POEMS 7   2
  into (big with unthings) tosses hello whirling whose rhyme . 751 95 POEMS 79   4

802

	PAGE	TITLE	LINE

TOSSING
on insulated brows (while tossing boms at uncle toms) . . . . 500 50 POEMS 14   15

TOTAL
much more is or total sun oceaning than any . . . . 502 50 POEMS 16   3
and was are night's total exploding millionminded Who / . . . 633 (CHAIRE) 35   16
/ / / a total stranger one black day . . . . 730 95 POEMS 58   1
no matter who, some total (preferably blonde of course) . . . 779 73 POEMS 7   5

TOTALLY
of tiniest forever--crazily from totally sprouted by alive . 480 NEW POEMS 18   23

TOTOUCH
g S uddenl Y totouch the curvedship of Her- . . . . 122 & SEVEN POEMS 1   6

TOTTER
large four gnarled lips totter Therefore, approaching my . . 255 IS 5 ONE 26   4

TOTTERED
gashing yellow yawn and tottered to a glass bumping . . . . . 132 & SON REAL 3   16

TOTTERING
i reined them in tottering before the throne and . . . . . . 30 T&C ORIENTALE 4   37
are dancing slowly are tottering up and down in . . . . . . 69 T&C POST IMPR 6   26
e n derl y tottering in sun-light THE nobody . . . . 101 & POST IMPR 11   78
kissed breast awake) slow tottering visions bigly come . . . 565 1 X 1 25   13

+TOTTERISH
FOR CONTEXT, SEE . . . . 495 50 POEMS 9   16

TOTTERS
wears velour trousers life totters, life has a beard" . . . . 102 & POST IMPR 12   9
to the kanoon she totters, slouches, with giggling hips . . . 143 & SON REAL 14   13
not care if time totters, light droops, all measures . . . . 446 NO THANKS 61   6

+TOTTERS
FOR CONTEXT, SEE . . . . 104 & POST IMPR 14   16

TOUCH
that reverently bent to touch the yellow wonder of . . . . . 8 T&C OF NICOL   32
such mysteries very simply touch me, whose heart-wholeness . 12 T&C SONGS 2   37
grass their wings will touch with her face and . . . . . . 16 T&C SONGS 6   12
there is one; to touch it is the fear . . . . 23 T&C PUELLA MEA   274
with elaborate fingers possibly touch the pink hollyhock . . 58 T&C PORTRAIT 6   16
prostitute. ducking always the touch of must and shall, . . . 74 T&C SON REAL 5   2
i have loved, should touch another's, and your dear . . . . . 76 T&C SON UNRE 1   2
"Yes" "why do you touch flowers as if they . . . . 91 & POST IMPR 3   8
i felt a mountain touch me where i stood . . . . 135 & SON REAL 6   11
the (i do but touch you) timid lewd moon . . . . 155 & SON ACTU 4   16
just not each other touch) seeking, some street which . . . . 174 & SON ACTU 23   5
brain irrevocably frigid to touch a merest shape which . . . 193 XLI PORTRAIT 1   15
of irrevocable nothing which touch and taste and smell . . . 199 XLI PORTRAIT 7   2
dawn loves most to touch wishing by willows, bending . . . . 211 XLI SONNETS 7   17
fooled the doctors, i touch you with hopes and . . . . 289 IS 5 FOUR 6   15
we everywhere do not touch) deep things; remembering ever . . 294 IS 5 FOUR 11   5
wiggles in considerable twilight touch (now) with a suddenly 302 IS 5 FIVE 1   5
strutting (very jerkily) not toucH- ing because separated by 335 VIVA 26   12
ing of just bells (touch) ing ? mind (moon . . . . 350 VIVA 41   8
(have you a wish?) touch me, before we perish . . . . 357 VIVA 48   3
or which i cannot touch because they are too . . . . 366 VIVA 57   4
/ i (meet) t (touch) ems crouch (lunge . . . . 388 NO THANKS 5   2
said she (may i touch said he how much . . . . 399 NO THANKS 16   5
ing) fall ing through touch less stillness (seized among . . 432 NO THANKS 49   9
slenderly i win (like touch all stars or to . . . . 433 NO THANKS 50   11
un der fog 's touch slo ings fin gering . . . . 463 NEW POEMS 1   4
climb their eyes to touch his dream / / . . . . 517 50 POEMS 31   14
first who, his april touch drove sleeping selves to . . . . 520 50 POEMS 34   10
who) descend -ing (mercifully) touch deathful earth's any . . 557 1 X 1 17   9
our most are selves) touch: forever (and so to . . . . 564 1 X 1 24   15
never and never into (touch me! love) forever --until . . . . 633 (CHAIRE) 35   14
out your eyes, and touch the black skin of . . . . 639 (CHAIRE) 41   13
feel and soul may touch --the great (my darling) . . . . . . 664 (CHAIRE) 66   4
shall never discover our touch and feel --for love . . . . . 664 (CHAIRE) 66   15
forever's long let beauty touch a blunder (called life) . . . 742 95 POEMS 70   13
of silence) and forever touch or until she and . . . . . . 758 95 POEMS 85   42
misers are poor) --let's touch the sky: with a . . . . 769 95 POEMS 95   5
is the year) --let's touch the sky: with a . . . . 769 95 POEMS 95   12
most by more) --let's touch the sky: with a . . . . 769 95 POEMS 95   19

TOUCH (CONTINUED)
    and as you're --let's touch the sky: with a . . . . 769 95 POEMS 95   26
    i) be care ful (touch noth ing) or it'll . . . . 797 73 POEMS 25   5
+TOUCH
    FOR CONTEXT, SEE . . . . 122 & SEVEN POEMS 1   6
    FOR CONTEXT, SEE . . . . 361 VIVA 52   12
TOUCHABLY
    night her trillion secrets touchably alive --while and all . 809 73 POEMS 37   4
TOUCHED
    say Perhaps her body touched me; and to face . . . . 82 T&C SON ACTU 1   14
    you feel when they touched you (but that's not . . . . . . 127 & SEVEN POEMS 5   38
    men feel when, you touched, them dead's sorry like . . . . 127 & SEVEN POEMS 5   40
    of Divinity avenue i touched the accelerator and give . . . 248 IS 5 ONE 19   22
    into my window it touched me with its small . . . . 284 IS 5 FOUR 1   2
    propagated when Miss G touched n.y. our skeleton stepped . 326 VIVA 18   10
    things whose slendering sweetness touched renown) suddenly . 414 NO THANKS 31   4
    so much tasted plus touched quite so And How . . . . 474 NEW POEMS 12   8
    rolled behind forever, we touched a shy animal called . . . . 612 (CHAIRE) 14   9
    / / / if (touched by love's own secret) . . . . 659 (CHAIRE) 61   1
TOUCHES
    moves) at sunset and who--touches--the hills without any . . 91 & POST IMPR 3   4
    a green dress, who; touches: the fields (at sunset) . . . . . 91 & POST IMPR 3   20
    white damn Whom it touches / / / / . . . . 328 VIVA 19   23
    dark places paints eyes touches hands with new- ness . . . . 437 NO THANKS 53   5
    flaming a coolly bell touches most mere until (eternally) . . 601 (CHAIRE) 3   14
TOUCHING
    of my dreams justly touching roses their fingers whitely . . 211 XLI SONNETS 7   11
    just outside this window, touching the glass boxes one . . . 282 IS 5 THREE 6   25
    / / / / touching you i say (it . . . . 303 IS 5 FIVE 2   1
    / / / our touching hearts slenderly comprehend (clinging . . 305 IS 5 FIVE 4   1
    i spirally understand What touching means or What does . . . 356 VIVA 47   20
    myself as Spring opens (touching skilfully, mysteriously) her 366 VIVA 57   8
    are (behind each no) touching every yes / / . . . . 373 VIVA 64   18
    earth) how should tasting touching hearing seeing breathing . 663 (CHAIRE) 65   9
+TOUCHING
    FOR CONTEXT, SEE . . . . 314 VIVA 6   17
    FOR CONTEXT, SEE . . . . 314 VIVA 6   18
TOUGH
    before one the vague tough exquisite flowers, whom hardens . 154 & SON ACTU 3   7
TOUJOURS
    femmes exactes qui dansent toujours in my head dis-donc, . . 121 & PORTRAIT 12   51
TOUS
    cheri? les anglais m'aiment tous, les americains aussi.... . 120 & PORTRAIT 12   13
TOUSLE
    slid steps parting the tousle of saxophonic brogue. / . . . . 140 & SON REAL 11   15
TOUT
    algebraic odour jigs et tout en face always wiggles . . . . . 134 & SON REAL 5   10
TOUTES
    joujoux, want nice sleep? toutes les petites femmes exactes . 121 & PORTRAIT 12   50
TOWARD
    whose scrupulous enchanted fronds toward all things intrinsic 19 T&C PUELLA MEA   112
    a booming smell waddles toward, me, dressed like a . . . . . 94 & POST IMPR 6   15
    fifteen. Then she came toward him on her knees . . . . 145 & SON REAL 16   3
    renewal my body turns toward thee again for the . . . . 184 XLI SONGS 6   8
    her body will come toward me with its hurting . . . . 214 XLI SONNETS 10   11
    (and drawing thy mouth toward my mouth, steer our . . . . . . 215 XLI SONNETS 11   16
    my youth has travelled toward her these years or . . . . . . 216 XLI SONNETS 12   4
    and Enters this church. toward which The Expectant stutter . 280 IS 5 THREE 4   32
    out of the east toward her a fragile light . . . . 284 IS 5 FOUR 1   17
    hands moves) why then toward morning he is a . . . . 299 IS 5 FOUR 16   11
    i note how fatally toward twilight the a little . . . . 345 VIVA 36   4
    time lessness; quietly turning toward me the guessable . . . 370 VIVA 61   9
    your (how luminous) life toward twilight will dissolve . . . 379 VIVA 70   11
    in sunset or thrushes toward dusk among whippoorwills or . . 512 50 POEMS 26   25
    resistless metal: and (stealing toward the blissful pair) . . 799 73 POEMS 27   20
+TOWARD
    FOR CONTEXT, SEE . . . . 385 NO THANKS 2   61

	PAGE	TITLE	LINE
TOWER			
of the steep unspeaking tower within whose brightening . . .	4	T&C EPITHALAM	50
so one high shining tower (which as a glass	8	T&C OF NICOL	17
from the shocked impossible tower i caught you strained . . .	30	T&C ORIENTALE 4	26
a magic, a discrete tower of magic and (as	83	T&C SON ACTU 2	10
fleet He'll not my tower, laborious, casual where the	83	T&C SON ACTU 2	13
TOWERFUL			
are mountains rivery forests towerful towns (queen poet king	586	1 X 1 46	8
+TOWERING			
FOR CONTEXT, SEE	351	VIVA 42	3
TOWERS			
night blossoming in white towers to the moon, soft	8	T&C OF NICOL	3
multitudes out of final towers; captured: in the narrow . . .	345	VIVA 36	8
TOWN			
offense to you, white town whose spires softly dare.	86	T&C SON ACTU 5	4
orange in the slowly. town, night featherly swifts the . . .	89	& POST IMPR 1	2
and colours of a town-- that i have perhaps	297	IS 5 FOUR 14	7
distance from the crooked town) a harbour fools the	319	VIVA 11	17
believes fragrance of a town (whose dormers choke and	340	VIVA 31	2
came slowly over the town / / / /	355	VIVA 46	21
have all come to town some like it shot	497	50 POEMS 11	4
that here was a town (and the town is	505	50 POEMS 19	3
a town (and the town is so aged the	505	50 POEMS 19	3
in a pretty how town (with up so floating	515	50 POEMS 29	1
i am wandering a town (if its houses turning	720	95 POEMS 48	1
+TOWN			
FOR CONTEXT, SEE	371	VIVA 62	8
FOR CONTEXT, SEE	681	95 POEMS 9	15
TOWNS			
IMPRESSIONS beyond the brittle towns asleep i look where . .	64	T&C POST IMPR 1	1
/ / mOOn Over tOwns mOOn whisper less creature	383	NO THANKS 1	1
THE MooN o VER ToWNS SLoWLY SPRoUTING SPIR IT	383	NO THANKS 1	10
mountains rivery forests towerful towns (queen poet king . .	586	1 X 1 46	8
TOY			
the slender paramour to toy with thy extraordinary lust, . .	3	T&C EPITHALAM	4
and floats like a toy on the end of	69	T&C POST IMPR 6	43
flesh like an old toy balloon) heavily swims to	219	XLI SONNETS 15	12
explO ded like a toy eloping to Ire (land	320	VIVA 12	12
being to enter a Toy and emerging (believably enlarged) . . .	337	VIVA 28	2
TOYLIKE			
the horror of her toylike head and vainly tried	53	T&C PORTRAIT 1	40
it, in his little toylike hand) and then he	69	T&C POST IMPR 6	18
TOYS			
and softly into irresponsible toys.) when this man with . . .	62	T&C PORTRAIT 10	22
and around the irresponsible toys circle wildly in the . . .	63	T&C PORTRAIT 10	30
(peers: body of aching toys in unsmooth sexual luminosity . .	159	& SON ACTU 8	12
....and little-dusk has his toys to play with ◇	169	& SON ACTU 18	9
grave) with all his toys (money men motors "my"	394	NO THANKS 11	3
wound up such pretty toys as themselves could not	451	NO THANKS 66	9
clutching their dolls wallow toys playing writhe with toys .	565	1 X 1 25	6
toys playing writhe with toys (than are all unworlds	565	1 X 1 25	6
TOYTOWN			
its invisibly skil ful toyTown which upups to dowNdown . . .	371	VIVA 62	8
TP			
forge with Sitting Bull's T.P. and the duckbilled platitude .	321	VIVA 13	14
TRACE			
light) only to trace with stiffening slow shrill	155	& SON ACTU 4	7
TRACKING			
an alert clumsily foolishwise (tracking the beast Tomorrow by	374	VIVA 65	7
+TRADESMEN			
FOR CONTEXT, SEE	405	NO THANKS 22	1
TRAFFIC			
inga ro undMe the traffic of lovely; muscles-sinke x	122	& SEVEN POEMS 1	3
limousine oozes in fashionable traffic, just a halfsmile (for	146	& SON REAL 17	10
much). How did the traffic get so jammed? bedad	245	IS 5 ONE 16	12
thumblike into pie is traffic this recalls hat gestures . . .	330	VIVA 21	6
red (the roar of traffic collapses: through west ninth . . .	800	73 POEMS 28	18

TRAFFICING
    sits hideously upon the trafficing hum of dusk each . . . . . 168 & SON ACTU 17   2
TRAGIC
    friends and foes my tragic tale concludes herewith: soldier, 799 73 POEMS 27   40
TRAIN
    waiting for the next train to grind me into . . . . 262 IS 5 ONE 32   3
    rail before the really train after all arrived. If . . . . . 263 IS 5 ONE 32   63
    door golf slam bridge train shriek chewing whistles hugest . 309 VIVA 1   18
    day) let's take the train for because dear whispered . . . . 316 VIVA 8   2
TRAIPSE
    trickling chins began to traipse into the cheeks "eet . . . . 73 T&C SON REAL 4   11
TRAITOR
    immeasurable fate) coward, clown, traitor, idiot, dreamer, . 562 1 X 1 22   9
TRAMP
    led by a Jumpy Tramp who played each card . . . . 194 XLI PORTRAIT 2   22
TRAMPLE
    together- ly singing ams trample (they flyingly silence / . . 482 NEW POEMS 20   12
TRAMPLED
    collapses singing knocked down trampled the kicked by flics . 274 IS 5 TWO 9   7
TRAMPLING
    upon a scarlet sunset trampling the night easily from . . . . 30 T&C ORIENTALE 4   24
TRANCE
    awakened from summer's green trance, would not adventure soon 675 95 POEMS 3   10
TRANCEWORLD
    an O of milky tranceworld writhes in twi nn . . . . 615 {CHAIRE} 17   17
TRANQUILLITIES
    us of our slow tranquillities and He without Whose . . . . . 210 XLI SONNETS 6   2
TRANSCENDS
    sweet strong final bird transcends the sight, O thou . . . . 7 T&C EPITHALAM   166
    spring; but april's day transcends november's year (eternity 765 95 POEMS 91   12
TRANSFERRED
    things newly which are transferred with dusk) wondering why . 428 NO THANKS 45   4
TRANSFIGURED
    and love from her transfigured face a queer pulp . . . . . . 55 T&C PORTRAIT 3   15
+TRANSFORMING
    FOR CONTEXT, SEE . . . . 343 VIVA 34   11
TRANSLATED
    can these moments be translated: i say that even . . . . . . 264 IS 5 ONE 33   6
TRANSLATION
    one tree, one svelte translation of eternity unto the . . . . 6 T&C EPITHALAM   123
TRANSPARENCY
    instant commits an impenetrable transparency. the harsh . . . 137 & SON REAL 8   12
    deaths Concentric geometries of transparency slightly joggled 311 VIVA 3   9
TRANSPARENT
    unease revealed of teasingly transparent folds-- with man's . 5 T&C EPITHALAM   95
    throughout that very proud transparent company of quivering . 6 T&C EPITHALAM   142
    of queens is more transparent than water, she is . . . . . . 33 T&C ORIENTALE 6   51
    self in) while a transparent blouse even recklessly juggles . 341 VIVA 32   18
    --and i perceive, within transparent walls how several . . . 376 VIVA 67   7
    because because because equals (transparent or science must . 478 NEW POEMS 16   3
+TRANSPARENT
    FOR CONTEXT, SEE . . . . 354 VIVA 45   18
TRANSPLENDENT
    automaton moon from the transplendent hand of sombre god . . 30 T&C ORIENTALE 4   40
TRANSPORTED
    what beneath breathing selves transported are into how . . . 454 NO THANKS 69   5
TRAPEZE
    swingthings of speeds of trapeze gush somersaults open ing . 536 50 POEMS 48   9
TRAPS
    unfools of unbeing set traps for his heart, lay . . . . 439 NO THANKS 55   17
TRATESMEN
    when muckers pimps and tratesmen delivered are of vicians . . 405 NO THANKS 22   1
TRAVEL
    be goes was) can travel this or i and . . . . 608 {CHAIRE} 10   12
TRAVELLED
    pleasant, my youth has travelled toward her these years . . . 216 XLI SONNETS 12   4
    be pitiful: because i've travelled all alone through the . . 216 XLI SONNETS 12   11
    somewhere i have never travelled, gladly beyond any . . . . . 366 VIVA 57   1

	PAGE	TITLE	LINE
TRAVELLER			
guest of merely me --traveller from eternity; in a	651	{CHAIRE} 53	2
TRAVELLING			
of quite unmitigated hate (travelling in a futile groove . .	413	NO THANKS 30	15
TRAVELS			
rapidly a reddish ant travels my fifth finger. a	281	IS 5 THREE 5	11
TREACHEROUS			
shunning the sudden moonbeam's treacherous snare she sought .	8	T&C OF NICOL	25
/ along the brittle treacherous bright streets of memory . .	304	IS 5 FIVE 3	1
TREAD			
shall pass. Our feet tread sleepless meadows sweet with . . .	9	T&C SONGS 1	27
the keen ecstatic actual tread (and thereto perfectly	19	T&C PUELLA MEA	125
accurate saints thickly which tread the serene nervous light	85	T&C SON ACTU 4	1
her heroes, sounds the tread of those vast armies	209	XLI SONNETS 5	2
TREADWATERING			
conway 's unstreet with treadwatering nonlegs (strictly) . .	616	{CHAIRE} 18	15
TREASURE			
weather (not either) my treasure, when violets appear love .	578	1 X 1 38	7
i'll give you a treasure of tiniest world a	586	1 X 1 46	2
a now of your treasure blithe each shameless blithe	763	95 POEMS 90	36
TREASURES			
one immaculate curving cool treasures of silence (slenderly .	156	& SON ACTU 5	4
all selfsubtracting hugely doom treasures of reeking	843	73 POEMS 71	8
TREE			
into silence, only one tree, one svelte translation of . . .	6	T&C EPITHALAM	122
eye shall sprout a tree fruit that dangles therefrom	16	T&C SONGS 6	2
a supple and young tree, her slim lascivious arms	20	T&C PUELLA MEA	156
flesh is an enchanted tree; with her lips' most	22	T&C PUELLA MEA	232
and hid in a tree of tall marble from	30	T&C ORIENTALE 4	20
going to utter a tree, Nobody shall stop me	67	T&C POST IMPR 4	1
dollar up into the tree? I didn't said the	125	& SEVEN POEMS 4	2
ripe melon into the tree? you got me said	125	& SEVEN POEMS 4	8
of violets into the tree? I dunno said the	125	& SEVEN POEMS 4	15
with blend ing the tree leaps a stiffened exquisite	182	XLI SONGS 4	7
/ / / little tree little silent Christmas tree	192	XLI CHANSONS 2	1
tree little silent Christmas tree you are so little	192	XLI CHANSONS 2	2
up at our beautiful tree we'll dance and sing	192	XLI CHANSONS 2	26
bird chirps in a tree, somewhere nowhere and a	281	IS 5 THREE 5	12
"duh Swede rolls down tree flights an Sam begins	332	VIVA 23	8
how at the yearhour tree- spires shout appalling deathmoney .	346	VIVA 37	14
things half daemon half tree among sunset dream acute	362	VIVA 53	7
-like finger of the tree / / /	480	NEW POEMS 18	27
open could that every tree or than all life	502	50 POEMS 16	7
do --time is a tree (this life one leaf)	511	50 POEMS 25	26
dusk among whippoorwills or tree field rock hollyhock forest	512	50 POEMS 26	26
when by now and tree by leaf she laughed	515	50 POEMS 29	13
leaf out of each tree (and every child was	521	50 POEMS 34	50
if a lit tle tree listens forever to always	525	50 POEMS 37	20
/ (sitting in a tree-) o small you sitting	535	50 POEMS 47	1
you sitting in a tree- sitting in a treetop	535	50 POEMS 47	3
leaf is wing and tree is voice more leastfully	583	1 X 1 43	19
of yes) not a tree can count his leaves	591	1 X 1 51	17
is a leaf so tree is a bough (and	594	1 X 1 54	19
un der a particular tree are all breathing bright	600	{CHAIRE} 2	7
the fingers of this tree (darling) have hands, and	667	{CHAIRE} 69	1
out of some dreaming tree (and how i'll stand	752	95 POEMS 80	2
snow moon dream wing tree leaf bird sun &	753	95 POEMS 81	16
bird singing in a tree, who never sings the	760	95 POEMS 87	2
evolving vision dreamtree, truthtree tree of jubilee: with .	763	95 POEMS 90	32
the sky of a tree called life; which grows	766	95 POEMS 92	12
dance you suddenly blossoming tree --i'll sing / /	767	95 POEMS 93	23
of that this and tree illimitably try to seize	822	73 POEMS 50	4
under are this wonderful tree smiling stand (all realms . . .	832	73 POEMS 60	4
+TREE			
FOR CONTEXT, SEE	632	{CHAIRE} 34	15
FOR CONTEXT, SEE	763	95 POEMS 90	1
FOR CONTEXT, SEE	763	95 POEMS 90	1
FOR CONTEXT, SEE	763	95 POEMS 90	31

	PAGE	TITLE	LINE
+TREE (CONTINUED)			
FOR CONTEXT, SEE	763	95 POEMS 90	31
FOR CONTEXT, SEE	764	95 POEMS 90	49
TREEBODIES			
writhe lurch faceflowers stutter treebodies wobbly- ing thing	436	NO THANKS 52	10
TREES			
continuous intercourse--through skies and trees the lilac's .	5	T&C EPITHALAM	91
possible nearaway from huge trees drenched by a rounding . .	10	T&C SONGS 1	45
thy legs are the trees of dreaming whose fruit	29	T&C ORIENTALE 3	22
the grass collides with trees and houses and finally, ...	47	T&C IMPRESS 1	9
earth and all the trees are put on edge	61	T&C PORTRAIT 9	21
leaves away, and the trees stand. I think i	80	T&C SON UNRE 5	3
the sky and the trees stand: the trees stand.	80	T&C SON UNRE 5	15
the trees stand: the trees stand. The trees, suddenly	80	T&C SON UNRE 5	16
the trees stand. The trees, suddenly wait against the	80	T&C SON UNRE 5	16
on whoseswooning edge black trees think (hear little knives .	99	& POST IMPR 10	11
chairs wait under the trees Fields slowly Elysian in	104	& POST IMPR 14	13
rin g from Hideous trees or Maybe Mandolins 1	122	& SEVEN POEMS 1	12
stands but as the trees, lay, which grow /	154	& SON ACTU 3	16
drea-mingly Is (not- quite trees hugging with the rash, . . .	155	& SON ACTU 4	5
without thinking under honest trees, a stream does. the . . .	160	& SON ACTU 9	2
of stark Picasso throttling trees hither my soul repairs . .	180	XLI SONGS 2	7
finished in the nobler trees and the language of	184	XLI SONGS 6	11
only chops hugest inherent Trees of Ego, from whose	195	XLI PORTRAIT 3	19
to stir, of thoughtful trees whom night hath pondered	205	XLI SONNETS 1	11
do complain earth's ghastlier trees by whom Time measured . .	207	XLI SONNETS 3	2
among the slow deep trees perpetual of sleep some	208	XLI SONNETS 4	13
/ / will suddenly trees leap from winter and	218	XLI SONNETS 14	1
and these (i notice) trees winterbrief surly old gurgle . . .	282	IS 5 THREE 6	11
a kite in the trees, here and here reflecting	283	IS 5 THREE 7	11
as i have seen trees (in whose black bod	354	VIVA 45	26
thousand thrusts squirms stars Trees, swift each with its . .	356	VIVA 47	8
then dearest the way trees are Made leaves open	359	VIVA 50	11
welcome the year and trees dance (and i guess	372	VIVA 63	14
o) greenthatpink) acrobata mong trees climbing on A pi . . .	385	NO THANKS 2	46
hills. listen. ,not, alive, trees, dream(ev: ery: wheres: .	416	NO THANKS 33	2
those skeletons of these trees) when sunbeams loot furnished	442	NO THANKS 57	9
born--pity poor flesh and trees, poor stars and stones, . . .	554	1 X 1 14	11
are mountains, roots are trees, it's they shall cry	560	1 X 1 20	15
Hills jump with brooks: trees tumble out of twigs	580	1 X 1 40	28
/ / / / trees were in (give give)	589	1 X 1 49	1
darling birds are in (trees are in) song when	589	1 X 1 49	16
leaping greenly spirits of trees and a blue true	663	{CHAIRE} 65	2
no you: and all trees are (any more than	667	{CHAIRE} 69	11
(stroll more slowly than trees) dodreamingly phantoms	681	95 POEMS 9	4
slogan may topple you (trees are their roots and	732	95 POEMS 60	3
leaves with all their trees and by forests with	754	95 POEMS 82	14
and in earth sky trees : every where a	835	73 POEMS 63	22
+TREES			
FOR CONTEXT, SEE	99	& POST IMPR 10	14
FOR CONTEXT, SEE	487	50 POEMS 1	7
FOR CONTEXT, SEE	511	50 POEMS 25	8
TREESOF			
l in gof throughof treesOf. (Fields Elysian the like, ...	104	& POST IMPR 14	5
TREESOUL			
wisdoming friend's --a fingery treesoul onlying from serene .	517	50 POEMS 31	6
TREETOP			
tree- sitting in a treetop riding on a greenest	535	50 POEMS 47	4
TREE3GHOSTS			
lliw og-dog) life ? tree3ghosts are Is A eyes	628	{CHAIRE} 30	8
TREMBLE			
jabbed jerked with ecstasy ....tremble (not knowing how much	153	& SON ACTU 2	12
/ / let us tremble) a personal radiance sits	168	& SON ACTU 17	1
fingers and your arms tremble remembering something squirming	279	IS 5 THREE 3	22
sally and nan they tremble and cower so pale:	509	50 POEMS 23	17
TREMBLES			
brief gesture of twilight trembles the imagined galleon of .	156	& SON ACTU 5	9
whose erect blood finally trembles, emerging to perceive . .	435	NO THANKS 51	39

		PAGE	TITLE	LINE

TREMBLING
    and lays bare her trembling heart, with beads of . . . . . .   8 T&C OF NICOL   15
    failure uncouth discovers a trembling and smooth Unstrength,   11 T&C SONGS 2   8
    my heart smote in trembling thirds of anguish quivers . . . .   11 T&C SONGS 2   16
    flower so glad) as trembling used to yield with . . . .   18 T&C PUELLA MEA   53
    in whose dome the trembling bliss of a kingdom . . . .   21 T&C PUELLA MEA   205
    fragile intense, which wholly trembling memory undertakes . .   82 T&C SON ACTU 1   2
    mia "he kissed wholly trembling" or so thought the . . . . .   84 T&C SON ACTU 3   16
    its bones, and the trembling -firm-smooth ness and which . . 175 & SON ACTU 24   6
    certain flowers resemble but trembling (cowards which fear to 293 IS 5 FOUR 10   5
    my each how my trembling where my still unvisible . . . . . . 372 VIVA 63   5
    angel's fart came one trembling out of huge each . . . . . . 506 50 POEMS 20   12
    now or this (young trembling any) into flame twig . . . . . . 583 1 X 1 43   10
+TREMBLING
    FOR CONTEXT, SEE . . . . 248 IS 5 ONE 19   34
    FOR CONTEXT, SEE . . . . 838 73 POEMS 66   10
TREMBLY
    and down in a trembly mist of atrocious melody.... . . . . .   69 T&C POST IMPR 6   26
TREMENDOUS
    inconceivable embrace of whose tremendous hair that blossom .   6 T&C EPITHALAM   146
    rest --turning from the tremendous lie of sleep i . . . . . .   78 T&C SON UNRE 3   13
    thy counted petals O tremendous flower on whose huge . . . .   79 T&C SON UNRE 4   3
    than naught, feels the tremendous yonder for his own-- . . .   81 T&C SON UNRE 6   12
    hair genuinely artificial, unpleasantly tremendous. under . . 103 & POST IMPR 13   14
    only always into the tremendous canyon the , tremendous . . . 202 XLI PORTRAIT 9   43
    tremendous canyon the , tremendous canyon always only exhales 202 XLI PORTRAIT 9   44
    on permament and slap tremendous sorrydaze bog triperight . . 333 VIVA 24   13
    flowers rise out of tremendous darkness into air) / . . . . . 559 1 X 1 19   14
    gives me a most tremendous hug knowing i feel . . . . 680 95 POEMS 8   25
TREMENDOUSLY
    of Cleopatra while easily tremendously floats in the bright . 112 & PORTRAIT 6   73
TREMONT
    frighteningly performed and at tremont and bromfield i paused   52 T&C PORTRAIT 1   11
TREMULOUS
    Helios the sweet wheels tremulous-- are there no kings . . .   4 T&C EPITHALAM   48
    (which dressed in various tremulous armor stun the eyes . . .   4 T&C EPITHALAM   68
    night amorous of waters tremulous, blinded with silence the .   37 T&C AMORES 2   6
    inextinguishable, taught by thy tremulous grace bravely to . 206 XLI SONNETS 2   3
TRENO
    this noth ing il treno per Roma si-gnori? jerk. . . . . 278 IS 5 THREE 2   19
+TRESPASSING
    FOR CONTEXT, SEE . . . . 729 95 POEMS 57   9
TRIANGLE
    and can play the triangle like the devil) my . . . . 253 IS 5 ONE 24   3
TRIANGULAR
    / / blue the triangular why of a dream . . . . 668 (CHAIRE) 70   1
TRIBUNE
    all up over the tribune dances crazily & & . . . . 267 IS 5 TWO 2   5
TRICK
    tried to repeat a trick of syncopation Europe has . . . . . . 135 & SON REAL 6   10
    which by some loveless trick sepa rate one stilled . . . . . 354 VIVA 45   19
    and by that little trick or this he shot . . . . 360 VIVA 51   16
    no power beyond the trick to seem their joys . . . . 776 73 POEMS 4   24
    / / / the trick of finding what you . . . . 807 73 POEMS 35   1
TRICKIEST
    fallingest fool in this trickiest if? why i'm by . . . . . . 590 1 X 1 50   15
TRICKLE
    hapsingly proregress heandshe-ingly people trickle . . . . . 330 VIVA 21   3
TRICKLED
    nondescript genie of trunk trickled firm- ly in to . . . . .   96 & POST IMPR 8   33
TRICKLES
    1 someThing street and trickles carefully into the park . . .   62 T&C PORTRAIT 10   26
    some street which easily trickles a brittle fuss of . . . . . 174 & SON ACTU 23   6
TRICKLING
    Dick Mid's the three trickling chins began to traipse . . . .   73 T&C SON REAL 4   11
    in outrageous sabots language trickling pried his black mouth 277 IS 5 THREE 1   13
+TRICKLING
    FOR CONTEXT, SEE . . . . 464 NEW POEMS 2   7

	PAGE	TITLE	LINE
TRICKS			
she's up to some tricks with my bill as	707	95 POEMS 35	9
TRICKSTERVILLAIN			
(swimfloatdrifting fragment of heaven) trickstervillain . . .	677	95 POEMS 5	12
+TRICKTRICKCLICKFLICK			
Pic-abian tricktrickclickflick-er garnished	180	XLI SONGS 2	4
+TRICKTRICKCLICKFLICK-ER			
Pic-abian tricktrickclickflick-er garnished	180	XLI SONGS 2	4
TRICKY			
you didn't lose (existing's tricky: but to live's a	807	73 POEMS 35	2
TRIED			
toylike head and vainly tried to catch one funny	53	T&C PORTRAIT 1	42
in her fierce laziness tried to repeat a trick	135	& SON REAL 6	9
was back in neutral tried and again slo-wly; bare, ...	248	IS 5 ONE 19	14
(little child who have tried who have failed who	393	NO THANKS 10	8
how hard he never tried) the great pink superme	635	{CHAIRE} 37	6
TRIES			
the dress. one nipple tries. playfully to peek into	143	& SON REAL 14	9
tangoing (while a feller tries to hold down the	242	IS 5 ONE 13	7
TRIFLE			
her perhaps only A trifle less (merely beyond how	453	NO THANKS 68	5
+TRIFLE			
FOR CONTEXT, SEE	611	{CHAIRE} 13	5
TRIG			
object-or his wellbeloved colonel (trig westpointer most . .	339	VIVA 30	4
TRIGGER			
a finger pulls a trigger a bird flies into	338	VIVA 29	23
TRIGLYPH'S			
a metope now that triglyph's here) / / /	257	IS 5 ONE 27	40
TRILL			
of alive with a trill like until / /	587	1 X 1 47	23
TRILLERS			
gently O sweetly melancholy trillers amid the thrillers these	230	IS 5 ONE 2	25
TRILLION			
through a million billion trillion stars / / /	258	IS 5 ONE 28	24
of summer night her trillion secrets touchably alive --while	809	73 POEMS 37	4
TRILLIONTH			
silence) give me a trillionth part of inquisitive merrily . .	678	95 POEMS 6	13
TRILLIONWORLDED			
discoverably disappearing floats at trillionworlded the . . .	517	50 POEMS 31	4
TRINIGHTLY			
(but four) gentlemen are trinightly entertained by a whore .	312	VIVA 4	3
TRIPERIGHT			
slap tremendous sorrydaze bog triperight election who so . .	333	VIVA 24	14
TRIPLE			
sea(while emanating the triple starred Hotel du Golf... . .	319	VIVA 11	20
TRISTRAM			
throat the lips of Tristram slowly dote, La beale	17	T&C PUELLA MEA	36
TRITE			
into a clutter of trite jewels now like a	47	T&C IMPRESS 1	6
to exactly kiss the trite worm of her nakedness	164	& SON ACTU 13	4
intelligent thighs, the electric trite thighs; the hair . . .	173	& SON ACTU 22	14
particular Love surround your trite how terrible selfhood . .	522	50 POEMS 35	10
daisy in the Dust (trite now and old) lie	690	95 POEMS 18	3
TRIUMPHED			
when over hate has triumphed darkly love and the	213	XLI SONNETS 9	5
of mind; thus virtue triumphed over vice and beauty	799	73 POEMS 27	36
TRIUMPHS			
twilight surrounded by their triumphs and listen well how . .	111	& PORTRAIT 6	38
TRIVIAL			
(wrist performs a thundering trivial) it. y protuberant . . .	159	& SON ACTU 8	5
O scrupulously take thy trivial toll, for whose cool	212	XLI SONNETS 8	3
screech of Broadway, the trivial stink of rich frail	220	XLI SONNETS 16	3
photographed, measured; disdains the trivial labelling of . .	377	VIVA 68	11
(the silly cause of trivial which thinkless unwishing doth .	411	NO THANKS 28	3
jubilee: with aeons of (trivial merely) existence, all when .	763	95 POEMS 90	33
+TRIVIAL			
FOR CONTEXT, SEE	193	XLI PORTRAIT 1	19

		PAGE	TITLE	LINE

+TRIVIALITY
    FOR CONTEXT, SEE . . . . 159 & SON ACTU 8   5
TROD
    her whose feet have trod the silly souls of . . . . 75 T&C SON REAL 6   10
TROIS
    quickly Not un deux trois der die Stood (apparition.) . . . . 348 VIVA 39   12
TROLL
    (essNessUn rolli) ngl yS troll s (who leO v . . . . 347 VIVA 38   14
TROLLEY
    over swill; one butting trolley imposingly empty; snickering 172 & SON ACTU 21   5
TROP
    mon cheri; il fait trop froid"-- they are gone: . . . . 304 IS 5 FIVE 3   10
    veux Dwrith il est trop fort le negre esn7othingish8s . . . . 430 NO THANKS 47   20
TROUBADOURS
    the tune of tiny troubadours, and (phantom-white) . . . . . . 8 T&C OF NICOL   5
TROUBLE
    i should say goodmorning trouble adds up all sorts . . . . . 287 IS 5 FOUR 4   2
TROUBLED
    swam upward from the troubled heart of May; a . . . . 8 T&C OF NICOL   8
    and definite houses are troubled. A sharp blue day . . . . . 62 T&C PORTRAIT 10   7
    and definite houses are troubled. in the sunset their . . . . 62 T&C PORTRAIT 10   12
+TROUBLED
    FOR CONTEXT, SEE . . . . 9 T&C SONGS 1   11
TROUBLES
    she couldn't remember her troubles, and milly befriended a . 682 95 POEMS 10   4
TROUBLING
    lust like a high troubling ship upon the fragrant . . . . . . 112 & PORTRAIT 6   96
TROUSERFLY
    dirt while the mute trouserfly confessed a button solemnly . 258 IS 5 ONE 28   19
    much its misbutt- oned trouserfly tumbling, faded five or . . 607 (CHAIRE) 9   6
TROUSERS
    young life wears velour trousers life totters, life has . . . 102 & POST IMPR 12   8
    and unlike shirts neckties trousers we cannot wear it . . . . 238 IS 5 ONE 9   10
    physiognomy his scientifically pressed trousers ejaculate . . 259 IS 5 ONE 29   24
    inside one pair of trousers (which had died) / . . . . 473 NEW POEMS 11   6
    mended his bright torn trousers (quite as if he . . . . 680 95 POEMS 8   16
TROY
    dispute as prove from Troy (N.Y.) to Cairo (Egypt) . . . . . 266 IS 5 TWO 1   6
    (flesh is grass) from Troy, n.y. the way of . . . . 320 VIVA 12   3
TROYS
    would not all the Troys of Helen's beauty: never . . . . . . 18 T&C PUELLA MEA   67
TRUCK
    his ZOOM DOOM icecoalwood truck a wistful little clown . . . 680 95 POEMS 8   5
TRUDGES
    toboggans into know and trudges up to ignorance again: . . . 579 1 X 1 39   2
TRUDGING
    flame of neat huge trudging kiss moistly climbing hideously . 67 T&C POST IMPR 4   25
TRUE
    i have been sometimes true to Nothing and which . . . . 43 T&C AMORES 7   11
    admitting i have been true only to the noise . . . . 43 T&C AMORES 7   21
    mightest conceive gods (but true to the incomparable couch . 46 T&C LA GUERRE 2   20
    you shall hear the true story of Mr Do . . . . 236 IS 5 ONE 7   2
    may truth opening encompass true) while your contriving fate, 373 VIVA 64   16
    sweet (i feel that's true) / / / / . . . . 475 NEW POEMS 13   25
    (in his mercy) your true lover spare: for that . . . . 484 NEW POEMS 22   10
    his sorrow was as true as bread: no liar . . . . 521 50 POEMS 34   45
    completely kind mindheart one true one generous child- man . 523 50 POEMS 36   41
    through unstrange synthetic now true histories plunge? rains 527 50 POEMS 39   27
    one) life's only and true value neither is love . . . . . . 531 50 POEMS 43   7
    they (not false not true not you not i) . . . . 542 1 X 1 2   6
    a sun with blue true two man neral rise . . . . 567 1 X 1 27   4
    fresh with blue come true from a funeral eyes . . . . 567 1 X 1 27   20
    with pain You so&so true wars are never won . . . . 570 1 X 1 30   10
    humbly heights below) kneeling, we--true lovers--pray that us 574 1 X 1 34   11
    / / / / true lovers in each happening . . . . 576 1 X 1 36   1
    both disprove by proving true (all doubts, all certainties, . 576 1 X 1 36   4
    an everywhere, even more true would truest lovers grow . . . 576 1 X 1 36   11
    / life is more true than reason will deceive . . . . 592 1 X 1 52   1

	PAGE	TITLE	LINE

TRUE (CONTINUED)
```
a brave and a true of a who have  . . . . . . . . . . . . . .   606 (CHAIRE) 8        8
my unreal in -credible true each new self) smile. . . . . . .   612 (CHAIRE) 14       6
feel that (false and true are merely to know) . . . . . . . .   631 (CHAIRE) 33      13
the hell yes it's true that was me but  . . . . . . . . . . .   638 (CHAIRE) 40      10
trees and a blue true dream of sky; and . . . . . . . . . . .   663 (CHAIRE) 65       3
this man's heart is true to his earth; so . . . . . . . . . .   676 95 POEMS 4        2
truest things always are true because they can't be . . . . .   697 95 POEMS 25      32
because they can't be true / / / /  . . . . . . . . . . . . .   697 95 POEMS 25      32
(except my life) the true time of year-- and  . . . . . . . .   717 95 POEMS 45       8
the arrival of everything true) and i'm no (if  . . . . . . .   720 95 POEMS 48      11
one (his song's so true) who sings for us . . . . . . . . . .   760 95 POEMS 87       8
are my world, my true) and it's you are . . . . . . . . . . .   766 95 POEMS 92       7
the new is the true and to lose is  . . . . . . . . . . . . .   767 95 POEMS 93      10
a strange (and a true) and a climbing fall  . . . . . . . . .   769 95 POEMS 95      20
warcry is I AM true to his mate his . . . . . . . . . . . . .   774 73 POEMS 2       13
(be it false or true) disposes me to shoot  . . . . . . . . .   798 73 POEMS 26      26
win or lose) good true beautiful things god how . . . . . . .   805 73 POEMS 33       3
and each most falsely true; or so subhuman superminds . . . .   817 73 POEMS 45       2
```
TRUEBEAUTIFULLY
```
is becom ing each truebeautifully more-than-thing (& falling   715 95 POEMS 43      18
```
TRUEST
```
even more true would truest lovers grow if out  . . . . . . .   576 1 X 1 36        11
appears. Because only the truest things always are true . . .   697 95 POEMS 25      31
```
TRULL
```
Her voice? gruesome: a trull leaps from the lungs . . . . . .   227 IS 5 ONE GERT    13
```
TRULY
```
cool writhe of gloom truly which syncopate some sunbeam's . .    19 T&C PUELLA MEA   85
i say body? follows truly through a dribbling moan  . . . . .   140 & SON REAL 11     4
prettiness you hew form truly / / / / . . . . . . . . . . . .   195 XLI PORTRAIT 3   24
thee (beloved) this and truly i would be near . . . . . . . .   215 XLI SONNETS 11    5
surely Cued motif smites truly to Beautifully retire through   311 VIVA 3            3
to jip hug behemoth truly pseudo yours podia of . . . . . . .   333 VIVA 24          25
lascivious caring eyes watches; truly, curvingly while reacts   344 VIVA 35           5
/ / into a truly curving form enters my . . . . . . . . . . .   419 NO THANKS 36      1
glad things or free truly which live always shall . . . . . .   441 NO THANKS 56     62
yourself so more than truly there's never been quite  . . . .   481 NEW POEMS 19     10
home come young so truly perfectly the skies by . . . . . . .   526 50 POEMS 38       9
young with mysteries (each truly his more than some . . . . .   617 (CHAIRE) 19      10
himself the sun --arriving truly, faithfully who goes (never   756 95 POEMS 84       2
world) one spirit serenely truly himself; and alone only  . .   808 73 POEMS 36       3
```
TRUMP
```
forgetfulness with the wild trump of April: witchery of . . .     4 T&C EPITHALAM    59
```
TRUMPETS
```
with victory and with trumpets thy legs are the . . . . . . .    29 T&C ORIENTALE 3  21
of Pure percussion colours- like-trumpets they (writhe they,   100 & POST IMPR 11    12
Lady hear the purple trumpets blow horses of gold . . . . . .   110 & PORTRAIT 6      33
glories move, the old trumpets cry; who gavest as . . . . . .   209 XLI SONNETS 5     12
forth to war with trumpets clap and syphilis / . . . . . . .   273 IS 5 TWO 8        24
```
TRUNK
```
wordless nondescript genie of trunk trickled firm- ly in  . .    96 & POST IMPR 8     33
the bottom of this trunk, under some dirty collars) . . . . .   296 IS 5 FOUR 13     11
by a finger of trunk, and singing out of  . . . . . . . . . .   631 (CHAIRE) 33       3
```
TRUNKS
```
these men's fingers toss trunks shuffle sacks spin kegs . . .   114 & PORTRAIT 7      7
```
TRUST
```
being kind because i trust him to your grace, . . . . . . . .    42 T&C AMORES 6     22
and then to slowly trust T upon H, and  . . . . . . . . . . .   650 (CHAIRE) 52       3
to be free just trust in the u s  . . . . . . . . . . . . . .   711 95 POEMS 39       8
and wind is wind) trust your heart if the . . . . . . . . . .   732 95 POEMS 60       5
(as doubt as can trust) they work and they  . . . . . . . . .   801 73 POEMS 29      26
```
TRUSTED
```
muting of seatides i trusted not, one night when . . . . . .    39 T&C AMORES 4     10
```
TRUTH
```
music Lady the noiseless truth of swirling worms is . . . . .   113 & PORTRAIT 6     117
growing and that's the truth, who threw the ripe . . . . . .   125 & SEVEN POEMS 4   6
the sacred flag of truth unfurled, in the bright . . . . . .   273 IS 5 TWO 8        14
to dreamings more than truth untrue, the best mouth . . . . .   344 VIVA 35           7
```

		PAGE	TITLE	LINE
TRUTH (CONTINUED)				
only Nobody knows where truth grows why birds fly		368	VIVA 59	19
stupendous is nor may truth opening encompass true) while . .		373	VIVA 64	16
ter sc ribbled lonely truth (from hang from droop		415	NO THANKS 32	10
a man? loudly for Truth have liars pled, their		438	NO THANKS 54	17
wrongsideout, sameness chokes oneness truth is confused with		446	NO THANKS 61	4
is a breakfastfood or truth can live with right		511	50 POEMS 25	2
quite so least as truth --i say though hate		521	50 POEMS 34	65
stern miraculous this every truth--beware of heartless them .		556	1 X 1 16	6
and the green whereless truth of an eternal now		558	1 X 1 18	4
a wind gives the truth to summer's lie; bloodies		560	1 X 1 20	2
fiend, if fiends speak truth; if angels burn by		562	1 X 1 22	5
must fly if a truth is a cry of		587	1 X 1 47	16
un till the god's truth stands art-naked: you and		605	{CHAIRE} 7	3
(mind murmurs; the fool) "truth would prove truthless and . .		625	{CHAIRE} 27	17
day: gay as only truth is gay (nothing's false, ...		651	{CHAIRE} 53	6
but by the sizeless truth of a dream whose		664	{CHAIRE} 66	22
of no rises a truth of yes (only herself		736	95 POEMS 64	2
(till mountains speak the truth) enter a cloverish silence .		745	95 POEMS 73	2
erect in the deathless truth of His presence (welcoming . . .		749	95 POEMS 77	19
wear sunlight. The whole truth not hid by matter;		765	95 POEMS 91	5
force is feebleness: the truth more first than sun		768	95 POEMS 94	12
/ / seeker of truth follow no path all		775	73 POEMS 3	1
all paths lead where truth is here / /		775	73 POEMS 3	4
shall be this only truth (a dream of a		776	73 POEMS 4	34
bird sings love's every truth beyond all since and		783	73 POEMS 11	3
gone. Tall as the truth was who: and wore		786	73 POEMS 14	5
less form all goodness truth and beauty lurk, simply		790	73 POEMS 18	9
beautiful; and Beautiful, who (truth to sing) could never . .		799	73 POEMS 27	12
and mine (or any truth beyond perceive) quivers this		809	73 POEMS 37	2
irrevocable time particular pure truth of patience heard . .		821	73 POEMS 49	5
oneness dream! ! joy truth! ! soul / /		841	73 POEMS 69	39
the beauty of the truth; and strolls the axis		845	73 POEMS 73	9
TRUTHED				
as we stood, one (truthed by wisping tinily the		572	1 X 1 32	7
TRUTHFUL				
but shall increase whole truthful infinite immediate us / . .		538	50 POEMS 50	14
you not possible; only truthful --truthfully, once if		564	1 X 1 24	11
go let them go--the truthful liars and the false		569	1 X 1 29	9
TRUTHFULLY				
not possible; only truthful --truthfully, once if strangers .		564	1 X 1 24	12
TRUTHLESS				
fool) "truth would prove truthless and life a mere		625	{CHAIRE} 27	17
TRUTHS				
air (and joyfully all truths of wing resuming) selves, . . .		659	{CHAIRE} 61	3
enormous near far silent truths of mountain (strolling is . .		755	95 POEMS 83	7
unders of dream adventure truths of skies-- darling of . . .		761	95 POEMS 88	8
TRUTHTREE				
precision evolving vision dreamtree, truthtree tree of . . .		763	95 POEMS 90	31
TRY				
frantic heart is fain; try me with thy perfumes		212	XLI SONNETS 8	5
cubes of tiny fragrance try; i have watched certain		214	XLI SONNETS 10	4
well behaved" ...and always try to not wonder how		229	IS 5 ONE FRAN	11
hand at some window try to understand the (through		305	IS 5 FIVE 4	10
through the gloominess of (try to imagine) whispering of . .		324	VIVA 16	13
in thick glass you try if we are a		326	VIVA 18	5
college, cambridge, mass. i try if you are a		327	VIVA 18	45
(faith -ful which -ly try are ing) al most		388	NO THANKS 5	13
could what the movies try to do because they		425	NO THANKS 42	5
these not eyes quite try almost their mind immeasurably . . .		479	NEW POEMS 17	4
us a pie (it's try, boys) mine is yours		513	50 POEMS 27	16
no other mind should try to fool has always		679	95 POEMS 7	7
no matter how he'll try to try) So wrong		685	95 POEMS 13	4
how he'll try to try) So wrong (wrong wrong)		685	95 POEMS 13	4
a few dim tombstones try to re (still u		695	95 POEMS 23	7
this and tree illimitably try to seize the doom		822	73 POEMS 50	5
+TRY				
FOR CONTEXT, SEE		333	VIVA 24	9

	PAGE	TITLE	LINE

TRYING
somewhere behind us always trying (or sometimes trying under 368 VIVA 59 10
always trying (or sometimes trying under us) to is . . . . . 368 VIVA 59 10
irketh sundry who are trying to find their minds . . . . . 410 NO THANKS 27 8

TRYST
its roundness: if swallows tryst in your barn be . . . . . 514 50 POEMS 28 6
whom i'll keep my tryst until that tide shall . . . . 843 73 POEMS 71 6

TRYSTS
upon the mouth there trysts curvingly a fragile smile . . . . 20 T&C PUELLA MEA 148

TSZE
wouldn't believe it) lao tsze certainly told him, and . . . . 553 1 X 1 13 7

TUBE
she was a silver tube of wise lust whose . . . . 110 & PORTRAIT 6 5

TUBULAR
imperceptible gesticulations threatens the tubular downward . 201 XLI PORTRAIT 9 9

TUCK
oon InG s ly) tuck. s its (ghostsoul sheshape) . . . . . . 495 50 POEMS 9 12

TUCKS
out his C.O.D. Abe tucks it up back inley . . . . 321 VIVA 13 8

+TUCKS
FOR CONTEXT, SEE . . . . 495 50 POEMS 9 12

TUG
the gentscoon coos gently: tug? g (ing intently it . . . . . 387 NO THANKS 4 9

TUGS
early single star which tugs weakly at twilight, caught . . . 305 IS 5 FIVE 4 5

TUH
in not disagreeable contras tuh dat not exacly fat . . . . . 240 IS 5 ONE 11 3
usil (age) ini sticks tuh de mans l (hutch) . . . . 325 VIVA 17 5
flask an offers it tuh duh whole gang accrost . . . . 332 VIVA 23 20

TUHMIH
butoiguttuh braikyooz, datswut eesez tuhmih. (Nowoi askyuh . 310 VIVA 2 5

TUM
of humorous, fury heapingandsqueezing tum-bling- . . . . . . 100 & POST IMPR 11 13
all born so Alive) ump-A-tum ; tee-die uM-tuM tidl . . . . . 426 NO THANKS 43 19
Alive) ump-A-tum ; tee-die uM-tuM tidl -id umptyumpty (OO-- . 426 NO THANKS 43 21

TUMBLE
of it sour gnomes tumble clumsily, the little box . . . . . . 69 T&C POST IMPR 6 3
Ignatz miraculously inhabits. (people tumble down. people . . 280 IS 5 THREE 4 5
oh my spirit you tumble climb and mightily fatally . . . . . 434 NO THANKS 51 27
jump with brooks: trees tumble out of twigs and . . . . . . 580 1 X 1 40 28

TUMBLED
(we do not speak) tumbled hushingly bits of downward . . . . 168 & SON ACTU 17 7
jewess shrieked the messiah tumbled successfully into the . . 241 IS 5 ONE 12 5

TUMBLEDISH
young Up floatingly clothes tumbledish olD (with sprouts o . 534 50 POEMS 46 5

TUMBLES
girl in white spins, tumbles; rolling in sand. across . . . . 281 IS 5 THREE 5 3

TUMBLING
/ / / / Tumbling-hair picker of buttercups violets . . . . . 26 T&C CHANSONS 3 1
dull volume of her tumbling face scribbled with a . . . . . 73 T&C SON REAL 4 5
each other humped to tumbling garble when a minute . . . . . 119 & PORTRAIT 11 12
loll the hands' will tumbling into shall --and Love's . . . . 131 & SON REAL 2 14
girl in white is tumbling in sand Clouds over . . . . 281 IS 5 THREE 5 13
undaunted moon's bright third tumbling slowly / / / . . . . . 305 IS 5 FIVE 4 15
its misbutt- oned trouserfly tumbling, faded five or so . . . 607 {CHAIRE} 9 6

+TUMBLING
FOR CONTEXT, SEE . . . . 100 & POST IMPR 11 13
FOR CONTEXT, SEE . . . . 319 VIVA 11 6
FOR CONTEXT, SEE . . . . 330 VIVA 21 7
FOR CONTEXT, SEE . . . . 835 73 POEMS 63 7

TUMBLING-HAIR
/ / / / Tumbling-hair picker of buttercups violets . . . . . 26 T&C CHANSONS 3 1

+TUMBLISH
FOR CONTEXT, SEE . . . . 655 {CHAIRE} 57 5

TUMTITUMTIDDLE
clenched. fists of tint. TUMTITUMTIDDLE if sometimes my eyes 100 & POST IMPR 11 17

TUMULT
while devouring the firm tumult of exquisitely in- secure . . 201 XLI PORTRAIT 9 19

TUMULT (CONTINUED)

(slowly) Voyaging tones intimate tumult (Into) bangs minds . 348 VIVA 39   7
none) so huge a tumult is the simplest wish: . . . . 609 (CHAIRE) 11   5

TUNE

passionate darkness to the tune of tiny troubadours, and . .   8 T&C OF NICOL   4
ears know the fuZZy tune that's played by the . . . . 100 & POST IMPR 11   36
glove, a soon forgotten tune, a house for lease. . . . . . 360 VIVA 51   9
date and played a tune) death's dollhead wandering under . . 479 NEW POEMS 17   9

+TUNE

FOR CONTEXT, SEE . . . . 310 VIVA 2   13
FOR CONTEXT, SEE . . . . 602 (CHAIRE) 4   2

TUNES

is waving moth- eaten tunes. a fattish hand turns . . . . .   69 T&C POST IMPR 6   2
atrocious melody.... tiniest dead tunes crawl upon my face .   69 T&C POST IMPR 6   27
mE as dea d tunes OR s-cra p-y leaVes . . . . 122 & SEVEN POEMS 1   11

TUNNEL

the dark long cool tunnel of raving colour, on . . . . . . 100 & POST IMPR 11   3

TURBANS

watches on their heads turbans of a hundred colours . . . . .   33 T&C ORIENTALE 6   37

TURBULENCE

flutter of stars a turbulence of forms delightful with . . .   31 T&C ORIENTALE 5   9

TURD

smoulders like a new turd in April his legs . . . . 198 XLI PORTRAIT 6   20
can but eat and turd ere with the dirt . . . . 360 VIVA 51   4

TURK

buying whiskies for a turk a waiter intones: bloo-moo-n . . . 108 & PORTRAIT 4   12

TURKISH

c discuss news in turkish x and y play . . . . 200 XLI PORTRAIT 8   21

TURN

If she a little turn her head i know . . . .   17 T&C PUELLA MEA   33
me. Then shall i turn my face, and hear . . . .   76 T&C SON UNRE 1   13
magnificent face the streets turn young with rain, spiral . .   93 & POST IMPR 5   4
kind large flesh i turn to the cruel-littleness of . . . . . 142 & SON REAL 13   2
should see when i turn to find her how . . . . 152 & SON ACTU 1   8
for the candle, it'll turn into a little curse . . . . 164 & SON ACTU 13   16
Life a formula: example, Turn Your Shirttails Into Drawers . 230 IS 5 ONE 2   33
so hairy-sturdy you may turn O turn that airy . . . . 233 IS 5 ONE 4   2
you may turn O turn that airy hurdysturdygurdy but . . . . . 233 IS 5 ONE 4   2
hurdysturdygurdy but when will turn backward O backward Time 233 IS 5 ONE 4   3
leaving my room i turn, and (stooping through the . . . . . 288 IS 5 FOUR 5   7
light after light) to turn, disappears the very swift . . . . 300 IS 5 FOUR 17   5
by who knows) only turn a little your. so. . . . . 303 IS 5 FIVE 2   15
folks with missians to turn us into rissions and . . . . . . 405 NO THANKS 22   6
the mike if Jew turn kike who dares to . . . . 438 NO THANKS 54   15
gering s wli whichs turn in to whos est . . . . 463 NEW POEMS 1   12
only if you should turn the infinite corner of . . . . 479 NEW POEMS 17   17
sell you a pound. Turn gert (spin! helen) the . . . . 513 50 POEMS 27   2
quisite theys of re turn a n d fall . . . . 536 50 POEMS 48   16
ghostly they doubting can turn men's see to stare . . . . . 580 1 X 1 40   8
lift a luminous whole; turn sheer despairing to most . . . . 649 (CHAIRE) 51   6
mortally immortal i can turn immense all time's because . . . 679 95 POEMS 7   14
wonder mere surprise (then turn the page) contentment read . 689 95 POEMS 17   4
a looking bird: the turn ing; edge, of life . . . . 712 95 POEMS 40   6
with out a body (turn ing silently to a . . . . 753 95 POEMS 81   6
my) words of words turn to a silence who's . . . . 761 95 POEMS 88   14
to seem their joys turn woes and right goes . . . . 776 73 POEMS 4   25
they do and they turn to a which though . . . . 801 73 POEMS 29   10
now cancels kind; friends turn to enemies) therefore lament, 834 73 POEMS 62   4
until that tide shall turn; and from all selfsubtracting . . 843 73 POEMS 71   6

+TURN

FOR CONTEXT, SEE . . . . 310 VIVA 2   6

TURNED

(which as a glass turned light to flame and . . . .   8 T&C OF NICOL   18
one by one are turned suddenly and softly into . . . .   62 T&C PORTRAIT 10   21
greasedlightning) just as we turned the corner of Divinity . 248 IS 5 ONE 19   21
with dignity square feet turned abruptly Miss Gay away: . . . 326 VIVA 18   26
which now O fear turned o Now handspring trans . . . . 343 VIVA 34   10
look men who are turned to seem) "stetti" and . . . . 387 NO THANKS 4   14

TURNED (CONTINUED)

    by raspail). But he turned into a fair y! . . . . 401 NO THANKS 18   15
    fair y!!! but she turned into a fair-y (and . . . . 401 NO THANKS 18   20
    this motionless forgetful where turned at his glance to . . . 520 50 POEMS 34   6
    a whisper, as time turned to dream "and poets . . . . 626 (CHAIRE) 28   11
    all the earth has turned to sky are flowers . . . . 630 (CHAIRE) 32   9

TURNING

    whiter than the rest --turning from the tremendous lie . . . 78 T&C SON UNRE 3   13
    the sallow street-lamps were turning snowy against a west . . 194 XLI PORTRAIT 2   2
    afternoon and warm air turning into January darkness up . . . 279 IS 5 THREE 3   2
    else carefully slowly fatally turning into ourselves... while 283 IS 5 THREE 7   25
    hopes, life to (carefully turning a corner) never bother . . 298 IS 5 FOUR 15   27
    of time lessness; quietly turning toward me the guessable . . 370 VIVA 61   8
    town (if its houses turning into themselves grow silent . . . 720 95 POEMS 48   2

+TURNING

    FOR CONTEXT, SEE . . . . 142 & SON REAL 13   4
    FOR CONTEXT, SEE . . . . 474 NEW POEMS 12   14

TURNS

    tunes. a fattish hand turns the crank; the box . . . . 69 T&C POST IMPR 6   2
    with renewal my body turns toward thee again for . . . . . . 184 XLI SONGS 6   8
    smiling you answer "everything turns into something else, and 303 IS 5 FIVE 2   5
    of times a wheel turns doesn't determine its roundness: . . . 514 50 POEMS 28   5
    lucky fifth of you turns people into eachs and . . . . 537 50 POEMS 49   7
    deathboard where all now turns when (love's a universe . . . 574 1 X 1 34   6
    last things (least all turns almost now; now almost . . . . . 633 (CHAIRE) 35   9
    since becomes why: old turns to young (winter goodbye) . . . 737 95 POEMS 65   6
    brain) more than machine turns less than beast at . . . . . . 787 73 POEMS 15   12
    on both knees" green turns red (the roar of . . . . 800 73 POEMS 28   17
    each dim inuti ve turns obv ious t o . . . . 829 73 POEMS 57   5
    makes this whenworld squirm turns houses to people and . . . 841 73 POEMS 69   17

TWAIN

    men whose subtle throne twain sphinxes bear each with . . . . 4 T&C EPITHALAM   42
    yet less than those twain perfect roses whose ambrosial . . . 6 T&C EPITHALAM   148
    in rareness: let thy twain eyes deeply wield a . . . . 10 T&C SONGS 1   42

TWANG

    Indians Youse n.b. ye twang of little joe (yankee) . . . . . 410 NO THANKS 27   7

TWAS

    in the rasberrypatch and 'twas me that she asked . . . . . . 707 95 POEMS 35   24
    hurt too much and 'twas me that looked up . . . . 707 95 POEMS 35   25

TWEAK

    cane and, mazurkas about tweak- ing his wing collar . . . . . 274 IS 5 TWO 9   32
    diminutive this opened drawer) tweak S with his brutebeak . . 697 95 POEMS 25   22

TWEAKED

    tired business man somewhat tweaked and dinted then did . . . 57 T&C PORTRAIT 5   33

TWEEDS

    hoppy happy toad in tweeds tweeds little itchy mousies . . . 25 T&C CHANSONS 2   10
    happy toad in tweeds tweeds little itchy mousies with . . . . 25 T&C CHANSONS 2   11

TWELVE

    umbrellas upon an elephant twelve feet high behind whose . . 32 T&C ORIENTALE 6   8
    / / PORTRAITS being twelve who hast merely gonorrhea . . . . 105 & PORTRAIT 1   2
    for the mother of twelve undershirts (we are told . . . . . 167 & SON ACTU 16   3

TWENTIETH

    died in more our twentieth will open wide a . . . . 537 50 POEMS 49   11

TWENTY

    he sees eight and twenty ladies in a line . . . . 15 T&C SONGS 5   3
    once permitted me for twenty iron men her common . . . . . . 52 T&C PORTRAIT 1   21
    the legs whereas, at twenty minutes to one, i . . . . 115 & PORTRAIT 8   25
    is need of just twenty five cents dear friends . . . . 196 XLI PORTRAIT 4   12
    Madam's best april the twenty nellie anyway and it's . . . . 251 IS 5 ONE 22   2
    arranging; sunlight with-ered unspea-king: tWeNtY, f i n g . 255 IS 5 ONE 26   3

TWENTYSEVEN

    / / / / twentyseven bums give a prostitute . . . . 150 & SON REAL 21   1

TWENTYSIX

    totter Therefore, approaching my twentysix selves bulging in 255 IS 5 ONE 26   5

TWIC

    linotypes gobblehobble our lightheavy twic twoc ingly attacks 259 IS 5 ONE 29   13

TWICE

    The babybreasted broad "kitty" twice eight --beer nothing, . 74 T&C SON REAL 5   12

		PAGE	TITLE	LINE

TWICE (CONTINUED)

gang got shot up twice, it operated in the . . . . 149 & SON REAL 20   8
a week. and slept twice a week with a . . . . 149 & SON REAL 20   12
with eyes and making twice the a week you . . . . 251 IS 5 ONE 22   7
Wing Wong, uninterred at twice fortyeight, succeeded in . . . 341 VIVA 32   1
a little more than twice all that so gently . . . . 370 VIVA 61   12
socalled if multiplied by twice infinity could never equal . 510 50 POEMS 24   10
never and never to twice (blow life to isn't: . . . . 560 1 X 1 20   21
every because is murdered twice / / / / . . . . 588 1 X 1 48   8
we glimpsed-- more likely twice that (once crammed into . . . 607 {CHAIRE} 9   2
of self pouring (alive twice) and becomes eithering dreams . 613 {CHAIRE} 15   10
egghead strutstrolls eager a (twice by Dizzying eyeplums pun 615 {CHAIRE} 17   5
let him kiss me twice but my lover has . . . . 684 95 POEMS 12   10
sings the same thing twice and still that singing's . . . . 760 95 POEMS 87   3
being so sans until twice i have lived forever . . . . 765 95 POEMS 91   14

TWICEUPONATIME

crumb of our Now) twiceuponatime wave-- put out your . . . . 639 {CHAIRE} 41   12

TWIDDLES

when autumn comes, who twiddles his white thumbs and . . . . 296 IS 5 FOUR 13   6

TWIDDLING

derbied creature, swaggers daintily twiddling his tiny cane . 274 IS 5 TWO 9   30

TWIG

at times the weary twig of a neckless nudity . . . . 134 & SON REAL 5   5
trembling any) into flame twig or limb explodes and . . . . . 583 1 X 1 43   11
littlest this the of twig three souls sit round . . . . . . 687 95 POEMS 15   2
any god) while leaf twig limb ask every question . . . . . . 818 73 POEMS 46   9

TWIGS

trees tumble out of twigs and sticks; / / . . . . 580 1 X 1 40   28

TWILIGHT

indolence simmer upon thinking twilight momently) as down the   6 T&C EPITHALAM 126
the implacable bassoon-- now Twilight seeks the thrill of . . 12 T&C SONGS 2   48
the beautiful nonsense of twilight and somebody Napoleon / . 63 T&C PORTRAIT 10 38
dawn, into the women-coloured twilight i smilingly glide. I . 66 T&C POST IMPR 3 8
of morning but in twilight becomes unutterably crisp a . . . 68 T&C POST IMPR 5 7
with mystic lips take twilight where i know: proving . . . . 71 T&C SON REAL 2 13
in the quick of twilight ....or if sunset utters . . . . . . 82 T&C SON ACTU 1   6
cautiously who prolongs unserious twilight) shadows have . . 84 T&C SON ACTU 3 10
heed the mauve of twilight (who slenderly descends, daintily 93 & POST IMPR 5   9
pearshaped lady in gluey twilight moving, suddenly is three . 95 & POST IMPR 7   2
borne neatly through enormous twilight surrounded by their . 111 & PORTRAIT 6   38
des negres (in the twilight of Paris Marie Louise . . . . . 121 & PORTRAIT 12   44
green brief gesture of twilight trembles the imagined galleon 156 & SON ACTU 5   8
stilled in the framing twilight of Spring.... and the . . . 158 & SON ACTU 7   11
naked lady framed in twilight is an accident whose . . . . . 162 & SON ACTU 11   2
live: and the empty twilight cannot grieve nor the . . . . . 165 & SON ACTU 14   8
are clean --this is twilight, a little puppy hopping . . . . 167 & SON ACTU 16   7
a Face (it is twilight) a Face playing on . . . . 169 & SON ACTU 18 16
heard a handorgan in twilight playing like hell / . . . . . 174 & SON ACTU 23 15
upon such peregrinations as twilight spon- taneously by . . . 197 XLI PORTRAIT 5 3
mere Music mounting unsurely twilight but here were something 211 XLI SONNETS 7   3
arms' bothness (say a twilight lifting the fragile skill . . 218 XLI SONNETS 14 4
the drunker applaud while twilight takes the sting out . . . 279 IS 5 THREE 3 18
or (between dawn and twilight) giving your eyes, present . . 285 IS 5 FOUR 2   14
eyes, gifted with green twilight) / / / / . . . . 291 IS 5 FOUR 8   27
dissolves when it is twilight (and looking up in . . . . . . 301 IS 5 FOUR 18   3
city wiggles in considerable twilight touch (now) with a . . 302 IS 5 FIVE 1   4
which tugs weakly at twilight, caught in thickening fear . . 305 IS 5 FIVE 4   6
note how fatally toward twilight the a little tilted . . . . 345 VIVA 36   5
a bat in this twilight") there one is look . . . . 353 VIVA 44   5
the green groove of twilight, striking into many a . . . . . 360 VIVA 51   19
(how luminous) life toward twilight will dissolve reintegrate 379 VIVA 70   11
to morning's beautiful friend twilight (and a first dream . . 424 NO THANKS 41   7
his climbing shoulders queerly twilight : never, no (body. . 490 50 POEMS 4   19
some dirty window every) twilight i feel (his lousy . . . . 501 50 POEMS 15   7
star one moving are twilight they beyond near) girlest . . . 518 50 POEMS 32   4
yes the wrists of twilight would rejoice keen as . . . . . . 520 50 POEMS 34   24
one by wonder (on twilight) they come until (over . . . . . 557 1 X 1 17   12
some ? i call twilight you 'll see an . . . . 571 1 X 1 31   4

TWILIGHT (CONTINUED)
    moo ving lump of twilight squirts a two ne . . . . 602 (CHAIRE) 4   2
    / if in beginning twilight of winter will stand . . . . . . 808 73 POEMS 36   1
    / faithfully tinying at twilight voice of deathless earth's `. 821 73 POEMS 49   1
+TWILIGHT
    FOR CONTEXT, SEE . . . . 122 & SEVEN POEMS 1 25
    FOR CONTEXT, SEE . . . . 349 VIVA 40   2
    FOR CONTEXT, SEE . . . . 350 VIVA 41   1
    FOR CONTEXT, SEE . . . . 627 (CHAIRE) 29   6
    FOR CONTEXT, SEE . . . . 823 73 POEMS 51   4
TWILIGHT'S
    of air not with twilight's first thrushes may awake . . . . . 577 1 X 1 37   6
    most ethereal silence through twilight's mystery made flesh-- 669 (CHAIRE) 71   8
+TWILIGHT'S
    FOR CONTEXT, SEE . . . . 448 NO THANKS 63   6
TWILIGHTS
    birds by daisies and twilights Deepen her, Recite upon . . . 65 T&C POST IMPR 2 10
TWIN
    e; seasays. Break snice-Ly in-twin K les Of, CleaN . . . . . 94 & POST IMPR 6   14
    became and was these twin imminent lisping bags of . . . . . 115 & PORTRAIT 8   21
TWINE
    begins to heave and twine about me, and to . . . . 147 & SON REAL 18   13
TWINED
    and the old vine twined this is a dog . . . . 647 (CHAIRE) 49   15
TWINGE
    quell me with the twinge of all living intense . . . . 19 T&C PUELLA MEA 100
TWINKLE
    whist little ghostthings tip-toe twinkle-toe little twitchy . 25 T&C CHANSONS 2   4
    i am we (pretty twinkle merry bells) Someone has . . . . . . 630 (CHAIRE) 32   13
TWINKLE-TOE
    whist little ghostthings tip-toe twinkle-toe little twitchy . 25 T&C CHANSONS 2   4
+TWINKLES
    FOR CONTEXT, SEE . . . . 94 & POST IMPR 6   14
TWINKLING
    before my eyes or twinkling over to my side . . . . 44 T&C AMORES 8   8
+TWINNINGLY
    FOR CONTEXT, SEE . . . . 615 (CHAIRE) 17   17
+TWIRL
    FOR CONTEXT, SEE . . . . 235 IS 5 ONE 6   18
    FOR CONTEXT, SEE . . . . 431 NO THANKS 48   8
TWIRLED
    that it mayn't be twirled around your little finger . . . . . 411 NO THANKS 28   6
+TWIRLING
    FOR CONTEXT, SEE . . . . 32 T&C ORIENTALE 6   11
TWIRLS
    pass Mr Tom Larsen twirls among pale lips the . . . . 252 IS 5 ONE 23   5
    s C omprises 6 twirls of do gsh it . . . . 789 73 POEMS 17   10
+TWIRLS
    FOR CONTEXT, SEE . . . . 94 & POST IMPR 6   2
TWIST
    poke if inch dimmer twist on permanent and slap . . . . 333 VIVA 24   12
TWISTANDTWIRL
    to be a fellow's twistandtwirl talk about your Sal- . . . . . 235 IS 5 ONE 6   18
TWISTED
    dead dollars and some twisted laws) it comes both . . . . . . 644 (CHAIRE) 46   5
TWISTI
    / / (one!) the wisti-twisti barber -pole is climbing . . . . 128 & SEVEN POEMS 6 2
TWISTS
    make an error, with twists spontaneously methodical. He . . . 170 & SON ACTU 19   11
+TWISTS
    FOR CONTEXT, SEE . . . . 676 95 POEMS 4   22
TWITCH
    with the lithe free twitch of scintillant space, with . . . . 18 T&C PUELLA MEA   83
    the six subjunctive crumbs twitch like mutilated thumbs: . . 117 & PORTRAIT 10   31
    brain harder than can twitch its terrors; the, mouth's, . . . 136 & SON REAL 7   7
    hips; or, your first twitch of crisp boy flesh . . . . 140 & SON REAL 11   7
    pompous ancient jews obscurely twitch through the bumping . . 219 XLI SONNETS 15   9
    deads (lovers grip sprawl twitch lovers) & one dog? . . . . . 384 NO THANKS 2   10

		PAGE	TITLE	LINE

TWITCH (CONTINUED)
a twot with a twitch like kingdom come (moon . . . . 469 NEW POEMS 7   4
TWITCHED
world wriggled like a twitched string. / / / . . . . 135 & SON REAL 6   17
TWITCHES
masturbation). A dirty wind, twitches the, clothes which are 167 & SON ACTU 16   6
know how and he twitches a liberal titty and . . . . 711 95 POEMS 39   23
TWITCHING
a worshipper prostrate within twitching shadow lolls sobbing 28 T&C ORIENTALE 2   14
of lazy jade and twitching eyelids finger their unquiet . . . 34 T&C ORIENTALE 6   78
in the last light twitching at the world / . . . . 64 T&C POST IMPR 1   12
mouth) --jazz, for whose twitching lips, between you and . . 227 IS 5 ONE GERT   6
+TWITCHING
FOR CONTEXT, SEE . . . . 445 NO THANKS 60   12
TWITCHY
ghostthings tip-toe twinkle-toe little twitchy witches and . 25 T&C CHANSONS 2   5
TWITTER
a pose : to twitter wickedly whereas the big . . . . 95 & POST IMPR 7   12
fragile his queer hands twitter before him, like foolish . . 198 XLI PORTRAIT 6   23
hands tease slim float twitter faces) only stand with . . . . 633 {CHAIRE} 35   5
th ey tangle in twitter y t wofroing chino . . . . 747 95 POEMS 75   15
+TWITTER
FOR CONTEXT, SEE . . . . 519 50 POEMS 33   1
+TWITTERING
FOR CONTEXT, SEE . . . . 28 T&C ORIENTALE 2   4
FOR CONTEXT, SEE . . . . 100 & POST IMPR 11   42
TWITTERS
utter ly churning witty, twitters upon Our (ta-te-ta in . . . 89 & POST IMPR 1   14
+TWITTERY
FOR CONTEXT, SEE . . . . 747 95 POEMS 75   15
TWO
her eyes which like two elves incredibly amuse themselves) . 17 T&C PUELLA MEA   39
(very slowly) one or two ladies like flowers made, ... 23 T&C PUELLA MEA 281
Paris moves with lovers, two and two bound for . . . . 71 T&C SON REAL 2   8
with lovers, two and two bound for themselves, when . . . . . 71 T&C SON REAL 2   8
showed how hair, in two fists of shrill colour, ... 73 T&C SON REAL 4   4
horribly suddenly; (of these two most early stars wincing . . 98 & POST IMPR 9   5
grave already three or two young stars with spades . . . . . 115 & PORTRAIT 8   2
were alive and number two took up the song, ... 117 & PORTRAIT 10   15
elevator but I bet two bits come seven come . . . . 125 & SEVEN POEMS 4 10
exactly the alarm tore two slits in her cheeks. . . . . 132 & SON REAL 3   13
this of the smile's two eyes.... too, since the . . . . 141 & SON REAL 12   4
against me, when for two dollars i fill her . . . . 148 & SON REAL 19   13
nights and chews a two-bit cigar waiting for the . . . . . . 149 & SON REAL 20   2
teeth leak smoke: remembering, two pink big lips curl.... . . 149 & SON REAL 20   15
slavver of spring chased two flights of squirrel-stairs into 194 XLI PORTRAIT 2   7
why he should blow two bits for the coming . . . . 196 XLI PORTRAIT 4   21
i drink, or sometimes two remarking cries of paklavah . . . . 217 XLI SONNETS 13   11
how these wooden big two feet conclude happeningly the . . . 229 IS 5 ONE FRAN   4
Waiter a drink waiter two or three drinks what's . . . . . . 233 IS 5 ONE 4   20
Freud a year or two and when Freud got . . . . 236 IS 5 ONE 7   7
are accustomed to accomplish two or three times, and . . . . 236 IS 5 ONE 7   14
/ weazened Irrefutable unastonished two, countenances seated 255 IS 5 ONE 26   2
keeping still; we were two alert lice in the . . . . 289 IS 5 FOUR 6   24
bluish; next Door but two occupy a man and . . . . 312 VIVA 4   10
here's looking at ourselves two solids in (all one . . . . . 323 VIVA 15   2
exhausted condition, i purchased two bags of lukewarm peanuts 326 VIVA 18   15
dumbly behind three or two partly tran sparent panes . . . . 354 VIVA 45   18
of his jacket were two glued uncarefully ears in . . . . . . 355 VIVA 46   7
ing; diskface, es (are two notSoft soft one are . . . . 388 NO THANKS 5   20
is by (with hope two eyes a memory this . . . . 402 NO THANKS 19   6
and) not bald. (Coughs.) Two pale slippery small eyes . . . . 406 NO THANKS 23   9
ring & all one two three rings are cake . . . . 470 NEW POEMS 8   17
squads right impatiently replied two billion pubic lice . . . 473 NEW POEMS 11   5
are both making silence two-made-of-one & nothing tells . . . 483 NEW POEMS 21   6
silently down more than two those that and that . . . . 491 50 POEMS 5   7
too and and nuns two nuns w an d . . . . 508 50 POEMS 22   7
a thousand pounds or two and he smote the . . . . 552 1 X 1 12   9

		PAGE	TITLE	LINE
TWO (CONTINUED)				
/ one's not half two. It's two are halves		556	1 X 1 16	1
not half two. It's two are halves of one:		556	1 X 1 16	1
by mortals told make two. Let liars wilt, repaying		556	1 X 1 16	10
bites this universe in two, peels forever out of		560	1 X 1 20	18
sun with blue true two man neral rise eyes		567	1 X 1 27	4
each first flower of two / / / /		573	1 X 1 33	24
how tinily of squir (two be tween sto nes)		581	1 X 1 41	4
awandering awondering but any two are perfectly alone there's		591	1 X 1 51	11
of twilight squirts a two ne like nothing verdi		602	{CHAIRE} 4	2
of time lessness; but two dim disks of stare		605	{CHAIRE} 7	13
e n s and two are wildstrawberries / /		614	{CHAIRE} 16	16
fascist beast boom boom) two eyes for an eye		635	{CHAIRE} 37	16
inch) grin ning heshaped two these (stroll more slowly		681	95 POEMS 9	3
into a crazy dream two were a hundred million		709	95 POEMS 37	3
only himself was him) two were the cleanest keenest		709	95 POEMS 37	5
the throat of one two came hurrying home to		709	95 POEMS 37	13
who (is? are) who (two faces at a dark		715	95 POEMS 43	2
/ / sentinel robins two guard me and you		746	95 POEMS 74	1
sky should break in two he'd make them one		760	95 POEMS 87	7
in huger always whom two tiny selves sleep (doll		777	73 POEMS 5	11
realms of hellas dwelt two very different sons of		799	73 POEMS 27	2
in a moon or two) / / / /		805	73 POEMS 33	8
+TWO				
FOR CONTEXT, SEE		60	T&C PORTRAIT 8	6
FOR CONTEXT, SEE		259	IS 5 ONE 29	14
FOR CONTEXT, SEE		388	NO THANKS 5	14
FOR CONTEXT, SEE		468	NEW POEMS 6	4
FOR CONTEXT, SEE		610	{CHAIRE} 12	1
FOR CONTEXT, SEE		725	95 POEMS 53	9
FOR CONTEXT, SEE		747	95 POEMS 75	16
TWO-BIT				
nights and chews a two-bit cigar waiting for the		149	& SON REAL 20	2
TWO-MADE-OF-ONE				
are both making silence two-made-of-one & nothing tells		483	NEW POEMS 21	6
TWOC				
gobblehobble our lightheavy twic twoc ingly attacks landing a		259	IS 5 ONE 29	13
TWOS				
doomed hurrying brains (by twos or threes which fiercely		354	VIVA 45	21
TWOT				
young queen with a twot with a twitch like		469	NEW POEMS 7	4
like it in the twot nine months young /		497	50 POEMS 11	7
TWURLS				
much Too. originally spontaneous twurls-of-excrement inanely		94	& POST IMPR 6	2
TWURLS-OF-EXCREMENT				
much Too. originally spontaneous twurls-of-excrement inanely		94	& POST IMPR 6	2
TYING				
and she coughed while tying strings / / /		132	& SON REAL 3	18
TYPEWRITER				
the other, each (a typewriter within his reach) upon		266	IS 5 TWO 1	20
the crackle of a typewriter, in the afternoon sky.		281	IS 5 THREE 5	7
TYRANNICALLY				
hair) the expensively democratic tyrannically dumb Awake,		337	VIVA 28	13
U				
here, inven ting air U) sing tw iligH		448	NO THANKS 63	4
/ / / mr u will not be missed		551	1 X 1 11	1
few not excluding mr u / / / /		551	1 X 1 11	4
+U S A				
FOR CONTEXT, SEE		711	95 POEMS 39	8
+U.S.A.				
FOR CONTEXT, SEE		549	1 X 1 9	2
UDDERS				
gums skidding on slippery udders she lifts an impertinent		151	& SON REAL 22	10
UGHHUH				
this very diminishing vicarious ughhuh world (the pertly		337	VIVA 28	11
mean the (o well ughhuh sure why not yuh		400	NO THANKS 17	9
but (it's Rilly yeh ughhuh yuh) i know (o		400	NO THANKS 17	14

UGLIES

    / e cco the uglies t s ub sub . . . . 788 73 POEMS 16   2
+UGLIEST
    FOR CONTEXT, SEE . . . . 788 73 POEMS 16   2
UGLINESS
    will pass the simple ugliness of exact tombs, where . . . . . 86 T&C SON ACTU 5   11
    from a a nnual (ugliness of) rinsed mind slowly: . . . . . . 99 & POST IMPR 10   21
    & spontaneous & difficult ugliness of themselves with a . . . 354 VIVA 45   15
    and beauty bowed to ugliness and logic thwarted life: . . . . 799 73 POEMS 27   37
+UGLINESS
    FOR CONTEXT, SEE . . . . 789 73 POEMS 17   5
UGLY
    idea (Listen drenches: earth's ugly) mind. , Rinsing with . . 99 & POST IMPR 10   3
    hat. the arms hung ugly. , the hands sharp . . . . 103 & POST IMPR 13   5
    puppy-faces to mouth her ugly nipples squirming in pretty . . 151 & SON REAL 22   9
    (all than were nevers ugly beautiful most is now) . . . . . . 565 1 X 1 25   15
    credibly (always are beautiful) ugly" / / / / . . . . 738 95 POEMS 66   17
    eyelashes-- the other, cunning ugly lame; but as you'll . . . 799 73 POEMS 27   5
    a marvellous artificer now Ugly was the husband of . . . . . 799 73 POEMS 27   8
UH
    play b cries "effendi" "Uh" "coffee" "uh" enter paperboy, . . 200 XLI PORTRAIT 8   10
    cries "effendi" "Uh" "coffee" "uh" enter paperboy, c buys . . 200 XLI PORTRAIT 8   11
    from the lungs "gimme uh swell fite like up . . . . 227 IS 5 ONE GERT   14
    Rektuz, Toysday nite; where uh guy gets gayn troze . . . . . 227 IS 5 ONE GERT   16
    guy gets gayn troze uh lobstersalad / / / . . . . 227 IS 5 ONE GERT   16
    oi dough un giv uh shid oi sez. Tom . . . . 310 VIVA 2   3
    do it it buy uh cupl un wait k . . . . 325 VIVA 17   8
    frum dem" --"somebody hung uh gun on Marcus"-- "duh . . . . . 332 VIVA 23   7
    face i hauls out uh flask an offers it . . . . 332 VIVA 23   20
    somebody is sittin in uh green field watchin four . . . . . . 332 VIVA 23   30
    drop into sunset, playin uh busted harmonica / / . . . . . . 332 VIVA 23   32
    the universe to a uh" pause "Cookie but" nonvisibly . . . . . 464 NEW POEMS 2   15
    rather as a" pause "uh" cough "Biscuit" (& so . . . . 464 NEW POEMS 2   23
+UKE
    FOR CONTEXT, SEE . . . . 310 VIVA 2   12
ULTIMA
    a Hyperluxurious Supersieve (which Ultima Thule Of Plumbing . 334 VIVA 25   3
ULTIMATE
    pearl! O indefinable frail ultimate pose! O visible beatitude   5 T&C EPITHALAM   109
    wounded us will becauseless ultimate earth accept and . . . . 745 95 POEMS 73   5
ULTRAMACHINATIONS
    woman who's (despite the ultramachinations of some loveless . 807 73 POEMS 35   10
ULTRAOMNIPOTENCE
    fine specimen of hypermagical ultraomnipotence. We doctors . 554 1 X 1 14   13
ULTRAWRISTS
    an infrafairy of floating ultrawrists who lullabylullaby (I . 317 VIVA 9   5
UM
    Alive) ump-A-tum ; tee-die uM-tuM tidl -id umptyumpty (OO-- . 426 NO THANKS 43   21
    wuman vive the millenni um three cheers for labor . . . . . . 492 50 POEMS 6   10
UM-TUM
    Alive) ump-A-tum ; tee-die uM-tuM tidl -id umptyumpty (OO-- . 426 NO THANKS 43   21
UMBRELLA
    our hero folded his umbrella. It seemed too beautiful. . . . 263 IS 5 ONE 32   57
UMBRELLAS
    of jasper beneath saffron umbrellas upon an elephant twelve . 32 T&C ORIENTALE 6   6
UMMM
    she (cccome? said he ummm said she) you're divine! . . . . . 399 NO THANKS 16   30
UMP
    all born so Alive) ump-A-tum ; tee-die uM-tuM tidl . . . . . 426 NO THANKS 43   19
UMP-A-TUM
    all born so Alive) ump-A-tum ; tee-die uM-tuM tidl . . . . . 426 NO THANKS 43   19
UMPTYUMPTY
    tee-die uM-tuM tidl -id umptyumpty (OO-- ! ting Bam- . . . . 426 NO THANKS 43   24
UN
    velocity commenting upon an un- clean table. and, whose . . . 97 & POST IMPR 8   37
    1 choc olate s. un der, a lo co . . . . 179 XLI SONGS 1   13
    however protest, anent the un -spontaneous and otherwise . . 230 IS 5 ONE 2   15
    nizmus tash, oi dough un giv uh shid oi . . . . 310 VIVA 2   3

	PAGE	TITLE	LINE

UN (CONTINUED)

ainnoughbudih gutnutntuhplai? HAI <> un duhyookuhsumpnruddur 310 VIVA 2 — 12

it buy uh cupl un wait k (relijinisde) o . . . . 325 VIVA 17 — 8

not to sense something un poco putrido when we . . . . . 327 VIVA 18 — 45

spiralS and Now (comes un, season of in: wardly . . . . . . 346 VIVA 37 — 20

dream (An) quickly Not un deux trois der die . . . . 348 VIVA 39 — 12

times vacantly gazing through un washed panes into a . . . . 354 VIVA 45 — 8

(you leSs) ly (un der the mi croscopic . . . . 361 VIVA 52 — 14

"stetti" and willbeishfully bursting un- eats wasvino . . . . 387 NO THANKS 4 — 17

snow) says! Says over un graves der, speaking (says. . . . . 417 NO THANKS 34 — 2

(says W I elds) un forgetting un. der (theys) . . . . 417 NO THANKS 34 — 18

I elds) un forgetting un. der (theys) the : . . . . 417 NO THANKS 34 — 20

/ / / / un der fog 's touch . . . . 463 NEW POEMS 1 — 1

est people be come un / / / / . . . . 463 NEW POEMS 1 — 19

A soursweet bedtime -less un- (wonderful) story atrickling a 464 NEW POEMS 2 — 5

she of the sea un der a who a . . . . 493 50 POEMS 7 — 6

when behind where under un) / / / / . . . . 505 50 POEMS 19 — 25

never's always until absolute un gulps the first knowledge . 517 50 POEMS 31 — 12

ids dare pain dares un no budy elses un . . . . 519 50 POEMS 33 — 23

un no budy elses un ids dare dare joy . . . . 519 50 POEMS 33 — 25

shoulder and thick stickingly un stride after glide massacre 522 50 POEMS 35 — 3

vanish under prodigies of un) "have you" the mountain, . . . 555 1 X 1 15 — 10

or command, reality or un-) proudly depths above why's . . . 574 1 X 1 34 — 8

together are standing together un der a particular tree . . . 600 (CHAIRE) 2 — 6

cocked eyebrow) subtracting cliches un by un till the . . . . 605 (CHAIRE) 7 — 2

subtracting cliches un by un till the god's truth . . . . . 605 (CHAIRE) 7 — 2

nic) like spring yoo un-air-stan? me crazy me like . . . . . 618 (CHAIRE) 20 — 28

do people say it's un lucky to break one) . . . . 623 (CHAIRE) 25 — 6

exactly than the other un good people stare for . . . . . . 662 (CHAIRE) 64 — 11

of window) may be un less it were (floati . . . . 668 (CHAIRE) 70 — 5

/ / / / un (bee) mo vi n . . . . 691 95 POEMS 19 — 1

some world not any un god manufacture might but . . . . . . 698 95 POEMS 26 — 3

history and finally The UN "be quiet little hungary . . . . 711 95 POEMS 39 — 16

breath es (over- ing un -derfully & a- rounding . . . . . . 719 95 POEMS 47 — 16

was of is and un of so) h . . . . 723 95 POEMS 51 — 10

ly which is every) un (star rain snow moon . . . . 753 95 POEMS 81 — 14

sit (hearing the rain) un til against my (where . . . . . . 785 73 POEMS 13 — 19

a life whats wh (un) ich (cur ling) s . . . . 795 73 POEMS 23 — 9

complained "is just" ("or un-" the just rejoined / . . . . . 806 73 POEMS 34 — 2

things or dreamed become un- / / / / . . . . 822 73 POEMS 50 — 8

t o s trange un til o urselve s . . . . 829 73 POEMS 57 — 9

never forever & when) un til one strict here . . . . 840 73 POEMS 68 — 26

UNACCOUNTABLE

eligible day under the unaccountable sun) Distinct Lady . . . 43 T&C AMORES 7 — 24

UNACQUAINTED

a certain Young Woman unacquainted with the libido and . . . 327 VIVA 18 — 42

UNALIVE

as if they were unalive, as if They were . . . . 91 & POST IMPR 3 — 9

/ / Lord John Unalive (having a fortune of . . . . 331 VIVA 22 — 1

UNANIMAL

believe in that incredible unanimal mankind (and not until) . 620 (CHAIRE) 22 — 14

UNASTONISHED

/ / weazened Irrefutable unastonished two, countenances . . . 255 IS 5 ONE 26 — 1

UNBE

and less it shall unbe than all the sea . . . . 530 50 POEMS 42 — 6

UNBEAUTIFUL

in furnished souls are unbeautiful and have comfortable minds 70 T&C SON REAL 1 — 2

UNBECAME

same it's time you unbecame where climbing was and . . . . . 834 73 POEMS 62 — 18

UNBECOMINGLY

die (becoming most buried unbecomingly very by most) people . 412 NO THANKS 29 — 16

UNBEHELD

yours the preposterous colour unbeheld --mine the unbought . 84 T&C SON ACTU 3 — 2

UNBEING

let all unfools of unbeing set traps for his . . . . 439 NO THANKS 55 — 16

army the gradual of unbeing (fro on stiffening greenly . . . 633 (CHAIRE) 35 — 3

UNBEINGDEAD

Swims Upstream & (5) unbeingdead isn't beingalive / / . . . . 803 73 POEMS 31 — 18

	PAGE	TITLE	LINE

UNBESIDE
   is wut ektyouelly metus. Unbeside which limps who might . . . 790 73 POEMS 18   14

UNBIG
   / / precisely as unbig a why as i'm . . . . 735 95 POEMS 63   1
   under teach-- precisely as unbig as i'm a why . . . . 735 95 POEMS 63   9

UNBOLD
   gloom, bad laughters, smiles unbold) also, tomorrow the daily 142 & SON REAL 13   8

UNBORN
   / ci-git 1 Foetus (unborn to not die safely . . . . 394 NO THANKS 11   1
   are obsolete; pasts are unborn (here less than nothing's . . 592 1 X 1 52   11

UNBOUGHT
   colour unbeheld --mine the unbought contemptuous intent till 84 T&C SON ACTU 3   3

UNBREATHINGLY
   firsts of wonder) child unbreathingly share (huge Perhaps by 757 95 POEMS 85   29

UNBROKEN
   other lulla wise by UnBroken LULLAlullabyBY the She-in-him . 317 VIVA 9   29

UNBUNGED
   (out of the black unbunged Something gushes vaguely a . . . . 195 XLI PORTRAIT 3   10

+UNBURIABLE
   FOR CONTEXT, SEE . . . . 309 VIVA 1   5

UNBURIED
   the window walk the unburied feet of the little . . . . 108 & PORTRAIT 4   36
   squirm newly as from unburied which floats the first . . . . 520 50 POEMS 34   9

+UNBUTTONING
   FOR CONTEXT, SEE . . . . 445 NO THANKS 60   14

UNCANNED
   soul and anything else uncanned for everyone carries . . . . 466 NEW POEMS 4   6

UNCAREFULLY
   jacket were two glued uncarefully ears in that face . . . . . 355 VIVA 46   7

UNCARING
   vilest mind and sweet uncaring earth by thoughtful war . . . 213 XLI SONNETS 9   3

UNCEASING
   surges a miracle of unceasing birth and glory and . . . . . 749 95 POEMS 77   9

UNCERTAIN
   a myth in the uncertain morning, with April feet . . . . . . 17 T&C PUELLA MEA   20

UNCHANGINGLY
   night into the street unchangingly the always old lady . . . 58 T&C PORTRAIT 6   20

UNCHASTITY
   warm long flower of unchastity, imperial Cytherea, from frail 7 T&C EPITHALAM   160

UNCLE
   time i had an uncle named Sol who was . . . . 239 IS 5 ONE 10   2
   vaudeville perhaps because my Uncle Sol could sing McCann . . 239 IS 5 ONE 10   5
   the fact that my Uncle Sol indulged in that . . . . 239 IS 5 ONE 10   7
   it needlessly added my Uncle Sol's farm failed because . . . 239 IS 5 ONE 10   14
   the vegetables so my Uncle Sol had a chicken . . . . 239 IS 5 ONE 10   17
   the chickens when my Uncle Sol had a skunk . . . . 239 IS 5 ONE 10   20
   died and so my Uncle Sol imitated the skunks . . . . 239 IS 5 ONE 10   24
   somebody who'd given my Uncle Sol a Victor Victrola . . . . . 239 IS 5 ONE 10   27
   the Missouri when my Uncle Sol's coffin lurched because . . . 239 IS 5 ONE 10   33
   (and down went my Uncle Sol and started a . . . . 239 IS 5 ONE 10   36
   / / / my uncle Daniel fought in the . . . . 253 IS 5 ONE 24   1
   like the devil) my uncle Frank has done nothing . . . . 253 IS 5 ONE 24   5
   breaks (or something) my uncle Frank breaks into tears. . . . 253 IS 5 ONE 24   8
   breaks into tears. my uncle Tom knits and is . . . . 253 IS 5 ONE 24   9
   the ears (but my uncle Ed that's dead from . . . . 253 IS 5 ONE 24   11
   (while tossing boms at uncle toms) is hows to . . . . 500 50 POEMS 14   15
   the freedoms pappy or uncle shylock not interested / . . . . 641 {CHAIRE} 43   8
   the quo pro quid" uncle sam shrugs his pretty . . . . 711 95 POEMS 39   21

+UNCLEAN
   FOR CONTEXT, SEE . . . . 97 & POST IMPR 8   37

UNCLENCHES
   a sharp indecent stir unclenches into fingers.... she too . . 131 & SON REAL 2   11

UNCLEVER
   stupid. mouth normal, large, unclever. hair genuinely . . . . 103 & POST IMPR 13   14

UNCLOSE
   slightest look easily will unclose me though i have . . . . . 366 VIVA 57   5

UNCLOSED
   foetal fragrance to rickety unclosed blinds inslants . . . . 144 & SON REAL 15   3

	PAGE	TITLE	LINE

UNCOMMON
  were young and death uncommon (forgiving not divine, to . . . 798 73 POEMS 26   2
UNCOMMONWEALTH
  babbitt (GOD SAVE THE UNCOMMONWEALTH OF HUMANUSETTS / / . . . 325 VIVA 17   22
UNCORRUPTED
  or prince upon his uncorrupted arse with all his . . . . . . 254 IS 5 ONE 25   20
UNCOUTH
  (over Selene's car closing uncouth) of Helios the sweet . . .   4 T&C EPITHALAM   47
  youth the exquisite failure uncouth discovers a trembling and 11 T&C SONGS 2   7
  your smile) a skilful uncouth prison, a precise clumsy . . .   83 T&C SON ACTU 2   5
  on sharp robes of uncouth odour, for an onion! . . . .   94 & POST IMPR 6   9
  us be a little uncouth and amorous in memory . . . .   111 & PORTRAIT 6   57
  seat itself (with the uncouth habitual dull jerk at . . . . . 227 IS 5 ONE GERT   9
  / / how this uncouth enchanted person, arising from . . . . . 300 IS 5 FOUR 17   1
  crisp todo of murdering uncouth faces which pass rap . . . . 354 VIVA 45   10
UNCOUTHLY
  luminosity spree. --dear) the uncouthly Her. thuglike stare . 159 & SON ACTU 8   14
  day inclined to be uncouthly erotic more particularly the . . 326 VIVA 18   23
UNCULTURED
  are not relatively speaking uncultured (who Very distinctly . 391 NO THANKS 8   19
+UNCURLING
  FOR CONTEXT, SEE . . . . 795 73 POEMS 23   9
UNDAUNTED
  melancholy, suddenly looming) accurate undaunted moon's . . . 305 IS 5 FIVE 4   14
  hope's own hope, receive (undaunted guest of dark most . . . 821 73 POEMS 49   11
UNDE
  United States Of America unde negant redire quemquam supp . . 392 NO THANKS 9   19
UNDEAD
  to prove he is undead who, living, noone is. . . . . 360 VIVA 51   29
  fly do? a notalive undead too-nearishness and shall we . . . 528 50 POEMS 40   5
  she and he lie (undead) / / / / . . . . 694 95 POEMS 22   8
+UNDEAD
  FOR CONTEXT, SEE . . . . 309 VIVA 1   29
UNDEATH
  of deeplyness rose to undeath) salute. and having worshipped 358 VIVA 49   13
  billion brains may coax undeath from fancied fact and . . . . 664 (CHAIRE) 66   19
UNDEATHS
  do cry unfools unfree undeaths who live nor shall . . . . . . 440 NO THANKS 56   34
  of) dirtpoor (popes emperors) undeaths through (slapsoothed . 681 95 POEMS 9   12
UNDECAYING
  stroll) exhumed most innocently undecaying friend hangs at . 546 1 X 1 6   4
UNDELUDED
  and particulary) live that undeluded notselfpitying lover of 607 (CHAIRE) 9   9
UNDENIABLE
  concupiscence the bright large undeniable disease of Life, . 193 XLI PORTRAIT 1   23
UNDER
  / Doll's boy's asleep under a stile he sees . . . . 15 T&C SONGS 5   2
  mine. Doll's boy's asleep under the stile for every . . . . . 15 T&C SONGS 5   18
  a fragile certain song under the window of your . . . . 43 T&C AMORES 7   5
  in the eligible day under the unaccountable sun) Distinct . . 43 T&C AMORES 7   24
  lips of incorruptible Nothing under the ample sun, under . . 43 T&C AMORES 7   38
  under the ample sun, under the insufficient day under . . . . 43 T&C AMORES 7   39
  under the insufficient day under the noise of worms . . . . . 43 T&C AMORES 7   40
  big feather is tied under myhis chin.) that climbs . . . . . 69 T&C POST IMPR 6   42
  People, cherie, who live under stones.) Don't be afraid . . . 86 T&C SON ACTU 5   10
  genuinely artificial, unpleasantly tremendous. under flat . . 103 & POST IMPR 13   15
  D and chairs wait under the trees Fields slowly . . . . 104 & POST IMPR 14   13
  eighteen hundred years.... exactly under the window under the 108 & PORTRAIT 4   33
  exactly under the window under the window under the . . . . . 108 & PORTRAIT 4   34
  window under the window under the window walk the . . . . . . 108 & PORTRAIT 4   35
  your legs Your arms under me around; my head . . . . 123 & SEVEN POEMS 2   11
  live suddenly without thinking under honest trees, a stream . 160 & SON ACTU 9   2
  like the thrill of under me you so quite . . . . 175 & SON ACTU 24   14
  done and said, and under the grass lies her . . . . 181 XLI SONGS 3   12
  her time looking picturesque under the as it happens . . . . 234 IS 5 ONE 5   3
  Lobster without feet mingle under the mercy. (exit the . . . 243 IS 5 ONE 14   14
  arms hopes feet hands under us the unspeaking Mediterranean . 283 IS 5 THREE 7   3
  flesh mind breathing beside under around myself) by and . . . 283 IS 5 THREE 7   17

		PAGE	TITLE	LINE

UNDER (CONTINUED)

awkward eyes pushing sleep under and thoroughly into all . . 293 IS 5 FOUR 10   29
bottom of this trunk, under some dirty collars) only . . . . 296 IS 5 FOUR 13   12
contours; within which "ladies&gentlemen" --under glass-- . . 319 VIVA 11   32
i met a man under the moon on Sunday. . . . . 355 VIVA 46   1
trying (or sometimes trying under us) to is it . . . . 368 VIVA 59   10
meanwhile this ghost goes under, his drowned girth are . . . 418 NO THANKS 35   12
to a leastful most under imagination. When (out of . . . . . 432 NO THANKS 49   14
silence for ifs diving under because) only who'll say . . . . 439 NO THANKS 55   24
things over blame things under praise glad things or . . . . 441 NO THANKS 56   60
are (whose selves abide under whatever shall discovered be) . 446 NO THANKS 61   10
/ / / we) under) over, the thing of . . . . 447 NO THANKS 62   1
tune) death's dollhead wandering under weakening stars Feels; 479 NEW POEMS 17   10
(beyond when behind where under un) / / / . . . . 505 50 POEMS 19   24
fred (jump! neddy) but under the wonder is over . . . . 513 50 POEMS 27   33
timid air is firm) under his eyes would stir . . . . 520 50 POEMS 34   8
--fear buries a tomorrow under woe and up comes . . . . 531 50 POEMS 43   3
is up and vanish under prodigies of un) "have . . . . 555 1 X 1 15   10
what over and which under burst lurch things phantoms . . . . 565 1 X 1 25   1
to every isn't that's under the spring --but if . . . . 580 1 X 1 40   5
song like not anything under skies over grass until . . . . . 587 1 X 1 47   11
(beingest growingest) over all under all hate all fear . . . 590 1 X 1 50   21
become if who'd) me under a opens (of petals . . . . 634 (CHAIRE) 36   5
infinite tomorrow steer --souls under whom flow (mountain . . 659 (CHAIRE) 61   5
of spring (over the under the gift of the . . . . 661 (CHAIRE) 63   8
we are (above and under all possible worlds) in . . . . 664 (CHAIRE) 66   18
can think) a learning under teach-- precisely as unbig . . . 735 95 POEMS 63   8
then that Star goes under the earth / / . . . . 752 95 POEMS 80   8
and whisper their joy under entirely the coming . . . . 754 95 POEMS 82   11
love is the voice under all silences, the hope . . . . 768 95 POEMS 94   9
over gladness and joy under care-- let's do as . . . . 769 95 POEMS 95   16
(doll by doll) motionless under magical foreverfully falling 777 73 POEMS 5   12
a day of may under more a blue than . . . . 778 73 POEMS 6   19
fact of fear; and under any silence of each . . . . 821 73 POEMS 49   7
/ of all things under our blonder than blondest . . . . 825 73 POEMS 53   1
whos (he and she) under are this wonderful tree . . . . 832 73 POEMS 60   3

+UNDER

FOR CONTEXT, SEE . . . . 179 XLI SONGS 1   13
FOR CONTEXT, SEE . . . . 361 VIVA 52   14
FOR CONTEXT, SEE . . . . 417 NO THANKS 34   2
FOR CONTEXT, SEE . . . . 417 NO THANKS 34   20
FOR CONTEXT, SEE . . . . 463 NEW POEMS 1   1
FOR CONTEXT, SEE . . . . 493 50 POEMS 7   6
FOR CONTEXT, SEE . . . . 600 (CHAIRE) 2   6

UNDER'S

what freedom's not some under's mere above but breathing . . 538 50 POEMS 50   1

UNDERCLOTHES

happy like the way underclothes All so differ- ently . . . . 126 & SEVEN POEMS 5   27

UNDERDRAWERS

a cigar-stub disintegrates, above, underdrawers club the . . 144 & SON REAL 15   5

+UNDERFULLY

FOR CONTEXT, SEE . . . . 719 95 POEMS 47   16

UNDERING

minds (out of some undering joy and overing grief . . . . . . 517 50 POEMS 31   9
bells glide seethe glow (undering proudly humbly overing) all 841 73 POEMS 69   25

UNDERLINED

and the word love underlined this is a girl . . . . 647 (CHAIRE) 49   5

UNDERNEATH

an old mop punching underneath conventions exposes hidden . . 203 XLI LA GUERRE 1   3

UNDERS

o sure) but nobody unders (no but Rully yes . . . . 400 NO THANKS 17   3
and wings are birds; unders of dream adventure truths . . . . 761 95 POEMS 88   8

UNDERSCREAM

i mean really th underscream of sudde nly perishing . . . . . 646 (CHAIRE) 48   9

UNDERSHIRTS

the mother of twelve undershirts (we are told by . . . . . . 167 & SON ACTU 16   3

UNDERSTAND

over the music i understand him i shove my . . . . 69 T&C POST IMPR 6   33

UNDERSTAND (CONTINUED)

	PAGE	TITLE	LINE
and always (i simply understand the gnashing petals of . . .	133	& SON REAL 4	10
to me before shutting.... understand i love you.... feel . .	157	& SON ACTU 6	5
an American, if you understand that i mean what	262	IS 5 ONE 32	13
life, for you. I understand. Once again....) sliding a . . .	282	IS 5 THREE 6	32
of fragile Marys will understand how smiling may be	294	IS 5 FOUR 11	12
your Heart possibly will understand; or why (in this	300	IS 5 FOUR 17	9
some window try to understand the (through pale miles	305	IS 5 FIVE 4	10
of afterwards-- i spirally understand What touching means or	356	VIVA 47	18
O 3rd Findingest whispers understand sobs bigly climb what .	358	VIVA 49	6
(why? or lest we understand) slightly i am hearing	375	VIVA 66	9
unreally; as this planet (understand) forgets the entire and	379	VIVA 70	8
feel opens but shuts understand G gladly forget little . . .	390	NO THANKS 7	5
he knows, he cannot understand (why Jones don't pay	406	NO THANKS 23	5
owes) because he cannot understand, he drinks (and he	406	NO THANKS 23	7
much sleep they only understand enormously which fail--look:	418	NO THANKS 35	8
(get me) babe not (understand me) lousy kid that's	475	NEW POEMS 13	23
and adding and (i understand) is hows to hump	500	50 POEMS 14	7
honest breadcrumb) say "i understand quite what you mean . .	546	1 X 1 6	12
worlds wanted us to understand they'd never close (and . . .	603	{CHAIRE} 5	8
part: Soul was (i understand) seduced by Life; whose	621	{CHAIRE} 23	2
bigger than not to understand "i'll never let you	622	{CHAIRE} 24	4
christ but you must understand why because i am	638	{CHAIRE} 40	14
than every world can understand and now you are	667	{CHAIRE} 69	4
wisest man will partly understand (although the wisest man .	685	95 POEMS 13	11
illimitably is) making fools understand (like wintry me) that	736	95 POEMS 64	5
and wore his (mountains understand how) life like a	786	73 POEMS 14	8
wise; and much could understand concerning no and yes: . . .	834	73 POEMS 62	15

+UNDERSTAND

	PAGE	TITLE	LINE
FOR CONTEXT, SEE	310	VIVA 2	2
FOR CONTEXT, SEE	400	NO THANKS 17	10
FOR CONTEXT, SEE	547	1 X 1 7	3
FOR CONTEXT, SEE	547	1 X 1 7	5
FOR CONTEXT, SEE	547	1 X 1 7	7
FOR CONTEXT, SEE	618	{CHAIRE} 20	28
FOR CONTEXT, SEE	739	95 POEMS 67	13

UNDERSTANDING

	PAGE	TITLE	LINE
weapon of your hair. Understanding why his eye laughs, . . .	161	& SON ACTU 10	11
(Dare until a flower, understanding sizelessly sunlight Open	453	NO THANKS 68	14

UNDERSTANDS

	PAGE	TITLE	LINE
man feels, no woman understands. / / / /	212	XLI SONNETS 8	14
only something in me understands the voice of your	366	VIVA 57	18
i mean is Nobody Understands Her RERLY / /	400	NO THANKS 17	18
and surely poets only understands) honour this loneliness of	456	NO THANKS 71	11
at poise, love alone understands: only for whom i'll	843	73 POEMS 71	5

+UNDERSTANDS

	PAGE	TITLE	LINE
FOR CONTEXT, SEE	400	NO THANKS 17	3

UNDERSTOOD

	PAGE	TITLE	LINE
curling infantile fingers it understood my eyes cheeks mouth	284	IS 5 FOUR 1	4
of others, be it understood) he does not have	406	NO THANKS 23	2

+UNDERSTOOD

	PAGE	TITLE	LINE
FOR CONTEXT, SEE	398	NO THANKS 15	1

UNDERTAKE

	PAGE	TITLE	LINE
so wholly burn, to undertake Medea's rescuing eyes; nor . . .	18	T&C PUELLA MEA	71

UNDERTAKES

	PAGE	TITLE	LINE
which wholly trembling memory undertakes --your kiss, the . .	82	T&C SON ACTU 1	2

UNDERWISH

	PAGE	TITLE	LINE
is the overlove & underwish of beauty; before keen	480	NEW POEMS 18	6

UNDIE

	PAGE	TITLE	LINE
infinite our) merely to undie / / / /	817	73 POEMS 45	14

UNDIGESTIBLY

	PAGE	TITLE	LINE
of) instru- ments, waltzing; undigestibly: groans. bounce ! .	442	NO THANKS 57	6

UNDIMISHIED

	PAGE	TITLE	LINE
this squirming cube of undimishied silence, supports while .	201	XLI PORTRAIT 9	18

UNDISCOVERABLE

	PAGE	TITLE	LINE
drunkenness) here's to one undiscoverable guess of whose mad	424	NO THANKS 41	12

UNDISCOVERED

	PAGE	TITLE	LINE
with mouth flower-faint and undiscovered eyes and dim slow .	5	T&C EPITHALAM	98

UNDO

. No doing shall undo (nor madness nor mere . . . . 577 1 X 1 37　　9

doing shall not quite undo such first amazement as . . . . . 762 95 POEMS 89　　4

UNDOOM

progress, and negation's dead undoom. I'd rather learn from . 484 NEW POEMS 22　12

UNDREAM

contemplate in raptures of undream that strictly (and how) . 544 1 X 1 4　　20

sold the reason, they undream a dream) one is . . . . 556 1 X 1 16　　8

UNDRESSED

upon one startling doll undressed in unripe green with . . . 55 T&C PORTRAIT 3　　9

UNDUBLCHECK

cumbine wid i (check undublcheck) babbitt (GOD SAVE THE . . . 325 VIVA 17　　20

UNDULOUS

blinded with silence the undulous heaven yearns where in . . 37 T&C AMORES 2　　8

+UNDULOUS

FOR CONTEXT, SEE . . . . 508 50 POEMS 22　12

UNDYING

. (to noone everyone) constitutes undying; or whatever this and 264 IS 5 ONE 33　　3

being alive (instead of undying) is not so much . . . . 664 (CHAIRE) 66　　2

UNE

with the body like une boite a joujoux, want . . . . 121 & PORTRAIT 12　49

UNEARTH

there here or on unearth / / / / . . . . 541 1 X 1 1　　12

UNEARTHLY

glorious snows, and the unearthly sweetness of a rose . . . . 8 T&C OF NICOL　　7

in the young lips unearthly slenderness / / / . . . . 156 & SON ACTU 5　15

UNEASE

of daisies--by what rare unease revealed of teasingly . . . . 5 T&C EPITHALAM　94

+UNEATS

FOR CONTEXT, SEE . . . . 387 NO THANKS 4　17

UNENDURED

showers its curls of unendured eternal gold over the . . . . 4 T&C EPITHALAM　38

UNEQUAL

great common divisor of unequal souls. / / / . . . . 74 T&C SON REAL 5　15

UNEXIST

young kiss only must unexist, solemnly and per rules . . . . 373 VIVA 64　　3·

UNEYES

when i contemplate her uneyes safely ensconced in thick . . . 326 VIVA 18　　4

when we contemplate her uneyes safely ensconced in thick . . 327 VIVA 18　46

UNFIRM

feet conclude happeningly the unfirm drooping bloated calves 229 IS 5 ONE FRAN　5

UNFLINCHINGLY

parties and because you unflinchingly applaud all songs . . . 204 XLI LA GUERRE 2　6

UNFOLDING

blazed with snowy fire) unfolding, gave the moon a . . . . . 8 T&C OF NICOL　19

UNFOOLS

to harness: let all unfools of unbeing set traps . . . . . 439 NO THANKS 55　16

here unpoets do cry unfools unfree undeaths who live . . . . 440 NO THANKS 56　33

+UNFORGETTING

FOR CONTEXT, SEE . . . . 417 NO THANKS 34　18

UNFREE

unpoets do cry unfools unfree undeaths who live nor . . . . . 440 NO THANKS 56　33

UNFURLED

sacred flag of truth unfurled, in the bright heyday . . . . . 273 IS 5 TWO 8　14

UNGENEROUS

may strut or creep ungenerous who ape deftly aims . . . . . 440 NO THANKS 56　20

+UNGOD

FOR CONTEXT, SEE . . . . 698 95 POEMS 26　　3

UNGROWS

down someone who's we ungrows) a dream in the . . . . 716 95 POEMS 44　35

UNGUESSED

through are gaze the unguessed whys by me at . . . . 613 (CHAIRE) 15　　3

UNHANDS

remember he who watched unhands describe what mimicry, with . 376 VIVA 67　　3

UNHAPPILY

not inobvious perturba- tions unhappily, the denizens of the 326 VIVA 18　23

UNHAPPY

single place dark or unhappy then when you're quite . . . . . 192 XLI CHANSONS 2　20

	PAGE	TITLE	LINE

UNHE
  (leaving a perfectly distinct unhe; a ticking phantom by . . 558 1 X 1 18   7

UNHEARD
  far lands perished of unheard of maladies including flu) . . 266 IS 5 TWO 1   14

UNHEARTS
  this heart could dare) unhearts can less unminds must . . . . 440 NO THANKS 56   4

UNHOLY
  imaginable gesture exact warm unholy / / / / . . . . 162 & SON ACTU 11   17

UNHURRIED
  if sunset utters one unhurried muscled huge chromatic fist . 82 T&C SON ACTU 1   8
  pledged to illimitable dissipation unhurried clouds of . . . 206 XLI SONNETS 2   14
  such were the not unhurried reflections to which my . . . . . 263 IS 5 ONE 32   32

UNIFORMS
  of captains in freshly-creased -uniforms with only-just- . . 274 IS 5 TWO 9   23

UNIMAGINABLE
  the valley thrills the unimaginable upward lark and drowns . 5 T&C EPITHALAM   79
  new flower with thy unimaginable wings, where dwells the . . 40 T&C AMORES 4   45
  hurt of praise the unimaginable night not known / . . . . . . 418 NO THANKS 35   14
  nothing--human merely being doubt unimaginable You? (now the 663 {CHAIRE} 65   12

UNIMAGINABLY
  morning have concealed so unimaginably young a star / . . . . 626 {CHAIRE} 28   14
  should never know are unimaginably ours to feel-- how . . . . 809 73 POEMS 37   8
  myself, i find selves unimaginably mine; beyond sorrow's own 810 73 POEMS 38   10

UNIMAGINED
  these whose lips smash unimagined sky deeper than heaven . . 563 1 X 1 23   11

UNIMMORTAL
  fee her eager body's unimmortal flower knew in the . . . . . 4 T&C EPITHALAM   55
  as reckoned by the unimmortal mind, these immeasurable . . . 721 95 POEMS 49   6

UNIMPORTANT
  of which is extremely unimportant) whereas Life matters if . 260 IS 5 ONE 30   12
  first to live makes unimportant what i and you . . . . 264 IS 5 ONE 33   19

UNINGSTROLL
  / / / innerly UningstrolL (stamens&pistil silent A s . . . . 342 VIVA 33   2

UNINTERESTING
  bLurting and cHuckling like uninteresting- landscapes made . 101 & POST IMPR 11   69

UNINTERRED
  / / Wing Wong, uninterred at twice fortyeight, succeeded . . 341 VIVA 32   1

UNIQUE
  and i mean the unique and nervously obscene need; . . . . . . 153 & SON ACTU 2   3
  which is loneliness, these unique dreams never shall soil . . 328 VIVA 19   3

UNITE
  idle vertical worthless self unite in a peculiarly momentary 260 IS 5 ONE 30   16

UNITED
  the fire's ruddy glow united) not less than sixteen . . . . . 254 IS 5 ONE 25   10
  The) president of the (united The president of the . . . . . 392 NO THANKS 9   16
  The president of the united states The president of . . . . . 392 NO THANKS 9   17
  The president of the united states of The President . . . . . 392 NO THANKS 9   17
  The President Of The) United States Of America unde . . . . . 392 NO THANKS 9   18
  dream to dreaming flame) united by perfect nothing: . . . . . 721 95 POEMS 49   4

UNIVERSAL
  (having thoroughly oiled the universal joint tested my gas . 248 IS 5 ONE 19   6

UNIVERSE
  foreverfully blend we a universe of gulls' drift Of . . . . . 371 VIVA 62   21
  splendor than our merely universe, love's also there: and . . 377 VIVA 68   6
  a supermetamathical subpreincestures pooped universe (of . . 425 NO THANKS 42   2
  lost) put on his universe and yawned: it looks . . . . 451 NO THANKS 66   1
  and through this opening universe will wraiths of doom . . . 454 NO THANKS 69   9
  "shapley has compared the universe to a uh" pause . . . . . . 464 NEW POEMS 2   13
  into hugeness world system universe and bang --fear buries . 531 50 POEMS 43   2
  hell of a good universe next door; let's go . . . . 554 1 X 1 14   15
  a dream bites this universe in two, peels forever . . . . . . 560 1 X 1 20   18
  turns when (love's a universe beyond obey or command, ... 574 1 X 1 34   7
  / / meet mr universe (who clean and jerked . . . . 645 {CHAIRE} 47   1
  supreme this complete doubtless universe we'd (and we alone . 675 95 POEMS 3   8
  soul may blast some universe to might have been, ... 714 95 POEMS 42   9
  particle is not a universe-- but if, with goldenly . . . . . 756 95 POEMS 84   8
  their smallest joy's a universe emerging from a wish) . . . . 768 95 POEMS 94   8
  white guardians of the universe of sleep safely may . . . . . 811 73 POEMS 39   1

UNIVERSE (CONTINUED)
    marvellously self diminutive whose universe a single leaf may 821 73 POEMS 49   13
    any thing (even a universe) might be so not . . . . 827 73 POEMS 55   5
    the axis of the universe --love. Each believing world . . . . 845 73 POEMS 73   10
UNIVERSES
    only, Queen among centuries universes between Who out of   . . 358 VIVA 49   12
UNIVERSITY
    obscure to be sure university spends her time looking . . . . 234 IS 5 ONE 5   2
UNJOYOUSLY
    moments are no more unjoyously bullied of vilest mind . . . . 213 XLI SONNETS 9   2
UNJUST
    / / "nothing" the unjust man complained "is just" . . . . . . 806 73 POEMS 34   1
UNKEEN
    unslender, what her big unkeen "Business is rotten" the . . . 225 IS 5 ONE LIZ   11
UNKEMPT
    Distinct Lady of my unkempt adoration if i have . . . . 43 T&C AMORES 7   2
UNKIND
    quitting only in the unkind dawn its muscle amorous . . . . . 165 & SON ACTU 14   3
+UNKIND
    FOR CONTEXT, SEE . . . . 554 1 X 1 14   1
UNKINDEST
    guess) perhaps the very unkindest way to kill each . . . . . 528 50 POEMS 40   11
UNKINDNESS
    exit a kind of unkindness exit little mr Big . . . . 389 NO THANKS 6   1
UNKNOWABLE
    wear all never guessed unknowable most joy) faithfully . . . 811 73 POEMS 39   7
UNKNOWN
    how slenderly the illustrious unknown (warily as their . . . 344 VIVA 35   11
    and what may be unknown most secret i will . . . . 428 NO THANKS 45   10
UNKNOWNNESS
    function is to fabricate unknownness (known being wishless; . 446 NO THANKS 61   1
UNLESS
    Olaf, too preponderatingly because unless statistics lie he . 339 VIVA 30   41
    for; not when or unless if or to prove, ... 386 NO THANKS 3   5
    there to where --name unless i'm mistaken chauvesouris-- . . 504 50 POEMS 18   9
    of hopefear sons of unless and children of almost) . . . . . 512 50 POEMS 26   3
    little while they live-- unless by your thinking forever's . 742 95 POEMS 70   11
    sweetness except Himself?" --"noone unless it's a smiling" . 748 95 POEMS 76   16
+UNLESS
    FOR CONTEXT, SEE . . . . 464 NEW POEMS 2   5
    FOR CONTEXT, SEE . . . . 668 {CHAIRE} 70   5
UNLIFE
    (life imitate gossip fear unlife mean -ness, and to . . . . . 452 NO THANKS 67   8
    hands hold his whose unlife bursts only so; only . . . . . . 479 NEW POEMS 17   15
    terrible cry "no slave's unlife shall murder me for . . . . . 711 95 POEMS 39   11
UNLIGHTED
    stolen (somewhere between our unlighted hearts lust lurks . . 322 VIVA 14   10
UNLIKE
    as is death and unlike shirts neckties trousers we . . . . . 238 IS 5 ONE 9   9
UNLIVES
    what filth is here unlives do cry on him . . . . 440 NO THANKS 56   8
UNLIVING
    breasts, forked in surprisable unliving eyes chopped by a . . 103 & POST IMPR 13   4
UNLOCKED
    empty; snickering shop doors unlocked by white-grub faces) . 172 & SON ACTU 21   6
UNLOVE
    world will pray so (unlove disappearing) only your less . . . 450 NO THANKS 65   10
UNLOVE'S
    / / / / unlove's the heavenless hell and . . . . 765 95 POEMS 91   1
UNLOVELY
    battered bodies the odd unlovely souls struggle slowly and . 55 T&C PORTRAIT 3   18
    peerless fantasies or the unlovely longness of the year . . . 207 XLI SONNETS 3   5
UNLUCKY
    it's lucky to be unlucky and the hitler lies . . . . 466 NEW POEMS 4   19
+UNLUCKY
    FOR CONTEXT, SEE . . . . 623 {CHAIRE} 25   6
UNMADE
    doubting have darkly themselves unmade makes love armies . . 580 1 X 1 40   14

	PAGE	TITLE	LINE

UNMAKE
themselves if all dreams unmake (when in a most . . . . 414 NO THANKS 31   5
UNMAN
shi ly glad old unman who is eye / . . . . 602 (CHAIRE) 4   6
UNMARKETABLE
the genuine daze of unmarketable excitation, whose careless . 150 & SON REAL 21   13
+UNMEANING
FOR CONTEXT, SEE . . . . 713 95 POEMS 41   3
UNMIND
-fed infantile eyes drooling unmind grim yessing childflesh . 337 VIVA 28   6
now man's most vast (unmind by brain) more than . . . . 787 73 POEMS 15   10
UNMINDS
dare) unhearts can less unminds must fear because and . . . . 440 NO THANKS 56   5
UNMIRACLE
keener appetite than mere unmiracle can quite appease-- . . . 714 95 POEMS 42   5
UNMITIGATED
continual stitch of the unmitigated systole purrs against my 136 & SON REAL 7   4
a bit of quite unmitigated hate (travelling in a . . . . . . 413 NO THANKS 30   14
UNMOTION
some sun; his least unmotion roams the youngest star) . . . . 609 (CHAIRE) 11   12
UNMOVING
sepa rate one stilled unmoving mind from a hun . . . . 354 VIVA 45   20
+UNMOVING
FOR CONTEXT, SEE . . . . 691 95 POEMS 19   1
UNMUTE
dithyrambs of large immaculate unmute antibolshevistic gents 266 IS 5 TWO 1   8
UNNAKED
was you naked amid unnaked things, your flesh, a . . . . . . 170 & SON ACTU 19   6
UNNATURAL
on your head your unnatural hair has in the . . . . 126 & SEVEN POEMS 5   9
UNNECESSARY
OH the bothering dear unnecessary hairless o ld / . . . . . . 250 IS 5 ONE 21   17
UNNOISE
a jazz Band? or unnoise men don't make soup . . . . 141 & SON REAL 12   18
UNNOTICED
/ / / / unnoticed woman from whose kind . . . . 142 & SON REAL 13   1
UNNOW
shall be immeasurable happenless unnow shuts more than open . 502 50 POEMS 16   6
UNOBSERVED
to peer through windows, unobserved --listen, for (out of . . 292 IS 5 FOUR 9   8
UNPAINFUL
these, were the not unpainful thoughts which occupied the . . 263 IS 5 ONE 32   60
UNPLEASANTLY
unclever. hair genuinely artificial, unpleasantly tremendous. 103 & POST IMPR 13   14
UNPOETS
what stink is here unpoets do cry unfools unfree . . . . . . 440 NO THANKS 56   32
UNPRECISELY
to inexactly pass and unprecisely to repass where flesh . . . 401 NO THANKS 18   11
UNPREPARED
and kindred questions inhibit unprepared digestions, come: . 266 IS 5 TWO 1   30
UNQUESTIONABLY
and a heart but unquestionably a soul-- by no . . . . 802 73 POEMS 30   18
UNQUIET
twitching eyelids finger their unquiet spears the queen of . 34 T&C ORIENTALE 6   82
UNQUOTE
gould's quote oral history unquote might (publishers note) be 410 NO THANKS 27   10
equals the quote and unquote loss of liberty my . . . . . . 544 1 X 1 4   15
stick some quote statue unquote to prove that a . . . . . . 636 (CHAIRE) 38   2
answer "no"? quote citizens unquote might otherwise forget . 636 (CHAIRE) 38   5
if the quote state unquote says "kill" killing is . . . . . 636 (CHAIRE) 38   7
his quote eye cue unquote. Much better than which, ... 807 73 POEMS 35   8
UNREAL
himself occasionally contrives an unreal precise intrinsic . 193 XLI PORTRAIT 1   24
up all sky (really unreal world, will you perhaps . . . . . . 558 1 X 1 18   14
whos (ex- plore my unreal in -credible true each . . . . . 612 (CHAIRE) 14   5
UNREALITIES
/ / / / SONNETS--UNREALITIES it may not always . . . . 76 T&C SON UNRE 1   T

		PAGE	TITLE	LINE

+UNREALITY
    FOR CONTEXT, SEE . . . . 574 1 X 1 34   8
UNREALLY
    spirits, you would disappear unreally; as this planet . . . . 379 VIVA 70   8
UNREASONED
    are neither reasoned nor unreasoned, his wisdom cancels . . . 683 95 POEMS 11   5
UNREASONING
    surprises with refrain of unreasoning summer that by . . . . 184 XLI SONGS 6   5
UNRECOGNIZABLE
    smith spouts cornucopiously not unrecognizable whats of t oo 465 NEW POEMS 3   10
UNRELUCTANT
    / EPITHALAMION Thou aged unreluctant earth who dost with . . 3 T&C EPITHALAM   1
UNREMEMBERED
    and hither myself struts unremembered (rememberingly with in 299 IS 5 FOUR 16   9
UNREPUTE
    signal perfume of whose unrepute focusses in the sweet . . . 74 T&C SON REAL 5   5
UNRIPE
    startling doll undressed in unripe green with nauseous . . . 55 T&C PORTRAIT 3   9
UNRIVALLED
    by word his own unrivalled brand of pyro -technic . . . . . . 266 IS 5 TWO 1   11
+UNROLLINGLY
    FOR CONTEXT, SEE . . . . 347 VIVA 38   13
UNSAID
    (now) with a suddenly unsaid gesture lightly my eyes? . . . . 302 IS 5 FIVE 1   5
UNSATED
    you, approve these firm unsated eyes which have beheld . . . 36 T&C AMORES 1   10
UNSAYS
    's wife) --does doesn't unsays says looks smiles or . . . . . 779 73 POEMS 7   19
UNSCENTED
    church's protestant blessings daughters, unscented shapeless 70 T&C SON REAL 1   4
UNSEEN
    Her green body among unseen things, things obscene (Whose . . 77 T&C SON UNRE 2   3
UNSELF
    squirming: now withered and unself her gnarled vomits a . . . 506 50 POEMS 20   4
    unwish returns on its unself. A world of made . . . . 554 1 X 1 14   8
    her nons- elf 's unself too -thf- ully lee . . . . 704 95 POEMS 32   4
UNSELLABLE
    one eager souldoll one unsellable not buyable alive one . . . 524 50 POEMS 36   45
UNSELVES
    not those who slave unselves to lend for hope . . . . 440 NO THANKS 56   16
UNSERIOUS
    shining hordes in sweet unserious dress ascends the golden . 4 T&C EPITHALAM   63
    care cautiously who prolongs unserious twilight) shadows have 84 T&C SON ACTU 3   10
UNSERIOUSLY
    then be with me: unseriously seem by the perusing . . . . . . 9 T&C SONGS 1   28
UNSHADOWING
    and does our fatally unshadowing fate put on one . . . . . . 454 NO THANKS 69   11
UNSHAPEFUL
    slender dimness in the unshapeful hour making dear moan . . . 9 T&C SONGS 1   5
UNSHEARED
    whose sheen of full unsheared fleece is mean beside . . . . . 11 T&C SONGS 2   12
UNSHY
    item a bounceless period unshy the empty house is . . . . . . 499 50 POEMS 13   7
UNSIGNED
    letter starting "dearest we" unsigned: remarkably brief but . 504 50 POEMS 18   2
UNSINGING
    is singing) silence: but unsinging. In spectral such hugest . 839 73 POEMS 67   2
UNSITS
    she does not stand-ing. unsits her (wrist performs a . . . . 159 & SON ACTU 8   3
UNSKILFUL
    May) --moving in the unskilful day my lady utterly . . . . . 17 T&C PUELLA MEA   23
UNSLAIN
    most smashed unworld stands unslain he which knows not . . . 414 NO THANKS 31   6
UNSLEEP
    blind fear --haunts all unsleep this cry of one . . . . 439 NO THANKS 55   6
UNSLENDER
    of this) her blunt unslender, what her big unkeen . . . . . . 225 IS 5 ONE LIZ   11

		PAGE	TITLE	LINE

UNSLOWLY
    mythical guests of Is unslowly more who (and here . . . . . . 557 1 X 1 17   7
UNSMALLER
    itself and no meanness unsmaller) armies can immensely meet . 580 1 X 1 40   16
UNSMILE
    largest nonglance the least unsmile or whatever weeds feel . 359 VIVA 50   17
UNSMOOTH
    of aching toys in unsmooth sexual luminosity spree. --dear) . 159 & SON ACTU 8   13
UNSOLEMNLY
    lumps of noise.... furniture unsolemnly : bur sting the . . . 159 & SON ACTU 8   9
UNSORRY
    never not have been unsorry, perhaps / / / . . . . 336 VIVA 27   11
UNSPEAKING
    silent, of the steep unspeaking tower within whose . . . . . 4 T&C EPITHALAM   50
    the night utter ripe unspeaking girls. / / / . . . . 45 T&C LA GUERRE 1   15
    by shores soundless, the unspeaking watcher who adores . . . 79 T&C SON UNRE 4   8
    ship upon the fragrant unspeaking ignorant darkness of New . 112 & PORTRAIT 6   98
    galleon of Spring) somewhere unspeaking sits my life; the . . 156 & SON ACTU 5   10
    hands under us the unspeaking Mediterranean bluer than we . . 283 IS 5 THREE 7   3
    mind (slightly smiling, patient, unspeaking with a sign on . 298 IS 5 FOUR 15   3
+UNSPEAKING
    FOR CONTEXT, SEE . . . . 255 IS 5 ONE 26   3
UNSPONTANEOUS
    skilled in quick softness. Unspontaneous. cute. the signal . 74 T&C SON REAL 5   4
    taps. "ready girls". the unspontaneous streets make bright . 108 & PORTRAIT 4   5
+UNSPONTANEOUS
    FOR CONTEXT, SEE . . . . 230 IS 5 ONE 2   15
UNSTRANGE
    might no patient mind unstrange learn (nor could all . . . . 420 NO THANKS 37   7
    may please? must through unstrange synthetic now true . . . . 527 50 POEMS 39   25
UNSTREET
    a long conway 's unstreet with treadwatering nonlegs . . . . 616 {CHAIRE} 18   14
UNSTRENGTH
    a trembling and smooth Unstrength, against the strong . . . . 11 T&C SONGS 2   9
UNSTROLLS
    shrieks bubble squirmwrithed staggerful unstrolls collaps . . 330 VIVA 21   4
UNSULLIED
    the upper class American unsullied stands, before the world: 273 IS 5 TWO 8   17
UNSURELY
    or mere Music mounting unsurely twilight but here were . . . 211 XLI SONNETS 7   2
UNSUSPECTING
    squirming sPine of the) unsuspecting street; THE YELLOW EYES 101 & POST IMPR 11   55
UNSUSPICIOUS
    a boy's body on unsuspicious legs of girl. his . . . . 148 & SON REAL 19   2
UNSWIFT
    blur of paleness; the unswift mouths of snow insignificantly 218 XLI SONNETS 14   14
UNTARNISHED
    shining girl of time untarnished! O small intimate gently . . 5 T&C EPITHALAM   106
UNTEACH
    a loudness called mankind unteach whole infinite the who . . 603 {CHAIRE} 5   3
UNTEACHES
    wise and each ignorant gladness--unteaches what despair . . . 764 95 POEMS 90   41
UNTHEKNOWNDULOUS
    in sin g ular untheknowndulous s pring / / . . . . 508 50 POEMS 22   12
UNTHING
    upward deep most invincible unthing --stern sexual . . . . . 351 VIVA 42   2
    them- selves this implacable unthing next, our illustrious . 799 73 POEMS 27   22
UNTHINGS
    of keen moon) dream unthings silent three like your . . . . . 687 95 POEMS 15   9
    moonday into (big with unthings) tosses hello whirling whose 751 95 POEMS 79   3
UNTHINKING
    laughsin- to Slivers of (unthinking. c'est l'heure exquise) i 94 & POST IMPR 6   18
UNTIDILY
    Flynn" the words drizzle untidily from released cheeks "I'll 226 IS 5 ONE MAME   9
UNTIL
    my indolent priceless smile, until this very frail enormous . 155 & SON ACTU 4   12
    worm of her nakedness until it go rapidly to . . . . 164 & SON ACTU 13   6
    with me slightly. or until with neat obscure obvious . . . . 165 & SON ACTU 14   10

	PAGE	TITLE	LINE

UNTIL (CONTINUED)
love-tooth on edge. So until light each having each . . . . . 173 & SON ACTU 22   11
sharpens and becomes crisper until i smile with knowing . . . 301 IS 5 FOUR 18   13
spirits starve and smother; until autumn abruptly wholly hugs 305 IS 5 FIVE 4   8
of Rish and Foses) until (finding one's self at . . . . 319 VIVA 11   14
did kick and curse until for wear their clarion . . . . 339 VIVA 30   25
in a tight balloon until the smallening world became . . . . 360 VIVA 51   14
deathless life with magic until peace outthunders silence. . 428 NO THANKS 45   16
prayers whom kneeling eyes (until perfectly their imperfect . 450 NO THANKS 65   7
Forever its freedom (Dare until a flower, understanding . . . 453 NO THANKS 68   13
gallant as they come) until she hit a mine . . . . 494 50 POEMS 8   3
the losing spectres mime until out of merely not . . . . . 502 50 POEMS 16   13
o yes to flower until so blithe a doer . . . . 509 50 POEMS 23   8
home through never's always until absolute un gulps the . . . 517 50 POEMS 31   12
(on twilight) they come until (over dull all nouns) . . . . . 557 1 X 1 17   13
/ / / / until and i heard a . . . . 587 1 X 1 47   1
joys of his voice until and who came with . . . . 587 1 X 1 47   7
under skies over grass until and until into flame . . . . . 587 1 X 1 47   13
over grass until and until into flame i can . . . . 587 1 X 1 47   13
whole of a soul until i awoke for the . . . . 587 1 X 1 47   19
with a trill like until / / / / . . . . 587 1 X 1 47   24
bell touches most mere until (eternally) with (now) luminous 601 {CHAIRE} 3   14
unanimal mankind (and not until) / / / / . . . . 620 {CHAIRE} 22   14
never let you go until you've made me white" . . . . 622 {CHAIRE} 24   6
all sweet things are until" "spring follows winter: as . . . 625 {CHAIRE} 27   8
love! against these its until you are and until . . . . . . 633 {CHAIRE} 35   7
until you are and until i am dreams until . . . . 633 {CHAIRE} 35   7
until i am dreams until comes vast dark until . . . . 633 {CHAIRE} 35   8
until comes vast dark until sink last things (least . . . . 633 {CHAIRE} 35   8
(touch me! love) forever --until is and shall be . . . . . 633 {CHAIRE} 35   15
behind yes) without or until no atom couldn't die . . . . . 634 {CHAIRE} 36   12
blossoming) for also then's until / / / / . . . . 667 {CHAIRE} 69   14
fellow'll play his handorgan until you say "i want . . . . . 697 95 POEMS 25   4
one with won der until (see the) with the . . . . 715 95 POEMS 43   11
dream is climbing sky (until his voice is more . . . . . . 752 95 POEMS 80   6
stillness beyond conceiving) dream until No least leaf almost 758 95 POEMS 85   37
and forever touch or until she and he become . . . . 758 95 POEMS 85   43
(eternity being so sans until twice i have lived . . . . . 765 95 POEMS 91   13
are poor-- let's love until noone could quite be . . . . . 769 95 POEMS 95   24
to live is without until: but pitiful they've (big . . . . 776 73 POEMS 4   20
some green mysterious land until my second dream begins-- . 777 73 POEMS 5   5
and they live for until though the sun in . . . . 801 73 POEMS 29   22
and enormously more less: until her-and-his nonexistence . 808 73 POEMS 36   11
i'll keep my tryst until that tide shall turn; . . . . . . 843 73 POEMS 71   6
+UNTIL
FOR CONTEXT, SEE . . . . 785 73 POEMS 13   19
FOR CONTEXT, SEE . . . . 829 73 POEMS 57   9
FOR CONTEXT, SEE . . . . 840 73 POEMS 68   26
UNTIMID
hand followed by gay untimid final flowers (which dressed . . 4 T&C EPITHALAM   67
the dusk with an untimid svelte subdued magic while . . . . . 138 & SON REAL 9   5
UNTO
lead forth thy love unto that bed prepared by . . . . 6 T&C EPITHALAM   113
with wordless worship absolute, unto the certain altar at . . 6 T&C EPITHALAM   116
svelte translation of eternity unto the pale meaning of . . . 6 T&C EPITHALAM   124
madness) --'tis a gate unto a palace intricate (whereof . . . 21 T&C PUELLA MEA   202
dead beauties, mine being unto me sweeter (of whose . . . . . 22 T&C PUELLA MEA   250
/ / / / unto thee i burn incense . . . . 31 T&C ORIENTALE 5   1
flutter the level litanies unto thee i burn incense, ... 31 T&C ORIENTALE 5   21
my heart discovers thee unto whom i burn olbanum . . . . . 31 T&C ORIENTALE 5   29
no backward- wondering be unto us O soul, but . . . . 41 T&C AMORES 5   27
that i may go unto him, and take his . . . . 76 T&C SON UNRE 1   11
with some shame whispered unto God, my name is . . . . . . 117 & PORTRAIT 10   22
/ / / when unto nights of autumn do . . . . 207 XLI SONNETS 3   1
hope (by cold espoused unto fear) in dreadful corners . . . 207 XLI SONNETS 3   7
their numbers are like unto the stars of Heaven. . . . . . . 256 IS 5 ONE 27   21
pride, his father's joy, unto whom duty whispers low . . . 273 IS 5 TWO 8   4
which had been presented unto you by a mystery? . . . . . . 279 IS 5 THREE 3   23

UNTO (CONTINUED)

rag upon what God unto him gave) responds, without . . . . . 339 VIVA 30   17

/ / / be unto love as rain is . . . . 372 VIVA 63   1

love as rain is unto colour; create me gradually . . . . . . 372 VIVA 63   1

why, then comes peace unto men who are always . . . . 414 NO THANKS 31   13

so on & so unto canned swoonsong came "I . . . . 464 NEW POEMS 2   26

UNTOUCH

early soul him shall untouch meaningless precision and . . . 402 NO THANKS 19   13

UNTRUE

dreamings more than truth untrue, the best mouth i . . . . . 344 VIVA 35   7

+UNTUMBLED

FOR CONTEXT, SEE . . . . 695 95 POEMS 23   7

FOR CONTEXT, SEE . . . . 695 95 POEMS 23   7

UNUNUNUN

sin uously&them&twi tching, begins unununun? butbutbut?? . . 445 NO THANKS 60   14

UNUTTERABLY

but in twilight becomes unutterably crisp a thing, which . . 68 T&C POST IMPR 5   8

UNVISIBLE

trembling where my still unvisible when. Wait if i . . . . . 372 VIVA 63   5

findingly Spring the Fragrance unvisible) ges -tured . . . . 482 NEW POEMS 20   9

UNVOICE

the & how <> Unvoice (which frightenS a noisy . . . . 726 95 POEMS 54   7

UNWARY

into crossing sidewalks the unwary june-bug and the frivolous 61 T&C PORTRAIT 9   3

UNWASHED

huge neck around whose unwashed sonorous muscle the filth . . 96 & POST IMPR 8   30

+UNWASHED

FOR CONTEXT, SEE . . . . 354 VIVA 45   8

UNWHORES

than more magnetic pink unwhores a wai ter lugs . . . . . . 629 {CHAIRE} 31   7

UNWIELDY

gas evil to feel. Unwieldy.... the bloodbeat in her . . . . . 135 & SON REAL 6   7

UNWINDING

what & vast solidities, unwinding dizzily & mirrors; sprung . 480 NEW POEMS 18   18

UNWISDOM

should wrest the rare unwisdom of thy eyes, and . . . . . . 205 XLI SONNETS 1   2

UNWISH

a mountainrange; lenses extend unwish through curving . . . . 554 1 X 1 14   7

through curving wherewhen till unwish returns on its unself. 554 1 X 1 14   7

UNWISHED

with their enormous fingers unwished / / / / . . . . 165 & SON ACTU 14   16

UNWISHING

of trivial which thinkless unwishing doth depend upon the . . 411 NO THANKS 28   4

UNWONDERING

fears or any when unwondering immense directionless horizon) 378 VIVA 69   14

UNWORLD

in a most smashed unworld stands unslain he which . . . . . . 414 NO THANKS 31   6

monstering horror swallows this unworld me by you as . . . . 711 95 POEMS 39   2

should some im probably unworld crash to 1 nonillion . . . . 728 95 POEMS 56   11

how numb can an unworld get? A: number / . . . . 791 73 POEMS 19   9

UNWORLD'S

let's, from some loud unworld's most rightful wrong climbing, 745 95 POEMS 73   1

UNWORLDS

toys (than are all unworlds hollow silence has deeper . . . . 565 1 X 1 25   7

all regular righteous comfortable) unworlds thief crook cynic 677 95 POEMS 5   8

UNWOUND

Will come (we being unwound & gone into the . . . . 361 VIVA 52   4

UNYEWKUNTEL

yew tea mis eyesucks unyewkuntel finglestein idstings yewrety 474 NEW POEMS 12   12

UP

harbouring dark, and (catching up her delicate silk) all . . 8 T&C OF NICOL   26

whom white-thighed Semiramis put up her mouth to wholly . . . 22 T&C PUELLA MEA   248

when i have offered up each fragrant night, when . . . . . . 39 T&C AMORES 4   30

to my side Looked up with impertinently exquisite faces . . . 44 T&C AMORES 8   9

tossed into delicious dancing up Up with the pale . . . . . . 44 T&C AMORES 8   13

into delicious dancing up Up with the pale important . . . . 44 T&C AMORES 8   14

/ the hours rise up putting off stars and . . . . 50 T&C IMPRESS 4   1

of gold i looked up and thought to myself . . . . 58 T&C PORTRAIT 6   12

	PAGE	TITLE	LINE

UP (CONTINUED)

the monkey will sit, up, and look at, you . . . . 69 T&C POST IMPR 6 14
dancing slowly are tottering up and down in a . . . . 69 T&C POST IMPR 6 26
my head i sit up and blink at you . . . . 69 T&C POST IMPR 6 34
side my sex sitting up- right on the stomach . . . . 101 & POST IMPR 11 59
poor girls that gets up god knows when every . . . . 109 & PORTRAIT 5 15
and number two took up the song, might i'm . . . . 117 & PORTRAIT 10 15
capering damned) --staring wildly up and down the here . . . 118 & PORTRAIT 10 39
once i was away up in the sky Blue, ... 123 & SEVEN POEMS 2 1
threw the silver dollar up into the tree? I . . . . 125 & SEVEN POEMS 4 2
is climbing people high, up-in tenements talk. in sawdust . . 128 & SEVEN POEMS 6 4
why then we'd go up higher with all the . . . . 129 & SEVEN POEMS 7 8
It's Nice To Get Up In, the slipshod mucous . . . . 130 & SON REAL 1 1
the dawn. she got up with a gashing yellow . . . . 132 & SON REAL 3 14
imply perspicuity, or? shut up. Seeing seeing her is . . . . 141 & SON REAL 12 10
him, and they cleaned up a few times--before she . . . . . . 145 & SON REAL 16 5
The gang got shot up twice, it operated in . . . . 149 & SON REAL 20 8
big horses; light feeling up streets; heels taking derbies . 172 & SON ACTU 21 2
the fluffy threads, put up your little arms and . . . . . . 192 XLI CHANSONS 2 17
take hands and looking up at our beautiful tree . . . . . . 192 XLI CHANSONS 2 26
and is hurriedly picked up and thrown on the . . . . 203 XLI LA GUERRE 1 15
because when you're hard up you pawn your intelligence . . . 204 XLI LA GUERRE 2 10
uh swell fite like up ter yknow, Rektuz, Toysday . . . . . . 227 IS 5 ONE GERT 15
it ◇ cranked her up, slipped the clutch (and . . . . 248 IS 5 ONE 19 10
nice she acted right up to the last minute . . . . 248 IS 5 ONE 19 26
frown Amy Lowell got up and all the little . . . . 249 IS 5 ONE 20 3
dead from the neck up is lead all over . . . . 253 IS 5 ONE 24 14
that means half- way up the Campanile, believe thou . . . . 256 IS 5 ONE 27 8
gollywog voice the kingdomofheaven up behind and crazily . . 259 IS 5 ONE 29 3
a onetwo which doubles up suddenly his bunged hinging . . . . 259 IS 5 ONE 29 15
frock coat (scrambling all up over the tribune dances . . . . 267 IS 5 TWO 2 5
cuss tenderly this side up handle with care fragile . . . . . 270 IS 5 TWO 5 15
getting dim freezing or up to your know . . . . 272 IS 5 TWO 7 9
bugs crawling right all up all everywhere over you . . . . . 272 IS 5 TWO 7 10
brave.... the communists pick up themselves friends & their . 275 IS 5 TWO 9 43
turning into January darkness up through which sprouting . . 279 IS 5 THREE 3 2
pink cliff back and up leaning out of yellowgreen . . . . . 281 IS 5 THREE 5 9
more than.) But look: up- raising, hoisting, a little . . . 282 IS 5 THREE 6 4
say goodmorning trouble adds up all sorts of quickly . . . . 287 IS 5 FOUR 4 3
is twilight (and looking up in fear i see . . . . 301 IS 5 FOUR 18 4
to sum it All Up god being Dead (not . . . . 315 VIVA 7 9
don't as pop weird up her hot ow you . . . . 316 VIVA 8 10
(& both all hopped up) prettily then which did . . . . . . 317 VIVA 9 34
C.O.D. Abe tucks it up back inley clamored Clever . . . . . 321 VIVA 13 8
swung roun an crawled up into itself, an awful . . . . . . 332 VIVA 23 25
"take hands" smiling "coming up these dark stairs. / . . . . 353 VIVA 44 31
season" think "finality lives up on them a little . . . . . 354 VIVA 45 12
am hearing somebody coming up stairs, carefully (carefully . 375 VIVA 66 11
dares to feel (but up with joy; and up . . . . 424 NO THANKS 41 10
up with joy; and up with laughing and drunkenness) . . . . . 424 NO THANKS 41 11
much i cannot) tear up the world: & toss . . . . 433 NO THANKS 50 2
Love (having found) wound up such pretty toys as . . . . . 451 NO THANKS 66 9
yells but who shot up grabbing had by my . . . . 496 50 POEMS 10 9
mouth) stumbling (can't keep up with how big very . . . . . 501 50 POEMS 15 10
dark the mountains grow up from the sky is . . . . 505 50 POEMS 19 10
shall go which and up come who breasts will . . . . 511 50 POEMS 25 23
moon in the man. Up sam (down! alice) a . . . . 513 50 POEMS 27 20
pretty how town (with up so floating many bells . . . . . . 515 50 POEMS 29 2
down they forgot as up they grew autumn winter . . . . . . 515 50 POEMS 29 10
forget to remember with up so floating many bells . . . . . 515 50 POEMS 29 24
/ / / / up into the silence the . . . . 529 50 POEMS 41 1
tomorrow under woe and up comes yesterday most green . . . . 531 50 POEMS 43 4
on hollow was young Up floatingly clothes tumbledish olD . . 534 50 POEMS 46 4
what it's pliz) then up rose bishop budge from . . . . 552 1 X 1 12 6
hair) 'd he picked up a thousand pounds or . . . . 552 1 X 1 12 9
the monster merde then up rose pride and up . . . . 552 1 X 1 12 11
up rose pride and up rose pelf and ghibelline . . . . 552 1 X 1 12 11
of the tomb then up rose mr lipshits pres . . . . 552 1 X 1 12 26

835

UP (CONTINUED)

till your if is up and vanish under prodigies . . . . 555 1 X 1 15   9

sing as easily creation up all sky (really unreal . . . . . . 558 1 X 1 18   13

into know and trudges up to ignorance again: but . . . . . . 579 1 X 1 39   2

eyes can learn look up to silence and completely . . . . . . 592 1 X 1 52   10

my (with a down up around again fly) forever . . . . 594 1 X 1 54   25

folds (but infinite) gently up the with a carroty . . . . . 629 (CHAIRE) 31   15

/ why must itself up every of a park . . . . 636 (CHAIRE) 38   1

notwithstanding with his censored up a wench's rock-a-bye . . 642 (CHAIRE) 44   26

yes! and (plunging rapturously up) we spill our masterpiece . 650 (CHAIRE) 52   19

geoffrey and all) come up from the never of . . . . 661 (CHAIRE) 63   11

stops: & pick ing up a magical stick t, ... 697 95 POEMS 25   8

/ jack's white horse (up high in the night . . . . 699 95 POEMS 27   1

who stag geri ng up some streetfu l of . . . . 703 95 POEMS 31   4

eye" "well maybe she's up to some tricks with . . . . 707 95 POEMS 35   9

'twas me that looked up at my willy and . . . . 707 95 POEMS 35   25

/ old age sticks up Keep Off signs) & . . . . 729 95 POEMS 57   2

here will who straight up into the where so . . . . 746 95 POEMS 74   7

sharp shrill shower bouncing up off burned earth but . . . . 754 95 POEMS 82   2

almost breathing me) --look up: and we'll (for what . . . . . 762 95 POEMS 89   9

O the sun comes up-up-up in the opening sky . . . . 773 73 POEMS 1   1

O the sun comes up-up-up in the opening sky . . . . 773 73 POEMS 1   1

O the sun comes up-up-up in the opening sky . . . . 773 73 POEMS 1   1

/ / / Me up at does out of . . . . 784 73 POEMS 12   1

(far from a grown -up i&you- ful world of . . . . 832 73 POEMS 60   10

is a voyage ? up upup: go ing downdowndown . . . . 840 73 POEMS 68   5

(down slowly swoop wholly up leaping through merciful . . . . 841 73 POEMS 69   31

+UP

FOR CONTEXT, SEE . . . . 100 & POST IMPR 11   40

FOR CONTEXT, SEE . . . . 234 IS 5 ONE 5   1

FOR CONTEXT, SEE . . . . 237 IS 5 ONE 8   16

FOR CONTEXT, SEE . . . . 259 IS 5 ONE 29   25

FOR CONTEXT, SEE . . . . 278 IS 5 THREE 2   8

FOR CONTEXT, SEE . . . . 330 VIVA 21   11

FOR CONTEXT, SEE . . . . 347 VIVA 38   8

FOR CONTEXT, SEE . . . . 387 NO THANKS 4   7

FOR CONTEXT, SEE . . . . 495 50 POEMS 9   9

FOR CONTEXT, SEE . . . . 726 95 POEMS 54   3

UP-IN

is climbing people high, up-in tenements talk. in sawdust . . 128 & SEVEN POEMS 6   4

UP-UP-UP

O the sun comes up-up-up in the opening sky . . . . 773 73 POEMS 1   1

UP'S

/ / / if up's the word; and a . . . . 769 95 POEMS 95   1

UPCLIMBEST

among) float withins he upclimbest And (sky she) . . . . . . 482 NEW POEMS 20   6

UPDIVES

are wintry handlebars glued) updives pursued by its . . . . . 585 1 X 1 45   7

UPDOWNWARDISHLY

fire of Thickness) points uPDownwardishly find everywheres . 311 VIVA 3   15

UPFALL

i downrise outwrithein- ing upfall and Am the glad . . . . . 449 NO THANKS 64   6

UPFLOATING

goldenly huge whole the upfloating moon. Time's a strange . . 750 95 POEMS 78   9

UPHILL

wouldn't creep one mile uphill to only see him . . . . 520 50 POEMS 34   32

UPLIFTING

her mind) supremely whole uplifting the, of each where . . . 533 50 POEMS 45   6

UPLIFTS

occur --see! now himself uplifts of stars the star . . . . . 582 1 X 1 42   13

UPLOOK

list, every nonelastic male-- uplook, all joybegotten whelps 398 NO THANKS 15   18

UPNOWGATH

w (e loo) k upnowgath PPEGORHRASS eringint (o- aThe) . . . . 396 NO THANKS 13   4

UPON

flowers --didst e'er depart upon more exquisite quest? and . 3 T&C EPITHALAM 20

with hooded day preening upon his hand followed by . . . . . 4 T&C EPITHALAM 66

whose expecting breath exults upon the tongue of flame . . . 6 T&C EPITHALAM 118

		PAGE	TITLE	LINE

UPON (CONTINUED)

	PAGE	TITLE	LINE
in winsome indolence simmer upon thinking twilight momently)	6	T&C EPITHALAM	126
the amazed doves flicker upon sunny wings as if	6	T&C EPITHALAM	138
cool incorrigible arms impaled upon delicious mystery, with .	7	T&C EPITHALAM	157
by one there fell upon the night, like angel's	8	T&C OF NICOL	10
whose white voices pass upon forgetting (fail me not)	9	T&C SONGS 1	2
shadowy sheep float free upon terrific pastures pale, whose .	9	T&C SONGS 1	9
purpled world will dance upon Between my lips which	16	T&C SONGS 6	4
and innocent very deftly upon which indolent miracles	19	T&C PUELLA MEA	95
loving) as invisibly when upon her palpable solitude a . . .	19	T&C PUELLA MEA	105
slow glories fleetly go.) Upon a keen and lovely	20	T&C PUELLA MEA	145
and lips consists --always upon the mouth there trysts . . .	20	T&C PUELLA MEA	148
of all things lovely--Time! upon whose watering lips the . .	23	T&C PUELLA MEA	267
which do crowd gaily upon oblivion sweeter than any	23	T&C PUELLA MEA	272
a tendril fleetly curled upon frailness) used to stroll . . .	23	T&C PUELLA MEA	280
swarms of white bees upon the bough of thy	29	T&C ORIENTALE 3	8
of defeat thy hair upon thy shoulders is an	29	T&C ORIENTALE 3	20
thy blood thy feet upon thy ankles are flowers	29	T&C ORIENTALE 3	29
and i came riding upon a horse of porphyry	30	T&C ORIENTALE 4	9
caught you clutched you upon my mouth listen beloved	30	T&C ORIENTALE 4	13
and i came riding upon a scarlet sunset trampling	30	T&C ORIENTALE 4	23
strained you broke you upon my blood listen beloved	30	T&C ORIENTALE 4	28
and i came riding upon a thousand crimson years	30	T&C ORIENTALE 4	36
incense the bowl crackles upon the gloom arise purple	31	T&C ORIENTALE 5	4
jasper beneath saffron umbrellas upon an elephant twelve feet	32	T&C ORIENTALE 6	7
earth and the rings upon their hands are from	33	T&C ORIENTALE 6	47
very amorous he reclines upon the couch of couches	33	T&C ORIENTALE 6	54
subtle body weaving insinuating upon the gold cloth	34	T&C ORIENTALE 6	87
ex- pending gathering pouring upon itself stiffenS to a . . .	34	T&C ORIENTALE 6	92
queens and white money upon her nakedness he nods	34	T&C ORIENTALE 6	102
all the earth writhe upon deep rugs / /	35	T&C ORIENTALE 6	116
lain with empty arms upon the giddy hills to	36	T&C AMORES 1	7
shall rise, slowly return upon the red elected lips	36	T&C AMORES 1	30
her forth to sleep upon the world and the	38	T&C AMORES 3	4
breaking of your soul upon my lips / /	38	T&C AMORES 3	18
floating hands were laid upon me I was whirled	44	T&C AMORES 8	11
have religions taken thee upon their scraggy knees squeezing	46	T&C LA GUERRE 2	15
wakes with a song upon her mouth having death	50	T&C IMPRESS 4	7
city sleeps with death upon her mouth having a	50	T&C IMPRESS 4	30
/ stinging gold swarms upon the spires silver chants	51	T&C IMPRESS 5	3
of parted lips dim upon the syrinx / /	54	T&C PORTRAIT 2	12
jouncing curtain. , rises upon one startling doll undressed .	55	T&C PORTRAIT 3	8
god's flowers were pulling upon bells of gold i	58	T&C PORTRAIT 6	10
infinite the erect deep upon me in the last	64	T&C POST IMPR 1	6
twilights Deepen her, Recite upon her flesh the rain's . . .	65	T&C POST IMPR 2	13
is spilling rancid elves upon neat sunlight into the	69	T&C POST IMPR 6	4
tiniest dead tunes crawl upon my face my hair	69	T&C POST IMPR 6	27
/ / god gloats upon Her stunning flesh. Upon	77	T&C SON UNRE 2	1
upon Her stunning flesh. Upon the reachings of Her	77	T&C SON UNRE 2	1
ly churning witty, twitters upon Our (ta-te-ta in a	89	& POST IMPR 1	15
(like some floating snake upon itself always and slowly . . .	95	& POST IMPR 7	9
head established It suddenly upon the huge neck around . . .	96	& POST IMPR 8	29
of ridiculous velocity commenting upon an un- clean table. .	97	& POST IMPR 8	37
most early stars wincing upon a single colour, i	98	& POST IMPR 9	6
hands move more simply upon the evening and a	98	& POST IMPR 9	8
of ice newly formed upon an old pool. Her	103	& POST IMPR 13	12
white squirming pipes wiggle upon the perfumed roman strength	110	& PORTRAIT 6	8
a high troubling ship upon the fragrant unspeaking ignorant .	112	& PORTRAIT 6	97
jetted music splashing fresh upon silence) i without fail . .	115	& PORTRAIT 8	20
Nothing has also carved upon her much too white	116	& PORTRAIT 9	9
bruising smile; as rapidly upon the jiggled norm of	137	& SON REAL 8	9
(when battling street-lamps fail upon the gold dawn, where .	142	& SON REAL 13	3
nibbles. another couches, weary, upon a flabby mattress of .	143	& SON REAL 14	12
vegetable of her mouth. Upon the whole he suddenly	148	& SON REAL 19	7
and this shall dance upon the nude and final	155	& SON ACTU 4	14
perfect agony. Waiting (always) upon a fragile instant when .	156	& SON ACTU 5	13
/ / / / upon the room's silence, i	164	& SON ACTU 13	1
rose of you, worn upon my mind all night, ...	165	& SON ACTU 14	2

                                                               PAGE   TITLE   LINE
UPON (CONTINUED)
    personal radiance sits hideously upon the trafficing hum of . 168 & SON ACTU 17   2
    closes her left hand upon a mirror. / / . . . . 170 & SON ACTU 19   14
    a quick bird (tenderly upon the dark's prodigious face   . . . 187 XLI SONGS 9   9
    more downy than street-lamps upon an almostclean plate . . . 194 XLI PORTRAIT 2   33
    pennies have been deposited upon the drum there is   . . . . 196 XLI PORTRAIT 4   10
    a numbing im- perfectness upon such peregrinations as . . . . 197 XLI PORTRAIT 5   3
    innovation of mus- cularity upon the most crimson assistance 197 XLI PORTRAIT 5   15
    flowers of silence curled upon a wish, to rapture . . . . . . 205 XLI SONNETS 1   4
    their exquisite dreams--O Love! upon thy dim shrine of . . . 206 XLI SONNETS 2   10
    pursed lips do blow upon cool flutes within wide . . . . . . 208 XLI SONNETS 4   6
    wishing by willows, bending upon streams? / / . . . . 211 XLI SONNETS 7   18
    made a pale fracas upon the accurate moon.... Across . . . . 214 XLI SONNETS 10   9
    noting flies, which jerk upon the weak colour of . . . . . . 217 XLI SONNETS 13   3
    painfully perpetually crouched, quivering, upon the sternly . 231 IS 5 ONE 3   50
    lived presented to him upon the auspicious occasion of . . . 239 IS 5 ONE 10   29
    idea n'est-ce pas? (whereas, upon the other hand, myself) . . 245 IS 5 ONE 16   15
    any king or prince upon his uncorrupted arse with . . . . . . 254 IS 5 ONE 25   20
    and kodaks --by night upon the Riva Schiavoni or . . . . . . 256 IS 5 ONE 27   17
    taken care to lie upon our abdomens for greater . . . . 261 IS 5 ONE 31   12
    typewriter within his reach) upon his fearless derriere . . . 266 IS 5 TWO 1   21
    come, gaze with me upon this dome of many . . . . 273 IS 5 TWO 8   1
    his stern blue eye, upon his firm white lips . . . . 273 IS 5 TWO 8   10
    heart and conscience free, upon the front steps of . . . . . 273 IS 5 TWO 8   19
    fat jibing lips, once upon a (that is over: . . . . 277 IS 5 THREE 1   17
    which The Expectant stutter (upon artificial limbs, with . . 280 IS 5 THREE 4   33
    watching (sprawling, in grass upon a cliff) what had . . . . 283 IS 5 THREE 7   23
    your body's whitest song upon my mind--if i have . . . . . . 306 IS 5 FIVE 5   5
    the top leaps bounding upon other tops to caroming . . . . . 311 VIVA 3   6
    demannd canned saounds) gloats upon the possession of quotes 331 VIVA 22   6
    and his reflection walking upon a mirror this is . . . . . . 335 VIVA 26   4
    and wanting any rag upon what God unto him . . . . 339 VIVA 30   17
    hot with heat-- Olaf (upon what were once knees) . . . . . . 339 VIVA 30   31
    of one small lady upon earth above; to whom . . . . 360 VIVA 51   33
    if a living dance upon dead minds why, it . . . . 377 VIVA 68   1
    slippery small eyes balanced upon one broken babypout (pretty 406 NO THANKS 23   10
    thinkless unwishing doth depend upon the texture of their . . 411 NO THANKS 28   5
    guest (as critics will upon a poet feast) meanwhile . . . . . 418 NO THANKS 35   11
    one hangs a hat upon her tit one carves . . . . 427 NO THANKS 44   5
    and; droops as if upon a thread invisible) A . . . . 434 NO THANKS 51   21
    mind, woven by always upon sunset, crickets within me . . . . 435 NO THANKS 51   35
    lewd shy New and upon the beyond imagining spasm . . . . . . 442 NO THANKS 57   21
    spits) int o immensity (upon once whom fiercely by . . . . . 465 NEW POEMS 3   6
    yes before angel curvings upon a mostless more of . . . . . . 480 NEW POEMS 18   12
    but all these hundreds upon thousands of people socalled . . 510 50 POEMS 24   9
    space-- life stands gradually upon four minds (out of . . . . 517 50 POEMS 31   8
    politician is an arse upon which everyone has sat . . . . . . 550 1 X 1 10   1
    silentness god ever breathed upon beginning) "beautiful o . . 572 1 X 1 32   10
    and slings his wheel upon his back and off . . . . 624 {CHAIRE} 26   19
    mys- tery (liftingly caught upon falling) silent! ly living . 627 {CHAIRE} 29   15
    to slowly trust T upon H, and smile could . . . . 650 {CHAIRE} 52   4
    father lays" "black hell upon you and all filthy . . . . . . 707 95 POEMS 35   21
    into themselves grow silent upon new perfectly blue) i . . . 720 95 POEMS 48   3
    and looks and leaps upon the air) / / . . . . 774 73 POEMS 2   16
    every now and then upon a merely human plane) . . . . 799 73 POEMS 27   10
    refer to thinking) rests upon a dismal misconception; namely 807 73 POEMS 35   5
    ght in g) is upon a gra v es . . . . 833 73 POEMS 61   11
+UPON
    FOR CONTEXT, SEE   . . . . 429 NO THANKS 46   6
    FOR CONTEXT, SEE   . . . . 610 {CHAIRE} 12   5
    FOR CONTEXT, SEE   . . . . 639 {CHAIRE} 41   12
    FOR CONTEXT, SEE   . . . . 796 73 POEMS 24   8
+UPONS
    FOR CONTEXT, SEE   . . . . 681 95 POEMS 9   8
UPPER
    of his youth the upper class American unsullied stands, . . . 273 IS 5 TWO 8   16
UPPERCUT
    sank him with an uppercut but everybody (i believe) . . . . . 706 95 POEMS 34   2

		PAGE	TITLE	LINE

+UPPERCUTS
    FOR CONTEXT, SEE . . . . 388 NO THANKS 5   16

+UPRAISING
    FOR CONTEXT, SEE . . . . 282 IS 5 THREE 6   4

UPREARING
    (slenderly wholly rising, herself uprearing wholly slowly, . 156 & SON ACTU 5   6

UPRIGHT
    a church stood perfectly upright but not piano item: . . . . 263 IS 5 ONE 32   51

+UPRIGHT
    FOR CONTEXT, SEE . . . . 101 & POST IMPR 11   59
    FOR CONTEXT, SEE . . . . 472 NEW POEMS 10   9

UPROAR
    and ridiculous a polite uproar of knuckling silent planes . . 68 T&C POST IMPR 5   14

UPROSE
    u s a" suddenly uprose hungary and she gave . . . . 711 95 POEMS 39   9

UPSETS
    the most expensive furniture upsets a crucifix which smashes 203 XLI LA GUERRE 1   12

UPSIDEDOWN
    clown whom somebody buried upsidedown in an ashbarrel so . . 680 95 POEMS 8   9

UPSOARINGS
    disks of graceful oath, upsoarings the break on ceiling- . . 96 & POST IMPR 8   9

UPSQUIRTINGLY
    And How replies the upsquirtingly careens the to collide . . 330 VIVA 21   9

UPSTAIRS
    racket. The horses sleep upstairs. And you can see . . . . . 171 & SON ACTU 20   6

UPSTANDING
    "I can!" --yon clean upstanding well dressed boy that . . . . 273 IS 5 TWO 8   6

+UPSTARE
    FOR CONTEXT, SEE . . . . 385 NO THANKS 2   48

UPSTREAM
    The Game Fish Swims Upstream & (5) unbeingdead isn't . . . . 803 73 POEMS 31   17

UPUP
    a voyage ? up upup: go ing downdowndown com; . . . . 840 73 POEMS 68   6

UPUPS
    skil ful toyTown which upups to dowNdown (and only . . . . . 371 VIVA 62   9

UPWARD
    valley thrills the unimaginable upward lark and drowns the . 5 T&C EPITHALAM   79
    of a rose swam upward from the troubled heart . . . . 8 T&C OF NICOL   8
    a cathedral before whose upward lean magnificent face the . . 93 & POST IMPR 5   3
    always and slowly which upward certainly is pouring) emits . 95 & POST IMPR 7   10
    from the world prettily upward, mock us....) and there . . . 133 & SON REAL 4   5
    this gorgeous rush of upward lips.... cleverly perching on . 201 XLI PORTRAIT 9   27
    of men called Love) upward doth leap from the . . . . 210 XLI SONNETS 6   4
    (who tensetendoned and with upward vacant eyes, painfully . . 231 IS 5 ONE 3   49
    editor cigarstinking hobgoblin swims upward in his . . . . . 259 IS 5 ONE 29   9
    miraculous challenge, devout am upward deep most invincible . 351 VIVA 42   2
    here's to opening and upward, to leaf and to . . . . 424 NO THANKS 41   1
    limps man crying silence upward --to have tasted Beautiful . 437 NO THANKS 53   11
    great small wish into upward deepness of less fear . . . . . 528 50 POEMS 40   8
    not wait) buds imitate upward each first flower of . . . . . 573 1 X 1 33   23
    ing swim snowing ly upward with Joy, no where . . . . 584 1 X 1 44   13
    their heartbeats dare some upward world of each more . . . . 757 95 POEMS 85   6

UPWARDCRINGING
    of my blood: with upwardcringing swiftness plunge these . . . 139 & SON REAL 10   5

UPWARDLOOKING
    inTerred) LONG LIVE that Upwardlooking Serene Illustrious and 315 VIVA 7   11

UPWRINKLED
    (with what was nose upwrinkled into nothing earthly, while . 226 IS 5 ONE MAME   3

URGENT
    belly's ample vase (that urgent urn which doth amass . . . . 21 T&C PUELLA MEA 198
    dumb dark svelte and urgent (again love i slowly . . . . . . 37 T&C AMORES 2   15

URINAL
    mind layed in a urinal howlessly and without why . . . . . . 387 NO THANKS 4   2

URN
    ample vase (that urgent urn which doth amass for . . . . . . 21 T&C PUELLA MEA 198

URSEAPPEAL
    jetsam are gentlemen poeds urseappeal netsam our spinsters . 492 50 POEMS 6   3

US

receptive earth, O let us descend take shimmering wind . . .	41	T&C AMORES 5	15
these fragile splendors from us crumple them hide them . . .	41	T&C AMORES 5	20
backward- wondering be unto us O soul, but straight	41	T&C AMORES 5	28
and glorygirded faces lead us into the serious steep	41	T&C AMORES 5	33
death dance cruelly for us and start the last	80	T&C SON UNRE 5	10
brain of air!) Let us as we have seen	80	T&C SON UNRE 5	12
swifts the Dark on us all; stories told returned	89	& POST IMPR 1	5
ostensible centuries therefore let us be a little uncouth . .	111	& PORTRAIT 6	56
is would don't punish us for we were good;	117	& PORTRAIT 10	20
world prettily upward, mock us....) and there was a	133	& SON REAL 4	6
i have loved, let us see if that's all.	154	& SON ACTU 3	1
what is dear to us; and by a gestured	158	& SON ACTU 7	9
/ / / let us tremble) a personal radiance	168	& SON ACTU 17	1
day it was Spring.... us drew lewdly the murmurous	174	& SON ACTU 23	1
/ Picasso you give us Things which bulge: grunting	195	XLI PORTRAIT 3	2
thick mind you make us shrill presents always shut	195	XLI PORTRAIT 3	5
am dying so let us come in together and	198	XLI PORTRAIT 6	31
dimension to occur about us and birds known, scarcely	205	XLI SONNETS 1	13
of sure sleep bereaves us of our slow tranquillities	210	XLI SONNETS 6	2
Time being not for us, purple roses were sweeter	213	XLI SONNETS 9	15
therefore my friends let us now sing each and	230	IS 5 ONE 2	36
hand, myself) but let us next demand wherefore yon	245	IS 5 ONE 16	15
and he said to us Kid. daze nutn like	259	IS 5 ONE 29	27
business.... even so, let us make haste --consider well . . .	260	IS 5 ONE 30	21
sleep by dolls let us not be continually astonished	261	IS 5 ONE 31	3
meantime in dreams let us investigate thoroughly each one . .	261	IS 5 ONE 31	10
seemed too beautiful. Let us perhaps excuse me if	263	IS 5 ONE 32	59
my little darlings, let us now passionately remember how--	266	IS 5 TWO 1	16
unprepared digestions, come: let us mildly contemplate . . .	266	IS 5 TWO 1	31
tidiyum necks begin) let us add that there are	274	IS 5 TWO 9	16
hopes feet hands under us the unspeaking Mediterranean bluer	283	IS 5 THREE 7	3
playing moving far below us perhaps one villa caught	283	IS 5 THREE 7	9
big fear Who held us deeply in His fist	289	IS 5 FOUR 6	3
which i suggest teach us a new terror always	289	IS 5 FOUR 6	10
Spring and night) "let us go a very little	303	IS 5 FIVE 2	2
if you'll notice follows us like a big yellow	303	IS 5 FIVE 2	10
(Along the sand behind us, a big yellow dog	303	IS 5 FIVE 2	12
are teased: let (however) us Walk very (therefore and) . . .	317	VIVA 9	17
brilliant pupil mated, let us not deem it miraculous	326	VIVA 18	8
hearts hugely squirm roots) us ly; though hither nosing . . .	361	VIVA 52	9
of Dreaming) somewhere behind us always trying (or sometimes	368	VIVA 59	9
(or sometimes trying under us) to is it find	368	VIVA 59	11
the whining rigging over us, i implore you to	378	VIVA 69	2
sun big moon (enter us) / / / /	393	NO THANKS 10	18
with missians to turn us into rissions and blokes	405	NO THANKS 22	6
come, what Being! open us open our selves. create	422	NO THANKS 39	12
smile, hands (an- onymo -Us / / / /	449	NO THANKS 64	18
inch looks good to us (and Ever-Ever Land is	466	NEW POEMS 4	16
greenness only dying makes us grow / / /	491	50 POEMS 5	16
place is now let us accept (the time forever, ...	504	50 POEMS 18	14
steak and they send us a pie (it's try, ...	513	50 POEMS 27	15
Whose blood was for us spilled) than all mankind	514	50 POEMS 28	9
of (not visible to us) whom only his dream	516	50 POEMS 30	15
so immediate is escorts us home through never's always . . .	517	50 POEMS 31	11
and will it tell us who we are and	528	50 POEMS 40	2
and will it tell us why we dream and	528	50 POEMS 40	3
and will it tell us how we drink crawl	528	50 POEMS 40	4
enough for both of us darling. And if i	531	50 POEMS 43	13
whole truthful infinite immediate us / / / /	538	50 POEMS 50	14
kneeling, we--true lovers--pray that us will ourselves . . .	574	1 X 1 34	11
there they'll scarcely find us (if they do, we'll	579	1 X 1 39	13
as if worlds wanted us to understand they'd never	603	(CHAIRE) 5	8
almighty for dying (forgive us, o life! the sin	604	(CHAIRE) 6	25
i'll sing while at us very deafly a most	659	(CHAIRE) 61	13
are in love: with us they've nothing times nothing	664	(CHAIRE) 66	11
from time shall set us free) forgetting me, remember	688	95 POEMS 16	14
space bowed to immortal us if in one little	694	95 POEMS 22	6

US (CONTINUED)

/ / / over us if (as what was . . . . 741 95 POEMS 69   1
miracle's to breathe) wounded us will becauseless ultimate . 745 95 POEMS 73   5
true) who sings for us for you for me . . . . 760 95 POEMS 87   9
the laziest creature among us a wisdom no knowledge . . . . . 769 95 POEMS 95   8
& i (be ca us e It's we) humble . . . . 782 73 POEMS 10   21
youths and maidens: let us pray / / / . . . . 794 73 POEMS 22   8

+US

FOR CONTEXT, SEE . . . . 310 VIVA 2   13

USE

careful painters love to use for their youngest angels   . . . 20 T&C PUELLA MEA 141
smile didst love to use in other days (drawing . . . . 213 XLI SONNETS 9   12
inexcusable of all to use a highfalootin phrase luxuries . . 239 IS 5 ONE 10   9
rious excu se (in use among pu rposive pu . . . . 477 NEW POEMS 15   6
a soul and couldn't use a mind / / . . . . 544 1 X 1 4   28
is over --it's no use demanding that lending be . . . . 625 (CHAIRE) 27   2

+USE

FOR CONTEXT, SEE . . . . 405 NO THANKS 22   10

USED

so glad) as trembling used to yield with dew . . . . 18 T&C PUELLA MEA   53
fleetly curled upon frailness) used to stroll (very slowly) . 23 T&C PUELLA MEA 280
like flowers made, softly used to wholly move slender . . . . 23 T&C PUELLA MEA 283
world and new sweetly used to laugh and love . . . . 23 T&C PUELLA MEA 286
Buffalo Bill's defunct who used to ride a watersmooth-silver 60 T&C PORTRAIT 8   3
this beach has been used too. much Too. originally . . . . . 94 & POST IMPR 6   1
Razor Blades having been used and reused to the . . . . 230 IS 5 ONE 2   21
wonder about guys you used to (and them slim . . . . 242 IS 5 ONE 13   4
ruined aqueduct lady, which used to lead something into . . . 260 IS 5 ONE 30   24
we was buddies i used to know him lift . . . . 270 IS 5 TWO 5   11
of course my father used to become hoarse talking . . . . . . 276 IS 5 TWO 10   15
we, you and i, used to move when i . . . . 289 IS 5 FOUR 6   19
which click) little gould used to amputate his appetite . . . 410 NO THANKS 27   3

USEFULLY

may myself do nothing usefully and love yourself so . . . . . 481 NEW POEMS 19   9

USELESS

answer Who with the useless flanks and cringing feet . . . . 374 VIVA 65   12

+USELESS

FOR CONTEXT, SEE . . . . 101 & POST IMPR 11   76

USES

or rather Somebody who uses roofs and streets skilfully . . . 92 & POST IMPR 4   12
of her indomitable body uses a careful fierceness. Her . . . 146 & SON REAL 17   3

+USING

FOR CONTEXT, SEE . . . . 448 NO THANKS 63   4

USUAL

/ / / as usual i did not find . . . . 197 XLI PORTRAIT 5   1
little more openly than usual hither, thither who briskly . . 354 VIVA 45   13

UTMOST

perfectly should disappear moon's utmost magic, or stones . . 377 VIVA 68   4
stand, so strictly (over utmost him so hugely) stood . . . . 520 50 POEMS 34   27
to freedom till her utmost secrecies and his (dreaming . . . 721 95 POEMS 49   10
of not knowable night's utmost nothing, wanders a little . . 810 73 POEMS 38   2

UTTER

vivid magical impetuous and utter ponds of dream; and . . . . 19 T&C PUELLA MEA 117
the snow will oft utter, whereof the year has . . . . 21 T&C PUELLA MEA 188
between barrages, the night utter ripe unspeaking girls. / . 45 T&C LA GUERRE 1 15
i am going to utter a tree, Nobody shall . . . . 67 T&C POST IMPR 4   1
who danc ing goes utter ly churning witty, twitters . . . . . 89 & POST IMPR 1   12
myself Hereupon helpless i utter lilac shrieks and scarlet . 199 XLI PORTRAIT 7   11
stone, how obsolete lips utter their extant smile.... remark 260 IS 5 ONE 30   6

UTTERABLE

strike the air in utterable coolness deeds of green . . . . . 163 & SON ACTU 12   7

UTTERANCE

mighty brightness dumbs the utterance of his soul--so even . 79 T&C SON UNRE 4   10

UTTERED

a single star is uttered, and i think of . . . . 186 XLI SONGS 8   20
(at our first) beasts uttered human words --our second . . . 844 73 POEMS 72   1

UTTERING

great writhing words as, uttering overmuch, stand helplessly 76 T&C SON UNRE 1   7

UTTERING (CONTINUED)
   harsh erecting breasts and uttering tits punish my hug . . . 137 & SON REAL 8   13
   is most herself while uttering one a third face, ... 813 73 POEMS 41   8
UTTERLY
   unskilful day my lady utterly alive, to me is . . . .   17 T&C PUELLA MEA   24
   skilful fingerings; it is utterly to lull with foliate . . .   19 T&C PUELLA MEA   87
   / / / / utterly and amusingly i am . . . . 155 & SON ACTU 4   1
   thou art of him utterly afraid, i love of . . . . 215 XLI SONNETS 11   3
   hands poising to again utterly disappear; rushing gently . . 369 VIVA 60   15
   as bright, bitter all utterly things sweet, maggoty minus . . 521 50 POEMS 34   62
   worlds of prose mind utterly beyond is brief that . . . . . 763 95 POEMS 90   20
   know than feel; mistrusting utterly that timelessness whose . 817 73 POEMS 45   12
+UTTERLY
   FOR CONTEXT, SEE . . . .   89 & POST IMPR 1   12
UTTERS
   tortured the base day utters at length her soft . . . . . .   6 T&C EPITHALAM 131
   twilight ....or if sunset utters one unhurried muscled huge . 82 T&C SON ACTU 1   7
   this April sunset completely utters utters serenely silently   93 & POST IMPR 5   1
   April sunset completely utters utters serenely silently a . . 93 & POST IMPR 5   2
   with an African gesture utters a frivolous intense half . . . 95 & POST IMPR 7   7
   sits between her cheeks utters a thud of scarlet. . . . . . 143 & SON REAL 14   6
   a slopcaked shrub painstakingly utters a slippery mess, a . . 144 & SON REAL 15   8
   spiritual cry of spring utters a striving flower, just . . . 213 XLI SONNETS 9   7
UVULA
   enclose me. a gigantic uvula with imperceptible . . . . . . 201 XLI PORTRAIT 9   8
V
   tw iligH (t's v va vas (vast . . . . 448 NO THANKS 63   9
   ; jimmy s: A V o (. : . . . . 471 NEW POEMS 9   27
   except yourselves r s v p" she cannot read . . . . 504 50 POEMS 18   5
VA
   iligH (t's v va vas (vast ness. . . . . 448 NO THANKS 63   10
VACANCY
   thuglike stare the pollenizing vacancy when, Thy patters? . . 159 & SON ACTU 8   15
   face (whose eyes inherit vacancy) will time extract his . . . 210 XLI SONNETS 6   10
VACANT
   tensetendoned and with upward vacant eyes, painfully . . . . 231 IS 5 ONE 3   49
   masturbates softly in the vacant lot of his physiognomy . . . 259 IS 5 ONE 29   22
VACANTLY
   dreams (or some times vacantly gazing through un washed . . . 354 VIVA 45   8
VACATION
   not any never no vacation here is hands is . . . . 523 50 POEMS 36   19
VACUUM
   Fran dictaphones wireless subways vacuum cleaners pianolas . 237 IS 5 ONE 8   9
+VACUUM
   FOR CONTEXT, SEE . . . . 549 1 X 1 9   11
VAGUE
   straining my lips are vague with ecstasy my palpitating . . .   31 T&C ORIENTALE 5   23
   one before one the vague tough exquisite flowers, whom . . . 154 & SON ACTU 3   7
   you. I occasionally feel vague how vague i don't . . . . . 160 & SON ACTU 9   14
   occasionally feel vague how vague i don't know tenuous . . . 160 & SON ACTU 9   15
VAGUELY
   black unbunged Something gushes vaguely a squeak of planes . 195 XLI PORTRAIT 3   11
   "The Madam?" I emitted; vaguely watching that mountainous . . 228 IS 5 ONE MARJ   11
VAIN
   existence has conversed in vain, O scrupulously take thy . . 212 XLI SONNETS 8   2
   sharp days slobber in vain: Nor am i afraid . . . . 293 IS 5 FOUR 10   21
   their beauties are in vain but though mankind persuades . . . 744 95 POEMS 72   4
VAINLY
   her toylike head and vainly tried to catch one . . . . . .   53 T&C PORTRAIT 1   41
   fingers brought her sleep: vainly no smallest voice might . . 520 50 POEMS 34   15
   Brave --wildly who rage, vainly who strive; and being . . . . 799 73 POEMS 27   29
VALENTINE
   die dream that your valentine makes happier me than . . . . . 718 95 POEMS 46   3
VALLEE
   croons canned a la vallee and preserved goldfishian gestures) 425 NO THANKS 42   3
VALLEY
   and suddenly from the valley thrills the unimaginable upward   5 T&C EPITHALAM   78
   does at a gold valley the famished arrow sang . . . .   14 T&C SONGS 4   19

VALLEY (CONTINUED)

of buds mattered. a valley spilled its tickling river . . . . 135 & SON REAL 6   14
but Coolitch wiped his valley forge with Sitting Bull's . . . 321 VIVA 13   13
a fragile heaven of lilies-of-the-valley but it will be . . . 352 VIVA 43   3
under whom flow (mountain valley forest) a million wheres . . 659 {CHAIRE} 61   5

VALLEYS

birch to make an acorn--valleys accuse their mountains of . . 520 50 POEMS 34   10
mountains grow. Lifting the valleys of the sea my . . . . . 520 50 POEMS 34   17
sleet and snow: strangles valleys by ropes of thing . . . . . 560 1 X 1 20   11

VALOR

past, and wed to valor, battle with heroic breeds; . . . . . 209 XLI SONNETS 5   8

VALUE

life's only and true value neither is love makes . . . . . . 531 50 POEMS 43   7

VAN

the philophilic name S.S. VAN MERDE) having first put . . . . 334 VIVA 25   4

VANISH

if is up and vanish under prodigies of un) . . . . 555 1 X 1 15   10
(like me like you) vanish in so --laughing to . . . . 716 95 POEMS 44   28
love, when such marvels vanish, will include --there by . . . 741 95 POEMS 69   10
this namelessness (completely fleetly) vanish, at the . . . . 819 73 POEMS 47   12

VANISHED

might "meet again sometime") vanished, gunwale awash. I . . . 327 VIVA 18   37
doll of an almost vanished me (for whom the . . . . 720 95 POEMS 48   9

VANISHES

cowardice called a world vanishes, teach disappearing also me 669 {CHAIRE} 71   12
less: until her-and-his nonexistence vanishes with also . . . 808 73 POEMS 36   12

VANISHING

of fairie hands and vanishing with dawn). Spring, that . . . 5 T&C EPITHALAM   88
to his perfect satisfaction vanishing from a this world . . . 516 50 POEMS 30   14

VANQUISHED

divine generosity, thus reason vanquished instinct and matter 799 73 POEMS 27   34

VARIOUS

flowers (which dressed in various tremulous armor stun the . 4 T&C EPITHALAM   68
(at Myself's height these various innocent ferocities are . . 202 XLI PORTRAIT 9   40
me into lifeless atoms various ab- surd thoughts slyly . . . 262 IS 5 ONE 32   3
always are kneeling the various deaths which are your . . . . 285 IS 5 FOUR 2   20
my lady, intricate imperfect various things chiefly which . . 306 IS 5 FIVE 5   2
more than all oceans various and while everywhere beneath . . 351 VIVA 42   7
an angel; or (as various worlds he'll spurn rather . . . . . 562 1 X 1 22   7

VAS

(t's v va vas (vast ness. Be) . . . . 448 NO THANKS 63   11

VASE

grasp the belly's ample vase (that urgent urn which . . . . . 21 T&C PUELLA MEA 197
eyes are as a vase of divine silence Come . . . . 27 T&C ORIENTALE 1   11
slippery contours of a vase inexpressibly fragile it is . . . 193 XLI PORTRAIT 1   14

VASES

ankles are flowers in vases of silver in thy . . . . 29 T&C ORIENTALE 3   29

VAST

of semiluminous nausea A vast wordless nondescript genie of . 96 & POST IMPR 8   33
fishe s s olemnandputrid vast, stomachs bLurting and . . . . 101 & POST IMPR 11   68
mor- sel is i. Vast cheeks enclose me. a . . . . 201 XLI PORTRAIT 9   7
in sorting from this vast nonchalant inward walk of . . . . . 201 XLI PORTRAIT 9   21
the tread of those vast armies of the marching . . . . 209 XLI SONNETS 5   3
immediate silliest and whose vast one function being to . . . 337 VIVA 28   2
v va vas (vast ness. Be) look now . . . . 448 NO THANKS 63   12
of bombast--papery what & vast solidities, unwinding dizzily 480 NEW POEMS 18   18
ecstatic ease with which vast my complexly wisdoming friend's 517 50 POEMS 31   5
am dreams until comes vast dark until sink last . . . . 633 {CHAIRE} 35   8
while crylessly drifting through vast most nothing's own . . 661 {CHAIRE} 63   13
hawk and veers the vast most crafty crow your . . . . 774 73 POEMS 2   8
4 now man's most vast (unmind by brain) more . . . . 787 73 POEMS 15   9

VASTLY

dirt death shall him vastly gird, a coward waiting . . . . . 360 VIVA 51   5
lightyears of pyjamastring) a (vastly and particulary) live . 607 {CHAIRE} 9   8

VASTNESS

ignorant disappearing me hurling vastness of love (sometimes 428 NO THANKS 45   8

+VASTNESS

FOR CONTEXT, SEE . . . . 448 NO THANKS 63   12

	PAGE	TITLE	LINE

VASTNESSES
ever provingly disprove eithering vastnesses of orish mind . 761 95 POEMS 88 — 4

VAUDEVILLE
should have gone into vaudeville perhaps because my Uncle . . 239 IS 5 ONE 10 — 5

VEERS
hugest heartless hawk and veers the vast most crafty . . . . 774 73 POEMS 2 — 8

VEGETABLE
amusing big vital vicious vegetable of her mouth. Upon . . . 148 & SON REAL 19 — 6

VEGETABLES
pe o pleLike hideous vegetaBles weasOned with-be- . . . . . . 101 & POST IMPR 11 — 65
the chickens ate the vegetables so my Uncle Sol . . . . . . 239 IS 5 ONE 10 — 16

VEILED
in black candy she veiled with candy white carrying . . . . . 470 NEW POEMS 8 — 5

VEILS
at length from palpitating veils. O still miraculous May! . . 5 T&C EPITHALAM — 104

VELOCITY
an- gle of ridiculous velocity commenting upon an un- . . . . 97 & POST IMPR 8 — 37
actuality), an orchid whose velocity is sculptural / / . . . 193 XLI PORTRAIT 1 — 26

VELOUR
is young life wears velour trousers life totters, life . . . 102 & POST IMPR 12 — 8

VELVET
perpetualness. When what's in velvet beyond doomed thought is 81 T&C SON UNRE 6 — 9

VENEZIA
stop look & listen Venezia: incline thine ear you . . . . . . 256 IS 5 ONE 27 — 2

VERB
queen: each is a verb, miraculous inflected oral devious, . . 21 T&C PUELLA MEA — 209

VERBAL
is at moon-cease soon verbal mist-flowers close ghosts on . . 90 & POST IMPR 2 — 14
nouns) begins a whole verbal adventure to illimitably Grow . 557 1 X 1 17 — 15

VERDI
two ne like nothing verdi slightly knu as and . . . . 602 (CHAIRE) 4 — 3

VERILY
/ o pr gress verily thou art m mentous . . . . 392 NO THANKS 9 — 2

VERMILION
I into the big vermilion departure swim, sayingly; (Do . . . 66 T&C POST IMPR 3 — 11
virginal pinks and wealthy vermilion and breathless-scarlet, 100 & POST IMPR 11 — 6
sting out of the vermilion jacket of nodding hairy . . . . . 279 IS 5 THREE 3 — 18

VERMOUTH
a tiny sunset of vermouth -colour. Hair. he put . . . . 148 & SON REAL 19 — 8

VERO
dodreamingly phantoms (exchanging) e vero madonna (nudge . . 681 95 POEMS 9 — 6

VERSES
at them, and made verses, through the sharp light . . . . . . 302 IS 5 FIVE 1 — 14

VERTICAL
sensual mysticism of entire vertical being, i am skilfully . 201 XLI PORTRAIT 9 — 23
the insane teeth the vertical grin give me the . . . . 220 XLI SONNETS 16 — 8
the your-and my- idle vertical worthless self unite in . . . 260 IS 5 ONE 30 — 15

VERTIGINOUSLY
whats of t oo vertiginously absorbed which a la . . . . 465 NEW POEMS 3 — 12

VERY
dead mouths throughout that very proud transparent company of 6 T&C EPITHALAM — 142
moment lose: haste) the very shadowy sheep float free . . . . 9 T&C SONGS 1 — 8
such and such mysteries very simply touch me, whose . . . . . 12 T&C SONGS 2 — 37
dexterous and fugitive my very frail lady drifting . . . . . 17 T&C PUELLA MEA — 18
surprise (it were so very new a flower, a . . . . 18 T&C PUELLA MEA — 51
(beings alert and innocent very deftly upon which indolent . 19 T&C PUELLA MEA — 95
ponds of dream; and very secret food its leaves . . . . 19 T&C PUELLA MEA — 118
all things amorous fashioned very curiously of roses and . . 20 T&C PUELLA MEA — 137
at flight --my lady's very singular and slenderest hands . . 20 T&C PUELLA MEA — 159
distinct foot (if whose very minuteness doth abuse reason, . 22 T&C PUELLA MEA — 218
in the moon) --fashioned very curiously of roses and . . . . 22 T&C PUELLA MEA — 229
of rhyme-- in life's very fragile hour (when the . . . . . . 23 T&C PUELLA MEA — 275
frailness) used to stroll (very slowly) one or two . . . . . 23 T&C PUELLA MEA — 281
whose fruit is the very eatage of forgetfulness thy . . . . . 29 T&C ORIENTALE 3 — 23
when the emperor is very amorous he reclines upon . . . . . . 33 T&C ORIENTALE 6 — 53
servant who in Thy very house silently sits looking . . . . . 57 T&C PORTRAIT 5 — 7
thighs i am so very glad that the soul . . . . 61 T&C PORTRAIT 9 — 26
in the alive coolness, very faintly and finally through . . . 92 & POST IMPR 4 — 15

		PAGE	TITLE	LINE

VERY (CONTINUED)

	PAGE	TITLE	LINE
the bed is not very big a sufficient pillow	134	& SON REAL 5	1
of a neckless nudity (very occasionally budding a flabby . .	134	& SON REAL 5	7
daffy, and which was very silly hocked the diamond	145	& SON REAL 16	8
say the breasts look very good: firmlysquirmy with a	150	& SON REAL 21	3
eyes smiles, one grin very distinctly wobbles from the . . .	151	& SON REAL 22	15
priceless smile, until this very frail enormous star (do . .	155	& SON ACTU 4	13
the spring of this very year (a spring of	158	& SON ACTU 7	3
forest and were you very sorry to come away?	192	XLI CHANSONS 2	6
oh but you'll be very proud and my little	192	XLI CHANSONS 2	24
portrait over the door very notable of the sultan's	198	XLI PORTRAIT 6	8
with far colours, thinking very much of nothing and	211	XLI SONNETS 7	16
cries of paklavah meeah. (Very occasionally three.) and i . .	217	XLI SONNETS 13	13
you if we're not very careful) O, the darling	250	IS 5 ONE 21	4
spits quickly into the very bright spittoon / /	252	IS 5 ONE 23	12
with Lord Rothermere billiards very well by moonlight with .	262	IS 5 ONE 32	22
piston and of pistil; very well provided an instant	264	IS 5 ONE 33	22
fla -me of the (very prettily indeed) arra- nged	267	IS 5 TWO 2	12
(the Flics, tidiyum, are very tidiyum reassuringly similar, .	274	IS 5 TWO 9	10
similar, they all have very tidiyum mustaches, and very . . .	274	IS 5 TWO 9	11
very tidiyum mustaches, and very tidiyum chins, and just . .	274	IS 5 TWO 9	12
and just above their very tidiyum ears their very	274	IS 5 TWO 9	14
very tidiyum ears their very tidiyum necks begin) let	274	IS 5 TWO 9	15
all the flics are very organically arranged and their . . .	274	IS 5 TWO 9	19
teeth the Communists have (very) fine eyes (which stroll . .	275	IS 5 TWO 9	48
ourselves... while in the very middle of fire all	283	IS 5 THREE 7	26
to turn, disappears the very swift and invisibly living . . .	300	IS 5 FOUR 17	6
walking beside me, my very lady, if scarcely the	302	IS 5 FIVE 1	2
"let us go a very little beyond the last	303	IS 5 FIVE 2	2
and i'm ever so very little afraid") i say	303	IS 5 FIVE 2	7
my singing slips the very skilful strangeness of your	306	IS 5 FIVE 5	7
and his wife: Both very young noisily who kiss	312	VIVA 4	11
let (however) us Walk very (therefore and) softly among . . .	317	VIVA 9	18
about "stuffed fauna" being "very interesting"... we	326	VIVA 18	33
his Its image strutting (very jerkily) not toucH- ing	335	VIVA 26	11
released for all this very diminishing vicarious ughhuh world	337	VIVA 28	10
and planets heard, rose very slowly in a tight	360	VIVA 51	13
my life will shut very beautifully, suddenly, as when	366	VIVA 57	10
this (shivering pale naked very poor) creature of shadow, . .	374	VIVA 65	13
relatively speaking uncultured (who Very distinctly confine .	391	NO THANKS 8	20
other courted both was very very thwarted) and when	401	NO THANKS 18	5
courted both was very very thwarted) and when which	401	NO THANKS 18	5
(becoming most buried unbecomingly very by most) people / . .	412	NO THANKS 29	17
less (merely beyond how very) closely than Nothing, remember	453	NO THANKS 68	6
a much less thin very much more big &	470	NEW POEMS 8	12
a much more than very much biggest & thickest	470	NEW POEMS 8	15
by alive green each very lifting & seriously voice	480	NEW POEMS 18	24
up with how big very them) now (it tears	501	50 POEMS 15	10
la moon. Employs a very crazily how clownlike that	504	50 POEMS 18	7
limber and lithe some very fine mower a tall;	509	50 POEMS 23	11
tall some jerry so very (and nellie and fan)	509	50 POEMS 23	13
dares to fear) i very humbly thank you which	522	50 POEMS 35	9
(you guess) perhaps the very unkindest way to kill	528	50 POEMS 40	11
am so glad and very merely my fourth will	537	50 POEMS 49	1
give and on forever's very now we stand nor	538	50 POEMS 50	12
heart the animal is very very kind so kind	544	1 X 1 4	26
the animal is very very kind so kind it	544	1 X 1 4	26
illimitably my --being so very born no bird can	558	1 X 1 18	12
we love each other very dearly , more than	577	1 X 1 37	1
year both is the very weather (not either) my	578	1 X 1 38	5
least your any most very amazing now or here)	580	1 X 1 40	3
/ which is the very (in sad this havingest	590	1 X 1 50	1
the floating in the very spirits singing in are	591	1 X 1 51	7
are slowly all together very magically smiling and if	600	{CHAIRE} 2	10
illimit able to speak very softly altogeth er miracu	600	{CHAIRE} 2	14
bringing this visitor their very oldest lives one pays . . .	624	{CHAIRE} 26	8
with some- thing sil -very ; bright, &: mys	632	{CHAIRE} 34	5
a child 's hand) very carefully bring -ing to	652	{CHAIRE} 54	3

		PAGE	TITLE	LINE

VERY (CONTINUED)

sing while at us very deafly a most stares . . . . 659 (CHAIRE) 61   13
with a look the very boldest man can scarcely . . . . 685 95 POEMS 13   2
himself's own self; his very him / / / . . . . 756 95 POEMS 84   14
(on tiptoe at the very quick of nowhere) we . . . . 758 95 POEMS 85   46
are one today) my very so gay young love . . . . 767 95 POEMS 93   15
annie slightly mad but very wonderful in bed --saints . . . . 794 73 POEMS 22   6
of hellas dwelt two very different sons of zeus: . . . . . . 799 73 POEMS 27   2
oneself alone but the very song of (as mountains . . . . . . 804 73 POEMS 32   13
of you whispers "is very pleasant" my ghost to . . . . 808 73 POEMS 36   15
moment it takes one very falling most (there: did . . . . . . 809 73 POEMS 37   11
own joys and hoping's very fears yours is the . . . . 810 73 POEMS 38   11
my darling (open the very secret of hope to . . . . 811 73 POEMS 39   4
in his arms my very life who's your --when . . . . 812 73 POEMS 40   12
voice your ways (o very most my shining love) . . . . 819 73 POEMS 47   4
sil e nce e very w here noon e . . . . 830 73 POEMS 58   6
angry skies and gently (very whiteness: absolute peace, never 839 73 POEMS 67   14

+VERY

FOR CONTEXT, SEE . . . . 122 & SEVEN POEMS 1   21
FOR CONTEXT, SEE . . . . 255 IS 5 ONE 26   8
FOR CONTEXT, SEE . . . . 287 IS 5 FOUR 4   7
FOR CONTEXT, SEE . . . . 398 NO THANKS 15   22

VEST

did nothing on the vest its wideflung friend clenched . . . . 258 IS 5 ONE 28   17
she let go my vest and crept through the . . . . 284 IS 5 FOUR 1   11

VEUX

droppe5 qu'est-ce que tu veux Dwrith il est trop . . . . . . 430 NO THANKS 47   18

VIBRANT

beyond shock blurted) strokes, vibrant with the purr of . . . 115 & PORTRAIT 8   14

VIBRATION

down flesh neither may vibration create voice if therefore . 425 NO THANKS 42   12

VICARIOUS

all this very diminishing vicarious ughhuh world (the pertly 337 VIVA 28   11

VICE

thus virtue triumphed over vice and beauty bowed to . . . . 799 73 POEMS 27   36

VICIANS

tratesmen delivered are of vicians and all the world . . . . 405 NO THANKS 22   2

VICINITY

or in the felicitous vicinity of the de l'Europe . . . . . . 256 IS 5 ONE 27   18
thought) otherwise immaculately tabulated vicinity) invei- . 267 IS 5 TWO 2   16

VICIOUS

the amusing big vital vicious vegetable of her mouth. . . . . 148 & SON REAL 19   5

VICTIM

suddenly his bunged hinging victim against the giving ropes . 259 IS 5 ONE 29   16
perpetual eyes each exact victim, how he does not . . . . . . 386 NO THANKS 3   11
a comfortable disease: your victim (death and life safely . . 554 1 X 1 14   3
hawked and scalped his victim , not to save . . . . 643 (CHAIRE) 45   2

VICTOR

my Uncle Sol a Victor Victrola and records while . . . . . . 239 IS 5 ONE 10   27

VICTORIAN

of squirrel-stairs into a mid-victorian attic which is known 194 XLI PORTRAIT 2   8

VICTORIOUS

saw their once again victorious Pantarkes (whose grace the . 4 T&C EPITHALAM   34
Jason (in impossible things victorious impossibly) so wholly 18 T&C PUELLA MEA   70

VICTORY

is an army with victory and with trumpets thy . . . . 29 T&C ORIENTALE 3   21

VICTROLA

Uncle Sol a Victor Victrola and records while he . . . . . . 239 IS 5 ONE 10   28

VIERGE

cul de Paris" (Marie Vierge Priez Pour Nous) with . . . . . . 120 & PORTRAIT 12   15

VIEWS

lives (may never cease views with smooth vigilant perpetual . 386 NO THANKS 3   10

VIGILANT

cease views with smooth vigilant perpetual eyes each exact . 386 NO THANKS 3   10

VILEST

more unjoyously bullied of vilest mind and sweet uncaring . . 213 XLI SONNETS 9   2

VILLA

below us perhaps one villa caught like pieces of . . . . . . 283 IS 5 THREE 7   10

```
                                                       PAGE     TITLE        LINE
VILLAGE
   amiable putrescence carpenters the village of her mind bodily 136 & SON REAL 7      2
   by black wine. a village does not move behind . . . . . . . 434 NO THANKS 51        8
+VILLAIN
   FOR CONTEXT, SEE . . . . . . . . . . . . . . . . . . . . . . 677 95 POEMS 5        12
VILLAINS
   doubts, all certainties, as villains strive and heroes  . . . 576 1 X 1 36          5
   a world with its villains or heroes (for god . . . . . . . . 732 95 POEMS 60       14
VILLAINY
   / / honour corruption villainy holiness riding in fragrance . 661 (CHAIRE) 63       1
VINAL
   OR BEAUTY HURTS MR. VINAL take it from me . . . . . . . . . . 230 IS 5 ONE 2        T
VINE
   legs just like a vine that's spent all of . . . . . . . . . . 147 & SON REAL 18    10
   tolled and the old vine twined this is a . . . . . . . . . . 647 (CHAIRE) 49       15
VINES
   i stride among the vines (my heart pursues against  . . . . . 434 NO THANKS 51     15
+VINO
   FOR CONTEXT, SEE . . . . . . . . . . . . . . . . . . . . . . 387 NO THANKS 4       18
VIOLENT
   Fields lying miraculous in violent silence fill with  . . . .  86 T&C SON ACTU 5    7
VIOLET
   to his innumerable whereabouts violet logic of annihi- lation 197 XLI PORTRAIT 5    6
   at red blue yellow violet white orange green- ness  . . . . . 437 NO THANKS 53     14
   none) "don't cry dear violet you may take mine" . . . . . . . 684 95 POEMS 12       3
   of mind equal one violet / / / / . . . . . . . . . . . . . . 736 95 POEMS 64       8
VIOLETFLAVOURED
   silently emit a tiny violetflavoured nuisance: Odor? ono. . . 231 IS 5 ONE 3       53
VIOLETS
   Tumbling-hair picker of buttercups violets dandelions And the  26 T&C CHANSONS 3    3
   threw the bunch of violets into the tree? I . . . . . . . . . 125 & SEVEN POEMS 4  14
   either) my treasure, when violets appear love is a . . . . . 578 1 X 1 38           8
+VIOLETS
   FOR CONTEXT, SEE . . . . . . . . . . . . . . . . . . . . . . 179 XLI SONGS 1       19
VIOLIN
   and thin despair of violin / / / / . . . . . . . . . . . . .  12 T&C SONGS 2       50
   rine, s And the violin spitting squeaky songs into . . . . . 100 & POST IMPR 11    43
   life, dollies of anyway VIOLIN / / / / . . . . . . . . . . . 101 & POST IMPR 11    84
VIOLINISTS
   the thrillers these crepuscular violinists among my and your 230 IS 5 ONE 2        26
VIOLINS
   normal melody of probable violins dance the square virtues .  43 T&C AMORES 7      33
VIRGINAL
   and pretty- lemons and virginal pinks and wealthy vermilion . 100 & POST IMPR 11    6
   nowhere from) querying affirmation; virginal immediacy of . . 669 (CHAIRE) 71       5
VIRGINITY
   (a recipe against Laughing Virginity Death) then dearest the 359 VIVA 50            9
VIRGINS
   don't --the substantial dollarbringing virgins "from the  . . 256 IS 5 ONE 27      29
VIRTUE
   for fear) of shadowy virtue and of sunful sin . . . . . . . . 607 (CHAIRE) 9       13
   slave of mind; thus virtue triumphed over vice and  . . . . . 799 73 POEMS 27      36
VIRTUES
   violins dance the square virtues and the oblong sins  . . . .  43 T&C AMORES 7      34
VISAGE
   myriad tints enrich a visage simple, terse, seated like . . . 254 IS 5 ONE 25      18
VISE
   her beauty is a vise whose stilling lips murder . . . . . . . 152 & SON ACTU 1     10
VISIBLE
   frail ultimate pose! O visible beatitude sweet sweet  . . . .   5 T&C EPITHALAM    110
   some out of (not visible to us) whom only . . . . . . . . . . 516 50 POEMS 30      15
+VISIBLY
   FOR CONTEXT, SEE . . . . . . . . . . . . . . . . . . . . . . 464 NEW POEMS 2       17
VISIBLYA
   jumps of THuNdeRB loSSo!MiN -visiblya mongban (gedfrag- ment 347 VIVA 38           12
VISION
   --by their precision evolving vision dreamtree, truthtree . . 763 95 POEMS 90      30
   half perceive. Only whose vision can create the whole . . . . 845 73 POEMS 73       5
```

	PAGE	TITLE	LINE

VISIONS
red elected lips scaleless visions) / / / / . . . . 36 T&C AMORES 1 32
breast awake) slow tottering visions bigly come crashing into 565 1 X 1 25 13
+VISIONS
FOR CONTEXT, SEE . . . . 405 NO THANKS 22 2
VISITED
city which nobody's ever visited, where always it's Spring) . 129 & SEVEN POEMS 7 12
VISITOR
widows wives bringing this visitor their very oldest lives . 624 {CHAIRE} 26 7
VITAL
slapped the amusing big vital vicious vegetable of her . . . 148 & SON REAL 19 5
a, fathoming jelly of vital futile huge light as . . . . . . 159 & SON ACTU 8 2
electric Distinct face haughtily vital clinched in a swoon . 193 XLI PORTRAIT 1 3
VIVA
springtime is lovetime and viva sweet love" (all the . . . . 591 1 X 1 51 4
springtime is lovetime and viva sweet love" / / . . . . 591 1 X 1 51 28
VIVE
that man isn't wuman vive the millenni um three . . . . 492 50 POEMS 6 9
VIVID
always dwells beside the vivid magical impetuous and utter . 19 T&C PUELLA MEA 116
the silence filled with vivid noiseless boys at Roupy . . . . 45 T&C LA GUERRE 1 11
see the large lips vivid, the face grey, and . . . . 75 T&C SON REAL 6 7
disappear and perfectly) nowhere vivid anonymous mythical . . 557 1 X 1 17 5
trickstervillain raucous rogue & vivid voltaire you beautiful 677 95 POEMS 5 14
can't answer: and such vivid nothing as green meteors . . . . 818 73 POEMS 46 11
+VIVID
FOR CONTEXT, SEE . . . . 615 {CHAIRE} 17 13
+VIVIDLY
FOR CONTEXT, SEE . . . . 703 95 POEMS 31 7
VOCAL
of her mind) --the vocal fern, always which feels . . . . . . 19 T&C PUELLA MEA 124
VOICE
/ Always before your voice my soul half-beautiful and . . . . 11 T&C SONGS 2 1
fern of her delicious voice (of her voice which . . . . 19 T&C PUELLA MEA 114
delicious voice (of her voice which always dwells beside . . 19 T&C PUELLA MEA 115
/ / your little voice Over the wires came . . . . 44 T&C AMORES 8 1
death leaping Sweetly your voice / / / / . . . . 44 T&C AMORES 8 24
seen death's clever enormous voice which hides in a . . . . . 45 T&C LA GUERRE 1 4
you sing in your whiskey-voice the grass rises on . . . . . . 61 T&C PORTRAIT 9 18
God in a tiny voice, i am may the . . . . 117 & PORTRAIT 10 11
/ / (the phonograph's voice like a keen spider . . . . 166 & SON ACTU 15 1
hot alley, a nigger's voice feels curiously cool . . . . . . 167 & SON ACTU 16 18
dark's prodigious face thy voice scattering perfume-gifted . 187 XLI SONGS 9 12
/ / the skinny voice of the leatherfaced woman . . . . 196 XLI PORTRAIT 4 1
for the thing. Her voice? gruesome: a trull leaps . . . . . . 227 IS 5 ONE GERT 12
them--then carefully the rolypoly voice squatting on a . . . 228 IS 5 ONE MARJ 9
with his big gollywog voice the kingdomofheaven up behind . . 259 IS 5 ONE 29 2
instead then shall the voice of liberty be mute?" . . . . . . 268 IS 5 TWO 3 13
the painter of your voice-- beyond these elements remarkably 291 IS 5 FOUR 8 15
in me understands the voice of your eyes is . . . . 366 VIVA 57 19
E eat of her voice in whose silence the . . . . 390 NO THANKS 7 4
neither may vibration create voice if therefore among foul . 425 NO THANKS 42 12
very lifting & seriously voice -like finger of the . . . . . 480 NEW POEMS 18 25
thick snake of a voice these root like legs . . . . 490 50 POEMS 4 11
a spinster's heart my voice feels who inquires is . . . . . . 506 50 POEMS 20 7
words but joy's the voice down shall go which . . . . 511 50 POEMS 25 22
sleep: vainly no smallest voice might cry for he . . . . . . 520 50 POEMS 34 15
sing you are my voice, / / / / . . . . 531 50 POEMS 43 14
the colours of your voice) from some complete existence . . . 559 1 X 1 19 5
wing and tree is voice more leastfully than i . . . . 583 1 X 1 43 19
the joys of his voice until and who came . . . . 587 1 X 1 47 6
first sunrise) and his voice is green like growing . . . . . 617 {CHAIRE} 19 5
have not okayed his voice --and any wave signs . . . . 620 {CHAIRE} 22 6
flower- soft bird -quick voice loves children and sunlight . 660 {CHAIRE} 62 21
ghost 's rainfaint windthin voice-which-is no-voice sobcries 697 95 POEMS 25 12
's rainfaint windthin voice-which-is no-voice sobcries "paw? 697 95 POEMS 25 13
a who but the voice-with-a-smile of democracy announces night 711 95 POEMS 39 5
grows most big a voice comes out of some . . . . 752 95 POEMS 80 2

	PAGE	TITLE	LINE

VOICE (CONTINUED)
climbing sky (until his voice is more than bird) . . . . . . 752 95 POEMS 80 6
a silence who's the voice of voice / / . . . . 761 95 POEMS 88 14
who's the voice of voice / / / / . . . . 761 95 POEMS 88 14
wish) love is the voice under all silences, the . . . . . . 768 95 POEMS 94 9
sixth avenue) "then" my voice marvels "what happened" as . . 800 73 POEMS 28 21
his kind sweet big voice: then a slender face . . . . 813 73 POEMS 41 2
of your eyes your voice your ways (o very . . . . 819 73 POEMS 47 3
faithfully tinying at twilight voice of deathless earth's . . 821 73 POEMS 49 1
+VOICE
FOR CONTEXT, SEE . . . . 385 NO THANKS 2 54
VOICE-WHICH-IS
ghost 's rainfaint windthin voice-which-is no-voice sobcries 697 95 POEMS 25 12
VOICE-WITH-A-SMILE
a who but the voice-with-a-smile of democracy announces night 711 95 POEMS 39 5
VOICELESS
) Whoshout (Ghost) atOne (voiceless) O ther or im) . . . . . 347 VIVA 38 22
+VOICELIKE
FOR CONTEXT, SEE . . . . 480 NEW POEMS 18 25
VOICES
those rivers whose white voices pass upon forgetting (fail . 9 T&C SONGS 1 2
brain clotted with loosely voices look look. Skilfully . . . 99 & POST IMPR 10 6
a. of, loosely ; voices / / / / . . . . 99 & POST IMPR 10 24
tenements talk. in sawdust Voices a: whispering drunkard . . 128 & SEVEN POEMS 6 5
skill of new leaves' voices, and sharp lips of . . . . 218 XLI SONNETS 14 5
with large legs rancid voices Baedekers Mothers and kodaks . 256 IS 5 ONE 27 16
/ / / / voices to voices, lip to . . . . 264 IS 5 ONE 33 1
/ / voices to voices, lip to lip i . . . . 264 IS 5 ONE 33 1
i have lips and voices which are for kissing . . . . 264 IS 5 ONE 33 25
out of ten fingers voices rise from down ever . . . . 281 IS 5 THREE 5 21
gestures bud plumptumbling hand voices Eye Doangivuh sud- . . 330 VIVA 21 7
for wear their clarion voices and boots were much . . . . . 339 VIVA 30 26
(among leaves Easily through voices womenlike telling of . . 356 VIVA 47 4
to leaf) but should voices (whom lure an eagerest . . . . . 362 VIVA 53 9
behind death's death whenless voices sing everywhere your . . 450 NO THANKS 65 17
small million of dark voices sing against the awful . . . . 454 NO THANKS 69 13
and three singing with voices made of earth and . . . . . . 507 50 POEMS 21 8
luminous they climb oblivion) voices who are dreams, less . . 810 73 POEMS 38 6
is ablaze with their voices) all shallbe and was . . . . . . 841 73 POEMS 69 8
+VOICES
FOR CONTEXT, SEE . . . . 448 NO THANKS 63 20
FOR CONTEXT, SEE . . . . 789 73 POEMS 17 22
VOIX
guerre. Mimi a la voix fragile qui chatouille Des . . . . . 120 & PORTRAIT 12 6
promene-t-elle, pourquoi eclate ta voix fragile couleur de . 121 & PORTRAIT 12 55
VOLSTEAD
lovely lambs, of Sumner Volstead Christ and Co. the . . . . 266 IS 5 TWO 1 2
VOLTAIRE
raucous rogue & vivid voltaire you beautiful anarchist (i . . 677 95 POEMS 5 14
VOLUME
colour, clutched the dull volume of her tumbling face . . . . 73 T&C SON REAL 4 5
+VOLUME
FOR CONTEXT, SEE . . . . 201 XLI PORTRAIT 9 21
VOMIT
frozen brook of pinkest vomit out of eyes which . . . . . . 258 IS 5 ONE 28 14
VOMITS
large he- shaped object vomits cleverly against a quai . . . 324 VIVA 16 6
and unself her gnarled vomits a rock of mindscream . . . . . 506 50 POEMS 20 5
VOTE
the golden rull to vote for me (all decent . . . . 500 50 POEMS 14 21
forth to exercise her vote (or made by threats . . . . 544 1 X 1 4 10
like the sight of vote and politics, as everyone . . . . . . 790 73 POEMS 18 12
VOULEZ
exactly in my brain voulez- vous coucher avec moi? . . . . . 120 & PORTRAIT 12 28
cinq rue Henri Mounier voulez-vous coucher avec moi? te . . . 121 & PORTRAIT 12 36
exactly dance si vous voulez chatouiller mon lezard ladies . 121 & PORTRAIT 12 40
VOULEZ-VOUS
cinq rue Henri Mounier voulez-vous coucher avec moi? te . . . 121 & PORTRAIT 12 36

	PAGE	TITLE	LINE

VOUS

in my brain voulez- vous coucher avec moi? Non? . . . . 120 & PORTRAIT 12   29

cinq rue Henri Mounier voulez-vous coucher avec moi? te . . . 121 & PORTRAIT 12   36

dead exactly dance si vous voulez chatouiller mon lezard . . 121 & PORTRAIT 12   40

VOW

thence swore many a vow but both made sense . . . . 316 VIVA 8   14

smashed word broken open vow or the oath cracked . . . . . . 569 1 X 1 29   3

VOYAGE

Gay during our return voyage, my pensive companion dimly . . 326 VIVA 18   31

bly warped by his voyage from every to no) . . . . 516 50 POEMS 30   3

/ what is a voyage ? up upup: go . . . . 840 73 POEMS 68   3

VOYAGING

& (grows) Slowly (slowly) Voyaging tones intimate tumult . . 348 VIVA 39   6

VULGARITY

the throat A meticulous vulgarity: a sodden fastidious normal 201 XLI PORTRAIT 9   11

W

proximity to a Y. W. c. a. she suddenly . . . . 326 VIVA 18   35

we) the g--d -ld w. isn't that it can't . . . . 411 NO THANKS 28   10

W'S

big dove on g w's wig so what he . . . . 545 1 X 1 5   13

WA

reaml essn esse s wa it sp i t) . . . . 488 50 POEMS 2   9

WADDLES

CleaN a booming smell waddles toward, me, dressed like . . . 94 & POST IMPR 6   15

WADDLING

/ / / the waddling madam star taps taps. . . . . 108 & PORTRAIT 4   1

with a sharp face waddling carefully the length of . . . . . 279 IS 5 THREE 3   9

WADE

/ / i will wade out till my thighs . . . . 189 XLI SONGS 11   1

WADSWORTH

small negro son, Henry Wadsworth Bryant. By this time, . . . 263 IS 5 ONE 32   53

WAFTED

the bursting of the wafted stars (in time to . . . . 36 T&C AMORES 1   20

the blissful pair) skilfully wafted over them- selves this . 799 73 POEMS 27   21

WAGE

to gain a living wage-- when thorns regard their . . . . . . 620 (CHAIRE) 22   2

WAGGED

with ripe eyes and wagged his tail that's the . . . . 125 & SEVEN POEMS 4   16

+WAGGONS

FOR CONTEXT, SEE . . . . 404 NO THANKS 21   4

WAGGY

came! along-along to the waggy silver dog and the . . . . . 125 & SEVEN POEMS 4   25

WAGON

cop's rung for the wagon but as i was . . . . 53 T&C PORTRAIT 1   38

WAGS

neck of the citharede wags in the dust the . . . . 34 T&C ORIENTALE 6   96

sheet on which distinctly wags at times the weary . . . . . 134 & SON REAL 5   4

horizontal large distinct ecstasy wags and. rages Laughters . 202 XLI PORTRAIT 9   36

WAIL

whose night three willows wail, a slender dimness in . . . . 9 T&C SONGS 1   4

things pure and hornets wail by children stung or . . . . . 511 50 POEMS 25   14

WAIST

the lover blest.) Her waist is a most tiny . . . . 21 T&C PUELLA MEA   193

a man squeezing her waist said the cop's rung . . . . 53 T&C PORTRAIT 1   36

three animals. The minute waist continually with an African . 95 & POST IMPR 7   5

WAIT

stand. The trees, suddenly wait against the moon's face. . . 80 T&C SON UNRE 5   17

nake; D and chairs wait under the trees Fields . . . . 104 & POST IMPR 14   13

a stiffened exquisite i wait the sweet annihilation of . . . 182 XLI SONGS 4   10

buy uh cupl un wait k (relijinisde) o (peemuvdepipl) . . . . 325 VIVA 17   9

no o god dear wait sh please o no . . . . 358 VIVA 49   5

my still unvisible when. Wait if i am not . . . . 372 VIVA 63   5

halt stop forget relax wait (little child who have . . . . 393 NO THANKS 10   6

are and do not wait) buds imitate upward each . . . . 573 1 X 1 33   21

+WAIT

FOR CONTEXT, SEE . . . . 488 50 POEMS 2   9

WAITER

for a turk a waiter intones: bloo-moo-n sirkusricky platzburg 108 & PORTRAIT 4   13

WAITER (CONTINUED)
    mauls Kneeland, and a waiter cleverly lugs indigestible . . . 217 XLI SONNETS 13   8
    a child, stout hurdysturdygurdyman waiter, make me a child. . 233 IS 5 ONE 4   15
    of Algernon Carl Swinburned. Waiter a drink waiter two . . . 233 IS 5 ONE 4   20
    Swinburned. Waiter a drink waiter two or three drinks . . . . 233 IS 5 ONE 4   20
    man is o so Waiter this; woman is please . . . . 243 IS 5 ONE 14   2
+WAITER
    FOR CONTEXT, SEE . . . . 629 (CHAIRE) 31   8
+WAITERS
    FOR CONTEXT, SEE . . . . 245 IS 5 ONE 16   7
WAITING
    by whitest hands of waiting years, curtained with wordless .   6 T&C EPITHALAM 114
    stooping by the coffinlid waiting for something to rise . . . 117 & PORTRAIT 10   6
    for Chicago. Eddie was waiting for him, and they . . . . . . 145 & SON REAL 16   5
    chews a two-bit cigar waiting for the bulls to . . . . 149 & SON REAL 20   4
    the year's perfect agony. Waiting (always) upon a fragile . . 156 & SON ACTU 5   12
    a cat. A cat waiting for god knows makes . . . . 166 & SON ACTU 15   9
    on the third rail waiting for the next train . . . . 262 IS 5 ONE 32   2
    vastly gird, a coward waiting clumsily to cease whom . . . . 360 VIVA 51   6
WAKE
    did their dance (sleep wake hope and then) they . . . . . . 515 50 POEMS 29   19
    of hope, and i wake to a perfect patience . . . . 749 95 POEMS 77   12
WAKED
    essential flame never which waked) & perfectingly We dive . . 373 VIVA 64   8
WAKES
    is extinguished the city wakes with a song upon . . . . . . 50 T&C IMPRESS 4   6
    pa) ris her flesh: wakes in little streets while . . . . . . 104 & POST IMPR 14   9
WAKING
    and so awake what waking calls asleep) so never . . . . . . 609 (CHAIRE) 11   8
    proclaim the aim of waking is to dream, remember . . . . . . 688 95 POEMS 16   5
WALES
    liked the prince of wales wife wants to die . . . . 499 50 POEMS 13   2
WALK
    and fair; who to walk with Master Gower in . . . . 20 T&C PUELLA MEA 166
    window under the window walk the unburied feet of . . . . . 108 & PORTRAIT 4   35
    din whose mouths distinctly walk your smiles accuse the . . . 138 & SON REAL 9   3
    / / cruelly, love walk the autumn long; the . . . . 190 XLI SONGS 12   2
    Comes the moon love, walk the autumn love, for . . . . 190 XLI SONGS 12   12
    love thou art frail --walk the longness of autumn . . . . . 190 XLI SONGS 12   19
    this vast nonchalant inward walk of vol- ume the . . . . . . 201 XLI PORTRAIT 9   21
    teased: let (however) us Walk very (therefore and) softly . . 317 VIVA 9   18
    moving (whose feet almost walk air). now who stops. . . . . 437 NO THANKS 53   17
    which only He may walk Who dares to call . . . . 438 NO THANKS 54   27
    we drink crawl eat walk die fly do? a . . . . 528 50 POEMS 40   4
    love though the stars walk backward) honour the past . . . . 732 95 POEMS 60   8
    she may above people walk in the air with . . . . 762 95 POEMS 89   8
WALKED
    / / / i walked the boulevard i saw . . . . 56 T&C PORTRAIT 4   1
    since your mind has walked into my kiss as . . . . 297 IS 5 FOUR 14   5
WALKING
    shall go my love walking in the grass their . . . . 16 T&C SONGS 6   11
    a stealthily frail flower walking with its fellows in . . . . 214 XLI SONNETS 10   2
    in bed will you walking beside me, my very . . . . 302 IS 5 FIVE 1   2
    / / / myself, walking in Dragon st one . . . . 313 VIVA 5   1
    fly and his reflection walking upon a mirror this . . . . . . 335 VIVA 26   4
    their breaths.) "people are walking deaths in this season" . 354 VIVA 45   11
    or else a life walking in the dark i . . . . 648 (CHAIRE) 50   3
WALKS
    of the sky light walks scattering poems on earth . . . . . . 50 T&C IMPRESS 4   3
    of the sky night walks scattering poems / / . . . . 50 T&C IMPRESS 4   33
    / / Spring (side walks are) is most (windows . . . . 436 NO THANKS 52   2
    to a which that walks like a who but . . . . 711 95 POEMS 39   4
WALL
    lustre from the castle wall glided, a drop of . . . . 8 T&C OF NICOL   23
    / of this wilting wall the colour drub souring . . . . 144 & SON REAL 15   1
    its life on a garden-wall, and is going to . . . . 147 & SON REAL 18   11
    taste. Jumped the quick wall of your smile into . . . . . . 154 & SON ACTU 3   4
    what's below. the singer. Wall. i want the perpendicular . . 220 XLI SONNETS 16   6

WALL (CONTINUED)

    cleverly against a quai wall almost spray -ing threecoloured 324 VIVA 16   7
    and because against this wall his white sincere small . . . . 355 VIVA 46   14
    (see just over this) wall the apples are (yes . . . . 543 1 X 1 3   2
    (see just over this) wall the red and the . . . . 543 1 X 1 3   26

WALLENDAS

    "fert ig" (tent-sky wholly wallendas) ready were all erect . 605 (CHAIRE) 7   10

WALLOPING

    a climbing dark exact walloping human noise of digestible . . 202 XLI PORTRAIT 9   45

WALLOW

    dolls clutching their dolls wallow toys playing writhe with . 565 1 X 1 25   5

WALLOWING

    deep his din of wallowing male (shock beyond shock . . . . . 115 & PORTRAIT 8   13

WALLS

    / between nose-red gross walls sprawling with tipsy tables . 55 T&C PORTRAIT 3   2
    and evil. the slobbering walls filthily push witless creases 96 & POST IMPR 8   3
    should you remark the walls have been repapered he . . . . . 198 XLI PORTRAIT 9   26
    am a wind-- your walls will not reckon how . . . . 292 IS 5 FOUR 9   5
    which isn't fond of walls) an electromagnetic (now I've . . . 315 VIVA 7   3
    i perceive, within transparent walls how several smoothly . . 376 VIVA 67   7

WALTZ

    warmlyish wetflat splurging smells waltz the glush of . . . . 96 & POST IMPR 8   12

WALTZING

    out of) instru- ments, waltzing; undigestibly: groans. bounce 442 NO THANKS 57   6

WAMPUM

    elsewhere; to blow incredible wampum / / / / . . . . 116 & PORTRAIT 9   17

WAN

    shores leaves his smile wan, and his blood stopped . . . . . 77 T&C SON UNRE 2   7
    with blood now accurately wan) keenly, to dreamings more . . 344 VIVA 35   6
    / nouns to nouns wan wan too nons too . . . . 508 50 POEMS 22   2
    nouns to nouns wan wan too nons too and . . . . 508 50 POEMS 22   3

WAND

    deepening thighs a greedier wand than even death's what . . . 454 NO THANKS 69   4
    steps (to mount the wand) a by no means . . . . 697 95 POEMS 25   17

WANDER

    broken babypout (pretty teeth wander into which and out . . . 406 NO THANKS 23   11
    curl (mouth seekingly lips wander a finding whom of . . . . . 565 1 X 1 25   3
    (opening) grow are (me wander and nows to the . . . . 612 (CHAIRE) 14   3

WANDERED

    felt of my necktie wandered against my shirt and . . . . . 284 IS 5 FOUR 1   5
    timelessness: we who have wandered down from fragrant . . . . 743 95 POEMS 71   11

WANDERER

    because the why --gracious wanderer, be thou gay / . . . . . 651 (CHAIRE) 53   12
    night, bring this beautiful wanderer home to a dream . . . . 811 73 POEMS 39   10

WANDEREST

    beat? Wind beautifully who wanderest over smooth pages of . . 3 T&C EPITHALAM   17

WANDERFULING

    must be off duty wanderfuling aft spits) int o . . . . 465 NEW POEMS 3   4

WANDERIN

    like a grey rock wanderin g through pasture wom . . . . 654 (CHAIRE) 56   3

WANDERING

    suppliant singer and his wandering word. / / / . . . . 7 T&C EPITHALAM   168
    king in the morning wandering. Through the young and . . . . 17 T&C PUELLA MEA   9
    astir my fragile lady wandering in whose perishable poise . . 17 T&C PUELLA MEA   13
    into his hat) go wandering after it with fingers; . . . . . . 298 IS 5 FOUR 15   21
    spoor) over the earth wandering hunter whom you knew . . . 374 VIVA 65   8
    a tune) death's dollhead wandering under weakening stars . . 479 NEW POEMS 17   10
    first knowledge of death's wandering guess) while children . 517 50 POEMS 31   13
    almost (do they beautifully wandering in merciful miracles . 582 1 X 1 42   2
    humblest and proudest eagerly wandering (equally all alive in 661 (CHAIRE) 63   5
    / someone i am wandering a town (if its . . . . 720 95 POEMS 48   1
    blind blissfully seething gift wandering deeply through . . . 754 95 POEMS 82   4

+WANDERING

    FOR CONTEXT, SEE . . . . 508 50 POEMS 22   8
    FOR CONTEXT, SEE . . . . 591 1 X 1 51   10

WANDERS

    the i am who wanders imminently across the renewed . . . . 91 & POST IMPR 3   17
    gums, a morsel prettily wanders buoyed on the murderous . . . 201 XLI PORTRAIT 9   4

WANDERS (CONTINUED)
    a black goat lookingly wanders There is nothing left . . . . 278 IS 5 THREE 2   16
    over the ripe world wanders with a near and . . . . 293 IS 5 FOUR 10   24
    of (perhaps) myself carefully wanders streets dark and, deep 300 IS 5 FOUR 17   13
    for his feet (who wanders through only white darkness . . . . 439 NO THANKS 55   19
    so aged the ocean wanders the streets are so . . . . 505 50 POEMS 19   5
    ver and) a- live wanders remembe r ing per . . . . 534 50 POEMS 46   10
    & & away wanders: exact ly; as if . . . . 655 {CHAIRE} 57   10
    knowable night's utmost nothing, wanders a little guess (only 810 73 POEMS 38   2
WANDLIKE
    your flesh, a succinct wandlike animal, a little strolling . 170 & SON ACTU 19   7
WANT
    man and what i want to know is how . . . . 60 T&C PORTRAIT 8   9
    by Effie's little, in (want a match or can . . . . 117 & PORTRAIT 10   29
    une boite a joujoux, want nice sleep? toutes les . . . . . 121 & PORTRAIT 12   49
    because you know you want it to dance with . . . . 126 & SEVEN POEMS 5   21
    see but you don't want to dead's happy like . . . . 126 & SEVEN POEMS 5   26
    thighs .... merci.... i want to die nous sommes . . . . . . 133 & SON REAL 4   17
    fattish drone of I Want a Doll, wispish-agile feet . . . . 140 & SON REAL 11   13
    / by god i want above fourteenth fifth's deep . . . . 220 XLI SONNETS 16   1
    the singer. Wall. i want the perpendicular lips the . . . . 220 XLI SONNETS 16   6
    don't you makes burst want to dear somehow quickyes . . . . 251 IS 5 ONE 22   12
    will know, they don't want to to no / / . . . . 272 IS 5 TWO 7   17
    hell with literature we want something redblooded lousy with 407 NO THANKS 24   3
    until you say "i want a fortune" . At . . . . 697 95 POEMS 25   5
    poor little peoples that want to be free just . . . . 711 95 POEMS 39   7
    fate, my sweet) i want no world (for beautiful . . . . . . 766 95 POEMS 92   6
+WANT
    FOR CONTEXT, SEE . . . . 310 VIVA 2   4
    FOR CONTEXT, SEE . . . . 398 NO THANKS 15   20
WANTED
    and <> because Who? wanted them, stomachslikEDead fishe s . . 101 & POST IMPR 11   67
    or as if worlds wanted us to understand they'd . . . . . . 603 {CHAIRE} 5   8
WANTING
    intents a corpse and wanting any rag upon what . . . . . . 339 VIVA 30   16
WANTS
    with you and it wants to and it can . . . . 126 & SEVEN POEMS 5   22
    prince of wales wife wants to die but the . . . . 499 50 POEMS 13   2
    freedom the common man wants) honey swoRkey mollypants / . . 635 {CHAIRE} 37   25
    no tice nobod y wants Less (not to men . . . . 727 95 POEMS 55   4
    ob serve no body wants Most (not putting it . . . . 727 95 POEMS 55   9
    be cause ever ybody wants more (& more & . . . . 727 95 POEMS 55   18
WAR
    boy god of everlasting war received the shuddering sacrament   7 T&C EPITHALAM   154
    great steeds moving to war across the smiling meads; . . . . 209 XLI SONNETS 5   5
    uncaring earth by thoughtful war heaped wholly with high . . 213 XLI SONNETS 9   3
    fought in the civil war band and can play . . . . 253 IS 5 ONE 24   3
    man goes forth to war with trumpets clap and . . . . 273 IS 5 TWO 8   23
    lucy during the recent war could and what is . . . . 276 IS 5 TWO 10   3
    warmest heart recoiled at war: a conscientious object-or his 339 VIVA 30   2
    / this mind made war being generous this heart . . . . . . 440 NO THANKS 56   1
    names (this poet made war whose naught and all . . . . . . 440 NO THANKS 56   24
    (bigger than cosmic rays war earthquakes famine or the . . . 475 NEW POEMS 13   19
    can't make it clearer war just isn't what we . . . . 638 {CHAIRE} 40   8
WARCRY
    a damn-- his royal warcry is I AM and . . . . 774 73 POEMS 2   3
    Makes Right --his royal warcry is I AM true . . . . 774 73 POEMS 2   12
WARDLY
    un, season of in: wardly of him (every) who . . . . 346 VIVA 37   21
WARILY
    slenderly the illustrious unknown (warily as their master's . 344 VIVA 35   12
WARLIKE
    the looser of the warlike zone of her that . . . .   4 T&C EPITHALAM   44
WARM
    ocean fondled o'er the warm long flower of unchastity, . . .   7 T&C EPITHALAM   160
    intense inhabitants; in whose warm superlative body do . . . 22 T&C PUELLA MEA   255
    it was thick slim warm moist built like an . . . . 110 & PORTRAIT 6   17
    a singular block her, rain-warm-naked exquisitely hashed . . 133 & SON REAL 4   2

WARM (CONTINUED)

dumbNess? her other, wet, warm lips limp, across my . . . . . 137 & SON REAL 8   7

an imaginable gesture exact warm unholy / / / . . . . 162 & SON ACTU 11   17

in the afternoon and warm air turning into January . . . . . 279 IS 5 THREE 3   2

body's suddenly curving entire warm questions / / / . . . . . 282 IS 5 THREE 6   35

young morning with a warm world in it (kiss . . . . 529 50 POEMS 41   5

her mind with a warm thick scream and a . . . . 647 {CHAIRE) 49   7

everywhere fairyair feelable heavenless warm sweet mistfully 755 95 POEMS 83   11

+WARMERS

FOR CONTEXT, SEE . . . . 276 IS 5 TWO 10   11

WARMEST

glad and big whose warmest heart recoiled at war: . . . . . . 339 VIVA 30   2

WARMING

to think that she's warming three worlds) who's ama . . . . . 827 73 POEMS 55   12

WARMLY

apt in my hand warmly to lie it is . . . . 21 T&C PUELLA MEA 195

WARMLYISH

of ripe silver with warmlyish wetflat splurging smells waltz 96 & POST IMPR 8   12

WARMTH

witless creases of screaming warmth chuck pil- lows are . . . 96 & POST IMPR 8   4

star link clauses of warmth (after dream who knows?) . . . . 168 & SON ACTU 17   15

WARPED

/ / / / warped this perhapsy stumbl i . . . . 495 50 POEMS 9   1

(he was terri bly warped by his voyage from . . . . 516 50 POEMS 30   3

all the girls (the warped ones, the lamed ones; . . . . . . 619 {CHAIRE) 21   17

+WARPING

FOR CONTEXT, SEE . . . . 415 NO THANKS 32   13

WARREN

errors "is dead" beautiful Warren Gamaliel Harding "is" dead 336 VIVA 27   6

WARRIOR

thy head is one warrior innocent of defeat thy . . . . 29 T&C ORIENTALE 3 18

WARRIORS

the emperor ten elected warriors with bodies of lazy . . . . 34 T&C ORIENTALE 6 76

the dust the ghastly warriors amber with lust breathe . . . . 34 T&C ORIENTALE 6 97

WARS

of failure more than wars of feet all things . . . . 414 NO THANKS 31   3

pain You so&so true wars are never won / . . . . 570 1 X 1 30   10

WART

old woman with the wart on her nose what . . . . 25 T&C CHANSONS 2 18

WARY

Why the chary the wary (as all as can . . . . 801 73 POEMS 29   7

WAS

WORD DELETED, APPEARED 210 TIMES

WASHED

the thrill of moon, washed with a wild and . . . . 12 T&C SONGS 2   49

blackening; the sky is washed with tone now for . . . . 282 IS 5 THREE 6   14

vacantly gazing through un washed panes into a crisp . . . . 354 VIVA 45   9

home & mrs dominic washed his sweet dirty face . . . . 680 95 POEMS 8   13

WASHES

among first light groping washes my nightmare from his . . . 374 VIVA 65   15

WASHING

and hands get red washing things and dishes) and . . . . . . 242 IS 5 ONE 13   15

WASHINGTON

an infantile phenomenon) George Washington almost . . . . . . 262 IS 5 ONE 32   11

me laft welates Wouldwoe Washington to Lydia E. McKinley . . 321 VIVA 13   5

+WASHINGTON'S

FOR CONTEXT, SEE . . . . 545 1 X 1 5   12

WASN'T

of a joy which wasn't and isn't and won't . . . . 631 {CHAIRE) 33   9

what knocked him over Wasn't (for instance) the Knowing . . . 702 95 POEMS 30   10

WASTES

that maidens whom passion wastes will lay between their . . . 16 T&C SONGS 6   7

WASVINO

willbeishfully bursting un- eats wasvino isspaghett (i / / . 387 NO THANKS 4   18

WATCH

song that we may watch together how behind the . . . . 43 T&C AMORES 7   28

lie of sleep i watch the roses of the . . . . 78 T&C SON UNRE 3   14

amid a monstrous din watch your step and follow . . . . . . 117 & PORTRAIT 10   27

WATCH (CONTINUED)

2 play backgammon, 3 watch a has gold teeth . . . . 200 XLI PORTRAIT 8   4
soul dangles from his watch-chain which would be embarrassing 204 XLI LA GUERRE 2   4
WATCH-CHAIN
soul dangles from his watch-chain which would be embarrassing 204 XLI LA GUERRE 2   4
WATCHED
fragrance try; i have watched certain petals rapidly wish . . 214 XLI SONNETS 10   5
must remember he who watched unhands describe what mimicry, . 376 VIVA 67   3
WATCHER
shores soundless, the unspeaking watcher who adores perceived 79 T&C SON UNRE 4   8
WATCHES
door a naked eunuch watches on their heads turbans . . . . . 33 T&C ORIENTALE 6 36
indolent lascivious caring eyes watches; truly, curvingly . . 344 VIVA 35   5
rubbish of guitars and watches only as this (which . . . . . 479 NEW POEMS 17   7
WATCHIN
in uh green field watchin four crows drop into . . . . . . 332 VIVA 23   31
WATCHING
Madam?" I emitted; vaguely watching that mountainous worthy . 228 IS 5 ONE MARJ 11
the ring on (and watching her face grow old . . . . 242 IS 5 ONE 13   13
each other, releasing lay, watching (sprawling, in grass upon 283 IS 5 THREE 7 21
and his child are watching snowflakes (falling & falling . . 715 95 POEMS 43   4
WATCHSPRING
moon, thinner than a watchspring / / / / . . . . 322 VIVA 14   14
WATER
roebuck at a white water the cruel bugle sang . . . . 14 T&C SONGS 4   9
ladies his lips drink water but his heart drinks . . . . . . 15 T&C SONGS 5   7
is more transparent than water, she is softer than . . . . . 33 T&C ORIENTALE 6 52
darker than little round water at one end of . . . . 126 & SEVEN POEMS 5 2
do you see that water flowerpots in windows but . . . . 126 & SEVEN POEMS 5 24
to hear, in darkness, water the lips of death . . . . 136 & SON REAL 7   17
the brain of cleverly-crinkling -water pursues the angry . . 160 & SON ACTU 9   5
of Just Add Hot Water And Serve-- from every . . . . 230 IS 5 ONE 2   12
not piano item: a water- melon causes indigestion to . . . . 263 IS 5 ONE 32   51
rapidly a glass of water / / / / . . . . 268 IS 5 TWO 3   14
you know what in water or with the bugs . . . . 272 IS 5 TWO 7   9
in sand. across this water, crowding tints: browns and . . . 281 IS 5 THREE 5   5
leaning out of yellowgreen water. they are building a . . . . 281 IS 5 THREE 5   9
please the talentgang and water most encourage flame as . . . 511 50 POEMS 25   7
earth in air in water and in fire, but . . . . 651 (CHAIRE) 53   8
WATERING
things lovely--Time! upon whose watering lips the world . . . 23 T&C PUELLA MEA 267
+WATERING
FOR CONTEXT, SEE . . . . 616 (CHAIRE) 18   15
+WATERMELON
FOR CONTEXT, SEE . . . . 263 IS 5 ONE 32   51
WATERS
me not) whose courseless waters are a gloat of . . . .   9 T&C SONGS 1   3
lily atilt on insolent waters but i was aware . . . . 30 T&C ORIENTALE 4 8
of porphyry into the waters i rode down the . . . . 30 T&C ORIENTALE 4 11
blue night amorous of waters tremulous, blinded with silence 37 T&C AMORES 2   5
from the noise of waters) one's eye perceives . . . . 319 VIVA 11   24
him) do through icy waters roll that helplessness which . . . 339 VIVA 30   9
WATERSMOOTH
used to ride a watersmooth-silver stallion and break . . . . 60 T&C PORTRAIT 8   4
WATERSMOOTH-SILVER
used to ride a watersmooth-silver stallion and break . . . . 60 T&C PORTRAIT 8   4
WATERTANK
drowning himself in the watertank but somebody who'd given . 239 IS 5 ONE 10   26
WAVE
some legally into Oblivion wave little flags weeping flatter 391 NO THANKS 8   7
me and shall who wave among your deepening thighs . . . . . . 454 NO THANKS 69   3
and strong one queerying wave will whitely yearn from . . . . 526 50 POEMS 38   7
more seldom than a wave is wet more frequent . . . . 530 50 POEMS 42   3
that grey mind by wave doom disappeared, out of . . . . 599 (CHAIRE) 1   6
his voice --and any wave signs on the dotted . . . . 620 (CHAIRE) 22   7
of our Now) twiceuponatime wave-- put out your eyes, ... 639 (CHAIRE) 41   12
+WAVE
FOR CONTEXT, SEE . . . . 310 VIVA 2   12

                                        PAGE   TITLE   LINE

	PAGE	TITLE	LINE

WAVES

there are none: and waves which only He may . . . . 438 NO THANKS 54   27

WAVING

a gasping organ is waving moth- eaten tunes. a . . . . 69 T&C POST IMPR 6   1

WAX

a little curse of wax. Something, distinct and. Amusing, . . 164 & SON ACTU 13   17

WAXWORKS

mindless He--and She-- shaped waxworks filled with dead ideas 250 IS 5 ONE 21   9

WAY

speak in her frail way, it is wholly to . . . . 18 T&C PUELLA MEA 77
marble from a great way i distinguished singing and . . . . . 30 T&C ORIENTALE 4   21
evening. We'll choose the way to the forest--no offense . . . 86 T&C SON ACTU 5   3
but I know the way-- (nervously Whose eyes approve . . . . . 117 & PORTRAIT 10   34
sheet back in this way. here is little Effie's . . . . 118 & PORTRAIT 10   42
dead's happy like the way underclothes All so differ- . . . . 126 & SEVEN POEMS 5   27
again all over the way men you liked made . . . . 127 & SEVEN POEMS 5   37
was spring by the way in the soiled canary-cage . . . . 197 XLI PORTRAIT 5   12
sall right in its way kiddo but as fer . . . . 237 IS 5 ONE 8   11
A sort of the way he smile) but and . . . . 251 IS 5 ONE 22   9
cammin' that means half- way up the Campanile, believe . . . 256 IS 5 ONE 27   8
applause) pronounced by the way Pay the extremely artistic . 267 IS 5 TWO 2   10
my lips hands the way i move my habits . . . . 285 IS 5 FOUR 2   6
hair, (your fingertips the way you move) the painter . . . . 291 IS 5 FOUR 8   13
(oh & by the way asked sis breath of . . . . 316 VIVA 8   18
from Troy, n.y. the way of (all flesh is . . . . 320 VIVA 12   5
i and by the way) ,which is not fly . . . . 335 VIVA 26   20
acruise and her quick way of slowly staring and . . . . 337 VIVA 28   8
pertly papped muchmouthed) her way of beginningly finishing . 337 VIVA 28   12
be; even remembering the way who looked at whom . . . . . . 338 VIVA 29   19
moon on Sunday. by way of saying nothing he . . . . . . 355 VIVA 46   3
Death) then dearest the way trees are Made leaves . . . . . 359 VIVA 50   11
a python over the way freezes a serpent becomes . . . . 384 NO THANKS 2   21
stay said he (which way said she like this . . . . 399 NO THANKS 16   14
and was built that way on purpose by simple . . . . 466 NEW POEMS 4   11
lover spare: for that way knowledge lies, the foetal . . . . 484 NEW POEMS 22   11
/ / / the way to hump a cow . . . . 500 50 POEMS 14   1
hump a cows the way to hump a cow . . . . 500 50 POEMS 14   9
hump a cows the way to hump a cow . . . . 500 50 POEMS 14   17
& mr across the way are kind of afraid) . . . . 501 50 POEMS 15   2
perhaps the very unkindest way to kill each of . . . . . . 528 50 POEMS 40   11
wrong --then all the way from perfect nowhere came . . . . . 599 (CHAIRE) 1   12
a guess) quite half way down to the earth . . . . 631 (CHAIRE) 33   10
/ a thrown a -way It with some- thing . . . . 632 (CHAIRE) 34   2
(a thrown a- way X -mas) ter- i . . . . 632 (CHAIRE) 34   8
should have thrown a- way (and whose brook -bright . . . . . 660 (CHAIRE) 62   17
sts , on its way to now -here / . . . . 676 95 POEMS 4   25
see it in the way he stands and looks . . . . 774 73 POEMS 2   15
(& not the other way round) because it 's . . . . 782 73 POEMS 10   6
and satyrs, go your way youths and maidens: let . . . . . . 794 73 POEMS 22   7
this is a beautiful way) / / / / . . . . 824 73 POEMS 52   8

WAYS

punctuated by the al- ways retchings of a worthless . . . . . 96 & POST IMPR 8   26
even than how many ways of sitting on your . . . . 126 & SEVEN POEMS 5   8
summer that by responding ways cloaked with renewal my . . . 184 XLI SONGS 6   7
surely known the furious ways and the peaceful, and . . . . 216 XLI SONNETS 12   14
striding) priests-and- slowly, al, ways; procession: and . . 280 IS 5 THREE 4   28
you are on our ways to dust of your . . . . 293 IS 5 FOUR 10   14
to the ant (al ways alingwaysing) go to the . . . . 403 NO THANKS 20   19
him of deceiving) whose ways are neither reasoned nor . . . . 683 95 POEMS 11   5
odd) can justify the ways of man to God . . . . 731 95 POEMS 59   2
can not justify the ways of God to man . . . . 731 95 POEMS 59   4
eyes your voice your ways (o very most my . . . . 819 73 POEMS 47   4

WC

/ / kind) YM& WC (of sort of) A . . . . 464 NEW POEMS 2   2

WE

soundless, saying of "alas we were chaste on earth . . . . . 9 T&C SONGS 1   22
were chaste on earth we ghosts: hark to the . . . . 9 T&C SONGS 1   22
day) do not fear, we will go amaying. thy . . . . 13 T&C SONGS 3   7

PAGE   TITLE   LINE

WE (CONTINUED)

	PAGE	TITLE	LINE
all shining things therefore we also blandly into receptive .	41	T&C AMORES 5	11
them in nothingness for we would sleep this is	41	T&C AMORES 5	23
you gave me when we loved the far- departed	42	T&C AMORES 6	3
fragile certain song that we may watch together how	43	T&C AMORES 7	28
a little harder last we on the groaning flame	67	T&C POST IMPR 4	23
air!) Let us as we have seen see doom's	80	T&C SON UNRE 5	12
In this at least we have got a bulge	84	T&C SON ACTU 3	13
Don't be afraid and we will pass the simple	86	T&C SON ACTU 5	11
get yer goat but we don't care do we	109	& PORTRAIT 5	6
we don't care do we dearie we should worry	109	& PORTRAIT 5	7
care do we dearie we should worry about the	109	& PORTRAIT 5	7
and of Antony and we will confuse hotly our	111	& PORTRAIT 6	60
don't punish us for we were good; and the	117	& PORTRAIT 10	20
and down the here we are now judgment day	118	& PORTRAIT 10	40
cement for her, merrily we became each other humped	119	& PORTRAIT 11	11
going to die. When we grimly go to bed	147	& SON REAL 18	12
and precise --and then we are I and She....	152	& SON ACTU 1	14
mother of twelve undershirts (we are told by is	167	& SON ACTU 16	3
the droll snowing delirium (we do not speak) tumbled	168	& SON ACTU 17	6
light each having each we promised to forget-- wherefore . .	173	& SON ACTU 22	12
murmurous minute clumsy smelloftheworld. We intricately . . .	174	& SON ACTU 23	3
of Nothing and Something, we heard a handorgan in	174	& SON ACTU 23	14
called spring, is what we stroke maybe asleep? do	191	XLI CHANSONS 1	11
ever so quietly when we weren't looking. / /	191	XLI CHANSONS 1	16
to sing (heart, could we bear the marvel of	205	XLI SONNETS 1	15
thou by whose page we break the precious bread	209	XLI SONNETS 5	6
(Case in point if we are to believe these	230	IS 5 ONE 2	24
there, over there. yet we scarcely fare much better--	233	IS 5 ONE 4	9
taxi smile or angle we do not sell and	238	IS 5 ONE 9	6
unlike shirts neckties trousers we cannot wear it out	238	IS 5 ONE 9	11
everything and i remember we all cried like the	239	IS 5 ONE 10	32
like greasedlightning) just as we turned the corner of . . .	248	IS 5 ONE 19	21
ride and believe i we was happy to see	248	IS 5 ONE 19	25
the Loggia where are we angels by O yes	257	IS 5 ONE 27	31
by O yes beautiful we now pass through the	257	IS 5 ONE 27	32
strikingly succulent getup but we knew a muffhunter and . . .	259	IS 5 ONE 29	27
yeggs and thirsties since we are spanked and put	261	IS 5 ONE 31	2
should call exactly extraordinary. We refer, of course, to .	263	IS 5 ONE 32	36
suppressed desire of shall we say: Idleness, while meaning .	263	IS 5 ONE 32	39
Heaven knows (yet are we mindful, though not as	264	IS 5 ONE 33	13
more what of it we should worry in every	268	IS 5 TWO 3	5
pal funny aint it we was buddies i used	270	IS 5 TWO 5	9
unspeaking Mediterranean bluer than we had imagined a few . .	283	IS 5 THREE 7	4
your eyes knew me, we smiled to each other, ...	283	IS 5 THREE 7	21
tail frisks) (gonE) "mouse", We are not the same	286	IS 5 FOUR 3	16
? (or was something we saw in the mirror)?	286	IS 5 FOUR 3	20
the damned table and we hold lips Eyes everything	287	IS 5 FOUR 4	17
possibly this dear, that we may resume impact with	289	IS 5 FOUR 6	6
brighten carefully these things we consider life. Dear i . .	289	IS 5 FOUR 6	12
with so and so: we are together, we will	289	IS 5 FOUR 6	16
so: we are together, we will kiss or smile	289	IS 5 FOUR 6	16
dear from moving as we, you and i, used	289	IS 5 FOUR 6	18
of not keeping still; we were two alert lice	289	IS 5 FOUR 6	23
eyelids' flutter which says we are for each other:	290	IS 5 FOUR 7	13
afraid that this, which we call autumn, cleverly dies	293	IS 5 FOUR 10	23
most certainly (of what we everywhere do not touch)	294	IS 5 FOUR 11	4
through new light hush we are made of the	299	IS 5 FOUR 16	15
you were in Paris we met here / /	304	IS 5 FIVE 3	15
man named Smith and we sailed on the Leviathan	313	VIVA 5	11
law preserved conTinuum (but we read that beFore) of	315	VIVA 7	6
thcared giggling lithped now we muthn't pleathe don't as . .	316	VIVA 8	8
to Theodore Odysseus Graren't we couldn't free the negro . .	321	VIVA 13	11
(at that just supposing we had met and just	323	VIVA 15	10
but you know supposing we just had let it	323	VIVA 15	12
that seem puzzling but we both might have found	323	VIVA 15	18
glass you try if we are a gentleman not	326	VIVA 18	5
fauna" being "very interesting"... we also discussed the . .	326	VIVA 18	33

WE (CONTINUED)

   (stating that she hoped we might "meet again sometime") . . . 326 VIVA 18   36
   un poco putrido when we contemplate her uneyes safely . . . . 327 VIVA 18   46
   duh good ole days we spent in '18 kickin . . . . 332 VIVA 23   14
   midmost o.c. an launch we a Hyperluxurious Supersieve (which 334 VIVA 25   2
   tyrannically dumb Awake, chaos: we have napped. / / . . . . . 337 VIVA 28   15
   roofs roar drownInsound(& (we (are like) dead) . . . . . . 347 VIVA 38   21
   i were a child "we can see a bat . . . . 353 VIVA 44   4
   wish?) touch me, before we perish (believe that not . . . . . 357 VIVA 48   4
   will it Will come (we being unwound & gone . . . . 361 VIVA 52   2
   Of complete dream if we love each (shyly) other, ... 363 VIVA 54   9
   i have no servants. We could almost live at . . . . 365 VIVA 56   6
   there's a free room. We almost could go (you . . . . 365 VIVA 56   8
   everywhere descending; nothing which we are to perceive in . 366 VIVA 57   13
   (but O gracefully) a we, entirely whose least breathing . . . 368 VIVA 59   13
   that so gently while we were alseep while we . . . . 370 VIVA 61   15
   we were alseep while we were each other disappeared: . . . . 370 VIVA 61   16
   : locking foreverfully blend we a universe of gulls' . . . . 371 VIVA 62   21
   which waked) & perfectingly We dive out of tinying . . . . . 373 VIVA 64   8
   slightly (why? or lest we understand) slightly i am . . . . . 375 VIVA 66   9
   / / that which we who're alive in spite . . . . 386 NO THANKS 3   1
   died beyond the clock) we, of ourselves who more . . . . . . 386 NO THANKS 3   2
   your shelves (that which we die for; not when . . . . 386 NO THANKS 3   5
   roses wince) that which we die for lives (may . . . . 386 NO THANKS 3   9
   leaps (and that which we die for lives as . . . . 386 NO THANKS 3   13
   wholly as that which we live for dies) / . . . . 386 NO THANKS 3   14
   that will Ever love) we 've hidden him in . . . . 397 NO THANKS 14   10
   begins stuttering each sentence we both consid (notb- notbr- 398 NO THANKS 15   10
   to hell with literature we want something redblooded lousy . 407 NO THANKS 24   3
   with (between me and we) the g--d -ld w. . . . . 411 NO THANKS 28   9
   beyond imagining spasm rise we you-with-me around (me) you . 442 NO THANKS 57   22
   / / / / we) under) over, the thing . . . . 447 NO THANKS 62   1
   by simple people like we) down with hell and . . . . 466 NEW POEMS 4   12
   am luck -y is we lucky luck- ier luck . . . . 467 NEW POEMS 5   12
   / / Q: dwo we know of anything which . . . . 468 NEW POEMS 6   2
   she or it never we you and they never . . . . 474 NEW POEMS 12   4
   open new (dark we all findingly Spring the . . . . 482 NEW POEMS 20   8
   got to smoke and we aint got nothing to . . . . 489 50 POEMS 3   2
   got to Sing and we aint got nothing to . . . . 489 50 POEMS 3   6
   got to die and we aint got Nothing to . . . . 489 50 POEMS 3   10
   got to dream and we aint got nothing to . . . . 489 50 POEMS 3   14
   stop damned fall all we go spill and chairs . . . . 496 50 POEMS 10   14
   only one snowflake (and we speak our names / . . . . 502 50 POEMS 16   14
   a letter starting "dearest we" unsigned: remarkably brief but 504 50 POEMS 18   1
   Give liz (take! tommy) we order a steak and . . . . 513 50 POEMS 27   14
   (it's now, boys) here we come / / / . . . . 513 50 POEMS 27   36
   id ar (now heer we kum dearie) bud hooz . . . . 519 50 POEMS 33   14
   moved through theys of we, singing each new leaf . . . . . . 521 50 POEMS 34   49
   though dull were all we taste as bright, bitter . . . . . . 521 50 POEMS 34   61
   and dumb death all we inherit, all bequeath and . . . . . . 521 50 POEMS 34   64
   it tell us who we are and will it . . . . 528 50 POEMS 40   2
   it tell us why we dream and will it . . . . 528 50 POEMS 40   3
   it tell us how we drink crawl eat walk . . . . 528 50 POEMS 40   4
   undead too-nearishness and shall we cry and shall we . . . . 528 50 POEMS 40   6
   we cry and shall we laugh and shall entirely . . . . 528 50 POEMS 40   6
   a wide open door we are so both and . . . . 537 50 POEMS 49   13
   on forever's very now we stand nor a first . . . . 538 50 POEMS 50   12
   has pulled (for he's we) such fruit from what . . . . 543 1 X 1 3   21
   him: i told him; we told him (he didn't . . . . 553 1 X 1 13   18
   specimen of hypermagical ultraomnipotence. We doctors know a 554 1 X 1 14   13
   repaying life they're loaned; we (by a gift called . . . . . 556 1 X 1 16   12
   who die, the more we live / / / . . . . 560 1 X 1 20   24
   a leaf opening) as we stood, one (truthed by . . . . 572 1 X 1 32   7
   humbly heights below) kneeling, we--true lovers--pray that us 574 1 X 1 34   11
   known and i've only we our least begin to . . . . 574 1 X 1 34   14
   / / / / we love each other very . . . . 577 1 X 1 37   1
   soul sunlight? yes (always we have heard them sing . . . . 582 1 X 1 42   6
   real, all imagining; and we who are we? surely . . . . . . 582 1 X 1 42   10

		PAGE	TITLE	LINE

WE (CONTINUED)

	PAGE TITLE	LINE
and we who are we? surely not i not	582 1 X 1 42	10
i am you , we are spring / /	583 1 X 1 43	21
leap and i'm born we 're sunlight of oneness	589 1 X 1 49	19
a run skip around we go yes) there's nothing	594 1 X 1 54	8
a what which around we come who) one's everyanything	594 1 X 1 54	17
a shout each around we go all) there's somebody	594 1 X 1 54	35
there's somebody calling who's we we're anything brighter . .	594 1 X 1 54	36
came (as easily as we forget something) livingest the	599 (CHAIRE) 1	13
magically smiling and if we are not perfectly careful	600 (CHAIRE) 2	11
of love himself: who's we --nor can you die	601 (CHAIRE) 3	17
& evil & legal) we thank thee god almighty	604 (CHAIRE) 6	22
/ / / / we miss you, jack--tactfully you	605 (CHAIRE) 7	1
and a circusheart and we miss them more than	605 (CHAIRE) 7	7
the round little man we loved so isn't no!	606 (CHAIRE) 8	3
/ / possibly thrice we glimpsed-- more likely twice	607 (CHAIRE) 9	1
self) smile. Eyes. & we remember: yes; we played	612 (CHAIRE) 14	7
& we remember: yes; we played with a piece	612 (CHAIRE) 14	8
it rolled behind forever, we touched a shy animal	612 (CHAIRE) 14	9
(friend the laughing grinning) we no (smiling) strike agains	618 (CHAIRE) 20	7
off he goes but we can hear him still	624 (CHAIRE) 26	21
you are i am we (pretty twinkle merry bells)	630 (CHAIRE) 32	12
bow) --and if, when we meet again, little he	631 (CHAIRE) 33	7
war just isn't what we imagine but please for	638 (CHAIRE) 40	9
breathed such miracle murdered we whom cannot kill more . . .	639 (CHAIRE) 41	9
great problem nearly solved we dare adorn the whole	650 (CHAIRE) 52	14
and (plunging rapturously up) we spill our masterpiece / . .	650 (CHAIRE) 52	20
by love's own secret) we, like homing through welcoming . . .	659 (CHAIRE) 61	1
remaking what other -wise we should have thrown a-	660 (CHAIRE) 62	14
that love are in we, that love are in	664 (CHAIRE) 66	6
that love are in we and here is a	664 (CHAIRE) 66	6
when times where-- that we are in love, that	664 (CHAIRE) 66	10
are in love, that we are in love: with	664 (CHAIRE) 66	10
(for love are in we am in i are	664 (CHAIRE) 66	12
--for love are in we are in love are	664 (CHAIRE) 66	16
in love are in we; for you are and	664 (CHAIRE) 66	16
and i am and we are (above and under	664 (CHAIRE) 66	17
in i are in we / / / /	664 (CHAIRE) 66	24
things cannot spring but we be they'll some or	666 (CHAIRE) 68	5
anyhow you 've (whoever we are) stepped carefully o	668 (CHAIRE) 70	16
doubtless universe we'd (and we alone had) made --yes; . . .	675 95 POEMS 3	8
knowing i feel that we & worlds are less	680 95 POEMS 8	29
as alone. For whatever we lose (like a you	682 95 POEMS 10	11
me) it's always ourselves we find in the sea	682 95 POEMS 10	12
now and old) lie we so must most lily	690 95 POEMS 18	4
kissing) till into themselves we fell-- how have all	694 95 POEMS 22	4
course of a shall we say somewhat diversified (putting . . .	699 95 POEMS 27	16
kind bear is angary we fear for the quo	711 95 POEMS 39	20
in snow-- a whom we make (of grin for	716 95 POEMS 44	5
(as down someone who's we ungrows) a dream in	716 95 POEMS 44	35
what the hell are we all morticians? / /	727 95 POEMS 55	21
a blunder (called life) we die to breathe, itself	742 95 POEMS 70	14
greenly hurl snow suppose we could not love, dear;	743 95 POEMS 71	4
whose home is timelessness: we who have wandered down	743 95 POEMS 71	11
the where so safe we are / / /	746 95 POEMS 74	8
of this snowy head we call old frank go	754 95 POEMS 82	5
thousand hundred nothing seem --we are himself's own self; . .	756 95 POEMS 84	14
very quick of nowhere) we --While one thrush sings	758 95 POEMS 85	47
(more near ourselves than we) is a bird singing	760 95 POEMS 87	1
the bough) how? why --we never we know (so	767 95 POEMS 93	6
how? why --we never we know (so kiss me)	767 95 POEMS 93	6
lose is to have --we never we know-- brave!	767 95 POEMS 93	12
to have --we never we know-- brave! brave (the	767 95 POEMS 93	12
young love why? how-- we never we know (with	767 95 POEMS 93	18
why? how-- we never we know (with a high	767 95 POEMS 93	18
there where) and away we go in even the	769 95 POEMS 95	7
who's some) one who's we / / / /	769 95 POEMS 95	28
ca us e It's we) humble one (gifted with	782 73 POEMS 10	22

	PAGE	TITLE	LINE
WE (CONTINUED)			
/ / everybody happy? WE-WE-WE & to hell with	791	73 POEMS 19	2
/ / everybody happy? WE-WE-WE & to hell with	791	73 POEMS 19	2
/ / everybody happy? WE-WE-WE & to hell with	791	73 POEMS 19	2
muchtheworseforwear shoes 'fair friend' we enlightened this .	800	73 POEMS 28	9
superstate ever knew (1) we sans love equals mob	803	73 POEMS 31	7
possibly may have shall we say guessed?" "we shall"	807	73 POEMS 35	13
shall we say guessed?" "we shall" quoth gifted she:	807	73 POEMS 35	14
believable) could only fancy we should never know are	809	73 POEMS 37	7
how should some world (we marvel) doubt, for just	809	73 POEMS 37	9
and you: when are we never, but forever now	817	73 POEMS 45	5
silently cries the (whom we call rose a) mystery	837	73 POEMS 65	16
+WE			
FOR CONTEXT, SEE	391	NO THANKS 8	11
FOR CONTEXT, SEE	396	NO THANKS 13	3
WE-WE-WE			
/ / everybody happy? WE-WE-WE & to hell with	791	73 POEMS 19	2
WE'D			
their balloon, why then we'd go up higher with	129	& SEVEN POEMS 7	8
this complete doubtless universe we'd (and we alone had) . .	675	95 POEMS 3	8
WE'LL			
silver minute of evening. We'll choose the way to	86	T&C SON ACTU 5	3
at our beautiful tree we'll dance and sing "Noel	192	XLI CHANSONS 2	27
in the mirror)? therefore we'll kiss; for maybe what	286	IS 5 FOUR 3	21
shall carve time so we'll before what's death come	433	NO THANKS 50	14
called one's self so we'll not have (but i	528	50 POEMS 40	12
only living thing) and we'll make yes / /	528	50 POEMS 40	14
rose and even (we'll adventure the into most	577	1 X 1 37	17
us (if they do, we'll move away still further:	579	1 X 1 39	14
as a saboteur then we'll believe in that incredible	620	{CHAIRE} 22	13
wherein all human curiosity we'll spend (gladly, as lovers .	675	95 POEMS 3	12
me) --look up: and we'll (for what were less	762	95 POEMS 89	9
WE'RE			
me and you if we're not very careful) 0, ...	250	IS 5 ONE 21	4
you can ! & we're NOT (oh-- --i say	269	IS 5 TWO 4	10
squirtnowing for o squirting we're replies (at which now . .	343	VIVA 34	9
gone yours mine . We're alive and shall be:	491	50 POEMS 5	10
one (and april's where we're) / / / /	578	1 X 1 38	12
somebody calling who's we we're anything brighter than even .	594	1 X 1 54	37
than even the sun (we're everything greater than books . . .	594	1 X 1 54	38
than books might mean) we're everyanything more than believe	594	1 X 1 54	41
a spin leap alive we're alive) we're wonderful one	594	1 X 1 54	44
leap alive we're alive) we're wonderful one times one	594	1 X 1 54	45
nothing and nonsense --alive; we're alive, dear: it's (kiss .	665	{CHAIRE} 67	11
i am now and we're a mystery which will	667	{CHAIRE} 69	5
and the moon are we're; but also nowhere /	686	95 POEMS 14	19
and joy's perfect wholeness we're / / / /	812	73 POEMS 40	14
+WE'RE			
FOR CONTEXT, SEE	547	1 X 1 7	15
FOR CONTEXT, SEE	589	1 X 1 49	19
WE'VE			
all her now: but we've such freedom such intense	491	50 POEMS 5	14
superfluous hair or Think We've Met subhuman rights Before .	549	1 X 1 9	14
timelessly alive all glories we've agreed with nothing deeper	741	95 POEMS 69	7
and i've agreed and we've (with one last more	741	95 POEMS 69	13
/ / SONG but we've the may (for you	776	73 POEMS 4	1
+WE'VE			
FOR CONTEXT, SEE	397	NO THANKS 14	10
WEAK			
tickling aches, and the weak noise of her eyes	147	& SON REAL 18	8
epitome of chuckling flesh. Weak thirsty fists of idiot . . .	151	& SON REAL 22	6
which jerk upon the weak colour of table-cloths, the	217	XLI SONNETS 13	3
WEAKENING			
death's dollhead wandering under weakening stars Feels; if &	479	NEW POEMS 17	10
WEAKLY			
its wideflung friend clenched weakly dirt while the mute . .	258	IS 5 ONE 28	18
single star which tugs weakly at twilight, caught in	305	IS 5 FIVE 4	6

	PAGE	TITLE	LINE

WEAKNESS
but, never doubt my weakness makes more than most . . . . . . 433 NO THANKS 50   6
dollarfull shea with a weakness for living literature . . . . 546 1 X 1 6   15
WEALTH
cannot fail having no wealth but love, who shall . . . . . . 394 NO THANKS 11   13
year extend less humbly wealth to foe and friend . . . . . . 521 50 POEMS 34   38
WEALTHIER
and history immeasurably is wealthier by a single sweet . . . 750 95 POEMS 78   7
WEALTHY
and virginal pinks and wealthy vermilion and . . . . 100 & POST IMPR 11   6
/ / / three wealthy sisters swore they'd never . . . . 621 (CHAIRE) 23   1
WEAPON
stuffs, phrase the immense weapon of your hair. Understanding 161 & SON ACTU 10   10
WEAPONS
Antimere Should words carry weapons) are not Less than . . . 395 NO THANKS 12   10
WEAR
to beer and lime, wear dark, and where your . . . . 71 T&C SON REAL 2   5
neckties trousers we cannot wear it out no sir . . . . 238 IS 5 ONE 9   11
LIVES AT THE RITZ WEAR earl & wilson COLLARS . . . . 244 IS 5 ONE 15   4
life, to peer and wear clothes. i am altogether . . . . . . 281 IS 5 THREE 5   18
and curse until for wear their clarion voices and . . . . . 339 VIVA 30   25
surround this throat) i wear your dearest fears beyond . . . 372 VIVA 63   10
young, whatever life you wear it will become you; . . . . . 484 NEW POEMS 22   2
time forever, and you'll wear your silver shoes / . . . . . 504 50 POEMS 18   16
the sun: who music wear burst icy known swim . . . . 533 50 POEMS 45   14
the brave? does mask wear face? have singings gone . . . . 538 50 POEMS 50   6
how could i ever wear it now when the . . . . 684 95 POEMS 12   6
spectres, happiness) lovers alone wear sunlight. The whole . 765 95 POEMS 91   5
her heart's each whisper wear all never guessed unknowable . 811 73 POEMS 39   6
+WEAR
FOR CONTEXT, SEE . . . . 800 73 POEMS 28   8
WEARILY
bumping things. she picked wearily something from the floor . 132 & SON REAL 3   17
WEARING
dressed in fifteenthrate ideas wearing a round jeer for . . . 258 IS 5 ONE 28   4
WEARS
fascination, when my breast wears the intolerant brightness . 78 T&C SON UNRE 3   11
"Death is young life wears velour trousers life totters, . . 102 & POST IMPR 12   8
/ / / Nobody wears a yellow flower in . . . . 296 IS 5 FOUR 13   1
selves more strangely made (wears pain at joy, come . . . . 394 NO THANKS 11   7
WEARY
wags at times the weary twig of a neckless . . . . 134 & SON REAL 5   5
squirm nibbles. another couches, weary, upon a flabby . . . . 143 & SON REAL 14   12
the laziest self of weary the hugest sea of . . . . 537 50 POEMS 49   3
+WEASEL
FOR CONTEXT, SEE . . . . 568 1 X 1 28   8
WEASONED
o pleLike hideous vegetaBles weasOned with-be- . . . . . . 101 & POST IMPR 11   65
WEATHER
a firm fragile stinging weather, (breathless with sharp . . . 140 & SON REAL 11   8
...the cathedral recedes into weather without answering / / . 279 IS 5 THREE 3   24
only half (through deep weather then or none let's . . . . . 364 VIVA 55   13
both is the very weather (not either) my treasure, ... 578 1 X 1 38   5
WEAVING
dancing her subtle body weaving insinuating upon the gold . . 34 T&C ORIENTALE 6   86
in the tide's acute weaving murmur / / / . . . . 369 VIVA 60   21
WEAVINGLY
deathful earth's any which Weavingly now one by wonder . . . 557 1 X 1 17   11
WEAZEL
a bear slickern a weazel how be you (sun . . . . 568 1 X 1 28   8
WEAZENED
/ / / / weazened Irrefutable unastonished two, countenances . 255 IS 5 ONE 26   1
WEB
then Cunning forged a web so subtle air is . . . . 799 73 POEMS 27   16
WED
with the past, and wed to valor, battle with . . . . 209 XLI SONNETS 5   7
a tart in it (wed) open the tart, lady . . . . 637 (CHAIRE) 39   9

		PAGE	TITLE	LINE
WEDDING				
death away at this wedding) never mind a world	. 732	95 POEMS 60	12
WEDNESDAY				
in hitler's window on wednesday next at 1 E.S.T.	. 514	50 POEMS 28	13
WEE				
balloonman whistles far and wee and eddieandbill come running	24	T&C CHANSONS 1	5
balloonman whistles far and wee and bettyandisbel come . . .	24	T&C CHANSONS 1	13
balloonMan whistles far and wee / / / /	24	T&C CHANSONS 1	24
shouting of merry flowers wee skipping high-heeled flames . .	44	T&C AMORES 8	6
littlest poem a (with wee ears and see? tail	286	IS 5 FOUR 3	12
ben jiffyclaus bug fainarain wee celibate amaranth clutch . .	333	VIVA 24	20
WEED				
chuckling rubbish of pearl weed coral and stones; lifted, . .	369	VIVA 60	6
popular the wise, a weed a tearose) and every	798	73 POEMS 26	11
WEED'S				
persuades itself that every weed's a rose, roses (you	744	95 POEMS 72	6
WEEDS				
least unsmile or whatever weeds feel and fish think	359	VIVA 50	18
WEEK				
stewed three times a week. and slept twice a	149	& SON REAL 20	11
and slept twice a week with a big toothless	149	& SON REAL 20	12
eaten peppers for a week. On this street the	219	XLI SONNETS 15	2
making twice the a week you kind of, know	251	IS 5 ONE 22	7
WEEKS				
prayed for months & weeks & days & years	702	95 POEMS 30	19
WEENESS				
Oldeyed child, to ambitious weeness of boots tiny add	105	& PORTRAIT 1	7
WEEP				
beloved; i shall not weep: when from the less-than-whiteness	210	XLI SONNETS 6	8
and why do i weep eat sleep--what does the	295	IS 5 FOUR 12	16
should some why completely weep my father's fingers brought .	520	50 POEMS 34	13
WEEPING				
heart's chatter riveted a weeping skyscraper in me i	132	& SON REAL 3	4
Oblivion wave little flags weeping flatter thoroughly	391	NO THANKS 8	8
WEEPINGS				
hungering whispers hear with weepings soundless, saying of .	9	T&C SONGS 1	21
WEIGH				
if a thought should weigh a star --dreads dying	446	NO THANKS 61	7
/ a (ncient) a weigh tless puppet of once	616	{CHAIRE} 18	2
WEIGHTLESS				
(god distinctly has) the weightless svelte drifting sexual .	140	& SON REAL 11	2
black muscles fools a weightless slowness (deftly muting the	299	IS 5 FOUR 16	3
out crushing) the papery weightless diminutive world with a .	652	{CHAIRE} 54	9
+WEIGHTLESS				
FOR CONTEXT, SEE	616	{CHAIRE} 18	2
WEIRD				
pleathe don't as pop weird up her hot ow	316	VIVA 8	9
keep though all the weird worlds must be opened?	377	VIVA 68	14
+WEIRD				
FOR CONTEXT, SEE	100	& POST IMPR 11	12
WELCOME				
of dream while wings welcome the year and trees	372	VIVA 63	14
blind and robins never welcome spring nor flatfolk prove . .	511	50 POEMS 25	16
wonderingly celebrate day and welcome earth's arrival with a	582	1 X 1 42	4
of an angel everywhere welcome (but chiefly at home	678	95 POEMS 6	9
sky --sunlight and singing welcome your coming although . . .	717	95 POEMS 45	4
honour the past but welcome the future (and dance	732	95 POEMS 60	10
or humble, equally they're welcome --as if the humble	763	95 POEMS 90	14
WELCOMES				
was is to be welcomes welcomes her dreams his	533	50 POEMS 45	9
is to be welcomes welcomes her dreams his face	533	50 POEMS 45	9
of an eternal now welcomes each was of whom	558	1 X 1 18	5
WELCOMING				
at these (each serenely welcoming his only and illimitably .	626	{CHAIRE} 28	7
we, like homing through welcoming sweet miracles of air . . .	659	{CHAIRE} 61	2
truth of His presence (welcoming humbly His light and	749	95 POEMS 77	20
and what a gently welcoming darkestness-- now i lay	816	73 POEMS 44	4

+WELCOMING
FOR CONTEXT, SEE . . . . 657 {CHAIRE} 59   8

WELL
one goddess loved too well? Chryselephantine Zeus Olympian .   3 T&C EPITHALAM 24
grave great sensual knees well might any monarch please.) . . 21 T&C PUELLA MEA 214
their triumphs and listen well how the dainty destroyed . . . 111 & PORTRAIT 6 40
sharply believe me, wholly, well --did (wisely suddenly into 115 & PORTRAIT 8   9
one end of the well it's too cool to . . . . 126 & SEVEN POEMS 5   3
(andwhyevernot) into the round well and see the kitten . . . 127 & SEVEN POEMS 5 46
While grip Hips simply. well fussed flesh does surely . . . . 136 & SON REAL 7 11
piece of eminent fragility. Well and when--Does . . . . 141 & SON REAL 12   7
minutes past six) the well-fed L's immaculate roar looped . . 219 XLI SONNETS 15   5
youse) "a bloke wot's well behaved" ...and always try . . . . 229 IS 5 ONE FRAN 11
kind of, know (kind well of A sort of . . . . 251 IS 5 ONE 22   8
a Irish, cook but well oh don't you makes . . . . 251 IS 5 ONE 22 11
us make haste --consider well this ruined aqueduct lady, . . 260 IS 5 ONE 30 22
this fundamental respect the well recognised regime of . . . 261 IS 5 ONE 31   8
almost incompletely surrounded by well- drawn icecakes beheld 262 IS 5 ONE 32 11
Lord Rothermere billiards very well by moonlight with Lord . 262 IS 5 ONE 32 22
and of pistil; very well provided an instant may . . . . . 264 IS 5 ONE 33 22
can!" --yon clean upstanding well dressed boy that with . . . 273 IS 5 TWO 8   6
kissed, by loving relatives well fed, and fully photographed 273 IS 5 TWO 8 22
kid you might as well toss him a few . . . . 298 IS 5 FOUR 15 13
/ y is a WELL KNOWn ATHLETE'S BRIDE (lullaby) . . . . 317 VIVA 9   1
/ / / / well) here's looking at ourselves . . . . 323 VIVA 15   1
course you must shake well) indolently dreaming puzzling over 323 VIVA 15   5
himself rattling for that well known suburb the bronx . . . . 326 VIVA 18 12
a new england sculptor (well on in life) re . . . . 327 VIVA 18 r39
concept O hairlesschested females, well attend! list, every . 398 NO THANKS 15 16
i mean the (o well ughhuh sure why not . . . . 400 NO THANKS 17   9
not yuh course yeh well naturally i und certain . . . . . . 400 NO THANKS 17   9
most daren't (sortof people well youknow kindof) aint & . . . 412 NO THANKS 29   7
laid him down. Sleep well / / / / . . . . 568 1 X 1 28 30
languages there's none but well she knows; and can . . . . . 575 1 X 1 35 29
but also dying (as well as to cry and . . . . 686 95 POEMS 14   2
you know (just as well as i do) what . . . . 701 95 POEMS 29 11
you're hunting for ann well i'm looking for will" . . . . . 707 95 POEMS 35   1
there" "and you couldn't well miss willy's carroty hair" . . 707 95 POEMS 35   4
knock out your eye" "well maybe she's up to . . . . 707 95 POEMS 35   9
say and fools, all's well / / / / . . . . 768 95 POEMS 94 14
or on the other well your oldest pal for . . . . 779 73 POEMS 7   9
plus --fare ill: fare well-- a frown would be . . . . 798 73 POEMS 26 13
young finelooking fellow, dressed well but not over, stopped 800 73 POEMS 28   5

WELL-FED
minutes past six) the well-fed L's immaculate roar looped . . 219 XLI SONNETS 15   5

WELLBELOVED
a conscientious object-or his wellbeloved colonel (trig . . . 339 VIVA 30   4

WELLCURB
haven't Marjorie isn't this wellcurb simply darling" --O . . 257 IS 5 ONE 27 36

WELLFILLED
contemplate beginning with his wellfilled pants earth's . . . 266 IS 5 TWO 1 32

WELLKNOWN
Mr Do -nothing the wellknown parvenu who (having dreamed . . 236 IS 5 ONE 7   4

WELLS
beyond the sweet instinctive wells, which make to flourish . 19 T&C PUELLA MEA 121
regressed. Kipling again H.G. Wells, and Anatole France shook 263 IS 5 ONE 32 43

WELLSWEEP
of hilltop (barn house wellsweep forest & clearing) gone . . 755 95 POEMS 83   3

WENCH'S
his censored up a wench's rock-a-bye (rub-her-bub) bub? . . . 642 {CHAIRE} 44 26

WENDING
slowly: from! the: A wending putrescence. a. of, loosely . . 99 & POST IMPR 10 23

WENT
white, with shining feet, went forth into the dew: . . . . . 8 T&C OF NICOL 28
cheek the beauteous colour went with every bough that . . . . 8 T&C OF NICOL 30
/ All in green went my love riding on . . . . 14 T&C SONGS 4   1
before. Horn at hip went my love riding riding . . . . 14 T&C SONGS 4 11
before. Bow at belt went my love riding riding . . . . 14 T&C SONGS 4 21

		PAGE	TITLE	LINE
WENT (CONTINUED)				
before. All in green went my love riding on		14	T&C SONGS 4	31
fled, who with Egypt went to bed, whom white-thighed		22	T&C PUELLA MEA	246
knew Eddie in Topeka, went clean daffy, and which		145	& SON REAL 16	7
/ / when you went away it was morning		172	& SON ACTU 21	1
wore no cloze an went runnin aroun wid eachudder		237	IS 5 ONE 8	18
a button (and down went my Uncle Sol and		239	IS 5 ONE 10	35
were O. K.) i went right to it ◇		248	IS 5 ONE 19	9
did not fall she went creeping along the air		284	IS 5 FOUR 1	14
/ poor But TerFLY went (flesh is grass) from		320	VIVA 12	2
cough better today? nn-nn went head face goes (if		506	50 POEMS 20	8
reaped their sowing and went their came sun moon		515	50 POEMS 29	35
and molly and may went down to the beach		682	95 POEMS 10	2
and clever and he went cruising into a crazy		709	95 POEMS 37	1
god down this stranger went on both knees" green		800	73 POEMS 28	16
WEPT				
mountain, while his maples wept air to blood, asked		555	1 X 1 15	11
And then this dreamer wept: and so she quickly		777	73 POEMS 5	14
WERE				
WORD DELETED, APPEARED 82 TIMES				
WEREN'T				
so quietly when we weren't looking. / / /		191	XLI CHANSONS 1	16
WERES				
things? Its noyesiyou he-she (Weres / / / /		417	NO THANKS 34	25
WEST				
N splashes-sink which is west eighth, a star or		169	& SON ACTU 18	2
turning snowy against a west of robin's egg blue		194	XLI PORTRAIT 2	3
(stealthily) in the alive west begin requiescat this six . .		277	IS 5 THREE 1	3
complain steadily against the west one Clock dimly cries . .		434	NO THANKS 51	13
of traffic collapses: through west ninth slowly cars pour . .		800	73 POEMS 28	19
+WEST				
FOR CONTEXT, SEE		699	95 POEMS 27	5
WEST'S				
as down the oblivious west's numerous dun magnificence . . .		6	T&C EPITHALAM	127
WESTPOINTER				
his wellbeloved colonel (trig westpointer most succinctly . .		339	VIVA 30	5
WET				
my dumbNess? her other, wet, warm lips limp, across		137	& SON REAL 8	7
lose herself where the wet stars softly are keeping		206	XLI SONNETS 2	9
picture goes he's a wet dream by Cezanne /		246	IS 5 ONE 17	12
than a wave is wet more frequent than to		530	50 POEMS 42	3
WETFLAT				
ripe silver with warmlyish wetflat splurging smells waltz the		96	& POST IMPR 8	12
WHALE				
like Jonah And The Whale : oiwun uhsoi roitee		398	NO THANKS 15	19
WHAT				
WORD DELETED, APPEARED 191 TIMES				
WHAT-IS-IT				
your electric fur, and what-is-it comes over parting		175	& SON ACTU 24	11
WHAT'S				
radiance of perpetualness. When what's in velvet beyond . . .		81	T&C SON UNRE 6	9
life (i pant for what's below. the singer. Wall.		220	XLI SONNETS 16	6
scarcely fare much better-- what's become of (if you		233	IS 5 ONE 4	10
two or three drinks what's become of Maeterlinck now		233	IS 5 ONE 4	21
peculiar form of sleep what's beyond logic happens beneath .		264	IS 5 ONE 33	5
to murder time (forgetting what's to know wholly imagining .		362	VIVA 53	14
too far said she what's too far said he		399	NO THANKS 16	11
your little finger is) what's right about the g.o.		411	NO THANKS 28	8
about the g.o. world what's wrong with (between me		411	NO THANKS 28	9
time so we'll before what's death come (in one		433	NO THANKS 50	15
those three disappear finally what's left behind is (just . .		501	50 POEMS 15	17
stead of everybodyelse's) but what's wholly marvellous my . .		782	73 POEMS 10	14
+WHAT'S				
FOR CONTEXT, SEE		229	IS 5 ONE FRAN	11
FOR CONTEXT, SEE		330	VIVA 21	10
WHATEVER				
everyone) constitutes undying; or whatever this and that . .		264	IS 5 ONE 33	3
that our souls inhabit whatever is between them) knowing . .		285	IS 5 FOUR 2	5

WHATEVER (CONTINUED)
    the least unsmile or whatever weeds feel and fish . . . . . . 359 VIVA 50   18
    (whose selves abide under whatever shall discovered be) whose 446 NO THANKS 61   10
    the secrets of living whatever they sing is better . . . . . 481 NEW POEMS 19   3
    For if you're young, whatever life you wear it . . . . 484 NEW POEMS 22   2
    or fears to dare whatever dares to fear) i . . . . 522 50 POEMS 35   8
    for half a when, whatever is less alive than . . . . 580 1 X 1 40   20
    large as alone. For whatever we lose (like a . . . . 682 95 POEMS 10   11
    all sweet things beyond whatever mind may comprehend, ... 688 95 POEMS 16   11
    dream sans meaning (or whatever kills) a giving who . . . . . 735 95 POEMS 63   5
    go, my dear; and whatever is done by only . . . . 766 95 POEMS 92   3
    and it's you are whatever a moon has always . . . . 766 95 POEMS 92   8
    has always meant and whatever a sun will always . . . . 766 95 POEMS 92   9
    to heaven with hell. Whatever sages say and fools, ... 768 95 POEMS 94   14
    any doubt he was whatever (first and last) mostpeople . . . . 802 73 POEMS 30   11
WHATEVER'S
    a piss they speak whatever's on their mind they . . . . 427 NO THANKS 44   17
    their mind they do whatever's in their pants the . . . . . . 427 NO THANKS 44   18
    if you are glad whatever's living will yourself become. . . . 484 NEW POEMS 22   4
    / / / / whatever's merely wilful, and not . . . . 742 95 POEMS 70   1
WHATHAVEWE
    minus news alimony blackmail whathavewe and propaganda (it is 391 NO THANKS 8   11
WHATS
    ness and these startled whats are a (piercing clothes . . . . 437 NO THANKS 53   6
    spouts cornucopiously not unrecognizable whats of t oo . . . 465 NEW POEMS 3   10
    (m id) a life whats wh (un) ich (cur . . . . 795 73 POEMS 23   8
WHATSES
    whoses diving into a whatses to rescue miss nobody's . . . . 475 NEW POEMS 13   21
WHEEEEE
    devil devil devil devil wheeEEE / / / / . . . . 25 T&C CHANSONS 2   31
WHEEL
    e rin g partner whEEl shi min chb yi . . . . 100 & POST IMPR 11   38
    guesser goose pin yessir wheel no sendwisp ben jiffyclaus . . 333 VIVA 24   18
    number of times a wheel turns doesn't determine its . . . . . 514 50 POEMS 28   5
    kiss and slings his wheel upon his back and . . . . 624 (CHAIRE) 26   19
    found one old blue wheel in a pasture / . . . . 753 95 POEMS 81   21
WHEELED
    subject his Earliest word wheeled out on the sunny . . . . . 197 XLI PORTRAIT 5   21
+WHEELING
    FOR CONTEXT, SEE . . . . 122 & SEVEN POEMS 1   16
    FOR CONTEXT, SEE . . . . 122 & SEVEN POEMS 1   18
WHEELS
    of Helios the sweet wheels tremulous-- are there no . . . . .   4 T&C EPITHALAM   48
    child skating on noisy wheels of joy pathetic dress . . . . . 56 T&C PORTRAIT 4   3
    coach with gilt hopeless wheels mired where sits rigidly . . 131 & SON REAL 2   15
    mi croscopic world's whens, wheels; wonders: murders. cries: 361 VIVA 52   17
WHEEZING
    crammed into someone's kitchenette) wheezing bulgily world of 607 (CHAIRE) 9   4
WHELPS
    male-- uplook, all joybegotten whelps whom soothe psychotic . 398 NO THANKS 15   18
WHEN
    Now is the time when all occasional things close . . . . . .   6 T&C EPITHALAM   121
    an opening lily drowsy-fair (when from her couch of . . . . .   8 T&C OF NICOL   13
    autumn of a year: When through the thin air . . . . 11 T&C SONGS 2   22
    / / / / when god lets my body . . . . 16 T&C SONGS 6   1
    to yield with dew when the world was young . . . . 18 T&C PUELLA MEA   54
    world had in Springtime when the world was mad . . . . 18 T&C PUELLA MEA   56
    heavy hung with silence when the world was young . . . . . . 18 T&C PUELLA MEA   59
    rescuing eyes; nor he when swooned the white egyptian . . . . 18 T&C PUELLA MEA   73
    and loving) as invisibly when upon her palpable solitude . . 19 T&C PUELLA MEA   104
    to make them glad, when the world was young . . . . 20 T&C PUELLA MEA   131
    did most exquisitely err.) When the world was like . . . . . 22 T&C PUELLA MEA   221
    lithe eyes and long (when the world was like . . . . 22 T&C PUELLA MEA   226
    Nineveh, in her eyes when day is gone are . . . . 23 T&C PUELLA MEA   260
    life's very fragile hour (when the world was like . . . . . . 23 T&C PUELLA MEA   276
    INNOCENTES in Just- spring when the world is mud- . . . . . . 24 T&C CHANSONS 1   2
    piracies and it's spring when the world is puddle-wonderful . 24 T&C CHANSONS 1   10
    is softer than birds when the emperor is very . . . . 33 T&C ORIENTALE 6   53

WHEN (CONTINUED)

	PAGE	TITLE	LINE
trusted not, one night when in my fingers drooped	39	T&C AMORES 4	12
drooped your shining body when my heart sang between	39	T&C AMORES 4	14
knew thee death. and when i have offered up	39	T&C AMORES 4	29
up each fragrant night, when all my days shall	39	T&C AMORES 4	31
flower you gave me when we loved the far-	42	T&C AMORES 6	3
crazy how i cried when i heard over time	44	T&C AMORES 8	19
be jerked into eternity. when over my head a	49	T&C IMPRESS 3	22
to bed of crocuses When you sing in your	61	T&C PORTRAIT 9	18
softly into irresponsible toys.) when this man with the . . .	62	T&C PORTRAIT 10	23
of you-- but that when light fails and this	71	T&C SON REAL 2	7
two bound for themselves, when passionately dusk brings . . .	71	T&C SON REAL 2	9
read? of a time when the beautiful most of	72	T&C SON REAL 3	11
/ / / / when you rang at Dick	73	T&C SON REAL 4	1
/ / / / when thou hast taken thy	75	T&C SON REAL 6	1
thy last applause, and when the final curtain strikes	75	T&C SON REAL 6	1
entertainment of your eyes, when (being fool to fancy) . . .	78	T&C SON UNRE 3	3
made wise; at moments when the glassy darkness holds	78	T&C SON UNRE 3	5
a little while; moments when my once more illustrious	78	T&C SON UNRE 3	9
are filled with fascination, when my breast wears the	78	T&C SON UNRE 3	10
/ / / / when citied day with the	79	T&C SON UNRE 4	1
splendor of this night when souls which have forgot	81	T&C SON UNRE 6	3
poised radiance of perpetualness. When what's in velvet . . .	81	T&C SON UNRE 6	9
makes my body sorry when the minute moon is	82	T&C SON ACTU 1	4
and (as i guess) when Farmer Death (whom fairies	83	T&C SON ACTU 2	11
your expression my love when most passionate. , my, ...	94	& POST IMPR 6	25
of a worthless lamp. when With a minute terrif	96	& POST IMPR 8	27
gets up god knows when every day of their	109	& PORTRAIT 5	16
/ / / / when the spent day begins	115	& PORTRAIT 8	1
are made of gingerbread when the judgment day comes	117	& PORTRAIT 10	3
humped to tumbling garble when a minute pulled the	119	& PORTRAIT 11	13
liked made you feel when they touched you (but	127	& SEVEN POEMS 5	37
you made, men feel when, you touched, them dead's	127	& SEVEN POEMS 5	39
riant belly's fooling bore --When The Sun Begins To	130	& SON REAL 1	3
eminent fragility. Well and when--Does susceptibility imply .	141	& SON REAL 12	7
the cruel-littleness of cold (when battling street-lamps fail	142	& SON REAL 13	3
the night before Christmas when all through the house	142	& SON REAL 13	12
mattress of jelly.... than when to the kanoon she	143	& SON REAL 14	13
/ / it started when Bill's chip let on	145	& SON REAL 16	1
a white shocking wire, when she smiles a hard	147	& SON REAL 18	5
is going to die. When we grimly go to	147	& SON REAL 18	12
a little against me, when for two dollars i	148	& SON REAL 19	13
/ / / SONNETS--ACTUALITIES when my love comes to	152	& SON ACTU 1	1
mind, you should see when i turn to find	152	& SON ACTU 1	8
throne of night slowly when several stars are opening	156	& SON ACTU 5	2
sails filled with dream-- when on a green brief	156	& SON ACTU 5	8
upon a fragile instant when herself me (slowly, wholly . . .	156	& SON ACTU 5	13
/ / / / when i have thought of	157	& SON ACTU 6	1
stare the pollenizing vacancy when, Thy patters? hands.... is	159	& SON ACTU 8	16
than anything have (almost when hugeness will shut quietly) .	163	& SON ACTU 12	20
odour these gross days when i think of you	165	& SON ACTU 14	7
/ / / / when you went away it	172	& SON ACTU 21	1
shy breasts tickle, laughing when i wilt and wince	172	& SON ACTU 21	15
i like my body when it is with your	175	& SON ACTU 24	1
/ / / / when life is quite through	181	XLI SONGS 3	1
flight in the blue; when love's had his tears	181	XLI SONGS 3	6
the poppies, the dears; when all's done and said, ...	181	XLI SONGS 3	11
time and his worms, when loveliness says sweetly Yes	183	XLI SONGS 5	9
away ever so quietly when we weren't looking. /	191	XLI CHANSONS 1	16
dark or unhappy then when you're quite dressed you'll	192	XLI CHANSONS 2	21
of a faultless languor when invisibly consult with some . . .	193	XLI PORTRAIT 1	6
of robin's egg blue when i entered a mad	194	XLI PORTRAIT 2	3
canary-cage of largest existence. (when he would extemporise	197	XLI PORTRAIT 5	14
like a coffin's inside when you die, pretentious and	198	XLI PORTRAIT 6	2
country home and mother when sung at the old	204	XLI LA GUERRE 2	8
i love you because when you're hard up you	204	XLI LA GUERRE 2	10
buy a drink and when you're flush pride keeps	204	XLI LA GUERRE 2	11
/ / / / when unto nights of autumn	207	XLI SONNETS 3	1

		PAGE	TITLE	LINE

WHEN (CONTINUED)

whom Time measured is when frost to dance maketh	207	XLI SONNETS 3	3
/ / / / when the proficient poison of	210	XLI SONNETS 6	1
i shall not weep: when from the less-than-whiteness of	210	XLI SONNETS 6	9
extract his inconsiderable doom, when these thy lips	210	XLI SONNETS 6	12
beautifully embrace nothing and when thy bashful hands assume	210	XLI SONNETS 6	14
/ / / / when my sensational moments are	213	XLI SONNETS 9	1
wilt of human rind-- when over hate has triumphed	213	XLI SONNETS 9	5
i would be near when his scythe takes crisply	215	XLI SONNETS 11	6
/ / / / when i am in Boston,	217	XLI SONNETS 13	1
of table-cloths, the electric When In Doubt Buy Of	217	XLI SONNETS 13	4
dat baby ached." and when i timidly hinted "novocaine?"	226	IS 5 ONE MAME	12
that airy hurdysturdygurdy but when will turn backward O	233	IS 5 ONE 4	3
she coitnly can shimmie when you see her shake	235	IS 5 ONE 6	7
her shake shake shake, when you see her shake	235	IS 5 ONE 6	10
year or two and when Freud got through with	236	IS 5 ONE 7	8
skunks ate the chickens when my Uncle Sol had	239	IS 5 ONE 10	19
cried like the Missouri when my Uncle Sol's coffin	239	IS 5 ONE 10	33
Joe agreeably cheerfully remarked when surrounded by fat	241	IS 5 ONE 12	2
wrong you know (whereas when i lie down i	245	IS 5 ONE 16	11
to dear somehow quickyes when (now, dark dear oh)	251	IS 5 ONE 22	13
but fly kites and when the string breaks (or	253	IS 5 ONE 24	7
Life matters if or when the your-and my- idle	260	IS 5 ONE 30	14
into your jolly tete when the jolly shells begin	269	IS 5 TWO 4	3
know what i mean when the first guy drops	272	IS 5 TWO 7	3
everybody feels sick or when they throw in a	272	IS 5 TWO 7	6
i, used to move when i thought you were	289	IS 5 FOUR 6	19
(but that doesn't matter) when you thought you were	289	IS 5 FOUR 6	21
dreamed this) only imagine, when day has thrilled you	292	IS 5 FOUR 9	2
me that strangers arrive when i have kissed you	295	IS 5 FOUR 12	9
as he is old when autumn comes, who twiddles	296	IS 5 FOUR 13	5
just as day dissolves when it is twilight (and	301	IS 5 FOUR 18	3
smiling chevaux de bois) when you were in Paris	304	IS 5 FIVE 3	15
and mesh witH Which when both march outward into	311	VIVA 3	13
Talks in the daytime, when who is asleep with	312	VIVA 4	4
to Lydia E. McKinley when Buch tooked out his	321	VIVA 13	7
slovenly and homeless and when a kiss departs our	322	VIVA 14	11
ye olde freudian wish; when i contemplate her uneyes	326	VIVA 18	4
who was hectocotyliferously propagated when Miss G touched	326	VIVA 18	10
something un poco putrido when we contemplate her uneyes	327	VIVA 18	46
why in (thundering) by When eaten spaces grouse rocket	346	VIVA 37	10
new . oh if when: & a nd O	350	VIVA 41	14
/ / / / when rain whom fear not	356	VIVA 47	1
somewhere is fragrantly, arrive (when Rain comes; predicating	356	VIVA 47	14
/ / / / when hair falls off and	359	VIVA 50	1
blur And thighs forget (when clocks whisper and night	359	VIVA 50	2
whisper and night shouts) When minds shrivel and hearts	359	VIVA 50	3
grow brittler every Instant (when of a morning Memory	359	VIVA 50	5
very beautifully, suddenly, as when the heart of this	366	VIVA 57	11
how girllike laughtering blocks when builds its invisibly	371	VIVA 62	5
where my still unvisible when. Wait if i am	372	VIVA 63	5
and fears or any when unwondering immense directionless	378	VIVA 69	13
we die for; not when or unless if or	386	NO THANKS 3	5
a bed bed bed) when each other courted both	401	NO THANKS 18	4
very very thwarted) and when which was aborted what	401	NO THANKS 18	6
/ / / / when muckers pimps and tratesmen	405	NO THANKS 22	1
if all dreams unmake (when in a most smashed	414	NO THANKS 31	6
they shake the mountains when they dance / /	427	NO THANKS 44	20
leastful most under imagination. When (out of sheer nothing)	432	NO THANKS 49	14
lost, believing; hushed with when / / / /	432	NO THANKS 49	20
/ at dusk just when the Light is filled	434	NO THANKS 51	2
punks of Progress shriek; when Souls are outlawed, Hearts	438	NO THANKS 54	21
/ / / / when from a sidewalk out	442	NO THANKS 57	1
skeletons of these trees) when sunbeams loot furnished rooms	442	NO THANKS 57	10
timelessness with chips of when) that's yours; i guess	451	NO THANKS 66	4
some feel more better when all ought to feel	466	NEW POEMS 4	24
needle) ask her ask when (ask and ask and	498	50 POEMS 12	7
/ / /) when what hugs stopping earth	502	50 POEMS 16	1

		PAGE	TITLE	LINE

WHEN (CONTINUED)

	PAGE	TITLE	LINE
people remember being born) when and if nothing disappears .	505	50 POEMS 19	17
who are am (beyond when behind where under un) . ?	505	50 POEMS 19	24
him more by more when by now and tree	515	50 POEMS 29	13
sure that spring danced when she heard my father	521	50 POEMS 34	52
which quacks will cure when pimps may please? must	527	50 POEMS 39	24
actual either hand is when for sale? forever is	538	50 POEMS 50	11
themselves these insects mean? when microscopic shriekings .	555	1 X 1 15	4
/ / / / when you are silent, shining	559	1 X 1 19	1
blow space to time) --when skies are hanged and	560	1 X 1 20	7
/ / / / when god decided to invent	566	1 X 1 26	1
circustent and everything began when man determined to . . .	566	1 X 1 26	5
where all now turns when (love's a universe beyond	574	1 X 1 34	6
(not either) my treasure, when violets appear love is	578	1 X 1 38	8
me for half a when, whatever is less alive	580	1 X 1 40	20
Joy, no where (no) when may breathe so sky	584	1 X 1 44	15
in (give give) bud when to me you made	589	1 X 1 49	3
with all beautiful things when to me you gave	589	1 X 1 49	12
(trees are in) song when to me you leap	589	1 X 1 49	18
more now than dying's when / / / /	592	1 X 1 52	14
Death were good: for when (instead of stopping to	604	(CHAIRE) 6	9
with a piece of when till it rolled behind	612	(CHAIRE) 14	8
/ / / / when serpents bargain for the	620	(CHAIRE) 22	1
gain a living wage-- when thorns regard their roses	620	(CHAIRE) 22	3
insured against old age when every thrush may sing	620	(CHAIRE) 22	5
is compelled to close when the oak begs permission	620	(CHAIRE) 22	9
he sharpens wrong and when their lives are keen	624	(CHAIRE) 26	17
neither why nor how when is now and which	630	(CHAIRE) 32	11
christmas bow) --and if, when we meet again, little	631	(CHAIRE) 33	7
/ / / / when your honest redskin toma	643	(CHAIRE) 45	1
from the never of when come into the now	661	(CHAIRE) 63	11
one times one than when times where-- that we	664	(CHAIRE) 66	9
/ / / / when faces called flowers float	665	(CHAIRE) 67	1
mountains are dancing together) when every leaf opens without	665	(CHAIRE) 67	8
are dancing, the mountains) when more than was lost	665	(CHAIRE) 67	15
ever wear it now when the boy who gave	684	95 POEMS 12	7
a mystery to be (when time from time shall	688	95 POEMS 16	14
If all blood And When / / / /	690	95 POEMS 18	8
ADHUC SUB JUDICE LIS when mack smacked phyllis on	706	95 POEMS 34	1
fell for a whore when he married his wife	707	95 POEMS 35	18
/ home means that when the certainly roof leaks	728	95 POEMS 56	2
/ / / / when any mortal (even the	731	95 POEMS 59	1
people be quite so (when flowers) in credibly (always	738	95 POEMS 66	14
(darling) never fear: love, when such marvels vanish, will .	741	95 POEMS 69	10
worth dying, if (and when) roses complain their beauties . .	744	95 POEMS 72	3
i am not sorry when sun and rain make	749	95 POEMS 77	4
i am not sorry when silence becomes singing winter	749	95 POEMS 77	16
more than bird) and when no am was ever	752	95 POEMS 80	7
(trivial merely) existence, all when may not measure a . . .	763	95 POEMS 90	35
to say and the when to do is exactly	776	73 POEMS 4	9
it's so damn sweet when Anybody-- yes; no matter	779	73 POEMS 7	2
ment) where what how when who why which (or	797	73 POEMS 25	21
as can feel) they when and they how and	801	73 POEMS 29	21
(at the magical hour when is becomes if) a	802	73 POEMS 30	3
absence of that moment when a stranger takes in	812	73 POEMS 40	11
very life who's your --when all fears hopes beliefs	812	73 POEMS 40	13
encompass me and you: when are we never, but	817	73 POEMS 45	5
realms of where and when beyond) now and here	832	73 POEMS 60	7
but never forever & when) un til one strict	840	73 POEMS 68	26
partially imagine whose despair when every silence will not .	842	73 POEMS 70	10
child will dance! and when he's plucked such mysteries . . .	843	73 POEMS 71	13

+WHEN

	PAGE	TITLE	LINE
FOR CONTEXT, SEE	237	IS 5 ONE 8	17
FOR CONTEXT, SEE	554	1 X 1 14	7

WHEN'S

	PAGE	TITLE	LINE
both made sense in when's haymow with young fore'er	316	VIVA 8	16

WHENCE

	PAGE	TITLE	LINE
flesh with delight) --immortally whence are the high gods . .	3	T&C EPITHALAM	8

		PAGE	TITLE	LINE

WHENCE (CONTINUED)
creation, lifts a flower-- whence is the world's insufferable   6 T&C EPITHALAM   135
eyes like new tools) whence i guessed that he . . . . 355 VIVA 46   12
WHENEVER
i be wrong for whenever men are right they . . . . 481 NEW POEMS 19   8
WHENLESS
while behind death's death whenless voices sing everywhere . 450 NO THANKS 65   17
WHENLINGS
/ / / wherelings whenlings (daughters of ifbut offspring . . 512 50 POEMS 26   1
WHENS
the mi croscopic world's whens, wheels; wonders: murders. . . 361 VIVA 52   17
into most immemorial of whens) before each heartbeat . . . . 577 1 X 1 37   18
+WHENS
FOR CONTEXT, SEE . . . . 721 95 POEMS 49   5
WHENWORLD
sound (which makes this whenworld squirm turns houses to . . 841 73 POEMS 69   16
WHERE
the undulous heaven yearns where in tense starlessness anoint 37 T&C AMORES 2   8
with thy unimaginable wings, where dwells the breath of . . . 40 T&C AMORES 4   46
placid obscure palpable carnival where to a normal melody . . 43 T&C AMORES 7   32
see in the street where strong men are digging . . . . 50 T&C IMPRESS 4   12
towns asleep i look where stealing needles of foam . . . . . 64 T&C POST IMPR 1   2
lime, wear dark, and where your meeting breasts are . . . . 71 T&C SON REAL 2   5
mystic lips take twilight where i know: proving to . . . . . 71 T&C SON REAL 2   13
god worships God-- (behold! where chaste stars writhe . . . . 77 T&C SON UNRE 2   17
smart of thrilled ecstasy, where sea and sky marry-- . . . . 79 T&C SON UNRE 4   13
my tower, laborious, casual where the surrounded smile hangs   83 T&C SON ACTU 2   15
ugliness of exact tombs, where a large road crosses . . . . . 86 T&C SON ACTU 5   12
is hushed in moan-loll where night gathers morte carved . . . 90 & POST IMPR 2   9
through the general noise Where is Effie who was . . . . . . 117 & PORTRAIT 10   10
my head, precisely dance where danced la guerre. Mimi . . . . 120 & PORTRAIT 12   4
skilfully dead precisely dance where has danced la guerre . . 121 & PORTRAIT 12   33
oh ver mYveRylitTle street where you will come, at . . . . . 122 & SEVEN POEMS 1   23
nice like a dance where you danced simple hours . . . . 127 & SEVEN POEMS 5   32
roof or some- thing where <> and nobody expects . . . . 127 & SEVEN POEMS 5   43
which nobody's ever visited, where always it's Spring) and . 129 & SEVEN POEMS 7   12
gilt hopeless wheels mired where sits rigidly her body's . . 131 & SON REAL 2   16
a mountain touch me where i stood (maybe nine . . . . 135 & SON REAL 6   11
upon the gold dawn, where teeth of slowturning streets . . . 142 & SON REAL 13   4
streets; heels taking derbies (where?) a pup hurriedly . . . 172 & SON ACTU 21   3
a street there is where strange birds purr / . . . . 180 XLI SONGS 2   20
rain he'll not tell where.) beauty makes terms with . . . . . 183 XLI SONGS 5   6
eyes the sweet earth where thou liest / / . . . . 184 XLI SONGS 6   17
and your drowsy lips where float flowers of kiss . . . . . . 186 XLI SONGS 8   12
shut your big eyes. where did you go? like . . . . 191 XLI CHANSONS 1   5
thrown on the ash-heap where lies what was once . . . . 203 XLI LA GUERRE 1   17
inimitably to lose herself where the wet stars softly . . . . 206 XLI SONNETS 2   9
curled, in other lands where other songs be sung; . . . . . . 208 XLI SONNETS 4   11
complain, whose seat is where revolving planets struggle to . 212 XLI SONNETS 8   10
a striving flower, just where strove the droll god-beasts . . 213 XLI SONNETS 9   8
across this dirtied pane where softly preys the grey . . . . 218 XLI SONNETS 14   10
of children gladly cricks where a hurdy-gurdy accurately . . 219 XLI SONNETS 15   8
the futile fooling labyrinth where noisy colours stroll.... . 220 XLI SONNETS 16   12
yknow, Rektuz, Toysday nite; where uh guy gets gayn . . . . . 227 IS 5 ONE GERT   16
virgins "from the Loggia where are we angels by . . . . . . 257 IS 5 ONE 27   30
conarefetti) ev eryflitter, inga. where mil (lions of . . . . 265 IS 5 ONE 34   2
spoons dance every- should where say over the damned . . . . 287 IS 5 FOUR 4   17
kiss this pillow, dear where our heads lived and . . . . . . 288 IS 5 FOUR 5   10
arms through a darkness where new lights begin and . . . . . 297 IS 5 FOUR 14   3
yellowsonofabitch into a dungeon, where he died Christ (of . 339 VIVA 30   37
him (every) who does (where) not move ; is . . . . 346 VIVA 37   24
skull of a baboon (where once good lips stalked . . . . 360 VIVA 51   2
(for only Nobody knows where truth grows why birds . . . . . 368 VIVA 59   19
to dowNdown (and only where remembers look, this was . . . . 371 VIVA 62   10
each how my trembling where my still unvisible when. . . . . 372 VIVA 63   5
(if Green invents because where might Where live can . . . . 395 NO THANKS 12   7
invents because where might Where live can fisherMen swim . . 395 NO THANKS 12   7
too far said he where you are said she) . . . . 399 NO THANKS 16   12

	PAGE	TITLE	LINE

WHERE (CONTINUED)

and unprecisely to repass where flesh is heiry montparnasse . 401 NO THANKS 18 12
teeth and doesn't know where to find them (and . . . . 410 NO THANKS 27 1
how dark and single, where he ends, the earth . . . . 418 NO THANKS 35 1
are) is most (windows where blaze naLOVEme crazily ships . . 436 NO THANKS 52 3
Freedom slaves will click; where Boobs are holy, poets . . . 438 NO THANKS 54 19
nor grief can go where goes this whyless soul . . . . 441 NO THANKS 56 44
and safe and known where it's lucky to be . . . . 466 NEW POEMS 4 19
lucky means finding Holes where pockets aren't lucky 's . . 467 NEW POEMS 5 2
or anybody don't know where it her his my . . . . 475 NEW POEMS 13 3
feet into immense no Where which to map while . . . . 479 NEW POEMS 17 3
coast of Sum precisely where a craft of cost . . . . 494 50 POEMS 8 5
scribbling from there to where --name unless i'm mistaken . . 504 50 POEMS 18 8
am (beyond when behind where under un) / / . . . . 505 50 POEMS 19 24
height this motionless forgetful where turned at his glance . 520 50 POEMS 34 5
uplifting the, of each where all was is to . . . . 533 50 POEMS 45 7
fic land of supernod where freedom is compulsory and . . . . 544 1 X 1 4 23
may: life's the deathboard where all now turns when . . . . 574 1 X 1 34 6
sweet one (and april's where we're) / / / . . . . 578 1 X 1 38 12
upward with Joy, no where (no) when may breathe . . . . . . 584 1 X 1 44 15
it our away beyond where what a wonderful thing . . . . . . 593 1 X 1 53 18
a shy animal called where and she disappeared. Out . . . . 612 (CHAIRE) 14 10
a white high night where his heartlike ears have . . . . . . 631 (CHAIRE) 33 5
hole in its life where the young bell tolled . . . . 647 (CHAIRE) 49 14
one than when times where-- that we are in . . . . 664 (CHAIRE) 66 9
they'll some or if where shall breathe a new . . . . 666 (CHAIRE) 68 6
straight up into the where so safe we are . . . . 746 95 POEMS 74 7
and peaceful hills (not where not here but neither's . . . . 750 95 POEMS 78 5
than love will end; where nothing is to breathe . . . . . . 768 95 POEMS 94 3
(and a here there where) and away we go . . . . 769 95 POEMS 95 7
path all paths lead where truth is here / . . . . 775 73 POEMS 3 3
mistrust) despair and right where soulless our (with all . . 780 73 POEMS 8 6
un til against my (where three dreams live) fore . . . . . . 785 73 POEMS 13 21
of a mo ment) where what how when who . . . . 797 73 POEMS 25 19
only (jesus) every (god) where (chr ist) what absolute . . . 823 73 POEMS 51 17
perfect this (almost invisible where of a there of . . . . 827 73 POEMS 55 8
a whis per a where a hidi ng) est . . . . 831 73 POEMS 59 13
stand (all realms of where and when beyond) now . . . . . . 832 73 POEMS 60 6
it's time you unbecame where climbing was and bright . . . . 834 73 POEMS 62 19
briefer each our bliss-- where seeing eyes go blind . . . . 834 73 POEMS 62 27
seeing eyes go blind (where lips forget to kiss) . . . . . 834 73 POEMS 62 28
lips forget to kiss) where everything's nothing --arise, my . 834 73 POEMS 62 29
sky trees : every where a miracle arrives (yes) . . . . . . 835 73 POEMS 63 24

+WHERE

FOR CONTEXT, SEE . . . . 265 IS 5 ONE 34 5

WHERE'S

/ / / / Where's Madge then, Madge and . . . . 183 XLI SONGS 5 1
/ / / / where's Jack Was General Was . . . . 642 (CHAIRE) 44 1
why (rub-her-bub) bub? (bubs) where's Jim Soon Admiral Soon . 642 (CHAIRE) 44 11
fly (rub-her-bub) bub? (bubs) where's John Big Doughgob Big . 642 (CHAIRE) 44 21

WHEREABOUTS

clue to his innumerable whereabouts violet logic of annihi- . 197 XLI PORTRAIT 5 6

WHEREAS

: to twitter wickedly whereas the big and firm . . . . . . 95 & POST IMPR 7 13
laughter, and the legs whereas, at twenty minutes to . . . . 115 & PORTRAIT 8 25
/ / / / whereas by dark really released, ... 146 & SON REAL 17 1
inhabit the Hotel Meurice (whereas i live in a . . . . . . 245 IS 5 ONE 16 4
goes wrong you know (whereas when i lie down . . . . 245 IS 5 ONE 16 11
cute idea n'est-ce pas? (whereas, upon the other hand, . . . 245 IS 5 ONE 16 15
enters abruptly Notre Dame (whereas de gustibus non . . . . 245 IS 5 ONE 16 23
which is extremely unimportant) whereas Life matters if or . 260 IS 5 ONE 30 12
in the legislat- ure whereas tommy so and so . . . . 266 IS 5 TWO 1 37
big little and all) whereas (my sweet) our summer . . . . . 776 73 POEMS 4 29
this hearty fellow'll exist --whereas that delicate creature 813 73 POEMS 41 7
day are) only loaned: whereas night is given (night . . . . 816 73 POEMS 44 7
Each believing world denies, whereas your lover (looking . . 845 73 POEMS 73 11

WHEREBY

a gesture of immaculate perfume--whereby (with fear aglow) my 19 T&C PUELLA MEA 108

		PAGE	TITLE	LINE

WHEREBY (CONTINUED)
    is a throbbing neck whereby to grasp the belly's . . . . . . 21 T&C PUELLA MEA 196
WHEREFORE
    we promised to forget-- wherefore is there nothing left . . . 173 & SON ACTU 22   13
    let us next demand wherefore yon mob an accident? . . . . . . 245 IS 5 ONE 16   16
    drift Of thickly starhums wherefore & wormSmile eternal; . . 371 VIVA 62   23
WHEREFROM
    bodies lightly desperate certainly wherefrom departed is . . 57 T&C PORTRAIT 5   39
WHEREFUL
    lost my dazed my whereful selves they put on . . . . 819 73 POEMS 47   16
+WHEREFUL
    FOR CONTEXT, SEE . . . . 534 50 POEMS 46   18
WHEREIN
'   a most swift radiance wherein slowly drift murmurous things . 18 T&C PUELLA MEA   80
    noone has suspected (but wherein silently always are kneeling 285 IS 5 FOUR 2   18
    magic: that white sleep wherein all human curiosity we'll . . 675 95 POEMS 3   11
WHERELESS
    whole and the green whereless truth of an eternal . . . . . . 558 1 X 1 18   4
WHERELESSLY
    more than immeasurable dream wherelessly spiralling) beyond . 454 NO THANKS 69   8
WHERELINGS
    / / / / wherelings whenlings (daughters of ifbut . . . . . . 512 50 POEMS 26   1
WHEREOF
    hair that blossom stands whereof is most desire, yet . . . .   6 T&C EPITHALAM   147
    smooth and awkward foal, whereof young moons begin the . . . 11 T&C SONGS 2   4
    snow will oft utter, whereof the year has perfect . . . . . . 21 T&C PUELLA MEA   189
    unto a palace intricate (whereof the luscious pillars rise . 21 T&C PUELLA MEA   203
    one kingdom the king whereof is darkness thy forehead . . . . 29 T&C ORIENTALE 3   3
    entirely melting sinuous lean... whereof this lady in some . 225 IS 5 ONE LIZ   16
WHEREON
    with a changeless grin whereon a dozen staunch and . . . . . 258 IS 5 ONE 28   9
WHERES
    the always beyond such wheres and fears or any . . . . 378 VIVA 69   13
    trees, dream(ev: ery: wheres: ex: tend: ing: hush . . . . . 416 NO THANKS 33   3
    valley forest) a million wheres which never may become . . . 659 {CHAIRE} 61   6
+WHERES
    FOR CONTEXT, SEE . . . . 480 NEW POEMS 18   10
WHERETO
    fatal flight of worlds whereto this earth's a hurled . . . . 81 T&C SON UNRE 6   5
    of geomet- rical putrescence whereto my invariably . . . . . 197 XLI PORTRAIT 5   20
WHEREUPON
    the first crumb said whereupon its fellow five crumbs . . . . 117 & PORTRAIT 10   13
    it an even dollar whereupon the Divine Average who . . . . . 196 XLI PORTRAIT 4   15
    was dead dead dead) whereupon mary quite contrary didn't . . 401 NO THANKS 18   8
    no-voice sobcries "paw? lee" --whereupon out (S1O wLy) steps 697 95 POEMS 25   15
WHEREVER
    really a dream-- here's, wherever you aren't or are, ... 605 {CHAIRE} 7   15
    my sweet) not only wherever the sun and the . . . . 686 95 POEMS 14   16
WHEREWHEN
    extend unwish through curving wherewhen till unwish returns . 554 1 X 1 14   7
WHEREWHENS
    by perfect nothing: millionary wherewhens distant, as . . . . 721 95 POEMS 49   5
WHETHER
    that stinks Excuse Me whether it's president of the . . . . . 549 1 X 1 9   2
    misder finger isn't important whether it's millions of other 549 1 X 1 9   4
    absolutely doesn't matter and whether it's in lonjewray or . 549 1 X 1 9   6
    stinks to please but whether to please itself or . . . . . . 549 1 X 1 9   9
    talking's talking to oneself (whether that oneself be sought 804 73 POEMS 32   3
WHEY
    picture His peering biggest whey coloured face on which . . . 117 & PORTRAIT 10   32
WHICH
    WORD DELETED, APPEARED 368 TIMES
WHICHFUL
    pin g dre ams whichful sarcasms papery deathfuls) awaits . . 415 NO THANKS 32   18
    / / / (nothing whichful about thick big this . . . . 658 {CHAIRE} 60   1
WHICHS
    bodies) squirm-of-frightened shy are whichs small its hungry 437 NO THANKS 53   7
    fin gering s wli whichs turn in to whos . . . . 463 NEW POEMS 1   11

		PAGE	TITLE	LINE

WHICHWHAT

ter lugs his copious whichwhat skilfully here & (simply . . . 629 (CHAIRE) 31   9
collap sing thatthis is whichwhat yell itfulls o f . . . . . 646 (CHAIRE) 48   6

WHIGH

six cents hit the whigh shaped hathole thangew yelps . . . . 602 (CHAIRE) 4   4

WHILE

who sees them pass) while hunted from his kingdom . . . . . .   4 T&C EPITHALAM   70
the flicker's laughing yet, while on the hills the . . . . .   5 T&C EPITHALAM   75
they would mistrust a while the moving of beauteous . . . . .   6 T&C EPITHALAM 140
folded soul shall know while on faint hills do . . . . 11 T&C SONGS 2   27
pale, a terror musical? while in an earthless hour . . . . . 12 T&C SONGS 2   41
face and all the while shall my heart be . . . . 16 T&C SONGS 6   13
like a flower lieth (while within the eyes is . . . . 20 T&C PUELLA MEA   14
which being a little while caressed its fragrance makes . . . 21 T&C PUELLA MEA 191
the fifty pillars listening while the queens of all . . . . . 35 T&C ORIENTALE 6 115
queer pulp of ecstasy while in the battered bodies . . . . . 55 T&C PORTRAIT 3   17
in pursuit pleasantly elephantine while nearby the father a . 56 T&C PORTRAIT 4   9
soft furious light, and while fire-escapes and roofs and . . 62 T&C PORTRAIT 10   15
roofs and chimneys and while roofs and fire-escapes and . . 62 T&C PORTRAIT 10   16
fire-escapes and chimneys and while chimneys and fire-escapes 62 T&C PORTRAIT 10   17
is it Poles? perhaps. While permanent faces coyly bandy . . . 70 T&C SON REAL 1   9
again, lingering a little while i see thee then . . . . 75 T&C SON REAL 6   5
was mine a little while; moments when my once . . . . 78 T&C SON UNRE 3   8
lame and begging colour) while there and here the . . . . . . 93 & POST IMPR 5   15
wakes in little streets while exactlygir lisHlegs; play; ing; 104 & POST IMPR 14   11
our moreover irrevocable bodies while the infinite . . . . . 111 & PORTRAIT 6   62
in memory of Cleopatra while easily tremendously floats in . 111 & PORTRAIT 6   71
eyes approve the blessed while His ears are crammed . . . . . 117 & PORTRAIT 10   36
into which people look (while people stare arranging and . . 124 & SEVEN POEMS 3   4
New and Old things, while people stare carefully moving . . . 124 & SEVEN POEMS 3   14
mussed, and she coughed while tying strings / / . . . . 132 & SON REAL 3   18
seriously. Dumb for a while. my god--a patter of . . . . . . 133 & SON REAL 4   13
my mouth occurs homelessly. While grip Hips simply. well . . 136 & SON REAL 7   11
untimid svelte subdued magic while in your eyes there . . . . 138 & SON REAL 9   7
pass a million years (while a bee dozes on . . . . 181 XLI SONGS 3   9
leaves repeats eventual perfection while east deserves of . . 184 XLI SONGS 6   14
of undimishied silence, supports while devouring the firm . . 201 XLI PORTRAIT 9   19
didst love the pen while others wrote in steel, ... 209 XLI SONNETS 5   10
the Baboon sniggering insipidities while. i sit, sipping . . 220 XLI SONNETS 16   13
upwrinkled into nothing earthly, while the slippery eyes . . 226 IS 5 ONE MAME   4
and me almost succeeds while toddle rings the bell. . . . . . 227 IS 5 ONE GERT   7
outward (amid <> tables) while softly along Kirkland Street . 232 IS 5 ONE 3   11
Victor Victrola and records while he lived presented to . . . 239 IS 5 ONE 10   28
to nothing on) tangoing (while a feller tries to . . . . . . 242 IS 5 ONE 13   7
friend clenched weakly dirt while the mute trouserfly . . . . 258 IS 5 ONE 28   19
one fist dangling scandal while five other fingers snitch . . 259 IS 5 ONE 29   9
shall we say: Idleness, while meaning its opposite? Nothing . 263 IS 5 ONE 32   39
being for a little while and which easily break . . . . 264 IS 5 ONE 33   15
like any other pastel. (While you and i have . . . . 264 IS 5 ONE 33   25
of pretty medals drew (while messrs jack james john . . . . . 266 IS 5 TWO 1   25
stare, the drunker applaud while twilight takes the sting . . 279 IS 5 THREE 3   18
fatally turning into ourselves... while in the very middle . 283 IS 5 THREE 7   26
to be a fool while Spring is in the . . . . 290 IS 5 FOUR 7   6
do neighbours re babies while; / / / / . . . . 309 VIVA 1   36
about the desertbyIts elf while) nextto Mesmoked eleven . . . 318 VIVA 10   14
harbour fools the sea(while emanating the triple starred . . 319 VIVA 11   19
" " aureally (yawning while all the dominoes) fall: . . . . . 331 VIVA 22   8
anent this muddy toiletbowl, while kindred intellects evoke . 339 VIVA 30   13
prettiest deaths without effort while hungering churches . . 340 VIVA 31   15
ly its self in) while a transparent blouse even . . . . 341 VIVA 32   17
eyes watches; truly, curvingly while reacts (sharp now with . 344 VIVA 35   5
all oceans various and while everywhere beneath thee and . . 351 VIVA 42   8
all that so gently while we were alseep while . . . . 370 VIVA 61   15
while we were alseep while we were each other . . . . 370 VIVA 61   15
singular kingdom (sleep) . while some thing else kisses . . . 370 VIVA 61   22
not born of dream while wings welcome the year . . . . 372 VIVA 63   14
truth opening encompass true) while your contriving fate, my 373 VIVA 64   17
slim curving mighty children while a python over the . . . . 384 NO THANKS 2   21

		PAGE	TITLE	LINE

WHILE (CONTINUED)

stars may not observe; while roses wince) that which . . . . 386 NO THANKS 3   8
progress or mainly awash while chiefly submerged or an . . . 410 NO THANKS 27   11
who are always men while a man shall which . . . . 414 NO THANKS 31   14
in the moon a while) and shall carve time . . . . 433 NO THANKS 50   13
your Tom is Dick; while Gadgets murder squawk and . . . . . 438 NO THANKS 54   11
dream, create and kill while the whole moves; and . . . . . . 446 NO THANKS 61   14
not know him (and while behind death's death whenless . . . . 450 NO THANKS 65   17
the earth tinily whirls; while daisies grow (and boys . . . . 451 NO THANKS 66   12
Where which to map while these not eyes quite . . . . 479 NEW POEMS 17   4
greath on insulated brows (while tossing boms at uncle . . . 500 50 POEMS 14   15
mystery of love become while every sun goes round . . . . . . 510 50 POEMS 24   14
of death's wandering guess) while children climb their eyes . 517 50 POEMS 31   14
at her diamond solitaire while guesswho nibbles his ton . . . 545 1 X 1 5   5
by matchabelli) tits as (while thumb a plus fingers . . . . . 546 1 X 1 6   10
"have you" the mountain, while his maples wept air . . . . . 555 1 X 1 15   11
and this mountain slept while his pines lifted their . . . . 555 1 X 1 15   16
the breathing for me while i am away?) / . . . . 558 1 X 1 18   15
every cannot stir imagining; while you are motionless-- whose 559 1 X 1 19   11
person) through musical shadows while hunted by daemons . . . 586 1 X 1 46   13
of me and only while your sweet eyes close . . . . 588 1 X 1 48   5
eternity floated a blossoming (while anyone might slowly . . 599 {CHAIRE} 1   9
could knock you down (while scotch was your breakfast . . . . 605 {CHAIRE} 7   5
of a rose easily (while will be goes was) . . . . 608 {CHAIRE} 10   10
mountains! how can each" while flame crashed "be so . . . . . 626 {CHAIRE} 28   9
eyes of elsewhere jabber while (infinite fog & puking . . . . 629 {CHAIRE} 31   5
and won't be words while possibly not (at a . . . . 631 {CHAIRE} 33   10
love, stand with me while silence sings not into . . . . . . 633 {CHAIRE} 35   12
a keen cold groan while the gadgets purred and . . . . 647 {CHAIRE} 49   9
over and lay still while he passed (as close . . . . 648 {CHAIRE} 50   8
stop (kneeling in doubt: while all skies fall) and . . . . . 650 {CHAIRE} 52   2
distinct grandiloquent deep D; while all skies fall at . . . 650 {CHAIRE} 52   16
come (s gruntsqueak , while, idling-is-grindstone one; what: 656 {CHAIRE} 58   6
alighting) and i'll sing while at us very deafly . . . . . . 659 {CHAIRE} 61   13
come riding alive down while crylessly drifting through vast 661 {CHAIRE} 63   13
breathing a fatal stillness; while enormous this how patient 674 95 POEMS 2   4
thing which raced sideways while blowing bubbles: and may . . 682 95 POEMS 10   8
hole swallows it self while nobody (and stars moon . . . . . 693 95 POEMS 21   17
a hundred million whos (while only himself was him) . . . . . 709 95 POEMS 37   4
you'd care to see (while a stuttering ghost that . . . . . . 709 95 POEMS 37   7
job to be done) while a wisp of why . . . . 709 95 POEMS 37   11
time space doom dream while floats the whole perhapsless . . 714 95 POEMS 42   7
eyes looking (alw ays) while earth and sky grow . . . . 715 95 POEMS 43   8
blue) i am any (while around him streets taking . . . . 720 95 POEMS 48   4
pigeons) squ -I- nts (while showe ring cigaretteash O . . . . 726 95 POEMS 54   12
outglory glory the little while they live-- unless by . . . . 742 95 POEMS 70   10
the ending earth-- and while a (huge which by . . . . 743 95 POEMS 71   2
omnipotent He feel sorry while these were blossoming) roses . 748 95 POEMS 76   10
/ all nearness pauses, while a star can grow . . . . 750 95 POEMS 78   1
sing to me and while this dream is climbing . . . . 752 95 POEMS 80   5
rej and lena smile (while looming darkly a kindness . . . . . 754 95 POEMS 82   9
quick of nowhere) we --While one thrush sings / . . . . 758 95 POEMS 85   48
and scratch-scrutch and scritch (while the no-she-yes-he . . 773 73 POEMS 1   15
to sing, my darling: while old worlds and young . . . . 776 73 POEMS 4   4
asking no favor but (while down come blundering proud . . . . 783 73 POEMS 11   6
be out of work while she can swarm. To . . . . 790 73 POEMS 18   8
but a person) and while never saying a word . . . . 802 73 POEMS 30   25
believe scarcely may) certainly while mute each inch of . . . 808 73 POEMS 36   9
trillion secrets touchably alive --while and all mysteries . 809 73 POEMS 37   5
creature is most herself while uttering one a third . . . . . 813 73 POEMS 41   8
that mountain, any god) while leaf twig limb ask . . . . . . 818 73 POEMS 46   9
/ / / / while a once world slips . . . . 822 73 POEMS 50   1

+WHILE

FOR CONTEXT, SEE . . . . 442 NO THANKS 57   8
FOR CONTEXT, SEE . . . . 611 {CHAIRE} 13   7

WHILEPIN

desert smoked bad me whilepin Kishcam elscasta? netsits Elf . 318 VIVA 10   21

WHIM
     scythe takes crisply the whim of thy smoothness. and . . . . 215 XLI SONNETS 11   6
     grab sicksilk soak sulksuck whim poke if inch dimmer . . . . 333 VIVA 24   11
WHIMPERED
     with of what manshaped whimpered how girllike laughtering . . 371 VIVA 62   3
WHIMS
     furiously puzzling through, prismatic, whims, the chattering 157 & SON ACTU 6   13
+WHINE
     FOR CONTEXT, SEE . . . . 795 73 POEMS 23   19
WHINING
     with wind, and the whining rigging over us, i . . . . 378 VIVA 69   2
WHINNIED
     woman in the crowd whinnied and a man squeezing . . . . . .   53 T&C PORTRAIT 1   35
WHIPALERT
     &Isdensekil-ling-whipAlert-floatScor ruptingly) . . . . 430 NO THANKS 47   14
WHIPPED
     backwardSpinning hoop returns fasterishly whipped the top . . 311 VIVA 3   6
WHIPPING
     ish' shead Or, the whipping of a blackSnake cu . . . . . .   101 & POST IMPR 11   52
WHIPPOORWILL
     on him sings a whippoorwill; heart was big as . . . . 568 1 X 1 28   15
     / / / / whippoorwill this moonday into (big . . . . 751 95 POEMS 79   1
WHIPPOORWILLS
     thrushes toward dusk among whippoorwills or tree field rock . 512 50 POEMS 26   25
WHIRL
     Frolic or the Century whirl? one's memory indignantly . . . .   72 T&C SON REAL 3   3
     yi nch along the whirl- ingPeaceful furious street people . . 100 & POST IMPR 11   38
     perfectly dear (and worlds whirl beyond worlds: immortal . .   376 VIVA 67   12
     thicker the thumb (it's whirl, girls) round and round . . . . 513 50 POEMS 27   7
     dancing swoop (and swooping whirl over a frightened boy . . . 777 73 POEMS 5   7
+WHIRL
     FOR CONTEXT, SEE . . . . 495 50 POEMS 9   18
WHIRL'S
     let's as silence, because Whirl's after all: (after me) . . . 160 & SON ACTU 9   12
WHIRLED
     upon me I was whirled and tossed into delicious . . . .   44 T&C AMORES 8   12
+WHIRLFULLY
     FOR CONTEXT, SEE . . . . 655 (CHAIRE) 57   7
WHIRLING
     start the last leaf whirling in the final brain . . . .   80 T&C SON UNRE 5   11
     people) reel (dark- ly) whirling in (b ellSB el . . . . 444 NO THANKS 59   15
     seethe firm swirl hips whirling climb to GIVE (yoursmine . .   445 NO THANKS 60   27
     nimbler than Really go whirling into gaily white thousands .   630 (CHAIRE) 32   3
     with unthings) tosses hello whirling whose rhyme (spilling .   751 95 POEMS 79   5
+WHIRLING
     FOR CONTEXT, SEE . . . . 447 NO THANKS 62   8
     FOR CONTEXT, SEE . . . . 487 50 POEMS 1   17
WHIRLING'S
     fragrance dances a honeydunce; whirling's a frantic struts a 763 95 POEMS 90   11
WHIRLINGEST
     givingest girl on this whirlingest earth? why you're by . . . 590 1 X 1 50   6
WHIRLS
     know: the earth tinily whirls; while daisies grow (and . . . 451 NO THANKS 66   11
+WHIRLS
     FOR CONTEXT, SEE . . . . 423 NO THANKS 40   16
WHIRLSWANS
     solemn dolls re -volve whirlswans rabbitsare: swimswim ⬦ . .   384 NO THANKS 2   29
WHIS-PER
     entities e. g. the) whis-per it (Living / . . . .   391 NO THANKS 8   26
WHISK
     and run and hidehidehide whisk whisk look out for . . . . . .   25 T&C CHANSONS 2   16
     run and hidehidehide whisk whisk look out for the . . . . . .   25 T&C CHANSONS 2   17
WHISKEY
     you sing in your whiskey-voice the grass rises on . . . . . .   61 T&C PORTRAIT 9   18
     the lady'll have a whiskey-sour-- whose least amazing smile .   74 T&C SON REAL 5   13
WHISKEY-SOUR
     the lady'll have a whiskey-sour-- whose least amazing smile .   74 T&C SON REAL 5   13

WHISKEY-VOICE
    you sing in your whiskey-voice the grass rises on . . . . . . 61 T&C PORTRAIT 9   18
WHISKIES
    a cockney is buying whiskies for a turk a . . . . 108 & PORTRAIT 4   12
WHISPER
    shrieking tightness solid screams whisper.) Lumberman of The 195 XLI PORTRAIT 3   15
    mouths of snow insignificantly whisper.... / / / / . . . . . 218 XLI SONNETS 14   15
    did something like a whisper, "even her." "The Madam?"   . . . 228 IS 5 ONE MARJ   10
    fasters by button of whisper sum blinked he belowtry . . . . 333 VIVA 24   8
    face with hands which whisper This is my beloved . . . . . . 352 VIVA 43   14
    thighs forget (when clocks whisper and night shouts) When . . 359 VIVA 50   2
    mOOn Over tOwns mOOn whisper less creature huge grO . . . . . 383 NO THANKS 1   2
    sunset, crickets within me whisper whose erect blood finally 435 NO THANKS 51   37
    purer than purest pure whisper of a whisper so . . . . 601 {CHAIRE} 3   2
    pure whisper of a whisper so (big with innocence) . . . . . . 601 {CHAIRE} 3   2
    grows" then in a whisper, as time turned to . . . . 626 {CHAIRE} 28   11
    opens around them) and whisper their joy under entirely . . . 754 95 POEMS 82   11
    fate and even Our whisper it Selves but don't . . . . 762 95 POEMS 89   13
    6 this bell 's whisper asks (of a world . . . . 787 73 POEMS 15   14
    (in that order) is wHISpEr it left; at the . . . . 792 73 POEMS 20   9
    let her heart's each whisper wear all never guessed . . . . . 811 73 POEMS 39   6
    before quite your whisper's whisper is subtracted from my . . 821 73 POEMS 49   9
    into winter twi light (whisper) "was my friend" reme   . . . . 823 73 POEMS 51   5
+WHISPER
    FOR CONTEXT, SEE . . . . 391 NO THANKS 8   26
    FOR CONTEXT, SEE . . . . 512 50 POEMS 26   22
    FOR CONTEXT, SEE . . . . 831 73 POEMS 59   12
WHISPER'S
    --now, before quite your whisper's whisper is subtracted from 821 73 POEMS 49   9
WHISPERED
    limbs reeking of the whispered deep, deliberate groping ocean   7 T&C EPITHALAM   158
    crumb with some shame whispered unto God, my name . . . . . . 117 & PORTRAIT 10   22
    or why her tiniest whispered invitation is like a . . . . . . 229 IS 5 ONE FRAN   14
    train for because dear whispered again in never's ear . . . . 316 VIVA 8   4
    boys and girls have whispered thus and so) and . . . . 451 NO THANKS 66   14
    skies by merciful love whispered were, completes its . . . . 526 50 POEMS 38   10
    do or be?" god whispered him a snowflake "yes: . . . . 555 1 X 1 15   14
WHISPERFUL
    pursued by its wigglesome whisperful body and almost isn't . 585 1 X 1 45   8
+WHISPERFULLY
    FOR CONTEXT, SEE . . . . 421 NO THANKS 38   4
WHISPERING
    flesh the rain's pearls singly-whispering. / / / / . . . . 65 T&C POST IMPR 2   16
    beautiful elephants (mingled in whispering thickly smooth . . 95 & POST IMPR 7   15
    in sawdust Voices a: whispering drunkard passes who knows . . 128 & SEVEN POEMS 6   6
    a dream myself speaks (whispering, suggesting that our souls 285 IS 5 FOUR 2   3
    ghost whom assault these whispering fists of hail (and . . . 299 IS 5 FOUR 16   12
    singing like an idiot, whispering like a drunken man . . . . 304 IS 5 FIVE 3   3
    of (try to imagine) whispering of a named Krassin . . . . . . 324 VIVA 16   14
    with newly murdered flowers whispering barns bulge a tiniest 340 VIVA 31   12
    man extracted hate from whispering grass? joy in time . . . . 527 50 POEMS 39   10
    heavenless warm sweet mistfully whispering rainlife) infinite 755 95 POEMS 83   12
+WHISPERING
    FOR CONTEXT, SEE . . . . 304 IS 5 FIVE 3   13
    FOR CONTEXT, SEE . . . . 423 NO THANKS 40   7
    FOR CONTEXT, SEE . . . . 430 NO THANKS 47   6
    FOR CONTEXT, SEE . . . . 710 95 POEMS 38   9
WHISPERINGLY
    by on whom glories whisperingly impinge (god's pretty mother) 85 T&C SON ACTU 4   5
WHISPERLESS
    the cold perfect night whisperless to mark, how that . . . . 205 XLI SONNETS 1   6
WHISPERS
    the pines deepen to whispers primeval and throw backward . .   5 T&C EPITHALAM   76
    who will their hungering whispers hear with weepings . . . .   9 T&C SONGS 1   20
    toys to play with windows-and-whispers, (will . . . . 169 & SON ACTU 18   10
    joy, unto whom duty whispers low "thou must!" and . . . . . . 273 IS 5 TWO 8   4
    no O 3rd Findingest whispers understand sobs bigly climb . . 358 VIVA 49   6
    bridges with mirrors from whispers to stars; climbing silence 439 NO THANKS 55   22

WHISPERS (CONTINUED)
    tables the and bitch whispers jill mopping too bad . . . . . 496 50 POEMS 10   16
    to do what must (whispers) be must be (the . . . . 543 1 X 1 3   13
    a blind stare, he whispers "i ran" / / . . . . 800 73 POEMS 28   24
    the ghost of you whispers "is very pleasant" my . . . . 808 73 POEMS 36   15
    wind in the dark) whispers. And i and my . . . . 813 73 POEMS 41   11
    it must be your" whispers that flower murmurs eager . . . . . 837 73 POEMS 65   6
+WHISPERS
    FOR CONTEXT, SEE . . . . 629 {CHAIRE} 31   17
WHISPERSHOUT
    e vero madonna (nudge whispershout) laugh matching onceupons 681 95 POEMS 9   7
WHIST
    / / / hist whist little ghostthings tip-toe twinkle-toe . . . 25 T&C CHANSONS 2   1
WHISTLE
    (ee) ps on his whistle somebody says here's luck . . . . . . 108 & PORTRAIT 4   19
    what i say is whistle that sing that yell . . . . 475 NEW POEMS 13   16
    they sing and they whistle (now here is a . . . . 709 95 POEMS 37   9
WHISTLES
    the little lame balloonman whistles far and wee and . . . . . 24 T&C CHANSONS 1   5
    the queer old balloonman whistles far and wee and . . . . . . 24 T&C CHANSONS 1   12
    and the goat-footed balloonMan whistles far and wee / . . . . 24 T&C CHANSONS 1   21
    bridge train shriek chewing whistles hugest to morrow from . 309 VIVA 1   19
WHITE
    lilied robe the sun's white hands emboss, betwixt whose . . . 3 T&C EPITHALAM   29
    of night blossoming in white towers to the moon, ... 8 T&C OF NICOL   3
    of tiny troubadours, and (phantom-white) dumb-blooming boughs 8 T&C OF NICOL   5
    lyre, a creature of white hands, who letting fall . . . . . . 8 T&C OF NICOL   22
    her delicate silk) all white, with shining feet, went . . . . 8 T&C OF NICOL   27
    between those rivers whose white voices pass upon forgetting 9 T&C SONGS 1   2
    between your thoughts more white than wool My thought . . . . 11 T&C SONGS 2   14
    red roebuck at a white water the cruel bugle . . . . 14 T&C SONGS 4   9
    he when swooned the white egyptian day who with . . . . . . 18 T&C PUELLA MEA   73
    inimitable find beyond the white authentic springs, beyond . 19 T&C PUELLA MEA   120
    went to bed, whom white-thighed Semiramis put up her . . . . 22 T&C PUELLA MEA   247
    a dream locked in white fragrance Come hither O . . . . . . 27 T&C ORIENTALE 1   19
    breasts are swarms of white bees upon the bough . . . . . . 29 T&C ORIENTALE 3   7
    spring thy thighs are white horses yoked to a . . . . 29 T&C ORIENTALE 3   11
    itself stiffenS to a white thorn of desire the . . . . . . 34 T&C ORIENTALE 6   94
    queen of queens and white money upon her nakedness . . . . 34 T&C ORIENTALE 6   102
    a certain face become white perfume only, from the . . . . . 39 T&C AMORES 4   34
    "kitty". sixteen, 5' 1", white, prostitute. ducking always . 74 T&C SON REAL 5   1
    marry-- to know the white ship of thy heart . . . . 79 T&C SON UNRE 4   15
    forest--no offense to you, white town whose spires softly . . 86 T&C SON ACTU 5   4
    / / SNO a white idea (Listen drenches: earth's . . . . 99 & POST IMPR 10   2
    air) don't speak A white idea, drenching. earth's brain . . . 99 & POST IMPR 10   19
    arms and legs like white squirming pipes wiggle upon . . . . 110 & PORTRAIT 6   7
    upon her much too white forehead a pair of . . . . 116 & PORTRAIT 9   10
    plunge these leopards of white dream in the glad . . . . . . 139 & SON REAL 10   6
    with surprise like a white shocking wire, when she . . . . . 147 & SON REAL 18   5
    with a speed of white speech (the simple instant . . . . . . 157 & SON ACTU 6   7
    agrin with memories (this white worm and i who . . . . . . 164 & SON ACTU 13   12
    amazingly, one pair is white (but you know that) . . . . . 171 & SON ACTU 20   9
    shop doors unlocked by white-grub faces) clothes in delicate 172 & SON ACTU 21   6
    to whom the musical white spring offers her lily . . . . . . 206 XLI SONNETS 2   1
    stabbing music of your white youth wounded by my . . . . . . 218 XLI SONNETS 14   2
    ponderous arms bedecked whose white thick wrists deliver . 225 IS 5 ONE LIZ   8
    eye, upon his firm white lips a smile, one . . . . 273 IS 5 TWO 8   10
    man, three cats, five white mice, and a baboon. . . . . . . 279 IS 5 THREE 3   8
    a little girl in white spins, tumbles; rolling in . . . . . 281 IS 5 THREE 5   3
    a little girl in white is tumbling in sand . . . . 281 IS 5 THREE 5   13
    moves, since Doom (with white longest hands neatening each . 288 IS 5 FOUR 5   3
    comes, who twiddles his white thumbs and frisks down . . . . 296 IS 5 FOUR 13   6
    / / after all white horses are in bed . . . . 302 IS 5 FIVE 1   1
    doesn't give a soft white damn Whom it touches . . . . 328 VIVA 19   22
    against this wall his white sincere small hands with . . . . 355 VIVA 46   14
    tinyness, the moon (with white wig and polished buttons) . . 365 VIVA 56   12
    of distinct sunset driving white spikes of silence into . . . 378 VIVA 69   9
    / this (that grey) white (man) horse floats on . . . . . . 408 NO THANKS 25   2

WHITE (CONTINUED)

huger than fear a white with madness wind and . . . . 432 NO THANKS 49 16
red blue yellow violet white orange green- ness o . . . . . . 437 NO THANKS 53 14
(who wanders through only white darkness who moves in . . . . 439 NO THANKS 55 19
/ a football with white eyebrows the 3 rd . . . . 465 NEW POEMS 3 1
she veiled with candy white carrying a bouquet of . . . . . . 470 NEW POEMS 8 5
are in) four are white (three singdance six dancesing . . . . 507 50 POEMS 21 16
green silence with a white earth in it you . . . . 529 50 POEMS 41 2
and stifles forests in white ago? Blow hope to . . . . 560 1 X 1 20 12
until you've made me white" so she did and . . . . 622 {CHAIRE} 24 6
sulky gob with entirely white eyes of elsewhere jabber . . . 629 {CHAIRE} 31 3
go whirling into gaily white thousands return by millions . . 630 {CHAIRE} 32 4
round cloud in a white high night where his . . . . 631 {CHAIRE} 33 4
known kind with one white eye and one black . . . . 647 {CHAIRE} 49 17
made flesh-- dreamslender exquisite white firstful flame . . 669 {CHAIRE} 71 9
a deeper magic: that white sleep wherein all human . . . . . 675 95 POEMS 3 11
by no means almost white morethanPerson; who (riding through 697 95 POEMS 25 19
/ / / jack's white horse (up high in . . . . 699 95 POEMS 27 1
now (dancing yes for) white ly (joy! joy! joy) . . . . 715 95 POEMS 43 14
my mother's greatgrandmother's rosebush white roses are . . . 748 95 POEMS 76 1
Himself as the little white rose of a child" . . . . 748 95 POEMS 76 17
prance with the three white its stimpstamps) the grintgrunt . 773 73 POEMS 1 10
/ / / / white guardians of the universe . . . . 811 73 POEMS 39 1

+WHITE
FOR CONTEXT, SEE . . . . 385 NO THANKS 2 60
FOR CONTEXT, SEE . . . . 487 50 POEMS 1 5
FOR CONTEXT, SEE . . . . 581 1 X 1 41 10

WHITE&GOLD
/ / / once White&Gold daisy in the Dust . . . . 690 95 POEMS 18 1

WHITE-GRUB
shop doors unlocked by white-grub faces) clothes in delicate 172 & SON ACTU 21 6

WHITE-THIGHED
went to bed, whom white-thighed Semiramis put up her . . . . 22 T&C PUELLA MEA 247

WHITEHOT
scarlet Goes with her whitehot face, gashed by hair's . . . . 106 & PORTRAIT 2 7
impetuous acute sentience whose whitehot lips however . . . . 193 XLI PORTRAIT 1 11

WHITELIEST
(joy! joy! joy) and whiteliest all wonderings are silence . . 715 95 POEMS 43 15

WHITELY
fear, across the harvest whitely peer empty of surprise . . . 11 T&C SONGS 2 23
mark, how that asleep whitely she seems whose lips . . . . . 205 XLI SONNETS 1 7
touching roses their fingers whitely live by? or better, . . 211 XLI SONNETS 7 11
immediately yeswind-faces peer skies; whiteLy are which . . . 346 VIVA 37 7
i) into a together whitely big there is but . . . . 365 VIVA 56 9
more flowering than stars whitely births of mind if . . . . . 450 NO THANKS 65 5
one queerying wave will whitely yearn from each last . . . . 526 50 POEMS 38 7

+WHITELY
FOR CONTEXT, SEE . . . . 715 95 POEMS 43 14

WHITEN
by tomb rosily gods whiten befall saith rain anguish . . . . 90 & POST IMPR 2 3

WHITENESS
weep: when from the less-than-whiteness of thy face (whose . 210 XLI SONNETS 6 9
skies and gently (very whiteness: absolute peace, never . . . 839 73 POEMS 67 14

WHITER
slow perfect body amorous (whiter than lilies which are . . . 5 T&C EPITHALAM 100
and cease for being whiter than this world) exhales . . . . . 5 T&C EPITHALAM 101
charms: one pierced moment whiter than the rest --turning . . 78 T&C SON UNRE 3 12

WHITERMUCH
eye nowbrow sangsung nee whitermuch grab sicksilk soak . . . 333 VIVA 24 10

WHITES
crowding tints: browns and whites shoving, the dotting . . . 281 IS 5 THREE 5 5

WHITEST
that bed prepared by whitest hands of waiting years, ... 6 T&C EPITHALAM 114
will go amaying. thy whitest feet crisply are straying. . . . 13 T&C SONGS 3 8
firm than your body's whitest song upon my mind--if . . . . . 306 IS 5 FIVE 5 4

WHITEWHOM
◇ ! throughwhich! brittlest! whitewhom! f l o a . . . . . . 416 NO THANKS 33 12

	PAGE	TITLE	LINE

WHITHERING
    silence fill with microscopic whithering ...(that's the Black 86 T&C SON ACTU 5   8
WHITHERS
    the exquisite froms and whithers of existence, as by . . . . 79 T&C SON UNRE 4   6
WHITTLES
    gesture of existence, continually whittles keen careful . . . 193 XLI PORTRAIT 1   21
    most gradual gesture, and whittles life to eternity --after . 297 IS 5 FOUR 14   13
WHO
WORD DELETED, APPEARED 351 TIMES
WHO-HORNS
    you and the gentle who-horns says-does moo-woo (the prance . 773 73 POEMS 1   8
WHO'D
    the watertank but somebody who'd given my Uncle Sol . . . . . 239 IS 5 ONE 10   27
    mountains flimsying become if who'd) me under a opens . . . . 634 {CHAIRE} 36   4
+WHO'D
    FOR CONTEXT, SEE . . . . 552 1 X 1 12   7
WHO'LL
    diving under because) only who'll say "and this be . . . . . 439 NO THANKS 55   25
    these (down pull & who'll shades / / . . . . 501 50 POEMS 15   24
    shall be and is --who'll solve the depths of . . . . 562 1 X 1 22   11
    be) the only man who'll never die / / . . . . 685 95 POEMS 13   16
+WHO'LL
    FOR CONTEXT, SEE . . . . 310 VIVA 2   7
    FOR CONTEXT, SEE . . . . 805 73 POEMS 33   6
WHO'RE
    / that which we who're alive in spite of . . . . 386 NO THANKS 3   1
    in eternal now if who're by the five nevers . . . . 561 1 X 1 21   9
    this girl and boy who're littler than (day disappears) . . . 757 95 POEMS 85   3
WHO'S
    point made glints squinting who's a wink bum-nothing and . . 96 & POST IMPR 8   18
    / / / / who's most afraid of death? . . . . 215 XLI SONNETS 11   1
    can fisherMen swim and who's myself's Antimere Should words . 395 NO THANKS 12   9
    doesn't know a thing who's much too busy being . . . . 504 50 POEMS 18   12
    "something a little child who's just as small as . . . . . . 555 1 X 1 15   13
    and possible is love (who's imagined, therefore limitless) . 574 1 X 1 34   2
    all) there's somebody calling who's we we're anything . . . . 594 1 X 1 54   36
    shadow of love himself: who's we --nor can you . . . . 601 {CHAIRE} 3   17
    pride involved (this i who's also you) and nothing . . . . . 650 {CHAIRE} 52   10
    face of the child who's every child (& therefore . . . . . 668 {CHAIRE} 70   11
    this how patient creature (who's never by never robbed . . . 674 95 POEMS 2   6
    by some that bum who's every one / / . . . . 698 95 POEMS 26   8
    lose (as down someone who's we ungrows) a dream . . . . . . 716 95 POEMS 44   35
    turn to a silence who's the voice of voice . . . . 761 95 POEMS 88   14
    me and an every (who's any who's some) one . . . . 769 95 POEMS 95   28
    an every (who's any who's some) one who's we . . . . 769 95 POEMS 95   28
    any who's some) one who's we / / / . . . . 769 95 POEMS 95   28
    than which, every woman who's (despite the ultramachinations 807 73 POEMS 35   9
    (an almost someone always who's noone) a noone who, ... 812 73 POEMS 40   4
    arms my very life who's your --when all fears . . . . 812 73 POEMS 40   12
    swiftly for the deathlessness who's beauty: reoccurs so . . . 818 73 POEMS 46   6
    she's warming three worlds) who's ama zingly Eye / . . . . . 827 73 POEMS 55   13
    thing: of a creature who's O cean (everywhere nothing . . . 840 73 POEMS 68   19
    the (myself's own self who's) child will dance! and . . . . 843 73 POEMS 71   12
+WHO'S
    FOR CONTEXT, SEE . . . . 519 50 POEMS 33   15
    FOR CONTEXT, SEE . . . . 590 1 X 1 50   10
WHO'VE
    which crazy they drink who've climbed steeper than hopes . . 563 1 X 1 23   2
    through joy and anguish) who've made her, outglory glory . . 742 95 POEMS 70   8
WHOCARES
    it can dance and Whocares dead's fine like hands . . . . . 126 & SEVEN POEMS 5 23
WHOEVER
    THE nobody (knows and WhoEver would)? dance lewd dollies . . 101 & POST IMPR 11 80
    Odour. (and here's what WhoEver will know Had you . . . . . 154 & SON ACTU 3   13
    invisible) anyhow you 've (whoever we are) stepped carefully 668 {CHAIRE} 70   15
    makes the oldest man (whoever he may be) the . . . . 685 95 POEMS 13   15
WHOING
    which huger than huge) whoing sea leaps to greenly . . . . . 743 95 POEMS 71   3

	PAGE	TITLE	LINE

WHOISIT
the scrumptious magdalene of whoisit and madame something by 198 XLI PORTRAIT 6   11

WHOLE
month for whom the whole year dies, risen at . . . .   5 T&C EPITHALAM 103
her mouth. Upon the whole he suddenly clapped a . . . . 148 & SON REAL 19   7
richly, darkness. On the whole possibly have i loved....? . . 154 & SON ACTU 3   10
which is worth the whole, an inch of nothing . . . . 161 & SON ACTU 10   13
seems whose lips the whole of life almost do . . . . 205 XLI SONNETS 1   8
eat sleep--what does the whole intend" they wonder. oh . . . 295 IS 5 FOUR 12   16
Gay away: "on the whole" (if you will permit . . . . 326 VIVA 18   27
offers it tuh duh whole gang accrost duh table-- . . . . . . 332 VIVA 23   20
will bow, & the whole garden will bow) / . . . . 352 VIVA 43   18
and kill while the whole moves; and every part . . . . 446 NO THANKS 61   14
overflow (am was) assassinating whole grassblades, five ideas 491 50 POEMS 5   12
soul love is the whole and more than all . . . . 521 50 POEMS 34   68
and why? take this whole tear. By handless hints . . . . . . 527 50 POEMS 39   16
is her mind) supremely whole uplifting the, of each . . . . . 533 50 POEMS 45   5
explodes but shall increase whole truthful infinite immediate 538 50 POEMS 50   14
his year. All lose, whole find / / / . . . . 556 1 X 1 16   15
all nouns) begins a whole verbal adventure to illimitably . . 557 1 X 1 17   14
his own paradise thankfully whole and the green whereless . . 558 1 X 1 18   4
a canoe and a whole world and then a . . . . 572 1 X 1 32   16
a cry of a whole of a soul until . . . . 587 1 X 1 47   17
loudness called mankind unteach whole infinite the who of . . 603 {CHAIRE} 5   4
lucky to break one) whole with sky / / . . . . 623 {CHAIRE} 25   8
growing is" erect her whole life smiled "was and . . . . . . 626 {CHAIRE} 28   5
actually lift a luminous whole; turn sheer despairing to . . 649 {CHAIRE} 51   5
we dare adorn the whole with a distinct grandiloquent . . . . 650 {CHAIRE} 52   14
our blood as if whole supreme this complete doubtless . . . . 675 95 POEMS 3   7
instance) the Knowing your whole (yes god damned) life . . . 702 95 POEMS 30   12
dream while floats the whole perhapsless mystery of paradise) 714 95 POEMS 42   7
secrecies comprise goldenly huge whole the upfloating moon. . 750 95 POEMS 78   9
alone wear sunlight. The whole truth not hid by . . . . 765 95 POEMS 91   5
if broken hearts were whole and cowards heroes (the . . . . . 798 73 POEMS 26   8
going to get one whole buck' not a word . . . . 800 73 POEMS 28   12
replied-- but as one whole buck became his (believe . . . . . 800 73 POEMS 28   14
completely alert and miraculously whole; with not merely a . 802 73 POEMS 30   16
nevermoving all nowhere) goldenly whole, prodigiously alive . 808 73 POEMS 36   6
to disappear, that hugest whole creation may be less . . . . 809 73 POEMS 37   13
absence would make your whole life and my (and . . . . 817 73 POEMS 45   13
vision can create the whole (being forever born a . . . . . . 845 73 POEMS 73   5
+WHOLE
FOR CONTEXT, SEE . . . . 347 VIVA 38   14
WHOLEAGAINST
picpac obviously scratches tomorrowlobs wholeagainst you . . 333 VIVA 24   6
WHOLENESS
simply touch me, whose heart-wholeness overmuch Expects of . 12 T&C SONGS 2   38
Everywhere and joy's perfect wholeness we're / / / . . . . . 812 73 POEMS 40   14
WHOLES
souls why souls are wholes not parts but all . . . . 510 50 POEMS 24   8
WHOLLY
and hour by hour wholly renews her pale flesh . . . .   3 T&C EPITHALAM   7
dream shall my love wholly taste thee as a . . . .   9 T&C SONGS 1   35
my soul half-beautiful and wholly droll is as some . . . . . 11 T&C SONGS 2   2
know that i am wholly dead: nor ever did . . . . 17 T&C PUELLA MEA 34
things victorious impossibly) so wholly burn, to undertake . 18 T&C PUELLA MEA 71
frail way, it is wholly to bewitch my smallest . . . . 18 T&C PUELLA MEA 78
my soul is wont wholly to know the poignant . . . . 19 T&C PUELLA MEA 109
bliss of a kingdom wholly is. Beneath her thighs . . . . . . 21 T&C PUELLA MEA 206
up her mouth to wholly kiss-- never boast your . . . . 22 T&C PUELLA MEA 248
made, softly used to wholly move slender ladies made . . . . 23 T&C PUELLA MEA 283
his soul--so even i wholly chained to a grave . . . . 79 T&C SON UNRE 4   11
complete fragile intense, which wholly trembling memory . . . 82 T&C SON ACTU 1   2
bocca mia "he kissed wholly trembling" or so thought . . . . 84 T&C SON ACTU 3   16
poem which will not wholly miss you; or if . . . . 92 & POST IMPR 4   19
begs, sharply believe me, wholly, well --did (wisely suddenly 115 & PORTRAIT 8   9
treasures of silence (slenderly wholly rising, herself . . . 156 & SON ACTU 5   5
wholly rising, herself uprearing wholly slowly, lean in the . 156 & SON ACTU 5   6

WHOLLY (CONTINUED)

   when herself me (slowly, wholly me) will press in . . . . . . 156 & SON ACTU 5   14
   intent of genius-- painting wholly feels ashamed before this 162 & SON ACTU 11   5
   by thoughtful war heaped wholly with high wilt of . . . . . . 213 XLI SONNETS 9   4
   of things will never wholly kiss you; wholly to . . . . 290 IS 5 FOUR 7   4
   never wholly kiss you; wholly to be a fool . . . . 290 IS 5 FOUR 7   5
   and with this flower wholly whom you do not . . . . 294 IS 5 FOUR 11   16
   somehow you are never wholly rid (and who does . . . . 298 IS 5 FOUR 15   8
   smother; until autumn abruptly wholly hugs our dying silent . 305 IS 5 FIVE 4   8
   is strictly fiercely and wholly dies his impeccable feathered 344 VIVA 35   1
   go) remembering only dare (Wholly consider how these . . . . 362 VIVA 53   4
   (forgetting what's to know wholly imagining fire) only . . . 362 VIVA 53   15
) therefore togethering our wholly lives Givehurling with . 371 VIVA 62   16
   die for lives as wholly as that which we . . . . 386 NO THANKS 3   14
   not every but any) heart--wholly, idiotically--before such . 480 NEW POEMS 18   4
   star (sing! every joy) --wholly now disappear night's not . 582 1 X 1 42   14
   a) "fert ig" (tent-sky wholly wallendas) ready were all . . . 605 (CHAIRE) 7   10
   a tooth (and the wholly babble open at blessed . . . . . . 635 (CHAIRE) 37   19
   never may become one (wholly strange; familiar wholly) . . . 659 (CHAIRE) 61   7
   one (wholly strange; familiar wholly) dearest more than . . . 659 (CHAIRE) 61   7
   of all beautiful selves wholly which and innocently are) . 745 95 POEMS 73   12
   of everybodyelse's) but what's wholly marvellous my Darling 782 73 POEMS 10   14
   thankful (hark) birds singing wholly are / / / . . . . 819 73 POEMS 47   20
   minds (down slowly swoop wholly up leaping through merciful . 841 73 POEMS 69   30
+WHOLLY
   FOR CONTEXT, SEE . . . . 722 95 POEMS 50   7
WHOM
   token of his coming whom her soul burns to . . . . 3 T&C EPITHALAM   11
   that one month for whom the whole year dies, ... 5 T&C EPITHALAM 103
   sight, O thou to whom belong the hearts of . . . . 7 T&C EPITHALAM 166
   a rain frailly raging whom the hills sink into . . . . 9 T&C SONGS 1   25
   the spring that maidens whom passion wastes will lay . . . . 16 T&C SONGS 6   7
   Egypt went to bed, whom white-thighed Semiramis put up . . . 22 T&C PUELLA MEA 247
   heart discovers thee whom i burn olbanum / . . . . 31 T&C ORIENTALE 5 30
   guess) when Farmer Death (whom fairies hate) shall crumble . 83 T&C SON ACTU 2 11
   important head-- by on whom glories whisperingly impinge . . 85 T&C SON ACTU 4 5
   lifted in singing--hands fragile whom almost tire the . . . 85 T&C SON ACTU 4 11
   egyptian noise. ladies with whom time feeds especially his . 138 & SON REAL 9 8
   / god pity me whom (god distinctly has) the . . . . 140 & SON REAL 11 1
   vague tough exquisite flowers, whom hardens richly, darkness 154 & SON ACTU 3 9
   belonging to my friend. Whom i salute, by what . . . . 158 & SON ACTU 7 9
   stir, of thoughtful trees whom night hath pondered o'er . . . 205 XLI SONNETS 1 11
   / O Thou to whom the musical white spring . . . . 206 XLI SONNETS 2 1
   earth's ghastlier trees by whom Time measured is when . . . 207 XLI SONNETS 3 2
   of hungering days for whom the old glories move, ... 209 XLI SONNETS 5 12
   much of nothing and whom dawn loves most to . . . . 211 XLI SONNETS 7 17
   felicities me wormperused by whom the hungering mouth of . 212 XLI SONNETS 8 8
   corners of her youth; whom, fiercely shy and gently . . . . . 214 XLI SONNETS 10 6
   (but a roof hugs whom) as the august evening . . . . 217 XLI SONNETS 13 6
   round young man to whom headwaiters bow so? hush--the . . . . 245 IS 5 ONE 16   7
   solemnly inert. Brushing from whom the stiffened puke i . . . 258 IS 5 ONE 28 21
   ofS hurl; edindodg: ing whom areEyes shy-dodge is bright . . 265 IS 5 ONE 34   4
   erring child of circumstance whom the bulls nabbed at . . . . 266 IS 5 TWO 1   39
   his father's joy, unto whom duty whispers low "thou . . . . 273 IS 5 TWO 8   4
   only sweeter frailer you whom certain flowers resemble but . 293 IS 5 FOUR 10 4
   all beautiful things) winter, whom Spring shall kill / . . . 293 IS 5 FOUR 10 31
   with this flower wholly whom you do not ever . . . . 294 IS 5 FOUR 11 16
   am this person of whom somehow you are never . . . . 298 IS 5 FOUR 15 7
   he is a ghost whom assault these whispering fists . . . . . 299 IS 5 FOUR 16 11
   with rain.... (he, slightly whom or cautiously this person . 300 IS 5 FOUR 17 16
   of cambridge, mass. to whom nobody seems to have . . . . . 326 VIVA 18   3
   the helen molle dancers, whom he considered "elevating--that 327 VIVA 18   40
   a soft white damn Whom it touches / / . . . . 328 VIVA 19   23
   way who looked at whom first, anyhow dancing" (a . . . . . . 338 VIVA 29   20
   / / when rain whom fear not children but . . . . 356 VIVA 47   1
   waiting clumsily to cease whom every perfect thing meanwhile 360 VIVA 51   7
   upon earth above; to whom i cry, remembering her . . . . . 360 VIVA 51   34
   of alWays)fiercely live whom on Large Darkness And . . . . . 361 VIVA 52   30

WHOM (CONTINUED)
    leaf) but should voices (whom lure an eagerest strict . . . . 362 VIVA 53   9
    is there a flower (whom i meet anywhere able . . . . 367 VIVA 58   1
    the earth wandering hunter whom you knew once? what . . . . . 374 VIVA 65   8
    the grave? from only Whom shall time no refuge . . . . 377 VIVA 68   13
    ing among who dreams whom mutterings dream & : . . . . 384 NO THANKS 2   6
    million yells they f-oo-1 (whom, blinds; blood) pa-nt stab . 388 NO THANKS 5   9
    that Ghost is dead (whom noone might inter fleeing . . . . . 394 NO THANKS 11   5
    each hates a Man whom both would call their . . . . 394 NO THANKS 11   9
    uplook, all joybegotten whelps whom soothe psychotic myths . 398 NO THANKS 15   18
    this ghost) humbly and whom for worst or best . . . . 441 NO THANKS 56   51
    if night's mostness (and whom did merely day close) . . . . . 450 NO THANKS 65   1
    air is throbbing prayers whom kneeling eyes (until perfectly 450 NO THANKS 65   6
    o immensity (upon once whom fiercely by pink mr . . . . . . 465 NEW POEMS 3   6
    her comma considers frood whom he pronounces young mistaken . 499 50 POEMS 13   4
    (not visible to us) whom only his dream ing . . . . 516 50 POEMS 30   15
    treesoul onlying from serene whom queries not suspected . . . 517 50 POEMS 31   7
    am the sun of whom / / / / . . . . 527 50 POEMS 39   32
    oUt of whe reful whom (leas tly) smiles the . . . . 534 50 POEMS 46   19
    welcomes each was of whom among not numerable ams . . . . . 558 1 X 1 18   6
    lips wander a finding whom of girl) dolls clutching . . . . 565 1 X 1 25   4
    / / / these (whom; pretends blue nothing) are . . . . 584 1 X 1 44   1
    to comprehend not numerable whom? / / / / . . . . 609 (CHAIRE) 11   14
    such miracle murdered we whom cannot kill more mostful . . . 639 (CHAIRE) 41   10
    pasture wom an creature whom than earth hers elf . . . . . . 654 (CHAIRE) 56   8
    feels everything; all around whom is perfectly a strange . . 657 (CHAIRE) 59   3
    tomorrow steer --souls under whom flow (mountain valley . . 659 (CHAIRE) 61   5
    never will share for whom create is less than . . . . 664 (CHAIRE) 66   8
    a wistful little clown whom somebody buried upsidedown in . . 680 95 POEMS 8   8
    except in snow-- a whom we make (of grin . . . . 716 95 POEMS 44   5
    almost vanished me (for whom the departure of everything . . 720 95 POEMS 48   9
    d than (a sleep) whom and tipto e t . . . . 733 95 POEMS 61   7
    greatest of living magicians (whom you and i some . . . . . 738 95 POEMS 66   5
    (except your fear to whom i give this little . . . . 762 95 POEMS 89   7
    grow it's love by whom (my beautiful friend) the . . . . . . 776 73 POEMS 4   17
    silence: in huger always whom two tiny selves sleep . . . . 777 73 POEMS 5   10
    nly this darkness (in whom always i do nothing) . . . . . . 785 73 POEMS 13   4
    there such a lay-- whom, among her dollies, dad . . . . . . 794 73 POEMS 22   3
    mercifully glorying keen star whom she-and-he-like ifs of am 808 73 POEMS 36   8
    if out of climbing whom begins to spill such . . . . 811 73 POEMS 39   12
    you" silently cries the (whom we call rose a) . . . . 837 73 POEMS 65   16
    moment born-- some for whom crumbs of colour can . . . . . 842 73 POEMS 70   3
    alone understands: only for whom i'll keep my tryst . . . . 843 73 POEMS 71   5
+WHOM
    FOR CONTEXT, SEE . . . . 333 VIVA 24   2
    FOR CONTEXT, SEE . . . . 416 NO THANKS 33   12
WHOMEVER'S
    if be damned with whomever's afraid down with ought . . . . . 424 NO THANKS 41   8
WHOMS
    nothing mean in tenderly whoms of sizeless a silence . . . . 658 (CHAIRE) 60   7
    quite such eagerly innocent whoms of merciful sweetness . . . 748 95 POEMS 76   13
WHORE
    joked to a girlish whore with busy rhythmic mouth . . . . . . 56 T&C PORTRAIT 4 13
    importantly banal, Kitty. a whore. Sixteen you corking brute 74 T&C SON REAL 5   8
    neck of this brittle whore delicately wobbles an improbably . 229 IS 5 ONE FRAN   2
    trinightly entertained by a whore who Talks in the . . . . . 312 VIVA 4   3
    soul? is death a whore with life's disease which . . . . . . 527 50 POEMS 39   21
    a thief by a whore dragged goes to meet . . . . 533 50 POEMS 45   22
    he fell for a whore when he married his . . . . 707 95 POEMS 35   18
+WHORES
    FOR CONTEXT, SEE . . . . 629 (CHAIRE) 31   7
WHORLCLOWN
    1) littlecrownGrave whose whorlclown of spreadnessed bE rich 342 VIVA 33   20
WHOS
    whichs turn in to whos est people be come . . . . 463 NEW POEMS 1   14
    the power of blueness) whos (ex- plore my unreal . . . . . 612 (CHAIRE) 14   4
    were a hundred million whos (while only himself was . . . . 709 95 POEMS 37   3
    through godthanking ground) bluest whos of this snowy head . 754 95 POEMS 82   5

WHOS (CONTINUED)
/ / 2 little whos (he and she) under . . . . 832 73 POEMS 60   1
WHOSE
but the imprint of whose cloven feet the shrieking . . . . .   3 T&C EPITHALAM   13
the mere echo of whose shining mirth the furious . . . . . .   3 T&C EPITHALAM   15
of that delicious boy whose serious grace one goddess . . . .   3 T&C EPITHALAM   24
of the Pheidian soul whose eagle frights creation, in . . . .   3 T&C EPITHALAM   27
eagle frights creation, in whose palm Nike presents the . . .   3 T&C EPITHALAM   27
crown sweetest to man, whose lilied robe the sun's . . . . .   3 T&C EPITHALAM   29
white hands emboss, betwixt whose absolute feet anoint with .   3 T&C EPITHALAM   30
smiling, the diadumenos in whose young chiseled eyes the . .   4 T&C EPITHALAM   33
once again victorious Pantarkes (whose grace the prince of .   4 T&C EPITHALAM   35
feet of awe), thunderer whose omnipotent brow showers its . .   4 T&C EPITHALAM   37
breast in bright degrees, whose pillow is the graces . . . .   4 T&C EPITHALAM   40
of gods and men whose subtle throne twain sphinxes . . . . .   4 T&C EPITHALAM   41
to her brazen breasts, whose foot-stool tells how fought . .   4 T&C EPITHALAM   43
tall Hippolytus, lord on whose pedestal the deep expels . . .   4 T&C EPITHALAM   46
steep unspeaking tower within whose brightening strictness .   4 T&C EPITHALAM   51
the certain altar at whose head stands that clear . . . . . .   6 T&C EPITHALAM   116
stands that clear candle whose expecting breath exults upon .   6 T&C EPITHALAM   117
meaning of heaven clings, (whose million leaves in winsome .   6 T&C EPITHALAM   125
incognizable amethyst. Lady at whose imperishable smile the .   6 T&C EPITHALAM   137
the inconceivable embrace of whose tremendous hair that . . .   6 T&C EPITHALAM   146
those twain perfect roses whose ambrosial grace, goddess, thy   6 T&C EPITHALAM   148
within the chancel of whose charms the tall boy . . . .   7 T&C EPITHALAM   153
sacrament of sleep, betwixt whose cool incorrigible arms . .   7 T&C EPITHALAM   156
nymphlike face, a form whose snowy symmetry of grace . . . .   8 T&C OF NICOL   20
praise between those rivers whose white voices pass upon . .   9 T&C SONGS 1   1
forgetting (fail me not) whose courseless waters are a . . .   9 T&C SONGS 1   3
gloat of silver; o'er whose night three willows wail, ...   9 T&C SONGS 1   4
upon terrific pastures pale, whose tall mysterious shepherd .   9 T&C SONGS 1   10
not known musics in whose careful eyes are dinned; . . . . .   9 T&C SONGS 1   18
as a single lamb whose sheen of full unsheared . . . .   11 T&C SONGS 2   11
surprise death's faultless eyes (whose hand my folded soul .   11 T&C SONGS 2   26
the feet of mowers whose bodies strong with love . . . . . .   11 T&C SONGS 2   34
very simply touch me, whose heart-wholeness overmuch Expects   12 T&C SONGS 2   38
are at kisses playing, whose strangeness much says; singing .   13 T&C SONGS 3   11
fragile lady wandering in whose perishable poise is the . . .   17 T&C PUELLA MEA   14
dote, La beale Isoud whose leman was. And if . . . .   17 T&C PUELLA MEA   37
the poignant instantaneous fern whose scrupulous enchanted .   19 T&C PUELLA MEA   111
for their youngest angels (whose praising bodies in a . . . .   20 T&C PUELLA MEA   142
of ladies goodly store whose beauty did in nothing . . . . .   21 T&C PUELLA MEA   174
and shapely thighs) in whose dome the trembling bliss . . . .   21 T&C PUELLA MEA   205
little distinct foot (if whose very minuteness doth abuse . .   22 T&C PUELLA MEA   217
any poem she of whose body words are afraid . . . .   22 T&C PUELLA MEA   240
unto me sweeter (of whose shy delicious glance things . . . .   22 T&C PUELLA MEA   251
are intense inhabitants; in whose warm superlative body do .   22 T&C PUELLA MEA   255
all things lovely--Time! upon whose watering lips the world .   23 T&C PUELLA MEA   267
me is April in whose armpits is the approach . . . .   29 T&C ORIENTALE 3   10
the trees of dreaming whose fruit is the very . . . .   29 T&C ORIENTALE 3   23
satraps in scarlet in whose kiss is the combining . . . . . .   29 T&C ORIENTALE 3   25
twelve feet high behind whose ear sits always a . . . .   32 T&C ORIENTALE 3   9
of a microscopic stage whose jouncing curtain. , rises . . .   55 T&C PORTRAIT 3   7
the pink hollyhock existence whose pansy eyes look from . . .   58 T&C PORTRAIT 6   17
reminiscence partaken softly at whose gate smile always the .   58 T&C PORTRAIT 6   25
tiny smiling, man in whose hand the crank goes . . . .   69 T&C POST IMPR 6   8
of must and shall, whose slippery body is Death's . . . . . .   74 T&C SON REAL 5   3
the signal perfume of whose unrepute focusses in the . . . .   74 T&C SON REAL 5   5
lady'll have a whiskey-sour-- whose least amazing smile is .   74 T&C SON REAL 5   14
street darkling awaiteth her whose feet have trod the . . . .   75 T&C SON REAL 6   10
unseen things, things obscene (Whose fingers young the caving   77 T&C SON UNRE 2   3
hideous Work most old Whose battening gesture prophecies a .   77 T&C SON UNRE 2   12
O tremendous flower on whose huge heart prospecting darkness   79 T&C SON UNRE 4   4
who adores perceived sails whose mighty brightness dumbs the   79 T&C SON UNRE 4   9
be known; and man, whose here is always worse . . . .   81 T&C SON UNRE 6   11
rout the young mouth whose lips begin a smile . . . .   85 T&C SON ACTU 4   7
to you, white town whose spires softly dare. Will . . . . .   86 T&C SON ACTU 5   4
silently a cathedral before whose upward lean magnificent . .   93 & POST IMPR 5   3

WHOSE (CONTINUED)
of delapida- tion bath-houses whose opened withins ejaculate.   94 & POST IMPR 6   4
delicate-swill tints of hair Whose (the lit-tle m-oo-n's o .   94 & POST IMPR 6   21
the huge neck around whose unwashed sonorous muscle the . . .   96 & POST IMPR 8   30
un- clean table. and, whose distended immense Both paws . . .   97 & POST IMPR 8   38
a Lone ly, flower whose secretloveliness hur. ts itse; . . . 101 & POST IMPR 11   73
there is a lady, whose name is Afterwards she . . . . 102 & POST IMPR 12   24
tube of wise lust whose arms and legs like . . . . 110 & PORTRAIT 6   6
darkness of New Lady whose kiss is a procession . . . . 112 & PORTRAIT 6   99
heaven i salute you whose body is Egypt whose . . . . 113 & PORTRAIT 6 110
whose body is Egypt whose hair is Nile) put . . . . 113 & PORTRAIT 6 112
the greenslim purse of whose face opens on a . . . . 114 & PORTRAIT 7   18
day begins to frail (whose grave already three or . . . . . . 115 & PORTRAIT 8   2
have not sinned in whose displeasure lives a kiss) . . . . . 115 & PORTRAIT 8   7
is little Effie's head whose brains are made of . . . . . . 117 & PORTRAIT 10   2
know the way-- (nervously Whose eyes approve the blessed . . 117 & PORTRAIT 10   35
is little Effie's head whose brains are made of . . . . . . 118 & PORTRAIT 10   44
from jumbling her flesh whose casual mouth's coy rooting . . 131 & SON REAL 2   7
her careful distinct sex whose sharp lips comb my . . . . . . 137 & SON REAL 8   1
slabs of tilting din whose mouths distinctly walk your . . . 138 & SON REAL 9   2
his immense lips On whose deep nakedness death most . . . . . 138 & SON REAL 9   10
girls marching to love whose bodies kiss me with . . . . . . 138 & SON REAL 9   12
dribbling moan of jazz whose arched occasional steep youth . 140 & SON REAL 11   5
/ unnoticed woman from whose kind large flesh i . . . . 142 & SON REAL 13   1
peek into the belly whose deep squirm nibbles. another . . . 143 & SON REAL 14   11
almost leans a lady whose still-born smile involves the . . 144 & SON REAL 15   13
lips a moist mistake, whose fragrance hurls me into . . . . . 148 & SON REAL 19   10
daze of unmarketable excitation, whose careless movements . . 150 & SON REAL 21   14
beauty is a vise whose stilling lips murder suddenly . . . . 152 & SON ACTU 1   11
twilight is an accident whose niceness betters easily the . . 162 & SON ACTU 11   3
the last flower in whose hair, thy lips are . . . . 190 XLI SONGS 12   3
doomed impetuous acute sentience whose whitehot lips however 193 XLI PORTRAIT 1   11
of actuality), an orchid whose velocity is sculptural / . . . 193 XLI PORTRAIT 1   26
entered a mad street whose mouth dripped with slavver . . . . 194 XLI PORTRAIT 2   4
Trees of Ego, from whose living and biggest bodies . . . . . 195 XLI PORTRAIT 3   20
silence that primeval exposure whose electric solidity . . . 197 XLI PORTRAIT 5   17
lozenge. a ruglike sentience whose papillae expertly drink . 201 XLI PORTRAIT 9   16
delicately experi- menting colossus whose irrefutable spiral 201 XLI PORTRAIT 9   25
of digestible mill- ions whose rich slovenly obscene . . . . 202 XLI PORTRAIT 9   46
of success than enquire whose soul dangles from his . . . . . 204 XLI LA GUERRE 2   3
asleep whitely she seems whose lips the whole of . . . . . . 205 XLI SONNETS 1   8
redolent shoulders, Thou from whose feet reincarnate song . . 206 XLI SONNETS 2   6
of intangible commemoration, (from whose faint close as some 206 XLI SONNETS 2   12
/ / Thou in whose swordgreat story shine the . . . . 209 XLI SONNETS 5   1
smiling meads; thou by whose page we break the . . . . . . 209 XLI SONNETS 5   6
tranquillities and He without Whose favour nothing is (being 210 XLI SONNETS 6   3
less-than-whiteness of thy face (whose eyes inherit vacancy) 210 XLI SONNETS 6   10
thy trivial toll, for whose cool feet this frantic . . . . 212 XLI SONNETS 8   4
him let me complain, whose seat is where revolving . . . . 212 XLI SONNETS 8   10
my Mes from sleep whose stranger dreams thy strangeness . . . 213 XLI SONNETS 9   14
death of light, against whose enormous curve of flesh . . . . 214 XLI SONNETS 10   3
pinkish ponderous arms bedecked whose white thick wrists . . 225 IS 5 ONE LIZ   8
moist mouth, --jazz, for whose twitching lips, between you . 227 IS 5 ONE GERT   6
of Women By Night whose latest Seeds Of Evil . . . . 245 IS 5 ONE 16   8
(by that bright flame whose myriad tints enrich a . . . . . . 254 IS 5 ONE 25   17
my shame: lady through whose profound and fragile lips . . . 306 IS 5 FIVE 5   13
a least crooking of Whose compassionate digit, earth's most 315 VIVA 7   15
serene immediate silliest and whose vast one function being . 337 VIVA 28   1
Olaf glad and big whose warmest heart recoiled at . . . . . . 339 VIVA 30   2
fragrance of a town (whose dormers choke and snore . . . . . 340 VIVA 31   2
in producing sixtyfour maxims whose) centripetal wisdom in . 341 VIVA 32   4
years of rapid animal whose swir -ling (not too . . . . 341 VIVA 32   12
patiently l) littlecrownGrave whose whorlclown of . . . . . 342 VIVA 33   20
(for) Please (tnights, on whose for eheads shone eternal . . 343 VIVA 34   15
the enchanted dike of whose lean lips, hovers how . . . . . . 344 VIVA 35   10
have seen trees (in whose black bod ies leaves . . . . 354 VIVA 45   27
did an archer spy (whose aim had erred never) . . . . 360 VIVA 51   15
of your intense fragility: whose texture compels me with . . 366 VIVA 57   14

		PAGE	TITLE	LINE
WHOSE (CONTINUED)

	PAGE	TITLE	LINE
gracefully) a we, entirely whose least breathing may surprise	368	VIVA 59	13
herself against the air--and whose do you suppose possibly	378	VIVA 69	5
of her voice in whose silence the music of	390	NO THANKS 7	4
to not die safely whose epoch fits him like	394	NO THANKS 11	2
(Moved more suddenly than) whose tiniest smile? may Be	397	NO THANKS 14	4
Husband to him (and whose what he conceives to	398	NO THANKS 15	6
childfully diminishing earth --never whose proudly life	402	NO THANKS 19	5
of feet all things whose slendering sweetness touched renown)	414	NO THANKS 31	4
he ends, the earth (whose texture feels of pride	418	NO THANKS 35	2
a mightily form moves whose passenger and whose pilot	419	NO THANKS 36	23
moves whose passenger and whose pilot my spirit is	419	NO THANKS 36	23
in november's may) from whose (if loud most howish	420	NO THANKS 37	5
flowering so new) self whose eyes smell of the	424	NO THANKS 41	3
one undiscoverable guess of whose mad skill each world	424	NO THANKS 41	13
of blood is made (whose fatal songs are moving	424	NO THANKS 41	14
crickets within me whisper whose erect blood finally	435	NO THANKS 51	38
a proud dreamhorse moving (whose feet almost walk air).	437	NO THANKS 53	16
is for them, them; whose death's to be born)	439	NO THANKS 55	3
(this poet made war whose naught and all sun	440	NO THANKS 56	25
loot furnished rooms through whose foul windows absurd clouds	442	NO THANKS 57	12
how lucky lovers are (whose selves abide under whatever	446	NO THANKS 61	9
whatever shall discovered be) whose ignorant each breathing	446	NO THANKS 61	11
meaningless secret on luminous whose selves and lives	456	NO THANKS 71	2
timeless souls (the not whose spiral hunger may appease	456	NO THANKS 71	4
and hands hold his whose unlife bursts only so;	479	NEW POEMS 17	15
entirely her only love whose any mystery makes every	484	NEW POEMS 22	7
ever had love loved whose his climbing shoulders queerly	490	50 POEMS 4	18
are gentlemen ppoyds even whose recktie are covered by	492	50 POEMS 6	15
unless i'm mistaken chauvesouris-- whose grammar is	504	50 POEMS 18	10
the dimension of him whose each foot likes the	512	50 POEMS 26	5
here of this earth whose both eyes love this	512	50 POEMS 26	9
and if (by Him Whose blood was for us	514	50 POEMS 28	9
/ / enters give whose lost is his found	533	50 POEMS 45	2
his found leading love whose heart is her mind)	533	50 POEMS 45	4
pure living complete love whose doom is beauty and	538	50 POEMS 50	4
while you are motionless-- whose moving is more april	559	1 X 1 19	12
and soul to mind) --whose hearts are mountains, roots	560	1 X 1 20	15
kneel lovers are these whose lips smash unimagined sky	563	1 X 1 23	10
continue to outgrow all whose mosts if you have	574	1 X 1 34	13
merely opening leaf (beyond whose nearness there is no	592	1 X 1 52	8
died again and again; whose golden, crimson dooms conceive	599	(CHAIRE) 1	2
understand) seduced by Life; whose brother married Heart, now	621	(CHAIRE) 23	3
are leapandswooping tinily birds whose magical gaiety makes	631	(CHAIRE) 33	12
/ / / / whose are these (wraith a	639	(CHAIRE) 41	1
thrown a- way (and whose brook -bright flower- soft	660	(CHAIRE) 62	17
truth of a dream whose sleep is the sky	664	(CHAIRE) 66	23
earth beguiles our spirits, whose miraculously disenchanted	675	95 POEMS 3	2
befriended a stranded star whose rays five languid fingers	682	95 POEMS 10	6
convict him of deceiving) whose ways are neither reasoned	683	95 POEMS 11	5
of his mother's smile --whose only secret all creation	714	95 POEMS 42	14
(of grin for smile whose head's his face with	716	95 POEMS 44	7
climbs the onlying world) whose silence are cries poems	719	95 POEMS 47	4
are you and i, whose home is timelessness: we	743	95 POEMS 71	10
laughing and crying) children whose any sadness or joy	749	95 POEMS 77	8
spire to merciful Him Whose only now is forever:	749	95 POEMS 77	18
unthings) tosses hello whirling whose rhyme (spilling his	751	95 POEMS 79	5
than are done; and whose last doing shall not	762	95 POEMS 89	4
a song to see: whose all (you're a sight	763	95 POEMS 90	2
chivalry in terror of whose furious beak (as sweetly	774	73 POEMS 2	5
murderers of high estate whose mongrel creed is Might	774	73 POEMS 2	11
skyline on earth between whose d owdy hou se	788	73 POEMS 16	8
To doubt that in whose form less form all	790	73 POEMS 18	8
mistrusting utterly that timelessness whose absence would	817	73 POEMS 45	13
a more than day whose sun is moon, and	818	73 POEMS 46	2
and marvellously self diminutive whose universe a single leaf	821	73 POEMS 49	13
ly this (merely and whose not numerable leaves are	826	73 POEMS 54	3
(silence is the blood whose flesh is singing) silence:	839	73 POEMS 67	1

WHOSE (CONTINUED)
    is) and partially imagine whose despair when every silence . 842 73 POEMS 70   9
    always half perceive. Only whose vision can create the   . . . 845 73 POEMS 73   5
+WHOSE
    FOR CONTEXT, SEE . . . . 100 & POST IMPR 11   37
    FOR CONTEXT, SEE . . . . 101 & POST IMPR 11   46
    FOR CONTEXT, SEE . . . . 101 & POST IMPR 11   47
    FOR CONTEXT, SEE . . . . 448 NO THANKS 63   18
    FOR CONTEXT, SEE . . . . 611 {CHAIRE} 13   10
    FOR CONTEXT, SEE . . . . 612 {CHAIRE} 14   4
WHOSES
    the ex prince of whoses diving into a whatses . . . . 475 NEW POEMS 13   20
WHOSESWOONING
    parenthesis the) pond on whoseswooning edge black trees think 99 & POST IMPR 10   10
WHOSHOUT
    (are like) dead) Whoshout (Ghost) atOne (voiceless) 0 . . . 347 VIVA 38   22
WHOSO
    perfect the most frail. (Whoso rideth in the tale . . . . . . 20 T&C PUELLA MEA   163
    with my lord Boccaccio-- whoso knocketh at the door . . . . . 20 T&C PUELLA MEA   171
    which doth amass for whoso drinks, a dizzier wine . . . . . . 21 T&C PUELLA MEA   199
WHOWHICH
    filthy some past imagining whowhich of mad rags strode   . . . 662 {CHAIRE} 64   6
WHY
    minuteness doth abuse reason, why then the artificer did . . 22 T&C PUELLA MEA   219
    You the wind?" "Yes" "why do you touch flowers . . . . 91 & POST IMPR 3   8
    cigars who jim him why gluey grins topple together . . . . .   96 & POST IMPR 8   17
    you never can and why have to? dead's nice . . . . 126 & SEVEN POEMS 5   31
    you into their balloon, why then we'd go up . . . . 129 & SEVEN POEMS 7   7
    of your hair. Understanding why his eye laughs, i . . . . . . 161 & SON ACTU 10   11
    (but i was thinking why the girl-and-bird of you . . . . . . 174 & SON ACTU 23   12
    / / CHANSONS INNOCENTES why did you go little . . . . 191 XLI CHANSONS 1   1
    will anyone tell him why he should blow two . . . . 196 XLI PORTRAIT 4   20
    entirely ask of god why on the alert neck . . . . 229 IS 5 ONE FRAN   1
    thickly to protrude-- or why her tiniest whispered invitation 229 IS 5 ONE FRAN   14
    which greets one (Everywhere Why) as divine poesy per . . . . 230 IS 5 ONE 2   17
    no sir which is why granted who discovered America . . . . . 238 IS 5 ONE 9   12
    have no doubts about why you put the ring . . . . 242 IS 5 ONE 13   11
    / / / / why are these pipples taking . . . . 245 IS 5 ONE 16   1
    in the same place. Why according to tomorrow's paper . . . . 262 IS 5 ONE 32   18
    nascitur, is not made...) why then to Hell with . . . . 264 IS 5 ONE 33   30
    by gosh by gum why talk of beauty what . . . . 268 IS 5 TWO 3   9
    because Nobody knows, or why jerks Here &, here, ... 286 IS 5 FOUR 3   7
    face to another and why do i weep eat . . . . 295 IS 5 FOUR 12   16
    --(and i wonder just why that should please him . . . . 296 IS 5 FOUR 13   9
    what he does) and why (at the bottom of . . . . 296 IS 5 FOUR 13   11
    pockets curled hands moves) why then toward morning he . . . 299 IS 5 FOUR 16   11
    possibly will understand; or why (in this most exquisite . . 300 IS 5 FOUR 17   10
    god was invented but why (captured by a policeman's . . . . . 324 VIVA 16   3
    which stumbling eyes which why in (thundering) by When . . . 346 VIVA 37   9
    been dancing: which is why something about me reminded . . . 355 VIVA 46   20
    / come a little further--why be afraid-- here's the . . . . . 357 VIVA 48   1
    knows where truth grows why birds fly and especially . . . . 368 VIVA 59   19
    park. Complete. and slightly (why? or lest we understand) . . 375 VIVA 66   9
    dance upon dead minds why, it is love; but . . . . 377 VIVA 68   2
    urinal howlessly and without why (quite minus gal or . . . . 387 NO THANKS 4   3
    if you d n't why g to yonder s . . . . 392 NO THANKS 9   7
    / / / / why why How many winds . . . . 395 NO THANKS 12   1
    / / / why why How many winds make . . . . 395 NO THANKS 12   1
    a lot said he) why not said she (let's . . . . 399 NO THANKS 16   8
    listen don't be sil why sure) i mean the . . . . 400 NO THANKS 17   8
    (o well ughhuh sure why not yuh course yeh . . . . 400 NO THANKS 17   9
    knows, he cannot understand (why Jones don't pay me . . . . . 406 NO THANKS 23   6
    futile groove god knows why) and so do i . . . . 413 NO THANKS 30   16
    mere one bursting soul why, then comes peace unto . . . . . . 414 NO THANKS 31   12
    transferred with dusk) wondering why this star does not . . . 428 NO THANKS 45   4
    a yellowandbluish cat (perched why Curvingly at this) window; 434 NO THANKS 51   32
    light dancing isn'ts on why, digging bridges with mirrors . . 439 NO THANKS 55   21
    must fear because and why what filth is here . . . . 440 NO THANKS 56   6

	PAGE	TITLE	LINE

WHY (CONTINUED)

	PAGE	TITLE	LINE
sunlight Open what thousandth why and discover laughing) / .	453	NO THANKS 68	15
to catch telescopes) why. Being is patience is	478	NEW POEMS 16	7
to multiply because and why dividing thens by nows	500	50 POEMS 14	5
green means face or why a quilt's pink stops	506	50 POEMS 20	10
and as for souls why souls are wholes not	510	50 POEMS 24	8
wonder is over the why (it's now, boys) here	513	50 POEMS 27	33
roots and should some why completely weep my father's	520	50 POEMS 34	13
say though hate were why men breathe-- because my	521	50 POEMS 34	66
soft worms of spiralling why and out of black	522	50 POEMS 35	13
the not because and why but (who stood within	523	50 POEMS 36	5
to mere because and why? take this whole tear.	527	50 POEMS 39	15
will it tell us why we dream and will	528	50 POEMS 40	3
goes to meet her why she his because /	533	50 POEMS 45	23
slow not since not why) both didn't know exeunt	542	1 X 1 2	3
as to find. Each why of a leaf says	543	1 X 1 3	7
shall and finding only why smashed it into because	566	1 X 1 26	7
wings of because; each why of star (afloat on	575	1 X 1 35	18
how their joy to why their stride and breathing	580	1 X 1 40	9
isn't small one littlest why, it into if shall	588	1 X 1 48	1
on this whirlingest earth? why you're by far the	590	1 X 1 50	8
in this trickiest if? why i'm by much the	590	1 X 1 50	17
my and foreverless thy? why our is love and	590	1 X 1 50	26
will somebody tell me why people let go /	593	1 X 1 53	24
one one hasn't a why or because or although	594	1 X 1 54	10
it, dying 's miraculous why? be cause dying is	604	(CHAIRE) 6	12
mirror lying are each (why do people say it's	623	(CHAIRE) 25	5
sky are flowers neither why nor how when is	630	(CHAIRE) 32	10
/ / / / why must itself up every	636	(CHAIRE) 38	1
but you must understand why because i am dead	638	(CHAIRE) 40	15
old forgotten full of why (rub-her-bub) bub? (bubs) where's .	642	(CHAIRE) 44	7
and give because the why --gracious wanderer, be thou	651	(CHAIRE) 53	11
/ blue the triangular why of a dream (with	668	(CHAIRE) 70	1
all time's because to why / / / /	679	95 POEMS 7	14
as spring and wonders why So gay gay gay	685	95 POEMS 13	8
the because of a why but our doom is	686	95 POEMS 14	12
is to grow) forgetting why, remember how in time	688	95 POEMS 16	3
/ / / / why from this her and	694	95 POEMS 22	1
got --ex cept what? why , what it Takes.	701	95 POEMS 29	7
while a wisp of why as thick as my	709	95 POEMS 37	11
/ / / / why do the fingers of	724	95 POEMS 52	1
precisely as unbig a why as i'm (almost too	735	95 POEMS 63	1
unbig as i'm a why (almost too small for	735	95 POEMS 63	9
is who. since becomes why: old turns to young	737	95 POEMS 65	5
/ / / "but why should" the greatest of	738	95 POEMS 66	1
on the bough) how? why --we never we know	767	95 POEMS 93	5
so gay young love why? how-- we never we	767	95 POEMS 93	17
star --do lovers love? why then to heaven with	768	95 POEMS 94	13
for instance (or ; why even i suppose one	779	73 POEMS 7	13
beyond all since and why asking no favor but	783	73 POEMS 11	4
/ / / / why don't be sil ly	793	73 POEMS 21	1
what how when who why which (or anything) /	797	73 POEMS 25	22
spare three cents please' --why guesswho nearly leaped out .	800	73 POEMS 28	7
in the steeple says Why the chary the wary	801	73 POEMS 29	6
him but myself; and why? because without any doubt	802	73 POEMS 30	9
dark who wings his why beyond because and sings	815	73 POEMS 43	5
finch please tell me why this summer world (and	836	73 POEMS 64	2

+WHY

	PAGE	TITLE	LINE
FOR CONTEXT, SEE	127	& SEVEN POEMS 5	45
FOR CONTEXT, SEE	413	NO THANKS 30	6
FOR CONTEXT, SEE	413	NO THANKS 30	11

WHY'S

	PAGE	TITLE	LINE
un-) proudly depths above why's first because (faith's last .	574	1 X 1 34	9

WHYCOL

	PAGE	TITLE	LINE
ular, (ppear ah! Star whycol our ed shy lurch	349	VIVA 40	11

WHYCOLOURED

	PAGE	TITLE	LINE
brook chickadee mountain. Mountain) whycoloured worlds of . .	512	50 POEMS 26	28

		PAGE	TITLE	LINE

WHYING

more (fingeryhands me and whying) seek than finds feeling . . 612 {CHAIRE} 14   12
tendril of celestial wish (whying diminutive bright . . . . . 669 {CHAIRE} 71   2

WHYLAUGHING

eyes Strange known Face (whylaughing! among: skydiamonds / / 628 {CHAIRE} 30   13

WHYLESS

go where goes this whyless soul a loneliest road . . . . . . 441 NO THANKS 56   45
earth accept and primeval whyless sky; healing our by . . . . 745 95 POEMS 73   6

WHYLESSNESS

<> some perpetually roaming whylessness-- autumn has gone: . 839 73 POEMS 67   7

WHYS

-er than all the whys which lurk between your . . . . 282 IS 5 THREE 6   21
time derange the silent whys of such a deathlessness) . . . . 420 NO THANKS 37   6
have disappeared a million whys; but opening if are . . . . . 588 1 X 1 48   6
are gaze the unguessed whys by me at look) . . . . 613 {CHAIRE} 15   3
feel nots are their whys stones become eyes locks . . . . . . 716 95 POEMS 44   22

WHYSPRIG

wt he n , whysprig sli nkil -Y- strol . . . . 430 NO THANKS 47   6

WICKED

it that birth was wicked and life is worse . . . . 545 1 X 1 5   10

+WICKED

FOR CONTEXT, SEE . . . . 519 50 POEMS 33   11

WICKEDLY

pose : to twitter wickedly whereas the big and . . . . . . 95 & POST IMPR 7   12
firstclassprivates on his rectum wickedly to tease by means . 339 VIVA 30   28
Own motion deeply to wickedly comprehend the innocently . . . 356 VIVA 47   9
all safely small big wickedly worlds of world disappear . . . 761 95 POEMS 88   12

WID

an went runnin aroun wid eachudder Hell Bent fer . . . . . 237 IS 5 ONE 8   18
motH) with a grass wid OW er who smelt . . . . 320 VIVA 12   17
hova in big cumbine wid i (check undublcheck) babbitt . . . . 325 VIVA 17   17
on duh boollevares an wid tears streamin down my . . . . . . 332 VIVA 23   18
runow dutmoi jak roids wid yooze Vury Sin Silly . . . . 398 NO THANKS 15   21
slipslouch twi tterstamp coon wid a plon kykerplung guit . . 519 50 POEMS 33   3

WIDE

shiny and not too wide dear god there's a . . . . 198 XLI PORTRAIT 6   5
upon cool flutes within wide glooms, and sing (of . . . . . . 208 XLI SONNETS 4   6
is a million griefs wide (it shall bury much . . . . 439 NO THANKS 55   11
our twentieth will open wide a wide open door . . . . 537 50 POEMS 49   12
will open wide a wide open door we are . . . . 537 50 POEMS 49   12

WIDEFLUNG

on the vest its wideflung friend clenched weakly dirt . . . . 258 IS 5 ONE 28   18

+WIDOWER

FOR CONTEXT, SEE . . . . 320 VIVA 12   17

WIDOWS

houses pour maids mothers widows wives bringing this visitor 624 {CHAIRE} 26   6

WIDTH

swims into a hair's width: into less? into not) . . . . . . 633 {CHAIRE} 35   10

WIELD

thy twain eyes deeply wield a noise of petals . . . . 10 T&C SONGS 1   42

WIELDS

with the superior dust-of-sleep. wields easily the pale club 163 & SON ACTU 12   4
of punctual brains... --Who wields a poem huger than . . . . 377 VIVA 68   12

+WIELDS

FOR CONTEXT, SEE . . . . 417 NO THANKS 34   15

WIFE

bed steals to his wife the sky and hour . . . . 3 T&C EPITHALAM   6
a man and his wife: Both very young noisily . . . . 312 VIVA 4   11
you captain) Memo 1 wife in impossibly hell Memo . . . . . . 389 NO THANKS 6   19
said he but your wife said she now said . . . . 399 NO THANKS 16   22
the prince of wales wife wants to die but . . . . 499 50 POEMS 13   2
knight and ploughman pardoner wife and nun merchant frere . . 661 {CHAIRE} 63   9
when he married his wife and here is a . . . . 707 95 POEMS 35   18
i suppose one 's wife) --does doesn't unsays says . . . . . . 779 73 POEMS 7   18

WIFELESS

seeing that i was wifeless and only half awake, ... 262 IS 5 ONE 32   7

WIG

the moon (with white wig and polished buttons) would . . . . 365 VIVA 56   12

	PAGE	TITLE	LINE

WIG (CONTINUED)
   dove on g w's wig so what he is . . . . 545 1 X 1 5   13
WIGGIN
   some difficulty sardines. Mr. Wiggin took Wrs. Miggin's harm 263 IS 5 ONE 32   48
+WIGGIN'S
   FOR CONTEXT, SEE . . . . 263 IS 5 ONE 32   48
WIGGLE
   like white squirming pipes wiggle upon the perfumed roman . . 110 & PORTRAIT 6   8
   what are parks for wiggle yes has are leap, ... 251 IS 5 ONE 22   20
+WIGGLE
   FOR CONTEXT, SEE . . . . 773 73 POEMS 1   11
WIGGLED
   square, little amorous-tadpole people wiggled battered by . . 173 & SON ACTU 22   4
WIGGLES
   tout en face always wiggles the perfectly dead finger . . . . 134 & SON REAL 5   11
   scarcely the somewhat city wiggles in considerable twilight . 302 IS 5 FIVE 1   4
WIGGLESOME
   updives pursued by its wigglesome whisperful body and almost 585 1 X 1 45   8
WILD
   from forgetfulness with the wild trump of April: witchery . .   4 T&C EPITHALAM   59
   moon, washed with a wild and thin despair of . . . .   12 T&C SONGS 2   49
   (sometimes a wonder of wild roses sometimes) with north . . . 512 50 POEMS 26   32
   begins-- the sky is wild with leaves; which dance . . . . . . 777 73 POEMS 5   6
   / / / / wild (at our first) beasts . . . . 844 73 POEMS 72   1
WILDLY
   into the dew: right wildly beat her heart at . . . .   8 T&C OF NICOL   28
   the irresponsible toys circle wildly in the slow-ly-in . . . 63 T&C PORTRAIT 10   31
   innumerable capering damned) --staring wildly up and down the 118 & PORTRAIT 10   39
   at Beautiful and Brave --wildly who rage, vainly who . . . . 799 73 POEMS 27   29
WILDSTRAWBERRIES
   s and two are wildstrawberries / / / / . . . . 614 (CHAIRE) 16   17
WILFUL
   / / whatever's merely wilful, and not miraculous (be . . . . 742 95 POEMS 70   1
WILL
   / / SONGS (thee will i praise between those . . . .   9 T&C SONGS 1   1
   fills his mind who will their hungering whispers hear . . . .   9 T&C SONGS 1   20
   do not fear, we will go amaying. thy whitest . . . . 13 T&C SONGS 3   7
   therefrom the purpled world will dance upon Between my . . . 16 T&C SONGS 6   4
   maidens whom passion wastes will lay between their little . . 16 T&C SONGS 6   8
   the grass their wings will touch with her face . . . . 16 T&C SONGS 6   12
   beauty of my lady will) --at her glance my . . . . 18 T&C PUELLA MEA   44
   speaking (sometimes as it will) the silence of her . . . . . 18 T&C PUELLA MEA   63
   there, nor he that will amaying go with my . . . . 20 T&C PUELLA MEA   169
   earlier flower, the snow will oft utter, whereof the . . . . 21 T&C PUELLA MEA   188
   the hungry star which will e -ven tu- al . . . . 49 T&C IMPRESS 3   14
   rain fell (as it will in spring) ropes of . . . . 58 T&C PORTRAIT 6   4
   to myself Death and will You with elaborate fingers . . . . . 58 T&C PORTRAIT 6   15
   with thin impulse i will have a dream i . . . . 67 T&C POST IMPR 4   6
   be roses and spring will bring her worms rushing . . . . . . 67 T&C POST IMPR 4   11
   easily at first, it will be leaves and a . . . . 67 T&C POST IMPR 4   19
   him a coin he will pick it cleverly from, ... 69 T&C POST IMPR 6   10
   and then his master will yell at him over . . . . 69 T&C POST IMPR 6   12
   string and the monkey will sit, up, and look . . . . 69 T&C POST IMPR 6   14
   or three, pennies he will be thrown a peanut . . . . 69 T&C POST IMPR 6   16
   a peanut (which he will open skilfully with his, ... 69 T&C POST IMPR 6   16
   hand) and then he will stiff-ly throw the shell . . . . 69 T&C POST IMPR 6   18
   do you get me?) will maybe dance and maybe . . . . 72 T&C SON REAL 3   13
   to the sun, nor will rain care cautiously who . . . . 84 T&C SON ACTU 3   8
   whose spires softly dare. Will take the houseless wisping . . 86 T&C SON ACTU 5   5
   be afraid and we will pass the simple ugliness . . . . 86 T&C SON ACTU 5   11
   minutely dead. Then you will slowly kiss me / . . . . 86 T&C SON ACTU 5   14
   in my mind blossom will stumble beneath a clumsiest . . . . . 91 & POST IMPR 3   11
   a millionth poem which will not wholly miss you; . . . . . . 92 & POST IMPR 4   19
   home then my mouth will go out into the . . . . 100 & POST IMPR 11   19
   tangerines and apples it will, Gorge indistinct palishflesh . 100 & POST IMPR 11   26
   first finger (i say "will he buy flowers" to . . . . 102 & POST IMPR 12   6
   roses les bluets yes, will He buy? Les belles . . . . 102 & POST IMPR 12   19
   / raise the shade will youse dearie? rain wouldn't . . . . . 109 & PORTRAIT 5   2

WILL (CONTINUED)

of Antony and we will confuse hotly our moreover	111	& PORTRAIT 6	60
judgment day comes God will find six crumbs stooping	117	& PORTRAIT 10	4
&: SEVEN POEMS i will be M o ving	122	& SEVEN POEMS 1	1
Her- ....kIss her: hands will play on, mE as	122	& SEVEN POEMS 1	10
mYveRylitTle street where you will come, at twi li	122	& SEVEN POEMS 1	24
biggish loll the hands' will tumbling into shall --and . . .	131	& SON REAL 2	14
asking Through her Muteness will slowly roam my dumbNess? . .	137	& SON REAL 8	5
tomorrow the daily papers will feature Peace And Good	142	& SON REAL 13	9
feature Peace And Good Will, and Mary with one	142	& SON REAL 13	10
it is funny, you will be dead some day.	153	& SON ACTU 2	1
need; it's funny. They will all be dead knead	153	& SON ACTU 2	4
funny, thing. And you will be and i and	153	& SON ACTU 2	9
much better than me will you like the rain's	153	& SON ACTU 2	13
(and here's what WhoEver will know Had you as	154	& SON ACTU 3	13
myth of body, which will make oddly to strut	155	& SON ACTU 4	10
me (slowly, wholly me) will press in the young	156	& SON ACTU 5	14
muscle, and what it will do to me before	157	& SON ACTU 6	4
body squirms kissingly, i will bring you every spring	161	& SON ACTU 10	7
his eye laughs, i will bring you every year	161	& SON ACTU 10	12
have (almost when hugeness will shut quietly) almost, your .	163	& SON ACTU 12	20
the room's silence, i will sew a nagging button	164	& SON ACTU 13	2
rapidly to bed: i will get in with it, ...	164	& SON ACTU 13	7
to feel what it will do in my bullying	164	& SON ACTU 13	13
to play with <> (will BigMorning get away with	169	& SON ACTU 18	11
ness and which i will again and again and	175	& SON ACTU 24	7
in the autumn she will never guess. but i	183	XLI SONGS 5	15
/ / / i will wade out till my	189	XLI SONGS 11	1
in burning flowers I will take the sun in	189	XLI SONGS 11	3
with chasteness of sea-girls Will i complete the mystery . .	189	XLI SONGS 11	11
of my flesh I will rise After a thousand	189	XLI SONGS 11	13
come away? see i will comfort you because you	192	XLI CHANSONS 2	7
smell so sweetly i will kiss your cool bark	192	XLI CHANSONS 2	9
little sister and i will take hands and looking	192	XLI CHANSONS 2	25
slenderly by it caressed will explode and spill the	193	XLI PORTRAIT 1	17
sister's howling moves off will anyone tell him why	196	XLI PORTRAIT 4	20
have been repapered he will nod like buddha or	198	XLI PORTRAIT 6	27
(whose eyes inherit vacancy) will time extract his	210	XLI SONNETS 6	10
important gardens her body will come toward me with	214	XLI SONNETS 10	11
/ / / / will suddenly trees leap from	218	XLI SONNETS 14	1
leap from winter and will the stabbing music of	218	XLI SONNETS 14	1
human comely thing? (or will the fleshless moments go	218	XLI SONNETS 14	9
GERT joggle i think will do it although the	227	IS 5 ONE GERT	1
airy hurdysturdygurdy but when will turn backward O backward	233	IS 5 ONE 4	3
this is Paris. i will sit in the corner	233	IS 5 ONE 4	16
known photographed, ourselves yawning will ask ourselves ou .	237	IS 5 ONE 8	2
/ / / / Will i ever forget that	262	IS 5 ONE 32	1
tomorrow's paper the proletariat will not rise yesterday. . .	262	IS 5 ONE 32	19
beyond logic happens beneath will; nor can these moments . .	264	IS 5 ONE 33	5
fixed so that it will not rub, like any	264	IS 5 ONE 33	24
let me see yes Will that was cleverest he	271	IS 5 TWO 6	5
don't and never never will know, they don't want	272	IS 5 TWO 7	16
/ / / / will out of the kindness	281	IS 5 THREE 5	1
laughter i say you will perhaps pardon, possibly you	285	IS 5 FOUR 2	9
perhaps pardon, possibly you will comprehend. and how this .	285	IS 5 FOUR 2	10
hands neatening each crease) will smooth entirely our minds .	288	IS 5 FOUR 5	5
we are together, we will kiss or smile or	289	IS 5 FOUR 6	16
the syntax of things will never wholly kiss you;	290	IS 5 FOUR 7	4
a wind-- your walls will not reckon how strangely	292	IS 5 FOUR 9	5
corners of your heart will never guess how much	292	IS 5 FOUR 9	15
which a poor wind will roam / / /	292	IS 5 FOUR 9	20
i give roses who will advise even yourself, lady	294	IS 5 FOUR 11	3
painter of fragile Marys will understand how smiling may . .	294	IS 5 FOUR 11	12
you being in love will tell who softly asks	295	IS 5 FOUR 12	2
plugged promise-- then he will maybe (hearing something fall	298	IS 5 FOUR 15	20
of your Heart possibly will understand; or why (in	300	IS 5 FOUR 17	9
horses are in bed will you walking beside me, ...	302	IS 5 FIVE 1	2
moving of your arm will do suddenly that will	302	IS 5 FIVE 1	9

WILL (CONTINUED)

will do suddenly that will do more than heroes	302	IS 5 FIVE 1	11
from death"-- you only will create (who are so	306	IS 5 FIVE 5	11
to oh no body will (can you give a)	314	VIVA 6	21
the whole" (if you will permit a metaphor savouring	326	VIVA 18	27
/ / / i will cultivate within me scrupulously	328	VIVA 19	1
smiles smiling) "but I will not everywhere be real	338	VIVA 29	12
without getting annoyed "I will not kiss your fucking	339	VIVA 30	19
is some shit I will not eat" our president, ...	339	VIVA 30	33
any heavens my mother will (all by herself) have	352	VIVA 43	1
herself) have one. It will not be a pansy	352	VIVA 43	2
of lilies-of-the-valley but it will be a heaven of	352	VIVA 43	4
blackred roses my father will be (deep like a	352	VIVA 43	5
(suddenly in sunlight he will bow, & the whole	352	VIVA 43	17
& the whole garden will bow) / / /	352	VIVA 43	18
/ / it) It will it Will come (we	361	VIVA 52	1
it) It will it Will come (we being unwound	361	VIVA 52	2
/ / / lady will you come with me	365	VIVA 56	1
your slightest look easily will unclose me though i	366	VIVA 57	5
i and my life will shut very beautifully, suddenly, ...	366	VIVA 57	10
its doom than you will smile) / / /	367	VIVA 58	12
your eyes are You will communicate a little more	370	VIVA 61	11
luminous) life toward twilight will dissolve reintegrate . .	379	VIVA 70	11
dying one life and will my rest to these	390	NO THANKS 7	13
wolfhounds women) and the will to shave that Ghost	394	NO THANKS 11	4
(or than everyone that will Ever love) we 've	397	NO THANKS 14	10
her guest (as critics will upon a poet feast)	418	NO THANKS 35	11
in) Spring a someone will lie (glued among familiar	428	NO THANKS 45	2
unknown most secret i will breathe such crude perfection . .	428	NO THANKS 45	10
mightily forgetting all which will forget him (emptying our .	428	NO THANKS 45	14
heels for Freedom slaves will click; where Boobs are	438	NO THANKS 54	18
such shoulders as cowards will scheme to harness: let	439	NO THANKS 55	14
than worlds immenser world will pray so (unlove disappearing)	450	NO THANKS 65	9
with boys to bed will go, / / /	451	NO THANKS 66	16
in not dying) Is will still occur; birds disappear	452	NO THANKS 67	13
through this opening universe will wraiths of doom rush . . .	454	NO THANKS 69	9
nothing tells anywhere "snow will come soon" & pretending . .	483	NEW POEMS 21	8
life you wear it will become you; and if	484	NEW POEMS 22	3
are glad whatever's living will yourself become. Girlboys may	484	NEW POEMS 22	4
/ / / / (will you teach a wretch	498	50 POEMS 12	1
decent mem and wonens will allows which if they	500	50 POEMS 14	22
if nothing disappears they will disappear always who are . .	505	50 POEMS 19	19
and just so long will being pay the rent	511	50 POEMS 25	5
and just so long will the impure think all	511	50 POEMS 25	13
just so long tomorrow will not be too late	511	50 POEMS 25	21
up come who breasts will be breasts thighs will	511	50 POEMS 25	24
will be breasts thighs will be thighs deeds cannot	511	50 POEMS 25	24
hole in the ocean will never be missed (it's	513	50 POEMS 27	24
conceiving mind of sun will stand, so strictly (over	520	50 POEMS 34	26
flame beckoned) as earth will downward climb, so naked . . .	521	50 POEMS 34	42
strong one queerying wave will whitely yearn from each . . .	526	50 POEMS 38	7
life's disease which quacks will cure when pimps may	527	50 POEMS 39	23
toomany-ness far too and will it tell us who	528	50 POEMS 40	2
who we are and will it tell us why	528	50 POEMS 40	2
why we dream and will it tell us how	528	50 POEMS 40	3
earth in it you will (kiss me) go out	529	50 POEMS 41	3
it (kiss me) you will go on into the	529	50 POEMS 41	6
day in it you will go (kiss me down	529	50 POEMS 41	9
memory i) kiss me (will go) / / /	529	50 POEMS 41	12
very merely my fourth will cure the laziest self	537	50 POEMS 49	2
in more our twentieth will open wide a wide	537	50 POEMS 49	11
breathing yes which fear will never no? measureless our . . .	538	50 POEMS 50	2
/ / mr u will not be missed who	551	1 X 1 11	1
huger than eternity, men will be saviours --flop grasshopper,	555	1 X 1 15	6
sky (really unreal world, will you perhaps do the	558	1 X 1 18	14
drowned, the single secret will still be man what	560	1 X 1 20	8
than dying's keener each will kissed breast awake) slow . . .	565	1 X 1 25	12
and (seeing something yes) will grin with pain You	570	1 X 1 30	8

		PAGE	TITLE	LINE
WILL (CONTINUED)				
dreams among) no year will fall this than, a		573	1 X 1 33	12
we--true lovers--pray that us will ourselves continue to . .		574	1 X 1 34	12
for you and close will shy wings of because;		575	1 X 1 35	16
more true than reason will deceive (more secret or		592	1 X 1 52	1
hill becomes nil) and will somebody tell me why		593	1 X 1 53	23
plan) the stupidest teacher will almost guess (with a . . .		594	1 X 1 54	5
space (was and be will) from beautiful obvious to		608	(CHAIRE) 10	5
a rose easily (while will be goes was) can		608	(CHAIRE) 10	11
thorniest question my roses will answer" "but dying's		625	(CHAIRE) 27	14
life smiled "was and will always remain: who i		626	(CHAIRE) 28	6
ever been, is, and will ever be, So /		631	(CHAIRE) 33	14
speak, a little innocence will make them sing; teach . . .		649	(CHAIRE) 51	2
reality of all nothing will actually lift a luminous		649	(CHAIRE) 51	5
less than excellent E will exactly do next (our		650	(CHAIRE) 52	12
a secret they never will share for whom create		664	(CHAIRE) 66	7
we're a mystery which will never happen again, a		667	(CHAIRE) 69	6
ex- actly what life will do) loves nothing as		676	95 POEMS 4	15
and hoping death himself will do the same because		679	95 POEMS 7	4
not the wisest man will partly understand (although the . . .		685	95 POEMS 13	11
well i'm looking for will" "did you look for		707	95 POEMS 35	1
murder me for i will freely die" she cried		711	95 POEMS 39	12
glimpse such sunlight as will leap higher than high		717	95 POEMS 45	11
love you, was and will be and my birthday		734	95 POEMS 62	4
after days of dark, will climb; will blossom: will		735	95 POEMS 63	13
of dark, will climb; will blossom: will sing (like		735	95 POEMS 63	13
will climb; will blossom: will sing (like april's own		735	95 POEMS 63	13
when such marvels vanish, will include --there by arriving .		741	95 POEMS 69	10
roses (you feel certain) will only smile / /		744	95 POEMS 72	8
to breathe) wounded us will becauseless ultimate earth accept		745	95 POEMS 73	5
of blue) of here will who straight up into		746	95 POEMS 74	6
which has been or will be told sings only--and		765	95 POEMS 91	8
and whatever a sun will always sing is you		766	95 POEMS 92	9
more begin than love will end; where nothing is		768	95 POEMS 94	2
rich (and a robin will sing his robin a		769	95 POEMS 95	22
(never did & never will) any damn thing :		793	73 POEMS 21	11
always done ; & will do alw -ays something		793	73 POEMS 21	21
nobody (including our selves) will reme mber (for 1		797	73 POEMS 25	14
is now and always will be or the ◇		803	73 POEMS 31	14
beginning twilight of winter will stand (over a snowstopped .		808	73 POEMS 36	1
moon alive sing more will wonderfully birds than are		811	73 POEMS 39	14
/ / your homecoming will be my homecoming-- my		812	73 POEMS 40	1
o urselve s are will be wor (magi c		829	73 POEMS 57	13
my darling but nobody will stop it With All		835	73 POEMS 63	30
murmurs eager this "i will give you five hopes		837	73 POEMS 65	8
whylessness-- autumn has gone: will winter never come? o . .		839	73 POEMS 67	8
despair when every silence will not make a dream		842	73 POEMS 70	10
own self who's) child will dance! and when he's		843	73 POEMS 71	12
+WILL				
FOR CONTEXT, SEE		347	VIVA 38	8
WILL'S				
mother i rather suppose" "will's dad never gave me		707	95 POEMS 35	17
WILLBEISHFULLY				
to seem) "stetti" and willbeishfully bursting un- eats . . .		387	NO THANKS 4	17
WILLED				
mire, scheming imagine, passion willed, freedom a drug that's		521	50 POEMS 34	55
WILLIAM				
melon causes indigestion to William Cullen Longfel- low's . .		263	IS 5 ONE 32	52
oke with him) one william shakespeare broke the silence . . .		552	1 X 1 12	24
WILLING				
of stuffs the alert willing myth of body, which		155	& SON ACTU 4	9
stick (in which a willing bulb of flame bubbles)		282	IS 5 THREE 6	27
said she) if you're willing said he (but you're		399	NO THANKS 16	19
WILLINGLY				
childhood and He said "willingly for the tale is		57	T&C PORTRAIT 5	15
WILLOWING				
of bottles, cats smoothly willowing out and in between . . .		279	IS 5 THREE 3	14

WILLOWS
   o'er whose night three willows wail, a slender dimness . . . 9 T&C SONGS 1   4
   to touch wishing by willows, bending upon streams? / . . . . 211 XLI SONNETS 7   18
WILLS&WERES
   hereanynoevery ing (danc) ing wills&weres / / / / . . . . . . 493 50 POEMS 7   18
WILLY
   looked up at my willy and you in the . . . . 707 95 POEMS 35   25
WILLY'S
   you couldn't well miss willy's carroty hair" "it seems . . . 707 95 POEMS 35   4
WILSON
   Ide and Earl & Wilson Collars) of you i . . . . 230 IS 5 ONE 2   9
   RITZ WEAR earl & wilson COLLARS / / / . . . . 244 IS 5 ONE 15   5
WILT
   the ashes then thou wilt rise and thou wilt . . . . 40 T&C AMORES 4   39
   wilt rise and thou wilt come to her and . . . . 40 T&C AMORES 4   40
   tickle, laughing when i wilt and wince / / . . . . 172 & SON ACTU 21 15
   heaped wholly with high wilt of human rind-- when . . . . . . 213 XLI SONNETS 9   4
   make two. Let liars wilt, repaying life they're loaned; . . . 556 1 X 1 16   11
+WILT
   FOR CONTEXT, SEE . . . . 388 NO THANKS 5   27
   FOR CONTEXT, SEE . . . . 646 {CHAIRE} 48   7
WILTED
   breasts the droll mouth wilted and not old, harry, ... 52 T&C PORTRAIT 1 32
   Memory stands, with clumsily wilted fingers emptying youth . 359 VIVA 50   6
WILTING
   / / of this wilting wall the colour drub . . . . 144 & SON REAL 15   1
WILTS
   nibbling timid teethful hours wilts the stern texture of . . 112 & PORTRAIT 6   80
   (! ye galleon wilts b: e; n, d . . . . 389 NO THANKS 6   9
WIN
   she said said She Win and you won't be . . . . 125 & SEVEN POEMS 4 23
   see their ears. Ears win- k, funny stable. In . . . . 171 & SON ACTU 20   7
   / / you in win ter who sit dying . . . . 354 VIVA 45   2
   with their breaths) in win ter you think, die . . . . 354 VIVA 45   23
   that was cling) on win ter sc ribbled lonely . . . . 415 NO THANKS 32   6
   i fail slenderly i win (like touch all stars . . . . . . 433 NO THANKS 50   11
   less always than to win less never than alive . . . . 530 50 POEMS 42   9
   all) but lose or win (come heaven, come hell) . . . . 776 73 POEMS 4   13
   they're few all (beyond win or lose) good true . . . . . . 805 73 POEMS 33   2
WINCE
   when i wilt and wince / / / / . . . . 172 & SON ACTU 21 15
   not observe; while roses wince) that which we die . . . . . . 386 NO THANKS 3   8
   they brood breeding they wince) his laugh is a . . . . 439 NO THANKS 55   10
   le sp, arrow, s wince among those skeletons of . . . . . . 442 NO THANKS 57   8
WINCES
   with the brittle legs winces swiflty out of number . . . . . 62 T&C PORTRAIT 10 24
   spirit prowls, its nose winces before a dissonance of . . . . 319 VIVA 11   11
WINCING
   door. a fang of wincing gas showed how hair, ... 73 T&C SON REAL 4   3
   two most early stars wincing upon a single colour, ... 98 & POST IMPR 9   6
WIND
   mountains ceased to beat? Wind beautifully who wanderest over 3 T&C EPITHALAM 17
   teartroubled to the momentary wind with guiding smile, lips . 9 T&C SONGS 1   11
   us descend take shimmering wind these fragile splendors from 41 T&C AMORES 5   18
   bells and a tall wind is dragging the sea . . . . 51 T&C IMPRESS 5   9
   / / / a wind has blown the rain . . . . 80 T&C SON UNRE 5 1
   have you to say, wind wind wind--did you love . . . . 80 T&C SON UNRE 5 6
   you to say, wind wind wind--did you love somebody . . . . . . 80 T&C SON UNRE 5 6
   to say, wind wind wind--did you love somebody and . . . . . . 80 T&C SON UNRE 5 6
   see doom's integration......... a wind has blown the rain . . 80 T&C SON UNRE 5 13
   / / / the wind is a Lady with . . . . 91 & POST IMPR 3   1
   person "Are You the wind?" "Yes" "why do you . . . . 91 & POST IMPR 3   8
   to me said the) wind being A lady in . . . . 91 & POST IMPR 3   19
   his coat against the wind / / / / . . . . 115 & PORTRAIT 8   28
   improbable hands of the Wind) / / / / . . . . 153 & SON ACTU 2   14
   pale club of the wind and swirled justly souls . . . . 163 & SON ACTU 12   5
   for masturbation). A dirty wind, twitches the, clothes which 167 & SON ACTU 16   6
   says sweetly Yes to wind and cold; and how . . . . 183 XLI SONGS 5   11

	PAGE	TITLE	LINE

WIND (CONTINUED)

hatless who (bent by wind) slammed hard- over the	277	IS 5 THREE 1	10
which i am a wind-- your walls will not	292	IS 5 FOUR 9	4
noone's fool; if this wind who i am prowls	292	IS 5 FOUR 9	11
around which a poor wind will roam / /	292	IS 5 FOUR 9	20
these gardens moves a wind bringing rain and leaves, ...	304	IS 5 FIVE 3	11
our eyes filled with wind, and the whining rigging	378	VIVA 69	1
a white with madness wind and broke oceans and	432	NO THANKS 49	16
fame, the harder the wind blows the taller i	439	NO THANKS 55	27
a which of a wind gives the truth to	560	1 X 1 20	1
keen of a lean wind flays screaming hills with	560	1 X 1 20	9
are their roots and wind is wind) trust your	732	95 POEMS 60	4
roots and wind is wind) trust your heart if	732	95 POEMS 60	4
do nothing) deepens with wind (and hark begins to	785	73 POEMS 13	6
the rain in the wind in the dark) whispers.	813	73 POEMS 41	11
with millionary knives of wind-- scatter his nothing all . .	839	73 POEMS 67	11

+WIND

FOR CONTEXT, SEE	346	VIVA 37	6

WIND'S

storms and rough cold, wind's menace and leaf's grieving: . .	207	XLI SONNETS 3	10

WINDMILLS

behind my eye the windmills are silent their flattened . . .	434	NO THANKS 51	10

WINDOW

certain song under the window of your soul it	43	T&C AMORES 7	5
sitting in her gentle window like a reminiscence partaken . .	58	T&C PORTRAIT 6	22
i (being at a window in this midnight) for	92	& POST IMPR 4	8
years.... exactly under the window under the window under . .	108	& PORTRAIT 4	33
the window under the window under the window walk	108	& PORTRAIT 4	34
the window under the window walk the unburied feet	108	& PORTRAIT 4	35
of Nowhere) arranging a window, into which people look . . .	124	& SEVEN POEMS 3	4
perhaps Hand in a window (carefully to and fro	124	& SEVEN POEMS 3	11
which in a putrid window every day almost leans	144	& SON REAL 15	12
of wines women and window-sills) i met that hideous	158	& SON ACTU 7	4
Something in the normal window. and a cat. A	166	& SON ACTU 15	8
palace --You, --in this window sits a Face (it	169	& SON ACTU 18	15
that's straightacross from my window, night air bothered with	171	& SON ACTU 20	3
you'll stand in the window for everyone to see	192	XLI CHANSONS 2	22
and before my doubting window leaves softly to stir, ...	205	XLI SONNETS 1	10
to stand at no window because i can't sleep	242	IS 5 ONE 13	20
blouse just outside this window, touching the glass boxes . .	282	IS 5 THREE 6	25
moon looked into my window it touched me with	284	IS 5 FOUR 1	1
and crept through the window she did not fall	284	IS 5 FOUR 1	12
lean out of this window is love, love and	295	IS 5 FOUR 12	23
i go to this window just as day dissolves	301	IS 5 FOUR 18	1
in hand at some window try to understand the	305	IS 5 FIVE 4	10
moon's round, through the window as you see and	365	VIVA 56	4
slowly i opened the window a most tinyness, the	365	VIVA 56	11
i lean from the window, behold ghosts, a man	375	VIVA 66	6
why Curvingly at this) window; yes women sturdily meander . .	434	NO THANKS 51	33
comes to some dirty window every) twilight i feel	501	50 POEMS 15	7
stalinist arse in hitler's window on wednesday next at . . .	514	50 POEMS 28	13
new moon outside your window saying if that's all, ...	572	1 X 1 32	2
(with crazily eyes of window) may be un less	668	(CHAIRE) 70	4
faces at a dark window) this father and his	715	95 POEMS 43	3
at an o pen window this fine morning) fly	724	95 POEMS 52	9
peering from some high window; at the gold of	824	73 POEMS 52	4

+WINDOW

FOR CONTEXT, SEE	171	& SON ACTU 20	2

WINDOW-SILLS

of wines women and window-sills) i met that hideous	158	& SON ACTU 7	4

WINDOWS

hangest canary-birds in parlor windows spring slattern of . .	61	T&C PORTRAIT 9	10
/ / POST IMPRESSIONS windows go orange in the	89	& POST IMPR 1	1
on either side the windows are packed with hardslippery . . .	100	& POST IMPR 11	4
side the street's DarkcOOllonGBody windows, are. clenched. . .	100	& POST IMPR 11	16
weasOned with-be- ing-put-too-long in windows and never sold	101	& POST IMPR 11	66
that water flowerpots in windows but they live higher	126	& SEVEN POEMS 5	25
melancholy delicacy night gargles windows. / / / /	168	& SON ACTU 17	19

WINDOWS (CONTINUED)

to play with windows-and-whispers, (will . . . . 169 & SON ACTU 18   10
He suddenly tasted worms windows and roses he laughed, . . . 170 & SON ACTU 19   12
the dotting millions of windows of thousands of . . . . . . 281 IS 5 THREE 5   6
is to peer through windows, unobserved --listen, for (out . . 292 IS 5 FOUR 9   8
hail (and a few windows awaken certain faces busily . . . . . 299 IS 5 FOUR 16   13
than mine" (opening the windows) "and there is a . . . . . . 328 VIVA 19   10
with rain) faces (at windows) do not speak and . . . . 340 VIVA 31   5
walks are) is most (windows where blaze naLOVEme crazily . . 436 NO THANKS 52   3
who buzz on) -lar (windows called sidewalks of houses . . . . 436 NO THANKS 52   16
rooms through whose foul windows absurd clouds cruise nobly . 442 NO THANKS 57   12

+WINDOWS-AND-WHISPERS

to play with windows-and-whispers, (will . . . . 169 & SON ACTU 18   10

WINDS

move beautifully in the winds of my lust like . . . . 112 & PORTRAIT 6   95
why why How many winds make wonderful and is . . . . 395 NO THANKS 12   2
con founds all itcreating winds / / / / . . . . 826 73 POEMS 54   17

WINDTHIN

a ghost 's rainfaint windthin voice-which-is no-voice . . . . 697 95 POEMS 25   11

WINDY

their hands scimitars like windy torches each is blacker . . 33 T&C ORIENTALE 6   39

WINE

thee as a new wine from steep hills by . . . . 9 T&C SONGS 1   36
but his heart drinks wine the tenth lady says . . . . 15 T&C SONGS 5   8
whoso drinks, a dizzier wine than should the grapes . . . . . 21 T&C PUELLA MEA   199
never quite taste the wine which their nearness evaporates . 193 XLI PORTRAIT 1   12
oft hath quaffed the wine of life and found . . . . 273 IS 5 TWO 8   8
hill, driven by black wine. a village does not . . . . . . 434 NO THANKS 51   7

WINES

year (a spring of wines women and window-sills) i . . . . . 158 & SON ACTU 7   4

WING

fluttering from night's outer wing strong silent greens . . . 208 XLI SONNETS 4   2
about tweak- ing his wing collar pecking at his . . . . . . 274 IS 5 TWO 9   33
houses (as the kno wing spirit prowls, its nose . . . . . . 319 VIVA 11   10
/ / / / Wing Wong, uninterred at twice . . . . 341 VIVA 32   1
fruit of eager bosoms" Wing Wong / / / . . . . 341 VIVA 32   22
(here) ingc r O wing; ly: cry. be, gi . . . . 423 NO THANKS 40   9
to sing) leaf is wing and tree is voice . . . . 583 1 X 1 43   18
thing and a gro Wing) silence, who; is: somE . . . . 657 (CHAIRE) 59   14
joyfully all truths of wing resuming) selves, into infinite . 659 (CHAIRE) 61   3
rain snow moon dream wing tree leaf bird sun . . . . 753 95 POEMS 81   16

WINGED

heart of May; a Winged Passion woke and one . . . . 8 T&C OF NICOL   9

WINGFEET

seethe luminous leopards (on wingfeet of thingfear) come . . 586 1 X 1 46   16

WINGING

spirits singing in are winging in the blossoming) lovers . . 591 1 X 1 51   8
(secretly adoring shyly tiny winging darting floating merry . 591 1 X 1 51   22

WINGLESS

and odour drives the wingless thing man forth into . . . . . 4 T&C EPITHALAM   60

WINGS

doves flicker upon sunny wings as if in terror . . . . 6 T&C EPITHALAM   138
in the grass their wings will touch with her . . . . 16 T&C SONGS 6   12
flower with thy unimaginable wings, where dwells the breath . 40 T&C AMORES 4   46
a moth with stumbling wings flutters and flops along . . . . 47 T&C IMPRESS 1   8
with grieving feet and wings mounts against the margins . . . 59 T&C PORTRAIT 7   12
in dusk her new wings then decently hanged himself, ... 170 & SON ACTU 19   3
thy voice scattering perfume-gifted wings suddenly escorts . 187 XLI SONGS 9   14
thunder of those hungering wings of His, into the . . . . . 210 XLI SONNETS 6   6
but he has little wings and here's my hotel . . . . 353 VIVA 44   10
born of dream while wings welcome the year and . . . . . . 372 VIVA 63   14
grow and the rain's wings the birds of snow . . . . 441 NO THANKS 56   55
(asleep who must go things-without-wings / / / / . . . . . . 483 NEW POEMS 21   12
and close will shy wings of because; each why . . . . 575 1 X 1 35   17
of which demons with wings would be streaming if . . . . . . 652 (CHAIRE) 54   13
and of love and wings: and of the gay . . . . 663 (CHAIRE) 65   7
shadows are substances and wings are birds; unders of . . . . 761 95 POEMS 88   7
all the dark who wings his why beyond because . . . . 815 73 POEMS 43   5

PAGE   TITLE   LINE

+WINGS
  FOR CONTEXT, SEE . . . .   64 T&C POST IMPR 1   10
  FOR CONTEXT, SEE . . . .   840 73 POEMS 68   32
WINK
  glints squinting who's a wink bum-nothing and money fuzzily .   96 & POST IMPR 8   18
  chimneys, my nerves sumptuously wink ....and little-dusk has 169 & SON ACTU 18   8
  others don't scream murmur wink at kid anaesthetize marry . . 391 NO THANKS 8   14
+WINK
  FOR CONTEXT, SEE . . . .   171 & SON ACTU 20   7
WINKED
  My how glad he winked and hope he'll do . . . .   126 & SEVEN POEMS 5   17
WINKING
  timeshaped face plus innocuous winking hands, carefully . . .   62 T&C PORTRAIT 10   3
WINKS
  never met who maybe winks at you in a . . . . 126 & SEVEN POEMS 5   15
  posture. (As an eye winks). and almost i refrain . . . . . . 131 & SON REAL 2   5
WINNER
  and life is the winner (and beggars are rich . . . .   769 95 POEMS 95   3
WINNING
  and losing's less than winning (but love is more . . . . .   684 95 POEMS 12   19
WINS
  persian at phonograph x wins exeunt ax: by; c, ...   200 XLI PORTRAIT 8   30
WINSOME
  (whose million leaves in winsome indolence simmer upon . . .   6 T&C EPITHALAM   125
  hinge of flesh, a winsome thing and strange; apt . . . . . .   21 T&C PUELLA MEA   194
  of Silence from the winsome cage of thy body . . . .   187 XLI SONGS 9   2
  square mur- mur, a winsome flatulence-- In the soft . . . . . 201 XLI PORTRAIT 9   13
WINTER
  hunted from his kingdom winter cowers, seeing green armies .   4 T&C EPITHALAM   70
  like Coney Island in winter / / / / . . . .   72 T&C SON REAL 3   15
  to the people, for winter who crookedly care. / . . . . 190 XLI SONGS 12   21
  suddenly trees leap from winter and will the stabbing . . . . 218 XLI SONNETS 14   1
  / / it is winter a moon in the . . . . 279 IS 5 THREE 3   1
  into all beautiful things) winter, whom Spring shall kill . . 293 IS 5 FOUR 10   31
  it away (his autumn's winter being summer's spring who . . . 420 NO THANKS 37   3
  down) spring summer autumn winter he sang his didn't . . . . 515 50 POEMS 29   3
  up they grew autumn winter spring summer) that noone . . . . 515 50 POEMS 29   11
  and ding) summer autumn winter spring reaped their sowing . . 515 50 POEMS 29   34
  neverless now and without winter spring? she'll spin that . . 531 50 POEMS 43   10
  she looked) "especially in winter" (like a leaf opening) . .   572 1 X 1 32   5
  then? all history's a winter sport or three: but . . . . . . 579 1 X 1 39   5
  are until" "spring follows winter: as clover knows, maybe" . 625 {CHAIRE} 27   9
  keeping is darkness and winter and cringing --it's spring . . 665 {CHAIRE} 67   17
  in snowily nowheres of winter his silence) give me . . . . . 678 95 POEMS 6   12
  welcome your coming although winter may be everywhere with .   717 95 POEMS 45   5
  old turns to young (winter goodbye) april hello, / . . . . .   737 95 POEMS 65   7
  when silence becomes singing winter by spring, i lift . . . . 749 95 POEMS 77   17
  here no then of winter equals now of spring; . . . . 765 95 POEMS 91   11
  in fall and in winter our spring is the . . . . 766 95 POEMS 92   31
  / / / / one winter afternoon (at the magical . . . . 802 73 POEMS 30   1
  in beginning twilight of winter will stand (over a . . . . . 808 73 POEMS 36   1
  he" i staring into winter twi light (whisper) "was . . . . . 823 73 POEMS 51   4
  autumn has gone: will winter never come? o come, ... 839 73 POEMS 67   8
+WINTER
  FOR CONTEXT, SEE . . . . 354 VIVA 45   2
  FOR CONTEXT, SEE . . . . 354 VIVA 45   23
  FOR CONTEXT, SEE . . . . 415 NO THANKS 32   6
  FOR CONTEXT, SEE . . . . 618 {CHAIRE} 20   23
WINTER'S
  to ignorance again: but winter's not forever, even snow . . . 579 1 X 1 39   3
WINTERBRIEF
  these (i notice) trees winterbrief surly old gurgle a . . . . 282 IS 5 THREE 6   11
WINTRY
  than (by yon sunset's wintry glow revealed) this tall . . . . 254 IS 5 ONE 25   1
  a pleasant country: if's wintry (my lovely) let's open . . . 578 1 X 1 38   2
  world (on which are wintry handlebars glued) updives pursued 585 1 X 1 45   5
  climb: ing i -nto wintry twi- light (all together . . . . . . 627 {CHAIRE} 29   5
  making fools understand (like wintry me) that not all . . . . 736 95 POEMS 64   6

	PAGE	TITLE	LINE

WINTRY (CONTINUED)
| an eggyellow smear of wintry sunse t / / . . . . | 788 73 POEMS 16 | 14 |
+WINTRY
| FOR CONTEXT, SEE . . . . | 789 73 POEMS 17 | 4 |
WIPED
| he ant but Coolitch wiped his valley forge with . . . . . . | 321 VIVA 13 | 13 |
WIRE
| like a white shocking wire, when she smiles a . . . . | 147 & SON REAL 18 | 5 |
WIRED
| dominic has a doll wired to the radiator of . . . . | 680 95 POEMS 8 | 2 |
WIRELESS
| an San Fran dictaphones wireless subways vacuum cleaners . . | 237 IS 5 ONE 8 | 9 |
WIRES
| little voice Over the wires came leaping and i . . . . . . | 44 T&C AMORES 8 | 2 |
WISDOM
plump left fist opening "wisdom." Flicker of gold. "Yep. . .	226 IS 5 ONE MAME	8
a better fate than wisdom lady i swear by	290 IS 5 FOUR 7	9
sixtyfour maxims whose) centripetal wisdom in thirtytwo . . .	341 VIVA 32	4
more than most fabulous wisdom fears to see (who	446 NO THANKS 61	12
reasoned nor unreasoned, his wisdom cancels conflict and . .	683 95 POEMS 11	6
gay and with a wisdom not the wisest man	685 95 POEMS 13	10
creature among us a wisdom no knowledge can kill	769 95 POEMS 95	9
spirit's ignorance by every wisdom knowledge fears to dare, .	843 73 POEMS 71	11
WISDOMING
which vast my complexly wisdoming friend's --a fingery . . .	517 50 POEMS 31	5
WISDOMS
flower than now (softlying wisdoms enter guess) childmoon . .	518 50 POEMS 32	9
WISE
mouth my heart made wise; at moments when the	78 T&C SON UNRE 3	4
a silver tube of wise lust whose arms and	110 & PORTRAIT 6	5
ruffian-rogue, laughing body with wise breasts half-grown, .	140 & SON REAL 11	11
her. Bill was put wise that she was coming	145 & SON REAL 16	9
absolutely into me.... a wise and puerile moving of	302 IS 5 FIVE 1	8
world say "his most wise music stole nothing from	306 IS 5 FIVE 5	9
lullaby and other lulla wise by UnBroken LULLAlullabyBY the .	317 VIVA 9	29
the feeble are so wise the people remember being	505 50 POEMS 19	15
to foolish and to wise offered immeasurable is proudly . . .	521 50 POEMS 34	39
shall hate confound the wise? doubt blind the brave?	538 50 POEMS 50	5
be must be (the wise fool) if living's to	543 1 X 1 3	14
the oath cracked length wise--let it go it was	569 1 X 1 29	5
you or i) were wise." "You mean worlds may	603 (CHAIRE) 5	10
for malice and too wise for fear) of shadowy	607 (CHAIRE) 9	12
ing remaking what other -wise we should have thrown	660 (CHAIRE) 62	14
of blossom --blissfully nonchalant wise and each ignorant .	764 95 POEMS 90	40
heroes (the popular the wise, a weed a tearose)	798 73 POEMS 26	10
who thought yourself so wise; and much could understand . . .	834 73 POEMS 62	14
+WISE
| FOR CONTEXT, SEE . . . . | 374 VIVA 65 | 6 |
| FOR CONTEXT, SEE . . . . | 845 73 POEMS 73 | 6 |
WISELY
with guiding smile, lips wisely minced for blown kisses, . .	9 T&C SONGS 1	12
me, wholly, well --did (wisely suddenly into a dangerous . .	115 & PORTRAIT 8	10
get in with it, wisely, pester skilfully, teasing its	164 & SON ACTU 13	8
WISER
early to better is wiser for worse. Give liz	513 50 POEMS 27	10
WISEST
lips are amused, no wisest painter of fragile Marys	294 IS 5 FOUR 11	10
a wisdom not the wisest man will partly understand	685 95 POEMS 13	10
partly understand (although the wisest man am i) So	685 95 POEMS 13	12
WISH
"and did you perhaps wish also shishkabob?" / /	194 XLI PORTRAIT 2	38
silence curled upon a wish, to rapture should surprise . . .	205 XLI SONNETS 1	4
watched certain petals rapidly wish in the corners of	214 XLI SONNETS 10	5
a shimmie how you wish that you was Jimmie.	235 IS 5 ONE 6	12
mentioned ye olde freudian wish; when i contemplate her . . .	326 VIVA 18	3
star (have you a wish?) touch me, before we	357 VIVA 48	2
rose or if your wish be to close me, ...	366 VIVA 57	9
(and i guess though wish and world go down, ...	372 VIVA 63	15

896

WISH (CONTINUED)
   deeply, rain (dream hugely) wish firmly. splendidly advancing 422 NO THANKS 39   3
   canned swoonsong came "I wish you good" the mechanical . . . 464 NEW POEMS 2   28
   anyone earth by april wish by spirit and if . . . . 515 50 POEMS 29   32
   steer his great small wish into upward deepness of . . . . . 528 50 POEMS 40   8
   so sky so . wish / / / / . . . . 584 1 X 1 44   19
   hill and threw his wish at blue with a . . . . 593 1 X 1 53   6
   dart out flew his wish (it dived like a . . . . 593 1 X 1 53   8
   tumult is the simplest wish: so pitiless a massacre . . . . . 609 (CHAIRE) 11   5
   eternity; in a single wish, receive all i am . . . . 651 (CHAIRE) 53   3
   luminous tendril of celestial wish (whying diminutive bright 669 (CHAIRE) 71   1
   than littlest they adventure (wish by·terror) steep not . . . 757 95 POEMS 85   20
   at birthdays each (a wish no bigger than) in . . . . 763 95 POEMS 90   7
   universe emerging from a wish) love is the voice . . . . . . 768 95 POEMS 94   8
+WISH
   FOR CONTEXT, SEE . . . . 480 NEW POEMS 18   6
WISHED
   no hungry man but wished him food; no cripple . . . . 520 50 POEMS 34   30
   the moon before God wished Himself into a rose . . . . . . 577 1 X 1 37   15
   thought or done or wished without a little innocence, ... 649 (CHAIRE) 51   9
WISHES
   lips always clenched faintly, wishes you with all her . . . . 72 T&C SON REAL 3   7
   worthy of more ponderous wishes or hopes less tall . . . . . 328 VIVA 19   8
   clothes thoughts kiss -ing wishes bodies) . . . . 437 NO THANKS 53   7
   breathing's to steal-- five wishes are five and one . . . . . 543 1 X 1 3   17
+WISHFUL
   FOR CONTEXT, SEE . . . . 415 NO THANKS 32   18
+WISHFULLY
   FOR CONTEXT, SEE . . . . 387 NO THANKS 4   17
WISHING
   i call rich beyond wishing if this thou catch, ... 13 T&C SONGS 3   17
   loves most to touch wishing by willows, bending upon . . . . 211 XLI SONNETS 7   18
   but love, all of wishing) though life's lived wrongsideout, . 446 NO THANKS 61   2
   ground and breathing is wishing and wishing is having-- . . . 665 (CHAIRE) 67   2
   breathing is wishing and wishing is having-- but keeping . . 665 (CHAIRE) 67   2
   without any sound and wishing is having and having . . . . . 665 (CHAIRE) 67   9
WISHLESS
   haunted with huddling infinite wishless melancholy, suddenly 305 IS 5 FIVE 4   13
   fabricate unknownness (known being wishless; but love, all of 446 NO THANKS 61   2
WISP
   -mas) ter- i -ous wisp A of glo- ry. . . . . 632 (CHAIRE) 34   12
   be done) while a wisp of why as thick . . . . 709 95 POEMS 37   11
+WISP
   FOR CONTEXT, SEE . . . . 333 VIVA 24   19
WISPILY
   completely thus or that wispily is to say according . . . . . 516 50 POEMS 30   12
WISPING
   Will take the houseless wisping rune of road lazily . . . . . 86 T&C SON ACTU 5   5
   stood, one (truthed by wisping tinily the silverest alive . . 572 1 X 1 32   8
WISPISH
   I Want a Doll, wispish-agile feet with slid steps . . . . . . 140 & SON REAL 11   14
WISPISH-AGILE
   I Want a Doll, wispish-agile feet with slid steps . . . . . . 140 & SON REAL 11   14
WISTFUL
   is dimly heard a wistful and precarious bird.) Springing . . 20 T&C PUELLA MEA 152
   / my strength becoming wistful in a glib girl . . . . 131 & SON REAL 2   1
   DOOM icecoalwood truck a wistful little clown whom somebody . 680 95 POEMS 8   6
WISTFULLY
   / / the (Wistfully dead seem generous) don't . . . . 391 NO THANKS 8   2
   thoroughly imploring threaten) the wistFully dead you . . . . 391 NO THANKS 8   10
   the so to speak wistfulLy dead are not relatively . . . . . . 391 NO THANKS 8   17
WISTI-TWISTI
   / / (one!) the wisti-twisti barber -pole is climbing . . . . 128 & SEVEN POEMS 6   2
WIT
   that is or to wit farming and be it . . . . 239 IS 5 ONE 10   11
   ar (ise) wi lt (wit (hprettyw) ith) mr jeff . . . . 388 NO THANKS 5   28
   give a shit for wit the boys i mean . . . . 427 NO THANKS 44   7
   ford) and eke to wit a human being --let's . . . . 607 (CHAIRE) 9   14

WITCHERY
wild trump of April: witchery of sound and odour . . . . . . 4 T&C EPITHALAM   59
me in the sacred witchery of almostness which May . . . . . . 10 T&C SONGS 1   37
WITCHES
tip-toe twinkle-toe little twitchy witches and tingling . . . 25 T&C CHANSONS 2   6
WITH
WORD DELETED, APPEARED 725 TIMES
WITHAL
shapely sharp cunning and withal delirious feet of the . . . 17 T&C PUELLA MEA   29
small, ardent, and perfectly withal smooth to stroke and . . 20 T&C PUELLA MEA 154
WITHDRAWS
approaches, sets down coffee withdraws a and c discuss . . . 200 XLI PORTRAIT 8   19
WITHDREW
crows had ceased. I withdrew my hands from the . . . . 263 IS 5 ONE 32   55
life the little hands withdrew, jerkily, themselves quietly . 284 IS 5 FOUR 1   8
WITHER
which is first to wither, to pass? shallowness of . . . . . . 190 XLI SONGS 12   6
it so skilful) must wither fail and cease --but . . . . 742 95 POEMS 70   4
WITHERED
they died squirming: now withered and unself her gnarled . . 506 50 POEMS 20   4
+WITHERED
FOR CONTEXT, SEE . . . . 255 IS 5 ONE 26   3
WITHERS
world and the earth withers the moon crumbles one . . . . . . 38 T&C AMORES 3   5
flower in the hair withers; thy hair is acold . . . . 190 XLI SONGS 12   15
WITHHOLDING
and (if you can withholding nothing) World, conceive a . . . 420 NO THANKS 37   14
WITHIN
fortunate fingers sometime dwell (within a greener shadow of   3 T&C EPITHALAM   22
the steep unspeaking tower within whose brightening . . . . .   4 T&C EPITHALAM   51
his doom-- O thou within the chancel of whose . . . .   7 T&C EPITHALAM 153
a flower lieth (while within the eyes is dimly . . . .   20 T&C PUELLA MEA 151
ness a worshipper prostrate within twitching shadow lolls . . 28 T&C ORIENTALE 2   14
i was considering how within night's loose sack a . . . . . . 49 T&C IMPRESS 3   2
of bloated rose coiled within cobalt miles of sky . . . . . . 93 & POST IMPR 5   6
blow upon cool flutes within wide glooms, and sing . . . . . 208 XLI SONNETS 4   6
other, each (a typewriter within his reach) upon his . . . . 266 IS 5 TWO 1   20
it sweet-- a tear within his stern blue eye, ... 273 IS 5 TWO 8   9
which fear to miss within your least gesture the . . . . . . 293 IS 5 FOUR 10   7
/ / / if within tonight's erect everywhere of . . . . 299 IS 5 FOUR 16   1
approaches) painfully sterilized contours; within which . . . 319 VIVA 11   29
/ i will cultivate within me scrupulously the Inimitable . . 328 VIVA 19   1
knees but something beats within my shirt to prove . . . . . 360 VIVA 51   28
forever --and i perceive, within transparent walls how . . . 376 VIVA 67   7
always upon sunset, crickets within me whisper whose erect . 435 NO THANKS 51   37
why but (who stood within his steam be- ginning . . . . . . 523 50 POEMS 36   7
/ this out of within itself moo ving lump . . . . 602 (CHAIRE) 4   1
WITHINS
tion bath-houses whose opened withins ejaculate. obscenity . 94 & POST IMPR 6   4
is prayer among) float withins he upclimbest And (sky . . . . 482 NEW POEMS 20   5
WITHOUT
have laughed their last; without, the street darkling . . . . 75 T&C SON REAL 6   9
sunset and who--touches--the hills without any reason (i have 91 & POST IMPR 3   5
--do not suppose these without any reason and otherwise . . . 91 & POST IMPR 3   15
fresh upon silence) i without fail entered became and . . . . 115 & PORTRAIT 8   20
of air there) and without breaking anything. / / . . . . . . 124 & SEVEN POEMS 3   19
off and squeeze- into-largeness without one word and you . . 127 & SEVEN POEMS 5   34
Mid's large bluish face without eyebrows sits in the . . . . 149 & SON REAL 20   1
/ let's live suddenly without thinking under honest trees, . 160 & SON ACTU 9   1
of downward flower flowing without or cease or time; . . . . 168 & SON ACTU 17   8
slow tranquillities and He without Whose favour nothing is . 210 XLI SONNETS 6   3
she attacks her Lobster without feet mingle under the . . . . 243 IS 5 ONE 14   13
a box of newly without exaggeration shot with some . . . . . 263 IS 5 ONE 32   46
cathedral recedes into weather without answering / / / . . . 279 IS 5 THREE 3   24
frisks down the boulevards without his coat and hat . . . . . 296 IS 5 FOUR 13   8
be socalled) memory Of (without more ado about less . . . . . 317 VIVA 9   22
unto him gave) responds, without getting annoyed "I will . . 339 VIVA 30   18
contains these prettiest deaths without effort while . . . . 340 VIVA 31   15

                                                      PAGE   TITLE   LINE
WITHOUT (CONTINUED)
    i am a birdcage without any bird, a collar . . . . 360 VIVA 51   25
    a dog, a kiss without lips; a prayer lacking . . . . 360 VIVA 51   27
    but being not amazing: without love separate, ... 374 VIVA 65   1
    a urinal howlessly and without why (quite minus gal . . . . 387 NO THANKS 4   3
    as a mind full without fear might faithfully lie . . . . . 418 NO THANKS 35   7
    birds of snow things without name beyond because things . . . 441 NO THANKS 56   57
    everybody gets a bellyful without lifting my finger i . . . . 475 NEW POEMS 13   8
    (asleep who must go things-without-wings / / / / . . . . . 483 NEW POEMS 21   12
    theres what immense live without every dancing. singless on- 491 50 POEMS 5   5
    eye of star and without was if minus and . . . . 502 50 POEMS 16   5
    death neverless now and without winter spring? she'll spin . 531 50 POEMS 43   10
    mean the an imal without a heart. Huge this . . . . 544 1 X 1 4   4
    only man is god. Without a heart the animal . . . . 544 1 X 1 4   25
    (yes but behind yes) without or until no atom . . . . 634 {CHAIRE} 36   12
    or done or wished without a little innocence, although . . . 649 {CHAIRE} 51   9
    when every leaf opens without any sound and wishing . . . . . 665 {CHAIRE} 67   8
    (my your and) self without, completely dare be beautiful . . 666 {CHAIRE} 68   13
    during which fingers are without hands; and i have . . . . 667 {CHAIRE} 69   10
    your heart but most (without the smallest doubt) because . . 679 95 POEMS 7   9
    mystery of paradise) mind without soul may blast some . . . . 714 95 POEMS 42   9
    her improbable world and without any doubt of impossible . . 748 95 POEMS 76   3
    heart) i am never without it (anywhere i go . . . . 766 95 POEMS 92   2
    amazing day it's brains without hearts have set saint . . . . 769 95 POEMS 95   15
    gift to live is without until: but pitiful they've . . . . 776 73 POEMS 4   20
    / / a grin without a face (a look . . . . 797 73 POEMS 25   1
    a face (a look without an i) be care . . . . 797 73 POEMS 25   3
    our hero is quite without change, you're going to . . . . . 800 73 POEMS 28   11
    myself; and why? because without any doubt he was . . . . . 802 73 POEMS 30   10
    have enough to do without confusing timelessness and time. . 817 73 POEMS 45   8
    / / / / without the mercy of your . . . . 819 73 POEMS 47   1
+WITHOUT
    FOR CONTEXT, SEE . . . . 753 95 POEMS 81   5
WITHS
    peopling places seeks play: withs of star link clauses . . . 168 & SON ACTU 17   14
    ofC omeg o CRINGE WITHS lilt (-ing- lyful . . . . 421 NO THANKS 38   15
WITLESS
    slobbering walls filthily push witless creases of screaming . 96 & POST IMPR 8   4
WITTILY
    mesh. New and eager. wittily peels the. ploop. --OOc . . . . 136 & SON REAL 7   13
WITTY
    goes utter ly churning witty, twitters upon Our (ta-te-ta . . 89 & POST IMPR 1   14
    sinuous globular slippery intense witty huge and its chords . 110 & PORTRAIT 6   24
    always talking individual, mysterious witty hatless. Cats . . 279 IS 5 THREE 3   12
WIVES
    pour maids mothers widows wives bringing this visitor their . 624 {CHAIRE} 26   6
+WIZENED
    FOR CONTEXT, SEE . . . . 101 & POST IMPR 11   65
WOBBLES
    one grin very distinctly wobbles from the thinning lips . . . 151 & SON REAL 22   15
    this brittle whore delicately wobbles an improbably distinct 229 IS 5 ONE FRAN   3
WOBBLY
    fuzzily mouths take big wobbly foot-steps every goggle cent . 96 & POST IMPR 8   20
    lurch faceflowers stutter treebodies wobbly- ing thing . . . 436 NO THANKS 52   10
WOE
    buries a tomorrow under woe and up comes yesterday . . . . . 531 50 POEMS 43   3
WOES
    seem their joys turn woes and right goes wrong . . . . . . 776 73 POEMS 4   25
WOKE
    May; a Winged Passion woke and one by one . . . . 8 T&C OF NICOL   9
    to swarm their fates woke dreamers to their ghostly . . . . . 520 50 POEMS 34   12
WOLF
    or disciple sheep or wolf) gush to it as . . . . 804 73 POEMS 32   4
WOLFHOUNDS
    men motors "my" yachts wolfhounds women) and the will . . . . 394 NO THANKS 11   4
WOMAN
    out for the old woman with the wart on . . . . 25 T&C CHANSONS 2   17
    / AMORES consider O woman this my body. for . . . . 36 T&C AMORES 1   2

                                        899

		PAGE	TITLE	LINE

WOMAN (CONTINUED)
not old, harry, a woman in the crowd whinnied	53	T&C PORTRAIT 1	34
the hoisting light any woman is smooth and ridiculous	68	T&C POST IMPR 5	13
thought is like a woman amorous to be known;	81	T&C SON UNRE 6	10
thinkingly) remind me of Woman and how between her	95	& POST IMPR 7	17
/ / / unnoticed woman from whose kind large	142	& SON REAL 13	1
/ / a blue woman with sticking out breasts	167	& SON ACTU 16	1
voice of the leatherfaced woman with the crimson nose	196	XLI PORTRAIT 4	3
no man feels, no woman understands. / / /	212	XLI SONNETS 8	14
o so Waiter this; woman is please shut that	243	IS 5 ONE 14	3
door opens by itself woman.) they so to speak	243	IS 5 ONE 14	9
tailor chuckles like a woman in a dream (but	287	IS 5 FOUR 4	13
cognomen of a Young Woman of cambridge, mass. to	326	VIVA 18	1
is a certain Young Woman unacquainted with the libido	327	VIVA 18	42
dead the only man woman or child who wrote	336	VIVA 27	3
a man hugging a woman in a park. Complete.	375	VIVA 66	8
bad cigar is a woman but a gland is	466	NEW POEMS 4	27
/ / / nor woman (just as it be	472	NEW POEMS 10	1
words im -prison a woman for all her now:	491	50 POEMS 5	14
better than which, every woman who's (despite the	807	73 POEMS 35	9
some loveless infraworld) a woman knows; and certain men	807	73 POEMS 35	11

+WOMAN
FOR CONTEXT, SEE	104	& POST IMPR 14	8
FOR CONTEXT, SEE	492	50 POEMS 6	8
FOR CONTEXT, SEE	654	(CHAIRE) 56	7
FOR CONTEXT, SEE	700	95 POEMS 28	4

+WOMANSELLINGBALLOON
| ott er s thesillyold WomanSellingBalloonS In theex qui site | 104 | & POST IMPR 14 | 17 |

WOMB
| suddenly into a dangerous womb of cringing air) the | 115 | & PORTRAIT 8 | 11 |
| history oped her teeming womb said demon for to | 552 | 1 X 1 12 | 21 |

WOMEN
yellow dawn, into the women-coloured twilight i smilingly	66	T&C POST IMPR 3	8
men and intotheslow hot women my Stomach ruBSiTSElf	101	& POST IMPR 11	62
(a spring of wines women and window-sills) i met	158	& SON ACTU 7	4
so? hush--the author of Women By Night whose latest	245	IS 5 ONE 16	8
motors "my" yachts wolfhounds women) and the will to	394	NO THANKS 11	4
at this) window; yes women sturdily meander in my	435	NO THANKS 51	34
he danced his did. Women and men (both little	515	50 POEMS 29	5
and if by yes. Women and men (both dong	515	50 POEMS 29	33
men must loaf and women must lay) and she	552	1 X 1 12	18
to the dearest little women alive (but jim stood	709	95 POEMS 37	14

+WOMEN
FOR CONTEXT, SEE	101	& POST IMPR 11	61
FOR CONTEXT, SEE	444	NO THANKS 59	7
FOR CONTEXT, SEE	500	50 POEMS 14	22
FOR CONTEXT, SEE	507	50 POEMS 21	21

WOMEN-COLOURED
| yellow dawn, into the women-coloured twilight i smilingly | 66 | T&C POST IMPR 3 | 8 |

WOMENLIKE
| leaves Easily through voices womenlike telling of death love | 356 | VIVA 47 | 4 |

WON
/ / / mouse) Won derfully is anyone else	397	NO THANKS 14	1
s(not a fraid of moon You) not-mere-ly-won-der-ing-&	469	NEW POEMS 7	20
true wars are never won / / / /	570	1 X 1 30	10
and (except nothing) nothing's won --but if a look	580	1 X 1 40	18
sky grow one with won der until (see the)	715	95 POEMS 43	10
ing downdowndown com; ing won der ful sun moon	840	73 POEMS 68	9

WON'T
ask of shad- ow won't you have a drink?	97	& POST IMPR 8	41
She Win and you won't be sorry And The	125	& SEVEN POEMS 4	23
its ring and there won't be a single place	192	XLI CHANSONS 2	20
therehere And) i say "won't you" (remembering) knowing that	353	VIVA 44	24
most (people simply can't) won't (most parent people mustn't	412	NO THANKS 29	4
kumrads don't and kumrads won't believe in life) and	413	NO THANKS 30	5
die but the doctors won't let her comma considers	499	50 POEMS 13	3
wasn't and isn't and won't be words while possibly	631	(CHAIRE) 33	9
to this dame: he won't be out of work	790	73 POEMS 18	7

		PAGE	TITLE	LINE
WONDER				
to touch the yellow wonder of her hair. /		8	T&C OF NICOL	32
and thou didst not wonder thy face is as		27	T&C ORIENTALE 1	17
girl eyes sincere with wonder a poise a wounding		54	T&C PORTRAIT 2	5
morning, O do not wonder that (just at the		92	& POST IMPR 4	17
god knows makes me wonder if i'm alive (eye		166	& SON ACTU 15	10
the night. makes me wonder if, if i am		166	& SON ACTU 15	12
always try to not wonder how let's say elation		229	IS 5 ONE FRAN	12
or never never to wonder about guys you used		242	IS 5 ONE 13	4
to never, never really wonder i mean about the		242	IS 5 ONE 13	16
he think about, i wonder as over this floor		286	IS 5 FOUR 3	3
the whole intend" they wonder. oh and they cry		295	IS 5 FOUR 12	17
and hat --(and i wonder just why that should		296	IS 5 FOUR 13	9
please him or i wonder what he does) and		296	IS 5 FOUR 13	10
time is it i wonder never mind consider rather		322	VIVA 14	1
/ / i'd think "wonder if" if i were		353	VIVA 44	1
persuade even silence: therefore wonder opens a gate; the		376	VIVA 67	9
& sunsmell (sometimes a wonder of wild roses sometimes)		512	50 POEMS 26	31
neddy) but under the wonder is over the why		513	50 POEMS 27	33
Weavingly now one by wonder (on twilight) they come		557	1 X 1 17	12
luckiest what of the wonder (beingest growingest) over all		590	1 X 1 50	19
nothing ignoble) everywhere wonder / / / /		658	{CHAIRE} 60	26
all in a singing wonder of blossoming yes riding)		661	{CHAIRE} 63	3
sing, my love and wonder) is something you have		686	95 POEMS 14	5
age-- read for sheer wonder mere surprise (then turn		689	95 POEMS 17	3
away from them (i wonder) or isn't she a		724	95 POEMS 52	15
breathe, itself becomes her wonder --and wonderful is death;		742	95 POEMS 70	15
through sleeping firsts of wonder) child unbreathingly share		757	95 POEMS 85	28
what despair preaches myriad wonder people of a person;		764	95 POEMS 90	43
and this is the wonder that's keeping the stars		766	95 POEMS 92	14
are through the (with wonder into colours all into		778	73 POEMS 6	3
all into singing) may wonder a with deep (A		778	73 POEMS 6	5
with deep (A so wonder pure) even than the		778	73 POEMS 6	6
dust expect hope doubt (wonder mistrust) despair and right		780	73 POEMS 8	3
eagerly tumbl ing through wonder ful sunlight --look--		835	73 POEMS 63	8
agony of time --small wonder such a monster's fellowmen		842	73 POEMS 70	13
timelessly celebrates the merciful wonder no world deny may		845	73 POEMS 73	14
+WONDER				
FOR CONTEXT, SEE		715	95 POEMS 43	10
WONDERED				
world.... But i have wondered since isn't it odd		172	& SON ACTU 21	9
april) must often have wondered "most people be quite		738	95 POEMS 66	11
WONDERFUL				
when the world is puddle-wonderful the queer old balloonman		24	T&C CHANSONS 1	10
daisies through the field wonderful with eyes a little		26	T&C CHANSONS 3	6
/ any man is wonderful and a formula a		68	T&C POST IMPR 5	1
space is a little wonderful, and say Perhaps her		82	T&C SON ACTU 1	13
my love emits a wonderful smell in my mind,		152	& SON ACTU 1	7
meanwhile these speak her wonderful But i (having in		162	& SON ACTU 11	8
through the forest of wonderful, and that my feet		216	XLI SONNETS 12	12
guess how much my wonderful jealousy is dark if		292	IS 5 FOUR 9	16
--but if yourself consider wonderful that your (how luminous)		379	VIVA 70	10
think it is less wonderful than this only by		379	VIVA 70	13
How many winds make wonderful and is luck The		395	NO THANKS 12	2
of one (ask super-) wonderful (mother) child is a		398	NO THANKS 15	5
raving city screamingly street wonderful flowers And o the		437	NO THANKS 53	3
soursweet bedtime -less un- (wonderful) story atrickling a		464	NEW POEMS 2	6
uirmwri th-ing out of wonderful thunder! of? ocean. a		469	NEW POEMS 7	9
(his lousy eyes roaming) wonderful all sky (a little		501	50 POEMS 15	8
beyond where what a wonderful thing is the end		593	1 X 1 53	19
alive we're alive) we're wonderful one times one /		594	1 X 1 54	45
Snowing Isn't That Perfectly Wonderful / / / /		629	{CHAIRE} 31	22
now & then my wonderful friend dominic depaola gives		680	95 POEMS 8	23
becomes her wonder --and wonderful is death; but more,		742	95 POEMS 70	16
slightly mad but very wonderful in bed --saints and		794	73 POEMS 22	6
she) under are this wonderful tree smiling stand (all		832	73 POEMS 60	4
+WONDERFUL				
FOR CONTEXT, SEE		835	73 POEMS 63	8

	PAGE	TITLE	LINE

+WONDERFUL (CONTINUED)
FOR CONTEXT, SEE . . . . 840 73 POEMS 68   9
WONDERFULLY
counting the moved myriads wonderfully loved, (hasten, it is   9 T&C SONGS 1   15
clumsy brightness of air wonderfully stumbled above the . . . 173 & SON ACTU 22   3
into the abyss --and wonderfully i fell through the . . . . . 360 VIVA 51   18
alive sing more will wonderfully birds than are / . . . . . . 811 73 POEMS 39   14
+WONDERFULLY
FOR CONTEXT, SEE . . . . 397 NO THANKS 14   1
WONDERING
no lingering no backward- wondering be unto us O . . . . . . 41 T&C AMORES 5   27
are transferred with dusk) wondering why this star does . . . 428 NO THANKS 45   4
of stare are still wondering if the stunt was . . . . 605 (CHAIRE) 7   14
+WONDERING
FOR CONTEXT, SEE . . . . 469 NEW POEMS 7   20
FOR CONTEXT, SEE . . . . 591 1 X 1 51   10
WONDERINGLY
wandering in merciful miracles wonderingly celebrate day and 582 1 X 1 42   3
in fragrance and song wonderingly come (brighter than . . . . 778 73 POEMS 6   13
WONDERINGS
joy) and whiteliest all wonderings are silence is becom . . . 715 95 POEMS 43   16
WONDERLESS
simply joining with the wonderless city's sublime cheap . . . 218 XLI SONNETS 14   6
WONDERS
croscopic world's whens, wheels; wonders: murders. cries: . . 361 VIVA 52   17
earth) a procession of wonders huger than prove our . . . . . 575 1 X 1 35   10
thing as spring and wonders why So gay gay . . . . 685 95 POEMS 13   8
WONDROUS
quite ennobling forsooth? One wondrous fine sonofabitch (to . 254 IS 5 ONE 25   5
WONENS
(all decent mem and wonens will allows which if . . . . . . 500 50 POEMS 14   22
WONG
/ / / Wing Wong, uninterred at twice fortyeight, ... 341 VIVA 32   1
of eager bosoms" Wing Wong / / / / . . . . 341 VIVA 32   23
WONT
aglow) my soul is wont wholly to know the . . . . 19 T&C PUELLA MEA 109
WOO
the gentle who-horns says-does moo-woo (the prance with the . 773 73 POEMS 1   8
WOOD
terminated in fists hair wood erect cursing hatless who . . . 277 IS 5 THREE 1   8
what yoo-gointa-doo? (ice coal wood man) nic he like . . . . 618 (CHAIRE) 20   20
+WOOD
FOR CONTEXT, SEE . . . . 680 95 POEMS 8   5
WOODEN
Jesus sags in frolicsome wooden agony). / / / . . . . 134 & SON REAL 5   16
face, and how these wooden big two feet conclude . . . . . . 229 IS 5 ONE FRAN   4
+WOODROW
FOR CONTEXT, SEE . . . . 321 VIVA 13   5
WOODS
and. press --in the woods which stutter and sing . . . . . . 163 & SON ACTU 12   12
WOOER
blithe a doer a wooer some limber and lithe . . . . 509 50 POEMS 23   9
WOOL
thoughts more white than wool My thought is sorrowful: . . . 11 T&C SONGS 2   14
WOOLWORTH
the tongue sits the Woolworth building a serene . . . . . . 201 XLI PORTRAIT 9   14
WOOLWORTHIAN
annihi- lation demonstrating from woolworthian pinnacle a . . 197 XLI PORTRAIT 5   7
WOOPSING
daughter item son a woopsing queer colon hobby photography . 499 50 POEMS 13   9
WOP
may say professor" asleep wop "shapley has compared the . . . 464 NEW POEMS 2   12
Big Boss (crying) jew wop rich poor (sing ing) . . . . 618 (CHAIRE) 20   11
WORD
singer and his wandering word. / / / / . . . . 7 T&C EPITHALAM 168
send me a little word; that i may go . . . . 76 T&C SON UNRE 1   10
squeeze- into-largeness without one word and you lie still . 127 & SEVEN POEMS 5   34
forever subject his Earliest word wheeled out on the . . . . 197 XLI PORTRAIT 5   21

		PAGE	TITLE	LINE
WORD (CONTINUED)				
's no sharpest neat word for the thing. Her		227	IS 5 ONE GERT	11
antibolshevistic gents (each manufacturing word by word his .		266	IS 5 TWO 1	10
(each manufacturing word by word his own unrivalled brand . .		266	IS 5 TWO 1	10
image of one fatal word; so that my life		360	VIVA 51	22
graves der, speaking (says. word Less) ly (goes folds? . . .		417	NO THANKS 34	5
let it go--the smashed word broken open vow or		569	1 X 1 29	2
more than any bright word may cry --even the		605	{CHAIRE} 7	7
a hand and the word love underlined this is		647	{CHAIRE} 49	4
/ if up's the word; and a world grows		769	95 POEMS 95	1
whole buck' not a word this stranger replied-- but		800	73 POEMS 28	13
for which i've no word except alive --that is, ...		802	73 POEMS 30	14
while never saying a word who was anything but		802	73 POEMS 30	25
+WORD				
FOR CONTEXT, SEE		240	IS 5 ONE 11	2
WORDLESS				
waiting years, curtained with wordless worship absolute, unto		6	T&C EPITHALAM	115
semiluminous nausea A vast wordless nondescript genie of . .		96	& POST IMPR 8	33
+WORDLESSLY				
FOR CONTEXT, SEE		417	NO THANKS 34	5
WORDS				
anguish quivers to your words, As to a flight		11	T&C SONGS 2	17
she of whose body words are afraid perfectly beautiful . . .		22	T&C PUELLA MEA	240
beautiful is, forgive these words which i have made.		22	T&C PUELLA MEA	242
or such great writhing words as, uttering overmuch, stand . .		76	T&C SON UNRE 1	7
all songs containing the words country home and mother . . .		204	XLI LA GUERRE 2	7
No gas. Flynn" the words drizzle untidily from released . . .		226	IS 5 ONE MAME	9
you with hopes and words and with so and		289	IS 5 FOUR 6	16
who's myself's Antimere Should words carry weapons) are not .		395	NO THANKS 12	10
swallow a man; three words im -prison a woman		491	50 POEMS 5	13
late worms are the words but joy's the voice		511	50 POEMS 25	22
isn't and won't be words while possibly not (at		631	{CHAIRE} 33	9
(like any these my) words of words turn to		761	95 POEMS 88	13
these my) words of words turn to a silence		761	95 POEMS 88	13
first) beasts uttered human words --our second coming made .		844	73 POEMS 72	1
+WORDS				
FOR CONTEXT, SEE		409	NO THANKS 26	4
WORE				
bangup time wen nobody wore no cloze an went		237	IS 5 ONE 8	17
truth was who: and wore his (mountains understand how) . . .		786	73 POEMS 14	7
WORK				
before this its hideous Work most old Whose battening		77	T&C SON UNRE 2	11
so naked for immortal work his shoulders marched against . .		521	50 POEMS 34	43
much cheap me i work i know i say		523	50 POEMS 36	16
here is hands is work since i am born		523	50 POEMS 36	20
won't be out of work while she can swarm.		790	73 POEMS 18	7
as can trust) they work and they pray and		801	73 POEMS 29	27
WORKED				
its point Jimmie's sister worked for Dick. And had		149	& SON REAL 20	7
WORKINGMAN				
/ / / / workingman with hand so hairy-sturdy		233	IS 5 ONE 4	1
already is the poorbuthonest workingman (by that bright flame		254	IS 5 ONE 25	16
WORKMEN				
you perhaps know these workmen? / / / /		378	VIVA 69	16
WORLD				
perpetual round a pale world gathers comfort to her		5	T&C EPITHALAM	82
being whiter than this world) exhales the hovering high . . .		5	T&C EPITHALAM	101
to strike the young world into smoking song-- as		7	T&C EPITHALAM	163
dangles therefrom the purpled world will dance upon Between .		16	T&C SONGS 6	4
moving, through the new world scarce astir my fragile		17	T&C PUELLA MEA	12
with dew when the world was young and new		18	T&C PUELLA MEA	54
flower such as the world had in Springtime when		18	T&C PUELLA MEA	55
in Springtime when the world was mad and Launcelot		18	T&C PUELLA MEA	56
with silence when the world was young and Diarmuid		18	T&C PUELLA MEA	59
them glad, when the world was young and mad, ...		20	T&C PUELLA MEA	131
exquisitely err.) When the world was like a song		22	T&C PUELLA MEA	221
and long (when the world was like a flower		22	T&C PUELLA MEA	226
greatest lovers in the world! who with Grania strangely . . .		22	T&C PUELLA MEA	244

WORLD (CONTINUED)

	PAGE	TITLE	LINE
whose watering lips the world poises a moment (futile, . . .	23	T&C PUELLA MEA	267
fragile hour (when the world was like a tale	23	T&C PUELLA MEA	276
dream (in the lazy world and new sweetly used	23	T&C PUELLA MEA	285
Just- spring when the world is mud- luscious the	24	T&C CHANSONS 1	2
it's spring when the world is puddle-wonderful the queer . .	24	T&C CHANSONS 1	10
to sleep upon the world and the earth withers	38	T&C AMORES 3	4
it is dawn the world goes forth to murder	50	T&C IMPRESS 4	10
feet incorrigible ragging the world, / / / /	61	T&C PORTRAIT 9	37
minute mind of the world. The lean and definite	62	T&C PORTRAIT 10	9
light twitching at the world / / / /	64	T&C POST IMPR 1	12
think?) the i do, world is probably made of	66	T&C POST IMPR 3	14
the perfume of the world (and just as smaller	71	T&C SON REAL 2	10
final curtain strikes the world away, leaving to shadowy . .	75	T&C SON REAL 6	2
imminently across the renewed world" to me said the)	91	& POST IMPR 3	18
loving around beers the world has these men's hands	114	& PORTRAIT 7	13
m m make the world safe for democracy it	125	& SEVEN POEMS 4	11
laughter splashed from the world prettily upward, mock . . .	133	& SON REAL 4	5
my eyes, the killed world wriggled like a twitched	135	& SON REAL 6	17
beautifully swims the fooling world in my huge blood, ...	157	& SON ACTU 6	11
of anything, maybe the world.... But i have wondered	172	& SON ACTU 21	9
darkness from our searched world should wrest the rare . . .	205	XLI SONNETS 1	1
silver-fingered fountain steals the world. / / / /	208	XLI SONNETS 4	14
throstles Art is O World O Life a formula:	230	IS 5 ONE 2	32
tumbled successfully into the world the animals continued . .	241	IS 5 ONE 12	5
people who rule this world (and me and you	250	IS 5 ONE 21	3
unsullied stands, before the world: with manly heart and . .	273	IS 5 TWO 8	17
nothing left of the world but into this noth	278	IS 5 THREE 2	17
of fire all the world becoming bright and little	283	IS 5 THREE 7	27
Spring is in the world my blood approves, and	290	IS 5 FOUR 7	6
and over the ripe world wanders with a near	293	IS 5 FOUR 10	24
your hair --let the world say "his most wise	306	IS 5 FIVE 5	9
think of (sh) the world renowned investigator of paper . . .	326	VIVA 18	6
very diminishing vicarious ughhuh world (the pertly papped .	337	VIVA 28	11
how dis (appeared cleverly) world iS Slapped: with; liGhtninG	347	VIVA 38	4
balloon until the smallening world became absurd; him did . .	360	VIVA 51	14
to perceive in this world equals the power of	366	VIVA 57	13
in the dark) this world has been Picked, like	370	VIVA 61	3
guess though wish and world go down, one poem	372	VIVA 63	15
how to run the world) A always don't there	390	NO THANKS 7	1
vicians and all the world howls stadesmen beware of	405	NO THANKS 22	3
right about the g.o. world what's wrong with (between	411	NO THANKS 28	8
you can withholding nothing) World, conceive a man /	420	NO THANKS 37	14
whose mad skill each world of blood is made	424	NO THANKS 41	13
night did the great world (in darkly taking rain)	432	NO THANKS 49	2
cannot) tear up the world: & toss it away;	433	NO THANKS 50	2
man? King Christ, this world is all aleak; and	438	NO THANKS 54	25
they spawn and a world is for them, them;	439	NO THANKS 55	3
places yes is a world & in this world	443	NO THANKS 58	6
world & in this world of yes live (skilfully	443	NO THANKS 58	7
steep fragrance of eternity) world by than worlds immenser .	450	NO THANKS 65	9
by than worlds immenser world will pray so (unlove	450	NO THANKS 65	9
riches of our pretty world sweetly who flourishes, swiftly .	456	NO THANKS 71	5
simplicity than makes a world) / / / /	506	50 POEMS 20	14
nor flatfolk prove their world is round nor dingsters	511	50 POEMS 25	17
vanishing from a this world into bigger much some	516	50 POEMS 30	14
laugh and build a world with snow. My father	521	50 POEMS 34	48
/ i say no world can hold a you	523	50 POEMS 36	1
nothing i say the world not fit you) he	523	50 POEMS 36	27
not (i say the world yes any world is	523	50 POEMS 36	29
the world yes any world is much too non	523	50 POEMS 36	30
morning with a warm world in it (kiss me)	529	50 POEMS 41	5
of despair into hugeness world system universe and bang . . .	531	50 POEMS 43	2
on its unself. A world of made is not	554	1 X 1 14	9
made is not a world of born--pity poor flesh	554	1 X 1 14	10
help murder save the world" what world? is it	555	1 X 1 15	1
save the world" what world? is it themselves these	555	1 X 1 15	2
all sky (really unreal world, will you perhaps do	558	1 X 1 18	14

904

	PAGE	TITLE	LINE
WORLD (CONTINUED)			
was big as the world aint square with room	568 1 X 1 28		17
canoe and a whole world and then a single	572 1 X 1 32		16
(if disappear should some world) selves . No doing	577 1 X 1 37		8
strawberry bang this blueeyed world (on which are wintry . .	585 1 X 1 45		4
a treasure of tiniest world a piece of forever	586 1 X 1 46		3
(in sad this havingest world) most merry most fair	590 1 X 1 50		3
one's everyanything so so world is a leaf so	594 1 X 1 54		19
or i and every world, before silence begins a	601 (CHAIRE) 3		19
someone's kitchenette) wheezing bulgily world of genial plac	607 (CHAIRE) 9		4
keen he throws the world a kiss and slings	624 (CHAIRE) 26		18
lives lurch a once world quickly from rises army	633 (CHAIRE) 35		2
tastes If as some world of a spark 's	639 (CHAIRE) 41		7
not to save a world for stalin was he	643 (CHAIRE) 45		3
the papery weightless diminutive world with a hole in	652 (CHAIRE) 54		10
dream: is amazing) a worlD. and in this world	657 (CHAIRE) 59		10
worlD. and in this world lies: smoothbeautifuL ly folded; . .	657 (CHAIRE) 59		11
are in you) this world (as timorous itsters all	664 (CHAIRE) 66		13
love) alive than every world can understand and now	667 (CHAIRE) 69		4
dull cowardice called a world vanishes, teach disappearing .	669 (CHAIRE) 71		12
his earth; so anyone's world does -n't interest him	676 95 POEMS 4		4
as small as a world and as large as	682 95 POEMS 10		10
& as loveless some world not any un god	698 95 POEMS 26		3
girl each brings a world to build our clown	716 95 POEMS 44		11
what calls itself a world should have the luck	717 95 POEMS 45		9
bloodlight climbs the onlying world) whose silence are cries	719 95 POEMS 47		3
one who feels a world crylaughingly float away leaving . . .	720 95 POEMS 48		7
wedding) never mind a world with its villains or	732 95 POEMS 60		13
roses of her improbable world and without any doubt	748 95 POEMS 76		3
(far from the frantic world with its rapture and	749 95 POEMS 77		14
gaining --love! if a world ends more than all	750 95 POEMS 78		15
heartbeats dare some upward world of each more most	757 95 POEMS 85		6
big wickedly worlds of world disappear all and (like	761 95 POEMS 88		12
sweet) i want no world (for beautiful you are	766 95 POEMS 92		7
beautiful you are my world, my true) and it's	766 95 POEMS 92		7
the word; and a world grows greener minute by	769 95 POEMS 95		1
of hate sometimes called world) to sing / /	783 73 POEMS 11		8
whisper asks (of a world born deaf) "heaven or	787 73 POEMS 15		15
(over a snowstopped silent world) one spirit serenely truly .	808 73 POEMS 36		2
feel-- how should some world (we marvel) doubt, for	809 73 POEMS 37		9
(only which is this world) more my life does	810 73 POEMS 38		3
longer blinded with a world; and let her heart's	811 73 POEMS 39		6
/ while a once world slips from few of	822 73 POEMS 50		1
chickadee to all the world, but to me some	828 73 POEMS 56		4
grown -up i&you- ful world of known) who and	832 73 POEMS 60		11
/ now does our world descend the path to	834 73 POEMS 62		1
The Policemen In The World / / / /	835 73 POEMS 63		31
me why this summer world (and you and i	836 73 POEMS 64		3
things appear) death's: any world must always half perceive.	845 73 POEMS 73		4
universe --love. Each believing world denies, whereas your .	845 73 POEMS 73		11
the merciful wonder no world deny may or believe	845 73 POEMS 73		14
+WORLD			
FOR CONTEXT, SEE	174 & SON ACTU 23		3
FOR CONTEXT, SEE	226 IS 5 ONE MAME		10
FOR CONTEXT, SEE	237 IS 5 ONE 8		16
FOR CONTEXT, SEE	310 VIVA 2		1
FOR CONTEXT, SEE	411 NO THANKS 28		10
FOR CONTEXT, SEE	411 NO THANKS 28		12
FOR CONTEXT, SEE	423 NO THANKS 40		37
FOR CONTEXT, SEE	503 50 POEMS 17		8
FOR CONTEXT, SEE	519 50 POEMS 33		9
FOR CONTEXT, SEE	519 50 POEMS 33		19
FOR CONTEXT, SEE	615 (CHAIRE) 17		17
FOR CONTEXT, SEE	807 73 POEMS 35		11
FOR CONTEXT, SEE	841 73 POEMS 69		16
WORLD'S			
flower-- whence is the world's insufferable clay clothed with	6 T&C EPITHALAM		135
the pride of the world's queen: each is a	21 T&C PUELLA MEA		208

WORLD'S (CONTINUED)
    eyes.... too, since the world's but a piece of . . . . 141 & SON REAL 12   5
    little dizzy did the world's smell (but i was . . . . 174 & SON ACTU 23   11
    slowness (deftly muting the world's texture with drifted . . 299 IS 5 FOUR 16   4
    der the mi croscopic world's whens, wheels; wonders: murders. 361 VIVA 52   16
    concession at the recent world's fair was the paytoilet . . . 425 NO THANKS 42   16
    neral rise eyes "this world's made 'bout right it's . . . . . 567 1 X 1 27   9
    (sh) who made the world's best one hand snatch . . . . 645 {CHAIRE} 47   4
    swim signals all some world's millionary mind never may . . . 818 73 POEMS 46   12
+WORLDED
    FOR CONTEXT, SEE . . . . 517 50 POEMS 31   4
WORLDS
    the fatal flight of worlds whereto this earth's a . . . . . . 81 T&C SON UNRE 6   5
    love You (thickness means worlds inhabited by roamingly stern 363 VIVA 54   3
    rare perfectly dear (and worlds whirl beyond worlds: immortal 376 VIVA 67   12
    (and worlds whirl beyond worlds: immortal yonder collidingly 376 VIVA 67   12
    though all the weird worlds must be opened?) . . . . 377 VIVA 68   14
    live (skilfully curled) all worlds / / / / . . . . 443 NO THANKS 58   10
    eternity) world by than worlds immenser world will pray . . . 450 NO THANKS 65   9
    my) heart before how worlds delicate of bombast--papery what 480 NEW POEMS 18   16
    chickadee mountain. Mountain) whycoloured worlds of because . 512 50 POEMS 26   28
    day of day are worlds collapsing? any was a . . . . 538 50 POEMS 50   9
    angel; or (as various worlds he'll spurn rather than . . . . 562 1 X 1 22   7
    open green those (dear) worlds of than great more . . . . . . 573 1 X 1 33   3
    than begin are, the worlds move in your (and . . . . 575 1 X 1 35   39
    million hundred more bright worlds than merely by doubting . 580 1 X 1 40   13
    so now million many worlds in each least less . . . . 603 {CHAIRE} 5   1
    life (hark! what silence)?" "Worlds? o no: i'm certain . . . 603 {CHAIRE} 5   5
    (look again) flowers." "Don't worlds open and worlds close?" 603 {CHAIRE} 5   6
    "Don't worlds open and worlds close?" "Worlds do, but . . . . 603 {CHAIRE} 5   7
    open and worlds close?" "Worlds do, but differently; or . . . 603 {CHAIRE} 5   7
    differently; or as if worlds wanted us to understand . . . . 603 {CHAIRE} 5   8
    were wise." "You mean worlds may have better luck, ... 603 {CHAIRE} 5   11
    day?" "Or worse! poor worlds; i mean they're possible . . . . 603 {CHAIRE} 5   12
    "only are quite what worlds merely might be / . . . . 603 {CHAIRE} 5   14
    and under all possible worlds in love a billion . . . . . . 664 {CHAIRE} 66   18
    feel that we & worlds are less alive than . . . . 680 95 POEMS 8   29
    ends more than all worlds begin to (see?) begin . . . . 750 95 POEMS 78   16
    compulsions doubts & corners) worlds are to dream now . . . . 755 95 POEMS 83   19
    safely small big wickedly worlds of world disappear all . . . 761 95 POEMS 88   12
    this: to feel) poor worlds must merely do, which . . . . . . 762 95 POEMS 89   3
    giving only) is living" worlds of prose mind utterly . . . . 763 95 POEMS 90   19
    my darling: while old worlds and young (big little . . . . . 776 73 POEMS 4   5
    (big little and all worlds) merely have the must . . . . . . 776 73 POEMS 4   7
    is exactly theirs (dull worlds or keen; big little . . . . . 776 73 POEMS 4   11
    right goes wrong (dim worlds or bright; big little . . . . . 776 73 POEMS 4   27
    not to die) but worlds are made of hello . . . . 776 73 POEMS 4   37
    that she's warming three worlds) who's ama zingly Eye . . . . 827 73 POEMS 55   12
    / / / all worlds have halfsight, seeing either . . . . 845 73 POEMS 73   1
+WORLDS
    FOR CONTEXT, SEE . . . . 829 73 POEMS 57   13
WORM
    have begun the hair's worm huge, ecstatic, rathe.... yours . 84 T&C SON ACTU 3   11
    exactly kiss the trite worm of her nakedness until . . . . . 164 & SON ACTU 13   5
    with memories (this white worm and i who love . . . . 164 & SON ACTU 13   12
    Sol and started a worm farm) / / / . . . . 239 IS 5 ONE 10   38
+WORMING
    FOR CONTEXT, SEE . . . . 100 & POST IMPR 11   14
WORMPERUSED
    feed with felicities me wormperused by whom the hungering . . 212 XLI SONNETS 8   7
WORMS
    to the noise of worms. in the eligible day . . . . 43 T&C AMORES 7   22
    under the noise of worms / / / / . . . . 43 T&C AMORES 7   40
    spring will bring her worms rushing through loam. (afterward 67 T&C POST IMPR 4   12
    minute hips, O press worms rushing slowly through loam . . . 67 T&C POST IMPR 4   30
    noiseless truth of swirling worms is tomorrow / / . . . . . 113 & PORTRAIT 6   118
    (Must be summer. Hush. Worms.) But It's Nicer To . . . . . . 130 & SON REAL 1   12
    handfuls of little normal worms. Dress deftly your flesh . . 161 & SON ACTU 10   8

WORMS (CONTINUED)

methodical. He suddenly tasted worms windows and roses he . . 170 & SON ACTU 19   12
with time and his worms, when loveliness says sweetly . . . . 183 XLI SONGS 5   8
moonlight ourselves against the worms hate laugh shimmy / . . 238 IS 5 ONE 9   20
him into nibbling final worms / / / / . . . . 277 IS 5 THREE 1   24
ground) but though with wormS eyes writhe amor (Though . . . 361 VIVA 52   6
men are caught by worms (love may not care . . . . 446 NO THANKS 61   5
not be too late worms are the words but . . . . 511 50 POEMS 25   22
Who from sharp soft worms of spiralling why and . . . . 522 50 POEMS 35   12

WORMSMILE

thickly starhums wherefore & wormSmile eternal; quite perhaps 371 VIVA 62   24

WORN

performing rose of you, worn upon my mind all . . . . 165 & SON ACTU 14   2

WORRY

we dearie we should worry about the rain huh . . . . 109 & PORTRAIT 5   8
of it we should worry in every language even . . . . 268 IS 5 TWO 3   5
full of an important worry) halt stop forget relax . . . . . 393 NO THANKS 10   4
cities --i do not worry if briefer days grow . . . . 749 95 POEMS 77   3
nature --i do not worry if longer nights grow . . . . 749 95 POEMS 77   15

WORSE

whose here is always worse than naught, feels the . . . . . . 81 T&C SON UNRE 6 11
boots were much the worse, and egged the firstclassprivates . 339 VIVA 30   26
ought to feel less worse (but only sameness is . . . . 466 NEW POEMS 4   24
better is wiser for worse. Give liz (take! tommy) . . . . . . 513 50 POEMS 27   10
wicked and life is worse squats a big dove . . . . 545 1 X 1 5   10
or what may be worse and what may be . . . . 568 1 X 1 28   22
luck, some day?" "Or worse! poor worlds; i mean . . . . 603 {CHAIRE} 5   12
no evil is so worse than worst you fall . . . . 679 95 POEMS 7   12
old swimminghole" "i'd be worse than a fool to . . . . 707 95 POEMS 35   3

+WORSE

FOR CONTEXT, SEE . . . . 544 1 X 1 4   11
FOR CONTEXT, SEE . . . . 800 73 POEMS 28   8

WORSHIP

years, curtained with wordless worship absolute, unto the . .   6 T&C EPITHALAM 115
Satan dead, do fearers worship Much and Quick; badness . . . 438 NO THANKS 54   2

WORSHIPPED

undeath) salute. and having worshipped for my doom pass . . . 358 VIVA 49   14

+WORSHIPPED

FOR CONTEXT, SEE . . . . 320 VIVA 12   9

WORSHIPPER

purple dark- ness a worshipper prostrate within twitching . . 28 T&C ORIENTALE 2 13

WORSHIPPING

/ / / / worshipping Same they squirm and . . . . 439 NO THANKS 55   1
ours for the mere worshipping (as calmly as if . . . . 617 {CHAIRE} 19   12

WORSHIPS

through moaned space god worships God-- (behold! where chaste 77 T&C SON UNRE 2 15
beautiful" her, my life worships and (night) then "everything 572 1 X 1 32   12

WORST

remember how-- braving the worst, of peril heedless, each . . 266 IS 5 TWO 1   18
humbly and whom for worst or best (and proudly . . . . 441 NO THANKS 56   52
is so worse than worst you fall in hate . . . . 679 95 POEMS 7   12

WORTH

year something which is worth the whole, an inch . . . . . . 161 & SON ACTU 10   13
much earth is Madge worth? Inquire of the flower . . . . . . 183 XLI SONGS 5   13
/ / IKEY (GOLDBERG)'S WORTH I'M TOLD $ SEVERAL . . . . 244 IS 5 ONE 15   1
who naked is is worth a million statues / . . . . 247 IS 5 ONE 18   8
by threats of something worth than death to change . . . . . 544 1 X 1 4   11
imagine life is not worth dying, if (and when) . . . . 744 95 POEMS 72   2

WORTHLESS

ways retchings of a worthless lamp. when With a . . . . 96 & POST IMPR 8   26
your-and my- idle vertical worthless self unite in a . . . . 260 IS 5 ONE 30   15

WORTHY

vaguely watching that mountainous worthy in the fragile act . 228 IS 5 ONE MARJ   12
such being a conduct worthy of more ponderous wishes . . . . 328 VIVA 19   6

WOULD

(or seeming that they would mistrust a while the . . . . . .   6 T&C EPITHALAM 140
thirsty blood of Paris would not all the Troys . . . . 18 T&C PUELLA MEA 67
if for fear you would espy the little distinct . . . . 22 T&C PUELLA MEA 216

		PAGE	TITLE	LINE

WOULD (CONTINUED)

	PAGE	TITLE	LINE
dreamed i thought you would have deceived me and	30	T&C ORIENTALE 4	31
in nothingness for we would sleep this is the	41	T&C AMORES 5	24
nobody (knows and WhoEver would)? dance lewd dollies pretty .	101	& POST IMPR 11	80
big brother who is would don't punish us for	117	& PORTRAIT 10	19
ands All the chips would kid Jimmie to give	149	& SON REAL 20	10
-over. fiftythree (and one would see if it could)	150	& SON REAL 21	2
just as your mother would, only don't be afraid	192	XLI CHANSONS 2	11
largest existence. (when he would extemporise the innovation	197	XLI PORTRAIT 5	14
love you because you would rather black the boots	204	XLI LA GUERRE 2	2
from his watch-chain which would be embarrassing for both . .	204	XLI LA GUERRE 2	4
this and truly i would be near when his	215	XLI SONNETS 11	5
But of all most would i be one of	215	XLI SONNETS 11	9
drooping bloated calves i would receive the answer more . . .	229	IS 5 ONE FRAN	7
radically defunct periodical. i would suggest that certain .	230	IS 5 ONE 2	18
my most intimate friends would never have gathered. A	262	IS 5 ONE 32	14
was horribly scared i would actually fall off the	263	IS 5 ONE 32	62
perfectly clear, it entirely would have been not my	263	IS 5 ONE 32	64
75 done this nobody would have believed would they	270	IS 5 TWO 5	3
nobody would have believed would they no kidding this	270	IS 5 TWO 5	5
mother hoped that i would die etcetera bravely of	276	IS 5 TWO 10	14
if I could, they would somehow not Be real"	338	VIVA 29	9
I had guessed everything would be; even remembering the . . .	338	VIVA 29	18
wig and polished buttons) would take you away --and	365	VIVA 56	13
--and all the clocks would run down the next	365	VIVA 56	14
our mingling spirits, you would disappear unreally; as this .	379	VIVA 70	7
a Man whom both would call their friend and	394	NO THANKS 11	9
envy neither; nor bewail (would rather make than have	394	NO THANKS 11	11
should he have anything would give a little more	420	NO THANKS 37	2
who laugh like they would fall apart and masturbate	427	NO THANKS 44	11
they kill like you would take a piss they	427	NO THANKS 44	16
imagined life adventuring who would feel if spring's least .	450	NO THANKS 65	13
his bread because he would not sell his head)	473	NEW POEMS 11	3
be? their socalled hearts would think these socalled people .	510	50 POEMS 24	2
had their minds socalled would not exist but if	510	50 POEMS 24	4
life could its breath would stink and as for	510	50 POEMS 24	7
thousand years. Expecting more would be neither fantastic nor	514	50 POEMS 28	3
firm) under his eyes would stir and squirm newly	520	50 POEMS 34	8
the wrists of twilight would rejoice keen as midsummer's . .	520	50 POEMS 34	24
comes here a man would have from madame death	531	50 POEMS 43	9
everywhere, even more true would truest lovers grow if . . .	576	1 X 1 36	11
all shall, their eyes would never miss a yes)	576	1 X 1 36	14
murmurs; the fool) "truth would prove truthless and life . .	625	{CHAIRE} 27	17
mean anything which everyone would rather not become; but . .	626	{CHAIRE} 28	4
which demons with wings would be streaming if something . . .	652	{CHAIRE} 54	13
from summer's green trance, would not adventure soon a . . .	675	95 POEMS 3	10
Less Than Nothing (which would have been Something) what . .	702	95 POEMS 30	22
me that she asked would it hurt too much	707	95 POEMS 35	24
each nearerness) everyone certainly would (my most beautiful	717	95 POEMS 45	13
(my mother's greatgrandmother surely would know) of purest .	748	95 POEMS 76	6
--dingdong: dongding-- to say would be to sing if	798	73 POEMS 26	7
fare well-- a frown would be a smile if	798	73 POEMS 26	14
nay: cry yea-- november would be may that you	798	73 POEMS 26	21
kiss --not though mankind would rather know than feel; . . .	817	73 POEMS 45	11
that timelessness whose absence would make your whole life .	817	73 POEMS 45	13

WOULDN'T

	PAGE	TITLE	LINE
will youse dearie? rain wouldn't that get yer goat	109	& PORTRAIT 5	4
he's "dead" if he wouldn't have eaten them Yapenese	336	VIVA 27	10
him food; no cripple wouldn't creep one mile uphill	520	50 POEMS 34	31
kind so kind it wouldn't like a soul and	544	1 X 1 4	27
(jesus told him; he wouldn't believe it) lao tsze	553	1 X 1 13	5
? o baby i wouldn't like Death if Death	604	{CHAIRE} 6	5
is one nor she wouldn't be seen with the	707	95 POEMS 35	12
i done that You wouldn't have / / /	784	73 POEMS 12	8

+WOULDN'T

	PAGE	TITLE	LINE
FOR CONTEXT, SEE	310	VIVA 2	6

WOULDWOE

	PAGE	TITLE	LINE
make me laft welates Wouldwoe Washington to Lydia E.	321	VIVA 13	5

	PAGE	TITLE	LINE
WOUND			
again. Love (having found) wound up such pretty toys	451	NO THANKS 66	9
stone these little children wound with stone flowers opening	525	50 POEMS 37	3
WOUNDED			
of your white youth wounded by my arms' bothness	218	XLI SONNETS 14	3
every miracle's to breathe) wounded us will becauseless . . .	745	95 POEMS 73	5
WOUNDING			
wonder a poise a wounding a beautiful suppression the	54	T&C PORTRAIT 2	6
WOUNDSMILE			
twi nn ingly scarlet woundsmile) / / / /	615	(CHAIRE) 17	21
WOVEN			
meander in my mind, woven by always upon sunset, ...	435	NO THANKS 51	35
WRAITH '			
/ whose are these (wraith a clinging with a	639	(CHAIRE) 41	1
a clinging with a wraith) ghosts drowning in supreme	639	(CHAIRE) 41	1
WRAITH'S			
note) be entitled a wraith's progress or mainly awash	410	NO THANKS 27	10
WRAITHISH			
eaching come ghostlike (inch) wraithish (by inch) grin ning .	681	95 POEMS 9	2
WRAITHS			
this opening universe will wraiths of doom rush (which . . .	454	NO THANKS 69	9
nothing which all soulless wraiths proclaim substance; all .	765	95 POEMS 91	3
WRAPPEDUPBODY			
into, the littletin-cup His wrappedupbody Queerly Has, my, .	100	& POST IMPR 11	40
WRATH			
nipples squirming in pretty wrath, gums skidding on slippery	151	& SON REAL 22	9
gently brutal, the prettiest wrath of blossoms dishevelling .	214	XLI SONNETS 10	7
WREATH			
bool to lay a wreath from ancient greath on	500	50 POEMS 14	13
WREATHED			
always children forever singing wreathed with singing	525	50 POEMS 37	14
WREATHS			
kiddo he's a palping wreaths of badly Yep cigars	96	& POST IMPR 8	16
+WRENCH			
FOR CONTEXT, SEE	263	IS 5 ONE 32	45
WREST			
our searched world should wrest the rare unwisdom of	205	XLI SONNETS 1	2
WRESTLED			
any (men's hells having wrestled with) man drops into	558	1 X 1 18	1
WRETCH			
(will you teach a wretch to live straighter than	498	50 POEMS 12	2
WRIGGLED			
eyes, the killed world wriggled like a twitched string. . . .	135	& SON REAL 6	17
WRIGGLING			
fright a comic tadpole wriggling in delicious mud /	157	& SON ACTU 6	15
WRIGLEY			
Spearmint Girl With The Wrigley Eyes (of you land	230	IS 5 ONE 2	6
WRING			
despot's goldenest gal did wring that dragon's tail (for . .	552	1 X 1 12	17
WRINKLING			
foot mired in silk wrinkling loth stocking begins queerly . .	225	IS 5 ONE LIZ	3
WRIST			
not stand-ing. unsits her (wrist performs a thundering . . .	159	& SON ACTU 8	4
WRIST'S			
his foot for his wrist's too fine the nineteenth	15	T&C SONGS 5	12
WRISTERS			
shirts fleaproof earwarmers etcetera wristers etcetera, my .	276	IS 5 TWO 10	12
WRISTS			
arms alight in skilful wrists which hint at flight	20	T&C PUELLA MEA	158
combining of kings thy wrists are holy which are	29	T&C ORIENTALE 3	26
beeg wun" her handless wrists did gooey severe shapes. . . .	73	T&C SON REAL 4	14
bedecked whose white thick wrists deliver promptly to a . . .	225	IS 5 ONE LIZ	8
the musician of your wrists; the poet who is	291	IS 5 FOUR 8	8
heads are legs think wrists argue) short (eyes do	309	VIVA 1	10
to rise these your wrists thighs feet hands poising	369	VIVA 60	12
now so yes the wrists of twilight would rejoice	520	50 POEMS 34	24
+WRISTS			
FOR CONTEXT, SEE	317	VIVA 9	5

	PAGE	TITLE	LINE

WRITE

poems i do not write. In this at least . . . . 84 T&C SON ACTU 3 12
speaking--a man wrongers who write what they are dine . . . . 334 VIVA 25 7
cannot read and cannot write who laugh like they . . . . . . 427 NO THANKS 44 10
she cannot read or write, la moon. Employs a . . . . 504 50 POEMS 18 6

WRITHE

space, with the cool writhe of gloom truly which . . . . . . 18 T&C PUELLA MEA 84
of all the earth writhe upon deep rugs / . . . . 35 T&C ORIENTALE 6 116
/ / / / writhe and gape of tortured . . . . 48 T&C IMPRESS 2 1
souls struggle slowly and writhe like caught. brave: flies; . 55 T&C PORTRAIT 3 19
(behold! where chaste stars writhe captured in brightening . 77 T&C SON UNRE 2 17
percussion colours- like-trumpets they (writhe they, ... 100 & POST IMPR 11 12
and snore the steeples writhe with rain) faces (at . . . . . 340 VIVA 31 4
cul t ke ylike writhe of brea Thing / . . . . 349 VIVA 40 18
though with wormS eyes writhe amor (Though through our . . . 361 VIVA 52 7
by darts pierced lazily writhe lurch faceflowers stutter . . 436 NO THANKS 52 8
dolls wallow toys playing writhe with toys (than are . . . . 565 1 X 1 25 6
sunlight --look-- selves, stir: writhe o-p-e-n-i-n-g are . . 835 73 POEMS 63 11

+WRITHED

FOR CONTEXT, SEE . . . . 330 VIVA 21 4

WRITHES

ly in 2 that, writhes... A.. lit. tleora basket . . . . 101 & POST IMPR 11 53
O of milky tranceworld writhes in twi nn ingly . . . . 615 (CHAIRE) 17 17

+WRITHES

FOR CONTEXT, SEE . . . . 430 NO THANKS 47 19

WRITHEWHO

clutch ed in a writhewho room) as hows of . . . . 795 73 POEMS 23 17

WRITHING

bear each with a writhing youth caught to her . . . . 4 T&C EPITHALAM 42
know, or such great writhing words as, uttering overmuch, . . 76 T&C SON UNRE 1 7
the black air with writhing alive skies--and in death's . . . 432 NO THANKS 49 18
star o- pening of (writhing your exploding my) heart . . . . 480 NEW POEMS 18 15

+WRITHING

FOR CONTEXT, SEE . . . . 449 NO THANKS 64 5
FOR CONTEXT, SEE . . . . 469 NEW POEMS 7 8

WRITING

things-- at the present writing one still finds delighted . . 70 T&C SON REAL 1 7

WRONG

called and did no wrong cried the third crumb, ... 117 & PORTRAIT 10 16
the girl who goes wrong you know (whereas when . . . . 245 IS 5 ONE 16 10
various things chiefly which wrong your eyes (frailer than . 306 IS 5 FIVE 5 2
the g.o. world what's wrong with (between me and . . . . . . 411 NO THANKS 28 9
sunday may i be wrong for whenever men are . . . . 481 NEW POEMS 19 7
live with right and wrong or molehills are from . . . . . . 511 50 POEMS 25 2
to never? you were wrong --then all the way . . . . 599 (CHAIRE) 1 11
so right he sharpens wrong and when their lives . . . . . . 624 (CHAIRE) 26 16
try to try) So wrong (wrong wrong) and with . . . . 685 95 POEMS 13 5
to try) So wrong (wrong wrong) and with a . . . . 685 95 POEMS 13 5
try) So wrong (wrong wrong) and with a smile . . . . 685 95 POEMS 13 5
loud unworld's most rightful wrong climbing, my love (till . 745 95 POEMS 73 1
which can never do wrong does (minute by second . . . . . . 769 95 POEMS 95 17
woes and right goes wrong (dim worlds or bright; . . . . . . 776 73 POEMS 4 26
from it; you 're wrong, my friend. But what . . . . 793 73 POEMS 21 16
quite tell right from wrong, took brother Fearless by . . . . 799 73 POEMS 27 13

WRONG'S

and to fall (now wrong's the only right since . . . . 834 73 POEMS 62 21

WRONGERS

all to--mendaciously speaking--a man wrongers who write what 334 VIVA 25 7

WRONGSIDEOUT

wishing) though life's lived wrongsideout, sameness chokes . 446 NO THANKS 61 3

WROTE

the pen while others wrote in steel, accept all . . . . . . 209 XLI SONNETS 5 10
woman or child who wrote a simple declarative sentence . . . 336 VIVA 27 3

WRS

sardines. Mr. Wiggin took Wrs. Miggin's harm in is, ... 263 IS 5 ONE 32 48

WUGGLEWIGGLE

its stimpstamps) the grintgrunt wugglewiggle . . . . 773 73 POEMS 1 11

WUSHYUHNAME
   to collide flatfooting with Wushyuhname a girl-flops to the . 330 VIVA 21   10
X
   suspenders c reads Atlantis x and y play b . . . . 200 XLI PORTRAIT 8   9
   finishes Helmar lights another x and y play, effendi . . . . 200 XLI PORTRAIT 8   17
   discuss news in turkish x and y play b . . . . 200 XLI PORTRAIT 8   21
   y play b spits x and y play, b . . . . 200 XLI PORTRAIT 8   22
   in persian at phonograph x wins exeunt ax: by; . . . . 200 XLI PORTRAIT 8   30
   (m c) t (m x x x ii) I . . . . 388 NO THANKS 5   36
   c) t (m x x x ii) I / . . . .   388 NO THANKS 5   37
   t (m x x x ii) I / / . . . . 388 NO THANKS 5   38
+X
   FOR CONTEXT, SEE . . . . 200 XLI PORTRAIT 8   30
XERXES
   somebody knew Lincoln somebody Xerxes this man: a narrow . .   62 T&C PORTRAIT 10   1
XMAS
   Was A Diver on Xmas Eve like Hell Itself . . . . 239 IS 5 ONE 10   6
+XMAS
   FOR CONTEXT, SEE . . . . 632 {CHAIRE} 34   9
Y
   a business and the Y her legs panting as . . . . 132 & SON REAL 3   9
   a thundering trivial) it. y protuberant through the room's . 159 & SON ACTU 8   5
   reads Atlantis x and y play b cries "effendi" . . . .   200 XLI PORTRAIT 8   9
   lights another x and y play, effendi approaches, sets . . .   200 XLI PORTRAIT 8   17
   in turkish x and y play b spits x . . . .   200 XLI PORTRAIT 8   21
   b spits x and y play, b starts armenian . . . .   200 XLI PORTRAIT 8   23
   / / / / y is a WELL KNOWn . . . .   317 VIVA 9   1
   / hanged if n y in a real hot . . . .   476 NEW POEMS 14   3
+Y
   FOR CONTEXT, SEE . . . . 200 XLI PORTRAIT 8   30
   FOR CONTEXT, SEE . . . . 602 {CHAIRE} 4   4
   FOR CONTEXT, SEE . . . . 635 {CHAIRE} 37   26
YACHTS
   (money men motors "my" yachts wolfhounds women) and the . .   394 NO THANKS 11   4
YALE
   for country and for Yale above his blond determined . . . .   273 IS 5 TWO 8   12
   1 son in improbably yale / / / / . . . .   389 NO THANKS 6   22
YANKEE
   twang of little joe (yankee) gould irketh sundry who . . .   410 NO THANKS 27   7
   yet invented by even yankee ingenu ity (out of . . . . . .   644 {CHAIRE} 46   3
YANKING
   squeal of soiling light yanKing from bushy obscurity a . .   96 & POST IMPR 8   28
YANKS
   thumblike index down- dragging yanks back skin "see" (i, . . 226 IS 5 ONE MAME   6
   leaves the sun and yanks immortal stars awry? Blow . . . . . 560 1 X 1 20   4
   Off signs) & youth yanks them down (old age . . . .   729 95 POEMS 57   5
YAOORTI
   PARTHENON) and having ordered yaoorti from Nicho' settled my 194 XLI PORTRAIT 2   11
YAWN
   with a gashing yellow yawn and tottered to a . . . .   132 & SON REAL 3   15
+YAWN
   FOR CONTEXT, SEE . . . . 442 NO THANKS 57   15
   FOR CONTEXT, SEE . . . . 442 NO THANKS 57   15
YAWNCHURCHES
   men selves-them inghurl) bangbells (yawnchurches suck people) 444 NO THANKS 59   13
YAWNED
   on his universe and yawned: it looks like rain . . . . . .   451 NO THANKS 66   2
YAWNING
   is rotten" the face yawning said what her mouth . . . . . .   225 IS 5 ONE LIZ   12
   murdered known photographed, ourselves yawning will ask . .   237 IS 5 ONE 8   2
   close " " aureally (yawning while all the dominoes) . . . .   331 VIVA 22   8
YE
   seems to have mentioned ye olde freudian wish; when . . . .   326 VIVA 18   3
   ness notman (! ye galleon wilts b: e; . . . .   389 NO THANKS 6   7
   Negroes Indians Youse n.b. ye twang of little joe . . . . .   410 NO THANKS 27   7
   the king of) hear ye! the godless are the . . . .   499 50 POEMS 13   14
   save man from himself ye duskiest despot's goldenest gal . . 552 1 X 1 12   16
   nothing's soon; scream, all ye screamers, till your if . . . 555 1 X 1 15   9

YEA
    demon for to doom yea (fresh complexions being oke . . . . . 552 1 X 1 12   23
    friend --cry nay: cry yea-- november would be may . . . . . . 798 73 POEMS 26   20
YEAH
    (correct you said it yeah) but listen but (it's . . . . 400 NO THANKS 17   12
YEAR
    for whom the whole year dies, risen at length . . . .   5 T&C EPITHALAM 103
    the autumn of a year: When through the thin . . . .   11 T&C SONGS 2   21
    oft utter, whereof the year has perfect bliss-- for . . . . .   21 T&C PUELLA MEA 189
    dead and the gold year a formal spasm in . . . .   41 T&C AMORES 5   6
    spring of this very year (a spring of wines . . . . 158 & SON ACTU 7   3
    will bring you every year something which is worth . . . . . 161 & SON ACTU 10   12
    that sleep all the year in a dark box . . . . 192 XLI CHANSONS 2 14
    unlovely longness of the year droops with things dead . . . . 207 XLI SONNETS 3   5
    studied with Freud a year or two and when . . . . 236 IS 5 ONE 7   7
    (comes but once er year) i'll tell de woild . . . . 237 IS 5 ONE 8   16
    was it perhaps a year) ago i found staring . . . . 296 IS 5 FOUR 13   15
    the earth with the year a cigarette between his . . . . 300 IS 5 FOUR 17   19
    are folded: but the year completes his life as . . . . 304 IS 5 FIVE 3   8
    huge disaster of the year: like this most early . . . . 305 IS 5 FIVE 4   4
    while wings welcome the year and trees dance (and . . . . . . 372 VIVA 63   14
    tic, Eternity's a Five Year Plan: if Joy with . . . . 438 NO THANKS 54   6
    grain septembering arms of year extend less humbly wealth . . 521 50 POEMS 34   37
    love only rides his year. All lose, whole find . . . . 556 1 X 1 16   14
    more april than the year (if all her most . . . . 559 1 X 1 19   12
    of dreams among) no year will fall this than, ... 573 1 X 1 33   11
    lovely) let's open the year both is the very . . . . 578 1 X 1 38   4
    breathing lives some planet's year, his longest life's a . . 609 (CHAIRE) 11   10
    the true time of year-- and if what calls . . . . 717 95 POEMS 45   8
    april's day transcends november's year (eternity being so . . 765 95 POEMS 91   12
    (for young is the year, for young is the . . . . 769 95 POEMS 95   11
    for young is the year) --let's touch the sky: . . . . 769 95 POEMS 95   11
    (and young is the year, dear) as living as . . . . 769 95 POEMS 95   25
    not forsake a failing year --now, before quite your . . . . . 821 73 POEMS 49   8
YEAR'S
    begins again, shares the year's perfect agony. Waiting . . . 156 & SON ACTU 5   12
YEARHOUR
    or how at the yearhour tree- spires shout appalling . . . . . 346 VIVA 37   14
YEARN
    toward all things intrinsic yearn, the immanent subliminal .   19 T&C PUELLA MEA 112
    queerying wave will whitely yearn from each last shore . . . 526 50 POEMS 38   7
YEARNING
    kinds of officers (a yearning nation's blueeyed pride) their 339 VIVA 30   23
YEARNS
    my fond soul seriously yearns beyond this fern of . . . . . .   12 T&C SONGS 2   42
    silence the undulous heaven yearns where in tense . . . . . .   37 T&C AMORES 2   8
YEARNSWOONS
    na (mite) : yearnswoons; &Isdensekil- ◇ ruptingly) ca-y-est 430 NO THANKS 47   12
YEARS
    whitest hands of waiting years, curtained with wordless . . .   6 T&C EPITHALAM 114
    upon a thousand crimson years arched with agony i . . . . . .   30 T&C ORIENTALE 4 36
    which was a million years building he takes the . . . .   32 T&C ORIENTALE 6 3
    elephant is a thousand years old the harem of . . . .   32 T&C ORIENTALE 6 18
    it is eighteen hundred years.... exactly under the window . . 108 & PORTRAIT 4   31
    shall pass a million years (while a bee dozes . . . . 181 XLI SONGS 3   8
    rise After a thousand years lipping flowers And set . . . . . 189 XLI SONGS 11   14
    travelled toward her these years or to snare the . . . . . . 216 XLI SONNETS 12   4
    done nothing for many years but fly kites and . . . . 253 IS 5 ONE 24   6
    from person Porous sits years its of self fee . . . . 312 VIVA 4   19
    coming once in seven years explO ded like a . . . . 320 VIVA 12   11
    a retired general) sixteen years of rapid animal whose . . . 341 VIVA 32   10
    every several fat thousand years. Expecting more would be . . 514 50 POEMS 28   3
    guess in fifty thousand years equals the quote and . . . . . 544 1 X 1 4   14
    more than some eighty years through which that memory . . . . 617 (CHAIRE) 19   11
    weeks & days & years & nights & forever) . . . . 702 95 POEMS 30   19
    still for a thousand years and then lay down . . . . 709 95 POEMS 37   15
    i (five or six years old) peering from some . . . . 824 73 POEMS 52   2
    time with all his years) he's free into the . . . . 845 73 POEMS 73   8

                                   912

		PAGE	TITLE	LINE

+YEARS
FOR CONTEXT, SEE . . . . 607 (CHAIRE) 9   7

YEGGS
/ / / poets yeggs and thirsties since we . . . . 261 IS 5 ONE 31   1

YEH
why not yuh course yeh well naturally i und . . . . 400 NO THANKS 17   9
listen but (it's Rilly yeh ughhuh yuh) i know . . . . 400 NO THANKS 17   13

YELL
then his master will yell at him over the . . . . 69 T&C POST IMPR 6   13
whistle that sing that yell that spell that out . . . . . . 475 NEW POEMS 13   17
sing thatthis is whichwhat yell itfulls o f . . . . 646 (CHAIRE) 48   6
(summoned by that savage yell from shining realms of . . . . 799 73 POEMS 27   26

YELLING
smiling shabby man is yelling over the music i . . . . 69 T&C POST IMPR 6   33

YELLOW
bent to touch the yellow wonder of her hair. . . . . 8 T&C OF NICOL   32
anoint with ardor the yellow lover stands in the . . . . . . 37 T&C AMORES 2   11
the hair-thin tints of yellow dawn, into the women-coloured . 66 T&C POST IMPR 3   7
the) unsuspecting street; THE YELLOW EYES AND --; i . . . . . 101 & POST IMPR 11   56
up with a gashing yellow yawn and tottered to . . . . 132 & SON REAL 3   15
/ Nobody wears a yellow flower in his buttonhole . . . . . . 296 IS 5 FOUR 13   1
the face a dead yellow small rose / / . . . . 296 IS 5 FOUR 13   16
us like a big yellow dog. You don't believe? . . . . 303 IS 5 FIVE 2   10
behind us, a big yellow dog that's.... now it's . . . . . . 303 IS 5 FIVE 2   12
point at red blue yellow violet white orange green- . . . . 437 NO THANKS 53   14

+YELLOW
FOR CONTEXT, SEE . . . . 547 1 X 1 7   14
FOR CONTEXT, SEE . . . . 788 73 POEMS 16   14

YELLOWANDBLUISH
Oxen distinctly move, a yellowandbluish cat (perched why . . 434 NO THANKS 51   32

YELLOWGREEN
up leaning out of yellowgreen water. they are building . . . 281 IS 5 THREE 5   9

YELLOWISH
fatal faded (pinkish or yellowish maybe) piece of pitiful . . 697 95 POEMS 25   25

YELLOWS
light with thinned newfragile yellows lurch and. press --in . 163 & SON ACTU 12   10
made compose curves and yellows, angles or silences to . . . 291 IS 5 FOUR 8   4

YELLOWSONOFABITCH
duly notified threw the yellowsonofabitch into a dungeon, . . 339 VIVA 30   36

YELLS
rinsed with thoroughly million yells they f-oo-1 (whom, . . . 388 NO THANKS 5   8
dropped o god alice yells but who shot up . . . . 496 50 POEMS 10   8

YELPS
whigh shaped hathole thangew yelps one shi ly glad . . . . 602 (CHAIRE) 4   5

YEP
palping wreaths of badly Yep cigars who jim him . . . . . . 96 & POST IMPR 8   16
"wisdom." Flicker of gold. "Yep. No gas. Flynn" the . . . . 226 IS 5 ONE MAME   8
them slowly) "I'm asleep. Yep. Youse is asleep kid . . . . 228 IS 5 ONE MARJ   4

YES
with my solemn eyeswhichneversmile yes, By god. for i . . . . 69 T&C POST IMPR 6   36
"Are You the wind?" "Yes" "why do you touch . . . . 91 & POST IMPR 3   8
les roses les bluets yes, will He buy? Les . . . . 102 & POST IMPR 12   18
intro- duced you say Yes because you know you . . . . 126 & SEVEN POEMS 5   21
my passionate anatomy oh yes! Large legs pinch, toes . . . . 146 & SON REAL 17   7
instant of perfect hunger Yes) how beautifully swims the . . 157 & SON ACTU 6   9
when loveliness says sweetly Yes to wind and cold; . . . . . 183 XLI SONGS 5   10
little countries to the yes of her youth. And . . . . 216 XLI SONNETS 12   7
are parks for wiggle yes has are leap, which, ... 251 IS 5 ONE 22   20
we angels by O yes beautiful we now pass . . . . 257 IS 5 ONE 27   31
is the more accurate, yes it delivers the goods, ... 264 IS 5 ONE 33   11
/ life hurl my yes, crumbles hand (ful released . . . . . . 265 IS 5 ONE 34   2
next let me see yes Will that was cleverest . . . . 271 IS 5 TWO 6   5
faintly blubbering pointing see yes) It here comes A . . . . 280 IS 5 THREE 4   17
on his breast BLIND) yes i am this person . . . . 298 IS 5 FOUR 15   6
me who said o yes Frost Something there is . . . . 315 VIVA 7   2
what is it oh yes chair but not Cassiopeia's . . . . 322 VIVA 14   5
each no) touching every yes / / / / . . . . 373 VIVA 64   18
unders (no but Rully yes i know) but what . . . . 400 NO THANKS 17   4

YES (CONTINUED)

	PAGE	TITLE	LINE
(o sure i know yes of course) but what	400	NO THANKS 17	16
and he might live) yes, partly nor some edgeless	414	NO THANKS 31	9
sarcasms papery deathfuls) awaits yes this alive secretly i .	415	NO THANKS 32	20
can't i mean move yes sir she jes was	425	NO THANKS 42	7
Curvingly at this) window; yes women sturdily meander in . .	434	NO THANKS 51	33
of peace) all places yes is a world &	443	NO THANKS 58	6
in this world of yes live (skilfully curled) all	443	NO THANKS 58	8
holy (soft briGht deep) yeS near sta? calm star	455	NO THANKS 70	8
sta? calm star big yEs alone (wHo Yes near	455	NO THANKS 70	8
big yEs alone (wHo Yes near deep whO big	455	NO THANKS 70	11
nothingly gushing tinsel; silently yes before angel curvings	480	NEW POEMS 18	12
house is full 0 Yes of guk rooms daughter	499	50 POEMS 13	8
busy being her beautiful yes. The place is now	504	50 POEMS 18	12
in all, all) o yes to flower until so	509	50 POEMS 23	7
do not stand against yes which is built by	512	50 POEMS 26	29
spirit and if by yes. Women and men (both	515	50 POEMS 29	32
now and now so yes the wrists of twilight	520	50 POEMS 34	23
among broken odds of yes terday's tomorrow (than today . . .	522	50 POEMS 35	6
a store too much yes what too much o	523	50 POEMS 36	14
(i say the world yes any world is much	523	50 POEMS 36	30
one fearless one good yes completely kind mindheart one . . .	524	50 POEMS 36	39
(but i imagine that yes is the only living	528	50 POEMS 40	13
thing) and we'll make yes / / / /	528	50 POEMS 40	14
mere above but breathing yes which fear will never	538	50 POEMS 50	2
wall the apples are (yes they're gravensteins) all as	543	1 X 1 3	3
told him, and general (yes mam) sherman; and even	553	1 X 1 13	10
whispered him a snowlflake "yes: you may sleep now, ...	555	1 X 1 15	14
and his angels too yes, sir what may be	568	1 X 1 28	20
No and (seeing something yes) will grin with pain	570	1 X 1 30	8
to keeping's give; as yes is to if, love	574	1 X 1 34	4
if, love is to yes must's a schoolroom in	574	1 X 1 34	4
more suns than are (yes; and if time should	576	1 X 1 36	13
would never miss a yes) / / / /	576	1 X 1 36	14
/ / / / yes is a pleasant country:	578	1 X 1 38	1
than never begins to yes but if a look	580	1 X 1 40	21
with a soul sunlight? yes (always we have heard	582	1 X 1 42	5
has come love (by yes every new bird no	583	1 X 1 43	15
said did o no yes earth was in (live	589	1 X 1 49	7
so many kinds of yes) not a tree can	591	1 X 1 51	16
skip around we go yes) there's nothing as something	594	1 X 1 54	8
Eyes. & we remember: yes; we played with a	612	(CHAIRE) 14	8
he's clever) "for all, yes for all sweet things	625	(CHAIRE) 27	7
did was always fall (yes but behind yes) without	634	(CHAIRE) 36	11
fall (yes but behind yes) without or until no	634	(CHAIRE) 36	11
O what the hell yes it's true that was	638	(CHAIRE) 40	10
as i'm to you yes closer made of nothing	648	(CHAIRE) 50	10
--but look: not sunlight? yes! and (plunging rapturously up)	650	(CHAIRE) 52	18
make each no thy yes: love; and give because	651	(CHAIRE) 53	10
singing wonder of blossoming yes riding) to him who	661	(CHAIRE) 63	3
is infinite which is yes (i who have died	663	(CHAIRE) 65	4
and never --it's april (yes, april; my darling) it's	665	(CHAIRE) 67	4
my darling) it's spring! yes the pretty birds frolic	665	(CHAIRE) 67	5
spry as can fly yes the little fish gambol	665	(CHAIRE) 67	6
glad as can be (yes the mountains are dancing	665	(CHAIRE) 67	7
if should sing (at yes of day) younger than	666	(CHAIRE) 68	17
we alone had) made --yes; or as if our	675	95 POEMS 3	9
as long as to (yes) forget (and longer dear)	686	95 POEMS 14	9
paradise) forgetting if, remember yes in time of all	688	95 POEMS 16	9
the Knowing your whole (yes god damned) life is	702	95 POEMS 30	12
your daughter i'm asking yes who but that sly	707	95 POEMS 35	13
/ / / / yes but even 4 or	708	95 POEMS 36	1
(little is) now (dancing yes for) white ly (joy!	715	95 POEMS 43	14
rises a truth of yes (only herself and who	736	95 POEMS 64	2
l0Ok (aliv e) e yes are (chIld) and wh	740	95 POEMS 68	5
the grintgrunt wugglewiggle champychumpchomps yes the	773	73 POEMS 1	12
and scritch (while the no-she-yes-he fluffies tittle tattle .	773	73 POEMS 1	16
our spring is the yes of yes love was	776	73 POEMS 4	32

		PAGE	TITLE	LINE

YES (CONTINUED)

is the yes of yes love was and shall	776	73 POEMS 4	32
damn sweet when Anybody-- yes; no matter who, some	779	73 POEMS 7	3
-ays something is (guess) yes you're right: my enemy	793	73 POEMS 21	23
(as if as can yes) they sell and they	801	73 POEMS 29	2
if of day to yes / / / /	815	73 POEMS 43	8
earth's innumerable doom: againing (yes by microscopic yes)	821	73 POEMS 49	3
againing (yes by microscopic yes) acceptance of irrevocable	821	73 POEMS 49	3
understand concerning no and yes: if they've become the	834	73 POEMS 62	16
where a miracle arrives (yes) you and i may	835	73 POEMS 63	25

+YES

FOR CONTEXT, SEE	251	IS 5 ONE 22	13
FOR CONTEXT, SEE	400	NO THANKS 17	9
FOR CONTEXT, SEE	400	NO THANKS 17	9
FOR CONTEXT, SEE	400	NO THANKS 17	12
FOR CONTEXT, SEE	400	NO THANKS 17	13
FOR CONTEXT, SEE	400	NO THANKS 17	14
FOR CONTEXT, SEE	417	NO THANKS 34	23
FOR CONTEXT, SEE	640	{CHAIRE} 42	3

YESMAM

| bloo-moo-n sirkusricky platzburg hoppytoad yesmam. the | 108 | & PORTRAIT 4 | 16 |

YESSING

| eyes drooling unmind grim yessing childflesh perpetually | 337 | VIVA 28 | 7 |

YESSIR

| slim guesser goose pin yessir wheel no sendwisp ben | 333 | VIVA 24 | 18 |

YESTERDAY

pillar is eaten by yesterday she was a silver	110	& PORTRAIT 6	4
proletariat will not rise yesterday. Inexpressible itchings	262	IS 5 ONE 32	19
woe and up comes yesterday most green and young	531	50 POEMS 43	4
and to -morrow and yesterday and everything except love	762	95 POEMS 89	14

+YESTERDAY

FOR CONTEXT, SEE	110	& PORTRAIT 6	31
FOR CONTEXT, SEE	111	& PORTRAIT 6	49
FOR CONTEXT, SEE	112	& PORTRAIT 6	77
FOR CONTEXT, SEE	112	& PORTRAIT 6	91

YESTERDAY'S

| / / / does yesterday's perfection seem not quite | 414 | NO THANKS 31 | 1 |

+YESTERDAY'S

| FOR CONTEXT, SEE | 522 | 50 POEMS 35 | 6 |

YESWIND

| shrink: as through immediately yeswind-faces peer skies; | 346 | VIVA 37 | 6 |

YESWIND-FACES

| shrink: as through immediately yeswind-faces peer skies; | 346 | VIVA 37 | 6 |

YET

hark! the flicker's laughing yet, while on the hills	5	T&C EPITHALAM	75
curved and curling thing, yet holds continuous	5	T&C EPITHALAM	90
whereof is most desire, yet less than those twain	6	T&C EPITHALAM	147
through meadows hugely move. yet what am i that	12	T&C SONGS 2	36
other songs be sung; yet stand They here enraptured,	208	XLI SONNETS 4	12
beautiful almost than you. Yet if not flower, tell	211	XLI SONNETS 7	6
purely with muted step, yet somewhat proudly too-- are	211	XLI SONNETS 7	9
over there, over there. yet we scarcely fare much	233	IS 5 ONE 4	9
shook hands again and yet again shook again hands	263	IS 5 ONE 32	44
the goods, Heaven knows (yet are we mindful, though	264	IS 5 ONE 33	13
mindful, though not as yet awake, of ourselves which	264	IS 5 ONE 33	13
lice; headaches: ifs.) yet shall our Not to	361	VIVA 52	22
go down, one poem yet shall swim / /	372	VIVA 63	15
bad dear sh not yet jesus what blood darling	496	50 POEMS 10	18
say? here youngest selves yet younger selves conceive here's	538	50 POEMS 50	7
one in another hides; yet man can, being all,	609	{CHAIRE} 11	4
most dangerous machine as yet invented by even yankee	644	{CHAIRE} 46	2
the mystery of freedom? yet, among their loud exactitudes	659	{CHAIRE} 61	10
might but man kind yet in park this grim	698	95 POEMS 26	5

YEWRETY

| eyesucks unyewkuntel finglestein idstings yewrety oride lesgo | 474 | NEW POEMS 12 | 13 |

YIELD

| as trembling used to yield with dew when the | 18 | T&C PUELLA MEA | 53 |
| cobalt miles of sky yield to and heed the | 93 | & POST IMPR 5 | 7 |

YIELDING
   of gradual hands and yielding to that fee her . . . . 4 T&C EPITHALAM 54
YM&
   / / / kind) YM& WC (of sort of) . . . . 464 NEW POEMS 2   2
YOKED
   thighs are white horses yoked to a chariot of . . . . 29 T&C ORIENTALE 3 11
YON
   us next demand wherefore yon mob an accident? somebody . . . 245 IS 5 ONE 16 16
   / / than (by yon sunset's wintry glow revealed) . . . . 254 IS 5 ONE 25   1
   these busted statues of yon motheaten forum be aware . . . . 260 IS 5 ONE 30   2
   who replies "I can!" --yon clean upstanding well dressed . . 273 IS 5 TWO 8   6
   undecaying friend hangs at yon gilty ceiling per both . . . . 546 1 X 1 6   5
YOND
   seemSwoop (whir -ling be, yond! thought are. more (Than . . . 447 NO THANKS 62   9
YONDER
   me of her Thy yonder servant who in Thy . . . . 57 T&C PORTRAIT 5   6
   naught, feels the tremendous yonder for his own-- on . . . . 81 T&C SON UNRE 6 12
   / / / / yonder deadfromtheneckup graduate of a . . . . 234 IS 5 ONE 5   1
   whirl beyond worlds: immortal yonder collidingly absorbs . . 376 VIVA 67 12
   n't why g to yonder s called newsreel s . . . . 392 NO THANKS 9   8
YONKERS
   big toothless girl in Yonkers. Dick Mid's green large . . . . 149 & SON REAL 20 13
YOO
   joy (eye kinely thank yoo) / / / / . . . . 519 50 POEMS 33 28
   gently herculanean my mortal) yoo make sno eye kil . . . . . 618 (CHAIRE) 20   4
   make sno eye kil yoo (friend the laughing grinning) . . . . . 618 (CHAIRE) 20   6
   no care so what yoo-gointa-doo? (ice coal wood man) . . . . . 618 (CHAIRE) 20 19
   old nic) like spring yoo un-air-stan? me crazy me . . . . . . 618 (CHAIRE) 20 27
YOO-GOINTA-DOO
   no care so what yoo-gointa-doo? (ice coal wood man) . . . . . 618 (CHAIRE) 20 19
YOOZE
   dutmoi jak roids wid yooze Vury Sin Silly : . . . . 398 NO THANKS 15 21
+YOOZWIDDUHPOIMNUNTWWAIV
   gutnutntuhplai? yoozwidduhpoimnuntwaiv un . . . . 310 VIVA 2 12
YORK
   outside it was New York and beautifully snowing. Inside . . . 96 & POST IMPR 8   2
   outside. (it was New York and beautifully, snowing.... / . . 97 & POST IMPR 8 45
   the mouth of New York. Be- tween its supple . . . . 201 XLI PORTRAIT 9   2
   Shikahgo Sain Looey Noo York aṛ. San Fran dictaphones . . . . 237 IS 5 ONE 8   8
YOU
   says to nine ladies you take his mouth for . . . . 15 T&C SONGS 5 15
   as if for fear you would espy the little . . . . 22 T&C PUELLA MEA 216
   boast your dead beauties, you greatest lovers in the . . . . 22 T&C PUELLA MEA 244
   dreamed it appeared that you thought to escape me . . . . . . 30 T&C ORIENTALE 4   4
   from splintering foam caught you clutched you upon my . . . . 30 T&C ORIENTALE 4 13
   foam caught you clutched you upon my mouth listen . . . . . . 30 T&C ORIENTALE 4 13
   dreamed in my dream you had desire to thwart . . . . 30 T&C ORIENTALE 4 17
   impossible tower i caught you strained you broke you . . . . 30 T&C ORIENTALE 4 27
   i caught you strained you broke you upon my . . . . 30 T&C ORIENTALE 4 27
   you strained you broke you upon my blood listen . . . . 30 T&C ORIENTALE 4 28
   i dreamed i thought you would have deceived me . . . . 30 T&C ORIENTALE 4 31
   and space i saw you close your eyes and . . . . 30 T&C ORIENTALE 4 34
   sombre god i picked you as an apple is . . . . 30 T&C ORIENTALE 4 41
   hills to dream of you, approve these firm unsated . . . . . . 36 T&C AMORES 1   8
   (in time to come you shall remember of this . . . . 36 T&C AMORES 1 21
   this it is because you have loved me, moon . . . . 39 T&C AMORES 4   5
   that on the flower you gave me when we . . . . 42 T&C AMORES 6   3
   myself Death and will You with elaborate fingers possibly . . 58 T&C PORTRAIT 6 15
   know is how do you like your blueeyed boy . . . . 60 T&C PORTRAIT 8 10
   spring slattern of seasons you have dirty legs and . . . . . 61 T&C PORTRAIT 9 11
   sticky with dreams and you have a sloppy body . . . . 61 T&C PORTRAIT 9 15
   bed of crocuses When you sing in your whiskey-voice . . . . . 61 T&C PORTRAIT 9 18
   departure swim, sayingly; (Do you think?) the i do, ... 66 T&C POST IMPR 3 13
   accurate silence.... But first you) press easily at first, . 67 T&C POST IMPR 4 17
   the queer monkey (if you toss him a coin . . . . 69 T&C POST IMPR 6 10
   up, and look at, you with his solemn blinky . . . . 69 T&C POST IMPR 6 14
   up and blink at you with my solemn eyeswhichneversmile . . . 69 T&C POST IMPR 6 35
   all i ask of you-- but that when light . . . . 71 T&C SON REAL 2   6

	PAGE	TITLE	LINE

YOU (CONTINUED)

begin to husk heaven) you, you exactly paled and	71	T&C SON REAL 2	12
to husk heaven) you, you exactly paled and curled	71	T&C SON REAL 2	12
always clenched faintly, wishes you with all her fragile . .	72	T&C SON REAL 3	7
here and This, do you get me?) will maybe	72	T&C SON REAL 3	12
/ / / when you rang at Dick Mid's	73	T&C SON REAL 4	1
sitting. --If they knew you at Dick Mid's the	73	T&C SON REAL 4	10
Kitty. a whore. Sixteen you corking brute amused from	74	T&C SON REAL 5	9
if this should be-- you of my heart, send	76	T&C SON UNRE 1	10
long (and what have you to say, wind wind	80	T&C SON UNRE 5	5
say, wind wind wind--did you love somebody and have	80	T&C SON UNRE 5	6
love somebody and have you the petal of somewhere	80	T&C SON UNRE 5	7
building a building around you, a frail slippery house, . . .	83	T&C SON ACTU 2	2
the forest--no offense to you, white town whose spires . . .	86	T&C SON ACTU 5	4
are minutely dead. Then you will slowly kiss me	86	T&C SON ACTU 5	14
and green person "Are You the wind?" "Yes" "why	91	& POST IMPR 3	8
wind?" "Yes" "why do you touch flowers as if	91	& POST IMPR 3	8
will not wholly miss you; or if i certainly	92	& POST IMPR 4	20
no sir hopping sawdust you kiddo he's a palping	96	& POST IMPR 8	15
ale, which never lets you grow old blinking at	96	& POST IMPR 8	24
of shad- ow won't you have a drink? (the	97	& POST IMPR 8	41
he buy flowers" to you and "Death is young	102	& POST IMPR 12	6
beard" i say to you who are silent. --"Do	102	& POST IMPR 12	10
who are silent. --"Do you see Life? he is	102	& POST IMPR 12	10
of their lives aint you, oo-oo. dearie not so	109	& PORTRAIT 5	19
day) O i tell you out of the minute	111	& PORTRAIT 6	51
black great god) Cleopatra you are eaten by yester-	112	& PORTRAIT 6	89
Lady Lady Of Ladies you who move beautifully in	112	& PORTRAIT 6	94
deadly heaven i salute you whose body is Egypt	113	& PORTRAIT 6	109
beauty i declare to you if what i am	115	& PORTRAIT 8	4
the other somethings did-- you imagine His surprise bellowing	117	& PORTRAIT 10	8
a match or can you see?) which the six	117	& PORTRAIT 10	29
ver mYveRylitTle street where you will come, at twi	122	& SEVEN POEMS 1	24
/ / i'll tell you a dream i had	123	& SEVEN POEMS 2	1
room for me in You my stomach goes into	123	& SEVEN POEMS 2	8
melon into the tree? you got me said the	125	& SEVEN POEMS 4	8
said She Win and you won't be sorry And	125	& SEVEN POEMS 4	23
who maybe winks at you in a streetcar and	126	& SEVEN POEMS 5	15
in a streetcar and you pretend you don't but	126	& SEVEN POEMS 5	15
streetcar and you pretend you don't but really you	126	& SEVEN POEMS 5	16
you don't but really you do see and you	126	& SEVEN POEMS 5	16
you do see and you are My how glad	126	& SEVEN POEMS 5	16
if it talks about you somewhere behind your back	126	& SEVEN POEMS 5	18
was never intro- duced you say Yes because you	126	& SEVEN POEMS 5	21
you say Yes because you know you want it	126	& SEVEN POEMS 5	21
Yes because you know you want it to dance	126	& SEVEN POEMS 5	21
it to dance with you and it wants to	126	& SEVEN POEMS 5	22
fine like hands do you see that water flowerpots	126	& SEVEN POEMS 5	24
in their house than you so that's all you	126	& SEVEN POEMS 5	26
you so that's all you see but you don't	126	& SEVEN POEMS 5	26
all you see but you don't want to dead's	126	& SEVEN POEMS 5	26
for your musiclesson and you like music and to	126	& SEVEN POEMS 5	30
play who can but you know you never can	126	& SEVEN POEMS 5	31
can but you know you never can and why	126	& SEVEN POEMS 5	31
like a dance where you danced simple hours and	127	& SEVEN POEMS 5	32
danced simple hours and you take all your prickley-clothes .	127	& SEVEN POEMS 5	33
without one word and you lie still as anything	127	& SEVEN POEMS 5	34
largeness begins to give you, the dance all over	127	& SEVEN POEMS 5	36
all over again and you, feel all again all	127	& SEVEN POEMS 5	36
over the way men you liked made you feel	127	& SEVEN POEMS 5	37
men you liked made you feel when they touched	127	& SEVEN POEMS 5	37
feel when they touched you (but that's not all)	127	& SEVEN POEMS 5	38
all) because largeness tells you so you can feel	127	& SEVEN POEMS 5	39
largeness tells you so you can feel what you	127	& SEVEN POEMS 5	39
you can feel what you made, men feel when, ...	127	& SEVEN POEMS 5	39
made, men feel when, you touched, them dead's sorry	127	& SEVEN POEMS 5	39
◇ and nobody expects you to anyway dead says	127	& SEVEN POEMS 5	44
and the rosebug and you say Sure you say	127	& SEVEN POEMS 5	48

YOU (CONTINUED)

and you say Sure you say (like that) sure . . . . 127 & SEVEN POEMS 5   48
sure i'll come with you you say for i . . . . 127 & SEVEN POEMS 5   49
i'll come with you you say for i like . . . . 127 & SEVEN POEMS 5   49
pretty people? (and if you and i should get . . . . 129 & SEVEN POEMS 7   4
take me and take you into their balloon, why . . . . 129 & SEVEN POEMS 7   6
minutes and love.... do you? and always (i simply . . . . . . 133 & SON REAL 4   8
i think , did you ever hear a jazz . . . . 141 & SON REAL 12   16
smell in my mind, you should see when i . . . . 152 & SON ACTU 1   8
/ it is funny, you will be dead some . . . . 153 & SON ACTU 2   1
dead some day. By you the mouth hair eyes, ... 153 & SON ACTU 2   2
a funny, thing. And you will be and i . . . . 153 & SON ACTU 2   9
better than me will you like the rain's face . . . . 153 & SON ACTU 2   13
that's all. Bit into you as teeth, in the . . . . 154 & SON ACTU 3   2
possibly have i loved....? you) sheath before sheath stripped 154 & SON ACTU 3   11
WhoEver will know Had you as bite teeth; i . . . . 154 & SON ACTU 3   14
teeth; i stood with you as a foal stands . . . . 154 & SON ACTU 3   15
frail enormous star (do you see it?) and this . . . . 155 & SON ACTU 4   13
(i do but touch you) timid lewd moon plunge . . . . 155 & SON ACTU 4   16
i have thought of you somewhat too much and . . . . 157 & SON ACTU 6   1
shutting.... understand i love you.... feel your suddenly . . 157 & SON ACTU 6   6
me) love, and after you. I occasionally feel vague . . . . . 160 & SON ACTU 9   13
kissingly, i will bring you every spring handfuls of . . . . 161 & SON ACTU 10   7
laughs, i will bring you every year something which . . . . . 161 & SON ACTU 10   12
i have found what you are like the rain, ... 163 & SON ACTU 12   1
ivory performing rose of you, worn upon my mind . . . . 165 & SON ACTU 14   2
when i think of you and do not live: . . . . 165 & SON ACTU 14   7
she says to me you big fool she says . . . . 167 & SON ACTU 16   12
also i think of you, getting mandolin-clink mixed with . . . 169 & SON ACTU 18   5
key to a palace --You, --in this window sits . . . . 169 & SON ACTU 18   15
thing he saw was you naked amid unnaked things, ... 170 & SON ACTU 19   5
horses sleep upstairs. And you can see their ears. . . . . . 171 & SON ACTU 20   7
pair is white (but you know that) they look . . . . 171 & SON ACTU 20   10
/ / / when you went away it was . . . . 172 & SON ACTU 21   1
in delicate hubbub as you stood thinking of anything, ... 172 & SON ACTU 21   8
isn't it odd of you you really to lie a . . . . 172 & SON ACTU 21   10
/ / / / you asked me to come: . . . . 173 & SON ACTU 22   1
terrible inches speech--it made you a little dizzy did . . . 174 & SON ACTU 23   11
why the girl-and-bird of you move.... moves.... and also, . . 174 & SON ACTU 23   13
this and that of you, i like, slowly stroking . . . . 175 & SON ACTU 24   9
thrill of under me you so quite new / . . . . 175 & SON ACTU 24   14
haste annihilator drawing into you my enchanting leaves / . . 182 XLI SONGS 4   17
her hair, (but if you ask the rain he'll . . . . 183 XLI SONGS 5   5
sit and think of you the holy city which . . . . 186 XLI SONGS 8   4
and i think of you / / / / . . . . 186 XLI SONGS 8   22
CHANSONS INNOCENTES why did you go little fourpaws? you . . . 191 XLI CHANSONS 1   1
you go little fourpaws? you forgot to shut your . . . . 191 XLI CHANSONS 1   3
big eyes. where did you go? like little kittens . . . . 191 XLI CHANSONS 1   5
stroke maybe asleep? do you know? or maybe did . . . . 191 XLI CHANSONS 1   13
little silent Christmas tree you are so little you . . . . . 192 XLI CHANSONS 2   3
you are so little you are more like a . . . . 192 XLI CHANSONS 2   4
a flower who found you in the green forest . . . . 192 XLI CHANSONS 2   5
green forest and were you very sorry to come . . . . 192 XLI CHANSONS 2   6
see i will comfort you because you smell so . . . . 192 XLI CHANSONS 2   7
will comfort you because you smell so sweetly i . . . . 192 XLI CHANSONS 2   8
cool bark and hug you safe and tight just . . . . 192 XLI CHANSONS 2   10
give them all to you to hold every finger . . . . 192 XLI CHANSONS 2   18
said Nicho' "and did you perhaps wish also shishkabob?" . . . 194 XLI PORTRAIT 2   38
/ / / Picasso you give us Things which . . . . 195 XLI PORTRAIT 3   2
of sharp thick mind you make us shrill presents . . . . 195 XLI PORTRAIT 3   5
lopped of every prettiness you hew form truly / . . . . 195 XLI PORTRAIT 3   24
a coffin's inside when you die, pretentious and shiny . . . . 198 XLI PORTRAIT 6   2
courteous of men should you remark the walls have . . . . . . 198 XLI PORTRAIT 6   26
/ Humanity i love you because you would rather . . . . 204 XLI LA GUERRE 2   1
i love you because you would rather black the . . . . 204 XLI LA GUERRE 2   2
both parties and because you unflinchingly applaud all songs 204 XLI LA GUERRE 2   5
howard Humanity i love you because when you're hard . . . . . 204 XLI LA GUERRE 2   9
when you're hard up you pawn your intelligence to . . . . . . 204 XLI LA GUERRE 2   10

			PAGE	TITLE	LINE

YOU (CONTINUED)

	PAGE	TITLE	LINE
you're flush pride keeps you from the pawn shop	204	XLI LA GUERRE 2	13
pawn shop and because you are continually committing	204	XLI LA GUERRE 2	14
house Humanity i love you because you are perpetually	204	XLI LA GUERRE 2	17
i love you because you are perpetually putting the	204	XLI LA GUERRE 2	17
on it and because you are forever making poems	204	XLI LA GUERRE 2	22
death Humanity i hate you / / / /	204	XLI LA GUERRE 2	25
more beautiful almost than you. Yet if not flower, ...	211	XLI SONNETS 7	5
whose twitching lips, between you and me almost succeeds . .	227	IS 5 ONE GERT	6
my country, 'tis of you, land of the Cluett	230	IS 5 ONE 2	4
The Wrigley Eyes (of you land of the Arrow	230	IS 5 ONE 2	6
& Wilson Collars) of you i sing: land of	230	IS 5 ONE 2	10
In His andsoforth do you get me?) according to	230	IS 5 ONE 2	30
i ca, I love, You. And there're a ◇	231	IS 5 ONE 3	41
◇ like all of you successfully if delicately gelded	231	IS 5 ONE 3	43
with hand so hairy-sturdy you may turn O turn	233	IS 5 ONE 4	2
what's become of (if you please) all the glory	233	IS 5 ONE 4	10
coitnly can shimmie when you see her shake shake	235	IS 5 ONE 6	7
shake shake shake, when you see her shake a	235	IS 5 ONE 6	11
shake a shimmie how you wish that you was	235	IS 5 ONE 6	12
how you wish that you was Jimmie. Oh for	235	IS 5 ONE 6	12
listen my children and you shall hear the true	236	IS 5 ONE 7	1
could do nothing which you and i are accustomed	236	IS 5 ONE 7	12
importance to me to you nothing is what particularly	238	IS 5 ONE 9	16
to wonder about guys you used to (and them	242	IS 5 ONE 13	4
no doubts about why you put the ring on	242	IS 5 ONE 13	11
of babies and how you know the dam rent's	242	IS 5 ONE 13	18
girl who goes wrong you know (whereas when i	245	IS 5 ONE 16	10
being Brand -new; and you know consequently a little	248	IS 5 ONE 19	2
world (and me and you if we're not very	250	IS 5 ONE 21	4
twice the a week you kind of, know (kind	251	IS 5 ONE 22	8
but well oh don't you makes burst want to	251	IS 5 ONE 22	12
children and of course you know their mother, of	254	IS 5 ONE 25	11
it isn't snowing snow you know it's snowing buttercups . . .	254	IS 5 ONE 25	23
cry of How do you find the sun, ladies?	255	IS 5 ONE 26	7
Venezia: incline thine ear you glassworks of Murano; pause .	256	IS 5 ONE 27	3
didn't Ruskin says about you got the haven't Marjorie	257	IS 5 ONE 27	35
: an American, if you understand that i mean	262	IS 5 ONE 32	13
unimportant what i and you believe; not for philosophy . . .	264	IS 5 ONE 33	19
any other pastel. (While you and i have lips	264	IS 5 ONE 33	25
To Name and General You know who a string	266	IS 5 TWO 1	23
god america i love you land of the pilgrims'	268	IS 5 TWO 3	2
forth oh say can you see by the dawn's	268	IS 5 TWO 3	3
begin dropping jolly fast you hear the rrmp and	269	IS 5 TWO 4	4
then ◇ and before you can ! & we're	269	IS 5 TWO 4	8
eyes i loved like you can't imagine Harry was	271	IS 5 TWO 6	9
/ / lis -ten you know what i mean	272	IS 5 TWO 7	3
the first guy drops you know everybody feels sick	272	IS 5 TWO 7	4
or up to your you know what in water	272	IS 5 TWO 7	9
up all everywhere over you all me everyone that's	272	IS 5 TWO 7	11
is more did tell you just what everybody was	276	IS 5 TWO 10	4
our lady what do you think of this? Do	279	IS 5 THREE 3	21
had been presented unto you by a mystery? ...the	279	IS 5 THREE 3	23
behind me I tell you; several, incredible, sleepy /	281	IS 5 THREE 5	24
hands the slim hinging you --because it's five o'clock . . .	282	IS 5 THREE 6	8
enough of life, for you. I understand. Once again....) . . .	282	IS 5 THREE 6	32
complete silent and everywhere you your kisses your flesh . .	283	IS 5 THREE 7	16
habits laughter i say you will perhaps pardon, possibly . . .	285	IS 5 FOUR 2	9
will perhaps pardon, possibly you will comprehend. and how .	285	IS 5 FOUR 2	10
are not the same you and i, since here's	286	IS 5 FOUR 3	16
lips Eyes everything hands you know what happens) but	287	IS 5 FOUR 4	19
/ / / / you are not going to, ...	289	IS 5 FOUR 6	1
not going to, dear. You are not going to	289	IS 5 FOUR 6	1
is no longer, can you imagine it i can't	289	IS 5 FOUR 6	4
and eat sunlight (do you believe it? i begin	289	IS 5 FOUR 6	9
put my eyes into you but that doesn't matter	289	IS 5 FOUR 6	13
than of old because you fooled the doctors, i	289	IS 5 FOUR 6	15
the doctors, i touch you with hopes and words	289	IS 5 FOUR 6	15

		PAGE	TITLE	LINE
YOU (CONTINUED)

from moving as we, you and i, used to . . . . 289 IS 5 FOUR 6 — 18
move when i thought you were going to (but . . . . 289 IS 5 FOUR 6 — 19
that doesn't matter) when you thought you were going . . . . 289 IS 5 FOUR 6 — 21
matter) when you thought you were going to America. . . . . . 289 IS 5 FOUR 6 — 21
will never wholly kiss you; wholly to be a . . . . 290 IS 5 FOUR 7 — 4
(your fingertips the way you move) the painter of . . . . . . 291 IS 5 FOUR 8 — 13
when day has thrilled you are a house around . . . . 292 IS 5 FOUR 9 — 3
around this house of you love being such, or . . . . 292 IS 5 FOUR 9 — 12
/ / / / you are like the snow . . . . 293 IS 5 FOUR 10 — 1
rain only sweeter frailer you whom certain flowers resemble . 293 IS 5 FOUR 10 — 3
thing) since i and you are on our ways . . . . 293 IS 5 FOUR 10 — 14
and death a marriage) you give me courage so . . . . 293 IS 5 FOUR 10 — 18
/ / / because you go away i give . . . . 294 IS 5 FOUR 11 — 2
this flower wholly whom you do not ever fear, ... 294 IS 5 FOUR 11 — 16
/ / / / you being in love will . . . . 295 IS 5 FOUR 12 — 1
length inexcusable, this inexplicable pleasure--you go from . 295 IS 5 FOUR 12 — 7
when i have kissed you into a memory slowly, ... 295 IS 5 FOUR 12 — 9
--that since and if you disappear solemnly myselves ask . . . 295 IS 5 FOUR 12 — 11
to? love? Love if you like and i like, ... 295 IS 5 FOUR 12 — 22
person of whom somehow you are never wholly rid . . . . . . 298 IS 5 FOUR 15 — 8
on) after all, kid you might as well toss . . . . 298 IS 5 FOUR 15 — 13
love preferably, anything which you can't pass off on . . . . 298 IS 5 FOUR 15 — 16
a corner) never bother you any more. / / . . . . 298 IS 5 FOUR 15 — 28
and dull compared with you, silently who are and . . . . . . 301 IS 5 FOUR 18 — 9
are in bed will you walking beside me, my . . . . 302 IS 5 FIVE 1 — 2
/ / / touching you i say (it being . . . . 303 IS 5 FIVE 2 — 1
be found" and smiling you answer "everything turns into . . . 303 IS 5 FIVE 2 — 4
a big yellow dog. You don't believe? look back. . . . . . . 303 IS 5 FIVE 2 — 10
chevaux de bois) when you were in Paris we . . . . 304 IS 5 FIVE 3 — 15
stole nothing from death"-- you only will create (who . . . . 306 IS 5 FIVE 5 — 11
to meet "how do you do" she smiling said . . . . 313 VIVA 5 — 5
she smiling said "thought you were earning your living . . . 313 VIVA 5 — 6
/ but mr can you maybe listen there's me . . . . 314 VIVA 6 — 1
no body will (can you give a) listen to . . . . 314 VIVA 6 — 22
listen to who may you be any how? down . . . . 314 VIVA 6 — 25
being just a Reflex you know since Everything is . . . . . . 315 VIVA 7 — 7
up her hot ow you hurt tho nithe steered . . . . 316 VIVA 8 — 11
(I could have been You, You might have been . . . . 317 VIVA 9 — 8
could have been You, You might have been I) . . . . 317 VIVA 9 — 8
is so interested but you make me laft welates . . . . 321 VIVA 13 — 4
it) solution (of course you must shake well) indolently . . . 323 VIVA 15 — 5
met and just but you know supposing we just . . . . 323 VIVA 15 — 11
that i and that you had carefully ourselves decided . . . . . 323 VIVA 15 — 23
at all like what you and what i (of . . . . 323 VIVA 15 — 27
ensconced in thick glass you try if we are . . . . 326 VIVA 18 — 5
"on the whole" (if you will permit a metaphor . . . . 326 VIVA 18 — 27
mass. i try if you are a gentleman not . . . . 327 VIVA 18 — 45
borrow contact from that you and from this you . . . . 328 VIVA 19 — 17
you and from this you sensations, imitating a few . . . . . 328 VIVA 19 — 18
im on duh koib" --you know alotta sweet bull . . . . 332 VIVA 23 — 10
obviously scratches tomorrowlobs wholeagainst you gringlehow 333 VIVA 24 — 6
/ / ohld song you Know a fly and . . . . 335 VIVA 26 — 2
of inter -vening) anyway You know Separated what i . . . . . 335 VIVA 26 — 15
song by ; neither you nor i and by . . . . 335 VIVA 26 — 19
everywhere be real to you in a moment" The . . . . 338 VIVA 29 — 14
me: more blond than you. / / / / . . . . 339 VIVA 30 — 42
And) i say "won't you" (remembering) knowing that you . . . . 353 VIVA 44 — 24
you" (remembering) knowing that you are afraid "go first" . . 353 VIVA 44 — 25
bats & mice (and you, you say "let's" going . . . . 353 VIVA 44 — 28
& mice (and you, you say "let's" going in . . . . 353 VIVA 44 — 29
/ / / / you in win ter who . . . . 354 VIVA 45 — 1
breaths) in win ter you think, die slow ly . . . . 354 VIVA 45 — 24
the earliest star (have you a wish?) touch me, ... 357 VIVA 48 — 2
I have never loved you dear as now i . . . . 360 VIVA 51 — 10
I have never loved you dear as now i . . . . 360 VIVA 51 — 20
I have never loved you dear as now i . . . . 360 VIVA 51 — 30
i have never loved you dear as now i . . . . 360 VIVA 51 — 35

	PAGE	TITLE	LINE
YOU (CONTINUED)			
soft-ly me and eye (you leSs) ly (un	361	VIVA 52	12
/ if i love You (thickness means worlds inhabited	363	VIVA 54	1
stern bright faeries if you love me) distance is	363	VIVA 54	5
/ / lady will you come with me into	365	VIVA 56	1
through the window as you see and really i	365	VIVA 56	5
We almost could go (you and i) into a	365	VIVA 56	8
polished buttons) would take you away --and all the	365	VIVA 56	13
closed myself as fingers, you open always petal by	366	VIVA 57	7
what it is about you that closes and opens;	366	VIVA 57	17
to its doom than you will smile) / /	367	VIVA 58	12
/ my darling since you and i are thoroughly	368	VIVA 59	2
/ because i love you) last night clothed in	369	VIVA 60	1
/ / / if you and i awakening discover	370	VIVA 61	1
which your eyes are You will communicate a little	370	VIVA 61	11
gladly seem firm for you: remember (as those pearls	372	VIVA 63	8
earth wandering hunter whom you knew once? what if	374	VIVA 65	8
somebody and with something) You are gone. there is	375	VIVA 66	4
over us, i implore you to notice how the	378	VIVA 69	2
the air--and whose do you suppose possibly are certain . . .	378	VIVA 69	5
immense directionless horizon) --do you perhaps know these .	378	VIVA 69	16
discuss our mingling spirits, you would disappear unreally; .	379	VIVA 70	7
than this only by you my heart always moves	379	VIVA 70	14
ov--in g over (moving) you beautifully also; at denfert . . .	384	NO THANKS 2	18
bad, like candy: & you are dead you captain)	389	NO THANKS 6	15
& you are dead you captain) Memo 1 wife	389	NO THANKS 6	17
threaten) the wistFully dead you directly perceive or minus .	391	NO THANKS 8	10
kn w & if you d n't why g	392	NO THANKS 9	6
squirmcurl ing homonomously metameric You / / / /	395	NO THANKS 12	16
far said he where you are said she) may	399	NO THANKS 16	12
this said he if you kiss said she may	399	NO THANKS 16	16
you're divine! said he (you are Mine said she)	399	NO THANKS 16	32
it comes to (listen you don't have to i	400	NO THANKS 17	6
but listen here's (correct you said it yeah) but	400	NO THANKS 17	12
anything is bad which you think good) because he	406	NO THANKS 23	4
something authentic and delirious you know something genuine	407	NO THANKS 24	12
whie (all good kumrads you can tell by their	413	NO THANKS 30	7
whoy the hope that you may mess your pance	413	NO THANKS 30	12
to fate and (if you can withholding nothing) World, ...	420	NO THANKS 37	13
art they kill like you would take a piss	427	NO THANKS 44	16
lives) oh my spirit you tumble climb and mightily	434	NO THANKS 51	26
imagining spasm rise we you-with-me around (me) you IYou . .	442	NO THANKS 57	23
we you-with-me around (me) you IYou / / /	442	NO THANKS 57	24
air rock day) : you; smile, hands (an- onymo	449	NO THANKS 64	14
take the hearse, see you again. Love (having found)	451	NO THANKS 66	8
/ / come (all you mischief- hatchers hatch mischief)	452	NO THANKS 67	1
hatchers hatch mischief) all you guilty scamper (you bastards	452	NO THANKS 67	3
all you guilty scamper (you bastards throw dynamite) let . .	452	NO THANKS 67	5
-rithmetic o- ver me you & all those &	464	NEW POEMS 2	9
swoonsong came "I wish you good" the mechanical dawn	464	NEW POEMS 2	28
"morning") & that those you i St ep into	464	NEW POEMS 2	30
sleep kill and have you am luck -y is	467	NEW POEMS 5	11
a fraid of moon You) <> / / /	469	NEW POEMS 7	19
Mind's (i never you never he she or	474	NEW POEMS 12	2
or it never we you and they never saw	474	NEW POEMS 12	4
but if somebody or you are beautiful or deep	475	NEW POEMS 13	13
i eu can have you rope / / /	476	NEW POEMS 14	13
only so; only if you should turn the infinite	479	NEW POEMS 17	17
/ / / / you shall above all things	484	NEW POEMS 22	1
you're young, whatever life you wear it will become	484	NEW POEMS 22	2
wear it will become you; and if you are	484	NEW POEMS 22	3
become you; and if you are glad whatever's living	484	NEW POEMS 22	3
take off time that you should ever think, may	484	NEW POEMS 22	9
/ / / If you can't eat you got	489	50 POEMS 3	1
If you can't eat you got to smoke and	489	50 POEMS 3	1
go to sleep if you can't smoke you got	489	50 POEMS 3	5
if you can't smoke you got to Sing and	489	50 POEMS 3	5
go to sleep if you can't sing you got	489	50 POEMS 3	9

	PAGE	TITLE	LINE

YOU (CONTINUED)

	PAGE	TITLE	LINE
if you can't sing you got to die and	489	50 POEMS 3	9
go to sleep if you can't die you got	489	50 POEMS 3	13
if you can't die you got to dream and	489	50 POEMS 3	13
perished later all hands (you may recall) being lost	494	50 POEMS 8	7
/ / / (will you teach a wretch to	498	50 POEMS 12	1
in the rain (did you kiss a girl with	498	50 POEMS 12	17
each eye look "thank you" nicely the lady's small	506	50 POEMS 20	13
and i am for you just so long and	511	50 POEMS 25	27
ounce and i'll sell you a pound. Turn gert	513	50 POEMS 27	1
there a peers at you) has (elephant the blue)	516	50 POEMS 30	9
/ / / / you which could grin three	522	50 POEMS 35	1
i very humbly thank you which could grin may	522	50 POEMS 35	9
world can hold a you shall see the not	523	50 POEMS 36	2
i know this suit you pay a store too	523	50 POEMS 36	12
the world not fit you) he is not (i	523	50 POEMS 36	28
shadowless they? i bring you peace the moon of	527	50 POEMS 39	3
and fiend? i give you man extracted hate from	527	50 POEMS 39	8
having and have is (you guess) perhaps the very	528	50 POEMS 40	10
white earth in it you will (kiss me) go	529	50 POEMS 41	3
in it (kiss me) you will go on into	529	50 POEMS 41	6
firm day in it you will go (kiss me	529	50 POEMS 41	9
And if i sing you are my voice, /	531	50 POEMS 43	14
a tree-) o small you sitting in a tree-	535	50 POEMS 47	2
a lucky fifth of you turns people into eachs	537	50 POEMS 49	6
sunful i am through you so i / /	537	50 POEMS 49	16
glove but i'm and you are actual either hand	538	50 POEMS 50	10
false not true not you not i) it comes	542	1 X 1 2	7
over our thief goes (you go and i) has	543	1 X 1 3	20
"i understand quite what you mean by" sold! to	546	1 X 1 6	13
it's president of the you were say or a	549	1 X 1 9	2
(believe it or not) you told him: i told	553	1 X 1 13	16
prodigies of un) "have you" the mountain, while his	555	1 X 1 15	11
him a snowflake "yes: you may sleep now, my	555	1 X 1 15	14
(really unreal world, will you perhaps do the breathing	558	1 X 1 18	14
/ / / when you are silent, shining host	559	1 X 1 19	1
cannot stir imagining; while you are motionless-- whose	559	1 X 1 19	11
nowhere with me and you? Blow soon to never	560	1 X 1 20	20
complete) i not not you not possible; only truthful	564	1 X 1 24	9
people that abuses it you can git anything you	567	1 X 1 27	11
you can git anything you like out of it	567	1 X 1 27	12
out of it if you gut a mind to	567	1 X 1 27	14
a weazel how be you (sun or snow) gone	568	1 X 1 28	9
like all them kings you read about and on	568	1 X 1 28	13
and the boths and neithers--you must let them go	569	1 X 1 29	12
haste I must be you no sunbeam ever lies	570	1 X 1 30	4
will grin with pain You so&so true wars are	570	1 X 1 30	9
? i call twilight you 'll see an in	571	1 X 1 31	4
i've come to ask you if there isn't a	572	1 X 1 32	1
all whose mosts if you have known and i've	574	1 X 1 34	13
may move may rest --you bring (out of dark	575	1 X 1 35	6
the moon open for you and close will shy	575	1 X 1 35	15
all of time) gives you skilful his flame so	575	1 X 1 35	23
me or simplify my you , darling sweet this	577	1 X 1 37	11
me; for me and you, exceedingly too small. Swoop	579	1 X 1 39	8
a gr eenes t you b ecome s whi	581	1 X 1 41	8
surely not i not you behold nor any breathing	582	1 X 1 42	10
leastfully than i am you , we are spring	583	1 X 1 43	20
/ / i think you like" a strawberry bang	585	1 X 1 45	1
your heart: i'll give you a treasure of tiniest	586	1 X 1 46	2
bud when to me you made for by love	589	1 X 1 49	4
things when to me you gave gave darling birds	589	1 X 1 49	14
song when to me you leap and i'm born	589	1 X 1 49	18
knew and neither did you and everybody never breathed	591	1 X 1 51	14
has anybody seen little you-i who stood on a	593	1 X 1 53	3
a string (murmurs little you-i as the hill becomes	593	1 X 1 53	21
now now i love you and you love me	594	1 X 1 54	28
i love you and you love me (and books	594	1 X 1 54	28

	PAGE	TITLE	LINE

YOU (CONTINUED)

count to soon) rose--did you see her? darling, did	599	{CHAIRE} 1	10
see her? darling, did you (kiss me) quickly count	599	{CHAIRE} 1	10
quickly count to never? you were wrong --then all	599	{CHAIRE} 1	11
careful be lieve me you and i'll go strolling	600	{CHAIRE} 2	12
who's we --nor can you die or i and	601	{CHAIRE} 3	18
fool called everyone (or you or i) were wise."	603	{CHAIRE} 5	10
or i) were wise." "You mean worlds may have	603	{CHAIRE} 5	11
of stopping to think) you begin to feel of	604	{CHAIRE} 6	9
/ / we miss you, jack--tactfully you (with one	605	{CHAIRE} 7	1
we miss you, jack--tactfully you (with one cocked eyebrow) .	605	{CHAIRE} 7	1
god's truth stands art-naked: you and the fact that	605	{CHAIRE} 7	3
brewed which could knock you down (while scotch was	605	{CHAIRE} 7	4
all day) a 3ringbrain you had and a circusheart	605	{CHAIRE} 7	6
a dream-- here's, wherever you aren't or are, good	605	{CHAIRE} 7	15
this or i and you / / / /	608	{CHAIRE} 10	13
ocean patient) dream's eternity (you feel behind this man . .	617	{CHAIRE} 19	4
understand "i'll never let you go until you've made	622	{CHAIRE} 24	5
Who and i am you are i am we	630	{CHAIRE} 32	12
against these its until you are and until i	633	{CHAIRE} 35	7
appeal from reason" (freud) --you pays your money and . . .	636	{CHAIRE} 38	13
pays your money and you doesn't take your choice.	636	{CHAIRE} 38	14
/ / i'm asking you dear to what else	638	{CHAIRE} 40	3
doesn't of course but you don't seem to realize	638	{CHAIRE} 40	6
me isn't me can't you see now no not	638	{CHAIRE} 40	12
not any christ but you must understand why because	638	{CHAIRE} 40	13
supreme thunder? ours (over you reels and me a	639	{CHAIRE} 41	3
close as i'm to you yes closer made of	648	{CHAIRE} 50	9
(this i who's also you) and nothing less than	650	{CHAIRE} 52	10
carefully bring -ing to you and to me (and	652	{CHAIRE} 54	6
/ / i thank You God for most this	663	{CHAIRE} 65	1
merely being doubt unimaginable You? (now the ears of . . .	663	{CHAIRE} 65	12
in i are in you) this world (as timorous	664	{CHAIRE} 66	12
are in we; for you are and i am	664	{CHAIRE} 66	17
For love are in you am in i are	664	{CHAIRE} 66	24
little fish quiver so you and so i (now	665	{CHAIRE} 67	13
so) moon, she is you nothing may, quite your	666	{CHAIRE} 68	10
can understand and now you are and i am	667	{CHAIRE} 69	5
and i have no you: and all trees are	667	{CHAIRE} 69	11
(& therefore invisible) anyhow you 've (whoever we are) . . .	668	{CHAIRE} 70	14
rogue & vivid voltaire you beautiful anarchist (i salute . .	677	95 POEMS 5	15
daunted by always nothing) you darling diminutive person . .	678	95 POEMS 6	3
/ / / because you take life in your	679	95 POEMS 7	1
do the same because you aren't afraid to kiss	679	95 POEMS 7	5
is quite so good you don't conceive a better;	679	95 POEMS 7	10
so worse than worst you fall in hate with	679	95 POEMS 7	12
we lose (like a you or a me) it's	682	95 POEMS 10	11
"don't cry dear violet you may take mine" "o	684	95 POEMS 12	4
who gave it to you is the tallest of	684	95 POEMS 12	8
and wonder) is something you have and i 've	686	95 POEMS 14	6
g are (th e) you (o nly) asl (rose)	691	95 POEMS 19	5
her and him did you and did i climb	694	95 POEMS 22	2
play his handorgan until you say "i want a	697	95 POEMS 25	4
what it Takes. now you know (just as well	701	95 POEMS 29	10
looking for will" "did you look for him down	707	95 POEMS 35	2
never looked there" "and you couldn't well miss willy's . . .	707	95 POEMS 35	4
your annabel screech have you hunted her round by	707	95 POEMS 35	6
long as there's haymows you never can tell" "as	707	95 POEMS 35	10
is a riddle for you red says it aint	707	95 POEMS 35	19
lays" "black hell upon you and all filthy men	707	95 POEMS 35	21
at my willy and you in the newmown hay	707	95 POEMS 35	25
hay and he telling you no" "than look you	707	95 POEMS 35	26
you no" "than look you down through the old	707	95 POEMS 35	27
this unworld me by you as the god of	711	95 POEMS 39	2
hungary and do as you are bid a good	711	95 POEMS 39	18
his pretty pink shoulders you know how and he	711	95 POEMS 39	22
blind (like me like you) except in snow-- a	716	95 POEMS 44	3
believe (like me like you) vanish in so --laughing	716	95 POEMS 44	27

		PAGE	TITLE	LINE

YOU (CONTINUED)

/ / i love you much (most beautiful darling) . . . . 717 95 POEMS 45 . . . 1
earth and i like you better than everything in . . . . . . 717 95 POEMS 45 . . . 3
(rounD) moon, how do you (rouNd er than roUnd) . . . . . . 722 95 POEMS 50 . . . 4
/ / / / you no tice nobod y . . . . 727 95 POEMS 55 . . . 1
a slogan may topple you (trees are their roots . . . . . . 732 95 POEMS 60 . . . 2
his dream; dancin g you Star / / / . . . . 733 95 POEMS 61 . . . 11
shall love, do love you, was and will be . . . . 734 95 POEMS 62 . . . 3
/ first robin the; you say something (for only . . . . . . 737 95 POEMS 65 . . . 2
of living magicians (whom you and i some times . . . . . . 738 95 POEMS 66 . . . 6
time --how fortunate are you and i, whose home . . . . . . 743 95 POEMS 71 . . . 10
weed's a rose, roses (you feel certain) will only . . . . . 744 95 POEMS 72 . . . 7
nonexistence millions call life, you and i may reverently . . 745 95 POEMS 73 . . . 10
two guard me and you and little house this . . . . 746 95 POEMS 74 . . . 2
sings for us for you for me for each . . . . 760 95 POEMS 87 . . . 9
dead) dance, i and you; high (are become more . . . . 762 95 POEMS 89 . . . 10
new (every more only you) most emanation creates creation . . 764 95 POEMS 90 . . . 46
it (anywhere i go you go, my dear; and . . . . 766 95 POEMS 92 . . . 3
fear no fate (for you are my fate, my . . . . 766 95 POEMS 92 . . . 6
no world (for beautiful you are my world, my . . . . 766 95 POEMS 92 . . . 7
my true) and it's you are whatever a moon . . . . 766 95 POEMS 92 . . . 8
will always sing is you here is the deepest . . . . 766 95 POEMS 92 . . . 9
is now) and dance you suddenly blossoming tree --i'll . . . . 767 95 POEMS 93 . . . 23
the sky: with a you and a me and . . . . 769 95 POEMS 95 . . . 27
and the me purrs you and the gentle who-horns . . . . 773 73 POEMS 1 . . . 7
because he cannot fear (you see it in the . . . . 774 73 POEMS 2 . . . 15
we've the may (for you are in love and . . . . 776 73 POEMS 4 . . . 2
dream of spring --how you and i are blossoming . . . . . . 777 73 POEMS 5 . . . 16
simply Is what makes you feel you aren't 6 . . . . 779 73 POEMS 7 . . . 22
what makes you feel you aren't 6 or 6 . . . . 779 73 POEMS 7 . . . 22
for once (imag -ine) You / / / / . . . . 779 73 POEMS 7 . . . 31
my Darling is that you & i are more . . . . 782 73 POEMS 10 . . . 17
i are more than you & i (be ca . . . . 782 73 POEMS 10 . . . 18
have i done that You wouldn't have / / . . . . 784 73 POEMS 12 . . . 8
who doesn't agree (if you can't dentham comma bentham; . . . 791 73 POEMS 19 . . . 5
: far from it; you 're wrong, my friend. . . . . 793 73 POEMS 21 . . . 15
would be may that you and i'd be quite . . . . 798 73 POEMS 26 . . . 22
perfection-- another i and you, is a deduction which . . . . 798 73 POEMS 26 . . . 24
thus-- but look around you, friends and foes my . . . . . . 799 73 POEMS 27 . . . 39
stopped me by 'could you spare three cents please' . . . . . 800 73 POEMS 28 . . . 6
blessed evil-- it is you (ne i) nobody else . . . . 804 73 POEMS 32 . . . 8
mankind dizzy with haranguing --you are deafened every . . . 804 73 POEMS 32 . . . 10
trick of finding what you didn't lose (existing's tricky: . . 807 73 POEMS 35 . . . 1
arriving at the place you never left (and i . . . . 807 73 POEMS 35 . . . 4
--"dying" the ghost of you whispers "is very pleasant" . . . 808 73 POEMS 36 . . . 14
mysteries which i or you (blinded by merely things . . . . . 809 73 POEMS 37 . . . 5
falling most (there: did you see it?) star to . . . . 809 73 POEMS 37 . . . 12
your kiss losing through you what seemed myself, i . . . . . 810 73 POEMS 38 . . . 9
of my soul's return --you are my sun, my . . . . 810 73 POEMS 38 . . . 14
my selves go with you, only i remain; a . . . . 812 73 POEMS 40 . . . 2
or any somebody or you can begin to begin . . . . 816 73 POEMS 44 . . . 11
times encompass me and you: when are we never, ... 817 73 POEMS 45 . . . 4
must call life are you / / / / . . . . 818 73 POEMS 46 . . . 14
/ / who are you, little i (five or . . . . 824 73 POEMS 52 . . . 1
that" i marvelled "be you?" and a chickadee to . . . . . . 828 73 POEMS 56 . . . 2
most endure all that you never were hide, poor . . . . . . 834 73 POEMS 62 . . . 12
the same it's time you unbecame where climbing was . . . . . 834 73 POEMS 62 . . . 18
a miracle arrives (yes) you and i may not . . . . 835 73 POEMS 63 . . . 26
this summer world (and you and i who love . . . . 836 73 POEMS 64 . . . 3
"if i should tell you anything" (that eagerly sweet . . . . 836 73 POEMS 64 . . . 7
name, three i'll give you sweet joys for each . . . . 837 73 POEMS 65 . . . 3
this "i will give you five hopes for any . . . . 837 73 POEMS 65 . . . 8
one dying, i'll give you" silently cries the (whom . . . . . 837 73 POEMS 65 . . . 15

+YOU

FOR CONTEXT, SEE . . . . 25 T&C CHANSONS 2 . . . 19
FOR CONTEXT, SEE . . . . 109 & PORTRAIT 5 . . . 2
FOR CONTEXT, SEE . . . . 109 & PORTRAIT 5 . . . 11
FOR CONTEXT, SEE . . . . 227 IS 5 ONE GERT . . . 15

		PAGE	TITLE	LINE

+YOU (CONTINUED)

FOR CONTEXT, SEE	228 IS 5 ONE MARJ	4
FOR CONTEXT, SEE	229 IS 5 ONE FRAN	10
FOR CONTEXT, SEE	237 IS 5 ONE 8	14
FOR CONTEXT, SEE	247 IS 5 ONE 18	1
FOR CONTEXT, SEE	247 IS 5 ONE 18	6
FOR CONTEXT, SEE	259 IS 5 ONE 29	20
FOR CONTEXT, SEE	287 IS 5 FOUR 4	7
FOR CONTEXT, SEE	310 VIVA 2	2
FOR CONTEXT, SEE	310 VIVA 2	5
FOR CONTEXT, SEE	310 VIVA 2	5
FOR CONTEXT, SEE	310 VIVA 2	12
FOR CONTEXT, SEE	398 NO THANKS 15	21
FOR CONTEXT, SEE	410 NO THANKS 27	6
FOR CONTEXT, SEE	417 NO THANKS 34	23
FOR CONTEXT, SEE	442 NO THANKS 57	25
FOR CONTEXT, SEE	474 NEW POEMS 12	12
FOR CONTEXT, SEE	474 NEW POEMS 12	13
FOR CONTEXT, SEE	519 50 POEMS 33	28
FOR CONTEXT, SEE	547 1 X 1 7	1
FOR CONTEXT, SEE	547 1 X 1 7	2
FOR CONTEXT, SEE	547 1 X 1 7	3
FOR CONTEXT, SEE	547 1 X 1 7	4
FOR CONTEXT, SEE	547 1 X 1 7	4
FOR CONTEXT, SEE	547 1 X 1 7	6
FOR CONTEXT, SEE	547 1 X 1 7	7
FOR CONTEXT, SEE	547 1 X 1 7	8
FOR CONTEXT, SEE	547 1 X 1 7	9
FOR CONTEXT, SEE	602 (CHAIRE) 4	5
FOR CONTEXT, SEE	618 (CHAIRE) 20	4
FOR CONTEXT, SEE	618 (CHAIRE) 20	6
FOR CONTEXT, SEE	618 (CHAIRE) 20	19
FOR CONTEXT, SEE	618 (CHAIRE) 20	27
FOR CONTEXT, SEE	629 (CHAIRE) 31	12
FOR CONTEXT, SEE	710 95 POEMS 38	7
FOR CONTEXT, SEE	832 73 POEMS 60	10

YOU-I

| has anybody seen little you-i who stood on a | 593 1 X 1 53 | 3 |
| a string (murmurs little you-i as the hill becomes | 593 1 X 1 53 | 21 |

YOU-WITH-ME

| imagining spasm rise we you-with-me around (me) you IYou | 442 NO THANKS 57 | 23 |

YOU'D

| sharpens say to sing you'd almost cut your thumb | 624 (CHAIRE) 26 | 15 |
| cleanest keenest bravest killers you'd care to see (while | 709 95 POEMS 37 | 6 |

YOU'LL

and said never mind, you'll find But the moon	125 & SEVEN POEMS 4	19
when you're quite dressed you'll stand in the window	192 XLI CHANSONS 2	22
they'll stare! oh but you'll be very proud and	192 XLI CHANSONS 2	24
road the moon if you'll notice follows us like	303 IS 5 FIVE 2	9
that's yours; i guess you'll have to loan me	451 NO THANKS 66	6
(the time forever, and you'll wear your silver shoes	504 50 POEMS 18	16
coat --which something as you'll never guess in fifty	544 1 X 1 4	13
his head, baby & you'll find a heart in	637 (CHAIRE) 39	2
that heart, mabel & you'll find a bed in	637 (CHAIRE) 39	5
this bed, sibyl & you'll find a tart in	637 (CHAIRE) 39	8
the tart, lady & you'll find his mind in	637 (CHAIRE) 39	11
are as lost as you'll find / / /	647 (CHAIRE) 49	20
loud exactitudes of imprecision, you'll (silently alighting)	659 (CHAIRE) 61	12
ugly lame; but as you'll shortly comprehend a marvellous	799 73 POEMS 27	6

+YOU'LL

| FOR CONTEXT, SEE | 571 1 X 1 31 | 4 |

YOU'RE

not so hard dear you're killing me / /	109 & PORTRAIT 5	23
or unhappy then when you're quite dressed you'll stand	192 XLI CHANSONS 2	21
love you because when you're hard up you pawn	204 XLI LA GUERRE 2	10
a drink and when you're flush pride keeps you	204 XLI LA GUERRE 2	12
and tired to which you're married and hands get	242 IS 5 ONE 13	15
answers (but now don't you're hurting o Me please	343 VIVA 34	5

YOU'RE (CONTINUED)
  hurting o Me please you're killing) death is like . . . . . . 343 VIVA 34   6
  love said she) if you're willing said he (but . . . . 399 NO THANKS 16   19
  willing said he (but you're killing said she but . . . . . . 399 NO THANKS 16   20
  he ummm said she) you're divine! said he (you . . . . 399 NO THANKS 16   31
  and young. For if you're young, whatever life you . . . . . . 484 NEW POEMS 22   2
  says (floating each how) you're which as to die . . . . 543 1 X 1 3   9
  green of a new) you're who as to grow . . . . 543 1 X 1 3   11
  as to grow but you're he as to do . . . . 543 1 X 1 3   12
  this whirlingest earth? why you're by far the darlingest . . 590 1 X 1 50   8
  / / / "so you're hunting for ann well . . . . 707 95 POEMS 35   1
  more by far than you're alive or i'm-- crying . . . . 716 95 POEMS 44   31
  / / rosetree, rosetree --you're a song to see: . . . . 763 95 POEMS 90   2
  to see: whose all (you're a sight to sing) . . . . 763 95 POEMS 90   3
  as i'm and as you're --let's touch the sky: . . . . 769 95 POEMS 95   25
  something is (guess) yes you're right: my enemy . . . . 793 73 POEMS 21   24
  is quite without change, you're going to get one . . . . . . 800 73 POEMS 28   11
  busy the millions (as you're as can i'm) they . . . . 801 73 POEMS 29   14
+YOU'RE
  FOR CONTEXT, SEE . . . . 793 73 POEMS 21   15
YOU'VE
  like the nicest man you've never met who maybe . . . . 126 & SEVEN POEMS 5   14
  hero, Dan who as you've guessed already is the . . . . 254 IS 5 ONE 25   15
  let you go until you've made me white" so . . . . 622 {CHAIRE} 24   6
  here-- an everywhere which you've and i've agreed and . . . . 741 95 POEMS 69   12
+YOU'VE
  FOR CONTEXT, SEE . . . . 668 {CHAIRE} 70   14
YOUAMIARE
  equals mob love being youamiare (2) the holy miraculous . . . 803 73 POEMS 31   8
YOUFUL
  / / / / youful larger of smallish) Humble . . . . 503 50 POEMS 17   1
YOUKNOW
  daren't (sortof people well youknow kindof) aint & even . . . 412 NO THANKS 29   8
YOUNG
  the diadumenos in whose young chiseled eyes the people . . .   4 T&C EPITHALAM   33
  nakedness to strike the young world into smoking song-- . . .   7 T&C EPITHALAM   163
  and awkward foal, whereof young moons begin the newness . . .   11 T&C SONGS 2   4
  morning wandering. Through the young and awkward hours my . .   17 T&C PUELLA MEA   10
  when the world was young and new (a flower . . . .   18 T&C PUELLA MEA   54
  when the world was young and Diarmuid looked in . . . .   18 T&C PUELLA MEA   59
  when the world was young and mad, in the . . . .   20 T&C PUELLA MEA   131
  as a supple and young tree, her slim lascivious . . . .   20 T&C PUELLA MEA   156
  beauty of sunset the young city putting off dimension . . . .   48 T&C IMPRESS 2   15
  / / / the young man sitting in Dick . . . .   57 T&C PORTRAIT 5   1
  always keep" always? the young man sitting in Dick . . . . .   57 T&C PORTRAIT 5   22
  things obscene (Whose fingers young the caving ages curiously   77 T&C SON UNRE 2   3
  hair nor rout the young mouth whose lips begin . . . .   85 T&C SON ACTU 4   7
  face the streets turn young with rain, spiral acres . . . . .   93 & POST IMPR 5   4
  the, stomachs, of the young (girls silky and lewd) . . . . . 101 & POST IMPR 11   77
  flowers on his head. young death sits in a . . . . 102 & POST IMPR 12   3
  you and "Death is young life wears velour trousers . . . . . 102 & POST IMPR 12   7
  she is sitting beside young death, is slender; likes . . . . 102 & POST IMPR 12   25
  like ships and like young girls and like butterflies . . . . 111 & PORTRAIT 6   65
  already three or two young stars with spades of . . . . 115 & PORTRAIT 8   3
  will press in the young lips unearthly slenderness / . . . . 156 & SON ACTU 4   15
  more or less deserved, Young fellow go in peace. . . . . . . 229 IS 5 ONE FRAN   8
  pale softish almost round young man to whom headwaiters . . . 245 IS 5 ONE 16   7
  / / / this young question mark man question . . . . 246 IS 5 ONE 17   1
  the high minded pure young girl much kissed, by . . . . 273 IS 5 TWO 8   20
  fine Eyes some are young some old none look . . . . 274 IS 5 TWO 9   4
  a queer fellow as young as he is old . . . . 296 IS 5 FOUR 13   4
  his wife: Both very young noisily who kiss throw . . . . . . 312 VIVA 4   11
  in when's haymow with young fore'er (oh & by . . . . 316 VIVA 8   17
  captivating cognomen of a Young Woman of cambridge, mass. . 326 VIVA 18   1
  Gay is a certain Young Woman unacquainted with the . . . . . 327 VIVA 18   42
  the all saving our young kiss only must unexist, ... 373 VIVA 64   2
  death's place new fragrantly young earth space opening was. . 432 NO THANKS 49   19
  perfectly Nothing hurled into young Now entirely arrives . . 456 NO THANKS 71   8

		PAGE	TITLE	LINE

YOUNG (CONTINUED)

thick in a hot young queen with a twot . . . . 469 NEW POEMS 7 3
right they are not young and may myself do . . . . 481 NEW POEMS 19 8
things be glad and young. For if you're young, ... 484 NEW POEMS 22 1
young. For if you're young, whatever life you wear . . . . . 484 NEW POEMS 22 2
the twot nine months young / / / / . . . . 497 50 POEMS 11 8
frood whom he pronounces young mistaken and cradles in . . . 499 50 POEMS 13 4
shore and home come young so truly perfectly the . . . . . . 526 50 POEMS 38 8
into the morning the young morning with a warm . . . . 529 50 POEMS 41 4
yesterday most green and young pleasure and pain are . . . . 531 50 POEMS 43 4
cing on hollow was young Up floatingly clothes tumbledish . . 534 50 POEMS 46 4
if now or this (young trembling any) into flame . . . . . . 583 1 X 1 43 9
nor sleeping) since he's young with mysteries (each truly . . 617 (CHAIRE) 19 9
nic like ot-am sum-air (young old nic) like spring . . . . . 618 (CHAIRE) 20 25
have concealed so unimaginably young a star / / . . . . . . 626 (CHAIRE) 28 14
its life where the young bell tolled and the . . . . 647 (CHAIRE) 49 14
of day) younger than young bird first for joy, ... 666 (CHAIRE) 68 18
man am i) So young young young and with . . . . 685 95 POEMS 13 13
am i) So young young young and with a . . . . 685 95 POEMS 13 13
i) So young young young and with a something . . . . 685 95 POEMS 13 13
/ / / / Young m oon: be kind . . . . 733 95 POEMS 61 1
why: old turns to young (winter goodbye) april hello, ... 737 95 POEMS 65 6
my very so gay young love why? how-- we . . . . 767 95 POEMS 93 16
eyes are keener (for young is the year, for . . . . 769 95 POEMS 95 11
is the year, for young is the year) --let's . . . . 769 95 POEMS 95 11
could quite be (and young is the year, dear) . . . . 769 95 POEMS 95 24
while old worlds and young (big little and all . . . . 776 73 POEMS 4 5
gay fair brave tall young come they) through the . . . . . . 778 73 POEMS 6 10
/ if seventy were young and death uncommon (forgiving . . . . 798 73 POEMS 26 1
(halting) "a tall strong young finelooking fellow, dressed . 800 73 POEMS 28 3

YOUNGER

threecoloured puke over this younger than i am newspaper . . 324 VIVA 16 9
here youngest selves yet younger selves conceive here's . . . 538 50 POEMS 50 7
november and april) who younger than begin are, the . . . . . 575 1 X 1 35 37
of forever with summitless younger than angels are mountains 586 1 X 1 46 5
(at yes of day) younger than young bird first . . . . 666 (CHAIRE) 68 18
the older he's the younger she's / / / . . . . 742 95 POEMS 70 18

YOUNGEST

to use for their youngest angels (whose praising bodies . . . 20 T&C PUELLA MEA 142
if a score of youngest angels suddenly should stretch . . . . 130 & SON REAL 1 5
was kilt and my youngest boy was kilt last . . . . 271 IS 5 TWO 6 7
gone to say? here youngest selves yet younger selves . . . . 538 50 POEMS 50 7
least unmotion roams the youngest star) --how should a . . . 609 (CHAIRE) 11 12
if the humble proud youngest bud testified "giving (and . . . 763 95 POEMS 90 16
slender their ladies (Each youngest) in sunlight / / . . . . 778 73 POEMS 6 24

YOUNGLY

(swooning) a pillar of youngly loveflesh topped with danc . . 615 (CHAIRE) 17 1

YOUR

/ / Always before your voice my soul half-beautiful . . . . . 11 T&C SONGS 2 1
the strong silences of your song; or as a . . . . 11 T&C SONGS 2 10
its lovelier friends, between your thoughts more white than . 11 T&C SONGS 2 14
of anguish quivers to your words, As to a . . . . 11 T&C SONGS 2 17
the snow, and before your dead face which sleeps, ... 11 T&C SONGS 2 29
heart-wholeness overmuch Expects of your hair pale, a terror 12 T&C SONGS 2 39
and Master Hafiz keep your dead beautiful ladies. Mine . . . 17 T&C PUELLA MEA 2
lovelier than any of your ladies were. In her . . . . 17 T&C PUELLA MEA 4
made. And never boast your dead beauties, you greatest . . . 22 T&C PUELLA MEA 243
wholly kiss-- never boast your dead beauties, mine being . . 22 T&C PUELLA MEA 249
Master Hafiz, to me your ladies are all one-- . . . . 23 T&C PUELLA MEA 264
are all one-- keep your dead beautiful ladies. Eater . . . . 23 T&C PUELLA MEA 265
city of Bagdad.) Keep your dead beautiful ladies Harun . . . 23 T&C PUELLA MEA 289
i saw you close your eyes and i came . . . . 30 T&C ORIENTALE 4 35
love, the breaking of your soul upon my lips . . . . 38 T&C AMORES 3 16
in my fingers drooped your shining body when my . . . . 39 T&C AMORES 4 13
my heart sang between your perfect breasts darkness and . . . 39 T&C AMORES 4 15
becoming steps to seek your face and i entreat, ... 42 T&C AMORES 6 14
come receive him as your lover sumptuously being kind . . . . 42 T&C AMORES 6 19
i trust him to your grace, and for in . . . . 42 T&C AMORES 6 23

YOUR (CONTINUED)

	PAGE	TITLE	LINE
under the window of your soul it is not	43	T&C AMORES 7	5
/ / / / your little voice Over the	44	T&C AMORES 8	1
and death leaping Sweetly your voice / / /	44	T&C AMORES 8	24
how do you like your blueeyed boy Mister Death	60	T&C PORTRAIT 8	10
muddy petticoat, drowsy is your mouth your eyes are	61	T&C PORTRAIT 9	13
drowsy is your mouth your eyes are sticky with	61	T&C PORTRAIT 9	14
When you sing in your whiskey-voice the grass rises	61	T&C PORTRAIT 9	18
and the slobber of your thighs i am so	61	T&C PORTRAIT 9	25
for thou comest and your hands are the snow	61	T&C PORTRAIT 9	28
of all i hear your stepping freakish feet feet	61	T&C PORTRAIT 9	34
don't remember me pencil your eyes dear and have	71	T&C SON REAL 2	2
at Tabari' s, keep your teeth snowy, stick to	71	T&C SON REAL 2	4
wear dark, and where your meeting breasts are round	71	T&C SON REAL 2	5
i say that if your lips, which i have	76	T&C SON UNRE 1	2
should touch another's, and your dear strong fingers clutch .	76	T&C SON UNRE 1	3
if on another's face your sweet hair lay in	76	T&C SON UNRE 1	5
the rare entertainment of your eyes, when (being fool	78	T&C SON UNRE 3	2
i have deemed with your peculiar mouth my heart	78	T&C SON UNRE 3	4
the genuine apparition of your smile (it was through	78	T&C SON UNRE 3	6
the intolerant brightness of your charms: one pierced moment	78	T&C SON UNRE 3	11
petal of somewhere in your heart pinched from dumb	80	T&C SON UNRE 5	7
wholly trembling memory undertakes --your kiss, the little .	82	T&C SON ACTU 1	3
the singular beginning of your smile) a skilful uncouth . . .	83	T&C SON ACTU 2	5
the reckless magic of your mouth) my love is	83	T&C SON ACTU 2	8
thousand selves who are your smile. / / /	92	& POST IMPR 4	21
flesh stalks the Momentinmyarms your expression my love when	94	& POST IMPR 6	23
people bells) i say your eyes can take day	98	& POST IMPR 9	3
i know only that your hands move more simply	98	& POST IMPR 9	7
moon, i somehow feel your smile slightly is a	98	& POST IMPR 9	11
the soaring silence (put your smallest ear against yester- .	110	& PORTRAIT 6	30
hair is Nile) put your ear to the ground	113	& PORTRAIT 6	113
lives a kiss) kneeling, your frequent mercy begs, sharply . .	115	& PORTRAIT 8	8
a monstrous din watch your step and follow me	117	& PORTRAIT 10	27
my stomach goes into your Little Stomach My legs	123	& SEVEN POEMS 2	9
My legs are in your legs Your arms under	123	& SEVEN POEMS 2	10
are in your legs Your arms under me around;	123	& SEVEN POEMS 2	10
fits (my head) in your Brain--my, head's big she	123	& SEVEN POEMS 2	12
(said laughing) with your head. all big /	123	& SEVEN POEMS 2	15
ways of sitting on your head your unnatural hair	126	& SEVEN POEMS 5	9
sitting on your head your unnatural hair has in	126	& SEVEN POEMS 5	9
about you somewhere behind your back it makes your	126	& SEVEN POEMS 5	18
your back it makes your neck feel pleasant and	126	& SEVEN POEMS 5	19
my dear, Time for your musiclesson and you like	126	& SEVEN POEMS 5	29
and you take all your prickley-clothes off and squeeze- . . .	127	& SEVEN POEMS 5	33
whose mouths distinctly walk your smiles accuse the dusk . .	138	& SON REAL 9	4
subdued magic while in your eyes there lives a	138	& SON REAL 9	7
drifting sexual feather of your shall i say body?	140	& SON REAL 11	3
of my hips; or, your first twitch of crisp	140	& SON REAL 11	7
lips pleasantly groan on your taste. Jumped the quick	154	& SON ACTU 3	4
the quick wall of your smile into stupid gardens	154	& SON ACTU 3	5
i love you.... feel your suddenly body reach for	157	& SON ACTU 6	6
firmer lips to take your new mouth in his	161	& SON ACTU 10	3
limp huddling string of your smile over his body	161	& SON ACTU 10	6
normal worms. Dress deftly your flesh in stupid stuffs, . . .	161	& SON ACTU 10	9
the immense weapon of your hair. Understanding why his . . .	161	& SON ACTU 10	10
inch of nothing for your soul. / / /	161	& SON ACTU 10	14
And the coolness of your smile is stirringofbirds between . .	163	& SON ACTU 12	17
will shut quietly) almost, your kiss / / /	163	& SON ACTU 12	22
i grieve, faint for your face O stay with	165	& SON ACTU 14	9
Nearness rapes laughter from your preferable, eyes / / . . .	166	& SON ACTU 15	16
getting mandolin-clink mixed with your hair; feeling your .	169	& SON ACTU 18	6
with your hair; feeling your knees among the supercilious .	169	& SON ACTU 18	6
naked amid unnaked things, your flesh, a succinct wandlike .	170	& SON ACTU 19	7
futile purr of blood; your sex squeaked like a	170	& SON ACTU 19	9
My crazy fingers liked your dress ....your kiss, your	173	& SON ACTU 22	8
fingers liked your dress ....your kiss, your kiss was	173	& SON ACTU 22	9
your dress ....your kiss, your kiss was a distinct	173	& SON ACTU 22	9

		PAGE	TITLE	LINE

YOUR (CONTINUED)

Text	PAGE	TITLE	LINE
when it is with your body. It is so	175 & SON ACTU 24	1
nerves more. i like your body. i like what	175 & SON ACTU 24	4
feel the spine of your body and its bones, ...	175 & SON ACTU 24	6
the, shocking fuzz of your electric fur, and what-is-it . . .	175 & SON ACTU 24	11
make me stern against your charming strength O haste	182 XLI SONGS 4	14
holy city which is your face your little cheeks	186 XLI SONGS 8	6
which is your face your little cheeks the streets	186 XLI SONGS 8	7
the streets of smiles your eyes half- thrush half-angel . . .	186 XLI SONGS 8	9
half- thrush half-angel and your drowsy lips where float . .	186 XLI SONGS 8	11
the sweet shy pirouette your hair and then your	186 XLI SONGS 8	15
your hair and then your dancesong soul. rarely-beloved a . .	186 XLI SONGS 8	17
you forgot to shut your big eyes. where did	191 XLI CHANSONS 1	4
sweetly i will kiss your cool bark and hug	192 XLI CHANSONS 2	9
and tight just as your mother would, only don't	192 XLI CHANSONS 2	11
fluffy threads, put up your little arms and i'll	192 XLI CHANSONS 2	17
Lumberman of The Distinct your brain's axe only chops	195 XLI CHANSONS 5	17
hard up you pawn your intelligence to buy a	204 XLI LA GUERRE 2	10
but more especially in your own house Humanity i	204 XLI LA GUERRE 2	16
secret of life in your pants and forgetting it's	204 XLI LA GUERRE 2	19
the stabbing music of your white youth wounded by	218 XLI SONNETS 14	2
violinists among my and your skyscrapers--Helen & Cleopatra .	230 IS 5 ONE 2	26
a formula: example, Turn Your Shirttails Into Drawers and . .	230 IS 5 ONE 2	33
O backward Time in your no thy flight and	233 IS 5 ONE 4	3
little child. In thy your ear: en amerique on	233 IS 5 ONE 4	5
fellow's twistandtwirl talk about your Sal- Sal- Sal-, talk .	235 IS 5 ONE 6	19
Sal- Sal-, talk about your Salo -mes but gimmie	235 IS 5 ONE 6	23
if or when the your-and my- idle vertical worthless	260 IS 5 ONE 30	14
for May --bring forth your flowers and machinery: sculpture .	264 IS 5 ONE 33	9
a damn... bring on your fireworks, which are a	264 IS 5 ONE 33	21
deafanddumb thy sons acclaim your glorious name by gorry . .	268 IS 5 TWO 3	7
odd what pops into your jolly tete when the	269 IS 5 TWO 4	3
freezing or up to your you know what in	272 IS 5 TWO 7	9
(dreaming, et cetera, of Your smile eyes knees and	276 IS 5 TWO 10	25
eyes knees and of your Etcetera) / / /	276 IS 5 TWO 10	26
think of this? Do your proud fingers and your	279 IS 5 THREE 3	21
your proud fingers and your arms tremble remembering	279 IS 5 THREE 3	22
whys which lurk between your naked shoulderblades. --Here . .	282 IS 5 THREE 6	23
downward, embrace me with your body's suddenly curving entire	282 IS 5 THREE 6	34
silent and everywhere you your kisses your flesh mind	283 IS 5 THREE 7	16
everywhere you your kisses your flesh mind breathing beside .	283 IS 5 THREE 7	16
and the sea ...finally your eyes knew me, we	283 IS 5 THREE 7	20
how this has arrived your mind may guess if	285 IS 5 FOUR 2	11
dawn and twilight) giving your eyes, present me also	285 IS 5 FOUR 2	15
various deaths which are your lover lady: together with . . .	285 IS 5 FOUR 2	21
brain is less than your eyelids' flutter which says	290 IS 5 FOUR 7	12
myself is sculptor of your body's idiom: the musician	291 IS 5 FOUR 8	7
idiom: the musician of your wrists; the poet who	291 IS 5 FOUR 8	8
mistranslate a rhythm in your hair, (your fingertips the . .	291 IS 5 FOUR 8	11
rhythm in your hair, (your fingertips the way you	291 IS 5 FOUR 8	12
move) the painter of your voice-- beyond these elements . . .	291 IS 5 FOUR 8	15
me carven thing provoke your gesture possibly or any	291 IS 5 FOUR 8	20
its own reason) in your lips slenderly should create	291 IS 5 FOUR 8	22
the distinct country of your eyes, gifted with green	291 IS 5 FOUR 8	26
i am a wind-- your walls will not reckon	292 IS 5 FOUR 9	5
the normal corners of your heart will never guess	292 IS 5 FOUR 9	14
fear to miss within your least gesture the hurting	293 IS 5 FOUR 10	7
ways to dust of your fragility (but chiefly of	293 IS 5 FOUR 10	15
fragility (but chiefly of your smile, most suddenly which . .	293 IS 5 FOUR 10	16
ever so tinily these, your crisp eyes actually shall	294 IS 5 FOUR 11	8
new faeries (and if your slim lips are amused, ...	294 IS 5 FOUR 11	10
ever fear, me in your heart softly; not all	294 IS 5 FOUR 11	18
am i separated from your body smile brain hands	295 IS 5 FOUR 12	3
begin and increase, since your mind has walked into	297 IS 5 FOUR 14	5
always who begs in your mind (slightly smiling, patient, . .	298 IS 5 FOUR 15	2
himself taptaptaps out of your brain, hopes, life to	298 IS 5 FOUR 15	26
invisibly living rhythm of your Heart possibly will	300 IS 5 FOUR 17	8
gradually) remembering badly, softly your kissed thrice . . .	300 IS 5 FOUR 17	23

	PAGE	TITLE	LINE

YOUR (CONTINUED)

and puerile moving of your arm will do suddenly	302	IS 5 FIVE 1	9
only turn a little your. so. And there's the	303	IS 5 FIVE 2	15
things chiefly which wrong your eyes (frailer than most . . .	306	IS 5 FIVE 5	3
songs less firm than your body's whitest song upon	306	IS 5 FIVE 5	4
very skilful strangeness of your smile the keen primeval . .	306	IS 5 FIVE 5	7
keen primeval silence of your hair --let the world	306	IS 5 FIVE 5	8
"thought you were earning your living or probably dead" . . .	313	VIVA 5	7
Jefferson to Injustice Taughed your story is so interested .	321	VIVA 13	3
hands with ludendorff and your humble moving through the . .	324	VIVA 16	12
admit i've died) seeing your bald intellect collywobbling on	329	VIVA 20	3
"I will not kiss your fucking flag" straightway the	339	VIVA 30	19
does a hand with your hair in my imagination	356	VIVA 47	22
how dreaming becomes if your heart's mine) i guess	364	VIVA 55	5
gladly beyond any experience, your eyes have their silence: .	366	VIVA 57	2
have their silence: in your most frail gesture are	366	VIVA 57	3
they are too near your slightest look easily will	366	VIVA 57	5
first rose or if your wish be to close	366	VIVA 57	9
equals the power of your intense fragility: whose texture . .	366	VIVA 57	14
understands the voice of your eyes is deeper than	366	VIVA 57	19
so quite softly as your hair what bird has	367	VIVA 58	4
rare quite who are your eyes (shall any dream	367	VIVA 58	8
sealace appeared to me your mind drifting with chuckling . .	369	VIVA 60	4
sinking) inward, fled; softly your face smile breasts gargled	369	VIVA 60	9
deepness to rise these your wrists thighs feet hands	369	VIVA 60	12
last night, all of your body with its spirit	369	VIVA 60	18
the guessable mirrors which your eyes are You will	370	VIVA 61	10
wholly lives Givehurling with your my most : locking	371	VIVA 62	17
this throat) i wear your dearest fears beyond their	372	VIVA 63	10
opening encompass true) while your contriving fate, my . . .	373	VIVA 64	17
love separate, smileless--merely imagine your sorrow a . . .	374	VIVA 65	2
/ / put off your faces, Death: for day	376	VIVA 67	1
come, Love, put on your faces / / /	376	VIVA 67	14
yourself consider wonderful that your (how luminous) life . .	379	VIVA 70	11
books could even be your shelves (that which we	386	NO THANKS 3	4
called theatre & with your wn eyes beh ld	392	NO THANKS 9	10
life said he but your wife said she now	399	NO THANKS 16	22
gutted with grace" squeeze your nuts and open your	407	NO THANKS 24	16
your nuts and open your face / / /	407	NO THANKS 24	16
mayn't be twirled around your little finger is) what's . . .	411	NO THANKS 28	7
that you may mess your pance every kumrad is	413	NO THANKS 30	12
mountains for friends --open your thighs to fate and	420	NO THANKS 37	13
to sap and to your (in my arms flowering	424	NO THANKS 41	2
space opening was. Were your eyes: lost, believing; hushed .	432	NO THANKS 49	20
knaves on Shadows fed, your Harry's Tom, your Tom	438	NO THANKS 54	10
fed, your Harry's Tom, your Tom is Dick; while	438	NO THANKS 54	10
so (unlove disappearing) only your less than guessed more . .	450	NO THANKS 65	10
whenless voices sing everywhere your selves himself	450	NO THANKS 65	18
shall who wave among your deepening thighs a greedier . . .	454	NO THANKS 69	3
o- pening of (writhing your exploding my) heart before . . .	480	NEW POEMS 18	15
and (in his mercy) your true lover spare: for	484	NEW POEMS 22	10
her alone she's not your gal jack spoke to	496	50 POEMS 10	3
is not to elevate your tool but drop a	500	50 POEMS 14	10
forever, and you'll wear your silver shoes / /	504	50 POEMS 18	16
feels who inquires is your cough better today? nn-nn	506	50 POEMS 20	7
equal one) which may your million selves and my	510	50 POEMS 24	12
if swallows tryst in your barn be glad; nobody	514	50 POEMS 28	7
guess) childmoon smile to your breathing doll / /	518	50 POEMS 32	12
stern particular Love surround your trite how terrible . . .	522	50 POEMS 35	10
out of black because your absolute courage with its	522	50 POEMS 35	14
completes its brightness with your eyes any illimitable star	526	50 POEMS 38	11
(kiss me down into your memory and a memory	529	50 POEMS 41	10
of shore so far your nearness reaches a lucky	537	50 POEMS 49	5
sticking fire my are your are birds our all	541	1 X 1 1	5
is a comfortable disease: your victim (death and life . . .	554	1 X 1 14	3
all ye screamers, till your if is up and	555	1 X 1 15	9
begin the colours of your voice) from some complete	559	1 X 1 19	5
a new moon outside your window saying if that's	572	1 X 1 32	2

YOUR (CONTINUED)

	PAGE	TITLE	LINE
/ / except in your honour, my loveliest, nothing	575	1 X 1 35	1
his flame so is your heart alert, of languages	575	1 X 1 35	25
the worlds move in your (and rest, my love)	575	1 X 1 35	40
who is la guerre) your me or simplify my	577	1 X 1 37	11
(and does with each your least your any most	580	1 X 1 40	2
with each your least your any most very amazing	580	1 X 1 40	3
life and strikes my your our blossoming sphere /	582	1 X 1 42	16
/ / / open your heart: i'll give you	586	1 X 1 46	1
me and only while your sweet eyes close have	588	1 X 1 48	5
/ "sweet spring is your time is my time	591	1 X 1 51	1
singing) "sweet spring is your time is my time	591	1 X 1 51	25
high bluer took it your but bluest took it	593	1 X 1 53	16
is away and so your is a my (with	594	1 X 1 54	23
down (while scotch was your breakfast every night all	605	(CHAIRE) 7	5
ready were all erect your yous to cross the	605	(CHAIRE) 7	12
/ / / hair your a brook (it through	613	(CHAIRE) 15	1
sing you'd almost cut your thumb so right he	624	(CHAIRE) 26	15
"or even a daisy-- your thorniest question my roses	625	(CHAIRE) 27	13
whose magical gaiety makes your beautiful name-- i feel . . .	631	(CHAIRE) 33	12
reason" (freud) --you pays your money and you doesn't	636	(CHAIRE) 38	13
and you doesn't take your choice. Ain't freedom grand	636	(CHAIRE) 38	14
twiceuponatime wave-- put out your eyes, and touch the . . .	639	(CHAIRE) 41	13
/ neither awake (there's your general yas buy gad)	640	(CHAIRE) 42	2
of a cannibal) there's your mineral general animal (five . .	640	(CHAIRE) 42	11
/ / / when your honest redskin toma hawked	643	(CHAIRE) 45	1
you nothing may, quite your my (my your and)	666	(CHAIRE) 68	12
quite your my (my your and) self without, completely	666	(CHAIRE) 68	12
(by the miracle of your sweet innocence refuted) clumsy . . .	669	(CHAIRE) 71	10
laughshriek ing at me your scorn of easily hatred	677	95 POEMS 5	4
of inquisitive merrily humble your livingest courage / / . .	678	95 POEMS 6	16
you take life in your stride (instead of scheming	679	95 POEMS 7	1
always failed to fool your heart but most (without	679	95 POEMS 7	8
than all (as all your more than eyes tell	683	95 POEMS 11	13
unthings silent three like your my life and our	687	95 POEMS 15	11
for curiosity (and close your eyes) / / /	689	95 POEMS 17	8
(for instance) the Knowing your whole (yes god damned) . . .	702	95 POEMS 30	11
like i just heard your annabel screech have you	707	95 POEMS 35	5
pink pinafore'd knock out your eye" "well maybe she's	707	95 POEMS 35	8
with the likes of your son" "and who but	707	95 POEMS 35	12
son" "and who but your daughter i'm asking yes	707	95 POEMS 35	13
have showed billy how" "your bastard boy must have	707	95 POEMS 35	15
--sunlight and singing welcome your coming although winter .	717	95 POEMS 45	4
gayest someone's heart at your each nearerness) everyone . .	717	95 POEMS 45	12
to die dream that your valentine makes happier me	718	95 POEMS 46	3
wind is wind) trust your heart if the seas	732	95 POEMS 60	5
the future (and dance your death away at this	732	95 POEMS 60	11
/ / / / your birthday comes to tell	734	95 POEMS 62	1
they live-- unless by your thinking forever's long let . . .	742	95 POEMS 70	11
/ / stand with your lover on the ending	743	95 POEMS 71	1
/ / / joyful your complete fearless and pure	761	95 POEMS 88	1
coming of pure joyful your fearless and complete love, . . .	761	95 POEMS 88	10
each creature new (except your fear to whom i	762	95 POEMS 89	6
measure a now of your treasure blithe each shameless	763	95 POEMS 90	36
of a person; joyful your any new (every more	764	95 POEMS 90	45
/ / i carry your heart with me (i	766	95 POEMS 92	1
by only me is your doing, my darling) i	766	95 POEMS 92	4
stars apart i carry your heart (i carry it	766	95 POEMS 92	15
ruffian of the sky your kingbird doesn't give a	774	73 POEMS 2	2
vast most crafty crow your kingbird doesn't give a	774	73 POEMS 2	9
on the other well your oldest pal for instance	779	73 POEMS 7	10
dad first ("don't tell your mother") had; making annie . . .	794	73 POEMS 22	4
--saints and satyrs, go your way youths and maidens:	794	73 POEMS 22	7
more nearest even than your fate and mine (or	809	73 POEMS 37	1
than with the mystery your smile sings or if	810	73 POEMS 38	4
my deeper death becomes your kiss losing through you	810	73 POEMS 38	8
safely may by imperishable your glory escorted through . . .	811	73 POEMS 39	2
/ / / / your homecoming will be my	812	73 POEMS 40	1

931

	PAGE	TITLE	LINE
YOUR (CONTINUED)			
who, till their and your returning, spends the forever . . .	812	73 POEMS 40	5
eyes have opened to your morning feeling their stars	812	73 POEMS 40	7
stars have risen through your skies: so, in how	812	73 POEMS 40	8
my very life who's your --when all fears hopes	812	73 POEMS 40	12
whose absence would make your whole life and my	817	73 POEMS 45	13
without the mercy of your eyes your voice your	819	73 POEMS 47	2
mercy of your eyes your voice your ways (o	819	73 POEMS 47	2
your eyes your voice your ways (o very most	819	73 POEMS 47	3
infinite precise thrill of your beauty, then my lost	819	73 POEMS 47	13
year --now, before quite your whisper's whisper is subtracted	821	73 POEMS 49	9
/ / / "though your sorrows not any tongue	837	73 POEMS 65	1
But it must be your" whispers that flower murmurs	837	73 POEMS 65	5
but it Must be your" perfectly alive blossom of	837	73 POEMS 65	10
"but it must be Your" / / / /	837	73 POEMS 65	18
believing world denies, whereas your lover (looking through .	845	73 POEMS 73	12
+YOUR			
FOR CONTEXT, SEE	109	& PORTRAIT 5	5
FOR CONTEXT, SEE	247	IS 5 ONE 18	6
FOR CONTEXT, SEE	310	VIVA 2	6
FOR CONTEXT, SEE	330	VIVA 21	10
YOUR-AND			
if or when the your-and my- idle vertical worthless	260	IS 5 ONE 30	14
YOURS			
/ / / / yours is the music for	84	T&C SON ACTU 3	1
music for no instrument yours the preposterous colour	84	T&C SON ACTU 3	2
worm huge, ecstatic, rathe.... yours are the poems i	84	T&C SON ACTU 3	12
heart has been with yours shut by our mingling	297	IS 5 FOUR 14	1
hug behemoth truly pseudo yours podia of radarw leschin . . .	333	VIVA 24	25
chips of when) that's yours; i guess you'll have	451	NO THANKS 66	5
our gone snow gone yours mine . We're alive	491	50 POEMS 5	9
try, boys) mine is yours ask me the name	513	50 POEMS 27	18
missed (it's in, girls) yours is mine either was	513	50 POEMS 27	27
and hoping's very fears yours is the light by	810	73 POEMS 38	12
which my spirit's born: yours is the darkness of	810	73 POEMS 38	13
+YOURS			
FOR CONTEXT, SEE	445	NO THANKS 60	29
YOURSELF			
it was i think yourself delivered into both my	57	T&C PORTRAIT 5	18
who will advise even yourself, lady in the most	294	IS 5 FOUR 11	3
perpetual sea --but if yourself consider wonderful that your	379	VIVA 70	10
nothing usefully and love yourself so more than truly	481	NEW POEMS 19	10
glad whatever's living will yourself become. Girlboys may . .	484	NEW POEMS 22	4
is not to get yourself a stool but draw	500	50 POEMS 14	2
dishonoured mind who thought yourself so wise; and much . . .	834	73 POEMS 62	14
YOURSELVES			
to become noone except yourselves r s v p"	504	50 POEMS 18	5
+YOURSELVES			
FOR CONTEXT, SEE	450	NO THANKS 65	18
YOURSMINE			
whirling climb to GIVE (yoursmine mineyours yoursmine ! i . .	445	NO THANKS 60	29
to GIVE (yoursmine mineyours yoursmine ! i ( )	445	NO THANKS 60	29
YOUS			
were all erect your yous to cross the chasm	605	{CHAIRE} 7	12
YOUSE			
raise the shade will youse dearie? rain wouldn't that	109	& PORTRAIT 5	2
slowly) "I'm asleep. Yep. Youse is asleep kid and	228	IS 5 ONE MARJ	4
Green River (here's to youse) "a bloke wot's well	229	IS 5 ONE FRAN	10
kid Christmas meant sumpn youse knows wot i refers	237	IS 5 ONE 8	14
/ / / mr youse needn't be so spry	247	IS 5 ONE 18	1
he-man's solid bliss for youse ideas i'll match youse	247	IS 5 ONE 18	6
youse ideas i'll match youse a pretty girl who	247	IS 5 ONE 18	6
People preferring Negroes Indians Youse n.b. ye twang of . .	410	NO THANKS 27	6
YOUTH			
each with a writhing youth caught to her brazen	4	T&C EPITHALAM	42
of my stupid sincere youth the exquisite failure uncouth . .	11	T&C SONGS 2	6
whose arched occasional steep youth swallows curvingly the .	140	& SON REAL 11	5
the corners of her youth; whom, fiercely shy and	214	XLI SONNETS 10	6

		PAGE	TITLE	LINE

YOUTH (CONTINUED)
    fins sharply pleasant, my youth has travelled toward her . . 216 XLI SONNETS 12   4
    the yes of her youth. And if somebody hears . . . . 216 XLI SONNETS 12   8
    music of your white youth wounded by my arms' . . . . 218 XLI SONNETS 14   2
    this tall strong stalwart youth, what sight shall human . . 254 IS 5 ONE 25   2
    bright heyday of his youth the upper class American . . . . 273 IS 5 TWO 8   15
    clumsily wilted fingers emptying youth colour and what was . 359 VIVA 50   7
    the with a carroty youth blonde whis (gorgedis reswal . . . . 629 {CHAIRE} 31   17
    prodigal read generous --for youth read age-- read for . . . 689 95 POEMS 17   2
    Keep Off signs) & youth yanks them down (old . . . . 729 95 POEMS 57   5
    No Tres) & (pas) youth laughs (sing old age . . . . 729 95 POEMS 57   10
    Must n't Don't &) youth goes right on gr . . . . 729 95 POEMS 57   17
YOUTH'S
    certainly wherefrom departed is youth's indispensable . . . .   57 T&C PORTRAIT 5   40
YOUTHS
    delicately crouching beneath silver youths the leaneyed . . . 110 & PORTRAIT 6   36
    satyrs, go your way youths and maidens: let us . . . . 794 73 POEMS 22   8
YUH
    ughhuh sure why not yuh course yeh well naturally . . . . . . 400 NO THANKS 17   9
    (it's Rilly yeh ughhuh yuh) i know (o sure . . . . 400 NO THANKS 17   14
YUNNUHSTAN
    / / ygUDuh ydoan yunnuhstan ydoan o yunnuhstan dem . . . . . 547 1 X 1 7   3
    ydoan yunnuhstan ydoan o yunnuhstan dem yguduh ged yunnuhstan 547 1 X 1 7   5
    yunnuhstan dem yguduh ged yunnuhstan dem doidee yguduh ged . 547 1 X 1 7   7
YURARSTOIN
    (Nowoi askyuh woodundat maik yurarstoin green? Oilsaisough.) 310 VIVA 2   6
YZ
    front; and there was yz SHOT AND KILLED her . . . . 317 VIVA 9   11
Z
    ATHLETE'S BRIDE (lullaby) & z = an infrafairy of . . . . . . 317 VIVA 9   3
+Z
    FOR CONTEXT, SEE . . . . 317 VIVA 9   12
ZAGFLASH
    zigging HE of a zagflash king poUnc es buzzsqueaking . . . . 747 95 POEMS 75   11
ZEAL
    then fired by hypercivic zeal sought newer pastures or . . . 258 IS 5 ONE 28   11
ZERO
    (his from daughter's mother's zero mind fahrenheit) old . . . 546 1 X 1 6   1
ZEUS
    loved too well? Chryselephantine Zeus Olympian sceptred . . .   3 T&C EPITHALAM   25
    very different sons of zeus: one, handsome strong and . . . . 799 73 POEMS 27   2
ZIGGING
    Bouncing, Bet the ruby&emerald zigging HE of a zagflash . . . 747 95 POEMS 75   9
ZINGLY
    three worlds) who's ama zingly Eye / / / . . . . 827 73 POEMS 55   14
ZITHER
    p ing the bigtwittering zither-and the mealy, ladies dancing 100 & POST IMPR 11   42
ZITHER-AND
    p ing the bigtwittering zither-and the mealy, ladies dancing 100 & POST IMPR 11   42
ZONE
    looser of the warlike zone of her that brought . . . .   4 T&C EPITHALAM   44
ZOO
    the denizens of the zoo were that day inclined . . . . 326 VIVA 18   23
    blue elephant at the zoo (jumbled to queer this . . . . 516 50 POEMS 30   7
ZOOM
    the radiator of his ZOOM DOOM icecoalwood truck a . . . . . . 680 95 POEMS 8   4
ZOOMS
    down again who but zooms through one perfectly beautiful . . 585 1 X 1 45   18
000000
    6 teen or sixty 000,000 anybodyelses-- but for once . . . . . 779 73 POEMS 7   26
1
    hands, carefully inhabits number 1 on something street Spring   62 T&C PORTRAIT 10   4
    swiflty out of number 1 someThing street and trickles . . . .   62 T&C PORTRAIT 10   25
    / "kitty". sixteen, 5' 1", white, prostitute. ducking always   74 T&C SON REAL 5   1
    gears being in A 1 shape passed from low . . . . 248 IS 5 ONE 19   18
    mirror this is friday 1 what 3 a fly . . . . 335 VIVA 26   6
    dead you captain) Memo 1 wife in impossibly hell . . . . . . 389 NO THANKS 6   18
    in impossibly hell Memo 1 son in improbably yale . . . . . . 389 NO THANKS 6   21

	PAGE	TITLE	LINE

1 (CONTINUED)

/ / / ci-git 1 Foetus (unborn to not . . . . 394 NO THANKS 11   1

on wednesday next at 1 E.S.T. bring the kiddies . . . . 514 50 POEMS 28   13

probably unworld crash to 1 nonillion (& so) nothings . . . . 728 95 POEMS 56   12

dentham comma bentham; or 1 law for the lions . . . . 791 73 POEMS 19   7

will reme mber (for 1 frac tion of a . . . . 797 73 POEMS 25   16

human superstate ever knew (1) we sans love equals . . . . . 803 73 POEMS 31   7

12

there are possibly 2 1/2 or impossibly 3 individuals . . . . 514 50 POEMS 28   1

14TH

meaning of the stars 14th st dis (because my . . . . 697 95 POEMS 25   29

16

/ / / / 16 heures l'Etoile the communists . . . . 274 IS 5 TWO 9   1

18

days we spent in '18 kickin duh guts outa . . . . 332 VIVA 23   15

+1932

FOR CONTEXT, SEE . . . . 388 NO THANKS 5   32

1944

christian love. "Nothing" in 1944 A D "can stand . . . . . . 636 {CHAIRE} 38   9

1956

/ / / THANKSGIVING (1956) a monstering horror swallows . . . 711 95 POEMS 39   T

2

cu tSudden ly in 2 that, writhes... A.. lit. . . . . 101 & POST IMPR 11   52

◇ smoke Helmar cigarettes 2 play backgammon, 3 watch . . . . 200 XLI PORTRAIT 8   3

about less than nothing) 2 boston Dolls; found with . . . . . 317 VIVA 9   24

(drooli ngly supp ort 2 be nt toothpick s) . . . . 408 NO THANKS 25   10

afternoon? (kow dow r 2 bul retoinis wus de . . . . 409 NO THANKS 26   3

n, r Eve aling 2 a -sprout eyelands) sin . . . . 445 NO THANKS 60   10

/ there are possibly 2 1/2 or impossibly 3 . . . . 514 50 POEMS 28   1

lish sparrows say then 2 or per (who can . . . . 787 73 POEMS 15   5

dnite also conce als 2 ph antoms clutch ed . . . . 795 73 POEMS 23   14

mob love being youamiare (2) the holy miraculous difference . 803 73 POEMS 31   8

/ / / / 2 little whos (he and . . . . 832 73 POEMS 60   1

known) who and who (2 little ams and over . . . . 832 73 POEMS 60   13

3

or an old man 3 thirds asleep, on his . . . . 102 & POST IMPR 12   13

cigarettes 2 play backgammon, 3 watch a has gold . . . . . . 200 XLI PORTRAIT 8   4

is friday 1 what 3 a fly & her . . . . 335 VIVA 26   8

with white eyebrows the 3 rd chief something or . . . . 465 NEW POEMS 3   2

2 1/2 or impossibly 3 individuals every several fat . . . . . 514 50 POEMS 28   1

& h ideou s 3 m aybe o nce . . . . 789 73 POEMS 17   19

second to tenth rate (3) as it was in . . . . 803 73 POEMS 31   13

+3

FOR CONTEXT, SEE . . . . 628 {CHAIRE} 30   8

+3-RING

FOR CONTEXT, SEE . . . . 605 {CHAIRE} 7   6

3RD

please o no 0 3rd Findingest whispers understand sobs . . . . 358 VIVA 49   6

+3RD

FOR CONTEXT, SEE . . . . 465 NEW POEMS 3   2

3RDTOES

horse floats on 4 3rdtoes P (drooli ngly supp . . . . 408 NO THANKS 25   6

3RINGBRAIN

night all day) a 3ringbrain you had and a . . . . 605 {CHAIRE} 7   6

300

(who clean and jerked 300 lbs) i mean observe . . . . 645 {CHAIRE} 47   2

33RD

the bulls nabbed at 33rd) pulled six months for . . . . . . 266 IS 5 TWO 1   39

4

(man) horse floats on 4 3rdtoes P (drooli ngly . . . . . . 408 NO THANKS 25   5

/ yes but even 4 or (& h ow) . . . . 708 95 POEMS 36   2

pigeons coo) haps even 4 now man's most vast . . . . 787 73 POEMS 15   8

sin cerity equals perspicuity (4) Only The Game Fish . . . . 803 73 POEMS 31   16

4TH

of Congressman Pudd 's 4th of July oration, with . . . . . . 249 IS 5 ONE 20   2

the end of doubleyou 4th) reminds me in spite . . . . 699 95 POEMS 27   6

5

/ / / / 5 ◇ smoke Helmar cigarettes . . . . 200 XLI PORTRAIT 8   1

	PAGE	TITLE	LINE
5 (CONTINUED)			
the ferocious phenomenon of 5 o'clock i find myself	201	XLI PORTRAIT 9	1
silence, it is) still 5 o'clock I stare only	202	XLI PORTRAIT 9	42
evening And it is 5 o'clock in the oblong	202	XLI PORTRAIT 9	49
/ / at just 5 a m i hear	787	73 POEMS 15	1
Fish Swims Upstream & (5) unbeingdead isn't beingalive / . .	803	73 POEMS 31	17
+5			
FOR CONTEXT, SEE	430	NO THANKS 47	17
5'			
/ / "kitty". sixteen, 5' 1", white, prostitute. ducking . . .	74	T&C SON REAL 5	1
50			
add that there are 50 (fifty) flics for every	274	IS 5 TWO 9	17
54			
Tartskids with thecas-tanets in 5/4; Time chick. chick but: .	318	VIVA 10	5
6			
/ / there are 6 doors. Next door (but	312	VIVA 4	1
elsewher e except me 6 e nglish sparrow s)	696	95 POEMS 24	8
you feel you aren't 6 or 6 teen or	779	73 POEMS 7	24
you aren't 6 or 6 teen or sixty 000,000	779	73 POEMS 7	24
less than beast at 6 this bell 's whisper	787	73 POEMS 15	13
nes s C omprises 6 twirls of do gsh	789	73 POEMS 17	9
6AROUND			
silent A s groupingThe 6around one darks to 7th	342	VIVA 33	6
69			
Seeds Of Evil sold 69 carloads before publication the	245	IS 5 ONE 16	9
+7			
FOR CONTEXT, SEE	430	NO THANKS 47	21
7TH			
6around one darks to 7th s o howpale) bluedmufFletomben . . .	342	VIVA 33	7
75			
look at this) a 75 done this nobody would	270	IS 5 TWO 5	2
8			
at the age of 8 ysomethi ng (imagine) with, ...	792	73 POEMS 20	13
+8			
FOR CONTEXT, SEE	430	NO THANKS 47	21
9			
pRaW, 1T; O: allons 9 & . (musically-who? pivoting)	430	NO THANKS 47	25

Index Words in
Order of Frequency

2740	THE	125	MAY	67	WHITE
2145	AND	123	WHILE	66	DID
1959	OF	120	SOME	66	MUCH
1921	A	119	NOTHING	66	NEW
996	TO	117	OUR	66	SWEET
836	IS	113	MAN	65	BEYOND
824	IN	112	SHALL	65	JUST
775	I	110	AM	65	SAID
725	WITH	110	MOON	63	SEE
559	YOU	109	GO	63	YOUNG
492	MY	108	DREAM	62	BODY
466	ARE	107	CAN	62	COULD
409	ALL	107	OUT	62	FLOWER
368	WHICH	105	ALWAYS	62	SOMETHING
367	AS	105	MIND	60	AIR
363	NOT	101	UP	60	FLOWERS
351	WHO	101	VERY	60	MADE
345	BUT	101	WHY	60	MUST
339	IT	99	BECAUSE	60	N
338	BY	98	THESE	60	QUITE
338	THAN	97	ANY	59	BEFORE
338	THAT	97	DEATH	59	DARK
335	THIS	97	HIM	59	KISS
322	FOR	96	OVER	59	LY
321	HIS	95	YES	59	RAIN
315	OR	94	SILENCE	59	TWO
303	YOUR	93	EVERY	58	LIGHT
299	IF	93	ING	58	TOO
293	ME	93	THY	57	HAIR
289	HER	93	WHERE	57	LADY
257	BE	92	TIME	57	SUN
252	ONE	90	DAY	57	UNDER
250	LIKE	89	HERE	57	WOULD
238	SO	88	HANDS	56	FLESH
235	ON	88	SHOULD	56	LET
230	MORE	87	DEAD	55	BEAUTIFUL
227	HE	87	ITS	55	EVEN
222	INTO	85	DOWN	55	NOR
218	LOVE	85	E	55	STARS
216	FROM	85	SPRING	55	THEM
215	WE	84	COME	54	FEAR
215	WILL	83	BEING	54	LOOK
211	WHEN	83	KNOW	54	MOUTH
210	WAS	83	WHOM	53	FIRST
205	&	82	WERE	53	HAD
202	LITTLE	81	THEN	52	DON'T
201	WHOSE	81	THERE	52	FEEL
196	EYES	81	THINGS	51	GREEN
192	HAVE	80	BIG	51	MEN
191	WHAT	77	FACE	51	SUDDENLY
187	AT	77	HEART	50	SLOWLY
183	O	76	THING	49	DEEP
172	NOW	76	LIPS	49	DOES
171	HOW	75	EARTH	49	FEET
167	NO	75	HAS	49	T
156	THEY	75	SMILE	49	THREE
149	AN	74	GOD	48	LIVE
148	NEVER	74	SAY	48	MAKE
143	DO	74	SING	48	THINK
143	THEIR	73	US	47	AGAINST
141	ONLY	72	SUCH	47	BETWEEN
138	MOST	70	LESS	47	GIVE
136	EACH	70	SKY	47	STAR
136	THROUGH	69	NIGHT	47	THOU
131	S	69	PEOPLE	47	WITHOUT
130	SHE	69	SOUL	46	AGAIN
130	WORLD	68	ALIVE	46	DIE
126	LIFE	68	OLD	46	EVER
126	UPON	67	IT'S	46	HEAD

46	SLEEP	34	OPEN	27	MOVING
46	UNTIL	34	PERHAPS	27	PERFECT
45	BRIGHT	34	RIGHT	27	SILENTLY
45	SMALL	33	BEGIN	27	SINCE
45	UN	33	BIRDS	27	SOMEBODY
44	DREAMS	33	CHILD	27	TALL
44	G	33	EVERYTHING	26	I'M
44	VOICE	33	FIVE	26	KNOWN
43	AWAY	33	HAVING	26	LAST
43	DARKNESS	33	M	26	LEGS
42	COMES	33	NOBODY	26	+LIKE
42	DEAR	33	TELL	26	OFF
42	LADIES	33	WINDOW	26	PUT
42	SILENT	32	ABOUT	26	SEA
42	SNOW	32	BEAUTY	26	STAND
42	TREES	32	CAREFULLY	26	THOUGH
42	TWILIGHT	32	GIRL	25	ALONE
41	FINGERS	32	L	25	ALSO
41	SINGING	32	LARGE	25	B
41	TOUCH	32	LIVING	25	BEHIND
41	WAY	32	MAKES	25	CANNOT
41	Y	32	OH	25	EVERYWHERE
40	ALMOST	32	R	25	FRAIL
40	AROUND	32	ROSES	25	GIRLS
40	GROW	32	WIND	25	IMAGINE
40	JOY	31	ASK	25	PRETTY
40	OTHER	31	BELIEVE	25	SMILING
40	ROUND	31	BREATHING	25	SOFTLY
40	SAYS	31	CHILDREN	25	SPEAK
40	WELL	31	HIGH	25	THEE
40	WHOLLY	31	ISN'T	25	W
39	BOTH	31	MOVE	25	WINTER
39	KNOWS	31	SILVER	24	ANYTHING
39	LONG	31	STILL	24	CAN'T
39	ONCE	30	APRIL	24	DARE
39	TREE	30	BEGINS	24	DAWN
39	+YOU	30	GAY	24	FLAME
38	AMONG	30	HIMSELF	24	GLAD
38	BORN	30	LET'S	24	LIVES
38	D	30	MORNING	24	LOVED
38	MEAN	30	RED	24	SUNSET
38	MERELY	30	SELF	24	WHO'S
38	STREET	30	TURN	23	AFRAID
38	TRUE	29	ARMS	23	AFTER
38	WHOLE	29	BLOOD	23	COLOUR
37	BEEN	29	CALLED	23	DANCING
37	DANCE	29	FIND	23	HEAVEN
37	LEAST	29	HELL	23	HOPE
37	ROSE	29	KEEN	23	HOUSES
37	SELVES	29	KIND	23	LIE
37	SONG	29	OPENING	23	MANY
37	WORLDS	29	SHARP	23	MINE
36	TRUTH	29	THAT'S	23	MYSELF
36	WONDER	28	BLACK	23	REALLY
35	FACES	28	DARLING	23	SOFT
35	FAR	28	FALL	23	STANDS
35	GOES	28	FRAGILE	23	THOSE
35	GOOD	28	GOT	23	WONDERFUL
35	PERFECTLY	28	GREAT	23	YOU'RE
35	SUNLIGHT	28	OWN	22	ABOVE
35	TAKE	28	UNDERSTAND	22	BED
34	BIRD	28	YEAR	22	BREASTS
34	BLUE	27	BECOME	22	COMING
34	EYE	27	CERTAIN	22	DOESN'T
34	FOREVER	27	CRY	22	DYING
34	GUESS	27	HUGE	22	ER
34	HAND	27	LEAF	22	FRAGRANCE
34	MIGHT	27	LEAVES	22	GOLD
34	MOUNTAINS	27	LOVERS	22	GONE

22	I'LL	19	THOUSAND	16	CLOSE
22	ITSELF	19	UNIVERSE	16	DOOR
22	MYSTERY	19	VOICES	16	DREAMING
22	NEXT	19	WENT	16	DULL
22	SHY	19	WITHIN	16	EARTH'S
22	SMILES	19	YEARS	16	ENORMOUS
22	THERE'S	19	YET	16	FATE
22	TINY	18	BRAIN	16	FILLED
22	WOMAN	18	FOOL	16	FULL
21	CALL	18	FRIEND	16	HARD
21	COLOURS	18	GRIN	16	HEARD
21	F	18	HALF	16	HOPES
21	FEW	18	HEAR	16	LAUGH
21	HOME	18	KID	16	LIFE'S
21	+I	18	LAND	16	MATTER
21	INFINITE	18	LEAN	16	MIRACLE
21	LAY	18	LOST	16	MISS
21	MAYBE	18	NEAR	16	PASS
21	MEMORY	18	NOONE	16	RISE
21	MERE	18	NOWHERE	16	SIMPLY
21	MILLION	18	P	16	SINGS
21	NEITHER	18	PLAY	16	STRONG
21	NESS	18	PLEASE	16	THEMSELVES
21	OURSELVES	18	RIDING	16	THEREFORE
21	POOR	18	SEEM	16	TRY
21	POSSIBLY	18	SMOOTH	16	U
21	QUICK	18	+SOMETHING	16	UPWARD
21	REMEMBER	18	STREETS	16	WHATEVER
21	SOMETIMES	18	THIGHS	16	WORD
21	THOUGHT	18	TILL	16	WRONG
21	UNTO	18	TIMES	15	AINT
21	WISH	18	UNCLE	15	ASLEEP
20	BACK	18	WHISPER	15	BECOMES
20	BREATHE	18	WISE	15	BLOSSOMING
20	C	17	AUTUMN	15	BOYS
20	DOOM	17	BLIND	15	BRITTLE
20	EARS	17	CAREFUL	15	COLD
20	EXCEPT	17	COOL	15	DIM
20	FIRE	17	DIED	15	DOUBT
20	FOUND	17	EASILY	15	DUMB
20	H	17	ELSE	15	FATHER
20	HOUSE	17	ENOUGH	15	FEELS
20	MEANS	17	FIRM	15	FINGER
20	MINUTE	17	FLOAT	15	FORGET
20	MOMENT	17	FLY	15	FOUR
20	MR	17	GET	15	GESTURE
20	MUSIC	17	HE'S	15	GRASS
20	SIT	17	HERE'S	15	HOT
20	THICK	17	HERSELF	15	IMMORTAL
19	BETTER	17	HUMAN	15	K
19	CAME	17	LAUGHING	15	KING
19	COMPLETE	17	LUMINOUS	15	LOOKING
19	DISAPPEAR	17	+MAN	15	+ONE
19	DISTINCT	17	MINDS	15	OO
19	EXACTLY	17	NAME	15	OPENS
19	FAIR	17	+OVER	15	PURE
19	FREEDOM	17	PINK	15	SEEN
19	GENTLY	17	RE	15	SHINING
19	GHOST	17	SECRET	15	SINGLE
19	HATE	17	SEEING	15	SIX
19	HEARTS	17	SKIES	15	SLOW
19	HILLS	17	SKILFULLY	15	SMELL
19	LISTEN	17	SPACE	15	SOULS
19	PALE	17	WINDOWS	15	SPIRIT
19	PER	17	WINGS	15	SURE
19	PROUD	16	BOY	15	TEETH
19	REASON	16	CARE	15	TOGETHER
19	SITTING	16	CLIMB	15	TOWARD
19	SLIGHTLY	16	CLIMBING	15	TWICE

15	WANT	13	LOVER	12	STOOD
15	WATER	13	LOW	12	SURELY
15	WORMS	13	MAGIC	12	TEARS
15	YOUTH	13	MOUNTAIN	12	TERROR
14	ALONG	13	MOVES	12	TH
14	BELLS	13	OCEAN	12	TOMORROW
14	BEST	13	PETALS	12	TREMBLING
14	BRAVE	13	RAPIDLY	12	TURNS
14	COURSE	13	RARE	12	V
14	CRIES	13	SOMEWHERE	12	WHAT'S
14	DAYS	13	SUMMER	12	WHISPERS
14	DEATH'S	13	SWIM	12	WRITHE
14	DOLL	13	TOOK	11	ACROSS
14	DRINK	13	UH	11	AMOROUS
14	DUH	13	USED	11	ANYONE
14	DUSK	13	VAST	11	AWAKE
14	ENTIRELY	13	VER	11	BOX
14	EVERYBODY	13	WALK	11	CRAZY
14	GAVE	13	WEAR	11	DEEPLY
14	IMMENSE	13	WHEREAS	11	DICK
14	LAUGHTER	13	+WORLD	11	DIS
14	LOOKED	12	2	11	DISTINCTLY
14	NG	12	ABSOLUTE	11	DOG
14	NOISE	12	ANOTHER	11	DREAMED
14	+OLD	12	BEGINNING	11	DUST
14	PLACE	12	BENEATH	11	EAT
14	POEM	12	BIGGER	11	EVERYONE
14	RATHER	12	BRING	11	EXACT
14	SIDE	12	COMPLETELY	11	FAIL
14	SITS	12	CREATE	11	FALLING
14	SLIM	12	DARES	11	FAT
14	SOON	12	DEEPER	11	FLOATS
14	STARE	12	DESPAIR	11	FUL
14	STOP	12	DIRTY	11	GODS
14	THIN	12	DIVINE	11	HITHER
14	TOLD	12	DONE	11	HOUR
14	TRULY	12	DOTH	11	LEAP
14	WE'RE	12	EAGER	11	LIVED
14	WORDS	12	END	11	MAKING
14	YOU'LL	12	EST	11	MERCY
13	1	12	FEELING	11	MURDERED
13	AMAZING	12	FLIGHT	11	NIGHT'S
13	BEAUTIFULLY	12	FLOATING	11	ONES
13	BECAME	12	FREE	11	OTHERS
13	+BELLS	12	GIVING	11	PLAYING
13	BLOW	12	GOD'S	11	POEMS
13	BODIES	12	GOING	11	POET
13	BREATH	12	GRAVE	11	PRESIDENT
13	CAUGHT	12	HIPS	11	READ
13	CERTAINLY	12	INSTANT	11	REAL
13	CITY	12	+ITSELF	11	ROOM
13	CREATURE	12	KEEP	11	SHOULDERS
13	DE	12	LEFT	11	SHUT
13	DER	12	LES	11	SIMPLE
13	ETERNAL	12	LIES	11	SMOKE
13	ETERNITY	12	LING	11	SON
13	EXQUISITE	12	LUCK	11	SORRY
13	FACT	12	MAD	11	SOUND
13	FEARS	12	MEET	11	STEEP
13	FINE	12	MIRACULOUS	11	STONE
13	FORTH	12	MOTHER	11	STRANGE
13	FRIENDS	12	NAKED	11	SWEETLY
13	GLASS	12	+NOTHING	11	TAKES
13	GLORY	12	PEACE	11	TER
13	IM	12	PERSON	11	THEY'RE
13	KILL	12	QUEEN	11	THINKING
13	LA	12	REMEMBERING	11	TOWN
13	LOSE	12	SAME	11	TURNED
13	LOVE'S	12	SOMEONE	11	WANDERING

11	WAR	10	X	9	SEVERAL
11	WARM	10	YELLOW	9	SH
11	WAYS	9	AFTERNOON	9	SIN
11	WE'LL	9	+ALIVE	9	SKILFUL
11	YOURS	9	+ALWAYS	9	STRANGER
10	ACCURATE	9	BELL	9	SUDDEN
10	ANGELS	9	BRAINS	9	TASTE
10	ANGUISH	9	BREAK	9	THUS
10	ANSWER	9	BUY	9	WALL
10	ART	9	CANDY	9	WIN
10	BAD	9	CARRY	9	WON'T
10	CLEVER	9	CHRIST	9	WORSE
10	CLUMSILY	9	CITIES	8	AGE
10	CRISP	9	CLEAN	8	AGONY
10	DEVIL	9	+COLOURED	8	AL
10	+DON'T	9	CONSIDER	8	+ALL
10	ECSTASY	9	CRAZILY	8	ANGEL
10	ENTER	9	DRESS	8	BESIDE
10	ES	9	EX	8	BLISS
10	FAINT	9	FINAL	8	BOW
10	FINALLY	9	FISH	8	BREAST
10	FOREST	9	FLEET	8	BRIEF
10	FORGETTING	9	FOOT	8	BUILDING
10	GHOSTS	9	FUNNY	8	BURIED
10	GIVEN	9	GENERAL	8	BUSY
10	HAT	9	GOLDEN	8	CLEVERLY
10	HOURS	9	GRACE	8	CLOCK
10	HUGEST	9	GROWS	8	CLOTHES
10	HUSH	9	GUESSED	8	CLOUDS
10	I'VE	9	HAPPENS	8	+COMRADES
10	IMMEASURABLE	9	HIGHER	8	CONCEIVE
10	KISSED	9	HOLD	8	COULDN'T
10	KNEW	9	HORSES	8	DELICIOUS
10	+LITTLE	9	HUMBLE	8	DESCEND
10	LUCKY	9	HUNDRED	8	DESIRE
10	LUST	9	INCENSE	8	DIDN'T
10	+ME	9	JOE	8	DIES
10	MIRROR	9	JOLLY	8	DISAPPEARS
10	+MOON	9	KNEES	8	DOLLS
10	MYSTERIOUS	9	LILY	8	DOWNWARD
10	NECK	9	LOOKS	8	DRESSED
10	NEWLY	9	LORD	8	DRINKS
10	NICE	9	LOVELY	8	EAR
10	NINE	9	LOVES	8	EATEN
10	PARIS	9	MERCIFUL	8	EITHER
10	PRECISELY	9	MET	8	EMPTY
10	PURPLE	9	MIDNIGHT	8	+EYED
10	QUICKLY	9	MILLIONS	8	FAINTLY
10	QUIETLY	9	MONEY	8	FIERCELY
10	RICH	9	MOVED	8	FIST
10	SINGULAR	9	MRS	8	FORM
10	SLENDER	9	MYSTERIES	8	+GIRL
10	SLIPPERY	9	NAMED	8	+GIVE
10	SONGS	9	+NOBODY	8	HERO
10	SPOKE	9	NOSE	8	HOLY
10	ST	9	+NOW	8	HORSE
10	STONES	9	ODD	8	HUGELY
10	STRING	9	OTHERWISE	8	HUGER
10	STROLL	9	PAIN	8	HURL
10	TEN	9	PARTICULAR	8	HURT
10	TIME'S	9	PAST	8	IMMACULATE
10	TOUCHED	9	PIECE	8	IMPORTANT
10	TREMENDOUS	9	PITY	8	INCH
10	+UP	9	PRIDE	8	INCREDIBLE
10	WANDERS	9	PROUDLY	8	JESUS
10	WHISPERING	9	PROVE	8	KUMRADS
10	WING	9	QUEENS	8	LEAPS
10	WOMEN	9	QUEER	8	LIFTING
10	WORLD'S	9	SERENE	8	LIFTS

8	LIKES	7	BELIEVING	7	IGNORANT
8	MERRY	7	BELOVED	7	ILLIMITABLE
8	MOMENTS	7	BENT	7	ILLIMITABLY
8	MOUSE	7	BEWARE	7	IMAGINABLE
8	MURDER	7	BIGGEST	7	IMAGINED
8	NE	7	BIRTH	7	IMMEDIATE
8	NONE	7	BLOSSOM	7	INDOLENT
8	NORMAL	7	BODY'S	7	INGLY
8	ONE'S	7	BOOKS	7	INNOCENCE
8	OPENED	7	BUD	7	INTENSE
8	OW	7	CANDLE	7	INVISIBLE
8	PERCEIVE	7	CAT	7	KEEPING
8	PERFUME	7	CEASE	7	KISSES
8	PICKED	7	CENTURIES	7	LAUGHED
8	PLUS	7	CHEEKS	7	LE
8	PUTTING	7	CLEOPATRA	7	LEARN
8	RING	7	CLOWN	7	LEWD
8	RIPE	7	CLUMSY	7	LIFT
8	SCARLET	7	CLUTCH	7	MAGICAL
8	SECOND	7	COMPREHEND	7	MAN'S
8	SEEMS	7	CREATION	7	MANKIND
8	SERIOUSLY	7	CRIED	7	MARVEL
8	SET	7	CRUEL	7	MASTER
8	SHADOW	7	DAMN	7	MEANING
8	SLEEPING	7	DAMNED	7	MEANWHILE
8	SMALLEST	7	DEER	7	MIDDLE
8	SOCALLED	7	DELICATE	7	MINUS
8	SOL	7	DIDST	7	MUSICAL
8	SOMEWHAT	7	DIFFERENT	7	NAKEDNESS
8	SPIRITS	7	DOING	7	NEARNESS
8	SQUARE	7	DRIFT	7	NOTHING'S
8	SQUIRMING	7	EAGERLY	7	O'CLOCK
8	STANDING	7	EARLY	7	PAIR
8	STINK	7	ECHO	7	+PEOPLE
8	STIR	7	ELF	7	PERPETUAL
8	STRICTLY	7	EMERGING	7	PERPETUALLY
8	SWEETNESS	7	ENDS	7	POETS
8	TE	7	EQUALS	7	POSSIBLE
8	THICKLY	7	ERECT	7	PRAISE
8	THINKS	7	EVENING	7	PRAY
8	THROAT	7	+EVERYWHERE	7	PROBABLY
8	THUNDER	7	EXISTENCE	7	PUTS
8	TIMELESSNESS	7	FATAL	7	QUESTION
8	TOM	7	FELL	7	+REALLY
8	TOUCHING	7	FELLOW	7	RISES
8	TOYS	7	FIELDS	7	ROAD
8	TWI	7	FIFTY	7	ROCK
8	UNCOUTH	7	FISTS	7	ROOFS
8	UTTERLY	7	FLAT	7	ROOM'S
8	UTTERS	7	+FLOAT	7	RUN
8	WAIT	7	FRAGILITY	7	SAFELY
8	WAITING	7	FURIOUS	7	SANG
8	WIFE	7	FUTILE	7	SAW
8	WISDOM	7	GAS	7	SCARCELY
8	WOULDN'T	7	GENEROUS	7	SHADOWS
8	WRISTS	7	GLADNESS	7	SHAKE
8	+YES	7	+GOT	7	+SHAPED
8	YOUSE	7	GROUND	7	SHIP
7	3	7	HAPPY	7	SHRILL
7	ABSURD	7	HARK	7	SIGHT
7	AGO	7	HE'LL	7	SLENDERLY
7	ALERT	7	HEARING	7	SMILED
7	+ALMOST	7	HEARTBEAT	7	SNOWING
7	ALTHOUGH	7	HOLE	7	SOMEHOW
7	ANIMALS	7	HUMBLY	7	SPEAKING
7	AR	7	HUMP	7	SPONTANEOUS
7	ASKED	7	HUNG	7	SQUIRM
7	BANG	7	ID	7	STERN
7	BEGAN	7	IDEAS	7	STOMACHS

7	STOPPED	6	COUNTRY	6	JERK
7	STRIKE	6	COURAGE	6	JIM
7	SUPPOSE	6	CREATURES	6	JIMMIE
7	SURPRISE	6	CRUMB	6	JOYS
7	SWIMS	6	CRUMBS	6	+JUST
7	TEACH	6	CRYING	6	+KILLED
7	TERRIBLE	6	CURIOUSLY	6	KILLING
7	THANK	6	CURLED	6	KILT
7	THITHER	6	CURVING	6	KINGDOM
7	THOROUGHLY	6	DANCED	6	KISSING
7	THOUGHTS	6	DEAD'S	6	KNOCKED
7	THOUSANDS	6	DELICATELY	6	+KNOW
7	THROWN	6	DEM	6	KNOWING
7	THUMB	6	DEW	6	LADY'S
7	TIDIYUM	6	DIMINUTIVE	6	LEAD
7	+TIME	6	DISAPPEARING	6	LEAPING
7	TIMID	6	DISTANCE	6	LENGTH
7	TUMBLING	6	DRIFTING	6	LIFTED
7	TURNING	6	EAST	6	LIKED
7	TWITCH	6	EATS	6	LITHE
7	+TWO	6	EDGE	6	LITTLER
7	UGLY	6	EMPEROR	6	LONELINESS
7	+UNDER	6	ENTERS	6	MADNESS
7	+UNDERSTAND	6	ETCETERA	6	MARK
7	UNSPEAKING	6	EV	6	MICROSCOPIC
7	UTTER	6	EVIL	6	MID'S
7	VARIOUS	6	+EXACTLY	6	MOON'S
7	WALKING	6	EXIST	6	MOTHER'S
7	WAVE	6	+FAIRY	6	MOUTHS
7	WELCOME	6	FALSE	6	MUTE
7	WHISPERED	6	FEARLESS	6	N'T
7	WHITELY	6	FEEBLE	6	NING
7	WHORE	6	FELT	6	+NO ONE
7	YOUNGEST	6	FIELD	6	+NOWHERE
7	YOURSELF	6	FINDING	6	OBSCENE
6	5	6	FRAGRANT	6	OCCUR
6	6	6	FRANTIC	6	+OTHER
6	ACCURATELY	6	FRUIT	6	OURS
6	ADVENTURE	6	GAL	6	PANTS
6	AMID	6	GARDEN	6	PAPER
6	ANIMAL	6	GAZE	6	PARK
6	ANT	6	GIFTED	6	PART
6	ARROW	6	GIVES	6	PARTICULARLY
6	ASKING	6	GLADLY	6	PASTURE
6	AWARE	6	GLOOM	6	PATIENT
6	BABY	6	GLORIES	6	PAY
6	BAR	6	GONDOLA	6	PLAYED
6	BEAT	6	+GOOD	6	PRECISE
6	BECOMING	6	GRADUAL	6	PRODIGIOUS
6	BELOW	6	GRADUALLY	6	QUOTE
6	BIT	6	GREY	6	RECEIVE
6	BLOND	6	GRIEF	6	RETURN
6	BLOSSOMS	6	GRIM	6	ROOTS
6	BRIGHTNESS	6	GROWING	6	RUB
6	BRUTAL	6	HAPPENED	6	RUSH
6	BUB	6	HEIGHT	6	SAFE
6	BUILT	6	HELLO	6	SAM
6	BULGE	6	HEROES	6	SANS
6	BURN	6	HIDEOUS	6	SAYING
6	BUSINESS	6	HISTORY	6	SCREECH
6	CALM	6	HUG	6	SE
6	CATHEDRAL	6	HUMANITY	6	SEND
6	CLENCHED	6	HURRY	6	SERIOUS
6	CLING	6	INNUMERABLE	6	SEVEN
6	CLOCKS	6	INSIDE	6	SHARPENS
6	CLOVER	6	IRREVOCABLE	6	SHE'S
6	COMMON	6	ITEM	6	SHEER
6	CORNER	6	IVORY	6	SHOT
6	CORNERS	6	JACK	6	SHYLY

6	SILLY	5	ANGRY	5	EXTREMELY
6	SINCERE	5	ANYBODY	5	+EYES
6	SINK	5	ANYWAY	5	FAITHFULLY
6	SIR	5	APPEAR	5	+FALLING
6	SKIN	5	APRIL'S	5	FATALLY
6	+SLOWLY	5	AREN'T	5	FED
6	SOLD	5	ARRIVE	5	FEMALE
6	SOLEMN	5	ARRIVING	5	FIEND
6	SONNETS	5	+ASS	5	FLAMING
6	SORT	5	BACKWARD	5	FLEETLY
6	SPILL	5	BEAST	5	FLICS
6	SPITE	5	+BEAUTIFUL	5	FLOWERING
6	SPLENDOR	5	BITE	5	FLUTTER
6	STAIRS	5	BLESSED	5	FOAM
6	+STAR	5	BLOWN	5	FOND
6	STEPS	5	BOUGH	5	FOOLISH
6	STOMACH	5	BREAD	5	FOOLS
6	STOPS	5	BREATHLESS	5	FORESTS
6	STRIKES	5	BROKEN	5	FORGOTTEN
6	STROKE	5	BROUGHT	5	FRANK
6	STROLLING	5	BUTTON	5	FUN
6	STRUT	5	CA	5	FURTHER
6	+SUNLIGHT	5	CAMBRIDGE	5	FUTURE
6	SWIFTLY	5	CATCH	5	GENTLEMEN
6	SWOOP	5	CAUSE	5	GESTURES
6	TABLE	5	CE	5	+GET
6	TAIL	5	CEILING	5	GHOSTLY
6	TALKING	5	CELESTIAL	5	GIFT
6	TEAR	5	CHIMNEYS	5	GLANCE
6	TEXTURE	5	CHURCH	5	GLOW
6	TING	5	CLIMBS	5	+GOING
6	TINIEST	5	CLOUD	5	GOLDENLY
6	TINILY	5	COAT	5	GOULD
6	TODAY	5	COLLAR	5	GRAND
6	TOE	5	COMPLAIN	5	+GREEN
6	TOP	5	CONTINUALLY	5	GUERRE
6	TOSS	5	COWARDS	5	HANDSOME
6	TRANSPARENT	5	CREEP	5	HARDER
6	+TREE	5	CRIMSON	5	HASTE
6	TRIVIAL	5	CROUCHED	5	HIDE
6	TWENTY	5	CROWD	5	HILL
6	UNITED	5	CURL	5	HOLES
6	UNLESS	5	DANGEROUS	5	HONOUR
6	UNQUOTE	5	+DEAD	5	HORRIBLY
6	USE	5	DEAREST	5	HOWEVER
6	VALLEY	5	DEARIE	5	HOWS
6	VIVID	5	DEATHS	5	HUDDLING
6	WAITER	5	DEFTLY	5	HUGENESS
6	WALLS	5	DEPTHS	5	HUNDREDS
6	WANTS	5	DIN	5	HUNGER
6	WATERS	5	DIRT	5	HUNGERING
6	WEE	5	DISAPPEARED	5	HUNTED
6	WH	5	DIZZILY	5	I'D
6	WHEREOF	5	DOLLIES	5	ILLUSTRIOUS
6	+WHOSE	5	DOMINIC	5	IMAGINING
6	WID	5	DOOMED	5	IMPOSSIBLE
6	WINE	5	DOUBTING	5	INNOCENT
6	WINTRY	5	DOUBTS	5	INSTEAD
6	WISHING	5	DROP	5	INTERESTED
6	WON	5	ELECTRIC	5	KEENER
6	WORK	5	ELEPHANT	5	KINGS
6	WORTH	5	ELSEWHERE	5	KNEELING
6	YE	5	EMBRACE	5	LAID
6	YOUNGER	5	EN	5	LANDS
5	ADD	5	ERR	5	LANGUAGE
5	+AGAINST	5	ET	5	LAYS
5	AH	5	EVER-EVER	5	LD
5	ALARM	5	+EVERYTHING	5	LEAVING
5	AMS	5	EXQUISITELY	5	LIGHTS

5	LILIES	5	REMEMBERS	5	TOY
5	LIMP	5	RHYTHM	5	TRAFFIC
5	LIT	5	RIDICULOUS	5	TRICK
5	LITTLEST	5	ROOT	5	TRIED
5	LOCKED	5	SALUTE	5	TRITE
5	LONELY	5	SAVE	5	TROUSERS
5	LONGER	5	SAWDUST	5	TRUMPETS
5	+LOOK	5	+SAYS	5	TRUST
5	LOUSY	5	SEASON	5	+TWILIGHT
5	LOVING	5	SEEK	5	UNDERSTANDS
5	LURCH	5	SELL	5	WATCH
5	LYING	5	SEX	5	WE'VE
5	MAGNIFICENT	5	SEXUAL	5	WEST
5	MARRIED	5	SHADOWY	5	WHEEL
5	MARVELS	5	SHAPE	5	WHETHER
5	MEASURED	5	SHAPED	5	WHI
5	MEMORIES	5	SHARE	5	WHIRL
5	MEN'S	5	SIL	5	WHIRLING
5	+MEN	5	SINUOUS	5	WHIS
5	MESH	5	+SMILE	5	WHOS
5	MIGHTILY	5	SMOOTHLY	5	WHYS
5	MILDLY	5	SNOWY	5	WIDE
5	MILE	5	+SONG	5	WILD
5	MILES	5	+SOUL	5	WILT
5	MIST	5	SPINE	5	WORRY
5	MO	5	SPIRALLING	5	YON
5	MOIST	5	SPITS	5	YONDER
5	MONKEY	5	SQUIRMS	5	YOO
5	MOTIONLESS	5	STICK	5	ACUTE
5	+MOVING	5	STIRS	4	4
5	MUD	5	STRANGENESS	4	+ABOUT
5	MUSCLES	5	STRENGTH	4	ABRUPTLY
5	NEARLY	5	STRIDE	4	ACCEPT
5	NEAT	5	STUCK	4	ACTUAL
5	NIGHTS	5	STUMBLING	4	ACTUALLY
5	NON	5	STUPID	4	AGAINS
5	NONSENSE	5	+SUDDENLY	4	ALICE
5	NOTICE	5	SUM	4	AMERICA
5	NUMB	5	SUPREME	4	AMERICAN
5	NUMBER	5	SURROUNDED	4	+AMONG
5	OBLIVION	5	SVELTE	4	ANNIE
5	OCCASIONALLY	5	SWALLOW	4	ANSWERS
5	ODOUR	5	SWALLOWED	4	+ANYTHING
5	OLAF	5	SWALLOWS	4	ANYWHERE
5	+ONCE	5	SWEETER	4	APPEARED
5	+ONLY	5	SWIFT	4	ARMIES
5	ORANGE	5	SWOON	4	+AROUND
5	+ORGAN	5	TA	4	ARRANGING
5	PAL	5	TABLES	4	ARSE
5	PALER	5	TAKING	4	ARTIFICIAL
5	PARTLY	5	TALK	4	ASKS
5	PAS	5	TELLS	4	+AWAY
5	PASSION	5	TENDERLY	4	BALD
5	PAUSE	5	TERRORS	4	BALLOON
5	PERFECTION	5	+THEMSELVES	4	BEACH
5	PETAL	5	THEY'LL	4	BEAR
5	PICK	5	THEY'VE	4	+BECOMES
5	PICTURE	5	THIRSTY	4	BEGS
5	PIGEONS	5	THREW	4	BEHOLD
5	PLEASANT	5	THROW	4	BET
5	POURING	5	THRUSH	4	+BETWEEN
5	PRESS	5	TI	4	BIGLY
5	PRETTILY	5	TICKLING	4	BILLION
5	PRIMEVAL	5	TIDE	4	BLITHE
5	PROGRESS	5	TINTS	4	BLUEEYED
5	PULLED	5	TIRED	4	BLUER
5	PULLING	5	TONGUE	4	BLUISH
5	RECENT	5	TOUCHES	4	BOSTON
5	RELEASED	5	TOWER	4	BREATHES

4	+BRIGHT	4	EE	4	HURRYING
4	BROKE	4	EGYPT	4	IDIOT
4	BROOK	4	EL	4	IGNORANCE
4	BROTHER	4	ENCHANTED	4	IMAGE
4	BURST	4	ENTIRE	4	IMAGINATION
4	BUSILY	4	ENTITLED	4	IMITATE
4	BUTTONS	4	ERE	4	IMPOSSIBLY
4	CALLS	4	ESCAPES	4	INFANTILE
4	CAPABLE	4	ESPECIALLY	4	INFINITY
4	CAPTAIN	4	EXCUSE	4	INSTANCE
4	CARPETED	4	EXIT	4	INT
4	CARVED	4	FABULOUS	4	INTIMATE
4	CEASED	4	FACTS	4	INTRICATE
4	CHEAP	4	FAILED	4	INVISIBLY
4	CHIEFLY	4	FAILURE	4	IRON
4	CHRISTMAS	4	FARM	4	JEW
4	CHUCKLES	4	FART	4	JOYFUL
4	CIGAR	4	FATTISH	4	JUMP
4	CLICK	4	FER	4	KILLED
4	CLOTHED	4	FERN	4	KINDNESS
4	CLUTCHED	4	FIENDS	4	KITTENS
4	COFFEE	4	FILTHY	4	KITTY
4	COLOURED	4	FIRE-ESCAPES	4	KNOWLEDGE
4	+COME	4	FIRMLY	4	LARGENESS
4	+COMING	4	FL	4	LARGEST
4	CON	4	FLAG	4	LAWS
4	CONTEMPLATE	4	FLIES	4	LAZILY
4	COOLNESS	4	FLOOR	4	LEANS
4	COUCH	4	FOLDED	4	LIARS
4	COUNT	4	FOLDS	4	LICE
4	CRASH	4	FOREHEAD	4	LIMBS
4	CREATES	4	FORGIVE	4	LINE
4	CRINGING	4	FRESH	4	LIVINGEST
4	CROON	4	FREUD	4	LOGIC
4	+CRUMBS	4	FRIGHTENED	4	LOSING
4	CUNNING	4	FROLIC	4	LOUD
4	CURIOUS	4	FROWN	4	+LOVE
4	CURVE	4	FUR	4	LOVELIER
4	CURVINGLY	4	FURNISHED	4	MADGE
4	DAD	4	GAILY	4	MALE
4	DAISIES	4	GAME	4	MARIE
4	DAISY	4	GARDENS	4	MARJ
4	+DANCE	4	GATE	4	MASS
4	+DANCING	4	GLIDE	4	MELANCHOLY
4	DARKER	4	+GO	4	MENTION
4	DARKLY	4	GOIL	4	MI
4	DAUGHTER	4	+GOLD	4	MIGHTY
4	DAZE	4	+GONE	4	MIL
4	DEARS	4	GORGE	4	+MILLIONS
4	DEATHLESSNE	4	GR	4	MINDLESS
4	DEFUNCT	4	GREENLY	4	MINGLING
4	DELIRIOUS	4	GRINS	4	MIRACLES
4	DESPITE	4	GROPING	4	MIRACULOUSLY
4	DISCOVERED	4	GUEST	4	MIRRORS
4	DISEASE	4	GURL	4	MISCHIEF
4	+DO	4	GUSH	4	MOAN
4	DOLLARS	4	GUYS	4	MOO
4	DOOMS	4	HAFIZ	4	MOONLIGHT
4	DOORS	4	HAIRY	4	+MORE
4	DOST	4	HANGING	4	+MORNING
4	+DOWN	4	HARDLY	4	+MOST
4	DROLL	4	HARUN	4	MOTH
4	DROOPS	4	HEARS	4	+MUCH
4	DROWNED	4	HEART'S	4	MURDERING
4	DURING	4	HEELS	4	MURMURS
4	DYING'S	4	HIDEOUSLY	4	MUSCLE
4	+EATEN	4	HOST	4	MYTH
4	ECSTATIC	4	HOUNDS	4	+NAME
4	ED	4	HUNGRY	4	NCE

948

4	NEED	4	RINGS	4	THRILLING
4	NEVERS	4	RISING	4	TIGHT
4	NOISY	4	ROAR	4	TLE
4	NOTH	4	ROBE	4	TOOTH
4	NOUS	4	ROBIN	4	TORTURED
4	NUMERABLE	4	ROLLS	4	TOTAL
4	OBSOLETE	4	ROYAL	4	TOTTERING
4	OCCURS	4	RUSHING	4	TOWNS
4	OCEANS	4	SAL	4	TRAIN
4	OMAR	4	SAND	4	TREAD
4	OMNIPOTENT	4	+SCREAM	4	TREMBLE
4	ONENESS	4	SCREAMS	4	TREMULOUS
4	OON	4	SEAT	4	TUMBLE
4	OUS	4	SEEMED	4	+TUMBLING
4	OUTSIDE	4	SENSE	4	TUNE
4	PAINTED	4	SENSUAL	4	TWIG
4	PALACE	4	SERENELY	4	TWITCHING
4	PARADISE	4	SHINE	4	TWITTER
4	PASSED	4	SHIPS	4	UGLINESS
4	PASSIONATE	4	SHOUT	4	UNIMAGINABLE
4	PATIENCE	4	SHRIEKING	4	UNWORLD
4	PEACEFUL	4	SICK	4	+UPON
4	PEARLS	4	+SILENTLY	4	UTMOST
4	PEER	4	SIMPLICITY	4	VAGUE
4	PEERS	4	SISTER	4	VANISH
4	PENNIES	4	SIXTEEN	4	VE
4	PERFUMED	4	SKIPPING	4	+VERY
4	PERPENDICUL	4	SLO	4	VICTIM
4	PHANTOM	4	SMITH	4	VIOLET
4	PHOTOGRAPHE	4	SMOKING	4	WALKS
4	PIECES	4	SMOOTHNESS	4	WAN
4	PILLAR	4	SNARE	4	WASHED
4	PILLOW	4	+SNOW	4	WATCHING
4	PLACES	4	SNOWFLAKE	4	WEARS
4	PLEASANTLY	4	SOLEMNLY	4	WEATHER
4	PLEASURE	4	SOM	4	WEEK
4	POCKETS	4	SORROW	4	WELCOMING
4	POINT	4	SOUGHT	4	WET
4	POLE	4	SPEAKS	4	WHATEVER'S
4	POUR	4	SPIN	4	WHEELS
4	POWER	4	SPIRES	4	WHERE'S
4	PRAYER	4	SPOIL	4	WHEREUPON
4	PRAYERS	4	SPROUTING	4	+WHISPERING
4	PRECISION	4	STARING	4	WHISTLES
4	PRETEND	4	START	4	WHO'LL
4	PRINCE	4	STEER	4	WHOEVER
4	PROCESSION	4	STILLNESS	4	WICKEDLY
4	PROFESSOR	4	STIRRING	4	WILDLY
4	PROFOUND	4	STOOPING	4	WINCE
4	PROSE	4	STORY	4	WINSOME
4	PU	4	STRANGELY	4	+WINTER
4	PULL	4	STRENUOUS	4	WISHES
4	PURR	4	STROLLS	4	WIT
4	PUSH	4	SUB	4	WO
4	PUTRESCENCE	4	SUBTLE	4	+WOMAN
4	QUIVERING	4	SUMMER'S	4	+WOMEN
4	RADIANCE	4	SUPPLE	4	WONDERFULLY
4	RAG	4	SWELL	4	WORM
4	+RAIN	4	TAKEN	4	WRITE
4	RAN	4	TALE	4	WRITHING
4	REACH	4	TAUT	4	YELL
4	REFINED	4	+THERE	4	YESTER
4	REJOICE	4	THEYS	4	YESTERDAY
4	REMARK	4	THIEF	4	+YESTERDAY
4	REPLIES	4	THINNER	4	YORK
4	REST	4	THIRD	4	YOU'VE
4	REVEALED	4	THREAD	4	+YOUR
4	RHYME	4	THRICE	3	ABSENCE
4	+RIGHT	4	THRILL	3	ACCORDING

3	ACCUSE	3	BRIGHTER	3	CRUMBLING
3	ADMIT	3	BRINGING	3	+CRUMBLING
3	ADVENTURING	3	BRINGS	3	CURB
3	AGED	3	BRUISED	3	CURE
3	AGREE	3	BRUSH	3	CURSE
3	ALAS	3	BUBBLES	3	CURTAIN
3	ALTOGETHER	3	BUBS	3	CURTAINS
3	ALW	3	BUCK	3	CURVED
3	AMERICAINS	3	BUDS	3	CURVES
3	AMERICANS	3	+BUGS	3	DANC
3	AMUSED	3	BUILD	3	DAT
3	AMUSING	3	BULB	3	+DAY
3	ANCIENT	3	BULLS	3	DEATHFUL
3	ANENT	3	BURSTING	3	DEATHLESS
3	ANKLES	3	CAGE	3	DECIDED
3	ANYONE'S	3	+CAN	3	DEED
3	APART	3	CANCELS	3	DEEDS
3	ARMY	3	CANNED	3	DEMOCRACY
3	ARRIVES	3	CAPTURED	3	DERBIES
3	+ASLEEP	3	CARRYING	3	DESCENDING
3	ATE	3	CARVE	3	DEY
3	AUTHENTIC	3	CATS	3	DIAMOND
3	AVENUE	3	CENTS	3	DIMENSION
3	AWFUL	3	CHAIN	3	DIMINISHING
3	AWKWARD	3	CHAIR	3	DIMLY
3	AYS	3	CHANGE	3	DIP
3	BABIES	3	CHAOS	3	+DIRTY
3	BABOON	3	CHARMS	3	DISCOVER
3	BALLOONMAN	3	CHEEK	3	DISPROVE
3	BARN	3	CHEERFULEST	3	DIVE
3	BATTERED	3	CHERI	3	DIZZY
3	BEASTS	3	CHICK	3	DOCTORS
3	BEATS	3	CHINS	3	DOME
3	BEAU	3	CHUCK	3	DRAWING
3	BEAUTEOUS	3	CHUCKLING	3	DRAWS
3	BEAUTIES	3	CIRCLE	3	DRE
3	+BECAUSE	3	CLIFF	3	DREA
3	+BECOME	3	CLIMBED	3	+DREAMING
3	+BECOMING	3	CLINGING	3	+DREAMINGLY
3	BEGGARS	3	CLOSED	3	DRIBBLING
3	+BEGIN	3	CLOSES	3	DRIFTS
3	BELIEVES	3	CO	3	DROPPING
3	BELLY'S	3	COLLAPSES	3	DROPS
3	BEND	3	COLLARS	3	DROWNING
3	BESTIAL	3	COLLIDE	3	DROWSY
3	BIRTHDAY	3	COM	3	+DUMB
3	BITCH	3	COMFORTABLE	3	DWELLS
3	+BITCH	3	COMMUNISTS	3	DY
3	BITS	3	COMPARED	3	EARLIEST
3	+BLADE	3	CONCEIVING	3	EASE
3	BLE	3	CONFUSE	3	EDDIE
3	BLEND	3	CONTENT	3	EDGELESS
3	BLINDED	3	CONTOURS	3	EFFENDI
3	BLINDS	3	COO	3	EFFIE'S
3	BLING	3	COUGH	3	EGO
3	BOAST	3	COUNTRIES	3	ELVES
3	BOO	3	COW	3	EMPEROR'S
3	BOOK	3	COWARD	3	ENDING
3	BOOM	3	COWS	3	+ENGLISH
3	BOOTS	3	CRANK	3	EQUAL
3	BOY'S	3	CREASING	3	ERRING
3	BRAND	3	CREATED	3	EVE
3	BRAVELY	3	CREEPING	3	+EVER
3	BREA	3	CROOKED	3	+EXCEPT
3	+BREAKING	3	CROSS	3	EXPECTING
3	BREAKS	3	CROSSING	3	EXPLODING
3	BREATHED	3	CROWN	3	EXTRAORDINARY
3	BRIDE	3	CROWNED	3	EYEBROWS
3	BRIEFNESS	3	CRUELLY	3	EYELIDS

3	FA	3	GRIP	3	INVENTED
3	FAILS	3	GRO	3	INWARD
3	FAIRIES	3	GROOM	3	IRREVOCABLY
3	FAITH	3	GROSS	3	ISE
3	FAITHFUL	3	+GROWING	3	ISH
3	FALLEN	3	GUY	3	JAZZ
3	FALLS	3	HAIR'S	3	JERKED
3	FANCY	3	HANDORGAN	3	JES
3	FARE	3	+HANDS	3	JEWELS
3	FATHER'S	3	HANGED	3	JIMMIE'S
3	+FEEBLY	3	HANGS	3	JOB
3	FEROCIOUS	3	HARRY	3	JOHN
3	FILLS	3	HAST	3	JOY'S
3	FINDS	3	HATH	3	JUMPING
3	FINGERED	3	HAUNTED	3	JUSTLY
3	FLAMES	3	HE'D	3	KEENLY
3	FLED	3	HEADS	3	KIDDO
3	+FLESH	3	HEARTLESS	3	KINDS
3	FLICKER	3	HEARTY	3	KNIVES
3	FLIGHTS	3	HEAVENLY	3	LAME
3	+FLOATING	3	HELEN	3	LAMPS
3	FLOWN	3	HELP	3	LARGER
3	+FLUNG	3	+HERE	3	LARK
3	FLUTTERING	3	HI	3	LASCIVIOUS
3	FLUTTERS	3	HIDING	3	+LEAF
3	FOE	3	+HIMSELF	3	LEANING
3	FOETAL	3	HINGING	3	+LEGS
3	FOLLOW	3	HIP	3	LEND
3	FOLLOWS	3	HOLDS	3	LETS
3	FOOLED	3	+HOLE	3	LI
3	FOOLING	3	+HOLY	3	LIBERTY
3	FORBID	3	HONEST	3	LIGHTLY
3	FORGOT	3	HOPED	3	LIMB
3	FORTUNATE	3	HOPELESS	3	LINGERING
3	FORTUNE	3	HOPING	3	LIONS
3	FOUL	3	HOPPING	3	LIP
3	FRAILER	3	HORIZONTAL	3	+LISTEN
3	FRAILLY	3	HORROR	3	LL
3	FRAN	3	HOTEL	3	LONGEST
3	FREQUENT	3	HUGS	3	LOT
3	FRIGHT	3	+HUNDRED	3	LOUDLY
3	FRIVOLOUS	3	HUR	3	LOVELESS
3	FRO	3	HURLED	3	+LUMINOUS
3	FRONT.	3	+HURLING	3	LUNGS
3	FULLY	3	HURRIEDLY	3	LUSCIOUS
3	FURY	3	HURTING	3	MACHINE
3	FUTURES	3	ICY	3	MADAM
3	FUZZY	3	IDEA	3	MAGICALLY
3	GAIN	3	IFS	3	MARBLE
3	GASPING	3	IL	3	MARCHING
3	GATHER	3	ILL	3	MARRY
3	GENTS	3	IMMEASURABLY	3	MATTERS
3	GENUINE	3	IMMENSITY	3	MEADOW
3	GETS	3	IMPERFECT	3	MEADOWS
3	GETTING	3	IMPLACABLE	3	MEASURE
3	GI	3	IMPRESSIONS	3	MEASURES
3	GIGANTIC	3	IMPROBABLE	3	MELODY
3	GIMME	3	INCALCULABLE	3	MENT
3	GLUED	3	+INCH	3	MERDE
3	GNOMES	3	INCLINED	3	MERRILY
3	GOAL	3	INCLUDING	3	METAPHOR
3	GOAT	3	INCREASE	3	MICE
3	+GOD	3	INHABITS	3	MILLIONARY
3	GODDESS	3	INNOCENTLY	3	MILLIONTH
3	GOODNESS	3	+INSTEAD	3	MIMI
3	GRANTED	3	INTENT	3	MIND'S
3	+GRASSHOPPER	3	INTERESTING	3	MINUTES
3	GREENER	3	INTRINSIC	3	+MISTER
3	GREENS	3	INVENT	3	MOB

3	MONG	3	PAINTING	3	RETURNS
3	MONTH	3	PANE	3	RIDE
3	MONTHS	3	PAPERY	3	RIVER
3	MOR	3	PARENTHESIS	3	RIVERS
3	MOREOVER	3	PARTING	3	ROAMING
3	MORSEL	3	PASSING	3	ROBES
3	MORTALS	3	PATIENTLY	3	ROD
3	MOSTS	3	PAUSES	3	ROOF
3	MOUNTS	3	PAYS	3	ROPES
3	MUTILATED	3	PEACEFULLY	3	ROTHERMERE
3	+MY	3	PEARL	3	ROTTEN
3	MYS	3	PEN	3	RUB-HER-BUB
3	MYSELF'S	3	PENNY	3	RUBBISH
3	MYSTERIOUSLY	3	+PERFECTLY	3	RUDDY
3	N'EST	3	+PERHAPS	3	RUE
3	N'EST-CE	3	PERISHED	3	RULE
3	NAMES	3	PERISHING	3	SACRED
3	NARROW	3	PERSONS	3	SAILING
3	NATURAL	3	PHENOMENON	3	SAILS
3	NAY	3	PILLARS	3	SAINT
3	ND	3	PIN	3	SALLY
3	NEARER	3	PINCH	3	SCATTERING
3	NEAREST	3	PITIFUL	3	SCIENCE
3	NEATLY	3	PITILESS	3	SCOTCH
3	NECESSARY	3	PLANES	3	SCRATCHES
3	NERVOUS	3	+PLEASE	3	SCREAM
3	+NEVER	3	PLUNGE	3	SCREAMING
3	+NEW	3	POINTING	3	SEAS
3	NEWER	3	POISE	3	SEATED
3	NGL	3	POMPOUS	3	SECRETLY
3	NIBBLING	3	POOL	3	SEEKS
3	NIC	3	PORTRAITS	3	SEETHE
3	NICHO'	3	POURQUOI	3	SEIZE
3	+NICK	3	POUT	3	SEIZED
3	+NIGHT	3	PRECARIOUS	3	SEPARATED
3	NLY	3	PRESENT	3	SHAME
3	NN	3	PRINCESS	3	SHARPENING
3	NOB	3	PRISON	3	SHE'LL
3	NOD	3	PRISONER	3	SHEEP
3	NONEXISTENCE	3	PROCLAIM	3	SHIRT
3	NOON	3	PROSTITUTE	3	SHOOK
3	NOUNS	3	PROVING	3	SHOP
3	NOVEMBER	3	PS	3	SHORE
3	NT	3	PUREST	3	SHORES
3	NUDGE	3	PUTRID	3	SHOUTING
3	NUDGING	3	PUZZLING	3	SHOVE
3	NY	3	QUE	3	SHRIEK
3	O'ER	3	QUEERLY	3	SHRIEKS
3	OBSCURE	3	QUESTIONS	3	SHUDDERING
3	OBSERVE	3	QUI	3	SIC
3	OBSERVED	3	QUIET	3	SIGNORE
3	OBVIOUS	3	QUIVERS	3	SILENCES
3	OCCULT	3	QUOTH	3	SILK
3	OCCURRED	3	RAGGED	3	+SILLY
3	OFFERING	3	RAH	3	+SINGULAR
3	OFFSPRING	3	RAIN'S	3	SKILL
3	OFT	3	RAPID	3	SKIP
3	OFTEN	3	+RATHER	3	SKUNKS
3	OI	3	REACHES	3	SLAVE
3	OLDEST	3	REALITY	3	SLEEPS
3	ONESELF	3	REALMS	3	SLEPT
3	OPPOSITE	3	RECEIVED	3	SLIPS
3	ORAL	3	REEKING	3	SLOBBER
3	ORDER	3	REMARKABLY	3	SMASHED
3	ORGAN	3	REMARKED	3	SMELLED
3	OUGHT	3	REMINDING	3	SMELLS
3	+OURSELVES	3	REMINDS	3	SNOWILY
3	+OUT	3	REPEAT	3	SOBS
3	PAINTER	3	REPLIED	3	+SOCALLED

3 SOFTER	3 +TOGETHER	3 +WHY
3 SOLE	3 TOMB	3 WILLING
3 SOMEBODY'S	3 TOOL	3 WINDS
3 SOMEONE'S	3 TORN	3 WINK
3 SONS	3 TOTTERS	3 WISELY
3 SORROWFUL	3 TRAVELLED	3 WISEST
3 SOUNDLESS	3 TREASURE	3 WISHED
3 SOUNDS	3 +TREES	3 WISTFUL
3 SP	3 TROUBLED	3 WISTFULLY
3 SPARE	3 TRUNK	3 WITTY
3 SPARK	3 TRUTHFUL	3 WONDERING
3 SPEND	3 TRUTHS	3 WONDERS
3 SPENT	3 TRYING	3 WORST
3 SPIRAL	3 TU	3 +Y
3 SPRINGTIME	3 TUH	3 YANKS
3 SPROUT	3 TUM	3 YAWNING
3 SPRY	3 TUMULT	3 YDOAN
3 STATES	3 TUNES	3 YEP
3 STAY	3 TWAIN	3 YGUDUH
3 STEAL	3 TWEEN	3 YUNNUHSTAN
3 STEALING	3 TWELVE	2 4TH
3 STEALS	3 TY	2 ABLAZE
3 STEEPLES	3 UGHHUH	2 ABLE
3 STEP	3 UL	2 ABSOLUTELY
3 STICKING	3 UNDAY	2 ABUSE
3 STICKS	3 UNDEAD	2 ABYSS
3 STILLED	3 UNHURRIED	2 ACCIDENT
3 STINGING	3 UNIMAGINABLY	2 ACHES
3 STINKS	3 UNLIFE	2 +ACROSS
3 STOUT	3 UNREAL	2 ACT
3 STRANGERS	3 UNSELF	2 ACTLY
3 STREET-LAMPS	3 +UNTIL	2 ACTUALITIES
3 STRICT	3 UTTERING	2 AF
3 STRIKING	3 VAIN	2 +AFRAID
3 STRIVING	3 VAINLY	2 AFTERWARDS
3 STRUCTURE	3 VALLEYS	2 AGES
3 STRUTS	3 VASE	2 AGILE
3 STUFF	3 VERMILION	2 AGLOW
3 STUTTER	3 VERTICAL	2 AGREED
3 STUTTERING	3 VING	2 AIM
3 SUIT	3 VIOLETS	2 AIMING
3 SUNBEAMS	3 VIOLIN	2 +AIR
3 SUNDAY	3 VITAL	2 ALGEBRAIC
3 SUNNY	3 VOTE	2 ALIGHTING
3 SUPERIOR	3 VOULEZ	2 ALL'S
3 SUPPOSING	3 VOUS	2 +ALONG
3 SWARM	3 VOYAGE	2 ALREADY
3 SWILL	3 WAGS	2 AMAYING
3 TADPOLE	3 WAIST	2 +AMERICAN
3 TALKS	3 WANDER	2 AMERIQUE
3 TAPS	3 WARPED	2 AMIABLE
3 TASTED	3 WATCHES	2 AMPLE
3 TEL	3 WEAK	2 AMY
3 TENSE	3 WEARY	2 ANDING
3 TERRIFIC	3 WEEP	2 ANG
3 THICKENING	3 WEIGHTLESS	2 ANGEL'S
3 THICKNESS	3 WELCOMES	2 ANGLAIS
3 THINE	3 WHATS	2 ANGLE
3 +THINGS	3 WHENCE	2 +ANIMAL
3 +THREE	3 WHEREFORE	2 ANN
3 THROBBING	3 WHEREIN	2 ANNABEL
3 THRONE	3 WHERES	2 ANNIHILATIO
3 THRUSHES	3 +WHISPER	2 ANNOUNCES
3 TIC	3 WHISTLE	2 ANOINT
3 TIL	3 +WHITE	2 ANOTHER'S
3 TIMELESSLY	3 WHITER	2 ANSWERED
3 TION	3 WHITEST	2 ANTICS
3 TIS	3 WHO'RE	2 ANYHOW
3 TOC	3 WHOSO	2 +ANYONE

2	AP	2	BELIEVABLY	2	BUTTERCUPS
2	APE	2	BELLY	2	BUTTERFLIES
2	APER	2	BELONG	2	BUTTS
2	APPARITION	2	BELONGING	2	C'EST
2	APPEARING	2	+BENDING	2	CADENCE
2	APPEARS	2	BETTY	2	CAFES
2	APPEASE	2	BETWIXT	2	CALIPH
2	APPETITE	2	+BIG	2	CANARY
2	APPLAUD	2	BIGNESS	2	CANCELLED
2	APPLAUSE	2	BILL	2	CANDLES
2	APPLE	2	BILL'S	2	CANYON
2	APPLES	2	BIRCH	2	CARES
2	APPROACHES	2	BISHOP	2	CARESS
2	APPROVE	2	BLACKER	2	CARESSED
2	APT	2	+BLADES	2	CARNIVAL
2	ARCHED	2	BLAME	2	CARROTY
2	ARISE	2	BLESSINGS	2	CARVEN
2	ARISING	2	BLISSFULLY	2	CASE
2	ARM	2	BLOATED	2	+CASTANETS
2	+AROUNDING	2	BLOKE	2	CASTLE
2	ARRIVAL	2	BLONDE	2	CASUAL
2	ARRIVED	2	BLOUSE	2	CAUSES
2	+ARRIVING	2	BLOWS	2	CAUTIOUSLY
2	ARTIFICER	2	BLUEST	2	CAVING
2	ARTISTS	2	BLUNDER	2	CENT
2	ASHES	2	BLUNT	2	CENTRIFUGALLY
2	ASTIR	2	BLUR	2	CEPT
2	ASTONISHMENT	2	BLY	2	+CERTAINLY
2	ATHLETE'S	2	+BODIES	2	CETERA
2	ATROCIOUS	2	+BODY	2	CHAIRS
2	ATTACKS	2	BOLD	2	+CHAIRS
2	ATTENTION	2	BON	2	CHANGING
2	ATTITUDE	2	BORROW	2	CHANSONS
2	AUGUST	2	BOTTLES	2	CHARGE
2	AUNT	2	BOTTOM	2	CHARMING
2	AUSSI	2	BOUNCING	2	CHASED
2	+AUTUMN	2	BOUT	2	CHASTE
2	AUTUMNAL	2	BOWED	2	CHATTER
2	AVEC	2	BOWL	2	CHATTERING
2	AWAKENED	2	+BOY	2	CHERIE
2	AWAKENING	2	+BREAK	2	CHEWED
2	AWASH	2	BREAKING	2	CHIC
2	AWL	2	+BREATHING	2	+CHICK
2	BABE	2	BREATHS	2	CHICKADEE
2	+BABY	2	BRIDGE	2	CHICKENS
2	BABYLON	2	BRIEFER	2	+CHILD
2	BADLY	2	BRIEFEST	2	CHILDFULLY
2	BAGDAD	2	BRIGHTENING	2	CHILDHOOD
2	BAGS	2	+BRINGING	2	+CHILDREN
2	BAIT	2	BROAD	2	CHIPS
2	BALL	2	BROW	2	CHISELS
2	BALLS	2	BROWN	2	CHOKE
2	BAND	2	BUBBLE	2	CHORDS
2	BARBAROUS	2	+BUBBLES	2	+CHRIST'S
2	BARE	2	BUG	2	CHUCKS
2	BARK	2	BULGING	2	CIGARETTE
2	BATTLE	2	+BULL	2	CIGARETTES
2	BEADS	2	BULLYING	2	CINQ
2	BEARD	2	BUM	2	CIRCULAR
2	+BEAUTIFULLY	2	BUMPING	2	CITIZENS
2	BECKONS	2	BUMS	2	+CITIZENS
2	BEE	2	BUR	2	CITY'S
2	BEER	2	BURIES	2	CLAP
2	BEGGAR	2	BURNING	2	CLEAR
2	+BEGINNING	2	BURNS	2	CLEARER
2	BEHELD	2	+BURSTING	2	CLINGS
2	+BEING	2	BURY	2	CLOTH
2	BELIEFS	2	+BUSINESS	2	+CLOWN
2	BELIEVABLE	2	BUSTED	2	CLUB

2	CLUTTERED	2	CULT	2	+DISAPPEAR
2	COARSE	2	CUP	2	DISAPPEARANCE
2	COBALT	2	+CURB	2	+DISAPPEARED
2	COCKED	2	CURIOSITY	2	+DISAPPEARING
2	COIN	2	CURLING	2	DISCOVERS
2	COLLAPSING	2	+CURLING	2	DISCRETE
2	COLLECTIVE	2	CURSED	2	DISCUSS
2	COLLEGE	2	CUT	2	DISCUSSED
2	COLLIDING	2	CUTE	2	DISDAIN
2	COLONEL	2	DAEMONS	2	+DISGORGE
2	COLOSSAL	2	DAINTILY	2	DISKS
2	COLOSSUS	2	DAM	2	DISSONANCE
2	COMEDY	2	DAME	2	DISTANT
2	COMFORT	2	+DAMN	2	DIVINELY
2	COMMA	2	DAN	2	DIVING
2	COMPANY	2	DANCES	2	DIZZYING
2	COMPELLED	2	DANCESING	2	+DOESN'T
2	COMPLETES	2	DANGLE	2	DOLL'S
2	COMPOSE	2	DANGLES	2	DOLLAR
2	COMPOSED	2	DAPPLED	2	+DOLLARS
2	CONCEIVES	2	+DARKNESS	2	DONG
2	CONCUPISCEN	2	DARLINGS	2	DOROTHY
2	CONFESSED	2	DAUGHTERS	2	DOTING
2	CONSEQUENTL	2	DAY'S	2	DOUTE
2	CONSIDERING	2	+DAYS	2	DOVE
2	CONTAIN	2	DEAF	2	DOW
2	CONTENTED	2	DECLARE	2	DR
2	CONTINUAL	2	DEEPEN	2	DRAGGED
2	CONTINUE	2	DEEPENING	2	DRAGGING
2	+CONTRAST	2	DEEPEST	2	DRAWN
2	CONTRIVES	2	DEEPNESS	2	DREAD
2	COOK	2	DEFEAT	2	DREAM'S
2	+COOL	2	DEFINITE	2	DREAMER
2	CORNERLESS	2	DELIVERED	2	DREAMHORSE
2	CORPSE	2	DEMAND	2	DREAMLIKE
2	CORRECT	2	DEMANDS	2	+DREAMS
2	COUCHER	2	+DEMOCRACY	2	DRED
2	COUCHES	2	DEMOCRATIC	2	DREW
2	COUGHED	2	DEMON	2	DRIVE
2	COURTESY	2	DENIES	2	DRIVEN
2	COVERED	2	DENIZENS	2	DROOPED
2	COWARDICE	2	DENY	2	DROPPED
2	COWERS	2	DEPART	2	+DROPPED
2	CR	2	DEPARTED	2	DROWN
2	CRACKED	2	DEPARTING	2	+DRUNK
2	CRACKLE	2	DEPARTURE	2	DUSTY
2	CRAMMED	2	DERFULLY	2	DUTY
2	CRASHED	2	DES	2	DYNAMITE
2	CRASHING	2	+DESCEND	2	EA
2	CRAWL	2	DESCENDS	2	EACHNESS
2	CREASE	2	DESCRIBE	2	EACHUDDER
2	CREDIBLE	2	DESPERATE	2	EARL
2	CREPT	2	DESPISE	2	EARTHQUAKES
2	CRINGES	2	DETERMINED	2	EARTHS
2	+CRINGING	2	DEVOURS	2	EATER
2	CRISPLY	2	DEVOUT	2	EATING
2	CROCUSES	2	DIARMUID	2	ECSTASIES
2	CROWDS	2	DIFFER	2	EDUCATION
2	CROWS	2	DIFFERENCE	2	EEL
2	CRU	2	DIFFICULT	2	EESEZ
2	CRUDE	2	DIFFICULTY	2	EFFIE
2	+CRUISING	2	DIG	2	EGYPTIAN
2	CRUM	2	DIGGING	2	EH
2	CRUMBLE	2	DIGNITY	2	EIGHT
2	CRUMBLES	2	+DIMINUTIVE	2	EIGHTEEN
2	+CRY	2	DING	2	EIGHTH
2	CU	2	DINGY	2	EITHERING
2	CUE	2	DINTED	2	EJACULATE
2	CUL	2	DIRTIED	2	+EL'S

2	ELE	2	+FACED	2	+FOREVER
2	ELECTED	2	+FACES	2	FOREVERFULLY
2	ELECTION	2	FADED	2	FOREVERING
2	ELEPHANTINE	2	FAERIE	2	FORGE
2	ELEPHANTS	2	FAERIES	2	FORGETFULNESS
2	ELEVATOR	2	+FALL	2	FORGETS
2	ELEVEN	2	FAMILIAR	2	FORGIVENESS
2	ELL	2	FAMOUS	2	FORMS
2	ELSES	2	FARTHEST	2	FORMULA
2	ELYSIAN	2	FASHIONED	2	FOUGHT
2	EMITS	2	FAULTLESS	2	+FOUR
2	EMPTIED	2	FE	2	FRACTION
2	EMPTINESS	2	+FEAR	2	FRAGMENT
2	+EMPTY	2	FEAST	2	FRAGRANTLY
2	EMPTYING	2	FEATHER	2	FRAMED
2	ENCLOSE	2	FEE	2	FRED
2	ENCOMPASS	2	+FEET	2	FREELY
2	ENDURE	2	FELLER	2	FREEZING
2	ENE	2	FELLOW'LL	2	FREQUENTLY
2	ENEMIES	2	+FELLOW	2	FRIEND'S
2	ENG	2	FELLOWS	2	FRISKS
2	+ENGLAND	2	FERAI	2	FROLICSOME
2	ENGLISH	2	FIDDLING	2	FROND
2	ENJOY	2	FIERCE	2	FROST
2	ENORMOUSLY	2	FIFTH	2	FROTH
2	ENSCONCED	2	FILL	2	FROZEN
2	ENTERED	2	FILTH	2	FRUM
2	ENTHUSIASTI	2	FIN	2	FU
2	ENTLY	2	+FIND	2	FUCK
2	ENVY	2	FINDINGLY	2	FUCKING
2	EP	2	FINGERING	2	FUNCTION
2	EPOCH	2	FIRMER	2	FUNERAL
2	EQUALLY	2	FISHERMEN	2	FURIOUSLY
2	+EQUALS	2	FISHING	2	FURNITURE
2	ERGO	2	FIT	2	FUSS
2	ESCAPE	2	FITS	2	FUTILITY
2	ESCORTS	2	+FIVE	2	GADGETS
2	ESTABLISHED	2	FLABBY	2	GAIETY
2	ETC	2	FLASH	2	GALLEON
2	EUNUCH	2	FLASHING	2	GANG
2	EUROPE	2	FLAYS	2	GARGLES
2	EVERLASTING	2	FLEE	2	GATHERS
2	+EVERY	2	FLEETER	2	GAYER
2	EVERYANYTHI	2	FLESHLESS	2	GED
2	+EVERYBODY'	2	FLEW	2	GEE
2	+EVERYONE	2	+FLICKER	2	GENIUS
2	EXAMPLE	2	FLINGER	2	GENTLE
2	EXCHANGING	2	+FLITTERING	2	GENTLEMAN
2	EXCLUDING	2	FLOATED	2	+GENTLEMEN
2	EXEUNT	2	FLOATINGLY	2	GERT
2	EXHALES	2	+FLOATINGLY	2	GES
2	EXHALING	2	FLOP	2	GETHER
2	EXHUMED	2	FLOPS	2	GH
2	EXISTS	2	FLUFFY	2	GHT
2	EXPAND	2	FLUTE	2	GIGGLING
2	+EXPANDING	2	FLUTES	2	GINGERBREAD
2	EXPANDS	2	+FLY	2	GIRL'S
2	EXPECTS	2	FOAL	2	+GIRL'S
2	EXPERIENCE	2	FOETUS	2	+GIRLISH
2	EXPLODE	2	FOG	2	+GIRLS
2	EXPLODES	2	FOLK	2	GIT
2	EXPLOSION	2	FOLKS	2	GLAND
2	EXPRESS	2	FOOD	2	GLIB
2	EXPRESSION	2	+FOOL	2	GLIMPSED
2	+EXQUISITE	2	+FOOLISH	2	GLOATS
2	EXTEND	2	FOOLISHWISE	2	GLORIOUS
2	EY	2	FORD	2	+GLORY
2	EYES'	2	FORE	2	GLOVE
2	EYESWHICHNEVERSMILE	2	FOREVER'S	2	GLUEY

956

2	GLY	2	HEAVENLESS	2	IMPERISHABLE
2	GNARLED	2	HEAVENS	2	IMPERTINENTLY
2	GOLF	2	HEIGHTS	2	IMPETUOUS
2	GOO	2	HELD	2	IMPINGE
2	GOODBYE	2	HELLAS	2	IMPORTANCE
2	GOODLY	2	HELMAR	2	+IMPOSSIBLY
2	GORGEOUS	2	HENRI	2	IMPRESSED
2	GRABBED	2	HEROIC	2	IMPRESSION
2	GRACEFULLY	2	+HERSELF	2	IMPROBABLY
2	GRAPES	2	+HEY	2	INCESSANT
2	GRASSHOPPER	2	HIC	2	INCHES
2	GRAVENSTEINS	2	HID	2	INCORRIGIBLE
2	GRAZE	2	HIDDEN	2	INDECENT
2	GREATER	2	HIDES	2	INDEFINABLE
2	GREATEST	2	HING	2	INDIGESTION
2	GREEDIER	2	HINTS	2	INDIGNANT
2	GREENNESS	2	+HIS	2	INDIVIDUAL
2	GREETS	2	HIT	2	INEXCUSABLE
2	GRIEFS	2	HO	2	INEXPLICABLE
2	GRIEVE	2	HOB	2	INGA
2	GRIEVING	2	HOB-A-NOB	2	INGS
2	GRINNING	2	HOISTING	2	INHABIT
2	GRIPPING	2	HOLDING	2	INHALING
2	GRIPS	2	HOLINESS	2	INHERIT
2	GROAN	2	HOLLOW	2	INHUMAN
2	GROOVE	2	HOLLYHOCK	2	INI
2	GROWN	2	HOMECOMING	2	INIMITABLE
2	GRUNTING	2	HOMELESS	2	INIMITABLY
2	GUARD	2	HOOP	2	INNOCENTES
2	GUD	2	HOP	2	INSANE
2	GUESSABLE	2	HORRIBLE	2	INSPIRED
2	GUESSWHO	2	+HORSE	2	INSTRUMENT
2	GUESTS	2	+HOT	2	INSTRUMENTS
2	GUM	2	+HOTEL	2	INTEGRATION
2	GUMS	2	HOU	2	INTENTS
2	GUN	2	+HOUSE	2	INTER
2	+GURDY	2	+HOUSES	2	INTOLERABLE
2	GUTS	2	HOVERING	2	INTRICATELY
2	HAIL	2	+HOW	2	INVARIABLY
2	HAIR-THIN	2	HOWDAH	2	INVENTS
2	HALVES	2	HOWLS	2	INVINCIBLE
2	HANDFUL	2	HUDDLED	2	INVITE
2	+HANDFUL	2	HUGGING	2	IRREFUTABLE
2	HANDLE	2	HUM	2	IRRESPONSIBLE
2	HANDLESS	2	+HUMAN	2	+ISN'T
2	HANG	2	HUMOROUS	2	ISN'TS
2	HAPPEN	2	HUN	2	IT'LL
2	HAPPENING	2	HUNGARY	2	ITY
2	HAPPINESS	2	HUNKS	2	J
2	HAPS	2	HUNTER	2	J'EN
2	HAREM	2	HURDY	2	JACKET
2	HARM	2	+HURT	2	JACKKNIVES
2	HARPS	2	HUSBAND	2	JAM
2	HARVARD	2	HUSHED	2	JAMES
2	HASSAN'S	2	+I'LL	2	JE
2	HATCH	2	ICE	2	JEALOUSY
2	HATE'S	2	IDIOM	2	JELLY
2	HATES	2	IDLY	2	JERKILY
2	HATLESS	2	IDS	2	JEWS
2	HATRED	2	IGNORANTLY	2	JIGGLED
2	HAUNTS	2	+IMAGINE	2	JIGS
2	HAVEN'T	2	IMITATION	2	JOINT
2	HAY	2	IMMACULATELY	2	JOLTS
2	HEAD'S	2	IMMEDIATELY	2	JONES
2	+HEAD	2	IMMENSELY	2	JOSTLE
2	+HEART	2	IMMORTALLY	2	JOUNCE
2	HEAT	2	IMPECCABLE	2	JOUNCING
2	HEAVEN'S	2	IMPERCEPTIBLE	2	JOVIAL
2	+HEAVEN	2	+IMPERCEPTIBLE	2	JUDGMENT

2	NELLIE	2	OST	2	PINCHED
2	NERVES	2	OT	2	PINE
2	NERVOUSLY	2	OTH	2	PINES
2	NES	2	+OTHERWISE	2	PINKISH
2	NEVER'S	2	OUCH	2	+PINKISH
2	NEVERLESS	2	OUTWARD	2	PINKS
2	+NEW YORK	2	OVE	2	PINNACLE
2	NEWNESS	2	OVERING	2	PIPES
2	+NEWNESS	2	+OVERING	2	PITYING
2	NEWS	2	OVERMUCH	2	PLACING
2	NGLY	2	+OWE	2	PLAN
2	NIBBLES	2	OWNED	2	PLANET
2	+NICE	2	OXEN	2	PLANETS
2	NICELY	2	PA	2	PLATO
2	NIGGER	2	PACKED	2	+PLAY
2	NIGGER'S	2	PAGE	2	PLAYS
2	NIGGERS	2	PAINFULLY	2	PLUMP
2	NILE	2	PAINTS	2	POCKET
2	NIMBLE	2	PALER-PALER	2	POETIC
2	NIPPLES	2	PALPABLE	2	+POETS
2	NITE	2	PALPITATING	2	POISED
2	NOBOD	2	PANES	2	POISES
2	NOBODY'LL	2	PANSY	2	POISON
2	NOBODY'S	2	+PANTS	2	POLICEMAN
2	NOEL	2	PAPERBOY	2	PONDER
2	NOISELESS	2	+PARIS	2	PONDEROUS
2	NONCHALANT	2	PARKS	2	POPPIES
2	NONS	2	PARTICLE	2	PORPHYRY
2	NOONE'S	2	PASH	2	PORTRAIT
2	NOSTRILS	2	PASSES	2	POS
2	NOTABLE	2	PASSIONATEL	2	POSE
2	NOTE	2	PASTURES	2	+POSITIVELY
2	NOTHINGNESS	2	+PATCH	2	POST
2	NOTICED	2	PATH	2	POUNDS
2	NOTING	2	PAUL	2	PR
2	NOVEMBER'S	2	PAW	2	PRAISING
2	NOWS	2	PAWN	2	PRE
2	NTO	2	PAWS	2	+PRECISELY
2	NUDE	2	PECULIAR	2	PREENING
2	NUM	2	PEDDLERS	2	PREFER
2	NUMBING	2	PEEK	2	PREFERABLY
2	NUNS	2	PEELS	2	PRESENCE
2	NUTN	2	PEERING	2	PRESENTED
2	NUTS	2	PENCIL	2	PRESENTLY
2	NUZZLE	2	PENCILS	2	PRESENTS
2	OAK	2	PERCEIVES	2	PRESERVED
2	OAT	2	PERCHING	2	PRESSED
2	OATH	2	PERFUMES	2	PRESUME
2	OBEY	2	PERISH	2	PRETENDING
2	OBJECT	2	PERMANENT	2	PRETTIEST
2	OBLONG	2	+PERMANENT	2	+PRETTY
2	OC	2	+PERSON	2	PRICELESS
2	OCCASIONAL	2	PERSONAL	2	PRIESTS
2	+OCEAN	2	PERSONALLY	2	PRO
2	OCEANING	2	PERSPECTIVE	2	PROBABLE
2	+OFF	2	PERSPICUITY	2	PROBLEM
2	OFFERED	2	PERSUADE	2	PROCESSIONS
2	OFFERS	2	PETALED	2	PRODDED
2	OG	2	PH	2	PROFFERS
2	OLDE	2	PHANTOMS	2	+PROGRESS
2	OLDER	2	PHILOSOPHER	2	PROPAGANDA
2	OLE	2	PHILOSOPHY	2	PROPPED
2	OM	2	PHONOGRAPH	2	PROVIDED
2	+ONENESS	2	PHRASE	2	PROWLS
2	ONION	2	PICASSO	2	PROXIMITY
2	ONLYING	2	PICKING	2	PUKE
2	ONO	2	PIE	2	PUMPING
2	OPAQUE	2	PIERCED	2	PUNISH
2	+OPENING	2	PIMPS	2	PUNISHED

959

2	PUNKS	2	ROAMS	2	SHAMELESS
2	PUP	2	ROBINS	2	+SHAPE
2	PUPPY	2	ROGUE	2	SHAPELY
2	PURELY	2	ROLL	2	SHARES
2	PURER	2	ROLLED	2	SHARPLY
2	PURRS	2	ROMAN	2	SHAT
2	PURSUES	2	+ROOM	2	SHAVE
2	Q	2	ROOMS	2	SHEATH
2	QUELL	2	ROPE	2	SHEET
2	QUERIES	2	+ROSE	2	SHELL
2	QUERYING	2	ROSEBUGS	2	SHEPHERD
2	+QUICKLY	2	ROSETREE	2	SHI
2	QUIPS	2	ROSILY	2	SHIMMIE
2	QUOTES	2	ROTTING	2	+SHIRT
2	RADIATOR	2	ROUNDING	2	SHIRTS
2	RAGING	2	ROUNDLY	2	SHIT
2	RAI	2	ROUNDTABLE	2	+SHIT
2	RAIL	2	ROUT	2	SHOCK
2	RAIMENT	2	ROWS	2	SHOCKING
2	RANCID	2	ROYCE	2	SHOES
2	+RAPIDLY	2	+RUBBER	2	SHOOTING
2	RAPTURE	2	RUFFIAN	2	SHORT
2	RASBERRYPATCH	2	RUINED	2	SHOULDER
2	RATE	2	RUNNING	2	+SHOUT
2	+RATE	2	RUNS	2	SHOUTS
2	RATH	2	SAD	2	SHOWED
2	RAVING	2	SAG	2	SHRINE
2	RAYS	2	SAGGING	2	SHRINK
2	REA	2	SAINTS	2	SHUDDERS
2	READY	2	SAKE	2	SHUTS
2	REALITIES	2	+SAKE	2	SHUTTING
2	REALNESS	2	SALESMAN	2	SI
2	REAPED	2	SALUTED	2	SIDEWALK
2	RECALL	2	SAMENESS	2	SIDEWALKS
2	RECENTLY	2	SAN	2	SIGNS
2	RECKLESS	2	+SAND	2	+SILENCE
2	+RED	2	SANK	2	SILVERLY
2	REEL	2	SAT	2	+SIMPLY
2	REFER	2	+SAY	2	+SING
2	REFRAIN	2	SCANDAL	2	SINGDANCE
2	REFUSED	2	SCARED	2	SINGER
2	REFUTED	2	SCATTER	2	+SINGING
2	REGARD	2	SCHEMING	2	SION
2	REGULAR	2	SCIENTIFIC	2	+SIX
2	RELAXING	2	+SCIENTIFIC	2	SIXTH
2	REMAIN	2	SCORN	2	SIZELESS
2	REMARKABLE	2	SCRATCH	2	SKATING
2	REME	2	SCRUMPTIOUS	2	SKELETON
2	+REMEMBERING	2	SCRUPULOUSLY	2	SKIDDING
2	REMEMBRANCE	2	SCULPTOR	2	+SKIDS
2	REMIND	2	SECRECIES	2	SKIL
2	RENEWS	2	SECRETS	2	+SKILFUL
2	REQUIESCAT	2	SEDUCED	2	SKIRT
2	RESEMBLE	2	SEEDS	2	+SKY
2	RESEMBLES	2	+SEEK	2	SKYSCRAPER
2	RESPONDS	2	SEEKING	2	SKYSCRAPERS
2	RESTS	2	SEEMING	2	SLABS
2	REVERENTLY	2	SEES	2	SLAMMED
2	RHYTHMIC	2	SEETHING	2	SLAPPED
2	RI	2	+SELF	2	SLAVES
2	RIBBON	2	SENTENCE	2	SLEEK
2	RICHLY	2	SENTIENCE	2	SLEEPY
2	RIDES	2	SEPARATE	2	SLENDERNESS
2	RIN	2	SERVANT	2	SLIPPED
2	RIND	2	SERVE	2	SLOPPY
2	RINSED	2	SEW	2	SLOVENLY
2	RISEN	2	SEZ	2	SLOWNESS
2	RO	2	SHABBY	2	SLY
2	ROAM	2	SHALLBE	2	SMACKED

2	SMALLER	2	SPROUTED	2	SUN'S
2	SMASH	2	SPROUTS	2	+SUN
2	SMELT	2	SPRUNG	2	SUNBEAM'S
2	SMILELESS	2	SPUN	2	SUNFUL
2	+SMILING	2	SPURTING	2	SUNG
2	SMITING	2	SQUATS	2	SUNRISE
2	SMOKED	2	SQUATTING	2	SUNS
2	SMOKES	2	SQUEAL	2	SUPP
2	SMOTE	2	SQUEEZE	2	SUPPRESSED
2	SNAKE	2	SQUEEZING	2	SUPREMELY
2	SNO	2	+SQUIRM	2	SURROUND
2	SNOWFLAKES	2	+SQUIRMING	2	SUSPECTED
2	SOAR	2	SQUIRTING	2	SWALLOWING
2	SOBBING	2	STAGE	2	SWARMS
2	SOL'S	2	STAGGERED	2	SWEAR
2	SOLDIER	2	STALLION	2	+SWEET
2	SOLID	2	+STANDS	2	SWI
2	SOLIDITY	2	STARK	2	SWIFTNESS
2	SOLIDS	2	STARTED	2	SWIMMING
2	SOLITUDE	2	STARTLED	2	SWIMMINGHOL
2	SOLUTION	2	STATE	2	SWIRL
2	+SOMEONE	2	STATUE	2	SWOONING
2	SOMES	2	STATUES	2	+SWOONING
2	SOMETIME	2	STEAD	2	+SWOOP
2	+SOMETIMES	2	STEADILY	2	SWOOPING
2	+SOMEWHERE	2	STEAK	2	SWORE
2	SOMMES	2	STEALTHILY	2	SYLLABLE
2	SONNET	2	STEM	2	SYMMETRY
2	SONOFABITCH	2	STEPPED	2	SYSTEM
2	SONOROUS	2	STERNLY	2	T'S
2	SONT	2	STICKY	2	+TABLE
2	SOONER	2	STIFF	2	TAC
2	SORROWS	2	STIFFENED	2	TALKING'S
2	SOUL'S	2	STIFFENING	2	TALLEST
2	SOULLESS	2	+STIFFLY	2	TAME
2	+SOUND	2	STILE	2	TANGERINES
2	SOUR	2	+STILLNESS	2	TANGLE
2	SPAN	2	STING	2	TART
2	SPANKED	2	+STIR	2	TASTES
2	+SPARE	2	STOCKING	2	TASTING
2	SPARROWS	2	STOCKINGS	2	TAXIS
2	+SPARROWS	2	STOLEN	2	TEA
2	SPASM	2	+STONES	2	TEASE
2	SPAT	2	STOOL	2	TEEM
2	SPATTERED	2	STOOPED	2	+TELL
2	SPAWN	2	STOPPING	2	TELLING
2	SPEAR	2	STORE	2	TEND
2	SPEARS	2	STRAIGHT	2	TENDRIL
2	SPECIALTY	2	STRAWBERRIES	2	TENT
2	SPECTRES	2	STREAMING	2	TENTH
2	SPEECH	2	STRINGS	2	TENUOUS
2	SPEED	2	STRIVE	2	TERMS
2	SPELL	2	+STROLLING	2	TERSE
2	SPENDS	2	+STROLLS	2	THANKFUL
2	SPIC	2	STRUGGLE	2	THANKFULLY
2	SPIKES	2	STUFFS	2	THANKS
2	SPILLED	2	STUMBLE	2	THATTHIS
2	SPILLING	2	STUPENDOUS	2	+THEIR
2	SPIRALLY	2	STURDILY	2	THEIRS
2	SPIRE	2	+STURDY	2	+THEN
2	SPIRIT'S	2	SUBHUMAN	2	THER
2	SPITTOON	2	SUBJECT	2	THERES
2	SPLENDORS	2	SUBLIME	2	THEY'D
2	SPOON	2	SUBLIMINAL	2	THICKER
2	SPRAWLING	2	SUCCEEDS	2	+THING
2	SPRAWLS	2	SUCCESSFULLY	2	THINGISH
2	SPRING'S	2	SUGGEST	2	THINNED
2	+SPRING	2	SUMPN	2	THIRDS
2	SPRINGS	2	SUMPTUOUSLY	2	THIRTEEN

961

2	THIRTY	2	+TUNE	2	VANISHED
2	THO	2	TURD	2	VANISHES
2	THORN	2	TURES	2	VANISHING
2	+THOU	2	+TURNING	2	VASTLY
2	THOUGHTFUL	2	TW	2	VEGETABLES
2	THREADS	2	TWAS	2	VELOCITY
2	THREATENS	2	TWEAK	2	VEN
2	THREATS	2	TWEEDS	2	VERBAL
2	THRICE-THREE-HUNDREDTH	2	TWILIGHT'S	2	VEST
2	THRILLED	2	TWIN	2	VI
2	THRILLS	2	TWINKLE	2	VICINITY
2	THROUGHOUT	2	+TWIRL	2	VICTORIOUS
2	THROWS	2	TWIRLS	2	VILLAGE
2	THUMBLIKE	2	TWITCHES	2	VILLAINS
2	THUMBS	2	+TWITTERING	2	VINE
2	THUNDERBOLT	2	TWOT	2	VIRGINAL
2	THUNDERING	2	TYPEWRITER	2	VIRTUE
2	THWARTED	2	ULAR	2	VISIBLE
2	TICKING	2	ULLY	2	VISION
2	TIFUL	2	ULTIMATE	2	VISIONS
2	TIMELESS	2	UM	2	VIVA
2	+TIMELESSNESS	2	UNALIVE	2	+VOICES
2	TIMIDLY	2	UNBEING	2	VOIX
2	TIMOROUS	2	UNBIG	2	VOMITS
2	TINGLING	2	UNBORN	2	VOW
2	TINSEL	2	UNBURIED	2	WADDLING
2	TINYING	2	UNCOUTHLY	2	WAFTED
2	TIP	2	UND	2	WAIL
2	TIPPING	2	UNDAUNTED	2	WAKE
2	TIPSY	2	UNDEATH	2	WAKES
2	TITS	2	UNDEATHS	2	WAKING
2	TOKEN	2	UNDERING	2	WALKED
2	TOMMY	2	UNDERS	2	WAND
2	+TOMORROW	2	UNDERSTANDING	2	WANDERED
2	TONE	2	UNDERSTOOD	2	WANDERER
2	TONES	2	UNDO	2	+WANDERING
2	TOOLS	2	UNDREAM	2	+WANT
2	TOOTHLESS	2	UNDYING	2	WANTED
2	+TOP	2	UNEARTHLY	2	WARCRY
2	TOPPED	2	UNEYES	2	WARMTH
2	TOPPLE	2	UNFOOLS	2	WARRIORS
2	TORE	2	UNIMMORTAL	2	WARS
2	TORSE	2	UNIMPORTANT	2	WASHINGTON
2	TOSSES	2	UNIQUE	2	WASN'T
2	+TOUCH	2	UNKNOWN	2	WATCHED
2	+TOUCHING	2	+UNLESS	2	WE'D
2	TOWERS	2	UNLOVELY	2	+WE'RE
2	+TOWN	2	UNMIND	2	+WE
2	TOYLIKE	2	UNMITIGATED	2	WEAKLY
2	TRANSCENDS	2	UNSERIOUS	2	WEAKNESS
2	TRANSPARENCY	2	UNSPONTANEOUS	2	WEALTH
2	TREACHEROUS	2	UNSTRANGE	2	WEALTHY
2	TREASURES	2	UNTHING	2	WEAVING
2	TREMBLES	2	UNTHINGS	2	WED
2	+TREMBLING	2	UNTIMID	2	WEED
2	TRES	2	+UNTUMBLED	2	WEEPING
2	TRICKLES	2	UNVISIBLE	2	WEIGH
2	TRICKLING	2	UNWISH	2	WEIRD
2	TRICKTRICKCLICKFLICK-ER	2	UNWORLDS	2	WELLS
2	TRIES	2	UPO	2	WEPT
2	TRILLION	2	+UPRIGHT	2	+WHAT'S
2	TRIUMPHED	2	URGENT	2	WHE
2	TROP	2	USES	2	+WHEE
2	TROUSERFLY	2	USUAL	2	+WHEELING
2	TROY	2	UTTERED	2	+WHEN
2	TRUEST	2	UV	2	WHENS
2	TRYST	2	VACANCY	2	WHEREBY
2	TTING	2	VACANT	2	WHERETO
2	TUMBLED	2	VAGUELY	2	WHEREVER

963

1	ADROIT	
1	ADVANCING	
1	ADVANTAGE	
1	ADVE	
1	ADVENTURES	
1	+ADVENTURING	
1	ADVISE	
1	AEONS	
1	AERONAUT	
1	AESTHETE	
1	AFAR	
1	AFFECTIONATE	
1	AFFIRM	
1	AFFIRMATION	
1	AFFORDS	
1	AFLAME	
1	AFLICKF	
1	AFLOAT	
1	+AFLOAT	
1	AFLUTTER	
1	AFRICAN	
1	AFT	
1	AFTERDAY	
1	AFTERGLOW	
1	+AFTERGLOW	
1	AFTERWARD	
1	AGAINING	
1	AGAINLESS	
1	AGGRESSIVE	
1	AGINES	
1	AGONIZING	
1	AGREEABLE	
1	AGREEABLY	
1	AGREEMENT	
1	AGRIN	
1	AHLBRHOON	
1	AID	
1	AIMS	
1	AIN	
1	AIN'T	
1	+AIN'T	
1	AINNOUGHBUDIH	
1	+AINT	
1	AIRSO	
1	AIRY	
1	AKIN	
1	AKING	
1	AKING-B	
1	AL-DOWN	
1	ALARM-CLOCK	
1	ALBUTNOTQUITEMOST	
1	ALCHEMIST	
1	ALE	
1	+ALE	
1	ALEAK	
1	+ALERT	
1	ALGEBRAS	
1	ALGERNON	
1	ALIGHT	
1	+ALIGHTING	
1	ALIKE	
1	ALIMONY	
1	ALING	
1	ALINGWAYSING	
1	ALIV	
1	ALIVEING	
1	ALLABOUT	
1	ALLBYITSELF	
1	ALLEGIANCE	

1	ALLEMAND	
1	ALLEN	
1	ALLEY	
1	ALLEZCIRCULEZ	
1	ALLGOTUPFITTOKILL	
1	ALLL	
1	ALLNESS	
1	ALLOFHER	
1	ALLONS	
1	ALLOTTED	
1	ALLOWED	
1	ALLOWS	
1	ALLS	
1	ALLWHERE	
1	ALLY	
1	ALMIGHTY	
1	ALMOND	
1	ALMOS	
1	ALMOSTCLEAN	
1	ALMOSTNESS	
1	ALONG-ALONG	
1	ALOTTA	
1	ALS	
1	ALSEEP	
1	ALTAR	
1	ALTER	
1	ALTERED	
1	ALTITUDE	
1	ALTOGETH	
1	+ALTOGETHER	
1	ALTOONA	
1	ALTRUISTIC	
1	ALWAYS-SO-MUCH-INTERESTED	
1	AMA	
1	AMARANTH	
1	AMASS	
1	AMAZE	
1	AMAZED	
1	AMAZEMENT	
1	AMAZINGLY	
1	+AMAZINGLY	
1	AMBER	
1	AMBIGUOUS	
1	AMBITIOUS	
1	AMBROSIAL	
1	AMEN	
1	+AMERICA	
1	AMETHYST	
1	AMINGFEEBLYOFF	
1	AMMUNICIONS	
1	+AMMUNITIONS	
1	AMONGOTHER	
1	AMONGS	
1	AMOR	
1	AMORAL	
1	AMORES	
1	AMOROUS-TAD	
1	+AMOROUSLY	
1	AMOUNT	
1	AMPLIFY	
1	AMPUTATE	
1	AMUS	
1	AMUSE	
1	AMUSINGLY	
1	AN-DORG-AN	
1	ANAESTHETIZ	
1	ANARCHIST	
1	ANATOLE	
1	ANATOMY	

1	ANC	
1	ANCHORED	
1	+ANCIENT	
1	AND-CLING	
1	ANDDARK	
1	ANDS	
1	ANDSOFORTH	
1	ANDTHEIR	
1	ANDWHYEVERN	
1	ANGARY	
1	+ANGEL	
1	ANGELFACES	
1	ANGER	
1	+ANGLE	
1	ANGLES	
1	ANGLEWORM	
1	ANGLICAN	
1	ANGRILY	
1	+ANGRY	
1	ANGUISHED	
1	ANISETTES	
1	ANKLE	
1	ANKUS	
1	ANNIHI	
1	+ANNIHILATI	
1	ANNIHILATOR	
1	ANNOUNCE	
1	ANNOYED	
1	ANNOYS	
1	ANNUAL	
1	+ANNUAL	
1	ANON	
1	ANONYMITY	
1	ANONYMOUS	
1	+ANONYMOUS	
1	+ANSWER	
1	ANSWEREST	
1	ANSWERING	
1	+ANTEATER	
1	ANTHOLOGIST	
1	ANTHROPOID	
1	ANTIBOLSHEVISTIC	
1	ANTIMERE	
1	ANTIQUITIES	
1	ANTIQUITIES--RELAXING	
1	ANTOMS	
1	ANTONY	
1	ANUS	
1	+ANY	
1	ANYBODYELSES	
1	ANYTHING'S	
1	AP-INGOF	
1	APES	
1	APIDLY	
1	APISH	
1	APP	
1	APPALLING	
1	+APPARELED	
1	APPARELLING	
1	APPEAL	
1	+APPEAL	
1	APPEARANCE	
1	+APPLAUSE	
1	APPLAWS	
1	APPLIED	
1	APPRECIATE	
1	APPRECIATION	
1	APPROACH	
1	+APPROACHED	

965

1 BEARS	1 BENDING	1 BLACKSHIRT
1 +BEAST	1 BENEVOLENT	1 BLACKSNAKE
1 +BEAT	1 +BENT	1 BLACKTREESTHINK
1 BEATIFIC	1 BENTHAM	1 BLADE
1 BEATITUDE	1 BEQUEATH	1 BLADES
1 BEAUT	1 BERCOLOURED	1 BLANDLY
1 BEAUTI	1 BEREAVES	1 BLANK
1 BEAUTIFOOL	1 BERINGED	1 BLASE
1 BEAUTIFUL-CURVEOFHUNGER	1 BERLESSN	1 BLAST
1 +BEAUTY	1 +BERLIN	1 BLAZE
1 BECAUSELESS	1 BERQ	1 BLAZED
1 BECKON	1 BESEECH	1 BLAZING
1 BECKONED	1 BESIDES	1 BLE-AT-SSW-EE-T-NOTH
1 BECKONINGLY	1 BESPANGLED	1 +BLEATS
1 BECOM	1 +BETH	1 BLESS
1 BECOMINGLY	1 BETRAYAL	1 BLEST
1 BEDAD	1 BETTERS	1 BLIEST
1 BEDBUGS	1 BETTYANDISBEL	1 BLINDLY
1 BEDDINGS	1 BEWAIL	1 BLINDMAN
1 BEDECKED	1 BEWITCH	1 BLINK
1 BEDFELLOWS	1 +BEYOND	1 BLINKED
1 BEDROOM	1 BEYONDS	1 BLINKING
1 BEDTIME	1 BI	1 BLINKY
1 BEEG	1 +BIBLE	1 BLISSFUL
1 BEERS	1 BICEPS	1 BLOAT
1 BEES	1 BID	1 BLOB
1 BEFALL	1 BIDDY	1 BLOCK
1 BEFRIENDED	1 BIEN	1 BLOCKS
1 BEFRIENDING	1 +BIGGER	1 BLOKES
1 +BEGAN	1 +BIGGEST	1 BLONDER
1 BEGET	1 BIGGISH	1 BLONDEST
1 BEGGING	1 BIGMORNING	1 BLOO
1 BEGI	1 BIGTWITTERING	1 BLOO-MOO-N
1 BEGINNINGLESS	1 +BILL	1 BLOOD'S
1 BEGINNINGLY	1 BILLIARD	1 BLOODBEAT
1 +BEGINNINGLY	1 BILLIARD-CUE	1 +BLOODED
1 BEGINNINGS	1 BILLIARDBALLS	1 BLOODIES
1 +BEGINS	1 BILLIARDS	1 BLOODLIGHT
1 +BEGOTTEN	1 BILLIKEN	1 BLOODSHED
1 BEGUILES	1 BILLS	1 BLOOMING
1 BEGUN	1 BILLY	1 +BLOSSOM
1 BEH	1 BINGBONGWHOM	1 BLOWING
1 BEHAVED	1 BIPEDS	1 BLU
1 BEHEMOTH	1 BIR	1 BLUBBERING
1 +BEHIND	1 +BIRD	1 +BLUE
1 +BEHOLD	1 BIRDCAGE	1 BLUEANDGREE
1 BEHOLDING	1 +BIRDS	1 BLUEDMUFFLE
1 BEINGALIVE	1 BIRTH'S	1 BLUENESS
1 BEINGEST	1 +BIRTHDAY	1 BLUES
1 BEINGS	1 BIRTHDAYS	1 BLUETS
1 BEL	1 BIRTHS	1 +BLUISH
1 BELCH	1 BISCUIT	1 BLUISH-OLD
1 BELCHES	1 BITES	1 BLUISHSUSPE
1 BELIEVAB	1 +BITS	1 BLUNDERING
1 +BELIEVABLY	1 BITTER	1 +BLUR
1 +BELIEVE	1 BITTEREST	1 BLURB
1 BELIEVED	1 BIZ	1 BLURTED
1 +BELL'S	1 BL	1 BLURTING
1 BELLE	1 BLAC	1 BLUSH
1 BELLES	1 +BLACK	1 BLUSHING
1 BELLOW	1 +BLACKBERRIES	1 BO
1 BELLOWING	1 BLACKENING	1 +BOARD
1 BELLOWINGS	1 +BLACKER	1 BOARDS
1 BELLYFUL	1 +BLACKEST	1 BOAT
1 +BELOVED	1 BLACKISH	1 BOCCA
1 BELOWTRY	1 BLACKMAIL	1 BOCCACCIO
1 BELT	1 BLACKNESS	1 BOD
1 BEN	1 +BLACKNESS	1 BODILY
1 +BEN	1 BLACKRED	1 BODYFEE

1 BOG
1 +BOIL
1 BOIS
1 BOIT
1 BOITE
1 BOLDEST
1 +BOLSHEVIST
1 BOMBAST
1 BOMBED
1 +BOMBS
1 BOMS
1 BONE
1 BONES
1 +BONG
1 BONNET
1 BOOBS
1 BOODLE'S
1 BOOL
1 BOOLLEVARES
1 BOOMING
1 BOOST
1 BOOSTS
1 BOOTED
1 BOOZING
1 BORE
1 BORED
1 BORNE
1 BOSOMS
1 +BOSOMY
1 BOSS
1 +BOSTON
1 BOTHATONCE
1 BOTHER
1 BOTHERED
1 BOTHERING
1 BOTHING
1 BOTHNESS
1 BOTHS
1 BOTTES
1 BOTTLE
1 BOTTOMLESS
1 BOTTOMS
1 BOU
1 BOUGHS
1 BOUGHT
1 BOULDER
1 +BOULDER
1 BOULEVARD
1 BOULEVARDS
1 +BOULEVARDS
1 BOUNCE
1 BOUNCELESS
1 BOUND
1 BOUNDING
1 BOUNDS
1 BOUQUET
1 BOWERS
1 BOWING
1 +BOWL
1 BOWS
1 BOXES
1 BOXIN
1 BOYGIRLS
1 +BOYISHNESS
1 +BOYS
1 BR
1 BRAG
1 BRAGGING
1 BRAIKYOOZ

1 BRAIN'S
1 +BRAIN
1 BRAINY
1 BRAKES
1 +BRAMBLIEST
1 BRASS
1 BRATTLE
1 +BRAVELY
1 BRAVER
1 BRAVEST
1 BRAVING
1 BRAWNY
1 BRAZEN
1 BRE
1 BREADCRUMB
1 BREAKFAST
1 BREAKFASTFOOD
1 +BREASTED
1 BREATHE-MOVE-AND-SEEM
1 +BREATHES
1 BREATHING'S
1 BREATHINGS
1 BREATHLESS-SCARLET
1 BRED
1 BREEDING
1 BREEDS
1 BRETISH
1 BRETON
1 BREVIS
1 BREWED
1 BRI
1 BRIDEGROOMS
1 BRIDGES
1 +BRIEF
1 BRIGGS
1 BRIGHTEN
1 BRIGHTEST
1 BRIGHTMILLION
1 BRIGHTSHADOWFULLY
1 BRILLIANT
1 BRILLIANTLY
1 BRISKLY
1 +BRITISH
1 BRITTLER
1 BRITTLEST
1 BROADWAY
1 BROGUE
1 BROMFIELD
1 BRONX
1 BROOD
1 BROOKS
1 +BROTHER
1 +BROW
1 BROWNS
1 BROWS
1 BRUD
1 BRUISING
1 BRUMMELL
1 BRUSHES
1 BRUSHING
1 BRUTE
1 BRUTEBEAK
1 BRYANT
1 BS
1 BUBBIES
1 BUCH
1 +BUCHANAN
1 BUCK'
1 BUCKS

1 +BUD
1 BUDDHA
1 BUDDIES
1 BUDDING
1 BUDGE
1 BUDGINGLY
1 BUDY
1 BUFFALO
1 BUFFETING
1 +BUG
1 BUGGER
1 BUGGY
1 BUGLE
1 BUGS
1 BUILDS
1 BUL
1 BULBOUS
1 BULBS
1 BULGES
1 BULGILY
1 BULGINGS
1 BULL
1 BULL'S
1 BULLET
1 BULLIED
1 BUM-NOTHING
1 BUMP
1 BUMPED
1 BUMPINGS
1 BUMPS
1 BUN
1 BUNCH
1 BUNCHA
1 +BUNCHES
1 BUNDL
1 +BUNDLE
1 BUNG
1 BUNGED
1 BUOYANT
1 BUOYED
1 BURLIN
1 BURNED
1 BURRS
1 BURS
1 +BURST
1 BURSTS
1 BUSHSCYTHEBLADE
1 BUSHY
1 BUSI
1 BUSIEST
1 +BUSINESSMAN
1 +BUSY
1 +BUSYING
1 BUTBUTBUT
1 BUTOIGUTTUH
1 +BUTS
1 +BUTTERFLY
1 BUTTING
1 +BUTTON
1 BUTTONED
1 BUTTONHOLE
1 +BUTTS
1 BUYABLE
1 BUYING
1 BUYS
1 BUZZ
1 BUZZSQUEAKING
1 BVD
1 BYE

1 BYS	1 CARPET	1 CHASSISED
1 C-A-T	1 CARRIES	1 CHASTENESS
1 C-URLIN-G	1 +CARRION	1 CHAT
1 CA-Y-EST	1 CARRY-TADPOLE	1 CHATOUILLE
1 CAESARS	1 CARS	1 CHATOUILLER
1 CAFE	1 +CARTS	1 +CHATTERING
1 +CAGE	1 CARVES	1 CHATTERISH
1 CAIRO	1 +CARVING	1 CHATTERS
1 CAKE	1 CASKET	1 CHAUCER
1 +CAKE	1 CASSIOPEIA'S	1 CHAUVESOURIS
1 +CAKED	1 CASTLES	1 CHB
1 +CAKES	1 CASTRATED	1 CHEAPLY
1 CALCHIDAS	1 CASTS	1 CHECK
1 CALENDARS	1 +CAT	1 +CHECK
1 CALIFORNIAN	1 CATASTROPHE	1 CHED
1 CALLING	1 CATCHING	1 CHEERFUL
1 CALMLY	1 CATHEDRALS	1 CHEERFULLY
1 CALVES	1 CAUSELESS	1 CHEERING
1 CAMEF	1 CAUSING	1 CHEERS
1 CAMELS	1 CAUTION	1 +CHEMISTRY
1 +CAMELS	1 CAVALIERS	1 CHERES
1 +CAMERA	1 CAVE	1 CHERISHED
1 CAMMIN'	1 CAVEAT	1 CHERRIES
1 CAMPANILE	1 +CAVING	1 CHESOFNEW
1 CAN'S	1 CCCOME	1 +CHESTED
1 +CAN'T	1 CCO	1 CHEVAUX
1 CAN'TS	1 CCOCOUCOUGCOUGHCOUGHI	1 CHEWCHOO
1 CANARY-BIRD	1 CEAN	1 CHEWING
1 CANARY-CAGE	1 CEASELESSLY	1 +CHEWING
1 CANDIDATE'S	1 CEASELESSNESS	1 CHEWS
1 CANDIES	1 CEASING	1 CHICAGO
1 CANDLELIGHT	1 CECILE	1 +CHICAGO
1 +CANDY	1 CED	1 CHICKEN
1 CANE	1 CELEBRATE	1 CHICKS
1 CANNIBAL	1 CELEBRATES	1 CHIEF
1 CANNON	1 CELIBATE	1 CHIEVE
1 CANNONADIN	1 CELLOPHANE	1 CHILD'S
1 +CANNONADIN	1 CELLOS	1 CHILD-HEAD
1 CANOE	1 CEMENT	1 CHILDFLESH
1 CANOPENERS	1 CEN	1 CHILDISH
1 CANOUNCHIR	1 CENSORED	1 CHILDLOST
1 CANT	1 CENTRIPETAL	1 CHILDMOON
1 CANTED	1 CENTURY	1 CHIME
1 CAP	1 CERITY	1 CHIMNEY
1 CAPERING	1 CERTAINTIES	1 CHIN
1 CAPTAINS	1 CESSATION	1 CHINESE
1 CAPTIVATING	1 CEZANNE	1 CHING
1 CAR	1 CEZANNE'S	1 CHINO
1 CARBURETOR	1 CH	1 +CHINOISERIES
1 CARCASS	1 CHAINED	1 CHIP
1 CARD	1 CHAINS	1 CHIPMUNK
1 CARDS	1 +CHAIR	1 CHIPPING
1 +CARE	1 CHAIRETE	1 CHIPPITY
1 CARED	1 CHALCEDONY	1 +CHIRPING
1 CAREENS	1 CHALKING	1 CHIRPS
1 CAREF	1 CHALLENGE	1 CHISEL
1 +CAREFUL	1 CHAMBERS	1 CHISELED
1 +CAREFULLY	1 CHAMPYCHUMPCHOMPS	1 CHIVALRY
1 CARELESS	1 CHANCEL	1 CHOC
1 +CARES	1 CHANGELESS	1 +CHOCOLATES
1 CARET	1 CHANTS	1 CHOICE
1 CARING	1 CHAP	1 CHOKED
1 CARL	1 CHAPPY	1 CHOKES
1 CARLOADS	1 CHARIOT	1 +CHOMPS
1 CARNIVOROUS	1 +CHARLES	1 CHOOSE
1 CAROLLING	1 CHARLIE	1 CHOPPED
1 CAROMING	1 CHARY	1 CHOPS
1 CAROUSE	1 CHAS	1 CHORD
1 CARPENTERS	1 CHASM	1 CHORES

1	CHOSEN	1	+CLAUS	1	COFFIN'S
1	CHR	1	CLAUSES	1	COFFINLID
1	CHREYESAKE	1	CLAY	1	COGITATING
1	+CHRIST	1	+CLEAN	1	COGNOMEN
1	CHRISTIAN	1	CLEANCORNER	1	COGNOSCENTI
1	CHRISTOPHER	1	CLEANED	1	COHERENT
1	CHROMATIC	1	CLEANERS	1	COHN
1	CHROME	1	+CLEANERS	1	COHORTS
1	CHROMES	1	CLEANEST	1	COIL
1	CHRYSELEPHANTINE	1	CLEANSHAVEN	1	COILED
1	CHUBBY	1	CLEARING	1	COINS
1	CHUCKING	1	CLEAT	1	COITNLY
1	+CHUCKING	1	CLEAVING	1	COL
1	CHUCKLED	1	+CLENCHED	1	COLDING
1	+CHUCKLING	1	CLERK	1	COLLAP
1	+CHUCKLINGS	1	CLEVEREST	1	COLLAPS
1	+CHUMP	1	CLEVERJERK	1	COLLAPSE
1	CHUNKLIKE	1	CLEVERLY-CR	1	+COLLAPSED
1	CHURCH'S	1	CLICHES	1	+COLLAPSING
1	CHURCHES	1	+CLICK	1	+COLLAPSINGLY
1	+CHURCHES	1	CLICKING	1	COLLARBUTTON
1	CHURNING	1	CLIM	1	COLLECT
1	CHUST	1	+CLIMB	1	COLLECTS
1	CHUTE	1	CLIMBI	1	+COLLEGE
1	CHUZD	1	+CLIMBING	1	+COLLIDE
1	CI	1	CLIMBINGLY	1	COLLIDES
1	CI-GIT	1	CLIMBSCR	1	COLLIDINGLY
1	CIBLE	1	CLINCHED	1	COLLISION
1	+CIGAR	1	+CLINGING	1	COLLYWOBBLING
1	CIGAR-STUB	1	CLINK	1	COLON
1	CIGARETTEAS	1	CLOAKED	1	COLOURLESS
1	CIGARETTEBU	1	CLOGS	1	COLUMN
1	CIGARS	1	CLOSELY	1	COMB
1	CIGARSTINKI	1	CLOSER	1	COMBINE
1	CIGERR	1	CLOSING	1	+COMBINE
1	CINCINGONDO	1	CLOTHE	1	COMBINING
1	+CINCINNATI	1	+CLOTHES	1	COME-SWARM
1	CINDERCOLOU	1	CLOTHS	1	COMELY
1	CING	1	CLOTTED	1	+COMES
1	CIRCLING	1	CLOTTINGSAND	1	COMEST
1	+CIRCULEZ	1	CLOUD-GLOSS	1	+COMFORTER
1	CIRCUMSTANC	1	CLOVEN	1	COMFORTS
1	CIRCUSHEART	1	CLOVERISH	1	COMIC
1	CIRCUSTENT	1	CLOWN'S	1	COMICS
1	CISE	1	CLOWNLIKE	1	COMMAND
1	CISEL	1	CLOZE	1	COMMEMORATION
1	CITHAREDE	1	+CLUCKING	1	COMMENDABLE
1	CITHERN	1	CLUE	1	COMMENTING
1	CITI	1	CLUETT	1	COMMERCE
1	CITIED	1	CLUMSIEST	1	COMMITS
1	CITIZEN	1	CLUSTERED	1	COMMITTING
1	+CIVIC	1	+CLUTCHED	1	COMMON'S
1	CIVIL	1	CLUTCHING	1	COMMUNICATE
1	CIVILIZATIO	1	CLUTTER	1	COMMUNION
1	+CIVILIZE	1	COACH	1	COMMUNIST
1	CK	1	COACHMAN	1	COMPANION
1	CL	1	COAL	1	COMPANIONS
1	CLAIM	1	+COAL	1	+COMPANY
1	CLAIMS	1	COAST	1	COMPARABLE
1	CLAMOR	1	COATS	1	COMPARATIVELY
1	CLAMORED	1	COAX	1	COMPASSIONATE
1	CLAMORS	1	COCKATOO	1	COMPEL
1	CLAMPS	1	COCKNEY	1	COMPELS
1	CLAPPED	1	COCODRILLO	1	COMPLACENT
1	CLARION	1	COD	1	COMPLAINED
1	CLASS	1	CODIFIED	1	+COMPLETELY
1	+CLASS	1	COEDS	1	COMPLEXIONS
1	CLATTERED	1	COERCION	1	COMPLEXITY
1	CLAUS	1	COFFIN	1	COMPLEXLY

1 COMPLICATED
1 COMPREHENDED
1 COMPREHENDS
1 COMPRISE
1 COMPRISES
1 +COMPRISES
1 COMPULSIONS
1 COMPULSORY
1 +COMRADE
1 CONAREFETTI
1 CONCE
1 CONCEALED
1 +CONCEALS
1 CONCEIVABLE
1 CONCEIVABLY
1 CONCENTRIC
1 CONCEPT
1 CONCERNED
1 CONCERNIN
1 CONCERNING
1 CONCESSION
1 CONCLUDE
1 CONCLUDES
1 CONCRETE
1 CONCUS
1 +CONCUSSION
1 CONDEMNATORY
1 CONDITION
1 CONDOMS
1 CONDUCT
1 CONEY
1 CONFESSIO
1 +CONFETTI
1 CONFINE
1 CONFLICT
1 CONFORM
1 CONFOUND
1 +CONFOUNDS
1 CONFUSED
1 CONFUSING
1 +CONFUSION
1 CONFUTE
1 CONFUTES
1 CONGRESSMAN
1 CONJUGATED
1 CONJURERS
1 CONNIVANCE
1 CONNOTATION
1 CONQUERS
1 CONSCIENCE
1 CONSCIENTIOUS
1 CONSCIOUS
1 CONSCIOUSNESS
1 CONSID
1 +CONSIDER
1 CONSIDERABLE
1 CONSIDERED
1 CONSIDERS
1 CONSISTS
1 CONSTITUTES
1 CONSTRUCTIV
1 CONSTRUED
1 CONSUBSTANT
1 CONSULT
1 CONSUMMATIO
1 CONTACT
1 CONTAINING
1 CONTAINS
1 CONTEMPTUOU

1 CONTENTMENT
1 CONTINUED
1 CONTINUOUS
1 CONTINUUM
1 +CONTRACTIN
1 CONTRADICT
1 CONTRARY
1 CONTRAS
1 CONTRIVE
1 CONTRIVED
1 CONTRIVING
1 CONTROL
1 CONVENTIONS
1 CONVERSATIO
1 CONVERSE
1 CONVERSED
1 CONVICT
1 CONVULSED
1 CONVULSIVE
1 CONWAY
1 COOKIE
1 COOKIES
1 COOLER
1 +COOLIDGE
1 COOLISH
1 COOLITCH
1 COOLLY
1 +COOLNESS
1 COON
1 +COON
1 COOS
1 COP'S
1 COPIOUS
1 COPPERS
1 COPS
1 COQUETTISHL
1 CORAL
1 CORDIALLY
1 CORKING
1 CORKSCREW
1 CORN
1 CORNERED
1 +CORNERED
1 +CORNERS
1 CORNUCOPIOU
1 CORPSECOLOU
1 CORRECTLY
1 +CORRUPTING
1 CORRUPTION
1 COSMIC
1 COST
1 COSTLIER
1 COSTLY
1 COSTUME
1 COUGHING
1 +COUGHING
1 COUGHS
1 COULDN'T-BE-GIVEN-AWAY
1 COULDNT
1 COULEUR
1 COUNTED
1 COUNTENANCES
1 COUNTING
1 COUNTLESS
1 COUNTRY'S
1 COUPLE
1 +COUPLE
1 COURSELESS
1 COURTE

1 COURTED
1 COURTEOUS
1 +COURTEOUS
1 COURTESIED
1 COVER
1 COVERING
1 +COW
1 COWER
1 COY
1 COYLY
1 +CRABS
1 +CRACK
1 CRACKING
1 CRACKLES
1 CRACKLING
1 CRACKSMAN
1 CRADLE
1 CRADLES
1 CRADLING
1 CRAFT
1 CRAFTY
1 CRANKED
1 CRANKIN
1 CRAPS
1 CRASHDIS
1 CRAVAT
1 CRAVEN
1 CRAWLED
1 CRAWLING
1 +CRAZED
1 CREA
1 CREANG
1 CREASED
1 CREASES
1 CREATING
1 +CREATING
1 CREATIVE
1 +CREATURES
1 CREDIBLY
1 CREDO
1 CREDOS
1 CREED
1 CREEPED
1 CREEPS
1 CREPUSCULAR
1 CRESCENDO
1 CRICKETS
1 CRICKS
1 +CRIED
1 +CRIES
1 CRIESWHICHAREWINGS
1 CRIGHT
1 CRIMBFLITTERINGISH
1 CRIME
1 CRIMINAL
1 CRINGE
1 CRINGEWILTDROOLERY
1 CRINKLING
1 CRIPPLE
1 CRIPPLED
1 CRISPER
1 CRISPING
1 CRITICS
1 CROCODILE
1 CROCUS
1 CROI
1 CRONE
1 CROOK
1 CROOKEDLY

1	DEMOTIC	1	+DIMENSIONAL	1	DISTRESS
1	DEMURE	1	DIMENSIONLESS	1	DITHYRAMBS
1	DEMURELY	1	DIMES	1	DIVED
1	DEN	1	DIMMER	1	DIVER
1	DENFERT	1	DIMNESS	1	DIVERSIFIED
1	DENIED	1	DINARILY	1	+DIVES
1	DENLY	1	DINARY	1	DIVIDES
1	DENOUNCES	1	DINE	1	DIVIDING
1	+DENSE	1	DINED	1	DIVINITIES
1	DENTHAM	1	+DING	1	DIVINITY
1	DEPAOLA	1	DINGDONG	1	DIVISIBLE
1	DEPARTS	1	DINGLE	1	DIVISOR
1	DEPEND	1	DINGSTERS	1	DIZZIER
1	DEPENDING	1	DINNED	1	DIZZIZ
1	DEPOSITED	1	DINT	1	DL
1	DEPRIVING	1	DINTS	1	DMORE
1	DERANGE	1	DIOCRI	1	DNIGHTEF
1	DERBIED	1	DIPS	1	DNITE
1	DERBIES-WITH-MEN-IN-THEM	1	DIR	1	+DO'S
1	DERL	1	DIRECTING	1	DOANCARE
1	DERRICKS	1	DIRECTIONLESS	1	DOANGIVUH
1	DERRIERE	1	DIRECTLY	1	DOCILE
1	DERS	1	DIRTIEST	1	DOCTOR
1	DESDEMONIAL	1	DIRTPOOR	1	DOD
1	DESERT	1	DIS-DONC	1	+DODDERING
1	DESERTBYITS	1	DISA	1	DODDERINGLY
1	DESERVED	1	DISAGREEABLE	1	DODDERS
1	DESERVES	1	DISAPP	1	DODGE
1	DESIRABLE	1	+DISAPPEARINGLY	1	DODGING
1	DESIRES	1	+DISAPPEARS	1	+DODGING
1	DESPAIRING	1	DISASTER	1	DODREAMING
1	DESPAIRS	1	DISCIPLE	1	DODREAMINGL
1	DESPERATELY	1	DISCOBOLUS	1	DOER
1	+DESPERATELY	1	DISCORDIA'S	1	DOER'S
1	DESPOT'S	1	DISCOVERABLY	1	+DOG
1	DESTINIES	1	DISCREETLY	1	DOGOODING
1	DESTINY	1	+DISCUSSING	1	DOGS
1	DESTROY	1	DISDAINS	1	DOI
1	DESTROYED	1	+DISEASE	1	DOIDEE
1	DESTRUCTIVITY	1	DISENCHANTED	1	DOITY
1	DETACHES	1	DISGUISE	1	+DOLL
1	DETACHING	1	+DISH	1	DOLL-ANGEL-LIFE
1	DETERMINE	1	DISHES	1	DOLL-LIKE
1	DEUX	1	DISHEVELLING	1	DOLLARBRINGING
1	DEVIOUS	1	DISHONOURED	1	DOLLARFULL
1	DEVOURING	1	+DISINTEGRA	1	DOLLHEAD
1	+DEXTERITY	1	DISINTEGRAT	1	DOLORES
1	DEXTEROUS	1	DISINTEGRATES	1	DOMAINS
1	DIADUMENOS	1	DISINTEREST	1	+DOMAINS
1	+DIAMONDS	1	DISKFACE	1	DOMESHAPED
1	DIAPHANOUS	1	DISMAL	1	DOMINOES
1	+DICKSON	1	DISMAY	1	DON
1	DICTAPHONES	1	DISPLACING	1	DONC
1	DICTUM	1	DISPLEASURE	1	+DONG
1	DID-HE-DOES-SHE	1	DISPOSES	1	DONGDING
1	DID-NOT-MOVE	1	DISPUTANDUM	1	DOO
1	+DIDDLES	1	DISPUTE	1	DOOM'S
1	DIFFERENTLY	1	DISSECT	1	DOOMFUL
1	+DIFFERENTLY	1	DISSECTED	1	+DOOMFUL
1	DIGESTIBLE	1	DISSIPATION	1	DOORWAY
1	DIGESTION	1	DISSOLUTE	1	DOOT
1	DIGESTIONS	1	DISSOLVE	1	DOOYUH
1	DIGGED	1	DISSOLVED	1	DORG
1	DIGIOUS	1	DISSOLVES	1	DORMERS
1	DIGIT	1	DISSONANT	1	DOS
1	DIH	1	DISTENDED	1	DOTE
1	DIKE	1	+DISTINCT	1	DOTTED
1	DILEMMA	1	DISTINGUISH	1	DOTTING
1	DIME	1	DISTORTING	1	+DOUBLE

1	DOUBLES	1	DROPPE	1	EARLIER
1	DOUBLEYOU	1	DROPPE5	1	EARN
1	DOUBTLESS	1	+DROPPING	1	EARNING
1	DOUCEMENT	1	DROPPINGLY	1	EARNS
1	DOUGH	1	DROPSIN	1	+EARS
1	DOUGHGOB	1	DROVE	1	+EARTH
1	DOVES	1	DROWNINSOUND	1	EARTHLESS
1	+DOWDY	1	DROWNS	1	EARTHLY
1	DOWNDOWN	1	DROWSY-FAIR	1	EARTHQUAKE
1	DOWNDOWNDOWN	1	DRUB	1	EARWARMERS
1	DOWNLIFE	1	DRUG	1	EASIER
1	DOWNRISE	1	DRUM	1	EASTMAN
1	+DOWNWARD	1	DRUN	1	EATAGE
1	DOWNWARDNESS	1	DRUNG	1	+EATERS
1	DOWNY	1	DRUNK	1	EBONY
1	DOZEN	1	DRUNKARD	1	EBYO
1	DOZES	1	DRUNKEN	1	ECCO
1	DRAB	1	+DRUNKENLY	1	+ECCO
1	DRAGON	1	DRUNKENNESS	1	ECEND
1	DRAGON'S	1	DRUNKER	1	ECKSHUN
1	DRANK	1	DRYAD	1	ECLATE
1	+DRAPER	1	DTOTHE	1	ECLIPSING
1	DRAW	1	DU	1	ECOME
1	DRAWER	1	DUCED	1	ECOMIN
1	DRAWERS	1	DUCKBILLED	1	ECONOMIC
1	DREA-MINGLY	1	DUCKING	1	ECSTATICALL
1	DREADFUL	1	DUDE	1	ECTL
1	DREADFULLY	1	DUHSIVILEYEZUM	1	EDA
1	DREADS	1	DUHYOOKUHSUMPNRUDDUR	1	EDDIEANDBIL
1	+DREAM	1	DULLNESS	1	EDGAR
1	DREAM-SEND	1	DULLY	1	EDGED
1	DREAMERS	1	DULUTH	1	EDGES
1	DREAMEST	1	DULY	1	EDIBLE
1	+DREAMFULLY	1	DUMB-BLOOMING	1	EDIFICE
1	DREAMFULS	1	DUMBLY	1	EDINDODG
1	DREAMIN	1	DUMBNESS	1	EDINWHO
1	DREAMINGS	1	+DUMBNESS	1	EDITOR
1	DREAMLESS	1	DUMBS	1	EDN
1	+DREAMLESSNESSES	1	DUMDAM	1	EDN-O
1	DREAMSEEMS	1	DUMP	1	EEBLE
1	DREAMSLENDER	1	DUN	1	EEBLY
1	DREAMSOUL	1	+DUNCE	1	EELING
1	DREAMTREE	1	DUNEYED	1	EEN
1	DREAMY	1	DUNGEON	1	EENES
1	DRENCHED	1	DUNNO	1	EEP
1	DRENCHES	1	DURATION	1	EERILY
1	DRENCHING	1	DUSKIEST	1	EET
1	DRIBBLES	1	DUST-OF-SLEEP	1	EEV
1	+DRIFT	1	DUSTILY	1	EEYEB
1	DRIFTED	1	DUTMOI	1	+EFFENDI
1	+DRIFTING	1	DWELL	1	EFFIGIES
1	DRINKING	1	DWELT	1	EFFIGY
1	DRIPPED	1	DWINDLED	1	EFFORT
1	DRIVES	1	DWO	1	+EFFORT
1	DRIVING	1	DWRITH	1	EFOURFI
1	DRIZZLE	1	DYGURDY	1	EFTSTHROWR
1	DROLLS	1	+DYING	1	EGG
1	DRONE	1	DYINGEST	1	EGGED
1	DROOL	1	DYINGS	1	EGGHEAD
1	+DROOL	1	+DYNAMITE	1	EGGYELLOW
1	+DROOLERY	1	E'ER	1	EGYPT'S
1	DROOLI	1	E-VER	1	EHEADS
1	DROOLING	1	EACHING	1	EHEU
1	+DROOLINGLY	1	EACHS	1	+EIGHT
1	DROOP	1	EAD	1	EIGHTY
1	DROOPING	1	EAGEREST	1	+EIGHTY
1	DROOPNEW	1	EAGLE	1	EINSTEIN
1	DROOPNEW-GREE	1	EAKSPEASIES	1	+EISENHOWER
1	DROPP	1	EANI	1	EKE

974

975

1 +FRAGMENTS	1 FUTURE'S	1 GEOMET
1 FRAID	1 FUTURING	1 +GEOMETRICAL
1 FRAILEST	1 FUZZ	1 GEOMETRIES
1 FRAILNESS	1 FUZZILY	1 GEORGE
1 FRAILTIES	1 FUZZY-PASH	1 +GEORGE WASHINGTON'
1 +FRAILTIES	1 GABOU	1 GER
1 FRAILTY	1 GACES	1 GERANIUMS
1 FRAME	1 GAD	1 GERI
1 FRAMES	1 GAI	1 GERING
1 FRAMING	1 GAINING	1 +GERMAN
1 FRANCE	1 GAINSBOROUG	1 GEST
1 FRANKLY	1 GAINST	1 GESTICULATE
1 FREAKISH	1 +GAITE	1 GESTICULATES
1 FREDERICK	1 GALLANT	1 GESTICULATIONS
1 FREEDOM'S	1 GALLANTLY	1 GESTURED
1 FREEDOMS	1 GALLOP	1 +GESTURED
1 FREEING	1 GAMALIEL	1 +GESTURES
1 FREEZES	1 GAMBOL	1 GESTURING
1 FRENZIEDLY	1 GAMMON	1 +GET-UP
1 FRENZY	1 GAN	1 GETUP
1 FRERE	1 +GANG	1 GG
1 FRESHLY	1 GANGSTERS	1 GHASTLIER
1 FRESHLY-CREASED	1 GAPE	1 GHASTLY
1 FRESHNESS	1 GARBLE	1 GHIBELLINE
1 +FREUD	1 GARDEN-WALL	1 GHOST-FLOWER
1 FREUDIAN	1 GARGLE	1 GHOST-LIPS
1 FRIDAY	1 GARGLED	1 GHOSTLIKE
1 FRIEND'	1 GARMENTS	1 +GHOSTS
1 FRIENDLESS	1 GARNISHED	1 GHOSTS-OF-LOVE
1 FRIENDLY	1 GARRET	1 GHOSTSOUL
1 FRIENDSHIP	1 GARTER	1 GHOSTTHINGS
1 FRIEZE	1 GARTERS	1 GIDDY
1 FRIGHTENING	1 GASHED	1 GIFTS
1 FRIGHTENS	1 GASHING	1 GIGGLY
1 FRIGHTS	1 GASPED	1 GILLETTE
1 FRIGID	1 GASTRONOMIC	1 GILT
1 +FRINGING	1 GATES	1 GILTY
1 +FRISK	1 GATHERED	1 GIMMIE
1 FRITZ	1 GATHERING	1 GING
1 FRIVOLITY	1 +GATHERING	1 +GINGER ALE
1 FROCK	1 GATHERINGLY	1 GINKS
1 FROGEATERS	1 GAUNT	1 GINNING
1 FROID	1 GAVEST	1 GINNINGLY
1 FROIDES	1 GAWD	1 GIRD
1 +FROING	1 GAWN	1 +GIRDED
1 FROISSART	1 +GAY	1 GIRL-AND-BIRD
1 FROM-SOFT	1 GAY-BE-GAY	1 GIRL-FLOPS
1 FROMS	1 GAYEST	1 GIRLBOYS
1 FRONDS	1 GAYN	1 GIRLEST
1 FROOD	1 GAZING	1 GIRLGOLD
1 FRUITS	1 GEARS	1 GIRLHOOD
1 FRYING	1 GEDDUP	1 GIRLISH
1 FTBLAC	1 GEDFRAG	1 GIRLLIKE
1 +FUCKING	1 GEDUP	1 GIRTH
1 +FUGACES	1 GELDED	1 GIV
1 FUGITIVE	1 GEMS	1 GIVEHURLING
1 +FULL	1 GEN	1 GIVERS
1 FULLA	1 GENERALISSIMO	1 GIVEST
1 +FULLS	1 GENEROSITIES	1 GIVESWOOP
1 +FULLY	1 GENEROSITY	1 GIVINGEST
1 FUNDAMENTAL	1 +GENEROUS	1 GIVUSUHTOONUNDUHPHUGNTING
1 +FUNERAL	1 GENEROUSLY	1 GL
1 FUNEREALLY	1 GENIAL	1 +GLANCE
1 FUNNILY	1 GENIE	1 +GLANDS
1 FUNNYGRAPHS	1 +GENTEELLY	1 GLARING
1 FURLED	1 GENTILS	1 GLASSWORKS
1 FURTIVE	1 GENTSCOON	1 GLASSY
1 FUSION	1 GENUINELY	1 GLAZED
1 FUSSED	1 GEOFFREY	1 GLE

1 GLEAM	1 +GOLLIWOG	1 GREEKS
1 GLES	1 +GOLLY	1 GREEN'S
1 GLIDED	1 GOLLYWOG	1 GREENEST
1 GLIDING	1 GONORRHEA	1 +GREENEST
1 GLIKE	1 GOO-DMORE-N	1 GREENISH
1 GLIMPSE	1 GOODBY	1 +GREENNESS
1 GLINGTH	1 GOODMORNING	1 GREENSLIM
1 GLINTS	1 GOODS	1 GREENTHATPINK
1 GLIT	1 GOOEY	1 GREENTWITTERING
1 +GLITTER	1 GOOSE	1 GREENWICH
1 GLO	1 +GOOSEBERRI	1 GREET
1 GLOAM	1 GOOSED	1 GREETING
1 GLOAMING	1 GORGEDIS	1 GRESS
1 +GLOAMING	1 GORRY	1 GREW
1 GLOAT	1 GOSH	1 +GREY
1 GLOBULAR	1 GOSSIP	1 GREYLY
1 +GLOOM	1 GOTTEN	1 GREYS
1 GLOOMINESS	1 GOULD'S	1 GRIMLY
1 GLOOMS	1 GOW	1 GRIND
1 GLORIED	1 GOWER	1 GRINDS
1 GLORYGIRDED	1 +GOWN	1 GRINDSTONE
1 GLORYING	1 GRA	1 GRINGLEHOW
1 GLOSS	1 GRAB	1 GRINNED
1 GLOVED	1 GRABBING	1 +GRINNING
1 GLOVES	1 GRACED	1 GRINTGRUNT
1 +GLOW	1 GRACEFUL	1 GRITTED
1 GLOWING	1 GRACES	1 GROANING
1 GLOWS	1 GRACIOUS	1 +GROANING
1 GLUE	1 +GRADUALLY	1 +GROANINGISHLY
1 GLUSH	1 GRADUALLYVERYGRADUALLY	1 GROANS
1 GLUTTED	1 GRADUATE	1 +GROOVING
1 GLUTTONOUS	1 GRAFTER	1 GROPEOFSTRENGTH
1 GLYT	1 GRAIN	1 +GROPING
1 GNASHING	1 GRAMMAR	1 +GROPINGNESS
1 GNESS	1 GRAMMATICAL	1 GROUPED
1 GNORI	1 +GRAND	1 GROUPINGTHE
1 GOAT-FOOTED	1 +GRANDEUR	1 GROUSE
1 GOATS	1 GRANDILOQUE	1 GROVELLING
1 GOB	1 GRANDJA	1 +GROW
1 +GOB	1 +GRANDMOTHE	1 GROWINGEST
1 GOBBLEHOBBLE	1 +GRANDMOTHE	1 +GROWL
1 +GOBLIN	1 GRANIA	1 +GROWLS
1 GOBLINS	1 GRANIA'S	1 GRREAPSPHOS
1 GOBS	1 +GRANT	1 GRUB
1 GOBULAR	1 GRAPPLE	1 GRUESOME
1 GOD-BEASTS	1 GRAREN'T	1 GRUMBLING
1 +GODDAMN	1 GRASP	1 +GRUNT
1 GODDAMNED	1 GRASSBLADE	1 GRUNTSQUEAK
1 GODDESSES	1 GRASSBLADES	1 GSH
1 GODIVA	1 +GRAVE	1 GSKY
1 GODLESS	1 GRAVES	1 GUARDIANS
1 GODLY	1 +GRAVESTONE	1 GUELPH
1 GODTHANKING	1 GRAVEYARD	1 GUENEVER
1 GODTOWN	1 GRAVYPISSING	1 GUESSER
1 +GOES	1 GRAY	1 GUESSING
1 GOETHE	1 +GRAZE	1 GUIDING
1 GOF	1 GREASEDLIGHTNING	1 GUILTY
1 GOGGLE	1 +GREAT	1 +GUILTY
1 GOILS	1 GREATGRANDMOTHER	1 GUINEA
1 GOIN	1 GREATGRANDMOTHER'S	1 GUISE
1 GOINTA	1 GREATH	1 GUIT
1 GOLD'S	1 GREATLY	1 +GUITAR
1 GOLD-FISH	1 GREATNESS	1 GUITARS
1 GOLDBERG'S	1 GREE	1 GUK
1 GOLDBERGER	1 GREECE	1 GULLS'
1 GOLDENEST	1 +GREECE	1 GULPED
1 +GOLDENLY	1 GREEDIEST	1 GULPS
1 +GOLDFISH	1 GREEDILY	1 GUMCHEWING
1 GOLDFISHIAN	1 GREEDY	1 GUNWALE

1 IMAGI
1 +IMAGINABLE
1 IMAGINABLY
1 +IMAGINATION
1 IMAGINATIONS
1 IMAGINES
1 +IMAGINES
1 IMAL
1 IMITATED
1 IMITATING
1 IMMANENT
1 IMMATERIAL
1 IMMEDIACY
1 +IMMEDIATELY
1 IMMEMORIAL
1 IMMEMORIALLY
1 IMMENS
1 +IMMENSELY
1 IMMENSER
1 IMMENSEST
1 IMMINENT
1 IMMINENTLY
1 +IMMOBILE
1 IMMORTALITY
1 +IMMORTALS
1 IMPACT
1 IMPALED
1 IMPART
1 IMPATIENCE
1 IMPATIENT
1 IMPATIENTLY
1 +IMPECCABLE
1 IMPECCABLY
1 IMPENETRABLE
1 IMPERCEPT
1 IMPERCEPTION
1 IMPERFECTLY
1 +IMPERFECTNESS
1 IMPERIAL
1 IMPERISHABLY
1 IMPERSONALLY
1 IMPERSONATES
1 IMPERTINENT
1 IMPLIES
1 IMPLORE
1 IMPLORING
1 IMPLY
1 IMPORTANTLY
1 IMPORTING
1 IMPOSINGLY
1 IMPOSTURE
1 IMPOTENCE
1 IMPOTENTLY
1 IMPRECISION
1 IMPREGNABLE
1 IMPRINT
1 +IMPRISON
1 IMPRISONED
1 +IMPROBABLY
1 IMPULSE
1 IMPURE
1 IN-EVERYBODY-ELSE'S-...
1 IN-STANT
1 IN-TWIN
1 INANE
1 INANELY
1 INANI
1 INANITY
1 INCAPABLE

1 INCESSANTLY
1 +INCISIONS
1 INCISIVE
1 INCITIONS
1 INCLINE
1 INCLUDE
1 INCLUDED
1 INCOGNIZABLE
1 INCOMPARABLE
1 INCOMPLETELY
1 INCONCEIVABLE
1 INCONSEQUENTIAL
1 INCONSIDERABLE
1 INCORRUPTIBLE
1 +INCREASING
1 +INCREDIBLE
1 INCREDIBLY
1 +INCREDIBLY
1 INCURIOUS
1 IND
1 INDECISION
1 INDEED
1 +INDEED
1 INDESTRUCTIBLE
1 INDEX
1 INDIA
1 INDIANS
1 INDIGENOUS
1 INDIGESTIBLE
1 INDIGNANTLY
1 INDISPENSABLE
1 INDISPUTABLY
1 INDISTINCT
1 INDIVIDUALS
1 INDIVISIBLE
1 INDOLENCE
1 INDOLENTLY
1 INDOMITABLE
1 INDUBITABLE
1 INDUBITABLY
1 INDULGED
1 INDULGES
1 INDUSTRY
1 INE
1 INERT
1 INESS
1 INEVITABLE
1 INEXACTLY
1 INEXISTENCE
1 INEXPRESSIBLE
1 +INEXPRESSIBLE
1 INEXPRESSIBLY
1 INEXTINGUISHABLE
1 INFIN
1 +INFINITE
1 +INFINITESIMALLY
1 INFLECTED
1 INFLICTED
1 INFO
1 INFRAFAIRY
1 INFRAWORLD
1 INFREQUENTLY
1 ING-PUT-TOO-LONG
1 ING-ROUNDLY-DIS
1 INGAND
1 INGC
1 INGD
1 INGENIOUS
1 INGENU

1 +INGENUITY
1 INGFALLALL
1 INGHARNESS
1 INGHURL
1 INGING
1 INGINT
1 INGOF
1 INGPEACEFUL
1 INGROUNDING
1 INGSEEKFIND
1 INGSPINSON
1 INGT
1 INGTHEM
1 INGW
1 INGWORMING
1 INHABITANTS
1 INHABITED
1 INHALE
1 INHERENT
1 INHIBIT
1 +INHUMANITA
1 ININ
1 INJUSTICE
1 INKABLE
1 INLEY
1 INNERLY
1 INNOCUOUS
1 INNOVATION
1 INNUMERABLY
1 INOBVIOUS
1 INQUIRE
1 INQUIRES
1 INQUIRY
1 INQUISITIVE
1 INS
1 INSCOL
1 INSCRUTABLE
1 INSECT
1 INSECTS
1 +INSECURE
1 INSENSIBLE
1 INSERTS
1 INSIGNIFICA
1 INSINUATING
1 INSIPID
1 INSIPIDITIE
1 INSIST
1 INSLANTS
1 INSOLENT
1 +INSTANT
1 INSTANTANEO
1 INSTIGATE
1 INSTINCT
1 INSTINCTIVE
1 INSTRU
1 INSTRUCT
1 INSTRUCTION
1 +INSTRUMENT
1 INSU
1 INSUFFERABL
1 +INSUFFICIE
1 INSUFFICIEN
1 INSULATED
1 INSURED
1 INTAGLIO
1 INTANGIBILITY
1 INTANGIBLE
1 INTELLECT
1 INTELLECTS

1	LIEST	1	LIVINGLY	1	LOUS
1	LIETH	1	+LIVINGLY	1	LOVE-CRUMBS
1	LIEVE	1	LLAROFCH	1	LOVE-TOOTH
1	LIF	1	LLED	1	LOVECRAZED
1	LIFELESS	1	LLEGE	1	LOVEFIST
1	LIFELESSNES	1	LLIW	1	LOVEFLESH
1	LIFELUMP	1	LLOLOA	1	LOVEHOUSE
1	LIFEPRESERV	1	LLOYD'S	1	LOVELIEST
1	LIFETIME	1	LLS	1	+LOVELINESS
1	+LIFT	1	LLSBE	1	LOVEST
1	LIFTINGLY	1	LLSBELL	1	LOVESTAR
1	LIGHT'S	1	LLSIDE	1	LOVETREE
1	+LIGHT	1	LLY	1	LOVINGLY
1	LIGHTHEAVY	1	LM	1	LOVINGS
1	+LIGHTNING	1	LMO	1	LOW'S
1	LIGHTNING-R	1	LMOST	1	LOWELL
1	LIGHTYEARS	1	LO	1	LOWEST
1	LIGIOUS	1	LOAF	1	LOWING
1	LIKE-TRUMPE	1	LOAMHOME	1	LOWLINESS
1	LIKEGREE	1	LOAN	1	LOWNECKED
1	LIKELY	1	LOAT	1	LOWS
1	LILAC'S	1	LOATHING	1	LOYALTEA
1	LILIED	1	LOATI	1	+LOYALTY
1	LILIES-OF-T	1	+LOBS	1	LOZENGE
1	LILT	1	LOBSTER	1	LPOUNCEUPCRACKW
1	+LILY	1	LOBSTERSALAD	1	LSB
1	LIMBER	1	LOCK	1	LUCENT
1	LIME	1	LOCKING	1	LUCINDA
1	LIMITLESS	1	LOCKS	1	+LUCKIER
1	LINESS	1	+LOCOMOTIVE	1	+LUCKIEST
1	LING-WHIPALERT-FLOATSCOR	1	LOGGIA	1	LUCKIH
1	LINGER	1	LOLLS	1	LUCKILY
1	+LINGERIE	1	+LONDON	1	+LUCKY'S
1	LINGS	1	LONE	1	LUDENDORFF
1	LINK	1	LONELIEST	1	LUDICROUS
1	LINOTYPES	1	+LONELINESS	1	LUDICROUSLY
1	LINTEL	1	+LONELY	1	LUFFED
1	LION	1	LONGFEL	1	LUG
1	LIONTAMER	1	LONGFELLOW	1	LUGBRIN
1	LIPPING	1	+LONGFELLOW'S	1	LUGU
1	LIPS'	1	LONGING	1	+LUGUBRIOUS
1	LIPSHITS	1	+LONGS	1	LUKEWARM
1	LIPSTICK	1	LONJEWRAY	1	LULL
1	LISBOA	1	LOO	1	LULLA
1	LISH	1	LOOEY	1	LULLABYLULLABY
1	LISHLEGS	1	LOOKINGLY	1	LULLALULLABYBY
1	+LISPED	1	+LOOM	1	LUMBERMAN
1	+LISPINGLY	1	+LOOMINGLY	1	LUMINOSITY
1	LISPS	1	+LOOMS	1	LUMINOUSLY
1	LIST	1	LOOP	1	+LUMP
1	LIT-TLE	1	LOOPED	1	LUMPS
1	LITERALLY	1	LOOPTHELOOP	1	LUN
1	LITHPED	1	LOOSE	1	LUNDUN
1	LITTER	1	LOOSENED	1	LUNE
1	LITTL	1	LOOSENESS	1	LUNG
1	LITTLE-DUSK	1	LOOSER	1	LUNGING
1	LITTLECROWNGRAVE	1	LOOT	1	+LUNGING
1	LITTLEEXACTLY	1	LOPPED	1	LURC
1	LITTLELIVERPILL	1	LOPSIDED	1	+LURCH
1	+LITTLENESS	1	LORETTA	1	LURCHE
1	LITTLETIN	1	LOSER	1	LURCHED
1	LITTLETIN-CUP	1	LOSES	1	LURE
1	LIV	1	LOSING'S	1	LUSH
1	LIVE'S	1	+LOSING	1	+LUSHLY
1	LIVELY	1	LOSSAL	1	LUSTFUL
1	+LIVER	1	LOSSOMIN	1	LUSTFULHUNCHED
1	+LIVES	1	+LOT	1	LUSTING
1	LIVIN	1	LOTH	1	LUSTRE
1	+LIVING	1	LOUDNESS	1	LUXURIES

985

1 MUSICALLY-WHO	1 NEARERANDNEARERANDNEARER	1 NGIS
1 MUSICIAN	1 NEARERNESS	1 NGLISH
1 MUSICLESSON	1 NEARING	1 NIB
1 MUSICS	1 NEARISHNESS	1 NIBBLE
1 MUSN'T	1 +NEARLY	1 +NIBBLING
1 +MUSN'T	1 NEARLY-OPAQUE	1 +NICELY
1 MUSSED	1 NEATENING	1 NICELYBITS
1 +MUSSOLINI	1 NEATEST	1 NICENESS
1 MUST'S	1 NEATT	1 NICER
1 +MUSTACHE	1 NECESSITY	1 NICEST
1 MUSTACHES	1 +NECK	1 NICHOLAS
1 MUSTN'T	1 +NECKED	1 NICKED
1 +MUSTN'T	1 NECKLESS	1 NICKELS
1 MUTED	1 +NECKTIE	1 NICKNAMED
1 MUTENESS	1 NECKTIES	1 NICOLETTE
1 MUTHN'T	1 NED	1 NIFTY
1 MUTTER	1 NEDDY	1 NIG
1 +MUTTERING	1 NEE	1 NIGHTFALL
1 MUTTERINGS	1 +NEEDING	1 NIGHTLY
1 MYEARS	1 NEEDLE	1 +NIGHTLY
1 MYHIS	1 NEEDLES	1 NIGHTMARE
1 MYRIADS	1 NEEDLESS	1 +NIGHTMARE
1 MYRON	1 NEEDLESSLY	1 NIKE
1 MYSELVES	1 NEEDN'T	1 NIL
1 MYSTERIEUSE	1 NEEDS	1 NIMBLER
1 +MYSTERIOUS	1 NEGANT	1 NIMBLEST
1 MYSTICISM	1 NEGATION'S	1 NINETEENTH
1 MYTHICAL	1 NEGATIVE	1 NINEVEH
1 MYTHS	1 NEGLECTED	1 NINTH
1 MYVERYLITTLE	1 NEGRE	1 NIPPLE
1 +N.B.	1 NEGRES	1 NIPPONIZED
1 N'S	1 NEGRESS	1 NIT
1 N-SAINT	1 NEGROES	1 NITHE
1 NABBED	1 NEIGES	1 NIVOROU
1 NABOR	1 +NEIGHBOR	1 NIX
1 NAGGING	1 NEIGHBOURS	1 NIZE
1 NAILS	1 NEIGHING	1 NIZE-ADAY
1 NAILYUH	1 NEITHER'S	1 NIZMUS
1 NAKE	1 NEITHERS	1 NK
1 +NAKED	1 NEL	1 NKIL
1 NAKEDEST	1 NER	1 NKS
1 NAKEDLY	1 NERAL	1 NL
1 NALOVEME	1 NERATIVENES	1 NLI
1 NAMELESS	1 +NERVE	1 NMOTIO
1 NAMELESSNESS	1 NESTING	1 NN-NN
1 NAMING	1 NETS	1 NNUAL
1 NAN	1 NETSAM	1 NO-SHE-YES-HE
1 +NAPKIN	1 NETSITS	1 NO-THING
1 NAPKINS	1 NEUTRAL	1 NO-VOICE
1 NAPOLEON	1 NEVERISH	1 NOBLE
1 NAPPED	1 NEVERMOVING	1 NOBLER
1 NARROWING	1 NEVERTHELES	1 NOBLEST
1 NATION'S	1 NEVERTOBEEXTINGUISHED	1 NOBLY
1 NATIONS	1 NEVERWHERES	1 NOBODIES
1 NATURE	1 +NEW ORLEAN	1 +NOD
1 NAUGHTY	1 +NEW DEAL	1 NODDING
1 NAUSEA	1 NEWBORN	1 NODS
1 NAUSEOUS	1 NEWENGLAND	1 NOGGED
1 NAVY	1 NEWFRAGILE	1 NOGRAPHISRUNN
1 NB	1 NEWLYS	1 NOHW
1 NC	1 NEWMOWN	1 NOING
1 NCI	1 NEWSPAPER	1 NOISECOLOURED
1 NCIENT	1 +NEWSPAPER	1 NOISES
1 NDA	1 NEWSREEL	1 NOISILY
1 NDERSTAN	1 NEWTON'S	1 +NOISY
1 NDESGINB	1 NEXTTO	1 NOIVE
1 NDN	1 NFACE	1 NOMBRIL
1 NEA	1 NGED	1 NONCOMS
1 NEARAWAY	1 NGFLOUNDERP	1 NONDESCRIPT

1	NONELASTIC	1	NUCLEUS	1	OFLIKE
1	+NONENTITIES	1	NUDG	1	OFOF
1	NONGLANCE	1	+NUDGING	1	OFPIECES
1	NONILLION	1	NUDITY	1	OFS
1	NONLEAF	1	NUDN	1	OG-DOG
1	NONLEGS	1	NUISANCE	1	OGLING
1	+NONSELF'S	1	NUISANCES	1	OGRE
1	NONSUFFICIENTLY	1	NUJOLNEEDING	1	+OH
1	NONSUN	1	+NUMB	1	OHLD
1	NONTH	1	NUMBERED	1	OHO
1	NONTHINGS	1	+NUMBERLESSNESS	1	OIDOUGHWUNT
1	+NONTHINKABLE	1	NUMBERS	1	OIL
1	NONVISIBLY	1	NUMERABLY	1	+OIL
1	NOO	1	NUMEROUS	1	OILED
1	NOOER	1	NUN	1	OILSAISOUGH
1	NOONES	1	NUPFLOATSW	1	OINIS
1	NORM	1	NVISIBLE	1	OIWUN
1	NORMALITY	1	NYMPH	1	+OK
1	+NORMANDY	1	NYMPHLIKE	1	+OKAY
1	NORTH	1	O-L-D	1	OKAYED
1	NOSE-RED	1	O-P-E-N-I-N-G	1	OKAYS
1	NOSING	1	O-RAS-OURH	1	OKE
1	NOSTER	1	OA	1	OL
1	NOT-MERE-LY-WON-DER-ING-&	1	OAKS	1	OLATE
1	NOTALIVE	1	OATTUMBLI	1	OLBANUM
1	NOTB	1	OB	1	+OLDER
1	NOTBR	1	OBEDIENT	1	OLDEYED
1	NOTBRE	1	OBJECT-OR	1	OLDISH
1	NOTBREA	1	OBJECTED	1	OLEMNANDPUT
1	NOTBREA-K	1	OBJECTIVELY	1	OLLAPSE
1	NOTBUSY	1	+OBJECTOR	1	OLLE
1	NOTCHING	1	OBLIVIONS	1	OLYMPIAN
1	+NOTE	1	OBLIVIOUS	1	OMA
1	NOTED	1	OBSCENELY	1	OMAHA
1	NOTGIRL'SWITH	1	OBSCENER	1	OMEG
1	NOTHARD	1	OBSCENITIES	1	+OMEGA
1	NOTHINGLY	1	OBSCENITY	1	OMELET
1	NOTHINGS	1	OBSCURELY	1	OMEN
1	+NOTHINGS	1	OBSCURITY	1	OMES
1	NOTHURT	1	+OBSERVE	1	OMETHING
1	+NOTICE	1	OBSERVES	1	OMFUL
1	NOTIFIED	1	OBSTRE	1	+OMICRON
1	NOTION	1	+OBSTREPERO	1	OMIEPSICRONLONO
1	NOTMAN	1	OBV	1	OMIT
1	NOTQU	1	+OBVIOUS	1	OMITS
1	NOTRE	1	OBVIOUSLY	1	+OMNIPOTENCE
1	NOTS	1	OCCASION	1	+OMNIVOROUS
1	NOTSELFPITYING	1	+OCCULT	1	OMPRISES
1	NOTSOFT	1	OCCUPATION	1	ON&OFF
1	NOTWITHSTANDING	1	OCCUPIED	1	ONA
1	NOUN	1	OCCUPY	1	ONC
1	NOURISH	1	OCTOBERING	1	ONCEUPONS
1	NOVOCAINE	1	OCTOPUS	1	ONDUMONDE
1	NOWBROW	1	ODDLY	1	+ONE'S
1	NOWH	1	ODDS	1	ONE-T
1	NOWHEREGOINGALWAYS	1	ODE	1	ONED
1	NOWHERES	1	ODOR	1	ONEEYED
1	NOWOI	1	ODOURS	1	ONEFUL
1	NOWORLD	1	ODY'S	1	ONEHUNDREDPERCENTORIGINAL
1	NOYESIYOU	1	ODYKNOWSWHO	1	ONESTHE
1	NS	1	ODYSSEUS	1	ONETWO
1	NSTRETCHY	1	OF-FACENESS	1	ONETWOTHREEFOURFIVE
1	NTD	1	OF-LOVE-AND	1	ONLY-JUST
1	NTS	1	OFA	1	ONTHETOPWHOSE
1	NTUMBLED	1	OFC	1	ONYMO
1	NTURIN	1	OFCRIN	1	OO-OO
1	NTY	1	OFFENSE	1	OOC
1	NU	1	OFFICERS	1	OOCH
1	NUCLEOLUS	1	+OFFSPRING	1	OOK

1	PEDESTAL	1	PEST	1	PINKTHISGREEN
1	PEEK-A-BOO	1	PESTER	1	PINN
1	PEELING	1	+PETALED	1	+PINNACLE
1	PEEMUVDEPIPL	1	PETER	1	+PINWHEELING
1	+PEEPS	1	PETITES	1	PINXIT
1	PEERED	1	PETITIONS	1	PIPEWRENCH
1	PEERLESS	1	PETRIFIED	1	PIPPLES
1	PELF	1	PETTICOAT	1	PIRACIES
1	PENDING	1	PHANTOM-WHITE	1	PIROUETTE
1	PENGUINSOUL	1	+PHANTOMS	1	+PIROUETTING
1	PENING	1	PHEIDIAN	1	PISS
1	+PENSE	1	PHENOMENA	1	+PISS
1	PENSIVE	1	PHILOPHILIC	1	+PISSING
1	PEOPL	1	PHILOSPHY	1	PISSOIR
1	PEOPLES	1	PHO	1	PISTIL
1	PEOPLESHAPED	1	PHOEBEING	1	+PISTIL
1	PEOPLING	1	PHONOGRAPH'S	1	PISTON
1	PEPPER	1	+PHONOGRAPH	1	PITCHFORK
1	PEPPERS	1	+PHONOGRAPHS	1	PITH
1	PERCEIVED	1	PHOTOGRAPH	1	PITHECOID
1	PERCENT	1	PHOTOGRAPHY	1	+PITYING
1	+PERCENT	1	PHRASING	1	PIVOINE
1	PERCEPTIBLE	1	PHYLLIS	1	PIVOTING
1	PERCHANCE	1	PHYSIOGNOMY	1	PLAC
1	PERCHED	1	PI	1	PLACID
1	PERCUSSION	1	PIANO	1	+PLACIDITY
1	PEREGRINATE	1	+PIANO	1	PLANE
1	PEREGRINATIONS	1	PIANOLAS	1	PLANET'S
1	PERFECTEST	1	PIC	1	PLANNED
1	PERFECTINGLY	1	+PICABIAN	1	PLANT
1	PERFECTNESS	1	PICCOLOS	1	PLANTS
1	PERFECTS	1	+PICKED	1	PLASTIC
1	PERFORM	1	PICKER	1	PLASTICITY
1	PERFORMED	1	+PICKING	1	PLATE
1	PERFORMING	1	PICKLES	1	PLATI
1	PERFORMS	1	PICKS	1	+PLATINUM
1	PERFUME-GIFTED	1	PICPAC	1	PLATITUDE
1	PERHAPSLESS	1	PICTURESQUE	1	PLATO-RABEL
1	PERHAPSY	1	PIDDLE	1	PLATZBURG
1	PERIL	1	PIDDLE-OF-DROPS	1	PLAYER
1	PERIOD	1	+PIECE	1	PLAYFUL
1	PERIODICAL	1	+PIECES	1	PLAYFULLY
1	PERISHABLE	1	PIERCING	1	PLAYIN
1	PERMAMENT	1	PIGEONSJUSTLIKETHAT	1	PLAYTHINGS
1	PERMANENTLY	1	PIGGISH	1	PLEASANTER
1	PERMISSION	1	PIGLIKE	1	PLEASE'
1	PERMIT	1	PIGS	1	PLEASED
1	PERMITTED	1	PIL	1	PLEASEDON'T
1	PEROUSTIMIDI	1	+PILE	1	PLEATHE
1	PERPE	1	PILGRIM	1	PLED
1	+PERPETUAL	1	PILGRIMS'	1	PLEDGED
1	PERPETUALNESS	1	+PILL	1	PLEEZ
1	PERPETUATING	1	+PILLAR	1	PLELIKE
1	PERS	1	PILLOW'S	1	PLENTY
1	PERSIAN	1	PILLOWS	1	PLIGHT
1	PERSIST	1	+PILLOWS	1	PLIZ
1	PERSISTING	1	PILLS	1	PLOC
1	PERSISTS	1	PILOT	1	PLON
1	PERSONNE	1	PIMPLES	1	PLOOP
1	PERSPIRATION	1	PIMPLY	1	PLORE
1	PERSUADES	1	PINAFORE'D	1	PLOUGHMAN
1	PERSUASIVE	1	PINCIAN	1	PLUCKED
1	PERT	1	PING	1	PLUCKINGS
1	PERTLY	1	PINGNESS	1	PLUGGED
1	PERTURBA	1	+PINK	1	PLUM
1	+PERTURBATIONS	1	PINK-FLAG	1	PLUMBED
1	+PERUSED	1	PINKEST	1	PLUMBING
1	PERUSING	1	PINKHAM	1	PLUMPTUMBLI
1	PERVERSE	1	PINKNESS	1	PLUMS

1 +PLUMS
1 PLUNGED
1 PLUNGES
1 PLUNGING
1 +PLUNKY
1 PLURAL
1 PLY
1 PO
1 POCO
1 PODIA
1 POEDS
1 POESY
1 POETRY
1 POF
1 POIGNANT
1 POILU
1 POINTS
1 POIS
1 +POISED
1 POISING
1 POISONED
1 POISONOUS
1 POKE
1 POKED
1 POLES
1 POLICE
1 POLICEMAN'S
1 POLICEMEN
1 POLISHED
1 POLITE
1 POLITELY
1 POLITICIAN
1 POLITICIANS
1 +POLITICIANS
1 POLITICS
1 POLITISIONS
1 POLLENIZING
1 POLLOI
1 +POLLY
1 POMP
1 POND
1 PONDERED
1 PONDS
1 POOPED
1 +POOR
1 POORBUTHONEST
1 POP
1 POPES
1 POPOT
1 POPPA
1 POPPY
1 POPPY'S
1 POPS
1 POPULAR
1 PORE
1 PORKIE
1 PORKY
1 POROUS
1 PORTALS
1 PORTS
1 POSED
1 POSI
1 POSITION
1 POSITIVE
1 POSOLUTELY
1 POSSESS
1 POSSESSION
1 POSSIBLILITY
1 POSTU

1 +POSTUME
1 POSTURE
1 +POTS
1 POUNC
1 +POUNCE
1 +POUNCES
1 POUND
1 +POUNDS
1 POURS
1 +POUT
1 +POUTING
1 +POWER
1 PPEAR
1 PPEARE
1 PPED
1 PPEGORHRASS
1 PPIN
1 PPOYDS
1 PRACTICING
1 PRANCE
1 PRATFALL
1 PRAW
1 PRAYED
1 PREACH
1 PREACHER
1 PREACHES
1 PRECIOUS
1 PREDICATING
1 PREDICTED
1 PREEXIST
1 PREFECT
1 PREFERABLE
1 PREFERRING
1 PREGNANT
1 PREHUMAN
1 PREPARED
1 PREPONDERATINGLY
1 PREPOSTEROUS
1 PRES
1 +PRESERVERS
1 +PRESIDENT
1 PRESTO
1 PRETENDED
1 PRETENDS
1 PRETENTIOUS
1 +PRETTILY
1 PRETTINESS
1 PRETTINESSES
1 PREVAIL
1 PREVENTED
1 PREY
1 PREYS
1 PRICE
1 +PRICKING
1 PRICKLEY
1 PRICKLEY-CLOTHES
1 PRICKS
1 PRIED
1 PRIES
1 PRIESTS-AND
1 PRIEZ
1 PRIGGED
1 PRIL
1 PRIMATES
1 PRIME
1 PRIMING
1 PRING
1 PRISMATIC
1 PRISMS

1 PRIVACY
1 +PRIVATES
1 PRIVILEGE
1 PROACHED
1 PROCES
1 +PROCESSION
1 PRODIGAL
1 PRODIGIES
1 PRODIGIOUSLY
1 PRODIGY
1 PRODUCING
1 PROFANE
1 PROFICIENT
1 PROFUSE
1 PROGRAM
1 PROJECTILE
1 PROLETARIAT
1 PROLONGS
1 PROMENE
1 PROMENE-T-ELLE
1 PROMENENT
1 PROMISE
1 PROMISED
1 PROMPTLY
1 PRONOUNCED
1 PRONOUNCES
1 PROOF
1 +PROOF
1 PROOV
1 PROP
1 PROPAGATED
1 PROPHECIES
1 PROPORTION
1 PROPOS
1 +PROPPED
1 PROPPING
1 PROREGRESS
1 PROSPECTING
1 PROSTITUTED
1 PROSTRATE
1 PROTECTED
1 PROTEST
1 PROTESTANT
1 PROTESTATIONS
1 PROTESTS
1 PROTRUDE
1 PROTUBERANT
1 PROUDER
1 PROUDEST
1 +PROUDESTLY
1 PROUDHUMBLE
1 +PROUST
1 +PROVING
1 PROVINGLY
1 PROVOKE
1 PROWL
1 PROWST
1 PRUNE
1 PRURIENT
1 +PSALMIST
1 PSEUDO
1 PSEUDOBEAST
1 PSH
1 PSTARETH
1 PSYCHOTIC
1 PUBIC
1 PUBLIC
1 PUBLICATION
1 PUBLISHERS

1 RECORD	1 RENEWED	1 RIDETH
1 RECORDS	1 +RENEWING	1 RIDUH
1 +RECTOR'S	1 RENOWN	1 RIED
1 RECTUM	1 RENOWNED	1 RIES
1 +RECTUMS	1 RENT	1 RIGGING
1 RED-RAG	1 RENT'S	1 RIGHTEOUS
1 REDBLOODED	1 REOCCURS	1 RIGHTEOUSNESS
1 REDDISH	1 REPAIRS	1 RIGHTER
1 REDIRE	1 REPAPERED	1 RIGHTEST
1 REDOLENT	1 REPAPERING	1 RIGHTFUL
1 REDSKIN	1 REPASS	1 RIGHTLY
1 REDSTONE	1 REPAYING	1 RIGHTS
1 REE	1 +REPEAT	1 +RIGHTS
1 REELING	1 REPEATS	1 RIGIDLY
1 +REELING	1 REPOS	1 RILE
1 REELS	1 RERLY	1 RILLY
1 REELY	1 RERUM	1 RINE
1 REENTER	1 RESCUE	1 +RING
1 REES	1 RESCUING	1 RINGAROM
1 REFERS	1 RESHARPENED	1 RINGING
1 REFLECTING	1 RESIST	1 RINSING
1 REFLECTION	1 RESISTLESS	1 RIOT
1 REFLECTIONS	1 RESOLVED	1 RIOUS
1 REFLEX	1 RESPECT	1 RIPEBLACKBERRIES
1 REFUGE	1 RESPECTER	1 RIS
1 REFUL	1 RESPECTS	1 RISH
1 REFUSE	1 RESPIRE	1 RISSIONS
1 REFUSES	1 RESPONDING	1 RITHMETIC
1 REGIME	1 RESPONSE	1 RITY
1 REGIONS	1 RESTAURANT	1 RITZ
1 +REGRESS	1 RESTROLL	1 RIVA
1 REGRESSED	1 RESUME	1 RIVE
1 REINCARNATE	1 RESUMING	1 RIVERLY
1 REINED	1 RESURRECTION	1 RIVERY
1 REINTEGRATE	1 RESWAL	1 RIVETED
1 REINTEGRATI	1 +RESWALLOWING	1 RIVING
1 REJ	1 RETCHINGS	1 RLETLYCAR
1 REJOINED	1 RETIRE	1 RLY
1 REKTUZ	1 RETIRED	1 ROADSIDE
1 +RELATES	1 RETOINIS	1 ROAMI
1 RELATIVE	1 +RETURN	1 ROAMINGLY
1 RELATIVELY	1 RETURNED	1 ROARING
1 RELATIVES	1 +RETURNEST	1 +ROARING
1 RELAX	1 RETURNING	1 ROASTED
1 RELEASE	1 REUSED	1 ROBBED
1 RELEASING	1 REVE	1 ROBERT
1 +RELIGION	1 REVEAL	1 ROBIN'S
1 RELIGIONS	1 +REVEALING	1 ROBINSON
1 RELIGIOUS	1 REVENGE	1 ROCK-A-BYE
1 +RELIGIOUS	1 REVERSE	1 ROCKER
1 RELIJINISDE	1 REVERSED	1 ROCKET
1 REMAINED	1 REVIEWING	1 RODE
1 REMAKING	1 REVOLV	1 ROEBUCK
1 +REMARKABLE	1 +REVOLVE	1 ROGUISH
1 REMARKING	1 REVOLVES	1 ROH
1 REMBLIN	1 REVOLVING	1 ROIDS
1 REMEMBE	1 +REVOLVINGLY	1 ROITEE
1 +REMEMBER	1 RHYMES	1 +ROLLED
1 REMEMBERED	1 RHYTHMS	1 ROLLI
1 REMEMBERING	1 +RHYTHMS	1 ROLLING
1 +REMIND	1 RIANT	1 ROLLINGEST
1 REMINDED	1 RIBBLED	1 ROLYPOLY
1 REMINISCENC	1 RICAL	1 ROMA
1 REMU	1 RICHES	1 ROMANTIC
1 +REMUNERATI	1 RICKETY	1 ROME
1 REN	1 RID	1 ROMP
1 RENDER	1 +RID	1 ROMTH
1 RENDERING	1 RIDDLE	1 ROOMUR
1 RENEWAL	1 +RIDES	1 +ROOSEVELT

1	+ROOSTER	1	S-CRA	1	SAYSTHESEA-BRE
1	ROOTED	1	S-P-I-R-A	1	SBELLS
1	ROOTING	1	SABLE	1	SC
1	+ROPER	1	SABOTEUR	1	SCALE
1	ROR	1	SABOTS	1	SCALELESS
1	ROSE'S	1	SACK	1	SCALPED
1	ROSEBUG	1	SACKS	1	SCALPEL
1	ROSEBUSH	1	SACRAMENT	1	SCAMPER
1	ROSENBLOOM	1	SADISTIC	1	SCARCE
1	+ROSES	1	SADNESS	1	SCARCELYEST
1	ROSY	1	SAFETYRAZOR	1	SCARE
1	ROTGUT	1	SAFFRON	1	SCARECROW
1	ROUGH	1	SAGE	1	+SCARED
1	ROUN	1	SAGES	1	+SCARLETLY
1	ROUN'	1	SAGEST	1	SCATTERED
1	+ROUND	1	SAGS	1	SCENTED
1	ROUNDAR	1	SAHARAS	1	SCENTS
1	ROUNDED	1	SAI	1	SCEPTRED
1	ROUNDER	1	+SAID	1	SCHEDULE
1	+ROUNDER	1	SAIK	1	SCHEME
1	+ROUNDEST	1	SAIL	1	SCHIAVONI
1	+ROUNDINGLY	1	SAILED	1	SCHOLARS
1	ROUNDNESS	1	SAILOR	1	SCHOOLCHILDREN
1	ROUNDTABLES	1	SAILORS	1	SCHOOLROOM
1	ROUPY	1	SAIN	1	SCIENCE2B
1	ROW	1	+SAINT	1	SCIENCE2B-N
1	ROWL	1	SAITH	1	SCIENTI
1	ROWSPEACH	1	+SALAD	1	SCIENTIF
1	ROWSTER	1	SALE	1	SCIENTIFICALLY
1	RPOSIVE	1	SALIVA	1	SCIENTIST
1	RR	1	SALL	1	SCIMITARS
1	RRAN	1	SALLOW	1	SCINTILLANT
1	RRMP	1	SALO	1	SCOLDS
1	RSM	1	SALOME	1	SCOOT
1	RSM-O	1	+SALOMES	1	SCORCHBEND
1	RST	1	+SALT	1	SCORE
1	RT	1	SALUTING	1	SCORNING
1	RUBBER	1	SALWAYS	1	SCORNS
1	RUBBERY	1	SAMES	1	SCOUT
1	RUBSITSELF	1	+SAN FRANCISCO	1	SCOWL
1	RUBY&EMERALD	1	SANDBURG	1	SCR
1	RUBYTHROAT'S	1	SANDPILE	1	SCRAGGY
1	RUFFIAN-ROGUE	1	SANDS	1	SCRAMBLE
1	RUGGED	1	SANE	1	SCRAMBLING
1	RUGLIKE	1	+SANG	1	+SCRAPY
1	RUGS	1	SANGSUNG	1	SCRATCH-SCRUTCH
1	+RUINING	1	SANTA	1	SCRATCHILY
1	+RULE	1	SAOUNDS	1	+SCRATCHING
1	RULES	1	SAP	1	SCRATCHINGCROWD
1	RULL	1	SARCASMS	1	SCRATCHINGS
1	RULLY	1	SARDINES	1	SCRE
1	+RUMOR	1	SATAN	1	SCREAMED
1	RUNE	1	SATANIC	1	SCREAMERS
1	RUNG	1	SATISFACTION	1	SCREAMGROA
1	RUNNIN	1	SATRAPS	1	+SCREAMING
1	+RUNNING	1	SATTER	1	SCREAMINGLY
1	RUNOW	1	+SATURNALIA	1	SCREECH-OWLS
1	RUPTINGLY	1	SATYRS	1	SCREECHING
1	RUSEFELT	1	SAUCERS	1	SCREETCHING
1	RUSHED	1	SAVAGE	1	SCRETCH
1	+RUSHES	1	SAVING	1	SCRIBBLED
1	RUSKIN	1	SAVIOUR	1	+SCRIBBLED
1	RUSSIA'S	1	SAVIOURS	1	SCRIBBLING
1	+RUSSIANS	1	+SAVO	1	SCRITCH
1	RUSTLE	1	SAVOURING	1	SCROLL
1	RUSTLING	1	SAXOPHONIC	1	SCRUPULOUS
1	RVENTLY	1	SAYINGLY	1	SCRUTCH
1	RY	1	SAYS-DOES	1	SCRUTINIZE
1	RYE	1	SAYSTHESEA	1	SCULPTURAL

1 SCULPTURE	1 SEVENTY	1 SHOULDERBLADES
1 SCUTTLING	1 SEVERE	1 +SHOULDERS
1 SCYTHE	1 SEVERED	1 SHOULDN'T
1 +SCYTHE	1 SEWING	1 SHOUTFLOWERED
1 +SEA'S	1 SEWS	1 SHOVELING
1 +SEA	1 SEXED	1 SHOVING
1 SEA-GIRLS	1 SEXES	1 SHOVINGS
1 SEALACE	1 SEXIS	1 SHOWE
1 SEARCHED	1 SHAD	1 SHOWER
1 SEASALT	1 SHADE	1 +SHOWERING
1 SEASAYS	1 SHADES	1 SHOWERS
1 SEASONS	1 +SHADOW	1 SHOWING
1 SEATIDES	1 SHADOWEATEN	1 SHRAPNEL
1 SEBERRIES	1 +SHADOWFULL	1 SHRIEKED
1 SECOND-IN-TO-HIGH	1 SHADOWLESS	1 +SHRIEKING
1 SECONDHAND	1 SHAKEN	1 SHRIEKINGS
1 SECONDS	1 SHAKES	1 SHRILLERNESS
1 SECRETLOVELINESS	1 SHAKESPEARE	1 SHRINES
1 SECU	1 SHAL	1 SHRIVED
1 SECURE	1 +SHALL	1 SHRIVEL
1 SECURELY	1 SHALLOWNESS	1 SHROUDS
1 +SECURITY	1 SHALT	1 SHRU
1 SED	1 SHAPELESS	1 SHRUB
1 SEDLY	1 SHAPES	1 SHRUG
1 SEDULOUSLY	1 +SHAPES	1 SHRUGGING
1 SEEKER	1 SHAPLEY	1 +SHRUGGING
1 SEEKINGLY	1 SHARPEN	1 SHRUGS
1 SEEMING'S	1 SHARPEST	1 SHSP
1 +SEEMS	1 SHAVED	1 SHUFFLE
1 SEEMSWOOP	1 +SHAVEN	1 SHUFFLES
1 SEETHES	1 SHAWL	1 SHUNNING
1 SEL	1 SHE-AND-HE-	1 SHUSH
1 SELDOM	1 SHE-IN-HIM	1 SHUTER
1 SELENE	1 SHEA	1 +SHY
1 SELENE'S	1 SHEAD	1 SHY-DODGE
1 SELFHOOD	1 SHEATHED	1 SHYBRIGHTEYES
1 SELFLESS	1 SHEBA	1 SHYER
1 SELFSUBTRACTING	1 SHEEN	1 +SHYEST
1 +SELL	1 SHEEREST	1 SHYLOCK
1 SELLING	1 SHELF	1 +SHYLY
1 +SELLING	1 SHELLS	1 SI-GNORI
1 SELLS	1 SHELVES	1 SIAM
1 +SELVES	1 SHERMAN	1 SIB
1 SELVES-THEM	1 SHES	1 SIBL
1 SELVES-U	1 SHESHAPE	1 SIBYL
1 SEMILUMINOUS	1 SHID	1 +SICKLY
1 SEMIRAMIS	1 SHIED	1 SICKNESS
1 SENDWISP	1 SHIES	1 SICKSILK
1 SENECKTIE	1 SHIFTING	1 +SIDE
1 SENSATIONAL	1 SHIKAHGO	1 SIDESTEPS
1 SENSATIONS	1 SHIMMERING	1 +SIDEWALKS
1 +SENSE	1 SHIMMY	1 SIDEWAYS
1 SENSIBLE	1 SHINED	1 +SIEVE
1 SENSUOUSLY	1 SHINES	1 SIGHED
1 SENT	1 SHINY	1 SIGHS
1 SENTIMENTS	1 +SHIP	1 +SIGHT
1 SENTINEL	1 SHIPPED	1 SIGN
1 SEPA	1 SHIRTTAILS	1 SIGNAL
1 +SEPARATE	1 SHISHKABOB	1 SIGNALLING
1 SEPARATING	1 +SHITS	1 SIGNALS
1 SEPTEMBERING	1 SHIVERING	1 SIGNIFI
1 SERENADE	1 SHIVERS	1 SIGNIFICANT
1 SERPENT	1 SHO	1 +SIGNIFICANT
1 SERPENTS	1 SHOCKED	1 SIGNIFY
1 SERVANTS	1 SHONE	1 +SIGNORI
1 SES	1 SHOOT	1 SIGNORIES
1 SESTET	1 SHOP-GIRLS	1 SILENC
1 SETS	1 SHORTLY	1 SILENCEOFSOUND
1 SETTLED	1 SHOUL	1 SILENTNESS

1	+SILK	1	SLANT	1	SLUT
1	SILKEN	1	+SLANTS	1	+SLY
1	SILKENLY	1	SLAP	1	SLYLY
1	SILKS	1	+SLAPPING	1	SMACK
1	SILKY	1	SLAPSOOTHED	1	SMALLENING
1	SILLIEST	1	SLATE	1	SMALLHEADED
1	SILLS	1	SLATTERN	1	SMALLISH
1	SILVER-FINGERED	1	SLAUGHTER	1	SMART
1	SILVEREST	1	SLAVE'S	1	SMARTING
1	+SILVERY	1	SLAVVER	1	SMASHES
1	SIM	1	SLEEP'S	1	SMEAR
1	SIMBULLY	1	SLEEPDEEP	1	SMEARED
1	SIMILAR	1	SLEEPILY	1	SMEESTAIRE
1	SIMMER	1	SLEEPLESS	1	+SMELL
1	SIMPLEST	1	SLEEPSHAPED	1	SMELLINGS
1	SIMPLIFY	1	SLEET	1	SMELLOFTHEW
1	SINCERELY	1	+SLENDER	1	SMI
1	+SINCERELY	1	SLENDEREST	1	SMILE'S
1	+SINCERITY	1	SLENDERING	1	SMILINGLY
1	SINFUL	1	+SLENDERLY	1	SMIRK
1	SINGERS	1	SLEUTHFULLY	1	SMIRKS
1	SINGING'S	1	SLI	1	SMITE
1	SINGINGS	1	SLICED	1	SMITES
1	SINGLESS	1	SLICED-NICELYBITS	1	+SMOKE
1	SINGLY	1	+SLICING	1	+SMOKED
1	SINGLY-WHISPERING	1	SLICKERN	1	SMOKY
1	+SINGULARLY	1	SLID	1	+SMOOTH
1	+SINISTER	1	SLIDING	1	SMOOTHANDUSELESS
1	SINKE	1	SLIGHT	1	SMOOTHBEAUTIFUL
1	SINKING	1	SLIGHTEST	1	SMOOTHDUMB
1	+SINKING	1	+SLIM	1	SMOOTHLOOMINGLY
1	+SINKINGLY	1	SLIME	1	+SMOOTHNESS
1	SINLESS	1	SLIMMER	1	SMOTHER
1	SINNED	1	+SLIMNESS	1	SMOULDERS
1	SINNER	1	SLINGS	1	SN
1	SINS	1	+SLINKILY	1	SNAIL'S
1	+SINUOUSLY	1	SLIPPERED	1	+SNAKE
1	SIPPING	1	+SLIPPERY	1	SNAKEOIL
1	+SIR	1	SLIPPING	1	+SNAPPING
1	SIRKUSRICKY	1	+SLIPS	1	+SNARE
1	SIS	1	SLIPSHOD	1	SNARES
1	SISTER'S	1	SLIPSLOUCH	1	SNARLED
1	SISTERS	1	SLITS	1	SNATCH
1	SIT-EX	1	SLITTED	1	SNICE
1	SITE	1	SLIVERS	1	SNICE-LY
1	+SITS	1	SLO-WLY	1	SNICK
1	SITSAT	1	SLOBBERING	1	+SNICKER
1	SITTIN	1	SLOGAN	1	SNICKERING
1	SITUATED	1	SLOP	1	SNIFFING
1	SIXEREIGHT	1	SLOPCAKED	1	SNIGGERING
1	+SIXTEEN	1	SLOPP	1	SNITCH
1	+SIXTH	1	SLOPPED	1	SNORE
1	SIXTY	1	+SLOPPIDY	1	SNOUT
1	SIXTYFOUR	1	SLOT	1	SNOWINGLY
1	SIZELESSLY	1	+SLOUCH	1	+SNOWINGLY
1	SKEIN	1	SLOUCHES	1	SNOWLFLAKE
1	SKELETONS	1	+SLOW	1	SNOWMAN
1	SKILLED	1	SLOW-LY-IN	1	SNOWS
1	+SKIN	1	+SLOWLIEST	1	SNOWSTOPPED
1	SKINFULL	1	SLOWLYSLOWL	1	SNUG
1	SKINNY	1	SLOWLYWITH	1	SNUGANDEVIL
1	SKULCH	1	SLOWQUICKLY	1	SO&SO
1	SKULL	1	SLOWTURNING	1	SOAK
1	SKUNK	1	SLUICE	1	SOARING
1	SKYDIAMONDS	1	+SLUM	1	+SOARINGS
1	SKYLESSNESS	1	+SLUMPING	1	SOB
1	SKYLINE	1	SLUS	1	SOBBINGS
1	SLAM	1	SLUSH	1	SOBCRIES
1	SLAMSLUM	1	+SLUSH	1	SOCA

1	STAINS	1	STIFF-LY	1	STRODE
1	STALE	1	STIFFENS	1	STROKABLE
1	STALIN	1	STIFLES	1	STROKED
1	STALINIST	1	STILL-BORN	1	STROKES
1	STALKED	1	STILLING	1	STROKING
1	STALKS	1	STIMPSTAMPS	1	STROL
1	STALWART	1	STIMULUS	1	STRONGMAN
1	STAMENS&PISTIL	1	+STING	1	STROPPING
1	STAMMER	1	STINK-BRAG	1	STROVE
1	+STAMP	1	STINKING	1	STRUCK
1	STAMPS	1	+STINKING	1	STRUGGLEINWEIRD
1	+STAMPS	1	+STINKS	1	STRUNSKY'S
1	STAN	1	STIRRED	1	STRUT-MINCE
1	STAND-ING	1	STIRRINGOFBIRDS	1	+STRUTS
1	STANDARDS	1	+STIRS	1	STRUTSTROLLS
1	STANDEST	1	STITCH	1	STRUTTING
1	+STANDING	1	STLY	1	STS
1	+STANDSTILL	1	STO	1	STUB
1	STANT	1	STOLE	1	STUDIED
1	STAR'S	1	STOMACHSCLENCHE	1	STUDY
1	STARES	1	STOMACHSLIKEDEAD	1	STUFFED
1	STARFISH	1	STOMACHSOFOLD	1	STUFFEDITALICS
1	STARHUMS	1	+STONE	1	STUFFEST
1	STARHUSHED	1	STOOPID	1	STUMBL
1	STARINGS	1	+STOOPING	1	STUMBLED
1	STARLESSNESS	1	STOOPS	1	+STUMBLING
1	STARRED	1	+STOPPED	1	STUMP
1	STARRILY	1	STORIES	1	STUN
1	+START	1	STORMS	1	STUNG
1	STARTING	1	STRAIGHTACROSS	1	STUNNING
1	STARTLING	1	STRAIGHTENS	1	STUNT
1	STARTS	1	STRAIGHTER	1	+STUPID
1	STARVE	1	STRAIGHTWAY	1	STUPIDEST
1	STARVED	1	STRAIN	1	STUPIDLY
1	+STATE	1	STRAINED	1	STURDY
1	+STATESMEN	1	STRAINING	1	STUTT
1	STATING	1	STRANDED	1	+STUTTERS
1	STATISTICS	1	STRANDS	1	STYLE
1	STAUNCH	1	+STRANGE	1	+SUB
1	+STEADY	1	+STRANGENESS	1	SUBCHEMISTR
1	STEALTH	1	STRANGLES	1	SUBDUED
1	STEAM	1	STRANGLING	1	+SUBHUMAN
1	STEEDS	1	+STRAWBERRIES	1	SUBJUNCTIVE
1	STEEL	1	STRAWBERRY	1	SUBLIMATED
1	STEEPED	1	STRAYING	1	SUBMERGED
1	STEEPER	1	STREAM	1	SUBMICROSCO
1	STEEPEST	1	STREAMIN	1	SUBMIT
1	STEEPLE	1	STREAMS	1	SUBMORONIC
1	STEEPNESS	1	STREE	1	SUBPREINCES
1	STEERED	1	STREET'S	1	SUBSTANCE
1	STEERING	1	+STREET'S	1	SUBSTANCES
1	STEEVENSUN	1	+STREET	1	SUBSTANTIAL
1	STENCH	1	STREETCAR	1	SUBTRACTED
1	+STEP	1	STREETFU	1	+SUBTRACTIN
1	STEPP	1	+STRENGTH	1	SUBTRACTING
1	STEPPING	1	STRETCH	1	SUBURB
1	STER	1	+STRETCH	1	+SUBURBAN
1	STERD	1	STRETCHANDSTRETCHAND...	1	SUBWAYS
1	STERILIZED	1	STREWED	1	SUCCEED
1	STETTI	1	STRICKEN	1	SUCCEEDED
1	STEVE	1	+STRICKEN	1	SUCCEEDING
1	+STEVENSON	1	+STRICTLY	1	SUCCESS
1	STEWED	1	STRICTNESS	1	SUCCESSFUL
1	STH	1	STRIDES	1	SUCCINCT
1	STIC	1	STRIDING	1	SUCCINCTLY
1	STIC-KY	1	STRIKER	1	SUCCULENT
1	STICKILY	1	STRIKINGLY	1	SUCK
1	STICKINGLY	1	+STRING	1	+SUCK
1	+STICKY	1	STRIPPED	1	+SUCKED

1 +SUCKING	1 SUPPOSEDLY	1 SWIVELCHAIR
1 +SUCKS	1 +SUPPOSEDLY	1 SWOLLEN
1 SUD	1 SUPPRESS	1 SWOONED
1 SUDDE	1 SUPPRESSING	1 +SWOONINGLY
1 SUDDENL	1 SUPPRESSION	1 SWOONS
1 SUDDENLY-LI	1 SUPS	1 +SWOONS
1 SUFFER	1 SURD	1 SWOONSONG
1 SUFFERS	1 +SURE	1 +SWOOPING
1 SUFFICE	1 +SURELY	1 SWOOPINGLY
1 SUFFICIENT	1 SURELYEYE	1 SWOOPS
1 SUGAREDELLI	1 SURELYFL	1 SWORD
1 SUGGESTING	1 SURFACES	1 SWORDGREAT
1 SUGGESTION	1 SURGES	1 SWORKEY
1 SUGGESTS	1 SURGING	1 SWORN
1 SUICIDE	1 SURLING	1 SWOT
1 SUIS	1 SURLY	1 SWUNG
1 SULKED	1 SURMISE	1 SYLLABLES
1 SULKSUCK	1 +SURPASS	1 SYMBOL
1 SULKY	1 SURPASSING	1 SYMBOLS
1 SULTAN'S	1 SURPRISABLE	1 SYNCOPATE
1 +SUM	1 SURPRISES	1 SYNCOPATION
1 SUM-AIR	1 SURPRISING	1 SYNOPSIS
1 +SUMMER	1 SURREPTITIOUSLY	1 SYNTAX
1 SUMMITLESS	1 SURVEYS	1 SYNTHETIC
1 SUMMONED	1 SUS	1 SYPHILIS
1 SUMNER	1 SUSCEPTIBILITY	1 SYRIANSANG
1 SUMPTUOUS	1 SUSPECT	1 SYRINX
1 SUN-LIGHT	1 +SUSPECT	1 SYSTOLE
1 SUN-SHEER	1 SUSPENDERS	1 T'AIME
1 SUN-STIRRING	1 +SUSPENDERS	1 TA-TE-TA
1 SUNBEAM	1 SUSPICIOUS	1 TABARI'
1 SUNDARK	1 SUSTA	1 TABLE-CLOTHS
1 +SUNDAY	1 +SUSTAININGNESS	1 +TABLES
1 SUNDRY	1 SWADDLED	1 TABLETS
1 +SUNG	1 SWAGGERING	1 TABULATED
1 SUNLIGH	1 SWAGGERS	1 TAC-TIC
1 SUNLIGHT'S	1 SWAM	1 TAC-TOC
1 SUNLY	1 SWANK	1 TACTFULLY
1 SUNNING	1 +SWANS	1 +TAFT
1 +SUNRISE	1 SWARMING	1 TAIL'S
1 SUNSE	1 +SWAT	1 TAILOR
1 SUNSET'S	1 SWAYING	1 TAILORED
1 +SUNSET	1 SWAYS	1 +TAILS
1 SUNSETS	1 SWEARS	1 TAINT
1 SUNSMELL	1 SWEAT	1 TAKIN
1 SUPER	1 SWEATING	1 TALENTGANG
1 SUPERB	1 SWEDE	1 TALKATIVE
1 SUPERBLY	1 +SWEEP	1 TALKIN
1 SUPERC	1 SWEETEST	1 TALLER
1 SUPERCILIOUS	1 SWEETLY-SALUTED	1 TAM
1 +SUPERCOLOSSAL	1 SWERVESCA	1 TAMARACK
1 SUPERFLUOUS	1 SWIFLTY	1 +TAMBOURINES
1 SUPERHUMAN	1 +SWIFTLY	1 +TAMER
1 SUPERIMPOSING	1 SWIFTLYENORMOUS	1 TANEOUSLY
1 SUPERLATIVE	1 SWIFTS	1 TANETS
1 SUPERLATIVELY	1 SWIG	1 TANG
1 SUPERME	1 SWIMFLOATDRIFTING	1 TANGIBLE
1 SUPERMETAMATHICAL	1 +SWIMMING	1 +TANGLE
1 SUPERMINDS	1 +SWIMMINGLY	1 TANGLED
1 SUPERNOD	1 SWIMSWIM	1 TANGOING
1 SUPERSEDED	1 SWINBURNED	1 +TANK
1 SUPERSIEVE	1 SWING	1 TANMIH
1 SUPERSNARE	1 SWINGTHINGS	1 TAPERING
1 SUPERSTATE	1 SWIR	1 +TAPPING
1 SUPPER	1 SWIRLED	1 TAPPINGPEOPLEONTHEBACK
1 SUPPLIANT	1 SWIRLING	1 +TAPS
1 +SUPPORT	1 +SWIRLING	1 TAPTAPTAPS
1 SUPPORTS	1 SWIRLS	1 +TART
1 SUPPOSED	1 SWIRLY	1 TARTSKIDS

1 TASH	1 TEXTURES	1 THISTLEFLUFF-THING
1 +TASTING	1 TFUL	1 THITHERHITHERING
1 TATOATLOATF	1 TH-ING	1 THIZ
1 TATTERDEMAL	1 THANGEW	1 +THOMAS
1 TATTLE	1 THANGZKEED	1 THORNIEST
1 TAUGHED	1 +THANK	1 THORNS
1 TAUGHT	1 THANKING	1 THOROUGHLY'S
1 TAXI	1 +THANKING	1 THOS
1 TAXIMAN	1 +THANKS	1 +THOSE
1 TAYLOR	1 THANKSGIVING	1 THOUSANDTH
1 TCH	1 THANKYOUVERYMUCH	1 THR
1 TCH-ING	1 THATANDTHIS	1 THREADED
1 TCHING	1 +THATCH	1 THREATEN
1 TEACHABLE	1 THATOFA	1 THREECOLOURED
1 TEACHER	1 THAZ	1 THREEDIMENSIONAL
1 TEAD	1 THCARED	1 THREEING
1 TEAROSE	1 THE-SEAT-OF-THE	1 THREES
1 TEARTROUBLE	1 THEA	1 THRESHOLD
1 +TEASE	1 THEATRE	1 THRILLERS
1 TEASED	1 THECAS	1 +THROAT'S
1 TEASING	1 THECAS-TANETS	1 THROB
1 TEASINGLY	1 THEEX	1 +THROB
1 TECHNIC	1 +THEIRS	1 THRONG
1 TEDDY	1 THEMA	1 THROSTLES
1 TEDDY-BEARS	1 THEN'S	1 THROTTLED
1 TEE	1 THEN-ARROWS	1 THROTTLING
1 TEE-DIE	1 THENCE	1 +THROUGH
1 TEEL	1 THENLIKE	1 THROUGHOF
1 TEEL-LY	1 THENS	1 THROUGHWHICH
1 TEEMING	1 THEODORE	1 +THROW
1 TEEN	1 THEOREMS	1 +THROWING
1 TEETERTIPTO	1 THEPINKISHT	1 +THROWS
1 TEETHE	1 THEQUEER	1 +THRUSHES
1 TEETHFUL	1 THERAINCOMING	1 THRUSHSONG
1 TELESCOPED	1 THERE'LL	1 THRUST
1 TELESCOPES	1 THERE'RE	1 THRUSTS
1 TELLURIAN	1 +THERE'S	1 THUD
1 TEMPO	1 THEREFROM	1 THUDDING
1 TEMPORAL	1 THEREHERE	1 THUGLIKE
1 TENDER	1 THERETO	1 THULE
1 +TENDONED	1 THEREUPON	1 THUMBPRINTS
1 TENDS	1 THERMOPYLAE	1 THUMPING
1 TENEMENTS	1 THERR	1 +THUMPS
1 TENNISRACKET	1 THESILLYOLD	1 +THUNDER
1 TENSETENDONED	1 THETHE	1 THUNDER-FORAGING
1 +TENT	1 THEWITH	1 THUNDERB
1 TENT-SKY	1 +THEY'RE	1 THUNDERER
1 TERDAY'S	1 THF	1 THUNDEROUS
1 TERFLY	1 THICKEST	1 +THUNDERS
1 TERIOUSLY	1 THICKISH	1 THURSDAY
1 TERMINATED	1 +THICKLY	1 +THURSDAY
1 TERRI	1 THICKLYFOOLISH	1 THURSDAYS
1 +TERRIBLE	1 THIEVES	1 THWART
1 TERRIBLY	1 THIGHED	1 THYSELF
1 +TERRIBLY	1 THIMBLES	1 TICE
1 TERRICOLOUS	1 +THIN	1 TICKLE
1 TERRIF	1 THINGFEAR	1 TICKLES
1 +TERRIFIC	1 THINGFULEST	1 TIDE'S
1 TERRIFYING	1 THINGLESS	1 +TIDES
1 TERRIFYINGLY	1 THINGS-WITHOUT-WINGS	1 TIDEWINGS
1 +TERROR	1 +THINK	1 TIDL
1 TERY	1 THINKINGLY	1 TIED
1 TES	1 THINKLESS	1 TIES
1 TESTED	1 THINNING	1 TIGERS
1 TESTIFIED	1 THIRD'S	1 TIGHTENED
1 +TESTIMONIAL	1 THIRSTIES	1 TIGHTENS
1 TETE	1 THIRSTILY	1 TIGHTNESS
1 TETHATR	1 THIRTYTWO	1 TILLER
1 TEW	1 THISTLEFLUFF	1 TILLNES

1 TILTED	1 TOMBS	1 TRANSLATED
1 TILTING	1 TOMBSTONES	1 TRANSLATION
1 TIM	1 TOMORROW'S	1 +TRANSPARENT
1 +TIMELESS	1 TOMORROWLOBS	1 TRANSPLENDENT
1 +TIMELESSLY	1 TOMS	1 TRANSPORTED
1 TIMELY	1 TON	1 TRAPEZE
1 TIMESHAPED	1 TONIGHT'S	1 TRAPS
1 +TIMIDITIES	1 TONISHING	1 TRAST
1 +TIN	1 TONTON	1 TRATESMEN
1 TINCT	1 +TOO	1 TRAVEL
1 TINGG	1 TOO-NEARISHNESS	1 TRAVELLER
1 TINKING	1 TOOKED	1 TRAVELLING
1 TINKLING	1 TOOMANY	1 TRAVELS
1 TINKLING-CHEERING-...	1 TOOMANY-NESS	1 TREADWATERING
1 TINT	1 TOOTH-PICK	1 TREE3GHOSTS
1 TINYNESS	1 +TOOTHFULLY	1 TREEBODIES
1 TIONS	1 TOOTHPICK	1 TREESOF
1 +TIP	1 TOOTHSOME	1 TREESOUL
1 TIP-TOE	1 TOPEKA	1 TREETOP
1 TIPTO	1 TOPPLES	1 TREMB
1 TIPTOE	1 TOPS	1 TREMBLY
1 +TIPTOE	1 TORCHES	1 TREMENDOUSLY
1 +TIPTOEING	1 +TORSO	1 TREMONT
1 TIPTOP	1 TORTURE	1 TRENO
1 TIRE	1 TORTURES	1 +TRESPASSING
1 TIREDNESS	1 TORTURES-PLEASANTLY	1 TRIANGLE
1 TIRF	1 TOSSED	1 TRIANGULAR
1 TISS	1 TOSSING	1 TRIBUNE
1 TIT	1 TOTALLY	1 TRICKIEST
1 TITTLE	1 TOTOUCH	1 TRICKLE
1 TITTY	1 TOTTER	1 TRICKLED
1 TIV	1 TOTTERED	1 +TRICKLING
1 TIVE	1 +TOTTERISH	1 TRICKS
1 TLADYF	1 +TOTTERS	1 TRICKSTERVILLAIN
1 TLEORA	1 TOU	1 TRICKY
1 TLESS	1 TOUCHABLY	1 TRIFL
1 TLOV	1 TOUGH	1 TRIFLE
1 TLY	1 TOUJOURS	1 +TRIFLE
1 TM	1 TOUS	1 TRIG
1 TNIGHTS	1 TOUSLE	1 TRIGGER
1 TOAD	1 TOUT	1 TRIGLYPH'S
1 +TOAD	1 TOUTES	1 TRILL
1 TOADSTOOLS	1 +TOWARD	1 TRILLERS
1 TOBACCO	1 TOWERFUL	1 TRILLIONTH
1 TOBOGGANS	1 +TOWERING	1 TRILLIONWORLDED
1 TODAY'S	1 TOYSDAY	1 TRINIGHTLY
1 TODDLE	1 TOYTOWN	1 TRIPERIGHT
1 TODO	1 TP	1 TRIPLE
1 TOENAILS	1 TR	1 TRISTRAM
1 TOES	1 TRACE	1 TRIUMPHS
1 +TOES	1 TRACKING	1 TRIVI
1 TOF	1 +TRADESMEN	1 +TRIVIAL
1 TOGETHERING	1 TRAFFICING	1 +TRIVIALITY
1 +TOGETHERLY	1 TRAGIC	1 TROD
1 TOHIM	1 TRAIPSE	1 TROIS
1 TOIL	1 TRAITOR	1 TROLL
1 +TOILET PAP	1 TRAMP	1 TROLLEY
1 TOILET	1 TRAMPLE	1 TROUBADOURS
1 +TOILET	1 TRAMPLED	1 TROUBLE
1 TOILETBOWL	1 TRAMPLING	1 +TROUBLED
1 TOILETWINDO	1 TRAN	1 TROUBLES
1 TOITSELFW	1 TRANCE	1 TROUBLING
1 TOLL	1 TRANCEWORLD	1 TROYS
1 TOLLED	1 TRANGE	1 TROZE
1 +TOM	1 TRANQUILLITIES	1 TRUCK
1 TOM-CAT	1 TRANS	1 TRUDGES
1 TOM-TOM	1 TRANSFERRED	1 TRUDGING
1 TOMA	1 TRANSFIGURED	1 TRUEBEAUTIFULLY
1 +TOMAHAWKED	1 +TRANSFORMING	1 TRULL

1003

1 WHENLINGS
1 +WHENS
1 WHENWORLD
1 +WHERE
1 WHEREABOUTS
1 WHEREFROM
1 WHEREFUL
1 +WHEREFUL
1 WHERELESS
1 WHERELESSLY
1 WHERELINGS
1 WHEREON
1 +WHERES
1 WHEREWHEN
1 WHEREWHENS
1 WHEY
1 WHIE
1 WHIGH
1 WHILEPIN
1 WHIMPERED
1 WHIMS
1 +WHINE
1 WHINING
1 WHINNIED
1 WHIPALERT
1 WHIPPED
1 WHIPPING
1 WHIPPOORWILLS
1 WHIR
1 WHIRL'S
1 +WHIRL
1 WHIRLED
1 +WHIRLFULLY
1 WHIRLING'S
1 WHIRLINGEST
1 WHIRLS
1 +WHIRLS
1 WHIRLSWANS
1 WHIS-PER
1 WHISKEY-SOUR
1 WHISKEY-VOICE
1 WHISKIES
1 WHISPER'S
1 WHISPERFUL
1 +WHISPERFULLY
1 WHISPERINGLY
1 WHISPERLESS
1 +WHISPERS
1 WHISPERSHOUT
1 WHIST
1 WHITE-GRUB
1 WHITE-THIGHED
1 WHITE&GOLD
1 WHITELIEST
1 +WHITELY
1 WHITEN
1 WHITERMUCH
1 WHITES
1 WHITEWHOM
1 WHITHERING
1 WHITHERS
1 +WHO'D
1 WHO-EVER-HEARD-OF-GROWING
1 WHO-HORNS
1 WHOCARES
1 WHOING
1 WHOISIT
1 +WHOLE
1 WHOLEAGAINST

1 WHOLES
1 +WHOLLY
1 WHOMEVER'S
1 +WHORES
1 WHORLCLOWN
1 WHOSES
1 WHOSESWOONING
1 WHOSHOUT
1 WHOWHICH
1 WHOY
1 WHY'S
1 WHYCOL
1 WHYCOLOURED
1 WHYLAUGHING
1 WHYLESSNESS
1 WHYSPRIG
1 WI
1 WICK
1 WICKED
1 +WICKED
1 WIDEFLUNG
1 +WIDOWER
1 WIDOWS
1 WIDTH
1 WIELD
1 +WIELDS
1 WIFELESS
1 WIGGIN
1 +WIGGIN'S
1 +WIGGLE
1 WIGGLED
1 WIGGLESOME
1 WILDSTRAWBERRIES
1 WILFUL
1 WILL'S
1 +WILL
1 WILLBEISHFULLY
1 WILLED
1 WILLINGLY
1 WILLOWING
1 WILLS&WERES
1 WILLY
1 WILLY'S
1 WILTING
1 WIND'S
1 +WIND
1 WINDMILLS
1 +WINDOW
1 WINDOW-SILLS
1 WINDOWS-AND-WHISPERS
1 WINDTHIN
1 WINDY
1 WINES
1 WINGED
1 WINGFEET
1 WINGLESS
1 +WINK
1 WINKED
1 WINKING
1 WINNER
1 WINNING
1 WINS
1 WINT
1 WINT-AIR
1 WINTER'S
1 WINTERBRIEF
1 WINTR
1 +WINTRY
1 WIPED

1 WIRE
1 WIRED
1 WIRELESS
1 WIRES
1 WISDOMING
1 WISDOMS
1 WISER
1 +WISH
1 +WISHFUL
1 +WISHFULLY
1 +WISP
1 WISPILY
1 WISPISH
1 WISPISH-AGI
1 WISTI
1 WISTI-TWIST
1 WITCHES
1 WITH-BE
1 WITH-ERED
1 WITHDRAWS
1 WITHERED
1 +WITHERED
1 WITHHOLDING
1 +WITHOUT
1 WITLESS
1 WITTILY
1 WIVES
1 +WIZENED
1 WLEDGE
1 WLI
1 WLYTHE
1 WN
1 WND
1 WO-L
1 WOE
1 WOES
1 WOFROING
1 WOID
1 WOIDS
1 WOIL
1 WOLF
1 WOLFHOUNDS
1 WOMANSELLIN
1 WOMEN-COLOU
1 WOMENLIKE
1 +WONDER
1 +WONDERFULL
1 WONDERINGS
1 WONDERLESS
1 WONDROUS
1 WONENS
1 WONT
1 WOO
1 +WOOD
1 +WOODROW
1 WOODS
1 WOODUNDAT
1 WOOER
1 WOOL
1 WOOLWORTH
1 WOOLWORTHIAN
1 WOOPSING
1 +WORD
1 +WORDLESSLY
1 +WORDS
1 WORKED
1 WORKMEN
1 +WORLDED
1 +WORLDS

1	+WORMING	1	+YEARS
1	WORMPERUSED	1	YEGGS
1	WORMSMILE	1	YELLING
1	WORN	1	YELLOWANDBLUISH
1	WORSHIPPED	1	YELLOWGREEN
1	+WORSHIPPED	1	YELLOWISH
1	WORSHIPPER	1	YELLOWSONOFABITCH
1	WOT	1	YELLUH
1	WOT'S	1	YELPS
1	WOTHRE	1	YESMAM
1	+WOULDN'T	1	YESSING
1	WOULDWOE	1	YESSIR
1	WOUNDING	1	YESTERDAY'S
1	WOUNDSMILE	1	+YESTERDAY'S
1	WOVEN	1	YESWIND
1	WRAITH'S	1	YESWIND-FACES
1	WRAITHISH	1	YEWRETY
1	WRAPPEDUPBODY	1	YFA
1	WREATH	1	YGURDYGUR
1	WREATHED	1	YHALF
1	WREATHS	1	YI
1	+WRENCH	1	YIELDING
1	WREST	1	YLIKE
1	WRESTLED	1	YM&
1	WRETCH	1	YOKED
1	WRIGGLED	1	YOND
1	WRIGGLING	1	YONKERS
1	WRIGLEY	1	YOO-GOINTA-DOO
1	WRING	1	YOOZE
1	WRINKLING	1	YOOZWIDDUHPOIMNUNTWAIV
1	WRIST	1	+YOU'LL
1	WRIST'S	1	+YOU'RE
1	WRISTERS	1	+YOU'VE
1	+WRISTS	1	YOU-WITH-ME
1	+WRITHED	1	YOUAMIARE
1	+WRITHES	1	YOUFUL
1	WRITHEWHO	1	YOUKNOW
1	WRITING	1	YOUNGLY
1	WRONG'S	1	YOUR-AND
1	WRONGERS	1	+YOURS
1	WRONGSIDEOUT	1	YOURSELVES
1	WRS	1	+YOURSELVES
1	WSP	1	YOUS
1	WT	1	YOUTH'S
1	WUGGLEWIGGLE	1	YS
1	WUMAN	1	YSOMETHI
1	WUN	1	YSTRUT
1	WUS	1	YURARSTOIN
1	WUSHYUHNAME	1	YW
1	+X	1	YZ
1	XERXES	1	Z
1	XMAS	1	+Z
1	+XMAS	1	ZAGFLASH
1	XPLODING	1	ZEAL
1	YACHTS	1	ZENS
1	YANKING	1	ZERO
1	YAOORTI	1	ZIGGING
1	YAPENESE	1	ZINGLY
1	YAS	1	ZITHER
1	YAW	1	ZITHER-AND
1	YAWN	1	ZONE
1	YAWNCHURCHES	1	ZOOM
1	YAWNED	1	ZOOMS
1	YBODY		
1	YEAH		
1	YEAR'S		
1	YEARHOUR		
1	YEARNING		
1	YEARNSWOONS